D1325782

CHRONOLOGY OF THE MODERN WORLD

1763 – 1992

Second Edition

Companion volumes

CHRONOLOGY OF THE ANCIENT WORLD,
10,000 B.C. – A.D. 799

By H.E.L. Mellersh

CHRONOLOGY OF THE MEDIEVAL WORLD
800–1491

By R.L. Storey

CHRONOLOGY OF THE EXPANDING WORLD
1492–1762

By Neville Williams

NEVILLE WILLIAMS
PHILIP WALLER

Chronology of the Modern World

1763-1992

Second Edition

Helicon

Chronology of the Modern World, Second Edition
by Neville Williams and Philip Waller

First Edition published in 1966
Second Edition published in 1994
Reprinted 1995

Helicon Publishing Ltd
42 Hythe Bridge Street
Oxford, OX1 2EP

Printed and bound in England

ISBN 0 09 178274 0

British Library Cataloguing in Publication Data
A catalogue record for this book
is available from the British Library

First Edition for
G.P. GOOCH
(1873-1968)

Second Edition for
J.M. ROBERTS

Contents

Introduction to the First Edition . . ix

Introduction to the Second Edition . xv

Chronology I

Index 933

Introduction to the First Edition

Chronology of the Modern World is a guide to the events and achievements in every walk of life of the past two centuries. The information is given chronologically, yet the volume incorporates a large-scale Index which readily provides specific references. Political and international events appear throughout on the left-hand page, year by year, in monthly paragraphs under precise calendar dates. The corresponding right-hand pages for each year are devoted to achievements in the Arts and Sciences, arranged under classified headings. Both the monthly paragraphs of the left-hand pages and the subject paragraphs of the right-hand pages bear individual letters, enabling speedy reference from the Index (A to N on the left; O to Z on the right). Thus the user will find the reference to Albert Schweitzer's death as '1965 Z', in fact the final paragraph in the volume.

1763 was chosen as the starting-point since the Treaty of Paris of that year, which concluded the Seven Years' War, marks the end of the long series of dynastic wars; the stage is set for the emergence of the New Europe and the New America. In 1763, too, we are on the threshold of the first great Industrial Revolution, and before long developments in science and technology come thick and fast. The tale has been carried forward from January 1763, year by year, with the increasing tempo of events in a gradually shrinking globe—and universe—to December 1965.

LEFT-HAND PAGES One or more of the chief events of the year have been selected to form head-lines. The January paragraph is given the reference 'A', February the reference 'B' and so on; but the letter 'I' has not been used to avoid possible confusion with 'J'. Those events for which no precise calendar date can be found have been placed at the end of the month in question, unless it is known that they took place early in the month. Beneath the December paragraph ('M') appears a final paragraph 'N', in which have been placed events that cannot be assigned to a particular month (e.g. a famine). Cross-references to the same or another year are included where appropriate; e.g. under 1807, Dec. 17th, 'Napoleon's Milan Decrees against British trade, extending Berlin Decrees (of Nov. 21st 1806).' To avoid unnecessary repetition in dates the convention —, has been used for indicating another event of the same date of the month as the previous entry. Each entry appears on a fresh line to make for clarity and quick reference.

RIGHT-HAND PAGES Here too, head-lines pick out the most significant achievements of the year. The paragraphs are classified under these headings:

- O Politics, Economics, Law and Education
- P Science, Technology, Discovery
- Q Scholarship (including archaeology and research in 'arts' subjects)
- R Philosophy and Religion
- S Art, Sculpture, Fine Arts and Architecture
- T Music
- U Literature (excluding plays)
- V The Press
- W Drama and Entertainment (including for the most modern period Films and Television programmes)
- X Sport
- Y Statistics (especially the populations of principal countries and cities, given at regular intervals, production figures for coal, steel and petroleum, the tonnage of merchant fleets, the size of armies and the demand for consumer goods)
- Z Births and Deaths of notabilities: exact calendar dates wherever known, including age at death and, if no longer living, adding death date in the birth entry, e.g. in paragraph 1792 Z under Aug. 4th we have 'Richard Arkwright d. (60) and Percy Bysshe Shelley b. (–1822)'

The titles of foreign works are given in translation whenever they have subsequently been translated into the English language. In works published anonymously the author's name is placed within square brackets, e.g. [A. and C. Tennyson], *Poems by Two Brothers*. Pseudonyms are noted and also works appearing posthumously.

On occasion an item might equally well have appeared in a different paragraph from the one in which it is placed; for example the first issue of the journal *The Musical Times* could be regarded as primarily a musical event or, alternatively, as a journalistic one. Again, comparative statistics for religious denominations could appear equally well under 'R' or under 'Y'. Any real problems raised by the choice of paragraphs for border-line cases and any unintentional oddities of arrangement that remain will be readily solved by means of the Index.

Though the selection of material for inclusion has not proved an easy task, the editor has throughout endeavoured to maintain a proper balance. In the last event the inclusion or omission of an item rested on personal choice; but he believes that though a score of different editors would all have included 95 per cent. of the same material, the final 5 per cent. would in each case have been very different. Nonetheless he holds that no major event has been omitted and no author, artist or musician of consequence has gone unrepresented. The editor and his assistants have always gone right to the sources to verify their facts and to resolve problems of inconsistency presented by different works of reference giving on occasion different dates for the same event. The number of common errors in various current works of reference has at times seemed alarming and every effort has been made to prevent their perpetuation in this volume. Opportunity has been taken in the long process of indexing of making further checks. In a work of this scope, however, it would be hypocritical to claim that no slips exist. Users of the *Chronology* are accordingly invited to inform the publisher of any entries in the text or index which they consider to be misleading or inaccurate and also to indicate any significant omissions. It is the aim of publisher and editor to provide the public with a work of reference of authority.

THE INDEX

Entries for Persons, Places and Subjects and titles of books are listed in one alphabetical sequence. Prefixes to surnames have been disregarded; e.g. de Gaulle appears under 'G'.

PERSONS The entries for Persons include full names and titles, dates of birth (and death), nationality and a brief description of their claim to fame (e.g. 'author', 'atomic physicist', 'soldier', 'Christian Democrat leader'). The nationality has been abbreviated: 'Am.' for American, 'B.' for British, 'F.' for French, 'G.' for German and 'R.' for Russian; for other countries abbreviations have been employed which avoid confusion—'Aus.' for Austrian and 'Austral.' for Australian. For important individuals there are classified sub-entries; in the case of a statesman, whose references are predominantly to the left-hand pages, these sub-entries are arranged chronologically and they give a conspectus of his entire career. For persons whose work features in right-hand pages the sub-entries are arranged by subjects (e.g. an important author's work will be subdivided 'as dramatist', 'as novelist' and 'as poet'). The entries for persons in fact form a Dictionary of Biography.

PLACES Places are assigned their country according to the current world map. Entries for major cities are for the sake of clarity divided into a series of sub-entries for events there, listed in date order, followed by a series for buildings and institutions in alphabetical order. For less important places there is only a chronological arrangement.

Prefixes such as 'New' or 'South' are taken as part of the place-name proper (e.g. New York appears under 'N' and South Africa under 'S'). Britain appears under 'B', and Russia under 'R'; but the United States of America appears under 'U'. The entries for countries are of two kinds. For minor states, such as Mexico or Poland, there is one chronological sequence of sub-entries; these show at a glance the country's history during these two centuries. For major states on the other hand, such as Britain, Russia and the United States, the sub-entries would be enormously bulky if the same system were followed. Accordingly, entries for major countries have been drastically pruned so that they relate to such topics as frontiers.

Someone primarily interested in the political history of a major country should turn to the classified Subject Entries mentioned below. For place-names the index entries provide a useful gazeteer.

SUBJECTS In this category the most important feature is the series in which political events are classified; these include entries for Administrations; Conferences and Congresses; Constitutions; Coup d'états; Elections; Legislation; Parliaments and other Elected Assemblies; Revolutions; Political Parties; Treaties. In each case the sub-entries are arranged by countries alphabetically and, within countries, chronologically. For example, to obtain the reference to the 20th amendment to the American Constitution the reader should turn to 'Constitutions, in US, Amendments to, 20th,' where he will see the reference= 1933 B. The entry 'Political Parties' lists all parties in each country from Algeria to Yugoslavia, alphabetically within the country. This approach forges a useful tool for the study of comparative history. In the same way there are general subject entries for such topics as Religious Denominations, and Wars.

TITLES OF WORKS All books and plays are indexed individually in the main alphabetical sequence; in each case the definite or indefinite article in the language of the title has been disregarded (e.g. *Importance of Being Earnest, The; Tale of Two Cities, A*. There are, however, general entries for Ballets; Films; Journals; Newspapers; Operas; and Overtures, within which these works are listed alphabetically.

OTHER SUBJECT ENTRIES such as Coal, Electricity, Epidemics, Photography and Universities are suitably subdivided. In the case of long entries this is by countries, otherwise it is alphabetical or chronological, as in each case seems most suitable.

CROSS-REFERENCES There are ample cross-references to guide the user, but without inflating the index unduly certain information is given in more than one place, to save the reader from unnecessary trouble (e.g. entries for the atomic bomb appear both under 'atom' and under 'bomb').

To sum up: the Index to the *Chronology* is almost an Encyclopaedia of Modern History. In not a few cases the user will find the index answers his problem without the necessity of turning to the text. (When did Goethe die? When was *Sunset Boulevard* filmed? What was Jerome K. Jerome's middle name? These and many kindred questions receive an immediate answer.) In many cases we predict that the user will be fascinated by the parallel entries in fields very different from his own and will become a happy browser.

* * *

The invitation to edit this *Chronology* came to me in April 1963 from Leopold Ullstein, who had for some time been pondering the possibilities of compiling a volume on the lines of Stein's *Kulturfahrplan* (first issued in Berlin in 1948). It at once became clear that to give adequate space both to political events and to all significant aspects of man's development in a single volume would mean concentrating on the last two centuries, compared with Stein's broad survey from the origins of civilisation. At a later stage we hope to prepare a further volume on the same scale, probably beginning in 1500. Much preliminary work and many discussions led to the adoption of the present scheme. For political events we aimed at giving precise, calendar dates, as a refinement on the method of presentation in G. P. Gooch's *Annals of Politics and Culture* (1st edition, 1901). Unlike S. H. Steinberg's *Historical Tables* (1st edition, 1939) we planned from the first to provide an index, and one which would feature as an integral part of the book. Our intention was that each entry in the text should be as concise as possible, that is to say self-explanatory, without superfluous comment. The compilation, checking and indexing of the entries in a work of this scope took far longer than either of us envisaged. That the work has not in fact been even longer delayed is due to the happy partnership between publisher and editor.

Many besides Mr. Ullstein have assisted in the genesis and progress of the work and it is not possible to thank them all individually. But I must acknowledge with gratitude the constant help of John Pattisson who has borne the brunt of my editorial problems, the assistance of Adrian Yendell in the preliminary compilation of material for the nineteenth century and in work on the index, and the advice which Mrs. Rosemary Proctor gave me in the fields of modern art, sculpture and architecture. As with all my books I owe a great deal to Mrs. D. Steer who typed the whole of the text and much of the index; the rest of the index was typed by Miss M. Whitmee. My wife, as always, gave me the encouragement to see the work to a conclusion and two of my children, Alison and Guy, helped in the sorting of index slips (a stack of slips which ultimately ran to over 30 feet).

Chronology of the Modern World is dedicated to George Gooch, doyen of British historians in stature as in age. My first of many visits to him at Upway Corner, Chalfont St. Peter, twenty years ago was one of the most memorable experiences of my life; and much of this book was compiled beneath the picture of Erasmus that came from him as a wedding present.

N. W.

Hampstead Garden Suburb
Whit Monday 1966

Introduction to the Second Edition

This new, enlarged edition of the *Chronology of the Modern World* requires no apologia. A generation of omnibus readers and others can attest to the original work's value and interest. Nevertheless, two principal criticisms may be anticipated. The first is ideological: the contention that no fact is free-standing, and that to include one item while discarding another involves tendentious judgement. Books of dates, so this argument commonly runs, are unduly orthodox in their criteria. They conform to canons established by complacently conservative, westernized white middle-class males. The second complaint is the specialist's: that abbreviation cannot be accomplished without distortion. Simplification inevitably means trivialization. To the expert, books of dates are at best worthless, at worst misleading. For instance, the expert might view a supposed scientific or industrial 'breakthrough' as merely the end-point of a complex process whose origins may lie 10 or more years before. The same view may be taken of a work of literature or art; and our political and economic life similarly comprises concatenations whose true sequence of causation and connection can scarcely be glimpsed by being captioned as a series of discrete 'events'.

There is substance in both of these objections, but if they are slavishly adhered to, both point towards paralysis more than productivity. They are as much arguments against attempting any compendium as against this one in particular. Moreover, it can be countered, as the original editor, Neville Williams, remarked, that the vast majority of entries included here would be admitted to any compilation. No narrow philosophy is involved in deciding that the resignation of President Nixon in 1974 was an event of some significance. It is not the purpose of this book to debate what that significance was. It is simply a journal of record, not an essay in comprehension. The aim is to bring together an accessible and reliable collection of data that are noteworthy. Hard-pressed scholars, teachers, journalists, and indeed anyone in public and private life who wants to save precious time and labour will be grateful for a volume to which they can turn to verify a date, just as a traveller consults a signpost or map.

As for its new editor, he is pleased to pay tribute to the firm foundations laid by his predecessor, and to laud the industry and intelligence of those who have assisted in producing this revised and extended edition. The organizational expertise of Robert Peberdy has been outstanding in assembling and collating the product of a zealous and scrupulous team of researchers and advisers: Ann Barrett, Lewis Baston, Julia Colman, Ingrid von Essen, Martin Goodman, Clare Griffiths, Trevor Griffiths, Ann Swailes, Jason Tomes, Trevor I. Williams.

A final pleasure is to dedicate this new edition to J.M. Roberts, saluting the achievement of the author of the *History of the World* (1976), the third edition of which inaugurated Helicon's publications list in 1992. More particularly, several members of the team involved in this *Chronology* have been drawn from Merton College, where John Roberts was Fellow and Tutor in Modern History from 1953 to 1979 and Warden from 1984. To all that, the Editor would like to add a personal note, glad to celebrate his friendship with an effervescent colleague stretching over twenty years.

Users of the *Chronology* are again invited to inform the publishers of any inaccuracies.

Philip Waller
Merton College, Oxford

CHRONOLOGY

1763 Peace of Paris ends Seven Years' War

A **Jan:**

B **Feb:** 10th, the Peace of Paris between Britain, France and Spain ends the Seven Years' War (called in America the French and Indian War), the last of the series of dynastic wars; by its terms (1) Britain secures Canada, Nova Scotia, Cape Breton, St. Vincent, Tobago, Dominica, Grenada, Senegal and Minorca from France, and Florida from Spain; (2) France regains Martinique, Guadaloupe, St. Lucia and Goree and is guaranteed fishing rights off Newfoundland; (3) the French settlements in India are restored, but no fortifications are to be built there; (4) Spain acquires Louisiana from France, exchanges Florida for Havana and recovers Manila and the Philippines;
15th, peace treaty of Hubertusburg between Prussia and Austria restores the *status quo* with Austria restoring Glatz and Silesia to Prussia and Prussia evacuating Saxony, and by a secret article Frederick the Great of Prussia undertakes to support the election of Archduke Joseph of Austria as King of the Romans.

C **Mar:**

D **Apr:** 7th, Earl of Bute's ministry falls in Britain and,
16th, George Grenville becomes prime minister and chancellor of Exchequer;
18th, Henry Fox's refusal to give up the lucrative post of paymaster-general, on elevation to peerage, provokes bitter ministerial conflict;
23rd, John Wilkes attacks the King's Speech, commending the terms of peace, in No. 45 of the *North Briton* and
30th, he is arrested on a general warrant.

E **May:** 6th, chief justice Pratt discharges Wilkes on ground of Parliamentary privilege and declares general warrants illegal;
7th, rising of Indians under Pontiac near Detroit spreads rapidly east (–1766);
25th, internal free trade in corn in France (–1766).

F **Jun:**

G **Jul:** Mir Kasim of Murshidabad, defeated by Thomas Adams and deposed, takes refuge in Oudh;
Act to prevent fraudulent votes in British elections;
'Whiteboys' revolt against agrarian hardships in Ireland.

H **Aug:**

J **Sep:** 9th, the group of Whigs led by John Duke of Bedford joins the government and the Earl of Shelbourne retires from the ministry on personal grounds.

K **Oct:** 3rd, Augustus III, elective King of Poland, dies;
7th, British proclamation provides for government of the new colonies of Quebec, East and West Florida and Grenada, while assignment of region west of the Alleghenies as an Indian reserve halts westward expansion and imperial government takes over regulation of trade with the Indians.

L **Nov:** 23rd, in Wilkes affair the Commons resolve that Parliamentary privilege does not extend to seditious libels.

M **Dec:** Patrick Henry delivers radical speech in 'the parson's cause' in Virginia, brought by an incumbent for restitution of salary, in which he denies right of British crown to disallow acts of colonial legislatures.

N Hyder Ali, Indian adventurer in Mysore, conquers Kanara.

O **Politics, Economics, Law and Education**

J. J. Rousseau in *Lettres de la Montagne* attacks the constitution and council of Geneva for condemning his *Émile* (1762).

Frederick the Great establishes village schools in Prussia.

P **Science, Technology, Discovery, etc.**

J. G. Kölreuter's experiments on the fertilisation of plants by animal pollen-carriers.

Q **Scholarship**

David Hume, *History of Great Britain.*

Almanack de Gotha first issued.

R **Philosophy and Religion**

Voltaire, *Treatise on Tolerance.*

John Campbell, *Dissertation on Miracles.*

Justinus Febronius (von Hontheim, Bishop of Treves), *De Statu Ecclesiae*, urges the supremacy of general councils (it is to be condemned by Pope Clement XIII in 1766).

Henry Venn, *Complete Duty of Man.*

S **Art, Sculpture, Fine Arts and Architecture**

Francesco Guardi, *Election of a Doge* (painting).

Étienne Falconet, *Pygmalion and Galathea* (sculpture).

Horace Walpole, *Catalogue of Engravers born and resident in England.*

The Madeleine, Paris, completed.

T **Music**

U **Literature**

Giuseppi Parini, *Il Mattino.*

James Boswell meets Samuel Johnson (*May* 16th).

V **The Press**

St. James's Chronicle issued.

W **Drama and Entertainment**

Almack opens a gaming-house in London (later becoming Brooks').

X **Sport**

Y **Statistics**

Z **Births and Deaths**

Mar. 21st 'Jean Paul' (Frederick Richter) b. (–1825).

Oct. 10th Xavier de Maistre b. (–1852).

A **Jan:** 19th, John Wilkes is expelled from Commons for having written seditious libel; riots in London in favour of Wilkes.

B **Feb:** 21st, court of King's Bench finds Wilkes guilty of reprinting No. 45 of the *North Briton* and printing the *Essay on Woman.*

C **Mar:**

D **Apr:** 11th, treaty between Russia and Prussia guarantees the present constitutions of Poland and Sweden, and provides for controlling election to Polish monarchy and joint action against Nationalists.

E **May:** 18th, British Parliament amends Sugar Act from a commercial to a fiscal measure, to tax American Colonists and establish a single Vice-Admiralty court for the thirteen colonies.

F **Jun:**

G **Jul:**

H **Aug:**

J **Sep:** 7th, Stanislas Poniatowski, the protégé of Russia, elected King of Poland.

K **Oct:** 23rd, Hector Munro defeats Nabwab of Oudh at Buxar, Bengal.

L **Nov:** 26th, suppression of Jesuits in France.

M **Dec:**

N Catharine II confiscates ecclesiastical lands in Russia, paying the clergy salaries, to deprive them of political power.
Hyder Ali usurps the throne of Mysore and takes Calcutta.
Réunion becomes a French crown colony.
De Bougainville claims Falkland Isles for France.

O **Politics, Economics, Law and Education**

C. Beccaria-Bonesana, *On Crimes and Punishments.*

Brown University, Providence, Rhode Island, founded.

P **Science, Technology, Discovery, etc.**

Joseph Black measures the latent heat of steam.

J. G. Zimmermann, *On Discovery in Medicine.*

James Hargreaves invents the spinning jenny.

P. M. J. Trésaguet develops three-tier method of road making in France.

Q **Scholarship**

J. A. Ernesti's edition of Polybius.

J. J. Winckelmann, *History of Ancient Art.*

The Dilettanti Society of London sends three members to Greece and Asia Minor to study antiquities.

Adam Anderson, *The Origins of Commerce.*

R **Philosophy and Religion**

Charles Bonnet, *Contemplation de la nature.*

Thomas Reid's *Inquiry in the Human Mind on the Principles of Common Sense* founds the philosophical school of natural realism.

F. M. A. de Voltaire, *Philosophical Dictionary.*

August Spangenberg reforms the Moravian Brethren.

S **Art, Sculpture, Fine Arts and Architecture**

J. A. Houdon, *St. Bruno* (sculpture).

Robert Adam, Kenwood House, Middlesex.

The Pantheon, Paris (–1790).

T **Music**

Joseph Haydn, 'The Philosopher' Symphony (No. 22 in E flat).

J. C. Bach gives recitals in London.

U **Literature**

Oliver Goldsmith, *The Traveller.*

Dr. Johnson founds The Literary Club, London, in which Edmund Burke, Edward Gibbon, Goldsmith and Joshua Reynolds are prominent.

Jeanne de Lespinasse and Suzanne Necker found salons in Paris.

V **The Press**

W **Drama and Entertainment**

X **Sport**

Y **Statistics**

Z **Births and Deaths**

Sept. 12th Jean Philippe Rameau d. (81).

Oct. 26th William Hogarth d. (67).

— John Kay d. (60).

1765 American colonists oppose Stamp Act—Clive's reforms in India

A **Jan:**

B **Feb:**

C **Mar:** 23rd, British Parliament passes Stamp Act, devised by Grenville for taxing the American colonies.

D **Apr:**

E **May:** 29th, In the Virginian assembly Patrick Henry challenges the right of Britain to tax the colonies;
Robert Clive begins administrative reforms in Bengal (–1767).

F **Jun:**

G **Jul:** 16th, Grenville resigns on collapse of ministry over a Regency bill, and Marquess of Rockingham forms a government.

H **Aug:** 13th, Archduke Leopold becomes ruler of Tuscany, and shortly abolishes the Inquisition in the duchy;
18th, Joseph II of Austria succeeds as Holy Roman Emperor on death of Francis I, but is co-regent with Maria Theresa in Bohemia and Hungary.

J **Sep:** British government acquires fiscal rights in Isle of Man from Duke of Atholl.

K **Oct:** 27 delegates from nine colonies attend Stamp Act Congress in New York and, 19th, draw up a declaration of rights and liberties.

L **Nov:**

M **Dec:** on death of the Dauphin, his son, Louis Augustus (future Louis XVI) becomes heir to French throne.

N

O Politics, Economics, Law and Education

First public restaurant opened in Paris.
A. R. J. Turgot, *Réflexions sur la formation et la distribution des richesses.*
William Blackstone, *Commentaries on the Laws of England* (–1769).
The first gymnasium opened, Breslau.

P Science, Technology, Discovery, etc.

L. Spallanzani pioneers preserving through hermetic sealing and argues against spontaneous generation.
James Watt invents a condenser (which leads to his construction of a steam engine, 7174, improved in 1775).

Q Scholarship

R Philosophy and Religion

A. Tucker, *The Light of Nature Pursued* (–1774).
C. F. Nicolai begins to edit the 'Universal German Library' as an organ for popular philosophy (–1792).

S Art, Sculpture, Fine Arts and Architecture

J. H. Fragonard, *Corésus et Callirhoé* (painting).
J. B. Greuze, *La Bonne Mère* and *Le Mauvais Fils Puni* (paintings).
F. Boucher is appointed court painter at Versailles and paints Mme de Pompadour.
A. J. Gabriel, Place de la Concorde, Paris.

T Music

U Literature

Henry Brooke, *The Fool of Quality; or The History of Henry Earl of Moreland* (–1770).
Thomas Chatterton forges the 'Rowley' poems.
Thomas Percy, aided by William Shenstone, *Reliques of Ancient English Poetry.*
Horace Walpole's *The Castle of Otranto* founds the English romantic school of fiction.
C. M. Wieland, *Comic Tales.*
Samuel Johnson's edition of the *Works of William Shakespeare* published.

V The Press

W Drama and Entertainment

M. J. Sedaine, *Philosophe sans le savoir.*

X Sport

Y Statistics

Z Births and Deaths

Apr. 5th Edward Young d. (82).
Dec. 8th Eli Whitney b. (–1825).
— Robert Fulton b. (–1815).

1766 Britain declares its right to tax American colonies

A **Jan:**

B **Feb:** 23rd, on death of Stanislaus Lesczcynski the duchy of Lorraine, then under his rule, is incorporated in France.

C **Mar:** British Parliament repeals the Stamp Act by 275–161 votes but, 18th, passes Declaratory Act, declaring Britain's right, among others, to tax the American colonies.

D **Apr:**

E **May:**

F **Jun:** Count Aranda becomes chief minister in Spain and introduces secular education.

G **Jul:** 12th, on Rockingham's dismissal by George III, Pitt, becoming Earl of Chatham, forms a ministry with Duke of Grafton; Henry Conway and Shelburne becoming secretaries of state and Charles Townshend chancellor of Exchequer (dubbed by Burke 'a tessellated pavement without cement').

H **Aug:**

J **Sep:**

K **Oct:**

L **Nov:** 12th, the Nizam Ali of Hyderabad cedes Northern Circars, Madras, to Britain.

M **Dec:**

N Russia and Prussia interfere in Polish affairs against the Nationalists.
Internal free trade in corn, in France, since 1763, abolished (re-introduced 1774).
John Byron, ignorant of de Bougainville's annexation in 1764, takes Falkland Isles for Britain and establishes Port Egmont.
Ali Bey assumes power in Egypt.

O **Politics, Economics, Law and Education**

Adam Ferguson, *Essay on the History of Civil Society.*

P **Science, Technology, Discovery, etc.**

Henry Cavendish discovers hydrogen is less dense than air and delivers papers to the Royal Society on the chemistry of gases.

John Byron returns (*May* 9th) from voyage of circumnavigation.

Louis de Bougainville's voyage of discovery in the Pacific (–*Mar.* 1769) on which he names the Navigators Islands.

Q **Scholarship**

G. E. Lessing, *Laocoön.*

R **Philosophy and Religion**

Francis Blackburne, *Confessional.*

The French clergy again required to observe the Gallican Articles, 1682, limiting papal authority.

Pope Clement XIII sanctions the celebration of the Sacred Heart (founded by Marguerite Alacoque, d. 1690).

Catherine the Great grants freedom of worship in Russia.

S **Art, Sculpture, Fine Arts and Architecture**

J. H. Fragonard, *The Swing* (painting).

E. M. Falconet, equestrian monument to Peter the Great, St. Petersburg (–1779).

Denis Diderot, *Essai sur la Peinture.*

T **Music**

J. Haydn, *Great Mass with Organ* (No. 4 in E flat).

U **Literature**

Heinrich Gerstenberg, *Letters on the Curiosities of Literature* (–1770), formulates the principles of *Sturm und Drang.*

Oliver Goldsmith, *The Vicar of Wakefield.*

C. M. Wieland, *The Story of Agathon.*

V **The Press**

W **Drama and Entertainment**

X **Sport**

Y **Statistics**

Z **Births and Deaths.**

Feb. 17th T. R. Malthus b. (–1834).

Mar. 9th William Cobbett b. (–1835).

Apr. 22nd Mme de Staël b. (–1817).

Sep. 26th John Dalton b. (–1844).

Dec. 29th Charles Macintosh b. (–1843).

1767 Taxation in American colonies

A **Jan:** Robert Clive leaves India, where chaos soon prevails, until the arrival of Warren Hastings in 1772.

B **Feb:** 29th, reduction of land tax in Britain from 4s. to 3s. in £ is forced on the government by back-benchers representing the landed interest.

C **Mar:** 1st, Charles III expels the Jesuits from Spain, later in year the Order is expelled from Parma and the Two Sicilies;
Chatham's illness prevents his attending Parliament until *Jan.* 1769.

D **Apr:** revised Russo-Prussian alliance, by which Frederick the Great undertakes to support the Polish Opposition factions, to enter Poland if Austria should invade it and to support Russia in the event of a war with Turkey.

E **May:**

F **Jun:** Townshend introduces taxes on imports of tea, glass, paper and dyestuffs in American colonies to provide revenue for colonial administration.

G **Jul:**

H **Aug:** Burmese invade Siam.

J **Sep:** at public meeting in Boston a non-importation agreement is framed in protest at the new taxes;
6th, Lord North becomes Chancellor of Exchequer on Townshend's death.

K **Oct:**

L **Nov:** Polish Diet meets, under Russian sway.

M **Dec:**

N Russian agents agitate in Montenegro and Bosnia against Turkish rule.

O **Politics, Economics, Law and Education**
James Steuart, *An Inquiry into the Principles of Political Œconomy.*

P **Science, Technology, Discovery, etc.**
P. S. Pallas, *Elenchus Zoophytorum.*
Nautical Almanac first issued, edited by Nevil Maskelyne, astronomer royal.
Joseph Priestley, *History of Electricity.*

Q **Scholarship**
C. Heyne, edits Vergil's *Opera.*
J. J. Winckelmann, *Monumenti antichi inediti* (–1768).

R **Philosophy and Religion**
Moses Mendelssohn, *Phaedon.*
J. F. Marmontel censured by Archbishop of Paris and the Sorbonne for dealing with religious toleration in his novel *Bélisaire.*

S **Art, Sculpture, Fine Arts and Architecture**
Allan Ramsay is appointed portrait painter to George III.
Christie's, London, founded.

T **Music**
C. W. Gluck, *Alceste* (opera).
J.-J. Rousseau, *Dictionnaire de Musique.*

U **Literature**
Michael Bruce, *Elegy Written in Spring.*
J. K. Lavater, *Swiss Songs.*
H. Gerstenberg, *Ariadne auf Naxos.*
L. Sterne completes *Tristram Shandy.*

V **The Press**

W **Drama and Entertainment**
O. Goldsmith, *The Good Natur'd Man.*
G. E. Lessing, *Minna of Barnhelm* and *Hamburgische Dramaturgie* (–1768).

X **Sport**

Y **Statistics**

Z **Births and Deaths**
Mar. 15th Andrew Jackson b. (–1845).
July 11th John Quincy Adams b. (–1848).
Sept. 8th August Schlegel b. (–1845).
Oct. 25th Benjamin Constant b. (–1830).

1768 Turkey declares war on Russia

A **Jan:** 20th, a Secretary of State for the Colonies is first appointed in Britain.

B **Feb:**

C **Mar:** 28th, John Wilkes is elected M.P. for Middlesex.

D **Apr:**

E **May:** 10th, riots in Westminster in favour of Wilkes on assembling of Parliament (and in *June* when he is sentenced for seditious libel).

F **Jun:**

G **Jul:** Massachusetts Assembly is dissolved for refusing to assist collection of taxes;
France purchases Corsica from Genoa.

H **Aug:** Confederation founded in Poland at Bar, aided by France, to counter Russian designs; attempts are made by the Confederates to kidnap King Stanislas and Civil War breaks out.

J **Sep:** Boston citizens refuse to quarter troops sent to quell riot.

K **Oct:** 19th, Shelburne resigns from Grafton's ministry in Britain;
Austria finally renounces all claims to Silesia;
Turkey, instigated by France, declares war on Russia in defence of Polish liberties.

L **Nov:** 7th, Frederick the Great of Prussia completes Political Testament.

M **Dec:** 3rd, Prince von Kaunitz, Austrian Chancellor, suggests to Joseph II of Austria the practicability of partitioning Poland.

N Pope Clement XIII confiscates Parma in retaliation for the expulsion of the Jesuits, whereupon the King of Naples invades the Papal States and France seizes Avignon.
The Gurkhas conquer Nepal.

O Politics, Economics, Law and Education
Joseph Priestley, *Essay on the First Principles of Government.*

P Science, Technology, Discovery, etc.
P. S. Pallas travels through Russia to the Chinese frontier to observe (1769) the transit of Venus.
James Cook sails (*May* 25th) on first voyage of discovery, on which he explores the Society Islands and charts the coasts of New Zealand and W. Australia (returns *June* 1771).

Q Scholarship
J. A. Ernesti, *Archaeologia litteraria.*

R Philosophy and Religion
Abraham Booth, *Reign of Grace.*
Emanuel Swedenborg, *Delititiae Sapientiae.*

S Art, Sculpture, Fine Arts and Architecture
The Royal Academy is founded, with Joshua Reynolds as president, who begins delivering fifteen discourses on art (–1790).
Augustin Pajou undertakes decorative sculpture on Opera House, Versailles.

T Music
W. A. Mozart, *Bastien and Bastienne* (opera).

U Literature
James Boswell, *Account of Corsica, Journal of a Tour of that Island and Memoir of Pascal Paoli.*
Thomas Gray, *Poems.*
L. Sterne, *A Sentimental Journey.*
Jean de Saint-Lambert, *Les Saisons.*

V The Press
'Junius' first appears in *The Public Advertiser* (Oct.).

W Drama and Entertainment
M. J. Sedaine, *La Gageure Imprévue.*

X Sport

Y Statistics

Z Births and Deaths
Mar. 18th Laurence Sterne d. (55).
Mar. 22nd Bryan Donkin b. (–1855).
Sept. 4th. François Chateaubriand b. (–1848).

1769 Britain retains tax on tea in America

A **Jan**: John Wilkes is elected an alderman of London.
The Letters of Junius begin attacks on George III, Grafton, Lord Chief Justice Mansfield and other ministers.
The Bourbons demand the dissolution of the Jesuits.

B **Feb**: 2nd, death of Pope Clement XIII;
4th, Wilkes is expelled from Parliament and, though thrice re-elected for Middlesex, the Commons declare his opponent to be the successful candidate (*Apr.* 15th).
Chatham returns to Lords.
Austria occupies Lemberg and the Zips region of Poland.

C **Mar**:

D **Apr**: 22nd, Mme du Barry becomes official mistress of Louis XV.

E **May**: 1st, Privy Council decides to retain the tea duty in American colonies after weeks of argument;
17th, the Virginia Assembly is dissolved after protesting about the practice of removing colonial treason trials to Westminster.
19th, after three-month struggle between pro and anti Jesuit factions in the College of Cardinals, the latter's candidate, Lorenzo Ganganelli, is elected Pope Clement XIV.

F **Jun**: Hyder Ali of Mysore compels British at Madras to sign treaty of mutual assistance.

G **Jul**:

H **Aug**: France expels Pasquale Paoli, the Corsican patriot, from the island;
Frederick II and Joseph II meet in Neisse to discuss partition of Poland.

J **Sep**: Russian troops occupy Moldavia.

K **Oct**: Prusso-Russian alliance is renewed until 1780; Joseph II guaranteeing Frederick II the reversion of Ansbach and Bayreuth, while Prussia guarantees to uphold the Swedish constitution.

L **Nov**: Russian troops occupy Bucharest.

M **Dec**: Russia signs treaty with Denmark to prevent the overthrow of the Swedish constitution.

N Serious famine in Bengal (–1770).
Burma acknowledges suzerainty of China.

O **Politics, Economics, Law and Education**

E. Burke, *Observations on a late Publication on the Present State of the Nation.*

Richard Price's observations on population and the expectancy of life draw attention to inadequate calculations of British insurance and benefit societies.

The first crêche is opened, at Steintal, Alsace.

P **Science, Technology, Discovery, etc.**

Richard Arkwright's spinning machine.

Joseph Black's condenser.

Nicolas Cugnot's steam road carriage.

Josiah Wedgwood opens 'Etruria' pottery works, near Burslem.

First lightning conductors on high buildings.

Q **Scholarship**

E. Forcellini, *Totius Latinitatis Lexicon.*

W. Robertson, *History of Charles V.*

Museum Pio-Clementiano, Rome, opened.

R **Philosophy and Religion**

Charles Bonnet, *Palingénésie philosophique* (–1770).

S **Art, Sculpture, Fine Arts and Architecture**

Robert Adam and his brothers, The Adelphi, London.

T **Music**

C. P. E. Bach, *Passion Cantata.*

U **Literature**

J. G. Herder, *Kritische Wälder.*

G. E. Lessing, *Wie die Alten den Tod gebildet.*

V **The Press**

The Morning Chronicle, London, issued.

W **Drama and Entertainment**

J. F. Ducis produces his adaptation of Shakespeare's *Hamlet* in Paris.

X **Sport**

Y **Statistics**

Z **Births and Deaths**

Mar. 29th Nicholas Jean Soult b. (–1851).

May 1st Arthur Wellesley, later Duke of Wellington, b. (–1852).

May 4th Thomas Lawrence b. (–1830).

June 18th Robert Stewart, later Viscount Castlereagh b. (–1822).

Aug. 15th Napoleon b. (–1821).

Aug. 23rd G. L. P. C. Cuvier b. (–1832).

Sept. 14th Alexander von Humboldt b. (–1859).

— Giovanni Tiepolo d. (77).

1770 North becomes British prime minister—Struensee's government in Denmark

A **Jan:** 28th, North becomes prime minister on Grafton's resignation, forming the ministry of 'The King's Friends'.

B **Feb:**

C **Mar:** 3rd, brawl between civilians and troops in Boston (annually celebrated as Boston Massacre).

D **Apr:** British Parliament repeals duties on paper, glass and dyestuffs in American colonies, but retains tea duty.

E **May:** 16th, Dauphin of France marries Marie Antoinette, daughter of the Empress Maria Theresa of Austria.

F **Jun:** 13th, the printers and publishers of *The Letters of Junius* are tried for seditious libel.

G **Jul:** 5th (–6th), Russian fleet, officered by British sailors, defeats Turkish navy at Tchesme.

H **Aug:** duc de Choiseul's intervention prevents war between Spain and Britain over possession of Falkland Isles.

J **Sep:** Joseph II of Austria and Frederick II of Prussia meet at Neustadt to discuss plans for halting Russia's expansion;
13th, J. F. Struensee, favourite of Queen Caroline Matilda, secures fall of Count Bernstorff in Denmark.

K **Oct:**

L **Nov:**

M **Dec:** 5th, Struensee abolishes the Council in Denmark and becomes supreme; begins far-reaching programme of reforms, introducing freedom of worship and of press;
24th, Choiseul falls from power in France through intrigues of Mme du Barry and of duc D'Aiguillon, who succeeds him as minister of foreign affairs, aided by René Maupeou.

N Marathas bring Delhi under their sway.

O **Politics, Economics, Law and Education**

E. Burke, *Thoughts on the Cause of the Present Discontents.*
Ferdinando Galiani, in *Dialogues sur le Commerce des Blés*, attacks the Physiocrats.
Elementary education in the Austrian Empire is organised.

P **Science, Technology, Discovery, etc.**

John Hill introduces method of obtaining specimens for microscopic study.
Leonhard Euler, *Introduction to Algebra.*
Jesse Ramsden's screw-cutting lathe.
James Cook discovers Botany Bay (*Apr.* 28th).

Q **Scholarship**

R **Philosophy and Religion**

James Beattie, *Essay on the Nature and Immutability of Truth in opposition to Sophistry and Scepticism.*
Immanuel Kant, *De mundi sensibilis et intelligibilis forma et principiis.*
Paul Holbach, *Système de la Nature*, attacking Christianity, is refuted by Voltaire and by Frederick the Great.

S **Art, Sculpture, Fine Arts and Architecture**

T. Gainsborough, *The Blue Boy* (painting).

T **Music**

Handel's *Messiah* is first performed in New York.

U **Literature**

O. Goldsmith, *The Deserted Village.*
J. F. Marmontel, *Sylvain.*

V **The Press**

The Massachusetts Spy is issued.

W **Drama and Entertainment**

Johannes Ewald, *Rolf Krage*, the first Danish tragedy.

X **Sport**

Y **Statistics**

Z **Births and Deaths**

Mar. 11th William Huskisson b. (–1830).
Apr. 7th William Wordsworth b. (–1850).
Apr. 11th George Canning b. (–1827).
May 30th François Boucher d. (67).
Aug. 25th Thomas Chatterton d. (18).
Aug. 27th Georg Hegel b. (–1831).
Nov. 19th Bertil Thorwaldsen b. (–1857).
Dec. 17th Beethoven b. (–1827).

1771 Russia takes Crimea

A **Jan**: 22nd, Spain agrees to cede the Falkland Isles to Britain, but makes no reparation for insult to British flag;
Prince Henry of Prussia visits Russia and proposes partition of Poland;
Maupeou overthrows the French Parlements, which he replaces by a simplified system of courts.

B **Feb**:

C **Mar**: 27th, Brass Crosby is taken into custody for breach of privilege over printing Parliamentary debates, the last attempt to prevent reporting of debates.

D **Apr**:

E **May**:

F **Jun**: Russia completes conquest of the Crimea.

G **Jul**: 6th, Austria and Turkey sign treaty with intention of forcing Russia to restore her conquests.

H **Aug**:

J **Sep**:

K **Oct**:

L **Nov**:

M **Dec**

N

O **Politics, Economics, Law and Education**
Richard Price, *Appeal to the Public on the subject of the National Debt.*
Abolition of serfdom in Savoy.

P **Science, Technology, Discovery, etc.**
Luigi Galvani discovers electric nature of nervous impulse.
J. A. Deluc establishes rules for measuring heights by the barometer.
The Smeatonian Club, a society of engineers, is founded in Britain.

Q **Scholarship**
Jacopo Facciolati, aided by Egidio Forcellini, *Totius Latinitatis Lexicon.*
A. H. Anquetil Duperron translates *The Zenda Avesta.*
W. Robertson, *History of America.*
Encyclopædia Britannica, first edition.

R **Philosophy and Religion**
J. S. Semler, *Studies in the Free Investigation of the Canon* (–1775).
J. W. Fletcher publishes under John Wesley's stimulus *Five Checks to Antinomianism.*
Wesley disowns justification by works.
John Jebb and other divines become Unitarians on the failure of a Parliamentary petition to free English clergy from subscription to the 39 Articles.

S **Art, Sculpture, Fine Arts and Architecture**
Benjamin West, *The Death of Wolfe* (painting).
J. A. Houdon, bust of Diderot.
Horace Walpole completes *Anecdotes of Painting.*

T **Music**
J. Haydn, the 'Sun' quartets (Nos. 31–6).
N. Piccini, *Antigone* (opera).

U **Literature**
Matthias Claudius publishes essays and poems in *The Wandsbeck Messenger* (–1775).
F. Klopstock, *Odes.*
T. Smollett, *The Expedition of Humphry Clinker.*
C. M. Wieland, *Der neue Amadis.*

V **The Press**

W **Drama and Entertainment**

X **Sport**

Y **Statistics**

Z **Births and Deaths**
Apr. 13th Richard Trevithick b. (–1833).
May 14th Robert Owen b. (–1858).
June 3rd Sydney Smith b. (–1845).
July 7th Thomas Gray d. (55).
Aug. 15th Walter Scott b. (–1832).
Sept. 17th Tobias Smollet d. (51).

1772 First Partition of Poland

A **Jan:** 17th, Ove Guldberg secures arrest of Struensee in Denmark.

B **Feb:** 28th, Boston assembly threatens secession from Britain unless rights of colonies are maintained.

C **Mar:** 24th, following the marriages to commoners of the Dukes of Cumberland and Gloucester, Parliament places all descendants of George II under terms of Royal Marriage Act;
30th, Robert Clive defends his administration of Bengal in the Commons.

D **Apr:** 13th, Warren Hastings appointed governor of Bengal (–1785).

E **May:**

F **Jun:** 10th, mob in Rhode Island burns revenue cutter *Gaspée*.

G **Jul:** Britain refuses to allow French fleet to enter Baltic, to support Gustavus III against his Swedish subjects.

H **Aug:** 5th, Frederick the Great, fearing Austria's concern at Russian conquests in Turkey will lead to a general war, engineers First Partition of Poland, Prussia taking West Poland (except Danzig) and Ermland, Austria taking East Galicia and Lodomerica and Russia taking lands east of Dvina and Dnieper;
19th, Gustavus III re-establishes full authority of monarchy in Sweden.

J **Sep:**

K **Oct:**

L **Nov:** 2nd (*–Jan.* 1773), Committees of Correspondence for action against British are formed in Massachusetts under Samuel Adams.

M **Dec:**

N

O **Politics, Economics, Law and Education**

Comte de Mirabeau, *Essai sur le Despotisme.*

Lord Mansfield's decision that a slave is free on landing in England (Somerset's Case).

F. S. Sullivan, *Lectures on the Feudal and English Laws.*

P **Science, Technology, Discovery, etc.**

Daniel Rutherford discovers nitrogen.

Henry Cavendish, *Attempts to Explain some of the Phenomena of Electricity.*

J. Priestley discovers that plants give off oxygen.

L. Euler expounds the principles of mechanics, optics, acoustics and astronomy in *Lettres à une princesse d'Allemagne.*

Jean Romé de Lisle, *Essai de Cristallographie.*

Thomas Coke begins reforms in animal husbandry at Holkham, Norfolk.

James Bruce explores Abyssinia and traces the Blue Nile to its confluence with the White Nile.

The Bromberg Canal, linking Rivers Oder and Vistula, begun (–1775).

First carriage-traffic on the Brenner Pass.

Q **Scholarship**

J. G. Herder's *On the Origins of Speech* begins the study of comparative philology.

R **Philosophy and Religion**

Albrecht von Haller, *Chief Truths of Revelation.*

S **Art, Sculpture, Fine Arts and Architecture**

T **Music**

J. Haydn, 'Farewell' Symphony (No. 45 in F sharp minor).

First German performance of Handel's *Messiah.*

U **Literature**

P. A. F. Choderlos de Laclos, *Les Liaisons Dangereuses.*

Hainbund, a society of young, patriotic poets, is formed at Göttingen.

V **The Press**

The Morning Post, London, issued (*Nov.* 2nd.).

W **Drama and Entertainment**

G. Bessenyei, *Tragedy of Agis.*

Lessing, *Emilia Galotti.*

X **Sport**

Y **Statistics**

British Textile Trade:

raw cotton imports	5·3 mill. lb.
exported linens	11·6 mill. yds.
exported silks	91,000 lb.

Z **Births and Deaths**

Mar. 29th Emanuel Swedenborg d. (84).

Apr. 11th Manuel Quintana b. (–1857).

Apr. 19th David Ricardo b. (–1823).

Sept. 30th James Brindley d. (56).

Oct. 21st S. T. Coleridge b. (–1834).

1773 Boston Tea Party

A **Jan:**

B **Feb:** Renewal of France's alliance with Sweden.

C **Mar:** 12th, Virginia House of Burgesses appoints a Provincial Committee of Correspondence for mutual action against British, and other colonies follow this lead.

D **Apr:**

E **May:** British East India Company Regulating Act provides for a governor-general and a council in India and officers are forbidden to trade for themselves.

F **Jun:**

G **Jul:** 21st, Pope Clement XIV by the bull *Dominus ac Redemptor* dissolves the Jesuits.

H **Aug:**

J **Sep:** Warren Hastings, first governor-general of India, makes alliance with the state of Oudh for campaign against the Mahrathas.

K **Oct:** 16th, Denmark cedes the duchy of Oldenburg to Russia.
Pugachoff, a pretender, leads revolt of Cossacks in S.E. Russia, which checks Russian advance in Turkey.

L **Nov:**

M **Dec:** 16th, Boston Tea Party.
France restores Avignon to Papacy.

N Spanish ordinance that an industrial occupation is not prejudicial to rank or prestige.

O **Politics, Economics, Law and Education**
John Erskine, *Institutes of the Law of Scotland.*

P **Science, Technology, Discovery, etc.**
T. F. Pritchard's cast-iron bridge at Ironbridge, near Coalbrookdale, Shropshire (–1779).
Veterinary and Agricultural College, Copenhagen, founded.

Q **Scholarship**
James, Lord Monboddo, *Origin and Progress of Language* (–1792).
Philadelphia Museum, Pennsylvania, founded.

R **Philosophy and Religion**

S **Art, Sculpture, Fine Arts and Architecture**
Joshua Reynolds, *The Graces Decorating Hymen* (painting).

T **Music**
Charles Burney, *The Present State of Music in Germany, the Netherlands and the United Provinces.*

U **Literature**
G. A. Bürger, *Leonore.*
A. von Haller, *Alfred.*
J. G. Herder, *Von deutscher Art und Kunst.*
G. F. Klopstock, *Messiah.*

V **The Press**
Der Deutsche Mercur (–1810), edited by C. M. Wieland.

W **Drama and Entertainment**
J. W. Goethe, *Goetz von Berlichingen.*
O. Goldsmith, *She Stoops to Conquer.*
Swedish national theatre is established in Stockholm.

X **Sport**

Y **Statistics**

Z **Births and Deaths**
Mar. 24th Philip Stanhope, Earl of Chesterfield d. (78).
May 9th Sismondi b. (–1842).
May 15th Clemens Prince Metternich b. (–1859).
Oct. 6th Louis Philippe b. (–1850).
Nov. 22nd Robert Clive d. (48).

1774 Philadelphia Congress of American Colonies

A **Jan:** accession of Abdul Hamid I as Sultan of Turkey.

B **Feb:** petition from Massachusetts asking for removal of governor-general Thomas Hutchinson is refused by British House of Commons.

C **Mar:** 28th, British Parliament passes Coercive Acts against Massachusetts, which include act closing port of Boston from *June* 1st.

D **Apr:** Quebec Act, establishing Roman Catholicism and Roman law in Canada, to secure Canada's loyalty to Britain;
Hastings seizes Rohilkhand, N.W. India, from Rohilla tribe.

E **May:** 10th, accession of Louis XVI of France, who appoints Jean Maurepas premier and Vergennes foreign secretary;
27th, Virginia House of Burgesses adopt resolution for calling a continental congress.

F **Jun:**

G **Jul:** Russians rout Turks at battle of Shumla and
21st, the peace of Kutchuk-Kainardji is signed, by which Turkey cedes to Russia the Crimea and mouth of River Dnieper, grants her free navigation for trade in Turkish waters and promises to protect Christians in Constantinople.

H **Aug:** 12th, Russia signs secret alliance with Denmark;
Louis XVI recalls the Parlements and appoints Turgot controller-general of France.

J **Sep:** 5th (–*Oct.* 26th), first Continental Congress of the thirteen American Colonies meets at Philadelphia with representatives from each colony except Georgia;
9th, Suffolk Convention in America resolves that the Coercive legislation of *Mar.* 28th be disregarded.
13th, Turgot re-introduces free trade in corn in France (suspended since 1766, but re-abolished 1776);
14th, the pretender Pugachoff is delivered by Cossacks to the Russian government, following a decisive defeat (executed *Jan.* 1775);
Austria occupies Bukovina.

K **Oct:**

L **Nov:** John Wilkes becomes lord mayor of London.

M **Dec:** 1st, by resolution of the Continental Congress non-importation of British goods comes into force in American colonies.

N With the insanity of Joseph I of Portugal, Pombal, the favourite of the Regent Queen Maria Anna, becomes all-powerful.
Rebellion in Shantung organised by the White Lotus Society.
Expulsion of the Jesuits from Poland.

O Politics, Economics, Law and Education

E. Burke, *On American Taxation.*
John Campbell, *A Political Survey of Great Britain.*
John Cartwright, *American Independence, the Glory and Interest of Great Britain.*
Charles, Earl of Stanhope, advocates Parliamentary Reform in pamphlets.
Arthur Young, *Political Arithmetic.*

P Science, Technology, Discovery, etc.

J. E. Bode founds *Astronomisches Jahrbuch*, Berlin.
J. Priestley discovers oxygen.
K. W. Scheele discovers chlorine and baryta.
T. Bergman's treatise on carbon dioxide and carbonic acid.
A. Lavoisier, *Opuscules physiques et chimiques.*
William Cullen, *First Lines of the Practice of Physics.*
William Hunter, *The Anatomy of the Gravid Uterus.*
N. Desmarest's essay on extinct volcanoes.
John Wilkinson builds boring mill which facilitates the manufacture of cylinders for steam engines.

Q Scholarship

O. Goldsmith, *The History of the Earth and Animated Nature.*

R Philosophy and Religion

Ann Lee of Manchester settles in New York City with a band of 'Shakers' to begin a spiritualists' revival.

S Art, Sculpture, Fine Arts and Architecture

T Music

C. W. Gluck, *Iphigenia in Aulis* (opera).

U Literature

Lord Chesterfield, *Letters to his Son.*
J. W. Goethe, *Clavigo* and *Sorrows of Werther.*
Thomas Warton, *History of English Poetry* (–1781).
C. M. Wieland, *Aberites.*

V The Press

W Drama and Entertainment

X Sport

Y Statistics

Z Births and Deaths

Mar. 16th Matthew Flinders b. (–1814).
Apr. 4th Oliver Goldsmith d. (46).
Aug. 12th Robert Southey b. (–1843).

1775 Beginning of War of American Independence

A **Jan:**

B **Feb:** 1st, Chatham introduces bill to conciliate American colonists, which is rejected, and repressive legislation follows;
Peasants in Bohemia revolt against servitude.

C **Mar:** 19th, Prusso-Polish commercial treaty.
Portuguese fleet is repulsed in attack on Monte Video.

D **Apr:** 19th, War of American Independence opens with defeat of British under Thomas Gage at Lexington and Concord.

E **May:** 7th, Turkey formally cedes Bukovina to Austria;
10th, Fort Ticonderoga, New York, and
12th, Crown Point fall to Americans;
10th, Second Continental Congress meets at Philadelphia;
31st, troops before Boston are adopted as the Continental Army.

F **Jun:** 15th, George Washington is appointed Commander-in-Chief of American forces (takes up command at Cambridge, Mass., *July* 3rd);
17th, British victory at Bunker Hill.

G **Jul:** 1st, failure of Spanish expedition to reduce pirate stronghold of Algiers leads to fall of d'Aranda;
6th, declaration of Philadelphia Congress under John Hancock sets out war aims;
19th, Chrétien Malesherbes appointed French minister of interior.

H **Aug:**

J **Sep:**

K **Oct:**

L **Nov:** 9th, Grafton resigns from North's ministry, disliking the war, and is succeeded as lord privy seal by Dartmouth, while Lord George Germain becomes colonial secretary.

M **Dec:** 31st, failure of Benedict Arnold's attack on Quebec.

N Nuncomar, who had accused Hastings of accepting bribes, is hanged at Calcutta.
Provincial administration in Russia is reformed.

Z **Births and Deaths**
Jan. 22nd André Ampère b. (–1836).
Jan. 30th W. S. Landor b. (–1864).
Feb. 10th Charles Lamb b. (–1834).
Apr. 23rd J. M. W. Turner b. (–1851).
Aug. 6th Daniel O'Connell b. (–1847).
Dec. 16th Jane Austen b. (–1817).

O **Politics, Economics, Law and Education**

E. Burke, *Speech on Conciliation with America.*
Thomas Spence advocates system of land nationalisation in England.
Justus Moser's *Patriotic Phantasies* plead for a national, organic state in Germany.
The study of Danish language and literature supplants German in Danish schools.
Pedro Campomanes, *Discourse on Popular Education.*

P **Science, Technology, Discovery, etc.**

K. W. Scheele, *Air and Fire.*
J. C. Fabricius classifies insects in *Systema Entomologiae.*
A. G. Werner inaugurates the modern study of geology.
James Watt perfects the invention of the steam engine at Matthew Boulton's Birmingham works.
James Cook returns to England (*July* 25th) after second voyage in South Seas, during which he discovered the Sandwich Islands and conquered scurvy.
Richard Chandler, *Travels in Asia Minor.*

Q **Scholarship**

J. J. Griesbach's critical edition of Greek New Testament.

R **Philosophy and Religion**

Louis St. Martin, *Des Erreurs et de la Verité.*

S **Art, Sculpture, Fine Arts and Architecture**

J. B. S. Chardin, self-portrait.
Ralph Earl, *Roger Sherman* (portrait).
Joshua Reynolds, *Miss Bowles* (portrait).
George Romney establishes himself in London as a portrait painter.
J. A. Houdon, busts of Turgot and Gluck.
Denis Diderot's accounts of the Salon, Paris, begin modern art criticism.
John Flaxman's neo-classical designs for friezes and medallion portraits for Josiah Wedgwood's pottery.

T **Music**

C. P. E. Bach, *The Israelites in the Wilderness* (oratorio).

U **Literature**

J. W. Goethe settles at Weimar and obtains a post at court for Herder.
S. Johnson, *A Journey to the Western Islands of Scotland.*

V **The Press**

W **Drama and Entertainment**

Vittorio Alfieri's first play, *Cleopatra*, produced in Turin.
P. A. C. Beaumarchais' *Barber of Seville* produced in Paris after two years' prohibition.
J. J. Eschenburg's German translation of Shakespeare's plays (–1781).
R. B. Sheridan, *The Rivals.*
Sarah Siddons's début at Drury Lane Theatre.

X **Sport**

Y **Statistics**

(*continued opposite*)

1776 American Declaration of Independence

A **Jan:** 6th, abolition of the *Corvée* (forced labour for repair of roads) in France (restored in *Aug.*).

B **Feb:** 5th, abolition of the *Jurandes*, or privileged corporations, by Turgot;
British Parliament passes Prohibitory Act placing colonies' external trade under interdict.

C **Mar:** 4th, Washington occupies Heights of Dorchester;
14th, Grafton unsuccessfully moves for suspension of Prohibitory Act in American Colonies in hope of peace;
15th, Congress resolves that the authority of the British Crown be suppressed;
17th, Washington forces British under William Howe to evacuate Boston;
American troops are driven from Canada.

D **Apr:** By treaty of Copenhagen with Denmark Russia cedes her claims to Holstein.

E **May:** 2nd, American mission to Paris obtains French loan of 1 mill. livres.
12th, Malesherbes resigns as French minister of the interior;
—, Turgot is dismissed by Louis XVI for attempting to make further financial reforms;
15th, Virginia convention instructs Richard Lee and other delegates to Congress to propose independence.

F **Jun:** 7th, Lee frames proposal that the United Colonies are of right independent states;
12th, Virginia publishes its Bill of Rights.

G **Jul:** 4th, American Declaration of Independence, drafted by Thomas Jefferson with revisions by Benjamin Franklin and John Adams, is carried by Congress;

H **Aug:** Britain recruits Hessian mercenaries for American war.

J **Sep:** free trade in corn (re-introduced 1774) abolished in France;
15th, Howe takes New York.

K **Oct:** 11th (and 13th), Benedict Arnold is defeated in engagements on Lake Champlain;
Congress retires to Baltimore;
Jacques Necker is appointed finance minister in France;
The Rockingham Whigs cease to attend Parliament in protest at the continuation of the American War.

L **Nov:** 20th, Fort Lee surrenders to Britain;
28th, Washington retreats across New Jersey to Pennsylvania.

M **Dec:** Rhode Island occupied;
26th, Washington defeats Hessians at battle of Trenton.

N Unified administration for Portuguese S. American colonies under viceroyalty of River Plate, with capital in Rio de Janeiro.
Potemkin, favourite of Catherine II, organises Russian Black Sea fleet and begins construction of Sebastopol harbour.

O **Politics, Economics, Law and Education**

Jeremy Bentham, *A Fragment on Government.*
John Cartwright's *Take Your Choice* advocates Parliamentary Reform.
T. Paine, *Common-Sense* (pamphlet).
Richard Price, *Observations on Civil Liberty and the Justice and Policy of the War with America.*
Adam Smith, *An Inquiry into the Nature and Causes of the Wealth of Nations.*
U.S. Congress institutes a national lottery.

P **Science, Technology, Discovery, etc.**

The machine-plane is invented.
James Cook's third voyage of discovery in the Pacific (-1779).

Q **Scholarship**

Edward Gibbon, *Decline and Fall of the Roman Empire* (-1788).
B. Kennicott, *Vetus Testamentum hebraicum cum variis lectionibus.*

R **Philosophy and Religion**

Soame Jenyns, *View of the Internal Evidence of the Christian Religion.*
The sect of Illuminati is formed in Bavaria (suppressed in 1786).
Denis Diderot's *Encyclopédie* completed by D'Alembert.

S **Art, Sculpture, Fine Arts and Architecture**

J. H. Fragonard, *The Washerwoman* (painting).
William Chambers begins building the new Somerset House, London.

T **Music**

Charles Burney, *History of Music* (-1789).
John Hawkins, *The General History of the Science and Practice of Music.*
Lord Sandwich founds the Concert of Antient Music, London.

U **Literature**

V **The Press**

W **Drama and Entertainment**

V. Alfieri, *Antigone.*
F. M. von Klinger, *Sturm und Drang.*
J. M. R. Lenz, *Die Soldaten.*

X **Sport**

Col. St. Leger establishes the St. Leger at Doncaster Races.

Y **Statistics**

Z **Births and Deaths**

Jan. 24th E. T. A. Hoffmann b. (-1822).
June 11th John Constable b. (-1837).
Aug. 25th David Hume d. (65).
Aug. 27th B. Niebuhr b. (-1831).

1777 Burgoyne capitulates at Saratoga

A **Jan:** 3rd, Washington defeats British at Princeton, New Jersey.

B **Feb:** 24th, accession of Maria I of Portugal leads to Pombal's dismissal.

C **Mar:**

D **Apr:** Marquis de La Fayette's French volunteers arrive in America.

E **May:**

F **Jun:**

G **Jul:**

H **Aug:** 16th, Americans defeat British force at Bennington, Vermont.

J **Sep:** 11th, William Howe defeats Americans under Nathaniel Greene at Brandywine, Pennsylvania;
19th, General Burgoyne suffers heavy casualties at Bemis Heights, New York;
27th, Howe occupies Philadelphia.

K **Oct:** 4th, Washington is defeated at Germantown, Pennsylvania;
7th, Burgoyne loses second battle of Bemis Heights and
17th, capitulates to Americans under Horatio Gates at Saratoga, New York.

L **Nov:** 15th, Congress adopts Confederation Articles of perpetual union of United States of America, which are sent to states for ratification (completed 1781) as first U.S. constitution;
20th, British secure control of Delaware.

M **Dec:** suspension of Habeas Corpus act in England.
30th, on death of Maximilian III Bavaria passes to Charles Theodore, Elector Palatine, but Joseph II of Austria lays claim to Lower Bavaria.

N The Swiss Cantons fearing Austrian aggression sign alliance with France.
Spain and Portugal settle disputes arising from S. American Colonies.

O **Politics, Economics, Law and Education**

V. Alfieri, *La Tirannide.*

E. Burke, *A Letter to the Sheriffs of Bristol,* on Parliamentary representation, and *Address to the King.*

James Anderson, *Nature of the Corn Laws.*

John Howard, *The State of the Prisons of England and Wales.*

A co-operative workshop for tailors is formed at Birmingham to employ men on strike.

P **Science, Technology, Discovery, etc.**

K. W. Scheele prepares sulphuretted hydrogen (hydrogen sulphide).

K. F. Wenzel's work on atomic theory.

C. A. Coulomb invents the torsion balance.

David Bushnell invents the torpedo.

The Botanical Magazine founded.

Q **Scholarship**

R **Philosophy and Religion**

Joseph Priestley, *Disquisition relating to matter and spirit.*

Hugh Blair, *Sermons.*

Lessing in *Ernst und Falk* pleads for broad understanding in questions of religion and politics.

S **Art, Sculpture, Fine Arts and Architecture**

T. Gainsborough, *The Watering-Place* (painting).

J. B. Greuze, *La Cruche Cassée* (painting).

T **Music**

J. Haydn, 'La Roxolane' Symphony (No. 63 in C).

C. W. von Gluck, *Armide* (opera).

U **Literature**

V **The Press**

W **Drama and Entertainment**

X **Sport**

Y **Statistics**

Z **Births and Deaths**

Apr. 30th Karl Gauss b. (–1855).

July 9th Henry Hallam b. (–1859).

1778 France supports American colonies—Beginning of War of Bavarian Succession

A **Jan:** 3rd, Palatinate recognises Austrian claim to Lower Bavaria.

B **Feb:** 6th, France and American Colonists sign offensive and defensive alliance and also a commercial treaty;
—, Britain declares war on France;
17th, North presents to Parliament his plan for conciliating the colonies.

C **Mar:**

D **Apr:** 5th, British commissioners are appointed to negotiate with Congress and in the meantime to suspend the obnoxious laws;
7th, Chatham delivers his last speech against continuing hostilities (he dies *May* 11th).

E **May:** 28th, Sir George Savile's act modifies British penal laws against Roman Catholics, while a further act relieves Protestant Dissenting ministers from making a declaration of faith.

F **Jun:** 17th, U.S. Congress rejects British peace offer;
18th, Henry Clinton evacuates British troops from Philadelphia;
28th, Washington defeats British at Monmouth, New Jersey.

G **Jul:** 3rd, Prussia declares war on Austria, with whom Saxony is allied, in the war of Bavarian Succession (lasting with minor skirmishes—*May* 1779);
3rd (-4th), Wyoming massacre by Indians in Pennsylvania;
8th, Comte d'Estaing's French fleet arrives off Delaware.

H **Aug:** 29th, Americans led by John Sullivan abandon siege of Newport, Rhode Island;
British force captures Savannah, Georgia.

J **Sep:** 4th, the States of Holland sign treaty of amity and commerce with American Colonies;
French seize Dominica, as a naval base.

K **Oct:**

L **Nov:** 11th, William Butler leads force of Indians to massacre the villagers of Cherry Valley in New York.
British force under Admiral Samuel Barrington takes St. Lucia, W. Indies, from the French.

M **Dec:**

N Warren Hastings takes Chandernagore, Bengal, and Hector Munro takes Pondichery from the French in India.
Jefferson champions the rights of slaves.
Portugal cedes Fernando Po and Annobon Islands, Gulf of Guinea, to Spain.

O **Politics, Economics, Law and Education**

P **Science, Technology, Discovery, etc.**

Benjamin Thompson experiments on heat by friction and with the explosive force of gunpowder.
G. L. L. Buffon, *Époques de la nature.*
J. A. Deluc, *Lettres physiques et morales sur les montagnes.*
Friedrich Mesmer first practises 'mesmerism' in Paris.
Joseph Bramah's improved water closet.
James Cook surveys the coasts of Bering's Strait.

Q **Scholarship**

E. Malone's studies in Shakespearian controversy.
A. H. Anquetil Duperron, *Législation orientale.*

R **Philosophy and Religion**

Commission des Réguliers appointed to reform French religious houses, which leads to edict regulating admissions and the size of monasteries.
G. E. Lessing replies to the attacks of the orthodox J. M. Goeze in *Anti-Goeze.*

S **Art, Sculpture, Fine Arts and Architecture**

J. S. Copley, *Brook Watson and the Shark* (painting).

T **Music**

U **Literature**

Fanny Burney (pseud.), *Evelina.*
J. G. Herder's collection of folk songs (–1779) leads to study of folklore in Germany.
F. M. A. de Voltaire, *Irène.*

V **The Press**

W **Drama and Entertainment**

R. B. Sheridan, *The School for Scandal.*

X **Sport**

Y **Statistics**

Z **Births and Deaths**

Jan. 10th Carl Linnaeus d. (70).
Jan. 26th Ugo Foscolo b. (–1827).
Mar. 5th Thomas Arne d. (67).
Apr. 10th William Hazlitt b. (–1830).
Apr. – John Hargreaves d. (*c.* 55).
May 11th William Pitt, Earl of Chatham, d. (60).
May 30th Voltaire d. (83).
July 2nd J. J. Rousseau d. (66).
Dec. 6th J. L. Gay-Lussac b. (–1850).
Dec. 17th Humphry Davy b. (–1829).
—, Joseph Lancaster b. (–1838).

1779 Spain declares war on Britain

A **Jan:** France defends Senegal, W. Africa, against British attack.

B **Feb:** 25th, George Clark completes American conquest of the Old Northwest, forcing the British to surrender at Vincennes.

C **Mar:** the Irish Protestant Volunteer movement for the defence of Ireland from French invasion soon numbers 40,000.

D **Apr:**

E **May:** 13th, by Peace of Teschen, ending War of Bavarian Succession, Austria obtains the Inn Quarter of Bavaria and Prussia acquires the reversionary rights to Ansbach and Bayreuth (which fall to her in *Jan.* 1792);
France abandons Goree, W. Africa, to Britain.

F **Jun:** 16th, Spain declares war on Britain (after France has undertaken to assist her in recovering Gibraltar and Florida), and the siege of Gibraltar opens (–1783);
18th, French force takes St. Vincent, W. Indies.

G **Jul:** 4th, French force takes Grenada, W. Indies.

H **Aug:** British repulse American attack on Penobscot, Maine.
Congress despatches force into Wyoming Valley against the Indian tribes who had harried Pennsylvania in *July* 1778;
French fleet dominates the English Channel.

J **Sep:** 23rd, John Paul Jones in *Serapis* defeats H.M.S. *Countess of Scarborough.*

K **Oct:**

L **Nov:**

M **Dec:** Britain ends restrictions on Irish trade in answer to demands of Henry Flood and Henry Grattan.

N War against Mahrattas in India (–1782).
John Acton reforms Neapolitan Navy and British influence replaces French in Naples.

O **Politics, Economics, Law and Education**

P **Science, Technology, Discovery, etc.**

C. A. Coulomb investigates the laws of friction.
L. Spallanzani shows that semen is necessary to animal fertilisation.
Samuel Crompton's spinning mule.
A 'velocipede' is constructed in Paris.
Royal Academy of Sciences, Lisbon, founded.
James Rennel, *Bengal Atlas.*

Q **Scholarship**

R **Philosophy and Religion**

David Hume, *Dialogues of Natural Religion.*
William Cowper and John Newton, *Olney Hymns.*
Robert Lowth's new translation of *Isaiah.*
Selina, Countess of Huntingdon, builds Spa Fields Chapel, London, but in face of clerical opposition takes shelter under the Toleration Acts to register the chapel as a dissenting place of worship.

S **Art, Sculpture, Fine Arts and Architecture**

J. A. Houdon, bust of Molière.
Antonio Canova, *Daedalus and Icarus* (sculpture).
James Gillray's earliest satirical cartoon.

T **Music**

C. W. Gluck, *Iphigenia in Tauris* (opera).
Battles between Gluck's and Nicola Piccini's supporters in Paris.
J. C. Bach, *Amadis de Gaule* (opera).

U **Literature**

S. Johnson, *Lives of the Poets* (–1781).

V **The Press**

W **Drama and Entertainment**

G. E. Lessing, *Nathan the Wise.*
R. B. Sheridan, *The Critic.*

X **Sport**

The Derby is established at Epsom Racecourse, Surrey; first winner Sir C. Bunbury's 'Diomed'.

Y **Statistics**

Z **Births and Deaths**

Jan. 15th David Garrick d. (61).
Feb. 13th James Cook d. (50).
Feb. 21st Savigny b. (–1861).
May 15th William Lamb, Lord Melbourne, b. (–1848).
May 28th Thomas Moore b. (–1852).
—, Thomas Chippendale d. (*c.* 60).

1780 League of Armed Neutrality—Gordon riots in London

A **Jan:** 16th, Admiral George Rodney defeats Spanish at Cape St. Vincent and temporarily relieves Gibraltar.

B **Feb:** 8th, Yorkshire petition for Parliamentary reform presented at Westminster.

C **Mar:** 10th, Russia's declaration of armed neutrality, to prevent British ships from searching neutral vessels for contraband of war, which is subsequently confirmed by France, Spain, Austria, Prussia, Denmark and Sweden.

D **Apr:** 17th, Rodney's indecisive action against the French at Martinique;
19th, Harry Grattan demands Home Rule for Ireland;
Dunning's resolution deploring the increased influence of the Crown leads Commons to affirm the principle of periodical scrutiny of the civil list.

E **May:** Charleston, S. Carolina, surrenders to the British under Sir Henry Clinton;
Burke introduces bill for economic reform, aiming at abolition of sinecures and redundant offices.

F **Jun:** 2nd, Duke of Richmond proposes manhood suffrage in England;
—, (–8th), Gordon riots in London, when Lord George Gordon heads procession for presenting petition to Parliament for repealing Catholic Relief act of 1778, and Roman Catholic chapels are pillaged;
Joseph II of Austria visits Catherine II of Russia for discussions leading to Austro-Russian treaty of 1781.

G **Jul:** French troops under Rochambeau arrive at Newport, Rhode Island.

H **Aug:** 16th, Cornwallis defeats American army under Horatio Gates at Camden;
18th, Sumpter's army is defeated by British under Tarleton.

J **Sep:** 10th, Hyder Ali of Mysore conquers the Carnatic;
23rd, John André, captured British agent, reveals Benedict Arnold's plot to surrender West Point to Clinton.

K **Oct:** 7th, British force under Ferguson is defeated at battle of King's Mountain, S. Carolina;
Serfdom in Bohemia and Hungary abolished.

L **Nov:** 20th, Britain declares war on Holland to prevent her joining the League of Armed Neutrality;
29th, Maria Theresa of Austria dies, succeeded by Joseph II (–1790).

M **Dec:** 13th, Ireland is granted free trade with Britain and is to enjoy advantages of the colonial trade.

N Abolition of British secretaryship for colonies and of Council of Trade and Plantations.
Jacques Necker abolishes farming of taxes in France.

O **Politics, Economics, Law and Education**
Gaetano Filangieri, *Science of Legislation.*

P **Science, Technology, Discovery, etc.**
A. Lavoisier concludes that respiration is a form of combustion.
L. Spallanzani, *Dissertation on Animal and Vegetable Science.*
A circular saw is invented.
Oliver Evans invents a mechanical lift for a flour mill.
Steel pens are first used in England.

Q **Scholarship**

R **Philosophy and Religion**
James Bandinel delivers first Bampton Lectures at Oxford University.
Robert Raikes's Sunday School at Gloucester.

S **Art, Sculpture, Fine Arts and Architecture**
J. Reynolds' portrait of Mary Robinson as 'Perdita'.
J. S. Copley, *Death of Chatham* (painting).

T **Music**
Haydn, 'Toy' Symphony.
Giovanni Paisiello, *Barber of Seville* (opera).
Karl von Dittersdorf, *Job* (oratorio).
Sébastien Érard makes his first pianoforte.

U **Literature**
Frederick the Great, *De la littérature allemande.*
C. M. Wieland, *Oberon.*

V **The Press**
The British Gazette and Sunday Monitor, the first Sunday newspaper issued (*Mar.* 26th).

W **Drama and Entertainment**

X **Sport**

Y **Statistics**
Roman Catholics in England, 70,000.

Z **Births and Deaths**
Feb. 14th William Blackstone d. (57).
Aug. 29th J. A. D. Ingres b. (–1867).
Robert Smirke b. (–1867).

1781 Cornwallis capitulates at Yorktown

A **Jan**: Daniel Morgan defeats Tarleton's British force at battle of the Cowpens, S. Carolina, and takes many prisoners, depriving Cornwallis of light troops.

B **Feb**: Conclusion of Russia's treaty with Austria, for driving the Turks out of Europe, restoring a Greek Empire under Catherine's grandson Constantine, forming a Kingdom of Dacia under an Orthodox prince and allocating Serbia and the western Balkans to Austria and the Morea, Candia and Cyprus to Venice.

C **Mar**: 15th, Cornwallis defeats Americans under Greene at battle of Guilford Courthouse, N. Carolina.

D **Apr**: 29th, de Grasse captures Tobago;
French fleet under Suffren prevents Britain from seizing Cape of Good Hope.

E **May**: 19th, Louis XVI of France dismisses Necker;
Prussia joins League of Armed Neutrality.

F **Jun**: Hastings deposes Rajah of Benares for refusing to contribute to war expenses.

G **Jul**: 1st, Eyre Coote defeats Hyder Ali at Porto Novo, saving Madras from destruction;
Spanish force takes Pensacola, Florida, from British.

H **Aug**: 30th, de Grasse occupies Chesapeake Bay.

J **Sep**: 8th, Cornwallis defeats Greene at Eutaw Springs in N. Carolina;
30th, Washington and La Fayette cut Cornwallis's communications, beginning siege of Yorktown, Virginia.

K **Oct**: 13th, Joseph II grants patent of religious tolerance in Austrian Empire and freedom of the press;
19th, Cornwallis capitulates at Yorktown with almost 8,000 men; the British evacuate Charleston and Savannah and land operations are virtually over.

L **Nov**: 13th, Dutch settlement at Negapatam, Madras, is captured by British;
26th, British fleet takes St. Eustacius, W. Indies, from Holland;
—, Joseph II abolishes serfdom in Austria and
28th, makes monastic orders independent of Rome.

M **Dec**:

N Hastings plunders the treasure of the Nabob of Oudh.
Portuguese gain Delagoa Bay, E. Africa, from Austria.

O **Politics, Economics, Law and Education**

J. Necker, *Compte rendu.*
J. H. Pestalozzi expounds his educational theory in *Leonard and Gertrude.*

P **Science, Technology, Discovery, etc.**

F. W. Herschel discovers the planet Uranus (*Mar.* 13th).
K. W. Scheele and T. O. Bergman discover the metallic element tungsten.
The Siberian highway is begun.

Q **Scholarship**

J. H. Voss, translation of Homer's *Odyssey.*
Clarendon Press, Oxford, founded.

R **Philosophy and Religion**

Immanuel Kant, *Critique of Pure Reason.*
G. J. Planck, *History of Protestant Dogma.*
Dissolution of a third of the monasteries of the Austrian Empire.
Moses Mendelssohn, *On the Civil Amelioration of the Condition of the Jews.*

S **Art, Sculpture, Fine Arts and Architecture**

John Opie, *The School* (painting).
J. A. Houdon, *Seated Voltaire* (sculpture).

T **Music**

J. Haydn, 'Russian' (or 'Maiden') string quartets (Nos. 37–42).
W. A. Mozart, *Idomeneo* (opera).
J. A. Hiller founds Gewandhaus concerts at Leipzig.

U **Literature**

G. Crabbe, *The Library.*
J.-J. Rousseau, *Confessions.*

V **The Press**

W **Drama and Entertainment**

F. Schiller, *Die Räuber*, produced at Mannheim.

X **Sport**

P. Beckford, *Thoughts on Hunting.*

Y **Statistics**

Z **Births and Deaths**

Feb. 13th Gotthold Ephraim Lessing d. (52).
Mar. 18th Anne Robert Jacques Turgot d. (53).
June 9th George Stephenson b. (–1848).
Oct. 17th Edward Hawke d. (76).

1782 Rodney defeats French fleet in battle of The Saints

A **Jan**: 11th, Dutch surrender Trincomalee, Ceylon, to British.

B **Feb**: 5th, Spanish capture Minorca from British;
12th, indecisive battle of Sadras, Madras, between British and French;
13th, French take St. Christopher, W. Indies;
22nd, Motion against government, deprecating the continuation of the war in America, is defeated in British House of Commons by one vote.

C **Mar**: 15th, motion of lack of confidence in Lord North's administration is defeated in Commons by nine votes;
19th, Lord North resigns and, 27th, Marquess of Rockingham forms Whig Coalition ministry with C. J. Fox, E. Burke, Lord Shelburne and, on George III's insistence, Thurlow;
Pope Pius VI visits Vienna but fails to persuade Joseph II to rescind patent of tolerance.

D **Apr**: 12th, Admiral George Rodney defeats de Grasse at battle of The Saints, saving the West Indies;
Joseph II abrogates Barrier treaty of 1715 and requires Dutch to abandon garrisons in barrier towns in Austrian Netherlands which are evacuated, 18th;
Gratton makes Irish Declaration of Rights, demanding complete legislative freedom.

E **May**: 3rd, Commons vote the earlier resolution rejecting Wilkes as an M.P. to be subversive of the electors' rights;
9th, Thomas Grenville is sent to Paris to open negotiations with Count de Vergennes and Benjamin Franklin for a peace;
17th, Fox introduces repeal of Ireland Act, 1720, thus granting Ireland legislative independence (–1800), but Gratton's Parliament is elected solely by Protestants;
—, treaty of Salbai ends Mahratta War;
30th, Henry Dundas carries motion for recalling Warren Hastings from India.

F **Jun**: Spain completes conquest of Florida.

G **Jul**: 6th, naval battle of Cuddalore, off Madras, between Britain and France;
11th, Shelburne forms ministry, following Rockingham's death, (1st) with William Pitt the Younger, chancellor of Exchequer and leader of Commons, but Fox and Burke are excluded from office;
Portugal joins League of Armed Neutrality.

H **Aug**:

J **Sep**:

K **Oct**: Howe relieves Gibraltar.

L **Nov**: 30th, peace preliminaries, arranged by Franklin and Adams, are accepted by Britain and America.

M **Dec**: 7th, Tippoo succeeds Hyder Ali in Mysore.

N Rama I founds new dynasty in Siam, with capital at Bangkok.

O **Politics, Economics, Law and Education**
Royal Irish Academy, Dublin, founded.

P **Science, Technology, Discovery, etc.**

Q **Scholarship**
Girolamo Tiraboschi, *History of Italian Literature* completed.

R **Philosophy and Religion**
Dugald Stewart, *Elements of the Philosophy of the Human Mind.*
Joseph Priestley, *A History of the Corruptions of Christianity.*

S **Art, Sculpture, Fine Arts and Architecture**
H. Fuseli, *The Nightmare* (painting).
F. Guardi, *Fêtes for the Archduke Paul of Russia* and *The Concert* (paintings).
A. Canova begins monument to Pope Clement XIV in Rome.

T **Music**
W. A. Mozart, 'Haffner' Symphony (K.385 in D) and *Il Seraglio* (opera).

U **Literature**
Fanny Burney, *Cecilia.*
William Cowper, *Poems* and *Table Talk.*
J. G. Herder, *The Spirit of Hebrew Poetry* (–1783).

V **The Press**

W **Drama and Entertainment**

X **Sport**

Y **Statistics**
British Textiles Trade

raw cotton imports	11·8 mill. lb.
exported linens	5·6 mill. yds.
exported silks	60,000 lb.

Z **Births and Deaths**
Jan. 29th Daniel Auber b. (–1871).
Jan. – J. C. Bach d. (47).
Apr. 7th Francis Legatt Chantrey b. (–1841).
May 15th Richard Wilson d. (67).
June 19th H. F. R. de Lamennais b. (–1854).

1783 The Peace of Versailles

A **Jan:**

B **Feb:** 14th, British and
20th, American proclamations for cessation of arms;
24th, Lord Shelburne resigns, following resolution censuring the peace preliminaries and lengthy negotiations begin in which William Pitt and Lord North in turn decline to form ministry.

C **Mar:**

D **Apr:** 1st, Duke of Portland becomes nominal premier of a Fox-North coalition;
9th, Tippoo forces British to surrender Bednore.

E **May:** 7th, Pitt brings forward scheme for Parliamentary Reform, which is supported by Charles James Fox and opposed by Lord North.

F **Jun:** Joseph II enforces the German language in Bohemia and suppresses the permanent committee of the Diet.

G **Jul:** 17th, Besançon Parlement demands the calling of the French States-General;
Russia annexes Kuban on the plea of restoring order;
Britain and Austria persuade Turkey against declaring war on Russia.

H **Aug:**

J **Sep:** 3rd, by Peace of Versailles between Britain, France, Spain and U.S.A. Britain recognises independence of U.S.A. and recovers her West Indian possessions; France recovers St. Lucia, Tobago, Senegal, Goree and East Indian possessions; Spain retains Minorca and receives back Florida; France may fortify Dunkirk (a separate treaty between Britain and Holland is signed *May* 20th, 1784).

K **Oct:** Joseph II of Austria delivers Summary of Claims to States General of Holland, bringing to a head the question of the navigation of the Scheldt;
Following the sack of Tiflis by a Persian chief, Russia intervenes in Georgia, takes Baku and forces Heraclius of Georgia to recognise Russian sovereignty.

L **Nov:** 10th, Charles Calonne is appointed French controller-general and raises loans.

M **Dec:** 17th, Fox's India Bill is defeated in Lords and Fox-North coalition resigns;
19th, William Pitt forms ministry (–1801) and
27th, as chancellor of Exchequer is sole member of cabinet in Commons.

N Famine in Japan.

o **Politics, Economics, Law and Education**

Civil marriage and divorce established in Austrian Empire.

P **Science, Technology, Discovery, etc.**

William Herschel writes *Motion of the Solar System in Space.*

J. M. and J. E. Montgolfier launch fire balloons at Annonay (*June* 5th), at Versailles (*Sept.* 19th) and, carrying a man, at Paris (*Nov.* 21st).

Marquis Jouffroy d'Abbans sails a paddle-wheel steamboat on the R. Sâone.

Henry Bell's copper cylinder for calico printing.

Q **Scholarship**

R **Philosophy and Religion**

I. Kant in *Prolegomena to any Possible Metaphysic* answers attacks on his *Critique of Pure Reason.*

Moses Mendelssohn pleads for freedom of conscience in *Jerusalem.*

J. G. Eichhorn completes *Introduction to Old Testament.*

Charles Simeon starts evangelical movement in Cambridge.

S **Art, Sculpture, Fine Arts and Architecture**

J. Opie, *Age and Infancy* (painting).

J. L. David, *Grief of Andromache* (painting).

J. A. Houdon, *Girl Shivering* (sculpture).

T **Music**

W. A. Mozart, Mass in C Minor.

L. van Beethoven publishes first composition (Variations on a march of Dressler).

U **Literature**

William Blake, *Poetical Sketches.*

Thomas Crabbe, *The Village.*

Joseph Dobrovsky, *Scriptores rerum Bohemicarum.*

V **The Press**

W **Drama and Entertainment**

X **Sport**

Y **Statistics**

Z **Births and Deaths**

Jan. 23rd Marie Henri Beyle ('Stendhal') b. (–1842).

Apr. 3rd Washington Irving b. (–1859).

July 24th Simon Bolivar b. (–1830).

Sept. 18th Leonhard Euler d. (75).

Oct. 29th Jean D'Alembert d. (65).

A **Jan:** 6th, by treaty of Constantinople Turkey acquiesces in Russia's annexation of the Crimea and Kuban.

B **Feb:**

C **Mar:** 8th, Parliamentary opposition to William Pitt dwindles to a majority of one;
11th, British sign peace treaty with Tippoo of Mysore;
20th, by Peace of Versailles Holland cedes Negapatam to Britain;
24th, Parliament is dissolved and in the ensuing election Pitt gains a large majority.

D **Apr:** 23rd, Thomas Jefferson's land ordinance passed, the basis for the Land Ordinance of 1787.

E **May:** Andreas Bernstorff, recalled to office in Denmark, abolishes serfdom, permits a free press and begins educational reforms.

F **Jun:** 21st, Pitt reduces duties on tea and spirits.

G **Jul:** 4th, following revolution in Transylvania Joseph II abrogates the constitution; he subsequently rides roughshod over Hungarian sentiment by removing the Crown of Hungary to Vienna and suppressing feudal courts;
12th, Hovering Act checks smuggling round coasts of Britain.

H **Aug:** 13th, Pitt's India Act places East India Company under a government-appointed Board of Control (–1858) and forbids interference in native affairs, to check territorial expansion.

J **Sep:**

K **Oct:** Joseph II breaks off diplomatic relations with Holland when two Austrian vessels, ordered to navigate the Scheldt, are fired on by the Dutch, causing a European crisis, in which Louis XVI offers to mediate (leads to treaty of Fontainebleau, *Nov.* 8th, 1785).

L **Nov:**

M **Dec:**

N Financial depression in U.S.

O Politics, Economics, Law and Education

Gustav III founds Swedish Academy of Arts and Sciences.
Valentine Haüy founds in Paris the first school for the blind.

P Science, Technology, Discovery, etc.

Henry Cavendish discovers that water is a compound of hydrogen and oxygen.
George Attwood's machine for proving the laws of accelerated motion.
Rene Haüy, *Essai d'une théorie sur la structure des cristaux.*
Henry Cort's puddling process revolutionises the manufacture of wrought iron.
Andrew Meikle's threshing machine.
Joseph Bramah's patent lock.
River Eider linked by canal to the Baltic.

Q Scholarship

William Mitford's *History of Greece* (–1810).
William Jones founds the Bengal Asiatic Society and his discourses (–94) mark a turning-point in the study of Sanskrit.

R Philosophy and Religion

I. Kant. *Notion of a Universal History in a Cosmopolitan Sense.*
J. G. Herder, *Ideas towards a Philosophy of History* (–91).
Bernardin de Saint-Pierre, *Études de la Nature.*
John Wesley signs deed of declaration (*Feb.* 28th) as the charter of Wesleyan Methodism, and ordains two 'Presbyters' for the American Mission (*Sept.* 1st).

S Art, Sculpture, Fine Arts and Architecture

J. Reynolds' portraits of Mrs. Siddons as 'The Tragic Muse' and of T. Warton.
T. Rowlandson's first political cartoon.

T Music

André Grétry, *Richard Cœur de Lion* (opera).
Antonio Salieri, *Les Danaïdes* (opera).

U Literature

V The Press

The Boston Centinel (Mass.) founded.

W Drama and Entertainment

P. A. C. Beaumarchais, *Le Mariage de Figaro.*
F. Schiller, *Kabale und Liebe.*

X Sport

Y Statistics

Z Births and Deaths

Feb. 18th Nicolo Paganini b. (–1840).
July 30th Denis Diderot d. (71).
Oct. 19th James Henry Leigh Hunt b. (–1859).
Oct. 20th Henry Temple, Viscount Palmerston b. (–1865).
Dec. 13th Samuel Johnson d. (74).

1785 The Bavarian Exchange

A **Jan:** Joseph II begins unsuccessful attempts to exchange Bavaria with Charles Theodore for the Austrian Netherlands, excepting Luxembourg and Namur.

B **Feb:**

C **Mar:**

D **Apr:** 18th, William Pitt's motion for Parliamentary reform is defeated.

E **May:**

F **Jun:** Hastings returns to England.

G **Jul:** 23rd, Frederick the Great forms Die Fürstenbund (League of German Princes) to oppose Joseph II's Bavarian exchange scheme.

H **Aug:** 15th, arrest of Cardinal de Rohan in Diamond Necklace Affair, which discredits Marie Antoinette.

J **Sep:** 10th, Prussia signs commercial treaty with U.S.

K **Oct:**

L **Nov:** 8th, by treaty of Fontainebleau, Holland recognises Joseph II's sovereignty over part of R. Scheldt, Joseph abandons his claim to Maestricht, renounces his right to free navigation of Scheldt outside his dominions and receives 10 mill. guilders;
10th, alliance between France and Holland, despite the efforts of the British envoy at The Hague.

M **Dec:**

N Parlement of Paris begins series of attacks on Charles de Calonne.

O **Politics, Economics, Law and Education**
J. H. Campe pioneers educational reforms in Germany.

P **Science, Technology, Discovery, etc.**
Henry Cavendish discovers the composition of nitric acid.
C. L. Berthollet uses chlorine ('eau de Javel') in bleaching.
C. A. Coulomb, *Recherches théoriques et expérimentales sur la force de torsion et sur l'élasticité des fils de métal.*
Steam engine with rotary motion installed by Matthew Boulton and James Watt in a cotton-spinning factory at Papplewick, Nottinghamshire.
Jean Blanchard and John Jeffries cross the English Channel in a balloon.
Russians settle in the Aleutian Isles, North Pacific.

Q **Scholarship**

R **Philosophy and Religion**
I. Kant, *Groundwork of the Metaphysic of Ethics.*
William Paley, *Principles of Moral and Political Philosophy.*
Samuel Johnson, *Prayers and Meditations* (posthm.).
London Society for the establishment of Sunday Schools is founded.
James Madison's religious freedom act (*Dec.* 26th) rescinds religious tests in Virginia.

S **Art, Sculpture, Fine Arts and Architecture**
J. Reynolds, *The Infant Hercules* (painting).
J. L. David, *Oath of the Horatii* (painting).
Alexander Cozens writes *New Methods of . . . Compositions of Landscape.*
J. A. Houdon visits U.S. to sculpt George Washington.

T **Music**
W. A. Mozart, six string quartets dedicated to J. Haydn.
Caecilian Society for the performance of sacred music founded in London (–1861).

U **Literature**
W. Cowper, *The Task* and *John Gilpin.*
C. F. D. Schubart, *Sämtliche Gedichte* (–86).
Moses Mendelssohn, *Morning Hours.*

V **The Press**

W **Drama and Entertainment**

X **Sport**

Y **Statistics**

Z **Births and Deaths**
Jan. 4th Jacob Grimm b. (–1863).
Mar. 7th Alessandro Manzoni b. (–1873).
Aug. 15th Thomas de Quincey b. (–1859).
Oct. 18th Thomas Love Peacock b. (–1866).
Nov. 18th David Wilkie b. (–1841).

A **Jan:**

B **Feb:** 24th, Charles Cornwallis is appointed Governor-General of India with power to override the council.

C **Mar:** 29th, William Pitt appoints commissioners for reducing the national debt through establishing a sinking fund (abolished 1828).

D **Apr:**

E **May:** Annapolis convention, under James Madison and Alexander Hamilton, attended by New York, Pennsylvania, Virginia, New Jersey and Delaware, draws attention to weakness of the Confederation.

F **Jun:** William Pitt establishes excise scheme and consolidates the militia.

G **Jul:**

H **Aug:** 11th, Penang ceded to Britain by Rajah of Kedah;
17th, Frederick the Great dies, succeeded by Frederick William II (–1797), brother of the Princess of Orange.

J **Sep:** 26th, Anglo-French commercial treaty, negotiated by William Eden, reduces many duties;
Rebellion of Daniel Shays in Massachusetts, aiming to prevent further judgments for debt until next state election; state troops are used to protect the arsenal and (*Nov.*) the revolt peters out.

K **Oct:** 16th, Joseph II's edict establishing a single seminary at Louvain for the entire Austrian Netherlands provokes wave of protest among clergy.

L **Nov:**

M **Dec:**

N Committee of Council of Trade is formed in Britain.
Dutch Patriot Party deprives William V of Orange of command of army.

O **Politics, Economics, Law and Education**
Thomas Clarkson, *Essay on Slavery.*

P **Science, Technology, Discovery, etc.**
W. Herschel's *Catalogue of Nebulae.*
E. F. F. Chladni founds the science of acoustics.
Edward Cartwright opens a cotton factory in Doncaster.
'Sea-island' cotton is planted in U.S.
Ezekiel Reed invents a nail-making machine in U.S.
Georges Buffon, *Histoire Naturelle des Oiseaux.*

Q **Scholarship**

R **Philosophy and Religion**
Lorenzo Ricci, Bishop of Pistoia and Prato, holds a diocesan synod, which adopts the Gallican articles of 1682, and celebrates the mass in Italian.
Leopold of Tuscany abolishes religious guilds.
German bishops, aiming at a national church, draw up the Punctation of Ems (*Aug.* 25th).
Members of the Mennonite sect from Central Europe settle in Canada.

S **Art, Sculpture, Fine Arts and Architecture**
John Hoppner, *Portrait of a Lady* (painting).

T **Music**
W. A. Mozart, *The Marriage of Figaro* (opera).
Karl von Dittersdorf, *Doctor und Apotheker* (opera).

U **Literature**
William Beckford, *An Arabian Tale, from an unpublished manuscript* (*The History of Caliph Vathek*).
Robert Burns, *Poems chiefly in the Scottish Dialect.*
G. A. Bürger, *Gedichte.*
J. K. A. Musäus's collection of stories, *Straussefedern.*
William Bilderdijck's *Elias* starts the Dutch Romantic Revival.

V **The Press**

W **Drama and Entertainment**
John Burgoyne's play, *The Heiress.*

X **Sport**
Baseball is first played, at Princeton.

Y **Statistics**
British merchant shipping, 1,150,000 registered tonnage.

Z **Births and Deaths**
Jan. 26th Benjamin Robert Haydon b. (–1846).
Feb. 24th Wilhelm Grimm b. (–1859).
Apr. 16th John Franklin b. (–1847).
May 21st K. W. Scheele d. (44).
June (–) G. Hepplewhite d. (60).
Aug. 17th Frederick the Great d. (74).
Dec. 18th Carl Maria von Weber b. (–1826).

1787 U.S. Constitution is signed—Turkey's war with Russia

A **Jan:** Joseph II constitutes Austrian Netherlands as a province of the Austrian monarchy, provoking riots in Louvain and Brussels, led by Van der Noot;
Catherine II visits the Crimea where she is joined, *Feb.*, by Joseph II, with whom she forms a defensive alliance.

B **Feb:** 13th, on Comte de Vergenne's death Armand Comte de Montmorin is appointed French minister of foreign affairs;
22nd, French notables meet at Versailles (*–May* 25th) and reject Charles de Calonne's proposals for financial reform.

C **Mar:**

D **Apr:** 11th, New York assembly imposes duties on foreign goods;
17th, Calonne is banished to Lorraine, succeeded as minister of finance by Cardinal Étienne Brienne, Archbishop of Toulouse.

E **May:** 10th, Edmund Burke impeaches Warren Hastings;
25th, Philadelphia convention meets under Washington to frame a constitution.

F **Jun:** 28th, Dutch insurgents arrest Princess Wilhelmina of Holland near Gouda.

G **Jul:** 6th, Parlement of Paris opposes Étienne Brienne and demands the summoning of the States-General.
Northwest Ordinance in U.S.; five states were eventually created out of old Northwest Territory.

H **Aug:** 10th, Turkey declares war against Russia, fearing designs on Georgia;
14th, Parlement of Paris is banished by Louis XVI to Troyes (recalled to Paris *Sept.* 24th).

J **Sep:** 17th, U.S. constitution is signed;
Prussian troops assist restoration of William V of Orange (*–Oct.*).

K **Oct:** 27th, Comte de Montmorin declares that France has no intention of interfering in Dutch affairs.

L **Nov:** 20th, Louis XVI declares that the States-General will be summoned for *July* 1792

M **Dec:**

N France begins trade to Annam.
Rebellion in Formosa (suppressed by China in 1788).

O **Politics, Economics, Law and Education**

Jeremy Bentham, *Defence of Usury*.

John Adams, *A Defence of the Constitutions of Government of the United States of America*, published in London, replies to Turgot's criticisms.

James Madison, *The Vices of the Political System of the United States*.

P **Science, Technology, Discovery, etc.**

A. L. Lavoisier, with collaborators, *Méthode de nomenclature chimique*.

Nicolas Leblanc's process for making soda (sodium carbonate).

John Fitch launches a steamboat on the Delaware.

Horace Saussure reaches the summit of Mt. Blanc (*Aug*. 2nd).

Q **Scholarship**

Jean Jacques Barthélemy completes his *Voyage du jeune Anacharsis en Grèce*.

Catharine II orders the compilation of an Imperial Dictionary, with 285 words translated into 200 languages.

R **Philosophy and Religion**

John Wesley's *Sermons*.

The Edict of Versailles grants religious freedom and legal status to French Protestants.

S **Art, Sculpture, Fine Arts and Architecture**

J. Reynolds' portrait of Lord Heathfield.

T **Music**

W. A. Mozart, *Don Giovanni*, 'Prague' Symphony and *Eine Kleine Nachtmusik*.

L. Boccherini's E major string quartet.

U **Literature**

Johann Heinse, *Ardinghello und die glückseligen Inseln*.

V **The Press**

W **Drama and Entertainment**

P. Beaumarchais, *Tarare*.

F. Schiller, *Don Carlos*.

J. W. Goethe, *Iphigenie auf Tauris*.

X **Sport**

M.C.C. move to Lord's cricket ground, in what is now Dorset Square, Marylebone.

Y **Statistics**

Z **Births and Deaths**

Mar. 10th William Etty b. (–1849).

Mar. 16th Georg Simon Ohm b. (–1854).

Mar. 17th Edmund Kean b. (–1833).

Oct. 4th François Pierre Guillaume Guizot b. (–1874).

Nov. 15th C. W. von Gluck d. (73).

Dec. 16th Mary Russell Mitford b. (–1855).

1788 Austria declares war on Turkey—Scandinavian War

A **Jan**: 20th, Parlement of Paris presents a list of grievances;
28th, first British penal settlement is founded at Botany Bay;
30th, death of Charles Edward Stuart, the Young Pretender, in Rome.

B **Feb**: 9th, Joseph II of Austria declares war on Turkey;
Trial of Warren Hastings, for high crimes and misdemeanours in India, begins (–1795).

C **Mar**:

D **Apr**: 15th, Anglo-Dutch alliance.

E **May**: 9th, British Parliamentary motion for abolition of Slave Trade.

F **Jun**: 9th, Joseph Banks founds Africa Association for arousing interest in exploration and trade;
21st, U.S. constitution comes into force, when ratified by the 9th state, New Hampshire;
Sweden declares war on Russia, invading Russian Finland.

G **Jul**: 17th, Russia destroys Swedish fleet.

H **Aug**: 8th, Louis XVI decides to summon the States-General for *May* 1789;
13th, Prussia joins the Anglo-Dutch alliance to form the Triple Alliance for preserving peace in Europe;
22nd, foundation of British settlement in Sierra Leone as an asylum for slaves;
25th, Loménie de Brienne, who has announced national bankruptcy, is dismissed and
27th, Jacques Necker is recalled as French minister of finance.

J **Sep**: 13th, New York is declared the federal capital of U.S.;
Denmark invades Sweden.

K **Oct**: Joseph II, having failed to take Belgrade, returns to Vienna;
6th, Last 4-years Diet meets in Poland.

L **Nov**: 6th, through the intervention of the Triple Alliance Denmark and Sweden sign the Convention of Uddevalla which provides for the evacuation of Danish troops;
George III's first derangement;
Louis XVI decides to summon the notables.

M **Dec**: 10th, Commons debate the Regency question;
17th, Russian army under Gregory Potemkin takes Ochákov.

N

O **Politics, Economics, Law and Education**

Hannah More, *Thoughts on the Importance of the Manners of the Great to General Society.*

P **Science, Technology, Discovery, etc.**

Pierre Laplace publishes his laws of the planetary system.

James Hutton expounds his dynamic theory of continual changes in the earth's features in *New Theory of the Earth.*

Linnean Society founded in London.

J. L. Lagrange, French mathematician, *Mécanique analytique.*

Q **Scholarship**

John Lemprière, *Classical Dictionary.*

F. Schiller, *History of the Revolt of the Netherlands under the Spanish Regime.*

R **Philosophy and Religion**

Thomas Reid, *Essays on the Active Powers of the Human Mind.*

I. Kant, *Critique of Practical Reason.*

Richard Porson's *Letters to Travis.*

Religious edict in Prussia imposes censorship in education and penalties for heresy (repealed 1797).

American Presbyterians revise the Westminster Catechism and introduce principles of religious liberty.

S **Art, Sculpture, Fine Arts and Architecture**

J. L. David, *Love of Paris and Helen* (painting).

T **Music**

J. Haydn, 'Oxford' Symphony (No. 92 in G).

W. A. Mozart, Symphonies 39 (E flat), 40 (G minor) and 41 ('Jupiter').

U **Literature**

V **The Press**

John Walter founds *The Times* (*Jan.* 1st).

W **Drama and Entertainment**

J. W. Goethe, *Egmont.*

X **Sport**

M.C.C. codifies the Laws of Cricket.

Y **Statistics**

Z **Births and Deaths**

Jan. 22nd George Lord Byron b. (–1824).

Feb. 5th Robert Peel b. (–1850).

Feb. 22nd Arthur Schopenhauer b. (–1860).

Apr. 15th George Louis Leclerk Buffon d. (80).

Aug. 2nd Thomas Gainsborough d. (61).

Dec. 14th Carl Philipp Emanuel Bach d. (74).

A **Jan:**

B **Feb:** 3rd, William Pitt introduces Regency bill, vesting Regency in Prince of Wales, but without power to create peers or grant offices;
19th, George III recovers;
20th, Gustavus III introduces act of Unity and Security in Sweden which grants him absolute powers (receives royal assent *Apr.* 3rd).

C **Mar:** 4th, first Congress meets at New York and during the session ten of the proposed twelve amendments to the constitution are made and sent to the states for ratification.

D **Apr:** 7th, accession of Selim III of Turkey (–1807);
30th, George Washington inaugurated as President of U.S. with John Adams vice-president, Thomas Jefferson secretary of state and Alexander Hamilton secretary of Treasury.

E **May:** 5th, States-General meet at Versailles.

F **Jun:** Spaniards attack British fishing vessels at Nootka Sound, W. Canada;
17th, third estate in France declares itself a National Assembly and undertakes to frame a constitution (–*Sept.* 30th, 1791);
20th, third estate takes tennis court oath, undertaking not to depart until a constitution is drawn up;
23rd, Honoré Mirabeau establishes his reputation in the Séance Royale;
27th, Union of the three estates in France.

G **Jul:** 4th, U.S. declare themselves to be an economic and customs union;
11th, Louis XVI's dismissal of Jacques Necker implies a royalist *coup d'état* and provokes the Paris mob
14th, to sack the Bastille;
17th, Jean Bailly becomes mayor of Paris and the Marquis de La Fayette commander of the National Guard;
31st, Austrian and Russian troops under Francis Duke of Coburg and Count Alexander Suvorov defeat Turks at Focshani.

H **Aug:** 4th, French feudal system is abolished;
27th, French National Assembly adopts Declaration of the Rights of Man.

J **Sep:** 22nd, Austrian and Russian troops under Duke of Coburg defeat Turks at Rimnik.

K **Oct:** 5th (–6th), march of women to Versailles to move Louis XVI and his court to Paris;
6th, Austrians take Belgrade;
9th, Coburg's army takes Bucharest;
Emigration of French royalists begins in earnest;
Revolution breaks out in Austrian Netherlands under Van der Noot, after Joseph II of Austria has revoked constitution of Brabant and Hainault.

L **Nov:** 2nd, nationalisation of property of church in France;
7th, National Assembly forbids any member to accept office under Louis XVI;
12th, France is divided into 80 administrative departments;
The Revolution Society, meeting in London, congratulates French National Assembly on fall of the Bastille.

M **Dec:** 13th, Austrian Netherlands declare independence as Belgium;
21st, issue of Assignats (paper money) in France;
29th, Tippoo of Mysore attacks the Rajah of Travancore.

N

O **Politics, Economics, Law and Education**

J. Bentham, *Introduction to the Principles of Morals and Legislation.*

E. J. Sièyes, *Qu'est-ce que le Tiers État?* and *Exposition des Droits de l'Homme.*

Pierre Malouet's *Considérations sur le Gouvernement* recommends a limited monarchy.

Journal des Débats founded in Paris.

Pierre Cabanis, *Observations sur les hôpitaux.*

P **Science, Technology, Discovery, etc.**

A. L. Lavoisier, *Traité élémentaire de chimie.*

Aloisio Galvani's observations on the muscular contraction of dead frogs, which he infers was caused electrically, prompts Alessandro Volta's assertion on the nature of electricity.

W. Herschel completes his reflecting telescope and discovers a seventh satellite ('Mimas') in the Saturnian system.

Antoine Jussieu begins the modern classification of plants in *Genera Plantarum.*

Gilbert White, *Natural History of Selborne.*

Q **Scholarship**

Jean Amiot, *Dictionnaire tartare-mantchou-français.*

Arabic studies in the western world come of age with Johann Reiske, *Adnotationes historicae* to his *Abulfeda* (posth.).

William Jones's translation of Kàlidàsa's drama, *Sakuntala.*

R **Philosophy and Religion**

Pope Pius VI admits the ninth-century decretals of Isidore, on which much papal authority was based, were forged.

The three ecclesiastical imperial electors recognise the Pope's right to send nuncios.

Pius VI refutes the Ems articles (of *Aug.* 1786).

S **Art, Sculpture, Fine Arts and Architecture**

François Gérard, *Joseph and his Brothers* (painting).

T **Music**

W. A. Mozart, *Così fan tutte* (opera).

U **Literature**

William Blake, *Songs of Innocence.*

William Bowles, *Fourteen Sonnets written chiefly on picturesque spots.*

J. H. B. de Saint-Pierre, *Paul et Virginie.*

F. Schiller, *Die Künstler.*

V **The Press**

W **Drama and Entertainment**

Joseph Chénier, *Charles IX.*

J. W. Goethe, *Tasso.*

X **Sport**

Y **Statistics**

Z **Births and Deaths**

Aug. 6th Friedrich List b. (–1846).

Sept. 15th James Fenimore Cooper b. (–1851).

— J. L. M. Daguerre b. (–1867).

1790 Austria suppresses revolution in Austrian Netherlands

A **Jan**: 9th, Britain, Prussia and Holland agree on a common policy over Belgium, but William Pitt subsequently refuses to recognise Belgian independence;
31st, Prussia withdraws from intervention in Russo-Turkish War.

B **Feb**: 20th, Leopold II of Austria becomes Holy Roman Emperor on Joseph II's death;
In British Parliament Edmund Burke condemns and Charles James Fox welcomes the developments in France;
French religious houses are suppressed and the municipality of Paris is reorganised;
Alexander Hamilton introduces Funding Bill in U.S.

C **Mar** 2nd, Edmund Burke secures defeat of C. J. Fox's bill for repeal of Test and Corporation Acts;
16th, Van der Noot drives the Democrats, or Vonckists, from power in Belgium;
29th, Poland cedes Thorn and Danzig to Prussia on the understanding that Prussia will obtain Austrian Galicia for her.

D **Apr**:

E **May**: Honoré Mirabeau becomes a secret agent of the Crown and begins series of Notes for the Court on proceedings in the National Assembly. The Assembly debates the right to declare war and make peace, which becomes a pertinent issue with the danger of war between Britain and Spain over Nootka Sound, in which France would be bound by the Family Compact to aid Spain.

F **Jun**: 1st, Britain forms alliance with Mahrathas in India;
At Reichenbach Conference Britain and Holland refuse to support Prussia, thus averting a war with Austria, and a treaty is signed between Austria and Prussia under which Frederick William II abandons his aggressive policy over Belgium, Sweden, Poland and Turkey.

G **Jul**: 4th, British alliance with the Nizam of Hyderabad;
12th, Civil constitution of the French clergy;
14th, festival of Champ de Mars, Paris; Louis XVI accepts the constitution.

H **Aug**: 14th, Treaty of Verela ends Swedish-Russian war, Russia acquiring part of Finland;
31st, mutiny is quelled in Nancy.

J **Sep**: 10th, Jacques Necker resigns.

K **Oct**: Wolfe Tone founds Society of United Irishmen as a political union of Roman Catholics and Protestants to further Irish Parliamentary reform;
28th, Spain yields to Britain's demands for reparation over Nootka Sound (see *June* 1789) and abandons claim to Vancouver Island.

L **Nov**: 27th, French clergy required to take oath to support the civil constitution;
William Pitt increases government majority in British election.

M **Dec**: 2nd, Austrians re-enter Brussels and suppress revolution;
10th, Austria renounces scheme for exchanging Bavaria for the Netherlands;
22nd, Alexander Suvorov captures Ismail from the Turks.

N Growing power of the Jacobins (Maximilien Robespierre), the Cordeliers (Georges Danton) and other political clubs in Paris.

O **Politics, Economics, Law and Education**

André de Chénier, *Avis au peuple français* and *Jeu de paume.*

E. Burke, *Reflections on the Revolution in France.*

Alexander Radistcheff's *Journey from St. Petersburg to Moscow* pleads for the emancipation of serfs.

P **Science, Technology, Discovery, etc.**

J. W. Goethe, *Versuch die Metamorphose der Pflanzen zu erklären.*

T. Clifford's nail-maker.

First steam-rolling-mill in England.

Firth-Clyde and Oxford-Birmingham canals begun.

George Vancouver explores the north-west coast of America.

First patent law in U.S.

James Bruce, *Travels to Discover the Source of the Nile, 1768–73.*

Q **Scholarship**

R **Philosophy and Religion**

I. Kant, *Critique of Judgment.*

Civil constitution of the clergy in France (July 12th). Jews in France are admitted to civil liberties.

John Carroll is consecrated as Roman Catholic bishop of Baltimore, the first bishop in America (becomes Archbishop of Baltimore in 1811).

S **Art, Sculpture, Fine Arts and Architecture**

Archibald Alison, *Essay on the Nature and Principles of Taste.*

T **Music**

U **Literature**

Robert Burns, *Tam O'Shanter.*

Karl Moritz completes *Anton Reiser.*

David Williams founds the Royal Literary Fund.

V **The Press**

W **Drama and Entertainment**

X **Sport**

Y **Statistics**

Z **Births and Deaths**

Apr. 17th Benjamin Franklin d. (84).

July 17th Adam Smith d. (63).

Sept. 26th Nassau William Senior b. (–1864).

Oct. 21st Alphonse de Lamartine b. (–1869).

— Théodore Géricault b. (–1824).

A **Jan**: 30th, Honoré Mirabeau elected President of French Assembly.

B **Feb**: Prussia and Austria guarantee a free constitution for Poland.

C **Mar**: 4th, Vermont becomes a state of U.S.;
28th, Britain increases navy, fearing a war with Russia over the Black Sea port of Ochákov, captured from the Turks.

D **Apr**: 2nd, death of Mirabeau;
18th, Louis XVI is prevented by riot from going to St. Cloud, which demonstrates he is a prisoner.

E **May**: 3rd, Polish constitution, converting an elective into a hereditary monarchy under the elector of Saxony, following the death of King Stanislas II;
6th, by Canada Constitution Act Canada is divided into two provinces, Upper (Ontario) and Lower (Quebec), with separate legislative assemblies;
14th, Lord Cornwallis overthrows Tippoo of Mysore at battle of Seringapatam.

F **Jun**: 20th (–25th), Louis XVI attempts to leave France, but is turned back at Varennes and taken to Paris.

G **Jul**: 5th, Frederick William II of Prussia dismisses Ewald Hertzberg;
6th, Leopold II of Austria issues letter calling on powers to support Louis XVI;
—, arrival of Comte d'Artois makes Coblenz the headquarters of French *émigrés*;
17th, massacre of Champ de Mars by Marquis de La Fayette restores order in Paris;
Rioters in Birmingham attack Joseph Priestley's house for his support of French Revolution.

H **Aug**: 4th, by peace of Sistova Turkey cedes Orsova to Austria, in defiance of treaty of Reichenbach (see *June* 1790);
22nd, Negro revolt in French part of San Domingo;
27th, by declaration of Pillnitz Austria and Prussia state they are ready to intervene in French affairs with consent of other powers, but William Pitt announces Britain will remain neutral; France interprets the declaration as a threat.

J **Sep**: 3rd, French Constitution is passed by National Assembly, making France a constitutional monarchy;
4th, France annexes Avignon;
30th, French National Assembly dissolves after decreeing that none of its members is eligible to serve in the Legislative Assembly.

K **Oct**: 1st, Legislative Assembly meets at Paris (–*Sept.* 1792); Jacques Brissot and others of the Girondist Party in France urge war against Austria.

L **Nov**: 9th, Louis XVI vetoes a decree of the Assembly demanding the return of the *émigrés* under pain of death.

M **Dec**: 15th, first ten amendments to U.S. constitution ratified;
Gustavus III of Sweden offers to head a crusade against France.

O Politics, Economics, Law and Education

E. Burke, *An Appeal from the New to the Old Whigs* and *Letter to a Member of the National Assembly.*
Thomas Paine, *The Rights of Man*, part I.
James Mackintosh, *Vindiciae Gallicae.*
K. W. von Humboldt, *Attempt to Determine the limits of the Frontier of the State.*
John Sinclair, *The Statistical Account of Scotland.*
Bank of North America founded (*July*).
Jeremy Bentham designs a 'panopticon' for the central inspection of convicts.
School for the Indigent Blind opened in Liverpool.

P Science, Technology, Discovery, etc.

Philippe Pinel, *Traité médico-philosophique de l'aliénation mentale.*
J. W. Goethe's optical studies (–92).
Ordnance Survey established in Britain.
Samuel Peel patents india-rubber cloth.

Q Scholarship

Constantin Volney's essay on the philosophy of history, *Les Ruines, ou méditations sur les révolutions des empires.*
George Martens, *Recueil des traités, 1671–1791* (–1801, Göttingen).

R Philosophy and Religion

Sulpicians found a Roman Catholic seminary in U.S.
Robert Hall, Baptist, *Sermons.*

S Art, Sculpture, Fine Arts and Architecture

George Morland, *The Stable* (painting).
Anguetin Pajou, *Psyche Abandoned* (sculpture).
Karl Langhans, Brandenburg Gate, Berlin.

T Music

W. A. Mozart, *Magic Flute* (opera) and Requiem.
J. Haydn, 'Surprise' Symphony.
Luigi Cherubini, *Lodoiska* (opera).

U Literature

Boswell, *Life of Johnson.*
Marquis de Sade, *Justine.*

V The Press

The Observer founded.

W Drama and Entertainment

Elizabeth Inchbald, *A Simple Story.*
Joseph Chénier's plays *Henry VIII* and *Jean Calas* produced in Paris.
Goethe becomes director of the Weimar theatre (–1817).

X Sport

Y Statistics

1791

N Washington, D.C., is laid out.
Odessa is founded.

z **Births and Deaths**

Jan. 15th Franz Grillparzer b. (–1872).
Apr. 2nd Honoré Gabriel Riquetti Mirabeau d. (42).
Apr. 27th S. F. B. Morse b. (–1872).
Sept. 5th Giacomo Meyerbeer b. (–1864).
Sept. 22nd Michael Faraday b. (–1867).
Dec. 5th Wolfgang Amadeus Mozart d. (35).

1792 France declares war on Austria and Prussia

A **Jan:** 9th, Russia, deserted by Austria and concerned over Prussian intrigues in Poland, ends her war with Turkey by the peace of Jassy, obtaining Ochákov and a boundary on the R. Dniester, but surrendering her conquests in Moldavia and Bessarabia;
18th, Prussia gains Ansbach and Bayreuth by escheat, under Treaty of Teschen (*May* 1779).

B **Feb:** 5th, Tippoo of Mysore, defeated in his war with British and Hyderabad, cedes half Mysore to Britain;
7th, Austro-Prussian alliance against France.

C **Mar:** 1st, Francis II of Austria succeeds his brother Leopold II as Holy Roman Emperor (–1835);
24th, Girondins under Jean Roland and Charles Dumouriez form ministry in France;
29th, Gustavus III of Sweden is assassinated.

D **Apr:** 20th, France declares war on Austria (the War of the First Coalition).

E **May:** 19th, Russia invades Poland, where the constitution is abrogated.

F **Jun:** 1st, Kentucky becomes a U.S. state;
20th, mob invades Tuileries.

G **Jul:** 8th, France declares war on Prussia and
18th, on Sardinia;
25th, Duke of Brunswick's manifesto threatens destruction of Paris if French royal family is harmed.

H **Aug:** Prussian and Austrian troops invade France;
9th, revolutionary Commune established in Paris;
10th, mob invades Tuileries, massacring the Swiss guard; the Legislative Assembly is suspended;
13th, French royal family is imprisoned.

J **Sep:** 2nd, Prussians take Longwy and Verdun; but
20th, the invaders are stopped at battle of Valmy;
21st, French National Convention meets;
22nd, French Republic proclaimed; the Revolutionary Calendar comes into force.

K **Oct:** 19th, French troops take Mayence and cross Rhine.

L **Nov:** 6th, French under Charles Dumouriez defeat Austrians at Jemappes, take Brussels and conquer Austrian Netherlands;
19th, French Convention offers assistance to all peoples wishing to overthrow their government;
27th, France annexes Savoy and Nice and opens R. Scheldt to commerce;
The Jacobins, under G. J. Danton, wrest power from the Girondins.

M **Dec:** 5th, trial of Louis XVI before the Convention opens;
—, revolutionary *coup d'état* in Geneva;
12th, William Pitt introduces an Aliens bill;
15th, French decree compelling all lands occupied by French troops to accept their institutions;
18th, Paine is tried in his absence for publishing *The Rights of Man.*

O Politics, Economics, Law and Education

J. B. ('Anacharsis') Cloots, *La République universelle.*
T. Paine, *Rights of Man*, part II (*Feb.*).
Arthur Young, *Travels in France.*
William Cobbett attacks U.S. institutions in his 'Peter Porcupine' pamphlets.
Mary Wollstonecraft, *Vindication of the Rights of Women.*
Slave trade abolished in Denmark.
Dollar coinage introduced in U.S., with the opening of a mint at Philadelphia.
Libel Act in Britain.
William Tuke reforms the treatment of lunatics at the York Retreat.

P Science, Technology, Discovery, etc.

The French government adopts Claude Chappe's system of semaphore.
George Cartwright's *Journal of Transactions . . . on the Coast of Labrador.*
Cable-making machine invented.

Q Scholarship

D. Lysons, *The Environs of London*, Vol. I.
Joseph Eckhel, *Doctrina numorum veterum* (–98).

R Philosophy and Religion

Dugald Stewart, *Elements of the Philosophy of the Human Mind*, Vol. I (continued 1814 and 1827).
J. G. Fichte, *Critique of Revelation.*
In France the religious orders are dissolved and civil marriage and divorce is instituted.
A Swedenborgian church is founded in Baltimore.
Baptist Missionary Society founded in London.

S Art, Sculpture, Fine Arts and Architecture

James Hoban begins the White House, Washington.
Rafaello Morghen's engraving of Leonardo's *Last Supper.*

T Music

D. Cimarosa, *The Secret Marriage* (opera).
C. J. Rouget de Lisle, *La Marseillaise* ('Chant de guerre de l'armée du Rhin').

U Literature

Samuel Rogers, *The Pleasures of Memory.*

V The Press

W Drama and Entertainment

J. W. Goethe, *Der Grosskophta.*

X Sport

Y Statistics

1792

N Sierra Leone company formed.

Denmark becomes the first state to abolish Slave Trade.

Differences in U.S. arising from Alexander Hamilton's financial policy lead to formation of political parties, namely Republican (Thomas Jefferson) and Federal (Hamilton and John Adams).

Alvarez Godoy becomes a dictator in Spain, and John, Prince of Portugal, regent for his insane mother, represses revolutionary tendencies.

z **Births and Deaths**

Feb. 23rd Joshua Reynolds d. (69).
Feb. 29th Carl von Baer b. (–1876) and
Gioacchino Rossini b. (–1868).
Mar. 3rd Robert Adam d. (64).
Apr. 25th John Keble b. (–1866).
May 13th Giovanni Mastai-Ferretti (later Pope Pius IX) b. (–1878).
Aug. 4th Richard Arkwright d. (60) and
Percy Bysshe Shelley b. (–1822).
Aug. 18th Lord John Russell b. (–1878).
Oct. 28th John Smeaton d. (68).

1793 First Coalition against France—Louis XVI executed—Second Partition of Poland

A **Jan**: 21st, Louis XVI is executed;
23rd, Russia and Prussia agree on second partition of Poland (effected May 7th).

B **Feb**: 1st, France declares war on Britain and Holland;
13th, first Coalition against France is formed by Britain, Austria, Prussia, Holland, Spain and Sardinia.

C **Mar**: 7th, France declares war on Spain; the Spanish invade Roussillon and Navarre;
11th, William Pitt issues Exchequer bills to raise funds for defence and for subsidies to Britain's allies;
15th, Traitorous Correspondence Act is passed and Habeas Corpus Act suspended in Britain;
18th, Charles Dumouriez is defeated at Neerwinden, leading to the liberation of Belgium;
26th, Holy Roman Empire declares war on France; Royalist revolt in La Vendée;
France annexes the bishopric of Basle;
Britain and Russia sign convention to interdict all Baltic trade with France.

D **Apr**: 4th, Charles Dumouriez deserts to the allies;
6th, Committee of Public Safety established in France with dictatorial power, dominated by G. J. Danton;
22nd, U.S. proclaim their neutrality (despite the 1778 alliance with France).

E **May**: 7th, second partition of Poland effected, Russia taking Lithuania and W. Ukraine, and Prussia taking Danzig, Thorn, Posen, Gnesen and Kalisch.

F **Jun**: 2nd, final overthrow of Girondins and arrest of Jacques Brissot begins Reign of Terror;
24th, revised French constitution is framed.

G **Jul**: 13th, Jean Marat is murdered by Charlotte Corday;
23rd, allies recapture Mayence and drive French troops from Germany;
British force occupies Corsica;
Maximilien Robespierre and Antoine St. Just join Committee of Public Safety.

H **Aug**: 23rd, levy of entire male population capable of serving in France;
28th, Alexander Hood occupies Toulon (recaptured *Dec.* 19th).

J **Sep**: new French offensive in Netherlands, where British army under Duke of York is defeated at Hondschoote, and in Rhineland.
17th, French law fixes wages and maximum prices.

K **Oct**: 5th, Christianity is abolished in France;
16th, Marie Antoinette is executed;
20th, Vendéans are defeated at Cholet;
31st, prominent Girondins are executed by guillotine in Place de la Concorde, Paris.

L **Nov**: Philippe Égalité (Duke of Orléans) is executed.

M **Dec**: 12th, Vendéans are defeated at Le Mans;
19th, Bonaparte takes Toulon;
26th, French victory at Weissenburg forces allies to retreat across Rhine.

N Britain seizes French settlements in India.
Lord Cornwallis promulgates code of justice in India on British model, reorganises finances, and organises 'Permanent Settlement' of Bengal.
U.S. Law compelling return of fugitive slave to his master.

O Politics, Economics, Law and Education

J. B. ('Anacharsis') Cloots, *Base constitutionelle de la république du genre humain.*
M. J. Condorcet, *Tableau du Progrès de l'Esprit humain.*
William Godwin, *The Inquiry Concerning Political Justice.*
Compulsory public education in France from the age of six.

P Science, Technology, Discovery, etc.

Kurt Sprengel's investigations into plant fertility.
Eli Whitney invents the cotton gin in U.S., which leads to the rapid growth of cotton exports from the southern states.
Samuel Bentham's woodworking machinery.
The Board of Agriculture established in Britain, with Arthur Young as Secretary.

Q Scholarship

Richard Porson is appointed Professor of Greek at Cambridge and, with Thomas Gaisford, leads a revival of classical scholarship.

R Philosophy and Religion

I. Kant, *Religion within the Boundaries of Reason.*
Jacques Hébert edits *Père Duchesne*, advocating atheism.
Hébert and Pierre Chaumette organise the Feast of Reason, celebrated in St. Eustache Church, Paris (*Nov.* 10th).

S Art, Sculpture, Fine Arts and Architecture

J. L. David, *Marat* (painting).
A. L. Girodet de Roussy, *Endymion* (painting).
A. Canova, *Cupid and Psyche* (sculpture).
Corner-stone of Capitol, Washington, laid (*Sept.* 18th), designed by William Thornton (completed 1830).
The Louvre, Paris, becomes a national art gallery.

T Music

N. Paganini makes his début as a virtuoso violinist.

U Literature

Jean Paul (pseud.), *Die Unsichtbare Loge.*
N. M. Karamzin (Russian short stories), *Poor Lisa* and *Natalia.*
Madame Jeanne Roland writes her *Appel à l'impartiale postérité* (published 1820).

V The Press

W Drama and Entertainment

X Sport

Y Statistics

Z Births and Deaths

June 26th Gilbert White d. (72).
July 3rd John Clare b. (–1864).
July 11th William Robertson d. (71).

1794 French invade Spain and Holland

A **Jan:**

B **Feb:**

C **Mar:** 5th, execution of partisans of Jacques Hébert (Hébertistes) in France;
Polish rising under T. A. Kosciuszko, which is suppressed by Russians (*Oct.*).

D **Apr:** 5th, execution of G. J. Danton and Camille Desmoulins;
19th, by treaty of The Hague Britain pays subsidies for 60,000 Prussian and Dutch troops in coalition against France.

E **May:** 18th, Charles Pichegru leads French to victory at Tourcoing.

F **Jun:** 1st, Lord Howe defeats French fleet in English Channel;
10th, power of revolutionary tribunals is increased by law of 22 Prairial, leading to mass executions;
25th, French troops take Charleroi;
26th, Austrians defeated by J. B. Jourdan at Fleurus; Duke of Coburg evacuates Belgium;
French force invades Spain.

G **Jul:** 11th, following the split of the Whig party on the issue of Parliamentary reform, Lord Portland and William Wyndham enter Pitt's cabinet, while C. J. Fox and Charles Grey lead a Whig rump of 40;
Lazare Hoche defeats *émigrés* at Quiberon Bay;
Conspiracy by Moderates of the Mountain and Dantonists against M. Robespierre, succeeds in abolishing the Commune of Paris (founded *Aug.* 1792) and
28th, Robespierre and A. St. Just are executed.

H **Aug:**

J **Sep:** 28th, alliance of St. Petersburg, of Britain, Russia and Austria against France.

K **Oct:** French troops reach the Rhine;
25th, Prussia withdraws her troops from the war.

L **Nov:** 9th, Russians enter Warsaw;
11th, Jacobin Club, Paris, is closed;
19th, following U.S. embargo on British shipping, John Jay negotiates treaty with Britain, by which Britain evacuates frontier posts in North-west and appoints commissioners to settle the boundary dispute.

M **Dec:** 8th, surviving Girondists are admitted to the Convention;
13th, in debate on the Address in British Parliament some members demand peace with France;
Prussia and Spain open separate negotiations for peace;
24th, a new issue of Assignats further depreciates the French currency;
27th, French troops under Charles Pichegru invade Holland.

N Britain takes the Seychelles, Martinique, St. Lucia and Guadaloupe, but Guadaloupe is later recaptured by the French.
Abolition of slavery in French colonies.
Whisky insurrections in Pennsylvania, occasioned by excise.
Eleventh amendment to U.S. constitution, closing federal courts to suits instituted against a state by citizens of another state or of foreign states.
Aga Mohammed founds Kajar dynasty in Persia.

O **Politics, Economics, Law and Education**
T. Paine, *The Age of Reason* (–95).
École Normale founded in France.
Stonyhurst College founded.

P **Science, Technology, Discovery, etc.**
Erasmus Darwin, *Zoonomia, or the laws of Organic Life* (–96).
John Hunter, *Treatise on the Blood, Inflammation and Gunshot Wounds* (posth.).
Adrien Legendre, *Éléments de Géométrie.*

Q **Scholarship**
James Stuart and Nicholas Revett, *The Antiquities of Athens, measured and delineated.*

R **Philosophy and Religion**
J. G. Fichte, *On the Notion of the Theory of Science* and *Vocation of a Scholar*
W. Paley, *A View of the Evidences of Christianity.*
M. Robespierre presides over the Feast of the Supreme Being in Paris (*June* 8th).

S **Art, Sculpture, Fine Arts and Architecture**
J. H. Dannecker, bust of F. Schiller.

T **Music**
J. Haydn, 'Clock' Symphony.

U **Literature**
W. Blake, *Songs of Experience.*
Anne Radcliffe, *The Mysteries of Udolpho.*
W. Godwin, *Caleb Williams, or Things as They are.*
William Gifford's satirical *Baviad.*
André de Chénier, *Jeune Captive* (poem).
Xavier de Maistre, *Voyage autour de ma chambre.*
J. W. Goethe, *Reinecke Fuchs.*
F. Schiller edits the *Horen* (–97).

V **The Press**

W **Drama and Entertainment**
S. T. Coleridge and R. Southey collaborate in *The Fall of Robespierre.*

X **Sport**

Y **Statistics**

Z **Births and Deaths**
Jan. 16th Edward Gibbon d. (57).
Apr. 8th Marie Jean Antoine Condorcet d. (50).
May 8th Antoine Laurent Lavoisier d. (50).
July 17th John Roebuck d. (76).
Nov. 17th George Grote b. (–1871).

A **Jan:** 3rd, secret treaty between Russia and Austria for third partition of Poland;
19th, Charles Pichegru is received with open arms in Amsterdam, captures the Dutch fleet in Texel and French troops overrun Holland.

B **Feb:** 9th, Tuscany makes peace with France;
15th, by peace of La Jaunaie the Vendéans come to terms with the French government;
21st, freedom of worship in France;
The Dutch surrender Ceylon to Britain.

C **Mar:** 11th, the Mahrathas defeat Mogul at Kurdla.

D **Apr:** 1st, bread riots in Paris;
5th, by peace of Basle France cedes to Prussia her conquests on the right bank of the Rhine, Frederick William II defends the interests of the N. German princes and subsequently Saxony, Hanover, the Bavarian Palatinate and Hesse-Cassel make terms with France;
23rd, Warren Hastings is acquitted of high treason.

E **May:** 16th, Batavian Republic established in Holland;
20th, The White Terror in Paris (–*June*).

F **Jun:** 25th, Luxembourg capitulates to French;
27th, British force lands at Quiberon to aid revolt in Brittany (suppressed in *Oct.*);
French recapture St. Lucia.

G **Jul:** 27th, Spain signs peace with France, ceding her part of San Domingo.

H **Aug:** 23rd, third French constitution, vesting power in Directory (effective *Nov.* 3rd);
Prussia joins Austro-Russian agreement over Poland.

J **Sep:** 6th, C. J. Jourdan crosses the Rhine;
20th, Charles Pichegru occupies Mannheim;
Austria reconquers right bank of Rhine;
British force under James Craig occupies Cape of Good Hope as a colony for Prince William V of Orange, who has taken refuge in England on the French invasion of Holland.

K **Oct:** 1st, Belgium is incorporated with France;
5th, Napoleon Bonaparte's whiff of grapeshot puts down insurrection on the Day of the Sections;
24th, in third Partition of Poland Prussia takes Warsaw and land between R. Bug and R. Niemen, Austria takes Cracow and Galicia, and Russia the area between Galicia and R. Dvina;
27th, Thomas Pinckney negotiates treaty of San Lorenzo between U.S. and Spain, which settles boundary with Florida and grants U.S. right to navigate Mississippi.

L **Nov:** 3rd, Directory in France;
25th, Stanislaus II of Poland abdicates;
Austrians defeated at Loano, Piedmont, by Barthélemi Schérer;
Following attack on George III, Pitt introduces Treasonable Practices Bill and Seditious Meetings Bill, forbidding meetings of more than 50 persons held without notice to a magistrate.

M **Dec:** 19th, and 31st, Austria signs armistice with France.

N

O Politics, Economics, Law and Education

École Polytechnique, Paris.

Institut National, Paris, with sections for natural science, moral and political science and the arts, to replace the abolished Academies.

Joseph Lakanal's plans for *écoles centrales* in France.

'Speenhamland' Act for poor relief in Britain.

P Science, Technology, Discovery, etc.

Joseph Bramah invents a hydraulic press.

Mungo Park explores the course of the River Niger.

Q Scholarship

Charles François Dupuis, *Origine de tous les cultes*, arouses an interest in Upper Egypt.

Friedrich Wolf, *Prolegomena to Homer.*

R Philosophy and Religion

I. Kant, *Zum ewigen Frieden.*

Maynooth College, a Roman Catholic seminary, founded by Act of Irish Parliament to prevent priests from travelling for instruction to the Continent, whereby they might come under the influence of revolutionary ideas.

S Art, Sculpture, Fine Arts and Architecture

F. Goya, *The Duchess of Alba* (painting).

A. J. Carstens, *Night with Her Children* and *Battle of Rossbach* (paintings).

John Soane begins the Bank of England (–1827).

T Music

Haydn 'Drum Roll' Symphony and first performance of 'London' Symphony (composed '91).

Paris Conservatoire de Musique founded.

U Literature

M. G. Lewis, *The Monk.*

Ann Radcliffe, *The Italian.*

J. W. Goethe, *Wilhelm Meister.*

F. Schiller, *Letters Concerning the Aesthetic Education of Mankind.*

Jean Paul (pseud.), *Hesperus.*

Ludwig Tieck, *William Lovell* (–96).

J. H. Voss, *Luise.*

V The Press

W Drama and Entertainment

X Sport

Y Statistics

Z Births and Deaths

Jan. 3rd Josiah Wedgwood d. (65).

May 10th Augustin Thierry b. (–1856).

May 19th James Boswell d. (56).

June 13th Thomas Arnold b. (–1842).

Oct. 31st John Keats b. (–1821).

Dec. 3rd Rowland Hill b. (–1879).

Dec. 4th Thomas Carlyle b. (–1881).

Dec. 20th Leopold von Ranke b. (–1886).

A **Jan:**

B **Feb:**

C **Mar:** 5th, final suppression of revolts in Vendée and Brittany;
9th, Napoleon Bonaparte marries Josephine de Beauharnais;
19th, freedom of the press in France;
William Pitt begins negotiations for peace with France through the Swiss Minister.

D **Apr:** Napoleon Bonaparte assumes command in Italy, 13th, defeating Austrians at Millesimo and, 22nd, the Piedmontese at Mondovi;
28th, Sardinia is forced to abandon the Austrian alliance.

E **May:** 10th, failure of François Babeuf's plot to restore French constitution of 1793;
—, Napoleon Bonaparte defeats Austrians at Lodi and
15th, enters Milan;
—, by peace of Cherasco Sardinia cedes Savoy and Nice to France;
16th, Lombardic Republic established.

F **Jun:** 1st, Tennessee becomes a U.S. state;
J. B. Jourdan invades Franconia, but is driven back;
Jean Moreau crosses the Rhine.

G **Jul:** Britain captures Elba.

H **Aug:** 5th, by treaty with France, Prussia yields lands on left bank of Rhine in exchange for Münster and other ecclesiastical territory;
15th, Napoleon Bonaparte defeats Wurmser at Castiglione delle Stiviere in his attempt to relieve Mantua;
19th, alliance of San Ildefonso between France and Spain against Britain, is virtually a renewal of the Family Compact;
J. B. Jourdan invades Germany, but Archduke Charles of Austria defeats him at Amberg.

J **Sep:** 3rd, Archduke Charles defeats J. B. Jourdan at Würzburg and Jourdan resigns his command;
17th, George Washington, who had refused to accept further nomination for election, delivers his farewell address.

K **Oct:** 5th, Spain declares war on Britain;
16th, Cispadane Republic is established from Bologna, Ferrara, Modena and Reggio.

L **Nov:** 15th (–17th), Napoleon Bonaparte defeats Austrians under Joseph Alvintzi at Arcole;
16th, Paul I succeeds as Emperor of Russia on Catherine II's death (–1801);
Royal Navy withdraws from Mediterranean;
John Adams defeats Thomas Jefferson in U.S. presidential election by 3 votes; Jefferson elected vice-president.

M **Dec:** 19th, Directory refuse further negotiations with Britain;
French expedition under Lazare Hoche to Bantry Bay fails through gales, but rumours of expedition cause run on provincial banks in England.

N Britain captures Demerara, Essequibo, Berbice, St. Lucia and Grenada, but abandons Corsica.
Aga Mohammed of Persia seizes Khorasan in Khuzistan.

O **Politics, Economics, Law and Education**

E. Burke, *Letters on a Regicide Peace*, and in *A Letter to a Noble Lord* castigates the Duke of Bedford for criticising him for accepting a pension.
Louis de Bonald, *Théorie du pouvoir politique et religieux.*
Joseph de Maistre, *Considérations sur la France.*
Jean Cambacérès *Projet de Code Civil* (taken as the basis for the Napoleonic Code in 1801).
J. G. Fichte, *Science of Rights.*

P **Science, Technology, Discovery, etc.**

Pierre Laplace enunciates the 'nebular hypothesis' in *Exposition du système du monde.*
Edward Jenner vaccinates against smallpox.
Drummond invents 'limelight'.
G. L. C. Cuvier's lectures at École Centrale du Panthéon found the science of comparative zoology.

Q **Scholarship**

Brockhaus, *Encyclopaedia* (first edition).
National Library, Lisbon, founded.

R **Philosophy and Religion**

Richard Watson, *An Apology for the Bible.*

S **Art, Sculpture, Fine Arts and Architecture**

F. Goya's *Los Caprichos*, which satirise the government and religion, are seized by the Inquisition.
J. Bacon sculpts Dr. Johnson's memorial in St. Paul's Cathedral.

T **Music**

J. Haydn, 'Kettledrum' Mass.
Benjamin Carr's opera *The Archers of Switzerland* given first performance in New York.

U **Literature**

Fanny Burney (pseud.), *Camilla.*
Jean Paul (pseud.), *Leben des Quintus Fixlein.*

V **The Press**

W **Drama and Entertainment**

August Iffland becomes director of the Prussian national theatre, Berlin.

X **Sport**

Y **Statistics**

Z **Births and Deaths**

Mar. 20th Edward Gibbon Wakefield b. (–1862).
May 4th William Hickling Prescott b. (–1859).
May 8th François Mignet b. (–1884).
June 25th Tsar Nicholas I b. (–1855).
July 26th Jean Baptiste Camille Corot b. (–1875).
July 31st Robert Burns d. (37).

1797 (Jan.–Nov.) Battle of Cape St. Vincent—Peace of Campo Formio

A **Jan:** 4th, Napoleon Bonaparte defeats Austrians under Joseph Alvintzi at Rivoli;
26th, final treaty of Polish partition.

B **Feb:** 2nd, Mantua surrenders to French;
14th, John Jervis and Horatio Nelson defeat Spanish fleet off Cape St. Vincent;
19th, Pius VI by treaty of Tolentino cedes the Romagna, Bologna and Ferrara to France, and Napoleon Bonaparte advances through Tyrol to Vienna;
Ralph Abercromby takes Trinidad;
Bank of England suspends cash payments.

C **Mar:** 4th, John Adams inaugurated President of U.S.;
Lord Lake quells rebellion in Ulster.

D **Apr:** 15th, naval mutiny at Spithead and
17th, government meets sailors' grievances;
18th, preliminary peace between Austria and France signed at Leoben.

E **May:** 2nd, naval mutiny at the Nore;
16th, Venetian constitution proclaimed;
Adam Duncan blockades the Texel.

F **Jun:** 6th, Napoleon Bonaparte founds the Ligurian Republic in Genoa;
28th, France occupies the Ionian Islands;
30th, suppression of the Nore mutiny.

G **Jul:** 9th, Cisalpine Republic proclaimed and
15th, Cispadane Republic is merged with it, comprising territories of Milan, Modena, Ferrara, Bologna and Romagna;
France puts forward peace-feelers to Britain;
Charles Talleyrand becomes French foreign minister (–*July* 1799).

H **Aug:**

J **Sep:** 4th, in *coup d'état* of 18 Fructidor a royalist reaction is prevented by Paul Barras;
Lazare Carnot flees.

K **Oct:** 4th, following expulsion of U.S. minister to France commissioners reach Paris to negotiate with Directory for preserving peace, but on refusing to give bribes are returned to U.S. (the 'XYZ Affair');
11th, Adam Duncan defeats Dutch off Camperdown (the Batavian Republic had declared war on Britain in *Feb.* 1795);
14th, France annexes the Valtelline and Chiavenna, Switzerland, to the Cisalpine Republic;
17th, by Peace of Campo Formio between France and Austria, Austria cedes Belgium and Lombardy to France and obtains Istria, Dalmatia and Venice; and by a secret agreement Austria agrees to future cession of left bank of Rhine, from Basle to Andernach, to France and the free navigation of the Rhine in return for French help to acquire archbishopric of Salzburg and part of Bavaria;
Napoleon Bonaparte is appointed to command forces for invasion of England.

L **Nov:** 16th, Frederick William III succeeds as King of Prussia and continues policy of neutrality (–1840).

O Politics, Economics, Law and Education

F. R. Chateaubriand, *Essai historique, politique et moral sur les Révolutions.*

F. Genz's open letter to Frederick William III pleads for freedom of the press and free trade in Prussia.

Andrew Bell advocates teaching by the monitorial system.

P Science, Technology, Discovery, etc.

Heinrich Olbers publishes a method of calculating the orbits of comets.

J. L. Lagrange, *Théorie des fonctions analytiques.*

Nicolas de Saussure, *Recherches Chimiques sur la Végétation.*

Henry Maudslay invents carriage lathe.

Thomas Bewick, *British Birds* (–1804).

Q Scholarship

Karl Schlegel, *Die Griechen und Römer.*

R Philosophy and Religion

I. Kant, *Metaphysical Foundations of the Theory of Right.*

F. Schelling, *Philosophy of Nature.*

William Wilberforce, *A Practical View of the Prevailing Religious System of Professed Christians.*

Methodist New Connexion leaves the Wesleyans.

S Art, Sculpture, Fine Arts and Architecture

J. M. W. Turner, *Millbank, Moonlight* (painting).

T. Girtin's first exhibition of water-colours.

Bertil Thorwaldsen settles in Rome.

T Music

J. Haydn, 'Emperor' quartet.

L. Cherubini, *Medea*, opera.

U Literature

S. T. Coleridge, *Kubla Khan* (published 1816).

Ludwig Tieck, *Tales of Peter Lebrecht.*

Johann Hölderlin, *Hyperion* (–99).

Wilhelm Wackenroden, *Outpourings of a Monk.*

V The Press

W Drama and Entertainment

George Colman, *The Heir at Law.*

August Kötzebue, *Menschenhass und Reue* (produced in London as *The Stranger*).

Ugo Foscolo, *Tieste.*

X Sport

Y Statistics

1797 (Dec.)

M Dec: 5th, Bonaparte arrives in Paris;
16th, peace conference to arrange terms between France and the Holy Roman Empire opens at Rastadt;
29th, French capture Mayence;
Ralph Abercromby arrives in Ireland as Commander-in-Chief.

N Paul I limits Russian peasants' work for their landlords to three days a week and decrees succession to property by strict seniority.

z **Births and Deaths**

Jan. 31st Franz Schubert b. (–1828).
Mar. 2nd Horace Walpole d. (80).
Mar. 27th Alfred de Vigny b. (–1863).
Apr. 16th Louis Adolphe Thiers b. (–1877).
July 8th Edmund Burke d. (68).
Aug. 30th Mary Wollstonecraft Shelley b. (–1851).
Oct. 16th James Brudenell, Earl of Cardigan, b. (–1868).
Dec. 13th Heinrich Heine b. (–1856).
Dec. 26th John Wilkes d. (70).

A **Jan**: 22nd, Directory established in Batavian Republic;
24th, Lemanic Republic proclaimed in Geneva;
Irish rebellion breaks out.

B **Feb**: 11th, French take Rome;
15th, Roman Republic proclaimed and Pius VI, refusing to surrender his temporal power, leaves Rome for Valence.

C **Mar**: 5th, France occupies Bern and
9th, annexes left bank of Rhine;
29th, Helvetian Republic proclaimed;
Alvarez Godoy is forced to resign in Spain, where the reforming party takes office.

D **Apr**: 26th, Geneva is annexed to France;
Publication in U.S. of the dispatches of the commissioners treating with the Directory in 1797 (the 'XYZ affair'), arouses war fever in U.S.

E **May**: Income tax is introduced in Britain, as a tax of 10 per cent. on all incomes over £200;
3rd, Navy Department created in U.S. to fit out squadrons to attack French shipping and possessions in West Indies.
19th, French expedition to Egypt sails from Toulon;
Marquess of Wellesley appointed governor-general of India.

F **Jun**: 12th, French force takes Malta;
21st, Lord Lake defeats Irish rebels at Vinegar Hill and enters Wexford, ending the Irish Rebellion.

G **Jul**: Napoleon Bonaparte occupies Alexandria and, 21st, at battle of the Pyramids becomes master of Egypt.

H **Aug**: 1st, Horatio Nelson destroys French fleet off Aboukir (battle of the Nile), cutting Bonaparte's communications with Europe;
19th, French alliance with Helvetian Republic;
22nd, French force lands in Ireland (fails, *Oct.*).

J **Sep**: 1st, treaty of Hyderabad between Britain and the Nizam;
5th, new law of conscription in France;
Turkey declares war on France.

K **Oct**: 27th, failure of French attempt to invade Ireland.

L **Nov**: Barthélemy Joubert occupies Piedmont;
29th, Ferdinand IV of Naples declares war against France and enters Rome;
Britain captures Minorca.

M **Dec**: 4th, France declares war on Naples;
9th, Charles Emmanuel of Sardinia is forced by Barthélemy Joubert to abdicate;
15th, French recapture Rome, and overrun the Kingdom of Naples;
24th, Anglo-Russian alliance, the foundation of a Second Coalition against France, is signed.

N Britain takes Honduras from Spain.
Following the passage of the Aliens and Seditions Acts, the Virginia and Kentucky legislatures pass resolutions, framed by James Madison and Thomas Jefferson respectively, to nullify any act of Congress in any state which considers it to be unconstitutional.

O Politics, Economics, Law and Education

T. R. Malthus, *Essay on the Principle of Population.*
Anton Thibaut, *Versuche über einzelne Theile der Theorie des Rechts.*

P Science, Technology, Discovery, etc.

Henry Cavendish determines the mean density of the earth.
Count Rumford discovers heat is generated by friction.
The Voltaic pile is invented.
Charles Tennant improves the manufacture of bleaching powder (chloride of lime).
N. L. Robert's paper-making machine.
Philippe Lebon's patent for systems of heating and lighting from coal-gas.
Alois Senefelder invents lithography.
George Bass proves Tasmania is an island.

Q Scholarship

K. W. F. Schlegel, *Geschichte der Poesie der Griechen und Römer.*

R Philosophy and Religion

J. G. Fichte, *System der Sittenlehre.*
I. Kant, *Strife of the Faculties.*
J. F. Saint-Lambert, *Principe des mœurs chez toutes les nations ou catéchisme universel.*

S Art, Sculpture, Fine Arts and Architecture

T Music

J. Haydn, *The Creation* (oratorio).
L. van Beethoven, 2nd Piano Concerto (op. 19).

U Literature

Charles Brockden Brown, *Wieland: or the Transformation.*
Ugo Foscolo, *Letters of Jacopo Ortis.*
W. S. Landor, *Gebir.*
W. Wordsworth and S. T. Coleridge, *Lyrical Ballads* (including *The Rime of the Ancient Mariner*).

V The Press

William Pitt increases the tax on British newspapers from 1½d. to 2½d. per copy and prohibits the import of foreign newspapers.
Johann Cotta founds *Allgemeine Zeitung* in Leipzig.

W Drama and Entertainment

X Sport

Y Statistics

Z Births and Deaths

Jan. 19th Auguste Comte b. (–1857).
Apr. 26th Ferdinand Delacroix b. (–1863).
June 29th Giacomo Leopardi b. (–1837).
Aug. 21st Jules Michelet b. (–1874).
Dec. 4th Luigi Galvani d. (61).

1799 Pitt forms second Coalition against France—Napoleon becomes First Consul

A **Jan**: 2nd, Britain joins the Russo-Turkish alliance;
—, Napoleon Bonaparte advances into Syria;
23rd (–*June* 19th), the Parthenopean Republic established in Piedmont.

B **Feb**:

C **Mar**: 1st, Turks and Russians complete the conquest of the Ionian Islands, which are organised as a Republic under Turkish protection;
12th, Austria declares war on France;
19th, Bonaparte begins siege of Acre, defended by Turks aided by Sidney Smith;
25th, Austrians under Archduke Charles defeat J. B. Jourdan's army at Stockach;
25th, French troops occupy Tuscany.

D **Apr**: 5th, French under B. Schérer defeated at Magnano by Austrians under Paul Kray;
8th, Conference of Rastadt (opened *Dec.* 1797), for settlement between France and the Holy Roman Empire, is dissolved;
27th, success of Austrians and Russians at battle of Cassano ends Cisalpine Republic;
—, Russians under A. Suvorov occupy Turin.

E **May**: 4th, Tippoo of Mysore is killed at Seringapatam and his kingdom is divided between Britain and the Nizam of Hyderabad;
20th, Napoleon Bonaparte abandons siege of Acre.

F **Jun**: 1st, William Pitt concludes formation of Second Coalition of Britain, Russia, Austria, Turkey, Portugal and Naples against France;
4th, Archduke Charles defeats André Masséna at Zürich;
17th (–19th), A. Suvorov recaptures Naples from the French in the battle of The Trebbia (N. Italy).

G **Jul**: 12th, political associations are forbidden in Britain;
20th, Charles Talleyrand retires from ministry of foreign affairs in France (reappointed *Nov.* 10th);
24th, Napoleon Bonaparte defeats the Turks at Aboukir.

H **Aug**: 15th, French are defeated at Novi by A. Suvorov, who then crosses the Alps;
22nd, Bonaparte leaves Egypt.

J **Sep**: 13th, Duke of York takes command of British army in Holland;
19th, Austro-Russian army is defeated at Bergen-op-Zoom;
25th (–27th), Russians under A. Korsakov are defeated by A. Masséna at Zürich; the main Russian army under A. Suvorov arrives too late and is forced to retreat across the Alps; Archduke Charles falls back on the River Danube.

K **Oct**: 9th, Napoleon Bonaparte lands at Fréjus;
18th, Duke of York capitulates at Alkmaar and Britain surrenders prisoners of war;
21st, Britain declares the entire coast of Holland under blockade;
22nd, Russia, disgusted with Austria, leaves Coalition.

L **Nov**: 9th, Bonaparte overthrows the Directory and
10th, appoints C. Talleyrand foreign minister (–1807);
13th, Austria occupies Ancona.

M **Dec**: 24th, Constitution of Year VIII establishes the Consulate, with Napoleon Bonaparte First Consul for ten years; Britain and Austria reject French offers of peace.

N James Madison's further Virginia Resolution, to reduce effects of acts of Congress in states.
The Carnatic, Mysore, is placed under British administration.

O **Politics, Economics, Law and Education**

James Mackintosh, *Introduction to the Law of Nature and Nations.*

Russian government grants the Russia-American company the monopoly of trade in Alaska.

P **Science, Technology, Discovery, etc.**

Count Rumford procures a charter for the Royal Institution, with Joseph Banks as first president.

Mungo Park, *Travels in the Interior of Africa.*

Q **Scholarship**

Sharon Turner, *History of England from the Earliest Period to the Norman Conquest* (–1805).

R **Philosophy and Religion**

J. G. Herder in *Metakritik* attacks the critical philosophy of I. Kant and J. G. Fichte.

F. Schleiermacher, *Reden über die Religion.*

Church Missionary Society and Religious Tract Society founded in London.

S **Art, Sculpture, Fine Arts and Architecture**

J. L. David, *Rape of the Sabine Women* (painting).

T **Music**

L. van Beethoven, 'Pathétique' Sonata in C Minor (op. 13).

F. Boïeldieu, *The Caliph of Baghdad* (opera).

U **Literature**

Thomas Campbell, *The Pleasures of Hope.*

Novalis (pseud.), *Heinrich von Ofterdingen.*

K. W. F. von Schlegel, *Lucinde.*

V **The Press**

W **Drama and Entertainment**

F. Schiller, *Wallenstein.*

X **Sport**

Y **Statistics**

Z **Births and Deaths**

Feb. 28th Ignaz von Döllinger b. (–1890).

May 18th Pierre Augustin Caron de Beaumarchais d. (67).

May 20th Honoré de Balzac b. (–1850).

June 7th Alexander Pushkin b. (–1837).

Oct. 18th Christian Friedrich Schönbein b. (–1868).

Dec. 14th George Washington d. (67).

A **Jan:** 17th, treaty of Montluçon ends disaffection in La Vendée, releasing troops for new French offensive in Europe.

B **Feb:** 19th, Napoleon Bonaparte as First Consul establishes himself in the Tuileries.

C **Mar:** 14th, election of Luigi Chiaramonti, the candidate of the French Cardinal Jean Maury, as Pope Pius VII (–1823);
20th, French army under J. B. Kléber defeats Turks at Heliopolis and advances to Cairo (where he is assassinated *June* 14th);
28th, Act of Union with England passes Irish Parliament.

D **Apr:** Paul von Kray succeeds Archduke Charles as commander of Austrian army.

E **May:** 9th, Jean Moreau defeats Austrians at Biberach;
15th (–20th), Napoleon Bonaparte's army crosses the Great St. Bernard Pass;
Alvarez Godoy returns to power in Spain.

F **Jun:** 2nd, Joachim Murat occupies Milan;
4th, Genoa capitulates;
14th, Napoleon Bonaparte defeats Austrians at battle of Marengo and reconquers Italy;
19th, Moreau defeats Austrians at Höchstedt;
U.S. Departments of State are moved from Philadelphia to Washington, the new seat of government.

G **Jul:**

H **Aug:**

J **Sep:** 5th, Britain captures Malta;
30th, William Pitt advocates Catholic Emancipation in Britain.

K **Oct:** 1st, by secret treaty of San Ildefonso Spain sells Louisiana to France;
Napoleon Bonaparte promises Tuscany, with the title of King, to the Duke of Parma, son-in-law of Charles IV of Spain.

L **Nov:** 7th, Paul I imposes embargo on British vessels in Russian ports until Britain restores Malta to the Knights of St. John;
In U.S. presidential election Thomas Jefferson and Aaron Burr (Republican) each secure 73 votes against John Adams, 65 and Charles Pinckney, 64 (Federalist) and House of Representatives determines election of Jefferson; downfall of Federalist Party.

O **Politics, Economics, Law and Education**

Paul Feuerbach, and others, *Encyclopaedia of Penal Jurisprudence.*
Arnold Heeren, *European Political Systems.*
J. G. Fichte, *Exclusive Commercial State.*
Robert Owen's model factory at New Lanark.
Combination Acts forbid trade associations in Britain.
Letter post is introduced in Berlin.
Library of Congress, Washington, established.

P **Science, Technology, Discovery, etc.**

Humphry Davy, *Researches, Chemical and Philosophical, Chiefly Concerning Nitrous Oxide.*
William Herschel discovers the existence of infra-red solar rays.
Alessandro Volta produces electricity from his cell.
Thomas Young, *Outlines and Experiments respecting Sound and Light.*
Richard Trevithick's light-pressure steam engine.
Earl of Stanhope's iron printing press.
Eli Whitney makes muskets with interchangeable parts, leading to the idea of mass production.
Henry Maudslay's precision screw-cutting lathe.
Royal College of Surgeons, London, founded.
French engineers begin carriage road over the Simplon Pass (-06).

Q **Scholarship**

Hervás y Panduro collects philological peculiarities of 300 languages and compiles grammars to 40 tongues in *Catalogue for the Languages of the Nations* (-05).

R **Philosophy and Religion**

F. W. Schelling, *System of Transcendental Idealism.*
Church of United Brethren in Christ founded in U.S.

S **Art, Sculpture, Fine Arts and Architecture**

J. L. David, *Portrait of Mme Récamier.*
Thomas Girtin, *White House at Chelsea* (painting).
F. Goya, *Portrait of a Woman.*

T **Music**

L. van Beethoven, 1st Symphony in C major (op.21), and 3rd Piano Concerto in C minor (op.37).
M. L. C. Cherubini, *The Water-Carrier* (opera).

U **Literature**

Robert Bloomfield, *The Farmer's Boy*, with Thomas Bewick's woodcuts, becomes first best-seller of English verse.
Maria Edgeworth, *Castle Rackrent.*
Novalis (pseud.), *To the Night.*
Jean Paul (pseud.), *Titan* (-03).
Mme de Staël, *On Literature.*
William Wordsworth's manifesto of romanticism as preface to 2nd edition of *Lyrical Ballads.*

V **The Press**

Many newspapers are suppressed in France.

M Dec: 3rd, J. Moreau defeats Austrians at Hohenlinden and advances on Vienna;
16th, Second Armed Neutrality of the North agreed between Russia, Sweden, Denmark and Prussia and St. Petersburg, to counter British right of search, imposes new criteria for a valid blockade;
24th, discovery in Paris of plot to assassinate Bonaparte enables him to deport democratic republicans to Guiana.

N

W **Drama and Entertainment**

F. Schiller, *Mary Stuart*.

Joseph Fouché establishes theatrical censorship in France.

X **Sport**

Y **Statistics**

Z **Births and Deaths**

Jan. 24th Edwin Chadwick b. (–1890).

Feb. 11th William Henry Fox Talbot b. (–1877).

Apr. 25th William Cowper d. (68).

May 9th John Brown b. (–1859).

July 31st Friedrich Wöhler b. (–1882).

Oct. 25th Thomas Babington Macaulay b. (–1859).

Oct. 26th Helmuth von Moltke b. (–1891).

Nov. 5th Jesse Ramsden d. (65).

A **Jan:** 1st, Act of Union of England and Ireland comes into force;
14th, Britain places embargo on vessels of Armed Neutrality of the North;
29th, Convention between France and Spain to issue an ultimatum to Portugal to break that country's traditional allegiance to Britain which, if not accepted, will lead to war (promulgated by the Treaty of Aranjuez, *Mar.* 21st, when Spain also agrees to cede Louisiana to France).

B **Feb:** 9th, Peace of Lunéville between Austria and France marks virtual destruction of Holy Roman Empire; France gains the left bank of the Rhine, Tuscany is ceded to Parma to form the new kingdom of Etruria, and recognition is given to Batavian, Cisalpine, Helvetian, and Ligurian Republics.

C **Mar:** 2nd, War of the Oranges with Portugal is declared by Spain;
4th Thomas Jefferson inaugurated as President of U.S. in new capital of Washington;
14th, William Pitt (having first tendered resignation *Feb.* 5th) resigns over question of Catholic Emancipation, and is replaced by Henry Addington;
21st, French defeated near Alexandria by Ralph Abercromby;
23rd, Assassination of Tsar Paul I who is succeeded by Alexander I (–1825);
28th, Peace of Florence between France and Naples, by which British vessels to be excluded from Neapolitan ports;
29th, embargo on British vessels in Danish ports; the Danes enter Hamburg in order to close the Elbe (and subsequently enter Lübeck);
Britain seizes Danish and Swedish islands in West Indies;
Prussia finally decides to join Armed Neutrality of North.

D **Apr:** 2nd, because of Danish actions on the Elbe, a British fleet is sent to Denmark where Horatio Nelson is victorious off Copenhagen and the Danes are forced, 9th, to consent to a truce;
3rd, Hanover is overrun by the Prussians;
14th, suspension of Habeas Corpus Act (previously suspended 1794) to allow detention in Britain of political suspects without trial; to continue during war and for first month of peace.

E **May:**

F **Jun:** 6th, by Treaty of Badajoz with Spain, Portugal cedes Olivenza, and agrees to shut ports to British ships;
17th, the Armed Neutrality of the North breaks up with the signing with Britain of Treaty of St. Petersburg, which recognises British right of search (Denmark signs *Oct.* 23rd, 1801, and Sweden, *Mar.* 30th, 1802);
19th, formal reconciliation between Russia and Britain;
23rd, Horne Tooke Act whereby clergy not eligible to sit in Parliament, although Tooke is allowed to retain seat until end of session;
27th, Cairo falls to English force.

G **Jul:** 15th, under French Concordat with Papacy French ecclesiastics are to be appointed by government and merely confirmed by Pope, who is allowed to keep the Papal States, with exception of Ferrara, Bologna, and Romagna (ratified by Napoleon 28th *Sept.*, but not fully ratified by France until *Apr.* 18th, 1802).

H **Aug:**

O Politics, Economics, Law and Education

J. H. Pestalozzi, *How Gertrude teaches her children.*
Foundation of the Bank of France.

P Science, Technology, Discovery, etc.

Giuseppe Piazzi discovers the first asteroid, Ceres (*Jan.* 1st).
K. F. Gauss, *Disquisitiones arithmeticae.*
Marie Bichat, *Anatomie générale.*
Robert Fulton constructs first practical submarine, *Nautilus*, at Brest.
Iron tram-road from Croydon to Wandsworth (–03).
John Dalton formulates the law of partial pressure in gases.

Q Scholarship

R Philosophy and Religion

G. W. F. Hegel and F. W. J. Schelling found *Critical Journal of Philosophy.*
Episcopal Church in U.S. adopts 39 Articles of Religion.

S Art, Sculpture, Fine Arts and Architecture

J. L. David, *Napoléon au Grand Saint-Bernard* (painting).
J. M. W. Turner, *Calais Pier* (painting).
Elgin marbles brought from Athens to London.

T Music

J. Haydn, *The Seasons.*
L. van Beethoven, 1st (op 15) Piano Concerto, and six string quartets (op. 18).

U Literature

Vicomte de Chateaubriand, *Atala.*
R. Southey, *Thalaba the Destroyer.*

V The Press

New York *Evening Post* issued.

W Drama and Entertainment

F. Schiller, *The Maid of Orleans.*

X Sport

Y Statistics

First accurate censuses taken in 1800 and 1801 provide population statistics for Italy, 17·2 mill.; Spain 10·5 mill.; Great Britain, 10·4 mill.; Ireland 5·2 mill.; and U.S., 5·3 mill.; London, 864,000; Paris, 547,756; Vienna, 231,050; Berlin, 183,294, and New York, 60,515.

1801 (Sep.–Dec.)

J **Sep:** 12th, Alexander I of Russia announces annexation of Georgia and George XIII (Regent of Georgia since *Jan.* 15th) recognises Russian decision instead of accepting traditional suzerainty of Persia;
29th, Treaty of Madrid between France and Portugal confirming Treaty of Badajoz;
France obtains part of Guiana;
French troops evacuate Egypt.

K **Oct:** 1st, peace preliminaries between Britain and France signed whereby Britain to restore all maritime conquests, except Trinidad and Ceylon, to France, Spain and Holland; France agrees to evacuate Naples; the integrity of Portugal is recognised; the independence of the Ionian Islands is agreed upon; both French and English armies are to evacuate Egypt which is to be restored to Turkey, and Malta is to be restored to the Knights by Britain (see Peace of Amiens, *Mar.* 27th, 1802);
9th, by treaty with France, Turkey formally recovers Egypt.

L **Nov:**

M **Dec:**

N

z **Births and Deaths**

Feb. 21st John Henry Newman b. (–1890).
Mar. 25th Friedrich von Hardenberg ('Novalis') d. (29).
Nov. 1st Vincenzo Bellini b. (–1835).

1802 Peace of Amiens

A **Jan:** 26th, Napoleon Bonaparte becomes President of Italian Republic (the former Cisalpine Republic).

B **Feb:**

C **Mar:** 27th, Peace of Amiens between Britain and France which achieves the complete pacification of Europe (for terms, see Preliminaries, *Oct.* 1st, 1801).

D **Apr:**

E **May:** 19th, Creation of Napoleon's Order of Legion of Honour.

F **Jun:**

G **Jul:**

H **Aug:** 2nd, Napoleon Bonaparte becomes First Consul for life, with right to appoint his successor;

4th, Introduction of Fifth Constitution in France in which the Senate, which is ruled by Napoleon, is enlarged, whereas the Tribunate and the legislative bodies lose influence.

J **Sep:** 21st, Napoleon Bonaparte annexes Piedmont.

K **Oct:** 23rd, in India Maharaja Holkar of Indore defeats both Peshwa of Poona and Sindhia of Gwalior at Poona;

Napoleon annexes the duchies of Parma and Piacenza.

L **Nov:**

M **Dec:** 31st, by Treaty of Bassein, Peshwa of Poona surrenders independence to East India Company.

N

O Politics, Economics, Law and Education

Jeremy Bentham's *Civil and Penal Legislation* introduces the theory of utilitarianism.
Daniel Webster, *The Rights of Neutral Nations in Time of War.*
Health and Morals of Apprentices Act in Britain pioneers the prevention of injury and the protection of labour in factories.
Dorpat University founded.

P Science, Technology, Discovery, etc.

William Herschel discovers that some stars revolve round one another.
Gottfried Treviranus first uses the term 'biology'.
Thomas Wedgwood makes the first photograph in copying paintings on glass.
Thomas Telford begins constructing roads in the Scottish Highlands.
John Truter and William Somerville explore Bechuanaland, almost reaching Lake Ngami.
Heinrich Olbers discovers the second asteroid, Pallas (*Mar.* 28th).
John Dalton compiles tables of atomic weights and states his atomic theory.

Q Scholarship

Richard Porson's revised edition of the *Hecuba* of Euripides.

R Philosophy and Religion

William Paley, *Natural Theology.*
F. Schelling, *Bruno.*

S Art, Sculpture, Fine Arts and Architecture

Antonio Canova, *Napoleon Bonaparte* (sculpture).
Thomas Girtin completes *The Eidometropolis.*

T Music

Beethoven, 'Moonlight' Sonata (op. 27, no. 2); and 2nd Symphony (D major, op. 36).

U Literature

Vicomte de Chateaubriand, *Le Génie du Christianisme.*
Heinrich Kleist, *The Broken Pitcher.*
Mme de Staël, *Delphine.*

V The Press

William Cobbet's *Weekly Political Register* (*Jan.*).
Edinburgh Review (*Oct.* –1929).

W Drama and Entertainment

To celebrate the Peace of Amiens, William Murdock illuminates the Soho foundry, Birmingham, with gas-burners.

X Sport

Duke of Richmond establishes horse-racing at Goodwood.

Y Statistics

Raw cotton imports	56 mill. lb.
Linen exports	15·7 mill. yds.
Silk exports	78,000 lb.

Z Births and Deaths

Feb. 26th Victor Hugo b. (–1885).
Apr. 18th Erasmus Darwin d. (71).
July 22nd M. F. X. Bichat d. (31).
July 24th Alexandre Dumas (père) b. (–1870).
Aug. 2nd Nicholas Wiseman b. (–1865).

1803 U.S.A. purchases Louisiana from France—Britain declares war on France

A **Jan:**

B **Feb:** 19th, Act of Mediation in Switzerland, whereby Cantons regain independence;
24th, U.S. Supreme Court in unanimous decision (*Marbury* v. *Madison*) for the first time declares an act of Congress to be unconstitutional and of no effect;
25th, Enactment of Delegates of the Empire at Diet of Ratisbon, which reconstructs German States under influence of France and Russia; most of the ecclesiastical estates and the free imperial cities are abolished and four new electorates are created.

C **Mar:** 1st, Ohio becomes a state of the Union (Congress having extended Federal laws to Ohio, *Feb.* 19th).

D **Apr:** 30th, U.S. purchases Louisiana Territory and New Orleans from the French.

E **May:** 17th, by Orders-in-Council Britain places her first embargo on all French and Dutch ships in British ports;
18th, renewal of hostilities between Britain and France because of Napoleon's interference in Italian and Swiss affairs, and because of Britain's refusal to part with Malta immediately.

F **Jun:** 10th, French occupation of Hanover completed;
Britain obtains St. Lucia and Tobago.

G **Jul:** 23rd, rebellion of Robert Emmet in Ireland, influenced by the French.

H **Aug:** 3rd, second Mahratha War against Sindhia of Gwalior begins when British troops open offensive.

J **Sep:** 23rd, Arthur Wellesley defeats Sindhia at Assaye; Britain takes Dutch Guiana.

K **Oct:** 19th, by convention with France, Spain is declared neutral and is to enforce Portugal's neutrality.

L **Nov:**

M **Dec:** 30th, Sindhia of Gwalior finally submits to the British.

N

O **Politics, Economics, Law and Education**

A. Coräes publishes *Present conditions of Civilisation in Greece* to interest the great powers in the cause of Greek independence.

J. B. Say, *Traité d'Économique politique.*

Joseph Lancaster, *Improvements in Education as it respects the industrious Classes.*

P **Science, Technology, Discovery, etc.**

W. H. Wollaston discovers the metallic elements rhodium and palladium in impure platinum.

Claude Berthollet, *Essai de Statique Chimique.*

J-B. Lamarck, *Recherches.*

Lazare Carnot, *Principes fondamentaux de l'équilibre et du mouvement.*

Robert Fulton propels a boat by steam power.

Caledonian Canal begun.

Henry Shrapnel's shell (invented 1784) is adopted by British army.

Q **Scholarship**

J. L. Tieck's translation of *Minnelieder* leads to the study of old Germanic literature.

R **Philosophy and Religion**

S **Art, Sculpture, Fine Arts and Architecture**

J. S. Cotman and J. B. Crome found Norwich School of artists.

Henry Raeburn, *The Macnab* (portrait).

Benjamin West, *Christ Healing the Sick* (painting).

John Soane, Governor's Court, Bank of England.

T **Music**

L. van Beethoven, 'Kreutzer' Sonata for piano and violin (op. 47).

U **Literature**

F. Schiller, *Die Braut von Messina.*

V **The Press**

The Globe founded.

W **Drama and Entertainment**

X **Sport**

Y **Statistics**

Z **Births and Deaths**

May 12th Justus von Liebig b. (–1873).

May 25th Edward George Bulwer-Lytton, Lord Lytton, b. (–1873); and Ralph Waldo Emerson b. (–1882).

June 2nd Michael Ivanovich Glinka b. (–1857).

July 5th George Borrow b. (–1881).

July 20th Thomas Lovell Beddoes b. (–1849).

Aug. 3rd. Joseph Paxton b. (–1865).

Sept. 28th Prosper Mérimée b. (–1870).

Oct. 8th Vittorio Alfieri d. (54).

Dec. 11th Hector Berlioz b. (–1869).

Dec. 18th Johann Gottfried von Herder d. (59).

1804 Napoleon Bonaparte crowned Napoleon I

A **Jan:**

B **Feb:** 16th, discovery of conspiracy against Napoleon.

C **Mar:** 20th, Duc d'Enghien, implicated in February plot, is executed.

D **Apr:** 16th, war between East India Company and Holkar of Indore opens;
26th, Henry Addington tenders resignation after the Irish Militia bill which shows William Pitt's opposition to the Ministry (his resignation is accepted, 29th).

E **May:** 10th, William Pitt forms Cabinet, but finds it necessary to exclude C. J. Fox;
16th, Napoleon proclaimed Emperor by Senate and Tribunate (–1815).

F **Jun:**

G **Jul:**

H **Aug:** 11th, Francis II assumes title of hereditary Emperor of Austrian possessions (though he still maintains title of Holy Roman Emperor).

J **Sep:** 25th, Twelfth Amendment added to American Constitution which provides for separate ballots for the Presidency and the Vice-Presidency.

K **Oct:** 9th, Hobart, Tasmania, founded;
27th, Heinrich Baron Stein appointed Prussian Minister of Trade.

L **Nov:** 13th–17th, defeats of Holkar's forces;
Austria and Russia make a declaration to maintain the Ottoman Empire against French expansion.

M **Dec:** 2nd, Napoleon Bonaparte is crowned Emperor as Napoleon I by Pope Pius VII in Paris;
12th, Spain declares war on Britain at instigation of France.

N

O **Politics, Economics, Law and Education**
Code Napoléon promulgated in France.
First British Savings Bank opened (at Tottenham).

P **Science, Technology, Discovery, etc.**
J. Leslie, *Experimental Inquiry into the Nature and Properties of Heat.*
François Appert opens bottling factory.

Q **Scholarship**
F. Hoelderlin's translations of the tragedies of Sophocles into German.

R **Philosophy and Religion**
Thomas Brown, *Inquiry into the Relation of Cause and Effect.*
K. C. F. Kreuse, *Philosophical Systems.*
British and Foreign Bible Society founded.

S **Art, Sculpture, Fine Arts and Architecture**
English Water Colour Society founded.
St. Petersburg Bourse built.

T **Music**
L. van Beethoven, 3rd ('Eroica') Symphony (op. 55).

U **Literature**
Jean Paul (pseud.), *Flegeljahre* (–05).
William Blake, *Jerusalem.*

V **The Press**

W **Drama and Entertainment**
F. Schiller, *Wilhelm Tell.*

X **Sport**

Y **Statistics**

Z **Births and Deaths**
Feb. 6th Joseph Priestley, d. (71).
Feb. 12th Immanuel Kant d. (80).
Apr. 5th Matthias Schleiden b. (–1881).
Apr. (–) Jacques Necker d. (72).
June 3rd Richard Cobden b. (–1865).
July 1st 'George Sand' (pseud. of Armandine Dupin, later Dudevant) b. (–1876).
July 4th Nathaniel Hawthorne b. (–1864).
Dec. 21st Benjamin Disraeli, Earl of Beaconsfield, b. (–1881).
Dec. 23rd C. A. Sainte-Beuve b. (–1869).

1805 Battles of Trafalgar and Austerlitz

A **Jan:**

B **Feb:** 24th, Arthur Wellesley resigns civil and military positions in India.

C **Mar:** 4th, Thomas Jefferson begins second term as President of U.S.

D **Apr:** 11th, by treaty of St. Petersburg, Britain and Russia agree to form a European league for the liberation of the northern German states, the Third Coalition against France.

E **May:** 26th, Napoleon is crowned King of Italy in Milan Cathedral.

F **Jun:** 4th, the Ligurian Republic is united with France, which thus gains Genoa.

G **Jul:**

H **Aug:** 9th, Austria joins signatories of Treaty of St. Petersburg.

J **Sep:**

K **Oct:** 20th, Austrians under Karl Mack are defeated by French at Ulm;
21st, Lord Nelson defeats combined Franco-Spanish fleet at Trafalgar, and is mortally wounded in the action.

L **Nov:** 23rd, peace treaty between East India Company and Sindhia.

M **Dec:** 2nd, Napoleon defeats combined Russo-Austrian forces at Austerlitz;
15th, by treaty of Schönbrunn with France, Prussia cedes Cleves, Neuchâtel and Ansbach, and is allowed to occupy Hanover in order to prevent her joining the coalition against Napoleon;
26th, by Peace of Pressburg between Austria and France, the Austrians give up the Tyrol and all possessions in Italy and in Dalmatia and, in addition, give up all possessions and influence in Southern Germany so that Bavaria and Württemberg become kingdoms, and Baden becomes a Grand Duchy.

N After *May*, England closes down on the American trade with the West Indies, resulting in loss of friendship with the U.S. practically leading to war.

O **Politics, Economics, Law and Education**
Lord Liverpool, *Treatise on the Coins of the Realm.*
Internal customs duties in Prussia are abolished.

P **Science, Technology, Discovery, etc.**
William Congreve's iron rockets used to bombard Boulogne (–06).
Thomas Telford's iron aqueduct over the Ellesmere Canal.
Mungo Park undertakes expedition to the Niger River.

Q **Scholarship**
H. T. Colebrooke, *Essay on the Vedas* and *Sanskrit Grammar.*

R **Philosophy and Religion**
Hosea Ballou, *A Treatise on Atonement.*

S **Art, Sculpture, Fine Arts and Architecture**
F. Goya, *Doña Isabel Cobos de Porcal* (portrait).
Philipp Runge, *The Morning* (painting).
J. M. W. Turner, *Shipwreck* (painting).
British Institution for the development of the Fine Arts.

T **Music**
L. van Beethoven, 4th Piano Concerto in G (op. 58); and *Fidelio* (opera).
Nicolò Paganini begins to tour Europe as a virtuoso violinist.

U **Literature**
Vicomte Chateaubriand, *René.*
Walter Scott, *The Lay of the Last Minstrel.*
Robert Southey, *Madoc.*
William Wordsworth completes *The Prelude.*

V **The Press**

W **Drama and Entertainment**

X **Sport**

Y **Statistics**
U.K. total state expenditure, £62·8 mill.

Z **Births and Deaths**
Mar. 4th Jean Baptiste Greuze d. (80).
Apr. 2nd Hans Christian Andersen b. (–1875).
June 22nd Giuseppe Mazzini b. (–1872).
July 29th Charles Alexis de Tocqueville b. (–1859).

A **Jan:** 8th, Britain finally occupies Cape of Good Hope;
23rd, death of William Pitt.

B **Feb:** 10th, Formation of 'Ministry of all the Talents' with Lord Grenville as Prime Minister and C. J. Fox as Foreign Secretary;
15th, French troops enter Naples;
—, Franco-Prussian Treaty against Britain, whereby Prussia is to close her ports to British ships.

C **Mar:** 30th, Joseph Bonaparte becomes King of Naples.

D **Apr:** 1st, Britain declares war on Prussia after the seizure of Hanover;
Britain begins blockade of French coast.

E **May:**

F **Jun:** 5th, Louis Bonaparte becomes King of Holland;
27th, Buenos Aires surrenders to a small British force (but is retaken by the Spanish in *Aug.*).

G **Jul:** 12th, establishment of Confederation of Rhine under protection of France, uniting Bavaria, Württemberg, Mainz, Baden, and eight lesser principalities.

H **Aug:** 6th, The Holy Roman Empire ends; Francis II formally resigns the Imperial Dignity and becomes Francis I, Emperor of Austria.

J **Sep:** 13th, death of Fox.

K **Oct:** 1st, Prussian ultimatum to France for retaining Hanover, which Napoleon intends to restore to Britain;
9th, Prussia declares war on France;

14th, Napoleon defeats Prussia at Jena and Saxony at Auerstädt;
16th, war between Turkey and Russia at instigation of French emissary at Constantinople, with Russia's occupation of Danubian Provinces;
24th, British Parliament dissolved in order to acquire more pro-Grenville supporters into Parliament by means of patronage;
27th, Napoleon occupies Berlin.

L **Nov:** 21st, by the Berlin Decrees, Napoleon begins the 'Continental System', closing continental ports to British vessels and declaring all British ports to be in a state of blockade;
28th, Joachim Murat leads a French force into Warsaw.

M **Dec:** 11th, by Peace of Posen with France, Saxony is made a kingdom and enters the Confederation of the Rhine;
15th, Napoleon enters Warsaw;
—, new British Parliament, in which Lord Grenville's ministry is returned with considerable majority.

N Burr Plot in the U.S., when Aaron Burr, having collected men at Blennerhasset's Island, after *Aug.*, forms an expedition to march into Louisiana (he is subsequently arrested, tried, and acquitted in 1807).

O Politics, Economics, Law and Education

Ernst Arndt, *Spirit of the Age* (–18) inspires the German national revival.
James Madison, *An Examination of the British Doctrine which subjects to Capture a Neutral Trade not open in Time of Peace.*
K. Zacharies von Lingerthel, *Legislation.*
J. F. Herbert, *German Education.*

P Science, Technology, Discovery, etc.

Humphry Davy isolates the metallic elements sodium and potassium by electrolysis.
P. A. Latreille, *Genera Crustaceorum et Insectorum.*
A nail-cutting machine is invented.

Q Scholarship

J. C. Adelung, *Mithridates*, a history of languages and dialects.
Wilhelm De Wette, *Introduction to the Old Testament.*

R Philosophy and Religion

J. G. Fichte, *Bericht über die Wissenschaftslehre.*
Napoleon convokes a Sanhedrin and establishes a consistorial organisation for Jews in France.

S Art, Sculpture, Fine Arts and Architecture

David Wilkie, *Village Politicians* (painting).
Brera Gallery, Milan, opened.
Claude Clodion begins Arc de Triomphe, Paris.

T Music

L. van Beethoven, 'Rasoumoffsky' string quartets (op. 59), 4th Symphony in B flat (op. 60) and Violin Concerto (op. 61).

U Literature

V The Press

W Drama and Entertainment

X Sport

Y Statistics

U.K. registered tonnage of merchant shipping, 2,080,000.
U.K. iron production, 243,851 tons.
U.K. cotton industry employs 90,000 factory workers and 184,000 handloom weavers.

Z Births and Deaths

Mar. 6th Elizabeth Barrett Browning b. (–1861).
Apr. 9th Isambard Kingdom Brunel b. (–1859).
May 20th John Stuart Mill b. (–1873).
Aug. 22nd Jean Honoré Fragonard d. (73).

1807 (Jan.–Oct.) Treaty of Tilsit leaves Britain alone against Napoleon

A **Jan**: 4th, dismissal of Baron Stein by Frederick William III of Prussia;
7th, Britain declares a blockade of coasts of France and of Napoleon's allies, and all ships trading in ports where Britain is excluded are liable to capture.

B **Feb**: 8th, indecisive battle of Eylau between France and combined Russo-Prussian army;
19th, British fleet forces way through Dardanelles, to support Russia in war against Turkey (but is forced to withdraw *Mar.* 2nd., suffering severe damage).

C **Mar**: 24th, fall of 'Ministry of all the Talents' over Lord Grenville's refusal to grant Catholic Emancipation at a future date, and the Whigs surrender seals of office, never to take office again under George III;
31st, Duke of Portland becomes Prime Minister with George Canning and Lord Castlereagh as Secretaries of State.

D **Apr**: 26th, by Convention of Bartenstein, Russia and Prussia form an alliance to drive France out of German States;
27th, Duke of Portland dissolves Parliament to test support for new Ministry.

E **May**: 29th, Sultan Selim III of Turkey is deposed by Mustapha IV.

F **Jun**: 14th, at the battle of Friedland France defeats combined Russian and Prussian force;
22nd, the new British Parliament assembles with a majority for the new ministry (as a result of the 'No-Popery' general election);
22nd, U.S. frigate *Chesapeake* is stopped by British vessel *Leopard*, and demands are made to hand over British deserters, which nearly causes war, averted by Thomas Jefferson's pacific policy;
27th, Britain joins Convention of Bartenstein (see *Apr.*).

G **Jul**: 7th, Napoleon meets Tsar Alexander and Frederick William II on the R. Niemen, and by Treaty of Tilsit with France, Russia agrees to establishment of Duchy of Warsaw, recognises Confederation of Rhine, agrees to close all ports to British ships, and, by a secret agreement, the Tsar agrees to coerce Denmark, Sweden, and Portugal into joining alliance against Britain, and is given a free hand in Finland;
9th, by a separate Treaty of Tilsit with France, Prussia loses all possessions west of Elbe and all Polish territories, which are to form Duchy of Warsaw under King of Saxony, and by a secret agreement, agrees to join the 'Continental System' and to exclude British ships from Prussian ports;
10th, Baron Stein becomes Prussia's principal minister.

H **Aug**: Jerome Bonaparte is created King of Westphalia (formed from former Prussian possessions west of R. Elbe), and Erfurt is incorporated in France.

J **Sep**: 2nd–5th, British bombardment of Copenhagen because of Napoleon's plan to use Danish fleet against Britain;
7th, the Danes surrender;
—, France obtains Hither Pomerania from Sweden;
Napoleon suppresses Tribunate, thus ensuring his dictatorship.

K **Oct**: 9th, Emancipation of Prussian serfs;
27th, by Treaty of Fontainebleau, Spain and France agree to conquer Portugal;
29th, Denmark joins France against Britain.

O Politics, Economics, Law and Education

Gottlieb Hufeland, *New Foundations of Political Economy.*
Comte de Saint-Simon, *Introduction aux Travaux Scientifiques du xix Siècle.*
Napoleon introduces Commercial Law Code in France.

P Science, Technology, Discovery, etc.

J. L. Gay-Lussac, *Observations on Magnetism.*
Alexander von Humboldt and Aimé Bonpland, in *Voyage aux régions équinoxiales du Nouveau Continent, 1799–1804*, study climate, volcanoes, etc., of Spanish America.
Charles Bell, *System of Comparative Surgery.*
Rolbert Fulton's steamboat *Clermont*, built by Boulton and Watt, plies on Hudson River.
Thomson patents aerated waters.

Q Scholarship

J. C. L. Sismondi, *History of the Italian Republics in the Middle Ages.*
Friedrich Wolf, *Science of Antiquity.*

R Philosophy and Religion

G. W. F. Hegel, *Phenomenology of Spirit.*
First Convention of U.S. Evangelical Association, or 'New Methodists', founded by Jacob Albright.

S Art, Sculpture, Fine Arts and Architecture

J. M. W. Turner, *Sun Rising in a Mist* (painting).
J. L. David completes *Coronation of Napoleon* (painting).

T Music

L. van Beethoven, *Leonora No. 3* and *Coriolanus* overtures; 'Appassionata' sonata.
G. L. P. Spontini, *The Vestal Virgin* (opera).
Étienne Méhul, *Joseph* (opera).
Thomas Moore's *Irish Melodies* with music by John Stevenson (–34).

U Literature

Lord Byron, *Hours of Idleness.*
B. Constant, *Adolphe* (published 1815).
Mme de Staël, *Corinne.*
Charles and Mary Lamb, *Tales from Shakespeare.*
Ugo Foscolo, *Carme sui sepolcri.*
Jean Paul, *Levana.*
William Wordsworth, *Ode on Intimations of Immortality.*

V The Press

W Drama and Entertainment

X Sport

Horse-racing: Ascot Gold Cup first given.

Y Statistics

1807 (Nov.–Dec.)

L Nov: 7th, Russia breaks off relations with Britain, amounting to declaration of war (as result of Treaty of Tilsit of *July* 7th);

11th, further British Orders-in-Council declaring blockade of Continental ports (extended *Nov.* 25th);

19th, France invades Portugal for refusing to enter 'Continental System';

29th, the Portuguese royal family, the Braganzas, flee to Brazil.

M Dec: 17th, Napoleon's Milan Decrees against British trade, extending Berlin Decrees (of *Nov.* 21st 1806);

22nd, U.S. Embargo Act as reprisal for French and British restrictions and for the *Chesapeake* Incident, by which the U.S. withholds raw materials and finished products with idea of forcing belligerents to end the wars.

N Buenos Aires is attacked by the British at the end of *June* but they are forced to withdraw *July*.

Military reforms in Prussia after Scharnhorst's Manifesto of *July*.

z **Births and Deaths**

Feb. 27th Henry Wadsworth Longfellow b. (–1882).
May 28th Jean Louis Rodolphe Agassiz d. (73).
July 4th Giuseppe Garibaldi b. (–1882).

1808 Napoleon's 'Continental System' at its height—British expedition to Portugal

A **Jan:** 1st, Sierra Leone becomes a British Crown Colony;
—, U.S. prohibits import of slaves from Africa.

B **Feb:** 2nd, a French force occupies Rome after Pope Pius VII refuses to recognise Kingdom of Naples and to join alliance against Britain;
16th, France invades Spain;
28th, Austria joins Napoleon's 'Continental System';
29th, French take Barcelona.

C **Mar:** 3rd, Joachim Murat occupies Madrid;
16th, Tsar Alexander I proclaims Finland to be a province conquered by Russia.

D **Apr:**

E **May:** 2nd, Spanish rising against the French begins in Madrid;
6th, Charles IV of Spain and Crown Prince Ferdinand renounce the Spanish throne;
30th, Napoleon annexes Tuscany, allowing it seats in the French Senate and legislature.

F **Jun:** 9th, Creation of Austrian *Landwehr*;
15th, Joseph of Naples becomes King of Spain (subsequently Joachim Murat becomes King of Naples);
17th, Tsar Alexander I, suspecting French intentions against Russia, promises to restore privileges in Finland.

G **Jul:** Mahamud II succeeds Mustapha IV, who is dethroned as Sultan of Turkey.

H **Aug:** 1st, British expedition is sent to Portugal;
—, King Joseph flees from Madrid, fearing Spanish rebels;
21st, Arthur Wellesley defeats French at Vimiero and subsequently returns to England;
30th, by convention of Cintra with the British commander Hew Dalrymple, Andache Junot withdraws French troops from Portugal.

J **Sep:** 8th, Napoleon forces Prussia to limit its army to 42,000 men.

K **Oct:** 12th, Napoleon holds Erfurt Congress with his vassals and Tsar Alexander to strengthen Franco-Russian alliance, particularly regarding the Eastern Question.

L **Nov:** 19th, Municipal Councils are introduced in Prussia.

M **Dec:** 13th, Madrid capitulates to Napoleon;
16th, fall of Baron Stein in Prussia, following Napoleon's criticisms of him.

N

O Politics, Economics, Law and Education

J. G. Fichte, *Addresses to the German Nation.*
Foundation of Tugendbund (Society of Virtue) in Königsberg.
Royal Lancasterian Institution for promoting education of the poor, on the model of Joseph Lancaster.

P Science, Technology, Discovery, etc.

John Dalton, *New System of Chemical Philosophy* (–27).
J. L. Gay-Lussac, *The Combination of Gases.*

Q Scholarship

K. F. Eichhorn, *History of German Law* (–23).
F. Schlegel, *Language and Wisdom of the Indians.*

R Philosophy and Religion

J. F. Fries, *New Critique of Reason.*
Alexander Humboldt, *Opinions of Nature.*
Napoleon abolishes the Inquisition in Spain and Italy.
Sydney Smith, *Peter Plymley's Letters*, attacks disabilities of Roman Catholics in Britain.

S Art, Sculpture, Fine Arts and Architecture

Antonio Canova, *Pauline Bonaparte Borghese as Venus* (sculpture).
Kaspar Friedrich, *The Cross on the Mountains* (painting).
F. Goya, *Execution of the Citizens of Madrid* (painting).
J. D. Ingres, *La Grande Baigneuse* (painting).

T Music

L. van Beethoven, 5th Symphony (op. 67) and 6th, 'Pastoral' Symphony (op. 68).

U Literature

Vicomte de Chateaubriand, *Les Aventures du dernier Abencérage* (published 1826).
W. Scott, *Marmion.*

V The Press

The Examiner founded with Leigh Hunt as editor.
The Times sends Henry Crabb Robinson as special correspondent to the Peninsular Campaign.

W Drama and Entertainment

J. W. Goethe, *Faust*, pt. 1.

X Sport

Y Statistics

Z Births and Deaths

Apr. 20th Charles Louis Napoleon Bonaparte (Napoleon III) b. (–1873).
— Honoré Daumier b. (–1879).

1809 (Jan.–Sep.) Death of Sir John Moore—Napoleon imprisons Pope Pius VII

A **Jan:** 5th, Britain concludes Treaty of Dardanelles with Turkey;
16th, Sir John Moore is killed at Corunna, having created diversion to distract Napoleon;
The Spanish Supreme Junta and Britain agree not to make separate peace with Napoleon.

B **Feb:** 8th, Francis I of Austria decides on war with France, fearing Napoleon will overrun Austria.

C **Mar:** 1st, The Non-Intercourse Act comes into force whereby U.S. refuses to trade with Britain and France, but will begin trade with the one which removes restrictions;
4th, James Madison becomes the fourth President of U.S.;
15th, U.S. Embargo Act (of *Dec.* 22nd 1807) expires;
29th, Gustavus IV of Sweden is forced to abdicate after military defeats in war with Denmark; is succeeded (*June* 5th) by Charles XIII (–1818).

D **Apr:** 22nd, Arthur Wellesley lands at Lisbon to take command in Portugal;
—, Austrian forces occupy Warsaw (but compelled to withdraw *June* 3rd);
25th, British conclude treaty of friendship with Sikhs at Amritsar;
26th, Britain restricts limits of blockade to Holland, France, and Italian states;
Britain agrees to provide Austria with a monthly subsidy of £150,000 and to send an expedition to the Scheldt.

E **May:** 12th, Arthur Wellesley defeats French under Soult at Oporto and forces them to retreat from Portugal;
13th, French army takes Vienna;
17th, Napoleon issues Imperial Decree annexing Papal States;
21st–22nd, after the battle of Aspern against Austrians, Napoleon is forced to recross the R. Danube. France calls on Russian support against Austria which is given ineffectively;
Russian offensive against the Turks is renewed.

F **Jun:** 19th, Curwen's Act is passed to prevent sale of Parliamentary seats, thus decreasing number of seats which British government can manipulate for its regular supporters.

G **Jul:** 5th (–6th), Napoleon defeats Austrians at Wagram;
6th, Pope Pius VII, having excommunicated Napoleon, is taken prisoner by the French;
16th, revolt in Upper Peru against Spanish authority;
28th, Arthur Wellesley is victorious at Talavera and is subsequently created Duke of Wellington;
—, (–*Dec.* 23rd), British expedition to Walcheren, to help Austrians by diverting Napoleon's attention from Danube, fails.

H **Aug:** 4th, Prince Metternich becomes Chief Minister of Austria.

J **Sep:** 6th, Duke of Portland resigns because of ill health;
17th, by Peace of Frederikshavn with Sweden, Russia obtains Finland, although Napoleon refuses to recognise this treaty;
21st, Castlereagh and Canning fight a duel over the latter's attempts to have Castlereagh removed from the War Office due to alleged incompetency, with particular regard to the Walcheren expedition;
26th, Turkey is defeated by Russians at Brailoff (and subsequently at Silestria).

O Politics, Economics, Law and Education
Joseph de Maistre, *Principe Générateur des Constitutions Politiques.*
David Ricardo, *The High Price of Bullion or Proof of the Depreciation of Bank Notes.*

P Science, Technology, Discovery, etc.
K. F. Gauss, *Theoria motus corporum coelestium.*
Étienne Malus discovers polarisation of light by reflection.
W. Maclure, *Observations on the Geology of the U.S.*
J-B. Lamarck, *Système des animaux sans vertèbres.*
S. T. Sömmering invents water voltameter telegraph.
John Heathcoat's bobbin net machine.
Pall Mall, London, is lit by gas.

Q Scholarship

R Philosophy and Religion
Evangelical revival begins in Germany.
Theological Seminary, St. Petersburg, founded.
Elizabeth Seton founds Sisters of Charity of St. Joseph in U.S.

S Art, Sculpture, Fine Arts and Architecture
John Constable, *Malvern Hall* (painting).
Kaspar Friedrich, *Mönch am Meer* (painting).
Henry Raeburn, *Mrs. Spiers* (portrait).

T Music
L. van Beethoven, 5th Piano Concerto, 'Emperor' in E flat (op. 73).
G. L. P. Spontini, *Ferdinand Cortez* (opera).

U Literature
Lord Byron, *English Bards and Scots Reviewers.*
Thomas Campbell, *Gertrude of Wyoming.*
Vicomte de Chateaubriand, *Les Martyrs.*
J. W. Goethe, *The Elective Affinities.*
Washington Irving, *Knickerbocker's History of New York.*
Ivan Kriloff, *Fables* (–1811).
Hannah More, *Coelebs in Search of a Wife.*
August Schlegel, *Lectures on Dramatic Art and Literature.*

V The Press
Quarterly Review founded (*Feb.*) by Walter Scott and other Tories.

W Drama and Entertainment

X Sport
2,000 Guineas established at Newmarket Races.

Y Statistics

1809 (Oct.–Dec.)

K **Oct**: 4th, Spencer Perceval forms an administration in Britain;
14th, by Peace of Schönbrunn, Austria cedes Trieste and Illyria to France, Galicia to Saxony and Russia, Salzburg and Inn District to Bavaria, and joins the Continental System.

L **Nov**: 19th, Spanish defeated at Ocana; French overrun all Andalusia, apart from Cadiz.

M **Dec**: 16th, Napoleon is divorced from Josephine by an act of Senate.

N Britain captures Martinique and Cayenne from the French.

z Births and Deaths

Jan. 15th Pierre Joseph Proudhon b. (–1865).
Jan. 19th Edgar Allan Poe b. (–1849).
Feb. 12th Charles Darwin b. (–1882) and Abraham Lincoln b. (–1865).
Mar. 31st Edward Fitzgerald b. (–1883) and Nicolai Gogol b. (–1852).
May 31st Joseph Haydn d. (77).
June 8th Thomas Paine d. (72).
June 14th Henry Keppel b. (–1904).
July 9th Friedrich Henle b. (–1885).
Aug. 6th Alfred Lord Tennyson b. (–1892).
Aug. 29th Oliver Wendell Holmes b. (–1894).
Nov. 3rd Felix Mendelssohn-Bartholdy b. (–1847).
Dec. 29th William Ewart Gladstone b. (–1898).

1810 Napoleon annexes Holland

A **Jan:** 6th, by Treaty of Paris, Sweden agrees to join 'Continental System' in return for Napoleon's recognition of Treaty of Frederikshavn (*Sept.* 17 1809), and recovers Pomerania.

B **Feb:** 11th, Napoleon marries Marie-Louise of Austria.

C **Mar:** 23rd, by the Rambouillet Decrees (kept secret until *May*) Napoleon orders sale of all U.S. ships which have been seized for violation of French decrees.

D **Apr:** 19th, under influence of Simon Bolivar, the Junta in Venezuela breaks from Spain, refusing to recognise Joseph Bonaparte, and proclaiming allegiance to Ferdinand VII.

E **May:** 1st, U.S. reopens commerce with Britain and France with various provisos;
21st, Whig Reform Bill, to provide for triennial parliaments and for extension of franchise, is defeated;
22nd, revolt in New Grenada against Spanish authority;
25th, revolt in Rio de la Plata, against Joseph Bonaparte's régime.

F **Jun:** K. A. von Hardenberg succeeds Stein in Prussia.

G **Jul:** 1st, Louis, King of Holland abdicates after pressure from Napoleon;
9th, Napoleon annexes Holland;
10th, Michel Ney takes Ciudad Rodrigo after long siege; British force takes Île de Bourbon and Mauritius in Indian Ocean.

H **Aug:** 5th, Trianon Tariff, whereby Napoleon places tax on all colonial imports into France;
18th, Charles XIII of Sweden adopts General Jean Bernadotte as heir.

J **Sep:** 16th, Revolt in Mexico in favour of independence from Spain;
18th, Junta in Chile revolts against Joseph Bonaparte and assumes authority;
20th, report of Bullion Committee in Britain, suggesting return to cash payments within two years, is not accepted.

K **Oct:** 18th and 25th, by Decrees of Fontainebleau Napoleon orders confiscation and burning of British goods found within Napoleonic states and establishes tribunals to try persons accused of introducing illicit wares;
Duke of Wellington holds the lines of Torres Vedras throughout the month, forcing the French to withdraw.

L **Nov:** 1st, Napoleon revokes Berlin and Milan Decrees with regard to U.S. trade (not published until *May* 11th 1812).

M **Dec:** 10th, Napoleon annexes northern Hanover, Bremen, Hamburg, Lauenburg, and Lübeck, in order to strengthen blockade to prevent smuggling of British goods;
31st, Tsar Alexander introduces new tariffs aimed at French goods, in violation of Treaty of Tilsit (*July* 1807).

N Obstinate fighting in Danubian Provinces between Turkey and Russia.
Guadaloupe, the last French colony in West Indies, is taken by the British.

O **Politics, Economics, Law and Education**

Lazare Carnot, *De la défense de places fortes.*

K. W. von Humboldt as Prussian minister of education reforms the gymnasia and institutes pre-university matriculation.

Berlin University founded with J. G. Fichte as rector.

P **Science, Technology, Discovery, etc.**

J. W. Goethe, *Theory of Colours.*

Samuel Hahnemann's *Organon of Therapeutics* founds homoeopathy.

Franz Gall and Johann Spurzheim, *Anatomie et physiologie du système nerveux.*

Krupp works opened at Essen.

Q **Scholarship**

G. F. Creuser, *Symbolism of the Ancients* (–12).

R **Philosophy and Religion**

John Milner opposes the right of the British government to veto the appointment of Roman Catholic bishops.

Protestant revivalists in Geneva form *Société des Amis.*

The Cumberland Presbytery, Kentucky, excluded from the Presbyterian Church.

S **Art, Sculpture, Fine Arts and Architecture**

Francisco Goya engraves *Los Desastres de la Guerra* (–13).

J. F. Overbeck founds the 'Nazarenes' to regenerate German religious art.

San Carlo Opera House, Naples (–12).

T **Music**

L. van Beethoven, incidental music to *Egmont.*

G. Rossini, *La Cenerentola* (opera).

U **Literature**

Mme de Staël, *De l'Allemagne.*

F. H. von der Hagen edits *Nibelungenlied* (–42).

Walter Scott, *The Lady of the Lake.*

V **The Press**

F. C. Perthes edits *Das deutsche Museum.*

W **Drama and Entertainment**

Heinrich von Kleist, *Das Kätchen von Heilbronn* and Prinze Friederick von Hambourg (publ. 1821).

X **Sport**

Y **Statistics**

Z **Births and Deaths**

Feb. 22nd Frédéric Chopin b. (–1849).

Feb. 24th Henry Cavendish d. (79).

Mar. 15th Charles de Montalembert b. (–1870).

June 8th Robert Schumann b. (–1856);

Aug. 10th Camillo Count Cavour b. (–1861).

Sept. 29th Elizabeth Cleghorn Gaskell (*née* Stevenson) b. (–1865).

Dec. 7th Theodor Schwann b. (–1882).

Dec. 11th Alfred de Musset b. (–1857).

1811 British victories in Portugal—Prince of Wales becomes Prince Regent

A **Jan:** 22nd, by annexing Oldenburg, Napoleon virtually alienates Tsar Alexander, since the heir apparent to that Duchy is his brother-in-law, and the annexation violates Treaty of Tilsit (*July* 1807).

B **Feb:** 2nd, U.S. renews Non-Intercourse Act against British commerce;
5th, George III's insanity necessitates Regency Act, whereby Prince of Wales becomes Prince Regent, but with limited powers for twelve months;
10th, Russians take Belgrade and capture Turkish army;
20th, Austria declares itself bankrupt.

C **Mar:** 1st, Mehemet Ali massacres Mamelukes at Cairo;
20th, birth of François-Charles-Joseph, heir to Napoleon's throne; he is given the title of King of Rome.

D **Apr:**

E **May:** 8th, Duke of Wellington defeats French at Fuentes d'Onoro;
16th, British check French under Nicolas Soult at Albuhera.

F **Jun:** 17th, National Council meets in Paris to settle disputes between Napoleon and Pope Pius VII (but is dissolved *July* 6th, when it refuses to support Napoleon's orders unless the Pope is freed).

G **Jul:** 5th, Venezuela becomes independent and adopts constitution under influence of Simon Bolivar and Francisco de Miranda, having disavowed allegiance to Ferdinand VII of Spain (lasts until *July* 1812).

H **Aug:** 14th, Paraguay declares itself independent of Spain (and later of Buenos Aires *Oct.* 12th);
British occupy Java in East Indies.

J **Sep:** 7th, K. von. Hardenberg's Edict in Prussia provides for peasant proprietorship.

K **Oct:** 29th, Napoleon threatens to invade Berlin unless Prussia cancels her military plans for rapprochement with Russia, and the French state the terms of proposed alliance with Prussia.

L **Nov:** 5th, James Madison recommends Congress to prepare U.S. for hostilities against Britain, in view of the British Orders-in-Council on trade and violation of the 30-mile limit.

M **Dec:**

N

Z **Births and Deaths**

Mar. 31st R. W. von Bunsen b. (–1899).
June 4th Harriet Beecher Stowe b. (–1896).
June 7th James Young Simpson b. (–1870).
July 18th W. M. Thackeray b. (–1863).
Aug. 31st Théophile Gautier b. (–1872).
Sept. 30th Thomas Percy d. (81).
Oct. 22nd Franz Liszt b. (–1886).
Oct. 29th Louis Blanc b. (–1882).
Nov. 16th John Bright b. (–1889).

O **Politics, Economics, Law and Education**

'Luddites' destroy machinery in Nottingham and Yorkshire towns (*Mar.*).

Hampden Clubs are formed in England to agitate against the government, particularly for extending the franchise.

Civil Code is introduced into Austrian Empire, excepting Hungary, after 50 years of preparation.

Joshua Watson founds National Society for Educating the Poor in the Principles of the Established Church.

University of Christiana, Oslo, founded.

P **Science, Technology, Discovery, etc.**

Charles Bell, *New Idea of the Anatomy of the Brain.*

Amadeo Avogadro states his hypothesis on the composition of gases.

Courtois discovers the element iodine and extracts it from kelp.

S. O. Poisson, *Traité de Mécanique* (–33).

J. R. Meyer climbs the Jungfrau.

Q **Scholarship**

Berthold Niebuhr, *Roman History* (–32).

R. C. Rask, *Icelandic and Old Norse Grammar.*

J. P. A. Récusat, *Essai sur la langue et la littérature chinoises.*

K. A. Böttiger, *Kunstmythologie.*

R **Philosophy and Religion**

Large numbers of Welsh Protestants leave Anglican Church in 'the Great Schism'.

S **Art, Sculpture, Fine Arts and Architecture**

T. Lawrence, *Benjamin West* (painting).

B. Thorwaldsen, *Procession of Alexander the Great* (sculpture).

J. Rennie, *Waterloo Bridge* (–17).

J. Nash begins Regent Street.

T **Music**

L. van Beethoven, piano sonata 'Les Adieux' (op. 81a).

Carl von Weber, *Abu Hassan* (opera).

U **Literature**

Jane Austen, *Sense and Sensibility.*

Friedrich Fouqué, *Undine.*

J. W. Goethe, *My Life*, *Poetry and Truth.*

V **The Press**

W **Drama and Entertainment**

X **Sport**

Y **Statistics**

Population of Great Britain 12·5 mill., an increase of 2·1 mill. in a decade. London's population exceeds 1 mill.

(*Continued opposite*)

1812 (Jan.–Sep.) U.S. declares war on Britain—Napoleon's retreat from Moscow

A **Jan**: 19th, Duke of Wellington takes Ciudad Rodrigo; French re-occupy Swedish Pomerania and Rügen to put pressure on Sweden to end clandestine trade and to prevent Russo-Swedish alliance.

B **Feb**: 11th, British Act of Parliament removes the restrictions on the Prince Regent (of *Feb.* 5th 1811);
24th, by alliance with France, Prussia agrees to allow free passage for French troops, to provide troops in event of war with Russia and to adhere to the 'Continental System'; August Scharnhorst and Gerhard von Gneisenau resign in disgust.

C **Mar**: 4th, Marquess Wellesley resigns as foreign secretary because of lack of support for the Peninsular campaign and is replaced by Lord Castlereagh;
16th, by alliance with France, Austria agrees to provide army for Napoleon, who guarantees integrity of Turkey and promises to restore Illyrian Provinces to Austria;
19th, Spanish Cortes passes liberal constitution under a hereditary monarch;
20th, by Act of Parliament frame-breaking becomes a capital offence in Britain.

D **Apr**: 4th, U.S. introduces ninety-day embargo to ensure that all U.S. ships are safely in port when war begins with Britain;
6th, British capture Badajoz (after siege since *March* 16th);
9th, by secret Treaty of Abo, Sweden agrees to aid Russia by creating diversion against the French in North Germany, while in return Tsar suggests Swedish annexation of Norway as compensation for loss of Finland (*Sept.* 17th 1809);
14th, Louisiana becomes a state of the U.S.

E **May**: 11th, Spencer Perceval is assassinated in House of Commons, and Lord Liverpool agrees to form an administration;
21st, Lord Liverpool resigns after vote of no confidence;
28th, by Treaty of Bucharest with Turkey, Russia obtains Bessarabia and withdraws demand for Moldavia and Wallachia, and the peace enables the Tsar to act against Napoleon.

F **Jun**: 8th, Tory administration under Liverpool resumes office;
18th, U.S. Congress approves war against Britain (the formal declaration is made 19th);
23rd, British Orders-in-Council of *Apr.* 26th 1809 restricting trade of U.S. are revoked;
24th, Napoleon crosses the R. Niemen and enters Russian territory;
26th, Polish Diet declares Poland independent (but Napoleon refuses to acknowledge Polish decision *July* 14th);
28th, Napoleon crosses the R. Vilna after Tsar's retreat.

G **Jul**: Britain makes peace with Russia and Sweden, and
18th, by Alliance of Orebro, Britain joins Sweden and Russia;
22nd, Wellington defeats French under Marshal Marmont at Salamanca;
31st, Venezuelan Republic falls to Spanish force and Francisco de Miranda is arrested.

H **Aug**: 12th, Duke of Wellington enters Madrid;
16th, General William Hull surrenders Detroit to British forces, thus postponing U.S. plan to invade Canada;
17th (–18th), Russia is defeated at Smolensk, which is occupied by the French.

J **Sep**: 7th, following their defeat at Borodino the Russians are obliged to retreat, and abandon Moscow;
14th, Napoleon enters Moscow, which burns until 19th (occupation lasts until *Oct.* 18th);
19th (–*Oct.* 19th), British are forced to withdraw from Burgos.

O Politics, Economics, Law and Education

W. M. Leake's *Greece* arouses interest in England in the political state of that country.

P Science, Technology, Discovery, etc.

Humphry Davy, *Elements of Chemical Philosophy.*
Pierre Laplace, *Théorie Analytique* (theory of probability).
Georges Cuvier, *Recherches sur les ossemens fossiles de quadrupèdes.*
Henry Bell's steamship *Comet* (25 tons) plies on the Clyde, maximum speed 7 knots.
Main streets of London lit by gas.
Philippe Girard invents machine for spinning flax.
Blenkinsop's railway locomotive, with toothed wheels, hauls coal wagons at a colliery near Leeds.

Q Scholarship

H. F. Gesenius, *Hebrew and Chaldaic Dictionary.*

R Philosophy and Religion

G. W. Hegel, *Logic.*
J. G. Fichte, *Transcendental Philosophy.*
Repeal of Conventicle Act eases position of Protestant dissenters in England.
Baptist Union of Great Britain formed.
Jews in Prussia emancipated.

S Art, Sculpture, Fine Arts and Architecture

Francisco Goya, *Duke of Wellington* (painting).

T Music

L. van Beethoven, 7th (op. 92) and 8th Symphonies (op. 93).
G. Rossini, *La Pietra del Paragone* (opera).

U Literature

Lord Byron, *Childe Harold's Pilgrimage* (–18).
J. and W. Grimm, *Fairy Tales.*

V The Press

W Drama and Entertainment

The Waltz is introduced to English ballrooms.
Mrs. Siddons's last appearance.

X Sport

Y Statistics

U.K. textile trade: raw cotton imports, 73 mill. lb.
linen exports, 15,275,000 yds.

K **Oct**: 13th, British under Isaac Brock defeat U.S. at Queenston Heights, preventing further attempted invasion of Canada;
19th, Napoleon's retreat from Moscow begins;
23rd, Malet's conspiracy to dethrone Napoleon, install Louis XVIII and end the wars, begins, but he is arrested and, 29th, executed.

L **Nov**: 26th (–28th), disaster for the French army retreating across the Beresina;
In U.S. presidential election James Madison (128 electoral votes) defeats De Witt Clinton (89 votes).

M **Dec**: 5th, Napoleon leaves his troops under command of Joachim Murat and sets out for Paris (where he arrives, 18th);
30th, by Convention of Tauroggen with Russia, unknown to Frederick William III, the Prussian General von York breaks away from French alliance and becomes temporarily neutral.

N

z **Births and Deaths**

Feb. 7th Charles Dickens b. (–1870).
Apr. 26th Alfred Krupp b. (–1887).
May 7th Robert Browning b. (–1889).
Dec. 23rd Samuel Smiles b. (1904).

1813 (Jan.–Sep.) Wellington's army enters France—Napoleon's defeat at Battle of Leipzig

A **Jan:**

B **Feb:** 28th, Prussia agrees, by Alliance of Kalisch with Russia, to conduct joint campaign in Saxony and Silesia against Napoleon and the Confederation of the Rhine.

C **Mar:** 3rd, Britain concludes Treaty of Stockholm with Sweden who agrees to supply army in return for British subsidies and for promise not to oppose union with Norway;
17th, Frederick William III of Prussia declares war against the French, appeals to the people to support the campaign, and begins formation of *Landwehr* and *Landsturm*;
18th, after patriotic outbreak in Hamburg against the French, the city is occupied by the Russians;
27th, combined Russo-Prussian force occupies Dresden, forcing King of Saxony to flee.

D **Apr:** 27th, U.S. force in search of British ships captures York (now Toronto).

E **May:** 2nd, Napoleon defeats the Prussian and Russian armies at Lützen (Gross-Gorschen);
20th (–21st), indecisive battle of Bautzen is fought with heavy losses on both sides;
24th, Catholic Relief Bill is abandoned in Parliament when the Speaker has the clause allowing Catholics to sit and vote in Parliament deleted, thus rendering the Bill ineffective;
27th, U.S. force occupies Fort St. George, and British abandon entire Niagara frontier.

F **Jun:** 1st, U.S. frigate *Chesapeake* is captured by H.M.S. *Shannon*;
4th, Armistice of Poischwitz between Prussia and France through the mediation of Prince Metternich (*Aug.* 10th);
14th (–15th), Britain undertakes to pay subsidies to Russia and Prussia;
21st, Wellington completely routs the French at Vittoria, forcing Joseph Bonaparte to flee from Spain to France;
26th, Metternich agrees to peace congress at interview with Napoleon at Dresden, though he is fully aware of Austria's impending alliances with Russia and Prussia;
27th, by Treaty of Reichenbach with Prussia and Russia, Austria agrees to declare war on *July* 20th, if the French refuse the conditions of peace.

G **Jul:** 28th, Congress of Prague between France, Prussia and Austria begins but is dissolved (*Aug.* 10th) with nothing achieved;
Venezuela becomes independent for second time with Simon Bolivar as virtual dictator.

H **Aug:** 12th, Austria declares war against Napoleon;
23rd, the French defeat by Friedrich von Bülow at Grossbeeren prevents march on Berlin;
26th, French are defeated at Katzbach by Gebhard von Blücher;
26th (–27th), in battle of Dresden, Napoleon defeats the allied army from Bohemia.

J **Sep:** 6th, Michel Ney is defeated by von Bülow at Dennewitz;
9th, Treaty of Teplitz confirms Reichenbach agreement (of *June* 27th) uniting Russia, Prussia and Austria against France;
—, San Sebastian finally capitulates to Wellington, after siege lasting since *Aug.* 31st;
10th, U.S. successes on Lake Erie;
29th, Detroit is re-occupied by U.S.

O Politics, Economics, Law and Education

Benjamin Constant, *De l'esprit de conquête et de l'usurpation dans les rapports avec la civilisation européene.*
Robert Owen, *A New View of Society.*
Elizabeth Fry begins to visit Newgate Prison.
East India Company's trade monopoly in India abolished, but its monopoly in China continues.

P Science, Technology, Discovery, etc.

Augustin de Candolle's agricultural and botanical survey of France.
Hedley's steam locomotive 'Puffing Billy', with smooth wheels running on smooth rails, at Wylam colliery.
George Clymer's 'Columbia' printing-press eliminates the screw process.
David Brewster discovers crystals with two axes of double refraction.
John Leslie, *Experiments and Instruments depending on the relations of air to heat and moisture.*

Q Scholarship

R. Southey, *Life of Nelson.*

R Philosophy and Religion

J. F. Herbart, *Introduction to Philosophy.*
Methodist Missionary Society founded.

S Art, Sculpture, Fine Arts and Architecture

J. M. W. Turner, *Frosty Morning* (painting).
David Cox, *Treatise on Landscape Painting and Effect in Water Colours* (–14).

T Music

G. Rossini, *Tancredi* and *The Italian Girl in Algiers* (operas).
Philharmonic Society founded in London, with regular concerts in the Argyll Rooms.

U Literature

Ernst Arndt, *Was ist das deutsche Vaterland?* and other patriotic songs.
Jane Austen, *Pride and Prejudice.*
Lord Byron, *The Giaour* and *The Bride of Abydos.*
A. von Chamisso, *Peter Schlemihl.*
Alessandro Manzoni, *Inni Sacri.*
P. B. Shelley, *Queen Mab.*

V The Press

W Drama and Entertainment

X Sport

Y Statistics

K **Oct**: 5th, U.S. victory at Battle of Thames River (Ontario);
8th, Wellington crosses Bidassoa and enters France;
—, Bavaria joins allies by Treaty of Ried with Austria, and leaves Confederation of Rhine (formal declaration of war against France, 14th);
12th, by Peace of Gulistan with Russia, Persia cedes Caucasus region;
16th (–19th), Napoleon's defeat in the 'Battle of the Nations' at Leipzig and retreat leads to dissolution of Confederation of the Rhine and of Kingdom of Westphalia;
26th, after a rising in Italian States the Austrians defeat Eugene de Beauharnais at Valsarno, thus regaining foothold in Italy;
31st, Pampeluna finally surrenders to British force.

L **Nov**: 6th, Mexico declares itself independent;
8th, Allies offer Frankfurt peace proposals to Napoleon by which France would be left with the boundaries of the Alps and the Pyrenees (but he replies evasively 16th);
10th, Wellington defeats Nicolas Soult in France and goes on to invest Bayonne (*Dec.* 10th);
11th, U.S. forces are defeated by an inferior British force at Chrysler's Farm, Montreal;
15th (–17th), French expelled from Holland after risings by Dutch people, and
30th, William of Orange returns to Holland.

M **Dec**: 1st, by Declaration of Frankfurt the allies resolve to invade France because of vague reply to peace terms by Napoleon;
10th, U.S. forces burn Newark;
11th, Napoleon agrees to restore Ferdinand VII of Spain, by Treaty of Valençay;
19th, British force takes Fort Niagara from U.S.;
21st, Karl Schwarzenberg's Austrian forces enter France through Switzerland;
29th, Swiss Diet votes restoration of old constitution and revokes Act of Mediation;
29th (–31st), British forces burn Buffalo as reprisal for U.S. attack on Newark;
31st, Prussians under Gebhard von Blücher cross the Rhine.

N

z **Births and Deaths**

Jan. 19th Henry Bessemer b. (–1898).
Mar. 19th David Livingstone b. (–1873).
Apr. 8th Joseph Lagrange d. (78).
May 5th Søren Kierkegaard b. (–1855).
May 22nd Richard Wagner b. (–1883).
July 12th Claude Bernard b. (–1878).
Oct. 10th Giuseppe Verdi b. (–1901).

A Jan: 11th, Joachim Murat deserts Napoleon and joins allies;
14th, by Treaty of Kiel with Sweden, Denmark cedes Norway in return for Western Pomerania and Rügen;
—, in separate treaty with Britain, Denmark regains her lost territories, with exception of Heligoland.

B Feb: 1st, in battle of La Rothière, Blücher first attacks the French and the Russians complete the victory;
5th, (– *Mar.* 19th), peace negotiations at Chatillon are futile as Napoleon refuses to accept 1792 frontier of France;
27th, Karl Schwarzenberg defeats French forces at Bar-sur-Aube.

C Mar: 9th, by Treaty of Chaumont, the allies agree not to negotiate separate peace with Napoleon;
9th (–10th), at battle of Laon the combined allied army compels Napoleon to withdraw;
12th, Wellington captures Bordeaux;
30th (–31st), allies triumphantly enter Paris.

D Apr: 1st, Senate, influenced by Talleyrand, names provisional French government in Paris;
8th, National Assembly in Norway meets to discuss constitution, as Norway has declared itself independent, in defiance of Treaty of Kiel (*Jan.* 14th), and decides on limited monarchy (Christian Frederick of Denmark is elected King on *May* 17th);
11th, by Treaty of Fontainebleau, Napoleon abdicates unconditionally and is banished to Elba.

E May: 3rd, Louis XVIII enters Paris;
4th, Ferdinand of Spain annuls Constitution of the Cortes;
30th, by First Peace of Paris, the French recognise frontier of 1792 and agree to recognise independence of the Netherlands and the Italian and the German States.

F Jun: 4th, Louis XVIII issues Constitutional Charter, taking up throne on his hereditary right, not by a contract with the people.

G Jul: 5th, a British force is compelled to retire after a defeat by the U.S. forces at Chippewa.

H Aug: 13th, Cape of Good Hope Province becomes a British Colony while other former Dutch colonies are restored, apart from Demerara, Essequibo and Berbice;
14th, by Convention of Moss, Sweden recognises Norwegian Constitution, with provision that King Frederick Christian must renounce his throne;
24th, a British force takes Washington and burns main buildings.

J Sep: 11th, U.S. force capture British flotilla on Lake Champlain.

K Oct: 26th, Hanover is proclaimed a kingdom by the Prince Regent in the name of George III;
Governor-General of India declares war on the Gurkhas of Nepal.

L Nov: 1st, Congress of Vienna formally opens;
4th, Norwegian constitution is established, and
11th, Charles XIII of Sweden is elected to the throne;
13th, Russia hands over Saxony to Prussia, an action opposed by Austria, the German States, and France, as the Tsar wishes to obtain Poland in exchange.

M Dec: 24th, Treaty of Ghent ends the war between Britain and U.S., the latter abandoning the main demands for an end to impressment and compensation for commercial losses.

N

O Politics, Economics, Law and Education

Vicomte de Chateaubriand, *Bonaparte et les Bourbons.*
Berthold Niebuhr, *Prussia's Right to Saxony.*
F. K. von Savigny, *The Claim of Our Age on Legislation.*
English Statute of Apprentices, 1563, repealed.

P Science, Technology, Discovery, etc.

J. J. Berzelius, *Theory of Chemical Proportions and the Chemical Action of Electricity.*
M. J. B. Orfila, *Toxicologie générale.*
George Stephenson constructs the first effective steam locomotive (*July* 25th).

Q Scholarship

R Philosophy and Religion

Pope Pius VII on returning to Rome (*May*) restores the Inquisition and revives the Index and the Jesuits.
First Anglican Bishop in India (Calcutta).

S Art, Sculpture, Fine Arts and Architecture

Francisco Goya, *2 May* and *3 May 1808* (paintings).
Dulwich Gallery is opened, the first collection accessible to the public in Britain.

T Music

John Field, *Nocturnes.*
Franz Schubert, *Gretchen am Spinnrade.*
L. van Beethoven, *Fidelio*, final two-act form.
J. N. Mälzel invents a metronome.

U Literature

Jane Austen, *Mansfield Park.*
Lord Byron, *The Corsair.*
Friedrich Rückert, *Poems.*
[Walter Scott], *Waverley.*
R. Southey, *Vision of Judgment* (published -21).
William Wordsworth, *The Excursion.*

V The Press

John Walter II begins to print *The Times* by steam.

W Drama and Entertainment

Edmund Kean's début at Drury Lane as Shylock.

X Sport

M.C.C. first play cricket on present Lord's Ground.

Y Statistics

Z Births and Deaths

Jan. 27th Johann Gottlieb Fichte d. (52).
Apr. 15th John Lothrop Motley b. (-1877).
Oct. 4th Jean François Millet b. (-1875).
Oct. 29th Joanna Southcott d. (65).
— Michael Bakunin b. (-1876).
— Mikhail Lermontov b. (-1841).

1815 (Jan.–Sep.) Napoleon's 'Hundred Days' end in Battle of Waterloo— The Congress of Vienna settles the map of Europe

A **Jan:** 3rd, by secret treaty, Austria, Britain and France form defensive alliance against Prusso-Russian plans to solve the Saxon and Polish problems;
8th, before news of peace of Ghent, the battle of New Orleans is fought and the British are defeated within half an hour;
10th, Britain declares war against King of Kandy, Ceylon.

B **Feb:**

C **Mar:** 1st, Napoleon lands in France forcing Louis XVIII to flee (19th);
2nd, Dominion of Kandyan Provinces is vested in the Sovereign of the British Empire, and exercised through Governor of Ceylon;
20th, Napoleon enters Paris and the 'Hundred Days' begin (until *June* 29th);
23rd, Corn Law is passed, prohibiting imports of foreign corn into Britain when average home price of wheat is below 80 shillings per quarter, but allowing duty-free imports when that price is exceeded;
25th, Austria, Britain, Prussia, and Russia form new alliance against Napoleon in order to maintain the established order in Europe.

D **Apr:** 10th, Austria sends a note to Joachim Murat, King of Naples, declaring war against him for occupying Rome, Florence and Bologna (although formal declaration not made until 12th).

E **May:** 3rd, Murat is defeated at Tolentino by the Austrians;
18th, Treaty of peace concluded by Prussia, Russia and Austria with King of Saxony;
25th, Frederick William III promises constitution in Prussia.

F **Jun:** 2nd, Napoleon issues the liberal constitution of 'Le Champ de Mai';
4th, Denmark cedes Pomerania and Rügen to Prussia in return for part of Duchy of Lauenburg;
9th, Congress of Vienna closes after Final Act is passed; Holland, Belgium and Luxembourg are united to form the Netherlands (by Act of *May* 31st), Switzerland is to be neutral, East Poland is ceded to Russia and the Western Provinces of Poland to Prussia, Cracow becomes an independent republic, Lombardy and Venetia are restored to Austria, Prussia gains the Rhineland and the northern region of Saxony, Hanover obtains East Friesland and Hildesheim, the German Confederation is established under Presidency of Austria (by Act of 8th *June*), the Bourbon monarch Ferdinand VII is restored in Spain, the Braganza dynasty returns to the Portuguese throne, Ferdinand IV is recognised as King of Two Sicilies, the Pope and the minor Italian princes are restored, and Britain retains the majority of her overseas conquests, including Malta and Heligoland;
18th, Duke of Wellington and Gebhard von Blücher defeat Napoleon at Waterloo;
22nd, Napoleon abdicates for second time, after being given choice of resignation or deposition by the French Chambers.

G **Jul:** 7th, Allies enter Paris, enabling Louis XVIII to return, 8th, to Tuileries;
White Terror begins in Southern France by fanatical royalists against revolutionary elements, Bonapartists and Protestants.

H **Aug:** 2nd, by agreement between Prussia, Austria, Britain and Russia, the imprisonment of Napoleon is left to the British decision and he is banished to St. Helena (where he arrives 17th).

J **Sep:** 26th, anti-Liberal Holy Alliance is formed between Austria, Russia and Prussia to maintain Vienna settlement.

O Politics, Economics, Law and Education

T. R. Malthus, *An Inquiry into the Nature and Progress of Rent.*
David Ricardo, *The Influence of a Low Price of Corn on the Profits of Stock.*
Apothecaries Act in Britain forbids unqualified doctors practising medicine.

P Science, Technology, Discovery, etc.

L. J. Prout's hypothesis on relation between specific gravity and atomic weight.
Augustin Fresnel's researches on the diffraction of light.
J-B. Lamarck, *Histoire naturelle des animaux* (–22).
Humphry Davy invents miner's safety lamp (–16).
John MacAdam's method of constructing roads of broken stone officially adopted in England.
U.S.N. *Fulton*, first steam warship (38 tons).
William Smith's geological map of England and Wales.

Q Scholarship

F. K. von Savigny, *History of Roman Law in the Middle Ages.*
G. J. Thorkelin's edition of *Beowulf.*

R Philosophy and Religion

Dugald Stewart, *Progress of Metaphysical, Ethical and Political Philosophy.*
Julius Wegschneider, *Institutiones theologicae dogmaticae.*

S Art, Sculpture, Fine Arts and Architecture

Francisco Goya, *Tauromaquia* (engravings).
J. M. W. Turner, *Crossing the Brook* (painting).
Antonio Canova, *Three Graces* (sculpture).
Pius VII sends Canova to Paris to secure the return to Rome of works of art looted by Napoleon.
John Nash, Brighton Pavilion (–23).

T Music

U Literature

Pierre Béranger, *Chansons.*
E. T. A. Hoffmann, *Die Elixiere des Teufels.*
Walter Scott, *Guy Mannering.*
William Wordsworth, *White Doe of Rylstone.*

V The Press

W Drama and Entertainment

The quadrille is first danced in England.

X Sport

Y Statistics

U.K. total state expenditure, £112·9 mill.

K **Oct**: 6th, Prince Regent supports principles of Holy Alliance but avoids any commitments involving Britain;
13th, Joachim Murat is shot after abortive attempt to regain Naples;
British occupy Ascension Island.

L **Nov**: 5th, by treaty with Russia, Austria and Prussia, Britain establishes protectorate over Ionian Islands;
20th, by Second Peace of Paris, France yields territory to Savoy and to Switzerland, and agrees to restore captured art treasures, while the Quadruple Alliance between Austria, Prussia, Russia, and Britain is renewed;
27th, Alexander I issues a Polish Constitution (having proclaimed Poland to be part of Russia, *May* 25th).

M **Dec**: 2nd, treaty of peace between Britain and Rajah of Nepal, but war is soon resumed;
7th, Michel Ney is shot, following trial for treason in aiding Napoleon at Waterloo.

N

z **Births and Deaths**

Mar. 5th Franz Mesmer d. (81).
Apr. 1st Otto von Bismarck b. (–1898).
Apr. 24th Anthony Trollope b. (–1882).
Dec. 8th Adolf Menzel b. (–1905).

1816 Argentina declares independence from Spain—Spa Fields Riots in London

A **Jan:** 16th, Brazil made an Empire under John, Prince Regent of Portugal.

B **Feb:** 7th, Simon Bolivar is entrusted by the Congress of New Grenada with political and military control in invasion of Venezuela from Haiti, but is subsequently defeated by the royalist Pablo Morillo.

C **Mar:** 20th, Maria I, the insane Queen of Portugal, dies, and is succeeded by her son, John VI (–1826).

D **Apr:**

E **May:** 5th, Carl August of Saxe-Weimar grants first German Constitution.

F **Jun:** 20th, George Canning returns to Cabinet as President of Board of Control for India; 21st, United Netherlands accedes to Holy Alliance.

G **Jul:** 9th, at Congress of Tucuman, independence of United Provinces of La Plata (Argentina) is declared.

H **Aug:** 8th, Bavaria joins the Holy Alliance.

J **Sep:** 5th, Louis XVIII dissolves the Chamber and reduces number of members so that Moderates obtained majority in ensuing election.

K **Oct:**

L **Nov:** 5th, Diet of German Confederation opened at Frankfurt-am-Main under Prince Metternich.

M **Dec:** 2nd, Spa Fields Riots take place when crowd, which assembles to hear demands for political reform, marches on London;
11th, Indiana becomes an American state.
Britain restores Java to the Netherlands.

N

O Politics, Economics, Law and Education

Protective tariff in U.S.
Distress in England causes large-scale emigration to Canada and U.S.
Friedrich Froebel starts an educational community at Keilhau, Thuringia.
Ghent university founded.

P Science, Technology, Discovery, etc.

David Brewster invents kaleidoscope.

Q Scholarship

Franz Bopp, *System of Conjugation.*
Nikolai Karamzin, *History of the Russian Empire.*
Berthold Niebuhr discovers the Institutes of Gaius in Verona.

R Philosophy and Religion

American Bible Society founded.

S Art, Sculpture, Fine Arts and Architecture

Francisco Goya, *Duke of Osuna.*
Leo Klenze, Glyptothek, Munich (–30).
Through the success of B. R. Haydon's campaign for public patronage of the arts the Elgin Marbles are bought for the British Museum.

T Music

L. van Beethoven, *Liederkreis* (op. 98).
Franz Schubert, *Erl King* and 5th Symphony in B flat.
G. Rossini, *Barber of Seville* (opera).

U Literature

Jane Austen, *Emma.*
Lord Byron, *The Siege of Corinth.*
S. T. Coleridge, *Kubla Khan* (written 1797).
Leigh Hunt, *The Story of Rimini.*
Count Leopardi, *Alle Pressamente alle Morte.*
T. L. Peacock, *Headlong Hall.*
Walter Scott, *The Antiquary* and *Old Mortality.*
P. B. Shelley, *Alastor.*

V The Press

William Cobbett's *Political Register*, published at 2d., the first cheap periodical.

W Drama and Entertainment

X Sport

Y Statistics

U.K. registered tonnage of merchant shipping, 2,504,000 (steamships 1,000).

Z Births and Deaths

Apr. 21st Charlotte Brontë b. (–1855).
July 17th R. B. Sheridan d. (65).
Dec. 13th E. W. Siemens b. (–1892).

1817 Unrest in Britain provokes repressive legislation—Independence of Venezuela under Bolivar

A **Jan:** 28th, Prince Regent is fired at on return from opening of Parliament.

B **Feb:** 5th, new electoral law, limiting franchise, is introduced in France;
10th, Britain, Prussia, Austria and Russia agree to first decrease in army of occupation in France.

C **Mar:** 4th, James Monroe is inaugurated fifth President of U.S.;
4th, Habeas Corpus Act is suspended after secret Parliamentary committee's report that insurrection is imminent (extended by Act of Parliament, *June* 30th to last until *March* 1st 1818);
10th, 'March of the Blanketeers' begins in Manchester to present petition in London in protest against suspension of Habeas Corpus Act, but majority are halted, 11th, at Stockport;
17th, Act of Parliament for protection of King and Prince Regent, that any acts against them will amount to treason;
31st, Act to prevent seditious meetings is passed;
—, Lord Sidmouth's 'Circular' sent to magistrates advising them to suppress seditious publications;
Establishment of Councils of State in Prussia to supervise separate provinces.

D **Apr:** 28th, Rush-Bagot Agreement is concluded between Britain and U.S. to limit naval forces on the Great Lakes.

E **May:** Sweden accedes to Holy Alliance.

F **Jun:** 9th, riots in Derbyshire against low wages and local unemployment.

G **Jul:**

H **Aug:**

J **Sep:** 23rd, by treaty with Britain, Spain agrees to end slave trade;
Ultra-Royalists lose ground in French election.

K **Oct:** 1st, Bank of England makes partial resumption of cash payments;
18th, Wartburg Festival reveals revolutionary tendencies of German students who meet at Jena to celebrate anniversaries of Luther's death and of Battle of Leipzig;
30th, Simon Bolivar organises independent government of Venezuela, but not on liberal lines.

L **Nov:** 5th, Third Mahratta War against the British in India with attacks at Poona, Nagpur and Indore;
Sultan of Turkey grants partial autonomy to Serbs after lengthy struggle for independence.

M **Dec:** 10th, Mississippi is admitted to the Union as an American state.

N

O **Politics, Economics, Law and Education**

David Ricardo, *Principles of Political Economy and Taxation.*

P **Science, Technology, Discovery, etc.**

Karl Ritter, *Geography in its relation to Nature and History* (-18).

Q **Scholarship**

Philipp Böckh, *The Public Economy of Athens.*

R **Philosophy and Religion**

G. W. F. Hegel, *Encyclopaedia of Philosophy.*

Joseph de Maistre, *Du Pape.*

H. F. R. de Lamennais, *Essai sur l'indifférence.*

Lutheran and Reformed Churches in Prussia unite in an Evangelical Union, which spreads to other states.

Juan Llorentz, late secretary of the Inquisition, publishes *History of the Inquisition in Spain.*

S **Art, Sculpture, Fine Arts and Architecture**

John Constable, *Flatford Mill* (painting).

Francis Chantrey, *Sleeping Children* (sculpture).

Braccio Nuova, Vatican Museum, Rome (-21).

St. Isaac's cathedral, St. Petersburg (-51).

T. Jefferson, University of Virginia, Charlottesville (-26).

T **Music**

M. Clementi, *Gradus ad Parnassum.*

G. Rossini, *La Gazza Ladra* (opera).

U **Literature**

W. C. Bryant, *Thanatopsis.*

Lord Byron, *Manfred.*

S. T. Coleridge, *Sybilline Leaves.*

G. Crabbe, *Tales of the Hall.*

Franz Grillparzer, *Die Ahnfrau.*

P. B. Shelley, *The Revolt of Islam.*

V **The Press**

Thomas Barnes edits *The Times* (-41).

The Scotsman founded (*Jan.*).

Blackwood's Magazine with John Wilson (under the pseudonym of 'Christopher North'), editor.

W **Drama and Entertainment**

X **Sport**

Y **Statistics**

Z **Births and Deaths**

Feb. 23rd George Frederick Watts b. (-1904).

July 12th Henry David Thoreau b. (-1862).

July 14th Madame de Staël d. (51).

July 18th Jane Austen d. (41).

Aug. 29th John Leech b. (-1864).

Nov. 22nd John Thadeus Delane b. (-1879).

Nov. 30th Theodor Mommsen b. (-1903).

A **Jan**: 6th, by Treaty of Mundoseer, the dominions of Holkar of Indore are annexed with the Rajput States and come under British protection;
31st, Act suspending Habeas Corpus is repealed, and suspension is never again introduced in Britain.

B **Feb**: 5th, on the death of Charles XIII of Sweden, Bernadotte succeeds to throne as Charles XIV, founding a new dynasty;
12th, Independence of Chile proclaimed in Santiago (and is safeguarded by defeat of Spanish Royalist forces, *April* 5th).

C **Mar**:

D **Apr**:

E **May**: 19th, defeat of Bill to repeal Septennial Act, in attempt to shorten duration of British Parliament from seven years;
26th, Bavarian Constitution, providing for Diet of two Chambers, for comparative freedom of speech and for legal equality, is proclaimed;
28th, Prussian Tariff Reform Act abolishes internal customs.

F **Jun**: 2nd, Francis Burdett's motion for parliamentary reform with annual parliaments and universal suffrage is overwhelmingly defeated;
3rd, Baji Rao, Peshwa of Poona and his dominions come under British control in Bombay presidency.
10th, Parliament is dissolved and in ensuing election (*July* 1st–25th) the Whig opposition increases its seats.

G **Jul**:

H **Aug**: 22nd, liberal Constitution introduced in Baden, providing for Diet of two Chambers, legal equality and fiscal reforms.

J **Sep**: 27th (–*Nov.* 21st), Conference at Aix-la-Chapelle is held between Austria, Prussia, Russia, France, and Britain to discuss French indemnity.

K **Oct**: 9th, Allies agree to evacuate their troops from France by *Nov.* 30th, as the indemnity is being paid;
20th, by convention between U.S. and Britain, the border between Canada and U.S. is defined as the 49th Parallel, and a joint occupation of Oregon is to take place for 10 years.

L **Nov**: 15th, France is invited to join European Concert;
15th, at same time the Quadruple Alliance between Russia, Austria, Prussia and Britain is renewed to watch over France in order to protect her against revolution; Britain refuses to make a formal alliance with her allies and with France;
20th, Simon Bolivar formally declares Venezuela independent of Spain.

M **Dec**: 3rd, Illinois becomes U.S. state, with population of approximately 40,000;
21st, Duc de Richelieu resigns in France and is succeeded by Élie Decazes, after October elections show increasing influence of the Left.

N

O Politics, Economics, Law and Education

Mme de Staël, *Considérations sur la Révolution* (posth.).
Bonn University founded.

P Science, Technology, Discovery, etc.

F. W. Bessel's *Fundamenta Astronomiae* codifies 3,222 stars on the basis of James Bradley's observations.
J. F. Encke discovers the circulation of 'Encke's comet'.
F. Stromeyer and K. S. L. Hermann discover the metallic element cadmium.
John Ross's expedition to discover North-West Passage.

Q Scholarship

Henry Hallam, *The View of the State of Europe in the Middle Ages.*
Joseph Dobrovsky, *History of the Czech Language.*

R Philosophy and Religion

G. W. Hegel succeeds J. G. Fichte as professor of philosophy at Berlin.

S Art, Sculpture, Fine Arts and Architecture

Edwin Landseer, *Fighting Dogs getting Wind* (painting).
Prado Museum, Madrid.
Piazza Vittorio Veneto, Turin.

T Music

G. Rossini, *Moses in Egypt.*
Franz Schubert, 6th Symphony in C.

U Literature

Jane Austen, *Northanger Abbey* and *Persuasion* (posth.).
Lord Byron, *Don Juan* (–23).
Jean Delavigne, *Les Messéniennes.*
F. Grillparzer, *Sappho.*
William Hazlitt, *Lectures on the English Poets* (–19).
John Keats, *Endymion.*
T. L. Peacock, *Nightmare Abbey.*
Walter Scott, *Heart of Midlothian* and *Rob Roy.*
Mary Wollstonecraft Shelley, *Frankenstein.*

V The Press

W Drama and Entertainment

X Sport

First professional horse-racing in U.S.

Y Statistics

U.K. iron production 325,000 tons.

Z Births and Deaths

Apr. 23rd James Anthony Froude b. (–1894).
May 5th Karl Marx b. (–1883).
May 25th Jacob Burckhardt b. (–1897).
June 17th Charles François Gounod b. (–1893).
July 11th William Edward Forster b. (–1886).
Dec. 24th J. P. Joule b. (–1889).
— Ivan Turgeniev b. (–1883).

1819 British settlement at Singapore—U.S. obtains Florida—Carlsbad Decrees and Six Acts

A **Jan:**

B **Feb:** 6th, East India Company, represented by Stamford Raffles, establishes a settlement at Singapore by treaty with local ruler (preliminary treaty having been concluded, 30th *Jan.*);
24th, U.S. Congress, ratifies treaty (Adams–Onis) that obtains Florida from Spain; after delays, ratifications are exchanged *Feb.* 24th, 1821.

C **Mar:** 23rd, August von Kötzebue, a reactionary and an alleged Russian agent, is assassinated by a student in Mannheim.

D **Apr:** 24th, after lengthy negotiations with Britain, Turkey obtains Parga from Ionian Islands.

E **May:** 1st, liberty of press introduced in France.

F **Jun:**

G **Jul:** 2nd, Robert Peel's Act for gradual resumption of cash payments, which must be totally resumed by *May* 1st 1823, is passed.

H **Aug:** 16th, 'Peterloo' Massacre takes place when a crowd which has gathered in St. Peter's Fields, Manchester, to listen to speeches on parliamentary reform and on repeal of Corn Laws, is charged on by the militia.

J **Sep:** 20th, after A. von Kötzebue's murder the Frankfurt Diet, instigated by Prince Metternich, sanctions the Carlsbad Decrees, whereby freedom of press is abolished, universities are placed under State supervision, all political agitation is to be suppressed, and a meeting to investigate rumours of conspiracy is to take place in attempt to check revolutionary and liberal movements in the German Confederation;
25th, Württemberg is given constitution similar to those recently established in other German States.

K **Oct:** first step towards *Zollverein* (Customs Union) taken when Prussia concludes tariff treaty with Schwarzburg-Sonderhausen.

L **Nov:** Prince Metternich uses influence to begin conference in Vienna to modify the Federal Act of the German States in order to fix the functions of the Diet, with idea of eliminating all elements of constitutional control in German States.

M **Dec:** 7th, Hanover given Constitution with two Chambers by Ordinance of Prince Regent of Britain;
14th, Alabama is admitted as a U.S. state;
—, Lord John Russell begins his parliamentary reform campaign after evidence of corruption at an earlier election;
17th, Simon Bolivar becomes President of newly-formed Republic of Colombia, created from Venezuela and New Granada;
British Parliament passes the 'Six Acts' to deal with disorders and provide for the speedy trial of offenders, for wider powers to enable magistrates to search for arms, for the increase in penalties for seditious libel, for the prohibition in the training in the use of weapons, for the greater curtailment of public meetings and for the introduction of stamp duty on newspapers.

N

O **Politics, Economics, Law and Education**

Simon Bolivar, *Discourse Before the Congress of Angostura.*

Jean Sismondi, *Nouveaux Principes d'Économie Politique.*

Twelve-hour day for juveniles in England.

In McCulloch *v.* Maryland, Chief Justice John Marshall gives judicial sanction to doctrine of centralisation of power, at expense of states.

P **Science, Technology, Discovery, etc.**

H. C. Oersted discovers electro-magnetism.

E. Mitscherlich propounds the theory of isomorphism from observations on the crystallisation of phosphates and arsenates.

Thomas Telford begins Menai suspension bridge (–21).

John Barrow enters 'Barrow's Straits' in N. Arctic (*Aug.*).

First ship fitted with steam engine to cross the Atlantic, the *Savannah*, makes crossing in 26 days.

Q **Scholarship**

Angelo Mai discovers Cicero's *De Republica* in Vatican Library.

Jakob Grimm's *German Grammar* establishes the permutation of consonants.

Horace Wilson, *Sanskrit Dictionary.*

R **Philosophy and Religion**

Arthur Schopenhauer, *World as Will and Idea.*

Georg Hermes, *Philosophical Introduction to Christian Theology* (–29).

S **Art, Sculpture, Fine Arts and Architecture**

Théodore Géricault, *Raft of the Medusa* (painting).

Francisco Goya, *Doña Antonia Zárate* (painting).

J. M. W. Turner, *Childe Harold's Pilgrimage* (painting).

Bertel Thorwaldsen, *Christ and the Apostles* (–38) (sculpture).

William Inwood, St. Pancras Church, London (–22).

K. F. Schinkel, Schauspielhaus, Berlin (–23).

T **Music**

Franz Schubert, 'Trout' Quintet (op. 114).

U **Literature**

Lord Byron, *Mazeppa.*

J. W. Goethe, *West-östlicher Divan.*

Victor Hugo, *Odes.*

John Keats, *Hyperion* (published 1856).

V **The Press**

W **Drama and Entertainment**

X **Sport**

Y **Statistics**

z **Births and Deaths**

Feb. 8th John Ruskin b. (–1900).
Feb. 22nd James Russell Lowell b. (–1891).
May 24th Princess Alexandrina Victoria (Queen Victoria) b. (–1901).
May 27th Julia Ward Howe b. (–1910).
May 31st Walt Whitman b. (–1892).
June 10th Gustave Courbet b. (–1877).
June 12th Charles Kingsley b. (–1875).
June 21st Jacques Offenbach b. (–1880).
July 19th Gottfried Keller b. (–1890).
Aug. 1st Herman Melville b. (–1891).
Aug. 19th James Watt d. (83).
Aug. 26th Albert, Prince Consort b. (–1861).
Nov. 22nd 'George Eliot' (pseud. of Mary Ann Evans) b. (–1880).

1820 (Jan.–Oct.) The Missouri Compromise—The Cato Street Conspiracy

A **Jan:** 1st, Revolution in Spain begins due to Ferdinand VII's failure to adhere to Constitution of 1812, also his sending troops to Spanish America to put down risings with which Spanish rebels are in sympathy;
29th, George III dies and is succeeded by Prince Regent as George IV (–1830).

B **Feb:** 13th, Duc de Berry, heir presumptive to French throne, is assassinated when proposals to modify Louis XVIII's Charter are being discussed;
20th, Duc de Decazes is dismissed after Berry's death, and succeeded by Duc de Richelieu;
23rd, Cato Street Conspiracy to murder Cabinet ministers is discovered and leaders later executed;
28th, following the accession of George IV Parliament is dissolved (resulting elections of *March* 6th–*April* 14th are mainly favourable to the Tory government).

C **Mar:** 3rd, Maine enters the Union as a free state to counteract impending entrance of Missouri as slave state;
6th, 'The Missouri Compromise' is decided by Congress, whereby Missouri to enter Union as slave state, but slavery is to be abolished in the remainder of Louisiana purchase;
7th, Ferdinand VII of Spain is forced to restore the Constitution of 1812 and to abolish Inquisition;
26th, liberty of the individual curtailed in France;
30th, Duc de Richelieu re-establishes censorship of French press.

D **Apr:** 4th, U.S. Land Law abolishes credit system, and establishes minimum price of land at $1·25 per acre.

E **May:** 15th, Final Act of the Conference at Vienna under Metternich (meeting since *Nov.* 1819) is passed authorising the German Confederation to interfere in the affairs of those states unable to maintain public order and the principles of despotic government (this is passed as law by Frankfurt Diet, *June* 8th).

F **Jun:** 6th, Caroline, Princess of Wales, whom George IV wishes to divorce, triumphantly enters London, demanding her recognition as Queen;
New electoral law in France regulates electoral colleges and introduces system of 'double-voting', resulting in increased strength of the Right.

G **Jul:** 2nd, revolt begins in Naples, due to misrule of Ferdinand IV, at the instigation of the Carbonari and other secret societies, resulting in promise of Constitution similar to that in Spain (by royal decree, 7th);
5th, Bill of Pains and Penalties against Princess Caroline, to deprive her of titles and to dissolve her marriage to King George IV, is introduced in Parliament.

H **Aug:** 24th, revolution in Portugal begins in Oporto and spreads to Lisbon (29th), caused by discontent at King John VI living in Brazil and at the Regency under English influence; the leaders demand a constitution.

J **Sep:** 29th, birth of Comte de Chambord as heir to French throne (son of late Duc de Berry).

K **Oct:** 23rd, Conference at Troppau begins to discuss policy against revolutionary tendencies in Europe and is attended by Austria, Russia, and Prussia, and by plenipotentiaries from France and Britain.

O Politics, Economics, Law and Education

T. R. Malthus, *Principles of Political Economy.*
J. J. von Görres, *Germany and the Revolution.*

P Science, Technology, Discovery, etc.

André Ampère's laws of electro-dynamic action.
Regent's Canal, London.
Rich deposits of platinum discovered in Urals.
First iron steamship is launched (makes maiden voyage 1822).

Q Scholarship

R Philosophy and Religion

Thomas Brown, *Lectures on the Philosophy of the Human Mind.*
Thomas Erskine, *Internal Evidence for the Truth of Revealed Religion.*

S Art, Sculpture, Fine Arts and Architecture

William Blake's illustrations to the Book of Job.
John Constable, *Harwich Lighthouse* (painting).
Bertel Thorwaldsen, *The Lion of Lucerne* (sculpture).
The Venus de Milo is discovered.

T Music

Franz Schubert, *Wanderer* fantasia.
G. Meyerbeer, *Margherita d'Anjou* (opera).

U Literature

Washington Irving, *The Sketch-Book of Geoffrey Crayon, Gent,* including *Rip Van Winkle.*
John Keats, *The Eve of St. Agnes* and *Ode to a Nightingale.*
Alphonse de Lamartine, *Méditations poétiques.*
C. Lamb, *Essays of Elia* (–23).
Alexander Pushkin, *Ruslan and Ludmila.*
P. B. Shelley, *Prometheus Unbound* and *Ode to the West Wind.*
Walter Scott, *Ivanhoe.*

V The Press

John Bull founded.

W Drama and Entertainment

Edmund Kean acts Richard III in New York (revisits U.S. in 1825–6).

X Sport

Y Statistics

L **Nov**: 10th, Bill against Queen Caroline is dropped and inquiry into her conduct also ends, due in part to popular sympathy for her;

19th, Preliminary Protocol issued by Austria, Russia and Prussia at Troppau, expelling those nations undergoing revolutions from the Concert of Europe and allowing other States to intervene to crush revolts by force if necessary (an agreement repudiated by Britain, *Dec.* 16th);

23rd, to avoid embarrassing discussions over Queen Caroline, Parliament is prorogued;

25th, temporary truce is concluded between Spain and Colombia as Ferdinand VII is faced with revolution, but he still refuses to uphold Colombian independence under Simon Bolivar so that war is soon resumed.

M **Dec**: 17th, Conference at Troppau is adjourned until *Jan.* 1821 when the powers are to meet at Laibach.

George Canning resigns from Lord Liverpool's Cabinet, after disagreeing with treatment of Queen Caroline.

N

z **Births and Deaths**

Feb. 28th John Tenniel b. (–1914).
Apr. 27th Herbert Spencer b. (–1900).
May 12th Florence Nightingale b. (–1910).
Sept. 16th Francis Parkman b. (–1893).
— Friedrich Engels b. (–1895).

1821 (Jan.–Jun.) Greek War of Independence begins—Independence of Mexico and Peru—First Free-Trade Legislation in Britain

A **Jan:** 12th, European powers meet at Laibach (–*May* 12th);
23rd, when Parliament reopens Queen Caroline is granted annuity of £50,000 and a house;
26th, Portuguese Cortes are established and discuss basis of Constitution whereby feudalism and the Inquisition are to be abolished; a single elective Chamber is to be established and the King is to have only a suspensory vote (this basis is decreed *May* 9th).

B **Feb:** 13th, at Laibach, Austria agrees to Ferdinand IV's request to send army into Naples to suppress revolt;
24th, John VI of Portugal promises to introduce equitable clauses of Portuguese Constitution into Brazil;
24th, proposals for independence of Mexico from Spain, and for the future of its government, are drawn up under Vicente Guerrero.

C **Mar:** 5th, James Monroe begins second term as U.S. President;
6th, revolt in Moldavia (after earlier outbreak in Wallachia in *Feb.*) against oppressive rule of the Turks; the rebels appeal to Tsar Alexander I for help, thus beginning Greek War of Independence;
7th, Neapolitan rebels are crushed at Rieti by the Austrians (who enter Naples, 23rd, and restore Ferdinand IV to the throne);
10th, Revolution, influenced by the Carbonari, begins in Piedmont to put Charles Albert Carignan on the throne;
13th, Victor Emmanuel of Piedmont abdicates and proclaims his brother Charles Felix, not Charles Albert, as his successor;
16th, Charles Felix issues decree forcing Charles Albert to renounce claim to throne of Piedmont.

D **Apr:** 8th, Austrian army intervenes in Piedmont and defeats supporters of Charles Albert at Novara;
17th, Roman Catholic Removal of Disability Bill is defeated in House of Lords on second reading;
22nd, John VI of Portugal issues decree in Brazil (confirming earlier decree of *Mar.* 27th) to agree to Regency there under his son and to remove the main government to Lisbon.
22nd, after several outbreaks in the Morea, in which the Greeks massacre Turks, the Greek Patriarch of Constantinople is murdered by the Turks as a reprisal, and a reign of terror begins.

E **May:** 7th, by Act of Parliament the Bank of England resumes cash payments two years earlier than previously stipulated, to avoid making drain on gold supplies of other countries;
7th, Africa Company is dissolved because of heavy expenses incurred, and Sierra Leone, Gambia, and Gold Coast are taken over by the British government to form British West Africa;
9th, Lord John Russell's motion for parliamentary reform is rejected;
28th, repeal of customs duties on certain timber imports begins British free trade legislation.

F **Jun:** 19th, Turks defeat Greek rebels at Dragashan;
24th, Simon Bolivar ensures independence of Venezuela by defeating Spanish army at Carabobo, but the subsequent Constitution of the Cortes severely curtails power of the President.

O **Politics, Economics, Law and Education**

George Grote, *Statement of the Question of Parliamentary Reform.*
J. J. von Görres, *Europe and the Revolution.*
James Mill, *Elements of Political Economy.*
Comte de St.-Simon, *Du Système industriel.*

P **Science, Technology, Discovery, etc.**

Michael Faraday discovers electro-magnetic rotation.
T. J. Seebeck discovers thermo-electricity.
First international congress on biology.

Q **Scholarship**

École des Chartes, Paris, founded for the study of historical documents.

R **Philosophy and Religion**

G. W. Hegel, *Philosophy of Right.*
B. Neibuhr brings about a concordat between Prussia and the Papacy.

S **Art, Sculpture, Fine Arts and Architecture**

John Constable, *Hay Wain* (painting).

T **Music**

C. M. von Weber, *Der Freischütz* (opera).

U **Literature**

James Fenimore Cooper, *The Spy.*
Thomas de Quincey, *Confessions of an English Opium Eater.*
John Galt, *Annals of the Parish.*
J. W. Goethe, *Wilhelm Meisters Wanderjahre.*
W. Hazlitt, *Table Talk* (–22).
Heinrich Heine, *Poems.*
Alessandro Manzoni, *Il Cinque Maggio.*
Walter Scott, *Kenilworth.*
P. B. Shelley, *Adonais.*
John Bowring's *Specimens of the Russian Poets* introduces Russian literature to England.

V **The Press**

Manchester Guardian founded.

W **Drama and Entertainment**

X **Sport**

Y **Statistics**

Populations (in millions): France, 30·4; Great Britain, 20·8 (of which Ireland, 6·8); Italian states, 18; Austria, 12; U.S. 9·6; combined populations of Prussia, Bavaria, Saxony, the duchies, principalities and free cities of Germany, 26·1.
Coal Production: U.K. 8 mill. tons; U.S. 3,650 tons.

G **Jul:** 19th, Coronation of George IV, but Queen Caroline not admitted to ceremony;
26th, relations severed between Turkey and Russia, after Turks' refusal to protect Christian subjects;
28th, Independence of Peru from Spain formally proclaimed.

H **Aug:** 7th, Queen Caroline dies;
10th, Missouri finally becomes member of the Union as a slave state (see *Mar.* 6th 1820).

J **Sep:** 15th, Guatemala is declared independent of Spain and aligns itself with Mexico;
29th, Portuguese Cortes decrees that King John's earlier acts with regard to Brazil are repealed and recalls the Regent in an attempt to reintroduce old colonial system.

K **Oct:** 5th, Greeks take Tripolitza in the Morea and massacre the Turkish population there.

L **Nov:** 28th, Panama is declared independent of Spain and joins Republic of Colombia.

M **Dec:** 1st, Republic of San Domingo is established independent of Spain;
12th, Duc de Richelieu succeeded by Jean Villèle in France, ending the rule of the Right Centre, and leading to a period of reaction under the Ultra-Conservatives.

N

z **Births and Deaths**

Feb. 23rd John Keats d. (26).
Feb. 26th Joseph de Maistre d. (66).
Apr. 9th Charles Pierre Baudelaire b. (–1867).
May 5th Napoleon I d. (52).
July 16th Mary Baker Eddy b. (–1910).
Aug. 31st Hermann Helmholtz b. (–1894).
Oct. 30th Feodor Dostoievsky b. (–1881).
Nov. 21st Henry Thomas Buckle b. (–1862).
Dec. 12th Gustave Flaubert b. (–1880).

1822 Brazil becomes independent of Portugal—Turks massacre Greeks at Chios

A **Jan**: 13th, liberal republican Constitution is adopted in Greece;
17th, Robert Peel enters Lord Liverpool's Cabinet as home secretary.
27th, Greek independence formally proclaimed.

B **Feb**: 5th, the assassination of Ali of Janina enables the Porte to concentrate forces against Greeks.

C **Mar**: 17th, in France new press law prohibits sale of newspapers unless they are approved by government, requiring offenders to be tried in royal courts, where magistrates take orders from government officials.

D **Apr**: 22nd, Turkish fleet captures island of Chios and massacres Christian inhabitants or sells them as slaves.

E **May**: 19th, Augustus de Iturbide is elected Emperor of Mexico by the Constitutional Congress.

F **Jun**: 18th, Greeks set fire to Turkish admiral's vessel, as reprisal for atrocities in Chios, and the rest of the fleet scatters;
24th, partial repeal of British Navigation Acts allows foreign ships to bring goods from European ports, provided that the ship is registered in the port in question; also opens up West Indies trade with the U.S.;
President of Council of French universities placed in charge of all education and of all teachers, a notable victory for Clerical party.

G **Jul**: 15th, Corn Law is amended, reducing price at which foreign wheat may enter Britain from 80 shillings to 70 shillings per quarter and fixing a sliding scale of duties (this Act never becomes effective).
Turkish invasion of Greece begins; the Turks overrun peninsula north of Gulf of Corinth (but are later forced to retreat).

H **Aug**: 12th, Lord Castlereagh commits suicide (aged 82).

J **Sep**: 16th, George Canning succeeds Castlereagh as Foreign Secretary and as leader of the House of Commons;
23rd, Portuguese Constitution is decreed, providing for liberty, legal equality, a single Chamber which the King may not dissolve until its period of four years has expired, and a constitutional monarchy.

K **Oct**: 12th, Brazil becomes formally independent of Portugal and Dom Pedro is proclaimed Emperor.
20th, Congress of Verona opens, attended by representatives of Austria, Prussia, France, Russia and Britain, for whom the Duke of Wellington is plenipotentiary, to discuss European problems.

L **Nov**: 19th, French plan for intervention in Spain is tentatively accepted by other powers at Verona after opposition from Austria, Prussia and Britain to an outright invasion by Louis XVIII; France may intervene in Spain if attacked or if the Spanish rebels depose Ferdinand VII.

M **Dec**: 2nd, San Salvador, Bahamas, not wishing to be united with Mexico, asks for incorporation with U.S.;
14th, Congress of Verona ends, having ignored Greek War of Independence;
—, Bottle Riots in Dublin, where Viceroy of Ireland is attacked by Orangemen, the violent element of Irish Protestants.

N Liberia is founded as a colony for freed American slaves.

O **Politics, Economics, Law and Education**

Francis Place, *Illustrations . . . of the Principles of Population*, advocates birth control.

P **Science, Technology, Discovery, etc.**

F. Fournier de Pescay, *Théorie Analytique de la Chaleur.*
J. V. Poncelet, *Traité des Propriétés projectives des figures.*
German Association for Science, founded by Oken, meets at Leipzig.
A. J. Fresnel perfects lenses for lighthouses.
Beaumont begins study of digestion in exposed human stomach.
Streets of Boston, Mass., lit by gas.

Q **Scholarship**

H. T. Colebrooke founds Royal Asiatic Society for study of eastern languages.

R **Philosophy and Religion**

S **Art, Sculpture, Fine Arts and Architecture**

F. Delacroix, *Dante and Virgil Crossing the Styx* (painting).
John Martin, *Destruction of Herculaneum* (painting).

T **Music**

L. van Beethoven, Mass in D (op. 123).
Franz Schubert, Symphony No. 8 in B minor ('Unfinished').
Royal Academy of Music, London, founded.
Franz Liszt, aged eleven, makes début as pianist in Vienna.

U **Literature**

Washington Irving, *Bracebridge Hall, or the Humourist.*
Alexander Pushkin, *Eugene Onegin* (–32).
Esias Tegner, *Axel.*
Alfred de Vigny, *Poèmes.*
Stendhal (pseud.), *De l'amour*, which sells only 17 copies in 11 years.

V **The Press**

The *Sunday Times* founded.

W **Drama and Entertainment**

X **Sport**

Y **Statistics**

U.K. Textiles trade:

raw cotton imports	145 mill. lb.
exports of cottons	304 mill. yds.
exports of woollens	1·7 mill. pieces.
exports of linen	33·8 mill. yds.
exports of silks	287,000 lb.

Z **Births and Deaths**

Mar. 24th Henri Murger b. (–1861).
Apr. 27th Ulysses Grant b. (–1885).
May 26th Edmond de Goncourt b. (–1896).
July 8th Percy Bysshe Shelley d. (29).
July 24th E. T. A. Hoffmann d. (46).
Aug. 25th William Herschel d. (88).
Oct. 13th Antonio Canova d. (64).
Dec. 10th César Franck b. (–1895).
Dec. 24th Matthew Arnold b. (–1888).

A **Jan:** 31st, William Huskisson enters British Cabinet as President of Board of Trade;
Russia, Austria, France, and Prussia demand abolition of Spanish Constitution of 1812, but Cortes refuses so that ambassadors of those countries leave Madrid.

B **Feb:**

C **Mar:** 19th, Augustus de Iturbide forced to abdicate in Mexico (and Mexico becomes a republic, *Oct.* 1824);
25th, British government recognises Greeks as belligerents in war with Turkey.

D **Apr:** 6th, French army crosses the Bidassoa and war with Spain begins.

E **May:** 12th, Warehousing of Goods Act allows foreigners to deposit goods for import in British warehouses without payment of duty, a victory for free trade principles;
12th, Catholic Association established in Ireland by Daniel O'Connell, virtually taking over government.

F **Jun:** 11th, Ferdinand VII of Spain refuses to leave Madrid in the face of French invasion and is declared to be temporarily incapacitated, a provisional Regency of the Cortes being established;
18th, John VI annuls Portuguese Constitution of 1822 after risings against his rule and against the loss of Brazil.

G **Jul:** 1st, Guatemala, San Salvador, Nicaragua, Honduras and Costa Rica form the Confederation of United Provinces of Central America;
4th, Robert Peel allows employment of transported convicts in colonies instead of placing them in hulks;
10th, British Act, due largely to Peel, sets pattern for prison reform;
14th, Switzerland refuses to grant asylum to foreign refugees;
18th, further British duties are repealed to modify Navigation Acts, providing equality of rights for all nations reciprocating these concessions, in order to develop trade.

H **Aug:** 31st, the French storm the Trocadero, and enter Cadiz.

J **Sep:** 10th, Simon Bolívar, having landed in Peru, is recognised as dictator and prepares to meet Royalist forces (he is formally proclaimed Emperor *Feb.* 10th 1824).

K **Oct:** 1st, Ferdinand VII of Spain, having been restored by the French who have crushed Spanish rebellion, issues Decree for execution of his enemies and reign of tyranny begins.

L **Nov:** 13th, Dom Pedro dissolves Brazilian Assembly after several conspiracies against him, and a Council of State is subsequently established to draw up a Constitution for Brazil.

M **Dec:** 2nd, Monroe Doctrine excludes European powers from interfering in politics of American Republics and closes American continent to colonial settlements by them.

N Provincial Diets are established in Prussia.

O **Politics, Economics, Law and Education**
William Huskisson begins to reduce British tariff.
Death penalty abolished for over 100 crimes in Britain.
Comte de St.-Simon, *Catéchisme des Industriels* (–24).
George Birkbeck founds Mechanics' Institute.

P **Science, Technology, Discovery, etc.**
Michael Faraday liquefies chlorine.
G. Amici observes pollen approaching plant ovary.
The Lancet first issued.
Charles Babbage begins construction of calculating machine.
Charles Macintosh invents waterproof fabric.
Lake Chad, Central Africa, discovered by Walter Oudney on an expedition from Tripoli.

Q **Scholarship**
George IV presents his father's library to British Museum.
Louis Thiers, *Histoire de la Révolution française* (–27).

R **Philosophy and Religion**
Friedrich Schleiermacher, *Christian Dogma.*

S **Art, Sculpture, Fine Arts and Architecture**
Jean Ingres, *La Source* (painting).
Louis Lebas, Notre Dame-de-Lorette, Paris.
Robert Smirke, General Post Office, St. Martin's-le-Grand, and British Museum (–47).

T **Music**
Franz Schubert, incidental music to *Rosamunde.*
Carl von Weber, *Euryanthe* (opera).
Sébastien Érard makes a grand piano with double escapement.

U **Literature**
James Fenimore Cooper, *The Pioneers* (first of the 'Leatherstocking' novels).
Alphonse de Lamartine, *Nouvelles Méditations Poétiques.*
Stendhal (pseud.), *Racine et Shakespeare* (–25).
The *Forget-me-not*, the first English illustrated annual.

V **The Press**

W **Drama and Entertainment**
Oxford Union Society founded.

X **Sport**
William Webb Ellis originates Rugby Football.

Y **Statistics**

Z **Births and Deaths**
Feb. 27th Ernest Renan b. (–1892).
Aug. 2nd Edward Augustus Freeman b. (–1892).
Aug. 11th Charlotte M. Yonge b. (–1901)

A **Jan:**

B **Feb:** 24th, Governor-General of India declares war against Burmese after the latter have violated territory of East India Company by capturing island of Shahpuri.

C **Mar:** 27th, Decree in Brazil for election of deputies to legislative assembly.

D **Apr:** 17th, frontier treaty, between Russia and U.S., defining respective rights in Pacific Ocean and on north-west coast of America;
19th, Lord Byron dies at Missolonghi (aged 36) aiding Greeks against Turkey;
30th, garrison of Lisbon revolts against John VI and recognises his younger son, Dom Miguel, as ruler;
Crete is captured by Egyptians.

E **May:** 3rd, John VI of Portugal sanctions son's actions but
9th, boards British warship, repudiates this decree and re-asserts his authority;
11th, British take Rangoon.

F **Jun:**

G **Jul:** in war with the Greeks, Turkey captures island of Ipsara.

H **Aug:** 6th, Simon Bolivar defeats Spanish forces at Junin in Peru.

J **Sep:** 16th, Louis XVIII dies and is succeeded by Charles X (–1830).
29th, Press Law, censoring French press (of *Mar.* 30th, 1820) suspended, but Charles' policy is generally illiberal.

K **Oct:** Greeks nearly annihilate Turks at Mitylene.

L **Nov:** in U.S. presidential election none of the four candidates has a majority; House of Representatives elect John Adams as president.

M **Dec:** 9th, at Battle of Ayacucho, Peru, the Spanish army is defeated and agrees to leave South America, 12th;
31st, George Canning recognises the independence of Buenos Aires, Mexico and Colombia.

N

O Politics, Economics, Law and Education

Repeal of the Combinations Acts of 1799–1800, due largely to Francis Place and Joseph Hume (*June* 21st), permits British workers to combine.

P Science, Technology, Discovery, etc.

Nicolas Carnot, *Puissance motrice du Feu*, a pioneer study of thermodynamics.
C. Prevost and J. B. Dumas show that the sperm is essential to animal fertilisation.
Joseph Aspdin makes Portland cement.

Q Scholarship

Philip Böckh edits *Corpus Inscriptionum Graecum* (–59).
Leopold von Ranke's *History of the Roman and Teutonic People, 1494–1514*, founds modern historiography.
Carlo Botta, *History of Italy*.
Sequoyah invents the Cherokee alphabet.

R Philosophy and Religion

J. F. Herbart, *Psychology as a Science* (–25).
American Sunday School Union founded.

S Art, Sculpture, Fine Arts and Architecture

Eugène Delacroix, *Les Massacres de Chios* (painting).
Jean Ingres, *Vow of Louis XIII* (painting).
John Flaxman, *Pastoral Apollo* (sculpture).
J. F. Overbeck, *Entry of Christ into Jerusalem* (painting).
National Gallery, London, founded with the collection of J. J. Angerstein.
Jeffry Wyatville, royal apartments, Windsor Castle (–28).
K. F. Schinkel, Atlas Museum, Berlin.

T Music

L. van Beethoven's 9th ('Choral') Symphony performed in Vienna; quartets (op. 127, 130, 131 and 135).

U Literature

W. S. Landor, *Imaginary Conversations* (–37).
Count Leopardi, *Canzoni e Versi*.
Mary Mitford, *Our Village* (–32).
Walter Scott, *Redgauntlet*.

V The Press

Westminster Review founded by J. Bentham.
Le Globe, Paris, issued.

W Drama and Entertainment

X Sport

Y Statistics

Z Births and Deaths

Mar. 2nd Friedrich Smetana b. (–1884).
June 26th William Thomson, Lord Kelvin b. (–1907).
Aug. 8th Friedrich August Wolf d. (65).
Sept. 4th Anton Bruckner b. (–1896).

1825 Independence of Bolivia and Uruguay—British Navigation Acts are modified

A **Jan:** 4th, Ferdinand I (IV) of Naples dies and is succeeded by Francis I.

B **Feb:** 24th, Egyptian forces land in the Morea, after call for help from Porte, and begin to subdue peninsula;
28th, Anglo-Russian Treaty over the latter's territory on north-west coast of America, and over respective rights in Pacific Ocean (similar to U.S.-Russian Treaty *Apr.* 17th 1824).

C **Mar:** 4th, John Quincy Adams is inaugurated sixth President of U.S.

D **Apr:** 15th, French law makes sacrilege a capital offence;
27th, French law of indemnity compensates nobles for losses in French Revolution.

E **May:** 17th, Roman Catholic Relief Bill rejected by House of Lords on second reading.

F **Jun:** 22nd, Act to regulate Cotton Mills and Factories, with particular regard to young people, is passed, whereby no one under sixteen years is to work more than twelve-hour day, excluding time for meals;
Greeks put forward proposals to place themselves under British protection (which are passed by Greek Provisional government, *July* 24th, but subsequently rejected by British government).

G **Jul:** 5th, Acts of Parliament passed modifying Navigation Acts permitting European goods to enter Britain in ships of country of origin;
6th, because of strikes and industrial disorder, the legislation repealing Anti-Combination Acts (*June* 21st 1824) is amended so that, although trade unions are still recognised as legal, violence is prohibited, which has effect of prohibiting strike action.

H **Aug:** 6th, Bolivia (Upper Peru) becomes independent of Peru;
25th, Uruguay becomes independent of Brazil;
29th, Portugal recognises Brazilian independence under Dom Pedro.

J **Sep:** 19th, Hungarian Diet reopened after 13 years, and Austrian Emperor, in face of discontent in Hungary, agrees to triennial meetings.

K **Oct:**

L **Nov:**

M **Dec:** 1st, Tsar Alexander I dies (aged 47) and is succeeded by Nicholas I, his younger brother (–1855).
10th, Brazil declares war against Argentina over question of Uruguay;
26th, Decembrist Rising in Russian army, aiming at assembly of national representatives, is easily crushed.

N

O **Politics, Economics, Law and Education**
Rapid expansion of trade unions in Britain.
Hungarian Academy of Sciences, Budapest, founded.

P **Science, Technology, Discovery, etc.**
Michael Faraday isolates benzene.
J. F. Herschel invents actinometer for measuring the heat of the sun's rays.
W. E. and E. H. Weber, *Treatise on Magnetic Waves.*
Stockton and Darlington railway is opened.

Q **Scholarship**
Lord Macaulay's 'Essay on Milton' in *Edinburgh Review.*
Augustin Thierry, *Histoire de la Conquête d'Angleterre par les Normands.*

R **Philosophy and Religion**
Joseph Smith, founder of Mormons, claims he had his vision.
Comte de St.-Simon, *Nouveau Christianisme.*

S **Art, Sculpture, Fine Arts and Architecture**
Samuel Morse, *Lafayette* (painting).
Thomas Cole founds Hudson River School of landscape painting, New York.
Peter von Cornelius's frescoes in Ludwigskirche, Munich.
John Nash, Buckingham Palace.

T **Music**
L. van Beethoven, *Grosse Fuge*; 9th Symphony first performed in England by Philharmonic Society who commissioned it.
Franz Schubert, 'Death and the Maiden' quartet (–26).

U **Literature**
W. Hazlitt, *The Spirit of the Age: or Contemporary Portraits.*
Alessandro Manzoni, *I Promessi Sposi.*
Esias Tegner, *Frithjofs Saga.*

V **The Press**

W **Drama and Entertainment**
Alexander Pushkin, *Boris Godunov.*

X **Sport**

Y **Statistics**
U.K. total state expenditure, £55·5 mill.
U.K. iron production, 581,367 tons.

Z **Births and Deaths**
Apr. 11th Ferdinand Lassalle b. (–1864).
May 4th Thomas Henry Huxley b. (–1895).
June 21st William Stubbs b. (–1901).
Oct. 10th Stephanis Johannes Paulus Kruger b. (–1904).
Oct. 25th Johann Strauss b. (–1899).
Nov. 14th Jean Paul Friederick Richter ('Jean Paul') d. (62).
Nov. 29th Jean Martin Charcot b. (–1893).
Dec. 29th Jacques Louis David d. (76).

1826 St. Petersburg Protocol for Autonomy of Greece—Russo-Persian war begins

A **Jan:**

B **Feb:** 24th, by treaty of Yandabu, ending Burmese War, Burmese pay indemnity and British resident is established at Ava.

C **Mar:** 10th, John VI of Portugal dies, succeeded by Dom Pedro of Brazil as Peter IV;
25th, promulgation of Brazilian Constitution with hereditary monarchy and general assembly of two chambers (which convenes *May* 6th).

D **Apr:** 4th, St. Petersburg Protocol between Britain and Russia respecting Greek problem, on the basis of complete autonomy of Greece under Turkish suzerainty (but does not become treaty until *July* 6th 1827 when France also joins);
5th, Russian ultimatum to Turkey over Serbia and Danubian Provinces;
22nd, Ibrahim, son of Mohammed Ali of Egypt, takes Missolonghi after long siege;
29th, liberal Constitution promulgated in Portugal for a hereditary monarchy with legislative power in hands of Cortes of two Chambers (which meets *Oct.* 30th).

E **May:** 2nd, Peter IV waives right of accession to Portuguese throne, in order to remain in Brazil; his daughter Maria is to become queen, provided Dom Miguel, his brother, marries her.

F **Jun:** 19th, Decree by Mahmud II, Sultan of Turkey, for dissolution of corps of janissaries after week of rioting;
20th, treaty of commerce between Siam and Britain, whereby Perak and Selangor are independent, Kedah becomes Siamese territory and Britain obtains Isle of Pangkor and Sembilan Islands;
22nd, Pan-American Congress meets in Panama under influence of Simon Bolivar in effort to unite American Republics (ends without effect *July* 15th).

G **Jul:**

H **Aug:**

J **Sep:** 28th, Russia declares war against Persia over latter's encroachment in Transcaucasia.

K **Oct:** 7th, Akkerman Convention (as result of Tsar's ultimatum to Sultan in *Apr.*) settles problem of Danubian Provinces and of Serbia to the advantage of Russia.

L **Nov:**

M **Dec:** George Canning's agreement to send troops to Portugal, to counteract Spanish threat of invasion in support of Dom Miguel, who is trying to obtain throne from Maria;
19th, treaty of commerce between Prussia and Mecklenburg-Schwerin develops the idea of the *Zollverein.*

N Secret authorisation from Charles X allows Jesuits to return to France and teach in State seminaries.

O Politics, Economics, Law and Education

University College, London, and Munich University founded.

P Science, Technology, Discovery, etc.

André Ampère, *Electrodynamics.*
Alcohol is synthesised.
Leopoldo Nobili invents galvanometer.
Stamford Raffles founds Zoological Society, London.
First railway tunnel (Liverpool-Manchester railway).

Q Scholarship

G. H. Pertz, under H. F. K. Stein's direction, edits *Monumenta Germaniae Historica.*

R Philosophy and Religion

S Art, Sculpture, Fine Arts and Architecture

F. W. Schadow becomes director of Düsseldorf Art Gallery.
U.S. National Academy of Design founded.

T Music

C. von Weber, *Oberon* (opera).
F. Mendelssohn, music for *A Midsummer Night's Dream.*

U Literature

E. B. Browning, *Essay on Mind, with Other Poems.*
James Fenimore Cooper, *The Last of the Mohicans.*
Alfred De Vigny, *Cinq Mars.*
Benjamin Disraeli, *Vivian Grey* (–27).
Heinrich Heine, *Pictures of Travel*, I.
Walter Scott, *Woodstock.*

V The Press

W Drama and Entertainment

X Sport

Y Statistics

U.K. registered tonnage of merchant shipping 2,411,000 tons (24,000 tons steamships).

Z Births and Deaths

Feb. 3rd Walter Bagehot b. (–1877).
Mar. 29th Johann H. Voss d. (75).
Apr. 6th Gustave Moreau b. (–1898).
June 5th Carl von Weber d. (39).
July 4th Thomas Jefferson d. (73).

A **Jan**: 26th, Peru secedes from Colombia in protest against Simon Bolivar's alleged tyranny;
British forces arrive at Lisbon in support of Portuguese Queen Maria.

B **Feb**: 17th, Lord Liverpool suffers a stroke and is forced to resign as Prime Minister;
20th, Brazilian forces defeated at battle of Ituziango by combined army of Uruguay and Argentina.

C **Mar**:

D **Apr**: 4th, Note from Russia, France and Britain to Sultan urging a truce in war with Greece;
10th, George Canning forms ministry of liberal Tories and moderate Whigs;
17th, French law to censor press is rejected by Peers;
29th, dissolution of French National Guard by decree of Charles X after unrest, a decision unpopular among the middle classes who dominated those forces;
Count Capo d'Istria elected President of Greece.

E **May**:

F **Jun**: 5th, Turks capture the Acropolis and enter Athens;
9th, Turkish Manifesto rejects allied Note (of *Apr.* 4th) for truce with Greece;
18th, Concordat between Netherlands and Pope Leo XII allowing the Dutch a preponderance in church affairs;
21st, Robert Peel reforms criminal law, by reducing number of capital offences, abolishing immunity of clergy from arrest in cases of felony, and by defining law of offences against property in a simplified form;
24th, Jean Villèle secures royal ordinance to censor French press.

G **Jul**: 3rd, Decree of Brazilian Emperor appointing Dom Miguel lieutenant of Portugal;
6th, Treaty of London whereby Russia, Britain, and France agree to recognise autonomy of Greece and to force truce on Sultan.

H **Aug**: 8th, death of George Canning (aged 56);
16th, Sultan rejects Note of Russian, French and British ambassadors demanding truce and power to negotiate is now placed in hands of admirals of the respective allied fleets;
31st, Lord Goderich forms Tory administration in Britain.

J **Sep**:

K **Oct**: 1st, Russia defeats Persian forces and takes Erivan in Armenia;
20th, Turkish and Egyptian fleets are destroyed at Battle of Navarino by allied squadrons (the Egyptians having arrived *Sept.*).

L **Nov**: 17th and 24th, in the French elections the Ultra-Conservatives are defeated by Liberal opposition.

M **Dec**: 8th (–12th), allied ambassadors leave Constantinople;
26th, Sultan Mahmud II rejects right of allies to mediate in war with Greece.

N

O **Politics, Economics, Law and Education**

Henry Brougham founds Society for the Diffusion of Useful Knowledge.

P **Science, Technology, Discovery, etc.**

George Ohm formulates Ohm's Law.
Friedrich Wöhler obtains metallic aluminium.
Joseph Niepce produces photographs on an asphalt-coated plate.
Karl von Baer, *Epistola de Ova Mammalium et Hominis Generis* (*Origin of the Ovum*).
Joseph Ressel invents the first practical ship's screw.
Friction matches ('Lucifers') introduced.

Q **Scholarship**

Henry Hallam, *Constitutional History of England*.

R **Philosophy and Religion**

John Keble, *The Christian Year*.
John Darby secedes from Church of England to found Plymouth Brethren.

S **Art, Sculpture, Fine Arts and Architecture**

John Constable, *The Cornfield* (painting).
J. M. W. Turner, *Ulysses Deriding Polyphemus* (painting).

T **Music**

Franz Schubert, *Die Winterreise*.
G. Bellini, *Il Pirata* (opera).

U **Literature**

John Clare, *The Shepherd's Calendar*.
Heinrich Heine, *Buch der Lieder*.
Giacomo Leopardi, *Operette morali*.
[E. A. Poe], *Tamerlane*.
[A. and C. Tennyson], *Poems by Two Brothers*.

V **The Press**

The Evening Standard, London, founded.

W **Drama and Entertainment**

X **Sport**

Y **Statistics**

Z **Births and Deaths**

Mar. 5th Pierre Simon Laplace d. (77), and Alessandro Volta d. (82).
Mar. 26th Ludwig van Beethoven d. (56).
Apr. 2nd William Holman Hunt b. (–1910).
Apr. 5th Joseph Lister b. (–1912).
Aug. 12th William Blake d. (69).
Oct. 10th Ugo Foscolo d. (49).
Oct. 16th Arnold Böcklin b. (–1901).

1828 Repeal of British Test and Corporation Acts—Russo-Turkish War begins

A **Jan**: 3rd, Jean Villèle resigns as French Prime Minister after election defeats (*Nov.* 1827) and Vicomte de Martignac succeeds, 5th, forming administration of moderates;
18th, commercial treaty between Bavaria and Württemberg abolishes customs duties on their common frontier;
25th, Duke of Wellington forms Tory administration, following resignation of Goderich, 8th, on question of appointing chairman of finance committee.

B **Feb**: 22nd, Peace of Turkmanchai by which Persia cedes part of Armenia, including Erivan, to Russia;
26th, Dom Miguel takes oath as Regent of Portugal.

C **Mar**: 3rd, Peter IV abdicates as King of Portugal.

D **Apr**: 14th, new press law in France suppresses censorship, but press trials are still held in government-influenced tribunals and are not conducted by juries;
26th, Russia declares war on Turkey;
British troops recalled by Duke of Wellington from Portugal.

E **May**: 9th, repeal of British Test and Corporation Acts so that Catholic and Protestant Nonconformists now allowed to hold public office in Britain;
29th, William Huskisson resigns as Secretary of State for War and the Colonies after friction with Wellington;
—, 'Tariff of Abominations' passed by Congress in attempt to make U.S. economically self-sufficient by obstructing and prohibiting entry of foreign goods and materials.

F **Jun**: 16th, attack on French Jesuits by Vicomte de Martignac, who prohibits religious orders from teaching unless sanctioned by State;
23rd, Dom Miguel is proclaimed King of Portugal, following peaceful *coup d'état*;
30th, in the Clare Election Daniel O'Connell stands as a Roman Catholic candidate (and is elected *July* 4th).

G **Jul**: 15th, new Corn Law allowing imports of corn at any price and using sliding scale;
19th, London Protocol issued by Britain, Russia, and France, allowing France to intervene in the Morea to evacuate hostile troops in order to secure Greek independence;
Union of Clerical and Liberal Parties in Belgium after King William I has estranged Clericals by concluding Concordat of 1827.

H **Aug**: 6th, Mehemet Ali agrees to British admiral's demand to quit Greece;
27th, Uruguay formally proclaimed independent at preliminary peace between Brazil and Argentina.

J **Sep**:

K **Oct**: 11th, Russians occupy Varna in war against Turkey.

L **Nov**: 16th, London Protocol, issued by France, Britain, and Russia, recognises independence of Greece when Morea and Cyclades Isles are guaranteed by those powers;
In U.S. presidential election, Andrew Jackson (178 electoral votes) defeats John Quincy Adams (83 votes).

M **Dec**:

N Working Men's Party founded in New York.
Prussia forms customs union with Hesse-Darmstadt.

O **Politics, Economics, Law and Education**

Thomas Arnold is appointed headmaster of Rugby School (–41).

P **Science, Technology, Discovery, etc.**

Friedrich Wöhler's synthesis of urea founds organic chemistry.

Niels Abel begins the study of elliptic functions.

Von Baer, *Ueber die Entwickelungsgeschichte der Thiere* (–37), establishes science of comparative embryology.

Nicholas von Dreyse invents a bolt-action needle gun.

Q **Scholarship**

J. G. Grimm, *German Legal Antiquities.*

Noah Webster's *Dictionary.*

W. F. P. Napier, *History of Peninsular War* (–40).

R **Philosophy and Religion**

Dugald Stewart, *Philosophy of the Active and Moral Powers of Man.*

S. T. Coleridge, *Constitution of Church and State.*

S **Art, Sculpture, Fine Arts and Architecture**

John Constable, *Dedham Vale* (painting).

William Dyce's *Madonna* introduces ideas of 'Nazarener' artists to Britain.

T **Music**

Franz Schubert, C. Major Symphony ('Great') and Klavierstücke.

Daniel Auber, *Masaniello* (opera).

G. Rossini, *Le Comte Ory* (opera).

U **Literature**

Thomas Carlyle's *Essay on Goethe* draws attention of English readers to German literature.

Alexander Pushkin, *Poltava.*

V **The Press**

The Spectator and *Athenaeum* are issued.

W **Drama and Entertainment**

X **Sport**

Y **Statistics**

Z **Births and Deaths**

Feb. 12th George Meredith b. (–1909).

Mar. 20th Henrik Ibsen b. (–1906).

Apr. 13th Josephine Butler b. (–1906).

Apr. 16th Francisco Goya y Lucientes d. (81).

Apr. 21st Hippolyte Taine b. (–1893).

May 12th Dante Gabriel Rossetti b. (–1882).

Aug. 28th Leo Tolstoy b. (–1910).

Nov. 19th Franz Schubert d. (31).

1829 Catholic Emancipation in Britain—Independence of Serbia and Danubian Provinces

A **Jan:**

B **Feb:**

C **Mar:** 4th, Andrew Jackson is inaugurated President of U.S.;
21st, Duke of Wellington challenges Earl of Winchilsea to a duel after latter's criticism of his support for Catholic Relief;
22nd, London Protocol on Greece modifies Protocol of *Nov.* 1828, extending guarantee of powers to include Continental Greece and Island of Euboea.

D **Apr:** 13th, Roman Catholic Relief Bill passes Lords (having passed Commons, *Mar.* 5th) allowing Catholics to sit and vote in Parliament, giving them right of suffrage and making them eligible for all military, civil and corporate offices except those of Regent, Lord Chancellor of England, and Lord Lieutenant of Ireland; they are to take an oath denying the Pope has power to interfere in domestic affairs and recognising Protestant succession.

E **May:** 27th, Prussia finally obtains support for commercial policy from Bavaria and Württemberg.

F **Jun:** 19th, Robert Peel's Act to establish new police force in London and its suburbs.

G **Jul:**

H **Aug:** 6th, dismissal of Vicomte de Martignac in France after alienating both extreme parties by proposals to change electoral law;
8th, Charles X appoints Prince de Polignac Prime Minister in France, an Ultra-Conservative who does not possess the confidence of the Chamber, which constitutes a departure from ministerial responsibility.

J **Sep:** 14th, treaty of Adrianople ends Russo-Turkish War and Sultan Mahmud II recognises London Protocol (*Mar.* 1829) which guarantees territory of Greece, the independence of Danubian Provinces and of Serbia, while Tsar Nicholas I obtains land south of Caucasus.

K **Oct:**

L **Nov:**

M **Dec:**

N

O **Politics, Economics, Law and Education**

Earl of Surrey, elected for Horsham (*May* 4th), becomes first Roman Catholic M.P.

Robert Peel founds the Metropolitan Police force.

Governor-General Lord Bentinck secures abolition of 'Suttee' in Bengal (extended to Bombay and Madras in 1830).

P **Science, Technology, Discovery, etc.**

Thomas Graham formulates law on diffusion of gases.

James Nelson invents process for pre-heating the blast air in blast furnaces, to produce very high temperatures.

George and Robert Stephenson's *Rocket* wins Liverpool and Manchester Railway competition (*Oct.*).

First steam locomotive runs in U.S. (Baltimore-Ohio, *Aug.* 9th).

Horse-drawn omnibus runs in London.

Q **Scholarship**

Archaeological Institute, Rome, founded.

F. Guizot, *Histoire de la Civilisation en France.*

H. H. Milman, *History of the Jews.*

R **Philosophy and Religion**

James Mill, *Analysis of the Human Mind.*

S **Art, Sculpture, Fine Arts and Architecture**

E. Delacroix, *Sardanapalus* (painting).

T **Music**

G. Rossini, *William Tell* (opera).

F. Mendelssohn revives interest in Bach's *St. Matthew Passion* through Berlin performance.

F. Damian invents the mouth organ and Charles Wheatstone the concertina.

U **Literature**

Honoré de Balzac, *Les Chouans* and *La Comédie Humaine* (–48).

William Cobbett, *Advice to a Young Man.*

Alfred de Musset, *Contes d'Espagne et d'Italie.*

Victor Hugo, *Les Orientales.*

[Charles Ste-Beuve], *Joseph Delorme.*

V **The Press**

Revue des Deux Mondes first issued (re-founded 1831).

W **Drama and Entertainment**

X **Sport**

Oxford and Cambridge boat race first rowed.

Y **Statistics**

Z **Births and Deaths**

Apr. 10th William Booth b. (–1912).

May 29th Humphry Davy d. (50).

June 8th John Everett Millais b. (–1896).

Sept. 7th Friedrich August Kekulé b. (–1897).

Dec. 18th Jean de Lamarck d. (63).

A **Jan**: Debate in U.S. Congress between Daniel Webster and Robert Y. Hayne on the nature of the Union, with Hayne supporting state rights.

B **Feb**: 3rd, at London Conference, Greece is declared independent under the protection of France, Russia and Britain.

C **Mar**: 18th, Charles X's appointment of Polignac is opposed by French Chambers in the answer to the address from the throne;
29th, Ferdinand VII of Spain publishes law of 1789 which abrogates Salic Law, thus allowing females to be heirs to throne.

D **Apr**: 27th, Simon Bolivar abdicates as President of Colombia.

E **May**: 16th, Charles X of France dissolves Chambers and calls for elections;
28th, U.S. act settles controversy between Georgia and Cherokee Indians in order ultimately to settle Indians on land west of the Missouri, if they give up lands east of that river.

F **Jun**: 26th, George IV dies and is succeeded by William IV (–1837).

G **Jul**: 5th, French begin invasion of Algeria and take Algiers;
19th, French elections finally held, after delays caused by Charles X, and the Liberal opposition obtains majority;
25th, Charles X issues five ordinances, for controlling press, dissolving Chambers and changing electoral system;
27th (–29th), Revolution in Paris and other areas of France on news of Charles's law;
31st, Louis Philippe is appointed Lieutenant-General of France.

H **Aug**: 2nd, abdication of Charles X;
7th, Louis Philippe is elected King of France by Chambers, and, 9th, accepts throne (–1848);
14th, Constitutional Charter in France, based on an elective monarchy, allowing for initiation of legislation in Chambers, for the permanent suppression of press censorship, and for end to Catholicism as State religion of France;
25th, Revolution in Belgium, against union with Dutch.

J **Sep**: 11th, Republic of Ecuador established and granted Constitution by Colombia under which it is to be part of Confederation of Colombia;
15th, William Huskisson killed by train at opening of Liverpool-Manchester Railway;
22nd, Venezuela secedes from Colombia and becomes an independent sovereign state;
Revolts in Saxony, Hesse and Brunswick where rulers are dethroned and constitution granted.

K **Oct**:

L **Nov**: 8th, accession of Ferdinand II of Naples on death of Francis I;
15th, Duke of Wellington resigns over the civil list and Lord Grey is asked to form a Liberal-Whig ministry, with Lord Palmerston as Foreign Secretary;
18th, National Congress in Belgium decrees independence;
22nd, Belgian Congress votes for monarchy (but excludes House of Orange, 24th *Nov.*);
29th, insurrection in Poland against Russian domination is brought to a head by intention of Tsar Nicholas to use Polish forces to march into France and Belgium to crush revolts there.

M **Dec**: 20th, London Conference of Britain, France, Austria, Prussia and Russia agree with Belgium on separation from Holland.

N

O Politics, Economics, Law and Education

H. F. R. de Lamennais advocates a free press and religious toleration in France.
F. J. Stahl, *Philosophy of Law*.
Count Mikhail Speranski codifies Russian law (45 vols. with commentaries).
King's College, London, founded.
First epidemic of cholera in Europe.

P Science, Technology, Discovery, etc.

Charles Lyell, *Principles of Geology* (–33).
Charles Bell, *The Nervous System of the Human Body*.
Nitrates first shipped from Chile and Peru.
Liverpool-Manchester Railway opened.
Richard and John Lander explore lower course of R. Niger.
Royal Geographic Society, London.
J. J. Audubon, *Birds of America*.

Q Scholarship

R Philosophy and Religion

Auguste Comte, *Course of Positive Philosophy* (–42).
Roman Catholicism no longer the State religion of France.
Joseph Smith, *Book of Mormon*; a Mormon church is established at Fayette, New York.

S Art, Sculpture, Fine Arts and Architecture

Franz Klenze, the Walhalla near Regensburg.
Honoré Daumier's drawings in *La Caricature*.

T Music

Hector Berlioz, *Symphonie Fantastique*.
Daniel Auber, *Fra Diavolo* (opera).

U Literature

William Cobbett, *Rural Rides*.
Victor Hugo, *Hernani*.
Stendhal (pseud.), *Le Rouge et le Noir*.
Alfred Lord Tennyson, *Poems chiefly Lyrical*.

V The Press

W Drama and Entertainment

X Sport

Y Statistics

Emigration from Great Britain to U.S., 1820–30, totals 27,489, and from Ireland to U.S., 54,338.

Z Births and Deaths

Jan. 7th Thomas Lawrence d.(60).
Feb. 3rd Robert Cecil, Marquess of Salisbury b. (–1903).
Sept. 8th Frédéric Mistral b. (–1914).
Sept. 18th William Hazlitt d. (51).
Dec. 8th Benjamin Constant d. (63).
Dec. 17th Simon Bolivar d. (47).

1831 (Jan.–Nov.) Separation of Belgium from Holland—Russia suppresses Polish revolt—Britain annexes Mysore

A **Jan:** 5th, a Constitution is granted in Hesse-Cassel;
20th (and 27th), two Protocols by powers in London for separation of Belgium and Holland and for limit of their boundaries, which is accepted by Holland but rejected by Belgium;
25th, Polish Diet declares independence of Poland, dethrones Nicholas and deposes Romanovs.

B **Feb:** 3rd, revolutionary outbreaks in Modena, Parma and Papal States influenced by French Revolution (of *July* 1830), and crisis worsens after election of a reactionary Pope, Gregory XVI;
3rd, Belgians elect French Duc de Nemours King (but this is subsequently rejected by Louis Philippe to prevent outcry in Britain);
7th, Belgian Constitution proclaimed assigning executive power to hereditary king who governs through Ministers, responsible to legislative body, with judiciary independent, and freedom of worship, of education and of the press.

C **Mar:** 8th, Constitution proclaimed in Hanover after unrest since revolution in France (*July* 1830);
21st, First Reform Bill, initiated by Lord John Russell, to redistribute seats and to extend franchise is defeated during committee stage;
Austrian troops enter Italian Peninsula to put down revolts.

D **Apr:** 7th, Pedro I of Brazil abdicates in favour of son, in order to return to Portugal to aid Maria I;
22nd, Dissolution of Parliament by Lord Grey after defeat of Reform Bill. Subsequent election, fought on question of support for whole Bill, gives majority to Whigs.

E **May:** 26th, Polish forces are defeated by Russian army at Ostrolenke.

F **Jun:** 4th, Belgian Congress proclaims Leopold of Saxe-Coburg King;
26th, London Conference issues Eighteen Articles for peace preliminaries between Belgium and Holland as substitute for January Protocols, but these are rejected by Dutch.

G **Jul:**

H **Aug:** 2nd, Dutch troops invade Belgium, but are forced to withdraw, 20th, when French army enters Belgian territory.

J **Sep:** 4th, Saxony is granted Constitution after revolt (of *Sept.* 1830);
8th, Russia takes Warsaw after two-day battle and Polish revolt collapses (Tsar proclaims peace *Oct.* 18th);
21st, Second Reform Bill passes House of Commons (but is rejected by Lords *Oct.* 7th).

K **Oct:** 9th, assassination of Count Capo d'Istria after hostility to his bureaucratic methods in Greece;
14th, London Conference issues Twenty-four Articles, which are rejected by Dutch as too advantageous to Belgians;
Bristol Riots after rejection of Reform Bill.

L **Nov:** 15th, treaty incorporating Twenty-four Articles for separation of Holland and Belgium is accepted by Austria, France, Britain, Prussia, Russia and Belgium (ratified 31 *Jan.* 1832).

O **Politics, Economics, Law and Education**

Ebenezer Elliott, *Corn Law Rhymes.*

William L. Garrison begins publishing *The Liberator*, an abolitionist periodical, in Boston.

P **Science, Technology, Discovery, etc.**

Michael Faraday and Joseph Henry independently discover electro-magnetic induction.

M. Melloni's discoveries in radiant heat through the thermomultiplier.

British Association for the Advancement of Science established.

R. Brown discovers nucleus in plant cells (publishes in 1833).

Charles Darwin's voyage on the *Beagle* (–36).

Q **Scholarship**

R **Philosophy and Religion**

Alexander Campbell deposed by General Assembly of Church of Scotland for teaching against atonement.

William Miller founds Second Adventists in U.S., predicting the end of the world in 1843.

S **Art, Sculpture, Fine Arts and Architecture**

E. Delacroix, *The Barricade* (painting).

H. Delaroche, *Princes in the Tower* (painting).

'Barbizon School' of artists, including Jean Millet and Pierre Rousseau, first exhibit in the salon.

T **Music**

L. J. F. Hérold, *Zampa* (opera).

V. Bellini, *La Sonnambula* and *Norma* (operas).

U **Literature**

Honoré de Balzac, *Peau de Chagrin* and *Le Chef-d'œuvre inconnu.*

Henri Barbier, *Les Iambes.*

V. Hugo, *Notre-Dame de Paris.*

T. L. Peacock, *Crotchet Castle.*

V **The Press**

W **Drama and Entertainment**

Catharine Gore, *School for Coquettes.*

X **Sport**

Y **Statistics**

Populations (in millions): Great Britain, 12·2; Ireland, 7·7; U.S., 12·8.

Coal production: U.K. 30,000,000 tons; France, 2,571,000 tons.

L **Nov**: 17th, Venezuela, Ecuador and New Granada dissolve Union of Colombia (of 1819) and New Granada becomes an independent state;
Riot of silk-weavers in Lyons, due mainly to low wages.

M **Dec**: 12th, Third Reform Bill introduced in House of Commons.

N East India Company annexes Mysore, after suppression of a peasants' revolt.

z **Births and Deaths:**

Jan. 2nd Berthold Niebuhr d. (54).
Mar. 21st Dorothea Beale b. (–1906).
June 8th Sarah Siddons d. (75).
July 4th James Monroe d. (73).
Nov. 9th Henry Labouchere b. (–1912).
Nov. 13th J. Clerk-Maxwell b. (–1879).
Nov. 14th Georg Wilhelm Friedrich Hegel d. (61).
— Camille Pissarro b. (–1903).

A **Jan**: 19th, Austrian troops, under Count Radetzky, occupy Ancona after fresh risings in Papal States (at end of 1831) and remain until 1838.

B **Feb**: 26th, Polish Constitution abolished and new organic statute imposed by Tsar Nicholas I allowing for partial autonomy which, however, remains a dead letter;
29th, New Granada's constitution is proclaimed providing for republican system of government with Congress of two Chambers.

C **Mar**: 23rd, Reform Bill passes Commons.

D **Apr**: 10th, French law excludes families of Charles X and of Napoleon from France;
Turkey declares war on Mohammed Ali, Khedive of Egypt, who demands Syria as reward for aid against Greece.

E **May**: 9th, William IV, having lost confidence in Grey over Reform Bill, forces him to resign, but he is recalled within a week as the Duke of Wellington is unable to form administration;
27th, Hambach Festival of South German Democrats advocates armed revolt;
—, Ibrahim, son of Mohammed Ali, takes Acre.

F **Jun**: 5th, Insurrection in Paris by Republicans attending funeral of their late leader, General Lamarque;
7th, Reform Bill becomes law (after King has agreed to create sufficient Whig Peers to out-vote Tory opposition in Lords if necessary). Over 140 seats redistributed, and in the boroughs all antiquated forms of franchise are eliminated and the franchise is extended to include leaseholders paying minimum of £10 rent per annum, while in counties the 40-shilling freehold qualification is retained and certain lease-holders acquire the vote;
28th, Prince Metternich's Six Articles to maintain despotic government in face of opposition within the German Confederation.

G **Jul**: 9th, Dom Pedro, with aid of France and Britain, takes Oporto and Dom Miguel's forces are defeated;
14th, U.S. Tariff Act (less rigid than that of *May* 1828) but subsequently rejected in South Carolina (*Nov.* 24th);
17th, Act for amendment of representation in Scotland extends Reform Act across border.

H **Aug**: 7th, Irish Reform Act passed;
8th, Greek National Assembly elects Prince Otto of Bavaria King as Otto I (–1862);
East India Company, under William Bentinck, annexes Cathar after residents ask for British protection.

J **Sep**:

K **Oct**: 11th, Marshal Soult forms ministry in France.

L **Nov**: 7th, Duchesse de Berry, a leading Legitimist conspirator in France, is arrested;
In U.S. presidential election, Andrew Jackson, who was nominated as candidate at the first Democratic Convention to be held, defeats Henry Clay (219 electoral votes to 49).

O **Politics, Economics, Law and Education**
Giuseppe Mazzini founds 'Young Italy' movement.
Slavery Abolition Society founded in Boston, Mass.
Silvio Pellico, *My Imprisonment.*
Zürich University founded.

P **Science, Technology, Discovery, etc.**
Diastase, the first enzyme, is separated from barley.
Justus Liebig investigates constitution of ether-alcohol mixtures.
Marshall Hall discovers reflex action of nerve centres.
Jakob Steiner founds synthetic geometry.
W. E. Weber and K. F. Gauss construct the needle telegraph at Göttingen.
First railway in mainland Europe (Budweis-Linz) is completed.
Göta Canal completed.

Q **Scholarship**

R **Philosophy and Religion**
Gregory XVI's encyclical condemning freedom of conscience and of the press.
Gustavus Adolphus Society founded to combat Roman Catholicism.
T. Arnold's *Essay on Church Reform.*

S **Art, Sculpture, Fine Arts and Architecture**
William Wilkins, National Gallery, London.

T **Music**
F. Chopin, Mazurkas (op. 6).
G. Donizetti, *L'Elisir d'Amore* (opera).

U **Literature**
Carl Almqvist, *Book of the Thorn and the Rose.*
Honoré de Balzac, *Contes Drôlatiques.*
Washington Irving, *A Town of the Prairie.*
Alexander Pushkin, *Eugene Onegin* completed.
George Sand (pseud.), *Indiana.*
Lord Tennyson, *The Lotus-Eaters* and *The Lady of Shalott.*
Book jackets are first used by British publishers.

V **The Press**
Penny Magazine started.

W **Drama and Entertainment**
Goethe, *Faust*, pt. ii.
V. Hugo, *Le Roi s'amuse.*

X **Sport**

Y **Statistics**
U.K. Textiles trade:

Raw cotton imports	277 mill. lb.
Cotton exports	461 mill. yds.
Woollen exports	2,297,000 pieces.
Linen exports	49,531,000 yds.

M **Dec:** 21st, at Battle of Konieh Egyptian forces rout Turkish army;
23rd, French take Antwerp, forcing Holland to recognise independence of Belgium (after siege since late *Nov.*).

N

z **Births and Deaths**

Jan. 23rd Édouard Manet b. (–1883).
Jan. 27th C. L. Dodgson ('Lewis Carroll') b. (–1898).
Feb. 3rd George Crabbe d. (78).
Mar. 22nd Johann Wolfgang Goethe d. (82).
May 13th G. L. P. C. Cuvier d. (62).
June 6th Jeremy Bentham d. (84).
June 17th William Crookes b. (–1919).
Aug. 16th Wilhelm Wundt b. (–1920).
Sept. 21st. Walter Scott d. (61).
Sept. 30th Frederick, Lord Roberts b. (–1914).
Nov. 28th Leslie Stephen b. (–1904).
Dec. 8th G. A. Henty b. (–1902).

1833 Prussia establishes *Zollverein*—Turkey recognises independence of Egypt—Factory inspection in Britain

A **Jan:** 1st, Britain proclaims sovereignty over Falkland Islands;
16th, Andrew Jackson asks Congress for legislation to enforce tariff (of *July* 14th 1832) in South Carolina.

B **Feb:** 20th, Russian ships enter Bosphorus on way to Constantinople to aid Turkey against Egypt (after conference with Porte *Dec.* 1832–*Feb.* 1833).

C **Mar:** 1st, Clay Tariff passed by U.S. Congress to amend tariff of *July* 1832 in order to appease South Carolina; Congress also passes Force Act, authorising President to use armed force to collect revenues if necessary;
4th, Jackson begins second term as U.S. President;
23rd, Prussia establishes *Zollverein* (customs union) in Germany by a series of treaties, but Austria is excluded.

D **Apr:** 3rd, attempt by revolutionaries in Germany to take over Frankfurt Diet in protest against articles of *June* 1832 is easily crushed.

E **May:** 3rd, Turkey recognises independence of Egypt and cedes Syria and Aden to Mehemet Ali;
21st, Dutch conclude armistice of indefinite length with Belgium;
22nd, constitution in Chile gives greater power to president and establishes Roman Catholicism as State religion.

F **Jun:** 28th, Primary Education Law in France gives effective control to Church.

G **Jul:** 8th, by treaty of Unkiar-Skelessi, a defensive alliance between Turkey and Russia, Sultan agrees to close Dardanelles to all but Russian warships;
24th, Lisbon evacuated by Miguelist forces and occupied by supporters of Dom Pedro and Queen Maria (who returns *Sept.* 22nd).

H **Aug:** 29th, British Factory Act passed, whereby no children under nine to work in factories, those between nine and 13 not to work more than nine-hour day and inspectors are to be appointed to ensure that regulations are carried out;
29th, Bank Charter Act allows Bank of England to retain exclusive possession of government balances, monopoly of limited liability, and to be only Joint-Stock Bank allowed to issue own notes within 65-mile radius of London.

J **Sep:** 10th (–20th), Conference at Münchengrätz between Russia, Prussia and Austria to discuss European problems, particularly with regard to Turkey;
26th, new liberal Constitution granted in Hanover by William IV;
29th, death of Ferdinand VII of Spain, who is succeeded by Queen Isabella II (–1868).

K **Oct:** 15th, at Berlin, Prussia, Russia and Austria agree to support the integrity of the Ottoman Empire and to further the Holy Alliance by promising to aid one another in the event of attack.

L **Nov:**

M **Dec:**

N General Trades Union in New York links all unions in one organisation (collapses 1837).
Beginning of Whig Party in U.S. which absorbs the National Republican Party, the former opposition, and attacks Andrew Jackson's democratic policies.

O **Politics, Economics, Law and Education**

End of East India Company's monopoly of China trade.
First State grant for education in England.
Académie des Sciences Morales et Politiques revived in France.
The charity bazaar becomes popular in England.

P **Science, Technology, Discovery, etc.**

Q **Scholarship**

Franz Bopp, *Comparative Grammar* (–52).
J. M. Kemble's edition of *Beowulf*.
Jules Michelet, *Histoire de France* (–67).

R **Philosophy and Religion**

John Keble, *National Apostasy* (Assize sermon at Oxford) begins Oxford Movement.
Tracts for the Times (–41).
Nonconformists allowed to celebrate marriages in chapels in Britain.
Orson Pratt begins Mormon mission in Canada.

S **Art, Sculpture, Fine Arts and Architecture**

T **Music**

F. Mendelssohn, 4th Symphony in A ('Italian').
F. Chopin, 12 Études (op. 10).

U **Literature**

Robert Browning, *Pauline*.
Thomas Carlyle, *Sartor Resartus*.
Alfred de Musset, *André del Sarto* and *Les Caprices de Marianne*.
Nicolai Gogol, *The Government Inspector*.
Alexander Pushkin, *Queen of Spades*.
George Sand (pseud.), *Lelia*.

V **The Press**

Knickerbocker Magazine.

W **Drama and Entertainment**

Edmund Kean's last appearance (*Mar.*) as Othello.

X **Sport**

Y **Statistics**

Z **Births and Deaths**

May 7th Johannes Brahms b. (–1897).
June 4th Garnet Wolseley b. (–1913).
Aug. 20th Benjamin Harrison b. (–1901).
Aug. 28th Edward Burne-Jones b. (–1898).
Oct. 21st Alfred Nobel b. (–1896).

1834 The Tolpuddle Martyrs—Slavery abolished in British Empire—Civil war in Spain

A **Jan**: formation of Grand National Consolidated Trades Union, led by Robert Owen, to organise general strike for eight-hour day (but collapses *Oct.*).

B **Feb**: Attempt by 'Young Italy' followers of Giuseppe Mazzini on Savoy fails.

C **Mar**: 18th, Tolpuddle labourers in Dorset sentenced to be transported for making illegal oath in forming lodge of Owen's Union.

D **Apr**: 9th, revolt of silk-weavers in Lyons, lasting four days, after attempts by French government to suppress trade union activities;
12th, 150 Republicans arrested in Paris from fear of insurrection and, 14th, rising crushed by army under Adolphe Thiers;
22nd, Britain, France, Spain and Portugal form Quadruple Alliance in support of liberal constitutions in Iberian Peninsula.

E **May**: 26th, Dom Miguel of Portugal finally surrenders and abdicates, allowing for restoration of Maria II;
Sikhs capture Peshawar.

F **Jun**:

G **Jul**: 9th, Lord Grey resigns over problem of tithes and coercion act in Ireland, and is succeeded, 16th, by Melbourne;
Beginning of civil war in Spain when Don Carlos, brother of late Ferdinand VII of Spain, claims throne (the Carlists are finally defeated, *Aug.* 1839).

H **Aug**: 15th, South Australia Act is passed allowing for establishment of colony there.

J **Sep**: 24th, Peter IV of Portugal dies, succeeded by Maria II.

K **Oct**: 16th, British Houses of Parliament practically destroyed by fire.

L **Nov**: Lord Melbourne resigns after King's refusal to allow Lord Russell to become leader of House of Commons and Robert Peel is asked to form Tory administration (he accepts, *Dec.* 9th).

M **Dec**: 17th, Robert Peel issues Tamworth Manifesto giving Tory Party a policy of liberal Conservatism, accepting Reform Act of 1832 and agreeing to pass more equitable reforms.

N

Z **Births and Deaths** (*cont.*)
July 10th James Whistler b. (–1903).
July 19th Edgar Degas b. (–1917).
July 25th Samuel Taylor Coleridge d. (61).
Sept. 15th Heinrich Treitschke b. (–1896).
Nov. 12th Alexander Borodin b. (–1887).
Dec. 23rd T. R. Malthus d. (68).
Dec. 27th Charles Lamb d. (59).
— Edwin Klebs b. (–1913).

O Politics, Economics, Law and Education

J. Bentham, *Deontology; or the Science of Morality* (posth.).
Poor Law Amendment Act forbids outdoor relief in Britain and establishes workhouses.
Abolition of slavery in British Empire (*Aug.* 1st).
Chimney Sweeps Act in Britain.
Liverpool Mechanics Institute is founded.

P Science, Technology, Discovery, etc.

J. F. Herschel begins astronomical observations at Cape of Good Hope.
Michael Faraday discovers electrical self-induction.
Jean Dumas formulates Law of Substitution.
Louis Braille perfects system of characters for the blind to read.
Cyrus McCormick's reaping machine.
'Hansom' cabs are introduced to London.

Q Scholarship

L. von Ranke, *History of the Popes* (–36).
George Bancroft, *History of the United States* (–74).

R Philosophy and Religion

H. F. R. Lamennais, *Paroles d'un croyant.*
Portuguese monasteries suppressed.

S Art, Sculpture, Fine Arts and Architecture

William Dunlap, *Rise and Progress of the Arts of Design in the United States.*

T Music

H. Berlioz, *Harold in Italy.*
R. Schumann, *Carnaval* (op. 9).

U Literature

Honoré de Balzac, *La Recherche de l'Absolu* and *Le Père Goriot.*
Franz Grillparzer, *Der Traum, ein Leben.*
Francesco Guerrazzi, *L'Assedio di Firenze.*
Edward Bulwer-Lytton, *The Last Days of Pompeii.*
Leopold Schefer, *Laienbrevier* (–35).

V The Press

Lloyd's Register of Shipping.

W Drama and Entertainment

X Sport

Royal and Ancient Golf Club, St. Andrews, is patronised by William IV.

Y Statistics

Z Births and Deaths

Jan. 10th John Dalberg Acton, Lord Acton b. (–1902).
Feb. 7th Dimitry Mendeléev b. (–1907)
Feb. 16th Ernst Haeckel b. (–1919).
Mar. 24th William Morris b. (–1896).

(*Continued opposite*)

1835 September Laws in France suppress radicalism—British Municipal Corporations reformed

A **Jan:**

B **Feb:**

C **Mar:** 2nd, Francis I of Austria dies, succeeded by Ferdinand I (–1848);
'Lichfield House Compact', a tacit agreement between Daniel O'Connell, leader of Irish Nationalists, and Whig opposition, whereby the Irish promise Parliamentary support provided Whigs vote against coercion acts.

D **Apr:** 8th, Robert Peel resigns after defeat when voting against resolution to appropriate surplus revenues of Irish Church for non-ecclesiastical objects and
18th, Lord Melbourne forms Whig ministry.

E **May:** 12th, Baden joins *Zollverein*.

F **Jun:**

G **Jul:** 28th, assassination attempt on Louis Philippe by the Corsican, Giuseppe Fieschi.

H **Aug:**

J **Sep:** 9th, British Municipal Corporations Act abolishes all old Charter privileges and establishes new governing body of councillors elected by ratepayers with aldermen elected by councillors, and a mayor elected for one year;
'September Laws' in France severely censor the press and suppress the radical movement.

K **Oct:**

L **Nov:**

M **Dec:**

N Juan de Rosas becomes Dictator in Argentina (–1852).
Milosh is forced to grant Constitution in Serbia but soon withdraws it at the Sultan's demand.

Z **Births and Deaths**

Feb. 4th Albert Venn Dicey b. (–1922).
June 16th William Cobbett d. (72).
Sept. 24th Vincenzo Bellini d. (33).
Oct. 3rd Charles Camille Saint-Saëns b. (–1921).
Nov. 25th Andrew Carnegie b. (–1919).
Nov. 30th 'Mark Twain' (pseud. of Samuel Langhorne Clemens) b. (–1910).
Dec. 4th Samuel Butler b. (–1902).

O **Politics, Economics, Law and Education**

A. de Tocqueville, *De la Démocratie en Amérique* (–40).

Richard Cobden's free trade pamphlet *England, Ireland and America* and, to combat Russophobia, *Russia*.

P **Science, Technology, Discovery, etc.**

S. D. Poisson, *Théorie mathématique de la Chaleur*.

L. A. J. Quételet, *Sur l'homme et le développement de ses facultés*, suggests the physique and intellect of the 'average man'.

Samuel Colt's revolver.

William Hooker establishes a botanical laboratory at Kew.

Q **Scholarship**

C. A. Brandis, *Handbook to the History of Graeco-Roman Philosophy* (–66).

Connor Thirlwall, *History of Greece* (–44).

J. Grimm, *German Mythology*.

R **Philosophy and Religion**

D. F. Strauss, *Life of Jesus*.

Revival of Sabbatarianism in England.

Papal Bull condemns rationalist teaching of Georg Hermes.

S **Art, Sculpture, Fine Arts and Architecture**

Casper Friedrich, *Rest during the Harvest* (painting).

T **Music**

G. Donizetti, *Lucy of Lammermoor* (opera).

U **Literature**

Hans Andersen, *Fairy Tales* (–72).

R. Browning, *Paracelsus*.

Georg Büchner, *Danton's Death*.

T. Gautier, *Mademoiselle de Maupin*.

N. Gogol, *Dead Souls*.

Bulwer-Lytton, *Rienzi*.

A. de Vigny, *Servitude et grandeur militaires*.

W. Wordsworth, *Yarrow Revisited*.

V **The Press**

New York Herald (*May*), founded as a 1-cent popular paper.

W **Drama and Entertainment**

The polka first danced in Prague.

X **Sport**

Y **Statistics**

U.K. total State expenditure, £48·9 mill.

U.K. iron production, 1 mill. tons.

(*Continued opposite*)

A **Jan:**

B **Feb:** 22nd, first ministry of Adolphe Thiers in France (–*Sept.*).

C **Mar:** 2nd, Texas declares itself independent of Mexico and
17th, proclaims republican constitution.

D **Apr:** 21st, Texan independence is ensured by defeat of Mexico at battle of San Jacinto.

E **May:**

F **Jun:** 15th, Arkansas becomes U.S. state;
16th, formation of London Working Men's Association begins Chartist Movement.

G **Jul:**

H **Aug:** 13th, Tithe Commutation Act commutes tithes for money payment equal to between 60 and 75 per cent of nominal value;
13th, British Stamp Duties are reduced from 4d. to 1d.;
17th, Parliament provides for registration of births, marriages and deaths in Britain.

J **Sep:** 6th, Adolphe Thiers is forced to resign in France after proposing invasion of Spain.

K **Oct:** 28th, Federation of Peru and Bolivia proclaimed (Constitution is promulgated *May* 1st 1837);
30th, Louis Napoleon fails to create a revolt among the garrison of Strasbourg as a first step to seizing power and is subsequently exiled to U.S.

L **Nov:** 11th, Chile declares war on Peru-Bolivian Federation.

M **Dec:**

N

O **Politics, Economics, Law and Education**
Communist league formed in Paris.
Victor Considérant, *Destinée sociale* (–38).
London University founded as an examining body.
Adelaide becomes capital of S. Australia.

P **Science, Technology, Discovery, etc.**
Acetylene is made.
First railway in Canada opened and first train in London.
Samuel Morse builds his first telegraph.

Q **Scholarship**
F. C. Diez, *Grammar of the Romance Languages* (–44).

R **Philosophy and Religion**
R. W. Emerson's *Nature* founds Transcendentalism.
Johann Görres, *Christian Mysticism* (–42).
E. B. Pusey's tract *On the Holy Eucharist.*
In England the Ecclesiastical Commissioners are incorporated.

S **Art, Sculpture, Fine Arts and Architecture**
Arc de Triomphe, Paris, completed.

T **Music**
M. I. Glinka, *A Life for the Czar* (opera).
G. Meyerbeer, *The Huguenots* (opera).

U **Literature**
Charles Dickens, *Sketches by Boz* and *Pickwick Papers* (–37).
A. Garcia-Gutiérrez, *El Trovador.*
Karl Immermann, *Epigonen.*
A. de Lamartine, *Jocelyn.*
Nikolas Lenau (pseud.), *Faust.*
F. Marryat, *Mr. Midshipman Easy.*

V **The Press**
Beginnings of cheap press in France with *La Presse* and *Le Siècle.*

W **Drama and Entertainment**
'The Lancers' is first danced in Paris.

X **Sport**
Prix du Jockey Club, France, first run.

Y **Statistics**
U.K. registered tonnage of merchant shipping 2,350,000 tons (60,000 tons of steamships).

Z **Births and Deaths**
Jan. 21st Léo Délibes b. (–1891).
Apr. 7th T. H. Greene b. (–1882).
May 24th Joseph Rowntree b. (–1925).
June 9th Elizabeth Garrett Anderson b. (–1917).
June 10th André Ampère d. (61).
June 20th Emmanuel Joseph Sieyès d. (78).
July 8th Joseph Chamberlain b. (–1914).
Sept. 7th Henry Campbell-Bannerman b. (–1908).
Nov. 18th W. S. Gilbert b. (–1911).

A **Jan:** 26th, Michigan becomes a U.S. state.

B **Feb:**

C **Mar:** 4th, Martin Van Buren is inaugurated President of U.S.

D **Apr:**

E **May:**

F **Jun:** 18th, liberal Constitution is proclaimed in Spain providing for national sovereignty, House of two Chambers, absolute veto of crown and restricted suffrage;
20th, on death of William IV Queen Victoria succeeds to British throne (–1901);
—, Hanover is automatically separated from Britain, as Salic Law forbids female succession, and the throne is taken up by Ernest Augustus, Duke of Cumberland, eldest surviving son of George III (–1851);
Natal Republic founded by Dutch settlers and a Constitution is proclaimed.

G **Jul:** Ernest Augustus suppresses the Constitution in Hanover.

H **Aug:**

J **Sep:**

K **Oct:**

L **Nov:** Louis Joseph Papineau's rebellion in Lower Canada, result of conflicts between governor and legislative councils, and the popularly-elected assemblies, and also due to opposition between French and British elements; the rebels are successful, 22nd, at St. Denis, but are routed, 24th, at St. Charles.

M **Dec:** 5th, similar revolt in Upper Canada under William Lyon Mackenzie;
13th, W. L. Mackenzie sets up provisional government for Upper Canada from headquarters on Navy Island in Niagara River and prepares for invasion of Canada;
29th, Canadian government forces burn U.S. steamer *Caroline* which is helping rebels;
King of Hanover dismisses seven professors of Göttingen University, including the brothers Grimm, who oppose his revocation of Constitution.

N

O **Politics, Economics, Law and Education**

F. W. A. Froebel opens first kindergarten near Blankenburg.
Horace Mann begins educational reforms in Massachusetts.

P **Science, Technology, Discovery, etc.**

René Dutrochet recognises that chlorophyll is necessary to photosynthesis.
F. G. W. Struve publishes micrometric measurements of 2,714 double stars.
K. F. Mohr's theory of conservation of energy.
James Dana, *System of Mineralogy*.
J. L. G. Agassiz's work on fossils.
Isaac Pitman invents shorthand.

Q **Scholarship**

Georg Grotefend deciphers cuneiform inscriptions in Persia.
Thomas Carlyle, *French Revolution*.
W. H. Prescott, *Ferdinand and Isabella*.

R **Philosophy and Religion**

Immanuel Fichte founds *Zeitschrift für Philosophie*.
Archbishops of Cologne, Gnesen and Posen imprisoned for refusing to compromise over mixed marriages in Prussia.
American Presbyterians split into 'old' and 'new' schools.

S **Art, Sculpture, Fine Arts and Architecture**

Fitzwilliam Museum, Cambridge.

T **Music**

Hector Berlioz, *Benvenuto Cellini* and *Requiem*.

U **Literature**

Hendrik Conscience, *In't Wonderjaar, 1566*.
C. Dickens, *Oliver Twist* (–38).
M. Y. Lermontov, *Elegy on the Death of Pushkin*.
N. Lenau (pseud.), *Savonarola*.

V **The Press**

W **Drama and Entertainment**

X **Sport**

Y **Statistics**

Methodists: in U.S., 650,678; in U.K., 318,716.

Z **Births and Deaths**

Feb. 10th Alexander Pushkin d. (37).
Mar. 1st William Dean Howells b. (–1920).
Mar. 18th Stephen Grover Cleveland b. (–1908).
Mar. 31st John Constable d. (59).
Apr. 5th Algernon C. Swinburne b. (–1909).
Apr. 17th J. Pierpont Morgan b. (–1913).
Dec. 25th E. T. Gerry b. (–1927).

A **Jan:** 13th, W. L. Mackenzie is arrested in U.S.

B **Feb:** 10th, temporary provision made by British government for Lower Canada after collapse of Constitution, forbidding meeting of legislative assembly.

C **Mar:**

D **Apr:**

E **May:** 29th, Lord Durham arrives in Quebec as Governor-in-Chief of all British North America.

F **Jun:**

G **Jul:** 31st, first Irish Poor Law based on English Act (*Aug.* 14th 1834).

H **Aug:**

J **Sep:** 18th, Anti-Corn Law League is established in Manchester by Richard Cobden.

K **Oct:** 1st, Britain's First Afghan War, to prevent increased influence of Russia, which constitutes threat to British position in India;
9th, Lord Durham resigns position in Canada after criticism of him for leniency towards rebels;
Austrian troops evacuate Papal States except for Ferrara (after occupation since *Jan.* 19th 1832).

L **Nov:** 30th, Mexico declares war on France after French occupation of Vera Cruz (*Nov.* 27th) in attempt to obtain compensation for French victims of civil disturbances in Mexico.

M **Dec:** 16th, Boers defeat Zulus on Blood River, Natal;
24th, Sultan of Turkey, supported by Russia, limits authority of Milosh in Serbia.

N

Y **Statistics**
Navies: Britain, 90 ships of the line; France, 49; Russia, 50; U.S., 15.

Z **Births and Deaths**
Feb. 6th Henry Irving b. (–1917).
Mar. 26th W. E. H. Lecky b. (–1903).
Apr. 2nd Léon Gambetta b. (–1882).
May 10th James Bryce b. (–1922).
May 17th Charles de Talleyrand-Périgord d. (84).
July 8th Ferdinand Zeppelin b. (–1905).
Oct. 24th Joseph Lancaster d. (60).
Oct. 25th Georges Bizet b. (–1875).
Dec. 3rd Octavia Hill b. (–1912).
Dec. 24th John Morley b. (–1923).

O Politics, Economics, Law and Education

Antoine Cournot, *The Mathematics of Commerce.*

F. Lieber, *Political Ethics.*

The Working Men's Association, led by F. O'Connor, draw up the People's Charter, demanding reform, including manhood suffrage, vote by ballot, annual parliaments and payment of members (*May* 8th).

Foundation of the Public Record Office, London, the first central national archives repository.

P Science, Technology, Discovery, etc.

Hugh Miller, *Crystallography.*

Mathias Schleiden's cellular theory of plants.

H. G. Dyer and J. Hemming invent ammonia process for making soda (sodium carbonate).

J. Liebig demonstrates that animal heat is due to respiration, founding the science of biochemistry.

Bruce's type-casting machine.

Great Western and *Sirius* cross the Atlantic to inaugurate regular steamship communication between U.K. and U.S.

Q Scholarship

T. Arnold, *History of Rome* (–43).

Camden Society for publishing historical documents founded in London.

R Philosophy and Religion

J. B. H. Lacordaire revives the Dominican Order in France.

S Art, Sculpture, Fine Arts and Architecture

National Gallery, London, opened.

The great palace of the Tsars, Moscow, rebuilt. (–49).

T Music

R. Schumann, *Nouvelletten* (piano).

H. Berlioz, dramatic symphony *Romeo and Juliet.*

U Literature

C. Dickens, *Nicholas Nickleby* (–39).

V. Hugo, *Ruy Blas.*

Karl Immermann, *Münchhausen.*

E. F. Mörike, *Poems.*

E. A. Poe, *Arthur Gordon Pym.*

R. S. Surtees, *Jorrocks' Jaunts and Jollities.*

W. M. Thackeray, *The Yellowplush Correspondence*, in *Frazer's Magazine.*

V The Press

Times of India founded.

Northern Star, edited by Feargus O'Connor, as a Chartist manifesto.

W Drama and Entertainment

Jenny Lind's début as Agathe in C. M. Weber's *Der Freischütz* in Stockholm.

Elisa Rachel's début as Camille in Corneille's *Horace* at the Théâtre Français begins the revival of French classical drama.

X Sport

(*Continued opposite*)

1839 Turkey invades Syria—Anglo-Chinese Opium War—Chartist riots in Britain

A **Jan:** 20th, Battle of Yungay, resulting in victory for Chile against Peru-Bolivian Federation, leads to dissolution of that union;
The Times declares in favour of free trade.

B **Feb:** 4th, National Convention of Chartists begins in London;
11th, Durham Report on North America debated in House of Lords;
24th, Uruguay declares war against Argentina.

C **Mar:** 9th, French forces withdraw from Mexico, whose government agrees to compensate French victims of civil riots;
Establishment of National Anti-Corn Law League in London.

D **Apr:** 19th, treaty of London whereby territorial arrangements between Belgium and Holland are finally accepted by King William I of Holland, so that Belgium is independent, Luxembourg becomes an independent Grand Duchy, and R. Scheldt is opened to commerce of both Dutch and Belgian nations;
21st, Turkish army invades Syria in opposition to Mehemet Ali (war continues until *Feb.* 1841).

E **May:** 6th, Bill to suspend Jamaican Constitution after riots due to emancipation of slaves, passes Commons by narrow majority;
7th, Lord Melbourne resigns because of small majority for Jamaican Bill and Robert Peel is asked to form Conservative administration, but he fails to do so because of 'Bedchamber Question' when Queen Victoria refuses to dismiss certain of her Whig ladies-in-waiting, so that, 13th, Melbourne's Whig administration returns.

F **Jun:** 13th, abdication of Milosh in Serbia who is succeeded by his son, Milan (who dies *July* 9th, and is succeeded by younger brother, Michael (–1842));
24th, at battle of Nezib, Ibrahim routs Turkish forces.

G **Jul:** 1st, death of Sultan Mahmud II who is succeeded by a boy, Abdul Mejid (–1861);
—, Turkish fleet voluntarily surrenders to Mehemet Ali at Alexandria;
12th, Chartist petition rejected by Parliament;
27th, note from the Powers to the Sultan of Turkey reserving their right to deal with Mehemet Ali;
Chartist riots in Birmingham and elsewhere throughout month;
Beginning of Opium War between China and Britain after Chinese authorities seize and burn British cargoes of opium.

H **Aug:** 17th, British Parliament establishes special council to make laws for Lower Canada;
23rd, Hong Kong taken by British in war with China.

J **Sep:**

K **Oct:**

L **Nov:** 3rd, Opium War flares up when British frigate sinks Chinese fleet of junks;
3rd, Reform Decree in Ottoman Empire guarantees life, liberty and property of all subjects;
4th, Chartist rising in Newport, Mon., in attempt to break open jail is easily crushed.

M **Dec:** 3rd, death of Frederick VI of Denmark who is succeeded by nephew Christian VIII (–1848).

N

O **Politics, Economics, Law and Education**

Louis Blanc, *L'Organisation du travail*, proposes system of national workshops.
Institute of Physiology founded in Breslau.

P **Science, Technology, Discovery, etc.**

Theodor Schwann, *Microscopic Investigations on the Accordance in the Structure and Growth of Plants and Animals*, founds modern cell theory.
Michael Faraday, *Researches in Electricity* (–1855).
W. H. Fox Talbot publishes a photographic negative (*Jan.* 25th), and Louis Daguerre perfects process for producing a silver image on a copper plate (*Mar.*)—the 'daguerreotype'.
K. G. Mosander discovers the metallic element lanthanum.
James Nasmyth designs steam hammer.
Charles Goodyear vulcanises rubber.
First tunnel kiln is made in Denmark.
S.S. *Great Britain* becomes first screw steamer to cross the Atlantic.
Robert Murchison's geological treatise, *The Silurian System.*
Charles Darwin, *Voyage of the 'Beagle'*.

Q **Scholarship**

L. von Ranke, *History of the Reformation in Germany* (–43).
Lowell Institute, Boston founded by John Lowell, junior, to provide free public lectures by eminent scholars.

R **Philosophy and Religion**

S **Art, Sculpture, Fine Arts and Architecture**

J. M. W. Turner, *Fighting Téméraire* (painting).
Thomas V. Walter, State Capitol, Columbus, Ohio (–61).

T **Music**

F. Chopin, 24 Preludes (op. 28).
F. Mendelssohn conducts F. Schubert's C Major Symphony ('Great') at Leipzig.

U **Literature**

M. Y. Lermontov, *A Hero of Our Time.*
H. W. Longfellow, *Voices of the Night.*
Stendhal (pseud.), *La Chartreuse de Parme.*
Rodolphe Töpffer, *Nouvelles genevoises.*

V **The Press**

W **Drama and Entertainment**

X **Sport**

Henley Royal Regatta instituted.
Grand National first run at Aintree and Cesarewitch at Newmarket.

Y **Statistics**

Z **Births and Deaths**

Jan. 19th Paul Cézanne b. (–1906).
Mar. 16th M. P. Moussorgsky b. (–1881).
July 8th John D. Rockefeller b. (–1937).
Aug. 4th Walter Pater b. (–1894).
Sept. 19th George Cadbury b. (–1922).

1840 Quadruple Alliance aids Turkey against Mehemet Ali

A **Jan:**

B **Feb:** 5th, by treaty of Waitangi, Maori chiefs surrender sovereignty to British;
10th, marriage of Queen Victoria to Prince Albert of Saxe-Coburg-Gotha;
26th, Adolphe Thiers forms second ministry in France (–*Oct.* 28th).

C **Mar:**

D **Apr:**

E **May:**

F **Jun:** 6th, Carlist Wars in Spain end when Carlist forces finally surrender, due mainly to negotiations of General Espartero;
7th, death of Frederick William III of Prussia, who is succeeded by Frederick William IV (–1861).

G **Jul:** 15th, Russia, Britain, Prussia and Austria form Quadruple Alliance in support of Turkey and by treaty of London offer Mehemet Ali Egypt, as hereditary possession, and southern Syria for life, provided he gives up Crete and northern Syria (but he refuses in hope of French aid);
23rd, act of Parliament for union of Upper and Lower Canada with equal representation for both of these former provinces.

H **Aug:** 6th, Louis Napoleon's attempted rising at Boulogne fails and he is subsequently sentenced to life imprisonment in Ham;
6th, Ernest Augustus of Hanover imposes new Constitution with increased powers for monarch;
10th, Municipal Act for Ireland gives right to vote to all paying £10 annual rent.

J **Sep:** 11th, bombardment of Beirut by British to force Mehemet Ali to submit.

K **Oct:** 7th, William I of Holland abdicates in favour of his son, William II (–1849);
12th, Queen Regent Cristina of Spain resigns after revolts and Espartero's influence increases;
28th, Adolphe Thiers forced to resign after attempting to obtain French aid for Mehemet Ali.

L **Nov:** 3rd, bombardment and capture of Acre by British forces Ibrahim to evacuate all Syria;
5th, by convention of Alexandria, Mehemet Ali agrees to terms of treaty of London (*July* 15th);
—, end of Afghan War when Afghan forces surrender to British.

M **Dec:** 15th, Napoleon I's remains brought to Les Invalides in Paris.

N

O Politics, Economics, Law and Education

P. J. Proudhon, *Qu'est-ce que la Propriété?*
Rowland Hill introduces penny post in Britain (*Jan.* 10th).
P. Shuttleworth founds first teachers' training college.

P Science, Technology, Discovery, etc.

J. E. Purkinje first uses the term 'protoplasm'.
J. P. Joule begins work on heat.
P. J. Liebig, *The Chemistry of Diet.*
J. L. G. Agassiz, *Études sur les glaciers.*
Botanical Gardens, Kew, opened.
R. Kölliker identifies spermatozoa as cells.
W. Whewell, *Philosophy of Inductive Sciences.*
J. W. Draper photographs the moon.

Q Scholarship

Augustin Thierry, *Récits des temps mérovingiens.*
J. Y. Akerman, *Numismatic Manual.*

R Philosophy and Religion

R. W. Emerson and Margaret Fuller edit *The Dial* as an organ of Transcendentalism.

S Art, Sculpture, Fine Art and Architecture

Charles Barry, Houses of Parliament (–52).
Heinrich Hübach, Trinkhalle, Baden-Baden.
George Kemp, Scott Museum, Edinburgh.

T Music

F. Chopin, two nocturnes (op. 37) and two polonaises (op. 40).
G. Donizetti, *La Fille du Régiment* (opera).
R. Schumann, *Dichterliebe* song cycle.
A. Sax invents saxophone.
R. Wagner, *Faust* overture.

U Literature

R. H. Barham, *Ingoldsby Legends* (–47).
J. F. Cooper, *The Pathfinder.*
C. Dickens, *Old Curiosity Shop.*
P. Mérimée, *Colomba.*
E. A. Poe, *Tales of the Grotesque and Arabesque.*
C. Sainte-Beuve, *Histoire de Port-Royal* (–60).

V The Press

The Tablet.

W Drama and Entertainment

X Sport

Y Statistics

Religions in U.S.: Roman Catholics, 1,000,000; Baptists, 850,000; Methodists, 870,000; Presbyterians, 228,600.
Railways in operation: U.S. 2,816 miles; U.K. 1,331 miles.

Y **Statistics** (*cont.*)

Industry: cotton textiles become leading U.S. industry with 1,778,000 spindles and 75,000 workers.

Emigration: 75,810 leave Great Britain for U.S., 1831–40, and 207,381 leave Ireland for U.S.

Z **Births and Deaths**

Jan. 6th Fanny Burney (Frances D'Arblay) d. (87).
Apr. 2nd Émile Zola b. (–1902).
Apr. 27th Edward Whymper b. (–1911).
May 7th Peter Iljitch Tchaikovsky b. (–1893).
May 13th Alphonse Daudet b. (–1897).
May 27th Nicolo Paganini d. (56).
June 2nd Thomas Hardy b. (–1928).
June 10th H. M. Stanley b. (–1904).
Sept. 2nd Austin Dobson b. (–1921).
Sept. 27th A. T. Mahan b. (–1914).
Nov. 14th Claude Oscar Monet b. (–1926), and Auguste Rodin b. (–1917).

1841 British sovereignty in New Zealand and Hong Kong—The Dardanelles are closed to warships

A **Jan**: 26th, British sovereignty proclaimed over Hong Kong.

B **Feb**: 13th, Sultan finally accepts treaty with regard to Mehemet Ali who obtains Egypt as a hereditary possession.

C **Mar**: 4th, W. H. Harrison inaugurated President of U.S.

D **Apr**: 4th, on Harrison's death, John Tyler becomes President of U.S.

E **May**: 3rd, New Zealand is formally proclaimed as British colony;
8th, Baldomero Espartero is appointed Regent of Spain.

F **Jun**:

G **Jul**: 13th, France joins Quadruple Alliance of *July* 1840 with regard to Turkey;
13th, by Convention of the Straits the powers guarantee Ottoman independence and the Dardanelles and Bosporus are closed to warships of all nations in peacetime (thus overthrowing treaty of Unkiar Skelessi, 1833).

H **Aug**: 30th, Robert Peel forms Conservative ministry when Lord Melbourne resigns after defeat over amendment to Address.

J **Sep**:

K **Oct**: Dorr Rebellion in Rhode Island, against decrepit form of government, fails (but new Constitution is granted 1842).

L **Nov**: 2nd, beginning of Second Afghan War when Afghans rise and massacre British army officers;
9th, birth of Prince of Wales, heir to British throne;
U.S. slave ship *Creole* is taken over by slaves who murder crew and put into port in British West Indies where slavery is not recognised; U.S. demands for their return are ignored by Britain.

M **Dec**:

N Pre-Emption Distribution Act in U.S. gives rights to squatters who take up locations on surveyed public lands.

X **Sport**
Tom Hyer becomes first recognised boxing champion in U.S. (–48).

Y **Statistics**
Populations: Great Britain, 18,534,000; Ireland, 8,175,000; U.S. 17,063,353.
Principal cities: London, 2,235,344; Paris, 935,261; Vienna, 356,870; New York, 312,710; Berlin, 300,000.
Coal production: Great Britain, 40,000,000 tons; France, 4,078,500 tons.
Iron production: Great Britain, 1,350,000 tons; France, 1,247,000 tons.

Z **Births and Deaths**
Jan. 25th John, Lord Fisher b. (–1920).
Feb. 26th Evelyn Baring, Lord Cromer b. (–1917).
May 14th Squire Bancroft b. (–1926).
July Mikhail Lermontov d. (27).
Sept. 2nd Hirobumi Ito b. (–1909).
Sept. 8th Anton Dvořák b. (–1904).
Sept. 28th Georges Clémenceau b. (–1929).
Nov. 20th Wilfred Laurier b. (–1919).
— Firmin Auguste Renoir b. (–1919).

O **Politics, Economics, Law and Education**

Louis Blanc attacks July monarchy in *Histoire de dix ans.*
Friedrich List, *National System of Political Economy.*
Degrees are granted to women in U.S.

P **Science, Technology, Discovery, etc.**

R. W. Bunsen invents carbon-zinc battery.
H. R. Worthington's direct-action steam pump.
Steam machinery applied to biscuit manufacture at Reading factory.
Demonstration of arc lamps for Paris streets.
J. B. Elie de Beaumont and Ours Dufrénoy, geological map of France.
David Livingstone discovers Lake Ngami.
James Ross discovers the Great Southern Continent.
William Hooker reforms Kew Gardens.
British Pharmaceutical Society founded.

Q **Scholarship**

L. van Ranke is appointed historiographer of Prussia.
London Library opened (*May*) as a private subscription circulating library.

R **Philosophy and Religion**

Rudolf Lotze, *Metaphysics.*
J. H. Newman is censured in Oxford for the doctrine of Tract 90 in which he explained the 39 Articles in a Catholic sense.
Ludwig Feuerbach, *Essence of Christianity.*
Oratory of St. Francis de Sales founded in Italy for work among poor youths.
David Livingstone begins missionary work in Africa.

S **Art, Sculpture, Fine Arts and Architecture**

H. Daumier's lithographs *Physionomies tragico-classiques.*
F. Chantrey's bequest to Royal Academy.

T **Music**

R. Schumann, Piano Concerto in A minor (op. 54; completed 1845).
Daniel Auber, *The Crown Diamonds* (opera).
G. Rossini, *Stabat Mater* (oratorio).
A. H. Hoffman, *Deutschland, Deutschland über Alles.*

U **Literature**

Honoré de Balzac, *Une Ténébreuse Affaire.*
T. Carlyle, *On Heroes and Hero-Worship.*
Charles Lever, *Charles O'Malley.*
Hugh Miller, *Old Red Sandstone.*

V **The Press**

Punch is issued, with Mark Lemon editor and John Leech chief illustrator.
The Jewish Chronicle, London, and *New York Tribune* founded.
J. T. Delane appointed editor of *The Times* (–77).
George Bradshaw's first *Railway Guide* (*Dec.*).

W **Drama and Entertainment**

Catherine Gore, *Cecil, or the Adventures of a Coxcomb.*
Thomas Cook leads first excursion (to Leicester).

(*Continued opposite*)

1842 Canadian-U.S. frontier settled—Chinese ports opened to British trade

A **Jan:** 1st, British forces capitulate at Kabul in war with Afghans and agree to withdraw to India, but majority are killed fighting on journey.

B **Feb:**

C **Mar:**

D **Apr:** 29th, Robert Peel's Budget modifies sliding scale to encourage imports of corn, reduces many duties and revives income tax.

E **May:** 3rd, Parliament rejects Chartist Petition.

F **Jun:**

G **Jul:**

H **Aug:** 9th, Webster-Ashburton Treaty between Britain and U.S. defines frontier between Canada and U.S.;
10th, Lord Ashley's Mines Act prevents women, and children below 10 years, working underground;
29th, by treaty of Nanking ending Anglo-Chinese War, Canton, Shanghai and Chinese ports are opened to British commerce with consular facilities, and Britain obtains large indemnity;
Chartist risings in manufacturing areas of England.

J **Sep:**

K **Oct:** 10th, Second Afghan War ends with British proclamation of victory;
Rising against Baldomero Espartero in Barcelona.

L **Nov:**

M **Dec:** 4th, Espartero bombards Barcelona and revolts are soon crushed;
19th, U.S. recognises independence of Hawaii.

N New Whig Tariff in U.S. replaces Compromise Tariff (1833) (but is itself replaced by Walker Tariff 1846).
War between the Boers and British in Natal (–43).

Z **Births and Deaths** (*cont.*)
Mar. 7th Henry Mayers Hyndman b. (–1921).
Mar. 18th Stéphane Mallarmé b. (–1898).
Mar. 20th Antonio Fogazzaro b. (–1911).
Mar. 23rd 'Stendhal' (Marie Henri Beyle), d. (59).
May 12th Jules Massenet b. (–1912).
May 13th Arthur Sullivan b. (–1900).
June 12th Thomas Arnold d. (46).
July 25th Charles Jean Sismondi d. (69).
July 26th Alfred Marshall b. (–1924).
Aug. 13th Albert Sorel b. (–1906).

O **Politics, Economics, Law and Education**

Étienne Cabet, *Voyage en Icarie.*

Edwin Chadwick's commission reports on the sanitary condition of the labouring population.

Act for inspection of asylums.

C. E. Mudie's circulating library.

P **Science, Technology, Discovery, etc.**

Crawford Long uses ether as an anaesthetic for minor operation in U.S.

Julius Mayer, *Law of Conservation of Energy.*

James Braid studies 'hypnotism'.

Great Western Railway converts some rails to standard gauge in Britain.

Q **Scholarship**

Bibliographical Society, London, founded.

R **Philosophy and Religion**

William Miller, *Evidence from Scripture of the Second Coming of Christ.*

Hippolytus, *Refutation of all Heresies*, is discovered at Mount Athos.

S **Art, Sculpture, Fine Arts and Architecture**

J. D. Ingres begins studies for 'Golden Age' wall-paintings.

F. W. Schadow, *Wise and Foolish Virgins* (painting).

T **Music**

F. Mendelssohn, Symphony in A minor ('Scottish', op. 36).

R. Wagner, *Rienzi* (opera).

M. Glinka, *Russlan and Ludmilla* (opera).

Philharmonic Society of New York founded under Ureli Hill.

U **Literature**

Théodore de Banville, *Les Cariatides.*

H. W. Longfellow, *Ballads and Other Poems.*

Lord Macaulay, *Lays of Ancient Rome.*

Lord Tennyson, *Morte d'Arthur and other Idylls.*

V **The Press**

Illustrated London News (*May*).

W **Drama and Entertainment**

X **Sport**

Ruff's *Guide to the Turf* first issued.

Y **Statistics**

British Textiles trade:

imports of raw cotton	435 mill. lb.
cotton exports	734 mill. yds.
woollen exports	75·3 mill. yds.
linen exports	69·2 mill. yds.
silk exports	369,000 lb.

Z **Births and Deaths**

Jan. 11th William James b. (–1910).

Feb. 4th Georg Brandes b. (–1927).

(*Continued opposite*)

A **Jan:** (*–Apr.*), British forces under Charles Napier conquer Sind, in lower valley of Indus (but war not declared until after Indian attack on British Residency, *Feb.* 15th).

B **Feb:**

C **Mar:**

D **Apr:** 11th, British Act of Parliament separates Gambia from Sierra Leone as Crown Colony.

E **May:** 4th, Natal is proclaimed a British Colony.

F **Jun:** 17th, Maori revolts against British in New Zealand.

G **Jul:** 15th, General Narvaez defeats Baldomero Espartero, who leaves Spain.

H **Aug:** Britain formally annexes Sind.

J **Sep:** 15th Otto I of Greece convokes National Assembly after popular rising against his misrule.

K **Oct:** 8th, Anglo-Chinese commercial treaties confirm Treaty of Nanking (of *Aug.* 1842).

L **Nov:** 8th, Queen Isabella II of Spain is declared of age;
28th, Britain and France recognise independence of Hawaii.

M **Dec:** 13th, Basutoland becomes a native state under British protection.

N

X **Sport**

Y **Statistics**

Z **Births and Deaths**
Jan. 20th Paul Cambon b. (–1924).
Feb. 19th Adelina Patti, b. (–1919).
Mar. 21st Robert Southey d. (68).
Apr. 15th Henry James b. (–1916).
June 15th Edvard Grieg b. (–1907).
Aug. 19th C. M. Doughty b. (–1926).

O **Politics, Economics, Law and Education**

August Haxthausen undertakes survey of land laws in Russia at invitation of Tsar Nicholas I.

Ethnological Society is founded.

P **Science, Technology, Discovery, etc.**

Michael Faraday coats metals with nickel by electrical process.

J. P. Joule, *Production of Heat by Voltaic Electricity*.

Georg Ohm analyses harmonic vibrations.

An aerostat is made.

J. B. Lawes and J. H. Gilbert at Rothamsted establish that nitrogen, potassium and phosphorus are necessary for plant growth, and Lawes opens superphosphate factory at Deptford Creek.

I. K. Brunel's Thames Tunnel opened.

Zola arched dam near Aix-en-Provence.

The export of machinery from Britain is legalised.

Charles Thurber invents 'chirographer' typewriter.

Q **Scholarship**

H. G. Liddell and R. Scott, *Greek-English Lexicon*.

R **Philosophy and Religion**

J. S. Mill, *Logic*.

S. Kierkegaard, *Either-or*.

Thomas Chalmers leads Scottish Disruption (*May* 18th), when 474 clergy withdraw from general assembly to form United Free Church of Scotland on the issue of lay patronage.

Joseph Smith authorises polygamy among Mormons.

Babist sect is founded in Persia.

S **Art, Sculpture, Fine Art and Architecture**

J. M. W. Turner, *The Sun of Venice Going to Sea* (painting).

J. Ruskin, *Modern Painters* (-60).

T **Music**

M. W. Balfe, *The Bohemian Girl* (opera).

G. Donizetti, *Don Pasquale* (opera).

R. Wagner, *Flying Dutchman* (opera).

F. Mendelssohn establishes Leipzig Conservatoire.

U **Literature**

George Borrow, *The Bible in Spain*.

Thomas Carlyle, *Past and Present*.

C. Dickens, *A Christmas Carol*.

J. R. Lowell, *Poems*.

Bulwer-Lytton, *The Last of the Barons*.

William Wordsworth is appointed poet laureate on Robert Southey's death.

V **The Press**

The Economist and *The News of the World* are first issued.

W **Drama and Entertainment**

Theatres Act ends monopoly of London managements.

(*Continued opposite*)

A **Jan:**

B **Feb:**

C **Mar:** 8th, accession of Oscar I in Sweden on death of Charles XIV (–1859);
16th, Greek Constitution with two Chambers, the Senate and the Deputies.

D **Apr:** 12th, J. C. Calhoun's treaty for annexation of Texas by U.S. is signed (but defeated in Senate, *June* 8th).

E **May:** Natal is combined with Cape Colony for administrative purposes.

F **Jun:** 6th, Factory Act in Britain restricts female workers to twelve-hour day and children between eight and 13 years limited to six-and-a-half hours;
Tsar Nicholas I visits London and suggests partition of Ottoman Empire based on memorandum of Count Karl Nesselrode.

G **Jul:** 19th, Bank Charter Act separates banking and note-issuing departments of Bank of England, note-issuing is to be covered by coin and bullion except for fiduciary sum of £14 mill.

H **Aug:** 6th, French, under Duc de Joinville, begin hostilities against Morocco.

J **Sep:** 10th, French War in Morocco ends with treaty of Tangier.

K **Oct:**

L **Nov:** 23rd, Holstein Estates resolve on independence of Duchies of Schleswig and Holstein from Denmark.
James K. Polk (Democrat) wins U.S. presidential election with 170 electoral votes over Henry Clay (Whig), 105 votes.

M **Dec:**

N

O **Politics, Economics, Law and Education**

J. S. Mill, *Unsettled Questions of Political Economy.*

Edward Miall founds Anti-State Church Association (later the Liberation Society) to increase number of Dissenters in Parliament.

'Ragged School' Union.

Rochdale pioneers found Co-operative Society (*Dec.*).

First public baths and wash-houses opened at Liverpool.

British Royal Commission on the health of towns.

P **Science, Technology, Discovery, etc.**

Robert Chambers, *The Vestiges of the Natural History of Creation.*

Samuel Morse transmits first message on U.S. telegraph line (Washington-Baltimore, *May* 24th).

Q **Scholarship**

Lobegott Tischendorf discovers part of the *Codex Sinaiticus* of the New Testament.

R **Philosophy and Religion**

John Thomas founds the Christadelphians.

Y.M.C.A. is founded.

S **Art, Sculpture, Fine Arts and Architecture**

T **Music**

F. Mendelssohn, violin concerto in E minor (op. 64).

G. Verdi, *Ernani* (opera).

J. Joachim's début in London, playing Beethoven's Violin Concerto under Mendelssohn.

H. Berlioz, *Traité de l'Instrumentation.*

The Musical Times is first issued.

U **Literature**

B. Disraeli, *Coningsby.*

Alexandre Dumas (père), *The Three Musketeers* and *The Count of Monte Cristo.*

H. Heine, *Deutschland, ein Wintermärchen.*

A. W. Kinglake, *Eothen.*

E. Sue, *The Wandering Jew* (–45).

José Zorilla y Moral, *Don Juan Tenorio.*

V **The Press**

Society of Women Journalists is founded in London.

W **Drama and Entertainment**

X **Sport**

Y **Statistics**

Z **Births and Deaths**

Mar. 18th Nicolai Rimsky-Korsakov b. (–1908).

Mar. 24th Bertel Thorwaldsen d. (73).

Mar. 30th Paul Verlaine b. (–1896).

Apr. 16th Anatole France b. (–1924).

July 27th John Dalton d. (77).

Oct. 15th Friedrich Wilhelm Nietzsche b. (–1900).

Oct. 23rd Robert Bridges b. (–1930).

Dec. 2nd Francis Carruthers Gould b. (–1925).

A **Jan:**

B **Feb:**

C **Mar:** 1st, U.S. Congress agrees to annexation of Texas and admission into the Union;
3rd, Florida becomes U.S. state;
4th, James K. Polk is inaugurated U.S. President;
11th, further Maori risings against British rule in New Zealand.

D **Apr:** Robert Peel's second 'Free-Trade' Budget repeals export duties entirely, and duties on many imports are limited or abolished.

E **May:** 23rd, new Spanish Constitution.

F **Jun:** 30th, Maynooth Grant increased to aid education in Ireland;
Anglo-French expedition sent to Madagascar against local ruler.

G **Jul:**

H **Aug:**

J **Sep:**

K **Oct:**

L **Nov:** 22nd, Whig leader, Lord John Russell, announces conversion to free trade in the 'Edinburgh Letter'.

M **Dec:** 6th, Robert Peel resigns, as Conservatives are not in favour of free trade, but he returns, 20th, as Russell is unable to form government;
11th, outbreak of Anglo-Sikh war when Sikhs cross Sutlej and surprise British;
—, the *Sonderbund*, a league of the seven Catholic Cantons in Switzerland, is formally established to protect Catholic interests;
29th, Texas becomes U.S. state.

N

O **Politics, Economics, Law and Education**

F. Engels, *The Condition of the Working Classes in England* (Leipzig).
College of Chemistry founded in London.

P **Science, Technology, Discovery, etc.**

A. von Humboldt, *Cosmos* (–58).
Arthur Cayley, *Theory of Linear Transformations.*
Adolphe Kolbe synthesises acetic acid.
William McNaught's compound steam engine.
Josué Heilmann's machine comb for combing cotton and wool.
E. B. Bigelow of Massachusetts invents Brussels power loom for making carpets.
W. G. Armstrong's hydraulic crane.
John Franklin leads expedition to discover North-West Passage.

Q **Scholarship**

A. H. Layard begins excavations at Nineveh.
Louis Thiers, *History of the Consulate and Empire* (–65).
T. Carlyle, *Cromwell's Letters and Speeches.*

R **Philosophy and Religion**

J. H. Newman is received into the Roman Catholic Church (*Oct.* 9th) and explains his step in *Essay on the Development of Christian Doctrine.*

S **Art, Sculpture, Fine Arts and Architecture**

British Museum (Robert Smirke).
The Madeleine, Paris, is completed by J. T. Huvé.
Restoration of Notre-Dame, Paris, revives Gothic style.

T **Music**

F. Chopin, Piano Sonata in B minor (op. 58).
F. Liszt, *Les Préludes.*
R. Wagner, *Tannhäuser* (opera).

U **Literature**

Honoré de Balzac, *Les Paysans.*
B. Disraeli, *Sybil, or the Two Nations.*

V **The Press**

W **Drama and Entertainment**

Henrick Hertz, *King René's Daughter.*

X **Sport**

Knickerbocker Club codifies rules of baseball.

Y **Statistics**

U.K. total State expenditure, £54·8 mill.

Z **Births and Deaths**

Feb. 15th Elihu Root b. (–1937).
Mar. 27th Wilhelm von Röntgen b. (–1923).
May 10th Benito Pérez Galdós b. (–1920).
June 18th Andrew Jackson d. (78).
Oct. 23rd Sarah Bernhardt b. (–1923).
Dec. 10th Frederick Pollock b. (–1937).

A **Jan:** 2nd, French troops defeat Algerian rebels but sustain heavy losses;
28th, East India Company's forces under Harry Smith defeat Sikhs at Aliwal.

B **Feb:** 10th, Hugh Gough defeats Sikhs at Sobrahan;
14th, rising in Cracow Republic swiftly spreads throughout Poland.

C **Mar:** 9th, by Treaty of Lahore ending First Sikh War Britain gains territory beyond the Sutlej River;
12th, Austrian and Russian troops occupy Cracow.

D **Apr:** 12th, on failure of U.S. negotiations with Mexico for purchasing New Mexico, President Polk sends troops into the disputed area;
23rd, U.S. Senate resolves to end British joint occupation of Oregon under the Convention of *Aug.* 1827.

E **May:** 8th, U.S. forces under Zachary Taylor defeat Mexicans at Palo Alto and, 9th, at Resaca de la Palma;
13th, formal declaration of war by U.S. against Mexico;
16th, Dom Miguel's supporters force Costa Cabral, the effective ruler of Portugal, into exile and Britain, under the terms of the Quadruple Alliance, 1834, sends a squadron to Oporto to suppress the rising;
25th, Louis Napoleon escapes from Ham to London;
26th, Robert Peel repeals the Corn Laws (royal assent given *June* 26th), splitting the Conservative Party;
German Professors meet at Frankfurt ('The Intellectual Diet of the German People') to discuss German reunification.

F **Jun:** 12th, mammoth meeting of Liberals in Brussels demands reforms;
15th, Treaty of Washington declares 49th Parallel the boundary between Oregon and Canada;
15th, election of Cardinal Mastai-Ferretti as Pope Pius IX (–1878);
30th, Robert Peel resigns on failing to secure passage of Coercion bill for preserving public order in Ireland, and Lord John Russell forms Liberal government, with Lord Palmerston as Foreign Secretary;
Mormons under Brigham Young leave Nauvoo City on trail for the Great Salt Lake.

G **Jul:** 8th, Christian VIII of Denmark declares the Danish State indivisible and heritable by females, thus excluding the Duchies of Schleswig-Holstein from becoming a separate province, with resultant tension in Germany.

H **Aug:** 8th, David Wilmot's proviso, that slavery should be excluded in any territory acquired from Mexico, introduced in House of Representatives but fails to pass U.S. Senate through opposition of South;
18th, U.S. forces capture Santa Fé;
22nd, U.S. annexes New Mexico;
28th, British Possessions Act gives Canada the right to fix tariffs.

J **Sep:** 17th, Germanic Confederation reserves its right in Schleswig-Holstein.

K **Oct:** 10th, Princess Luisa Fernanda, sister of Isabella II of Spain, marries Duc de Montpensier, Louis Philippe's youngest son, contrary to François Guizot's undertaking to Lord Aberdeen in 1843, which threatens Anglo-French relations and weakens the Orléanist monarchy in France.

O Politics, Economics, Law and Education

Massino D'Azeglio attacks the Papacy in *Degli ultimi casa de Romagna* and is expelled from Tuscany.
P. J. Proudhon, *Philosophie de la misère.*
Smithsonian Institution, Washington, founded.

P Science, Technology, Discovery, etc.

Johann Galle discovers the planet Neptune (*Sept.* 23rd) on the basis of Urbain Leverrier's calculations.
R. Owen, *British Fossils* (–1884).
E. Galois's research on the resolubility of algebraic equations published posth.
H. von Mohl discovers protoplasm, overthrowing Mathias Schleiden's theory of free-cell formation.
G. B. Amici establishes circulation of the sap in plants.
A. Sobrero prepares nitroglycerine.
Auguste Laurent correctly determines the formula of water as H_2O.
Christian Schönbein invents gun-cotton.
Morton uses ether as an anaesthetic in an operation.
F. G. J. Henle, *Manual of Rational Pathology.*
Zeiss optical factory opened at Jena.
Elias Howe patents sewing machine in U.S.
John Deere makes plough with steel mould board.
Rapid development of railways in Britain on introduction of a standard gauge.

Q Scholarship

F. C. Baur traces the composition of the synoptic Gospels.
Henry Rawlinson opens up Assyrian history by deciphering Persian cuneiform inscriptions at Behistan.
George Grote, *History of Greece.*
W. H. Prescott completes *The Conquest of Peru.*

R Philosophy and Religion

William Whewell, *Elements of Systematic Morality.*
Friedrich Vischer, *Aesthetics.*
Theodor Waitz, *Foundations of Psychology.*
Evangelical Alliance founded in London to oppose Romanism.
British Presbyterian mission to Nigerian coast.

S Art, Sculpture, Fine Arts and Architecture

F. Delacroix decorates library of the Luxembourg, Paris.
J. F. Millet, *Oedipus Unbound* (painting).
G. F. Watts, *Paolo and Francesca* (painting).
Franz Klenze, Propylaea, Munich (–62).
J. B. Bunning, London Coal Exchange.

T Music

H. Berlioz, *Damnation of Faust.*
F. Liszt, 1st Hungarian Rhapsody.
F. Mendelssohn, *Elijah* (oratorio, in Birmingham).
R. Schumann, 2nd Symphony (C major).

U Literature

Ferdinand Freiligrath's revolutionary poetic cycle, *Ça Ira.*
Gottfried Keller, *Poems.*

L **Nov**: 6th, Austria annexes Cracow Republic in violation of Treaty of Vienna, provoking protests from Britain, France, Sweden and Turkey.

M **Dec**: 28th, Iowa becomes a state of U.S.
Duke of Lucca, forced to grant administrative reforms, decides to sell his duchy to Leopold of Tuscany.

N The Irish potato crop again fails and famine increases despite organised relief.
Agricultural and industrial depression in France causes widespread distress.
Beginnings of native segregation in Natal where the first location commission sets up preserves for immigrant Zulus.
Commodore James Biddle of U.S. visits Edo Bay, Japan, but is refused facilities for trade.

U **Literature** (*cont.*)

Edward Lear, *Book of Nonsense.*
H. W. Longfellow, *The Belfry of Bruges.*
J. G. Whittier, *Voices of Freedom.*
Honoré de Balzac, *La Cousine Bette.*
George Sand (pseud.), *La Marc au diable.*
F. Dostoievsky, *Poor Folk.*
M. Jokai, *Working Days.*
H. Melville, *Typee; a Peep at Polynesian Life.*

V **The Press**

Daily News, first cheap English newspaper founded (*Jan.* 21st), with C. Dickens as editor.

W **Drama and Entertainment**

X **Sport**

Kennington Oval is first used as a cricket ground.

Y **Statistics**

U.K. registered tonnage of merchant shipping 3,200,000 tons (131,000 steamships).

Z **Births and Deaths**

Jan. 30th F. H. Bradley b. (–1924).
Mar. 17th Friedrich Wilhelm Bessel d. (61).
Oct. 6th George Westinghouse b. (–1914).
Nov. 4th Felix Mendelssohn-Bartholdy d. (38).
Nov. 30th Friedrich List d. (57).

1847 Liberia becomes independent republic

A **Jan:**

B **Feb:** 3rd, United Diet summoned in Prussia by Frederick William IV.

C **Mar:** Liberals in Hungary obtain majority to the Table of Deputies, and March laws provide for a ten-point programme of responsible government.

D **Apr:**

E **May:**

F **Jun:** 8th, Factory Act providing for ten-hour day for women and for young people between ages of 13 and 18.

G **Jul:** 4th, Adolphe Thiers holds first reform banquet held in Paris, demanding wider franchise;
17th, Austrian troops occupy Ferrara after unrest caused by disappointment at Pius IX not undertaking reforms;
24th, Convention of Gramido ends war in Portugal.

H **Aug:** 26th, Liberia is proclaimed independent republic.

J **Sep:** 3rd, Baldomero Espartero is recalled to Spain;
14th, U.S. forces capture Mexico City;
François Guizot becomes French premier at critical time when France is subjected to severe political and economic unrest.

K **Oct:** 21st, *Sonderbund* War begins in Switzerland after Catholic Cantons refuse to dissolve union in face of liberal majority in Diet (*July* 20th), the *Sonderbund* is dissolved after defeat of Catholic Cantons (*Nov.* 29th);
Charles Albert of Piedmont dismisses reactionary ministers and proceeds with more liberal policy.

L **Nov:**

M **Dec:**

N

Z **Births and Deaths** (*cont.*)
Mar. 3rd Alexander Graham Bell b. (–1922).
May 7th Archibald Philip Primrose, Lord Rosebery b. (–1929).
May 15th Daniel O'Connell d. (71).
June 11th Millicent Garrett Fawcett b. (–1929).
Oct. 2nd Paul von Hindenburg b. (–1934).

O **Politics, Economics, Law and Education**

Louis Blanc's partisan *History of the French Revolution* (-62).
Karl Marx attacks P. J. Proudhon in *The Poverty of Philosophy*.

P **Science, Technology, Discovery, etc.**

H. Helmholtz, *On the Conservation of Energy*.
George Boole, *Mathematical Logic*.
Sir James Simpson uses chloroform as an anaesthetic.
Evaporated milk first made.
Gold is discovered in California (*Sept.*) and leads to the first 'gold rush'.
Improvements to the St. Lawrence completed, Lake Ontario to Montreal.
Samuel Colt opens an armoury at Hartford, Conn., U.S.

Q **Scholarship**

Jules Michelet, *Histoire de la Révolution française* (-53).
L. von Ranke, *Neun Bücher preussischer Geschichte* (-1848).

R **Philosophy and Religion**

Giuseppe Ferrari, *Philosophy of History*.
United Presbyterian Church of Scotland is formed from the United Secession Church of 1733 and the Relief Church of 1752.
H. Ward Beecher begins ministry at Plymouth Congregational Church, Brooklyn, making its pulpit a national platform.
The Mormons found Salt Lake City.
First Roman Catholic working-men's club, at Cologne.

S **Art, Sculpture, Fine Arts and Architecture**

Thomas Couture, *Romans of the Decadence*.

T **Music**

G. Verdi, *Macbeth* (opera).
Friedrich von Flotow, *Martha* (opera).

U **Literature**

Charlotte Brontë, *Jane Eyre*.
Emily Brontë, *Wuthering Heights*.
A. H. Hoffmann, *Struwwelpeter*.
G. Sand (pseud.), *Le Péché de M. Antoine*.
W. M. Thackeray, *Vanity Fair* (-48).

V **The Press**

W **Drama and Entertainment**

P. Mérimée, *Carmen*.
N. Ostrovsky, *The Bankrupt* (for which he is dismissed the Russian government service and the play is prohibited).

X **Sport**

Y **Statistics**

Z **Births and Deaths**

Jan. 14th Wilson Carlile b. (-1942).
Feb. 11th Thomas Alva Edison b. (-1931).

(*Continued opposite*)

1848 (Jan.–May) Year of Revolutions—Louis Napoleon elected French President

A **Jan:** 12th, Earl of Dalhousie becomes Governor-General of India;
—, revolt in Palermo, Sicily, against corruption of Bourbons; is completely successful by end of month;
20th, Christian VIII of Denmark dies, succeeded by Frederick VII (–1863).

B **Feb:** 2nd, treaty of Guadaloupe Hidalgo ends Mexican-U.S. War;
3rd, Harry Smith annexes country between Orange and Vaal rivers;
10th, constitution in Naples proclaimed by Ferdinand II (after demonstration against him over loss of Sicily);
15th, decree for constitution in Tuscany published;
22nd (–24th), revolt in Paris due to failure of Louis Philippe's reign, the economic depression and prohibition of reform banquets;
24th, Louis Philippe abdicates in favour of grandson, Comte de Paris, but Republican Provisional government is proclaimed under Alphonse de Lamartine;
27th, National Workshops are erected in France on Louis Blanc's plan to provide relief in Paris.

C **Mar:** 4th, Constitution in Piedmont and Sardinia, proclaimed by Charles Albert;
12th (–15th), revolution in Vienna begins with university demonstrations; 13th, Prince Metternich resigns and calling of States-General is promised;
14th, Constitution in Rome promulgated by Pope Pius IX;
15th, Hungarian Diet adopts reforms of *Mar.* 1847;
17th, revolution in Venice under Daniele Manin, after knowledge of success of Italian, French and Viennese Revolts, and Republic is proclaimed (22nd);
—, William II of Holland appoints committee to revise Constitution (power of Parliament is increased by Constitutional amendment, *Nov.*);
—, (–19th), in revolution in Berlin, Frederick William IV agrees to grant constitution, but, 21st, is forced to parade in streets of Berlin;
18th (–22nd), five-day revolution in Milan (*Cinque Giornate*) against Austrian rule, and Joseph Radetzky forced to abandon city;
20th, revolt in Parma;
—, Second Sikh War begins, arising out of Sikh aristocracy's discontent at British administration and murder of two British officers;
21st, Frederick VII of Denmark announces decision to incorporate Schleswig;
24th, German elements in Duchies of Schleswig and Holstein form government and Prussia recognises autonomy of Duchies;
—, Sardinia declares war on Austria;
31st, German Ante-Parliament (*Vorparlement*) meets at Frankfurt (–*Apr.* 4th).

D **Apr:** 8th, Austrians defeated by Piedmontese (Sardinian) troops at first battle of Goito;
10th, Chartist Petition to Parliament fails;
13th, Sicily is declared independent of Naples;
25th, Constitution in Austria with responsible government (repealed *May* 15th);
—, Papacy joins Sardinia against Austria;
—, Austrians suppress revolt in Cracow;
29th, Pius IX disassociates himself from Italian National Movement;
30th, Austrians are defeated at Pastrengo and Radetzky retreats.

E **May:** 2nd, Prussians invade Denmark over position of Schleswig-Holstein;
4th, French National Assembly meets, after elections based on universal male suffrage, with majority for moderate Republicans;
7th, Polish rebels surrender after Prussian troops put down insurrection in Warsaw;

O Politics, Economics, Law and Education

Karl Marx and Friedrich Engels issue *Communist Manifesto* (*Feb.*).
Marx's pamphlet, *Wage, Labour and Capital.*
J. S. Mill, *Principles of Political Economy.*
Public Health Act inaugurates sanitary legislation in Britain.

P Science, Technology, Discovery, etc.

Richard Owen, *On the Archetypes and Homologies of the Vertebrate Skeleton.*
Foundation of American Association for the Advancement of Science at Philadelphia (*Sept.* 20th).

Q Scholarship

Jakob Grimm, *History of the German Language.*
Lord Macaulay, *History of England* (–61).
J. C. Hart in *The Romance of Yachting* inaugurates the Shakespeare-Bacon controversy.

R Philosophy and Religion

J. A. Froude, *Nemesis of Faith.*
Frédéric Monod founds the *Église Libre* seceding from the French National Church.
Spiritualism gains ground in U.S.

S Art, Sculpture, Fine Arts and Architecture

H. Holman Hunt, J. Millais and D. G. Rossetti found the Pre-Raphaelite Brotherhood.
J. E. Millais, *Ophelia* (painting).
J. F. Millet, *The Winnower* (painting).

T Music

Carl Nicolai, *The Merry Wives of Windsor* (opera).
Friedrich Smetana opens music school in Prague.

U Literature

Vicomte de Chateaubriand, *Mémoires d'Outre-tombe.*
Alexandre Dumas (fils), *La Dame aux Camélias.*
Elizabeth Gaskell, *Mary Barton.*
J. R. Lowell, *The Biglow Papers.*
H. Merger, *Scènes de la Vie de Bohème.*
Juan Valera, *Pepita Jimenez.*

V The Press

W Drama and Entertainment

X Sport

Y Statistics

Z Births and Deaths

Feb. 5th Joris Karl Huysmans b. (–1907).
Feb. 27th Ellen Terry b. (–1928), and C. H. H. Parry b. (–1918).
Mar. 31st William Waldorf, Viscount Astor b. (–).
Apr. 7th Randall Davidson b. (–1930).
Apr. 8th G. Donizetti d. (51).
June 14th Bernard Bosanquet b. (–1923).

E May: 15th, Communist rising in Paris, after news of suppression of Polish revolt; workmen overturn government and set up provisional administration which immediately collapses;
—, second rising in Vienna against new Austrian Constitution which is thereupon repealed;
—, collapse of Naples revolt;
17th, Ferdinand I of Austria flees from Vienna to Innsbruck;
18th, German National Assembly meets at Frankfurt and suspends German Confederation;
22nd, Prussian National Assembly meets in Berlin;
29th, Wisconsin becomes U.S. state;
—, Austrian victory at Curtatone against Tuscany;
30th, delay caused by Tuscan forces, however, allows Sardinian troops to defeat Austrians at second battle of Goito;
—, Treaty of Guadaloupe Hidalgo (*Feb.* 2nd) ratified by Mexico so that U.S. obtains Texas, New Mexico, California, Nevada, Utah, Arizona, parts of Colorado and of Wyoming from Mexico in return for large indemnity.

F Jun: 2nd, Pan-Slav Congress meets at Prague under Presidency of Francis Palacky;
10th, Austrians victorious at Vicenza, despite vigorous defence;
17th, Austrian troops under Prince Windischgrätz suppress Czech revolt in Prague;
23rd (–24th), 'June Days' in France, when Louis Cavaignac suppresses Paris workmen in effort to close workshops, killing thousands;
29th, Archduke John of Austria is elected Regent of the Reich which is to replace German Confederation.

G Jul: 22nd, Austrian Reichstag (Constituent Assembly) meets;
25th, Austrian army under Joseph Radetzky victorious at Custozza, enabling him to drive Sardinian forces from Milan and rest of Lombardy (*Aug.* 4th–5th);
—, Habeas Corpus Act suspended in Ireland, which leads to insurrection in Tipperary, led by Smith O'Brien;
27th, formal union of Venice, Sardinia and Lombardy;
Russians invade Danubian Principalities at request of Turkey to put down revolts there.

H Aug: 9th, Armistice between Austria and Sardinia is concluded at Vigevano, by which Sardinia gives up Lombardy and recognises *status quo* in Italy apart from in Venice before revolutions;
11th, Sardinian troops are expelled from Venice;
12th, Ferdinand I returns to Vienna;
26th, Truce of Malmö between Denmark and Prussia;
29th, Boers defeated at Boomplatz by British forces, and retire across the Vaal, thus ensuring Orange River sovereignty.

J Sep: 7th, abolition of serfdom in Austria;
11th, Bourbons of Naples accept armistice with Sicily at instigation of British and French admirals;
12th, new constitution by which Switzerland becomes federal union with strong central government;
24th, Louis Kossuth proclaimed president of committee for national defence of Hungary.

(*Continued opposite*)

Z **Births and Deaths** (*cont.*)

July 4th François de Chateaubriand d. (79).
July 18th W. G. Grace b. (–1915).
July 25th A. J. Balfour b. (–1930).
Aug. 12th George Stephenson d. (67).
Nov. 24th William Lamb, Viscount Melbourne, d. (69).
Dec. 8th Joel Chandler Harris ('Uncle Remus') b. (–1908).
— Paul Gauguin b. (–1903).

K **Oct**: 6th, third revolution in Vienna at news that government is to crush revolt in Hungary;
13th, Nasir Ud-Din becomes Shah of Persia;
31st, Prince Windischgrätz takes Vienna.

L **Nov**: 4th, Republican Constitution in France is promulgated with single Chamber, strong President and direct election under universal suffrage;
10th, Ibrahim, Viceroy of Egypt, dies and is succeeded by Abbas (–1854);
15th, Count Rossi, Papal Premier, assassinated by fanatical democrat;
16th, popular insurrection in Rome;
24th, Pius IX flees to Gaeta.

M **Dec**: 2nd, Emperor Ferdinand I of Austria abdicates in favour of nephew Franz Joseph I (–1916);
5th, Prussian National Assembly is dissolved and Constitution granted, but ultimate authority of King maintained;
10th, Louis Napoleon is elected President of France by a massive majority;
27th, German National Assembly proclaims fundamental rights.

N

1849 (Jan.–Jul.) Austrians defeat Sardinians at Novara—Britain annexes Punjab—Failure of German reunification by parliamentary means

A **Jan:** 13th, Sikhs defeated at Chillianwalla, but British lose many troops;
23rd, Prussian dispatch suggests German Union without Austria;
29th, French National Assembly announces own dissolution (but lingers on till end of *May*).

B **Feb:** 7th, Grand Duke of Tuscany flees to Gaeta;
9th, Rome proclaimed Republic under Giuseppe Mazzini;
21st, British defeat Sikhs at Gujerat;
22nd, Benjamin Disraeli becomes leader of Conservative Party (following death of Lord George Bentinck, *Sept.* 1848).

C **Mar:** 4th, proclamation of Austrian Constitution whereby all national groups to have own rights and Reichstag of two Chambers to be established, but this is immediately replaced by Constitution in which territories are indivisible and, 7th, Assembly is dissolved;
4th, Zachary Taylor inaugurated President of U.S.;
12th, Sardinia ends truce with Austria (of *Aug.* 9th, 1848);
—, Sikhs surrender at Rawalpindi;
13th, Neapolitan Parliament finally dissolved;
23rd, on Austrian victory at Novara, Charles Albert of Sardinia abdicates in favour of Victor Emmanuel II;
27th, German National Assembly passes Constitution and
28th, elects Frederick William IV of Prussia 'Emperor of the Germans';
29th, Britain annexes Punjab by treaty with Maharajah of Lahore.

D **Apr:** 3rd, Frederick William IV is unwilling to take crown from the people but wishes to receive it from the German Princes, and his vague reply is taken by German National Assembly as a refusal;
12th, Tuscany recalls Grand Duke Leopold;
14th, Hungarian Diet proclaims independence, with Louis Kossuth as Governor-President;
25th, French expedition lands in Papal States;
Rebellion in Montreal against British rule.

E **May:** 1st, Convention of Balta Liman by which joint Russo-Turkish occupation of Danubian Principalities is established for seven years;
3rd (–8th), revolts in Dresden, suppressed by Prussians;
11th (–13th), military revolt in Baden which causes Grand Duke to flee;
15th, Palermo is entered by Neapolitan forces and Sicily is forced to submit to Naples;
26th, 'Three-Kings' League' of Prussia, Saxony and Hanover to promote closer unity (but not recognised by Austria; and Saxony withdraws *Oct.* 19th).

F **Jun:** 5th, liberal Constitution in Denmark provides for limited monarchy, and civil liberties are guaranteed;
6th, German National Assembly (a 'rump') moves to Stuttgart and, 18th, is dissolved by troops; marks failure of attempt at German unification under a Parliamentary system;
13th, Communist riots in Paris are easily defeated and lead to repressive legislation;
26th, British Navigation Acts finally repealed.

G **Jul:** 3rd, French enter Rome, despite heroic resistance by Giuseppe Garibaldi, and restore Pope Pius IX;

O Politics, Economics, Law and Education

Agricultural co-operative land banks are founded in Germany.
Bedford College for Women, London, founded.
Amelia Bloomer begins to reform women's dress.

P Science, Technology, Discovery, etc.

Armand Fizeau measures the velocity of light.
Edward Frankland isolates metal alkyls.
Joseph Monier's reinforced concrete.
C. E. Minié invents an expanding-base bullet.
Krupp's steel gun bursts during tests.
Tubular railway bridge over Menai Straits (–50).
Robert Stephenson's cast-iron bridge at Newcastle upon Tyne opened.

Q Scholarship

J. M. Kemble, *The Saxons in England.*

R Philosophy and Religion

Papal encyclical condemns socialism and communism.
Charles Kingsley and F. D. Maurice teach Christian Socialism.
F. W. Faber founds the Oratory, London.

S Art, Sculpture, Fine Arts and Architecture

Gustave Courbet, *After Dinner at Ornans* (painting).
E. Delacroix paints ceiling of Salon d'Apollon in the Louvre.
Alfred Rethel's wood-engravings, *The Dance of Death.*
John Ruskin, *The Seven Lamps of Architecture.*

T Music

G. Meyerbeer, *The Prophet* (oratorio).
F. Liszt, *Tasso.*
R. Schumann, music for *Manfred.*

U Literature

Matthew Arnold, *The Strayed Reveller.*
C. Dickens, *David Copperfield* (–50).
Charles Kingsley, *Alton Locke.*
Charles Sainte-Beuve begins his 'Causeries du Lundi' series in *Le Constitutionnel.*

V The Press

W Drama and Entertainment

X Sport

Y Statistics

1849 (Jul.–Dec.)

G **Jul:** 10th, peace preliminaries between Denmark and Prussia;
23rd, Baden insurgents capitulate to Prussian troops.

H **Aug:** 2nd, death of Mehemet Ali;
6th, Peace of Milan ends war between Sardinia and Austria;
13th, Hungarian army capitulates at Vilagos when Russians aid Austria;
28th, Venice submits to Austria after long siege (which began *July* 20th).

J **Sep:**

K **Oct:** *October Manifesto* by Canadians in support of union with U.S. after repeal of Navigation Act (*June* 26th) increases economic depression.

L **Nov:** 22nd, Cape Colony forbids landing of convicts and forces ship from Britain to sail to Tasmania.

M **Dec:**

N Beginning of Russian advance into Persia.

z **Births and Deaths**

Jan. 22nd August Strindberg b. (–1912).
Mar. 19th Alfred von Tirpitz b. (–1930).
May 22nd Aston Webb b. (–1930).
July 5th W. T. Stead b. (–1912).
Oct. 7th Edgar Allan Poe d. (40).
Oct. 17th Frédéric Chopin d. (39).

1850 (Jan.–Oct.) Anglo-Kaffir War—French troops restore Pius IX to Rome

A **Jan:** 15th, British fleet blockades the Piraeus to force Greece to compensate Don Pacifico, a Moorish Jew who was a British subject, for damages sustained in Athens;
29th, Henry Clay's compromise resolutions about slavery, boundaries, California and Texas laid before U.S. Senate;
31st, liberal Constitution granted in Prussia.

B **Feb:** 23rd, Hanover follows the lead of Saxony in leaving the Three Kings' alliance with Prussia;
27th, Austria, Bavaria, Saxony and Württemberg agree to uphold German union.

C **Mar:** 20th, a German Parliament is summoned by Frederick William IV of Prussia to Erfurt to form a new confederation in opposition to Austria;
Further Anglo-Kaffir war breaks out (–1853);
Improvement in Anglo-Spanish relations.

D **Apr:** 12th, French troops restore Pius IX and garrison Rome; Pius revokes the Constitution;
19th, Clayton-Bulwer agreement by which Britain and U.S. agree not to obtain exclusive control of a proposed Panama canal;
27th, the Greek Government submits to British demands for compensation;
29th, Erfurt Parliament is prorogued.

E **May:** 10th, Austria revives the old Bundestag at Frankfurt under Prince Félix Schwarzenberg to counter Prussian attempts at German unification;
31st, universal suffrage in France is abolished.

F **Jun:** Lord Palmerston survives a Parliamentary attack on his conduct of foreign affairs with the *Civis Romanus sum* speech;
Tenant Right league is founded in Ireland.

G **Jul:** 2nd, peace of Berlin between Prussia and Denmark; Schleswig to be governed by Denmark while Holstein to be ruled by an administrator;
9th, death of U.S. President Zachary Taylor who is succeeded by Millard Fillmore;
24th, Schleswig-Holstein insurgents defeated at Idstedt.

H **Aug:** 2nd, Treaty of London between Britain, France, Russia, Denmark and Sweden on Schleswig-Holstein;
5th, Australia Government act grants representative government to South Australia, Tasmania and Victoria (which is separated from New South Wales);
9th, Texas surrenders her claim to New Mexico;
17th, Britain buys forts on the Gold Coast from Denmark;
26th, bill for the more effective recovery of fugitive slaves in U.S.;
Death of Louis Philippe; Orléanist claim to French throne is now upheld by Comte de Paris.

J **Sep:** 9th, California is admitted to the Union as a free state;
12th, rising in Hesse-Cassel in which Austria supports the Elector, Prussia the insurgents;
16th, the slave trade is forbidden in the District of Columbia;
26th, liberty of the press is restricted in France.

K **Oct:** 11th, Camillo Cavour is appointed minister in Piedmont where he begins economic reforms;

O Politics, Economics, Law and Education

Herbert Spencer, *Social Studies*, founds sociology.
Austro-Hungarian customs union.
Single coinage in Switzerland.
Mines Inspection Act in U.K.
Sunday rest introduced in Austria, and old-age insurance in France.
William Ewart's Public Libraries Act in Britain; first public libraries in Berlin.
School of Mines, London, founded (origin of Imperial College of Science and Technology).
Natural Science Honours School established at Oxford.
University extension lectures begin in New York.
Secondary education in Belgium.
Frances Buss founds North London Collegiate School.

P Science, Technology, Discovery, etc.

Rudolf Clausius enunciates the second law of thermodynamics and founds the kinetic theory of gases.
M. Melloni discovers that heat rays vary in wavelength.
R. W. von Bunsen's burner.
P. L. Chebichev, *On Primary Numbers.*
R. Remak, *Development of the Frog.*
H. Helmholtz establishes speed of nervous impulse.
Claude Bernard demonstrates glycogenic function of the liver.
E. C. Carré invents vacuum freezing machine.
J. W. Brett lays first submarine telegraph cable between Dover and Calais.
Royal Meteorological Society founded.
Heinrich Barth undertakes expedition to Central Africa.
Francis Galton explores Damaraland.
Arctic expedition under Erasmus Ommanney to search for John Franklin (–51); subsequent expeditions make known the north coast of Canada.

Q Scholarship

A. F. F. Mariette discovers the ruins of the Serapeum and the catacombs of the Apis bulls.
Karl Lachmann's edition of Lucretius.

R Philosophy and Religion

Re-establishment of the Roman Catholic hierarchy in Britain (*Sept.*).
Privy Council's judgment in George Gorham's case, denying the regenerative power of baptism, leads H. E. Manning and others to join Roman Church.
Abolition of the Church's jurisdiction in matters of heresy and sacrilege in Victor Emmanuel's dominions.
Frederick William IV entrusts the management of Prussian evangelical churches to a church council.
Civita Cattolica founded in Rome as the organ of the Curia and the Jesuits.

S Art, Sculpture, Fine Arts and Architecture

J. B. Corot, *Une Matinée* (painting).
Gustave Courbet, *The Stone-Breakers* (painting).
J. E. Millais, *Christ in the House of his Parents* (painting).

K Oct: 26th, Russian intervention in Germany in Austria's favour;
Taiping rebellion in China under Hung Siu-tsuen, who takes Nanking and Shanghai, proclaims himself emperor and attacks Peking.

L Nov: 1st, Austrian and Bavarian troops occupy Hanau in Hesse-Cassel while Prussia prepares for war;
28th, as a result of Russian mediation, Prince Schwarzenberg of Austria and Otto von Manteuffel of Prussia sign the Punctation of Olmütz, by which Prussia subordinates herself to Austria and recognises the Frankfurt Diet;
29th, Austria and Prussia unite to restore order in Hesse-Cassel.

M Dec: 23rd (–*Mar.* 1851), Dresden conference, to settle the constitutional problems of Germany, proves fruitless.

N

S **Art, Sculpture, Fine Arts and Architecture** (*cont.*)

F. Goya's *Proverbios* engravings (posth.).
Joseph Paxton, Crystal Palace (–51).

T **Music**

F. Liszt produces R. Wagner's opera *Lohengrin.*
R. Schumann, 3rd Symphony ('The Rhenish') in E flat.

U **Literature**

E. B. Browning, *Sonnets from the Portuguese.*
R. W. Emerson, *Representative Men.*
N. Hawthorne, *The Scarlet Letter.*
Alexander Hertzen, *From Another Shore.*
Lord Tennyson publishes *In Memoriam* and succeeds William Wordsworth as poet laureate.
W. M. Thackeray, *Pendennis* completed.

V **The Press**

Reynolds Weekly News (*May*).

W **Drama and Entertainment**

H. Ibsen, *Catalina.*
Otto Ludwig, *Die Erbförster*,
P. T. Barnum persuades Jenny Lind to tour U.S.

X **Sport**

Y **Statistics**

Railways in operation: U.S. 9,015 miles; U.K. 6,635 miles.
Emigration to U.S. (1841–50): From Britain, 267,044; from Ireland, 780,719.

Z **Births and Deaths**

Jan. 14th 'Pierre Loti' (Julien Viaud) b. (–1923).
Jan. 29th Ebenezer Howard b. (–1928).
Mar. 7th Thomas Masaryk b. (–1937).
Apr. 23rd William Wordsworth d. (80).
May 9th J. L. Gay-Lussac d. (71).
May 28th F. W. Maitland b. (–1906).
June 24th Horatio, Lord Kitchener b. (–1916).
July 2nd Robert Peel d.(62).
Aug. 5th Guy de Maupassant b. (–1893).
Aug. 17th Honoré de Balzac d. (51).
Aug. 26th Louis Philippe d. (76).
Nov. 13th R. L. Stevenson b. (–1894).

1851 Louis Napoleon's *coup d'état*

A **Jan:**

B **Feb:** 22nd, Lord John Russell resigns after defeat, 20th, when voting against motion to assimilate county and borough franchises, but as Lord Stanley is unable to form Conservative administration, he returns on same day.

C **Mar:** 16th, Spanish Concordat with Papacy by which Catholicism becomes sole faith in Spain and Church gains control of education and the press.

D **Apr:**

E **May:** 16th, Prussia again recognises German Confederation at Conference at Dresden; Censorship of Prussian press is revived.

F **Jun:**

G **Jul:** 1st, Victoria proclaimed separate colony;
24th, abolition of British window-tax encourages construction of windows in buildings.

H **Aug:** 1st, Ecclesiastical Titles Act prevents Roman Catholic bishops taking titles from territory within Britain.

J **Sep:** 7th, Prussia concludes commercial treaty with Hanover.

K **Oct:**

L **Nov:** 18th, death of Ernest Augustus of Hanover; succeeded by George V (–1866).

M **Dec:** 2nd, Louis Napoleon carries out *coup d'état* in order to change constitution of France, risings break out 3rd (–4th), but are easily suppressed;
19th, Lord Palmerston resigns as Foreign Secretary, after his unauthorised approval of Louis Napoleon's actions, and is succeeded, 26th, by Lord Granville;
21st, result of plebiscite in France supports new constitution to be drawn up by Louis Napoleon;
31st, Austrian Constitution is abolished.

N German Diet appoints Reaction Committee to control small states and abolishes Fundamental Rights.

Y **Statistics**

Populations (in millions): China, 430; German States and free cities, 34; France, 33; Great Britain, 20·8; Ireland, 6·5; Italy, 24; U.S. 23; Austria, 16.
Coal production (in million tons): Great Britain, 60; France, 11·8; U.S. 7; German States, 1·7.
Iron production: Great Britain, 3 million tons; France, 2,414,000 tons; Russia, 400,000 tons.

Z **Births and Deaths**

May 27th Vincent D'Indy b. (–1931).
May 29th Léon Bourgeois b. (–1925).
June 11th Mrs. Humphrey Ward (Mary Augusta Arnold) b. (–1920).
July 8th Arthur Evans b. (–1941).
July 12th Louis Daguerre d. (62).
Sept. 14th James Fenimore Cooper d. (61).
Oct. 2nd Ferdinand Foch b. (–1929).
Nov. 21st Leslie Ward ('Spy') b. (–1922).
Nov. 26th Nicolas Jean Soult d. (82).
Dec. 19th J. M. W. Turner d. (76).

O **Politics, Economics, Law and Education**
Vincenzo Gioberti, *Il Rinnovamento Civile d'Italia.*
French government begins transportation of convicts to French colonies.
Illinois follows Maine in enforcing Prohibition, but Ohio abandons liquor licensing.
Owens College, Manchester, founded.
Mary Carpenter, *Reformatory Schools for . . . Juvenile Offenders.*

P **Science, Technology, Discovery, etc.**
Franz Neumann states the mathematical laws of magnetic-electric induction.
William Thomson's papers on the laws of conservation and dissipation of energy.
George Bond photographs the moon at Cambridge, Mass.
William Kelly's steel-making converter.
James Bogardus constructs a cast-iron-frame building.
Isaac Singer's sewing machine.
Hermann Helmholtz's ophthalmoscope.
Gold is found in Australia.

Q **Scholarship**
Francis Parkman, *The Conspiracy of Pontiac.*

R **Philosophy and Religion**
Philip Schaff, *History of the Apostolic Church.*

S **Art, Sculpture, Fine Arts and Architecture**
J. B. Corot, *Danse des Nymphes* (painting).
C. D. Rauch and K. F. Schinkel complete equestrian monument to Frederick the Great, Berlin.
J. Tenniel draws for *Punch.*
J. Ruskin, *The Stones of Venice* (–53).
Joseph Cubitt, King's Cross Station, London (–52).
Thomas Walter begins building wings and dome of the Capitol, Washington (–65).

T **Music**
G. Verdi, *Rigoletto* (opera).
R. Wagner attacks G. Meyerbeer in *Opera and Drama.*

U **Literature**
G. Borrow, *Lavengro.*
N. Hawthorne, *The House of the Seven Gables.*
H. Heine, *Romanzero.*
G. Keller, *Der grüne Heinrich* (–53).
H. Melville, *Moby Dick.*
H. W. Longfellow, *The Golden Legend.*

V **The Press**
New York Times (*Sept.*).

W **Drama and Entertainment**
The Great Exhibition, Hyde Park.
William Macready retires from the London stage.

X **Sport**

(*Continued opposite*)

A **Jan:** 14th, French Constitution gives President monarchical power;
17th, Sand River Convention establishes South African Republic (Transvaal);
22nd, Orléans family is banished from France by Presidential decree.

B **Feb:** 3rd, Juan de Rosas is overthrown in Argentina at battle of Caseros;
17th, repressive measures in France, including censorship of press;
23rd, Lord John Russell resigns, after defeat on amendment to Militia Bill and, 27th, a Conservative administration is formed under Lord Derby, with B. Disraeli chancellor of Exchequer (*–Dec.* 20th).

C **Mar:**

D **Apr:** 1st, Second Burmese War breaks out after British ultimatum to King of Burma, for compensation following outrages.

E **May** 6th, Leopold II of Tuscany abolishes Constitution;
8th, treaty of London by Britain, France, Russia, Prussia, Austria and Sweden guarantees integrity of Denmark.

F **Jun:** 30th, British Act of Parliament gives new Constitution providing for representative government for New Zealand.

G **Jul:**

H **Aug:**

J **Sep:**

K **Oct:**

L **Nov:** 4th, Count Cavour becomes Prime Minister of Piedmont;
21st, plebiscite is held in France in support of revival of French Empire;
In U.S. presidential election Franklin Pierce (Democrat) defeats Winfield Scott (Whig) by 254 electoral votes to 42.

M **Dec:** 2nd, French (Second) Empire is proclaimed with Napoleon III Emperor;
16th, B. Disraeli's first budget is defeated and
20th, Derby's government resigns, when a Coalition of Whigs and Peelites is formed under Lord Aberdeen, with W. E. Gladstone as chancellor of Exchequer;
—, British forces annex Pegu (Lower Burma) in war with Burmese.

N Russia obtains territory at mouth of River Amur; expansion in this coastal area of Pacific continues (–1860).

Z **Births and Deaths** (*cont.*)
Mar. 3rd Nicolai Gogol d. (41).
Sept. 5th Paul Bourget b. (–1935).
Sept. 12th Herbert Henry Asquith b. (–1928).
Sept. 14th Arthur Wellesley, Duke of Wellington, d. (83).
Sept. 30th Charles Villiers Stanford b. (–1924).
Oct. 9th Emil Fischer b. (–1919).
Dec. 15th Henri Becquerel b. (–1908).

O **Politics, Economics, Law and Education**

P **Science, Technology, Discovery, etc.**

C. F. Gerhardt formulates new theory of organic compounds.
James Sylvester discusses the calculus of forms.
Herbert Spencer coins the term 'evolution' in *The Development Hypothesis.*
Heinrich Barth explores Lake Chad.
David Livingstone embarks on expedition to explore Zambesi (-56).
Niagara Falls Suspension Bridge.

Q **Scholarship**

Léopold Delisle begins the modern study of palaeography at the Bibliothèque Impériale, Paris.
L. von Ranke, *History of France, Principally in the Sixteenth and Seventeenth Centuries.*

R **Philosophy and Religion**

Kuno Fischer, *History of Modern Philosophy* (-93).
Convocation of the Church of England, dormant since 1741, is revived through the efforts of Bishops Wilberforce and Phillpotts.
First biennial (later annual) Conference at Eisenach of Protestants from each German state.
First Plenary Council of Roman Catholics in U.S., held at Baltimore.

S **Art, Sculpture, Fine Arts and Architecture**

F. M. Brown, *The Last of England* (painting).
Charles Méryon's series of etchings 'Eaux-fortes sur Paris'.
I. K. Brunel and T. H. Wyatt, Paddington Station (-54).

T **Music**

U **Literature**

M. Arnold, *Empedocles on Etna.*
H. Beecher Stowe, *Uncle Tom's Cabin.*
T. Gautier, *Émaux et Camées.*
W. M. Thackeray, *History of Henry Esmond.*
Ivan Turgeniev, *A Sportsman's Sketches.*

V **The Press**

W **Drama and Entertainment**

Charles Reade, *Masks and Faces.*

X **Sport**

Y **Statistics**

British Textiles trade:

imports of raw cotton	740 mill. lb.
exports of cottons	1,524 mill. yds.
exports of woollens	165,527,000 yds.
exports of linens	133,193,000 yds.
exports of silks	1,131,000 lb.

Z **Births and Deaths**

Jan. 4th Joseph Joffre b. (-1931).
Feb. 24th George Augustus Moore b. (-1933).
Feb. 25th Thomas Moore d. (72).
Mar. 1st Théophile Delcassé b. (-1923).

(*Continued opposite*)

1853 Russia occupies Danubian Principalities—Gladstone's Free Trade Budget

A **Jan**: 29th, Napoleon III marries Eugénie de Montijo at Tuileries.

B **Feb**: 19th, commercial treaty between Prussia and Austria.

C **Mar**: 4th, Franklin Pierce inaugurated President of U.S.

D **Apr**: 4th, Oldenburg and Hanover join *Zollverein*;
18th, W. E. Gladstone introduces first Budget which abolishes most of duties on partially manufactured goods and foodstuffs and halves most duties on manufactured products;
19th, Prince Alexander Menshikov, Russian emissary to Turkey, claims protectorate for Russia over Christian subjects of Ottoman Empire.

E **May**: 1st, new Constitution in Argentina is not accepted by Buenos Aires;
21st, Turks reject Russian ultimatum (of *Apr.* 19th) and Menshikov leaves Constantinople.
31st, Tsar Nicholas I orders occupation of the Danubian Principalities.

F **Jun**: 2nd, British fleet ordered to assemble off Dardanelles (arriving there 13th, and is joined by French squadron 14th);
20th, peace between Britain and Burma, but Burmese King refuses to sign a treaty.

G **Jul**: 1st, Cape Colony obtains Constitution with elective Legislative Council (first Parliament meets *June* 30th 1854);
2nd, Russian army crosses the Pruth and invades Danubian Provinces;
28th, Vienna Note to solve Eastern Question, drawn up by French ambassador, is submitted to Russia by Austria (and subsequently is approved by Russia *Aug.* 3rd, amended by Turkey *Aug.* 19th, the amendments being rejected by Russia, *Sept.* 7th).

H **Aug**:

J **Sep**: 24th, France annexes New Caledonia.

K **Oct**: 4th, Turkey declares war on Russia.

L **Nov**: 15th, death of Maria II of Portugal who is succeeded by Pedro V;
30th, Turkish fleet destroyed by Russia off Sinope.

M **Dec**: 11th, Britain annexes Nagpur, one of leading Mahratha States.

N German Navy of 1848 is sold by auction.
Britain discontinues transportation of convicts to Tasmania.

Z **Births and Deaths**
Feb. 9th Leander Starr Jameson b. (–1917).
May 14th Hall Caine b. (–1931).
June 3rd William Flinders Petrie b. (–1942).
July 5th Cecil Rhodes b. (–1902).
Nov. 5th Marcus Samuel b. (–1927).
Nov. 27th Frank Dicksee b. (–1928).
Dec. 17th Herbert Beerbohm Tree b. (–1917).
— Vincent Van Gogh b. (–1890).

O **Politics, Economics, Law and Education**

Repeal of advertisement tax in Britain.

The Mayor of Mulhausen sponsors an 'artisan's town' of 1,200 model dwellings intended for owner-occupiers.

P **Science, Technology, Discovery, etc.**

Samuel Colt opens armoury in London.

I. K. Brunel, Saltash Bridge (-59).

Vienna-Trieste railway through the Alps.

Destruction of Turkish wooden frigates by Russian shells at Sinope emphasises the need for armour plating.

The *Wellingtonia gigantea*, the largest tree in the world, is discovered in California.

Q **Scholarship**

T. Mommsen, *History of Rome* (-56).

H. von Sybel, *History of the French Revolution.*

H. Taine, *La Fontaine et ses Fables* (-60).

R **Philosophy and Religion**

Johann Herzog, *Encyclopaedia of Protestant Theology* (-68).

F. D. Maurice is expelled from his professorship at King's College, London, for questioning the doctrine of eternal punishment in *Theological Essays.*

C. H. Spurgeon begins preaching at Exeter Hall, London.

Roman Catholic hierarchy is established in Holland.

W. A. Muhlenberg's memorial urging the Episcopal Church in U.S. to widen its activities in social work.

S **Art, Sculpture, Fine Arts and Architecture**

Georges Haussmann begins reconstruction of Paris and lays out the Bois de Boulogne.

T **Music**

G. Verdi, *Il Trovatore* and *La Traviata* (operas).

Johannes Brahms, Piano Sonata in C (op. 1).

R. Schumann's article 'New Paths'.

R. Wagner issues his text of *The Ring.*

William Steinway begins to make pianos in New York.

U **Literature**

M. Arnold, *The Scholar Gipsy* and *Sohrab and Rustum.*

Elizabeth Gaskell, *Cranford.*

N. Hawthorne, *Tanglewood Tales.*

Charles Kingsley, *Hypatia.*

Leconte de Lisle's *Poèmes Antiques* founds the 'Parnassus School' of poets.

C. M. Yonge, *The Heir of Redclyffe.*

V **The Press**

The Field, London.

W **Drama and Entertainment**

Gustave Freytag, *The Journalist.*

X **Sport**

Y **Statistics**

(*Continued opposite*)

A **Jan:** 3rd, British ambassador in Constantinople, Stratford Canning, receives order to send British fleet into Black Sea, which is subsequently carried out.

B **Feb:** 23rd, at Convention of Bloemfontein, British agree to leave territory north of Orange River which allows for establishment of Constitution for Orange Free State.

C **Mar:** 12th, Britain and France conclude alliance with Turkey against Russia;
26th, Charles III, Duke of Parma, is murdered;
27th, France and, 28th, Britain declare war on Russia;
31st, U.S. makes first treaty with Japan, negotiated by Commodore Perry.

D **Apr:** 12th, Buenos Aires adopts separate Constitution from Argentina;
20th, Austria and Prussia conclude defensive alliance against Russia;

E **May:** 26th, France and Britain occupy the Piraeus after declaring blockade of Greece for attempting to attack Turkey, and Greece subsequently promises neutrality;
30th, Kansas-Nebraska Act repeals Missouri Compromise (of 1820) and provides for settlement of these territories under popular sovereignty, a situation which immediately leads to 'War for Bleeding Kansas' between free-states and pro-slavery elements;
Britain declares Monroe Doctrine not binding on European countries.

F **Jun:** 3rd, Austrian ultimatum to Russia against carrying the war across the Balkans;
5th, Elgin Treaty between Britain and U.S. establishes reciprocity for trade between U.S. and Canada (and is made act of Canadian Legislature *Sept.* 23rd);
14th, Austro-Turkish treaty, for Austria to occupy the Danubian Principalities until the end of the war;
29th, U.S. possessions in Far West are completed when Senate ratifies Gadsden Purchase (of *Dec.* 1853) which comprises area which is now southern New Mexico and southern Arizona.
Colonial Secretaryship is separated from the Secretaryship for War in Britain.

G **Jul:** 6th, Republican Party formally established in U.S. in opposition to Kansas-Nebraska Act (title having first been adopted *Feb.* 28th);
7th, manifesto is published in Spain which begins liberal revolt led by General O'Donnell;
13th, Abbas I, Viceroy of Egypt, is murdered; succeeded by Mohammed Said (–1863).

H **Aug:** 3rd, B. Espartero becomes premier of Spain (and Regent Maria Christina is exiled, 28th);
8th, Vienna Four Points by Britain, Austria and France state conditions of peace to be Russia's abandonment of claim to protectorate over Sultan's Christian subjects, revision of Straits settlement in interests of European powers, free passage of mouths of Danube and guarantee of integrity of Danubian principalities and of Serbia;
22nd, Austria occupies Danubian Principalities after Russians withdraw.

J **Sep:** 14th, allied powers land unopposed in Crimea;
20th, at the battle of the Alma British and French troops are victorious but do not press advantage to its conclusion.

K **Oct:** 17th, English and French forces begin siege of Sebastopol but assault is postponed after ineffective allied bombardment;
18th, Ostend Manifesto, signed by U.S. ambassadors to Britain, France and Spain, is dispatched to Washington advising acquisition of Cuba by force if Spain refuses to cede it to U.S.;

O **Politics, Economics, Law and Education**

Report by Stafford Northcote and Charles Trevelyan leads to foundation of Civil Service Commission.

Juvenile Offenders Act in U.K.

John Bowring's *The Decimal System* leads to the introduction of the florin in U.K.

F. D. Maurice founds the Working Men's College, London.

University College, Dublin, founded.

P **Science, Technology, Discovery, etc.**

Christian Ehrenberg, *Microgeology*.

Georg Riemann, *On the Hypotheses forming the Foundation of Geometry*.

H. J. S. Smith investigates the theory of numbers (–64).

Claude Bernard makes known the function of the vasodilator nerves.

Abraham Gesner manufactures kerosene.

Richard Burton and John Speke travel to the interior of Somaliland.

Q **Scholarship**

J. Grimm, *German Dictionary*, vol. 1.

R **Philosophy and Religion**

George Boole, *The Laws of Thought on which are founded the Mathematical Theories of Logic and Probabilities*.

Pius IX declares the dogma of Immaculate Conception of Blessed Virgin Mary to be an article of faith (*Dec.* 8th).

Jewish seminary founded at Breslau.

S **Art, Sculpture, Fine Arts and Architecture**

Moritz Schwind's frescoes at Wartburg Castle depicting the life of St. Elisabeth of Hungary.

T **Music**

F. Liszt, *Mazeppa*.

H. Berlioz, *The Childhood of Christ* (oratorio).

U **Literature**

F. D. Guerazzi, *Beatrice Cenci*.

C. Kingsley, *Westward Ho!*

Frédéric Mistral founds the Félibrige Society for the revival of Provençal culture.

G. de Nerval, *Les Filles du feu*.

Coventry Patmore, *Angel in the House*.

H. D. Thoreau, *Walden, or Life in the Woods*.

M. Tompa, *Legends or Flowers*.

V **The Press**

Le Figaro, Paris, issued.

W **Drama and Entertainment**

G. V. Angier and L. S. J. Sandeau, *Le Gendre de M. Poirier*.

X **Sport**

Y **Statistics**

K Oct: 25th, battle of Balaclava is begun by Russians and results in allied victory at great loss after Charges of the Heavy Brigade and of the Light Brigade;
Prussian Upper House reconstituted with increased influence of great landowners and repressive legislation is subsequently carried out.

L Nov: 5th, at battle of Inkerman allies defeat Russians who suffer heavy losses;
14th, storm bursts over Sebastopol wrecking allied supply ships, leading to chaos and loss of life.

M Dec: 2nd, Austria concludes alliance with Britain and France whereby her Italian possessions are guaranteed during war in return for Austrian defence of Danubian Principalities.

N

z **Births and Deaths**

Jan. 1st James George Frazer b. (–1941).
Feb. 9th Edward Carson b. (–1935).
Feb. 27th H. F. R. de Lamennais d. (71).
Mar. 23rd Alfred Milner b. (–1925).
Apr. 28th Johann Ludwig Tieck d. (80).
June 10th G. E. Buckle b. (–1935).
July 12th George Eastman b. (–1932).
Aug. 20th Friedrich Schelling d. (79).
Sept. 1st Engelbert Humperdinck b. (–1921).
Oct. 20th Arthur Rimbaud b. (–1891).

A **Jan**: 26th, Piedmont joins allies against Russia.

B **Feb**: 6th, Lord Palmerston undertakes to form Liberal ministry after resignation of Lord Aberdeen (1st), due to popular dissatisfaction with war policy;
Panama given federal status by constitutional amendment.

C **Mar**: 2nd, Tsar Nicholas I of Russia dies (aged 58) and is succeeded by Alexander II (–1881);
30th, by treaty of Peshawar Britain and Afghanistan form alliance against Persia;
End of Taiping Rebellion in China.

D **Apr**:

E **May**: King George V of Hanover abolishes liberal institutions at demand of Federal Diet.

F **Jun**: 15th, abolition of stamp duty on newspapers in Britain.

G **Jul**: 16th, British Parliament establishes responsible government throughout Australian States, except for Western Australia.

H **Aug**: 18th, Austrian Concordat with Pope gives clergy control of education, censorship and of matrimonial law (revoked 1867).

J **Sep**: 11th, Sebastopol entered by allies after capitulation of Russians.

K **Oct**:

L **Nov**: 21st, Swedish alliance with Britain, France and Turkey against Russia;
28th, Kars, on Asiatic front, is taken by Russian forces.

M **Dec**: 29th, Austrian ultimatum to Russia threatens war unless Russia accepts 'Vienna Points' (of *Aug.* 8th 1854), with addition of neutrality of Black Sea and cession of Bessarabia.

N Victoria government restricts Chinese immigration.

X **Sport**

Y **Statistics**
U.K. total State expenditure, £69·1 mill.

Z **Births and Deaths**
Feb. 23rd K. F. Gauss d. (77).
Mar. 31st Charlotte Brontë d. (39).
May 17th Timothy Healy b. (–1931).
May 24th Arthur Wing Pinero b. (–1934).
Aug. 7th Stanley J. Weyman b. (–1928).
Nov. 5th Eugene Debs b. (–1926).
Nov. 11th Søren Kierkegaard d. (42).
— 'Marie Corelli' (pseud. of Mary Mackay) b. (–1924).

O **Politics, Economics, Law and Education**

Administrative Reform Association founded in London (*May* 5th), as protest against the muddles and disasters of the Crimean War.

Pierre Le Play, *Les Ouvriers européens*, the first comparative study of working-class incomes.

Chair of Technology founded at Edinburgh University.

P **Science, Technology, Discovery, etc.**

Franz Köller makes tungsten-steel.

É. St. Claire Deville's process for extracting aluminium.

R. S. Lawrence constructs turret lathe.

Powdered milk.

Electric telegraph between London and Balaclava is completed (*Apr.*).

Matthew Mauray, *Physical Geography of the Sea.*

D. Livingstone discovers Victoria Falls of the Zambesi River (*Nov.*).

Q **Scholarship**

Johann Droysen, *History of Prussian Policy* (–86).

H. Milman, *History of Latin Christianity.*

W. H. Prescott, *Philip II.*

R **Philosophy and Religion**

Alexander Bain, *Sense and the Intellect.*

H. Spencer, *Principles of Psychology.*

Auguste Gratry, *Connaissance de Dieu*, opposing Positivism.

Religious Worship Act in U.K.

Sardinian Monastic Law dissolves all contemplative orders.

S **Art, Sculpture, Fine Arts and Architecture**

G. Courbet's *Pavillon du Réalisme* at Paris World Fair, including his *L'Atelier* (painting).

Jacob Burckhardt's treatise on art history, *Der Cicerone.*

T **Music**

H. Berlioz, *Sicilian Vespers*, and *Te Deum.*

George Bristow, *Rip Van Winkle* (opera).

R. Wagner conducts orchestral concerts in London, where the Crystal Palace concerts are also established.

U **Literature**

H. W. Longfellow, *The Song of Hiawatha.*

G. de Nerval's *La Rêve et la Vie* (posth.) begins the Symbolist Movement.

Lord Tennyson, *Maud and Other Poems.*

W. M. Thackeray, *The Rose and the Ring.*

Anthony Trollope, *The Warden.*

Ivan Turgeniev, *Rudin.*

Walt Whitman, *Leaves of Grass.*

V **The Press**

Newspaper tax abolished in Britain.

Foundation of *The Daily Telegraph* (June 29th) and *The Saturday Review.*

W **Drama and Entertainment**

Adelaide Ristori takes Paris by storm in S. Pellico's *Francesca da Rimini.*

Paris World Fair.

(*Continued opposite*)

Treaty of Paris ends Crimean War—Second Anglo-Chinese War

A **Jan**: 29th, Queen Victoria institutes the Victoria Cross.

B **Feb**: 13th, Britain annexes Oudh, which increases hostility of India to British rule;
18th, Reform Edict in Turkish Empire guarantees life, honour and property of all subjects, abolishes civil power of heads of Christian Churches, ends torture and provides for large-scale reform of prisons, and for religious freedom;
25th, Peace conference at Paris (–*Mar*. 30th) attended by representatives of Britain, France, Austria, Turkey, Sardinia and Russia (Prussian delegate is allowed to attend later).

C **Mar**: 16th, birth of Prince Imperial in France (Eugène Louis Jean Joseph) ensures succession to throne;
30th, the integrity of Turkey is recognised by the powers in the Treaty of Paris who guarantee Danubian Principalities, Russia cedes Bessarabia, the Black Sea is to be neutral, and the R. Danube is to be free.

D **Apr**: 15th, Britain, France and Austria guarantee integrity and independence of Turkey in a further treaty;
16th, Declaration of Paris abolishes privateering, defines nature of contraband and blockade and recognises principle of 'free ships, free goods'.

E **May**: 24th, Massacre of Pottawatomie Creek by John Brown in war for 'Bleeding Kansas' in which pro-slavers are murdered by free-staters;
27th, Tsar Alexander II grants amnesty for Polish insurgents.

F **Jun**:

G **Jul**: 12th, Austria grants amnesty for Hungarian insurgents of 1848–9;
—, Natal is established as a separate British Crown Colony with an elected assembly.

H **Aug**:

J **Sep**: 3rd, unsuccessful rising of Prussian royalists in Neufchâtel Canton, Switzerland, a possession of the King of Prussia, which had proclaimed a republic in 1848;
15th, re-establishment of Spanish Constitution of 1845 with additional provision for annual assembly of Cortes, by Leopold O'Donnell (who replaced Baldomero Espartero, *July*).

K **Oct**: 8th, *Arrow* Incident, when ship flying British flag is boarded by Chinese, who arrest members of crew; provokes second Anglo-Chinese War (–1858);
14th, Spanish Constitutional amendment annulled after O'Donnell's dismissal.

L **Nov**: 1st, war between Britain and Persia after latter occupies Herat (–1857);
3rd (–4th), British fleet bombards Canton;
James Buchanan (Democrat) wins U.S. presidential election (174 electoral votes) over John C. Frémont (Republican, 114 votes) and Millard Fillmore (American [Know-Nothing] Party, 8 votes).

O **Politics, Economics, Law and Education**

Christian von Bunsen's *Signs of the Times* revives Liberal movement in Prussia.

P **Science, Technology, Discovery, etc.**

Hermann Helmholtz, *Physiological Optics* (-66).
Nathaniel Pringsheim observes sperm entering ovum.
Henry Bessemer's process for making steel brings down prices.
William Siemens makes ductile steel for boiler plating.
W. H. Perkins prepares first aniline dye ('mauve').
Richard Burton and John Speke set out to find source of the Nile and (1858) discover Lake Tanganyika and Lake Victoria Nyanza.
Neanderthal skull found in Quaternary bed in Feldhofen Cave near Hochdal.

Q **Scholarship**

J. A. Froude, *History of England from the Death of Wolsey to the Defeat of the Armada* (-70).
J. R. Motley, *Rise of the Dutch Republic.*
C. A. de Tocqueville, *L'Ancien Régime et la Révolution.*
Theodor Goldstücker, *Sanskrit Dictionary.*

R **Philosophy and Religion**

Friedrich Schelling's Berlin lectures on philosophy published posth. (-58).
Rudolf Lotze, *Mikrokosmus* (-64).
H. Taine, *Les Philosophes Français du XIX siècle* (serially).
G. A. Denison is acquitted by the Judicial Committee of the Privy Council, after condemnation by the Court of Arches, for favouring the Real Presence.
Wilhelm Ketteler, Bishop of Mainz, founds *The Catholic*, an Ultramontane journal, to oppose Ignaz von Döllinger and the Munich School.

S **Art, Sculpture, Fine Arts and Architecture**

J. D. Ingres completes *La Source* (painting).
H. von Ferstel, Votivkirche, Vienna (-79).

T **Music**

Alexander Dargomijsky, *Russalka* (opera).

U **Literature**

Gustave Flaubert, *Madame Bovary* (-57).
Victor Hugo, *Les Contemplations.*
Charles Reade, *It Is Never Too Late to Mend.*

V **The Press**

Harper's Weekly, New York.
Frankfurter Zeitung.

W **Drama and Entertainment**

Henry Irving's début on the London stage.
Thomas Cook leads first travel tour to Europe.

X **Sport**

M **Dec:** 2nd, frontier between France and Spain is defined;
16th, The South African Republic (Transvaal) is organised under Marthinius Pretorius.

N During the year Britain grants self-government to Tasmania and allows responsible government in New Zealand.

Y **Statistics**

U.K. registered tonnage of merchant shipping 4,367,000 (387,000 steamships).
U.K. cotton industry employs 379,000 factory workers and 23,000 handloom weavers.

Z **Births and Deaths**

Jan. 12th J. S. Sargent b. (–1925).
Feb. 17th Heinrich Heine d. (58).
Apr. 26th W. F. Massey b. (–1925) and Henry Morgenthau b. (–1946).
May 6th Sigmund Freud b. (–1939) and Robert Edwin Peary b. (–1920).
May 22nd Augustin Thierry d. (61).
June 22nd H. Rider Haggard b. (–1925).
July 26th George Bernard Shaw b. (–1950).
July 29th Robert Schumann d. (46).
Aug. 15th Keir Hardie b. (–1915).
Oct. 15th Oscar Wilde b. (–1900).
Dec. 18th J. J. Thomson b. (–1940).
Dec. 22nd Frank Billings Kellogg b. (–1937).
Dec. 28th Woodrow Wilson b. (–1924).

1857 Indian Mutiny begins—Garibaldi founds Italian National Association

A **Jan:**

B **Feb:**

C **Mar:** 4th, Peace of Paris ends Anglo-Persian War and Shah recognises independence of Afghanistan;
4th, James Buchanan inaugurated President of U.S.;
7th, the decision of the Supreme Court in the Dred Scott case in connection with position of a slave in a free state renders the Missouri compromise unconstitutional.

D **Apr:**

E **May:** 10th, Revolt of Sepoys at Meerut begins Indian Mutiny against British rule (–1858);
26th, Prussia renounces sovereignty over Neufchâtel.

F **Jun:** 1st, Royal Navy destroys Chinese fleet;
14th, commercial treaty between France and Russia (promulgated by France, 30th *July*);
27th, Massacre of Cawnpore when British soldiers and male residents are executed after promise of safe-conduct.

G **Jul:** 15th, women and children, taken by Indians at Cawnpore, are brutally murdered.

H **Aug:** Italian National Association formed by Giuseppe Garibaldi for unification under Piedmont.

J **Sep:** 20th, Delhi is captured by British after siege since June;
25th, Henry Havelock and James Outram temporarily relieve Lucknow.

K **Oct:** Irish Republican Brotherhood (Fenians) founded in New York; soon spreads to Ireland;
Frederick William IV of Prussia suffers a stroke.

L **Nov:** 17th, Colin Campbell relieves Lucknow;
20th, Tsar Alexander II appoints committee to study the problem of emancipation of serfs (Emancipation Edict is approved *Mar.* 1861).

M **Dec:** 6th, British forces recapture Cawnpore;
29th, British and French forces take Canton.

N

Z **Births and Deaths** (*cont.*)
Sept. 5th Auguste Comte d. (59).
Sept. 15th William Howard Taft b. (–1930).
Sept. 30th Hermann Sudermann b. (–1928).
Dec. 3rd. Joseph Conrad b. (–1924).
— Max Klinger b. (–1920).

O **Politics, Economics, Law and Education**
Matrimonial Causes Act establishes divorce courts in England and Wales.
Science Museum, South Kensington, is founded.
Widespread cattle disease in Europe.

P **Science, Technology, Discovery, etc.**
Louis Pasteur demonstrates that lactic fermentation is due to a living organism.
E. G. Otis installs first safety elevator which, with the development of cheaper steel, makes possible the skyscraper.
Transatlantic cable is laid (–65).

Q **Scholarship**
C. T. Newton discovers remains of the mausoleum of Halicarnassus.
'Rolls Series' of edited texts of chronicles and memorials of the Middle Ages is begun.
H. T. Buckle, *History of Civilisation* (–61).

R **Philosophy and Religion**
Ernest Renan, *Études d'histoire religieuse.*
First ritualistic cases in English church courts.

S **Art, Sculpture, Fine Arts and Architecture**
J. F. Millet, *The Gleaners* (painting).
E. Delacroix, decorations for S. Sulpice, Paris (–60).
Gavarni (pseud.), *Masques et Visages* (lithographs –58).
National Portrait Gallery, London, opened.

T **Music**
F. Liszt, *A Faust Symphony.*

U **Literature**
Charles Baudelaire, *Les Fleurs du Mal.*
B. Björnson, *Synnöve Solbakken.*
George Borrow, *The Romany Rye.*
E. B. Browning, *Aurora Leigh.*
George Eliot (pseud.), *Scenes from Clerical Life* in *Blackwood's Magazine.*
Thomas Hughes, *Tom Brown's Schooldays.*
Dinah Mulock (later Mrs. Craik), *John Halifax Gentleman.*
W. M. Thackeray, *The Virginians* (serially).
Anthony Trollope, *Barchester Towers.*

V **The Press**
Birmingham Post.
Atlantic Monthly founded, with J. R. Lowell as editor.

W **Drama and Entertainment**

X **Sport**

Y **Statistics**

Z **Births and Deaths**
Feb. 2nd Michael Ivanovich Glinka d. (54).
Feb. 22nd Robert Baden-Powell b. (–1941).
Feb. 26th Émile Coué (–1926).
Mar. 2nd Alfred de Musset d. (47), and Paul Doumer b. (–1932).
Mar. 18th Rudolf Diesel b. (–1913).
May 13th Ronald Ross b. (–1932).
June 2nd Edward Elgar b. (–1934).

(*Continued opposite*)

1858 British Crown takes over powers of East India Company— Napoleon III and Cavour plan unification of Italy

A **Jan:** 14th, Felice Orsini's plot to assassinate Napoleon III.

B **Feb:** 19th, Lord Palmerston resigns after defeat on Conspiracy to Murder bill following Orsini plot and
26th, Lord Derby forms Conservative administration.

C **Mar:**

D **Apr:** 1st, Granadian Confederation formed from provinces in former Colombian Federation (Republican Constitution promulgated *May* 22nd).

E **May:** 11th, Minnesota becomes U.S. state.

F **Jun:** 26th, Treaty of Tientsin ends Anglo-Chinese War; China opens further ports to British commerce and legalises opium trade (similar treaty with France by Chinese *June* 27th).

G **Jul:** 8th, proclamation of peace in India by British;
20th, Napoleon III and Cavour begin meetings at Plombières to plan unification of Italy;
23rd, Act of Parliament removes disabilities of Jews;
O'Donnell returns to power in Spain.

H **Aug:** 2nd, British Columbia organised as Colony;
2nd, powers of East India Company are transferred to the British Crown;
19th, Austria, Prussia, France, Britain, Russia, Turkey and Sardinia decide to unite Moldavia with Wallachia;
21st (–*Oct.* 15th), debates between Abraham Lincoln and Stephen Douglas in Senatorial campaign in Illinois, which Douglas ultimately wins;
26th, Anglo-Japanese commercial treaty providing for unsupervised trade and for setting up British residency.

J **Sep:**

K **Oct:** 7th, William, Prince of Prussia, declared Regent for the insane King Frederick William IV.

L **Nov:** 8th, boundaries of Montenegro fixed by France, Britain, Prussia, Russia and Turkey, after friction between Montenegro and Turkish Empire.

M **Dec:** 7th, notification of Franco-Spanish blockade of Cochin-China (–1862);
23rd, Serbian Diet deposes Alexander Karageorgevitch and declares Milosh Obrenovitch (who abdicated in *June* 1839) King again.

N

Z **Births and Deaths** (*cont.*)
Sept. 16th Andrew Bonar Law b. (–1923).
Oct. 20th John Burns b. (–1943).
Nov. 4th F. R. Benson b. (–1939).
Nov. 17th Robert Owen d. (87).
Nov. 20th Selma Lagerlöf b. (–1940).
Dec. 23rd Giacomo Puccini b. (–1924).

O **Politics, Economics, Law and Education**

Abolition of property qualification for Members of British Parliament. Lionel de Rothschild becomes first Jewish M.P.
Henry Carey, *Principles of Social Science.*
Alexander II begins emancipation of Russian serfs.
Prussian army is entirely equipped with needle-guns.
Ottawa is appointed the capital of Canada.

P **Science, Technology, Discovery, etc.**

Hermann Helmholtz propounds vortex motion theory.
William Thomson invents the mirror galvanometer (patented '67).
Charles Darwin and Alfred Wallace contribute joint paper on variation of species.
T. H. Huxley lectures to Royal Society on the theory of vertebrate skulls.
Göransson improves Bessemer steel-making process.
South Foreland lighthouse is lit by electricity.
I. K. Brunel's S. S. *Great Eastern* launched.

Q **Scholarship**

Henry Rawlinson, *The History of Herodotus* (–60).
Thomas Carlyle, *Frederick the Great* (–65).

R **Philosophy and Religion**

Blessed Virgin Mary is reputed to have appeared to Bernadette Soubirous at Lourdes, which becomes a centre of pilgrimage.
Stundist Sect, on Lutheran lines, is founded in Russia.
Isaac Hecker founds the Paulist Fathers in U.S.

S **Art, Sculpture, Fine Arts and Architecture**

Édouard Manet, *Le Concert aux Tuileries* (painting).
W. P. Frith, *Derby Day* (painting).
Alfred Stevens begins monument to Wellington.
Covent Garden Opera House built by Charles Barry.
Ringstrasse, Vienna, is begun.

T **Music**

Peter Cornelius, *The Barber of Baghdad* (opera).
Jacques Offenbach, *Orpheus in the Underworld* (opera).
César Franck, *Messe Solennelle.*

U **Literature**

Octave Feuillet, *Roman d'un jeune homme pauvre.*
O. W. Holmes, *The Autocrat of the Breakfast Table.*
William Morris, *The Defence of Guenevere.*

V **The Press**

W **Drama and Entertainment**

X **Sport**

Y **Statistics**

Z **Births and Deaths**

Jan. 22nd Beatrice Webb (*née* Potter), Lady Passfield, b. (–1943), and Frederick Lugard b. (–1945).
May 8th Ruggiero Leoncavallo b. (–1919).
May 31st Graham Wallas b. (–1932).
July 26th Edward Mandell House b. (–1938).

(*Continued opposite*)

1859 John Brown raids Harpers Ferry—Austrian defeats in Italy

A **Jan:** 19th, treaty of alliance between France and Sardinia.

B **Feb:** 14th, Oregon becomes a U.S. state.

C **Mar:** 31st, Lord Derby's ministry is defeated over B. Disraeli's Reform Bill.

D **Apr:** 17th, French decree for amnesty for political offenders and extension of political rights;
19th, Austrian ultimatum to Sardinia to disarm (rejected by Count Cavour, 26th);
27th, peaceful revolution in Tuscany demanding that House of Lorraine choose between Austria and Italy (followed by similar peaceful risings in Modena and Parma);
29th, Austrian forces cross Sardinian frontier.

E **May:** 3rd, France declares war on Austria;
22nd, death of Ferdinand II of the Two Sicilies, succeeded by Francis II.

F **Jun:** 4th, Austrians defeated at Magenta by French who free Milan;
10th, Lord Derby resigns after further defeat and Lord Palmerston subsequently forms Liberal administration;
14th, Prussia begins to mobilise against France;
24th, Austrians defeated at Solferino by French and Sardinian forces.

G **Jul:** 8th, death of Oscar I in Sweden; succeeded by Charles XV (–1872);
8th, Franco-Austrian armistice;
11th, preliminary Peace of Villafranca (confirmed *Nov.*) by which Austria is to cede Parma and Lombardy to France, for subsequent cession to Sardinia; Tuscany and Modena are to be restored and Venice is to remain Austrian, a treaty which causes Count Cavour to resign in disgust.

H **Aug:**

J **Sep:** Formation of German National Association by Rudolf von Bennigsen to work for German unity under Prussia.

K **Oct:** 16th (–18th), John Brown, American abolitionist, makes abortive raid on Harpers Ferry, site of a federal arsenal (he is hanged *Dec.* 2nd);
22nd, Spain declares war against the Moors in Morocco (–1860);
—, Buenos Aires, having seceded from the Argentine Confederation 1853–4, is defeated by federal troops (and agrees to reunion *Nov.* 10th).

L **Nov:** 10th, Treaty of Zürich confirms the preliminary peace of Villafranca (*July*).

M **Dec:** Albert von Roon is appointed Minister of War in Prussia to carry out military reforms.

N Queensland is separated from New South Wales and Brisbane becomes its capital.

O **Politics, Economics, Law and Education**

Carlo Passaglia, under Cavour's influence, attacks Pope's temporal power in *Epistola ad Episcopos Catholicos pro causa Italica.*

F. Lassalle, *Italian War and the Mission of Prussia.*

J. S. Mill, *On Liberty.*

K. Marx, *Criticism of Political Economy.*

Reforms of curriculum in Prussian secondary schools.

P **Science, Technology, Discovery, etc.**

R. L. G. Planté invents electric accumulator.

R. W. von Bunsen and G. R. Kirchhoff by elaborating the spectrum analysis forge a vital weapon for the chemist and astronomer.

Charles Darwin, *The Origin of Species by Natural Selection.*

Edwin Drake drills the first oil well, at Titusville, Pennsylvania.

The steam-roller is invented.

Q **Scholarship**

L. von Ranke, *History of England Principally in the Seventeenth Century* (–68).

Pasquale Villari, *Life of Savonarola.*

L. Tischendorf, with the Tsar's support, gains access to the remainder of the *Codex Sinaiticus.*

R **Philosophy and Religion**

E. Renan, *Essais de monde et de critique.*

Moritz Lazarus and Heymann Steinthal found a journal of comparative psychology.

S **Art, Sculpture, Fine Arts and Architecture**

J. B. Corot, *Macbeth* (painting).

J. A. Ingres, *Le Bain Turc* (painting).

É Manet, *Absinthe Drinker* (painting).

J. F. Millet, *L'Angélus* (painting).

Wilhelm Busch invents the captionless strip cartoon.

Parliament House, Ottawa (–67).

T **Music**

C. F. Gounod, *Faust* (opera).

R. Wagner, *Tristan und Isolde* (opera).

U **Literature**

Pedro Alarcón, *Diary of a Witness of the War in Africa.*

Charles Dickens, *A Tale of Two Cities.*

George Eliot (pseud.), *Adam Bede.*

Edward Fitzgerald, *Rubáiyát of Omar Khayyám.*

Ivan Goncharov, *Oblomov.*

Victor Hugo, *La Légende des siècles* (–1883).

George Meredith, *The Ordeal of Richard Feverel.*

George Sand (pseud.), *Elle et Lui.*

Lord Tennyson, *Idylls of the King.*

V **The Press**

W **Drama and Entertainment**

Adelina Patti's début in New York as Lucia in Donizetti's *Bride of Lammermoor.*

Blondin (pseud.) crosses Niagara Falls on a tightrope (*June* 30th).

X **Sport**

Y **Statistics**

Z **Births and Deaths**

Jan. 6th Samuel Alexander b. (–1938).
Jan. 21st Henry Hallam d. (81).
Jan. 27th William Hickling Prescott d. (62).
Feb. 21st George Lansbury b. (–1940).
Apr. 3rd Washington Irving d. (76).
Apr. 16th Charles Alexis de Tocqueville d. (53).
May 2nd Jerome K. Jerome b. (–1927).
May 6th Alexander von Humboldt d. (89).
May 22nd Arthur Conan Doyle b. (–1930).
May 26th A. E. Housman b. (–1936).
June 11th Clemens, Prince Metternich d. (86).
Aug. 28th Leigh Hunt d. (74).
Sept. 3rd Jean Léon Jaurès b. (–1914).
Sept. 7th Isambard Kingdom Brunel d. (53).
Oct. 18th Henri Bergson b. (–1941).
Oct. 27th Theodore Roosevelt b. (–1919).
Nov. 24th Cass Gilbert b. (–1934).
Dec. 5th Sidney Lee b. (–1926).
Dec. 8th Thomas de Quincey d. (74).
Dec. 18th Francis Thompson b. (–1907).
Dec. 28th Thomas, Lord Macaulay d. (59).

1860 Garibaldi proclaims Victor Emmanuel King of Italy—Abraham Lincoln elected U.S. President

A **Jan:** 20th, Count Cavour is recalled as Prime Minister in Sardinia;
23rd, Cobden-Chevalier Treaty establishes substantial degree of free trade between Britain and France.

B **Feb:** 2nd, Jefferson Davis introduces Resolutions, in favour of federal slave trade, in U.S. Congress.

C **Mar:** 5th, size of Austrian Imperial Council (*Reichsrat*) increased by March Patent;
11th (–15th), Plebiscites in Tuscany, Emilia, Parma, Modena and Romagna in favour of union with Sardinia;
17th, Second Maori War breaks out in New Zealand (–1870);
24th, Sardinia cedes Nice and Savoy to France by treaty of Turin.

D **Apr:** 2nd, first Italian Parliament meets in Turin;
3rd, Pretoria becomes capital of Transvaal;
26th, peace between Spain and Morocco.

E **May:** 5th, G. Garibaldi and Redshirts sail for Genoa, land, 11th, and, 27th, take Palermo.

F **Jun:** 6th, formal reunion of Argentina and Buenos Aires.

G **Jul:** Russians found Vladivostok in vicinity of Korean border.

H **Aug:** 22nd, Garibaldi crosses the Straits, with British connivance;
25th, Anglo-French troops take Tientsin in war with China.

J **Sep:** 5th, treaty between Britain, Austria, France, Prussia, Russia and Turkey, to restore order in Syria after massacre of Christians by Druses;
7th, G. Garibaldi enters Naples; Francis II of Naples flees;
11th, Victor Emmanuel, King of Sardinia, invades Papal States, after rising of 8th;
18th, Cavour defeats Papal troops at Castelfidardo;
21st, Anglo-French troops defeat Chinese at Pa-li-Chau.

K **Oct:** 20th, October Diploma amends Austrian Constitution, providing for federation with wide autonomy for separate territories;
21st (–22nd), plebiscites in Naples and Sicily in support of union with Sardinia;
24th, treaty of Peking by which Chinese ratify Treaty of Tientsin with Britain (of *June* 26th 1858) and recognise treaty with France (of *June* 27th 1858);
26th, G. Garibaldi meets Victor Emmanuel and proclaims him King of Italy.

L **Nov:** 4th (–5th), plebiscites in Umbria and Legations for union with Sardinia;
6th, in U.S. presidential election, Abraham Lincoln (Republican) opposing further extension of slavery secures a majority of popular votes, but only 180 out of 303 electoral votes; John C. Breckinidge (Southern Democrat) has 72 votes, John Bell (Constitutional Union), 39, and Stephen A. Douglas (Northern Democrat), 12 votes;
24th, Napoleon III extends power of French legislature.

M **Dec:** 20th, South Carolina secedes from Union, in protest at Abraham Lincoln's election.

N

O Politics, Economics, Law and Education

J. S. Mill, *Treatise on Representative Government.*
Russians found Vladivostok.
Food and Drugs Act in U.K.
Degrees in Science are established at London University.

P Science, Technology, Discovery, etc.

Chemical congress at Karlsruhe settles problem of atomic weights.
G. T. Fechner, *Elements of Psycho-Physics.*
Rhinoscope invented.
Exploitation of potassium deposits at Stassfurt, near Magdeburg.

Q Scholarship

Charles de Montalembert, *Moines d'Occident.*
J. L. Motley, *History of the United Netherlands* (-67).

R Philosophy and Religion

Frederick Temple, Mark Pattison and others contribute to *Essays and Reviews*, which is condemned by Convocation.
English Church Union is founded to counter the High Church movement in England.
Russian Orthodox Church establishes monastery and hospice at Jerusalem.

S Art, Sculpture, Fine Arts and Architecture

É Manet, *The Guitarist* (painting).
W. Holman Hunt, *The Discovery of Our Saviour in the Temple* (painting).
J. Burckhardt, *The Culture of the Renaissance in Italy.*

T Music

U Literature

Wilkie Collins, *The Woman in White.*
George Eliot (pseud.), *The Mill on the Floss.*
Ivan Turgeniev, *On the Eve.*

V The Press

The Cornhill Magazine founded under W. M. Thackeray's editorship.
Charles Bradlaugh founds and edits *The National Reformer.*
The Catholic Times first issued.

W Drama and Entertainment

Dion Boucicault, *The Colleen Bawn.*
Eugène Labiche, *Le Voyage de M. Perrichon.*
Alexander Ostrovsky, *The Tempest.*

X Sport

Open Golf Championship started (first won by W. Park).
Prize fight at Farnborough (*Apr.*) between Tom Sayers (U.K.) and John C. Heenan (U.S.), the last contest with bare fists in England.

Y Statistics

Railway mileage in operation: U.S. 30,600; U.K. 10,410; Russia, 900.
Oil production: U.S., 500,000 barrels; Rumania, 8,542 barrels.
Emigration to U.S. (1851-60): from Britain, 423,964; from Ireland, 914,119.
Pig-iron production (in mill. tons): Gt. Britain, 3·9; France, 0·9; U.S., 0·8.

z **Births and Deaths**

Jan. 17th Anton Chekhov b. (–1904).
Mar. 13th Hugo Wolf b. (–1903).
May 9th J. M. Barrie b. (–1937).
July 7th Gustave Mahler b. (–1911).
July 20th Margaret McMillan b. (–1931).
Aug. 20th Raymond Poincaré b. (–1934).
Sept. 21st Arthur Schopenhauer d. (72).
Nov. 6th Ignaz Paderewski b. (–1941).
Dec. 14th George Hamilton Gordon, Earl of Aberdeen, d. (76)
Dec. 28th Philip Wilson Steer b. (–1942).

1861 (Jan.–Nov.) Outbreak of American Civil War—Death of Prince Consort

A **Jan**: 2nd, Frederick William IV of Prussia dies and is succeeded by William I (–88);
29th, Kansas is created U.S. state.

B **Feb**: 4th, Peace Convention at Washington in effort to preserve Union;
4th, Congress of Montgomery at which South Carolina, Georgia, Alabama, Mississippi, Florida, and Louisiana decide, 8th, to elect Jefferson Davis as President of Confederate States of America which is formed 9th (five more states join—*Apr.–May*);
13th, Francis II of Naples surrenders at Gaeta to Garibaldi;
18th, Italian Parliament proclaims Victor Emmanuel King (and Kingdom of Italy proclaimed *Mar.* 17th);
26th, Austrian constitution centralised by 'February Patent' which is unpopular in Hungary;
27th, Warsaw Massacre when crowd fired on by Russian troops during demonstration against Russian rule.

C **Mar**: 2nd, Morrill Tariff, precipitated by panic in 1857, is beginning of several tariff increases in U.S.;
3rd, emancipation of Russian serfs proclaimed (*Feb.* 19th, old style);
4th, Abraham Lincoln inaugurated President of U.S.;
18th, Spain annexes San Domingo at latter's request;
19th, end of Maori War in New Zealand.

D **Apr**: 10th, Finland obtains constitution from Russia;
12th (–13th), Confederates take Fort Sumter, Charleston, S. Carolina after 40-hour bombardment, marking outbreak of American Civil War;
15th, A. Lincoln calls for Militia to suppress Confederacy;
19th, blockade of Confederate forts decreed (and extended, 27th).

E **May**:

F **Jun**: 6th, Count Cavour dies in Italy (aged 50);
25th, Sultan Abdul Mejid dies and is succeeded as Sultan of Turkey by brother Abdul Aziz.

G **Jul**: 21st, indecisive victory of Confederates at Bull Run.

H **Aug**: 21st, Hungarian Diet is dissolved after opposition to 'February Patent', and government carried out by Imperial Commission;
28th (–29th), Unionists capture Forts Clark and Hatteras on North Carolina coast.

J **Sep**: 2nd, Prussia concludes commercial treaty with China at Tientsin.

K **Oct**: 31st, London Convention of Britain, Spain and France to protect their interests on Mexico's suspension of payments of foreign debts.

L **Nov**: 8th, *Trent* affair, when Confederate Commissioners to Great Britain and France are taken off British ship by Unionists, but given up when Britain subsequently protests;
11th, Pedro V of Portugal dies and succeeded by Louis I;
Financial powers of French legislature extended.

O Politics, Economics, Law and Education

F. Lassalle, *System of Assigned Rights.*
H. Spencer, *Education, Moral, Intellectual, Physical.*
Paper duties in U.K. are repealed.

P Science, Technology, Discovery, etc.

R. W. von Bunsen detects the alkali metals caesium and rubidium by their spectra, and identifies them as new elements.
William Crookes discovers thallium.
Louis Pasteur develops the germ theory of disease.
William Thomson persuades British Association to appoint committee to determine electrical standards.
William Siemens in U.K. and Pierre and Émile Martin in France simultaneously develop the open-hearth process for making steel with a regenerative gas-fired furnace, which effects a rapid rise in steel production and a reduction in the coal used.
Ernest Solvay's process for making soda (sodium carbonate).
Philipp Reis makes first practical instrument capable of transmitting sound.
First machine-chilled cold store built by T. S. Mort at Sydney.
H.M.S. *Warrior*, the first all-iron warship, is completed (steam screw, but also rigged for sail).

Q Scholarship

A. P. Stanley, *Lectures on the Eastern Church.*
H. Maine, *Ancient Law.*
Vladimir Dahl, *Dictionary of the Living Russian Tongue.*

R Philosophy and Religion

Ignaz von Döllinger, in *The Church and the Churches*, declares war on Ultramontane party.

S Art, Sculpture, Fine Arts and Architecture

Jean Garnier builds Paris Opera House (–75).
T. Hansen, Heinrichshof, Vienna (–63).
William Morris begins to make wallpapers and tapestries.

T Music

Johannes Brahms, Piano Concerto no. 1 in D minor (op. 15).

U Literature

Charles Dickens, *Great Expectations.*
George Eliot (pseud.), *Silas Marner.*
O. W. Holmes, *Elsie Venner* (or *The Professor*).
Charles Reade, *The Cloister and the Hearth.*
Mrs. Henry Wood, *East Lynne.*

V The Press

W Drama and Entertainment

X Sport

1861 (Dec).

M Dec: 14th, death of Prince Consort (aged 42);
23rd, Sultan of Turkey agrees to unification of Moldavia and Wallachia as Roumania (and assemblies meet in Bucharest, *Feb.* 5th 1862).

N

Y **Statistics**

Populations (in millions): Russia, 76; U.S., 32; Great Britain, 23·1; Ireland, 5·7; Italy, 25.
Coal production (in mill. tons): Great Britain, 83·6; France, 6·8; Russia, 0·3.
Iron production (in mill. tons): Great Britain, 3·7; France, 3; U.S., 2·8; Germany, 0·2.

Z **Births and Deaths**

Jan. 28th Henri Murger d. (38).
Feb. 15th A. N. Whitehead b. (–1947).
Apr. 23rd Edmund Allenby b. (–1936).
May 6th Rabindranath Tagore b. (–1941).
May 19th Nellie Melba b. (–1931).
June 19th Douglas, Earl Haig, b. (–1928).
June 30th Elizabeth Barrett Browning d. (55).
Oct. 10th Fridtjof Nansen b. (–1930).
Oct. 16th J. B. Bury b. (–1927).
— Elmer Ambrose Sperry b. (–1930).

1862 Lincoln declares all slaves to be free—Bismarck's 'Blood and Iron' speech

A Jan:

B Feb: 6th, Ulysses S. Grant captures Fort Henry on Tennessee River from Confederates;
8th, Unionists take Roanoke Isle and, 10th, Elizabeth City, North Carolina;
15th (-16th), U. S. Grant captures Fort Donelson;
France purchases Mentone and Roquebrune from Monaco.

C Mar: 3rd (-4th), Unionists take Amelia Island, Florida;
8th, Confederate frigate *Merrimack* sinks *Cumberland* in Hampton Roads, Virginia, but, 9th, is forced to withdraw by Unionist vessel *Monitor*;
10th, Britain and France recognise independence of Zanzibar;
12th, Jacksonville, Florida, is taken by Unionists.
14th, Newbern, N. Carolina, is captured by Unionists.

D Apr: 7th, Confederates forced to withdraw after initial success at Shiloh, Tennessee;
24th (-25th), Unionists lay siege to New Orleans, Louisiana (taken *May* 1st).

E May:

F Jun: 5th, treaty of Saigon between France and Annam; France annexes Cochin-China;
15th, Turks bombard Belgrade after Serb rising there;
25th (-*July* 1st), Seven Days battle results in withdrawal of Federal troops from the Peninsula;
U.S. recognises independence of Liberia.

G Jul: *Alabama* case after British fail to stop new vessel sailing to aid Confederates, which causes considerable damage to Unionist fleets (settled 1872).

H Aug: 2nd, commercial treaty between France and Prussia;
18th, Sioux rising begins in Minnesota but is subsequently defeated;
29th, G. Garibaldi plans to take Rome but is captured by Royalist troops at Aspromonte;
—, (-30th), second battle of Bull Run, where Thomas ('Stonewall') Jackson defeats Union Army.

J Sep: 17th, indecisive battle of Antietam, Maryland, but Confederates forced to withdraw;
22nd, A. Lincoln declares all slaves to be free from *Jan.* 1st 1863;
—, Otto von Bismarck becomes Prussian premier;
29th, Bismarck's 'Blood and Iron' speech.

K Oct: 7th, Prussian Diet rejects increase in military budget, but subsequently passed by Peers, and Diet is adjourned so that Bismarck rules without budget for four years;
8th, indecisive battle of Perryville, Kentucky, in American Civil War;
22nd, garrison in Athens revolts and forces King Otto I to resign, 24th.

L Nov:

M Dec: 13th, Confederate army under Robert E. Lee gains victory over Ambrose Burnside, at Fredericksburg.

N

O Politics, Economics, Law and Education

J. S. Mill, *Utilitarianism.*
John Ruskin, *Unto this Last.*
Herbet Spencer, *First Principles.*
F. Lassalle's Working-Class Programme advocates a system of State socialism.
Foundation of colleges in each U.S. state in which science and technology is placed on a par with arts subjects.

P Science, Technology, Discovery, etc.

Julius Sachs proves that starch is produced by photosynthesis.
F. Wöhler finds that water decomposes calcium carbide into lime and acetylene.
F. W. A. Argelander completes the Bonn catalogue of stars visible in the Northern Hemisphere.
Johann von Lamont discovers earth current.
H. Helmholtz, *Sensations of Tones.*
Joseph Brown constructs a universal milling machine.
Richard Gatling's ten-barrel gun.

Q Scholarship

August Potthast, *Bibliotheca Historia Medii Aevi.*
Henry Rawlinson, *The Five Great Monarchies of the Ancient Eastern World* (–67).

R Philosophy and Religion

J. W. Colenso, Bishop of Natal, denies authenticity of The Pentateuch.
Joseph Lyne (Fr. Ignatius) forms a monastic community in Suffolk, preparatory to founding Llanthony Abbey, first post-Reformation religious house in England.

S Art, Sculpture, Fine Arts and Architecture

É. Manet, *Lola de Valence* (painting).
Gilbert Scott designs Albert Memorial.

T Music

G. Verdi, *La Forza del Destino* (opera).

U Literature

G. Flaubert, *Salammbô.*
V. Hugo, *Les Misérables.*
George Meredith, *Modern Love* and *Poems of the English Roadside.*
Ivan Turgeniev, *Fathers and Sons.*
[C. F. Browne], *Artemus Ward, His Book.*
J. G. Whittier, *Snow-Bound.*

V The Press

W Drama and Entertainment

Sarah Bernhardt's début at Comédie Française.
International Exhibition, London.

X Sport

An English cricket team tours Australia.

Y **Statistics**

British Textile trade:

imports of raw cotton	452 mill. lb.
exports of cottons	1,681 mill. yds.
exports of woollens	167 mill. yds.
exports of linens	156·8 mill. yds.
exports of silks	2·6 mill. yds.

Z **Births and Deaths**

Apr. 25th Edward Grey b. (–1933).
May 6th Henry David Thoreau d. (44).
May 16th Edward Gibbon Wakefield d. (66).
May 28th Henry Thomas Buckle d. (40).
June 6th Henry Newbolt b. (–1938).
July 2nd William Bragg b. (–1942).
Aug. 17th Maurice Barrès b. (–1923).
Aug. 22nd Claude Debussy b. (–1918).
Aug. 29th Maurice Maeterlinck b. (–1949).
Sept. 22nd Louis Botha b. (–1919).
Nov. 15th Gerhart Hauptmann b. (–1946).
— Aristide Briand b. (–1932).
— Edith Wharton (*née* Jones) b. (–1937).

1863 (Jan.–Nov.) Confederates defeated at Gettysburg—Denmark incorporates Schleswig

A **Jan**: 22nd, Polish insurrection begins when National Committee publishes manifesto;
On death of Mohammed Said, Ismail becomes Khedive of Egypt (–79).

B **Feb**: 3rd, Greek Assembly elects Prince Alfred, second son of Queen Victoria, King, but British government rejects decision;
8th, Prussia allies with Russia to suppress Polish Revolt at Convention made by Count Alvensleben;
24th, Arizona organised as territory of U.S.;
25th, National Banking Act in U.S. to provide uniform system and to create market for State Bonds (revised *June* 3rd 1864).

C **Mar**: 3rd, Idaho organised as territory of U.S.;
30th, William, Prince of Denmark, recognised as King of Greece and takes title of George I (–1919);
—, Denmark incorporates Schleswig by March Patent;
Poland divided into provinces by Russia.

D **Apr**:

E **May**: 4th, new Maori risings in New Zealand;
5th, Confederate victory at Chancellorsville, Virginia, after five-day battle, but 'Stonewall' Jackson dies of wounds, 10th.

F **Jun**: 20th, West Virginia created U.S. state;
Civil War in Afghanistan after death of Dost Mohammed.

G **Jul**: 1st (–3rd), Robert E. Lee's Confederate army defeated by General Meade's force at Gettysburg, Pennsylvania;
4th, Confederate defeat at Vicksburg, Mississippi;
9th, Confederates surrender Fort Hudson, Missouri, to Unionists, which cuts off Texas, Arkansas and Louisiana from rest of Confederacy.

H **Aug**: 11th, French protectorate established over Cambodia;
16th, Frankfurt meeting of German princes to reform Confederation, but Prussia opposes this and meeting ends *Sept.* with nothing achieved.

J **Sep**:

K **Oct**: 1st, German Diet votes for federal action against Denmark.

L **Nov**: 13th, Schleswig incorporated in New Danish Constitution;
14th, conference between Britain, France, Austria, Russia and Prussia to decide on position of Ionian Islands (see *Mar.* 29th 1864);
15th, Frederick VII of Denmark dies and is succeeded by Christian IX;
18th, Christian IX of Denmark signs new constitution;
23rd (–25th), Confederates defeated at Chattanooga, Tennessee;
A. Thiers forms opposition Third Party in France.

O Politics, Economics, Law and Education

P Science, Technology, Discovery, etc.

T. H. Huxley, *Man's Place in Nature.*
Charles Lyell, *The Antiquity of Man.*
Max Schultze propounds cell theory.
Thomas Graham's process for separating gases by atmolysis.
A. Nadar makes ascents (*Oct.*) in his balloon '*Le Géant*', in Paris and starts a newspaper, *L'Aéronaute*, devoted to aeronautics.

Q Scholarship

T. Mommsen issues first part of *Corpus Inscriptionum Latinum.*
S. R. Gardiner, *History of England, 1603–56* (–1903).
Paul Littré, *Dictionnaire de la langue française* (–72).
A. W. Kinglake, *History of the Crimean War* (–87).

R Philosophy and Religion

E. Renan, *Vie de Jésus* and *Histoire des origines du christianisme.*
Church of England congress at Manchester.
J. W. Colenso, Bishop of Natal, is deposed by South African bishops in conclave for denying doctrine of eternal punishment and condoning polygamy (*Dec.*); on his appeal the Privy Council decides his deposition was *ultra vires.*

S Art, Sculpture, Fine Arts and Architecture

É. Manet, *Luncheon on the Grass* (painting).
Napoleon III orders a special exhibition of works refused by the Academy ('the Salon des Refusés).
C. Baudelaire's essay on Constantin Guy, 'Le Peintre de la vie moderne'.
D. G. Rossetti, *Beata Beatrix* (painting).
James Whistler, *Symphony in White* (painting).

T Music

H. Berlioz, *The Trojans,* pt. i—*The Taking of Troy* (opera).
G. Bizet, *The Pearl Fishers* (opera).
W. H. Fry, *Notre Dame de Paris* (opera).

U Literature

Charles Kingsley, *The Water Babies.*

V The Press

Le Petit Journal, first cheap newspaper in France issued.

W Drama and Entertainment

X Sport

Football Association founded.
Grand Prix de Paris is first run at Longchamp.

Y Statistics

U.S. crude petroleum production, 2,611,000 barrels.

1863 (Dec.)

M **Dec**: 24th, Saxon and Hanoverian federal troops enter Holstein.

N

z **Births and Deaths**

Jan. 18th Constantin Stanislavsky b. (–1938).
Jan. 19th Werner Sombart b. (–1941).
Jan. 29th Frederick Delius b. (–1934).
Feb. 9th Anthony Hope Hawkins (A. Hope) b. (–1933).
Feb. 20th Lucien Pissarro b. (–1944).
Mar. 12th Gabriele D'Annunzio b. (–1938).
Mar. 27th Frederick Henry Royce b. (–1933).
May 31st Francis Younghusband b. (–1942).
July 17th David Lloyd George b. (–1945).
Aug. 13th Eugène Delacroix d. (64).
Aug. 14th Colin Campbell, Lord Clyde, d. (70).
Sept. 17th Alfred de Vigny d. (66).
Sept. 20th Jacob Grimm d. (78).
Nov. 21st Arthur Quiller-Couch ('Q') b. (–1944).
Dec. 12th Edvard Munch b. (–1944).
Dec. 23rd W. M. Thackeray d. (52).

1864 (Jan.–Nov.) W. Sherman marches Union Army through Georgia—Austria and Prussia declare war on Denmark over Schleswig and Holstein

A **Jan:** 13th, Zemstvo Law in Russia establishing provincial councils (*Jan.* 1st, old style);
16th, Austria and Prussia send ultimatum to Denmark for repeal of constitution for the incorporation of Schleswig and form alliance in case of its rejection.

B **Feb:** 1st, Austro-Prussian troops enter Schleswig.

C **Mar:** 29th, Ionian Islands ceded by Britain to Greece.

D **Apr:** 10th, Archduke Maximilian of Austria accepts title of Emperor of Mexico;
18th, Danish forces defeated at Düppel and German troops invade Denmark;
25th, Lord John Russell calls London Conference of Britain, Russia, France, Austria and Prussia to solve Danish Question.

E **May:** 5th, William Sherman leaves Chattanooga, Tennessee, to march army through Georgia;
5th (–6th), U. S. Grant and R. E. Lee fight indecisive battle of the Wilderness, Virginia, in American Civil War;
8th (–21st), at battle of Spotsylvania Courthouse in Civil War, Grant is unable to defeat Lee;
26th, territory of Montana organised in U.S.

F **Jun:** 3rd, revised National Banking Act in U.S.;
25th, through Bismarck's astuteness London Conference on Denmark ends with nothing achieved and, 26th, war resumes.

G **Jul:** 22nd, Sherman defeats Confederate army of John Hood at Atlanta.

H **Aug:**

J **Sep:** 1st, Confederates abandon Atlanta, Georgia, which is occupied, 2nd, by Sherman;
5th (–8th), British, French and Dutch fleets attack Japan in Shimonoseki Straits in reprisal for closing ports and expelling foreigners (a truce, 14th, is followed by peace convention, *Oct.* 22nd, when Japan pays indemnity);
15th, Franco-Italian Treaty whereby Italy renounces claim to Rome and Florence becomes Italian capital (–1870) in place of Turin;
The reactionary Ramon Narvaez becomes premier of Spain.

K **Oct:** 30th, Peace of Vienna by which Denmark cedes Schleswig, Holstein and Lauenburg to Austria and Prussia;
31st, Nevada created U.S. state.

L **Nov:** 8th, re-election of Abraham Lincoln as U.S. President;
Andrew Johnson elected Vice-President;
28th, new democratic Constitution, with one Chamber of Deputies, in Greece;
29th, massacre of Cheyenne and Arapahoe Indians at Sand Creek, Colorado, by Col. Chivington's troops.

O Politics, Economics, Law and Education

Geneva Convention prescribes immunity for the Red Cross League, founded by Henri Dunant, in time of war.
Le Play, *La Réforme Sociale.*
Octavia Hill begins reform of tenement dwellings in St. Marylebone.
International Working-Men's Association founded in London.
Universities of Belgrade and Bucharest founded.

P Science, Technology, Discovery, etc.

Louis Pasteur invents pasteurisation (for wine).
Joseph Bertrand, *Treatise on Differential and Integral Calculus.*
Robert Whitehead constructs torpedo.
Metropolitan Railway, London, opened.

Q Scholarship

James Bryce, *The Holy Roman Empire.*
N. Fustel de Coulanges, *La Cité Antique.*
Michele de Rossi begins exploration of the Catacombs, Rome.

R Philosophy and Religion

J. H. Newman, *Apologia pro vita sua.*
Pius IX issues Syllabus of Errors, claiming the Church's control over culture, science and education (*Dec.* 8th), and provokes a discussion of papal infallibility.
Episcopally ordained Scottish ministers are permitted to hold English benefices.

S Art, Sculpture, Fine Arts and Architecture

Arnold Böcklin, *Villa at the Sea* (painting).
Auguste Rodin, *Man With the Broken Nose* (sculpture).

T Music

Anton Bruckner, Mass No. 1 in D minor.
P. I. Tchaikovsky, Overture *Romeo and Juliet.*

U Literature

Charles Dickens, *Our Mutual Friend.*
J. Goncourt, *Renée Mauperin.*
Wilhelm Raabe, *Der Hungerpastor.*
Leo Tolstoy, *War and Peace* (–69).
A. Trollope, *The Small House at Allington.*
A. de Vigny, *Les Destinées* (posth.).

V The Press

Neue Freie Presse, Vienna.

W Drama and Entertainment

H. Ibsen, *The Pretenders.*

X Sport

Y Statistics

M Dec: 1st, Russian judiciary reformed (*Nov.* 20th, old style);
22nd, W. T. Sherman occupies Savannah, Georgia, after its surrender to Union army.

N

z **Births and Deaths**

Feb. 14th Israel Zangwill b. (–1926).
Apr. 9th Sebastian de Ferranti b. (–1930).
May 2nd Giacomo Meyerbeer d. (73).
May 19th Nathaniel Hawthorne d. (59).
May 20th John Clare d. (71).
June 4th Nassau William Senior d. (74).
July 15th Marie Tempest b. (–1942).
July 24th Frank Wedekind b. (–1918).
Aug. 28th Ferdinand Lassalle d. (39).
Sept. 17th Walter Savage Landor d. (89).
Oct. 28th John Leech d. (47).
— Henri Toulouse-Lautrec b. (–1901).

1865 Assassination of Lincoln—End of U.S. Civil War—Bismarck meets Napoleon III at Biarritz

A **Jan:** 27th, treaty between Spain and Peru virtually recognises Peruvian independence.

B **Feb:** 17th, Unionists take Columbia, South Carolina;
18th, Unionist fleet takes Charleston after long siege.

C **Mar:** 18th, Paraguay begins war against Argentina, Brazil and Uruguay (–*Mar.* 1st 1870);
27th, the independent British Colony of Kaffaria is incorporated with Cape Colony.

D **Apr:** 3rd, Richmond, Virginia, surrenders to Grant;
9th, Lee, Confederate C.-in-C., capitulates to Grant at Appomattox Courthouse;
14th, Abraham Lincoln assassinated by J. W. Booth and is succeeded by Andrew Johnson as President of U.S.;
26th, Confederate force under Joseph E. Johnston surrenders at Durham, North Carolina.

E **May:** 5th, revolt in San Domingo forces Spain to renounce sovereignty;
10th, Jefferson Davis, president of the Confederacy, is captured near Florida border and imprisoned;
26th, surrender of last Confederate army at Shreveport, near New Orleans, ends U.S. Civil War;
30th, commercial treaty between Britain and *Zollverein.*

F **Jun:** 29th, Ramon Narvaez dismissed in Spain and replaced by Leopold O'Donnell.

G **Jul:**

H **Aug:** 14th, Convention of Gastein by which Austria receives Holstein, whereas Prussia obtains Schleswig and Kiel, and purchases Lauenburg.

J **Sep:** 2nd, end of Maori War in New Zealand when Governor issues proclamation of peace;
20th, Austrian constitution temporarily annulled.

K **Oct:** 4th (and 11th), Otto von Bismarck and Napoleon III meet at Biarritz when the French Emperor agrees to Prussian supremacy in Germany, and to a united Italy;
18th, Lord Palmerston dies (aged 80) and Lord John Russell becomes Prime Minister, with W. E. Gladstone leader of House of Commons;
U.S. demands recall of French troops from Mexico.

L **Nov:**

M **Dec:** 10th, Leopold I of Belgium dies and is succeeded by his son, Leopold II (–1909);
18th, 13th Amendment to U.S. Constitution abolishes slavery;
Kolozsvár Diet, dominated by Hungarians, decrees for the incorporation of Transylvania in Hungary (completed 1868);
New constitution in Sweden abolishing traditional four Estates which are replaced by two Chambers.

N Capital of New Zealand is moved from Auckland to Wellington.

O **Politics, Economics, Law and Education**

Henri Baudrillant, *La Liberté du travail.*
W. S. Jevons, *The Coal Question.*
Commons Preservation Society founded in U.K.
Foundation of Massachusetts Institute of Technology and of Odessa University.
Jean Duruy organises French secondary education.

P **Science, Technology, Discovery, etc.**

Julius Plückner invents line geometry.
Friedrich Kekulé propounds ring theory of the structure of benzene.
Karl Ludwig devises the kymograph for recording blood pressure.
Paul Schutzenberger invents 'celanese' acetate rayon (not commercially produced until 1904).
Pierre Lallement constructs the 'bone-shaker' pedalled bicycle.
First carpet sweeper and first mechanical dish-washer.
Atlantic cable finally successful.

Q **Scholarship**

F. Parkman, *France and England in the New World* (–92).
W. E. H. Lecky, *A History of the Rise and Influence of Rationalism in Europe.*

R **Philosophy and Religion**

J. S.Mill, *Auguste Comte and Positivism.*
E. B. Pusey in *Eirenicon* trys to find a basis for reunion with Rome.
William Booth founds Salvation Army.
China Inland Mission founded.

S **Art, Sculpture, Fine Arts and Architecture**

Winslow Homer, *Prisoners from the Front* (painting).
É. Manet, *Olympia* (painting).
H. Taine, *La Philosophie de l'art* (–69).

T **Music**

Nicholas Rimsky-Korsakov, 1st Symphony in E minor.
R. Wagner's opera *Tristan und Isolde* is performed in Munich.

U **Literature**

M. Arnold, *Essays in Criticism.*
Lewis Carroll (pseud.), *Alice's Adventures in Wonderland.*
John Ruskin, *Sesame and Lilies.*
A. C. Swinburne, *Atalanta in Calydon.*

V **The Press**

Pall Mall Gazette.
Fortnightly Review.

W **Drama and Entertainment**

X **Sport**

W. G. Grace's début as cricketer in Gentlemen *v.* Players.
Edward Whymper climbs the Matterhorn (*July* 13th).

Y **Statistics**

U.K. total State expenditure £70·3 mill.

Z **Births and Deaths**

Jan. 16th Pierre Joseph Proudhon d. (56).
Feb. 9th Beatrice Tanner (Mrs. Patrick Campbell) b. (–1940).
Feb. 15th Nicholas Wiseman, Cardinal d. (62).
Mar. 21st Richard Cobden d. (60), and H. A. L. Fisher b. (–1940).
Apr. 9th Erich Ludendorff b. (–1937).
Apr. 15th Abraham Lincoln d. (56).
June 8th Joseph Paxton d. (59).
June 13th W. B. Yeats b. (–1939).
July 15th Alfred Harmsworth, Viscount Northcliffe, b. (–1922).
Aug. 10th Alexander Glazounov b. (–1936).
Oct. 1st Paul Dukas b. (–1935).
Nov. 2nd Warren Gamaliel Harding b. (–1923).
Nov. 12th Elizabeth Gaskell d. (55).
Dec. 30th Rudyard Kipling b. (–1936).

1866 (Jan.–Sep.) Prussia defeats Austria at Sadowa—War between Austria and Italy

A **Jan:** 14th, Peru declares war on Spain in resentment at clauses in the treaty (of *Jan.* 1865).

B **Feb:** 17th, Habeas Corpus Act suspended in Ireland after unrest;
23rd, Alexander Cuss, Prince of Roumania, dethroned, succeeded by Charles, Prince of Hohenzollern, as Carol I (–1914) (who is recognised by Sultan of Turkey *Oct.* 24th).

C **Mar:**

D **Apr:** 8th, Italy concludes offensive and defensive alliance with Prussia against Austria with promise of Venezia as reward.

E **May:** 27th, Sultan grants rights of primogeniture to Ismail, Khedive of Egypt.

F **Jun:** 7th, Prussian troops march into Holstein and
8th, annex that Duchy;
12th, secret treaty between Austria and France, whereby Napoleon III promises French neutrality provided that Austria cedes Venezia, which France will in turn hand over to Italy;
13th, U.S. 14th Amendment concerns citizenship, representation and public debt.
14th, Federal Diet in Germany votes for mobilisation against Prussian intervention in Holstein, at which Prussian delegates declare the German Confederation at an end;
15th (–16th), Prussia invades Saxony, Hanover and Hesse during the night;
20th, Italy declares war on Austria;
24th, Austrian forces under Archduke Albert defeat Italians at Custozza, northern Italy;
25th, Japan concludes tariff convention with Britain, France, Holland and U.S.;
26th, Russell's ministry resigns after defeat on Reform Bill;
29th, Prussians defeat Hanoverian army at Langensalza.

G **Jul:** 3rd, Prussians defeat Austrians at Sadowa (Königgrätz);
4th, Napoleon III announces cession of Venezia by Austria;
6th, Lord Derby forms Conservative administration, with B. Disraeli leader of the House of Commons;
20th, Italian fleet destroyed by Austrians off Lissa;
26th, preliminary peace treaty between Prussia and Austria at Nikolsburg;
28th, Danish constitution altered in favour of King and Upper House.

H **Aug:** 10th, treaty between Bolivia and Chile whereby territory between Andes and the Pacific is ceded to Chile;
12th, Austro-Italian armistice;
13th, Prussia concludes treaty of peace with Württemberg, with secret military alliance against France, and similar treaties are made, 7th, with Baden, and 22nd, with Bavaria;
23rd, Peace of Prague confirms preliminary peace of Nikolsburg (*July* 26th), whereby Austria to be excluded from Germany, while Hanover, Hesse, Nassau and Frankfurt are to be incorporated with Prussia, South German States to be independent, but States north of the Main to form Confederation under Prussia, which also obtains Austrian Silesia and territory from Saxony and from South German States.

J **Sep:** 2nd, after long discontent against Turkish authority Crete revolts and decrees union with Greece;

O **Politics, Economics, Law and Education**

Cobden Club, London, founded by Thomas Potter.
'Black Friday' (*May* 11th) scenes of commercial panic in London following the stoppage of Overend and Gurney.
People's Bank, Milan, is founded.
Gottenberg system of State control of sales of spirits in Sweden.
Elizabeth Garrett Anderson opens dispensary for women and children in Euston Road, London.
Dr. T. J. Barnardo opens home for waifs in Stepney.

P **Science, Technology, Discovery, etc.**

Gregor Mendel's papers (–1869) establish the laws of heredity.
Alfred Nobel invents dynamite.
French army is equipped with Chassepot rifle.

Q **Scholarship**

William Stubbs is appointed Professor at Oxford and founds the study of medieval English history.
Pierre Larousse, *Grand Dictionnaire Universel du XIX siècle* (–1876).
Charles Wilson begins to excavate environs of Jerusalem.

R **Philosophy and Religion**

Friedrich Lange, *History of Materialism* (neo-Kantian).
J. R. Seeley, *Ecce Homo.*
American Evangelical Alliance founded.

S **Art, Sculpture, Fine Arts and Architecture**

Claude Monet, *Camille* (painting).
Gustave Moreau, *Head of Orpheus* (sculpture).
Edgar Degas begins to paint scenes of ballet dancers.
Act to facilitate public exhibitions in Britain.
Joseph Poelaert, Palace of Justice, Brussels (–83).

T **Music**

Friedrich Smetana, *The Bartered Bride* (opera).
Ambrose Thomas, *Mignon* (opera).

U **Literature**

Charles Baudelaire, *Les Épaves.*
Alphonse Daudet, *Lettres de Mon Moulin.*
Fyodor Dostoievsky, *Crime and Punishment.*
Victor Hugo, *Les Travailleurs de la Mer.*
J. H. Newman, *Dream of Gerontius.*
A. C. Swinburne, *Poems and Ballads.*
P. Verlaine, *Poèmes saturniens.*
Walt Whitman, *Drum Taps.*

V **The Press**

W **Drama and Entertainment**

H. Ibsen, *Brand.*
Squire Bancroft and Henry Irving act on the London stage.

J **Sep**: 3rd, Bismarck obtains indemnity from Prussian Diet for having ruled unconstitutionally with regard to Budget;
20th, Prussia annexes Hanover, Hesse, Nassau and Frankfurt (as agreed at Prague *Aug.* 23rd).

K **Oct**: 3rd, war between Austria and Italy ended by treaty of Vienna;
21st (–22nd), plebiscites in Venezia result in support for union with Italy;
—, peace between Prussia and Saxony.

L **Nov**: after split in North German Liberal Party, Rudolf von Bennigsen forms a new National Liberal Party.

M **Dec**: 24th, Schleswig-Holstein is incorporated in Prussia.

N

x **Sport**

J. G. Chambers founds Amateur Athletic Club.
The Marquess of Queensberry codifies boxing rules.

Y **Statistics**

U.K. registered tonnage of merchant shipping, 5,779,000 (876,000 steamships).

Z **Births and Deaths**

Jan. 15th Massimo d'Azeglio d. (67).
Jan. 23rd Thomas Love Peacock d. (80).
Jan. 29th Romain Rolland b. (–1944).
Mar. 29th John Keble d. (73).
Apr. 3rd James Hertzog b. (–1942).
Sept. 21st H. G. Wells b. (–1946).
Oct. 12th James Ramsay MacDonald b. (–1937).
Nov. 8th Herbert, Lord Austin b. (–1941).
Dec. 14th Roger Fry b. (–1934).

1867 (Jan.–Nov.) Canada becomes a Dominion—Formation of North German Confederation—Garibaldi's march on Rome—Fenian outrages

A **Jan:**

B **Feb:** 13th, Fenian outrages occur in Kerry, and a separate attempt is made at Chester Castle;
17th, Hungarian Diet is opened, and subsequently the Constitution of 1848 is restored so that *Ausgleich* (Compromise) takes place allowing for Dual Monarchy, whereby Magyars dominate Hungary and German element dominates rest of Austrian territories, though to be single foreign and war policies.

C **Mar:** 1st, Nebraska becomes a U.S. state;
2nd, Basic Reconstruction Act in U.S. dividing southern states into five military districts; to re-enter Union these districts are to draw up constitutions passed by state conventions, and they must recognise 14th Amendment (of *June* 1866);
—, Tenure-of-Office Act passed in U.S., over President's veto, to restrict powers of the President to dismiss and appoint;
5th, abortive Fenian risings in Ireland;
12th, Napoleon III withdraws French support for Maximilian of Mexico;
29th, British North America Act establishes Dominion of Canada comprising Quebec, Ontario, Nova Scotia and New Brunswick;
30th, U.S. purchases Alaska from Russia;
Last French troops quit Mexico.

D **Apr:** 1st, end of rule of East India Company in Straits Settlements which now become Crown Colony;
16th, formation of North German Confederation with Prussia at head.

E **May:** 11th, London Conference guarantees neutrality of Luxembourg which Napoleon III was trying to buy from the King of the Netherlands (treaty signed *Sept.* 9th) and Prussia is to forgo her right to garrison the Luxembourg fortresses.

F **Jun:** 8th, Francis Joseph I of Austria is crowned King of Hungary at Budapest;
19th, Emperor Maximilian executed in Mexico.

G **Jul:** 23rd, Russia forms governor-generalship over Turkestan.

H **Aug:** 15th, Parliamentary Reform Act in Britain extends suffrage in boroughs to all householders paying rates and all lodgers paying £10 rent annually, in counties to landowners with land at value of £5 p.a. and tenants paying £12 rent annually; redistribution of seats takes place;
15th, British Factory Act, whereby terms of previous acts extended to cover other premises, manufactures or processes;
21st, Act of Parliament regulates hours and conditions of work for children, young persons and women in workshops;
First Socialist, Ferdinand Bebel, elected to North German Reichstag.

J **Sep:** 18th, Fenian outrage in Manchester when prison van attacked and policeman killed.

K **Oct:** 27th, G. Garibaldi begins march on Rome;
28th, French force lands at Civita Vecchia.

L **Nov:** 3rd, G. Garibaldi, defeated by French and Papal troops at Mentana, is sent as captive to Caprera;
5th, death of General O'Donnell in Spain.

O Politics, Economics, Law and Education

Walter Bagehot, *The English Constitution.*
Karl Marx, *Das Kapital*, vol. I.
W. T. Torrens secures passage of Artisans' Dwellings Act in Britain.
J. S. Mill and Mark Pattison urge reform of English education.

P Science, Technology, Discovery, etc.

William Thomson invents siphon recorder.
Pierre Michaux manufactures bicycles.
Gold is discovered in Wyoming.
Joseph Lister announces practice of antiseptic surgery using phenol (carbolic acid).

Q Scholarship

E. A. Freeman, *History of the Norman Conquest* (–76).
Von Sickel, *Acta Karolinorum.*

R Philosophy and Religion

Archbishop A. C. Tait holds first Pan Anglican Synod (*Sept.*).
Holders of civil office in U.K. no longer required to make declarations against transubstantiation.
Pius IX celebrates 18th centenary of death of SS. Peter and Paul and announces intention of holding a Council.

S Art, Sculpture, Fine Arts and Architecture

Paul Cézanne, *Rape* (painting).
É. Manet and G. Courbet hold one-man shows at Paris World Fair in defiance of the Salon.
The Paris World Fair introduces Japanese art to the West.

T Music

Georges Bizet, *Fair Maid of Perth* (opera).
G. Verdi, *Don Carlos* (opera).
J. Strauss, The 'Blue Danube' Waltz.

U Literature

Charles de Coster, *Légende d'Uylenspiegel.*
Adam Lindsey Gordon, *Sea Spray and Smoke Drift* introduces the first Australian poet.
O. W. Holmes, *The Guardian Angel.*
Ouida (pseud.), *Under Two Flags.*
Anthony Trollope, *Last Chronicle of Barset.*
Ivan Turgeniev, *Smoke.*
Émile Zola, *Thérèse Raquin.*

V The Press

W Drama and Entertainment

H. Ibsen, *Peer Gynt.*
Paris World Fair.

X Sport

Y Statistics

M Dec: 13th, Fenian outrage at Clerkenwell kills 12 people;
21st, new Austrian Constitution accepts Dual System with regard to Hungary.

N

z **Births and Deaths**

Jan. 17th Jean Dominique Ingres d. (87).
Mar. 25th Arturo Toscanini b. (–1957).
Apr. 10th G. W. Russell ('A.E.') b. (–1935).
Apr. 18th Robert Smirke d. (86).
May 26th Princess Mary of Teck (Queen Mary) b. (–1953).
May 27th Arnold Bennett b. (–1931).
June 28th Luigi Pirandello b. (–1936).
Aug. 3rd Philipp August Böckh d. (81), and Stanley, Earl Baldwin, b. (–1947).
Aug. 14th John Galsworthy b. (–1933).
Aug. 25th Michael Faraday d. (76).
Aug. 31st Charles Pierre Baudelaire d. (46).
Nov. 7th Marie Sklodowska (Marie Curie) b. (–1934).
— Sun Yat-Sen b. (–1925).
— Arturo Toscannini b. (–1957).

1868 Revolution in Spain—Britain annexes Basutoland

A **Jan:** 2nd, British expedition to Ethiopia, led by Sir Robert Napier, after ruler has imprisoned British consul;
3rd, Shogunate abolished in Japan and restoration of Meiji dynasty.

B **Feb:** 24th, President A. Johnson is impeached for violating the Tenure-of-Office Act of *Mar.* 1867;
25th, Lord Derby resigns through ill health and
28th, B. Disraeli replaces him as Prime Minister.

C **Mar:** 12th, Britain annexes Basutoland;
Prussia confiscates territory of King of Hanover.

D **Apr:** 13th, Robert Napier captures Magdala in Ethiopia.

E **May:** 11th, freedom of press granted in France;
12th, Samarkand is occupied by Russians;
16th, President A. Johnson is acquitted by Senate.

F **Jun:** 10th, Michael III, King of Serbia, is murdered; succeeded by Milan IV (–1889);
11th, limited right of public meeting allowed in France.

G **Jul:** 28th, 14th Amendment to U.S. Constitution, concerned with civil rights;
Third Maori War breaks out in New Zealand (–1870).

H **Aug:** 8th, France concludes commercial treaty with Madagascar.

J **Sep:** 17th, Liberal revolution against Queen Isabella II in Spain under Marshal Juan Prim and, 18th, Admiral Topete issues a Liberal manifesto in Cadiz;
30th, Queen Isabella of Spain flees to France, and is declared deposed.

K **Oct:**

L **Nov:** In U.S. presidential election U. S. Grant (Republican) has 214 electoral votes over Horatio Seymour (Democrat), with 80 votes.

M **Dec:** 2nd, following Liberal victory (387 seats) over Conservatives (272 seats) in British general election, B. Disraeli resigns without waiting for Parliament's re-assembly. W. E. Gladstone, who lost his seat in south-west Lancashire, forms a Liberal ministry with Lord Clarendon as Foreign Secretary and Robert Lowe as chancellor of Exchequer;
11th, Turkish ultimatum to Greeks to leave Crete (accepted *Feb.* 1869);
22nd, W. E. Gladstone is elected M.P. for Greenwich.

N

O Politics, Economics, Law and Education

Alexander Hamilton Stephens, *A Constitutional View of the War Between the States* (-70).
Hospital for epileptics founded near Bielefeld, Germany.
Austrian schools are freed from clerical control.

P Science, Technology, Discovery, etc.

Charles Darwin, *Variations of Animals and Plants under Domesticisation.*
Ernst Haeckel, *The History of Creation.*
George Westinghouse's brake.
P. D. Armour's meat-packing factory at Chicago opened.

Q Scholarship

Royal Historical Society and Cambridge Philological Society are founded.

R Philosophy and Religion

Abolition of compulsory church rates in England and Wales.

S Art, Sculpture, Fine Arts and Architecture

E. Degas, *L'Orchestre* (painting).
É. Manet, *Zola* (painting).
P. A. Renoir, *Lise* (painting).
Renoir and Manet begin to paint continually out of doors.
George Street, The Law Courts, London (-82).

T Music

J. Brahms, *A German Requiem*, op. 45 (additions made, 1872).
E. Grieg, Piano Concerto in A minor (op. 16).
R. Wagner, *The Mastersingers of Nuremberg* (opera).

U Literature

L. A. Alcott, *Little Women.*
G. Brandes, *Aesthetic Studies.*
R. Browning, *The Ring and the Book* (-69).
W. Collins, *The Moonstone.*
F. Dostoievsky, *The Idiot.*
W. Morris, *The Early Paradise.*

V The Press

Press Association, London, founded.
The Overland Monthly (San Francisco), with Bret Harte as editor.

W Drama and Entertainment

X Sport

The Cincinnati Red Stockings, first U.S. professional baseball club, founded.

Y Statistics

Z Births and Deaths

Mar. 14th Maxim Gorki b. (-1936).
Apr. 1st Edmond Rostand b. (-1918).
Apr. 12th J. L. Garvin b. (-1947).
Apr. 26th Harold Harmsworth, Lord Rothermere, b. (-1940).
May 7th Henry, Lord Brougham, d. (89).
June 6th Robert Falcon Scott b. (-1912).
July 12th Stefan George b. (-1933).
July 14th Gertrude Bell b. (-1926).
Aug. 29th Christian Friedrich Schönbein d. (68).
Nov. 13th Gioacchino Rossini d. (76).

1869 Red River rebellion in Canada—Suez Canal opened

A **Jan:**

B **Feb:** 6th, Greece agrees to leave Crete (after Turkish ultimatum of *Dec.* 1868).

C **Mar:** 4th, General U. S. Grant, Republican, is inaugurated President of U.S.

D **Apr:**

E **May:**

F **Jun:** 1st, new Spanish Constitution promulgated, providing for continuation of monarchical form of government.

G **Jul:** 12th, Parliamentary system adopted by Napoleon III, based on programme of Third Party;
26th, Disestablishment of Irish Church whereby Episcopal Church to end its existence from beginning of 1871.

H **Aug:**

J **Sep:** National Prohibition Party formed in Chicago to agitate for temperance.

K **Oct:** 11th, Red River Rebellion begins in Canada when half-breeds, led by Louis Riel, stop survey team near Winnipeg.

L **Nov:** 17th, opening of Suez Canal;
19th, Canadian Government purchases territories in north-west belonging to Hudson Bay Company.

M **Dec:**

N Tunis accepts control by Britain, Italy and France because of bankruptcy.

Y **Statistics**

Roman Catholics in Britain number 950,000, of whom 750,000 are Irish immigrants.

Z **Births and Deaths**

Feb. 28th Alphonse de Lamartine d. (79).
Mar. 9th Hector Berlioz d. (66).
Mar. 20th Neville Chamberlain b. (–1940).
Mar. 26th Edwin Lutyens b. (–1944).
Mar. 31st Henry J. Wood b. (–1944).
June 8th Frank Lloyd Wright b. (–1959).
Oct. 2nd Gandhi b. (–1948).
Oct. 13th Charles Augustin Sainte-Beuve d. (65).
Oct. 23rd Edward Stanley, Earl of Derby, d. (70).
Dec. 30th Stephen Leacock b. (–1944).
Dec. 31st Henri Matisse b. (–1954).
— André Gide b. (–).

O Politics, Economics, Law and Education

Walter Bagehot, *Physics and Politics.*
J. S. Mill, *The Subjection of Women.*
The State of Wyoming enfranchises women and gives them the right to hold office.
M. Bakunin founds the Social Democratic Alliance.
W. T. Thornton, *On Labour.*
Uriah Stephens founds Knights of Labor.
M. Arnold, *Culture and Anarchy.*
Girton College, Cambridge, founded.

P Science, Technology, Discovery, etc.

Dimitry Mendeleeff's periodic law for the classification of the elements.
Francis Galton, *Hereditary Genius, its Laws and Consequences*, founds the science of eugenics.
H. Mège-Mouries invents margarine.
Hyatt invents celluloid.
Alizarin, synthetic dye, is prepared.
'Cup and cone' ball-bearings are invented.
The first electric washing-machine.
Gustave Nachtigal explores the Sahara and the Sudan.

Q Scholarship

W. E. H. Lecky, *A History of European Morals from Augustus to Charlemagne.*
Karl Lehr's edition of *Horace's Odes.*

R Philosophy and Religion

Eduard Hardtmann, *The Philosophy of the Unconscious.*
James Knowles founds the Philosophical Society, London.
The Vatican Council meets (*Dec.*) and H. E. Manning advocates a definition of papal infallibility.
I. Döllinger, J. N. Huber and J. Friedrich, in the *Letters of Janus*, oppose the doctrine and the tendencies of the Syllabus of Errors.
The Church of England revives suffragan bishops.
The Irish Church is disestablished.

S Art, Sculpture, Fine Arts and Architecture

Claude Monet, *The Balcony* (painting).
Joseph Boehm, marble statue of Queen Victoria at Windsor Castle.

T Music

J. Brahms, *Hungarian Dances* Nos. 1 and 2 (as piano duets).
R. Wagner, *The Rhinegold* (opera).

U Literature

R. D. Blackmore, *Lorna Doone.*
G. Flaubert, *L'Éducation sentimentale.*
Bret Harte, *The Outcasts of Poker Flat.*
V. Hugo, *L'Homme qui rit.*
M. Twain, *The Innocents Abroad.*
P. Verlaine, *Fêtes galantes.*
Jules Verne, *Twenty Thousand Leagues Under the Sea.*

V The Press

W Drama and Entertainment

W. Halévy, *Frou-frou.*

X Sport

(*Continued opposite*)

1870 (Jan.–Sep.) Franco-Prussian War begins—Napoleon III capitulates at Sedan

A **Jan**: 2nd, Olivier Ollivier becomes French premier;
Baden decides to seek entry to North German Confederation.

B **Feb**:

C **Mar**: 1st, end of war between Paraguay and combined forces of Brazil, Argentina and Uruguay;
30th, 15th Amendment in U.S. ratified, whereby suffrage not to be revoked, particularly Negro suffrage.

D **Apr**: 20th, Senate in France made an Upper House, sharing legislative powers with Assembly.

E **May**: 12th, Manitoba made Canadian province, which helps to end Red River Rebellion;
Fenian attack from Vermont, U.S., on Quebec, Canada, fails.

F **Jun**: 4th, Order-in-Council reforms British Civil Service so that most departments, apart from Foreign Office, open to competitive examination;
20th, British War Office Act subordinates Commander-in-Chief to Secretary of State;
25th, Isabella of Spain abdicates in Paris in favour of Alfonso XII;
28th, decree in Russia for reform of municipal government.

G **Jul**: 2nd, news reaches France of acceptance of Spanish throne by Leopold, Prince of Hohenzollern;
12th, Leopold's acceptance is withdrawn by his father;
13th, French ultimatum to Prussia not to renew Spanish candidature results in 'Ems Telegram';
19th, France declares war on Prussia;
30th, Austria revokes Concordat with Papacy (of 1855) after decree of Papal Infallibility (18th).

H **Aug**: 1st, Irish Land Act provides for loans to peasants to buy land and for compensation for eviction and for improvements;
4th, French, led by Marie MacMahon, are defeated at Weissenberg by Crown Prince Frederick;
6th, further French defeats at Worth and Spicheren;
9th, Married Women's Property Act in Britain gives wives greater power over own property;
—, Prussia guarantees Belgian neutrality in war with France and, 11th, Britain and France also guarantee this;
16th, Prussian forces victorious at Vionville and Mars-la-Tour;
18th, French defeated at Gravelotte and St. Privat;
Western Australia granted representative government.

J **Sep**: 1st, French defeated at battle of Sedan, France;
2nd, Napoleon III capitulates at Sedan;
4th, defeat leads to revolt in Paris, provisional government of national defence is set up and a Republic proclaimed;
19th, Siege of Paris by Prussian forces begins;
20th, Italians enter Rome.

O **Politics, Economics, Law and Education**

W. E. Forster's education act establishes board schools.
Benjamin Jowett becomes Master of Balliol.
Keble College, Oxford, founded.
University Extension Lectures at Cambridge.
Royal Commission on Science under Duke of Devonshire.

P **Science, Technology, Discovery, etc.**

T. H. Huxley's address to British Association on spontaneous generation.
Z. T. Gramme invents dynamo with ring armature.
Walter Weldon's process for making bleaching powder increases output fourfold.
Adolf Nordenskjöld explores interior of Greenland.
J. D. Rockefeller founds Standard Oil Company.
Adolf von Bayer synthesises the dye indigo.

Q **Scholarship**

Heinrich Schliemann begins to excavate Troy.
Dictionary of American Biography begun.

R **Philosophy and Religion**

Vatican Council declares (*July* 18th) dogma of papal infallibility in matters of faith and morals by 533 votes to 2.
Convocation of Church of England appoints committees (*May*) to revise the Old and New Testaments, which lead to the 'Revised Version'.
J. H. Newman, *Grammar of Assent.*
I. D. Sankey joins D. L. Moody in Chicago mission.

S **Art, Sculpture, Fine Arts and Architecture**

Jean Corot, *Femme à la Perle* (painting).
H. Fantin-Latour, *Hommage à Manet* (painting).

T **Music**

Clément Delibes, *Coppélia* (ballet).
R. Wagner, *Die Walküre* (opera).
R. Wagner's *Essay on Beethoven* studies the metaphysics of music in terms of A. Schopenhauer's philosophy.

U **Literature**

C. Dickens, *Mystery of Edwin Drood* (unfinished).
B. Disraeli, *Lothair.*
F. Dostoievsky, *The House of the Dead.*
Ivan Goncharov, *The Precipice.*
D. G. Rossetti, *Poems.*

V **The Press**

W **Drama and Entertainment**

X **Sport**

W. G. Grace and his brothers found Gloucestershire Cricket Club.

Y **Statistics**

Coal production (in mill. tons): U.K. 110·4; U.S. 35; Germany, 29·4; Austria, 13; France, 12.
Iron production (in mill. tons): U.K. 5·9; U.S. 1·6; Germany, 1·3; France, 1·2; Russia, 0·4.

K Oct: 2nd, Rome made capital of Italy by Decree of 9th, and King of Italy formally incorporates Rome and Roman provinces in Italy;
27th, French troops surrender Metz, France;
28th, Strasbourg surrenders to Prussian forces.

L Nov: 16th, Amadeus, Duke of Aosta, elected King of Spain;
23rd, alliance treaty between North German Confederation and Bavaria (following similar North German treaty with Württemberg, *Nov.* 15th).

M Dec: 30th, Marshal Prim dies in Spain, after being wounded by assassin;
German Centre Party (Catholic) is established.

N Diamonds discovered in Orange Free State.

Y **Statistics** (*cont.*)

World Steel production: 560,000 tons (half by U.K.).
Railway mileage: U.K., 15,310.
Emigration to U.S. (1861–70): from Britain, 606,896; from Ireland, 435,779.
436,000 tons of shipping use Suez Canal, 71 per cent British.
Defence Estimates in £ mill.: Great Britain, 23·4; France, 22; Russia 22; Germany, 10·8; Austria-Hungary, 8·2; Italy, 7·8.

Births and Deaths

Feb. 12th 'Marie Lloyd' (pseud. of Matilda Wood) b. (–1922).
Mar. 4th Thomas Sturge Moore b. (–1944).
Mar. 13th Charles, Count de Montalembert d. (60).
Apr. 9th Nikolai Lenin b. (–1924).
May 6th James Young Simpson d. (59).
May 24th J. C. Smuts b. (–1950).
June 9th Charles Dickens d. (58).
Aug. 4th Harry Lauder b. (–1950).
Sept. 23rd Prosper Mérimée d. (66).
Oct. 27th Roscoe Pound b. (–1965).
Nov. 6th Herbert, Viscount Samuel b. (–1963).
Dec. 5th Alexandre Dumas (père) d. (67).

1871 German Empire is incorporated—Rising of Commune in Paris

A **Jan:** 18th, William I of Prussia proclaimed German Emperor at Versailles;
19th, French defeated at St. Quentin;
28th, Paris capitulates and armistice with Germany is signed.

B **Feb:** 1st, French Eastern Army crosses Swiss frontier and is disarmed;
13th, French National Assembly meets at Bordeaux;
17th, L. A. Thiers becomes head of French executive;
26th, preliminary peace of Versailles between France and Germany.

C **Mar:** 13th, London Conference between great powers repudiates Black Sea clauses of 1856 (after Russian repudiation of clauses, *Oct.* 1870);
18th, rising of Commune begins in Paris;
26th, Commune is formally set up.

D **Apr:** 16th, German Empire receives Constitution remodelled from that of North German Confederation.

E **May:** 8th, Treaty of Washington settles existing difficulties between Britain and U.S., over the north-west boundary, the fisheries and the *Alabama* claims;
10th, Franco-German Peace of Frankfurt by which France cedes Alsace-Lorraine, pays indemnity of 5 milliards of francs, and is to be subjected to army of occupation until payment completed;
13th, Law of Guarantees in Italy declares the Pope's person inviolable and allows him the possession of the Vatican;
21st (–28th), 'Bloody Week' in Paris ends with defeat of the Commune.

F **Jun:** 16th, University Test Acts allow students to enter Oxford and Cambridge without religious tests;
29th, British Act of Parliament for legalising trade unions.

G **Jul:** 20th, British Columbia joins Dominion of Canada (after Imperial Order-in-Council of *May*);
31st, discovery that William Tweed's Ring in New York has systematically defrauded City treasury;
Germany begins *Kulturkampf* (cultural struggle) with Catholic Church, when Otto von Bismarck suppresses the Roman Catholic Department for spiritual affairs.

H **Aug:** 14th, Local government boards created in England;
17th, Edward Cardwell's Army reforms reorganise British army and the introduction of short service provides for trained reserve forces;
31st, L. A. Thiers elected French President;
Basutoland is united with Cape Colony.

J **Sep:**

K **Oct:** 27th, Britain annexes diamond fields of Kimberley, Griqualand West.

L **Nov:**

M **Dec:**

N

O Politics, Economics, Law and Education

W. S. Jevons, *Theory of Political Economy.*
John Ruskin, *Fors Claveriga.*
Germany adopts gold standard (*Dec.* 4th).
Purchase of commissions in British Army abolished.
Adolph Wagner, *The Social Question.*
Anne Clough provides house of residence for first women students at Cambridge which becomes (1880) Newnham College.

P Science, Technology, Discovery, etc.

Charles Darwin, *The Descent of Man.*
Discovery of the element gallium.
Chair of experimental physics is founded at Cambridge University.
Mt. Cenis tunnel opened (*Sept.* 17th).
H. M. Stanley meets D. Livingstone at Ujiji (*Nov.* 10th).

Q Scholarship

T. Mommsen, *Roman Constitutional Law* (–88).

R Philosophy and Religion

Ignaz Döllinger is excommunicated by Archbishop of Munich for refusing to accept Vatican decrees.
First Congress of Old Catholics meets at Munich.
Repeal of Ecclesiastical Titles Act of 1851 against 'papal aggression'.
Jehovah's Witnesses founded.

S Art, Sculpture, Fine Arts and Architecture

James Whistler, *The Artist's Mother* (painting).

T Music

Anton Bruckner, 2nd Symphony.
G. Verdi *Aïda* (opera).
Camille Saint-Saëns, symphonic poem *Le Rouet D'Omphale* (op. 35).

U Literature

L. Carroll (pseud.), *Through the Looking-Glass.*
George Eliot (pseud.), *Middlemarch* (–72).
Walt Whitman, *Democratic Vistas.*
É. Zola, *Les Rougon-Macquart* series of novels (–93).

V The Press

W Drama and Entertainment

Bank holidays introduced in England and Wales.
P. T. Barnum and J. A. Bailey open their circus at Brooklyn as the 'greatest show on earth'.

X Sport

F.A. Cup established.

Y Statistics

Populations (in millions): Germany, 41; U.S., 39; France, 36·1; Japan, 33; Great Britain, 26, and Ireland, 5·4; Italy, 26·8.

Y **Statistics** (*cont.*)

Coal production (in mill. tons): Great Britain, 117·4; U.S., 35; Germany, 29·4; France, 13·3; Austria, 12·5.

Iron production (in mill. tons): Great Britain, 6·6; France, 2·5; Germany, 1·4.

Z **Births and Deaths**

Jan. 17th David, Earl Beatty, b. (–1936).
Feb. 4th Friedrich Ebert b. (–1925).
May 11th John Herschel d. (79).
May 14th Daniel Auber d. (89).
June 18th George Grote d. (76).
July 10th Marcel Proust b. (–1922).
Aug. 27th Theodore Dreiser b. (–1945).
Aug. 30th Ernest Rutherford b. (–1937).
Sept. 6th Montagu Norman b. (–1950).
Oct. 2nd Cordell Hull b. (–1955).
Nov. 1st Stephen Crane b. (–1900).
— Paul Valéry b. (–1945).

A **Jan:** 6th, assassination of Fisk, the 'Erie Ring' speculator, in New York, draws attention to corruption under the Grant régime;
25th, Henri Comte de Chambord's Antwerp Declaration, countering the suggestions of 'a Revolution Monarchy'.

B **Feb:** 2nd, Holland sells trading posts on the Gold Coast to Britain;
8th, murder of Earl of Mayo, Viceroy of India;

C **Mar:** 19th, Charles Dilke, declaring himself a Republican, moves for an inquiry into Queen Victoria's expenditure.

D **Apr:** 26th, proclamation of Don Carlos as Charles VII of Spain leads to civil war.

E **May:** 4th, defeat of Carlist forces and Don Carlos escapes to France;
Liberal Republicans at the Cincinnati Convention decide to run Horace Greeley, editor of the *New York Tribune*, as presidential candidate against U. S. Grant.

F **Jun:** 25th, the Jesuits are expelled from Germany.

G **Jul:** 1st, T. F. Burgers is elected President of Transvaal Republic;
18th, Ballot Act in Britain introduces voting by secret ballot;
28th, France adopts conscription.

H **Aug:**

J **Sep:** 7th, meeting of the three emperors in Berlin leads to an *entente* between Germany, Russia and Austria-Hungary;
14th, Geneva court of arbitration finds Britain legally responsible for depredations of the *Alabama* and other Confederate cruisers, awarding U.S. $15,500,000 damages.

K **Oct:** 21st, German emperor, called on to adjudicate between Britain and U.S. over disputed ownership of St. Juan, decides in favour of U.S.;
Responsible government in Cape Colony, with J. C. Molteno first premier;
George Berkeley, governor of Cape Colony, annexes Griqualand West.

L **Nov:** 5th, Anglo-French commercial treaty, modifies the treaty of 1860;
5th, re-election of Ulysses Grant, the Republican candidate (286 electoral votes) as President, over Horace Greeley (62 votes), who dies, 29th;
22nd, Comte de Paris accepts compensation for confiscation of his estates.

M **Dec:** 9th, Otto von Bismarck's County Organisation bill, for remodelling local government in Prussia at expense of nobles' powers, passes Upper House after special creation of 25 peers.

N Compulsory military service in Japan.
First rebellion against Spain in Philippines.

O Politics, Economics, Law and Education

M. Bakunin is expelled from the International at the Hague Conference.
National Agricultural Labourers' Union founded in Britain by Joseph Arch.
German Criminal Code in force.
Strasbourg University founded.

P Science, Technology, Discovery, etc.

Albert Billroth makes first resection of the oesophagus.
Thomas Edison perfects the 'duplex' telegraph.
William Thomson's sounding-machine (the 'Kelvin') for determining depth at sea.
The Challenger undertakes world oceanographic survey (–76).
New York-Brooklyn bridge opened (*July*).
Electric filament lighting installed in St. Petersburg docks.

Q Scholarship

T. Mommsen edits *Corpus Juris Civilis.*
G. Brandes, *Main Streams of XIXth Century Literature* (–75).

R Philosophy and Religion

D. F. Strauss, *The Old Faith and the New.*
Père Hyacinthe attempts to found national church in France.
General Assembly of French Protestants holds first meeting since 1659.

S Art, Sculpture, Fine Arts and Architecture

A. Böcklin, *Battle of the Centaurs* (painting).
E. Degas, *Le Foyer de la Danse* (painting).
P. Cézanne and C. Pissarro paint at Pontoise.

T Music

G. Bizet's incidental music to Alphonse Daudet's *L'Arlésienne.*
C. Franck, *Les Béatitudes* (oratorio).
Alexandre Lecocq, *Madame Angot's Daughter* (opera).

U Literature

Samuel Butler, *Erewhon, or Over the Range.*
Charles Stuart Calverley, *Fly Leaves.*
Alphonse Daudet, *Aventures Prodigieuses de Tartarin de Tarascon.*
Thomas Hardy, *Under the Greenwood Tree.*
Ivan Turgeniev, *A Month in the Country.*
Jules Verne, *Around the World in 80 Days*, appears in *Le Temps.*

V The Press

C. P. Scott edits *Manchester Guardian* (–1929).

W Drama and Entertainment

Eleanora Duse's début.
Royal Albert Hall, London, opened.
Alexandre Ostrovsky, *The Snow Maiden.*

X Sport

1st International Association football match, England *v.* Scotland (*Nov.* 30th).

Y **Statistics**

British Textiles trade:

imported raw cotton	1,181 mill. lb.
cottons exported	3,538 mill. yds.
woollens exported	412,541,000 yds.
linens exported	245,019,000 yds.
silks exported	4,417,000 yds.

Z **Births and Deaths**

Jan. 10th Alexander Scriabin b. (–1915).
Jan. 21st Franz Grillparzer d. (81).
Mar. 10th Giuseppe Mazzini d. (66).
Mar. 19th Serge Diaghilev b. (–1929).
Apr. 9th Léon Blum b. (–1950).
May 18th Bertrand Russell b. (–1970).
May 31st Heath Robinson b. (–1944).
July 1st Louis Blériot b. (–1936).
July 4th Calvin Coolidge b. (–1933).
July 12th F. E. Smith, Lord Birkenhead b. (–1930).
July 16th Roald Amundsen b. (–1928).
Aug. 24th Max Beerbohm b. (–1956).
Oct. 4th Roger Keyes b. (–1945).
Dec. 23rd Théophile Gautier d. (61).

A Jan: 9th, Napoleon III dies at Chislehurst, England (aged 64) leaving an only son aged 17.

B Feb: 11th, abdication of Amadeo I of Spain;
16th, Republic proclaimed in Spain.

C Mar: 13th, W. E. Gladstone resigns following defeat of Irish University bill in which forty-three Liberals vote against government, but as B. Disraeli refuses to take office with a minority administration Gladstone returns;
Judicature Act reforms system of central courts in England by establishing a Supreme Court of Judicature with its separate divisions, and a Court of Appeal.

D Apr: 2nd, reform of Austrian franchise in favour of Germans;
23rd, massive monarchist demonstrations in Madrid;
Ashanti War breaks out;
Dutch War against Sultan of Achin in north-west Sumatra.

E May: 6th, military convention between Germany and Russia;
11th (–14th), Paul Falk, Prussian minister of public worship, introduces the May Laws, subjecting the clergy to State control;
24th, L. A. Thiers falls and M. MacMahon is elected French president;
Financial crisis begins in Vienna, spreading to other European capitals and leading to withdrawal of foreign investments from U.S.A.

F Jun: 5th, abolition of slave markets and export of slaves by Sultan of Zanzibar, under pressure from Sir John Kirk.

G Jul: 1st, Prince Edward Island joins the Dominion of Canada;
Dissolution of monasteries in Italy.

H Aug: 5th, reconciliation of Comte de Chambord and Comte de Paris;
12th, Russia assumes suzerainty of Khiva and Bokhara;
W. E. Gladstone reforms his ministry, himself becoming chancellor of Exchequer.

J Sep: 8th, during Carlist risings Emilio Castelar is made ruler of Spain to restore order under a centralised republic;
15th, Germans evacuate France;
Marco Minghetti forms ministry in Italy following break-up of Giovanni Lanza's government;
Financial panic in U.S. caused by speculation, over-production and withdrawal of foreign capital.

K Oct: 17th, Comte de Chambord's Frohsdorf letter of uncompromising Legitimism;
20th, Ecuador becomes a theocracy (–75).
22nd, alliance of the emperors of Germany, Russia and Austria-Hungary;
27th, Comte de Chambord ends hope of restoration of French monarchy by refusing to accept tricolour.

L Nov: 20th, French monarchists confer M. MacMahon with presidential powers for seven years;
Croats are granted internal self-government;
Rival cities of Buda and Pesth are statutorily united to form capital of Hungary.

M Dec: Papal nuncio is expelled from Switzerland.

N The Flemish language is admitted in courts of Flanders.
Abolition of the Office of Statholder (or King of Sweden's lieutenant) in Norway.
Andrew Clarke, governor of Straits Settlements, places British residents in the several Malay states.
Famine in Bengal.

O Politics, Economics, Law and Education

H. Taine, *Les Origines de la France contemporaine.*
H. Spencer, *The Study of Sociology.*
National Federation of Employers founded in Britain.
Economic crises in Europe, U.S. and Australia.
Germany adopts the Mark coinage and U.S. adopts the gold standard.

P Science, Technology, Discovery, etc.

W. K. Clifford, *Preliminary Sketch of Bi-quaternions.*
Jean Charcot, *Le cours sur les maladies du système nerveux.*
J. Clerk-Maxwell, *A Treatise on Electricity and Magnetism.*
W. Thomson reforms the mariner's compass.
G. Drayton's oil engine.
First oil well sunk in Baku.
Philo Remington's company produce typewriter designed by C. L. Scholes.
Julius Payer and Karl Weyprecht discover Franz Joseph Land (*Aug.* 13th).
Introduction of colour sensitising makes possible colour photography.

Q Scholarship

Walter Pater, *Studies in the History of the Renaissance.*

R Philosophy and Religion

Christoph Sigwart, *Logic.*
D. L. Moody and I. Sankey begin revivalist meetings in England (–75).

S Art, Sculpture, Fine Arts and Architecture

Paul Cézanne, *Straw Hat* (painting).
Jean Corot, *Souvenir d'Italie* (painting).
É. Manet, *Le Bon Bock* (painting).

T Music

N. Rimsky-Korsakov, *Ivan the Terrible* (opera).

U Literature

Paul Heyse, *Kinder der Welt.*
J. S. Mill, *Autobiography.*
Arthur Rimbaud, *Une Saison en Enfer.*
Leo Tolstoy, *Anna Karenina* (–75).

V The Press

W Drama and Entertainment

X Sport

Y Statistics

U.S. Petroleum production: 9,894,000 barrels.
Crime: 14,893 convictions for offences in England and Wales (of which 123 for murder and 943 for manslaughter); 2,721 convictions in Scotland.

Z Births and Deaths

Jan. 15th Edward Bulwer-Lytton, Lord Lytton, d. (69).
Feb. 1st Clara Butt b. (–1936), and Fedor Chaliapin b. (–1938).
Feb. 10th Justus von Liebig d. (69).
Feb. 28th John Simon b. (–1954).
Mar. 26th Gerald du Maurier b. (–1934).
Apr. 1st Sergei Rachmaninoff b. (–1943).
May 8th John Stuart Mill d. (67).
Dec. 17th Ford Madox Hueffer (F. M. Ford) b. (–1939).

1874 (Jan.–Oct.) *Kulturkampf* in Germany—Conservatives win British General Election

A **Jan**: 2nd, Emilio Castelar retires in Spain and
3rd, Marshal Francisco Serrano becomes dictator;
13th, conscription is introduced in Russia;
23rd, Prince Alfred, Duke of Edinburgh, marries Princess Marie Alexandrovna in St. Petersburg;
In Reichstag elections the Ultramontane Catholic Centre increases its seats through hatred of the May Laws.

B **Feb**: 2nd, in British general election W. E. Gladstone holds out the promise of abolition of income tax; election riots at Dudley, Hanley and Wolverhampton, Staffs.;
4th, Garnet Wolseley burns Kumasi, ending Ashanti War and, 13th, by treaty of Fommenah King Koffee of Ashanti promises free trade, an open road to Kumasi and undertakes to pay indemnity to Britain and stop human sacrifices;
17th, British general election results in Conservative majority of 83 (the first clear Conservative majority since 1841), W. E. Gladstone resigns and
18th, B. Disraeli forms ministry, with Stafford Northcote chancellor of Exchequer, 15th Earl of Derby as foreign secretary and Richard Cross as home secretary;
Strike of agricultural workers in eastern England (–*Aug.* 10th).

C **Mar**: 15th, France assumes protectorate over Annam, which breaks off its vassalage to China.

D **Apr**:

E **May**: 20th, end of civil disturbances in Arkansas caused by disputed election of governorship;
23rd, G. O. Trevelyan's bill for extension of household suffrage to the counties is defeated;
25th, Marco Minghetti resigns in Italy, following the defeat of Quintino Sella's financial proposals, but the King refuses to accept his resignation;
Further May Laws in Germany against Ultramontane clergy (which provoke Pius IX's bull *Quod Nunquam* annulling them, in *Mar.* 1875);
At the Gotha Conference German Marxians and Lassalleans unite to form Socialist Working-Men's Party;
The Swiss Constitution is revised to centralise authority and the federal court receives more power.

F **Jun**: Federal forces reinstate U. P. Kellogg, Republican governor of Louisiana, after S. D. McEnery, Democrat, claimed to be installed as rival governor.

G **Jul**: Denmark grants Iceland self-government with a representative Althing.

H **Aug**: Bolivia-Chile boundary is fixed as parallel 24°S.

J **Sep**: 15th, Prince of Wales visits France.

K **Oct**: 4th, Count Arnim, lately German ambassador in Paris, is arrested in Germany, on charge of embezzling State papers, but in reality because of his attacks on the French Republic, and subsequently a Conservative plot is uncovered in Germany for replacing Bismarck by Arnim;
25th, Britain annexes the Fiji Islands.

o Politics, Economics, Law and Education

Union Générale des Postes established at Berne.

Building Societies Act in Britain protects small investors and encourages home ownership.

E. T. Gerry founds Society for the Prevention of Cruelty to Children in New York.

Civil marriage made compulsory in Germany.

Arthur Orton, the Tichborne Claimant, found guilty of perjury (*Feb.* 28th).

Yorkshire College (later Leeds University) founded.

p Science, Technology, Discovery, etc.

Ernst Haeckel, *Anthropogenia.*

W. S. Jevons constructs an 'abecedarium' (or logical machine).

Solomon introduces pressure-cooking method for canning foods.

q Scholarship

J. R. Green, *Short History of the English People.*

W. Stubbs, *Constitutional History of England* (–78).

Augustus Pitt-Rivers exhibits his collections relating to primitive peoples at Bethnal Green Museum (he presents them to Oxford University in 1883).

r Philosophy and Religion

Henry Sidgwick, *Methods of Ethics.*

Wilhelm Wundt, *Physiological Psychology.*

Disraeli's Public Worship Regulation Act aims at curbing ritualistic practices.

W. E. Gladstone attacks papal infallibility in his pamphlet, *The Vatican Decrees.*

The Old Catholics permit the use of the vernacular and the marriage of priests.

s Art, Sculpture, Fine Arts and Architecture

First Impressionist Exhibition, Paris, includes works by P. Cézanne, E. Degas, C. Pissarro and A. Sisley.

C. Monet's painting, *Impression: Sunrise* gives rise to the derisive title 'Impressionism'.

A. Renoir, *La Loge* (painting).

t Music

M. P. Moussorgsky, *Boris Godunov* (opera), and *Pictures from an Exhibition.*

J. Strauss, *Die Fledermaus* (opera).

R. Wagner completes *Götterdämmerung.*

G. Verdi, *Requiem.*

F. Smetana, symphonic poem *My Fatherland.*

u Literature

P. Alarcón, *The Three-cornered Hat.*

G. Flaubert, *La Tentation de Saint Antoine.*

A. Fogazzaro, *Miranda.*

T. Hardy, *Far from the Madding Crowd.*

V. Hugo, *Ninety-Three.*

P. Verlaine, *Romances sans Paroles.*

v The Press

w Drama and Entertainment

x Sport

Wingfield invents lawn tennis ('Sphairistike').

L Nov: 2nd (–3rd), Democrats make sweeping gains in U.S. state elections;
24th, Alfonso, son of Queen Isabella, comes of age and declares for a constitutional monarchy in Spain.

M Dec: 29th (–31st), Spanish generals rally to Alfonso who is proclaimed King as Alfonso XII (–85).

N Financial collapse of Turkey through heavy borrowing abroad.
Canada adopts voting by ballot on a single day.

Y **Statistics**

Z **Births and Deaths**

Jan. 25th W. Somerset Maugham b. (–1965).
Feb. 3rd Gertrude Stein b. (–1946).
Feb. 9th Jules Michelet d. (75).
Feb. 15th Ernest Shackleton b. (–1922).
Mar. 26th Robert Frost b. (–1964).
Apr. 25th Guglielmo Marconi b. (–1937).
May 29th Gilbert Keith Chesterton b. (–1936).
Aug. 10th Herbert Hoover b. (–1964).
Sept. 12th François Guizot d. (86).
Sept. 13th Arnold Schönberg b. (–1951).
Sept. 21st Gustav Holst b. (–1934).
Oct. 25th Geoffrey Dawson b. (–1944).
Nov. 27th Chaim Weizmann b. (–1953).
Nov. 30th Winston Churchill b. (–1965).
Dec. 17th William Mackenzie King b. (–1950).

1875 Revised Constitution in France—Britain buys Suez Canal Shares —Risings in Bosnia and Herzegovina

A **Jan**: 9th, Alfonso XII lands at Barcelona, but Carlist War continues;
12th, Kwang-su becomes Emperor of China (-1908);
13th, W. E. Gladstone resigns Liberal leadership in House of Commons;
30th, Republican Constitution in France, with Wallon amendment, is passed by one vote.

B **Feb**: 3rd, Marquess of Hartington is elected Liberal leader as Gladstone's successor;
24th (-25th), enactment of laws on the organisation of the Public Powers and of the Senate of France;
In the face of deteriorating relations with France Otto von Bismarck endeavours to preserve Germany's *entente* with Russia.

C **Mar**: Kálmár Tisza, leader of the Left, forms ministry in Hungary on break-up of Deak party.

D **Apr**: 8th, article 'Is War Safe?' in *Berlin Post* starts war scare;
Louis Decazes, French foreign minister, appeals to Britain and Russia for support against Bismarck, and war is averted;
14th, reforms of Japanese courts of law;
House of Commons decides to exclude strangers by majority vote of the House alone.

E **May**: 10th, Tsar Alexander and his foreign minister, Prince Gorchakov, visit Berlin;
Religious orders abolished in Prussia.

F **Jun**:

G **Jul**: 16th, law on the relation of the Public Powers completes the French Constitution of 1875;
Risings in Bosnia and Herzegovina against Turkish rule.

H **Aug**: Prince of Wales visits India;
Public Health Act in Britain;
Lord Carnarvon holds informal conversations in London on South African federation.

J **Sep**: 29th, B. Disraeli overrules Admiralty ruling requiring the restitution of fugitive slaves within territorial waters;
Rebellion in Cuba leads to deterioration of U.S.-Spanish relations.

K **Oct**: 12th, in New Zealand provincial governments are abolished and the government centralised, through efforts of Julius Vogel.

L **Nov**: 25th, Britain buys 176,602 shares in Suez Canal from the Khedive of Egypt.

M **Dec**: 12th, the Sultan of Turkey promises reforms throughout the Ottoman Empire to meet the rebels' demands;
Julius Andrássy, on behalf of the Eastern powers, calls for religious freedom in Bosnia and Herzegovina, which Disraeli accepts as the basis for reform;
Stanley Cave is sent to Egypt to inquire into its finances.

O Politics, Economics, Law and Education

Labourers' Dwellings Act.
Agricultural Holdings Act, allowing compensation for unexhausted improvements.
Food and Drugs Act.
S. Plimsoll's Merchant Shipping Act in Britain.
Reichsbank founded in Germany.
London Medical School for Women founded.

P Science, Technology, Discovery, etc.

Caton begins experiments on electrical responses of brain.
H. M. Stanley traces the Congo to the Atlantic.
London's main-drainage system completed.

Q Scholarship

F. Max Müller edits *The Sacred Books of the East* (51 vols. –1903).
Dictionary of German Biography is begun.

R Philosophy and Religion

Émile Laveleye, *L'Avenir des Peuples Catholiques.*
Helena Blavatsky founds Theosophical Society in New York.
Mary Baker Eddy, *Science and Health.*

S Art, Sculpture, Fine Arts and Architecture

Adolf Menzel, *The Forge* (painting).
Claude Monet, *Boating at Argenteuil* (painting).
The *Hermes* of Praxiteles is found at Olympia.

T Music

P. I. Tchaikovsky, 1st Piano Concerto in B flat minor (op. 23).
G. Bizet, *Carmen* (opera).
Karl Goldmark, *Queen of Sheba* (opera).
Trial by Jury begins W. S. Gilbert and A. Sullivan partnership.

U Literature

M. Twain (pseud.), *The Adventures of Tom Sawyer.*

V The Press

W Drama and Entertainment

Gabrielle Réjane's début in Paris.

X Sport

Matthew Webb is the first man to swim the English Channel.

Y Statistics

Production of pig iron (in thousand tons): Great Britain, 6,365; Germany, 2,029; France, 1,416.
Production of steel (in thousand tons): Great Britain, 536; Germany, 370; France, 258.
Strength of armies: Russia, 3,360,000; Germany, 2,800,000; France, 412,000; Great Britain, 113,649.
U.K. State expenditure: £73 mill.

1875

N President MacMahon arbitrates in the Delagoa Bay dispute, recognising Portuguese claims against Britain.
Treaty of friendship between Japan and Korea, after various incidents.

z **Births and Deaths**

Jan. 14th Albert Schweitzer b. (–1965).
Jan. 20th J. F. Millet d. (60).
Jan. 23rd Charles Kingsley d. (55).
Feb. 22nd Jean-Baptiste Camille Corot d. (78).
Mar. 7th Maurice Ravel b. (–1937).
June 3rd Georges Bizet d. (36).
Aug. 4th Hans Christian Andersen d. (70).
Aug. 13th Samuel Coleridge-Taylor b. (–1912),
Aug. 26th John Buchan, Lord Tweedsmuir, b. (–1940).
Dec. 4th Rainer Maria Rilke b. (–1926).
— M. I. Kalinin b. (–1946).

A **Jan:** 31st, Sultan Abdul Aziz agrees to adopt reform programme of Andrássy Note (of *Dec.* 1875) in Ottoman Empire, but this is rejected by the insurgents;
Cortes adopt new Constitution in Spain providing for two-chamber legislature, elected on limited suffrage.

B **Feb:** 26th, China declares Korea to be an independent state;
28th, end of Carlist War with flight of Don Carlos.

C **Mar:** 5th (–7th), Egyptians defeated at Gura by Ethiopians;
8th, rule of National Assembly in France ends with summoning of a new Senate (Conservative) and a Chamber (overwhelmingly Republican);
9th (–16th), Turkish troops massacre Bulgarians;
28th, Agostino Depretis forms ministry of the Left in Italy, following Marco Minghetti's fall;
Stephen Cave's report on Egyptian finances published.

D **Apr:**

E **May:** 10th, the Liberal Midhat Pasha forms ministry in Constantinople;
13th, Berlin Memorandum of Germany, Russia and Austria to Turkey, calling for an armistice, the re-establishment of the insurgents and the supervision of Turkish reforms by the powers, but Britain refuses to approve;
30th, deposition of Sultan Abdul Aziz, whose nephew is proclaimed as Murad V.

F **Jun:** 15th, several members of Ottoman government assassinated;
30th, Serbia, under the nationalist Jovan Ristich, declares war on Turkey.

G **Jul:** 2nd, Montenegro declares war on Turkey.

H **Aug:** 1st, Colorado becomes a U.S. state;
12th, Disraeli leaves the Commons on being created Earl of Beaconsfield;
31st, Murad V of Turkey, Sultan since *May*, is deposed on plea of insanity, succeeded by Abdul Hamid II (–1909).

J **Sep:** 1st, Serbs defeated at Alexinatz;
6th, W. E. Gladstone's *The Bulgarian Horrors and the Question of the East.*

K **Oct:** 31st, Turkey agrees to 6-week armistice as result of a Russian ultimatum.

L **Nov:** 1st, Appellate Jurisdictions Act in Britain restores jurisdiction of House of Lords and of Judicial Committee of the Privy Council;
7th, in U.S. Presidential election S. J. Tilden, Democrat, secures 184 out of the 185 electoral votes required, against R. B. Hayes, Republican, with 165, but 20 votes are in dispute (settled by electoral commission, *Jan*, 1877);
G. J. Goschen and Joubert visit Egypt to establish dual control;
Russia prepares for war against Turkey.

O Politics, Economics, Law and Education

First International (International Working Men's Association) dissolved at Philadelphia Congress (*July*),

M. Bakunin organises 'Land and Liberty', a secret society in Russia, which becomes spearhead of the Populist Movement.

German Conservative Party founded.

Industrial and Provident Societies Act in Britain.

Lembroso, *The Criminal*, founds criminology.

Z. R. Brockway founds reformatory at Elmira, New York, for juvenile offenders.

Reichsbank opened (*Jan.*).

Johns Hopkins University, Baltimore, founded, the first graduate school in U.S.

P Science, Technology, Discovery, etc.

A. G. Bell patents the telephone.

Formation of chromosomes first observed.

T. A. Edison invents the phonograph.

Rich deposits of nickel ores are found in New Caledonia.

Q Scholarship

R Philosophy and Religion

F. H. Bradley, *Ethical Studies.*

Felix Adler founds Society for Ethical Culture, New York.

A. Bain founds *Mind.*

Presbyterian Churches in England unite with the English congregations of United Presbyterian Church of Scotland to form the Presbyterian Church of England.

S Art, Sculpture, Fine Arts and Architecture

A. Renoir, *Au Théâtre* and *Le Moulin de la Galette* (paintings).

P. Gauguin exhibits landscapes at the Salon, Paris.

T Music

J. Brahms, 1st Symphony in C Minor (op. 68).

P. I. Tchaikovsky, *Francesca da Rimini.*

R. Wagner, *Siegfried* (opera).

Bayreuth Festspielhaus opens for first complete performance of Wagner's *The Ring.*

Léo Delibes, *Sylvia* (opera).

Hans Richter conducts concerts in London.

Purcell Society is founded.

U Literature

Julius Dahn, *Ein Kampf.*

Henry James, *Roderick Hudson.*

S. Mallarmé, *L'Après-midi d'un faune.*

B. Pérez-Galdós, *Doña Perfecta.*

W. Morris, *Sigurd the Volsung.*

V The Press

W Drama and Entertainment

X Sport

W. G. Grace scores two triple centuries in successive county cricket matches.

U.S. National Baseball League is founded.

M **Dec**: 5th, Ulysses Grant's last message to Congress;
12th (–*Jan.* 20th 1877), Constantinople Conference, called at Britain's suggestion, to consider Turkish problem;
23rd, proclamation of Ottoman Constitution, embodying parliamentary government, freedom of worship and a free press.

N New Zealand Constitution sweeps away provincial councils.
Coup d'état in Bolivia leads to Hilarión Daza's presidency.

Y **Statistics**

U.K. Merchant Shipping tonnage: 6,263,000 (2,005,000 steamships).

Z **Births and Deaths**

Jan. 5th Konrad Adenauer b. (–1967).
Feb. 16th G. M. Trevelyan b. (–1964).
June 8th 'George Sand' (Amandine Dudevant, *née* Dupin) d. (71).
Nov. 28th Carl von Baer d. (84).
Dec. 29th Pablo Casals b. (–1973).
Dec. 30th Michael Bakunin d. (62).

1877 (Jan.–Nov.) Russia declares war on Turkey—Britain annexes Transvaal

A **Jan:** 1st, Queen Victoria proclaimed Empress of India;
15th, by Budapest convention Austria undertakes to remain neutral in event of a Russo-Turkish War, and is to occupy Bosnia and Herzegovina when she sees fit, thereafter Serbia, Montenegro and Herzegovina are to form a neutral zone;
20th, failure of the powers at the Constantinople Conference to effect accord between Russia and Turkey in the Balkans;
29th, U.S. electoral commission decides in favour of R. B. Hayes, the Republican candidate.

B **Feb:** 5th, dismissal of Midhat Pasha, leader of the Turkish Liberals;
28th, peace signed between Turkey and Serbia.

C **Mar:** 3rd, U.S. Desert Land bill;
4th, R. B. Hayes inaugurated U.S. President;
12th, Britain annexes Walvis Bay on south-west African coast;
18th, additional Russo-Austrian convention that no large state be erected in the Balkans;
19th, first Turkish Parliament meets;
31st, London Protocol of great powers demands Turkey to undertake reforms;
Bartle Frere appointed High Commissioner of South Africa with instructions to work towards federation.

D **Apr:** 12th, Sultan of Turkey refuses London Protocol;
—, Theophilus Shepstone annexes South African Republic of Transvaal for Britain on grounds of bankruptcy and danger from Basutos and Zulus, but annexation violates Sand River convention of 1852;
24th, Russia declares war on Turkey and invades Roumania.

E **May:** 2nd, Porfirio Diaz becomes President of Mexico (–1911);
6th, British note to Russia warning her against attempted blockade of Suez or occupation of Egypt;
16th, crisis of *Seize Mai* in France when M. MacMahon, annoyed at Jules Simon's failure to stand up to the anti-clerical Left, dismisses him, appointing de Broglie to form a Monarchist ministry, which, 19th, is given a vote of no confidence in the Chamber;
Roumania enters war against Turkey.

F **Jun:** 27th, Russians cross the Danube.

G **Jul:** 20th, first Russian reverses;
21st, British Cabinet decides to declare war on Russia if she were to occupy Constantinople.

H **Aug:** first Kaffir War (–78).

J **Sep:** suppression of Satsuma Rebellion in Japan.

K **Oct:** Britain signs treaty of commerce with Madagascar, which agrees to liberate slaves.

L **Nov:** 18th, Russians storm Kars;
19th, Duc de Broglie's ministry forced to resign and is succeeded by General Rochebouet's, which also fails to enjoy confidence of the Chamber.

O Politics, Economics, Law and Education

Protection for patents in Germany.
Compulsory education in Italy, six–nine years.

P Science, Technology, Discovery, etc.

Asaph Hall discovers two satellites of Mars at Washington (*Aug.* 11th and 18th).
Lord Rayleigh, *Treatise on Sound.*
Koch demonstrates techniques of fixing and straining bacteria.
Joseph Monier's reinforced concrete beams.
Carl Laval invents cream separator.
First public telephone.
Frozen meat is shipped from Argentina to France.

Q Scholarship

R Philosophy and Religion

Truth first issued.

S Art, Sculpture, Fine Arts and Architecture

P. Cézanne shows 16 pictures at 3rd Impressionist Exhibition.
É. Manet's painting *Nana* is rejected by the Salon.
Winslow Homer, *The Cotton-Pickers* (painting).
A. Rodin, *The Bronze Age* (sculpture).
Society for the Protection of Ancient Buildings from Injudicious Restoration founded in London.
P. J. H. Cuyper, Rijksmuseum, Amsterdam.

T Music

Alexander Borodin, Symphony No. 2 in B minor.
J. Brahms, Symphony No. 2 in D (op. 75).
P. I. Tchaikovsky, Symphony No. 4 in F minor (op. 36).
C. Saint-Saëns, *Samson and Delilah* (opera).

U Literature

Henry James, *The American.*
Sarah Jewett, *Deephaven.*
É. Zola, *L'Assommoir.*

V The Press

The Nineteenth Century issued (edited by J. Knowles).

W Drama and Entertainment

H. Ibsen, *The Pillars of Society.*

X Sport

All-England Lawn Tennis championships first played at Wimbledon; 1st champion, Spencer Gore.

Y Statistics

1877 (Dec.)

M **Dec:** 10th, fall of Plevna, Bulgaria, to Russian army;
12th, Turks appeal to powers to mediate, but Bismarck declines and the British cabinet is divided;
13th, Jules Dufaure forms ministry in France;
14th, Serbia, siding with Russia, declares war on Turkey.

N Famine in India.

z **Births and Deaths**

Jan. 22nd Hjalmar Schacht b. (–1970).
Feb. 17th André Maginot b. (–1932).
Mar. 24th Walter Bagehot d. (51).
May 29th John Lothrop Motley d. (63).
July 27th Ernest Dohnányi b. (–1960).
Sept. 3rd Louis Adolphe Thiers d. (80).
Sept. 11th James Jeans b. (–1946).
Oct. 29th Wilfred Rhodes b. (–1973).
Nov. 25th Harley Granville-Barker b. (–1946).
Dec. 31st Gustave Courbet d. (58).
— Lev Trotsky b. (–1940).

1878 (Jan.–Jul.) Congress of Berlin settles Eastern Question—Anti-Socialist legislation in Germany

A **Jan**: 9th, on Victor Emmanuel's death, Humbert I succeeds as King of Italy (–1900);
9th, Turks capitulate at Shipka Pass and appeal to Russia for an armistice;
16th, U.S. signs treaty of friendship with Samoa;
20th, Russians take Adrianople;
23rd, British cabinet sends fleet to Constantinople at Sultan Abdul Hamid II's request, Lord Derby resigns in protest but later withdraws as fleet is recalled; 'Jingoist' war fever in Britain;
28th, risings in Thessaly;
28th, Count Andrássy proposes calling a European conference, meanwhile, 31st, Turkey signs armistice with Russia.

B **Feb**: 2nd, Greece declares war on Turkey;
7th, election of Cardinal Joachim Pecci as Pope Leo XIII, who soon opens negotiations with Germany for abrogation of May Laws of 1873 and 1874;
8th, Britain again decides to send fleet to Constantinople, but Sultan, under Russian pressure, refuses permission to enter the Straits (notwithstanding the fleet arrives, 15th);
10th, by convention of El Zanjóu, ending the Ten Years War, Spain promises reforms in Cuba;
28th, Bland-Allison bill reintroduces silver standard in U.S.

C **Mar**: 3rd, by preliminary treaty of San Stefano between Russia and Turkey, Montenegro to be enlarged, with port of Antivari; Roumania, Montenegro and Serbia to be independent; reforms to be undertaken in Bosnia and Herzegovina; Bulgaria to be enlarged with a seaboard on Aegean and most of Macedonia; Russia to receive Ardaham, Kars and Batum, while Turkey to pay Russia a huge indemnity;
25th, Nikolai Ignatiev, Russian diplomat, on mission to Vienna fails to reconcile Austria to treaty of San Stefano;
27th, fearing further Russian aggression British cabinet calls out reserves and drafts Indian troops to Malta.

D **Apr**: 2nd, Derby resigns and is succeeded as foreign minister by Lord Salisbury;
8th, Austria evades Salisbury's suggestions for common action against Russia.

E **May**: 8th, Peter Shuvalov, Russian ambassador in London, undertakes mission to St. Petersburg to divide Bulgaria;
11th (and *June* 2nd), radical attempt to assassinate Emperor William I of Germany;
18th, Colombia grants French company a nine-year concession to build Panama Canal;
24th, Reichstag rejects Bismarck's proposed repressive legislation against radicals;
30th, secret Anglo-Russian agreement to reduce the size of Bulgaria.

F **Jun**: 4th, secret Anglo-Turkish agreement to check Russian advance in Asia Minor, by which Britain promises to defend Turkey against further attack and Britain is allowed to occupy Cyprus;
6th, Anglo-Austrian agreement on Bulgaria;
13th (*July* 13th), Berlin Congress attended by Count Andrássy, Otto von Bismarck, Peter Shuvalov, W. H. Waddington, L. Corti, B. Disraeli and Lord Salisbury to discuss Eastern Question.

G **Jul**: 13th, by Treaty of Berlin Bulgaria is split into (a) autonomous Bulgaria, north of Balkans, (b) Eastern Rumelia with a special organisation under Turkey and (c) Macedonia where reforms are to be undertaken; Austria is given mandate to occupy Bosnia and Herzegovina; Roumania is awarded Dobrudja but has to hand over South

O **Politics, Economics, Law and Education**

H. Treitschke draws attention to growth of Jewish influence in Germany.
Flemish becomes the official language in Flanders.

P **Science, Technology, Discovery, etc.**

The sphygmograph is invented.
Sidney Thomas and Percy Gilchrist perfect the 'basic' process for steel production by lining the Bessemer furnace with dolomite.
Swan's carbon filament lamp.
David Hughes invents the microphone.
New Eddystone Lighthouse.
Earliest electric street lighting in London.
A. A. Pope manufactures first American bicycles.

Q **Scholarship**

W. E. H. Lecky, *History of England in the XVIIIth Century* (–90).

R **Philosophy and Religion**

William Booth founds Salvation Army in Britain.
F. Max Müller delivers first Hibbert Lectures on Comparative Religion.
Georges Romanes, *A Candid Examination of Theism.*
Roman Catholic hierarchy is restored in Scotland.

S **Art, Sculpture, Fine Arts and Architecture**

Albert Bierstadt, *Sierra Nevada.*
Pierre Puvis de Chavannes, *Life of St. Geneviève.*
James Whistler awarded ¼d. damages in libel action with John Ruskin for disparaging remarks on his painting, *Nocturne in Black and Gold.*
Cleopatra's Needle from Heliopolis, given to England in 1819, is removed from Alexandria to London.

T **Music**

Anton Dvořák, *Three Slavonic Rhapsodies* (op. 45).
A. Sullivan, *H.M.S. Pinafore.*
George Grove edits *Dictionary of Music and Musicians* (–79).
P. I. Tchaikovsky *Swan-Lake* (ballet).

U **Literature**

Theodor Fontane, *Vor dem Sturm.*
T. Hardy, *The Return of the Native.*
H. James, *Daisy Miller.*
René Sully-Prudhomme, *La Justice.*
A. C. Swinburne, *Poems and Ballads.*

V **The Press**

W **Drama and Entertainment**

Ellen Terry joins Irving's Company at the Lyceum Theatre.

X **Sport**

Bicycle Touring Club founded in England.

Y **Statistics**

G **Jul**: 13th, Bessarabia to Russia; Montenegro is given Antivari; Montenegro, Roumania and Serbia become independent states; Russia receives Batum, Kars and Ardaham; British occupation of Cyprus is confirmed; Italian and Greek demands are shelved; promises for reforms in Macedonia and Asia Minor lead to agitation;
30th, in Reichstag elections Conservatives gain seats at expense of National Liberals.

H **Aug**: 15th, Nubar Pasha forms ministry in Egypt, with Rivers Wilson as minister of finance.

J **Sep**:

K **Oct**: 11th, Germany and Austria annul clause in Peace of Prague, 1866, over plebiscite in North Schleswig;
17th, J. A. MacDonald becomes premier of Canada on Conservatives winning general election on protectionist platform;
18th, anti-Socialist law in Germany (–1890), prohibits public meetings, publications and collections, thus driving Socialism underground;
21st, Irish National Land League founded with C. S. Parnell as president.

L **Nov**: 25th, Comité d'Études du Haut-Congo formed to organise Belgian advance in Congo.

M **Dec**: 11th, Bartle Frere, British High Commissioner in South Africa, delivers ultimatum to Zulus;
Franco-British dual control in Egypt is suspended on the Khedive's introduction of ministerial government.

N Beginning of Irredentist agitation in Italy to obtain Trieste and other Italian-speaking areas.

z **Births and Deaths**

Jan. 23rd Rutland Boughton b. (–1963).
Feb. 7th Pope Pius IX d. (85).
Feb. 10th Claude Bernard d. (64).
May 10th Gustav Stresemann b. (–1929).
May 28th Lord John Russell, Earl Russell d. (85).
Sept. 20th Upton Sinclair b. (–1968).
Oct. 8th A. J. Munnings b. (–1959).
Oct. 15th Paul Reynaud b. (–1966).
Nov. 27th William Orpen b. (–1931).
— John Masefield b. (–1967).
— Martin Buber b. (–1965).

1879 Zulu War

A **Jan**: 1st, resumption of specie payments in U.S., suspended since 1873;
5th, Republicans gain in French senatorial elections;
12th, British-Zulu War (*–July*);
22nd, Zulus massacre British troops at Isandhlwana, Zululand;
24th, Germany signs commercial treaty with Samoa;
30th, on M. MacMahon's resignation, Jules Grévy, a Conservative Republican, is elected President of France.

B **Feb**: 4th, W. H. Waddington becomes French premier;
18th, fall of Nubar ministry in Egypt after army demonstration;
22nd, constitution granted in Bulgaria, with a national assembly.

C **Mar**:

D **Apr**: 29th, Alexander of Battenberg is elected Prince Alexander I of Bulgaria (–1866).

E **May**: 26th, by treaty of Gandamak Britain occupies the Khyber Pass and pays the Amir of Afghanistan an annual subsidy.

F **Jun**: 25th, Ismael Khedive of Egypt is deposed by the Sultan, succeeded by Tewfik (–1892);
Law against Jesuits in France.

G **Jul**: 1st, primary education in Belgium is secularised;
12th, protectionist laws for industry and agriculture in Germany split the Liberal Party.

H **Aug**: 4th, Alsace-Lorraine is declared an integral part of the German *Reich* under a governor-general;
17th, French Panama Canal Company is organised under Ferdinand de Lesseps;
28th, in Zulu War British troops capture Cetywayo;
Count Taaffe forms Austrian ministry (–1893) and ends German predominance in Austria-Hungary in favour of Slavs.

J **Sep**: 1st, Britain signs peace with Zulu chiefs;
3rd, Afghan troops massacre the British legation at Kabul;
4th, Anglo-French dual control of Egypt re-established (suspended in *Dec.* 1878);
15th, treaty of Livadia between Russia and China gives Russia key points in Ili Valley.

K **Oct**: 7th, Austro-German dual alliance for five years (renewed until 1918);
Britain invades Afghanistan and, 19th, Yakub the Amir abdicates and surrenders to Britain;
P. A. Saburov's mission to Berlin for renewal of Russo-German alliance fails.

L **Nov**: 24th (*–Dec.* 9th), W. E. Gladstone in Midlothian Campaign denounces Conservative government for imperialism and mishandling of domestic affairs;
27th, French Chamber is moved from Versailles to Paris.

M **Dec**: 16th, Transvaal Republic is proclaimed.

N

O **Politics, Economics, Law and Education**

Henry George, *Progress and Poverty.*
Robert Giffen, *Essay on Finance.*
W. L. Blackley proposes scheme for old-age pensions.
The radical, terrorist, Will of the People Society is founded in Russia.
Afrikander Bond is founded in South Africa to work for the recognition of the Dutch language.

P **Science, Technology, Discovery, etc.**

The element scandium is discovered.
Saccharin is discovered.
Researches of the Hon. Henry Cavendish (posth., ed. J. Clerk Maxwell.)
Dugald Clerk uses an electric arc to heat steel furnace.
W. E. Ayrton pioneers electricity as a motive power, and W. E. Siemens exhibits an electric railway in Berlin.
London's first telephone exchange.
First Pullman dining-car in Britain.
Australian frozen meat is on sale in London.

Q **Scholarship**

W. W. Skeat, *Etymological English Dictionary* (–82).
H. Treitschke, *History of Germany in the XIXth Century* (–95).

R **Philosophy and Religion**

A. J. Balfour, *Defence of Philosophic Doubt.*
H. Spencer, *Principles of Ethics* (–93).
Papal Encyclical (*Aug.* 4th) protesting against modern metaphysics.
Mary Baker Eddy becomes pastor of a Church of Christ, Scientist, Boston.

S **Art, Sculpture, Fine Arts and Architecture**

J. Bastien-Lepage, *Portrait of Sarah Bernhardt.*
A. Renoir, *Mme Charpentier and her children.*
A. Rodin, *John the Baptist* (sculpture).

T **Music**

J. Brahms, Violin Concerto in D (op. 77) played by J. Joachim.
P. I. Tchaikovsky, *Eugen Onegin* (opera).
A. Bruckner, 6th Symphony.

U **Literature**

G. Meredith, *The Egoist.*
B. Pérez-Galdós, *Episodios Nacionales* (–83).
R. L. Stevenson, *Travels with a Donkey.*
Juan Valera, *Doña Luz.*

V **The Press**

W **Drama and Entertainment**

H. Ibsen, *A Doll's House.*
A. Strindberg, *The Red Room.*
The public granted unrestricted admission to the galleries of the British Museum.

X **Sport**

z **Births and Deaths**

Jan. 13th William Reid Dick b. (–1961).
Mar. 14th Albert Einstein b. (–1955).
May 5th William Beveridge b. (–1963).
May 25th William Maxwell Aitken, Lord Beaverbrook, b. (–1964).
Aug. 27th Rowland Hill d. (83).
Nov. 5th James Clerk Maxwell d. (48).
Nov. 22nd John Thadeus Delane d. (59).
Dec. 21st Joseph Stalin b. (–1953).
— Honoré Daumier d. (71).
— Edward Morgan Forster b. (–1970).

1880 Liberals in power in Britain—Transvaal declares itself an independent republic

A **Jan:**

B **Feb:**

C **Mar:** 8th, Lord Beaconsfield appeals to electorate on issue of Irish Home Rule;
24th, Britain, U.S. and Germany recognise the King of Samoa and provide for an executive with European representation;
29th (-30th), decrees in France for non-authorised religious associations to regularise their positions and for dispersal of Jesuits.

D **Apr:** 18th, in British elections Liberals secure majority of 137 over Conservatives and Irish Nationalists win 65 seats, so Beaconsfield resigns;
28th, W. E. Gladstone forms Liberal ministry in which he is also chancellor of Exchequer, with Lord Granville foreign secretary, William Harcourt home secretary and Joseph Chamberlain president of Board of Trade.

E **May:** 3rd, Charles Bradlaugh, M.P. for Northampton, claims rights to affirm at swearing-in of Commons, instead of taking oath (for persistent refusal to take oath he is taken into custody, *June* 23rd, and is subsequently excluded from the House); during the Bradlaugh affair Henry Wolff, John Gorst, Lord Randolph Churchill and sometimes H. H. Asquith associate as a group independent of the Conservative leadership, nicknamed the Fourth Party;
Acute rivalry between France and Italy begins in Tunis;
Michael Loris-Melikov becomes Russian minister of interior, with wide powers for dealing with Nihilists; the problem of constitutional reform is shelved.

F **Jun:** 25th, Cape Parliament rejects scheme for South African federation;
29th, France annexes Tahiti;
—, Papal nuncio is expelled from Belgium during crisis over educational policy;
Clericals defeat Liberals in Belgian elections and begin long era of power (-1914).
France, alarmed at Stanley's advance in Congo for Leopold II of Belgium, sends de Brazza to treat with chiefs on north side of river.

G **Jul:** 11th, French law grants amnesty to Marquis de Rochefort and other Communards of 1871;
17th, Egyptian finances are reorganised;
New penal code in Japan, based on that of France.

H **Aug:** 2nd, Relief of Distress Act for Ireland.

J **Sep:**

K **Oct:** 13th, Transvaal declares itself independent of Britain.

L **Nov:** 2nd, Irish Land League is prosecuted (results in acquittal of Parnellites in *Jan.* 1881 through disagreement of jury);
8th, civil war in Samoa;
26th, Turkey yields to the powers and permits Montenegro to occupy Dulcigno, in place of the territory assigned by the Berlin Congress of 1878.

M **Dec:** 30th, Transvaal Boers under Kruger declare a Republic.

O **Politics, Economics, Law and Education**

Employers' Liability Act grants workmen compensation for accidents caused by employers' negligence.
Walter Bagehot, *Economic Studies* (posth.).
Parcel post introduced in England.
Owens College becomes Manchester University.
First girls' high schools in England.
De Beers Mining Corporation is formed by Cecil Rhodes.

P **Science, Technology, Discovery, etc.**

Louis Pasteur discovers streptococcus.
Laveran observes the malarian parasite.
Andrew Carnegie's first large steel furnace.
T. A. Edison and J. W. Swan independently make the first practical electric light.
Beginning of street lighting by electricity in New York.
Tinned salmon, meat and fruit are available.

Q **Scholarship**

R **Philosophy and Religion**

John Caird, *Philosophy of Religion.*
Jesuits in France disbanded and military chaplains are abolished.
Burials Bill enables dissenters to hold services in parish churchyards in Britain.

S **Art, Sculpture, Fine Arts and Architecture**

Cologne Cathedral completed.

T **Music**

A. Dvořák, Symphony No. 1 in D (op. 60).
P. I. Tchaikovsky, *1812 Overture* and *Italian Capriccio.*
C. Franck, piano quintet.
A. Sullivan, *Pirates of Penzance* (opera).

U **Literature**

B. Disraeli, *Endymion.*
F. Dostoievsky, *The Brothers Karamazov* (-81).
Jens Jacobsen, *Niels Lyhne.*
H. W. Longfellow, *Ultima Thule.*
G. de Maupassant, *Boule de Suif.*
J. H. Shorthouse, *John Inglesant.*
Lewis Wallace, *Ben Hur.*
É. Zola, *Nana.*

V **The Press**

Half-tone block used in *New York Daily Graphic.*

W **Drama and Entertainment**

X **Sport**

First test match between England and Australia.
Society of American Wheelmen founded.

N Captain C. C. Boycott, land agent in Mayo, is 'boycotted' for refusing to take rents at the figures fixed by tenants.

War of the Pacific, Chile against Bolivia and Peru (–1884).

First federal confederation assembly meets at Sydney, New South Wales, under Henry Parkes.

Y Statistics

Coal production (in mill. tons): Great Britain, 149; U.S., 64·9; Germany, 59; France, 19·4; Russia, 3·2.

Pig-iron production (in mill. tons): Great Britain, 7·8; U.S., 3·9; Germany, 2·5; France, 0·5; Russia, 0·4.

Railway mileage in operation: U.S., 87,801; Great Britain, 17,935; France, 16,430; Russia, 12,200.

Emigration to U.S. (1871–80): from U.K., 548,043; from Ireland, 436,871.

Suez Canal: used by 4,344,000 tons of shipping, 70 per cent British.

Telephones: 50,000 private telephones in use in U.S.

Z Births and Deaths

Jan. 26th Douglas MacArthur b. (–1964).
Mar. 1st Giles Lytton Strachey b. (–1932).
May 8th Gustave Flaubert d. (58).
July 24th Ernest Bloch b. (–1959).
Oct. 5th Jacques Offenbach d. (61).
Dec. 22nd 'George Eliot' (Mary Ann Evans) d. (61).
Dec. 28th R. H. Tawney b. (–1962).
— Jacob Epstein b. (–1959).

1881 (Jan.–Nov.) Repressive legislation for Ireland—France occupies Tunis—Three Emperors' league formed

A **Jan:** 28th, Transvaal Boers in their revolt repulse a British force under George Colley at Laing's Nek;

31st (–*Feb.* 2nd), Irish members at Westminster obstruct passage of repressive Coercion bill for Ireland in Commons, which sits for 41 hours continuously when, *Feb.* 2nd, Speaker, H. B. W. Brand, takes division on first reading.

B **Feb:** 1st, first signs of nationalist movement in Egypt with rising of officers;

24th, by treaty of St. Petersburg China pays indemnity to Russia for return of Ili Valley;

27th, Boers defeat British under G. Colley at Majuba Hill.

C **Mar:** 2nd, suspension of Habeas Corpus Act in Ireland;

4th, James A. Garfield, Republican, is inaugurated U.S. President;

12th, following raids of Krumir tribe into Algiers, France occupies Tunis;

13th, Alexander II signs Ukase calling an assembly of Russian nobles and the same day is assassinated by terrorists. Alexander III succeeds (–1894).

D **Apr:** 5th, Britain concludes treaty of Pretoria with Boers, recognising independence of South African Republic of Transvaal;

19th, on death of Lord Beaconsfield, Lord Salisbury becomes leader of Conservatives in Lords, Stafford Northcote in Commons;

30th, French navy seizes Bizerta and troops invade Tunis from Algeria.

E **May:** 12th, by treaty of Bardo with the Bey Tunis accepts French protectorate.

F **Jun:** 18th, Three Emperors' League, a secret alliance between Germany, Austria and Russia for three years;

28th, Austro-Serbian alliance;

Immigration Act in New Zealand restricts Japanese immigration.

G **Jul:** 2nd, President Garfield is shot; he dies *Sept.* 19th, and is succeeded by Chester Arthur;

3rd, Britain persuades Turkey to sign convention with Greece, granting Greece Thessaly and part of Epirus, as was promised at Berlin Congress;

13th, constitution revised in Bulgaria, where a new ministry of Russian officers is formed;

28th, Serbia becomes virtual protectorate of Austria by secret treaty;

Rising against the French in Algeria (–83).

H **Aug:** 16th, W. E. Gladstone's Irish Land Act fixes tenures, and establishes a land court to deal with excessive rents.

J **Sep:** 9th, Nationalist rising in Egypt under Arabi Pasha.

K **Oct:** 13th, C. S. Parnell is imprisoned for inciting Irish to intimidate tenants taking advantage of Land Act.

L **Nov:** 14th, Léon Gambetta forms ministry in France (–*Jan.* 1882), following Jules Ferry's resignation on attack of his Tunisian policy.

O **Politics, Economics, Law and Education**

Natural History Museum, South Kensington, opened (*Apr.*).
Freedom of press in France.
American Federation of Labor founded at Pittsburgh.
Flogging is abolished in British Army following abolition in Royal Navy in 1879.
University College, Liverpool, founded.
Postal orders are issued in Britain.

P **Science, Technology, Discovery, etc.**

L. Pasteur attenuates anthrax virus by vaccine.
S. P. Langley invents bolometer for determining minute changes of temperature.
Edward Tylor, *Anthropology.*
A. A. Common in England and H. Draper in U.S. each photograph a comet (*June* 24th).

Q **Scholarship**

B. F. Westcott and F. J. A. Hort, *Greek New Testament.*

R **Philosophy and Religion**

Revised Version of New Testament.
Anti-papal demonstrations on the removal of the remains of Pius IX.
C. P. Pobédonostsev, procurator of the Holy Synod, persecutes Jews in Russia.

S **Art, Sculpture, Fine Arts and Architecture**

Max Liebermann, *An Asylum for Old Men* (painting).
C. Monet, *Sunshine and Snow* (painting).

T **Music**

J. Brahms, *Academic Festival* (op. 80) and *Tragic* (op. 81) overtures.
Jacques Offenbach, *The Tales of Hoffmann* (opera).

U **Literature**

G. Flaubert, *Bouvard et Pecuchet.*
A. France (pseud.), *Le Crime de Sylvestre Bonnard.*
H. James, *Portrait of a Lady.*
G. de Maupassant, *La Maison Tellier.*
D. G. Rossetti, *Ballads and Sonnets.*
S. C. F. Schandorph, *The History of Thomas Friis.*
R. L. Stevenson, *Virginibus Puerisque.*
P. Verlaine, *Sagesse.*

V **The Press**

Evening News and *The People* are issued.

W **Drama and Entertainment**

H. Ibsen, *Ghosts.*
Édouard Pailleron, *Le Monde ou l'on s'ennuie.*
Sarah Bernhardt leaves the *Comédie Française.*
D'Oyly Carte builds the Savoy Theatre, the first public building in England lit by electricity.

X **Sport**

First U.S. lawn tennis championships (R. D. Sears champion until 1888).

M **Dec**: Canadian Pacific Railway Company founded.

N Moderate extension of Italian franchise.
Foundation of political parties in Japan, following imperial decree that an assembly will be convened in 1890.

Y **Statistics**

Population (in millions): U.S., 53; Germany, 45·2; France, 37·6; Italy, 28·4; Great Britain, 29·7; Ireland, 5·1.

Populations of chief cities: London, 3·3; Paris, 2·2; New York, 1·2; Berlin, 1·1; Vienna, 1·0; Tokio, 0·8; St. Petersburg, 0·6; Brussels, 0·1.

Z **Births and Deaths**

Feb. 4th Thomas Carlyle d. (86).
Feb. 9th Feodor Dostoievsky d. (60).
Mar. 9th Ernest Bevin b. (–1951).
Mar. 16th M. P. Moussorgsky d. (42).
Apr. 19th Benjamin Disraeli, Earl of Beaconsfield, d. (77).
May 4th Alexander Kerensky b. (–1970).
May 25th Béla Bartók b. (–1945).
July 26th George Borrow d. (78).
Aug. 2nd Ethel M. Dell (Savage) b. (–1939).
Aug. 6th Alexander Fleming b. (–1955).
Oct. 15th William Temple b. (–1944).
— P. G. Wodehouse b. (–1975).
Oct. 25th Pablo Picasso b. (–1973).
— Clive Bell b. (–1964).
— Kemel Atatürk b. (–1938).

1882 Phoenix Park Murders—Italy joins German-Austrian Alliance—Battle of Tel-el-Kebir

A **Jan**: 8th, Léon Gambetta's note to Egypt by France and Britain, to strengthen Khedive's hands against Nationalists;
22nd, Italian electoral reform lowers tax requirements and age limit of electors;
27th, Léon Gambetta falls and Charles Freycinet forms ministry in France.

B **Feb**: 5th, Khedive is forced to appoint a Nationalist ministry in Egypt;
Pan Slav speech by Russian General M. D. Skobelev in Paris alarms Germany.

C **Mar**: 6th, Prince Milan proclaims himself King of Serbia, with Austrian support;
29th, primary education in France to be free, compulsory and non-sectarian.

D **Apr**: 4th, the Prussian legation at the Vatican is restored.

E **May**: 2nd, Kilmainham 'treaty' between C. S. Parnell and British government for an amnesty on condition that Parnell seeks to end disorders; Lord Cowper, Lord Lieutenant of Ireland, and his chief secretary resign;
6th, Fenians murder new Irish chief secretary, Lord Frederick Cavendish, and T. H. Burke, Irish under-secretary, in Phoenix Park, Dublin;
—, U.S. bans Chinese immigrants for ten years;
20th, Italy joins Austro-German alliance, which becomes Triple Alliance, for five years (renewed until 1915); this assures Italy of support in event of French attack, but secures no guarantee of her possession of Rome;
22nd, U.S. secures trading rights in Korea.

F **Jun**: 6th, Hague convention fixes three-mile limit for territorial waters;
12th, anti-foreign riots in Alexandria led by Arabi Pasha;
28th, Anglo-French agreement on boundaries of Sierra Leone and French Guinea.

G **Jul**: 9th, Royal Navy bombards Alexandria and John Bright resigns from Gladstone's cabinet in protest;
23rd, Koreans attack Japanese legation in Seoul, provoking Chinese intervention;
Repressive Prevention of Crimes bill for Ireland suspends trial by jury and grants police wide powers of search and arrest.

H **Aug**: 17th, Massacre of Irish family at Maamtrasna, by the 'Invincibles', a secret Irish terrorist society.

J **Sep**: 13th, Garnet Wolseley defeats Egyptians at Tel-el-Kebir, Lower Egypt, and proceeds to occupy Egypt and the Sudan;
15th, British force occupies Cairo; Arabi surrenders and is banished to Ceylon.

K **Oct**:

L **Nov**: 9th, Franco-British dual control of Egypt established.

M **Dec**: Italy takes over Assab Bay in Red Sea and establishes colony of Eritrea.

N During the year there are 2,590 agrarian outrages in Ireland and 10,457 families are evicted.

O Politics, Economics, Law and Education

M. Bakunin, *Dieu et l'État* (posth.).
W. Besant, *All Sorts and Conditions of Men.*
W. S. Jevons, *The State in Relation to Labour.*
Primrose League is founded in Britain to foster Conservative Party principles.
Married Women's Property Act in Britain gives married women the right of separate ownership of property of all kinds.
Republican Party is founded in Portugal.
American Colonial Society founded.
London Chamber of Commerce first meets (*Jan.* 25th).
Cotton duties abolished in India.
Bank of Japan founded.
Bohemian National University, Prague.
Regent Street Polytechnic opened in London.

P Science, Technology, Discovery, etc.

Ralph Copeland observes transit of Venus in Jamaica.
George Kynoch's brass cartridge-case.
Gottlieb Daimler builds petrol engine.
T. A. Edison's generating station at Pearl Street, New York, and the first hydro-electric plant at Appleton, Wisconsin.
Society for Psychical Research founded, with Henry Sidgwick president.
The idea of a Channel Tunnel is first discussed in Britain, but military authorities disapprove.

Q Scholarship

R Philosophy and Religion

Leslie Stephen, *Science of Ethics.*
Wilson Carlile founds Church Army.

S Art, Sculpture, Fine Arts and Architecture

É. Manet, *Le Bar aux Folies-Bergères* (painting).
J. S. Sargent, *El Jaleo* (painting).
O. Wilde's *Lectures on the Decorative Arts* explains the aesthetic movement.

T Music

J. Brahms, Piano Concerto No. 2 in B flat (op. 83).
F. Gounod, *The Redemption* (oratorio).
N. Rimsky-Korsakov, *The Snow Maiden* (opera).
A. Sullivan, *Iolanthe* (opera).
R. Wagner, *Parsifal* (opera).
Berlin Philharmonic Orchestra founded.

U Literature

W. D. Howells, *A Modern Instance.*
F. Nietzsche, *Die fröhliche Wissenschaft.*

V The Press

Berliner Tageblatt.

W Drama and Entertainment

H. F. Becque, *Les Corbeaux.*
H. Ibsen, *An Enemy of the People.*

W Drama and Entertainment (*cont.*)

H. A. Jones, *The Silver King*.
V. Sardou, *Féodora*.

X Sport

American Baseball Association founded.

Y Statistics

British Textiles trade:

imports of raw cotton	1,458 mill. lb.
exports of cotton	4,349 mill. yds.
exports of woollens	265,211,000 yds.
exports of linens	176,451,000 yds.
exports of silks	7,662,000 yds.

Z Births and Deaths

Jan. 11th Theodor Schwann d. (72).
Jan. 25th Virginia Woolf b. (–1941).
Jan. 26th Léon Gambetta d. (43).
Jan. 30th F. D. Roosevelt b. (–1945).
Feb. 2nd James Joyce b. (–1941).
Feb. 22nd Eric Gill b. (–1940).
Mar. 24th Henry Wadsworth Longfellow d. (75).
Mar. 26th T. H. Green d. (46).
Apr. 9th D. G. Rossetti d. (54).
Apr. 19th Charles Darwin d. (71).
Apr. 27th Ralph Waldo Emerson d. (78).
June 1st John Drinkwater b. (–1937).
June 2nd Giuseppe Garibaldi d. (74).
June 5th Igor Stravinsky b. (–1971).
Aug. 27th Samuel Goldwyn b. (–1974).
Sept. 23rd Friedrich Wöhler d. (82).
Oct. 14th Eamon de Valéra b. (–1975).
Nov. 18th Jacques Maritain b. (–1973).
Dec. 6th Louis Blanc d. (71) and Anthony Trollope d. (67).
Dec. 11th Max Born b. (–1979).
Dec. 16th J. B. Hobbs b. (–1964).
Dec. 28th Arthur Stanley Eddington b. (–1944).
— Georges Braque b. (1963).

1883 Paul Kruger becomes President of Transvaal—French protectorate over Annam and Tonkin

A **Jan**: 3rd, Lord Granville's circular to the powers on Britain's desire to withdraw forces from Egypt as soon as the state of the country permits;
16th, Pendleton act begins reform of U.S. civil service (completed 1901);
30th, Clement Fallières forms ministry in France, lasting three weeks.

B **Feb**: 21st, Jules Ferry forms second ministry in France (–1885).

C **Mar**: 15th, Irish-American terrorists attempt to blow up *The Times* office and the Local Government Board, London.

D **Apr**: 16th, Paul Kruger becomes President of South African Republic;
24th, Germany begins settlements in South-West Africa and Angra Pequeña, which prompts Britain to state that any claims to sovereignty in territory between Cape Colony and Angola will be regarded as an infringement of her rights.

E **May**: 1st, Otto von Bismarck introduces sickness insurance schemes in Germany;
—, the Organic Law in Egypt, based on Lord Dufferin's report of *Feb.* 6th, establishes a legislative Council and a general assembly, though authority remains vested in the British agent.

F **Jun**: 1st (–*Dec.* 1885), French war with Madagascar;
8th, by convention of Marsa with the Bey of Tunis, France gains effective control of Tunisia.

G **Jul**:

H **Aug**: 18th, Corrupt and Illegal Practices Act limits spending of all parties in a British general election to £800,000 and limits spending of individual candidates;
24th, Comte de Chambord, French pretender, dies without heir;
25th, France acquires protectorate over Annam and Tonkin, Indo-China.

J **Sep**: 11th, Evelyn Baring lands in Egypt as British agent;
30th, Alexander of Bulgaria restores the constitution of 1879, alienating Russia;
Boer republic of Stellaland founded in Bechuanaland.

K **Oct**: 20th, by peace of Ancór Peru cedes territory to Chile, who is to occupy Tacna and Arica for ten years, when a plebiscite is to be held;
30th, secret Austro-Rumanian alliance (–1914), through Rumanian fear of Russia.

L **Nov**: 5th, the Madhi defeats Egyptian force under William Hicks at El Obeid and Britain decides to evacuate the Sudan;
Nationalist Radical party revolts against Serbian government.

M **Dec**: 14th, Portuguese government grants concession for a railway from Delagoa Bay to Transvaal to a U.S. promoter.

N French troops begin conquest of the Upper Niger.
Queensland's request to annex New Guinea is declined by Britain.

O **Politics, Economics, Law and Education**

Lester Ward, *Dynamic Sociology.*
Boys' Brigade founded.

P **Science, Technology, Discovery, etc.**

W. Thomson's discourse to Royal Institution on the size of atoms.
R. Koch discovers preventive inoculation against anthrax.
L. A. Bertillon, *Ethnographie moderne des races sauvages.*
Electrical exhibition, Munich.
Northern Pacific Railroad constructed.
First skyscraper, Chicago.
Sydney-Melbourne railway opened.
Orient Express first runs (*Oct.* 4th).

Q **Scholarship**

Heinrich Brugsch, *Inscriptiones Aegypticae.*
J. R. Seeley, *The Expansion of England.*

R **Philosophy and Religion**

F. H. Bradley, *The Principles of Logic.*
F. Nietzsche, *Thus Spake Zarathustra.*
Franz Reusch, *History of the Index of Forbidden Books.*

S **Art, Sculpture, Fine Arts and Architecture**

P. Cézanne, *Rocky Landscape* (painting).
A. Renoir, *Dance at Bougival* and *Umbrellas* (paintings).

T **Music**

J. Brahms, Symphony No. 3 in F (op. 90).
A. E. Chabrier, *España* Rhapsody.
A. Dvořák, *Stabat Mater* (oratorio).
Metropolitan Opera, New York, founded.
Royal College of Music, London, founded under George Grove.

U **Literature**

H. F. Amial, *Journal Intime* (posth.) (trans. 1885 by Mrs. Humphry Ward).
B. Björnson, *Beyond Human Endurance.*
Paul Bourget, *Essais de Psychologie contemporaine.*
G. de Maupassant, *Une Vie.*
E. Renan, *Souvenirs d'enfance et de jeunesse.*
R. L. Stevenson, *Treasure Island.*
E. Verhaeren, *Les Flamandes.*

V **The Press**

La Tribune.

W **Drama and Entertainment**

X **Sport**

Y **Statistics**

U.S. petroleum production, 23,450,000 barrels.

z **Births and Deaths**

Jan. 3rd Clement, Lord Attlee, b (–1967).
Jan. 17th Compton Mackenzie b. (–1972).
Feb. 18th Richard Wagner d. (70).
Feb. 23rd Karl Jaspers b. (–1969).
Mar. 14th Karl Marx d. (65).
May 5th Archibald, Lord Wavell, b. (–1950).
May 18th Walter Gropius b. (–1969).
June 5th John Maynard Keynes b. (–1946).
June 14th Edward Fitzgerald d. (74).
July 19th Benito Mussolini b. (–1945).
Aug. 19th Coco Chanel b. (–1971).
Sept. 4th Ivan Turgeniev d. (65).
— Pierre Laval b. (–1945).

1884 The Mahdi takes Omdurman—Germany occupies S.W. Africa and Cameroons—Third British Reform Bill

A **Jan**: 31st, Russians take Merv from the Amir of Afghanistan;
Poll tax, a relic of serfdom, is abolished in Russia.

B **Feb**: 18th, C. G. Gordon reaches Khartoum, but the Mahdi rejects his offer of negotiations;
26th, Britain recognises Portugal's right to territory at mouth of Congo, in order to frustrate Belgian designs but, in the face of protests from France and Germany, Britain abandons the treaty (*June* 26th);
27th, London convention regulates the status of Transvaal.

C **Mar**: 17th, Germany, Austria and Russia renew Three Emperors' Alliance (of *June* 1881);
21st, trades unions in France are legalised.

D **Apr**: 4th, Bolivia cedes Atacama to Chile by treaty of Valparaiso;
German occupation of South-West Africa, Togoland and Cameroons (–*Aug.*).

E **May**: 17th, Organic Act applies laws of Oregon to Alaska after interim term of government under U.S. war department.

F **Jun**: 6th, by treaty of Hué the Emperor of Annam recognises French protectorate;
28th (–*Aug.* 2nd), international conference on Egyptian finance in London, at which Otto von Bismarck and Jules Ferry oppose Britain's attempts to use Egyptian revenues for paying costs of Sudanese campaign.

G **Jul**: 27th, divorce (abolished in 1816) is re-established in France.

H **Aug**: 5th, in France members of former dynasties are excluded from the presidency and life senatorships are abolished.

J **Sep**:

K **Oct**: 13th, the Mahdi takes Omdurman.

L **Nov**: In U.S. presidential election Grover Cleveland, Democrat, wins 219 electoral votes against James G. Blaine, Republican, with 182, who is deserted by the Mugwumps, the reformist Republicans;
Britain annexes St. Lucia Bay to Natal, to prevent the Boers in Zululand gaining access to the east coast;
15th, Berlin conference of 14 nations on African affairs, organised by Otto von Bismarck and Jules Ferry, provides for free trade on Congo river and the abolition of slavery and the slave trade.

M **Dec**: 10th, Porfirio Diaz becomes President of Mexico (–1911);
British Franchise bill passes, after W. E. Gladstone undertakes to meet Conservative demands to introduce a further measure for redistributing seats, with uniform male suffrage in counties and boroughs for householders and lodgers, increasing the electorate to 5 million;
16th, Britain, following earlier recognition by U.S. and Germany, recognises International Association of the Congo.

N The Norwegian Constitution is reformed.
Britain establishes protectorate over section of Somali coast from the port of Zeila.

Births and Deaths (*cont.*)
May 12th Friedrich Smetana d. (60).
June 30th Georges Duhamel b. (–1915).
Nov. 5th J. E. Flecker b. (–1915).
— Damon Runyon b. (–1946).

O Politics, Economics, Law and Education

P. A. Kropotkin, *Paroles d'un Revolté.*
H. Spencer, *The Man versus the State.*
Fabian Society founded.
Royal Commission on the housing of the working classes (Dilke chairman).
Imperial Federation League founded in Canada.
Charlottenburg Technical High School, Berlin.

P Science, Technology, Discovery, etc.

Nikolaier discovers tetanus bacillus.
Cocaine is used as an anaesthetic.
Charles Parsons constructs first practical steam turbine for making electricity.
Oliver Lodge discovers electrical precipitation.
Hiram Maxim's recoil-operated gun.
Edwin Lankester founds Marine Biological Association.

Q Scholarship

Oxford English Dictionary (ed. James Murray–1928).

R Philosophy and Religion

S Art, Sculpture, Fine Arts and Architecture

'Les Vingt' exhibiting society founded by James Ensor in Brussels, supported by Georges Seurat, Paul Gauguin, Paul Cézanne and Vincent van Gogh (–94).
G. Seurat, *Bathers at Asnières* (painting).
E. Burne-Jones, *King Cophetua and the Beggar Maid* (painting).
A. Rodin, *Burghers of Calais* (sculpture) (–95).

T Music

A. Bruckner, Symphony No. 7, and *Te Deum.*
C. Franck, *Les Djinns* (opera).
J. Massenet, *Manon* (opera).
C. V. Stanford, *Savonarola* (opera).

U Literature

E. Amicis, *An Italian Schoolboy's Journal.*
G. D'Annunzio, *Il Libro delle Vergini.*
C. M. Leconte de Lisle, *Poèmes tragiques.*
Jean Moréas, *Les Syrtes.*
Mark Twain (pseud.), *Huckleberry Finn.*
P. Verlaine, *Jadis et naguère.*

V The Press

Le Matin issued.

W Drama and Entertainment

H. Ibsen, *The Wild Duck.*

X Sport

Y Statistics

Z Births and Deaths

Jan. 19th Ivan Maisky b. (–1975).
Feb. 1st Hugo von Hofmannsthal b. (–1929).
Mar. 24th François Mignet d. (88).
Mar. 31st Sean O'Casey b. (–1964).
May 8th Harry S. Truman b. (–1972).

(Continued opposite)

1885 (Jan.–Nov.) Death of Gordon at Khartoum—Leopold II establishes Congo State—Germany annexes Tanganyika and Zanzibar

A **Jan**: 9th, Spain proclaims protectorate over Spanish Guinea;
22nd, treaty of friendship between Germany and South African Republic;
26th, the Mahdi takes Khartoum and General Charles Gordon dies;
28th, British relief force arrives at Khartoum; the Sudan is evacuated.

B **Feb**: 5th, Congo State is established under Leopold II of Belgium, as a personal possession;
6th, Italy occupies Massawa, Eritrea;
12th, German East Africa Company is chartered;
25th, Germany annexes Tanganyika and Zanzibar.

C **Mar**: 4th, Grover Cleveland, Democrat, is inaugurated U.S. President;
30th, Russian occupation of Penjdeh, Afghanistan, provokes crisis in Anglo-Russian relations;
31st, fall of Jules Ferry's ministry in France, following French reverse at Hanoi in war with China;
Britain proclaims protectorate over North Bechuanaland, ending the Stellaland Republic.

D **Apr**: 26th, Britain occupies Port Hamilton, Korea (–*Feb.* 1887).

E **May**: 17th, Germany annexes Northern New Guinea and the Bismarck Archipelago.

F **Jun**: 5th, British establish protectorate over Niger River region;
9th, treaty of Tientsin between France and China recognises French protectorate in Annam;
—, W. E. Gladstone resigns, following hostile amendment to budget;
21st, death of Mahdi;
25th, Lord Salisbury forms Conservative ministry (–*Jan.* 1886), himself taking foreign secretaryship, with Michael Hicks Beach chancellor of Exchequer and Richard Cross home secretary;
British Redistribution of Seats Bill, introduced in *Feb.*, enacted, providing London with 37 additional seats, Liverpool 6 and Yorkshire industrial towns 16 and merging boroughs with population of under 15,000 with counties.

G **Jul**: 30th, Dervishes take Kassala, extending their control to the whole Sudan except Red Sea forts.

H **Aug**: 14th, a secretary of state for Scotland is appointed;
—, Lord Ashburne's Act authorises loans for Irish tenants to buy holdings on easy terms.

J **Sep**: 10th, Britain makes compromise settlement with Russia over Afghanistan frontier;
18th, disturbances in Eastern Rumelia in favour of union with Bulgaria.

K **Oct**: 22nd, Britain sends ultimatum to King Thibaw of Burma concerning his interference with trade and his refusal to comply leads to Third Burmese War.

L **Nov**: 11th, boundary between Sierra Leone and Liberia is defined;
13th, Serbia invades Bulgaria, following the union with Eastern Rumelia;
17th, Serbs defeated at Slivnitza, but Austrian intervention saves Serbia from invasion;
21st, C. S. Parnell calls on Irish in Britain to vote Conservative;
23rd, in British general election Liberals win 335 seats, Conservatives 249, Irish Home-Rulers 86; Lord Salisbury remains premier;

O **Politics, Economics, Law and Education**
Henry Maine, *Popular Government.*
Karl Marx, *Das Kapital*, vol. 2.
Gustav Cohn, *Foundations of Political Economy.*
The Pope excommunicates the Knights of Labor, but later withdraws his censure.

P **Science, Technology, Discovery, etc.**
Louis Pasteur cures hydrophobia.
F. Galton proves permanence and individuality of fingerprints.
Gottlieb Daimler invents internal combustion engine and Karl Benz builds single-cylinder engine for motor-car.
Starley's 'Rover' safety bicycle.
George Eastman's machine for manufacturing coated photographic paper.
Ney Elias crosses the Pamirs from east to west.
Gold is discovered in Transvaal.

Q **Scholarship**
Dictionary of National Biography is begun under Leslie Stephen.
Albert Sorel, *Europe and the French Revolution* (–1904).

R **Philosophy and Religion**
Leo Tolstoy, *My Religion.*
The Mormons split into polygamic and monogamic sections.

S **Art, Sculpture, Fine Arts and Architecture**
E. Degas, *Woman Bathing* (pastel).

T **Music**
J. Brahms, Symphony No. 4 in E minor (op. 98).
César Franck, *Symphonic Variations.*
A. Sullivan, *The Mikado* (opera).

U **Literature**
Paul Bourget, *Cruelle Énigme.*
Richard Burton, *The Arabian Nights* (–88).
A. Daudet, *Tartarin the Mountaineer.*
Jules Laforgue, *Complaintes.*
G. de Maupassant, *Bel Ami.*
George Meredith, *Diana of the Crossways.*
George Moore, *A Mummer's Wife.*
Walter Pater, *Marius the Epicurean.*
Leo Tolstoy, *The Power of Darkness.*
Émile Zola, *Germinal.*

V **The Press**

W **Drama and Entertainment**
H. F. Becque, *La Parisienne.*

X **Sport**

Y **Statistics**
U.K. total State expenditure: £88·5 mill.
Steel production (in mill. tons): Great Britain, 2·4; Germany, 1·2; France, 0·5.

L Nov: 27th, Bulgarians take Pirot, but are forced to withdraw from Serbia;
28th, British troops occupy Mandalay;
—, Cape railway reaches to Kimberley.

M Dec: 17th, France acquires control of Madagascar's foreign relations;
19th, Jules Grévy is re-elected President of France;
Germany's dispute with Spain over the Carolines is settled by papal arbitration in favour of Spain.

N British protectorate over Southern New Guinea is proclaimed, following German annexation in the north.
Belgian Labour Party is founded, with demand for universal suffrage.

z **Births and Deaths**

Feb. 7th Alban Berg b. (–1935).
Apr. 13th György S. von Lukács b. (–1971).
May 13th Friedrich Henle d. (74).
May 14th Otto Klemperer b. (–1973).
May 22nd Victor Hugo d. (83).
July 23rd Ulysses Grant d. (63).
Aug. 23rd Henry Tizard b. (–1959).
Sept. 11th D. H. Lawrence b. (–1930).
Oct. 11th François Mauriac b. (–1970).
Oct. 30th Ezra Pound b. (–1972).
Nov. 11th George Smith Patton b. (–1945).

1886 (Jan.–Nov.) Liberals defeated on Irish Home Rule Bill—Revolution in Eastern Rumelia

A **Jan:** 1st, Britain annexes Upper Burma, though guerilla warfare continues;
7th, General Georges Boulanger, who embodies French revenge on Germany for the Franco-Prussian War, becomes war minister in Charles Freycinet's cabinet;
13th, Lagos becomes separate British colony from Nigeria;
27th, Lord Salisbury resigns, after defeat on 'three acres and a cow' amendment of Jesse Collings to Address.

B **Feb:** 1st, W. E. Gladstone forms third Liberal ministry (*–Jul.* 20th), with Lord Rosebery foreign minister and W. V. Harcourt chancellor of Exchequer;
7th, H. M. Hyndman holds rally of Social Democratic Federation in Trafalgar Square.

C **Mar:** 3rd, peace of Bucharest between Serbia and Bulgaria.

D **Apr:** 5th, Abdul Hamid II, Sultan of Turkey, appoints Alexander of Bulgaria governor of Eastern Rumelia;
8th, Gladstone introduces Home Rule bill for Ireland;
26th, the major powers send ultimatum to Greece to stop support for revolution in Eastern Rumelia;
—, Prussian government expropriates Polish land-owners in West Prussia and Posen;
27th, de Brazza is appointed commissioner-general of French Congo.

E **May:** 1st (*–July* 1887), Japanese foreign minister calls conference in Tokio, but fails to abolish extra-territorial concessions;
4th, Anarcho-Communists riot in Chicago;
8th (*–June*), the powers blockade Greece, compelling her to maintain *status quo* in Eastern Rumelia;
Presidential Succession law in U.S., providing for succession to presidency in the event of the deaths of both the President and the Vice-President.

F **Jun:** 8th, W. E. Gladstone's Liberal government is defeated on second reading of Irish Home Rule bill, with 93 Liberals, including John Bright, Joseph Chamberlain and the Marquess of Hartington, voting with the Opposition;
23rd, Bonaparte and Orléans families are banished from France.

G **Jul:** 10th, British Royal Niger Company is chartered;
14th, Anglo-German agreement on frontiers of Gold Coast and Togoland;
24th, Anglo-Chinese agreement recognises British position in Burma;
In British general election Conservatives win 316 seats, dissident Liberals 78; Liberals 191 and Irish Nationalists 85; and 26th Lord Salisbury forms Conservative ministry (*–Aug.* 1892).

H **Aug:** 20th (–21st), military *coup d'état* in Sofia.

J **Sep:** 4th, Alexander of Bulgaria abdicates and Stephen Stambulov becomes Regent.

K **Oct:** 2nd, Lord Randolph Churchill's speech at Dartford outlines bold programme of domestic reform.

L **Nov:** 1st, Anglo-German agreement delimiting respective spheres of influence in East Africa;
10th, Prince Waldemar of Denmark is elected King of Bulgaria, but refuses to serve;
20th, 'Plan of Campaign', drawn up by William O'Brien and John Dillon, calls on Irish tenants to organise themselves.

O **Politics, Economics, Law and Education**

A. Carnegie, *Triumphant Democracy.*
Karl Marx, *Capital* (first English edition of vol. 1).
American Federation of Labor founded (*Dec.* 8th).
A. V. Dicey, *The Law of the Constitution.*
Charles Dilke appears as co-respondent (*Feb.* 12th) in sensational divorce suit.

P **Science, Technology, Discovery, etc.**

The element germanium discovered.
Henri Moissan isolates fluorine.
The synthetic drugs pyramidon and antifebrin discovered.
R. Krafft-Ebing, *Psychopathia Sexualis.*
C. A. von Welsbach invents gas mantle.
Canadian Pacific Railway completed (*Nov.* 7th).
The Severn Tunnel opened.
Niagara Falls hydro-electric installations begun.
The French army is equipped with the Lebel rifle, using smokeless powder.
H. Y. Castner patented his electrolytic process for making caustic soda.

Q **Scholarship**

English Historical Review founded under Mandell Creighton's editorship.
British School of Archaeology, Athens, opened (*Nov.*).

R **Philosophy and Religion**

A. Harnack, *History of Dogma.*

S **Art, Sculpture, Fine Arts and Architecture**

J. S. Sargent, *Carnation, Lily, Lily, Rose* (painting).
G. Seurat, *Sunday on the Island of Grande Jatte* (painting).
Eighth and last Impressionist Exhibition.
J. Whistler, P. W. Steer and W. Sickert found New English Art Club.
Statue of Liberty.

T **Music**

U **Literature**

George Gissing, *Demos.*
H. Rider Haggard, *King Solomon's Mines.*
Henry James, *The Bostonians* and *The Princess Casamassima.*
Pierre Loti (pseud.), *Pêcheurs d'Islande.*
F. Nietzsche, *Beyond Good and Evil.*
A. Rimbaud, *Les Illuminations.*
R. L. Stevenson, *Dr. Jekyll and Mr. Hyde.*
A. Strindberg, *The Son of a Servant* (–87).
E. Vogüé, *Le Roman Russe.*

V **The Press**

Jean Moréas and Gustave Kahn found *Le Symboliste*, a literary review of the Symbolist Movement.
Linotype is first used by the *New York Tribune.*

W **Drama and Entertainment**

H. Ibsen, *Rosmersholm.*
Stephens of San Francisco completes world trip on a 'penny-farthing' cycle.

M Dec: 15th, René Goblet forms ministry in France on C. Freycinet's fall;
23rd, Lord Randolph Churchill resigns through faltering support of cabinet for his budget, calling for army and naval economies;
30th, German-Portuguese agreement on boundaries between Angola and German South-West Africa;
Conflict in Reichstag over army bill (–*Mar.* 1887), with Liberals attempting to secure control over appropriations.

N First Indian National Congress meets, but lacks Moslem support.

X Sport

Amateur Golf Championship started; Horace Hutchinson first champion.

Y Statistics

U.K. merchant shipping tonnage 7,362,000 (3,965,000 steamships).

Z Births and Deaths

Feb. 15th Edward Cardwell d. (72).
Mar. 1st Oskar Kokoschka b. (–1980).
Mar. 8th E. C. Kendall b. (–1972).
Mar. 27th Ludwig Mies van der Rohe b. (–1969).
Apr. 5th William Edward Forster d. (67).
May 10th Karl Barth b. (1965).
May 23rd Leopold von Ranke d. (91).
June 5th Kurt Hahn b. (–1974).
July 23rd Salvador de Madariaga b. (–1978).
July 31st Franz Liszt d. (75).
Oct. 16th David Ben-Gurion b. (–1973).
— Mily Alexeivich Balakirev b. (–1910).
Dec. 18th Chu Teh b. (–1976).

1887 (Jan.–Nov.) Britain annexes Zululand and holds first Colonial Conference

A **Jan**: 11th, Otto von Bismarck advocates a larger German army;
14th, G. J. Goschen is appointed chancellor of the Exchequer in succession to Lord Randolph Churchill, and W. H. Smith, leader of House;
A drastic Irish Crimes Act is introduced; its passage is aided by articles in *The Times* on 'Parnellism and Crime' (see *July* 1888);
20th, New Zealand annexes Kermadec Isles, Pacific.

B **Feb**: 4th, U.S. Interstate Commerce Act regulates railways;
8th, H. L. Dawes's Act empowers U.S. President to terminate tribal government and divide lands amongst Indians;
12th, Anglo-Italian agreement to maintain *status quo* in Mediterranean;
20th, Triple Alliance between Germany, Austria and Italy renewed for three years.

C **Mar**: 24th, Austria becomes signatory to Anglo-Italian agreement on Mediterranean.

D **Apr**: 4th, first Colonial Conference in London opens;
20th, tension between France and Germany following a German court's conviction of Schnaebele, a French frontier official, for espionage.

E **May**: 4th, Spain supports Anglo-Italian agreement on Mediterranean;
16th, René Goblet's cabinet falls in France and,
18th, Maurice Rouvier forms ministry from which Georges Boulanger is excluded;
22nd, Henry Drummond Wolff signs convention with Egypt, by which Britain agrees to evacuate Egypt in three years, with the right to return if there are further disorders, an agreement nullified by French opposition;
26th, British East Africa Company is chartered.

F **Jun**: 17th, reform of suffrage in Holland;
18th, Germano-Russo Reinsurance treaty (–1890) to replace expiring Three Emperors' Alliance, which Russia had refused to renew;
21st, Queen Victoria's Golden Jubilee;
—, Britain annexes Zululand, blocking the attempt of Transvaal to gain communication with coast;
25th (–*July* 26th), U.S., Britain and Germany confer in Washington on Samoa.

G **Jul**: 4th, Bulgaria elects Prince Ferdinand of Saxe-Coburg King (–1918) but he is not immediately recognised by the powers;
Anglo-Russian agreement on Afghanistan;
31st, Francesco Crispi forms ministry in Italy (–1891) on A. Depreti's death.

H **Aug**:

J **Sep**:

K **Oct**: 1st, Baluchistan is united with India;
G. Boulanger's *coup d'état* fails in France, but his popularity increases with revelations of scandals connected with President Grévy's family.

L **Nov**: 13th, 'Bloody Sunday' with casualties and arrests in Trafalgar Square at Socialist meeting attended by Irish agitators;
16th, Anglo-French condominium over New Hebrides.

O **Politics, Economics, Law and Education**

Allotments and Copyhold Acts in England.
First Congress of criminal anthropologists, held at Rome.
L. Zamenhof founds 'Esperanto'.

P **Science, Technology, Discovery, etc.**

Joseph Lockyer, *The Chemistry of the Sun.*
Phenacetin, an analgesic drug, is discovered.
Emil Fischer and Tafel synthesise fructose.
Commercial preparation of aluminium by electrolysis, in Switzerland.
Cyanide process for extracting gold and silver.
Heinrich Hertz produces radio waves and demonstrates that they are reflected as are light waves.
Hilaire Comte de Chardonnet invents a process for making artificial silk.
Emil Berliner invents his version of the gramophone.
Carl Laval's turbine.
H. M. Stanley discovers the Lake Albert Edward Nyanza (*Dec.* 13th).

Q **Scholarship**

F. W. Maitland, *Bracton's Notebook.*

R **Philosophy and Religion**

Canonisation of Sir Thomas More, John Fisher and other English Roman Catholic martyrs.

S **Art, Sculpture, Fine Arts and Architecture**

T **Music**

J. Brahms, Concerto in A minor (op. 102) for violin and 'cello.
A. Borodin, *Prince Igor* (opera—unfinished).
G. Verdi, *Otello* (opera).
J. Stainer, *The Crucifixion* (oratorio).
A. Sullivan, *Ruddigore* (opera).
I. Paderewski gives first recitals in Vienna.

U **Literature**

T. Hardy, *The Woodlanders.*
Konrad Meyer, *Temptation of Pescara.*
Hermann Sudermann, *Frau Sorge.*

V **The Press**

W **Drama and Entertainment**

Victorien Sardou, *La Tosca.*
André Antoine founds Théâtre Libre in Paris for production of plays by H. F. Becque.

X **Sport**

Y **Statistics**

M **Dec**: 1st, Portugal secures cession of Macao from China;
2nd, Jules Grévy resigns presidency of France owing to financial scandals connected with his son-in-law, Wilson, who trafficked in medals of the Legion of Honour; Marie Sadi-Carnot is elected President;
12th, Britain, Austria and Italy sign treaty for maintenance of *status quo* in Near East.

N Central American states, under leadership of Guatemala, sign treaty of amity and consider draft federal constitution.
France organises Cochin China, Cambodia, Annam and Tonkin as Union Indo-Chinoise.

z **Births and Deaths**

Jan. 5th Bernard Leach b. (–1979).
Jan. 28th Artur Rubinstein b. (–1982).
Feb. 20th Vincent Massey b. (–1967).
Feb. 28th Alexander Borodin d. (53).
June 22nd Julian Huxley b. (–1975).
July 7th Marc Chagall b. (–1985).
July 14th Alfred Krupp d. (75).
Sept. 26th Barnes Wallis b. (–1979).
Oct. 6th Charles Édouard Jeanneret ('Le Corbusier') b. (–1965).
Oct. 31st Chiang Kai-shek b. (–1975).
Nov. 1st L. S. Lowry (–1976).
Nov. 17th Bernard, Viscount Montgomery, b. (–1976).

1888 Turkey's concession to Germany for first stage of Baghdad Railway

A **Jan**: 28th, military agreement between Germany and Italy provides for use of Italian troops against France in the event of a Franco-German war.

B **Feb**: 3rd, Bismarck publishes the Germano-Austrian alliance of 1879, as a warning to Russia, and, 6th, speaks in Reichstag on Russian designs;
11th, King Lobengula of Matabele accepts British protection;
Tension in Franco-Italian relations, Italy fearing the French fleet will attack Spezia.

C **Mar**: 9th, Frederick III succeeds as Emperor of Germany on William I's death;
17th, British protectorate over Sarawak;
27th, Boulanger is retired from French army, becoming eligible for election to Chamber.

D **Apr**: 15th, on election to French Chamber G. Boulanger begins campaign for revision of constitution. Charles Floquet forms French cabinet (–*Feb.* 1889);
G. J. Goschen reduces interest on Britain's national debt;
Agrarian rising in Rumania.

E **May**: 12th, British protectorate over North Borneo and Brunei;
13th, serfdom abolished in Brazil.

F **Jun**: 15th, William II becomes Emperor of Germany, on death of his father, Frederick I.

G **Jul**: 2nd, *The Times* is sued by a former Irish Nationalist M.P. over publication of letters of C. S. Parnell, later proved as forgeries (settled by a special commission in *Feb.* 1890).

H **Aug**: 9th, Local Government Act establishes county councils in Britain.

J **Sep**: Arab rising in German East Africa.

K **Oct**: 6th, Turkey grants concession to Germany to build a railway to Ankara, the first stage of Baghdad Railway;
14th, Hamburg and Bremen join German customs union;
29th, by Suez Canal convention, signed at Constantinople, the powers declare the canal open to all nations in war as in peace;
30th, King Lobengula grants Rhodes mining rights in Matabeleland;
France floats Russian loan, the beginnings of a Franco-Russian *entente*.

L **Nov**: In U.S. presidential election, fought on tariff issue, Benjamin Harrison, Republican, wins 233 electoral votes, Grover Cleveland, Democrat, 168; his loss is ascribed to treachery of Tammany Hall, the Democratic organisation in New York City.

M **Dec**: 11th, French colony of Gabon united with French Congo;
Italy supports Menelek of Shoa in his revolt against Johannes IV of Ethiopia.

N Protective tariffs in New Zealand and Sweden.

O **Politics, Economics, Law and Education**

James Bryce, *American Commonwealth.*
Cecil Rhodes amalgamates Kimberley diamond companies.

P **Science, Technology, Discovery, etc.**

The word 'chromosome' is first used.
Pasteur Institute, Paris, founded.
N. Tesla invents A.C. electric motor which is manufactured by George Westinghouse.
E. J. Marey's *chambre chronophotographique*, forerunner of the cinematograph.
George Eastman's 'Kodak' box camera.
J. B. Dunlop invents pneumatic tyre.
First refrigerated railway truck; first railway in China.
Aeronautical exhibition, Vienna (*Apr.*).
F. Nansen crosses Greenland.
C. M. Doughty, *Travels in Arabia Deserta.*

Q **Scholarship**

University of Pennsylvania equips expedition to excavate Babylonian remains at Nippu, Iraq.

R **Philosophy and Religion**

Bernard Bosanquet, *Logic or the Morphology of Thought.*
G. J. Romanes, *Mental Evolution in Man.*
James Martineau, *A Study of Religion.*

S **Art, Sculpture, Fine Arts and Architecture**

James Ensor, *Entry of Christ into Brussels* (painting).
V. van Gogh, *Sunflowers* and *The Yellow Chair* (paintings).

T **Music**

N. Rimsky-Korsakov, symphonic suite *Scheherezade* (op. 35).
Richard Strauss, tone poem *Don Juan.*
Hugo Wolf, *Der Gärtner* and other lieder.
Gustav Mahler directs the Budapest opera.

U **Literature**

Maurice Barrès, *Sous l'Œil des Barbares.*
Edward Bellamy, *Looking Backwards, 2000–1887.*
Rolf Boldrewood (pseud.), *Robbery under Arms.*
A. France (pseud.), *La Vie littéraire* begins.
R. Kipling, *Plain Tales from the Hills.*
G. de Maupassant, *Pierre et Jean.*
A. Quiller-Couch, *Astonishing History of Troy Town.*
Mark Rutherford (pseud.), *The Revolution in Tanner's Lane.*
P. Verlaine, *Amour.*
É. Zola, *La Terre.*

V **The Press**

The Financial Times, *The Star* (ed. O'Connor –1960), and *Collier's Weekly* are first issued.

W **Drama and Entertainment**

A. W. Pinero, *Sweet Lavender.*
A. Strindberg, *Miss Julie.*
First beauty contest, at Spa, Belgium (*Sept.*).

X **Sport**

Football League founded.
Lawn Tennis Association established.

Y **Statistics**

Value of World Production: percentages contributed by U.S., 31·8; Great Britain, 17·8; Germany, 13·3; France, 10·7; Russia, 8·1; Austro-Hungary, 5·6; Italy, 2·7; Belgium, 2·2; Spain, 1·9; other countries, 5·9.

Z **Births and Deaths**

Feb. 20th Dame Marie Rambert b. (–1982).
Apr. 15th Matthew Arnold d. (65).
May 11th Irving Berlin b. (–1989).
July 10th Giorgio de Chirico b. (–1978).
July 30th Werner Jaeger b. (–1961).
Aug. 13th J. L. Baird b. (–1946).
Aug. 15th T. E. Lawrence b. (–1935).
Sept. 5th Sarvepalli Radhakrishnan b. (–1975).
Sept. 12th Maurice Chevalier b. (–1972).
Oct. 14th Katherine Mansfield (*née* Beauchamp, pseud. of Kathleen Murry) b. (–1923).
Nov. 9th Jean Monnet b. (–1979).
Nov. 11th A. N. Tupolev b. (–1972).
Nov. 18th Frank Dobson b. (–1963).
— T. S. Eliot b. (–1965).

1889 French protectorate over Ivory Coast—Italy claims protectorate over Ethiopia

A **Jan:** 10th, France establishes protectorate over Ivory Coast;
30th, Crown Prince Archduke Rudolf of Austria commits suicide at Mayerling.

B **Feb:** 11th, Constitution granted in Japan, with two-chamber Diet, but Emperor retains extensive powers;
22nd, North and South Dakota, Montana and Washington are created U.S. states;
Pierre Tirard forms ministry in France (*–Mar.* 1890).

C **Mar:** 4th, Benjamin Harrison, Republican, inaugurated as U.S. President;
6th, Milan of Serbia abdicates in favour of his son and Jovan Ristich acts as Regent.

D **Apr:** 8th, G. Boulanger, fearing trial for treason, flees from France and in the subsequent elections the Republicans triumph;
22nd, Oklahoma is opened to settlement.

E **May:** 2nd, by treaty of Ucciali with Menelek of Ethiopia, Italy claims protectorate over Ethiopia;
31st, Naval Defence Act in Britain inaugurates extensive naval building programme;
German old-age insurance law.

F **Jun:** Brussels Conference for abolition of slave trade and suppression of traffic in arms and liquor to undeveloped peoples.

G **Jul:** 17th, French law forbidding multiple candidates in elections;
23rd, British Board of Agriculture founded;
Crisis in Italian-Vatican relations.

H **Aug:** 19th (*–Sept.* 14th), London dock strike.

J **Sep:**

K **Oct:** 2nd, first Pan-American conference at Washington rejects J. G. Blaine's plan for reciprocity;
29th, British South Africa Company, headed by Cecil Rhodes, is granted royal charter with extensive powers for expanding its territory at the expense of Transvaal;
Antonio Blanco, President since 1870, is deprived of office in Venezuela.

L **Nov:** 15th, on Pedro II's abdication Brazil is proclaimed a republic;
Menelek, through Italian support, becomes King of Ethiopia, following disputed succession on death (*Mar.* 12th) of Johannes IV.

M **Dec:** 6th, Calvinist-Catholic coalition in Holland, following fall of Liberals.

N Manhood suffrage in New Zealand.

Z **Births and Deaths** (*cont.*)
May 25th Igor Sikorsky b. (–1972).
July 5th Jean Cocteau b. (–1963).
July 20th J. C. Reith b. (–1971).
Sept. 26th Martin Heidegger b. (–1976).
Oct. 11th J. P. Joule d. (71).
Nov. 16th George S. Kaufman b. (–1961).
Dec. 12th Robert Browning d. (77).
Dec. 18th Gladys Cooper b. (–1971).
Jomo Kenyatta b. (–1978).

O Politics, Economics, Law and Education

G. B. Shaw, *Fabian Essays.*

London County Council is formed (–1965). Lord Rosebery is elected first chairman (*Feb.* 12th).

Welsh Intermediate Education Act founds secondary education in Wales.

Catholic University, Washington, founded.

P Science, Technology, Discovery, etc.

G. V. Schiaparelli determines the synchronous rotation of the planet Mercury.

Frederick Abel invents cordite.

George Eastman produces a celluloid roll-film.

Institution of Electrical Engineers is founded in London.

Q Scholarship

H. Bresslau, *Handbuch der Urkundenlehre für Deutschland und Italien.*

R Philosophy and Religion

S. Alexander, *Moral Order and Progress.*

H. Bergson, *Les Données immédiates et la conscience.*

T. H. Huxley, *Agnosticism.*

S Art, Sculpture, Fine Arts and Architecture

V. van Gogh, *Landscape with Cypress Tree* (painting).

P. Puvis de Chavannes decorates Hôtel de Ville, Paris (–93).

Eiffel Tower, Paris, built.

T Music

A. Dvořák, Symphony No. 4 in G (op. 88).

C. Franck, Symphony in D minor.

R. Strauss, symphonic poem *Death and Transfiguration* (op. 31).

P. I. Tchaikovsky, Symphony No. 5 in E minor (op. 64).

A. Sullivan, *The Gondoliers* (opera).

The 'Red Flag' is written in London after a dock strike.

U Literature

J. M. Barrie, *A Window in Thrums.*

A. Gide begins *Journal* (–1949).

Gerhardt Hauptmann, *Before Dawn.*

J. K. Jerome, *Three Men in a Boat.*

M. Maeterlinck, *Serres chaudes.*

W. B. Yeats, *The Wanderings of Oisin.*

W Drama and Entertainment

P. T. Barnum and J. A. Bailey's show at Olympia (*Nov.*).

X Sport

Y Statistics

Z Births and Deaths

Mar. 27th John Bright d. (76).

Apr. 8th Sir Adrian Boult b. (–1983).

Apr. 14th Arnold Toynbee b. (–1975).

Apr. 16th Charles Chaplin b. (–1977).

Apr. 20th Adolf Hitler b. (–1945).

Apr. 24th Stafford Cripps b. (–1952).

Apr. 28th Antonio Salazar b. (–1970).

May 11th Paul Nash b. (–1946).

(*Continued opposite*)

1890 (Jan.–Nov.) William II dismisses Bismarck—Anti-Trust Laws in U.S.—Bechuanaland and Uganda come under British control

A **Jan:**

B **Feb:**

C **Mar:** 15th (–28th), international congress for Protection of Workers held in Berlin;
20th, Otto von Bismarck is dismissed by William II and Georg Caprivi becomes German chancellor (–94);
27th, universal suffrage in Spain.

D **Apr:** Conservatives defeated in New Zealand elections by Labour and Liberal parties.

E **May:** 24th, by Mackinnon treaty between Leopold of Belgium and British East Africa Company, the latter recognises Leopold's rights on the west bank of the Upper Nile in return for territory near Lake Tanganyika;
Italy reorganises her Red Sea territories as the Colony of Eritrea.

F **Jun:** 18th, Germany allows Reinsurance treaty (see *June* 1887) with Russia to lapse, despite Russian attempts to open negotiations for a renewal;
19th, U.S. Force bill, for federal control of elections, especially to protect Negro voters in the South, passes House of Representatives but is not adopted by Senate;
Swiss federal government introduces social insurance.

G **Jul:** 1st, by Anglo-German convention Britain exchanges Heligoland for Zanzibar and Pemba;
2nd, John Sherman's anti-trust law enacted in U.S.;
—, Brussels act passed by international conference to eradicate African slave trade and liquor traffic with primitive peoples;
3rd, Idaho becomes a U.S. state;
10th, Wyoming becomes a U.S. state;
17th, Cecil Rhodes becomes premier of Cape Colony;
29th, industrial courts established in Germany to adjust wage disputes;
First general election in Japan.

H **Aug:** 5th, Anglo-French convention defines spheres of influence in Nigeria, the British Protectorate in Zanzibar and Pemba and the French Protectorate in Madagascar;
17th, Tsar Alexander III fails to persuade Germany to make an *entente* with Russia at his meeting with the Emperor William II at Narva.

J **Sep:** 12th, British South Africa Company founds Salisbury in Mashonaland.

K **Oct:** 1st, German anti-socialist law of 1878 expires and, 21st, Social Democrats adopt Marxist programme at Erfurt congress;
22nd, responsible government in Western Australia;
28th, German East Africa Company cedes its territorial rights to Germany;
Following McKinley tariff, Liberals in Canada urge reciprocity with U.S.

L **Nov:** 12th, Cardinal Charles Lavigerie's 'Algiers Toast', calling on all Frenchmen to rally to the constitution, an attempt to reconcile the Roman Catholic Church with the Republic;
14th, Anglo-Portuguese agreement on Zambesi and the Congo grants Britain the control of the Lower Zambesi and the right to colonise central territory up to the Congo;
23rd, on accession of Queen Wilhelmina the Grand Duchy of Luxembourg is separated from the Netherlands;
29th, first Japanese Diet opened.

O **Politics, Economics, Law and Education**

Alfred Marshall, *Principles of Economics.*
William Booth, *In Darkest England and the Way Out.*
Act for the housing of the working classes in Britain.
First May Day labour celebrations in Germany.
Failure of Baring's Bank, London.
L. A. Bertillon describes identification of criminals in *Photographie judiciare.*
Free elementary education in England.
W. H. O'Shea is granted a decree nisi against C. S. Parnell (*Nov.* 17th).
Daughters of the American Revolution founded in Washington.

P **Science, Technology, Discovery, etc.**

T. Curtius obtains azoimide (compound of hydrogen and nitrogen) from organic sources.
First English electrical power station, at Deptford.
First 'tube' railway, City and South London Railway, passing beneath River Thames.
Earliest corridor-train.
Forth Bridge completed.
Building entirely steel-framed erected in Chicago.

Q **Scholarship**

J. G. Frazer, *The Golden Bough* (–1914).
A. T. Mahan, *The Influence of Sea Power upon History, 1660–1783.*

R **Philosophy and Religion**

William James, *The Principles of Psychology.*
Lux Mundi, edited by Charles Gore.
Privy Council upholds judgment of the Archbishop of Canterbury's court against Bishop Edward King of Lincoln for ritualistic practices.

S **Art, Sculpture, Fine Arts and Architecture**

P. Cézanne, *The Cardplayers* (painting).
Frederick Leighton, *The Bath of Psyche* (painting).
P. Puvis de Chavannes leads secession of artists from the Salon to exhibit in the Champ de Mars.
William Morris founds Kelmscott Press.

T **Music**

A. Borodin, *Prince Igor* (opera).
P. Mascagni, *Cavalleria Rusticana* (opera).
P. I. Tchaikovsky, *Queen of Spades* (opera).

U **Literature**

Knut Hamsun (pseud.), *Hunger.*
Leo Tolstoy, *The Kreutzer Sonata.*
J. G. Whittier, *At Sundown.*

V **The Press**

W. T. Stead edits *Review of Reviews.*
Daily Graphic, first fully-illustrated English newspaper (*Jan.* 4th).
Stefan George founds *Blätter fur die Kunst.*

W **Drama and Entertainment**

H. Ibsen, *Hedda Gabler.*

1890 (Dec.)

M **Dec:** 12th, C. S. Parnell resigns and is succeeded as leader of Irish Nationalists by Justin McCarthy;
18th, Frederick Lugard occupies Uganda for the British East Africa Company.

N Bechuanaland is placed under a British governor.
Beginnings of Armenian nationalist revolutionary movement.

X Sport

English county cricket clubs officially classified, with seven 1st-class counties.

Y Statistics

Railway mileage in operation: U.S.; 125,000; France, 20,800; Great Britain, 20,073; Russia, 19,000.

Coal production (in mill. tons): Great Britain, 184; U.S., 143; Germany, 89; France, 26·1; Austro-Hungary, 26; Russia, 6.

Steel production (in mill. tons): U.S., 4·3; Great Britain, 3·6; Germany, 2·3; France, 0·7; Austro-Hungary, 0·5; Russia, 0·4.

Emigration to U.S. (*1881–90*): from Great Britain, 807,357; from Ireland, 655, 482.

Z Births and Deaths

Jan. 9th Karel Čapek b. (–1938).
Jan. 14th Ignaz von Döllinger d. (91).
Mar. 9th Vyacheslav Molotov b. (–1986).
Mar. 29th Harold Spencer Jones b. (–1960).
Mar. 31st W. L. Bragg b. (–1971).
Apr. 6th Anthony Fokker b. (–1939).
May 19th Ho Chi Minh b. (–1969).
July 15th Gottfried Keller d. (71).
Aug. 5th Naum Gabo b. (–1977).
Aug. 11th John Henry Newman d. (89).
Aug. 27th Man Ray b. (–1976).
Sept. 15th Agatha Christie b. (–1976).
Sept. 24th A. P. Herbert b. (–1971).
Oct. 14th Dwight D. Eisenhower b. (–1969).
Nov. 8th César Franck d. (67).
Nov. 10th Arthur Rimbaud d. (37).
Nov. 22nd Charles de Gaulle b. (–1970).
— Harry L. Hopkins b. (–1946).
— Vincent van Gogh d. (37).
Dec. 5th Fritz Lang b. (–1976).

1891 British Liberals adopt 'Newcastle Programme'—Renewal of Triple Alliance

A **Jan:** 31st, Marquis de Rudin, of the Right, forms coalition in Italy on F. Crispi's resignation; Civil War in Chile.

B **Feb:** 9th, Menelek, Emperor of Ethiopia, denounces Italian claims to a protectorate; 24th, federal Constitution in Brazil.

C **Mar:** 24th, Anglo-Italian agreement over Ethiopia, defining the frontiers of their Red Sea colonies (further convention, *Apr.* 15th);
Sydney Convention under Henry Parkes draws up a federal Constitution for Australia (*–July*), but the scheme is dropped through opposition of New South Wales.

D **Apr:** 15th, The Katanga Company is formed under Leopold of Belgium's direction to exploit copper deposits.

E **May:** 6th, Triple Alliance of Germany, Austria and Italy is renewed for twelve years.

F **Jun:** 1st, thorough factory inspection in force in Germany;
10th, L. Starr Jameson becomes administrator of South Africa Company's territories;
11th, further Anglo-Portuguese convention on territories north and south of Zambesi: Portugal assigns Barotseland to Britain. Nyasaland is subsequently proclaimed a British Protectorate;
16th, John Abbot becomes premier of Canada on Macdonald's death (premier since 1878);
20th, Britain and Holland define their boundaries in Borneo.

G **Jul:** 4th, William II visits London, hoping Britain might accede to Triple Alliance;
23rd, French squadron visits Kronstadt and a French loan is floated to finance Trans-Siberian railway.

H **Aug:** 27th, Franco-Russian *entente.*

J **Sep:** 19th, José Balmaceda driven from office in Chile;
30th, Georges Boulanger commits suicide in exile in Brussels.

K **Oct:** British Liberal party adopts the 'Newcastle Programme', advocating Irish Home Rule, Disestablishment of Welsh Church, reform of Lords, triennial parliaments, abolition of plural franchise and local veto on sales of liquor.

L **Nov:** 23rd, Deodoroda Fonseca, first President, driven from office in Brazil by naval revolt, is succeeded by Florians Peixoto who governs dictatorially.

M **Dec:** Joseph Chamberlain becomes leader of Liberal Unionists in Commons on Lord Hartington's succession to the dukedom of Devonshire.

N Felix Méline introduces rigid Protection in France.
Social legislation in Denmark.

O **Politics, Economics, Law and Education**

Charles Booth, *Life and Labour of the People in London* (–1903).
Goldwin Smith, *The Canadian Question.*
Public Health Act in Britain.
Pan-German League is founded (*Apr.*).
The Prince of Wales, giving evidence in libel action Gordon-Cumming *v.* Lycett Green, concerning cheating at cards at Tranby Croft, admits he played baccarat for high stakes.

P **Science, Technology, Discovery, etc.**

Johnstone Stoney introduces the term 'electron'.
Trans-Siberian Railway begun (–1904).

Q **Scholarship**

R **Philosophy and Religion**

R. W. Church (posth.), *History of the Oxford Movement.*
Cardinal R. W. Vaughan denies the validity of Anglican Orders (*Oct.* 5th).
Papal encyclical *Rerum novarum* on condition of working classes (*May* 15th), earns Leo XIII the name of 'the working man's Pope'.
Union of General and Particular Baptists in England under John Clifford.

S **Art, Sculpture, Fine Arts and Architecture**

P. Gauguin settles in Tahiti.
Retrospective Vincent van Gogh exhibition at *Salon des Indépendents.*
Henri Toulouse-Lautrec's first posters for Montmartre music halls.
Giovanni Segantini, *Ploughing of the Engadine* (painting).
William Richmond undertakes interior decorations and glass mosaics for St. Paul's Cathedral.

T **Music**

P. I. Tchaikovsky's *Casse-Noisette* ballet music.
Carnegie Music Hall, New York, opened.

U **Literature**

M. Barrès, *Le Jardin de Bérénice.*
J. M. Barrie, *The Little Minister.*
A. C. Doyle's *Adventures of Sherlock Holmes* begin in *Strand Magazine.*
G. Gissing, *New Grub Street.*
T. Hardy, *Tess of the D'Urbervilles.*
J. K. Huysmans, *Là-bas.*
Francis Thompson, *The Hound of Heaven.*
F. Wedekind, *Spring's Awakening.*
O. Wilde, *The Picture of Dorian Gray.*

V **The Press**

Il Mattino issued.

W **Drama and Entertainment**

V. Sardou, *Thermidor.*
J. T. Grein founds the Independent Theatre Society, London, for introducing plays by Henrik Ibsen and other continental dramatists to the English stage.
E. Duse's début in Vienna.

X **Sport**

Y **Statistics**

Populations (in mills.): U.S. 65; Germany, 49·4; Japan, 40·7; France, 38·3; Great Britain, 33; Ireland, 4·7; Italy, 30·3; Austria, 23·8.

Z **Births and Deaths**

Jan. 16th Léo Delibes d. (55).
Mar. 19th Earl Warren b. (–1974).
Mar. 29th Georges Seurat d. (32).
Apr. 2nd Max Ernst b. (–1976).
Apr. 7th David Low b. (–1964).
June 20th John A. Costello b. (–1976).
Aug. 2nd Arthur Bliss b. (–1975).
Aug. 12th James Russell Lowell d. (72).
Aug. 22nd Jacques Lipchitz b. (–1973).
Sept. 16th Karl Dönitz b. (–1980).
Sept. 28th Herman Melville d. (72).
Oct. 26th Helmuth Count von Moltke d. (90).
Nov. 15th Averell Harriman b. (–1986).
— Ilya Ehrenburg b. (–1967).
Dec. 26th Henry Miller b. (–1980).

A **Jan**: 7th, Abbas, aged 18, succeeds Tewfik as Khedive of Egypt (–1914) and is hostile to British influence.

B **Feb**: 1st, Germany signs commercial treaties with Austria-Hungary, Italy, Switzerland and Belgium;
22nd, U.S. Populist party is organised at St. Louis;
29th, Anglo-U.S. treaty on Bering Sea seal fishery.

C **Mar**: 26th Labour Department formed in Germany;
In Prussia a bill for religious education of children by the clergy is withdrawn after acrimonious debate.

D **Apr**:

E **May**: Giovanni Giolitti replaces Marquis di Rudin as premier of Italy.

F **June**: 30th, iron and steel workers begin strike in U.S.;
Prince Ito becomes premier of Japan.

G **Jul**: in British general election Liberals win 273 seats, Irish Home Rulers 81, Labour 1 against Conservatives 269, and Liberal Unionists 46, but Lord Salisbury awaits Parliament's re-assembly before resigning;
At Omaha the Populist Party convention nominates James B. Weaver for presidency.

H **Aug**: 11th, Lord Salisbury resigns and W. E. Gladstone forms Liberal ministry (*–Mar.* 9th), with Lord Rosebery foreign secretary, W. V. Harcourt chancellor of exchequer and H. H. Asquith home secretary;
17th, Franco-Russian military convention.

Sep: Sergei Witte becomes Russian finance minister;
First trains arrive at Johannesburg from the Cape.

K **Oct**: 15th, Anglo-German convention over Cameroons.

L **Nov**: 8th, Grover Cleveland, Democrat, wins U.S. presidential election with 277 electoral votes, on platform opposing the McKinley tariff and the Force bill, against Benjamin Harrison, Republican, 145, and James B. Weaver, Populist, 22;
10th, the Panama scandal breaks in France and Ferdinand de Lesseps and associates are committed for trial for corruption and mismanagement;
22nd, Belgians suppress rising of Arab slave-holders in Upper Congo.

M **Dec**: 5th, John Thompson becomes premier of Canada on John Abbott's resignation (*–Dec.* 1894);
12th, Pan-Slav conference at Cracow.

N French War against King Dahomey in West Africa.
Serious famine in Russia.

Z **Births and Deaths** (*cont.*)
Aug. 15th Duc Louis de Broglie b. (–1987).
Aug. 17th Mae West b. (–1980).
Oct. 4th Engelbert Dolfuss b. (–1934).
Oct. 6th Alfred Lord Tennyson d. (83).
Oct. 12th Ernest Renan d. (69).
Oct. 14th Sumner Welles b. (–1961).
Nov. 6th J. W. Alcock b. (–1919).
Dec. 6th E. W. Siemens d. (76).
Dec. 15th J. Paul Getty b. (–1976).
Dec. 21st Rebecca West b. (–1983).

O Politics, Economics, Law and Education

Émile Faguet, *Politiques et Moralistes français du XIX siècle.*
California earthquake disaster (*Apr.* 19th).
Age of marriage for Italian girls raised to twelve.
Pioneer Club for Ladies founded in London.
Pan-Slav Conference at Cracow (*Dec.*).

P Science, Technology, Discovery, etc.

Auriga, a new star, observed in Milky Way (*Feb.* 1st).
C. F. Cross discovers viscose, making possible the manufacture of rayon.
Rudolf Diesel patents a petrol engine.
First automatic telephone switchboard.
Pineapples are canned.

Q Scholarship

James Darmesteter edits the Zend-Avesta (–93).
W. E. Gladstone delivers first Romanes Lecture at Oxford.

R Philosophy and Religion

G. J. Romanes, *Darwin and After Darwinism.*
Charles Gore founds the Community of the Resurrection.

S Art, Sculpture, Fine Arts and Architecture

Claude Monet begins pictures of Rouen Cathedral (–95).
Henri Toulouse-Lautrec, *At the Moulin Rouge* (painting).

T Music

A. Bruckner, *Psalm 150.*
C. H. H. Parry, *Job* (oratorio).
R. Leoncavallo, *I Pagliacci* (opera).
A. Dvořák becomes director of New York National Conservatory.

U Literature

R. Kipling, *Barrack Room Ballads.*
I. Zangwill, *The Children of the Ghetto.*
É. Zola, *La Débâcle.*

V The Press

W Drama and Entertainment

M. Maeterlinck, *Pelléas et Mélisande*, with C. Debussy's music.
G. B. Shaw, *Widower's Houses.*
O. Wilde, *Lady Windermere's Fan.*
Lottie Collins sings Ta-ra-ra-boom-de-ay in London.

X Sport

Y Statistics

U.K. Trades union membership, 1,576,000.

Z Births and Deaths

Jan. 3rd. J. R. R. Tolkien b. (–1973).
Jan. 14th Martin Niemöller b. (–1984).
Feb. 18th Wendell Wilkie b. (–1944).
Mar. 27th Walt Whitman d. (72).
Apr. 13th Arthur Harris b. (–1984).
— Robert Watson-Watt b. (–1973).
May 7th Josip Broz Tito b. (–1980).
May 16th Edward Augustus Freeman d. (68).
July 23rd Haile Selassie b. (–1975).

(*Continued opposite*)

1893 (Jan.–Nov.) Franco-Russian rapprochement

A **Jan:** 13th, Independent Labour Party formed at conference in Bradford under Keir Hardie;
17th, Hawaii proclaimed a republic with the connivance of the resident U.S. minister;
Franco-Russian alliance is signed;
Abbas Khedive of Egypt dismisses pro-British ministers, but Lord Cromer asserts his authority.

B **Feb:** 14th, Hawaii is annexed by treaty to U.S. (but the treaty is withdrawn by President Grover Cleveland, *Mar.* 9th, in hope of restoring the monarchy and James Blount is sent to investigate the affair).

C **Mar:** 8th, trial of Ferdinand de Lesseps and associates for corruption over Panama Canal opens in Paris (the sentences, 21st, are set aside, *June* 15th, by *cour de cassation* under the statute of limitations);
10th, French colonies of French Guinea and Ivory Coast formally established;
Anarchist outrages in Paris;
Gerald Portal hoists British flag in Uganda, which British East Africa Company evacuates.

D **Apr:** 14th, Alexander I of Serbia, now eighteen, declares himself of age and dissolves Regency Council;
22nd, Paul Kruger is re-elected in Transvaal for third time;
General strike in Belgium.

E **May:** 10th, Natal is granted self-government.

F **Jun:** Franco-Russian commercial treaty;
Alarmed at Belgian advance in the Congo, France sends an occupying force to forestall further annexations.

G **Jul:** 13th, army bill increases size of German army but reduces military service to two years;
15th, French note to Siam provokes crisis in Franco-British relations, and 31st, France agrees to maintain Siam as buffer state;
Matabeles rise against rule of British South Africa Company.

H **Aug:**

J **Sep:** 1st, the Second Irish Home Rule bill, proposing that 80 Irish representatives should sit at Westminster, passes the Commons but is rejected, 8th, by the Lords.

K **Oct:** 13th (–29th), Russian fleet visits Toulon;
29th, Count Taaffe, premier of Austria-Hungary, resigns when the question of universal suffrage splits his coalition.

L **Nov:** 1st, under Grover Cleveland, Congress repeals Sherman bill on compulsory silver purchase;
13th, by Pretoria convention Britain agrees to the annexation of Swaziland by the Transvaal;
15th, Anglo-German agreement defines Nigeria-Cameroons boundary, and leases territory east of Lake Chad to within 100 miles of the Nile to Germany;
17th, Dahomey becomes a French protectorate;
L. Starr Jameson crushes Matabele revolt and occupies Bulawayo.

O **Politics, Economics, Law and Education**

C. H. Pearson, *National Life and Character, a Forecast.*
Imperial Institute, South Kensington, and the University of Wales are founded.
Franchise in New Zealand is extended to women.
Universal suffrage in Belgium with plural voting, on basis of wealth and education.

P **Science, Technology, Discovery, etc.**

Robert Armstrong-Jones begins modern treatment of mental diseases at London County Council's Claybury Asylum.
Karl Benz's four-wheel car.
Automatic railway signals are installed at Liverpool.
Manchester Ship Canal completed.
New Croton aqueduct tunnel, New York, completed.
Egbert Judson invents zip fastener.
F. Nansen leads expedition to North Pole (–96).
Corinth Canal is opened (*Aug.* 6th).

Q **Scholarship**

R **Philosophy and Religion**

F. H. Bradley, *Appearance and Reality.*
W. T. Stead, *If Christ Came to Chicago.*
Leslie Stephen, *Agnostic's Apology.*

S **Art, Sculpture, Fine Arts and Architecture**

The Studio, with Aubrey Beardsley's drawings, spreads the ideas of *art nouveau* in architecture and interior decoration.
Copenhagen Town Hall (–1902).

T **Music**

A. Dvořák, Symphony no. 5 ('From the New World', op. 95).
J. Sibelius, *Karelia Suite* (op. 10).
P. I. Tchaikovsky, Symphony no. 6 in B minor ('Pathétique', op. 74).
E. Humperdinck, *Hansel and Gretel* (opera).
G. Puccini, *Manon Lescaut* (opera).
G. Verdi, *Falstaff* (opera).

U **Literature**

A. France (pseud.), *La Rôtisserie de la Reine Pédauque.*
José de Heredia, *Les Trophées.*
M. Rutherford (pseud.), *Catherine Furze.*

V **The Press**

The Sketch issued.

W **Drama and Entertainment**

Georges Courteline, *Boubouroche.*
A. W. Pinero, *The Second Mrs. Tanqueray.*
O. Wilde, *A Woman of No Importance.*
Chicago World Exhibition.

X **Sport**

M **Dec**: 4th, Anglo-French agreement on Siam, but Britain's concessions to French designs dismay Germany;
9th, the anarchist, Auguste Vailland, explodes bomb in the Paris Chamber of Deputies;
10th, on fall of G. Giolitti's ministry through bank scandals, F. Crispi forms cabinet in Italy (*–Mar.* 96);
Italians defeat Mahdists in attack on Eritrea.

N France acquires protectorate over Laos.
Tariff war between France and Switzerland.
Germany signs further commercial treaties with Balkan states.
Internal Macedonia Revolutionary Organisation founded in Bulgaria to work for independence for Macedonia.
Anti-Saloon League founded in U.S. to further the cause of Prohibition.

Y **Statistics**

U.S. crude petroleum production: 48,431,000 barrels.

Z **Births and Deaths**

Jan. 12th Hermann Goering b. (–1946).
Feb. 12th Omar Bradley b. (–1981).
Feb. 21st Andrés Segovia b. (–1987).
Mar. 5th Ivon Hitchens b. (–1979).
— Hippolyte Taine d. (65).
Apr. 8th Mary Pickford b. (–1979).
Apr. 11th Dean Acheson b. (–1971).
Apr. 20th Harold Lloyd b. (–1971).
— Joan Miró b. (–1983).
Apr. 29th Harold Clayton Urey b. (–1981).
June 9th Cole Porter b. (–1964).
June 30th Harold Laski b. (–1950).
— Walter Ulbricht b. (–1973).
July 6th Guy de Maupassant d. (43).
Aug. 16th J. M. Charcot d. (67).
Aug. 30th Huey Pierce Long b. (–1935).
Oct. 18th Charles François Gounod d. (75).
Nov. 6th Peter Iljich Tchaikovsky d. (53).
Nov. 8th Francis Parkman d. (73).
Dec. 1st Ernst Toller b. (–1939).
Dec. 26th Mao Tse-tung b. (–1976).

A **Jan**: L. Starr Jameson completes occupation of Matabeleland.

B **Feb**: 10th, Germany signs commercial treaty with Russia;
W. E. Gladstone withdraws Employers' Liability bill on Lords' amendments.

C **Mar**: 3rd, W. E. Gladstone resigns, having split Liberal Party over Home Rule, and Lord Rosebery, a Liberal Unionist, becomes prime minister, with W. V. Harcourt as leader of the Commons;
15th, Franco-German agreement on boundaries between French Congo and the Cameroons.

D **Apr**: 11th, Uganda is declared a British protectorate;
H. V. Harcourt introduces death duties in budget.

E **May**: 5th, Anglo-Italian agreement over East Africa, by which Italy is assigned Harar;
12th, Anglo-Belgian agreement assigning Leopold territory on the left bank of the Upper Nile;
21st, restoration of Serbian constitution of 1869.

F **Jun**: 22nd, Dahomey proclaimed a French Colony;
23rd, Colonial Conference in Ottawa (–*July* 10th);
24th, President M. F. Sadi-Carnot of France is assassinated by an Italian anarchist at Lyons; succeeded by Jean Casimir-Périer;
Germany thwarts Lord Rosebery's attempts to draw Britain closer to the Triple Alliance.

G **Jul**: 11th, laws suppressing anarchist and socialist organisations in Italy;
17th, Italians take Kassala, Sudan, from the Dervishes;
23rd, Japanese troops seize the palace in Seoul, Korea;
27th, Regent of Korea declares war on China.

H **Aug**: 1st, Japan declares war on China over question of Korea;
14th, on protest from France, Leopold II of Belgium abandons claims to Upper Nile territory;
18th, Carey Act in U.S. grants lands in Colorado, Idaho and six other states to encourage irrigation;
28th, Wilson-Gorman tariff, embodying a 2 per cent income tax, becomes law in U.S. without President Cleveland's signature; replaces McKinley tariff.
Glen Grey act in Cape Colony embarks on a new natives policy.

J **Sep**: 25th Britain annexes Pondoland, connecting Cape Colony with Natal.

K **Oct**: 15th, Alfred Dreyfus is arrested on treason charge;
26th, Prince Hohenlohe succeeds Count Caprivi as German chancellor; the unpopularity of the commercial treaty with Russia (*Feb.*) contributes to Caprivi's fall.

L **Nov**: On Alexander III's death Nicholas II becomes Tsar (–1917);
10th, French troops begin conquest of Madagascar (–*Jan.* 96);
21st, Japanese victory over Chinese at Port Arthur;
Banks in Newfoundland fail.

O Politics, Economics, Law and Education

Benjamin Kidd, *Social Revolution.*
S. and B. Webb, *History of Trade Unionism.*
Parish Councils are established in England.
Dutch Labour Party is founded.

P Science, Technology, Discovery, etc.

Lord Rayleigh and William Ramsay discover argon.
James Dewar liquefies oxygen.
First railway over the Andes.

Q Scholarship

F. Pollock and F. W. Maitland, *History of English Law.*

R Philosophy and Religion

Lord Halifax opens discussions on reunion of Anglican Church with Rome.
Freedom of worship in Austria, where civil marriage becomes compulsory.

S Art, Sculpture, Fine Arts and Architecture

Matthew Corbett, *Morning Glory* (painting).
Gustave Caillebotte collection of Impressionist paintings is rejected by Luxembourg Museum, Paris.
The Yellow Book, with Aubrey Beardsley as art editor.
Ashendene Press is established by Charles St. John Hornby.

T Music

Claude Debussy, *L'Après-midi d'un Faune.*
Jules Massenet, *Thaïs* (opera).
Hugo Wolf, *Italian Serenade.*

U Literature

Hall Caine, *The Manxman.*
Anthony Hope (pseud.), *Prisoner of Zenda.*
R. Kipling, *The Jungle Book.*
G. Moore, *Esther Waters.*
S. Weyman, *Under the Red Robe.*
É. Zola, *Les Trois Villes* (–98).

V The Press

W Drama and Entertainment

G. B. Shaw, *Arms and the Man.*
T. A. Edison's Kinetoscope Parlour, New York.

X Sport

Paris-Rouen trial run for motor-cars.
New York Jockey Club founded.

Y Statistics

M **Dec:** 21st, MacKenzie Bowell becomes Canadian premier, following John Thompson's death;
22nd, A. Dreyfus is convicted by a court martial *in camera*, and imprisoned in Devil's Island, French Guiana.

N Lord Spencer's naval programme in England.
Standing Committee of Commons appointed to consider measures for Scotland.
Riots in Sicily.
Risings of Christians against Turks in Crete (–97).
Revolts in Dutch East Indies.

z **Births and Deaths**

Feb. 10th Harold Macmillan b. (–1986).
Apr. 10th Ben Nicholson b. (–1982).
Apr. 17th Nikita Khrushchev b. (–1971).
Apr. 26th Rudolf Hess b. (–1987).
Apr. 30th Herbert Evatt b. (–1965).
May 6th Alan Cobham b. (–1973).
June 23rd Duke of Windsor b. (–1972).
June 26th Peter Kapitza b. (–1984).
July 9th Dorothy Thompson b. (–1961).
July 26th Aldous Huxley b. (–1963).
July 30th Walter Pater d. (55).
Sept. 8th Hermann Helmholtz d. (73).
Oct. 7th Oliver Wendell Holmes d. (85).
Oct. 20th James Anthony Froude d. (76).
Dec. 3rd Robert Louis Stevenson d. (44).
Dec. 8th James Thurber b. (–1963).
Dec. 20th Robert Menzies b. (–1978).
— J. B. Priestley b. (–1984).

A **Jan**: 1st, British Niger Company proclaims protectorate over Busa, on middle Niger, and Nikki, near Dahomey;
French Trades Union Congress at Nantes adopts principle of general strike and
13th, President Casimir-Périer resigns in disgust;
17th, succeeded by Jules Faure (–99) and Alexandre Ribot forms ministry.

B **Feb**: 12th, resounding Japanese victory at Wei-hai-wei.

C **Mar**: 25th, Italian troops advance into Ethiopia;
28th, Edward Grey announces that Britain would regard a French occupation of Upper Nile as an unfriendly act.

D **Apr**: 17th, by treaty of Shimonoseki China and Japan recognise independence of Korea, China opens seven new ports and cedes Formosa, Port Arthur and the Liao Tung peninsula to Japan;
23rd, Russia, France and Germany (with Britain at last moment abstaining) protest against cession of mainland to Japan.

E **May**: 2nd, British South Africa Company territory South of Zambesi is organised as Rhodesia;
8th, by revised treaty Japan surrenders Liao Tung peninsula and Port Arthur to China in return for huge indemnity;
15th, Agenor Goluchowski becomes Austrian foreign secretary;
20th, U.S. income tax declared unconstitutional.

F **Jun**: 10th, Henry Campbell-Bannerman, British War Secretary, forces Queen Victoria to accept the resignation of Duke of Cambridge as Commander-in-Chief;
11th, Lord Rosebery is defeated on a vote relating to cordite supply;
—, Britain annexes Togoland to block Transvaal's access to sea;
25th, Lord Salisbury forms Unionist ministry, with Joseph Chamberlain as colonial secretary (–*July* 1902);
28th, union of Nicaragua, Honduras and El Salvador (ended in 1898 by El Salvador's opposition);
Raids from Bulgaria into Macedonia are made following foundation of External Macedonian Revolutionary Organisation at Sofia.

G **Jul**: 1st, East African Protectorate organised on dissolution of British East Africa Company;
8th, opening of Delagoa Bay railway gives Transvaal an outlet;
15th, Stephen Stambulov, Bulgarian premier, murdered;
20th, U.S. note to Britain that a modification by force of British Guiana's boundary with Venezuela would be a violation of the Monroe doctrine;
British general election confirms Lord Salisbury's majority, with Unionists majority of 152 (Conservatives 340; Liberal Unionists 71; Liberals 177; Irish Nationalists 82).

H **Aug**: 1st (–8th), Kaiser William II's conversations at Cowes with Lord Salisbury, who proposes the partition of Turkey, but there is misunderstanding and, subsequently, profound mutual distrust;
30th, compulsory Roman Catholic instruction in Belgian State schools.

J **Sep**: Leopold II of Belgium agrees to co-operate with French on Upper Nile;
Casimir Badeni forms ministry in Austro-Hungary and attempts to pacify Czechs.

O Politics, Economics, Law and Education

T. G. Masaryk, *The Czech Question.*
K. Marx, *Das Kapital*, volume 3.
London School of Economics and Political Science founded.
National Trust founded.
Oscar Wilde brings unsuccessful libel action against Marquess of Queensberry and in a sensational trial (*May*) is found guilty of homosexual charges.

P Science, Technology, Discovery, etc.

W. Röntgen discovers X-rays.
J. H. Northrop's automatic loom.
G. Marconi invents wireless telegraphy.
Auguste and Louis Lumière invent the cinematograph.
First main-line railway is electrified.
Kiel Canal opened (*June* 20th).
W. Ramsay detects, by spectroscope, helium from a terrestrial source.

Q Scholarship

American Historical Review issued.

R Philosophy and Religion

Sigmund Freud in *Studien über Hysterie* founds psychoanalysis.
A. J. Balfour, *The Foundations of Belief.*
Bible Conference of conservative evangelicals at Niagara defines 'fundamentalism'.
World Student Christian Federation founded.
Cardinal Herbert Vaughan lays foundation stone of Westminster Cathedral.

S Art, Sculpture, Fine Arts and Architecture

T Music

G. Mahler, Symphony no. 2.
R. Strauss, *Till Eulenspiegel's Merry Pranks* (symphonic poem).
Robert Newman arranges first series of Promenade Concerts at Queen's Hall, under Henry J. Wood.

U Literature

Hilaire Belloc, *Verses and Sonnets.*
Joseph Conrad, *Almayer's Folly.*
J. K. Huysmans, *En Route.*
Henry James, *The Middle Years* (autobiography).
George Moore, *The Celibates.*
A. Rimbaud, *Le Bateau Ivre.*
Henry Sienkiewicz, *Quo Vadis?*
H. G. Wells, *The Time Machine.*
W. B. Yeats, *Poems.*

V The Press

W Drama and Entertainment

O. Wilde, *The Importance of Being Earnest.*

X Sport

Peter Latham becomes world champion of both lawn tennis and racquets.

K **Oct**: 1st, massacre of Armenians in Constantinople;
8th, assassination of Queen of Korea with Japanese connivance;
17th, Sultan Abdul Hamid II of Turkey is forced by the powers to agree to undertake reforms, yet the massacres continue;
Britain sends a squadron to the Dardanelles and Austria recommends international naval action against Turkey.

L **Nov**: 7th, Russia plans to seize Constantinople but, owing to France being unwilling to risk a general war, postpones action;
11th, 'British' Bechuanaland is annexed to Cape Colony;
26th, Lord Salisbury rejects U.S. plan for arbitration in British Guiana–Venezuela boundary dispute;
Léon Bourgeois forms Radical ministry in France on defeat of Alexandre Ribot.

M **Dec**: 7th, Ethiopians defeat Italians at Amba Alagi;
17th, President Cleveland asks Congress to appoint commission to obtain facts in Venezuelan boundary question;
29th, L. Starr Jameson's raid into Transvaal from Bechuanaland.

N Native risings in Mozambique (–99).
Risings in Cuba against Spain, aiming at independence.

Y **Statistics**

Coal production (in mill. tons): Great Britain, 190; U.S., 179; Germany, 120; France, 28.

Iron production (in mill. tons): U.S., 11·3; Great Britain, 8·9; Germany, 5·7; France, 2·0.

U.K. total State expenditure: £100·9 mill.

Z **Births and Deaths**

Jan. 1st J. Edgar Hoover b. (–1972).
Feb. 1st John Ford b. (–1973).
Feb. 18th Semyon Timoshenko b. (–1970).
Feb. 21st Henrik Dam b. (–1976).
Mar. 28th Christian Herter b. (–1966).
Apr. 16th Ove Arup b. (–1988).
June 24th Jack Dempsey b. (–1983).
June 29th T. H. Huxley d. (70).
July 12th R. Buckminster Fuller b. (–1983).
— Oscar Hammerstein b. (–1960).
July 14th F. R. Leavis b. (–1978).
July 24th Robert Graves b. (–1985).
Sept. 18th John Diefenbaker b. (–1979).
Sept. 28th Louis Pasteur d. (73).
Oct. 8th Juan Perón b. (–1974).
Oct. 19th Lewis Mumford b. (–1990).
Nov. 16th Paul Hindemith b. (–1963).
Nov. 29th W. V. S. Tubman b. (–1971).
Dec. 1st Henry Williamson b. (–1977).
— Nikolai Bulganin b. (–1975).
— Friedrich Engels d. (75).
— Georgi K. Zhukov b. (–1974).

A **Jan**: 2nd, L. Starr Jameson surrenders at Doornkop;
3rd, William II sends 'Kruger telegram', congratulating Transvaal leader on suppressing the Raid, which provokes crisis in Anglo-German relations;
4th, Utah becomes a U.S. state;
6th, Cecil Rhodes resigns premiership of Cape Colony; a committee of Cape Assembly reports, subsequently, that Rhodes engineered the Jameson Raid. Transvaal orders munitions from Europe and fortifies Pretoria and Johannesburg;
15th, Anglo-French agreement over Siam;
18th, Francis Scott takes Kumasi in Britain's 4th Ashanti War, imprisoning King Prempeh.

B **Feb**: Beginning of Cretan revolution against Turkey, inspired by Greeks;
Reconciliation of Russia and Bulgaria when Crown Prince Boris is converted to Orthodox faith;
19th, Ferdinand I of Bulgaria is recognised by Russia, subsequently by the other powers.

C **Mar**: 1st, Ethiopians defeat Italians at Adowa, forcing Italy to sue for peace;
5th, F. Crispi's ministry falls in Italy, through indignation at failure of Ethiopian War, and Antonio Rudini forms ministry with support from Radicals under Felice Cavalotti;
12th, Britain decides on re-conquest of Sudan, to protect the Nile from French advance;
17th, Transvaal and Orange Free State conclude offensive and defensive alliance;
Further Matabele rising in Rhodesia (*–Oct.*);
New evidence favourable to Dreyfus is suppressed in France.

D **Apr**: Félix Méline, Progressive, forms ministry in France.

E **May**: 1st, murder of Nasir-Ud-Din, Shah of Persia.

F **Jun**: 3rd, treaty signed in Moscow by which China and Russia form defensive alliance for 15 years and China grants Russia the right to operate railway in North Manchuria;
9th, Russo-Japanese agreement recognises Russia's position in Korea;
29th, Liberal government in Holland widens the franchise, but leaves working-class dissatisfied;
Expedition under Major Marchand leaves France to advance to Fashoda and claim Sudan.

G **Jul**: 1st, treaty of federation of Straits Settlements;
3rd, Abdul Hamid II, Sultan of Turkey, agrees to introduce self-government in Crete and as Greek support of insurgents continues, Austria proposes international blockade of the island which, 29th, is rejected by Britain;
11th, Wilfred Laurier forms Liberal ministry in Canada;
Land bill for Ireland extends tenants' rights with regard to improvements.

H **Aug**: 16th, British protectorate in Ashanti proclaimed;
18th, France annexes Madagascar whose external treaties with other states are annulled;
25th, ambassadors of the powers draw up revised scheme for Crete under a Christian governor, approved by Turkey (which is accepted by insurgents *Sept.* 12th);
26th, native insurrection in Philippines;
—, Armenian revolutionaries attack Ottoman Bank, Constantinople, which provokes a three-day massacre.

O Politics, Economics, Law and Education

Nobel Prizes established.

P Science, Technology, Discovery, etc.

Ernest Rutherford's magnetic detection of electrical waves.
S. P. Langley's flying machine makes successful flights (*May* 6th, *Nov.* 28th)
Power plant at Niagara Falls opened.
An electric submarine is constructed in France.
Martin Conway crosses Spitzbergen.

Q Scholarship

R Philosophy and Religion

Henri Bergson, *Matière et Mémoire.*

S Art, Sculpture, Fine Arts and Architecture

Frederic Leighton, *Clytie* (painting).
W. Morris and E. Burne-Jones make designs for *Kelmscott Chaucer.*
National Portrait Gallery moved from Bethnal Green to permanent home in Westminster.

T Music

J. Brahms, *Four Serious Songs* (op. 121).
R. Strauss, tone poem *Thus Spake Zarathustra.*
G. Puccini, *La Bohème* (opera).
H. Wolf, *The Corregidor* (opera).
The Grand Duke ends Gilbert and Sullivan partnership of 'Savoy' operas.

U Literature

A. France (pseud.), *L'Histoire contemporaine* (–1901).
T. Hardy, *Jude the Obscure.*
A. E. Housman, *A Shropshire Lad.*
R. L. Stevenson, *Weir of Hermiston* (unfinished).

V The Press

Alfred Harmsworth founds the *Daily Mail*, selling at ½d.
Phil May joins *Punch.*

W Drama and Entertainment

H. Ibsen, *John Gabriel Borkman.*
A. Chekhov, *The Seagull.*

X Sport

First Olympiad of modern era held at Athens.
Persimmon, owned by Prince of Wales, wins the Derby.

Y Statistics

Steel production (in mill. tons): U.S., 5·2; Germany, 4·7; Great Britain, 4·1; France, 1·1.
U.K. merchant shipping tonnage: 9,020,000 (of which 284,000 steamships).

1896 (Sep.–Dec.)

J **Sep:** 21st, Horatio Kitchener takes Dongola in Sudan;
24th, W. E. Gladstone's last speech, at Liverpool, on Armenian massacres, pleads for isolated action by Britain;
30th, Russia and China sign convention over Manchuria;
—, Franco-Italian convention over Tunis, by which Italy surrenders many claims.

K **Oct:** 4th, Lord Rosebery resigns Liberal leadership on account of party's view of Armenian question, being succeeded in Lords by Lord Kimberley and in Commons by W. V. Harcourt;
24th, Otto von Bismarck publishes the secret Russo-German Re-insurance treaty of 1887, which was unknown to Austria;
26th, by treaty of Addis Ababa Italian protectorate of Ethiopia is withdrawn;
Robert Baden-Powell puts down Matabele rising;
Tsar Nicholas II visits Paris and London.

L **Nov:** In U.S. presidential election William McKinley, Republican, on gold-standard platform, gains 271 electoral votes against William Jennings Bryan, Democratic and Populist candidate, standing for policy of free silver coinage, with 176 votes;
26th, Aliens Immigration Act in Transvaal restricts liberty of press and public meetings (it is repealed in 1897 on Joseph Chamberlain's protest that it violates convention of 1884);
Russia plans to seize Constantinople if Britain intervenes in Crete.

M **Dec:**

N Revival of Young Turk movement.

z **Births and Deaths**

Jan. 8th Paul Verlaine d. (51).
Jan. 14th John Dos Passos b. (–1970).
Apr. 21st Henry de Montherlant b. (–1972).
July 1st Harriet Beecher Stowe d. (85).
July 16th Edmond de Goncourt d. (74).
— Trygve Lie b. (–1968).
Aug. 9th Jean Piaget b. (–1980).
Aug. 13th John. E. Millais d. (67).
Oct. 3rd William Morris d. (62).
Oct. 11th Anton Bruckner d. (72).
Oct. 12th Eugenio Montale b. (–1981).
Nov. 16th Oswald Mosley b. (–1980).
Dec. 10th Alfred Nobel d. (63).

1897 (Jan.–Oct.) War between Turkey and Greece

A Jan: Federal convention, with representatives from each Australian colony except Queensland, meets at Hobart to discuss draft federal constitution.

B Feb: 2nd, Cretan insurrection resumed;
6th, Crete proclaims union with Greece;
15th, the powers land troops in the island but
17th, Britain rejects Austro-Russian proposal for blockade of Piraeus.

C Mar: 4th, William McKinley inaugurated president of U.S. (–1901);
18th, blockade of Crete by the powers begins on Greece's refusal to withdraw troops;
20th, France, now preponderant influence in Addis Ababa, obtains treaty with Ethiopia defining Somali frontier;
28th, Japan adopts gold standard.

D Apr: 5th, the Czech language is granted equality with German in Bohemia;
6th, Sultan of Zanzibar abolishes slavery;
7th, Turkey declares war on Greece;
30th, Austro-Russian agreement to maintain *status quo* in the Balkans.

E May: 8th, Greece begs powers to intervene; intervention follows Turkish defeat of Greeks, 12th, in Thessaly;
14th, by treaty with Ethiopia Britain abandons certain claims in Somaliland but Emperor Menelek refuses to surrender his claims to lands near the Nile;
19th, armistice in Graeco-Turkish war.

F Jun: 15th, Alfred von Tirpitz appointed German naval secretary;
Second Colonial Conference, London, presided over by Joseph Chamberlain (–*July*).

G Jul: 7th, Nelson Dingley's tariff increases U.S. protection;
10th, French force under Marchand occupies Fashoda;
Britain denounces treaties with Belgium and Germany which would prevent Canadian preference;
Report of Parliamentary committee into Jameson Raid censures Cecil Rhodes, but acquits Joseph Chamberlain and the Colonial Office.

H Aug: 7th, Egyptian force takes Abu Hamed in Sudan;
Franco-Russian alliance extended;
French expedition to Sudan under Marchand reaches River Bahr-el-Ghazal;
Alfred Milner becomes high commissioner for South Africa.

J Sep: Rising of Batetelas on Upper Congo;
Mutiny of Sudanese troops in Uganda (–98).

K Oct: 20th, Prince Bernhard von Bülow becomes German foreign secretary;
King of Korea proclaims himself emperor and Russia and Japan intervene to preserve order, but leave the emperor independent.

O **Politics, Economics, Law and Education**
S. & B. Webb, *Industrial Democracy.*
Workmen's Compensation Act in Britain.

P **Science, Technology, Discovery, etc.**
Ronald Ross discovers malaria bacillus.
J. J. Thomson's work on cathode rays; evaluation of ratio of charge and mass of the electron.
Monotype type-setting machine.
Julius Hann, *Handbook of Climatology.*
The discovery of gold at Bonanza Creek, Yukon, Canada, leads to Klondike Gold Rush.

Q **Scholarship**

R **Philosophy and Religion**
Havelock Ellis, *Studies in the Psychology of Sex* (–1900).
Zionist Conference held at Basle, under Theodor Herzl and Max Nordau.

S **Art, Sculpture, Fine Arts and Architecture**
P. Gauguin, *Where do we come from? What are we? Where are we going?* (painting).
M. Klinger, *Christus in Olymp* (painting).
C. Pissarro, *Boulevard des Italiens* (painting).
Tate Gallery, London, opened (*Aug.* 16th).
Bing's *Art Nouveau* Gallery opens in Paris with exhibition of Edvard Munch's paintings.
Whitechapel Art Gallery built (–99).

T **Music**
Vincent d'Indy, *Fervaal* (opera).

U **Literature**
M. Barrès, *Le Déracinéa* (1st vol. of triology, *Le Roman de l'énergie nationale* –1902).
Joseph Conrad, *The Nigger of the Narcissus.*
John Galsworthy, *From the Four Winds.*
Stefan George, *Das Jahr der Seele.*
R. Kipling, *Captains Courageous* and *Recessional.*
A. Strindberg, *Inferno.*
H. G. Wells, *The Invisible Man.*

V **The Press**

W **Drama and Entertainment**
Edmond Rostand, *Cyrano de Bergerac.*
G. B. Shaw's *Candida* produced (written 1894).
Forbes Robertson's *Hamlet* at the Lyceum.
Diamond Jubilee Celebrations throughout Britain.

X **Sport**

Y **Statistics**

L **Nov:** 4th, Cape railway reaches Bulawayo in Southern Rhodesia;
15th, Mathieu Dreyfus discovers the document on which his brother, Alfred Dreyfus, was convicted, to be in the writing of Major M. C. Esterházy;
28th, Count Badeni is forced to resign in Austria through German opposition to the language ordinance (of *Apr.* 1897), and the Austro-Hungarian monarchy weathers the crisis with difficulty;
—, Germany occupies Kiao-chow, North China, in retaliation for the murder of German missionaries.

M **Dec:** 1st, Zululand is annexed to Natal;
13th, Russia occupies Port Arthur;
16th, Peace of Constantinople between Greece and Turkey (the problem of Crete settled in *Nov.* 1898);
25th, Italy cedes Kassala to Egypt.

N British troops occupy Benin, Nigeria, in protest at human sacrifices.
Plague in Poona.
Severe famine in India.
Austro-Hungarian Socialist party splits into six nationalist groups.

z **Births and Deaths**

Feb. 4th Ludwig Erhard b. (–1977).
Apr. 3rd Johannes Brahms d. (63).
Apr. 23rd Lester Pearson b. (–1972).
May 27th John Cockcroft b. (–1967).
June 12th Anthony Eden, Viscount Avon b. (–1977).
July 28th Kingsley Martin b. (–1969).
Aug. 8th Jacob Burckhardt d. (79).
Aug. 11th Enid Blyton b. (–1968).
Sept. 26th Pope Paul VI (Giovanni Montini) b. (–1978).
Nov. 12th Aneurin Bevan b. (–1960).
Dec. 14th Kurt von Schuschnigg b. (–1979).
Dec. 17th Alphonse Daudet d. (57).

1898 (Jan.–Sep.) Fashoda crisis—Battle of Omdurman—First German Navy Bill

A **Jan:** 11th, acquittal of Major M. C. Esterházy in trial for alleged forgery of document in Dreyfus case, provokes Zola's *J'accuse*, 13th, an open letter to the French President (for which, *Feb.* 23rd, he is imprisoned);
Anglo-Russian crisis over loan to China and
25th, Lord Salisbury suggests compromise which Russia declines to accept.

B **Feb:** 9th, Paul Kruger's re-election as President of Transvaal with massive majority;
15th, destruction of U.S.S. *Maine* in Havana;
After Greece has defaulted on obligations an international commission is appointed to control Greek finances.

C **Mar:** Finding neither U.S., 8th, nor Japan, 17th, will support her in the conflict with Russia over the loan to China, Britain decides against pressing her case to the brink of war;
27th, Russia obtains lease of Port Arthur and Britain is leased Wei-hai-wei and Kowloon;
28th, First German navy bill, introduced by Alfred von Tirpitz, begins Germany's naval expansion;
29th, Joseph Chamberlain suggests an Anglo-German alliance;
Bohemia is divided into Czech, German and mixed districts.

D **Apr:** 8th, Horatio Kitchener's victory at Atbara River;
10th, France obtains concessions in China;
19th, U.S. ultimatum to Spain to relinquish authority in Cuba;
25th, U.S. declares war on Spain, retroactive to *Apr.* 21st.

E **May:** 1st, George Dewey destroys Spanish fleet at Manila;
3rd (–8th), bread riots in Milan are put down with heavy loss of life;
13th, Joseph Chamberlain, in Birmingham speech, criticises Russia and bids for friendship of U.S. and Germany, which creates unfavourable impression in Britain and overseas.

F **Jun:** 11th (–*Sept.* 16th), Emperor Te Tsung of China's 100 days of Reform, under guidance of K'ang Yu-wei;
14th, Anglo-French convention defines boundaries in Nigeria and Gold Coast;
28th, Luigi Pelloux forms ministry in Italy on Count Rudini's resignation.

G **Jul:** 3rd, U.S. naval victory at Santiago;
25th, U.S. invades Porto Rico, and, 26th, Spain asks for terms;
30th, Théophile Delcassé appointed French foreign secretary (–*June* 1905).

H **Aug:** 12th, transfer of islands of Hawaii to U.S.;
13th, U.S. forces capture Manila;
24th, Tsar invites powers to co-operate in reducing armaments;
30th, Anglo-German secret agreement on future of the African territories of Portugal, who is bankrupt; Britain to obtain lease of Delagoa Bay and Germany to receive parts of Mozambique and Angola;
—, Col. Henry admits the forgery of a document in the Dreyfus case.

J **Sep:** 2nd, Horatio Kitchener defeats Dervishes at Omdurman;
10th, Empress Elizabeth of Austria is murdered by an Italian anarchist at Geneva;
19th, Kitchener reaches Fashoda;
21st, Tzu-hsi, Dowager Empress of China, seizes power and revokes reforms.

O Politics, Economics, Law and Education

Otto von Bismarck, *Reflections and Memoirs.*

British Committee on Old-Age Pensions, chairman Lord Rothschild, is unable to accept any of the schemes proposed to it. Old-Age pensions are, however, introduced in New Zealand.

Public outcry against the meat supplied for U.S. troops fighting in the Spanish War leads to the passage of the first Food and Drugs Act.

London University bill establishes a teaching university.

P Science, Technology, Discovery, etc.

Pierre and Marie Curie discover radium and polonium.

W. Ramsay and M. W. Travers discover neon and metargon.

The discovery of phosphorus sesquisulphide makes possible the safety match.

The word 'photosynthesis' is introduced.

M. J. Owen's automatic bottle-making machine.

C. von Linde's machine for the liquefaction of air.

The first flash-light photograph is taken.

Count F. von Zeppelin makes an airship.

First petrol tractor, built at Marion, Ohio.

Paris Métro system started.

Q Scholarship

R Philosophy and Religion

The U.K. Benefices Act forbids the sale of advowsons and increases the power of Anglican bishops.

S Art, Sculpture, Fine Arts and Architecture

Jules Dalou, *The Triumph of the Republic* (sculpture).

A. Rodin, *The Kiss* (sculpture).

T Music

S. Coleridge-Taylor, *Hiawatha's Wedding Feast.*

Umberto Giordano, *Fedora* (opera).

U Literature

T. Hardy, *Wessex Poems.*

J. K. Huysmans, *La Cathédrale.*

H. James, *The Turn of the Screw.*

H. G. Wells, *The War of the Worlds.*

O. Wilde, *Ballad of Reading Gaol.*

V The Press

W Drama and Entertainment

G. B. Shaw, *Caesar and Cleopatra.*

X Sport

Y Statistics

K **Oct**: William II visits Palestine and Syria (–*Nov.*).

L **Nov**: 4th, French evacuate Fashoda after Britain protests;
26th, Franco-Italian commercial treaty ends tariff war (since 1886);
—, following the Turkish evacuation of Crete, Prince George of Greece is appointed high commissioner in the island;
27th, Deutsche Bank secures preliminary concessions for Baghdad Railway.

M **Dec**: 10th, treaty of Paris between U.S. and Spain by which Spain cedes Cuba, Porto Rico and Guam and also the Philippines, as yet to be conquered, for $20 million.

N Foundation of the Boxers, an anti-foreign society in China to resist westernisation and combat Christianity.

z Births and Deaths

Jan. 9th Gracie Fields b. (–1979).
Jan. 14th C. L. Dodgson ('Lewis Carroll') d. (65).
Feb. 3rd Alvar Aalto b. (–1976).
Feb. 9th Steen Rasmussen b. (–1990).
Feb. 18th Enzo Ferrari b. (–1988).
Mar. 15th Henry Bessemer d. (85).
Apr. 9th Paul Robeson b. (–1976).
Apr. 18th Gustave Moreau d. (72).
May 3rd Golda Meir b. (–1978).
May 19th W. E. Gladstone d. (89).
June 26th Willy Messerschmitt b. (–1978).
July 19th Herbert Marcuse b. (–1979).
July 30th Henry Moore b. (–1986).
July 31st Otto von Bismarck d. (83).
Sept. 9th Stéphane Mallarmé d. (56).
Sept. 24th Howard Florey b. (–1968).
Chou En-lai b. (–1976).

1899 (Jan.–Oct.) Anglo-Boer War begins—Germany secures Baghdad Railway contract

A **Jan:** 5th, Aguinaldo demands Philippine independence from U.S.;
19th, Anglo-Egyptian convention on Sudan;
Campbell-Bannerman succeeds Harcourt as leader of Liberals in Commons.

B **Feb:** 4th, Filipinos revolt;
6th, ratification of Treaty of Paris;
12th, Germany buys the Pacific islands of Marianas, Caroline and Pelew from Spain;
15th, Tsar Nicholas II suppresses liberties in Finland;
18th, Émile Loubet is elected President of France (–1906), following Félix Faure's death;
China opposes Italy's demands for concessions at Chekiang.

C **Mar:** 4th, J. G. Schurman's Commission offers representative government to the Filipinos, but the revolt continues;
21st, Anglo-French convention on hinterland of Tripoli ends Fashoda crisis, but Italy protests at large concessions to France in Sahara;
24th, Petition of Johannesburg Uitlanders to Queen Victoria, reciting their grievances against the Boers;
31st (–*June* 5th), at Bloemfontein Conference Alfred Milner and Paul Kruger fail to reach agreement on Transvaal franchise.

D **Apr:**

E **May:** 18th (–*July* 21st), at first Peace Conference 26 nations meet at the Hague, at the Tsar Nicholas II's suggestion, to extend Geneva Convention to naval warfare, explosive bullets and poison gas and authorise the establishment of a permanent Court of Arbitration.

F **Jun:** 3rd, *cour de cassation* annuls Alfred Dreyfus's first trial and orders a retrial;
10th, U.S. Congress appoints canal commission to report on routes through Panama;
22nd, René Waldeck-Rousseau, a moderate, becomes French premier.

G **Jul:** 11th, Transvaal government decides immigrants in Transvaal to be enfranchised after seven years residence;
27th, Joseph Chamberlain proposes a joint British-Boer enquiry into the Transvaal franchise bills, which is unacceptable to Kruger.

H **Aug:** 9th, Britain purchases the possessions of the Niger Company (Protectorate proclaimed, *Jan.* 1900);
9th, Théophile Delcassé, visiting St. Petersburg, extends the Franco-Russian alliance.

J **Sep:** 6th, John Hay, U.S. Secretary of State, sends 'open door' note to Britain, Germany and Russia against interference in China's treaty ports;
9th, at retrial at Rennes court martial Alfred Dreyfus is condemned 'with extenuating circumstances', but, 19th, is pardoned by presidential decree, which with premier Waldeck-Rousseau's intervention in the Le Creusot strike, helps to heal divisions in France;
'Mad Mullah' raids on British and Italian Somaliland.

K **Oct:** 3rd, settlement of British Guiana-Venezuelan boundary dispute, largely favourable to Britain;
9th, Paul Kruger's ultimatum, which is supported, 11th, by Orange Free State, provokes, 12th, Anglo-Boer War;

O **Politics, Economics, Law and Education**
H. S. Chamberlain, *The Foundations of the XIXth Century* (published in Vienna).
London Borough Councils are established.
Board of Education takes charge of education in England and Wales.
John Dewey, *School and Society*.

P **Science, Technology, Discovery, etc.**
The magnetic recording of sound is devised.
Dortmund-Ems Canal is completed.
Aspirin is invented.
Ernst Haeckel, *The Riddle of the Universe*.
A motor 'bus runs in London (*Oct.* 9th).

Q **Scholarship**
Lord Acton plans *The Cambridge Modern History*.
John Rylands Library, Manchester, opened.

R **Philosophy and Religion**
A. Bain, *The Realisation of the Possible*.
T. H. Green, *Prolegomena to Ethics* (posth.).
James Ward, *Naturalism and Agnosticism*.
Leo XIII's bull *Testem Benevolentiae* condemns erroneous opinions, including the 'Americanism' of Isaac Hecker.

S **Art, Sculpture, Fine Arts and Architecture**
Jules Dalou, monument to Alphard.
W. H. Thornycroft, statue of Cromwell.

T **Music**
H. Berlioz, *The Trojans at Carthage*, being pt. 2 of *The Trojans* (opera).
Edward Elgar, *Enigma Variations*.
J. Sibelius, Symphony no. 1 in E minor.

U **Literature**
Stefan George, *Der Teppich des Lebens*.
A. Gide, *Le Prométhée mal enchaîné*.
M. Gorki, *Foma Gordeyev*.
R. Kipling, *Stalky and Co*.
Edith Nesbit, *The Story of the Treasure Seekers*.
L. Tolstoy, *Resurrection*.

V **The Press**

W **Drama and Entertainment**
A. W. Pinero, *The Gay Lord Quex*.
National Norwegian Theatre is founded.

X **Sport**

Y **Statistics**

K **Oct**: 14th, by secret treaty of Windsor Portugal undertakes to prevent passage of munitions from Dclagoa Bay to Transvaal;
17th, Boers defeated at Glencoe;
—, Bohemian language ordinances of *Apr.* 1897 are repealed;
23rd, Cipriano Castro assumes power in Venezuela;
30th, Piet Joubert wins battle of Nicholson's Nek, against British force under George White.

L **Nov**: 1st, Ladysmith, Natal, surrenders to Piet Joubert;
14th, Britain and Germany settle Togoland-Gold Coast frontier and the question of Samoa, with Britain taking Tonga and Savage Islands (confirmed *Dec.* 2nd);
19th (–25th), Kaiser William II and von Bülow visit England to discuss possible Anglo-German alliance, but Joseph Chamberlain's Leicester speech, 30th, ends rapprochement;
The Khalifa of Sudan is killed by Reginald Wingate on the White Nile.

M **Dec**: 10th, British defeat at Stromberg;
11th, British under Lord Methuen repulsed by Piet Cronje at Magersfontein, Orange Free State, and 15th, the 'Black week' ends with Louis Botha's repulse of Redvers Buller at Colenso, Natal;
—, Bülow in Reichstag rejects British advances for an alliance;
23rd, Germany secures Baghdad Railway contract;
24th, Netherlands adopts Proportional Representation;
Canadian and Australian Volunteers land in South Africa.

N Revisionist German Social Democrats abandon strict Marxism.
Modification of plans for federal government of Australia by conference of premiers, to meet criticism of New South Wales.

z **Births and Deaths**

Jan. 7th Francis Poulenc b. (–1963)
Feb. 15th Georges Auric b. (–1983).
Feb. 18th Sir Arthur Bryant b. (–1985).
Feb. 23rd Erich Kästner b. (–1974).
Apr. 22nd Vladimir Nabokov b. (–1977).
Apr. 29th Duke Ellington b. (–1974).
May 8th F. A. von Hayek b. (–1992).
May 10th Fred Astaire b. (–1987).
June 3rd Johann Strauss d. (74).
June 7th Elizabeth Bowen b. (–1973).
June 11th Yasunari Kawabata b. (–1972).
July 1st Charles Laughton b. (–1965).
Aug. 13th Alfred Hitchcock b. (–1980).
Aug. 16th R. W. Bunsen d. (88).
Aug. 24th Jorge Luis Borges b. (–1986).
Dec. 16th Noël Coward b. (–1973).
— Paul Spaak b. (–1972).

1900 (Jan.–Aug.) Relief of Ladysmith and of Mafeking—Boxer Rising in China

A **Jan:** 1st, Frederick Lugard becomes high commissioner in Nigeria;
10th, Frederick Roberts lands in South Africa as Commander-in-Chief of British army, with Lord Kitchener as chief of staff;
Tension in Anglo-German relations through Britain's seizure of a German vessel on suspicion of carrying contraband but, 16th, Britain gives way;
Francis Joseph of Austria appoints a bureaucratic ministry under Ernst von Körber to resolve the conflict between German and Czech parties in Austria.

B **Feb:** 18th, in South African War Piet Cronje surrenders to British at Paardeberg;
22nd, bitter Parliamentary conflict in Italy following the declaration by the Court of Cassation that the constitutional decrees of June 1899 are invalid;
27th, British Labour Party founded, with Ramsay MacDonald secretary;
28th, Redvers Buller relieves Ladysmith;
—, Count Muraviev, Russian foreign minister, suggests France and Germany put joint pressure on Britain to end South African War, but Germany rejects this (*Mar.* 3rd) while France takes advantage of Britain's plight to advance her interests in Morocco.

C **Mar:** 10th, Britain signs treaty with Uganda for regulating the government with the advice of a British commissioner;
13th, Frederick Roberts captures Bloemfontein;
14th, U.S. Currency Act declares paper and other money redeemable in gold;
Russian attempts to secure a naval base at Masampo in South Korea are vigorously opposed by Japan.

D **Apr:** 7th, President William McKinley appoints W. H. Taft commission to report on the Philippines;
30th, Hawaii is organised as a territory of U.S.;
Republican bloc formed in France to defend the Republic against anti-Dreyfusard opponents.

E **May:** 1st, the Foraker Act for establishing civil government in Puerto Rico takes effect;
17th, Relief of Mafeking;
19th, Britain annexes the Tonga Islands and
24th, annexes the Orange Free State.

F **Jun:** 5th, Pretoria taken by Redvers Buller;
12th, second German Naval Act aims at a fleet of 38 battleships in 20 years;
13th (–*Aug.* 14th), Boxer rising in China against Europeans;
18th, General Pelloux resigns following the success of the Left in Italian elections;
19th, Republican National Convention at Philadelphia re-nominates McKinley for presidency and nominates Theodore Roosevelt for vice-presidency;
20th, assassination of the German ambassador at Peking, begins the siege of the legations.

G **Jul:** 4th, armies of Roberts and Buller join forces at Vlakfontein;
14th, international expedition, including U.S. and Japan, takes Tientsin, and U.S. secretary of state, John Hay, restates policy of 'open door' in China;
29th, Humbert I of Italy assassinated by an anarchist;
French government aid wine-growers by reducing retail duties.

H **Aug:** 14th, international force relieves legations in Peking;
27th, Louis Botha is defeated at Bergendal;
31st, Frederick Roberts occupies Johannesburg.

O Politics, Economics, Law and Education

German Civil Law Code in force (*Jan.* 1st).
George Cadbury founds Bournville Village Trust.
Amalgamation of Castle and Union Steamship Companies.
Leslie Stephen, *The Utilitarians.*

P Science, Technology, Discovery, etc.

Max Planck elaborates quantum theory.
William Crookes separates uranium.
Lord Rayleigh, *Scientific Papers.*
Rediscovery by Hugo de Vries and others of Gregor Mendel's work on heredity.
The acetylene lamp is perfected.
Browning revolver invented.
R. A. Fessenden first transmits speech by wireless.
First Zeppelin trial-flight (*July* 2nd).
Elbe-Trave Canal opened.

Q Scholarship

Arthur Evans begins to discover Minoan culture through excavations in Crete.
Paul Claudel, *Discovery of the East.*
Victoria History of the Counties of England started.

R Philosophy and Religion

Henri Bergson, *On Laughter.*
Sigmund Freud, *The Interpretation of Dreams.*
Bertrand Russell, *Critical Exposition of the Philosophy of Leibniz.*
Wilhelm Wundt, *Comparative Psychology.*
C. H. Spurgeon, *Autobiography* (posth.).

S Art, Sculpture, Fine Arts and Architecture

Painting:

Lawrence Alma-Tadema, *Vain Courtship.*
Paul Cézanne, *Still Life With Onions.*
Claude Monet, *Water Lilies, Harmony in Rose.*
Auguste Renoir, *Nude in the Sun* (pastel).
J. S. Sargent, *The Sitwell Family.*
Toulouse-Lautrec, *La Modiste.*

Sculpture:

Auguste Rodin exhibition at La Place de l'Alma establishes his reputation.

Architecture:

Charles Rennie Mackintosh, Glasgow School of Art.
Edwin Lutyens, Deanery Gardens, Sonning, Berks.
The Wallace Collection, Manchester Square, London, opened.

T Music

Gustave Charpentier, *Louise* (opera).
E. Elgar, *Dream of Gerontius* (oratorio).
G. Mahler, Fourth Symphony.
G. Puccini, *Tosca* (opera).
J. Sibelius, *Finlandia* (overture).
J. S. Bach Festival established in Bethlehem, Pennsylvania.

J Sep: 17th, proclamation of Commonwealth of Australia as a federal union of the six colonies (to come into force *Jan.* 1st 1901);
U.S. Taft Commission begins to exercise legislative power in Philippines, appropriating sums for road and harbour works.

K Oct: 6th, President Kruger, having fled to Europe, is denied an audience by Kaiser William II;
16th, in the 'Khaki' election in Britain, the Conservatives, organised by Joseph Chamberlain, remain in power, with a majority of 134 (Conservatives and Unionists 334 seats, Liberal Unionists 68; Liberals 186, Irish Nationalists 82; Labour 2). Lord Salisbury reconstructs ministry, appointing Lord Lansdowne foreign secretary;
—, Yangtze agreement between Britain and Germany to restrain foreign aggression in China and maintain open door for trade;
17th, Bernhard von Bülow succeeds Prince Hohenlohe as German chancellor;
25th, Transvaal is formally annexed by Britain at Pretoria.

L Nov: 5th, Cuban constitutional convention begins to sit at Havana;
6th, in U.S. presidential election William McKinley, Republican (292 electoral votes), defeats William Jennings Bryan, Democrat (with 155 votes), on an anti-imperialist platform;
—, Boer guerrilla raids on communications and British outposts grow in intensity in Orange River Colony and Transvaal;
9th, Russia, having completed the occupation of Manchuria with 100,000 troops, agrees with the Chinese governor to restore civil administration, but this agreement is abrogated by both central governments;
Rising of the Ashanti suppressed by British.

M Dec: 14th, secret Franco-Italian agreement to maintain French influence in Morocco and Italian interests in Tripoli.

N Beginnings of Hejaz railway to the Holy Places in Arabia, built by popular subscription as a Pan-Islamic project (–1908).
Civil War in Colombia (–1903).

U Literature

Colette (pseud.), first 'Claudine' novel.
J. Conrad, *Lord Jim.*
M. Gorki, *Three People.*
Charles Péguy launches *Les Cahiers de la Quinzaine* (–14).
E. Rostand, *L'Aiglon.*
G. B. Shaw publishes *Three Plays for Puritans* with prefaces.
L. Tolstoy, *The Living Corpse.*

V The Press

The Daily Express is founded by Arthur Pearson.

W Drama and Entertainment

A. Chekhov, *Uncle Vanya.*
The cake-walk dance.

X Sport

D. F. Davis presents international challenge cup for lawn tennis.

Y Statistics

Z Births and Deaths

Jan. 20th John Ruskin d. (81).
Feb. 4th Jacques Prévert b. (–1977).
Feb. 22nd Luis Buñuel b. (–1983).
Feb. 29th George Seferis b. (–1971).
Mar. 23rd Erich Fromm b. (–1980).
June 5th Stephen Crane d. (28).
June 25th Lord Louis Mountbatten b. (–1979).
— Dennis Gabor b. (–1979).
Aug. 19th Gilbert Ryle b. (–1976).
Aug. 25th Hans Krebs b. (–1981).
— Friedrich Nietzsche d. (56).
Sept. 20th Willem Visser't Hooft b. (–1992).
Nov. 14th Aaron Copland b. (–1990).
Nov. 30th Oscar Wilde d. (44).
Dec. 22nd Alan Bush b. (–).

1901 (Jan.–Aug.) Death of Queen Victoria—Australia becomes a dominion

A **Jan:** 1st, Commonwealth of Australia comes into being with Edmund Barton, federalist and protectionist, as prime minister;
19th, William II visits England for Victoria's last days;
22nd, death of Queen Victoria; accession of Edward VII;
To combat guerrilla actions of Boers Lord Kitchener builds chain of blockhouses and starts denuding country of its farms.

B **Feb:** 8th, on receiving Russia's proposals for evacuation of Manchuria China appeals to the major powers and is supported by Britain, Japan and, with hesitancy, by Germany;
11th, death of Milan, father of Alexander I of Serbia;
23rd, Anglo-German agreement on boundary between German East Africa and Nyasaland;
27th, Russian minister of propaganda is murdered to avenge repression of student agitation;
Giuseppe Saracco overthrown for policy towards strikers in Genoa and Giuseppe Zanardelli forms ministry which is dependent on support of extreme Left;
Failures of Louis Botha's raid on Natal and Christian de Wet and James Hertzog's invasion of Cape Colony;
Botha meets Kitchener, 26th, at Middelburg, but negotiations founder on amnesty for Cape rebels.

C **Mar:** 2nd, in U.S. Orville Platt's amendment on Cuban constitution and J. C. Spooner's amendment calling for civil government in Philippines are added to Army Appropriations bill;
15th, in the Reichstag Prince von Bülow declares the Yangtze agreement of 1900 with Britain did not apply to Manchuria, and as a result the London discussions on the possibility of an Anglo-German-Japanese bloc against Russia end abruptly.

D **Apr:** 6th, on protests from Britain and Japan Russia drops draft convention with China;
18th, in the British budget proposals of Hicks Beach a higher revenue is anticipated from direct than indirect taxes for the first time.

E **May:** 29th, Lord Salisbury's confidential memorandum upholding policy of isolation marks the end of discussions for Anglo-German alliance.

F **Jun:** 12th, Cuban convention making the country virtually a protectorate of the U.S. is incorporated in the Cuban constitution as condition of the withdrawal of U.S. troops;
Moroccan mission to Paris, London and Berlin seeking an Anglo-German pact on Morocco.

G **Jul:** 1st, in France the Association Law is promulgated for compulsory regulation of all congregations and associations and the dissolution of those not authorised by the State;
4th, civil government in Philippines with W. H. Taft governor-general, who proclaims amnesty to rebels taking oath of allegiance to U.S.;
16th, Liberal ministry in Denmark;
20th, Morocco grants France control of frontier police;
22nd, Lords deliver Taff Vale judgment that a trade union can be sued in its registered name as a corporate body;
Negotiations begin in London for an Anglo-Japanese alliance;
Clerical Party in power in Holland (–1905).

H **Aug:** 17th, as expression of imperialist sentiment the Royal Titles Act adds the words 'and of the British Dominions beyond the Seas' to Edward VII's style.

O **Politics, Economics, Law and Education**

Final Pendleton Act creates U.S. Civil Service (see *Jan.* 1883).
B. S. Rowntree, *Poverty: a study of town life.*
J. P. Morgan founds United States Steel Corporation.

P **Science, Technology, Discovery, etc.**

Max Planck, *Laws of Radiation.*
W. Normann discovers process for hardening liquid fats.
Adrenalin is first manufactured.
G. Marconi transmits messages by wireless telegraphy from Cornwall to Newfoundland.
First petrol-engined motor-bicycle in Britain.
Trans-Siberian Railway reaches Port Arthur.

Q **Scholarship**

James Bryce, *Studies in History and Jurisprudence.*
Max Weber, *The Protestant Ethic and the Birth of Capitalism.*
British Academy founded.

R **Philosophy and Religion**

L. T. Hobhouse, *Mind in Evolution.*
S. Freud, *The Psychopathology of Everyday Life.*

S **Art, Sculpture, Fine Arts and Architecture**

Painting:
Paul Gauguin, *The Gold in Their Bodies.*
Edvard Munch, *Girls on the Bridge.*

T **Music**

A. Dvořák, *Russalka* (opera).
E. Elgar, Overture *Cockaigne* (op. 40).
M. Ravel, *Jeux d'Eaux*, for piano.
S. Rachmaninov, piano concerto no. 2.

U **Literature**

S. Butler, *Erewhon Revisited.*
H. Caine, *The Eternal City.*
R. Kipling, *Kim.*
Selma Lagerlöf, *Jerusalem.*
M. Maeterlinck, *Life of the Bee.*
Thomas Mann, *Buddenbrooks.*
G. W. Russell, W. B. Yeats and others, *Ideals in Ireland.*

V **The Press**

The Tatler issued.

W **Drama and Entertainment**

A. Strindberg, *Dance of Death.*
A. Chekhov, *Three Sisters.*

X **Sport**

J **Sep:** 7th, by Peace of Peking ending the Boxer Rising, China is to pay indemnity to the great powers;
14th, on death of President William McKinley, following shooting by anarchist Leon Czolgosz, Theodore Roosevelt succeeds;
25th, Ashanti Kingdom annexed to Gold Coast Colony;
Visit of Russian Emperor to France provokes anti-militarist demonstrations.

K **Oct:** 16th, Anglo-Japanese negotiations reopened in London by Baron Hayashi;
25th, Joseph Chamberlain's anti-German speech at Edinburgh leads (*Dec.* 27th) to breakdown in negotiations for Anglo-German alliance.

L **Nov:** 11th, Turkey accepts French ultimatum on violation of treaties;
20th, second Hay-Pauncefoote treaty provides for U.S. construction of Panama Canal with a neutral canal zone to be under U.S. supervision (ratified by Senate *Dec.* 16th);
25th, Prince Ito of Japan, visiting St. Petersburg, seeks Japanese concessions in Korea.

M **Dec:** 2nd, U.S. Supreme Court decides Puerto Ricans are not U.S. citizens;
7th, Japan drops negotiations with Russia deciding instead to conclude an alliance with Britain;
—, Anglo-Italian agreement for settling Sudan frontier;
26th, completion of Uganda railway from Mombasa to Lake Victoria.

N The Social Revolutionary Party is organised in Russia.
Italian Socialists extend their political influence through strike action.
Strikes and anarchist outrages in Belgium.
French miners, with many abstentions, vote for a general strike, but it is not carried into effect.

Y **Statistics**

Populations (in millions): China, 350; India, 294; Russia, 146; U.S., 75·9; Germany, 56·3; Japan, 45·4; Great Britain and Ireland, 41·4; France, 38·9; Italy, 32·4; Austria, 26·1.

Coal production (in mill. tons): U.S., 268; Great Britain, 219; Germany, 112; Austria, 34; Belgium, 23; Russia, 15.

Steel production (in mill. tons): U.S., 10·1; Germany, 6·2; Great Britain, 4·9; France, 1·5.

Crude petroleum production: U.S., 69·3 mill. barrels.

Z **Births and Deaths**

Jan. 15th Arnold Boecklin d. (73).
Jan. 16th Fulgencio Batista y Zaldívar b. (–1973).
Jan. 27th Giuseppe Verdi d. (88).
Feb. 20th Louis Isadore Kahn b. (–1974).
Feb. 27th Marino Marini b. (–1980).
Mar. 13th Benjamin Harrison d. (68).
Mar. 24th Charlotte M. Yonge d. (78).
Mar. 27th Eisaku Sato b. (–1975).
Apr. 22nd William Stubbs d. (76).
Apr. 29th Hirohito b. (–1989).
May 23rd Edmund Rubbra b. (–1986).
June 6th Achmad Sukharno b. (–1970).
Sept. 21st Learie Constantine b. (–1971).
Oct. 23rd George von Siemens d. (62).
Nov. 3rd André Malraux b. (–1976).
Nov. 18th G. H. Gallup b. (–1984).
Dec. 5th Walt Disney b. (–1966).
Dec. 16th Margaret Mead b. (–1978).
— Henri Toulouse-Lautrec d. (37).
Dec. 27th Marlene Dietrich b. (–1992).

1902 (Jan.–Nov.) Triple Alliance renewed—End of Boer War

A **Jan**: 30th, Britain ends isolation by signing treaty with Japan, providing for the independence of China and Korea. Neither State to enter separate agreements with other powers without consulting its ally.

B **Feb**: 6th, French agreement with Ethiopia to finance Jibouti-Addis Ababa railway provokes protests from Britain and Italy;
Italian government prevents general strike through calling up all railwaymen on the reserve.

C **Mar**: 20th, Franco-Russian declaration approving the principles of the Anglo-Japanese alliance, but reserving their rights to safeguard their interests.

D **Apr**: 8th, Russo-Chinese agreement for the evacuation of Manchuria;
15th, Britain adjusts the Sudanese frontier with Ethiopia;
—, murder of Sipyengin, Russian minister of interior, succeeded by Viacheslav Plehve who suppresses peasants' revolt and despoils Armenian Church.

E **May**: 12th, coal strike in U.S. (–*Oct.* 13th);
15th, national bankruptcy in Portugal;
31st, Peace of Vereeniging ends Boer War, in which British casualties numbered 5,774 killed (and 16,000 deaths from disease) against 4,000 Boers killed in action. Boers accept British sovereignty and are promised representative government and £3 million from Britain for restocking farms.

F **Jun**: 2nd, in France René Waldeck-Rousseau resigns, despite his majority in the Chamber, through lack of sympathy with extremists, and is succeeded by Émile Combes who directs a vigorous anti-clerical policy;
28th, renewal of Triple Alliance between Germany, Austria and Italy for six years;
—, Congress authorises Theodore Roosevelt to buy rights of the French Panama Company and to acquire from Colombia perpetual control of the canal zone;
30th (–*Aug.* 11th), Colonial Conference in London resolves in favour of Imperial Preference.

G **Jul**: 12th, Arthur Balfour becomes British prime minister on Lord Salisbury's retirement;
Australian Parliament passes Immigration Restriction Act and enfranchises women in federal elections, which gives women the preponderance of votes in Melbourne and Sydney constituencies.

H **Aug**:

J **Sep**: 5th, Anglo-Chinese commercial treaty;
27th, Crown Lands ordinance inaugurates white settlement of East African uplands.

K **Oct**: 13th, Theodore Roosevelt ends U.S. coal strike by threatening to work the mines with federal troops and the owners agree to the appointment of a commission to investigate miners' claims.

L **Nov**: 1st, Franco-Italian Entente, in which Italy assures France of her neutrality if France is attacked;
8th, Spain holds back from signing agreement on Morocco with France from fear of antagonising England;
13th, Persia concludes favourable tariff with Russia, discriminating against British goods.

O Politics, Economics, Law and Education

J. A. Hobson, *Imperialism.*
The Order of Merit established by Edward VII.
The Pilgrims, Anglo-American Association, founded.
Congress limits substitution of oleo-margarine for butter.
Reclamation Force established in U.S. for opening up the arid west, with funds for irrigation works.

P Science, Technology, Discovery, etc.

Oliver Heaviside states his conception of a layer in the atmosphere to aid transmission of wireless waves.
A. Cushing begins work on the pituitary body.
William Bayliss and Ernest Starling discover hormones.
C. Richet discovers cases of 'maphylaxis', or abnormal sensitiveness to anti-diphtheria serum.
F. Poulsen's arc generator.
J. M. Bacon crosses Irish Channel in balloon (*Nov.*).

Q Scholarship

R Philosophy and Religion

William James, *The Varieties of Religious Experience.*
Paul Hoensbroech, *The Papacy in its Social and Cultural Influence.*

S Art, Sculpture, Fine Arts and Architecture

Painting:
P. Gauguin, *Horsemen on the Beach.*
C. Monet, *Waterloo Bridge.*
J. S. Sargent, *Lord Ribbesdale.*
Sculpture:
A. Rodin, *Romeo et Juliette.*
Architecture:
Cass Gilbert, New York Customs House (–07).

T Music

C. Debussy, *Pelléas et Mélisande* (opera).
Edward German, *Merrie England* (operetta).
F. Delius, *Appalachia.*

U Literature

H. Belloc, *The Path to Rome.*
J. Conrad, *Youth.*
A. Conan Doyle, *The Hound of the Baskervilles.*
A. Gide, *The Immoralist.*
R. Kipling, *Just So Stories.*
M. Gorki, *Night's Lodging.*
J. Masefield, *Salt Water Ballads.*
Émile Verhaeren, *Les Forces Tumultueuses.*

V The Press

The Times Literary Supplement issued.

W Drama and Entertainment

Gabriele D'Annunzio, *Francesca da Rimini.*
J. M. Barrie, *The Admirable Crichton.*

1902 (Dec.)

M Dec: 18th, in London the Committee of Imperial Defence holds first meeting;
—, Education Act for England and Wales provides for secondary education, places schools under Committees of local authorities and brings denominational schools into the State system;
19th, Germany, Britain and Italy blockade Venezuela in protest at Cipriano Castro's refusal to meet claims for injuries caused during revolution;
25th, German protectionist tariff;
Aswan dam opened.

N Increasing disturbance in Macedonia by Bulgarian, Serbian and Greek bands.
Beginnings of educational and economic reform in China.

X **Sport**

Y **Statistics**

Trade union membership (in mill.): U.K., 1·9; U.S., 2·0.

U.K. textiles trade:

Imports of raw cotton	1,633 mill. lb.
Exports of cottons	5,332 mill. yds.
Exports of woollens	158 mill. yds.
Exports of linens	163 mill. yds.
Export of silks	9.5 mill. yds.

Z **Births and Deaths**

Jan. 30th Niklaus Pevsner b. (–1983).
Feb. 4th Charles Lindbergh b. (–1974).
Feb. 11th Arne Jacobsen b. (–1971).
Feb. 23rd S. R. Gardiner d. (72).
Feb. 27th John Steinbeck b. (–1968).
Mar. 26th Cecil Rhodes d. (41).
Mar. 29th William Walton b. (–1983).
Apr. 9th Lord David Cecil b. (1986).
May 21st Marcel Lajos Breuer b. (–1981).
June 18th Samuel Butler d. (66).
June 19th Lord Acton d. (68).
June 28th Richard Rodgers b. (–1979).
July 5th Henry Cabot Lodge b. (–1985).
July 28th Karl Popper b. (–).
Aug. 9th Solomon b. (–1988).
Sept. 20th Stevie Smith b. (–1971).
Sept. 29th Émile Zola d. (62).
Nov. 14th G. A. Henty d. (70).
Dec. 9th R. A. Butler b. (–1982).
Dec. 13th Talcott Parsons b. (–1979).
Ruhollah Khomeini b. (–1989).

1903 (Jan.–Oct.) Beginning of the 'Entente Cordiale'

A Jan: 22nd, Hay-Herrán pact for U.S. acquisition of the Panama Canal Zone, but Colombia delays ratification.

B Feb: Germany, Britain and Italy lift Venezuelan blockade (*Dec.* 1902) on the Hague Tribunal appointing a commission to investigate claims;
Russia and Austria call for programme of reforms for pacifying Macedonia;
Anti-trust laws in U.S. reinforced;
Joseph Chamberlain visits South Africa and, convinced of the impracticability of Alfred Milner's policy of establishing British supremacy, aims at conciliation with Boers.

C Mar: 15th, British conquest of Northern Nigeria completed;
18th, dissolution of French religious orders.

D Apr: Britain and France refuse support for construction of Baghdad Railway;
Dutch government ends railway and dock strikes by calling in troops;
Increased sickness benefits for German workers.

E May: 1st (–4th), Edward VII's visit to Paris begins improvement in Anglo-French relations;
15th, Joseph Chamberlain announces his conversion to Imperial Preference, which divides the Conservatives;
—, to counter Russian designs Lord Lansdowne declares that Britain would resist the establishment by any power of a fortified base on the Persian Gulf;
E. D. Morel and Roger Casement begin agitation against atrocities in Belgian Congo.

F Jun: 10th, murders of King Alexander I and Queen Draga of Serbia and, 15th, the Serbian Assembly elects Peter Karageorgevitch King (Peter I –1921) and restores the 1889 constitution.

G Jul: 6th (–9th), London visit of President Émile Loubet and Théophile Delcassé begins conversations leading to *Entente Cordiale*;
20th, following death of Leo XIII, Giuseppe Sarto is elected Pope Pius X;
21st, Irish Land Purchase Act;
25th, Arthur Henderson wins Barnard Castle, Co. Durham, by-election for Labour in three-cornered fight.

H Aug: 12th, Japanese note to Russia on failure to evacuate Manchuria;
29th, dismissal of Count Witte, Russian finance minister, is taken as a victory for the group favouring Russian expansion in Manchuria and Korea;
Regulation of motor-cars in Britain, with 20 m.p.h. speed limit.

J Sep: 16th, Francis Joseph's aim to bring Hungarian regiments into a unified army system provokes Magyar opposition;
18th, Joseph Chamberlain resigns to test feeling in country on Imperial Preference; leading free-traders also resign and Arthur Balfour reconstructs ministry with Austen Chamberlain as chancellor of exchequer.

K Oct: 1st (–3rd), Austro-Russian agreement at Mürzstag for reforms in Macedonia is approved by powers;
20th, settlement of Alaskan frontier by 3-power commission, in which British representative gives casting vote in favour of U.S., embitters Canada;
Anglo-Russian conversations break down through Russian unwillingness to sacrifice interests in Persia.

O **Politics, Economics, Law and Education**

Mrs. Emmeline Pankhurst founds Women's Social and Political Union (*Oct.*).
Royal Naval College, Dartmouth, established.
An infants' welfare centre opened in Ghent.
Act for controlling livestock disease in U.S.
Ebenezer Howard establishes Letchworth Garden City.

P **Science, Technology, Discovery, etc.**

Agnes Clerke, *Problems in Astrophysics.*
W. Ramsay discovers the gases krypton and xenon in the atmosphere.
J. J. Thomson, *The Conduction of Electricity Through Gases.*
Orville and Wilbur Wright make successful flight in aeroplane with a petrol engine (*Dec.* 17th).
C. T. R. Wilson's sensitive electroscope.
R. A. Zsigmondy invents the ultramicroscope.
Krupps Works, Essen, founded.
Detroit becomes the 'motor capital' of the world.
First motor taxis in London.

Q **Scholarship**

German Museum, Munich, opened.

R **Philosophy and Religion**

G. E. Moore, *Principia Ethica.*
Royal Commission on Ecclesiastical Discipline in England.
Johannes Haller, *The Papacy and Church Reform.*
Carl Munth founds Roman Catholic periodical *Hochland.*

S **Art, Sculpture, Fine Arts and Architecture**

Painting:
P. W. Steer, *Richmond Castle.*
L. Alma-Tadema, *Silver-favorites.*
National Art Collections Fund formed to prevent works of art leaving Britain.

Architecture:
J. F. Bentley, Westminster Cathedral (Campanile 273 ft.).
Giles Gilbert Scott, Liverpool Cathedral begun.
New York Chamber of Commerce and Stock Exchange built.

T **Music**

Eugène D'Albert, *Tiefland* (opera).
F. Delius, *Sea Drift.*

U **Literature**

S. Butler, *The Way of All Flesh* (posth.).
G. R. Gissing, *The Private Papers of Henry Ryecroft.*
Hugo von Hofmannsthal, *Electra.*
Henry James, *The Ambassadors.*

V **The Press**

B. Croce founds *La Critica.*

W **Drama and Entertainment**

Oscar Hammerstein builds Drury Lane Theatre, New York (later the Manhattan Opera House).
Arthur Schnitzler, *Reigen.*
G. B. Shaw, *Man and Superman.*

1903 (Nov.–Dec.)

L **Nov:** 3rd, fearing U.S. would choose alternative canal route if Colombia delayed further, a group of Colombians proclaims independence of Panama;

17th, by treaty of Petropolis Bolivia cedes territory to Brazil in return for rail and water outlet to the east;

Commission in Transvaal favours immigrant Chinese labour for Rand mines, which is later sanctioned by Arthur Balfour;

At London Congress the Russian Social Democratic Party splits into Menshevists, led by G. V. Plecharoff, and Bolshevists, led by N. Lenin and Leon Trotsky.

M **Dec:** 18th, U.S.-Panama treaty places Canal Zone in U.S. hands in perpetuity for annual rent.

N In U.S. regulation of child labour is introduced, and Elkins Act strengthens Interstate Commerce Act, 1887, by requiring railways to keep to published charges.

Foundation of Union of Liberation in Russia, supported by members of the professions, aiming at a liberal constitution.

New Zealand tariff favours British goods.

X Sport

Y Statistics

Naval strength (numbers of battleships in service): Great Britain, 67; France, 39; U.S., 27; Germany, 27; Italy, 18; Russia, 18; Japan, 5.

Petroleum production (in mill. barrels): U.S., 88·7 (being 49% of world production); Russia, 80·5.

Z Births and Deaths

Jan. 10th Barbara Hepworth b. (–1975).
Jan. 11th Alan Paton b. (–1988).
Feb. 22nd Hugo Wolf d. (43).
May 12th Lennox Berkeley b. (–1989).
July 2nd Lord Home b. (–).
July 10th Kenneth Clark b. (–1983).
July 17th James Whistler d. (70).
Aug. 7th Louis Leakey b. (–1972).
Aug 22nd Robert Cecil, third Marquess of Salisbury d. (73).
Aug. 24th Graham Sutherland b. (–1980).
Sept. 25th Marc Rothko b. (–1970).
Oct. 22nd W. E. H. Lecky d. (87).
Oct. 28th Evelyn Waugh b. (–1966).
Oct. 31st Joan Robinson b. (–1983).
Nov. 1st Theodor Mommsen d. (87).
Dec. 8th Herbert Spencer d. (83).
Dec. 13th John Piper b. (–1992).
— Paul Gauguin d. (55).
— Camille Pissarro d. (72).

1904 (Jan.–Nov.) Russo-Japanese War

A **Jan:**

B **Feb:** 4th, outbreak of Russo-Japanese War. Japan begins siege of Port Arthur and soon occupies Seoul, forcing Korea to annul her concessions to Russia.

C **Mar:** 8th, German anti-Jesuit law, 1872, revised to permit the return of individual members of the order;
11th, army bill is passed in Hungary, despite Magyar obstruction, through using guillotine;
14th, judgment in U.S. Northern Securities case declares attempted mergers of railway interests as violation of anti-Trust Act.

D **Apr:** 8th, *Entente Cordiale* settles Anglo-French differences in Morocco, Egypt and Newfoundland fishery, and Britain recognises Suez Canal Convention and surrenders claim to Madagascar;
23rd, U.S. acquires property of French Panama Canal company;
24th (–27th), visit of Émile Loubet and Théophile Delcassé to Victor Emmanuel III annoys Papacy.

E **May:** 17th, French ambassador at Vatican is recalled;
30th, Japanese occupy Dalny (Dairen), Russia.

F **Jun:**

G **Jul:** 28th, assassination of Viacheslav Plehve, Russian minister of interior;
28th, Germany signs commercial treaties with Belgium, Switzerland, Sweden and Austria-Hungary;
Rafael Reyes becomes dictator in Colombia and attempts to reorganise finances.

H **Aug:** 10th, Japanese cripple Russian fleet off Port Arthur;
11th, alteration to the drink licensing laws in Britain generates controversy but fails to deal with problem of drunkenness;
26th (–*Sept.* 3rd), Japanese defeat Russians at Liaoyang, China.

J **Sep:** 7th, on expedition to Lhasa, Francis Younghusband signs treaty with Tibet by which the Dalai Lama will not concede territory to a foreign power;
General strike in Italy, culminating in violent incidents in Milan.

K **Oct:** 3rd, Insurrection of Hereros and Hottentots in German South-West Africa (–1908);
3rd, Franco-Spanish treaty for preserving independence of Morocco, with secret clauses aiming at ultimate partition;
20th, Bolivia and Chile settle differences by treaty;
21st, Russian fleet, bound for the Far East, fires on British trawlers in Dogger Bank area of North Sea, provokes
23rd, wave of indignation in Britain, but Arthur Balfour and Lord Lansdowne remain cool and
28th, Tsar Nicholas II agrees to refer question of compensation to Hague international commission;
In Italian elections the Socialists, discredited by strike action, lose heavily.

L **Nov:** 8th, Theodore Roosevelt (Republican, with 336 electoral votes wins U.S. presidential election against Alton B. Parker (Democrat, with 133 votes);
18th, Émile Combes introduces bill for separation of Church and State in France, ending the 1801 Concordat (promulgated *Dec.* 1905);

O Politics, Economics, Law and Education

L. T. Hobhouse, *Democracy and Reaction.*
Workers' Educational Association founded by Albert Mansbridge.
Ten-hour day in France.
Protectionist tariff in Canada.
Paris Conference on White Slave Trade.

P Science, Technology, Discovery, etc.

Ernest Rutherford and F. Soddy state general theory of radioactivity.
J. P. L. T. Elster devises photo-electric cell.
An ultra-violet lamp is made.
Safety razor blades.
Work on Panama Canal begins (*May* 4th).
New York, Broadway Subway open, with electric trains from City Hall.
Rolls-Royce is founded.

Q Scholarship

Henry Adams, *Mont St. Michel and Chartres.*

R Philosophy and Religion

S Art, Sculpture, Fine Arts and Architecture

Painting:
Frank Brangwyn paints decorative panel in Skinners' Company Hall, London.
Max Beerbohm, 'Poets Corner' (drawings of literary men).
P. Cézanne, *Mont Sainte Victoire.*
William Nicholson's sets for first production of Barrie's *Peter Pan.*
Henri Rousseau, *The Wedding.*
Architecture:
C. R. Mackintosh, The Willow Tea Rooms, Glasgow.

T Music

F. Delius, *Koanga* (opera).
G. Puccini, *Madama Butterfly* (opera).

U Literature

G. K. Chesterton, *The Napoleon of Notting Hill.*
J. Conrad, *Nostromo.*
W. H. Hudson, *Green Mansions.*
M. R. James, *Ghost Stories of an Antiquary.*
Jack London, *Sea Wolf.*
R. Rolland, *Jean-Christophe* (–12).

V The Press

Alfred Harmsworth founds *The Daily Mirror.*

W Drama and Entertainment

J. M. Barrie, *Peter Pan.*
A. Chekhov, *The Cherry Orchard.*
T. Hardy, *The Dynasts.*
Luigi Pirandello, *Il fu Mattia Pascal.*
J. M. Synge, *Riders to the Sea.*
Abbey Theatre, Dublin, founded.
First J. E. Vedrenne-Granville-Barker season at Court Theatre, London.

L Nov: 23rd, German-Russian negotiations for an alliance break down through Russia's unwillingness to sign before consulting France;
Zemstvo Congress at St. Petersburg demands a republican constitution and civil liberties.

M Dec: 10th, nationalist, anti-Austrian ministry takes office in Serbia.

N Reorganisation of French possessions as French West Africa, with capital at Dakar.
Canadian protectionist tariff.

X Sport

The American Walter J. Travis wins British amateur golf championship.

Y Statistics

In U.S. two-fifths of manufacturing capital is contributed by 'trusts'.

Z Births and Deaths

Jan. 9th George Melitonovich Balanchine b. (–1983).
Jan. 14th Cecil Beaton b. (–1980).
Jan. 17th Henry Keppel d. (95).
Feb. 21st Alexei Nikolaevich Kosygin b. (–1980).
Feb. 22nd Leslie Stephen d. (72).
Apr. 16th Samuel Smiles d. (92).
Apr. 27th C. Day-Lewis b. (–1972).
May 1st Anton Dvořák d. (62).
May 2nd Bing Crosby b. (–1977).
May 10th H. M. Stanley d. (63).
June 2nd Johnny Weissmuller b. (–1984).
July 1st G. F. Watts d. (87).
July 2nd Anton Chekhov d. (44).
July 12th Pablo Neruda b. (–1973).
July 14th S. J. P. Kruger d. (79).
July 27th Anton Dolin b. (–1983).
Aug 7th Ralph Bunche b. (–1971).
Aug. 21st Count Basie b. (–1984).
Aug. 22nd Teng Hsiao-ping b. (–).
Aug. 26th Christopher Isherwood b. (–1986).
Oct. 1st Otto Frisch b. (–1979).
Oct. 2nd Graham Greene b. (–1991).
Nov. 14th Michael Ramsey b. (–1988).
Nov. 17th Isamu Noguchi b. (–1988).
Dec. 10th Antonin Novotný b. (1975).
Dec. 27th Marlene Dietrich b. (–1992).

A Jan: 1st, Russians surrender Port Arthur to Japanese;
22nd, 'Bloody Sunday' in St. Petersburg when workers in revolt are fired upon;
Louis Botha forms *Het Volk* organisation to agitate for responsible government in Transvaal.

B Feb: Insurrection in Welle District of Belgian Congo.

C Mar: 1st (–9th), Japanese defeat Russians at Mukden;
3rd, Tsar Nicholas II promises to undertake religious and other reforms and to call a consultative assembly;
21st, Anglo-Persian agreement to counter Russian designs in the Near East;
30th, Greeks in Crete revolt against Turkish rule;
31st, Kaiser William II's visit to Tangier sets off first Moroccan crisis.

D Apr: 25th, Transvaal is granted a constitution which Louis Botha regards as inadequate;
30th, Anglo-French military conversations.

E May: 1st (–5th), Maurice Rouvier, French premier, fails to settle Moroccan question with Germany;
8th, Union of Unions in Russia, under Paul Miliukov, combines various liberal elements demanding parliamentary institutions;
17th, Britain proposes full discussions on Morocco;
27th, Japanese annihilate Russian fleet in Tsushima Straits.

F Jun: 6th, Théophile Delcassé, French foreign minister since 1898, resigns under pressure from Germany;
7th, Norwegian Storting decides on separation from Sweden (ratified by plebiscite, *Aug.*).

G Jul: 8th, France, assured of U.S. support against unreasonable demands by Germany, agrees to a conference on Morocco;
23rd (–4th), William II and Nicholas II sign treaty of Björkö, for mutual aid in Europe (Prince von Bülow objects to the limitation to Europe and threatens to resign);
Chinese boycott U.S. goods.

H Aug: 12th, Anglo-Japanese alliance is renewed for ten years;
19th, Tsar Nicholas II creates an Imperial Duma, elected on limited franchise, and with only deliberative powers.

J Sep: 1st, Provinces of Alberta and Saskatchewan formed in Canada;
5th, by treaty of Portsmouth, mediated by Theodore Roosevelt, Russia cedes Port Arthur and Talienwan to Japan and recognises Japan's interests in Korea, but Japan fails to obtain an indemnity;
24th, Sweden acquiesces in Norway's independence;
28th, France and Germany agree to call a conference on Morocco.

K Oct: 20th (–30th), general strike in Russia;
26th, workers in St. Petersburg form first Soviet; mutiny on battleship *Potemkin*;
—, by Treaty of Separation between Norway and Sweden, Oscar II abdicates Norwegian crown;
30th, by 'October Manifesto' the Tsar capitulates to demands for the Duma to have legislative powers, a wider franchise for its election and civil liberties.

O Politics, Economics, Law and Education

N. Lenin (pseud.), *Two Tactics.*
New York state investigates insurance houses following charges of corrupt practices.
International Agricultural Institute founded in Rome.
Automobile Association, London, founded.

P Science, Technology, Discovery, etc.

Albert Einstein states his first theory of relativity.
Austin Motor Company founded.
Regular motor 'bus service in London, where the Bakerloo and Piccadilly undergrounds are opened.
Neon signs are first displayed.

Q Scholarship

R Philosophy and Religion

Wilhelm Dilthey, *Experience and Poetry.*
G. Santayana, *Life of Reason.*
S. Freud, *Three Treatises on the Theory of Sex.*
Baptist World Alliance founded in London.

S Art, Sculpture, Fine Arts and Architecture

Painting:
P. Cézanne, *Les Grandes Baigneuses.*
Louis Vauxcelles coins the name 'Les Fauves' (Wild Beasts) for the group of French artists led by Henri Matisse.
Die Brücke ('The Bridge') group of artists is formed in Dresden by Ernst Kirchner to revive interest in the graphic arts (–13).
H. Matisse, *La Joie de Vivre.*
Pablo Picasso, *Boy With Pipe.*
Henri Rousseau, *The Hungry Lion.*
J. S. Sargent, *The Marlborough Family.*

Sculpture:
Thomas Brock, memorial to Queen Victoria, outside Buckingham Palace; the posts and pedestal by Aston Webb.
W. Holman Hunt, *Pre-Raphaelitism.*

Architecture:
Flagg, Singer Building, New York (–08).
Antoni Gaudi, Casa Milà, Barcelona (–10).

T Music

C. Debussy, *La Mer.*
F. Delius, *A Mass of Life.*
F. Léhar, *The Merry Widow* (operetta).
R. Strauss, *Salome* (opera).
L. A. Coerne's *Zenobia*, first European production of an American opera.
A. Schweitzer, *J. S. Bach, the Musician Poet.*

U Literature

A. Strindberg, *Historical Miniatures.*
H. G. Wells, *Kipps.*
Edith Wharton, *House of Mirth.*
Oscar Wilde, *De Profundis.*

L Nov: 16th, Count Sergei Witte appointed premier of Russia;
18th, Prince Charles of Denmark is elected King Haakon VII of Norway;
—, Japanese exercise protectorate over Korea;
25th, Lord Rosebery attacks Henry Campbell-Bannerman's idea of Irish Home Rule, but Liberals close ranks;
28th, Sinn Fein party is founded in Dublin;
Report of Commission of Inquiry into Congo atrocities excuses Leopold II.

M Dec: 4th, Arthur Balfour resigns and, 5th, Henry Campbell-Bannerman forms Liberal ministry with Edward Grey foreign secretary, Herbert Asquith as chancellor of exchequer and R. B. Haldane as war secretary;
9th, separation of Church and State in France (as established by the 1801 Concordat); complete liberty of conscience;
12th, Tsar Nicholas II grants constitution in Montenegro;
22nd, insurrection of Moscow workers (–*Jan.* 1st 1906);
Revolution in Persia begins.

N Deterioration of Roumanian-Greek relations over Macedonian problem (–1911).
Serbia's tariff war with Austria (–1907).
Sun Yat-sen organises a union of secret societies to expel the Manchus from China.
Moslem rising in German East Africa.

V The Press

W Drama and Entertainment

Tristram Bernard, *Triplepatte*.
H. von Hofmannsthal, *Das gerettete Venedig*.
A five-cent cinema in Pittsburg shows *The Great Train Robbery*.

X Sport

Y Statistics

Religious denominations (in thousands):
(a) *Britain:* Roman Catholics, 5,800; Church of England, 2,450; Presbyterian Church of Scotland, 1,170; Wesleyan Methodists, 521; Primitive Methodists, 212; Congregationalists, 498; Baptists, 426; Presbyterians, 80; Unitarians, 75; Episcopal Church of Scotland, 50; Quakers, 18; Jews, 240.
(b) *U.S.:* Roman Catholics, 12,079; Baptists, 6,166; Episcopal Methodists, 6,305; Congregational Methodists, 296; Presbyterians, 1,830; Mormons, 350; Unitarians, 90; Quakers, 90; Jews, 177.
U.K. total State expenditure: £149.5 mill.
Convictions for drunkenness in U.K.: 207,171.

Z Births and Deaths

Jan. 2nd Michael Tippett b. (–).
Feb. 6th Wladyslaw Gomulka b. (1982).
Feb. 9th Adolf Menzel d. (89).
Mar. 29th Edward Burra b. (–1976).
Apr. 2nd Serge Lifar b. (–1986).
May Bill Brandt b. (–1983).
May 24th Mikhail Sholokov b. (–1984).
June 21st Jean-Paul Sartre b. (–1980).
July 1st John Hay d. (67).
Sept. 5th Arthur Koestler b. (–1983).
Sept. 18th Greta Garbo b. (–1990).
Oct. 13th Henry Irving d. (67).
Oct. 15th C. P. Snow b. (–1980).
Nov. 25th Patrick Devlin b. (–).
Dec. 9th Richard Jebb d. (64).
— Dag Hammarskjöld b. (–1961).
Dec. 21st Anthony Powell b. (–).
Dec. 24th Howard Hughes b. (–1976).

1906 (Jan.–Nov.) Liberals' landslide in Britain

A **Jan**: 1st, Helmuth von Moltke becomes chief of German general staff;
10th, Anglo-French military and naval conversations;
12th, Liberal landslide in British general election (Liberals, 377 seats, with majority of 84 over all parties; Unionists, 157; Irish Nationalists, 83; Labour, 53); Henry Campbell-Bannerman's cabinet embarks on sweeping social reforms;
16th, Algeciras conference on Morocco opens (–*Apr.*);
17th, Clément Fallières elected President of France, through Georges Clemenceau's influence;
Viscount Katsura, premier of Japan, resigns.

B **Feb**: 24th, Liberal revolt in Cuba on President Tomás Palma's re-election; Theodore Roosevelt intervenes to establish a provisional government which will carry out reforms.

C **Mar**: 16th, nationalisation of Japanese railways.

D **Apr**: 5th, Count Friedrich Holstein's dismissal by William II ends fear of German war with France over Morocco;
8th, Algeciras Act signed, giving France and Spain chief control in Morocco.

E **May**: 5th, fall of Count Witte in Russia, who is succeeded by the Conservative Ivan Goremykin;
6th, Fundamental Laws promulgated in Russia;
7th, Alaska allowed to elect a delegate to U.S. Congress;
9th, Chinese decide to take over administration of Imperial Customs Service (of which Robert Hart inspector-general since 1863);
10th, first Duma meets in Russia (–*July* 21st), resulting in deadlock through the Cadets' Party's criticism of Fundamental Laws;
11th, Isvolsky becomes Russian foreign secretary;
19th, João Franco becomes premier of Spain with dictatorial powers;
30th, Giovanni Giolitti forms ministry in Italy (–*Dec.* 1909);
Turkey yields to British pressure over Egypt's frontier with Palestine.

F **Jun**: 5th, third German naval bill provides for increases in construction of battleships;
Peter Stolypin becomes premier of Russia.

G **Jul**: 4th, Britain, France and Italy guarantee the independence of Abyssinia;
12th, Alfred Dreyfus is rehabilitated;
21st, on dissolution of Duma the Cadets adjourn to Finland and issue Viborg Manifesto, calling on Russians to refuse paying taxes;
Universal suffrage bill introduced in Hungary.

H **Aug**: 15th, Edward VII's discussions with William II at Cronberg;
Anglo-Chinese convention on Tibet.

Sep:

K **Oct**:

L **Nov**: 22nd, Peter Stolypin introduces agrarian reforms in Russia.

O Politics, Economics, Law and Education

British Patents Act secures greater protection for patentees, while Merchant Shipping Act restricts pilots' certificates to British subjects and reforms conditions in merchant navy.
School care committees established in Britain.
London *Daily News* stages Sweated Industries Exhibition to demand reforms.
Night shift work for women internationally forbidden.
Confederazione Generale de Lavoro founded in Italy.
U.S. Pure Food and Drugs Act passed, following revelations in Upton Sinclair's *Jungle* of conditions in Chicago stockyards, which prompted a federal investigation.
U.S. National Forests Commission established.

P Science, Technology, Discovery, etc.

J. J. Thomson undertakes work on gamma rays.
Arthur Harden and W. J. Young discover cases of catalysis among enzymes.
Automatic railway coupling first used.
Beginnings of Zuider Zee drainage scheme.
Simplon Tunnel (begun in 1898) is opened.
H.M.S. *Dreadnought* with entirely large-calibre armament is launched.

Q Scholarship

Hugo Winckler leads archaeological expedition to North Cappadocia.
P. S. Allen, *Erasmi Epistolae* (–58).
W. S. Churchill, *Lord Randolph Churchill.*

R Philosophy and Religion

The English Hymnal (ed. Percy Dearmer and R. Vaughan Williams).

S Art, Sculpture, Fine Arts and Architecture

Painting:
A. Derain, *Port of London.*
G. Rouault, *At the Mirror.*
Sculpture:
Aristide Maillol, *Chained Action.*
Architecture:
Edwin Lutyens designs two churches and an institute for Hampstead Garden Suburb, founded by Henrietta Barnett.

T Music

Jules Massenet, *Ariane* (opera).
Ethel Smyth, *The Wreckers* (opera).
A Mozart Festival is held in Salzburg.

U Literature

A. Blackwood, *The Empty House.*
J. Galsworthy, *The Man of Property.*
P. Valéry, *Monsieur Teste.*
'Everyman's Library' begun.

V The Press

W Drama and Entertainment

P. Claudel, *Partage de Midi.*
A. W. Pinero, *His House in Order.*

1906 (Dec.)

M Dec: 6th, self-government is granted to Transvaal and Orange River Colonies;
13th, through revolt of Centre Party the Reichstag opposes expenses on colonial wars; von Bülow dissolves Reichstag and in subsequent elections the Socialists suffer losses;
Trades Disputes Act legitimises peaceful picketing in Britain.

N Crisis in French wine industry caused by declining prices.
Aga Khan founds All India Moslem League.

X **Sport**

Y **Statistics**

U.S. makes 23,000 motor vehicles (more than France) and produces 124·4 mill. barrels of petroleum.

Populations (in mill.): China, 438; Russia, 149·2; U.S., 85; Germany, 62; Great Britain, 38·9; Ireland, 4·3; France, 39·2.

Populations of cities (in mill.): London, 4·5; New York, 4; Paris, 2·7; Berlin, 2; Tokio, 1·9; St. Petersburg, 1·4; Vienna, 1·3.

Army strengths (in mill.): Russia, 13; Germany, 7·9; Austro-Hungary, 7·4; France, 4·8; Italy, 3·1; Great Britain, 0·8, with 0·4 from colonial forces.

Z **Births and Deaths**

Jan. 15th Aristotle Onassis b. (–1975).
Mar. 13th Oscar Nemon b. (–1985).
Mar. 25th A. J. P. Taylor b. (–1990).
Apr. 9th Hugh Gaitskell b. (–1963).
Apr. 13th Samuel Beckett b. (–1989).
Apr. 19th Pierre Curie d. (46).
Apr. 28th Kurt Gödel b. (–1978).
May 23rd Henrik Ibsen d. (78).
June 29th Albert Sorel d. (64).
Aug. 7th Marcello Caetano b. (–1980).
Aug. 28th Sir John Betjeman b. (–1984).
Sept. 25th Dimitry Shostakovich b. (–1975).
Nov. 2nd Luchino Visconti b. (–1976).
Nov. 18th Alec Issigonis b. (–1988).
Dec. 19th Leonid Brezhnev b. (–1982).
— F. W. Maitland d. (56).
Dec. 30th Josephine Butler d. (78).
— Paul Cézanne d. (67).

A **Jan:** 10th, universal direct suffrage in Austria.
14th, earthquake in Jamaica, Kingston destroyed, 1,000 killed.

B **Feb:** war between Honduras and Nicaragua (*–Dec.*).

C **Mar:** 5th, Second Duma meets in Russia (*–June* 16th);
Roumanian army puts down Moldavian revolt with brutality.

D **Apr:** 8th, Anglo-French convention confirms independence of Siam;
30th, Edward VII visits Rome.

E **May:** 2nd, Edward VII visits President Fallières in Paris;
14th, Imperial Conference, London;
—, Sweden adopts proportional representation for elections to both chambers and manhood suffrage for Second Chamber;
16th, Pact of Cartagena between Britain, France and Spain to counter German designs on Balearic and Canary Islands;
23rd, legislative council is erected in Mozambique.

F **Jun:** 10th, Franco-Japanese agreement to preserve 'open door' in China;
14th, female suffrage in Norway;
15th (*–Oct.* 18th), Peace Conference at the Hague, originally called at Theodore Roosevelt's suggestion in 1904, but postponed owing to war in Far East, reassembles; attempt at stopping the arms race fails, but progress is made in direction of voluntary arbitration of disputes, despite German opposition;
16th, reactionary party in Russia forces Tsar Nicholas II to dissolve the Second Duma; an electoral edict increases representation of propertied classes and reduces representation of national minorities;
26th, Commons pass Henry Campbell-Bannerman's resolution that the power of the Lords to prevent passage of bills must be restricted.

G **Jul:** 1st, revised constitution for Orange River Colony;
19th, Emperor of Korea abdicates and
25th, Japan obtains protectorate over Korea;
30th, Russo-Japanese agreement over China;
—, elections for first assembly in Philippines;
Triple alliance between Germany, Austria and Italy is renewed for six years, despite the coolness of Italy.

H **Aug:** 3rd, Kaiser William II and Tsar Nicholas II meet at Swinemünde to discuss Baghdad Railway;
4th, French fleet bombards Casablanca following anti-foreign outbreaks;
31st, Anglo-Russian Convention on Persia, Afghanistan and Tibet is signed, aligning Russia with Britain and France against the Central Powers.

J **Sep:** 5th, Edward VII meets Alexander Izvolski, Russian foreign minister, at Marienbad;
21st, risings in German South-West Africa suppressed.

K **Oct:**

L **Nov:** 14th, the Third Duma meets in Russia (–1912), elected on a restricted franchise: leads to the suppression of revolutionary outbreaks;
16th, Oklahoma is admitted as a U.S. state.

O Politics, Economics, Law and Education

First British census of production.
Medical inspection of school children in Britain.
R. Baden-Powell founds Boy Scouts.
U.S. restricts immigration.
Henry Deterding founds Royal Dutch Shell Group.

P Science, Technology, Discovery, etc.

C. Pirquet's method for diagnosing tuberculosis.
Alexis Pavlov studies conditional reflexes.
C. Ross Harrison develops tissue culture techniques.
Emil Fischer, *Researches on the Chemistry of Proteins.*
Richard Anschütz and Max Schuler perfect the gyro-compass.
A. Lumière's improved process for colour reproduction through auto-chrome plates.
Leo Bäkeland invents Bakelite.
S.S. *Lusitania* and *Mauritania* launched.

Q Scholarship

Henry Adams, *The Education of Henry Adams: a study of XXth Century Multiplicity* (privately printed).
Maurice Bloomfield, *Vedic Concordance.*
Cambridge History of English Literature (-27).

R Philosophy and Religion

H. Bergson, *L'Évolution créatrice.*
W. James, *Pragmatism.*
C. Gore, *The New Theology and the Old Religion.*
Pius X condemns modernism in encyclical *Pascendi gregis.*

S Art, Sculpture, Fine Arts and Architecture

Painting:
Exhibition of Cubist paintings, Paris.
A. Derain, *Blackfriars Bridge* and *The Bathers.*
P. Picasso, *Les Demoiselles d'Avignon.*
H. Matisse, *Luxe, Calme et Volupté.*
E. Munch, *Amor and Psyche.*
H. Rousseau, *The Snake Charmer.*
National League of Handicrafts Societies leads to extension of 'arts and crafts' movement in U.S.
Architecture:
Edward Mountford, New Central Criminal Court, London.

T Music

F. Delius, *A Village Romeo and Juliet* (opera) and *Brigg Fair* (rhapsody).
P. Dukas, *Ariadne and Bluebeard* (opera).
E. Elgar, March '*Pomp and Circumstance*' no. 4 in G (op. 39).
M. Ravel, *Spanish Rhapsody.*
R. Strauss, *Elektra* (opera).
R. Vaughan Williams, *Towards the Unknown Region.*

U Literature

J. Conrad, *Secret Agent.*
M. Gorki, *Mother.*
R. M. Rilke, *Neue Gedichte* (-08).
F. Wedekind, *Such is Life.*

1907 (Dec.)

M Dec: 6th, frontier between Uganda and East Africa is defined;
7th, first Nationalist Congress in Egypt under Mustapha Kemal;
8th, on Oskar II's death, Gustavus V succeeds as King of Sweden (-1950).

N Nicolai Lenin (pseud.) leaves Russia.

V The Press

W Drama and Entertainment

G. B. Shaw, *Major Barbara.*
J. M. Synge, *Playboy of the Western World.*
Julius Caesar and *The Tunnel Under the Canal* (films).

X Sport

Y Statistics

Railway mileage in operation (in thousand miles): U.S., 236·9; Russia, 44·6; Germany, 36; India, 29·8; France, 29·7; Austro-Hungary, 25·8; Great Britain and Ireland, 23·1; Canada, 22·4.

Z Births and Deaths

Jan. 11th Pierre Mendès-France b. (–1982).
Feb. 2nd Dmitry Mendeléev d. (73).
Feb. 21st W. H. Auden b. (–1973).
May 12th J. K. Huysmans d. (59).
May 14th Mohammed Ayub Khan b. (–1974).
May 22nd Lawrence Olivier b. (–1989).
May 26th John Wayne b. (–1979).
June 1st Frank Whittle b. (–).
June 20th Lillian Hellman b. (–1984).
Aug. 1st Eric Shipton b. (–1977).
Aug. 13th Basil Spence b. (–1976).
Aug. 15th Joseph Joachim d. (76).
Sept. 4th Edvard Grieg d. (64).
Sept. 6th Sully Prudhomme d. (67).
Sept. 12th Louis Macneice b. (–1964).
Nov. 28th Alberto Moravia b. (–1990).
Dec. 15th R. H. S. Crossman b. (–1974).
Dec. 16th Francis Thompson d. (47).
Dec. 17th William Thomson, Lord Kelvin, d. (84).
Dec. 18th Christopher Fry b. (–).

1908 (Jan.–Nov.) Anglo-German tension—Austria annexes Bosnia and Herzegovina

A **Jan:** 4th, Mulai Hafid is proclaimed Sultan of Morocco at Fez;
27th, Count Alois Aehrenthal, Austrian foreign minister, announces the Austrian government will build railway towards Salonika.

B **Feb:** 1st, King Carlos I of Portugal and the Crown Prince are murdered in Lisbon and Manuel II becomes King (–1910).

C **Mar:**

D **Apr:** 8th, H. H. Asquith becomes British prime minister on Henry Campbell-Bannerman's resignation through ill health and David Lloyd George becomes chancellor of exchequer.

E **May:** Labour government in Australia under Andrew Fisher.

F **Jun:** 9th, Edward VII meets Nicholas II at Reval and the Tsar agrees to introduce extensive reforms in Macedonia;
14th, fourth German navy bill authorises expenditure on four further capital ships;
23rd, Shah Mohammed Ali overthrows Persian constitution of *Dec.* 1906;
—, U.S. severs diplomatic relations with Venezuela on Cipriano Castro's refusal to compensate U.S. citizens for injuries.

G **Jul:** 6th, Young Turks under Niazi Bey stage revolt at Resina in Macedonia, the government troops sent to quell them desert and, 24th, Sultan Abdul Hamid II restores the constitution of 1876;
Pan Slav Conference in Prague.

H **Aug:** 20th, Leopold II hands over Congo to Belgium (confirmed by act of Belgian Parliament, *Oct.* 18th);
23rd, Baltic Convention between Germany, Sweden, Denmark and Russia, and North Sea Convention between Britain, Germany, Denmark, France and the Netherlands to maintain the *status quo* on the shores of the two seas;
—, Abdul Aziz of Morocco is defeated at Marrakesh by Mulai Hafid, the new Sultan.

J **Sep:** 13th, German Social Democrat rally at Nuremberg;
16th, Buchlau conference between Count Aehrenthal and Alexander Izvolski, at which Austria undertakes not to oppose opening of the Straits to Russian warships and Russia agrees to Austrian annexation of Bosnia and Herzegovina;
25th, Casablanca incident, when German deserters from the French Foreign Legion are taken by force from a German consular official.

K **Oct:** 5th, Declaration of Independence of Bulgaria by Ferdinand I, who assumes the title of Tsar of Bulgaria;
6th, Austria annexes Bosnia and Herzegovina by decree;
7th, Crete proclaims union with Greece;
12th, South Africa constitutional convention meets at Durban, later removes to Capetown (–*Feb.* 1909), agreeing on a Union of South Africa;
28th, *Daily Telegraph* publishes interview with Kaiser William II in which he states the German people are hostile to Britain while he is a friend.

L **Nov:** 3rd, in U.S. presidential election William Howard Taft, Republican, with 321 electoral votes, defeats William Jennings Bryan, Democrat, with 162 votes;
9th, Alexander Izvolski, Russian foreign minister, visits London;

O **Politics, Economics, Law and Education**

F. Meinecke, *Cosmopolitanism and the National State.*
G. Sorel, *Reflections on Violence.*
Graham Wallas, *Human Nature in Politics.*
Port of London Authority established.
Berlin Copyright Convention.
Labour insurance in Russia.
Britain prohibits the manufacture and importation of phosphorus matches.

P **Science, Technology, Discovery, etc.**

Hermann Minkowski elaborates four-dimensional geometry, the mathematics of relativity.
Fritz Haber invents his industrial process for synthesising ammonia.
Two further subway lines opened in New York.

Q **Scholarship**

R **Philosophy and Religion**

Federal Council of Churches founded in U.S.

S **Art, Sculpture, Fine Arts and Architecture**

Painting:
Marc Chagall, *Nu Rouge.*
Maurice Vlaminck, *The Red Trees.*
Augustus John, *The Lord Mayor of Liverpool.*
C. Monet, *The Ducal Palace, Venice.*
Pierre Bonnard, *Nude against the Light.*
Maurice Utrillo's 'White Period' (–1914).

Sculpture:
Jacob Epstein, 'Figures', for the British Medical Association, The Strand, causes a furore of indignation.
Constantin Brancusi, *The Kiss.*

Architecture:
Peter Behrens, A.E.G. Turbine Factory, Berlin (first building of steel and glass).

T **Music**

B. Bartók, first string quartet.
E. Elgar, Symphony no. 1 in A flat (op. 55).

U **Literature**

A. Bennett, *The Old Wives' Tale.*
G. K. Chesterton, *The Man Who Was Thursday.*
Colette (pseud.), *La Retraite Sentimentale.*
W. H. Davies, *Autobiography of a Super-tramp.*
E. M. Forster, *A Room With a View.*
A. France (pseud.), *L'Île des pingouins.*
K. Grahame, *The Wind in the Willows.*

V **The Press**

Lord Northcliffe buys *The Times.*
J. L. Garvin edits *The Observer* (–42).
Ford Madox Ford founds *English Review.*

L Nov: 10th (–11th), Reichstag debate on *Daily Telegraph* interview further embitters Anglo-German relations;
14th, Liberal victory in Cuban elections leads to José Gómez's presidency (–1913).

M Dec: 2nd, revolt in Bohemia;
4th, abortive London naval conference of the powers to regulate conditions of warfare;
9th, regulation of hours of factory work for women and young persons in Germany;
17th, first meeting of Ottoman Parliament with large Young Turk majority;
28th, disastrous earthquake in South Calabria and Sicily.

N.

W **Drama and Entertainment**

The Tiller Girls dance on the London Stage.

X **Sport**

Olympic Games held in London.
Jack Johnson becomes the first negro world boxing champion.

Y **Statistics**

Z **Births and Deaths**

Jan. 9th Simone de Beauvoir b. (–1986).
Jan. 25th 'Ouida' (Louise de la Ramée) d. (67).
Feb. 11th Vivian Fuchs b. (–).
Mar. 11th Edmondo de Amicis d. (61).
Apr. 22nd Henry Campbell-Bannerman d. (72).
May 22nd W. G. Hoskins b. (–1992).
May 28th Ian Fleming b. (–1964).
June 20th Nicolai Rimsky-Korsakov d. (63).
June 24th Stephen Grover Cleveland d. (71).
July 6th Joel Chandler Harris ('Uncle Remus') d. (60).
July 8th Nelson Rockefeller b. (–1979).
Aug. 5th Harold Holt b. (–1967).
Aug. 25th Henri Becquerel d. (56).
Aug. 27th Donald Bradman b. (–).
— Lyndon Baines Johnson b. (–1973).
Oct. 9th Jacques Tati b. (–1982).
Dec. 10th Olivier Messiaen b. (–1992).
Dec. 11th Elliott Carter b. (–).
Dec. 17th W. F. Libby b. (–1980).

1909 (Jan.–Nov.) Lords reject Lloyd George's budget

A **Jan:** 1st, Old-age pensions payable to all British subjects over 70;
2nd, dismissal of Yüan Shih-kai places Chinese administration in Manchu hands;
Anglo-Persian Oil Co. formed.

B **Feb:** 9th, Germany recognises France's special interests in Morocco in return for economic concessions;
13th, Kiamil Pasha, Grand Vizier of Turkey, forced to resign by the Turkish nationalists;
21st, Ferdinand I of Bulgaria visits Russia to obtain financial aid;
26th, Turkey recognises Austria's annexation of Bosnia and is paid compensation.

C **Mar:** 2nd, the powers intervene to prevent a Serbo-Austrian war;
4th, W. H. Taft inaugurated as President of U.S. (–1913);
12th, British alarm at growth of German navy leads to passage of naval bill;
25th, press censorship imposed in Egypt to control Nationalists;
31st, Serbia yields to Austria in Bosnian dispute.

D **Apr:** 9th, Payne-Aldrich tariff in U.S. maintains protection, despite party pledges.
13th, army counter-revolution in Constantinople against rule of Mohammedan Union;
19th, Turkey recognises Bulgarian independence;
24th, army of liberation captures Constantinople from rebels and, 27th, Young Turks depose Sultan Abdul Hamid who is succeeded by Mohammed V (–1918);
Strike of Paris postal workers (–*May*).

E **May:** 25th, Indian Councils Act gives greater powers to legislative councils, whose members are mostly directly elective, and ensures appointment of an Indian to the Viceroy's executive council.

F **Jun:**

G **Jul:** 14th, Theobald von Bethmann-Hollweg becomes German chancellor on Bernhard von Bülow's resignation;
15th, Mahommed Ali, Shah of Persia, deposed in favour of Sultan Ahmad Shah, aged 12;
24th, on Georges Clemenceau's resignation, Aristide Briand forms ministry in France;
26th, general strike in Barcelona with rioting throughout Catalonia (–*Sept.* 26th).

H **Aug:**

J **Sep:**

K **Oct:** 13th, Francisco Ferrer Guardia, leader of militant anti-clericals in Spain, executed;
21st, Liberal ministry in Spain;
24th, Russia and Italy sign Racconigi agreement for preserving *status quo* in Balkans;
25th, murder of Prince Ito of Japan by a Korean fanatic, leads to Japanese dictatorship in Korea.

L **Nov:** 5th, Commons pass D. Lloyd George's budget but, 30th, it is rejected by Lords.
Anglo-German conversations on control of Baghdad Railway (–*Dec.*).

O **Politics, Economics, Law and Education**

N. Lenin (pseud.), *Materialism and Empiric Criticism.*
William Beveridge, *Unemployment.*
Trade Boards Act ends 'sweating' in British industry.
Women are admitted to German universities.
Girl Guides founded in Britain.
Political action branch of Industrial Workers of the World is founded at Detroit.
House of Lords upholds Osborne Judgment (*Dec.* 2nd), making compulsory levies by trades unions for party political purposes illegal.

P **Science, Technology, Discovery, etc.**

Paul Ehrlich prepares salvarsan as cure for syphilis.
T. H. Morgan begins research in genetics.
Karl Hofmann produces synthetic rubber from butadiene.
Henry Ford's 'Model T' car.
Louis Blériot crosses the English Channel by monoplane.
R. E. Peary reaches North Pole (*Apr.* 6th).

Q **Scholarship**

R **Philosophy and Religion**

H. Bergson, *Time and Freewill, Matter and Memory.*
S. Freud lectures in U.S. on psychoanalysis.
W. James, *A Pluralistic Universe.*

S **Art, Sculpture, Fine Arts and Architecture**

Painting:
H. Matisse, *The Dance.*
P. Bonnard, *Standing Nude.*
O. Kokoschka, *Princess Montesquieu-Rohan.*
A. John, *Robin.*
W. Orpen, *Hommage à Monet.*
H. Rousseau, *Flowers in a Vase.*
E. Munch, Mural for Oslo University (–11).
Filippo Marietti first uses the term 'Futurism'.

Sculpture:
Antoine Bourdelle, *Hercules the Archer.*
H. Matisse, *The Backs* (first of four 6-ft. reliefs –1930).

Architecture:
Frank Lloyd Wright, Robie House, Chicago.

T **Music**

Sergei Diaghilev produces his Russian ballet in Paris including M. Fokine's *Les Sylphides* (to Chopin's music).
G. Mahler, Symphony no. 9.
I. J. Paderewski directs the Warsaw Conservatory.
R. Vaughan Williams, *Fantasia on a Theme by Tallis.*

U **Literature**

G. Apollinaire (pseud.), *L'Enchanteur pourrissant.*
A. Gide, *La Porte Étroite.*
H. G. Wells, *Tono-Bungay.*

V **The Press**

Daily Sketch and *Nouvelle Revue Française* issued.

1909 (Dec.)

M Dec: 2nd, H. H. Asquith denounces Lords for breach of constitution over finance bill and obtains dissolution of Parliament;
—, Giovanni Giolitti is overthrown in Italy and Baron Sonnino forms a government,
17th, on Leopold II's death, Albert I succeeds as King of the Belgians (–1934);
19th, Juan Gómez seizes power in Venezuela;
Civil War in Honduras (–1911).

N Compulsory military service in Australia.

W Drama and Entertainment

M. Maeterlinck, *The Blue Bird.*
J. M. Synge, *Deirdre of the Sorrows.*
Birmingham Repertory Company founded.
D. W. Griffiths transforms child actress Gladys Smith into Mary Pickford.
Carmen (French film).
Cinematograph Licensing Act for controlling cinemas exhibiting films in Britain.

X Sport

Edward VII's *Minoru* wins the Derby.

Y Statistics

Jewish population (in thousands): Russia, 5,215; Austro-Hungary, 2,084; U.S., 1,777; Germany, 607; Turkish Empire, 463; Britain, 240; France, 95.
Coffee production (in mill. lb.): Brazil, 1,852; Venezuela, 96; Guatemala, 82; Colombia, 79; West Indies, 70; Mexico, 68.
Tea production (in mill. lb.): India, 254; China, 208; Ceylon, 182.

Z Births and Deaths

Jan. 1st Barry Goldwater b. (–).
Jan. 14th Joseph Losey b. (–1984).
Feb. 9th Dean Rusk b. (–).
Feb. 28th Stephen Spender b. (–).
Mar. 30th Ernst Gombrich b. (–).
Apr. 9th Robert Helpmann b. (–1986).
Apr. 10th Algernon Swinburne d. (72).
May 18th George Meredith d. (81).
June 6th Isaiah Berlin b. (–).
June 24th William Penney b. (–1991).
Sept. 21st Kwame Nkrumah b. (–1972).
Oct. 9th Donald Coggan b. (–).
Oct. 28th Francis Bacon b. (–1992).

1910 (Jan.–Nov.) Union of South Africa becomes a dominion—Japan annexes Korea

A **Jan**: 15th, British general election on issues of D. Lloyd George's budget, the power of the Lords and Irish Home Rule, resulting in reduced Liberal majority (Liberals, 275 seats; Labour, 40; Irish Nationalists, 82; Unionists, 273);
15th, reorganisation of French Congo as French Equatorial Africa;
Military League forces Greek assembly to refuse constitution.

B **Feb**: 10th, Swedish constitution is revised;
20th, Butros Ghali, premier of Egypt, who is a Copt, is assassinated by Nationalist fanatic.

C **Mar**: 19th, Republicans reduce power of Speaker of U.S. House of Representatives;
Luigi Luzzatti succeeds Baron Sonnino as Italian premier.

D **Apr**: 27th, Louis Botha and James Hertzog found South African party;
28th, British finance bill is finally passed;
Albanian revolt is suppressed by Turkish army.

E **May**: 6th, accession of George V on death of Edward VII (–1936);
10th, British House of Commons resolves that the Lords should have no power to veto money bills, and limited powers to postpone other bills and that the maximum lifetime of Parliament be reduced from seven to five years;
14th, Anglo-Belgian agreement assigns west shore of Lake Albert to Belgian Congo;
24th, L. Starr Jameson founds Unionist party in South Africa on imperialist platform;
26th, Pius X issues encyclical *Editio saepe*, which angers German Protestants;
27th, Prussian diet rejects reform of suffrage.

F **Jun**: 11th, Pius X, on representations by Prussia, stops circulation of encyclical of *May* 26th in Germany.

G **Jul**: 1st, Union of South Africa becomes a dominion;
4th, Russo-Japanese agreement on Manchuria and Korea.

H **Aug**: 22nd, Japan formally annexes Korea;
28th, Montenegro is proclaimed an independent kingdom under Nicholas I;
31st, Theodore Roosevelt propounds his concept of 'The New Nationalism';
Austro-Hungarian commercial treaty with Serbia.

J **Sep**: 7th, International Court of arbitration at The Hague settles Newfoundland fisheries question (referred to it in *Oct.* 1906);
15th, South African party wins first South African elections and Louis Botha becomes premier.

K **Oct**: 4th, King Manuel II of Portugal flees to England on outbreak of revolution in Lisbon and, 5th, Portugal is proclaimed a republic under Theophilo Braga;
10th, Aristide Briand calls out troops in French railway strike, a general strike is averted and, 18th, the railwaymen resume work;
18th, Eleutherios Venizelos becomes premier of Greece and begins financial reforms.

L **Nov**: 4th (–5th), Tsar Nicholas II with his new foreign minister, Sergei Sazonov, agrees with William II at Potsdam to cease opposition to the Baghdad Railway on condition that Russia is given a free hand in North Persia (Britain is dismayed by Russia's negotiations with Germany on the railway question without consultation);
28th, H. H. Asquith again appeals to the electorate.

O **Politics, Economics, Law and Education**

Norman Angell, *The Great Illusion.*

First Labour Exchanges opened in Britain (*Feb.* 1st).

Development Commission instituted (*May*) to advise British Treasury on loans for developing agriculture and rural areas.

Irving Fisher, *National Vitality.*

The Industrial Syndicalist, ed. Tom Mann, runs for 10 issues.

International motor-car convention.

U.S. Postal Savings Bank established.

Season tickets are first issued on railways in Britain, which withdraw second class accommodation.

H. H. Crippen is hanged.

P **Science, Technology, Discovery, etc.**

Marie Curie, *Treatise on Radiography.*

Charles Parsons' speed-reducing gear extends use of geared turbines.

First roller bearings.

Mount Wilson 100-inch reflecting telescope completed.

Manhattan Bridge, New York, opened.

Germany's machine-tool industry overtakes Britain's.

Electrification of part of Magdeburg-Halle main-line railway.

Q **Scholarship**

Arthur Evans excavates Cnossos.

R **Philosophy and Religion**

B. Russell and A. W. Whitehead, *Principia Mathematica.*

A. Schweitzer, *In Quest of the Historical Jesus.*

E. Underhill, *Mysticism.*

S **Art, Sculpture, Fine Arts and Architecture**

Painting:

'Futurist Manifesto' signed by V. Boccioni, C. Carra, G. Balla and G. Severini.

Fernand Léger, *Nues dans le forêt.*

Amedeo Modigliani, *Cellist.*

Henri Rousseau, *Yadwiga's Dream.*

Roger Fry organises Post-Impressionist exhibition, London.

The Turner Wing at the Tate Gallery opened.

Exhibition of Islamic Art, Munich.

National Federation of Arts in U.S.

Architecture:

Max Berg, Jahrhunderthall, Breslau (–12).

T **Music**

E. Elgar, violin concerto.

G. Puccini, *The Girl of the Golden West* (opera).

N. Rimsky-Korsakov, *The Golden Cockerel* (opera).

R. Vaughan Williams, *A Sea Symphony* (Symphony no. 1).

I. Stravinsky, *The Firebird* (ballet).

Thomas Beecham's first opera season at Covent Garden.

Pianist Solomon makes London debut at age of eight.

U **Literature**

A. Bennett, *Clayhanger.*

P. Claudel, *Cinq grandes odes.*

E. M. Forster, *Howard's End.*

C. Péguy, *Le Mystère de la charité de Jeanne d'Arc.*

H. G. Wells, *The History of Mr. Polly.*

1910 (Dec.)

M Dec: in British general election Liberals win 272 seats; Labour, 42; Irish Nationalists, 84; Unionists, 272 (making a majority for a Parliament Bill and Home Rule 126, an increase of 4 since *Jan.*).

N Swiss railways are nationalised.
Royal Canadian Navy is formed.

V The Press

Lord Lothian founds *The Round Table*.

W Drama and Entertainment

Gerald du Maurier manages Wyndham's Theatre (–25).
A Child of the Ghetto (film).
Faust (film).
Messaline (film).
Lucretia Borgia (film).

X Sport

Jack Johnson's defeat of J. J. Jefferies in U.S. national boxing championship.

Y Statistics

Defence estimates (in £ mill.): Great Britain, 68; Germany, 64; Russia, 63; France, 52; Italy, 24; Austria-Hungary, 17.
Battleships in commission (and under construction): Great Britain, 56 (9); Germany, 33 (8); U.S., 30 (4); France, 17 (6); Japan, 14 (3); Italy, 10 (2); Russia, 7 (8).
Cotton production (in 500-lb. bales): U.S., 11·6 mill.; India, 3·8 mill.; Egypt, 1·5 mill.; China, 1·2 mill.
Wool production (in mill. lb.): Australia and New Zealand, 833; Argentina, 414; U.S., 321; Russia, 320; U.K., 141; Uruguay, 130.
Silk production (in mill. lb.): Japan, 19; China, 14; Italy, 8; Levant, 6; Austria, 0·7.
Telephones: 122,000 in use in Great Britain.

Z Births and Deaths

Feb. 9th J. L. Monod b. (–1976).
Mar. 9th Samuel Barber b. (–1981).
Apr. 21st Mark Twain (Samuel Langhorne Clemens) d. (74).
May 12th Dorothy Hodgkin b. (–).
June 7th Pietro Annigoni b. (–1988).
June 22nd John Hunt b. (–).
June 23rd Jean Anouilh b. (–1987).
Aug. 13th Florence Nightingale d. (90).
Aug. 27th William James d. (68).
— Mother Teresa b. (–).
Sept. 7th William Holman Hunt d. (83).
Oct. 17th Julia Ward Howe d. (91).
Oct. 29th A. J. Ayer b. (–1989).
Nov. 10th Leo Tolstoy d. (82).
Dec. 4th Mary Baker Eddy d. (89).

1911 (Jan.–Jul.) Parliament Bill—Agadir Crisis—Chinese Republic proclaimed

A **Jan**: 7th, Carnegie Trust Co., New York, closed by state supervisor of banks;
17th, attempted assassination of Aristide Briand in French Chamber of Deputies;
20th, Ecuador refuses to submit her dispute with Peru to Hague Tribunal;
21st, National Progressive Republican League founded under Robert La Follette in U.S.;
25th, U.S. cavalry sent to preserve neutrality of Rio Grande in Mexican Civil War.

B **Feb**: 6th, British Labour Party elect Ramsay MacDonald chairman;
10th, Persia appoints W. Morgan Shuster to reorganise finances;
21st, U.S.-Japanese commercial treaty signed at Washington;
22nd, Canadian Parliament resolves to preserve union within British Empire, with control of own fiscal policy;
23rd, French Chamber of Deputies votes for building two battleships;
24th, Reichstag passes army bill;
27th, resignation of Aristide Briand's ministry;
28th, Andrew Fisher, Australian premier, plans to nationalise monopolies.

C **Mar**: 18th, Luzzatti resigns in Italy.

D **Apr**: 3rd, progress of Parliament bill accelerated by use of 'Kangaroo' clause;
3rd, Anglo-Japanese commercial treaty;
4th, U.S. Congress meets in extra-ordinary sessions to deal with Reciprocity agreement with Canada (ratified by Senate *July* 22nd);
11th, Jean-Jaurès announces scheme for socialist organisation of France;
13th, U.S. House of Representatives votes in favour of direct election of senators;
19th, Separation of Church and State in Portugal;
23rd (–7th), armistice in Mexican Civil War;
24th, Commons reject amendment to Parliament bill providing for referendum.

E **May**: 4th, D. Lloyd George introduces National Health Insurance bill;
8th, Lord Lansdowne introduces Unionist reconstruction of House of Lords bill in Lords;
15th, Commons passes Parliament Bill;
—, U.S. Supreme Court orders dissolution of Standard Oil Co.;
23rd, Russia warns Turkey to withdraw troops from Montenegro frontier;
—, H. H. Asquith opens Imperial Conference, London;
25th, Porfirio Diaz resigns presidency of Mexico;
26th, Reichstag grants Alsace-Lorraine its own legislature and large measure of autonomy.

F **Jun**: 8th, Birkbeck Bank, London, crashes;
11th, revised Greek constitution;
13th, reversal for Christian Socialists in Austrian election;
22nd, George V's coronation;
28th, Joseph Caillaux forms ministry in France;
—, Japanese sign commercial treaty with France.

G **Jul**: 1st, arrival of German gunboat *Panther* in Agadir creates international tension;
6th, Anglo-U.S. treaty for arbitration of disputes;
10th, Russia warns Germany of her support for France in Moroccan crisis;
13th, renewal of Anglo-Japanese alliance for four years;
24th, while Commons debate Lords amendments to Parliament Bill, H. H. Asquith is shouted down and Speaker adjourns the House;
26th, W. H. Taft signs Reciprocity bill with Canada.

O Politics, Economics, Law and Education

Copyright Act requires copies of all British publications to be given to the British Museum and five other 'copyright libraries'.
Shops Act introduces compulsory weekly half-day holidays for employees.
Coal Mines Act makes radical changes in control and management of British mines.
First British Official Secrets Act.
Investigation of alleged corruption in Ohio state reveals that a quarter of the electorate sold their votes.
A. Carnegie endows international peace foundation (*Dec.*).
Brussels Conference to control liquor supplies to backward countries.

P Science, Technology, Discovery, etc.

Ernest Rutherford and Frederick Soddy devise scheme for achieving the transmutation of elements.
Aeronautical map of France published.
Roald Amundsen reaches South Pole (*Dec.* 15th).
Buenos Aires to Valparaiso Railway completed.

Q Scholarship

British Museum's expedition to excavate Carchemish.
Cambridge Medieval History (–36).

R Philosophy and Religion

Hans Vaihinger, *The Philosophy of 'as If'*.
J. M. Thompson, *Miracles in the New Testament.*
World Missionary Conference, Edinburgh.

S Art, Sculpture, Fine Arts and Architecture

Painting:
A. Renoir, *Gabrielle with a Rose.*
Georges Braque, *Man with a Guitar.*
H. Matisse, *The Red Studio.*
Wassily Kandinsky and Franz Marc found *Blauen Reiter* ('Blue Rider') group of artists in Munich.
Da Vinci's *Mona Lisa* is stolen from the Louvre.
Sculpture:
J. Epstein, Tomb of Oscar Wilde, France.
Architecture:
Walter Gropius, Fagus Factory, Germany.

T Music

E. Elgar, Symphony no. 2 in E flat (op. 63).
G. Mahler, *The Song of the Earth.*
M. Ravel, *Daphnis and Chloë* (ballet).
R. Strauss, *Der Rosenkavalier* (opera).
Ermanno Wolf-Ferrari, *The Jewels of the Madonna* (opera).
A. Schönberg's manual of harmony.
Irving Berlin's *Alexander's Ragtime Band.*

U Literature

Max Beerbohm, *Zuleika Dobson.*
Rupert Brooke, *Poems.*
T. Dreiser, *Jennie Gerhardt.*

H **Aug**: 1st, London dockers strike and, 7th, refuse to return until other transport workers' claims are satisfied;
10th, Lords pass Parliament bill, deciding (131–114 votes) not to insist on their amendments;
—, Commons vote to pay M.P.s £400 p.a.
14th, South Wales miners end strike after ten months;
15th, British railwaymen, under John Burns, strike (–19th);
20th, Portugal adopts a Liberal constitution;
21st, William II speaks at Hamburg on Germany's 'place in the sun' which her navy will secure for her;
31st, Franco-Russian military conversations.

J **Sep**: 11th, attempt to repeal Maine prohibition laws defeated;
14th, assassination of Peter Stolypin, Russian premier, and 19th, Vladimir Kokovtsoff appointed premier;
21st, in Canadian general election the Liberals, standing for Reciprocity with U.S., are defeated (the agreement is later annulled);
29th, Italy declares war on Turkey and Italian fleet bombards Tripoli coast;
—, first election in Sweden under Proportional Representation.

K **Oct**: 9th, H.M.S. *King George V* launched;
10th, Robert K. Borden forms Conservative ministry in Canada;
11th, revolution breaks out in Central China;
17th, Turkey promises Bulgaria to withdraw her troops and demobilise;
23rd, British cabinet changes, with Winston Churchill at Admiralty and Reginald McKenna home secretary;
26th, Chinese Republic proclaimed.

L **Nov**: 1st, amalgamation of London General Omnibus Co., Metropolitan and District Railway Co. and Underground Electric Railways of London;
4th, convention by which Germany allows France a free hand in Morocco in return for territory in the Congo;
5th, Italy annexes Tripoli and Cyrenaica;
6th, Francisco Madero becomes President of Mexico;
8th, A. J. Balfour resigns Unionist leadership (succeeded, 13th, by Andrew Bonar Law);
16th, Yüan Shi-kai forms cabinet in China;
—, Russia sends troops to Kazvin, Persia, on receiving no reply to ultimatum of 11th to Persia, and, 23rd, Persia concedes demands;
21st, Suffragette riots in Whitehall;
25th, Chinese revolutionaries bomb Nanking;
26th, Italy's decisive victory in Tripoli.

M **Dec**: 7th, Chinese edict abolishing pigtails and ordering reform of calendar;
11th, settlement of British railwaymen's dispute;
12th, George V holds Delhi Durbar;
30th, Sun Yat-sen elected president of United Provinces of China by a revolutionary assembly in Nanking.

N

U **Literature** (*cont.*)

H. von Hofmannsthal, *Jedermann*.
D. H. Lawrence, *The White Peacock*.
K. Mansfield (pseud.), *In a German Pension*.
J. Masefield, *The Everlasting Mercy*.
Saki (pseud.), *The Chronicles of Clovis*.
R. M. Rilke, *Duimo Elegies* (–22).
Hugh Walpole, *Mr. Perrin and Mr. Traill*.
H. G. Wells, *The New Macchiavelli*.
Edith Wharton, *Ethan Frome*.
Georgian Poetry (ed. Edward Marsh, –22).

V **The Press**

W **Drama and Entertainment**

Basil Dean opens Liverpool Repertory Theatre.
Anna Karenina (film).
The Fall of Troy (film).
Spartacus (film).
Pinocchio (film).

X **Sport**

Gordon-Bennett International Aviation Cup first given.

Y **Statistics**

Populations (in mill.): China, 325; India, 315; Russia, 167; U.S., 94; Germany, 65; Japan, 52; Great Britain, 40·8; Ireland, 4·3; France, 39·6; Italy, 34·6.
Steel production (in mill. tons): U.S., 23·6; Germany, 14·7; Great Britain, 6·4; France, 3·8; Russia, 3·8; Austria-Hungary, 2·3; Belgium, 1·9.
Rubber production (in thousand tons): Brazil and Peru, 39; West Africa, 15; Central America and Mexico, 11·7; Malaya, 9·2; East Africa, 5·3.
Petroleum production: U.S., 220·4 mill. barrels.

Z **Births and Deaths**

Feb. 2nd Jussi Bjoerling b. (–1960).
Feb. 6th Ronald Reagan b. (–).
Mar. 7th Antonio Fogazzaro d. (68).
May 18th Gustav Mahler d. (50).
May 27th Hubert Humphrey b. (–1978).
May 29th W. S. Gilbert d. (75).
July 5th Georges Pompidou b. (–1974).
July 21st Marshall McLuhan b. (–1980).
Aug. 16th E. F. Schumacher b. (–1977).
Aug. 29th John Charnley b. (–1982).
Sept. 16th Edward Whymper d. (71).

A **Jan**: 3rd, Ulster Unionists resolve to repudiate authority of any Irish Parliament set up under Home Rule Bill;
6th, New Mexico becomes a U.S. state;
10th, Joseph Caillaux resigns in France and
14th, Raymond Poincaré forms cabinet;
18th, British miners ballot in favour of strike action;
Elections to German Reichstag leave the Socialists the strongest party.

B **Feb**: 6th, Nanking assembly endorses Yüan Shih-kai's proposals for constitutional reform;
10th, French senate ratifies Moroccan agreement;
12th, Manchu dynasty abdicates in China and a provisional republic is established;
14th, Arizona becomes a U.S. state;
15th, Labour amendment to Address, favouring a minimum wage, is rejected in Commons;
26th, British coal strike begins in Derbyshire (becoming general, *Mar.* 1st);
29th, Maurice Hankey appointed Secretary to the Committee of Imperial Defence.

C **Mar**: 9th, the powers ask Italy to state terms on which she would accept arbitration to end Turkish war;
14th, W. H. Taft forbids shipments of arms from U.S. to Mexico;
19th, H. H. Asquith introduces minimum wage bill to settle coal strike;
—, Tom Mann, British Syndicalist leader, arrested for inciting soldiers to mutiny;
—, U.S. excise bill, taxing net income from business sources;
28th, Commons reject women's franchise bill;
29th, government defeat in Reichstag on Post Office estimates;
—, U.S. Senate passes Reed Smoot's pension bill;
30th, Sultan of Morocco signs treaty making Morocco a French protectorate.

D **Apr**: 4th, Chinese Republic proclaimed in Tibet;
9th, Canadian-West Indies preferential agreement;
18th, Turkey closes Dardanelles to shipping (–*May* 1st);
19th, Dillingham Immigration bill makes literacy a condition of entrance to U.S. (later modified to meet Japanese representations);
20th, U.S. House of Representatives resolves that election expenses of presidential and vice-presidential candidates be published;
23rd, Welsh Church Disestablishment bill is introduced in Commons;
27th, Anglo-Belgian loan to China is cancelled after representations by other powers.

E **May**: 14th, Clayton bill, to prohibit issue of injunctions without notice, passes House of Representatives;
22nd, Count Tisza elected president of Hungarian Chamber after wild scenes;
—, Reichstag is adjourned following Socialist attacks on German emperor;
23rd, London dock strike;
28th, House of Representatives passes naval appropriations bill without provision for new battleships.

F **Jun**: 2nd, Clericals win Belgian elections on schools issue;
5th, U.S. marines land in Cuba;
11th, national strike of transport workers in Britain;
17th, W. H. Taft vetoes army appropriations bill;
22nd, Taft is nominated Republican presidential candidate at Chicago convention, where Theodore Roosevelt makes proposals for a new Progressive Republican Party;
25th, George Lansbury protests in Commons against forcible feeding of Suffragettes.

O Politics, Economics, Law and Education

Reports of Royal Commissions on Divorce and on Vivisection.
R. Casement's report on Putumayo atrocities, Peru (*July* 13th).
French *Code du Travail* promulgated.
Royal Flying Corps established.
U.S. Parcels Post inaugurated.
G.P.O. takes over British telephone systems.

P Science, Technology, Discovery, etc.

Albert Einstein formulates the law of photochemical equivalence.
Casimir Funck introduces word 'vitamine'.
X-ray crystallography begins.
L. O. Howard, *The House Fly, Disease Carrier.*
Drinking water is sterilised by ultra-violet rays in Manila.
Cellophane, invented by Edwin Brandenberger in 1900, is manufactured.
Henry Brearley invents a type of stainless steel.
R. F. Scott reaches the South Pole (*Jan.* 18th).
First regular air service, between Berlin and Friedrichshaven, in rigid airships *Victoria Luise* and *Hansa*; G. H. Curtiss constructs the first sea-plane.
S.S. *Titanic* lost on maiden voyage (*Apr.* 15th), with 1,513 drowned.
Remains of Piltdown Man 'found'; later proved to be a scientific hoax.

Q Scholarship

E. Maude Thompson, *Introduction to Latin and Greek Palaeography.*

R Philosophy and Religion

E. Troeltsch, *Socialism and the Christian Church.*
B. M. Streeter, and others, *Foundations: a Statement of Christian Belief in Terms of Modern Thought.*
Church of Scotland revises Prayer Book.

S Art, Sculpture, Fine Arts and Architecture

Painting:
W. Orpen, *Café Royal.*
M. Chagall, *The Cattle Dealer.*
P. Picasso, *The Violin.*
F. Léger, *Woman in Blue.*
Franz Marc, *Tower of Blue Horses.*
Marcel Duchamp, *Nude Descending A Staircase.*
Albert Gleizes and Jean Metzinger publish *Du Cubisme.*

Sculpture:
A. Modigliani, *Stone Head.*
A. Bourdelle, frescoes and bas-reliefs for the Théâtre des Champs-Élysées.
George Frampton's *Peter Pan* in Kensington Gardens.

Architecture:
E. Lutyens, Viceroy's House, New Delhi.
Grand Central Railway Station, New York.

T Music

F. B. Busoni, *Die Brautwahl* (opera).
F. Delius, *On Hearing the First Cuckoo in Spring.*
A. Schönberg's song-cycle, *Pierrot Lunaire.*
R. Strauss, *Ariadne auf Naxos* (opera).
I. Stravinsky, *Petruschka* (ballet).

G **Jul**: 2nd, Woodrow Wilson nominated as Democratic presidential candidate at Baltimore convention;
7th, Theobald von Bethman-Hollweg visits St. Petersburg;
9th, W. F. Massey forms ministry in New Zealand on Thomas Mackenzie's resignation;
10th, elections for French Chamber on principle of Proportional Representation;
15th, British National Health Insurance Act in force;
18th, Tewfik Pasha becomes Grand Vizier of Persia, following fall of Said Pasha's ministry;
24th, riots in London docks and at Ben Tillett's Tower Hill meeting.

H **Aug**: 2nd, U.S. Senate resolves to extend Monroe doctrine to foreign corporations holding territory on American continent;
5th (–16th), Raymond Poincaré visits Russia;
—, Theodore Roosevelt holds Progressive Republican Convention at Chicago;
7th, Russo-Japanese agreement determining spheres of influence in Mongolia and Manchuria;
17th, British note to restrain China from sending military expedition to Tibet;
—, Britain protests to U.S. that Panama Canal rates infringe Hay-Pauncefoote treaty of *Nov.* 1901;
19th, Britain accepts Count Berchtold's project for Balkan conversations.

J **Sep**: 6th, British Trades Union Congress votes against Syndicalism;
13th, revolution in Santo Domingo;
18th, Ulster Anti-Home Rule demonstrations begin at Enniskillen under Edward Carson;
23rd, Chinese government declines 6-powers loan in favour of loan by Birch, Crisp and Company of London;
29th, British and French forces pacify riots in Samos (*Sept.* 4th, Turks withdraw troops);
30th, Bulgarian and Serbian armies mobilise for war against Turkey.

K **Oct**: 6th, great powers back French proposals for averting Balkan war;
8th, Montenegro declares war on Turkey;
12th, Turkey declines to undertake reforms in Macedonia on which the powers insist;
14th, a fanatic wounds T. Roosevelt in Wisconsin;
16th, rebels under Porfirio Diaz occupy Vera Cruz;
17th, Turkey declares war on Bulgaria and Serbia;
18th, Italy and Turkey sign peace treaty at Lausanne by which Tripoli and Cyrenaica are granted autonomy under Italian suzerainty, and Italy restores Dodecanese Islands to Turkey.

L **Nov**: 3rd, Turkey asks powers to intervene to end Balkan war;
5th, Woodrow Wilson, Democrat, wins U.S. presidential election, with 435 electoral votes over T. Roosevelt, Progressive, with 88 votes, and W. H. Taft, Republican, with 8; Arizona, Kansas and Wisconsin adopt women's suffrage;
11th, government defeat in Commons on amendment to Home Rule bill;
—, Chile resumes diplomatic relations with Peru (after thirty months);
21st, Turkey declares terms of Balkan allies for a peace unacceptable;
26th, George Lansbury, who had resigned to test feeling of electorate on women's suffrage, is defeated in Bow by-election;
27th, run on savings banks in central and east Europe.

(*Continued opposite*)

U **Literature**

E. M. Dell, *The Way of an Eagle.*
C. J. R. Hauptmann, *Atlantis.*
P. Loti, *Le Pèlerin d'Angkor.*
Compton Mackenzie, *Carnival.*
R. Tagore, *Gitanjali.*
'New Poetry' movement in U.S.

V **The Press**

G. Dawson edits *The Times.*
The Daily Herald first issued.
H. Monro founds *Poetry Review.*

W **Drama and Entertainment**

P. Claudel, *L'Annonce faite à Marie.*
Five million Americans visit cinemas daily.
London has 400 cinemas (90 in 1909).
Quo Vadis? (film).
Sarah Bernhardt in *Queen Elizabeth* (film).
Charles Pathé produces first new film.

X **Sport**

Olympic Games held at Stockholm, in which races are timed electrically.

Y **Statistics**

Armies, including Reservists (in mill.): Russia, 5·5; Germany, 4·1; France, 3·9; Austria-Hungary, 2·3; Italy, 1·2; Japan, 1·0; British Empire, 0·9; U.S., 0·1.
Trades union membership: U.K., 3,416,000.

Z **Births and Deaths**

Jan. 15th Henry Labouchere d. (80).
Feb. 6th Christopher Hill b. (–).
Feb. 10th Joseph, Lord Lister d. (85).
Mar. – Robert Falcon Scott d. (41).
Mar. 23rd Werner von Braun b. (–1977).
Mar. 26th Tennessee Williams b. (–1983).
Mar. 27th James Callaghan b. (–).
Apr. 15th W. T. Stead d. (63).
May 14th Johann A. Strindberg d. (63).
May 28th Patrick White b. (–1990).
Aug. 13th Octavia Hill d. (74) and Jules Massenet d. (70).
Aug. 20th William Booth d. (83).
Sept. 1st Samuel Coleridge-Taylor d. (37).
Sept. 5th John Cage b. (–1992).

M **Dec:** 2nd, U.S. Supreme Court orders dissolution of Union Pacific and Southern Pacific railways merger;
3rd, armistice between Turkey, Bulgaria, Serbia and Montenegro (Greece abstains);
14th, Louis Botha resigns South African premiership to form new cabinet, 20th, without James Hertzog;
19th, Prince Katsura forms cabinet in Japan;
20th, at London peace conference between Turkey and Balkan states, ambassadors of great powers accept principle of Albanian autonomy, providing Serbia has canal access to Adriatic.

1913 (Jan.–Jul.) Second Balkan War

A **Jan**: 2nd, Turkish garrison at Chios surrenders to Greeks;
5th, Gottlieb von Jagow becomes German foreign minister (–1916);
6th, London peace conference between Turkey and Balkan states suspended;
16th, Irish Home Rule bill passes Commons (but, 30th, is rejected by Lords);
17th, Raymond Poincaré elected President of France (–1920);
18th, Graeco-Turk naval battle off Tenedos;
21st, Aristide Briand forms cabinet in France;
23rd, Nazim Pasha is murdered in Turkish *coup* and Shevket Pasha forms ministry;
28th, Suffragettes demonstrate in London on withdrawal of franchise bill.

B **Feb**: 3rd, Bulgarians renew Turkish War (–*Apr.* 16th);
5th, Welsh Church Disestablishment bill passes Commons but, 13th, is rejected by Lords;
13th, Franco-U.S. agreement to extend 1908 arbitration convention for five years;
25th, federal income tax introduced in U.S.

C **Mar**: 4th, Woodrow Wilson inaugurated as U.S. President;
11th, Anglo-German agreement on frontier between Nigeria and Cameroons;
14th, Balkan allies accept mediation of great powers, but on unacceptable terms;
18th, King George I of Greece is murdered at Salonika;
26th, Bulgarians take Adrianople;
28th, Belgian army bill introduces universal military service;
31st, Turkey accepts recommendations of great powers for a peace.

D **Apr**: 3rd, Mrs. E. Pankhurst sentenced for inciting persons to place explosives outside D. Lloyd George's house;
8th, first Parliament of Chinese Republic opens;
16th, Turkey signs armistice with Bulgaria.

E **May**: 6th, King Nicholas of Montenegro yields Scutari to the powers until an Albanian government is created (in *Dec.*);
6th, women's franchise bill is rejected in Commons;
8th, U.S. House of Representatives passes tariff bill;
26th, Miss Emily Dawson appointed first woman magistrate in England;
30th, Canadian Senate rejects naval bill;
—, peace treaty between Turkey and Balkan states signed in London;
31st, Seventeenth Amendment to U.S. constitution, on popular election of senators.

F **Jun**: 10th, U.S. Supreme Court decides states have right to fix inter-state rail rates;
18th, Commons debate Marconi Report which acquits D. Lloyd George and other ministers of corruption in assigning imperial wireless contract to the Marconi Company;
24th (–7th), President Poincaré of France visits England;
26th, Bulgaria signs defensive treaty with Austria-Hungary;
28th, Roumania warns Bulgaria she will not remain neutral in a war;
30th, Second Balkan War opens, with Bulgaria attacking Serbian and Greek positions;
—, Reichstag passes bill to increase German army.

G **Jul**: 1st, Zanzibar is incorporated with British East Africa;
— (–9th), Hague opium conference;
7th, Commons pass Irish Home Rule bill (rejected, 15th, by Lords);
8th, Commons pass Welsh Church bill (rejected, 22nd, by Lords);
10th, Russia declares war on Bulgaria;

O Politics, Economics, Law and Education

Prince Bernhard von Bülow, *Imperial Germany*.
Federal Reserve Act reconstructs U.S. banking and currency system by creating federal banks.
Old-age and sickness insurance introduced in U.S., France and Holland.
Judge Archibald of U.S. federal commercial court is found guilty of corruption.
Rockefeller Foundation established.

P Science, Technology, Discovery, etc.

J. J. Thomson, *Rays of Positive Electricity and Their Application to Chemical Analysis*.
W. Geiger's research on radiation.
Niels Bohr's model of the atom.
F. Soddy coins term 'isotope'.
Bela Schick discovers test for immunity from diphtheria.
Richard Willstätter discovers composition of chlorophyll.
McCollum isolates vitamin A.
Diesel-electric railway opened in Sweden.
H. Ford pioneers progressive assembly technique by means of conveyor belts.

Q Scholarship

G. P. Gooch, *History and Historians of the Nineteenth Century*.

R Philosophy and Religion

Edmund Husserl, *Phenomenology*.
S. Freud, *Totem and Taboo*.
James Moffatt, *New Translation of the New Testament*.

S Art, Sculpture, Fine Arts and Architecture

Painting:
Armory Show, New York, introduces Post-Impressionist art to U.S.
Harold Gilman, Walter Sickert and Wyndham Lewis form London Group of artists.
Walter Sickert, *Ennui*.
Stanley Spencer, *Self-Portrait*.
F. Marc, *Deer in the Forest*.
J. S. Sargent, Portrait of Henry James.
G. Apollinaire's appraisal, *The Cubist Painters*.
Sculpture:
J. Epstein, *Rock Drill*.
Eric Gill, Stations of the Cross, Westminster Cathedral.
Architecture:
Cass Gilbert, Woolworth Building, New York.

T Music

Alexander Scriabin, *Prometheus*.
Igor Stravinsky, *The Rite of Spring* (ballet).
Guitarist Andrés Segovia makes his debut in Madrid (1924, in Paris; 1928, in U.S.).

U Literature

Alain-Fournier (pseud.), *Le Grand Meaulnes*.
D. H. Lawrence, *Sons and Lovers*.
T. Mann, *Death in Venice*.
Ch. Péguy, *La Tapisserie de Notre-Dame*.
M. Proust, *Du côté de chez Swann* (1st part of *À la recherche du temps perdu* –17).
E. Wharton, *The Custom of the Country*.

1913 (Jul.–Dec.)

G **Jul:** 12th, Turkey re-enters war, and 20th, recaptures Adrianople from Bulgaria;
23rd, 'Second Revolution' in South China (*–Sept.*);
28th, ambassadors of powers regulate establishment of Albanian principality;
31st, Balkan states sign armistice in Bucharest.

H **Aug:** 7th, French army bill, imposing 3 years military service;
10th, peace is signed in Bucharest.

J **Sep:** 3rd, Nanking falls to Yüan Shih-kai;
16th, Japan sends flotilla to Yangtze river, on China's failure to honour reparations agreement;
18th, Bulgarian-Turkish treaty settles frontier in Thrace;
24th, Ulster Unionists appoint provisional government to come into force on Home Rule bill taking effect.

K **Oct:** 6th, Yüan Shih-kai elected President of Chinese Republic;
17th, Serbs invade Albania;
21st, failure of royalist rising in Portugal;
28th, Britain, France and Germany withhold recognition of Victoriano Huerta's government in Mexico until U.S. defines its policy;
—, Germano-Turkish military conversations.

L **Nov:** 1st, naval convention of Triple Alliance;
3rd, U.S. demands withdrawal of General Huerta from Mexico;
5th, joint declaration by Russia and China recognising the autonomy of Outer Mongolia under Chinese suzerainty;
6th, Mahatma Gandhi, leader of Indian Passive Resistance movement, is arrested;
13th, Graeco-Turkish peace treaty;
17th, first vessel passes through Panama Canal;
20th, Zabern incident, in which a German officer in Alsace-Lorraine insults Alsatian recruits, embitters Franco-German relations.

M **Dec:** 5th, British proclamation forbids sending of arms to Ireland;
13th, Britain and France oppose Germano-Turkish military convention;
14th, Greece formally annexes Crete.

N

V The Press

S. and B. Webb found *The New Statesman* (edited by Clifford Sharp).

W Drama and Entertainment

Barry Jackson and John Drinkwater open Birmingham Repertory Theatre.
L. Pirandello, *Se non Così*.
The Vampire (film).
The Squaw Man (film).
The Student of Prague (film).
The foxtrot sweeps to popularity.

X Sport

Y Statistics

Industrial output: increases per cent, since 1893:

	U.S.	Germany	Great Britain
Coal	210	159	75
Pig iron	337	287	50
Steel	715	522	136
Exports of raw materials	196	243	238
Exports of manufactures	563	239	121

Steel production (in mill. tons): Germany, 14; U.S., 10; Great Britain, 6; Russia, 4·2; France, 2·8.

Divorces: U.K., 801; U.S., 14,000.

Z Births and Deaths

Jan. 9th Richard Nixon b. (–).
Jan. 10th Gustáv Husák b. (–1991).
Jan. 18th Danny Kaye b. (–1987).
Mar. 25th Garnet Lord Wolseley d. (80).
Mar. 31st J. Pierpont Morgan d. (76).
Apr. 21st Richard Beeching b. (–1985).
May 16th Woody Herman b. (–1987).
May 25th Donald Maclean b. (–1983).
June 2nd Alfred Austin d. (78).
July 14th Gerald Ford b. (–).
Aug. 11th Angus Wilson b. (–1991).
Aug. 13th Makarios III b. (–1977).
Aug. 16th Menachem Begin b. (–1992).
Sept. 12th Jesse Owens b. (–1980).
Oct. 1st Rudolf Diesel d. (56).
Nov. 22nd Benjamin Britten b. (–1976).
— Albert Camus b. (–1960).
Dec. 18th Willy Brandt b. (–1992).

1914 (Jan.–Jul.) Outbreak of First World War

A **Jan:** 1st, Northern and Southern Nigeria amalgamated;
8th, Gaston Calmette, editor of *Figaro*, makes charges against Joseph Caillaux, French finance minister;
11th, Yüan Shih-kai governs without Parliament in China;
27th, President Oreste of Haiti abdicates during revolt and U.S. marines land to preserve order (General Zamon elected President, *Feb.* 8th).

B **Feb:** 4th, U.S. House of Representatives passes Burnett Immigration bill;
15th, Franco-German agreement on Baghdad Railway.

C **Mar:** 1st, unrest in Brazil, with Rio de Janeiro in state of siege;
8th, Monarchist party win Spanish elections;
10th, Suffragettes damage 'Rokeby Venus' by Velasquez, in National Gallery;
14th, Turko-Serbian peace treaty;
16th, Mme Caillaux assassinates Gaston Calmette, editor of *Figaro*, for publishing love-letters;
30th, H. H. Asquith combines post of war secretary with premiership in Britain.

D **Apr:** 1st, Civil government established in Panama Canal Zone;
14th, President Wilson sends U.S. fleet to Tampico, Mexico, to enforce salute to flag and
21st, following ultimatum to Mexico, troops occupy Vera Cruz customs house.

E **May:** 6th, Lords reject women's enfranchisement bill;
10th, Liberal Unionists unite with Conservatives;
20th, Argentina, Brazil and Chile arbitrate at Niagara Falls between U.S. and Mexico;
22nd, Britain acquires control of oil properties in Persian Gulf from Anglo-Persian Oil Company;
25th, Commons pass Irish Home Rule bill;
31st, General Carranza becomes provisional president of Mexico.

F **Jun:** 11th, Niagara Falls delegates approve new Mexican government (peace with U.S. signed, 24th);
13th, René Viviani forms ministry in France;
—, Greece annexes Chios and Mytilene;
15th, Anglo-German agreement on Baghdad Railway and Mesopotamia;
28th, Archduke Francis Ferdinand of Austria and his wife assassinated at Sarajevo by a Bosnian revolutionary.

G **Jul:** 5th, General V. Huerta re-elected President of Mexico (he resigns 15th, and is succeeded by Carbajal);
10th, Ulster provisional government re-affirms Ulster's determination to resist Home Rule;
20th (–29th), President Raymond Poincaré visits Russia;
21st (–24th), British and Irish parties fail to agree at Buckingham Palace Conference;
23rd, Austro-Hungarian ultimatum to Serbia;
24th, Edward Grey proposes four-power mediation of Balkan crisis, but Serbia appeals to Russia;
26th, Austrians mobilise on Russian frontier;
—, Irish rising in Dublin;
28th, Austria-Hungary declares war on Serbia;
30th, Germany requires Russia to cease mobilisation;
—, Jean-Jaurès (aged 55) is murdered in Paris.

O Politics, Economics, Law and Education

Richard Huch, *The Great War in Germany.*
Edwin Cannan, *Wealth.*
Currency and Bank Notes Act, repealing Bank Charter Act, 1844, empowers Bank of England to issue £1 and 10/- notes.
French hoarding of gold, silver and copper coinage leads to Bank of France issuing 5, 10 and 20 Franc notes.
German War Raw Material Department established.
Maternity benefits for German women.

P Science, Technology, Discovery, etc.

A. Eddington, *Stellar Movement and the Structure of the Universe.*
J. H. Jeans, *Report on Radiation and the Quantum Theory.*
Work of National Physical Laboratory is extended to include the testing and certification of radium preparations.
James Dewar elucidates the composition of air.
Bottomley discovers fertilisation through peat.
Canadian Grand Trunk Pacific Railway completed (*Apr.* 7th).
Panama Canal officially open to traffic (*Aug.* 15th).
E. Shackleton leads Antarctic expedition (–17).

Q Scholarship

Edward VII Gallery of British Museum opened.
Austin Dobson, *Eighteenth-Century Studies.*
Journal of Egyptian Archaeology issued.
T. Roosevelt, *History as Literature.*

R Philosophy and Religion

C. D. Broad, *Perception, Physics and Psychical Research.*
Bertrand Russell, *Knowledge of the External World as a Field for Scientific Method in Philosophy.*

S Art, Sculpture, Fine Arts and Architecture

Painting:
A. John, *George Bernard Shaw.*
H. Matisse, *The Red Studio.*
G. Braque, *The Guitarist.*
O. Kokoschka, *The Vortex.*
Architecture:
Henry Bacon, The Lincoln Memorial, New York.
E. F. Carritt, *Theory of Beauty.*

T Music

Rutland Boughton, *The Immortal Hour* (opera).
F. B. Busoni, *Symphonic Nocturne.*
R. Vaughan Williams, *A London Symphony* (no. 2) and *Lark Ascending.*

U Literature

F. Brett Young, *Deep Sea.*
J. Conrad, *Chance.*
Henry James, *The Golden Bowl.*
James Joyce, *Dubliners.*
Miguel de Unamuno y Jugo, *Niebla.*
George Moore, *Hail and Farewell.*

H **Aug:** 1st, Germany declares war on Russia; France mobilises and Italy declares her neutrality;
—, German-Turkish treaty signed at Constantinople;
2nd, Germany occupies Luxembourg and sends ultimatum to Belgium to allow passage of troops;
—, Russians invade East Prussia;
3rd, Germany declares war on France and invades Belgium;
4th, Britain declares war on Germany;
—, U.S. declares her neutrality;
5th, Austria-Hungary declares war on Russia;
6th, Serbia and Montenegro declare war on Germany;
8th, British troops land in France;
—, Britain and France occupy Togoland;
10th, France declares war on Austria;
—, Germans occupy Liège;
—, *Breslau* and *Goeben* escape through Dardanelles;
12th, Britain declares war on Austria-Hungary;
14th, Russia promises autonomy to Poland in return for Polish aid;
15th, Japanese ultimatum to Germany for evacuation of Kiau-Chow;
16th, Constitutionalist army occupies Mexico City;
20th, Germans occupy Brussels;
22nd (–23rd), battles of Namur and Mons;
23rd, Russian victory at Frankenau, East Prussia;
24th, Allies retreat from Mons (–*Sept.* 7th);
26th, French cabinet reconstructed;
—, Germans cross R. Meuse and, 27th, occupy Lille;
— (–28th), Germans defeat Russians at Tannenberg;
28th, R.N. under David Beatty raids Bight of Heligoland;
—, Austria-Hungary declares war on Belgium;
30th, Germans take Amiens.

J **Sep:** 1st, name of St. Petersburg changed to Petrograd;
3rd, French government moved to Bordeaux;
—, Germans cross R. Marne and, 4th, occupy Rheims;
4th, Pact of London between France, Russia and Britain against a separate peace;
5th (–12th), battle of Marne, 9th (–15th), German retreat;
9th (–12th), in battle of Masurian Lakes, East Prussia, the Russians are driven back;
10th, *Emden* cruises in Bay of Bengal;
14th, Allies reoccupy Rheims;
—, Erich von Falkenhayn succeeds Helmuth von Moltke as German Commander-in-Chief;
15th (–18th), in battle of Aisne Germans withstand Allied attacks;
—, German capitulation in New Guinea;
—, bill suspends operation of Home Rule and Welsh Church bills for duration of war;
—, U.S. troops withdraw from Vera Cruz;
18th, Paul von Hindenburg appointed to command German armies in the East;
26th (–8th), battle of the R. Niemen;
27th, Russians cross Carpathians and invade Hungary;
—, Duala in Cameroons surrenders to British and French;
28th, Germans and Austrians advance towards Warsaw.

K **Oct:** 1st, Turkey closes Dardanelles;
9th, Antwerp surrenders to Germans;

V The Press

W Drama and Entertainment

Charlie Chaplin in *Making a Living* (film).
The Little Angel (film).
L. Baylis first produces Shakespeare at the Old Vic.

X Sport

Y Statistics

Defence estimates (in £ mill.): Germany, 110·8; Russia, 88·2; Great Britain, 76·8; France, 57·4; Austria-Hungary, 36·4; Italy, 28·2.
Army strengths (at mobilisation in mill.): Germany, 4·2; France, 3·7; Russia, 1·2; Austria-Hungary, 0·8; Great Britain, 0·7; Italy, 0·7.

Navies:

	Britain	Germany	France	Russia	Italy	U.S.	Japan
Dreadnoughts	19	13	6	6	6	8	3
Pre-Dreadnoughts	39	22	20	8	8	22	13
Battle Cruisers	8	5	—	3	—	—	2
Cruisers	63	7	19	6	10	15	13
Light Cruisers	35	33	7	8	7	14	16
Destroyers	180	163	80	100	35	48	64
Submarines	44	38	75	35	20	36	14

Merchant Shipping (in mill. tons): British Empire, 21·0; Holland, 5·6; Germany, 5·5; U.S., 5·4; Norway, 2·5; France, 2·3; Italy, 1·7; Japan, 1·7; Sweden, 1·1.
Merchant shipping losses by Britain (Aug.–Dec.): 696,542 tons.
Foreign investments (in £ mill.): Great Britain, 3,600; France, 1,740; Germany, 1,080; (U.S. has debit on account $3,000 mill.).
World aluminium production: 30,000 tons.
U.S. Motor vehicle production: 1·7 mill.

Z Births and Deaths

Feb. 25th John Tenniel d. (93).
Mar. 12th George Westinghouse d. (67).
Mar. 25th Frédéric Mistral d. (84).
May 13th Joe Louis b. (–1981).
May 18th Pierre Balmain b. (–1982).
May 19th Max Perutz b. (–).
July 2nd Joseph Chamberlain d. (78).
Sept. 2nd George Brown b. (–1985).
Oct. 25th John Berryman b. (–1972).
Oct. 28th Jonas Edward Salk b. (–).
Nov. 14th Frederick, Earl Roberts, d. (82).
Dec. 1st A. T. Mahan d. (74).

1914 (Oct.–Dec.)

K **Oct:** 12th, Germans occupy Ghent and Lille;
13th, Boer rebellion against British in South Africa under Christian de Wet;
14th, first Canadian troops land in England;
15th, Clayton anti-trust act in U.S.;
— (–20th), battle for Warsaw; Germans under von Mackensen are driven back by Russians;
17th (–30th), battle of Yser prevents Germans from reaching Channel ports;
26th, Russians break through in Ivangorod;
27th, Germans retreat from Poland;
29th, John A. Fisher becomes First Sea Lord;
—, Turkish warships bombard Odessa and Sebastopol;
30th (–*Nov.* 21st), first battle of Ypres; Germans fail to break through.

L **Nov:** 1st, Maximilius von Spee defeats R.N. under Christopher Cradock at battle of Coronel, Chile;
2nd, Russia declares war on Turkey;
3rd, large Republican gains in U.S. elections;
5th, France and Britain declare war on Turkey;
—, Britain annexes Cyprus which she has occupied since *June* 1878;
9th, *Emden* sunk off Cocos I.;
18th, Germans break Russian line at Kutno;
21st, Indian troops occupy Basra;
23rd, R.N. bombard Zeebrugge.

M **Dec:** 2nd, Austrians take Belgrade (reoccupied by Serbians, 14th);
5th (–17th), Austrians defeat Russians at battle of Limanova, but fail to break Russian lines before Cracow;
6th, Germans take Łódź;
8th, Admiral Frederick Sturdee destroys German squadron off Falkland Islands;
10th, French government returns to Paris;
17th, British protectorate proclaimed in Egypt;
18th, Abbas II is deposed and Prince Hussein Kemel becomes Khedive of Egypt.

N Mahatma Gandhi returns to India and supports the government.

1915 (Jan.–May) Italy enters the war—Dardanelles Campaign—Second battle of Ypres

A **Jan:** 1st, H.M.S. *Formidable* sunk in English Channel;
3rd (–4th), rebellion in Albania;
8th (–*Feb.* 5th), heavy fighting in Bassée Canal and Soissons area;
12th, House of Representatives defeats proposal for women's suffrage in U.S.;
13th, South African troops occupy Swakopmund in German South-West Africa;
18th, Japan's secret ultimatum to China regarding rights in Shantung and leases in Manchuria;
19th, German airship bombs East Anglian ports;
24th, cruiser *Blücher* sunk in battle of Dogger Bank;
28th, President Wilson vetoes U.S. Immigration bill;
30th, first German submarine attack without warning off Le Havre.

B **Feb:** 4th, Turks repulsed from Suez Canal;
— (–27th), Germans advance following battle in Masuria, East Prussia;
—, Foreign Office announces that any vessel carrying corn to Germany will be seized;
11th, U.S. note to Britain on use of U.S. flag on British vessels, such as *Lusitania*, and U.S. note to Germany on sinking of neutral ships;
16th (–26th), French bombard Champagne;
17th, Germans take Memel;
18th, German blockade of England comes into force with intensive submarine warfare;
19th, British and French fleets bombard Dardanelles;
27th, Russians evacuate East Prussia.

C **Mar:** 6th, Demetrios Gournaris forms ministry in Greece on resignation of Eleutherios Venizelos;
10th, British launch battle of Neuve Chapelle;
11th, British blockade of Germany comes into effect;
18th, cotton declared an article of contraband;
—, Anglo-French naval attack on Dardanelles fails;
22nd, Russians take Przemysl.

D **Apr:** 22nd (–*May* 25th), German offensive leads to second battle of Ypres;
22nd, Germans first use poison gas on Western Front;
24th, battle of St. Julien;
25th, Anglo-French forces land at Gallipoli;
26th, Britain, France and Italy sign secret convention;
—, German offensive in Courland and, 27th, in Lithuania.

E **May:** 1st, U.S. vessel *Gulflight* sunk by German submarines without warning;
2nd, Austro-German offensive in Galicia breaks Russian lines;
4th, Italy denounces the Triple Alliance (renewed in *Dec.* 1912);
7th, Germans sink *Lusitania* off Irish coast, with loss of 1,198 lives and U.S. is brought to verge of war with Germany;
12th, Louis Botha occupies Windhoek, capital of German South-West Africa;
13th, names of Emperors of Germany and Austria are struck off roll of Knights of the Garter;
14th, Portuguese cabinet resigns after insurrection;
15th, John Fisher, First Sea Lord, resigns, disapproving of cabinet's Dardanelles policy;
21st, Italian ambassador in Vienna is warned that Austria cannot admit nullification of Triple Alliance;
23rd, Italy declares war on Austria-Hungary;
25th, China accepts Japanese ultimatum (of *Jan.* 18th);

O **Politics, Economics, Law and Education**

Defence of Realm Act (*Mar.* 9th) to mobilise Britain's resources.
Ministry of Munitions established.
Robert La Follette's Seamen's Act to improve conditions in U.S. merchant fleet.
Sale of absinthe is prohibited in France.
Women's Institute founded in Britain.

P **Science, Technology, Discovery, etc.**

Albert Einstein's general theory of relativity.
W. and L. Bragg devise crystal method for the diffraction of X-rays.
Kendall isolates thyroxine from thyroid gland; the dysentery bacillus is isolated.
Outbreaks of tetanus in the trenches are controlled through serum injections.
Thorburn's *British Birds* (–16).
Hugo Junkers makes first all-metal aeroplane.
Royal Navy uses paravanes as protection of vessels against mines (*Oct.*).
Wegener's theory of continental drift.
Leipzig railway station, the largest in Europe, completed.

Q **Scholarship**

Aurel Stein, on his expedition to South Mongolia, discovers the remains of Marco Polo's 'city of Etzina'.

R **Philosophy and Religion**

S **Art, Sculpture, Fine Arts and Architecture**

Painting:
M. Duchamp, *The Bride Stripped Bare by Her Bachelors Even* (the first Dada-style painting).
P. Picasso, *Harlequin*.
U.S. collectors purchase many works of art at Christie's London sales to aid British Red Cross.
Hugh Lane's bequest to English and Irish National Galleries.

T **Music**

Frank Bridge, *Lament*.
M. de Falla, *Love, The Magician*.
Gustav Holst, *The Planets* (symphonic suite).
John Ireland, *The Forgotten Rite*.
Max Reger, 'Variations on a Theme of Mozart'.
Clara Butt sings in aid of Red Cross.
Remains of R. de Lisle, composer of *La Marseillaise*, brought to the Invalides (*July* 4th).

U **Literature**

John Buchan, *The Thirty-Nine Steps*.
P. Claudel, *Corona*.
J. Conrad, *Victory*.
D. H. Lawrence, *The Rainbow*.
W. S. Maugham, *Of Human Bondage*.
F. Neumann, *Mitteleuropa*.
Ezra Pound, *Cathay* (poems).

V **The Press**

Sunday Pictorial issued.
Lord Beaverbrook buys the *Daily Express*.
The Globe is suppressed (*Nov.* 6th–20th) for spreading false rumour about Lord Kitchener's resignation.

E **May**: 26th, H. H. Asquith forms Coalition, with A. J. Balfour First Lord of Admiralty and R. McKenna Chancellor of Exchequer; W. S. Churchill leaves Admiralty for Chancellorship of Duchy of Lancaster;
29th, Theophilo Braga elected President of Portugal.

F **Jun**: 1st, first Zeppelin attack on London;
3rd, Russian southern front collapses with German recapture of Przemysl;
—, British take Amarah on R. Tigris and Mesopotamia surrenders to British;
5th, women's suffrage in Denmark;
8th, Allies take Neuville;
9th, riots in Moscow;
10th, Russian victory on R. Dniester;
15th, battle of Givenchy;
16th, D. Lloyd George appointed first minister of munitions;
21st, Christian de Wet surrenders at Bloemfontein;
23rd, Robert Lansing becomes U.S. secretary of state after W. J. Bryan's resignation, 8th;
—, German Social Democrats' manifesto asking for a peace to be negotiated;
—, Austro-German forces take Lemberg;
29th (–*July* 7th), in first battle of Isonzo Italians try to force bridgeheads held by Austrians.

G **Jul**: 9th, German forces in South-West Africa surrender to Louis Botha;
12th, German government takes over control of coal industry;
14th, British National Registration Act (National Register taken *Aug.* 15th);
18th (–*Aug.* 10th), second battle of Isonzo;
27th, revolution in Haiti.

H **Aug**: 4th, National Ministry in New Zealand;
5th, Germans enter Warsaw;
6th, fresh Allied landings at Suvla Bay, Gallipoli;
—, Bernadino Machado elected President of Portugal;
20th, Germans take Novo-Georgievsk;
—, Italy declares war on Turkey;
26th, Germans capture Brest-Litovsk.

J **Sep**: 6th, Russians check Germans at Tarnopol;
—, Bulgaria signs military alliances with Germany and Turkey;
8th, Nicholas Nicolaievich relieved of his command, which Tsar Nicholas II takes over in person;
9th, U.S. asks Austria to recall her ambassador (who leaves New York, *Oct.* 5th);
18th, Germany gives undertaking that her submarines will cease attacking merchant shipping until end of war;
—, Germans capture Vilna;
22nd, Joseph Joffre opens battle of Champagne but the Germans hold their own;
23rd, Greek army is mobilised;
25th (–*Oct.* 8th), in battle of Loos the British drive the Germans back towards Lens and Loos;
—, U.S. loans $500 mill. to Britain and France.
28th, British defeat Turks at Kut-el-Amara in Mesopotamia;

K **Oct**: 5th, Allies land troops at Salonika;
9th, Austro-German troops occupy Belgrade;

(*Continued opposite*)

W **Drama and Entertainment**

Felix Powell and George Asaf write 'Pack Up Your Troubles in Your Old Kit Bag'.
D. W. Griffiths, *Birth of a Nation* (film).
C. B. de Mille's *Carmen* (film).
Douglas Fairbanks in *The Lamb* (film).

X **Sport**

Y **Statistics**

Merchant shipping losses by Britain (in tons): Jan.–Mar., 215,905; Apr.–June, 223,767; July–Sept., 356,659; Oct.–Dec., 307,139.

Z **Births and Deaths**

Jan. 3rd James Elroy Flecker d. (31).
Apr. 14th Alexander Scriabin d. (43).
May 20th Moshe Dayan b. (–1981).
June 10th Saul Bellow b. (–).
Aug. 26th Humphrey Searle b. (–1982).
Sept. 26th James Keir Hardie d. (59).
Oct. 17th Arthur Miller b. (–).
Oct. 23rd W. G. Grace d. (67).
Oct. 24th Tito Gobbi b. (–1984).
Nov. 12th Roland Barthes b. (–1980).

K **Oct**: 9th, conference of Latin American states recognises Venustiano Carranza as chief of *de facto* government in Mexico (recognised by U.S. 19th);
11th, Bulgarian offensive against Serbia;
—, execution of Edith Cavell in Brussels;
12th, Allies declare they will assist Serbia under Bucharest treaty of *Aug.* 10th 1913;
—, Greece refuses Serbian appeal for aid under Serbo-Greek treaty of 1913;
13th, T. Delcassé, French foreign minister, resigns;
15th, Britain declares war on Bulgaria;
18th (–*Nov.* 3rd), third battle of Isonzo;
19th, Japan signs treaty of London, undertaking not to make a separate peace;
20th, J. B. Hertzog's Nationalist Party's successes in South African elections leave South African Party government in a minority in the House;
28th, René Viviani resigns and
29th, Aristide Briand forms ministry in France.

L **Nov**: 5th, Chinese princes vote for monarchy, with Yüan Shih-kai as emperor;
6th, Sophocles Skouloudis forms ministry in Greece favourable to Allies;
10th (–*Dec.* 10th), fourth battle of Isonzo;
12th, Britain annexes Gilbert and Ellice Islands;
13th, W. S. Churchill resigns from British cabinet;
21st, Italy agrees not to make a separate peace;
22nd, indecisive battle of Ctesiphon, Mesopotamia, between Turks and British.

M **Dec**: 3rd, Joseph Joffre becomes French Commander-in-Chief;
16th, Douglas Haig succeeds John French as British Commander-in-Chief in France and Flanders;
19th (–*Jan.* 8th 1916), British withdrawal from Suvla and Anzac in Gallipoli;
21st, William Robertson becomes British chief of staff;
28th, British cabinet agrees on principle of compulsory service.

1916 (Jan.–Jun.) Lloyd George forms coalition—Easter Rebellion in Dublin

A Jan: 19th, Russian offensive in Galicia opens;
24th, U.S. Supreme Court rules income tax law is constitutional;
27th, British Labour Party conference votes against conscription;
—, 'Spartacus' Communist group founded in Berlin;
29th, first Zeppelin raid on Paris.

B Feb: 2nd, Boris Stürmer becomes Russian premier;
9th, British military service act in force;
14th, Allies guarantee Belgium a place at the peace conference;
16th, Russians take Erzurum;
—, U.S. refuses to recognise Germany's claims to sink armed merchantmen without warning;
18th, last German garrison in Cameroons surrenders;
21st (–*Dec.* 16th), battle of Verdun;
22nd, Tsar Nicholas II opens Duma in person;
29th, first 'Black List' of firms in neutral countries, with whom trade is forbidden, is issued in Britain;
—, German order for sinking armed merchantmen at sight comes into force.

C Mar: 2nd, Russians take Bitlis (reconquered by Turks *Aug.* 7th);
9th, Germany declares war on Portugal;
15th, U.S. punitive expedition to Mexico;
—, Alfred von Tirpitz, German Minister of Marine, resigns;
—, fifth battle of Isonzo;
17th (–*Apr.* 4th) strike of Clydeside munitions workers;
20th, Allies agree on partition of Turkey;
—, Allied air attack on Zeebrugge;
22nd, Yüan Shih-kai dies;
27th, Aristide Briand opens Paris inter-allied war conference.

D Apr: 9th, German attack before Verdun;
18th, Russians take Trebizond;
21st, Roger Casement lands in Ireland (is arrested, 24th, and executed *Aug.* 3rd);
24th, Sinn Fein Easter Rebellion in Dublin (–*May* 1st);
29th, Kut-el-Amara falls to Turks.

E May: 8th, Anzacs arrive in France;
31st (–*June* 1st), in battle of Jutland, Royal Navy losses exceed those of German fleet.

F Jun: 2nd, second battle of Ypres;
4th, Alexei Brusilov begins Russian offensive;
5th (–6th), H.M.S. *Hampshire* sunk, with Lord Kitchener aboard;
6th (–24th), Allies blockade Greece;
—, Arab Revolt in Hedjaz begins;
9th, Grand Sheriff of Mecca revolts against Turkey;
10th, Republican Convention nominates Charles E. Hughes as presidential candidate;
13th, Jan Smuts captures Wilhemsthal in German East Africa;
14th, Allied economic conference in Paris;
15th, Woodrow Wilson is re-nominated Democratic presidential candidate at St. Louis convention;
17th, Italian coalition formed under Paolo Boselli;
18th, Russians take Czernowitz;
21st, battle of Carrizal between U.S. and Mexican troops;

O Politics, Economics, Law and Education

G. Lowes Dickinson, *The European Anarchy*.
Lionel Curtis, *The Problem of the Commonwealth*.
New Ministries Act in Britain leads to establishment of Ministry of National Service.
Cabinet Secretariat is formed (*Dec.*) in Britain.
Report of Bryce Committee on German Atrocities (*May*).
Report of Royal Commission on Irish Rebellion, under Lord Hardinge (*July* 3rd).
Report of Royal Commission on Venereal Diseases states that 10 per cent of British urban population is infected (*Mar.* 3rd).
National Savings Movement founded in Britain.
Severe rationing of food in Germany. Shortages in Paris lead to milk queues.
U.S. Shipping Board is established.
U.S. Rural Credits Law.
Products of child labour are excluded from U.S. inter-state commerce.
School of Oriental and African Studies, London University, founded.
Summer Time (daylight saving) introduced in Britain (*May* 21st).

P Science, Technology, Discovery, etc.

G. N. Lewis states a new valency theory, which is later stated independently by Kossel.
The Committee on the Neglect of Science, led by Ray Lankester, starts press campaign (*Feb.* 2nd) demanding greater awareness of science in Britain's schools, universities and civil service.
A Board of Scientific Societies is sponsored by the Royal Society to promote co-operation in pure and applied science and promote the application of science for the service of Britain.
The government establishes a Department of Scientific and Industrial Research (*Nov.*).
Herbert Jackson succeeds in making optical glasses of the same standard as those of the Zeiss works at Jena.
Treatment of war casualties leads to development of plastic surgery.
F. W. Mott's theory of shell-shock.
First military tanks used (*Sep.*).

Q Scholarship

Closure of many British museums and galleries to save manpower, but the press campaigns successfully for keeping the British Museum Reading Room and the Natural History Museum open.

R Philosophy and Religion

Pareto, *Treatise of General Sociology*.

S Art, Sculpture, Fine Arts and Architecture

Painting:
Claude Monet, *Water Lilies* (murals at the Musée d'orangerie, Paris).
Georges Rouault's etchings *Guerre* and *Misère* (–27).
H. Matisse, *Bouquet*.
Man Ray, *The Rope Dancer Accompanies Herself with Her Shadow*.
Dadaist anti-art cult flourishes in Zürich, headed by Tristan Tzara, Hans Arp and Giacomo Balla (movement lasts –21).

Architecture:
Eugène Freyssinet, Airship Hangars at Orly, France (first giant structure in reinforced concrete).

T Music

Arnold Bax, *The Garden of Fand* (orchestral work).
Leoš Janáček, *Jenufa* (opera).

F **Jun**: 23rd, Greece accepts Allies' demands for demobilisation;
—, Convention of Ulster Nationalists agrees to exclude Ulster under Government of Ireland act;
25th, Austrians evacuate positions in South Tirol;
26th, T. Roosevelt declines nomination as Progressive Republican presidential candidate.

G **Jul**: 1st, French and British troops begin Somme offensive (–*Nov*. 8th);
6th, D. Lloyd George becomes War Secretary in succession to Lord Kitchener;
9th, German commercial submarine *Deutschland* reaches U.S.;
25th, Sergei Sazonov, Russian foreign minister, resigns;
26th, U.S. protests against British 'Black List' forbidding trading with certain U.S. firms.

H **Aug**: 4th, Denmark sells West Indian Islands to U.S.;
—, (–6th), sixth battle of Isonzo;
19th, Royal Navy torpedoes and damages German battleship *Westfalen* in North Sea;
—, Germans bombard English coast;
20th, Allied offensive in Mesopotamia begins;
27th, Roumania declares war on Austria-Hungary, and begins offensive in Transylvania;
28th, Italy declares war on Germany;
30th, Turkey declares war on Russia;
—, Paul von Hindenburg appointed German chief of general staff.

J **Sep**: 1st, Bulgaria declares war on Roumania;
4th, British troops take Dar-es-Salaam;
6th, Supreme War Council of Central Powers established;
14th (–18th), seventh battle of Isonzo;
15th, British first use tanks on Western Front;
18th, Greek army surrenders to Germans at Kavalla;
Alexei Brusilov's offensive checked by Germans.

K **Oct**: 4th, Austro-German counter-offensive in Roumania;
9th (–12th), eighth battle of Isonzo;
11th, Greece accepts Allies' ultimatum to hand over Greek fleet;
16th, Allies occupy Athens;
19th, Franco-British conference at Boulogne recognises Venizelist government of Greece at Salonika;
21st, Count Carl Stürgkh, Austrian premier, assassinated;
24th (–*Nov*. 5th), French offensive east of Verdun;
31st (–*Nov*. 4th), ninth battle of Isonzo.

L **Nov**: 5th, Central Powers proclaim Kingdom of Poland;
7th, Woodrow Wilson, Democrat, re-elected U.S. president with 277 electoral votes against Charles E. Hughes, Republican with 254 votes;
—, Miss Jeanette Rankin returned by Montana as first woman member of Congress;
13th, Cardinal Mercier protests against deportation of Belgians to Germany for forced labour;
21st, Emperor Francis Joseph of Austria dies, succeeded by his grand-nephew as Charles I (–1918);
—, Arthur Zimmermann becomes German foreign minister;
24th, U.S.-Mexican protocol signed at Atlantic City (but, *Dec*. 18th, President Carranza refuses to ratify);

T Music (*cont.*)

Erich Korngold, *Violanta* (opera).
E. Smyth, *The Boatswain's Mate* (opera).
Campaign against performing works by German composers makes slight headway in England.
Jazz sweeps U.S.

U Literature

J. Buchan, *Greenmantle.*
G. D'Annunzio, *La Leda Senza Gigno* (–18).
J. Joyce, *Portrait of the Artist as a Young Man.*
G. Moore, *The Brook Kerith.*
A. Quiller-Couch, *The Art of Writing.*
G. B. Shaw publishes 'Prefaces' to *Androcles and the Lion, Overruled* and *Pygmalion.*

V The Press

Le Populaire, French Socialist organ, issued.
Forward, British Labour newspaper, suppressed for inciting Clydeside workers to refuse making munitions.

W Drama and Entertainment

Leonid Andreyev, *He Who Gets Slapped.*
Algernon Blackwood, *Starlight Express.*
Harold Brighouse, *Hobson's Choice.*
Eugene O'Neill, *Bound East.*
The Bing Girls (revue).

X Sport

Y Statistics

Merchant shipping losses by Britain (in tons): Jan.–Mar., 325,237; Apr.–June, 270,690; July–Sept., 284,358; Oct.–Dec., 617,563.
U.S. Petroleum production: 300,767,000 tons.
Coal production (in mill. tons): U.S., 590; Great Britain, 256·4.

Z Births and Deaths

Feb. 28th Henry James d. (72).
Mar. 11th Harold Wilson b. (–).
Apr. 22nd Yehudi Menuhin b. (–).
May 20th Owen Chadwick b. (–).
June 5th Horatio, Lord Kitchener, d. (66).
July 9th Edward Heath b. (–).
Sept. 29th Michael Wallace-Hadrill b. (–1985).
Oct. 26th François Mitterand b. (–).

L Nov: 29th, Hussein is proclaimed King of the Arabs;
—, British government takes over South Wales coalfield under Defence of Realm Act because of strikes;
—, David Beatty appointed Commander-in-Chief of British fleet and John Jellicoe First Sea Lord.

M Dec: 3rd, Robert Nivelle succeeds Joseph Joffre as French Commander-in-Chief;
5th, D. Lloyd George resigns from H. H. Asquith's cabinet;
6th, Germans take Bucharest;
7th, H. H. Asquith resigns and D. Lloyd George becomes prime minister of coalition government, and (11th) forms war cabinet, including A. J. Balfour, George Curzon, Arthur Henderson and Alfred Milner;
12th, Aristide Briand forms French War Ministry;
—, U.S. Senate passes Immigration bill, with literacy test clause amended to meet Japanese criticism;
—, Germany's peace note to Allies saying the Central Powers were prepared to negotiate (reply sent 30th, via U.S. ambassador in Paris);
13th, new British offensive in Mesopotamia;
15th (–17th), French offensive between Meuse and Woëvre Plain;
19th, British government takes control of shipping and of mines;
20th, Woodrow Wilson's peace note to all belligerents;
31st, Allied ultimatum to Greece for withdrawal of forces from Thessaly.

N

1917 (Jan.–May) February and Bolshevist Revolutions in Russia—U.S. declares war on Central Powers—Germans intensify submarine warfare

A **Jan**: 1st, Britain, France and Italy recognise Kingdom of Hedjaz;
—, Turkey denounces treaties of Paris, 1856, and Berlin, 1878;
5th, Allies evacuate Dobrudja;
8th, Austrians take Foscani;
16th, Greece accepts Allied ultimatum of *Dec.* 1916;
31st, Germany's declaration to neutrals announces policy of unrestricted naval warfare.

B **Feb**: 2nd, bread rationing in Britain;
3rd, U.S. and Germany break off diplomatic relations;
4th (–23rd), Germans' preliminary withdrawal between Arras and Soissons;
12th, Woodrow Wilson refuses to reopen negotiations with Germany until she abandons unrestricted naval warfare;
15th, William Hughes becomes premier of Australia.

C **Mar**: 4th (–*Apr.* 5th), German main withdrawal on Western Front;
8th, Woodrow Wilson orders arming of U.S. merchant ships without special authority of Congress;
—, U.S. marines land at Santiago, Cuba, at request of civil government;
— (–14th) (old style, *Feb.* 23rd.–*Mar.* 1st), February Revolution in Russia;
11th, British capture Baghdad;
16th, Tsar Nicholas II abdicates and Prince George Lvov, Paul Milivkov and Alexander Kerensky form ministry in Russia;
17th (–18th), British capture Bapaume and Péronne on Western Front;
19th, Alexandre Ribot forms cabinet in France;
—, Allies raise Greek blockade;
20th, Imperial war cabinet first meets in London;
26th (–*Apr.* 8th), Archibald Murray defeats Turks at Gaza;
30th, Russian provisional government guarantees independence of Poland;
31st, U.S. takes over Virgin Islands from Denmark.

D **Apr**: 2nd, Woodrow Wilson calls special sessions of Congress for declaration of war and
6th, U.S. declares war on Germany;
7th, Cuba declares war on Germany;
—, Kaiser William II promises universal suffrage in Prussia;
9th (–*May* 4th), in battle of Arras British third army advances 4 miles;
— (–21st), Canadians take Vimy Ridge;
11th, German Independent Labour Party founded;
14th, U.S. House of Representatives authorises 'Old Glory Loan';
16th (–20th), Germans halt French advance in second battle of Aisne;
—, food strikes in Berlin;
18th (–19th), in second battle of Gaza Turks, with German support, repulse British;
20th, U.S. and Turkey sever relations;
29th, Henri Pétain becomes chief of French staff;
30th, Frederick Maude defeats Turks at Shatt-el-Adhaim.

E **May**: 3rd (–5th), fresh British attack at Arras breaks Hindenburg Line;
5th, A. J. Balfour addresses U.S. House of Representatives;
— (–9th), battle of Chemin des Dames;
14th, tenth battle of Isonzo;
15th, Henri Pétain succeeds R. G. Nivelle as French Commander-in-Chief and Ferdinand Foch becomes chief of staff;
18th, U.S. selective military conscription bill;
—, Prince Lvov reforms cabinet in Russia to include Socialists;

O Politics, Economics, Law and Education

Herman Fernau, *The Coming Democracy*.

Establishment of British Ministry of Labour and of a Civil Aerial Transport Committee.

Impact of the war rapidly changes the social and administrative structure of Britain.

Women in munitions factories cut their hair short as a safety precaution, and 'bobbed hair' sweeps Britain and U.S.

Reports of the Commissions on the Dardanelles (*Mar.* 8th) and on Mesopotamia Campaign (*June* 26th).

British merchant ships first sail in organised convoys (*Feb.*).

Companion of Honour and Order of British Empire founded.

P Science, Technology, Discovery, etc.

Radioactive element protoactinium is discovered.

Q Scholarship

History (Journal of the Historical Association).

Hrozny, *The Hittite Language*.

R Philosophy and Religion

C. Jung, *The Unconscious*.

Maude Royden becomes assistant preacher at the City Temple, London, the first Englishwoman to have a permanent pulpit.

S Art, Sculpture, Fine Arts and Architecture

Painting:

P. Picasso's sets and costumes for Diaghilev's ballet *Parade* are described by G. Apollinaire as 'Surrealist'—first use of the term.

P. Bonnard, *Nude at the Fireplace*.

A. Modigliani, *Crouching Female Nude*.

J. S. Sargent, *John D. Rockefeller*.

W. Orpen, W. Rothenstein and E. Kennington are commissioned as British war artists.

Piet Mondrian launches *de Stijl* magazine in Holland.

Carlo Carrà and Giorgio de Chirico found the Metaphysical School in Italy.

Sculpture:

P. A. Renoir, *The Washerwoman*.

T Music

Arnold Bax, *Tintagel* (symphonic poem).

G. Holst, *Hymn of Jesus* (choral work).

Hans Pfitzner, *Palestrina* (opera).

Serge Prokofiev, 'Classical' Symphony.

Ottorino Respighi, *The Fountains of Rome* (symphonic poem).

Albert Roussel, *Les dieux dans l'ombre des Cavernes* (orchestral work).

Igor Stravinsky's music for *The Soldier's Tale* (mime with narrative).

E. Satie's music for the ballet *Parade*.

U Literature

Norman Douglas, *South Wind*.

T. S. Eliot, *Prufrock and Other Observations*.

L. Feuchtwanger, *Jew Süss* (Eng. translation 1922).

Knut Hamsun, *Growth of the Soil*.

Henry James, *The Middle Years*.

Frank Swinnerton, *Nocturne*.

Paul Valéry, *La jeune parque*.

Mary Webb, *Gone to Earth*.

Pulitzer Prizes are first awarded in U.S.

E May: 20th, mutinies in French army in Champagne;
22nd, Count Tisza, Hungarian premier, resigns;
23rd, Tuan Ch'i-jui, premier of China, dismissed.

F Jun: 2nd, Brazil revokes her neutrality and seizes German ships;
3rd, Albanian independence under Italian protection is proclaimed;
7th, battle of Messines;
10th, Sinn Fein riots in Dublin;
12th, King Constantine I of Greece abdicates in favour of second son, Alexander (–1920);
14th, U.S. mission under E. Root arrives in Petrograd;
15th, amnesty for prisoners of Irish Rebellion, 1916;
16th, first all-Russian congress of Soviets;
19th, British royal family renounces German names and titles, having adopted name of Windsor;
24th, Russian Black Sea fleet mutinies at Sebastopol;
26th, Alexander Kerensky launches Russian counter-attack;
—, first U.S. division arrives in France;
29th, Edward Allenby takes over Palestine command;
—, Greece severs relations with Central Powers.

G Jul: 1st (–9th), Russians break through at Zborov and on R. Dniester;
9th, government control of fuel and food in U.S.;
12th, Tuan Ch'i-jui resumes Chinese premiership;
13th, George Michaelis appointed German chancellor on resignation of T. von Bethmann-Hollweg;
16th (–18th), V. Lenin and other Bolsheviks fail to seize power in Petrograd;
19th, German-Austrian counter-attack in Galicia;
—, Zeppelins attack English industrial areas;
—, Reichstag passes motion for peace;
— (–*Aug.* 2nd), mutinies in German fleet;
20th, Prince Lvov resigns in Russia (succeeded 22nd, by Alexander Kerensky);
—, Corfu pact for union of Serbs, Croats and Slovenes;
25th, Irish convention meets under Horace Plunkett;
31st, Douglas Haig's offensive in third battle of Ypres (or Passchendaele) begins (–*Nov.* 10th).

H Aug: 1st, Richard von Kühlmann becomes German foreign minister;
3rd, Russians take Czernowitz;
6th, failure of German offensive at Foscani;
13th, revolt in Spain for home rule for Catalonia;
14th, China declares war on Germany and Austria;
—, Pope Benedict XV's peace note;
20th (–*Dec.* 15th), French gain positions in second battle of Verdun;
21st, Germans attack on Riga front;
25th (–8th), all-Russian conference at Moscow.

J Sep: 3rd, Germans take Riga;
8th, Lavr Kornilov, dismissed as Russian Commander-in-Chief, marches on Petrograd as leader of counter-revolutionary movement;
12th, Paul Painlevé forms cabinet in France;
15th, Russian republic proclaimed under Alexander Kerensky;
20th, British offensive near Ypres;
29th (–*Oct.* 1st), German aircraft attack London on successive nights.

V The Press

W Drama and Entertainment

G. Apollinaire, *Les Mamelles de Tirésias.*
J. M. Barrie, *Dear Brutus.*
L. Pirandello, *Liola.*
Bubbly, with George Robey (revue).
A society is formed to produce Eugène Brieux's *Damaged Goods* in London, and the production is licensed by the Lord Chamberlain.
Mater dolorosa (film).
The Little American (film).

X Sport

Y Statistics

Merchant shipping losses by Britain (in tons): Jan.–Mar., 911,840; Apr.–June, 1,361,870; July–Sept., 952,938; Oct.–Dec., 782,889.

Z Births and Deaths

Jan. 29th Evelyn Baring, Earl of Cromer, d. (76).
Mar. 1st Robert Lowell b. (–1977).
Mar. 8th Ferdinand, Count Zeppelin, d. (79).
May 20th Richard Cobb b. (–).
May 29th John Fitzgerald Kennedy b. (–1963).
July 2nd Herbert Beerbohm Tree d. (65).
Aug. 9th Ruggiero Leoncavallo d. (59).
Aug. 30th Denis Healey b. (–).
Sept. 26th Edgar Degas d. (83).
Nov. 17th François Auguste Rodin d. (77).
Nov. 19th Indira Gandhi b. (–1984).
Nov. 26th Leander Starr Jameson d. (64).
Dec. 17th Elizabeth Garrett Anderson d. (81).
— W. F. Cody ('Buffalo Bill') d. (71).

K **Oct**: 15th, Germans renew offensive in East Africa at battle of Mahiwa;
22nd, Soviet congress passes resolution for armistice;
23rd, French victory on Aisne forces Germans back to Oise-Aisne canal;
24th, rout of second Italian army, in the Caporetto campaign;
28th, Vittorio Orlando becomes Italian premier.

L **Nov**: 1st, Count von Hertling appointed German chancellor;
2nd, A. J. Balfour's declaration on Palestine that Britain favoured the establishment of a national home for the Jewish people;
5th (–9th), Allied conference at Rapallo decides on Supreme Allied War Council (which first meets, 29th, at Versailles);
6th, Canadians and British capture Passchendaele Ridge;
7th (old style, *Oct.* 26th), Lenin leads Bolsheviks against A. Kerensky at Petrograd (October Revolution), and
8th, becomes chief of commissars of people and Leon Trotsky is appointed premier;
7th, British take Gaza;
10th (–12th), Kerensky's counter-revolution fails;
11th, Italians fall back on R. Piave;
16th, Georges Clemenceau forms cabinet in France on Paul Painlevé's fall;
17th, British take Jaffa;
20th, first notable tank battle in British advance at Cambrai;
—, Ukrainian republic proclaimed;
26th, Soviets offer armistice to Germany and Austria.

M **Dec**: 1st, German East Africa cleared of German troops;
5th, German and Russian delegates sign armistice at Brest-Litovsk (where peace negotiations begin 21st);
6th, Finnish republic proclaimed;
7th, U.S. declares war on Austria-Hungary;
9th, Roumania signs armistice with Central Powers at Foscani;
—, Turks surrender Jerusalem to Edmund Allenby;
10th, Italians torpedo Austrian battleship *Wien* in Trieste;
17th, Robert Borden becomes Canadian premier after Unionist election victory;
28th, Bessarabia proclaims its independence as the Moldavian republic;
—, U.S. government takes control of railways;
31st, prohibition in Canada.

N

Wilson's 14 Points—Treaty of Brest-Litovsk —The Armistice

A **Jan**: 8th, Woodrow Wilson propounds Fourteen Points for world peace in message to Congress;
14th, Joseph Caillaux, former premier of France, arrested for treason (sentenced to imprisonment *Apr.* 1920);
16th, strike begins in Vienna;
18th, Russian constitutional assembly opens in Petrograd but
19th, is dissolved by Bolsheviks;
20th, *Breslau* sunk in Dardanelles;
21st, Edward Carson resigns from War Cabinet;
24th, Germany and Austria decline British-U.S. peace proposals;
27th, Russia denounces Anglo-Russian treaty of 1907;
28th (–*Feb.* 3rd), strike in Berlin;
—, Bolsheviks occupy Helsinki.

B **Feb**: 5th, separation of Church and State in Russia;
9th, Ukraine signs peace with Central Powers;
18th, German offensive opens on Russian front;
20th (–23rd), inter-allied Labour and Socialist conference in London;
21st, Australians occupy Jericho;
25th, meat and butter rationed in London and Southern England.

C **Mar**: 1st, Germans occupy Kiev and, 2nd, Narva;
3rd, peace treaty of Brest-Litovsk between Russia and Central Powers, and 7th, between Germany and Finland;
12th, Turks occupy Baku (–*May* 14th);
21st, German offensive begins second battle of the Somme;
23rd, Germans shell Paris from 75 miles away;
—, Lithuania proclaims its independence;
26th, Doullens agreement for united command on Western Front, under Ferdinand Foch, signed by Georges Clemenceau and Alfred Milner.

D **Apr**: 1st, R.A.F. formed, replacing R.F.C.;
8th (–10th), Rome meeting of representatives of Czecho-Slovaks, Roumanians, Yugoslavs and Poles;
9th (–29th), battle of the Lys;
—, Latvia proclaims her independence;
12th, Germans take Armentières;
14th, Germans occupy Helsingfors, on Russians' withdrawal;
19th, Alfred Milner becomes British war secretary;
22nd (–23rd), Zeebrugge raid blocks entrance to Bruges Canal;
24th, British victory at Villers-Bretonneux;
29th, German major offensive on Western Front ends.

E **May**: 1st, Germans occupy Sebastopol;
6th, Allied break-through in Albania;
7th, Roumania signs peace treaty with Central Powers;
9th, Maurice debate in Commons on military manpower threatens D. Lloyd George's leadership;
— (–10th), British attack on Ostend;
14th, Overman bill empowers U.S. President to reorganise executive departments;
23rd, Georgia proclaims its independence;
27th (–*June* 5th), intensive German offensive on Western Front;
29th, Germans capture Soissons and Rheims.

O **Politics, Economics, Law and Education**

Oswald Spengler, *The Decline of the West* (–22).
A. F. Pollard, *The League of Nations: an Historical Argument.*
Women over 30 gain the vote in Britain.
Food shortage in Britain leads to establishment of National Food Kitchens (*Mar.*) and Rationing (*July* 14th). Prime Minister appeals to women to help with the harvest (*June* 25th).
Standard Clothing for male civilians is made by Board of Control of Textile Industries.
Ministry of Labour established in Germany (*Oct.*).
Daylight Saving introduced in U.S.

P **Science, Technology, Discovery, etc.**

Arthur Eddington, *Gravitation and the Principle of Relativity.*
Mount Wilson telescope first used.
Three-colour traffic lights installed in New York.
Influenza epidemic (*May–June* and *September*).

Q **Scholarship**

H. R. H. Hall and Leonard Woolley begin Babylonian excavations.

R **Philosophy and Religion**

Bertrand Russell, *Mysticism and Logic.*

S **Art, Sculpture, Fine Arts and Architecture**

Painting:
Paul Klee's abstract *Gartenplan.*
John Nash, *The Cornfield.*
Paul Nash, *We are making a New World.*
Architecture:
A. Ozenfant and Le Corbusier (pseud.), *Après le Cubisme*, a manifesto on 'Purism'.
David Low's cartoons in *The Star*, newspaper.

T **Music**

B. Bartók, *Bluebeard's Castle* (opera).
E. Elgar, 'cello concerto.
G. Puccini, *Il Trittico* (operas).
S. Diaghilev's ballet company visits London.

U **Literature**

Alexander Blok, *The Twelve.*
Rupert Brooke, *Collected Poems* (posth. ed. Edward Marsh).
G. M. Hopkins, *Poems* (posth.).
Laurence Housman, *The Sheepfold.*
Lytton Strachey, *Eminent Victorians.*

V **The Press**

W **Drama and Entertainment**

James Joyce, *The Exiles.*
Luigi Pirandello, *Six Characters in Search of an Author.*
European tour of the 'Original Dixieland Jazz Band'.
The Lilac Domino (musical).

F **Jun**: 9th (–13th), German offensive near Compiègne;
21st, British government announces abandonment of Home Rule and conscription for Ireland.

G **Jul**: 6th, Montagu-Chelmsford Report on Constitution of India published;
13th, Turkish offensive in Palestine checked;
15th (–*Aug.* 4th), second battle of the Marne;
16th, execution of ex-Tsar Nicholas II and family on orders of Ural Regional Council;
18th, great Allied counter-attack opens;
22nd, Allies cross R. Marne.

H **Aug**: 2nd, French recapture Soissons;
—, Japanese advance into Siberia;
3rd, British force lands at Vladivostok;
8th, H. A. L. Fisher introduces Education bill for England and Wales;
15th, U.S. and Russia sever diplomatic relations;
20th, British offensive on Western Front opens;
31st, Bolshevist troops attack British embassy at Petrograd.

J **Sep**: 1st, British take Péronne;
4th, Hsu Shi-chang elected President of Chinese Republic;
—, Germans retreat to Siegfried Line;
10th, Mahommedan riots in Calcutta;
12th, U.S. offensive at St. Mihiel salient;
14th, Austro-Hungarian peace offer (which Allies refuse, 20th);
15th, Allied break-through in Bulgaria;
22nd, collapse of Turkish resistance in Palestine;
29th, Belgians capture Dixmude;
—, Bulgaria signs armistice with Allies;
—, Paul von Hindenburg demands immediate peace offer;
30th, George, Count Hertling, German chancellor, resigns.

K **Oct**: 1st, British and Arab forces occupy Damascus;
—, French take St. Quentin;
3rd, Prince Max of Baden appointed German chancellor;
— (–4th), German-Austrian note to U.S., via Switzerland, for armistice;
6th, French occupy Beirut;
9th, British take Cambrai and Le Cateau;
12th, Germany and Austria agree to Woodrow Wilson's terms, that their troops should retreat to their own territory before armistice is signed;
13th, Laon falls to French and, 17th, Lille to British troops;
17th, republic of Yugoslavia formally established;
19th, Belgians recapture Zeebrugge and Bruges;
20th, Germany suspends submarine warfare;
22nd, influenza epidemic in Britain at its height;
26th, Ludendorff dismissed;
30th, Allies sign armistice with Turkey;
—, Czechoslovakia proclaimed as an independent republic in Prague;
31st, Hungarian premier, Count Tisza, assassinated.

L **Nov**: 1st, Anglo-French forces occupy Constantinople;
3rd, Allies sign armistice with Austria-Hungary (to come into force 4th);

W **Drama and Entertainment** (*cont.*)

The Bing Boys on Broadway (revue).
Veritas Vincit (film).
Charlie Chaplin in *Shoulder Arms* and *A Dog's Life* (films).

X **Sport**

Y **Statistics**

Merchant shipping losses by Britain (in tons): Jan.–Mar., 697,668; Apr.–June, 630,862; July–Sept., 512,030; Oct.–Dec., 83,952.
World total of shipping losses, 1914–1918, 15 mill. tons of which 9 mill. was British.

Naval Losses, 1914–18

	Dread-noughts	Pre-Dread-noughts	Battle Cruisers	Cruisers	Light Cruisers	De-stroyers	Sub-marines
British Empire	2	11	3	13	12	64	54
France	—	4	—	5	—	13	12
Germany	—	1	1	6	17	68	200
Austria	2	1	—	—	3	6	11
Turkey	—	1	—	—	1	3	—
Italy	1	3	—	1	2	9	7
Russia	2	2	—	2	—	18	15
Japan	1	—	1	—	2	1	—
U.S.	—	—	—	1	—	2	2

Casualties, 1914–18 (in thousands):

	Killed	*Wounded*	*Missing*
British Empire	767	2,090	132
France	1,383	2,560	—
U.S.	81	179	1
Italy	564	1,030	—
Germany	1,686	4,211	991
Russia*	1,700	2,500	—

* To Peace of Brest-Litovsk.

Z **Births and Deaths**

Jan. 15th Gamal Abdel Nasser b. (–1970).
Jan. 26th Nicolae Ceauşescu b. (–1989).
Mar. 6th J. E. Redmond d. (62).
Mar. 26th Claude Debussy d. (56).
May 11th Richard Feynman b. (–1988).
Aug. 25th Leonard Bernstein b. (–1990).
Sept. 27th Martin Ryle b. (–1984).
Oct. 7th Charles Hubert Hastings Parry d. (70).
Nov. 7th Billy Graham b. (–).
Dec. 2nd Edmund Rostand d. (50).
Dec. 11th Alexander Solzhenitsyn b. (–).
Dec. 23rd Helmut Schmidt b. (–).
Dec. 25th Anwar Sadat b. (–1981).
Nelson Mandela b. (–).

L **Nov**: 3rd, German grand fleet mutinies at Kiel;
4th, Allied conference at Versailles agrees on peace terms for Germany;
5th, U.S. Congressional elections result in Republican majority of 43;
6th, Polish republic proclaimed in Cracow;
—, U.S. troops occupy Sedan;
8th, British take Maubeuge;
9th, republic proclaimed in Bavaria;
—, revolution in Berlin, Prince Max resigns, William II abdicates and a council of People's Delegates assumes power;
11th, armistice signed between Allies and Germany;
12th, Emperor Charles I abdicates in Austria (and, 13th, in Hungary);
—, Austria proclaims union with Germany;
13th, Soviet government annuls treaty of Brest-Litovsk;
14th, British Labour Party decides to secede from Coalition;
— (–21st), German fleet surrenders at sea;
—, German troops in Northern Rhodesia surrender;
—, T. Masaryk elected President of Czechoslovakia;
18th, Latvian independence;
—, Belgian troops enter Brussels and Antwerp;
22nd, D. Lloyd George and A. Bonar Law issue Coalition election manifesto;
29th, Nicholas King of Montenegro deposed and his kingdom united with Serbia under King Peter;
30th, Transylvania proclaims union with Roumania.

M **Dec**: 1st, Iceland becomes a sovereign state;
4th, Serbo-Croatian-Slovene Kingdom of Yugoslavia is proclaimed;
5th, Germans blockade Baltic;
6th, Allies occupy Cologne;
8th, Bolshevik rule in Estonia;
14th, in British general election Coalition have majority of 262 (Conservatives and Unionists, 395, Liberals, 163; Labour, 59, Sinn Fein, 73, others, 16);
—, Sidonio Paes, President of Portugal, assassinated;
—, Woodrow Wilson arrives in Paris for peace conference;
20th, Berlin conference of workers' and soldiers' delegates demands nationalisation of industries;
27th, Poles occupy Posen.

N

1919 (Jan.–Apr.) The Versailles Peace Conference—Mussolini founds Italian Fascist Party

A **Jan**: 3rd, Herbert Hoover becomes director-general of international organisation for relief of Europe;
4th, Bolsheviks take Riga;
5th (–11th), Communist (Spartacist) revolt in Berlin;
—, National Socialist Party formed in Germany;
7th, British Labour Party decide to go into opposition;
10th, British army takes over administration of Baghdad Railway;
— (–*Feb.* 4th), Soviet Republic of Bremen;
11th, Roumania annexes Transylvania;
16th, prohibition amendment to U.S. Constitution ratified by last of states;
17th, Ignace Paderewski premier of Poland (resigns *May* 18th);
18th, Peace Conference at Versailles opens under Georges Clemenceau's chairmanship;
21st, Sinn Fein Congress, Dublin, adopts declaration of independence;
23rd, Socialist victory in German elections;
25th, Allies withdraw from Shenkunsk after Bolshevik attack;
—, Peace Conference adopts principle of League of Nations;
29th, Czechoslovakians defeat Poles in Galicia.

B **Feb**: 2nd, monarchy proclaimed in Portugal;
3rd (–9th), Anton Denikin's White Russian Army routs Bolsheviks in Caucasus;
—, Woodrow Wilson presides at first League of Nations meeting, Paris;
—, international Socialist conference, Berne;
—, Bolsheviks capture Kiev;
11th, Friedrich Ebert elected President of German republic;
13th, Philipp Scheidemann, Socialist, forms cabinet in Germany;
14th, Woodrow Wilson lays League of Nations Covenant before Peace Conference (adopted *Mar.* 25th);
—, Bolsheviks invade Estonia;
20th, Ameer of Afghanistan murdered;
21st, Kurt Eisner, Bavarian premier, assassinated in Munich;
23rd, Benito Mussolini founds Fasci del Combattimento;
26th, Britain sets up Coal Commission under Lord Sankey (reports *June* 23rd);
28th, H. C. Lodge begins campaign in U.S. against League of Nations.

C **Mar**: 9th, bankruptcy of Canadian Grand Trunk Pacific Railway (is nationalised 1920);
10th, U.S. Supreme Court upholds conviction of Eugene V. Debs for espionage;
—, Nationalist riots in Cairo, following deportation of Said Zaghlul Pasha;
16th, Karl Renner, Socialist, appointed chancellor of Austria;
21st, Danube is thrown open to navigation;
—, Edmund Allenby becomes high commissioner in Egypt;
22nd, Soviet government formed in Budapest.

D **Apr**: 4th, Philippines demand independence;
—, Soviet Republic established in Bavaria (–*May* 1st).
5th, Éamon de Valéra is elected president of the Sinn Fein Dáil executive (suppressed *Sept.*);
7th, Allies evacuate Odessa and
8th, Red Army enters Crimea;
10th (–14th), riots in Portugal;
11th, referendum in New Zealand declares against Prohibition;
20th, King Nicholas is dethroned in Montenegro, which votes for union with Serbo-Croat-Slovene State (Yugoslavia);

O **Politics, Economics, Law and Education**

International Labour Organisation established.
Communist Third International founded.
J. M. Keynes, *The Economic Consequences of the Peace.*
Irving Fisher, *Stabilising the Dollar in Purchasing Power.*
British Housing Act empowers local authorities to raise money by issuing bonds.
Women over 20 are enfranchised in Germany.
German Ministry of Economics is established.

P **Science, Technology, Discovery, etc.**

Observations of the total eclipse of the sun (*May* 29th) bear out Albert Einstein's theory of relativity.
Ernest Rutherford's 'transmutation', producing a simpler atom from a complex one.
F. W. Aston builds mass-spectrograph and establishes the phenomena of isotopy.
Hans Vogt experiments with sound film system.
J. W. Alcock and A. W. Brown fly across the Atlantic in 16 hrs. 27 mins. (*June* 14th).
Ross Smith flies from London to Australia in 135 hours (*Dec.* 10th).
First successful helicopter flight; first motor scooter.
E. Shackleton, *South*, an account of his 1914–17 expedition.
Severe influenza epidemic (*Mar.*).

Q **Scholarship**

J. B. Huizinga, *The Waning of the Middle Ages.*
H. L. Mencken, *The American Language.*

R **Philosophy and Religion**

Henri Bergson, *L'énergie spirituelle.*
Havelock Ellis, *The Philosophy of Conflict.*
Dean W. R. Inge, *Outspoken Essays.*
Karl Barth, *The Epistle to the Romans.*
Enabling Act in Britain brings the Church Assembly into existence.

S **Art, Sculpture, Fine Arts and Architecture**

Painting:
P. Picasso, *Pierrot and Harlequin;* and sets for the *Three-Cornered Hat.*
A. Modigliani, *The Marchesa Casati.*
E. Munch, *The Murder.*
A. Munnings, *Zennor Hill.*
John Ruskin Centenary Exhibition, Royal Academy.

Sculpture:
Wax and plaster figures of dancers and horses, created by E. Degas 1890–1912, are cast in bronze.

Architecture:
The Bauhaus (School of Design, Building and Crafts) founded by W. Gropius in Weimar; transferred to Dessau, 1925.
E. Lutyens submits design for the Cenotaph, Whitehall.

T **Music**

M. de Falla, *Three-cornered Hat* (ballet).
La boutique fantasque (Diaghilev's production).
André Messager's *Monsieur Beaucaire* (operetta) with Maggie Teyte.
A. Busch founds string quartet.

D **Apr**: 28th, German delegates arrive at Peace Conference;
30th, Peace Conference grants German concession in Shantung to Japan, whereupon China leaves the Conference.

E **May**: 1st, great strike in Winnipeg (–*June* 15th);
—, Bavarian government troops capture Munich from Communists;
3rd, war between British India and Afghanistan (–*Aug.* 3rd);
6th, Peace Conference disposes of Germany's colonies, assigning German East Africa as a mandate to Britain, and German South-West Africa as a mandate to South Africa;
28th, Armenia declares its independence;
29th, Germany's counter-proposals to Peace Conference;
30th, Britain agrees on transfer of part of German South-West Africa to Belgium.

F **Jun**: 3rd, British reinforcements reach Archangel;
6th, Finland declares war on U.S.S.R.;
8th, Nicaragua asks U.S. for protection against Costa Rica;
9th, Red Army takes Ufa;
10th, Austria protests against terms of Peace Conference;
21st, Gustave Bauer, Socialist, forms cabinet in Germany, following P. Scheidemann's fall, 20th, for decision against signing Peace Treaty;
—, Francesco Nitti becomes premier of Italy;
—, German fleet is scuttled in Scapa Flow;
22nd, German national assembly at Weimar authorises signature of Peace Treaty (signed at Versailles, 28th);
28th, Britain and U.S. guarantee France in event of an unprovoked German attack, which U.S. later refuses to ratify.

G **Jul**: 12th, Britain and France authorise resumption of commercial relations with Germany;
12th, Edward Carson demands repeal of Home Rule and threatens to call out volunteers;
19th, peace celebrations in Britain;
26th, Indian government and Afghanistan peace conference at Rawalpindi (treaty signed *Aug.* 8th);
27th (–31st), race riots in Chicago;
31st, Germany adopts Weimar Constitution.

H **Aug**: 1st, Hungarian Socialist régime under Bela Kun overthrown;
4th, Roumanians enter Budapest;
5th, Mackenzie King elected Canadian Liberal leader;
—, Mustapha Kemal at Turkish Nationalist Congress declares himself independent of Istanbul, aiming to prevent further dismemberment of Turkey;
6th, Archduke Joseph becomes 'state governor' of Hungary (resigns 23rd, on Allies' demand);
9th, Anglo-Persian agreement at Teheran to preserve integrity of Persia;
10th, Anglo-White Russian forces defeat Soviet forces in North Dvina;
14th, revised Bavarian constitution;
15th (–*Nov.*), Prince of Wales visits Canada and U.S.;
22nd, Imperial Preference Provisions Act passed;
—, Joseph Ward resigns on break-up of Coalition in New Zealand;
23rd, U.S. Senate committee rejects Shantung clause of Versailles Treaty;
31st, press censorship abolished in Ireland.

U **Literature**

Sherwood Anderson, *Winesburg, Ohio.*
M. Beerbohm, *Seven Men.*
A. Gide, *La Symphonie pastorale.*
T. Hardy, *Collected Poems.*
V. Blasco Ibáñez, *The Four Horsemen of the Apocalypse.*
W. S. Maugham, *The Moon and Sixpence.*

V **The Press**

Arthur Mee founds *Children's Newspaper.*

W **Drama and Entertainment**

G. B. Shaw, *Heartbreak House.*
Arnold Bennett and Nigel Playfair manage the Birmingham Repertory Theatre.
J'Accuse (film).
Madame Dubarry (film).
Hedda Gabler (film).
The Mystery Man (film).
Growth of broadcasting by amateurs in U.S.

X **Sport**

Suzanne Lenglen dominates Wimbledon Lawn Tennis Championships.
U.S. boxer Jack Dempsey defeats Jess Willard to win World Heavy-weight title.

Y **Statistics**

Merchant fleets (in mill. tons): British Empire, 18·6; U.S., 13·1; Germany, 3·5; Japan, 2·3; France, 2·2; Norway, 1·9; Holland, 1·6; Italy, 1·4; Sweden, 1·0.

Z **Births and Deaths**

Jan. 5th Theodore Roosevelt d. (61).
Jan. 14th Giulio Andreotti b. (–).
Feb. 17th Wilfrid Laurier d. (78).
Apr. 4th William Crookes d. (86).
May 16th Liberace b. (–1987).
May 18th Margot Fonteyn b. (–1991).
June 6th Lord Carrington b. (–).
July 15th Iris Murdoch b. (–).
July 20th Edmund Hillary b. (–).
July 31st Primo Levi b. (–1987).
Aug. 8th Ernst Haeckel d. (85).
Aug 11th Andrew Carnegie d. (84).
Aug. 27th Louis Botha d. (57).
Aug. 28th G. N. Hounsfield b. (–).
Sept. 27th Adelina Patti d. (76).
Oct. 17th Henry Irving d. (49).
Oct. 18th Pierre Trudeau b. (–).
Oct. 22nd Doris Lessing b. (–).
Oct. 26th Mohammed Reza Shah Pahlevi b. (–1980).
Nov. 23rd P. F. Strawson b. (–).
Dec. 3rd Pierre Auguste Renoir d. (78).

1919 (Sep.–Dec.)

J **Sep**: 2nd, Anton Denikin's force enters Kiev;
10th, Allied peace treaty with Austria at St. Germain;
12th, Gabriele d'Annunzio leads unofficial Italian army to seize Fiume;
15th, China terminates war with Germany;
22nd, U.S. steel strike (–*Jan.* 1920);
25th, Peace Conference grants Norway sovereignty over Spitzbergen;
27th, British troops enter Archangel.

K **Oct**: 6th, Prohibition in Norway;
10th, Luxembourg referendum in favour of monarchy, with economic union with France;
12th, British withdraw from Murmansk;
13th, New York dock strike;
17th, Austria ratifies peace treaty;
22nd, Nicolai Yudenich, Russian counter-revolutionary, defeated by Red Army near St. Petersburg;
27th, George Curzon succeeds A. J. Balfour as British foreign secretary;
— (–8th), Woodrow Wilson vetoes Volstead Prohibition Enforcement bill, but House and Senate pass it;
28th, British War Cabinet ends;
29th, International Labour Conference at Washington.

L **Nov**: 7th, Allied Supreme Council demands withdrawal of Roumanian troops from Hungary;
11th, first 2-minutes' silence in Britain;
13th, U.S. Senate's resolution on article X of League of Nations Covenant amounts to virtual rejection of Peace Treaty;
15th, Red Army takes Omsk;
17th, Belgo-Dutch agreement on River Scheldt;
21st, Supreme Council gives Poland mandate over Galicia for 25 years;
27th, Peace of Neuilly between the Allies and Bulgaria;
28th, Latvia declares war on Germany;
—, Lady Astor elected first British woman M.P.

M **Dec**: 5th, Serbo-Croat-Slovene Kingdom agrees to peace treaties with Austria and Bulgaria;
9th, U.S. delegates leave Peace Conference;
13th, Soviets capture Kharkov from Anton Denikin;
15th, Fiume declares her independence;
16th, German troops evacuate Latvia and Lithuania;
19th, Liberals defeated in New Zealand elections;
20th, House of Representatives moves to curtail immigration;
31st, Britain, U.S., and Japan sign agreement over East Siberia.

N

A **Jan:** 5th, Poles and Letts capture Dvinsk from Bolsheviks;
8th, Admiral Alexander Koltchak defeated at Krasnoyarsk (he is executed by Bolsheviks *Feb.* 7th);
10th, The League of Nations comes into being;
—, Eupen and Malmédy united with Belgium;
13th, Argentina admitted to League;
16th, first meeting of Council of League in Paris;
—, Prohibition comes into force in U.S.;
—, U.S. Senate votes against joining League;
17th, Paul Deschanel becomes President of France;
23rd, Holland declines to surrender ex-Kaiser William II as demanded by Supreme Allied War Council;
28th, Turkish national pact of Ankara signed at Constantinople.

B **Feb:** 2nd, Estonia signs peace with U.S.S.R. and declares its independence;
8th, Bolsheviks capture Odessa;
9th, Allies cede Spitzbergen to Norway;
10th, plebiscite in Schleswig north zone favours uniting with Denmark (middle zone favours Germany, *Mar.* 14th);
13th, Switzerland is admitted to League;
15th, Allies take over Memel;
25th, Bainbridge Colby becomes U.S. secretary of state, following Robert Lansing's resignation, 13th;
26th, League takes over the Saar;
—, U.S.S.R. sends Allies new peace offer;
27th, Allies announce that Turkey will retain Constantinople, but Dardanelles to be under international control;
28th, Hungarian and, 29th, Czechoslovak constitutions are adopted.

C **Mar:** 1st, Nicholas Horthy elected Regent of Hungary;
—, U.S. government returns railways to companies;
5th, Norway, 8th, Denmark and 10th, Netherlands are admitted to League;
10th, Ulster votes to accept Home Rule bill;
11th, Emir Feisal proclaimed King of an independent Syria;
13th (–17th), Wolfgang Kapp attempts pro-monarchist *coup d'état* in Berlin;
16th, Allies occupy Constantinople;
19th, U.S. Senate finally rejects Versailles Treaty;
28th, Bolsheviks take Novorossiisk on Black Sea; collapse of Anton Denikin's White Russian army.

D **Apr:** 6th (–*May* 17th), French troops occupy Frankfurt, Darmstadt and Hanau until Germany evacuates Ruhr;
25th, Supreme Allied Council assigns mandates of Mesopotamia and Palestine to Britain and of Syria and the Lebanon to France;
—, Polish offensive in the Ukraine under Josef Pilsudski against U.S.S.R. (–*Oct.* 12th);
30th, conscription abolished in Britain.

E **May:** 5th, Woodrow Wilson rules that Communist Labor Party of America is outside scope of U.S. deportation laws;
5th, treaty of Berlin between Germany and Latvia;
8th, Poles and Ukrainians enter Kiev;
11th, Turkish national assembly meets at Ankara;
20th, President Carranza of Mexico assassinated; succeeded by Adolfo de la Huerta;

O Politics, Economics, Law and Education

Prohibition in U.S. (*Jan.* 16th).
German National Economic Council established.
W. Sombart, *Der Moderne Kapitalismus.*
Oswald Spengler, *Prussianism and Socialism.*
Slump in U.S.
Welwyn Garden City is established.
Royal Institute of International Affairs, London, founded.

P Science, Technology, Discovery, etc.

Baade discovers the asteroid Hidalgo, which orbits farthest from the sun.
J. T. Thompson invents sub-machine gun.
The decade of 'lighter than air' airships begins.
Discovery of the skeletons of Peking Man ('*Sinanthropus*').

Q Scholarship

H. G. Wells, *Outline of History.*

R Philosophy and Religion

C. G. Jung, *Psychological Types.*
J. Maritain, *Art et scolastique.*

S Art, Sculpture, Fine Arts and Architecture

Painting:
Juan Gris, *Guitar, Book and Newspaper.*
S. Spencer, *Christ Bearing the Cross* and *The Last Supper.*
H. Matisse, *The Odalisque.*
A. Modigliani, *Reclining Nude.*
Spectators at Cologne Exhibition of Dadaist art allowed to smash paintings.
Antoine Pevsner and Naum Gabo issue the *Realistic Manifesto*, containing the principles of European Constructivism.
Bernard Leach establishes Leach Pottery at St Ives, Cornwall.

T Music

Vincent D'Indy, *The Legend of St. Christopher* (oratorio).
Erik Satie, *Socrate* (opera).
I. Stravinsky's ballet *Pulcinella* and *Le Chant du Rossignol.*
Marie Rambert founds the Rambert School of Ballet in London, leading to the establishment of the Marie Rambert Dancers.
Louis Durey, Darius Milhaud, Germaine Tailleferre, Arthur Honegger, Georges Auric and Francis Poulenc form 'Les Six'.

U Literature

Colette, *Chéri.*
J. Galsworthy, *In Chancery.*
Franz Kafka, *The Country Doctor.*
Sinclair Lewis, *Main Street.*
Katherine Mansfield (pseud.), *Bliss.*
Sigrid Undset, *Kristin Lavransdatter* (–22).
P. Valéry, *Le Cimetière marin.*

V The Press

Time and Tide issued.

W Drama and Entertainment

J. Galsworthy, *The Skin Game.*
E. O'Neill, *Beyond the Horizon.*

E **May**: 27th, Woodrow Wilson vetoes Knox peace resolution terminating state of war with Germany;
—, Leonid Krassin, Soviet trade delegate, arrives in London.

F **Jun**: 4th, treaty of Trianon between the Allies and Hungary;
12th, Republican Convention at Chicago nominates Warren G. Harding for presidency and Calvin Coolidge for vice-presidency;
20th, federal water power act in U.S.;
21st, Konstantin Fehrenback becomes chancellor of Germany;
—, Supreme Allied Council agrees that Germany shall make 42 annual reparations payments largely to France, Britain, Italy and Belgium;
24th, Greek offensive in Asia Minor against Turkish nationalists;
25th, The Hague selected as seat of International Court of Justice.

G **Jul**: 1st, Robert Borden resigns in Canada (succeeded as premier, 10th, by Arthur Meighen);
5th, Democratic convention nominates James M. Cox for presidency, F. D. Roosevelt for vice-presidency;
— (–16th), Spa Conference between Allies and Germany on reparations;
—, Schleswig is transferred to Denmark;
6th, Britain evacuates Batum;
—, U.S.S.R. offensive against Poland opens;
8th, Britain annexes East African Protectorate as Kenya Colony;
11th, plebiscite in East and West Prussia 97 per cent for Germany;
12th, U.S.S.R.-Lithuanian peace treaty;
21st, Sinn Feiners and Unionists riot in Belfast;
—, King Feisal recognises French mandate in Syria;
24th, treaty of St. Germain (signed *Sept.* 1919), comes into force;
25th, France occupies Damascus;
Greeks under King Alexander occupy Adrianople;
27th, Russians take Pinsk and cross into Poland;
28th, Teschen agreement between Czechoslovakia and Poland signed in Paris.

H **Aug**: 8th, U.S.S.R. again rejects proposal for armistice with Poland;
9th, British Labour organisations appoint Council of Action to arrange general strike if Britain declares war on U.S.S.R.;
10th, New States treaty between Allies, Roumania, Czechoslovakia and Poland; and frontier treaty with Roumania, Czechoslovakia and the Serbo-Croat-Slovene Kingdom (Yugoslavia);
—, Graeco-Italian treaty assigns Dodecanese Isles to Greece;
—, Constantinople government signs the Treaty of Sèvres, representing a break between the Nationalists and the Sultan;
11th, Riga treaty between U.S.S.R. and Latvia;
14th, Yugoslav-Czechoslovak alliance, which is joined, 17th, by Roumania to form 'Little Entente';
— (–16th), Poles defeat Russians at Warsaw;
18th, Milner-Zaghlul conversations provide for recognition of Egyptian independence;
19th, Poles enter Brest-Litovsk;
26th, Nineteenth Amendment gives women the vote in U.S.

J **Sep**: 5th, Alvaro Obregón becomes President of Mexico;
7th, Franco-Belgian military convention;
10th, Russo-British negotiations are suspended owing to Russian attempt to subsidise *Daily Herald*;

W **Drama and Entertainment (*cont.*)**

First public broadcasting station in Britain opened by G. Marconi at Writtle (*Feb.*); first broadcasting station in U.S. opened at East Pittsburgh (*Nov.* 2nd) by Westinghouse Company to give Harding-Cox election results.

Paul Whiteman's band visits Europe and the rage for jazz becomes universal.

British Board of Film Censors established.

The Cabinet of Dr. Caligari with Conrad Veidt (film).

The Mother and *Polyanna* with Mary Pickford (films).

Mary Pickford marries Douglas Fairbanks.

X **Sport**

Olympic Games held at Antwerp.

William T. Tilden, America, wins Wimbledon Lawn Tennis Championships.

English cricketer Percy Fender achieves 100 runs in 35 minutes.

Y **Statistics**

Coal production (in mill. tons): U.S., 645·5; Great Britain, 229·5; Germany, 107·5.

Petroleum production (in mill. barrels): U.S., 443; Mexico, 163; Russia, 25; Dutch East Indies, 17; Persia, 12; India, 7; Roumania, 7; Poland, 5.

Motor vehicles licensed: U.S., 8,887,000; Great Britain, 663,000.

Strikes:

	No. of workers involved	No. of working-days lost
Great Britain	1,932,000	27,011,000
U.S.	1,463,054	—
France	1,487,996	24,563,527

The Courts: In Britain 3,747 divorces are granted; 95,763 convictions for drunkenness.

Z **Births and Deaths**

Jan. 2nd Isaac Asimov b. (–1992).
Jan. 4th Benito Pérez Galdós d. (75).
Jan. 20th Federico Fellini b. (–).
Feb. 19th Robert Edwin Peary d. (64).
Mar. 24th Mrs. Humphry Ward d. (69).
May 11th William Dean Howells d. (82).
May 18th John Paul II b. (–).
July 4th Max Klinger d. (63).
July 10th John, Lord Fisher, d. (79).
July 11th Empress Eugénie d. (94).
Sept. 1st Wilhelm Wundt d. (88).
Oct. 10th Thelonius Monk b. (–1982).
Nov. 20th Jesse Collings d. (89).

J **Sep**: 23rd, Alexandre Millerand elected President of France as successor to Paul Deschanel, resigned from ill health, 16th.

K **Oct**: 1st, new Austrian constitution;
9th, Poland annexes Vilna;
10th, plebiscite in Carinthia favours Austria;
12th, U.S.S.R.-Polish peace treaty signed at Tartu;
20th, treaty of Ankara between France and Turkey;
—, U.S.-Chinese tariff treaty;
27th, Poland signs treaty with Danzig;
—, League of Nations headquarters are moved to Geneva.

L **Nov**: 2nd, Warren G. Harding, Republican, elected President of U.S. with 404 electoral votes against James M. Cox, Democrat, 127;
7th (–*Dec.* 21st), serious famine in China;
12th, by treaty of Rapallo Italy obtains Istria and cedes Dalmatia to Serbo-Croat-Slovene Kingdom (Yugoslavia) while Fiume is to be independent;
14th, Red Army takes Sebastopol;
15th, Danzig is declared a free city;
16th, end of Russian counter-revolution;
17th, Dowager Queen Olga becomes Regent of Greece;
19th, convention between Nicaragua, Honduras and Costa Rica.

M **Dec**: 2nd, by treaty of Alexandropol, Armenia cedes territory to Turkey;
3rd, Austria joins the League;
5th, plebiscite in Greece favours return of King Constantine (who returns 19th);
9th, Michael Hainisch elected first President of Austria;
10th, Woodrow Wilson and Léon Bourgeois awarded Nobel Peace Prize;
12th, martial law in Cork;
15th (–22nd), Brussels conference on Germany's reparations;
16th, Bulgaria, Costa Rica, Finland and Latvia, and
17th, Albania are admitted to the League;
23rd, Government of Ireland Act passed; Northern and Southern Ireland each to have own parliament;
—, Franco-British convention on boundaries of Syria and Palestine;
29th, French Socialist Conference votes for adhesion to Moscow International.

N

A **Jan**: 3rd, first Indian Parliament meets;
10th, Leipzig war trials before German supreme court begin;
16th, Aristide Briand forms ministry in France;
22nd, deportation of Mantes, self-styled U.S.S.R. ambassador to U.S.;
24th (–29th), Paris conference of the Allies fixes Germany's reparation payments;
25th, U.S. Senate adopts resolution on suspension of naval contracts.

B **Feb**: 4th, James Craig elected United Ulster leader;
8th, Jan C. Smuts gains majority of 20 in South African elections;
9th, peace treaty of Riga between U.S.S.R. and Poland;
12th, W. S. Churchill becomes colonial secretary;
18th, recall of U.S. representative from Reparation Commission;
21st, London conference of Allies on the Near East;
26th, U.S.S.R. signs treaties with Persia and, 28th, with Afghanistan;
27th, riots between Communists and Fascists in Florence.

C **Mar**: 1st, Turkish treaty with Afghanistan;
4th, President Warren G. Harding inaugurated;
5th, U.S. warns Costa Rica and Panama to settle frontier dispute by arbitration;
8th, French troops occupy Düsseldorf and other towns in Ruhr on grounds of Germany's failure to make preliminary reparations payment;
11th, France in treaty with Turkey renounces Cilicia;
15th, Ruanda, East Africa, ceded to Britain by Belgian convention;
16th, Anglo-U.S.S.R. trade agreement and British trade mission visits Moscow;
17th, A. Bonar Law resigns Unionist leadership in Commons;
—, Polish Constitution established;
18th, by treaty of Riga with U.S.S.R., Poland abandons claim to the Ukraine;
20th, in Upper Silesian plebiscite 63 per cent vote for incorporation with Germany;
21st, Austen Chamberlain elected Unionist leader;
23rd, Germany announces she will be unable to pay £600 mill. due as reparations on *May* 1st;
24th, British Reparation Recovery act imposes 50 per cent duties on German goods (reduced, *May* 20th, to 26 per cent);
—, Communist riots in Hamburg;
25th, U.S. refuses U.S.S.R. request to resume trading;
27th, ex-Emperor Charles's *coup* in Hungary fails;
28th, British I.L.P. refuses to affiliate with Communists;
31st, strike of British miners.

D **Apr**: 12th, President Harding declares U.S. could play no part in the League;
19th, Government of Ireland Act in force;
23rd, Czechoslovak-Roumanian alliance;
24th, plebiscite in Tyrol favours Germany;
—, Germany unsuccessfully asks U.S. to mediate in reparations controversy;
General Erich von Ludendorff is acquitted of breaches of laws of war by Leipzig court;
27th, Reparations Commission fixes Germany's total liability at £6,650 mill.

E **May**: 2nd, French troops are mobilised for occupation of Ruhr;
5th, Allied Supreme Council warns Germany that failure to pay reparations, by 12th, will lead to occupation of Ruhr;
6th, German-U.S.S.R. peace treaty signed;
8th, capital punishment is abolished in Sweden;
10th, in German cabinet crisis Julius Wirth, Catholic Centre Party, becomes chancellor;

O **Politics, Economics, Law and Education**

James Bryce, *Modern Democracies.*
Gilbert Murray, *The Problem of Foreign Policy.*
Bertrand Russell, *The Prospects of Industrial Civilisation.*
Stern-Rubarth, *Propaganda as a Political Weapon.*
'Chequers', presented to the nation by Lord Lee of Fareham, becomes the official country residence of the Prime Minister (*Jan.* 8th).
British Broadcasting Company founded.
British Legion founded (*May* 24th).
National Institute of Industrial Psychology, London, founded.
Belgium and Luxembourg form a customs union, though in the rest of Europe high tariffs return.
New Economic Policy in U.S.S.R. (*Mar.*) witnesses a partial return of capitalism.

P **Science, Technology, Discovery, etc.**

Ernest Rutherford and James Chadwick disintegrate all the elements, except carbon, oxygen, lithium and beryllium, as preliminary to splitting the atom (–24).
First medium-wave wireless broadcast, in U.S.

Q **Scholarship**

Institute of Historical Research, London, founded, with A. F. Pollard as director.
Lytton Strachey, *Queen Victoria.*

R **Philosophy and Religion**

H. Hartmann, *Philosophy of Knowledge.*
John M'Taggart, *The Nature of Existence.*
Teschner, *Telepathy and Clairvoyance.*

S **Art, Sculpture, Fine Arts and Architecture**

Painting:
P. Klee, *The Fish.*
Georges Braque, *Still Life with Guitar.*
Fernand Léger, *Three Women.*
E. Munch, *The Kiss.*
P. Picasso, *Three Musicians.*
Architecture:
Micheal de Klerk, Eigen Haard flats, Amsterdam.

T **Music**

Arthur Honegger, *King David* (opera, later revised as oratorio).
Serge Prokofiev, *Love of Three Oranges* (opera).
Musicians' Union founded, London.

U **Literature**

Agatha Christie, *The Mysterious Affair at Styles.*
A. Huxley, *Crome Yellow.*
D. H. Lawrence, *Women in Love.*
John Galsworthy, *To Let.*
George Moore, *Héloïse and Abelard.*
John Dos Passos, *Three Soldiers.*
Italo Svevo, *The Confessions of Zeno.*
P. Valéry, *L'Âme de la danse.*

V **The Press**

E **May**: 11th, Germany accepts Allies' ultimatum on reparations;
14th, 29 Fascists returned in Italian elections;
19th, U.S. Emergency Quota Immigration act;
20th, Germany and China resume diplomatic relations;
28th, Walter Rathenau appointed German minister for reparations;
—, Egyptian Nationalist riots at Alexandria;
30th, plebiscite in Salzburg favours union with Germany.

F **Jun**: 5th, Italy, Serbia and Yugoslavia agree on control of Fiume;
7th, U.S. refuses to recognise Mexican government until international obligations are honoured;
—, first Parliament of Northern Ireland opens;
—, Roumanian-Yugoslav alliance;
19th, the powers agree to mediate between Turkey and Greece (but, 25th, Greece refuses the offer);
20th, London Imperial Conference;
22nd, Labour Conference of Great Britain rejects affiliation with Communists;
27th, Afghanistan-Persian treaty.

G **Jul**: 1st, Safeguarding of Industries Act in Britain to prevent dumping of foreign manufactures;
11th, British truce with Sinn Fein;
16th, Greeks defeat Turks at Kutahia;
23rd, convention for internationalisation of Danube;
25th, Belgium and Luxembourg sign 50-year economic pact;
29th, All-India Congress decides to boycott Prince of Wales's visit.

H **Aug**: 11th, U.S. invites powers to conference on Far East and the limitation of armaments;
12th, Allied Supreme Council refers Upper Silesia question to League;
23rd, Dáil rejects British peace offer;
24th, U.S. signs peace treaties with Austria;
—, (–*Sept.* 16th), in battle of the Sakkaria, the Turks prevent Greek forces from reaching Ankara;
25th, U.S. signs peace treaties with Germany, and 29th, with Hungary;
26th, German finance minister Mathias Erzberger assassinated;
29th (–*Dec.* 16th), state of emergency proclaimed in Germany in the face of economic crisis.

J **Sep**: 9th, constitution of Central American Union signed by republics of Guatemala, Honduras and San Salvador;
22nd, Estonia, Latvia and Lithuania are admitted to the League;
30th, Anglo-Russian commercial agreement;
—, French troops evacuate Ruhr.

K **Oct**: 6th, Franco-German agreement for supply of reparations in kind;
18th, U.S.S.R. central executive grants independence to Crimea;
19th, revolution in Lisbon;
20th, Franco-Turkish agreement signed at Ankara;
25th (–6th), Poland and Germany accept League proposal for partition of Upper Silesia;
—, ex-Emperor Charles is expelled from Hungary on failure of further attempted *coup*;
27th, Germany agrees to accept Allies' conditions on reparations.

(*Continued opposite*)

W **Drama and Entertainment**

Gabriel Marcel, *La Grâce*.
Eugene O'Neill, *The Emperor Jones*.
Jean Sarment, *Le Pêcheur d'ombres*.
Rapid development of night clubs.
Charles Chaplin in *The Kid* (film).
Hunger! Hunger! Hunger! (film).
Anne Boleyn (film).
The Adventuress from Monte Carlo (film).

X **Sport**

Australia wins the Ashes.

Y **Statistics**

Populations (in mill.): U.S.S.R., 136; U.S., 107; Japan, 78; Germany, 60; Great Britain, 42·7; France, 39·2; Italy, 38·7.
Petroleum production: U.S., 472 mill. barrels.

Z **Births and Deaths**

Jan. 1st César b. (–).
Mar. 25th Mary Douglas b. (–).
May 2nd Satyajit Ray b. (–1992).
May 12th Joseph Beuys b. (–1986).
Aug. 17th G. R. Elton b. (–).
Sept. 2nd Austin Dobson d. (81).
Sept. 27th Engelbert Humperdinck d. (67).
Oct. 2nd Robert Runcie b. (–).
Nov. 27th Alexander Dubček b. (–1992).
Dec. 16th Camille Saint-Säens d. (86).

L **Nov:** 1st, Otto Braun, Socialist, forms ministry in Prussia;
4th, Takashi Hara, premier of Japan, assassinated;
5th, U.S.S.R. treaty with government of Mongolia;
12th, powers recognise Albanian government;
— (–*Feb.* 6th, 1922), Washington Conference on disarmament;
Rapid fall of the German Mark.

M **Dec:** 6th, Britain signs peace with Ireland;
6th, Liberals defeat Conservatives in Canadian election;
7th, U.S. and Austria resume diplomatic relations;
11th, British arrest president of Indian National Congress;
13th, U.S., British Empire, France and Japan sign Washington treaty to respect each other's rights over insular possessions in the Pacific, and by this treaty the U.S. is drawn into consultation with other powers in matters of common concern;
14th, in Ödenburg plebiscite 65 per cent vote for union with Hungary, as against Czechoslovakia;
15th, Germany applies for moratorium for payments;
21st, U.S.S.R.-Turkish alliance;
—, William Hughes becomes premier of Australia in Nationalist cabinet reconstruction;
27th, Italian-U.S.S.R. commercial agreement;
29th, U.S., British Empire, France, Italy and Japan sign Washington treaty to limit naval armaments;
—, Mackenzie King, Liberal, becomes premier of Canada.

N

1922 (Jan.–Jun.) Irish Rebellion—Mussolini's march on Rome—Fall of Lloyd George

A **Jan**: 7th, The Dáil approves treaty with Britain and
9th, motion for re-election of Éamon de Valéra as president is defeated;
10th, Arthur Griffith elected head of provisional government of Southern Ireland;
—, strike in Rand gold mines;
13th, Cannes conference decides to postpone Germany's reparation payments;
15th, Raymond Poincaré forms ministry in France (following Aristide Briand's resignation, 12th);
—, Irish government formed under Michael Collins;
26th, legislative council of Southern Rhodesia accepts draft constitution conferring limited self-government;
31st, Walter Rathenau becomes German foreign minister.

B **Feb**: 1st, Washington conference approves treaties restricting submarine warfare and poison gas;
4th, Japan agrees to restore Shantung to China;
6th, Cardinal Achille Ratti elected Pope Pius XI, following Benedict XV's death, *Jan.* 22nd;
11th, nine-power treaty of Washington for securing China's independence and maintaining the 'open door';
—, U.S.-Japanese naval agreement;
—, Honduras becomes an independent republic;
15th, Permanent Court of International Justice holds first sessions at The Hague;
21st, British protectorate in Egypt ended.

C **Mar**: 1st, U.S.S.R.-Swedish trade agreement;
6th, U.S. prohibits export of arms to China;
10th, strikes and martial law in Johannesburg;
15th, modified reparations agreement, for Germany to pay with raw materials, signed by France and Germany (approved by Commission, 31st);
—, de Valéra organises a Republican Society, to fight Nationalists;
16th, Britain recognises Kingdom of Egypt under Fuad I, with joint Anglo-Egyptian sovereignty over Sudan;
17th, Baltic states and Poland sign agreement on neutrality;
18th, Mahatma Gandhi sentenced to six years' imprisonment for civil disobedience;
20th, President W. Harding orders return of U.S. troops from Rhineland.

D **Apr**: 1st, U.S. coal strike (–*Aug.* 15th);
—, South Africa denounces Mozambique Convention;
7th, Britain concedes to Standard Oil Co. rights in Palestine;
10th (–*May* 19th), economic conference of European powers at Genoa;
14th, Irish rebels seize the Four Courts, Dublin, from the Free State government;
16th, treaty of Rapallo between Germany and U.S.S.R. recognises U.S.S.R. as 'a great power' and leads to the resumption of diplomatic and trade relations.

E **May**: 10th, Genoa convention between U.S.S.R. and the Vatican;
15th, Germany cedes Upper Silesia to Poland;
24th, Italy signs commercial treaty with U.S.S.R.

F **Jun**: 5th, Medal of Congress presented to people of Verdun;
10th, bankers' committee of Reparations Commission declines to recommend international loan for Germany;
16th, polling in Southern Ireland gives majority to Pro-Treaty candidates;
20th, independent citizenship for U.S. women marrying aliens;

O **Politics, Economics, Law and Education**

Herbert Hoover, *American Individualism.*
C. E. Montague, *Disenchanted.*
Lady Rhondda is permitted to take a seat in House of Lords by Committee of Privileges, but this judgment is later reversed.
Report of Geddes Economy Committee leads to severe cuts in expenditure on British armed and civil services and on education.
Revival of Ku-Klux-Klan in U.S.
Fordney-McComber Act drastically raises U.S. tariff.
C. Pestalozzi, *The Argument about Co-education.*
International Union for Cultural Co-operation, Vienna.
U.S. forms 'Prohibition Navy' to prevent widespread liquor smuggling.
Marie Stopes holds series of meetings in Queen's Hall, London, advocating birth control.

P **Science, Technology, Discovery, etc.**

Niels Bohr's theory that electrons travel in concentric orbits round the atomic nucleus.
P. S. M. Blackett's experiments in transmutation of elements.
The element hafnium discovered.
Heyrowsky's electro-chemical analysis.
Frederick Banting and Best isolate insulin and a diabetic patient in Toronto receives an insulin injection.
First ionamide dyes are prepared.
John Harwood invents self-winding wrist-watch.
The 'Austin Seven' popularises motoring in Britain.

Q **Scholarship**

Lord Carnarvon and Howard Carter discover the tomb of Tutankhamūn at Luxor (*Nov.*).

R **Philosophy and Religion**

James Dewey, *Human Nature.*
Étienne Gilson, *The Philosophy of the Middle Ages.*
E. Troeltsch, *Historismus.*
Ludwig Wittgenstein writes *Tractatus Logico-Philosophicus.*

S **Art, Sculpture, Fine Arts and Architecture**

Painting:
Paul Klee, *The Machine Song.*
Joan Miró, *The Farm.*
P. W. Steer, *Mrs. Raynes* and *Victor Lecour.*
Max Beerbohm, *Rossetti and his Circle* (drawings of artists).
M. Chagall, *Dead Souls* (85 etchings, published 1948).
Clive Bell publishes *Since Cézanne.*
David Low, *Lloyd George and Co.* (a book of political cartoons).
Architecture:
E. Freyssinet, Bridge of St. Pierre-du-Vauvray.
L.C.C. County Hall opened.

T **Music**

A. Bliss, 'Colour' Symphony.
P. Hindemith, *St. Susanna* (opera).
F. Lehár, *Frasquita* (operetta).

F **Jun**: 24th, Walter Rathenau (aged 55) is murdered by Nationalists;
26th, emergency decree in Germany to protect the economy of the republic;
28th, dispute between the Reich and Bavaria;
—, British Labour Party declines to reconsider affiliation with Communist Party;
—, siege of Four Courts, Dublin, and
30th, rebel forces surrender to Free State troops.

G **Jul**: 2nd (–5th), heavy fighting in Dublin;
8th, Chile and Peru agree to submit Tacna-Arica dispute to arbitration;
20th, League Council approves mandates for Togoland, the Cameroons and Tanganyika and
24th, for Palestine and Egypt;
29th, ultimatum of Allied Powers forbidding Greek occupation of Constantinople;
30th, Nationalists capture Tipperary.

H **Aug**: 1st, Balfour Note circulated to Allies, stating that Britain would only expect to recover from her European debtors the sum which the U.S. expected from her, thus placing the odium of war debts on U.S.;
—, Britain, France and Italy warn Greece against attempted occupation of Palestine;
4th (–8th), fighting between Fascists and Socialists in Italian cities;
22nd, Michael Collins (aged 30), chairman of Irish Provisional Government, killed by Republican ambush;
24th, Arab Congress at Nablus rejects British mandate for Palestine;
31st, Czecho-Serbo-Croat alliance signed at Marienbad;
—, Reparations Commission adopts Belgian proposal for Germany's payments by instalments on Treasury bills.

J **Sep**: 9th, William T. Cosgrave elected President of Irish Free State (following Arthur Griffith's death, *Aug.* 12th);
10th, Anglo-U.S.S.R. commercial treaty, which U.S.S.R. refuses in *Oct.* to ratify;
11th, British mandate proclaimed in Palestine while Arabs declare a day of mourning;
13th, Franco-Polish 10-year military convention;
18th, Hungary is admitted to the League;
21st, U.S. protectionist tariff;
27th, King Constantine of Greece abdicates;
30th, conscription in U.S.S.R.

K **Oct**: 4th, Austria receives international loan;
10th, Graeco-Turkish armistice;
11th, Mundania conference between Allies and Turkey ends in agreement regarding neutral zones, with Greece undertaking to evacuate Thrace;
17th, unemployed workers leave Glasgow on hunger march to London;
19th, fall of D. Lloyd George's Coalition;
23rd, A. Bonar Law forms Conservative ministry in Britain;
24th, Dáil adopts a Constitution for Irish Free State;
—, Friedrich Ebert re-elected Reich President;
27th, Italian cabinet resigns;
—, referendum in Southern Rhodesia votes against joining Union of South Africa;
28th, Benito Mussolini marches on Rome, and
30th, forms Fascist government.

L **Nov**: 1st, Kemal Pasha proclaims Turkish republic;
—, civil war renewed in China;

T **Music** (*cont.*)

M. Ravel, sonata for violin and 'cello.
O. Respighi, 'Gregorian' violin concerto.
I. Stravinsky, *Mavra* (opera).
R. Vaughan Williams, 3rd Symphony ('Pastoral').

U **Literature**

John Buchan, *Huntingtower*.
R. M. du Gard, *Les Thibault* (–40).
T. S. Eliot, *The Waste Land*.
James Joyce, *Ulysses* (published in Paris).
D. H. Lawrence, *Aaron's Rod*.
Sinclair Lewis, *Babbitt*.
Katharine Mansfield (pseud.), *The Garden Party*.
R. M. Rilke, *Sonette am Orpheus*.
Hugh Walpole, *The Cathedral*.
P.E.N., London, founded by Mrs. Dawson Scott.

V **The Press**

Criterion issued.

W **Drama and Entertainment**

B. Brecht, *Drums in the Night*.
A. A. Milne, *The Dover Road*.
George Grossmith introduces cabaret entertainment.
The debut of the 'cocktail'.
Launch of Chanel No. 5 perfume.
Lilac Time (G. H. Clutsam—musical).

Films:
The Last of the Mohicans.
Glorious Adventure.
Pharaoh's Wife.
Dr. Mabuse.

British Broadcasting Company founded (*Dec.* J. C. Reith appointed General Manager).

X **Sport**

English cricketer Percy Fender achieves 50 runs off 14 balls.

Y **Statistics**

British Textile trade:

Imports of raw cotton	1,409 mill. lb.
Exports of cottons	4,313 mill. yds.
Exports of linens	77 mill. yds.
Exports of silks	5 mill. sq. yds.

T.U. membership: 5,625,000 in Great Britain.

Strikes:

	No. of workers involved	No. of working-days lost
Great Britain	552,000	19,850,000
France	307,056	3,385,902
U.S.	1,608,321	—

L **Nov**: 2nd (–7th), Berlin conference of monetary experts on German currency;
7th, reduced Republican majority in U.S. Congressional elections;
17th, Far Eastern Republic votes for union with U.S.S.R.;
—, in British general election Conservatives win 344 seats, Labour 138 and Liberals 117;
22nd, Wilhelm Cuno becomes German chancellor;
24th, execution of Erskine Childers in Ireland;
28th, six ex-ministers of Greece executed.

M **Dec**: 1st, Josef Pilsudski, President of Poland, resigns;
6th, Irish Free State officially proclaimed;
7th, Northern Ireland Parliament votes for non-inclusion in Irish Free State;
15th, Franco-Canadian trade agreement;
16th, in Australian elections Nationalists win 27 seats, Labour 29 and the Country Party 14;
17th, last British troops leave Irish Free State;
26th, Reparations Commission, against British vote, declares Germany has made a voluntary default in payments.

N

z **Births and Deaths**

Jan. 5th Ernest Shackleton d. (48).
Jan. 22nd James Viscount Bryce d. (84).
Feb. 24th Richard Hamilton b. (–).
Apr. 7th A. V. Dicey d. (87).
Apr. 16th Kingsley Amis b. (–).
Apr. 22nd Charlie Mingus b. (–1979).
May 15th Leslie Ward ('Spy'), d. (71).
Aug. 1st Alexander Graham Bell d. (75).
Aug. 14th Alfred Harmsworth, Lord Northcliffe, d. (57).
Aug. 18th W. H. Hudson d. (81).
Oct. 7th 'Marie Lloyd' (pseud. of Matilda Wood) d. (76).
Nov. 8th Christiaan Barnard b. (–).
Nov. 15th Marcel Proust d. (51).

A **Jan**: 1st, The Union of Soviet Socialist Republics established, a confederation of Russia the Ukraine, White Russia and Transcaucasia (comes into force *July* 6th);
10th, Memel, under Allied occupation, is seized by Lithuania;
11th, French and Belgian troops occupy Ruhr in consequence of Germany's failure over reparations;
19th, Germany declares policy of passive resistance, which provokes further boycott by the French, and the German economy slows to a standstill;
28th, French troops completely encircle the Ruhr;
31st, Britain accepts terms of commission for funding her war debt to U.S.

B **Feb**: 1st, Allied ultimatum to Lithuania to evacuate Memel;
2nd, Central American Republics sign treaty of amity at Washington;
—, Stanley Bruce becomes premier of Australia;
4th, Lausanne conference on the Near East breaks down through Turkey's refusal to accept proposals;
10th, Turkey's alliance with Afghanistan;
16th, conference of ambassadors assigns Memel to Lithuania, with safeguards for Poland;
24th, U.S. Labor Party convention repudiates Communism.

C **Mar**: 3rd, U.S. Senate rejects proposal to join International Court of Justice;
14th, Allies recognise Vilna and East Galicia as Polish;
21st, Secretary of State Charles Hughes declares U.S. will not recognise U.S.S.R. unless she acknowledges her foreign debts and restores alien property.

D **Apr**: 11th, Conservative government defeated (by 145 votes to 138) in Commons on motion on ex-Servicemen;
20th, Egyptian Constitution adopted;
26th, Mexico recognises oil concessions granted before 1917;
30th, Irish rebels suspend offensive operations following acceptance of terms of Éamon de Valéra's proclamation of 27th by the government.

E **May**: 8th, British note to U.S.S.R. on dissemination of anti-British propaganda;
10th, Vaslav Vorovski, U.S.S.R. delegate at Lausanne, murdered;
20th, A. Bonar Law resigns on grounds of ill health and
22nd, Stanley Baldwin forms Conservative ministry, with Neville Chamberlain as Chancellor of Exchequer;
25th, Britain, France, Italy and Belgium agree to reimburse U.S. cost of U.S. army of the Rhine;
—, independence of Transjordan under Amir Abdullah is proclaimed;
29th, Palestine Constitution suspended by British order in Council through refusal of Arabs to co-operate.

F **Jun**: 1st, New York State Prohibition Enforcement Act repealed;
9th, *coup d'état* in Bulgaria leads to fall of Alexander Stambolisky (who is assassinated, 15th);
10th, Swiss-Liechtenstein customs union;
19th, Stanley Baldwin and Andrew Mellon sign Anglo-U.S. war debt convention;
26th, German-Estonian commercial treaty.

G **Jul**: 2nd (–*Aug.* 20th), London dock strike;
10th, dissolution of non-Fascist parties in Italy;
18th, British Matrimonial Causes Act gives women equality in divorce suits;
24th, peace treaty of Lausanne between Greece, Turkey and the Allies.

O **Politics, Economics, Law and Education**

Alfred Marshall, *Money, Credit and Commerce.*
W. A. Appleton, *Unemployment.*
Labour and Socialist International founded (*May*).
A birth control clinic is opened in New York.

P **Science, Technology, Discovery, etc.**

Frederick Lindemann investigates the size of meteors and the temperature of the upper atmosphere.
L. A. Bauer analyses the earth's magnetic field.
E. N. da C. Andrade, *The Structure of the Atom.*
John B. Tytus invents continuous hot-strip rolling of steel.
Heape and Grylls make a rapid filming machine.

Q **Scholarship**

The Cambridge Ancient History (ed. J. B. Bury), Vol. I.
S. de Madariaga, *The Genius of Spain.*

R **Philosophy and Religion**

György S. von Lukacs, *History and Class Consciousness.*

S **Art, Sculpture, Fine Arts and Architecture**

Painting:
M. Beckmann, *The Trapeze.*
P. Picasso, *Seated Woman.*
Stanley Spencer, *The Resurrection* (–1927).
M. Utrillo, *Ivry Town Hall.*
Sculpture:
Frank Dobson, *Sir Osbert Sitwell.*
Architecture:
Raymond Hood, Chicago Tribune Building.
Royal Fine Art Commission is formed in Britain to advise the government on design and siting of buildings and memorials.

T **Music**

B. Bartók, *Dance Suite.*
M. de Falla, *Master Pédros* (opera).
G. Holst, *The Perfect Fool* (opera).
A. Honegger, *Pacific 231.*
Z. Kodály, *Háry János* and *Psalmus Hungaricus.*
F. Poulenc, *The House Party* (ballet).
A. Roussel, *Le Festin de l'Araignée.*
William Walton, *Façade* music to accompany reading of Edith Sitwell's poems, later arranged as a ballet.
Robert Mayer founds Children's Concerts in London.

U **Literature**

Arnold Bennett, *Riceyman Steps.*
E. E. Cummings, *Enormous Room.*
John Drinkwater, *Collected Poems.*
Scott Fitzgerald, *Tales of the Jazz Age.*
D. H. Lawrence, *Kangaroo.*
F. Mauriac, *Génitrix.*
D. L. Sayers, *Whose Body?*

H **Aug:** 2nd, President W. G. Harding dies (aged 57), succeeded, 3rd, by Calvin Coolidge;
6th, Gustav Stresemann becomes German chancellor and foreign minister;
10th (–13th), strikes and riots in Germany;
13th, Mustapha Kemal elected President of Turkey by Angora assembly;
15th, Irish Free State troops arrest Éamon de Valéra;
27th, in Irish elections Nationalists win 63 seats, Republicans 44;
31st, Italy occupies Corfu;
— (–*Sept.* 17th), U.S. coal strike.

J **Sep:** 1st, earthquake in Japan;
3rd, U.S. recognises Mexican government;
—, Greece appeals to League over Corfu;
10th, Irish Free State admitted to League;
14th, Miguel Primo de Rivera assumes dictatorship in Spain;
15th, Germany's bank rate raised to 90 per cent;
26th, Germany abandons passive resistance;
27th, martial law in Germany;
28th, Abyssinia is admitted to League;
29th, Palestine mandate begins.

K **Oct:** 1st, failure of Black Reichswehr *coup d'état* in Germany;
—, responsible government in Southern Rhodesia;
11th, value of German Mark drops to rate of 10,000 million to £;
13th, Ankara (formerly Angora) becomes new capital of Turkey;
21st, France recognises separatist government in the Palatinate;
26th (–*Nov.* 8th), British Empire conference in London recognises the right of Dominions to make treaties with foreign powers;
29th, revised Turkish republican Constitution under Kemal Pasha.

L **Nov:** 8th (–9th), Adolf Hitler's *coup d'état* in Munich fails;
20th, German currency temporarily stabilised;
29th, Reparations Commission appoints two committees of experts under Charles Dawes and Reginald McKenna to investigate German economy;
30th, separatist riots in Rhineland end.

M **Dec:** 6th, in British general election the Conservatives, standing on platform of protective tariff to relieve unemployment, lose heavily (Conservatives, 258, Labour, 191, Liberal, 158);
8th, U.S. treaty of friendship and commerce with Germany;
17th, Greek army deposes George II;
18th, Britain, France and Spain sign convention on Tangier.

N

W Drama and Entertainment

Karel Čapek, *R.U.R.*
J. E. Flecker, *Hassan.*
Eugene O'Neill, *Anna Christie.*
Luigi Pirandello, *The Late Mattia Pascal.*
Elmer Rice, *The Adding Machine.*
G. B. Shaw, *Back to Methuselah.*
Sutton Vane, *Outward Bound.*

Films:
A Woman of Paris (directed by Charles Chaplin).
Public Opinion.
Love on the Dole.
I.N.R.I.
Skyscraper.
The Pilgrim.
Robin Hood.
Safety First, with Harold Lloyd.

X Sport

First F.A. Cup Final played at Wembley Stadium, won by Bolton Wanderers.

Y Statistics

	Strikes: No. of workers involved	No. of working-days lost
Great Britain	405,000	10,670,000
U.S.	744,948	—
Holland	22,200	3,119,000

In Germany between 1919 and 1923 an annual average of 23,158,000 working-days lost.

Z Births and Deaths

Jan. 9th 'Katherine Mansfield' (pseud. of Kathleen Murry *neé* Beauchamp) d. (35).
Feb. 1st Ernst Troeltsch d. (57).
Feb. 8th Bernard Bosanquet d. (75).
Feb. 10th Wilhelm von Röntgen d. (78).
Mar. 2nd Basil Hume b. (–).
Mar. 26th Sarah Bernhardt d. (77).
June 10th 'Pierre Loti' (pseud. of Julien Viaud) d. (73).
— Robert Maxwell b. (–1991).
Sept. 1st Rocky Marciano b. (–1969).
Sept. 23rd John Lord Morley d. (84).
Oct. 30th Andrew Bonar Law d. (65).
Dec. 2nd Maria Callas b. (–1977).
Dec. 4th Maurice Barrès d. (61).
Dec. 27th Gustav Eiffel d. (91).

1924 (Jan.–Jun.) First Labour Government in Britain—Dawes Report on German reparations

A **Jan:** 11th, Eleutherios Venizelos accepts premiership of Greek national assembly (–*Feb.* 4th);
21st, N. Lenin dies;
—, first Kuomin Tang (Nationalist) Congress at Canton admits Communists to the party and welcomes Russian advisers;
22nd, Stanley Baldwin resigns;
23rd, Ramsay MacDonald forms first Labour government in Britain, with Philip Snowden Chancellor of Exchequer;
24th, non-Fascist trade unions abolished in Italy;
25th, Franco-Czechoslovak alliance.

B **Feb:** 1st, Britain recognises U.S.S.R.;
2nd Caliphate abolished by Turkish national assembly;
3rd, Alexei Rykoff elected president of Council of People's Commissars in U.S.S.R.;
16th, British dock strike (–26th);
18th, Edwin Denby, U.S. navy secretary, forced to resign through connection with oil leases;
19th, Shah Ahmad of Persia deposed;
23rd, Britain reduces reparation recovery duties on German goods to 5 per cent;
28th, U.S. troops land in Honduras.

C **Mar:** 3rd, Germany signs treaty of friendship with Turkey;
9th, Italy annexes Fiume but abandons her claims to Yugoslavia's Dalmatian coast;
24th, Greece is proclaimed a republic.

D **Apr:** 1st, Adolf Hitler is sentenced to 5 years' imprisonment (but is released *Dec.* 20th);
9th, Committees under Charles Dawes and Reginald McKenna make reports on reparations issue;
11th, Socialist government in Denmark;
14th, Anglo-U.S.S.R. conference in London;
18th, League reorganises Hungary's finances;
24th, Irish boundary conference in London fails.

E **May:** 4th, in Reichstag elections Nationalists and Communists win many seats from moderates;
11th, in French elections the National bloc is defeated by a cartel of the Left;
15th, international conference on immigration held at Rome;
19th, Pan-American treaty signed to prevent conflicts between states;
26th, Calvin Coolidge signs bill limiting immigration into U.S. and entirely excluding Japanese;
—, W. Marx ministry in Germany resigns on breakdown of negotiations for coalition of Nationalists and Moderates;
31st, China recognises U.S.S.R.

F **Jun:** 10th, on murder of Giacomo Matteotti, Italian Socialist deputy, the opposition leave the Chamber;
—, Republican Convention at Cleveland nominates Calvin Coolidge for U.S. presidency and Charles Dawes for vice-presidency;
—, Alexandre Millerand, President of France, resigns;
13th, Gaston Doumergue is elected his successor and
15th, Édouard Herriot becomes premier;
24th, Democratic Convention in New York nominates J. W. Davis for presidency and Charles W. Bryan for vice-presidency;

O Politics, Economics, Law and Education

Ramsay MacDonald in House of Commons claims the executive is immune from judicial criticism, a reply to Mr. Justice McCardie's judgment in O'Dwyer *v.* Nairn.

Sweden returns to the gold standard.

J. Edgar Hoover appointed Director of the U.S. Bureau of Investigation (later the F.B.I.).

Four universities are founded in Italy.

P Science, Technology, Discovery, etc.

Arthur Eddington discovers that the luminosity of a star is approximately a function of its mass.

Louis de Broglie argues that particles can also behave as waves, laying the foundations for wave mechanics.

The first insecticide.

'Fonofilm' system of talking pictures is developed.

World Power Conference at Wembley (*June*).

Q Scholarship

Ancient Monuments Society founded in England.

R Philosophy and Religion

S Art, Sculpture, Fine Arts and Architecture

Painting:

Gwen John, *The Convalescent.*

Sculpture:

Charles Wheeler, *The Infant Christ* (bronze bust).

Architecture:

E. Lutyens, Britannic House, Finsbury.

T Music

Ernest Bloch, piano quintet.

George Gershwin, *Rhapsody in Blue.*

P. Hindemith's song-cycle *Das Marienleben.*

G. Puccini, *Turandot* (opera).

O. Respighi, *The Pines of Rome.*

A. Schönberg's music monodrama *Erwartung* and *Die glückliche Hand* (opera).

I. Stravinsky, wind octet.

Anton Webern, three religious songs.

S. Koussevitsky conducts Boston Symphony Orchestra.

U Literature

E. M. Forster, *A Passage to India.*

John Galsworthy, *The White Monkey.*

David Garnett, *A Man at the Zoo.*

T. Mann, *The Magic Mountain.*

Pablo Neruda, *Twenty Love Poems and a Song of Despair.*

St. John Perse (pseud.), *Anabase.*

Mary Webb, *Precious Bane.*

V The Press

F. M. Ford founds *Transatlantic Review.*

W Drama and Entertainment

Noël Coward, *The Vortex.*

F Jun: 25th, Britain states she will not abandon the Sudan, despite Egyptian demands for complete evacuation;
30th, J. B. Hertzog, Nationalist Party leader, forms ministry in South Africa with Labour support, following defeat of J. C. Smuts' South African Party in elections.

G Jul: Ramsay MacDonald refuses to sign treaty of mutual assistance prepared by League;
11th (–15th), rioting between Hindus and Moslems in Delhi;
16th, at London conference on reparations, attended by Gustave Stresemann and Édouard Herriot, the Dawes Report, which removes reparations from the sphere of political controversy, is approved.

H Aug: 6th, Lausanne treaty for re-establishing world peace comes into force;
16th, French delegates at London conference agree to evacuate Ruhr within a year and
18th, French troops leave Offenburg region;
29th, Reichstag approves Dawes Plan, which comes into force *Sept.* 1st.

J Sep: 17th, Italy abrogates treaty of Rapallo (*Nov.* 12th 1920);
20th, Britain brings Mosul controversy before the League;
29th, Germany states terms on which she will join the League, including a permanent seat on the Council;
30th, naval control of Germany abolished.

K Oct: 2nd, League adopts Geneva Protocol for the peaceful settlement of international disputes;
3rd, King Hussein abdicates throne of Hejaz in favour of his son Ali;
9th, Parliament is dissolved following Labour defeat on question of prosecution of *Workers' Weekly*;
—, Irish Free State bill receives royal assent (and, 17th, passes Dáil);
10th, international loan to Germany arranged in London;
25th, Foreign Office publishes the Zinoviev Letter, in which the Third International allegedly instructs Britons to provoke revolution;
—, Tsao Kun, President of China, resigns;
28th, France recognises U.S.S.R.;
29th, Conservatives win British general election with 413 seats against Labour 151, and Liberals 40.

L Nov: 4th, Calvin Coolidge, Republican, wins U.S. presidential election with 382 electoral votes, over J. W. Davis, Democrat, 136, and La Follette, Progressive, 13;
—, Ramsay MacDonald resigns and
6th, Stanley Baldwin forms Conservative government with Austen Chamberlain as foreign secretary and Winston Churchill as Chancellor of Exchequer;
19th, murder of Lee Stack in Cairo;
20th, revolt of Kurds in Turkey is put down with ferocity;
21st, Stanley Baldwin informs U.S.S.R. that Britain will not proceed with the treaties negotiated by the Labour government;
30th, last French and Belgian troops are withdrawn from the Ruhr;
—, Egyptian premier accepts British terms over Stack's murder.

M Dec: 2nd, Anglo-German commercial treaty;
7th, in German elections Nationalists and Communists lose seats to Socialists;
15th (–*Jan.* 15th 1925), cabinet crisis in Germany;
24th, Albania is proclaimed a republic.

N

W Drama and Entertainment (*cont.*)

H. R. Lenormand, *L'Homme et ses Fantômes.*
G. B. Shaw, *St. Joan.*
British Empire Exhibition, Wembley.

Films:
The Ten Commandments.
Reveille.
The Great Wall.
Fernand Léger's abstract *Le Ballet Mécanique.*
Wanderer of the Wasteland, a nature feature in colour.
The Admiralty film *Zeebrugge.*
John Ford's *The Iron Horse.*

X Sport

Olympic Games, Paris.
New Zealand 'All Blacks' Rugby Football team make undefeated tour of Britain.

Y Statistics

Coal production (in mill. tons): U.S., 485; Great Britain, 267·1; Germany, 124·6; France, 44·9.
Steel production (in mill. tons): U.S., 45; Germany, 9·3; Great Britain, 8·2; France, 6·9.
Strikes: 10 million days lost in U.S., and 8 million lost in Great Britain.

Z Births and Deaths

Jan. 21st Nikolai Lenin (pseud. of Vladimir Ilyich Ulyanov) d. (54).
Feb. 3rd Woodrow Wilson d. (67).
Mar. 8th Anthony Caro b. (–).
Apr. 21st 'Marie Corelli' (pseud. of Mary Mackay) d. (59) and Eleonora Duse d. (64).
Apr. 28th Kenneth Kaunda b. (–).
May 12th Tony Hancock b. (–1968).
May 29th Paul Cambon d. (78).
June 12th George Bush b. (–).
June 14th James Black b. (–).
July 13th Alfred Marshall d. (81).
July 27th Ferruccio Busoni d. (58).
Aug. 2nd James Baldwin b. (–1987).
Aug. 3rd Joseph Conrad (Korzeniowski) d. (67).
Aug. 15th Robert Bolt b. (–).
Sept. 18th F. H. Bradley d. (78).
Oct. 1st James Earl ('Jimmy') Carter b. (–).
Oct. 13th Anatole France (pseud. of J. A. A. Thibaud) d. (79).
Nov. 29th Giacomo Puccini d. (66) and C. V. Stanford d. (71).

A **Jan**: 1st, Christiania, Norwegian capital, resumes name of Oslo;
5th, Mrs. Ross of Wyoming becomes first woman governor in U.S.;
6th, Allies inform Germany they will not now evacuate Cologne area on 10th;
11th, on Charles Hughes's resignation F. B. Kellogg becomes U.S. secretary of state;
15th, Hans Luther, Independent, succeeds Wilhelm Marx as German chancellor, with Gustav Stresemann as foreign minister;
16th, Leon Trotsky is dismissed from chairmanship of Russian Revolutionary Military Council;
20th, Russo-Japanese alliance;
—, Anglo-Chinese treaty of Pekin;
29th, D. Lloyd George succeeds Lord Oxford as Liberal leader.

B **Feb**: 10th, U.S.-Canadian fishing agreement;
28th, President Friedrich Ebert of Germany dies.

C **Mar**: 5th, Labour Opposition in Commons leave the House on suspension of David Kirkwood;
9th, Calvin Coolidge arbitrates in Chilean-Peruvian dispute;
12th, Britain refuses to sign Geneva protocol (of *Oct.* 1924) for the peaceful settlement of international disputes;
29th, Japanese suffrage widened.

D **Apr**: 3rd, Britain repeals Reparation Recovery Act and re-establishes sterling on a gold basis at its pre-1914 rate;
3rd, Holland and Belgium sign convention on the navigation of the Scheldt;
4th, Japan evacuates Sakhalin;
10th, Paul Painlevé becomes premier of France on Édouard Herriot's defeat;
23rd, Franco-Spanish war in Morocco against Kabyles;
25th, Paul von Hindenburg elected President of Germany.

E **May**: 1st, Cyprus is declared a British Crown Colony;
4th (–*June* 17th), Geneva Conference on arms traffic and use of poison gas in war;
12th, U.S.S.R. Constitution ratified by Soviet Congress;
30th, Joseph Coates, Reform Party, becomes premier of New Zealand, following W. F. Massey's death, 10th;
Shooting of Chinese students by municipal police in Shanghai and other incidents in Canton provokes Chinese boycott of British goods.

F **Jun**: 8th, Britain and France accept in principle Germany's proposals (of *Feb.* 9th) for a security pact to guarantee Franco-German and Belgo-German boundaries;
25th, Theodore Pangalos becomes premier of Greece in Athens *coup d'état*.

G **Jul**: 7th, South African Senate rejects colour-bar bill;
9th, revolution in Ecuador;
13th, French troops begin evacuation of Rhineland;
—, British government enquiry into coal-miners' dispute;
16th, first elected Parliament of Iraq opens in Baghdad;
18th, insurrection of the Druses in Syria (–*June* 1927);
—, Italian-Yugoslav treaty of Netturno on Dalmatian question;
31st, Unemployment Insurance Act in Britain;
—, provisional settlement of British miners' dispute.

O **Politics, Economics, Law and Education**

Lord Beaverbrook, *Politicians and the Press.*
Adolf Hitler, *Mein Kampf,* Vol. 1.
Harold Laski, *Grammar of Politics.*
Dominions Office established.
French National Economic Council appointed.
Disaster to U.S. dirigible *Shenandoah* draws public attention to air defence.
State of Tennessee forbids teaching of human evolution in schools.

P **Science, Technology, Discovery, etc.**

R. A. Millikan discovers the presence of penetrating radiations in the upper atmosphere.
A. N. Whitehead, *Science and the Modern World.*
Goldberger isolates vitamins B and B_2.
Collip obtains extract of the parathyroid gland for treating tetanus.
Daventry high-power broadcasting transmitter in operation.
Clarence Birdseye extends deep-freezing process to pre-cooked foods.
Marcel Breuer designs the tubular steel chair.

Q **Scholarship**

Hilaire Belloc, *History of England.*
Viscount Grey of Fallodon, *Twenty-Five Years, 1892–1916.*

R **Philosophy and Religion**

H. Hardtman, *Psychology and the Church.*
Songs of Praise (ed. Percy Dearmer).
United Church of Canada is founded.

S **Art, Sculpture, Fine Arts and Architecture**

Painting:
Max Ernst develops the *frottage* technique, rubbing on paper over natural textures.
Alfred Munnings, *Their Majesties returning from Ascot.*
P. Picasso, *Three Dancers.*
G. Rouault, *The Apprentice.*

Sculpture:
Constantin Brancusi, *Bird in Space.*
Jacob Epstein, *Rima* and *The Duke of Marlborough.*
Eric Gill, *Deposition.*
Alfred Gilbert, *The Shaftesbury Memorial* ('Eros').

Architecture:
W. Gropius, The Bauhaus, Dessau.

T **Music**

Ernest Bloch, *Concerto Grosso.*
F. Busoni, *Dr. Faustus* (opera).
Aaron Copland, Symphony no. 1.
Franz Lehár, *Paganini* (operetta).

U **Literature**

E. E. Cummings, *XLI Poems.*
John Dos Passos, *Manhattan Transfer.*
Scott Fitzgerald, *The Great Gatsby.*
Richard Garnett, *Twilight of the Gods.*
André Gide, *Les Faux-Monnayeurs.*

H Aug: 7th, League advises against partition of Mosul;
15th, Norway annexes Spitzbergen;
18th, U.S. agreement with Belgium on war debts;
26th, Henri Pétain takes command of French troops in Morocco;
28th, Britain resumes diplomatic relations with Mexico, after eight years;
29th, amnesty for Kapp, pro-monarchical, conspirators in Germany of *Mar.* 1920.

J Sep: 29th, republican Constitution in Greece.

K Oct: 5th (–16th), Locarno Conference, discussing question of security pact, strikes a balance between French and German interests by drafting treaties (a) guaranteeing the Franco-German and Belgo-German frontiers, (b) between Germany and France, Belgium, Czechoslovakia and Poland respectively, and (c) a mutual guarantee between France, Czechoslovakia and Poland;
12th, U.S.S.R.-German commercial treaty;
—, risings in Syria;
18th (–20th), French fleet bombards Damascus;
19th, Italy completes occupation of Italian Somaliland under terms of 1889 Protectorate;
26th, Chinese customs conference at Peking;
29th, Conservatives win seats in Canadian elections but Mackenzie King maintains precarious Liberal government with support of Progressives;
31st, Reza Khan usurps Persian throne;
Greek army invades Bulgaria in reprisal for a soldier's murder and Bulgaria appeals to League.

L Nov: 12th, U.S. agreement with Italy on war debts;
22nd, Free State representative on Irish boundary commission resigns;
27th, Aristide Briand forms ministry in France.

M Dec: 1st, Locarno treaties signed in London;
—, British troops evacuate Cologne;
3rd, Irish boundary settled after long negotiations;
5th (–*Jan.* 20th 1926), cabinet crisis in Germany;
6th, Italy's agreement with Egypt on Cyrenaica;
15th, Greece agrees to League's penalties over her dispute with Bulgaria;
16th, League settles Mosul question in favour of Iraq;
17th, U.S.S.R. signs defensive alliance with Turkey.

N

U **Literature** (*cont.*)

Aldous Huxley, *Those Barren Leaves.*
Franz Kafka, *The Trial* (posth.).
Eugenio Montale, *Cuttlefish Bones.*
Gertrude Stein, *The Making of Americans* (written 1906–8).
Jules Supervielle, *Gravitations* (poems).
P. G. Wodehouse, *Carry on, Jeeves.*
Virginia Woolf, *Mrs. Dalloway.*

V **The Press**

The New Yorker is issued.

W **Drama and Entertainment**

Noël Coward, *Hay Fever.*
Ashley Dukes, *The Man With a Load of Mischief.*
Sean O'Casey, *Juno and the Paycock.*
The Charleston.

Films:
The Gold Rush.
Greed.
Miracle of the Wolves.
Owd Bob.
The Last Laugh.
The Only Way.

X **Sport**

Y **Statistics**

Railway mileage in operation: U.S., 261,871; Great Britain, 29,300; Russia, 26,255.
Wireless licences: Great Britain, 1,654,000.
Strikes: In Denmark 4 mill. working days are lost.

Z **Births and Deaths**

Mar. 12th Sun Yat-sen d. (58).
Mar. 20th George, Marquess of Curzon, d. (66).
Mar. 26th Pierre Boulez b. (–).
Apr. 14th J. S. Sargent d. (69).
May 12th Alfred, Lord Milner, d. (71).
May 14th H. Rider Haggard d. (69).
May 22nd John French, Earl of Ypres, d. (73).
June 27th Michael Dummett b. (–).
Aug. 29th Richard Attenborough b. (–).
Sept. 7th Laura Ashley b. (–1985).
Sept. 8th Peter Sellers b. (–1980).
Sept. 16th Charles Haughey b. (–).
Sept. 29th Léon Bourgeois d. (74).
Oct. 3rd Gore Vidal b. (–).
Oct. 13th Margaret Thatcher b. (–).
Oct. 24th Luciano Berio b. (–).
Nov. 10th Richard Burton b. (–1984).
Nov. 20th Queen Alexandra d. (80).
— Robert Kennedy b. (–1968).

A **Jan**: 3rd (–*Aug.* 22nd), Theodore Pangalos usurps power as dictator of Greece;
4th, Moderate ministry takes office in Bulgaria, offering amnesty to all political prisoners except Communists;
8th, Ibn Saud becomes King of Hejaz on King Hussein's expulsion and changes name of Kingdom to Saudi Arabia;
14th (–30th), series of agreements between Denmark, Sweden, Norway and Finland for peaceful settlement of disputes;
20th, Hans Luther, Socialist, again becomes German chancellor;
New Code of laws in Turkey.

B **Feb**: 10th, Germany applies for admission to League of Nations;
Tension between Italy and Germany over Germanisation of South Tyrol.

C **Mar**: 11th, Éamon de Valéra resigns as head of Sinn Fein; subsequently founds Fianna Fáil;
12th, Denmark disarms;
17th, Brazil and Spain prevent Germany's admission to League;
26th, Roumanian-Polish alliance.

D **Apr**: 3rd, foundation of the *Ballilla* in Italy, a Fascist youth organisation;
7th, first of several attempts to assassinate Benito Mussolini;
22nd, Persia, Turkey and Afghanistan sign treaty for mutual security;
24th, Berlin treaty of friendship and neutrality between Germany and U.S.S.R.

E **May**: 1st (–*Nov.*), British coal strike;
2nd, U.S. troops land to preserve order in Nicaraguan revolt;
3rd (–12th), General Strike in Britain;
8th, French fleet bombards Damascus in the Revolt of Druses;
10th, Vincent Witos, leader of Peasants' Party, forms ministry in Poland;
12th, Josef Pilsudski's *coup d'état* in Poland;
17th, Wilhelm Marx, Centre, becomes German chancellor, following Hans Luther's resignation, 12th;
18th (–26th), preparatory Disarmament Conference meets, attended by U.S., but not by U.S.S.R.;
23rd, the Lebanon is proclaimed a republic by France;
26th, Riff war ends, with Abd-el-Krim's surrender to France;
31st, Gomes da Costa leads *coup d'état* in Portugal.

F **Jun**: 1st, Ignace Moscicki becomes President of Poland;
5th, Anglo-Turkish agreement on Mosul, with most of the area assigned to Iraq in accordance with League's award of *Dec.* 1925;
7th, Liberal ministry replaces Socialist government in Sweden;
10th, Spain announces her withdrawal from League, but later rescinds this;
—, Franco-Roumanian treaty;
12th, Brazil leaves the League;
26th, McNary-Haugen bill for tariff on agricultural products is defeated in U.S. Senate;
28th, W. L. Mackenzie King resigns as result of Canadian customs scandals and Arthur Meighen becomes premier of Liberal ministry.

G **Jul**: 1st, Anglo-Portuguese agreement on South-West Africa-Angola boundary;
2nd, anti-clerical legislation in Mexico;

O **Politics, Economics, Law and Education**

J. M. Keynes, *The End of Laissez-Faire.*
The Intimate Papers of Colonel House.
B. Webb, *My Apprenticeship.*
British General Electricity Board established.
Reading University founded.
Council for the Preservation of Rural England founded.
France returns to gold standard.
Kenneth Lindsay, *Social Progress and Educational Waste.*
Adoption is made legal in England and Wales.

P **Science, Technology, Discovery, etc.**

F. Lindemann, *The Physical Significance of the Quantum Theory.*
Max Born and Werner Heisenberg formulate a mathematical theory to explain quantum theory.
J. L. Baird demonstrates television in Soho (*Jan.* 26th).
Liver extract first used for treating pernicious anaemia.
Alan Cobham flies from Croydon to Cape Town and back (*Mar.*) to discover possibilities of long-distance air routes.
Flights over North Pole by Roald Amundsen and by Richard Byrd.
Scott Polar Research Institute, Cambridge, opened.

Q **Scholarship**

M. Rostovziev, *Social and Economic History of the Roman Empire.*
Speculum, a Journal of Medieval Studies issued.
G. M. Trevelyan, *History of England.*

R **Philosophy and Religion**

R. H. Tawney, *Religion and the Rise of Capitalism.*
Essays Catholic and Critical.

S **Art, Sculpture, Fine Arts and Architecture**

Painting:
M. Chagall, *Lovers' Bouquet.*
A. John, *Lady Ottoline Morrell.*
S. Spencer, Murals for Burghclere Chapel, Berkshire (–1932).
J. S. Sargent Exhibition, Royal Academy.

Sculpture:
J. Epstein, *The Visitation.*
H. Moore, *Draped reclining figure.*

Architecture:
A. Gaudí, Church of the Sagrada Familia, Barcelona completed (begun 1883).
Le Corbusier (pseud.), *The Coming Architecture* published.

T **Music**

Alban Berg, *Wozzeck* (opera).
Arthur Honegger, *Judith* (opera).
Constant Lambert becomes first English composer to be commissioned to write music for Diaghilev's ballet with *Romeo and Juliet.*

U **Literature**

Theodore Dreiser, *An American Tragedy.*
William Faulkner, *Soldiers' Pay.*
André Gide, *Si le grain ne meurt.*

G **Jul**: 9th, Gomes da Costa is overthrown in Portugal by General Antonio de Fragoso Carmona;
15th, fall of Aristide Briand's ministry through financial crisis;
23rd, Raymond Poincaré becomes premier of French National Union Ministry (–1929);
26th, Philippines legislature calls for plebiscite on independence, which is vetoed by the governor;
28th, U.S.-Panama alliance to protect the canal in wartime;
—, Belgian financial crisis: Franc is devalued and King Albert I is given dictatorial powers for six months;
30th, Albania's frontiers are fixed internationally;
31st, Afghanistan signs non-aggression pact with U.S.S.R.

H **Aug**: 10th, following devaluation of the French Franc, a sinking fund is established to redeem the national debt;
17th, Greece signs treaty of friendship with Yugoslavia;
22nd, Theodore Pangalos is overthrown and President George Kondylis is recalled to Greece.

J **Sep**: 1st, civil marriage is established in Turkey;
2nd, Italy's treaty with the Yemen begins Italian attempt to dominate east coast of Red Sea;
6th, Chiang Kai-shek reaches Hankow in his northern campaign in Chinese Civil War;
8th, Germany is admitted to the League, and in consequence
11th, Spain leaves;
16th, Italian-Roumanian treaty;
18th, Yugoslavia signs treaty of friendship with Poland;
23rd, Aristide Briand and Gustav Stresemann discuss the Rhineland and reparations at Thoiry;
25th, international convention on slavery;
—, campaign against the Mafia begins in Sicily;
—, W. L. Mackenzie King forms Liberal ministry in Canada after general election.

K **Oct**: 15th, Ignaz Seipel, Christian Socialist, forms ministry in Austria, replacing Rudolf Ramek;
19th (–*Nov.* 18th), Imperial Conference in London decides that Britain and the Dominions are autonomous communities, equal in status;
Expulsion of Leon Trotsky and Grigori Zinoviev from the Politbureau, following Josef Stalin's victory over Leftist opposition;
Union of National Peasants' Party founded in Roumania.

L **Nov**: 8th, British Parliament appoints the Simon Commission on India;
10th, Vincent Massey becomes first Canadian minister to Washington;
11th, the Hungarian Upper House, representing the landed aristocracy, is re-established;
19th, British miners call off strike (begun *May* 1st);
27th, treaty of Tirana between Italy and Albania;
Communist revolt in Java (–*July* 1927).

M **Dec**: 2nd, Liberal government in Denmark, following Socialist losses in election;
17th (–*Jan.* 28th 1927), cabinet crisis in Germany.

N British legation in Peking declares Britain's sympathy with Chinese Nationalist movement (Kuo Min Tang).

U **Literature** (*cont.*)

F. Kafka, *The Castle* (posth.).
D. H. Lawrence, *The Plumed Serpent.*
T. E. Lawrence, *Seven Pillars of Wisdom.*
W. S. Maugham, *The Casuarina Tree.*
A. A. Milne, *Winnie the Pooh.*

V **The Press**

W **Drama and Entertainment**

Paul Green, *In Abraham's Bosom.*
Margaret Kennedy and Basil Dean, *The Constant Nymph.*
Sean O'Casey, *The Plough and the Star.*

Films:
Fritz Lang's *Metropolis.*
Renoir's *Nana.*
The Last Days of Pompeii.
Ben Hur with Ramon Navarro.
John Barrymore in *Don Juan.*
Rudolph Valentino's death.

X **Sport**

J. B. Hobbs scores 16 centuries in first-class cricket.

Y **Statistics**

Populations (in mill.): U.S.S.R., 148; U.S., 115; Japan, 85; Germany, 64; Great Britain, 45; France, 41; Italy, 40.
Petroleum production: U.S. 770·8 mill. barrels.
British merchant fleet: 11·9 mill. tons (629,000 tons motor).
Strikes in Great Britain: 162,233,000 working-days lost.

Z Births and Deaths

Jan. 20th Charles Montagu Doughty d. (73).
Feb. 2nd Valéry Giscard d'Estaing b. (–).
Feb. 9th Garret Fitzgerald b. (–).
Mar. 3rd Sidney Lee d. (67).
Mar. 6th Andrzej Wajda b. (–).
Apr. 8th Jürgen Moltmann b. (–).
Apr. 19th Squire Bancroft d. (84).
Apr. 21st Queen Elizabeth II b. (–).
May 15th Peter Shaffer b. (–).
June 3rd Allen Ginsburg b. (–).
July 2nd Émile Coué d. (69).
Aug. 1st Israel Zangwill d. (62).
Oct. 15th Michel Foucault b. (–1984).
Dec. 5th Claude Oscar Monet d. (66).
Dec. 20th Geoffrey Howe b. (–).
Dec. 29th Rainer Maria Rilke d. (51).

1927 (Jan.–Aug.) German financial crisis—Washington Naval Disarmament Conference

A **Jan:** 1st, Chinese Kuo Min Tang (Nationalist) government established at Hankow;
29th, German cabinet crisis is resolved with Wilhelm Marx becoming chancellor;
31st, inter-Allied military control of Germany ends.

B **Feb:** 3rd (–13th), revolt in Portugal against the military dictatorship of General Carmona;
19th, Chinese Nationalists extract from Britain a reduction of the concessions at Hankow and Kiukiang.

C **Mar:** 9th, revocation of self-government in Libya;
24th, Chinese Communists seize Nanking.

D **Apr:** 5th, treaty of friendship between Italy and Hungary;
11th, Charles Ibáñez becomes dictator in Chile;
15th, Chiang Kai-shek organises government at Nanking;
—, U.S.S.R. and Switzerland resume diplomatic relations;
17th, bank crisis in Japan forces resignation of R. Wakatsuki's ministry;
18th, split in Kuo Min Tang between Chiang Kai-shek and the Radicals;
21st, Italian labour charter issued.

E **May:** 2nd (–23rd), economic conference at Geneva, attended by 52 nations, including U.S.S.R.;
4th, Henry Stimpson, U.S. secretary of state, brings together factions in Nicaragua, and U.S. is asked to supervise elections;
9th, Parliament House, Canberra, is opened;
13th, 'Black Friday' with collapse of Germany's economic system;
20th, by treaty of Jeddah Britain recognises independence of Saudi Arabia;
26th, Britain annuls trade agreement with U.S.S.R. and
27th, breaks off diplomatic relations after discovery of documents relating to Soviet intrigues against British Empire;
27th, Thomas Masaryk is re-elected President of Czechoslovakia;
Japan intervenes in Shantung, blocking advance of Chinese Nationalists on Peking.

F **Jun:** 2nd, revised Greek Constitution;
20th (–*Aug.* 4th), Britain, U.S. and Japan confer at Washington on naval disarmament, but fail to reach agreement;
Rupture of Yugoslav-Albanian relations following frontier incidents;
Druse revolt in Syria ends.

G **Jul:** 10th, assassination of Kevin O'Higgins (Nationalist minister) provokes denunciation of tactics of Irish Republicans;
15th (–16th), Socialist riots and general strike in Vienna, following acquittal of Nationalists for political murders;
27th, Belgium and Portugal make territorial adjustments in the Congo;
28th, British Trades Union Act declares certain strikes and lock-outs illegal;
Unrest in Samoa, fomented by Europeans (–*Aug.*).

H **Aug:** 7th, international Peace Bridge between U.S. and Canada opened;
12th, Éamon de Valéra and other Irish Republican leaders agree to take oaths and their seats in the Dáil;
22nd, Allied military control of Hungary abolished;
23rd, Nahas Pasha becomes leader of the Wafd in Egypt.

O Politics, Economics, Law and Education

Kemal Atatürk, *The New Turkey*.
Adolf Hitler, *Mein Kampf*, Vol. II.
T. E. Lawrence, *Revolt in the Desert*.
British Broadcasting Corporation takes over from British Broadcasting Company (*Jan.* 1st).
C. K. Ogden founds Orthological Institute.

P Science, Technology, Discovery, etc.

Heisenberg propounds 'the uncertainty principle' in quantum-physics.
W. Heitler and F. London make discoveries on the wave mechanics of valency.
W. Muller's work on genetics and radiation.
Siegfried Junghans's process for continuous casting of non-ferrous metal.
Albert W. Hall's improvements to fluorescent lamps.
Charles A. Lindbergh flies from New York to Paris in 37 hours (*May* 20th, 21st).
Gino Watkins leads expedition to Edge Island, Spitzbergen.

Q Scholarship

Leonard Woolley's discoveries at Ur.
Economic History Review issued.

R Philosophy and Religion

J. W. Dunne, *An Experiment with Time*.
S. Freud, *The Future of an Illusion*.
Heidegger, *Sein und Zeit*.
B. Russell, *Analysis of Matter*.
World Conference on Faith and Order, at Lausanne.

S Art, Sculpture, Fine Arts and Architecture

Painting:
M. Chagall, *Fables of La Fontaine* (100 etchings, published 1952).
L. S. Lowry, *Coming Out of School*.
H. Matisse, *Figures with Ornamental Background*.
Rex Whistler, frescoes for the Tate Gallery Restaurant.

Sculpture:
J. Epstein, *Madonna and Child* and *Paul Robeson*.
Eric Gill, *Mankind*; also designs the 'Sans Serif' alphabet.

T Music

Arthur Honegger, *Antigone* (opera with Jean Cocteau's libretto).
Ernst Křenek, *Johnny Strikes Up* (opera).
M. Ravel, violin sonata.
Dmitry Shostakovich, 1st Symphony.
I. Stravinsky, *Œdipus Rex* (opera).
Jaromir Weinberger, *Schwanda the Bagpiper* (opera).
George Antheil's 'ballet mécanique', scored for aeroplane propellers, anvils, motor horns, etc.
Otto Klemperer appointed Dircctor of the Kroll Opera, Berlin.

U Literature

Ernest Hemingway, *Men Without Women*.
Sinclair Lewis, *Elmer Gantry*.
Henri Michaux, *Qui je fus*.

J **Sep:** 2nd, in Turkish elections Mustapha Kemal is empowered to nominate all candidates, giving the People's Party a monopoly;
15th, in Irish elections Nationalists fail to win clear majority over Republicans;
16th, Paul von Hindenburg, dedicating the Tannenburg memorial, repudiates Germany's responsibility for the War (art. 231 of Versailles Treaty);
22nd, slavery abolished in Sierra Leone.

K **Oct:** 1st, U.S.S.R.-Persian non-aggression pact;
17th, first Labour government in Norway.

L **Nov:** 11th, Franco-Yugoslav treaty of friendship;
15th, Canada is elected to a seat on League Council;
22nd, Albania signs defensive alliance with Italy, in reply to the Franco-Yugoslav treaty;
—, Persia claims Bahrein Island;
30th, Maxim Litvinov, U.S.S.R. commissar for foreign affairs, proposes immediate disarmament at Geneva, but this is rejected as a 'Communist trick'.

M **Dec:** 13th, Lithuanian-Polish dispute is referred to League;
14th, Britain recognises Iraq's independence and promises to support her application for membership of League in 1932;
—, China and U.S.S.R. break off relations;
18th, Chiang Kai-shek overthrows Hankow government;
27th, Josef Stalin's faction is victorious at All-Union Congress and Leon Trotsky is expelled from Communist Party as a deviationist;
Amendment to Mexican petroleum law brings improvement in relations with U.S.

N

U **Literature** (*cont.*)

Marcel Proust, *Le Temps retrouvé* (posth.).
Dorothy Richardson, *Oberland*.
Virginia Woolf, *To The Lighthouse*.
Henry Williamson, *Tarka the Otter*.

V **The Press**

W **Drama and Entertainment**

Paul Claudel, *Protée*.
Thornton Wilder, *The Bridge of San Luis Rey*.
Ben Travers, *Thark*.
The slow foxtrot.

Films:

Sound films, popularised by *The Jazz Singer*, with Al Jolson.
Underworld.
Love, with Greta Garbo.
C. B. de Mille's *King of Kings*.

X **Sport**

Helen Wills wins Ladies Tennis Championship at Wimbledon.
J. Weismüller swims 100 yards in 51 seconds.

Y **Statistics**

Z **Births and Deaths**

Feb. 18th Elbridge Thomas Gerry d. (89).
Feb. 19th Georg Brandes d. (85).
Feb. 24th Edward Marshall Hall d. (68).
May 6th Hudson Maxim d. (74).
June 1st J. B. Bury d. (76).
June 14th J. K. Jerome d. (68).
July 31st Harry Hamilton Johnston d. (69).
Aug. 4th John Dillon d. (76).
Oct. 8th César Milstein b. (–).

1928 (Jan.–Sep.) Kellogg-Briand Pact—Complete Women's Suffrage in Britain—Japan occupies Shantung

A **Jan:** 13th, Allied military control of Bulgaria abolished;
14th, first Conservative administration in Latvia;
29th, treaty between Germany and Lithuania provides for arbitration over Memel.

B **Feb:** 20th, Britain recognises independence of Transjordan.

C **Mar:** 16th, Nahas Pasha premier of Egypt (–*June* 25th);
25th, General Antonio Carmona elected President of Portugal;
28th, military service in France reduced to a year.

D **Apr:** 6th, Palmas Island, near Philippines, is awarded to Holland in arbitration of dispute with U.S.;
9th, Islam no longer recognised as State religion of Turkey;
13th, F. B. Kellogg submits his plan for renunciation of war to Locarno powers (Pact signed *Aug.*);
19th, Japan occupies Shantung;
21st, Aristide Briand puts forward his draft treaty for outlawing war;
22nd, National Union of the Left triumph in French elections;
27th, Oliveira Salazar becomes minister of finance in Portugal with wide powers;
29th, British ultimatum forces Egypt to provide for freedom of public meetings.

E **May:** 3rd (–11th), Sino-Japanese clashes at Tsinan;
6th, National Peasants' Party Congress in Roumania demands responsible government;
7th, women's suffrage in Britain reduced from age of 30 to 21;
12th, Italian electoral law reduces electorate from 10 million to 3 million;
20th, in German elections Socialists win at expense of Nationalists;
31st, Eleutherios Venizelos returns to Greece as premier.

F **Jun:** 9th, France convenes constituent assembly in Syria, with a Nationalist majority;
23rd, explanatory note on Kellogg-Briand pact is sent to the powers;
24th, the French Franc is again devalued;
28th, Hermann Müller, Socialist, is appointed German chancellor (following resignation of Wilhelm Marx's ministry, 13th).

G **Jul:** 17th, Obregón, President of Mexico, assassinated; succeeded by Emilio Portes Gil;
19th, King Fuad's *coup d'état* in Egypt, where Parliament is dissolved for three years and freedom of press is suspended;
—, China annuls 'unequal treaties';
25th, Italy becomes a signatory to Tangier statute, giving Spain greater control there.

H **Aug:** 2nd, Italy signs 20-year treaty of friendship with Ethiopia;
8th, the Croats withdraw from Yugoslav Parliament to set up a separatist assembly in Zagreb;
27th, Kellogg-Briand Pact, outlawing war and providing for pacific settlement of disputes, signed in Paris;
28th, all-party conference at Lucknow votes for dominion status for India, bút radical members, 30th, form the Independence of India League.

J **Sep:** 1st, Albania is proclaimed a Kingdom and Zog I is elected King;
10th, Argentina nationalises oil;
11th, Portuguese treaty with South Africa regulates problems of transport and labour recruitment;
23rd, Italy signs treaty of friendship with Greece;
26th, act of League Assembly, embodying Kellogg-Briand Pact, is signed by 23 nations.

O Politics, Economics, Law and Education

Émile Chartier (pseud.), *Le Citoyen contre les pouvoirs.*
Benito Mussolini, *My Autobiography.*
G. B. Shaw, *The Intelligent Woman's Guide to Socialism and Capitalism.*
U.S.S.R. first Five-year Plan.
Italy returns to gold standard.
Over-production of coffee causes collapse of Brazil's economy.

P Science, Technology, Discovery, etc.

H. Geiger and W. Müller construct the 'Geiger counter'.
A. Fleming discovers penicillin.
The constitution of thyroxine is discovered.
T. H. Morgan, *The Theory of Sex.*
J. L. Baird gives transatlantic television transmission and demonstrates colour television in Britain.
Graf Zeppelin completes the flight Friedrichshafen to New Jersey in 4 days 15½ hours.
First east-west transatlantic flights by Köhl and by Fitzmaurice.

Q Scholarship

Completion of *New English Dictionary* (begun 1884).

R Philosophy and Religion

Revised Prayer Book of Church of England rejected by Parliament.
L. Pastor completes his *History of the Popes* (begun 1886).
Pope Pius XI's encyclical *Mortalium animus.*
Ecumenical Missionary Conference, held in Jerusalem, stresses partnership in a common undertaking.

S Art, Sculpture, Fine Arts and Architecture

Painting:
Max Beckmann, *Black Lilies.*
Henri Matisse, *Seated Odalisque.*
Edvard Munch, *Girl on a Sofa.*
Kenwood, Hampstead, housing Lord Iveagh's art collection, opened.
Amédée Ozenfant coins the term 'purism' in his treatise *Art.*
Architecture:
E. Scott, Shakespeare Memorial Theatre, Stratford-on-Avon.
Congrès Internationaux d'Architecture Moderne, founded in Switzerland.

T Music

Arnold Bax, 3rd Symphony.
George Gershwin, *An American in Paris.*
M. Ravel, *Bolero.*
A. Roussel, piano concerto.
I. Stravinsky, *Capriccio.*
Kurt Weil and Bertolt Brecht, *The Threepenny Opera.*

U Literature

Stephen V. Benét, *John Brown's Body.*
Aldous Huxley, *Point Counter Point.*
Christopher Isherwood, *All the Conspirators.*
D. H. Lawrence, *Lady Chatterley's Lover.*
T. F. Powys, *Mr. Weston's Good Wine.*
Upton Sinclair, *Boston.*

K Oct: 2nd, Arvid Lindman forms Conservative ministry in Sweden;
4th (–16th), plebiscite in Germany against building new battleships fails;
6th, Chiang Kai-shek is elected President of China.

L Nov: 3rd, Turkey adopts Latin alphabet;
6th, Herbert Hoover, Republican, elected U.S. President with 444 electoral votes against Alfred E. Smith, Democrat, 87;
14th, in New Zealand elections United (Liberal) Party under Joseph Ward wins 29 seats, Reform 28 and Labour 19;
15th, Fascist Grand Council becomes part of Italian constitution, with right of nominating candidates to Chamber.

M Dec: 5th, Wilhelm Miklas elected President of Austria, in succession to Michael Hainisch;
6th, war between Bolivia and Paraguay;
12th, Peasants' Party wins Roumanian elections;
20th, Britain recognises Nanking government (Kuo Min Tang) of China;
22nd, Committee under Owen D. Young appointed to examine reparations question;
Arrest of a Slovak deputy in Czechoslovakia for irredentist agitation in favour of Hungary provokes ill feeling.

N Strikes in India.
Extensive railway development in East Africa.

U **Literature** (*cont.*)
Edgar Wallace, *The Squeaker*.
Virginia Woolf, *Orlando*.
W. B. Yeats, *The Tower*.

V **The Press**
Life and Letters first issued.

W **Drama and Entertainment**
Jean Giraudoux, *Siegfried*.
J. Van Druten, *Young Woodley*.

Films:
Walt Disney makes first 'Mickey Mouse' film in colour.
Charles Chaplin's *Circus*.
Eisenstein's *October*.
The Woman in the Moon.
The Patriot.

X **Sport**
Learie Constantine is the first West Indian cricketer in England to achieve 1,000 runs and 100 wickets in a season.

Y **Statistics**

Z **Births and Deaths**
Jan. 1st Thomas Hardy d. (87).
Jan. 29th Douglas, Earl Haig, d. (66).
Feb. 15th H. H. Asquith, Earl of Oxford and Asquith, d. (75).
Mar. 12th Edward Albee b. (–).
Mar. 19th Hans Küng b. (–).
Apr. 10th Stanley John Weyman d. (72).
May 1st Ebenezer Howard d. (78).
June 14th Che Guevara b. (–1967).
July 19th John Bratby b. (–).
July 21st Ellen Terry d. (80).
July 26th Stanley Kubrick b. (–).
Aug. 19th R. B. Haldane, Viscount Haldane, d. (72).
Sept. 3rd Roald Amundsen d. (56).
Oct. 17th Frank Dicksee d. (85).
Nov. 12th Grace Kelly b. (–1982).
Nov. 21st Herman Sundermann d. (71).
Dec. 7th Noam Chomsky b. (–).

A **Jan**: 5th, King Alexander I suppresses Yugoslav Constitution and establishes dictatorship;
—, inter-American treaty of arbitration, analogous to Kellogg-Briand Pact, signed in Washington;
21st, Croat party in Yugoslavia is dissolved;
31st, Leon Trotsky is expelled from U.S.S.R.

B **Feb**: 6th, Germany accepts Kellogg-Briand Pact;
9th, Litvinov Protocol, or Eastern Pact, between U.S.S.R., Estonia, Latvia, Poland and Roumania for renunciation of war;
11th, Lateran Treaty establishes an independent Vatican City;
27th, Turkey signs Litvinov Protocol.

C **Mar**: 6th, Bulgarian-Turkish treaty of friendship;
17th, Spanish government closes Madrid University to stifle student agitation;
24th, Fascists 'win' single-party elections in Italy;
27th, Graeco-Yugoslav pact of friendship;
28th, new Constitution in Ecuador ends military régime.

D **Apr**: 3rd, Persia signs Litvinov Protocol;
12th, Indian Trade Disputes Act and Public Safety Act to reduce radical Labour unrest;
24th, Socialist ministry formed in Denmark, following defeat of Liberals in election;
30th, Ernst Streeruwitz appointed chancellor of Austria.

E **May**: 16th, restoration of Greek Senate, abolished in 1862, in hope of stabilising republican régime;
20th, Japan evacuates Shantung;
22nd, Amir Amanullah flees from Afghanistan (Nadir Khan proclaimed King, *Oct.* 15th);
26th, Catholic Party wins Belgian elections;
30th, in British general election Labour wins 287 seats, Conservatives, 261, Liberals, 59, others, 8.

F **Jun**: 3rd, settlement of Arica-Tacna dispute, originating in 1910, by which Chile is awarded Arica, Peru gains Tacna and Bolivia acquires railway rights;
5th, Ramsay MacDonald forms Labour ministry, with Arthur Henderson Foreign Secretary, Philip Snowden Chancellor of Exchequer and J. R. Clynes Home Secretary;
7th, Young Committee recommends that Germany should pay annuities, secured on mortgage of German railways, to an international bank until 1988;
27th, Reichstag repeals Protection of Republic Act;
Kemal Atatürk suppresses Communist propaganda in Turkey.

G **Jul**: 2nd, fall of Tanarka ministry in Japan;
24th, Kellogg-Briand Pact comes into force;
25th, Pope Pius XI, no longer 'a voluntary prisoner', leaves Vatican for first time;
27th, Raymond Poincaré resigns from ill health and Aristide Briand becomes premier of France.

H **Aug**: Saudi Arabia signs treaty of friendship with Turkey (and, 24th, with Persia);
6th (–13th), at Reparations Conference at the Hague, Germany accepts Young Plan and the Allies agree to evacuate the Rhineland by June 1930;
11th, Iraq and Iran sign treaty of friendship;

O Politics, Economics, Law and Education

Margaret Bondfield becomes first woman privy councillor.
Collapse of U.S. Stock Exchange begins world economic crisis, bringing an era of depression and unemployment (*Oct.* 28th).
Colonial Development Fund established.
Leon Trotsky leaves U.S.S.R. for Turkey.
The term *Apartheid* is first used.

P Science, Technology, Discovery, etc.

Albert Einstein, *Unitary Field Theory*.
James Jeans, *The Universe Around Us*.
Adrian and Matthews, using an ultra-sensitive galvanometer, are able to follow a single impulse in a single nerve fibre.
Kodaks develop a 16 mm. colour film.
Tootal's discover a crease-resisting cotton fabric.
Graf Zeppelin airship flies round the world.
New Tilbury Dock, London, opened.
Richard Byrd flies over the South Pole.

Q Scholarship

14th edition of *Encyclopædia Britannica*.
Journal of Modern History issued.

R Philosophy and Religion

John Dewey, *The Quest for Certainty*.
Heidegger, *What is Philosophy?*
Walter Lippmann, *Preface to Morals*.
The Presbyterian Churches in Scotland unite to form The Church of Scotland.
World Conference of Lutherans at Copenhagen.

S Art, Sculpture, Fine Arts and Architecture

Painting:
P. Klee, *Fool in a Trance* (in one continuous line).
P. Mondrian, *Composition with Yellow and Blue*.
P. Picasso, *Woman in Armchair*.
Grant Wood, *Woman with Plants*.
Second Surrealist Manifesto. The Surrealist group is joined by Salvador Dali.
Opening of Museum of Modern Art, New York, with exhibitions of works by Cézanne, Gauguin, Seurat and Van Gogh.

Sculpture:
J. Epstein, *Night and Day*, London Transport Building, St. James's Park.

T Music

Paul Hindemith, *Neues von Tage* (opera).
Constant Lambert, *Rio Grande*.
William Walton, viola concerto.
A. Toscanini directs New York Philharmonic Orchestra.
Oxford History of Music begun.

U Literature

Robert Bridges, *The Testament of Beauty*.
Jean Cocteau, *Les Enfants terribles*.
William Faulkner, *The Sound and the Fury*.
Robert Graves, *Goodbye To All That*.

H Aug: Arab attacks on Jews in Palestine, following disputes over Jewish use of the Wailing Wall, Jerusalem.

J Sep: 5th, A. Briand proposes a European federal union;
12th, Count Grandi is appointed Italian foreign minister;
14th, U.S. joins the International Court;
16th, peace is signed between Bolivia and Paraguay;
26th, Johann Schober forms ministry in Austria supported by Christian Socialists and Nationalists.

K Oct: 3rd, name of Serbo-Croat-Slovene Kingdom changed to Yugoslavia;
3rd, Britain resumes relations with U.S.S.R.;
—, Julius Curtius appointed German foreign minister on Gustav Stresemann's death;
12th, Labour Party wins Australian elections and
22nd, James H. Scullin forms ministry;
31st, Egyptian constitution is restored;
Cessation of U.S. loans to Europe, following Wall Street Crash.

L Nov: 13th, Basle Bank for International Settlements is founded to deal with Germany's reparation payments under the Young Plan;
17th, Nikolai Bukharin and other members of the Right opposition in U.S.S.R. are expelled;
30th, second Rhineland Zone is evacuated.

M Dec: 6th, female suffrage in Turkey;
22nd, referendum in Germany upholds the adoption of the Young Plan;
—, U.S.S.R. signs agreement with China over Chinese Eastern railway;
Round-table conference between Viceroy and Indian party leaders on Dominion status.

N

U **Literature** (*cont.*)

Ernest Hemingway, *A Farewell to Arms.*
Hugo von Hofmannsthal, *Poems.*
Sinclair Lewis, *Dodsworth.*
Charles Morgan, *Portrait in a Mirror.*
J. B. Priestley, *The Good Companions.*
Erich Remarque, *All Quiet on the Western Front.*
A. de St. Exupéry, *Courrier Sud.*
Thomas Wolfe, *Look Homeward Angel.*
Virginia Woolf, *A Room of One's Own.*

V **The Press**

W **Drama and Entertainment**

P. Claudel, *Le Soulier de satin* (first performed in 1943).
Noël Coward, *Bitter Sweet.*
Jean Giraudoux, *Amphitryon 38.*
Elmer Rice, *See Naples and Die.*
G. B. Shaw, *The Apple Cart.*
R. C. Sherriff, *Journey's End.*

Films:

Bull-Dog Drummond.
Jun and the Paycock.
The Love Parade.
Die Generallinie.
Warner Bros. announce they will make no more 'black and white' films.

X **Sport**

Y **Statistics**

Value of world production, percentages contributed by: U.S., 34·4; U.K., 10·4; Germany, 10·3; U.S.S.R., 9·9; France, 5·0; Japan, 4·0; Italy, 2·5; Canada, 2·2; Poland, 1·7.

Z **Births and Deaths**

Jan. 12th A. MacIntyre b. (–).
Jan. 15th Martin Luther King b. (–1968).
Feb. 15th Graham Hill b. (–1975).
Mar. 20th Ferdinand Foch d. (78).
Mar. 23rd Roger Bannister b. (–).
Apr. 29th Jeremy Thorpe b. (–).
May 1st Audrey Hepburn b. (–).
May 20th Archibald Primrose, Earl of Rosebery, d. (82).
July 15th Hugo von Hofmannsthal d. (55).
Aug. 5th Millicent Garrett Fawcett d. (82).
Aug. 19th Serge Diaghilev d. (57).
Sept. 3rd Gustav Stresemann d. (51).
Sept. 15th Murray Gell-Man b. (–).
Sept. 17th Stirling Moss b. (–).
Nov. 24th Georges Benjamin Clemenceau d. (88).
Dec. 9th Bob Hawke b. (–).
Dec. 12th John Osborne b. (–).

1930 (Jan.–Jul.) Allied occupation of Rhineland ends—Gandhi begins civil disobedience campaign

A **Jan:** 1st, Powers agree to future abolition of extra-territorial privileges in China;
—, Nahas Pasha again premier of Egypt;
23rd, Wilhelm Frick, Nazi, becomes minister in Thuringia;
28th, dictatorship of Primo de Rivera ends in Spain and General Damaso Berenguer forms ministry.

B **Feb:** 6th, Austro-Italian treaty of friendship;
18th (–*Mar.* 24th), Geneva tariff conference;
U.S. Commission in Haiti recommends reforms and the appointment of Stenio Vincent as president.

C **Mar:** 8th, U.S.-League commission reports that slavery exists in Liberia;
12th, Mahatma Gandhi opens civil disobedience campaign in India;
27th, Hermann Müller's Socialist cabinet resigns in Germany;
28th, name of Constantinople changed to Istanbul and of Angora to Ankara;
30th, Heinrich Brüning, Centre, forms a coalition of the Right in Germany, replacing the Socialists, but without a majority in Reichstag;
31st, revolt in Ethiopia, led by the empress's brother;
Publication of Reuben J. Clark's Memorandum of 1928 on Monroe doctrine.

D **Apr:** 3rd, Ras Tafari becomes Emperor Haile Selassie of Abyssinia;
22nd, Britain, U.S., France, Italy and Japan end London Conference (held since *Jan.* 21st), with signing of a treaty on naval disarmament, regulating submarine warfare and limiting aircraft carriers;
30th, Italian naval programme begun;
30th, Workman's Insurance law in France.

E **May:** 2nd, Dunning tariff in Canada imposes high duties, but gives Britain preferential treatment;
6th, Japan recognises China's tariff autonomy;
8th, breakdown of London talks on Egypt and Sudan;
17th, Young Plan for reparations in force;
19th, white women enfranchised in South Africa;
24th, Benito Mussolini champions revision of Versailles Treaty;
28th, George W. Forbes becomes premier of United Party ministry in New Zealand on Joseph Ward's retirement;
Opposition party founded in Turkey, favouring greater ties with the West.

F **Jun:** 1st, Carl Ekman forms Liberal ministry in Sweden;
8th, Crown Prince Charles is elected King of Roumania;
17th, Herbert Hoover signs Smoot-Hawley high tariff, in spite of economists' protests that it will lead to reprisals;
21st, Ismail Sidky Pasha becomes premier of Egypt;
24th, Simon Report on India published;
27th, treaty of arbitration signed by Scandinavian powers;
30th, Britain recognises independence of Iraq;
—, last Allied troops leave Rhineland.

G **Jul:** 16th, Paul von Hindenburg authorises German budget by decree on failure of Reichstag to pass it;
21st, Maxim Litvinov becomes U.S.S.R. foreign minister;
30th, National Union party (neo-Fascist), founded in Portugal;
Kurd rising on Persian-Turkish frontier.

O **Politics, Economics, Law and Education**

Albert Einstein, *About Zionism.*
Ortega y Gasset, *The Revolt of the Masses.*
C. S. Johnson, *The Negro in American Civilisation.*
J. M. Keynes, *Treatise on Money.*
Harold Laski, *Liberty and the Modern State.*
F. R. Leavis, *Mass Civilisation and Minority Culture.*
Rosenberg, *Myths of the 20th Century.*
Leon Trotsky, *Autobiography.*
Pilgrim Trust founded.
France begins construction of Maginot Line.
In U.S.S.R. 55 per cent of agricultural workers are employed on collective farms.
Smoot-Hawley Act raises U.S. tariff.
Youth Hostels Association founded in Britain.

P **Science, Technology, Discovery, etc.**

The planet Pluto discovered (*Mar.* 18th).
Debye investigates the structure of molecules with X-rays.
J. H. Northrop makes pepsin and trypsin in crystallised form.
Reppe makes artificial fabrics from acetylene base.
Acrylic plastics are invented (U.K. Perspex; U.S. Lucite).
Picture telegraphy service between Britain and Germany opened (*Jan.* 7th).
The photoflash bulb is invented.
Turkestan-Siberian railway completed.
Amy Johnson's solo flight, London to Australia, in 19½ days (arrives *May* 24th).
Crash of airship R.101 near Beauvais (*Oct.* 7th).
British Arctic Air Route expedition (–31).

Q **Scholarship**

L. Woolley, *Digging Up the Past.*
R. W. Chambers, *William Shakespeare.*
G. M. Trevelyan, *England Under Queen Anne* (–32).

R **Philosophy and Religion**

S. Freud, *Civilisation and its Discontents.*

S **Art, Sculpture, Fine Arts and Architecture**

Painting:
Rex Whistler, illustrations for *Gulliver's Travels.*
Grant Wood, *American Gothic.*
Van Doesburg first uses term 'Concrete Art'.
Sculpture:
H. Matisse, *Tiaré.*
Architecture:
R. Hood, Daily News Building, New York.
Shreve, Lamb and Harmon, Empire State Building, New York.
E. Lutyens, Gledstone, Skipton, Yorks.
Cecil Beaton, *The Book of Beauty* (photographs).

T **Music**

Arnold Schönberg, *Vom Heute auf Morgen* (opera).
I. Stravinsky, *Symphony of Psalms.*
Adrian Boult becomes musical director of B.B.C.

1930 (Aug.–Dec.)

H **Aug**: 7th, Conservative ministry under R. B. Bennett replaces Liberals in Canada;
25th, Josef Pilsudski forms ministry in Poland (–*Nov.* 28th) to break down Left opposition and Radical Leaders are imprisoned;
25th, Augusto Legúia resigns presidency in Peru during revolt.

J **Sep**: 5th, Argentina revolution, with José Uriburu as the new President;
8th (–22nd), special sessions of Canadian Parliament to enact emergency laws dealing with depression;
14th, in German elections Socialists win 143 seats and Communists 77, but National Socialists (Nazis), denouncing Versailles Treaty, gain 107 seats from Moderates;
15th, removal of press censorship in Spain brings independent demands for a republic.

K **Oct**: 1st, Britain restores Wei-hai-wei to China;
— (–*Nov.* 14th), Imperial Conference in London, in which Britain rejects Canadian proposal for preferential tariff to help Dominion wheat;
4th, Brazilian revolution, with Getulio Vargas as the new President;
5th (–12th), conference of Balkan powers in Athens, origin of Balkan Entente (leading to pact of *Feb.* 1934);
14th, attempted Fascist *coup d'état* in Finland;
20th, Passfield White Paper on Palestine stresses Arab land hunger and suggests halt in Jewish immigration while Arab unemployment remains, which shakes Jewish confidence in Britain;
30th, treaty of friendship between Turkey and Greece signed at Ankara.

L **Nov**: 11th, repressive legislation in Finland against Communism;
12th (–*Jan.* 19th 1931), Round-table conference on India in London;
14th, assassination of premier Hamaguchi of Japan;
17th (–28th), Geneva Economic Conference discusses the world depression.

M **Dec**: 3rd, Otto Ender, Christian Socialist, forms Austrian ministry;
9th, Preparatory Commission on Disarmament adopts draft convention for discussions at League Conference in *Feb.* 1932, but Germany and U.S.S.R. disapprove of draft;
12th, last Allied troops leave the Saar;
30th, Scandinavian states, Holland, Belgium and Luxembourg, sign Oslo agreements (–1938), against raising tariffs without prior consultation.

Z **Births and Deaths** (*cont.*)
Mar. 6th Alfred von Tirpitz d. (81).
Mar. 8th William Howard Taft d. (72).
Mar. 19th A. J. Balfour d. (82).
Apr. 3rd Helmut Kohl b. (–).
Apr. 21st Robert Bridges d. (85).
May 13th Fridtjof Nansen d. (68).
May 15th Jasper Johns b. (–).
June 16th Elmer Ambrose Sperry d. (69).
July 7th Arthur Conan Doyle d. (71).
July 15th Jacques Derrida b. (–).
Aug. 15th Tom Mboya b. (–1969).
Aug. 16th Ted Hughes b. (–).
Sept. 30th F. E. Smith, Lord Birkenhead, d. (58).
Oct. 10th Harold Pinter b. (–).

T **Music** (*cont.*)

Thibaud, Cortot and Casals form a trio.
B. Gigli's début.
Camargo Ballet Society founded to encourage British ballet.

U **Literature**

W. H. Auden, *Poems*.
E. M. Delafield, *Diary of a Provincial Lady*.
T. S. Eliot, *Ash Wednesday*.
William Faulkner, *As I Lay Dying*.
Robert Frost, *Collected Poems*.
John Dos Passos, *42nd Parallel*.
J. C. Powys, *In Defence of Sensuality*.
Salvatore Quasimodo, *Acque e terre*.
Sigrid Undset, *Burning Bush*.
Hugh Walpole, *Rogue Herries*.
Evelyn Waugh, *Vile Bodies*.

V **The Press**

Daily News and *Daily Chronicle* amalgamate as *News Chronicle* (–60).
Daily Worker is first issued.
William Randolph Hearst owns 33 newspapers with total circulation of 11 mill.

W **Drama and Entertainment**

Noël Coward, *Private Lives*.
W. S. Maugham, *The Breadwinner*.
Elmer Rice, *Street Scene*.
Films:
Anthony Mann's *The Blue Angel* with Marlene Dietrich.
René Clair's *Sous les Toits de Paris*.
Alfred Hitchcock's *Murder*.
Journey's End.
Hell's Angels.
All Quiet on the Western Front.
The Big House.
Hallelujah.
Advent of the wider screen.

X **Sport**

Donald Bradman scores 334 runs for Australia in the Leeds Test Match (and in 1930/1 season makes 425 not out for New South Wales against Queensland).
Max Schmeling becomes world heavyweight boxing champion.

Y **Statistics**

Religious denominations in Great Britain (in thousands): Roman Catholics, 6,024; Church of England, 2,285; Methodists, 548; Congregationalists, 480; Baptists, 406; Presbyterians, 84; Presbyterian Church of Scotland, 1,270; Episcopal Church of Scotland, 60.
Wireless licences in U.K.: 3,092,000.
Telephone subscribers in U.K.: 1,996,000.

Z **Births and Deaths**

Jan. 13th Sebastian de Ferranti d. (66).
Jan. 23rd Derek Walcott b. (–).
Mar. 2nd D. H. Lawrence d. (45).

(*Continued opposite*)

1931 (Jan.–Aug.) The Hoover Moratorium—Britain abandons gold standard

A **Jan:** 12th, Allied military control committee is dissolved;
26th, Mahatma Gandhi is released for discussions with government;
27th, Pierre Laval becomes premier of France.

B **Feb:** Oswald Mosley breaks away from British Labour Party to form New Party (which is left in the wilderness in the general election, in *Oct.*).

C **Mar:** 4th, by Delhi Pact between Viceroy (Lord Irwin) and Gandhi, civil disobedience campaign is suspended, Congress Party promises to recognise Round-table Conference and political prisoners are released;
8th, U.S.S.R.-Turkish agreement on naval reductions in Black Sea;
21st, Austro-German customs union is projected and on protests by France, Italy and Czechoslovakia is referred to the International Court in *May*, which decides against it;
26th, treaty of friendship between Iraq and Transjordan.

D **Apr:** 14th, King Alfonso flees in Spanish revolution and Alcalá Zamora becomes President of provisional government;
22nd, treaty of friendship between Egypt and Iraq, the first pact between Egypt and an Arab state.

E **May:** 5th, People's National Convention in Nanking adopts provisional constitution;
8th, Farmers' Party in power in Norway;
11th, bankruptcy of Credit-Anstalt in Austria begins financial collapse of Central Europe;
13th, Paul Doumer is elected French President (–*May* 1932).

F **Jun:** 15th, U.S.S.R.-Polish treaty of friendship and commerce;
16th, Bank of England advances money to Austria, but France withholds support;
20th, Herbert Hoover's plan for one-year moratorium for reparations and war debts;
21st, Karl Buresch, Christian Socialist, forms Austrian ministry;
24th, U.S.S.R.-Afghanistan treaty of neutrality.

G **Jul:** 1st, opening of Benguella-Katanga railway completes first trans-African railway;
—, anti-Chinese riots in Korea;
10th, Norway's annexation of East Greenland provokes Danish protest (referred to League which adjudicates against Norway in *Apr.* 1933);
13th, bankruptcy of German Danatbank leads to closure of all German banks until *Aug.* 5th;
25th, Cárlos Ibañez, President of Chile, resigns (succeeded *Oct.* 4th, by Juan Montero);
May Committee reports estimated budget deficit in Britain of £100 million and proposes drastic economies, which splits cabinet.

H **Aug:** 1st, Franco-U.S. loan to Britain;
3rd, Austria and Germany renounce customs union, Julius Curtius resigns in disgrace and Chancellor Heinrich Brüning takes over foreign affairs;
11th, London Protocol on Hoover moratorium;
19th, French loan to Hungary;
—, Layton-Wiggin report calls for six-month extension of foreign credit to Germany;
24th, Ramsay MacDonald resigns and, 25th, forms National Government to balance the budget; Labour party subsequently expels MacDonald, Philip Snowden and J. P. Thomas, who serve with him; Arthur Henderson becomes leader of rump of Labour Party.

O **Politics, Economics, Law and Education**

Norman Angell and Harold Wright, *Can Governments Cure Unemployment?*
B. Mussolini and G. Forzano, *The 100 Days.*
R. H. Tawney, *Equality.*
Political and Economic Planning (P.E.P.) founded in London.

P **Science, Technology, Discovery, etc.**

Publication of 'Gödel's proof', Kurt Gödel's questioning of the possibility of establishing dependable axioms in mathematics.
J. Cockcroft develops high-voltage apparatus for atomic transmutations.
Ernest O. Lawrence devises the cyclotron (an 'atom-smasher').
A. Eddington, *The World of Physics.*
O. P. Karrer isolates vitamin A.
Julius A. Nieuwland invents 'Neoprene' synthetic rubber process.
I.C.I. produce petrol from coal.
Spicer-Dufay process of natural colour photography.
Zoological Gardens, Whipsnade, opened.

Q **Scholarship**

R **Philosophy and Religion**

J. Dewey, *Philosophy and Civilisation.*
Neurath, *Empirical Sociology.*
O. Spengler, *Mankind and Technology.*
Papal Encyclical *Quadragesimo Anno* on social questions.

S **Art, Sculpture, Fine Arts and Architecture**

Painting:
P. Bonnard, *The Breakfast Room.*
Otto Dix, *Girls.*
E. Hopper, *Route 6, Eastham.*
H. Matisse, *The Dance*, murals at the Barnes Foundation, Pennsylvania.
P. Nash, *Kinetics.*

Sculpture:
C. Brancusi, *Mlle Pognany.*
J. Epstein, *Genesis* (marble).

Architecture:
Rockefeller Center, New York (–39).

T **Music**

Hans Pfitzner, *The Heart* (cantata).
W. Walton, *Belshazzar's Feast* (choral work).
S. Rachmaninov's music is banned in U.S.S.R. as 'decadent'.

U **Literature**

G. Bernanos, *La Grande Peur des bien-pensants.*
Pearl Buck, *The Good Earth.*
Theodore Dreiser, *Dawn.*
A. de St.-Exupéry, *Vol de nuit.*
V. Sackville-West, *All Passion Spent.*
George Seferis, *The Turning Point.*
Lytton Strachey, *Portraits in Miniature.*
Tristan Tzara, *L'Homme approximatif.*

1931 (Sep.–Dec.)

J Sep: 7th (–*Dec.* 1st), Gandhi attends second India Round-table Conference in London, but the Conference fails to reach agreement on the representation of religious minorities;
10th, government's economy measures provoke riots in London and Glasgow and, 15th, naval mutiny at Invergordon over pay cuts;
12th, Mexico is admitted to League;
13th, Heimwehr *coup d'état* in Austria under Fascist leader Dr. Pfrimer fails;
18th, United and Reform parties form coalition in New Zealand;
—, Japan begins siege of Mukden, using bomber seaplanes, and occupies other strategic points in Manchuria;
21st, Britain abandons gold standard, the £ falling from $4·86 to $3·49.

K Oct: 11th, Adolf Hitler's alliance with the commercial magnate, Hugenberg, to support the National Socialists;
16th, U.S. delegates attend League Council to discuss Japan;
20th, Protection of Republic law in Spain;
27th, in British general election National Government wins 558 seats, Opposition 56.

L Nov: Ramsay MacDonald forms second National Government, with Neville Chamberlain Chancellor of Exchequer and John Simon Foreign Secretary.

M Dec: 9th, Spanish republican Constitution with
10th, election of Alcalá Zamora President and Manuel Azaña premier;
11th, Japan abandons gold standard;
Statute of Westminster defines Dominion status.

N Joseph A. Lyons founds United Australia Party from Nationalists and Labour dissidents.
National Coffee Department is established in Brazil and begins official destruction of surplus stocks.

V **The Press**

Kingsley Martin edits *The New Statesman* (–60), with which the *Nation* and *Athenaeum* are amalgamated.

W **Drama and Entertainment**

J. Bridie, *The Anatomist*.
Noël Coward's *Cavalcade*.
E. O'Neill, *Mourning Becomes Electra*.
Dodie Smith, *Autumn Crocus*.
Lilian Baylis reopens Sadlers Wells.

Films:
Charlie Chaplin in *City Lights*.
Congress Dances.
René Clair's *The Million*.
Fritz Lang's *M*.
Sagan's *Mädchen in Uniform* with Dorothea Wieck.
Lamprecht's *Emil and the Detectives*.
Frankenstein with Boris Karloff.
Trader Horn.
Gracie Fields in *Sally in Our Alley*.

X **Sport**

Y **Statistics**

Populations (in mill.): China, 410; India, 338; U.S.S.R., 168; U.S., 122; Japan, 75; Germany, 64; Great Britain, 46; France, 42.
Petroleum production (in mill. barrels): U.S., 851; Venezuela, 116.

Z **Births and Deaths**

Jan. 3rd Joseph Joffre d. (78).
Jan. 22nd Anna Pavlova d. (49).
Jan. 31st Christopher Chataway b. (–).
Feb. 1st Boris Yeltsin b. (–).
Feb. 23rd Nellie Melba d. (72).
Mar. 2nd Mikhail Gorbachev b. (–).
Mar. 11th Rupert Murdoch b. (–).
Mar. 26th Timothy Healy d. (76).
Mar. 27th Arnold Bennett d. (64).
Mar. 29th Margaret McMillan d. (70).
Aug. 17th E. A. Wrigley b. (–).
Aug. 31st Hall Caine d. (78).
Sept. 24th J. M. G. M. Adams b. (–1985).
Sept. 29th William Orpen d. (52).
Oct. 7th Desmond Tutu b. (–).
Oct. 18th Thomas Alva Edison d. (84).
Dec. 3rd Vincent D'Indy d. (80).

A **Jan**: 2nd, Manchukuo republic proclaimed in Manchuria;
4th, Japanese reach Shanhaikwan on Great Wall;
—, Indian government granted emergency powers for six months, Indian National Congress is declared illegal and Mahatma Gandhi is arrested;
7th, Stimpson Doctrine, set out in note protesting against Japanese aggression in Manchuria, that U.S. will recognise no gains made by armed force;
—, Heinrich Brüning declares Germany cannot, and will not, resume reparations payments;
15th, France completes pacification of French Morocco;
22nd, U.S.S.R. second Five-year Plan begins;
25th, U.S.S.R.-Polish non-aggression pact;
28th, Japanese occupy Shanghai (*–May*).

B **Feb**: 2nd (*–July*), sixty states, including U.S. and U.S.S.R., attend Geneva Disarmament Conference, at which French proposal for international police force is opposed by Germany;
6th, Fascist *coup d'état* in Memel;
7th, by Oslo convention, Scandinavian countries, Belgium and Netherlands undertake economic co-operation;
8th, Bulgaria renounces further reparations payments;
16th, Republican majority in Irish elections;
21st, André Tardieu forms ministry in France;
27th, reorganisation of U.S. federal reserve system;
29th (*–Mar.* 3rd), Nazi revolt in Finland.

C **Mar**: 1st, Protection in Britain, with corn subsidies;
3rd, Chinese forces are driven back from Shanghai;
9th, Emperor Pu Yi, who had abdicated Chinese throne in 1912, is installed as President of Manchukuo;
—, Éamon de Valéra is elected President of Ireland;
13th, in German presidential election Paul von Hindenburg receives 18 million votes against Adolf Hitler, 11 million, and a Communist, 5 million, but below the majority required for election (new election *Apr.* 10th).

D **Apr**: 6th (–8th), London four-power conference on Danube founders since Germany and Italy decline to leave the problem to the Danubian states;
6th, British Minister of Health's circular to local authorities urging vigorous policy of slum clearance;
10th, Paul von Hindenburg (19 million votes) re-elected German President, against Hitler (13 million) and a Communist (3 million);
24th, Nazi successes in elections in Prussia, Bavaria, Württemberg and Hamburg.

E **May**: 1st, Left parties win French elections;
6th, President Paul Doumer of France murdered by Russian *émigré*;
10th, Albert Lebrun elected his successor;
16th, murder of Inukai, Japanese premier;
19th, Dáil votes for abolition of oath of loyalty to British crown, but the opposition in the Senate succeeds in preventing enactment;
20th, Engelbert Dollfuss, Austrian chancellor, forms a coalition of Christian Socialists and Agrarians;

F **Jun**: 1st, on Heinrich Brüning's resignation Franz von Papen forms a ministry in Germany with Constantin von Neurath foreign minister, from which the Nazis are excluded;

O **Politics, Economics, Law and Education**

W. Lewis, *Doom of Youth.*
John Strachey, *The Coming Struggle for Power.*
B.B.C. takes over responsibility for developing television from J. L. Baird's company.
Basic English founded as a prospective international language.
Commissioner for creating employment is appointed in Germany.
Aristotle Onassis purchases six freight ships, the start of his shipping fortune.
New Procedure rules in Supreme Court of Judicature in Britain to obviate attendance of witnesses through having facts proved by affidavits.
Kidnapping of C. A. Lindbergh's infant son.

P **Science, Technology, Discovery, etc.**

Chadwick's discovery of the neutron.
Harold C. Urey and Washburn discover that electrolysed water is denser than ordinary water, leading to the discovery of deuterium ('heavy hydrogen').
Edwin Land discovers the synthetic light polariser.
Karl Jansky pioneers radio-astronomy.
Vitamin D discovered.
Hans Krebs describes the citric acid cycle in cells, which converts sugars, fats and proteins into carbon dioxide, water and energy.
Balloon-tyre produced for farm tractors.
Zuider Zee drainage scheme completed.
Cologne-Bonn autobahn opened.
Opening of Lambeth Bridge, London, and Sydney Harbour Bridge.
Codos flies from Paris to Hanoi in 3 days 5 hrs. 40 mins. (*Jan.*).

Q **Scholarship**

Centenary celebrations of Goethe's death include the institution of the Goethe Medal for scholarship and art.
The Folger Library, Washington, opened.

R **Philosophy and Religion**

Henri Bergson, *Les deux sources de la monde et de la religion.*
Karl Jaspers, *Philosophie.*
Karl Barth, *Christian Dogmatics.*
Reunification of the Methodist Churches in England.

S **Art, Sculpture, Fine Arts and Architecture**

Painting:
Max Beckmann, *Seven Triptychs* (–1950).
Stanley Spencer, *May Tree, Cookham.*
Sculpture:
E. Gill, *Prospero and Ariel* for Broadcasting House, London (–1937).
Alexander Calder exhibits 'stabiles' (sculptures moved by engines) soon followed by 'mobiles' (sculptures moved by air currents).
Architecture:
Liverpool Metropolitan Cathedral begun on E. Lutyens' plans (later abandoned for F. Gibberd's).
Meyer and Hand, Broadcasting House, London (–1937).

T **Music**

Arnold Bax, 'cello concerto.
M. Ravel, Piano Concerto in G.
Dmitry Shostakovich, *Lady Macbeth of Mtsensk* (opera).
Thomas Beecham founds the London Philharmonic Orchestra.

F **Jun**: 4th, second ministry of Édouard Herriot in France;
6th (–18th), revolt in Chile ends in appointment of Socialist government;
13th, Anglo-French pact of friendship signed at Lausanne;
16th (–*July* 9th), at Lausanne reparations conference Germany accepts proposal for a final conditional payment of 3,000 million Rm.;
—, ban in Germany on Nazi Storm Troopers (in operation since *Apr.*) is lifted;
27th, Constitution proclaimed in Siam.

G **Jul**: 5th, Oliveira Salazar elected premier of Portugal and establishes Fascist régime;
11th (–*Oct.* 3rd), revolution in Brazil;
15th, by Geneva protocol Austria is granted loan on condition she renounces *Anschluss* until 1952;
18th, by new language regulations in Belgium French becomes official language of Walloon provinces, Flemish the language of Flanders;
—, Turkey is admitted to the League;
20th, Franz von Papen removes Socialist premier of Prussia by show of force;
21st (–*Aug.* 20th), Imperial Economic Conference at Ottawa favours moderate imperial preference;
31st, in Reichstag elections Nazis win 230 seats, Socialists 133, Centre 97 and Communists 89, producing stalemate, since neither Nazis nor Socialists would enter a coalition;
—, war begins between Bolivia and Paraguay (the Chaco War –*June* 1935).

H **Aug**: 10th, revolt of Gen. José Sanjurjo in Seville is suppressed;
13th, Adolf Hitler refuses President Hindenburg's request to serve as vice-chancellor under Franz von Papen.

J **Sep**: 1st, in war between Peru and Colombia over Leticia harbour, Colombia appeals to the League (which in *Mar.* 1933 orders Peru to withdraw);
14th, Germany leaves disarmament conference;
—, Belgian government is granted wide powers to deal with financial crisis;
25th, Catalonia is granted autonomy, with its own flag, language and Parliament;
28th, Herbert Samuel and other Liberal free-traders resign from Cabinet over policy of imperial preference; John Simon becomes leader of Liberals supporting government.

K **Oct**: 2nd, Lytton Report to League on Manchuria recognises Japan's special interests and recommends an autonomous State under Chinese sovereignty, but Japanese controlled;
3rd, on end of British mandate, Iraq joins League;
4th, Julius Gömbös, anti-Semite Nationalist, forms ministry in Hungary;
31st, Eleutherios Venizelos resigns in Greece, succeeded, *Nov.* 4th, by Panyoti Tsaldaris, a moderate Royalist.

L **Nov**: 6th, German elections produce further deadlock, with some Communist gains from Nazis;
8th, F. D. Roosevelt wins U.S. presidential election in Democrat landslide with 472 electoral votes over Herbert Hoover, Republican, with 59;
14th, Croat party demands new Yugoslav constitution;
17th, Franz von Papen resigns, and, 24th, Adolf Hitler rejects German chancellorship;
19th (–*Dec.* 24th), third India Conference in London;
29th, Franco-U.S.S.R. non-aggression pact;
29th, Persia annuls Anglo-Persian Oil Co. agreement of 1901.

T Music (*cont.*)

Duke Ellington is recognised as the first composer of jazz, and the first Negro musician of distinction.

U Literature

W. H. Auden, *The Orators.*
L. F. Céline, *Voyage au bout de la Nuit.*
William Faulkner, *Light in August.*
Ernest Hemingway, *Death in the Afternoon.*
Aldous Huxley, *Brave New World.*
F. R. Leavis, *New Bearings in English Poetry.*
R. Lehmann, *Invitation to the Waltz.*
Rose Macaulay, *They Were Defeated.*
Henri Michaux, *Un Barbare en Asie.*
Charles Morgan, *The Fountain.*
Boris Pasternak, *Second Birth* (poems).
Jules Romains, *Les Hommes de bonne volonté* (–47).
G. B. Shaw, *The Adventures of the Black Girl in Her Search for God.*

V The Press

Scrutiny issued (–1953).

W Drama and Entertainment

B. Brecht, *The Mother.*
J. Bridie, *Tobias and the Angel.*
J. B. Priestley, *Dangerous Corner.*
Shakespeare Memorial Theatre, Stratford-on-Avon, opened.

Films:
The Blue Light
René Clair's *À Nous La Liberté.*
Gary Cooper in *A Farewell to Arms.*
Marlene Dietrich in *Shanghai Express.*
La Maternelle.
Morning Glory.
Grand Hotel.
First 'Tarzan' film.
Shirley Temple's début.
127 sound films made (8 in 1929).
The Cinema Quarterly is issued.

X Sport

Olympic Games held at Los Angeles.
D. R. Jardine's 'body-line' bowling in M.C.C. tour of Australia.

Y Statistics

Unemployment: U.S., 13·7 mill.; Germany, 5·6 mill.; Great Britain, 2·8 mill.
U.K. Textiles trade:

Raw cotton imports	1,257 mill. lb.
Exports of cottons	2,303 mill. yds.
Exports of linens	65 mill. yds.
Exports of silks	4 mill. sq. yds.

Trades union membership: Great Britain, 4,443,000.

M **Dec:** 4th, Gen. K. von Schleicher forms ministry in Germany, attempting to conciliate the Centre and the Left;
9th, Japanese invade Jehol;
11th, No Force Declaration of Britain, France, Germany and Italy against resorting to force for settling differences; and, with signing of Geneva Protocol on Germany's equality of rights with other nations, Germany returns to Disarmament Conference;
15th, Mexico leaves the League;
16th, National Union in Lithuania adopts Fascist programme;
18th, Édouard Herriot resigns, after defeat in Chamber of proposal to pay debt to U.S., and Paul-Boncour forms cabinet;
27th, South Africa leaves gold standard;
28th, U.S. Congressional resolution against cancellation of Germany's war debt.

N Oswald Mosley founds British Union of Fascists.
Famine in U.S.S.R.
Australian federal government is strengthened by passage of Financial Agreement Enforcement Act.
Hunger Marches by British unemployed are organised.

Y **Statistics** (*cont.*)

U.S.S.R. production (in mill. tons): pig iron, 6·2; steel, 5·9; coal, 64·4; oil, 21·4; fertilisers, 0·9; cement, 3·5.

Z **Births and Deaths**

Jan. 7th André Maginot d. (54).
Jan. 21st Giles Lytton Strachey d. (51).
Feb. 6th François Truffaut b. (–1984).
Feb. 10th Edgar Wallace d. (57).
Feb. 18th Miloš Forman b. (–).
Mar. 7th Aristide Briand d. (69).
Mar. 14th George Eastman d. (77).
Mar. 18th John Updike b. (–).
May 7th Paul Doumer d. (75).
May 24th Arnold Wesker b. (–).
June 11th Athol Fugard b. (–).
July 6th Kenneth Grahame d. (73).
Aug. 9th Graham Wallas d. (74).
Aug. 17th V. S. Naipaul b. (–).
Sept. 16th Ronald Ross d. (75).
Oct. 27th Sylvia Plath b. (–1963).
Nov. 29th Jacques Chirac b. (–).

1933 (Jan.–Apr.) Hitler becomes German Chancellor—Japanese advances in China—'New Deal' in U.S.

A **Jan:** 2nd (–12th), rising in Barcelona of anarchists and syndicalists;
13th, U.S. Congress votes independence for Philippines after period of transition, which passes over President Hoover's veto, but is rejected, *Oct.*, by Philippine legislature;
16th, E. Venizelos again premier of Greece (–*Mar.* 10th);
24th, Éamon de Valéra's Fianna Fáil gains majority of one in Irish elections;
25th, Liberal ministry formed in Norway;
28th, Kurt von Schleicher's ministry falls in Germany, after failure to conciliate Centre and Left and
30th, Adolf Hitler is appointed Chancellor, forming a Nazi cabinet with Franz von Papen vice-chancellor, Constantin von Neurath foreign minister, Hermann Göring and Wilhelm Frick;
31st, Édouard Daladier becomes premier of France.

B **Feb:** 3rd, settlement of Anglo-Persian oil dispute;
6th, Twentieth Amendment to U.S. Constitution advances the President's inauguration to *Jan.* 20th, while senators and representatives are to take office on *Jan.* 3rd;
16th, fearing German threats the Little Entente (Czechoslovakia, Roumania and Yugoslavia) is reorganised, with a permanent council;
23rd (–*Mar.* 12th), Japanese occupy China north of Great Wall;
24th, League adopts Lytton Report on Manchuria, despite its rejection by Japan;
27th, Nazis engineer the Reichstag Fire, which Adolf Hitler denounces as a Communist plot, and suspends civil liberties and freedom of press.

C **Mar:** 4th, F. D. Roosevelt's inauguration speech, 'The only thing we have to fear is fear itself'; beginnings of the New Deal;
5th, in German elections Nazis win 288 seats, Socialists, 120, Communists, 81, Centre, 74, and Nationalists, 52;
6th, Poland occupies Danzig;
— (–9th), U.S. banks closed;
7th, Engelbert Dollfuss suspends Parliamentary government in Austria;
9th, U.S. Congress grants President Roosevelt wide powers concerning currency and credit;
16th, Britain's disarmament plan for reduction in size of armies fails, as Germany insists that Storm Troopers should not be included in total;
19th, Benito Mussolini proposes pact with Britain, France and Germany (signed *July* 15th);
23rd, enabling law in Germany grants Adolf Hitler dictatorial powers until *Apr.* 1937;
26th, new Constitution in Portugal;
27th, Japan announces she will leave the League (takes effect 1935);
30th, James B. M. Hertzog forms National Coalition in South Africa and is joined by Jan C. Smuts.

D **Apr:** 1st, persecution of Jews begins in Germany, with national boycott of all Jewish businesses and professions;
8th, Western Australia, irritated by federal taxation, votes to secede from Commonwealth;
10th, British Labour Party moves vote of censure on government for driving thousands of unemployed to seek Poor Law assistance;
25th, Canada, and, 30th, U.S. abandon gold standard;
27th, Anglo-German trade agreement.

O Politics, Economics, Law and Education

Norman Angell, *The Great Illusion Now.*
Joan Robinson, *The Economics of Imperfect Competition.*
Leon Trotsky, *History of the Russian Revolution.*
British Agricultural Marketing Scheme and U.S. Agricultural Adjustment tariff.
Oxford Union Society passes motion refusing to fight for King and Country.
German four-year plan for abolishing unemployment.
London Passenger Transport Board established.

P Science, Technology, Discovery, etc.

Anderson and R.A. Millikan, while analysing cosmic rays, discover positive electrons ('positrons').
De Haas's work on very low temperatures.
The discovery of the Steinheim skull leads to the rejection of the theory that Neanderthal Man was in the line of descent of *Homo sapiens.*
An all-metal wireless valve is made by Marconiphone Company.
The first commercially-produced synthetic detergent is made by I.C.I.
Polythene discovered.

Q Scholarship

Winston Churchill, *Marlborough: His Life and Times* (–38).

R Philosophy and Religion

A. N. Whitehead, *Adventures of Ideas.*
E. W. Barnes, *Scientific Theory and Religion.*
Nathan Söderblom, *The Living God* (Gifford Lectures).
Amalgamation of Protestant Churches in Germany as the German Evangelical Church (*July*).

S Art, Sculpture, Fine Arts and Architecture

Painting:
Herbert Read publishes *Art Now.*
Wassily Kandinsky and Paul Klee leave Germany for France and Switzerland respectively.
Sculpture:
A. Giacometti, *The Palace at 4 a.m.*
Architecture:
Ove Arup, Highpoint 1, Highgate, London.
W. Holden, Senate House, London University.
The Warburg Institute is transferred from Hamburg to London (is incorporated in London University, 1944).

T Music

R. Strauss, *Arabella* (opera).
Balanchine and Kirstein found School of American Ballet.

U Literature

G. Duhamel, *The Pasquier Chronicle* (–45).
T. S. Eliot, *The Use of Poetry and the Use of Criticism.*
A. Malraux, *La Condition humaine.*
Thomas Mann, *The Tales of Jacob* (first volume of 'Joseph and his Brothers' –43).
G. Orwell (pseud.), *Down and Out in Paris and London.*
G. Santayana, *The Last Puritan.*
Gertrude Stein, *The Autobiography of Alice B. Toklas.*
Helen Waddell, *Peter Abelard.*

E **May**: 2nd, German trades unions are suppressed;
3rd, oath of allegiance to British Crown removed from Irish Constitution and Irish appeals to Privy Council made illegal;
10th, Paraguay declares war on Bolivia;
12th, U.S. agricultural adjustment act and federal emergency relief act;
—, Franco-Canadian tariff agreement;
17th, in South African elections National Coalition wins 138 seats, Opposition, 12;
—, Associations law in Spain nationalises church property and closes church schools;
18th, Tennessee Valley Authority created in U.S. to develop the valley's resources;
26th, Australia claims a third of Antarctic continent;
27th, U.S. securities act to protect investors by providing information on new security issues;
28th, Nazis win Danzig elections.

F **Jun**: 12th (–*July* 27th), 64 countries attend World Monetary and Economic Conference in London but fail to reach agreement on currency stabilisation, through F. D. Roosevelt's opposition (*July* 3rd), leading to rampant economic nationalism and, in Britain, to the 'buy British' campaign;
16th, U.S. National Industrial Recovery Act and Farm Credit Act;
19th, Nazi party in Austria is dissolved, but terrorist agitation continues;
20th, army *coup d'état* in Siam.

G **Jul**: 3rd, London convention defining the aggressor signed by U.S.S.R., the Baltic and Balkan states;
14th, political parties, other than Nazi, suppressed in Germany;
15th, Rome Pact binds Britain, France, Germany and Italy to the League Covenant, the Locarno treaties and the Kellogg-Briand Pact;
20th, concordat with Papacy defines position of Catholic Church in Germany;
23rd, National Guard ('Blue Shirts') formed in Eire to oppose É. de Valéra's Republican Army;
27th, British Commonwealth declaration on monetary and economic affairs;
—, Saudi Arabia and Transjordan sign treaty of friendship;
Assyrian Christians massacred by Iraqui (–*Aug.*).

H **Aug**: 5th, Polish agreement with Danzig;
25th, Canada, U.S., U.S.S.R., Australia and Argentina sign wheat agreement.

J **Sep**: 3rd, Irish opposition parties of National Guard and the Centre form United Ireland Party under Owen O'Duffy (but led by William Cosgrave from 22nd);
14th, Graeco-Turkish ten-year non-aggression pact.

K **Oct**: 11th, Latin American countries sign Rio de Janeiro non-aggression pact;
14th, Germany leaves disarmament conference and the League;
16th, Labour Party wins Norwegian elections;
23rd, Albert Sarraut forms ministry in France;
Unrest in Palestine grows.

L **Nov**: 12th, Nazis dominate German elections, with 92 per cent of electorate voting for Nazi candidates;
16th, British Liberal Party joins opposition;
—, President Getulio Vargas of Brazil acquires dictatorial powers;
17th, U.S. recognises U.S.S.R. and resumes trade;
19th, Right wins Spanish elections for the Cortes;
22nd, Camille Chautemps forms ministry in France.

(*Continued opposite*)

V **The Press**

Arthur Christiansen edits *The Daily Express* (–57).

W **Drama and Entertainment**

J. Bridie, *A Sleeping Clergyman.*
Gordon Daviot, *Richard of Bordeaux.*
Merton Hodge, *The Wind and the Rain.*
Eugene O'Neill, *Ah Wilderness.*
British Film Institute founded.
Odeon cinema circuit formed in Britain.

Films:

Alexander Korda's *The Private Lives of Henry VIII* with Charles Laughton;
Greta Garbo in *Queen Christina.*
The Testament of Dr. Mabuse.
René Clair's *14 Juli.*
Cavalcade.
King Kong.
She Done Him Wrong with Mae West.

X **Sport**

National Playing Fields Association founded in London.

Y **Statistics**

Z **Births and Deaths**

Jan. 1st Joe Orton b. (–1967).
Jan. 2nd Keith Thomas b. (–).
Jan. 5th Calvin Coolidge d. (60).
Jan. 21st George Augustus Moore d. (80).
Jan. 31st John Galsworthy d. (66).
Mar. 19th Philip Roth b. (–).
Apr. 22nd Frederick Henry Royce d. (60).
July 8th 'Anthony Hope' (pseud. of Anthony Hope Hawkins) d. (60).
July 23rd Richard Rogers b. (–).
Sept. 7th Edward Grey, Viscount Grey of Fallodon, d. (81).
Dec. 4th Stefan George d. (65).
Dec. 23rd Akihito b. (–).

M **Dec**: 5th, Twenty-first amendment to U.S. Constitution repeals prohibition;
9th, radical rising in Spain;
18th, Newfoundland Constitution suspended on mismanagement of economic affairs and
21st, Newfoundland loses dominion status, reverting to Crown Colony;
28th, Britain makes final payment to U.S. for war debts;
29th, Ion Duca, Liberal premier of Roumania, is murdered by Iron Guard and is succeeded by George Tartarescu;
Flight of Alexandre Stavisky, a Russian promoter, involved in fraudulent transactions in France, is exploited by Royalists and Fascists;
Jews protest at immigration restrictions in Palestine.

N

1934 (Jan.–Jun.) Dollfuss murdered—Hitler becomes Führer—Purge of Russian Communist Party begins

A **Jan:** 14th, Catalan elections won by Left, while in rest of Spain the Right predominates;
26th, Germany signs ten-year non-aggression pact with Poland;
30th, Édouard Daladier forms ministry in France;
—, U.S. Gold Reserve Act authorises President to revalue the dollar;
31st, Federal Farm Mortgage Corporation set up in U.S.
Turkey's five-year plan for industry begins.

B **Feb:** 1st (–16th), Austrian decree dissolving all political parties except Engelbert Dollfuss's Fatherland Front leads to risings; the Christian Socialists forfeit support from working classes;
5th, Corporations act in Italy;
6th (–7th), riots in Paris, and, 8th, Paul Doumergue forms National Union ministry of all parties, except Royalists, Socialists and Communists, to avert civil war;
9th, Balkan pact signed between Roumania, Greece, Yugoslavia and Turkey, as a counterpart to the Little Entente, to prevent Balkans from encroachment by the great powers, but Bulgaria is not a signatory;
12th (–13th), general strike in France;
15th, Civil Works Emergency Relief act in U.S.;
16th, Anglo-Russian trade pact;
21st (–*Mar.* 16th), French troops combat Berbers in South-West Morocco.

C **Mar:** 1st, Pu Yi assumes title of Emperor of Manchukuo;
8th, Labour Party for first time wins clear majority on L.C.C. over Municipal Reform and Liberal Parties;
16th (–17th), Rome protocols signed between Italy, Austria and Hungary to form Danubian bloc against Little Entente (Czechoslovakia, Roumania and Yugoslavia);
24th, Tydings-McDuffie act declares independence of the Philippines from 1945;
26th, Road Traffic Act introduces driving tests in Britain.

D **Apr:** 7th, Gandhi suspends civil disobedience campaign;
7th, extension of U.S.S.R.-Finnish non-aggression pact for ten years;
Socialists lead strike in Barcelona.

E **May:** 14th, British Unemployment bill given third reading;
15th, Karlis Ulmanis becomes dictator in Latvia;
24th, Colombia and Peru settle dispute over Leticia.

F **Jun:** 5th, J. C. Smuts's South African Party unites with J. B. M. Hertzog's followers in Nationalist Party to form United South African Nationalists, while other Nationalists re-form under D. F. Malan;
8th, Oswald Mosley addresses mass meeting of British Union of Fascists at Olympia;
9th, U.S.S.R. renews relations with Czechoslovakia and, 10th, with Roumania;
11th, Disarmament Conference ends in failure;
12th, political parties banned in Bulgaria;
—, Congress grants F. D. Roosevelt powers to conclude agreements for reducing tariffs;
—, Cape Parliament retains right to secede from Commonwealth in South African Status bill;
14th (–15th), Venice meeting between Hitler and Mussolini fails to bring about closer relations owing to divergent interests in the Danube Valley;
19th, U.S. Silver Purchase bill authorises President to nationalise silver;
20th, agreement on frontier between Sudan and Libya;

O **Politics, Economics, Law and Education**

Lewis Mumford, *Technics and Civilisation.*
John Wheeler-Bennett, *The Disarmament Deadlock.*
Bertrand Russell, *Freedom and Organisation.*
Peace Pledge Union founded in Britain.
British Iron and Steel Federation.
Hendon Police College founded.
Wavelengths of chief European broadcasting stations are altered, to conform with recommendations of Lucerne Committee (*Jan.* 14th).
German law for the regulation of labour.
Dr. H. Schacht's plan for the control of Germany's foreign trade (*Sept.*).
Kurt Hahn founds Gordonstoun School, Scotland.

P **Science, Technology, Discovery, etc.**

F. Joliot and I. Curie-Joliot discover induced radioactivity.
Ernest O. Lawrence's cyclotron, for producing high-velocity particles.
Enrico Fermi suggests that neutrons and protons are the same fundamental particles in two different quantum states.
Alexander Fleming and Petrie, *Recent Advances in Vaccine and Serum Therapy.*
Reichstein makes pure Vitamin C.
Phthalacyamine dyes are prepared.
Chilling process for meat cargoes discovered.
U.S.S.R. balloon *Osoaviakhim* ascends 13 miles into stratosphere (*Jan.* 30th).
Beebe descends 3,028 feet into ocean off Bermuda (*Aug.* 16th).
S.S. *Queen Mary* launched (*Sept.* 26th), and Southern Railway's first train ferry launched.
Regular air-mail service, London to Australia (*Dec.*).

Q **Scholarship**

Arnold Toynbee, *A Study of History* (–54).
Oxford History of England, ed. G. N. Clark (–65).
J. E. Neale, *Queen Elizabeth.*
Harold Nicolson, *Curzon, the Last Phase.*

R **Philosophy and Religion**

Lionel Curtis, *Civitas Dei.*
Albert Einstein, *My Philosophy.*
R. Niebuhr, *Moral Man and Immoral Society.*
William Temple, *Nature, Man and God.*

S **Art, Sculpture, Fine Arts and Architecture**

Painting:
J. Piper, *Rye Harbour.*
Stanley Spencer, *The Angel, Cookham Church.*

Architecture:
Cambridge University Library.
Wornum, Royal Institute of British Architects Building, London.
Gustav Adolf Kirche, Berlin.

T **Music**

P. Hindemith completes *Mathis der Maler* (opera), but its performance is banned in Germany.
A. Honegger's ballet, *Sémiramis.*
I. Stravinsky, *Persephone*, an opera-ballet.
John Christie founds Glyndebourne operatic festival.

F **Jun:** 22nd, Ramsay MacDonald, ordered to rest, delegates duties to Stanley Baldwin;
23rd, Saudi Arabia and the Yemen sign peace after war of six weeks;
30th, Nazi purge in Germany with summary executions of Kurt von Schleicher, Ernst Roehm and other party leaders for alleged plot against Hitler.

G **Jul:** 1st, Germany suspends all cash transfers on debts abroad;
2nd, Lazaro Cárdenas elected President of Mexico;
7th, Keisuke Okada forms ministry in Japan;
12th, Belgium prohibits uniformed political parties;
14th, oil pipeline Mosul to Tripoli opened;
19th, Stanley Baldwin announces increase in size of R.A.F.;
25th, E. Dollfuss is murdered in attempted Nazi *coup* in Austria;
30th, Kurt Schuschnigg is appointed Austrian chancellor.

H **Aug:** 1st, Australia's prohibitive duty on imported cottons provokes boycott of Australian produce in Lancashire;
2nd, death of Paul von Hindenburg (aged 87);
19th, German plebiscite approves vesting of sole executive power in Adolf Hitler as Führer.

J **Sep:** 9th, Fascist and anti-Fascist demonstrations in Hyde Park, London;
12th, Baltic states sign treaty of collaboration;
17th, United Australian Party wins general election;
18th, U.S.S.R. is admitted to the League.

K **Oct:** 2nd, Royal Indian Navy founded;
4th, Alejandro Lerroux forms ministry of Right in Spain, provoking, 5th, strike called by the Left;
9th, King Alexander of Yugoslavia is assassinated in Marseilles;
23rd (–*Dec.* 19th), London Naval Disarmament Conference meets, but no agreement is reached;
24th, Gandhi withdraws from Indian National Congress;
—, German Labour Front founded;
30th, dissolution of Graeco-Turkish Commission of 1923.

L **Nov:** 3rd, Syrian Parliament is indefinitely prorogued;
7th, Joseph Lyons, United Australian Party, forms coalition ministry with Country Party in Australia;
9th, Pierre Flandin forms coalition in France;
13th, Sedition bill introduced in Britain;
20th, Depressed Areas bill introduced in Britain;
26th, abolition of titles in Turkey;
28th, Winston Churchill warns Parliament of German air menace;
30th, Egyptian Constitution of 1930 suspended;
Moroccan nationalist movement founded.

M **Dec:** 1st, assassination of Serge Kirov, close collaborator of Josef Stalin, leads to O.G.P.U. purge in Russian Communist Party;
5th, clashes between Italian and Ethiopian troops on Somaliland frontier;
14th, enfranchisement of women in Turkey;
16th, National Union Party provides only candidates in Portuguese elections;
19th, Japan denounces Washington treaties of 1922 and 1930;
21st, Anglo-Irish coal and cattle pact;
Daniel Salamanca, President of Bolivia, overthrown by military *coup*.

N

U **Literature**

Louis Aragon, *Hourra l'Oural* (poem).
Scott Fitzgerald, *Tender is the Night*.
Robert Graves, *I, Claudius*.
Dorothy L. Sayers, *The Nine Tailors*.
Sholokhov, *Quiet Flows the Don*.
First Soviet Writers' Conference held in Moscow under M. Gorki.

V **The Press**

Left Review (–1938).

W **Drama and Entertainment**

Jean Cocteau, *La Machine infernale*.
Sean O'Casey, *Within the Gates*.
J. B. Priestley, *Eden End*.

Films:
René Clair's *The Last Millionaire*.
Forgotten Men.
The Scarlet Pimpernel.
The Thin Man.

X **Sport**

Henry Cotton ends U.S. golfers' dominance by winning open championship at Sandwich.

Y **Statistics**

Z **Births and Deaths**

Feb. 23rd Edward Elgar d. (76).
Apr. 11th Gerald du Maurier d. (61).
May 9th Alan Bennett b. (–).
May 17th Cass Gilbert d. (74).
May 25th Gustav Holst d. (59).
June 10th Frederick Delius d. (71).
July 4th Marie Curie d. (66).
Sept. 9th Roger Fry d. (67).
Sept. 20th Sophia Loren b. (–).
Oct. 14th Arthur Schuster d. (83).
Oct. 15th Raymond Poincaré d. (74).
Nov. 23rd Arthur Wing Pinero d. (79).

1935 (Jan.–Jun.) The Saar is restored to Germany—Stresa Conference—Italy invades Abyssinia

A **Jan**: 1st, Mustapha Kemal, President of Turkey, adopts name of Kemal Atatürk when National Assembly makes family names obligatory;
4th, British cotton-spinners vote to reduce the productive capacity of the industry;
7th, Franco-Italian agreement of Marseilles, intended as preliminary to a general treaty of co-operation;
9th, Britain signs trade pact with India;
13th, Saar plebiscite favours incorporation with Germany;
15th (–17th), Grigori Zinoviev and other U.S.S.R. leaders are convicted of treason and imprisoned (Zinoviev is re-tried as a Trotskyist and sentenced to death, *Aug.* 1936);
17th, David Lloyd George's 'New Deal' speech at Bangor (*July* 22nd, the government replies to his programme);
28th, George Lansbury leads Commons storm over means test.

B **Feb**: 1st (–3rd), Anglo-German conference in London to discuss Germany's rearmament; Italy sends troops to East Africa.

C **Mar**: 1st (–11th), rising of E. Venizelos in Greece is suppressed;
7th, restoration of Saar to Germany marks beginning of Germany's expansion;
12th, 30-m.p.h. speed limit enforced in built-up areas of Britain;
16th, Germany repudiates disarmament clauses of Versailles Treaty;
20th, Labour ministry takes office in Norway;
23rd, U.S.S.R. sells her interest in Chinese Eastern Railway to Japan;
25th, Paul Van Zeeland forms ministry of National Unity in Belgium and devalues Belgian Franc.

D **Apr**: 11th (–14th), Britain, France and Italy confer at Stresa, to establish a common front against Germany;
23rd, Polish Constitution is adopted after nine years discussion.

E **May**: 2nd, Franco-U.S.S.R. treaty of mutual assistance for five years;
16th, U.S.S.R.-Czechoslovakia pact of mutual assistance;
19th, Sudete (Nazi) Party strengthens position in Czechoslovakian election;
27th, U.S. Supreme Court declares National Industrial Recovery Act to be unconstitutional;
31st, ministry of Pierre Flandin, who had demanded extensive powers, is overthrown in France.

F **Jun**: 3rd, Croats boycott Yugoslav Parliament;
4th, Pierre Laval forms ministry in France;
7th, Stanley Baldwin, Conservative, forms National Government in Britain, with Ramsay MacDonald Lord President of Council, John Simon Home Secretary and Samuel Hoare Foreign Secretary;
14th, end of Chaco War between Paraguay and Bolivia;
18th, by Anglo-German Naval Agreement Germany undertakes that her navy shall not exceed a third of tonnage of Royal Navy;
23rd, Anthony Eden offers Benito Mussolini concessions over Abyssinia, which he rejects;
27th, League of Nations Union peace ballot in Britain shows strong support for ideals of League;
—, D. Lloyd George forms Council of Action for peace and reconstruction.

O Politics, Economics, Law and Education

S. and B. Webb, *Soviet Communism: A New Civilisation.*
Victor Gollancz founds Left Book Club (first publication in *May* 1936).
Germany reintroduces compulsory military service (*Mar.* 16th).
New Deal Social Security legislation in U.S.
G. H. Gallup founds the American Institute of Public Opinion and conducts the first Gallup Polls of public opinion.
British Council founded.
Persia changes its name to Iran; and a University is founded at Teheran.
Bank of Canada founded (*Mar.* 11th).
L.C.C. Green Belt Scheme in operation (*Apr.* 1st).

P Science, Technology, Discovery, etc.

Robert Watson-Watt builds first practical radar equipment for detecting aircraft.
Domagk discovers prontosil for treating streptococcal infections.
J. C. Kendall isolates the steroid hormone Cortisone from the adrenal cortex.
The 35 mm. 'Kodachrome' film devised.
Hydrogenerator plant, for making petrol from coal, opened at Billingham, Co. Durham (*June*).
Oil pipelines from Kirkuk in Iraq to Haifa and Tripolis opened (*Jan.*).
Lower Zambesi railway bridge, the longest in world, opened to traffic (*Jan.* 14th).
M. Campbell at Daytona Beach, Florida, drives his car *Bluebird* at 276·8 m.p.h.
S.S. *Normandie* crosses Atlantic in 107 hours 33 mins.
Pan-American Airways start trans-Pacific service from California.

Q Scholarship

Brockhaus Encyclopaedia completed.
R. H. Hodgkin, *History of the Anglo-Saxons.*
T. E. Lawrence, under pseudonym of T. E. Shaw, publishes translation of *The Odyssey of Homer.*

R Philosophy and Religion

J. B. S. Haldane, *Philosophy of a Biologist.*
Karl Jaspers, *Suffering and Existence.*
Margaret Mead, *Growing up in New Guinea.*
Karl Barth, *Credo.*
F. H. Hinsley appointed Cardinal Archbishop of Westminster (*Apr.*).

S Art, Sculpture, Fine Arts and Architecture

Painting:
Salvador Dali, *Giraffe on Fire.*
E. Munch, *The Modern Faust.*
S. Spencer, *Workmen in the House.*
T. W. Earp, *Modern Movements in Painting.*
David Gascoyne, *Short Survey of Surrealism.*
Sculpture:
J. Epstein, *Ecce Homo.*
Architecture:
E. Mendelssohn and Chermeyeff, The De la Warr Pavilion, Bexhill, Sussex.

T Music

Alban Berg, violin concerto.
George Gershwin, *Porgy and Bess* (folk opera).

G **Jul**: 4th, Austria, encouraged by Mussolini, abolishes anti-Hapsburg laws and restores in part imperial property;

13th, U.S.S.R.-U.S. trade pact;

25th (–*Aug.* 20th), Third International meeting declares that Communists in democratic countries should support their governments against Fascist states;

27th, French government is granted emergency financial powers;

Anti-Roman Catholic riots in Belfast.

H **Aug**: 2nd, Government of India Act reforms governmental system, separates Burma and Aden from India, grants provincial governments greater self-government and creates a central legislature at Delhi (to come into force *Apr.* 1st 1937);

14th, F. D. Roosevelt signs Social Security act;

30th, U.S. Coal Stabilization Act and Wealth Tax, which increases surtax;

31st, U.S. Neutrality Act.

J **Sep**: 10th, assembly of white settlers in Kenya denounces government policy and advocates closer union with Uganda and Tanganyika;

15th, Nuremberg laws outlaw the Jews and make Swastika the official flag of Germany.

K **Oct**: 2nd, Italy invades Abyssinia;

7th, League Council declares Italy the aggressor;

— (–17th), Kurt Schuschnigg's 'bloodless *coup d'état*' in Vienna in collaboration with Prince Starhemberg against Emil Fey, minister of interior, and his Nazi allies;

19th, League imposes sanctions against Italy;

23rd, Mackenzie King forms Liberal ministry in Canada.

L **Nov**: 3rd, Greek plebiscite favours George II;

3rd, French Socialist groups merge as Socialist and Republican Union, under Léon Blum; this soon forms close relations with Radical Socialists and Communists to found a Popular Front;

4th, German-Polish economic agreement;

5th, Milan Hodza, Agrarian party, forms ministry in Czechoslovakia;

7th, U.S.S.R.-Turkish treaties extended for ten years;

14th, in British general election Government parties win 428 seats, Opposition, 184 (Conservatives, 385, National Liberal, 32, Liberal, 17, Labour, 154, I.L.P., 4, and Communist, 1); Ramsay MacDonald is defeated by Emmanuel Shinwell at Seaham Harbour;

15th, Commonwealth of Philippines is inaugurated;

—, Canadian-U.S. reciprocal trade agreement;

20th, British miners ballot to press for wage increase;

29th, Michael Savage forms first Labour ministry in New Zealand.

T **Music** (*cont.*)

Sergei Rachmaninov, *Rhapsody on a Theme of Paganini.*
Dmitry Shostakovich, Symphony no. 1 (op. 10).
I. Stravinsky's ballet, *Game of Cards.*
William Walton, Symphony.
D. F. Tovey, *Essays in Musical Analysis* (–39).
The term 'swing' is coined.
Jazz of Negro or Jewish origin is banned from German radio (*Oct.*).

U **Literature**

W. H. Auden and C. Isherwood, *The Dog Beneath the Skin.*
Ivy Compton-Burnett, *A House and its Head.*
Cyril Connolly, *The Rock Pool.*
C. Day-Lewis, *A Time to Dance.*
Walter de la Mare, *Poems, 1919–34.*
Christopher Isherwood, *Mr. Norris Changes Trains.*
A. Malraux, *Le Temps du mépris.*
William Saroyan, *The Daring Young Man on the Flying Trapeze.*

V **The Press**

W **Drama and Entertainment**

T. S. Eliot, *Murder in the Cathedral.*
Clifford Odets, *Waiting for Lefty.*
Robert Sherwood, *The Petrified Forest.*
Emlyn Williams, *Night Must Fall.*
Ivor Novello's *Glamorous Night.*
To appease demand for American-style films, U.S.S.R. plans to found a Crimean Hollywood.

Films:

Greta Garbo in *Anna Karenina.*
D. Selznick's *David Copperfield.*
Jean Renoir's *Toni.*
Cyrano de Bergerac.
Becky Sharp.
Lives of a Bengal Lancer.
Top Hat with Fred Astaire and Ginger Rogers.

Silver Jubilee Celebrations in Britain (*May* 6th).
Germany has regular television services.
First broadcast quiz programme, in Canada (*May* 15th).

X **Sport**

Y **Statistics**

Railway mileage in operation: U.S., 254,347; Great Britain, 62,502; U.S.S.R., 52,687; Germany, 27,218; France, 26,580.
Illiteracy: percentages of population: Egypt, 85; India, 80; Brazil, 67; Mexico, 58; Turkey, 55; Greece, 32; Spain, 31; Portugal, 30; Poland, 21; Italy, 19; U.S.S.R., 13.

M **Dec:** 1st, Chiang Kai-shek elected president of Chinese (Kuo Min Tang) executive;
9th, Hoare-Laval proposals on Abyssinia, which favour Italy, are wrecked by public indignation in Britain and France;
12th, Nationalists demand restitution of Egyptian Constitution of 1923;
13th, E. Beneš succeeds T. Masaryk as President of Czechoslovakia;
18th, Samuel Hoare resigns and, 23rd, Anthony Eden is appointed Foreign Secretary.

N

z **Births and Deaths**

Feb. 8th Max Liebermann d. (86).
Mar. 13th George Earle Buckle d. (80).
Apr. 8th Edwin Cannan d. (74).
May 18th Paul Dukas d. (69).
May 19th T. E. Lawrence d. (46).
June 1st Norman Foster b. (–).
June 13th Christo b. (–).
June 21st 'Françoise Sagan' (pseud. of Françoise Quoirez) b. (–).
July 17th G. W. Russell ('A.E.') d. (68).
Sept. 10th Huey Pierce Long d. (42).
Sept. 16th Carl Andre b. (–).
Oct. 20th Arthur Henderson d. (72).
Oct. 22nd Edward, Lord Carson, d. (61).
Nov. 5th Lester Piggott b. (–).
Nov. 13th George Carey b. (–).
Nov. 20th John, Earl Jellicoe, d. (75).
Dec. 1st Woody Allen b. (–).
Dec. 24th Alban Berg d. (50).
Dec. 25th Paul Bourget d. (83).

1936 (Jan.–Jun.) Germans troops enter Rhineland—Popular Front in France—Spanish Civil War begins—Abdication of Edward VIII

A **Jan:** 15th, Japan leaves London naval conference;
20th, accession of Edward VIII on death of George V;
22nd, Albert Sarraut forms ministry on fall of Pierre Laval through public indignation at Italian policy.

B **Feb:** 16th, in Spanish elections Popular Front wins 265 seats against 142 for the Right and 66 for the Centre parties; Manuel Azaña becomes premier and re-establishes constitution of 1931;
17th, Anglo-Irish trade pact ends tariff war;
26th, military *coup d'état* in Japan places Koki Hirota as premier.

C **Mar:** 3rd, British defence budget leaps from £122 million to £158 million, to increase Fleet Air Arm, add 250 aircraft for home defence and 4 new infantry battalions;
7th, Germany violates Treaty of Versailles by occupying demilitarised zone of Rhineland;
23rd, Italy, Austria and Hungary sign Rome pact;
25th, Britain, U.S. and France sign London naval convention;
29th, 99 per cent of electorate vote for official Nazi candidates in German elections;
31st, Lord Eustace Percy resigns from cabinet, a symptom of general dissatisfaction with Stanley Baldwin, especially for his tergiversation over the Hoare-Laval pact;
Britain's first civil defence anti-gas school opened.

D **Apr:** 1st, Austria reintroduces conscription;
7th, Cape Parliament passes Native Representation bill, permitting natives to elect three Europeans to represent them in Union Parliament, and establishing a native representative council with only advisory powers;
8th, U.S.S.R.-Mongolia treaty of mutual assistance;
10th, Cortes dismisses President Zamora of Spain;
13th, General John Metaxas becomes Greek premier;
28th, accession of King Farouk in Egypt;
Arab High Committee formed to unite Arabs against Jewish claims.

E **May:** 3rd, Popular Front wins 387 seats in French elections, other parties, 231;
5th, Italians occupy Addis Ababa, ending Abyssinian war and, 9th, Abyssinia is formally annexed by Italy;
10th, Nahas Pasha forms all-Wafdist ministry in Egypt;
—, Manuel Azaña elected President of Spain;
21st, Kurt Schuschnigg becomes leader of Austrian Fatherland Front;
22nd, J. H. Thomas, dominions secretary, resigns over budget leakage;
24th, Rexists (Fascist) win 21 seats in Belgian elections;
28th, Irish Senate is abolished.

F **Jun:** 4th, Léon Blum, Socialist, forms Popular Front ministry in France;
9th, Count Nobile Ciano appointed Italian foreign minister;
12th, 40-hour week in France;
17th, Canadian supreme court nullifies most of 'New Deal' legislation of R. B. Bennett's government in 1935;
23rd, Clement Attlee moves vote of censure on Stanley Baldwin's government for irresponsible foreign policy (defeated by 214 votes);
24th, Paul van Zeeland introduces social improvements programme in Belgium;
30th, suppression of French Fascist Party.

O **Politics, Economics, Law and Education**

A. Carr-Saunders, *World Population.*
Lancelot Hogben, *Political Arithmetic; Mathematics for the Million.*
J. M. Keynes, *General Theory of Employment, Interest and Money.*
M'Gonighe and Kirby, *Poverty and Public Health.*
J. Strachey, *The Theory and Practice of Socialism.*
Reorganisation of Bank of France.
The Ford Foundation is established.
London University moves from Kensington to Bloomsbury.

P **Science, Technology, Discovery, etc.**

Solar eclipse (*June* 19th) observed by expeditions in Kamishari, North Japan, and Omsk, Siberia.
Mrs. A. Mollison flies from England to Cape Town in 3 days 6 hrs. 25 mins. (*May* 4th–7th).
The *Wupperthal*, first diesel-electric vessel, launched.

Q **Scholarship**

A. J. Carlyle completes *History of Medieval Political Theory in the West.*
H. A. L. Fisher, *History of Europe.*
F. Meinecke, *The Origin of Historismus.*

R **Philosophy and Religion**

A. J. Ayer, *Language, Truth and Logic.*
S. Freud, *Autobiography.*
W. Sombart, *Sociology.*

S **Art, Sculpture, Fine Arts and Architecture**

Painting:
Laura Knight, *Ballet.*
P. Mondrian, *Composition in Red and Blue.*
R. Whistler, frescoes at Plas Newydd, Anglesey (–1938).
The cleaning of Velasquez's *Philip of Spain* by the National Gallery provokes controversy.

Sculpture:
Marino Marini, *The Horseman* (painted wood).
Isamu Noguchi, *History of Mexico.*

Architecture:
W. Gropius and E. M. Fry, Film Studios, Denham, Bucks.
F. L. Wright, Kaufman House, 'Falling Water', Bear Run, Pennsylvania, and office block (with umbrella columns), Racine, Wisconsin.
Crystal Palace, Sydenham, destroyed by fire.

T **Music**

C. Lambert, *Summer's Last Will and Testament.*
S. Prokofiev, *Peter and the Wolf.*
Woody Herman founds 'The Band that Played the Blues'.

U **Literature**

W. H. Auden, *Look, Stranger!*
Georges Bernanos, *Journal of a Country Priest.*
Aldous Huxley, *Eyeless in Gaza.*
Margaret Mitchell, *Gone With the Wind.*
H. de Montherlant, *Les Jeunes Filles* (–39).

G **Jul:** 11th, Austro-German convention acknowledges Austria's independence;
15th, League raises sanctions against Italy;
17th, munitions industry in France is nationalised;
18th, army revolt under Emilio Mola and Francisco Franco begins Spanish Civil War;
20th, by Montreux convention Turkey recovers sovereignty over Dardanelles and Bosporus;
21st, revised means-test regulations in Britain;
24th, Junta de Defensa Nacional set up at Burgos;
Failure of Jarrow special development area scheme.

H **Aug:** 2nd, France suggests to Britain a policy of non-intervention in Spain;
4th, Franco's army captures Badajoz and advances eastwards;
11th, Chiang Kai-shek enters Canton;
24th, Germany adopts two-year compulsory military service;
26th, treaty ends British military occupation of Egypt, except Canal Zone, and forms Anglo-Egyptian alliance for 20 years.

J **Sep:** 9th, conference in London on non-intervention in Spanish Civil War;
—, France signs treaties of friendship with Syria, where mandate is to end in 1939, and, 19th, with the Lebanon;
10th, Joseph Goebbels accuses Czechoslovakia of harbouring U.S.S.R. aircraft;
27th, France, Switzerland and Holland abandon gold standard;
Japan's secret demands to China about employment of Japanese in Chinese government and presenting united front against Communists are rejected by Nanking.

K **Oct:** 1st, U.S.S.R. accedes to London naval convention of *Mar.* 25th;
—, Spanish insurgents appoint General Francisco Franco chief of state;
2nd, France devalues the Franc;
5th, Italy devalues the Lira;
6th, British Labour Party Conference rejects application of Communist Party for affiliation;
10th, Kurt Schuschnigg dissolves Heimwehr, absorbing remaining members in Fatherland Front;
12th, Oswald Mosley leads anti-Jewish march along Mile End Road, London;
14th, alarmed at German occupation of Rhineland, Belgium denounces military alliance with France and resumes liberty of action;
19th, Germany's four-year plan begins, with Hermann Goering as economic minister;
20th, Stanley Baldwin warns Edward VIII that gossip about himself and Mrs. Wallis Simpson is undermining respect for the throne;
22nd, martial law in Belgium, to combat the Rexists.

L **Nov:** 1st, following Count Ciano's visit to Berlin, Benito Mussolini proclaims Rome-Berlin axis;
3rd, in U.S. presidential election F. D. Roosevelt, Democrat, is re-elected, with 523 electoral votes over A. M. Landon, Republican, with 8, and carries every state except Maine and Vermont;
6th, siege of Madrid begins, Spanish government moves to Valencia;
9th, Vienna conference between Italy, Austria and Hungary consolidates Italian position in Danube basin;
14th, Germany denounces clauses of Versailles Treaty about internationalisation of her waterways;
16th, Stanley Baldwin warns Edward VIII that if he marries Mrs. Simpson he would offend public opinion and damage prestige of the throne;

U **Literature** (*cont.*)
Stevie Smith, *Novel on Yellow Paper.*
Dylan Thomas, *Twenty-five Poems.*
Criticism of works of art, literature and music is forbidden in Germany.
Allen Lane founds Penguin Books, starting the paperback revolution.

V **The Press**
John and Rosamund Lehmann found *New Writing.*

W **Drama and Entertainment**
B.B.C. starts television service from Alexandra Palace (*Nov.* 2nd).
Ian Hay (pseud.), *The Housemaster.*
Terence Rattigan, *French Without Tears.*

Films:
Charlie Chaplin in *Modern Times.*
Mr. Deeds Comes to Town.
Things to Come.
As you Like It.
The Great Ziegfeld.
Shirley Temple signs five-year contract for £1,000 per week.

X **Sport**
Olympic Games in Berlin, in which the black U.S. athlete Jesse Owens wins four gold medals.
Max Schmeling beats Joe Louis for world heavyweight championship.

Y **Statistics**
Populations (in mill.): China, 422; India, 360; U.S.S.R., 173; U.S., 127; Japan, 89; Germany, 70; Great Britain, 47; France, 44.
Religious Denominations in U.S. (in mill.): Roman Catholics, 19·9; Baptists, 8·2; Methodists, 7; Lutherans, 4·2; Presbyterians, 2·5; Protestant Episcopal, 1·7; Mormons, 0·7.

Z **Births and Deaths**
Jan. 18th Rudyard Kipling d. (70).
Jan. 19th Zia ur-Rahman b. (–1981).
Jan. 23rd Clara Butt d. (62).
Mar. 4th James ('Jim') Clark b. (–1968).
Mar. 11th David, Earl Beatty, d. (65).
Mar. 18th F. W. de Klerk b. (–).
Mar. 21st Alexander Glazounov d. (71).
Apr. 30th Alfred Edward Housman d. (77).
May 8th Oswald Spengler d. (55).
May 12th Frank Stella b. (–).
June 14th Gilbert Keith Chesterton d. (62).
June 18th Maxim Gorky d. (68).
July 10th Herbert Boyer b. (–).
July 28th Garry Sobers b. (–).
Aug. 1st Louis Blériot d. (64).
Oct. 5th Václav Havel b. (–).
Dec. 10th Luigi Pirandello d. (69).
— Erich Weiss ('Houdini') d. (52).

L Nov: 18th, Germany and Italy recognise Franco's government in Spain;
23rd, Expropriation law in Mexico empowers government to seize private property;
24th, Germany and Japan sign Anti-Comintern Pact.

M Dec: 1st (–16th), Pan-American peace conference in Buenos Aires;
5th, new constitution in U.S.S.R., with a Supreme Council and a two-chamber Parliament;
10th, Edward VIII abdicates, becoming Duke of Windsor;
11th, accession of George VI;
12th, Chiang Kai-shek is forced to declare war on Japan;
—, abolition of office of governor-general of Ireland;
16th, protocol signed in London for non-intervention in Spain.

N Reserve Bank of New Zealand is nationalised.

1937 (Jan.–Jun.) Japanese take Peking, Shanghai and Nanking—Rebel victories in Spain—Italy leaves the League

A **Jan**: 2nd, Anglo-Italian agreement on Mediterranean and for maintaining independence of Spain;
7th, Poland signs agreement with Danzig;
14th, Communists, I.L.P. and Socialist League form United Front in Britain, aiming to transform Labour movement;
15th, amnesty for Austrian Nazis;
23rd, trial of Karl Radek and other political leaders in Moscow purge;
24th, Bulgaria and Yugoslavia sign treaty of perpetual peace.

B **Feb**: 8th, Spanish rebels take Malaga with Italian aid;
14th, Kurt Schuschnigg claims right to decide on question of the Hapsburg restoration in Austria;
15th (–18th), conference of Balkan powers in Athens;
20th, Paraguay withdraws from the League;
27th, French defence plan creates ministry of defence, extends Maginot Line and nationalises Schneider-Creusot arms factory;
All-India Congress most successful party in Indian elections.

C **Mar**: 1st, Adam Koc forms Camp of National Unity in Poland; a Workers' and Peasants' Camp is formed in opposition to him;
2nd, nationalisation of oil in Mexico;
16th, Benito Mussolini visits Libya;
18th, defeat of Italian legionaries at Brihuega checks rebel threat to Madrid;
25th, Italy and Yugoslavia sign Belgrade Pact of assistance for five years.

D **Apr**: 1st, Indian Constitution in force; All-India Party abstains from forming government, demanding complete independence;
2nd, South Africa prohibits political activity by foreigners in South-West Africa;
22nd, Kurt Schuschnigg meets Benito Mussolini in Venice;
24th, Britain and France release Belgium from obligations under Locarno treaty of 1925;
27th, Spanish rebels destroy Guernica.

E **May**: 1st, F. D. Roosevelt signs U.S. Neutrality act;
8th, Montreux convention abolishes Egyptian capitulations;
10th (–23rd), London bus strike;
14th (–*June* 15th), Imperial Conference, London;
15th, Moslem rising in Albania;
26th, Egypt joins the League;
28th, on Stanley Baldwin's retirement Neville Chamberlain forms National ministry, with John Simon Chancellor of Exchequer;
31st, German fleet bombards Almeria as reprisal for Loyalists' air attack on *Deutschland*.

F **Jun**: 1st, Prince Konoye becomes Japanese premier of a national union ministry, with Koki Hirota foreign minister;
12th, purge of U.S.S.R. generals;
14th, Dáil passes Constitution for Ireland;
18th, Spanish rebels take Bilbao;
21st, on French Senate refusing Léon Blum's demands for emergency fiscal powers he resigns and Camille Chautemps forms Radical-Socialist ministry;
23rd, Germany and Italy withdraw from non-intervention committee;
26th, Spanish rebels take Santander;
Duke of Windsor marries Mrs. Wallis Simpson in France.

O Politics, Economics, Law and Education

Walter Lippmann, *The Good Society*.
Talcott Parsons, *The Structure of Social Action*.
S. Rowntree, *The Human Needs of Labour*.
Stephen Spender and others, *The Mind in Chains; Socialism and the Cultural Revolution*.
First comprehensive wages agreement in Britain made by Lewis Ltd.
Romansch recognised as fourth national language in Switzerland (*Dec.*).
First sit-down strikes in U.S. and Canada, in General Motors Strike.

P Science, Technology, Discovery, etc.

Skull of *Pithecanthropus* found in Java.
Dirac, Milne and Dingle engage in controversy about the age of the world.
Zinc protamine insulin is successfully used in cases of diabetes.
Crystalline Vitamin A and Vitamin K concentrate are obtained.
Aneurin synthesises Vitamin B.
Wallace H. Carothers makes nylon stockings.
F. Whittle's first jet engine.
U.S.S.R. establishes observation station on an ice floe near the North Pole.
Sphinx Rock meteorological station in Bernese Oberland is opened (*Oct.* 31st).
The L.M.S. Railway's 'Coronation Scot'.

Q Scholarship

National Maritime Museum, Greenwich, opened.

R Philosophy and Religion

A. Huxley, *Ends and Means*.
M. Buber, *I and Thou*.
Oxford Conference on 'Church, Community and State'.
Papal Encyclical on Atheistic Communism (*Mar.* 18th).

S Art, Sculpture, Fine Arts and Architecture

Painting:
Joan Miró, murals, R. Dufy's decor and P. Picasso's mural *Guernica* for Paris World Fair.
William Coldstream and Lawrence Gowing found Euston Road group of artists, advocating a return to a realistic conception of painting.
Duveen Gallery, Tate Gallery, opened.
Paul Mellon endows National Gallery of Art, Washington.
Nazi exhibition of 'Degenerate Art' in Munich.
Sculpture:
J. Epstein, *Consummatum Est*.

T Music

Frederick Ashton's ballet *Les Patineurs* to G. Meyerbeer's music.
Arthur Bliss, ballet *Checkmate*.
Dmitry Shostakovich, 5th Symphony.
Jaromir Weinberger, *Wallenstein* (opera).
Pianist Artur Rubinstein makes successful tour of U.S.

U Literature

W. H. Auden and C. Isherwood, *The Ascent of F.6*.
Ernest Hemingway, *To Have and Have Not*.

G **Jul:** 7th, Japanese troops on manœuvres near Peking clash with Chinese; fighting spreads rapidly;
7th, Royal Commission on Palestine recommends end of mandate and establishment of Arab and Jewish states;
8th, Afghanistan, Iran, Iraq and Turkey sign non-aggression pact;
17th, naval agreements between Britain and Germany and Britain and U.S.S.R.;
22nd, Irish elections result in stalemate but Éamon de Valéra is again premier;
23rd, Matrimonial Causes bill, introduced by A. P. Herbert, facilitates divorce proceedings in England and Wales;
28th, Japanese seize Peking and, 29th, Tientsin.

H **Aug:** 6th, U.S.-U.S.S.R. trade pact;
11th, Bakr Sidqi, dictator of Iraq, assassinated;
15th, Mackenzie King appoints commission to study amendments to British North America Act.

Sep: F. D. Roosevelt signs Wagner-Steagall act to provide finance for housing;
3rd, British Labour Party's declaration that war is not inevitable, reiterates Britain's role in League;
10th (–14th), at Nyon Conference, convoked by Britain, nine nations adopt system of patrol in Mediterranean to deal with piracy arising from Spanish Civil War;
25th (–28th), Benito Mussolini visits Berlin;
26th, Arabs murder British district commissioner for Galilee.

K **Oct:** 1st, Higher Arab Committee in Palestine declared illegal;
13th, Germany guarantees inviolability of Belgium;
16th, Fascist groups in Hungary form National Socialist Party;
17th, riots in Sudeten area of Czechoslovakia;
21st, Spanish rebels take Gijón, completing conquest of the North-West;
23rd, Labour defeated in Australian elections by United Australian and Country parties;
24th, Paul van Zeeland, premier of Belgium, resigns on charges of corruption over National Bank, and is succeeded by Paul Janson, Liberal;
28th, Spanish government moves to Barcelona.

L **Nov:** 3rd (–24th), Brussels conference of powers discusses Sino-Japanese War;
5th, Air Raid Precautions bill introduced in Commons;
6th, Italy joins German-Japanese Anti-Comintern Pact;
9th, Japanese take Shanghai;
15th, extraordinary session of Congress opens to promote legislative programme, but little is accomplished;
17th (–21st), Lord Halifax's visit to Adolf Hitler, to attempt peaceful settlement of Sudeten problem, marks beginning of policy of appeasement;
18th, discovery of Fascist plot in Paris;
20th, Italo-Austro-Hungarian pact is extended;
24th, Walter Funk replaces Dr. Schacht as German minister of economics;
28th, General Franco begins naval blockade of Spanish coast;
29th, Sudeten Germans leave Czech Parliament following ban on political meetings.

U **Literature** (*cont.*)

A. Malraux, *L'Espoir*.
J. P. Marquand, *The Late George Apley*.
George Orwell (pseud.), *The Road to Wigan Pier*.
J. P. Sartre, *La Nausée*.
Stevie Smith, *A Good Time Was Had By All*.
John Steinbeck, *Of Mice and Men*.

V **The Press**

Morning Post merged in *The Daily Telegraph*.

W **Drama and Entertainment**

B. Brecht, *A Penny for the Poor*.
Jean Giraudoux, *Elektra*.
L. Housman, *Victoria Regina*.
J. B. Priestley, *Time and the Conways*.
Paris World Fair.

Films:
Jean Renoir's *The Great Illusion*.
Lost Horizon.
A Star is Born.
Camille.
The Edge of the World.

'Singing Mice' perform on U.S. radio.
Harold Rome's revue *Pins and Needles*.

X **Sport**

Y **Statistics**

Oil production (in mill. barrels): U.S., 1,277; U.S.S.R., 196; Venezuela, 182; Iran, 73; Roumania, 53; Dutch East Indies, 50; Mexico, 46.
Consumption of petroleum products (in mill. barrels) (motor fuel in brackets): U.S., 1,167 (517); U.S.S.R., 158 (24); Great Britain, 85 (43); France, 50 (25); Canada, 43 (21); Germany, 43 (20); Japan, 34 (10).
Refrigerators: U.S. has 2 mill. domestic refrigerators; Great Britain, 3,000.

M Dec: 2nd, far-reaching changes in high command of British Army imposed by Leslie Hore-Belisha;
5th (–19th), Spanish Loyalists' offensive near Teruel;
11th, Italy withdraws from the League;
12th (–13th), Japanese troops take Nanking;
14th, political parties banned in Brazil;
16th, Franco-Syrian convention;
24th, Japanese capture Hangchow;
28th, Octavian Goga, anti-Semite, forms ministry in Roumania, on fall of Nicholas Titulescu;
29th, new Irish Constitution; Irish Free State becomes Eire;
30th, Liberal Constitution Party forms ministry in Egypt;
C. R. Attlee visits Spain to encourage Republican leaders.

N

z **Births and Deaths**

Jan. 18th Frederick Pollock d. (91).
Jan. 30th Vanessa Redgrave b. (–).
Feb. 6th Elihu Root d. (91).
Mar. 16th Austen Chamberlain d. (73).
Mar. 20th John Drinkwater d. (54).
June 19th J. M. Barrie d. (77).
July 3rd Tom Stoppard b. (–).
July 9th David Hockney b. (–).
July 20th Guglielmo Marconi d. (63).
Aug. 11th Edith Wharton d. (75).
Sept. 14th T. G. Masaryk d. (87).
Oct. 19th Ernest, Lord Rutherford, d. (66).
Nov. 9th James Ramsay MacDonald d. (71).
Dec. 20th Erich Ludendorff d. (72).
Dec. 21st Frank Billings Kellogg d. (80).
Dec. 28th Maurice Ravel d. (62).

A **Jan**: 4th, Britain postpones scheme for partition of Palestine and appoints commission under John Woodhead, which is boycotted by Arabs, to study boundaries (reports *Nov.* 9th);
10th, Japanese enter Tsingtao;
14th, Socialists leave French cabinet, which Camille Chautemps reorganises as a Radical Socialist ministry.

B **Feb**: 4th, Adolf Hitler assumes office of war minister and appoints Joachim von Ribbentrop foreign minister;
12th, Hitler forces Kurt Schuschnigg to promise release of Nazis in Austria;
15th, General Franco recaptures Teruel and drives towards the coast;
18th, French Chamber cancels Labour code;
20th, Anthony Eden resigns in protest at Neville Chamberlain's determination to seek agreement with Italy before settlement of Spanish question and is succeeded as Foreign Secretary, 25th, by Lord Halifax;
21st, Winston Churchill leads outcry against Chamberlain and, 22nd, 25 ministerialists vote against government in censure motion.

C **Mar**: 2nd (–15th), trial of Nikolai Bukharin and other political leaders in U.S.S.R.;
11th, German troops enter Austria, which, 13th, is declared part of the Reich;
13th, Léon Blum forms Popular Front ministry in France (–*Apr.* 10th);
19th, Lithuania capitulates to Poland's demands to reopen the frontier;
—, Mexico expropriates British and U.S. oil properties;
28th, Japanese install puppet government of Chinese Republic at Nanking.

D **Apr**: 10th, Édouard Daladier, Radical Socialist, forms ministry in France, supported by Léon Blum;
15th, General Franco takes Vinaroz;
16th, by Anglo-Italian pact Britain recognises Italian sovereignty over Ethiopia and Italy undertakes to withdraw troops from Spain (in force *Nov.* 16th);
23rd, Sudeten Germans demand full autonomy;
25th, British three-year agreement with Eire settles outstanding disputes;
27th, Graeco-Turkish treaty of friendship.

E **May**: 3rd (–9th), Adolf Hitler visits Benito Mussolini in Rome;
4th, Douglas Hyde, a Protestant, becomes first President of Eire under new Constitution;
12th, Germany recognises Manchukuo;
13th, Paul Spaak, Socialist, forms coalition in Belgium;
17th, Anglo-Turkish agreement;
18th, United Party under J. B. M. Hertzog confirmed in power in South African elections;
19th (–20th), in first Czechoslovak crisis France and Britain stand firm against Adolf Hitler's demands.

F **Jun**: 17th, in Eire elections Fianna Fáil win 77 seats, the Opposition, 61.

G **Jul**: 11th (–*Aug.* 11th), U.S.S.R. troops clash with Japanese on border of Manchukuo;
19th (–21st), George VI visits Paris;
25th, Walter Runciman visits Prague and reports in favour of Nazi claims in Czechoslovakia;
31st, Bulgaria signs non-aggression pact with Greece and other powers of Balkan Entente.

O **Politics, Economics, Law and Education**

D. Lloyd George, *The Truth About the Peace Treaties.*

National Institute of Economic and Social Research, London, founded.

Wages and Hours bill in U.S. provides for minimum wages and a maximum working week and prohibits child labour.

British Ministry of Labour Committee under Lord Amulree recommends a week's holiday with pay as a national standard.

Women's Voluntary Service founded in Britain.

P **Science, Technology, Discovery, etc.**

Pyotr Kapitza publishes studies on Helium II, about the state of Helium at −456°F.

Werner von Braun appointed technical director at the German rocket research centre at Peenemünde.

Ewins and Phillips synthesise sulphapyridine ('M. and B. 693').

Karrer synthesises vitamin E.

Polyamide plastic 'Perlon' (similar to American nylon) is discovered in Germany.

J. Ladisla and Georg Biro invent the ball-point pen.

Howard Hughes in monoplane *New York World Fair* flies round world in 3 days 19 hrs. 17 mins. (*July* 10th–14th).

S.S. *Queen Elizabeth* launched (*Sept.* 27th).

Trolleybuses begin to replace trams in London (*Mar.* 6th).

Q **Scholarship**

J. B. Huizinga, *Homo Ludens.*

L. Mumford, *The Culture of Cities.*

R **Philosophy and Religion**

S **Art, Sculpture, Fine Arts and Architecture**

Painting:

Raoul Dufy, *Regatta.*

Pablo Picasso, *Woman in Easy Chair.*

Georges Rouault, *Ecce Homo.*

Sculpture:

Eric Gill, 50-ft. relief for League of Nations Building, Geneva.

Architecture:

F. L. Wright, Taliesin West, Phoenix, Arizona.

T **Music**

Béla Bartók, Violin Concerto.

Aaron Copland, *Billy the Kid* (opera).

Benny Goodman's band dominates Broadway.

Count Basie and his band achieve prominence in New York.

U **Literature**

Elizabeth Bowen, *The Death of the Heart.*

Cyril Connolly, *Enemies of Promise.*

Graham Greene, *Brighton Rock.*

C. Isherwood, *Goodbye to Berlin.*

Paul Valéry, *Degas, Danse, Dessein.*

V **The Press**

Edward Hulton starts *Picture Post* (–1958).

H **Aug:** 12th, Germany mobilises;
21st (–23rd), Little Entente recognises right of Hungary to rearm.

J **Sep:** 7th, Sudeten Germans break off relations with Czech government after clashes between rival parties and France calls up reservists;
15th, Neville Chamberlain visits Adolf Hitler at Berchtesgaden (and, 27th, at Godesberg) and Hitler states his determination to annex Sudetenland on principle of self-determination;
18th, Anglo-French proposals for Czechs to accept Germany's terms;
22nd, Milan Hodza's cabinet resigns in Prague;
27th, Royal Navy is mobilised;
—, League pronounces Japan to be the aggressor in China;
29th, at Munich conference Neville Chamberlain, Édouard Daladier, Adolf Hitler and Benito Mussolini agree to transfer Sudetenland to Germany, while the remaining frontiers of Czechoslovakia are guaranteed; Germany becomes the dominant power in Europe and both the Little Entente and the French system of alliances in Eastern Europe are shattered.

K **Oct:** 1st, Czechs accept Polish ultimatum for cession of Teschen;
— (–10th), Germany occupies Sudetenland;
—, Alfred Duff Cooper resigns as First Lord of Admiralty;
—, League of Nations separates Covenant from Versailles Peace Treaty;
2nd, Japan withdraws from the League;
4th, end of Popular Front in France when Socialists and Communists abstain from vote of confidence;
5th, Eduard Beneš resigns in Czechoslovakia;
6th, Slovakia and, 8th, Ruthenia are granted autonomy;
21st, Japanese take Canton and, 25th, Hankow;
25th, Libya is declared to be part of Italy;
29th, Belgium withdraws from non-intervention committee.

L **Nov:** 2nd, Hungary annexes Southern Slovakia;
8th (–14th), anti-Semitic pogroms in Germany;
—, U.S. elections result in Democrats having 69 seats in Senate and 261 in House, while Republicans have 23 in Senate and 168 in House;
10th, anti-Semitic legislation in Italy;
11th, Inönü elected President of Turkey on Kemal Atatürk's death;
26th, U.S.S.R.-Polish declaration of friendship renews non-aggression pact;
30th, speeches in Italian Chamber claim Nice and Corsica for Italy;
—, Corneliu Codreanu and other members of Roumanian Iron Guard shot in government's attempts to destroy Fascism;
—, Emil Hacha elected Czech President.

M **Dec:** 1st, British national register for war service;
6th, Franco-German pact on inviolability of existing frontiers;
14th, Italian Chamber of Deputies is replaced by Chamber of Fasces and Corporations;
17th, Italy denounces 1935 agreement with France;
23rd, General Franco begins main offensive in Catalonia;
26th, Pan-American Conference makes Declaration of Peru against all foreign intervention;
28th, Iraq severs relations with France.

N

W **Drama and Entertainment**

Jean Anouilh, *Le Voyageur sans bagage.*
Philip Barry, *Here Come the Clowns.*
Jean Cocteau, *Les Parents terribles.*
Thornton Wilder, *Our Town.*
Emlyn Williams, *The Corn is Green.*

Films:
Anthony Asquith's *Pygmalion* with Leslie Howard.
Eisenstein's *Alexander Newski.*
Dance from the Volcano.
The Lady Vanishes.
Walt Disney's *Snow White and the Seven Dwarfs.*

New York World Fair.
Empire Exhibition, Glasgow.
The Lambeth Walk (dance).

X **Sport**

Len Hutton scores 364 runs against Australia at the Oval Test Match (*Aug.*).

Y **Statistics**

Coal production (in mill. tons): Great Britain, 230; Germany, including Saar, 153; U.S.S.R., 150; France, 46.
Pig-iron production (in mill. tons): U.S., 29,130; Germany, including Saar, 16,111; U.S.S.R., 14,479; Great Britain, 7,781; France, 6,679; Belgium, 3,143.
Steel production (in mill. tons): U.S., 42,906; Germany, including Saar, 20,573; U.S.S.R., 17,380; Great Britain, 11,908; France, 6,946; Belgium, 31,103.
Private cars (in mills.): U.S., 19; Great Britain, 1·7; Germany, including Austria, 1·3; Italy, 1·1; France, 0·8.
Immigration to Great Britain: 504,527.
Emigration from Great Britain: 1,609,847 British and 491,176 aliens.

Z **Births and Deaths**

Jan. 5th King Juan Carlos b. (–).
Mar. 1st Gabriele D'Annunzio d. (75).
Mar. 7th David Baltimore b. (–).
Mar. 28th Edward Mandell House d. (79).
Apr. 12th Fedor Chaliapin d. (65).
Apr. 19th Henry Newbolt d. (75).
July 4th Otto Bauer d. (57).
Aug. 7th Constantin Stanislavsky d. (75).
Sept. 13th Samuel Alexander d. (79).
Nov. 10th Kemal Atatürk d. (57).
Dec. 25th Karel Čapek d. (48).

1939 (Jan.–Jul.) Italy invades Albania—Dismemberment of Czechoslovakia —End of Spanish Civil War—German invasion of Poland begins World War II

A **Jan:** 1st (–6th), Édouard Daladier visits Algiers, Tunisia and Corsica to counter Benito Mussolini's demands for colonies in North Africa;
4th, F. D. Roosevelt asks Congress for $552 million for defence;
10th, Neville Chamberlain and Lord Halifax visit Rome for conversations with Benito Mussolini;
21st, Adolf Hitler dismisses Dr. H. Schacht, president of Reichsbank, replacing him by Walter Funk, minister of economics;
26th, Franco with Italian aid takes Barcelona.

B **Feb:** 10th, Japanese troops occupy Hainan;
27th, Britain and France recognise General Franco's government in Spain (U.S. recognition *Apr.* 1st).

C **Mar:** 10th, Joseph Tiso, premier of Slovakia, is deposed by Prague government and appeals to Hitler;
15th, German troops occupy Bohemia and Moravia, which become a protectorate ruled by Constantin von Neurath;
16th, Slovakia is placed under German 'protection', while Hungary annexes Ruthenia;
17th, Édouard Daladier is granted wide powers by French Assembly to speed rearmament;
20th, U.S. ambassador is recalled from Berlin in protest at the dismemberment of Czechoslovakia;
21st, Germany annexes Memel from Lithuania;
28th, Madrid's surrender to General Franco ends Spanish Civil War;
—, Adolf Hitler denounces Germany's non-aggression pact with Poland of *Jan.* 1934;
31st, Britain and France pledge to support Poland.

D **Apr:** 7th, Italy invades Albania;
7th, Spain joins Germany, Italy and Japan in the Anti-Comintern Pact;
11th, Hungary withdraws from League of Nations;
13th, Britain and France guarantee the independence of Roumania and Greece;
15th, F. D. Roosevelt asks Adolf Hitler and Benito Mussolini for assurances that they will not attack 31 named states;
16th, U.S.S.R. proposes a defensive alliance with Britain;
24th, Robert Menzies becomes premier of Australia, following death of J. A. Lyons (*Apr.* 7th);
27th, conscription in Britain for men aged 20–21;
—, Adolf Hitler denounces 1935 Anglo-German naval agreement.

E **May:** 4th, Vyacheslav Molotov appointed commissar of foreign affairs in place of Maxim Litvinov;
8th, Spain leaves the League;
12th, Anglo-Turkish pact of mutual assistance;
17th, Sweden, Norway and Finland reject Germany's offer of non-aggression pacts, but Denmark, Estonia and Latvia accept;
22nd, Adolf Hitler and Benito Mussolini sign ten-year political and military alliance (the 'Pact of Steel');
23rd, Parliament approves British plan for an independent Palestine by 1949, which is later denounced by Jews and by Arabs in Palestine.

F **Jun:** 8th (–11th), George VI visits U.S. at end of tour of Canada;
14th, Japanese blockade of British concession at Tientsin.

G **Jul:** 9th, Winston Churchill urges military alliance with U.S.S.R.;
26th, U.S. denounces 1911 trade pact with Japan.

O Politics, Economics, Law and Education

E. H. Carr, *The Twenty Years' Crisis.*
M. Oakeshott, *The Social and Political Doctrines of Contemporary Europe.*
B.O.A.C. is established.
Ministry of Supply is established (*July* 11th) and Ministry of Information (*Sept.* 5th) in Britain.

P Science, Technology, Discovery, etc.

Hahn and Strassman discover nuclear fission by bombarding uranium with neutrons.
Joliot demonstrates the possibility of splitting the atom of uranium isotope 235.
Paul Müller invents D.D.T.
I.C.I. begin commercial production of polythene.
Lincoln Ellsworth surveys a large part of eastern Antarctica.
First flight of the first helicopter, Igor Sikorsky's VS-300 (*Sept.* 14th).
John Cobb at Bonneville Salt Flats, Utah, drives at 368·85 m.p.h. (*Aug.* 23rd).
Malcolm Campbell's water speed record of 141·7 m.p.h.
Streamlined diesel train achieves 133·6 m.p.h. between Hamburg and Berlin.
Opening of Trans-Iranian Railway, Caspian Sea to Persian Gulf (*Jan.*).
Pan-American Airways begin regular commercial flights between U.S. and Europe (*May* 20th).
The first Messerschmitt military plane, the Me 109, sets a world speed record of 481 m.p.h.

Q Scholarship

R Philosophy and Religion

John Dewey, *Culture and Freedom.*
Arthur Eddington, *The Philosophy of Physical Science.*
Charles Sherrington, *Man on His Nature.*
Frank Buchman re-founds 'Oxford Group' as Moral Rearmament.

S Art, Sculpture, Fine Arts and Architecture

Painting:
Laura Knight, *Golden Girl.*
P. Picasso, *Night Fishing at Antibes.*
S. Spencer, first of the series *Christ in the Wilderness* (–1953).
G. Sutherland, *Entrance to a Lane.*
'Grandma Moses' (Anna M. Robertson) becomes famous overnight in Unknown American Painters Exhibition.

Sculpture:
J. Epstein, *Adam* (marble).

T Music

William Walton, Violin Concerto.
Myra Hess organises National Gallery lunch-time concerts (*Oct.*) which popularise pianoforte and chamber music in Britain.

U Literature

Robert Graves, *The Long Week-end.*
James Joyce, *Finnegans Wake* (written from 1922).
Richard Llewellyn, *How Green Was My Valley.*
T. Mann, *Lotte in Weimar.*
John Steinbeck, *The Grapes of Wrath.*
Jan Struther, *Mrs. Miniver.*

H Aug: 5th, British military mission leaves for Moscow (arriving there, 11th);
18th, U.S.S.R.-German commercial agreement;
23rd, U.S.S.R.-German non-aggression pact; the 'Anti-Comintern Pact' collapses;
—, Neville Chamberlain warns Adolf Hitler that Britain will stand by Poland and pleads for settlement of Danzig question;
24th, British Parliament approves Emergency Powers bill;
25th, Anglo-Polish treaty of mutual assistance signed in London;
26th (–31st), attempts by Daladier and Chamberlain to negotiate with Hitler fail;
31st, evacuation of women and children from London begins;
—, U.S.S.R. Supreme Soviet ratifies non-aggression pact with Germany.

J Sep: 1st, Germany invades Poland and annexes Danzig;
2nd, British National Service bill, calling up men aged 18–41, in force;
3rd, Britain and France declare war on Germany;
—, British ministerial changes, with Winston Churchill First Lord of Admiralty;
—, Germans sink *Athenia* off Ireland;
4th, Franco-Polish agreement;
5th, J. C. Smuts premier of South Africa;
7th, Germans overrun Pomerania and Silesia and, by 10th, control western Poland;
13th, Édouard Daladier reforms ministry becoming foreign secretary himself;
17th, Germans reach Brest-Litovsk;
—, U.S.S.R. invades Poland from east;
19th, H.M.S. *Courageous* sunk;
—, R.A.F. begins 'leaflet' raids on Germany;
—, Polish government withdraws to Roumania, and Ignace Moscicki, the premier, resigns;
21st, Armand Calinescu, premier of Roumania, assassinated by the Iron Guard;
27th, emergency Budget raises standard rate of income tax in Britain to 7s. 6d. in £;
28th, Germans reach Warsaw;
—, U.S.S.R. pact with Estonia;
29th, national registration in Britain;
30th, German-U.S.S.R. treaty of amity settles partition of Poland; by 30th, British Expeditionary Force of 158,000 men sent to France.

K Oct: 5th, U.S.S.R. pact with Latvia;
6th, Adolf Hitler's peace-feelers are summarily rejected by Britain and France;
8th, Germany incorporates western Poland into the Reich;
10th, U.S.S.R. cedes Vilna to Lithuania;
—, deportation of Polish Jews to Lublin reserve begins;
14th, H.M.S. *Royal Oak* sunk in Scapa Flow.

L Nov: 4th, F.D. Roosevelt signs bill enabling Britain and France to purchase arms in U.S. on 'cash and carry' basis, amending the Neutrality Act of *May* 1937;
7th, sovereigns of Belgium and Holland approach George VI advocating peace with Germany;
17th, Britain and France co-ordinate their economic efforts;
18th, magnetic mines, laid by U-boats, sink 60,000 tons of shipping on English east coast in a week;
30th, U.S.S.R. invades Finland, with main offensive to north of Lake Ladoga.

M Dec: 13th, battle of River Plate, ends 17th, with scuttling of *Graf Spee* off Montevideo;
14th, U.S.S.R. expelled from League of Nations.

N

V The Press

W Drama and Entertainment

New York Exhibition.
T. S. Eliot, *The Family Reunion.*
Lillian Hellman, *The Little Foxes.*
George S. Kaufman and Moss Hart, *The Man Who Came to Dinner.*

Films:
Gone With the Wind.
Goodbye Mr. Chips.
The Stars Look Down.
Dawn Patrol.
Jean Renoir's *The Rules of the Game.*
Stagecoach with John Wayne.

Ivor Novello's *The Dancing Years* (revue).
'*Roll out the Barrel*' and '*Hang Out the Washing on the Siegfried Line*' (popular songs).
Jerome Kern '*The Last Time I Saw Paris*' (song).

X Sport

Enzo Ferrari founds his car company, Auto Avio Construzione.

Y Statistics

Merchant fleets (in mill. tons): Great Britain, 17·8; U.S., 11·4; Japan, 5·6; Norway, 4·8; Germany, 4·4; Italy, 3·4; Netherlands, 2·9; France, 2·9.
Of 29 mill. tons of shipping passing through the Suez Canal 51 per cent was British. Of 27 mill. tons using the Panama Canal 35 per cent was U.S., 26 per cent British.
Machine tools in use: Germany, 1,177,600; U.S., 942,000; Japan, 67,260.
Aluminium: World production, 647,000 tons; Germany the chief producer, with 240,000.
Criminal offences: U.S., 1,484,811 (21,401 crimes against the person); England and Wales, 303,771 (2,899 crimes against the person).
Housing: on *May* 1st the four millionth house to be built in Britain, since *Nov.* 1918, was completed.
British war production (*Sept.–Dec.*)*:* 2,924 aircraft; 314 tanks; 17 major vessels with total tonnage 22,780.
Shipping losses (*Sept.–Dec.*, in thousand tons): Great Britain, 498; Allied, 90; Neutral, 347.
U.K. total State expenditure: £1,005 mill.

Z Births and Deaths

Jan. 28th William Butler Yeats d. (73).
Mar. 20th Brian Mulroney b. (–).
Apr. 12th Alan Ayckbourn b. (–).
May 22nd Ernst Toller d. (45).
June 26th Ford Madox Ford d. (66).
July 8th Havelock Ellis d. (80).
Sept. 17th Ethel M. Dell d. (58).
Sept. 23rd Siegmund Freud d. (83).
Dec. 23rd Anthony Fokker d. (49).
Dec. 31st F. R. Benson d. (81).

1940 (Jan.–Jun.) Germany invades Norway and Denmark—Churchill becomes Prime Minister—Dunkirk—Fall of France—Battle of Britain—The Blitz

A **Jan:** 1st, Oliver Stanley replaces Leslie Hore-Belisha as British War Secretary in government reconstruction;
8th, bacon, butter and sugar rationed in Britain;
21st, W. S. Churchill advises neutrals to side with Britain before they suffer German aggression.

B **Feb:** 1st, U.S.S.R. launches attacks on Karelian Isthmus and near Lake Kuhmo;
8th, British Labour Party delegation to Finland calls for substantial aid for Finns;
11th, U.S.S.R. attack on Mannerheim Line;
16th, H.M.S. *Cossack* rescues British prisoners from the *Altmark* in Norwegian waters;
21st, British women to receive old-age pension at 60.

C **Mar:** 3rd, U.S.S.R. troops capture Viborg;
12th, Finland signs peace treaty with U.S.S.R., ceding the Karelian Isthmus and shores of Lake Ladoga;
19th, R.A.F. raids Isle of Sylt;
20th, Paul Reynaud forms ministry in France on É. Daladier's resignation.

D **Apr:** 3rd, ministerial changes in Britain, with Lord Woolton as Food Minister;
4th, Treasury finances a company for trading with Balkans to intensify blockade of Germany;
9th, Germany invades Norway and Denmark;
14th, British naval forces land in Norway, but fail to take Trondheim through lack of air power.

E **May:** 2nd, British forces evacuate Namsos;
7th, Neville Chamberlain under fire in Commons and, 10th, resigns, when W. S. Churchill forms National government, with Clement Attlee as Lord Privy Seal, A. V. Alexander as First Lord of Admiralty and Ernest Bevin as Labour Minister;
10th, Germany invades Holland, Luxembourg and Belgium;
—, L.D.V. (later 'Home Guard') formed in Britain;
13th, W. S. Churchill's 'blood and toil' speech rallies confidence in his leadership;
14th, Dutch army surrenders, German troops turn the line of the Albert Canal and pierce French defences near Sedan;
21st, Germans capture Amiens and Arras;
22nd, British Government granted wide emergency powers;
28th, Belgium capitulates;
29th (–*June* 3rd), British forces evacuated from Dunkirk;
30th, Stafford Cripps leads trade mission to Moscow.

F **Jun:** 10th, Italy declares war on France and Britain;
13th, W. S. Churchill visits Paul Reynaud at Tours;
14th, Germans enter Paris;
15th, U.S. declines France's appeal for aid;
16th, France is offered union with Britain;
—, Marshal Pétain replaces Paul Reynaud as head of French administration;
17th (–23rd), Russians occupy Baltic states;
22nd, France concludes armistice with Germany;
24th, terms of French Vichy Government's armistice with Italy include the withdrawal of French colonies from the war;
27th, U.S.S.R. invades Roumania on refusal of King Carol to cede Bessarabia and Bukovina; Roumania appeals for German aid in vain.

O **Politics, Economics, Law and Education**

British Government appoints Scientific Advisory Committee under Lord Hankey to consider the advances of science in relation to national welfare.

British Colonial Development and Welfare Act for providing funds for approved development plans.

Barlow Report on the location of industry (published *Jan.*).

The George Cross is instituted (*Sept.* 23rd).

P **Science, Technology, Discovery, etc.**

Albert Einstein states in his paper to the American Scientific Congress at Washington that there is as yet no theory which can provide a logical basis for physics.

Rockefeller grant for University of California to build a giant cyclotron, under E. O. Lawrence's direction, for producing mesons from atomic nuclei.

Howard Florey develops penicillin as an antibiotic.

Edwin McMillan and Abelson discover neptunium (element 93).

Q **Scholarship**

R **Philosophy and Religion**

A. J. Ayer, *The Foundations of Empirical Knowledge.*

C. Jung, *The Interpretation of Personality.*

George Santayana, *The Realm of Spirit.*

S **Art, Sculpture, Fine Arts and Architecture**

Painting:

M. Beckmann, *Circus Caravan.*

W. Kandinsky, *Sky Blue.*

H. Matisse, *Rumanian blouse.*

J. Piper, *St. Mary le Port, Bristol.*

R. Whistler, *Miss Laura Ridly.*

Augustus John Exhibition, Tate Gallery.

Edward Ardizzone, Muirhead Bone, Henry Lamb, John and Paul Nash and Eric Ravillous appointed official British war artists.

T **Music**

Lennox Berkeley, Introduction and Allegro for two pianos and orchestra.

Elizabeth Lutyens, Three Pieces.

Darius Milhaud, *Médéa* (opera).

Igor Stravinsky, Symphony in C.

M. Tippett, *A Child of Our Time* (oratorio).

Agnes de Mille's ballet, *Rodeo.*

U **Literature**

Graham Greene, *The Power and the Glory.*

Ernest Hemingway, *For Whom the Bell Tolls.*

Eugene O'Neill, *Long Day's Journey into Night* (written, not produced until 1956).

Michael Sadleir, *Fanny by Gaslight.*

Upton Sinclair, *Between Two Worlds.*

Dylan Thomas, *Portrait of the Artist as a Young Dog.*

V **The Press**

W **Drama and Entertainment**

Robert Ardrey, *Thunder Rock.*

B.B.C. Radio Newsreel begun.

1940 (Jul.–Dec.)

G **Jul**: 3rd, Royal Navy sinks French fleets in Oran and North Africa;
5th, Vichy Government breaks off relations with Britain;
9th, R.A.F. begins night bombing of Germany;
—, Roumania places herself under German protection;
15th (–21st), 90 German bombers shot down over Britain;
18th, at Japan's request Britain prohibits the passage of war materials for China passing through Burma;
21st, Britain recognises Czechoslovak National Committee in London as a provisional government;
23rd, purchase tax imposed in Britain.

H **Aug**: 4th, Italians advance from Abyssinia into British Somaliland;
5th, Britain signs agreements with Polish Government in London and, 7th, with Free French under Charles de Gaulle;
8th, Indian Congress Party rejects the Viceroy's invitation to serve on War Advisory Council;
11th (–18th), Battle of Britain at its peak;
15th, 180 German planes shot down;
19th, British withdraw from British Somaliland;
23rd, all-night raid on London begins the 'Blitz'.

J **Sep**: 3rd, U.S. sends destroyers to Britain in exchange for leased bases in Newfoundland and the Caribbean;
6th, Ion Antonescu assumes dictatorial powers in Roumania; King Carol flees;
15th, heavy raid on London with 103 German planes destroyed;
16th, Italians reach Sidi Barrani;
16th, Selective Training and Service Act in U.S.;
27th, British and Free French forces fail to occupy Dakar in Senegal;
—, Germany, Italy and Japan sign ten-year economic and military pacts;
During month Britain loses 160,000 tons of shipping.

K **Oct**: 2nd, *Empress of Britain* with child evacuees for Canada sunk;
3rd, cabinet changes following Neville Chamberlain's retirement;
4th, Adolf Hitler meets Benito Mussolini in Brenner Pass;
7th, Germans seize Roumanian oilfields;
13th (–21st), heavy raids on London;
18th, Britain reopens Burma Road;
22nd, Germany's U-boat warfare is intensified;
28th, Italy demands cession of strategic points in Greece, and Britain, answering Greece's appeal for aid, postpones offensive in Middle East.

L **Nov**: 3rd, British forces occupy Suda Bay, Crete;
4th, H.M.S. *Jervis Bay* sunk in Atlantic;
5th, F. D. Roosevelt, Democrat, is re-elected President for a third term, against Wendell L. Willkie, Republican;
11th, British attack on Taranto cripples Italian fleet;
12th (–14th), V. Molotov in Berlin refuses to co-operate with Germany in Balkans;
20th, Anglo-U.S. agreement for partial standardisation of weapons and pooling of technical knowledge;
—, Hungary and, 23rd, Roumania, endorse German-Italian-Japanese treaty of *Sept.* 27th;
In the month's air raids, 4,558 persons killed in Britain.

(*Continued opposite*)

W **Drama and Entertainment** (*cont.*)

Films:

Charlie Chaplin in *The Great Dictator.*
Alfred Hitchcock's *Rebecca.*
Walt Disney's *Fantasia.*
Gaslight.
Derrière la Façade.
The Postmaster.
A Day in the New World.
German army sings 'Lili Marlene'.

X **Sport**

Y **Statistics**

Merchant shipping losses (in thousand tons): British, 2,725; Allied, 822; Neutral, 1,002.
War production in Great Britain: aircraft, 15,049; tanks, 1,397; major warships, 106 (totalling 221,935 tons).
Production in U.S.S.R. (in mill. tons): pig iron, 14·9; steel, 18·3; coal, 165·9; oil, 31·1; cement, 3·5; mineral fertilisers, 0·9.
Private cars (in mill.): U.S., 32·4; Great Britain, 2·4; France, 2·3; Canada, 1·4.
In Britain there are 3·3 mill. *telephones* and 8·9 mill. *wirelesses* in use.
Divorces: U.S., 264,000; Great Britain, 8,396.

Z **Births and Deaths**

Feb. 1st John Buchan, Lord Tweedsmuir, d. (63).
Mar. 16th Selma Lagerlöf d. (63).
Apr. 9th Beatrice, Mrs. Patrick Campbell, d. (75).
Apr. 18th H. A. L. Fisher d. (75).
May 7th George Lansbury d. (81).
Aug. 21st Lev Trotsky d. (61).
Aug. 30th J. J. Thomson d. (83).
Oct. 9th John Lennon b. (–1980).
Oct. 23rd Pele b. (–).
Nov. 9th Neville Chamberlain d. (71).
Nov. 17th Eric Gill d. (58).
Nov. 26th Harold Harmsworth, Lord Rothermere, d. (72).

M **Dec:** 9th, Eighth Army under Archibald Wavell opens offensive in North Africa by attacking Sidi Barrani;
15th, Italians driven across Libyan border;
16th, Italians driven from El Wak in Italian Somaliland;
22nd, air raid on Manchester;
—, Lord Halifax is appointed British Ambassador in Washington;
23rd, Anthony Eden becomes British Foreign Secretary.

N

1941 (Jan.–May) Lend-Lease—Germany invades Russia—Atlantic Charter—Japanese bomb Pearl Harbor and U.S. enters the war

A **Jan:** 3rd, Italians surrender Bardia;
6th, F. D. Roosevelt sends Lend-Lease Bill to Congress;
10th, H.M.S. *Southampton* is sunk and H.M.S. *Illustrious* crippled by German bombers on Greek convoy;
19th, British forces take Kassala, Sudan;
26th, British forces take Biscia in Eritrea;
30th, Archibald Wavell takes Derna and advances towards Benghazi;
—, South Africans drive Italians from Kenya;
—, pro-British rising in Abyssinia.

B **Feb:** 6th, British occupy Benghazi;
9th, bombardment of Genoa and raids on Leghorn fail to stop German troops under General Rommel from crossing from Italy to North Africa;
19th, British troops invade Italian Somaliland from Kenya;
27th, Britain signs pact of friendship with Hungary.

C **Mar:** 4th, Royal Navy raids Lofoten Islands;
5th, Britain withdraws her minister from Belgrade in protest at Bulgarian collaboration with Germany;
7th, British troops invade Abyssinia;
11th, Lend-Lease Bill signed after two months' controversy in U.S.;
19th, German air raids on London resumed;
20th, Yugoslavia comes to terms with Germany;
24th, U.S.S.R. undertakes to support Turkey if she is the victim of aggression;
27th, British forces take Keren and Harar;
—, Prince Paul of Yugoslavia deposed in *coup d'état* following his pact with Adolf Hitler;
28th, three Italian cruisers sunk in battle off Cape Matapan;
31st, German counter-offensive in North Africa opens;
U-boat attacks intensified;
Pacifists in Britain, including leading Communists, organise a People's Convention to end the war.

D **Apr:** 5th, U.S.S.R.-Yugoslav treaty of friendship;
—, British forces take Addis Ababa and, 6th, Massawa in Eritrea;
6th, German ultimatum to Greece and Yugoslavia; Britain sends 60,000 men to Greece;
7th, Archibald Wavell evacuates Benghazi;
—, British Budget raises standard rate of income tax to 10s. in £;
11th, Blitz on Coventry;
13th, Josef Stalin signs neutrality pact with Japan;
—, Germans recapture Bardia;
18th, Yugoslav opposition collapses;
20th, Erwin Rommel attacks Tobruk;
22nd (–*May* 2nd), British evacuate Greece.

E **May:** 2nd, Iraq, siding with Germany, demands withdrawal of British forces;
6th, J. Stalin becomes head of Soviet government;
9th, U.S.S.R. withdraws recognition of Yugoslavia;
10th, House of Commons destroyed in London's heaviest air raid;
—, Rudolf Hess lands in Scotland;
14th, Vichy government endorses Admiral J. F. Darlan's agreement with Adolf Hitler for aiding Germany;
20th, Germans invade Crete;

O Politics, Economics, Law and Education

John Masefield's account of Dunkirk, *The Nine Days' Wonder*.
Edmund Wilson, *To The Finland Station*.
Double Summer Time is introduced in Britain.
Air Raid Precautions services reformed as Civil Defence (*Sept.* 4th).
Germany abandons Gothic type for Roman (*May* 31st).
B. S. Rowntree, *Poverty and Progress: A Second Social Survey of York*.
Oxford University holds degree ceremony at Harvard to honour F. D. Roosevelt (*June* 19th).
'Utility' clothing and furniture in Britain, where clothes are rationed (*June* 1st).

P Science, Technology, Discovery, etc.

'Manhattan Project' of atomic research begun in Chicago and Los Angeles under Pegram and H. C. Urey (*Dec.*).
Therapeutic Research Corporation of Great Britain founded to rationalise research.
The National War Formulary is compiled.
J. R. Whinfield and J. T. Dickson develop the synthetic polyester fibre 'Terylene' ('Dacron' in U.S.A.).
A Ferry Command aircraft crosses the Atlantic from the west in 8 hr, 23 mins.

Q Scholarship

Cambridge Economic History of Europe, Volume I (–).
B. Croce, *History as the Story of Liberty*.

R Philosophy and Religion

Rudolf Bultmann, *New Testament and Mythology*.
Étienne Gilson, *God and Philosophy*.
Nathaniel Micklem, *The Theology of Politics*.
R. Niebuhr, *The Nature and Destiny of Man* (–43).

S Art, Sculpture, Fine Arts and Architecture

Painting:
F. Léger, *Divers against a Yellow Background*.
P. Nash, *Bombers over Berlin*.
Henry Moore's drawings in crayon of refugees in air-raid shelters during the London Blitz and Felix Topolski's drawings of the armed forces.
S. Spencer, *Shipbuilding in the Clyde* (–1947).
Sickert Exhibition at National Gallery.

T Music

Benjamin Britten, Violin Concerto.
Ernst Křenek, *Tarquin* (opera).
William Walton, *Scapino* overture.
Council for the Encouragement of Music and the Arts (C.E.M.A.) concerts begin in Britain.

U Literature

L. Aragon, *Le Crève-Cœur*.
I. Ehrenberg, *The Fall of Paris*.
Scott Fitzgerald, *The Last Tycoon*.
F. Werfel, *The Song of Bernadette*.
Rebecca West, *Black Lamb and Grey Fox: A Journey Through Yugoslavia in 1937*.

V The Press

R. Barrington-Ward succeeds Geoffrey Dawson as editor of *The Times*.
Daily Worker is suppressed (*Jan.* 21st).

E **May**: 20th, Abyssinian campaign ends;
22nd, Rachid Ali, ruler of Iraq, flees;
24th, H.M.S. *Hood* sunk by *Bismarck* off Greenland;
27th, *Bismarck* is sunk by Royal Navy west of Brest, but *Prinz Eugen* escapes;
29th, British evacuate Candia.

F **Jun**: 3rd, U.S.S.R. withdraws recognition of Greece;
8th, British and Free French Forces invade Syria to prevent establishment of Axis bases;
12th, first conference of Allies in London pledged to mutual assistance;
22nd, Germany invades Russia;
—, Finns invade Karelia;
27th, Hungary declares war on Russia;
28th, Germans capture Minsk.

G **Jul**: 1st, Claude Auchinleck succeeds General A. Wavell in Middle East;
6th, U.S.S.R. troops abandon occupied Poland and Baltic states, retiring to 'Stalin Line' on former frontier with Poland;
7th, U.S. troops relieve British in occupation of Iceland;
11th, cease-fire in Syria, which is administered by Allies;
12th, Anglo-Russian agreement of mutual assistance signed in Moscow;
16th, Germans pierce Stalin Line and take Smolensk;
20th, British ministerial changes, with Brendan Bracken as Minister of Information and R. A. Butler as President of Board of Education;
25th, Germans take Tallinn;
26th, Britain and U.S. freeze Japanese assets to counter Japan's claims to bases in Indo-China;
27th, Japanese troops land in Indo-China;
—, Germans enter the Ukraine;
29th, Russian Army invading Roumania withdraws to the Dniester.

H **Aug**: 11th, W. S. Churchill and F. D. Roosevelt, meeting in the western Atlantic, sign the Atlantic Charter;
12th, Anglo-Soviet trade agreement;
18th, National Fire Service established in Britain;
25th, Britain and U.S.S.R. invade Iran following the Shah's refusal to reduce numbers of resident Germans.

J **Sep**: 3rd, Germans advance to outskirts of Leningrad and, 8th, take Schülsselburg, completing land blockade of Leningrad;
19th, Germans take Kiev;
22nd (–27th), 'Russian Tank Week' in British arms factories;
24th, Allied conference in London endorses Atlantic Charter;
29th (–*Oct.* 10th), Lord Beaverbrook and Averell Harriman visit Moscow to arrange for war supplies;
Movement in Britain for a Second Front.

K **Oct**: 1st, Germans advance from Smolensk towards Moscow;
2nd, Germans take Orel;
13th, R.A.F. bombs Nuremberg;
16th, as Germans 60 miles from Moscow the U.S.S.R. government is transferred to Kuibishev, but J. Stalin stays in Moscow;
—, Odessa falls and, 22nd, Perekop on Sea of Azov;

W Drama and Entertainment

B. Brecht, *Mother Courage and her Children.*
Joyce Cary, *Herself Surprised.*
Noël Coward, *Blithe Spirit.*
Piscator's Studio Theatre, New York, founded to present social drama.
B.B.C. *Brains Trust* first broadcast.
Sanger's Circus (founded 1820) closes down.

Films:
Orson Welles's *Citizen Kane.*
Leslie Howard in *The First of the Few.*
49th Parallel.
Kipps.
Marx Brothers' last film, *The Big Store.*
Nous les Gosses.
Friedmann Bach.
Das andere Ich.

X Sport

Y Statistics

Populations (in mill.): China, 450; India, 389; U.S.S.R., 182; U.S., 131; Germany, including Austria, Slovakia, West Poland, etc., 110; Japan, 105; Great Britain, 47; Brazil, 41; France, 40.
War production in Great Britain: coal, 206 mill. tons; pig iron, 7·3 mill. tons; steel, 12·7 mill. tons. 20,093 aircraft; 4,844 tanks; 170 major war vessels totalling 346,416 tons.
Merchant shipping losses (in thousand tons): Great Britain, 3,047; Allied, 1,290; Neutral, 347.
Private cars: U.S., 38.8 mill.; Great Britain, 2.2 mill.

Z Births and Deaths

Jan. 5th Henri Louis Bergson d. (81).
Jan. 8th Robert, Lord Baden-Powell, d. (83) and Amy Johnson d. (38).
Jan. 13th James Joyce d. (58).
Mar. 8th Sherwood Anderson d. (65).
Mar. 13th Tom Mann d. (84).
Mar. 28th Virginia Woolf d. (59).
May 7th James George Frazer d. (87).
May 18th Werner Sombart d. (78).
June 4th Kaiser William II d. (82).
June 15th Evelyn Underhill d. (66).
June 29th Ignaz Jan Paderewski d. (80).
July 11th Arthur Evans d. (90).
Aug. 7th Rabindranath Tagore d. (80).

1941 (Oct.–Dec.)

K **Oct**: 22nd, Britain resumes diplomatic relations with Mexico (broken since *May* 1938);
24th, Germans take Kharkov;
25th, failure of first German offensive against Moscow.

L **Nov**: 3rd, Germans take Kursk;
12th, H.M.S. *Ark Royal* sunk near Gibraltar;
16th, second German offensive against Moscow;
18th, British begin attack in Western Desert;
25th, H.M.S. *Barham* sunk in Mediterranean;
27th, Marshal Timoshenko launches Russian counter-offensive, forcing Germans to evacuate Rostov-on-Don (taken, 23rd);
29th, Russian counter-offensive in Moscow sector.

M **Dec**: 5th, Britain declares war on Finland, Hungary and Roumania on their refusing to withdraw from the war against U.S.S.R.;
5th, Anthony Eden visits Moscow;
7th, Japanese bomb Pearl Harbor, Hawaii and British Malaya;
8th, Britain and U.S. declare war on Japan;
9th, National Service Bill in Britain lowers age of call-up to 18½ and renders single women aged 20–30 liable to military service;
—, Japanese land on Luzon; Russians recapture Tikhvin, saving Leningrad;
10th, H.M.S. *Prince of Wales* and H.M.S. *Repulse* sunk by Japanese aircraft;
11th, U.S. declares war on Germany and Italy;
17th, heavy penalties for British black-marketeers;
18th, Rommel retreats in North Africa;
19th, Penang evacuated by British;
22nd (–28th), W. S. Churchill visits Washington and Ottawa;
24th, British re-occupy Benghazi and regain control of Cyrenaica;
25th, Hong Kong surrenders to Japanese;
26th, British commandos raid Lofoten Islands and, 27th, Vaagso, near Trondheim;
30th, Russians recapture Kaluga.

N

1942 (Jan.–Jun.) Fall of Singapore—Germans reach Stalingrad—Battle of El Alamein

A **Jan**: 2nd, Britain, U.S., U.S.S.R., China and 22 other Allies pledge themselves not to make separate peace treaties with the enemy;
9th, British recapture Bardia;
10th, Japanese invade Dutch East Indies;
11th, Japanese take Kuala Lumpur;
19th, Japanese invade Burma;
21st, Rommel launches new offensive in Western Desert;
29th, Anglo-Soviet alliance with Iran.

B **Feb**: 1st, British forces in Malaya withdraw to Singapore;
—, Vidkun Quisling becomes premier of Norway;
3rd, Eighth Army evacuates Derna;
11th, German battleships leave Brest for Baltic;
15th, Singapore surrenders;
19th (–22nd), W. S. Churchill reconstructs ministry, with C. R. Attlee deputy Prime Minister, Stafford Cripps Leader of House and James Grigg War Secretary;
24th, U.S. task force raids Wake Islands;
28th, Japanese land in Java.

C **Mar**: 10th, Rangoon falls to Japanese;
28th, British commandos raid St. Nazaire;
—, R.A.F. bombs Lübeck;
31st, Japanese successes in Burma and Andaman Islands threaten east coast of India.

D **Apr**: 4th, Japanese sink 3 British warships in Bay of Bengal;
6th, end of white bread in Britain;
8th (–15th), General George Marshall and Harry Hopkins in London discussing aid for Russia by launching a Second Front;
9th, Bataan surrenders to Japanese;
14th, British Budget doubles entertainment tax;
16th, Indian Congress rejects terms of self-government offered by Stafford Cripps;
23rd (–30th), German 'Baedeker' raids on Exeter, Bath, etc.;
Continuous intensive air raids on Malta while reinforcements from Italy are sent to General Rommel in North Africa.

E **May**: 1st, Japanese take Mandalay, while British withdraw along Chindwin Valley to India;
5th, British troops invade Madagascar;
6th, Corregidor surrenders;
8th, Germans attack Kerch Peninsula;
—, Germans attack in East Crimea;
13th, Russian gains in Kharkov region;
20th, Germans take Kerch Peninsula;
26th, V. Molotov in London signs closer Anglo-Soviet treaty for prosecuting the war;
—, Rommel resumes offensive with massive tank support (–*June* 2nd);
—, Anglo-Soviet 20-year alliance signed in London;
29th, further U.S.-U.S.S.R. lend-lease agreement;
30th, British convoy reaches Russia despite heavy air attacks;
—, mammoth R.A.F. raid on Cologne;
31st, Czech patriots assassinate Gestapo leader Heydrich.

F **Jun**: 2nd, British abandon Gazala-Bir Hakeim Line;
3rd, indecisive U.S.-Japanese battle in Midway Islands;

O Politics, Economics, Law and Education

William Beveridge, *Report on Social Security* (*Dec.* 1st).
E. H. Carr, *Conditions of Peace.*
L. B. Namier, *Conflicts; Studies in Contemporary History.*
Anglo-American Caribbean Commission is established.
Malta is awarded the George Cross in token of the heroism of the islanders under constant German air attack (*Apr.* 16th).
James Burnham, *The Managerial Revolution, or What is Happening in the World Now.*
Uthwatt Report on land development in Britain (*Sept.* 9th).
Gilbert Murray founds Oxfam.

P Science, Technology, Discovery, etc.

E. Fermi at Chicago initiates a controlled chain-reaction in the first nuclear reactor. (*Dec.* 2nd).
American scientists develop ENIAC, the first electronic brain or automatic computer.
Magnetic tape is invented.
Germans launch the V-2 rocket.
The Alaska Highway is opened (*Oct.*).

Q Scholarship

G. M. Trevelyan, *English Social History.*
The Mildenhall hoard is discovered.

R Philosophy and Religion

R. G. Collingwood, *The New Leviathan.*
E. Fromm, *The Fear of Freedom.*
Reichenbach, *Philosophy Foundations of Quantum Mechanics.*
C. S. Lewis, *The Screwtape Letters.*
William Temple, appointed Archbishop of Canterbury (*Feb.* 23rd), publishes *Christianity and the Social Order.*
Kenneth Walker, *The Diagnosis of Man.*

S Art, Sculpture, Fine Arts and Architecture

Painting:
Pierre Bonnard, *L'Oiseau bleu.*
John Piper, *Windsor Castle.*
Graham Sutherland, *Red Landscape.*
Artists Aid Russia Exhibition at Hertford House.

T Music

Benjamin Britten, *Sinfonia da Requiem.*
Aaron Copland, *Lincoln Portrait.*
Roy Harris, 5th Symphony.
Carlo Menotti, *The Island God* (opera).
Edmund Rubbra, 4th Symphony.
Dmitry Shostakovich, 7th Symphony ('Leningrad').

U Literature

A. Camus, *L'Étranger.*
T. S. Eliot, *Little Gidding.*
John Steinbeck, *The Moon is Down.*

V The Press

J. L. Garvin resigns from *The Observer* (*Feb.* 28th; editor since 1928).
Stars and Stripes, daily paper for U.S. forces in Europe, published from *The Times* office (*Nov.* 2nd).

F **Jun**: 6th, Nazis burn Lidice in Bohemia;
10th, Free French garrison at Bir Hakeim surrenders;
13th, British lose 230 tanks in desert fighting and
19th, withdraw to Sollum-Sidi Omar Line, along Egyptian frontier;
21st, Rommel takes Tobruk;
—, heavy British losses on convoy to Malta;
25th, Eighth Army retreats to Mersa Matruh;
—, R.A.F. 1,000-bomber raid on Bremen;
28th, Eighth Army retreats to El Alamein;
Germans launch counter-attack in Kharkov region.

G **Jul**: 1st, vote of censure debate in Commons on direction of war;
—, Coal Commission takes over colliery leases in Britain under 1938 Act;
3rd, Germans take Sebastopol;
26th, R.A.F. raids Hamburg;
27th, Second Front demonstration in Trafalgar Square;
28th, Germans take Rostov and overrun northern Caucasus;
Gregory Zhukov replaces Timoshenko as Commander of U.S.S.R. southern armies.

H **Aug**: 7th, Americans land in Guadalcanal;
12th (–15th), W. S. Churchill, A. Harriman and J. Stalin confer in Moscow;
15th, H.M.S. *Eagle* and H.M.S. *Manchester* lost on Malta convoy;
19th, Dieppe raid, casualties include 3,500 Canadians;
—, General Alexander replaces Auchinleck as Commander-in-Chief Middle East, while B. L. Montgomery is given command of Eighth Army;
26th, Germans reach Stalingrad;
31st, Rommel renews offensive at Alam Halfa, but is driven back to original lines.

J **Sep**: 12th, British convoy to Russia survives German bombing off Norway;
13th, German all-out attack on Stalingrad begins;
U.S. bombers raid France daily.

K **Oct**: 21st, J. C. Smuts addresses assembly of both Houses of Parliament, Westminster;
23rd, Eighth Army's attack on Rommel's line begins battle of El Alamein;
U.S. national labour service act.

L **Nov**: 4th, Rommel in full retreat;
8th, Allied landings in French North Africa under Dwight D. Eisenhower;
9th, Germans move into unoccupied France;
10th, Egypt is cleared of Germans;
11th, General D. Eisenhower's recognition of Admiral François Darlan as French Chief-of-State in North Africa arouses British indignation;
13th, British retake Tobruk;
—, U.S. task force at Guadalcanal beats off Japanese;
19th, Russian counter-offensive from Stalingrad surrounds besieging German Army;
22nd, British ministerial changes, with Herbert Morrison replacing Stafford Cripps in cabinet.

M **Dec**: 12th (–23rd), von Manstein fails to relieve Stalingrad;
16th (–20th), rout of Italians on R. Don;
19th, British and Indian troops begin advance in Burma;
21st, Eighth Army reoccupies Benghazi;
24th, Admiral F. Darlan assassinated in Algiers;
31st, Royal Navy beats off massive German air attack on convoy to Russia.

N U.S. war factories achieve maximum production.

W **Drama and Entertainment**

Jean Anouilh, *Antigone*.
Sean O'Casey, *Red Roses For Me*.
T. Rattigan, *Flare Path*.

Films:
Mrs. Miniver, with Gree Garson.
Coastal Command.
Holiday Inn with Bing Crosby.
How Green Was My Valley.
The Evening Visitor.
Loveletter.
Diesel.
Rembrandt.

B.B.C., Tommy Handley in *ITMA*.

X **Sport**

Warmerdam's record pole-jump.

Y **Statistics**

Steel production: World total, 175 mill. tons (U.S. leads with 70 mill.).
Great Britain's war production: 23,671 aircraft; 8,611 tanks; 173 major vessels, totalling 299,920 tons.
Merchant shipping losses (in thousand tons): Great Britain, 3,695; Allied, 4,394; Neutral, 249.

Z **Births and Deaths**

Jan. 8th Stephen Hawking b. (–).
Jan. 17th Muhammad Ali b. (–).
Jan. 22nd Walter Richard Sickert d. (81).
Jan. 31st Derek Jarman b. (–).
Mar. 12th William Bragg d. (79).
Mar. 21st Philip Wilson Steer d. (81).
Mar. 28th Neil Kinnock b. (–).
July 28th William Flinders Petrie d. (89).
July 31st Francis Younghusband d. (79).
Aug. 23rd Michel Fokine d. (62).
Sept. 26th Wilson Carlile d. (92).
Oct. 14th Marie Tempest d. (78).
Nov. 17th Martin Scorcese b. (–).
Nov. 21st James B. M. Hertzog d. (76).
Nov. 27th Jimi Hendrix b. (–1970).
Moamer al Khaddafi b. (–).

1943 (Jan.–May) Russian victory at Stalingrad—Germans surrender in North Africa—Allies invade Italy—Mussolini falls

A **Jan**: 2nd, German withdrawal from Caucasus begins;
11th, British treaty with China renouncing extra-territorial rights;
14th (–24th), W. S. Churchill and F. D. Roosevelt confer at Casablanca on grand strategy;
15th, Japanese are driven from Guadalcanal;
18th, German air attack on London renewed;
23rd, Eighth Army enters Tripoli;
26th, Russian victory at Voronezh;
27th, civil conscription of women in Germany;
30th, Russians destroy German Army south-west of Stalingrad;
31st, Paulus surrenders at Stalingrad.

B **Feb**: 8th, Russians take Kursk;
10th, Eighth Army reaches Tunisian frontier;
14th, Russians recapture Rostov and, 16th, Kharkov;
18th, Labour M.P.'s, disobeying C. R. Attlee and H. Morrison, protest at Government's policy over Beveridge Report;
21st, George VI announces on 25th anniversary of Red Army the presentation of sword of honour to Stalingrad (handed by W. S. Churchill to J. Stalin at Teheran in *Nov.*);
—, Allied armies in North Africa come under General Dwight D. Eisenhower's supreme command;
24th, von Arnim withdraws forces through Kasserine Pass;
28th, heavy R.A.F. raid on Berlin.

C **Mar**: 1st, R.A.F. begins systematic bombing of European railway system;
7th (—11th), Eighth Army repulses heavy German counter-attacks in Tunisia;
15th, Russians forced to evacuate Kharkov;
Growing support in by-elections for candidates of Commonwealth Party, founded by Richard Acland, indicates dissatisfaction with Government's social policy, but W. S. Churchill's broadcast, 22nd, advocating four-year plan for post-war reconstruction, retrieves Government's popularity;
29th, B. L. Montgomery breaks through Mareth Line into Southern Tunisia.

D **Apr**: 6th, Rommel's retreat north from Gabes Gap enables British and U.S. armies, 8th, to link up;
8th, General S. von Arnim succeeds Rommel as Commander of Afrika Korps;
10th, Eighth Army occupies Sfax;
20th, Massacre in Warsaw ghetto;
24th, O. Wingate's commandos return to base after three months in Burmese jungle and Japanese resume offensive;
26th, U.S.S.R. breaks off diplomatic relations with London Polish Government;
Heavy air raids on Ruhr;
Bermuda Conference on refugee problem.

E **May**: 1st, compulsory arbitration in British coal industry;
—, U.S. coal-miners' strike (settled *Nov.* 3rd);
7th, Allies take Tunis and Bizerta, while Germans retire to Cap Bon Peninsula;
11th, U.S. force lands at Attu, Aleutian Islands;
12th, German Army in Tunisia surrenders;
17th, R.A.F. bombs Ruhr dams using spinning bombs designed by Barnes Wallis;
22nd, Third Communist International (formed 1919) dissolved;
Air offensive on Germany becomes more destructive.

O **Politics, Economics, Law and Education**

D. W. Brogan, *The American Political Scene.*
Harold Laski, *Reflections on the Revolution of Our Time.*
A. D. Lindsay, *The Modern Democratic State.*
Walter Lippmann, *U.S. Foreign Policy.*
Peter Nathan, *The Psychology of Fascism.*
U.S. Office of Economic Warfare created (*July*).
J. M. Keynes's plan for an international currency union.
First Henry Kaiser 'Liberty' ships.
United Nations Relief and Rehabilitation Administration is established.
The Nuffield Foundation formed.
Cambridge University founds a professorship of American History and Institutions.
Board of Education's *Sex Education in Schools and Youth Organisations* published to reduce venereal disease.
Forshaw and Abercrombie, *The County of London Plan.*
R. A. Brady, *Business as a System of Power.*

P **Science, Technology, Discovery, etc.**

Penicillin is successfully applied to treat chronic diseases.
Selman A. Waksman and A. Schatz discover streptomycin.
'Big inch' oil pipeline from Texas to U.S. eastern seaboard opened.
Fully-laden glider is towed across Atlantic from Montreal in 28 hrs.

Q **Scholarship**

Pilgrim Trust purchases Sir Isaac Newton's library.
J. M. Thompson, *The French Revolution.*

R **Philosophy and Religion**

J.-P. Sartre, *L'Être et le néant.*
Jacques Maritain, *Christianity and Democracy.*
C. E. Raven, *Science, Religion and the Future.*
Bertrand Griffin appointed Archbishop of Westminster as Cardinal Arthur Hinsley's successor.
Archbishop Suhard of Paris founds worker-priest movement.
Archbishop of Moscow is elected Patriarch of All Russia.

S **Art, Sculpture, Fine Arts and Architecture**

Sculpture:
H. Moore, *Madonna and Child*, Northampton.
H. G. Adam, *Reclining Figure.*

T **Music**

Arnold Bax, Violin Concerto.
Lennox Berkeley, *Divertimento.*
W. Bush, 'cello concerto.
Khachaturian, *Ode to Stalin.*
R. Vaughan Williams, Symphony no. 5 in D.
'La Pléiade' formed to finance concerts of music by French composers in Paris.

U **Literature**

Henry Green, *Caught.*
Henri Michaux, *Exorcismes.*

F **Jun**: 4th, French Committee of National Liberation is formed, including General Charles de Gaulle and General Henri Giraud;
11th, island of Pantelleria surrenders to Allies after bombardment;
—, agreement on post-war relief signed at end of Hot Springs Conference;
29th, U.S. forces land in New Guinea.

G **Jul**: 5th, German offensive on Russian front opens with battle of Kursk;
10th, Allies land in Sicily;
12th (–15th), Russian counter-offensive against Orel salient;
19th, first Allied air raid on Rome;
23rd, Palermo occupied;
26th, Benito Mussolini falls from power. Victor Emmanuel asks Marshal Badoglio to form a government;
U.S. Congress passes anti-strike act over F. D. Roosevelt's veto.

H **Aug**: 5th, Russians take Orel;
5th, capture of Catania gives Allies command of Sicilian Straits;
10th (–24th), W. S. Churchill, F. D. Roosevelt and Mackenzie King confer at Quebec on Far Eastern operations;
16th, U.S. troops occupy Messina;
23rd, Russians recapture Kharkov;
24th, Britain and U.S. recognise French Committee for National Liberation in Algiers;
27th, Japanese evacuate New Georgia Island.

Sep: 3rd, Allies invade Italy;
8th, Allied landings in Salerno Bay;
—, Dwight D. Eisenhower announces Italy's unconditional surrender (made, 3rd);
10th, Eighth Army takes Taranto;
24th, Russians cross Dnieper north of Kiev;
25th, Russians take Smolensk;
30th, Fifth Army takes Naples.

K **Oct**: 4th, Fitzroy Maclean undertakes military mission to Marshal Tito;
6th, Kuban Peninsula in Russian hands;
12th, Portugal grants Britain facilities in the Azores;
13th, Italy declares war on Germany;
18th (–30th), Moscow Conference of Allied foreign ministers;
19th, Germans in Italy retire from Volturno river;
27th, Russians break into Nogaisk steppes.

L **Nov**: 1st, U.S. force lands at Bougainville in Solomons;
2nd, Moscow declaration of Allied foreign ministers on international security sets up European Advisory Commission;
4th, Eighth Army takes Isernia;
6th, Russians take Kiev;
11th, Lord Woolton appointed first British Minister of Reconstruction;
19th, release on health grounds of Oswald Mosley, imprisoned since 1940 under Defence Regulations, divides British Labour Party;
22nd, W. S. Churchill, F. D. Roosevelt and Chiang Kai-shek agree at Cairo to measures for defeating Japan;
23rd, U.S. troops occupy Makin in Gilbert Islands;
26th, Russians take Gomel;
28th (–*Dec.* 1st), W. S. Churchill, F. D. Roosevelt and J. Stalin meet at Teheran for planning overthrow of Germany.

(Continued opposite)

U **Literature** (*cont.*)

Ricardo Molinari, *Mundos de la Madrugada* (poems).
Romain Rolland, *Péguy*.
New Writing and Daylight, ed. J. Lehmann.

V **The Press**

Frankfurter Zeitung is suppressed by Adolf Hitler.

W **Drama and Entertainment**

J. Bridie, *Mr. Bolfry*.
Noël Coward, *This Happy Breed*.
J.-P. Sartre, *Les Mouches*.
Rogers and Hart, *Oklahoma!* (musical).
Dorothy Sayers's B.B.C. radio serial *The Man Born to be King*.

Films:
For Whom the Bell Tolls.
Orson Welles's *Jane Eyre*.
Colonel Blimp.
The Gentler Sex.
Stage-Door Canteen.
Stalingrad: One Day of War.
Summer Light.

Frank Sinatra becomes first pop idol of the teenager.

X **Sport**

Y **Statistics**

British war production: 26,263 aircraft; 8,611 tanks; 168 major vessels, totalling 292,450 tons.
Merchant shipping losses (in thousand tons): Great Britain, 1,678; Allied, 1,886; Neutral, 82.

Z **Births and Deaths**

Jan. 9th R. G. Collingwood d. (54).
Jan. 24th John Burns d. (84).
Mar. 10th Laurence Binyon d. (73).
Mar. 28th Sergei Rachmaninov d. (69).
Mar. 29th John Major b. (–).
Apr. 30th Beatrice Webb, Lady Passfield, d. (85).
June 17th Annie S. Swan (Mrs. Burnett Smith) d. (83).
July 4th Wladyslaw Sikorski d. (62).
July 10th Arthur Ashe b. (–1993).
Sept. 1st W. W. Jacobs d. (80).
Sept. 29th Lech Walesa b. (–).
Nov. 22nd Billie Jean King b. (–).

M **Dec:** 12th, U.S.S.R.-Czechoslovak treaty for post-war co-operation;
26th, *Scharnhorst* sunk;
Russians succeed in recapturing two-thirds of the territory captured by Germans.

1944 (Jan.–Jul.) Normandy landings—Germans driven from Russia—V-bombs on England

A **Jan**: 4th, Fifth Army launches attack east of Cassino;
9th, U.S. troops take San Vittore;
—, Commonwealth Party wins Skipton by-election;
20th, R.A.F. drops 2,300 tons of bombs on Berlin (provoking, *Feb.* 9th, protests in House of Lords on bombing of German cities);
22nd, Allied landings at Nettuno and Anzio;
27th, Leningrad completely relieved.

B **Feb**: 4th, Allied troops reach Monte Cassino;
4th, Conservative majority slashed at Brighton by-election;
7th (–29th), German assaults on Anzio bridgehead;
10th, Pay-as-you-earn income tax introduced;
15th, Monte Cassino monastery bombed;
—, U.S. troops complete reconquest of Solomons;
19th (–26th), heaviest air raids on London since May 1941;
22nd, Russians take Krivoi Rog, Ukraine;
28th, British begin operations in Upper Burma;
South Wales miners' strike.

C **Mar**: 4th, Russian offensive in Ukraine begins;
6th, U.S. bombers begin daylight attacks on Berlin;
15th, Allies launch heavy attack on Monte Cassino;
19th, Russians force the Dniester;
31st, Japan transfers mineral concessions in North Sakhalin to U.S.S.R.;
Japanese troops advance on Imphal.

D **Apr**: 2nd, Russians enter Roumania;
11th, liberation of Crimea begins;
18th, Aneurin Bevan agitates for annulment of powers conferred on Minister of Labour for dealing with strikes;
22nd, Allies land at Hollandia, New Guinea.
During the month Allies drop 81,400 tons of bombs on Germany and occupied Europe.

E **May**: 1st (–16th), London conference of Dominion premiers;
—, Anglo-Spanish agreement to reduce Spain's exports of wolfram to Germany;
9th, Sebastopol liberated;
12th, Allies assault Gustav Line in Italy;
18th, Monte Cassino is taken;
21st, Allies break through the Hitler Line in Italy.

F **Jun**: 4th, Fifth Army enters Rome;
6th, 'D-Day' landings in Normandy;
10th, Russian offensive against Finland opens;
12th, Allies call on Germany's satellites to side with them;
13th, first flying-bomb dropped on London;
15th, Fifth Army takes Orvieto;
19th, U.S. troops take Saipan;
23rd (–28th), Germans encircled at Vitebsk;
27th, Allies take Cherbourg.

G **Jul**: 1st, U.S. monetary and financial conference at Bretton Woods, New Hampshire;
3rd, Russians take Minsk, capturing 100,000 Germans;
5th, British capture of Ukhrul removes threat to Imphal;

O Politics, Economics, Law and Education

Norman Bentwich, *Judea Lives Again.*
William Beveridge, *Full Employment in a Free Society.*
John Hilton, *Rich Man, Poor Man.*
Elspeth Huxley and Margery Perham, *Race Relations.*
Julian Huxley, *On Living in a Revolution.*
Sumner Welles, *The Time for Decision.*
R. A. Butler introduces British Education Act.
The Fleming Report recommends that British independent schools should accept selected pupils paid for by public authorities.
I.C.I. endow 80 fellowships at nine British universities.
'Black-out' restrictions are relaxed in Britain (*Sept.*).
Thomas Sharpe's plan for Greater London.
U.S.S.R. substitutes 'Hymn of the Soviet Union' for 'The Internationale'.

P Science, Technology, Discovery, etc.

Second uranium pile built at Clinton, Tennessee, for manufacturing plutonium for an atomic bomb.
New cyclotron of Department of Terrestrial Magnetism, Carnegie Institution, Washington, completed.
Quinine is synthesised.
Blalock successfully operates on 'blue babies'.
First non-stop flight London-Canada (*Sept.* 8th).

Q Scholarship

F. M. Stenton, *Anglo-Saxon England.*
B. H. Sumner, *Survey of Russian History.*

R Philosophy and Religion

F. A. von Hayek, *The Road to Serfdom.*
C. Jung, *Psychology and Religion.*
L. Mumford, *The Condition of Man.*
W. Temple, *The Church Looks Forward.*
Roger Schutz founds Protestant community of Taize, near Cluny.

S Art, Sculpture, Fine Arts and Architecture

Painting:
G. Sutherland, *Christ on the Cross*, Northampton.
M. Beckmann, *Self-Portrait.*

T Music

Béla Bartók, Violin Concerto.
Paul Hindemith, *Herodias* (opera).
Ernest Moeran, *Sinfonietta.*
Dmitry Shostakovich, 8th Symphony.
Oxford University founds a faculty of music.

U Literature

H. E. Bates, *Fair Stood the Wind for France.*
Ivy Compton-Burnett, *Elders and Betters.*
T. S. Eliot, *Four Quartets.*
A. Huxley, *Time Must Have a Stop.*
R. Lehmann, *The Ballad and the Source.*

G **Jul**: 9th, Caen captured;
16th, Germans withdraw from Arezzo;
18th, General Tojo resigns in Japan;
19th, Leghorn and Ancona fall to Allies;
20th, attempt to assassinate Hitler;
23rd, Russian troops cross 'Curzon Line' in Poland;
26th, U.S.S.R. recognises the Lublin Committee of Polish Liberation in Moscow as the authority for liberated Poland;
28th, Russians take Brest-Litovsk.

H **Aug**: 8, 1st, Warsaw rising begins;
—General Omar Bradley appointed commander of U.S. 12th Army Group (largest ever U.S. force); U.S. troops break through at Avranches;
13th (–20th), German Seventh Army exterminated in Falaise Gap;
15th, British land on French Riviera;
19th, Eighth Army takes Florence;
20th, Russian offensive in Bessarabia and Roumania;
25th, Charles de Gaulle enters Paris in the wake of the Allied troops and, 30th, seat of French provisional government is transferred from Algiers to Paris;
26th, Eighth Army opens attack in Adriatic sector;
30th, Russians enter Bucharest.

J **Sep**: 4th, Allies capture Antwerp and destroy flying-bomb sites in Pas de Calais;
—, cease-fire on Finnish front;
5th, U.S.S.R. declares war on Bulgaria;
—, Brussels is liberated;
8th, first V-2 rocket lands in Britain;
10th (–17th), W. S. Churchill and F. D. Roosevelt meet in Quebec;
11th, Americans cross German frontier near Trier;
12th, Roumanian armistice signed;
17th, British airborne forces land at Eindhoven and Arnhem, but fail to outflank the German defence of the Westwall and are withdrawn after heavy casualties;
19th, Finnish armistice signed;
29th, Russians invade Yugoslavia.

K **Oct**: 3rd, Canadians reach R. Maas;
9th (–18th), W. S. Churchill visits Moscow;
19th, U.S. troops land in Philippines;
20th, Russians and Yugoslavs enter Belgrade;
23rd, Allies recognise General Charles de Gaulle's administration as the provisional government of France;
The Red Army advances into Hungary.

L **Nov**: 3rd, Flushing falls to the Allies and the port of Antwerp is reopened to shipping;
7th, F. D. Roosevelt, Democrat, wins U.S. Presidential election, for a fourth term, with 25,610,946 votes against 22,018,177 for Thomas Dewey, Republican, who fails to carry his own state of New York;
12th, *Tirpitz* sunk;
24th, Strasbourg is taken;
27th, Edward Stettinius appointed U.S. secretary of state on Cordell Hull's resignation (secretary since 1933).

(*Continued opposite*)

U **Literature** (*cont.*)
W. S. Maugham, *The Razor's Edge.*
A. Moravia, *Agustino.*

V **The Press**

W **Drama and Entertainment**
T. Rattigan, *Love in Idleness.*
J.-P. Sartre, *Huis Clos.*
Tennessee Williams, *The Glass Menagerie.*

Films:
Laurence Olivier's *Henry V.*
The Way Ahead.
Alfred Hitchcock's *Lifeboat.*
The White Cliffs of Dover.
Zola.
Justice is Coming.

X **Sport**

Y **Statistics**
British Commonwealth armed forces total 8·7 mill. of which Britain provides 4·5 mill.
U.S. armed forces total 7·2 mill.
Britain's electrical output totals 38·3 mill. units (increase of 12 mill. from 1939).
U.S. synthetic rubber: 763,000 tons manufactured.
Gold production (in thousand ounces): South Africa, 12,227; Canada, 2,900; U.S., 1,000; Mexico, 750.

Z **Births and Deaths**
Jan. 1st Edwin Landseer Lutyens d. (75).
Jan. 18th Paul Keating b. (–).
Jan. 23rd Edvard Munch d. (80).
Mar. 28th Stephen Leacock d. (74).
May 9th Ethel Smyth d. (86).
May 12th Arthur Quiller-Couch ('Q') d. (80).
July 11th Lucien Pissarro d. (81).
July 18th Thomas Sturge Moore d. (74).
Aug. 19th Henry J. Wood d. (75).
Sept. 13th Heath Robinson d. (72).
Oct. 8th Wendell Wilkie d. (52).
Oct. 26th William Temple d. (63).
Nov. 7th Geoffrey Dawson d. (70).
Nov. 22nd Arthur Stanley Eddington d. (61).
Dec. 30th Romain Rolland d. (78).

M **Dec:** 3rd, police action against E.A.M. (Republican) demonstrations in Athens raises criticisms of British policy in Greece, and to restore confidence W. S. Churchill visits Athens (24th);
5th, Allies take Ravenna;
16th, German offensive in Ardennes ('Battle of the Bulge',—*Jan.* 5th) begins;
18th, North Burma is cleared of Japanese;
27th, Russians surround Budapest.

1945 (Jan.–Apr.) Germany surrenders—Roosevelt dies—Attlee forms Labour Government—The atom bomb—Japan surrenders

A Jan: 1st, 14th Army opens offensive in Burma;
3rd, Americans counter-attack Ardennes salient;
8th, Egyptian elections, boycotted by the Wafd, result in majority for Ahmed Pasha, the premier;
11th, truce in Greek civil war;
12th, Representation of the People bill, to settle problems of British service voters;
13th, Russian forces begin offensive in Silesia;
17th, Russians take Warsaw; 19th, Cracow, 23rd, Tilsit;
20th, provisional Hungarian government under General Miklos concludes armistice with Allies;
22nd, 14th Army take Monywa on Chindwin River;
23rd, Russians reach the Oder;
U-boats using homing torpedoes take heavy toll of British shipping in Atlantic.

B Feb: 3rd, Allies capture Colmar;
4th (–11th), W. S. Churchill, F. D. Roosevelt and J. Stalin confer at Yalta to plan for Germany's unconditional surrender, settle the Polish question and arrange for U.N. Conference at San Francisco;
5th, General Douglas MacArthur's troops enter Manila;
6th, world T.U. conference in London;
8th, Canadian offensive south-east of Nijmegen towards Rhine;
10th, Elbing captured;
13th, Budapest falls;
15th, British troops reach Rhine on ten-mile front;
16th, massive U.S. air raids on Tokyo begin;
19th, invasion of Iwo Jima (–*Mar.* 17th);
24th, Ahmed Pasha, premier of Egypt, assassinated after announcing Egypt's declaration of war against Germany.

C Mar: 2nd, Petru Groza forms a pro-Russian government in Roumania;
7th, Cologne captured;
—, 14th Army enters Mandalay;
13th, Allies command west bank of Rhine (Nijmegen to Coblenz);
19th, U.S.S.R. denounces Turko-Soviet non-aggression pact of 1925;
23rd, General Dempsey's 2nd Army crosses Rhine;
28th, last of 1,050 V-rockets falls on Britain;
29th, Russians cross Austrian frontier;
30th, Danzig captured.

D Apr: 1st, Americans begin invasion of Okinawa (–*June* 21st);
3rd, Eduard Beneš appoints a National Front government in Czechoslovakia with Zdenek Fierlinger as premier;
5th, U.S.S.R. denounces non-aggression pact with Japan of *Apr.* 1941;
—, U.S. Army takes Osnabrück;
6th, U.S. naval victory over Japanese at Kyushu;
10th, U.S. troops take Hanover, but Germans resist attack on Bremen;
11th, 8th Army reaches R. Santerno;
12th, F. D. Roosevelt dies (aged 63) and is succeeded by Harry S. Truman;
14th, Allies enter Arnhem;
17th, Paasikivi forms new coalition in Finland;
20th, Russians reach Berlin;
22nd, Bologna falls;
23rd, Allies reach River Po;
—, junction of U.S. and U.S.S.R. forces at Torgau;

O **Politics, Economics, Law and Education**

D. W. Brogan, *The Free State* (intended for re-education of Germany).
E. Cammaerts, *The Peace That Was Left.*
L. Curtis, *World War; Its Cause and Cure.*
Lord Moran, *The Anatomy of Courage.*
'Black Markets' for food, cigarettes and clothing in Europe.
France enfranchises women.
Bank of France is nationalised.
Family allowances are introduced in Britain.
Shintoism is disestablished in Japan by Allied Control Commission.

P **Science, Technology, Discovery, etc.**

The dropping of the atomic bomb (*Aug.* 6th) reveals the discovery of releasing and controlling atomic energy.
Henry Dale pleads for the abolition of secrecy in science.
Developments in radar and other wartime scientific inventions are made known.
Jánossy investigates cosmic radiation.
Synthesis of vitamin A.

Q **Scholarship**

R **Philosophy and Religion**

R. G. Collingwood, *The Idea of Nature.*
K. Popper, *The Open Society and Its Enemies.*
M. Buber, *For the Sake of Heaven.*
Sperry, *Religion in America.*
C. J. Webb, *Religious Experience.*

S **Art, Sculpture, Fine Arts and Architecture**

Painting:
S. Spencer, series of *Resurrection* pictures (–1950).
M. Chagall, sets and costumes for *The Firebird* ballet.
E. W. Tristram, *English Medieval Wall-Painting.*

Sculpture:
A. Calder, *Red Pyramid* (mobile).
H. Moore, *Family Group.*

T **Music**

Benjamin Britten, *Peter Grimes* (opera).
Arthur Honegger, *Sinfonie Liturgique.*
R. Strauss, *Metamorphosen.*
Igor Stravinsky, Symphony in three movements.
S. Prokofiev, *Sluts* (ballet).

U **Literature**

Henry Green, *Loving.*
John Hersey, *A Bell for Adano.*
P. J. Jouve, *La Vierge de Paris.*
Carlo Levi, *Christ Stopped at Eboli.*
S. Lewis, *Cass Timberlane.*
G. Orwell (pseud.), *Animal Farm.*
J.-P. Sartre, *The Age of Reason.*
E. Waugh, *Brideshead Revisited.*
K. Winsor, *Forever Amber.*

D **Apr**: 25th, Karl Renner becomes chancellor of provisional Austrian government;
— (–*June* 26th), U.N. Conference attended by Anthony Eden, Vyacheslav Molotov, J. C. Smuts and Edward Stettinius in San Francisco;
26th, Bremen surrenders;
—, U.S. and U.S.S.R. forces take Torgau;
27th, 5th Army takes Genoa and Verona;
28th, Allies cross Elbe;
—, Benito Mussolini killed by partisans;
29th, Venice falls;
30th, death of Adolf Hitler in Berlin.

E **May**: 1st, surrender of German Army on Italian front;
2nd, Berlin surrenders to Russians;
3rd, Allies enter Hamburg and, 4th, Rangoon;
7th, General Jodl makes final capitulation of Germany to General Dwight Eisenhower near Reims;
8th, 'V.E.' Day; Wilhelm von Keitel surrenders to Zhukov near Berlin;
—, Nationalist riots in Algeria;
—, Spain breaks off diplomatic relations with Germany;
9th, Russians take Prague;
10th, purge of collaborators begins in Prague;
14th, Democratic Republic of Austria established;
25th, W. S. Churchill forms Conservative 'Caretaker' ministry;
28th, French shelling of Damascus angers W. S. Churchill who requires Charles de Gaulle to order a cease-fire in Syria and the Lebanon.

F **Jun**: 5th, Allied Control Commission assumes control throughout Germany, which is divided into four occupation zones;
10th, José Bustamente becomes President of Peru;
11th, Liberals under Mackenzie King win Canadian elections;
15th, British Parliament prorogued;
20th, Spain is excluded from U.N.;
25th, Sean O'Kelly becomes President of Eire on Douglas Hyde's retirement;
26th, Einar Gerhardsen, Labour, forms coalition in Norway;
28th, Osobka-Morawski forms National Unity government in Poland;
29th, Czechoslovakia cedes Ruthenia to U.S.S.R.

G **Jul**: 1st, James F. Byrnes succeeds Edward Stettinius as U.S. secretary of state;
3rd, three-power occupation of Berlin takes effect;
5th (–12th) polling in British general election, with 1,675 candidates for 637 seats;
12th, Joseph Chifley becomes premier of Australia on John Curtin's death;
17th (–*Aug.* 2nd), Potsdam Conference, attended by J. Stalin, H. S. Truman, W. S. Churchill and C. R. Attlee, to settle the occupation of Germany;
26th, Labour landslide in British election with 412 seats, against Conservatives and supporters 213, Liberals 12;
—, Britain, U.S. and China demand Japan's unconditional surrender as the terms of peace;
27th, C. R. Attlee forms ministry with Ernest Bevin as Foreign Secretary and Hugh Dalton as Chancellor of Exchequer;
31st, Per Hansson forms Social Democrat cabinet in Sweden.

H **Aug**: 3rd, Germans and Hungarians in Czechoslovakia deprived of citizenship;
6th, U.S. drops atomic bomb on Hiroshima;

V **The Press**

W **Drama and Entertainment**

Ronald Duncan, *This Way to the Tomb.*

Films:

George Eisenstein's *Ivan the Terrible.*
Jean Renoir's *The Man from the South.*
Roberto Rossellini's *Rome, Open City.*
Billy Wilder's *The Lost Week-end.*
G. Gershwin, *Rhapsody in Blue.*

'Bebop' dancing in U.S.

X **Sport**

Y **Statistics**

War casualties, 1939–45: Great Britain, 244,723 killed; 277,090 wounded. Rest of British Commonwealth, 109,929 killed; 197,908 wounded. U.S., 230,173 killed; 613,611 wounded. Germany, 3,000,000 military and civilian dead or missing; *c.* 1,000,000 wounded. U.S.S.R., estimated 20,000,000 military and civilian dead.

Naval losses: Royal Navy: 5 battleships, 8 aircraft carriers, 26 cruisers, 128 destroyers, 77 submarines.

U.S. Navy: 2 battleships, 5 aircraft carriers, 6 escort cruisers, 10 cruisers, 71 destroyers, 52 submarines.

Germany: 7 battleships; 2 heavy cruisers 5 light cruisers; 25 destroyers and 974 U-boats.

Japan: 12 battleships, 15 aircraft carriers, 4 escort carriers, 16 heavy cruisers, 20 light cruisers, 126 destroyers, 125 submarines.

Merchant shipping losses (in thousand tons): Great Britain, 11,380; U.S., 3,310; Allied, 5,030; Neutral, 1,420; Germany, 8,320.

Railway mileage in operation: U.S., 240,156; U.S.S.R., 52,687; Great Britain, 50,555; France, 6,900.

Religions (in millions): *Christian*, 692 (Roman Catholics, 331; Anglican Communion and Protestant, 206; Orthodox, 144; Coptic, 10). *Non-Christian:* Confucians and Taoists, 351; Hindus, 230; Mohammedans, 209; Buddhists, 230; Animists, 136; Shintoists, 25; Jews, 16.

Z **Births and Deaths**

Jan. 26th Jacqueline du Pré b. (–1987).
Mar. 26th David, Earl Lloyd George, d. (81).
Apr. 11th Frederick, Lord Lugard, d. (87).
Apr. 12th Franklin Delano Roosevelt d. (63).
Apr. 28th Benito Mussolini d. (61).
Apr. 30th Adolf Hitler d. (56)
July 20th Paul Valéry d. (74).
Sept. 26th Béla Bartók d. (64).
Oct. 15th Pierre Laval d. (62).
Dec. 21st George Smith Patton d. (60).
Dec. 26th Roger, Lord Keynes, d. (73).
Dec. 28th Theodore Dreiser d. (74).

H **Aug**: 6th, U.S.S.R. declares war on Japan and invades Manchuria;
9th, atomic bomb dropped on Nagasaki;
13th, World Zionist Congress demands admission of 1 million Jews to Palestine;
14th, Japan's surrender ends Second World War;
—, U.S.S.R. treaty with Nationalist China for recognising the independence of Outer Mongolia;
—, General Henri Pétain sentenced to death (commuted to life imprisonment) for collaborating with Hitler;
17th, Dutch refuse to recognise Independent Indonesian Republic;
22nd, Charles de Gaulle's visit to Washington improves Franco-U.S. relations;
24th, Harry S. Truman orders cessation of lend-lease which has cost U.S. $48·5 billion.
28th, U.S. forces land in Japan, with General George Marshall supreme commander of Allied occupation.

J **Sep**: 2nd, Japan signs capitulation on board U.S.S. *Missouri;* Korea is placed under U.S. and U.S.S.R. occupation until a democratic government is established; Outer Mongolia is recognised as under Soviet control, while China regains sovereignty over Inner Mongolia and Manchuria, Formosa and Hainan;
2nd, independent Vietnam Republic formed with Ho Chi minh President;
10th, Vidkun Quisling sentenced to death in Norway for collaboration;
11th, Allied foreign ministers in London begin drafting peace settlement for Germany;
13th, Iran requests withdrawal of British, U.S. and U.S.S.R. forces;
20th (–23rd), All-India Congress Committee under Gandhi and Pandit Nehru rejects British proposals for self-government and calls on Britain to quit India;
23rd, Egypt demands revision of Anglo-Egyptian 1936 treaty, the end of military occupation and the return of the Sudan;
27th, Congress Party and Muslim League win most seats in elections for Indian Central Legislative Assembly.

K **Oct**: 7th, Oliveira Salazar permits formation of opposition parties in Portugal but, 14th, reimposes press censorship;
9th, Pierre Laval sentenced to death for collaboration;
11th, breakdown of negotiations between Chiang Kai-shek and Mao Tse-tung leads to fighting between Nationalists and Communists in North China for control of Manchuria;
15th, Labour and Dominion parties in South Africa withdraw from coalition, leaving J. C. Smuts premier of a United Party government;
—, British government takes emergency powers for five years to deal with balance of payments crisis provoked by ending of lend-lease;
20th, Egypt, Iraq, Syria and Lebanon warn U.S. that the creation of a Jewish state in Palestine would lead to war; foundation of Arab League;
21st, swing to Left in elections for French Constituent Assembly, with Communists 152 seats and Socialists 151;
24th, U.N. comes into formal existence with ratification of Charter by 29 nations;
25th, Liberals in Brazil secure resignation of Getulio Vargas and the election of José Linhares as President;
30th, Danish elections leave Social Democrats the strongest single party, but Erik Eriksen forms coalition of Liberals and Conservatives.

L **Nov**: 3rd, Zoltan Tildy, Smallholders Party, forms coalition in Hungary;
10th, Communist-dominated government of Albania, under Enver Hoxha, recognised by Western powers;
11th, Marshal Tito's National Front wins elections to Yugoslav Constituent Assembly;

(*Continued opposite*)

L Nov: 13th, Charles de Gaulle elected President of French Provisional Government;
—, Sukarno becomes President of Indonesia;
18th, Communist rising in Azerbaijan province, Iran; troops sent to quell it are stopped by U.S.S.R. forces at Kazvin;
—, O. Salazar's National Union Party win Portuguese elections, boycotted by opposition;
—, Communist-dominated Fatherland Front wins Bulgarian elections;
20th, trial of Nazi war criminals before Allied tribunal opens at Nuremberg;
—, Allied Control Commission approves transfer of 6 million Germans from Austria, Hungary and Poland to West Germany pending a peace settlement;
25th, People's Party win Austrian elections;
29th, Federal People's Republic of Yugoslavia proclaimed;
30th, Alcide de Gasperi, leader of Christian Democrats, forms new coalition in Italy following Ferrucio Parri's resignation;
Strikes in U.S. (–*Mar.* 46) hamper production.

M Dec: 2nd, Enrico Dutra elected President of Brazil;
4th, Senate approves U.S. participation in U.N.;
6th, U.S. loan to Britain of $3·75 billion;
13th, France and Britain pledge to evacuate troops from Syria;
14th, U.S. sends George Marshall to mediate in Chinese Civil War;
18th, in Austria Leopold Figl, People's Party, forms coalition cabinet with Socialists;
27th, foreign ministers of Britain, U.S. and U.S.S.R., meeting in Moscow, call for provisional democratic government in Korea;
28th, Karl Renner elected President of Austria.

N

1946 (Jan.–May.) First meeting of U.N. General Assembly—The Nuremberg Trials

A Jan: 7th, Austrian Republic with 1937 frontiers is recognised by Western powers;
10th, truce in Chinese Civil War (*–Apr.* 14th);
—, U.N. General Assembly's first session opens in London, with Paul Spaak of Belgium president;
11th, constituent assembly in Albania proclaims a People's Republic;
20th, Charles de Gaulle resigns presidency of French provisional government through continued Communist opposition and is succeeded, 22nd, by the Socialist Félix Gouin;
31st, new Constitution in Yugoslavia, modelled on U.S.S.R.

B Feb: 1st, Trygve Lie, Norwegian Socialist, elected U.N. Secretary-General;
—, Hungarian Republic proclaimed, with Zoltan Tildy, leader of Smallholders Party, President;
13th, Trades Disputes Act, 1927, which had declared certain strikes and lockouts illegal, is repealed in Britain;
14th, Bank of England is nationalised;
17th, Christian Socialists win Belgian elections, but the position of the monarchy hampers the formation of a coalition;
24th, Juan Perón elected President of Argentina;
Strikes of steel and electrical workers in U.S. spread to other industries.

C Mar: 4th, Britain, U.S. and France appeal to the Spanish to depose General Franco;
5th, W. S. Churchill's Fulton speech appeals to the West to stand up to U.S.S.R.;
6th, France recognises Vietnam as a free State within the Indo-Chinese Federation;
10th, Britain and France begin evacuating Lebanon;
15th, U.S.S.R. adopts fourth Five-year Plan;
19th, Soviet council of ministers, with Josef Stalin chairman, replaces council of people's commissars;
22nd, Britain recognises independence of Transjordan (proclaimed *May* 25th);
26th, Allied Control Commission limits level of German production;
29th, new Constitution in Gold Coast, which becomes first British African colony with a majority of Africans in the legislature.

D Apr: 5th, U.S.S.R. agrees to withdraw troops from Iran on promise of reforms in Azerbaijan;
10th, Japanese election favours Moderate parties;
18th, League of Nations assembly dissolves itself;
19th, U.S. recognises Yugoslavia Republic;
21st, Social Democrats in East Germany merge with Communists;
29th, Anglo-U.S. committee advises against partition of Palestine.

E May: 5th, French draft constitution rejected by referendum;
9th, Victor Emmanuel III of Italy abdicates and Umberto II proclaims himself king;
17th, Mitri Antonescu, wartime premier of Roumania, sentenced to death;
—, U.S. government takes over control of railways, dislocated by strikes, and, 20th, coal mines;
20th, bill for nationalisation of coal mines in Britain passes Commons;
26th, Klement Gottwald becomes premier of Czechoslovakia following Communist victories in elections;
30th, Catholic People's Party win Dutch elections and J. Beel forms new coalition.

O **Politics, Economics, Law and Education**

F. Meinecke, *The German Catastrophe.*

Étienne Mantoux, *The Carthaginian Peace.*

Monnet plan for modernising French industry and agriculture.

In Britain the Reith committee reports on the establishment of new towns and the government sets up working parties for various industries.

U.S. Supreme Court rules (*June* 3rd) the segregation of negroes on interstate buses unconstitutional.

The Privy Council maintains the validity of a Canadian bill discontinuing appeals from Canadian courts.

Removal of social disabilities of untouchables in Bombay.

Italy enfranchises women.

P **Science, Technology, Discovery, etc.**

Edward Appleton and Donald Hay discover that sun-spots emit radio waves.

Discovery of carbon-13, an isotope for curing metabolic diseases.

Fairey Aviation Co. construct a pilotless radio-controlled rocket missile.

Electronic brain is built at Pennsylvania University.

Chester Carlson invents xerography.

The magnetic north pole observed by aircraft to be 250 miles north of charted position.

The Williamson diamond mine, Tanganyika, is found to be the world's largest.

Q **Scholarship**

R. A. Knox's translation of New Testament.

New Bodleian Library, Oxford, opened.

R **Philosophy and Religion**

Aldous Huxley, *The Perennial Philosophy.*

Bertrand Russell, *History of Western Philosophy.*

R. G. Collingwood, *The Idea of History* (posth.).

Pope Pius XII creates 32 new cardinals (*Feb.* 8th).

Committee of World Council of Churches drafts plans for a reconstructed world International Assembly.

International Christian Conference at Cambridge aims at closer relations between Protestant and Orthodox Churches.

S **Art, Sculpture, Fine Arts and Architecture**

Painting:

G. Sutherland, *Head of Thorns.*

Ben Nicholson, *Painted Relief, West Penrith.*

Sculpture:

P. Picasso founds the pottery at Vallauris.

T **Music**

The Arts Council is inaugurated in Britain.

B. Britten, *The Rape of Lucretia* (opera).

C. Menotti, *The Medium* (opera).

S. Prokofiev, *War and Peace*; *The Duenna* (operas).

D. Milhaud, 2nd Symphony.

D. Shostakovich, 9th Symphony.

Salzburg Festival reopened (*Aug.* 2nd).

F. Ashton, *Symphonic Variations* (ballet).

G. M. Balanchine, *Night Shadow* (ballet).

Jerome Robbins, *Interplay* and *Fancy Free* (ballets).

F **Jun**: Mouvement Républicain Populaire secures most votes in French elections for constituent assembly, with Communists second;
2nd, Britain and U.S. restore Azores bases to Portugal;
—, Italian referendum in favour of a republic;
3rd, South African Asiatic Land Tenure and Indian Representation bill passed;
—, Umberto II leaves Italy and Alcide de Gasperi, the premier, becomes provisional head of state;
19th, Georges Bidault elected president of French provisional government;
27th, foreign ministers of Britain, U.S., U.S.S.R. and France transfer Dodecanese Islands from Italy to Greece and areas of Northern Italy to France;
28th, Enrico de Nicola elected President of Italy;
—, widespread dismissals for incompetence in U.S.S.R. industries;
30th, referendum in Poland favours a single-house assembly and wide nationalisation.

G **Jul**: 4th, Philippine Republic inaugurated;
7th, election of Miguel Alemán, a civilian, as Mexican President leads to closer ties with U.S.;
14th, anti-Jewish pogrom in Kielce, Poland;
15th, President Truman signs bill of credit for $3.75 billion for Britain.
—, Canadian commission reports on Soviet espionage;
21st, world wheat shortage leads to bread rationing in Britain;
27th, British National Insurance Act consolidates social services;
29th (–*Oct.* 15th), Peace Conference of 21 nations that had opposed the Axis meets in Paris to draft peace treaties.

H **Aug**: 20th, Allied Control Commission dissolves Wehrmacht;
25th, 'closed shop' dispute in British transport industry begins.

J **Sep**: 1st, Greek plebiscite favours the monarchy (and, 28th, George II returns to Athens);
6th, J. F. Byrnes's speech at Stuttgart makes U.S. bid for German co-operation;
15th, People's Republic formed in Bulgaria following a referendum against the monarchy;
18th, Archbishop Stephinac of Croatia imprisoned in Yugoslavia;
30th, in verdicts of Nuremberg Tribunal, Joachim von Ribbentrop, Hermann Göring (who subsequently commits suicide) and ten other leading Nazis sentenced to death; Rudolf Hess and Walter Funk sentenced to life imprisonment; five others receive long sentences, but Dr. H. Schacht and Franz von Papen are acquitted;
London conference on Palestine meets (–*Dec.*), but is boycotted by Zionists.

K **Oct**: 5th, Tage Erlander, Social Democrat, becomes premier of Sweden on Per Hansson's death;
13th, revised French Constitution adopted with many abstentions;
—, Siam accepts U.N. verdict for returning territory to Indo-China;
23rd, U.N. General Assembly meets in New York;
30th, Britain co-ordinates armed services under a single defence committee;
Spain signs commercial agreement with Argentina following Perón's visit to Franco.

U **Literature**

Simone de Beauvoir, *Tous les hommes sont mortels.*
J. J. Gautier, *Histoire d'un fait divers.*
André Gide, *Journal, 1939–42.*
Jacques Prévert, *Paroles.*
Dylan Thomas, *Deaths and Entrances.*
Robert Penn Warren, *All the King's Men.*

V **The Press**

Le Temps exonerated from the charge of collaborationist activities.
New governing body established to maintain independence of *The Observer.*

W **Drama and Entertainment**

Jean Cocteau, *L'Aigle à deux têtes.*
Eugene O'Neill, *The Iceman Cometh.*
T. Rattigan, *The Winslow Boy.*
J.-P. Sartre, *Morts sans sépulture.*

Films:

Frank Capra, *It's a Wonderful World.*
Marcel Carné, *Les Portes de la Nuit.*
J. Cocteau, *La Belle et la Bête.*
Vittorio de Sica, *Shoeshine.*
David Lean, *Great Expectations.*
Roberto Rossellini, *Paisa.*
William Wyler, *The Best Years of Our Lives.*
British TV service resumed (*June* 7th), with under 12,000 viewers.
B.B.C. Third Programme (for cultural entertainment) inaugurated (*Sept.* 29th).

X **Sport**

Joe Louis successfully defends title as world heavyweight champion for 23rd time.
Australia under Donald Bradman retain ashes in M.C.C. tour (–*Mar.* 1947).

Y **Statistics**

Populations (in mill.): China, 455; India, 311; U.S.S.R., 194; U.S., 140; Japan, 73; West Germany, 48; Italy, 47; Britain, 46; Brazil, 45; France, 40; Spain, 27; Poland, 24; Korea, 24; Mexico, 22; East Germany, 18; Egypt, 17.
European coal production (in mill. tons): Britain, 189; West Germany, 67; France, 53; Poland, 48; Belgium, 25; Holland, 9.
Petroleum production (in mill. tons): U.S., 250; Central and South America, 82; U.S.S.R., 26; Persia, 20; Saudi Arabia, 12; other Middle East states, 9; Roumania, 4.
Merchant fleets (tonnage in mill.): U.S., 57; British Empire, 20; Norway, 4; Holland, 2·1; Greece, 1·7; France, 1·3; U.S.S.R., 1·2.

L Nov: 3rd, power in Japan transferred from Emperor to elected assembly;
4th, Chinese-U.S. treaty of friendship and commerce;
—, Republicans (246 seats) win U.S. Congressional elections (with Democrats holding 188 seats);
6th, British National Health Act in force;
—, Royal Commission favours equal pay for women in Britain;
9th, President Truman removes controls, excepting those on certain food stocks and rent;
10th, elections to French national assembly give Communists 186 seats, M.R.P. 166 and Socialists 103, resulting in political deadlock;
15th, Holland recognises Indonesian Republic;
21st, Georgi Dimitrov returns from Moscow to become premier of Bulgaria;
26th, Labour retains power in New Zealand elections;
28th, nationalisation of transport bill published in London.

M Dec: 2nd, J. F. Byrnes and Ernest Bevin agree to economic fusion of British and U.S. zones of Germany;
5th, New York City is chosen as permanent headquarters of U.N.;
9th, Indian constituent assembly, boycotted by Moslem League, discusses independence;
11th, U.N. bars Spain from its activities and
14th, rejects South African proposal for incorporation of South-West Africa;
16th, Léon Blum forms Socialist government in France;
30th, U.N. Atomic Energy Commission approves U.S. plan for control.

N Douglas MacArthur purges extreme nationalists in Japan and orders Japanese war criminals to be tried by military tribunals.
During massive strikes 116 million working-days lost in U.S., compared with 2·2 million in Britain.

z **Births and Deaths**

Jan. 29th Harry L. Hopkins d. (56).
Feb. 13th Rainer Fassbinder b. (–1982).
Mar. 2nd Logan Pearsall Smith d. (80).
Apr. 17th George Köhler b. (–).
Apr. 21st John Maynard, Lord Keynes, d. (60).
June 3rd Michael Ivanovich Kalinin d. (71).
June 8th Gerhart Hauptmann d. (83).
June 14th John Logie Baird d. (58).
July 29th Gertrude Stein d. (72).
Aug. 13th Herbert George Wells d. (70).
Aug. 19th William J. ('Bill') Clinton b. (–).
Aug. 31st Harley Granville-Barker d. (69).
Sept. 16th James Jeans d. (69).
Oct. 16th Granville Bantock d. (78).
Dec. 10th Damon Runyan d. (62).

1947 (Jan.–Jun.) The Truman Doctrine—Marshall Aid—Independence of India and Pakistan— The Cominform founded

A **Jan**: 1st, British coal industry becomes nationalised;
—, Nigeria acquires modified self-government;
7th, George Marshall succeeds John F. Byrnes as U.S. secretary of state;
16th, Vincent Auriol elected President of France;
21st, J. C. Smuts refuses to place South-West Africa under U.N. trusteeship;
—, P. Ramadier forms coalition in France, on Léon Blum's resignation;
26th, Egypt breaks off diplomatic relations with Britain, for revising 1936 treaty, and for stating she will prepare the Sudan for self-government, and refers the question to the U.N.;
27th, Regional Advisory Commission for the Pacific established;
29th, U.S. abandons efforts at mediation in China.

B **Feb**: 1st, in Italy Alcide de Gasperi forms new ministry of Christian Democrats, Communists and Left Socialists;
7th, British proposal for dividing Palestine into Arab and Jewish zones with administration as a trusteeship is rejected by Arabs and Jews;
10th, by the peace treaties, signed in Paris, (i) Italy loses Adriatic Islands and part of Venezia Giulia to Yugoslavia, the Dodecanese Islands to Greece and small frontier regions to France, renounces her sovereignty over North African colonies, agrees to the establishment of Trieste as a free territory, pays reparations and reduces her forces to 300,000 men; (ii) Roumania loses Bessarabia and North Bukovina to U.S.S.R., but regains Transylvania; (iii) Bulgaria retains South Dobrudja; (iv) Hungary is reassigned 1938 frontiers; and (v) Finland cedes Petsamo to U.S.S.R.;
(*–Apr.*), fuel crisis in Britain.

C **Mar**: 3rd, N. I. Bulganin replaces Josef Stalin as U.S.S.R. defence minister;
4th, Anglo-French treaty of alliance;
10th (*–Apr.* 24th), Moscow Conference of foreign ministers fails through division between the West and U.S.S.R. over problem of Germany;
12th, Harry S. Truman in message to Congress outlines the Truman Doctrine of economic and military aid to states threatened by Communism, in announcing plan to aid Greece and Turkey;
19th, Paul Spaak forms coalition of Catholics and Socialists in Belgium;
—, Chinese Nationalists capture Communist capital of Yenan;
29th, nationalist revolt against France in Madagascar (*–July*).

D **Apr**: 2nd, U.N. Security Council appoints U.S. Trustee for Pacific islands formerly under Japanese mandate;
—, Britain refers Palestine question to U.N.;
14th, Charles de Gaulle assumes control of Rassemblement du Peuple Français (R.P.F.), to rally non-Communists in France to unity and reform;
16th, ex-President Joseph Tiso of Slovakia executed.

E **May**: 29th, Indian constituent assembly outlaws 'untouchability';
31st, Alcide de Gasperi forms government of Christian Socialists and Independents in Italy (following resignation, 13th, through friction with the Left);
—, Ferenc Nagy, premier of Hungary, falls; succeeded by Lajos Dinnyes, Smallholder;
Serious strikes in France.

F **Jun**: 2nd, German Economic Council is established;
5th, George Marshall calls for a European Recovery Programme (Marshall Aid) in Harvard speech;
17th, Burmese constituent assembly resolves for an independent republic of Burma;

O Politics, Economics, Law and Education

L. S. Amery, *Thoughts on the Constitution.*
G. D. H. Cole, *The Intelligent Man's Guide to the Post-War World.*
Oliver Franks, *Central Planning and Control in War and Peace.*
R. B. McCallum and Alison Readman, pioneer analysis, *The British General Election of 1945.*
Commonwealth Relations Office and Colonial Development Corporation established.
Rationing abolished in U.S.S.R. (*Dec.* 14th).
U.S. Air Force becomes independent of Army.
Old People (ed. Seebohm Rowntree).
Basic English Foundation promoted by C. K. Ogden.

P Science, Technology, Discovery, etc.

Britain's first atomic pile at Harwell comes into operation (*Aug.*).
British government sets up Advisory Committee on Scientific Policy.
P. M. S. Blackett's theory that all massive rotating bodies are magnetic.
The reflecting microscope is developed.
L. Essen determines the speed of radio waves in a vacuum.
Dennis Gabor invents holography, the production of three-dimensional images.
W. F. Libby invents the Carbon-14 dating system.
First supersonic air flight.
First transatlantic automatic flight.
Capt. Odom flies round world in 73 hrs. 5 mins. (*Aug.*).
John Cobb's ground world speed record of 394·196 m.p.h. (*Sept.* 16th).

Q Scholarship

Discovery of main series of Dead Sea Scrolls.
H. W. Garrod, *Scholarship; Its Meaning and Value.*
F. M. Powicke, *King Henry III and the Lord Edward.*
Documents on British Diplomatic History, 1919–39, Vol. I.
H. R. Trevor-Roper, *The Last Days of Hitler.*

R Philosophy and Religion

A. Ruggiero, *Existentialism.*
Bishop E. W. Barnes, *The Rise of Christianity.*
C. S. Lewis, *Miracles.*
Michael Polanyi, *Science, Faith and Society.*

S Art, Sculpture, Fine Arts and Architecture

Painting:
M. Vlaminck, *A Bunch of Flowers.*
The cleaning of Rembrandt's *Woman Bathing* and other pictures in the National Gallery provokes controversy on the principles of cleaning canvases.

Sculpture:
H. Moore, *Three Standing Figures.*
A. Giacometti, *Main Pointing.*

Architecture:
Le Corbusier (pseud.), Unité d'habitation, Marseilles.

T Music

Benjamin Britten, *Albert Herring* (opera).
William Walton, String Quartet in A minor.

F **Jun**: 23rd, U.S. Congress passes Taft-Hartley act over President Truman's veto, prohibiting use of union funds for political purposes, outlawing the 'closed shop' and strengthening the government's hands in strikes and lockouts.

G **Jul**: 6th, Spanish bill of succession for changing government to a monarchy on General Franco's death or resignation;
12th (–15th), 16 West European nations meet in Paris to discuss Marshall Plan for economic recovery;
20th, Dutch troops launch new offensive in Java against Indonesian forces;
28th, National Peasant Party is dissolved in Roumania.

H **Aug**: 1st, U.N. Security Council calls for cease-fire in Indonesia (leads to truce *Jan.* 17th 1948);
15th, Independence of India proclaimed, partitioning India; Pandit Nehru premier of India and L. Ali Khan premier of Pakistan; British authority in remaining states ends; acts of violence in Punjab between Moslems and Hindus follow;
31st, Communist successes in Hungarian elections.

J **Sep**: 2nd, American republics sign treaty of mutual assistance at Rio de Janeiro;
14th, Poland denounces concordat with Catholic Church;
26th, Stephen Senanayake becomes premier of Ceylon;
30th, Pakistan and the Yemen are admitted to U.N.

K **Oct**: 5th, Warsaw Communist conference establishes the Cominform (Communist Information Bureau) to co-ordinate activities of European Communist Parties;
19th (–26th), Charles de Gaulle's R.P.F. becomes strongest group in French municipal elections;
21st, U.N. General Assembly calls on Greece and Balkan powers to settle disputes by peaceful means;
26th, Kashmir is admitted into Indian Union, provoking crisis with Pakistan;
29th, Belgium, Netherlands and Luxembourg ratify customs union (Benelux), which becomes effective *Nov.* 1st.

L **Nov**: 1st, Conservative gains in British municipal elections;
13th, Social Democrats form minority cabinet in Denmark;
14th, U.N. General Assembly recognises Korea's claim to independence;
19th, P. Ramadier resigns, and 23rd, Robert Schuman forms ministry supported by Socialists and M.R.P.;
20th, Princess Elizabeth marries Philip Mountbatten, Duke of Edinburgh;
22nd, Iran assembly nullifies oil agreement with U.S.S.R.;
25th (–*Dec.* 16th), London Conference of powers on Germany fails through U.S.S.R. demands for reparations;
27th, nationalisation of Australian banks;
29th, U.N. announces plan for partition of Palestine, with Jerusalem under U.N. Trusteeship.

M **Dec**: 14th, Rómulo Gallegos, Democratic Action, elected President of Venezuela;
16th, U.S.S.R. currency devalued;
19th, Roumanian-Yugoslav treaty of friendship;
22nd, new Constitution in Italy centralises government and provides for popularly elected Senate;
27th, Greek government dissolves Communist Party and E.A.M.;
30th, Kashmir conflict referred to U.N.;
30th, King Michael of Roumania abdicates, under Communist pressure.

N

U **Literature**

Thomas Armstrong, *King Cotton.*
Nigel Balchin, *Lord I Was Afraid.*
Albert Camus, *The Plague.*
Kathleen Knott, *Landscapes and Departures.*
Primo Levi, *If This is a Man.*
St. John Perse (pseud.), *Vents.*

V **The Press**

Size of British newspapers reduced and publication of magazines curtailed through fuel crisis (*Feb.* 17th–*Mar.* 3rd). Further reductions in size enforced on *July* 21st.

W **Drama and Entertainment**

Edinburgh Festival of the Arts is established.
Christopher Fry and Jean Anouilh, *Ring Round the Moon* (English version of the latter's *L'Invitation au Château*).
W. Douglas Home, *The Chiltern Hundreds.*
J. B. Priestley, *The Linden Tree.*
Tennessee Williams, *A Streetcar Named Desire.*

Films:
Charlie Chaplin's *Monsieur Verdoux.*
René Clair's *Le Silence est d'or.*
Henri Clouzot's *Quai des Orfèvres.*
Carol Reed's *Odd Man Out.*
Robert Hamer's *It Always Rains on Sunday.*

X **Sport**

Y **Statistics**

Religious denominations in U.S. (in mill.): Roman Catholics, 25·2; Baptists, 15; Methodists, 10·3; Lutherans, 5·2; Protestant Episcopal, 2·1; Mormons, 1.

Z **Births and Deaths**

Apr. 7th Henry Ford d. (82).
May 8th Henry Gordon Selfridge d. (90).
June 6th James Agate d. (69).
June 19th Salman Rushdie b. (–).
Aug. 8th Anton Denikin d. (74).
Aug. 21st Ettore Bugatti d. (65).
Sept. 20th Fionello Henry La Guardia d. (64).
Oct. 4th Max Planck d. (89).
Oct. 31st Sidney Webb, Lord Passfield, d. (88).
Dec. 14th Stanley, Earl Baldwin, d. (80).
Dec. 30th A. N. Whitehead d. (86).

1948 (Jan.–Jul.) Brussels Treaty—End of British Mandate in Palestine—Berlin blockade

A **Jan**: 1st, nationalisation of British Railways in force;
4th, Union of Burma proclaimed as an independent republic;
17th, Netherlands and Republic of Indonesia sign truce;
20th, Mahatma Gandhi is assassinated by a Hindu.

B **Feb**: 2nd, U.S. and Italy sign ten-year treaty of friendship and commerce;
4th, Ceylon becomes a self-governing dominion;
25th, Communist *coup d'état* in Czechoslovakia.

C **Mar**: 17th, Britain, France, Belgium, Netherlands and Luxembourg sign Brussels Treaty, for 50-year alliance against armed attack in Europe and providing for economic, social and military co-operation;
20th, U.S.S.R. delegates walk out of Allied Control Commission for Germany;
26th, Franco-Italian customs union concluded;
29th, Chiang Kai-shek, re-elected President of China by Nanking Assembly, is granted dictatorial powers;
31st, U.S. Congress passes Marshall Aid Act, contributing $5·3 billion for European recovery.

D **Apr**: 1st, U.S.S.R. begins to interfere with traffic between Berlin and West Germany;
6th, Central Legislature of British East Africa holds first sessions at Nairobi;
—, U.S.S.R. treaty of mutual assistance with Finland, aimed at Germany;
13th, Roumanian Constitution is remodelled on Soviet lines;
16th, Paris meeting of nations of European Recovery Programme sets up Organisation for European Economic Co-operation (O.E.E.C.);
18th, Christian Democrats win absolute majority in Italian elections.

E **May**: 7th, Hague congress of movement for European unity under W. S. Churchill;
11th, Luigi Einaudi elected President of Italy;
14th, as British mandate in Palestine ends a Jewish provisional government is formed in Israel with Chaim Weizmann President and David Ben-Gurion premier; the Arab Legion of Transjordan invades Palestine and enters Jerusalem;
15th, Egyptian troops intervene in Palestine on side of Arabs;
26th, in South African election J. C. Smuts's coalition of United and Labour parties is defeated by Nationalist Afrikander bloc, standing on *apartheid* platform;
28th, North Korea boycotts national constitutional assembly at Seoul.

F **Jun**: 1st, Britain, U.S., France and Benelux countries call for German representation in European Recovery Programme and for drafting of a federal constitution for Germany;
3rd, Daniel F. Malan forms Nationalist-Afrikander ministry in South Africa;
14th, Klement Gottwald elected President of Czechoslovak People's Republic;
18th, reform of West German currency;
19th, U.S. selective service bill for men aged 19 to 25;
24th, U.S.S.R. stops road and rail traffic between Berlin and the West forcing Western powers to organise airlifts (*–Sept.* 1949);
28th, Yugoslavia is expelled from Cominform for hostility to U.S.S.R.

G **Jul**: 8th, William Drees, Labour, forms coalition in Holland;
15th, U.N. Security Council orders truce in Palestine;
29th, Marshal Tito denies Cominform charges and is given vote of confidence by Yugoslav Communist Party, which is later purged of Cominform supporters;
30th, British Citizenship Act confers status of British subjects on all Commonwealth citizens;

O **Politics, Economics, Law and Education**

P. M. S. Blackett, *Military and Political Consequences of Atomic Energy.*
J. Jewkes, *Ordeal by Planning.*
First annual British Economic Survey.
Belgium enfranchises women; abolition of plural voting in Britain ends 'University seats'.
First World Health Assembly, Geneva (*June*).
Bread rationing in Britain ends (*July* 25th).
Institute of Advanced Legal Studies, London, founded.
British Electricity Authority takes over electrical industry.

P **Science, Technology, Discovery, etc.**

T. D. Lysenko's denunciation of non-Michurin geneticists in U.S.S.R. leads to purges of scientific committees.
H. J. Fleure, *Some Aspects of British Civilisation.*
L. Jánossy, *Cosmic Rays and Nuclear Physics.*
Arthur Keith, *A New Theory of Human Evolution.*
Preparation of antibiotics aureomycin and chloromycetin.
Peter Goldmark invents the long-playing record.
Transistor invented by Bell Telephone Company scientists.
Port radar installation at Liverpool Docks to supervise shipping approaches in fog, etc.
International Conference for redistribution of wavelengths (*Sept.* 15th).
Auguste Piccard constructs bathyscaphe for deep descents.
Wilfred Thesiger crosses Arabian desert and penetrates Oman Steppes.
A. C. Kinsey (and others), *Sexual Behaviour in the Human Male.*

Q **Scholarship**

J. W. Carter and Graham Pollard, *Thomas J. Wise in the Original Cloth* (investigations of Wise's literary forgeries).
W. S. Churchill, *The Gathering Storm* (first volume of *The Second World War*).
The White House Papers of Harry L. Hopkins.
L. B. Namier, *Diplomatic Prelude, 1938–9.*

R **Philosophy and Religion**

G. K. A. Bell, *Christian Unity.*
W. R. Inge, *Mysticism in Religion.*
Representatives of 147 churches from 44 countries meet in Amsterdam to inaugurate the World Council of Churches.
World Jewish Congress, Montreux.

S **Art, Sculpture, Fine Arts and Architecture**

Painting:
F. Léger, *Homage to David.*
Jackson Pollock, *Composition No. 1* (tachisma).
Sculpture:
Henry Moore, *Family Group* for Stevenage New Town.
Architecture:
Pier Luigi Nervi, Exhibition Hall, Turin (single-roof structure, in undulating pre-fabrication).
Construction of the first sizeable geodesic dome at Black Mountain College, Carolina, designed by Buckminster Fuller.
Bill Brandt, *Camera in London* (photographs).

T **Music**

1948 (Jul.–Dec.)

G **Jul**: 30th (–*Aug*. 18th), Conference of ten nations meets in Belgrade to consider the future of the R. Danube;
—, Zoltan Tildy is forced to resign in Hungary;
Amnesty is proclaimed in the Philippines, but the rebels refuse to comply.

H **Aug**: 10th, Gaston Eyskens, Christian Socialist, forms coalition in Belgium with Liberal support;
15th, Republic of Korea proclaimed in Seoul, with Syngman Rhee President;
25th, U.S.S.R. breaks off relations with U.S. for refusing to surrender a Soviet citizen against her will.

J **Sep**: 1st, Communists announce formation of a North China People's Republic;
4th, Queen Wilhelmina abdicates in Netherlands for health reasons; succeeded, 6th, by Queen Juliana;
5th, Wladyslaw Gomulka, leader of Communist Polish Workers' Party, is forced to resign for deviations;
9th, Korean People's Democratic Republic formed in North Korea, claiming authority over entire country;
10th, Henri Queuille, Radical, forms ministry in France, with Robert Schuman foreign minister;
17th, Count Folke Bernadotte, U.N. mediator in Palestine, assassinated by Jewish terrorists;
—, Hyderabad surrenders to Indian forces and agrees to join Indian Union;
18th, Indonesian Communists set up a Soviet government in Java, but are forced to withdraw;
24th, first conference in London of representatives from Britain's African colonies.

K **Oct**: 7th, Democratic-Liberal government formed in Japan by Shigeru Yoshida;
25th, U.S.S.R. vetoes proposal of non-permanent members of U.N. Security Council for ending Berlin blockade;
29th, military junta ends José Bustamente's government in Peru.

L **Nov**: 2nd, in U.S. presidential election, Harry S. Truman, Democrat, wins 303 electoral votes against Thomas E. Dewey, Republican, 189, confounding public opinion polls, and Democrats gain majority in both Houses;
7th, Charles de Gaulle's R.P.F. gains large number of seats in French elections for the Council of the Republic;
12th, Hideki Tojo and other Japanese war criminals sentenced by international military tribunal;
27th, C. R. Attlee appoints Lynskey tribunal to investigate charges of corruption against minister and officials.

M **Dec**: 1st, Arab Congress at Jericho proclaims Abdullah of Transjordan as King of Palestine;
5th, Ernst Reuter, Social Democrat, elected mayor of Berlin;
9th (–10th), U.N. General Assembly adopts convention on prevention and punishment of genocide and the declaration of human rights;
12th, conscription in Britain for men aged 18 to 26;
18th, following breakdown of negotiations the Dutch renew the offensive in Indonesia and capture the Sukarno government;
27th, refusal of Catholics in Hungary to make concessions to government leads to arrest of Cardinal Mindszenty;

(*Continued opposite*)

U **Literature**

Harold Acton, *Memoirs of An Aesthete*.
T. S. Eliot, *Notes Towards the Definition of Culture*.
Graham Greene, *The Heart of the Matter*.
A. Huxley, *Ape and Essence*.
Yasunari Kawabata, *Snow Country*.
Norman Mailer, *The Naked and the Dead*.
Howard Spring, *There is no Armour*.
Alan Paton, *Cry, the Beloved Country*.

V **The Press**

W **Drama and Entertainment**

Entertainment tax on British theatres is halved.
Christopher Fry, *The Lady's Not for Burning*.
Aldous Huxley, *The Gioconda Smile*.
T. Rattigan, *The Browning Version*.

Films:
Frank Capra's *The State of the Union*.
Jules Dassin's *The Naked City*.
Vittorio de Sica's *Bicycle Thieves*.
Carol Reed's *The Fallen Idol*.
Giuseppe de Santi's *Bitter Rice*.
Laurence Olivier's *Hamlet*.

B.B.C.'s 'Any Questions?'

X **Sport**

Y **Statistics**

Pig-iron production (in thousand tons): U.S., 55,085; U.S.S.R., 14,000; Great Britain, 9,425; France, 6,625; West Germany, 4,670 (with Saar, 1,125): Belgium, 3,943.
Steel production (in thousand tons): U.S., 80,285; U.S.S.R., 16,500; Great Britain, 15,116; France, 7,255; West Germany, 5,278 (with Saar, 1,212); Belgium, 3,917.

Z **Births and Deaths**

Jan. 30th Gandhi d. (79), and Orville Wright d. (76).
Mar. 8th Jonathan Sacks b. (–).
Sept. 3rd Edouard Beneš d. (65).
Sept. 11th Ali Jinnah d. (71).
Oct. 18th Walther von Brauchitsch d. (67).
Nov. 14th Prince Charles b. (–).

M **Dec**: 28th, U.S., Britain, France and Benelux countries constitute themselves an International Ruhr Authority;
—, Nokrashy Pasha, premier of Egypt, assassinated.

N

1949 (Jan.-May.) North Atlantic Treaty—Apartheid—Sterling devalued —Establishment of Communist Republic of China

A **Jan:** 7th, Dean Acheson succeeds George Marshall as U.S. secretary of state;
15th, Tientsin falls to the Communists;
18th, Council for Mutual Economic Assistance formed in Moscow to further economic co-operation between U.S.S.R. and her satellites (Poland joins the Council, 25th);
20th, President Harry S. Truman, in inaugural address, states Four-Point programme, including economic aid for underdeveloped countries;
—, U.N. Security Council calls for end of hostilities in Burma;
21st, Chiang Kai-shek resignes presidency of China, following succession of reversals for Nationalist Armies.

B **Feb:** 1st, clothes rationing ends in Britain;
8th, Eire declares she is unable to participate in N.A.T.O. while Ireland remains divided.

C **Mar:** 4th, A. Vyshinsky replaces V. Molotov as U.S.S.R. foreign minister;
8th, France recognises non-Communist Viet-Nam Nationalists under Bao Dai as an independent state within the French Union;
13th, Belgium, Netherlands and Luxembourg agree to implement full economic union as soon as possible, and, 26th, France and Italy sign corresponding agreement;
31st, Newfoundland joins Dominion of Canada as tenth province.

D **Apr:** 4th, North Atlantic Treaty signed in Washington by foreign ministers of Britain, France, Belgium, Netherlands, Italy, Portugal, Denmark, Iceland, Norway, U.S. and Canada for mutual assistance against aggression in North Atlantic;
9th, U.N. International Court of Justice delivers first decision, holding Albania responsible for incidents in Corfu Channel in 1946 and awarding damages to Britain;
18th, Republic of Eire is formally proclaimed in Dublin;
19th, U.S. Foreign Assistance bill authorises $5·43 billion for European Recovery Programme.

E **May:** 5th, Statute of Council of Europe, establishing Committee of Ministers and a Consultative Assembly, signed in London by Belgium, Denmark, France, Britain, Ireland, Italy, Luxembourg, the Netherlands, Norway and Sweden (and subsequently by Greece, Iceland and Turkey); Strasbourg is chosen as seat of Council;
11th, Israel is admitted to U.N.;
—, Siam changes name to Thailand;
12th, Berlin blockade is officially lifted;
—, Far Eastern Commission terminates Japan's reparation payments to aid Japanese recovery;
14th, U.N. General Assembly invites India, Pakistan and South Africa to discuss alleged discrimination against Indian races in South Africa;
17th, Britain recognises independence of Eire, but re-affirms position of Northern Ireland within the U.K.;
23rd, German Federal Republic comes into force, with capital at Bonn;
—, Communist Armies in China, commanded by Chu Teh, resume offensive, to drive Nationalist Armies off the mainland.

O Politics, Economics, Law and Education

J. D. Bernal, *The Freedom of Necessity*.

Bertrand Russell's Reith Lectures, *Authority and the Individual*.

UNESCO symposium on *Human Rights* (ed. J. Maritain).

Walter Moberly, *The Crisis in the University*.

University College of North Staffordshire founded under Lord Lindsay (becomes Keele University, 1962).

Saudi Arabian government grants a 60-year oil concession to the Getty Oil Company, controlled by J. P. Getty.

P Science, Technology, Discovery, etc.

Philip Hench discovers Cortisone (compound E) as treatment of rheumatism.

Selman A. Waksman isolates neomycin.

First atomic bomb tests in U.S.S.R.

U.S. physicist Richard Feynman publishes his re-casting of the theory of quantum electrodynamics.

Q Scholarship

J. E. Neale, *The Elizabethan House of Commons*.

W. K. Hancock and M. M. Gowing, *British War Economy* (Official History, Civil Series).

R Philosophy and Religion

E. Fromm, *Man for Himself*.

A. Koestler, *Insight and Outlook*.

Paul Tillich, *The Shaking of the Foundations*.

The Bible in Basic English.

S Art, Sculpture, Fine Arts and Architecture

Painting:

V. Pasmore, *Spiral Motives*.

Graham Sutherland's portrait of W. S. Maugham.

Sculpture:

J. Epstein, *Lazarus*.

Architecture:

F. L. Wright, Laboratory tower for S. C. Johnson & Son, Wisconsin.

T Music

G. Finzi, Clarinet Concerto.

A. Rawsthorne, concerto for string orchestra.

E. Rubbra's Mass *In Honorem Sancti Domini*.

U Literature

H. E. Bates, *The Jacaranda Tree*.

S. de Beauvoir, *The Second Sex*.

Enid Blyton's first Noddy books published.

Elizabeth Bowen, *The Heat of the Day*.

Joyce Cary, *A Fearful Joy*.

Paul Eluard, *Une Leçon de morale*.

Nancy Mitford, *Love in a Cold Climate*.

Charles Morgan, *The River Line*.

George Orwell (pseud.), *Nineteen Eighty-four*.

V The Press

F **Jun**: 2nd, Transjordan is renamed the Hashemite Kingdom of Jordan;
14th, Viet-Nam State is established at Saigon under Bao Dai, but conflict with Communists continues;
16th, Communist purge in Hungary;
27th, Liberal majority in Canadian elections;
29th, U.S. completes withdrawal of occupying forces from South Korea;
British dock strike;
South African Citizenship Act suspends automatic granting of citizenship to Commonwealth immigrants after five years, and ban on mixed marriages between Europeans and non-Europeans begins *Apartheid* programme.

G **Jul**: 16th, Chinese Nationalists organise Supreme Council under Chiang Kai-shek, which begins to remove forces to Formosa (completed, *Dec.* 8th);
18th, fresh agreement between Iran and Anglo-Iranian Oil Company (but is later rejected by Iran assembly);
29th, U.N. Atomic Energy Commission suspends meetings until a broader basis for agreement among powers is reached.

H **Aug**: 5th, U.S. aid to Nationalist China ceases;
10th, U.S. Defense Department is statutorily established;
—, Christian Socialists and Liberals form coalition ministry in Belgium;
15th, emergency legislation, authorising troops to work mines, ends Australian coal strike (begun *June* 27th).

J **Sep**: 2nd, U.N. Commission warns of danger of civil war in Korea;
15th, Theodor Heuss, Free Democrat, elected President and Konrad Adenauer, Christian Democrat, chancellor of West Germany;
18th, Britain devalues £ (from exchange rate of $4·03 to $2·80), and subsequently most European states devalue their currencies;
21st, Allied High Commission in Germany takes over functions of Allied Military Government;
27th, U.S.S.R. denounces treaty with Yugoslavia;
30th, Berlin Airlift ends, after 277,264 flights.

K **Oct**: 1st, Communist People's Republic of China proclaimed at Peiping under Mao Tse-tung, with Chou En-lai premier and foreign minister;
—, Bulgaria and, 21st, Roumania denounce treaties of friendship with Yugoslavia;
6th, President Truman signs Mutual Defense Assistance Act for military aid to N.A.T.O. countries;
7th, Democratic Republic established in East Germany with Wilhelm Pieck President and Otto Grotewohl minister-president;
9th, Socialist losses in Austrian elections;
14th, American Communist Party leaders convicted of conspiracy;
16th, defeat of rebels ends Greek Civil War (since *May* 1946);
28th, Georges Bidault forms coalition in France, following Henri Queuille's resignation over financial crisis.

L **Nov**: 11th (–13th), Polish United Workers' Party is purged of members with Titoist leanings;
21st, U.N. General Assembly votes for ultimate independence of Italy's former colonies;
24th, nationalisation of British iron and steel industries in force;
—, Allied High Commission makes further economic concessions to West Germany on her joining International Ruhr Authority;
26th, India adopts Constitution as a federal republic, remaining within the Commonwealth.

(*Continued opposite*)

W **Drama and Entertainment**

T. S. Eliot, *The Cocktail Party.*
Arthur Miller, *Death of a Salesman.*
Berliner Ensemble formed.

Films:
Anthony Asquith's *The Winslow Boy.*
Carol Reed's *The Third Man*, with Orson Welles.
Jean Melville's *Les Enfants terribles.*
Robert Rossen's *All The King's Men.*

X **Sport**

Y **Statistics**

Z **Births and Deaths**

Jan. 9th Thomas Handley d. (55).
Jan. 21st J. H. Thomas d. (74).
Feb. 11th Axel Munthe d. (91).
May 6th Maurice Maeterlinck d. (86).
Sept. 8th Richard Strauss d. (85).
Oct. 30th Edward R. Stettinius d. (49).

M **Dec:** 5th, U.N. General Assembly requires member states to submit information on armaments and armed forces, and
8th, calls on powers to recognise political independence of China;
14th, Israeli government moves capital from Tel Aviv to Jerusalem, disregarding U.N. resolution for internationalisation of Jerusalem;
15th, West Germany becomes full member of Marshall Plan;
16th, British Parliament bill reduces power of Lords to veto legislation;
17th, Robert Menzies, Liberal, forms new coalition in Australia;
27th, Holland transfers sovereignty to United States of Indonesia;
30th, France transfers sovereignty to Vietnam.

N

1950 (Jan.–May) Korean war begins—The Colombo Plan—The Schuman Plan

A **Jan:** 3rd, Wafdists return to power in Egyptian election;
5th, Alexander Diomedes, premier of Greece, resigns and his successor, Theotokis, experiences great difficulty throughout the year in forming stable government;
6th, Britain recognises Communist China;
—, Franco-German parliamentary conference in Basle;
9th, Colombo Conference of Commonwealth foreign ministers meets to prepare plans for co-operating in the economic development of Asiatic states;
12th, Nahas Pasha forms Egyptian government which includes all ministers dismissed in 1944;
—, state of emergency in Gold Coast caused by strikes;
—, capital punishment reintroduced in U.S.S.R.;
14th, Mohammed Said forms Iranian government;
25th, Alger Hiss found guilty in U.S. of perjury in concealing membership of Communist Party;
27th, N.A.T.O. bilateral agreement by which U.S. provides arms to its associates signed in Washington;
—, Alcide de Gasperi forms new coalition in Italy on the withdrawal of Liberal support;
29th, first series of riots in Johannesburg provoked by racial policy;
30th, Britain, Norway, Denmark and Sweden sign agreement for economic co-operation;
31st, President Truman instructs U.S. Atomic Energy Commission to proceed with development of the hydrogen bomb.

B **Feb:** 1st, Vlko Chervenkov becomes premier of Bulgaria on Vasil Kolarov's death;
13th, Bangkok conference of heads of U.S. missions in Asiatic countries for supporting moves for independence;
14th, U.S.S.R. and Communist China sign 30-year treaty in Moscow;
20th, U.S. severs relations with Bulgaria;
23rd, British general election results in a reduced Labour majority (315 seats, Conservatives 298, Liberals 9);
28th, C. R. Attlee reconstructs his ministry.

C **Mar:** 1st, Klaus Fuchs found guilty of betraying atomic secrets to U.S.S.R. agents;
—, Chiang Kai-shek resumes presidency of Nationalist China;
3rd, France confirms autonomy of the Saar;
8th, Marshal Voroshilov states U.S.S.R. possesses the atomic bomb;
12th, Belgian referendum in favour of King Leopold III's return (government resigns, 18th, through disagreement on the question of his return);
16th, Dean Acheson's suggestions to U.S.S.R. for ending the cold war;
21st, Konrad Adenauer advocates economic union between France and Germany;
31st, House of Representatives passes foreign aid bill of $3,100 million.

D **Apr:** 1st, Britain transfers Somaliland trusteeship to Italy;
8th, Delhi pact between India and Pakistan on treatment of minorities;
11th, U.S.S.R. note to U.S. about a U.S. bomber over the Baltic;
19th, London dock strike (–*May* 1st);
27th, Communist Party is outlawed in Australia;
—, Britain recognises Israel.

E **May:** 9th, Schuman plan, for placing French and German coal industry and iron and steel production under a single authority, announced;

A. Koestler (ed.), *The God that Failed.*
Congress for Cultural Freedom meets in West Berlin.
Legal Aid comes into force in Britain (*Oct.* 2nd).
London Stock Exchange starts compensation fund to guarantee investors against the default of member firms.
Wealthy U.S. industrialist Howard Hughes becomes a recluse.

P **Science, Technology, Discovery, etc.**
U.S. Atomic Energy Commission separates plutonium from pitchblende concentrates.
Existence of 'V'-particles is confirmed in Pasadena, California, and on the Pic du Midi d'Ossau.
New calculations for the speed of light obtained through radio waves at National Physical Laboratory, Teddington, and at Stanford University.
G. T. Seaborg of California University discovers element 98 (californium).
A jet-propelled, pilotless aircraft constructed in Australia.
Danish deep-sea expedition in *Galathea* to investigate fauna.
T. Heyerdahl, *The Kon-Tiki Expedition.*

Q **Scholarship**
A. L. Rowse, *The England of Elizabeth.*
Boswell's London Journal, 1762–3 (ed. F. A. Pottle).

R **Philosophy and Religion**
Nicholas Berdyaev, *Dreams and Reality.*
R. A. Knox, *Enthusiasm.*
A. Malraux, *Psychology of Art.*
Margaret Mead, *Social Anthropology.*
Gilbert Ryle, *The Concept of Mind.*
J.-P. Sartre, *La Mort dans l'âme.*
Holy Year of Roman Catholic Church.
Papal decree *Humani Generis* (*Aug.* 17th), against Existentialism and erroneous scientific theories.
Pope Pius XII pronounces dogma on bodily Assumption of Virgin Mary (*Nov.* 1st).
National Council of Churches of Christ is established in U.S.

S **Art, Sculpture, Fine Arts and Architecture**
Painting:
Marc Chagall, *King David.*
V. Pasmore, *Inland Sea.*
B. Berenson publishes *Aesthetics and History.*
Sculpture:
P. Picasso, *The Goat.*
A. Giacometti, *Seven Figures and a Head.*
F. Léger, series of Flower ceramics.
Architecture:
U.N. Building, New York, completed.
Powell and Moya, Pimlico Housing Estate, Westminster.
Eugenio Montiori, Rome Railway Station.
Mario Pani and Enrique del Moral, The University City, Mexico.

T **Music**
Béla Bartók, viola concerto.

E **May**: 11th, foreign ministers of Britain, France and U.S. confer in London on the future of Germany;
22nd, Peking government offers Tibet regional autonomy if she joins Communist system;
30th, Albania and Yugoslavia sever relations.

F **Jun**: 6th, Trygve Lie, appointed to a fresh term of office as U.N. Secretary-General, announces 20-year peace plan;
15th, West Germany joins Council of Europe;
24th, Georges Bidault, French premier, resigns after a vote of confidence against his ministry;
25th, North Korean forces invade South Korea;
27th, Trygve Lie urges U.N. members to assist South Korea to repel attacks and restore peace;
28th, North Koreans capture Seoul.

G **Jul**: 2nd, Henri Queuille, Radical, attempts to form French government;
8th, Douglas MacArthur appointed commander of U.N. forces in Korea;
11th René Pleven forms French government in which Guy Mollet and other Socialists serve;
19th, President Truman's message to Congress urging vast military budget;
20th, U.S. Senate committee denies Senator Joseph McCarthy's charges of Communist infiltration of State Department;
22nd, King Leopold III returns to Belgium after six years' exile;
23rd, Socialist demonstrations in Brussels against Leopold.

H **Aug**: 1st, Leopold III abdicates in favour of Prince Baudouin;
—, U.N. Security Council, with Jacob Malik (U.S.S.R.) as chairman, discusses Korea;
11th, W. S. Churchill carries motion at Strasbourg Congress of European Movement for a European army;
15th, Paul van Zeeland forms Christian Socialist ministry in Belgium.

J **Sep**: 1st, North Koreans attack across Naktong River;
6th, new constitution in Syria;
7th, Hungarian decree dissolving religious orders;
12th, emergency sessions of British Parliament for defence measures for Korean War;
—, George Marshall succeeds Louis A. Johnson as U.S. Defense Secretary;
15th, U.N. forces land at Inchon, South Korea;
— national service in Britain is extended to two years;
19th, European Payments Union established;
20th, Control of Communists bill in U.S.;
26th, U.N. forces recapture Seoul;
—, N.A.T.O. Council decides to form an integrated European defence force;
28th, Indonesia is admitted to U.N.

K **Oct**: 1st, South Korean troops cross 38th parallel;
4th, Turkey agrees to co-operate with N.A.T.O. defence plans for the Mediterranean;
7th, Acheson plan for strengthening U.N.'s powers to resist aggression (adopted, 19th);
15th, East German elections result in 99 per cent support for National Front;
19th, Hugh Gaitskell succeeds Stafford Cripps as Chancellor of Exchequer;
21st, Prague conference of U.S.S.R. satellites under V. Molotov on future of Germany;

T Music (*contd.*)

P. Hindemith, *Harmony of the World* (symphony).
A. Honegger, 5th Symphony.
Carlo Menotti, *The Consul* (opera).
A. Rawsthorne, Symphony no. 1.
W. Walton, violin sonata.
J. S. Bach bicentenary celebrations.
Petit-Chabrier, *Ballabile* (ballet).
N. de Valois-Gerhard, *Don Quixote* (ballet).
Robbins-Bernstein, *Age of Anxiety* (ballet).

U Literature

E. Hemingway, *Across the River and Into the Trees.*
Pablo Neruda, *General Song.*
Ezra Pound, *Seventy Cantos.*
Anthony Powell, *A Question of Upbringing.*

V The Press

W Drama and Entertainment

J. Anouilh, *La Répétition.*
Films:
René Clair's *La Beauté du diable.*
Jean Cocteau's *Orphée.*
John Ford's *Rio Grande.*
Akira Kurosawa's *Rashomon.*
Luciano's *Sunday in August.*
Max Ophuls' *La Ronde.*
Billy Wilder's *Sunset Boulevard.*
Irving Berlin, *Call Me Madam* (musical).
Fred Hoyle's Reith Lectures, *The Nature of the Universe* (broadcasting).
'Bebop' dancing.

X Sport

Uruguay wins World Cup football final.

Y Statistics

Populations of cities (in mill.): London, 8·3; New York, 7·8; Tokio, 5·3; Moscow, 4·1; Chicago, 3·6; Shanghai, 3·6; Calcutta, 3·5; Berlin, 3·3.
Motor cars (in mill.): U.S., 51·9; Great Britain, 4·4; West Germany, 3.
Crime: England and Wales, 461,435 crimes (of which 6,249 were crimes of violence); U.S., 1,790,030 crimes (of which 18,930 were crimes of violence).
Divorces: U.S., 385,000; Great Britain, 32,516.
Armies: U.S.S.R., 3,000,000; U.S., 591,700; France, 456,000; Italy, 250,000; Great Britain, 143,500; Egypt, 20,000.
Religious denominations in Britain (in thousands): Roman Catholics, 3,884; Church of England, 1,867; Presbyterian Church of Scotland, 1,273; Methodists, 776; Congregationalists, 387; Baptists, 338; Presbyterians, 82; Episcopal Church of Scotland, 57; Jews, 450.

1950 (Oct.–Dec.)

K **Oct**: 21st, Chinese forces occupy Tibet;
28th, Liberal-Agrarian ministry in Denmark under Erik Eriksen;
30th, nationalist rising in Puerto Rico.

L **Nov**: 3rd, French forces withdraw from frontier of N. Indo-China;
4th, U.N. Assembly revokes 1946 resolutions on relations with Spain;
5th, Douglas MacArthur reports the massing of Chinese Communists in North Korea;
7th, in U.S. elections Republicans gain 30 seats in House of Representatives;
13th, Tibet appeals to U.N. against Chinese aggression;
27th, U.N. troops forced to withdraw in Korea;
—, Peking delegates attend U.N. as observers;
28th, Poland and East Germany proclaim the Oder–Neisse line as the frontier.

M **Dec**: 4th, C. R. Attlee visits Washington;
13th, Marshall Aid to Britain ceases;
—, S. Africa refuses to place South-West Africa under U.N. trusteeship;
16th, state of emergency proclaimed in U.S. following reversals of U.N. forces in Korea;
27th, China refuses U.N. appeal for a cease-fire;
—, U.S. and Spain resume diplomatic relations;
28th, Chinese forces cross 38th parallel in Korea.

N

z **Births and Deaths**

Jan. 9th Alec Jeffreys b. (–).
Feb. 4th Montagu, Lord Norman, d. (78).
Mar. 6th Albert Lebrun d. (79).
Mar. 24th Harold J. Laski d. (56).
Mar. 30th Léon Blum d. (77).
July 9th Ismail Sidky Pasha d. (75).
July 22nd W. L. Mackenzie King d. (75).
Sept. 11th Jan Christian Smuts d. (80).
Nov. 2nd George Bernard Shaw d. (94).

1951 (Jan.–Jul.) Conservatives return to power in Britain—The Six sign Paris Treaty for single coal and steel authority

A **Jan**: 1st, North Korean and Chinese Communists break through U.N. lines on 38th parallel and, 4th, take Seoul;
17th, Communist China rejects U.N. Truce Committee's peace proposals for Far East;
—, Aneurin Bevan appointed British Minister of Labour;
24th, fall of Wilhelm Drees's coalition in Netherlands.

B **Feb**: 8th, President Truman orders army to control U.S. railways during strike;
13th, British Commonwealth Consultative Committee meets at Colombo to discuss development plan for S. and S.E. Asia;
14th, dissolution of David Ben-Gurion's government in Israel, following defeat in Knesset on problem of religious education;
28th, René Pleven's coalition in France falls on issue of electoral reform.

C **Mar**: 2nd, purge of Czechoslovak Communist Party;
5th, (–*June* 21st), deputy foreign ministers of Britain, France, U.S. and U.S.S.R. meet in Paris to prepare agenda for future conference, but problem of disarmament hampers progress;
7th, premier of Iran is assassinated;
9th, Herbert Morrison succeeds Ernest Bevin as British Foreign Secretary;
10th, Henri Queuille forms ministry in France, ending political deadlock;
12th, U.S. Senate Committee under Kefauver investigates crime in interstate commerce;
29th, U.S. completes draft peace treaty with Japan which she circulates to the powers;
—, Chinese government rejects Douglas MacArthur's offer of truce discussions but, 31st, India and, *Apr.* 2nd, Britain again urge truce in Korean War.

D **Apr**: 11th, President Truman relieves General MacArthur of command in Far East; succeeded by Matthew Ridgway (and, 19th, MacArthur argues against administration's policies in address to joint session of Congress);
18th, France, W. Germany, Italy, Belgium, Netherlands, and Luxembourg ('the Six'), sign Paris treaty, embodying the Schuman Plan to set up a single coal and steel authority;
22nd, Aneurin Bevan and Harold Wilson resign from Labour cabinet in protest at imposition of health service charges to meet increasing defence spending and this Bevanite revolt splits British Labour Party;
28th, Dr. Musaddiq appointed premier of Iran.

E **May**: 7th (–*June* 25th), George Marshall and other witnesses testify before Foreign Relations Committee and Armed Services Committee of U.S. Senate on Douglas MacArthur's removal;
15th, North Korean forces launch offensive.

F **Jun**: 3rd, Indian Socialist Party's mammoth demonstration in Delhi in protest at the government's food and housing policies;
13th, Éamon de Valéra returns to power in Eire on defection of members of John Costello's coalition;
17th, in elections for French National Assembly Gaullists win 117 seats, Socialists, 104, Communists, 101, Independents, 99, Radicals, 95, and Popular Republicans, 86;
23rd (–29th), further attempts to negotiate armistice in Korea fail;
Guy Burgess and Donald Maclean, 'missing diplomats', flee to U.S.S.R.

G **Jul**: 3rd, India complains to U.N. Security Council against Pakistan for violating cease-fire agreement in Kashmir;

O **Politics, Economics, Law and Education**

Lord Radcliffe's Reith Lectures, *Power and the State.*

London Congress on Space Travel establishes an International Astronautical Federation (*Sept.*).

Report of Royal Commission on Betting, Lotteries and Gaming (*Apr.* 17th).

Communist-sponsored World Peace Council meets in East Berlin (*Feb.*).

P **Science, Technology, Discovery, etc.**

The 'flying spot' microscope is devised.

Krilium, a synthetic chemical, is developed from acrylonitrile for use in fertilisation.

Electric power is satisfactorily produced from atomic energy at Arcon, Idaho (*Dec.*).

Second British plutonium pile, at Sellafield, Cumberland, in operation.

Dutch-Norwegian joint atomic energy research establishment opened at Hjeller, near Oslo.

John Brown and Co. make a peat-fired gas turbine on Clydebank.

Q **Scholarship**

E. H. Carr, *A History of Soviet Russia; the Bolshevik Revolution*, Vol. I.

Stephen Runciman, *History of the Crusades* (–58).

R **Philosophy and Religion**

Talcott Parsons, *The Social System.*

J.-P. Sartre, *The Psychology of Imagination.*

David Riesman, *The Lonely Crowd.*

Fraudulent Medium Act repeals provisions of Witchcraft Act, 1735, in Britain.

S **Art, Sculpture, Fine Arts and Architecture**

Painting:

S. Dali, *Christ of St. John on the Cross.*

Graham Sutherland, *Lord Beaverbrook.*

Sculpture:

Kenneth Armitage, *People in a Wind.*

Architecture:

Gerald Barry's plan for centenary of the 1851 'Great Exhibition', on the South Bank, London, with Hugh Casson director of architecture; Robert Matthew, Royal Festival Hall; Ralph Tubbs, Dome of Discovery.

Basil Spence's design for Coventry Cathedral wins award open to Commonwealth architects.

T **Music**

B. Britten, *Billy Budd* (opera).

I. Stravinsky, *The Rake's Progress* (libretto by W. H. Auden and Chester Kallman).

R. Vaughan Williams, *A Pilgrim's Progress* (opera).

Mackerras-Sullivan, *Pineapple Poll* (ballet).

U **Literature**

Isaac Asimov, *I, Robot.*

Robert Frost, *Complete Poems.*

N. Monsarrat, *The Cruel Sea.*

J. D. Salinger, *The Catcher in the Rye.*

C. P. Snow, *The Masters.*

Herman Wouk, *The Caine Mutiny.*

G **Jul:** 5th, International Court rules against Iran in dispute with Britain over nationalisation of Iranian oil industry and, 15th, President Truman sends Averell Harriman to Iran to urge a compromise settlement;
20th, King Abdullah of Jordan assassinated in Jerusalem.

H **Aug:** 5th, Matthew Ridgway breaks off armistice talks in Korea, charging Communists with violation of demilitarisation rules, and further negotiations fail;
—, mammoth Communist Youth Rally in Berlin;
7th, U.S. Congress rejects U.S.S.R. proposal for agreement on arms and atomic weapons, advising her first to honour existing obligations;
11th, French ministerial crisis (since elections on *June* 17th) ends with René Pleven forming a coalition of the Centre;
30th, U.S.-Philippines mutual defence pact.

J **Sep:** 8th, peace treaty with Japan signed at San Francisco by representatives of 49 powers, though U.S.S.R. and her satellites boycott final session of peace conference;
10th, foreign ministers of Britain, France and U.S. discuss plans to combat Soviet aggression and to use West German troops in N.A.T.O. army;
13th, U.N. Conciliatory Commission discusses Palestine problem with Israeli and Arab delegates, but by *Nov.* 21st the talks fail;
23rd, U.N. forces in Korea capture 'Heartbreak Ridge', north of Yanggu.

K **Oct:** 5th, House of Representatives approves $56.9 billion armed forces appropriation bill;
6th, Henry Gurney, British High Commissioner in Malaya, assassinated;
9th, David Ben-Gurion ends eight months' ministerial crisis in Israel by forming coalition;
16th, premier Ali Khan of Pakistan assassinated;
25th, in British general election Conservatives win 321 seats (net gain 23) over Labour 295 (net loss 20) and Liberal 6 (net loss 3), Irish Nationalist 2 and Irish Labour 1; and
27th, W. S. Churchill forms ministry, with Anthony Eden Foreign Secretary and R. A. Butler Chancellor of Exchequer;
25th, negotiations for armistice in Korea are renewed at Panmunjom;
27th, Egypt abrogates 1936 treaty of alliance with Britain and 1899 agreement over Sudan.

L **Nov:** 8th, Dean Acheson presents disarmament proposals to U.N. General Assembly, which U.S.S.R. counters with rival plan;
10th, France, Britain, U.S. and Turkey announce security programme for Near East;
11th, Juan Perón is re-elected President of Argentina;
14th, U.S. allegations of Communists killing Korean prisoners of war;
16th, Egypt offers to let future of Sudan be decided by plebiscite under U.N. supervision;
29th, military *coup d'état* in Syria.

M **Dec:** 6th, East and West Germany agree to send representatives to U.N. to discuss holding of free elections in Germany, but U.S.S.R. opposes the project;
13th, French National Assembly ratifies Schuman Plan (see *May* 1950) by 377 to 233 votes;
19th, Marshal Vishinsky demands U.N. to require U.S. to revoke her Mutual Security Act;
20th, Greece elected to U.N. Security Council over the U.S.S.R. candidate;

(*Continued opposite*)

V **The Press**

History Today first issued.

W **Drama and Entertainment**

J. Anouilh, *Colombe.*
Christopher Fry, *A Sleep of Prisoners.*
J.-P. Sartre, *Le Diable et le Bon Dieu.*
Peter Ustinov, *The Love of Four Colonels.*
John Whitney, *Saint's Day.*
South Pacific (musical).
The Festival of Britain.
Foundation stone of the National Theatre laid at South Bank.
British Film Censors introduce 'X certificate' classification for films totally unsuitable for anyone under 16.
Waller invents Cinerama.
Films:
Vittorio de Sica's *Miracle in Milan.*
Alfred Hitchcock's *Strangers on a Train.*
John Huston's *The African Queen.*
Max Ophuls's *Le Plaisir.*
Carol Reed's *Outcast of the Islands.*
'The Archers' (B.B.C. Light Programme).

X **Sport**

Y **Statistics**

Populations (in mill.): China, 490; India, 357; U.S.S.R., 190; U.S., 153 (of whom 136 whites, 16 negro and 0·7 other races); Japan, 85; Pakistan, 76; Great Britain, 50; West Germany, 48; Italy, 47; France, 42. S. Africa has 2·4 Europeans and 9·3 non-Europeans.
Merchant shipping (in mill. tons): U.S. 60; Gt. Britain, 12; Norway, 5·3; Greece, 3·5; Italy, 3·3; Netherlands, 2·9; France, 2·9; Japan, 2·7; U.S.S.R. 2.
80 mill. tons use Suez Canal (33·5 per cent British).
30 mill. tons use Panama Canal.
Oil production: U.S., 2,725 mill barrels; U.S.S.R., 266 mill. barrels.
Coal production (in mill. tons): U.S., 430; Great Britain, 222; U.S.S.R. 270; West Germany, 119; France, 53.

Z **Births and Deaths**

Jan. 27th Carl Mannerheim d. (83).
Feb. 19th André Gide d. (81).
Apr. 14th Ernest Bevin d. (70).
Apr. 23rd Charles Dawes d. (85).
July 13th Arnold Schönberg d. (76).
July 23rd Henri Philippe Pétain d. (95).
Aug. 21st Constant Lambert d. (45).

M **Dec**: 24th, Libya becomes an independent federation under King Idris I;
27th, failure of Korean armistice talks on exchange of prisoners and building of airfields in North Korea;
31st, Mutual Security Agency replaces Economic Co-operation Administration of Marshall Plan.

N

1952 (Jan.–Jun.) Arab League Security Pact—Mau Mau—Eisenhower elected U.S. President

A **Jan**: 5th, U.S. five-year loan to India;
7th, René Pleven's ministry falls through adverse Socialist vote on social security policy; and
22nd, Edgar Faure forms coalition;
14th, Tunisia unsuccessfully appeals to U.N. Security Council to state her case for autonomy;
18th, (–27th), anti-British riots in Egypt end with King Farouk's appointment of Aly Maher Pasha as premier (–*Mar.* 1st);
24th, Vincent Massey becomes first Canadian to serve as Governor-General of Canada;
25th, (–*Feb.* 4th), Franco-German crisis over administration of the Saar.

B **Feb**: 6th, death of George VI and accession of Queen Elizabeth II;
20th (–25th), N.A.T.O. Council, meeting in Lisbon, approves European defence project, agrees to raise 50 divisions by *Dec.* and to bring Morocco and Tunisia into the alliance;
26th, W. S. Churchill announces that Britain has produced her own atomic bomb;
29th, Edgar Faure's ministry falls, on failing to obtain National Assembly's assent to tax increases, and Antoine Pinay forms cabinet with some Gaullist support.

C **Mar**: 1st, in India's first national elections Pandit Nehru's Congress Party wins 364 of 489 seats in the National Assembly;
—, Aly Maher Pasha resigns in Egypt;
4th, Chinese Communists accuse U.S. forces in Korea of using germ warfare;
10th, U.S.S.R. note proposing four-power conference on unification and rearmament of Germany, to which the Western Powers reply, 23rd, that free elections would be a prerequisite, that Germany should not be empowered to rearm and that her boundaries, as settled by the Potsdam Conference, 1945, would be subject to revision;
20th, S. Africa Supreme Court invalidates race legislation of D. F. Malan;
30th, H. S. Truman announces he will not be a candidate in the presidential election;
— anti-French riots in Tangier.

D **Apr**: 8th, President Truman orders seizure of the steel industry to avert a strike;
10th, U.S.S.R. proposes that all-German elections be held under a four-power commission, instead of under U.N. supervision, and rejects the West's views on Germany's frontiers;
15th, Britain declares she will sign a mutual defence treaty with the European Defence Community;
22nd, D. F. Malan introduces bill to make S. African Parliament a high court, in order to prevent Supreme Court from invalidating race legislation;
28th, Dwight D. Eisenhower is relieved of his post as Supreme Allied Commander in Europe at his own request and succeeded by Matthew Ridgway (who is succeeded in Far East by Mark Clark).

E **May**: 6th, Rajendra Prasad elected President of India; and
13th, Pandit Nehru forms government;
20th, rioting of Communist prisoners of war at Koje Island prison camp, South Korea;
27th (–31st), European Defence Community treaty signed in Paris, with reciprocal N.A.T.O.-E.D.C. guarantees;
28th, Communist demonstrations in Paris.

F **Jun**: 1st, United National Party under Dudley Senanayake wins Ceylon elections;
18th, British scheme for Central African Federation published;

O **Politics, Economics, Law and Education**

Alan Moorehead, *The Traitors* (a discussion of the cases of atomic scientists Fuchs, Nunn May and Pontecorvo).

Arnold Toynbee's Reith Lectures, *The World and the West.*

P **Science, Technology, Discovery, etc.**

Rapid extension of use of radio-isotopes in scientific research, medicine and industry; Britain becomes the chief exporter of isotopes.

A contraceptive tablet of phosphorated hesperidin is made.

Britain's first atomic bomb tests, in Monte Bello Islands, N.W. Australia (*Oct.* 3rd).

U.S. explodes the first hydrogen bomb, at Eniwetok Atoll, Pacific (*Nov.* 6th).

President Truman lays keel of first atomic-powered submarine, *U.S.S. Nautilus.*

French hydro-electro power station and dam opened at Donzère-Mondragon in the Rhône Valley (*Oct.* 25th).

John Cobb is killed establishing a water speed record of 206·89 m.p.h. at Loch Ness (*Oct.* 5th).

'Smog' in London (*Dec.*).

The last London tram runs (*Jul.* 6th).

Q **Scholarship**

Kathleen Kenyon excavates the site of Jericho.

Ventris deciphers 'Linear B'.

Archaeologists use radioactive carbon tests for dating finds.

Harold Nicolson, *King Geroge V, His Life and Reign.*

J. M. Wallace-Hadrill, *The Barbarian West, 400–1000.*

R **Philosophy and Religion**

R. Niebuhr, *Christ and Culture.*

S **Art, Sculpture, Fine Arts and Architecture**

Painting:

Edward Burra, *John Deth.*

Jackson Pollock, *Convergence.*

Augustus John publishes *Chiaroscuro.*

Sculpture:

Reg Butler, *Young Girl 52,53.*

Jacob Epstein, *Madonna and Child*, Cavendish Square, London.

M. Marini, *The Horseman.*

H. Moore, *Time-Life* Screen, London.

Architecture:

Skidmore, Owings and Merrill, Lever House, New York.

Juan O'Gorman and others, University Library, Mexico City.

The proposals of the Waverley Committee, restricting the export of works of art from Britain, are broadly accepted by the government.

T **Music**

Arthur Bliss, *The Enchantress.*

Igor Stravinsky, *Babel* (opera).

S. Prokofiev, 7th Symphony ('Symphony of Youth').

R. Vaughan Williams, *Romance* for harmonica (for Larry Adler).

Robbins-Stravinsky, *The Cage* (ballet).

Cranko-Gardner, *Reflection* (ballet).

U **Literature**

Ray Bradbury, *The Illustrated Man.*

Ernest Hemingway, *The Old Man and the Sea.*

F **Jun**: 20th, President Truman signs foreign aid bill;
23rd, bombing of hydro-electric plants in North Korea by U.S. Air Force;
27th, London conference of U.S., France and Britain on Western foreign policy.

G **Jul**: 6th, Ruiz Cortines elected President of Mexico;
22nd, Dr. Musaddiq is re-appointed premier of Iran with emergency powers for six months;
—, Hague Court rules it has no jurisdiction in case between Iran and Anglo-Iranian Oil Co.;
23rd, General Mohammed Neguib seizes power in Egypt (forms a government *Sept.* 7th);
24th, Indian agreement with Kashmir government;
25th, European Coal and Steel Community in force;
26th, King Farouk abdicates in Egypt in favour of infant son, Fuad.

H **Aug**: 4th (–*Sept.* 25th), Honolulu Conference of three-power Pacific Council, Australia, New Zealand and U.S., as set up by Pacific Security Treaty of *Sept.* 1951;
5th, Japan resumes diplomatic relations with Nationalist China;
11th, Prince Hussain is proclaimed King of Jordan on termination of reign of King Talal, a schizophrenic;
14th, Matyas Rakosi is appointed premier of Hungary;
17th, Chinese delegates under Chou En-lai arrive in Moscow;
20th, death of Kurt Schumacher, leader of German Social Democratic Party;
23rd, Arab League Security Pact comes into force.

J **Sep**: 1st, William Drees, Labour, re-forms coalition in Netherlands after general election;
4th, General Carlos Ibáñez elected President of Chile;
5th, Britain, France and U.S. send notes to U.S.S.R. on peace treaty with Austria;
11th, federation of Eritrea with Ethiopia ratified;
18th, Finland completes reparation payments to U.S.S.R.;
21st, Conservatives and Liberals gain over Democrats and Agrarians in Swedish elections;
24th, revised Constitution in Roumania;
30th, Council of Europe adopts Eden plan, for making the Council a framework into which the Coal and Steel Community and Defence Community can be fitted.

K **Oct**: 2nd, Chinese government holds 'Asia and Pacific Peace Conference' in Peking;
3rd, U.S.S.R. demands recall of George Kennan, U.S. ambassador, for his comments about isolation of Western diplomats in Moscow;
4th, China and Mongolia sign ten-year agreement;
5th, U.S.S.R. Communist Party holds 1st Congress since 1939 and, 10th, adopts 1951–6 plan;
13th, Egyptian agreement with Sudan over waters of Nile;
17th, Council of Socialist International meets in Milan;
20th, state of emergency proclaimed in Kenya because of Mau Mau disturbances, and arrest of leaders of Kenya African Union;
22nd, Iran breaks off diplomatic relations with Britain over oil dispute;
28th, Dr. L. Figl forms coalition in Austria.

(*Continued opposite*)

U **Literature** *(cont.)*
F. R. Leavis, *The Common Pursuit.*
Doris Lessing, *Martha Quest.*
Dylan Thomas, *Collected Poems.*
Evelyn Waugh, *Men at Arms.*
Angus Wilson, *Hemlock and After.*

V **The Press**
William Haley becomes editor of *The Times.*

W **Drama and Entertainment**
Agatha Christie, *The Mousetrap.*
Films:
This is Cinerama opens on Broadway (*Sept.*).
Ingmar Bergman's *Summer With Monika.*
Charlie Chaplin's *Limelight* with Claire Bloom.
John Ford's *The Quiet Man*, with John Wayne.
Orson Welles's *Othello.*
J. Ferrer in *Moulin Rouge.*
The Liberace Show is a nation-wide success on U.S. television.

X **Sport**
Rocky Marciano defeats Jersey Joe Walcott to win World Heavy-weight title.

Y **Statistics**

Z **Births and Deaths**
Mar. 4th Charles Scott Sherrington d. (94).
Apr. 21st Stafford Cripps d. (63).
Jul. 26th Eva Perón d. (30).
Nov. 9th Chaim Weizmann d. (77).
Nov. 20th Benedetto Croce d. (86).

L **Nov**: 4th, Republican landslide in U.S. presidential election with Dwight D. Eisenhower 442 electoral votes, in record poll, over Governor Adlai Stevenson, Democrat, 89;
16th, Field-Marshal Papagos forms ministry in Greece following success of Greek Rally in elections;
20th, Bierut elected premier of Poland;
27th, London Commonwealth Economic Conference;
Trials of Rudolf Slansky, former secretary of Czech Communist Party, and of Vladimir Clementis, former foreign minister, in Czechoslovakia for treason.
Bill to denationalise iron and steel introduced in Britain.

M **Dec**: 2nd, Dwight D. Eisenhower visits Korea;
3rd, U.N. General Assembly adopts Indian proposal for Korean armistice;
4th, W. S. Churchill states Britain will curtail defence expenditure;
7th, riots in French Morocco;
8th, Itzhak Ben-Zvi becomes President of Israel, following Chaim Weizmann's death, *Nov.* 9th;
10th, Egypt abolishes 1923 Constitution;
12th, Communist world conferene in Vienna;
15th, China rejects Indian plan for Korean armistice;
23rd, Antoine Pinay, French premier, resigns.

N

1953 (Jan.–Jun.) Death of Stalin—Korean armistice—Egypt becomes a republic—Rise of Khrushchev

A **Jan:** 1st, London conference on federation of Northern and Southern Rhodesia and Nyasaland (scheme published *Feb.* 5th);
5th, W. S. Churchill visits Dwight D. Eisenhower;
6th, Asian Socialist conference at Rangoon;
8th, riots in Karachi, Pakistan;
10th, European Coal and Steel Community first meets;
12th, Yugoslav National Assembly adopts new constitution and, 14th, Marshal Josip Tito elected first President of Yugoslav Republic;
14th, Consultative Assembly of Council of Europe meets in Strasbourg to draft constitution for European Political Community (adopted *Feb.* 10th);
16th, dissolution of political parties in Egypt;
20th, Dwight D. Eisenhower is inaugurated President of U.S.;
21st, electoral reform bill passes Italian Chamber, with Communists abstaining.

B **Feb:** 10th, General M. Neguib is voted dictatorial powers in Egypt for three years;
12th, Anglo-Egyptian agreement on Sudan;
—, U.S.S.R. severs relations with Israel;
16th, S. African government takes emergency powers under Public Safety bill;
22nd, People's Party and Socialists win seats in Austrian elections;
24th, Rome Conference of foreign ministers of the European Defence Community countries;
28th, treaty of friendship between Greece, Turkey and Yugoslavia.

C **Mar:** 5th, J. Stalin dies (aged 73);
6th, G. M. Malenkov succeeds as Chairman of Council of Ministers;
16th, Marshal Tito visits London;
19th, W. German Bundestag approves Bonn agreement and Paris agreement establishing a European Defence Community;
30th, a new Danish Constitution; the Upper House is abolished and voting age reduced to 23;
31st, Dag Hammarskjöld, Sweden, elected Secretary-General of U.N. by Security Council (*Apr.* 7th elected Secretary of U.N. Assembly).

D **Apr:** 2nd, Julius Raab, People's Party, forms coalition in Austria;
6th, Konrad Adenauer visits New York (and, *May* 14th, London);
8th, Jomo Kenyatta and five other Kikuyu convicted of managing Mau Mau;
11th, U.N. force and Communists arrange for exchange of prisoners in Korea;
—, Vietnamese insurgents renew offensive on Laos;
13th, London conference on British West Indian federation opens;
15th, Nationalists secure clear majority in S. African elections;
18th, Mohammed Ali forms new ministry in Pakistan;
21st, Social Democrats gain clear majority in Danish elections;
30th, People's Progressive Party win first elections in British Guiana.

E **May:** 12th, General Gruenther (U.S.) appointed Supreme Allied Commander in Europe;
20th, France signs agreement with the Saar;
21st, Yoshida forms ministry in Japan;
25th, President Eisenhower states principles on which U.N. peace proposals for Korea were based.
Denationalisation of road transport in Britain.

F **Jun:** 2nd Coronation of Queen Elizabeth II;

O Politics, Economics, Law and Education

British Ministry of Agriculture inquiry into the disposal of Crichel Down, after prolonged agitation, eases tension between Civil Service and public.
Report of Royal Commission on Capital Punishment in Britain.
A Royal Commission is appointed to inquire into the law governing the certification and detention of mental patients.
The Beaver Committee on air pollution reports.
London Stock Exchange opens public galleries.

P Science, Technology, Discovery, etc.

Astronomers in Australia, S. Africa and U.S. discover a new scale of space outside the solar system.
Cosmic ray observatory is established on Mt. Wrangell, Alaska.
The Royal Observatory is moved from Greenwich to Herstmonceux, Sussex (–56).
R. Oppenheimer's Reith Lectures, *Science and the Common Understanding.*
International laboratory for nuclear research opened at Meyrin, near Geneva.
U.S.S.R. explodes a hydrogen bomb (*Aug.* 29th).
W. Le Gros Clark and others prove the Piltdown Man to have been a hoax.
The 'Jindivik' pilotless 'plane.
Experimental colour TV in U.S. (*Dec.*).
Edmund Hillary and Norkey Tenzing from John Hunt's expedition climb Mt. Everest (*May* 29th).
Austro-German expedition climbs Nanga Parbat in Himalayas (*July* 4th).
Myxomatosis spreads from continental Europe to Britain, killing millions of rabbits.

Q Scholarship

J. Wheeler-Bennett, *Nemesis of Power; the German Army in Politics.*
Cultural Patterns and Technical Change (ed. Margaret Mead).

R Philosophy and Religion

Karl Jaspers, *Tragedy is not Enough.*
Rhine, *The New World of the Mind.*
Skinner, *Science and Human Behaviour.*

S Art, Sculpture, Fine Arts and Architecture

Painting:
B. Nicholson, *September 1953.*
Mexican Art Exhibition, Royal Academy.
Sculpture:
Henry Moore, *King and Queen*, Middleheim, Antwerp.
Barbara Hepworth, *Monolith Empyrean*, Kenwood, London.
Institute of Contemporary Art, London, holds competition for sculpture of *The Unknown Political Prisoner*, which is won by Reg Butler.
Architecture:
P. Nervi and others, UNESCO Conference Hall, Paris (–1957).

T Music

M. Bloch, Concerto Grosso.
B. Britten, *Gloriana* (opera).
D. Milhaud, *David* (opera).
R. Vaughan Williams, Symphony no. 7.
Thomas Beecham produces F. Delius's opera *Irmelin* (composed 1892).
Homage to the Queen (ballet; score by Malcolm Arnold).

F **Jun**: 3rd, London Conference of Commonwealth premiers;
7th, in Italian elections Christian Democrats and their allies win seats from Socialists and Communists;
8th, Kenya African Union is proscribed;
17th, rising against Communist government in E. Berlin;
18th, Republic proclaimed in Egypt, with General M. Neguib President;
—, South Korea releases 26,000 non-Communist North Korean prisoners;
19th, the Rosenbergs, sentenced as atomic spies in 1951, are executed in U.S.;
26th, Joseph Laniel forms ministry in France;
29th, Alcide de Gasperi resigns as premier of Italy.

G **Jul**: 2nd, vote of confidence in Dáil for É. de Valéra's government following setbacks in by-elections;
4th, International Confederation of Free Trade Unions meets in Stockholm;
5th, Imre Nagy forms ministry in Hungary;
10th, dismissal of L. P. Beria, U.S.S.R. minister of internal affairs (he is shot as a traitor on *Dec.* 23rd);
—, British, French and U.S. foreign ministers meet in Washington;
12th, Brigadier Chichekli becomes President of Syria;
14th, defeat of Dr. Olivier's coalition in Malta on vote of confidence;
15th, Alcide de Gasperi forms new coalition (but resigns again, 28th);
—, Kenya Supreme Court quashes Jomo Kenyatta's conviction (upheld, *Sept.* 22nd, by E. African Court of Appeal);
—, Britain proposes four-power conference on Germany;
20th, U.S.S.R. and Israel resume diplomatic relations;
27th, Korean armistice is signed at Panmunjom;
30th, Britain signs alliance with Libya.

H **Aug**: 6th, widespread strikes begin in France;
8th, U.S.-Korean mutual defence treaty;
10th, Liberals return to power in Canadian elections;
15th, Giuseppe Pella forms Christian Democrat ministry in Italy;
16th (–19th), attempted royalist *coup d'état* in Persia;
20th, Dr. Musaddiq, premier of Persia arrested;
—, demonstration against federation in Nyasaland by Nyasaland African Congress;
—, France deposes Sultan of Morocco;
23rd, U.S.S.R. cancels E. German reparations;
24th, Kenya government calls on Mau Mau to surrender;
30th, Hungary and Yugoslavia resume relations.

J **Sep**: 6th, Christian Democratic Union wins W. German elections;
12th, N. Khrushchev appointed First Secretary of Central Committee of U.S.S.R. Communist Party;
27th, Japan establishes a national defence force;
28th, Cardinal Wyszynski, primate of Poland, arrested;
30th, Social Democratic ministry formed in Denmark.

K **Oct**: 6th, Britain sends forces to British Guiana to prevent *coup* by the Communist People's Progressive Party;
8th, Anglo-U.S. decision to hand over administration of Zone A of Trieste to Italy;
9th, Arab Liberation movement wins Syrian elections;
12th, Labour majority in Norwegian elections;
13th, John Kotalawala forms ministry in Ceylon on D. Bandaranaike's retirement;

(*Continued opposite*)

U **Literature**

W. Faulkner, *Requiem for a Nun.*
Ian Fleming, *Casino Royale* (first 'James Bond' thriller).
Gerald Hanley, *The Year of the Lion.*
C. Day-Lewis, *An Italian Visit.*
John Wain, *Hurry on Down.*

V **The Press**

British Press Council first meets.

W **Drama and Entertainment**

Coronation of Queen Elizabeth II televised.
T. S. Eliot, *The Confidential Clerk.*
Graham Greene, *The Living Room.*
N. C. Hunter, *A Day by the Sea.*
Arthur Miller, *The Crucible.*
Films:
Federico Fellini's *I Vitelloni.*
William Wyler's *Roman Holiday* with Audrey Hepburn.
Fred Zinnemann's *From Here to Eternity.*
The Robe (first film in 'Cinemascope').
B'wana Devil (first 3-dimensional film).
Four Chimneys.

X **Sport**

England win the Ashes from Australia.

Y **Statistics**

Z **Births and Deaths**

Mar. 14th Klement Gottwald d. (56).
Mar. 24th Queen Mary d. (85).
June 16th Margaret Bondfield d. (80).
July 16th Hilaire Belloc d. (82).
Oct. 30th Arnold Bax d. (69).

K **Oct**: 20th, Konrad Adenauer forms new government in W. Germany;
23rd, federal Constitution of Rhodesias and Nyasaland in force;
26th, U.S. publishes report of Communist outrages in Korea;
30th, general strike in Austria, as protest against occupation.

L **Nov**: 8th, all seats in Portuguese elections won by Salazar's União Nacional;
17th, non-party government in Finland under the governor of the Bank of Finland.

M **Dec**: 4th, W. S. Churchill, President Eisenhower and Joseph Laniel meet in Bermuda;
5th, Britain and Persia resume diplomatic relations;
7th, D. Ben-Gurion resigns in Israel after prolonged tension in coalition; succeeded, 9th, by Moshe Sharett;
8th, Eisenhower proposes to U.N. General Assembly an international control of atomic energy;
18th, Godfrey Huggins, Federal Party, forms ministry in Rhodesia-Nyasaland;
20th, Fatherland Front is the sole party in Bulgarian elections;
21st, Dr. Musaddiq is sentenced to three years' confinement;
23rd, René Coty elected President of France.

N

1954 (Jan.–May) Nasser gains power in Egypt—Fall of Dien Bien Phu—Terrorism in Algeria

A **Jan:** 8th (–15th), Commonwealth finance ministers meet at Sydney, under R. G. Menzies, to consolidate economic progress of the sterling area and Commonwealth;
17th, expulsion of Milovan Djilas, who had pleaded for greater freedom of expression, from Yugoslav Communist Party;
18th, Amintore Fanfani forms ministry of Christian Democrats in Italy following Giuseppe Pella's resignation, 5th;
23rd, Report of Randall Commission on U.S. foreign economic policy;
24th, Moshe Sharett forms new coalition in Israel;
25th (–*Feb.* 18th), foreign ministers of Britain, France, U.S. and U.S.S.R. meet in Berlin to reduce world tension, but U.S.S.R. rejects proposals of the West for the reunification of Germany through free elections;
30th, A. Fanfani resigns after vote of confidence against him.

B **Feb:** 10th, Mario Scelba forms coalition of Christian Democrats, Social Democrats and Liberals in Italy, with Parliamentary support from Republicans;
18th, Berlin Conference of foreign ministers ends with proposal for a further conference in *Apr.* at Geneva with Chinese and Korean representatives;
25th, Colonel Nasser usurps power as premier of Egypt but, 27th, General Mohammed Neguib again in control;
—, President Chichekli of Syria flees, following army revolt (and *Mar.* 1st, Sabri el Assali forms government).

C **Mar:** 1st, conference of the Organization of American States, in Caracas, Venezuela;
8th, U.S.-Japanese mutual defence agreement;
9th, Centre and Right gain in Finnish election;
23rd, Israel withdraws from U.N. mixed armistice commission;
31st, U.S.S.R. offers to join N.A.T.O.

D **Apr:** 5th, Dwight D. Eisenhower broadcasts on the H-bomb and the Communist threat;
12th, in Belgian elections Christian Socialists lose absolute majority to Socialists and Liberals (22nd, van Acker, Socialist, forms coalition);
13th, Vladimir Petrov of the U.S.S.R. embassy in Canberra is granted asylum in Australia;
—, Dr. Jagan, former prime minister, is sentenced and British Guiana becomes a 'proclaimed area';
16th, President Eisenhower pledges support to the six E.D.C. countries;
18th, General Nasser becomes premier and military governor of Egypt;
21st, U.S. Air Force flies a French battalion to Indo-China to defend Dien Bien Phu;
—, General Zahedi becomes premier of Persia;
26th (–*July* 21st), at Geneva conference on Korea and Indo-China U.N. powers insist on free elections in Korea;
27th, G. M. Malenkov elected premier of U.S.S.R.;
28th, premiers of India, Pakistan, Burma, Indonesia and Ceylon confer at Colombo;
—, India signs commercial and cultural agreement with China;
29th, first election in Honduras.

E **May:** 7th, Dien Bien Phu falls to Communist Vietnamese;
13th, President Eisenhower signs St. Lawrence Seaway bill;
15th, Queen Elizabeth and Prince Philip begin Commonwealth Tour;
18th, European Convention on Human Rights in force;
29th, Thailand complains to U.N. Security Council that Communists in Indo-China threaten her security;
—, R. G. Menzies forms coalition of Liberal and Country parties in Australia;

O Politics, Economics, Law and Education

A. Koestler, *The Invisible Writing*.
Richard Wright, *Black Power*.
Atomic Energy Authority and Independent Television Authority are established in Britain.
Landlord and Tenant Act provides security of tenure for tenants of premises outside the scope of the Rent Act.
International Convention for preventing pollution of the sea by oil.
High Court of Chivalry sits for the first time since 1731 and rules that Manchester Palace of Varieties cannot use the arms of Manchester Corporation (*Dec.* 21st).

P Science, Technology, Discovery, etc.

U.S. hydrogen bomb tests at Bikini in Marshall Islands reveal the bomb's powers of destruction (*Mar.* 1st).
Composite photograph of the night sky completed by Lisk Observatory, California.
Central Observatory of U.S.S.R. Academy of Sciences, near Leningrad, opened (*May* 21st).
Bell Telephone Company develops solar battery capable of converting the sun's radiation into electricity.
Widespread public concern about the disposal of radioactive waste.
The connection between smoking and lung cancer is first seriously suggested.
John Charnley starts research that leads to effective hip replacement operations (from 1961).
The Eurovision network is formed.
First 'flying bedstead' aircraft, with vertical take-off.
Series of 'Comet' disasters perturb British aircraft industry.
Italian expedition under Desio climb Mt. Godwin Austen (K. 2) in the Himalayas (*July* 31st).

Q Scholarship

Temple of Mithras is uncovered during excavations for rebuilding in City of London.
Mortimer Wheeler, *The Indus Civilization*.
Isaac Deutscher, *The Prophet Armed* (Vol. I; a study of Trotsky –63).

R Philosophy and Religion

Gilbert Ryle, *Dilemmas*.
A. Schweitzer, *The Problem*.
C. E. Raven, *Natural Religion and Christian Theology*.
P. Tillich, *Love, Power and Justice*.
Billy Graham's mammoth evangelistic meetings in London, Berlin and New York.

S Art, Sculpture, Fine Arts and Architecture

Painting:
- John Bratby, *Dustbins*.
- P. Picasso, *Sylvette*.
- G. Sutherland, portrait of *Churchill*.

Sculpture:
- Kenneth Armitage, *Seated Group Listening to Music*.
- Barbara Hepworth, *Two figures, Menhirs*.

Architecture:
- E. Bedford's design for G.P.O. Tower, London, accepted (–1965).
- New Barbican scheme, for development N.E. of St. Paul's Cathedral, proposed.
- Historic Buildings Councils for England and Wales make public grants for repairs.

E **May**: 31st, state of emergency in Buganda, Uganda;
31st, Marshal Tito visits Greece.

F **Jun**: 2nd, John Costello (Fine Gael) forms coalition in Ireland;
12th, French government defeated in National Assembly;
15th, Convention People's Party wins Gold Coast elections and, 21st, Dr. K. Nkrumah forms government;
18th, Pierre Mendès-France becomes premier of France;
29th, following the meeting of President Eisenhower and W. S. Churchill in Washington the Potomac Charter, or six-point declaration of western policy, is issued.

G **Jul**: 2nd, French evacuate southern part of Red River delta, Indo-China;
17th, Theodor Heuss is elected President of W. Germany;
—, Finnish-U.S.S.R. trade pact;
20th, armistice for Indo-China signed in Geneva by which France evacuates N. Vietnam, the Communists evacuate S. Vietnam, Cambodia and Laos, and France undertakes to respect the independence of Cambodia, Laos and Vietnam;
23rd, Indo-China settlement is approved by French National Assembly.

H **Aug**: 9th, Greece, Yugoslavia and Turkey sign treaty of mutual assistance;
22nd, Brussels negotiations on E.D.C. treaty break down through French unwillingness to make concessions.

J **Sep**: 8th, S.E. Asian Defence treaty and Pacific Charter signed in Manila by Britain, France, U.S., Australia, New Zealand, Pakistan, Thailand and Philippines;
15th, All-China People's Congress in Peking;
27th, U.S. Senate Select Committee reports that Joseph McCarthy has acted improperly in making government employees hand over documents.

K **Oct**: 3rd, nine-power conference in London on European unity agrees that W. Germany should enter N.A.T.O.;
5th, Britain, U.S., Italy and Yugoslavia agree that the Free Territory of Trieste should be divided into Italian and Yugoslav zones;
8th, Communist forces occupy Hanoi;
11th, China appeals to U.N. against U.S. aggression over Formosa;
18th, W. S. Churchill reconstructs cabinet, with Harold Macmillan as Minister of Defence;
19th, Anglo-Egyptian agreement on evacuation of troops from Suez Canal zone;
23rd, Britain, France, U.S. and U.S.S.R. agree to end occupation of Germany, and nine-power agreement on W. European union signed;
24th, state of emergency in Pakistan; the Governor-General declares the Constituent Assembly has lost the people's confidence;
26th, France and W. Germany sign economic and cultural agreement.

L **Nov**: 3rd, outbreak of terrorism in Algeria leads to dissolution of Algerian Nationalist Movement for the Triumph of Democratic Liberties;
4th, High Court judgment supports legality of Uganda government in withdrawing recognition of the Kabaka;
5th, Burma signs peace treaty with Japan;
13th, success of Social Credit Party in New Zealand elections reduces National government's majority;
17th, General Nasser becomes head of state in Egypt, following fall of President Neguib, 14th;

T Music

Darius Milhaud's *La Rivière Endormie* uses 'musique concrète'.
E. Rubbra, 6th Symphony.
D. Shostakovich, 10th Symphony.
Lennox Berkeley, *Nelson* (opera).
B. Britten, *The Turn of the Screw* (opera).
A. Copland, *The Tender Land* (opera).
A. Schönberg, *Moses and Aaron* (opera).
C. Menotti, *The Saint of Bleecker Street* (opera).
W. Walton, *Troilus and Cressida* (opera).
Paris radio gives first complete performance of S. Prokofiev's *The Flaming Angel* (opera).
Richard Buckle stages Diaghilev Exhibition at Edinburgh Festival.

U Literature

Kingsley Amis, *Lucky Jim*.
Saul Bellow, *The Adventures of Augie March*.
John Betjeman, *A Few Late Chrysanthemums*.
William Golding, *Lord of the Flies*.
J. Masters, *Bhowani Junction*.
F. Sagan (pseud.), *Bonjour Tristesse*.
C. P. Snow, *The New Men*.
J. R. R. Tolkien, *The Lord of the Rings* (I and II).

V The Press

The London Magazine founded.

W Drama and Entertainment

Dylan Thomas's dramatic poem *Under Milk Wood* (broadcasting).
Enid Bagnold, *The Chalk Garden*.
J. van Druten, *I am a Camera* (from Christopher Isherwood).
Christopher Fry, *The Dark is Light Enough*.
Tennessee Williams, *Cat on a Hot Tin Roof*.
Sandy Wilson, *The Boy Friend* (revue).
Julian Slade, *Salad Days* (musical).
Films:
Henri Clouzot's *Les Diaboliques*.
Federico Fellini's *La Strada*.
Elia Kazan's *On the Waterfront*.
Alfred Hitchcock's *Rear Window*.
Andrzej Wajda's *A Generation*.
The Divided Heart.
The Seven Samurai.
Voyage in Italy.
White Christmas, with Danny Kaye.
Hancock's Half-Hour on B.B.C. radio.

X Sport

Roger Bannister runs a mile in 3 mins. 59·4 secs. (*May* 6th).
Miss D. Leather of Birmingham University becomes first woman to run a mile in under 5 mins. (*May* 30th).
West Germany wins World Cup football final.

L **Nov:** 29th, Moscow Conference of representatives of Soviet satellite states opens; attended by observers from Communist China.

M **Dec:** 1st, U.S. signs pact of mutual security with Nationalist China;
2nd, U.S. Senate condemns Joseph McCarthy;
—, J. G. Strijdom, Nationalist, forms ministry in S. Africa on D. F. Malan's retirement;
13th, Siróky forms ministry in Czechoslovakia;
14th, Enosis issue over Cyprus provokes riots in Athens;
17th, Marshal Tito visits Delhi;
20th, U.S.S.R. threatens to annul treaty of 1942 with Britain if Paris agreement of *Oct.* 23rd on Germany is ratified;
France sends 20,000 troops to Algeria.

N

Y **Statistics**

Z **Births and Deaths**

Jan. 11th John, Viscount Simon d. (80).
Oct. 7th Seebohm Rowntree d. (83).
Nov. 3rd Henri Matisse d. (84).

1955 (Jan.–May) Treaty for European Union ratified—West Germany enters N.A.T.O.—Emergency in Cyprus

A **Jan**: 10th, President Eisenhower asks Congress to extend Trade Agreement Act;
—, federal council of Nigeria first meets;
18th, Kenya government issue terms for surrender of Mau Mau;
21st, Einar Gerhardsen, Labour, forms ministry in Norway;
24th, President Eisenhower's message to Congress on defence of Formosa;
25th, U.S.S.R. decrees end of state of war with Germany;
—, Jacques Soustelle, Left Republican, appointed governor-general of Algeria for restoring order.

B **Feb**: 5th, Pierre Mendès-France resigns on vote of confidence;
8th, G. M. Malenkov, premier of U.S.S.R., resigns; succeeded by N. A. Bulganin;
23rd, foreign ministers of S.E.A.T.O. countries (established in *Sept.* 1954) confer at Bangkok;
—, Edgar Faure, Radical, forms ministry in France;
24th, Turkey and Iraq sign treaty of alliance, the Baghdad Pact.

C **Mar**: 2nd, defensive alliance between Egypt and Syria;
3rd, Greece, Yugoslavia and Turkey set up a representative parliamentary council;
11th, Italy, 18th, West Germany and, 27th, France ratify Paris agreement of *Oct.* 1954 for establishing European Union;
24th, new constitution in force in Tanganyika;
27th, state of emergency in Pakistan;
31st, purge of Chinese Communist Party.

D **Apr**: 1st, U.S. Senate ratifies Paris agreement;
4th, Britain signs treaty with Iraq, and Parliament decides to adhere to the Baghdad Pact (of *Feb.* 24th);
5th, W. S. Churchill resigns, succeeded, 6th, by Anthony Eden who, 7th, re-forms Conservative ministry, with Harold Macmillan Foreign Secretary and R. A. Butler Chancellor of the Exchequer;
14th, Chou En-lai visits Rangoon;
15th, U.S.S.R.-Austrian economic agreement;
17th, Vietnam appeals to U.N. over alleged breach of Geneva agreement by the Viet Minh;
20th, President Eisenhower asks Congress for $3,530 million for foreign aid appropriations;
29th, Giovanni Gronchi elected President of Italy.

E **May**: 5th, end of occupation régime in W. Germany;
6th, Britain submits dispute with Argentina and Chile over ownership of Falkland Islands to International Court; but those countries refuse to present counter-claims;
7th, U.S.S.R. annuls treaties with Britain and France in retaliation for the ratification of the Paris agreement on European Union;
9th, W. Germany is admitted a member of N.A.T.O.;
15th, Britain, France, U.S. and U.S.S.R. sign Vienna treaty restoring Austria's independence;
26th, in British general election Conservatives and supporters win 345 seats over Labour 277, Liberal 6 and Sinn Fein 2;
—, N. A. Bulganin and N. Khrushchev visit Yugoslavia (sign treaty of friendship *June* 2nd);
29th (–*June* 14th), railway strike in Britain;
30th, Sa'id al-Mufti forms ministry in Jordan, following resignation of Tawfig Anu'l-Huda.

O Politics, Economics, Law and Education

Yarmolinsky Report, financed by Ford Foundation, reveals absurdities of various U.S. security precautions.

Judicial ruling that loyalty oath could not be required from tenants of New York Housing Authority.

P.E.P. Report on *World Population and Resources.*

The execution of Ruth Ellis, for murdering her lover, and new evidence in the Evans-Christie murders (1950) strengthen movement in Britain for abolishing capital punishment.

First Commonwealth Law Conference, Westminster (*July*).

Cambridge Conference of Vice-Chancellors from 88 European universities discusses specialisation (*July*).

Universal Copyright Convention comes into force (*Sept.*).

Duke of Edinburgh's Award Scheme for Young People.

P Science, Technology, Discovery, etc.

Audouin Dolfus ascends 4½ miles above the earth to make photo-electric observations of Mars.

B. F. Burk discovers that Jupiter emits radio waves.

Radio-physicists of Massachusetts Institute of Technology develop use of Ultra High-Frequency waves.

First use of atomically-generated power in U.S., at Schenectady (*July* 18th).

Growing concern at dangers to health and heredity of nuclear radiation.

Jonas E. Salk prepares vaccine against poliomyelitis at Pittsburgh University.

Dorothy Hodgkin discovers composition of Vitamin B12 (a liver extract for treating pernicious anaemia).

F. Sanger establishes the structure of the molecule of insulin.

Walter Gibb, in a Canberra, flies at altitude of 65,876 feet.

U.S. and U.S.S.R. announce they will attempt launching of earth satellites in International Geophysical Year (1957–8).

Charles E. Singer, E. J. Holmyard and A. R. Hall, *A History of Technology.*

Phenomenon of 'flying saucers' attracts attention.

First flight in U.S.S.R. of A. N. Tupolev's Tu-104 jet passenger aircraft.

Q Scholarship

Stephen Runciman, *The Eastern Schism.*

Interrelations of Cultures: their Contribution to International Understanding (UNESCO).

R Philosophy and Religion

R. Bergmann, *The Metaphysics of Logical Positivism.*

Herbert Marcuse, *Eros and Civilization.*

H. J. Paton, *The Modern Predicament.*

S Art, Sculpture, Fine Arts and Architecture

Painting:

Pietro Annigoni, *H. M. The Queen.*

S. Dali, *The Lord's Supper.*

J. Bratby, *Still Life with Chip-Fryer.*

B. Buffet, *Circus.*

Oskar Kokoschka, *Thermopylae* (triptych).

F **Jun**: 6th, Western Powers propose a summit conference at Geneva to ease tension and U.S.S.R. agrees to meeting *July* 18th;
11th, President Eisenhower proposes financial and technical aid to all non-Communist countries to develop atomic energy;
15th, Britain and U.S. sign atomic energy agreement;
22nd, resignation of Scelba's coalition in Italy; Antonio Segni, Christian Democrat, forms coalition;
30th, U.S.-West Germany military aid agreement.

G **Jul**: 4th, British dock strike ends after four weeks;
—, Britain undertakes to return Simonstown naval base to S. Africa while retaining right to use it;
5th, Assembly of Western European Union holds first meeting at Strasbourg;
18th (–23rd), at Geneva summit conference of Britain, U.S., France and U.S.S.R., Anthony Eden proposes Germany should be reunified;
20th, headquarters of International Armistice Commission in Saigon sacked;
21st, Greece proposes the Cyprus question be put before U.N. General Assembly;
24th, N. A. Bulganin and N. Khrushchev visit E. Germany;
30th, conscription introduced in China;
31st, devaluation of the Pakistan rupee.

H **Aug**: 1st, Communist Youth Congress held in Warsaw;
8th, Geneva Conference on peaceful uses of atomic energy;
—, barter agreement between Egypt, U.S.S.R. and Roumania;
11th, Muslim-dominated Right wing ministry takes office in Indonesia;
13th, Irish Republican Army raids army training centre at Arborfield, Berkshire;
15th, Buganda transitional agreement signed in Kampala;
—, Indians attempt to enter Goa;
20th, riots in Morocco;
30th, London conference of foreign ministers of Britain, Greece and Turkey on Cyprus and E. Mediterranean.

J **Sep**: 6th, anti-Greek riots in Istanbul and Izmir;
16th, rising in Córdoba under General Eduardo Lonardi spreads throughout Argentina;
19th, Juan Perón resigns, going into exile; and
23rd, Lonardi assumes presidency of Argentina;
—, Bundestag votes for resumption of relations of W. Germany with U.S.S.R.
24th, President Eisenhower suffers a heart attack;
25th, John Harding appointed governor of Cyprus.

K **Oct**: 2nd, France withdraws from U.N. General Assembly meeting through hostile interference over Algeria;
12th, goodwill visits of Royal Navy to Leningrad and U.S.S.R. Navy to Portsmouth; disappearance of Commander Crabbe, frogman, at Portsmouth;
17th, following withdrawal of Sultan of Morocco to Tangier, a Council of the Throne is instituted;
—, the Kabaka returns to Buganda;
23rd, referendum in S. Vietnam advocates deposition of Emperor Bao Dai and, 26th, republic is proclaimed under Ngo Dinh Diem;
26th, R. A. Butler introduces autumn Budget, embodying credit squeeze, to deal with Britain's unfavourable balance of payments;

S **Arts, Sculpture, Fine Arts and Architecture** *(cont.)*

Sculpture:

Lynn Chadwick, *Winged figures*.

H. G. Adam, Concrete sculpture for Le Havre Museum, forecourt.

Architecture:

Le Corbusier (pseud.), La Torette, Eveaux-sur-l'Arbresle, Lyons.

Frederick Gibberd, London Airport Buildings.

Eero Saarinen, General Motors Technical Center, Michigan.

T **Music**

Rolf Liebermann, *School for Wives* (opera).

Michael Tippett, *The Midsummer Marriage* (opera).

U **Literature**

James Baldwin, *Notes of a Native Son*.

J. Cary, *Not Honour More*.

R. Church, *Over the Bridge*.

I. Ehrenburg, *The Thaw*.

The Diary of Anne Frank.

Robert Graves, *The Crowning Privilege*.

Julian Green, *The Enemy*.

Graham Greene, *The Quiet American*.

J. Lehmann, *The Whispering Gallery*.

Vladimir Nabokov, *Lolita*.

V **The Press**

W **Drama and Entertainment**

S. Beckett, *Waiting for Godot*.

Ugo Betti, *The Queen and the Rebels*.

S. Lawler, *The Summer of the Seventeenth Doll*.

A. Miller, *A View from the Bridge*.

Ronald Duncan founds English Stage Company.

Commercial television in Britain (*Sept.*).

Films:

Juan Bardem's *Death of a Cyclist*.

Ingmar Bergman's *Smiles of a Summer Night*.

René Clair's *Les Grandes Manœuvres*.

Nicholas Ray's *Rebel Without a Cause*.

Satyajit Ray's *Panther Panchali*.

Sergei Samsonov's *The Grasshopper*.

Le Mystère Picasso.

Wild Birds.

Bill Haley's *Rock Around the Clock*.

The Court Jester, with Danny Kaye.

X **Sport**

Y **Statistics**

Railway mileage in operation: U.S., 234,342; Great Britain, 20,120; West Germany, 18,950; Japan, 17,200; China, 8,000.

K Oct: 27th (–*Nov.* 16th), four-power Geneva conference of foreign ministers on security and position of Germany;
30th, Sultan of Morocco abdicates.

L Nov: 1st, John Foster Dulles visits General Franco and, 6th, Marshal Tito;
2nd, D. Ben-Gurion forms ministry in Israel;
3rd, Iran joins Iraq-Turkey (Baghdad) Pact;
9th, S. Africa withdraws from U.N. General Assembly, since U.N.O. decides to continue consideration of Cruz Report of 1952 on *apartheid*;
16th, J. F. Dulles, H. Macmillan and A. Pinay issue statement on Germany in opposition to V. Molotov who had refused to discuss the question of Germany's reunification;
26th, John Harding proclaims state of emergency in Cyprus.

M Dec: 9th, Adnan Menderes forms ministry in Turkey;
13th, Hugh Gaitskell is elected leader of Labour Party, following C. R. Attlee's retirement;
14th, Albania, Austria, Bulgaria, Cambodia, Ceylon, Finland, Hungary, Ireland, Italy, Jordan, Laos, Libya, Nepal, Portugal, Roumania, and Spain, elected to U.N.;
20th, Anthony Eden re-forms ministry, with Harold Macmillan Chancellor of the Exchequer and Selwyn Lloyd Foreign Secretary.

N Border raids between Israel and Jordan increase in intensity.

z Births and Deaths

Mar. 11th Alexander Fleming d. (73).
Apr. 18th Albert Einstein d. (76).
July 24th Cordell Hull d. (83).
Aug. 12th Thomas Mann d. (80).
Nov. 24th Lionel Curtis d. (83).

1956 (Jan.–Apr.) Suez crisis—Hungarian Revolution—S. African Treason Trial begins

A **Jan:** 1st, Sudan is proclaimed an independent democratic republic;
2nd, Communists and Poujadists (Union et Fraternité Française) gain seats in French elections;
3rd, U.S.S.R. extends technical assistance to China;
5th, Marshal Tito meets Colonel Nasser in Cairo;
8th, first U.S.S.R. ambassador to W. Germany;
18th (–*Feb.* 8th), conference on Malayan federation, recommends independence by *Aug.* 1957;
—, National People's Army formed in E. Germany;
19th, Sudan joins Arab League, as ninth member;
23rd, N. A. Bulganin proposes 20-year U.S.S.R.-U.S. pact of friendship;
24th, Jordan and Israel accept U.N. truce proposals to ease Middle East tension;
25th, Guillebaud Committee reports on British Health Service.

B **Feb:** 1st, S. Africa requests U.S.S.R. to withdraw all consulates;
—, Anthony Eden and President Eisenhower issue Declaration of Washington, reaffirming joint policy in Middle East;
—, Guy Mollet, Socialist, forms ministry in France;
3rd, U.S.S.R. provides economic aid to Bulgaria;
4th, U.S.S.R. protests to U.S. about launching of balloons with photographic equipment over Soviet territory;
11th, referendum in Malta favours integration with Britain;
12th, U.S.S.R. states that the dispatch of U.S. or British troops to the Middle East would violate U.N. Charter;
14th, at 20th Soviet Communist Party Conference, N. Khrushchev denounces policies of Stalin;
15th (–*Mar.* 23rd), lock-out in British printing industry forces many periodicals to be printed abroad;
16th, British bank rate raised to 5½ per cent, highest rate since 1932, to curb inflation;
28th, India and Indonesia sign mutual aid treaty;
29th, Pakistan becomes an Islamic Republic (*Mar.* 2nd, decides to stay in Commonwealth).

C **Mar:** 2nd, France recognises independence of Morocco (Spanish recognition, *Apr.* 7th);
—, King Hussein of Jordan dismisses General J. B. Glubb from command of Arab Legion;
5th, Britain begins jamming Athens broadcasts to Cyprus;
7th, unrest in Georgia fomented by Stalinist faction;
8th, West German Constitution amended to permit introduction of conscription;
9th, Archbishop Makarios is deported from Cyprus to the Seychelles;
12th, Greece asks Cyprus question to be put before U.N. General Assembly;
15th, G. M. Malenkov visits British electrical installations;
20th, France recognises independence of Tunisia, with Bourguiba first President;
28th, Iceland calls for revision of 1951 agreement with U.S. and withdrawal of troops.

D **Apr:** 9th, U.S.S.R.-Mongolian Republic economic pact;
10th, People's United Front, led by D. Bandaranaike, wins Ceylon elections;
17th, Cominform dissolved;
—, Harold Macmillan introduces premium savings bonds in Budget;
18th (–28th), N. A. Bulganin and N. Khrushchev visit Britain;
21st, Egypt, Saudi Arabia and Yemen sign military alliance at Jedda;
22nd, China appoints Dalai Lama chairman of committee to prepare Tibet for regional autonomy within Chinese People's Republic;

O Politics, Economics, Law and Education

C.N.D. members and sympathisers march from Aldermaston in protest against nuclear arms and the dangers of radiation; such dangers are discussed in a World Health Organisation report (*Aug.* 16th).

Department of Scientific and Industrial Research Act establishes a new research council with wider powers. The Department's report on *Automation* puts into perspective the impact of automatic methods on industry.

F. Pollock and A. Weber, *Revolution of the Robots.*

Britain decides to spend an extra £100 million on technological education.

Norman St. John-Stevas, *Obscenity and the Law.*

Clinton Rossiter, *Conservatism in America.*

W. H. Whyte, *The Organization Man.*

Desegregation conflict in southern states of U.S. on schooling culminates in the case of A. Lucy at Alabama University.

P Science, Technology, Discovery, etc.

H. P. Wilkins and P. Moore, *The Moon.*

Edward Appleton's Reith Lectures, *Science and the Nation.*

Detection of the neutrino (a particle of no electric charge) at Los Alamos Laboratory, U.S.

Discovery of the anti-neutron at California University.

'Dido' reactor at Harwell opened (*Nov.* 21st).

Calder Hall, the largest nuclear power station, opened (*Oct.* 17th) and by the end of year supplies 65,000 kW.

F. W. Müller develops the ion microscope.

Tube Investments Ltd. brings into operation the first multi-purpose industrial high-energy plant in Europe.

Mullard image-dissector camera, capable of taking very rapid photographs.

Bell Telephone Company develops 'visual telephone', transmitting pictures simultaneously with sound.

Transatlantic telephone service inaugurated (*Sept.* 25th).

Peter Twiss flies at 1,132 m.p.h. in a Fairey Delta (*Mar.* 10th).

Scientists from seven countries encamp in Antarctica in preparation for International Geophysical Year.

Q Scholarship

Harold Acton, *The Bourbons of Naples.*

Lord Beaverbrook, *Men and Power, 1917.*

W. S. Churchill, *History of the English-Speaking Peoples* (–58).

Margery Perham, *Lugard: The Years of Adventure (1858–98).*

R Philosophy and Religion

A. J. Ayer, *The Revolution in Philosophy.*

R. Bultmann, *Essays Philosophical and Theological.*

Karl Mannheim, *Essays on the Sociology of Culture.*

Jean Mouroux, *The Christian Experience.*

Colin Wilson, *The Outsider.*

The German Evangelistic Churches begin revision of Lutheran text of New Testament.

The Buddhist Council, Rangoon, ends (*May*), the sixth council since 483 B.C.

S Art, Sculpture, Fine Arts and Architecture

Painting:

John Bratby publishes *A Painter's Credo.*

D **Apr:** 29th, cease-fire between Israel and Jordan, arranged by Dag Hammarskjöld, in force.

E **May:** 1st, Lebanon-Israel and, 2nd, Syrian-Israel cease-fires;
1st, Peronista Constitution revoked in Argentina;
9th, British Togoland plebiscite votes for integration with Gold Coast;
11th, European Coal and Steel Community adopts resolutions on a European common market and Euratom;
14th, U.S.S.R. complains U.S. 'planes have violated her air space;
22nd, Said el-Mufti forms ministry in Jordan;
—, Pandit Nehru announces plan for solving Algerian problem;
27th, India claims suzerainty over Chitral, which has been under Pakistani administration since 1947;
28th, France cedes former French settlements in India to Indian Union;
30th, life insurance nationalised in India;
31st, U.N. decides to withdraw inspection teams from Korea through frustration of their activities by North Koreans and Chinese.

F **Jun:** 1st, D. M. Shepilov succeeds V. Molotov as U.S.S.R. foreign minister;
2nd, Marshal Tito visits Moscow;
4th, Egypt declares she will not extend Suez Canal Company's concession after expiry in 1968;
6th, N. A. Bulganin calls on powers to match U.S.S.R.'s cuts in armed forces;
7th, in Tonbridge by-election Conservative majority drops by 8,594 votes in straight fight with Labour;
13th, last British troops leave Suez Canal base;
14th, U.S. and Britain sign agreement on atomic co-operation;
22nd, Julius Raab forms new coalition of Right in Austria;
24th, Colonel Nasser elected President of Egypt;
27th, Pakistan-U.S.S.R. trade pact;
28th, Sydney Silverman's bill for abolition of death penalty passes Commons (defeated in Lords, *July* 10th);
—, labour riots at Poznań, Poland, put down with heavy loss of life;
30th, Leeward Islands federation dissolved to enable islands to enter Caribbean federation.

G **Jul:** 7th, Sinhalese becomes official language in Ceylon;
9th, Duke of Edinburgh's Oxford conference on industry begins;
—, Restrictive Practices Act sets up Restrictive Practices Court in Britain;
11th, Finno-Karelian Republic abolished through incorporation in U.S.S.R. as Karelian Autonomous Republic;
17th, Kwame Nkrumah, People's Party, increases majority in Gold Coast elections;
19th (–20th), U.S. and Britain inform Egypt they cannot at present participate in financing Aswan High Dam project;
23rd, Royal Navy's first guided-missile vessel, H.M.S. *Girdle Ness*, commissioned;
26th, President Nasser seizes Suez Canal, under decree outlawing the company, provoking
26th (–31st), financial retaliations against Egypt by Britain, France and U.S.;
31st, British-West German ten-year agreement on atomic co-operation.

H **Aug:** 2nd, British and French nationals leave Egypt;
—, Britain rejects request of Federation of Rhodesia and Nyasaland for status as separate state within Commonwealth;

S **Art, Sculpture, Fine Arts and Architecture** *(cont.)*

Sculpture:

Lynn Chadwick, *Teddy Boy and Girl.*

Barbara Hepworth, *Orpheus*, Mullard House, London.

Architecture:

E. Saarinen's design for U.S. Embassy, London, wins open competition (–1960).

William Holford's plan for St. Paul's area published.

P. Nervi and Vitellozi, Palazzo dello Sport, Rome.

Jørn Utzon, Opera House, Sydney.

T **Music**

Heiss, song-cycle *Expression K* (Kafka).

Jean Martinu, *Hecube* (opera).

I. Stravinsky, *Canticum sacrum ad horem Sancti Marci nominis.*

F. Ashton-Malcolm Arnold, *Birthday Offering* (ballet).

Humphrey Searle, *Noctambules* (ballet).

U **Literature**

John Berryman, *Homage to Mistress Bradstreet.*

Kathleen Raine, *Collected Poems.*

Angus Wilson, *Anglo-Saxon Attitudes.*

V **The Press**

W **Drama and Entertainment**

J. Anouilh, *Poor Bitos* and *The Waltz of the Toreadors.*

J. Osborne, *Look Back in Anger.*

Angus Wilson, *The Mulberry Bush.*

English Stage Company's productions at Royal Court Theatre begin.

B. Brecht's Berliner Ensemble visits England for first London production of *The Threepenny Opera.*

Films:

Ingmar Bergman's *The Seventh Seal.*

Elia Kazan's *Baby Doll* with script by Tennessee Williams.

Alain Resnais, *Nuit et Brouillard.*

Satyajit Ray's *Aparajito.*

A Town Like Alice.

The King and I with Yul Brynner and Deborah Kerr.

Prince Rainier of Monaco marries Grace Kelly.

'Rock and Roll' dominates dance-floors.

X **Sport**

Olympic Games at Melbourne.

Y **Statistics**

Z **Births and Deaths**

Feb. 10th Hugh, Viscount Trenchard d. (83).

May 20th Max Beerbohm d. (83).

June 11th Frank Brangwyn d. (89).

June 22nd Walter de la Mare d. (83).

Sept. 22nd Frederick Soddy d. (79).

H Aug: 3rd, Gold Coast League Assembly adopts Kwame Nkrumah's resolution demanding independence, which is granted by Britain, *Sept.* 18th;
4th, Indonesia repudiates debts to Netherlands;
9th, airlift of British families from Suez Canal zone;
16th, first London conference on Suez boycotted by Nasser;
21st, J. F. Dulles's plan on Suez accepted by 18 nations, but U.S.S.R., India, Indonesia and Ceylon back alternative scheme by Pandit Nehru;
22nd, John Harding, governor of Cyprus, offers surrender terms which EOKA rejects;
25th, Greece and Roumania resume diplomatic relations.

J Sep: 10th, Nasser rejects 18-nation proposals for Suez Canal;
19th, second London conference on Suez meets; and
21st, establishes Canal Users' Association (which first meets in London, *Oct.* 18th);
23rd, Britain and France refer Suez dispute to U.N. Security Council;
29th, bread subsidy ends in Britain after 15 years;
—, Joseph Grimond succeeds Clement Davies as leader of British Parliamentary Liberal Party;
30th, Admiral Karl Doenitz released from Spandau prison, Berlin.

K Oct: 2nd, Aneurin Bevan elected treasurer of British Labour Party;
8th, Israel withdraws from Israeli-Jordan mixed armistice commission;
12th, Britain informs Israel she will be obliged to assist Jordan, if attacked, under 1948 treaty;
13th, Security Council adopts Anglo-French resolution on Suez, but U.S.S.R. vetoes this;
22nd, demonstrations in Hungary call for democratic government, the return of Imre Nagy to power, the withdrawal of U.S.S.R. troops and the release of Cardinal Mindszenty;
24th, Imre Nagy is appointed minister-president of Hungary and re-elected to Politburo; state of emergency; U.S.S.R. troops intervene;
25th, unified Egyptian-Jordanian-Syrian military command;
27th, new Hungarian government under Imre Nagy, including non-Communists;
—, Franco-German agreement on Saar;
28th, release of Cardinal Wyszynski, primate of Poland;
29th, Israeli troops invade Sinai Peninsula but Britain is assured they will not attack Jordan;
– , János Kádár becomes leader of Central Committee of Hungarian Workers' Party;
30th, Anglo-French ultimatum to Egypt and Israel calls for cease-fire and withdrawal ten miles from Suez, which is accepted only by Israel;
—, Cardinal Mindszenty is released; but Soviet troops invade N.E. Hungary;
31st, Anglo-French troops bomb Egyptian airfields; public outcry in Britain over the Suez War;
—, Roy Welensky succeeds Lord Malvern as premier of Federation of Rhodesia and Nyasaland;
—, U.S. sends aid to Israel.

L Nov: 1st, Jordan disallows use of R.A.F. bases in operations against Egypt;
2nd, Gaza falls to British;
—, Hungarian government renounces Warsaw treaty and appeals to U.N. and the powers against U.S.S.R. invasion;
—, U.S.S.R. vetoes Western powers request for U.N. Security Council to consider critical state in Hungary;

(*Continued opposite*)

L **Nov**: 3rd, Britain and France accept Middle East cease-fire if U.N. force will keep the peace;
4th, U.N. General Assembly adopts Canadian resolution to send international force to Middle East, with Britain and France abstaining;
—, Soviet forces attack Budapest. Imre Nagy takes refuge in Yugoslav Embassy; defection of János Kádár who forms a 'revolutionary peasant-worker' government;
5th, British paratroops land at Port Said;
—, U.S.S.R. threatens use of rockets unless Britain and France accept cease-fire;
6th, in U.S. presidential election, Dwight D. Eisenhower, Republican, re-elected with 457 electoral votes over Adlai Stevenson, Democrat, 74 votes, but Republicans fare badly in state elections;
7th, Anglo-French cease-fire in Egypt, but Britain declares she will evacuate troops only on arrival of U.N. force;
8th, U.N. General Assembly demands withdrawal of U.S.S.R. troops from Hungary;
9th, S. Vietnam's Constituent Assembly inaugurated;
10th, Baghdad Pact boycotts Britain (*–Mar.* 1957);
12th, János Kádár refuses entry to Hungary for U.N. observers but accepts U.N. relief;
13th, Alfred Gruenther, Supreme Allied Commander Europe, warns U.S.S.R. of retaliation if she uses rockets;
15th, U.N. emergency force arrives in Egypt;
—, U.S.S.R. loan to India;
17th, Kashmir votes to be an integral part of India;
20th, Lauris Norstad succeeds Alfred Gruenther as Supreme Allied Commander Europe;
21st, U.N. General Assembly censures U.S.S.R. over Hungary;
23rd (*–Dec.* 14th), Anthony Eden leaves London for recuperation in Jamaica, with R. A. Butler deputising for him.

M **Dec**: 3rd, U.S. suspends cultural exchange programme with U.S.S.R.;
5th, mass arrests on treason charges in S. Africa of Europeans, Africans and Natives;
—, Anglo-French forces begin withdrawal from Egypt;
—, Paul Spaak appointed Secretary-General of N.A.T.O. Council;
8th, call for a general strike in Hungary leads to proclamation of martial law and mass arrests;
17th, petrol rationing in Britain;
18th, Japan is admitted to U.N.;
19th, Lord Radcliffe's proposals for Cyprus constitution published;
—, preliminary hearing against over 150 accused in Johannesburg treason trial;
22nd, last Anglo-French forces leave Port Said;
27th, U.N. fleet begins clearance of Suez Canal;
31st, President Sukarno proclaims state of siege in S. Sumatra.

N

A **Jan**: 7th, Chou En-lai, premier of Chinese People's Republic, visits Moscow;
8th (–*Feb.* 26th), Syrian conspiracy trials, resulting in life sentences on ex-President Chichekli and others;
9th, Anthony Eden resigns;
10th, Harold Macmillan becomes Premier and, 13th, forms Conservative ministry with R. A. Butler Home Secretary, Selwyn Lloyd Foreign Secretary and Peter Thorneycroft Chancellor of the Exchequer;
20th, S. Africa denies port facilities to Indian vessels in retaliation for Indian sanctions against S. Africa.
22nd, Israeli forces complete withdrawal from Sinai Peninsula, but remain in Gaza strip;
24th, British Minister of Defence is given enlarged powers of control over defence services;
26th, Kashmir Constitution for incorporation with India in force, provoking demonstrations;
30th, U.N. General Assembly calls on S. Africa to reconsider *apartheid* policies;
31st, Trans-Iranian pipeline, Abadan–Teheran, completed.

B **Feb**: 2nd, Austria closes down offices of World Peace Council in Vienna;
9th, Japan and Poland resume diplomatic relations;
11th, Franco-U.S.S.R. trade pact;
12th, industrial rates in Britain raised to 50 per cent of net annual value (remained at 25 per cent since 1929);
14th, Labour wins Lewisham by-election from Conservatives;
—, Britain states she will reduce forces in Germany;
15th, Andrei Gromyko replaces D. T. Shepilov as U.S.S.R. foreign minister;
26th, U.N. General Assembly calls for a peaceful, democratic solution in Cyprus.

C **Mar**: 2nd (–14th), state of emergency in E. Indonesia and Thailand;
6th, Israeli troops hand over Gaza strip to U.N. force;
—, Ghana becomes independent State within the Commonwealth and, 8th, is admitted to U.N.;
7th, U.S. Senate approves Eisenhower's doctrine for U.S. forces to protect political independence of states of Middle East;
11th (–*Apr.* 11th), Singapore Constitutional Conference in London, agrees on internal self-government during 1958;
12th, Indian loan to Burma;
13th, expiration of Anglo-Jordan treaty of 1948;
14th, EOKA offers to suspend terrorist activities on release of Archbishop Makarios;
20th, Britain accepts N.A.T.O. offer to mediate in Cyprus, but rejected by Greece;
21st, Dag Hammarskjöld, U.N. Secretary-General, visits President Nasser;
— (–24th), President Eisenhower and Harold Macmillan at Bermuda Conference re-establish special relationship between Britain and U.S., which had been strained by Suez Crisis, and U.S. undertakes to make certain guided missiles available to Britain;
24th, Baghdad Pact ends boycott of Britain;
25th, Belgium, France, W. Germany, Italy, Luxembourg and Netherlands (the 'Six') sign Rome treaties for Common Market and Euratom;
27th, French company is formed to exploit mineral resources of Sahara;
28th, Britain releases Archbishop Makarios who is free to travel, except to Cyprus, and General Grivas is offered safe conduct to Greece;
29th, ships of small draught begin using Suez Canal (open to ships of maximum draught, *Apr.* 9th).

O Politics, Economics, Law and Education

Lord Hailey, *An African Survey* (revised).
Trevor Huddleston, *Naught for Your Comfort.*
V. P. Menon, *The Transfer of Power in India.*
W. Sargent's *The Battle for the Mind*, discusses brain-washing.
Declaration, a symposium by 'Angry Young Men'.
Desegregation crisis in Little Rock, Arkansas.
International Atomic Energy Agency is inaugurated at Vienna Conference.
Five-day week in British Civil Service.
Richard Hoggart, *The Uses of Literacy.*

P Science, Technology, Discovery, etc.

International Geophysical year begins (*July* 1st), with scientists concentrating on Antarctic exploration, oceanographic and meteorological research and the launching of satellites into space.
U.S.S.R. launches Sputnik I (*Oct.* 4th) to study the cosmosphere; weighing 180 lb., it circles the globe in 95 mins. Sputnik II is sent into orbit (*Nov.* 3rd) carrying an Eskimo dog, for studying living conditions in space.
Manchester University Jodrell Bank radio-telescope, under Bernard Lovell, tracks the Sputnik I's progress.
A new radio-telescope is built for the Mullard Observatory, Cambridge.
Artificial rain in New South Wales increases rainfall by 25 per cent and in Queensland saves crops.
Giberellin, a growth-producing hormone, is isolated.
Nobelium (element 102) is discovered at Stockholm.
H.M.C.S. *Labrador* discovers new north-west passage.
U.S.S.R. non-magnetic ship *Star* sets sail on expedition to take magnetic recordings.
U.S. expedition is flown in to South Pole.

Q Scholarship

Kathleen Kenyon, *Digging up Jericho.*
H. W. Parke and D. Wormell, *The Delphic Oracle.*
New Cambridge Modern History begins publication.
Arthur Bryant, *The Turn of the Tide.*
A. M. Schlesinger, *The Crisis of the Old Order, 1919–33.*

R Philosophy and Religion

A. J. Ayer, *The Problem of Knowledge.*
Roland Barthes, *Mythologies.*
Fred Hoyle, *Man and Materialism.*
Alec Vidler, *Essays in Liberality.*
First conference of European Rabbis, under Israel Brodie.

S Art, Sculpture, Fine Arts and Architecture

Painting:
  Francis Bacon, *Screaming Nurse.*
  K. Clark's survey, *The Nude.*
  Graham Sutherland, *Princess Gourielli.*
Sculpture:
  H. G. Adam, *Beacon of the Dead*, monument for Auschwitz (–1958).
  J. Epstein, *Christ in Majesty* for Llandaff Cathedral.
  L. Whistler, *seven glasses* for U.K. Atomic Energy Authority.

D **Apr**: 12th, W. German nuclear physicists refuse to co-operate in production or testing of atomic weapons;
13th, demonstrations in Jordan against Eisenhower doctrine;
17th, Pandit Nehru forms new Indian Congress movement, with Krishna Menon minister of defence;
18th, representatives of Burma, Ceylon, India, Indonesia, Iraq, Japan and Syria attend first meeting in New Delhi of Asian Legal Consultative Committee;
20th, U.S. resumes aid to Israel (suspended *Oct.* 1956);
—, Japan protests to U.S.S.R. over nuclear tests;
23rd, Albert Schweitzer's letter to Norwegian Nobel Committee urging mobilisation of world opinion against nuclear tests;
24th, Ibrahim Hashem forms Right wing ministry in Jordan, following demonstrations of Committee of National Guidance;
25th, U.S. 6th Fleet sails for E. Mediterranean (provokes U.S.S.R. protest, 29th);
—, King Hussein proclaims martial law in Jordan and seals frontiers;
29th, Hussein and King Saud of Saudi Arabia state the crisis in Jordan is an internal affair.

E **May**: 2nd, *Die Stem Van Suid Afrika* to be S. African national anthem;
5th, Adolf Schärf elected President of Austria;
10th, U.S.S.R. appeals to U.S. and Britain to cease nuclear tests;
15th, Britain explodes first British thermonuclear bomb in megaton range in Central Pacific;
19th, Adoni Zoli forms ministry in Italy, following resignation of Segni's coalition, 6th, on withdrawal of Social Democrats' support;
21st, Guy Mollet, Socialist, resigns premiership of France;
23rd (–*June* 26th), Nigerian Constitutional Conference in London;
30th, Britain relaxes restrictions on trade with Communist China.

F **Jun**: 1st, ERNIE draws first premium bond prizes in Britain;
4th, increase in British tourist travel allowance to dollar area;
5th, Britain and U.S. atomic authorities agree on exchange of information;
6th, Rent Act, de-restricting many previously controlled rents, receives royal assent; Labour displays hostility in refusing to join procession to Lords;
10th, Progressive Conservatives win Canadian elections (17th, Louis St. Laurent, Liberal, resigns, and 21st, John Diefenbaker forms ministry);
12th, Maurice Bourgès-Manoury, Radical, forms ministry in France;
22nd, three British subjects sentenced to imprisonment in Cairo espionage trial.

G **Jul**: 4th, V. Molotov, D. J. Shepilov and G. M. Malenkov expelled from Presidium of Central Committee of Soviet Communist Party;
15th, Franco announces that the Spanish monarchy would be restored on his death or retirement;
19th (–*Aug.* 14th), the Imam of Oman revolts against the Sultan of Oman, who requests British aid;
— (–26th) bus strike in Britain;
29th, International Atomic Energy Agency comes into being;
—, Western Powers and W. Germany issue declaration on German reunification and call for free elections;
30th, Royal Commission on Local Government in Greater London Area appointed.

H **Aug**: 8th, President Bourguiba of Tunisia appeals to Egypt for arms;

S **Art, Sculpture, Fine Arts and Architecture** (*cont.*)

Architecture:

Lucio Costa prepares plans for Brasilia, new capital of Brazil.

F. Gibberd, Hinkley Point Atomic Power Station, Somerset.

Le Corbusier (pseud.), Tokio Museum (–60).

T **Music**

Malcolm Arnold, 3rd Symphony.

Elliott Carter, *Variations for Orchestra.*

Jean Françaix, *King Midas* (opera).

John Gardner, *The Moon and Sixpence* (opera).

P. Hindemith, *The Harmony of the World* (opera).

Francis Poulenc, *Dialogues des Carmélites.*

William Walton, 'cello concerto.

I. Stravinsky, *Agon* (ballet).

B. Britten, *Prince of the Pagodas* (ballet).

U **Literature**

Sibylle Bedford, *A Legacy.*

John Braine, *Room at the Top.*

Jack Kerouac, *On the Road.*

C. Day-Lewis, *Pegasus.*

Iris Murdoch, *The Sandcastle.*

Roger Vailland, *The Law.*

P. White, *Voss.*

V **The Press**

W **Drama and Entertainment**

Entertainment duty abolished on living theatre in Britain and reduced on films.

S. Beckett, *Endgame.*

Robert Bolt, *The Flowering Cherry.*

John Osborne, *The Entertainer.*

My Fair Lady (musical).

Films:

Ingmar Bergman's *Wild Strawberries.*

Charlie Chaplin's *A King in New York.*

Mikhail Kalatozov, *The Cranes are Flying.*

David Lean's *The Bridge on the River Kwai*, with Alec Guinness.

Laurence Olivier's *The Prince and the Showgirl*, with Marilyn Monroe.

Otto Preminger's *Bonjour Tristesse.*

Porte des Lilas.

Quiet Flows the Don.

X **Sport**

Y **Statistics**

Production of electric power (in mill. kilowatts): U.S., 715,706; U.S.S.R. 209,480; Great Britain, 105,536; W. Germany, 91,773; Canada, 90,249; Japan, 81,303; France, 57,433.

Production of motor vehicles (in thousands): U.S., 7,200; W. Germany, 1,211; Great Britain, 1,149; France, 927; U.S.S.R., 495; Italy, 352; Japan, 45.

Rubber production (in thousand metric tons): U.S., 1,136 (synthetic); Indonesia, 696; Malaya, 648; Thailand, 135; Canada, 134 (synthetic); Cambodia and Vietnam, 101; Ceylon, 100.

H **Aug:** 15th, Cheddi Jagan forms government in British Guiana, following success of People's Progressive Party in elections;
30th, All-African Federal Executive Council formed in Nigeria;
31st, independence of Malayan Federation in force.

J **Sep:** 4th, Wolfenden Report on homosexual offences and prostitution published in Britain;
—, economic union of Egypt and Syria;
11th, U.S.S.R. complains to Turkey of concentrations of Turkish troops on Syrian borders;
14th, special session of U.N. General Assembly adopts U.N. report on Hungary;
15th, sweeping victory for Konrad Adenauer's Christian Democratic Union in W. German elections;
16th–17th, *coup d'état* in Thailand places Pote Sarasin, the new Secretary-General of S.E.A.T.O., as premier;
19th, British bank rate raised from 5 to 7 per cent;
20th, K. J. Holyoake becomes premier of New Zealand on Sidney Holland's retirement;
21st, accession of Olaf V of Norway on death of King Haakon;
23rd, Roumanian request to join Balkan Pact is refused by Greece;
26th, Dag Hammarskjöld, Sweden, re-elected Secretary-General of U.N. for further five years.

K **Oct:** 2nd, Rapacki Plan for a denuclearised zone in Central Europe presented to U.N. General Assembly by Polish People's Republic, supported by Czechoslovakia and E. Germany;
4th, Milovan Djilas, former Vice-President of Yugoslavia, sentenced to further term of imprisonment for spreading hostile propaganda;
7th, Labour Party returns to power in Norway;
12th, N. Khrushchev's letters to Labour and Socialist Parties in Britain and Europe urging them to prevent aggression of U.S. and Turkey in Middle East;
— (–21st), Queen Elizabeth visits Canada and U.S., and, 21st, addresses U.N. General Assembly;
16th, Syria declares state of emergency;
—, J. F. Dulles, U.S. secretary of state, warns U.S.S.R. against attack on Turkey;
19th, W. Germany severs relations with Yugoslavia, on the latter's recognition of E. Germany;
22nd, Hugh Foot appointed to succeed John Harding as governor of Cyprus;
23rd, Harold Macmillan visits Washington and, 26th, Ottawa;
26th, Marshal Zhukov, U.S.S.R. minister of defence, relieved of duties;
29th, Fulgencio Batista suspends Cuban constitution;
30th, Felix Gaillard, Radical Socialist, forms ministry in France.

L **Nov:** 11th, full internal self-government in Jamaica;
14th, Britain and U.S. send token consignments of arms to Tunisia provoking, 15th, French delegations to leave N.A.T.O. Conference;
—, Britain declares Bahrein an independent Arab State under British protection;
26th, International Court of Justice declares itself competent to adjudicate in India-Portuguese dispute over Portuguese enclaves in India;
27th, Pandit Nehru appeals to U.S. and U.S.S.R. to bring about effective disarmamen t

(*Continued opposite*)

z **Births and Deaths**

Jan. 16th Arturo Toscanini d. (89).
Feb. 9th Nicholas Horthy d. (88).
Mar. 11th Richard Evelyn Byrd d. (68).
Mar. 26th Édouard Herriot d. (84).
May 2nd Joseph McCarthy d. (47).
July 3rd Frederick Lindemann, Lord Cherwell d. (71).
July 11th Aga Khan d. (79)
Aug. 24th Ronald A. Knox d. (69).
Sept. 20th Jean Sibelius d. (91).
Nov. 30th Beniamino Gigli d. (67).
Dec. 18th Dorothy L. Sayers d. (64).

M Dec: 1st, retaliatory measures against Dutch in Indonesia following attempt on President Sukarno's life;
2nd, Bank Rate Tribunal under Lord Parker considers allegations of leakage of information;
8th, merger of four small Left wing parties in France as Union de la Gauche Socialiste;
15th, Greek resolution that Cyprus is entitled to self-determination fails to gain two-thirds majority in U.N.
19th, regular London–Moscow air service opens;
20th, European Nuclear Energy Agency inaugurated;
21st, U.S.S.R. proposals for summit conference;
30th, Maltese Legislative Assembly resolves that Malta has no obligations to Britain unless employment is found for discharged dockyard workers.

N

1958 (Jan.–Apr.) Khrushchev in power in Russia—Election of Pope John XXIII—De Gaulle elected President of France

A **Jan:** 1st, European Common Market and Euratom in force;
—, W. German forces handed over to N.A.T.O. command;
3rd (–14th), notes from British, U.S. and other powers objecting to Indonesian proclamation extending territorial waters;
—, West Indies Federation in force;
6th, Peter Thorneycroft, Enoch Powell and E. N. C. Birch resign from Harold Macmillan's government on cabinet refusing to prune estimates and
7th, D. H. Amory appointed Chancellor of the Exchequer;
8th, Marshal Bulganin again proposes summit conference;
20th, U.S.S.R. threatens Greece with economic sanctions if she agrees to installation of N.A.T.O. missile bases on her territory.

B **Feb:** 1st, Egypt and Sudan proclaim union as the United Arab Republic (and, 21st, plebiscite for President Nasser as head of state);
3rd, Benelux economic treaty signed;
5th, North Korea proposes withdrawal of all foreign troops from North and South Korea (completed *Oct.* 28th);
11th, Tunisia informs France that French warships will no longer be allowed to use Bizerta;
12th, Labour wins Rochdale by-election, with Conservatives at bottom of poll;
14th, Rapacki Plan for denuclearised zone of Central Europe delivered to foreign envoys in Warsaw (rejected by U.S., *Apr.* 14th, and by Britain, *May* 18th);
—, union of Kingdoms of Iraq and Jordan in Arab Federation with King Feisal as head of state;
15th, Britain and U.S. propose summit talks be preceded by meeting of foreign ministers or of ambassadors;
17th, Edgar Whitehead forms ministry in S. Rhodesia, when Garfield Todd, former premier, was ousted from leadership of United Federal Party on account of his stand on the franchise for Africans;
—, France and Tunisia accept mediation of Britain and U.S.;
19th, Anglo-Spanish trade pact;
20th, Kwame Nkrumah sets up foundation for mutual assistance in Africa south of the Sahara;
25th, Ceylon-U.S.S.R. agreement on technical co-operation;
27th, Umma Party wins Sudanese elections.

C **Mar:** 3rd, Nuri-es-Said forms ministry in Iraq;
5th, Syria accuses King Saud of organising plot to overthrow Syrian régime and prevent union with Egypt;
14th, Marshal Bulganin, in letter to H. Macmillan about summit talks, criticises agreement for establishing U.S. missile bases in Britain;
21st, Hungarian-Chinese economic pact;
27th, Liberals win Torrington by-election from Conservatives;
—, N.K hrushchev succeeds N. A. Bulganin as chairman of U.S.S.R. Council of Ministers (Bulganin is dismissed from Communist Party Presidium, *Sept.* 6th);
31st, John Diefenbaker leads government to victory in Canadian elections.

D **Apr:** 5th, Fidel Castro begins 'total war' against President Batista's government in Cuba;
8th, President Eisenhower proposes mutual inspection as means of enforcing atomic test ban;
15th, British Budget makes 'dividend stripping' illegal;
—, confederation of independent African states meets at Accra;
16th, sweeping victory for Nationalists in S. African elections:

O Politics, Economics, Law and Education

J. K. Galbraith, *The Affluent Society.*

J. D. Stewart, *British Pressure Groups.*

Under First Offenders Act no adult to be imprisoned by British magistrates court if there is a more appropriate method of dealing with him.

The case of the London members of the Chemists' Federation, the first to be referred to Restrictive Practices Court, found to be against the public interest.

British Public Records Act provides for inspection of records when 50 years old.

Geneva Conference on law of the sea.

First parking meters in London.

In Morocco women are permitted to choose own husbands and polygamy is restricted.

U.S. recession continues, with peak of 5 million unemployed in March.

P Science, Technology, Discovery, etc.

International Geophysical Year ends (*Dec.* 31st).

Volcanic eruption on the moon observed by U.S.S.R. scientist (*Nov.* 3rd).

U.S. artificial earth satellite *Explorer I* launched at Cape Canaveral (*Jan.* 31st) to study cosmic rays, Vanguard I rocket (*Mar.* 17th) to test solar cells, and Atlas (*Dec.* 18th) to investigate radio relay.

U.S.S.R. launches Sputnik III (*May* 15th) for aerodynamic studies, and puts in orbit two dogs in a rocket to a height of 279 miles (*Aug.* 27th).

U.S. nuclear submarine *Nautilus* passes under ice cap at North Pole (*Mar.* 4th), demonstrating the practicability of shortening commercial sea routes.

U.S.S.R. launches nuclear-powered ice-breaker *Lenin.*

Discovery of submarine current in equatorial Pacific.

British Section of Commonwealth Transantarctic Expedition under Vivian Fuchs reaches South Pole (*Jan.* 20th) overland from Shackleton Base and reaches Scott Base (*Mar.* 2nd).

Stereophonic gramophone recordings.

The Rotocycle, an aerial motor-scooter, is invented.

Q Scholarship

Stephen Runciman, *Sicilian Vespers.*

R. H. Tawney, *Lionel Cranfield.*

J. Wheeler-Bennett, *King George VI, His Life and Reign.*

R Philosophy and Religion

R. S. Peters, *The Concept of Motivation.*

Ludwig Wittgenstein, *The Blue Book* and *The Brown Book* (posth.).

Conversations between Church of England and the Methodist Church, an interim report.

Church of the Brethren at 250th meeting at Des Moines, Iowa, approves ordination of women. Evangelical Church of the Palatinate decides to admit women to ordination. Legislation to admit women to Swedish Lutheran pastorate is hotly contested by the Church Assembly.

United Presbyterian Church in U.S. formed (*May*) to become the fourth largest denomination, with 3 million members.

U.S. Congregationalists and Evangelicals form United Church of Christ (*June*) with 2 million members.

Supreme Religious Centre for World Jewry is dedicated in Jerusalem (*May* 8th).

S Art, Sculpture, Fine Arts and Architecture

Lord Bridges' Romanes Lecture, *The State of the Arts.*

Gulbenkian Fund's Committee reviews the needs of the arts in Britain.

D **Apr:** 16th, Felix Gaillard resigns as French premier on defeat of Tunisian policy;
18th, U.S.S.R. asks U.N. Security Council to take steps to end flights of military aircraft across her Arctic frontiers;
21st, on resignation of Labour ministry in Malta the governor assumes control;
23rd, Garfield Todd leaves Edgar Whitehead's cabinet to found a new United Rhodesian Party;
26th, N. African Nationalist parties meet in Tangier.

E **May:** 2nd, state of emergency in Aden colony;
3rd, President Eisenhower proposes demilitarisation of Antarctica, subsequently accepted by the countries concerned;
5th (–*June* 21st), London bus strike;
8th, J. F. Dulles states in Berlin House of Representatives that an attack on Berlin would be regarded as an attack on the Allies;
12th, U.S. and Canada establish N. American Air Defense Command;
13th, Europeans in Algiers stage demonstrations;
14th, M. Pflimlin (M.R.P.) forms ministry in France (–28th);
15th, General Charles de Gaulle states his readiness to assume the powers of the republic; and, 19th, praises the achievements of the army of Algeria;
25th, Christian Democrats win most seats in Italian elections but have not an absolute majority;
27th, state of emergency in Ceylon;
29th, Charles de Gaulle forms government of national safety in France.

F **Jun:** 1st, Iceland extends fishery limits to 12 miles;
9th (–10th), Harold Macmillan meets President Eisenhower and J. F. Dulles in Washington;
13th, A. Gromyko, Russian foreign minister, holds discussions with ambassadors in Moscow as preliminary to summit talks;
16th, U.S.-Japanese ten-year agreement on atomic energy;
17th, announcement of execution of Imre Nagy after secret trial in Hungary;
18th, President Eisenhower admits imprudence of Sherman Adams, assistant to the President, after hearings of Senate Committee on bribery charges involving Bernard Goldfine;
19th, British plan for Cyprus involves co-operation of Greek and Turkish governments in island's administration;
20th, Indonesia bans operations of Royal Dutch Shell Oil group;
25th, Amintore Fanfani, Christian Democrat, forms Italian coalition in succession to Zoli.

G **Jul:** 1st (–*Aug.* 21st), eight-power conference of experts at Geneva on detection of nuclear explosions;
—, Sudan diverts Nile waters as first stage of Managil project;
2nd, W. German Bundestag calls on powers to solve problem of Germany's reunification;
3rd, Anglo-U.S. agreement for co-operation in development of atomic weapons;
6th, Alaska becomes 49th state of U.S. (admitted *Jan.* 1959);
14th, in Baghdad *coup d'état*, King Feisal, his heir, and premier Nuri-es-Said are murdered, and King Hussein assumes power as head of Arab Federation;
15th, at request of President Chamoun, U.S. despatches forces to Lebanon;
—, S. Africa resumes full membership of U.N.;
17th, British paratroops land in Jordan at request of King Hussein;

S **Art, Sculpture, Fine Arts and Architecture** *(cont.)*

Victorian Society founded to safeguard Victorian and Edwardian buildings threatened by demolition

Painting:

J. Bratby, paintings for the film *The Horse's Mouth*.

Sidney Nolan, *Gallipoli* series.

Mark Rothko, monochrome canvases for the chapel at Houston, Texas (later named the Rothko Chapel).

Sculpture:

A. Calder, *Monumental Mobile* and *The Dog* (stabile).

H. Moore, *Reclining Figure*, UNESCO Building, Paris.

Architecture:

P. L. Nervi and G. Ponti, Pirelli Building, Milan.

O. Niemeyer, President's Palace, Brasilia.

Eero Saarinen, Yale Hockey Rink, U.S.

Mies Van der Rohe and Philip Johnson, Seagram Building, New York.

Arthur Ling, Belgrade Theatre, Coventry.

T **Music**

S. Barber, *Vanessa* (opera).

B. Britten, *Noye's Fludde*.

R. Vaughan Williams, Symphony no. 9 in E minor.

Humphrey Searle, *Diary of a Madman* (opera).

Van Cliburn of U.S. wins Moscow pianoforte competition.

Jeunesses Musicales meet in Brussels (*July*).

Magne, after Françoise Sagan, *Broken Date* (ballet).

L. Salzedo-Jack Carter, *Witchboy* (ballet).

F. Ashton-H.W. Henze, *Ondine* (ballet).

Macmillan-Martin, *The Burrow* (ballet).

U **Literature**

Lawrence Durrell, *Justine*.

Aldous Huxley, *Brave New World Revisited*.

B. Pasternak, *Dr. Zhivago*.

T. H. White, *The Sword in the Stone*.

Angus Wilson, *The Middle Age of Mrs. Eliot*.

The 'Beatnik' Movement, originating among young poets of California, spreads to Britain; devotees are unkempt, penurious and take drugs.

V **The Press**

W **Drama and Entertainment**

T. S. Eliot, *The Elder Statesman*.

Graham Greene, *The Potting Shed*.

Harold Pinter, *The Birthday Party*.

Leonard Bernstein, *West Side Story* (musical).

Brussels World Exhibition.

Films:

Marcel Carné, *Les Tricheurs*.

Jacques Tati, *Mon Oncle*.

Orson Welles, *Touch of Evil*.

Andrzej Wajda's *Ashes and Diamonds*.

The Wind Cannot Read.

G **Jul:** 19th, United Arab Republic and Iraq sign treaty of mutual defence;
20th, United Arab Republic severs relations with Jordan;
22nd, Harold Macmillan rejects Khrushchev's proposal for immediate summit talks on Middle East and suggests special meeting of Security Council;
24th, first life peerages in Britain;
26th, Prince Charles is created Prince of Wales;
—, last débutantes presented at British court;
31st, N. Khrushchev visits Peking.

H **Aug:** 1st, King Hussein dissolves the Federation of Jordan with Iraq;
5th, N. Khrushchev withdraws support for Security Council meeting on Middle East and proposes meeting of U.N. General Assembly, which is accepted by Britain and U.S.;
14th, Britain, France and other N.A.T.O. countries announce relaxation for trade with Soviet bloc and Communist China; but U.S. mantains embargo with China, North Korea and North Vietnam;
23rd, Communist China begins bombarding Quemoy;
—, racial disturbances in Nottingham and, 31st, in Notting Hill.

J **Sep:** 1st, Icelandic patrols board British fishing vessels within 12-mile limit;
3rd, Hendrik Verwoerd becomes S. African premier on J. G. Strijdom's death;
5th, Lord Parker succeeds Lord Goddard as Lord Chief Justice;
7th, N. Khrushchev states that any U.S. attack on China will be regarded as an attack on U.S.S.R.;
12th, U.S. Supreme Court orders Little Rock High School, Arkansas, to admit negroes;
—, Britain states that, though not committed to defend Formosa, she supports U.S. plan;
14th, General de Gaulle meets Konrad Adenauer;
15th (–26th), Commonwealth Trade and Economic Conference, Montreal;
18th, President Eisenhower signs extension of Reciprocal Trade Agreements Act;
19th, U.N. rejects Indian proposal to consider question of China's admission to U.N.;
—, provisional government of Algeria proclaimed in Cairo;
28th, French Constitution of the Fifth Republic, submitted to referendum in France, Algeria and territories overseas (–*Oct.* 5th), gives President greater powers and strengthens position of the government in the Assembly;
30th, U.S.S.R. resumes nuclear tests (suspended since *June*).

K **Oct:** 7th, President Iskander Mirza proclaims martial law in Pakistan;
20th, successful military *coup d'état* in Siam;
23rd, U.S.S.R. loan to United Arab Republic for building Aswan Dam;
24th, Ayub Khan forms cabinet in Pakistan;
28th, Cardinal Roncalli elected Pope John XXIII on death of Pius XII.

L **Nov:** 2nd, last British troops leave Jordan;
4th, Democratic victory in U.S. mid-term Congressional elections, leaving Democrats with 62 seats in Senate (Republicans, 34) and 280 seats in House of Representatives (Republicans, 152);
10th, ten-power Geneva conference on measures against surprise attack;
12th, United Federal Party of Roy Welensky wins Rhodesian Federal elections;
—, E. Germany demands recognition by powers;
17th, Sudanese army suppresses Constitution, and Ibrahim Abboud becomes premier of Sudan;

(*Continued opposite*)

W **Drama and Entertainment** (*cont.*)

Films (*cont.*):

Vertigo.

Coronation of Pope John XXIII (on television).

X **Sport**

Water-ski-ing becomes popular.

Brazil wins World Cup football final.

Y **Statistics**

Electronic computers: 1,000 in use in U.S.; 160 in use in Europe.

Z **Births and Deaths**

June 17th Imre Nagy d. (62).

Aug. 26th Ralph Vaughan Williams d. (85).

Oct. 2nd Marie Stopes d. (78).

Oct. 9th Pope Pius XII d. (82).

Oct. 24th G. E. Moore d. (85).

L Nov: 23rd, Ghana and Guinea announce they will form nucleus of a union of W. African states;

30th, Neo-Gaullist Union for a New Republic (U.N.R.) gains decisive victory in French elections.

M Dec: 3rd, nationalisation of Dutch businesses in Indonesia;

8th (–13th), All-Africa People's Conference in Accra;

11th, J. M. Beel, Catholic People's Party, forms coalition in Netherlands on resignation of William Drees, Labour;

12th, General Salan is appointed inspector-general of national defence in Algeria;

15th, O.E.E.C. Council fails to reach agreement on European free trade area;

16th, N.A.T.O. Council rejects U.S.S.R. proposals on Berlin;

21st, Charles de Gaulle elected President of French Republic with 78·5 per cent of votes, the Communist candidate 13·1 and the Union des Forces démocratiques candidate 8·4;

22nd, Franco-Egyptian trade pact;

27th, Britain announces convertibility of sterling for non-resident holders;

—, France devalues the Franc and makes it convertible to non-resident holders;

30th, French W. African states decide to form a federation within the French Community;

31st, amnesty proclaimed in the Lebanon.

N

A **Jan:** 1st, Batista, President of Cuba, flees to Dominica and, 2nd, Manuel Urrutia becomes provisional governor, but Fidel Castro strengthens position by purges and postponement of elections;
4th, disturbances at Léopoldville, Belgian Congo, which force Belgium, 13th, to grant reforms;
6th, W. German loan to India;
8th, General de Gaulle is proclaimed President of Fifth Republic, with Michel Debré premier;
10th, U.S.S.R. proposes conference to draw up German peace treaty (West replies by suggesting four-power foreign ministers' conference, *Feb.* 16th, which meets in Geneva, *May* 11th);
17th, Federal State of Mali formed by union of Republics of Senegal and French Sudan;
19th, S. African treason trial of the accused in *Dec.* 1956 reopens;
25th, Britain signs trade pact with E. Germany;
26th, A. Fanfani, Italian premier, resigns through dissensions in Christian Democrat Party.

B **Feb:** 1st, Swiss referendum rejects female suffrage in federal elections;
4th, Britain and Euratom agree to co-operate in peaceful uses of atomic energy;
6th, Antonio Segni, Christian Democrat, forms Italian ministry which is supported by Liberals and Monarchists;
7th, U.S.S.R. agreement to aid Chinese industry;
9th, U.S. supply arms to Indonesia;
11th, Laos announces will recognise U.N. as sole arbiter of disputes, provoking denunciation by North Vietnam;
16th, Fidel Castro becomes premier of Cuba;
19th, agreement signed in London by premiers of Greece, Turkey and Britain for independence of Cyprus;
20th, disturbances in Nyasaland where, *Mar.* 3rd, Hastings Banda and other leaders of Nyasaland African Congress are arrested;
21st, Harold Macmillan and Selwyn Lloyd visit U.S.S.R.;
—, British one-year trade pact with Spain;
23rd (–28th), first meeting of European Court of Human Rights at Strasbourg;
26th (–*May* 20th), state of emergency in Southern Rhodesia;
28th, Anglo-Egyptian agreement on settlement of claims arising from Suez crisis.

C **Mar:** 1st, Archbishop Makarios returns to Cyprus from exile;
— (–9th), unsuccessful army revolt in Mosul;
9th (–23rd), Harold Macmillan and Selwyn Lloyd visit General de Gaulle, Konrad Adenauer, John Diefenbaker and President Eisenhower;
10th, U.N. Geneva Conference approves international wheat agreement;
11th, Britain signs ten-year commercial treaty with Persia;
16th, U.S.S.R. loan to Iraq;
17th, U.S.S.R. and Australia resume diplomatic relations (severed in *Apr.* 1954);
—, Colonel Grivas, EOKA leader, returns to Athens from Cyprus;
—, in Tibetan rising against Chinese garrison the Dalai Lama escapes to receive, 31st, asylum in India and, *Sept.* 9th, appeals to U.N.;
24th, Iraq withdraws from Baghdad Pact, thus the Anglo-Iraq agreement of 1956 lapses;
27th, U.S. aircraft first 'buzzed' in Berlin air corridor by U.S.S.R. jet fighters;

O Politics, Economics, Law and Education

World Refugee Year begins (*June* 1st)
TV coverage of British general election (*Oct.*).
Vance Packard, *The Waste-Makers.*
C. Wright Mills, *The Causes of World War III.*
Legislation in Britain to reorganise Lancashire cotton industry, to reform system for detaining mental patients and to enable a child to be legitimised by its parents' subsequent marriage. The Street Offences Act clears prostitutes from streets.
Home Secretary allows scholars to inspect the Casement Diaries.
Obscene Publications Act permits publication of V. Nabokov's *Lolita* in Britain.
The Post Office Court in U.S. decides D. H. Lawrence's *Lady Chatterley's Lover* is not objectionable.
First British drive-in bank, in Liverpool.

P Science, Technology, Discovery, etc.

Launchings of U.S.S.R. cosmic rocket Lunik I (*Jan.* 2nd) and rocket with two monkeys aboard (*May* 28th).
U.S. artificial planet Pioneer IV (*Mar.* 3rd) and British rocket Black Knight IV at Woomera (*June* 29th).
U.S.S.R. sends dogs in orbit (*July* 6th); Lunik II reaches the moon (*Sept.* 12th) and Lunik III photographs moon (*Oct.* 4th).
Alvarez discovers the neutral *xi*-particle.
Benoit's experiments with ducks are claimed to modify the laws of inheritance.
De Beers of Johannesburg manufacture a synthetic diamond (*Nov.* 17th).
Louis B. Leakey finds the skull of 'the Nutcracker Man', 600,000 years old, in Tanganyika.
Launchings in U.S. of first atomic submarine (*June* 9th) and of first atomic-powered passenger-cargo ship, *Savannah* (*July* 21st).
British hovercraft crosses the Channel in two hours (*July* 25th).
Discovery of the Arctic submarine plateau.
First section of M.1 (London–Birmingham motorway) opened (*Nov.* 1st).

Q Scholarship

Remains of Nonsuch Palace are excavated successfully during Britain's driest summer for 200 years.
Garrett Mattingly, *The Defeat of the Armada.*
I. and P. Opie, *The Lore and Language of Schoolchildren.*

R Philosophy and Religion

Pope John XXIII announces the calling of the first Vatican Council since 1870, for promoting the search for Christian unity (*Jan.* 25th).
The Vatican orders the French Worker-Priest Movement (founded 1943) to discontinue (*July* 3rd; this ban is lifted in 1965).
Karl Barth, *Dogmatics in Outline.*
Pierre Teilhard de Chardin, *The Phenomena of Man.*
G. M. Mure, *Retreat from Truth.*

S Art, Sculpture, Fine Arts and Architecture

Painting:
John Bratby, *Coach-House Door.*
Joan Mirò's murals for UNESCO Building, Paris.
Sculpture:
Barbara Hepworth, Meridian, State House, London.

C **Mar**: 28th, J. E. de Quay forms Catholic People's Party ministry in Holland.
Deaths of Mau Mau prisoners at Hola Camp, Kenya.

D **Apr**: 4th (–*May* 30th), Ivory Coast signs series of agreements with Niger, Haute Volta and Dahomey to form Sahel-Bénin Union;
16th, Turkey's treaty of perpetual peace with Spain;
17th, Malaya and Indonesia sign treaty of friendship;
18th, Christian A. Herter succeeds J. F. Dulles as U.S. secretary of state (Dulles dies, *May* 24th);
20th, United Federal Party win Northern Rhodesian elections and African National Congress is suppressed;
26th, Cuba invades Panama;
27th, Liu Shao-chi elected Chairman of Chinese Republic in succession to Mao Tse-tung, who remains as head of Communist Party;
30th, Anglo-French trade pact.

E **May**: 2nd, Afro-Asian Organisation for Economic Co-operation in Cairo states exclusion of U.S.S.R.;
4th, U.S.S.R. note to Japan urges end of U.S. bases and offers to guarantee Japan permanent neutrality;
5th, Shah of Iran visits Britain; Iran replies to U.S.S.R. protest about her defence agreement with U.S. that she would agree to denuclearised zone in Middle East if the great powers agreed;
—, W. S. Tubman, True Whig, re-elected President of Liberia;
7th, Anglo-U.S. agreement enabling Britain to purchase components of atomic weapons other than warheads from U.S.;
10th, Austrian general election leads to coalition of People's Party and Socialists, *July* 16th, under Julius Raab;
11th (–*Aug.* 5th), Foreign Ministers' Conference, Geneva, to discuss Berlin and a German peace treaty;
22nd, Canadian-U.S. agreement for co-operation in use of atomic energy for mutual defence;
24th, Anglo-U.S.S.R. five-year trade pact;
25th (–*June* 4th), N. Khrushchev visits Albania;
28th, Britain announces removal of controls on imports of many consumer goods from dollar area, with increased import quotas of other goods;
30th, Iraq terminates U.S. military assistance agreements on grounds that such conflicted with Iraqi policy of neutrality.

F **Jun**: 3rd, Singapore becomes self-governing;
—, Iraq Petroleum Co and Lebanon settle dispute;
4th, U.S.-owned sugar mills and plantations in Cuba expropriated;
5th (–10th), Atlantic Congress, London, sponsored by N.A.T.O. Parliamentarians' Conference;
13th, Communist China's trade pact with Ceylon;
14th, U.S. agrees to provide Greece with nuclear information and supply ballistic rockets;
17th, Éamon de Valéra resigns as premier to become third President of Eire in succession to Sean O'Kelly, and, 23rd, Sean Lemass forms ministry;
20th, beginning of six-week printing strike in Britain, which affects all publications except London newspapers;
23rd, Iraq withdraws from sterling area;

S Art, Sculpture, Fine Arts and Architecture *(cont.)*

Architecture:

Arne Jacobsen, SAS Building, Copenhagen's first skyscraper.

Frank Lloyd Wright, Guggenheim Art Museum, New York, and Beth Shalom Synagogue, Elkin Park, Pa.

T Music

Pierre Boulez, *Livre du Quattuor* quartet.

Pousseur, *Rhymes from Various Sonorous Sources* (employs electronic music and two orchestras).

Francis Poulenc, *La Voix Humaine* (opera).

Purcell, Handel and Haydn anniversary concerts.

J. Cranko's *Antigone* to score by M. Theodorakis (ballet).

J. Robbins, *L'Après-midi d'un Faune* (ballet).

Peter Maxwell Davies, *St. Michael* Sonata.

Jazz musician Thelonius Monk forms his own big band.

U Literature

Saul Bellow, *Henderson the Rain King.*

Ivy Compton-Burnett, *A Heritage and Its History.*

William Faulkner, *The Mansion.*

Norman Mailer, *Advertisement for Myself.*

V. S. Naipaul, *Miguel Street.*

C. P. Snow's Rede Lecture, *The Two Cultures and the Scientific Revolution.*

Muriel Spark, *Memento Mori.*

James Thurber, *The Years with Ross.*

V The Press

Manchester Guardian renamed *The Guardian* (*Aug.* 24th).

W Drama and Entertainment

Bernard Miles opens Mermaid Theatre, the first in City of London for 300 years.

Peter Hall appointed Director of Shakespeare Memorial Theatre, Stratford.

Brendan Behan, *The Hostage.*

Arnold Wesker, *Roots.*

Films:

Carl Bresson's *Pickpocket.*

Jean Cocteau's *Le Testament d'Orphée.*

Donskoi's *Foma Gordeyev.*

Howard Hawks's *Rio Bravo*, with John Wayne.

Otto Preminger's *Anatomy of a Murder.*

Satyajit Ray's *The World of Apu.*

Carol Reed's *Our Man in Havana.*

Resnais' *Hiroshima, mon Amour.*

Tony Richardson's *Look Back in Anger.*

Gigi with Audrey Hepburn.

The Rickshaw Man.

S. Eisenstein's *Notes of a Film Director* published.

Face to Face and *Monitor* series in Britain (television).

Quiz scandal in U.S., where a prize-winner admitted being supplied with answers.

S. Africa decides against introducing TV.

Regular colour TV in Cuba.

X Sport

F **Jun:** 25th, U.S.S.R. proposals for denuclearised zone in Balkans and Adriatic (rejected by West, *July* 11th–13th);
26th, Queen Elizabeth opens St. Lawrence Seaway.

G **Jul:** 1st, Heinrich Lübke elected President of W. Germany in succession to Dr. Heuss (K. Adenauer's opposition prevented Dr. Erhard standing as Christian Democrat candidate);
4th, Jamaica is granted internal self-government within West Indies Federation;
5th, Ghana boycotts S. African goods;
—, Saar is incorporated in W. German economic system;
—, President Sukarno dissolves Indonesian constituent assembly;
8th, U.S.-Liberian defence agreement;
16th, Kwame Nkrumah of Ghana and W. S. Tubman of Liberia propose holding a conference of independent African states;
17th, N. Khrushchev reaffirms guarantee of Oder-Neisse frontier and calls for European denuclearised zone;
20th, cabinet government introduced to Trinidad and Tobago;
28th, Indian police party seized by Communist Chinese in Jammu and Kashmir area.

H **Aug:** 7th, Communist Chinese invade N.E. frontier of India;
—, increase in Soviet aid to Hungary;
16th, United Arab Republic restores diplomatic relations with Jordan (severed *July* 20th, 1958);
21st, Baghdad Pact changes name to Central Treaty Organisation (CENTO);
—, Hawaii becomes 50th state of U.S.;
26th, President Eisenhower visits Bonn and, 27th, Britain.

J **Sep:** 4th, emergency in Laos, with alleged aggression of North Vietnamese;
7th, four-power statement on decision to establish new disarmament committee;
16th, President de Gaulle broadcasts on future of Algeria;
18th, N. Khrushchev addresses U.N. General Assembly on disarmament;
22nd, U.N. vote against admission of Communist China;
25th, N. Khrushchev visits Peking;
—, S. Bandaranaike, premier of Ceylon, assassinated, succeeded by W. Dahanayake.

K **Oct:** 8th, in British general election Conservatives under Harold Macmillan win 366 seats, Labour 258, and Liberals, 8;
20th, Inter-American Nuclear Energy Commission holds first meeting in Washington;
26th, Basic Democracies Order promulgated in Pakistan; Rawalpindi is chosen as provisional capital.

L **Nov:** 8th, United Arab Republic and Sudan sign agreement on sharing the Nile waters after construction of Aswan High Dam;
—, President Bourguiba's Neo-Destour Party win all seats in Tunisian assembly;
10th, U.N. General Assembly condemns *apartheid* in S. Africa and racial discrimination in any part of the world;
—, announcement of ending of emergency in Kenya after ten years;
13th, S. African Progressive Party established at Johannesburg congress;
20th (–29th), European Free Trade Association (the 'Seven'), consisting of Britain, Norway, Portugal, Switzerland, Austria, Denmark and Sweden, ratify treaty.

M **Dec:** 3rd, President Eisenhower's tour of European capitals (–23rd);
6th, U.N. General Assembly resolves Togoland trusteeship territory should achieve independence in *Apr.* 1960;

(*Continued opposite*)

Y **Statistics**

Cement production (in mill. metric tons): U.S., 66·8; U.S.S.R., 42·7; W. Germany, 25·1; Japan, 19; France, 14·7; Great Britain, 13·8.

Aluminium production (in mill. tons): U.S., 1·9; U.S.S.R., 0·7; Canada, 0·6; France, 0·2;

Fertilisers (in mill. tons): U.S., 45; U.S.S.R., 12; Germany, 1; Great Britain, 0·7.

Television sets: U.S., 36 mill.; Great Britain, 10 mill.; France, 1,500,000.

Z **Births and Deaths**

July 15th Ernest Bloch d. (78).
July 17th Alfred Munnings d. (80).
Aug. 19th Jacob Epstein d. (78).
Oct. 9th Henry Tizard d. (74).
Oct. 16th George Marshall d. (78).
Dec. 14th Stanley Spencer d. (68).

M **Dec:** 9th, Britain and United Arab Republic resume diplomatic relations (severed in *Nov.* 1956);

10th, U.S. begins withdrawal of troops from Iceland;

13th, U.N. decides not to intervene in question of Algeria;

19th, Western powers at Paris meeting invite N. Khrushchev to attend summit conference in *Apr.* 1960;

24th, anti-Semitic incidents in Cologne;

25th, U.S.S.R. agrees to give financial and technical aid to Syria.

N

1960 (Jan.–Apr.) Summit Meeting—Sharpeville shootings—Congo Crisis—Kennedy elected U.S. President

A **Jan**: 1st, independent Republic of the Cameroons proclaimed;
6th (–*Feb.* 5th), Harold Macmillan visits Ghana, Nigeria, Rhodesia and S. Africa;
9th, work on Aswan High Dam begins;
11th, U.S. protests to Cuba against expropriation of U.S. property;
12th, E.F.T.A. countries (the 'Seven') hold first ministerial meeting in Paris;
—, President Sukarno forms National Front in Indonesia;
18th, London Conference on Cyprus breaks down;
—, Kenya Constitutional Conference, London, at first boycotted by African elected members, who take their places, 25th;
19th, U.S.-Japanese treaty of mutual security;
20th, Belgian Congo conference in Brussels agrees on full independence in *June*;
24th (–*Feb.* 1st), rioting by European extremists in Algiers;
28th, Burma signs treaty of friendship with Communist China.

B **Feb**: 2nd, Negro sit-in campaign in U.S. lunch-counters begins;
3rd, Harold Macmillan's 'wind of change' speech in Cape Town Parliament;
5th, Anastas Mikoyan, deputy premier of U.S.S.R., opens Soviet exhibition in Havana;
8th, Queen Elizabeth announces all her descendants, except those enjoying the style of Royal Highness, to bear the name of Mountbatten-Windsor;
10th (–*Mar.* 5th), N. Khrushchev visits India, Burma and Indonesia;
14th, Ayub Khan wins presidential ballot in Pakistan;
17th, U.S.-Britain agreement to build ballistic missile early warning station at Fylingdales;
19th, Prince Andrew born (first birth to a reigning sovereign since 1857);
24th, Signor Segni resigns in Italy, and, after various other attempts, Amintore Fanfani succeeds in forming ministry, *July* 22nd;
29th, Agadir earthquake.

C **Mar**: 3rd, Guillebaud Committee's report on railwaymen's pay embodies principle of fair comparison with other employment;
4th, N. Khrushchev protests against likelihood of Spain granting military bases to W. Germany;
5th, Harold Macmillan elected Chancellor of Oxford University over Oliver Franks;
—, President Sukarno suspends Indonesian Parliament;
15th, ten-power disarmament committee meets in Geneva (–*June* 27th, when Communists walk out);
16th, British Labour Party executive issues declaration of objectives, which include 'clause 4' on nationalisation;
21st, D. Senanayake, United National Party, forms ministry in Ceylon following elections;
—, Pan-African demonstration against pass laws in S. Africa leads to shooting of 67 Africans at Sharpeville, and a state of emergency is proclaimed (–*Aug.* 31st); world opinion against *apartheid* is intensified;
26th, U.S. loan to United Arab Republic;
27th, President Eisenhower and Harold Macmillan issue joint statement in Washington on nuclear test negotiations;
—, General Kassem, premier of Iraq, founds Palestinian Army for the proposed independence of a Palestine Republic.

D **Apr**: 1st, S. African government bans African National Congress and Pan-African Congress;
4th, Sultan of Selangor becomes head of Malayan Federation;

O **Politics, Economics, Law and Education**

Anti-Jewish incidents in W. Germany lead to the banning of neo-Nazi political groups and a review of textbooks.

R. M. Nixon-John F. Kennedy confrontations on TV during U.S. presidential election campaign.

Brasilia becomes new capital of Brazil (*Apr.*).

240 Spanish authors plead for reform of censorship.

Churchill College, Cambridge, founded.

P **Science, Technology, Discovery, etc.**

Twenty artificial satellites are in orbit.

U.S. Air Force recovers Discoverer satellite from Pacific, and U.S.S.R. recovers dogs that made 17 orbits of the earth.

U.S. launch a radio-reflector satellite (*Aug.* 12th).

R. L. Mossbauer's discoveries in gamma rays.

An optical micro-wave laser (maser) is constructed.

Surgeons at Birmingham develop a pacemaker for the heart.

Chlorophyll is synthesised simultaneously by Martin Strell of Munich and R. B. Woodward of Harvard University.

K. H. Hoffman synthesises pituitary hormone.

G. N. Robinson discovers methicillin, antibiotic drug.

J. C. Kendrew and M. Perutz elucidates three-dimensional structure of the protein myoglobin.

U.S. bathyscaphe *Trieste*, designed by Professor Piccard, dives to the bottom of Challenger Deep, 35,800 ft.

Q **Scholarship**

Archaeologists begin to save treasures in Aswan High Dam region of Nubia before flooding begins.

Excavations at Stonehenge by officials of Ministry of Works.

Further Biblical texts are discovered in Dead Sea region.

Gavin de Beer, *The Sciences Were Never at War*.

R **Philosophy and Religion**

A. J. Ayer, *Logical Positivism*.

'Kneel-in' campaign by Negroes in segregated churches in U.S. Southern States.

Archbishop Fisher of Canterbury visits Jerusalem, Istanbul and Rome (*Nov.* 22nd–*Dec.* 2nd).

A church at Herne Bay, Kent, is dedicated for use jointly by Anglicans and Methodists.

Three women are admitted to pastorate of Swedish Lutheran Church.

S **Art, Sculpture, Fine Arts and Architecture**

Painting:

P. Picasso Exhibition, Tate Gallery.

S. Nolan 'Leda and the Swan' series (since 1945).

Arthur Boyd, *Half-Caste Bride* and William Dobell create interest in Australian artists.

J. Bratby, *Gloria with Sunflower*.

Sculpture:

Musée Léger opened at Biot with the 'Children's Garden' in the forecourt.

Architecture:

R. L. Davies, Times Building, Printing House Square (–64).

Louis I. Khan, Research Laboratory, Pennsylvania University.

O. Niemeyer, Museum and Congress Building, Brasilia, opened.

D **Apr**: 4th, British budget ends 'golden handshake' and increases profits tax to 12½ per cent;
9th, Hendrik Verwoerd wounded by David Pratt;
10th, Civil Rights bill for safeguarding negroes' voting rights passes U.S. Senate;
14th, collectivisation of E. Germany's agriculture completed;
27th, Sierra Leone constitutional conference in London proposes independence in *Apr.* 1961;
—, British Labour Opposition move vote of censure on government for lack of judgment over Blue Streak missile;
—, Syngman Rhee resigns South Korean presidency;
—, Togo becomes an independent republic;
28th (–*May* 25th), student demonstrations in Ankara and Istanbul.

E **May**: 1st, U.S. U-2 aircraft, flown by Francis Gary Powers, shot down by U.S.S.R.;
3rd, E.F.T.A. comes into force, with 20 per cent tariff cuts between members from *July*;
—, Commonwealth Prime Ministers' Conference in London at which Eric Louw represents S. Africa;
6th, Princess Margaret marries Antony Armstrong-Jones;
7th, Leonid Brezhnev replaces Marshal Voroshilov as President of U.S.S.R.;
16th (–19th), summit meeting in Paris of N. Khrushchev, H. Macmillan, D. Eisenhower, and C. de Gaulle, which fails through U-2 affair;
17th, Kariba Dam, Rhodesia, opened;
23rd, Israel announces the arrest of Adolf Eichmann, former Gestapo chief;
27th, Adnan Menderes is overthrown in Turkey; General Cemal Gürsel assumes presidency;
—, U.S. ends aid to Cuba.

F **Jun**: 9th, Hong Kong struck by typhoon;
12th (–26th), President Eisenhower's Far East tour;
14th, President de Gaulle renews offer to Algerian provisional government to negotiate cease-fire, to which *Front de la Libération Nationale* agrees, but rejects subsequent French conditions;
15th, Japanese students riot in protest against Mutual Co-operation and Security Treaty with U.S. and Eisenhower's visit is postponed (19th, Japanese Diet ratifies treaty);
21st, Britain, France, Netherlands and U.S. provide for a Caribbean organisation for economic co-operation;
23rd, 'credit squeeze' with bank rate raised to 6 per cent in Britain;
24th, Greece, Yugoslavia and Turkey dissolve Balkan alliance of *Aug.* 1954;
25th, Mutual Co-operation Parliament meets in Indonesia;
26th, Madagascar proclaimed independent as the Malagasy Republic;
—, British Somaliland becomes independent and, 27th, joins Somalia;
30th, Bantu self-government bill in force in S. Africa;
—, independence of Congolese Republic under President Kasavubu with Patrice Lumumba premier.

G **Jul**: 1st, U.N. Food and Agriculture Organisation launches Freedom from Hunger Campaign;
—, U.S.S.R. shoots down U.S. aircraft over Barents Sea;
—, Britain and Cyprus reach agreement on British bases;
4th, Britain protests to Cuba over 'intervention' in Havana Shell Oil refinery;
5th (–6th), Congolese national army mutinies, and Europeans flee from Léopoldville area to Brazzaville;
6th, Aneurin Bevan, Deputy Leader of British Labour Party, dies (aged 62);

T **Music**

Arthur Bliss, *Tobias and the Angel.*
Pierre Boulez, *Portrait of Mallarmé.*
Hans W. Henze, *Der Prinz von Hamburg* (opera).
Ernst Křenek, *Whitsun Oratorio.*
Humphrey Searle, Symphony no. 3.

U **Literature**

John Betjeman, *Summoned by Bells.*
Lawrence Durrell, *Clea.*
Alain Robbe-Grillet, *Dans la labyrinthe.*
John Updike, *Rabbit Run.*

V **The Press**

Sunday Telegraph is issued.
The News Chronicle and *The Star* cease publication.

W **Drama and Entertainment**

Robert Bolt, *A Man For All Seasons.*
Lillian Hellman, *Toys in the Attic.*
E. Ionesco, *The Rhinoceros.*
John Mortimer, *The Wrong Side of the Park.*
Harold Pinter, *The Caretaker.*
Terence Rattigan, *Ross.*
Arnold Wesker, *I'm Talking About Jerusalem.*
Fings Ain't Wot They Used T'Be (musical).
Japan begins regular colour TV.
Films:
Federico Fellini's *La Dolce Vita.*
Alfred Hitchcock's *Psycho.*
Michelangelo Antonioni's *L'Avventura.*
Otto Preminger's *Exodus.*
Karel Reisz's *Saturday Night and Sunday Morning.*
Luchino Visconti's *Rocco and his Brothers.*
Black Orpheus.
The Entertainer.
The Lady With the Little Dog.
Shadows, the cinema of improvisation.

X **Sport**

Olympic Games at Rome.
Go-Karting becomes popular.
Barbara Moore, aged 56, sets off, *Jan.* 13th, to walk from John o'Groats to Land's End; next month Billy Butlin sponsors a walk over the same course which is won by James Musgrave of Doncaster and Wendy Lewis of Liverpool.

Y **Statistics**

Total weekly hours of broadcasts to other countries: East European countries, 1,094; U.S.S.R., 1,002; China, 724; Voice of America, 602; B.B.C., 589; W. Germany, 315; France, 314.
Ownership of private cars (in mill.): U.S., 75; France, 7·3; Great Britain, 6·5; Canada, 5; W. Germany, 4·5; U.S.S.R., 3·8.
Population of Cities (in mill.): Tokio, 9·6; London, 8·1; New York, 7·7; Shanghai, 6·2; Moscow, 5; Mexico City, 4·8; Buenos Aires, 4·5; Bombay, 4·1.

G **Jul**: 7th, Belgium sends troops to Congo;
8th, Lumumba appeals to U.N.
11th, Moise Tshombe, premier of Katanga, proclaims independence of that province;
— (–12th), France agrees to independence from *Aug.* of the Republics of Dahomey, Niger, Upper Volta, Ivory Coast, Chad, Central Africa and the Congo;
14th, Léopoldville government severs relations with Belgium;
15th, U.N. emergency force arrives in Congo;
—, W. Germany agrees to compensate French victims of Nazi persecution;
18th, Hayato Ikeda, Liberal Democrat, premier of Japan;
19th, U.S.S.R. protests at U.S. proposal to equip Bundeswehr with Polaris missile;
20th, Poland asks N.A.T.O. powers to acknowledge Oder-Neisse line (*Aug.* 12th, Britain states that Germany's frontiers depended on a peace treaty);
21st, Mrs. Sirimavo Bandaranaike, Freedom Party, premier of Ceylon after elections (the first woman premier of the Commonwealth);
25th, Nyasaland Constitutional Conference in London;
27th, on Heathcoat Amory's retirement Selwyn Lloyd becomes Chancellor of the Exchequer and Lord Home Foreign Secretary.

H **Aug**: 8th, U.N. demands evacuation of Belgian troops from Congo (last leave, *Sept.* 2nd);
9th, *coup d'état* in Laos;
12th, Ceylon government takes over press;
—, Dag Hammarskjöld and U.N. troops enter Katanga;
16th, Cyprus becomes an independent republic with Archbishop Makarios President;
19th, U.S. prohibits aid funds to be used for purchasing Cuban sugar;
25th (–31st), independent African states confer at Léopoldville;
—, Russian Communist Party's manifesto condemns dogmatism of Mao Tse-tung;
29th, assassination of Hazza el-Majali, premier of Jordan;
30th, E. Germany imposes partial blockade of W. Berlin (further restrictions on entry, *Sept.* 8th).

J **Sep**: 2nd, U.S.S.R. provides aircraft for Patrice Lumumba in the Congo;
—, Cuba recognises Communist China and denounces 1952 military aid treaty with U.S.;
5th, President Kasavubu of Congo dismisses P. Lumumba and Joseph Ileo forms a ministry;
12th, George Woodcock elected T.U.C. secretary;
19th, India and Pakistan treaty on Indus waters development;
20th, Commonwealth African Assistance Plan founded;
22nd, St. Pancras rent riots by tenants hit by 1957 Rent Act;
23rd, N. Khrushchev addresses U.N. General Assembly on colonial peoples and disarmament (–*Oct.* 13th);
28th, N.A.T.O. unified system of air defence command;
29th, Harold Macmillan addresses U.N.

K **Oct**: 1st, independence of Nigerian Federation;
5th, Hugh Gaitskell battles against Labour unilateralists at Scarborough Conference;
—, S. African referendum favours republic;
11th, Lord Monckton's Report on federation of the Rhodesias and Nyasaland;
15th, trial of 800 members of Menderes' régime in Turkey.
19th, U.S. embargo on shipments to Cuba;
20th, Harold Wilson unsuccessfully opposes Hugh Gaitskell in election for leadership of Parliamentary Labour Party.

Continued opposite)

Y **Statistics** (*cont.*)

TV sets (in mill.): U.S., 85; Great Britain, 10·4; W. Germany, 2; France, 1·5.

Crime in Great Britain, 398,180 indictable offences, of which 14,257 are crimes against the person. 57,363 juveniles, under 17, are indicted in U.S. total of 1,861,300 indictable offences, of which 154,930 are crimes against the person.

Britain's daily prison population totals 30,206.

Z **Births and Deaths**

Feb. 10th Aloizje Stephinac d. (62).
Feb. 11th Ernest Dohnányi d. (82).
May 30th Boris Pasternak d. (69).
May 31st Walter Funk d. (69).
July 16th Albert Kesselring d. (74).
Aug. 19th Lewis Namier d. (72).
Aug. 23rd Oscar Hammerstein d. (65).
Sept. 7th Wilhelm Pieck d. (84).
Sept. 9th Jussi Bjoerling d. (49).
Sept. 27th Sylvia Pankhurst d. (78).
Nov. 3rd Harold Spencer Jones d. (70).

L **Nov:** 1st, Harold Macmillan announces bill for facilities for U.S. Polaris submarines at Holy Loch;

8th, in U.S. presidential election, John F. Kennedy, Democrat, wins 303 votes over Richard Nixon, Republican, with 209, but Democrats lose 21 seats in House of Representatives; L. B. Johnson, Vice-President; 34,221,531 votes for Kennedy, 34,108,474 for Nixon and 502,773 for minor candidates; Kennedy subsequently nominates C. D. Dillon as secretary of treasury and R. S. McNamara defence secretary;

10th, Provisional People's Consultative Congress meets in Indonesia;

26th, National Party defeats Labour in New Zealand elections (*Dec.* 12th, K. J. Holyoake forms ministry);

28th, Mauritania becomes an independent Islamic republic.

M **Dec:** 2nd, Britain refuses request of Buganda for independence;

13th, Patrice Lumumba arrested and Antoine Gizenga forms ministry in Congo;

—, some 50 Labour back-benchers refuse to follow Hugh Gaitskell in defence debate;

—, revolution in Ethiopia (collapses, 19th);

14th, convention of Organisation for Economic Co-operation and Development (O.E.C.D.) signed in Paris by Canada, U.S. and 18 O.E.E.C. member countries to provide an Atlantic economic community;

—, King Baudouin of Belgium marries Doña Fabiola of Spain;

21st, King Saud takes over Saudi Arabian government on resignation of premier, Emir Faisal;

23rd, resignation of J. E. de Quay, Netherlands premier, following Protestant Parties siding with Labour on housing motion;

31st, Cuba requests U.N. Security Council to consider its complaint of U.S. aggression.

N

1961 (Jan.–Apr.) Army revolt in Algeria—S. Africa leaves the Commonwealth—The Berlin Wall—Dag Hammarskjöld dies in Congo

A **Jan**: 1st, farthings no longer legal tender in Britain;
3rd, U.S. severs relations with Cuba;
6th, Dag Hammarskjöld visits S. Africa to discuss *apartheid*;
—, (–8th), massive support in France for President de Gaulle's referendum on Algiers though 40 per cent of the electorate in Algeria abstain;
7th, Casablanca Conference of heads of state in Africa issues African Charter;
19th, Michael Ramsey appointed Archbishop of Canterbury on retirement of Archbishop Fisher;
20th, Queen Elizabeth II begins tour of India, Pakistan, Persia and Cyprus;
—, J. Kennedy inaugurated President of U.S.
26th, Britain and United Arab Republic resume full relations;
28th, Ruanda provisional government proclaims Republic, and is placed under U.N. trusteeship;
30th, civil disobedience campaign in Ceylon.

B **Feb**: 1st, Enoch Powell, British Minister of Health, increases health service charges;
4th, terrorist outbreaks in Angola;
9th, Leonid Brezhnev's 'plane intercepted by French fighter over Mediterranean;
—, President Kasavubu establishes a Central Congolese government with Joseph Ileo premier;
—, Royal Commission on British Press appointed;
10th, U.S. relinquishes rights in many defence bases in W. Indies under 1941 agreement;
11th, in Cameroons plebiscite, supervised by U.N., N. Cameroons vote for joining Nigeria, S. Cameroons for joining Cameroun;
13th, U.N. Security Council urges use of force to prevent civil war in Congo and demands enquiry into P. Lumumba's death (*Jan.* 17th);
14th, S. Africa's new decimal coinage, the Rand, in force;
16th, Cyprus votes to apply for membership of Commonwealth;
22nd, Konrad Adenauer visits London;
—, N. Khrushchev wages campaign against Dag Hammarskjöld, U.N. Secretary-General, and calls on commission of African states to supervise restoration of an independent Congo;
27th, Britain and Iceland settle fisheries dispute.

C **Mar**: 1st, John F. Kennedy establishes Peace Corps of Young Americans for overseas service;
7th, Lord Salisbury's attack on Iain Macleod, Colonial Secretary, for his liberal African policy;
8th (–17th), at meeting of Commonwealth Prime Ministers in London, H. Verwoerd announces S. Africa will leave Commonwealth on *May* 31st;
—, Congolese leaders agree on confederation under President Kasavubu;
9th, Dalai Lama appeals to U.N. to restore independence of Tibet;
21st (–*Sept.* 9th), three-power conference on discontinuance of nuclear tests;
26th, in Belgian elections Christian Socialists win most seats and form coalition with Socialists;
—, Harold Macmillan meets John F. Kennedy at Key West, Florida;
29th, in S. Africa treason trial all 28 accused are acquitted.

D **Apr**: 7th, U.N. General Assembly condemns S. African policies in South-West Africa (a U.N. Committee is later refused entry-permit to the territory);
11th, Conservative back-bench revolt by supporting amendment for bringing back the birch to R. A. Butler's Criminal Justice bill;
—, Nigeria imposes total boycott on S. African trade;

O **Politics, Economics, Law and Education**

Leon Radzinowycz, *In Search of Criminology*.

Raymond Williams, *The Long Revolution*.

Election Court rules that A. N. Wedgwood Benn is disqualified to serve as an M.P. through succession to Stansgate peerage.

Adolf Eichmann is found guilty of crimes against the Jewish people in trial in Israel (*Dec.*).

Trials in London of the spies Gordon Lonsdale and the Krogers (*Mar.*) and George Blake (*May*).

Sit-down demonstrations by C.N.D. members in Trafalgar Square, where police make 1,314 arrests (*Sept.* 17th–18th).

Freedom rides of young Negroes in U.S. southern states to protest against segregation.

New Towns Commission established under Andrew Duncan.

Five Welsh counties vote for Sunday opening of public houses.

University of Sussex founded.

P **Science, Technology, Discovery, etc.**

Major Yuri Gagarin of U.S.S.R. becomes first space-man, being orbited in a 6-ton satellite (*Apr.* 12th).

Alan Shepard of U.S. makes re-entry in capsule through atmosphere (*May* 5th).

Martin Ryle concludes from radio-astronomical observations that the universe changes with time. His burial of 'the steady state' theory is challenged by Fred Hoyle.

Claus and Nagy of New York conclude from study of organisms on meteorites in museums that life in the universe must be common.

Crick and Brenner claim to determine the structure of deoxyribonucleic acid (DNA), thus breaking the genetic code.

Leucotomy operation begins controversy.

New operation for treating deafness.

The Barnet Ventilation electric lung pump.

The national electrical grids of France and Britain are connected by cable.

Britain imports methane from the Sahara to supplement coal-gas.

The Atlas computer, the world's largest, is installed at Harwell, to aid atomic research and weather forecasting.

Conference in Tanganyika (*Sept.*) for preserving African wildlife.

Q **Scholarship**

New English Bible, New Testament, appears on 350th anniversary of Authorised Version.

Lord Hankey, *The Supreme Command*.

R **Philosophy and Religion**

Stephen Neil, *Christian Faith and Other Faiths*.

R. Niebuhr, *The Self and the Dramas of History*.

Papal Encyclicals on Catholic social doctrine (*July* 14th) and for Christian reconciliation under Rome's primacy (*Aeterna Dei*, *Dec.*).

Prepai tions for Vatican Council.

Delhi meeting of World Council of Churches (*Nov.* 19th) is joined by members of Russian Orthodox Church and of Pentecostal Churches of Chile and is attended by Roman Catholic observers.

The International Missionary Council is integrated with the World Council of Churches.

Closure of Synagogues in Moscow.

D **Apr:** 11th Alphons Gorbach, People's Party, succeeds Julius Raab as Austrian chancellor;
13th, U.N. General Assembly condemns *apartheid*;
17th, Cuba invaded by rebel forces, which are defeated by Fidel Castro;
—, Selwyn Lloyd's Budget raises starting-point of surtax to £4,000;
18th, Kenya African Democratic Union agrees to form government providing a house is built for Jomo Kenyatta in Kiambu district (Kenyatta is released by governor, *Aug.* 14th);
21st, U.N. calls for elections in Ruanda and Urundi;
—, army revolt in Algeria under General Maurice Challe (collapses, 26th, rebel leaders are tried, including General Salan, *July* 11th, and sentenced *in absentia* to death);
24th, Britain and U.S.S.R. appeal for cease-fire in Laos (where the international control commission arrives, *May* 8th);
—, at Coquilhatville conference of Congolese delegates, President Tshombe of Katanga denounces President Kasavubu's agreement with U.N. and is arrested after walking out of conference;
27th, Sierre Leone becomes independent within the Commonwealth.

E **May:** 1st, Tanganyika achieves full internal self-government with Julius Nyerere as premier;
—, Kwame Nkrumah takes over control of Convention People's Party in Ghana;
9th, Ali Amini, the new premier of Iran, dissolves Parliament and bans political meetings;
11th, following sentence of 42 years on the spy George Blake, Lord Radcliffe is appointed to review security procedures;
12th, foundation of a United States of the Congo, with Léopoldville the federal capital;
24th, Cyprus becomes 16th member of Council of Europe;
25th, President Kennedy presents an extra-ordinary state of Union message to Congress for increased funds urgently needed for U.S. space, defense and air programmes;
27th, Constituent Assembly proposes new Turkish constitution;
—, Tunku Abdul Rahman, Malayan premier, proposes a Greater Malaysian Federation;
28th, last journey of 'Orient Express', Paris–Bucharest, after 78 years;
29th, Western European Union agrees that W. Germany be allowed to build destroyers equipped to fire nuclear weapons;
30th, United Arab Republic breaks off relations with S. Africa;
31st, S. Africa becomes an independent republic outside the Commonwealth, with C. R. Swart President;
—, Ghana refuses to recognise S. Africa;
—, John F. Kennedy visits France, Vienna and London.

F **Jun:** 1st (–8th), rioting during Zanzibar elections;
2nd, Latin America free trade association in force;
4th, N. Khrushchev proposes to President Kennedy a German peace conference to conclude a treaty and establish Berlin as a free city and also proposes that disarmament discussions should proceed simultaneously with test ban talks (rejected by the West, *July* 17th);
5th, U.S. Supreme Court rules that Communist Party should register as a foreign-dominated organisation (Party refuses, *Nov.* 17th);
7th, U.S.S.R.-Italian trade pact;
9th, U.N. calls on Portugal to cease repressive measures in Angola;
13th, Austria refuses application of Archduke Otto of Hapsburg to return as a private individual;

S Art, Sculpture, Fine Arts and Architecture

Painting:

Theft of Goya's *Duke of Wellington* from National Gallery (*Aug.* 21st).

Sculpture:

F. E. McWilliam, *Resistance*.

Architecture:

E. Maufe, Guildford Cathedral completed.

A. and P. Smithson, *The Economist* group of buildings, London (–63).

E. Saarinen, T.W.A. Building, Kennedy (Idlewild) Airport, completed.

G. Maunsell and others, Hammersmith Flyover road bridge (prestressed concrete, precast sections, with electric road surface heating cables).

Hardwick's Euston portico is demolished, despite protests.

Bill Brandt, *Perspectives of Nudes* (photographs).

T Music

B. Britten, *A Midsummer Night's Dream* (opera).

Hans W. Henze, *Elegy for Young Lovers*.

Zoltan Kodály, Symphony.

Luigi Nono, *Intoleranza*.

F. Ashton's new production of *Les Deux Pigeons* (Messager—ballet).

Royal Ballet visits U.S.S.R.

Cellist Jacqueline du Pré makes her debut as a soloist, in London.

U Literature

John Masefield, *The Bluebells and Other Verse*.

Iris Murdoch, *A Severed Head*.

J. D. Salinger, *Franny and Zooey*.

V The Press

W Drama and Entertainment

J. Anouilh, *Becket*.

J. Osborne, *Luther*.

Harold Pinter, *The Collection*.

Lionel Bart, *Oliver* (musical).

Beyond the Fringe (revue).

Films:

M. Antonioni's *La Notte*.

Anthony Mann's *El Cid*.

Alain Resnais' *L'Année dernière à Marienbad*.

Tony Richardson's *A Taste of Honey*.

François Truffaut's *Jules et Jim* with Jeanne Moreau.

Breakfast at Tiffany's with Audrey Hepburn.

Elektra.

Whistle down the Wind.

The Age of Kings (Shakespeare's historical plays—television).

'Children's Hour' ends (*Apr.*—broadcasting).

X Sport

Roger Maris hits 61 home runs.

Y Statistics

Populations (in mill.): China, 660; India, 435; U.S.S.R., 209; U.S., 179 (of which 159 white, 19 negro and 1 other races); Japan, 95; Pakistan, 94; Brazil, 66; West Germany, 54; Great Britain, 53; Italy, 50; France, 47.

F **Jun**: 19th, Britain abrogates Anglo-Kuwait agreement of 1899;
—, U.S. and U.S.S.R. representatives begin disarmament talks in Washington;
20th, Kuwait admitted to Arab League, but membership of U.N. vetoed by U.S.S.R.;
22nd, President Tshombe is freed;
25th, Abdul Karim Kassem declares Kuwait an integral part of Iraq;
30th, Britain answers Kuwait's request for troops (withdrawn, *Aug.* 13th);
—, Konrad Adenauer appeals for a German peace treaty based on right of self-determination;
Hugh Gaitskell's final victory over Labour Party unilateralists.

G **Jul**: 7th, U.S.S.R. trade fair in London;
10th (–25th), Kwame Nkrumah visits U.S.S.R.;
17th, new Constitution in force in British Guiana;
22nd, U.N. orders cease-fire after clashes between French and Tunisians in Tunisia;
23rd, referendum for new constitution in S. Rhodesia;
25th, Selwyn Lloyd's emergency Budget begins wages pause; and bank rate is raised from 5 to 7 per cent.

H **Aug**: 10th, Britain applies for membership of E.E.C.;
13th, E. Germany seals off border between E. and W. Berlin, closing the Brandenburg Gate;
15th, Hastings Banda's Malawi Congress Party victorious in Nyasaland elections;
17th (–18th), Berlin Wall constructed and the Western Powers in alarm reinforce garrison;
19th, John F. Kennedy sends Vice-President Johnson to Berlin;
21st, Cheddi Jagan's party returns to power in British Guiana elections;
25th, President de Gaulle states France will not evacuate Bizerta until international crisis is over;
27th, Ben Khedda forms provisional government in Algeria;
31st, last Spanish troops leave Morocco.

J **Sep**: 1st, U.N. breaks off relations with Katanga government; attempts of U.N. to arrest members of the government lead to heavy fighting in Elisabethville and Jadotville;
— (–6th), non-aligned powers meet in Belgrade under President Nehru and Kwame Nkrumah;
10th, Pope John XXIII appeals in TV broadcast for world peace;
14th, New Zealand introduces compulsory selective national service;
17th, Christian Democratic Union and allies lose overall majority in W. German elections;
— (–18th), Dag Hammarskjöld killed in air crash in Congo (aged 56); (U Thant acting Secretary-General from *Nov.* 3rd);
19th, Jamaican referendum to secede from W. Indies Federation;
28th, Kwame Nkrumah detains leading members of Ghana opposition;
—, army *coup* in Damascus;
29th, Syria secedes from United Arab Republic and forms Syrian Arab Republic.

K **Oct**: 5th, Shah of Iran hands over properties to Pahlevi Foundation to be used for educational and charitable purposes;
9th, Uganda Constitutional Conference ends with agreement for internal self-government in *Nov.* 1962;
10th, statement of Edward Heath, Lord Privy Seal, to E.E.C. Council of Ministers on Britain's approach to Common Market (negotiations begin, *Nov.* 8th);
—, volcanic eruption in Tristan da Cunha;
21st, President Nasser confiscates property of wealthy Egyptians;

(*Continued opposite*)

Y **Statistics** (*cont.*)

Petroleum production (in mill. barrels): U.S., 2,600 (being 60 per cent of world total); U.S.S.R., 1,075.

Cotton yarn production (percentages of world total): U.S., 28; U.S.S.R., 16; India, 12; Japan, 10; Germany, 6; Great Britain, 5.

Z **Births and Deaths**

Jan. 17th Patrice Lumumba d. (35).
Jan. 31st Dorothy Thompson d. (66).
Mar. 8th Thomas Beecham d. (81).
June 2nd George S. Kaufman d. (71).
June 6th Carl Gustav Jung d. (85).
July 1st Lady Diana Spencer b. (–).
July 2nd Ernest Hemingway d. (61).
Sept. 17th A. Menderes d. (62).
Sept. 24th Sumner Welles d. (68).
Oct. 1st William Reid Dick d. (82).
Oct. 14th Paul Ramadier d. (73).
Oct. 19th Werner Jaeger d. (73).
Oct. 30th Luigi Einaudi d. (87).

K **Oct**: 27th, Mauritania and Mongolia admitted to U.N.

29th, C. Karamanlis forms new ministry in Greece after victory of National Radical Union in elections.

L **Nov**: 2nd, David Ben Gurion forms new coalition in Israel after long negotiations;

8th (–*Dec.* 16th), Queen Elizabeth visits Ghana and other African territories;

16th, R. A. Butler introduces Commonwealth Immigration bill;

19th, Garfield Todd holds inaugural meeting of Rhodesian New African Party;

21st, British government fails to stop Electricity Council granting substantial wage increase, which mocks wages pause;

24th, President de Gaulle visits Harold Macmillan;

—, U.N. General Assembly resolves to treat Africa as a denuclearised zone; and

28th, calls for independence of remaining colonial peoples.

M **Dec**: 4th, Barbados Labour Party led by Grantley Adams, premier of W. Indies Federation, loses seats in Barbados elections;

4th, People's National Movement led by Eric Williams returns to power in Trinidad;

5th, U.N. force launches attack in Katanga;

6th, Order-in-Council for Southern Rhodesian Constitution; to come into effect after holding of new elections;

9th, R. G. Menzies' Liberal-Country Party returns to power in Australia following general election;

—, U.S.S.R. breaks off relations with Albania;

15th, U.N. General Assembly rejects U.S.S.R. proposal to admit Communist China to U.N., though Britain votes in favour;

16th, U.S. loan to Ghana for Volta River project;

18th, Indian forces invade Goa (which surrenders, 19th);

—, U.N. cease-fire in Katanga; and

21st, Tshombe agrees to end secession of Katanga;

— (–22nd), Harold Macmillan meets John F. Kennedy in Bermuda;

31st, Lebanese army prevents *coup* of Syrian Popular Party in Beirut.

A **Jan**: 1st, Western Samoa becomes first sovereign independent Polynesian State;
3rd, President Sukarno proclaims West New Guinea an independent province;
5th (–16th), work-to-rule by Civil Service Clerical Association in protest at withdrawal of arbitration through pay pause;
6th, Princes of Laos invited to Geneva for joint negotiations;
9th, U.S.S.R.-Cuban trade pact;
14th, E.E.C. agrees on agricultural policy;
22nd, Julius Nyerere resigns in Tanganyika and Rashidj Kawawa forms ministry;
25th, African heads of state of Monrovia group (Liberia, Togo, Nigeria and Cameroun) issue Lagos Charter for pan-African co-operation;
29th, three-power conference on weapon tests at Geneva collapses.

B **Feb**: 8th, U.S. military council established in South Vietnam;
—, anti-O.A.S. riots in Paris;
10th, N. Khrushchev proposes 18-nation disarmament committee should meet at summit level;
12th, six members of C.N.D. Committee of 100 found guilty of breach of Official Secrets Act in conspiring to enter an R.A.F. base, and sentenced to imprisonment;
14th, T.U.C. agrees to join National Economic Development Council;
—, Kenya constitutional conference opens in London;
16th, anti-government riots in Georgetown, British Guiana;
23rd, U.N. Trusteeship Committee resolves to consider whether Southern Rhodesia has attained full self-government (see *Oct.* 31st).

C **Mar**: 1st, Uganda attains full internal self-government, with Benedicte Kiwanuka premier;
2nd, Britain applies to join European Coal and Steel Community;
—, in Burmese military *coup* Ne Win overthrows U Nu;
3rd, Borg Olivier, Nationalist, forms ministry in Malta;
5th, Britain applies to join Euratom;
14th, 17 foreign ministers attend Geneva disarmament conference, but France refuses to participate;
—, Eric Lubbock, Liberal, wins Orpington by-election with 7,855 majority (in 1959 election Conservative majority of 14,760);
18th, cease-fire in Algeria and establishment of *Front de la Libération Nationale* provisional government;
19th, W. Germany agrees to contribute to costs of B.A.O.R.;
23rd, Scandinavian States of Nordic Council sign Helsinki convention;
28th, Syrian army revolt fails;
31st, end of pay pause in Britain.

D **Apr**: 1st, Swiss referendum rejects manufacture or import of atomic weapons;
9th, British Budget introduces levy on speculative gains;
11th, Alexander Bustamante, Labour, forms ministry in Jamaica;
14th, M. Debré resigns in France; and
15th, Georges Pompidou forms ministry;
18th, end of West Indies Federation;
20th, O.A.S. leader Raoul Salan captured in Algiers;
22nd, renewed fighting in Laos;
25th, N. Khrushchev heads commission to draft new U.S.S.R. Constitution;
27th, United Federal Party is returned in Central African Federation elections which are boycotted by the European Opposition and all the African political parties.

O **Politics, Economics, Law and Education**

National Incomes Commission established in Britain (*Nov.* 5th)

Anthony Sampson, *The Anatomy of Britain.*

T. H. White, *The Making of the President.*

Commonwealth Immigrants Act in Britain to control immigration, especially from West Indies and Pakistan (in force *July* 1st).

British Net Book Agreement is upheld by Restrictive Practices Court.

Reorganisation of internal structure of London Stock Exchange.

Washington Supreme Court rules the reading of prayers in New York schools unconstitutional.

Annan Committee's Report on Teaching of Russian in British Schools (*June* 7th).

Rochdale Committee's Report on British Docks (*Sept.* 26th).

P **Science, Technology, Discovery, etc.**

U.S. astronauts John Glenn (*Feb.*) and M. Scott Carpenter (*May*) are put in orbit.

Satellite Telstar, launched at Cape Canaveral (*July* 10th), circles the earth every 157·8 mins., enabling live TV pictures transmitted from Andover, Maine, to be received at Goonhilly Down, Cornwall, and in Brittany (*July* 11th).

U.S. also launch the rocket Mariner, to explore Venus, and the British satellite Aerial, to study cosmic radiation.

Further advances in molecular biology, under Max Perutz.

Chudinov claims to have revived fossil algae some 250 million years old.

Twenty years after the beginning of the nuclear age U.S. has 200 atomic reactors in operation, Great Britain, 39 and U.S.S.R., 39.

Congenital malformation of babies due to side effects of thalidomide drug.

Report of Royal College of Physicians on Smoking and Health.

British weather reports give temperatures in centigrade as well as Fahrenheit (from *Jan.* 15th).

Q **Scholarship**

F. W. Deakin, *The Brutal Friendship.*

R **Philosophy and Religion**

J. L. Austin, *Sense and Sensibilia.*

Pope John XXIII insists on retention of Latin as the language of the Roman Catholic Church (*Apr.* 1st).

Vatican Council opens in Rome (*Oct.* 11th), with observer delegates from other Christian churches. Pope John orders the controversial document on Sources of Revelation to be revised.

1,100 Mormon missionaries campaign in England. Negroes are refused admission to Mormon priesthood.

8,000 English members of the Exclusive Brethren are expelled through unwillingness to accept decree forbidding contact with non-members.

S **Art, Sculpture, Fine Arts and Architecture**

Painting:

Royal Academy sells Leonardo da Vinci's cartoon of *The Virgin and Child*, which is ultimately purchased for the National Gallery.

A gallery is opened at Buckingham Palace to exhibit royal treasures.

S. Nolan, 'Kelly' series.

O. Kokoschka's autobiography, *Ringed With Vision.*

E **May**: 6th, Antonio Segni elected President of Italy on 9th ballot;
11th, Sarvepalli Radhakrishnan elected President of India (to 1967);
12th, S. African General Law Amendment bill imposes death penalty for sabotage;
—, British dock-workers awarded 9 per cent pay increase;
14th, Milovan Djilas, former Vice-President of Yugoslavia, given further sentence for publishing *Conversations with Stalin*;
24th, Conference of Barbados, Windward and Leeward Islands in London ends with proposal of 'Little Eight' to form new West Indies federation;
29th, state of emergency in W. Nigerian political crisis;
31st, Adolf Eichmann hanged after Israeli Court rejects appeal.

F **Jun**: 14th, European Space Research Organisation established at Paris;
14th, Conservative candidate loses deposit at W. Lothian by-election;
18th, Progressive Conservatives lose overall majority in Canadian elections, but John Diefenbaker remains as premier;
21st, U.S. concern at Chinese concentrations on mainland opposite Quemoy;
26th, Portuguese in Mozambique require Indian nationals to leave within three months of release from internment camps.

G **Jul**: 1st, Robert Soblen, sentenced to life imprisonment in U.S.A. for spying, arrives in London, following deportation from Jordan (British Home Secretary refuses to grant asylum and Soblen commits suicide, *Sept.* 11th);
—, independence of Ruanda Republic and of Kingdom of Burundi;
3rd, France proclaims independence of Algeria, following referendum of 99 per cent in favour, and the provisional government in exile returns;
4th, President Kennedy's speech envisaging partnership between U.S. and a United Europe;
12th, Conservatives at bottom of poll in Leicester North by-election;
13th, Harold Macmillan dismisses seven of his cabinet, including Lord Kilmuir, Selwyn Lloyd, David Eccles and Harold Watkinson, in an attempt to retrieve Conservative fortunes, and Reginald Maudling becomes Chancellor of the Exchequer;
20th, Laotian neutrality is guaranteed at Geneva conference;
22nd, Union movement under Oswald Mosley holds meeting in London;
31st, Britain agrees to establish a wider Malaysian Federation.

H **Aug**: 1st, attempted assassination of Kwame Nkrumah in Ghana;
6th, Jamaica becomes independent within the Commonwealth;
7th, Britain and United Arab Republic sign agreement for compensating British subjects whose property was seized after Suez;
13th, Ghana expels Archbishop of West Africa;
15th, Netherlands and Indonesia settle West New Guinea dispute;
16th, agreement signed in London for Aden to enter the Federation of S. Arabia;
—, Algeria is admitted to the Arab League;
20th, Malta requests independence within Commonwealth on breakdown of talks for financial aid;
22nd, President de Gaulle escapes assassination;
—, Arab League meets to discuss Syrian allegations of interference in internal affairs by United Arab Republic;
31st, Trinidad and Tobago become an independent nation within the Commonwealth.

J **Sep**: 1st, Singapore, and 12th, North Borneo, vote to join Malaysian Federation;
—, Iranian earthquake disaster;
2nd, U.S.S.R. agrees to send arms to Cuba;

S Art, Sculpture, Fine Arts and Architecture *(cont.)*

Architecture:

Coventry Cathedral is consecrated (*May* 25th); architect, Basil Spence; engraved windows, John Hutton; sculpture, J. Epstein; baptistery window, J. Piper; ten nave windows, Lawrence Lee; tapestry, Graham Sutherland.

Pan-American Airways Building, New York, provides world's largest office accommodation.

T Music

Michael Tippett, *King Priam* (opera).

Aaron Copland-Carter, *Improvisations* (ballet).

U Literature

W. Faulkner, *The Reivers* (posth.).

F. R. Leavis's Richmond Lecture attacks C. P. Snow's view of the Two Cultures.

Henry Miller's *Tropic of Capricorn* is published in England.

B. Pasternak, *In the Interlude* (poems).

Alexander Solzhenitsyn, *One day in the Life of Ivan Denisovich.*

V The Press

Private Eye is issued.

The Sunday Times issues a colour supplement.

W Drama and Entertainment

Edward Albee, *Who's Afraid of Virginia Woolf?*

Arnold Wesker, *Chips with Everything.*

B.B.C. Television, *That Was The Week That Was.*

Pilkington Report on Broadcasting in Britain (*June* 27th) strongly supports B.B.C.

New York broadcasting station (WBAI) performs Wagner's *Ring* in its entirety without a break.

Films:

Ingmar Bergman's *Winter Night.*

Jules Dassin's *Phaedra.*

John Ford's *How the West Was Won.*

John Frankenheimer's *The Manchurian Candidate.*

David Lean's *Lawrence of Arabia.*

Orson Welles's *The Trial.*

Advise and Consent.

A Kind of Loving.

The Birds.

Cleopatra, starring Elizabeth Taylor and Richard Burton.

X Sport

Brazil wins World Cup football final.

British driver Graham Hill wins world Grand Prix championship.

Y Statistics

Of the 230 mill. population of Africa, 29 mill. are Roman Catholics, 19 mill. Protestants, and 5 mill. from Coptic and Orthodox Churches. The religions of Africa total 2,000 sects.

Z Births and Deaths

Jan. 16th R. H. Tawney d. (81).

Jul. 20th G. M. Trevelyan d. (86).

J **Sep**: 3rd, Katanga government accepts U Thant's plan for Congolese reunification;
7th, Laos establishes diplomatic relations with Communist China and North Vietnam;
8th, Chinese troops cross McMahon line on Indian frontier;
9th (–13th), France resumes relations with Syria, Jordan and Saudi Arabia;
19th, Commonwealth premiers endorse Britain's resumed negotiations with E.E.C. to enter Common Market;
20th, Southern Rhodesia declares Zimbabwe African People's Union an unlawful body;
25th, Fidel Castro states U.S.S.R. intends to establish a base for its fishing fleet in Cuba;
26th, Ahmed Ben Bella elected premier of Algeria;
27th, army *coup* in Yemen; Colonel Abdulla el-Sallah becomes premier;
28th, United Arab Republic amends Constitution to provide for presidential council.

K **Oct**: 1st, U.N. takes over administration of West New Guinea from British;
5th, French National Assembly censures proposed referendum to sanction future president's election by popular mandate; and Georges Pompidou resigns but de Gaulle asks him to continue in office;
9th, Uganda becomes independent within the Commonwealth;
10th, *Der Spiegel* publishes article on N.A.T.O. exercise criticising weakness of Bundeswehr (the offices of the paper are occupied by the police, 16th);
11th, Congress passes U.S. Trade Expansion Act;
—, Hugh Foot resigns as Britain's U.N. representative on colonial questions in protest against British defence of Southern Rhodesian government;
16th, cease-fire in Congo;
20th, China launches offensive on Indian border positions;
22nd, John F. Kennedy announces in broadcast the installation of U.S.S.R. missile base in Cuba;
—, William Vassall, Admiralty clerk, sentenced for spying;
24th, U.S. blockade of Cuba;
26th, Khrushchev offers to withdraw missiles if U.S. removes bases from Turkey, a condition which Kennedy rejects;
28th, French referendum favours election of president by universal suffrage;
30th, U.N. General Assembly rejects U.S.S.R. proposal to admit Communist China;
31st, Krishna Menon, Indian defence minister, resigns;
—, U.N. General Assembly requests Britain to suspend enforcement of new Constitution in Southern Rhodesia (but Constitution comes into effect, *Nov.* 1st).

L **Nov**: 2nd, President Kennedy announces U.S.S.R. has been dismantling bases in Cuba;
—, Julius Nyerere elected President of Tanganyika;
—, Greville Wynne is arrested on espionage charge in Budapest and is later extradited to U.S.S.R.;
3rd, Anastas Mikoyan visits Cuba in connection with removal of missiles;
5th, Walter Strauss, W. German defence minister, dismissed over *Der Spiegel* affair (and 19th, five Free Democrat ministers resign);
—, U.N. General Assembly demands that all nuclear tests cease by *Jan.* 1st 1963;
—, U.S. Congressional elections leave Democrats in control of both houses;
—, Saudi Arabia severs relations with United Arab Republic;
8th, Thomas Galbraith, Civil Lord of Admiralty, resigns over Vassall affair;
—, George Brown defeats Harold Wilson in election for Labour Party deputy leadership;
9th, British Guiana constitutional conference in London breaks down;
10th, President of Yemen accuses Britain of plotting to overthrow régime;

(*Continued opposite*)

Z **Births and Deaths** (*cont.*)

Nov. 7th Eleanor Roosevelt d. (78).
Nov. 18th Niels Bohr d. (77).
Nov. 22nd René Coty d. (80).
Nov. 28th Queen Wilhelmina of the Netherlands d. (82).
Dec. 7th Kirsten Flagstad d. (67).

L **Nov**: 14th, Britain resumes negotiations with E.E.C.;
—, Harold Macmillan appoints Radcliffe tribunal to inquire into security;
20th, U.S.S.R. agrees to withdraw Ilyushin bombers from Cuba and U.S. announces end of blockade;
21st, China agrees to cease-fire on Sino-Indian border and forces subsequently withdraw;
22nd, Labour wins S. Dorset by-election through intervention of anti-common market candidate;
27th, Britain signs agreement to provide India with arms to resist Chinese aggression;
28th, President de Gaulle reprieves death sentence on Edmund Jouhaud for O.A.S. crimes;
29th, Anglo-French agreement to develop 'Concord' supersonic airliner;
30th, U Thant is elected U.N. Secretary-General.

M **Dec**: 4th, Western European Union Assembly in Paris calls for single N.A.T.O. nuclear force;
5th, U.S.-U.S.S.R. agreement on co-operation for peaceful uses of outer space;
—, Dean Acheson in West Point speech suggests Britain is 'just about played out'.
8th, Brunei rebellion collapses after British intervention;
9th, Tanganyika becomes a republic within the Commonwealth, with Julius Nyerere President;
11th, West German coalition of Christian Democrats, Christian Socialists and Free Democrats;
14th, Edgar Whitehead's United Federal Party defeated in Southern Rhodesia elections by Winston Field's right-wing Rhodesian Front;
—, Northern Rhodesia's first African-dominated government, under Kenneth Kaunda;
17th, committee on Lords reform recommends that an heir be able to disclaim his peerage;
18th, at Nassau meeting President Kennedy and Harold Macmillan agree that U.S. shall provide Britain with Polaris missiles instead of Skybolt;
19th, Britain acknowledges Nyasaland's right to secede from the Central African Federation;
27th, India and Pakistan reopen talks on Kashmir;
28th, U.N. troops engaged in heavy fighting in Katanga and, 29th, occupy Elisabethville.

N

1963 (Jan.–May) Britain refused entry to Common Market—Test Ban Treaty—Assassination of President Kennedy

A **Jan**: 2nd, General Lemnitzer succeeds General Norstad as Supreme Allied Commander Europe;
3rd, U.N. force captures Jadotville in Katanga;
9th, Lord Hailsham appointed minister for the North-East;
14th, President de Gaulle states objections to Britain's entry into Common Market and rejects U.S. offer of Polaris missiles;
15th, President Tshombe accepts U.N. plan for secession of Katanga;
18th, Hugh Gaitskell, Leader of British Labour Party, dies (aged 56);
22nd, President de Gaulle and Konrad Adenauer sign Franco-German treaty of co-operation;
24th, Italy accepts U.S. plan for multilateral nuclear force;
29th, Britain is refused entry into Common Market.

B **Feb**: 1st, Nyasaland becomes self-governing with Hastings Banda premier;
6th, U.S. places shipping restrictions on Cuba;
8th, rebels in Baghdad assassinate premier Abdul Karim Kassem and Abdul Salam Arif replaces him;
9th, U.S.S.R. releases Archbishop of Lvov after 18 years imprisonment;
14th, Harold Wilson is elected Leader of British Labour Party;
19th, U.S.S.R. agrees to withdraw troops from Cuba;
20th, U.S. recommends that surface ships should be used to carry Polaris missiles in N.A.T.O. force;
21st, Royal Society Committee reports of emigration of British scientists;
28th, L.C.C. offers 100 per cent loans for houses.

C **Mar**: 4th, British government proposes a unified ministry of defence;
17th, typhoid epidemic breaks out in Zermatt;
22nd, John Profumo, British Secretary of State for War, makes personal statement in Commons in face of rumours (on *June* 4th admits its untruthfulness);
25th, Terence O'Neill succeeds Lord Brookeborough as prime minister of Northern Ireland;
26th, British Consumer Council appointed under Lady Elliot;
26th, demonstration by unemployed outside Parliament.

D **Apr**: 1st, end of New York newspaper strike after 114 days;
3rd, Reginald Maudling abolishes Schedule A taxation and increases investment allowances in Budget;
6th, Britain and U.S. sign Polaris missile agreement;
9th, Winston Churchill becomes an honorary citizen of U.S.;
12th, first armed attack by Indonesian forces on Malaysia;
15th, disorder breaks out in last stages of C.N.D. Aldermaston March;
17th, United Arab Republic, Syria and Iraq agree to federate;
20th, first report of National Incomes Commission rejects 40-hour agreement in Scottish building industry;
22nd, Lester B. Pearson, Liberal, forms ministry in Canada, following John Diefenbaker's resignation, 17th;
22nd (–*July* 8th), general strike in British Guiana with rioting and terrorism;
25th, report of Radcliffe tribunal on Vassal spy case;
28th, Fidel Castro visits U.S.S.R.

E **May**: 9th, Labour gains 544 seats in England and Wales borough elections;
16th, Chief Enahoro of Nigeria is deported from Britain (*Sept.* 7th he is sentenced in Lagos; the Attorney-General, John Hobson, is later charged unsuccessfully before his Inn for his share in the deportation);

O **Politics, Economics, Law and Education**

Graham Wootton, *The Politics of Influence.*

Beeching Report on *The Reshaping of British Railways* proposes development of freight traffic and the closure of many lines.

Buchanan Report, *Traffic in Towns.*

Campaign in London against rapacious landlords of slum tenements ('Rachmanism').

Newsom Committee's Report on education recommends raising school-leaving age to 16.

Robbins Report on higher education recommends six new universities and a new ministry.

Nobel Committee inquires into moral impact of TV on the young.

Teaching machines first used in British schools.

Supreme Council of National Economy established in U.S.S.R. (*Mar.* 13th).

Campaigns against trading stamps in Britain.

P **Science, Technology, Discovery, etc.**

Discovery of anti-xi-zero, a fundamental atomic particle of anti-matter.

U.S.S.R. puts in orbit Valentina Tereshkova (*June* 16th) for three-day flight in space to study the problem of weightlessness in a woman. Another cosmonaut launched the same day makes 82 orbits.

U.S. astronaut Gordon Cooper, launched in an Atlas rocket, makes 22 orbits (*May* 15th).

U.S. orbit a belt of copper needles as test for secure system of global radio communications.

Space research provides much data on conditions on Mars and Venus.

Vaccine for measles is perfected.

Alan Hodgkin and John Eccles make discoveries in the transmission of nerve impulses.

Rachel Carson in her book *The Silent Spring* draws attention to the dangers of chemical pest control.

Natural gas deposits in Groningen are developed.

Friction welding is invented.

Construction of the Victoria Underground line, London, begun.

Britain endures coldest *Jan.* and *Feb.* since 1740.

Queen Elizabeth Hospital, Hong Kong, the largest in the Commonwealth, completed.

Q **Scholarship**

Alvar Ellegård, *A Statistical Method for Determining Authorship.*

A computer is used to investigate the authorship of St. Paul's Epistles.

Edward Crankshaw, *The Fall of the House of Hapsburg.*

A. Deutscher, *The Prophet Outcast; Trotsky, 1929–40.*

R **Philosophy and Religion**

John Robinson, Bishop of Woolwich, *Honest to God*, arouses widespread interest. Discussion of it includes Archbishop Ramsey's *Image Old and New.*

Alec Vidler and others, *Objections to Christian Belief.*

G. M. Carstair's Reith Lectures, *This Island Now.*

Towards a Quaker View of Sex.

Anglican-Methodist *Conversations* towards unity.

G. H. von Wright, *The Varieties of Goodness.*

John XXIII's encyclical *Pacem in Terris* (*Apr.* 11th) deals with peaceful settlement of disputes and with relations with non-Catholics and with Communists.

Vatican Council approves use of vernacular liturgies.

Mary Lusk appeals to be ordained in ministry of Church of Scotland.

E **May:** 16th, Indian-Pakistani talks on Kashmir break down;
—, Geneva Conference on General Agreement on Tariffs and Trade (G.A.T.T.) begins 'Kennedy round' negotiations for tariff cuts.

F **Jun:** 3rd, death of Pope John XXIII (aged 81); (30th, Cardinal Montini is enthroned as Pope Paul VI);
4th, John Profumo resigns from Parliament, admitting he misled the House of Commons (on *Mar.* 22nd);
11th, Constantine Karamanlis, Greek premier, resigns in protest against King Paul's state visit to Britain;
18th, new constitution for Press Council (*Dec.* 11th, Lord Devlin becomes chairman);
19th, John F. Kennedy addresses Congress on civil rights;
20th, U.S.-U.S.S.R. agreement on a 'hot line' from the White House to the Kremlin;
21st, France withdraws naval Atlantic forces from N.A.T.O.;
25th, President Tshombe is forced to resign as Katanga premier;
29th, President Kennedy visits Harold Macmillan.

G **Jul:** 9th, demonstrations occur during state visit of King and Queen of Hellenes;
10th, Edward Boyle, British Minister of Education, imposes Remuneration of Teachers Act on the Burnham Committee;
20th, end of U.S.S.R.-Chinese ideological talks in Moscow;
22nd, agreement reached for British Guiana to be granted internal self-government in 1964;
23rd, Stephen Ward found guilty at Central Criminal Court of living on immoral earnings of Christine Keeler and others;
26th, Skopje earthquake in Yugoslavia;
30th, H. A. R. Philby, British journalist who disappeared from Beirut in *Jan.*, is granted asylum in U.S.S.R.;
31st, Peerage bill receives royal assent and A. N. Wedgwood Benn disclaims peerage.

H **Aug:** 1st, Britain agrees to grant independence to Malta in 1964;
—, minimum prison age raised to 17 by Criminal Justice Act;
5th, Britain, U.S. and U.S.S.R. sign nuclear test ban treaty (subsequently signed by 96 states, but not France, before coming into force, *Oct.* 1st);
8th, Glasgow–London mail train robbery of £2½ million near Cheddington, Bucks.;
21st, Buddhists arrested and martial law imposed in South Vietnam;
28th, 200,000 Negroes take part in peaceful demonstration for civil rights in Washington;
—, Congress compels the acceptance of arbitration in U.S. rail strike;
30th, release of Kenneth Abrahams who alleges he has been abducted from Bechuanaland by South African police.

J **Sep:** 4th, riots over school desegregation in Birmingham, Alabama;
15th, Negroes killed by bomb in Birmingham, Alabama;
16th, Malaya, North Borneo, Sarawak and Singapore form Federation of Malaysia which, 17th, breaks off relations with Indonesia, following Sukarno's increased hostility;
18th, U.N. Special Committee on *Apartheid* calls for prohibition of arms and petroleum traffic with South Africa;
19th, Anglo-French report favours Channel Tunnel project;
21st, V. Široký, premier of Czechoslovakia, is dismissed;
26th, Lord Denning's Report on the Profumo affair.

S Art, Sculpture, Fine Arts and Architecture

Painting:

Leonardo da Vinci's *Mona Lisa* exhibited in New York.

Goya Exhibition at Royal Academy.

Renewed interest in the 'Art Nouveau' period influences fabrics and design.

Sculpture:

F. E. McWilliam, 'Dame Ninette de Valois', sculpture for Covent Garden Opera House.

Architecture:

G. Bunshaft, Beinecke Library, Yale University (a windowless building).

Le Corbusier (pseud.), Carpenter Center for the Visual Arts, Harvard University.

Rohe, Museum of the 20th Century, Berlin.

James Bunning's London Coal Exchange is demolished.

Roebuck House, Victoria Street, a skyscraper overlooking Buckingham Palace Gardens.

T Music

A. Bliss, *Mary of Magdala*.

R. Smith-Brindle, *Homage to H. G. Wells*.

B. Britten, *War Requiem*.

M. Tippett, concerto for orchestra.

U Literature

James Baldwin, *The Fire Next Time*.

Günter Grass, *The Tin Drum*.

Louis MacNeice, *The Burning Perch*.

Mary McCarthy, *The Group*.

Iris Murdoch, *The Unicorn*.

John Updike, *The Centaur*.

New York court allows publication of John Cleland's *Fanny Hill*, but in England magistrates courts oppose publication.

V The Press

Two journalists appearing before the Radcliffe tribunal are imprisoned for refusing to reveal the sources of their information for tales about the spy Vassall (*Feb.* 4th).

W Drama and Entertainment

John Arden, *The Workhouse Donkey*.

Rolf Hochhuth, *The Representative*.

E. Ionescu, *Exit the King*.

H. de Montherlant, *Le Chaos et la Nuit*.

Films:

Ingmar Bergman's *The Silence*.

Stanley Donen's *Charade*.

Joseph L. Mankiewicz's *Cleopatra*, costing some £12 million, with Elizabeth Taylor.

Otto Preminger's *The Cardinal*.

Carol Reed's *The Running Man*.

Tony Richardson's *Tom Jones*.

Luchino Visconti's *The Leopard*.

Billy Wilder's *Irma La Douce*.

The Beatles make the Liverpool sound international.

Capri bans transistor radios.

K **Oct:** 1st, Nigeria becomes a republic within the Commonwealth, with Dr. Azikiwe President;
—, Britain agrees to join discussions about a N.A.T.O. mixed-manned nuclear fleet;
3rd, successful army *coup* in Honduras;
4th, release of Archbishop Beran of Prague after 14 years imprisonment;
—, devastating hurricane in Caribbean;
7th, U.N. Trusteeship Committee calls on Britain not to transfer armed forces of Rhodesian Federation to Southern Rhodesia;
9th, the Kabaka of Buganda becomes first President of Uganda;
11th, U.N. condemns repression in South Africa by 106 votes to 1;
15th, Ludwig Erhard becomes chancellor of West Germany on Konrad Adenauer's resignation;
18th, Harold Macmillan resigns premiership for reasons of health, and 19th, Earl of Home becomes premier (later disclaims peerage and, *Nov.* 8th, is elected M.P.);
20th, Iain Macleod and Enoch Powell refuse to serve in new Conservative ministry;
21st, government loan to Cunard Company for new liner agreed upon;
25th, Vatican Council approves principle of a fixed Easter;
26th, N. Khrushchev states U.S.S.R. would not race U.S. to the moon;
31st, Britain suspends aid to Indonesia.

L **Nov:** 1st, army *coup* in South Vietnam; President Ngo Dinh Diem assassinated;
22nd, President John F. Kennedy is assassinated by Lee H. Oswald in Dallas and L. B. Johnson is sworn in as President of U.S.;
24th, Oswald is shot by Jack Ruby;
30th, Liberal and Country Party coalition increases majority in Australian elections.

M **Dec:** 3rd, Lord Mancroft resigns from board of Norwich Union Insurance Society through Arab pressure;
4th, U.N. Security Council votes for partial embargo on arms to South Africa;
6th, Christine Keeler is sentenced for perjury in 'Lucky' Gordon case;
10th, Zanzibar becomes independent within the Commonwealth;
11th, Kwame Nkrumah dismisses Chief Justice of Ghana following acquittals in treason trials;
12th, Kenya becomes independent republic within the Commonwealth;
18th, African students riot in Red Square, Moscow, after the death of a Ghanaian;
19th, British Monopolies Commission recommends the abolition of price maintenance on car electrical equipment;
22nd, clashes in Cyprus between Greeks and Turks and, 30th, following visit by Duncan Sandys, a neutral zone is agreed upon;
—, Greek liner *Lakonia* catches fire and sinks in North Atlantic with loss of 150 lives;
25th, state of emergency in Somalia frontier region of Kenya;
31st, dissolution of Central African Federation of Rhodesia and Nyasaland.

N

X **Sport**

Y **Statistics**

Indian religious denominations (in mill.): Hindu, 366; Moslem, 47; Christian, 10; Buddhist, 3.

Z **Births and Deaths**

Jan. 29th Robert Lee Frost d. (88).
Jan. 30th Francis Poulenc d. (64).
Mar. 16th William Henry Beveridge d. (84).
Aug. 22nd William Richard Morris, Lord Nuffield d. (85).
Aug. 31st Georges Braque d. (81).
Oct. 11th Jean Cocteau d. (74).
Nov. 18th Frank Dobson d. (74).
Nov. 22nd Aldous Huxley d. (69) and John Fitzgerald Kennedy d. (46).
Dec. 30th Paul Hindemith d. (68).

1964 (Jan.–Apr.) U.S. Civil Rights Bill—Fall of Khrushchev—China explodes atom bomb—Indonesian landings in Malaya

A **Jan**: 7th, Cuba orders 400 British buses;
8th, L. B. Johnson's state of Union message proposes reduced spending on defence;
9th, anti-American riots in Panama which, 10th, breaks off diplomatic relations with U.S.;
12th, rebellion in Zanzibar, which is declared a republic, and the Sultan is banished;
15th, Cyprus constitutional conference opens in London, but fails to reach agreement
20th (–24th), mutinies of Tanganyika Rifles and of troops in Uganda and Kenya, which are quelled by British forces;
21st (–*Sept.* 17th), sixth session of 17-nation disarmament conference in Geneva;
22nd, Kenneth Kaunda, United National Independent Party, becomes first premier of Northern Rhodesia;
27th, France establishes diplomatic relations with Communist China;
28th, riots in Salisbury, Southern Rhodesia.

B **Feb**: 3rd, China challenges leadership of U.S.S.R.;
6th, Anglo-French agreement on a rail Channel Tunnel;
11th, fighting between Greeks and Turks at Limassol, Cyprus;
20th, Balzan International Foundation makes controversial award of peace prize to U.N., and Switzerland later blocks the Foundation's funds;
21st, attempted assassination of Ismet Inönü, Turkish premier;
22nd, Ghana becomes a one-party Socialist State;
23rd, Britain recognises President Abdul Amari Karume's régime in Zanzibar;
27th, Plowden Committee recommends union between Foreign Office and Commonwealth Relations Office overseas staff.

C **Mar**: 4th, government changes August Bank Holiday to last Monday in month from 1965;
6th, death of King Paul I of the Hellenes; succeeded by Constantine II;
9th, fighting in Ktima, Cyprus;
11th, South Africa withdraws from International Labour Organisation;
16th, L. B. Johnson submits £344 mill. bill to combat poverty;
19th, study on South-East of England anticipates considerable rise in population by 1981;
22nd, outbreaks of anti-Muslim violence in India;
25th, Sakari Tuomioja, Finland, appointed mediator in Cyprus dispute;
—, violence spreads in British Guiana after eight-week strike of sugar-workers (strike ends, *July* 26th);
27th, U.N. peace force under General Gyani, India, takes over in Cyprus;
30th, Easter week-end outbreaks of Mods *v.* Rockers disturbances in Clacton and other British resorts.

D **Apr**: 1st (–18th), strike of Belgian doctors;
2nd, Yemen alleges British air attack on *Mar.* 28th;
4th, Archbishop Makarios abrogates 1960 treaty between Greece, Turkey and Cyprus and heavy fighting occurs in the north-west of the island;
8th, India releases Shaikh Abdullah, former premier of Kashmir;
9th, in first elections for Greater London Council Labour win 64 seats; Conservatives, 36;
11th, Humberto Branco elected President of Brazil, following deposition of Sr. Goulart;
13th, Winston Field resigns premiership of Southern Rhodesia on policy grounds and Ian Smith forms ministry;
14th, National Development Bonds introduced in British Budget;

O Politics, Economics, Law and Education

Ministry of Technology formed in Britain to direct the application of science to industry (*Oct.*).

British White Paper on *Monopolies, Mergers and Restrictive Practices* (*Mar.* 5th).

In Rookes, *v.* Barnard (*Jan.* 21st), the House of Lords rules that trade union officials are liable to damages claimed by a former member dismissed from employment as a result of resigning from his Union, and that the officials are not protected by the Trade Disputes Act 1906.

London Stock Exchange makes new demands on companies for information (*Aug.*).

National Commercial Bank of Scotland opens 'women only' branch in Edinburgh.

Oxford University appoints Franks Commission to examine the University's role in higher education.

Randolph Churchill, *The Fight for the Leadership of the Conservative Party.*

Warren Report on the assassination of President Kennedy (*Sept.* 17th).

Marshall McLuhan, *Understanding the Media.*

P Science, Technology, Discovery, etc.

Brookhaven scientists discover the fundamental particle omega-minus through using the 'Nimrod' cyclotron.

Fred Hoyle and J. V. Narlikar of Cambridge University propound new theory of gravitation, which solves the problem of inertia.

Britain's 'Blue Streak' is launched.

Ranger VII, launched from Cape Kennedy, succeeds in obtaining close-up photographs of the moon's surface (*July* 31st).

U.S. Mariner IV and U.S.S.R. Zond II are launched with equipment for photographing Mars.

U.S. develops unmanned satellites 'Syncom' for relaying pictures of Olympic Games from Tokio, and 'Nimbus'.

Dorothy Hodgkin wins Nobel prize for work on X-ray crystallography.

The living brain of a rhesus monkey is isolated from its body by neurosurgeons at Cleveland General Hospital.

U.S. Surgeon-General's report *Smoking and Health* links lung cancer with cigarette smoking.

U.S. divers live on 'Sealab' for nine days, 192 feet down, off Bermuda coast, to study effects of depth on man's mind and body.

Britain grants licences to drill for oil and gas in the North Sea.

Emigration of British scientists, principally to U.S. (the 'Brain Drain') alarms British government.

Britain's military aircraft, TSR–2, maiden flight (*Sept.* 28th).

Opening of the Forth Road Bridge (*Sept.* 4th), and of the Verrazano-Narrows Bridge (the world's longest).

Q Scholarship

The building of Stonehenge is explained as a means of predicting the eclipse of the moon.

A. H. M. Jones, *The Later Roman Empire.*

Leslie Hotson, *Mr. W. H.*

Roy Jenkins, *Asquith.*

Alexander Werth, *Russia at War.*

R Philosophy and Religion

A. Koestler, *The Act of Creation.*

Herbert Marcuse, *One-Dimensional Man.*

D **Apr**: 16th, the Committee of Public Accounts criticises Ferranti Ltd.'s profit on the Bloodhound missile as excessive (*July* 28th, a committee of investigation also criticises the Ministry of Aviation; Ferranti later offers to refund over £4 mill.);
16th, sentences totalling 307 years passed on 12 mail-train robbers;
—, Joshua Nkomo placed under restriction in Southern Rhodesia;
22nd, Greville Wynne, sentenced in Moscow, 1963, is exchanged with U.S.S.R. for Gordon Lonsdale, sentenced in London for espionage, 1961;
27th, Tanganyika and Zanzibar are united, with Julius Nyerere President (*Oct.* 29th the State is named Tanzania).

E **May**: 4th, further 'Kennedy round' G.A.T.T. talks in Geneva;
6th, South Africa passes Bantu Laws amendment bill;
14th, N. Khrushchev opens the Aswan Dam;
18th, Nationalist riots in Quebec;
19th, U.S. complains to Moscow about microphones concealed in Moscow embassy;
20th, outbreak of Aberdeen typhoid epidemic;
22nd, state of emergency in British Guiana;
24th, 300 spectators at football match in Lima die in riot;
27th, death of Pandit Nehru (aged 74); (Lala Bahadur Shastri appointed to succeed him, *June* 2nd).

F **Jun**: 9th, West Germany agrees to pay £1 mill. compensation for British victims of Nazi persecution;
11th, Greece rejects direct talks with Turkey over Cyprus;
12th, Nelson Mandela and seven others sentenced to life imprisonment for acts of sabotage in the Rivonia trial, Pretoria;
12th, U.S.S.R. and East Germany sign 20-year treaty of friendship;
13th, arrest of deputy premier of British Guiana;
19th, Congolese rebels take Albertville;
21st, breakdown of Malaysian-Indonesian talks;
30th, U.N. military operations in Congo end;
—, Spain terminates negotiations with Britain for constructing warships.

G **Jul**: 2nd, L. B. Johnson signs Civil Rights Act;
6th, Nyasaland Protectorate, renamed Malawi, becomes independent within the Commonwealth;
7th, France adopts selective military service;
8th (–15th), Commonwealth premiers meet in London;
10th, Moïse Tshombe succeeds C. Adoula as premier of the Congo;
15th, Anastas Mikoyan succeeds Leonid Brezhnev as President of U.S.S.R.;
16th, Resale Prices Act comes into force in Britain;
18th, race riots in Harlem, New York;
26th, U.S.S.R. calls for new 14-power meeting on Laos;
—, strike of British Guiana sugar-workers is called off;
27th (–30th), disturbances in Northern Rhodesia involving Lumpa Church, led by Alice Lenshina (death toll rises to 491);
—, Winston Churchill's last appearance in House of Commons;
30th, agreement for Gambia's independence in *Feb.* 1965.

H **Aug**: 2nd, a U.S. destroyer is attacked off North Vietnam; U.S. aircraft attack North Vietnam bases in reprisal;
4th, bodies of three Mississippi civil rights workers are found;
5th, Congolese rebels capture Stanleyville;
7th, People's Republic of the Congo is declared;

R Philosophy and Religion *(cont.)*

Howick Committee, appointed by Archbishop of Canterbury, favours retaining system of Crown appointments to bishoprics and deaneries (*Dec.* 1st).

Leslie Paul, *The Deployment and Payment of the Clergy.*

Pope Paul VI makes pilgrimage to the Holy Land (*Jan.* 4th–7th).

Roman Catholic hierarchy in England and Wales rules against use of contraceptive pill (*May* 7th); but authorises joint prayers with other churches (*Dec.* 6th).

S Art, Sculpture, Fine Arts and Architecture

'Op' art—geometric designs which give illusion of change of pattern.

Painting:

P. Cézanne's *Les Grandes Baigneuses* acquired by the National Gallery.

'Art of a Decade' exhibition, Tate Gallery.

Sculpture:

F. E. McWilliam, sculpture, *The Hampstead Figure*, Swiss Cottage Redevelopment Centre, London.

Architecture:

The Bull Ring, Birmingham, costing £1 mill., opened.

Arne Jacobsen, St Catherine's College, Oxford.

Basil Spence, Library and Swimming Pool at Swiss Cottage, London, opened, and his buildings for University of Sussex, near Brighton, near completion.

Ascot Racecourse new grandstand.

Shakespeare Quatercentenary Exhibition at Stratford-on-Avon and Edinburgh.

Sotheby, London, and Parke-Bernet, New York, merge.

T Music

Richard Rodney Bennett, *Aubade.*

Leonard Bernstein, 3rd Symphony (*Kaddish*).

B. Britten, symphony with solo 'cello.

John Cage, *Atlas Elipticales With Winter Music* (electronic version).

Gustav Mahler, 10th Symphony (posth.), completed by Deryck Cooke.

Michael Kennedy, *The Works of Ralph Vaughan Williams.*

Wilfred Mellers, *Music in a New Found Land.*

U Literature

Saul Bellow, *Herzog.*

John Berryman, *77 Dream Songs.*

William Burroughs, *The Naked Lunch.*

William Golding, *The Spire.*

E. Hemingway, *A Moveable Feast* (posth.).

C. Isherwood, *A Single Man.*

Philip Larkin, *The Whitsun Weddings.*

J.-P. Sartre, *Les Mots.*

C. P. Snow, *Corridors of Power.*

Gore Vidal, *Julian.*

V The Press

T.U.C. sells shares in *Daily Herald*, which last appears *Sept.* 14th. *The Sun* takes its place, *Sept.* 15th.

W Drama and Entertainment

TV: B.B.C. 2 opened (*Apr.* 21st); 'The Great War' Series.

Joan Littlewood's Theatre Workshop, Stratford E., and The Windmill Theatre (non-stop vaudeville) close.

H **Aug**: 8th, Turkish planes attack Cyprus and, 9th, U.N. orders cease-fire;
11th, Alice Lenshina surrenders in Northern Rhodesia, but further incidents occur;
12th, mail-train robber Charles Wilson is rescued from Winson Green prison;
13th, General Grivas assumes command of Greek Cypriot forces;
17th, Greece withdraws units from N.A.T.O.;
24th, white mercenaries arrive in Congo to fight the rebels;
26th, Nationalist movements, People's Caretaker Council and Zimbabwe African National Union are banned in Rhodesia;
28th, an English teacher is kidnapped from Lusaka and transported to Johannesburg, where he is later released.

J **Sep**: 2nd, Indonesian army lands in Malaya and, 4th, Commonwealth troops move in;
15th, the Vatican signs an accord with Hungary;
21st, Malta becomes an independent State within the Commonwealth;
24th, Berlin Passes agreement is signed for one year.

K **Oct**: 5th (–12th), Queen Elizabeth II visits Canada, with great security precautions in Quebec;
5th (–11th), Cairo conference of 58 non-aligned states, but Moïse Tshombe, Congo, is not permitted to attend;
7th, Hastings Banda obtains fresh powers of detention in Malawi;
14th, Martin Luther King, U.S. Negro leader, is awarded Nobel peace prize;
15th, in British general election Labour win 317 seats, Conservatives, 303, with Liberals, 9; (Labour receives 44·1 per cent of votes cast, Conservatives, 43·4, and Liberals, 9·0; overall national swing to Labour 3·2 per cent);
16th, Alec Douglas-Home resigns and Harold Wilson forms Labour ministry, with Patrick Gordon Walker, defeated at Smethwick, as Foreign-Secretary, George Brown Secretary of State for Economic Affairs, James Callaghan Chancellor of the Exchequer, and Lord Gardiner Lord Chancellor;
15th, Nikita Khrushchev is replaced as First Secretary of Soviet Communist Party by Leonid Brezhnev and as prime minister by Aleksei Kosygin;
16th, China explodes an atomic bomb;
24th, Northern Rhodesia, renamed Zambia, becomes an independent republic within the Commonwealth, with Kenneth Kaunda President;
26th, British government impose 15 per cent surcharge on imports except raw materials, to close £800 mill. balance of payments gap;
27th, Harold Wilson states that a declaration of independence by Rhodesia would be an open act of defiance;
29th, further Indonesian landings on west coast of Malaya, but Commonwealth troops capture the invaders.

L **Nov**: 2nd, deposition of King Saud of Saudi Arabia, and Faisal proclaimed King;
3rd, in U.S. elections President L. B. Johnson, Democrat, with 486 electoral votes, has sweeping victory over Barry Goldwater, Republican, with 52; popular vote: Johnson, 43,126,233; Goldwater, 27,174,989; the Democrat gains in House of Representatives leave them with 295 seats against the Republicans with 140;
5th, in Rhodesian referendum 90 per cent (of a 61 per cent poll) favour independence;
—, Chou En-lai visits Moscow for summit talks of Communist states;
7th, Ian Smith rejects proposed visit of Commonwealth Secretary to Southern Rhodesia;
8th, cease-fire in force in the Yemen;
9th, Eisaku Sato is elected Prime Minister of Japan;
10th, Kenya becomes a single-party State;

W **Drama and Entertainment** (*cont.*)

Arthur Miller, *After the Fall.*
John Osborne, *Inadmissible Evidence.*
Peter Shaffer, *The Royal Hunt of the Sun.*
Crathorne Committee supports Sunday theatres and entertainment, but not professional sport.
Stratford-on-Avon governors support Peter Hall when attacked for producing 'Theatre of Cruelty' and *avant-garde* foreign plays at the Aldwych.
Michael Balcon's group after long struggle buys British Lion Films.

Films:
Peter Brooks's *Lord of the Flies.*
Stanley Kubrick's *Dr. Strangelove.*
Andrzej Munk's *The Passenger.*
Alain Resnais's *Muriel.*
François Truffaut's *Silken Skin.*
The Beatles in *A Hard Day's Night.*
Goldfinger.
The Pumpkin Eater.

X **Sport**

In Tokyo Olympic Games U.S.S.R. wins 41 gold medals; U.S., 37; Japan, 16; Germany, 13; Italy and Hungary, 10; Poland, 7; Australia and Finland, 6; Britain, Czechoslovakia and Sweden, 5.
Cassius Clay defeats Sonny Liston in World Heavy-weight Championship.
In America's Cup *Constellation* (U.S.) beats *Sovereign* (Britain).

Y **Statistics**

Merchant shipping (tonnages):
U.S., 22,430,249; U.K., 21,489,948; Liberia; 14,549,645; Norway, 14,477,112; Japan, 10,813,228; U.S.S.R., 6,957,512; Greece, 6,887,624; Italy, 5,707,817; West Germany, 5,159,186; France, 5,116,232; Netherlands, 5,110,022; Sweden, 4,308,042; Panama, 4,269, 462; British Commonwealth (excluding U.K., Canada and India), 2,783,166; Denmark, 2,431,020; Spain, 2,047,715; Canada, 1,823,387.
Oil tankers (tonnage):
Liberia, 8,619,449; U.K., 8,002,203; Norway, 7,663,906; U.S., 4,505,274; Japan, 3,145,051; Panama, 2,253,418; France, 2,208,763; Italy, 1,982,485; U.S.S.R., 1,715,956; Netherlands, 1,638,419; Greece, 1,603,082; Sweden, 1,462,796; Denmark, 883,853; West Germany, 838,740; Spain, 590,882; Argentina, 509,526.

Z **Births and Deaths**

Jan. 8th Julius Raab d. (72).
Mar. 20th Brendan Behan d. (41).
Apr. 5th Douglas MacArthur, d. (84).
June 9th Maxwell William Aitken, Lord Beaverbrook d. (85).
Aug. 12th Ian Fleming d. (56).
Sept. 18th Clive Bell d. (83) and Sean O'Casey d. (84).
Sept. 20th Herbert Hoover d. (90).
Sept. 21st Otto Grotewohl d. (70).
Oct. 15th Cole Porter d. (71).
Dec. 9th Edith Sitwell d. (77).

1964 (Nov.-Dec.)

L **Nov:** 11th, food shortage in India provokes riots in Kerala;

—, James Callaghan introduces economy Budget in Britain with increased petrol tax, and announces higher old-age pensions, increase of 6d. in standard rate of income tax and capital gains and corporation taxes in 1965;

12th, Rhodesian High Court rules Joshua Nkomo's detention illegal; he and other African leaders are released, 16th, and taken to restrictive areas;

16th, British government accepts Lawrence Commission's recommendations for increasing M.P.s' salaries to £3,250;

—, Johannesburg trial begins under suppression of Communism act, of 14 whites, including Abraham Fischer, who had led defence in Rivonia trial;

17th, Britain states its intention of banning exports of arms to South Africa;

20th, pressure on the pound increases;

23rd, Britain's bank rate increased to 7 per cent;

24th, Belgian paratroopers, the Congolese army and white mercenaries capture Stanleyville from rebels and rescue hostages (and, 26th, rescue hostages from Paulis);

25th, riots in Saigon;

26th, Britain borrows $3,000 mill. from foreign bankers to save pound;

30th, Winston Churchill's 90th birthday.

M **Dec:** 1st, Gustavo Ordaz succeeds López Mateos as President of Mexico;

2nd, Juan Perón is detained in Brazil on way to Argentina;

4th, Federal agents in Mississippi arrest a sheriff and others in connection with the murder of civil rights workers;

6th, Harold Wilson visits L. B. Johnson in Washington;

—, Antonio Segni, President of Italy, resigns for health reasons; succeeded by Giuseppe Saragat, 28th;

—, riots in Khartoum;

8th, heavy fighting in Vietnam;

11th, Machinery of Government bill published, to permit an increased number of ministers in British House of Commons;

12th, Kenya becomes a republic within the Commonwealth with Jomo Kenyatta first President; ministers include Tom Mboya;

14th, the governor of British Guiana dismisses Cheddi Jagan, following elections, in which his People's Progressive Party lost overall majority, and appoints Forbes Burnham, People's National Congress, premier;

16th, British government, T.U.C. and employers sign a statement on productivity, prices and incomes, the first stage in incomes policy;

17th, announcement of free prescriptions in British Health Service in *Feb.* 1965;

18th, L. B. Johnson offers Panama a new canal treaty and announces that U.S. would plan a new canal;

18th, U.N. extends mandate for force in Cyprus to *Mar.* 1965;

21st, Sidney Silverman introduces bill abolishing death penalty;

—, Control of Office and Industrial Development bill published;

23rd, cyclone in Ceylon and Southern India;

30th, Cunard Q4 contract is placed with John Brown, Clydebank.

N

 U.S. Offensive in Vietnam—India–Pakistan War—Rhodesian Unilateral Declaration of Independence

A **Jan:** 1st, amalgamation of the British Foreign and Commonwealth Services as the Diplomatic Service;
2nd, President Ayub Khan gains clear victory over Miss Jinnah in Pakistan's presidential elections;
7th, Indonesia withdraws from U.N. and 8th, fresh Indonesian landings in Malaya;
14th, Prime Ministers of Northern Ireland and of Eire meet for the first time in 43 years;
—, demonstrations in London by aircraft workers against the government's policy for industry;
20th, inauguration of Lyndon Baines Johnson as 36th President of U.S.;
21st, Patrick Gordon Walker, Foreign Secretary, is defeated in Leyton by-election; he resigns, 22nd, succeeded by Michael Stewart;
30th, State Funeral of Winston Churchill;
31st, R. A. Butler retires from politics.

B **Feb:** 2nd, Royal Commission on Trade Unions and Employers' Associations is appointed;
7th, U. S. aircraft bomb North Vietnam, following attacks on American areas in South Vietnam;
11th, British Medical Association advises family doctors to resign from health service; (doctors vote in favour of government's proposals for new pay structure, *Nov.* 5th);
18th, Gambia becomes independent within the Commonwealth;
21st, Malcolm X, Black Muslim leader, is shot dead in Manhattan;
23rd, Roger Casement's remains are sent to the Irish Republic for reinterment;
24th, British government rejects Robbins Committee's recommendations for creating new universities;
25th, Regional Economic Planning Councils are set up in Britain.

C **Mar:** 3rd, Seretse Khama becomes first premier of Bechuanaland;
7th, violence breaks out at Selma, Alabama (9th, whites kill a white civil rights worker);
8th, landing of 3,500 U.S. marines in S. Vietnam;
11th, Britain's February trade figures show surplus for first time since *Aug.* 1963;
17th, Aubrey Jones is appointed first chairman of National Board for Prices and Incomes;
21st, Martin Luther King heads procession of 4,000 civil rights demonstrators from Selma to Montgomery, Alabama, to deliver petition on negro grievances;
25th, Ku Klux Klan shoot Viola Liuzzo, a white civil rights worker, in Selma;
—, Dudley Senanayake forms ministry in Ceylon following defeat of Mrs. Bandaranaike in elections;
—, West Germany extends time limit for Nazi trials from *May* 1965 to *Dec.* 1969;
28th, serious earthquake in Chile;
30th, bomb explodes in U.S. embassy, Saigon.

D **Apr:** 4th, North Vietnamese MIG aircraft shoot down U.S. jets;
6th, British Budget introduces 30 per cent capital gains tax and disallows expenses incurred in business entertainment; James Callaghan, Chancellor of the Exchequer, also announces the cancellation of the TSR-2 aircraft;
7th, President Johnson proposes aid for vast development programme in South-East Asia, which Hanoi and Peking governments reject;
8th, British White Paper sets 3 to 3½ per cent as the norm for pay increases;
9th, clashes between Indian and Pakistani forces on Kutch-Sind border;
11th, tornadoes in mid-western U.S.;
17th, student demonstrations in Washington against U.S. bombing of North Vietnam;

O **Politics, Economics, Law and Education**

British White Papers on *The Parliamentary Commissioner for Administration* (the 'Ombudsman', *Oct.* 12th), *A Policy for the Arts*, and *The Land Commission* (*Sept.* 22nd), which proposes 40 per cent levy on development values.

The 750th anniversary of Magna Carta and the 700th anniversary of Parliament are celebrated.

The Greater London Council (chairman, Harold Shearman) and 32 London Borough Councils come into being (*Apr.* 1st).

The Milner Holland Report on London Housing (*Mar.* 11th).

Hindi becomes official language of India (*Jan.* 26th).

Teach-Ins are held in American and British universities on Civil Rights, Vietnam and Southern Rhodesia.

George Brown introduces *The National Plan*, which aims at 25 per cent increase in Britain's output by 1970 (*Sept.* 16th).

The Queen's Awards to Industry are instituted.

The award of the M.B.E. to the Beatles in the Queen's Birthday Honours provokes controversy.

Britain agrees to adopt the metric system over ten years.

Law Commission under Mr. Justice Scarman is appointed.

Judge Elizabeth Lane is appointed first woman High Court Judge in England.

British White Paper recommends family courts (*Aug.* 24th).

Universities of Kent and Warwick are established.

University College, Cambridge, with men and women graduates, is founded.

Ministry of Education circular asks local authorities to submit plans for comprehensive schools.

P **Science, Technology, Discovery, etc.**

Soviet cosmonaut Alexei Leonov leaves spacecraft Voskhod II and floats in space for 20 minutes (*Mar.* 18th).

U.S. space-ship Gemini III is pilot-manœuvred during orbit by Virgil Grissom and John Young (*Mar.* 23rd).

Edward White walks for 20 minutes in space from U.S. Gemini IV (*June* 3rd), and Gemini V makes 120 orbits (*Aug.* 21st–29th).

Gemini VII, launched *Dec.* 4th, meets Gemini VI in orbit and returns, 18th, after record flight.

U.S. satellite Mariner IV transmits close-up photographs of Mars (*July* 15th).

First French satellite is launched (*Nov.* 26th).

Early Bird, U.S. commercial communications satellite, is first used by TV, *May* 2nd.

Soviet Antonov AN-22 makes flight with 720 passengers.

British Petroleum Company strikes oil in North Sea (*Sept.* 21st), but rig collapses, *Dec.* 27th.

Dungeness Atomic Power Station opened.

Q **Scholarship**

Yale University Press claims the 'Vinland Map' proves America was discovered by Leif Ericsson in eleventh century.

Identification of a coffin found in Stepney as containing the remains of Anne Mowbray, Duchess of York (d. 1481).

George Painter, *Marcel Proust*, Vol. II.

Arthur Schlesinger Jr., *Thousand Days*.

D **Apr:** 21st, 114-nation Disarmament Commission resumes talks in New York after five-year interval;
23rd, large-scale U.S. raid over North Vietnam;
27th, Britain's 15 per cent import surcharge is reduced to 10 per cent;
29th, Australia decides to send troops to Southern Vietnam.

E **May:** 7th, Ian Smith's Rhodesian Front has sweeping victory in Rhodesian elections;
10th, Frank Bosard and Percy Allen are sentenced in London for espionage;
11th, cyclone in East Pakistan;
12th, West Germany establishes diplomatic relations with Israel; Arab states break off relations with Bonn;
13th, Conservative gains in British borough elections;
18th (–28th), Queen Elizabeth II visits West Germany;
—, first reference on wage increase is made to Prices and Incomes Board (printing industry);
13th, Franz Jonas is elected President of Austria.

F **Jun:** 2nd, following a tie in Commons division on Opposition amendment to defer Corporation Tax, the Speaker gives casting vote for the government;
2nd, European hostages are reported killed by Congolese rebels;
3rd, British bank rate is cut to 6 per cent (raised to 7 per cent, *Nov.* 1964);
8th, U.S. troops are authorised to engage in offensive operations in Vietnam;
17th, at Commonwealth Prime Ministers' conference, London, a Commonwealth Secretariat is established;
19th, Ben Bella, President of Algeria, is deposed; Houari Boumedienne heads revolutionary council;
24th, South Vietnam breaks off relations with France;
30th, India-Pakistan cease-fire signed.

G **Jul:** 6th, French representatives withdraw from Common Market meetings in Brussels;
8th, Harold Davies arrives in Hanoi in attempt to open peace talks;
15th, King Constantine of Greece dismisses premier Papandreou (after weeks of unrest M. Stephanopoulos becomes premier, *Sept.* 17th);
28th, Edward Heath is elected Leader of British Conservative Party, following resignation of Alec Douglas-Home, 22nd, under a new voting procedure;
30th, Medical Care for the Aged bill signed by President Johnson.

H **Aug:** 2nd, British White Paper on Commonwealth immigration imposes annual limit of 8,500 on work permits;
5th, Devlin Committee recommends British dockers be employed on regular weekly basis;
7th, breakdown of constitutional talks on Aden and the South Arabian federation;
9th, by mutual agreement Singapore leaves Malaysia;
11th, race riots in Los Angeles;
19th, Frankfurt court, after 20-month trial of Auschwitz prison officials, sentences six men to life imprisonment;
24th, United Arab Republic and Yemen sign cease-fire agreement.

J **Sep:** 1st, Pakistani troops cross Kashmir cease-fire line;
—, terrorists in Aden shoot the Speaker of the Legislative Council; (26th, Britain suspends the Constitution);
2nd, death of Harry Hylton-Foster, Speaker of the House of Commons (*Oct.* 26th, Horace King elected Speaker);

R **Philosophy and Religion**

Pope Paul VI visits New York to address U.N. General Assembly (*Oct.* 4th) and, before the Vatican Council closes, promulgates document exonerating the Jews from the death of Christ.

The Orthodox Church annuls its excommunication of the Church of Rome in 1054.

The Vatican allows the resumption of worker-priests in France (suspended 1959).

Westminster Abbey's 900th anniversary celebrations (begin *Dec.* 28th).

S **Art, Sculpture, Fine Arts and Architecture**

Painting:

M. Beckmann Exhibition, Tate Gallery.

P. Bonnard Exhibition, Royal Academy.

Goya's portrait of the Duke of Wellington (stolen in 1961) is returned to the National Gallery.

Mondrian designs dominate young dress fashions.

Dame Laura Knight, *Autobiography.*

Rembrandt's portrait of *Titus* is sold at Christie's for 760,000 guineas.

Sculpture:

A. Giacometti Exhibition, Tate Gallery.

Michelangelo's *Pietà* on show in New York.

Architecture:

General Post Office Tower, London, opened.

New Aviary, London Zoo, designed by Lord Snowdon.

T **Music**

A. Schönberg's *Moses and Aaron* is given first complete performance, London.

L. Bernstein, *Chichester Psalms.*

W. Walton, *The Twelve.*

Malcolm Williamson, *Julius Caesar Jones* (opera with libretto by Geoffrey Dunn).

U **Literature**

Wolf Biermann, *Die Drahtharfe.*

Günter Grass, *Dog Years.*

Norman Mailer, *An American Dream.*

Robert Lowell, *Union Dead.*

V **The Press**

Circulation figures of British daily newspapers:

Daily Express, 3,981,110; *Daily Mail*, 2,424,810; *Daily Mirror*, 4,956,997; *Daily Sketch*, 826,440; *Daily Telegraph*, 1,350,529; *Daily Worker*, 60,246; *Financial Times*, 152,149; *The Guardian*, 275,900; *The Sun*, 1,361,090; *The Times*, 257,922.

W **Drama and Entertainment**

E. Bagnold, *The Chinese Prime Minister.*

J. Osborne, *A Patriot for Me.*

Frank Marcus, *The Killing of Sister George.*

Films:

Rita Tushingham in *The Knack.*

Samantha Eggar in *The Collector.*

The Beatles in *Help!*

Dr. Who and the Daleks.

Television:

The State Funeral of Sir Winston Churchill.

Sep: 3rd, civil war breaks out in Dominica;
6th, India invades West Pakistan and bombs Lahore;
8th, Southern Rhodesia appoints an 'accredited representative' in Lisbon;
10th, British agreement with the central banks arranges for massive support for the pound;
22nd, cease-fire in war between India and Pakistan, which is subsequently violated by both sides;
24th, Mauritius constitutional conference ends with promise of independence in 1966;
29th, U.S.S.R. admits supplying arms to Hanoi.

K Oct: 1st, attempted *coup d'état* in Indonesia;
4th (–11th), Ian Smith attends talks in London on Rhodesia;
13th, President Kasavubu dismisses Moise Tshombe, Congolese premier;
17th, demonstrations in U.S. and in London against the war in Vietnam;
19th, Un-American Activities Committee begins public hearing on Ku Klux Klan;
24th, Archbishop of Canterbury states that if the British government had to use force in Rhodesia this would have the support of Christians;
25th (–30th), Harold Wilson visits Salisbury for talks with Ian Smith and African leaders;
Kidnapping in Paris of Mehdi Ben Barka, Left Moroccan leader.

L Nov: 8th, in Canadian elections Lester Pearson again fails to obtain overall majority;
9th, Act for abolition of the death penalty in force in Britain;
11th, Ian Smith makes Rhodesian Declaration of Independence; Britain declares the régime illegal and introduces exchange and trade restrictions;
19th, British Guiana constitutional congress ends with agreement for independence in *May* 1966;
25th, General Mobutu deposes President Kasavubu of the Congo.

M Dec: 5th, General de Gaulle fails to obtain clear majority in election for the French presidency;
8th, new Rent Act in force in Britain, gives greater security to tenants;
9th, Nikolai Podgorny replaces A. Mikoyan as President of U.S.S.R.;
16th, Plowden Committee recommends British government has shareholding in aircraft firms;
17th, Britain imposes oil embargo on Rhodesia; (19th, beginning of airlift of oil to Zambia);
18th, nine African states break off diplomatic relations with Britain for not using force against Rhodesia;
19th, General de Gaulle defeats François Mitterand in election for French presidency;
22nd, British government appoints a Public Schools Commission under John Newsom;
29th, President Ho Chi Minh of North Vietnam rejects unconditional peace talks offered by U.S.;
—, independence for Bechuanaland announced for *Sept.* 1966;
31st, the executives of the Common Market Commission, The European Coal and Steel Community and Euratom merge into one executive authority.

N

W Drama and Entertainment (*cont.*)

Television (*cont.*)

Ban on cigarette advertising on commercial TV in Britain (from *Aug.* 1st).

'Radio Caroline' and other offshore pirate commercial radio stations are established.

X Sport

Ten professional British footballers are found guilty of 'fixing' matches (*Jan.* 26th).

Cassius Clay knocks out Sonny Liston in first minute of fight at Lewiston, Maine (*May* 25th).

Mme Vaucher, the first woman to climb the Matterhorn, climbs the north wall of the Matterhorn on centenary of first ascent (*July* 14th).

Karen Muir, aged 12, sets up swimming record for women's 110 yards backstroke (*Aug.* 10th).

Jim Clark wins Indianapolis 550 race and six other Grand Prix titles to become world motor racing champion.

Robert Manry reaches Falmouth after 11-week Atlantic voyage in $13\frac{1}{2}$-ft. craft.

Y Statistics

Use of land (area in acres per head of population):

	Total area	Potentially usable	Actually used
U.S.	12·0	6·0	3·5
Canada	125·0	22·0	4·0
Great Britain	1·1	0·6	0·55
England and Wales	0·8	0·6	0·55
Japan	1·1	0·2	0·17
India	2·5	0·8	0·75

British households owning electrical goods (*1955 percentages in brackets*):

TV set	88 (40)
Vacuum cleaner	82 (45)
Washing-machine	56 (20)
Refrigerator	29 (10)
Telephone	22 (21)

Z Births and Deaths

Jan. 4th Thomas Stearns Eliot d. (76).

Jan. 24th Winston Leonard Spencer Churchill d. (90).

Feb. 15th Nat 'King' Cole d. (45).

Mar. 6th Herbert, Lord Morrison d. (77).

Mar. 17th Farouk, ex-King of Egypt d. (45).

Apr. 21st Edward Appleton d. (72).

May 21st Geoffrey de Havilland d. (82).

June 13th Martin Buber d. (86).

June 20th Bernard Baruch d. (94).

Aug. 27th Charles Édouard Jeanneret (Le Corbusier) d. (77).

Sept. 4th Albert Schweitzer d. (90).

Nov. 2nd Herbert Evatt d. (71).

1966 (Jan.– Apr.) France withdraws from N.A.T.O. command structure —Cultural Revolution in China

A **Jan**: 1st, Pope Paul VI appeals for peace in Vietnam;
—, Colonel Jean-Bédel Bokassa seizes power in the Central African Republic;
—(–13th), transport strike in New York;
8th, major U.S. offensive against the Iron Triangle, stronghold of the Viet Cong;
10th, Tashkent peace agreement between India and Pakistan;
11th, death of Lal Bahandra Shastri, Prime Minister of India; succeeded by Indira Gandhi, 19th;
13th, Robert Weaver appointed Secretary of Housing and Urban Development, the first negro in U.S. Cabinet;
16th, General Ironsi takes power in Nigeria after military coup;
20th, Robert Menzies retires as Prime Minister of Australia; succeeded by Harold Holt, 25th;
27th (–*Aug.* 25th), 18-nation disarmament conference in Geneva;
30th, France ends boycott of E.E.C. meetings;
31st, U.S. resumes bombing of North Vietnam after 37-day pause;
—, Britain bans trade with Rhodesia.

B **Feb**: 1st, China protests to Britain about U.S. warships in Hong Kong;
—, British government tightens credit squeeze;
7th (–8th), President Johnson meets South Vietnamese leaders in Honolulu;
18th, Dean Rusk states that U.S. has exhausted every procedure for bringing peace to Vietnam;
19th, British Navy Minister Christopher Mayhew resigns in protest at proposed reduction in commitments east of Suez (contained in White Paper published on 22nd);
21st, President de Gaulle calls for dismantling of N.A.T.O.;
23rd, military junta seizes power in Syria;
24th, British government publishes Prices and Incomes Bill;
—, overthrow of President Nkrumah of Ghana by military coup while away on tour of Asia.

C **Mar**: 1st, rebellion in Eastern Assam;
2nd, Britain protests to Portugal about oil supplies reaching Rhodesia via Mozambique;
5th, Organization of African Unity urges Britain to use force against Rhodesia;
6th (–12th), food riots in West Bengal, spreading to Calcutta and Delhi;
8th, Australia triples its forces in Vietnam to 4,500 men;
10th, France requests removal of N.A.T.O. bases from French territory;
11th, after anti-Communist demonstrations, President Sukarno of Indonesia transfers all political powers to General Raden Suharto;
—, Canadian government orders inquiry into involvement of former Cabinet ministers with East German spy Gerda Munsinger;
30th, National Party wins sweeping victory in South African general election;
31st, in British general election Labour win 363 seats, Conservatives, 253, with Liberals, 12 (Labour receives 47.9 per cent of votes cast, Conservatives, 41.9, and Liberals, 8.5).

D **Apr**: 2nd, unrest breaks out in Saigon, as protesters demand end of military rule in South Vietnam; (14th, government promises elections within 3–5 months);
6th (–8th), increased ferry tolls spark riots in Hong Kong;
9th, Spain eases press censorship;
—, U.N. authorizes Britain to prevent oil shipments to Rhodesia by force;

O Politics, Economics, Law and Education

British government proposes supplementary benefits for unemployed, widows, sick, and disabled (*Jan.* 26th).
Opening of British Parliament televised for first time (*Apr.* 1st).
Australia introduces decimal currency (*Feb.* 14th).
E.F.T.A countries abolish tariffs on industrial goods, creating customs union (*Dec.* 31st).
U.S. Supreme Court rules poll tax unconstitutional as a voting requirement (*Mar.* 25th).
U.S. Supreme Court, in Miranda v. Arizona, upholds restrictions on police interrogation of suspects (*June* 13th).
Lord Chancellor rules that British House of Lords need not always be bound by its own judicial precedents (*July* 26th).
In Britain, establishment of Wolfson College in Oxford; foundation of Clare Hall and Fitzwilliam College in Cambridge.

P Science, Technology, Discovery, etc.

U.S.S.R. spacecraft Luna IX makes the first soft landing on the moon (*Feb.* 3rd), followed by U.S. Surveyor I (*June* 2nd).
U.S.S.R. Venera III crashes on Venus (*Mar.* 1st), the first man-made object to land on another planet.
U.S. Gemini VIII achieves the first link-up of a manned space craft with another object, an Agena rocket (*Mar.* 16th).
U.S.S.R. Luna XI goes into orbit around the moon (*Aug.*)
U.S. Lunar Orbiter I enters moon orbit (Aug. 10th) and transmits pictures of the dark side.
U.S.S.R. Luna XIII lands on the moon and sends back data about the soil.
Gemini XII, the last of the Gemini two-man space missions (launched *Nov.* 11th).
Astronomers at the U.S. Naval Research Laboratory discover powerful X-rays emitted from within the constellation Cygnus.
Molecular biologists discover that DNA is not confined to chromosomes but is also contained within cells in the mitochondria.
A French medical group defines death as brain inactivity rather than heart stoppage.
U.S. scientists Harry M. Meyer and Paul D. Parman develop a live virus vaccine for rubella (German measles), which reduces the incidence of the disease.
Konrad Lorenz, *On Aggression.*
David Lack, *Population Studies of Birds.*
C-12 isotope of carbon adopted as international standard of atomic atoms.
Structure of ecdysone (insect moulting hormone) determined.

Q Scholarship

K.V. Flannery and associates begin detailed survey of the Valley of Oaxaca, Mexico.
M. Coe and associates from Yale begin detailed study of Olmec culture, Mexico.
E. Le Roy Ladurie, *The Peasants of Languedoc.*
E.A. Wrigley, *An Introduction to English Historical Demography.*
Robert Blake, *Disraeli.*
Owen Chadwick, *The Victorian Church*, Vol. I (Vol. II, 1970).
R. Carr, *Spain, 1808–1939.*
A.J.P. Taylor, *From Sarajevo to Potsdam.*

R Philosophy and Religion

Theodor Adorno, *Negative Dialectics.*
Jacques Lacan, *Ecrits.*

D **Apr**: 14th, Sandoz Pharmaceuticals Inc. withdraws drug L.S.D. after widespread misuse;
15th, wave of anti-Chinese violence begins in Indonesia;
16th, General Abdul Rahman Arif succeeds his brother as President of Iraq;
—, Rhodesia demands departure of British diplomats from Salisbury (withdrawal suspended, 28th);
18th, People's Party forms a government in Austria;
27th (–*May* 20th), clashes between police and students at Spanish universities;
28th, President Johnson asks Congress for new civil rights legislation to end discrimination in housing and jury service.

E **May**: 3rd, British Budget introduces selective employment tax and corporation tax at 40 per cent;
—, U.S. admits shelling Cambodia;
4th, British Government accepts Kindersley Report's recommendation for £1,000 p.a. increase in doctors' pay;
7th, Nicolae Ceauşescu declares that Romania recognizes no supreme authority within international Communist movement;
9th (–20th), talks between British and Rhodesian officials in London (second round in Salisbury, *June* 2nd–*July* 5th);
16th (–*July* 1st), British seamen's strike (23rd, state of emergency proclaimed to allow government control of ports);
18th, Spain and Britain begin discussions on future of Gibraltar (talks end without agreement, *July* 14th);
23rd, South Vietnamese troops crush Buddhist rebellion in Da Nang after a week of fighting;
24th, Ugandan army drives out the King of Buganda (kingdom dissolved, *June* 10th);
26th, British Guiana becomes independent as Guyana;
28th, violent protests against creation of unitary state in Nigeria.

F **Jun**: 2nd, Eamon de Valera re-elected President of Ireland;
3rd, purge of 'rightists' in Chinese leadership begins;
7th, demonstrators in East Pakistan demand greater autonomy;
20th (–30th), President de Gaulle visits U.S.S.R.;
22nd, South Vietnamese army moves into Quang Tri, last stronghold of Buddhist opposition;
26th, major civil rights rally in Jackson, Mississippi;
29th, U.S. bombs Hanoi and Haiphong; Britain dissociates itself from bombing of populated areas.

G **Jul**: 1st, France withdraws its forces from N.A.T.O. command structure;
—, British Steel Renationalisation Bill published;
3rd, Frank Cousins, the first British Minister of Technology, resigns over prices and incomes policy; succeeded by A.N. Wedgwood Benn;
6th, North Vietnamese parade 50 captured U.S. airmen through streets of Hanoi;
11th, U.S.S.R. announces further aid to North Vietnam;
12th (–23rd), race riots in Chicago, Cleveland and Brooklyn;
14th, British bank rate rises from 6 to 7 per cent;
—, Israeli jets raid Syria in retaliation for border incursions;
20th, British government announces six-month wage and price standstill, dividend curbs, and credit and exchange controls;
24th, E.E.C. reaches agreement on Common Agricultural Policy;

R **Philosophy and Religion** (*cont.*)

Mary Douglas, *Purity and Danger.*
T.J.J. Altizer, *The Gospel of Christian Atheism.*
Billy Graham's Greater London Crusade.
Archbishop Michael Ramsey pays official visit to Pope Paul VI.
Red Guards in Peking close churches and fly red flags on the Roman Catholic Cathedral.
Office of Inquisitor abolished in Rome.
Index of books prohibited to Roman Catholics is abolished.
Publication of *The Jerusalem Bible.*

S **Art, Sculpture, Fine Arts and Architecture**

Severe floods in Florence leave the Renaissance centre under six feet of water (*Nov.* 4th).
Multi-part homage to Picasso in Paris, with exhibitions at the Bibliothèque Nationale, Grand Palais and Petit Palais.

Painting:

Term 'Arte Povera' coined by Germano Celant, Italy.
Allan Kaprow, *Gas – Collective Happening.*
Joseph Kosuth, *Titled (Art as an Idea).*
Malcom Morley, *SS 'Amsterdam' in Front of Rotterdam.*

Sculpture:

Carl André, *Equivalent 8.*

Architecture:

John Andrews and Page and Steele, Scarborough College, University of Toronto, Canada.
Marcel Breuer and Hamilton Smith, new building for the Whitney Museum, New York.
Gio Ponti, Secretariat Buildings, Islamabad, Pakistan.

T **Music**

Milton Babbitt, Sextets.
S. Barber, *Antony and Cleopatra* (opera).
B. Britten, *The Burning Fiery Furnace* (opera).
Hans Werner Henze, *The Bassarids* (opera).
György Ligeti, *Aventures et Nouvelles Aventures.*

U **Literature**

Truman Capote, *In Cold Blood.*
John Fowles, *The Magus.*
Graham Greene, *The Comedians.*
P.J. Kavanagh, *The Perfect Stranger.*
Yukio Mishima, *The Sailor who fell from Grace with the Sea.*
Vladimir Nabokov, *Despair.*
Sylvia Plath, *Ariel.*
Thomas Pynchon, *The Crying of Lot 49.*
Jean Rhys, *The Wide Sargasso Sea.*
Martin Walser, *The Unicorn.*
Patrick White, *The Solid Mandala.*

G **Jul**: 25th, Chinese newspapers carry front-page photos of Mao Tse-tung during 9-mile 65-minute swim down the Yangtse on 16th;
29th, General Yakubu Gowon succeeds General Ironsi as ruler of Nigeria after army mutiny;
31st, British Colonial Office dissolved; remaining responsibilities assumed by Commonwealth Office.

H **Aug**: 10th, George Brown replaces Michael Stewart as British Foreign Secretary;
11th, three-year-old undeclared war between Indonesia and Malaysia ends with agreement to decide status of Sarawak and Sabah by referendum;
13th, Central Committee of Chinese Communist Party, in first plenary session since 1962, endorses the 'Great Proletarian Cultural Revolution', the movement to 'purify' Chinese Communism through young Red Guards violently removing members of the intelligentsia;
15th, Israeli and Syrian forces clash around Sea of Galilee;
16th (–19th), disorderly hearings of U.S. Un-American Activities Committee on bill to penalise U.S. citizens aiding Viet Cong;
18th, Red Guards make their first appearance in Peking; four days of anti-Western demonstrations follow;
19th, earthquake in eastern Turkey kills 2,000.

J **Sep**: 6th, H.F. Verwoerd, Prime Minister of South Africa, is stabbed to death in Parliament in Cape Town; succeeded by B.J. Vorster, 13th;
—(–14th), Commonwealth conference in London commits Britain to seeking U.N. mandatory sanctions against Rhodesia;
9th, Rhodesian High Court rules that Smith's regime is unlawful but the only effective administration;
16th, China accuses U.S. of bombing Chinese territory near North Vietnamese frontier;
19th, U.S. Civil Rights Bill to end housing discrimination defeated by Senate filibuster;
23rd, U.S. discloses that its planes are defoliating jungle areas in central Vietnam to deny cover to enemy;
26th, British Motor Corporation announces dismissal of 10,000 workers (anti-redundancy strike, *Nov.* 2nd–14th);
27th, race riots in San Francisco after shooting of negro boy;
30th, Bechuanaland becomes independent as Botswana, with Sir Seretse Khama as President;
—, Albert Speer and Baldur von Schirach released from Spandau Prison, West Berlin, after serving 20 years for war crimes.

K **Oct**: 1st, Chinese Defence Minister, Lin Piao, accuses U.S.S.R. of plotting with U.S. over Vietnam;
4th, Basutoland becomes independent as Lesotho under King Moshoeshoe II;
5th, Prices and Incomes Act gives British government powers to freeze wages and prices;
—, Spain closes frontier with Gibraltar to all traffic except pedestrians (refuses to accept Gibraltar passports from *Nov.* 12th);
7th, U.S.S.R. expels all Chinese students;
14th, heaviest U.S. air raids on North Vietnam to date;
17th, U.S. President Lyndon Johnson begins 17-day tour of Far East and Pacific;
21st, slag heap at Aberfan, Glamorgan, South Wales, slips and engulfs school, killing 116 children and 28 adults;

V The Press

The Times of London appears in new format with news on front page (*May* 3rd); Lord Thomson buys *The Times* from Gavin Astor (*Sept.*).

The Daily Worker in Britain changes its name to *Morning Star* (*May*).

Three New York newspapers merge to form the *World Journal Tribune* (*Sept.*).

W Drama and Entertainment

Edward Albee, *A Delicate Balance*.

Emilio Carballido, *I, Too, Speak of the Rose*.

Aimé Césaire, *A Season in the Congo*.

Jorge Díaz, *The Toothbrush*.

Joe Orton, *Loot*.

Films:

- Robert Bolt's *A Man for All Seasons*.
- Claude Lelouch's *A Man and a Woman*.
- Andrei Tarkovsky's *Andrei Rublev*.
- *Alfie*.
- *Georgy Girl*.

Television:

- *Cathy Come Home*.
- First episodes of *Batman*; *Thunderbirds*; *The Monkees*; *Star Trek*
- Laurence Olivier's *Othello*.

Popular music:

- Motown outpace all other U.S. record companies in sales of singles.
- Avant-garde rock band the Velvet Underground does multi-media shows with Pop artist Andy Warhol.
- The Beach Boys, 'Good Vibrations'.
- The Byrds, *Fifth Dimension*.
- Bob Dylan, *Blonde on Blonde*.
- John Lennon speculates that the Beatles are more popular than Jesus.

X Sport

Arkle, ridden by Pat Taaffe, wins the Cheltenham Gold Cup in Britain for the third successive year (*Mar.* 17th).

Following a court case, the British Jockey Club allows women to hold licences for training race horses.

Alan Ball is the first British soccer player to be transferred for £100,000 (from Blackpool to Everton).

Host nation England wins soccer's World Cup, beating West Germany in the final 4–2 after extra time (*July* 30th).

In lawn tennis, Australia wins the Davis Cup for the third successive year, beating India in the final.

Australian Jack Brabham wins the World Formula One motor racing championship in a car manufactured by his own company (*Sept.* 4th).

Y Statistics

Z Births and Deaths

Sept. 21st Paul Reynaud d. (87).

Dec. 15th Walt Disney d. (65).

Dec. 30th Christian Herter d. (71).

K **Oct:** 22nd, George Blake, serving 42 years for espionage, escapes from Wormwood Scrubs prison, London;

24th (–25th), Manila Conference of Vietnam war allies: South Vietnam, U.S., Australia, New Zealand, Philippines, South Korea, Thailand;

27th, China announces successful test-firing of a guided nuclear missile;

—, U.N. Assembly ends South Africa's mandate over South-West Africa; South Africa refuses to accept the decision;

28th, President de Gaulle calls for U.S. withdrawal from Vietnam;

—, Britain and France agree plans for Channel Tunnel.

L **Nov:** 2nd, Enver Hoxha allies Albania with China and denounces U.S.S.R.;

4th, extensive flooding in central and northern Italy;

7th, riots in Delhi over cow slaughter laws;

8th, in U.S. mid-term elections, Democrats retain control of Congress with reduced majorities;

10th, Harold Wilson declares Britain's determination to become a member of the E.E.C.;

13th, Israeli forces attack Hebron area of Jordan (25th, U.N. censures Israel);

22nd, Spanish Cortes passes new constitution proposed by General Franco (95 per cent approval in referendum, *Dec.* 14th);

23rd, Red Guards demand dismissal of Chinese Head of State, Liu Shao-chi, and Party Secretary, Teng Hsiao-ping;

30th, Barbados becomes independent within Commonwealth;

—, Britain abolishes 10 per cent surcharge on imports.

M **Dec:** 1st, Kurt Kiesinger becomes Chancellor of West Germany, following resignation of Ludwig Erhard;

2nd, U.N. unanimously elects U Thant for second term as Secretary-General;

—(–4th), Harold Wilson and Ian Smith meet aboard H.M.S. *Tiger* and prepare plan for settlement of Rhodesian dispute (5th, Rhodesia rejects the plan);

7th, Arab Defence Council in Cairo co-ordinates military response to any Israeli attack;

8th, Syria seizes Iraq Petroleum Company pipeline;

13th, U.S. raid on Hanoi suburbs kills over 100 civilians;

16th, U.N. Security Council approves selective mandatory sanctions against Rhodesia;

20th, Britain rules out legal independence for Rhodesia except under black majority rule;

22nd, Ian Smith declares Rhodesia a republic;

24th, Cardinal Spellman, Archbishop of New York, in sermon at U.S. base near Saigon, says Vietnam is a war for civilisation and anything less than victory is inconceivable;

30th, Britain invites U.S., South Vietnam, and North Vietnam to meet on British territory to arrange ceasefire;

31st, Yugoslavia releases Communist dissident, Milovan Djilas, from prison.

1967 (Jan. – Apr.) Greek military coup—Six-Day War—France vetoes British entry into E.E.C.

A **Jan:** 6th, U.S. and South Vietnamese forces launch major offensive in Mekong Delta;
10th, President Johnson's state of Union address proposes 6 per cent war tax surcharge (increased to 10 per cent, *Aug.* 3rd);
—, U.S. Supreme Court upholds right of travel to Communist countries regardless of State Department prohibitions;
15th (–24th), Harold Wilson and George Brown tour E.E.C. capitals to argue for British membership;
18th, Jeremy Thorpe succeeds Jo Grimond as leader of the British Liberal Party;
26th (–*Feb.* 12th), Red Guards besiege Soviet embassy in Peking alleging mistreatment of Chinese students in Moscow;
28th, U.S.S.R. sends note to Potsdam signatories accusing West Germany of neo-Nazism and militarism;
30th, France abolishes exchange controls and frees the gold market.

B **Feb:** 2nd, President Johnson offers to halt U.S. bombing of North Vietnam, if North Vietnamese cease infiltration of South Vietnam (Ho Chi Minh rejects proposals, *Mar.* 15th);
—, General Somoza Jnr. becomes President of Nicaragua;
6th (–13th), Soviet Prime Minister Kosygin visits Britain and discusses Vietnam with Harold Wilson;
10th, curfew imposed in Aden after nationalist riots;
11th, Chinese army takes over Public Security Ministry and places Peking under military rule;
14th, 21 nations sign treaty in Mexico City prohibiting nuclear weapons from Latin America;
15th (–21st), ruling Congress Party sustains heavy losses in Indian general election;
21st, 18-nation disarmament conference re-opens in Geneva;
22nd, U.S. and South Vietnamese forces begin Operation Junction City;
26th, Chinese Premier Chou En-lai calls for return to order and discipline;
28th (–*Mar.* 12th), Anglo-Maltese conference in London on rundown of British forces in Malta.

C **Mar:** 2nd, accidental U.S. bombing of Lang Vei kills 80 South Vietnamese civilians;
6th, Svetlana Alliluyeva, Stalin's daughter, requests asylum at U.S. embassy in Delhi;
12th, French general election reduces Gaullist-led coalition government's majority in National Assembly to one;
13th (–21st), student 'sit-in' at London School of Economics in protest over disciplinary action;
18th, Liberian tanker *Torrey Canyon* runs aground off Land's End, south-west England; oil extends over 100 square miles;
19th, French Somaliland rejects independence in referendum;
28th, U Thant discloses his Vietnam peace plan, accepted by U.S., but rejected by North Vietnam;
29th, U.S. Court of Appeals in New Orleans orders complete desegregation of schools in Alabama, Florida, Georgia, Louisiana, Texas, and Mississippi;
31st, supreme headquarters of N.A.T.O. moves from France to Casteau in Belgium.

D **Apr:** 1st, Sir Edmund Compton takes office as Britain's first Parliamentary Commissioner for Administration (Ombudsman);
—, President Thieu of South Vietnam promulgates new constitution;

O Politics, Economics, Law and Education

60 nations, including U.S., U.S.S.R. and Britain, sign treaty banning nuclear weapons from outer space (*Jan.* 27th).

Latey Committee report recommends lowering age of majority in Britain from 21 to 18 (*July* 20th).

First landing of North Sea gas in Britain (*Mar.* 7th).

Thailand, Indonesia, Singapore, Philippines and Malaysia found the Association of South-East Asian States (A.S.E.A.N.) to promote regional growth and provide security against China.

Sexual Offences Act 1967 comes into operation, decriminalizing homosexual acts betweeen consenting adult males in Britain (*July* 27th).

Criminal Justice Act introduces majority verdicts in English criminal trials.

Sweden changes to driving on the right (*Sept.* 3rd).

British Road Safety Act introduces breath tests (from *Oct.* 10th).

Leasehold Reform Act enables tenants of houses in Britain held on long lease at low rent to acquire freehold or extended lease.

Publication of the 'Plowden Report' on primary education (*Jan.* 10th), *Children and their Primary Schools*; advocates extra expenditure on primary education in deprived areas of Britain and nation-wide provision of nursery education.

P Science, Technology, Discovery, etc.

S. Manabe and R.T. Wetherald warn that the increase in carbon dioxide in the atmosphere, produced by human activities, is causing a 'greenhouse effect', which will raise atmospheric temperatures and cause a rise in sea levels.

People's Republic of China explodes its first hydrogen bomb (announced on June 17th).

Invention of Dolby noise-reduction system for use in tape recording.

Introduction of direct dialling from New York to Paris and London (*Mar.* 1).

U.S. scientist Gene Amdahl proposes the use of parallel processors in computers to produce faster processing speeds.

Three U.S. astronauts die in a fire during a training exercise on the Apollo spacecraft (*Jan.* 27th).

Soviet cosmonaut dies during the descent of his Soyuz I spacecraft (*Apr.* 24th).

U.S.S.R. Venera IV lands on Venus (Oct. 18th), the first soft landing on another planet.

Jocelyn Bell and Anthony Hewish discover the first pulsar (*July*; announced in 1968); later shown to be a collapsed neutron star emitting bursts of radio energy.

Installation of a tank containing 100,000 gallons of cleaning fluid in a former gold mine in South Dakota, U.S., to detect neutrinos from the Sun.

Sheldon Lee Glashow, Abdus Salam and Steven Weinberg separately develop the electroweak unification theory, explaining 'electromagnetic' interactions and the 'weak' nuclear force.

U.S. scientist Charles T. Caskey and associates demonstrate that identical forms of messenger RNA produce the same amino acids in a variety of living beings, showing that the genetic code is common to all life forms.

Dr. Christiaan Barnard performs the first heart transplant operation, in South Africa (*Dec.* 3rd); the patient, Louis Washkansky, survives for 18 days.

Rene Favaloro in Cleveland, U.S., develops the coronary bypass operation.

Introduction of mammography (an X-ray technique) for the detection of breast cancer.

Desmond Morris, *The Naked Ape*.

'Crown' ethers discovered by C.J. Pedersen.

D **Apr**: 2nd (–7th), U.N. diplomatic mission to Aden; general strike and terrorist campaign by Arab nationalists;
7th, border clashes between Syria and Israel around Lake Tiberias;
8th, fighting resumes between Greek and Turkish Cypriots near Limassol;
13th, heavy Labour losses in British county council elections; in Greater London, Conservatives have 82 seats and Labour 18;
21st; military coup in Athens establishes the regime of the 'Greek Colonels';
27th (–*Oct.* 29th), 'Expo 67' exhibition in Montreal marks centenary of Canadian confederation.

E **May**: 2nd (–10th), Bertrand Russell International War Crimes Tribunal in Stockholm finds U.S. guilty of aggression in Vietnam;
4th, British bank rate down to 5.5 per cent (lowest since 1964);
6th, outbreak of rioting in Hong Kong;
10th, Greek military junta takes control of Greek Orthodox Church;
11th, Britain, Denmark and Ireland formally apply to join E.E.C.;
—, Conservatives make net gain of 535 seats in British borough elections;
12th, British government chooses Stansted for third London airport (local protestors win fresh inquiry, *Feb.* 1968);
16th, President de Gaulle, in press conference, virtually vetoes British entry into E.E.C.;
18th, 100,000 Chinese demonstrate in Peking against British possession of Hong Kong;
19th, U.N. withdraws peace-keeping force from Israeli-Egyptian border at request of U.A.R.;
20th, Arab League Council declares that an attack on one Arab State would be an attack on all;
22nd, President Nasser of U.A.R. closes Gulf of Aqaba to Israeli shipping; Israel and U.A.R. call up reserves;
23rd, U.S. tells U.A.R. to respect freedom of international waterways; U.S.S.R. warns Israel against aggression;
28th, secession of Biafra under Colonel Chukwuemeka Odumegwu Ojukwu provokes civil war in Nigeria.

F **Jun**: 5th, war breaks out between Israel and Arab States (U.A.R., Syria, Jordan, Lebanon and Iraq); Arab states declare oil embargo on Britain and U.S.; Israel destroys over 300 enemy aircraft;
6th, President Nasser closes Suez Canal and alleges that U.S. and British forces are aiding Israel;
7th, Duchess of Windsor makes first official appearance in Britain at unveiling of plaque to Queen Mary;
8th, Israel wins control of Sinai Peninsula, Gaza strip and Old Jerusalem; U.A.R. and allies agree to ceasefire;
9th, Israel attacks Syria after breach of ceasefire;
10th, end of Six-Day War; U.S.S.R. breaks off diplomatic relations with Israel;
11th, rioting in Florida signals a summer of racial violence in U.S. cities;
17th, China announces explosion of its first hydrogen bomb;
20th, Arab mutineers in Aden kill 22 British soldiers;
21st, Soviet President Podgorny visits Cairo to discuss re-armament of U.A.R.;
23rd (–25th), summit talks between President Johnson and Soviet Premier Kosygin at Glassboro, New Jersey;
30th, 46 nations sign Final Acts of 'Kennedy Round' of General Agreement on Tariffs and Trade.

Q Scholarship

Start of excavation of Mycenaean palace (and frescoes) at Akrotiri on the Aegean island of Thera.
Henry Chadwick, *The Early Church.*
Peter Brown, *Augustine of Hippo.*
Sheppard Frere, *Britannia.*
R.H.C. Davis, *King Stephen.*
Maurice Beresford, *New Towns of the Middle Ages.*
The Agrarian History of England and Wales (–).
P. Collinson, *The Elizabethan Puritan Movement.*
J.H. Plumb, *The Growth of Political Stability in England, 1675–1725.*
B. Bailyn, *The Ideological Origins of the American Revolution.*
Christopher Hill, *Reformation to Industrial Revolution.*
G.R. Elton, *The Practice of History.*

R Philosophy and Religion

Jacques Derrida, *Of Grammatology.*
Order of deacons revived in Roman Catholic Church.
Roman Catholics forbidden to attend prayers for unity in All Saints' Anglican Church, Rome.
Occupation of Old City of Jerusalem by Jews for the first time since C.E. 135.
Consecration of the Roman Catholic Cathedral of Christ the King in Liverpool, England.

S Art, Sculpture, Fine Arts and Architecture

Alfred Barr retires as Director of Collections, Museum of Modern Art, New York.
Tate Gallery purchases Roy Lichtenstein's *Whaam* of 1963.
David Hockney, *A Neat Lawn.*
Andy Warhol, *Marilyn Monroe.*

Sculpture:
Anthony Caro, *Prairie.*
Richard Long, *A Line Made by Walking.*
Robert Morris, *Untitled (Felt sculpture, soft).*
George Segal, *Execution.*

Architecture:
Paul Koralek, Trinity College Library, Dublin.
Le Corbusier, Centre Le Corbusier Heidi-Weber, Zurich.
Frederick Gibberd, Metropolitan Cathedral Church of Christ the King, Liverpool.

T Music

R.R. Bennett, *A Penny for a Song* (opera).
John Cage, *Musicircus.*
Aaron Copland, *Inscape.*
Alexander Goehr, *Arden Must Die* (opera).
Witold Lutoslawski, 2nd Symphony.
Karlheinz Stockhausen, *Hymnen.*
Toru Takemitsu, *November Steps.*

G **Jul:** 1st, commissions of E.E.C., European Coal and Steel Community and Euratom merge into a Commission of the European Communities (E.C.);
2nd, fighting begins in Eastern Congo between army and white mercenaries (mercenaries flee to Rwanda, *Nov.* 4th);
14th, U.N. orders Israel to desist from unifying Jerusalem;
16th, Hong Kong government arrests 600 Communists (assumes emergency powers, 20th);
18th, British Defence White Paper announces drastic reduction in commitments in Far East;
24th, President de Gaulle angers Canadian government by shouting 'Vive le Québec libre!' during visit to Montreal;
25th, Margaret Herbison, British Minister for Social Security, resigns over spending curbs;
27th, outbreak of race riots in Detroit; President Johnson appoints commission to investigate causes.

H **Aug:** 15th, Martin Luther King urges U.S. blacks to launch a campaign of massive civil disobedience;
22nd, Red Guards set fire to British embassy in Peking;
24th, U.S. and U.S.S.R. present draft nuclear non-proliferation treaty to Geneva disarmament conference;
25th, British troops start withdrawal from Aden;
28th, British Prime Minister Harold Wilson takes direct command of Department of Economic Affairs;
—, Belgium suspends all aid to Congo.

J **Sep:** 1st, Arab summit conference lifts boycott on oil to Britain and U.S. imposed during Six-Day War;
5th, Britain appeals for negotiations with nationalist forces in Aden;
10th, referendum in Gibraltar: 12,138 vote for retaining links with Britain, 44 for union with Spain;
12th (–15th), Indian and Chinese troops clash on Tibet–Sikkim frontier;
18th, end of casual dock labour in British ports; several unofficial strikes follow;
20th, mid-west Nigeria proclaims itself independent as Benin;
—, Queen Elizabeth launches liner *Queen Elizabeth II* at Clydebank, Scotland;
25th, nationalists call for ceasefire in Aden and Federation of South Arabia.

K **Oct:** 9th, revolutionary guerrilla Che Guevara is executed in Bolivia;
13th, Communists plant over 100 bombs in Hong Kong;
19th, Arab nationalists kill British administrator in Aden;
21st, U.A.R. navy sinks Israeli destroyer off Sinai (24th, Israeli artillery destroys Suez oil refineries);
—, demonstrations against Vietnam War in Washington, London and other capitals;
25th, epidemic of foot-and-mouth disease begins in Britain (ends, *Mar.* 1968);
26th, Shah Mohammad Reza Pahlevi formally crowns himself at ceremony in Teheran;
27th, U.N. Trusteeship Committee condemns British failure to overthrow Smith regime in Rhodesia;
28th, Kenya and Somalia end four-year border conflict.

L **Nov:** 2nd (–7th), rival nationalist groups fight in streets of Aden;
3rd, Greek military government abolishes trial by jury for all common and political crimes;
7th, U.S.S.R. celebrates 50th anniversary of Bolshevik Revolution;

U **Literature**

J.P. Donleavy, *The Saddest Summer of Samuel F.*
Robert Lowell, *Near the Ocean.*
Najob Mahfouz, *Miramar.*
Gabriel García Márquez, *One Hundred Years of Solitude.*
Flann O'Brien, *The Third Policeman.*
Michel Tournier, *Friday.*
Thornton Wilder, *The Eighth Day.*
The National Library, Ottawa, Ontario established.

V **The Press**

Closure of the British co-operative movement's paper *The Sunday Citizen.*
New York's *World Journal Tribune* ceases publication.

W **Drama and Entertainment**

Griselda Gambaro, *Los Siameses.*
Peter Nichols, *A Day in the Death of Joe Egg.*
Harold Pinter, *The Homecoming.*
George Ryga, *The Ecstasy of Rita Joe.*
Tom Stoppard, *Rosencrantz and Guildenstern are Dead.*
Derek Walcott, *Dream on Monkey Mountain.*
Martin Walser, *Home Front.*
Charles Wood, *Dingo.*
Films:
Robert Aldrich's *The Dirty Dozen.*
Joseph Losey's *Accident.*
Arthur Penn's *Bonnie and Clyde.*
John Schlesinger's *Far from the Madding Crowd.*
Television:
Ironside.
The Forsyte Saga.
Laugh-In.
The Prisoner.
B.B.C.2 makes Europe's first television broadcasts in colour.
B.B.C. starts local radio.
Four numbered stations replace B.B.C.'s Light, Home and Third Services.
Opening of first Laura Ashley shop in London.
Popular music:
First rock festivals held, in California.
'Pirate' radio stations become illegal in Britain.
The Beatles, *Sergeant Pepper's Lonely Hearts Club Band.*
The Doors, *The Doors.*
The Jimi Hendrix Experience, *Are You Experienced?*

X **Sport**

Queen's Park Rangers becomes first British Third Division side to win a Wembley soccer final, beating West Bromwich Albion 3–2 in the League Cup (*Mar.* 14th).
Foinavon, ridden by John Buckingham, wins the British Grand National at odds of 100–1 (*Apr.* 8th).
The World Boxing Association strips Muhammad Ali (formerly Cassius Clay) of his World Heavy-weight title for refusing the U.S. Army draft (*Apr.* 28th).
Glasgow Celtic is first Scottish team to win soccer's European Cup, beating Inter Milan 2–1 in Lisbon (*May* 25th).

L **Nov**: 9th, British bank rate rises to 6.5 per cent (to 8 per cent, 18th);
14th, Britain borrows $90 million from Bank of International Settlements;
8th, British Commonwealth Secretary, George Thomson, holds talks with Ian Smith in Salisbury;
18th, devaluation of sterling from $2.80 to $2.40;
21st (–29th), negotiations in Geneva between Britain and nationalists on transfer of power in South Arabia;
25th, Cyprus asks U.N. Security Council to prevent Turkish invasion (Turkey, Greece and Cyprus agree peace formula, *Dec.* 3rd);
26th, proclamation of People's Republic of South Yemen (last British troops leave Aden, 29th);
29th, Roy Jenkins replaces James Callaghan as British Chancellor of the Exchequer;
30th, Britain accepts $1.4 billion loan from International Monetary Fund.

M **Dec**: 6th, demonstrations in New York as part of 'Stop the Draft Week';
7th, Nicolae Ceauşescu becomes Roumanian head of state as well as Party General Secretary;
13th, King Constantine of Greece attempts to oust military junta (14th, goes into exile);
16th, U.N. General Assembly demands South African withdrawal from South-West Africa;
17th, Harold Holt, Prime Minister of Australia, drowns near Portsea, Victoria;
19th, at E.C. Council, France vetoes negotiations for British entry; Britain states application will not be withdrawn.

X Sport (*cont.*)

The British Lawn Tennis Association abolishes the distinction between amateurs and professionals (*Oct.* 5th) – as does the International Lawn Tennis Federation in 1968).

After 226 days (starting *Aug.* 27th 1966), Francis Chichester, in his yacht *Gipsy Moth IV*, completes the first solo round-the-world voyage (*Dec.* 12th).

Y Statistics

Religious denominations in U.S. (in mill.): Roman Catholics, 47.9; Baptists, 24.7; Methodists, 13.2; Lutherans, 8.7; Presbyterians, 4.1; Protestant Episcopal, 3.4; Mormons, 2.1; Greek Orthodox, 1.8; Jews, 5.7.

Z Births and Deaths

Apr. 19th Konrad Adenauer d. (91).
May 12th John Masefield d. (88).
Aug. 9th Joe Orton d. (34).
Aug. 31st Ilya Ehrenburg d. (75).
Sept. 18th John Cockcroft d. (70).
Oct. 8th Clement Attlee d. (84).
Oct. 9th Che Guevara d. (39).
Dec. 17th Harold Holt d. (59).
Dec. 30th Vincent Massey d. (80).

1968 (Jan. – Apr.) Assassination of Martin Luther King — 'May Events' in Paris — Soviet invasion of Czechoslovakia

A **Jan**: 4th, number of U.S. troops in Vietnam reaches 486,000;
5th, Alexander Dubček becomes First Secretary of Czechoslovak Communist Party;
8th, battle between Israeli and Jordanian forces south of Sea of Galilee;
10th, John Grey Gorton becomes 20th Prime Minister of Australia;
12th, U.S.S.R. dissidents Yuri Galanskov and Alexander Ginsburg sentenced in Moscow to hard labour ;
16th, British government re-introduces prescription charges, cuts capital spending, and proposes military withdrawal from east of Suez (except Hong Kong);
17th, Leyland Motors merges with British Motor Corporation;
21st, 31 North Koreans raid Seoul in attempt to assassinate President Park of South Korea;
23rd, North Korea seizes U.S. intelligence ship Pueblo (crew released, *Dec.* 23rd);
30th, Viet Cong launches Tet offensive against South Vietnamese cities;
—, students in Warsaw demonstrate against political censorship;
31st, U.N. trust territory of Nauru becomes independent (population 6,000).

B **Feb**: 7th, Flemish campaign against French-speakers at University of Louvain brings down Belgian government;
8th, three black students killed in Orangeburg, South Carolina, after attempt to desegregate bowling alley;
9th, Transvaal Supreme Court imprisons 30 men accused of terrorism in South-West Africa;
18th, in Britain, adoption of British Standard Time, one hour ahead of Greenwich Mean Time;
21st, bomb explodes at Soviet embassy, Washington;
25th, President Makarios of Cyprus re-elected by huge majority;
26th (–*Mar.* 5th), meeting in Budapest to plan World Communist Summit;
27th, Arab Emirates of Persian Gulf announce intention to federate when British troops leave in 1971.

C **Mar**: 1st, speculative flight from U.S. dollar into gold starts to destabilise international monetary system (London Gold Market closed, 15th–*Apr.* 1st);
—, emergency legislation restricts immigration of Kenyan Asians into Britain;
2nd, Queen Elizabeth reprieves three Africans sentenced to death in Rhodesia (6th, they are hanged in Salisbury);
11th, major U.S. and South Vietnamese offensive in Saigon area;
15th, George Brown resigns as British Foreign Secretary; replaced by Michael Stewart;
16th, U.S. Senator Robert Kennedy announces candidacy for Democratic Presidential nomination;
18th, heavy fighting in northern Rhodesia between government forces and African nationalists;
19th, British Budget increases duties and introduces special levy on unearned income to raise extra £923 million;
21st, British bank rate cut to 7.5 per cent (7 per cent, *Sept.* 19th);
22nd, President Novotný of Czechoslovakia resigns (succeeded by General Ludvik Svoboda, 30th);
31st, President Johnson announces decision not to seek re-election and restricts U.S. bombing of North Vietnam.

D **Apr**: 3rd, U.S. and North Vietnam agree to establish direct contact;
4th, assassination of Martin Luther King in Memphis, Tennessee;

O Politics, Economics, Law and Education

Race Relations Act outlaws discrimination in Britain.

Prescription charges re-imposed in Britain with some exceptions (announced *Jan.* 16th).

Royal Commission on Trade Unions and Employers' Associations urges end to national wage agreements and formation of labour tribunals in Britain (*June* 13th).

Fulton Committee criticises rigid class structure and lack of professionalism of British civil service (*June* 26th).

Central Banks agree two-tier system for gold: official dealings at $35 per ounce, commercial dealings at free price (*Mar.* 17th).

Major discoveries of oil made in Alaska on land fronting the Arctic Ocean.

Post Office in Britain introduces second class mail (*Sept.* 16th).

Abortion becomes lawful in Britain when pregnancy endangers physical or mental health of woman or child (*Apr.* 27th).

U.S. Supreme Court overturns precedents to broaden rights of criminal defendants and convicts (*May*).

British law case 'Conway v. Rimmer' gives courts power to inspect government documents privately to see if suppression for security reasons would prejudice the administration of justice.

Newsom Commission calls for integration of British independent schools with state schools (*July* 22nd).

P Science, Technology, Discovery, etc.

Inauguration of the Aswan High Dam on the River Nile in Egypt.

First demonstration flight of U.S.S.R. Tupolev Tu-144, the world's first supersonic airliner (*Dec.* 31st).

The first 'supertanker' for carrying oil goes into service.

Regular hovercraft services begin across the English Channel.

Completion of tidal power station on the Rance, France.

U.S.S.R. spacecraft Zond V (launched *Sept.* 14th) flies around the moon and returns to earth.

First manned U.S. Apollo space mission, Apollo VII, tests Apollo spacecraft (*Oct.* 11th–22nd); Apollo VIII makes the first manned mission to the moon; it completes 10 orbits and returns to earth (*Dec.* 21st–27th).

Mark Ptashne and Walter Gilbert separately identify the first repressor genes.

New fertility drugs cause a British woman to give birth to sextuplets.

Oral contraceptives are shown to cause blood clots in some women.

M. Arnstein develops a vaccine against meningitis.

Dr. Christiaan Barnard performs his second heart transplant operation; the patient lives for 74 days.

J.D. Watson, *The Double Helix*, about Crick and Watson's discovery of DNA.

First experimental fusion reactors (Tokomaks) built.

Glomar Challenger drills cores in sea bed as part of the Deep Sea Drilling Project.

Elso S. Barghoorn and associates report the discovery of remains of amino acids in rocks 3 billion years old.

Q Scholarship

The Cambridge History of Iran (–91).

J.J. Scarisbrick, *Henry VIII*.

Carl Bridenbaugh, *Vexed and Troubled Englishmen*.

M.R.D. Foot, H.C.G. Matthew (eds.), *The Gladstone Diaries* (–).

D **Apr**: 5th, Mrs. Barbara Castle becomes British Minister of Employment and Productivity, responsible for prices and incomes policy;
8th, new Czechoslovak government takes office under Oldřich Černik;
9th, East Germany adopts new constitution;
—, British Race Relations Bill published;
10th, President Johnson signs Civil Rights Bill prohibiting racial discrimination in housing;
11th, riots in Berlin follow attempted assassination of student leader Rudi Dutschke;
19th, Josef Smrkovský Chairman of Czechoslovak National Assembly, promises freedom of press, assembly and religion;
20th, Enoch Powell attacks coloured immigration to Britain: 'like the Roman, I seem to see the River Tiber foaming with much blood' (dismissed from Shadow Cabinet, 21st);
21st, Pierre Trudeau succeeds Lester Pearson as Prime Minister of Canada;
—, U.S. Vice-President Hubert Humphrey announces candidacy for Democratic Presidential nomination;
30th, Nelson Rockefeller announces candidacy for Republican Presidential nomination.

E **May**: 2nd, violent clashes between students and police begin in Latin Quarter of Paris;
5th, Spain further restricts access to and from Gibraltar;
9th, Conservatives take control of 27 out of 32 London boroughs in local elections;
10th, 'Night of the Barricades' in Paris (11th, French government makes concessions to student demands);
13th, U.S. and North Vietnamese negotiators begin peace talks in Paris;
14th, Czechoslovak government announces wide range of liberalising reforms;
17th, students and strikers occupy factories and hold protest marches in French cities;
—, Soviet Premier Kosygin and Defence Minister Marshal Grechko visit Prague;
24th, rioters set fire to Paris Bourse; President de Gaulle asks for vote of confidence in referendum;
26th, French government raises minimum wage by 33.3 per cent;
30th, President de Gaulle postpones referendum and calls general election, as riots continue;
31st, Nigerian–Biafran peace talks in Kampala break down.

F **Jun**: 5th, Senator Robert Kennedy shot in Los Angeles after winning California primary election (he dies, 6th);
10th, General Westmoreland hands over U.S. command in Vietnam to General Abrams;
11th, East Germany announces that West Berliners will require visas to cross its territory;
12th, French government bans demonstrations and dissolves 11 student organisations;
18th, British House of Lords rejects Rhodesian Sanctions Order (20th, Harold Wilson promises radical reform of Upper House);
19th, India accuses Pakistan and China of aiding rebels in Nagaland and Mizo;
20th, total U.S. combat deaths in Vietnam exceed 25,000;
24th (–*July* 25th), negotiations between Greek and Turkish Cypriots in Nicosia (second round, Aug. 29th–Dec. 9th);
26th, Earl Warren announces resignation as Chief Justice of U.S. Supreme Court;
27th, Czechoslovak National Assembly passes laws abolishing censorship and rehabilitating political prisoners;
30th, Gaullists win landslide victory in second round of French general election.

R **Philosophy and Religion**

Max Black, *The Labyrinth of Language.*
Michel Foucault, *The Archaeology of Knowledge.*
Jürgen Habermas, *Knowledge and Human Interests.*
Publication of Papal Encyclical *Humanae Vitae* (July 29th), prohibiting use of artificial contraception by Roman Catholics.
Fourth Assembly of the World Council of Churches meets in Uppsala, Sweden.
Tenth Lambeth Conference of Anglican bishops meets at Westminster, London.
All laws dealing with Church–State relations in Albania are abrogated, implying that religious bodies have been eliminated and that Albania has therefore become the world's first complete atheist state.
The South African Council of Churches declares the doctrine of racial separation to be 'truly hostile' to Christianity.

S **Art, Sculpture, Fine Arts and Architecture**

Painting:

Henry Moore exhibition held in the Tate Gallery and worldwide.
'Art of the Real' exhibition at the Museum of Modern Art, New York.
Supports/Surfaces movement, France.
Richard Hamilton, *Swinging London.*

Sculpture:

Anselmo, *Structure Which Eats Salad.*
Barry Flanagan, *Heap 3.*
César, *Compressions.*
Sol Lewitt, *Untitled Cube (6).*

Architecture:

Hubert Bennett and architects of Greater London Council, Hayward Gallery, London.
Mies van der Rohe, National Gallery, West Berlin.
Skidmore, Owings and Merrill, John Hancock Building, Chicago.
James Stirling, History Faculty Building, Cambridge University, Cambridge.

T **Music**

Malcolm Arnold, *Peterloo.*
Luciano Berio, *Sinfonia.*
Harrison Birtwistle, *Punch and Judy* (opera).
Pierre Boulez, *Domaines.*
B. Britten, *The Prodigal Son* (opera).
Luigi Dallapiccola, *Ulisse* (opera).
Gian Carlo Menotti, *Help, Help, the Globolinks!* (opera).
John Tavener, *The Whale.*

U **Literature**

Lawrence Durrell, *Tunc.*
Allen Ginsberg, *Airplane Dreams.*
Thom Gunn, *Touch.*
Ursula Le Guin, *A Wizard of Earthsea.*
Czeslaw Milosz, *Native Realm.*
Gore Vidal, *Myra Breckinridge.*
Marguerite Yourcenar, *The Abyss.*
Yasunari Kawabata awarded Japan's first Nobel Prize for Literature.

G **Jul:** 1st, 61 nations, including Britain, U.S. and U.S.S.R. sign Treaty on Non-Proliferation of Nuclear Weapons;
2nd, Britain offers famine relief to Nigeria and Biafra (4th, Biafra refuses it while Britain sells arms to Nigeria);
9th, Couve de Murville succeeds Georges Pompidou as French Premier;
—, Czechoslovakia rejects Soviet demand for meeting of Communist Party leaders;
14th, U.S.S.R. halts withdrawal of troops from Czechoslovakia after Warsaw Pact exercises;
15th, Malaysia rejects Philippine claim to Sabah in North Borneo;
16th, Soviet, East German, Hungarian, Polish and Bulgarian leaders declare Czechoslovak reforms unacceptable;
24th, conference of Spanish bishops proclaims workers' right to strike and form independent trade unions;
27th, Dubček states that Czechoslovakia will continue on its chosen road and not retreat one step;
29th (–*Aug.* 1st), Czechoslovak and Soviet leaders hold talks at Cierna-nad-Tisou.

H **Aug:** 4th, Israeli aircraft bomb Palestinian guerrilla bases in Jordan;
5th, Spain declares state of emergency in Guipuzcoa after Basque separatists murder police chief;
8th, Richard Nixon secures Republican nomination for U.S. Presidency and chooses Spiro Agnew as running-mate for Vice-Presidency;
15th, Nigeria forbids International Red Cross to fly relief supplies to starving Biafrans from neutralised air-strip;
20th, Soviet and allied forces invade Czechoslovakia and arrest reform leaders;
21st, Congress of Czechoslovak Communist Party, meeting in secret, rejects collaboration and re-elects Dubček;
23rd, President Svoboda of Czechoslovakia flies to Moscow for talks (secures release of Dubček, 25th);
24th, Yugoslavia and Roumania jointly condemn invasion of Czechoslovakia;
25th, France explodes hydrogen bomb in South Pacific, thus becoming fifth thermonuclear Power;
28th, Democratic Party convention in Chicago nominates Hubert Humphrey as Presidential candidate; violent demonstrations against the Vietnam War take place around the convention hall;
—, Czechoslovak National Assembly declares Soviet occupation illegal;
31st, earthquakes in Iran kill 12,000.

J **Sep:** 2nd, U.S.S.R. tells West Germany to stop exerting itself in Eastern Europe and hints at possible invasion (17th, U.S., Britain and France warn U.S.S.R. against attacking West Germany);
5th, British T.U.C. massively rejects statutory incomes policy and approves voluntary wage restraint only by narrow margin;
6th, Swaziland becomes independent under King Sobhuza II;
12th, Albania formally quits Warsaw Pact;
15th, Organization of African Unity appeals to Biafra to abandon independence struggle;
—, severe flooding in south-east England;
18th, President Marcos proclaims Philippine sovereignty over most of Sabah (19th, Malaysia withdraws diplomats from Manila);
26th, Antonio Salazar resigns as Prime Minister of Portugal after 36 years; succeeded by Marcello Caetano;
27th, U.S.S.R. postpones World Communist Summit planned for *Nov.*

v **The Press**

Sir William ('Pissing Billy') Carr sells a 51 per cent stake in *The News of the World* to Rupert Murdoch, having rejected an offer from Robert Maxwell.

w **Drama and Entertainment**

End of theatre censorship in Britain (*Sept.* 26th).
Peter Barnes, *The Ruling Class.*
Alan Bennett, *Forty Years On.*
Peter Handke, *Kaspar.*
Israel Horovitz, *The Indian Wants the Bronx.*
Thomas Kilroy, *The Death and Resurrection of Mr Roche.*
Arthur Miller, *The Price.*
Peter Terson, *Zigger Zagger.*
Michel Tremblay, *The Sisters-in-Law.*
Cabaret.
Hair.

Films:
Lindsay Anderson's *If...*
Stanley Kubrick's *2001, A Space Odyssey.*
Sergio Leone's *The Good, The Bad and the Ugly.*
Mike Nichols' *The Graduate.*
In the Heat of the Night.
Planet of the Apes.

Television:
Dad's Army.
Hawaii Five - O.

Popular music:
Transcendental Meditation tour in the U.S. by the Maharishi Mahesh Yogi and The Beach Boys.
The Band, *Music from Big Pink.*
James Brown, 'Say it Loud, I'm Black and I'm Proud'.
The Rolling Stones, *Beggar's Banquet.*
Van Morrison, *Astral Weeks.*

x **Sport**

Former world champion racing driver Jim Clark killed in accident at Hockenheim circuit, West Germany (*Apr.* 7th).

Manchester United becomes the first English soccer team to win the European Cup, beating Benfica of Portugal by 4–1 in the final in London (*May* 29th).

At the first 'open' Wimbledon the Singles titles are won by Rod Laver of Australia and Billie Jean King of the U.S.A.

In Olympic Games in Mexico City U.S. wins 45 gold medals; U.S.S.R., 29; Japan, 11; East Germany, 9; France and Czechoslovakia, 7; West Germany, Britain and Poland, 5; Rumania, 4; Bob Beamon of the U.S.A. establishes a new Long Jump world record of 29 feet 2 ½inches).

In Britain, Garry Sobers, batting for Nottinghamshire against Glamorgan at Swansea, hits six sixes in one over off Malcolm Nash (*Aug.* 31st).

The M.C.C. tour to South Africa is cancelled after the South African Government objects to the inclusion of the coloured player Basil D'Oliveira in the touring party (*Sept.* 24th).

K **Oct**: 4th, Czechoslovak leaders visiting Moscow agree to dismantle remnants of reform;
5th (–6th), crowds in Londonderry, Northern Ireland, clash with police during civil rights march;
9th (–13th), talks about Rhodesia problem between Harold Wilson and Ian Smith aboard H.M.S. *Fearless* at Gibraltar;
—(–12th), Conservative Party conference at Blackpool exposes divisions between 'Powellites' and leadership;
12th, Equatorial Guinea wins independence from Spain;
16th, U.S.S.R. and Czechoslovakia sign treaty on eventual withdrawal of Warsaw Pact forces;
—, British Commonwealth Office merges with Foreign Office.
21st, anti-U.S. demonstrations in Tokio;
27th, big protest march in London against Vietnam War;
28th, West German government initiates security review after spate of suicides of top Secret Service and military officials with access to secret information;
31st, President Johnson halts bombing of North Vietnam and announces agreement on Vietnamese delegations for peace talks;
—, Chinese Communist Party expels President Liu Shao-chi.

L **Nov**: 1st, White Paper on British House of Lords proposes abolition of hereditary element;
—, in Britain, merger creates Department of Health and Social Security;
5th, in U.S. elections Richard Nixon, Republican, with 302 electoral votes, wins narrow victory over Hubert Humphrey, Democrat, with 191, and George Wallace, Independent, with 45; popular vote: Nixon, 31,770,237; Humphrey, 31,270,533; Wallace, 9,906,141; Democrats keep control of Congress.
—, South Vietnam objects to composition of planned Paris peace talks (agrees to attend, 26th);
15th, new Greek constitution in force, with articles on personal freedom suspended;
16th, in Northern Ireland, 5,000 civil rights marchers defy ban on demonstrations in Londonderry;
17th, Anglo-Rhodesian talks in Salisbury end in deadlock;
20th, European exchange markets close after heavy speculation against French franc (President de Gaulle refuses to devalue, 23rd);
22nd, British government increases indirect taxes and introduces import deposits;
—, Northern Ireland government proposes reforms in housing and local franchise;
29th, Arab guerrillas attack potash plant on Dead Sea (*Dec.* 1st, Israeli jets blow up two bridges in Jordan);
30th, violence erupts between Catholic and Protestant demonstrators in Armagh, Northern Ireland.

M **Dec**: 2nd, Iraqi artillery in Jordan shells Israeli villages (4th, Israel bombs Iraqi bases);
6th, rumours of coalition government and Queen's abdication cause panic selling on London stock market;
9th, U.S.S.R. objects to cruise of two U.S. destroyers in Black Sea;
13th, President Costa e Silva of Brazil assumes emergency powers to prevent left-wing coup;
16th, Spain annuls 1492 decree expelling Jews;
18th, U.N. General Assembly declares colonial rule in Gibraltar incompatible with U.N. Charter;
23rd, U.S. proposes to close, re-locate, or share control of 50 military bases in Japan;
26th, two Arabs attack Israeli airliner in Athens (28th, Israel bombs Beirut airport, wrecking 13 aircraft).

Y **Statistics**

Motor cars (in mill.): U.S., 83.3; West Germany, 11.3; Great Britain, 10.9; Italy, 8.1; Japan 5.2; Spain, 1.6; Brazil, 1.5; India, 0.5; world total, 170.

Armed forces: U.S., 3,500,000; other N.A.T.O., 3,020,000; Warsaw Pact, 4,310,000; other Europe, 740,000; Middle East, 770,000; South Asia, 1,470,000; Far East (inc. China), 6,560,000; Oceania, 100,000; Africa, 400,000; Central America, 250,000; South America, 660,000.

Z **Births and Deaths**

Feb. 21st Howard Florey d. (69).
Apr. 4th Martin Luther King d. (39).
Apr. 7th Jim Clark d. (32).
June 6th Robert Kennedy d. (42).
June 25th Tony Hancock d. (44).
Nov. 26th Upton Sinclair d. (90).
Nov. 28th Enid Blyton d. (71).
Dec. 20th John Steinbeck d. (66).
Dec. 30th Trygve Lie d. (72).

1969 (Jan. – Apr.) Nixon becomes U.S. President—Resignation of deGaulle—Disturbances in Northern Ireland

A **Jan**: 1st, Czechoslovakia becomes a two-state federation;
3rd, in Northern Ireland, Roman Catholic and Protestant demonstrators clash in Londonderry (in Newry, 11th);
6th, France bans sale of military supplies to Israel;
10th, Sweden becomes first Western government to recognise North Vietnam;
16th, Czech student, Jan Palach, publicly burns himself to death in Prague in protest at Soviet occupation;
17th, British government issues *In Place of Strife: A Policy for Industrial Relations*;
18th, South Vietnamese and National Liberation Front join expanded peace talks in Paris;
20th, Richard Nixon takes oath as 37th U.S. President;
24th, General Franco imposes martial law in Spain;
—(–*Feb.* 19th), London School of Economics closed after student disorders;
27th, Iraq executes 14 men accused of spying for Israel.

B **Feb**: 1st, Yugoslavia and Roumania jointly refute Brezhnev doctrine on supremacy of international Communist interests;
3rd, Palestine Liberation Organisation elects Yassir Arafat as chairman;
7th, Anguilla votes to break all ties with Britain;
12th, Ndabaningi Sithole, leader of Zimbabwe African National Union, convicted of incitement to murder Ian Smith;
18th, Palestinian terrorists attack El Al airliner at Zurich airport;
22nd, France disputes British account of talks with President de Gaulle on future of the E.C.;
23rd (–*Mar.* 2nd), President Nixon tours Western European capitals;
24th, Northern Ireland general election reveals Unionists' divisions over reform;
—(–*Mar.* 19th), in Britain, strike at Ford plant involving 42,000 workers;
26th, death of Levi Eshkol, Premier of Israel (suceeded by Golda Meir, *Mar.* 11th);
27th, British bank rate rises from 7 to 8 per cent.

C **Mar**: 1st, in Laos the Pathet Lao opposition rejects the government's offer of talks to end civil war;
—, Soviet–Chinese border conflict at Ussuri River;
3rd, British House of Commons approves *In Place of Strife* White Paper despite 49 Labour Noes and 40 Labour abstentions;
5th, London gangsters Ronald and Reginald Kray sentenced to life-imprisonment;
10th, James Earl Ray convicted of murdering Martin Luther King in *Apr.* 1968;
12th, British emissary to Anguilla forced to leave at gun-point (19th, 250 British troops land and re-establish control);
25th, military government takes over in Pakistan amid escalating political violence; President Ayub Khan is replaced by General Yahya Khan.
27th, Harold Wilson arrives in Nigeria for talks with General Gowon;
—, in Britain, Conservatives take Walthamstow, East from Labour in by-election;
28th, anti-Soviet demonstrations in Prague.

D **Apr**: 4th (–*July* 1st), U.N. representatives of U.S., U.S.S.R., Britain and France hold talks on Middle East in New York;
8th, Arab guerrillas attack Eilat; Israeli jets retaliate with attack on Aqaba;
10th, King Hussein of Jordan proposes six-point Middle East peace plan (rejected by Palestinian organisations, 16th);
15th, British Budget increases corporation tax, selective employment tax and petrol duty;

O **Politics, Economics, Law and Education**

Representation of the People Act 1969 (*May* 12th) reduces voting age in Britain from 21 to 18.

Redcliffe-Maud Report of Royal Commission on Local Government in Britain recommends thorough re-organisation (*June* 11th).

Japanese Gross National Product exceeds that of West Germany for first time (*Mar.*).

British House of Commons approves permanent abolition of death penalty (*Dec.* 16th).

P **Science, Technology, Discovery, etc.**

U.S.A. in effect bans use of DDT pesticide.

Thirty-nine nations meet in Rome to discuss pollution.

Creation of 'bubble memory' device, which enables computers to retain information after electrical power is switched off.

Maiden flights of Boeing's 747 'jumbo jet' airliner and the prototype of the French-British supersonic airliner Concorde (*Mar.* 2nd).

Two U.S.S.R. space craft (Soyuz IV and V) are locked together for four hours to form the first experimental space station (*Jan.* 16th).

U.S. Apollo IX mission (*Mar.* 3rd–13th) tests Apollo moon vehicles in earth orbit, followed by Apollo X mission in which the lunar module descends to within 50,000 feet of the moon's surface (*May* 22nd).

U.S. Apollo XI space mission (*July* 16th–24th) leads to the first manned landing on the moon and first walk on the moon (*July* 20).

Foundation of Fermi National Accelerator Laboratory ('Fermilab') near Chicago.

Astronomers identify a visible star with a pulsar known from radio surveys.

Jonathan Beckwith and associates at Harvard Medical School isolate a single gene for the first time.

R.G. Edwards of the Cambridge Physiological Laboratory in Britain makes the first in vitro fertilisation of human egg cells (*Feb.* 15th).

Development and implant of the first effective artificial human heart, used as a temporary device for patients requiring transplants.

Dorothy Hodgkin announces the structure of insulin (*Aug.*).

Publication of *The Red Book* by James Fisher, listing animals and plants in imminent danger of extinction.

World production of polypropylene tops 1 million tons per annum.

'Cryptates' discovered, making salts soluble in organic solvents such as chloroform.

Q **Scholarship**

Kenneth Clark, *Civilisation.*

M. Wilson, L. Thompson (eds.), *The Oxford History of South Africa*, Vol. I (Vol. II, 1971).

C.A. Macartney, *The Habsburg Empire, 1790–1918.*

A.J.P. Taylor, *War by Timetable.*

K.D. Bracher, *The German Dictatorship.*

Angus Calder, *The People's War.*

R **Philosophy and Religion**

Isaiah Berlin, *Four Essays on Liberty.*

Herbert Marcuse, *An Essay on Liberation.*

J.R. Searle, *Speech Acts.*

A scheme for Anglican–Methodist union in England fails to reach the necessary 75 per cent majority in the Convocations of Canterbury and York.

D **Apr:** —, North Korea shoots down U.S. naval intelligence plane;
17th, Gustáv Husák succeeds Alexander Dubček as First Secretary of Czechoslovak Communist Party;
—, British government drops Bill to reform House of Lords;
—, in Northern Ireland 21-year-old civil rights activist Bernadette Devlin wins Mid-Ulster by-election;
20th, British troops guard public utilities in Northern Ireland after post offices bombed;
22nd, Nigerian forces capture Umuahia, the administrative capital of Biafra;
23rd, Northern Ireland government concedes universal adult suffrage in local elections;
27th, referendum in France narrowly rejects constitutional reforms;
28th, resignation of President de Gaulle; Alain Poher becomes interim President.

E **May:** 1st, James Chichester-Clark succeeds Terence O'Neill as Premier of Northern Ireland (6th, grants amnesty to arrested rioters);
9th, wave of currency speculation peaks with West German refusal to revalue mark;
10th, local elections leave Labour in control of only 28 out of 342 borough councils in England and Wales;
11th, Viet Cong launch rocket and ground attacks throughout South Vietnam;
14th, President Nixon suggests mutual withdrawal of U.S., allied and North Vietnamese troops from South Vietnam;
15th, violence in Kuala Lumpur between Malays and Chinese;
20th, government of Laos offers to halt U.S. bombing of Pathet Lao opposition if North Vietnamese withdraw from Laos;
21st, President Nixon nominates Warren Burger as Chief Justice of U.S. Supreme Court;
30th, Gibraltar's constitution comes into effect (general election, *July* 30th);
—, West Germany ends policy of automatically severing relations with governments which recognise East Germany.

F **Jun:** 2nd, Australian aircraft carrier *Melbourne* collides with U.S.S. *Frank E. Evans* during manoeuvres in China Sea;
5th (–17th), delegates from 75 countries attend World Communist Conference in Moscow;
8th, President Nixon announces withdrawal of 25,000 U.S. troops from Vietnam (further 35,000, *Sept.* 16th);
—, Spain completely closes land frontier with Gibraltar (suspends ferry service from Algeciras, 27th);
9th, in Britain Enoch Powell calls for repatriation of coloured immigrants;
15th, Georges Pompidou becomes President of France (appoints Jacques Chaban-Delmas as Prime Minister, 20th);
18th, British government abandons Trade Union Reform Bill in return for T.U.C. pledge to deal with unofficial strikes;
20th, Rhodesia votes to become a republic (24th, Britain cuts last official links);
25th, U.S. Senate passes resolution calling on President not to commit troops to foreign countries without Congressional approval;
26th (–*Aug.* 24th), strike at Port Talbot steel works, South Wales;
30th, Nigerian government takes control of all relief operations in Nigeria–Biafra war.

G **Jul:** 1st, formal investiture of Prince Charles as Prince of Wales at Caernarvon Castle;
4th, General Franco offers Spanish citizenship to all Gibraltarians;

R **Philosophy and Religion** (*cont.*)

Catherine McConnochie is ordained at the Presbytery of Aberdeen as the first woman minister in the Church of Scotland.

The Al-Aqsa Mosque, adjacent to the Dome of the Rock in Jerusalem, is damaged by fire.

The papal decree *Paschalis Mysterii* published.

S **Art, Sculpture, Fine Arts and Architecture**

Painting:

'When Attitude Becomes Form' exhibition, Institute of Contemporary Art, London.

Lichtenstein and David Smith retrospectives at the Guggenheim, New York.

Georg Baselitz, *The Wood on its Head.*

Sculpture:

Dan Flavin, *Monument for V. Tatlin.*

Michael Heizer, *Double Negative.*

Donald Judd, *Untitled* (minimal sculpture, vertically arranged metal and glass boxes).

Niki de Saint Phalle, *Black Nana.*

Architecture:

Denys Lasdun and Partners, First Phase of University of East Anglia, Norwich.

Wurster, Bernardi and Emmons, Skidmore, Owings and Merrill, and Pietro Belluschi as consultant, Bank of America World Headquarters, San Francisco.

T **Music**

Boris Blacher, *Zweihunderttausend Thaler* (opera).

Elliott Carter, Concerto for Orchestra.

Peter Maxwell Davies, *Eight Songs for a Mad King.*

Olivier Messiaen, *The Transfiguration of Our Lord Jesus Christ.*

Thea Musgrave, *Night Music.*

Krzysztof Penderecki, *The Devils of Loudon* (opera).

D. Shostakovich, 14th Symphony.

U **Literature**

First Booker Prize for fiction awarded in Britain.

Robert Coover, *Pricksongs and Descants.*

Michael Crichton, *The Andromeda Strain.*

John Fowles, *The French Lieutenant's Woman.*

Philip Roth, *Portnoy's Complaint.*

Kurt Vonnegut, *Slaughterhouse Five.*

Robert Penn Warren, *Audubon: A Vision.*

V **The Press**

Rupert Murdoch buys *The Sun*, which is relaunched as a tabloid (*Nov.*).

The Daily Telegraph prints news on the front page (*Oct.*)

W **Drama and Entertainment**

Mart Crowley, *The Boys in the Band.*

Arthur Kopit, *Indians.*

Joe Orton, *What the Butler Saw.*

G **Jul:** 13th, border incidents follow defeat of Honduras by El Salvador in qualifying round of World Cup;
14th, El Salvador invades Honduras (agrees to withdraw, 30th);
19th, car driven by U.S. Senator Edward Kennedy plunges into river at Chappaquiddick Island; his passenger, Mary Jo Kopechne, drowns;
—, Mrs. Gandhi issues ordinance for nationalisation of 14 major Indian banks;
20th, Neil Armstrong becomes first man to walk on the Moon;
22nd, in Spain, General Franco names Prince Juan Carlos as his eventual successor;
23rd (–*Aug.* 3rd), President Nixon visits southern Asia, Roumania and Britain;
24th, U.S.S.R. exchanges British spy Gerald Brooke, arrested 1965, for 'Portland spies', Peter and Helen Kroger;
—, heaviest fighting between U.A.R. and Israel since Six-Day War;
27th, North Vietnam denies military intervention in Laos.

H **Aug:** 8th, France devalues the franc by 12 per cent;
11th, in Zambia President Kenneth Kaunda announces nationalisation of copper mines;
12th, in Northern Ireland, arson and street-fighting in Belfast and Londonderry (14th, British troops intervene to separate rioters);
13th, U.S.S.R. forces cross Chinese border in Sinkiang;
15th, Eire mobilises reserves and moves troops near Northern Ireland frontier;
17th, Ulster Unionists rule out coalition government for Northern Ireland;
19th, British army assumes full responsibility for security in Northern Ireland;
21st, 50,000 protesters in Prague mark anniversary of Soviet invasion;
25th, Arab League meets in Cairo to plan 'holy war' against Israel;
28th, Irish Premier, John Lynch, proposes federation of Eire and Northern Ireland;
29th, British and Northern Ireland governments agree on civil rights reforms;
31st, military junta takes power in Brazil following illness of President Costa e Silva.

J **Sep:** 1st, Colonel Moamer al Khaddhafi deposes King Idris of Libya;
3rd, death of President Ho Chi Minh of North Vietnam (succeeded by Ton Dac Thang, 23rd);
7th, Laos, with U.S. aid, begins offensive against North Vietnamese on Plain of Jars;
9th, Israel attacks U.A.R. military bases south of Suez;
10th, British troops start to dismantle barricades in Belfast and Londonderry;
11th, Soviet Premier Kosygin makes surprise visit to Peking;
17th, week of violence between Hindus and Moslems breaks out in Gujarat, India;
22nd, World Islamic Conference opens at Rabat to consider consequences of arson attack on Al Aqsa mosque, Jerusalem, on *Aug.* 21st;
27th, purge of reformers in Czechoslovak government;
—, President Thieu of South Vietman says U.S. withdrawal will take 'years and years' as his country has 'no ambition' to take over the fighting;
28th, in West German elections Christian Democrats wins 46 per cent of votes, Social Democrats 43 per cent.

K **Oct:** 3rd, Greek government restores press freedom, abolishes arbitrary arrest and limits military powers;
4th, President Marcos recalls Philippine troops from Vietnam;
5th, British government abolishes Department of Economic Affairs and creates Ministry of Local Government and Regional Planning;
10th, Lord Hunt's committee recommends disarming Royal Ulster Constabulary and disbanding part-time police, the 'B' specials (11th, intense rioting in Belfast);
—, Czechoslovakia imposes drastic restrictions on foreign travel;

W **Drama and Entertainment** (*cont.*)

Films:

Richard Attenborough's *Oh! What a Lovely War.*
Costa-Gavras's *Z.*
Federico Fellini's *Satyricon.*
Pier Paolo Pasolini's *Theorem.*
Sam Peckinpah's *The Wild Bunch.*
Ken Russell's *Women in Love.*
John Schlesinger's *Midnight Cowboy!.*
Butch Cassidy and the Sundance Kid.

Television:

The Bill Cosby Show.
Kenneth Clark, *Civilisation.*
Monty Python's Flying Circus.
Sesame Street.

Popular music:

Half a million attend the three-day Woodstock Music and Arts Fair in the U.S.
Captain Beefheart and the Magic Band, *Trout Mask Replica.*
Cream, *Goodbye.*
The MC5, *Kick Out the Jams.*
The Stooges, *The Stooges.*
The Who, *Tommy.*
Frank Zappa, *Hot Rats.*

X **Sport**

Robin Knox-Johnston wins the first single-handed round-the-world yacht race (*Apr.* 22nd).

Graham Hill wins the Monaco Grand Prix for a record fifth time (*May* 18th).

Ann Jones wins the Women's Singles title at Wimbledon (*July* 4th), beating Billie Jean King of the U.S. in the Final; she is the first British winner of the title since 1961.

Tony Jacklin wins the British open gold championship (July 12th), the first Briton to win since Max Faulkner in 1951.

Rod Laver of Australia achieves his second Grand Slam (*Sept.* 8th), winning all four major tennis championships (the Australian Open, the French Open, Wimbledon, and the U.S. Open) in the same calendar year.

Y **Statistics**

Immigrant workers in western European countries (with immigrants as percentage of total population in brackets): Austria, 68,000 (0.9); Belgium, 679,000 (7.1); France, 3,177,000 (6.4); West Germany, 2,977,000 (4.8); Great Britain, 2,603,000 (5.0); Holland, 72,000 (0.6); Luxembourg, 28,000 (8.3); Sweden, 173,000 (2.2); Switzerland, 972,000 (16.0).

Z **Births and Deaths**

Feb. 16th Kingsley Martin d. (71).
Feb. 25th Karl Jaspers d. (86).
Mar. 28th Dwight D. Eisenhower d. (78).
July 5th Walter Gropius d. (86).
—Tom Mboya d. (38).
Aug. 17th Ludwig Mies van der Rohe d. (86).
Aug. 31st Rocky Marciano d. (45).
Sept. 3rd Ho Chi Minh d. (79).

1969 (Oct. – Dec.)

K **Oct**: 14th, in Britain, 50 new pence coin replaces 10 shilling note as prelude to decimalisation;
15th, millions demonstrate across U.S. in peaceful 'moratorium' against Vietnam War;
21st, Social Democrat Willy Brandt becomes Chancellor of West Germany;
26th, Portuguese government holds every seat in first significantly contested elections since 1926 (*Nov.* 8th, opposition parties dissolved);
28th, U.S. submits new Middle East peace plan (rejected by Israel, *Dec.* 22nd);
29th, new Cabinet of young 'technocrats' takes office in Spain;
—, U.S. Supreme Court demands immediate integration of 30 schools in Mississippi;
30th, Libya requests early closure of British bases.

L **Nov**: 1st, Congress Party of India formally splits into two factions;
3rd, President Nixon promises complete withdrawal of U.S. ground forces from Vietnam on secret time-table (50,000 more troops withdrawn, *Dec.* 15th);
8th, U.A.R. navy shells Israeli positions in Sinai (11th, air battle over Suez Canal);
11th, U.N. General Assembly rejects admission of Communist China for 20th time;
17th, U.S.-Soviet talks on strategic arms limitation (S.A.L.T.) open in Helsinki;
19th, details emerge of shooting of over 100 Vietnamese civilians by U.S. troops at My Lai on *Mar.* 16th, 1968;
—, Ghana expels 500,000 alien immigrants;
21st, U.S. agrees to return Okinawa to Japan in 1972 and remove all nuclear weapons;
24th, U.S. and U.S.S.R. ratify nuclear non-proliferation treaty;
25th, President Nixon orders destruction of U.S. germ warfare stocks;
29th, National Party wins fourth successive victory in New Zealand general election.

M **Dec**: 2nd, E.C. summit agrees to prepare for negotiations on British entry;
8th, Soviet Foreign Minister Gromyko begins talks with West German Ambassador in Moscow on mutual renunciation of force;
9th, U.S. calls on Israel to withraw from occupied territories in return for binding peace agreement;
12th, Greece withdraws from Council of Europe to pre-empt expulsion for abrogating democratic freedoms;
15th, Alexander Dubček becomes Czechoslovak Ambassador to Turkey;
18th, East Germany proposes diplomatic relations with West Germany as between foreign states;
19th, U.S. partially lifts embargo on trade with Communist China;
25th, Israel launches heavy attack on U.A.R. positions around Suez;
27th, U.A.R., Libya and Sudan form alliance.

1970 (Jan. – Apr.) West German Ostpolitik—U.S. Offensive in Cambodia—Palestinian Terrorism

A **Jan:** 1st, Britain abolishes limit of £50 for use during foreign travel;
—, Mao Tse-tung accuses U.S.S.R. of 'Fascist dictatorship' and 'moribund neo-colonialism';
5th, in Britain, teachers' pay talks break down (selective strikes until *Mar.* 3rd);
7th, British government revises rules for pay increases; practical end of statutory incomes policy;
11th, Biafran leader, General Ojukwu, flies into exile (15th, Nigeria accepts unconditional surrender of Biafra);
19th, British anti-apartheid campaigners raid cricket grounds due to be visited by South African team;
20th, abortive coup d'etat in Iraq (40 executed in following days);
30th, severe fighting between Israel and Syria on Golan Heights.

B **Feb:** 4th, British government proposes making introduction of comprehensive schools compulsory;
6th, U.A.R. frogmen sink Israeli supply ship at Eilat; Israeli jets sink U.A.R. minesweepers in Gulf of Suez;
10th, publication of White Paper *Britain and the European Communities: An Economic Assessment*;
—, Jordan places tighter controls on Palestinian guerrilla movement;
12th, Israeli air raid on factories near Cairo kills 70 civilians;
—, North Vietnamese offensive in north-east Laos;
18th, President Nixon presents document to Congress entitled *U.S. Foreign Policy for the 1970s: A New Strategy for Peace*;
21st, Swiss airliner crashes near Baden, killing 47 passengers; Palestinian terrorists claim responsibility;
23rd, Guyana becomes a republic within the Commonwealth.

C **Mar:** 1st, Socialists win unexpected victory in Austrian general election;
2nd, Rhodesia formally declares itself a republic (Clifford Dupont becomes President, *Apr.* 14th);
5th, British bank rate falls from 8 to 7.5 per cent (to 7 per cent, *Apr.* 14th);
8th, group of Greek Cypriots attempt to assassinate President Makarios;
10th, Knesset defines what constitutes a Jew under Israeli law;
11th, Iraq recognises Kurdish autonomy, thus ending nine-year war;
12th (–*May* 3rd), Queen Elizabeth tours New Zealand and Australia as part of Cook bi-centenary celebrations;
18th, overthrow of Prince Norodom Sihanouk of Cambodia;
19th, first ever meeting of East and West German heads of government takes place at Erfurt (*May* 21st, Willi Stoph and Willy Brandt meet again at Kassel);
23rd, U.S. refuses to supply 25 Phantom fighter-bombers to Israel (sale of 18 agreed, *Sept.* 9th);
29th, in Northern Ireland, attack on a police station in Londonderry (riots in Belfast, *Apr.* 1st);
30th, Japanese students hijack a Boeing 727 and fly to North Korea;
31st, Guatemalan guerrillas kidnap West German Ambassador, Count von Spreti.

D **Apr:** 1st, France proposes international conference on Vietnam, Laos and Cambodia;
—, Viet Cong launch major assaults throughout South Vietnam after six-month lull;
3rd, 500 British troops fly to Northern Ireland to reinforce 6,000 already there;
7th, U.S. Senator Edward Kennedy is spared legal action in respect of Chappaquiddick car crash of July 1969;

O Politics, Economics, Law and Education

New York state introduces abortion on demand.
Family Law Reform Act lowers British age of majority from 21 to 18 (*Jan.* 1st).
British Petroleum makes major oil discovery in North Sea (*Oct.* 19th).
Administration of Justice Act re-organises British High Court and abolishes imprisonment for debt.
Equal Pay Act makes wage and conditions of employment discrimination on ground of sex illegal in Britain from 1975.
Divorce becomes legal in certain cases in Italy (*Dec.* 1st).
First desegregated classes in over 200 school districts in southern U.S. (*Aug.* 31st).

P Science, Technology, Discovery, etc.

Japan (*Feb.* 11th) and the People's Republic of China (*Apr.* 24th) launch artificial satellites.
The Boeing 747 'jumbo jet' airliner begins scheduled flights.
I.B.M. develops the 'floppy disc' for storing computer data.
Carbon dioxide lasers first used for industrial cutting and welding.
U.S. Apollo XIII (launched *Apr.* 11) aborts planned moon landing because of explosion in the Command module (*Apr.* 13th).
U.S.S.R. un-manned Luna XVI lands on the moon, collects soil and returns to earth (*Sept.*); Luna XVII lands on the moon and deploys the Lunokhod I moon vehicle.
Scientists at the University of Wisconsin, U.S.A., assemble a gene from its chemical components.
Howard Temin and David Baltimore separately discover that RNA (ribonucleic acid) can be converted into DNA by the reverse transcriptase enzyme.
First successful nerve transplant achieved in West Germany.
P.R. and A.H. Ehrlich, *Population, Resources, and Experimental Issues in Human Ecology*.

Q Scholarship

The Cambridge History of Islam.
Roland Bainton, *Erasmus of Christendom.*
Christopher Hill, *God's Englishman: Oliver Cromwell and the English Revolution.*
R.C. Latham, W. Matthews (eds.), *The Diary of Samuel Pepys* (–83).
Richard Cobb, *The Police and the People.*

R Philosophy and Religion

Kate Millett, *Sexual Politics.*
Willard Quine, *Philosophy of Logic.*
T.S. Kuhn, *The Structure of Scientific Revolution.*
Publication of the complete *New English Bible*, an entirely new translation.
The General Synod of the Church of England is inaugurated.
The World Council of Churches holds its first consultation on 'Dialogue with Men of Living Faiths'.

S Art, Sculpture, Fine Arts and Architecture

Painting:
Record price for a Warhol *Campbell's Soup Tin* – £25,000.
David Hockney, *Mr and Mrs Ossie Clark and Percy.*
On Kawara, *I Am Still Alive.*
Denis Oppenheim, *Reading Position for a Second Degree Burn.*

D **Apr**: 8th, Israeli bombs fall on primary school in Nile delta killing 30 children;
10th, Greek government relaxes martial law (frees 332 political prisoners, 14th);
19th, Pathet Lao advances on Phnom Penh (Cambodian government appeals for U.S. assistance, 20th);
20th, President Nixon announces withdrawal of a further 150,000 U.S. troops from Vietnam;
22nd, U.S.S.R. celebrates centenary of Lenin's birth;
24th, Gambia becomes a republic within the Commonwealth;
30th, U.S. and South Vietnamese forces attack Communist sanctuaries in Cambodia.

E **May**: 2nd, U.S. bombs North Vietnam for first time since *Nov.* 1968;
4th, U.S. National Guardsmen shoot dead four anti-war demonstrators at Kent State University, Ohio;
6th, Irish Finance Minister, Charles Haughey, dismissed for alleged association with I.R.A. gun-running (acquitted by High Court, *Oct.* 23rd);
9th, demonstrations in Washington against U.S. intervention in Cambodia;
15th, International Olympic Committee expels South Africa;
21st, heavy floods cause extensive damage and loss of life in Roumania;
22nd, British Cricket Council cancels tour by South Africans at government request;
—, Palestinian terrorists ambush Israeli school bus and kill 12 people;
23rd, Portuguese forces attack African guerrilla headquarters in Angola;
25th (–27th), New York Stock Exchange extremely volatile;
27th, Opposition wins general election in Ceylon (Mrs. Bandaranaike becomes Prime Minister, 31st);
31st, earthquake in northern Peru kills over 50,000.

F **Jun**: 5th, France ends 15-month boycott of Western European Union;
7th, fighting breaks out between Jordanian army and Palestinian guerrillas (King Hussein and Yassir Arafat agree ceasefire, 10th);
15th, 12 Russians, mainly Jews, attempt hijack at Leningrad airport;
18th, in British general election, Conservatives win 330 seats, Labour, 287, and Liberals, 6 (Conservatives win 46·4 per cent of votes cast, Labour, 43, and Liberals, 7·4);
19th, Harold Wilson resigns as British Prime Minister and Edward Heath forms Conservative ministry, with Sir Alec Douglas-Home as Foreign Secretary, Iain Macleod as Chancellor of the Exchequer and Reginald Maudling as Home Secretary;
25th, U.S. proposes 'Rogers Plan' for ceasefire and U.N. mediation in Middle East (accepted by U.A.R., *July* 23rd, and Israel, *Aug.* 4th);
26th, in Northern Ireland, violence in Belfast as Bernadette Devlin M.P. starts prison sentence for incitement to riot;
—, Czechoslovak Communist Party expels Alexander Dubček;
28th, U.S. ground troops withdraw from Cambodia;
30th, Britain, Denmark, Norway and Eire open negotiations for E.C. membership.

G **Jul**: 3rd, in Northern Ireland, security forces begin search for arms in Falls Road area of Belfast;
6th, Irish Foreign Minister, Dr. Hillery, makes secret visit to Northern Ireland and criticises behaviour of British troops;
10th, U.S. Roman Catholic missionary, Bishop James Walsh, released after 12 years in Shanghai prison;
12th, China agrees loan to Tanzania and Zambia to build 'TanZam' railway;
16th (–29th), British national dock strike over pay; government declares State of Emergency;

Sculpture:
John De Andrea, *Standing Man.*
Sol Lewitt, *Five Modular Units.*
Mario Merz, *Igloo Fibonacci.*
Robert Smithson, *Spiral Jetty.*

Architecture:
Belluschi and Nervi, Roman Catholic Cathedral, San Francisco.
Kisho Kurokawa, Takara Beautillon, Expo '70, Osaka, Japan.
Yamasaki, World Trade Center, first tower topped out, New York.

T **Music**

Luciano Berio, *Opera.*
Leonard Bernstein, *Mass.*
Alexander Goehr, *Shadowplay-2* (opera).
Witold Lutoslawski, Cello Concerto.
Krzysztof Penderecki, *Utrenia.*
Terry Riley, *A Rainbow in Curved Air.*
Michael Tippett, *The Knot Garden* (opera).

U **Literature**

Maya Angelou, *I Know Why the Caged Bird Sings.*
Richard Bach, *Jonathan Livingston Seagull.*
Elizabeth Bowen, *Eva Trout.*
Ted Hughes, *Crow.*
Iris Murdoch, *Bruno's Dream.*
Michel Tournier, *The Erl King.*
Eudora Welty, *Losing Battles.*
Yukio Mishima commits ritual suicide.

V **The Press**

National newspaper strike in Britain (*June* 10th–15th).

W **Drama and Entertainment**

Antonio Buero Vallejo, *The Sleep of Reason.*
Dario Fo, *Accidental Death of an Anarchist.*
Athol Fugard, *Boesman and Lena.*
Christopher Hampton, *The Philanthropist.*
David Mercer, *After Hegarty.*
Peter Nichols, *The National Health.*
David Storey, *The Contractor and Home.*

Films:
Ken Loach's *Kes.*
Five Easy Pieces.
Love Story.

Television:
The Mary Tyler Moore Show.
On the Buses.
Upstairs Downstairs.

Popular music:
Third and final Isle of Wight Festival of pop music in Britain.
The Beatles officially split up, all four of them releasing solo albums.
Death from drug overdose of superstar guitarist Jimi Hendrix.

G **Jul**: 20th, Britain expresses readiness to supply arms to South Africa for maritime defence;
—, death of British Chancellor Iain Macleod (Anthony Barber becomes Chancellor of the Exchequer, 25th);
22nd, Tanzania, Uganda and Zambia threaten to leave Commonwealth if Britain sells arms to South Africa;
23rd, Northern Ireland government bans all marches for six months;
—, tear-gas bombs thrown from gallery force evacuation of British House of Commons.

H **Aug**: 7th, start of 90-day truce between Israel, U.A.R. and Jordan (renewed for further 90 days, *Nov*. 5th);
12th, West Germany and U.S.S.R. sign treaty in Moscow renouncing use of force;
13th, I.R.A. bomb store found in Tooting, London;
25th, U.N. mediator, Gunnar Jarring, meets representatives of Israel, U.A.R. and Jordan in New York.

J **Sep**: 3rd, Panama rejects U.S. draft treaties on status of Canal Zone;
5th, Marxist candidate, Salvador Allende, wins Chilean Presidential election (Chilean Congress ratifies his election, *Oct*. 24th);
6th, Palestinian terrorists hijack four aircraft, one to Cairo, two to Dawson's Field, Jordan, one to Heathrow, near London, where hijacker Leila Khaled is arrested;
7th, Indian presidential decree abolishes titles and privileges of Ruling Princes (deemed unconstitutional, *Dec*. 15th);
9th, Palestinians hijack B.O.A.C. airliner to Dawson's Field, Jordan;
12th, hijackers blow up three aircraft at Dawson's Field (30th, remaining hostages go free, after Britain, West Germany and Switzerland release Palestinian prisoners);
16th, King Hussein orders Jordanian army to disband Palestinian militia (17th, house-to-house fighting begins in Amman);
19th, Syrian tanks invade Jordan in support of Palestinians;
27th, King Hussein, Yassir Arafat and other Arab leaders sign agreement in Cairo to end civil war in Jordan;
28th, President Nasser of Egypt dies (succeeded by Anwar Sadat, 29th).

K **Oct**: 5th, Quebec separatists kidnap Jasper Cross, British Trade Commissioner in Canada (released, *Dec*. 3rd);
7th, President Nixon proposes five-point peace plan for Indo-China (rejected by North Vietnam, 14th);
9th, Cambodia declares itself the Khmer Republic;
10th, Fiji becomes independent within the Commonwealth;
11th, in Canada, Quebec separatists kidnap Pierre Laporte, Minister of Labour (body found, 17th);
13th, China establishes diplomatic relations with Canada (with Italy, *Nov*. 6th);
15th, British governmental re-organisation creates Department of Trade and Industry and Department of the Environment;
27th, in Britain, Anthony Barber introduces mini-Budget: 6d. cut in standard rate of income tax, lower corporation tax, higher charges for some welfare services;
28th, British government announces retention of 4,500 troops in Far East.

L **Nov**: 1st, in Britain, *The Sunday Times* alleges that Jack the Ripper was Albert Victor, Duke of Clarence;
2nd, abolition of British Prices and Incomes Board;

W **Drama and Entertainment** (*cont.*)

Creedence Clearwater Revival, *Cosmo's Factory.*
The Grateful Dead, *Workingman's Dead and American Beauty.*
Joni Mitchell, *Ladies of the Canyon.*
Simon and Garfunkel, *Bridge Over Troubled Water.*

X **Sport**

Joe Frazier becomes boxing's undisputed World Heavy-weight Champion, beating Jimmy Ellis in 4 rounds in New York (*Feb.* 16th).

Under pressure from British Home Secretary Callaghan, the Cricket Council cancels the South African tour of England (*May* 22nd).

Brazil is victorious in the soccer World Cup, held in Mexico, for the third time (beating Italy by 4–1 in the final); it wins the Rimet Trophy outright (*June* 21st).

Tony Jacklin wins the U.S. Open at Hazeltine Golf Club, Minnesota (*June* 21st); he is the first Briton to win since Ted Ray in 1920.

Nijinsky, ridden by Lester Piggott, wins the Derby in the fastest time since 1936 (*June* 4th). In the same season Piggott also wins the 2,000 Guineas, the King George VI and Queen Elizabeth Diamond Stakes and the St. Leger, completing the first Triple Crown of major British races since 1935.

Margaret Court of Australia becomes only the second woman, after Maureen Connolly in 1953, to win the Grand Slam of all four major tennis tournaments (*Sept.* 13th).

Y **Statistics**

Populations of cities (in mill.): New York, 11.5; Tokio, 11.4; Shanghai, 10.8; Buenos Aires, 8.8; Mexico City, 8; London, 7.4; Moscow, 7.1; Los Angeles, 7.

European populations working in agriculture (percentages): Belgium, 4.5; Bulgaria, 23.6; Czechoslovakia, 10.6; Denmark, 10.6; Eire, 25.1; France, 15.1; East Germany, 11.7; West Germany, 7.5; Great Britain, 2.7; Greece, 40.6; Holland, 6.1; Hungary 24.5; Italy, 16.4; Poland, 38.6; Romania, 36.8; Spain, 24.8; Sweden, 7.9; Yugoslavia, 44.6.

TV sets (per thousand of population): U.S., 412; France, 201; West Germany, 272; Great Britain, 293; Italy, 181; Japan, 215.

Social and educational composition of British Conservative Cabinet: aristocrats, 4, middle class, 14, working class, 0; attendance at public school, 15 (inc. 4 at Eton); attendance at University 15 (all Oxford or Cambridge).

Composition of British House of Lords: Dukes, 29; Marquesses, 30; Earls, 163; Viscounts, 110; Barons, 530; Life Peers, 163; Law Lords, 11; Archbishops and Bishops, 26.

Z **Births and Deaths**

Feb. 2nd Bertrand Russell d. (98).
Feb. 25th Marc Rothko d. (66).
Apr. 1st Semyon Timoshenko d. (75).
June 4th Hjalmar Schacht d. (93).
June 7th Edward Morgan Forster d. (90).
June 11th Alexander Kerensky d. (89).
June 21st Achmad Sukharno d. (69).
July 27th Antonio Salazar d. (81.)
Sept. 1st François Mauriac d. (84).
Sept. 18th Jimi Hendrix d. (27).
Sept. 28th John Dos Passos d. (74).
—Gamal Abdel Nasser d. (52).
Nov. 9th Charles de Gaulle d. (79).

1970 (Nov. – Dec.)

L **Nov**: 3rd, in U.S. Congressional elections, Republicans gain one Senator, but lose 10 Representatives;
8th, U.A.R., Libya and Sudan agree to federate (joined by Syria, 27th);
9th, preliminary Anglo-Rhodesian talks begin in Pretoria to seek basis for settlement;
11th, British government lends £48 million to Rolls Royce Ltd. to offset losses;
12th, cyclone and tidal wave kill 150,000 in East Pakistan;
20th, U.N. General Assembly votes to admit Communist China, but majority is less than required two-thirds;
22nd, Portuguese mercenaries attempt to invade Guinea.

M **Dec**: 2nd, Portugal grants a measure of autonomy to Angola and Mozambique;
3rd, British government publishes Industrial Relations Bill to make collective agreements enforceable at law;
—(–28th), in Spain, trial of Basque separatists at Burgos prompts strikes and demonstrations;
7th, West Germany and Poland sign treaty recognising Oder-Neisse Line as frontier;
—, Awami League of Bengali nationalists wins first free elections in Pakistan since 1948;
—, nationwide power-cut in Britain due to industrial action (work-to-rule ends, 14th);
13th, Polish government sharply increases food, fuel and clothing prices (14th, strikes, riots and arson begin in Gdansk, spreading to other Baltic ports);
20th, Edward Gierek replaces Wladyslaw Gomulka as First Secretary of Polish Communist Party;
30th, Vietnam peace talks in Paris end second full year with all sides agreeing there had been no progress.

1971 (Jan. – Mar.) War in Pakistan—Industrial Relations Act in Britain—United Nations admits China

A **Jan:** 2nd, stampede at Ibrox Park football stadium, Glasgow, Scotland, crushes 66 people to death (the ensuing Wheatley Report recommends that all stadia with capacities of 10,000 or more be licensed by the local authority);
3rd, Mujibur Rahman, leader of Awami League, pledges to seek full autonomy for East Pakistan in proposed new constitution;
4th, Lord Robens resigns as Chairman of British National Coal Board in protest at plans to sell parts of nationalised industries;
5th, Israel, Egypt and Jordan resume indirect peace talks with U.N. mediator;
8th, left-wing Tupamaros guerrillas kidnap Geoffrey Jackson, British Ambassador to Uruguay (released, *Sept.* 9th);
12th, 'Angry Brigade' anarchists bomb home of British Employment Secretary, Robert Carr;
—, Selwyn Lloyd succeeds Horace King as Speaker of British House of Commons;
15th, President Sadat of Egypt and U.S.S.R. President Podgorny inaugurate the Aswan High Dam;
20th (–*Mar.* 8th), nation-wide strike by British postal workers;
25th, in Uganda General Idi Amin deposes President Obote and seizes power;
31st, telephone service between East and West Berlin re-established after 19 years.

B **Feb:** 1st (–*Mar.* 31st), strike halts Ford car production in Britain;
4th, Egypt extends ceasefire and offers to re-open Suez Canal if Israel withdraws from Sinai;
5th, Robert Curtis is first British soldier to be killed on duty in Northern Ireland;
8th, South Vietnam invades Laos to close Ho Chi Minh Trail to North Vietnamese (withdraws, *Mar.* 24th);
14th, international oil companies accept higher prices demanded by Gulf States;
—, U.S.S.R. announces ninth Five Year Plan, with high priority for consumer goods;
15th, Britain introduces decimal currency;
20th, emergency warning of nuclear attack broadcast by mistake in U.S.;
23rd, in Britain, nationalisation of aero-engine and marine divisions of Rolls Royce Ltd.;
24th, British government publishes Immigration Bill to restrict rights of abode of Commonwealth citizens.

C **Mar:** 1st, postponement of Pakistani Constituent Assembly provokes general strike in East Pakistan;
7th, expiry of Middle East ceasefire, but accompanied by decision to withhold fire along Suez Canal;
10th, U.S.S.R. Jews, demanding emigration permits, occupy offices of Supreme Soviet;
—, three off-duty British soldiers murdered in public house near Belfast;
—, Mrs. Gandhi's Congress Party wins landslide victory in Indian general election;
—, William MacMahon succeeds John Gorton as Prime Minister of Australia;
12th, demonstrators in Belfast demand internment of I.R.A. leaders (1,300 more British troops sent, 18th);
23th, Brian Faulkner becomes Prime Minister of Northern Ireland;
26th, Awami League declares independence of East Pakistan as Bangladesh; troops from West Pakistan fight separatists;
—, renewal of conflict between Jordanian army and Palestinians;
30th, British Budget halves selective employment tax, increases child allowances and old age pensions, and reforms taxation of high incomes, reducing top rate to 75 per cent;
31st, U.S. Lieutenant William Calley sentenced to life imprisonment for My Lai massacre of *Mar.* 1968 (reduced to 20 years, *Aug.* 20th).

O Politics, Economics, Law and Education

Swiss referendum approves the introduction of female suffrage (*Feb.* 7th).

Environmental campaigners found the pressure group 'Greenpeace'.

26th amendment of U.S. constitution extends full voting rights to 18 year-olds (*June* 30th).

Provisional results of 1971 British census show considerable decrease in populations of London and other large cities (*Aug.*).

63 nations, including U.S., U.S.S.R. and Britain, sign treaty banning atomic weapons from the sea-bed (*Feb.* 11th).

Two-tier income tax and surtax system in Britain to be replaced by a single graduated tax (from 1973).

End of dollar convertibility and the floating of sterling signify the demise of the Bretton Woods system of agreed exchange rates (*Aug.*).

English courts of assize and quarter sessions replaced by the Crown Court.

Divorce Reform Act in Britain permits dissolution of marriage by consent after two-year separation (*Jan.*).

Department of Education in Britain allocates £132 million to get rid of 6,000 slum primary schools (*June* 25th).

P Science, Technology, Discovery, etc.

Introduction of quadraphonic sound reproduction system.

Japan launches world's largest supertanker, the *Nisseki Maru* (372,000 tons).

Canada inaugurates world's first nuclear power station with cooling by ordinary water.

Intel in the U.S. introduces the microprocessor, a minute device on a single 'chip' for processing information within a computer.

Niklaus Wirth develops the computer language Pascal.

U.S. Apollo XIV mission (*Jan.* 31st–*Feb.* 9th) collects 98lb of moon rock; astronauts on the Apollo XV mission (*July* 26th–*Aug.* 7th) drive around the moon on the lunar rover.

U.S.S.R launches Salyut I space station (*Apr.* 19th) which is visited by a three-man crew in *June* (7th–29th); the cosmonauts die during their descent to earth when a faulty valve causes their capsule to lose pressure.

U.S. space probe Mariner IX becomes first man-made object to orbit another planet (Mars) on Nov. 12th; it transmits 7,329 photographs of the planet.

U.S.S.R. craft Mars II goes into orbit around Mars (*Nov.* 27th); a capsule from Mars III lands on the planet, but its transmitters go dead after 20 seconds.

Surgeons develop the fibre-optic endoscope for looking inside the human body.

Choh Hao Li and associates at the University of California Medical Centre announce the synthesis of a human growth hormone, somnatotropin (*Jan.* 6th).

Jacques Monod, *Chance and Necessity*.

Q Scholarship

C.W. Ferguson of the University of Arizona establishes a tree-ring chronology dating back to c. 6000 B.C.

Cambridge Ancient History, Vols. I, II, 3rd edn (–77).

Peter Brown, *The World of Late Antiquity*.

Norman Davis, *Paston Letters and Papers of the 15th Century*, Pt I (Pt II, 1976).

Keith Thomas, *Religion and the Decline of Magic*.

Geoffrey Best, *Mid-Victorian Britain, 1851–1870*.

B. Harrison, *Drink and the Victorians*.

Mark Girouard, *The Victorian Country House*.

P.F. Clarke, *Lancashire and the New Liberalism*.

D **Apr**: 1st, British bank rate falls from 7 to 6 per cent (to 5 per cent, *Sept.* 2nd);
2nd, Pakistan protests at Indian support for East Pakistani separatism;
5th (–23rd), violent left-wing rebellion in Ceylon;
7th, President Nixon announces withdrawal of 100,000 more troops from Vietnam;
10th, U.S. table tennis team arrives in China (14th, U.S. relaxes restrictions on Chinese trade and travel);
13th, riots in East Belfast after I.R.A. in Northern Ireland, fire on Orange parade;
15th, Britain restores telephone link with China (cut in 1949);
17th, Egypt, Syria and Libya sign Benghazi Agreement to establish Federation of Arab Republics;
19th, Sierra Leone becomes a republic within the Commonwealth;
—, British unemployment, at 3.4 per cent, reaches highest level since 1940;
21st, death of President François Duvalier of Haiti (known as 'Papa Doc'); succeeded by his teenage son, Jean-Claude Duvalier;
25th, 200,000 demonstrate in Washington, D.C., against Vietnam War (12,000 protestors arrested during following week);
26th, British government decides to build third London airport at Foulness;
29th, U.S. combat deaths in Vietnam exceed 45,000.

E **May**: 3rd, Erich Honecker succeeds Walter Ulbricht as First Secretary of Socialist Unity Party of East Germany;
5th, European currency markets close after flight from U.S. dollar into marks (9th, West Germany and Holland float their currencies);
6th, Greece and Albania re-establish diplomatic relations;
11th, 120 Labour M.P.s declare opposition to British entry into E.C.;
13th, in British borough elections, Conservatives lose 1,943 seats;
14th, plot to overthrow President Sadat of Egypt foiled;
18th, British government proposes museum entrance charges (introduction postponed, *Dec.* 9th);
19th, in Britain, Queen Elizabeth II requests review of the Civil List (fixed at £475,000 per year since 1952);
20th, Leningrad court sentences nine Jews to hard labour for anti-Soviet activities;
—(–21st), British Prime Minister Edward Heath and President Pompidou, meeting in Paris, reach general agreement on terms for British membership of E.C.;
27th, Egypt signs 15-year treaty of friendship with U.S.S.R.;
28th, Chile and U.S.S.R. sign agreement on economic co-operation;
31st, India requests international aid for millions of refugees from war in East Pakistan.

F **Jun**: 7th, deals between Britain and E.C. on Commonwealth sugar and status of sterling (final agreement on British entry, 23rd);
10th, U.S. ends embargo on trade with China;
13th, *The New York Times* begins publication of secret Pentagon Papers detailing U.S. government deception in handling of Vietnam War (U.S. Supreme Court upholds right to publish, 30th);
21st, International Court of Justice rules South African administration of South-West Africa illegal;
22nd, Dom Mintoff, Prime Minister of Malta, demands resignation of Governor-General and re-negotiation of British-Maltese defence agreement;
25th, British Education Secretary, Mrs. Margaret Thatcher, announces end of free milk for primary school children;
30th, Yugoslav Federal Assembly passes 23 amendments to 1963 constitution, devolving power to constituent republics.

Q Scholarship (*cont.*)

F.S.L. Lyons, *Ireland since the Famine.*

Valerie Eliot (ed.), *The Waste Land: A Facsimile and Transcript of the Original Drafts.*

R Philosophy and Religion

Germaine Greer, *The Female Eunuch.*

Alasdair MacIntyre, *Against the Self-Images of the Age.*

Jean Piaget, *Structuralism.*

John Rawls, *A Theory of Justice.*

Hans Küng, *Infallible? An Enquiry.*

General Synod of the Church of England allows baptized members of other Christian denominations to receive communion in Anglican churches.

President Tito of Yugoslavia is first Communist head of state to be received officially by the Pope.

Joyce Bennett and Jane Hwang Hsien Yuen are ordained priests by the Anglican Bishop of Hong Kong.

S Art, Sculpture, Fine Arts and Architecture

Conceptual art dominates Paris Biennale, Prospect 71, Düsseldorf, and 6th Guggenheim International, New York.

Painting:

Tate Gallery acquires by gift from A. McAlpine 59 works by Turnbull, Tucker, King and Scott.

'Art in Revolution' exhibition at Hayward Gallery, London.

David Hockney, *Rubber Ring Floating in a Swimming Pool.*

Anselm Kiefer, *Mann im Wald.*

Sculpture:

Gilbert and George, *Underneath the Arches.*

Architecture:

Marcel Breuer and Hamilton Smith, Cleveland Musuem of Art, Cleveland, Ohio.

Nervi, Audience Hall, The Vatican.

Destruction of Pruitt Igoe public housing blocks in St. Louis (architect Minoru Yamasaki), heralds end of modern architecture.

T Music

B. Britten, *Owen Wingrave* (opera).

Cornelius Cardew, *The Great Learning.*

Gottfried von Einem, *Der Besuch der alten Dame* (opera).

Mauricio Kagel, *Staatstheater* (opera).

Arvo Pärt, 3rd Symphony.

D. Shostakovich, 15th Symphony.

Karlheinz Stockhausen, *Trans.*

U Literature

Albert Camus, *A Happy Death.*

E.L. Doctorow, *The Book of Daniel.*

Geoffrey Hill, *Mercian Hymns.*

Alexander Solzhenitsyn, *August 1914.*

V The Press

In Britain, *The Daily Sketch* is merged into *The Daily Mail* (*May*), which is then relaunched as a tabloid.

G **Jul**: 3rd, Indonesian government wins clear victory in first general election for 16 years;

7th: White Paper, entitled *The United Kingdom and the European Communities*, outlines terms for British entry;

9th, in Northern Ireland, troops shoot dead two rioters in Londonderry (15th, nationalist S.D.L.P. withdraws from Stormont Parliament after inquiry is refused);

10th, abortive coup against King Hassan of Morocco (13th, 10 leaders executed);

13th, heavy fighting between Jordanian army and Palestinian guerrillas (1,500 guerrillas captured by 19th);

15th, President Nixon announces he will visit China in 1972;

18th, Iraq closes border with Jordan in protest at suppression of Palestinian guerrilla movement (Syria closes border, 23rd);

19th, British government cuts purchase tax, raises capital allowances, and abolishes hire purchase restrictions;

25th, East Caribbean states sign Declaration of Grenada on political union;

28th, National Executive of British Labour Party votes to oppose E.C. membership on current terms.

H **Aug**: 5th, in Britain, Industrial Relations Bill receives Royal Assent;

—, at Geneva Disarmament Conference, U.S. and U.S.S.R. present draft treaty to ban biological weapons;

9th, Northern Ireland government introduces internment and forbids processions;

—(–11th), in Northern Ireland, over 22 people die in fighting between troops and I.R.A. in Belfast, Newry and Londonderry; Eire opens refugee camps for Catholics;

14th, Bahrain declares independence from Britain (Qatar becomes independent, *Sept.* 6th);

15th, President Nixon suspends conversion of dollars into gold and imposes 90-day price freeze and 10 per cent import surcharge in response to first U.S. trade deficit since 1894;

16th (–23rd), closure of European currency markets, after which sterling finds its own level (28th, Japan floats the yen);

18th, Australia and New Zealand announce withdrawal of their forces from Vietnam;

19th, N.A.T.O. transfers Mediterranean naval headquarters from Malta to Naples;

—, sharp exchanges between Edward Heath and Prime Minister Lynch of Eire over Northern Ireland bring Anglo-Irish relations close to breaking point (border incidents, 29th);

20th, Britain's first auction of North Sea oil and gas concessions;

24th, cabinet changes strengthen power of Greek Premier Georgios Papadopoulos;

31st, British Government orders inquiry into alleged ill-treatment of internees in Northern Ireland.

J **Sep**: 3rd, Britain, France and U.S.S.R. sign Berlin Agreement on communications between West Berlin and West Germany;

6th, over 100 Tupamaros guerrillas escape from prison in Bolivia;

8th, T.U.C. rejects terms for British membership of E.C.;

9th (–13th), riots in Attica prison, New York, leave 42 dead;

22nd (–23rd), recall of British House of Commons for emergency debate on Northern Ireland;

24th, Britain requests departure of 105 Soviet officials for alleged espionage (*Oct.* 8th, U.S.S.R. expels or bars 18 Britons);

27th (–28th), Edward Heath, John Lynch and Brian Faulkner meet at Chequers to discuss Northern Ireland; they agree only to condemn violence;

—, Cardinal Mindszenty leaves Hungary after 15 years as refugee in U.S. embassy.

W **Drama and Entertainment**

Edward Bond, *Lear*.
John Guare, *The House of Blue Leaves*.
Wole Soyinka, *Madmen and Specialists*.
David Williamson, *The Removalists*.

Films:
Stanley Kubrick's *A Clockwork Orange*.
Joseph Losey's *The Go–Between*.
Mike Nichols' *Carnal Knowledge*.
John Schlesinger's *Sunday Bloody Sunday*.
Vittorio de Sica's *The Garden of the Finzi-Continis*.
Luchino Visconti's *Death in Venice*.
The French Connection.

Television:
Columbo.

Popular music:
Marvin Gaye, *What's Goin' On*.
Janis Joplin, *Pearl*.
Carole King, *Tapestry*.
T. Rex, *Electric Warrior* – glam rocks starts in Britain.
Rod Stewart, *Every Picture Tells a Story*.
Led Zeppelin, *Led Zeppelin IV*.

X **Sport**

First limited-overs one-day cricket international; Australia beats England in Melbourne (*Jan.* 5th).
England regain the Ashes after 12 years from Australia (*Feb.* 17th).
Joe Frazier beats Muhammad Ali over 15 rounds at Madison Square Garden, New York, and retains the World Heavy-weight title (*Mar.* 8th).
Britain and Ireland's amateur golfers win the Walker Cup match against the U.S. (*May* 27th) – Britain and Ireland's first Walker victory since 1938.
The British Lions win a rugby Test series in New Zealand for the first time.

Y **Statistics**

Populations (in mill.): China, 786.8; India, 547.9; U.S.S.R., 244.1; U.S., 205.1; Japan, 106.0; Brazil 94.9; Bangladesh, 63.3; Pakistan, 62.1; West Germany, 61.1; Nigeria, 56.6; Great Britain and Northern Ireland, 55.5; Italy, 54.0; France, 51.2; Mexico, 50.6.

Z **Births and Deaths**

Jan. 10th Coco Chanel d. (87).
Mar. 7th Stevie Smith d. (68).
Mar. 8th Harold Lloyd d. (77).
Mar. 24th Arne Jacobsen d. (69).
Apr. 6th Igor Stravinsky d. (88).
June 4th György S. von Lukács d. (86).
June 16th J.C. Reith d. (81).
July 1st W.L. Bragg d. (81).
— Learie Constantine d. (69).
July 23rd W.V.S. Tubman d. (75).

K **Oct:** 1st, Joseph Luns succeeds Manlio Brosio as Secretary-General of N.A.T.O.;
3rd, President Thieu of South Vietnam retains office after all other candidates withdraw in protest at rigged elections;
4th, in Britain, Labour Party conference passes anti-E.C. resolution;
5th, Emperor Hirohito of Japan visits Britain for first time since Second World War;
12th, Iran celebrates 2,500th anniversary of Persian monarchy;
13th, in Britain, Conservative Party conference votes 8 to 1 in favour of E.C. entry;
20th, West German Chancellor Willy Brandt awarded Nobel Peace Prize;
25th, U.N. General Assembly votes to admit Communist China and expel Taiwan (China takes its seat, *Nov.* 15th);
27th, President Mobutu changes name of Congo to Zaire;
28th, British House of Commons votes 356 to 244 in favour of E.C. entry; 69 Labour M.P.s vote with Government, 39 Conservative M.P.s vote with Opposition;
31st, Britain reverts to Greenwich Mean Time after three years of British Standard Time.

L **Nov:** 3rd, Britain annexes Rockall in north Atlantic (area 5,500 square feet);
10th (–*Dec.* 4th), Cuban Premier Fidel Castro visits Chile;
12th, President Nixon proclaims end of U.S. offensive role in Vietnam War and withdraws 45,000 more troops;
15th, British Foreign Secretary Sir Alec Douglas-Home opens talks with Ian Smith in Salisbury (24th, agreement on new Rhodesian constitution);
16th, Compton Report rejects allegations of brutality in internment camps in Northern Ireland;
17th, military coup in Thailand;
22nd, Pakistan accuses India of invading East Pakistan;
25th, Harold Wilson, Leader of Opposition in British House of Commons, proposes unification of Ireland in 15 years;
28th, Palestinian terrorists murder Wasfi Tell, Prime Minister of Jordan (*Dec.* 1st, King Hussein rules out further talks with Palestinian guerrillas);
30th, Iran occupies Tunbs Islands in Persian Gulf one day before British protectorate expires; Iraq severs diplomatic relations with Iran and Britain, alleging collusion.

M **Dec:** 1st, Abu Dhabi, Sharjah, Dubai, Umm al Qaiwain, Ajman and Fujairah form United Arab Emirates;
—, President Tito purges Croat leadership of nationalists;
2nd, Report of Select Committee on Civil List proposes doubling Queen's income;
3rd, Pakistan bombs Indian air-fields;
4th, in Northern Ireland, explosion in Belfast public house kills 15 (subsequent reprisals bring annual death-toll to 173, including 43 troops);
6th, India recognises independence of Bangladesh; war breaks out along border between India and West Pakistan;
16th, East Pakistan forces surrender to India; India orders ceasefire on West Pakistan front;
—, Zimbabwe leaders form African National Council with aim of rejecting Anglo-Rhodesian settlement;
17th, end of Indo-Pakistan War; East Pakistan becomes independent as Bangladesh;
18th, U.S. devalues dollar by 7.9 per cent and lifts import surcharge; realignment of other major currencies;
20th, Zulfikar Ali Bhutto replaces Yahya Khan as President of Pakistan;
22nd, Mujibur Rahman is released from prison in West Pakistan to become President of Bangladesh;

z **Births and Deaths** (*cont.*)

Sept. 11th Nikita Khrushchev d. (77).
Sept. 20th George Seferis d. (71).
Oct. 12th Dean Acheson d. (78).
Nov. 11th A.P. Herbert d. (81).
Nov. 17th Gladys Cooper d. (82).
Dec. 9th Ralph Bunche d. (67).

M **Dec**: 24th, Maltese ultimatum to Britain: pay £18 million for use of naval bases or withdraw by end of year (*Dec.* 31st, Malta extends deadline);
31st, Kurt Waldheim takes office as U.N. Secretary-General.

1972 (Jan. – Mar.) President Nixon visits China—Direct Rule in Northern Ireland—East-West Detente

A **Jan**: 9th, British coal-miners' strike begins (state of emergency proclaimed, *Feb.* 9th);
10th, President Mujibur Rahman of Bangladesh arrives in Dacca (12th, resigns presidency in order to become Prime Minister);
11th (–*Mar.* 12th), Lord Pearce heads British Commission to Rhodesia to assess opinion on proposed new constitutional arrangements (agreed on *Nov.* 24th 1971; report issued on *May* 23rd);
14th, talks between British Defence Secretary, Lord Carrington, and Maltese Premier, Dom Mintoff, in Rome (16th, withdrawal of British forces from Malta suspended);
14th, death of King Frederik IX of Denmark; succeeded by Margarethe II;
20th, number of unemployed in Britain exceeds 1 million;
22nd, Britain, Denmark, Ireland and Norway sign Treaty of Accession to E.C. in Brussels;
25th, President Nixon reveals that his national security adviser, Henry Kissinger, has been conducting secret peace negotiations with North Vietnam since 1969;
30th, 'Bloody Sunday' in Northern Ireland: British troops shoot dead 13 civilians when violence erupts at anti-internment march in Bogside, Londonderry;
—, Pakistan leaves the Commonwealth in anticipation of British recognition of Bangladesh (on *Feb.* 4th).

B **Feb**: 2nd, demonstrators burn down the British Embassy in Dublin;
7th, Sir Keith Holyoake retires as Prime Minister of New Zealand; succeeded by John Marshall;
11th, Greece demands that Cyprus surrender secret armaments and accept coalition government (*Mar.* 14th, Cyprus yields arms to U.N. peace-keepers but refuses ministerial changes);
11th, British House of Commons approves second reading of European Communities Bill by 309 votes to 301;
18th, Wilberforce Commission recommends pay increases for British miners of up to £6 per week (equivalent to 22 per cent; 28th, coal strike ends after further government concessions);
21st (–27th), President Nixon visits China;
22nd, in Britain, I.R.A. bomb kills 7 people at Aldershot;
27th, Israel attacks south Lebanon in reprisal for Palestinian raids;
28th, Japan acknowledges China's territorial rights over Taiwan.

C **Mar**: 2nd, British Prime Minister Edward Heath forbids use of 'intensive' interrogation techniques in Northern Ireland, following Parker Report on security forces;
4th, in Northern Ireland, bomb explosion in restaurant in Belfast kills 2 and injures 136;
13th, Britain resumes ambassadorial relations with China and closes its consulate in Taiwan;
15th, King Hussein of Jordan proposes creation of autonomous Palestinian state on West Bank (*Apr.* 6th, Egypt breaks off relations in protest);
19th, India and Bangladesh sign mutual defence pact;
21st, British Budget includes tax cuts amounting to £1,200 million and increases in National Insurance benefits of 12.5 per cent;
22nd, British government establishes Industrial Development Executive, to direct government money into industrial investment (Christopher Chataway appointed Minister for Industrial Development);
26th, Britain and N.A.T.O. agree to pay Malta £14 million per year for use of military bases;

O Politics, Economics, Law and Education

Local Government Act provides for first full-scale re-organisation of local government in Britain since 1889 (to be effective from 1974).

Franks Committee recommends reform of the British Official Secrets Act to clarify the law on leakage of official information (*Sept.* 29th).

Bank of England replaces fixed bank rate with fluctuating minimum lending rate (M.L.R.) tied to discount rate of Treasury bills (*Oct.* 13th).

Thomas Cook travel agency, owned by British government, is sold to private sector (*May* 26th).

Community service, deferred sentences and criminal bankruptcy orders are introduced in Britain as alternatives to imprisonment.

Criminal Law Revision Committee recommends new limitations on rights of accused persons in British judicial system (*June* 27th).

U.S. Supreme Court rules that death penalty is contrary to Constitution (*June* 29th).

British White Paper, *Education: A Framework for Expansion* (*Dec.* 6th), proposes provision of nursery education for 90 per cent of four-year-old children within 10 years.

P Science, Technology, Discovery, etc.

First home video-cassette recorders introduced.

The B.B.C. launches CEEFAX, a TV information system.

U.S. craft Pioneer X is launched (*Mar.* 2nd), destined to travel beyond the solar system (which it leaves on *June* 13th 1983).

U.S.S.R. craft Venus VIII (launched *Mar.* 27th) makes a soft landing on Venus (*July* 22nd).

U.S. Apollo XVI moon mission (*Apr.* 16th–27th), followed by Apollo XVII (*Dec.* 7th–19th), the final Apollo manned mission to the moon.

Launch of Landsat I (*July* 23rd), the first of a series of satellites for surveying earth's resources from space.

U.S. scientist Murray Gell-Man presents the theory of quantum chromodynamics (QCD), which envisages that quarks interact according to their 'colour'; strongly interacting particles consist of quarks, which are bound together by gluons.

CAT (computerized axial tomography) scanning introduced to provide cross-sectional X-rays of human brain.

Q Scholarship

'Treasures of Tutankhamun' exhibition at the British Museum, to celebrate the 50th anniversary of the discovery of Tutankhamun's tomb.

Discovery of tomb of Han dynasty prince south of Peking, including jade suits.

Mark Elvin, *The Pattern of the Chinese Past.*

Henry Mayr-Harting, *The Coming of Christianity to Anglo-Saxon England.*

Michael Baxandall, *Painting and Experience in Fifteenth Century Italy.*

G.R. Elton, *Policy and Police: The Enforcement of the Reformation in the Age of Thomas Cromwell.*

Christopher Hill, *The World Turned Upside Down: Radical Ideas during the English Revolution.*

J.D. Chambers, *Population, Economy, and Society in Pre-Industrial England.*

Joyce M. Bellamy and John Saville (eds.), *Dictionary of Labour Biography*, Vol. I.

José Harris, *Unemployment and Politics: A Study in English Social Policy, 1886–1914.*

A.J.P. Taylor, *Beaverbrook.*

C **Mar:** 29th, in Britain, National Industrial Relations Court (N.I.R.C.) fines Transport and General Workers' Union £5,000 for failure to stop 'blacking' Liverpool docks (*Apr.* 20th, further fine of £50,000 for contempt);
—, North Vietnamese launch major offensive in Quang Tri province;
30th, Britain assumes direct rule over Northern Ireland, with William Whitelaw as Secretary of State.

D **Apr:** 4th, U.S.S.R. refuses visa to Swedish Academy official due to deliver Nobel Prize for Literature to Alexander Solzhenitsyn;
6th, President Allende of Chile vetoes constitutional amendment that would have made expropriation of property subject to congressional approval;
7th, British Cabinet reshuffle heralds more interventionist industrial policy;
—, release of 73 internees in Northern Ireland;
10th, Britain, U.S. and U.S.S.R. sign multilateral convention prohibiting the stockpiling of biological weapons;
—, Roy Jenkins resigns as deputy leader of the British Labour Party after Shadow Cabinet calls for referendum on E.C. membership;
17th (–*June* 12th), British Rail disrupted by work-to-rule in support of 16 per cent pay claim;
19th, Widgery Report on 'Bloody Sunday' shootings in Londonderry, Northern Ireland, concludes that I.R.A. fired first;
—, North Vietnamese aircraft attack U.S. 7th Fleet in Gulf of Tonkin;
23rd, in French referendum, 67.7 per cent vote in favour of enlargement of E.C.;
27th, British government lifts ban on marches in Northern Ireland and declares amnesty for 283 convicted of participating in illegal marches;
—, U.S. Senator Edmund Muskie withdraws from contest for Democratic presidential nomination.

E **May:** 1st, Quang Tri city falls to North Vietnamese (recaptured by South Vietnamese, *Sept.* 15th);
4th, Labour gains 1,519 seats in British borough elections;
8th, President Nixon orders blockade and mining of North Vietnamese ports;
10th, referendum in Eire records 83 per cent support for E.C. membership;
14th, Ulster Defence Association sets up first Protestant 'no go' areas in Belfast;
—(–20th), demonstrations in Kaunas demand freedom for Lithuania;
15th, candidate for Democratic presidential nomination, George Wallace, shot and paralysed in Maryland;
17th, West German Bundestag ratifies 1970 treaties with U.S.S.R. and Poland with Christian Democrats abstaining;
22nd (–29th), Richard Nixon becomes first U.S. President to visit U.S.S.R. (26th, signs treaty limiting anti-ballistic missile sites);
—, Ceylon ceases to be a British dominion and becomes a republic within the Commonwealth as Sri Lanka;
23rd, Britain abandons Rhodesian settlement proposals after Pearce Commission reports that black opinion is unfavourable;
30th, three pro-Palestinian Japanese terrorists kill 26 Israelis at Lod airport.

F **Jun:** 1st (–15th), West German police round up Baader-Meinhof urban guerrilla group;
10th, in Northern Ireland, battle between troops, Catholics and Protestants in Belfast leaves 6 dead;
13th, in Britain, Court of Appeal overturns judgement of N.I.R.C. and sets aside T.G.W.U. fines (*July* 26th, House of Lords reverses judgement and restores fines);
16th, start of heavy selling of sterling on currency markets (22nd, British bank rate rises to 6 per cent);

R **Philosophy and Religion**

Karl Popper, *Objective Knowledge*.
Stephen Toulmin, *Human Understanding*.
John V. Taylor, *The Go-Between God*.
Formation of United Reformed Church by union of Congregational Church in England and Wales and Presbyterian Church in England.
Dimitrios, Metropolitan of Imroz and Tenedos, is elected as Ecumenical Patriarch of Constantinople.
The first meeting held in London of the Standing Conference of Jews, Christians and Moslems.

S **Art, Sculpture, Fine Arts and Architecture**

'Inquiry into Reality: Images of Today' 5th Documenta, Kassel, Germany.

Sculpture:
Michelangelo's Pietà in St. Peter's Basilica, Rome, is attacked with a hammer by lunatic.
Tate Gallery purchases Carl André's 'bricks' (*Equivalent 8*, 1966).
Stuart Brisley, *And for Today – Nothing*.
Christo, *Valley Curtain, Colorado*.
Bruce Nauman, *Run From Fear / Fun From Rear*.
Nam June Paik, *Paik-Abe Video Synthesizer*.
Richard Serra, *Shift*.

Architecture:
Alvar Aalto, North Jutland Museum at Aalborg, Denmark.
Louis Kahn, Kimbell Art Museum, Fort Worth, Texas.
Kisho Kurokawa, Nagakin Capsule Tower, Tokio.
James Stirling, Florey Building, The Queen's College, Oxford.

T **Music**

Harrison Birtwistle, *The Triumph of Time*.
Sylvano Busotti, *Lorenzaccio* (opera).
John Cage, *Bird Cage*.
P.M. Davies, *Taverner* (opera).
M. Tippett, 3rd Symphony.

U **Literature**

John Berger's *G* wins the Booker prize; the author gives half the proceeds to the Black Panthers (American black urban guerrilla group) in protest at the source of the money.
Margaret Drabble, *The Needle's Eye*.
Frederick Forsyth, *The Day of the Jackal*.
V S. Naipaul, *In a Free State*.
Eudora Welty, *The Optimist's Daughter*.
Sir John Betjeman appointed Britain's Poet Laureate.

V **The Press**

Rupert Murdoch purchases the *Sydney Daily Telegraph* and *Sunday Telegraph* (*June*).
Closure of *Life* magazine (last issue *Dec.* 29th).

F **Jun:** 17th, U.S. police arrest five intruders planting electronic 'bugs' at the Democratic Party headquarters in the Watergate apartment complex, Washington;
18th, B.E.A. Trident airliner crashes at Staines, west of London, killing 118;
23rd, British government temporarily floats the pound to halt drain on reserves;
26th (–*July* 9th), I.R.A. ceasefire in Northern Ireland;
27th, French Socialist and Communist Parties agree on a common programme.

G **Jul:** 2nd, India and Pakistan agree to renounce force in settlement of disputes;
5th, Pierre Messmer succeeds Jacques Chaban-Delmas as Prime Minister of France;
—, Kakuei Tanaka succeeds Eisaku Sato as Prime Minister of Japan;
7th, William Whitelaw holds secret talks with I.R.A. in London;
8th, President Nixon announces that U.S.S.R. will purchase $750 million worth of U.S. grain over three years;
12th, Democratic Party convention in Miami nominates George McGovern as presidential candidate (14th, approves Thomas Eagleton for Vice-Presidency);
17th (–*Aug.* 11th), trials of Czechoslovak dissidents in Prague and Brno;
18th, Reginald Maudling resigns as British Home Secretary as consequence of connections with John Poulson, an architect facing bankruptcy and a police investigation for suspected corruption; succeeded by Robert Carr;
—, President Sadat of Egypt expels 20,000 Soviet advisers after accusing U.S.S.R. of failing to supply promised armaments;
21st, in Northern Ireland, 22 bombs explode in Belfast shopping centres and bus stations, killing 13 and injuring 130;
—, in Britain, five dockers go to prison for contempt of court after refusing to stop 'blacking' container depots at Hackney (released, 26th);
28th (–*Aug.* 16th), nation-wide dock strike in Britain, after union rejects Jones-Aldington proposals to ease unemployment resulting from 'containerisation';
31st, in Northern Ireland, army destroys Catholic and Protestant barricades to end 'no go' areas in Belfast and Londonderry.

H **Aug:** 1st, in Britain, T.U.C. and C.B.I. agree to set up independent conciliation service;
—, Egypt and Sudan announce plans for full union by *Sept.* 1973;
4th, President Amin asserts that Ugandan Asians are frustrating the involvement of Africans in Uganda's business and commercial life; he gives them 90 days to leave the country;
5th, Sargent Shriver becomes Democratic candidate for U.S. Vice-Presidency after revelation of psychiatric treatment prompts withdrawal of Thomas Eagleton;
12th, heavy U.S. air-raids on North Vietnam accompany departure of U.S. combat infantry from South Vietnam;
—, Chinese Communist Party accuses U.S.S.R. of complicity in plot to assassinate Chairman Mao;
16th, British government offers £50,000 reward for information on murders without motive in Northern Ireland;
—, Moroccan fighter pilots attempt to shoot down airliner carrying King Hassan (Moroccan defence minister commits suicide, 17th);
22nd, Republican Party convention in Miami nominates President Nixon for a second term (23rd, re-nominates Vice-President Agnew);
25th, China vetoes admission of Bangladesh to U.N.

J **Sep:** 1st, Iceland unilaterally extends its fishing limit from 12 to 50 miles (5th, Icelandic gunboat cuts fishing gear of British trawler);
4th (–9th), in Britain, T.U.C. conference at Blackpool suspends 32 unions for registering under Industrial Relations Act;

W Drama and Entertainment

Samuel Beckett, *Not I.*
David French, *Leaving Home.*
Athol Fugard, *Sizwe Banzi is Dead.*
Dorothy Hewett, *The Chapel Perilous.*
Jack Hibberd, *A Stretch of the Imagination.*
Franz Kroetz, *Farmyard.*
David Rabe, *The Basic Training of Pavlo Hummel.*
Sam Shepard, *The Tooth of Crime.*
Tom Stoppard, *Jumpers.*
Jesus Christ Superstar.

Films:
Luis Buñuel's *The Discreet Charm of the Bourgeoisie.*
Ford Coppola's *The Godfather.*
Rainer Werner Fassbinder's *The Bitter Tears of Petra Von Kant.*
Bob Fosse's *Cabaret.*
Pier Paolo Pasolini's *The Decameron.*
The Concert for Bangladesh.

Television:
Mash.
Ingmar Bergman's *Six Scenes from a Marriage.*
The Waltons.

Radio:
The last Goon Show.

Popular music:
David Bowie, *The Rise and Fall of Ziggy Stardust and the Spiders from Mars.*
The Rolling Stones, *Exile on Main Street.*
The Wailers, *Catch a Fire* – reggae spreads from Jamaica.
Stevie Wonder, *Innervisions.*

X Sport

Eddie Merckx of Belgium wins his fourth consecutive Tour de France.
Bob Massie of Australia takes 16 England wickets in the second Test at Lord's (*June* 22nd–26th) – a record for an Australian bowler.
In Olympic Games in Munich (*Aug.* 26th–*Sept.* 11th) U.S.S.R. wins 50 gold medals; U.S., 33: East Germany, 20; West Germany and Japan, 13; Australia, 8; Poland, 7; Hungary and Bulgaria, 6; Italy, 5; Sweden and Britain, 4; Mark Spitz of the U.S. wins 7 gold medals in swimming, all in world record times.
Bobby Fischer of the U.S. beats Boris Spassky of the U.S.S.R. in World Chess Championship in Reykjavik (*Sept.* 1st).
The British Jockey Club allows women jockeys to compete in horse-racing.

Y Statistics

Z Births and Deaths

Jan. 1st Maurice Chevalier d. (83).
Jan. 7th John Berryman d. (57).
Apr. 16th Yasunari Kawabata d. (72)
Apr. 27th Kwame Nkrumah d. (62).

J **Sep**: 5th, Arab terrorists murder 11 members of Israeli Olympic team at Munich; West German police kill 5 terrorists in gun battle;
7th, South Korea withdraws its 37,000 troops remaining in Vietnam;
11th, U.S. Democratic Party accuses Republican campaign finance chairman, Maurice Stans, of political espionage;
17th, Ugandan exiles attempt to invade Uganda from Tanzania;
18th, first plane-load of expelled Ugandan Asians arrives in Britain (22nd, President Amin orders 8,000 Asians to leave within 48 hours);
21st, William Whitelaw ends internment without trial in Northern Ireland;
24th, 53.5 per cent vote against E.C. membership in Norwegian referendum;
25th, three-day conference on future of Northern Ireland opens at Darlington;
26th, British government proposes wage and price restraint to T.U.C. and C.B.I. (tripartite talks continue until *Nov.* 2nd);
27th (*–Oct.* 13th), border fighting between North and South Yemen;
29th, Japan and China agree to end the legal state of war existing since 1937.

K **Oct**: 1st, Danish referendum approves E.C. entry;
3rd, U.S. and U.S.S.R. sign final S.A.L.T. accords limiting submarine-carried and land-based missiles (S.A.L.T. II talks begin in Geneva, *Nov.* 21st);
—, pro-E.C. Labour M.P. for Lincoln, Dick Taverne, at odds with his constituency party over British membership of E.C., announces his intention to stand down and fight by-election as independent 'Democratic Labour' candidate;
7th, Britain names Christopher Soames and George Thomson as its first E.C. Commissioners;
17th, Queen Elizabeth II begins a State visit to Yugoslavia, the first to a Communist country;
21st, E.C. summit in Paris approves principle of economic and monetary union by 1980;
26th, North Vietnam publishes ceasefire agreement with U.S.; Henry Kissinger says peace is at hand in Indo-China;
—, in Britain, Liberals win Rochdale from Labour in by-election, with Cyril Smith as new M.P. (win Sutton and Cheam from Conservatives, *Dec.* 7th);
29th, Palestinian hijackers of Lufthansa flight secure release of Arab terrorists held in West Germany since Sept. 5th;
—(*–Nov.* 2nd), British Foreign Secretary Sir Alec Douglas-Home visits China;
30th, Pierre Trudeau's Liberal Party wins narrow victory in Canadian general election;
—, Britain promises greater political power for Catholics in Northern Ireland.

L **Nov**: 1st, President Thieu of South Vietnam rejects U.S. ceasefire plan;
5th, in Britain, Peter Walker becomes Secretary of State for Trade and Industry; James Prior becomes Leader of the Commons;
6th, British government imposes 90-day freeze on price, pay, rent and dividend increases as Phase One of anti-inflation programme;
7th, in U.S. elections Richard Nixon, Republican, with 520 electoral votes, wins landslide victory over George McGovern, Democrat, with 17; popular vote: Nixon, 47,168,963; McGovern, 29,169,615; Republicans lose 2 Senators and gain 12 Representatives; Democrats keep control of both Houses;
8th, deadline for Asians to leave Uganda (25,000 go to Britain by end of year);
—, in Britain, N.I.R.C. fines Amalgamated Union of Engineering Workers £5,000 for excluding a member (29th, sequestration of A.U.E.W. funds follows refusal to pay);
9th, Bank of England demands special deposits from clearing banks in attempt to control money supply;

z **Births and Deaths** (*cont.*)

May 2nd J. Edgar Hoover d. (77).
May 4th E.C. Kendall d. (86).
May 22nd C. Day-Lewis d. (68).
May 28th Duke of Windsor d. (77).
July 31st Paul Spaak d. (72).
Sept. 21st Henry de Montherlant d. (76).
Oct. 1st Louis Leakey d. (69).
Oct. 26th Igor Sikorsky d. (83).
Nov. 1st Ezra Pound d. (87).
Nov. 30th Compton Mackenzie d. (89).
Dec. 23rd A.N. Tupolev d. (84).
Dec. 26th Harry S. Truman d. (88).
Dec. 27th Lester Pearson d. (75).

L **Nov**: 19th, West German general election returns Social Democrats with increased majority;
21st, eight-hour battle between Israel and Syria on Golan Heights;
22nd, rebel British Conservative M.P.s defeat government on new immigration rules favouring E.C. citizens over white Commonwealth;
—, preparatory talks for European Security Conference begin in Helsinki;
24th, Finland is first western nation formally to recognise East Germany;
25th, Norman Kirk becomes Prime Minister of New Zealand after Labour Party wins sweeping electoral victory;
28th, Anglo–Icelandic talks on fisheries dispute break down.

M **Dec**: 2nd, Australian Labour Party wins general election (Gough Whitlam becomes Prime Minister, 5th);
6th, in Britain, four 'Angry Brigade' anarchists gaoled for conspiracy to cause explosions after record 111-day trial;
11th, British Trade and Industry Secretary Peter Walker announces £175 million subsidy for National Coal Board and writes off £475 million deficit;
—, India and Pakistan agree on truce line in Jammu and Kashmir;
13th, in Britain, Conservative Party nominates its 18 members of E.C. Parliament; Labour refuses to send any representatives;
18th (–30th), heavy U.S. bombing of North Vietnam;
20th, Diplock Commission recommends wider powers of arrest in Northern Ireland and suspension of trial by jury in certain cases;
21st, West and East Germany sign Basic Treaty to establish 'neighbourly relations on the basis of equality';
23rd, earthquake devastates Managua, capital of Nicaragua;
27th, Britain ignores Maltese ultimatum demanding 10 per cent increase in rent for military bases;
31st, Northern Ireland Office reports total of 467 killings in 1972.

1973 (Jan. – Mar.) U.S. withdrawal from Vietnam—Yom Kippur War—Energy crisis

A **Jan:** 1st, Britain, Ireland and Denmark become members of the E.C.;
4th, Australia abandons colour bar in admission of new settlers;
6th, Portuguese revolutionaries explode 12 bombs in Lisbon in protest at colonial wars;
8th, trial opens in Washington of seven men accused of bugging Democratic Party headquarters in the Watergate apartment complex;
9th, Rhodesia closes its border with Zambia after terrorist attacks;
15th, U.S. suspends all military action against North Vietnam;
17th, in Britain, Edward Heath announces creation of Pay Board and Prices Commission;
—, President Marcos of Philippines proclaims new constitution under which he will rule indefinitely;
20th, inauguration of Richard Nixon for second term as U.S. President;
27th, U.S., North and South Vietnam, and Viet Cong sign ceasefire in Paris.

B **Feb:** 7th, protest strikes, arson and gun battles in Northern Ireland, following first detention of Protestant terrorist suspects;
8th, Archbishop Makarios returned unopposed as President of Cyprus;
12th, North Vietnam and Viet Cong release first U.S. prisoners of war;
13th, U.S. devalues dollar by 10 per cent by raising gold price to $42.22 per ounce;
14th (–*Mar.* 23rd), strike by British gas workers cuts off supplies in some areas;
19th, French right-wing extremists steal body of Marshal Pétain from Ile d'Yeu;
21st, 104 die when Libyan airliner crashes in Sinai after interception by Israeli jets;
—, government of Laos and Pathet Lao sign ceasefire agreement in Vientiane;
22nd, China and U.S. agree to establish liaison offices in Washington and Peking;
27th (–*May* 8th), 200 Ogdala Sioux occupy hamlet of Wounded Knee, South Dakota, and hold residents hostage in protest at treatment of U.S. Indians;
—, first ever full strike by British civil servants.

C **Mar:** 1st, in Eire, Fine Gael coalition wins general election (Liam Cosgrave becomes Prime Minister, 14th);
—, in Britain, Dick Taverne, independent Democratic Labour candidate, defeats official Labour candidate in Lincoln by-election, achieving majority of over 13,000 votes;
—(–*Apr.* 14th), British hospital ancillary workers strike for higher pay;
2nd (–19th), closure of European exchange markets in face of new currency crisis;
—, Palestinian terrorists murder U.S. ambassador to Sudan after invading reception at Saudi Arabian Embassy in Khartoum;
6th, neutral British Budget introduces V.A.T. at 10 per cent (supplanting other excise duties and the Selective Employment Tax) and increases pensions;
8th, I.R.A. car bombs at Great Scotland Yard and Old Bailey in London kill 1 and injure 238;
—, in Northern Ireland referendum, 591,820 (59 per cent turn-out) vote to remain in United Kingdom, and 6,463 to join Eire;
10th, following period of political tension, Sir Richard Sharples, Governor of Bermuda, is assassinated in Hamilton;
11th, Peronist candidate, Héctor Campora, wins Argentinian general election (*July* 13th, resigns to make way for General Perón);
16th, finance ministers from 14 countries, meeting in Paris, agree to establish floating exchange rate system;
20th, British White Paper on Northern Ireland proposes new assembly, power-sharing executive, and talks on an all-Ireland council;
29th, last U.S. troops leave Vietnam and last U.S. prisoners of war are released.

O Politics, Economics, Law and Education

Queen Elizabeth, on Australian tour, assents to change title there to 'Queen of Australia' (*Oct.* 19th).

Kilbrandon Report of Royal Commission on the Constitution recommends devolution for Scotland and Wales (*Oct.* 31st).

Foundation of European Trade Union Confederation with 29 million members in 14 E.C. and E.F.T.A. countries (*Feb.*)

E.F. Schumacher, *Small is Beautiful, a Study of Economics as if People Mattered.*

U.S. Supreme Court upholds right to abortion during first six months of pregnancy (*Jan.* 27th).

British Lord Chief Justice rules that physical obstruction on picket lines is unlawful (*Apr.* 10th).

British school-leaving age raised to 16.

P Science, Technology, Discovery, etc.

Bar codes first used in supermarkets.

Opening of pipeline for transmission of natural gas from Ukraine to West Germany.

Start of construction of Thames Flood Barrier, London.

U.S. launches the first Skylab space station (*May* 14th), which is visited by a three-man crew (*May* 25th–*June* 22nd); the third mission to Skylab (launched *Nov.* 16th) lasts a record 84 days and gathers data relevant to long space flights.

U.S. probe Pioneer X passes within 81,000 miles of Jupiter and transmits pictures and data.

Researchers at C.E.R.N. find some confirmation for the electroweak force when they discover neutral currents in neutrino reactions.

Herbert Boyer develops the technique of recombinant DNA, whereby different strands of DNA can be joined together and inserted into living organisms.

The first calf is produced from a frozen embryo.

Paul Lauterbur obtains the first NMR (nuclear magnetic resonance) image.

Q Scholarship

The Cambridge History of China (–).

M.I. Finley, *The Ancient Economy.*

G.R. Elton, *Reform and Renewal: Thomas Cromwell and the Common Weal.*

L.A. Marchand (ed.), *Byron's Letters and Journals* (–82).

H.J. Dyos and M. Wolff (eds.), *The Victorian City: Images and Realities.*

Theodore Zeldin, *France, 1848–1948*, Vol. I (Vol. II, 1977).

Allardyce Nicoll, *English Drama 1900–1930: The Beginnings of the Modern Period* (a companion to Nicoll's six-volume *History of the English Drama, 1660–1900*).

R Philosophy and Religion

Michael Dummett, *Frege: Philosophy of Language.*

Saul Kripke, *Naming and Necessity.*

G. Vermes, *Jesus the Jew.*

Mother Teresa of Calcutta receives the first Templeton Prize for Progress in Religion.

The Pope condemns 'Christian fratricide' in Ulster.

Golda Meir becomes the first Prime Minister of Israel to visit the Vatican.

Cypriot Orthodox bishops announce the deposition of Archbishop Makarios.

S Art, Sculpture, Fine Arts and Architecture

Auctioneers Christie's offer shares to the public.

1973 (Apr. – Jun.)

D **Apr**: 1st, Phase Two of British government's anti-inflation programme limits pay rises to £1 per week plus 4 per cent;

4th, British government provides £15 million subsidy to prevent mortgage rate exceeding 9.5 per cent for next three months;

9th, Palestinian terrorists attack home of Israeli ambassador to Cyprus (10th, Israeli commandos raid Beirut and kill three Palestinian guerrilla leaders);

12th, in Britain, Labour wins control of Greater London Council and six new metropolitan councils;

16th, British Embassy opens in East Germany;

17th, President Nixon drops ban on White House staff appearing before Senate Committee on Watergate affair (hearings begin, *May* 17th);

23rd, Henry Kissinger, head of U.S. National Security Council, in major speech in New York calls for new 'Atlantic Charter' governing relations between America, Europe and Japan;

27th, Andrei Gromyko and Yuri Andropov enter Soviet Politburo in first major reshuffle since 1964;

30th, President Nixon accepts responsibility for bugging of Watergate building but denies any personal involvement.

E **May**: 1st, in Britain, T.U.C. calls one-day protest strike against pay policies;

7th, British government introduces butter subsidies after outcry at E.C. sales of surplus butter to U.S.S.R.;

11th, U.S. court dismisses all charges against *The New York Times* in Pentagon Papers trial because of 'Government misconduct';

—, Joop den Uyl becomes Dutch Premier after record 164-day ministerial crisis;

18th (–21st), Soviet leader, Leonid Brezhnev, visits West Germany;

22nd, Antony Lambton, British Under-Secretary for Defence, resigns after revelations about cannabis and call-girls (24th, Lord Jellicoe, Lord Privy Seal, also resigns);

—, Britain and U.S. veto U.N. resolution to extend Rhodesian sanctions to South Africa and Portuguese colonies for breaking embargo;

23rd, Greek government foils naval mutiny;

26th, Icelandic gunboat shells British trawler *Everton*;

30th, Erskine Childers succeeds Eamon de Valera as President of Eire;

31st, U.S. Senate votes to cut off funds for bombing of Cambodia and Laos (bombing ends, *Aug*. 15th).

F **Jun**: 1st, British Honduras changes name to Belize;

7th, Labour Party announces plans to nationalise Britain's top 25 companies; Harold Wilson publicly repudiates the policy;

—, Icelandic coastguard vessel rams British warship in escalation of 'Cod War';

9th, General Franco confers Spanish premiership on Admiral Carrero Blanco;

15th, second official ceasefire begins in Vietnam;

20th, in Argentina, 35 die in riots at Buenos Aires airport as Juan Perón returns from 18-year exile;

24th, Leonid Brezhnev, during visit to U.S., declares that the Cold War is over;

25th, former White House counsel, John Dean, informs Senate Committee of President Nixon's complicity in Watergate cover-up;

26th, in Northern Ireland, newly formed 'Ulster Freedom Fighters' murder Senator Paddy Wilson of S.D.L.P. in Belfast;

28th, election by proportional representation of new Northern Ireland Assembly leaves official Unionists dependent on S.D.L.P. and Alliance support.

S Art, Sculpture, Fine Arts and Architecture (*cont.*)

Painting:

Pablo Picasso dies.
Richard Estes, *Paris Street Scene*.

Sculpture:

Barry Flanagan, *3rd February 1973*.
Robert Smithson, *Amarillo Ramp*.

Architecture:

Patrick Hodgkinson, Brunswick Centre, London.
John Portman and Associates, Hyatt—Regency Hotel, San Francisco.
Jorn Utzon, Hall, Todd and Littlemore, Sydney Opera House.
Minoru Yamasaki and Associates, World Trade Centre, New York.

T Music

Malcolm Arnold, 7th Symphony.
Pierre Boulez, *...explosante-fixe....*
B. Britten, *Death in Venice* (opera).
Aaron Copland, *Night Thoughts*.
György Ligeti, *Clocks and Clouds*.
Krzysztof Penderecki, 1st Symphony.
Steve Reich, *Music for Pieces of Wood*.

U Literature

Richard Adams, *Watership Down*.
Graham Greene, *The Honorary Consul*.
Richard Hughes, *The Wooden Shepherdess*.
Iris Murdoch, *The Black Prince*.
Thomas Pynchon, *Gravity's Rainbow*.
Derek Walcott, *Another Life*.
Patrick White, *The Eye of the Storm*.

V The Press

W Drama and Entertainment

Alan Ayckbourn, *The Norman Conquests*.
Edward Bond, *Bingo*.
Hugh Leonard, *Da*.
John McGrath, *The Cheviot, The Stag, and the Black, Black Oil*.
Peter Shaffer, *Equus*.

Films:

Lindsay Anderson's *O Lucky Man*.
Bernardo Bertolucci's *Last Tango in Paris*.
Rainer Werner Fassbinder's *Fear Eats the Soul*.
Pier Paolo Pasolini's *The Canterbury Tales*.
Nicolas Roeg's *Don't Look Now*.
Martin Scorcese's *Mean Streets*.
François Truffaut's *Day for Night*.
Enter the Dragon.

Television:

Kojak.

G **Jul**: 3rd, European Security Conference opens in Helsinki with 35 foreign ministers in attendance;
5th, terrorists kidnap 273 people from mission school in Rhodesia (17th, only 8 remain missing);
10th, in Britain, *The Times* alleges that Portuguese troops massacred 400 people in Mozambique in 1972;
—, the Bahamas become independent within the Commonwealth;
16th, parents of British children disabled by thalidomide drug accept £25 million compensation from Distillers Company;
—, Alexander Butterfield tells Senate Committee that President Nixon secretly tape-records all conversations in his office;
17th, bloodless coup deposes King Mohammed Zahir Shah of Afghanistan;
19th, British government announces weekly cash payments to mothers of £2 per child;
21st, France resumes nuclear tests at Mururoa Atoll despite protests from Australia and New Zealand;
26th, in Cyprus, E.O.K.A. terrorists blow up Limassol police station in continuing campaign for Enosis (union with Greece);
—, in by-election in Britain, Liberals win Ripon from Conservatives;
31st, militant Protestants, led by Rev. Ian Paisley, disrupt first sitting of Northern Ireland Assembly.

H **Aug**: 3rd (–7th), race riots at University of Rhodesia;
5th, Arab terrorist attack at Athens airport kills four people;
6th (–8th), accidental U.S. bombing of friendly Laotian villages causes hundreds of casualties;
10th, Israeli fighters force down Iraqi airliner, but wanted Palestinian guerrilla is not on board;
14th, new Pakistani constitution takes effect, with Zulfikar Ali Bhutto as President;
19th, abolition of Greek monarchy; Georgios Papadopoulos becomes President;
24th, Scotland Yard blames I.R.A. for week of letter-bomb incidents in Britain;
29th, Presidents Sadat and Khaddafi proclaim unification of Egypt and Libya, including plan for a joint Constituent Assembly (first meeting held, *Oct.* 3rd);
30th, Kenya bans hunting of elephants and trade in ivory.

J **Sep**: 3rd, Henry Kissinger becomes U.S. Secretary of State;
—, British T.U.C. expels 20 unions for registering under Industrial Relations Act;
5th (–8th), Jordanian terrorists hold 13 hostages in Saudi Arabian Embassy in Paris;
7th, Iceland threatens to break off diplomatic relations with Britain over fishing dispute;
11th (–12th), military junta, headed by General Augusto Pinochet, seizes power in Chile; over 2,500 die in fighting; President Allende reportedly commits suicide;
13th, major air battle between Israel and Syria;
14th, British mortgage rate reaches unprecedented 11 per cent;
15th, death of King Gustaf VI Adolf of Sweden; succeeded by King Carl XVI Gustaf;
17th, Edward Heath meets Prime Minister Cosgrave of Eire at military airfield near Dublin; first official visit to Eire by a British Prime Minister;
18th, U.N. admits East and West Germany;
23rd, Juan Perón and wife Isabel are elected President and Vice-President of Argentina (inaugurated *Oct.* 12th);
29th, Austria closes transit camp for emigrating Soviet Jews on demand of Arab kidnappers.

W **Drama and Entertainment** (*cont.*)

Popular music:

Pink Floyd, *The Dark Side of the Moon.*

Elton John, *Goodbye Yellow Brick Road.*

The New York Dolls, *New York Dolls.*

Lou Reed, *Berlin.*

X **Sport**

George Foreman defeats Joe Frazier to win world Heavy-weight title in Kingston, Jamaica (*Jan.* 22nd).

Sunderland becomes the first second-division side to win British F.A. Cup Final since 1931, beating Leeds United 1–0 (*May* 5th).

Members of the Association of Tennis Professionals boycott Wimbledon.

The first women's cricket World Cup (final *July* 28th).

Y **Statistics**

Numbers of tourists visiting selected countries: Australia, 472,124; Canada, 14,453,000; Eire, 1,284,000; Great Britain, 7,724,000; Japan, 688,481; New Zealand, 297,581; Spain, 34,558,943; Turkey, 1,341,527; U.S. 13,955,164.

Z **Births and Deaths**

Jan. 22nd Lyndon Baines Johnson d. (64).
Feb. 22nd Elizabeth Bowen d. (73).
Mar. 26th Noel Coward d. (73).
Apr. 8th Pablo Picasso d. (91).
Apr. 28th Jacques Maritain d. (90).
May 26th Jacques Lipchitz d. (81).
July 6th Otto Klemperer d. (88).
July 8th Wilfred Rhodes d. (95).
Aug. 1st Walter Ulbricht d. (80).
Aug. 6th Fulgencio Batista y Zaldívar d. (72).
Aug. 31st John Ford d. (78).
Sept. 2nd J.R.R. Tolkien d. (81).
Sept. 23rd Pablo Neruda d. (69).
Sept. 28th W.H. Auden d. (66).
Oct. 21st Alan Cobham d. (79).
Oct. 22nd Pablo Casals d. (96).
Dec. 1st David Ben-Gurion d. (87).
Dec. 5th Robert Watson-Watt d. (81).
Dec. 25th Ismet Inönü d. (84).

K **Oct:** 6th, full-scale war in Middle East, as Egypt and Syria attack Israel while Jews are observing Yom Kippur;

10th, U.S.S.R. starts airlift of military supplies to Arab states; Iraq joins war against Israel (as do Saudi Arabia and Jordan, 13th);

—, U.S. Vice-President Spiro Agnew resigns after pleading guilty to tax evasion;

11th, counter-attacking Israelis break through on Golan Heights and invade Syria;

12th, U.S. Court of Appeals orders President Nixon to hand over Watergate tapes;

15th, Britain and Iceland end 'Cod War' with agreement on fishing rights;

16th, Israelis cross Suez Canal and invade Egypt (19th, President Nixon asks Congress to approve $2,000 million worth of military aid for Israel);

17th, 11 Arab states agree to cut oil production by 5 per cent each month until U.S. changes its Middle Eastern policy;

20th, President Nixon dismisses Special Prosecutor in Watergate case; U.S. Attorney-General, Elliot Richardson, resigns in protest;

21st, Henry Kissinger and Leonid Brezhnev, meeting in Moscow, agree plan to stop war in Middle East (22nd, Egypt and Israel accept U.N. ceasefire, but fighting continues);

23rd, U.S. House of Representatives orders judiciary committee to assess evidence for impeachment of President Nixon;

24th, Syria accepts ceasefire and fighting halts on both fronts;

25th, U.S. puts its forces on precautionary alert in response to fears of Soviet intervention in Middle East;

28th, U.N. reports that drought has caused up to 100,000 deaths in Ethiopia.

L **Nov:** 1st, Phase Three of British government's anti-inflation programme limits pay rises to 7 per cent or £2.25 per week;

5th (–9th), Henry Kissinger tours Arab capitals on peace mission;

7th, U.S. Congress overturns presidential veto on Bill limiting Executive powers to wage war without congressional approval;

8th, in by-elections in Britain, Scottish Nationalists (S.N.P.) win Govan from Labour, Liberals win Berwick-on-Tweed from Conservatives;

11th, Israel and Egypt accept U.S. plan for ceasefire observance and prisoner exchange;

12th, British coal-miners begin over-time ban in protest at pay offer;

13th, energy crisis prompts British government to declare state of emergency (10 per cent cut in fuel and petrol supplies, 19th);

—, British minimum lending rate rises to 13 per cent after record balance of payments deficit;

14th, in Britain, Princess Anne marries Captain Mark Phillips in Westminster Abbey;

21st, British National Union of Mineworkers (N.U.M.) rejects any pay deal under Phase Three;

—, Northern Ireland parties agree on formation of new power-sharing Executive;

25th, General Phaidon Gizikis ousts President Papadopoulos of Greece;

29th, distribution of petrol rationing coupons begins in Britain (50 m.p.h. speed limit and widespread extinguishing of street-lights, *Dec.* 6th).

M **Dec:** 2nd, William Whitelaw becomes British Secretary of State for Employment; Francis Pym succeeds him as Northern Ireland Secretary;

6th, Gerald Ford takes oath as 40th Vice-President of U.S.;

—, in Britain, Financial Times Share Index records most drastic fall since first compiled in 1935;

M **Dec**: 9th, talks at Sunningdale, England, between Irish and British governments reach agreement on formation of a Council of Ireland with representatives from both governments; it is also agreed that the status of Northern Ireland will not be changed without majority support in the province;

11th, West Germany and Czechoslovakia agree to invalidate Munich Agreement of 1938 and establish diplomatic relations;

12th, British train-drivers' over-time ban starts to disrupt British Rail;

13th, Edward Heath orders British industry to work three-day week from *Dec.* 31st to save energy;

17th, Arab terrorists kill 32 in attack on Rome airport;

—, British Chancellor Anthony Barber's emergency Budget cuts spending by £1,200 million and restores hire purchase controls;

18th, I.R.A. launches Christmas bombing campaign in London;

20th, assassination of Spanish Premier, Carrero Blanco, in Madrid (29th, succeeded by Carlos Arias Navarro);

21st (–22nd), Middle East peace conference in Geneva sets up working party to discuss disengagement of troops on Egyptian front;

23rd, Shah of Iran announces that Gulf states will increase oil price from $5.10 to $11.65 a barrel from *Jan.* 1st.

1974 (Jan. – Mar.) Labour minority government—Portuguese revolution —Resignation of President Nixon—Partition of Cyprus

A **Jan:** 1st, Brian Faulkner takes office as Chief Executive of Northern Ireland (resigns leadership of Unionist Party, 7th);

2nd, introduction of entrance charges at British national museums and galleries (abolished *Mar.* 30th);

8th, in Britain, establishment of Department of Energy under Lord Carrington;

10th, British train-drivers begin series of one-day strikes;

14th, talks between Edward Heath and T.U.C. on miners' dispute in Britain break down (28th, Heath accuses Mick McGahey of N.U.M. of aiming to bring down government);

15th, riots in Jakarta, Indonesia, against visit by Japanese Premier;

18th, Israel and Egypt agree on disengagement of forces along Suez Canal;

25th, Britain offers industrial goods worth £110 million to Iran in exchange for 5 million extra tons of oil;

30th, President Nixon makes slip of tongue in State of Union address, mentioning need 'to replace discredited president – er, present – system...'.

B **Feb:** 4th, in Britain, I.R.A. bomb kills 12 people (servicemen and their families) on bus from Manchester to Catterick;

7th, Prime Minister Heath announces general election to be held on *Feb.* 28th, on the issue 'Who Governs Britain?';

—, Grenada becomes independent within the Commonwealth;

10th, British mineworkers begins all-out strike in support of pay claim of 30–40 per cent;

11th, John Poulson, a British architect who undertook numerous contracts for local authorities and other public bodies, is sentenced to five years' imprisonment for corruption (*Mar.* 15th, sentenced to another seven years on further charges);

13th, U.S.S.R. deports dissident author Alexander Solzhenitsyn;

17th, Harold Wilson announces 'social contract' between British Labour Party and T.U.C., whereby a Labour government will sponsor social legislation in return for wage restraint;

22nd, Pakistan recognises Bangladesh at start of Islamic summit at Lahore;

23rd, Enoch Powell urges anti-E.C. Conservatives to vote Labour in British election;

26th, Confederation of British Industry calls for repeal of Industrial Relations Act;

27th, new constitution strips Swedish monarchy of all remaining powers;

28th, British general election produces no overall majority, as Labour win 301 seats, Conservatives, 297, Liberals, 14, Scottish Nationalists, 7, Plaid Cymru, 2 (Conservatives win 37.9 per cent of votes cast, Labour, 37.1, and Liberals, 19.3).

C **Mar:** 3rd, 347 die when Turkish airliner crashes near Paris;

4th, Edward Heath resigns as British Prime Minister after Liberals refuse to enter coalition;

—, E.C. proposes economic co-operation with 20 Arab countries;

5th, in Britain, Harold Wilson forms minority Labour government, with James Callaghan as Foreign Secretary, Denis Healey as Chancellor of the Exchequer, Roy Jenkins as Home Secretary and Michael Foot as Secretary for Employment;

9th, British industry returns to five-day working week;

11th, British state of emergency ends after miners' union accepts £103 million pay deal;

14th, heavy fighting between Kurdish rebels and Iraqi forces on IraqiTurkish border;

19th, food riots in Bihar, India;

20th, in London, Princess Anne escapes kidnap attempt in the Mall;

26th, British Budget increases income tax by 3p, raises pensions and allocates £500 million for food subsidies;

O Politics, Economics, Law and Education

First observance of New Year's Day as public holiday in England and Wales.

New management structure for British National Health Service (*Apr.* 1st).

B.O.A.C. and B.E.A.C. merge to form British Airways.

Rehabilitation of Offenders Act in Britain makes it an offence to refer to criminal convictions after a certain lapse of time.

Rent Act extends indefinite security of tenure to furnished tenants without a resident landlord.

Reg Prentice, British Education Secretary, proposes abolition of 11-plus exam and establishment of fully comprehensive school system (*Mar.* 11th).

Creation of National Health Service family planning service in Britain (*Mar.* 28th).

P Science, Technology, Discovery, etc.

U.S. firm Hewlett Packard introduces the first programmable pocket calculator.

M. Molina and F.S. Rowland warn that chlorofluorocarbons (used in fridges and as propellants in sprays) may be damaging the atmosphere's ozone layer (which filters out much of the ultraviolet radiation from the Sun).

U.S. probe Mariner X (launched *Nov.* 3rd 1973) photographs the upper atmosphere of Venus (*Feb.*) and then takes photographs of Mercury (*Mar.* and *Sept.*).

U.S. probe Pioneer XI reaches Jupiter (*Dec.*).

U.S. astronomer Charles T. Kowal discovers and names Leda, the 13th moon of Jupiter (announced in *Sept.*).

U.S. physicists Burton Richter and Samuel Chao Chung Ting separately discover a new subatomic particle, later called the J/psi particle (announced *Nov.* 16th).

H.M. Georgi and S.L. Glashow propose the first Grand Unified Theory about the origins of the Universe.

Q Scholarship

Discovery of the 'terracotta army' – over 6,000 life-size model soldiers – guarding the tomb of China's first Emperor, Ch'in Shih-huang-ti, near Hsi-an in central China.

Colin Renfrew, *Before Civilization: The Radiocarbon Revolution and Prehistoric Europe*.

Robert Fogel and Stanley Engerman, *Time on the Cross: The Economics of American Negro Slavery*.

Ross McKibbin, *The Evolution of the Labour Party, 1910–24*.

Jennifer Sherwood and Niklaus Pevsner, *Oxfordshire*, the final volume in Pevsner's 'Buildings of England' series.

Encyclopaedia Britannica, 15th edn, in three sections: Propaedia, Micropaedia, Macropaedia.

R Philosophy and Religion

J.L. Mackie, *The Cement of the Universe*.

Robert Nozick, *Anarchy, State, and Utopia*.

P.F. Strawson, *Freedom and Resentment*.

Maurice Wiles, *The Remaking of Christian Doctrine*.

Pope Paul VI inaugurates a Holy Year.

Donald Coggan, Archbishop of York, appointed as Archbishop of Canterbury on the retirement of Michael Ramsey.

Brother Roger Schutz of Taizé is awarded the Templeton Prize.

Roman Catholics are permitted to become Freemasons in countries where this does not involve anti-clericalism.

D **Apr**: 1st, re-organisation of local government in England and Wales re-draws county boundaries;
2nd, Alain Poher becomes interim President of France on death of Georges Pompidou;
3rd, President Nixon agrees to pay $432,787 in unpaid income tax;
11th, Palestinian terrorists kill 18 Israelis, mostly women and children, at Kiryat Shemona;
—(–13th), strike by 6 million Japanese workers;
17th, number of killings in Northern Ireland since 1969 reaches 1,000;
19th, Israeli–Syrian air battle over Golan Heights;
25th, General Antonio de Spinola effects military coup in Portugal (26th, junta vows to dismantle authoritarian state and end wars in Angola, Mozambique and Guinea);
30th, President Nixon releases 1,308-page edited transcript of Watergate tapes to Judiciary Committee of House of Representatives.

E **May**: 1st, release of political prisoners and end of censorship in Portugal;
5th, in Britain, Harold Wilson condemns N.I.R.C. sequestration of A.U.E.W. funds (anonymous industrialists pay outstanding A.U.E.W. fines to end protest strike, 8th);
8th, Willy Brandt resigns as West German Chancellor after aide, Günther Guillaume, admits to spying;
15th, 20 children die when Israeli troops storm school occupied by Palestinian terrorists at Ma'alot (16th, Israel bombs Palestinian refugee camps in Lebanon);
17th, three bomb explosions in Dublin kill 32 people;
18th, atomic bomb test makes India the world's sixth nuclear power;
19th, Valéry Giscard d'Estaing wins second round of French Presidential election with 50.8 per cent of votes to François Mitterrand's 49.2;
—, Protestant strike begins in Northern Ireland against Sunningdale agreement and power-sharing (22nd, Executive postpones Council of Ireland till after 1977);
24th (–*Apr.* 4th), Edward Heath visits China (two giant pandas presented by China arrive at London Zoo, *Sept.* 14th);
27th, Jacques Chirac becomes Prime Minister of France;
28th, Northern Ireland Executive collapses when all Unionist members resign (29th, Britain re-imposes direct rule and general strike ends);
31st, Henry Kissinger secures agreement between Syria and Israel to disengage forces on Golan Heights.

F **Jun**: 1st, in Britain, 29 die when Nypro chemical plant at Flixborough blows up;
3rd, I.R.A. hunger-striker Michael Gaughan dies in Parkhurst prison in England;
4th, James Callaghan presents British conditions for re-negotiation of E.C. entry;
—, Itzhak Rabin succeeds Golda Meir as Prime Minister of Israel;
12th (–19th), President Nixon tours the Middle East (27th–*July* 3rd, in U.S.S.R.);
13th, Prince of Wales makes maiden speech in British House of Lords on leisure facilities;
15th, student dies in fighting between left-wing and right-wing demonstrators in Red Lion Square, Holborn, London;
17th, I.R.A. explodes bomb outside Westminster Hall, London, injuring 11 people (*July* 17th, bomb at Tower of London kills 1 and injures 37);
20th, British House of Commons rejects plans for greater state control over industry (one of over 20 government defeats between *Mar.* and *Oct.*);
28th, Ethiopian armed forces take control of government buildings and broadcasting;
—, President Makarios asks Greek officers to leave Cypriot National Guard.

S Art, Sculpture, Fine Arts and Architecture

Venice Biennale cancelled.

First major exhibition of photography by Arts Council in London, looks at work of American Diane Arbus.

Painting:

Anselm Kiefer, *Resumptio*.

Sculpture:

Art Gallery of Ontario, Toronto, opens extended building including Henry Moore Sculpture Centre.

Joseph Beuys, *I Like America and America Likes Me*.

Richard Long, *A Line in Ireland*.

Architecture:

John Andrews and Webb Zerata, Canadian National Tower, Toronto, is topped out, world's tallest freestanding structure.

Arata Isozaki, Gunma Prefectural Museum of Fine Arts, Japan.

Kenzo Tange, two new wings for Minneapolis Institute of Art.

T Music

Gordon Crosse, *The Story of Vasco* (opera).

Hans Werner Henze, *Tristan*.

György Ligeti, *San Francisco Polyphony*.

Olivier Messiaen, *Des canyons aux étoiles*.

Karlheinz Stockhausen, *Inori*.

Iannis Xenakis, *Cendrées*.

U Literature

John le Carré, *Tinker, Tailor, Soldier, Spy*.

Erica Jong, *Fear of Flying*.

Philip Larkin, *High Windows*.

Elsa Morante, *History*.

Alexander Solzhenitsyn expelled from the U.S.S.R. after publication of *The Gulag Archipelago, 1918–56*.

V The Press

World-wide shortage of newsprint.

W Drama and Entertainment

Thomas Bernhard, *The Force of Habit*.

Howard Brenton, *The Churchill Play*.

Alexander Buzo, *Norm and Ahmed*.

Dario Fo, *Can't Pay? Won't Pay!*

John Romeril, *The Floating World*.

Ntozake Shange, *For Coloured Girls who have Considered Suicide when the Rainbow is enuf*.

Tom Stoppard, *Travesties*.

Films:

Bernardo Bertolucci's *Last Tango in Paris*.

Francis Ford Coppola's *Godfather II*.

Federico Fellini's *Amarcord*.

Louis Malle's *Lacombe Lucien!*

Roman Polanski's *Chinatown*.

Jacques Rivette's *Celine and Julie Go Boating*.

G **Jul:** 1st, Isabel Perón becomes President of Argentina on the death of her husband;
2nd, start of sporadic industrial action against pay beds in British N.H.S. hospitals;
14th, left-wing government takes office in Portugal under Colonel Vasco Goncalves;
15th, Cypriot National Guard, with Greek support, overthrows President Makarios and installs former E.O.K.A. terrorist Nicos Sampson in his place;
20th, Turkey invades Cyprus, claiming right of intervention under 1960 treaty (ceasefire, 22nd);
22nd, British mini-Budget reduces V.A.T. to 8 per cent and allots £150 million for rate rebates;
23rd, Greek military government resigns (24th, Constantine Karamanlis returns from exile to form civilian administration);
—, nationalisation of Harland and Wolff shipyard in Belfast, Northern Ireland, to save 12,000 jobs;
24th, U.S. Supreme Court orders President Nixon to surrender all Watergate tapes to Special Prosecutor;
25th (–30th), foreign ministers of Britain, Turkey and Greece discuss future of Cyprus in Geneva;
26th, U.S. House Judiciary Committee recommends impeachment of President Nixon;
31st, in Britain, repeal of Industrial Relations Act and abolition of N.I.R.C.

H **Aug:** 1st, restoration of 1952 constitution in Greece;
5th, President Nixon admits complicity in the Watergate cover-up;
8th, British White Papers propose capital transfer tax and wealth tax;
9th, President Nixon resigns; Gerald Ford becomes 38th U.S. President;
11th, severe flooding in Bangladesh kills over 2,000;
12th, Turkey issues 24-hour ultimatum demanding creation of autonomous Turkish cantons in Cyprus (14th, Turkish forces resume offensive);
14th, Greece withdraws from N.A.T.O. in protest at failure to oppose Turks;
16th, second ceasefire leaves 40 per cent of Cyprus under Turkish control;
18th, 19 I.R.A. terrorists blow their way out of Portlaoise prison in Eire;
31st, death of Norman Kirk, Prime Minister of New Zealand (succeeded by Wallace Rowling, *Sept.* 6th).

J **Sep:** 4th, British T.U.C. conference in Brighton endorses 'social contract';
—, U.S. and East Germany establish diplomatic relations;
5th, Sir Keith Joseph, Shadow Home Secretary, questions whole basis of post-war British economic policy in speech at Preston;
8th, President Ford pardons Richard Nixon for any offences committed in office;
10th, Guinea-Bissau wins independence from Portugal;
12th, military coup deposes Emperor Haile Selassie of Ethiopia;
13th, Japanese 'Red Army' terrorists take French diplomats hostage at The Hague (17th, France and Netherlands pay ransom);
19th, Hurricane 'Fifi' kills 8,000 in Honduras;
20th, nationalist government takes office in Mozambique under Joaquim Chissano;
30th, General Francisco Costa Gomes succeeds General Spinola as Portuguese President.

K **Oct:** 5th, I.R.A. bombs kill 5 and injure 65 in two public houses in Guildford, England;
10th, British general election gives Labour an overall majority of 3, with 319 seats to Conservatives, 277, Liberals, 13, Scottish Nationalists, 11, Plaid Cymru 3 (Labour take 39.2 per cent of votes, Conservatives, 35.8, and Liberals, 18.3);
15th, riots and arson at Maze prison, Northern Ireland;

W Drama and Entertainment (*cont.*)

Television

The Family – the B.B.C.'s 'fly-on-the-wall' documentary about living with the Wilkins family.

Happy Days.

Porridge.

Radio:

The Prairie Home Companion with Garrison Keillor.

700 million video-cassettes rented in the U.S.

Popular music:

Bob Dylan and The Band undertake a classic U.S. tour, giving 39 shows.

Can, *Soon Over Babaluma.*

Kraftwerk, *Autobahn* – seminal techno music.

Mike Oldfield, *Tubular Bells.*

Steely Dan, *Pretzel Logic.*

X Sport

Sir Alf Ramsey is sacked as manager of the English soccer team (*May* 1st).

Host nation West Germany wins the World Cup, defeating Holland by 2–1 in the Final in Munich (*July* 7th).

Garry Sobers retires from Test cricket, holding the record for the number of runs: 8,032, from 93 Tests.

The British Lions win their first Test series in South Africa.

Muhammad Ali beats George Foreman to regain the World Heavy-weight title in Kinshasa, Zaire (*Oct.* 29th).

Y Statistics

Coal consumption in Great Britain (percentage of total output, with figures for 1947 in brackets): power stations, 57.4 (14.3); coke ovens and gasworks 16.0 (22.4); domestic, 10 (19.3); other inland, 14.4 (41.3); exports, 1.7 (2.8).

Social and educational composition of British Labour Cabinet: aristocrats, 1, middle class, 16, working class, 4; attendance at public school, 7 (none at Eton); attendance at University 16 (inc. 11 at Oxford or Cambridge).

Z Births and Deaths

Mar. 17th Louis Isadore Kahn d. (73).

Apr. 2nd Georges Pompidou d. (62).

Apr. 5th Richard Crossman d. (66).

Apr. 20th Mohammed Ayub Khan d. (66).

May 24th Duke Ellington d. (75).

June 18th Georgi K. Zhukov d. (77).

July 1st Juan Perón d. (78).

July 10th Earl Warren d. (83).

July 13th P.M.S. Blackett d. (76).

July 29th Erich Kästner d. (75).

Aug. 26th Charles Lindbergh d. (72).

Dec. 14th Kurt Hahn d. (88).

K **Oct**: 15th, violent protests in Boston, U.S., against integration of schools by 'busing';
18th, U.S. Senator Henry Jackson announces informal deal linking U.S. trade concessions to freedom of emigration from U.S.S.R.;
28th, 20 Arab nations recognise the Palestine Liberation Organisation (P.L.O.) as sole legitimate representative of Palestinian people;
—(–30th), Chancellor Schmidt of West Germany holds talks with Leonid Brezhnev in Moscow;
31st, Britain, France and U.S. veto motion to expel South Africa from U.N.

L **Nov**: 6th, Democrats gain 4 Senators and 43 Representatives in U.S. mid-term elections;
12th, British emergency Budget provides £1,500 million relief aid for industry;
13th, P.L.O. leader, Yassir Arafat, addresses U.N. General Assembly;
14th, Henry Kissinger proposes international co-operation to reduce price of oil;
20th, British Labour M.P. John Stonehouse disappears in Miami (arrested with false passport in Australia, *Dec.* 24th);
21st, I.R.A. bombs two public houses in Birmingham, England, killing 21 people and injuring 120;
23rd (–25th), President Ford and Leonid Brezhnev discuss arms control at Vladivostok;
24th, Ethiopian military government executes 60 politicians and nobles without trial;
26th, Kakuei Tanaka resigns as Japanese premier amid allegations of corruption (succeeded by Takeo Miki, Dec. 9th);
28th, following spate of I.R.A. outrages in Britain, the Prevention of Terrorism Bill is passed through Parliament in 24 hours; police are given power to hold terrorist suspects for five days without charge and suspects can be banned from the British mainland or deported to Northern Ireland.

M **Dec**: 2nd, Israel announces that it possesses means to manufacture nuclear weapons;
3rd, British government proposes defence cuts to save £4,700 million over 10 years;
7th, President Makarios returns to Cyprus after five months in exile;
8th, in Greece 62 per cent vote in referendum against restoration of monarchy;
9th (–10th), E.C. summit in Paris reaches agreement on revised British contribution to budget;
11th, Ian Smith calls constitutional conference to end guerrilla war in Rhodesia;
13th, British annual inflation rate reaches 18.3 per cent;
25th, cyclone devastates Darwin, Australia;
29th, A.N. Wedgwood Benn, Secretary for Industry, attacks British membership of E.C.
31st, during 1974 British retail prices have risen by 19 per cent, wage rates by 29 per cent, while total industrial production fell by 3 per cent (each sum a post-war record).

1975 (Jan. – Apr.) Communist victory in Vietnam—'Emergency' in India—First British North Sea Oil

A **Jan:** 1st, Nixon aides H.R. Haldeman, John D. Ehrlichman and John N. Mitchell are found guilty of Watergate offences (*Feb.* 21st, sentenced to $2\frac{1}{2}$ to 8 years in prison);
2nd, British hospital consultants start work-to-rule over new contracts;
4th, Phuoc Binh province of South Vietnam falls to North Vietnamese;
6th, Financial Times Share Index falls to 145.5 (having been at 339 on 28 *Feb.* 1974), the lowest level since 1954 (by *Dec.* 31st London shares gain over 150 per cent);
15th, Portugal agrees to grant independence to Angola;
—, British government proposes to nationalise the aircraft construction industry;
—, President Ford reports that the State of the Union is 'not good';
20th, British government abandons the Channel Tunnel project;
23rd, government decides to hold a referendum on the revised terms for British membership of the E.C.;
24th, Donald Coggan enthroned as Archbishop of Canterbury in Canterbury Cathedral, England;
31st, Industry Bill published, establishing a National Enterprise Board to facilitate state intervention in British industry.

B **Feb:** 4th, in Britain, in the first ballot of the Conservative leadership election Mrs. Margaret Thatcher wins 130 votes, Edward Heath 119 and Hugh Fraser 16; Heath resigns;
6th, 500 Spanish civil servants sign a pro-democracy manifesto;
11th, Mrs. Thatcher elected leader of the British Conservative Party, with 146 votes (William Whitelaw wins 79 votes, with 49 for three other challengers);
13th, Northern Cyprus declares separate existence as the Turkish Federated State of Cyprus;
24th, Bangladesh becomes a one-party state;
27th, Peter Lorenz, Chairman of West Berlin Christian Democratic Union, is kidnapped by terrorists (*Mar.* 5th, released after his captors' demands are met: five terrorists are released from goal in West Germany and flown out of the country);
28th, 43 die in crash of London Underground train at Moorgate station;
—, Lomé Convention signed, giving 46 developing countries preferential access to E.C. markets.

C **Mar:** 2nd, Iran becomes a one-party state;
18th, British government decides to recommend a 'Yes' vote in the E.C. referendum,
25th, King Faisal of Saudi Arabia assassinated, succeeded by King Khalid;
27th, in Britain, collective Cabinet responsibility suspended for the first time for the duration of the E.C. referendum campaign;
30th, North Vietnamese forces capture the central city of Da Nang.

D **Apr:** 5th, Chiang Kai-shek dies (6th, succeeded by Yen Chia-kan as President of Taiwan);
9th, British House of Commons vote confirms E.C. membership, by 396 to 170;
13th, civil war starts in Lebanon when clashes between Palestinians and Christian Falangists outside a Beirut church leave 30 dead;
15th, British Chancellor Denis Healey's 'rough and tough' Budget raises income tax by 2p and cuts spending by £900m;
17th, in Cambodia Khmer Rouge revolutionaries capture Phnom Penh; there is considerable brutality as people flee the city;
18th, N.H.S. consultants stop industrial action in British hospitals after being granted a pay rise of 30 per cent;

O Politics, Economics, Law and Education

Foundation of Ecology Party in Britain.

Sex Discrimination Act in Britain outlaws discrimination in employment or education on grounds of sex or marital status and establishes Equal Opportunities Commission.

I.M.F. abandons gold's remaining role in world monetary affairs (*Aug.* 31st).

Appeal Court rules that Sikhs living in Britain can have only one wife (*May* 9th).

Adopted children in Britain over 18 granted right to information about their natural parents.

P Science, Technology, Discovery, etc.

The first 'personal computer' is marketed in the U.S.

Liquid crystals first used for display purposes in electronic devices.

U.S.-German space probe Helios I passes the Sun at a distance of 28.7 million miles (*Mar.* 15th).

U.S. Apollo XVIII and U.S.S.R. Soyuz XIX spacecraft dock in earth orbit (*July* 17th–19th).

U.S.S.R. craft Venera IX and X land on Venus (*Oct.* 22nd and 25th) and transmit the first pictures from the surface.

Foundation of European Space Agency (*Aug.* 1st).

U.S. astronomer Charles T. Kowal discovers the 14th moon of Jupiter.

Astronomers at Leiden University estimate that the 'radio galaxy' spans a distance of 18 million light years.

Discovery of tau lepton or tauon atomic particle (*Aug.*).

Production of 'U' sub-atomic particles at the Stanford accelerator.

C. Milstein and G. Köhler produce the first monoclonal antibodies (identical micro-organisms), in Cambridge, England.

Oxford scientist Derek Brownhall produces the first clone of a rabbit.

J. Hughes discovers endorphins (morphine-like chemicals) in the brain.

Swiss scientists publish details of the first chemically directed synthesis of insulin.

EMI introduces the CAT body-scanner.

Q Scholarship

Discovery of 'Lucy', the remains of a hominid about 3 million years old, at Hadar in Ethiopia.

20,000 clay tablets with cuneiform texts found at Tell Mardikh (ancient Ebla) in Syria.

The Cambridge History of Africa (–86).

John Matthews, *Western Aristocracies and Imperial Court, A.D. 364–425*.

C.N.L. Brooke, G. Keir, *London 800–1216: The Shaping of a City*.

R.H. Hilton, *The English Peasantry in the Later Middle Ages*.

Carl Bridenbaugh, *The Spirit of '76: The Growth of American Patriotism Before Independence, 1607–1776*.

E.P. Thompson, *Whigs and Hunters*.

Paul Fussell, *The Great War and Modern Memory*.

A.J.P. Taylor, *The Second World War: An Illustrated History*.

Paul Addison, *The Road to 1945*.

R Philosophy and Religion

Paul Feyerabend, *Against Method*.

M. Foucault, *Discipline and Punish*.

H.-G. Gadamer, *Truth and Method*.

Paul Feyerabend, *Against Method*.

Archbishop Coggan of Church of England issues a 'call to the nation' for moral and spiritual renewal.

D **Apr**: 24th, British government decides to take a majority shareholding in British Leyland motors;

25th, the first free elections in Portugal since the 1920s produce no overall majority, the Socialists under Mario Soares emerge as the largest party;

—, South African government decides to abolish many measures of 'petty apartheid';

29th, last U.S. personnel flee Saigon by helicopter from the U.S. Embassy compound;

30th, publication of bill to establish British National Oil Corporation;

—, President Minh of South Vietnam surrenders Saigon to Communist forces.

E **May**: 1st, British government takes 50 per cent stake in Ferranti Electronics;

—, Ulster Unionists win majority in elections for Northern Ireland Constitutional Convention;

5th, Mrs. Castle announces the British government's intention to abolish pay beds in N.H.S. hospitals;

9th, British Environment Secretary Anthony Crosland tells local authority leaders that 'the party's over' for further expansion of local welfare services;

12th, Cambodian navy seizes the U.S.S. *Mayaguez* (recaptured by U.S. forces, 15th).

F **Jun**: 4th, first live radio broadcast of British parliament;

5th, consultative referendum approves Britain's membership of E.C.; turn-out is 64.5 per cent, of whom 67.2 per cent vote in favour;

—, Suez Canal reopened;

9th (–Aug 15th), trial in Lancaster of the 'Birmingham Six' charged with the 1974 pub bombings in Birmingham, England; all are found guilty and sentenced to life imprisonment;

10th, in U.S. report of Rockefeller Commission into C.I.A. activities reports illegal domestic operations and extensive mail-opening programme;

—, Municipal Assistance Corporation formed to help New York City escape bankruptcy;

11th, Uganda-based British lecturer Denis Hills, who had referred to President Amin in an unpublished text as a 'village tyrant', is sentenced to death (*July* 10th, released following interventions by several parties and visit by British Foreign Secretary Callaghan);

12th, Indira Gandhi found guilty of electoral corruption but remains Indian Prime Minister pending appeals;

18th, first North Sea Oil pumped ashore in Britain;

25th, Mozambique becomes independent with Samora Machel as President;

26th, Indira Gandhi declares a state of emergency in India; censorship is imposed and opposition leaders, including Morarji Desai, are imprisoned.

G **Jul**: 2nd, Australian Deputy Prime Minister Cairns dismissed because of his involvement in a loans scandal;

5th, Cape Verde Islands gain independence;

6th, Comoro Islands declare independence;

11th, White Paper *The Attack on Inflation* is published, proposing an incomes policy for 1975–76 which would allow only a flat rate £6 per week increase;

12th, São Tomé Principe gains independence;

24th, Reg Prentice, British Education Secretary, is refused renomination by his local Labour Party in Newham North-East constituency;

29th, coup in Nigeria replaces General Gowon with Brigadier Murtala Mohammed;

—, Organization of American States lifts ban on relations with Cuba.

S **Art, Sculpture, Fine Arts and Architecture**

'British Photography 1840–1950' exhibition at Hayward Gallery, London.
500th anniversary of Michelangelo's birth.

Painting:
Rebecca Horn, *Unicorn*.

Sculpture:
John De Andrea, *Woman in Bed*.

Architecture:
Foster Associates, Willis, Faber, Dumas Building, Ipswich, England.
I.M. Pei, John Hancock Tower, Boston, Massachusetts.
Kevin Roche, John Dinkeloo and Associates, Lehman Pavilion, Museum of Modern Art, New York.

T **Music**

Pierre Boulez, *Rituel*.
Elliott Carter, *A Mirror on Which to Dwell*.
Joonas Kokkonen, *The Last Temptations* (opera).
Witold Lutoslawski, *Les Espaces du sommeil*.
Luigi Nono, *Al gran sole carico d'amore* (opera).
Aulis Sallinen, *The Horseman* (opera).

U **Literature**

Saul Bellow, *Humboldt's Gift*.
Jorge Luis Borges, *The Book of Sand*.
Joyce Carol Oates, *Assassins*.
Primo Levi, *The Periodic Table*.
Anthony Powell, *Hearing Secret Harmonies* – the 12th and final volume of *A Dance to the Music of Time*, begun in 1951.
Paul Theroux, *The Great Railway Bazaar*.
Michel Tournier, *Gemini*.
P.G. Wodehouse is knighted, just before his death.

V **The Press**

Scottish Daily News launched by workers' co-operative (*May* 5th), but later fails (*Oct*.), following an attempt by Robert Maxwell to save the paper.

W **Drama and Entertainment**

Peter Hall becomes Director of Britain's National Theatre.
Michael Cook, *Jacob's Wake*.
Athol Fugard, *Statements*.
Trevor Griffiths, *Comedians*.
David Mamet, *American Buffalo*.
Harold Pinter, *No Man's Land*.
James Reeney, *Handcuffs* – completes *The Donnelly Trilogy*.
Tadeusz Rozewicz, *Mariage Blanc*.
Wole Soyinka, *Death and the King's Horseman*.

Films:
Milos Forman's *One Flew Over the Cuckoo's Nest*.
Werner Herzog's *Every Man for Himself and God Against All*.
Sidney Lumet's *Dog Day Afternoon*.
Steven Spielberg's *Jaws*.

H **Aug:** 1st, Helsinki Conference on Security and Co-operation in Europe issues 'Final Act', signed by 30 states: states are to respect each other's equality and individuality, avoid use of force in disputes, and respect human rights;
12th, British inflation peaks at 26.9 per cent;
15th, President Mujibur Rahman of Bangladesh is murdered; his successor is Khandakar Mushtaq Ahmed;
19th, in Britain supporters of imprisoned robber George Davis damage pitch of Headingley cricket ground in protest at Davis's imprisonment and prevent play in Test Match;
23rd, Greek colonels found guilty of treason and sentenced to death (25th, sentence commuted).

J **Sep:** 3rd, T.U.C. supports the British government's incomes policy;
4th, introduction of school busing for desegregation in Louisville, Kentucky, is followed by riots;
5th, Miss Lynette 'Squeaky' Fromme, a follower of murderer Charles Manson, attempts to assassinate President Ford (*Nov.* 26th, found guilty of attempted assassination);
16th, Papua New Guinea becomes independent from Australia;
17th, New York City narrowly averts bankruptcy through last-minute loan of $150m from the teachers' union;
18th, kidnapped U.S. heiress Patricia Hearst arrested for armed robbery;
22nd, Miss Sara Jane Moore attempts to asssassinate President Ford;
—, 15 die in bombings in nine Northern Ireland towns;
23rd, Israel and Egypt reach agreement on Israeli withdrawal from the Sinai peninsula;
29th, British Labour Party conference supports the new incomes policy.

K **Oct:** 1st, the British Lord Chief Justice rules that the first volume of *The Crossman Diaries* can be published;
8th, fighting resumes in Lebanon;
10th, part of Israeli-occupied Sinai returned to Egypt;
15th, the Liberal and National opposition decides to use its Senate majority to block the Australian government's supply of finance;
—, start of the 'Cod War', when Iceland increases its territorial waters from 50 to 200 miles and confronts German trawlers with gunboats;
21st, British unemployment breaches 1 million for first time since 1940s;
—, New York financial crisis leads to large cuts and a loss of power by elected officials;
22nd, the 'Guildford Four' are sentenced to life imprisonment after being found guilty of planting I.R.A. bombs in pubs in Guildford and Woolwich, England;
24th, one-day general strike of women in Iceland;
—, Young Liberal leader Peter Hain accused of robbing a London bank;
26th, Transkei becomes the first nominally independent South African black 'homeland';
27th, British House of Commons votes to abolish grants to 'direct grant' schools;
29th, British House of Lords passes the Community Land Bill, putting development land under control of local authorities.

L **Nov:** 1st (–*Dec.* 29th), British doctor Sheila Cassidy is imprisoned and tortured in Chile (*Dec.* 30th, British ambassador in Santiago recalled in protest);
3rd, Queen Elizabeth makes formal opening of Britain's North Sea Oil pumps;
—, Bangladesh government imposes martial law;

W **Drama and Entertainment** (*cont.*)

Television:

Starsky and Hutch.
The World at War.

Popular music:

Bob Dylan, *Blood on the Tracks.*
Queen, 'Bohemian Rhapsody' – the first major rock video.
Patti Smith, *Horses.*
Bruce Springsteen, *Born to Run.*

X **Sport**

Australia regains the Ashes (*Jan.* 9th).
Anatoly Karpov of the U.S.S.R. becomes world chess champion when Bobby Fischer fails to meet the deadline for their match in Manila (*Apr.* 3rd).
Stable boys in England strike in pursuit of a pay rise; they picket Ascot on Gold Cup day (*June* 19th).
Arthur Ashe of the U.S. becomes the first black Men's Singles champion at Wimbledon (*July* 5th).
Muhammad Ali beats Joe Frazier on points in Manila to retain the world Heavyweight boxing title (*Sept.* 30th).

Y **Statistics**

Average annual increase in per capita gross national product, 1970–80: Japan, 3.5; France, 3.1; Belgium, 2.8; Canada, 2.7; Germany, 2.7; Italy, 2.4; U.S., 2.3; Holland, 2.0; Great Britain, 1.8; Sweden, 1.7.

Z **Births and Deaths**

Jan. 28th Antonin Novotný d. (70).
Feb. 14th Julian Huxley d. (87).
— P.G. Wodehouse d. (93).
Feb. 24th Nikolai Bulganin d. (79).
Mar. 15th Aristotle Onassis d. (69).
Mar. 27th Arthur Bliss d. (83).
Apr. 5th Chiang Kai-shek d. (87).
Apr. 16th Sarvepalli Radhakrishnan d. (86).
May 20th Barbara Hepworth d. (72).
June 3rd Eisaku Sato d. (74).
Aug. 9th Dmitry Shostakovich d. (68).
Aug. 27th Haile Selassie d. (83).
Aug. 29th Eamon de Valera d. (92).
Sept. 4th Ivan Maisky d. (91).
Oct. 22nd Arnold Toynbee d. (86).
Nov. 29th Graham Hill d. (46).

1975 (Nov. – Dec.)

L **Nov**: 6th (–9th), unarmed Moroccan invasion of Spanish Sahara;
7th, electoral corruption verdict on Indira Gandhi quashed by the Supreme Court (after India's parliament, the Lok Sabha, retrospectively legalised her actions);
10th, Angola becomes independent with Agostinho Neto as President, but civil war breaks out between the government party, the Popular Movement for the Liberation of Angola (M.P.L.A.), and U.N.I.T.A.;
11th, Sir John Kerr, the Governor-General of Australia, dismisses Prime Minister Whitlam and appoints the Opposition leader, Malcolm Fraser;
12th, the British House of Lords passes laws on industry, planning and sex disrimination but rejects trade union law reform because it would allow journalists to establish closed shops, which is seen as a threat to freedom of the press;
14th, Spain agrees with Morocco and Mauritania to pull out of the Sahara by February 1976 and organise consultations about the area's future;
15th, Scottish Development Agency established;
20th, General Franco dies (22nd, the monarchy is restored and Juan Carlos becomes King of Spain);
—, interim U.S. Senate report reveals that the C.I.A. had plotted to kill foreign leaders, including Castro and Lumumba;
25th, Surinam (former Dutch Guyana) becomes independent;
—, British government sends three frigates to protect trawlers in Icelandic fishing grounds;
26th, attempted coup by left-wing Portuguese soldiers defeated;
27th, White Paper *Our Changing Democracy* proposes devolution for Scotland and Wales;
—, I.R.A. murders British publisher and right-wing activist Ross McWhirter;
28th, Fretilin liberation movement declares Portuguese (East) Timor independent;
29th, New Zealand National Party defeats the Labour government; Robert Muldoon becomes Prime Minister.

M **Dec**: 2nd (–14th), train hijack in Holland by South Moluccan terrorists;
3rd, Communist forces take control of Laos; the King abdicates;
5th, last 46 Northern Ireland internees released;
6th (–12th), I.R.A. gang is besieged at Balcombe Street in London and eventually surrenders;
7th, Indonesian forces invade East Timor and commit numerous atrocities;
11th, first shots fired in the Cod War around Iceland;
13th, general election in Australia gives large majority to the newly installed Fraser government;
16th, the British government bails out the Chrysler U.K. car company with £162.5 million in assistance;
21st, terrorists capture some O.P.E.C. oil ministers at their conference in Vienna;
23rd, Richard Welch, head of C.I.A. operations in Greece, is shot dead in Athens following his exposure by newspaper as a spy;
27th, Indian general election postponed, for a year, until 1977;
30th, former dictator of Greece, Colonel Papadopoulos, is imprisoned for a further 25 years for shootings at Athens Polytechnic in November 1973.

1976 (Jan. – Mar.) Death of Chairman Mao—Jimmy Carter elected U.S. President—I.M.F. crisis in Britain

A **Jan:** 1st, Venezuelan government nationalises its oil industry;
4th (–5th), 15 die in sectarian murders in South Armagh, Northern Ireland (6th, the elite S.A.S. – Special Air Service – is sent in to control the situation);
7th, government of Aldo Moro in Italy resigns after the Socialist Party withdraws support;
8th, Chou En-lai, Premier of China, dies and is replaced by Hua Kuo-feng (*Feb.* 9th);
13th, Argentina suspends diplomatic ties with Britain over Falkland Islands;
14th, British government commissions the Berrill Report on representation overseas;
18th, Labour M.P.s Jim Sillars and John Robertson launch the Scottish Labour Party (S.L.P.) to campaign for greater devolution for Scotland;
21st, inaugural Concorde flights from London to Bahrain and from Paris to Rio de Janeiro;
23rd, following an anti-Communist speech delivered by Mrs. Margaret Thatcher, a report in the U.S.S.R. newspaper *Red Star* brands her the 'Iron Lady';
28th, Spanish Prime Minister proposes lifting ban on political parties (enacted *July* 14th);
29th, a male model, Norman Scott, alleges in court that he was the homosexual lover of British Liberal Party leader Jeremy Thorpe in the 1960s; a Department of Trade report criticises Thorpe's judgement in becoming involved with a crashed 'secondary bank';
31st, population of the world reaches 4 billion.

B **Feb:** 4th, Lockheed bribery scandal exposed, with serious consequences for politicians and officials in Japan, Italy and Holland;
11th, in Italy Aldo Moro forms a minority Christian Democrat government;
13th, the Head of State of Nigeria, General Murtala Mohammad, is killed during an unsuccessful coup and succeeded by General Olusegun Obasanjo;
17th, M.P.L.A. forces secure control over most Angolan territory;
19th, Iceland breaks off diplomatic relations with Britain over the 'Cod War';
24th, Governor Jimmy Carter emerges as the surprise winner of the New Hampshire Democratic primary;
—(–*Mar.* 5th), 25th Congress of the Communist Party of the Soviet Union (27th, Italian Communist leader Enrico Berlinguer announces to the conference that a communist Italy would stay in N.A.T.O. and remain pluralist);
27th, Polisario Front declares the independence of Western Sahara, but an assembly of tribal chiefs votes for union with Morocco.

C **Mar:** 5th, the pound sterling falls below $2 for the first time ever;
9th, British Prime Minister Harold Wilson alleges that there had been 'South African participation' in allegations made against Jeremy Thorpe;
—, British House of Lords passes the Trade Union and Labour Relations Bill;
12th, Lebanese army leaders set up an interim military council until political control of country is restored;
15th, the French franc is forced out of the European currency 'snake';
16th, Harold Wilson announces that he is to resign as British Prime Minister;
20th, U.S. heiress Patricia Hearst found guilty of armed robbery with the 'Symbionese Liberation Army';
24th, military coup deposes President Isabel Perón of Argentina; all political parties and unions are 'suspended';
25th, Michael Foot wins the first ballot for the British Labour Party leadership with 90 votes; Callaghan wins 84, Jenkins 56, Wedgwood Benn 37, Healey 30, Crosland 17; a second ballot follows (30th) with three contestants only, giving Callaghan 141, Foot 133, and Healey 38.

O **Politics, Economics, Law and Education**

President Giscard d'Estaing publishes *La Démocratie Française.*

Layfield Report on local government finance in Britain (*May* 19th).

California allows the terminally ill to authorise the removal of life-support equipment (introduced on *Jan.* 1st 1977).

U.S. Supreme Court rules that capital punishment is not unconstitutional (*July* 2nd).

Death penalty is abolished in Canada (*July* 14th).

In Britain, Salmon Commission on Standards of Conduct in Public Life publishes report (*July* 15th).

Police Complaints Board is established in Britain.

Race Relations Act passed in Britain, establishing Commission for Racial Equality.

British government requires all Local Education Authorities without comprehensive education to submit plans for comprehensivization.

P **Science, Technology, Discovery, etc.**

The Monotype company in Britain introduces laser typesetting.

Anglo-French supersonic airliner Concorde begins regular passenger service across the Atlantic.

The German company Keuffel und Esser makes its last slide-rule.

A massive release of poisonous dioxin gas from a pesticide plant near Seveso in Italy kills domestic and farm animals in the surrounding region (*July* 26th).

U.S. space craft Viking I and Viking II soft-land on Mars (*July* 20th, *Sept.* 3rd) and transmit detailed pictures of the surface and scientific data.

Astronomers at Harvard College Laboratory discover bursts of X-rays coming from a star cluster 30,000 light years from earth.

Japanese molecular biologist Susumu Tonegawa demonstrates that antibodies are produced by large numbers of genes working in combination.

R.B. Woodward and A. Eschenmoser synthesize Vitamin B12.

Foundation of Genentech, the world's first genetic engineering company, in San Francisco.

A mystery disease afflicts people who attended the meeting of the American Legion in Philadelphia; 29 die within a month; the disease becomes known as Legionnaire's disease.

Q **Scholarship**

J.M. Roberts, *The Hutchinson History of the World.*

W.G. Hoskins, *The Age of Plunder: King Henry's England, 1500–1547.*

Peter Clark and Paul Slack, *English Towns in Transition, 1500–1700.*

E.S. de Beer (ed.), *The Correspondence of John Locke* (–89).

R **Philosophy and Religion**

Louis Althusser, *Essays in Self-Criticism.*

Noam Chomsky, *Reflections on Language.*

Imre Lakatos, *Proofs and Refutations.*

Episcopalian Church in U.S. approves ordination of women to the priesthood.

Report on *Christian Believing* by the Doctrine Commission of the Church of England.

Basil Hume appointed Roman Catholic Archbishop of Westminster, London.

Cardinal Suenens is awarded the Templeton Prize.

The Roman Catholic Bishop of Umtali, Rhodesia, is sentenced to 10 years' imprisonment for anti-government activities.

D **Apr**: 2nd, a new Portuguese constitution with a commitment to socialism is promulgated;
3rd, James Callaghan wins final ballot of Labour leadership election with 176 votes to 137 for Foot (5th, Callaghan becomes Prime Minister of Britain);
4th, government of Thailand defeated in general election (18th, new coalition formed);
—, Prince Sihanouk retires as head of state of Cambodia, replaced by Khieu Samphan of the Khmer Rouge;
5th, rioting in China over the removal by 'ultra-leftists' of wreaths laid in memory of Chou En-lai;
7th, British Labour government loses its overall majority with the defection of John Stonehouse to the 'English National Party';
9th, in Britain, Peter Hain, leader of the Young Liberals, is acquitted of bank robbery – evidence emerges that South Africans had tried to frame him;
14th, Western Sahara is divided between Morocco and Mauritania;
16th, India and Pakistan normalise diplomatic relations, for the first time since the war of 1971;
26th (–*Aug.* 5th), in Britain, trial of John Stonehouse, resulting in seven years' imprisonment for fraud, theft and forgery;
30th, new Moro government in Italy collapses and an election is called.

E **May**: 5th, British government announces its pay policy for 1976–77, recommending 4½ per cent for wage rises;
9th, German terrorist leader Ulrike Meinhof commits suicide in prison;
11th, in Britain, following supporters' campaign George Davis, imprisoned for armed robbery, is released because of faulty identification evidence;
12th, Jeremy Thorpe resigns as leader of British Liberal Party and is replaced by Jo Grimond as interim leader;
—, Icelandic gunboat attacks British trawler;
27th, in Britain, Harold Wilson's resignation Honours List causes controversy;
—, Michael Heseltine, an opposition front bench spokesman, causes the suspension of the British House of Commons by whirling the mace around his head;
31st, Syrian soldiers and tanks enter Lebanon.

F **Jun**: 1st, Cod War ends with agreement between Iceland and Britain about fishing;
8th (–12th), Polish leader Edward Gierek visits Bonn and decides to normalise relations between Poland and West Germany;
10th, Arab countries meeting in Cairo call for Syrian withdrawal for Lebanon;
16th (–25th), South African police kill 76 students in Soweto and other townships during protests and riots about teaching in Afrikaans (*July* 6th, Afrikaans education plan dropped);
—, British T.U.C. approves the new incomes policy;
—, U.S. ambassador to Lebanon kidnapped and murdered;
20th, Italian general election produces a major advance for the Communist Party;
21st, Arab Protection Force troops under the aegis of the Arab League arrive in Lebanon to take control from the Syrians;
24th, Polish government announces big price rises, causing rioting in factory areas (*Sept.* 9th, price rises suspended);
25th, Idi Amin is declared Uganda's President for life;
27th, Palestinian terrorists hijack an Air France plane and force it to fly to Entebbe, Uganda (*July* 4th, Israeli paratroopers rescue the 110 hijack victims at Entebbe);
29th, Seychelles gains independence.

S Art, Sculpture, Fine Arts and Architecture

Venice Biennale rehabilitated.
'Sand Circles', exhibition at Hayward Gallery, London.
Claude Viallat, *Window in Tahiti, Homage to Matisse.*

Sculpture:
Daniel Buren, *On Two Levels With Two Colours.*
César, *Le Pouce.*
Christo, *Running Fence.*

Architecture:
Tadao Ando, Row House Sumiyoshi, Osaka, Japan.
Arata Isozaki, Kaijima House, Kichijoji, Musashino City.
Denys Lasdun, National Theatre, South Bank Centre, London.
Roche and Dinkeloo, One UN Plaza, New York.

T Music

Malcolm Arnold, *Philharmonic Concerto.*
Luciano Berio, *Coro.*
B. Britten, 3rd String Quartet.
Philip Glass, *Einstein on the Beach* (opera).
Hans Werner Henze, *We Come to the River* (opera).

U Literature

Alex Haley, *Roots.*
Ryu Murakami, *Almost Transparent Blue.*
Patrick White, *A Fringe of Leaves.*
The Diaries of Evelyn Waugh.

V The Press

Death of Lord Thomson, owner of *The Times* and other newspapers (*Aug.* 4th).
U.S. Supreme Court rules against 'gag' orders whereby courts restrict press coverage of criminal trials.

W Drama and Entertainment

Britain's National Theatre opens on the South Bank
David Edgar, *Destiny.*
Barry Humphries, *Housewife – Superstar!*
Alexander Vampilov, *Duck Hunting.*

Films:
Derek Jarman's *Sebastiane.*
John Schlesinger's *Marathon Man* with Laurence Olivier and Dustin Hoffman.
Wim Wenders' *Kings of the Road.*
The Outlaw Josey Wales with Clint Eastwood.
Rocky.

Television:
I, Claudius.
The Muppet Show.

Popular music:
Pop group Abba become Sweden's biggest export earner after Volvo.
The Eagles, *Hotel California.*
The Ramones, *The Ramones.*
Tom Waits, *Small Change.*

G **Jul**: 1st, Adolfo Suarez becomes Prime Minister of Spain;
2nd, North and South Vietnam are formally unified;
4th, in U.S. bicentenary of Declaration of Independence is marked by nation-wide celebrations;
7th, in Britain, David Steel wins the Liberal leadership election, defeating John Pardoe;
14th, Jimmy Carter is nominated as Presidential candidate at the Democratic convention in New York;
—, Drought Bill published in Britain to deal with water shortages, with fines for excessive use of water;
18th, cash worth a record £6 million is stolen when thieves tunnel from sewers into the vaults of a bank in Nice, France;
21st, I.R.A. assassinates Christopher Ewart-Biggs, British ambassador in Dublin;
26th, S.L.P. breaks away from the British Labour Party;
27th, former Japanese Prime Minister Kakuei Tanaka is charged with accepting bribes from U.S. company Lockheed;
28th, earthquake in Tangshan, China, kills 650,000;
—, Britain breaks off relations with Uganda over the disappearance of a former Entebbe hostage;
29th, formation of new Italian government, led by Giulio Andreotti and dependent on Communist acquiescence;
30th, amnesty for political prisoners in Spain.

H **Aug**: 1st, Trinidad and Tobago becomes independent;
2nd, British House of Lords rules that Tameside council, near Manchester, can defy a government directive to introduce comprehensive schools;
4th (–*Sept.* 13th), further rioting in Soweto and Port Elizabeth, South Africa;
19th, Gerald Ford narrowly wins renomination against a challenge from Ronald Reagan at the Republican convention in Kansas City;
24th, Denis Howell appointed British Minister for Drought;
25th, Jacques Chirac, Prime Minister of France, resigns suddenly;
27th, Howell claims success when rain falls in eastern England;
28th, peace marches held all over Ireland – 25,000 march in Belfast;
30th (–*Sept.* 2nd), violence mars the Notting Hill Carnival in London.

J **Sep**: 9th, Mao Tse-tung, Chairman of the Chinese Communist Party, dies;
19th, Swedish general election ends 40 years of government by Social Democrats (*Oct.* 7th, Thorbjörn Fälldin becomes Conservative prime minister);
—, Ian Smith accepts the principle of majority rule in Rhodesia;
28th, British Chancellor Denis Healey, at Heathrow Airport en route to a conference, turns back to deal with a steep fall in the value of the pound;
29th, British government approaches the International Monetary Fund for a $3.9 billion standby loan.

K **Oct**: 3rd, Helmut Schmidt's Social Democrat-led coalition returns to power in West Germany with reduced majority;
4th, U.S. Agriculture Secretary Earl Butz resigns after making racist comments;
6th, military coup in Thailand;
—, President Ford declares 'there is no Soviet domination of Eastern Europe';
7th, Hua Kuo-feng succeeds Mao as Chairman; the 'Gang of Four', including Mao's widow, are arrested and denounced for plotting to take power;
11th, more colour than black and white TV licences in Britain;
17th, Riyadh summit of Arab countries produces ceasefire plan for Lebanon (21st, implemented);

X Sport

Liverpool wins the British Football League Championship for record ninth time (*May* 4th).

The Olympic Games in Montreal are boycotted by 20 African nations, Iraq and Guyana following New Zealand's rugby tour of South Africa; Taiwan withdraws after the Canadian government refuses to recognize it as the Republic of China. The U.S.S.R. wins 49 gold medals; East Germany, 40; U.S.A., 34; West Germany, 10; Japan, 9; Poland, 7; Bulgaria and Cuba, 6; Roumania, Hungary, Finland and Sweden, 4. Nadia Comaneci of Roumania achieves 7 'perfect' scores of 10 in the gymnastics events.

Sue Barker is first Briton to win the Women's Singles final in the French Open Championships since 1966.

First women's cricket match is played at Lord's, London (*Aug.* 4th).

Viv Richards of the West Indies scores a record 1,710 Test runs in a calendar year.

Y Statistics

Main components of British government spending (mill. pounds with percentages in brackets): social security, 16.2 (19.9); education, science, arts, libraries, 11.3 (14.0); health and personal social services, 10.6 (13.1); defence, 9.4 (11.6); housing, 7.4 (9.1); industry, energy, trade, employment, 5.1 (6.3); transport, 4.8 (5.9); environmental services, 4.7 (5.9); miscellaneous, 3.1 (3.8); law and order, 3.0 (3.8); agriculture, fisheries, food, 2.4 (3.0); government lending to nationalised industries, 1.7 (2.1); overseas aid, 1.1 (1.4).

Z Births and Deaths

Jan. 5th John A. Costello d. (84).
Jan. 8th Chou En-lai d. (77).
Jan. 12th Agatha Christie d. (85).
Jan. 23rd Paul Robeson d. (77).
Feb. 23rd L.S. Lowry d. (88).
Mar. 17th Luchino Visconti d. (69).
Mar. 24th Bernard L. Montgomery d. (88).
Apr. 1st Max Ernst d. (84).
Apr. 5th Howard Hughes d. (70).
Apr. 24th Henrik Dam d. (81).
May 11th Alvar Aalto d. (78).
May 26th Martin Heidegger d. (86).
May 31st J.L. Monod d. (66).
June 6th J. Paul Getty d. (83).
July 6th Chu Teh d. (90).
Aug. 2nd Fritz Lang d. (85).
Sept. 9th Mao Tse-tung d. (83).
Oct. 6th Gilbert Ryle d. (76).
Oct. 22nd Edward Burra d. (71).
Nov. 18th Man Ray d. (86).
Nov. 19th Basil Spence d. (69).
Nov. 23rd André Malraux d. (75).
Dec. 4th Benjamin Britten d. (63).

1976 (Oct. – Dec.)

K **Oct:** 18th, in Britain, Callaghan launches the 'great debate' about education;

28th (–*Dec.* 12th), conference on Rhodesia in Geneva, at which the parties led by Joshua Nkomo and Robert Mugabe form the Patriotic Front (*Nov.* 26th, tenuous agreement on an independence plan);

29th, Chairman Hua repudiates congratulations from Soviet bloc countries.

L **Nov:** 2nd, in U.S. presidential election Jimmy Carter, Democrat, defeats Republican President Gerald Ford, with 297 electoral college votes to 241; popular vote: Carter, 40,828,587; Ford, 39,147,613; Congress retains large Democratic majorities in both Houses of Congress.

4th, in Britain, Conservatives gain Workington and Walsall North (Stonehouse's former seat) in by-elections with large swings;

11th, political parties are legalised in Egypt;

15th, Parti Québecois wins large victory in Quebec provincial elections and new Premier René Lévesque promises a vote on independence by 1980;

—, Syrian troops take control of Beirut;

26th, Catholicism ceases to be the state religion of Italy;

30th, British government publishes bill for devolution in Scotland and Wales.

M **Dec:** 4th, Swiss voters reject proposal to cut the working week to 40 hours;

5th, Japan's ruling Liberal Democratic Party suffers losses in general election;

—, Jacques Chirac re-founds the Gaullist party as the R.P.R. (Rassemblement pour la République);

—, Jean-Bédel Bokassa proclaims the Central African Republic an Empire;

15th, mini-Budget in Britain cuts £2.5 billion from public spending in accordance with terms for the I.M.F. loan;

—, referendum in Spain approves transition to democracy;

20th, Rabin coalition in Israel breaks up and calls an election;

—, death of Richard Daley, Mayor of Chicago since 1955;

21st, Reg Prentice, British Minister for Overseas Development, resigns out of dissatisfaction with British government policy;

24th, Takeo Fukuda replaces Takeo Miki as Prime Minister of Japan.

1977 (Jan. – Apr.) Gandhi and Bhutto lose power—Panama Canal Treaty—Lib-Lab Pact

A **Jan:** 1st, U.S. Episcopal Church ordains its first women priests;
3rd, I.M.F. lends Britain $3.9 billion;
6th, Roy Jenkins takes office as President of the E.C. Commission;
7th, advocates of human rights in Czechoslovakia publish 'Charter 77' manifesto, pressing for implementation of human rights guarantees given at Helsinki conference in 1975;
17th, Gary Gilmore is first person to be executed in the U.S. since 1967;
18th, in India Indira Gandhi calls an election and releases opposition leaders from prison;
20th, inauguration of Jimmy Carter as the 39th President of the U.S.;
21st, Carter pardons people who evaded the draft for the Vietnam War;
24th, Ian Smith's government rejects British proposals on Rhodesia.

B **Feb:** 1st, Khmer Rouge incursion into Thailand kills 30;
3rd, Colonel Mengistu Haile Mariam becomes leader of Ethiopia after killing eight fellow members of the ruling military council;
9th, in Britain, Balcombe Street I.R.A. gang sent to prison for at least 30 years;
16th, Archbishop Janani Luwum, a Ugandan human rights advocate who had denounced abuse of power by security forces, is killed by Amin's forces;
17th, bill to nationalise British aircraft manufacture and shipbuilding is declared a 'hybrid bill' because it includes provision to nationalise some ship-repairing companies (*Mar.* 2nd, provisions concerning ship repair companies are dropped);
19th, Anthony Crosland, British Foreign Secretary, dies in office (21st, Dr. David Owen appointed);
22nd, in British House of Commons, guillotine motion on the Devolution Bill fails after 22 Labour Noes and 21 abstentions; the Bill is dropped.

C **Mar:** 2nd, Euro-communist leaders in France, Italy and Spain meet in Madrid;
4th, earthquake in Roumania kills 1,500 and wrecks much of Bucharest;
7th, Zulfikar Ali Bhutto claims massive victory in Pakistan's general election;
9th (–11th), Hanafi Moslem gunmen seize three buildings in Washington, D.C.;
11th (–23rd), widespread violent protests in Pakistan allege that Bhutto's election victory is fraudulent;
12th, political parties in Chile banned and censorship tightened;
15th, British government nationalises aircraft and shipbuilding industries;
16th, Lebanese Moslem leader Kamal Jumblatt assassinated; violence follows;
20th, Congress Party defeated in Indian election and Indira Gandhi loses her seat (24th, Morarji Desai becomes Prime Minister of a Janata Party government);
—, large gains for the Left in French local elections, but conservative Jacques Chirac becomes the first elected Mayor of Paris since the 1870s;
23rd, British Prime Minister Callaghan and Liberal leader David Steel agree a pact between Labour and Liberals (the 'Lib-Lab Pact') to avoid defeat in a confidence motion;
27th, world's worst air disaster in Tenerife kills 582 when two 747 'jumbo jets' collide;
29th, British Budget cuts income tax by 2p in return for another year of pay restraint.

D **Apr:** 7th, Baader-Meinhof terrorists assassinate Siegfried Buback, the chief prosecutor of West Germany;
—, in Israel Yitzhak Rabin withdraws as Prime Ministerial candidate after being investigated for banking violations;
9th, Spanish Communist Party is legalised;

O Politics, Economics, Law and Education

Richard Nixon gives David Frost extended interviews and discusses Watergate (*May*).

Publication of Annan Report on broadcasting in Britain (*Mar.* 24th).

Sixth E.C. Value Added Tax Directive unifies V.A.T. throughout the Community (apart from rates charged).

Adam Smith Institute founded in London to research and promote free market policies.

Nationalisation of British Aerospace and British Shipbuilders.

E.C. and E.F.T.A. agree to free trade in industrial goods (from *July* 1st).

Publication of Bullock Report on industrial democracy (*Jan.* 26th), recommending that British companies with over 2,000 employees should be run by boards comprising equal numbers of employee representatives, ownership representatives and co-opted directors.

Criminal Law Act allows British magistrates to try more cases.

Anti-obscenity campaigner Mrs. Mary Whitehouse secures conviction of British homosexual newspaper *Gay News* for blasphemy.

British Department of Education announces plans for national testing of children in mathematics, reading and writing (*Oct.* 26th).

Foundation of Robinson College, Cambridge, England.

P Science, Technology, Discovery, etc.

Bell Telephone Company in the U.S. transmits television signals over distance of 1½ miles using fiber optics.

Inauguration of 800-mile trans-Alaska oil pipeline (*June* 20th).

British Gas completes conversion of 40 million appliances from coal gas to North Sea gas.

Introduction of the Apple II, the first mass produced personal computer.

In the U.S. the human-powered aircraft *Gossamer Condor* makes its first flight.

Netherlands scientists discover that the wastes from incinerators are contaminated by dioxins – chemicals thought to cause cancer.

Launches of the U.S. spacecraft Voyager I (*Sept.* 5th) and II (*Aug.* 20th), intended to explore Jupiter and the outer planets of the solar system.

Several groups of astronomers discover rings around Uranus (*Mar.*)

Leon Lederman discovers the upsilon sub-atomic particle.

Cambridge scientist L.F. Sanger describes the full sequence of bases in a viral DNA.

Tomas G.M. Hökfelt discovers that most neurons contain not one but several neurotransmitters.

Production of images of human tissues using N.M.R. (nuclear magnetic resonance) scanning.

In New York two homosexual men are diagnosed as having the rare cancer Karposi's sarcoma; they are thought to have been the first victims of AIDS (Acquired Immune Deficiency Syndrome) in New York.

A baby mammoth, 40,000 years old, is found frozen in ice in the U.S.S.R.

Q Scholarship

Fergus Millar, *The Emperor in the Roman World, 31 B.C. – A.D. 337*.

H.C. Darby, *Domesday England*.

Lawrence Stone, *The Family, Sex and Marriage, 1500–1800*.

Simon Schama, *Patriots and Liberators*.

Mark Girouard, *Sweetness and Light: The 'Queen Anne' Movement, 1860–1900*.

D **Apr**: 20th, U.S. President Carter proposes a radical energy conservation plan;
21st, Zia ur-Rahman inaugurated as President of Bangladesh;
28th, Andreas Baader and two other terrorists imprisoned;
—, in British by-elections, Conservatives gain Ashfield on a 20 per cent swing but fail in more marginal Grimsby.

E **May**: 2nd (–13th), unsuccessful Protestant general strike in Northern Ireland;
5th, in Britain, huge Conservative gains in county elections and a strong National Front vote in Greater London;
11th, Peter Jay (son-in-law of Prime Minister Callaghan) appointed British ambassador in Washington, D.C.;
13th, in Britain, six members of the Metropolitan Police Obscene Publications Squad are jailed for 3–12 years on corruption charges;
17th, Likud bloc wins Israeli elections for the first time (*June* 21st, Menachem Begin becomes Prime Minister);
23rd (–*June* 11th), South Moluccan terrorists hijack a Dutch train;
25th, Labour gains in the Dutch general election;
30th, U.S. and Cuba agree to exchange diplomats with effect from *Sept.* 1st.

F **Jun**: 4th, fourth constitution of the U.S.S.R. published, making explicit the leading role of the Communist Party (adopted *Oct.* 7th);
5th (–11th), Jubilee week in Britain celebrates 25 years of reign of Queen Elizabeth II;
—, Albert René takes power in coup in the Seychelles;
8th, Uganda excluded from Commonwealth conference for human rights abuses;
14th (–*July* 11th), violence outside Grunwick photographic processing plant in London in bitter industrial dispute;
15th, Adolfo Suarez wins small majority in Spain's first elections since 1936;
16th, in U.S.S.R., Leonid Brezhnev combines post of head of state with that of Communist Party secretary;
—, Fianna Fail wins large victory over the governing coalition in Eire;
19th, *The Daily Mail* publishes a forged document alleging that a British minister had nodded through bribe payments by British Leyland;
27th, Djibouti gains independence from France;
30th, S.E.A.T.O. dissolved.

G **Jul**: 5th, General Zia ul-Haq takes power in coup in Pakistan;
12th, Sir John Kerr to resign as Australian Governor-General from *Dec.* 1977;
13th, electricity blackout in New York leads to chaos and looting;
14th, three British M.P.s criticised by report on the Poulson scandal (22nd, John Cordle resigns from the Commons);
15th, in Britain, mini Budget declares 10 per cent pay policy but rescinds half of March's tax cut;
21st (–25th), border war between Libya and Egypt;
—, Junius Jayawardene defeats the Bandaranaike government in Sri Lankan elections;
22nd, 'Gang of Four' expelled from the Chinese Communist Party and Teng Tsiao-ping reinstated as Deputy Premier;
23rd, Somali forces invade Ogaden area of Ethiopia;
30th, allegations surface that the British security services plotted against Harold Wilson (*Aug.* 31st, call for an inquiry rejected);
31st, Tamil separatist M.P.s in Sri Lanka start drafting a new constitution.

Q Scholarship (*cont.*)

David Marquand, *Ramsay MacDonald.*
José Harris, *William Beveridge: A Biography.*
J.K. Galbraith, *The Age of Anxiety.*
H. Orton, S. Sanderson, J. Widdowson (eds.), *The Linguistic Atlas of England.*

R Philosophy and Religion

Ronald Dworkin, *Taking Rights Seriously.*
Thomas Kuhn, *The Essential Tension.*
John Hick (ed.), *The Myth of God Incarnate.*
The Anglican-Roman Catholic Commission advises that the Church of England should recognize the primacy of the Pope.
10,000 copies of the Torah are shipped from the United States to the Moscow Synagogue for the first time since 1917.

S Art, Sculpture, Fine Arts and Architecture

Extra Venice Biennale devoted to art of dissent and dissidents, especially in Eastern Europe and Russia.
Exhibition of unofficial Soviet art at Institute of Contemporary Art, London.
Duchamp exhibition, Pompidou Centre, Paris.

Sculpture:
Walter De Maria, *Lightening Field.*
Richard Long, *Throwing a Stone Around MacGillycuddy's Rocks.*

Architecture:
Louis Kahn; Pellechia and Myers, Yale Centre for British Art, New Haven, Connecticut.
Renzo Piano, Richard Rogers and Gio Franco Franchini, Centre National d'Art et de Culture Georges Pompidou ('Pompidou Centre'), Paris.

T Music

John Cage, *Freeman Etudes.*
Elliott Carter, *A Symphony for Three Orchestras.*
George Crumb, *Star Child.*
Thea Musgrave, *Mary Queen of Scots* (opera).
Michael Tippett, *The Ice Break* (opera).

U Literature

John Cheever, *Falconer.*
Joan Didion, *A Book of Common Prayer.*
Patrick Leigh Fermor, *A Time of Gifts.*
Leonardo Sciascia, *Candido.*
Paul Scott, *Staying On.*

V The Press

In Britain, circulation of *The Sun* overtakes that of *The Daily Mirror.*
Max Aitken sells the *Express* group of newspapers to the British business conglomerate Trafalgar House (*June* 30th).
Rupert Murdoch acquires *The New York Post* (*Nov.*).

W Drama and Entertainment

Steven Berkoff, *East.*
John Murrell, *Waiting for the Parade.*

H **Aug:** 1st, a total ban on alcohol by 1981 is proposed in India;
4th, U.S. President Carter creates a Department of Energy;
13th, a National Front march in Lewisham, south London, sparks violent scenes;
16th, Elvis Presley dies at home in Memphis;
18th, 11th Chinese Communist Party Congress indicates a swing away from hardline Maoism towards economic improvement;
25th, in Britain Scarman Report recommends reinstatement of Grunwick strikers but is ignored by the management;
26th, French becomes the only official language of Quebec;
31st, Smith's Rhodesian Front wins all 50 white seats in the 66-seat Parliament.

J **Sep:** 1st, Cyrus Vance and David Owen propose peace plan for Rhodesia, recommending a large role for Nkomo and Mugabe's Patriotic Front;
5th, West German business leader Hans-Martin Schleyer kidnapped (*Oct.* 19th, found dead in France);
7th, U.S. and Panama sign the Panama Canal Treaty which returns the canal zone to Panama;
10th (–20th), national strike of bakery workers in Britain;
12th, South African black leader Steve Biko is killed in police custody;
21st, Bert Lance resigns as Carter's Budget Director after allegations are made about dubious bank loans;
—, alliance between Socialists and Communists in France breaks up;
26th, first Laker 'Skytrain' flight from London to New York, for $102 a ticket;
28th, in Britain, Liberal Assembly votes to support the Lib-Lab Pact.

K **Oct:** 1st, General Zia cancels the elections due in Pakistan on 18th;
8th, British M.P. Reg Prentice defects from Labour to Conservative;
18th, German commandos storm a hijacked plane in Mogadishu;
—, Andreas Baader and two other German terrorists kill themselves in prison;
20th, military coup in Thailand;
27th, in Britain Jeremy Thorpe denies involvement in alleged plot to harm Norman Scott;
—(–*Nov.* 11th), unofficial action by British power station workers causes sporadic blackouts.

L **Nov:** 1st, U.S. quits the International Labour Organisation, but Carter raises the minimum wage;
4th, U.N. imposes strict arms embargo on South Africa;
8th, Ed Koch wins Mayoral election in New York City;
9th, President Sadat of Egypt makes peace overtures to Israel, alienating other Arab states and his own Foreign Minister but winning acceptance from Israeli Prime Minister Begin;
11th, Anti-Nazi League set up to combat the apparent growth of the National Front in Britain;
14th, British firemen go on strike (to *Jan.* 12th 1978);
17th, in Britain, publication of Third Report of Royal Commission on the Distribution of Income and Wealth;
19th (–21st), Sadat visits Israel and addresses the Knesset;
24th, Ian Smith proposes a new Rhodesian constitution with equal votes;
30th, ruling National Party wins record majority in South African elections.

W Drama and Entertainment (*cont.*)

Peter Nichols, *Privates on Parade*.
Kid Stakas, *The Doll Trilogy*.
The Lindsay Kemp Company, *Flowers and Salome*.

Films:
Woody Allen's *Annie Hall*.
Luis Buñuel's *That Obscure Object of Desire*.
George Lucas' *Star Wars*.
Steven Spielberg's *Close Encounters of the Third Kind*.
Paolo and Vittorio Taviani's *Padre Padrone*.
The Last Waltz – Bob Dylan and The Band.

Television:
Lou Grant.
Tom Stoppard's *Professional Foul*.
Roots.

Radio:
Last edition of B.B.C.'s The Navy Lark, running since 1959.

Popular music:
Punk group The Sex Pistols' 'God Save the Queen' becomes Britain's top-selling single despite being banned from radio.
Elvis Costello, *My Aim is True*.
Iggy Pop, *Lust for Life*.

X Sport

Australia beats England by 45 runs in the Centenary Test Match at Melbourne, exactly the same result as in the first match (*Mar.* 12th–17th).
In Britain, *Red Rum*, ridden by Tommy Stack, wins its third Grand National (*Apr.* 2nd).
Virginia Wade is first British woman since 1969 to win a Wimbledon Singles title (*July* 1st).
England regains the Ashes (*Aug.* 15th).
After failing to win the rights to televise Test cricket in Australia, Kerry Packer, owner of Channel Nine Television, signs up 66 leading players to participate in his own series of matches; all are barred from Test cricket.

Y Statistics

Religious Denominations in U.S. (in mill.): Roman Catholics, 49.8; Baptists, 24.9; Methodists, 12.8; Lutherans, 8.0; Presbyterians, 3.4; Protestant Episcopal, 2.8; Mormons, 2.5; Greek Orthodox, 1.9; Jews, 5.8.
Oil production (in thousand barrels per day): U.S.S.R., 10,995; U.S., 9,797; Saudi Arabia, 9,017; Iran, 5,663; Iraq, 2,348; Venezuela, 2,238; Nigeria, 2,085; Libya, 2,063; Algeria, 1,152; Mexico, 1,050; Great Britain, 776; Kuwait, 368; Norway, 279.
Coffee production (in thousand metric tons): Brazil, 975.4; Colombia, 639.4; Ivory Coast, 291.3; Indonesia, 198.5; Ethiopia, 191.4; Mexico, 182.0; Uganda, 155.9; El Salvador, 150.7; Guatemala, 148.3; India, 102.3; Kenya, 101.2; Madagascar, 91.5.

Z Births and Deaths

Jan. 14th Anthony Eden d. (79).
Feb. 4th Ludwig Erhard d. (80).
Mar. 28th Eric Shipton d. (69).

M **Dec:** 2nd (–4th), Tripoli conference of Arab states condemns Egypt;
4th, Bophuthatswana, a black homeland in South Africa, becomes nominally independent;
—, coronation of Emperor Bokassa of Central Africa;
5th, strike of U.S. coal miners begins (8th, violent incidents in Ohio and Utah);
10th, Fraser government wins another large majority in Australian federal elections;
16th, opening of London Underground extension to Heathrow Airport, making Heathrow the first airport in the world to be connected to a city rail system;
24th (–25th), Israeli Prime Minister Begin visits Egypt;
31st, violent deaths in Northern Ireland fall sharply in 1977, with 111 killed compared with 297 in 1976.

z **Births and Deaths** (*cont.*)
Apr. 11th Jacques Prévert d. (77).
June 16th Werner von Braun d. (65).
July 2nd Vladimir Nabokov d. (78).
Aug. 3rd Makarios III d. (63).
Aug. 13th Henry Williamson d. (82).
Aug. 23rd Naum Gabo d. (87).
Sept. 4th E.F. Schumacher d. (66).
Sept. 12th Robert Lowell d. (60).
Sept. 16th Maria Callas d. (53).
Oct. 14th Bing Crosby d. (73).
Nov. 18th Kurt von Schuschnigg d. (79).
Dec. 25th Charles Chaplin d. (88).

1978 (Jan. – Apr.) Year of three Popes—Camp David Agreement—Murder of former Italian Prime Minister

A **Jan:** 3rd, Indian Congress Party splits (from *Feb.* 25th the rump led by Mrs. Gandhi is called the Congress (I) Party);
6th, picket killed in violent incidents during U.S. coal mines dispute;
12th, end of firemen's strike in Britain;
—, Andreotti government collapses in Italy;
16th (–18th), talks in Jerusalem between Egypt and Israel;
18th, European Court of Human Rights clears British government of torture but finds it guilty of inhuman and degrading treatment of prisoners in Northern Ireland;
23rd (–*Feb.* 7th), general strike in Nicaragua;
—, Sweden bans aerosol sprays because of damage to environment, the first country to do so;
24th, the Superior Court in Quebec rejects important parts of the language law enforcing use of French;
25th, amendment passed to Scottish and Welsh devolution bill requiring approval of 40 per cent of electorate in consultative referenda for devolution to take effect;
30th, Mrs. Thatcher, in an interview, refers to the legitimate fears of white Britons concerning 'swamping' by immigrants.

B **Feb:** 1st, start of 'Information scandal' or 'Muldergate' in South Africa when the Auditor General reports to Parliament that the Department of Information had made unauthorized expenditure in attempt to counter the country's negative image abroad; Justice Anton Mostert is appointed to undertake inquiry;
3rd, E.C. and China conclude their first trade agreement;
4th, Junius Jayawardene becomes President of Sri Lanka;
14th, President Carter proposes the sale of 50 jet fighters to Egypt;
16th, British House of Commons passes Bill establishing direct elections to European Assembly.

C **Mar:** 3rd, in Rhodesia Ian Smith and three black leaders sign agreement for a power-sharing government and eventual majority rule, but Mugabe and Nkomo's Patriotic Front is excluded;
5th, new Chinese constitution affirms the rule of law, in contrast to the policies under the Cultural Revolution;
11th, in Italy, in the 'Historic Compromise', a new government led by Giulio Andreotti is installed with the support of the Communist Party;
12th (and 19th), National Assembly elections in France return the Right to power with diminished majority;
14th, Israel invades southern Lebanon;
16th, *Amoco Cadiz* oil tanker runs aground off Brittany;
—, Red Brigade terrorists kidnap former Italian Prime Minister Aldo Moro;
18th, death sentence passed on former Pakistani Prime Minister Zulfikar Ali Bhutto;
22nd, first United Nations 'UNIFIL' ('UN Interim Force in Lebanon') troops arrive in Lebanon;
25th, U.S. coal-miners' strike ends.

D **Apr:** 6th, U.S. mandatory retirement age raised from 65 to 70;
7th, German Chancellor Schmidt proposes European currency stabilisation plan; later enacted as the European Monetary System (E.M.S.);
18th, Panama Canal Treaty ratified by the U.S. Senate;
25th, European Court of Human Rights condemns judicial birching in Isle of Man as degrading;
27th, Communist and Islamic forces take power in Afghanistan.

O Politics, Economics, Law and Education

Start of regular radio broadcasts of British Parliament (*Apr.* 3rd).

Ford Motors in U.S. fined $125 million in California for installing dangerous fuel tanks (*Feb.* 7th).

British government White Paper on Broadcasting proposes the establishment of a fourth television channel (*July* 26th).

Decision to construct new nuclear re-processing plant at Windscale in north-west England prompts much debate about the safety of the nuclear industry.

European Court affirms superiority of Community law over national law.

U.S. Supreme Court rules (in Regents of the University of California v. Bakke) that the University of California Medical School was wrong to discriminate in favour of applicants from ethnic minorities (*June* 28th).

Waddell Committee recommends new examination in England and Wales to replace 'O' level and C.S.E.

P Science, Technology, Discovery, etc.

Konica introduces the first camera with automatic focus.

U.S. bans use of chlorofluorocarbons (CFCs) as spray propellants in order to reduce damage to the ozone layer.

Launch of U.S. satellite Seasat I to measure temperature of sea surfaces, wind and wave movements, ocean currents, and icebergs.

Two U.S.S.R. cosmonauts spend a record 139 days and 14 hours in space (*June* 15th–*Nov.* 2nd).

Launches of U.S. space probes Pioneer I (*May* 20th) and II (*Aug.* 8th); they go into orbit around Venus on *Dec.* 4th and 9th.

U.S.S.R. space craft Venera XI and XII soft-land on Venus.

Discovery of Charon, a moon orbiting Pluto.

W. Paul measures the life of a neutron – about 15 minutes.

W. Gibson and associates at Harvard make bacteria manufacture insulin in response to instructions from synthetic DNA.

Birth of the first 'test tube' baby, Louise Brown, in England (*July* 25th).

Cyclosporin A introduced as immunosuppressant drug in organ transplant surgery.

Q Scholarship

Footprints of a hominid, made 3.6 million years ago, found near Laetoli, Tanzania.

Excavation of tomb of Philip of Macedon (died 337 B.C.) at Vergina in northern Greece.

Discovery of the foundations of the Aztec great temple under the centre of Mexico City.

Geoffrey Barraclough (ed.), *The Times Atlas of World History.*

Richard Bradley, *The Prehistoric Settlement of Britain.*

Howard Colvin, *A Biographical Dictionary of British Architects, 1600–1840.*

Alan Macfarlane, *The Origins of English Individualism.*

Mark Girouard, *Life in the English Country House.*

J.M. Roberts, *The French Revolution.*

Paul Thompson, *The Voice of the Past: Oral History.*

Arthur Schlesinger Jnr, *Robert Kennedy and his Times.*

R Philosophy and Religion

Daniel Dennett, *Brainstorms.*

Nelson Goodman, *Ways of Worldmaking.*

Jürgen Moltmann, *The Church in the Power of the Spirit.*

E **May**: 1st, Britain's first May Day public holiday;
8th, opposition amendment to Budget passed in British House of Commons, reducing income tax by 1p (10th, amendment is carried against the government to raise the threshold for higher tax rates from £7,000 to £8,000);
—, in South Africa, Prime Minister Vorster accepts responsibility for unauthorized expenditure of Information Department;
9th, Aldo Moro found dead in Rome after Italian government refuses to make concessions to his captors;
10th, nine people die in Islamic fundamentalist riots in Qom, Iran;
16th, Rhodesian forces kill 94 at a black political meeting;
18th, Yuri Orlov, Soviet human rights campaigner, is sentenced to seven years in a labour camp;
25th, in Britain, David Steel announces end of the Lib–Lab Pact.

F **Jun**: 6th, 'Proposition 13' to cut local property taxes in California passed in a referendum by large majority;
13th, Roumanian President Nicolae Ceauşescu visits Britain, staying with the Queen at Buckingham Palace;
—, Israelis pull out of south Lebanon but fighting erupts in the north;
15th, President Leone of Italy resigns after financial scandal (*July* 8th, Alessandro Pertini sworn in);
—, President Vorster abolishes South Africa's Information Department; Information Secretary Eschel Rhoodie resigns;
24th, South Yemeni parcel bomb kills President of North Yemen;
26th, the President of South Yemen is assassinated, by the faction who murdered the President of North Yemen.

G **July**: 5th, coup in Ghana replaces General Acheampong with his Fred Akuffo;
7th, Solomon Islands gain independence;
14th, Soviet dissident Anatoly Shcharansky sentenced to 13 years in jail;
21st, British Chancellor Denis Healey announces a 5 per cent guideline for wage increases in the next year;
24th, in Britain, George Davis, released from prison after a campaign in 1975–76, is sentenced to 15 years for armed robbery after being caught in the act and pleading guilty;
26th, British T.U.C. resolves not to support Chancellor Healey's 5 per cent pay policy;
31st, Queen Elizabeth gives Royal Assent to Devolution bill for Scotland and Wales.

H **Aug**: 3rd, De Lorean Motor Company announces intention to build a factory in Belfast, Northern Ireland, for production of sports cars;
4th, former British Liberal Party leader Jeremy Thorpe and three others are charged with conspiracy to murder Norman Scott between 1968 and 1977; Thorpe is also charged with incitement to murder;
6th, death of Pope Paul VI;
12th, Japan and China sign Treaty of Peace and Friendship;
22nd (–24th), Sandinista guerrillas seize the parliament building in Managua, Nicaragua;
—, death of President Kenyatta of Kenya (*Oct.* 10th, succeeded by Daniel arap Moi);
25th, Spain abolishes the death penalty in peacetime;
26th, Albino Luciani, Patriarch of Venice, is elected Pope; he takes the name John Paul I;
27th, new Iranian government of Sharif-Emami lifts ban on political parties.

R Philosophy and Religion (*cont.*)

Deaths of Pope Paul VI (*Aug.* 6th) and his successor John Paul I (*Sept.* 28th); John Paul's successor, John Paul II (Karol Wojtyla, Archbishop of Cracow), is the first non-Italian Pope since 1522.

General Synod of the Church of England rejects the ordination of women to the priesthood and episcopate.

S Art, Sculpture, Fine Arts and Architecture

Painting:

'Paris-Berlin', exhibition at the Pompidou Centre, Paris.
'The State of British Art', Institute of Contemporary Art, London.
Sandro Chia, *Perpetual Motion.*
Anselm Kiefer, *Untitled.*

Sculpture:

Christo, *Wrapped Walkways.*
Barry Flanagan, *As Night.*

Architecture:

Norman Foster, Sainsbury Centre, University of East Anglia, England.
I.M. Pei, extension to the National Gallery, Washington, D.C.

T Music

György Ligeti, *Le Grand Macabre* (opera).
Andrzej Panufnik, *Metasinfonia.*
Krzysztof Penderecki, *Paradise Lost* (opera).
Aribert Reimann: *Lear* (opera).

U Literature

J.G. Farrell, *The Singapore Grip.*
Graham Greene, *The Human Factor.*
Armistead Maupin, *Tales of the City.*
Iris Murdoch, *The Sea, The Sea.*
Yuri Trifonov, *Starik.*

V The Press

150th anniversary of British weekly *The Spectator.*
Re-launch of *Life* magazine in U.S. (*Oct.*).
Launch of *The Daily Star* (*Nov.* 2nd), a new British tabloid newspaper.
In Britain, suspension of *The Times*, *The Sunday Times* and *Times* supplements as a result of an industrial dispute (*Nov.* 30th).

W Drama and Entertainment

Brian Clark, *Whose Life is it Anyway.*
David Hare, *Plenty.*
Harold Pinter, *Betrayal.*
Evita.

Films:

Alan Parker's *Midnight Express.*
The Deer Hunter.
Superman.

J **Sep**: 5th (–17th), summit between Carter, Sadat and Begin at Camp David, Maryland; concludes with a 'framework' peace treaty ending 30 years of hostility between Israel and Egypt;

7th, British Prime Minister James Callaghan makes surprise announcement that there will be no General Election in 1978;

8th, demonstrations in Teheran lead to 95 deaths;

11th, exiled Bulgarian author Georgi Markov dies in London (*Jan.* 2nd 1979, inquest finds that he was unlawfully killed by the injection of a poison pellet through an umbrella);

15th, Spanish Parliament recognises Basque demand for autonomy,

16th, earthquake in Iran kills 21,000;

—, Rhodesian executive council starts conscripting blacks to fight the Patriotic Front;

19th, in Britain, Bingham Report reveals that B.P. and Shell had broken oil sanctions against Rhodesia and that British ministers concealed knowledge of this;

20th, B.J. Vorster resigns as Prime Minister of South Africa, on grounds of ill health (29th, P.W. Botha replaces him; *Oct.* 10th, Vorster becomes President);

21st, in Nigeria the outgoing military regime promulgates a new constitution based on that of the U.S.;

22nd, strike over pay begins at major Ford car plants in Britain;

28th, sudden death of Pope John Paul I;

—, Camp David accord approved by the Israeli Parliament, the Knesset;

30th, Tuvalu, formerly the Ellice Islands, gains independence.

K **Oct**: 2nd, British Labour Party conference votes against the Labour government's pay policy;

4th, renewed battles in Beirut kill 500;

5th, Swedish centre-right government collapses over nuclear power (13th, replaced by a minority Liberal government under Ola Ullsten);

10th, British unions and government fail to resolve their differences on pay during talks at 10 Downing Street;

12th, border clashes between Uganda and Tanzania caused by President Amin's expansionist claims on Tanzanian territory;

16th, Karol Wojtyla, Archbishop of Cracow, is elected Pope; he takes the name John Paul II;

24th, U.S. airline industry deregulated;

26th, World Health Organisation announces that smallpox has been eradicated except for laboratory stocks;

29th, in South Africa a newspaper reveals that the former Information Department funded *The Citizen*, a pro-government English-language newspaper;

31st, Iranian oil workers commence strike action.

L **Nov**: 1st, U.S. dollar rises sharply after President Carter announces a major support plan, including higher interest rates;

2nd, in South Africa Justice Mostert, against request from Prime Minister Botha for confidentiality, releases information from his inquiry into the former Information Department (7th, former Information Minister C.P. 'Connie' Mulder resigns from cabinet; Botha dismisses Mostert and appoints Justice Rudolf Erasmus to conduct new inquiry);

3rd, Dominica gains independence;

5th, referendum in Austria stops Zwentersdorf nuclear power station from being switched on;

6th, military government appointed in Iran;

W Drama and Entertainment (*cont*)

Television:

Dallas.

Holocaust.

Pennies from Heaven.

Taxi.

667th and last episode of B.B.C.'s *Z Cars.*

Last *Black and White Minstrel Show*, on B.B.C. (started in 1958).

Popular music:

Disco music popular: the Bee Gees' *Saturday Night Fever* becomes the biggest-selling soundtrack album yet.

Blondie, *Parallel Lines.*

Talking Heads, *More Songs About Buildings and Food.*

X Sport

New Zealand beats England in a Test match for the first time, after 48 years of matches (*Feb.* 15th).

Leon Spinks beats Muhammad Ali on points to win the World Heavy-weight title (*Feb.* 15th); seven months later, Ali regains the W.B.A. version of the title, beating Spinks on points in New Orleans (*Sept.* 17th); meanwhile Larry Holmes beats Ken Norton on points in Las Vegas (*June* 10th) and wins the W.B.C. crown.

The Cambridge boat sinks in the English University Boat Race (*Mar.* 25th).

Naomi James completes her solo round-the-world voyage (*June* 8th), taking two days fewer than Sir Francis Chichester in 1967.

Host nation Argentina wins the soccer World Cup, beating Holland in the Final 31 (*June* 25th).

European golfers are allowed to compete alongside British and Irish players in Ryder Cup matches against the U.S., in an attempt to produce a more even contest.

Y Statistics

Hours worked in manufacturing per week: Switzerland, 44.4; Great Britain, 43.5; Eire, 42.3; West Germany, 41.6; Greece, 41.2; Holland, 41.1; France, 41.0; Spain, 40.1; Luxembourg, 39.8; Portugal, 39.3; Norway, 38.6; Finland, 38.5; Belgium, 35.2; Austria, 33.4; Denmark, 32.6.

Composition of British House of Lords: Dukes, 28; Marquesses, 30; Earls, 160; Viscounts, 106; Barons, 494; Life Peers, 298; Law Lords, 18; Archbishops and Bishops, 26.

Z Births and Deaths

Jan. 13th Hubert Humphrey d. (66).

Jan. 14th Kurt Gödel d. (71).

Apr. 14th F.R. Leavis d. (82).

May 15th Robert Menzies d. (83).

Aug. 6th Pope Paul VI d. (80).

Aug. 22nd Jomo Kenyatta d. (89).

Sept. 17th Willy Messerschmitt d. (80).

Nov. 15th Margaret Mead d. (76).

Nov. 18th Giorgio de Chirico d. (90).

Dec. 8th Golda Meir d. (80).

Dec. 14th Salvador de Madariaga d. (92).

L Nov: 7th, U.S. mid-term elections produce small Democratic losses in Congress;
—(–*Dec.* 17th), bakery workers' strike in Britain;
8th, Uganda drops territorial claim on Tanzania;
—, Indira Gandhi returns to the Lok Sabha in a by-election;
18th, British tanker drivers start an overtime ban;
19th, in Guyana 911 die in mass suicide at the People's Temple in the Jim Jones cult centre;
20th (–*Dec.* 13), in Britain, committal hearings in Minehead concerning charges against Jeremy Thorpe and others produce lurid publicity;
22nd, Ford workers in Britain accept 17 per cent pay offer, a flagrant breach of the 5 per cent pay policy;
25th, Robert Muldoon returns to power in New Zealand with much reduced majority for the National Party;
27th, Japanese Prime Minister Takeo Fukuda resigns (*Dec.* 7th, succeeded by Masayoshi Ohira);
—, Tanzanian troops move into Ugandan border areas;
30th, in Britain, Times Newspapers suspend publication of their papers indefinitely because of industrial dispute.

M Dec: 5th, in South Africa the Erasmus Commission issues report on the Information scandal, but ignores allegations that President Vorster knew about the unauthorized expenditure;
6th, Callaghan announces that Britain will not join the new European Monetary System;
13th, government commercial sanctions against Ford for breaching the pay policy voted down in British Parliament;
15th, U.S. and China normalise diplomatic relations (effective from *Jan.* 1st 1979);
—, Cleveland, Ohio, defaults on its debt, the first U.S. city to do so since the 1930s;
17th, O.P.E.C. decides to raise oil prices by 14.5 per cent by the end of 1979;
19th (–26th), Indira Gandhi is expelled from the Lok Sabha for contempt and imprisoned;
25th, Vietnam begins full-scale invasion of Cambodia;
30th, committee of U.S. House of Representatives concludes that a second gunman was involved in the assassination of President John F. Kennedy in 1963;
31st, government of Iran admits that nearly all production and export of oil has been halted.

1979 (Jan. – Mar.) Iranian Revolution—Mrs. Thatcher elected British Prime Minister—Settlement of Rhodesia problem—U.S.S.R. invasion of Afghanistan

A **Jan:** 1st, U.S. and China open diplomatic relations;

3rd (–*Feb.* 7th), lorry drivers go on strike in Britain, causing widespread interruption of supplies;

4th, the Shah of Iran appoints Dr. Shakpur Bakhtiar Prime Minister as concession to popular discontent;

7th, Vietnamese troops and Cambodian rebels capture Phnom Penh and oust the Khmer Rouge regime;

10th, in Britain most petrol tanker drivers return to work;

11th (–14th), state of emergency in Northern Ireland because of tanker strike;

16th, the Shah of Iran and his family flee Iran for Egypt;

20th, Tanzanian troops invade Uganda after border clashes;

22nd, in Britain one-day strike of public sector workers closes schools and hospitals (–*Mar.* 6th, continuing industrial action by local authority workers such as dustmen and grave-diggers; –*Mar.* 20th, health service workers take industrial action; *The Sun* labels the surge of strikes 'the winter of discontent', an allusion to Shakespeare's 'Now is the winter of our discontent...');

26th (–29th), Islamic revolutionary violence in Teheran;

31st, in Italy the Andreotti government resigns, ending the 'Historic Compromise' between Christian Democrats and Communists.

B **Feb:** 1st, Ayatollah Khomeini returns to Iran from exile in Paris (since 1964);

8th, U.S. cuts off aid to Somoza regime in Nicaragua for human rights violations;

12th, Dr. Bakhtiar flees Iran; a Revolutionary Council loyal to Ayatollah Khomeini is created, with Mehdi Bazargan as Premier-designate;

14th, the U.S. Embassy in Teheran briefly seized by protesters;

—, British government and T.U.C. sign a Concordat to end the 'winter of discontent' strikes;

17th (–*Mar.* 5th), China makes punitive incursions into Vietnam;

19th, President Zia ur-Rahman's Bangladesh Nationalist Party wins elections in Bangladesh;

20th, in Northern Ireland, 11 members of a loyalist gang known as the 'Shankill butchers' are sentenced for 19 sectarian murders in Belfast following a sensational trial;

22nd, St. Lucia becomes independent;

23rd (–*Mar.* 16), war between North and South Yemen;

—, Rhodesian planes attack rebel camps in Zambia.

C **Mar:** 1st, referenda on devolution in Scotland and Wales; devolution is approved in Scotland by 51.6 per cent of voters but those approving fall short of the required 40 per cent of the electorate (32.9 per cent of electorate voted Yes, 30.8 per cent No, 36.3 per cent did not vote); 79.8 per cent of voters in Wales reject devolution (11.9 per cent voted Yes, 46.9 per cent No, 41.2 per cent did not vote);

7th, in Britain, the Callaghan government establishes the Clegg Commission on Comparability to examine the grievances of public sector workers;

10th, general strike begins in Nicaragua;

12th, New Jewel movement under Maurice Bishop seizes power in Grenada;

13th, European Monetary System (E.M.S.) becomes operational;

15th, civilian government committed to democratisation takes office in Brazil;

—, C.E.N.T.O. defence pact collapses;

22nd, I.R.A. assassinates British ambassador to Holland in The Hague;

26th, Egypt and Israel sign peace treaty in Washington, D.C.;

27th, Hafizullah Amin becomes Prime Minister of Afghanistan;

O Politics, Economics, Law and Education

British House of Commons establishes new structure of 14 Select Committees to examine the expenditure, administration and policies of principal government departments.

Andrew Boyle, *The Climate of Treason.*

Successful completion of Tokio Round of the General Agreement on Tariffs and Trade (G.A.T.T.).

France imposes prohibitive tariff on British lamb exports in defiance of the European Court.

In Britain, publication of Williams Report on obscenity (*Nov.* 28th).

British Local Education Authorities are freed from compulsion to introduce comprehensive education system.

Inner London Education Authority votes to ban corporal punishment from its 1,000 schools by Feb. 1981 (*Sept.* 18th).

Overseas students at British universities are required to pay the full cost of their courses.

Foundation of Green College, Oxford, England.

P Science, Technology, Discovery, etc.

Major accident at the Three Mile Island nuclear power station in Pennsylvania, U.S. (*Mar.* 28).

Start in Canada of TV broadcasting via a satellite.

The Philips Company launches the LaserVision video disc system.

First spreadsheet programme for personal computers – expands business use of PCs.

Matsushita in Japan develops a pocket-size flat-screen TV set.

The human-powered aircraft *Gossamer Albatross* crosses the English Channel.

First successful launch of the European Space Agency's Ariane rocket (*Dec.* 4th).

The U.S. space station Skylab I falls back to Earth after travelling 87 million miles in orbit since 1973.

U.S. space probes Voyager I and II explore the moons of Jupiter; Voyager I discovers a ring around Jupiter and two moons (the 15th and 16th).

U.S. space probe Pioneer XI travels through the rings of Saturn, which are found to be made of ice-covered rocks.

U.S.S.R. cosmonauts Vladimir A. Lyakhov and Valery V. Ryumin set new record for time spent in space of 175 days, 36 mins. (*Feb.* 25th–*Aug.* 19th).

The satellite HEAO2 (High Energy Astronomy Observatory – later renamed the Einstein Observatory) discovers a possible 'black hole' in the constellation Cygnus X-1.

U.S. astronomers John A. Eddy and Aram A. Boornazian announce that the Sun is shrinking at a rate of 5 feet per hour.

Physicists in Hamburg at DESY (Deutsches Elektron Synchroton) observe gluons – particles that carry the strong nuclear force which holds quarks together.

Inauguration of the European Molecular Biology Laboratory at Heidelberg, West Germany.

The U.S. Surgeon-general publishes a 1,200-page report confirming that cigarette smoking causes cancer and is linked with numerous other diseases.

Q Scholarship

E.H. Gombrich, *The Sense of Order: A Study in the Psychology of Decorative Art.*

M.T. Clanchy, *From Memory to Written Record: England 1066–1307.*

Charles Phythian-Adams, *Desolation of a City: Coventry and the Urban Crisis of the Late Middle Ages.*

1979 (Mar. – Jun.)

C **Mar**: 28th, British Labour government loses a motion of no confidence by 310–311 in the House of Commons; Prime Minister Callaghan calls a general election;
30th, in Britain, bomb planted by Irish National Liberation Army kills Airey Neave, Conservative spokesman on Northern Ireland, in the House of Commons car park;
31st, Malta cuts military links with Britain.

D **Apr**; 1st, Iran is declared an Islamic Republic by Ayatollah Khomeini;
2nd, publication of interim Erasmus report on the Information scandal in South Africa which clears serving politicians;
4th, Zulfikar Ali Bhutto is executed in Pakistan for conspiracy to murder;
7th, former Prime Minister Hovaida becomes a victim of a purge of the Shah's former officials in Iran;
10th (–20th), multi-racial elections held in Rhodesia;
11th, Kampala falls to Tanzanian and rebel forces; Idi Amin flees (13th, Yusufu Lule is inaugurated as President of Uganda);
16th, in South Africa Connie Mulder is expelled from the National Party following the information scandal;
18th, 100 children killed in demonstration against school uniforms in Bangui, Central African Empire;
23rd, violence at National Front election meeting in Southall, London, leaves dead a teacher, Blair Peach.

E **May**: 2nd, riots in Longwy, France, over proposed closure of steel plants;
3rd, Conservatives win British general election with 339 seats; Labour wins 269, Liberals, 11, Unionists, 12, Scottish Nationalists, 2, Plaid Cymru 2 (Conservatives win 43.9 per cent of votes cast, Labour, 36.9, Liberals, 13.8);
4th, Mrs. Margaret Thatcher becomes Britain's first woman Prime Minister;
5th, rebel guerrillas in El Salvador capture the French, Venezuelan, and Costa Rican embassies (last embassy recaptured *June* 1st);
8th (–*June* 22nd), in Britain, trial of former Liberal leader Jeremy Thorpe and three others for alleged plot to murder Norman Scott; all are acquitted, but Thorpe never resumes his political career;
10th, U.S. President Carter's plan for petrol rationing is rejected by Congress;
15th, British government abolishes Prices Commission and price controls;
22nd, in Canada Trudeau's Liberal government loses the general election; Joe Clark is appointed Prime Minister of Progressive Conservative minority government;
25th, crash of DC-10 aircraft at Chicago kills 273 and causes the grounding of DC-10s in U.S. from *May* 29th to *July* 13th;
28th, Greece signs Treaty of Accession to E.C., for entry in 1981.

F **Jun**: 1st, Bishop Abel Muzorewa, a black leader, is appointed Prime Minister of the renamed Zimbabwe Rhodesia;
3rd (–4th), Italian general election, in which the Communist Party loses ground;
4th, President Vorster of South Africa resigns after the final Erasmus Report shows that he knew about illegal activities at Information Department;
—, Flight-Lieutenant Jerry Rawlings leads military coup that deposes President F. Akuffo of Ghana;
7th (and 10th), first direct elections for the European Parliament; low turnout and results influenced by popularity of national governments; in Britain the Conservatives win 60 seats, Labour, 17, Liberals, 0 (Conservatives win 48.4 per cent of votes cast, Labour, 31.6, and Liberals, 12.6); the Scottish Nationalists win 1 seat, the Ulster Unionists, 3.

Q Scholarship (*cont.*)

F.H. Hinsley et al., *British Intelligence in the Second World War* (–90).
Christopher Lasch, *The Culture of Narcissism.*

R Philosophy and Religion

Jean-François Lyotard, *The Post-modern Condition.*
Thomas Nagel, *Mortal Questions.*
Publication of *The New International Version of the Bible.*
Richard Rorty, *Philosophy and the Mirror of Nature.*
Mother Teresa awarded the Nobel Peace Prize.
Robert Runcie appointed to replace Donald Coggan as Archbishop of Canterbury.
General Synod of the Church of England refuses to allow women priests ordained abroad to celebrate holy communion.

S Art, Sculpture, Fine Arts and Architecture

Painting:
French government accepts large gift of works from the Picasso estate (museum to be established in Paris).
Paris-Moscou, exhibition at Pompidou Centre, Paris.
Velázquez, portrait of *Juan de Pareja* sold at Christie's for $5.5 million, the most expensive painting bought at auction.
Jennifer Durrant is first woman artist in residence at Oxford University, England.
Rome art critic Achille Bonito Olivia coins term 'Transavanguardia' to denote painters who had gone beyond modernism and had established a broader attitude to art.
Philip Guston, *The Rug.*

Sculpture:
Joseph Beuys retrospective at Guggenheim Museum, New York, installed by the artist himself.
Judy Chicago, *The Dinner Party.*

Architecture:
B.E.P. Akitek (with I.M. Pei as consultant), Overseas Chinese Banking Corporation Headquarters, Singapore.
Aldo Rossi, Teatro del Mondo, Venice.

T Music

Alban Berg, *Lulu* (posth. opera), first complete performance.
Harrison Birtwistle, *...agm....*
John Cage, *Roaratorio.*
Brian Ferneyhough, *La terre est un homme.*
Michael Tippett, 4th String Quartet.

U Literature

Italo Calvino, *If on a Winter's Night a Traveller.*
Odysseus Elytis, *Maria Nefeldi.*
Nadine Gordimer, *Burger's Daughter.*
Milan Kundera, *The Book of Laughter and Forgetting.*
Norman Mailer, *The Executioner's Song.*
Peter Matthiessen, *The Snow Leopard.*
V.S. Naipaul, *A Bend in the River.*
Alain Robbe-Grillet, *Le Rendez-vous.*
Philip Roth, *The Ghost Writer.*
William Styron, *Sophie's Choice.*

F **Jun:** 12th, British Chancellor Geoffrey Howe's first Budget reduces income tax from 33p to 30p and the top rate from 83p to 60p, and increases V.A.T. from 8 per cent and 12½per cent to 15 per cent;

14th (–26th), in Nicaragua, Sandinista rebels close in on the capital, Managua;

15th (–18th), summit meeting in Vienna of Carter and Brezhnev ends with the signing of the S.A.L.T. II treaty limiting nuclear weapons;

20th, President Lule of Uganda loses confidence vote in Parliament and is replaced by Godfrey Binaisa.

G **Jul:** 2nd, in Germany the Bavarian Christian Social Union leader Franz Josef Strauss is designated opposition candidate for Chancellor for the 1980 general election;

5th, Iran nationalises its industries;

9th, Hilla Limann elected President of Ghana;

11th, Kiribati (formerly the Gilbert Islands) becomes independent;

—, International Whaling Commission bans the hunting of sperm whales;

—, in India the Janata Party loses overall control of the Lok Sabha through defections;

13th, Palestinian guerrillas attack the Egyptian embassy in Ankara, killing three;

15th, Morarji Desai resigns as Indian Prime Minister (28th, replaced by Charan Singh);

16th, Saddam Hussein becomes President of Iraq;

—, President Carter proposes radical measures to deal with the energy crisis and speaks of 'a crisis... of our national will';

17th, Anastasio Somoza, dictator of Nicaragua, flees to the U.S.;

19th, members of Carter's cabinet resign, to facilitate a major reshuffle;

—, in Nicaragua, Sandinista rebels take Managua and set up a new government;

29th, Argentina and Britain re-establish diplomatic relations at ambassadorial level.

H **Aug:** 1st, the British government accepts the Clegg Commission's recommendation of large pay rises for some public sector workers;

(–8th), Commonwealth Conference in Lusaka proposes a conference to settle the Zimbabwe Rhodesia problem;

3rd, in Iran supporters of Ayatollah Khomeini dominate the new constitutent assembly;

—, a military coup in Equatorial Guinea deposes President Macias Nguema;

5th, Mauritania renounces claims to Western Sahara and makes peace with the Polisario guerrillas of Western Sahara;

10th (–24th), in Britain, a strike closes down I.T.V.;

—, workers in the British engineering industry impose a four-day week;

14th, 17 die when a hurricane hits boats participating in the Fastnet yacht race;

15th, Andrew Young, U.S. ambassador to the U.N., resigns when it is revealed that he had unauthorised contact with the P.L.O.;

27th, Earl Mountbatten and three others killed by an I.R.A. bomb while boating in County Sligo in Eire;

—, 18 soldiers and a civilian are killed in an I.R.A. attack at Warrenpoint in Northern Ireland.

J **Sep:** British engineering workers step up industrial action by imposing a three-day week;

6th, 30,000 'boat people' who have fled from Vietnam are allowed to settle in the U.S.;

7th, death toll from Hurricane David in the Dominican Republic reaches 1,100;

v The Press

Financier James Goldsmith launches *Now!* magazine in Britain (*Sept.*).

One of Canada's most important newspapers, the 111-year-old *Montreal Star*, ceases publication eight months after a lengthy strike over the introduction of new technology and manning practices (*Sept.* 25th).

Offices of *The Times of Malta* are fire-bombed by demonstrators celebrating 30 years of Dom Mintoff as leader of the Labour Party and Prime Minister; a Church daily, *Il Hajja*, also has its offices destroyed (*Oct.* 15th).

In Britain, resumption of publication of *The Times*, *The Sunday Times* and supplements (*Nov.* 13th).

w Drama and Entertainment

Caryl Churchill, *Cloud Nine.*
Dorothy Hewett, *The Man from Mukinupin.*
Peter Shaffer, *Amadeus.*
Martin Sherman, *Bent.*
David Williamson, *Travelling North.*

Films:
- Ridley Scott's *Alien.*
- *The Getting of Wisdom.*
- *Mad Max.*
- *Monty Python's Life of Brian.*

Television:
- Sir David Attenborough, *Life on Earth.*
- *Tales of the Unexpected.*
- *Testament of Youth.*

Popular music:
- The Clash, *London Calling.*
- Elvis Costello, *Oliver's Army.*
- The Police, 'Message in a Bottle' and 'Walking on the Moon'.
- Neil Young, *Rust Never Sleeps.*
- At a pop concert in Cincinnati, Ohio, given by the British group The Who, 11 people are crushed to death and 28 injured (*Dec.* 3rd).

x Sport

Trevor Francis moves from Birmingham City to Nottingham Forest in the first £1 million transfer deal in English football (*Feb.* 14th); the record is broken again when Steve Daley of Wolverhampton Wanderers moves to Manchester United for £1.45 million and Andy Gray from Aston Villa to Wolverhampton for £1.47 million.

Wales wins the rugby Triple Crown for the fourth successive year (*Mar.* 17th) and the Five Nations Championship for the second year running.

West Indies retain the cricket World Cup, beating England by 92 runs in the Final at Lord's (*June* 23rd).

British athlete Sebastian Coe is the first man to hold three indoor world records simultaneously, for the 800 metres, the mile and the 1,500 metres (*Aug.* 15th).

The 'Packer dispute' is settled when the Australian Cricket Board grants Channel Nine exclusive rights to televise Test cricket in Australia.

Black U.S. boxer John Tate wins the W.B.A. Heavy-weight title in Pretoria, defeating the white South African Gerrie Coetzee on points over 15 rounds before 80,000 spectators, the largest ever live audience for a heavy-weight title fight (*Oct.* 20th).

J **Sep**: 10th (*–Dec.* 21st), Lancaster House conference held in London to seek settlement of the Rhodesia problem;
—, British Leyland motor manufacturing company announces 25,000 redundancies;
11th, death of President Agostinho Neto of Angola (20th, replaced by José Eduardo dos Santos);
12th, telephone division of the British Post Office is established as separate company, British Telecommunications;
16th, in Swedish general election, non-Socialist parties retain power with majority of one seat;
—, overthrow of President Nur Mohammad Taraki of Afghanistan, replaced by Hafizullah Amin;
20th, in the Central African Empire, former President David Dacko overthrows his uncle Emperor Bokassa; the Empire reverts to Republic status;
24th (–29th), trial of Macias Nguema, former President of Equatorial Guinea, who is found guilty of genocide and executed;
26th, British government announces that the Metrication Board will be wound up;
29th (*–Oct.* 1st), Pope John Paul II makes first papal visit to Ireland.

K **Oct**: the U.S. hands over the Panama Canal zone to Panama;
—, a civilian government takes power in Nigeria after 13 years of military rule;
2nd, the conference of the British Labour Party votes for mandatory reselection of sitting M.P.s;
4th, British engineering strike ends with compromise agreement;
7th, Liberal Democrat Party wins a narrow victory in Japan's general election;
8th, Eschel Rhoodie of South Africa's Information Department is sentenced to six years' imprisonment for fraud;
14th, Israeli Foreign Minister, General Moshe Dayan, resigns in protest against Israel's stand on Palestinian autonomy;
16th, President Zia of Pakistan cancels elections and bans political activity;
—, British government announces plans to sell 5 per cent of its holding in British Petroleum, in order to raise £290 million, leaving the government with just over 25 per cent of B.P.;
23rd, in a surprise move (after Chancellor Howe has had a sleepless night) the British government abolishes exchange controls;
—, the former Shah of Iran is flown to the U.S. for medical treatment;
—, Václav Havel and five other Czech dissidents are convicted of subversion;
25th, referenda in Spain approve devolution of power to Catalonia and Euzkadi (the Basque provinces);
26th, President of South Korea, Park Chung-Hee, is assassinated by his secret service;
27th, St. Vincent and Grenadines gains independence;
30th, Robert Boulin, French Minister of Labour, accused of a scandal over property purchases, commits suicide.

L **Nov**: 1st, British government announces spending cuts for 1980–81 financial year of £3.5 billion;
4th, Iranian students seize the U.S. embassy in Teheran, taking 63 U.S. citizens and 40 others hostage; they demand the return of the Shah for trial;
6th, Ayatollah Khomeini's Islamic Revolutionary Council takes power in Iran from the provisional government;
7th, Senator Edward Kennedy announces challenge to President Carter for the Democratic nomination for the 1980 Presidential election (8th, Governor Jerry Brown of California announces candidacy for Democratic nomination; 13th, Ronald Reagan, former Governor of California, declares candidacy for Republican nomination);

x **Sport** (*cont.*)

International Olympic Committee decides (by 62 votes to 17) to admit athletes from China to the next Olympic Games (*Nov.* 26th).

Stewards agree to stage women's races at the Henley Royal Regatta in England from 1981 (*Dec.* 12th).

Scottish and English Football Associations decide that tickets for future England v. Scotland matches at Wembley will not be sold north of the border, to prevent drunken Scottish fans from causing disorder in London (*Dec.* 20th); the same day the Pools Promoters Association announces annual donations of £3.5 million to a trust investigating crowd behaviour and other social problems associated with soccer.

Y **Statistics**

Social and educational composition of British Conservative Cabinet: aristocrats, 3, middle class, 19, working class, 0; attendance at public school, 20 (inc. 6 at Eton); attendance at University 18 (inc. 17 at Oxford or Cambridge).

Z **Births and Deaths**

Jan. 5th Max Born d. (96).
—Charlie Mingus d. (56).
Jan. 26th Nelson Rockefeller d. (70).
Feb. 9th Dennis Gabor d. (78).
Mar. 16th Jean Monnet d. (90).
May 6th Bernard Leach d. (92).
May 8th Talcott Parsons d. (76).
May 29th Mary Pickford d. (86).
June 11th John Wayne d. (72).
July 29th Herbert Marcuse d. (81).
Aug. 16th John Diefenbaker d. (83).
Aug. 27th Lord Louis Mountbatten d. (79).
Sept. 22nd Otto Frisch d. (74).
Sept. 27th Gracie Fields d. (81).
Oct. 30th Barnes Wallis d. (92).
Dec. 30th Richard Rodgers d. (77).

L **Nov:** 12th, in response to the seizure of U.S. hostages in Iran, Carter imposes an embargo on Iranian oil (14th, Iranian assets in the U.S. are frozen);

13th, in Britain, publication of *The Times* is resumed after a stoppage of almost a year;

15th, following the publication of Andrew Boyle's *The Climate of Treason*, alleging that a senior British figure had been a U.S.S.R. agent, Mrs. Thatcher announces that the agent was Professor Sir Anthony Blunt, Surveyor of the Queen's Pictures and her art adviser; Blunt is stripped of his knighthood;

—, Minimum Lending Rate in Britain reaches a record 17 per cent;

19th (–28th), strikes at some British Leyland car plants following the dismissal of 'Red Robbo', alias Derek Robinson, a union shop steward;

—, U.S. House of Representatives votes $1.56 billion aid to the Chrysler Car Corporation;

20th, about 200 armed militants seize the Grand Mosque in Mecca, apparently in protest at corruption of Saudi regime (23rd, seige ended by Saudi Arabian troops);

22nd, former British Labour Party Chancellor Roy Jenkins floats the idea of a realignment of centre-left politics in his Dimbleby Lecture on B.B.C. television;

28th, Syrian Ambassador to the U.N., Hammoud El-Choufi, resigns from his post, accusing the government of President Hafez al Assad of corruption, repression and opportunism;

29th (–30th), E.C. summit in Dublin, at which Mrs. Thatcher demands a rebate against British contributions to the Community;

30th, British Steel announces loss of 50,000 jobs.

M **Dec:** 2nd, mob burns U.S. embassy in Tripoli;

5th, Jack Lynch resigns as Prime Minister of Eire (7th, replaced by Charles Haughey);

10th, the rebel parliament in Zimbabwe Rhodesia winds itself up, ending U.D.I.;

12th, Lord Soames arrives in Zimbabwe Rhodesia to oversee formal end of British rule;

13th, the Canadian government of Prime Minister Joseph Clark is defeated in a confidence debate; Clark calls an election;

18th, Canadian Liberal Pierre Trudeau reverses decision to retire from party leadership;

21st, Lancaster House agreement signed in London, providing for an end to Rhodesian civil war and introduction of majority rule (28th, ceasefire in Rhodesia);

25th, U.S.S.R. invasion of Afghanistan, in bid to halt civil war and protect U.S.S.R. interests;

27th, President Amin of Afghanistan killed and replaced by Babrak Karmal;

31st, at year end oil prices are 88 per cent higher than at the start of 1979;

—, publication of British New Year's Honours List in which Prime Minister Thatcher bestows political honours for the first time since 1974.

1980 (Jan. – Mar.) Independence of Zimbabwe—Recession in Britain—Start of Iran-Iraq War—Emergence of 'Solidarity' in Poland

A **Jan:** 1st, U.N. Secretary-General Kurt Waldheim visits Teheran to seek release of U.S. hostages;
2nd (–*Apr.* 2nd), British national steel strike;
3rd, Congress (I) Party wins sweeping victory in Indian general election;
6th, total death-toll in Northern Ireland since 1969 exceeds 2,000;
8th, President Carter describes Soviet invasion of Afghanistan as greatest threat to peace since the Second World War (23rd, warns U.S.S.R. against interference in Persian Gulf);
22nd, U.S.S.R. sends dissident physicist Andrei Sakharov into internal exile at Gorky;
23rd, Israel completes withdrawal from 7,000 square miles of Sinai peninsula;
25th, Abolhassan Bani-Sadr becomes President of Iran;
29th, Canada announces escape of four U.S. diplomats from Iran on Canadian passports;
30th, Department of Employment reports more working days lost in Britain through strikes in 1979 than in any year since 1926.

B **Feb:** 12th, International Olympic Committee rejects U.S. demand for cancellation or relocation of Moscow Olympics;
14th, polling begins in Rhodesia for 20 white seats in new parliament (polling for 80 black seats begins, 27th);
18th, Liberals defeat Progressive Conservatives in Canadian general election; Pierre Trudeau becomes Prime Minister;
19th, in Britain, publication of Employment Bill outlawing secondary picketing and requiring unions to hold secret ballots before strikes;
22nd, proclamation of martial law in Kabul as resistance to U.S.S.R. invaders continues;
24th (–*Mar.* 11th), U.N. Commission visits Iran but fails to see U.S. hostages;
26th, Israel and Egypt exchange ambassadors for first time.

C **Mar:** 4th, Z.A.N.U. wins Rhodesian general election (11th, Robert Mugabe forms coalition government with Joshua Nkomo as Minister of Home Affairs);
11th, President Zia crushes attempted military coup in Pakistan;
14th, British Leyland discloses annual loss of £144 million;
16th, proclamation of martial law in Aleppo as political violence sweeps Syria;
17th, free House of Commons vote approves government appeal for British boycott of Moscow Olympics (British Olympic Association decides to send team, 25th);
18th, U.S. bans sale of high technology equipment to U.S.S.R.;
19th, British government declares that private consortium may construct Channel Tunnel, but no public money will be forthcoming;
20th, Lord Underhill, former national agent of the British Labour Party, publishes documents detailing methods by which the Party had been infiltrated by the Trotskyite Revolutionary League under the name 'Militant Tendency';
24th, Archbishop Oscar Romero shot dead while celebrating mass in San Salvador (30th, 40 die in violence at funeral);
26th, British Budget increases spending on defence, police and pensions, and raises duties and prescription charges;
27th, 147 British and Norwegian workers die when Alexander Kielland oil-platform collapses in North Sea;
31st, Basque regional parliament opens in Guernica.

O Politics, Economics, Law and Education

The 'Brandt Report', *North–South: A Programme for Survival*, calls for radical change in relations between rich and poor countries (*Feb.* 12th).

Housing Act gives British council tenants the right to buy their homes.

Publication of government White Paper *The Interception of Communications in Great Britain*; Home Secretary William Whitelaw tells the House of Commons that police and secret services will continue to employ telephone-tapping and interception of mail in the fight against espionage, subversion, and terrorism; a senior judge will check and monitor operations (*Apr.* 1st).

Privatization of Ferranti, Fairey and British Aerospace.

Britain becomes a net exporter of oil (*June*).

Companies Act in Britain makes 'insider dealing' in shares a criminal offence.

Assisted Places Scheme provides financial support for selected children at British independent schools.

P Science, Technology, Discovery, etc.

Japanese Company Sony launches the 'Walkman', a small portable, personal tape recorder/player.

Launch of 10-year World Climate Research Program to study prediction of climate changes and human influence on climate change.

Intelsat-V communication satellite launched, capable of relaying 12,000 telephone calls and two colour TV channels.

Intelpost, the first public international electronic facsimile service.

People's Republic of China launches its first inter-continental ballistic missile.

U.S.S.R. cosmonauts Valery V. Ryumin and Leonid I. Popov set another record for time spent in space, 185 days.

Very Large Array (VLA) satellite at Socorro, New Mexico, enters service; its 27 dishes are equivalent to one dish 17 miles in diameter.

U.S. space probe Voyager I flies past Saturn (*Nov.* 12th); it discovers the planet's 13th, 14th, and 15th moons and transmits information about the planet and its moons and rings.

Astronomers Uwe Fink and associates report the discovery of a thin atmosphere on Pluto.

A new vaccine for prevention of hepatitis B is tested in the U.S.; it has a success rate of 92 per cent.

The Swiss firm Biogen produces human interferon in bacteria for the treatment of diseases.

Munich firm develops the lithotripter, a machine that uses sound waves to break up kidney stones.

A team at the Washington University School of Medicine (St Louis, Missouri) transplants insulin-producing pancreatic islets from a rat to a mouse, opening up the possibility of making similar transplants from animals to humans.

A gene is transferred from one mouse to another.

The U.S. Supreme Court rules that a microbe created by genetic engineering can be patented.

M. Ikeya and T. Liki of Yamaguchi University, Japan, announce a new method of dating fossil remains: electron spin resonance spectroscopy, which measures the amount of natural radiation received by such remains.

Q Scholarship

John Baines and Jaromír Málek, *Atlas of Ancient Egypt*.

Michael Baxandall, *The Limewood Sculptors of Renaissance Germany*.

D **Apr**: 2nd, in Britain, young blacks riot in St. Paul's district of Bristol after police raid on a club used by the coloured community;

6th, 10,000 Cubans seek political asylum in Peruvian embassy in Havana;

7th, U.S. bans trade with Iran, breaks off relations and expels Iranian diplomats;

—, Iraqi artillery bombards Iranian border town of Oweisa;

9th, major Israeli raid on Palestinian positions in southern Lebanon;

10th, Spain agrees to re-open border with Gibraltar (closed 1969);

14th, Israel and Egypt decide to hold negotiations on Palestinian autonomy;

18th, Rhodesia gains legal independence as Zimbabwe under President Canaan Banana;

23rd, Saudi Arabia expels British Ambassador in protest at a British television programme about execution of a Saudi princess and her lover for adultery;

25th, U.S. commando mission to rescue hostages in Iran fails with loss of eight lives (29th, Cyrus Vance resigns as U.S. Secretary of State; succeeded by Edmund Muskie);

28th, E.C. summit in Luxembourg fails to reach agreement on Britain's demand for rebate payment against contributions;

30th, Queen Juliana of Holland abdicates in favour of Crown Princess Beatrix;

—, terrorists seize Iranian embassy in London, demanding release of political prisoners in Iran (Special Air Service storms embassy, *May* 5th).

E **May**: 1st, U.S.S.R.'s traditional May Day parade is boycotted by ambassadors of 15 countries because of invasion of Afghanistan;

—, Sweden is practically at a standstill as pay negotiations crumble amidst strikes and lock-outs;

4th, death of President Tito of Yugoslavia; replaced by eight-man collective presidency;

10th, Franco-African agreement to form 30-nation French-speaking commonwealth;

14th, President Sadat of Egypt discontinues talks with Israel on Palestinian autonomy;

—, T.U.C. 'day of action' against British government policies evokes little response;

18th, E.C. imposes trade sanctions against Iran;

20th, referendum in Quebec on possible separation from Canada produces a 59.9 per cent vote against;

26th, George Bush abandons bid for Republican nomination for U.S. Presidency;

28th, first Islamic parliament (Majlis) opens in Iran;

30th, New Hebrides appeals for British and French help to suppress rebellion on Espiritu Santo (*July* 24th, Anglo-French force occupies the island);

—, E.C. foreign ministers agree on a rebate to Britain of £710 million.

F **Jun**: 3rd, U.S. nuclear alert when computer error indicates missile attack by U.S.S.R.;

9th, Roy Jenkins floats idea of creating new radical centre party in British politics;

11th, Colonel Khadaffi halts 'liquidation' of Libyan exiles, except those collaborating with U.S., Israel or Egypt;

12th, death of Masayoshi Ohira, Prime Minister of Japan (Zenko Suzuki succeeds, *July* 17th);

17th, British Ministry of Defence announces plan to deploy U.S. Cruise missiles at Greenham Common and Molesworth military bases;

—(–21st), over 30 die in clashes with police in coloured townships around Cape Town;

22nd, tribal violence in Tripura, India, claims 1,000 lives;

25th, Basque terrorists explode bombs on Costa Blanca to disrupt Spanish tourist trade;

26th, French President Giscard d'Estaing discloses France's capability to produce neutron bomb;

30th, sixpence piece ceases to be legal tender in Britain.

Q Scholarship (*cont.*)

Jerome J. McGann (ed.), *Lord Byron: The Complete Poetical Works* (–93).
W.A. McCutcheon, *The Industrial Archaeology of Northern Ireland.*
Norbert Lynton, *The Story of Modern Art.*
Bernard Crick, *George Orwell: A Life.*
Stanley Sadie (ed.), *The New Grove Dictionary of Music and Musicians.*

R Philosophy and Religion

Donald Davidson, *Essays on Action and Events.*
Richard Rorty, *Philosophy and the Mirror of Nature.*
Dr. Anthony Kenny, Master of Balliol College, Oxford, is expelled from Czechoslovakia following a police raid on the flat of the Czech dissident philosopher Dr. Julius Tomin (*Apr.* 12th); Dr. Kathleen Wilkes, Tutor in Philosophy at St. Hilda's College, Oxford, is arrested and expelled for the same reason on *May* 20th.
The Alternative Service Book 1980 is published as the first authorised prayer book of the Church of England since 1662.
The South African government withdraws Bishop Desmond Tutu's passport.
Following the U.S.S.R. invasion of Afghanistan, the Conference of Islamic Foreign Ministers calls on Moslems to boycott the Moscow Olympics.
The British television programme *Death of a Princess*, about the enforcement of Islamic law in Saudi Arabia, causes widespread controversy in the Islamic world.

S Art, Sculpture, Fine Arts and Architecture

Painting:
Interest in figurative painting revived in contemporary art.
Picasso exhibition at the Museum of Modern Art, New York.
'The Avant-Garde in Russia', exhibition at Los Angeles County Museum, Los Angeles.
Sandro Chia, *Excited Pastoral.*
Cindy Sherman, *Untitled* no. 66.

Sculpture:
Georg Baselitz, *Model For a Sculpture.*
Tony Cragg, *Plastic Palette I.*
Richard Deacon, *If the Shoe Fits.*

Architecture:
Francisco Saenz de Oiza, The Bank, Madrid.

T Music

Elliott Carter, *Night Fantasies.*
Peter Maxwell Davies, *The Lighthouse* (opera).
Philip Glass, *Satyagraha* (opera).
Oliver Knussen, *Where the Wild Things Are* (opera).
Krzystof Penderecki, 2nd Symphony.

U Literature

Joseph Brodsky, *A Part of Speech.*
Anthony Burgess, *Earthly Powers.*
Truman Capote, *Music for Chameleons.*
John le Carré, *Smiley's People.*
Umberto Eco, *The Name of the Rose.*

G **Jul**: 1st, increase in meat prices prompts industrial unrest in Poland (24th, Polish government approves wage rises);
—, John Anderson announces independent candidature for U.S. Presidency;
2nd, South Africa withdraws from Angola after three-week raid on guerrilla bases;
3rd, Bank of England reduces minimum lending rate from 17 to 16 per cent;
10th, British Labour Party issues radical proposals for nationalisation and price controls;
15th, British government decides to replace Polaris with U.S. Trident-1 nuclear missile system in mid-1980s;
17th, U.S. Republican Party convention in Detroit nominates Ronald Reagan as Presidential candidate; he chooses George Bush as running-mate for Vice-President;
18th, British annual inflation rate stands at 21 per cent after first fall in two years;
19th, Olympic Games open in Moscow, boycotted by 45 nations;
27th, inauguration of President Fernando Belaunde Terry ends 12 years of military rule in Peru;
29th, British Steel announces record losses of £545 million;
30th, New Hebrides becomes independent as Vanuatu;
—, Knesset proclaims unified Jerusalem the capital of Israel.

H **Aug**: 2nd, right-wing Italian terrorists kill 82 with bomb at Bologna railway station;
4th, abolition of Clegg Commission on pay comparability in British public sector;
5th, Belgian parliament passes Bill dividing country into three autonomous linguistic regions;
12th, Senator Edward Kennedy withdraws from contest for Democratic Presidential nomination after Carter wins vote in the rules committee by 545 votes;
13th (–28th), French fishermen blockade Channel ports in campaign for government aid;
14th, Polish strikers occupy Lenin shipyard in Gdansk;
—, Democratic Party convention in New York nominates President Carter and Vice-President Mondale for second term;
20th, U.S.S.R. jams Western radio broadcasts for first time in seven years to prevent news of widespread strikes in Poland;
26th, leadership changes in China consolidate power of pragmatic reformers led by Teng Tsiao-ping;
27th, British unemployment total exceeds 2 million;
31st, Lech Walesa, leader of Gdansk strikers, signs agreement with Polish government allowing formation of independent trade unions and granting release of political prisoners.

J **Sep**: 1st, conference of British T.U.C. at Brighton deplores Employment Act and calls for campaign of non-co-operation with government;
5th, Stanislaw Kania succeeds Edward Gierek as First Secretary of Polish Communist Party;
9th, closure of British Embassy in Teheran;
10th, Libya and Syria proclaim themselves a single state;
11th, referendum in Chile approves eight-year extension of Pinochet's military government;
12th, General Kenan Evren heads military take-over in Turkey;
—, Ayatollah Khomeini sets out conditions for release of U.S. hostages in Iran;
22nd, Iraq invades Iran in attempt to gain control of Shatt al-Arab waterway;
—, Indian government assumes powers to combat violence in southern India;
28th, President Zia of Pakistan visits Teheran and Baghdad in attempt to mediate in Iran–Iraq War.

U Literature (*cont.*)

Zhang Jie, *Leaden Wings.*
Shiva Naipaul, *Black and White.*
Patrick White, *The Twyborn Affair.*
Tom Wolfe, *The Right Stuff.*

V The Press

London's *Evening News* is merged into *The Evening Standard* (*Oct.* 31st).
Japan's leading newspaper, *Asahi Shimbun*, is produced by use of new technology - 'untouched by human hands' (*Sept.* 24th).

W Drama and Entertainment

Howard Brenton, *The Romans in Britain*, at the National Theatre, London, causes controversy on account of scenes involving nudity and sexual violence; prosecution for obscenity is threatened (all tickets are sold).
David Edgar (adaptor), *Nicholas Nickleby.*
Brian Friel, *Translations.*
Ronald Harwood, *The Dresser.*
Greg McGee, *Foreskin's Lament.*
Mark Medoff, *Children of a Lesser God.*
Sam Shepard, *True West.*

Films:
Gillian Armstrong's *My Brilliant Career.*
Michael Cimino's *Heaven's Gate*, which is withdrawn, after expenditure of $40 million.
Akira Kurosawa's *Kagemusha.*
David Lynch's *Elephant Man.*
Martin Scorcese's *Raging Bull.*
Ordinary People.
The Shining.

Television:
Hill Street Blues.

Popular music:
Ska revival by British bands, e.g. Madness and The Specials.
Joy Division, *Closer.*

X Sport

Nigel Short, age 14, from Bolton in Britain becomes youngest International Master in the history of chess (*Jan.* 11th).
Alan Minter is the first British fighter to win a world title in the U.S. since Ted 'Kid' Lewis in 1917 when he wins the World Middle-weight title (beating Vito Antuofermo in Las Vegas, *Mar.* 16th).
Liverpool Football Club wins the British League Championship for the second year running, the fourth time in five years, and the 12th time in all – a record (*May* 3rd).
Cliff Thorburn of Canada is first non-British player to win the world snooker championship (*May* 5th).
A.C. Milan, one of Italy's top football teams, is relegated to the second division by a Disciplinary Commission of the Italian League; it found the President and several key players guilty of fraud, bribe-taking and fixing games (*May* 18th).

K **Oct**: 1st, British Labour Party conference in Blackpool votes for unilateral nuclear disarmament, withdrawal from E.C. and mandatory re-selection of M.P.s;
5th, West Germany re-elects Chancellor Helmut Schmidt's coalition;
6th, British prison officers begin work-to-rule, refusing to admit new prisoners;
—, Transport Act ends National Express monopoly on long-distance coach travel in Britain;
10th, Mrs. Thatcher tells Conservative Party conference of her determination to persist with monetarist policies: 'U-turn if you want to; the Lady's not for turning';
—, earthquake in Algeria kills 20,000;
15th, James Callaghan resigns as leader of the British Labour Party;
17th, Queen Elizabeth II pays first State visit to Vatican by British monarch (22nd, the Pope annuls 1633 condemnation of Galileo);
21st, sterling exchange rate reaches $2.45 for first time since 1973;
23rd, Nikolai Tikhonov succeeds Alexei Kosygin as Soviet Prime Minister;
24th, Polish authorities register a new independent trade union, named 'Solidarity';
26th, London protest march by Campaign for Nuclear Disarmament attracts 50,000;
27th (*Dec.* 18th), seven I.R.A. prisoners in the Maze prison in Northern Ireland, on hunger strike, demanding 'political status'.

L **Nov**: 4th, in U.S. Presidential election, Republican Ronald Reagan wins a sweeping victory over President Carter; Reagan wins 489 electoral votes, Carter, 49; popular vote: Reagan, 43,899,248; Carter, 35,481,435; John Anderson (Independent), 5,719,437; Republicans win control of the Senate and gain 33 seats in the House of Representatives;
10th, Michael Foot defeats Denis Healey to become leader of the British Labour Party, winning 139 votes to Healey's 129 in the second ballot;
—(–*Dec.* 11th), British firemen work to rule in pay dispute;
20th, treason trial of former Chinese leaders, the 'Gang of Four', opens in Peking;
24th, British Chancellor Sir Geoffrey Howe announces £1.06 billion reduction in public spending and £3 billion increase in taxation;
27th, four Welsh nationalist extremists gaoled for arson attacks on holiday homes;
—, British government announces aim of cutting 100,000 jobs from civil service;
30th, Syria masses troops on Jordanian border; Jordan calls up reserves.

M **Dec**: 2nd, E.C. warns U.S.S.R. against military intervention in Poland;
3rd, start of major Soviet offensive against Afghan resistance fighters;
4th, Francisco Sá Carneiro, Prime Minister of Portugal, dies in air crash (21st, Francisco Pinto Balsemão succeeds);
8th, Mrs. Thatcher and Charles Haughey, meeting in Dublin, agree to establish commission to examine Anglo-Irish links respecting Northern Ireland;
—, former Beatle John Lennon is murdered in New York;
10th, President Brezhnev calls on West and China to make Persian Gulf and Indian Ocean 'a zone of peace';
15th, Milton Obote becomes President of Uganda after first elections in 18 years;
16th, O.P.E.C. increases crude oil prices by 10 per cent;
—, unveiling of memorial in Gdansk, Poland, to workers killed in riots of *Dec.* 1970;
21st, Iran demands 'deposit' of $24,000 million for release of U.S. hostages (29th U.S. refuses to pay);
27th, violent anti-U.S.S.R. demonstrations in Teheran on anniversary of invasion of Afghanistan.

X Sport *(cont.)*

The European Football Association (E.U.F.A.) fines the British Football Association £8,000 because of the 'violent and dangerous conduct of English supporters' who rioted during England's opening match against Belgium in Turin (*June* 12th); police had used tear gas to break up the rioting and the match was stopped for five minutes when players became affected by gas.

Bjorn Borg of Sweden wins his fifth consecutive Wimbledon Men's Singles title (*July* 5th); during the championships electronic fault-finding equipment is introduced for use by line judges.

The centenary Test match between England and Australia is held at Lord's (*Aug.* 28th–*Sept.* 2nd); the match is drawn after 10 hours are lost to rain – on the Saturday M.C.C. members assault the umpires.

Following the Soviet invasion of Afghanistan, the XXII Olympic Games in Moscow are boycotted by 65 countries, most notably the U.S., West Germany, Japan and Kenya. The U.S.S.R. wins 80 gold medals; East Germany, 47; Bulgaria, Cuba and Italy, 8; Hungary, 7; Roumania and France, 6; United Kingdom, 5; Poland, Sweden and Finland, 3. Allan Wells is the first Briton since 1924 to win the 100 metres gold.

Y Statistics

Populations of cities (in mill.): Tokio, 11.6; Shanghai, 10.0; Buenos Aires, 9.7; Mexico City, 8.9; Peking, 8.7; Seoul, 8.4; Cairo, 8.1; Moscow, 8.0; New York, 7.1; Tientsin, 7.0.

Jewish population (main centres): U.S., 5,750,000; Israel, 3,283,000; U.S.S.R., 1,811,000; France, 600,000; Great Britain, 350,000; Canada, 308,000; Argentina, 242,000; Brazil, 110,000; South Africa, 108,000.

Z Births and Deaths

Jan. 18th Cecil Beaton d. (76).
Feb. 17th Graham Sutherland d. (76).
Feb. 22nd Oskar Kokoschka d. (93).
Mar. 18th Erich Fromm d. (79).
Mar. 26th Roland Barthes d. (64).
Mar. 31st Jesse Owens d. (66).
Apr. 15th Jean-Paul Sartre d. (74).
Apr. 29th Alfred Hitchcock d. (80).
May 4th Tito (Josip Broz) d. (87).
June 7th Henry Miller d. (88).
July 1st C.P. Snow d. (74).
July 24th Peter Sellers d. (54).
July 27th Mohammed Reza Shah Pahlevi d. (60).
Aug. 6th Marino Marini d. (79).
Sept. 8th W.F. Libby d. (71).
Sept. 17th Jean Piaget d. (84).
Oct. 26th Marcello Caetano d. (74).
Nov. 22nd Mae West d. (88).
Dec. 3rd Oswald Mosley d. (84).
Dec. 8th John Lennon d. (40).
Dec. 18th Alexei Nikolaevich Kosygin d. (76).
Dec. 22nd Karl Doenitz d. (89).
Dec. 31st Marshall McLuhan d. (69).

1981 (Jan. – Mar.) Foundation of Social Democratic Party in Britain—Brixton and Toxteth Riots—Socialist government in France—Martial law in Poland

A **Jan:** 1st, Greece becomes 10th member of E.C.;

5th, British Prime Minister Mrs. Thatcher sacks Norman St John–Stevas as Leader of the Commons; Francis Pym becomes Leader of the Commons, John Nott replaces him as Defence Secretary;

6th, Gaston Thorn succeeds Roy Jenkins as President of European Commission;

13th, Namibian peace conference breaks up without agreement in Geneva;

15th, the Pope receives official 'Solidarity' delegation led by Lech Walesa;

20th, inauguration of Ronald Reagan as 39th President of U.S.;

—, Iran releases all 52 U.S. hostages (held since *Nov.* 4th 1979) after agreement is signed in Algiers releasing Iranian financial assets in U.S.;

24th, in Britain, special Labour Party conference at Wembley votes for electoral college of M.P.s, constituency parties and trade unions to elect leader;

25th, former British Labour ministers Roy Jenkins, Dr. David Owen, William Rodgers and Mrs. Shirley Williams issue the 'Limehouse Declaration', advocating a new central political position to pursue radical change, and form the 'Council for Social Democracy';

—, show trial in Peking convicts 'Gang of Four' of treason; Chiang Ch'ing, widow of Chairman Mao, receives suspended death sentence;

26th, British government announces £990 million aid for British Leyland;

29th, Adolfo Suarez resigns as Spanish Prime Minister (*Feb.* 10th, succeeded by Leopoldo Calvo–Sotelo).

B **Feb:** 3rd, Mrs. Gro Harlem Brundtland becomes first woman Prime Minister of Norway;

6th, Rev. Ian Paisley stages midnight parade of 500 Protestants with fire-arm certificates on his 'Carson trail' in Northern Ireland;

9th, General Wojciech Jaruzelski replaces Jozef Pinkowski as Prime Minister of Poland;

12th, fighting breaks out between rival ex-guerrilla forces in Zimbabwe (16th, Joshua Nkomo persuades his supporters to lay down their arms);

18th, British National Coal Board withdraws pit closure plan to avert strike by miners;

—, President Reagan proposes spending cuts of $49,000 million and 30 per cent reduction in taxation over three years;

20th, U.S. accuses U.S.S.R. and Cuba of attempting to subvert El Salvador;

23rd, 200 civil guards storm Spanish Parliament and hold M.P.s at gun-point in coup attempt (24th, guards surrender after denunciation by King Juan Carlos);

27th, release of three British missionaries detained in Iran since *Aug.* 1980.

C **Mar:** 2nd, 12 British M.P.s and nine Peers resign Labour whip to sit as Social Democrats (16th, one Conservative M.P. joins them);

5th, Mrs. Thatcher gives assurances to Unionists that the constitutional position of Northern Ireland will not be compromised;

9th (–*July* 30th), British civil servants take industrial action in pursuit of pay claim;

10th, austere British Budget raises duties and freezes income tax allowances;

22nd, U.S.S.R. extends Warsaw Pact manoeuvres in Poland until *Apr.* 7th;

26th, in Britain official launch of Social Democratic Party (S.D.P.), with programme of incomes policy, proportional representation and support for E.C. and N.A.T.O.;

27th, U.S.S.R. brands Polish trade union 'Solidarity' counter-revolutionary;

29th, former British Prime Minister Harold Wilson confirms reports of planned coup against his government in late 1960s but denies involvement of Lord Mountbatten;

O **Politics, Economics, Law and Education**

Milton Friedman, *Monetary Trends in the United States and the United Kingdom.*

Bank of England issues £50 note (*Mar.* 20th).

British Nationality Act replaces universal British subjecthood with three status categories (British citizenship with right of abode, citizenship of dependent territory, overseas citizenship).

Royal Commission on Criminal Procedure recommends extension of police powers of arrest and search in Britain (*Jan.* 8th).

European Court rules that dismissal for refusing to join union 'closed shop' is a violation of human rights (*Aug.* 13th).

French National Assembly abolishes the death penalty and thereby use of the guillotine (*Sept.* 30th).

British government reduces grant to universities by 3 per cent (*Mar.* 13th).

P **Science, Technology, Discovery, etc.**

French railways introduce their high-speed train, the Train à Grande Vitesse (T.G.V.).

Opening of bridge over the River Humber – the world's longest suspension bridge.

IBM launches its personal computer, using the Microsoft disc-operating system (MS-DOS) which becomes a standard programme throughout the computer industry.

Launch of two-dimensional fluorescent lamp.

First pocket-size TV produced, by Sir Clive Sinclair.

The *Solar Challenger* aircraft, powered by solar cells, crosses the English Channel.

First flight of the American reusable space shuttle (*Apr.* 12th–14th), using the orbiter *Columbia* (second shuttle flight *Nov.* 12th–14th).

U.S. space probe Voyager II photographs the rings and moons of Saturn and transmits scientific data (*Aug.*).

Astronomers at the University of Wisconsin discover the most massive star yet known, R136a, which is 100 times brighter than the Sun and 2,500 times larger.

U.S. Center for Disease Control recognises AIDS (Acquired Immune Deficiency Syndrome), thought to be caused by HIV virus.

The U.S. Food and Drug Administration grants permission to Eli Lilley and Co. to market insulin produced by bacteria, the first genetic engineering product to go on sale.

Scientists at Ohio University transfer a gene into a mouse – the first transfer of a gene from one animal species to another.

Chinese scientists make the first clone of a fish (a golden carp).

Chemists devise a way of giving polymers some of the properties of metals; this enables scientists at the University of Pennsylvania to construct the first 'plastic battery'.

Q **Scholarship**

UNESCO, *General History of Africa* (–).

Peter Salway, *Roman Britain.*

David Hill, *An Atlas of Anglo-Saxon England.*

Anthony Fletcher, *The Outbreak of the English Civil War.*

E.A. Wrigley and R.S. Schofield, *The Population History of England, 1541–1871: A Reconstruction.*

Mark Girouard, *The Return to Camelot: Chivalry and the English Gentleman.*

Stephen Koss, *The Rise and Fall of the Political Press*, Vol. I (Vol. II, 1984).

G.E. Mingay (ed.), *The Victorian Countryside.*

C **Mar:** 30th, President Reagan wounded in assassination attempt in Washington, D.C.
—, 364 academic economists sign memorial calling on British government to abandon hard-line monetarism.

D **Apr:** 1st, introduction of food rationing in Poland;
—, heavy fighting in Beirut between Arab peace-keeping force and Christian militias;
7th, referendum in Philippines grants sweeping powers to President Marcos;
9th, Bobby Sands, imprisoned I.R.A. hunger-striker, wins by-election in Fermanagh and South Tyrone, Northern Ireland;
10th (–12th), severe riots in inner London area of Brixton;
17th, Polish farmers win right to form independent trade union;
23rd, British unemployment exceeds 2.5 million;
28th, Foreign Office advises British nationals to leave Lebanon as conflict intensifies between clients of Syria and Israel;
30th, Central Committee of Polish Communist Party approves programme of moderate reforms.

E **May:** 5th, riots in Northern Ireland, following the death of I.R.A. hunger-striker Bobby Sands in Maze prison;
6th, U.S. expels all Libyan diplomats because of Libyan support for international terrorism;
8th (–27th), U.S. peace envoy, Philip Habib, tours Middle East;
10th, François Mitterrand becomes first Socialist President of France with 51.7 per cent of vote to Valéry Giscard d'Estaing's 48.3 per cent;
13th, gun man seriously wounds Pope John Paul II in assassination attempt in St. Peter's Square (*July* 22nd, Mehmet Ali Agca gaoled for life in Italy);
17th, Syrian artillery shells Christian suburbs of Beirut;
21st, President Mitterrand appoints Pierre Mauroy as French Premier;
22nd, in Britain, conviction of Peter Sutcliffe, 'the Yorkshire Ripper', for murder of 13 women;
26th, Italian government falls after revelations of infiltration by Masonic Lodge 'Propaganda 2' (Italy bans secret societies, *July* 24th);
30th, assassination of President Zia ur-Rahman of Bangladesh (succeeded by Vice-President Abdus Sattar).

F **Jun:** 8th, Israeli air force bombs Osirak nuclear reactor under construction near Baghdad (19th, U.N. Security Council condemns attack after Iraq denies military use);
11th, Fianna Fail loses general election in Eire (30th, Garret FitzGerald becomes Prime Minister at head of Fine Gael-Labour coalition);
12th, General Jaruzelski reconstructs Polish government to tackle economic crisis;
16th, in Britain, Liberals and S.D.P. issue joint statement of principles, *A Fresh Start for Britain*;
21st, Socialists win landslide victory in second round of elections to French National Assembly (23rd, new government includes three Communists);
22nd, in Iran, Ayatollah Khomeini denounces President Bani-Sadr (who flees to France, 29th);
28th, in Iran, bomb attack on offices of Islamic Republican Party kills 74 in Teheran, including Chief Justice Ayatollah Beheshti.
30th, British government announces that the armed survey ship H.M.S. *Endurance*, on patrol in the South Atlantic, will be withdrawn and not replaced.

Q Scholarship (*cont.*)

P.J. Waller, *Democracy and Sectarianism: A Political and Social History of Liverpool, 1868–1939*.
Kenneth O. Morgan, *Rebirth of a Nation: Wales 1880–1980*.
Avner Offer, *Property and Politics 1870–1914*.
Martin J. Wiener, *English Culture and the Decline of the Industrial Spirit, 1850–1980*.

R Philosophy and Religion

Jürgen Habermas, *The Theory of Communicative Action*.
R.M. Hare, *Moral Thinking*.
Alasdair MacIntyre, *After Virtue*.
The General Synod of the Church of England votes overwhelmingly to recognise the sacraments of the Free Churches and their women ministers and to allow women to be ordained to the Anglican diaconate.
The Unification Church ('Moonies') loses a libel action against *The Daily Mail* concerning an article about church treatment of members and the wealth of founder Sun Myung Moon.
The Salvation Army withdraws from the World Council of Churches because of its financial support for African guerrilla movements.

S Art, Sculpture, Fine Arts and Architecture

Painting:

Following the restoration of democracy in Spain, Picasso's *Guernica* is taken from the Museum of Modern Art, New York, to the Prado in Madrid.
'20th-century British Sculpture' exhibition at the Whitechapel Gallery, London.
'A New Spirit in Painting', exhibition at the Royal Academy, London.
Figuration Libre movement, France, based on comic strips and graffiti.
Francesco Clemente, *Toothache*.
Richard Long, *Terracotta Circle*.
David Salle, *An Illustrator Was There*.

Sculpture:

Carl André, *Niner*.
Tony Cragg, *Britain Seen From the North*.

Architecture:

Denys Lasdun, Redhouse and Softly, European Investment Bank, Luxembourg.
Tom Wolfe, *From Bauhaus to Our House*.

T Music

György Kurtag, *Messages of the Late Miss R.V. Troussova*.
Arvo Pärt, *Passio domini nostri Jesu Christi secundum Johannem*.
Alfred Schnittke, 3rd Symphony.
Karlheinz Stockhausen, *Donnerstag aus Licht* (opera).

U Literature

William Golding, *Rights of Passage*.
Alasdair Gray, *Lanark*.
Minoru Oda, *Hiroshima*.
Salman Rushdie, *Midnight's Children*.
Martin Cruz Smith, *Gorky Park*.
Paul Theroux, *The Mosquito Coast*.
D.M. Thomas, *The White Hotel*.

G **Jul**: 3rd, clashes between National Front supporters and Asian immigrants in Southall, London;

4th (–6th), in Britain, arson and riots in Toxteth district of Liverpool; disturbances follow in Manchester, Brixton (London), Reading, Hull and elsewhere;

16th, in Britain, Roy Jenkins narrowly fails to win Warrington by-election for the S.D.P.;

17th, Israeli jets attack Palestinian areas of Beirut (29th, Israel and P.L.O. agree ceasefire after two weeks of fighting in southern Lebanon);

23rd, Polish government announces plans to cut rations and quadruple food prices;

24th, Muhammad Ali Rajai elected President of Iran;

—, flood in Szechuan province of China makes up to 1.5 million people homeless;

27th, British Prime Minister, Mrs. Thatcher assigns £500 million to special employment measures and job training schemes;

29th, the Prince of Wales and Lady Diana Spencer marry in St. Paul's Cathedral, London.

H **Aug**: 3rd (–5th), 'Solidarity' blockades Warsaw city centre in protest at food shortages;

—, strike by U.S. air traffic controllers;

6th, U.S. air traffic controllers are dismissed for not complying with Presidential order to return to work;

9th, President Reagan announces decision to manufacture neutron bomb;

13th, East Germany officially celebrates 20th anniversary of Berlin Wall;

16th, U.S.S.R. postpones Polish debt repayments and increases supplies of raw materials and consumer goods to Poland;

19th, U.S. air force shoots down two Libyan fighters during naval exercises off the coast of Libya in the Gulf of Sirte;

20th, Bank of England abolishes the Minimum Lending Rate;

23rd, Soviet Politburo exhorts Polish government to adhere to Leninist principles;

26th, P.W. Botha confirms that South African troops are fighting guerrillas in Angola;

30th, bomb in Teheran kills President Rajai and Prime Minister Bahonar of Iran.

J **Sep**: 4th, Warsaw Pact begins largest military exercises in Baltic since the Second World War;

—, anti-government demonstrations by Moslem fundamentalists in Cairo;

—, assassination of French ambassador to Lebanon in Beirut;

5th (–10th), first national congress of 'Solidarity' union in Gdansk;

9th, French government announces nationalisation of 36 banks and 11 industrial groups;

14th, Norman Tebbit becomes British Employment Secretary and James Prior Northern Ireland Secretary in reshuffle to diminish influence of 'Wets' in Cabinet;

16th, British Liberal Party conference votes for electoral alliance with S.D.P.;

20th, Belize becomes independent within the Commonwealth;

25th, Mrs. Sandra Day O'Connor appointed the first woman Justice of U.S. Supreme Court;

27th, Denis Healey narrowly defeats A.N. Wedgwood Benn in vote for deputy leadership of British Labour Party (Healey wins 50.426 per cent of votes, Benn 49.574 per cent);

28th, panic falls in share prices in Hong Kong, Tokyo and London.

K **Oct**: 2nd, Hojatoleslam Ali Khameini elected President of Iran (29th, Hosein Musavi becomes Prime Minister);

3rd, I.R.A. hunger-strike at Maze prison, Northern Ireland, ends after 10 deaths;

4th, in Britain, first national conference of S.D.P. opens at Perth;

U **Literature** (*cont.*)

Mario Vargas Llosa, *The War of the End of the World.*

Publication of Terence Kilmartin's reworking of Scott Moncrieff's translation of Proust's *Remembrance of Things Past.*

V **The Press**

Rupert Murdoch buys *The Times* and other *Times* newspapers in Britain.

Now! magazine in Britain is closed after 18 months (*Mar.*).

Rupert 'Tiny' Rowland's Lonrho company purchases *The Observer* in Britain (effective from *July*).

The Washington Star ceases publication (*Aug.*).

W **Drama and Entertainment**

Edward Bond, *Restoration.*

Nell Dunn, *Steaming.*

Harvey Fierstein, *Torch Song Trilogy.*

Charles Fuller, *A Soldier's Play.*

Tom Kempinski, *Duet for One.*

Ariane Mnouchkine, *Mephisto.*

Sharon Pollock, *Blood Relations.*

Arnold Wesker, *Caritas.*

Cats.

Films:

Jean-Jacques Beneix's *Diva.*

Yilmaz Guney's *Yol.*

Louis Malle, *Atlantic City, My Dinner with Andre.*

Karel Reisz's *The French Lieutenant's Woman.*

Andrzej Wajda's *Man of Iron.*

Chariots of Fire.

On Golden Pond.

Television:

Brideshead Revisited.

Cagney and Lacey.

Dynasty.

Only Fools and Horses.

Popular music:

Grandmaster Flash and the Furious Five, 'Adventures on the Wheels of Steel', a seminal hip-pop single.

Brian Eno, *My Life in the Bush of Ghosts.*

Suicide, *Half Alive.*

X **Sport**

First London Marathon held, with 7,055 competitors (*Mar.* 29th).

In Britain, *Shergar*, ridden by Walter Swinburn, wins the Derby by 10 lengths, the longest winning distance yet in the 20th century (*June* 3rd).

In the Third Test at Headingley, England beat Australia by 18 runs after being forced to follow on, only the second time this has happened in 104 years of Test cricket (*July* 21st).

In nine days (*Aug.*), Steve Ovett and Sebastian Coe establish three new world records for the mile. The record is cut by over 1 second to 3 minutes 47.53 seconds.

First English soccer League match to be played on artificial turf (at Loftus Road ground of Queen's Park Rangers, London).

1981 (Oct. – Dec.)

K **Oct:** 6th, assassination of President Sadat of Egypt (succeeded by Hosni Mubarak, 14th);
18th, Panhellenic Socialist Movement wins Greek general election (21st, Andreas Papandreou forms first Socialist government in Greek history);
—, General Jaruzelski, Prime Minister of Poland, succeeds Stanislaw Kania as First Secretary of Polish Communist Party;
19th, British government sells National Freight Corporation to management-led consortium (sells 50 per cent of shares in Cable and Wireless Ltd., 30th);
22nd (–23rd), world summit on North-South relations on Cancun Island, Mexico, fails to agree measures to help developing countries;
23rd, Presbyterian Church of South Africa conducts mixed race marriages in defiance of apartheid laws;
24th, 150,000 attend Campaign for Nuclear Disarmament rally in London.

L **Nov:** 1st, Antigua and Barbuda become independent within the Commonwealth;
—, Tunisian government wins all seats in first multi-party elections since 1959;
4th, crisis talks in Poland between General Jaruzelski, Lech Walesa and Polish primate Cardinal Glemp;
6th, Mrs. Thatcher and Garret FitzGerald, meeting in London, agree to establish Anglo-Irish Inter-governmental Council (23rd, protest strikes in Northern Ireland);
14th, in Northern Ireland, I.R.A. murder Rev. Robert Radford, Unionist M.P. for Belfast South;
—, Gambia and Senegal form confederation of Senegambia;
18th, President Reagan offers to cancel deployment of Cruise and Pershing missiles in Europe if U.S.S.R. dismantles missiles targeted on Western Europe;
20th, U.S.S.R. contracts to supply Siberian natural gas to West Germany;
25th, Arab summit conference in Fez quickly reaches deadlock over Saudi Arabian peace plan for Middle East;
26th, in Britain, Mrs. Shirley Williams wins Crosby by-election for S.D.P.;
28th, National Party wins very narrow victory in New Zealand general election;
29th, terrorist bomb kills 64 in Damascus, Syria.

M **Dec:** 1st, U.S.–Soviet talks on arms limitation open in Geneva;
2nd, British Chancellor Sir Geoffrey Howe announces public spending increases to be financed by higher national insurance contributions, N.H.S. charges and rates;
—, Canadian House of Commons passes resolution to 'patriate' Canadian constitution from Britain;
9th, U.S.S.R. allows Lisa Alekseeva to emigrate after 17-day hunger-strike by her step-father Andrei Sakharov;
13th, imposition of martial law in Poland: mass detention and curbs on civil liberties and trade unions;
14th, Israel formally annexes the Golan Heights, occupied in 1967;
17th, British House of Lords rules that Greater London Council may not charge supplementary rate to subsidise public transport;
18th, reported suicide of Mehmet Shehu, Prime Minister of Albania (later denounced as U.S.-Soviet-Yugoslav spy);
22nd, General Leopoldo Galtieri becomes President of Argentina;
29th, President Reagan introduces economic sanctions against U.S.S.R. for compelling Poland to adopt martial law;
31st, Lieutenant Jerry Rawlings stages his second military coup in Ghana.

T **Statistics**

Populations (in mill.): China, 991.3; India, 690.2; U.S.S.R., 268.0; U.S., 229.8; Indonesia, 149.5; Brazil 120.5; Japan, 117.6; Bangladesh, 90.7; Nigeria, 87.6; Pakistan, 84.5; Mexico, 71.2; West Germany, 61.7; Italy, 56.2; Great Britain and Northern Ireland, 56.0; France, 54.0.

Z **Births and Deaths**

Jan. 5th Harold Clayton Urey d. (87).
Jan. 23rd Samuel Barber d. (70).
Apr. 8th Omar Bradley d. (88).
Apr. 12th Joe Louis d. (66).
May 30th Zia ur-Rahman d. (45).
July 1st Marcel Lajos Breuer d. (79).
Sept. 12th Eugenio Montale d. (84).
Oct. 6th Anwar Sadat d. (62).
Oct. 16th Moshe Dayan d. (66).
Nov. 22nd Hans Krebs d. (81).

1982 (Jan. – Mar.) Martial Law in Poland—Anglo-Argentine War over the Falkland Islands—Israel invades Lebanon

A **Jan**: 4th, E.C. foreign ministers denounce imposition of martial law in Poland;
8th, Spain agrees to end blockade of Gibraltar (*Dec.* 15th, frontier opened);
15th, chiefs of Spain's armed forces replaced;
16th, Britain and the Vatican resume full diplomatic relations after break of over 400 years;
19th, Polish authorities announce increases in food prices of between 200 per cent and 400 per cent from *Feb.* lst;
21st, members of Britain's National Union of Mineworkers (N.U.M.) vote to accept a wage increase of 9.3 per cent;
24th, Egypt's President Mubarak announces policy of non-alignment and seeks assistance from U.S.S.R. on industrial projects;
26th, according to government statistics, unemployment in Britain passes 3 million;
29th, U.S. government agrees to cover Poland's debt payments;
31st, Israel agrees to U.N. peace-keeping force in Sinai;
—, curfew imposed in Gdansk following riots over price increases.

B **Feb**: 1st, President Reagan announces emergency assistance for government of El Salvador;
2nd, anti-government rising by Moslem Brotherhood in Hamah, Syria;
4th, British company Laker Airways, providing cheap trans-Atlantic flights, collapses with debts of £270 million;
9th, E.C. and U.S. announce end to East–West talks in Madrid until martial law in Poland is lifted;
—, British Prime Minister Thatcher, in House of Commons, defends plan to scrap the South Atlantic survey ship H.M.S. *Endurance*;
13th, five former National Guardsmen are held in El Salvador pending further investigations into murder of three Catholic nuns and a lay woman worker in 1980;
17th, Joshua Nkomo dismissed from Zimbabwe government;
—, 4,000 arrested in raids by security services in Poland;
19th, court martial opens in Spain of 32 officers charged with involvement in 1981 attempted coup (*June* 3rd, sentenced to 30 years' imprisonment);
—, receivers appointed to failed government-supported De Lorean Car Company in Northern Ireland;
23rd, Japanese government refuses Poland new credits;
—, members of Ugandan Freedom Movement attack capital Kampala;
25th, U.N. votes to increase peace-keeping force in southern Lebanon;

C **Mar**: 1st, General Jaruzelski visits Moscow for talks on situation in Poland;
4th, President Mitterrand indicates support for Palestinian state in speech to Israeli Knesset;
9th, British Chancellor Howe in Budget increases tax allowances, raises pensions by 11 per cent, increases excise duties, reduces employers' National Insurance surcharge and announces Public Sector Borrowing Requirement of £9,500 million (3.5 per cent of G.D.P.);
10th, U.S. imposes embargo on Libyan oil imports and on exports of high-technology goods to Libya;
11th, British government announces intention to purchase Trident II submarine-launched missile system to replace Polaris;
15th, President Daniel Ortega suspends Nicaraguan constitution and declares one-month state of siege;
16th, President Brezhnev announces halt of deployment of SS-20 missiles west of Urals;

O Politics, Economics, Law and Education

British White Paper *Northern Ireland: A Framework for Devolution* (*Apr.* 4th).

Local Government Finance Act increases British central government's control over local authority spending.

Braniff International Corp. is first U.S. airline to file for bankruptcy (*May* 13th).

U.N. Law of Sea Conference agrees international convention governing use and exploitation of sea and seabed (*Apr.* 30th).

Equal Rights Amendment fails to secure ratification of sufficient number of states to ensure inclusion in U.S. constitution (*June* 30th).

U.S. Supreme Court overturns judgement making N.A.A.C.P. liable for damages arising from business boycott (*July* 2nd).

British Criminal Justice Act creates new system of custodial offences for young offenders, but removes imprisonment and Borstal detention as punishments.

European Court of Human Rights ruling allows British parents to refuse use of corporal punishment on children at school (*Feb.* 25th).

European Court of Human Rights condemns use of the tawse in Scottish schools.

P Science, Technology, Discovery, etc.

C.D. (compact disc) players go on sale.

The first 'clone' of an IBM computer is produced, using the same operating system as the IBM personal computer.

First flight by Boeing 757 airliner.

Soft landings on Venus by U.S.S.R. space probes Venera XIII (*Mar.* 1st) and XIV (*Nov.* 4th).

U.S. orbiter Columbia makes the first deployment of a satellite from the shuttle (*Nov.* 11th).

Astronomers at Villanova University in Pennsylvania announce the discovery of rings around Neptune.

A gene controlling growth is transferred from a rat to a mouse; the mouse grows to double size.

A new kind of artificial heart keeps a patient alive at the University of Utah Medical Center for 112 days (implanted in *Dec.*).

Scientists at Darmstadt announce the production of element 109 (*Aug.* 29th).

Q Scholarship

The Cambridge Ancient History, Vol. III–, 2nd edn (–).

The Cambridge History of Classical Literature, Vol. II (Vol. I, 1985).

Jacques Gernet, *A History of Chinese Civilization.*

James Campbell (ed.), *The Anglo-Saxons.*

K. Wrightson, *English Society, 1580–1680.*

Roy Porter, *English Society in the Eighteenth Century.*

R.C.O. Matthews, C.H. Feinstein, J.C. Odling-Smee, *British Economic Growth 1856–1973.*

R Philosophy and Religion

A.J. Ayer, *Philosophy in the Twentieth Century.*

Richard Rorty, *The Consequences of Pragmatism.*

Final Report of the Anglican-Roman Catholic International Commission (ARCIC).

Church of England working party produces the report *The Church and the Bomb*, supporting unilateral nuclear disarmament.

General Synod of the Church of England fails to gain necessary majority for a proposed covenant of unity with the Methodists, the United Reformed Church and the Moravians.

C **Mar:** 17th, Zimbabwe Prime Minister Robert Mugabe orders drafting of new constitution;
19th, Argentine scrap metal dealer lands on island of South Georgia and raises Argentine flag;
21st, rioting on occupied West Bank when Israel decides to disband elected Palestinian council of El Bireh;
23rd, military coup in Guatemala;
24th, military coup in Bangladesh;
25th, in Britain, Roy Jenkins of S.D.P. wins Glasgow Hillhead in by-election from Conservatives.

D **Apr:** 2nd, Argentine troops invade Falkland Islands; Britain breaks diplomatic relations with Argentina;
3rd, U.N. Security Council Resolution 502 demands withdrawal of Argentine forces from Falklands;
4th, Lord Carrington resigns as British Foreign Secretary, succeeded by Francis Pym;
—, first ships of British Royal Navy Task Force sail for Falklands;
7th, U.S. Secretary of State Alexander Haig offers to mediate in Falklands dispute;
11th, E.C. imposes economic sanctions on Argentina;
12th, Britain declares 200-mile maritime exclusion zone round Falkland Islands;
15th, five Moslem fundamentalists executed in Cairo for involvement in assassination of President Sadat;
16th, Queen Elizabeth proclaims new Canadian constitution, severing Canada's last colonial links with Britain;
19th, British government rejects Haig plan to resolve Falklands conflict (29th, Argentine government follows suit);
25th, British forces recapture South Georgia;
28th, Poland's Military Council of National Salvation announces release of 800 detainees;
30th, Reagan administration imposes economic sanctions on Argentina and offers to supply war materials to Britain.

E **May:** 1st, 50,000 Solidarity supporters demonstrate against martial law (4th, military controls tightened);
—, British air force bombs Port Stanley airport on Falkland Islands;
2nd, British submarine H.M.S. *Conqueror* sinks Argentine cruiser *General Belgrano*, killing 368;
3rd, Israeli Prime Minister Begin announces that Israel will assert sovereignty over occupied West Bank;
4th, Argentine missiles sink British destroyer H.M.S. *Sheffield*; 20 killed;
6th, Conservatives make large gains in British local elections;
7th, British government warns that all Argentine forces more than 12 miles off Argentina are liable to attack;
17th, eight E.C. countries renew sanctions against Argentina; lifted by Italy and Ireland;
18th, President Brezhnev proposes freeze on strategic arms;
21st, British troops land on East Falkland Island and establish bridgehead at Port San Carlos;
22nd, Pope celebrates Mass for Peace in Rome with British and Argentine cardinals;
28th, British troops recapture Port Darwin and Goose Green, taking 1,400 Argentines prisoner;
—, (–*June* 2nd), first-ever Papal visit to Britain.

R **Philosophy and Religion** (*cont.*)

A federal court in Little Rock, Arkansas declares it unconstitutional to teach creationism on a par with evolutionary theory.

Israeli invasion of Lebanon produces mixed reactions in both Israel and in the world Jewish community.

S **Art, Sculpture, Fine Arts and Architecture**

Painting:

Young British sculptors gain notoriety – Tony Cragg, Richard Deacon, Bill Woodrow, Barry Flanagan.

'Zeitgeist', exhibition at the Martin Gropius Bau, Berlin.

Switzerland and Britain collaborate on largest retrospective exhibition of the works of Jean Tinguely.

Georg Baselitz, *Last Supper in Dresden*.

Anish Kapoor, *White Sand, Red Millet, Many Flowers*.

Julian Schnabel, *Humanity Asleep*.

Sculpture:

Daniel Buren, *Installation*, for the Kassel Documenta.

Jenny Holzer, *Times Square*.

Architecture:

Kisho Kurokawa, Saitama Prefectural Museum of Art, Japan.

Richard Rogers, Inmos Microprocessor Factory, Gwent, Wales.

T **Music**

Luciano Berio, *La vera storia* (opera).

M. Kagel, *Rrrrrrr...*

William Mathias, *Lux Aeterna*.

Udo Zimmermann, *Die wundersame Schustersfrau* (opera).

U **Literature**

Isabel Allende, *The House of the Spirits*.

Andre Brink, *A Chain of Voices*.

Saul Bellow, *The Dean's December*.

Carlos Fuentes, *Distant Relations*.

Thomas Keneally, *Schindler's Ark*.

Primo Levi, *If Not Now, When?*

Harry Mulisch, *The Assault*.

V.S. Pritchett, *Collected Stories*.

John Updike, *Rabbit is Rich*.

Edmund White, *A Boy's Own Story*.

V **The Press**

Launch of *The Mail on Sunday* (*Oct.*).

W **Drama and Entertainment**

John Byrne, *The Slab Boys*.

Tadeusz Cantor, *The Dead Class*.

Caryl Churchill, *Top Girls*.

Michael Frayn, *Noises Off*.

Julian Mitchell, *Another Country*.

Neil Simon, *Brighton Beach Memoirs*.

F **Jun**: 3rd, Israel's Ambassador to Britain, Shlomo Argov, is shot and wounded in London street;
—, in Britain, Conservatives gain Merton, Mitcham and Morden in by-election;
4th, Israeli jets bomb guerrilla targets in Lebanon in retaliation for Argov shooting;
5th, Israeli armed forces invade Lebanon (6th, Israeli and Syrian forces clash in southern Lebanon; U.N. Security Council calls for halt to fighting);
7th, Israel carries out air attacks on Beirut, Sidon and Tyre;
—, rebel forces in Chad capture capital, Ndjamene, overthrowing regime of President Goukouni Oueddei;
8th, British landing ships *Sir Tristram* and *Sir Galahad* attacked in Bluff Cove, 40 killed;
11th, Israeli forces defeat Syrian armour around Lake Karoun;
13th, French government announces freeze of prices and incomes following devaluation of franc (to last until *Oct.* 31st);
14th, Argentine forces surrender at Port Stanley, ending Falklands War; 255 Britons and 652 Argentines died in Falklands conflict;
—, Israeli forces surround 6,000 P.L.O. guerrillas in West Beirut;
17th, President Galtieri resigns; replaced by General Alfredo Saint Jean;
22nd, leaders of three Kampuchean factions meet in Kuala Lumpur to form opposition government-in-exile;
—, U.S. government extends prohibition on supplying materials for Euro-Siberian gas pipeline to overseas companies manufacturing under licence;
23rd, Argentine air force and navy commanders resign from military junta on appointment of General Reynaldo Bignone as President;
25th, U.S. Secretary of State, Alexander Haig resigns; succeeded by George Shultz;
27th, Israel demands surrender of P.L.O guerrillas in West Beirut (29th, offers to allow them to leave Beirut with arms).

G **Jul**: 2nd, in Britain, Roy Jenkins elected leader of S.D.P.;
4th (–18th), British rail drivers belonging to A.S.L.E.F. union on strike in dispute about introduction of 'flexible rosters' (union eventually accepts rosters);
6th, Lord Franks appointed to chair committee of British Privy Councillors to investigate background to Falklands invasion;
11th, Argentina recognizes de facto cessation of hostilities with Britain (12th, British government declares end to hostilities in South Atlantic);
13th, Iranian troops enter Iraq aiming, to take Basra; offensive is repulsed;
16th, General Jaruzelski announces changes in leadership of Polish Communist Party;
17th, Israeli Prime Minister Begin gives P.L.O guerrillas in West Beirut 30 days to leave the city;
20th, P.L.O. offers acceptance of U.N. Security Council Resolution 242 (recognizing Israel's right to exist) in return for U.S. recognition of P.L.O. (25th, Palestinian leader Arafat signs document accepting Resolution 242; 26th, U.S. refuses to recognize P.L.O.);
—, 10 British soldiers killed in I.R.A. bomb attacks in Hyde Park and Regent's Park, London;
21st, Polish government releases 1,227 people from detention but rules out early end to martial law;
23rd, International Whaling Commission votes for complete ban on commercial whaling by 1985;
26th, Falklands Thanksgiving Service at St. Paul's Cathedral, London, after which Archbishop Runcie is criticized for his even-handed sermon;
29th, Arab League announces P.L.O.'s intention to leave West Beirut.

W **Drama and Entertainment** (*cont.*)

Tom Stoppard, *The Real Thing*.

Britain's Royal Shakespeare Company moves into its new London home, the Barbican Theatre.

Films:

Richard Attenborough's *Gandhi*, which sets a world record for the number of extras.

Ingmar Bergman's *Fanny and Alexander*.

Jean-Luc Godard's *Passion*.

Werner Herzog's *Fitzcarraldo*.

Ridley Scott's *Bladerunner*.

Steven Spielberg's *ET*.

Daniel Vigne's *The Return of Martin Guerre*.

Television:

Cheers.

Alan Bleasdale's *Boys from the Blackstuff*.

St. Elsewhere.

Alec Guinness in *Smiley's People*.

Start of broadcasts by Britain's Channel 4 television station (*Nov.* 2nd); also of S4C, a station transmitting some programmes in Welsh.

Popular music:

Simon and Garfunkel's reunion concert in Central Park.

Laurie Anderson, *Big Science*.

Michael Jackson, *Thriller*.

Prince, *1999*.

Richard and Linda Thompson, *Shoot Out the Lights*.

X **Sport**

15 England cricketers banned from Test cricket for three years for participation in a cricket tour of South Africa, breaking an international ban on sporting links.

The Australia rugby team wins all 22 matches on its tour of Britain and France.

The soccer World Cup is held in Spain; Italy beats West Germany 3–1 in the Final.

Daley Thompson of Britain wins the European decathlon title in Athens, setting a new world record of 8,743 points; he simultaneously holds the Olympic, Commonwealth and European decathlon titles.

Y **Statistics**

Railway mileage in operation: U.S., 168,000; U.S.S.R., 89,042; France, 21,364; West Germany, 17,657; Great Britain, 11,107; Italy, 10,039; Spain, 8,415; Sweden, 7,046; Turkey, 5,090; Finland, 3,785; Austria, 3,610; Norway, 2,635.

Number of civil aircraft: U.S., 1,136; Great Britain, 187; West Germany, 121; Spain, 88; Finland, 86; Italy, 61; Holland, 52; Switzerland, 50; Greece, 44; France, 36; Portugal, 31; Belgium, 26; Turkey, 22; Eire, 19; Austria, 16; Iceland, 14; Luxembourg, 9.

Unemployment rates (percentage of working population): Australia, 7.2; Belgium, 13.8; Canada, 11.0; Denmark, 10.0; Eire, 16.5; Finland, 5.9; France, 8.0; West Germany, 7.5; Great Britain and Northern Ireland, 13.1; Greece, 3.2; Holland, 12.6; Italy, 9.1; Japan, 2.4; Spain, 16.3; Sweden, 3.2; Yugoslavia, 12.4; U.S., 9.7.

H **Aug**: 4th, Israel intensifies bombardment of West Beirut;
6th, Italian authorities order liquidation of country's largest privately owned bank, the Banco Ambrosiano of Milan;
9th, gunmen attack Jewish restaurant in Paris, killing six;
12th, E.C. protests against President Reagan's embargo on use of U.S. technology in construction of West European-Soviet gas pipeline;
13th, in Poland riot police break up demonstrations by Solidarity supporters;
17th, China and U.S. agree gradual reduction in U.S. arms sales to Taiwan;
19th, Israeli Cabinet accepts U.S. plan to evacuate P.L.O. guerrillas and Syrian troops from Beirut (21st, first convoys of guerrillas leave for Cyprus; 30th, Yassir Arafat leaves for Tunisia);
23rd, Lebanese Chamber of Deputies elects leader of Christian Phalangists, Bashir Gemayel, President;
26th, in Poland Cardinal Glemp calls for release of Lech Walesa;
—, Argentine government lifts ban on political parties;
31st, demonstrations in Polish cities on second anniversary of founding of Solidarity.

J **Sep**: 1st, U.S. announces new Middle East peace proposals (2nd, rejected by Israel);
— (–12th), 12th Congress of Chinese Communist Party in Peking; Hua Kuo-feng, who had succeeded Chairman Mao, is removed from Politburo;
6th (–9th), Polish dissidents occupy Polish embassy in Berne, taking 13 hostages and demanding end to martial law; siege ended by Swiss commandos;
—, troops in El Salvador accused of killing 300 unarmed civilians during anti-guerrilla campaign in San Vicente province;
10th, Argentine Navy and Air Force agree to rejoin military junta;
13th, report by Lord Shackleton on scope for economic development of the Falkland Islands recommends investment of £100 million;
14th, President-elect Bashir Gemayel of Lebanon killed in Beirut bomb explosion (23rd, brother Amin sworn in as President);
15th, President Brezhnev puts forward six-point plan for peace in Middle East;
16th, former Iranian Foreign Minister Sadeq Qotbzadeh executed for plotting overthrow of government;
17th, West German government collapses following withdrawal of Free Democrat ministers (*Oct.* 1st, Christian Democrat-Free Democrat coalition government formed under Helmut Kohl);
18th, over 800 Palestinians killed after Christian Phalangist militiamen enter West Beirut refugee camps (25th, protests in Israel over Beirut massacre; 28th, Prime Minister Begin agrees to independent three-man board of inquiry into massacre);
19th, Social Democrats win Swedish general election;
25th, Mrs. Thatcher attends talks in Peking on future of Hong Kong;
26th, Israeli troops withdraw from West Beirut; replaced by peace-keeping force of French, Italian and U.S. troops.

K **Oct**: 2nd, Inland Telegram service in U.K. ends;
5th, Lebanese army moves through Beirut; 1,441 arrested;
7th, record day's trading on New York Stock Exchange; 147,070,000 shares change hands;
8th, new law in Poland bans Solidarity and forbids setting up of new trade unions;
10th, U.S. imposes trade sanctions on Poland;
11th, Sikhs besiege Indian Parliament in New Delhi following murders of Sikhs in Punjab state;
12th, P.L.O. leader Arafat holds talks with King Hussein of Jordan over proposed establishment of Palestinian state confederated with Jordan;

z **Births and Deaths**

Feb. 6th Ben Nicholson d. (87).
Feb. 17th Thelonius Monk d. (61).
Mar. 8th R.A. Butler d. (79).
May 12th Humphrey Searle d. (66).
June 10th Rainer Fassbinder d. (36).
June 12th Dame Marie Rambert d. (94).
June 29th Pierre Balmain d. (68).
Aug. 5th John Charnley d. (70).
Sept. 1st Wladyslaw Gomulka d. (77).
Sept. 14th Grace Kelly d. (53).
Oct. 18th Pierre Mendès-France d. (75).
Nov. 5th Jacques Tati d. (74).
Nov. 10th Leonid Brezhnev d. (75).
Dec. 20th Artur Rubinstein d. (95).

K **Oct**: 13th, strikes in Polish ship yards end when military law enforced;
19th, Northern Ireland Office announces closure of De Lorean car plant; John De Lorean arrested in Los Angeles on drugs charges;
20th, Sinn Fein wins five seats in elections to Northern Ireland Assembly;
28th, Socialists win Spanish general election;
30th, new Portuguese constitution comes into force, military influence in government ended.

L **Nov**: 2nd, Democrats make large gains in U.S. mid-term elections; Republicans retain control of Senate;
—, British N.U.M. votes 61 per cent against strike action over pay and pit closures;
7th, military coup in Upper Volta;
10th, President Brezhnev dies (12th, Yuri Andropov elected First Secretary of Soviet Communist Party);
—, I.M.F. agrees credits of $3,480 million over three years to Mexico;
11th, bomb destroys Israeli military H.Q. in Tyre, Lebanon; 100 killed;
—, S.D.L.P. and Sinn Fein boycott opening of new Northern Ireland Assembly;
12th, Solidarity leader Lech Walesa released from detention;
16th, Sino–Soviet talks open in Moscow, first since 1969;
22nd, Ramiz Alia becomes new Albanian head of state, replacing Haxhi Lleshi;
26th, Central Council of P.L.O. rejects U.S. scheme for confederation with Jordan.

M **Dec**: 5th, Greater London Council invites Danny Morrison and Gerry Adams of Sinn Fein to London (8th, government bans them from entering the British mainland);
6th, in Northern Ireland, 17 killed in bomb explosion at public house in Ballykelly, County Londonderry;
7th, House of Representatives rejects President Reagan's request for $988 million to build and deploy first five of 100 M.X. missiles;
8th, military coup in Surinam;
12th, in Britain, 20,000 women encircle Greenham Common air base in protest against proposed siting of U.S. Cruise missiles there;
14th, British Defence White Paper proposes expenditure of £1,000 million to make good equipment losses in Falklands War;
—, in Eire, Dr. Garret Fitzgerald is elected Prime Minister at head of Fine Gael–Labour coalition government;
15th, Health Service unions in Britain call off eight-month pay dispute;
—, I.M.F. agrees credits of $4.5 billion to Brazil to enable it to service its foreign debts;
16th, anti-government rally in Buenos Aires;
19th, Poland's Council of State announces suspension of martial law from 31st;
20th. O.P.E.C. meeting in Vienna ends without agreement on production quotas; differences between Iran and Saudi Arabia;
21st, Soviet leader Andropov offers to reduce number of intermediate-range missiles in Europe if U.S. abandons plans to deploy Cruise and Pershing II missiles in West Germany.

Cruise Missiles deployed in Britain—U.S.S.R. shoots down Korean jumbo jet—U.S. invades Grenada

A **Jan:** 1st, Britain bans Danish trawlers from fishing in British waters (7th, Captain Kent Kirk, fisherman and M.E.P., fined £30,000 for breaking ban; 18th, dispute settled);
6th, in reshuffle of British cabinet Michael Heseltine becomes Defence Secretary;
—, Indian government announces elections for state of Assam, despite opposition from local Hindus;
13th, Saudi Arabia re-establishes diplomatic links with Libya;
16th, U.S.S.R. Foreign Minister visits West Germany;
17th, Nigeria orders expulsion of 2 million illegal immigrants;
18th, in Britain, Franks Report published; exonerates Mrs. Thatcher's government of blame for Argentine junta's decision to invade Falklands Islands on 2 April 1982;
—, Group of Ten leading countries agree increase in funds of 'General Arrangements to Borrow' unit of I.M.F. from $7.1 billion to $19 billion;
19th, South Africa re-imposes direct rule on South-West Africa (Namibia);
24th, 32 Italian Red Brigade terrorists jailed for kidnap and murder of Aldo Moro in 1978;
27th, U.S.–Soviet talks resume in Geneva with U.S.S.R. proposing nuclear-free zone for central Europe;
31st, President Reagan proposes summit meeting with Soviet leader Andropov; rejected.

B **Feb:** 8th, Kahane Commission on Beirut massacre (*Sept.* 18th, 1982) condemns Israeli government and recommends dismissal of Defence Minster Sharon; (11th, Sharon resigns);
—, Hitachi Ltd. pleads guilty in U.S. federal court to charges of conspiracy to obtain classified information on I.B.M. computers;
10th, Church of England General Synod votes against unilateral nuclear disarmament;
—, European leaders urge flexibility in arms talks between U.S. and U.S.S.R.;
15th, Christian Phalangist militia withdraws from Beirut, giving Lebanese government control over the city;
19th, Joshua Nkomo held by Zimbabwean police;
21st, Soviet Prime Minister Tikhonov and Greek Prime Minister Papandreou hold talks; issue joint communique in support of nuclear-free zones in Europe;
24th, in India, 1,500 reported dead in violence during local elections in Assam;
—, in Britain, Liberals win Bermondsey by-election from Labour;
—, western banks underwrite $5 billion loan to Mexico; also short-term loan of $433 million;
28th, in Britain, Yorkshire and South Wales miners called out on strike to protest against planned pit closures;
—, I.M.F. grants Brazil loan of $5.4 billion.

C **Mar:** 1st, Sino–Soviet talks resume;
3rd, British National Union of Mineworkers executive calls ballot for national strike;
5th, Labour Party wins Australian general election;
6th, Christian Democrats win general election in West Germany; Green Party wins 24 seats in Bundestag;
9th, Joshua Nkomo flees Zimbabwe (*Aug.* 15th, returns);
10th, shipyard workers in Gdansk demand restoration of Solidarity union;
14th, O.P.E.C. agrees to cut oil prices for first time since formation in 1961; price of Saudi light crude reduced from $34 a barrel to $29;

O Politics, Economics, Law and Education

Number of British M.P.s increases to 650; pay of M.P.s is linked to civil service rates.

British government White Paper proposes abolition of Greater London Council and metropolitan counties (*Oct.* 7th).

N.H.S. hospitals in Britain are obliged to allow private contractors to tender for cleaning, catering and laundry services (*Sept.* 5th).

British government announces end to opticians' monopoly on sale of spectacles (*Nov.* 28th).

Decision of U.S. Supreme Court limits power of state and local governments to restrict access to legal abortions (*June* 15th).

U.S. Congress votes to make birthday of Martin Luther King Jr. a federal holiday (*Oct.* 19th).

Wearing of seat belts by front-seat car passengers made compulsory in Britain (*Jan.* 31st).

P Science, Technology, Discovery, etc.

IBM produces the first personal computer with a built-in hard disc.

Apple devises a computer programme featuring 'pull-down' menus with instructions given by means of a 'mouse' control box.

Japan launches the 'fifth generation' computer project, aiming to produce a machine capable of 1 billion computations per second.

Launch of Infrared Astronomical Satellite (*Jan.* 25th), designed to detect infrared radiation from objects in space.

U.S. space probe Pioneer X is first man-made object to leave solar system (*June* 13th).

A mission by space shuttle *Challenger* (*June* 18th–24th) includes first U.S. woman to go into space, Sally Ride.

U.S.S.R. probes Venera XV and XVI (launched on *June* 5th and 7th) enter orbit around Venus (*Oct.* 10th and 14th).

Observation of 'W' and 'Z' sub-atomic particles in experiments at C.E.R.N., Switzerland (*June*); the existence of these particles had been predicted as carriers of the weak nuclear force.

First experiments with Joint European Torus equipment at Culham, England, attempting to generate electricity by means of nuclear fusion.

A research team at the University of California at Los Angeles performs the first successful transfer of a human embryo.

Researchers isolate the hormone (produced by the heart) that regulates blood pressure (*June*; synthesized in *Aug.*).

Andrew W. Murray and Jack W. Szostak create the first artificial chromosome.

Fernand Daffos extracts the blood from a foetus and diagnoses disease in the foetus.

Researchers at the U.S. National Cancer Institute and at the Pasteur Institute in Paris isolate the virus thought to cause AIDS; it becomes known as the HIV virus.

Q Scholarship

Paul Ratchnevsky, *Genghis Khan: His Life and Legacy*.

Peter Clark, *The English Alehouse: A Social History 1200–1830*.

Maldwyn A. Jones, *The Limits of Liberty: American History 1607–1980*.

Final (48th) volume of W.S. Lewis (ed.), *Horace Walpole's Correspondence*.

C.A. Bayly, *Rulers, Townsmen and Bazaars: North Indian Society in the Age of British Expansion, 1770–1870*.

P.J. Waller, *Town, City, and Nation: England 1850–1914*.

John Campbell, *F.E. Smith*.

Alan Bullock, *Ernest Bevin: Foreign Secretary*.

C **Mar**: 15th, British Budget raises tax allowances by 14 per cent, 1.75 million people taken out of paying income tax, mortgage tax relief raised, Public Sector Borrowing Requirement projected at £8 billion;

17th, Chad seeks assistance of U.N. in border dispute with Libya;

21st, drought and famine reported over large parts of Ethiopia;

23rd, President Reagan proposes 'Star Wars' defence system for U.S., using satellites to detect enemy missiles and effect destruction;

28th, Chairman of British Steel, Ian MacGregor, appointed Chairman of National Coal Board;

31st, President Reagan halts sale of F-16 fighter aircraft to Israel until its troops are fully withdrawn from Lebanon.

D **Apr**: 10th, U.S. Middle East peace plan collapses when Jordan withdraws from talks;

12th, Vietnam claims victory over Kampuchean rebels;

13th, Harold Washington elected first black Mayor of Chicago;

18th, 39 die in bomb explosion at U.S. embassy in Beirut;

22nd, U.S. government announces readiness to negotiate long-term grain sales to U.S.S.R. in place of annual deals;

—, leader of Polish Solidarity trade union Lech Walesa returns to work at Lenin Shipyard, Gdansk;

24th, Socialist Party loses majority in Austrian elections (*May* 11th, coalition government formed under Dr. Fred Sinowatz);

—, Turkey's military government permits formation of political parties; ban remains on 150 leading politicians.

E **May**: 1st, police break up May Day demonstrations by Solidarity supporters across Poland;

4th, Iran outlaws Tudeh, Iranian Communist Party, and expels 18 Soviet diplomats;

—, President Reagan declares support for aim of Nicaraguan Contras to overthrow Sandinista government;

6th, Israel accepts U.S. plan for simultaneous withdrawal of Israeli and Syrian forces from Lebanon (13th, rejected by Syria);

16th, British Labour Party's election manifesto pledges to create 2.5 million jobs over five years, calls for unilateral nuclear disarmament and Britain's withdrawal from E.C. (18th, Conservative Party election manifesto promises further reforms in trade-union law, local government and nationalized industries);

17th, Israel and Lebanon sign agreement providing for withdrawal of Israeli troops from Lebanon within three months;

25th, U.S. agrees to export high-technology items to China;

—, U.S. Senate votes to release funds for M.X. missile project;

30th, 60-day state of emergency declared in Peru following increased terrorism.

F **Jun**: 1st, civilian members of Palestinian Al Fatah faction declare opposition to Arafat's leadership of P.L.O.;

3rd, in Britain, 752 arrested in protest outside U.S. Air Force Base at Upper Heyford, Oxfordshire;

7th, U.S. closes consulates in Nicaragua following expulsion of three U.S. diplomats;

9th, Conservatives win overall majority of 144 seats in British general election, taking 397 seats, against Labour, 209, Liberal-S.D.P. Alliance, 23, others 21 (Conservatives win 42.4 per cent of votes cast, Labour, 27.6, Liberal-S.D.P. Alliance, 25.4);

—, new centre-left coalition government under Mario Soares takes office in Portugal;

R Philosophy and Religion

Karl Popper, *Realism and the Aim of Science*.

General Synod of the Church of England rejects support for unilateral nuclear disarmament.

United Reformed Church becomes the first church in Britain officially to support unilateral nuclear disarmament.

A referendum in the Republic of Ireland results in a two to one majority for enshrining the existing legal ban on abortion in the national constitution.

In Iran Ayatollah Khomeini declares that Islam is a 'religion of the sword' and sends armed pilgrims to Mecca.

S Art, Sculpture, Fine Arts and Architecture

Painting:

Auctioneers Sotheby's bought by American Alfred Taubman.

'The Temporary Contemporary', exhibition at Los Angeles Museum of Contemporary Art, Los Angeles.

'The Essential Cubism', exhibition at the Tate Gallery, London.

Cindy Sherman, *Untitled* No. 131.

Sculpture:

Joseph Beuys, *Untitled Vitrine*.

Richard Deacon, *For Those Who Have Ears*.

Jenny Holzer, *New York City*.

Niki de Saint Phalle, Jean Tinguely, Fountain, Pompidou Centre, Paris.

Architecture:

Tadao Ando, Rokko Housing, Hyogo, Japan.

Sir Leslie Martin, Gulbenkian Foundation for Modern Art, Lisbon.

T Music

Leonard Bernstein, *A Quiet Place* (opera).

Harrison Birtwistle, *The Mask of Orpheus* (opera).

Pierre Boulez, *Répons*.

Hans Werner Henze, *The English Cat* (opera).

Witold Lutoslawski, 3rd Symphony.

Olivier Messiaen, *Saint Franc¸ois d'Assise* (opera).

U Literature

Isaac Asimov, *Foundation's Edge*.

Malcolm Bradbury, *Rates of Exchange*.

Ariel Dorfman, *Widows*.

Gabriel Garcia Márquez, *Chronicle of a Death Foretold*.

William Least-heat Moon, *Blue Highways*.

R.K. Narayan, *A Tiger for Malgudi*.

Salman Rushdie, *Shame*.

Alice Walker, *The Color Purple*.

V The Press

Stern magazine in Germany publishes extracts from 'The Hitler Diaries' (*May*), which are considered authentic by historian Hugh Trevor-Roper but are later exposed as a fake produced by a dealer in Nazi memorabilia.

Eddie Shah launches the Messenger group of free newspapers in Warrington, England, produced by nonunion workers; *Nov.* 29th, police break union picket.

F **Jun**: 11th, British Cabinet reshuffle: Nigel Lawson becomes Chancellor of the Exchequer;
Sir Geoffrey Howe, Foreign Secretary; Leon Brittan, Home Secretary; Cecil Parkinson, Trade and Industry Secretary.
12th, Michael Foot announces intention to resign as leader of British Labour Party;
14th, Roy Jenkins resigns leadership of British S.D.P. (21st, Dr. David Owen named as successor);
16th, Pope begins eight-day visit to Poland and has talks with General Jaruzelski and Lech Walesa (19th, Polish government warns Church to stay out of politics);
—, Yuri Andropov elected Chairman of Presidium of Supreme Soviet of U.S.S.R.;
17th, British annual rate of inflation falls to 3.7 per cent, lowest in 15 years;
24th, Yassir Arafat is ordered out of Syria; Syrian tanks besiege P.L.O. guerrilla bases in Lebanon;
27th, British Defence Secretary announces plan to build £215 million airport for Falkland Islands.

G **Jul**: 6th, British Defence White Paper re-states government's plan to deploy Cruise missiles at Greenham Common and Molesworth;
7th, British Chancellor announces cuts of £500 million in public expenditure;
12th, Secretary of State for Employment announces further reforms in British Trade Union law, including compulsory strike ballots;
—, China and Britain hold talks in Peking on future of Hong Kong;
16th, nine-nation committee of Organization of African Unity calls on foreign countries to end involvement in civil war in Chad;
18th, Presidents of Mexico, Colombia, Venezuala and Panama (Contadora Group) issue peace proposals for Central America;
19th, seven members of Greenpeace detained in Siberia in protest against whaling;
20th, Israeli Cabinet agrees on partial withdrawal of troops from Lebanon, redeployed south of Chouf Mountains;
21st, Polish government announces end to martial law and amnesty for political prisoners;
25th, Sri Lankan government imposes curfew following attacks on Tamil community (28th, ban imposed on political parties advocating partition);
26th, U.S.S.R. announces economic reforms allowing factory managers greater autonomy over wages, bonuses and technical innovations;
28th, U.S. House of Representatives votes to end covert aid to Nicaraguan contras by *Sept*. 30th.

H **Aug**: 2nd, Libyan planes bomb Faya-Largeau in Chad (7th, France sends paratroops to supplement 500 'military instructors' in Chad);
5th, evidence of 'supergrass' informer leads to jail sentences for 22 members of I.R.A. cell in Northern Ireland;
8th, military coup in Guatemala;
11th, Faya-Largeau in Chad falls to Libyan troops (19th, further 3,500 French troops sent to assist President Habre);
12th, President Zia of Pakistan announces elections for March 1985 and lifting of martial law;
—, Argentine government releases British assets frozen during Falklands War;
14th, French police seize large consignment of arms bound for I.R.A.;
19th, 40,000 Argentines protest at proposed amnesty for military personnel involved in human rights' violations during 1970s;
20th, President Reagan lifts ban on export of pipe-laying equipment to U.S.S.R.;
21st, Philippines opposition leader Benigno Aquino assassinated at Manila airport;

W Drama and Entertainment

Howard Barker, *Victory*.
Howard Brenton, *The Genius*.
David Hare, *A Map of the World*.
David Mamet, *Glengarry Glen Ross*.
Sam Shepard, *Fool for Love*.

Films:
Bill Forsyth's *Local Hero*.
Lawrence Kasdan's *The Big Chill*.
Gregory Nava's *El Norte*.
Euzhan Parcy's *Rue Cases Negres*.
Andrzej Wajda's *Danton*.

Television:
Alan Bennett's *An Englishman Abroad*.
Blackadder.
The Winds of War.
Launch of 'TV AM' breakfast-time station.

Popular music:
Frankie Goes to Hollywood, 'Relax'.
The Fall, *Perverted by Language*.
R.E.M., *Murmur*.
Z.Z. Top, *Eliminator*.

X Sport

Australia regains the Ashes (*Jan.* 7th).
In England, Lester Piggott, riding *Teenoso*, wins a record ninth Derby (*June* 1st).
The first five horses home in the Cheltenham Gold Cup in England are all trained by Michael Dickinson.
The first World Athletics Championships are held in Helsinki, free of boycotts. 157 nations compete; the U.S. leads the gold medal table with 8.
The U.S. fails to win the America's cup for the first since the race series began in 1870; the victor is the Australian yacht *Australia II*.

Y Statistics

Illiteracy in selected countries (percentage of adult population): Afghanistan, 81.8; Angola, 59.0; Argentina, 6.1; Bangladesh, 70.8; Brazil, 22.2; China, 34.5; Egypt, 61.8; Ethiopia, 37.6; India, 59.2; Indonesia, 32.7; Iran, 45.2; Israel, 8.2; Malaysia, 30.4; Mexico, 17.0; Pakistan, 73.8; Peru, 18.1; Saudia Arabia, 48.9; Sri Lanka, 13.2; Sudan, 68.6; Tunisia, 49.3.

Z Births and Deaths

Feb. 23rd Adrian Boult d. (93).
Feb. 25th Tennessee Williams d. (71).
Mar. 3rd Arthur Koestler d. (77).
Mar. 6th Donald Maclean d. (69).
Mar. 8th William Walton d. (80).
Mar. 15th Rebecca West d. (90).
Apr. 30th George Melitonovich Balanchine d. (79).
May 21st Kenneth Clark d. (82).
May 31st Jack Dempsey d. (87).

H **Aug**: 26th, President Andropov offers to destroy large number of SS-20 missiles in return for U.S. not deploying new missiles in Europe;

28th, Israeli Prime Minister Menachem Begin announces intention to resign (*Sept.* 15th, succeeded by Yitzhak Shamir).

J **Sep**: 1st, 269 killed when South Korean Boeing 747 airliner is shot down by Soviet fighter after straying into Soviet air space near Sakhalin Island (5th, West European nations impose 14-day ban on Aeroflot flights);

4th, civil war breaks out in Lebanon's Chouf mountains following withdrawal of Israeli troops;

6th, final document of European Conference on Security and Co-operation adopted in Madrid, pledging governments to continue 'Helsinki process' of peaceful settlement of disputes and increased respect for human rights;

—, U.S.S.R. admits military chiefs ordered fighters to stop flight of stray Korean airliner (8th, U.S. Secretary of State Shultz describes Soviet response to South Korean airliner disaster as inadequate);

11th, violent protests in Chile on 10th anniversary of military coup;

—, in Britain, S.D.P. conference votes against merger with Liberals for at least five years;

16th, C.I.A. denies South Korean airliner was engaged in spying;

19th, Caribbean islands of St. Kitts-Nevis achieve independence from Britain;

20th, Soviet Foreign Minister Gromyko refuses to attend U.N. General Assembly meeting in New York;

21st, demonstrators in Philippines demand resignation of President Marcos (29th, Marcos orders closure of any newspaper alleging army officers involved in murder of Aquino);

25th, 38 Republican prisoners escape from Maze Prison in Northern Ireland; 17 recaptured;

26th, ceasefire agreed in Lebanon; government agrees to conference of national reconciliation.

K **Oct**: 2nd, Neil Kinnock elected leader of British Labour Party;

5th, Nobel Peace Prize awarded to Lech Walesa;

6th, Indian government takes control of Punjab in response to growing violence;

10th, in Philippines commission investigating Aquino murder resigns (22nd, Marcos appoints new commission);

12th, Chinese Communist Party commences biggest purge of membership since Cultural Revolution; qualifications of 40 million party members to be reviewed;

—, President Reagan approves bill keeping U.S. Marines in Beirut for further 18 months;

14th, British Trade and Industry Secretary Cecil Parkinson resigns following revelations of adultery with his secretary, Miss Sarah Keays (16th, succeeded by Norman Tebbit);

19th, left-wing military coup in Grenada, in which Prime Minister Maurice Bishop is killed;

22nd, anti-nuclear protests held across Europe against deployment of U.S. Pershing II and Cruise missiles;

23rd, attacks by suicide bombers kill 242 U.S. and 62 French troops in peace-keeping force in military compound, Beirut, Lebanon;

25th, U.S. Marines invade Grenada to depose military government (28th, U.S. vetoes U.N. resolution deploring invasion);

31st, Governor-General of Grenada, Sir Paul Scoon, confirms that he requested assistance from East Caribbean forces and indirectly from U.S.;

z **Births and Deaths** (*cont.*)

July 1st R. Buckminster Fuller d. (87).
July 24th Georges Auric d. (84).
July 29th Luis Buñuel d. (83).
Aug. 5th Joan Robinson d. (79).
Aug. 18th Niklaus Pevsner d. (81).
Nov. 25th Anton Dolin d. (79).
Dec. 20th Bill Brandt d. (78).
Dec. 25th Joan Miró d. (90).

K **Oct**: 30th, Radical Party, led by Raoul Alfonsin, gains absolute majority in Argentine elections;

31st, national reconciliation conference on Lebanon opens in Geneva.

L **Nov**: 1st, British Defence Secretary Heseltine warns that demonstrators who approach Cruise missile bunkers at Greenham Common are liable to be shot;

2nd, all-white referendum in South Africa approves new constitution extending limited political rights to Coloureds and Asians;

4th, suicide bombers attack Israeli military headquarters in Tyre, Lebanon, killing 60;

—, Governor of Grenada declares state of emergency;

9th, China's Foreign Ministry announces intention to declare unilateral policy on Hong Kong in *Sept.* 1984 if no agreement has been reached with Britain;

14th, British Defence Secretary Heseltine announces arrival of first Cruise missiles at Greenham Common (15th, 141 arrested at demonstration outside Greenham Common airbase);

—, Turkish Cypriot Legislative Council issues unilateral proclamation of independence of Turkish part of island (18th, U.N. Security Council Resolution 541 declares action illegal);

21st, Official Unionist Party withdraws from Northern Ireland Assembly;

22nd, West German Bundestag votes for deployment of Pershing II missiles in country;

23rd, U.S.S.R. walks out of arms limitation talks in Geneva following deployment of U.S. missiles in Europe (24th, President Andropov announces U.S.S.R. to increase number of submarine missiles targeted at U.S.);

24th, P.L.O and Israel exchange prisoners captured during war in Lebanon: 4,800 Palestinians for 6 Israeli soldiers.

M **Dec**: 6th, Turkey's National Security Council dissolved, ending three years of military rule;

8th, British House of Lords votes for televising of debates for experimental period;

9th, former British Foreign Secretary Lord Carrington named as successor to Dr. Joseph Luns as Secretary-General of N.A.T.O. from 1984;

10th, Raoul Alfonsin installed as President of Argentina, ending eight years of military rule;

17th, I.R.A. car bomb explodes outside Harrods department store in London, killing six;

20th, Yassir Arafat and 4,000 supporters evacuated from Lebanon;

25th, Egypt and Jordan sign accord restoring economic relations;

29th, U.S. announces intention of withdrawing from UNESCO at end of 1984, alleging that the organisation 'exhibited hostility towards the basic institutions of a free society';

31st, coup led by Major-General Mohammed Buhari ousts government of President Shagari of Nigeria.

1984 (Jan. – Apr.) Miners' strike in Britain—I.R.A. bombs British government—Indira Gandhi assassinated

A **Jan:** 1st, Brunei becomes independent after 95 years as British Protectorate;
—, 19-member Supreme Military Council assumes power in Nigeria;
10th, 'amity talks' convened in Sri Lanka between Tamil and Sinhalese representatives;
17th, 35-nation conference on disarmament in Europe opens in Stockholm;
18th, President of American University in Beirut, Malcolm Kerr, is shot dead by pro-Iranian group;
19th, Islamic Conference Organization votes to invite Egypt back to membership (suspended since Camp David accord);
—, U.S. partly lifts trade sanctions on Poland;
25th, British government announces that staff at Government Communications Headquarters (G.C.H.Q.) in Cheltenham to be deprived of right to belong to trades unions (*Feb.* 21st, government announces that most G.C.H.Q. workers have accepted offer of £1,000 to surrender union rights).

B **Feb:** 1st, Nissan announces plan to build pilot car assembly plant in England;
6th, in Lebanon President Gemayel orders 24-hour curfew as Shi'ite Moslem and Druze militias over-run West Beirut;
7th, President Reagan orders U.S. Marines to withdraw from Beirut (26th, last U.S. Marines leave);
9th, President Andropov of U.S.S.R. dies (13th, Konstantin Chernenko named First Secretary of Soviet Communist Party);
11th, Iraq commences bombing of non-military targets in Iran;
27th, Iraq announces blockade of main Iranian oil terminal at Kharg Island and threatens to attack oil tankers loading there.

C **Mar:** 1st, joint South African–Angolan monitoring commission begins supervision of South African troop withdrawal from southern Angola;
—, A.N. Wedgwood Benn, out of British Parliament since 1983 election, wins Chesterfield by-election for Labour;
4th, Speaker of Iranian Parliament claims 400 Iranian soldiers killed by Iraqi chemical weapons;
7th, Polish students stage sit-in at Stanislaw Staszic College in Mietne to demand restoration of crucifixes in classrooms;
8th, leaders of British N.U.M. support planned strikes in Yorkshire and Scotland over proposed pit closures;
12th (–20th), new Lebanon reconciliation conference in Lausanne;
—, British miners' strike spreads to 100 pits (15th, 21 pits working, most in Nottinghamshire);
13th, British Budget raises income tax allowances, abolishes employers' National Insurance surcharge, begins reduction of Corporation Tax to 35 per cent over three years, and plans Borrowing Requirement of £7,250 million (2.5 per cent of G.D.P.);
23rd, Sarah Tisdall, junior British Foreign Office clerk, jailed for leaking secret documents on arrival of Cruise missiles in Britain to The Guardian newspaper;
31st, Indian government agrees to amend Punjabi constitution to acknowledge Sikhism as religion distinct from Hinduism.

D **Apr:** 3rd, Indian state of Punjab is declared 'dangerously disturbed area' (5th, government imposes detention without trial);
4th, in Britain, bailiffs clear women's peace camp at Greenham Common;
5th, in Britain, Nottinghamshire miners reject N.U.M. Executive Committee's recommendation not to cross picket lines;

O Politics, Economics, Law and Education

U.N. Conference on Population in Mexico, recommends agreement over means of slowing rate of population growth (*Aug.* 7th–16th).

British Data Protection Act gives people the right of access to computerised information about themselves.

American Telephone and Telegraph Co. (A.T.& T.) broken up (*Jan.* 1st).

Texaco Inc. acquires Getty Oil Co. in largest business merger in U.S. history (*Feb.*).

British Police and Criminal Evidence Act ('PACE') reforms police powers of entry, search and arrest, and revises rules on treatment and interrogation of suspects.

British House of Commons passes new divorce law, allowing couples to end marriage after one year (*June* 14th).

Report of Committee of Inquiry into Human Fertilization and Embryology, chaired by Dame Mary Warnock, recommends control of research into 'test-tube' babies and ban on surrogate motherhood agencies in Britain (*July* 18th).

Brenda Dean becomes first woman to lead major British union; elected leader of print union S.O.G.A.T.'82 (*Mar.*)

British Parliament approves new G.C.S.E. ('General Certificate of Secondary Education') examination, to replace O-Level and C.S.E. (*June.* 20th).

P Science, Technology, Discovery, etc.

Two U.S. shuttle astronauts make untethered space walks, using jet-propelled back packs to move in space.

An Indian astronomer discovers two more rings around Saturn.

U.S. astronomers working in Chile photograph a partial ring system around Neptune.

U.S. astronomers photograph a planet system around the star Beta Pictoris.

An Australian woman gives birth to a child created by in vitro fertilization of her husband's sperm with another woman's egg (*Jan.*).

An Australian woman give birth to a child developed from a previously frozen fertilized embryo.

William H. Clewall of the University of Colorado performs the first successful operation on an unborn foetus.

Surgeons at Loma Linda University Medical Center in California transplant the heart of a baboon into a two-week-old girl; the patient survives for 20 days.

From studies of DNA, Charles G. Sibley and Jon E. Ahlquist argue that humans are more closely related to chimpanzees than to other great apes; that humans and apes diverged approximately 5–6 million years ago.

Dr. Alec Jeffreys of the University of Leicester, Britain, discovers that a core sequence of DNA is unique to each person; this examination of DNA, known as 'genetic fingerprinting', can be used to establish family relationships and in criminal investigations.

Allan Wilson and Russell Higuchi of the University of California at Berkeley clone genes from an extinct animal, the zebra-like quagga.

Element 108 synthesized.

Q Scholarship

Kenneth O. Morgan (ed.), *The Oxford Illustrated History of Britain.*

J. Catto, *The Early Oxford Schools*, the first volume in *The History of the University of Oxford* (–).

Leslie Bethell (ed.), *The Cambridge History of Latin America* (–91).

David Hempton, *Methodism and Politics in British Society, 1750–1850.*

Kenneth O. Morgan, *Labour in Power, 1945–1951.*

D **Apr**: 6th, Polish government and Catholic church agree compromise on display of crucifixes in state schools and other public places;
12th, British N.U.M. President, Arthur Scargill, vetoes proposed national ballot on continuation of pit strike;
17th, W.P.C. Yvonne Fletcher killed and 11 others injured when gunmen inside Libyan People's Bureau in London fire on demonstrators (22nd, Britain breaks diplomatic relations with Libya; siege of building ends on 27th);
20th, demonstrations in West Germany against deployment of U.S. missiles in Europe.

E **May**: 2nd, publication of report of New Ireland Forum, formed by three main parties in Eire and the S.D.L.P. in Northern Ireland; advocates creation of united Ireland by federation of Eire and Northern Ireland or by government of Northern Ireland under joint authority of Britain and Eire;
—, dissident Soviet physicist Andrei Sakharov begins hunger strike when authorities refuse to allow wife, Yelena Bonner, to travel abroad for medical treatment (*Aug.* 6th, ends);
3rd, opposition parties gain seats in British local elections;
10th, International Court of Justice at The Hague rules that U.S. should cease blockade of Nicaraguan ports;
—, Danish Parliament votes to halt payments to N.A.T.O. for deployment of Pershing II and Cruise missiles in Europe;
14th, opposition makes gains in Philippine elections;
23rd, talks between Arthur Scargill and Ian MacGregor on British pit closures break down;
24th, five former El Salvador National Guardsmen found guilty of murder of three U.S. nuns and female lay assistant in 1980;
—, U.S. House of Representatives votes to continue military aid to El Salvador, but against further aid to Nicaraguan Contras;
—, Iranian war planes attack oil tankers off coast of Saudi Arabia (27th, U.S. sends Stinger anti-aircraft missiles to Saudi Arabia in case of Iranian attack);
29th, in Britain, 64 injured and 84 arrested in confrontation between pickets and police at Orgreave coke works (30th, Arthur Scargill arrested and charged with obstruction).

F **Jun**: 1st, U.S. Secretary of State Shultz calls on Nicaraguan government to stop support for rebels in El Salvador;
6th, 250 Sikh extremists killed when Indian troops storm Golden Temple at Amritsar (11th, Sikh soldiers mutiny at eight army bases in protest at attack);
10th, Iraq seeks U.N. supervision of agreement with Iran to stop attacks on civilian areas;
14th, Dutch parliament approves cabinet decision to delay final decision on deployment of Cruise missiles;
—, in Britain, S.D.P. wins Portsmouth South from Conservatives at by-election;
25th (–26th), summit conference of E.C. heads of government at Fontainebleau reaches agreement on British budget contribution;
27th, British unions hold 'day of action' in support of striking miners;
29th, Indian Prime Minister Indira Gandhi dismisses governor and police chief of Punjab.

G **Jul**: 4th, Lebanese Army units take over positions in Beirut from militias;
5th, former Nigerian Transport Minister Umaru Dikko, exiled in Britain, found inside crate at Stansted airport (12th, Britain expels two Nigerian diplomats);

R **Philosophy and Religion**

Donald Davidson, *Inquiries into Truth and Interpretation.*

N. Goodman, *Of Mind and Other Matters.*

G.A. Lindbeck, *The Nature of Doctrine.*

Appointment of Rev. Professor David Jenkins as Bishop of Durham in England arouses controversy because of the Bishop-elect's views on Christian doctrine; after the Bishop's consecration in York Minster (*July* 6th) lightning strikes the Minster (*July* 9th), prompting discussion about a possible act of God.

The Roman Catholic church in Chile officially backs demonstrations against violations of human rights for the first time under the Pinochet regime.

Billy Graham and Luis Palau hold missions in Britain.

Concordat of 1929 between Vatican City State and Italy is revised, with Roman Catholicism losing its status as official state religion of Italy.

The Roman Catholic Sacred Congregation for the Doctrine of the Faith publishes *An Instruction on Certain Aspects of the Theology of Liberation*, warning against acceptance of Marxist ideology (*Sept.* 3rd).

Leading proponent of liberation theology, Father Leonardo Boff, appears before the Doctrinal Office of the Vatican, accompanied by two Brazilian cardinals.

U.S. Supreme Court rules that the public financing of Nativity scenes does not violate principle of separation of Church and State in U.S. (*Mar.* 5th).

In India troops lay siege to the Golden Temple in Amritsar where Sikh militants had barricaded themselves in an attempt to secure special status for Amritsar and constitutional recognition for Sikhism.

S **Art, Sculpture, Fine Arts and Architecture**

Painting:

First Turner Prize for Painting awarded in Britain to Malcolm Morley.

Frank Stella is first visual artist to hold post of Charles Eliot Norton Professor of Poetry at Harvard University.

'Primitivism in the Twentieth Century', exhibition at Museum of Modern Art, New York.

Neo-Geo movement in the U.S.

Hans Haacke, *Taking Stock.*

Sculpture:

Tony Cragg, *St. George and the Dragon.*

Architecture:

High Tech, Classicism – two extremes in architectural design.

Philip Johnson, John Burgee, AT&T Building, New York

James Stirling, Neue Staatsgalerie, Stuttgart, Germany

The Prince of Wales, in an address to the Royal Institute of British Architects at Hampton Court, London (*May* 30th), attacks Modern Architecture (describing the proposed extension to the National Gallery as 'a carbuncle on the face of an old friend').

T **Music**

Robert Ashley, *Perfect Lives* (television opera).

Luciano Berio, *Un re in ascolta* (opera).

Philip Glass, *Akhnaten* (opera).

A. Sallinen, *The King Goes Forth to France* (opera).

Alfred Schnittke, 4th Symphony.

Karlheinz Stockhausen, *Samstag aus Licht* (opera).

John Tavener, *Ikon of Light.*

Michael Tippett, *The Mask of Time.*

G **Jul**: 10th (–20th), national dock strike in Britain over use of non-registered labour;
14th, Labour Party defeats ruling National Party in New Zealand general election;
16th, British High Court rules ban on union membership at G.C.H.Q. illegal (*Aug.* 6th, Court of Appeal overturns ruling; *Nov.* 22nd, House of Lords upholds ban);
18th, Democratic Party Convention in San Francisco selects Walter Mondale and Geraldine Ferraro (first woman to be nominated) as Party candidates for President and Vice-President;
19th, Jacques Delors named President of European Commission from *Jan.* 1985;
21st, James F. Fixx, author of *The Complete Guide to Running*, the 'Joggers' Bible', dies of a heart attack while jogging.

H **Aug**: 1st, legal moves begun to seize assets of South Wales miners after they fail to meet deadline for payment of fine;
3rd, Upper Volta renamed Burkina Faso ('land of upright men');
4th, violent clashes between Tamils and Sinhalese in Sri Lanka;
8th, Robert Mugabe announces plan for one-party state in Zimbabwe;
13th, federation established between Libya and Morocco;
16th, John De Lorean acquitted in U.S. of eight charges of drug-trafficking;
22nd, Republican Party Convention in Dallas nominates President Reagan and Vice-President Bush as party's nominees for November election;
23rd, Yelena Bonner, wife of U.S.S.R. dissident physicist Sakharov, sentenced to five years' internal exile;
24th (–*Sept.* 18th), national dock strike in Britain, sparked by Hunterston dockers attempting to block coal supplies to Ravenscraig steel works in support of miners;
31st, Yitzhak Shamir and Shimon Peres agree to form government of national unity in Israel and to alternate in post of Prime Minister.

J **Sep**: 3rd, 14 die in rioting in Sharpeville and other black townships around Johannesburg;
4th, Progressive Conservatives defeat ruling Liberals in Canada's general election;
9th, British Coal Board Chairman Ian MacGregor arrives for talks with Arthur Scargill in Edinburgh with carrier bag over his head;
12th, in Britain, High Court grants eviction order against Greenham Common peace camp;
14th, South African Prime Minister Botha sworn in as country's first Executive President (17th, first 19-member multi-racial Cabinet sworn in);
17th, France reaches agreement with Libya for withdrawal of both countries' forces from Chad by mid-November;
20th, bomb explodes at U.S. embassy in Beirut killing 23;
22nd, in Britain, the new Bishop of Durham, Dr. David Jenkins, describes Ian MacGregor as an 'imported, elderly American' (27th, Archbishop of Canterbury expresses regret at remarks);
25th, Jordan restores full diplomatic relations with Egypt;
26th, draft agreement for return of Hong Kong to China in 1997 signed in Peking.

K **Oct**: 10th, British N.U.M. fined £200,000 for contempt of court for attempting to discipline non-striking members;
12th, in Britain, I.R.A. bomb explodes at Grand Hotel, Brighton, during Conservative Party Conference, killing 4, injuring 32, and nearly killing Mrs. Thatcher (*Nov.* 13th, fifth person dies);
16th, British pit deputies' union N.A.C.O.D.S. votes for strike (24th, called off);
20th, Central Committee of Chinese Communist Party agrees programme of economic reforms, giving factory managers greater autonomy;

U Literature

J.G.Ballard, *The Empire of the Sun.*
S.S. Bhoosnurmath, *The Grand Man* (Bhavya Manava).
J.M. Coetzee, *The Life and Times of Michael K.*
Jan Drzezdzon, *God's Face* (Twarz Boga).
Stefan Heym, *The Wandering Jew.*
F. Sionil Jose, *Po-on* (5th and final volume of *The Pretenders*)
Milan Kundera, *The Unbearable Lightness of Being.*
Graham Swift, *Waterland.*
Ibrahim Tahir, *The Last Imam.*
William Trevor, *Fools of Fortune.*
New edition of James Joyce's *Ulysses*, correcting 5,000 errors.
Start of public lending right (P.L.R.) in Britain: payments to authors on library loans.

V The Press

Robert Maxwell buys the Mirror group of newspapers in Britain (*July* 13th).
Stock market flotation of Reuters news agency.
The News of the World in Britain is relaunched as a tabloid paper.

W Drama and Entertainment

Grupa Chwilowa, *A Miraculous Story.*
Teatr Nowy, *The End of Europe* wins 'Grand Prix' at Theatre of Nations, Nancy.
Terry Johnson, *Cries from the Mammal House.*
Sharman Macdonald, *When I was a Girl I used to Scream and Shout.*
Neil Simon, *Biloxi Blues.*
Starlight Express.

Films:
David Lean's *A Passage to India.*
Andrei Tarkovsky's *Nostalgia.*
Bertrand Tavernier's *A Sunday in the Country.*
Wim Wenders' *Paris, Texas.*
Terminator.
End of capital allowances on films in Britain – producers announce they will leave.

Television:
The Jewel in the Crown.
The Living Planet.
Miami Vice.
Edgar Reitz's *Heimat*, an epic lasting almost 16 hours.
In the U.S. 75 million people watch *The Day After*, about the effects of nuclear attack.
Threads dramatizes the presumed effects of a nuclear explosion over Sheffield, England.

Popular music:
'Strategien gegen Architekturen' by the German industrial band Einsturtzende Neubauten creates controversy in Britain.
'Do They Know It's Christmas?' single raises £8 million for famine relief in Africa.
Madonna, *Like a Virgin.*
Prince, *Purple Rain.*
Bruce Springsteen, *Born in the U.S.A.*

K **Oct**: 23rd, in Philippines, official report into Aquino murder (*Aug.* 21st, 1983) claims 26 people, including top military officials, involved;

27th, Polish authorities admit that missing pro-Solidarity priest, Father Jerzy Popieluszko, was murdered by members of security police (30th, priest's body found in reservoir; 31st, three officers to be charged);

31st, Indian Prime Minister Indira Gandhi assassinated by Sikh bodyguards; son Rajiv sworn in as Prime Minister; communal violence follows.

L **Nov**: 2nd, Angola offers to reduce number of Cuban troops in country if South Africa agrees to reliquish control of Namibia;

4th, Sandinista Front wins Nicaraguan elections; Daniel Ortega elected President with 63 per cent of popular vote;

—, British air force begins airlift of food supplies to famine-stricken Tigre province of Ethiopia;

6th, in U.S. Presidential election Republican President Ronald Reagan, with 525 electoral college votes, wins landslide victory over Democrat Walter Mondale, with 13 college votes; Reagan wins all states bar Minnesota and District of Columbia; Republicans retain majority in Senate and increase representation in House of Representatives; popular vote: Reagan, 54,455,075 (58.8 per cent); Mondale, 37,577,185 (40.6);

12th (–15th), Organization of African Unity summit in Addis Ababa calls for massive international aid for Africa;

16th, President Mitterrand acknowledges Libyan troops still in Chad in defiance of agreement;

20th, shares in British Telecom offered to public; issue is four-times over-subscribed (*Dec.* 3rd, trading opens with premium of 45p above offer price of £1.30p);

—, in Britain, North Wales branch of N.U.M. votes to end strike;

26th, U.S. restores full diplomatic relations with Iraq (severed in 1967);

30th, two striking miners charged with murder of cab driver in South Wales, by dropping block on car from bridge (*May* 1985, convicted of murder; *Oct.*, reduced to manslaughter).

M **Dec**: 1st, King Hussein of Jordan holds talks with Egypt's President Mubarak in Cairo on peace initiatives for West Bank;

3rd, leak of toxic gas from Union Carbide pesticide plant near Bhopal, India, kills 2,500 and injures 200,000;

7th, front page article in China's *People's Daily* argues that Marxist theory is not solution to all country's economic problems (10th, 'correction' criticizes article for failure to emphasize continued importance of Marxist principles);

—, Tamil terrorists attack Sri Lankan army convoy, killing 100;

15th, Soviet Politburo member Mikhail Gorbachev visits London; states U.S.S.R. willing to negotiate large reductions in nuclear weapons; Mrs. Thatcher declares 'I like Mr. Gorbachev; we can do business together';

18th, British government announces plan to privatize the Trustee Savings Bank;

22nd, Dom Mintoff resigns as Prime Minister of Malta; succeeded by Dr. Carmello Mifsud Bonnici;

24th, Congress (I) Party of Rajiv Gandhi wins large majority in Indian general election;

28th, sterling falls to $1.1627, down 27 cents on year.

X Sport

Before the English University Boat Race, the Cambridge boat collides with a stationary barge (*Mar.* 17th).

Sweden wins Lawn Tennis's Davis Cup for the first time, beating the U.S. 4–1 in the Final.

In three competitions (European Championships, Winter Olympics, World Championships) the British ice dancers Jayne Torvill and Christopher Dean are awarded 59 'perfect' scores of 6.

XXII Olympic Games held in Los Angeles, boycotted by the Soviet bloc, with the exception of Roumania, and by Iran and Libya, in retaliation for the American boycott in 1980. The U.S. wins 83 gold medals; Roumania, 20; West Germany, 17; China, 15; Italy, 14; Canada and Japan, 10; New Zealand, 8; Yugoslavia, 7; South Korea, 6; Britain, France and Holland, 5. In the athletics, Carl Lewis of the U.S. wins four gold medals.

Y Statistics

Cotton production (mill. metric tonnes): China, 6,258; U.S., 2,827; U.S.S.R., 2,343; India, 1,446; Pakistan, 1,009; Brazil, 723; Turkey, 580; Egypt, 399; Mexico, 280; Sudan, 219; Argentina, 180; Syria, 150; Greece, 142; Australia, 141; Iran, 111; Paraguay, 105; others, 1,044.

Z Births and Deaths

Jan. 20th Johnny Weissmuller d. (79).
Feb. 20th Mikhail Sholokov d. (78).
Mar. 5th Tito Gobbi d. (68).
Mar. 6th Martin Niemöller d. (92).
Apr. 5th Arthur Harris d. (91).
Apr. 8th Pyotr Kapitza d. (89).
Apr. 16th Count Basie d. (79).
May 19th John Betjeman d. (76).
June 22nd Joseph Losey d. (75).
June 25th Michel Foucault d. (57).
June 30th Lillian Hellman d. (77).
July 26th G.H. Gallup d. (82).
Aug. 5th Richard Burton d. (58).
Aug. 14th J.B. Priestley d. (89).
Oct. 14th Martin Ryle d. (66).
Oct. 21st François Truffaut d. (52).
Oct. 31st Indira Gandhi d. (66).

1985 (Jan. – Mar.) Sinking of *Rainbow Warrior*—T.W.A. and *Achille Lauro* hijacks —Anglo-Irish Agreement signed

A **Jan:** 7th (–8th), U.S. Secretary of State Shultz and U.S.S.R. Foreign Minister Gromyko hold talks in Geneva over resumption of arms control negotiations;
12th, state of emergency declared in New Caledonia following shooting of separatist leader Eloi Machoro by security forces;
14th, Israeli Cabinet agrees three-stage withdrawal from occupied Lebanon, commencing Feb.;
—, Hun Sen elected Prime Minister of Kampuchea in succession to late Chan Sy;
17th (–20th), summit conference at U.N. between President Kyprianu of Cyprus and Turkish-Cypriot leader Rauf Denktaş fails to resolve differences;
18th, in Britain, F.T. 100 Share Index exceeds 1,000 points for first time;
—, panel of prosecutors in Philippines announces sufficient evidence to charge 26 with involvement in murder of Benigno Aquino (*Feb.* 1st, trial opens);
25th, President Botha opens South Africa's new three-chamber Parliament for Whites, Indians, and Coloureds;
29th, in Britain, dons at Oxford University vote to refuse Mrs. Thatcher (an Oxford graduate) an honorary doctorate.

B **Feb:** 4th, Reagan administration's defence budget calls for tripling of expenditure on 'Star Wars' research programme;
5th, Gibraltar's frontier gates with Spain re-opened after 16 years;
—, in Britain, 200 evicted from protest outside Cruise missile base in Molesworth, Cambridgeshire;
7th, four Polish secret police officers found guilty of murder of Father Jerzy Popieluszko, sentenced to between 14 and 25 years in jail;
10th, imprisoned A.N.C. leader Nelson Mandela refuses South African government's offer of freedom, conditional on him renouncing violence;
11th, former British Ministry of Defence official Clive Ponting acquitted of charges of leaking documents relating to the sinking of Argentine cruiser *General Belgrano* during Falklands War;
19th, Irish Dail passes emergency law enabling government to seize up to IR£10 million from Provisional I.R.A. bank accounts;
27th, N.C.B. announces that over 50 per cent of Britain's miners are back at work.

C **Mar:** 1st, Julio Sanguinetti takes office as Uruguay's first elected President in 12 years;
3rd, British N.U.M. delegates' conference votes to return to work without settlement of strike;
10th, President Chernenko of U.S.S.R. dies;
11th, Mikhail Gorbachev is named First Secretary of Soviet Communist Party; he calls for more *glasnost* ('openness') in Soviet life and later pursues policy of *perestroika* ('reconstruction');
12th (–23rd), further round of U.S.–U.S.S.R. arms talks in Geneva;
15th, military rule ends in Brazil;
18th, Britain closes embassy in Beirut following kidnap of two Britons and one U.S. journalist;
19th, British Budget raises personal tax thresholds by more than inflation, raises excise duties, proposes major changes in National Insurance, announces borrowing requirement of £7 billion (2 per cent of G.D.P.);
20th, Belgian Parliament approves deployment of Cruise missiles;
21st, South African police fire on crowds at Uitenhage on 25th anniversary of Sharpeville massacre, killing 18 (22nd, judicial commission of inquiry announced);
29th (–30th), summit of E.C. heads of government in Brussels agrees terms for admission of Spain and Portugal on *Jan.* 1st, 1986;

O **Politics, Economics, Law and Education**

Major famine in Ethiopia.

Proceedings in British House of Lords televised for first time (*Jan.* 23rd).

U.S. Supreme Court rejects legal limits on spending of Political Action Committees (*Mar.* 18th).

Deposit required from any candidate in British general elections is increased from £150 to £500.

British Ecology Party changes its name to the Green Party (*Sept.*)

European Court of Human Rights finds Britain guilty of sex discrimination in immigration policy (*May* 28th).

Irish Dail legalizes shop sales of contraceptives (*Feb.* 20th).

Japanese Diet approves bill to remove restrictions on women's work (*May* 17th).

British House of Lords rules that doctors can prescribe contraceptive pills to girls aged under 16 without parents' consent (*Oct.* 17th).

International Whaling Commission bans commercial whaling.

World Bank sets up fund for Africa (*Feb.* 1st).

Nissan negotiates single-union deal with Amalgamated Union of Engineering Workers at new car construction plant at Washington in north-east England (*Apr.* 22nd).

P **Science, Technology, Discovery, etc.**

The British Antarctic Survey detects a hole in the ozone layer over Antarctica.

U.S. space shuttle *Discovery* (launched *Aug.* 27th) deploys three satellites; the crew also retrieve, repair and redeploy an orbiting satellite.

Crew of the shuttle *Atlantis* undertake construction exercises to develop skills for building a large orbiting space station.

Launch of European, Japanese and U.S.S.R. probes to rendezvous with Halley's comet in 1986.

Astronomers at Cornell University report the discovery of eight infrared galaxies located by the Infrared Astronomical Satellite.

Two groups of researchers discover rings around Neptune.

U.S. film star Rock Hudson is the first celebrity to die of AIDS (*Oct.* 2nd); on Dec. 16th it is reported that 8,000 Americans have died from the disease.

A woman in the U.S. treated for infertility gives birth to septuplets (*May*); three survive, but with medical problems.

In the U.S. lasers are used in surgery, to clean out clogged arteries.

Researchers locate gene markers on chromosomes for cystic fibrosis and polycystic kidney disease.

Evidence found for the existence of fullerenes (buckyballs), a new elemental form of carbon.

Q **Scholarship**

J.J. Scarisbrick, *The Reformation and the English People*.

Paul Slack, *The Impact of Plague in Tudor and Stuart England*.

Alan Everitt, *Landscape and Community in England*.

Cyril Ehrlich, *The Music Profession in Britain since the Eighteenth Century: A Social History*.

Margaret Drabble (ed.), *The Oxford Companion to English Literature*, 5th edn.

J.M. Winter, *The Great War and the British People*.

Judith M. Brown, *Modern India: The Origins of an Asian Democracy*.

R **Philosophy and Religion**

Jürgen Habermas, *The Philosophical Discourse of Modernity*.

P.F. Strawson, *Scepticism and Naturalism*.

D **Apr:** 2nd, Israeli Army removes 1,100 Lebanese prisoners from detention camps in southern Lebanon to Israel;
6th, coup in Sudan led by General Swar al-Dahab;
7th, Soviet leader Gorbachev announces moratorium on missile deployments in Europe until *Nov.* and offers to hold summit talks with President Reagan;
11th, Enver Hoxha, First Secretary of Albanian Communist Party and national leader for more than 40 years, dies; Ramiz Alia named new First Secretary;
12th, Islamic Jihad claims responsibility for bomb explosion in Madrid which kills 18 and injures 82;
15th, South African accepts recommendations of Parliamentary committee to abolish laws forbidding inter-racial marriage and sexual intercourse;
—, President Botha announces that South African forces in Angola will leave by 18th;
17th, anti-discrimination section of Canada's federal constitution (Charter of Rights and Freedoms) incorporated into law;
22nd, trial opens in Argentina of nine former military leaders, including General Galtieri;
26th, Warsaw Pact leaders agree to renew military alliance for further 30 years;
30th, Bernie Grant elected leader of Haringey Council, Britain's first black council leader; Venerable Wilfred Wood consecrated Bishop of Croydon, Britain's first black bishop.

E **May:** 1st, U.S. imposes financial and trade sanctions on Nicaragua;
—, 10,000 Solidarity supporters clash with police during May Day demonstrations in Gdansk;
2nd, large gains for opposition parties in British county council elections; Liberal–S.D.P. Alliance holds balance of power in 27 shire counties;
10th (–13th), Sikh extremists bomb three Indian cities, 84 reported dead;
14th, 146 die in Tamil attack on Sri Lankan city of Anuradhapura;
19th, Shi'ite Moslem militia attempts to drive Palestinians from refugee camps of Sabra, Shatila and Bourj-el-Barajneh in Beirut;
20th, Israel releases 1,150 prisoners under supervision of International Red Cross in exchange for last three soldiers held by Palestinians;
25th, 10,000 die as cyclone hits southern Bangladesh.

F **Jun:** 2nd, President Jayawardene of Sri Lanka discusses violence in his country with Indian Prime Minister Gandhi;
6th, skeleton thought to be remains of Auschwitz doctor Josef Mengele exhumed in Brazil (21st, identity confirmed by team of forensic experts);
10th, Israel completes withdrawal from all bar 'security zone' in southern Lebanon;
12th, Spain and Portugal sign treaty of accession to E.C.;
14th, two Shi'ite Moslem gunmen hijack T.W.A. jet with 145 passengers and crew of eight, demanding release of 700 prisoners held by Israel; one passenger, a U.S. Navy diver, is shot dead (17th, hostages removed from jet, in Beirut, Lebanon, and held in south Beirut);
15th, South Africa's first mixed marriage celebrated;
—, South Africa names multi-racial adminstration for Namibia but retains control of foreign policy and defence;
23rd, Air India Boeing 747 crashes into Atlantic off Irish coast killing all 329 on board; terrorist bomb suspected;
25th (–27th), Comecon summit in Warsaw proposes to develop links with E.C.;
30th, 39 U.S. hostages from T.W.A. jet taken to Damascus, released following Syrian intervention.

R **Philosophy and Religion** (*cont.*)

Bernard Williams, *Ethics and the Limits of Philosophy*.

D. Brown, *The Divine Trinity*.

Doctrinal Office of the Vatican imposes one year's silence on Leonardo Boff, leading exponent of 'liberation theology'.

General Synod of the Church of England approves ordination of women to the diaconate by large majority.

Methodist Conference in Britain votes against its members becoming Freemasons, and bans Masonic meetings on its premises.

Rev. Dr. Allan Boesak, President of the World Alliance of Reformed Churches, is arrested during a demonstration in Cape Town, South Africa.

S **Art, Sculpture, Fine Arts and Architecture**

Painting:

Picasso Museum opens in Paris.

Saatchi Collection opens in London.

Turner Prize in Britain awarded to Howard Hodgkin.

Exhibition 'German Art in the Twentieth Century 1905–1985', Royal Academy, London.

Cindy Sherman, *Untitled* No. 140.

Sculpture:

Arman, public sculpture: a heap of suitcases outside Gare St. Lazare, Paris.

Christo wraps Pont Neuf, Paris.

Anselm Kiefer, *The High Priestess*.

Architecture:

Richard Meier, Museum für Kunsthandwerk, Frankfurt am Main.

Norman Foster, Hong Kong and Shanghai Bank Headquarters, Hong Kong.

Richard Rogers, Lloyds Building, City of London.

T **Music**

Peter Maxwell Davies, *An Orkney Wedding, with Sunrise*.

Alexander Goehr, *Behold the Sun* (opera).

Oliver Knussen, *Higglety-Pigglety Pop* (opera).

Luigi Nono, *Prometeo-Tragedia dell'ascolto*.

Henri Pousseur, *Nacht der Nachte*.

Alfred Schnittke, *(K)ein Sommernachtstraum*.

Toru Takemitsu, *Riverrun*.

U **Literature**

Aas Foss Abrahamren, *The Bird and the White Tablecloth*.

Julian Barnes, *Flaubert's Parrot*.

Angela Carter, *Nights at the Circus*.

Alexander Kaletski *Metro, A Novel of the Moscow Underground*.

Ivan Klima, *My First Loves*.

Lars Lundkvist, *Korn*.

Doris Lessing, *The Good Terrorist*.

Grace Paley, *Later the Same Day*.

Patrick Suskind, *Perfume*.

Kurt Vonnegut, *Galapagos*.

Ted Hughes is appointed Britain's Poet Laureate.

G **Jul:** 2nd, Andrei Gromyko named President of U.S.S.R.; Edvard Shevardnadze becomes Foreign Minister;

4th, in Britain, Liberals win Brecon and Radnor at by-election from Conservatives, who come third;

11th, explosion sinks Greenpeace ship *Rainbow Warrior* in Auckland harbour, New Zealand, killing one man – ship was in South Pacific to disrupt French nuclear tests (two people later charged with explosion and discovered to be French agents);

15th, 12-day conference opens in Nairobi to mark end of U.N. Decade for Women;

18th (–20th), Organization of African Unity Conference in Addis Ababa declares that most African countries on verge of economic collapse;

20th, South African government declares state of emergency in 36 districts in response to increased violence;

24th, Indian Prime Minister Rajiv Gandhi announces agreement with Sant Harchand Singh Longowal, leader of Sikh community in Punjab, aimed at reducing tension in state;

27th, coup in Uganda, led by Brigadier Tito Okello, ousts President Milton Obote.

H **Aug:** 4th, black miners in South Africa's gold and coal mines vote for indefinite strike, demanding end to state of emergency;

15th, President Botha of South Africa re-states commitment to apartheid and rules out Parliamentary representation for blacks;

22nd, in Britain 54 die in fire on board jet at Manchester airport;

23rd, West German counter-espionage official Hans Joachim Tiedge seeks asylum in East Germany (28th, head of West German Secret Service sacked);

26th, report exonerates French government of involvement in sinking of *Rainbow Warrior*; findings rejected by New Zealand government (27th, French Prime Minister Laurent Fabius orders further investigations);

27th, South African civil rights activist Rev. Dr. Allan Boesak arrested on eve of leading march to prison where Nelson Mandela held (28th, violence when police seek to prevent march);

—, military coup in Nigeria, led by Major-General Ibrahim Babangida.

J **Sep:** 2nd, Cabinet reshuffle in Britain: Douglas Hurd becomes Home Secretary, Leon Brittan, Trade Secretary;

—, Pol Pot resigns as Commander of Khmer Rouge Army; replaced by Sol Senn;

9th, U.S. announces selective economic sanctions against South Africa;

—, riots in Handsworth area of Birmingham, England;

10th, E.C. Foreign Ministers approve sanctions against South Africa (Britain delays decision until 25th);

13th, Britain expels 25 Soviet diplomats and officials for alleged espionage activities (14th, U.S.S.R. expels 25 Britons; another round of expulsions follows);

16th, 10 Politburo members and 64 members of Central Committee of Chinese Communist Party resign, to make way for younger men;

17th, in West Germany, secretary in Chancellor Kohl's office defects to East Germany;

19th, over 7,000 die in earthquake in Mexico City;

20th, French Defence Minister Charles Hernu resigns and Admiral Pierre Lacoste, head of Foreign Service, is dismissed over *Rainbow Warrior* affair;

22nd, French Prime Minister Fabius admits that *Rainbow Warrior* was sunk by French secret service agents;

26th, elections held for Hong Kong's Legislative Council; first in 100 years of colonial rule;

28th (–29th), riots in Brixton, London, following police wounding of black woman, Mrs. Cherry Groce.

V The Press

Express newspapers in Britain are bought by United Newspapers.
Canadian Conrad Black takes control of Telegraph newspapers in Britain (*Dec.*).

W Drama and Entertainment

Howard Brenton and David Hare, *Pravda*.
Jean-Claude Carriere and Peter Brook, *The Mahabharata*.
Christopher Hampton, *Les Liaisons Dangereuses*.
Louis Nowra, *The Golden Age*.
Les Misérables.
Me and My Girl – the updated 'Lambeth Walk' musical.

Films:
Akira Kurosawa's *Ran*.
Istvan Szabo's *Colonel Redl*.
Back to the Future.
Kiss of the Spider Woman.
Out of Africa.
1985 sees cinema audiences in U. K. rise by 33 per cent to 70 million.

Television:
EastEnders.
The Golden Girls.
John Roberts, *The Triumph of the West*.
Taggart.
Troy Kennedy Martin, *Edge of Darkness*.
The War Game broadcast by the B.B.C. after 20 years' suppression
B.B.C. bans *At the Edge of the Union* for its interviews of I.R.A. members – TV journalists strike.

Popular music:
Live-Aid – televised concerts in U.S. and Britain to raise funds for famine relief.
Dire Straits, *Brothers in Arms*.
The Jesus and Mary Chain, *Psychocandy*.
The Pogues, *Rum, Sodomy and the Lash*.
The Smiths, *Meat is Murder*.
Sonic Youth, *Bad Moon Rising*.

X Sport

Dennis Taylor of Northern Ireland beats Steve Davis on the last ball of the 35th and final frame to win the Embassy World Professional Championship in Sheffield, England (*Apr.* 28th); 18.5 million people watch the final stages on television.
In England, 55 die when fire destroys the main stand at Bradford City's Valley Parade ground (*May* 11th).
39 people are killed at the Heysel Stadium in Brussels following a riot by Liverpool fans before the European Cup Final between Liverpool and Juventus of Italy (*May* 29th); as a consequence, English football clubs are banned from all European competitions.
Boris Becker, at 17 years and 227 days, wins the Wimbledon Men's Singles title (*July* 7th): he becomes the youngest winner, the first West German winner and the first unseeded player to win the title.
England regains the Ashes, beating Australia 3–1 in the six-Test series (*Sept.* 2nd).
Europe's golfers, captained by Tony Jacklin, win the Ryder Cup at the Belfry, England (*Sept.* 15th), the first European victory since 1957.

K **Oct:** 1st, Israel attacks P.L.O. headquarters in Tunis killing 60; revenge attack for murder of three Israelis in Cyprus;

6th, riots in Tottenham, London, during which P.C. Keith Blakelock is murdered;

7th, four Palestinian guerrillas hijack Italian cruise liner *Achille Lauro* with 450 people on board in Mediterranean (9th, hijackers surrender to Egyptian authorities after killing one U.S. passenger, Leon Klinghoffer, a crippled elderly Jew);

10th, U.S. jets intercept plane carrying hijackers from Egypt to Tunis and force it to land in Sicily; President Mubarak accuses U.S. of 'piracy';

12th, U.S. protests when Italian authorities release Mohammed Abbas, terrorist alleged to have been behind *Achille Lauro* hijack;

18th, British miners in Nottinghamshire and South Derbyshire vote to disaffiliate from the N.U.M. and form the Union of Democratic Mineworkers (U.D.M.);

27th, Julius Nyerere retires as President of Tanzania after 24 years; succeeded by Ali Hassan Mwinyi.

L **Nov:** 2nd, South African government imposes emergency restrictions on reporting of unrest;

4th, in New Zealand, two French secret service agents plead guilty to manslaughter and sabotage in sinking of *Rainbow Warrior* (21st, sentenced to 10 years in prison);

6th, General Jaruzelski resigns as Prime Minister of Poland to become Chairman of Council of State; Professor Zbigniew Messner named new Prime Minister;

13th, estimated 25,000 killed when Nevado del Ruiz volcano in Colombia erupts;

15th, Anglo–Irish Agreement signed at Hillsborough Castle, giving Eire a consultative role in the affairs of Northern Ireland; British Treasury Minister Ian Gow resigns in protest;

19th (–21st), U.S.–U.S.S.R. summit meeting in Geneva;

20th, British House of Commons votes against televising of proceedings;

24th, Egyptian commandos storm hijacked Egyptian airliner at Malta airport; 60 killed;

—, synod held in Rome to assess impact of reforms of Second Vatican Council;

29th, black union leaders in South Africa form new union covering 500,000 workers: Congress of South African Trade Unions.

M **Dec:** 2nd, court in Philippines acquits 26 accused of complicity in Aquino murder; Aquino's widow, Corazon, announces she will run for presidency against Marcos;

3rd, Church of England publishes report *Faith in the City*, critical of government policies on inner cities; government spokesmen denounce it as 'Marxist';

6th, U.S. agrees to allow Britain active role in 'Star Wars' research programme;

9th, five former members of Argentina's military junta found guilty of human rights' violations;

11th, in Northern Ireland, police and Loyalist demonstrators clash as first conference under Anglo–Irish Agreement held in Belfast;

17th, Ulster Unionist M.P.s all resign from British House of Commons over Anglo–Irish Agreement;

—, in Uganda General Tito Okello and Yoweri Museveni of National Resistance Army sign peace accord;

21st, South African police forcibly remove Winnie Mandela from home in Soweto;

—, Haitians demonstrate against government of Jean-Claude Duvalier;

25th, fighting breaks out on border between Mali and Burkina Faso;

30th, General Zia ends martial law in Pakistan;

31st, King Hussein of Jordan meets President Assad of Syria – first meeting for six years.

Y **Statistics**

Percentage of population living in towns and cities: Australia, 86; Bangladesh, 18; Brazil, 73; Chile, 83; China, 22; Denmark, 86; Egypt, 46; France, 73; West Germany, 86; Great Britain, 92; Holland, 88; India, 25; Iran, 54; Israel, 90; Italy, 67; Japan, 76; Kenya, 20; Mexico, 69; Nigeria, 30; Pakistan, 29; South Africa, 56; Sweden, 86; U.S., 74; U.S.S.R., 66; Zambia, 48.

Z **Births and Deaths**

Jan. 22nd Arthur Bryant d. (85).
Feb. 27th Henry Cabot Lodge d. (82).
Mar. 11th J.M.G.M. Adams d. (53).
Mar. 23rd Richard Beeching d. (71).
Mar. 28th Marc Chagall d. (97).
Apr. 13th Oscar Nemon d. (79).
June 2nd George Brown d. (70).
Sept. 17th Laura Ashley d. (60).
Nov. 3rd J.M. Wallace-Hadrill d. (69).
Dec. 2nd Philip Larkin d. (63).
Dec. 7th Robert Graves d. (90).

1986 (Jan. – Apr.) U.S. bombs Tripoli—Chernobyl nuclear power accident—State of Emergency in South Africa

A **Jan**: 1st, Spain and Portugal become 11th and 12th members of E.C.;
7th, U.S. imposes sanctions on Libya for involvement in international terrorism;
9th, Michael Heseltine resigns as British Defence Secretary following Cabinet disagreement over future of ailing Westland helicopter company (known as 'Westland affair'); succeeded by George Younger (24th, Trade Secretary Leon Brittan also resigns, over leak of letter; 25th, replaced by Paul Channon);
—, U.S.S.R. leader Gorbachev proposes 15-year timetable for elimination of all nuclear weapons;
20th, President Mitterand and Mrs. Thatcher meet in Lille and announce plans for Channel Tunnel rail link to open in 1993;
22nd, in India, three Sikhs sentenced to death for murder of Indira Gandhi;
23rd, polling in 15 Northern Irish constituencies following resignations of Ulster Unionists; all former M.P.s are re-elected except for Enoch Powell;
26th, National Resistance Army takes over Ugandan capital (29th, Yuweri Museveni sworn in as Uganda's President);
28th, U.S. space shuttle *Challenger* explodes shortly after take-off, killing crew of seven.

B **Feb**: 7th, presidential election in Philippines (9th, computer operators from Commission on Elections protest, claiming vote rigging);
—, President Jean-Claude Duvalier of Haiti flees to France following anti-government demonstrations; General Henri Namphy forms new government;
11th, U.S.S.R. Jewish dissident Anatoly Shcharansky and three others are released in exchange for five East Europeans;
12th, Channel Tunnel Treaty signed at Canterbury, England;
15th, opposition members walk out of Philippines Parliament when President Marcos declares himself victor in election;
19th, Iran takes Iraqi oil port of Faw, giving it control of mouth of Shatt al-Arab waterway;
22nd, Defence Minister Juan Ponce Enrile and Deputy Chief of Staff Fidel Ramos take over headquarters of Philippines Defence Ministry and declare opposition to President Marcos and support for Corazon Aquino;
24th, President Marcos flees Philippines; Corazon Aquino sworn in as President;
28th, Sweden's Prime Minister Olof Palme assassinated in Stockholm street.

C **Mar**: 2nd, Queen Elizabeth signs Australia Bill in Canberra, severing remaining legal ties with Britain;
6th, U.S.S.R. Communist Party Congress agrees sweeping changes in membership of Central Committee and Politburo;
7th, South African government lifts state of emergency imposed in *July* 1985;
12th, Spain votes in referendum to remain in N.A.T.O., but not in command structure;
16th, opposition parties win narrow majority in French general election, ending five years of Socialist rule (20th, Jacques Chirac, Gaullist leader, appointed Prime Minister);
18th, British Budget cuts basic rate of income tax to 29 per cent, raises excise duties on tobacco and petrol and announces borrowing requirement of £7 billion;
31st, Greater London Council and six metropolitan counties cease to exist;
—, fire severely damages Hampton Court Palace.

D **Apr**: 1st, price of North Sea oil falls below $10 a barrel for first time;
4th (–7th), Contadora group, meeting in Panama, fails to reach agreement on ending fighting in Central America;

O Politics, Economics, Law and Education

British Government Green Paper proposes introduction of poll tax in place of domestic rates (*Jan.* 28th).

Liechtenstein allows women to vote for first time in elections to National Diet (*Feb.* 2nd).

After 37 years, U.S. Senate ratifies U.N. Convention on the Prevention and Punishment of the Crime of Genocide (*Feb.* 19th).

In Britain representatives of the *Independent* and *Guardian* newspapers withdraw from daily briefings by government press officers to accredited 'lobby' journalists.

U.S. companies sell off or close subsidiaries in South Africa, including General Motors (ceases operations *Oct.* 22nd).

Nissan of Japan opens car assembly plant in Sunderland, north-east England (*Sept.* 8th).

British Defence Secretary announces Britain to scrap G.E.C. Nimrod early-warning aircraft programme and to order six U.S.-built Boeing 'AWACS' planes (*Dec.* 18th).

U.S. Supreme Court rules that Georgia law prohibiting oral and anal intercourse is not unconstitutional (*June* 30th).

U.S. Supreme Court supports preferential minority hiring quotas (*July* 2nd).

U.S. Senate votes for change in immigration laws, making employers who knowingly hire illegal aliens subject to civil fines (*Oct.* 17th).

British House of Commons votes to abolish corporal punishment in state schools (*July* 22nd).

N.S.P.C.C. reports doubling in number of reported cases of child sex abuse over year in Britain (*Dec.* 9th).

P Science, Technology, Discovery, etc.

Foundation of the Museum of Science and Industry at La Villette, Paris.

Jeana Yeager and Dick Rutan fly round the world in their *Voyager* aircraft without refuelling (*Dec.*).

The first 'lap size' computer introduced in the U.S.

U.S. space probe Voyager II passes close to Uranus (*Jan.*); photographs taken by the probe reveal 10 unknown satellites.

Explosion of U.S. space shuttle *Challenger* (*Jan.* 28th) leads to suspension of shuttle flights.

Launch of U.S.S.R. Mir I space station (*Feb.* 19th), intended to be permanently manned.

Return of Halley's Comet; it is photographed by five space probes, including the European probe Giotto, which flies into the comet's tail (*Mar.* 14th).

British surgeons perform the first heart, lung and liver transplant.

Surgeons develop an operation for removing tissue from the cornea by laser.

The U.S. government announces a structure for the supervision of research and applications in the field of genetic engineering (*June*).

Scientists at Massachusetts Institute of Technology announce discovery of the first gene that inhibits growth; it inhibits the cancer retinoblastoma.

Announcement of the approximate location of a gene causing Duchenne muscular dystrophy; this makes possible screening to find carriers of the gene.

U.S. Department of Agriculture permits the Biological Corporation of Omaha to market a virus produced by genetic engineering.

U.S. Food and Drug Administration approves use of the monoclonal antibody OKT3 in organ transplant surgery.

German physicists Johannes Bednorz and K.A. Müller announce discovery of a new superconducting material, in which superconductivity occurs at a higher temperature (30°K) than hitherto known; the potential for use of superconductivity is increased.

D **Apr**: 5th, bomb attack on 'La Belle' discotheque in West Berlin, frequented by U.S. servicemen, kills two and injures 200; Libyan involvement suspected;
10th, in Britain, Labour wins Fulham from Conservatives at by-election;
11th, in Lebanon, Brian Keenan, lecturer at American University of Beirut, is taken hostage;
14th, British House of Commons rejects bill to deregulate Sunday trading in England and Wales;
15th, bombers from U.S. warships and bases in Britain attack targets in Libya; 100 killed, 1 plane shot down;
17th, in Lebanon, bodies of two kidnapped Britons and one American found near Beirut; they had been murdered after the U.S. raid on Libya;
—, John McCarthy, acting bureau chief for Worldwide Television in Beirut, is taken hostage;
18th, President Botha of South Africa announces end to country's pass laws, restricting movement within the country;
—, in Britain, bomb discovered in El Al passenger's luggage at Heathrow airport; Jordanian, Nezar Hindawi, arrested for attempted bombing;
26th, major accident at Chernobyl nuclear power station near Kiev, U.S.S.R., announced after abnormally high levels of radiation reported in Sweden, Denmark and Finland;
30th, 2,000 police and commandos enter Sikh Golden Temple at Amritsar, India, to expel militants who had proclaimed an independent state of Khalistan.

E **May**: 3rd, 175 police and 150 demonstrators injured in violent protests outside News International's plant at Wapping, London;
4th, Babrak Karmal resigns as general secretary of People's Democratic (Communist) Party of Afghanistan; replaced by Najibullah, former head of Afghan secret police;
8th, British Labour Party makes large gains in local elections; Liberals win Ryedale from Conservatives in by-election;
10th, Britain expels three Syrian diplomats for alleged involvement in terrorism (11th, Syria expels three British diplomats);
18th, Sri Lankan forces seek to establish control over Jaffna peninsula in north, held by Tamil insurgents;
24th (–26th), Presidents of Nicaragua, Guatemala, El Salvador, Honduras and Costa Rica sign Declaration of Esquipulas at summit in Guatemala, endorsing Contadora peace treaty and calling for end to U.S. military intervention in area;
25th, in South Africa, 30,000 blacks expelled from homes in Crossroads squatter camp near Cape Town.

F **Jun**: 2nd, in India, 1,000 Sikhs arrested in Punjab during protests;
8th, former U.N. Secretary-General Kurt Waldheim elected President of Austria;
10th, in Britain, Patrick Magee convicted of murder of five people through bombing of Grand Hotel in Brighton (23rd, jailed for life);
12th, President Botha announces state of emergency throughout South Africa in response to deteriorating security situation; 1,000 black activists arrested;
—, report of Commonwealth Eminent Persons Group published, calls for economic sanctions against South Africa;
—, Northern Ireland Secretary announces dissolution of Northern Ireland Assembly set up in 1982;
20th, conference of 120 nations in Paris organized by U.N. Special Committee against Apartheid, O.A.U. and Non-Aligned Movement, calls for sanctions against South Africa;

Q Scholarship

M. Chibnall, *Anglo-Norman England, 1066–1166.*
David Morgan, *The Mongols.*
Oliver Rackham, *The History of the Countryside.*
G.R. Elton, *The Parliament of England, 1559–81.*
Stanley Wells, Gary Taylor (eds.), *William Shakespeare: The Complete Works.*
D.E. Underdown, *Revel, Riot and Rebellion: Popular Politics and Culture in England, 1603–60.*
Final volume of *The Collected Works of Walter Bagehot*, edited by Norman St John-Stevas.
Leon Radzinowicz, Roger Hood, *The Emergence of Penal Policy in Victorian and Edwardian England* (final volume in Leon Radzinowicz, *History of English Criminal Law and its Administration*).
Adrian Hastings, *A History of English Christianity, 1920–1985.*
Robert Rhodes James, *Anthony Eden.*
Arthur M. Schlesinger Jnr, *The Cycles of American History.*
Final volume of the *Supplement to the Oxford English Dictionary.*

R Philosophy and Religion

D.K. Lewis, *On the Plurality of Worlds.*
T. Nagel, *The View from Nowhere.*
A major Vatican document, *Instruction on Christian Freedom and Liberation*, recommends passive resistance against injustice and countenances armed struggle as 'a last resort to put an end to obvious and prolonged tyranny.'
The Vatican declares Father Charles Curran unfit to teach Catholic theology because of his writings on divorce, contraception, abortion and homosexuality.
Anglicans and Methodists in Britain are urged to support 'effective economic sanctions' against South Africa.
The Dutch Reformed Church in South Africa declares that racism is a sin.

S Art, Sculpture, Fine Arts and Architecture

Painting:
Opening of Palazzo Grassi, Venice; first exhibition: 'Futurism and Futurisms'.
Frank Auerbach, *Head of Catherine Lampert.*
Lucien Freud, *Painter and Model.*

Sculpture:
Turner Prize awarded to Gilbert and George.
Jeff Koons, *Rabbit.*

Architecture:
First show of British Architecture at Royal Academy, London, devoted to Richard Rogers, Norman Foster and James Stirling.
Gae Aulenti and international team of architects, Musée d'Orsay, Paris.
Arata Isozaki, Museum of Contemporary Art, Los Angeles.

T Music

Harrison Birtwistle, *Yan Tan Tethera* (opera).
John Cage, *But What About the Noise of Crumpling Paper....*
Elliott Carter, 4th String Quartet.
Helmut Lachenmann, *Ausklang.*
Krzysztof Penderecki, *Die schwarze Maske* (opera).
Aribert Reimann, *Troades* (opera).

F **Jun:** 26th (–27th), E.C. summit conference at The Hague appoints Sir Geoffrey Howe to lead peace mission to South Africa;
29th, General Jaruzelski announces amnesty for 300 political prisoners at Congress of Polish Communist Party.

G **Jul:** 5th, leader of Turkish Cypriots, Rauf Denktaş, refuses U.N. request for talks on re-opening of border dividing island;
7th, French agents jailed for sinking of *Rainbow Warrior* released into French custody;
11th, inflation in Britain falls to 2.5 per cent, lowest since *Dec.* 1967;
—, British newspapers banned from printing extracts from *Spycatcher*, the memoirs of former M.I.5 officer, Peter Wright;
17th, U.S. senate approves treaty allowing extradition of suspected I.R.A. terrorists to Britain;
24th, British government appoints advisory council to administer Turks and Caicos islands following resignation of Chief Minister and two others over alleged constitutional malpractice;
29th, Howe mission to South Africa fails to secure release of Nelson Mandela or lifting of ban on A.N.C.

H **Aug:** 3rd (–5th), special conference in London of seven Commonwealth leaders to consider policies on South Africa; Britain is only country to oppose sanctions programme;
11th, 154 Tamil refugees from Sri Lanka rescued from lifeboats off Newfoundland coast;
12th, U.S. suspends defence obligations to New Zealand following Labour government's espousal of anti-nuclear policy and denial of access for U.S. warships and military aircraft;
13th, ceremonies in Berlin to mark 25th anniversary of construction of Wall;
18th, Israel and U.S.S.R. hold talks in Helsinki on plight of Jews in U.S.S.R;
22nd, 1,700 die in Cameroon when toxic gas erupts from volcanic Lake Nyas;
23rd, Gennady F. Zakharov, U.S.S.R. diplomat accredited to U.N., arrested by F.B.I. and charged with spying (30th, U.S. newspaper correspondent Nicholas Daniloff arrested in Moscow and charged with spying).

J **Sep:** 6th, President Pinochet of Chile survives assassination attempt; state of siege declared;
7th, in South Africa, Rt. Rev. Desmond Tutu enthroned as first black Archbishop of Cape Town;
11th, share prices on Wall Street register biggest fall since 1929 due to renewed fears of inflation;
—, Israeli Prime Minister Peres holds talks with President Mubarak in Egypt;
16th, E.C. foreign ministers agree to prohibit new investment in South Africa;
17th, U.S. State Department orders 25 members of U.S.S.R. mission to U.N. out of the country by *Oct.* 1st;
21st, Prince of Wales admits he talks to plants;
23rd, British junior Health Minister Mrs. Edwina Currie blames poor health of northern Britons on ignorance;
24th, 4 million in Britain apply for shares in Trustee Savings Bank;
30th, British Labour Leader Neil Kinnock pledges a future Labour government will close all U.S. nuclear bases in Britain.

K **Oct:** 2nd, Indian Prime Minister Rajiv Gandhi survives assassination attempt in New Delhi;

U **Literature**

Peter Ackroyd, *Hawksmoor*.
Fleur Adcock, *The Incident Book*.
Yuz Aleshkovsky, *Kangaroo*.
Louise Erdrich, *The Beet Queen*.
William Gaddis, *Carpenter's Gothic*.
Günter Grass, *The Rat*.
David Grossman, *Smile of the Lamb*.
Garrison Keillor, *Lake Wobegon Days*.
Vikram Seth, *The Golden Gate*.
Endu Shusaku, *Scandal*.

V **The Press**

Production of *The Times*, *Sunday Times*, *The Sun* and *The News of the World* is moved overnight from central London premises to a new plant in Wapping, East London (*Jan.* 24th–25th).
Eddie Shah launches *Today*, Britain's first full-colour, low-cost tabloid newspaper (*Mar.* 4th); sales fail to achieve target levels, the paper is sold to 'Tiny' Rowland's Lonrho company.
Andreas Whittam-Smith and associates launch *The Independent* in Britain (*Oct.* 7th).

W **Drama and Entertainment**

Larry Kramer, *The Normal Heart*.
Richard Nelson, *Principia Scriptoriae*.
August Wilson, *Fences*.
The Phantom of the Opera.

Films:
Woody Allen's *Hannah and her Sisters*.
Jean-Jacques Beneix's *Betty Blue*.
Claude Berri's *Jean de Florette*.
Frears/Kureishi, *My Beautiful Laundrette*.
Jaime Hermosillo's *Dona Herlinda and her Son*.
David Lynch's *Blue Velvet*.
Oliver Stone's *Platoon*.
Andrei Tarkovsky's *Sacrifice*.

Television:
Inspector Morse.
Dennis Potter, *The Singing Detective*.

Popular music:
Husker Du, *Candy Apple Grey*.
Peter Gabriel, *So*.
Paul Simon, *Graceland*.
The Smiths, *The Queen is Dead*.

X **Sport**

After 10 successive defeats, Cambridge wins the English University Boat Race.
30 million people take part in Sportaid's 'Race Against Time', a series of fun runs held around the world to raise money for the starving of Africa (*May* 25th).
In the soccer World Cup, held in Mexico, Argentina beats West Germany 3–2 in the Final (*June* 29th).

K **Oct**: 2nd, U.S. Senate votes to impose economic sanctions on South Africa, overturning presidential veto;

5th, U.S.S.R. human rights campaigner Dr. Yuri Orlov released from Siberian exile and flown to U.S.;

11th (–12th), U.S.-U.S.S.R. mini-summit in Reykjavik fails to reach agreement on arms control, after President Reagan refuses to abandon Strategic Defense Initiative ('Star Wars');

12th, Queen Elizabeth II begins week-long visit to China, first by reigning British monarch;

19th, President Machel of Mozambique and 28 government officials killed in air crash in South Africa;

20th, Yitzhak Shamir succeeds Shimon Peres as Israeli Prime Minister under terms of 1984 rotation agreement;

—, Israeli nuclear technician Mordechai Vanunu kidnapped in London (*Dec.* 9th, Israelis admit to holding Mordechai Vanunu);

24th, Britain breaks off diplomatic relations with Syria for alleged involvement in plot to bomb El Al jet (*Apr.*).

L **Nov**: 2nd, U.S. hostage David Jacobsen freed in Beirut following intervention of British envoy Terry Waite;

3rd, Joaquim Chissano elected President of Mozambique;

—, details of U.S. arms deal with Iran to secure release of Beirut hostages appears in Lebanon magazine;

4th, Democrats gain control of Senate in U.S. mid-term elections;

6th, British Chancellor of Exchequer, Nigel Lawson, announces increase of £4.6 billion in government spending;

10th, President Ershad announces end to martial law in Bangladesh;

13th, U.S. President Reagan admits to secret arms deal with Iran, but denies involvement in hostage deal;

14th, U.S. securities dealer Ivan F. Boesky fined $100 million for illegal insider dealing;

25th, President Reagan's National Security Adviser, Vice-Admiral John Poindexter, resigns and aide, Lieutenant-Colonel Oliver North, is dismissed from National Security Council after revelation that money from arms sales was channelled to Contra rebels in Central America (26th, Reagan appoints former Senator John Tower to head inquiry into role of National Security Council in 'Iran-Contra scandal');

27th, French high school and university students protest at government education reforms (*Dec.* 8th, reform bill withdrawn).

M **Dec**: 3rd, British Gas floated on Stock Exchange; 4.5 million applications had been received for shares;

8th (–11th), food riots force Zambian government to reverse decision to double price of maize flour;

19th, U.S.S.R. authorities announce Andrei Sakharov and Yelena Bonner to return to Moscow after seven years' internal exile;

—, in U.S. Lawrence E. Walsh appointed special prosecutor to investigate Iran-Contra scandal;

30th, Esso announces withdrawal from South Africa.

X **Sport** (*cont.*)

Britain and Eire's women golfers win the Curtis Cup at Prairie Dunes, Kansas, their first victory in the U.S. and their first in the series since 1956.

Mike Tyson beats Trevor Berbick of Canada in two rounds to win the W.B.C. World Heavy-weight title in Las Vegas (*Nov.* 22nd); at 20 years, he is the youngest ever champion.

Y **Statistics**

Religious denominations in U.S. (in mill.): Roman Catholics, 52.9; Baptists, 23.7; Methodists, 12.6; Lutherans, 7.8; Mormons, 3.8; Presbyterians, 3.6; Protestant Episcopal, 2.5; Greek Orthodox, 1.9; Jews, 5.8.

Z **Births and Deaths**

Jan. 1st Lord David Cecil d. (83).
Jan. 4th Christopher Isherwood d. (81).
Jan. 23rd Joseph Beuys d. (64).
Feb. 16th Edmund Rubbra d. (84).
Apr. 14th Simone de Beauvoir d. (78).
June 14th Jorge Luis Borges d. (86).
July 26th Averell Harriman d. (94).
Aug. 31st Henry Moore d. (88).
Sept. 28th Robert Helpmann d. (77).
Nov. 8th Vyacheslav Molotov d. (96).
Dec. 16th Serge Lifar d. (81).
Dec. 29th Harold Macmillan d. (92).

1987 (Jan. – Apr.) Iran–Contra hearings — Naval action in Gulf — Agreement to eliminate intermediate nuclear forces

A **Jan:** 6th, Portuguese Council of State agrees to restore Macao to China before 2000 (*Apr.* 13th, Portugal signs agreement to return Macao in 1999);
9th, South African government bans all reporting of activities of A.N.C.;
15th, U.S.–U.S.S.R. arms control talks resume in Geneva;
20th, in Lebanon, Archbishop of Canterbury's envoy Terry Waite disappears in Beirut (*Feb.* 2nd, reported to be 'under arrest' in Beirut);
21st, new coalition government takes office in Austria under Dr. Franz Vranitzky;
24th, 162 police and 33 demonstrators injured in clashes outside Rupert Murdoch's News International plant at Wapping, London;
27th, U.S.S.R. leader Gorbachev proposes reforms, including secret ballots for election of party officials.

B **Feb:** 5th, S.O.G.A.T. ends picket of newspaper plant at Wapping, London;
—, Iran launches missile attack on Baghdad (19th, truce agreed in 'war of cities');
9th, Sino–U.S.S.R. talks on border held in Moscow, first since 1979;
10th, U.S.S.R. government announces release of 140 political dissidents;
—, Robert McFarlane, former U.S. National Security Adviser, attempts suicide after implicated in Iran–Contra scandal;
17th, in Eire Fianna Fail is returned as largest party in general election;
22nd, in Lebanon, 4,000 Syrian troops enter West Beirut in effort to end fighting between Shi'ite Moslem and Druze forces;
26th, report of Tower Commission, which investigated the management of the White House during the period of the 'Iran–Contra affair', is critical of Chief of Staff, Donald Regan (27th, Regan replaced by former Senator Howard Baker);
—, in Britain, S.D.P. wins Greenwich at by-election from Labour;
28th, U.S.S.R. leader Gorbachev proposes separate agreement abolishing intermediate-range nuclear weapons in Europe and drops insistence on curtailment of U.S. 'Star Wars' programme.

C **Mar:** 2nd (–4th), U.S.-U.S.S.R. proposals on medium-range missiles tabled at Geneva;
4th, President Reagan accepts full responsibility for Iran–Contra scandal;
6th, Townsend Thoresen cross-channel ferry, *Herald of Free Enterprise*, capsizes off Zeebrugge, killing 187;
10th, Charles Haughey elected Prime Minister of Eire;
13th, in Britain, Liberals retain Truro at by-election (called as consequence of death of M.P. David Penhaligon in car crash);
17th, British Budget reduces basic rate of income tax to 27 per cent, introduces new personal pension scheme, announces borrowing requirement of of £7 billion;
19th, Czechoslovak leader Gustáv Husák announces political and economic reforms;
25th, 6th National People's Congress opens in Peking; Premier Chao Tzu-yang confirms new liberal economic policies.

D **Apr:** 7th (–8th), in Lebanon, Syrian forces relieve Palestinian refugee camps of Shatila and Bourj-el-Barajneh after five-month siege by Shi'ite Amal militia;
8th, state of siege allowed to lapse in Paraguay, in force since 1947;
10th, Gorbachev announces that U.S.S.R. is prepared to negotiate on short- as well as intermediate-range missiles;
12th, general election in Fiji won by Indian-dominated coalition;
17th (–19th), rebellion by Argentine army officers;
—, Tamil terrorists ambush buses near Trincomale, killing 129;
20th (–26th), Palestinian National Council meets in Algiers; re-elects Arafat leader, but reduces his authority;

O Politics, Economics, Law and Education

Japan's National Railways transferred to seven private companies (*Apr.* 1st).
British Airways acquires British Caledonian for £237 million (*July* 16th).
U.S. Supreme Court upholds California law obliging employers to grant pregnant women up to four months' unpaid leave (*Jan.* 13th).
Court of Appeal in Britain rejects appeal by man to prevent a woman carrying his child from having an abortion (*Feb.* 23rd).
Vatican document, *Instruction on Respect for Human Life in its Origin and on the Dignity of Procreation: Replies to Certain Questions of the Day*, condemns artificial methods of fertilization and calls for ban on experiments on living embryos (*Mar.* 10th).
Superior Court Judge in 'Baby M.' case in U.S. denies parental rights to surrogate mother (*Mar.* 31st).
House of Lords in Britain approves sterilization of 17-year subnormal girl (*Apr.* 30th).
Formal announcement that world population has reached 5,000,000,000, double level of 1950 (*July* 11th).
British government announces intention to abolish Inner London Education Authority (*Sept.* 11th).
Allan Bloom, *The Closing of the American Mind.*

P Science, Technology, Discovery, etc.

An advanced supercomputer enters service, the Numerical Aerodynamic Simulation Facility, able to do 1,720,000,000 computations a second.
First suspect is convicted in Britain of two murders by evidence derived from genetic fingerprinting.
First glass-fibre optic cable laid across the Atlantic Ocean.
Digital audio tape cassettes, producing high-quality sound, go on sale.
International protocol to limit use of damaging CFCs.
Start of construction of Channel Tunnel between England and France (*Nov.*).
Launch of the U.S.S.R.'s Energia superbooster, the world's most powerful space launcher with thrust of 6.6 million lb.
U.S.S.R. cosmonaut Yuri V. Romanenko spends a record 326 days in the Mir space station (*Feb.* 6th–*Dec.* 29th).
Observation of radio waves from 3C326, believed to be a galaxy in the process of formation.
Discovery of the first supernova (explosion of a star) to be observed since 1604 (*Feb.* 24th).
Harvey Butcher of Groningen estimates that the Universe is younger than 10 billion years.
First successful five-organ transplant, in which a three-year-old girl in the U.S. receives a new liver, pancreas, small intestine and parts of the stomach and colon.
Surgeons at the University of Pennsylvania Hospital transplant an entire human knee.
Canadian surgeons use a laser to clear a blocked coronary artery.
A South African woman gives birth to triplets formed from her daughter's transplanted embryos.
The U.S. Patent and Trademark Office announces its intention to allow the patenting of animals produced by genetic engineering (*Apr.*).
Sir Walter Bodmer and associates announce the discovery of a marker for a gene that causes cancer of the colon.
David C. Page and associates announce the discovery of a gene that initiates the development of male features in mammals.

D **Apr**: 25th, in Northern Ireland, I.R.A. car bomb kills Lord Justice Maurice Gibson and Lady Gibson;
27th, U.S. Justice Department bars President Waldheim of Austria from entering U.S. for alleged involvement in Nazi atrocities.

E **May**: 1st, Quebec agrees to sign amended Canadian constitution recognizing it as a 'distinct society';
6th, ruling National Party wins sweeping victory in South African general election; Conservatives become second-largest party;
7th, Conservatives make gains in British local elections;
8th, in Northern Ireland, nine I.R.A. men killed in battle with police and troops after attempted bomb attack on police station in Loughall, Co. Armagh;
10th, Nationalist Party defeats ruling Labour Party in Malta's general election;
11th, Indian government imposes direct rule on Punjab;
14th, coup in Fiji led by Colonel Sitiveni Rabuka;
—, Egypt breaks off diplomatic relations with Iran over financing of Islamic fundamentalism;
17th, Iraqi Exocet missile hits U.S.S. *Stark* in Gulf, killing 37;
29th, 19-year-old West German, Mathias Rust, lands small plane in Moscow's Red Square (30th, Commander-in-Chief of U.S.S.R. Air Defences dismissed).

F **Jun**: 1st, Lebanese Prime Minister, Rashid Karami, killed by bomb on helicopter;
4th, West German Bundestag endorses U.S.–U.S.S.R. plan to eliminate medium-range missiles from Europe;
11th, Conservatives win British general election with overall majority of 101, winning 375 seats, against Labour, 229, Liberal-S.D.P. Alliance, 22; (Conservatives win 42.3 per cent of votes cast, Labour, 30.8, Liberal-S.D.P. Alliance, 22.6);
14th, large gains for Socialists in Italian general election;
18th, unemployment in Britain falls below 3 million;
21st, multi-candidate lists introduced in 5 per cent of constituencies in U.S.S.R. local elections;
25th, Károly Grósz, a reactionary, becomes Hungary's Prime Minister and later introduces an austerity programme to deal with economic problems.

G **Jul**: 1st, Single European Act in force, improving E.C. procedures and introducing qualified majority voting in Council of Ministers;
—, directors of London merchant bank Morgan Grenfell fined £25,000 for insider dealing;
7th, in evidence before Iran–Contra hearings, Colonel Oliver North claims his actions were sanctioned by superiors;
14th, opposition parties become legal in Taiwan;
17th, Vice-Admiral John Poindexter states that he authorized diversion of funds to Contra rebels;
20th, U.N. Security Council adopts Resolution 598 calling on Iran and Iraq to implement ceasefire;
21st, U.S. offers naval protection to Kuwaiti tankers in Gulf;
22nd, U.S.S.R. leader Gorbachev offers to dismantle all short- and medium-range missiles in U.S.S.R.;
24th, report of inquiry into *Herald of Free Enterprise* disaster (on *Mar.* 6th) critical of Townsend Thoresen company management;
29th, President Jayawardene and Prime Minister Gandhi sign agreement aimed at ending communal violence in Sri Lanka.

P **Science, Technology, Discovery, etc.** (*cont.*)

Chinese scientists insert genes controlling human growth hormones into goldfish and loach; they grow to four times the normal size.

Discovery of ceramics with superconducting properties.

Q **Scholarship**

R.R. Davies, *Conquest, Co-existence and Change: Wales 1063–1415*.

Maurice Howard, *The Early Tudor Country House: Architecture and Politics, 1490–1550*.

David Cressy, *Coming Over: Migration and Communication between England and New England in the Seventeenth Century*.

Simon Schama, *The Embarrassment of Riches*.

Robert Gildea, *Barricades and Borders: Europe 1800–1914*.

Charles Phythian-Adams, *Re-thinking English Local History*.

Richard Ellman, *Oscar Wilde*.

R **Philosophy and Religion**

Jacques Derrida, *Of Spirit: Heidegger and the Question*.

Hilary Putnam, *The Many Faces of Realism*.

Doctrine Commission of the Church of England publishes the report *We Believe in God*.

General Synod of Church of England debates homosexuality; published report states that sexual intercourse belongs properly within marriage, and that homosexuals should be met with compassion and a call to repentance.

The anonymous preface to the new edition of *Crockford's Clerical Directory* (published *Dec.* 2nd) is strongly critical of the Archbishops of Canterbury and York, and of the general leadership of the Church of England; its author, Dr. Gareth Bennett of New College, Oxford, commits suicide (*Dec.* 7th).

Patriarch Demetrios I of Constantinople joins in blessing crowds in St Peter's Square, Rome.

The Vatican announces plans to renew contact with the dissident Archbishop Marcel Lefebvre.

S **Art, Sculpture, Fine Arts and Architecture**

Painting:

Christie's sells van Gogh's *Irises* for £30 million, a world record sale price for art of any kind.

Turner Prize in Britain awarded to Richard Deacon.

'British Art of the Twentieth Century', exhibition at the Royal Academy, London.

Barbara Kruger, *I Shop Therefore I Am*.

Andres Serrano, *Piss Christ*.

Jeff Stultiens, *His Eminence, Cardinal Basil Hume, O.S.B., Archbishop of Westminster*.

Sculpture:

Richard Deacon, *The Back of my Hand*.

Architecture:

Le Corbusier retrospective exhibitions held at the Hayward Gallery, London, and Pompidou Centre, Paris.

Renzo Piano, de Menil Museum, Houston, Texas.

H **Aug:** 4th, Tamil rebels in Sri Lanka agree to surrender arms to Indian peacekeeping force;
6th, in Britain, Dr. David Owen resigns leadership of S.D.P., following vote in favour of merger negotiations with Liberals (28th, succeeded by Robert Maclennan);
7th, Arias Plan for peace in Central America signed by Presidents of Guatemala, El Salvador, Honduras, Nicaragua and Costa Rica;
12th, President Reagan insists he was not told of diversion of funds from arms sales to Nicaraguan Contras;
19th, gunman Michael Ryan kills 16 in English town of Hungerford, before shooting himself (*Sept.* 22nd, government bans automatic weapons of kind used by Ryan);
—, Zimbabwe's House of Assembly agrees change to constitution abolishing 20 seats reserved for whites;
—, U.S. announces restoration of full diplomatic relations with Syria;
30th, in Britain, Dr. David Owen announces formation of 'continuing' S.D.P.;

J **Sep:** 3rd, coup in Burundi; Military Committee for National Redemption formed;
6th, Radical Civic Union Party loses majority in Argentina's Chamber of Deputies;
7th, East German leader Honecker begins five-day official visit to West Germany; first by East German leader;
11th, U.N. Secretary-General begins peace mission to end Iran–Iraq War;
15th, diplomatic relations established between Albania and West Germany;
—(–17th), U.S. Secretary of State Shultz and U.S.S.R. Foreign Minister Shevardnadze reach agreement in principle on elimination of intermediate-range nuclear weapons;
17th, British Liberal Party Assembly votes for merger talks with S.D.P.;
—, constitutional affairs committee of President's Council in South Africa recommends repeal of 1953 Separate Amenities Act and relaxation of 1950 Group Areas Act;
25th, second coup in year in Fiji led by Colonel Sitiveni Rabuka.

K **Oct:** 1st, violent demonstrations against Chinese rule in Tibetan capital, Lhasa;
3rd, Canada and U.S. agree moves to reduce tariffs and economic barriers;
6th, Colonel Rabuka declares Fiji a republic;
8th, in Britain, inquest jury returns verdict of unlawful killing on 187 victims of Zeebrugge disaster;
13th (–17th), Commonwealth Conference in Vancouver; Britain dissents from declaration on South Africa;
15th, military coup in Burkina Faso;
—, Queen Elizabeth accepts resignation of Ratu Sir Penaia Ganilau as Governor-General of Fiji, ending 113-year colonial link;
16th, 'Great Storm' sweeps across south-east England, felling 15 million trees; reckoned to be worst storm in Britain for 300 years;
19th, Dow Jones Average falls 508.32 points (23 per cent), precipitating large falls in share values across world;
—, U.S. destroyers and commandos attack Iranian oil installations in Gulf;
25th (–*Nov.* 1st), 13th Communist Party Congress in Peking; Teng Hsiao p'ing retires as General Secretary and Politburo member.

L **Nov:** 1st, French authorities uncover arms haul on trawler *Eksund*, thought to be bound for I.R.A.;
2nd, U.S.S.R. leader Gorbachev, in speech to mark 70th anniversary of Russian Revolution, criticizes Stalin for political errors;

S **Art, Sculpture, Fine Arts and Architecture** (*cont.*)

James Stirling and Michael Willford, Clore Gallery, Tate Gallery, London.

Olympia and York property company takes over development of Canary Wharf, London Docklands; architects: Cesar Pelli, Adamson Associates, Frederick Gibberd and Partners.

T **Music**

John Adams, *Nixon in China* (opera).

George Benjamin, *Antara*.

Philip Glass, *The Making of the Representative for Planet 8* (opera).

Nigel Osborne, *The Electrification of the Soviet Union* (opera).

Judith Weir, *A Night at the Chinese Opera* (opera).

Iannis Xenakis, *Horos*.

U **Literature**

Chinua Achebe, *Anthills of the Savannah*.

Margaret Atwood, *The Handmaid's Tale*.

Bruce Chatwin, *Songlines*.

Robertson Davies, *What's Bred in the Bone*.

Kazuo Ishiguro, *An Artist of the Floating World*.

Haruki Marukami, *Norwegian Wood*.

Toni Morrison, *Beloved*.

Michael Ondaatje, *In the Skin of a Lion*.

Christopher Ricks (ed.), *The New Oxford Book of Victorian Verse*.

V **The Press**

Attempt made to establish *The News on Sunday*, a new left-wing British Sunday newspaper (*Apr.–Nov.*)

Robert Maxwell launches *The London Daily News* (*Feb.*), a new London evening newspaper; it is foiled by a temporary relaunch of the *Evening News* and closes in *July*.

Lonrho sells the British tabloid *Today* to Rupert Murdoch (*July*).

W **Drama and Entertainment**

Caryl Churchill, *Serious Money*.

Alma de Groen, *The Rivers of China*.

Lanford Wilson, *Burn This*.

Films:

Bille August's *Pelle the Conqueror*.

Bernardo Bertolucci's *The Last Emperor*.

Peter Gardos' *Whooping Cough*.

Brian de Palma's *The Untouchables*.

Wim Wenders' *Wings of Desire*.

Fatal Attraction.

Wall Street.

Italy lifts ban on *Last Tango in Paris*.

Popular music:

New Order, *Substance*.

U2, *The Joshua Tree*.

The Sugarcubes, 'Birthday'.

L Nov: 8th, in Northern Ireland, I.R.A. bombs explode at Remembrance Day service in Enniskillen, Co. Fermanagh, killing 11 (15th, Catholic Bishops in Northern Ireland and Republic denounce I.R.A. violence);

— (–11th), Arab summit meeting in Jordan; Syria's President Assad agrees to end political and military support of Iran;

11th, Boris Yeltsin dismissed as chief of Moscow Communist Party following criticism of slow pace of reforms;

18th, report of joint Senate/House of Representatives Iran–Contra Committee blames President Reagan for abuse of law; eight Republicans refuse to sign report;

—, Ethiopian government announces that 5 million people are facing starvation in northern provinces;

—, 30 die in fire at King's Cross Underground Station, London;

23rd (–24th), Secretary of State Shultz and U.S.S.R. Foreign Minister Shevardnadze agree treaty to eliminate all intermediate-range nuclear (I.N.F.) weapons;

24th, Li P'eng succeeds Chao Tzu-yang as China's Prime Minister;

—, government of Eire agrees new extradition arrangements with Britain, removing right to claim exemption for politically motivated crime.

M Dec: 7th (–10th), U.S.–U.S.S.R. Summit in Washington; Reagan and Gorbachev agree to eliminate intermediate nuclear forces;

17th, Gustáv Husák resigns as General Secretary of Czechoslovak Communist Party; succeeded by Milos Jakeš;

21st, 2,000 killed in ferry disaster in Philippines;

22nd, in Zimbabwe, Prime Minister Mugabe and Joshua Nkomo agree to unite ZANU (P.F.) and ZAPU parties;

—, U.N. Security Council criticizes Israeli action against Palestinians protesting on West Bank and Gaza Strip;

28th, Tunisia and Libya restore diplomatic relations;

31st, U.S. dollar reaches all-time low against major currencies.

X Sport

Sunil Gavaskar of India, playing in his 124th Test match, becomes the first batsman to score 10,000 Test runs (*Mar.* 7th).

Stephen Roche is the first Irishman and the second rider from beyond continental Europe to win the Tour de France (*July* 26th).

Laura Davies is the first British golfer to win the U.S. Women's Open Championship (*July* 28th).

Europe's golfers win the Ryder Cup in the U.S. for the first time (*Sept.* 27th).

Y Statistics

Divorces (as percentage of marriages contracted): Australia, 34; Belgium, 31; Canada, 43; Czechoslovakia, 32; Denmark, 44; Finland, 38; France, 31; West Germany, 30; Great Britain and Northern Ireland, 41; Greece, 13; Holland, 28; Italy, 8; Japan, 22; Norway, 40; Sweden, 44; U.S., 48.

Z Births and Deaths

Feb. 4th Liberace d. (67).
Mar. 3rd Danny Kaye d. (74).
Mar. 19th Duc Louis de Broglie d. (94).
Apr. 11th Primo Levi d. (67).
June 2nd Andrés Segovia d. (93).
June 22nd Fred Astaire d. (88).
Aug. 17th Rudolf Hess d. (93).
Oct. 3rd Jean Anouilh d. (77).
Oct. 19th Jacqueline du Pré d. (42).
Oct. 29th Woody Herman d. (74).
Nov. 30th James Baldwin d. (63).

1988 (Jan. – Apr.) U.S.S.R. withdrawal from Afghanistan—Election of George Bush as U.S. President

A **Jan**: 2nd, Canada and U.S. sign free trade agreement;
3rd, Mrs. Thatcher becomes longest serving British Prime Minister in 20th century;
8th, New York stock market registers third largest one-day fall in history, with Dow Jones average closing 140.58 points down on the day;
17th, presidential elections held in Haiti amidst allegations of voting irregularities;
22nd, U.S. submits draft space defence treaty at U.S.–U.S.S.R. disarmament talks in Geneva;
25th, Ramsewak Shankar is inaugurated as President of Surinam, bringing end to eight years of military rule;
26th, celebrations in Sydney mark bicentenary of arrival of European settlers in Australia;
29th, talks in Luganda achieve agreement for Cuban military withdrawal from Angola.

B **Feb**: 2nd, 2,000 nurses and other health workers in London hospitals hold a one-day strike over pay;
7th, Leslie Manigat inaugurated as President in Haiti, ending two years of military rule;
8th, Gorbachev announces that U.S.S.R. troops will begin withdrawal from Afghanistan on *May* 15th;
—, International Commission finds that Kurt Waldheim, President of Austria, knew about wartime atrocities in the Balkans, but clears him of war crimes;
10th, over 100 people die in violence during local elections in Bangladesh;
20th, Regional Soviet in Nagorno-Karabakh votes for region to be transferred from Azerbaijan to Armenia;
23rd, torrential rain in Brazil leaves 275 reported dead and 25,000 homeless;
—, U.S. Secretary of State George Shultz arrives in Israel at start of Middle East peace mission;
26th, Gorbachev makes unprecedented television appeal for calm after week of nationalist demonstrations in Armenia;
29th, in South Africa, Archbishop Desmond Tutu and 100 clergy detained in Cape Town while protesting at curbs imposed (on *Feb.* 24th) on anti-apartheid organisations.

C **Mar**: 1st, U.S.S.R. troops enforce curfew in Sumgait in Azerbaijan following deaths in ethnic violence;
6th, three suspected I.R.A. terrorists are shot dead by S.A.S. team in Gibraltar;
14th, three days of clashes begin between China and Vietnam over the disputed Spratly Islands;
15th, in the Budget, Chancellor Nigel Lawson reduces standard rate of income tax in Britain to 25 per cent and replaces all higher rates with single rate of 40 per cent;
20th, elections to National Assembly in El Salvador won by right-wing Nationalist Republican Alliance;
23rd, Contra commanders and Government officials sign 60-day ceasefire agreement in Nicaragua;
29th, British Secretary for Trade and Industry Lord Young announces sale of Rover car group to British Aerospace.

D **Apr**: 2nd, Indian forces seal border with Pakistan against infiltration of Sikh extremists after 120 deaths in week of violence in the Punjab;
3rd, peace agreement between Ethiopia and Somalia ends 11 years of border conflict;

O Politics, Economics, Law and Education

U.S.S.R. Supreme Court approves posthumous judicial rehabilitation of Nikolai Bukharin and nine other Soviet leaders executed or imprisoned at 1938 'show trial' (*Feb.* 4th).

British House of Commons votes to allow its proceedings to be televised (*Feb.* 9th).

British Local Government Act requires local authorities to put more services out to competitive tendering.

In Britain, Liberals and Social Democrats merge to form a new party (*Mar.*).

In bid to reduce overproduction of foodstuffs, E.C. starts to pay farmers to 'set aside' land from production.

In Britain, persistent disagreement between Prime Minister Thatcher and Chancellor Nigel Lawson on exchange rate policy unsettles money markets.

British Education Reform Act allows state schools to 'opt out' of local authority control and become 'grant-maintained schools' receiving funds from central government.

First pupils in England, Wales and Northern Ireland sit G.C.S.E. (General Certificate of Secondary Education) examinations, which replace the G.C.E. 'ordinary level' and C.S.E.

P Science, Technology, Discovery, etc.

The *Daedalus 88* sets new record for man-powered flight, covering 74 miles in 3 hours and 54 minutes.

U.S. 'Stealth bomber', invisible to radar and heat-seeking missiles, goes on public display (*Nov.*).

Serious damage is done to computer systems world-wide by 'viruses' implanted by 'hackers' breaking into computer networks.

Launch of two U.S.S.R. Phobos space probes (*July* 7th and 12th), to study Phobos, one of the moons of Mars; Phobos I is accidentally sent a 'suicide' instruction.

Israel launches a satellite (*Sept.* 19th), for geophysical studies.

First mission of the U.S. shuttle for almost three years (*Sept.* 29th–*Oct.* 3rd).

U.S.S.R. unmanned space shuttle *Buran* ('blizzard') makes its inaugural flight, under radio control (*Nov.* 15th).

Simon J. Lilly of the University of Hawaii reports the location of a galaxy about 12 billion light years from Earth, adding to evidence about the date of galaxy formation.

Stephen Hawking, *A Brief History of Time*.

A French company markets the abortion-inducing drug RV486; anti-abortion groups protest.

U.S. scientists announce a project to compile a complete 'map' of human genes; establishment of the Human Genome Organization (HUGO) in Washington, D.C.

U.S. Patent and Trademark Office grants Harvard University a patent for a mouse developed by genetic engineering (*Apr.*).

R. Jaenisch and associates implant a human gene, connected with a hereditary disorder, into a mouse.

The first dairy cattle are produced by cloning embryos.

Q Scholarship

A rich tomb of c. A.D. 300 is found near Sipan in Peru.

John Cannon et al. (eds.), *The Blackwell Dictionary of Historians*.

C. Brooke, R. Highfield and W. Swaan, *Oxford and Cambridge*.

D **Apr:** 5th, Shi'ite Moslem extremists hijack a Kuwait Airways 747 airliner, forcing it to fly to Iran and to Cyprus, where two hostages are shot dead (20th, hijack ends in Algiers);
10th, hundreds of deaths in explosion at army ammunition dump near Islamabad in Pakistan, for which Afghan agents are believed responsible;
16th, assassination of military commander of P.L.O., Abu Jihad, in Tunis;
18th, U.S. planes and warships destroy two Iranian oil platforms and attack ships in the Gulf in retaliation for damage to a U.S. frigate;
22nd, France flies in military reinforcements when three gendarmes are killed and others captured by Kanak separatists in New Caledonia;
25th, in Israel, John Demjanjuk ('Ivan the Terrible') is sentenced to death for war crimes in the gas chambers in the Treblinka concentration camp.

E **May:** 2nd, thousands of shipyard workers go on strike in Poland and seven Solidarity leaders are detained;
3rd, Islamic Jihad free three French hostages in Lebanon amidst allegations that France had done a deal with Iran;
6th, Pope John Paul II begins a 13-day tour of Uruguay, Bolivia, Peru and Paraguay;
8th, President Mitterrand (Socialist) defeats Jacques Chirac (Gaullist) in French Presidential elections, with over 54 per cent of poll;
10th, Chirac resigns as French Prime Minister and is replaced by Michel Rocard (Socialist);
15th, U.S.S.R. troops begin withdrawal from Afghanistan after eight and a half years;
19th, in India, Sikh rebels surrender after occupying Golden Temple in Amritsar;
23rd, in Britain, the second largest turn-out of peers in the 20th century secures majority of 134 for the Government's Poll Tax Bill in the House of Lords;

F **Jun:** 1st, Reagan and Gorbachev sign Intermediate-range Nuclear Forces (I.N.F.) treaty at Moscow Summit (*May* 29th–*June* 2nd);
2nd, Canberra High Court dismisses British Government's appeal against sale of Peter Wright's book *Spycatcher*, after 18 months of legal proceedings;
5th, in Moscow, leading world churchmen celebrate 1,000 years of Christianity in Russia;
19th, civilian President of Haiti, Leslie Manigat, is deposed by a military coup and replaced by General Henri Namphy;
23rd, U.S.S.R. troops move into parts of Armenia, Azerbaijan and the disputed region of Nagorno-Karabakh, as ethnic violence enters its fifth month;
28th (–*July* 1st), at 19th Communist Party conference in Moscow, Gorbachev outlines plans for changes in the administrative structure of the U.S.S.R., intended to make the Party more democratic and businesses more autonomous.

G **Jul:** 3rd, U.S. warship *Vincennes* shoots down Iranian civilian airliner in the Gulf, with loss of 290 lives;
6th, explosion on North Sea Piper Alpha oil platform kills 167;
—, presidential elections in Mexico won by Carlos Salinas de Gortari, of the ruling Institutional Revolutionary Party;
11th, Nicaragua expels U.S. ambassador and seven colleagues, on charge of inciting violent anti-government incidents;
18th, 70th birthday of A.N.C. leader Nelson Mandela marked by worldwide protests calling for his release from prison in South Africa;
28th, Israeli representative makes first official visit to U.S.S.R. since 1967;
31st, King Hussein of Jordan announces plans to cut legal and administrative ties with the occupied West Bank.

Q Scholarship

E.A. Wrigley, *Continuity, Chance, and Change: The Character of the Industrial Revolution in England.*
James McPherson, *Battle Cry of Freedom.*
John Sutherland, *Longman Companion to Victorian Fiction.*
Colin Holmes, *John Bull's Island: Immigration and British Society, 1871–1971.*
J.M. Winter, *The Experience of World War I.*
Eighth and final volume of the official biography of Winston Churchill by Martin Gilbert.
Sir Henry Phelps Brown, *Egalitarianism and the Generation of Inequality.*
Neil Sheehan, *A Bright Shining Lie: John Paul Vann and America in Vietnam.*

R Philosophy and Religion

Ted Honderich, *The Consequences of Determinism.*
Alisdair MacIntyre, *Whose Justice? Which Rationality?*
The Lambeth Conference of Anglican Bishops is held in Canterbury, England.
Rev. Barbara Harris, a divorcee, is elected as first woman bishop in the Anglican communion (*Sept.* 25th), to serve as suffragan Bishop of Massachusetts (consecrated *Feb.* 11th 1989).
In the Apostolic Letter *Mulieris Dignitatem* Pope John Paul II reiterates his opposition to women priests.
The film *The Last Temptation of Christ* is widely regarded as blasphemous.
The Holy Shroud of Turin, claimed by some to be Christ's mortuary cloth, is shown by carbon dating to date from the 14th century.
Archbishop Lefebvre consecrates four bishops in his traditionalist movement and is automatically excommunicated by Rome.
The South African Council of Churches headquarters is bombed.

S Art, Sculpture, Fine Arts and Architecture

Painting:

Jasper Johns's *False Start* sold for $17,050,000, a world record for contemporary art and for a work by a living artist.
Turner Prize awarded to Tony Cragg.
Francesco Clemente, *Paradigm.*
Peter Halley, *Red Cell.*

Sculpture:

Tony Cragg, *Generations.*
Anish Kapoor, *Mother as Void.*
Rachel Whiteread, *Closet.*

Architecture:

'Deconstructivist Architecture' exhibition at the Museum of Modern Art, New York.

T Music

Luciano Berio, *Ofanim.*
György Ligeti, Concerto for Piano and Orchestra.
Witold Lutoslawski, Piano Concerto.
Meredith Monk, *Book of Days.*
Karlheinz Stockhausen, *Montag aus Licht* (opera).

H **Aug**: 7th, over 1 million people in Sudan are homeless after widespread flooding in Khartoum and surrounding provinces;

8th, Iraq and Iran announce ceasefire;

17th, President Zia ul-Haq and the U.S. ambassador to Pakistan are killed when plane carrying them explodes in mid-air; state of emergency is declared;

25th, in Portugal, centre of Lisbon gutted by fire;

31st, Lech Walesa holds first talks with Polish authorities since the banning of Solidarity in 1981;

—, widespread flooding in Bangladesh leaves 25 million homeless.

J **Sep**: 4th, demonstrations by Serbs and Montenegrins in Yugoslavia calling for martial law in Kosovo and protection from Albanian separatists;

18th, in Haiti General is deposed in military coup;

20th, in speech to Council of Europe at Bruges, Mrs. Thatcher warns against the folly of moves towards political and economic union of Europe;

21st, state of emergency declared in Nagorno-Karabakh, U.S.S.R.;

22nd, Brazil concludes agreement with creditor banks, rescheduling debts of US$62,100 million;

29th, Nobel Peace Prize awarded to U.N. Peacekeeping forces;

30th, major changes are made in U.S.S.R. Politburo, including retirement of President Andrei Gromyko and dismissal of leading figures.

K **Oct**: 1st, Mikhail Gorbachev is elected President of U.S.S.R. by Supreme Soviet;

2nd, founding of Estonian Popular Front;

3rd, Chad and Libya end war and establish diplomatic relations;

6th, Algerian government introduces emergency measures, following rioting against rising prices and unemployment;

11th, Ladislav Adamec replaces Lubomir Štrougal as Prime Minister of Czechoslovakia as part of major changes in government and Communist Party;

19th, British Home Secretary announces ban on broadcasting of interviews with 11 terrorist organisations, including Sinn Fein;

26th, simultaneous elections to white, black, coloured and Indian local councils held for first time in South Africa;

31st, Polish Government announces closure of Gdansk shipyard.

L **Nov**: 1st, Israeli elections produce no clear winner;

2nd, Mrs. Thatcher begins three-day visit to Poland, in which she holds talks with the Prime Minister and meets Lech Walesa at Gdansk shipyard;

8th, in U.S. Presidential elections Republican George Bush, with 426 electoral college votes, defeats Democrat Michael Dukakis, with 112 votes, but the Democratic Party increases its majority in the Senate and House of Representatives; popular vote: Bush, 48,886,097; Dukakis, 41,809,074;

15th, P.L.O. Parliament in exile declares an independent state of Palestine;

16th, Parliament in Estonia votes to give itself rights to veto laws from Moscow;

—, Benazir Bhutto's Pakistan People's Party win 94 seats in general election (*Dec.* 2nd, she is sworn in as Prime Minister of Pakistan);

21st, general election in Canada won by Progresive Conservative Party led by Prime Minister Brian Mulroney;

22nd, Queen's Speech at State Opening of British Parliament announces Bills for Privatisation of Water and Electricity services;

23rd, two regions of Azerbaijan placed under state of emergency following ethnic clashes;

24th, Egypt and Algeria restore diplomatic relations.

U Literature

Kobo Abe, *The Ark Sakura.*
Saul Bellow, *More Die of Heartbreak.*
Peter Carey, *Oscar and Lucinda.*
Gabriel García Márquez, *Love in the Time of Cholera.*
Eduardo Mendoza, *The City of Marvels.*
Brian Moore, *The Colour of Blood.*
Milorad Pavic, *Dictionary of the Khazars.*
Salman Rushdie, *The Satanic Verses.*
Anatoli Rybakov, *Children of the Arbat* (published after a 20-year ban in the U.S.S.R.).

V The Press

The British weekly *New Society* is merged into *New Statesman* (*Feb.*).
The Sun pays £1 million to British singer Elton John to settle the pop singer's libel claim out of court.
Eddie Shah launches a new British daily paper, *The Post*, but it folds after 33 issues (*Nov.–Dec.*).

W Drama and Entertainment

David Henry Hwang, *M. Butterfly.*
David Mamet, *Speed-the-Plow.*
Gieve Patel, *Mister Behram.*
Sam Shepard, *A Lie of the Mind.*
Timberlake Wertenbaker, *Our Country's Good.*
Richard Eyre replaces Peter Hall as Director of Britain's National Theatre.

Films:
David Cronenberg's *Dead Ringers.*
Krzysztof Kieslowski, *Dekalog.*
Louis Malle's *Au Revoir les Enfants.*
Martin Scorcese's *The Last Temptation of Christ.*
A Fish Called Wanda.
Rain Man.

Popular music:
Rock stars make world-wide tour to give concerts in aid of Amnesty International.
Concert held at Wembley Stadium, London, to celebrate the 70th birthday of Nelson Mandela.
k d lang, *Shadowland.*
My Bloody Valentine, *Isn't Anything.*
The Pixies, *Surfer Rosa.*
Sonic Youth, *Daydream Nation.*

X Sport

'Sandy' Lyle is first British golfer to win the U.S. Masters, held at Augusta, Georgia (*Apr.* 10th).
Tottenham Hotspur Football Club, London, pays record £2 million transfer fee for Paul Gascoigne (*July* 7th).

M **Dec:** 7th, in New York, Gorbachev announces plans to reduce U.S.S.R. armed forces and conventional weapons;

12th, 34 die in rail crash at Clapham Junction in South London, the worst rail accident in Britain for 20 years;

14th, Spain has 24-hour general strike, the first such for 50 years;

15th, U.S. resumes contacts with P.L.O. after 13-year boycott;

16th, Mrs. Edwina Currie, Under-Secretary of State for Health, resigns after allegation of widespread salmonella infection in British egg production leads to collapse in egg sales;

21st, terrorist bomb explodes on Pan Am Boeing 747 airliner flying over Lockerbie in Scotland, killing all on board and 11 on the ground;

22nd, agreement reached at U.N. for Namibian independence, with phased withdrawal of Cuban forces;

30th, Government of Yugoslavia, led by Branko Mikulic, resigns as parliament blocks economic reform package.

X **Sport** *(cont.)*

XXIII Olympic Games in Seoul, South Korea, is free of boycotts. The U.S.S.R. wins 55 gold medals; East Germany, 37; U.S., 36; South Korea, 12; West Germany and Hungary, 11; Bulgaria, 10; Roumania, 7; France and Italy, 6; China, United Kingdom and Kenya, 5. In the Athletics, Ben Johnson of Canada wins the 100 metres in a world record time of 9.79 seconds; he is then stripped of the title when drug tests reveal traces of the anabolic steroid, stanozol.

Steffi Graf of West Germany becomes only the third woman to win the Grand Slam of all four major tennis tournaments; she also wins an Olympic gold, following the restoration of tennis to the Olympic Games at Seoul.

India refuses entry to cricket players who had sporting contacts with South Africa, forcing England to call off winter tour (*Sept.* 9th).

Y **Statistics**

Production of passenger cars (thousands): Japan, 8,198; U.S., 7,105; West Germany, 4,312; France, 3,228; Italy, 1,883; Spain, 1,498; U.S.S.R., 1,262; Great Britain, 1,227; Canada, 1,008; South Korea, 868; Brazil, 782; Sweden, 407; Others, 2,167.

Z **Births and Deaths**

Feb. 2nd Solomon d. (85).
Feb. 5th Ove Arup d. (92).
Feb. 15th Richard Feynman d. (69).
Apr. 12th Alan Paton d. (85).
Apr. 23rd Michael Ramsey d. (83).
Aug. 14th Enzo Ferrari d. (90).
Oct. 2nd Alec Issigonis d. (81).
Oct. 28th Pietro Annigoni d. (78).
Dec. 30th Isamu Noguchi d. (84).

1989 (Jan. – Mar.) Massacre in T'ien–an Men Square—Collapse of communism in Eastern Europe

A **Jan**: 2nd, Ranasinghe Premadasa sworn in as President of Sri Lanka;
6th, U.S.S.R. announces mass rehabilitation of thousands of citizens who were victims of Stalin's purges 1930–1950;
7th, Emperor Hirohito of Japan dies after a 62-year reign; his son, Crown Prince Akihito, succeeds him;
10th, Cuban troops begin withdrawal from Angola;
11th, 149 countries agree declaration outlawing use of poison gas, toxic and bacteriological weapons;
—, Hungarian Parliament passes law allowing formation of political parties;
15th, riot police in Prague break up demonstration marking 20th anniversary of Jan Palach's suicide in protest at Soviet invasion of Czechoslovakia;
19th, Ante Marković is named Prime Minister of Yugoslavia;
20th, George Bush inaugurated as 41st President of U.S.;
23rd, 274 die in earthquake in Tajikistan, U.S.S.R.;
31st, trial begins of Colonel Oliver North, U.S. Marines officer at centre of Iran–Contra affair.

B **Feb**: 2nd, President Botha resigns as leader of ruling National Party in South Africa, following a stroke; F.W. de Klerk succeeds him;
—, Carlos Andrés Pérez sworn in as President of Venezuela;
3rd, 35-year-old regime of President Alfredo Stroesner in Paraguay is overthrown by military coup led by General Andrés Rodríguez, who replaces him as President (*May* 1st, Rodríguez gains landslide victory in elections);
9th, in Jamaican general election, Michael Manley's People's National Party wins landslide victory over ruling Jamaica Labour Party;
—, in Bermuda, United Bermuda Party wins third successive election victory, but with reduced majority;
14th, Ayatollah Khomeini issues fatwa against British author Salman Rushdie, calling for his death for blasphemy in his book *The Satanic Verses*; Rushdie goes into hiding;
17th, leaders of Morocco, Libya, Algeria, Tunisia and Mauritania form economic bloc called Arab Maghreb Union;
18th, President Najibullah imposes state of emergency in Afghanistan;
21st, Václav Havel, dissident playwright, is imprisoned for inciting public disorder in Prague in *Jan*.

C **Mar**: 5th, cabinet resigns in Sudan; Prime Minister Sadiq al-Mahdi agrees to form coalition government and introduce a peace plan to end civil war;
7th, Iran formally breaks off diplomatic relations with Britain over the Rushdie affair;
—, China imposes martial law in Lhasa, Tibet;
15th, demonstration in Budapest calling for democracy and national independence;
19th, Alfredo Cristiani (Arena party) gains outright victory over Dr. Fidel Chavez Mena (Christian Democrats) in El Salvador presidential election;
24th, *Exxon Valdez* oil tanker runs aground in Prince William Sound, Alaska, spilling estimated 11 million gallons of oil (27th, U.S. declares state of emergency);
26th, voters have a choice of candidates for first time in elections for Congress of People's Deputies in U.S.S.R.; Boris Yeltsin, dismissed from the Politburo 17 months before, gains 89 per cent of vote in his Moscow constituency, while many senior Party officials fail to get elected;
28th, Solomon Mamaloni, new Prime Minister of the Solomon Islands, announces intention of turning the Islands into a republic, ending 100-year link with British Crown.

O **Politics, Economics, Law and Education**

South African law commission publishes working paper calling for the abolition of apartheid and introduction of universal franchise (*Mar.* 11th).

Proceedings of the British House of Commons are televised for first time (*Nov.* 21st).

British Security Services Act places M.I.5 and M.I.6 under a degree of judicial supervision; reform of Official Secrets Act creates clear categories of secret information, disclosure of which would be a criminal offence.

E.C. summit adopts Social Charter on workers' rights with Britain dissenting (*Dec.* 9th).

Court of First Instance established to relieve the over-burdened European Court of Justice of some cases.

British Court of Appeal is given power to review sentences considered lenient.

Following complaints from Moslems about Salman Rushdie's novel *The Satanic Verses*, the British Home Office announces that Blasphemy Law will not be extended to cover Islam.

In Britain, on appeal, the 'Guildford Four' are cleared of bombing convictions after serving 14 years of their life sentences (*Oct.* 17th).

Children Act compels British parents in divorce cases to consider the interests of their offspring in divorce settlements.

National Curriculum is introduced into schools in England and Wales.

P **Science, Technology, Discovery, etc.**

U.S. space shuttle launches the probe Magellan (*May* 4th), to map the surface of Venus using radar.

Launch of the European Space Agency's Hipparcos satellite, carrying two telescopes for measuring the distance of stars.

U.S. space probe Voyager II reaches Neptune and transmits pictures (*Aug.* 25th); it discovers a great dark spot on the planet.

U.S. shuttle launches the probe Galileo (*Oct.* 18th) to explore Jupiter.

Launch of the U.S. COBE (Cosmic Background Explorer) satellite to study microwave background radiation, thought to be a vestige of the 'big bang'.

Inauguration of LEP (Large Electron Positron Collider) at the C.E.R.N. research centre in Switzerland (*July* 14); the new accelerator has a circumference of 16.8 miles.

Stanley Pons and Martin Fleischmann announce (*Mar.*) that they have achieved nuclear fusion at room temperature; other scientists fail to replicate their experiment.

M. Harrison and colleagues remove a foetus from its mother's womb, operate on its lungs, and return it to the womb.

Researchers in Toronto and Michigan identify a gene responsible for cystic fibrosis.

Scientists in Britain introduce genetically engineered white blood cells into cancer patients, to attack tumours.

Q **Scholarship**

The Cambridge History of Japan (–).

Remains of the Rose and Globe Theatres uncovered in London, where Shakespeare's plays were originally performed.

Colin Morris, *The Papal Monarchy*.

Christopher Dyer, *Standards of Living in the Later Middle Ages: Social Change in England, c.1200–1520*.

C.N.L. Brooke, *The Medieval Idea of Marriage*.

D **Apr**: 2nd, government of General Prosper Avril in Haiti survives attempted coup;
5th, Lech Walesa and Polish Government sign agreement for political and economic reforms;
6th (–13th), in trial of Oliver North in U.S., North says that he acted on orders in arranging arms deals with Iran and diverting the profits to Nicaraguan Contras (*May* 4th, found guilty);
9th, Soviet troops disperse pro-independence demonstrators in Georgian capital, Tbilisi;
17th, Solidarity is legalised in Poland;
—, students march on Peking's T'ien-an Men Square to call for democracy;
20th, first multi-party elections in Czechoslovakia since 1946;
25th, Japanese Prime Minister, Noboru Takeshita, resigns over bribery scandal; replaced by Sosuke Uno;
26th, anti-Senegalese violence in Mauritius leaves 400 dead (28th, revenge killings in Senegal).

E **May**: 2nd, Hungarian troops start to dismantle 218-mile-long security fence along border with Austria;
3rd, centre-right coalition under Ruud Lubbers in Holland becomes first European government to resign over an environmental issue, when Liberal Democrats refuse support for proposals for financing of anti-pollution measures;
6th, elections held in Panama, subsequently annulled by General Noriega;
14th, Carlos Menem (Peronist) defeats Eduardo Angeloz (ruling Radical party) in Argentinian presidential elections (*July* 8th, Menem takes over as President on resignation of Alfonsín);
16th, Sheikh Hassan Khaled, Grand Mufti of Lebanon, dies in car bomb explosion in West Beirut;
17th, over 50 senior military officers die in unsuccessful coup in Ethiopia;
—, in Poland, Roman Catholic Church is given status unparalleled in Eastern Europe, with restoration of property confiscated in the 1950s and the right to run schools;
19th, Ciriaco De Mita announces resignation of his centre-left government in Italy (*July* 23rd, Giulio Andreotti becomes Prime Minister of similar coalition);
20th, in Spain, 13 are convicted for their part in distributing cooking oil in 1981 which killed more than 600 people;
29th, at N.A.T.O. summit in Brussels, President Bush proposes that both U.S. and U.S.S.R. cut forces in Europe and that N.A.T.O. should have a new role in opening up Eastern Europe to Western freedoms.

F **Jun**: 3rd, in China People's Army tanks move into T'ien-an Men Square in Peking killing 2,000 pro-democracy demonstrators;
—, Ayatollah Khomeini, spiritual and political leader of Iran, dies;
4th, Solidarity achieves landslide victory in elections to Polish Parliament;
12th, Gorbachev and Chancellor Kohl of West Germany sign Bonn Document affirming right of European states to determine their own political systems;
18th, Andreas Papandreou's Pasok Government loses overall majority in general election in Greece (*July* 2nd, interim government of New Democracy and Communists, led by Tzannis Tzannetakis, is sworn in);
23rd, President Jose Eduardo dos Santos of Angola and Dr. Jonas Savimbi, leader of U.N.I.T.A. rebels, sign declaration ending 14-year civil war in Angola;
28th, Tamil Tigers in Sri Lanka agree to ceasefire; lasts until *Nov.* 5th;
29th, government of Sadiq al-Mahdi in Sudan is overthrown in coup.

Q **Scholarship** (*cont.*)

Lyndal Roper, *The Holy Household: Women and Morals in Reformation Augsburg.*
Paul Langford, *A Polite and Commercial People: England 1727–1783.*
Simon Schama, *Citizens.*
Richard Holt, *Sport and the British.*
Avner Offer, *The First World War: An Agrarian Interpretation.*
Paul Fussell, *Wartime.*
Hugo Young, *One of Us.*
The Victoria History of the Counties of England celebrates 200 volumes with exhibition 'Particular Places' at the British Library and accompanying book (same title) by Christopher Lewis.
J.A. Simpson, E.S.C. Weiner (eds.), *The Oxford English Dictionary*, 2nd edn.

R **Philosophy and Religion**

David Armstrong, *A Combinatorial Theory of Possibility.*
Gilbert Harman, *Skepticism and the Definition of Knowledge.*
W. Quine, *Pursuit of Truth.*
Peter Brown, *The Body and Society.*
Mikhail Gorbachev is first U.S.S.R. leader to visit the Vatican; he and John Paul II agree to reestablish diplomatic relations between the U.S.S.R. and the Vatican.
Václav Havel attends a thanksgiving mass in St Vitus' Cathedral, Prague, after his inauguration as President of Czechoslovakia.
Pastor Lázló Tökes of Timişoara plays a prominent part in the Roumanian Revolution.
Six Jesuit priests, their housekeeper and her 15-year-old daughter are tortured and murdered at the University of Central America, San Salvador, El Salvador.

S **Art, Sculpture, Fine Arts and Architecture**

Painting:
'Italian Art in the Twentieth Century' exhibition at the Royal Academy, London.
Therese Oulton, *Passage.*

Sculpture:
Turner Prize awarded to Richard Long.
Richard Deacon, *Kiss and Tell.*

Architecture:
I.M. Pei, Pyramid, Louvre, Paris.
Johann Otto von Spreckelsen and Paul Andreu, La Grande Arche, La Défense, Paris.
H.R.H. The Prince of Wales, *A Vision of Britain: A Personal View of Architecture.*

T **Music**

John Cage, *Europera III/IV.*
Colin Matthews, *Cortege.*
Andrzej Panufnik, *Harmony.*
Alfred Schnittke, *Peer Gynt* (ballet).
John Tavener, *The Protecting Veil.*
Michael Tippett, *New Year* (opera).

1989 (Jul. – Oct.)

G **Jul**: 2nd, I.R.A. car bomb explodes in Hanover, the first of a series of attacks on British army personnel stationed in West Germany;

3rd, Britain states that there will be no automatic right of abode in Britain for Hong Kong residents worried about the colony's future under Chinese rule;

12th, in South Africa, Nelson Mandela makes first public statement since detention 25 years before;

14th, celebrations held to mark 200th anniversary of start of French Revolution;

19th, Polish Parliament elects General Jaruzelski (the only candidate) to new post of President, by just one vote;

23rd, elections for the Upper House in Japan end 34-year-old Liberal Democrat majority;

28th, Hojatoleslam Ali Rafsanjani is elected first executive President of Iran.

H **Aug**: 1st, state price controls are abolished in Poland, and food prices rise by up to 500 per cent;

7th, David Lange resigns as Prime Minister of New Zealand and is succeeded by Geoffrey Palmer;

8th, resignation of Japanese Prime Minister Sosuke Uno as result of sex scandal; succeeded by Toshiki Kaifu (sworn in on 9th);

18th, leading presidential candidate in Colombia is assassinated; government instigates crackdown against drug barons;

19th, Communists agree to join a Solidarity-led coalition in Poland;

24th, Solidarity candidate Tadeusz Mazowiecki is elected Prime Minister of Poland;

23rd, over 2 million people in Baltic republics of U.S.S.R. form human chain in nationalist demonstration marking 50th anniversary of U.S.S.R.–German non-aggression pact;

31st, in Britain, Buckingham Palace announces separation of the Princess Royal (Princess Anne) and Captain Mark Phillips.

J **Sep**: 1st, U.S. breaks off diplomatic relations with Panama;

6th, in whites-only election in South Africa, National Party is returned with reduced majority and F.W. de Klerk is elected President;

—, in Dutch general election Christian Democrats led by Ruud Lubbers remain largest party (7th, form coalition with Labour);

10th, Hungary allows East Germans to cross freely to the West;

11th, Norwegian elections take place under new system, which favours small parties (*Oct.* 16th, Conservative-led coalition takes office);

—, creation of New Forum opposition group in East Germany;

12th, Solidarity-dominated government takes office in Poland, the first government in Eastern Europe since 1940s not under Communist control;

14th, Sam Nujoma, president of S.W.A.P.O., returns to Namibia after nearly 30 years of exile;

17th, north-east Caribbean is hit by Hurricane Hugo;

24th, in Lebanon, Arab League ceasefire enables civilians to return to homes in Beirut;

26th, Vietnamese troops withdraw from Kampuchea;

27th, national parliament of Slovenia approves constitutional amendments giving right to secede from Federation of Yugoslavia;

28th, Ferdinand Marcos, former ruler of Philippines, dies in exile in Hawaii.

K **Oct**: 3rd, General Noriega survives attempted coup in Panama;

4th, mass demonstration in Leipzig demands political reform in East Germany;

7th, Hungarian Socialist Workers' Party votes for its own dissolution;

9th, Rezso Nyers is elected President of newly-formed Hungarian Socialist Party;

U Literature

Breyten Breytenbach, *Memory of Snow and Dust.*
Annie Dillard, *The Writing Life.*
David Grossman, *See Under: Love.*
Shusha Guppy, *The Blindfold Horse.*
John Irving, *A Prayer for Owen Meany.*
Kazuo Ishiguro, *Remains of the Day.*
Cheng Naishen, *The Piano Tuner.*
Amy Tan, *The Joy Luck Club.*

V The Press

Launch of *The Sunday Correspondent* in Britain (*Sept.* 17th); closed in *Nov.* 1990.

W Drama and Entertainment

Matsuyo Akimoto, *Suicide for Love.*
David Mamet, *A Life in the Theatre.*
Joshua Sobol, *Ghetto.*
Aspects of Love.
Miss Saigon.
8 million attend Broadway theatres in New York, an increase of 25.4 per cent on 1988; half attend musicals imported from Britain.

Films:
Woody Allen's *Crimes and Misdemeanours.*
Spike Lee's *Do the Right Thing.*
Steven Soderbergh's *Sex, Lies and Videotape.*
Batman.
My Left Foot.

Television:
David Lynch, *Twin Peaks.*
Round the World in Eighty Days, featuring Michael Palin.
Death on the Rock.
Tumbledown.
Launch of satellite station Sky TV in Britain.

Popular music:
Acid-house rave parties attract tens of thousands in England despite a clampdown by police.
The Neville Brothers, *Yellow Moon.*
Public Enemy, *It Takes a Nation of Millions to Hold Us Back.*
Lou Reed, *New York.*

X Sport

Cycling's first World Cup is won by Sean Kelly of Eire.
96 Liverpool fans die in a crush during the F.A. Cup semi-final against Nottingham Forest at Hillsborough, Sheffield, England (*Apr.* 15th).
Australia regains the Ashes, beating England 4–0 in the six-Test series (*Aug.* 1st).
Britain and Ireland's amateur golfers win the Walker Cup for the first time since 1971 (*Aug.* 17th); their victory is their first in the United States.
During the 1988–89 English horse-racing season, Peter Scudamore becomes the first National Hunt jockey to saddle 200 winners in one season; on *Nov.* 18th he sets a new record of 1,139 wins over jumps.
Martine le Moignan is the first British player to win the women's squash World title.

K **Oct:** 8th, Latvian Popular Front announces intention to seek independence from U.S.S.R.;
9th, Soviet Parliament bans strikes in all key industries;
11th, Poland opens borders with East Germany and declares it will accept refugees;
16th, Convention on International Trade in Endangered Species agrees total ban on trading in ivory;
17th, earthquake in San Francisco kills at least 273;
18th, Erich Honecker resigns from leadership of Party and State in East Germany; Egon Krenz succeeds him;
19th, Britain and Argentina declare formal cessation of hostilities, seven years after end of Falklands War;
23rd, new Hungarian Republic is declared, with a constitution allowing multi-party democracy;
24th, U.S. television evangelist Jim Bakker sentenced to 45 years imprisonment for fraud;
26th, Nigel Lawson resigns as Chancellor of the Exchequer in Britain; John Major replaces him;
29th, Socialist Workers' Party is re-elected for third term in Spanish general election, with reduced majority;
31st, Turgut Özal is elected President of Turkey in succession to General Kenan Evren.

L **Nov:** 1st, President Ortega's Sandinista regime in Nicaragua ends 19-month ceasefire with Contra rebels;
5th, Greece holds second election of year (23rd, new government sworn in, led by Prof. Xenophon Zolotas);
7th, East German Government led by Willi Stoph resigns amid continuing pro-reform demonstrations;
—, Namibia begins five days of polling to elect first independent government of Africa's last colony;
8th, Jordan holds first parliamentary election since 1967;
9th, East Germany announces opening of its border with West Germany; the authorities begin demolishing sections of the Berlin Wall the following day;
—, China's senior statesman, Teng Hsiao-p'ing, resigns as Chairman of Central Military Commission;
10th, Petar Mladenov replaces Todor Zhivkov as General Secretary of Communist Party in Bulgaria, ending Zhivkov's 35-year dictatorship;
13th, Hans Modrow elected Prime Minister in East Germany;
16th, F.W. de Klerk announces end of Separate Amenities Act in South Africa;
17th, fighting in San Salvador as rebel guerrillas win over parts of the city;
—, police break up peaceful demonstration in Prague;
22nd, in India's general election, Congress Party led by Rajiv Gandhi loses parliamentary majority (*Dec.* 2nd, new multi-party government is sworn in under V.P. Singh);
—, President René Muawad of Lebanon (elected 5th) dies in bomb explosion (24th, succeeded by Elias Hrawi);
27th, general strike in Czechoslovakia calls for end to Communist rule;
28th, Czechoslovak Prime Minister, Ladislav Adamec, formally renounces Communist monopoly on power.

Y **Statistics**

Ethnic composition of the U.S.S.R. (percentage of population): Russian, 51.6; Ukrainian, 15.8; Uzbek, 6.0; Belorussian, 3.5; Kazakh, 2.9; Azaibaijani, 2.4; Tatar, 2.4; Armenian, 1.7; Tajik, 1.5; Georgian, 1.4; Moldavian, 1.2; Turkmen, 0.9; Kyrgyz, 0.9; German, 0.7; Others, 7.1.

Z **Births and Deaths**

Jan. 7th Hirohito d. (87).
June 3rd Ruhollah Khomeini d. (87).
June 27th A.J. Ayer d. (78).
July 11th Laurence Olivier d. (82).
Sept. 22nd Irving Berlin d. (101).
Dec. 22nd Samuel Beckett d. (83).
Dec. 25th Nicolae Ceauşescu d. (71).
Dec. 26th Lennox Berkeley d. (86).

M **Dec**: 2nd, Bush and Gorbachev declare end of Cold War;

3rd, Politburo and Communist Party Central Committe resign in East Germany after revelations of widespread corruption (8th, former leader Erich Honecker charged with abuse of office);

10th, new government takes power in Czechoslovakia, led by Marian Calfa, with non-Communist majority;

11th, forcible repatriation begins of Vietnamese boat people from Hong Kong;

14th, Patricio Aylwin (Christian Democrat) wins overwhelming victory in presidential elections in Chile;

17th, army fires on demonstration in Timişoara, Roumania, killing about 100 people, but rumours report far higher figure (20th, President Ceauşescu declares state of emergency as protests spread);

—, Fernando Collor de Mello (Conservative) narrowly wins presidential election in Brazil;

19th, U.S. troops invade Panama to overthrow regime of General Noriega;

22nd, army joins forces with anti-government demonstrators in Roumania and overthrows President Ceausescu (25th, Nicolae and Elena Ceauşescu are captured, given summary trial and executed by the army);

—, ceremonial opening of the Brandenburg Gate;

26th, in Roumania interim government is formed by National Salvation Front; it announces constitutional changes, guarantees rights of national minorities, allows for freedom of worship and a free market economy, and promises free elections;

27th, Egypt and Syria resume full diplomatic relations;

29th, Václav Havel is elected Czechoslovakia's first non-Communist President for 41 years;

31st, riots break out along border between Soviet Azerbaijan and Iran.

A **Jan:** 1st, David Dinkins becomes first black mayor of New York;
3rd, in Panama General Noriega surrenders to U.S. authorities and is taken to Florida to face charges of drug-smuggling;
15th, Soviet troops are sent into Nagorno-Karabakh to quell continuing ethnic violence;
—, Bulgarian National Assembly votes to end Communist monopoly on power;
18th, Azerbaijan declares war on Armenia;
19th, Soviet troops fire on demonstrators in Baku, Azerbaijan;
22nd, Yugoslavia's Communist Party votes to abolish Party's monopoly on power;
26th, Indian troops bring Kashmir under direct rule and enforce curfew, following deaths in separatist violence and the resignation of the state government.

B **Feb:** 1st, Bulgarian government resigns (8th, new all-Communist government is formed);
—, Yugoslav government sends troops to Kosovo province in attempt to end clashes between ethnic Albanians and Serbian authorities;
2nd, in South Africa, President de Klerk ends 30 year ban on A.N.C.;
7th, Central Committee of Communist Party in U.S.S.R. votes to end Party's monopoly on political power;
11th, Nelson Mandela is released after 27 years in prison in South Africa;
15th, Social Democrat government in Sweden resigns (26th, leader Ingvar Carlsson is reappointed as Prime Minister of new Social Democrat government);
—, publication of research suggesting link between exposure to radiation at Sellafield nuclear plant in Britain and cases of leukaemia in employees' children;
16th, S.W.A.P.O. leader, Sam Nujoma, is elected first president of independent Namibia (21st, Republic of Namibia becomes an independent sovereign state);
19th, ruling Liberal Democrat Party wins general election in Japan;
21st, authorities in Kenya ban demonstrations after protests calling for President Moi's resignation and demanding an inquiry into the murder of the Foreign Minister;
24th, nationalists defeat Communist candidates in Lithuanian elections;
25th, in elections in Nicaragua, U.S.-backed coalition under Violeta Chamorro defeats Ortega's Sandinista government;
26th, U.S.S.R. agrees to withdraw troops from Czechoslovakia by *July* 1991.

C **Mar:** 6th, in Afghanistan, government of President Najibullah puts down attempted coup;
10th, General Avril resigns as President of Haiti (12th, Ertha Pascal-Trouillot succeeds him);
11th, Lithuania declares independence from U.S.S.R.;
12th, Dr. Vitautis Landsbergis is elected Lithuanian President;
13th, Israel's national unity coalition government collapses after dismissal of Shimon Peres by President Yitzhak Shamir;
15th, Gorbachev sworn in as first executive president of U.S.S.R.;
—, Fernando Collor de Mello takes office as President of Brazil;
18th, in East Germany's first free elections since 1933, 'Alliance for Germany' wins 48 per cent of vote;
24th, ruling Labour Party is returned for fourth term in Australian general election;
25th, Soviet authorities send tanks to Vilnius, capital of Lithuania, to discourage proponents of secession;
30th, Estonia suspends Soviet constitution on its territory;
31st, huge anti-poll tax demonstration in Trafalgar Square, London, ends in confrontations with the police, and rioting and looting in the West End;

O Politics, Economics, Law and Education

British government bans broadcast of interviews with members of the I.R.A. and Sinn Fein.

In Britain, David Owen's Social Democratic Party is wound up (*June* 3rd).

Britain introduces separate taxation for married women (*Apr.* 6th).

National Health Service and Community Care Act introduces self-managing trust hospitals and fund-holding general practitioners into British National Health Service (*June*).

Trial arising from Guinness company's takeover of Distillers Group (*Feb.* 12th–*Aug.* 27th) becomes the most expensive in British history.

European Court of Justice is report to be taking one and a half years to deal with references from national courts and two and a half to process direct actions.

Clean Air Act in U.S. raises standards for emissions made by utilities and industrial concers.

Chief Inspector of Schools in Britain reports that one in three children is 'getting a raw deal' from the state education system (*Feb.* 5th).

British Education Secretary John MacGregor states that new national curriculum for history should greater emphasis on dates and facts (*July* 26th).

Levels of British student grants are frozen and supplemented by 'top-up' loans (*Sept.*).

Inauguration of collegiate status of Rewley House, Oxford, England.

P Science, Technology, Discovery, etc.

Japan launches the first probe to be sent to the moon since 1976 (*Jan.* 24th); it places a small satellite in lunar orbit (*Mar.*).

The space shuttle *Discovery* places the Hubble Space Telescope in Earth orbit (*Apr.* 24th); the main mirror proves to be defective.

Launch of the German-built X-ray Röntgensatellite (*June* 1st).

The U.S. Magellan radar mapper arrives in orbit around Venus (*Aug.* 10th); it transmits the most detailed pictures of the planet's surface yet produced.

U.S. astronomer Mark R. Showalter discovers an 18th moon of Saturn when researching pictures transmitted by Voyager II.

Surgeons at Guy's Hospital in London perform the first surgery on a baby in its mother's womb (*Jan.* 30th).

Pierre Chambon and associates announce the discovery of gene that may be important in the development of breast cancer.

Bowel and liver grafts are transplanted at the University of Western Ontario, enabling the patient to resume a normal diet for the first time ever.

First human gene experiment: defective white blood cells are taken from a four-year-old girl, given a gene that controls a enzyme in the immune system, and reinserted.

Six institutions are selected to participate in the project for mapping the genes of selected human chromosomes.

Chemists at the Louis Pasteur University, Strasbourg, announce the creation of nucleohelicates, compounds that mimic the double helix structure of DNA.

Canadian scientists discover fossils of the oldest known multi-cellular animals, dating from 600 million years ago.

Q Scholarship

Maurice Keen, *English Society in the Later Middle Ages, 1348–1500.*

Conrad Russell, *The Causes of the English Civil War.*

F.M.L. Thompson (ed.), *The Cambridge Social History of Britain 1750–1950.*

David Cannadine, *The Decline and Fall of the British Aristocracy.*

D **Apr**: 1st, in Britain, 1,000 inmates riot in Strangeways Prison, Manchester, and take over large parts of the prison (25th, last prisoners surrender after storming of the prison by specially trained officers);
—, Robert Mugabe gains decisive victory in presidential election in Zimbabwe, and ruling Z.A.N.U.-P.F. wins 117 of the 120 seats;
3rd, King Baudouin of Belgium steps down from throne temporarily to allow passing of new law legalising abortion, which he refused to sign on principle;
4th, Chinese People's Congress approves the Basic Law, a mini constitution for Hong Kong after the 1997 take-over;
8th, New Democracy Party gains narrow majority in Greek general election; Constantine Mitsotakis takes office as Prime Minister, 11th;
—, centre-right Democratic Forum and allies win landslide victory in Hungarian general election;
11th, parts for a 'supergun' destined for Iraq detained by Customs officers on Teesside, Britain;
—, three hostages released in Lebanon after a French arms deal with Libya in contravention of the E.C. embargo;
12th, Lothar de Maizière sworn in as Prime Minister of coalition in East Germany;
18th, U.S.S.R. cuts off oil supplies to Lithuania;
19th, ceasefire is signed in Nicaragua.

E **May**: 1st, opposition demonstrations disrupt May Day parade in Red Square, Moscow;
4th, Latvia declares itself an independent sovereign state;
—, Constantine Karamanlis is re-elected President of Greece;
8th, Estonia declares independence from U.S.S.R.;
15th, home-produced beef is banned in U.K. schools and hospitals as result of concern over 'mad-cow disease' (bovine spongiform encephalopathy, or B.S.E.);
20th, Roumania holds first free elections since 1937; National Salvation Front wins two-thirds of seats and Ion Iliescu wins landslide victory in presidential elections;
22nd, North and South Yemen merge to form Yemen Republic.
24th, Princess Anne, the Princess Royal, visits U.S.S.R. in first official British royal visit since 1917 Revolution;
27th, National League for Democracy wins multi-party elections in Burma, though army later refuses to hand over power;
—, Cesar Gaviria Trujillo of ruling Liberals is chosen as President-elect in elections in Colombia;
29th, Boris Yeltsin elected President of Russian Federation, defeating Gorbachev's candidate;
31st, 40 die in ethnic clashes around Karachi in Pakistan.

F **Jun**: 5th, Communist hardliner, Vladimir Ivashko, elected President of Ukraine;
7th, President de Klerk lifts four-year state of emergency from all parts of South Africa except Natal province;
8th, Civic Forum triumphs in first free elections in Czechoslovakia since 1946;
—, Russian Parliament votes that its laws should take precedence over those of U.S.S.R. (12th, Russian Federation formally declares itself a sovereign state);
11th, Alberto Fujimori defeats author Mario Vargas Llosa in presidential election in Peru;
12th, Yitshak Shamir forms new right-wing coalition government in Israel;
—, in Algerian local elections, fundamentalist Islamic Salvation Front wins control of most municipal and provincial assemblies
14th, mobs of miners patrol the streets of Bucharest, attacking anti-government demonstrators;

Q Scholarship (*cont.*)

Peter Ackroyd, *Dickens.*
Ross McKibbin, *The Ideologies of Class: Social Relations in England 1880–1950.*
Kenneth O. Morgan, *The People's Peace: British History 1945–1990.*

R Philosophy and Religion

Donald Davidson, *Structure and Content of Truth.*
Karl Popper, *A World of Propensities.*
John MacQuarrie, *Jesus Christ in Modern Thought.*
Law forbidding religious propaganda in Albania is repealed.
A new Council of Churches for Britain and Ireland replaces the British Council of Churches; Roman Catholics and Black-led churches participate for the first time.
The World's largest cathedral is consecrated by the Pope in Yamoussoukro, Ivory Coast.
In Saudi Arabia approximately 1,400 Moslem pilgrims are crushed to death in stampede in overcrowded tunnel leading from Mecca to hill outside.

S Art, Sculpture, Fine Arts and Architecture

Painting:
Jenny Holzer is the first woman to represent the U.S. at the Venice Biennale.
'Monet in the '90s' exhibition at the Royal Academy, London
John Greenwood, *That's My Bus.*
Andres Serrano, *Red Pope I, II, III.*

Sculpture:
Damian Hirst, *My Way.*
Jeff Koons, *Jeff and Ilona (Made in Heaven).*
Rachel Whiteread, *Valley.*

Architecture:
Terry Farrell, practical completion of Charing Cross redevelopment, London.

T Music

Alexander Goehr, 4th String Quartet.
Hans Werner Henze, *Das verratene Meer* (opera).
György Ligeti, Concerto for Violin and Orchestra.
Alfred Schnittke, Second Concerto for Cello and Orchestra.
Judith Weir, *The Vanishing Bridegroom* (opera).

U Literature

Martin Amis, *London Fields.*
Nicholson Baker, *Room Temperature.*
A.S. Byatt, *Possession.*
Ian McEwan, *The Innocent.*
V.S. Naipaul, *India.*
Thomas Pynchon, *Vineland.*
Mordechai Richler, *Solomon Gursky Was Here.*
Alexander Solzhenitsyn is awarded the Russia State Literature Prize for *The Gulag Archipelago.*

V The Press

Launch in Britain of *The Independent on Sunday* (*Jan.*)
Robert Maxwell publishes *The European*, a weekly English-language newspaper for circulation throughout Europe (*May*).

F **Jun**: 20th, Uzbekistan declares independent sovereignty;
21st, major earthquake in north-west Iran;
22nd, in Canada, Manitoba and Newfoundland refuse to ratify Meech Lake Accord recognising Quebec as a 'distinct society';
29th, Lithuania suspends declaration of sovereignty during negotiations with Soviet government.

G **Jul**: 1st, East Germany cedes sovereignty over economic, monetary and social policy to West German government and Bundesbank; Deutschmark becomes official currency;
2nd, Imelda Marcos is acquitted of plotting to steal funds from the Philippines for private use;
6th, Petar Mladenov resigns as President of Bulgaria;
8th, Indian army takes direct control of Kashmir after separatist violence;
11th, demonstrations held in Kenya against one-party rule;
12th, Boris Yeltsin and other reformers resign from Communist Party in U.S.S.R.;
16th, Ukranian Parliament votes for sovereignty and to become a neutral state;
19th, Iraqi troops start massing on the border with Kuwait, following threats over disputed territory;
20th, I.R.A. bomb explodes at Stock Exchange in London;
25th, George Carey, Bishop of Bath and Wells in England, is named as successor to Robert Runcie as Archbishop of Canterbury;
27th (–*Aug*. 1st), Moslem extremists attempt coup in Trinidad and Tobago;
29th, free elections held in Mongolia;
—, troops loyal to President Doe in Liberia massacre at least 600 refugees sheltering in a church in the capital Monrovia (*Aug*. 5th, U.S. sends marines to evacuate U.S. citizens from Monrovia);
30th, in Britain, Ian Gow, Conservative M.P. for Eastbourne, is murdered by I.R.A. car bomb.

H **Aug**: 2nd, Iraqi forces invade Kuwait; deposed Emir flees to Saudi Arabia;
3rd, Arpád Göncz sworn in as President of new Democratic Republic of Hungary;
4th, Iraqi troops mass on border with Saudi Arabia;
6th, U.N. Security Council imposes sanctions against Iraq, including oil embargo;
—, President of Pakistan dismisses government of Benazir Bhutto on charges of corruption and ineptitude;
7th, President Bush sends U.S. forces to Saudi Arabia to prevent Iraqi invasion;
8th, West African states send multi-national force to end civil war in Liberia;
9th, Iraq announces annexation of Kuwait;
14th, Gorbachev issues decrees rehabilitating those repressed by Stalin and restoring citizenship to exiled dissidents including Alexander Solzhenitsyn;
15th, Iraq makes peace with Iran, accepting all Iranian terms;
19th, coalition government in East Germany collapses;
—, Iraq rounds up Western nationals in Kuwait and deports them to Iraq to serve as 'human shields' at military installations;
21st, 400 die in clashes between A.N.C. and Zulu Inkatha movement in Transvaal townships in South Africa;
24th, hostage Brian Keenan, held in Lebanon since 1986, is released;
31st, East and West Germany sign reunification treaty.

J **Sep**: 3rd, ethnic Albanians in Kosovo stage 24-hour strike, following imprisonment of trade union leader Hajrullah Gorani;

V **The Press** (*cont.*)

To improve voluntary regulation of the British press, the Press Council is abolished, to be replaced on *Jan.* 1st 1991 by the Press Complaints Commission.

W **Drama and Entertainment**

Robert Lepage, *Tectonic Plates.*
Yuri Trifonov, *Exchange.*
Derek Walcott, *Remembrance.*
Temporary closure of the Royal Shakespeare Company's London theatres due to lack of funds.

Films:
Denys Arcand's *Jesus of Montreal.*
Jean-Paul Rappeneau's *Cyrano de Bergerac.*
Giuseppe Tornatore, *Cinema Paradiso.*
Hou Xiaoxian's *City of Sorrows.*

Popular music:
Babes in Toyland, *Spanking Machine.*
Happy Mondays, *Pills 'n' Thrills and Bellyaches.*
Ice Cube, *Amerikkka's Most Wanted.*
Jane's Addiction, *Ritual De Lo Habitual.*
Concert held at Wembley, London, to celebrate the release of Nelson Mandela.
Pink Floyd perform *The Wall* in Berlin.

X **Sport**

Richard Hadlee of New Zealand becomes the first bowler to take 400 Test wickets (*Feb.* 4th).
James Buster Douglas wins the world Heavy-weight title, knocking out Mike Tyson in the 10th round of their fight in Tokio (*Feb.* 11th); Douglas later loses the title to Evander Holyfield (*Oct.* 25th).
Lester Piggott returns to the saddle five years after retiring and two years after completing a jail sentence for tax avoidance; he becomes the oldest ever flatrace jockey in Britain.
Martina Navratilova of the U.S. wins her ninth Wimbledon Women's Singles title (*July* 7th), beating the record of Helen Wills Moody, set between 1927 and 1938.
In the soccer World Cup, held in Italy, West Germany beats Argentina 1–0 in the Final (*July* 8th).
Yorkshire Cricket Club in England lifts ban on players born outside the county (*Nov.* 27th).

Y **Statistics**

Populations of cities (in mill.): Mexico City 18.7; Cairo, 14.0; Shanghai, 12.8; Tokio, 11.9; Peking, 10,4; São Paulo, 10.1; Seoul, 10.0; Calcutta, 9.2; Paris, 9.1; Moscow, 8.9.
Life expectancy at birth: Australia, 76.5; Belgium, 75.2; Canada, 77.0; Czechoslovakia, 71.8; Denmark, 75.8; Finland, 75.5; France, 76.4; West Germany, 75.2; Great Britain and Northern Ireland, 75.7; Greece, 76.1; Holland, 77.2; Ireland, 74.6; Italy, 76.0; Japan, 78.6; Norway, 77.1; Sweden, 77.4; U.S., 75.9.

Z **Births and Deaths**

Jan. 26th Lewis Mumford d. (94).
Apr. 15th Greta Garbo d. (84).

J **Sep:** 4th, Geoffrey Palmer resigns as Labour Prime Minister of New Zealand; Michael Moore replaces him;

8th, on final day of Labour Party Conference, British Conservative government announces entry of sterling into the European Exchange Rate Mechanism;

10th, President Samuel Doe of Liberia dies after being captured by rebel faction; Prince Johnson takes over government;

—, Cambodian factions agree on peace formula to end civil war;

18th, in South Africa, Winnie Mandela is charged with kidnapping and assault;

27th, Britain and Iran resume diplomatic relations broken over the Rushdie affair;

28th, Serbian parliament adopts new constitution stripping province of Kosovo of its autonomy;

29th, World Summit for Children is held in New York.

K **Oct:** 2nd, German Democratic Republic ceases to exist at midnight; on 3rd, East and West Germany are reunited;

4th, France and Belgium send troops to Rwanda to guarantee safety of nationals during invasion from Uganda;

5th, U.S. House of Representatives rejects federal budget; non-essential federal services begin to close down after Bush refuses to grant emergency funding; 9th, emergency bill is signed; 27th and 28th, budget is passed by both Houses;

7th, Socialists remain dominant in Austrian parliamentary elections (17th, form new coalition with People's Party);

8th, Israeli police fire on demonstrators at Temple Mount, Jerusalem; Israel later refuses to co-operate with U.N. attempts to carry out inquiry into the incident;

15th, Nobel Peace Prize is awarded to Gorbachev;

19th, ruling South African National Party formally opens its membership to all races;

24th, Benazir Bhutto's Pakistan People's Party suffers overwhelming defeat to Islamic Democratic Alliance in Pakistan general election (*Nov.* 6th, Nawaz Sharif is sworn in as Prime Minister);

27th, E.C. Summit opens in Rome; with exception of Britain, members vote to begin second stage of economic and monetary union by 1994 and to achieve single currency by 2000;

—, National Party led by James Bolger defeats ruling Labour Party in New Zealand elections;

28th, non-Communist parties triumph in elections in Georgia, U.S.S.R. with calls for independence and a market economy;

29th, coalition government in Norway resigns (30th, Mrs. Gro Harlem Brundtland forms minority Labour government);

30th, Hindu militants attack mosque built on Hindu holy site in Ayodhya;

—, British and French halves of the Channel Tunnel meet up.

L **Nov:** 1st, Geoffrey Howe, Leader of the House of Commons, resigns from British government over differences with Mrs. Thatcher on approach to E.C.;

7th, Mrs. Mary Robinson wins Irish elections to become first woman president of Republic of Ireland;

—, government of V.P. Singh resigns in India;

12th, enthronement of Emperor Akihito of Japan;

18th, Socialist Party of Labour, a recreated Communist Party, is founded in Roumania;

19th, Conference on Security and Cooperation in Europe summit opens in Paris; N.A.T.O. and Warsaw Pact sign treaty to eliminate thousands of weapons and tanks;

20th, Hungarian Prime Minister announces that Warsaw Pact will be scrapped by 1992;

Z **Births and Deaths** (*cont.*)

June 20th Steen Rasmussen d. (92).
Sept. 7th A.J.P. Taylor d. (84).
Sept. 26th Alberto Moravia d. (82).
Sept. 30th Patrick White d. (78).
Oct. 14th Leonard Bernstein d. (72).
Dec. 2nd Aaron Copland d. (90).

L **Nov:** 20th, election held for leadership of British Conservative Party, with Michael Heseltine as challenger to Mrs. Thatcher; Thatcher fails to secure the margin needed for re-election, with 204 M.P.s' votes against Heseltine's 152 (22nd, Mrs. Thatcher stands down from second ballot);

23rd, Soviet Parliament grants Gorbachev emergency powers to maintain order in U.S.S.R.;

25th, Christian militias withdraw from East Beirut in agreement to create reunified city policed by government troops and Syrian soldiers;

26th, Lee Kuan Yew resigns as Singapore's leader after 31 years as Prime Minister;

27th, John Major wins second ballot for leadership of Conservative Party with 185 votes to 131 for Heseltine and 56 for Hurd; Heseltine and Hurd withdraw from third ballot; John Major becomes Conservative leader;

28th, Mrs. Thatcher resigns, and John Major takes over as British Prime Minister;

29th, U.S.A. begins airlift of food supplies to U.S.S.R.

M **Dec:** 1st, President Habre of Chad is overthrown by Popular Salvation Front;

2nd, Helmut Kohl is returned as Chancellor in election in united Germany;

5th, first ever presidential and National Assembly elections are held in Haiti;

6th, Saddam Hussein announces freeing of all Western hostages in Kuwait and Iraq;

9th, Lech Walesa achieves landslide victory in Polish presidential election;

—, Slobodan Milosevic (Serbian Socialist Party) is elected president in Serbia's first free elections for 50 years;

12th, Zimbabwean Parliament legislates for nationalisation of white-owned farms at fixed compensation;

—, opposition Social Democrats make substantial gains in Danish general election, but Prime Minister Schlüter continues to lead minority coalition;

14th, Polish government of Tadeusz Mazowiecki resigns (29th, Lech Walesa nominates Jan Krzystof Bielicki as Prime Minister);

16th, Fr. Jean-Bertrand Aristide wins presidential election in Haiti;

17th, Lothar de Maizière resigns from German government after allegations that he worked for the Stasi (secret police);

20th, Eduard Shevardnadze resigns as U.S.S.R. foreign minister declaring that the U.S.S.R. is heading for dictatorship;

23rd, Slovenia votes for independence in plebiscite.

1991 (Jan. – Mar.) Disintegration of Yugoslavia—Coup against Gorbachev—Demise of the U.S.S.R.

A **Jan:** 6th, in Guatemala Jorge Serrano Elias is elected successor to President Vinicio Cerezo;
7th, 5,000 ethnic Greek Albanians flee to Greece amid chaos in Albania;
8th, government of Mrs. Kazimiera Prunskiene in Lithuania resigns over price increases;
13th, Soviet troops storm television station in Vilnius, Lithuania;
—, Mario Soares elected President of Portugal for second term;
15th, Iraq fails to meet U.N. deadline for withdrawal from Kuwait;
16th, U.S.-led coalition commences air offensive 'Operation Desert Storm' to liberate Kuwait from Iraqi occupation;
17th, King Olav of Norway dies aged 87; his son succeeds as Harald V;
—, Richard Branson and Per Lindstrand complete first hot-air balloon crossing of Pacific Ocean;
18th, Iraq launches Scud missiles against Israel;
25th, Iraq pumps oil into the Gulf causing largest ever slick;
26th, rebels in Somalia overrun Mogadishu; President Barre flees to Kenya and United Somali Congress appoints Ali Mahdi Mohammed as Prime Minister.

B **Feb:** 1st, President F.W. de Klerk announces plans for repeal of laws underpinning apartheid in South Africa;
7th, I.R.A. mortar bombs cause damage at 10 Downing Street in London, where a Cabinet meeting was in progress;
9th, Lithuanian referendum approves proposal for independence;
14th, Peruvian cabinet resigns in split over economic crisis;
22nd, hundreds of Kuwait oil wells are set alight by Iraqi soldiers as they face defeat (*Nov.* 3rd, last fire extinguished);
23rd, martial law declared in Thailand, following the overthrow of the government of Chatichai Choonhavan;
24th, U.S.-led coalition in Gulf launches ground offensive against Iraqi forces;
27th, coalition forces enter Kuwait City and declare Kuwait liberated;
28th, President Bush announces suspension of hostilities;

C **Mar:** 1st, in Iraq popular revolt against government begins in Basra and spreads to other Shi'ite cities; separate Kurdish revolt starts in the north;
3rd, Latvia and Estonia vote for independence in referenda;
6th, Chandra Shekhar resigns as Prime Minister of India;
7th, Albanian refugees land at Italian ports in defiance of the authorities;
11th, trial begins of former Greek Prime Minister, Andreas Papandreou, on bribery charges;
14th, in Britain the 'Birmingham Six' are released after successful appeal against their conviction in 1975 for I.R.A. pub bombings in Birmingham;
17th, referendum in U.S.S.R. gives slim majority for Gorbachev's proposal for renewed federation of socialist sovereign republics;
—, Serbia suspends the provincial Kosovo constitution and use of Albanian for official purposes is declared illegal;
24th, Nicephore Soglo defeats President Kerekou in Benin's first democratic elections for 20 years;
26th, Iraqi government forces bomb Kirkuk, held by Kurdish rebels; by 30th, Iraqi government has recovered most of the country;
31st, ruling Communist Party of Labour wins majority in free elections in Albania;
—, military structure of Warsaw Pact is dissolved.

O Politics, Economics, Law and Education

British government announces emergency legislation to control dangerous dogs, after public concern at a spate of savage attacks (*May* 28th).

Legal framework for apartheid in South Africa is destroyed with repeal of Land Acts, Group Areas Act and 1950 Population Registration Act. (*June* 4th and 17th).

Belgian Parliament changes constitution to allow women to accede to the throne (*June* 13th).

British Prime Minister, John Major, launches the 'Citizen's Charter', a scheme for setting standards of public services and providing for compensation when standards are not met (*July* 22nd).

Opening of the European Bank for Reconstruction and Development, to provide funds for enterprises in Eastern Europe and former U.S.S.R. (*Apr.* 5th).

Closure of Bank of Credit and Commerce International in western countries after discovery of widespread fraud (*July*).

Criminal Justice Act in Britain introduces income-related fines and prevents judges from taking previous convictions into account when passing sentence.

British House of Lords rules that a husband can be guilty of marital rape (*Oct.* 23rd).

British Department of Education announces results of first nation-wide tests (of seven-year-olds) under national curriculum (*Dec.* 19th).

P Science, Technology, Discovery, etc.

World Ocean Experiment (W.O.C.E.) programme set up to monitor ocean temperatures, circulation and other parameters.

The U.S. space shuttle deploys the 17-ton Arthur Holly Gamma Ray Observatory in Earth orbit (*Apr.* 7th).

A mission by the U.S. shuttle *Columbia* carries the Space Life Sciences-1 laboratory, in which astronauts conduct experiments on themselves, rats, and jellyfish polyps.

Chemist Helen Sharman is the first Briton to go into space, as a participant in a U.S.S.R. space mission (*May* 18th–26th).

The U.S. space probe Galileo takes the first high-quality picture of an asteroid, called Gaspra (*Oct.*).

The Jodrell Bank radio astronomy centre near Manchester reports the possible discovery of a planet orbiting pulsar star PSR 1829-10.

Astronomers at Mt. Palomar, California, announce the discovery of the most distant object yet seen, a quasar.

Launch of the European Space Agency's first Remote-sensing satellite (ERS-1) into polar orbit to monitor Earth's temperature from space.

First production of a significant amount of power by atomic fusion by JET (Joint European Torus) at Culham near Oxford.

Heart surgeons develop a way of repairing damaged hearts using muscles from the patient's body.

Researchers announce the discovery of a gene responsible for mental handicap.

Chemists isolate fullerenes – a new form of elemental carbon.

Q Scholarship

Discovery in the Italian Alps of the preserved body of a man from c.3,300 B.C., with clothes, bow, arrows, axe and other implements.

Alexander P. Kazhdan et al. (eds.), *The Oxford Dictionary of Byzantium.*

Henry Mayr-Harting, *Ottonian Book Illumination: An Historical Study.*

Felipe Fernández-Armesto, *Columbus.*

Euan Cameron, *The European Reformation.*

Conrad Russell, *The Fall of the British Monarchies, 1637–1642.*

D **Apr**: 9th, parliament of Georgia votes to assert independence from U.S.S.R.;
11th, Iraqi forces attack Kurdish refugees within U.S. exclusion zone;
17th, British, French and U.S. troops start to enter northern Iraq to establish and guard camps for Kurdish rebels;
13th, Giulio Andreotti forms a new government in Italy;
19th, in Britain, enthronement of Dr. George Carey as Archbishop of Canterbury;
22nd, agreement is reached on a 50-year moratorium on mineral exploration in Antarctica;
23rd, British government announces proposals for a new 'council tax' to replace the community charge ('poll tax') in 1993;
30th, Kurdish refugees begin to move into Western-protected havens;
—, Major-General Justin Lekhanya, military leader in Lesotho, is overthrown by Colonel Elias Ramaema.

E **May**: 4th, President Bush taken ill while jogging (6th, leaves hospital);
9th, Yugoslavia's Collective State Presidency grants special powers to Yugoslav National Army for operations in Croatia, freeing it from effective government control;
12th, multi-party elections in Nepal won by Congress Party;
14th, in South Africa, Winnie Mandela, wife of A.N.C. leader Nelson Mandela, sentenced to six years imprisonment for kidnap and accessory to assault;
15th, Mme. Edith Cresson appointed Prime Minister of France, after resignation of Michel Rocard;
—, ceasefire begins in Angola;
16th, Karl Otto Pöhl, President of the Bundesbank resigns after differences with German government over monetary policy;
—, in Britain, Labour candidate overturns 9,000 Conservative majority in Monmouth by-election, largely on fears about future of National Health Service;
17th, Somali National Movement declares north of Somalia independent;
21st, former Indian Prime Minister, Rajiv Gandhi, is assassinated by a Tamil suicide bomber during India's general elections campaign;
—, President Mengistu of Ethiopia flees to Zimbabwe as rebel forces close in on Addis Ababa;
28th, Ethiopian People's Revolutionary Democratic Front capture Addis Ababa and end 17 years of Marxist rule;
26th, Zviad Gamsakhurdia elected President of Georgia;
31st, President Dos Santos and Jonas Savimbi, leader of U.N.I.T.A., sign peace agreement in Lisbon to end Angolan civil war.

F **Jun**: 4th, Albanian government resigns after three-week general strike;
—, Mouloud Hamrouche, Prime Minister of Algeria, resigns after security forces fire on Islamic Salvation Front rioters in Algiers;
7th, Islamic Salvation Front ends protests in exchange for promise of elections;
10th, ticker-tape parade in New York to celebrate victory in the Gulf;
12th, Blaise Compaore, military leader of Burkina Faso, dissolves revolutionary government and calls for new constitution;
—, Boris Yeltsin becomes first ever directly elected leader of the Russian Federation;
17th, Population Registration Act repealed in South Africa, bringing end apartheid system;
20th, German government votes to move government from Bonn to Berlin;
—, P.V. Narasimha Rao is appointed Indian Prime Minister at head of minority government;
25th, republics of Croatia and Slovenia declare independence from Yugoslavia.

Q Scholarship (*cont.*)

Jack P. Greene, J.R. Pole (eds.), *The Blackwell Encyclopedia of the American Revolution.*

John Harriss (ed.), *The Family: A Social History of the Twentieth Century.*

R Philosophy and Religion

Michael Dummett, *The Logical Basis of Metaphysics.*

T. Nagel, *Equality and Partiality.*

Jürgen Moltmann, *History and the Triune God.*

Royal representation at the multi-faith Commonwealth Day service in Westminster Abbey, London (*Mar.* 8th).

Dr. George Carey succeeds Dr. Runcie as Archbishop of Canterbury; his enthronement service (*Apr.* 19th) includes modern informal music, reflecting the new archbishop's more evangelical vision of the Church of England;

Rabbi Dr. Jonathan Sacks is invested as British chief rabbi.

Pope John Paul II awards the title 'Venerable' to Cardinal John Henry Newman.

S Art, Sculpture, Fine Arts and Architecture

Painting:

Thyssen Collection of paintings opened in Madrid.

Turner Prize in Britain awarded to Anish Kapoor.

'High and Low' exhibition at the Museum of Modern Art, New York.

'Metropolis' exhibition, Martin Gropius Bau, Berlin

'Pop Art' exhibition at the Royal Academy, London.

Architecture:

Sir Norman Foster, Sackler Galleries, Royal Academy, London.

Sir Norman Foster, Stansted Airport, Essex.

Robert Venturi and Denise Scott Brown, Sainsbury Wing, National Gallery, London.

T Music

Malcolm Arnold, 9th Symphony.

Harrison Birtwistle, *Sir Gawain and the Green Knight* (opera).

John Corigliano, *The Ghosts of Versailles* (opera).

William Mathias, 3rd Symphony.

John Tavener, *The Repentant Thief.*

U Literature

William Boyd, *Brazzaville Beach.*

Angela Carter, *Wise Children.*

Bret Easton Ellis, *American Psycho.*

Ben Okri, *The Famished Road.*

Jean Rouaud, *Les Champs d'Honneur.*

John Updike, *Rabbit at Rest* (concluding volume of *Rabbit* quartet).

Derek Walcott, *Omeros.*

In Britain, Nicholas Mosley resigns from Booker Prize jury in protest at the absence of a 'novel of ideas' from thc shortlist.

V The Press

Closure of *The Listener* magazine in Britain.

A consortium led by Conrad Black takes over the Fairfax Group of newspapers in Australia.

G **Jul:** 1st, protocol signed in Prague marks formal end to Warsaw Pact;
—, E.C. ministers order total arms embargo on Yugoslavia and agree to send monitoring mission;
18th, floods in China submerge over 50 million acres of farmland;
24th, Indian government abandons centralized planning and introduces reforms to liberalize the economy;
31st, Bush and Gorbachev sign Strategic Arms Reduction Treaty (S.T.A.R.T.) to reduce arsenals of long-range nuclear weapons by a third.

H **Aug:** 6th, Bangladesh abandons presidential system of government and returns to parliamentary rule;
8th, John McCarthy, British journalist held hostage in Lebanon, is released after 1,943 days in captivity;
15th, U.N. Security Council condemns Iraq for hindering work of U.N. inspectors by denying access to nuclear facilities;
18th, remains of Frederick the Great of Prussia re-interred in Potsdam, Germany;
19th, Communist hardliners, led by Gennady Yanayev, stage coup in U.S.S.R. against President Gorbachev, who is placed under house arrest in the Crimea; radio and television stations are shut down and military rule imposed in many cities;
20th, Estonia declares independence;
21st, coup in U.S.S.R. collapses following widespread popular resistance led by Boris Yeltsin (22nd, Gorbachev returns to Moscow);
—, Latvia declares independence;
24th, Gorbachev resigns as First Secretary of U.S.S.R. Communist Party (29th, Parliament suspends Communist Party and seizes its assets);
27th, Croatian town of Vukovar falls to Serb-dominated army after 86-day siege;
28th, Soviet government is dismissed and K.G.B. collegium disbanded;
30th, Azerbaijan declares independence.

J **Sep:** 2nd, central government in U.S.S.R. is suspended pending formulation of new constitution;
6th, Soviet authorities make formal grant of independence to Latvia, Lithuania and Estonia;
7th, E.C.-sponsored peace conference on Yugoslavia opens in The Hague, chaired by Lord Carrington;
11th, withdrawal of Soviet troops from Cuba is announced;
15th, ruling Social Democrats lose general election in Sweden and Swedish Prime Minister Ingvar Carlsson resigns (*Oct.* 4th, Carl Bildt forms right-wing coalition);
17th, ceasefire negotiated between Croats and Serbs is quickly broken;
22nd, Armenia declares independence;
25th, U.N. imposes mandatory arms embargo on Yugoslavia;
—, peace accord is signed in El Salvador to end 11-year civil war;
26th, troops are deployed in Roumania after two days of riots by miners demanding higher wages; government led by Petre Roman resigns and Teodor Stolojan is named Prime Minister on *Oct.* 1st;
30th, President Aristide is overthrown in coup in Haiti (*Oct.* 8th, military install Judge Joseph Norette as provisional president).

K **Oct:** 1st, Leningrad reverts to name St. Petersburg;
—, Yugoslav federal army begins siege of Dubrovnik (7th, federal jets attack Croatian capital, Zagreb);
3rd, British Director of Public Prosecutions, Sir Allan Green, resigns after being stopped by police for alleged kerb crawling;

V **The Press** (*cont.*)

Robert Maxwell purchases *The New York Daily News* (*Mar.* 13th).

Circulation figures of British daily newspapers: Daily Express, 1,518,764; *Daily Mail*, 1,683,768; *Daily Mirror*, 3,641,269; *The Sun*, 3,665,006; *Today*, 459,621; *Daily Telegraph*, 1,058,082; *The Independent*, 372,240; *Financial Times*, 287,120; *The Guardian*, 409,660; *The Times*, 387,386.

Following the death of Robert Maxwell, the Mirror group in Britain is taken over and run by receivers; *The European* ceases publication (revived in 1992).

W **Drama and Entertainment**

Alan Bennett, *The Madness of George III*.

Steven Berkoff, *Kvetch*.

Ariel Dorfman, *Death and the Maiden*.

Kuniu Shimuzu (adapted by Peter Barnes), *Tango at the End of Winter*.

James Stock, *Blue Night in the Heart of the West*.

Films:

Joel and Ethan Coen's *Barton Fink*.

Jeunet and Caro's *Delicatessen*.

Walt Disney's *Beauty and the Beast*.

Agnieszka Holland's *Europa Europa*.

Krzysztof Kieslowski's *The Double Life of Veronique*.

Jacques Rivette's *Le Belle Noiseuse*.

Ridley Scott's *Thelma and Louise*.

Silence of the Lambs.

Terminator 2.

Television:

Alan Bleasdale, *GBH*.

Linda La Plante, *Prime Suspect*.

Sir David Attenborough, *The Trials of Life*.

Sonic the Hedgehog leads Sega's computer game war against Nintendo.

Popular music:

Guns n' Roses, *Use Your Illusion II*.

Nirvana, *Nevermind* – emergence of grunge music from Seattle, U.S.

Primal Scream, *Screamadelica*.

X **Sport**

On *Mar.* 3 Runcorn Highfield of the English Rugby League Second Division beats Dewsbury 9–2, ending a run of 75 League and Cup matches without a win, stretching back to *Oct.* 30th, 1988.

England beats the West Indies in a Test match in England for the first time in 22 years (*June* 10th).

South Africa is re-admitted to the International Olympic Committee (*July* 9th) and to the International Cricket Conference (*July* 10th).

In the third World Athletics Championships in Tokio, Mike Powell of the U.S. sets a new world record for the Long Jump of 8.95 metres (29 feet 4½ inches) (*Aug.* 30th), beating the record set by Bob Beamon in 1968 – the oldest in track and field athletics.

22 soccer clubs break away from the English Football League, under the auspices of the Football Association, to form a 'premier league'; it commences in *Aug.* 1992.

The English club Liverpool returns to European football (*Sept.* 18th) after six-year ban imposed after Heysel stadium disaster.

K **Oct:** 6th, ruling Social Democratic Party in Portugal gains outright majority in general elections;
8th, Abdur Rahman Biswas is elected President of Bangladesh;
13th, Bulgarian Socialist Party suffers overwhelming defeat in elections (*Nov.* 8th, Filip Dimitrov becomes first non-communist Prime Minister since 1944);
15th, Parliament in Bosnia-Herzegovina votes to declare independence;
20th, peace agreement is signed in Rome to end civil war in Mozambique;
—, Suleyman Demirel's True Path Party tops the poll in general election in Turkey;
21st, President Mobutu of Zaire sacks Prime Minister Etienne Tshisekedi, provoking violent rioting (31st, opposition movement forms rival government);
23rd, four factions in Cambodia sign peace accord in Paris to end civil war;
27th, Poland holds first free parliamentary elections since Second World War, but result is inconclusive, with no party polling more than 12 per cent;
31st, President Kaunda suffers defeat in Zambian elections.

L **Nov:** 1st, in Britain, the Quorn Hunt is banned from National Trust land in Derbyshire and Leicestershire after revelations of cruelty by the hunt's members;
5th, Robert Maxwell, publishing tycoon, dies after falling overboard from his yacht off the Canary Islands;
6th, Philippines hit by severe floods and landslides;
8th, E.C. foreign ministers decide to impose immediate economic and trade sanctions against Yugoslavia and suspend the peace conference (*Dec.* 2nd, sanctions are dropped against all republics except Serbia and Montenegro);
13th, hundreds of civilians evacuated from Dubrovnik, Croatia, under U.N. cease-fire;
14th, Prince Sihanouk returns to Cambodia after 13 years' exile;
18th, Terry Waite, envoy to the Archbishop of Canterbury and the last British hostage in Lebanon, is freed after 1,763 days in captivity;
24th, rock star Freddie Mercury dies of A.I.D.S.;
—, general election in Belgium produces gains to Flemish extremists and Green Party.

M **Dec:** 2nd, Joseph Cicipio, U.S. hostage in Lebanon is released, followed by Alan Steen (3rd) and Terry Anderson (4th);
3rd, general assembly of Kenya votes to end one-party state;
4th, Pan Am airline (founded 1927), burdened with massive debts, is closed down;
5th, Robert Maxwell's business empire collapses with huge debts and revelations about misappropriation of money in pension funds;
8th, leaders of Russia, Belarus and Ukraine agree to formation of Commonwealth of Independent States (C.I.S.) (21st, eight of the nine other U.S.S.R. republics sign the agreement);
9th (–10th), summit of E.C. heads of government at Maastricht in Holland agree treaty on closer economic and political union;
13th, U.N. ends ban on sporting, scientific and academic links with South Africa;
16th, British government announces appointment of Mrs. Stella Rimington as head of M.I.5;
19th, Paul Keating replaces Bob Hawke as Prime Minister and leader of Australian Labor Party;
20th, Ante Marković resigns as federal Prime Minister of Yugoslavia;
25th, Mikhail Gorbachev resigns as President of U.S.S.R.; the U.S.S.R. officially ceases to exist;
26th, Islamic Salvation Front defeats ruling National Liberation Front in first round of Algerian elections.

Y **Statistics**

Populations (in mill.): China, 1,149.7; India, 871.2; U.S.S.R., 291.0; U.S., 252.0; Indonesia, 181.5; Brazil 153.3; Pakistan, 126.4; Japan, 123.9; Nigeria, 123.8; Bangladesh, 115.6; Mexico, 82.2; Germany, 79.0; Vietnam, 67.6; Philippines, 62.4; Italy, 57.6; Great Britain and Northern Ireland, 57.6; Turkey, 57.3; Iran, 57.0; France, 56.9.

Illegitimacy rates (percentage of live births): Australia, 20.0; Belgium, 7.8; Bulgaria, 10.5; Czechoslovakia, 7.3; Denmark, 44.7; Eire, 12.6; Finland, 19.2; France, 28.2; Germany, 15.5; Great Britain and Northern Ireland, 28.7; Greece, 2.1; Holland, 10.6; Hungary, 12.4; Italy, 6.1; Norway, 36.4; Sweden, 51.8; U.S., 23.4; U.S.S.R., 10.2.

Religious affiliation in U.S.S.R. (percentage of population): Christian, 37.3 (Orthodox, 32.0; Protestant, 3.4; Roman Catholic, 1.9); Moslem, 13.4; Jewish, 0.8; non-religious, 29.1; atheist, 19.1; others, 0.3.

Z **Births and Deaths**

Feb. 21st Margot Fonteyn d. (71).
Mar. 3rd William Penney d. (81).
Apr. 3rd Graham Greene d. (86).
Apr. 28th Olivier Messiaen d. (83).
May 31st Angus Wilson d. (77).
Aug. 12th John Cage d. (79).
Nov. 5th Robert Maxwell d. (68).
Nov. 18th Gustáv Husák d. (78).

1992 (Jan. – Mar.) Bill Clinton wins U.S. Presidential election—British Conservatives elected for fourth consecutive term—Divorce and separation in British royal family

A **Jan:** 1st, Boutros Boutros Ghali becomes U.N. Secretary-General on retirement of Javier Pérez de Cuéllar;

—, Serbia and Croatia agree U.N. plan for deployment of peacekeeping forces;

2nd, price controls are lifted in Russia, Ukraine and many other C.I.S. republics;

—, opposition Democratic Party forms in Kenya under Mwai Kibaki;

6th, President Zviad Gamsakhurdia of Georgia flees to Armenia at end of two-week siege of government buildings in Tbilisi by rebel forces (16th, Gamsakhurdia declares war on rebels);

7th, army in Chad defeats attempted coup by forces loyal to deposed President Habre;

—, President Bush collapses at state dinner in Tokyo;

8th, Laurent Fabius replaces Pierre Mauroy as Socialist Party leader in France;

11th, President Chadli Benjedid of Algeria resigns as armed forces take control to thwart electoral victory by Islamic Salvation Front (12th, High Security Council cancels second round of poll);

12th, Russia and Ukraine agree to divide Black Sea fleet;

15th, E.C. recognises Croatia and Slovenia as independent republics;

19th, Zhelyu Zhelev elected President of Bulgaria;

21st, Serbia announces plans to create a new Yugoslav state;

23rd, U.N. imposes arms embargo on Somalia in attempt to end civil war;

—, resignation of government in Estonia over inability to deal with fuel and food shortages;

26th, E.C. lifts economic sanctions on South Africa;

30th, Charles Haughey, Prime Minister of Eire, resigns after allegations are made of telephone-tapping (*Feb.* 6th, Albert Reynolds succeeds as Prime Minister).

B **Feb:** 1st, U.N.-negotiated truce comes into effect in El Salvador;

2nd, Serbs accept U.N. peace plan;

4th, Yitshak Shamir loses parliamentary majority as Tehiya and Moledet parties leave the government;

6th, Queen Elizabeth II celebrates 40th anniversary of accession;

9th, Algerian government declares state of emergency after two days of clashes between fundamentalists and security forces;

—, first democratic local elections in Roumania for 45 years bring end to one-party rule;

13th, Carl Bildt announces end of Sweden's policy of neutrality;

18th, Sikh militants murder 17 people in Indian Punjab in attempt to enforce boycott of state elections;

22nd, ruling Nationalist Party wins general election in Malta;

23rd, ceasefire agreed in Somalia;

27th, Paul Keating, Prime Minister of Australia, accuses Britain of abandoning Australia to Japan in World War II;

28th, I.R.A. bomb explodes at London Bridge station; London's mainline and underground stations are closed for much of the day;

—, U.N. Security Council votes to send peacekeeping forces to Cambodia.

C **Mar:** 1st, referendum in Bosnia-Herzegovina, boycotted by Bosnian Serbs, decides in favour of becoming an independent sovereign state;

2nd, violent clashes take place in Sarajevo between militant Serbs, Croats and Moslems;

3rd, former U.S.S.R. troops begin withdrawal from Lithuania;

O Politics, Economics, Law and Education

Mrs. Barbara Mills, Q.C., is appointed first woman Director of Public Prosecutions in England and Wales (*Feb.* 6th).

King Fahd of Saudi Arabia grants 'Basic Law' giving new constitutional rights (*Mar.* 1st).

Baltic states create Council of Baltic Sea States to aid economic development and strengthen links with E.C. (*Mar.* 5th).

Miss Betty Boothroyd becomes first woman Speaker of British House of Commons (*Apr.* 27th).

John Bannon, Premier of South Australia, resigns after acknowledging responsibility for huge losses by State Bank of South Australia (*Sept.* 1st).

British Moslems inaugurate their self-styled 'Parliament' in London.

Dealers use the trading floor of the London stock exchange for the last time (*Jan.* 31st).

Takeover of Midland Bank by Hong Kong and Shangai Banking Corporation. (*Mar.*).

Lloyd's of London announces record loss of £2 billion on one year's trading.

Peter Clowes, former head of Barlow Clowes investment group in Britain and Channel Islands, is convicted of fraud and theft involving over £113 million (*Feb.* 10th).

European Court rules that almost all E.C. legislation adopted since 1957 could be invalid because of technical problem concerning signatures on documents (Feb. 28th).

John Gotti, head of largest Mafia family in New York, is convicted of murder and racketeering (*Apr.* 2nd).

Polytechnics in Britain are given university status.

P Science, Technology, Discovery, etc.

President Bush announces (*Feb.* 11th) that the U.S. will phase out CFCs by 1995, five years earlier than planned; Michael Heseltine makes a similar announcement for Britain (*Feb.* 14th).

The U.N. holds a Conference on Environment and Development in Rio de Janeiro attended by delegates from 178 countries (*June* 3rd–14th); most countries sign binding conventions on prevention of climate change and preservation of biodiversity.

Launch of *Endeavour*, a new-type U.S. space shuttle orbiter (*May*).

Astronauts on the U.S. space shuttle fit a new motor to a satellite (Intelsat-6) and fire it into a new orbit (*May* 14th).

The U.S. space probe Ulysses flies over the north and south poles of Jupiter, to enter a trajectory for reaching the south pole of the Sun; it transmits data about Jupiter's magnetosphere (*Feb.* 8th).

The COBE (Cosmic Background Explorer) satellite detects ripples thought to originate in the formation of galaxies.

Sperm cells are discovered to have odour receptors and may therefore reach eggs by detecting scent.

The first transplant of a baboon liver into a human.

Q Scholarship

The Cambridge History of the English Language (–).

Eamon Duffy, *The Stripping of the Altars: Traditional Religion in England, 1400–1580*.

Andrew Pettegree, *Emden and the Dutch Revolt: Exile and the Development of Reformed Protestantism*.

C **Mar**: 5th, Christian Democrat Jean-Luc Dehaene agrees to form coalition government in Belgium after three-month political crisis;
12th, Mauritius becomes a republic within the Commonwealth;
17th, Finnish parliament votes to apply for E.C. membership;
18th, white electorate in South Africa votes for constitutional and political reform;
19th, in Britain, Buckingham Palace announces the separation of Duke and Duchess of York (married 1986);
22nd, Socialist Party in France suffers crushing defeat in regional elections;
—, opposition Democrat Party in Albania wins absolute majority in general election, ending 45 years of Communist rule;
31st, U.N. votes to impose sanctions on Libya after refusal to hand over two men suspected of involvement in Lockerbie bombing (*Apr.* 15th, sanctions come into effect).

D **Apr**: 2nd, Mme. Edith Cresson resigns as Prime Minister of France and is replaced by Pierre Bérégovoy;
5th, President Alberto Fujimori of Peru suspends the constitution and dissolves Congress with military backing (22nd, after international criticism Fujimori promises to return Peru to democracy within 12 months);
6th, in Italy's general election, established parties suffer losses to the Lombard League, the Greens, and the anti-Mafia La Rete Party;
7th, E.C. formally recognises independence of Bosnia-Herzegovina; fighting escalates as federal air force aids Serb forces;
8th, Serb and federal army forces begin bombardment of Sarajevo;
9th, British General Election confounds predictions of opinion pollsters by returning the Conservatives for a fourth term, though with a reduced majority of 21; Conservatives win 336 seats, Labour, 271, with the Liberal Democrats, 20 (Conservatives receive 41.9 per cent of votes cast, Labour, 34.4 per cent, and Liberal Democrats, 17.8 per cent);
—, Manuel Noriega, former ruler in Panama, is convicted in Miami of drug trafficking and racketeering;
13th, Neil Kinnock and Roy Hattersley resign as leader and deputy leader of British Labour Party;
—, in South Africa, Nelson Mandela announces separation from his wife Winnie whose apparent involvement in criminal activity was damaging the A.N.C.'s reputation;
16th, President Najibullah of Afghanistan is overthrown; Mujaheddin rebels close in on Kabul;
23rd, in Britain, Princess Royal is granted divorce from Captain Mark Phillips;
23rd (–*May* 7th), disruptive public service strike in Germany; unions seek higher pay to compensate for economic conditions arising from reunification (dispute ends with agreement on 5.4 per cent increase);
29th, four white policemen in Los Angeles are acquitted of beating a black motorist, despite video-tape evidence; 30th–*May* 3rd, 58 people die in riots and looting which break out in protest at the acquittals.

E **May**: 6th, Lebanese government resigns over worsening economic situation;
8th, demonstrators clash with police in Bangkok, Thailand, as they call for resignation of unelected Prime Minister General Kraprayaon (20th, King promises constitutional amendments in return for an end to the demonstrations);
20th, Papua New Guinea reaches peace agreement with secessionists on Bougainville Island;
25th, Oscar Scalfaro is elected President of Italy;

Q Scholarship (*cont.*)

Bruce Redford (ed.), *The Letters of Samuel Johnson* (–94).
Anthony Huxley et al. (eds.), *The New Royal Horticultural Society Dictionary of Gardening*.

R Philosophy and Religion

N.T. Wright, *The New Testament and the People of God.*
A Methodist Church report in England supports inclusive language in publications and condemns patriarchy as deep sin.
Ten women are ordained to the Anglican priesthood in Australia, despite a ruling against by the New South Wales Court of Appeal.
Unconfirmed children are allowed to receive communion in the Church of Scotland.
Senior Church of England bishops device a two-tier system of episcopal oversight to enable opponents of women priests to stay within the Church in the event of the General Synod voting in favour of women's ordination.
The Church of England General Synod votes to allow women to be ordained to the priesthood (*Nov.* 11th).
Roman Catholic Church introduces new catechism (*Nov.* 16th).

S Art, Sculpture, Fine Arts and Architecture

Painting:
Turner Prize awarded to Grenville Davey.
'Matisse' exhibition at the Museum of Modern Art, New York.
'The Russian Utopia' exhibition at the Guggenheim Museum, New York.
Sculpture:
Damian Hirst, *The Physical Impossibility of Death in the Mind of Someone Living*.

T Music

Philip Glass, *The Voyage* (opera).
Andrzej Panufnik, Cello Concerto.
Aulis Sallinen, *Kullervo* (opera).
Alfred Schnittke, *Life with an Idiot* (opera).
John Tavener, *Mary of Egypt* (opera).
Michael Tippett, 5th String Quartet.

U Literature

Harold Brodkey, *The Runaway Soul.*
Jung Chang, *Wild Swans.*
Robertson Davies, *Murther and Walking Spirits.*
Martin Goodman, *On Bended Knees.*
Ian McEwan, *Black Dogs.*
Michael Ondaatje, *The English Patient.*
Adam Thorpe, *Ulverton.*
Foundation of the British Literature Prize as Britain's premier literary award.

V The Press

David and Frederick Barclay purchase the title of *The European* and re-launch the paper.
Closure of *Punch* in Britain (*Apr.* 8th).

W Drama and Entertainment

Jim Cartwright, *The Rise and Fall of Little Voice.*
John Guare, *Six Degrees of Separation.*

E **May**: 28th, Australian entrepreneur Alan Bond is sentenced to two and half years' imprisonment for dishonest business dealings (*Aug*. 27th, conviction is quashed);
30th, U.N. imposes ban on trade, air and sporting links and an oil embargo on new Yugoslav state because of continuing Serbian agression in Bosnia-Herzegovina.

F **Jun**: 2nd, Danish referendum votes against ratification of the Maastricht Treaty;
5th, Polish government is voted out of office by parliament; Waldemar Pawlak replaces Jan Olszewski as Prime Minister;
6th, elections in Czechoslovakia result in victory for pro-independence parties in Slovakia and for pro-federal parties in the Czech lands;
16th, Fidel Ramos wins Philippines presidential election;
18th, referendum in Eire endorses ratification of Maastricht;
—, 39 people are killed in 'Boipatong massacre' in South Africa, allegedly by Inkatha supporters (20th, police fire on black residents in Boipatong);
23rd, A.N.C. withdraws from constitutional discussions in protest at the violence;
23rd, Labour Party wins convincing victory over ruling Likud Party in Israeli general election;
29th, President Mohammed Boudiaf of Algeria assassinated by Islamic fundamentalists (*July* 2nd, Ali Kafi becomes new President).

G **Jul**: 5th, U.N. military observers arrive in Somali capital, Mogadishu, to help distribute food aid;
7th, Abdul Sabbur Fareed becomes new Prime Minister of Afghanistan;
9th, Chris Patten sworn in as 28th Governor of Hong Kong, replacing Lord Wilson of Tillyorn;
15th, in Algeria, president and vice-president of Islamic Salvation Front sentenced to 12 years' imprisonment for conspiracy against the state;
17th, President Havel of Czechoslovakia resigns after Slovak deputies vote to declare their republic a sovereign state;
18th, in Britain, John Smith is elected leader of the Labour Party and Mrs. Margaret Beckett deputy leader;
28th, Italian government forces through emergency legislation to cut federal budget and prevent bankruptcy;
29th, Erich Honecker, former East German leader, is forced to leave Chilean embassy in Moscow, to face trial in Germany on manslaughter charges for the killing of people who tried to escape over the Berlin Wall.

H **Aug**: 3rd, A.N.C. begins 'mass action' protest campaign in South Africa;
—, Russia and the Ukraine agree on joint command and control of Black Sea fleet;
7th, agreement reached in Rome to end civil war in Mozambique;
13th, U.N. condemns the Serbs' 'ethnic cleansing' (i.e. forced removal) programme as a war crime;
8th, passengers are evacuated from the *Queen Elizabeth II* cruise liner after it is holed by uncharted object off north-east coast of U.S.A.;
19th, Sir Lynden Pindling loses general election and resigns as President of Bahamas after 25 years;
20th, in Britain, *The Daily Mirror* publishes compromising photographs of the Duchess of York on holiday in France with a so-called 'financial adviser' (24th, newspapers carry transcript of a telephone conversation allegedly between Princess of Wales and an intimate male friend);
22nd (–26th), five nights of serious rioting at a reception centre for asylum seekers in Rostock marks resurgence of anti-foreigner violence in eastern Germany;

W **Drama and Entertainment** (*cont.*)

Tony Kushner, *Angels in America.*
Théâtre de Complicité, *Street of Crocodiles.*

Films:
Bille August's *The Best Intentions.*
Robert Altman's *The Player.*
Alain Corneau's *Tous les Matins du Monde.*
Merchant/Ivory's *Howard's End.*
Spike Lee's *Malcolm X.*
Sally Potter's *Orlando.*
Baz Luhrmann's *Strictly Ballroom.*

Television:
Sylvania Waters fly-on-the-wall documentary about Sydney's Donaher family.
Pole to Pole with Michael Palin.
Cable TV reaches 60 per cent of U.S. households.

Popular music:
AIDS awareness benefit concert held at Wembley, in memory of Queen's Freddie Mercury.
P.J. Harvey, *Dry.*
The Orb, *U.F. Orb* – ambient house music.
R.E.M., *Automatic for the People.*

X **Sport**

Aldershot becomes the first English League club to fold since Accrington Stanley in 1962.
Denmark win European football championship, having qualified for the competition only by taking the place which would have gone to Yugoslavia (*June* 26th).
Cricketer David Gower breaks Geoffrey Boycott's record of runs scored for England, reaching a total of 8,154 while playing in Test against Pakistan (*July* 6th).
XXIV Olympic Games in Barcelona. The Unified Team (comprising the 11 nations of the Commonwealth of Independent States and Georgia) wins 45 gold medals; U.S., 37; Germany, 33; China, 16; Cuba, 14; Spain, 13; South Korea, 12; Hungary, 11; France, 8; Australia, 7; Italy and Canada, 6. Chris Boardman, in the 4,000 metres individual pursuit, becomes the first Briton to win an Olympic cycling gold since 1908.
Nigel Mansell, driving a Williams-Renault, wins the Formula One Drivers' World Championship (*Aug.* 16th), setting a new record of nine Grand Prix victories in one season.
Riddick Bowe wins the World Heavy-weight boxing title, out-pointing Evander Holyfield in Las Vegas (*Nov.* 13th).

Y **Statistics**

Merchant shipping (tonnages): Liberia, 52,622,000; Panama, 46,128,000; Greece, 23,004,000; Norway, 21,298,000; Cyprus, 20,746,000; former U.S.S.R., 17,233,000; U.S., 15,466,000; British dependent territories, 14,132,000; China, 13,407,000; Malta, 8,705,000.

Z **Births and Deaths**

Jan. 11th W.G. Hoskins d. (83).
Mar. 9th Menachem Begin d. (78).

H **Aug**: 24th, Hurricane Andrew hits Bahamas and coast of Florida; insurance claims make this the most expensive natural disaster in U.S. history;
27th, Lord Owen replaces Lord Carrington as E.C.'s chief mediator on Yugoslav crisis;
—, U.S., Britain and France impose air exclusion zone in southern Iraq to protect Shi'ite Moslems from air attacks;
29th, ceasefire begins in Afghanistan after three weeks of heavy fighting between pro-government forces and the Mujaheddin faction.

J **Sep**: 4th, Todor Zhivkov, former Communist leader of Bulgaria, is convicted for misappropriation and embezzlement;
7th, troops from Ciskei homeland fire on A.N.C. demonstators marching towards Bisho in South Africa;
—, President Rakhmon Nabiyev is forced to resign in Tajikistan;
12th, Ramiz Alia, former president of Albania, is arrested on charge of misuse of state funds and abuse of power;
13th, Italian lira is devalued by 7 per cent within E.R.M.;
16th, sterling crisis: British Chancellor of the Exchequer, Norman Lamont, increases base rate from 10 per cent to 12 per cent, then to 15 per cent in attempt to defend the pound against speculative selling; sterling is withdrawn from the E.R.M. and allowed to 'float'; base rate returns to 12 per cent (22nd, cut to 9 per cent);
20th, French referendum produces vote narrowly in favour of ratification of Maastricht Treaty;
—, right-wing parties win strong position in parliament in Estonia's first post-independence elections;
23rd, German cabinet approves emergency plan to support east German industry and protect jobs;
—(–24th), over 80 are killed in flash floods in France;
24th, thousands of citizens flee north-western Liberia as battles rage following breakdown of peacekeeping;
—, David Mellor, first British National Heritage Secretary, resigns after tabloid press reveals affair with an actress and acceptance of gifts from daughter of a senior P.L.O. official;
25th, ceasefire between Azerbaijan and Armenia over disputed region of Nagorno-Karabakh, but each side accuses the other of breaking it before the end of *Sept*.
29th (–30th), first multi-party elections held in Angola; *Oct*. 17th, results give victory for ruling Popular Movement for Liberation of Angola Workers' Party.

K **Oct**: 5th, general election in Guyana results in narrow victory for People's Progressive Party, ending 28 year rule of People's National Congress;
11th, Ion Iliescu wins further four-year term in Romanian Presidental elections;
—, President Paul Biya wins slim majority in Cameroon's first multi-party elections;
12th, demonstrations held in many Latin American countries against celebrations of 500th anniversary of arrival of Columbus in the Americas;
13th, in Britain, announcements are made that coal production will cease at 31 of the country's 50 pits (19th, government postpones some of the closures after huge outcry and public support for the miners);
26th, Canadian referendum rejects Charlottetown reform agreement which would grant concessions to French-speaking Quebec;
31st, Vatican formally rehabilitates Galileo Galilei, forced by the Inquisition in 1633 to recant his assertion that the Earth orbits the sun.

z **Births and Deaths** (*cont.*)

May 8th F.A. von Hayek d. (92).
Apr. 6th Isaac Asimov d. (72).
Apr. 23rd Satyajit Ray d. (70).
Apr. 27th Olivier Messiaen d. (83).
Apr. 28th Francis Bacon d. (82).
May 6th Marlene Dietrich d. (90).
June 28th John Piper d. (88).
July 4th Willem Visser't Hooft d. (91).
Aug. 12th John Cage d. (79).
Oct. 8th Willy Brandt d. (78).
Nov. 7th Alexander Dubček d. (70).

L **Nov:** 1st (–5th), serious fighting breaks out in Luanda, Angola, in which senior figures in U.N.I.T.A. are killed;

3rd, Democrat William Jefferson ('Bill') Clinton, Governor of Arkansas, wins the U.S. Presidential election with 370 electoral college votes; President Bush (Republican) gains 168 electoral votes and H. Ross Perot (Independent) fails to win any, although he took 19 per cent of the popular vote; in the Congressional elections, Democrats retain control of both chambers; popular vote: Clinton, 43,728,375; Bush, 38,167,416; Perot, 19,237,247.

12th, results of referendum (3rd–5th) among Inuit people in northern Canada endorse creation of Nunavut, a semi-autonomous Inuit territory;

16th, Goldstone Commission in South Africa exposes evidence of state 'dirty tricks' campaign against the A.N.C.;

18th, in Pakistan Benazir Bhutto is tear-gassed by government forces as she leads march to Islamabad calling for fresh elections;

20th, in Britain, fire ravages Windsor Castle, the monarch's second main residence;

22nd, in legislative elections in Peru, parties supporting President Fujimori achieve absolute majority in the new Democratic Constituent Congress, though only 38 per cent of the vote; elections are boycotted by main opposition parties;

24th, last U.S. military personnel withdraw from the Philippines;

26th, in Britain, Prime Minister John Major announces that the Queen has offered to pay tax on her personal income;

27th, Dos Santos and Savimbi issue Namibia Declaration committing themselves to acceptance of Bicesse Peace Accord and continuing U.N. presence in Angola;

—, Lipizzaner stallions are evacuated during fire at Hofburg in Vienna;

30th (–*Dec.* 4th), S.W.A.P.O. win landslide victory in elections in Namibia.

M **Dec:** 2nd, Prime Minister of Greece, Constantine Mitsotakis, dismisses entire cabinet after facing dissent over austerity measures and his moderate position over Macedonia (3rd, new cabinet is appointed);

6th, Hindu extremists demolish 16th-century mosque at Ayodhya, provoking sectarian violence throughout India which claims over 1,200 lives;

—, Germany's asylum law is tightened to give powers to refuse entry to economic migrants;

9th, U.S. troops arrive in Mogadishu, Somalia, to oversee delivery of international food aid, in operation 'Restore Hope';

—, in Britain, separation is announced of Prince and Princess of Wales (married 1981);

11th (–12th), Edinburgh summit of E.C. heads of state meets Danish objections to Maastricht treaty;

16th, Israeli cabinet approves order to deport 415 Palestinians to Lebanon; Lebanon refuses to accept the deportees, who are forced to set up camp in 'no man's land' in security zone in south Lebanon;

—, Czech National Council adopts Constitution for the new, separate, Czech Republic to come into being on *Jan.* 1st 1993;

20th, Slobodan Milosevic is re-elected to Serbian presidency and his Socialist Party of Serbia wins gains in legislative elections;

21st, High Court rules that British government's decision to close 31 pits was illegal and had ignored right of mineworkers and trade unions to be consulted;

29th, Fernando Collor de Mello resigns as President of Brazil as impeachment proceedings begin against him in the Senate (30th, found guilty of corruption and official misconduct, and banned from public office for eight years).

INDEX

Attention is drawn here to the main series of Subject Entries.

Abdications
Administrations, in Britain
Administrations, in US
Aid
Aircraft
Air Forces
Archaeology
Armies
Arms
Assassinations
Atomic Energy
Ballet
Broadcasting
Canals
Civil Wars
Coal
Commissions, Royal
Committees
Concertos
Conferences and Congresses
Constitutions
Coups d'état
Currency
Dances
Demonstrations
Dictionaries
Education
Elections
Electricity
Exhibitions
Exploration
Films
Franchise, The
Galleries and Museums
Journals
League of Nations
Legislation
Machines
Manifestoes
Massacres
Monarchies
Motor Car, The
Navies
Newspapers
Opera
Oratorios
Overtures, Symphonic Poems, etc.
Pacts
Parliaments and other elected assemblies
Political Parties
Plebiscites
Population
Railways
Rebellions and Revolutions
Religious Denominations
Reports
Riots and Risings
Satellites, Artificial
Steel
Strikes
Symphonies
Treaties
United Nations
Universities
Wars

A

Aalborg, Denmark, North Jutland Museum, 1972 S
Aalto, Alvar, Finnish architect (1898–1976), 1898 Z, 1972 S, 1976 Z
Aaron's Rod (D. H. Lawrence), 1922 U
Abba, Swed. pop group, 1976 W
Abbas I, Khedive of Egypt (1848–54), 1848 L, 1854 G
Abbas Hilmi II, Khedive of Egypt (1892–1914), 1892 A, 1893 A; deposed, 1914 M
Abbott, Sir John Joseph Caldwell, Can. Conservative politician (1821–93), premier, 1891 F, 1892 M
Abd-el-Krim, Riff leader, 1926 E
Abdication Crisis in Britain, 1936 K, M
Abdications:
  Alexander Prince of Bulgaria, 1886 J
  Amadeo I of Spain, 1873 B
  Bolívar, Simón, in Colombia, 1830 D
  Charles I, Emperor of Austria, 1918 L
  Charles IV of Spain, 1808 E
  Charles Albert of Sardinia, 1849 C
  Charles Emmanuel of Sardinia, 1798 M
  Constantine I of Greece, 1922 J
  Edward VIII of Great Britain, 1936 M
  Farouk I of Egypt, 1952 G
  Ferdinand I of Austria, 1848 M
  Gustavus IV of Sweden, 1809 C
  Hussein of Hejaz, 1924 K
  Isabella II of Spain, 1870 F
  Korean Emperor, 1907 G
  Leopold III of Belgium, 1950 H
  Louis Philippe of France, 1848 B
  Manchu dynasty in China, 1912 B
  Michael of Rumania, 1947 M
  Milan of Serbia, 1889 C
  Otto I of Greece, 1862 K
  Pedro I of Brazil, 1831 D
  Pedro II of Brazil, 1889 L
  Pedro IV of Portugal 1828 C
  Stanislas II of Poland, 1795 6
  Victor Emmanuel of Piedmont, 1821 C
  Victor Emmanuel III of Italy, 1946 E
  Wilhelmina Queen of Netherlands, 1948 J
  William I of Netherlands, 1840 K
  William II of Germany, 1918 L
Abdul Aziz, Sultan of Morocco (1894–1908), 1908 H
Abdul Aziz, Sultan of Turkey (1861–76), 1861, F, 1866 B, E; agrees to unify Moldavia and Wallachia, 1861 M, agrees to adopt Andrássy reforms, 1876 A; deposed and murdered, 1876 E, F
Abdul Hamid I, Sultan of Turkey (1774–89), 1774 A
Abdul Hamid II, Sultan of Turkey (1876–1909), 1876 H, 1886 D, 1896 G, 1908 G, 1909 D; deposes Ismail, Khedive of Egypt, 1879 F; is forced to undertake reforms, 1895 K
Abdul Mejid I, Sultan of Turkey (1839–61), 1839 G, 1861 F
Abdul Rahman Putra, Tunku, Malay. Alliance party (1903–90), becomes premier, 1961 E
Abdullah, King of Jordan (1881–1951), proclaimed king of Palestine, 1948 M; accession as king of Jordan, 1949 E; assassinated, 1951 G
Abdullah-al-Sallal, premier of the Yemen, 1962 K
Abe, Kobo, Japanese author (b. 1924), 1988 U
Abecedarium, or logical machine, 1874 P
Abel, Sir Frederick, B. inventor of cordite (1827–1902), 1889 P
Abel, Niels Henrik, Nor. mathematician (1802–79), 1828 P
Abelson, F., Am. scientist, 1940 P
Abercrombie, Sir Patrick, B. engineer and town planning consultant (1879–1957), 1943 O
Abercromby, Sir Ralph, B. general (1734–1801), 1797 B, M, 1801 C
Aberdeen, Scotland, typhoid epidemic in, 1964 E
Aberdeen, earl of. *See* Gordon George Hamilton
Aberites (C. M. Wieland), 1774 U
Åbo (now Turku), Finland, Treaty of, Sweden with Russia, 1812 D
Aberfan, South Wales, slag heap slip, 1966 K
Abortion:
  legalized in Britain, 1968 O
  on demand, New York State, US, 1970 O
  US Supreme Court upholds right to, 1973 O
  in US, 1983 O
  in Republic of Ireland, refendum supports ban, 1983 R
  British man ruled unable to prevent abortion of his child, 1987 O
  RV486 abortion-inducing drug, 1988 P
  legalized in Belgium, 1990 D
Aboukir, Egypt, Nelson's victory at, 1798 H; Turks defeated at, 1799 G
About Zionism (A. Einstein), 1930 O
Abrahamren, Aas Foss, author, 1985 U
Abrahams, Kenneth, B., alleges abduction by S. African police, 1963 H
Abrams, Creighton Williams, Am. soldier (1914–74), 1968 F
Absinthe, sale prohibited in France, 1915 O
Abstract Art, treatise on, 1912 S
Abu Hamed, Sudan, taken by Egyptians, 1897 H
Abu Jihad (real name, Khalil al-Waza), PLO military commander (1935–88), 1988 D
Abulfeda (J. Reiske), 1789 Q
Abyss, The (M. Yourcenar), 1968 U
Abyssinia. *See* Ethiopia
Academies:
  British, 1901 Q
  French, replaced by Institut National, 1795 O
  Royal, London. *See under* Galleries and Museums
  Swedish, 1784
  US National Academy of Design, 1826 S
Academies of Science:
  France, Académie des Sciences Morales et Politiques, 1833 O
  Hungary, 1825 O
  Russia, observatory of, 1954 P
Accelerated motion, laws of, 1784 P
Accidental Death of an Anarchist (D. Fo), 1970 W
Account of Corsica ... (J. Boswell), 1768 U
Accra, Ghana, Confederation of Independent African States at, 1958 D;
All-Africa People's Conference at, 1958 M
Accumulator, electric, 1859 P
Acetate rayon ('Celanese'), invented, 1865 P
Acetic acid, synthesis of, 1845 P
Acetylene, 1836 P, 1861 P; lamp, 1900 P
Acheampong, Ignatius Kutu, Ghana leader (1931–79), 1978 G
Achebe, Chinua, Nigerian author (b. 1930), 1987 U
Acheson Plan, to strengthen UN power to resist aggression, 1950 K
Acheson, Dean, Am., lawyer and politician (1893–1971), 1893 Z, 1950 C; becomes US secretary of state, 1949 A; presents disarmament proposals to UN, 1951 L; West Point speech, 1962 M; 1971 Z
Achille Lauro cruise liner, hijack, 1985 K
Achin, N. W. Sumatra, Indonesia, Dutch war against Sultan of, 1873 D
Acid-house rave parties, 1989 W
Acker, M. van, Bel. Socialist, 1954 D
Ackroyd, Peter, B. author (b. 1949), 1986 U, 1990 Q
Acland, Sir Richard, B. politician (1906–1990), forms Commonwealth Party, 1943 C
Acoustics (E. F. F. Chladni), 1802 P
Acoustics, science of, founded, 1786 P; principles of, discussed, 1772 P
Acque e terre (S. Quasimodo), 1930 U
Acquired Immune Deficiency Syndrome (AIDS)
  first victims of, 1977 P
  recognized, 1981 P
  HIV virus isolated, 1983 P
  first celebrity death (Rock Hudson), 1985 P
  statistics, in United States, 1985 P
Acre, Israel, bombarded by British, 1840 L
Across the River and Into the Trees (E. Hemingway), 1950 U
Act of Creation, The (A. Koestler), 1964 R
Acta Karolinorum (ed. von Sickel), 1867 Q
Actinometer, invented, 1825 P
Action, Council of, 1920 H
Acton, Harold Maris, B. author (b. 1904), 1948 U, 1956 Q
Acton, John Dalberg, lord Acton, B. historian (1834–1902), 1834 Z, 1899 Q, 1902 Z
Acton, Sir John Francis Edward, B. administrator (1736–1811), prime minister of Naples, 1799 N
Adam Bede (George Eliot), 1859 U
Adam, Henri Georges, F. sculptor (1904–67), 1943 S, 1955 S, 1957 S
Adam, Robert, B. architect (1728–92), 1744 S, 1769 S., 1792 Z
Adamec, Ladislav, Prime Minister of Czechoslovakia (b. 1926)
  replaces Štrougal as Prime Minister, 1988 K
  Communist monopoly on power formally renounced, 1989 L
Adams, Gerry, N. Ir. politician (b. 1948), 1982 M
Adams, Henry, Am. author (1838–1918), 1904 Q, 1907 Q
Adams, John Michael Geoffrey Manningham, Prime Minister of Barbados (1931–85), 1931 Z, 1985 Z
Adams, John Quincy, Am. statesman, 6th president of US, Democratic Republican (1767–1848), 1767 Z; signs treaty with Spain over Florida, 1819 B; elected president, 1824 L; inaugurated, 1825 C; defeated by Jackson, 1827 L
Adams, John, Am. musician (b. 1920), 1987 T
Adams, John, Am. statesman, 2nd president of US, Federalist (1735–1826), 1787 O, 1792 N; vice-president, 1789 D; elected president, 1796 L; inaugurated, 1797 C; defeated by Jefferson, 1800 L
Adams, Richard George, B. author (b. 1920), 1973 U
Adams, Samuel, Am. statesman (1722–1803), 1772 L, 1776 G, 1782 L
Adams, Sherman, Am. administrator (b. 1899), assistant to president Eisenhower, 1958 F
Adams, Sir Grantley Herbert, Barbadian Labour politician, premier of West Indies Federation, 1961 M
Adams, Thomas, B. soldier (?1730–64), 1763 G
Adamson Associates, architects, 1987 S
Adcock, Fleur, New Zealand author (b. 1934), 1986 U
Adding-Machine, The (E. Rice), 1923 W
Addington, Henry, viscount Sidmouth, B. Tory politician (1757–1844), becomes premier, 1801 C; resigns, 1804 D; as home secretary suppresses seditious publications, 1817 C

Addis Ababa, Abyssinia: Treaty of, withdraws Italian protectorate, 1896 K; French influence in, 1897 C; railway to Jibouti, 1902 B; Italians occupy, 1936 E; British take, 1941 D; Organization of African Unity Conference, 1984 L, 1985 G
captured by Ethiopian People's Revolutionary Democratic Front, 1991 E
Addison, Paul, B. historian (b. 1943), 1975 Q
Addresses to the German Nation (J. G. Fichte), 1808 O
Address to the King (E. Burke), 1777 O
Adelaide, S. Australia, 1836 O
Adelung, Johann Christoph, G. philologist (1732–1806), 1806 Q
Aden:
ceded by Turkey, 1833 E; government of, is separated from India, 1935 H; state of emergency in, 1958 E; agreement for entering S. Arabia Federation, 1962 H; constitutional talks break down, 1965 H; terrorists shoot the Speaker; 1965 J; British suspends constitution, 1965 J. *See also* Yemen, South
curfew imposed following nationalist riots, 1967 B
UN diplomatic mission, 1967 D
general strike and terrorist campaign, 1967 D
Arab mutineers kill 22 British soldiers, 1967 F
Britain appeals for negotiations with nationalist forces, 1967 J
nationalists call for ceasefire, 1967 J
Arab nationalists kill British administrator, 1967 K
rival nationalist groups, conflict between, 1967 L
People's Republic of South Yemen declared, 1967 L
British withdrawal, 1967 H, 1967 L
Adenauer, Konrad, G. statesman, Christian Democrat (1876–1967), 1876 Z, 1963 A, 1967 Z; becomes chancellor of W. Germany, 1949 J; advocates Franco-German economic union, 1950 C; meets foreign leaders, 1953 D, 1958 J, 1959 C, 1961 B; reforms ministry, 1953 K; election successes, 1957 J; prevents Erhard's candidature for presidency, 1959 G; appeals for peace treaty based on self-determination, 1961 F; retires, 1963 K
Adler, Felix, Am. formerly G. religious leader (1851–1933), 1876 R
Adler, Larry, Am. harmonica player (b. 1914), 1952 T
Administrations, in Britain:
George Grenville (Whig), 1763 D
Marquess of Rockingham (Whig), 1765 G
Earl of Chatham (Whig), 1766 G
Duke of Grafton (Whig), 1768 K
Lord North (Tory), 1770 A
Marquess of Rockingham (Whig), 1782 C
Earl of Shelburne (Whig), 1782 G
Duke of Portland ('Fox-North Coalition'), 1783 D
William Pitt (Tory), 1783 M
Henry Addington (Tory), 1801 C
William Pitt (Tory), 1804 E
Lord Grenville (Whig) ('All the Talents'), 1806 B
Duke of Portland (Tory), 1807 C
Spencer Perceval (Tory), 1809 K
Earl of Liverpool (Tory), 1812 F
George Canning (Tory), 1827 D
Viscount Goderich (Tory), 1827 H
Duke of Wellington (Tory), 1828 A
Earl Grey (Whig), 1830 L
Viscount Melbourne (Whig), 1834 G
Sir Robert Peel (Tory), 1834 L
Viscount Melbourne (Whig), 1835 D
Sir Robert Peel (Tory), 1841 H
Lord John Russell (Whig), 1846 F
Earl of Derby (Tory), 1852 B
Earl of Aberdeen (Whig Coalition), 1852 M
Viscount Palmerston (Whig-Liberal), 1855 B
Earl of Derby (Conservative), 1858 B
Viscount Palmerston (Whig-Liberal), 1859 F
Earl Russell (Whig-Liberal), 1865 K
Earl of Derby (Conservative), 1866 F
Benjamin Disraeli (Conservative), 1868 B
William Ewart Gladstone (Liberal), 1868 M
Benjamin Disraeli, later Earl of Beaconsfield (Conservative), 1874 B
William Ewart Gladstone (Liberal), 1880 D
Marquess of Salisbury (Conservative), 1885 F
William Ewart Gladstone (Liberal), 1886 B
Marquess of Salisbury (Conservative), 1886 G
William Ewart Gladstone (Liberal), 1892 H
Earl of Rosebery (Liberal), 1894 C
Marquess of Salisbury (Conservative), 1895 F
Arthur James Balfour (Conservative), 1902 G
Sir Henry Campbell-Bannerman (Liberal), 1905 M
Herbert Henry Asquith (Liberal), 1908 D
Herbert Henry Asquith (Coalition), 1915 E
David Lloyd George (Coalition), 1916 M
Andrew Bonar Law (Conservative), 1922 K
Stanley Baldwin (Conservative), 1923 E
James Ramsay MacDonald (Labour), 1924 A
Stanley Baldwin (Conservative), 1924 L
James Ramsay MacDonald (Labour), 1929 F
James Ramsay MacDonald (National Government), 1931 H
Stanley Baldwin (National Government), 1935 F
Arthur Neville Chamberlain (National Government), 1937 E
Winston Leonard Spencer Churchill (Coalition), 1940 E
Winston Leonard Spencer Churchill (Conservative 'Caretaker'), 1945 E
Clement Richard Attlee (Labour), 1945 G
Winston Leonard Spencer Churchill (Conservative), 1951 K
Sir Robert Anthony Eden (Conservative), 1955 D
Maurice Harold Macmillan (Conservative), 1957 A
Sir Alec Douglas-Home (Conservative), 1963 K
Harold Wilson (Labour), 1964 K
Edward Heath (Conservative), 1970 F
Harold Wilson (Labour), 1974 C
James Callaghan (Labour), 1976 D
Margaret Thatcher (Conservative), 1979 E
John Major (Conservative), 1990 L
Administrations, in US:
George Washington (Federalist), 1789 D
John Adams (Federalist), 1797 C
Thomas Jefferson (Democratic Republican), 1801 C
James Madison (Democratic Republican), 1809 C
James Monroe (Democratic Republican), 1817 C
John Quincy Adams (Democratic Republican), 1825 C
Andrew Jackson (Democrat), 1829 C
Martin Van Buren (Democrat), 1837 C
William Henry Harrison (Whig), 1841 C
John Tyler (Whig), 1841 D
James Knox Polk (Democrat),1845 C
Zachary Taylor (Whig), 1849 C
Millard Fillmore (Whig), 1850 G
Franklin Pierce (Democrat), 1853 C
James Buchanan (Democrat), 1857 C
Abraham Lincoln (Republican), 1861 C
Andrew Johnson (Republican), 1865 D
Ulysses Simpson Grant (Republican), 1869 C
Rutherford Richard Hayes (Republican), 1877 C
James Abram Garfield (Republican), 1881 C
Chester Alan Arthur (Republican), 1881 G
Grover Cleveland (Democrat), 1885 C
Benjamin Harrison (Republican), 1889 C
Grover Cleveland (Democrat), 1893 C
William McKinley (Republican), 1897 C
Theodore Roosevelt (Republican), 1901 J
William Howard Taft (Republican), 1909 C
Woodrow Wilson (Democrat), 1913 C
Warren Gamaliel Harding (Republican), 1921 C
Calvin Coolidge (Republican), 1923 H
Herbert C. Hoover (Republican), 1929 C
Franklin Delano Roosevelt (Democrat), 1933 C
Harry S. Truman (Democrat), 1945 D
Dwight D. Eisenhower (Republican), 1953 A
John F. Kennedy (Democrat), 1961 A
Lyndon B. Johnson (Democrat), 1963 L
Richard Nixon (Republican), 1969 A
Gerald Ford (Republican), 1974 H
Jimmy Carter (Democrat), 1977 A
Ronald Reagan (Republican), 1981 A
George Bush (Republican), 1988 L
Bill Clinton (Democrat), 1992 L
Administrative Reform Association, 1855 O
Admirable Crichton, The (J. M. Barrie), 1902 U
Adolphe (B. Constant), 1807 U
Adonais (P. B. Shelley), 1821 U
Adopted children, right to information on natural parents, B., 1975 O
Adoption, in Britain, legalised, 1926 D
Adorno, Theodor, G. philosopher (1903–69), 1966 R
Adoula, Mr., Congolese premier, 1964 G
Adowa, N. Ethiopia, Italian defeat at, 1896 C
Adrenalin, manufacture of, 1901 P
Adrian, Edgar Douglas, Lord Adrian, B. physiologist (1889–1977), 1929 P
Adrianople (now Edirne), Turkey: Treaty of, between Russia and Turkey, 1829 J; Russians capture, 1878 A; Bulgarians take, 1913 C; Turks capture, 1913 G; Greeks occupy, 1920 G
Adriatic Islands, Italy cedes to Yugoslavia, 1947 B
Advancement of Science, British Association for the, 1831 P; American Association for the, 1848 P
Adventures of Augie March, The (S. Bellow), 1954 U
Adventures of Ideas (A. N. Whitehead), 1933 R
Adventures of Sherlock Holmes, The (A. C. Doyle), 1891 U
Adventures of Tom Sawyer, The (M. Twain), 1875 U
Adventures of a Black Girl in Her Search for God, The (G. B. Shaw), 1932 U
Advertisement for Myself (N. Mailer), 1959 U
Advertising, British tax on, repealed, 1853 O; of cigarettes on TV banned in Britain, 1965 W
Advice to a Young Man (W. Cobbett), 1829 U
'AE'. *See* Russell, George William
Aehrenthal, Count Alois, Aus. foreign minister, 1908 A, J
Aerated waters, 1807 P
Aeronautical map, 1911 P
Aeronautics, 1783 P, 1785 P, 1900 P. *See also* Aircraft, Aviation
Aeroplanes. *See* Aircraft

Aerostat, 1843 P
Aesthetic Studies (G. Brandes), 1868 U
Aesthetic and History (B. Berenson), 1950 S
Aesthetic movement, 1882 S
Aesthetics (F. Vischer), 1846 R
Affluent Society, The (J. K. Galbraith), 1958 O
Afghanistan
  Persia recognises independence, 1857 C
  Ameer of, British subsidy to, 1879 E; murdered, 1919 B
  Russian conquest in, 1884 A
  frontier, Anglo-Russian compromise over, 1885 J
  Communist and Islamic forces take power, 1978 D
  overthrow of Taraki, 1979 J
  Amin killed and replaced by Karmal, 1979 M
  Soviet invasion, 1979 M, 1980 B, M
  Soviet invasion condemned by US, 1980 A
  Soviet May Day parade boycotted by ambassadors in protest against Soviet invasion, 1980 E
  Moslems called on to boycott Moscow Olympics, 1980 R
  illiteracy, 1983 Y
  Najibullah replaces Karmal, 1986 E
  Soviet withdrawal, 1988 B, E
  explosion at Pakistan army ammunition dump blamed on Afghan agents, 1988 D
  state of emergency imposed, 1989 B
  attempted coup, 1990 C
  Najibullah overthrown and Mujaheddin rebels close on Kabul, 1992 D
  fighting between pro-government and Mujaheddin faction, 1992 H
Africa Association, founded, 1788 F
Africa Company, British, 1820 E, 1893 G
Africa, exploration of, 1799 P, 1850 P. *See also* Central Africa; East Africa; South-west Africa; South Africa
African Assistance Plan, 1960 J
African National Congress (ANC), 1992 D, F, J
  banned, 1986 G
  Howe mission fails to lift ban, 1986 G
  reporting of activities of banned, 1987 A
  ban lifted, 1990 B
  Mandela released from prison, 1990 B
  clashes with Zulu Inkatha movement, 1990 H
  mass action protest campaign, 1992 H
  Goldstone Commission on state dirty tricks campaign against, 1992 L
African Survey, An (Lord Hailey), 1957 O
Afrikander Bond, founded, 1879 O
Afro-Asian Organisation for Economic Co-operation, 1959 D
After Hegarty (D. Mercer), 1970 W
After the Fall (A. Miller), 1964 W
After Virtue (A. MacIntyre), 1981 R
Aga Khan, 1906 N
Aga Mohammed, of Persia (d. 1797), 1794 N, 1796 N
Agadir, Morocco: Incident, 1911 G; earthquake, 1960 B
Against Method (P. Feyerabend), 1975 R
Against the Self-Images of the Age (A. MacIntyre), 1971 R
Agassiz, Jean Louis Rodolphe, Swi. naturalist and geologist (1734–1807), 1837 P, 1840 P
Agca, Mehmet Ali, Turkish terrorist (b. 1958)
  assassination attempt on Pope John Paul II, 1981 E
Age of Anxiety, The (J.K. Galbraith), 1977 Q
Age of Kings, The, television programme, 1961 W
Age of Plunder, The: King Henry's England, 1500–1547 (W.G. Hoskins), 1976 Q
Age of Reason, The (T. Paine), 1794 O
Age of Reason, The (J.-P. Sartre), 1945 U
Aggression, On (K. Lorenz), 1966 P
...agm... (Birtwistle), 1979 T
Agnew, Spiro Theodore, Am. Republican politician (b. 1919)
  vice-presedential nomination, 1968 H
  vice-presidential re-nomination, 1972 H
  resignation from vice-presidency, 1973 K
Agnostic's Apology (L. Stephen), 1893 R
Agnosticism (T. H. Huxley), 1889 R
Agrarian History of England and Wales, The, 1967 Q
Agrarian reforms, in Russia, 1906 L
Agricultural Institute, International, 1905 O
Agricultural Labourers' Union, National British, 1872 O
Agricultural Marketing Scheme, British, 1933 O
Agricultural adjustment Tariff, US, 1933 O
Agriculture, British Board of, 1793 P, 1889 G
Agriculture, EC Common Agricultural Policy, 1966 G 1988 O
Agriculture, in Britain, reforms of holdings, 1875 O loans for, 1910 O
Agustino (A. Moravia), 1944 U
Ahlquist, Jon E., 1984 P
Ahmed Pasha, Egyp. premier, 1945 A, B
Ahmed Shah, of Persia (1909–24), 1909 G; deposed, 1924 B
Ahmed, Khandaker Mushtaq, President of Bangladesh, 1975 H
Ahnfrau, Die (F. Grillparzer), 1817 U
Ah Wilderness (E. O'Neill), 1933 W
Aid:
  Belgian aid to Congo suspended, 1967 H
  famine relief to Biafra, 1968 G, H
  famine relief to Nigeria, 1968 G
  to India refugees from war with East Pakistan, 1971 E
  famine relief to Ethiopia, 1984 L
  OAU summit calls for international aid for Africa, 1984 L
  'Do They Know It's Christmas' single, 1984 W
  Live Aid concerts, 1985 W
  famine relief to Somalia, 1992 G, M
Aid, British:
  to China, 1898 A, C, 1912 D, J
  to Austria, 1932 G, K
  to Indonesia, suspended, 1963 K
    See also Subsidies
  British Commonwealth, plan for Africa, 1960 J
    plan for S.E. Asia, 1950 A
  French, to Hungary, 1931 H
    to Russia, 1888 K, 1891 G
  W. German, to India, 1959 A
  Indian, to Burma, 1957 C
  Russian, for Bulgaria, 1956 B
    for China, 1959 B
    for Hungary, 1959 H
    for India, 1956 L
    for Iraq, 1959 C
    for Syria, 1959 M
    for United Arab Republic, 1958 K
    technical assistance for China, 1956 A
  US, to Britain, 1915 J, 1931 H, 1945 M, 1946 G
    to Europe, 1929 K
    to France, 1931 H
    to Ghana, 1961 M
    to India, 1952 A
    foreign aid, under Truman Doctrine, 1947 C, 1949 A
    Marshall Aid, for European Recovery, 1947 F, G, 1948 D
      to Britain ends, 1950 M
    aid under Foreign Assistance Bill, 1949 D, 1950 C, 1952 F, 1955 D, 1961 E
    to Nationalist China ends, 1949 H
    to Cuba ends, 1960 E, H
    to Israel ends, 1956 K; resumed, 1957 D
    to non-Communist countries for developing atomic energy, 1955 F
    is offered to S.E. Asia, 1965 L
    See also Lend-Lease; Loans; Marshall Plan
      military, to Iraq ends, 1959 E
    to NATO countries, 1949 K
    to W. Germany, 1955 F
Aid, Legal, 1950 O
Aid, industrial
  in Britain, 1970 L, 1974 L, 1981 A
  in US, 1979 L
Aigle a deux têtes, L' (J. Cocteau), 1946 W
Aiglon, L' (Rostand), 1900 U
Aiguillon, Emmanuel Armand de Wignerod du Plessis de Richelieu, duc d', F. statesman (1720–1782), 1770 M
Aintree, Liverpool, Eng., race course, 1839 X
Air and Fire (K. W. Scheele), 1775 P
Air defence, US, 1925 O
Air pollution, Beaver Committee on, 1953 O
Air, composition of, 1914 P
Air, liquefaction of, 1898 P
Airborne troops, British, 1944 J
Aircraft
  Antonov AN–22, 1965 P
  Blériot's, 1909 P
  Boeing 747 'jumbo jet', 1969 P, 1970 P
  Boeing 757 airliner, 1982 P
  Concorde, 1969 P, 1976 A, 1976 P
  Concord supersonic airliner, 1962 L
  Daedalus 88 sets new record for man-powered flight, 1988 P
  DC-10, grounded in US after Chicago crash, 1979 E
  flying bedstead, 1954 P
  Gossamer Albatross, 1979 P
  Gossamer Condor, 1977 P
  Langley's, 1896 P
  Me 109 sets world speed record, 1939 P
  petrol engine, 1903 P
  pilotless, 1950 P, 1953 P
  Solar Challenger, 1981 P
  Stealth bomber, 1988 P
  supersonic, 1968 P, 1969 P
  TSR–2, cancelled, 1965 D
  Tu-104 jet passenger aircraft, 1955 P
  Tupolev Tu-144, 1968 P
  vertical take-off, 1954 P
  Voyager flies round world without refuelling, 1986 P
  VS-300 helicopter, 1939 P
  Wright brothers', 1903 P
Aircraft carriers, limited by London Conference, 1930 D
Aircraft detection, by Radar, 1935 P
Aircraft industry, British, Plowden Report on, 1965 M
Aircraft workers, demonstration by, 1965 A
Aircraft, attacks on
  Palestinian terrorists attack El Al airliner at Zurich airport, 1969 B
  South Korean Boeing 747 shot down in Soviet air space, 1983 J
  bomb discovered in El Al passenger's luggage, Heathrow airport, 1986 D, K
  Iranian civilian airliner shot down by US, 1988 G
  Lockerbie air crash, 1988 M, 1992 C
  hijackings. *See* Hijackings

Air Crashes:
  Swiss airliner at Baden, 1970 B
  BEA Trident crashes at Staines, 1972 F
  Turkish airliner crashes near Paris, 1974 C
  at Tenerife, 1977 C
  DC-10 at Chicago, 1979 E
  Air India Boeing 747, 1985 F
  Pan Am Boeing 747 crashes at Lockerbie, 1988 M
Air Defence Council, North American, 1958 E
Air Forces:
  British. *See* Royal Air Force
  German, Zeppelin raids, on England, 1915 A, F, 1917 G, J
    on France, 1916 A
    Churchill's warning on, 1934 L
    bomber raids on Britain, 1940 G
    in Battle of Britain, 1940 H, J
    begin 'the Blitz' of Britain, 1940 H
    attack British convoy to Greece, 1941 A
    bomb London, 1941 C, E, 1943 A, 1944 B
    destruction of Coventry, 1941 D
    'Baedeker' raids on Britain, 1942 D
    continuous bombing of Malta, 1942 D
    attack British convoys to Russia, 1942 J, M
  Japanese, bomb Pearl Harbor, 1941 M
    sink *Prince of Wales* and *Repulse*, 1941 M
  Royal, formed, 1918 D
    increases in, 1934 G, 1936 C
    begins bombing of Germany, 1940 G
    bombs Lübeck, 1942 C
    bombs Cologne, 1942 E
    thousand-bomber raid on Bremen, 1942 F
    bombs Hamburg, 1942 G
    bombs Berlin, 1943 B
    bombs European railway system, 1943 C
    bombs Ruhr, 1943 D, E
    bombs Rome, 1943 G
    bombing of German cities, protests in Parliament at, 1944 A
    bombs occupied Europe, 1944 D
    production of aircraft for, 1939 Y, 1940 Y, 1941 Y, 1942 Y, 1943 Y, 1944 Y
  Russian, aircraft reported to be in Czechoslovakia, 1936 J
  United Nations, bombs North Korean plants, 1952 C
  US (formerly US Army Air Force), daily raids on occupied France, 1942 J; daylight raids on Berlin, 1944 C, 1944 D; bombing of occupied Europe, 1944 D; becomes independent of Army, 1947 O; incidents involving aircraft of, 1950 D, 1960 E; bombing of North Vietnam, 1965 B, D
Air Mail, 1934 P
Air Raid Precautions (ARP) in Britain, legislation, 1937 L; reorganised as Civil Defence, 1941 O
Air Raids, in Britain, casualties, statistics of, 1940 L; physics of, 1941 P
Air Services, first regular (by airship), 1912 P; regular Trans-Pacific, 1935 P; regular Trans-Atlantic, 1939 P; regular London–Moscow, 1957 M
Airlines
  Braniff International Corp., 1982 O
  Laker Airways, collapse of, 1982 B
  US industry deregulated, 1978 K
Airplane Dreams (A. Ginsberg), 1968 U
Airports
  Falkland Islands, 1983 F
  London, 1955 S
  London's third, 1971 D
  London, Heathrow, 1977 M
  London, Stanstead, 1967 E, 1991 S
  New York, Kennedy, 1961 S
Airships: rigid, 1912 P; lighter than air, 1920 P; *R. 101* disaster, 1930 P; US *Shenandoah*, 1925 O; Count Zeppelin's, 1898 P, 1900 P; *Graf Zeppelin*, 1928 P, 1929 P
Aisne, River, France, battles of, 1914 J, 1917 D, 1917 N
Aitken, Sir John William Max, B. newspaper proprietor (1910–85), 1977 V
Aitken, William Maxwell, Lord Beaverbrook, B. newspaper proprietor and politician (1879–1965), 1879 Z, 1915 V, 1924 O, 1941 J, 1951 S, 1956 Q, 1964 Z
Aix-la-Chapelle (now Aachen, W. Germany), Conference at, 1818 J
Akerman, John Yonge, B. antiquarian (1806–73), 1840 Q
Akihito, Emperor of Japan (b. 1933), 1933 Z, 1989 A, 1990 L
Akimoto, Matsuyo, 1989 W
Akitek, B.E.P., architect, 1979 S
Akkerman Convention, between Russia and Turkey, 1826 N
Akrotiri, Thera, excavations, 1967 Q
Akuffo, Fred, President of Ghana (1937–79), 1978 G, 1979 F
À la recherche du temps perdu (M. Proust), 1913 U
Al fatah, opposition to Arafat, 1983 F
Alabama, State, US: becomes a US state, 1819 M; as a Confederate State, 1861 B; University, desegregation crisis in, 1956 O
Alabama, The, depredations by, 1862 G, 1872 J
Alain-Fournier, Henri Alban (originally Fournier), F. author (1886–1914), 1913 U
Alarcón, Pedro Antoine de, Sp. author (1833–91), 1859 U, 1874 U
Alaska highway, 1942 P
Alaska, US state: trade monopoly in, 1799 O; purchased by US from Russia, 1867 C; law and administration of, 1884 E; frontier settled, 1903 K; elects delegates to Congress, 1906 E; becomes a US state, 1958 G; oil discoveries, 1968 O
Alastor (P. B. Shelley), 1816 U
Albania: autonomy for, accepted by peace conference, 1912 M; powers agree on establishing principality of, 1913 G; rebellion in, 1915 A; independence of, 1917 F; allied advance in, 1918 E; independence recognised, 1921 L; proclaimed a republic, 1924 M; frontier settlement, 1926 G; proclaimed a kingdom, 1928 J; Italy invades, 1939 D; republic proclaimed, 1946 A
  laws dealing with Church–State relations abrogated, 1968 R
  diplomatic relations established with West Germany, 1987 J
  law forbidding religious propaganda repealed, 1990 R
  Greek Albanians flee to Greece, 1991 A
  refugees land in Italy, 1991 C
  elections, 1991 C
  government resignation following general strike, 1991 F
  Democrat Party election victory ends Communist rule, 1992 C
Albanian separatists, Yugoslavia, 1988 J, 1990 B, 1990 J, 1991 C
Albee, Edward Franklin, Am. dramatist (b. 1928), 1928 Z, 1962 W, 1966 W
Albert Canal, Belgium, Germans turn line of, 1940 E
Albert Edward Nyanza, Lake, Central Africa, 1887 P
Albert I, king of Belgians (1909–34), 1909 M; given dictatorial powers, 1926 R
Albert, Eugène Francis Charles D', B. composer (1864–1932), 1903 T
Albert Francis Charles Augustus Emmanuel, of Saxe-Coburg Gotha, Prince Consort of Great Britain (1819–61), 1819 Z, 1840 B, 1861 Z; memorial to, 1862 S
Albert, Lake, Uganda/Congo, Anglo–Belgian pact on, 1910 E
Albert, archduke of Austria, 1866 F
Alberta, province, Canada, formed, 1905 J
Albertville, Congo, Congolese rebels take, 1964 F
Albright, Jacob, Am. religious leader (1759–1808), founds Evangelical Association, 1807 R
Albuera, Spain, Soult defeated at, 1811 E
Alcock, Sir John William, B. aviator (1892–1919), 1919 P
Alcohol, synthesis of, 1826 P
Alcott, Louisa May, Am. authoress (1832–88), 1868 U
Aldermaston March, 1956 O
Aldershot, England
  IRA bomb kills seven people, 1972 B
  League club folds, 1992 X
Aldrich, Robert, Am. film director (1918–83), 1967 W
Alekseeva, Lisa, R. dissident, 1981 M
Alemán, Miguel, president of Mexico, 1946 G
Alembert, Jean Le Rond D' (1717–83), F. mathematician, 1783 Z
Aleppo, Syria, martial law proclaimed, 1980 C
Aleshkovsky, Yuz, R. author (b. 1929), 1986 U
Aleutian Isles, N. Pacific, settled by Russians, 1785 P
Alexander (Karageorgevitch), prince of Serbia, deposed, 1858 M
Alexander Cuza, prince of Rumania, 1866 B
Alexander I of Greece (1917–20), 1917 F
Alexander I, Tsar of Russia (1778–1825), 1778 Z, 1825 M; annexes Georgia, 1801 J; meets Napoleon at Tilsit, 1807 G; designs on Finland, 1808 F; Napoleon alienates, 1811 A; issues Polish constitution, 1815 L; supports Greek rebels, 1821 C
Alexander I, king of Serbia (1889–1903), 1893 D, 1901 B, 1903 F
Alexander I, king of Yugoslavia (1921–34), establishes dictatorship, 1929 A; assassinated, 1934 K
Alexander II, Tsar of Russia (1855–81), 1855 C, 1858 O; studies emancipation of serfs, 1857 L; visits Berlin, 1875 E; assassinated, 1881 C
Alexander III, Tsar of Russia (1881–94), 1881 C, 1894 L; fails to secure *entente* with Germany, 1890 H
Alexander of Battenberg (1879–86): elected prince of Bulgaria, 1879 D, 1883 J; appointed governor of E. Rumelia, 1886 D; abdicates, 1886 J
Alexander, Albert Victor, Lord Alexander of Hillsborough, B. Co-operative Party politician (1885–1965), becomes First Lord of Admiralty, 1940 E
Alexander, Harold Rupert Leofric George, B. field-marshal (1891–1969), replaces Auchinleck as c.-in-c. Middle East, 1942 H
Alexander, Samuel, B. philosopher (1859–1938), 1859 Z, 1889 R, 1938 Z
Alexandra Caroline Mary Charlotte Louise Julie, princess of Denmark, Queen-consort of Edward VII of Great Britain (1844–1925), 1844 Z, 1925 Z
Alexandria, Egypt: French defeated near, 1801 C; powers sign Convention of, with Mehemet Ali, 1840 L; Cleopatra's Needle removed from,

1878 S; anti-foreign riots in, 1882 F, G; Nationalist riots in, 1921 E
Alexandrina Victoria, princess. *See* Victoria, Queen
Alexandropol, Turkey, Treaty of, between Armenia and Turkey, 1920 M
Alexinatz, Serbia, battle, 1876 J
Alfieri, Vittorio, It. dramatist (1749–1803), 1775 W, 1776 W, 1770 O, 1803 Z
Alfonsín, Dr. Raoul, President of Argentina (b. 1926), 1983 K, M, 1989 E
Alfonso XII of Spain (1875–85), 1870 F, 1874 L, M, 1875 A
Alfonso XIII of Spain (1886–1931), flees, 1931 D
Alfred (A. von Haller), 1773 U
Alfred Ernest Albert, duke of Edinburgh (1844–1900); elected to Greek throne, 1863 B; marries Princess Marie of Russia, 1874 A
Algebra, studies in, 1770 P
Algeciras, Conference on Morocco, 1906 A, D
Algeria: French conquest begins, 1830 G; French provisional government at, 1944 H; terrorism in, 1953 M, 1955 K, 1958 M; Nehru's plan for, 1956 E; demonstrations in, 1958 E; provisional government proclaimed, 1958 J; de Gaulle's broadcast on, 1959 J; UN declines to intervene, 1959 M; riots in, 1960 A; de Gaulle offers surrender terms to rebels, 1960 F; referendum on, 1961 A; cease-fire in, 1962 C; F.L.N. provisional government for, 1962 C; independence of, 1962 G; admitted to Arab League, 1962 H
earthquake, 1980 K
rioting against rising prices and unemployment, 1988 K
diplomatic relations with Egypt restored, 1988 L
Arab Maghreb Union, 1989 B
Islamic Salvation Front, 1990 F, 1991 F
elections, 1991 M
electoral victory by Islamic Salvation Front thwarted by military, 1992 A
state of emergency declared, 1992 B
Boudiaf assassinated, 1992 F
president and vice-president of Islamic Salvation Front imprisoned, 1992 G
Algiers, Algeria: Spanish expedition to, 1775 G; French take, 1830 G; rebels in, 1846 A
agreement on US hostages' release in Iran, 1981 A
Palestinian National Council meeting, 1987 D
Kuwaiti airliner hijack ended, 1988 D
Islamic Salvation Front riot, 1991 F
'Algiers Toast', by Cardinal Lavigerie, 1890 L
Ali Khan, premier of Pakistan, 1951 K
Ali of Janina, Turkish pasha, assassinated, 1822 B
Ali, Muhammad, Am. boxer (b. 1942), 1942 Z, 1964 X, 1965 X
stripped of World Heavy-Weight title for refusing draft, 1967 X
beaten by Frazier, 1971 X
regains World Heavy-weight title, 1974 X
retains World Heavy-Weight title, 1975 X
beaten by Spinks, 1978 X
regains WBA title, 1978 X
Alia, Ramiz, President of Albania (b. 1925), 1982 L, 1985 D, 1992 J
Alice's Adventures in Wonderland (L. Carroll), 1865 U
Alison, Archibald, B. author (1757–1839), 1790 S
Aliwal, India, battle, 1846 A
Alizarin, synthetic dye, 1869 P
Alkmaar, N. Holland, British capitulate at, 1799 K
All Passion Spent (V. Sackville-West), 1931 U
All Quiet on the Western Front (E. Remarque), 1929 U
All Sorts and Conditions of Men (W. Besant), 1882 W
All the Conspirators (C. Isherwood), 1928 U
All the King's Men (R. Penn Warren), 1946 U
All-Africa Federal Executive Committee, 1957 H
All-Africa People's Conference, Accra, 1958 M
All-Blacks, N. Zeal., Rugby tour, 1924 X
All-India Moslem League, 1906 N
Alle Pressements alle Morte (Leobardi), 1816 U
Allen, Percy Stafford, B. classical scholar (1869–1933), 1906 Q
Allen, Percy, B. spy, 1965 E
Allen, Woody, Am. film actor and director (b. 1935), 1935 Z, 1977 W, 1986 W, 1989 W
Allenby, Edmund, Lord Allenby, B. soldier (1861–1936), 1861 Z, 1917 F, M, 1919 C, 1936 Z
Allende, Isabel, Chilean (formerly Peruv.) author, 1982 U
Allende, Salvador, President of Chile (1908–73)
elected President, 1970 J
constitutional amendment on expropriation of property vetoed, 1972 D
reported suicide, 1973 J
Alliances. *See* Treaties of Alliance
Allied occupation of Germany, 1945 E; ends 1955 E; military government superseded by Allied High Commission, 1949 J
Alliluyeva, Svetlana, R., daughter of Stalin (b. 1926), 1967 C
al-Mahdi, Sadiq (also known as Sadiq Abdul Rahman), Prime Minister of Sudan (b. 1936), 1989 C
overthrow, 1989 F
Allotments, British, 1887 O
Allowances, family, 1945 O
Alma, USSR, battle, 1854 J
Alma-Tadema, Sir Lawrence, B. artist (1836–1912), 1900 S, 1903 S
Almanack de Gotha, 1763 Q
Almanack, nautical, 1767 P
Almayer's Folly (J. Conrad), 1895 U
Almeria, Spain, German fleet bombards, 1937 E
Almost Transparent Blue (R. Murakami), 1976 U
Almquist, Carl Jonas Love, Swe. author (1793–1846), 1832 U
Alphabet, Roman, adopted by Turkey, 1928 L
Alps, the, Europe, mountain range:
Brenner Pass through, 1772 P
Napoleon's campaigns in, 1799 H, J, 1800 E
Simplon Pass, carriage road through, 1800 P
railway through, 1853 P
Alsace-Lorraine, France: ceded to Germany, 1871 E; declared part of the Reich, 1879 H; Reichstag grants measure of autonomy to, 1911 E; returned to France, 1919 B
Alternative Service Book 1980, The, 1980 R
Althusser, Louis, French philosopher (b. 1918), 1976 R
Altizer, Thomas Jonathan Jackson, Am. theologian (b. 1927), 1966 R
Altman, Robert, Am. film writer and director (b. 1925), 1992 W
Altmark incident, 1940 B
Alton Locke (C. Kingsley), 1849 U
Aluminium, 1827 P; produced electrically, 1887 P; statistics of production, 1914 Y, 1939 Y 1959 Y
Alvarez, Am. atomic physicist, 1959 P
Alvensleben, Constantin von, Count, G. Diplomat, 1863 B
Alvintzi, Joseph, Aus. general (1735–1810), 1796 L defeated at Rivoli, 1797 A
Aly Maher Pasha, Egypt. politician, appointed premier, 1952 A; resigns, 1952 C
Amadeus (P. Shaffer), 1979 W
Amadeus I, king of Spain, formerly duke of Aosta (1845–73): elected king, 1870 L; abdicates, 1873 B
Amalgamated Union of Engineering Workers (AUEW)
fined for excluding member, 1972 L
Nissan negotiates single-union deal, 1985 O
Amanullah, Emir of Afghanistan, flees, 1959 E
Amarah, on R. Tigris, British take, 1915 F
Amarillo Ramp (R. Smithson), 1973 S
Amateur Athletic Club, 1866 X
Ambassadors, The (H. James), 1903 U
Amberg, Bavaria, W. Germany, 1796 H
Ambia Alagi, Abyssinia, Italians defeated at, 1895 M
Amdahl, Gene, Am. scientist, 1967 P
Amelia Island, Florida, US, taken by Unionists, 1862 C
America's Cup races, 1964 X
America, North-West coast, exploration of, 1790 P
America, Spanish, natural features of, studied, 1807 P
America, discovery by Leif Ericsson proved, 1965 Q
American Association for the Advancement of Science, 1848 P
American Bible Society, 1816 R
American Buffalo (D. Mamet), 1975 W
American Colonies, under British rule:
alliance with France, 1778 B
British plans to conciliate, 1775 B, O, 1778 B, D
rejected, 1778 F
British prohibitory act against trade with, 1776 B, C,
coercive legislation against, 1774 C, H
Continental Congress, first, 1774 E, J
second, 1775 E
Indians in, reserve for, 1763 K
rising of, 1763 E
trade with, 1763 K
resolution against import of British goods, 1774 M
suppression of British authority in, 1776 C
taxation by Britain, 1764 E, 1765 C, 1766 C, 1767 E, 1769 E, 1770 D
disputed, 1765 K, 1767 E, J, 1768 G, 1772 F
tracts on, 1774 O, 1775 O
vice-admiralty court on, 1764 E
American Declaration of Independence, 1776 G
American Dream, An (N. Mailer), 1965 U
American Federation of Labor, 1886 O
American Independence, the Glory and Interest of Gt. Britain (J. Cartwright), 1774 O
American Individualism (H. Hoover), 1922 O
American Institute of Public Opinion, 1935 O
American Language, The (H. L. Mencken), 1919 Q
American Political Scene, The (D. W. Brogan), 1943 O
American Psycho (B.E. Ellis), 1991 U
American Telephone and Telegraph Co. (AT&T) broken up, 1984 O
American Tragedy, An (T. Dreiser), 1926 U
American Wheelmen, Society of, 1880 X
Amery, Leopold Stennett, B. Conservative politician and author (1873–1955), 1947 O
Amici, Giovanni Battista, It. astronomer and microscopist (1786–1863), 1823 P, 1846 P
Amicis, Edmondo de, It. author (1846–1908), 1884 U

Amiel, Henri Frédéric, Swi. author (1821–81), 1883 U
Amiens, France: Peace Treaty of, 1802 C, W; Germans capture, 1914 H, 1940 E
Amin, Hafizullah, Afghan. leader (1929–79)
  Prime Minister, 1979 C
  President, 1979 J
  death, 1979 M
Amin, Idi, President of Uganda (b. 1925), 1971 A 1975 F
  Ugandan Asians expelled, 1972 H, J, L
  declared president for life, 1976 F
  expansionist claims on Tanzanian territory, 1978 K
Amini, Ali, Persian premier, 1961 E
Amiot, Jean Joseph Marie, F. Jesuit missionary and orientalist (1718–93), 1789 Q
Amir Abdullah, of Transjordan, 1923 E
Amis, Kingsley, B. author (b. 1922), 1954 U
Amis, Martin Louis, B. author (b. 1949), 1990 U
Amman, Jordan, house-to-house fighting after army ordered to disband Palestinian militia, 1970 J
Ammonia, soda made from, 1838 P; synthesis of, 1908 P
Amnesties:
  in Austria, for Nazis, 1937 A
  in Bulgaria, for political prisoners, 1926 A
  in France, for political offenders, 1859 D
  in Germany, for Kapp conspirators, 1925 H
  in Hungary, for rebels, 1856 E
  in India, for political prisoners, 1931 C
  in Ireland, for prisoners after rebellion, 1917 F
  in Lebanon, 1958 M
  in Poland, for rebels, 1856 E
  in the Philippines, for rebels, 1901 G; rejected, 1948 G
Amnesty International, world wide tour of rock concerts in aid of, 1988 W
Amory, Derick Heathcote, Viscount Amory, B. Conservative politician (1899–1981), appointed Chancellor of Exchequer, 1958 A; retires, 1960 G
Amour (P. Verlaine), 1888 U
Ampère, André Marie, F. physicist (1775–1836), 1775 Z, 1820 P, 1826 P, 1836 Z
Amphitryon 38 (J. Giraudoux), 1929 W
Amritsar, India, Golden Temple
  troops storm, 1984 F, R
  militants expelled from, 1986 D
  occupying Sikh rebels surrender, 1988 E
Amritsar, India, Treaty, 1809 D
Amsterdam, Holland: Pichegru welcomed in, 1795A; World Council of Churches founded at, 1948 R; Eigen Haard flats, 1921 S; Rijksmuseum, 1877 S
Amulree, Lord. *See* Mackenzie, William
Amundsen, Roald, Nor. explorer (1872–1928), 1872 Z, 1911 P, 1926 P, 1928 Z
Amur, River, USSR, 1852 N
Amyl, is isolated, 1849 P
Anabase (St-John Perse), 1924 U
Anaemia, pernicious, treatment for, 1926 P
Anaesthetics:
  chloroform, 1847 P
  cocaine, 1884 P
  ether, 1842 P
Analysis of Matter (B. Russell), 1927 R
Analysis of the Human Mind (James Mill), 1829 Q
Analysis, electrochemical, 1922 P
Anarchists:
  in Belgium, 1901 N
  in France, 1893 C, M
  in Italy, 1894 F, G, 1898 J, 1900 G
  in Spain, 1933 A
  in US, 1901 J
Anarchy, State and Utopia (R. Nozick), 1974 R
Anatomie et physiologie du système nerveux (Gall and Spurzheim), 1810 P
Anatomie générale (M. Bichat), 1801 P
Anatomist, The (J. Bridie), 1931 W
Anatomy of Britain, The (A. Sampson), 1962 O
Anatomy of Courage (Lord Moran), 1945 O
Anatomy of the Gravid Uterus (W. Hunter), 1774 P
Ancien Régime et la Révolution, L' (de Tocqueville), 1856 Q
Ancient Economy, The (M.I. Finley), 1973 Q
Ancient Law (H. Maine), 1861 Q
Ancient Monuments Society, 1924 Q
Ancona, Italy: Austrians occupy, 1799 L, 1832 A; Allies take, 1944 G
And Quiet Flows the Don (Sholokhov), 1934 U
And for Today—Nothing (S. Brisley), 1972 S
Andaman Islands, Indian Ocean, Japanese successes in, 1942 C
Andernach, W. Germany, 1797 K
Andersen, Hans Christian, D. author (1805–75), 1805 Z, 1835 U, 1875 Z
Anderson, Adam, B. historian (1692–1765), 1764 Q
Anderson, Elizabeth Garrett, B. Physician (1836–1917), 1836 Z, 1866 O, 1917 Z
Anderson, James, B. economist (1739–1808), 1777 O
Anderson, John Bayard, Am. presidential candidate (b. 1922), 1980 G, L
Anderson, Laurie, Am. artist (b. 1947), 1982 W
Anderson, Lindsay, B. film director (b. 1923), 1968 W, 1973 W
Anderson, Sherwood, Am. author (1876–1941), 1919 U
Anderson, Terry, Am. hostage, 1991 M
Ando, Tadao, Jap. architect (b. 1941), 1976 S, 1983 S
Andover, Maine, US, TV transmitter at, 1962 P
André del Sarto (A. de Musset), 1833 U
André, John, B. soldier (1751–80), 1780 J
Andrássy, Julius, count, Hung. statesman (1823–90), 1876 A, 1878 A F
  Note of religious freedom in Bosnia, etc., 1875 M
Andrade, Edward Neville da Costa, B. scientist (1887–1971), 1923 P
André, Carl, Am. sculptor (b. 1935), 1935 Z, 1966 S, 1972 S, 1981 S
Andrea, John De, Am. sculptor (b. 1941), 1970 S, 1975 S
Andreotti, Giulio, It. political leader (b. 1919), 1919 Z, 1976 G, 1978 A, 1989 E, 1991 D
  'Historic Compromise', 1978 C, 1979 A
Andreu, Paul, F. architect, 1989 S
Andrew, Prince, of Gt. Britain (Andrew Albert Christian Edward, b. 1960), 1960 B
  Duke of York, 1992 C
Andrews, John Hamilton, Austral. architect (b. 1933), 1966 S, 1974 S
Andreyev, Leonid N., R. dramatist (1871–1919), 1916 W
Androcles and the Lion (G. B. Shaw), 1916 U
Andromeda Strain, The (M. Crichton), 1969 U
Andropov, Yuri, R. politician (1914–84), 1973 D, 1982 L, 1983 A, L
  bargains with US on disarmament, 1982 M
  Chairman of Presidium of Supreme Soviet, 1983 F
  arms reduction proposals, 1983 H
  death, 1984 B
Aneurin, J. Am. scientist, 1937 P
Angel in the House (C. Patmore), 1854 U
Angell, Sir Norman, B. economist (1874–1967), 1931 O, 1933 O
Angelou, Maya, Am. author (b. 1928), 1970 U
Angeloz, Eduardo César (b. 1931), Argent. politician, 1989 E
Angels in America (T. Kushner), 1992 W
Angerstein, John Julius, B. philanthropist and art collector (1735–1823), 1824 S
Anglo-Iranian Oil Company (formerly Anglo-Persian), 1909 A, 1914 E, 1932 L; new agreement with Iran, 1949 G; Iran's dispute with, 1951 G, 1952 G, K
Anglo-Irish Inter-governmental Council, establishment of, 1981 L
Anglo-Norman England (M. Chibnall), 1986 Q
Anglo-Saxon Attitudes (A. Wilson), 1956 U
Anglo-Saxon England (F. M. Stenton), 1944 Q
Anglo-Saxons, The (J. Campbell), 1982 Q
Angola (or Portuguese West Africa), 1883 D: boundary with German South-west Africa, 1886 M, 1926 G; German designs on, 1898 H; UN calls on Portugal to cease repression in, 1961 F
  Portuguese forces attack guerrilla HQ, 1970 E
  Portugal grants measure of autonomy, 1970 M
  independence, 1975 L
  MPLA forces gain control of most of Angola, 1976 B
  South African involvement, 1980 G, 1981 H, 1985 D
  illiteracy, 1983 Y
  South African troop withdrawal from Southern, 1984 C
  Cuban troops in, 1984 L
  Cuban withdrawal, 1988 A, 1989 A
  civil war, 1989 F, 1992 L
  ceasefire, 1991 E
  peace agreement, 1991 E
  Bicesse Peace Accord and Namibia Declaration, 1992 L
  multi-party elections, 1992 J
  UN presence, 1992 L
Angora. *See* Ankara
'Angry Young Men', 1957 O
Angry Brigade anarchists, 1971 A, 1972 M
Anguilla
  votes to break ties with Britain, 1969 B
  British emissary forced to leave, 1969 C
  British re-establish control, 1969 C
Animal Farm (G. Orwell), 1945 U
Animal husbandry, 1772 P
Ankara (formerly Angora), Turkey: Turkish National Pact of, 1920 A; Turkish National Assembly at, 1920 E; Treaty of, with France, 1920 K; Greek attack on, repulsed, 1921 H; becomes capital, 1923 K; name is changed from Angora, 1930 C; riots in, 1960 D; Egyptian embassy attacked, 1979 G
Anna Christie (E. O'Neill), 1923 W
Anna Karenina (L. Tolstoy), 1873 U
Annals of the Parish (Galt), 1821 U
Annam, Viet-Nam: French trade with, 1787 N
  French treaty with, 1862 F; French protectorate in, 1874 C, 1883 H, 1884 F, 1885 F, 1887 N
Annan Committee on teaching of Russian, 1962 O
Annapolis, Maryland, US, convention at, 1786 E
Anne, Princess (Anne Elizabeth Alice Louise, HRH The Princess Royal), (b. 1950)
  first marriage, 1973 L
  escapes kidnap attempt, 1974 C
  separation from Captain Mark Phillips, 1989 H
  visits Soviet Union, 1990 E
  divorce granted, 1992 D

Annigoni, Pietro, It. artist (1910–88), 1910 Z, 1955 S; 1988 Z
Annobon Island, Gulf of Guinea, ceded by Portugal to Spain, 1778 N
Annonce faite à Marie, L' (P. Claudel), 1912 W
Annuals, illustrated, the first, 1823 U
Annunzio, Gabriele D', It. author (1863–1938), 1863 Z, 1884 U, 1902 W, 1916 U, 1919 J, 1938 Z
Another Country (J. Mitchell), 1982 W
Another Life (D. Walcott), 1973 U
Anouilh, Jean, F. dramatist (1910–87), 1910 Z, 1938 W, 1947 W, 1950 W, 1951 W, 1956 W, 1961 W, 1987 Z
Anquetil Duperron, Abraham Hyacinthe, F. orientalist (1731–1805), 1771 Q, 1778 Q
Ansbach, principality, Bavaria, W. Germany, 1769 K, 1779 E; Prussia acquires, 1792 A; ceded to France, 1805 M
Anschütz, Richard, G. scientist, 1907 P
'Anstey, F.' *See* Guthrey, Thomas Anstey
Anselmo (Anselmo Francesceni), It. artist (b. 1921), 1968 S
Antara (G. Benjamin), 1987 T
Antarctica: exploration of, 1841 P. *See also* Polar Exploration; Australian claims to, 1933 E; demilitarisation of, 1958 E; 50-year moratorium on mineral exploration agreed, 1991 D
Antheil, George, Am. musician (1900–59), 1927 T
Anthems, National:
  France, Marseillaise, 1792 T
  Russia, substitutes 'Hymn of Soviet Union' for 'Internationale', 1944 O
Anthills of the Savannah (C. Achebe), 1987 U
Anthony Eden (R. Rhodes James), 1986 Q
Anthrax, vaccine for, 1881 p, 1883 P
Anthropogénie (E. Haeckel), 1874 P
Anthropologists, Criminal, congress of, 1887 O
Anthropology:
  Nutcracker Man, 1959 P
  Peking Man, 1920 Q
  Piltdown Man, proved a hoax, 1953 P
  Steinheim skull, 1933 P
Anti-clericalism:
  in Belgium, 1880 F
  in France, 1792 L, 1877 E, 1879 F, 1880 C, 1881 R, 1902 F, 1904 L
  in Mexico, 1926 G
  in Prussia, 1873 E
Anti-Comintern Pact, between Germany and Japan 1936 L; Italy joins, 1937 L; collapse of, 1939 H
Anti-Corn Law League, Manchester, 1838 J; National 1839 C
Anti-Gas School, in Britain, 1936 C
Anti-Goeze (Lessing), 1778 R
Anti-Jesuit law, in Germany, 1904 R
Anti-militarism, in France, 1901 J
Anti-Nazi League, 1977 L
Anti-neutron, discovered, 1956 P
Anti-Semitism:
  in Britain, 1936 K
  in Germany, 1878 O 1933 D, 1935 J 1938 L, 1959 M, 1960 O
  in Hungary, 1932 K
  in Italy, 1938 L
  in Poland, 1939 K, 1946 G
  in Rumania, 1937 M
  in Russia, 1881 R
Anti-Slavery, tract on, 1786 O; movement in US, 1831 O; International Congress, Brussels, 1890 O
Anti-State Church Association, 1844 O
Anti-Trust Laws in US, 1903 B, O; railway mergers adjudged a violation of, 1904 C; other actions under, 1911 A, E, 1912 M
Anti-xi-zeno, discovered, 1963 P
Antibiotics:
  aureomycin, 1948 P
  chloromycetin, 1948 P
  methicillin, 1960 P
  penicillin, 1927 P, 1940 P
Antietam, Maryland, US, battle, 1862 J
Antigone (J. Anouilh), 1942 W
Antigone (V. Alfieri), 1776 W
Antigua and Barbuda, independence within Commonwealth, 1981 L
Antiquary, The (W. Scott), 1816 U
Antiquities of Athens, The (J. Stuart and N. Revett), 1794 Q
Antiquity of Man (C. Lyell), 1863 P
Antiseptic surgery, 1865 P
Antivari, Montenegro, S. Yugoslavia, 1878 C, G
Antoine, André, F. actor-manager (1858–1920),
Anton Reiser (K. Moritz), 1790 U
Antonescu, Ion, sentenced to death, 1946 E; becomes dictator in Rumania, 1950 J
Antonioni, Michaelangelo, It. film director (b. 1912), 1960 W, 1961 W
Antuofermo, Vito, It. boxer (b. 1953), 1980 X
Antwerp, Belgium: French capture, 1832 M; surrenders to Germans, 1914 K; Belgian troops enter, 1918 L; Olympic Games, at 1920 X; Allies recapture, 1944 J; port reopened, 1944 L
Anuradhapura, Sri Lanka, Tamil attack, 1985 E
Any Questions?, radio series, 1948 W
Anzac troops (Australia and New Zealand Army Corps), 1916 E
Anzac, Gallipoli, British withdraw from, 1915 M
Anzio, Italy, Allied landings at, 1944 A; Germans assault allied bridgehead, 1944 B
Apartheid, in S. Africa: Nationalists win election on platform of, 1948 E; programme inaugurated, 1949 F; provokes riots in Johannesburg, 1950 A; bill to make Parliament a high court, to implement, 1952 D; UN considers Cruz Report on, 1955 L; UN calls on S. Africa to reconsider, 1957 A; UN General Assembly condemns, 1959 L, 1961 D; treason trial, 1959 A, 1956 M; Bantu self-government bill in force, 1960 F; world opinion against is intensified by Sharpeville incidents, 1960 C; D. Hammarskjöld visits S. Africa to discuss, 1961 A; UN special committee on, calls for sanctions, 1963 J; Bantu Laws Amendment bill, 1964 E
  South African Council of Churches declares racial separation hostile to Christianity, 1968 R
  MCC tour of South Africa cancelled, 1968 X
  cricket grounds raided by Anti-apartheid campaigners, 1970 A
  'petty apartheid' measures abolished, 1975 D
  Parliamentary committee recommends abolition of laws forbidding inter-racial marriage and sexual intercourse, 1985 D
  Botha re-states S. African commitment to, 1985 H
  pass laws abolished, 1986 D
  international sanctions against South Africa, 1986 F, H, J, K, R
  Dutch Reformed Church declares racism a sin, 1986 R
  Group Areas Act, 1987 J
  Separate Amenities Act, 1987 J, 1989 L
  curbs imposed on anti-apartheid organizations, 1988 B
  law commission calls for abolition of apartheid and introduction of universal franchise, 1989 O
  repeal of legal framework, 1991 B, O
  system ended, 1991 F
Ape and Essence (A. Huxley), 1948 U
Apollinaire, Guillaume (pseud. of Wilhelm Apollinaris de Kostrowitsky), F. formerly Pol. author (1880–1918), 1909 U, 1913 S, 1917 S, W
Apology for the Bible, An (R. Watson), 1796 R
Appeal from the New to the Old Whigs, An (E. Burke), 1791 O
Appeal to the Public on the Subject of the National Debt (R. Price), 1771 O
Appeals, from Canadian Courts to Privy Council, discontinued, 1946 O
Appearance and Reality (F. H. Bradley), 1893 R
Appeasement, policy of, origins, 1937 L
Appel à l'impartiale postérité (Mme Roland), 1793 U
Apple Cart, The, (G. B. Shaw), 1929 W
Apple Computers, 1983 P
Appleton, Sir Edward, B. scientist (1893–1965), 1946 P, 1956 P, 1965 Z
Appleton, William Archibald, B. trade union leader (1859–1940), 1923 O
Appleton, Wisconsin, US, hydro-electric plant, 1882 P
Appomattox, Virginia, US, Lee's surrender at, 1865 D
Après-midi d'un faune, L' (Mallarmé), 1876 U
Après le Cubisme (Ozenfant and Le Corbusier), 1918 S
Aqaba, Gulf of
  closed to Israeli shipping, 1967 E
Aqaba, Israeli attack, 1969 D
Aqueduct tunnel, 1893 P
Aqueduct, iron, at Port Cyllstan, 1805 P
Aquino, Benigno, Philippine politician (1932–83)
  assassination, 1983 H, K, 1984 K
  trial of accused murderers, 1985 A, M
Aquino, Maria Corazon, President of the Philippines (b. 1933), 1985 M, 1986 B
Arab Emirates of Persian Gulf, intention to federate announced, 1968 B
Arab Federation, formed by Iraq and Jordan, 1958 B; Hussein assumes power in, 1958 G; dissolves, 1958 H
Arab League, founded, 1945 K; Security Pact, 1952 H; Algeria admitted to, 1962 H; Sudan joins 1956 A; discusses Syrian allegations of UAR interference, 1962 H
  Arab League Council declares attack on one Arab state would be attack on all, 1967 E
  holy war planned against Israel, 1969 H
  announces PLO's intention to leave West Beirut, 1982 G
  ceasefire in Beirut, 1989 J
Arab Maghreb Union, 1989 B
Arab–Israeli conflict. *See* Middle East
Arabi Pasha, Egypt. nationalist leader, 1881 J; leads anti-foreign riots, 1882 F; is banished, 1882 J
Arabian Desert, exploration of, 1948 P
Arabian Nights, The (Burton), 1885 U
Arabic studies, 1789 Q
Arabs:
  rising in German E. Africa, 1888 J
  rising of slave-holders in Congo, 1892 L
  in Palestine, attack Jews, 1929 H
    Passfield White Paper on, 1930 K
    Higher Committee, 1936 D, 1937 K
    boycott Woodhead Commission, 1938 A
    denounce plans for independent Palestine, 1939 E

warn US over Palestine, 1945 K
Arafat, Yassir, PLO leader (b. 1929), 1969 B
ceasefire with Jordan agreed, 1970 F
Cairo agreement, 1970 J
addresses UN General Assembly, 1974 L
signs acceptance of UN Resolution 242, 1982 G
leaves for Tunisia, 1982 H
talks with Jordan on proposed Palestinian state confederated with Jordan, 1982 K
civilian members of Al fatah oppose, 1983 F
ordered out of Syria, 1983 F
Arafat and supporters evacuated from Lebanon, 1983 M
re-election, 1987 D
Aragon, Louis, F. poet (1897–1982), 1934 U, 1941 U
Aranda, Don Pedro Pablo Abarca y Bolea, count of, S. statesman (1719–98), 1766 F, 1775 G
Aranjuez, Madrid, Spain, Treaty of, 1801 A
Arapahoe Indians, massacre of, 1864 L
Arbitration of disputes, international, 1907 F; agreements for peaceful settlement, signed by Scandinavian states, 1926 A
Arblay, Frances D' (Fanny Burney), B. author (1752–1840), 1778 U, 1782 U, 1796 U
Arborfield, Berkshire, Eng., 1955 H
Arbus, Diane, Am. photographer (1923–71), 1974 S
Arc lamps, for street-lighting, 1841 P
Arcand, Denys, Canad. film director (b. 1941), 1990 W
Arch, Joseph, B. trade unionist and Liberal politician (1826–1919), 1872 O
Archaeologia litteraria (J. A. Ernesti), 1768 Q
Archaeology:
Abu Simbel treasures in Aswan High Dam region rescued, 1960 Q
Akrotiri excavations, Thera, 1967 Q
Ankara, British Institute at, 1948 Q
Athens, British School at, 1886 Q
Aztec great temple foundations discovered, Mexico City, 1978 Q
Babylonian excavations, 1918 Q
Cappadocia, Winckler's expedition to, 1906 Q
Carbon-14 dating system, 1947 P
Carchemish, excavations, 1911 Q
Cnossos, excavations, 1910 Q
Crete, finds in, 1900 Q
cuneiform texts found at Tell Mardikh, Syria, 1975 Q
Emperor Ch'in Shih-huang-ti's tomb, with terracotta army, discovered in China, 1974 Q
Etzina, S. Mongolia, 1915 Q
frozen mammoth found, Soviet Union, 1977 P
Halicarnassus, mausoleum of, 1857 Q
hominid discovery at Hadar, Ethiopia, 1975 Q
hominid footprints discovered, Tanzania, 1978 Q
Japanese research into dating of fossil remains, 1980 P
Jericho, excavations, 1952 Q, 1857 Q
Jerusalem, excavations, 1866 Q
London, Temple of Mithras excavated, 1954 Q
remains of Anne Mowbray identified, 1965 Q
Mildenhall hoard, 1942 Q
Neanderthal skull found, 1856 Q
Nineveh, discoveries at, 1845 Q
Nippur, excavations, 1888 Q
Nonsuch Palace, Surrey, excavated, 1959 Q
Olmec culture studied, 1966 Q
Philip of Macedon's tomb excavated in Greece, 1978 Q
preserved body of man from *c.* 3,300 BC discovered in Italian Alps, 1991 Q
Rome, Institute opened, 1829 Q
Serapeum, discovered, 1850 Q
Stonehenge, Wiltshire, excavations, 1950 Q, 1964 Q
tomb of Han dynasty prince discovered, China, 1972 Q
tree-ring chronology, 1971 Q
Troy, excavations, 1870 Q
Tutankhamun's tomb discovered, 1922 Q
Ur, discoveries at, 1927 Q
Valley of Oaxaca, Mexico, surveyed, 1966 Q
Archaeology of Knowledge (M. Foucault), 1968 R
Archangel, Russia, British forces in, 1919 F, J
Archers, The, radio serial, 1951 W
Architecture
Prince of Wales's attack on modern, 1984 S
'Deconstructivist Architecture' exhibition, Museum of Modern Art, New York, 1988 S
Archives, British National, 1838 O, 1958 O
Arcole, Veneto, Italy, 1796 L
Arcon, Idaho, US, atomic power station at, 1951 P
Arctic exploration, 1819 P, 1845 P, 1850 P; for air route, 1930 P. *See also* Polar exploration
Ardahan, N.E. Asiatic Turkey, transferred to Russia, 1878 C, G
Arden, John, B. dramatist (b. 1930), 1963 W
Ardennes, Europe, mountain range, 'Battle of the Bulge' in, 1944 M
Ardinghello (J. Heinse), 1787 U
Ardizzone, Edward, B. artist (1900–1979), 1940 S
Ardrey, Robert, Am. dramatist (1908–1980), 1940 W
Arezzo, Italy, Germans withdraw from, 1944 G
Argelander, Friedrich Wilhelm August, G. astronomer (1799–1875), 1862 P
Argentina: United Provinces of La Plata, independence of, 1816 G; Buenos Aires reunited with, 1860 F; frozen meat from, 1877 P
military coup deposes president, 1976 C
diplomatic relations with Britain re-established, 1979 G
Galtieri becomes President, 1981 M
invades Falkland Islands, 1982 D
withdrawal from Falklands demanded by UN, 1982 D
EC economic sanctions imposed on, 1982 D
US economic sanctions imposed on, 1982 D
EC economic sanctions, renewal of, 1982 E
armed forces resign from military junta, 1982 F
recognizes de facto cessation of hostilities with Britain, 1982 G
armed forces rejoin military junta, 1982 J
Falklands War. *See* Wars
British assets released, 1983 H
proposed amnesty for military personnel involved in human rights violations, 1983 H
military rule ended, 1983 M
Radical Party gains absolute majority, 1983 K
illiteracy, 1983 Y
cotton production, 1984 Y
trial of former military leaders, 1985 D
former members of military junta found guilty of human rights violations, 1985 M
rebellion by army officers, 1987 D
presidential elections, 1989 E
Argon, discovered, 1894 P
Argov, Shlomo, Israeli diplomat (b. 1929), Ambassador to Britain
wounded in London, 1982 F
Argument about Co-education, The (Pestalozzi), 1922 O
Ariadne auf Naxos (H. Gerstenberg), 1767 U
Ariadne auf Naxos (R. Strauss), 1912 T
Arias, Dame Margot Fonteyn de (Margot Fonteyn), B. prima ballerina (1919–91), 1919 Z, 1991 Z
Arias Navarro, Carlos, Sp. Premier (1908–89), 1973 M
Arias Plan, 1987 H
Arica-Tacna, S. America, dispute between Chile and Peru over, 1883 K; settled, 1929 F
Ariel (S. Plath), 1966 U
Arif, Abdul Salam Muhammad, President of Iraq (1921–66), 1966 D
Aristide, Jean-Bertrand, President of Haiti (b. 1953), 1990 M, 1991 J
Arizona, State, US: US obtains, 1848 E; Gadsden Purchase, 1854 D; as a US territory, 1863 B; conditions for statehood, 1911 H; becomes a US state, 1912 B; adopts women's suffrage, 1912 L
Ark Sakura, The (K. Abe), 1988 U
Arkansas, State, US: becomes a US state, 1836 F; disturbances in, 1874 E
Arkle, B. racehorse, 1966 X
Arkwright, Sir Richard, B. engineer (1732–92), 1769 P, 1792 Z
Armagh, Northern Ireland, violence between Catholic and Protestant demonstrators, 1968 L
Armaments
Russia proposes reduction in, 1898 H
failure to stop arms race, 1907 F
production in Britain, 1939 Y, 1940 Y, 1941 Y, 1942 Y, 1943 Y, 1944 Y
standardisation of, British–US agreement on, 1940 L
Ruhr dams bombed with spinning bombs, 1943 E
Strategic Arms Limitation Talks (SALT), 1969 L, 1972 K, 1979 F, 1983 C
biological weapons, 1971 H, 1989 A
Strategic Defense Initiative (SDI; Star Wars programme), 1983 C, 1985 B, M, 1986 K, 1987 B
MX missile, 1983 E
chemical weapons, 1984 C, 1989 A
AWACS planes, 1986 O
GEC Nimrod early-warning programme scrapped by Britain, 1986 O
traffic in, embargoes on:
Britain to Ireland, 1913 M
UN votes for embargo to S. Africa, 1963 M
US to China, 1922 C
US to Mexico, 1912 C
traffic in, regulation of, 1889 F, 1925 E, 1949 M
traffic in, supplied by, Britain to India, 1962 L; to Tunisia, 1957 L
Russia to Cuba, 1962 J
to Egypt, 1955 H
US to Indonesia, 1959 B
France bans sale of military supplies to Israel, 1969 A
Britain to S. Africa, 1970 G
US halts sale of F-16 fighters to Israel, 1983 C
'supergun' parts destined for Iraq detained in Britain, 1990 D
release of French hostages after arms deal with Libya, 1990 D
See also Arms, Small
Arman, (Armand Fernandez), F. sculptor (b. 1928), 1985 S
Armed Neutrality of the North, 1800 M, 1801 F
Armenia: parts of ceded to Russia, 1827 B; massacres in, 1895 K, L, 1896 H; revolution in, 1896 H; independence declared, 1919 E
Nagorno-Karabakh votes for transfer to, 1988 B
nationalist demonstrations, 1988 B, F
Soviet troops enter, 1988 F

Azerbaijan declares war, 1990 A
independence, 1991 J
dispute over Nagorno-Karabakh, 1992 J
Armentières, France, Germans take, 1918 D
Armies, Private:
Irish Republican Army (I.R.A.), 1933 G
National Guard, Eire, 1933 G
Nazi Storm Troopers, Germany, 1932 F, 1933 C
Armies:
comparative casualties in, World War I, 1918 Y
World War II, 1945 Y
comparative strengths of, 1875 Y, 1906 Y, 1912 Y, 1914 Y, 1950 Y, 1968 Y
Australian, volunteers in S. Africa, 1899 M
conscription for, 1909 N
ANZACS, 1916 E
Austrian, Landwehr created, 1808 F
unified regimental system, 1903 J, 1904 C
mobilisation, 1914 G
Belgium, universal military service for, 1913 C
British, C.-in-C. of, subordinated to Secretary of State for War, 1870 F
Cardwell's reforms, 1871 H
purchase of commissions in, abolished, 1871 O
flogging in, abolished, 1881 O
expeditionary force lands in France, 1914 H
increased spending on, 1936 C
changes in higher command, 1937 M
expeditionary force lands in France, 1939 J
in Germany, reduced, 1957 B
W. Germany to contribute to cost of BAOR, 1962 C
Bulgarian, intervenes in politics, 1886 H
mobilisation of, 1912 K
Canadian, volunteers in S. Africa, 1899 M
lands in Europe, 1914 K
losses in Dieppe Raid, 1942 H
in offensive towards Rhine, 1945 B
Egyptian, intervenes in politics, 1879 B, 1881 B, 1954 C
European, Churchill proposes formation of, 1950 H
French, conscription for, 1793 H, 1798 J, 1872 G, 1913 H
equipped with Chassepot rifles, 1866 P
Lebel rifles, 1886 P
chaplains in, abolished, 1880 R
mobilises, 1914 H
mutinies, in, 1917 E
German, evacuates France, 1872 J
Bismarck advocates enlargement of, 1887 A
size of, increased, 1893 G, 1911 B, 1913 F
length of service in, reduced, 1893 G
Von Moltke as C.-in-C. of, 1906 A
mobilised for Czech crisis, 1938 H
See also Prussian Army
East German, National People's Army formed, 1956 A
West German, command of, given to NATO, 1958 A
Russian protests at proposals to equip with Polaris missiles, 1960 G
Greek, mobilised, 1915 J
intervenes in politics, 1923 M
Hungarian, rearmament of, 1938 H
Indian, sent to Malta, 1878 C
Italian, fights in Spanish Civil War, 1937 B, C
reduction in, 1947 B
Japanese, National Defence Force formed, 1953 J
NATO, plans for W. German troops to serve in, 1951 J
New Zealand, service in France, 1916 E
Palestinian, founded by Gen. Kassem, 1960 C
Prussian, reformed by Scharnhorst, 1807 N
Napoleon I limits size of, 1808 J
Landwehr and Landsturm formed, 1813 C
needle-guns for, 1858 O
Von Roon's reforms, 1859 M
See also German Army
Roumanian, brutality of, 1907 C
Russian, conscription for, 1874 A
mobilisation of, 1914 G
White Russian, collapse of, 1920 C
Serbian, mobilisation of, 1912 K
Spanish, intervention of, in politics, 1936 G
Turkish, intervention of, in politics, 1909 D
US, outcry against meat supplied to, 1898 O
troops land in France, 1917 F
first engagement with Germans, 1917 L
occupy Rhine, 1923 E
selective training and service for, 1940 J
Armitage, Kenneth, B. sculptor (b. 1916), 1951 S, 1954 S
Armour plating, of battleships, 1853 P
Armoured vehicles, 1916 P
Arms and the Man (G. B. Shaw), 1894 W, 1898 W
Arms, Small:
Browning revolver, 1900 P
Chassepot rifle, 1866 P
Colt's armoury for, 1853 P
Gatling, machine-gun, 1862 P
Lebel rifle, 1886 P
Maxim, 1884 P
Minié rifle, 1849 P
needle-guns, 1858 O
steel gun, Krupp's, 1849 P
Thompson sub-machine gun, 1920 P
Armstrong, David Malet, Austral. philosopher (b. 1926), 1989 R
Armstrong, Gillian, Austral. film director (b. 1950), 1980 W
Armstrong, Neil, Am. astronaut (b. 1930), 1969 G
Armstrong, Thomas, B. novelist (1899–1978), 1947 U
Armstrong, Sir William George, B. engineer (1810–1900), 1845 P
Armstrong-Jones, Antony earl of Snowdon (b. 1930), 1960 E, 1965 S
Armstrong-Jones, Sir Robert, B. alienist (1857–1943), 1893 P
Arndt, Ernst Moritz, G. author (1769–1860), 1806 O, 1813 U
Arne, Thomas, B. musician (1711–78), 1778 Z
Arnhem, Holland, British airborne forces land, 1944 J; Allies enter, 1945 D
Arnim, Harry Karl Kurt Eduard, Count, G. diplomat (1824–81), 1874 K
Arnim, Sixt von, G. general, 1943 B, D
Arnold, Benedict, Am. soldier (1741–1804), 1775 M, 1776 K; treason of, 1780 L
Arnold, Malcolm, B. musician (b. 1921), 1953 T, 1956 T, 1957 T, 1968 T, 1973 T, 1976 T, 1991 T
Arnold, Mary Augusta. *See* Ward, Mrs. Humphrey
Arnold, Matthew, B. author (1822–88), 1822 Z, 1849 U, 1852 U, 1853 U, 1865 U, 1869 O, 1888 Z
Arnold, Thomas, B. educationalist and historian (1795–1842), 1795 Z, 1828 O, 1832 R, 1838 Q, 1842 Z
Arnstein, M., 1968 P
Arof, Abdul Salan, Iraqi premier, 1963 B
Around the World in Eighty Days (J. Verne), 1872 U
Arp, Jean, F. artist (1877–1966), 1916 S
Arras, France: German withdrawal from, 1917 B; battle, 1917 D, E; Germans take, 1940 E
Arrow incident, 1856 K
Art Collections Fund, National, 1903 S
Art Criticism, 1775 S
Art Market
Velázquez's *Juan de Pareja* sold at record auction price for art work, 1979 S
Van Gogh's *Irises* sold for £30 million, 1987 S
world record paid for work by living artist, 1988 S
Art Now (H. Read), 1933 S
Art et Scolastique (J. Maritain), 1920 R
Art history, treatise on, 1855 S
Art of Writing, The (A. Quiller-Couch), 1916 U
Art: figurative painting revived, 1980 S; treatises on, 1813 S, 1865 S; works of, export from Britain controlled, 1952 S; France undertakes to restore looted, 1815 L
Arte Povera, 1966 S
Artemus Ward, His Book (C. F. Browne), 1862 U
Arthur Gordon Pym (E. A. Poe), 1838 U
Arthur Holly Gamma Ray Observatory, 1991 P
Arthur, Chester Alan, Am. politician, 21st president of US (1830–86), Republican, 1881 G
Articles of Religion, subscription to, 1771 R
Artificial rain, 1957 P
Artificial silk, 1887 P
Artist of the Floating World, An (K. Ishiguro), 1987 U
Artists, British War, 1916 S, 1940 S
'Art Nouveau', 1893 S; influences fabrics and designs, 1963 S
Artois, Comte d'. *See* Charles X
Arts Council, 1946 T
Arts and crafts movement in US, 1907 S
Arts, US National Federation of, 1910 S
Arts, in Britain, financial support for, 1958 S, 1965 O
Arup, Ove Nyquist, B. architect (1895–1988), 1895 Z, 1933 S, 1988 Z
As I Lay Dying (W. Faulkner), 1930 U
As Night (B. Flanagan), 1978 S
Asaf, George, B. librettist, 1915 W
Ascension Island, 1815 K
Ascent of F6 (Auden and Isherwood), 1937 U
Ascot, Berks., Eng., horseracing at, 1807 W; grandstand for, 1964 S
Ash Wednesday (T. S. Eliot), 1930 U
Ashanti, W. Africa: British protectorate in, 1896 H; war, 1824 B; kingdom is annexed to Gold Coast, 1901 J
Ashbourne, Lord. *See* Gibson, E.
Ashburton, Lord. *See* Baring, Alexander
Ashe, Arthur Robert, Am. tennis player (1943–93), 1943 Z, 1975 X
Ashendene Press, 1894 S
Ashley, Laura, B. designer and entrepreneur (1925–85), 1925 Z, 1985 Z
opening of first Laura Ashley shop, 1967 W
Ashley, Robert Reynolds, Am. musician (b. 1930), 1984 T
Ashton, Frederick William Mallandine, B. choreographer (1904–88), 1937 T, 1946 T, 1956 T, 1958 T, 1961 T
Asia Legal Consultative Committee, 1957 D
Asiatic Society, Royal, 1822 Q
Asimov, Isaac, Am. author (1920–92), 1920 Z, 1951 U, 1983 U, 1992 Z
Aspdin, Joseph, B. inventor of cement (1779–1855), 1824 P
Aspern, Austria, battle, 1809 E
Aspirin, 1899 P

Aspromonte, Calabria, S. Italy, Garibaldi captured at, 1862 H
Asquith (R. Jenkins), 1964 Q
Asquith, Anthony, B. film director (1902–68), 1938 W, 1949 W
Asquith, Herbert Henry, earl of Oxford and Asquith, B. statesman (1852–1928), 1852 Z, 1880 E, 1911 G, 1925 A, 1928 Z; as home secretary, 1892 H; as chancellor of Exchequer, 1905 M; becomes premier, 1908 D; denounces House of Lords, 1909 M; appeals to electorate, 1910 A, M; opens Imperial Conference, 1911 E; introduces minimum wage bill, 1912 L; combines war secretaryship with premiership, 1914 C; forms coalition, 1915 E; resigns premiership of coalition, 1916 M
Asquith, Margot, Countess of Oxford and Asquith (*née* Tennant), B. Liberal politician, 1864 Z, 1945 Z
Assab Bay, Eritrea, 1882 M
Assad, Hafez al, President of Syria (b. 1928), 1979 L, 1985 M, 1987 L
Assam, Eastern, rebellion, 1966 C
Assam, India, elections, 1983 A, B
Assassinations:
Abbas I of Egypt, 1854 G
Abdullah of Jordan, 1951 G
Abu Jihad, 1988 D
Ahmen Pasha of Egypt, 1945 B
Alexander of Yugoslavia, 1934 K
Tsar Alexander III of Russia, 1881 C
Ali Khan, 1951 K
Benigno Aquino, 1983 H, K, 1984 K
S. Bandaranaike, premier of Ceylon, 1959 J
Count Bernadotte, 1948 J
Duc de Berry, 1820 B
Bogoliepoff, 1901 B
Mohammed Boudiaf, 1992 F
British ambassador to Holland, 1979 C
Siegfried Buback, chief prosecutor of W. Germany, 1977 D
A. Calinescu, of Roumania, 1931 J
G. Calmette, 1914 B
Carlow I of Portugal, 1908 B
President Carranza, 1920 E
Carrero Blanco, Spanish premier, 1973 M
Charles III of Parma, 1854 C
Colombian presidential candidate, 1989 H
Constantinople, Patriarch of, 1821 D
Admiral Darlan, 1942 M
President Diem of South Vietnam, 1963 L
E. Dollfuss , 1934 G
President Paul Doumer, 1932 E
I. Duca, 1933 M
Kurt Eisner of Bavaria, 1919 B
Empress Elizabeth of Austria, 1898 J
M. Erzberger, 1921 H
Christopher Ewart-Biggs, British ambassador in Dublin, 1976 G
King Faisal of Saudi Arabia, 1975 C
King Feisal of Iraq, 1948 G
Francis Ferdinand of Austria, 1914 F
French ambassador to Lebanon, 1981 J
Galilee high commissioner, 1937 J
Gandhi, 1948 A
Rajiv Gandhi, Indian Prime Minister, 1991 E
President Garfield of US, 1881 G
George I of Greece, 1913 C
Premier Ghali of Egypt, 1910 B
H. Gurney, high commissioner in Malaya, 1951 K
Gustavus III of Sweden, 1792 C
Premier Hamaguchi of Japan, 1930 L
Premier Hara of Japan, 1921 L
Hazza-el-Majali, premier of Jordan, 1960 H
Heydrich, by Czech patriots, 1942 E
Humbert I of Italy, 1900 G
Premier Inukai of Japan, 1932 E
Prince Ito of Japan, 1909 K
Jean Jaurès, 1914 G
Kamal Jumblatt, Lebanese Moslem leader, 1977 C
Premier Kassim of Iraq, 1963 B
President Kennedy of US, 1963 L, 1978 M
R. Kennedy, 1968 F
Malcolm Kerr, President of American University in Beirut, 1984 A
Sheikh Hassan Khaled, 1989 E
Martin Luther King, 1968 D
J. B. Kléber, 1800 C
Korea, Queen of, 1895 K
Kotzebue, 1819 L
Abraham Lincoln, 1865 D
Archbishop Janani Luwum of Uganda, 1977 B
Malcolm X, 1965 B
Marat, 1793 G
G. Matteotti, 1924 F
Earl of Mayo, 1872 B
President McKinley, 1901 J
René Muawad, 1989 L
Nasr-ed-Din, Shah of Persia, 1896 E
Nazim Pasha of Turkey, 1913 A
Nokrashy Pasha of Egypt, 1948 M
Premier Nuri-es-Said of Iraq, 1958 G
K. O'Higgins, 1927 G
President Obrégon of Mexico, 1928 G
President Paes of Portugal, 1918 M
Olof Palme, Swedish Prime Minister, 1986 B
Park Chung-Hee, S. Korean president, 1979 K
Paul I, Tsar of Russia, 1801 C
Phoenix Park Murders, 1882 E
V. Plehve, 1904 G
Father Jerzy Popieluszko, 1985 B
President of S. Yemen, 1978 F
Marshal Prim, 1870 M
Rashid Karami, 1987 F
Walter Rathenau, 1922 F
Rossi, Papal premier, 1848 L
President Sadat of Egypt, 1981 K, 1982 D
President Sadi Carnot of France, 1894 F
Sir Richard Sharples, Bermudan Governor, 1973 B
Sipyengin, Russian minister of interior, 1902 D
Sir Lee Stack, 1924 L
A. Stambolisky , 1923 F
Stambulov, Bulgarian premier, 1895 G
P. Stolypin , Russian premier, 1911 J
Count Stürgkh, 1916 K
Wasfi Tell, Jordanian Prime Minister, 1971 L
Count Tisza, 1918 K
H.F. Verwoerd, 1966 J
V. Vorovski, 1923 E
Richard Welch, CIA agent in Athens, 1975 M
Zia ul-Haq, Pakistani President, 1988 H
Assassinations, attempted:
A. Briand, 1911 A
R. Dutschke, 1968 D
Gerald Ford, Am. President, 1975 J
Rajiv Gandhi, Indian Prime Minister, 1986 K
General de Gaulle, 1962 H
King Hassan of Morocco, 1972 H
A. Hitler, 1944 G
Inönü, Turkish premier, 1964 B
John Paul II, 1981 E
Louis Philippe, 1835 G
Makarios III, President of Cyprus, 1970 C
Mao Tse-tung, Chinese leader, 1972 H
B. Mussolini, 1926 D
Napoleon I, 1800 M, 1804 B
Napoleon III, 1858 A
K. Nkrumah, 1962 H
Park, South Korean President, 1968 A
Pinochet, 1986 J
Ronald Reagan, Am. President, 1981 C
President Sukarno of Indonesia, 1957 M
H.Verwoerd, 1960 D
GeorgeWallace, 1972 E
William I of Germany, 1878 E
Assault, The (H. Mulisch), 1982 U
Assaye, N. W. Hyderabad, India, battle, 1803 J
Assedio di Firenze, L', (Guerrazzi), 1834 U
Assembly techniques in factories, 1913 P
Association of South-East Asian States (ASEAN), 1967 O
Associations, in France, regulation of, 1901 G
Assommoir, L' (E. Zola), 1877 U
Assyriology, 1864 Q
Astaire, Fred, Am. actor and dancer (1899–1987), 1899 Z, 1935 W, 1987 Z
Aston, Francis William, B. physicist (1877–1945), 1919 P
Astonishing History of Troy Town, The (A. Quiller-Couch), 1888 U
Astor, Gavin, 2nd Baron Astor of Hever, B. newspaper proprietor (1918–84), 1966 V
Astor, Nancy Viscountess (1880–1964), B. Conservative politician, 1919 L
Astronautical Federation, International, 1951 O
Astronauts, *See under* Space flights
Astronomy, advances in, 1783 P, 1786 P, 1788 P, 1789 P, 1797 P, 1862 P, 1881 P, 1882 P, 1889 P, 1892 P, 1914 P, 1920 P, 1937 P, 1961 P; Jeans' stellar theory, 1926 P; new scale of space, 1953 P; composite photograph of night sky, 1954 P
Cygnus constellation, X-ray emissions discovered,1966 P
neutrino detected, 1967 P
pulsar discovered, 1967 P
13th moon of Jupiter discovered, 1974 P
14th moon of Jupiter discovered, 1975 P
radio galaxy estimated to span 18 million light years, 1975 P
Harvard College Laboratory research, 1976 P
rings around Uranus discovered, 1977 P
black hole, 1979 P
atmosphere on Pluto discovered, 1980 P
R136a discovered, 1981 P
researchers discover rings around Neptune, 1982 P
Infrared Astronomical Satellite, 1983 P
Venera XV and XVI probes enter orbit around Venus,1983 P
additional rings of Saturn discovered, 1984 P
partial ring around Neptune photographed, 1984 P
planet system around Beta Pictoris photographed, 1984 P
infrared galaxies discovered, 1985 P
rings around Neptune discovered, 1985 P
Halley's Comet photographed by space probes,1986 P
satellites of Uranus discovered, 1986 P
radio waves from 3C326 observed, 1987 P
supernova observed, 1987 P
Universe estimated to be younger than 10 billion years, 1987 P
galaxy located 12 billion light years from Earth, 1988 P
Cosmic Background Explorer (COBE), 1989 P, 1992 P
dark spot discovered on Neptune, 1989 P
surface of Venus mapped, 1989 P
18th moon of Saturn discovered, 1990 P
Hubble Space Telescope, 1990 P

Magellan probe, 1989 1990 P, P
Röntgensatellite, 1990 P
Arthur Holly Gamma Ray Observatory, 1991 P
asteroid photographed, 1991 P
discovery of most distant object yet seen, 1991 P
possible discovery of planet orbiting PSR 1829–10, 1991 P
Ulysses probe, 1992 P
Astrophysics, treatise on, 1903 P; Eddington's discovery on luminosity of stars, 1924 P
Aswan Dam, Egypt, 1902 M; High Dam, projected, 1956 G; Russian loan for, 1958 K; work begins, 1960 A; rescue of archaeological treasures near, 1960 Q; opened, 1964 E
Asylums, Mental, in Britain, inspection, 1842 O; treatment in, 1893 P; detention of patients in, reformed, 1959 O
At Sundown (J. G. Whittier), 1890 U
Atala (Chateaubriand), 1801 U
Atalanta in Calydon (A. C. Swinburne), 1865 U
Atatürk, Kemal. *See* Kemal Atatürk
Atbara, River, Sudan, Kitchener's victory at, 1898 D
Atheism, advocated, 1793 R
Athenia, sinking of, 1939 J
Athens, Greece: antiquities of, 1794 Q; Elgin Marbles brought from, 1801 S; Turks enter, 1827 F; garrison revolts, 1862 K; British School of Archaeology at, 1886 Q; Allies occupy, 1916 K; Conferences of Balkan Powers in, 1930 K; 1937 B; E.A.M. demonstrations in, 1944 M; riots over Cyprus issue, 1954 M
military coup, 1967 D
Arab terrorist attack at airport, 1973 H
European Championships, 1982 X
Athletics: track events timed electrically, 1912 X; pole-jump record, 1942 X; mile record, 1954 X
indoor world records, 1979 X
British world records, 1981 X
World Athletics Championships, Helsinki, 1983 X
Atholl, John Murray, duke of (1720–74), B. owner of Isle of Man, 1765 J
Atlanta, Georgia, US: Confederate defeat at, 1864 G; Sherman occupies, 1864 J
Atlantic Charter, 1941 H, J
Atlantic Charter, new, 1973 D
Atlantic City, Mexico, 1916 L
Atlantic Economic Community, 1960 M
Atlantic Ocean: first steamship crossing, 1818 P; regular steamship crossings, 1838 P; notable crossings, 1839 P, 1935 P; first flight across, 1919 P; notable flights across, 1928 P, 1941 P; crossing in small craft, 1965 X
Atlantic cable, 1865 P
Atlantis (C. J. R. Hautmann), 1912 U
Atlantis space shuttle, 1985 P
Atlas Elipticales With Winter Music (J. Cage), 1964 T
Atlas computer, 1961 P
Atlas of Ancient Egypt (J. Baines and J. Málek), 1980 Q
Atlas of Anglo-Saxon Britain, An D. Hill), 1981 Q
Atmolysis, gases separated by, 1863 P
Atmosphere, discovery of gases in, 1903 P; Heaviside layer in, 1902 P, 1924 P; Upper, radiation in, 1925 P; temperature of, 1923 P; A. Shepard's flight through, 1961 P; British Antarctic Survey detects hole in ozone layer, 1985 P
Atomic Bomb Test Ban. *See* Nuclear Test Ban
Atomic Bomb:
manufacture of plutonium for, 1944 P
dropped on Japan, 1945 H, P
Russia, first tests, 1949 P, 1950 C
British, first tests, 1952 B, P
thermonuclear, 1957 E
China, explodes first, 1964 K
Atomic Energy Authority, British, 1954 O; International, 1957 O, G
Atomic Energy Commission, UN, 1946 M
meetings of, suspended, 1949 G
US, ordered to develop hydrogen bomb, 1950
separates plutonium, 1950 P
Atomic Energy for Defence, Canada's agreement with US, 1959 E; treatise on military consequences, 1948 O
Atomic Energy, 1945 P
Britain's agreement with Euratom on peaceful uses, of, 1959 B
with W. Germany, 1956 G
with US on co-operation and exchange of information, 1955 F, 1956 F, 1957 F
Geneva Conference on peaceful uses of, 1955 H
Netherlands agreement with Norway for joint research, 1951 P
Proposals for international control of, 1953 M
US aid to non-Communist states to develop, 1955 F
Atomic Physics, 1934 P, 1939 P, 1940 P, 1941 P, 1948 P, 1959 P
atom size, 1883 P
atom structure, 1913 P
transmutation of atoms, 1919 P
Bohrs' theory of electron circulation, 1921 P
'Smasher', 1931 P
cyclotron, 1931 P
atom split, 1942 P
C-12 isotope of carbon adopted as international standard of atomic atoms, 1966 P
electroweak unification theory, 1967 P, 1973 P
neutrino detected, 1967 P
Fermi National Accelerator Laboratory (Fermilab), 1969 P
gluon, 1972 P
quantum chromodynamics (QCD), 1972 P
quark, 1972 P
nuclear magnetic resonance (NMR), 1973 P 1977 P
Grand Unified Theory, 1974 P
J/psi particle, 1974 P
'U' sub-atomic particles, 1975 P
discovery of tau lepton, 1975 P
Stanford accelerator, 1975 P
upsilon particle, 1977 P
neutron's life measured, 1978 P
Deutsches Elektron Synchroton (DESY), 1979 P
Electron spin resonance spectroscopy, 1980 P
Joint European Torus (JET), 1983 P, 1991 P
'W' and 'Z' sub-atomic particles observed, 1983 P
CERN, 1983 P
nuclear fusion, 1983 P
weak nuclear force, 1983 P
LEP (Large Electron Positron Collider), 1989 P
nuclear fusion at room temperature announced, 1989 P
atomic fusion, 1991 P
Atomic Power Stations: electricity first produced from, 1951 P; in Britain, 1957 S, 1965 P; in US, 1955 P
Atomic Reactors: at Harwell, 1956 P; numbers in operation, 1962 P
Atomic Scientists, betrayal of secrets by, 1950 C, 1952 O, 1953 F
Atomic Theory of Chemistry, 1830 P; studies in 1777 P
Atomic Transmutations, 1931 P
Atomic Weapons:
Britain's agreement with US for co-operation, 1958 G
for purchasing components, 1959 E
W. German physicists refuse to test, 1957 D
Swiss referendum against manufacture of, 1962 D
US Congress rejects Russian proposal for, 1951 H
See also Nuclear Test Ban
Atomic Weights: table of, 1803 P; theories about, 1815 P; settled by Karlsruhe Conference, 1860 P
Atomic-powered locomotive designed, 1954 P; passenger-cargo ship, 1959 P; submarine, 1952 P, 1959 P
Atonement, doctrine of, minister deposed for teaching against, 1831 R
Atrocities:
in Belgian Congo, 1903 E, 1905 L
in Brazil, 1912 O
by Germany, Bryce Report on, 1916 O
in US, murder of civil rights worker, 1965 C
in Poland, at Auschwitz Prison, 1965 H
Attack on Inflation, The, White Paper, 1975 G
Attempt to Determine the Limits of the Frontier of the State (K. W. von Humbold), 1791 O
Attempts to Explain some of the Phenomena of Electricity (H. Cavendish), 1772 P
Attenborough, Sir David, B. zoologist, television producer and director (b. 1926), 1979 W, 1991 W
Attenborough, Sir Richard Samuel, B. film director (b. 1923), 1923 Z, 1969 W, 1982 W
Attlee, Clement Richard, Earl Attlee, B. statesman and Labour Party leader (1883–1967), 1883 Z, 1936 F, 1967 Z; visits Spain, 1937 M; becomes Lord Privy Seal in Churchill's Coalition, 1940 E; becomes Deputy Premier, 1942 B; at Potsdam Conference, 1945 G; forms Labour ministry, 1945 G; reconstructs ministry, 1950 B; visits Washington, 1950 M; retires from Labour Party leadership, 1955 M
Attu, Aleutian Islands, US force lands, 1943 E
Attwood, George, B. mathematician, 1784 P
Atwood, Margaret, Canad. author (b. 1939), 1987 U
Auber, Daniel François Esprit, F. musician (1782–1871), 1782 Z, 1830 T, 1941 T
Auchinleck, Sir Claude, B. general (1884-1981), succeeds Wavell, 1941 G
replaced by Alexander, 1942 H
Auckland, Lord. *See* Eden, William
Auckland, N. Zeal., 1865 N; *Rainbow Warrior* sunk by French agents, 1985 G, H, J, L, 1986 G
Auden, Wystan Hugh, B. poet (1907–73), 1907 Z, 1930 U, 1932 U, 1935 U, 1936 U, 1937 U, 1951 T, 1973 Z
Audubon, John James, Am. naturalist (1780–1851), 1830 P
Audubon: A Vision (R.P. Warren), 1969 U
Auerbach, Frank, B. painter (b. 1931), 1986 S
Augier, Guillaume Victor, F. dramatist (1820–89), 1854 W
August 1914 (A. Solzhenitsyn), 1971 U
August, Bille, Dan. film director (b. 1948), 1987 W, 1992 W
Auguste Comte and Positivism (J. S. Mill), 1865 R
Augustine of Hippo (P. Brown), 1967 Q
Augustus III of Poland (1696–1763), elector of Saxony, 1763 K
Aulenti, Gaetana, It. architect (b. 1927), 1986 S
Aureomycin, 1948 P

Auric, Georges, F. musician (1899–1983), 1899 Z, 1920 T, 1983 Z
Auriga, star in Milky Way, 1892 P
Auriol, Vincent, F. statesman (1884–1965), elected F. president, 1947 A
Aurora Leigh (R. Browning), 1857 U
Auschwitz (or Oswiecim), Poland, Prison Camp, trial of officials, 1965 H
Mengele exhumed in Brazil, 1985 F
Ausklang (H. Lachenmann), 1986 T
Austen, Jane, B. novelist (1775–1817), 1775 Z, 1811 U, 1813 U, 1814 U, 1816 U, 1818 U, 1817 Z
Austerlitz, Czechoslovakia, battle, 1805 M
Austin, Herbert, Lord Austin, B. motor manufacturer (1866–1941), founds motor company, 1905 P
'Austin Seven' motor car, 1922 P
Austin, John Langshaw, B. philosopher (1911–60), 1962 R
Australia: representative government in, 1850 H; gold discovered, 1851 P; meat trade to London, 1879 P; federal confederation assembly, 1880 N; federal convention, 1897 A; federation, plans for, 1899 N; as a federal Commonwealth, 1900 J, 1901 A. *See also* Botany Bay
Queen Elizabeth's visit for Cook bi-centenary celebrations, 1970 C
Queen of Australia, Queen Elizabeth assents to change title to, 1973 O
general election, 1975 M, 1983 C
cotton production, 1984 Y
urbanization, 1985 X
legal ties with Britain severed, 1986 C
divorce statistics, 1987 Y
bicentenary of arrival of European settlers celebrated, 1988 A
life expectancy, 1990 Y
illegitimacy rates, 1991 Y
Australia, South, act for establishing colony, 1834 H
Australia, Western, 1870 H; votes to secede from Commonwealth, 1933 D
Austria:
union with Germany proclaimed, 1918 L
becomes part of Reich, 1938 C
Russians enter, 1945 C
Democratic Republic established, 1945 E
Allied occupation, 1945 F
Indent:protests at, 1953 K
frontiers of 1937 recognised, 1946 A
People's Party forms government, 1966 D
Arab kidnappers demand closure of transit camp for Soviet Jews, 1973 J
coalition government formed, 1983 D
Austrian Netherlands: Barrier towns, 1782 D; independence declared, 1789 M. *See also* Belgium
Authority and the Individual (B. Russell), 1949 O
Auto Avio Construzione, 1939 X
Auto-chrome plates, 1907 P
Autobahn, Cologne–Bonn, 1932 P. *See also* Motorways
Autobiography of Alice B. Toklas, The (G. Stein), 1933 U
Autobiography of a Super Tramp (W. H. Davies), 1908 U
Autocrat of the Breakfast-Table, The (O. W. Holmes), 1858 U
Automation:
aircraft, 1947 P, 1950 P
bottle-making machine, 1898 P
computers, 1942 P, 1958 Y, 1961 P
D.S.I.R. Report on, 1956 O
electronic brain, 1946 P
loom, 1895 P
railway couplings, 1906 P
railway signals, 1893 P
telephone switchboard, 1892 P
See also Machines
Automobile Association, 1905 O
Automobiles. *See* Motor Cars
Autumn Crocus (D. Smith), 1931 W
Ava, Burma, British resident at, 1826 B
Avenir des Peuples Catholiques, L' (Laveleye), 1875 R
Aventures du dernier Abencérage, Les (Chateaubriand), 1808 U
Aventures et Nouvelles Avęntures (G. Ligeti), 1966 T
Aventures Prodigieuses de Tartarin de Tarascon (A. Daudet), 1872 U
'Average Man', concept of the, 1835 P
Aviation:
Civil Aerial Transport Committee, British, 1917 O
Flights:
Alcock and Brown, 1919 P
Croydon to Cape Town, 1926 P
glider towed from Montreal, 1943 P
Graf Zeppelin's transatlantic, 1928 P
helicopter, 1919 P
high altitude, 1955 P
Howard Hughes', 1938 P
Amy Johnson, 1930 P
Lindberg's, 1927 P
London–Canada non-stop, 1944 O
Mrs. Mollison, 1936 P
Odom's world, 1947 P
Paris-Hanoi, 1932 P
Polar, 1926 P, 1929 P
Ross Smith, to Australia, 1919 P
sea-plane, 1912 P
Transatlantic, first east-west, 1928 P
by Ferry Command, 1941 P
automatic, 1947 P
US–Europe, regular commercial, 1939 P
Wiley Post, 1933 P
Gordon-Bennett Cup, 1911 X
Space Travel, congress on, 1951 O
Avignon, France: papal estates in, seized by France, 1768 N; restored to Papacy, 1773 M; annexed by France, 1791 J
Avis au peuple français (A. Chénier), 1790 O
Avogadro, Amadeo, Conte di Quaregna, It. chemist (1776–1856), 1811 P
Avon, Viscount. *See* Eden, Anthony
Avranches, France, US break-through in, 1944 H
Avril, General Prosper, President of Haiti, 1989 D, 1990 C
AWACS planes replace Nimrod early-warning system, B., 1986 O
Axel (E. Tegner), 1822 U
Ayacucho, Peru, battle, 1824 M
Ayckbourn, Alan, B. playwright (b. 1939), 1939 Z, 1973 W
Ayer, Sir Alfred Jules, B. philosopher (1910–89), 1910 Z, 1936 R, 1940 R, 1956 R, 1957 R, 1982 R, 1989 Z
Aylwin, Patricio, President of Chile (b. 1919), 1989 M
Ayodhya, India, mosque built on Hindu holy site
Hindu militants attack, 1990 K
mosque destroyed, 1992 M
Ayrton, William Edward, B. electrical engineer (1847–1908), 1879 P
Ayub Khan, Mohammed, President of Pakistan (1907–74), 1907 Z, 1969 C, 1974 Z; forms ministry, 1958 K; elected president, 1960 B
Azaña, Manuel, Sp. politician, as premier, 1931 M, 1936 B; elected president, 1936 E
Azeglio, Massimo Taparelli d', It. political philosopher and statesman (1798–1868), 1798 Z, 1846 O, 1868 Z
Azerbaijan:
risings in, 1945 L
reforms promised, 1946 D
Nagorno-Karabakh votes for transfer from, 1988 B
curfew imposed, 1988 C
Soviet troops enter, 1988 F
states of emergency declared, 1988 J, L
riots on Iranian border, 1989 M
percentage of Azerbaijanis in Soviet population, 1989 Y
Soviet troops fire on demonstrators, 1990 A
war declared on Armenia, 1990 A
independence, 1991 H
dispute over Nagorno-Karabakh, 1992 J
Azikiwe, Dr., president of Nigeria, 1963 K
Azoimide, obtained from organic source, 1890 P
Azores, Atlantic, Portugal grants Britain use of bases, 1943 K; bases restored to Portugal, 1946 F

B

Baader, Andreas, W. German terrorist (1943–77)
imprisoned, 1977 D
suicide, 1977 K
Baader-Meinhof group, 1972 F, 1977 D
Babangida, Major-General Ibrahim, Nigerian leader (b. 1941), 1985 H
Babbage, Charles, B. mathematician (1792–1871), 1823 P
Babbitt (S. Lewis), 1922 U
Babbitt, Milton Byron, Am. musician (b. 1916), 1966 T
Babes in Toyland, Am. pop group, 1990 W
Babeuf, François Noel, F. political agitator (1760–97), 1796 E
Babist Sect, in Persia, 1843 R
Babylonian remains, 1888 Q
Baccarat, 1891 O
Bach, Carl Philipp Emanuel, G. musician (1714–88), 1769 T, 1775 T, 1788 Z
Bach, Johann Christian, G. musician (1735–82), 1764 T, 1782 Z
Bach, Johann Sebastian, G. musician (1685–1750), choral works, revival of interest in, 1829 T
festivals of music of, 1900 T, 1950 T
Schweitzer's study of, 1905 T
Bach, Richard, Am. author, 1970 U
Back of my Hand, The (R. Deacon), 1987 S
Back to Methusaleh (G. B. Shaw), 1923 W
Bacon, Francis, B. artist (1909–92), 1909 Z, 1957 S, 1992 Z
Bacon, Francis, lord Verulam, suggested as author of Shakespeare's plays, 1848 Q
Bacon, Henry, Am. sculptor, 1917 S
Bacon, J. M., B. balloonist, 1902 P
Bacon, John, B. sculptor (1740–99), 1796 S
Bacteria, Koch's techniques for fixing, 1877 P
Badajoz, Spain:
Treaty, 1801 F
British capture, 1812 D
Baden, Switzerland, Swiss airliner crashes, 1970 B
Baden-Baden, Baden-Württemberg, Germany:
Trinkhalle in, 1840 S
as a Grand Duchy, 1805 M
enters N. German Confederation, 1870 A
Baden-Powell, Robert, lord Baden-Powell, B.

soldier and founder of scouting movement (1857–1941), 1857 Z, 1896 K, 1907 O, 1941 Z
Badeni, Casimir, Count, Aus. politician, 1895 J, 1897 L
Badoglio, Pietro, duke of Addis Ababa, It. soldier (1870–1956), forms government on Mussolini's fall, 1943 G
'Baedeker' raids on Britain, 1942 D
Baekeland, Leo Hendrik, G. inventor (1863–1944), 1907, P
Baer, Carl von, G. physiologist (1792–1874), 1792 Z, 1827 P, 1828 P, 1874 Z
Baeviad (W. Gifford), 1794 U
Bagehot, Walter, B. economist and author (1826–77), 1826 Z, 1867 O, 1869 O, 1877 Z, 1880 O
Baghdad, Iraq:
  British capture, 1917 C
  coups d'état in, 1958 G, 1963 B
  Osirak nuclear reactor bombed, 1981 F
  Pact, between Iraq and Turkey, 1955 B
    Britain joins, 1955 D
    Iran joins, 1955 L
    boycotts Britain, 1956 L, end of boycott, 1957 C
    name changed to Central Treaty Organisation, 1959 H
  Railway: Germany secures contract for, 1888 K, 1899 M, 1903 D; German discussions on, 1907 H, 1909 L; Russia ceases opposition to, 1910 L; Franco-German agreement on, 1914 B; Anglo-German agreement on, 1914 F; British army administers, 1919 A
Bagnold, Enid (Lady Jones), B. dramatist, 1954 W, 1965 W
Bahaan, Burma, Japanese take, 1942 D
Bahamas, The:
  independence, 1973 G
  election, 1992 H
  hurricane Andrew, 1992 H
Bahonar, Mohammad Javad, Prime Minister of Iran (1933–81), 1981 H
Bahr el Ghazal, River, Sudan, 1897 H
Bahrein Islands, Persian Gulf:
  Persia claims, 1927 L
  declared an independent Arab state, 1957 L
  declares independence, 1971 H
Bailey, James Anthony, Am. showman (1847–1906), 1871 W, 1889 W
Bailly, Jean Sylvain, F. revolutionary leader (1736–1793), 1789 G
Bailyn, Bernard, Am. historian (b. 1922), 1967 Q
Bain, Alexander, B. philosopher (1818–1903), 1855 R, 1876 R, 1899 R
Baines, John Robert, B. Egyptologist (b. 1946), 1980 Q
Bainton, Roland Herbert, Am. theologian (1894–1984), 1970 Q
Baird, John Logie, B. inventor of television (1888–1946), 1888 Z, 1926 P, 1928 P, 1932 O, 1946 Z
Baji Rao, Peshwa of Poona, 1818 F
Bakelite, 1907 P
Baker, Howard Henry, Am. politician (b. 1925), 1987 B
Baker, Nicholson, Am. author (b. 1957), 1990 U
Bakhtiar, Dr. Shakpur, Prime Minister of Iran (1914–91), 1979 A
  flees Iran, 1979 B
Bakker, Jim, Am. television evangelist (b. 1940), 1989 K
Baku, Azerbaijan, Russians take, 1783 K; oil wells in, 1873 P; Turks occupy, 1918 C; nationalist demonstrations, 1990 A
Bakunin, Michael, R. anarchist (1814–76), 1814 Z, 1869 O, 1872 O, 1876 N, Z
Balaclava, Crimea, Russia: battle, 1854 K; telegraph to London, 1855 P
Balakirev, Mily Alexeivich, R. musician (1886–1910), 1886 Z, 1910 Z
Balanchine, George Melitonovich, R.-born Am. choreographer (1904–83), 1904 Z, 1946 T, 1983 Z; founds American School of Ballet, 1933 T
Balchin, Nigel Marlin, B. author (1908–70), 1947 U
Balcon, Sir Michael, B. film director (1896–1977), 1964 W
Baldwin, James Arthur, Am. author (1924–87), 1924 Z, 1955 U, 1963 U, 1987 Z
Baldwin, Stanley, earl Baldwin, B. Conservative leader (1867–1947), 1867 Z, 1947 Z; becomes premier, 1923 E; resigns, 1924 A; becomes premier, 1924 L; MacDonald delegates duties to, 1934 F; forms National Government, 1935 F; dissatisfaction with, 1936 C; role in Abdication Crisis, 1936 K, L; retires, 1937 E
Balearic Islands, pact to counter German designs in, 1907 E
Balfe, Michael William, Ir. musician (1808–70), 1843 T
Balfour, Arthur James, earl of Balfour, B. statesman, Conservative politician and philosopher (1848–1930), 1848 Z, 1903 J, L, 1904 K, 1916 M, 1919 K, 1930 Z; forms ministry, 1902 G; resigns, 1905 M; resigns Unionist leadership, 1911 L; as First Lord of Admiralty, 1915 E; in US, 1917 E; Declaration on Palestine, 1917 L; Balfour Note, 1922 H; as philosopher, 1879 R, 1895 R
Balkans: Russia's agreement with Italy on preserving *status quo* in, 1909 K; Count Berchtold's conversations on, 1912 H; War of Turkey against Bulgaria, Serbia, Montenegro and Greece, 1912 K, L, M, 1913 C, E; Montenegro renews, 1913 B; Pact, 1934 P; Britain forms company to trade in, 1940 D; Rumania refused accession to Pact, 1957 J
Ball, Alan, B. soccer player (b. 1945), 1966 X
Ball-bearings, 'cup and cone', invented, 1869 P
Ball-point pen, 1938 P
Balla, Giacomo, It. artist (1871–1958), 1910 S, 1916 S
Ballad and the Source, The (R. Lehmann), 1944 U
Ballad of Reading Gaol, The (O. Wilde), 1898 U
Ballads and Other Poems (H. W. Longfellow), 1842 U
Ballads and Sonnets (D. G. Rossetti), 1881 U
Ballard, James Graham, B. writer (b. 1930), 1984 U
Ballet:
  Age of Anxiety, 1950 T
  Agon (Stravinsky), 1957 T
  American School of, 1933 T
  Antigone (Cranko), 1959 T
  Après-midi d'un faune, L' (Robbins), 1959 T
  Ballabile (Petit-Chabrier), 1950 T
  Ballet mécanique, 1927 T
  Birthday Offering (Ashton-Arnold), 1956 T
  Boutique Fantasque, La (Diaghilev), 1919 T
  Broken Date (Magne), 1958 T
  Burrow, The (Macmillan-Martin), 1958 T
  Cage, The (Robbins-Stravinsky), 1952 T
  Casse-Noisette (Tschaikovsky), 1891 T
  Chant de Rossignol, Le (Stravinsky), 1920 T
  Checkmate (Bliss), 1937 T
  Daphnis and Chlo (Ravel), 1911 T
  Deux Pigeons, Les (Ashton-Messenger), 1961 T
  Don Quixote, 1950 T
  Façade (Walton), 1923 T
  Fancy Free (Robbins), 1946 T
  Festin de l'Araign, Le (Roussel), 1923 T
  Game of Cards (Stravinsky), 1935 T
  Homage to the Queen (M. Arnold), 1953 T
  House Party, The (Poulenc), 1923 P
  Improvisations (Copland-Carter), 1962 T
  Interplay (J. Robbins), 1946 T
  Night Shadow (Balanchine), 1946 T
  Nobilissima Visiona (Hindemith), 1938 T
  Noctambules (Searle), 1956 T
  Ondine (Ashton-Henze), 1958 T
  Parade (Diaghilev-Satie), 1917 S, T
  Patineurs, Les (Ashton), 1937 T
  Peer Gynt (A. Schnittke), 1989 T
  Petruschka (Stravinsky), 1912 T
  Pineapple Poll, 1951 T
  Prince of the Pagodas (Britten), 1957 T
  Pulcinello (Stravinsky), 1920 T
  Rambert School of Ballet, London, 1920 T
  Reflection (Cranko-Gardner), 1952 T
  Rite of Spring, The (Stravinsky), 1913 T
  Rodeo (de Mille), 1940 T
  Royal, visits Russia, 1961 T
  Russian, under Diaghilev, visits Paris, 1909 T
  Sémiramis (Honegger), 1934 T
  Sluts (Prokofiev), 1945 T
  Soldier's Tale, The (Stravinsky-Diaghilev), 1917 T
  Swan-Lake (Tschaikovsky), 1878 T
  Sylphides, Les (Fokine-Chopin), 1909 T
  Symphonis Variations (Ashton), 1946 T
  Three-cornered Hat (de Falla), 1919 S, T
  Witchboy (J. Carter), 1958 T
Ballila, Italian Fascist youth organisation, 1926 D
Balloons: ascents by, 1783 P, 1785 P, 1863 P, 1902 P, 1934 P; photography from, Russian protests to US about, 1956 B
Ballou, Hosea, Am. Universalist minister (1771–1852), 1805 R
Ballykelly, Co. Londonderry, N. Ireland, bomb explosion, 1982 M
Balmaceda, José, Chilean president, 1891 J
Balmain, Pierre, F. couturier (1914–1982), 1914 Z, 1982 Z
Balsemão, Francisco Pinto, Prime Minister of Portugal (b. 1937), 1980 M
Balta Liman, treaty between Russia and Turkey, 1849 E
Baltic Convention, 1908 H
Baltic Sea, Britain bars French fleet from, 1772 G
Baltic States Russian occupation of, 1940 F
Baltic States, Council of, 1992 O
Baltimore, David, Am. scientist (b. 1938), 1938 Z, 1970 P
Baltimore, Maryland, US: Congress at, 1776 K; Roman Catholic Bishop, 1790 R; Swedenborgian Church in, 1792 R; steam engine from, 1829 P; Roman Catholic Council at, 1852 R; Democrat Convention at, 1912 G
Baluchistan, N. W. Pakistan, is united with India, 1887 K
Balzac, Honoré de, F. author (1799–1850), 1799 Z, 1829 U, 1831 U, 1832 U, 1834 U, 1841 U, 1845 U, 1846 U, 1850 Z
Balzan International Foundation, 1964 B
Bampton Lectures, Oxford, 1780 R
Banana, Rev. Dr. Canaan Sodindo, President of Zimbabwe (b. 1936), 1980 D
Bancroft, George, Am. historian (1800–91), 1834 Q
Bancroft, Sir Squire, B. actor-manager (1841–1926), 1841 Z, 1866 W, 1926 Z
Band, The, Canad. pop group, 1968 W
Banda, Hastings, premier of Malawi (b. 1905),

arrested as leader of African Congress Party in Nyasaland, 1959 B; becomes premier of Nyasaland, 1963 A; acquires powers of detention, 1964 K
Bandaranaike, Dudley, Ceyl. politician, 1953 K, 1956 D
Bandaranaike, Mrs. Sirimavo Ratwatte Dias, Prime Minister of Ceyl./Sri Lanka (b. 1916), becomes premier, 1960 F; is defeated, 1965 C; re-elected 1970 E; defeated, 1977 G
Bandaranaike, Solomon, Ceyl. politician (1899–1959), 1959 J
Bandinel, James, B. divine (1734–96), 1780 R
Bangkok, Thailand, 1782 N; Conference of heads of US Asiatic missions at, 1950 B; SEATO Conference at, 1955 B; riots, 1992 E
Bangladesh
  Rahman pledges full autonomy, 1971 A
  general strike, 1971 C
  independence, 1971 M
  Rahman becomes President, 1971 M
  population, 1971 Y, 1981 Y, 1991 Y
  Pakistan leaves Commonwealth in anticipation of British recognition of, 1972 A
  mutual defence pact with India, 1972 C
  China vetoes Bangladeshi membership of UN, 1972 H
  Pakistan recognizes, 1974 B
  floods, 1974 H, 1988 H
  becomes one-party state, 1975 B
  Rahman murdered, 1975 H
  Ahmed becomes President, 1975 H
  martial law imposed, 1975 L
  Zia ur-Rahman becomes President, 1977 D
  Zia ur-Rahman assassinated, 1981 E
  military coup, 1982 C
  illiteracy, 1983 Y
  Cyclone, 1985 E
  urbanization, 1985 Y
  martial law ended, 1986 L
  return to parliamentary rule, 1991 H
  See also Pakistan (East)
Bangor, N. Wales, 1935 A
Bangui, Central African Empire, children killed in demonstrations, 1979 D
Bani-Sadr, Abolhassan, President of Iran (b. 1933), 1980 A
  flees to France, 1981 F
Bankrupt, The (Ostrovsky), 1847 W
Bankruptcy. *See* Crises, Financial
Banks and Banking:
  Bank of International Settlements, loan to Britain, 1967 L
  western banks underwrite loan to Mexico, 1983 B
  Bank of Credit and Commerce International (BCCI), closure, 1991 O
  European Bank for Reconstruction and Development, 1991 O
  in Australia, nationalisation of, 1947 L
  in Austria, failure of Credit-Anstalt, 1931 D
  in Belgium, scandal over National Bank, 1937 K
  in Britain:
    Baring Bros., failure of, 1890 O
    Birkbeck Bank fails, 1911 F
    England, Bank of, buildings for, 1795 S, 1803 S
      suspends cash payments, 1797 B
      resumes cash payments, 1817 K, 1821 E
      Bank Charter Act for, 1833 H, 1844 G
        repealed, 1914 O
      issues Treasury notes, 1914 O
      advances money to Austria, 1931 F
      is nationalised, 1946 B
      agrees with central banks for support for, 1965 J
    Minimum Lending Rate abolished, 1981 H
    50 pound note issued, 1981 O
    provincial banks, run on, 1796 M
    bank holidays, 1871 W, 1964 C
    bank rate, notable changes in, 1957 J, 1960 F, 1961 G, 1964 L, 1965 F, 1970 C, 1971 D, 1973 L, 1979 L, 1980 G
    bank rate tribunal, 1957 M
    'women only' branch, in Edinburgh, 1964 O
    drive-in, in Liverpool, 1959 O
    International Monetary Fund (IMF) loan, 1967 L, 1976 J, M, 1977 A
    Trustee Savings Bank privatization, 1984 M, 1986 J
    Midland Bank taken over by Hong Kong and Shangai Banking Corporation, 1992 O
  in Canada, bank of Canada, 1935 O
    Newfoundland Bank fails, 1894 L
  in France, Bank of France, 1801 O
    issues Franc notes, 1914 O
    reorganised, 1936 O
    is nationalised, 1945 O
  nationalization, 1981 J
  in Germany, Agricultural Co-operative land, 1849 O
    Deutsche, 1898 L
    Reichsbank, 1875 O, 1876 O
      Schacht is dismissed from, 1939 A
    Danatbank, fails, 1931 G
    bank rate raised to 90 per cent, 1923 J
  in Italy, Milan People's Bank, 1866 O
    Banco Ambrosiano of Milan, liquidation of, 1982 H
  in Japan, 1882 O, 1927 D
  in New Zealand, Reserve Bank nationalised, 1936 N
  in Switzerland, Basel Bank, for Germany's reparations payments, 1929 L
  in Turkey, Ottoman Bank, Constantinople, attacked, 1896 H
  in US, Bank of North America, 1791 O
    uniform banking system provided, 1863 B, 1864 F
    Federal Bank created, 1913 O
    Postal Savings Bank, 1910 O
    closure of banks in crisis, 1933 C
Banks, Sir Joseph, B. scientist (1743–1820), 1788 F, 1799 P
Bannister, Roger Gilbert, B. athlete (b. 1929), 1929 Z, 1954 X
Bannon, John Charles, Premier of South Australia (b. 1944), 1992 O
Banting, Frederick, Can. biochemist (1891–1941), 1922 P
Bantry Bay, Cork, Eire, Hoche's expedition to, 1796 M
Bantu self-government bill, S. Africa, 1960 F
Banville, Thodore de, F. author (1823–91), 1842 U
Bao Dai, ex-emperor of Viet-Nam (b. 1913), 1949 C; establishes Viet-Nam state, 1949 F; deposed, 1955 K
Bapaume, N.E. France, British capture, 1917 C
Bar Code, introduction, 1973 P
Bar, in Podolia, formerly Poland, now Russia, Confederation, 1768 H
Bar-sur-Aube, France, French defeat at, 1814 B
Baraalam and Yearsef (ed. Budge), 1924 Q
Barbados, independence, 1966 L
Barbare en Asie, Un (H. Michaux), 1932 U
Barbarian West, The, 400–1000 (J.M. Wallace-Hadrill), 1952 Q
Barber of Serville (P. Beaumarchais), 1775 W
Barber, Anthony Perrinot Lysberg, Lord Barber, B. Conservative politician (b. 1920)
  Chancellor of Exchequer, 1970 G
  introduces mini-budget, 1970 K
Barber, Samuel, Am. musician (1910–81), 1910 Z, 1958 T, 1961 T, 1966 T, 1981 Z
Barbier, Henri Auguste, F. poet and dramatist (1805–82), 1831 U
Barbizon School of French Artists, 1831 S
Barbuda
  See Antigua and Barbuda
Barcelona, Spain: French capture, 1808 B; risings in, 1842 K; Alfonso XII at, 1875 A; general strike in 1909 G; rising by Monarchists, 1933 A; strike by Socialists, 1934 D; government moves to, 1937 K; Olympics, 1992 X; places: Casa Mila, 1905 S; Church of the Sagrada Familia, 1926 S
Barchester Towers (A. Trollope), 1857 U
Barclay, David and Frederick (both b. 1934), B. businessmen,
  purchase of *The European*, 1992 V
Bardem, Juan Antonio, Span. film director (b. 1922), 1955 W
Bardia, Cyrenaica, Libya: Italians surrender, 1941 A; Germans recapture, 1941 D; British take, 1942 A
Bardo, Tunisia, Treaty of, 1881 E
Barghoorn, Elso Sterrenberg, Am. scientist (b. 1915), 1968 P
Barham, Richard Harris, B. author (1788–1845), 1840 U
Baring, Alexander, lord Ashburton, B. diplomat (1774–1848), 1842 H
Baring, Evelyn, Lord Cromer, B. statesman and diplomat (1841–1917), as British agent in Egypt, 1883 J, 1893 A
Barker, Howard, B. playwright (b. 1946), 1983 W
Barker, Sue, B. tennis player (b. 1956), 1976 X
Barlow Clowes affair, 1992 O
Barlow, Sir Montague, B. economist, 1940 O
Barnard Castle, Durham, by-election, 1903 G
Barnard, Dr. Christiaan, South African surgeon (b. 1922), 1922 Z, 1967 P, 1968 P
Barnardo, Thomas John, B. philanthropist (1845–1905), 1865 O
Barnes, E. W., B. churchman and scientist, Bishop of Birmingham (1874–1953), 1933 R, 1947 R
Barnes, Julian Patrick, B. author (b. 1946), 1985 U
Barnes, Peter, B. dramatist (b. 1931), 1968 W, 1991 W
Barnes, Thomas, B. journalist (1784–1841), 1817 V
Barnett, Dame Henrietta Octavia Weston, B. social reformer (1851–1936), 1906 S
Barnum, Phineas Taylor, Am. showman (1810–91), 1850 W, 1871 W, 1889 W
Barometer, 1771 P
Barotseland, N. Rhodesia, 1891 F
Barrès, Maurice, F. author (1862–1923), 1862 Z, 1888 U, 1891 U, 1897 U, 1913 U, 1923 Z
Barr, Alfred, Am. art historian (1908–84), 1967 S
Barrack Room Ballads (R. Kipling), 1892 U
Barraclough, Geoffrey, Br. historian (1908–84), 1978 Q
Barras, Paul François Nicolas, Comte de, F. revolutionary (1755–1829), 1797 J
Barre, Siad, President of Somalia (b. 1920), 1991 A
Barricades and Borders: Europe 1800–1914 (R. Gildea), 1987 Q
Barrie, Sir James Matthew, B. dramatist (1860–1937), 1860 Z, 1889 U, 1891 U, 1902 W,

1917 W, 1937 Z
Peter Pan, 1904 S, W
Barrier Towns, Austrian Netherlands, 1782 D
Barrington, Samuel, B. admiral (1729–1800), 1778 L
Barrington-Ward, Robert McGowan, B. journalist (1891–1948), 1941 V
Barrow, Sir John, B. Arctic explorer (1764–1848), 1919 P
Barry, Sir Charles, B. architect (1795–1860), 1840 S, 1858 S
Barry, Sir Gerald Reid, B. journalist (1898–1968), as director-general of Festival of Britain, 1951 S
Barry, Philip, Am. dramatist (1896–1949), 1938 W
Barrymore, John, Am. film actor (1882–1942), 1926 W
Bart, Lionel, B. musician (b. 1930), 1961 W
Bartenstein, Russo-Prussian Convention of, 1807 D Britain joins, 1807 F
Barthélemy, Jean-Jacques, F. educationalist (1716–1795), 1787 Q
Barth, Heinrich, G. explorer (1821–65), 1850 P, 1852 P
Barth, Karl, Swi. theologian (1886–1965), 1886 Z, 1919 R, 1932 R, 1935 R, 1959 R
Barthes, Roland, Fr. author (1915–80), 1957 R, 1980 Z
Bartók, Béla, Hung. musician (1881–1945), 1881 Z, 1908 T, 1918 T, 1923 T, 1938 T, 1944 T, 1945 Z, 1950 T
Barton, Sir Edmund, Australian Federalist, premier, 1901 A
Baruch, Bernard, Am. financier (1870–1965), 1870 Z, 1965 Z
Baryta, discovered, 1774 P
Base constitutionelle de la république de genre humain (Cloots), 1793 O
Baseball:
first played, 1839 X
rules codified, 1845 X
first US professional club, 1868 X
US National League founded, 1876 X
American Association 1882 X
Baselitz, Georg, G. artist (b. 1938), 1969 S, 1980 S, 1982 S
Basic English, 1932 O
Foundation, 1947 O
Basic Training of Pavlo Hummel, The (D. Rabe), 1972 W
Basie, Count (born William Basie), Am. jazz musician (1904–84), 1904 Z, 1938 T, 1984 Z
Basle, Switzerland: bishopric annexed by France, 1793 C; Peace of, between France and Prussia, 1795 D; Austro-French secret agreement on, 1797 K; Zionist Conference at,1897 R; FrancoGerman Parliamentary Conference at, 1950 A
Basque region
trial of Basque separatists, 1970 M
Basque separatists demand for autonomy recognized, 1978 J
devolution of power to Basque provinces approved, 1979 K
Basque regional parliament opens, 1980 C
Basque separatists explode bombs on Costa Blanca, 1980 F
Basra, S.E. India, occupied by Indians, 1914 L
Bassée Canal, Belgium, 1915 A
Bass, George, B. naval surgeon (d. 1812), 1798 P
Bassein, Bombay, India, treaty, 1802 M
Bastien-Lepage, Jules, F. artist (1848–84), 1879 S
Basutoland, S. Africa: comes under British protection, 1843 M; annexed by Britain, 1868 C; is united with Cape Colony, 1871 H; independence as Lesotho, 1966 K
Basutos, tribe, S. Africa, 1877 D
Batavian Republic (Holland), 1795 E, 1797 K, 1801 B
Directory established in, 1798 A
Bateau Ivre, Le (A. Rimbaud), 1895 U
Bates, Herbert Ernest, B. author (1905–74), 1944 U, 1949 U
Batetelas, in Upper Congo, rising of, 1897 J
Bath, Somerset, Eng., bombed, 1942 D
Baths and wash-houses, public, 1844 O
Bathyscape, 1948 P, 1960 P
Batista, Fulgencio, Cuban politician (1901–73), 1901 Z, 1957 K, 1958 D, 1973 Z; flees, 1959 A
Batman, television series, 1966 W
Battery:
carbon-zinc, 1841 P
solar, 1954 P
Battle Cry of Freedom (J. McPherson), 1988 Q
Battle for the Mind, The (W. Sargent), 1957 O
Batum, S.W. Georgia, Russia: transferred to Russia, 1878 C, G; British evacuate, 1920 G
Baudelaire, Charles Pierre, F. author (1821–67), 1821 Z, 1857 U, 1863 S, 1866 U, 1867 Z
Baudouin I, King of the Belgians (1930–93), succeeds Leopold III, 1950 H; marries, 1960 M; 1990 D
Baudrillant, Henri Joseph Léon, F. economist (1821–1892), 1865 O
Bauer, Ferdinand Christian, G. theologian (1792–1860), 1846 Q
Bauer, Gustav, G. Socialist leader, 1919 F
Bauer, L. A., G. physicist, 1923 P
Bauer, Otto, Aus. Socialist leader (1881–1938), 1938 Z
Bautzen, E. Germany, battle, 1813 E
Bavaria: Austrian claims to, 1777 M, 1778 A, 1797 K; passes to Elector Palatine, 1777 M; War of Succession, 1778 G, 1779 E; Joseph II attempts to exchange Austrian Netherlands for, 1785 A, G, 1790 M; becomes a kingdom, 1805 M; alliance with N. German Confederation, 1870 L; republic proclaimed, 1918 L
Bax, Sir Arnold Edward Trevor, B. musician (1883–1953), 1916 T, 1917 T, 1928 T, 1932 T, 1943 T
Baxandall, Michael David Kighley, art historian (b. 1933), 1972 Q, 1980 Q
Bayer, Adolf von, G. chemist (1835–1917), 1880 P
Bayliss, Lilian, B. theatrical manager (1874–1937), 1914 W, 1931 W
Bayliss, Sir William Maddock, B. physiologist (1866–1924), 1902 P
Bayly, Christopher A., B. historian, 1983 Q
Bayonne, France, siege of, 1813 L
Bayreuth, Bavaria, W. Germany: principality, 1769 K, 1779 E; Prussia acquires, 1792 A; Festspielhaus in, 1876 T
Bazargan, Mehdi, Iran. Premier-designate (b. 1907), 1979 B
Bérégovoy, Pierre, Prime Minister of France (1925–93), 1992 D
Beach Boys, Am. pop group, 1966 W, 1968 W
Beaconsfield, Earl of. *See* Disraeli, Benjamin
Beale, Dorothea, B. educationalist (1831–1906), 1831 Z, 1906 Z
Beamon, Bob, Am. athlete (b. 1946), 1968 X, 1991 X
Beardsley, Aubrey, B. artist (1872–98), 1893 S, 1894 S
Bearings, roller, 1910 P
Beatles, The, B. pop group, 1963 W, 1964 W, 1965 O, W, 1966 W, 1967 W, 1970 W
Beatnik Cult, The, 1958 U
Beaton, Sir Cecil, B. photographer and designer (1904–80), 1904 Z, 1930 S, 1980 Z
Beatrice Cenci (F. D. Guerazzi), 1854 U
Beatrix, Queen of the Netherlands (b. 1938), 1980 D
Beattie, James, B. poet and philosopher (1735–1803), 1770 R
Beatty, David, Earl Beatty, B. naval officer (1871–1936), 1871 Z, 1914 H, 1916 L, 1936 Z
Beauharnais, Eugène de, F. soldier (1781–1824), stepson of Napoleon 1, 1813 K
Beauharnais, Josephine de (*née* Marie Rose Josephine Tascher de la Pagerie; married Napoleon 1). *See* Josephine
Beaumarchais, Pierre Augustin Caron de, F. dramatist (1732–99), 1775 W, 1784 W, 1787 W, 1799 Z
Beauty contest, first, 1888 W
Beauvoir, Simone de, F. author (1908–86), 1908 Z, 1946 U, 1949 U, 1986 Z
Beaver Committee on air pollution in Britain, 1953 O
Beaverbrook (A.J.P. Taylor), 1972 Q
Beaverbrook, Lord. *See* Aitken, William Maxwell
Bebel, Ferdinand August, G. Socialist (1840–1913), 1867 H
Bebop dancing, 1945 W, 1950 W
Beccaria-Bonesana, Cesare, Marchese de, It. publicist (1735–94), 1764 O
Bechuanaland, S. Africa: exploration of, 1802 P; British protectorate in, 1885 C; under a British governor, 1890 N; annexed to Cape Colony, 1895 L; to be independent, 1965 M; independence as Botswana, 1966 J
Becker, Boris, G. tennis player (b. 1967), 1985 X
Becket (J. Anouilh), 1961 W
Beckett, Mrs. Margaret Mary, B. Labour politician (b. 1943), 1992 G
Beckett, Samuel, Ir. dramatist (1906–89), 1906 Z, 1955 W, 1957 W, 1972 W, 1989 Z
Beckford, Peter, B. sportsman (1740–1811), 1781 X
Beckford, William, B. author (1759–1844), 1786 U
Beckmann, Max, G. artist (1884–1950), 1923 S, 1928 S, 1932 S, 1940 S, 1944 S, 1965 S
Beckwith, Jonathan, Am. biologist (b. 1935), 1969 P
Becque, Henri François, F. dramatist (1837–99), 1882 W, 1885 W, 1887 W
Becquerel, Henri, F. chemist (1852–1908), 1852 Z, 1908 Z
Bedchamber Question, 1839 E
Bedford, Dukes of. *See under* Russell
Bedford, Eric, B. architect, 1954 S
Bedford, Sibylle, Am. author (b. 1911), 1957 U
Bednore (now Nagar), in Mysore, India, 1783 D
Bednorz, Johannes Georg, G. physicist (b. 1950), 1986 P
Bee Gees, The, pop group, 1978 W
Beebe, William, Am. marine biologist (1877–1962), 1934 P
Beecham, Sir Thomas, B. musician (1879–1961), 1910 T, 1932 T, 1953 T, 1961 Z
Beecher Stowe, Harriet, Am. author (1811–96), 1852 U
Beecher, Henry Ward, Am. preacher (1813–76), 1847 R
Beeching, Richard, B. administrator (1913–85), 1913 Z, 1963 O, 1985 Z
Beel, J. M., Du. politician, leader of Catholic People's Party, 1958 M
Beer, Esmond Samuel de, B. historian (1895–1990), 1976 Q

Beer, Jacob. *See* Meyerbeer, Giacomo
Beer, Sir Gavin de, B. scientist and administrator (1899–1972), 1960 Q
Beerbohm, Sir Max, B. author and artist (1872–1956), 1872 Z, 1904 S, 1911 U, 1919 U, 1922 S, 1956 Z
Beet Queen, The (L. Erdrich), 1986 U
Beethoven, Ludwig van, G. musician (1771–1827), 1771 Z, 1783 T, 1827 Z
  Fidelio, 1805 T, 1814 T
  Liederkreis, 1816 T
  Mass in D, 1822 T
  overtures, 1807 T, 1810 T
  piano concertos, 1800 T, 1801 T, 1805 T, 1809 T
  piano sonatas, 1799 T, 1802 T, 1807 T, 1811 T
  string quartets, 1801 T, 1806 T
  symphonies, 1800 T, 1802 T, 1806 T, 1808 T, 1812 T
    Choral, 1824 T, 1825 T
  violin concerto, 1806 T, 1844 T
  Wagner's essay on, 1870 T
Before Civilization: The Radiocarbon Revolution and Prehistoric Europe (C. Renfrew), 1974 Q
Before Dawn (G. Hauptmann), 1889 U
Begin, Menachem, Prime Minister of Israel (1913–92), 1913 Z, 1977 E, 1983 H, 1992 Z
  peace negotiations with Sadat, 1977 L
  visits Egypt, 1977 M
  announces sovereignty over occupied West Bank, 1982 E
  ultimatum for PLO guerrillas, 1982 G
  agrees to Beirut massacre inquiry, 1982 J
Behan, Brendan, Ir. dramatist (1923–64), 1959 W, 1964 Z
Beheshti, Ayatollah Mohammad Hossein, Iranian Chief Justice (1929–81), 1981 F
Behrens, Peter, G. architect (1868–1940), 1908 S
Beirut, The Lebanon:
  British bombard, 1840 J
  French occupy, 1918 K
  airport bombed, 1968 M
  Israeli commandos kill Palestinian guerrilla leaders, 1973 D
  civil war starts, 1975 D
  Syrian intervention, 1976 L, 1987 B
  renewed fighting, 1978 K
  fighting between Arab peace-keeping force and Christian militia, 1981 D
  Christian suburbs shelled by Syria,1981 E
  Israelis attack Palestinian areas, 1981 G
  French ambassador assassinated, 1981 J
  Israeli air attacks on, 1982 F
  PLO guerrillas surrounded by Israeli forces, 1982 F
  Israel demands surrender of PLO guerrillas, 1982 F
  PLO guerrillas given 30 days to leave, 1982 G
  Israeli bombardment intensifies, 1982 H
  Israel accepts US plan to evacuate PLO guerrillas, 1982 H
  Palestinian refugee camp massacre, 1982 J, 1983 B
  Israeli troops withdrawn from West Beirut, 1982 J
  French, Italian and US peace-keeping force in, 1982 J
  Lebanese army moves through, 1982 K
  Christian Phalangist militia withdraw, 1983 B
  bomb explosion at US embassy, 1983 D
  suicide attack on UN peace-keeping force, 1983 K
  Kerr shot dead by pro-Iranian group, 1984 A
  curfew imposed as Shi'a Muslim and Druze militia overrun West, 1984 B
  US marines withdraw, 1984 B
  army takes over positions from militias, 1984 G
  US embassy bombed, 1984 J
  British embassy closed, 1985 C
  Shi'a Muslim militia attempts to drive Palestinians from refugee camps, 1985 E
  hostages, 1985 F, 1986 D, L, 1987 A, 1990 H, 1991 H, L
  Terry Waite's mission to free hostages, 1986 L
  US arms deal with Iran to secure release of hostages, 1986 L
  David Jacobsen freed 1986 , L
  Sheikh Hassan Khaled killed, 1989 E
  Arab League ceasefire, 1989 J
  Brian Keenan released, 1990 H
  Christian militias withdraw, 1990 L
  John McCarthy released, 1991 H
  Terry Waite released, 1991 L
Bel Ami (G. de Maupassant), 1885 U
Belarus, Commonwealth of Independent States (CIS), 1991 M
Belfast, Northern Ireland:
  riots in 1920 G, 1935 G
  rioting, 1969 H, K, 1971 D
  troops dismantle barricades, 1969 J
  security forces search for arms, 1970 G
  off-duty soldiers murdered, 1971 C
  demonstrations against IRA leaders, 1971 C
  British troop reinforcements, 1971 C
  Orange parade shootings, 1971 D
  deaths from fighting between IRA and troops, 1971 H, 1972 F
  terrorist attacks, 1971 M, 1972 C, G
  Protestant 'no go' areas, 1972 E, G
  Ulster Freedom Fighters murder SDLP Senator Paddy Wilson, 1973 F
  peace march, 1976 H
  'Shankill butchers' sentenced, 1979 B
  Unionist MP murdered, 1981 L
  Anglo-Irish Agreement conference, 1985 M
Belfry of Bruges, The (H. W. Longfellow), 1846 U
Belgium: declared independent of Austria, 1789 M; Britain withholds recognition, 1790 A; revolution in, suppressed, 1790 M; French liberate, 1793 C; incorporated with France, 1795 K; ceded to France, 1797 K; independence, 1830 L; Holland forced to recognise, 1832 M; recognised by Treaty of London, 1839 D; neutrality, guaranteed by Prussia, 1870 H; Germany invades, 1914 H, 1940 E; capitulates to Germany, 1940 E; Allies liberate, 1944 L
  division of, 1980 H
  Parliament approves deployment of Cruise missiles, 1985 C
  divorce statistic, 1987 Y
  abortion legalized, 1990 D
  life expectancy, 1990 Y
  Flemish extremists, 1991 L
  general election, 1991 L
  constitution changed to allow women to accede to the throne, 1991 O
  illegitimacy rate, 1991 Y
  coalition government formed following political crisis, 1992 C
Belgrade, Yugoslavia: Joseph II fails to capture, 1788 K; Austrians take, 1789 K; Russians capture, 1811 B; bombarded by Turkey, 1862 F; Austrians capture, 1914 M; occupation by Austrians and Germans, 1915 K; Pact of Assistance, 1937 C; British minister withdrawn from, 1941 C; liberated, 1944 K; Conference on R. Danube, 1948 G; meeting of non-aligned powers at, 1961 J; university, 1964 O
Bélisaire (J. F. Marmontel), 1767 R
Belize (formerly British Honduras), 1973 F
  independence within commonwealth, 1981 J
Bell Telephone Company, 1848 P, 1954 P, 1956 P
Bell for Adano, A (J. Hersey), 1945 U
Bell, Andrew, B. educationalist (1750–1832), 1797 O
Bell, Sir Charles, B. neurologist (1774–1842), 1807 P, 1811 P, 1830 P
Bell, Clive, B. art critic (1881–1964), 1881 Z, 1922 S, 1964 Z
Bell, George Kennedy Allen, B. churchman, bishop of Chichester (1883–1958), 1948 R
Bell, Gertrude Margaret Lowthian, B. traveller and archaeologist (1868–1926), 1868 Z, 1926 Z
Bell, Graham Alexander, Am. inventor and physicist (1847–1922), 1847 Z, 1876 P, 1922 Z
Bell, Henry, B. marine engineer (1767–1830), 1783 P, 1812 P
Bell, John, Am. politician, Constitutional Unionist (1797–1869), 1860 L
Bell, Susan Jocelyn, B. astronomer (b. 1943), 1967 P
Bellamy, Edward, Am. author (1850–98), 1888 U
Bellamy, Joyce M., B. historian, 1972 Q
Bellini, Vincenzo, It. musician (1810–35), 1801 Z, 1827 T, 1831 T, 1835 Z
Belloc, Hilaire, B. author (1870–1953), 1895 U, 1902 U, 1925 Q
Bellow, Saul, Am. author (b. 1915), 1954 U, 1959 U, 1964 U, 1975 U, 1982 U, 1988 U
Belluschi, Pietro, Am. architect (b. 1899), 1970 S
Belorussians, percentage in Soviet population, 1989 Y
Beloved (T. Morrison), 1987 U
Bemis Heights, New York, US, battles, 1777 J, K
Ben Barka, Mehdi, Moroccan Left leader, kidnapped, 1965 K
Ben Bella, Ahmed, premier of Algeria, 1962 J; deposed, 1965 F
Ben-Gurion, David, Israeli statesman (1886-73), 1886 Z, 1973 Z; becomes premier, 1948 E; resigns, 1951 B; forms coalition, 1951 K; resigns, 1953 M; forms ministries, 1955 L, 1961 L
Ben-Zvi, Itzhak, president of Israel, 1952 M
Benares, India, Rajah of, deposed, 1781 F
Bend in the River, A (V.S. Naipaul), 1979 U
Benedict XV, Pope (1914–22), Giacomo della Chiesa, It., 1917 H, 1922 B
Benefit Societies, 1769 O
Benefit of Clergy, in Britain, abolished, 1827 F
Beneix, Jean-Jacques, film director, 1981 W, 1986 W
Benelux countries, full economic union of Belgium, Netherlands and Luxembourg, 1949 C
Beneš, Eduard, Czech statesman (1884–1948), 1935 M, 1938 K, 1945 D
Benét, Stephen Vincent, Am. poet (1898–1943), 1928 U
Benfica, Port. soccer team, 1968 X
Bengal Asiatic Society, 1784 Q
Bengal Atlas (J. Rennell), 1779 P
Bengal, India: Clive's reforms, 1765 E; British settlement of, 1793 N
Benghazi, Cyrenaica, Libya: British occupy, 1941 A, B; evacuate, 1941 D; recapture, 1941 M; occupation by 8th Army, 1942 M
Benin, Nigeria
  British occupation, 1897 N
  declaration of independence, 1967 J
Benjamin, George William John, musician (b. 1960), 1987 T
Benjedid, Chadli, Algerian President, 1992 A

Benn, Anthony Neil Wedgwood (formerly Viscount Stansgate), B. Socialist politician (b. 1925), 1966 G, 1984 C; election court rules disqualification through succession to peerage, 1961 O; disclaims peerage, 1963 G
attacks British EEC membership, 1974 M
defeated in deputy leadership election, 1981 J
Bennett, Alan, B. dramatist (b. 1934), 1934 Z, 1968 W, 1983 W, 1991 W
Bennett, Arnold, B. novelist (1867–1931), 1867 Z, 1908 U, 1910 U, 1919 W, 1923 U, 1931 Z
Bennett, Dr. Gareth Vaughan, B. historian and clergyman (1929–87), 1987 R
Bennett, Joan, Am. film actress (1910–1990), 1910 Z
Bennett, Richard Rodney, B. musician (b. 1936), 1964 T, 1967 T
Bennett, Richard, Viscount Bennett, Canad. Conservative politician (1870–1947), 1930 H, 1936 F
Bennett, Sir Hubert, B. architect, 1968 S
Bennigsen, Rudolf von, G. Liberal leader (1824–1902), 1859 G, 1866 L
Bennington, Vermont, US, battle, 1777 H
Benoit, biologist, 1959 P
Benson, Sir Francis ('Frank') Robert, B. actor-manager (1858–1939), 1858 Z, 1939 Z
Bent (M. Sherman), 1979 W
Bentham, Jeremy, B. writer on jurisprudence (1748–1832), 1776 O, 1787 O, 1789 O, 1791 O, 1802 O, 1824 V, 1832 Z, 1834 O
Bentham, Sir Samuel, B. engineer (1787–1831), 1793 P
Bentinck, Lord George Cavendish, B. Tory politician (1802–48), 1849 B
Bentinck, Lord William Cavendish, B. Indian administrator (1774–1834), as governor-general, 1829 O, 1832 H
Bentinck, William Henry Cavendish, Duke of Portland, B. Tory leader, becomes nominal premier, 1783 D; becomes premier, 1807 C, D; resigns, 1809 J
Bentley, John Francis, B. architect (1839–1902), 1903 S
Bentwich, Norman, B. lawyer and Jewish leader (1883–1965), 1944 O
Benz, Karl, G. motor manufacturer (1844–1929), 1885 P, 1893 P
Benzene, is isolated, 1824 P; structure of, 1865 P
Beowulf, editions of, 1815 Q, 1833 Q
Beran, Archbishop of Prague, release of, 1963 K
Béranger, Pierre Jean de, F. poet (1780–1857), 1815 U
Berbers, in Morocco, French action against, 1934 B
Berbice, B. Guiana, taken by British, 1796 N; retained by Britain, 1814 H
Berbick, Trevor, Canad. boxer (b. 1952), 1986 X
Berchtesgaden, Bavaria, W. Germany, Chamberlain visits, 1938 J
Berchtold, Count, Aus. foreign minister, 1912 H
Berdyaev, Nicolas, B. philosopher, 1950 R
Berenguer, Damaso, Sp. general and politician, 1930 A
Berenson, Bernhard, Am. art critic (1865–1959), 1950 S
Beresford, Maurice, B. historian (b. 1920), 1967 Q
Beresina, River, Russia, French disaster at, 1812 L
Berg, Alban, Aus. musician (1885–1935), 1885 Z, 1926 T, 1935 T, Z, 1979 T
Berg, Max, G. architect, 1910 S
Bergen-op-Zoom, Holland, 1799 J
Bergendal, S. Africa, Botha's defeat at, 1900 H
Berger, John, B. author (b. 1926), Booker Prize, 1972 U
Bergman, Ingmar, Swe. film director (b. 1918), 1952 W, 1955 W, 1956 W, 1957 W, 1962 W, 1963 W, 1964 W, 1972 W, 1982 W
Bergman, Torbern Olof, Swe. chemist (1735–84), 1774 P
Bergmann, R., G. philosopher, 1955 R
Bergson, Henri, F. philosopher (1859–1941), 1859 Z, 1889 R, 1896 R, 1900 R, 1907 R, 1909 R, 1919 R, 1932 R
Beria, Leonid, R. minister of internal affairs, 1953 G
Bericht über die Wissenschaftslehre (J. G. Fichte), 1806 Q
Bering Sea, N. Pacific, seal fishery, 1892 B
Bering Strait, survey of coasts, 1778 P
Berio, Luciano, It. musician (b. 1925), 1925 Z, 1968 T, 1970 T, 1976 T, 1982 T, 1984 T, 1988 T
Berkeley, Sir George, B. colonial administrator (1819–1905), 1872 K
Berkeley, Sir Lennox Randal Francis, B. musician (1903–89), 1903 Z, 1940 T, 1943 T, 1954 T, 1989 Z
Berkoff, Steven, B. film and theatre director (b. 1937), 1977 W, 1991 W
Berlin, Germany:
Napoleon occupies, 1806 K
Napoleon's decrees, 1806 L
revoked, 1810 L
Napoleon threatens to invade, 1811 K
Conference between Prussia, Russia and Austria on integrity of Ottoman Empire, 1833 K
revolution in, 1848 E
Treaty, between Prussia and Denmark, 1850 G
meeting of Three Emperors at, 1872 J
Memorandum on armistice in Bulgaria, 1876 E
Congress on Eastern Question, 1878 F, G
Treaty on Eastern Question, 1878 G
adjustment to, 1880 L, 1881 G
Conference on Africa, 1884 L
Congress for protection of workers, 1890 C
Copyright Convention, 1908 O
air service to, 1912 P
political parties in, 1916 A
strikes in, 1918 A
revolution in, 1918 L
Spartacist revolt in, 1919 A
Kapp's attempted coup in, 1920 C
Treaty, between Germany and Latvia, 1920 E
Conference on German currency, 1922 L
Treaty between Germany and Russia, 1926 D
Olympic Games in, 1936 X
Mussolini visits 1937 J
bombing of, 1943 B, 1955 A, C
protests in Parliament against, 1944 A
Russians reach, 1945 D
surrenders to Allies, 1945 E
Allied occupation of, 1945 G
interference to communications, 1948 D
Russian blockade and Anglo-US airlift, 1948 G, K, 1949 E, J
E. Reuter as mayor, 1948 M
Cultural Freedom Congress, 1950 O
Communist Youth Rally, 1951 H
World Peace Council, 1951 O
anti-Communist rising, 1953 F
foreign ministers meet in, 1954 A
Dulles's speech in, 1958 E
NATO Council rejects Russian proposals on, 1958 M
US aircraft buzzed in air corridor, 1959 C
blockade by E. Germany, 1960 H
Wall constructed, 1961 H
passes agreement for crossing, 1964 J
Brandenburg Gate closed, 1961 H
attempted assassination of Rudi Dutschke, 1968 D
visas required by West Berliners to cross to East Germany, 1968 F
National gallery, 1968 S
telephone service re-established, 1971 A
anniversary celebrations of Wall, 1981 H, 1986 H
Martin Gropius Bau, 1982 S
'La Belle' discotheque bomb attack, West Berlin, 1986 D
Wall demolished, 1989 L
Brandenburg Gate reopened, 1989 M
vote to return government to, 1991 F
musical events in, 1829 T, 1882 T
places in:
A.E.G. Turbine factory, 1908 S
Atlas Museum, 1824 S
Brandenburg Gate, 1719 S, closure of, 1961 H
Charlottenburg Technical High School, 1884 O
Frederick the Great monument, 1851 S
Gustav Adolf Kirche, 1934 S
Museum of Twentieth Century, 1963 S
National Theatre in, 1796 W
Schauspielhaus, 1819 S
University, 1810 O, 1818 Q
population, 1801 Y, 1941 Y, 1881 Y, 1906 Y, 1950 Y
Berlin, Irving, Am. musician (1888–1989), 1888 Z, 1911 T, 1950 W, 1989 Z
Berlin, Sir Isaiah, B. philosopher (b. 1909), 1909 Z, 1969 R
Berliner Ensemble, 1949 W
Berliner, Emil, G. inventor (1851–1929), 1887 P
Berlinguer, Enrico, It. Communist leader (1922–84), 1976 B
Berlioz, Hector, F. musician (1803–69), 1803 Z, 1834 T, 1837 T, 1838 T, 1846 T, 1844 T, 1854 T, 1855 T, 1863 T, 1869 Z, 1899 T
Bermuda (or Somers Islands):
Conference on Refugees, 1943 D
Churchill and Eisenhower meet in, 1953 M
governor assassinated, 1973 C
election victory for United Bermuda Party, 1989 B
Bernadotte, Folke, Count, Swe. statesman (d. 1948), as UN mediator in Palestine, 1948 J
Bernadotte, Jean, F. general, as heir to Charles XIII of Sweden, 1810 H, 1818 B. *See also* Charles XIV
Bernal, John Desmond, B. physicist (1901–64), 1949 O
Bernanos, Georges, F. author (1888–1948), 1931 U, 1936 U
Bernard, Claude, F. physiologist (1813–78), 1813 Z, 1850 P, 1854 P, 1878 Z
Bernard, Tristram, F. dramatist (1866–1947), 1905 W
Berne, Switzerland: French occupy, 1798 C, Union general des postes at, 1874 O; International Socialist Conference at, 1919 B; Polish embassy seige, 1982 J
Bernhard, Thomas, Aus. dramatist (b. 1931), 1974 W
Bernhardt, Sarah, F. actress (1845–1923), 1845 Z, 1862 W, 1881 W, 1923 Z; as film actress, 1912 W; portrait, 1879 S
Bernstein, Leonard, Am. musician (1918–90) , 1918 Z, 1950 T, 1958 W, 1964 T, 1965 T, 1970 T, 1983 T, 1990 Z

Bernstorff, Andreas Peter, Count, Da. statesman (1735–97), 1784 E
Bernstorff, Johann Hartwig Ernst, Count von (1712–72), 1770 J
Berri, Claude, F. film director (b. 1934), 1986 W
Berry, Charles Ferdinand, Duc de, heir to French throne, 1820 B, J
Berry, Duchesse de, F. Legitimist, 1832 L
Berryman, John, Am. author (1914–72), 1914 Z, 1956 U, 1964 U, 1972 Z
Berthollet, Claude Louis, F. chemist (1748–1822), 1785 P, 1803 P
Bertillon, Louis Adolphe, F. statistician (1821–83), 1883 P, 1890 O
Bertolucci, Bernardo, It. film director (b. 1940), 1973 W, 1974 W, 1987 W
Bertrand, Joseph Louis François, F. mathematician (1822–85), 1864 P
Berzelius, Jöns Jacob, Swe. chemist (1779–1848), 1814 P
Besançon, Doubs, France, Parlement of, 1783 G
Besant, Sir Walter, B. author (1836–1901), 1882 W
Bessarabia, Russia: Russia restores conquests in, to Tukey, 1792 A; Russia obtains, 1812 E; Austria demands Russian cession of, 1855 M; ceded by Russia, 1856 C; disturbances in, 1878 G; proclaims independence, 1917 M; Russia demands cession of, 1940 F; Russian offensive in, 1944 H; Rumania cedes to Russia, 1947 B
Bessel, Friedrich Wilhelm, G. astronomer (1784–1846), 1818 P
Bessemer, Sir Henry, B. engineer (1813–98), 1813 Z, 1856 P, 1859 P, 1878 P, 1898 Z
Bessenyei, György, Hun. dramatist (1747–1811), 1772 W
Best, Geoffrey Francis Andrew, B. historian (b. 1928), 1971 Q
Beta Pictoris, star, planet system photographed, 1984 P
Bethell, Leslie Michael, B. historian (b. 1937), 1984 Q
Bethlehem, Pa., US, Bach Festival in, 1900 T
Bethmann-Hollweg, Theobald von, G. statesman (1856–1921), as Chancellor, 1909 G, 1912 G; resigns, 1917 G
Betjeman, Sir John, B. poet (1906–84), 1906 Z, 1954 U, 1960 U, 1972 U, 1984 Z
Betrayal (H. Pinter), 1978 W
Betti, Ugo, It. dramatist, 1955 W
Betting, lotteries and gaming, Royal Commission on, 1951 O
Between Two Worlds (U. Sinclair), 1940 U
Beuys, Joseph, G. artist (1921–86), 1921 Z, 1974 S, 1979 S, 1983 S, 1986 Z
Bevan, Aneurin, B. Socialist (1897–1960), 1897 Z, 1944 D; becomes Minister of Labour, 1951 A; resigns from Cabinet, 1951 D; elected Treasurer of Labour Party, 1956 J; death, 1960 G
Beveridge, William Henry, lord Beveridge, B. economist (1879–1963), 1879 Z, 1909 O, 1944 O, 1963 Z
  Plan for Social Security, 1942 O
    policy over, 1943 B
Bevin, Ernest, B. trade union leader and statesman (1881–1951), 1881 Z, 1946 M, 1951 Z; becomes Minister of Labour, 1940 E; becomes Foreign Secretary, 1945 G; resigns, 1951 C
Bewick, Thomas, B. wood-engraver (1753–1823), 1797 P, 1800 U
Bexhill, Sussex, England, 1935 S
Beyle, Marie Henri, F. author under pseudonym 'Stendhal' (1783–1842), 1783 Z, 1822 U, 1823 U, 1830 U, 1839 U, 1842 Z
Beyond Good and Evil (F. Nietzsche), 1886 U
Beyond Human Endurance (B. Björnson), 1883 U
Beyond the Horizon (O'Neill), 1920 W
Bhoosnurmath, S.S., writer, 1984 U
Bhopal, India, Union Carbide accident, 1984 M
Bhowani Junction (J. Masters), 1954 U
Bhutto, Benazir, Prime Minister of Pakistan (b. 1953), 1990 K, 1992 L
  elected Prime Minister, 1988 L
  dismissal, 1990 H
Bhutto, Zulfikar Ali, Pakis. leader (1928–79), 1971 M, 1973 H
  claims election victory, but fraud alleged, 1977 C
  death sentence passed on, 1978 C
  executed, 1979 D
Biafra
  secession from Nigeria leads to civil war, 1967 E
  leader exiled on surrender to Nigeria, 1970 A
Biarritz, France, Napoleon III meets Bismarck at, 1865 K
Biberach, Bad-Württ., Germany, Austrian defeat at, 1800 E
Bible in Spain, The (G. Borrow), 1843 U
Bible, The:
  New Testament, editions:
    Basic English, 1949 R
    Greek (ed. Westcott and Hort), 1881 Q
    Knox translation, 1946 Q
    Lutheran revision, 1956 R
    Moffatt's translation, 1913 R
    New English Bible, 1961 Q
    Revised Version, 1870 R, 1881 R
    studies and commentaries, 1775 Q, 1846 Q, 1919 R, 1941 R
  Old Testament, studies, 1776 Q, 1779 R, 1783 R, 1862 R
    Codex Sinaiticus, 1844 Q, 1859 Q
    Dead Sea Scrolls, 1947 Q, 1960 Q
Bibliographical Society, 1842 Q
Bibliotheca Historica Medii Aevi (ed. G. Potthast), 1862 Q
Bicess Peace Accord, 1992 L
Bichat, Marie François Xavier, F. anatomist and physiologist (1771–1802), 1771 Z, 1801 P, 1802 Z
Bicycle, Motor, 1901 P
Bicycle: 'bone-shaker', 1865 P; P. Michaux's, 1867 P; American, 1878 P; 'Rover' safety 1885 P; pennyfarthing, world tour on, 1886 W
Bidassoa, Spain, River, 1813 K
Bidault, Georges, F. politician (1899–1983), elected president of provisional government, 1946 F; forms coalition, 1949 K; resigns premiership, 1950 F
Biddle, James, Am. naval officer (1783–1848), 1846 N
Bielefeld, N. Rhine, Germany, epileptic hospital, 1868 O
Bielicki, Jan Krzysztof, Prime Minister of Poland (b. 1951), 1990 M
Biermann, Wolf, G. poet (b. 1936), 1965 U
Bierstadt, Albert, Am. formerly G. artist (1830–1902), 1878 S
Bierut, M., Pol. Communist, forms ministry, 1952 L
Bigelow, E. B., Am. inventor (1814–79), 1845 P
Biglow Papers, The (J.R. Lowell), 1848 U
Bignone, General Reynaldo Benito, President of Argentina (b. 1928), 1982 F
Bihar, India, food riots, 1974 C
Bikini, Marshall Islands, Pacific, US hydrogen bomb tests, in, 1954 P
Biko, Steve, S. African leader (1946–77), killed in police custody, 1977 J
Bilbao, Spain, rebels take, 1937 F
Bilderdijck, Willem, Du. poet (1756–1831), 1786 U
Bildt, Carl, Prime Minister of Sweden (b. 1949), 1991 J, 1992 B
Bill Cosby Show, The, television series, 1969 W
Billingham, Co. Durham, England, 1935 P
Billroth, Albert Christian Theodor, Aus. surgeon (1829–94), 1872 P
Biloxi Blues (N. Simon), 1984 W
Binaisa, Godfrey Lukwongwa, President of Uganda (b. 1920), 1979 F
Bing Girls, The, a revue, 1916 W
Bingo (E. Bond), 1973 W
Biochemistry, science of, founded, 1838 P
Biogen, Swiss laboratory, 1980 P
Biographical Dictionary of British Architects, A, 1600–1840 (H. Colvin), 1978 Q
Biological Sciences
  citric acid cycle in cells described, 1932 P
  Cortisone isolated, 1935 P
  structure of ecdysone determined, 1966 P
  in vitro fertilization of human egg cells, 1969 P
  molecular biology, 1976 P
  European Molecular Biology Laboratory, Heidelberg, 1979 P
  monoclonal antibody OKT3, 1986 P
  fossils of oldest known multi-cellular animals discovered, 1990 P
  sperm cells discovered to have odour receptors, 1992 P
  Deoxyribonucleic acid (DNA). *See* Deoxyribonucleic acid
  genetics. *See* Genetics
Biological Weapons, 1971 H
  destruction of US stocks ordered, 1969 L
  multilateral convention prohibiting stock-piling, 1972 D
  international declaration outlawing, 1989 A
Biology, term first used, 1802 P; first International Congress on, 1821 P
Biot, France, 1960 S
Bir Hakeim, Cyrenaica, Libya, French surrender at, 1942 F
Birch, Evelyn Nigel Chetwode, B. Conservative politician (1906–81), resigns, 1958 A
Bird Cage (J. Cage), 1972 S
Bird and the White Tablecloth, The (A.F. Abrahamren), 1985 U
Bird of Dawning, The (J. Masefield), 1933 U
Birds of America (J. J. Audubon), 1830 P
Birdseye, Clarence, Am. pioneer of frozen food, 1925 P
Birkbeck Bank, London, fails, 1911 F
Birkbeck, George, B. founder of mechanics' institutes (1776–1841), 1823 O
Birkenhead, Earl of. *See* Smith, Frederick Edwin
Birmingham Six, 1975 F
  released, 1991 C
Birmingham, Alabama, US, school desegregation riots in, 1963 J
Birmingham, England: Boulton's works at, 1775 P, 1802 W; co-operative workshop at, 1777 O; riots, 1791 G; Chartist rising, 1839 G; Repertory Company, 1909 W, 1913 W, 1919 W; surgery at, 1960 P; riots, 1985 J
Biro, Georg, Hun. inventor, 1938 P
Birth Control: F. Place advocates, 1822 O; M. Stopes's campaign, 1922 O; New York clinic, 1923 O; through phosphorated hesperidin in tablets ('the pill'), 1952 P; Roman Catholic rulings against use of, 1964 R, 1968 R
Birthday Party, The (H. Pinter), 1958 W

Births, Registration of, in Britain, 1836 H
Birtwistle, Sir Harrison, B. musician (b. 1934), 1968 T, 1972 T, 1979 T, 1983 T, 1986 T, 1991 T
Biscia, Eritrea, British take, 1941 A
Biscuit manufacture, by steam process, 1841 P
Bishop, Maurice, Prime Minister of Grenada (1944–83), 1979 C, 1983 K
Bismarck Archipelago, N.E. New Guinea, annexed by Germany, 1885 E
Bismarck, Otto Eduard Leopold von, Prince, G. statesman (1815–98), 1815 Z, 1864 K, 1898 Z; becomes minister president of Prussia, 1862 J; 'Blood and Iron' speech, 1862 J; rules without budget, 1862 K; meets Napoleon III, 1865 K; indemnified for unconstitutional rule, 1866 J; begins *Kulturkampf*, 1871 G; remodels Prussian local government, 1872 M; plot against, 1874 K; preserves *entente* with Russia, 1875 B; declines to mediate in Russo-Turkish War, 1877 M; proposes legislation against Radicals, 1878 E; at Congress of Berlin, 1878 F; introduces sickness insurance, 1883 E; organises Berlin Conference on Africa, 1884 L; advocates larger army, 1887 A; publishes Germano-Austrian alliance, 1888 B; dismissed, 1890 C; memoirs, 1898 O
Biswas, Abdur Rahman, President of Bangladesh, 1991 K
Bitlis, Turkey, Russians take, 1916 C
Bitter Sweet (N. Coward), 1929 W
Biya, Paul, President of Cameroon (b. 1933), 1992 K
Bizerta, Tunisia: seized by French, 1881 D; accepts French protectorate, 1881 E; Allies take, 1943 E; banned to French warships, 1958 B; de Gaulle states French will not evacuate until end of crisis, 1961 H
Bizet, Georges, F. musician (1838–75), 1838 Z, 1867 T, 1872 T, 1875 Z
Björkö, Treaty, between Germany and Russia, 1905 G
Björnson, Björnstjerne, Nor. author (1832–1910), 1857 U, 1883 U, 1889 U
Bjoerling, Jussi, Swe. opera singer (1911–60), 1911 Z, 1960 Z
Blacher, Boris, G. musician (1903–75), 1969 T
Black Dogs (I. McEwan), 1992 U
Black Force (R. Wright), 1954 O
Black Lamb and Grey Fox: A Journey Through Yugoslavia in 1937 (R. West), 1941 U
Black List, British, for war-time trade, 1916 B, G
Black Market, 1941 M, 1945 O
Black Nana (N. de Saint Phalle), 1969 S
Black Panthers, 1972 U
Black Prince, The (I. Murdoch), 1973 U
Black Reichwehr *coup d'état* fails, 1923 K
Black Sea: Russian Fleet for, 1776 N; Royal Navy sent into, 1854 A; neutrality of, 1855 M, 1856 C; repudiated, 1871 C
Black and White (S. Naipaul), 1980 U
Black and White Minstrel Show, 1978 W
Black, Conrad, Canad. newspaper proprietor (b. 1944)
Telegraph newspapers, 1985 V
Fairfax Group, 1991 V
Black, Sir James Whyte, B. pharmacologist (b. 1924), 1924 Z
Black, Joseph, B. engineer (1728–99), 1764 P, 1769 P
Black, Max, Am. philosopher (b. 1909), 1968 R
Black-out, in Britain, relaxed, 1944 O
Blackadder, television series, 1983 W
Blackburne, Francis, B. divine (1705–87), 1766 R
Blackett, Patrick Maynard Stuart, Baron Blackett, B. physicist (1897–1974), 1897 Z, 1922 P, 1947 P, 1948 O, 1974 Z
Blackley, William Lewery, B. churchman and advocate of old-age pensions (1830–1902), 1879 O
Blackmore, Richard Doddridge, B. novelist (1825–1900), 1869 T
Blackstone, Sir William, B. judge (1723–80), 1765 O, 1780 Z
Blackwell Dictionary of Historians, The (Cannon, J., et al. eds.), 1988 Q
Blackwell Encyclopedia of the American Revolution, The (J.P. Greene, J.R. Pole eds.), 1991 Q
Blackwood, Algernon, B. author (1869–1951), 1906 U, 1916 W
Blackwood, Frederick Temple Hamilton-Temple, Marquess of Dufferin and Alva, B. statesman (1826–1902), report on Egypt, 1883 E
Blaine, James Gillespie, Am. Republican politician (1830–93), loses presidential election, 1884 L
Blair, Eric, B. author under pseudonym of 'George Orwell' (1903–50), 1937 U, 1945 U, 1949 W
Blair, Hugh, B. Presbyterian divine (1718–1800), 1777 R
Blake, George, B. spy (b. 1922), 1961 E, O, 1966 K
Blake, William, B. poet and artist (1757–1827), as poet, 1783 U, 1789 U, 1794 U, 1804 U; as artist, 1820 S
Blakelock, Keith, B. policeman, murdered, 1985 K
Blanc, Louis, F. politician and economist (1811–82), 1811 Z, 1839 O, 1841 O, 1847 O, 1848 B, 1882 Z
Blanchard, Jean Pierre, F. balloonist (1753–1809), 1785 P
Blanco, Antonio Guzman, president of Venezuela, 1889 K
Blanco, Luis Carrero, Sp. vice-premier (1903–73), 1973 F
assassination, 1973 M
Bland, R. P., Am. Congressman, 1878 B
Blankenburg, Germany, kindergarten at, 1837 O
Blanketeers, March of, 1817 C
Blasco, Ibáñez, Sp. author, 1919 U
Blauer Reiter ('Blue Rider'), group of artists, 1911 S
Blavatsky, Helena Petrovina, R. theosophist (1831–1891), 1875 R
Bleach, Chlorine used as a, 1785 P
Bleaching powder, process for making, 1870 P
Bleasdale, Alan, B. dramatist (b. 1946), 1982 W, 1991 W
Blennerhasset's Island, US, 1806 N
Blériot, Louis, F. aviator (1872–1936), 1872 Z, 1909 P, 1936 Z
Blind, schools for, 1791 O
Blindfold Horse, The (S. Guppy), 1989 U
Bliss (K. Mansfield), 1920 U
Bliss, Arthur, B. musician (1891–1975), 1891 Z, 1922 T, 1937 T, 1952 T, 1960 T, 1963 T, 1975 Z
Blithe Spirit (N. Coward), 1941 W
Bloch, Ernest, Am. musician (1880–1959), 1880 Z, 1924 T, 1925 T, 1953 T, 1959 Z
Blockade, defined, 1856 D
Blockades:
by Britain, of France and her Allies, 1806 D, 1807 A, L, 1809 D
of Germany, 1915 B, C, 1940 D
of Greece, 1916 F
of US, 1811 L, 1812 F
Bloemfontein, S. Africa: Convention, 1854 B; Roberts captures, 1900 C
Blok, Alexander, R. poet (1880–1921), 1918 U
Blond on Blond (B. Dylan), 1966 W
Blondie, Am. pop group, 1978 W
Blondin, pseudonym of Jean François Gravelet, F. tight-rope walker and acrobat (1824–97), 1859 W
Blood Relations (S. Pollock), 1981 W
Blood River, Natal, Zulus defeated at, 1838 M
Blood pressure, recorded by kymograph, 1865 P
Blood, treatise on the, 1794 P
Bloom, Allan, Am. philosopher and critic (1930–93), 1987 O
Bloom, Claire, B. actress (b. 1931), 1952 W
Bloomer, Amelia Jenks, Am. reformer of women's clothes (1818–94), 1849 O
Bloomfield, Maurice, B. orientalist, 1907 Q
Bloomfield, Robert, B. rustic poet (1766–1823), 1800 U
Blount, James H., Am. diplomat, 1893 B
Blücher, Gebhard Leberecht von, Prussian general (1742–1819), 1813 H, 1814 B; crosses Rhine, 1813 M; at Waterloo, 1815 F
'Blue babies', operations, 1944 O
Blue Bird, The (M. Maeterlinck), 1909 W
Blue Highways (W.L. Moon), 1983 U
Blue Night in the Heart of the West (J. Stock), 1991 W
Blue Streak, missile, 1964 P
Bluebells and other verse, The (J. Masefield), 1961 U
Bluebird, driven by M. Campbell, 1935 P
'Blue Shirts', in Ireland, 1933 G
Bluff Cove, Falkland Islands, 1982 F
Blum, Léon, F. Socialist (1872–1950), 1872 Z, 1935 L, 1950 Z; forms Popular Front ministry, 1936 F; resigns, 1937 F; forms Popular Front ministry, 1938 C; supports Daladier, 1938 D; becomes premier, 1946 M; resigns, 1947 A
Blunt, Anthony, B. art expert and Soviet spy (1907–83), 1979 L
Blyton, Enid, B. author (1897–1968), 1897 Z, 1949 U, 1968 Z
Boat Race, Oxford and Cambridge, 1829 W, 1978 X, 1984 X, 1986 X
'Bobbed hair', 1917 O
Bobbin net machine, 1809 P
Boccherini, Luigi, It. musician (1743–1805), 1787 T
Boccioni, Umberto, It. sculptor (1882–1916), 1910 S
Böckh, Philipp August, G. classical scholar (1785–1867), 1817 Q, 1824 Q
Böcklin, Arnold, Swi. artist (1827–1901), 1827 Z, 1864 S, 1872 S, 1901 Z
Bode, Johann Elert, G. astronomer (1747–1826), 1774 P
Bodmer, Sir Walter, B. scientist (b. 1936), 1987 P
Body and Society, The (P. Brown), 1989 R
Boehm, Sir Joseph Edgar, B. formerly Aust. sculptor (1834–90), 1869 S
Boeing 747 'jumbo jet', 1969 P, 1970 P
Boers, in Natal, defeat Zulus, 1838 M
J. Chamberlain aims at conciliation, 1903 B
Boesak, Rev. Allan, S. Afr. churchman (b. 1946), arrest, 1985 H, R
Boesky, Ivan F., Am. securities dealer, 1986 L
Boesman and Lena (A. Fugard), 1970 W
Boff, Father Leonardo Genezia Darci, Brazilian theologian (b. 1938), 1984 R, 1985 R
Bogardus, James, Am. civil engineer (1800–74), 1851 P
Bohemia: ruled by Maria Theresa, 1765 H; Peasants' Revolt in, 1775 B; serfdom abolished, 1780 K; Germans occupy, 1939 C

Bohr, Niels, Da. physicist (1885–1962), 1913 P, 1922 P
Boïeldieu, François Adrien, F. musician (1775–1834), 1799 T
Boiler plating, by ductile steel, 1856 P
Boipatong massacre, South Africa, 1992 F
Bokassa, Colonel Jean-Bédel, Emperor of Central Afr. Repub. (b. 1921)
seizes power, 1966 A
proclaims Empire, 1976 M
coronation, 1977 M
overthrow, 1979 J
Bokhara, Russia, 1873 H
Boldrewood, Rolf. *See* Browne, T. A.
Bolger, James Brendan, Prime Minister of New Zealand (b. 1935), 1990 K
Bolívar, Simón, leader of S. American independence (1783–1830), 1783 Z, 1810 D, 1811 G, 1813 G, 1819 O, 1830 Z, invades Venezuela, 1816 B; organises independent Venezuela, 1817 K; declares Venezuela independent, 1818 L; in Colombia, 1820 L; defeats Spanish, 1821 F, 1824 H; as emperor of Peru, 1823 J; attempts to unite S. American republics, 1826 F; alleged tyranny of, 1827 A, abdicates in Colombia, 1830 D
Bolivia (or Upper Peru): becomes independent of Peru, 1825 H; federation with, Peru, 1836 K; dissolved, 1839 A; boundary with Chile settled, 1874 H
Tupamaros guerrillas escape prison, 1971 J
Pope John Paul II visits, 1988 E
Bologna, Italy, in Napoleonic campaigns, 1797 B, G, 1801 H; terrorist bomb, 1980 H
Bolometer, invented, 1881 P
Bolshoi Ballet, visits London, 1956 T
Bolt, Robert Oxton, B. dramatist (b. 1924), 1924 Z, 1957 W, 1960 W, 1966 W
Bomb, Atomic: plutonium for, 1944 P; dropped on Japan, 1945 H, P; Britain produces own, 1952 P; Russia's, 1949 P, 1950 C. *See also* Atomic Research; Nuclear Warfare; Test Ban
Bomb, Flying, 1944 F. *See also* Rockets
sites for launching, destroyed, 1944 J
Bomb, Hydrogen, 1950 A, 1952 L, 1954 D, 1953 P, 1954 P
Bombay, India: untouchables in, 1946 O; population, 1960 Y
Bon, Cape, Tunisia, Germans retire to, 1943 E
Bonald, Louis Gabriel Ambroise, Vicomte de, F. philosopher and politician (1754–1840), 1796 O
Bonanza Creek, Yukon, Canada, gold discovered at, 1897 P
Bonaparte Family, banished from France, 1886 F
Bonaparte et les Bourbons (Chateaubriand), 1814 O
Bonaparte, Charles Louis Napoleon. *See* Napoleon III
Bonaparte, Jerome, appointed King of Westphalia, 1807 H
Bonaparte, Joseph, King of Naples, 1806 C
Bonaparte, Louis, King of Holland, 1806 F
Bonaparte, Napoleon. *See* Napoleon I
Bond, Alan, Austral. entrepreneur (b. 1938), 1992 E
Bond, Edward, B. dramatist (b. 1934), 1971 W, 1973 W, 1981 W
Bond, George Phillips, Am. astronomer (1825–65), 1851 P
'Bond, James', 1953 S
Bondfield, Margaret Grace, B. Labour politician (1873–1953), 1873 Z, 1929 O, 1953 Z
Bone, Sir Muirhead, B. artist (1876–1953), 1940 S
Bonjour Tristesse (F. Sagan), 1954 U
Bonn Catalogue of Stars, 1862 P
Bonn Document, 1989 F
Bonn, Germany: university, 1818 O; becomes capital of Federal Republic, 1949 E; Eisenhower visits, 1959 H; vote to move government to Berlin from, 1991 F
Bonnard, Pierre, F. artist (1867–1947), 1908 S, 1909 S, 1942 S, 1965 S
Bonner, Yelena, R. dissident (b. 1923), 1984 E, 1986 M
sentenced to internal exile, 1984 H
Bonnet, Charles, Swi. naturalist and philosopher (1720–93), 1764 R, 1769 R
Bonneville Salt Flats, Utah, US, 1939 P
Bonnici, Dr. Carmello Mifsud, Prime Minister of Malta (b. 1933), 1984 M
Bonpland, Aimé Jacques Alexandre, F. traveller and botanist (1783–1858), 1807 P
Book of Common Prayer, A (J. Didion), 1977 U
Book of Daniel, The (E.L. Doctorow), 1971 U
Book of Days (M. Monk), 1988 T
Book of Laughter and Forgetting, The (M. Kundera), 1979 U
Book of Mormon (J. Smith), 1830 R
Book of Nonsense (E. Lear), 1846 U
Book of Sand, The (J.L. Borges), 1975 U
Book of the Thorn and the Rose (C. Almquist), 1832 U
Booker Prize for Fiction, 1969 U
Mosley resigns from jury, 1991 U
Boole, George, B. mathematician and philosopher (1815–64), 1847 P, 1854 R
Boomplatz, S. Africa, Boer defeat at, 1848 H
Boornazian, Aram A., Am. astronomer, 1979 P
Booth, Abraham, B. Baptist minister (1734–1806), 1768 R
Booth, Charles, B. sociologist (1840–1916), 1891 O
Booth, William, B. Evangelical leader (1829–1912), 1829 Z, 1865 R, 1878 R, 1890 O, 1912 Z
Boothroyd, Miss Betty, B. Labour politician (b. 1929), Speaker of House of Commons, 1992 O
Bophuthatswana, S. Africa, nominal independence, 1977 M
Bopp, Franz, G. philologist (1791–1867), 1816 Q, 1833 Q
Bordeaux, France: Wellington takes, 1814 C; National Assembly meets at, 1871 B; Government moved to, 1914 J
Borden, Sir Robert, Can. Unionist politician (1854–1937), as premier, 1911 K, 1917 M; resigns, 1920 G
Border Disputes and Conflicts:
Chad–Libya, 1983 C
Ethiopia–Somalia, 1988 D
Honduras–El Salvador, following World Cup qualifying round, 1969 G
Kenya–Somalia, 1967 K
Libya–Egypt border war, 1977 G
Mali–Burkina Faso, 1985 M
Syria–Israel, 1967 D
Tibet–Sikkim, 1967 J
USSR–China, 1969 C, 1969 H, 1987 B
Yemen, North–South Yemen, 1972 J
Borg, Bjorn, Swe. tennis player (b. 1956), 1980 X
Borges, Jorge Luis, Argent. author (1899–1986), 1899 Z, 1975 U, 1986 Z
Boring mill, 1774 P
Boris Godunov (Pushkin), 1825 U
Boris III, King of Bulgaria (1918–43), as Crown Prince, 1896 B
Born, Max, G. physicist (1882–1979), 1882 Z, 1926 P, 1979 Z
Borneo, North: British protectorate over, 1888 E; Philippines claim to, 1962 F; votes to join Malaysian Federation, 1962 J
Borodin, Alexander, R. musician (1834–87), 1834 Z, 1877 T, 1887 T, Z, 1890 T
Borodino, Russia, 1812 J
Borrow, George, B. author (1803–81), 1803 Z, 1843 U, 1851 U, 1857 U, 1881 Z
Bosanquet, Bernard, B. philosopher (1848–1923), 1888 R, 1923 Z
Boselli, Paolo, It. politician, forms coalition, 1916 F
Bosnia and Herzegovina, Yugoslavia: Russia agrees to Austrian annexation, 1908 J; Austria annexes, 1908 K; Turkey recognises, 1909 B
independence, 1991 K, 1992 C
independence formally recognized by EC, 1992 D
Serbian agression, 1992 E
Yugoslavian civil war. *See* Civil Wars
Bosnia, Yugoslavia: Russian intrigues in, 1767 N; rebellion in, 1875 G, M; reforms in, 1878 C
Bosphorus, The: closed to warships, 1841 G; Turkey recovers sovereignty over, 1936 G
Bossard, Frank, B. spy, 1965 E
Boston (U. Sinclair), 1928 U
Boston, Mass., US: riot, 1768 J; massacre, 1770 C; assembly threatens secession from Britain, 1772 B; 'Tea Party', 1773 M; Continental Army at, 1775 E; British evacuate, 1776 C; street-lighting in, 1822 P; Slavery Abolition Society, 1832 O; Lowell Institute, 1839 Q; Church of Christ Scientist, 1879 R; Symphony Orchestra, 1924 T; John Hancock Tower, 1975 S
Bostonians, The (H. James), 1886 U
Boswell's London Journal (ed. Pottle), 1950 Q
Boswell, James, B. author (1740–95), 1786 U, 1791 U, 1795 Z; meets Johnson, 1763 U
Botany Bay, Australia: discovered, 1770 P; penal settlement in, 1788 A
Botha, Louis, S. Afr. soldier and statesman (1862–1919), 1862 Z, 1899 M, 1900 H, 1915 G, 1919 Z; raid on Natal fails, 1901 B; meets Kitchener, 1901 B; forms *Het Volk*, 1905 A; on Transvaal constitution, 1905 D; founds S. African Party, 1910 D; becomes premier, 1910 J; ministerial changes, 1912 M; occupies Windhoek, 1915 E
Botha, Pieter Willem, S. African politician (b. 1916)
Prime Minister, 1978 J
confirms conflict in Angola, 1981 H
visits Britain, 1984 F
Executive President, 1984 J
President, 1985 A
SA commitment to apartheid re-stated and Parliamentary representation for blacks ruled out, 1985 H
pass laws abolished, 1986 D
state of emergency imposed, 1986 F
resignation as leader of National Party, 1989 B
Botswana, independence, 1966 J
Botta, Carlo Giuseppe Guglielmo, It. historian (1766–1837), 1824 Q
Böttinger, Karl August, G. archaeologist (1760–1835), 1811 Q
Bottle-making machine, 1898 P
Boubouroche (G. Courteline), 1893 W
Boucher, François, F. artist (1703–70), 1765 S, 1770 Z
Boucicault, Dion, Ir. actor and dramatist (1822–90), 1860 W
Boudiaf, Mohammed, President of Algeria, assassination, 1992 F
Bougainville, Louis Antoine de, F. navigator

(1729–1811), 1764 N, 1766 N, P
Bougainville, Solomon Isles, US task force at, 1943 L; peace agreement with secessionists, 1992 E
Boughton, Rutland, B. musician (1878–1960), 1878 Z, 1914 T
Boulanger, George Ernest Jean Marie, F. general (1837–91), 1887 K, 1888 C, D, 1889 A; becomes War minister, 1886 A; excluded from Rouvier's ministry, 1887 E; flight, 1889 D; suicide, 1891 J
Boule de Suif (G. de Maupassant), 1880 U
Boulez, Pierre, F. musician (b. 1925), 1925 Z, 1959 T, 1960 T, 1968 T, 1973 T, 1975 T, 1983 T
Boulin, Robert, F. politician (1920–79), 1979 K
Boulogne, France: Louis Napoleon's attempted rising, 1840 H; Conference at, 1916 K
Boult, Sir Adrian, B. musician (1889–1983), 1889 Z, 1930 T, 1983 Z
Boulton, Matthew, B. engineer (1728–1809), 1775 P, 1785 P, 1807 P
Boumedienne, Houari, Algerian general, 1965 F
Bound East (O'Neill), 1916 W
Bourbons of Naples, The (H. Acton), 1956 Q
Bourdelle, Antoine, F. sculptor (1861–1929), 1909 S, 1912 S
Bourgeois, Léon Victor Auguste, F. Radical politician and author (1851–1925), 1851 Z, 1895 L, 1920 M, 1925 Z
Bourgès-Manoury, F. Radical politician, forms ministry, 1957 F
Bourget, Paul Charles Joseph, F. author (1852–1935), 1883 U, 1885 U
Bourguiba, President of Tunisia and leader of Neo-Destour Party, 1956 C, 1957 H, 1959 L
Bourj-el-Barajneh refugee camp, Beirut, 1985 E, 1987 D
Bourke, Richard Southwell, Earl of Mayo, B. administrator (1822–72), viceroy of India, 1872 B
Bournville Village Trust, 1900 O
Boutros Ghali, Boutros, UN Secretary-General (b. 1922), 1992 A
Bouvard et Pécuchet (G. Flaibert), 1881 U
Bovine spongiform encephalopathy (BSE), 1990 E
Bowe, Riddick, Am. boxer (b. 1967), 1992 W
Bowell, Sir Mackenzie, Can. statesman, 1894 M
Bowen, Elizabeth Dorothea Cole, B. author (1899–1973), 1899 Z, 1938 U, 1949 U, 1970 U, 1973 Z
Bowie, David (born David Robert Jones), B. musician (b. 1947), 1972 W
Bowles, William Lisle, B. poet and antiquary (1762–1850), 1789 U
Bowring, Sir John, B. author and traveller (1792–1872), 1821 U, 1854 O
Boxer Rising, 1898 N, 1900 F, 1901 J
Boxing, world championships, 1970 X
Boxing:
with bare fists, 1860 X
Queensberry codifies rules, 1866 X
US national championship, 1910 X
world championships, 1908 X, 1930 X, 1936 X, 1965 X
Boy Scouts, 1907 O
Boy's Own Story, A (E. White), 1982 U
Boycott, Charles Cunningham, Ir. land-agent (1832–1897), 1880 N
Boycotts:
of British goods, by China, 1935 E
of S. African goods, by Ghana, 1959 G
by India, 1957 A
by Nigeria, 1961 D
Boyd, Arthur, Austral. artist (b. 1920), 1960 S
Boyd, William Andrew Murray, B. author (b. 1952), 1991 U
Boyer, Herbert, Am. scientist (b. 1936), 1936 Z, 1973 P
Boyle, Andrew Philip, B. author (1919–91), 1979 L, O
Boyle, Sir Edward Charles Gurney, B. Conservative politician (1923–1981), 1963 G
Boys from the Blackstuff, television programme, 1982 W
Boys in the Band, The (M. Crowley), 1969 W
Boys' Brigade, The, founded, 1883 O
Brabant, Belgium, constitution of, revoked, 1789 K
Brabham, Sir Jack, Austral. motor racing champion (b. 1926), 1966 X
Bracebridge Hall, or the Humourist (W. Irving), 1822 U
Bracher, Karl Dietrich, G. historian (b. 1922), 1969 Q
Bracken, Brendan, Viscount Bracken, B. journalist and Conservative politician (1901–58), 1941 G
Bradbury, Malcolm Stanley, author (b. 1932), 1983 U
Bradbury, Ray, Am. author (b. 1920), 1952 U
Bradford, Yorks, England, Independent Labour Party founded at, 1893 A
first SDP national conference, 1981 K
football stadium fire, 1985 X
Bradlaugh, Charles, B. politician and free-thinker (1833–91), 1860 V; refuses to take Parliamentary oath, 1880 E
Bradley, Francis Herbert, B. philosopher (1846–1924), 1846 Z, 1876 R, 1883 R, 1893 R, 1924 Z
Bradley, James, B. divine and astronomer (1693–1762), 1818 P
Bradley, Omar Nelson, Am. soldier (1893–1981), 1893 Z, 1944 H, 1981 Z
Bradley, Richard John, B. historian (b. 1946), 1978 Q
Bradman, Sir Donald, Austral. cricketer (b. 1908), 1908 Z, 1930 X, 1946 X
Bradshaw, George, B. originator of railway guides (1801–53), 1841 V
Braga, Theophilo, President of Portugal, 1910 K, 1915 E
Braganza, house of, flee from Portugal, 1807 L; return to Portugal, 1815 F
Bragg, Sir Lawrence, B. scientist (1890–1971), 1890 Z, 1915 P, 1971 Z
Bragg, Sir William, B. scientist (1862–1942), 1862 Z 1915 P, 1942 Z
Brahms, Johannes, G. musician (1833–97), 1833 Z, 1853 T, 1868 T, 1869 T, 1897 Z
double concerto, 1887 T
overtures, 1881 T
piano concertos, 1861 T, 1882 T
requiem, 1873 T
songs, 1896 T
symphonies, 1876 T, 1877 T, 1883 T, 1885 T
violin concerto, 1879 T
Braid, James, B. surgeon (?1795–1860), 1842 P
Braille, Louis, F. inventor of Braille system (1809–1852), 1934 P
Brailoff, Russia, battle, 1809 J
Brain drain, 1963 B, 1964 P
Brain, John Gerard, B. author (b. 1922), 1957 U
Brain, electric responses of, 1875 P
Brain, electronic, 1942 P, 1946 P
Brains Trust, BBC, 1941 W
Brainstorms (D. Dennett), 1978 R
Brainwashing, 1957 O
Brake, Westinghouse railway, 1868 P
Bramah, Joseph, B. locksmith (1748–1914), 1778 P, 1784 P, 1795 P
Branco, Humberto, President of Brazil, 1964 D
Brancusi, Constantin, It. sculptor (1876–1957), 1908 S, 1925 S, 1931 S
Brand (H. Ibsen), 1866 W
Brand, Henry Bouverie William, Viscount Hampden, B. politician and Speaker of the House of Commons (1814–92), 1881 A
Brandenberger, Edwin, Swi. inventor, 1912 P
Brandes, Georg, Dan. author (1842–1927), 1842 Z, 1868 U, 1872 Q, 1927 Z
Brandis, Christian August, G. philosopher and philologist (1790–1867), 1835 Q
Brandt, William, 'Bill', B. photographer (1905–83), 1905 Z, 1948 S, 1961 S, 1983 Z
Brandt, Willy, W. German leader (1913–92), 1913 Z, 1969 K, 1970 C
Nobel Peace Prize, 1971 K
resigns as Chancellor, 1974 E
Brandywine, Pa., US, battle, 1777 J
Brangwyn, Sir Frank, B. artist (1867–1956), 1904 S
Braniff International Corp., 1982 O
Branson, Richard, B. entrepreneur (b. 1950), 1991 A
Braque, Georges, F. artist and sculptor (1882–1963), 1911 T, 1914 S
Braschi, Giovanni Angelo, Pope Pius VI (1775–99), 1782 C
Brasilia, Brazil, becomes capital, 1960 O
buildings, 1957 S, 1958 S, 1960 S
Bratby, John Randall, B. artist (b. 1928), 1928 Z, 1954 S, 1955 S, 1956 S, 1958 S, 1959 S, 1960 S
Bratton, G., Am. engineer, 1873 P
Braun, Otto, G. politician, premier of Prussia, 1921 L
Braun, Werner von, G. scientist (1912–77), 1912 Z, 1938 P, 1977 Z
Braut von Messina, Die (F. Schiller), 1803 U
Brave New World (A. Huxley), 1932 U
Brave New World Revisited (A. Huxley), 1958 U
Brazil: becomes an empire, 1816 A; independence, 1822 K, 1823 F; recognised by Portugal, 1825 H; Dom Pedro's tyranny in, 1823 L; becomes a republic, 1889 L; coffee production in, 1909 Y
military junta takes control, 1969 H
population, 1971 Y, 1981 Y, 1991 Y
democratic government takes office, 1979 C
International Monetary Fund loan, 1983 B
illiteracy, 1983 Y
cotton production, 1984 Y
military rule ended, 1985 C
Mengele exhumed, 1985 F
urbanization, 1985 Y
torrential rain storm, 1988 B
debts rescheduled, 1988 J
presidential elections, 1989 M
Brazza, Pierre Paul François de, Count, F. explorer of Africa (1852–1905), 1880 F, 1886 D
Brazzaville Beach (W. Boyd), 1991 U
Brazzaville, Congo, 1960 G
Bread:
rationed in Britain, 1917 B, 1946 G, 1948 O
subsidy in Britain ends, 1956 J
white, baking of, ends in Britain, 1942 D
Breadwinner, The (W. S. Maugham), 1930 W
Brearley, Henry, B. metallurgist, 1912 P
Breath Test, introduction in Britain, 1967 O
Brecht, Bertolt, G. dramatist (1898–1956), 1922 W, 1928 T, 1932 W, 1937 W, 1941 W; Berliner Ensemble of, 1956 W

Breckinridge, John Cabell, Am. S. Democrat politician (1821–75), opposes Lincoln, 1860 L
Bremen, Germany: annexed by Napoleon, 1810 M; Soviet republic formed, 1919 A; surrenders to Allies, 1945 D
Brenner Pass, through Alps, 1772 P
Brenner, Sydney, S. Afr. chemist (b. 1927), 1961 P
Brenton, Howard, B. dramatist (b. 1942), 1974 W, 1980 W, 1983 W, 1985 W
Breslau (now Wroclaw), Poland: gymnasium, 1765 O; Institute of Physiology, 1839 O; Jewish Seminary, 1854 R; Jahrhunderthalle, 1910 S
Bresslau, H., G. student of diplomatic, 1889 Q
Bresson, Carl, film director, 1959 W
Brest, France, first submarine at, 1801 P
Brest-Litovsk, Russia: Germans take, 1915 H; Russia's armistice with Germany at, 1917 M; Peace Treaty, between Russia and Central Powers, 1918 O; annulled, 1918 L; Poles enter, 1920 H; Germans reach, 1939 J; Russians capture, 1944 G
Brett, John Watkins, B. telegraphic engineer (1805–1862), 1850 P
Bretton Woods, New Hampshire, US, UN Monetary Conference at, 1944 G
Breuer, Marcel Lajos, Hung. designer and architect (1902–1981), 1902 Z, 1925 P, 1966 S, 1971 S, 1981 Z
Brewster, Sir David, B. scientist (1781–1868), 1813 P, 1816 P
Breytenbach, Breytan, S. Afr. author (b. 1939), 1989 U
Brezhnev Doctrine, 1969 B
Brezhnev, Leonid, R. leader (1906–82), 1906 Z; becomes USSR president, 1960 E; 'Plane intercepted, 1961 B; Mikoyan succeeds, 1964 G; becomes first secretary of Soviet Communist Party, 1964 K
visits West Germany, 1973 E
visits US and declares Cold War over, 1973 F
agrees Middle East plan with Kissinger, 1973 K
talks with West German Chancellor Schmidt, 1974 K
discusses arms control with Ford, 1974 L
combines roles head of state and Communist Party secretary, 1977 F
SALT II treaty, 1979 F
'zone of peace' proposal, 1980 M
announces halt of deployment of SS-20 missiles, 1982 C
proposes freeze on strategic arms, 1982 E
Middle East peace plan, 1982 J
death, 1982 L, Z
Briand, Aristide, F. statesmen (1862–1932), 1862 Z, 1925 L, 1932 Z; becomes premier, 1909 G; averts strike, 1910 K; attempted assassination, 1911 A; resigns, 1911 B; forms cabinet, 1913 A; at Allied Conference, 1916 C; forms War Ministry, 1916 M; as premier, 1921 A; resigns, 1922 A; meets Streseman, 1926 J; proposals for outlawing war, 1928 D; again premier, 1929 G; proposes European federal union, 1929 J. *See also* Kellogg-Briand Pact
Bride of Abydos (Byron), 1813 U
Bridenbaugh, Carl, Am. historian (1903–92), 1968 Q, 1975 Q
Brideshead Revisited (E. Waugh), 1945 U
Brideshead Revisited, television programme, 1981 W
Bridge of San Luis Rey, The (T. Wilder), 1927 W
Bridge, Frank, B. musician (1879–1941), 1915 T
Bridges, Edward, Lord Bridges, B. civil servant (1892–1969), 1958 S
Bridges, Robert, B. poet (1844–1930), 1844 Z, 1929 U, 1930 Z
Bridges:
Forth, 1890 P, 1964 P
Humber, 1981 P
Lambeth, 1932 P
Lower Zambesi, 1935 P
Manhattan, 1910 P
Menai, 1819 P, 1849 P
New York-Brooklyn, 1872 P
Niagara Falls Suspension, 1852 P
Peace, 1927 H
Saltash, 1853 P
Sydney Harbour, 1932 P
Verrazano Narrows, 1964 P
cast-iron, 1773 P, 1850 P
tubular, 1849 P
Bridie, James (pseud. of Osborne Henry Mavor), B. dramatist (1888–1951), 1931 W, 1932 W, 1933 W, 1943 W
Bridport, Lord. *See* Hood, Alexander
Brief History of Time, A (S. Hawking), 1988 P
Brienne, Etienne Charles de Loménie de, Cardinal Archbishop of Toulouse, F. ecclesiastic and statesman (1727–94), 1787 D, 1787 G, 1788 H
Brieux, Eugène, F. dramatist (1868–1932), 1917 W
Brighouse, Harold, B. author (1882–1958), 1916 W
Bright Shining Lie, A.: John Paul Vann and America in Vietnam (N. Sheehan), 1988 Q
Bright, John, B. Liberal politician (1811–89), 1811 Z, 1882 G, 1886 F, 1889 Z
Brighton Rock (G. Greene), 1938 U
Brighton Rock Memoirs (N. Simon), 1982 W
Brighton, Sussex, England: Pavilion, 1815 S; by-election, 1944 B
Conservative Party members killed in IRA bomb attack, 1984 K
Brihuega, Spain, 1937 C
Brindle, Arthur, Am. musician (b. 1920), 1963 T
Brindley, James, B. engineer (1712–72), 1772 Z
Brink, André Philippus, S. Afr. author (b. 1935), 1982 U
Brisbane, Queensland, Australia, 1859 N
Brisley, Stuart, B. sculptor (b. 1933), 1972 S
Brissot, Jacques Pierre, F. revolutionary (1754–93), 1791 K, 1793 F
Bristol, England: roads in, 1815 P; riots in, 1831 K; St Paul's district riots, 1980 D
Bristow, George Frederick, Am. musician (1825–98), 1855 T
Britain Seen From the North (T. Cragg), 1981 S
Britain and the European Communities—An Economic Assessment, White Paper, 1970 B
Britannia (S. Frere), 1967 Q
British Aerospace
privatization, 1980 O
purchase of Rover car group, 1988 C
British Airways, 1974 O, 1987 O
British Caledonian acquired, 1987 O
British Antarctic Survey detects hole in ozone layer, 1985 P
British Army of Rhine (BAOR), W. Germany agrees to assist costs of, 1962 C
British Association for the Advancement of Science, 1831 P, 1861 P, 1870 P
British Birds (T. Bewick), 1797 P
British Birds (Thorburn), 1915 P
British Broadcasting Company, 1921 O
British Broadcasting Corporation:
Boult becomes musical director, 1930 T
develops TV, 1932 O
TV service begun, 1936 W; resumed, 1946 W
Third Programme, 1946 W
BBC Two, 1964 W
colour television broadcasts, 1967 W
local radio broadcasts, 1967 W
CEEFAX, 1972 P
Dimbleby Lecture, 1979 L
Reith Lectures. *See* Reith Lectures
British Caledonian, acquired by British Airways, 1987 O
British Columbia: becomes British colony, 1858 H; joins Dominion of Canada, 1871 G
British Council of Churches, 1990 R
British Council, 1935 O
British Economic Growth 1856–1973 (R.C.O. Matthews, C.H. Feinstein, J.C. Odling-Smee), 1982 Q
British Economic Survey, 1948 O
British Fossils (R. Owen), 1846 P
British Gas, privatization, 1986 M
British General Election of 1945, The (McCallum and Readman), 1947 O
British Guiana: British capture, 1796 N, 1803 J; Britain retains, 1814 H; boundary with Venezuela, 1895 G, L, M, 1899 K; forces sent to restore order, 1953 J; becomes a proclaimed area, 1954 D; state of emergency in, 1964 E; deputy premier arrested, 1964 F; to be independent in 1966, 1965 M; independence as Guyana, 1966 E
British Honduras. *See* Honduras
British Institution for the Development of the Fine Arts, 1805 S
British Intelligence in the Second World War (F.H. Hinsley et al.), 1979 Q
British Legion, 1921 O
British Leyland
merger with British Motor Corporation, 1968 A
government majority shareholding, 1975 D
redundancies, 1979 J
discloses annual loss, 1980 C
government aid, 1981 A
British Lion Films, 1964 W
British Literature Prize, 1992 U
British Medical Association, advises doctors to resign from health service, 1965 B
British Motor Corporation
dismissal of 10,000 workers, 1966 J
merger with Leyland Motors, 1968 A
British Museum. *See under* London
British National Coal Board
Lord Robens resigns, 1971 A
pit closure plan withdrawn, 1981 B
British Overseas Airways Corporation, 1939 O
British Petroleum Company, strikes oil in North Sea, 1965 R, 1970 O
government plans sale of shares, 1979 K
British Pressure Groups (J. D. Stewart), 1958 O
British Standard Time, adoption, 1968 B
British Steel
job losses announced, 1979 L
strike, 1980 A
record losses, 1980 G
British Telecom, privatization, 1984 L
British Telecommunications, establishment, 1979 J
British War Economy (Hancock and Gowing), 1949 Q
British West Indian Federation, London Conference on, 1953 L
British and Foreign Bible Society, 1804 R
Brittan, Sir Leon, B. Conservative politician (b. 1939), 1983 F
Trade Secretary, 1985 J
resignation over Westland affair, 1986 A

Britten, (Edward) Benjamin, Lord Britten, B. musician (1913–76), 1913 Z, 1941 T, 1942 T, 1945 T, 1946 T, 1947 T, 1951 T, 1953 T, 1957 T, 1958 T, 1961 T, 1966 T, 1968 T, 1971 T, 1973 T, 1976 T, Z
Brixton, London, England, riots, 1981 D, G, 1985 J
Brno, Czechoslovakia, dissidents tried, 1972 G
Broad, Charlie Dunbar (1887–1971), B. philosopher, 1914 R
Broadcasting:
wavelengths, settled, 1934 O; redistributed, 1948 P; comparative survey of foreign broadcasts, 1960 Y
in Britain
first station, 1920 W
medium wave, 1921 P
from Marconi House, 1922 W
Daventry transmitter, 1925 P
BBC chartered, 1927 O
Pilkington Report, 1962 W
pirate radio stations, 1965 W
Annan Report, 1977 O
of parliament, 1975 F, 1978 O
White Paper on, 1978 O
S4C radio station, 1982 W
ban on broadcasts of interviews with 11 terrorist organizations, 1988 K
See also British Broadcasting Corporation
in Canada, TV via satellite, 1979 P
in France, operatic first performance, 1954 T
in Greece, Britain jams Athens broadcasts to Cyprus, 1956 C
in US:
by amateurs, 1919 W
East Pittsburgh station, 1920 W
of election results, 1920 W
mistaken nuclear attack warning, 1971 B
in USSR, jams Western broadcasts, 1980 H
Brock, Sir Isaac, B. soldier (1769–1812), 1812 K
Brock, Sir Thomas, B. sculptor (1847–1922), 1905 S
Brockden Brown, Charles, Am. author (1771–1810), 1798 U
Brockhaus, Friedrich Arnold, G. publisher (1772–1823), 1796 Q
Brockway, Zebulon Reed, Am. penologist (1827–1920), 1876 O
Brodie, Sir Israel, B. Rabbi (1895–1979), 1957 R
Brodkey, Harold, Am. author (b. 1930), 1992 U
Brodsky, Joseph Aleksandrovich, R. author (b. 1940), 1980 U
Brogan, Sir Denis William, B. political scientist (1900–74), 1943 O, 1945 O
Broglie, Duc Louis de, F. physicist (1892–1987), 1892 Z, 1924 P, 1987 Z
Broken Pitcher, The (H. Kleist), 1811 U
Bromberg Canal, Germany, 1772 P
Brontë, Charlotte (afterwards Nicholls), B. novelist (1816–55) 1816 Z, 1847 U, 1855 Z
Brontë, Emily, B. novelist (1818–48), 1847 U
Brook Kerith, The (G. Moore), 1916 U
Brook, Peter Stephen Paul, B. director (b. 1925), 1964 W, 1985 W
Brooke, Basil, Lord Brookeborough, N. Ir. premier (1888–1973), 1963 C
Brooke, Christopher Nugent Lawrence, B. historian (b. 1927) 1975 Q, 1988 Q, 1989 Q
Brooke, Gerald, B. spy, 1969 G
Brooke, Henry, Ir. author (?1703–83), 1765 U
Brooke, Rupert, B. poet (1887–1915), 1911 U, 1918 U
Brookeborough, Lord. *See* Brooke, Basil
Brooklyn, New York, US, Plymouth Congregational Church, 1847 R
race riots, 1966 G
Brosio, Manlio, It. Secretary-General of NATO (1897–1980), 1971 K
Brougham, Henry, Lord Brougham, B. Whig politician (1779–1868), 1779 Z, 1827 O, 1868 Z
Brown University, Providence, Rhode Island, US, 1764 O
Brown, (Edmund Gerald) 'Jerry', Am. Democratic politician (b. 1938), 1979 L
Brown, David William, B. theologian (b. 1948), 1985 R
Brown, Ford Madox, B. artist (1821–93), 1852 S
Brown, George Alfred, Lord George-Brown, B. Labour politician (1914–85), 1914 Z, elected deputy leader of Party, 1962 L; minister of Economic Affairs, 1964 K, 1965 O; Foreign Secretary, 1966 H; resignation as Foreign Secretary, 1968 C; 1967 A, 1985 Z
Brown, James, Am. singer (b. 1933), 1968 W
Brown, John, Am. abolitionist (1800–59), 1800 Z, 1859 Z; at Pottawatomie Creek, 1856 E; raid on Harper's Ferry, 1859 K
Brown, John, and Company, Clydebank shipbuilders, 1951 P, 1964 M
Brown, Joseph Rogers, Am. inventor (1810–76), 1862 P
Brown, Judith Margaret, B. historian (b. 1944), 1985 Q
Brown, Peter Robert Lamont, B. historian (b. 1935), 1967 Q, 1971 Q, 1989 R
Brown, Sir (Ernest) Henry Phelps, B. economist (b. 1906), 1988 Q
Brown, Sir Arthur Whitten, B. aviator, 1919 P
Brown, Thomas, B. philosopher (1778–1820), 1804 R, 1820 R
Browne, C. F., Am. author under pseudonym 'Artemus Ward' (1834–67), 1862 U
Browne, Thomas Alexander, Austral. author under pseudonym 'Rolf Boldrewood' (1826–1915), 1888 U
Brownhall, Derek, Oxford research scientist, 1975 P
Browning Version, The (T. Rattigan), 1948 W
Browning, Elizabeth Barrett, B. poet (1806–61), 1806 Z, 1826 U, 1850 U, 1857 U, 1861 Z
Browning, John Moses, Am. inventor (1855–1926), 1900 P
Browning, Robert, B. poet (1812–89), 1833 U, 1835 U, 1868 U
Bruce, James, B. explorer (1730–94), 1772 P, 1790 P
Bruce, Michael, B. poet (d. 1767), 1767 U
Bruce, Stanley, Lord Bruce, Austral. statesman (1883–1967), 1923 B
Brücke, Die ('The Bridge'), group of artists, 1905 S
Bruckner, Anton, Aus. musician (1824–96), 1824 Z, 1864 T, 1871 T, 1879 T, 1884 T, 1892 T, 1896 Z
Brudenell, James, Earl of Cardigan, B. soldier (1797–1868), 1797 Z
Bruges, Belgium, Canal, blockaded, 1918 D
Belgians recapture, 1918 K
Brugsch, Heinrich Karl, G. Egyptologist (1827–94), 1883 Q
Brundtland, Gro Harlem, Prime Minister of Norway (b. 1939), 1981 B, 1990 K
Brunei, Borneo, British protectorate over, 1888 E
independence, 1984 A
Brunel, Isambard Kingdom, B. engineer (1806–59), 1806 Z, 1843 P, 1852 S, 1853 P, 1859 Z
Brüning, Heinrich, G. Centre Party politician (1885–1970), forms ministry, 1930 C, 1931 H; resolves to end reparations payments, 1932 A; resigns, 1932 F
Bruno (F. Schelling), 1802 R
Bruno's Dream (I. Murdoch), 1970 U
Brunswick, Karl Wilhelm Ferdinand, Duke of, Aus. general (1735–1806), issues manifesto, 1792 G
Brusilov, Alexei, R. general, 1916 F, J
Brussels, Belgium: riots, 1787 A; revolution in suppressed, 1790 M; French capture, 1792 L; Liberal meeting in, 1846 F; Palais de Justice in, 1866 S; population, 1881 Y; Conference on Slave Trade, 1889 F, 1890 O; Conference on liquor traffic, 1911 O; Germans occupy, 1914 H; Edith Cavell executed in, 1915 K; Belgian troops enter, 1918 L; Conference on Sino-Japanese War, 1937 L; Germans invade, 1940 E; liberated, 1944 J; Treaty, 1948 C; Socialist demonstrations in, 1950 G; Common Market meeting at, 1950 G
Heysel Stadium disaster, 1985 X
North Atlantic Treaty Organization summit, 1989 E
Brutal Friendship, The (F. W. Deakin), 1962 Q
Bryan, William Jennings, Am. Democrat politician (1860–1925), 1915 F; defeated in presidential elections, 1896 L, 1900 L, 1908 L; nominated for vice-presidency, 1924 F
Bryant, Sir Arthur, B. historian (1899–1985), 1899 Z, 1957 Q, 1985 Z
Bryant, William Cullen, Am. author (1794–1878), 1817 U
Bryce, James, Lord Bryce, B. jurist, historian and politician (1838–1922), 1838 Z, 1864 Q, 1888 O, 1901 Q, 1916 O, 1921 O, 1922 Z
Brynner, Yul, Am. film actor (1915–1985), 1956 W
Buber, Martin, Israeli philosopher (1878–1965), 1878 Z, 1937 R, 1945 R, 1965 Z
Buch der Lieder (H. Heine), 1827 U
Buchan, John, Lord Tweedsmuir, B. author and diplomat (1875–1940), 1875 Z, 1915 U, 1916 U, 1922 U, 1940 Z
Buchanan Report on Traffic in Towns, 1963 O
Buchanan, James, Am. Democrat (1791–1868), president of US (1857–61), elected, 1856 L; inaugurated, 1857 C
Bucharest, Rumania: occupied by Russians, 1769 L; Austrians capture, 1789 K; Treaty, between Turkey and Russia, 1812 E; legislative assembly at, 1861 M; University, 1864 O; Peace Treaty, 1886 C; armistice at, 1913 G; peace signed at, 1913 H; Germans take, 1916 M; Russians enter, 1944 H
earthquake, 1977 C
anti-government demonstrations, 1990 F
Buchlau Conference, 1908 J
Buchman, Frank, Am. founder of Moral Rearmament (1878–1961), 1939 R
Büchner, Georg, G. author (1813–37), 1835 U
Buck, Pearl S., Am. author, 1931 U
Buckingham Palace Conference, 1914 G
Buckingham, John, B. jockey (b. 1940), 1967 X
Buckle, George Earle, B. journalist (1854–1935), 1854 Z, 1935 Z
Buckle, Henry Thomas, B. historian (1821–62), 1821 Z, 1857 Q, 1862 Z
Buckle, Richard, B. author (b. 1916), 1954 T
Buckyballs, evidence found for existence of, 1985 P
Buda, Hungary, united with Pesth, 1873 L
Budapest, Hungary: Hungarian Academy of Sciences, 1825 O; becomes capital, 1873 L; Convention on Eastern Question, 1877 A; opera in, 1888 T; Soviet government formed in, 1919 C; Roumanians enter, 1919 H; Russians

surround, 1944 M; Russians take, 1945 B; Russian attack on, 1956 L
meeting to plan World Communist Summit, 1968 B
demonstration calling for democracy and national independence, 1989 C
Buddenbrooks (T. Mann), 1901 U
Buddhist Council, Rangoon, 1956 R
Budgets, notable:
in Britain, 1980 C, 1981 C, 1982 C, 1983 C, 1984 C
Peel's free trade, 1842 D
Gladstone's, 1853 D
Hicks-Beach's, 1901 D
Lloyd George's, 1909 L
deficit, 1931 G, H
increased defence spending, 1936 C
leakage, 1936 E
emergency, 1939 J
standard rate of income tax raised to ten shillings, 1941 D
entertainment tax doubled, 1942 D
defence spending curtailed,1952 M
emergency, 1955 K
increased profits tax, 1960 D
starting-point of surtax raised, 1961 D
emergency, 1961 G, 1964 L
corporation tax, 1965 D
Barber's mini-budget, 1970 K
tax reforms, 1971 C
VAT introduced, 1973 C
Barber's emergency budget, 1973 M
Healey's first, 1974 C
mini-budget, 1974 G, 1976 M, 1977 G
emergency, 1974 L
Healey's 'rough and tough' budget, 1975 D
public spending cuts, 1976 M
income tax cut, 1977 C
opposition amendment passed,1978 E
VAT increased,1979 F
in Germany, Reichstag fails to pass, 1930 G
in US, defence spending, 1939 A, 1950 G, 1951 K
Johnson proposes reduction in, 1964 A
Buenos Aires, Argentina: surrenders to British 1806 F; British attack, 1807 N; independence, 1811 H; recognised, 1824 M; separated from Argentina, 1854 D; enters Argentine Confederation, 1859 K; reunited with Argentina, 1860 F; railway to, 1911 P; Pan American Conference at, 1936 M; population, 1960 Y
population, 1970 Y
Juan Perón returns to riots, 1973 F
anti-government rally, 1982 M
Buero Vallejo, Antonio, Sp. dramatist (b. 1916), 1970 W
Buffalo Bill (W. F. Cody), Am., 1917 Z
Buffalo, N.Y., US, British burn, 1813 M 1936 M; population, 1960 Y
Buffet, Bernard, F. artist (b. 1928), 1955 S
Buffon, Georges Louis Leclerk, Comte de, F. naturalist (1707–88), 1778 P, 1786 P, 1788 Z
Bug, River, Russia and Poland, 1795 K
Buganda, Uganda: state of emergency, 1954 E; agreement for, signed, 1955 H; request for independence refused, 1960 M; dissolved, 1966 E
Bugatti, Ettore, It. racing-car designer, 1947 Z
Buhari, Major-General Mohammed, Nig. soldier and politician (b. 1942), 1983 M
Building Societies, in Britain, 1874 O
Building Techniques:
cast-iron frame building, 1851 P
reinforced concrete, 1910 S, 1916 S
steel and glass, 1908 S
steel-frame, 1890 P
undulating prefabrication, 1948 S
Buildings of England Series (N. Pevsner et al.), 1974 Q
Bukharin, Nikolai, R. politician (1888–1938), expelled, 1929 L; tried, 1938 C
posthumous rehabilitation, 1988 O
Bukovina, Austria, formerly in Moldavian principality: occupied by Austria, 1774 J; ceded to Austria, 1775 E
Bukovina, now in Russia: Russia demands cession of, 1940 F; Rumania cedes to Russia, 1947 B
Bulawayo, Rhodesia:
British occupy, 1893 L
Cape railway to, 1897 L
Bulganin, Nikolai Aleksandrovich, R. soldier and politician (1895–1975), 1895 Z, 1947 L; becomes premier, 1955 B; visits Yugoslavia, 1955 E; visits E. Germany, 1955 G; proposes pact with US, 1956 A; visits Britain, 1956 D; calls for reduction in armed forces, 1956 F; proposes Summit Conference, 1958 A; criticises Anglo-US agreement on bases, 1958 C; 1975 Z
Bulgaria: risings in, 1876 A, 1877 A; massacres by Turks, 1876 C; autonomy agreed, 1878 G; boundaries reduced, 1878 E–G; independence declared, 1908 K; recognised by Turkey, 1909 D; Russia declares war on, 1944 J; Republic proclaimed, 1946 J
Zhivkov dictatorship ended, 1989 L
National Assembly votes to end Communist monopoly on power, 1990 A
government resigns and is replaced by new all-Communist government, 1990 B
elections, 1991 K
illegitimacy rate, 1991 Y
presidential elections, 1992 A
Bulgarian Horrors, The (W.E. Gladstone), 1876 J
Bull Run, Virginia, US, battles of, 1861 G, 1862 H
Buller, Sir Redvers, B. soldier (1839–1908), 1899 M, 1900 F, G; relieves Ladysmith, 1900 B
Bullock, Alan Louis Charles, Lord Bullock (b. 1914), 1983 Q
Bulls, papal. *See* Papal Bulls
Bülow, Bernhard von, Prince, G. statesman (1849–1929), 1849 Z, 1901 C, 1905 G, 1913 O, 1929 Z; as Foreign Secretary, 1897 K; rejects British advances for alliance, 1899 M; becomes Chancellor, 1900 K
Bülow, Friedrich Wilhelm, baron von, Pruss. general, 1813 H, J
Bultmann, Rudolf, G. theologian (1884–1976), 1941 R, 1956 R
Bulwer, William Henry Lytton Earle, lord Bulwer, B. diplomat (1801–72), 1850 D
Bulwer-Lytton, Edward George, lord Lytton, B. novelist (1803–73), 1803 Z, 1834 U, 1835 U, 1843 U, 1873 Z
Buñuel, Luis, Sp. film director (1900–83), 1900 Z, 1972 W, 1977 W, 1983 Z
Bunbury, Sir Thomas Charles, B. racehorse owner (1740–1821), 1779 X
Bunche, Ralph J., Am. diplomat, (1904–71), 1904 Z, 1971 Z
Bunker Hill, Mass., US, battle, 1775 F
Bunning, James Bunstone, B. architect (1802–63), 1846 S, 1863 S
Bunsen, Christian Charles Josias, baron von, G. diplomat (1791–60), 1856 O
Bunsen, Robert Wilhelm von, G. chemist (1811–99), 1811 Z, 1841 P, 1850 P, 1859 P, 1861 P, 1899 Z
Bunshaft, Gordon, Am. architect (1909–52), 1963 S
Burckhardt, Jacob, Swi. art historian (1818–97), 1818 Z, 1855 S, 1860 S, 1897 Z
Burdett, Sir Francis, B. Whig politician (1770–1844), 1818 F
Bureau of Investigation, Am., Hoover appointed Director, 1924 O
Buren, Daniel, F. artist (b. 1938), 1976 S, 1982 S
Buren, Martin van, Am. Democrat (1782–1862), president of US (1837–41), inaugurated, 1837 C
Buresch, Karl, Aus. Christian Socialist, forms ministry, 1932 F
Burgee, John Henry, Am. architect (b. 1933), 1984 S
Burger's Daughter (N. Gordimer), 1979 U
Bürger, Gottfried August, G. poet (1748–94), 1773 U, 1786 U
Burger, Warren Earl, Am. Chief Justice (b. 1907), 1969 E
Burgess, Anthony, B. author (b. 1917), 1980 U
Burgess, Guy, B. diplomat and spy (1911–63), flees to Russia, 1951 F
Burgess, Thomas, François, Boer politician (1834–81), president of Transvaal, 1872 G
Burghclere Chapel, Berkshire, England, 1926 S
Burgos, Spain, British withdraw from, 1812 J
Basque separatists trial, 1970 M
Burgoyne, John, B. soldier and dramatist (1722–92), 1777 J, 1786 W; surrenders at Saratoga, 1777 K
Burk, B.F., Am. scientist, 1955 P
Burke, Arleigh Albert, Am. admiral, 1901 Z
Burke, Edmund, B. statesman (1729–97), 1764 U, 1782 G, 1790 C, 1797 Z; proposes economic reform, 1780 E; in Rockingham's coalition, 1782 C; impeaches W. Hastings, 1787 E; condemns French Revolution, 1790 B; writings, 1769 O, 1770 O, 1774 O, 1775 O, 1777 O, 1790 O, 1791 O, 1796 O
Burke, Thomas Henry, B. administrator (1829–82), 1882 E
Burkina Faso
Upper Volta renamed, 1984 H
border conflict with Mali, 1985 M
coup d'état, 1987 K
revolutionary government dissolved, 1991 F
Burma Road, S.E. Asia, 1940 G, K
Burma: war with Siam, 1767 H; acknowledges suzerainty of China, 1769 N; British Wars with, 1852 D, M, 1853 F, 1885 K; Britain annexes, 1886 A; British occupation recognised by China, 1886 G; government of, separated from India, 1935 H; Japanese invade, 1942 A; North region is cleared of Japanese, 1944 M; independent Republic proclaimed, 1948 A; multi-party elections, 1990 E
Burn This (L. Wilson), 1987 W
Burne-Jones, Sir Edward Coley, B. artist (1833–98), 1833 Z, 1884 S, 1896 S, 1898 Z
Burney, Charles, B. musicologist (1726–1814), 1773 T, 1776 T
Burney, Fanny. *See* Arblay, Frances D'
Burnham, Forbes, Guianian, People's National Congress, forms ministry, 1964 M
Burnham, James, Am. author, 1942 O
Burning Bush (S. Undset), 1930 U
Burning Peach, The (L. MacNeice), 1963 U
Burns, John, B. trade union leader (1858–1943), 1858 Z, 1911 H, 1943
Burns, Robert, Scottish poet (1759–96), 1786 U, 1790 U, 1796 Z
Burnside, Ambrose Everitt, Am. Unionist general (1824–81), 1862 M

Burra, Edward, B. artist (1905–76), 1905 Z, 1952 S, 1976 Z
Burroughs, William, Am. author, 1964 U
Burslem, Staffs., England, 1769 P
Burton, Richard, B. actor (1925–84), 1925 Z, 1962 W, 1984 Z
Burton, Sir Richard Francis, B. explorer and scholar (1821–90), 1854 P, 1856 P, 1885 U
Burundi
independence proclaimed, 1962 G
Military Committee for National Redemption, 1987 J
coup d'état, 1987 J
Bury, John Bagnell, B. classical scholar and historian (1861–1927), 1861 Z, 1923 Q, 1927 Z
'Bus. *See* Omnibus
Busa, Nigeria, British protectorate over, 1895 A
Busch, Wilhelm, G. caricaturist (1832–1908), 1859 S
Bush, Alan, B. musician, (b. 1900), 1900 Z, 1943 T
Bush, George Herbert Walker, Am. statesman, Republican (b. 1924), 41st President of US (1989–93),1924 Z, 1991 E, 1992 L, 1992 P
abandons presidential nomination bid, 1980 E
vice-presidential candidacy, 1980 G
vice-presidential re-nomination, 1984 H
elected President, 1988 L
presidential inauguration, 1989 A
NATO summit, Brussels, 1989 E
Cold War declared over, 1989 M
Gulf War, 1990 H, 1991 B
federal budget, emergency bill, 1990 K
Strategic Arms Reduction Treaty (START), 1991 G
collapses at state dinner in Tokyo, 1992 A
Bushnell, David, Am. inventor of torpedo (1750–1824), 1777 P
Business as a System of Power (R. A. Brady), 1943 O
Busoni, Ferruccio Benvenuto, It. musician (1866–1924), 1912 T, 1925 T
Busotti, Sylvano, It. musician (b. 1931), 1972 T
Buss, Frances Mary, B. educationalist (1827–94), 1850 O
Bustamante, Alexander, Jamaic. Labour leader, 1962 D
Bustamente, José, Peruv. president, 1945 F, 1948 K
But What About the Noise of Crumpling Paper ... (J. Cage), 1986 T
Butadiene, synthetic rubber from, 1909 P
Butcher, Harvey, astronomer, 1987 P
Bute, John Stuart, Earl of, B. Tory (1713–92), becomes prime minister, 1763 D
Butler, Josephine Elizabeth (*née* Grey), B. social reformer (1828–1906), 1828 Z, 1906 Z
Butler, Reg, B. sculptor (1913–81), 1952 S, 1953 S
Butler, Richard Austen, Lord Butler of Saffron Walden, B. Conservative politician (1902–1982), 1902 Z, 1941 G; introduces Education Act, 1944 O; becomes Chancellor of Exchequer, 1951 K; introduces credit squeeze, 1955 K; deputises for Eden, 1956 L; becomes Home Secretary, 1957 A; introduces Criminal Justice bill, 1961 D; introduces Commonwealth Immigration bill, 1961 L; retires from politics, 1965 A; 1982 Z
Butler, Samuel, B. author (1835–1902), 1835 Z, 1872 U, 1901 U, 1902 Z, 1903 U
Butler, William, B. soldier (d. 1781), 1778 L
Butlin, Sir William Edmund ('Billy'), B. founder of holiday camps (1899–1980), 1937 W
Butt, Clara, B. singer (1873–1936), 1873 Z, 1915 T, 1936 Z
Butter, substitute for, statutory limit to, 1902 O
Butterfield, Alexander, Am. soldier and public official (b. 1926), Nixon tape-recordings, 1973 G
Butz, Earl, Am. politician (b. 1909), resignation, 1976 K
Buxar, Bengal, India, battle, 1764 K
Buzo, Alexander John, Austral. dramatist (b. 1944), 1974 W
Byatt, Antonia Susan, B. author (b. 1936), 1990 U
Byrd, Richard, Am. admiral and explorer (1888–1957), 1926 P, 1929 P
Byrds, The, Am. pop group, 1966 W
Byrne, John, B. playwright (b. 1940), 1982 W
Byrnes, James F., Am. statesman (1879–1972), becomes US secretary of state, 1945 G; bids for German co-operation with US, 1946 J; retires, 1947 A
Byron's Letters and Journals (L.A. Marchand ed.), 1973 Q
Byron, George Gordon, Lord Byron, B. poet (1788–1824), 1788 Z, 1807 U, 1809 U, 1813 U, 1814 U, 1816 U, 1817 U, 1818 U, 1819 U, 1824 D
Byron, John, B. navigator (1723–86), 1766 N, P

C

C-12 isotope of carbon adopted as international standard of atomic atoms, 1966 P
Ca Ira! (F. Freiligrath), 1846 U
Cabanis, Pierre, F. physiologist (1757–1808), 1789 O
Cabaret entertainment, 1922 W
Cabaret, 1968 W
Cabet, Etienne, F. author and politician (1788–1856), 1842 O
Cabinet Secretariat, British, formed, 1916 O
Cabinet, War, end of British, 1919 K
Cable and Wireless Ltd., privatization of, 1981 K
Cable, submarine, 1850 P
Cable, transatlantic, 1857 P, 1865 P
Cable-making machine, 1792 P
Cabral, Costa, Count of Thomar, Port. dictator (1796–1854), 1846 E
Cadbury, George, B. chocolate manufacturer and social reformer (1839–1922), 1900 O
Cadiz, Spain, French troops enter, 1823 H
Cadmium, a metallic element, 1818 P
Caecilian Society for Performance of Sacred Music, 1785 T
Caen, France, Allies take, 1944 G
Caernarvon Castle, Wales, investiture of Prince of Wales, 1969 G
Caesar and Cleopatra (G. B. Shaw), 1898 W
Caesium, an element, is isolated, 1861 P
Caetano, Marcello, Port. prime minister (1906–80), 1906 Z, 1968 J, 1980 Z
Cage, John, Am. musician (1912–92), 1912 Z, 1964 T, 1967 T, 1972 T, 1977 T, 1979 T, 1986 T, 1989 T, 1991 Z, 1992 Z
Cagney and Lacey, television series, 1981 W
Cahiers de la Quinzaine, Les (C. Péguy), 1900 U
Caillaux, Joseph, F. Republican (1863–1940), forms ministry, 1911 F; resigns, 1912 A; becomes finance minister, 1914 A; wife of, kills G. Calmette, 1914 C; arrested for treason, 1918 A
Caillebotte, Gustave, F. art collector, 1894 S
Caine Mutiny, The (H. Wouk), 1951 U
Caine, Sir Thomas Henry Hall, B. novelist (1853–1931), 1853 Z, 1894 U, 1901 U, 1931 Z
Caird, John, B. theologian and philosopher (1820–1898), 1880 R
Cairns, Dr. James Ford, Austral. politician (b. 1914), 1975 G
Cairo, Egypt, 1811 C; J. B. Kléber in, 1800 C; falls to British, 1801 F; British occupation, 1882 J; Nationalist riots in, 1919 C; Stack's murder in, 1924 L; Conference of Allies on war in Far East, 1943 L; Afro-Asian Organisation meets in, 1959 D; Conference of non-aligned states at, 1964 K
Arab League leaders plan holy war against Israel, 1969 H
Israeli air raid near, 1970 B
Moslem demonstrations, 1981 J
Moslem fundamentalists executed, 1982 D
population, 1990 Y
Calais, France: submarine cable from, 1850 P; is liberated, 1944 J
Calcium carbonate, decomposition of, 1862 P
Calculating machine, 1823 P
Calculus, 1852 P, 1864 P
Calcutta, India
food riots, 1966 C
population, 1990 Y
Calcutta, India: E. India Company in, 1764 N, 1775 N; Anglican bishop appointed, 1814 R; riots, 1918 J; population, 1950 Y
Calder Hall, Cumb., England, nuclear power station, 1956 P
Calder, Alexander, Am. sculptor (b. 1898), 1932 S, 1945 S, 1958 S
Calder, Angus, B. historian (b. 1942), 1969 Q
Caleb Williams (W. Godwin), 1794 U
Caledonian Canal, Scotland, 1803 P
Calendars:
Chinese, reformed, 1911 M
French Revolutionary, 1792 J
Vatican Council approve principle of fixed Easter, 1963 K
Calfa, Marian, Czech. leader (b. 1946), 1989 M
Calhoun, John Caldwell, Am. statesman (1782–1850), 1844 D
Calico, printing by copper cylinder, 1783 P
California, State, US: gold rush, 1847 P; US obtains, 1848 E; admitted to Union, 1850 G; *Wellingtonia gigantea* in, 1853 P; earthquake, 1892 O; University, cyclotron at, 1940 P
Californium, element, 1950 P
Calinescu, Armand, Rum. premier, assassinated, 1939 J
Callaghan, (Leonard) James, Lord Callaghan of Cardiff, B. Labour leader (b. 1912), 1912 Z
chancellor of Exechequer, 1964 K, L
replaced as Chancellor of Exchequer, 1967 L
Foreign Secretary, 1974 C,
re-negotiates EC entry, 1974 F
wins second ballot for Party leadership, 1976 C
Prime Minister, 1976 D
'great debate' on education, 1976 K
'Lib–Lab Pact', 1977 C
election announcement, 1978 J
calls general election, 1979 C
resigns as Labour Party leader, 1980 K
Callas, Maria (G.B. Meneghini), Am. prima donna (1923–77), 1923 Z, 1977 Z
Calley, William Laws, US soldier (b. 1943), 1971 C
Calmette, Gaston, F. journalist (1858–1914), 1914 A, C
Calonne, Charles Alexandre de, F. statesman (1734–1802), 1783 L, 1785 N; financial reforms rejected, 1787 B; is banished, 1787 D
Calverley, Charles Stuart, B. poet and parodist (1831–84), 1872 U

Calvino, Italo, It. author (1923–87), 1979 U
Calvo-Sotelo, Leopoldo Bustelo, Prime Minister of Spain (b. 1926), 1981 A
Camargo Ballet Society, 1930 T
Cambacérès, Jean Jacques Régis de, duke of Parma, F. politician (1753–1824), 1796 O
Cambodia: as French Protectorate, 1863 H; as French Colony, 1887 N; independence, 1954 G
  Sihanouk overthrown,1970 C
  appeals for US assistance, 1970 D
  attacks on Communist sanctuaries, 1970 D
  proposed international conference on, 1970 D
  becomes Khmer Republic, 1970 K
  bombing ends after US funding cut off, 1973 E
  Phnom Penh captured by Khmer Rouge, 1975 D
  Sihanouk retires, 1976 D
  Khieu Samphan of the Khmer Rouge replaces Prince Sihanouk, 1976 D
  full-scale invasion by Vietnam, 1978 M
  Khmer Rouge regime ousted, 1979 A
  Vietnam claims victory over Kampuchean rebels, 1983 D
  Vietnamese withdrawal,1989 J
  civil war, 1990 J
  peace accord, 1991 K
  Sihanouk returns, 1991 L
  UN votes to send peacekeeping force, 1992 B
Cambon, Paul, F. statesman (1843–1924), 1843 Z, 1924 Z
Cambrai, France: British advance on, 1917 L; British take, 1918 K
Cambridge Ancient History, The (ed. Bury), 1923 Q
Cambridge Ancient History, 1971 Q, 1982 Q
Cambridge Economic History of Europe, 1941 Q
Cambridge History of Africa, 1975 Q
Cambridge History of China, 1973 Q
Cambridge History of Classical Literature, Vol. II, 1982 Q
Cambridge History of English Literature, The, 1907 Q
Cambridge History of Iran, 1968 Q
Cambridge History of Islam, 1970 Q
Cambridge History of Japan, 1989 Q
Cambridge History of Latin America (L. Bethell ed.), 1984 Q
Cambridge History of the English Language, 1992 Q
Cambridge Medieval History, The, 1911 Q
Cambridge Modern History, The New, 1957 Q
Cambridge Modern History, The, 1899 Q
Cambridge Philological Society, 1868 Q
Cambridge Social History of Britain 1750–1950, The (F.M.L. Thompson ed.), 1990 Q
Cambridge, England, University:
  Evangelical movement, 1783 R
  religious tests abolished, 1871 O
  residence for women, 1871 O
  professorship of experimental physics, 1871 P
  Institutions:
    Churchill College, 1960 O
    Fitzwilliam Museum, 1837 S
    Girton College, 1869 O
    Library, 1934 S
    Mullard Observatory, 1957 P
    Richmond Lectures, 1959 U, 1962 U
    Robinson College, 1977 O
    Scott Polar Research Institute, 1926 P
    University Extension Lectures, 1870 O
  History Faculty Building, 1968 S
Cambridge, Mass., US: moon photographed from, 1851 P; Harvard University, Carpenter Center, 1963 S
Cambridge, duke of. *See* George William Frederick
Camden Society, 1838 Q
Camden, S. Carolina, US, 1780 H
Camera:
  image-dissector, 1956 P
  photo'-flash bulb, 1930 P
  See also Photography
Cameron, Euan, B. historian, 1991 Q
Cameroons, The S.W. Africa: German occupation, 1884 D; Anglo-German convention, 1892 K; frontier with Nigeria, 1893 C, 1913 C; frontier with French Congo, 1894 C; Germans surrender, 1916 B; League mandate for, 1922 G; becomes independent republic, 1960 A; North, plebiscite for joining Nigeria, 1961 B; South, plebiscite for joining Cameroun, 1961 B; Lake Nyas gas eruption, 1986 H; multi-party elections, 1992 K
Camilla (F. Burney), 1796 U
Camp David, Maryland, US
  'framework' peace treaty between Israel and Egypt, 1978 J
Campaign for Nuclear Disarmament (CND), 1980 K, 1981 K
  Aldermaston March, 1956 O, 1963 O
  sit-down demonstrations, 1961 O
  trial of Committee of 100 members, 1962 B
Campbell's Soup Tin (Warhol), 1970 S
Campbell, Alexander, Scot, minister, founder of 'Campbellites' (1788–1866), 1831 R
Campbell, Colin, lord Clyde, B. soldier (1792–1863), 1792 Z, 1863 Z; relieves Lucknow, 1857 L
Campbell, James, B. historian (b. 1935), 1982 Q
Campbell, John Malcolm, B. historian (b. 1947), 1983 Q
Campbell, John, Scot, author (1708–75), 1763 R, 1774 O
Campbell, Sir Malcolm, B. racing-champion (1885–1945), 1935 P, 1939 P
Campbell, Mrs. Patrick (Beatrice, *née* Tanner), B. actress (1865–1940), 1865 Z, 1940 Z
Campbell, Thomas, B. poet (1777–1844), 1799 U, 1809 U
Campbell-Bannerman, Sir Henry, B. Liberal statesman (1836–1908), 1836 Z, 1905 L, 1906 A; as War Secretary, 1895 F; leader of Liberal Party, 1899 A; becomes premier, 1905 M; moves to restrict Lords' powers, 1907 F; retires, 1908 D
Campe, Joachin Heinrich, G. educationalist (1746–1818), 1785 O
Camperdown, N. Holland, battle, 1797 K
Camperdown, lord. *See* Duncan, Adam
Campo Formio, N. Italy, Peace between France and Austria, 1797 K
Camponanes, Pedro Rodriguez, It. author (1723–1802), 1775 O
Campora, Hector Jose, Argent. politician (1909–80), 1973 C
Camps, holiday, 1937 W
Camus, Albert, F. author (1913–1960), 1913 Z, 1942 U, 1947 U, 1971 U
Can Government Cure Unemployment? (Angell and Wright), 1931 O
Can't Pay? Won't Pay! (D. Fo), 1974 W
Can, G. pop group, 1974 W
Canada:
  ceded to Britain, 1763 B
  Quebec Act for, 1774 D
  American troops driven from, 1776 C
  Upper and Lower, established, 1791 E
  emigration to, 1816 O
  frontier with US, defined, 1818 K, 1842 H, 1846 F
  railways in, 1836 P, 1886 P
  Council for, 1839 H
  Union of Upper and Lower, 1840 G
  discovery of northern coasts, 1850 P
  Dominion established, 1867 C
  Purchase of Hudson's Bay Co. territories, 1869 L
  British Columbia joins Dominion, 1871 G
  Confederation, 1872 G
  resolution on preserving union with Britain, 1911 B
  diplomatic relations established with China, 1970 K
  death penalty abolished, 1976 O
  government defeat brings election call, 1979 M
  new constitution, 1982 D
  general election, 1984 J, 1988 L
  Charter of Rights and Freedoms, 1985 D
  Quebec to be recognized as 'distinct society', 1987 E
  Canadian–US agreement on tariffs and economic barriers, 1987 K
  divorce statistics, 1987 Y
  Quebec, Meech Lake Accord, 1990 F
  life expectancy, 1990 Y
  Charlottetown reform agreement rejected, 1992 K
  Nunavut, 1992 L
Canadian Question, The (G. Smith), 1891 O
Canals:
  Bromberg, 1772 P
  Bruges, blocked, 1918 D
  Caledonian, 1803 P
  Corinth, 1893 P
  Dortmund–Ems, 1899 P
  Eider to Baltic, 1784 P
  Elbe–Trave, 1900 P
  Ellesmere, 1805 P
  Firth–Clyde, 1790 P
  Göta, 1832 P
  Kiel, 1895 P
  Manchester Ship, 1893 P
  Oxford–Birmingham, 1790 P
  Panama, opened, 1914 P. For negotiations, building, traffic, etc., *see under* Panama
  Regent's, London, 1820 P
  Suez, opened, 1869 L
    Britain purchases shares in, 1875 L. For negotiations, building, traffic, etc., *see under* Suez
Canary Islands, Pact to counter German designs in, 1907 E
Canberra, Australia, 1954 D
  Parliament House, 1927 E
Cancer Research:
  lung cancer, 1954 P
  mammography, 1967 P
  cancer linked to cigarette smoking, 1979 P
  gene inhibiting retinoblastome discovered, 1986 P
  gene marker for cancer of colon discovered, 1987 P
  genetically engineered white blood cells introduced into cancer patients, 1989 P
  link between radiation and leukaemia at Sellafield suggested, 1990 B
  gene which may be important in breast cancer discovered, 1990 P
Cancun Island, Mexico, summit meeting on North–South relations, 1981 K
Candia. *See* Crete
Candid Examination of Theism, A (G. Romanes), 1878 Q
Candida (G. B. Shaw), 1897 W
Candido (L. Sciascia), 1977 U

Candolle, Augustin de, F. botanist (1778–1841), 1813 P
Cannadine, David, B. historian (b. 1950), 1990 Q
Cannan, Edwin, B. economist (1861–1935), 1914 O
Canned Foods, 1874 P, 1880 P, 1892 P
Cannes, France, Conference on Reparations, 1922 A
Canning, George, B. statesman, Tory (1770–1827), 1770 Z, 1807 C; duel with Castlereagh, 1809 J; returns to Cabinet, 1816 F; resigns, 1820 M; becomes foreign secretary, 1822 J; role in independence of S. American states, 1924 M; sends troops to Portugal, 1826 M; becomes premier, 1827 D; death, 1827 G
Canning, Stratford de, Lord Stratford de Canning, B. diplomat (1786–1880), 1854 A
Cannon, John Ashton, B. historian (b. 1926), 1988 Q
Canonisations, 1887 R
Canova, Antonio, It. sculptor (1757–1822), 1779 S, 1782 S, 1793 S, 1802 S, 1808 S, 1815 S, 1822 Z
Canton, China: opened to British commerce, 1842 H; falls to British and French, 1851 M; R.N. bombards, 1856 L; anti-British incidents, 1925 E; Chiang Kai-shek enters, 1936 H; Japanese take, 1938 K
Cantor, Tadeusz, 1982 W
Canzoni e Versi (Leopardi), 1824 U
Cape Breton Island, Canada, ceded to Britain, 1763 B
Cape Verdi Islands, independence, 1975 G
Cape of Good Hope (Cape Colony), S. Africa: British seizure prevented, 1781 D; British occupation, 1795 J, 1806 A; becomes British Colony, 1814 H; astronomical observations from, 1834 P; landing of convicts forbidden, 1849 L; Basutoland added to, 1871 H; responsible government in, 1872 K
Čapek, Karel, Czech. author (1890–1938), 1890 Z, 1923 W, 1938 Z
Capetown, S. Africa, 1908 K; Macmillan's speech in Parliament, 1960 B; deaths in clashes with police, 1980 F; Tutu enthroned as Archbishop, 1986 J
Capital (Marx, English edition), 1886 O
Capital Punishment:
in Britain, royal commission, 1953 O
movement for abolition, 1955 O
Silverman's bill, 1956 P, 1964 M
abolition, 1965 L
in Canada, abolished, 1976 O
in France, National Assembly abolishes, 1981 O
in Russia, reintroduced, 1950 A
in Spain, abolished in peacetime, 1978 H
in Sweden, abolished, 1921 E
in US, 1976 O, 1977 A
See also Death Penalty
Capitalism, study of, 1901 Q
Capitals:
Australia (Canberra), 1927 E
Brazil (Brasilia), 1957 A, 1960 O
Canada (Ottawa), 1858 O
Congo (Léopoldville), 1961 E
French W. Africa (Dakar), 1904 N
Hungary (Budapesth), 1873 L
Italy (Florence), 1864 J; (Rome), 1870 K
New Zealand (Wellington), 1865 N
Norway (Oslo), 1925 A
Pakistan (Rawalpindi), 1959 K
Queensland (Brisbane), 1859 N
Transvaal (Pretoria), 1860 D
Turkey (Ankara), 1923 K
U.S.A. (New York), 1788 J; (Washington), 1800 F, 1801 C
Viet-Nam (Saigon), 1949 F
W. Germany (Bonn), 1949 E
Capo d'Istria, Count, elected president of Greece, 1827 D; assassinated, 1831 K
Caporetto Campaign, Italy, Italians routed, 1917 K
Capote, Truman, Am. author (1924–84), 1966 U, 1980 U
Cappadocia, North, archaeological expedition to, 1906 Q
Cappellari, Bartolommeo Alberto. *See* Gregory XVI, Pope
Capra, Frank, Am. film director (1897–1991), 1946 W, 1948 W
Caprera, Isle, off Sardinia, 1867 L
Caprices de Marianne, Les (A. de Musset), 1833 U
Caprivi, Georg Leo von, G. chancellor and general (1831–99), 1890 C, 1894 K
Captain Beefheart and the Magic Band, Am. pop group, 1969 W
Captains Courageous (R. Kipling), 1897 U
Car-racing, 1965 X
Carabobo, Venezuela, 1821 F
Caracas, Venezuela, Conference of Organisation of American States, 1954 C
Carbajal, president, of Mexico, 1914 G
Carballido, Emilio, Mex. dramatist (b. 1925), 1966 W
Carbon dioxide, 1774 P
Carbon-zinc battery, 1841 P
Carbon–13, isotope, 1946 P
Carbon–14 dating system, 1947 P
Carbonari, Italian secret society, 1820 G, 1821 C
Carbonic acid, 1774 P
Carchemis, Turkey, archaeological expedition to, 1911 Q
Cárdenas, Lazaro, president of Mexico, 1934 G
Cardew, Cornelius, B. musician (1936–81), 1971 T
Cardigan, earl of. *See* Brundenell, J
Cardwell, Edward, lord Cardwell, B. Liberal politician (1813–86), 1813 Z, 1871 H, 1886 Z
Caretaker, The (H. Pinter), 1960 W
Carey, Dr. George, Archbishop of Canterbury (b. 1935), 1935 Z, 1990 G, 1991 D, R
Carey, Henry Charles, Am. economist (1793–1879), 1858 O
Carey, Joseph Maull, Am. Republican politician (1845–1924), 1894 H
Carey, Peter, Austral. author (b. 1943), 1988 U
Cariatides, Les (T. de Banville), 1842 U
Caribbean:
British bases leased to US, 1940 J
Declaration of Grenada, 1971 G
St Kitts–Nevis Islands, independence, 1983 J
Hurricane Hugo, 1989 J
Caribbean Commission, 1942 O
Caribbean Organisation for Economic Co-operation, 1960 F
Carinthia, plebiscite in, 1920 H
Caritas (A. Wesker), 1981 W
Carl August, elector of Saxe-Weimar (1758–1828), 1816 E
Carl XVI Gustaf, King of Sweden (b. 1946), 1973 J
Carlile, Wilson, B. evangelical leader (1847–1942), 1847 Z, 1882 R, 1942 Z
Carlist War, in Spain, 1834 G
Carlos I, King of Portugal, 1907 B
Carlos, Don, proclaimed King of Spain, 1872 D, 1876 B
Carlsbad Decrees, 1819 J
Carlson, Chester, Am. inventor of xerography, 1946 P
Carlsson, Ingvar Gästa, Prime Minister of Sweden (b. 1934), 1990 B, 1991 J
Carlyle, Alexander James, B. historian of philosophy (1861–1943), 1936 Q
Carlyle, Thomas, B. essayist and historian (1795–1881), 1795 Z, 1828 U, 1833 U, 1837 Q, 1841 U 1843 U, 1845 U, 1858 Q, 1881 Z
Carme sui sepolcri (U. Foscolo), 1807 U
Carmen (P. Mérimée), 1847 W
Carmona, Antonio de Fragosa, Sp. general and dictator, 1926 G, 1927 B, 1928 C
Carné, Marcel, F. film director (b. 1909), 1946 W, 1958 W
Carnarvon, earl of. *See* Herbert
Carnatic, The, region of Madras, S. India, 1799 N; Hyder Ali conquers, 1780 J
Carnegie Trust Co., 1911 A
Carnegie, Andrew, B. steel manufacturer and philanthropist (1835–1919), 1835 Z, 1880 P, 1886 O, 1911 O, 1919 Z
Carneiro, Dr. Francisco Sa, Prime Minister of Portugal (1934–80), 1980 M
Carnival (C. Mackenzie), 1912 U
Carnot, Lazare Nicolas Marguerite, F. soldier (1753–1823), 1797 J, 1803 P, 1810 O
Carnot, Nicolas Léonard Sadi, F. physician (1796–1832), 1824 P
Caro, Sir Anthony, B. sculptor (b. 1924), 1924 Z, 1967 S
Caro, Marc, F. film director, 1991 W
Carol I, King of Rumania (1866–1914), formerly Charles of Hohenzollern, 1866 B
Carol II, King of Rumania, 1940 F; flees, 1940 J
Carol, Joyce, author, 1975 U
Carolina, South, state, US: tariff problems in, 1833 A, C; leaves Union, 1860 M
Caroline Islands, Pacific: Germany's dispute with Spain, 1885 M; Germany purchases, 1899 B
Caroline Matilda, Queen of Denmark (1751–75), sister of George III, 1770 J
Caroline Princess of Wales (1768–1821), 1820 M, 1821 A, G, H; demands recognition as Queen, 1820 F; bill to dissolve marriage with George IV, 1820 G, L; enquiry into conduct of, 1820 L
Carothers, Wallace, H., Am. inventor of nylon stockings, 1937 P
Carpenter's Gothic (W. Gaddis), 1986 U
Carpenter, Malcolm Scott, Am. cosmonaut, 1962 P
Carpenter, Mary, B. philanthropist (1807–77), 1851 O
Carpet-sweeper, 1865 P
Carpets, manufacture by Brussels loom, 1845 P
Carr, Benjamin, Am. musician (1769–1831), 1796 T
Carr, Edward Hallett, B. historian (1892–1982), 1939 O, 1942 O, 1951 Q
Carr, Raymond, B. historian (b. 1919), 1966 Q
Carr, (Leonard) Robert, Lord Carr of Hadley, B. Conservative politician (b. 1916), 1971 A, 1972 G
Carr, Sir William ('Pissing Billy'), B. newspaper proprietor (1912–77), 1968 V
Carr-Saunders, Sir Alexander, B. economist (b. 1886), 1936 O
Carrà, Carlo, It. painter (1881–1966), 1910 S, 1917 S
Carranza, Venustiano, president of Mexico, 1914 E, 1915 K, 1916 L, 1920 E
Carré, E. C., F. inventor of freezing-machine, 1850 P
Carré, John le (pseudonym of David John Moore Cornwell), B. author (b. 1931), 1974 U, 1980 U
Carriage-lathe, 1797 P

Carriere, Jean-Claude, Fr. screen-writer (b. 1931), 1985 W
Carrington, Peter Alexander Rupert, 6th Baron Carrington, B. Conservative politician (b. 1919), 1919 Z, 1972 A, 1974 A, 1992 H
resigns as British Foreign Secretary, 1982 D
NATO Secretary-General, 1983 M
Hague peace conference, 1991 J
Carritt, Edgar Frederick, B. philosopher (1876–1961), 1914 S
Carrizal, Mexico, battle, 1916 F
Carroll, John, Am. Roman Catholic bishop (1735–1815), 1790 R
Carroll, Lewis. *See* Dodgson, Charles
Carry on, Jeeves (P. G. Wodehouse), 1925 U
Carson, Edward, lord Carson, B. Unionist politician (1854–1935), 1854 Z, 1912 J, 1935 Z; resigns from Cabinet, 1918 A; demands repeal of Home Rule, 1919 G
Carson, Rachel, Am. author (1907–64), 1963 P
Carstairs, George, B. philosopher (b. 1916), 1963 R
Carstens, Armus Jacob, G. artist (1754–98), 1795 S
Cartagena Pact, between Britain, France and Spain against Germany, 1907 E
Carte, Richard D'Oyly, B. promoter of opera (1844–1901), 1881 W
Carter, Angela, B. author (1940–92), 1985 U, 1991 U
Carter, Elliott, Am. musician (b. 1908), 1908 Z, 1957 T, 1969 T, 1975 T, 1977 T, 1980 T, 1986 T
Carter, Howard, B. artist and archaeologist (1874–1939), 1922 Q
Carter, Jack, Am. musician, 1958 T
Carter, James Earl, 'Jimmy', Am. statesman, Democrat (b. 1924), 39th president of US (1977–81), 1924 Z
wins New Hampshire Democratic primary, 1976 B
presidential nomination, 1976 G
becomes President, 1976 L
inauguration, 1977 A
energy conservation plan, 1977 D
creates Department of Energy, 1977 H
proposed sale of fighters to Egypt, 1978 B
signs SALT II treaty with USSR, 1979 F
Cabinet reshuffle, 1979 G
warns USSR, 1980 A
presidential re-nomination, 1980 H
wins vote in rules committee, 1980 H
loses election, 1980 L
Carter, John Waynflete, B. bibliographer (1905–75), 1948 Q
Carthaginian Peace, The (E. Mantoux), 1946 O
Cartography, 1779 P
Cartoons:
political, 1784 S, 1918 S, 1922 S
satirical, 1779 S
strip, 1859 S
Cartridge-cases, brass, 1882 P
Cartwright, Edmund, B. dissenting minister and cotton-spinning pioneer (1743–1823), 1786 P
Cartwright, George, B. explorer, 1798 P
Cartwright, Jim, B. playwright (b. 1958), 1992 W
Cartwright, John, B. political reformer (1740–1824), 1774 O, 1776 O
Casals, Pablo, Sp. musician (1876–1973), 1876 Z, 1973 Z
Cask, The (F. Wills Crofts), 1920 T
Caskey, Charles Thomas, Am. scientist (b. 1938), 1967 P
Cass Timberlane (S. Lewis), 1945 U
Cassidy, Sheila Anne, B. doctor (b. 1937), imprisonment and torture in Chile, 1975 L
Casson, Sir Hugh, B. architect (b. 1910), 1951 S
Cast-iron bridge, 1773 P
Casteau, Belgium, NATO headquarters, 1967 C
Castelar y Ripoli, Emilio, Sp. statesman (1832–99), 1873 J, 1874 A
Castelfidardo, Italy, Cavour's victory at, 1860 J
Castiglione delle Stiviere, Lombardy, Italy, 1796 H
Castle Rackrent (M. Edgeworth), 1800 U
Castle of Otranto, The (H. Walpole), 1765 U
Castle, Barbara Anne, Baroness Castle of Blackburn, B. Labour politician (b. 1911), 1968 D
Castle, The (Kafka), 1926 U
Castlereagh, viscount. *See* Stewart, Robert
Castner, H. Y., Am. chemist (1858–99), 1894 P
Castro, Cipriano, Venezuelan leader, 1899 K, 1902 M, 1908 F
Castro, Fidel, Cuban politician (b. 1927), 1958 D, 1959 A, 1961 D, 1971 L; becomes premier, 1959 B; states Russia will establish base in Cuba, 1962 J; visits Russia, 1963 D; CIA plot to kill, revealed, 1975
Casuarina Tree, The (W. S. Maugham), 1926 U
Cat on a Hot Tin Roof (T. Williams), 1954 W
Catalina (H. Ibsen), 1850 W
Catalogue of Nebulae (W. Herschel), 1786 P
Catalogue of the Languages of the Nations (Hervás y Panduro), 1800 Q
Catalonia, Spain, 1979 K
Catalonia, Spain: home rule movement, 1917 H; autonomy granted, 1932 J
Catalysis among enzymes, 1906 P
Catania, Sicily, Allies capture, 1943 H
Catcher in the Rye, The (J. D. Salinger), 1951 U
Cateau, Le, France, 1918 K
Catéchism des Industriels (St. Simon), 1823 O
Cathar, India, annexed by E. India Company, 1832 H
Cathay (E. Pound), 1915 U
Cathédrale, La (J. K. Huysmans), 1898 U
Cathedral, The (H. Walpole), 1922 U
Catherine Furze (M. Rutherford), 1893 U
Catherine II ('The Great') empress of Russia (1762–96), 1764 N, 1766, 1780 F, 1781 B, 1787 A, Q, 1796 L
Cathode rays, experiments with, 1897 P
Catholic Association, in Ireland, 1823 E
Catholic Emancipation, in Britain: Pitt advocates 1800 J; Pitt resigns on issue of, 1801 C; Grenville refuses to grant, 1807 C; bills for, defeated, 1813 E, 1821 D, 1825 E; Wellington supports, 1829 C; achieved, 1829 D
Catholic Parties. *See under* Political Parties
Cathy Come Home, television play, 1966 W
Cato Street conspiracy, 1820 B
Caton, H., F. electrical engineer, 1875 P
Cats, 1981 W
Catto, Jeremy., B. historian, 1984 Q
Caucasus, Russian acquisitions south of, 1829 J
Caught (H. Green), 1943 U
Causes of World War III (C. Wright Mills), 1959 O
Causes of the English Civil War, The (C. Russell), 1990 Q
Cavaignac, Louis, F. general (1802–57), 1848 F
Cavalcade (N. Coward), 1931 W
Cavalotti, Felice, It. Radical, 1896 C
Cave, Sir Stephen, B. politician (1820–80), 1875 M, 1876 C
Cavell, Edith, B. nurse (1865–1915); executed, 1915 K
Cavendish, lord Frederick Charles, B. administrator (1836–82), chief secretary for Ireland, murdered, 1882 Z
Cavendish, Henry, B. natural philosopher (1731–1810), 1766 P, 1784 P, 1785 P, 1789 P, 1798 P, 1810 Z
Cavendish, Spencer, Compton, marquess of Hartington, duke of Cambridge, B. Liberal (1833–1908); elected leader, 1875 B; notes against Liberal government, 1886 F
Cavendish, William, duke of Devonshire (1808–91), 1870 O, 1891 M
Cavour, Camillo, Count, It. statesman (1810–61), 1810 Z, 1859 O, 1861 Z; as minister of Piedmont, 1850 K, 1852 L; meets Napoleon III, 1858 G; rejects Austrian ultimatum for Sardinia to disarm, 1859 D; recalled to Sardinia, 1860 A; defeats papal troops, 1860 J
Cawnpore, India: British massacred, 1857 F, G; British recapture, 1857 M
Cayenne, F. Guiana, 1809 N
Cayley, Arthur, B. mathematician (1821–95), 1845 P
Ceauşescu, Elena, Rouman. politician (1919–89), 1989 M
Ceauşescu, Nicolae, Rouman. politician (1918–89), 1918 Z, 1989 Z
declares Roumania recognizes no supreme authority within international Communist movement, 1966 E
head of state, 1967 M
visits Britain, 1978 F
declares state of emergency, 1989 M
overthrow, 1989 M
Cecil, Lord David, B. author (1902–86), 1902 Z, 1986 Z
Cecil, Robert, Arthur Talbot Gascoyne, 3rd marquess of Salisbury, B. Conservative statesman (1830–1903), 1830 Z, 1885 L, 1895 L; becomes foreign secretary, 1878 D; attends Berlin Conference, 1878 F; becomes Conservative leader, 1881 D; becomes prime minister and foreign minister, 1885 F; resigns, 1886 A; forms ministry, 1886 G; resigns, 1892 G, H; forms ministry, 1895 F; proposes partition of Turkey, 1895 H; reforms ministry, 1900 K; upholds British isolation, 1901 E; retires, 1902 G
Cecil, Robert Arthur James Gascoyne, 5th marquess of Salisbury, B. Conservative politician (1893–1972), attacks British policy on Africa, 1961 C
Cecil, or the Adventures of a Coxcomb (C. Gore), 1841 U
Cecilia (F. Burvey), 1782 U
Celanese, invented, 1865 P
Celant, Germano, It. critic (b. 1940), 1966 S
Celibates, The (G. Moore), 1895 U
Céline, L. F., F. author, 1932 U
Cell theories, 1839 P, 1863 P
Cell, photo-electric, 1904 P
Cellophane, invented, 1912 P
Cellular, theory of plants, 1838 P
Celluloid, invented, 1869 P; roll-films, 1889 P
Cement of the Universe, The (J.L. Mackie), 1974 R
Cement production, statistics of, 1932 Y, 1940 Y, 1959 Y
Cement, Portland, 1824 P
Cendres (I. Xenakis), 1974 T
Censorship:
At the Edge of the Union banned by the BBC, 1985 W
Czechoslovak National Assembly abolishes, 1968 F
War Game, The finally broadcast by the BBC, 1985 W
of art and criticism, in Germany, 1936 U

of books, Roman Catholic index of prohibited books abolished, 1966 R
of films, in Britain, 1920 W, 1951 W
of films, in Italy, 1987 W
of music, in Germany, 1934 T, 1935 T in Russia, 1931 T
of plays, in France, 1775 W, 1800 W
of press. *See* Press, censorship of
of theatre in Britain, 1968 W
on broadcast interviews with political organizations in Britain, 1988 K, 1990 O
political
in Philippines, 1983 J
in Poland, student demonstrations against, 1968 A
in South Africa, reporting of ANC activities banned, 1987 A
Census of population: first accurate, 1801 Y; 1971 O
Census of production, British, first, 1907 O
Centaur, The (J. Updike), 1963 U
Central African Federation (of Northern and Southern Rhodesia and Nysaland): scheme for, 1952 F; Britain rejects request for status as separate state within Commonwealth, 1956 H; elections for, boycotted by European opposition and all African parties, 1962 D; Nyasaland's right to secede acknowledged, 1962 M; UN asks Britain to transfer forces of, to Southern Rhodesia, 1963 K; Dissolved, 1963 M. *See also* Malawi: Rhodesia; Zambia
Central African Republic:
becomes independent, 1960 G
Empire declared, 1976 M
reverts to republic status, 1979 J
Central America, Confederation of United Provinces of, 1823 G
Central American Union (of Guatemala, Honduras and San Salvador), constitution, 1921 J
Central Planning and Control in War and Peace (O. Franks), 1947 O
Central Treaty Organisation (CENTO), name changed from Baghdad Pact, 1959 H; 1979 C
Centre Parties. *See under* Political Parties
Ceres, first asteroid, discovered, 1801 P
Cerezo, Mario Vinicio, President of Guatemala (b. 1942), 1991 A
CERN (Organization Européenne pour la Recherche Nucléaire, Switzerland), 'W' and 'Z' sub-atomicparticles observed, 1983 P
Cernik, Oldrich, Czech. leader (b. 1921), 1968 D
Césaire, Aimé Fernand, F. dramatist (b. 1913), 1966 W
César, (César Baldaccini), F. artist (b. 1921), 1921 Z, 1968 S, 1976 S
Cetywayo, Zululand, captured, 1879 H
Ceylon: Dutch surrender to Britain, 1795 B; Britain retains, 1801 K, 1815 C; tea production in, 1909 Y; becomes self-governing dominion, 1948 B; state of emergency in, 1958 E
Bandaranaike becomes Prime Minister, 1970 E
left-wing rebellion, 1971 D
name changed to Sri Lanka, 1972 E
republic, status changed to, 1972 E
Cézanne, Paul, F. artist (1839–1906), 1839 Z, 1867 S, 1872 S, 1873 S, 1874 S, 1877 S, 1883 S, 1884 S, 1890 S, 1900 S, 1904 S, 1905 S, 1906 Z, 1964 S
Chaban-Delmas, Jacques, Prime Minister of France (b. 1915), 1969 F, 1972 G
Chabrier, Alexis Emmanuel, F. musician (1841–94) 1883 T, 1950 T
Chad Republic, becomes independent, 1960 G
rebel forces overthrow Oueddi regime, 1982 F
border dispute with Libya, 1983 C
OAU calls for end to foreign involvement in civil war, 1983 G
French military instructors and troops, 1983 H
Libyan capture of Faya-Largeau, 1983 H
Libyan planes bomb Faya-Largeau, 1983 H
France and Libya agree to withdraw forces from, 1984 J, L
war with Libya ended, 1988 K
Habre overthrown by Popular Salvation Front, 1990 M
attempted coup, 1992 A
Chad, Lake, Cen. Africa: explored, 1823 P, 1852 P; land east of, leased to Germany, 1893 L
Chadwick, Lynn Russell, B. sculptor (b. 1914), 1955 S, 1956 S
Chadwick, Sir Edwin, B. sanitary reformer (1800–95), 1800 Z, 1842 O, 1890 Z
Chadwick, Professor Sir Henry, B. historian and theologian (b. 1920), 1967 Q
Chadwick, Sir James, B. physicist (1891–1974), 1921 P, 1932 P
Chadwick, Professor Sir Owen, B. historian (b. 1916), 1916 Z, 1966 Q
Chagall, Marc, R. -born F. artist (1887–1985), 1887 Z, 1908 S, 1912 S, 1922 S, 1926 S, 1927 S, 1945 S, 1950 S, 1985 Z
Chain of Voices, A (A. Brink), 1982 U
Chaliapin, Feodor Ivanovich, R. bass singer (1873–1938), 1873 Z, 1938 Z
Chalk Garden, The (E. Bagnold), 1954 W
Challe, Maurice, F. soldier, leads Algerian revolt, 1961 D
Chalmers, Thomas, Scot. church leader (1780–1847), 1843 R
Chamber Music, notable, by:
Bartók, 1908 T
Beethoven, 1806 T
Bloch, 1924 T
Boccherini, 1787 T
Boulez, 1959 T
Britten, 1976 T
Carter, 1986 T
Franck, 1880 T
Goehr, 1990 T
Haydn, 1771 T, 1781 T, 1797 T
Mozart, 1785 T
Schubert, 1819 T, 1825 T
Stravinsky, 1924 T
Tippett, 1979 T, 1992 T
Walton, 1947 T
Trio to perform, formed by Thibaud, Cortot and Casals, 1930 T
Chamber of Commerce, London, 1882 O
Chamberlain, Austen, B. Conservative and Unionist leader (1863–1937), 1863 Z, 1937 Z; becomes chancellor of Exchequer, 1903 J; elected Unionist leader, 1921 C; becomes foreign secretary, 1924 L
Chamberlain, Houston Stewart, B. political author (1855–1927), 1899 O
Chamberlain, Joseph, B. Liberal Unionist leader (1836–1914), 1836 Z, 1896 L, 1897 G, 1914 Z; becomes president of Board of Trade, 1880 D; votes against Liberal government, 1886 F; becomes Liberal Unionist leader, 1891 M; as Colonial Secretary, 1895 F, 1897 F; bids for *entente* with Germany, 1898 C, E; stand on issue of Transvaal franchise, 1899 G; Leicester speech, 1899 L; organises Conservative electoral victory, 1900 K; anti-German speech, 1901 K; visits S. Africa, 1903 B; is converted to Imperial Preference, 1903 E; resigns to test feeling on Imperial Preference, 1903 J
Chamberlain, Neville, B. Conservative politician (1869–1940), 1869 Z, 1940 Z; as Chancellor of Exchequer, 1923 E, 1931 L; forms National ministry, 1937 E; censured for appeasement of Italy, 1938 B; visits Hitler, 1938 J; at Munich Conference, 1938 J; meets Mussolini, 1939 A; fails in negotiations over Poland, 1939 H; resigns from premiership, 1940 E; retires, 1940 K
Chambers, John Graham, B. athlete and journalist (1843–83), 1866 X
Chambers, Jonathan David, B. historian (1898–1970), 1972 Q
Chambers, Raymond William, B. author (1874–1942), 1830 P
Chambers, Robert, B. publisher and author (1802–1871), 1844 P
Chambers, Sir William, B. architect (1726–96), 1776 S
Chambon, Pierre, F. geneticist (b. 1931), 1990 P
Chambord, Henri Charles Ferdinand, comte de, F. pretender as 'King Henri V' (1820–83), 1820 J, 1873 H, 1883 H; Antwerp Declaration, 1872 A; Frohsdorf Letter, 1873 K; refuses to accept tricolour, 1873 K
Chambre Chronophotographique, 1888 P
Chamiso, Adalbert von, G. poet (1781–1838), 1813 U
Chamorro, Violeta Barrios de, Nicaraguan leader (b. 1939), 1990 B
Chamoun, President of Lebanon, 1958 G
Champagne, France, 1917 E; French bombardment, 1915 B; Joffre's offensive, 1915 J
Champlain, Lake, N. America, 1776 K; 1814 J
Champs d'Honneur, Les (J. Rouaud), 1991 U
Chan Sy, Prime Minister of Kampuchea, 1985 A
Chance (J. Conrad), 1914 U
Chance and Necessity (J. Monod), 1971 P
Chancellorsville, Va., US, Confederate victory at, 1863 E
Chandernagore, Bengal, India, French settlement, 1778 N
Chandler, Richard, B. antiquary and traveller (1738–1810), 1775 P
Chanel No. 5 perfume, 1922 W
Chanel, Gabrielle 'Coco', F. couturier (1883–1971), 1883 Z, 1971 Z
Chang, Jung, Chinese author (b. 1952), 1992 U
Channel Tunnel:
first proposed, 1882 O
Report on, 1963 J
rail, Anglo-French agreement on, 1964 B
Britain and France agree plans, 1966 K
Britain abandons project, 1975 A
possible private construction of, 1980 C
rail link plan announced, 1986 A
Treaty signed, 1986 B
construction started, 1987 P
British and French halves, joined up 1990 K
Channon, Henry Paul Guinness, B. Conservative politician (b. 1935), 1986 A
Chansons (Béranger), 1815 U
Chantrey, Sir Francis Legatt, B. sculptor (1782–1841), 1782 Z, 1817 S; bequest, 1841 A
Chao Tzu-yang, Chinese politician (b. 1918), 1987 C, 1987 L
Chaos et la Nuit, 1963 W
Chapel Perilous, The (D. Hewett), 1972 W
Chaplin, Charles, Am. film actor and director (1889–1977), 1889 Z, 1914 W, 1918 W, 1921 W, 1923 W, 1928 W, 1931 W, 1936 W, 1940 W, 1947 W, 1952 W, 1957 W, 1977 Z
Chappaquiddick Island, US, Edward Kennedy plunges car and passenger into river, 1969 G
Kennedy spared legal action, 1970 D

Chappe, Claude, F. engineer (1763–1805), 1793 P
Charcot, Jean Martin, F. physician (1825–93) 1825 Z, 1873 P, 1893 Z
Chardin, Jean Baptiste Simeon, F. artist (1699–1779), 1775 S
Chardonnet, Hilaire, Comte de, F. inventor (1839–1924), 1887 P
Charge of the Light Brigade, 1854 K
Charity bazaars, 1833 O
Charleroi, S.W. Belgium, 1794 F
Charles Albert, King of Sardinia (1831–49), 1847 K; grants constitution, 1848 B; abdicates, 1849 C
Charles Albert, Prince of Carignan, 1821 C, D
Charles Edward Louis Philip Casimir, the 'Young Pretender' to British throne (1720–88), 1788 A
Charles Emmanuel II, King of Sardinia (1796–1802), 1798 M
Charles Felix, King of Sardinia (1821–31), 1821 C
Charles I, emperor of Austria (1916–18), 1916 L; abdicates, 1918 L; *coup d'état* fails, 1921 C, K
Charles III, King of Spain (1759–88), 1767 C
Charles III, duke of Parma, 1854 C
Charles IV, King of Spain (1788–1808), 1800 K; abdicates, 1808 E
Charles IX (J. Chénier), 1789 W
Charles O' Malley (C. Lever), 1841 U
Charles Theodore, elector Palatine, King of Bavaria (1777–99), 1777 M, 1778 M, 1785 A
Charles X, King of France (1757–1836), 1826 N, as Comte d'Artois, 1791 G; accession, 1824 J, dissolves National Guard, 1827 D; appoints Polignac premier, 1829 H; dissolves chambers, 1830 E, ordinances of, 1830 G; abdicates, 1830 H
Charles XIII, King of Sweden (1809–18), 1809 C, 1818 B; adopts Bernadotte as heir, 1810 H; becomes King of Sweden and Norway, 1814 L
Charles XIV, King of Sweden (1818–44), 1818 B, 1844 C. *See also* Bernadotte, Jean
Charles XV, King of Sweden (1859–72), 1859 G
Charles, Crown Prince of Roumania, elected King, 1930 F
Charles, Prince of Denmark, elected King Haakon of Norway, 1905 L
Charles, Prince of Hohenzollern, becomes Carol I of Rumania, 1866 B
Charles, Prince of Wales (Charles Philip Arthur George), (b. 1948), 1948 Z
 created Prince of Wales, 1958 G
 investiture, 1969 G
 maiden speech in House of Lords, 1974 F
 marriage, 1981 G
 attack on modern architecture, 1984 S
 admits talking to plants, 1986 J
 Vision of Britain, A: A Personal View of Architecture, 1989 S
 separation from Princess of Wales, 1992 M
Charles, archduke of Austria (1771–1847), general, 1796 H, 1799 F, J, 1800 D
Charleston, S. Carolina, US, 1781 K; surrenders to British, 1780 E; siege of, 1865 B
Charlottesville, Va., US, university, 1817 S
Charnley, Sir John, B. surgeon (1911–82), 1911 Z, 1954 P, 1982 Z
Charpentier, Gustave, F. musician (1860–1956) 1900 T
'Charter 77' manifesto, 1977 A
Chartier, Emile, F. author (pseud.), 1928 O
Chartism: beginnings, 1836 F; points, 1838 O; London Convention, 1839 B; Parliament rejects petition, 1839 G, 1842 D; riots, 1839 G, L, 1842 H
Chartreuse de Parme, La (Stendhal), 1839 U
Chassepot, A. A., F. gunsmith (1833–1905), 1866 P
Chataway, Christopher John, B. Conservative politician (b. 1931), 1931 Z, 1972 C
Chateaubriand, François René, vicomte de, F. author (1768–1848), 1768 Z, 1797 O, 1801 U, 1802 U, 1805 U, 1809 U, 1814 O, 1848 T, Z
Chatham, Earl of. *See* Pitt, William
Châtillon, France, peace negotiations, 1814 B
Chattanooga, Tenn., US: Confederate defeat at, 1863 L; Sherman's march from, 1864 E
Chatterton, Thomas, B. poet (1752–70), 1765 U 1770 Z
Chatwin, Bruce, B. author (1940–89), 1987 U
Chaumette, Pierre Gaspard, F. revolutionary (1763–1794), 1793 R
Chaumont, France, treaty between Allies, 1814 C
Chautemps, Camille, F. Radical Socialist, 1933 L, 1937 F, 1938 A
Chavez Mena, Dr. Fidel, El Salvadorean politician, 1989 C
Chebichev, Pafnutiy Lvovich, R. mathematician (1821–94), 1850 P
Cheddington, Bucks, England, mail train robbery near, 1963 H
Cheers, television series, 1982 W
Cheever, John, Am. author (1912–82), 1977 U
Chef-d'oeuvre inconnu, Le (H. de Balzac), 1831 U
Chekhov, Anton, R. dramatist (1860–1904), 1860 Z, 1896 W, 1900 W, 1902 W, 1904 W, Z
Chekiang, E. China, Italy demands concessions in, 1899 B
Chemical weapons
 Iran–Iraq War, 1984 C
 international declaration outlawing, 1989 A
Chemical analysis, 1913 P
Chemical terms, treatise on, 1787 P
Chemin des Dames, France, battle, 1917 E
Chemistry:
 Kapitza's studies on Helium II, 1938 P
 synthesis of insulin by Swiss chemists, 1975 P
 synthesis of Vitamin B12, 1976 P
 synthetic DNA, 1978 P
 plastics research, 1981 P
 element 108 synthesized, 1984 P
 fullerenes, evidence found for existence of, 1985 P
 nucleohelicates, 1990 P
 fullerenes isolated, 1991 P
Chemistry of Diet, The (J. Liebig), 1840 P
Chemistry of the Sun, The (J. N. Lockyer), 1887 P
Chemistry, College of London, 1845 O
Chemistry, Organic, Wöhler founds study of, 1828 P
Chemistry, treatise on 1789 P
Chemists' Federation, British, 1958 O
Cheng Naishen, author, 1989 U
Chénier, André Marie de, F. author (1762–94), 1790 O, 1794 U
Chénier, Marie Joseph Blaise de, F. dramatist (1764–1811), 1789 W, 1791 W
Chequers, Bucks, England, becomes official residence of prime minister, 1921 O
Cherasco, Piedmont, N. Italy, peace signed at, 1796 E
Cherbourg, France, Allies take, 1944 F
Chéri (Colette), 1920 U
Chermayeff, Serge Ivan, Am. architect (b. 1900), 1935 S
Chernenko, Konstantin, R. leader (1911–85), 1984 B, 1985 C
Chernobyl USSR, nuclear accident, 1986 D
Cherokee alphabet, 1824 Q; Indians, 1830 E
Cherry Orchard, The (Chekhov), 1904 W
Cherry Valley, N. York, US, massacre, 1778 L
Cherubini, Maria Luigi Carlo, It. musician (1760–1842), 1791 T, 1797 T, 1800 T
Chervenkov, Vulko, Bulg. premier, 1950 B
Cherwell, Lord. *See* Lindemann, F.
Chesapeake Bay, Maryland, US, French occupy, 1781 H
Chesapeake and *Shannon*, naval action, 1813 F
Chess
 Karpov wins World championship, 1975 X
 Short becomes International Master, 1980 X
Chester, Ches., England, Fenian outrages in, 1867 L
Chesterfield, earl of. *See* Stanhope
Chesterton, Gilbert Keith, B. author (1874–1936), 1904 U, 1908 U
Chevalier, Maurice, F. actor and singer (1888–1972), 1888 Z, 1972 Z
Chevalier, Sulpice Guillaume, F. caricaturist under pseudonym of Gavarni (1801–66), 1857 S
Cheviot, The Stag and The Black, Black Oil, The (J. McGrath), 1973 W
Cheyenne Indians, massacred, 1864 C
Chia, Sandro, It. artist (b. 1946), 1978 S, 1980 S
Chiang Ch'ing, Chinese politician (b. 1914), sentenced at 'Gang of Four' trial, 1981 A
Chiang Kai-shek, Chin. Nationalist leader (1887–1975), 1887 Z; northern campaign, 1926 J; opposes Radicals in Kuo Min Tang, 1927 D; overthrows Hankow government, 1927 M; elected president of China, 1928 K; elected Kuo Min Tang president, 1935 M; enters Canton, 1936 H, declares war on Japan, 1936 M; meets Churchill, 1943 L; negotiations with Mao Tse-tung founder, 1945 K; Nanking Assembly grants dictatorial powers, 1948 C; resigns presidency of China, 1949 A; removes forces to Formosa, 1949 G; resumes presidency of Nationalist China, 1950 C; death, 1975 D, Z
Chiaramonti, Luigi Barnaba, It., Pope Pius VII (1800–23), 1800 C, 1814 R
Chiaroscuro (A. John), 1952 S
Chiavenna, Switzerland, France annexes, 1797 K
Chibnall, Marjorie McCallum, B. historian (b. 1915), 1986 Q
Chicago, Ill., US: Sankey and Moody mission, 1870 R; labour riots, 1886 E; world exhibition, 1893 W; stockyards, exposure of conditions in, 1906 O; Republican convention at, 1912 F; Progressive Republican convention at, 1912 H; race riots, 1919 G; university, atomic research, 1941 P, 1942 P
 race riots, 1966 G
 Fermi National Accelerator Laboratory (Fermilab), 1969 P
 DC-10 crash, 1979 E
 first black Mayor, 1983 D
 buildings in, 1890 P
  Chicago Tribune building, 1923 S
  John Hancock Building, 1968 S
  Skyscraper, the first, 1883 P
 population, 1950 Y
Chicago, Judy, American artist (b. 1939), 1979 S
Chichekli, President of Syria, 1953 G, 1954 B, 1957 A
Chichester, Sir Francis, B. yachtsman (1901–72), 1967 X, 1978 X
Chichester-Clark, James Dawson, Baron Moyola, Northern Irish Premier (b. 1923), 1969 E
Chief Truths of Revelation (A. von. Haller), 1772 R
Chiesa, Giacomo della, It. Pope Benedict XV (1854–1922), 1917 H
Chifley, Joseph, Austral. premier, 1945 G
Child allowance, introduction in Britain, 1973 G

Childe Harold's Pilgrimage (Byron), 1812 U
Childers, Erskine Hamilton, President of Eire (1905–74), 1973 E
Childers, Robert Erskine, Ir. author and Republican politician (1870–1922), 1922 L
Children of a Lesser God (M. Medoff), 1980 W
Children of the Arbat (A. Rybakov), 1988 U
Children of the Ghetto, The (I. Zangwill), 1897 U
Children's Hour, radio series, 1961 W
Chile: revolts against Joseph Bonaparte, 1810 J; independence proclaimed, 1818 B; nitrates trade, 1830 P; state religion, 1833 E; territorial settlements with Bolivia, 1866 H, 1874 H; relations with Peru, 1912 L; dispute with Argentine, 1925 C
  Castro visits, 1971 L
  constitutional amendment on expropriation of property vetoed by Allende, 1972 D
  military junta seizes power, 1973 J
  British doctor tortured, 1975 L
  political parties banned, 1977 C
  extension of military government, 1980 J
  protests mark 10th anniversary of military coup, 1983 J
  Catholic church backs demonstrations against human rights violations, 1984 R
  urbanization, 1985 Y
  state of siege declared after attempted assassination of Pinochet, 1986 J
  presidential election, 1989 M
Chillianwalla, Punjab, battle, 1849 A
Chiltern Hundreds, The (W. Douglas-Home), 1947 W
Chimney-sweeps act, in Britain, 1834 O
China: Inland mission, 1865 R; open ports, 1895 D; loans to, 1895 A, C; French concessions in, 1898 D; 'open-door', note, 1899 J; policy, 1800 G, 1900 K; customs service, 1906 E; tea production, 1909 Y; Republic proclaimed, 1911 K; Kuo Min Tang (Nanking) government, recognised by Britain, 1928 M; extra-territorial rights, Britain renounces, 1943 A; North China People's Republic, 1948 J; Communist offensive to drive Nationalist Armies off mainland, 1949 E; People's Republic proclaimed, 1949 K; UN calls for recognition of, 1949 M; Britain recognises, 1950 A
  purge of 'rightists', 1966 F
  Great Proletarian Cultural Revolution, 1966 H
  Red Guards, 1966 H, L, R, 1967 A, H
  army take-over of Public Security Ministry, 1967 B
  United Nations rejects admission of Communist, 1969 L
  diplomatic relations established with Canada, 1970 K
  Britain restores telephone link, 1971 D
  US restrictions relaxed, 1971 J
  population, 1971 Y, 1981 Y, 1991 Y
  Nixon visits, 1972 B
  Britain resumes ambassadorial relations, 1972 C
  Japan and China end legal state of war, 1972 J
  Hua Kuo-feng replaces Chou En-Lai as premier, 1976 A
  arrest and trial of 'Gang of Four', 1976 K, 1977 G, 1980 L, 1981 A
  new constitution affirms rule of law, 1978 C
  relations normalized with US, 1978 M
  diplomatic relations with US opened, 1979 A
  leadership changes, 1980 H
  floods, 1981 G, 1991 G
  scientific research, 1981 P
  Sino–Soviet talks, 1982 L, 1983 C
  US agrees to export high-technology items to, 1983 E
  Sino–British talks on future of Hong Kong, 1983 G
  purge of Communist Party membership, 1983 K
  announces intention to declare unilateral policy on Hong Kong, 1983 L
  illiteracy, 1983 Y
  draft agreement for return of Hong Kong, 1984 J
  economic reforms, 1984 K
  newspaper article on Marxist theory, 1984 M
  cotton production, 1984 Y
  Communist Party Central Committee members resign, 1985 J
  Politburo members resign, 1985 J
  urbanization, 1985 Y
  liberal economic policies, 1987 C
  clash with Vietnam over Spratly Islands, 1988 C
  T'ien-an Men Square demonstration and massacre, 1989 D, F
  merchant shipping tonnage statistics, 1992 Y
Chindwin Valley, Burma, operations in, 1942 E
Chinese Prime Minister, The (E. Bagnold), 1965 W
Chios, Island: Turks capture, 1822 D; massacre, 1822 D, F; garrison surrenders to Greece, 1912 A; Greece annexes, 1914 F
Chippendale, Thomas, B. furniture-maker (d. 1779), 1779 Z
Chippewa, Wis., US, battle, 1814 G
Chips with Everything (A. Wesker), 1962 W
Chirac, Jacques René, F. politician (b. 1932), 1932 Z
  Prime Minister, 1974 E, 1986 C
  resignation as Prime Minister, 1976 H, 1988 E
  re-founds Gaullist party, 1976 M
  Mayor of Paris, 1977 C
  defeated in Presidential elections, 1988 E
Chirico, Giorgio de, It. artist (1888–1978), 1888 Z, 1917 S, 1978 Z
Chissano, Joaquim Alberto, President of Mozambique (b. 1939), 1974 J, 1986 L
Chitral, Pakistan, India claims suzerainty over, 1956 E
Chivalry, High Court of, 1954 O
Chivington, Colonel, Am. soldier, 1864 L
Chladni, E. F. F., It. physicist (1756–1827), 1786 P, 1802 R
Chlorine: discovered, 1774 P; used as bleach, 1785 P; is liquefied, 1823 P
Chlorofluorocarbons (CFCs):
  ozone damage warning, 1974 P
  Swedish ban, 1978 A
  US bans use of, as spray propellants, 1978 P
  international protocol to limit use, 1987 P
  US and UK announce plans to cease using, 1992 P
Chloroform, 1847 P
Chloromycetin, 1948 P
Chlorophyll: pronounced necessary for photosynthesis, 1837 P; composition discovered, 1913 P; synthesis of, 1960 P
Choderlos de Laclos, Pierre Ambroise François (1741–1803), F. author, 1772 U
Choiseul, Etienne François, duc de, F. statesman (1719–85), 1770 H, M
Cholera epidemic, 1830 O
Cholet, N.W. France, Vendéan defeat at, 1793 H
Chomsky, Noam, Am. author (b. 1928), 1928 Z, 1976 R
Choonhavan, Chatichai, Thai leader, 1991 B
Chopin, Frédéric, Pol. musician (1810–49), 1810 Z, 1832 T, 1833 T, 1839 T, 1840 T, 1845 T, 1909 T
Choral Works:
  Appalachia (Delius), 1902 T
  Belshazzar's Feast (Walton), 1931 T
  Canterbury Pilgrims, The (Dyson), 1932 T
  Heart, The (Pfitzner), 1931 T
  Hiawatha's Wedding Feast (Coleridge-Taylor), 1898 T
  Hymn of Jesus (Holst), 1917 T
  Mass of Life, A (Delius), 1905 T
  Rio Grande (Lambert), 1929 T
  Sea Drift (Delius), 1903 T
  Seasons, The (Haydn), 1801 T
  Song of the Earth (Mahler), 1911 T
  Summer's Last Will and Testament (Lambert), 1936 T
  Symphony of Psalms (Stravinsky), 1930 Y
  Towards the Unknown Region (Vaughan Williams), 1907 T
  Twelve, The (Walton), 1965 T
  See also under Mass, settings of; Operas; Oratorios
Chou En-Lai, Chinese politician (1898–1976), 1898 Z, 1967 B, 1976 A, Z; as premier and foreign minister, 1949 K; visits Moscow, 1952 H, 1957 A, 1964 L; visits Rangoon, 1955 D
Chouans, Les (Balzac), 1829 U
Christ Stopped at Eboli (Levi), 1945 U
Christ and Culture (R. Niebuhr), 1952 R
Christian Democrats. *See under* Political parties
Christian Dogmatics (K. Barth), 1932 R
Christian Experience (J. Monroux), 1956 R
Christian Faith and other Faiths (S. Neill), 1961 R
Christian Frederick of Denmark, elected King of Norway, 1814 D
Christian IX, of Denmark (1863–1906), 1863 L
Christian Mysticism (J. Görres), 1836 R
Christian Scientists. *See under* Religious Denominations
Christian Socialism, 1849 R
Christian Socialists. *See under* Political parties
Christian Unity (G. K. A. Bell), 1948 R
Christian VIII, of Denmark (1839–48), 1839 M, 1846 G, 1848 A
Christian Year, The (J. Keble), 1827 R
Christiania, Norway. *See* Oslo
Christianity and Democracy (J. Maritain), 1943 R
Christianity and the Social Order (W. Temple), 1942 R
Christiansen, Arthur, B. journalist (1904–63), 1933 V
Christie, Agatha Mary Clarrisa Christie, B. author (1890–1976), 1890 Z, 1921 U, 1952 W, 1976 Z
Christie, John, founder of Glyndebourne Festival (1882–1962), 1934 T
Christie, Manson and Co., London, art sales at, 1915 S, 1979 S
  share offer, 1973 S
Christmas Carol, A (C. Dickens), 1843 U
Christo, (Christo Javacheff), Am. sculptor (b. 1935), 1935 Z, 1972 S, 1976 S, 1978 S, 1985 S
Chrome Yellow (A. Huxley), 1921 U
Chromosomes, term coined, 1888 P; observed, 1876 P
Chronicle of a Death Foretold (G.G. Márquez), 1983 U
Chronicles of Clovis, The (Saki), 1911 U
Chrysler Car Corporation, US government aid, 1979 L
Chrysler UK, government aid, 1975 M
Chrysler's Farm, Montreal, Canada, US defeat at, 1813 L
Chu Teh, Chinese soldier and statesman (1886–1976), 1886 Z, 1949 E, 1976 Z
Chudinov, Dr. K., R. scientist, 1962 P

Church Army, founded, 1882 R
Church Looks Forward, The (W. Temple), 1944 R
Church and the Churches, The (Döllinger), 1861 R
Church in the Power of the Spirit, The (J. Moltmann), 1978 R
Church of England. *See under* Religious Denominations
Church, Richard William, B. churchman (1815–90), 1891 R
Church, Richard, B. author (1893–1972), 1955 U
Churchill College, Cambridge, 1960 O
Churchill Play, The (H. Brenton), 1974 W
Churchill, Caryl, B. playwright (b. 1938), 1979 W, 1982 W, 1987 W
Churchill, Randolph Frederick Edward Spencer, B. journalist (1911–67), 1964 O
Churchill, Randolph Henry Spencer, lord Randolph Churchill, B. Conservative statesman (1849–94), 1887 A; a member of the 'Fourth Party', 1880 E; Dartford speech, 1886 K; resigns chancellorship of Exchequer, 1886 M; life, by W. S. Churchill, 1906 Q
Churchill, Sir Winston Leonard Spencer, B. statesman, orator and historian (1874–1965), 1874 Z
  First Lord of Admiralty, 1911 K
  becomes Chancellor of Duchy of Lancaster, 1915 E
  resigns from Cabinet,1915 L
  appointed Colonial Secretary, 1921 B
  becomes chancellor of Exchequer, 1924 L
  warns of German air manace, 1934 L
  opposes Chamberlain over Italy, 1938 B
  urges military alliance with Russia, 1939 G
  appointed First Lord of Admiralty, 1939 J
  advises neutrals to side with Britain,1940 A
  forms National Ministry, 1940 E
  'blood and toil' speech, 1940 E
  visits Reynaud, 1940 F
  offers France union with Britain, 1940 F
  meets Roosevelt in W. Atlantic, 1941 H
  visits Washington and Ottawa, 1941 M
  reconstructs ministry, 1942 B
  confers in Moscow, 1942 H
  at Casablanca Conference, 1943 A
  presents Stalingrad sword, 1943 B
  speech on post-war reconstruction, 1943 C
  at Quebec conference, 1943 H
  at Cairo conference, 1943 L
  meets Roosevelt and Stalin at Teheran, 1943 L
  in Quebec, 1944 J
  visits Moscow, 1944 K
  visits Athens, 1944 M
  at Yalta Conference,1945 B
  forms Conservative 'Caretaker' ministry, 1945 E
  requires de Gaulle to order cease-fire in Syria, 1945 E
  at Potsdam Conference, 1945 G
  resigns, 1945 G
  Fulton speech, 1946 C
  at Hague Congress for European Unity, 1948 E
  favours a European army, 1950 H
  forms Conservative ministry, 1951 K
  announces Britain has own atom bomb, 1952 B
  visits Eisenhower, 1953 A, 1954 F
  at Bermuda Conference, 1953 M
  reforms ministry, 1954 K
  portrait, 1954 T
  resigns, 1955 D
  becomes honorary US citizen, 1963 D
  last appears in Commons, 1964 G
  90th birthday, 1964 L
  death, 1965 Z
  state funeral, 1965 A, W
  as artist, 1947 S, 1948 S
  official biography, 1988 Q
  as author:
    life of father, 1906 Q
    Marlborough, 1933 Q
    Second World War, 1948 Q
    History of English-speaking Peoples, 1956 Q
Chwilowa, Grupa, 1984 W
CIA, US Senate interim report reveals CIA plots, 1975 L
Ciano, Count Nobile, It. foreign minister (1903–44), 1936 F, L
Cicero, manuscripts of, discovered, 1819 Q
Cicipio, Joseph, Am. hostage, 1991 M
Cierna-nad-Tisou, Czech., Czechoslovak–Soviet talks, 1968 G
Cigarette advertising, on TV, banned, 1965 W. *See also under* Diseases, lung cancer
Cigarette manufacturers, in Britain, required to state tar yield, 1975 O
Cigarettes, black market in, 1945 O
Cimarosa, Domenico, It. musician (1749–1801), 1792 T
Cimetière marin, Le (P. Valéry), 1920 U
Cimino, Michael, Am. film director (b. 1943), 1980 W
Cincinnati, Ohio, US: Democrat convention at, 1872 E; Red Stockings baseball club, 1868 X; pop concert, 1979 W
Cinema, The: forerunners of, 1888 P, 1894 W; cinematograph invented, 1895 P; sound films, 1927 W; wide screen, 1930 W; 'Cinerama', 1951 W; 'Cinemascope', 1953 W
  in Britain, licensing, 1909 W
    picture theatres in London, 1912 W
    Odeon circuit, 1933 W
  in US, five-cent, 1905 W
    attendances, 1912 W
  audience statistics, 1985 W
  capital allowances on films in Britain ended, 1984 W
  See also Films
Cinq grandes odes (P. Claudel), 1910 U
Cinq-mars (A. de Vigny), 1826 U
Cinque Maggio, Il (A. Manzoni), 1821 U
Cintra, Convention of, 1808 H
Circumnavigation, voyage of, 1766 P
Circus, the, 1941 W
Cisalpine Republic (Italy), 1797 G, K 1799 D, 1801 B 1802 A
Cispadane Republic (Italy), 1796 K; merged with Cisalpine Republic, 1797 G
Cité Antique, La (Fustel de Coulanges), 1864 Q
Citizens (S. Schama), 1989 Q
Citoyen contre les pouvoirs, Le (E. Chartier), 1828 O
City of Dreadful Night, The (F. Thompson), 1880 U
City of Marvels, The (E. Mendoza), 1988 U
Ciudad Rodrigo, Spain, battles, 1810 G, 1812 A
Civil Aerial Transport Committee, British, 1917 O
Civil Defence, in Britain, 1936 C, 1941 O
Civil Disobedience:
    in Ceylon, 1961 A
    in India, 1922 C, 1930 C, 1931 C, 1934 D
Civil List, British, scrutiny of, 1780 D
  Queen Elizabeth requests review, 1971 E
  Select Committee report, 1971 M
Civil Rights, in Northern Ireland, civil rights reforms agreed, 1969 H
Civil Rights, in US: 14th Amendment to secure, 1866 F, 1867 C, 1870 C; Kennedy's speech on, 1963 F; Negroes' peaceful demonstrations, 1963 H; Act signed, 1964 G; Workers, murder of, 1964 H, M, 1965 C; Workers' procession to Montgomery, 1965 C
  legislation to end discrimination in housing and jury service, 1966 D, J
  Jackson, Mississippi, rally, 1966 F
  civil disobedience campaign, 1967 H
Civil Service, in Britain, Commission founded, 1854 O
  posts open to competition, 1870 F, O
  Pendleton Act for, 1901 D
  effect of Crichel Down inquiry on, 1953 O
  five-day week in, 1957 O
  clerical officers work to rule, 1962 A
  first full strike, 1973 B
  job cuts announcement, 1980 L
  in US, reform of, 1883 A
Civil Wars
  in Afghanistan, 1863 F, 1979 M
  in Angola, 1975 L, 1989 F, 1992 L
    MPLA forces gain control of most of Angola, 1976 B
    Cuban withdrawal, 1988 A, 1989 A
    ceasefire, 1991 E
    peace agreement 1991 E
  in Cambodia, 1990 J
    peace accord, 1991 K
  in Chad, 1983 H, J, L
    OAU calls for end to foreign involvement, 1983 G
    France and Libya agree to withdraw forces, 1984 J
  in Chile, 1891 A
  in China, 1922 L, 1926 J, 1927 C, D, M, 1945 K, 1946 A
    Japanese intervention, 1927 E, 1928 E
    Britain recognises Nanking government, 1928 M
    Marshall attempts mediation, 1945 M
    US abandons mediation, 1947 A
    Nationalist reversals, 1949 A
    Tientsin falls to Communists, 1949 A
    Communists resume offensive, 1949 E
    Nationalists remove to Formosa, 1949 G
  in Colombia, 1900 N
  in Congo, 1967 G
  in Dominica, 1965 J
  in El Salvador, 1991 J, 1992 B
  in Ethiopia, 1991 E
  in Greece, 1944 M, 1945 A, 1946 E, 1949 K
  in Honduras, 1909 M
  in Indonesia, 1947 G, M
  in Jordan, 1970 J
  in Korea, 1949 J
  in Lebanon, 1975 D, 1978 K, 1983 J
    Beirut airport bombed, 1968 M
    Syrian intervention, 1976 L, 1981 E, 1987 B
    Christian suburbs shelled by Syria, 1981 E
    Israelis attack Palestinian areas, 1981 G
    French ambassador assassinated, 1981 J
    Christian Phalangist militia withdraw from Beirut, 1983 B
    massacre, 1983 B
    ceasefire, 1983 J
    British embassy closed, 1985 C
    Shi'a Muslim militia attempts to drive Palestinians from refugee camps, 1985 E
    hostages, 1985 F, 1986 D, L, 1987 A, 1990 H, 1991 H, L
    Syrian troops enter Beirut, 1987 B
    Amal militia, 1987 D
    Palestinian refugee camps relieved by Syrian forces, 1987 D
    Arab League ceasefire, 1989 J
    Christian militias withdraw from Beirut, 1990 L

in Liberia, 1990 H, J
in Mexico, 1911 A, D 1912 C, K, 1914 D
in Mozambique, 1991 K, 1992 G, H
in Nicaragua, 1988 C, 1989 L, 1990 D
in Nigeria, 1967 E
in Portugal, 1847 G
in Rhodesia, 1979 M
in Samoa, 1880 L
in Somalia, 1991 A, 1992 M
UN arms embargo, 1992 A
ceasefire agreement, 1992 B
in Spain (Carlist), 1834 G, 1840 F, 1872 D, E, 1875 A, 1876 B
(Franco's), opens, 1936 G
non-intervention in, 1936 H, J, M, 1938 K
siege of Madrid, 1936 L
Italian troops in, 1937 B, C, 1938 D, 1938 A
destruction of Guernica, 1937 D
Bilbao falls, 1937 E
German fleet bombards Almeria, 1937 E
piracy resulting from, 1937 J
government moves to Barcelona, 1937 K
rebels take Gijn, 1937 K
Attlee visits, 1937 M
Franco's naval blockade, 1937 M
withdrawal of Italian troops, 1938 D
Franco's Caledonian offensive, 1938 M
Franco takes Barcelona, 1939 A
Madrid surrenders, 1939 C
in Sri Lanka, 1986 E, 1986 H
Tamil terrorists ambush buses near Trincomala, 1987 D
ceasefire, 1989 F
Indian–Sri Lankan agreement, 1987 G
Indian peacekeeping force, 1987 H
in Switzerland, 1847 K
in US: War for Bleeding Kansas, 1854 E, 1856 E
War of 1861–5, opens, 1861 D
battle of Bull Run, 1861 G
Trent affair, 1861 L
Grant takes Fort Henry, 1862 B
Alabama case, 1862 G
Jackson's victory over Unionists at Bull Run, 1862 H
Lee's victory at Fredericksburg, 1862 M
Confederate victory at Chancellorsville, 1863 E
Lee defeats Confederates at Gettysburg, 1863 G
Sherman marches Unionist Army through Georgia, 1864 E, G
Savannah surrenders to Unionists, 1864 M
Richmond surrenders to Grant, 1865 D ends, 1865 E
Civil and Penal Legislation (J. Bentham), 1802 C
Civilisation (K. Clark), 1969 Q
Civilisation, television series, 1969 W
Civilisation and its Discontents (S. Freud), 1930 R
Cività Vecchia, Italy, French troops at, 1867 K
Civitas Dei (L. Curtis), 1934 R
Clacton, Essex, England, Mod *v.* Rockers at, 1964 C
Claim of Our Age to Legislation, The (F. Savigny), 1814 O
Clair, René, F. film director (1898–1981), 1930 W, 1931 W, 1932 W, 1933 W, 1934 W, 1947 W, 1950 W, 1955 W
Clairvoyance, studies in, 1921 R
Clanchy, Michael Thomas, B. historian (b. 1936), 1979 Q
Clapham Junction, B., rail crash, 1988 M
Clare, John, B. poet (1793–1864), 1793 Z, 1827 U, 1864 Z
Clare, county, Ireland, election, 1828 F
Clarence, Prince Albert Victor, Duke of (1864–92), 1970 L
Clarendon Press, Oxford, 1781 Q
Clarendon, Lord. *See* Villiers, G. W. F.
Clark, Brian Robert, B. playwright (b. 1932), 1978 W
Clark, Charles Joseph, 'Joe', Prime Minister of Canada (b. 1939), 1979 E, M
Clark, Sir George Norman, B. historian (1890–1979), 1934 Q
Clark, George Rogers, Am. soldier (1752–1818), 1779 B
Clark, James ('Jim'), B. racing driver (1936–68), 1936 Z, 1965 X, 1968 X, Z
Clark, Sir Kenneth Mackenzie, Baron Clark, B. art historian (1903–83), 1902 Z, 1957 S, 1969 Q, 1969 W, 1983 Z
Clark, Mark Wayne, Am. general (1896–1984), 1952 D
Clark, Peter, B. historian (b. 1944), 1976 Q, 1983 Q
Clark, Reuben J., Am. politician, writes memo on Monroe Doctrine, 1930 C
Clark, Sir Wilfred le Gros, B. anatomist (1895–1971), 1953 P
Clarke, Sir Andrew, B. Colonial official (1824–1902), 1873 N
Clarke, Peter Frederick, B. historian (b. 1942), 1971 Q
Clarkson, Thomas, B. anti-slavery agitator (1760–1846), 1786 O
Clash, The, B. pop group, 1979 W
Classical scholarship, 1796 Q, 1802 Q, 1850 Q, 1869 Q
Classicism, architectural design, 1984 S
Claudel, Paul, F. author (1868–1955), 1900 Q, 1906 W, 1910 U, 1912 W, 1915 U, 1927 W, 1929 W
Claudius, Matthias, G. author (1740–1815), 1771 U
Claus, Am. scientist, 1961 P
Clausius, Rudolf, Julius Emmanuel, G. physicist (1822–88), 1850 P
Clavigo (Goethe), 1774 U
Clay, Cassius. *See* Ali, Muhammad
Clay, Henry, Am. Whig politician (1777–1852), 1833 C, 1844 L; defeated by Jackson for presidency, 1832 C; compromise resolution on slavery, 1850 A
Claybury, Essex, England, asylum at, 1893 P
Clayhanger (A. Bennett), 1910 U
Clayton-Bulmer treaty, 1850 D
Clea (L. Durrell), 1960 U
Cleland, John, B. novelist (1709–89), 1963 U
Clemenceau, Georges, F. statesman (1841–1929), 1841 Z, 1906 A, 1909 G, 1918 C, 1929 Z; becomes premier, 1917 L; as Chairman of Peace Conference, 1919 A
Clemens, Samuel Langhorne, Am. writer under pseudonym of 'Mark Twain' (1835–1910), 1835 Z, 1869 U, 1875 U, 1884 U, 1910 Z
Clement XIII, Pope (1758–69), It. Cardinal (Carlo della Torre Rezzonico), 1763 R, 1764 R, 1766 R, 1769 B
Clement XIV, Pope (1769–74), It. Cardinal (Lorenzo Ganganelli), 1768 N, 1769 E, 1773 G
Clemente, Francesco, It. artist (b. 1952), 1981 S, 1988 S
Clementi, Muzio, It. musician (1752–1832), 1817 T
Clementis, Vladimir, Czech. foreign minister, executed, 1952 C
Cleopatra (V. Alfieri), 1775 W
Cleopatra's Needle, 1878 S
Clerical Parties. *See under* Political Parties
Clerk, Sir Dugold, B. engineer (1831–79), 1879 P
Clerk-Maxwell, James, B. physicist (1831–79), 1831 Z, 1873 P, 1879 P, Z
Clerke, Agnes May, B. historian of anatomy (1842–1907), 1903 P
Cleveland, Grover Stephen, Am. Statesman (1837–1903) Democrat, president of US (1885–8, 1893–6), 1837 Z, 1895 M, 1908 Z; wins presidential election, 1884 L; inaugurated, 1885 C; defeated, 1888 C; elected, for further term, 1892 L; withdraws treaty annexing Hawaii, 1893 B; repeals Sherman silver act, 1893 L; repeals McKinley tariff, 1894 E; opposes Wilson-Gormann tariff, 1894 H
Cleveland, Ohio, US: Republican convention at, 1924 F; hospital, surgery at, 1964 P
race riots, 1966 G
Cleveland Museum of Art, 1971 S
defaults on its debt, 1978 M
Cleves, ceded to France, 1805 M
Clewall, William H., Am. surgeon, 1984 P
Cliburn, Van, Am. pianist, 1958 T
Clifford, John, B. Baptist (1836–1923), 1891 R
Clifford, Thomas, B. inventor, 1790 P
Clifford, William Kingston, B. mathematician (1845–79), 1873 P
Climate of Treason, The (A. Boyle), 1979 L, O
Climate, research into, 1980 P
Clinton, De Witt, Am. Republician (1769–1828), 1812 L
Clinton, Sir Henry, B. general (?1738–95), 1778 F, 1780 E, J
Clinton, Tenn., US, uranium pile at, 1944 P
Clinton, William Jefferson, 'Bill', Am. statesman, Democrat (b. 1946), 42nd president of US (1993–),1946 Z, 1992 L
Clive, Robert, lord Clive, B. governor of Bengal (1725–73), 1765 E, 1767 A, 1772 C, 1773 Z
Clocks and Clouds (G. Ligeti), 1973 T
Clodin, Claude Michel, F. sculptor (1745–1814), 1806 S
Cloister and the Hearth, The (C. Reade), 1861 U
Cloots, Jean Baptiste du Val de Grace, baron ('Anacharsis'), F. politician (1755–94), 1792 O, 1793 O
'Closed shop' dispute, in Britain, 1946 H; in US, outlawed, 1947 F
Closet (R. Whiteread), 1988 S
Closing of the American Mind, The (A. Bloom), 1987 O
Clothes-rationing in Britain, 1941 O; ends, 1949 B
Clothing, standard, in Britain, 1918 O, 1941 O
Cloud Nine (C. Churchill), 1979 W
Clough, Anne Jemima, B. educationalist (1820–92), 1871 O
Clouzot, Henri, F. film director (1907–77), 1947 W, 1954 W
Clowes, Peter, B. investment adviser (b. 1942), 1992 O
Clubs: Left Book, 1935 O
for women, 1892 O
night, 1921 W
political, in France, 1790 N
Clutsam, G. H., composer of light opera, 1922 W
Clyde, River, Scotland, 1812 P
Clyde, lord. *See* Campbell, Colin
Clydeside, Scotland, munition workers in, 1916 V
Clymer, George, B. inventor (1754–1834), 1813 P
Clynes, John Robert, B. Labour politician (1869–1949), as home secretary, 1929 F
Cnossos, Crete, excavations at, 1910 Q
Coal Questions, The (W. S. Jevons), 1865 O
Coal:
extraction of petrol from, 1931 P, 1935 P

gas. *See* Gas, coal
mines, in Australia, strike, 1949 H
in Britain, statutory control, 1911 O
Sankey commission, 1919 B, 1919 O
strikes, 1922 D, 1944 B
enquiry into, 1925 G
Commission takes over colliery leases, 1942 G
compulsory arbitration, 1943 E
nationalisation, 1946 E, 1947 A
Aberfan Disaster, 1966 K
British National Coal Board, 1971 A, 1981 B
strikes, 1972 A, B, 1973 L, 1974 A, B, 1981 B, 1983 B, C, 1984 C-F, H, J-L, 1985 B, C
Wilberforce Commission, 1972 B
government subsidy, 1972 M
National Union of Mineworkers (NUM), pay bargaining, 1973 K, L, 1974 C
over-time ban, 1973 L
TUC talks on dispute break down, 1974 A
consumption of coal, statistics, 1974 Y
pit closure plan withdrawn, 1981 B
pit closures, 1983 B, 1984 C, 1992 K, M
NACODS votes for strike, 1984 K
Union of Democratic Mineworkers (UDM), 1985 K
in France and Germany, Schuman plan for, 1950 E
in Germany, government control, 1915 G
in US, stabilisation act for, 1935 H
strike, 1943 E
production, statistics of, in Austria, 1870 Y, 1871 Y, 1890 Y, 1901 Y
in Belgium, 1901 Y, 1946 Y
in Britain, 1821 Y, 1831 Y, 1841 Y, 1851 Y, 1861 Y, 1870 Y, 1871 Y, 1880 Y, 1890 Y, 1895 Y, 1901 Y, 1913 Y, 1916 Y, 1920 Y, 1924 Y, 1928 Y, 1941 Y, 1946 Y, 1951 Y
in France, 1831 Y, 1841 Y, 1851 Y, 1861 Y, 1870 Y, 1871 Y, 1880 Y, 1890 Y, 1895 Y, 1924 Y, 1938 Y, 1946 Y, 1951 Y,
in Germany, 1851 Y, 1870 Y, 1871 Y, 1880 Y, 1890 Y, 1895 Y, 1901 Y, 1913 Y, 1920 Y, 1924 Y, 1938 Y, 1946 Y, 1951 Y
in Holland, 1946 Y
in Poland, 1946 Y
in Russia, 1861 Y, 1880 Y, 1890 Y, 1901 Y, 1932 Y, 1938 Y, 1940 Y, 1951 Y
Coal, mines, in South Africa, strike, 1985 H
in US, 1821 Y, 1851 Y, 1870 Y, 1871 Y, 1880 Y, 1890 Y, 1895 Y, 1901 Y, 1913 Y, 1916 Y, 1920 Y, 1924 Y, 1946 Y, 1951 Y
used in steel production, 1861 P
traffic, Anglo-Irish pact for, 1934 M
Coalbrookdale, Salop, England, bridge, 1773 P
Coates, Joseph, N.Z. politician, Reform Party, 1925 E
Cobb, John, B. racing-driver (1899–1952), 1939 P, 1947 P, 1952 P
Cobb, Richard Charles, B. historian (b. 1917), 1917 Z, 1970 Q
Cobbett, William, B. essayist and politician (1766–1835), 1792 O, 1802 V, 1816 V, 1829 U, 1830 U, 1835 Z
Cobden Club, London, founded, 1866 O
Cobden, Richard, B. Liberal and free-trader (1804–1865), 1804 Z, 1835 O, 1865 Z; founds Anti-Corn Law League, 1838 J; signs commercial treaty with France, 1860 A
Cobham, Sir Alan John, B. aviator (1894–1973), 1894 Z, 1926 P, 1973 Z
Coblenz, Germany, French *émigrés* at, 1791 G
Coburg, Francis Josiah, duke of, general (d. 1806), 1789 G, J, K, 1794 F
Cocaine, used as anaesthetic, 1884 P
Cochin-China: Franco-Spanish blockade, 1858 M; France annexes, 1862 F; France organises, 1887 N
Cockcroft, Sir John Douglas, B. physicist (1897–1967), 1897 Z, 1931 P, 1967 Z
Cockcroft, Sir John, B. atomic physicist (b. 1897),
Cocktail Party, The (T. S. Eliot), 1949 W
Cocktail, the, 1922 W
Cocteau, Jean, F. author and film producer (1889–1963), 1889 Z, 1927 T, 1929 U, 1934 W, 1938 W, 1946 W, 1950 W, 1959 W, 1963 Z
Code du Travail, 1912 O
Codes of Law:
in Austria, civil, 1811 O
in Britain, criminal, reformed by Peel, 1827 F
in France, treatise on, 1796 O
Napoleonic, 1807 O
in Germany, civil, 1900 O
criminal, 1872 O
in Japan, penal, 1880 G
in Turkey, 1926 A
Codex Sinaiticus, 1844 Q, 1859 Q
Codos, Paul, Am. aviator, 1932 P
Codreanu, Corneliu, Rum. politician, 1938 L
Cody, William Frederick ('Buffalo Bill'), Am. (1846–1917), 1917 Z
Coe, Michael Douglas, Am. historian (b. 1929), 1966 Q
Coe, Sebastian, B. athlete (b. 1956), 1979 X, 1981 X
Coeducation, study of, 1922 O
Coelebs in Search of a Wife (H. More), 1809 U
Coen, Joel (b. 1955) and Ethan (b. 1958), Am. film directors, 1991 W
Coerne, Louis Adolphe, Am. musician (1870–1922), 1905 T
Coetzee, Gerrie, S. Afr. boxer (b. 1955), 1979 X
Coetzee, John M., S. Afr. author (b. 1940), 1984 U
Coffee production, statistics, 1977 Y
Coffee:
in Brazil, over-production, 1928 O, 1931 N
world production, 1909 Y
Coggan, Frederick Donald, Lord Coggan of Canterbury and Sissinghurst, Archbishop of Canterbury (b. 1909), 1909 Z, 1974 R, 1975 A, 1979 R
'call to the Nation', 1975 R
Cohn, Gustav, G. economist (1840–1918), 1885 O
Coinage:
in Britain, treatises on, 1805 O, 1854 O, 1930 O
florins introduced, 1854 O
farthings no longer legal tender, 1961 A
in Germany, 1873 O
in S. Africa, the Rand introduced, 1961 B
in Switzerland, 1850 O
in US, the dollar introduced, 1792 O
policy of free silver, 1896 L
See also Currency
Coke, Thomas, William, earl of Leicester, B. agriculturist (1752–1842), 1772 P
Colby, Bainbridge, Am. secretary of state, 1920 B
Cold War
bomb explosion at US Soviet embassy, 1968 B
Bush and Gorbachev declare end, 1989 M
Coldstream, Sir William Menzies, B. artist (1908–87), 1937 S
Cole, George Douglas Howard, B. economist (1889–1959), 1947 O
Cole, Nat 'King', Am. jazz singer (1920–65), 1965 Z
Cole, Thomas, Am. artist (1801–48), 1825 S
Colebrooke, Henry Thomas, B. orientalist (1765–1837), 1805 Q, 1822 Q
Colenso, John William, B. churchman, bishop of Natal (1814–83), 1862 R, 1863 R
Colenso, Natal, S. Africa, Bullers repulsed at, 1899 M
Coleridge, Samuel Taylor, B. poet and philosopher (1772–1834), 1772 Z, 1794 W, 1798 U, 1816 U, 1817 U, 1828 R, 1834 Z
Coleridge-Taylor, Samuel, B. musician (1875–1912), 1875 Z, 1898 T, 1912 Z
Colette, Sidonie Gabrielle, F. author (1873–1954), 1900 U, 1908 U, 1920 U
Collected Stories (V.S. Pritchett), 1982 U
Collected Works of Walter Bagehot, The (N. St John-Stevas ed.), 1986 Q
Collection, The (H. Pinter), 1961 W
Collective farms:
in E. Germany, 1960 D
in Russia, 1939 O
Colleen Bawn, The (D. Boucicault), 1860 W
Colley, Sir George Pomeroy, B. soldier (1835–81), 1881 A, B
Collings, Jesse, B. Liberal (1831–1920), 1831 Z, 1886 A, 1920 Z
Collingwood, Robin George, B. philosopher and historian (1889–1943), 1889 Z, 1942 R, 1943 Z, 1945 R, 1946 R
Collins, Lottie, B. music-hall artiste, 1892 W
Collins, Michael, Ir. revolutionary leader (1890–1922), 1890 Z, 1922 H
forms government, 1922 A
Collins, William Wilkie, B. novelist (1824–89), 1860 U, 1868 U
Collinson, Patrick, B. historian (b. 1929), 1967 Q
Collip, James Bertram, B. pathologist (1892–1965), 1925 P
Collor de Mello, Fernando, President of Brazil (b. 1949), 1992 M
Colman, George, the younger, B. dramatist (1762–1836), 1797 W
Colmar, E. France, 1945 B
Cologne, W. Germany: archbishop, 1837 R; Roman Catholic working-men's club, 1847 R; Cathedral, 1880 S; Allies occupy, 1918 M, 1925 A; art in, 1920 S; British evacuate, 1925 M; bombing, 1942 E; Allies take, 1945 C; anti-Semitism in, 1959 M
Colomba (P. Mérimée), 1840 U
Colombe (J. Anouilh), 1951 W
Colombia: Republic formed from Venezuela and New Grenada, 1819 M; truce with Spain, 1820 L; Panama joins, 1821 L; Britain recognises independence, 1824 M; Venezuela secedes from, 1830 J; dissolution of Union, 1831 L; grants Panama Canal concession, 1878 E; delays ratification of Hay-Herrán Pact, 1903 E, L; coffee production in, 1909 Y
Contadora Group, 1983 G
Nevado del Ruiz erupts, 1985 L
drug trade, 1989 H
presidential candidate assassinated, 1989 H
presidential elections, 1990 E
Colombo, Ceylon: Conference of Commonwealth foreign ministers, 1950 A; Plan, 1951 B; Conference of Asian premiers, 1954 D
Colonial Conference, British, first, 1887 D. *See also under* Conferences
Colonial Development Corporation, 1947 O
Colonial Development Fund, 1929 O
Colonial Secretaryship, British, 1768 A; revived, 1854 F

Colonial Society, German, 1882 O
Color Purple, The (A. Walker), 1983 U
Colorado State, US: US obtains, 1848 E; becomes a US state, 1876 H; grants for irrigation in, 1894 H
Colour Bar. *See* Apartheid; Civil Rights
Colour TV, 1953 P
Colour film, 16 mm., 1929 P
Colour films, 1929 W
Colour of Blood, The (B. Moore), 1988 U
Colour photography, Spier-Dufay process, 1931 P
Colour reproduction, process for, 1907 P
Colour sensitising, 1873 P
Colours, theory of, 1810 P
Colt, Samuel, Am. gunsmith (1814–62), 1835 P, 1853 P
Columbia, S. Carolina, US, Unionists take, 1865 B
Columbo, television series, 1971 W
Columbus (F. Fernández-Armesto), 1991 Q
Columbus, Ohio, US, state capital, 1839 S
Colvin, Howard Montagu, B. historian (b. 1919), 1978 Q
Comaneci, Nadia, Rouman. gymnast (b. 1956), 1976 X
Combes, Emile, F. anti-clerical, 1902 F, 1904 L
Combination of Gases, The (J. L. Gay-Lussac), 1808 P
Combinatorial Theory of Possibility, A (D. Armstrong), 1989 R
Comecon, proposed links with EC, 1985 F
Comedians (T. Griffiths), 1975 W
Comedians, The (G. Greene), 1966 U
Comédie humaine, La (Balzac), 1829 U
'Comet' aircraft, 1954 P
Comets:
calculation of orbits, 1797 P
Encke's, 1818 P
photography of, 1881 P
Comic Tales (C. M. Wieland), 1765 U
Comics, horror, 1952 V
Cominform (Communist Information Bureau): established, 1947 K; Yugoslavia expelled from, 1948 F; dissolved, 1956 D
Coming Architecture, The (Le Corbusier), 1926 S
Coming Democracy, The (Fernau), 1917 D
Coming Out of School (L.S. Lowry), 1927 S
Coming Over: Migration and Communication between England and New England in the Seventeenth Century (D. Cressy), 1987 Q
Coming Struggle for Power (J. Strachey), 1932 O
Coming of Christianity to Anglo-Saxon England, The (H. Mayr-Harting), 1972 Q
Comité d'Etudes du Haut-Congo, 1878 L
Commandos and Task Forces:
British, raid Norway, 1941 M
raid Wake Islands, 1942 B
raid St. Nazaire, 1942 C
raid Dieppe. 1942 H
Wingate's, in Burma, 1943 D
raid Aleutian Islands, 1943 E
raid Solomon Islands, 1943 F
raid New Guinea, 1943 F
in Philippines, 1944 K
Commentaries on the Laws of England (W. Blackstone), 1765 O
Commission for Racial Equality, 1976 O
Commissions, Anglo-US, for Caribbean, 1942 O
US-League, on slavery in Liberia, 1930 C
Kahane, on Beirut massacre, 1983 B
Philippines, investigating assassination of Aquino, 1983 K
Commissions, British
Anglican–Roman Catholic International Commission (ARCIC), 1977 R
Final Report of, 1982 R
Clegg, on pay comparability, 1979 C, H, 1980 H
Diplock, on Northern Ireland, 1972 M
Doctrine Commission of the Church of England, 'We Believe in God' report, 1987 R
Newsome, on public schools, 1968 O
on Anglo–Irish links, to be established, 1980 M
Pearce, on Rhodesia, 1972 A, E
Redcliffe-Maud, on Local Government, 1969 O
Salmon, on Standards of Conduct in Public Life, 1976 O
Wilberforce, on miners' pay, 1972 B
Commissions, British Royal:
betting, lotteries and gaming, 1951 O
capital punishment, 1953 O
criminal procedure, 1981 O
Dilke on housing, 1884 O
distribution of Income and wealth, 1977 L
divorse, 1912 O
ecclesiastical discipline, 1903 R
equal pay for women, 1946 L
fine arts, 1923 S
Greater London, 1957 G
land, 1965 O
law, 1965 O
Lawrence, on M.P.s salaries, 1964 L
mental patients, 1953 O
mines, 1842 O
monopolies, 1963 M
National Incomes, 1962 O
Newson, public schools, 1965 W
new towns, 1961 O
Palestine, 1937 G, 1938 A
press, the, 1961 B
science, 1870 O
Simon, on India, 1926 L
Trades Unions and Employers' Associations, 1965 B, 1968 O
vivisection, 1912 O
Woodhead, on Palestine, 1938 A
Commissions, South African
Erasmus, on Information Department scandal, 1978 M, 1979 D, F
calling for abolition of apartheid and introduction of universal franchise, 1989 O
Goldstone, on state dirty tricks campaign against ANC, 1992 L
Commissions, US:
Taft, on Philippines, 1900 B
for Haiti, 1930 B
Tower, on Iran-Contra affair, 1987 B
Commissions, international
International Whaling Commission, 1979 G
UN commission to Iran, 1980 B
Committees, British:
Amultree, on holidays with pay, 1938 O
Beaver, on air pollution, 1953 O
Burnham, on teachers' pay, 1963 G
Craythorne, on Sunday entertainment, 1964 W
Criminal Law Revision Committee, 1972 O
Devlin, on docks, 1965 H
Franks, on reform of Official Secrets Act, 1972 O
Fraser, on TV and the young, 1963 O
Guillebaud, on health service, 1956 A
Guillebaud, on railwaymen's pay, 1960 C
Hankey, scientific advisory, 1940 O
Howick, on ecclesiastical appointments, 1964 R
Hunt, on Northern Irish policing, 1969 K
Latey, on age of majority, 1967 O
May, on budget deficit, 1931 G
neglect of science, 1916 P
Newsom, on education, 1963 O
Plowden, on aircraft industry, 1965 M
Plowden, on diplomatic service, 1964 B
Reith, on new towns, 1946 O
Royal Society, on emigration of scientists, 1963 B
Uthwatt, on land development, 1942 O
Waddell, on examinations, 1978 O
Waverley, on export of works of art, 1952 S
Committees, US, Un-American Committee, hearing on Ku-Klux-Klan, 1965 K
Committees, international:
Lucerne, on wavelengths, 1934 O
Young, on reparations, 1928 M, 1929 F
See also under United Nations
Common Market or European Economic Community (EEC), ('The Six'): resolution on, adopted by European Coal and Steel Community 1956 E; Rome Treaty for, 1957 C; in force, 1958 A; Britain applies for membership, 1961 H; Heath's statement to, 1961 K; agreement on agriculture, 1962 A; Commonwealth premiers endorse Britain's attempt to enter, 1962 J; Britain resumes negotiations, 1962 L; de Gaulle's objection to British entry, 1963 A; France leaves council meeting, 1965 G; merger of executive authority of, with Euratom and ECSC, 1965 M
Common Pursuit, The (F. R. Leavis), 1952 U
Common Sense (T. Paine), 1776 O
Common, Andrew Ainslie, B. astronomer (1841–1903), 1881 P
Commons Preservation Society, 1865 O
Commonwealth Party. *See under* Political Parties
Commonwealth Relations Office: established, 1942 O; overseas staff amalgamated with foreign service, 1964 B, 1965 A
Commonwealth of Independent States (CIS), 1991 M
price controls lifted, 1992 A
Commonwealth, British:
S. Africa retains right to secede, 1934 F
citizens of, become British subjects, 1948 G
foreign ministers of, confer in Colombo, 1950 A
London economic conference,1952 L
premiers of, confer in London, 1953 F, 1960 E, 1961 C 1962 J, 1964 G, 1965 F
finance ministers of, meet at Sydney, 1954 A
trade and economic conference, Montreal, 1958 J
Cyprus votes to apply for membership, 1961 B
S. Africa leaves, 1961 E
Common Market, 1962 J
secretariat established, 1965 F
limit imposed to immigrants to Britain from, 1965 H
African states leave, 1965 M
British Colonial Office responsibilities assumed by Commonwealth Office, 1966 G
Conference seeks mandatory UN sanctions againt Rhodesia, 1966 J
Barbados becomes independent within, 1966 L
British Commonwealth Office merges with Foreign Office, 1968 K
Guyana becomes republic within, 1970 B
Gambia becomes republic within, 1970 D
Tanzania, Uganda and Zambia threaten withdrawal, 1970 G
Fiji becomes independent within, 1970 K
Immigration Bill restricts rights of abode, 1971 B
Sierra Leone becomes republic within, 1971 D
Pakistan leaves in anticipation of British recognition of Bangladesh,1972 A
Sri Lanka becomes republic within, 1972 E

British government defeated on new immigration rules favouring EC over Commonwealth citizens, 1972 L
Bahamas becomes independent within, 1973 G
Grenada beomes independent within, 1974 B
Conference on human rights, 1977 F
Conference on Zimbabwe Rhodesia, 1979 H
Antigua and Barbuda become independent within, 1981 L
Belize becomes independent within, 1981 J
sanctions against South Africa called for, 1986 F, G
premiers of, endorse Britain's attempt to enter Conference declaration on South Africa, 1987 K
Mauritius becomes republic within, 1992 C
Communards, French, 1871 G
Communications:
telephone service in Berlin re-established, 1971 A
Berlin Agreement, 1971 J
British telephone link with China restored, 1971 D
Intelpost, electronic facsimile service, 1980 P
Intelsat-V satellite launched, 1980 P
British Inland Telegram service ended, 1982 K
fibre optic cable laid across Atlantic Ocean, 1987 P
See also Broadcasting; Radio; Satellites; Television
Communism:
International, 1876 O, 1919 O, 1943 E
Russo-Chinese ideological talks, 1963 G, 1964 B
in Indonesia, 1966 C
Roumania recognizes no supreme authority within international Communist movement, 1966 E
in China, 1966 H
US Supreme Court upholds right of travel to Communist countries, 1967 A
World Communist Summit, Budapest, planned and postponed, 1968 B, J
Brezhnev Doctrine, 1969 B
World Communist Conference, Moscow, 1969 F
in Iran,1983 E
in Czechoslovakia, 1989 L
in E. Germany, 1989 M
in Bulgaria, 1990 A, B
in Yugoslavia, 1990 A
in Soviet Union, 1990 B, G, 1991 H
See also under Communist; Deviations; International; Political Parties
Communist International, 1876 O; Third, 1919 O, 1943 E
Communist League, founded in Paris, 1836 O
Communist Manifesto, 1848 O
Communists. *See under* Political Parties
Comoro Islands, declaration of independence, 1975 G
Compact Disc Player (CD), 1982 P
Compaore, Blaise, Burkina Faso military leader (b. 1951), 1991 F
Comparative Grammar (F. Bopp), 1833 Q
Comparative Psychology, 1859 R, 1900 R
Comparative Zoology, 1796 P
Compass, gyro, 1907 P
mariners, reform of, 1879 P
Compensation:
Austria, to Turkey, for annexing Bosnia, 1909 B
W. Germany, to Britain, for victims of Nazi persecution, 1964 F
in Britain, workmen's, 1897 O
in France, for nobility, 1825 D
Compiègne, France, German offensive near, 1918 F
Complaintes (J. Laforgue), 1885 U
Complete Duty of Man (H. Venn), 1763 R
Compound E. (Cortisone), discovered, 1949 P
Comprehensive schools, in Britain, 1965 O
Compressions (César), 1968 S
Compte Rendu (J. Necker), 1781 O
Compton, Sir Edmund Gerald, B. ombudsman (b. 1906), 1967 D
Compton-Burnett, Ivy, B. author, 1935 U, 1944 U, 1959 U
Computer
statistics of machines in use, 1958 Y
Atlas,1961 P
used for investigating authorship, 1963 Q
parallel processor, 1967 P
bubble memory device, 1969 P
'floppy disc',1970 P
microprocessor, 1971 P
Pascal language, 1971 P
Computerized axial tomography (CAT), 1972 P
programmable pocket calculator, 1974 P
personal, 1975 P
Apple II introduced, 1977 P
spreadsheet programme for personal, 1979 P
MS-DOS, 1981 P
first 'clone' of an IBM, 1982 P
'fifth generation' project launched, 1983 P
mouse control box, 1983 P
personal computer with hard disc, 1983 P
pull-down menu, 1983 P
Data Protection Act, 1984 B, O
lap size, 1986 P
Numerical Aerodynamic Simulation Facility, 1987 P
hackers, 1988 P
viruses, 1988 P
games, 1991 W
See also under Automation
Comte, Auguste, F. philosopher (1798–1857), 1798 Z, 1830 R, 1865 R, 1957 Z
Concept of Mind (G. Ryle), 1950 R
Concept of Motivation (R. S. Peters), 1958 R
Concertina, invented, 1829 T
Concertos:
clarinet, Finzi, 1949 T
orchestra
Arnold, 1976 T
Carter, 1969 T
pianoforte, Beethoven, 1800 T, 1801 T, 1805 Y, 1809 T
Brahms, 1861 T, 1882 T
Grieg, 1868 T
Ligeti, 1988 T
Lutoslawski, 1988 T
Rachmaninov, 1901 T, 1935 T
Ravel, 1932 T
Roussel, 1928 T
Schumann, 1841 T
Tchaikovsky, 1875 T
viola, Bartók, 1950 T
Walton, 1922 T
violin and 'cello, Brahms, 1887 T
violin, Bartók, 1938 T
Bax, 1943 T
Beethoven, 1806 T
Berg, 1935 T
Brahms, 1879 T
Britten, 1941 T
Elgar, 1910 T
Ligeti, 1990 T
Malipiero, 1952 T
Mendelssohn, 1844 T
Respighi, 1922 T
Walton, 1932 T
violoncello, Bax, 1932 T
Busch, 1943 T
Elgar, 1918 T
Lutoslawski, 1970 T
Panufnik, 1992 T
Schnittke, 1990 T
Walton, 1957 T
Concord, Mass., US, battle, 1775 D
Concordats of Papacy:
with Austria, 1855 H
with Belgium, 1828 G
with France, 1801 G; ended, 1905 M
with Germany, 1933 G
with Hungary, 1964 H
with Netherlands, 1827 F
with Poland, denounced, 1947 J
Concorde supersonic airliner, 1962 L, 1969 P, 1976 A, P
Concrete, reinforced, 1849 P, 1877 P
'Concrete Art', 1930 S
Condenser, invented, 1765 P, 1769 P
Condition humaine, La (A. Malraux), 1933 U
Condition of Man (L. Mumford), 1944 R
Condition of the Working Classes in England (F. Engels), 1845 O
Conditions for Peace (E. H. Carr), 1942 O
Condorcet, Marie Jean Antoine Nicholas Caritat, marquis de, F. mathematician, philosopher and revolutionary (1743–94), 1793 O, 1794 Z
Conduction of Electricity through Gases, The (J. J. Thomson), 1903 P
Confederate States, US, formed, 1861 B
Confederation of British Industry (CBI), 1972 H, J, 1974 B
Confederation of Independent African States, 1958 D
Confederation of the Rhine, 1806 K; dissolved, 1813 K
Confederazione Generale de Lavoro, 1906 O
Conferences, and Congresses:
African Wild Life, 1961 P
Aix-la-Chapelle, 1818 J
Algeciras, on Morocco, 1905 G, J, 1906 A
All-African People's, Accra, 1958 M
Allied, War of 1914–18, 1916 C
Allied, War of 1939–45 for allied leaders:
Cairo, 1943 L
Casablanca, 1943 A
London, 1941 F, J
Moscow, 1942 H, 1943 K
Potsdam, 1945 G
Quebec, 1943 H
Teheran, 1943 L
Yalta, 1945 B
Anglo–Irish Agreement, 1985 M
Arab summit, 1967 J
Architecture, Modern, 1928 S
Athens, of Balkan powers, 1930 K, 1937 B
Atlantic, of NATO Parliamentarians, 1959 F
Bangkok, of heads of US Asiatic missions, 1950 B
of SEATO, 1955 B
Basle, Franco-German Parliamentary, 1950 A
Belgrade, on R. Danube, 1948 G
Berlin, on Eastern Question, 1878 F, G
on protection of workers, 1890 C
on workers and soldiers, 1918 M
on Germany's currency, 1922 L
on cultural freedom, 1950 O
of foreign ministers, 1954 A, B
Bermuda, on refugees, 1943 D
between Eisenhower and Macmillan, 1957 C
Berne, of International Socialists, 1919 B

Bloemfontein, on Transvaal franchise, 1899 C
Bretton Woods, UN monetary and financial, 1944 G
British Colonial London, 1887 D, 1902 F
in Ottawa, 1894 F
British Commonwealth, of Dominion premiers, 1944 E
Economic, London, 1952 L
Law, London, 1955 O
Premiers, London, 1953 F, 1960 E, 1961 C, 1964 G, 1965 F
British Guiana, constitutional, 1962 L, 1965 L
British Imperial, London, 1907 E, 1911 E, 1921 F, 1923 K, 1926 K, 1930 K, 1937 E
Brussels, on Abolition of Slave Trade, 1889 F
on Germany's reparations, 1920 M
on Sino-Japanese War, 1937 K
on Belgian Congo, 1960 A
Buchlau, 1908 J
Buckingham Palace, on Irish Home Rule, 1914 G
Buenos Aires, Pan American, 1936 M
Cairo, of non-aligned states, 1964 K
Cambridge, of International Christians, 1946 R
of European vice-chancellors of universities, 1955 O
Camp David Summit, 1978 J
Cannes, on reparations, 1922 A
Caracas, of Organisation of American States, 1954 C
Casablanca, of Allied leaders, 1943 A
of heads of African states, 1961 A
Chinese Communist Party Congress, 1977 H, 1982 J
Chinese Customs Service, 1925 K
Colombo, of Commonwealth foreign ministers, 1950 A
of Asian premiers, 1954 D
Commonwealth, 1966 J, 1977 F, 1979 H, 1987 K
Copenhagen, of Lutherans, 1929 R
Coquilhatville, on Congo, 1961 D
Cracow, Pan-Slav, 1892 O
Darlington, on future of Northern Ireland, 1972 J
Dublin, of Sinn Fein, 1919 A
Erfurt, held by Napoleon, 1808 K
European Conference on Security and Co-operation, 1983 J
European Rabbis, 1957 R
Geneva, on arms traffic, 1925 E
on disarmament, 1926 E
economic, 1927 E, 1930 L
on tariffs, 1930 B
disarmament, 1932 B
Germany leaves, 1932 J
returns, 1932 M
No Force Declaration by, 1932 M
Germany leaves, 1933 K
ends, 1934 F
monetary, 1933 F
on world health, 1948 O
on Korea and Indo-China, 1954 D
Summit, 1955 F, G
on atomic energy, 1955 H
on detection of nuclear explosions, 1958 G
on surprise attack, 1958 L
on law of the sea, 1958 O
on Germany, 1959 E
disarmament, 1962 C, 1964 A, 1966 A, 1967 B, H, 1971 H, 1985 A, C, L, 1987 A, C, D, J, L, 1988 A
France, boycotts, 1962 C
on Laos, 1962 G
GATT, 1963 E
Genoa, on economic affairs, 1922 D
Hague, The, Peace, 1899 E
for European Unity, 1948 E
EC Conference, 1986 F
Hague peace conference on Yugoslavia, 1991 J, L
Honolulu, of Pacific Council, 1952 H
Hot Springs, on post-war relief, 1943 F
Islamic Foreign Ministers Conference, 1980 R
Jerusalem, on missions, 1928 R
Jews, Christians and Muslims, Standing Conference of 1972 R
Lahore, Islamic summit, 1974 B
Laibach, 1820 L, 1821 A, B
Lambeth Conference, 1968 R, 1988 R
Lancaster House, London, on Rhodesia, 1979 J, M
Latin American states, on Mexico, 1915 K
Lausanne, on Near East, 1923 B
on Faith and Order, 1927 R
Lebanon reconciliation conference, Lausanne, 1984 C
Léopoldville, of independent African states, 1960 H
'Little Eight', for new West Indies federation, 1962 E
Locarno, 1925 K
London
on Belgium, 1830 M, 1831 A, C, F, K
on Danish question, 1864 D
on neutrality of Luxembourg, 1867 E
on Black Sea clauses of 1856 Treaty, 1871 C
of Russian Social Democratic Party, 1903 L
naval, 1908 M
on Turkey and Balkans, 1912 M, 1913 A
of Allied Labour and Socialist Parties, 1918 B
on Near East, 1921 B
Anglo-Russian, 1924 D
on reparations, 1924 G
Round Table on India, 1929 M, 1930 L, 1931 C, 1931 J, 1932 L
on Greek independence, 1930 B
naval disarmament, 1930 D, 1934 K
Japan leaves, 1936 A
monetary, 1933 F
on rearmament, 1935 B
on non-intervention in Spain, 1936 J
world trades unions, 1945 B
on Palestine, 1946 J
on Germany, 1947 L, 1950 E
on British Africa, 1948 J
on space travel, 1951 O
to combat Russian aggression, 1951 J
on Western foreign policy, 1952 F
on British W. Indian federation, 1953 D
on Rhodesias and Nyasaland, 1953 A
on European unity, 1954 K
of foreign ministers of Britain, Greece and Turkey, 1955 H
on Nigerian constitution, 1957 E
on Singapore constitution, 1957 C
on Cyprus, 1960 A, 1964 A
on Kenya constitution, 1960 A, 1962 B
on Nyasaland constitution, 1960 G
on Sierra Leone constitution, 1960 D
on Uganda constitution, 1961 K
on Mauritius constitution, 1965 J
on rundown of British forces in Malta, 1967 B
Lucknow, all party, on India's status, 1928 H
Lusaka, Commonwealth, on Zimbabwe Rhodesia, 1979 H
Manila, of Vietnam War allies, 1966 K
Milan, of Socialist International, 1952 K
Montreal, on Commonwealth trade, 1958 J
Moscow, All-Union Soviet, 1927 M
of Soviet writers, 1934 U
of foreign ministers, 1947 C
of Russian Communist Party, 1952 K
on Soviet satellites, 1954 L
Münchengratz, 1833 J
Mundania, between Allies and Turkey, 1922 K
Munich, on Czechoslovakia, 1938 J
invalidated, 1973 M
Nablus, of Arabs on Palestine, 1922 H
Nairobi, to end UN Decade for Women, 1985 G
Namibian peace conference, 1981 A
National Reconciliation Conference on Lebanon, Geneva, 1983 K
New Grenada, 1816 B
Nyon, on Mediterranean, 1937 J
on Cyprus, 1974 G, 1985 A
on Middle East, 1973 M
on Rhodesia, 1976 K
on Security and Co-operation in Europe, 1972 L, 1973 G, 1975 H, 1977 A, 1990 L
Organization of African Unity (OAU), 1984 L, 1985 G
Oxford, on Church, Community and State, 1937 R
Duke of Edinburgh's, on Industry, 1956 G
Panama, Pan American, under Bolivar, 1826 F
Paris, Peace, 1856 B, 1946 G
achieved, 1960 E
Summit, preliminary negotiations for, 1958 A, B, F, 1959 M
Peking, Asia and Pacific, 1952 K
All-China People's, 1954 J
Peru, Pan-American, makes Declaration of Peru, 1938 M
Prague, between France, Germany and Austria, 1813 G
Pan-Slav, 1848 F, 1908 G
of Soviet satellites, 1950 K
Rangoon, of Asian Socialists, 1953 A
Rastadt, 1797 M, 1799 D
Reichenbach, 1790 F
Rio de Janeiro, on Environment and Development, 1992 P
Rome, on immigration, 1924 E
of EDC foreign ministers, 1953 B
Russia, Communist Party, 25th Congress, 1976 B
San Francisco, 1945 B, D
Peace between Allies and Japan, 1951 J
Spa, on reparations, 1920 G
Stockholm, of free trade unions, 1953 G
Stresa, between Britain, France and Italy, 1935 D
Tangier, N. African Nationalists, 1958 D
Tripoli, of Arab states, 1977 M
Troppau, 1820 K, L, M
Tucuman, 1816 G
UN Conference on the Law of the Sea, 1982 O
Verona, 1822 K, L, M
Versailles, Peace, 1918 L, 1919 A
Belgium guaranteed place at, 1916 B
adopts principle of League of Nations, 1919 A
League Covenant laid before, 1919 B
Vienna, 1814 L, 1815 F, 1820 E
on Danube basin, 1936 L
World Communist, 1952 M
OPEC, 1975 M
Warsaw, Communist, 1947 K
Communist Youth, 1955 H
Washington, on Samoa, 1887 F
Pan-American, 1889 K
International Labour, 1919 K

on disarmament, 1921 L
scientific, 1940 P
Wavelengths, redistribution of, 1948 P
Wembley, Power, 1924 P
World Communist Conference, 1969 F
World Council of Churches, Fourth Assembly of 1968 R
Zemstvo, 1904 L
Zionist, 1945 H
Confessional (F. Blackburne), 1766 R
Confessions (Rousseau), 1781 U
Confessions of Zeno (I. Svevo), 1921 U
Confessions of an Opium Eater (T. de Quincey), 1821 U
Confidential Clerk, The (T. S. Eliot), 1953 W
Conflicts (L. B. Namier), 1942 O
Congo, Belgian: Colonisation, 1878 L; rivalry with Portuguese, 1884 B; colony established, 1885 B; Belgian advances in, 1893 F; atrocities in, 1903 E, 1905 L; revolt in, 1905 B; Leopold II hands over to Belgium, 1908 H; frontier settled, 1927 G; Brussels conference promises independence, 1960 A; independence as Congolese Republic, 1960 F; Belgium suspends aid to, 1967 H; renamed Zaire, 1971 K. *See also* Congolese Republic
Congo, French: de Brazza in, 1886 D, 1888 M; boundary with Cameroons settled, 1894 C; reorganised, 1910 A
Congo, International Association of, recognised, 1884 M
Congo, River, Stanley traces source of, 1875 P; explorations of Stanley and de Brazza, 1880 F; Portuguese designs near, 1884 B; free trade on, 1884 L; Anglo-Portuguese agreement on, 1890 L
Congo, Upper, Arab rising in, 1892 L, 1897 J
Congolese Republic:
independence, 1960 F
army mutinies, 1960 G
Belgium sends troops to, 1960 G
Lumumba appeals to UN,1960 G
Léopoldville government severs relations with Belgium, 1960 G
UN demands evacuation of Belgian troops, 1960 G
UN troops enter Katanga, 1960 H
Kasavubu dismisses Lumumba, 1960 J
Russia provides aircraft for Lumumba, 1960 J
Lumumba arrested, 1960 M
Kasavubu establishes central government, 1961 B
Khrushchev calls for supervised restoration of independent Congo, 1961 B
Lumumba's death, 1961 B
UN urges use of force, 1961 B
Congolese leaders agree on Confederation under Kasavubu, 1961 C
Coquilhatville conference,1961 D
Tshombe arrested, 1961 D
United States of Congo formed, 1961 E
Tshombe freed, 1961 F
UN breaks with Katanga government, 1961 J
Hammarskjöld killed in air crash,1961 J
UN force attacks Katanga, 1961 M
cease-fire in Katanga, 1961 M
Tshombe ends secession of Katanga, 1961 M
UN plan for reunification of Congo, 1962 J
cease-fire, 1962 K
UN troops occupy Elisabethville, 1962 M
capture Jadotville, 1963 A
Tshombe accepts plan for Katanga secession, 1963 A
Tshombe is forced to resign, 1963 F
rebels take Albertville, 1964 F
UN operations end, 1964 F
People's Republic proclaimed, 1964 H
rebels take Stanleyville, 1964 H
white mercenaries in, 1964 H
Stanleyville recaptured from rebels, 1964 L
Kasavubu dismisses Tshombe, 1965 K
Mobutu deposes Kasavubu, 1965 L
Congregationalists. *See under* Religious Denominations
Congresses. *See* Conferences
Coningsby (B. Disraeli), 1844 U
Connaissance de Dieu (A. Gratry), 1855 R
Connolly, Cyril Vernon, B. author and journalist (1903–74), 1935 U, 1938 U
Conquest of Peru, The (W. H. Prescott), 1846 Q
Conquest, Co-existence and Change: Wales 1063–1415 (R.R. Davies), 1987 Q
Conrad, Joseph (Tedor Josef Konrad Korzeniowski), B. formerly Pol. novelist (1857–1924), 1857 Z, 1895 U, 1897 U, 1900 U, 1904 U, 1907 U, 1914 U, 1915 U, 1924 Z
Conscience, Hendrik, Belg. poet (1812–83), 1837 U
Conscription (military service): in Austria, 1936 D
in Britain, cabinet favours, 1915 M
Labour Party opposes, 1916 A
Act in force, 1916 B
ministry of, 1916 O
ends, 1920 D
for men of 20, 1929 D
for men between 19 and 41, 1939 J
for men, lowered to 18, 1941 M
for women, 1941 M
for men between 18 ½ and 26, 1948 M
extended for two years, 1950 J
in China, 1955 G
in France, 1872 G
reduced, 1928 C
selective, adopted, 1964 G
in Germany, reintroduced, 1935 O, 1936 H
West German constitution amended to permit, 1956 C
in Japan, 1872 N
in New Zealand, selective, 1961 J
in Russia, 1874 A, 1922 J
in US, selective, 1917 E
under National Labor Service Act, 1942 K
Selective Service bill, 1948 F
See also Armies
Consequences of Determinism, The (T. Honderich), 1988 R
Consequences of Pragmatism, The (R. Rorty), 1982 R
Conservation of energy, theory of, 1837 P, 1842 P
Conservatism in America (C. Rossiter), 1956 O
Conservative Parties. *See under* Political Parties
Considérations sur la France (J. de Maistre), 1796 O
Considérations sur la Revolution franaise (A. de Staël), 1818 O
Considérations sur le Gouvernment (P. Malouet), 1789 O
Considérant, Victor Prosper, F. Socialist (1809–93), 1836 O
Conspiracy of Pontiac, The (F. Parkman), 1851 Q
Constable, John, B. artist (1776–1837), 1776 Z, 1809 S, 1817 S, 1820 S, 1821 S, 1827 S, 1828 S, 1837 Z
Constant Nymph, The (M. Kennedy), 1926 W
Constant de Rebecque, Henri Benjamin, F. author and politician (1767–1830), 1767 Z, 1807 U, 1813 O, Z
Constantine I, King of Greece (1913–17, 1920–22), 1917 F; plebiscite favours return, 1920 M; abdicates, 1922 J
Constantine II, King of Greece (b. 1964); accession, 1964 C; dismisses Papandreou, 1965 G; attempt to oust military junta, 1967 M; exile, 1967 M
Constantine, Learie, W. Indian cricketer (1901–71), 1901 Z, 1928 X, 1971 Z
Constantine, prince, grandson of Catherine II of Russia, 1781 B
Constantinople, Turkey: protection of Christians in 1724 G; treaty, 1784 A; conference, 1876 M, 1877 A; Britain resolves to declare war, if Russia occupies, 1877 G; Armenians in, massacred, 1895 K, L; Russians propose to seize, 1895 K, 1896 L; Armenian revolution in, 1896 H; Peace, between Greece and Turkey, 1897 M; army revolt, 1909 D; Allies occupy, 1918 L, 1920 C; Turkey to retain, 1920 B; Allies forbid Greek occupation, 1922 G; name changed to Istanbul, 1930 C. *See also* Istanbul
Constitution of Church and State (S. T. Coleridge), 1828 Q
Constitutional History of England (H. Hallam), 1827 Q
Constitutional History of England (W. Stubbs), 1874 Q
Constitutional View of the War Between the States (A. H. Stephens), 1868 O
Constitutions:
Aden, suspended, 1965 J
Aden and S. Arabia Federation, talks break down, 1965 H
Argentina, 1853 E, 1956 E
Australia, representative government in, 1850 H, 1855 G
responsible government in W. Australia, 1870 H, 1890 K
federal, opposed, 1891 C
discussed, 1897 A, 1899 N
achieved, 1900 J
Austria, 1848 D, E, 1849 C
abolished, 1851 M
amended by October Diploma to provide for federation, 1860 K
is centralised by February Patent, 1861 B
opposition to, 1861 H
annulled, 1865 J
revised, 1867 M, 1920 K
Austrian Netherlands, revoked, 1789 K
Baden, 1818 H
Bavaria, 1818 E, 1919 H
Belgium, 1831 B, 1991 O
Brazil, promised, 1821 B
plans for, 1823 L
in force, 1826 C, 1891 B
British Guiana, in force, 1961 G
conference breaks down, 1962 L
agreement for internal self-government, 1963 G
conference, 1965 L
Brunswick, 1830 J
Bulgaria, 1879 B, 1881 G, 1883 J
Canada, legislative assemblies for Upper and Lower, 1791 E; 1981 M, 1982 D, 1985 D, 1987 E
Cape Colony, 1853 G
responsible government in, 1872 K
Central American Union, 1921 J
Chile, 1833 E, 1972 D
China, provisional, adopted, 1931 E, 1978 C
Croatia, internal self-government, 1873 L
Cuba, convention for framing, 1900 L
Platt amendment on, 1901 C
in force, 1901 F
suspended, 1957 K
Cyprus, proposals for, 1956 M

conference, 1964 A
Czechoslavakia, 1920 B
autonomy for Slovakia and Ruthenia, 1938 K
Czech Republic, 1992 M
Denmark, 1842 F, 1863 L
ultimatum for repeal, 1864 A
revised, 1866 G
for single chamber, 1953 C
Ecuador, 1830 J, 1929 C
Egypt, responsible goverment in, 1878 M
by Organic law, 1883 E
suspended, 1923 D
restored, 1929 K
suspended, 1934 L
Nationalists demand revision, 1935 M
abolished, 1952 M
Eire, 1922 K
oath of allegiance to British Crown removed from, 1933 E
passes Dáil, 1937 F
Finland, 1861 D
suppressed, 1899 B
France, Estates General summoned, 1788 H
Third Estate undertakes to frame, 1789 F
Louis XVI accepts, 1790 G
constitutional monarchy, 1791 J
revised, 1793 F
for Directory, 1795 H
of Year VIII (Consulate), 1799 M
Fifth, 1802 H
First Empire, 1804 E
Louis XVIII's Charter 1814 F
Napoleon's 'Champ de Mai', 1815 F
Constitutional Charter, 1830 H
Republican, 1848 L
revised, 1851 M
Louis Napoleon given monarchical powers, 1852 A
Second Empire, 1852 M
Senate becomes an Upper House, 1870 C
Walloon amendment, 1875 A
Republican, 1875 A, B, G
National Assembly summons new Senate and Chamber, 1876 C
Chamber is moved from Versailles to Paris, 1879 L
exclusion from presidency of members of former dynasties, 1884 H
life senatorships abolished, 1884 H
Boulanger campaigns for revision, 1888 D
draft, rejected by referendum, 1946 E
revised, adopted, 1946 K
Fifth Republic, 1958 J
Germany, 1849 C
Empire, 1871 D
Weimar Republic, 1919 G
W. Germany's amended to permit conscription, 1956 C
E. Germany, 1968 D
Gibraltar, 1969 E
Greece, adopted, 1822 A
revised, 1844 C
democratic, 1864 L
revised, 1910 A, 1911 F
Republican, 1924 C
further revisions, 1925 J, 1927 F, 1929 E
Gold Coast, 1946 L
Hanover, 1819 M, 1831 C, 1833 J
suppressed, 1837 G
new, imposed, 1840 H, 1855 E
Hesse-Cassel, 1830 J, 1831 A
Holland, 1848 C
Hong Kong, Basic Law, 1990 D
Hungarian 1867 B, 1920 B, 1989 K
Iceland, self-government for, 1874 G
India, Montagu-Chelmsford Report on, 1918 G
1937 D
as federal republic, 1949 L
Italy, conflict over, 1900 B
Fascist grand council becomes part of 1928 L
revised, 1938 M
Republican, 1946 F, 1947 M
Jamaica, suspended, 1839 D
self-government for, 1957 L, 1959 G
Japan, 1889 B, 1946 L
Kashmir, for incorporation in India, 1957 A
Kenya, conference, 1960 A, 1962 B
Libya, self-government revoked, 1927 C
Mauritius, conference, 1965 J
Mexico, congress for framing, 1822 E
Montenegro, 1905 M
Mozambique, legislative council in, 1907 E
Naples, promised, 1820 G, 1848 B
Natal, 1837 F, 1893 E
Newfoundland, suspended, 1933 M
New Granada, 1832 B
New Zealand, representative government in, 1852 F, 1856 N
centralised, 1875 K, 1876 N
Nicaragua, suspended, 1982 C
Nigeria, 1978 J, modified self-government for, 1947 A
Conference, 1957 E
Norway, 1814 D, L, 1884 N
Nyasaland, Conference, 1960 G
Orange River Colony, self-government for, 1906 M, 1907 G
Palestine, suspended, 1923 E
Pakistan, 1973 H
Persia, overthrown, 1908 F
Peru, 1836 K
Philippines, offered by US, 1899 C, 1973 A
Piedmont, 1848 C
Poland, guaranteed by Russia and Prussia, 1764 D
Diet, 1788 K
a free, 1791 B, E
abrogated, 1792 E
revised, 1815 L
abolished, 1832 B
revised, 1921 C, 1935 D
Portugal, 1821 A, 1822 J, 1976 D, 1982 K
annulled, 1823 F
revised, 1826 D
Liberal, supported by Quadruple Alliance, 1834 D
revised, 1911 H, 1933 E
Prussia, promised, 1815 E
granted, 1848 C, M
Liberal, 1850 A
Punjabi amended to acknowledge Sikhism as religion distinct from Hinduism, 1984 C
Rhodesia, 1971 L, 1974 M, 1977 L
S. Rhodesia, 1922 A, 1923 K
referendum for, 1961 G
new, in force, 1962 K
Rome, 1848 C
revoked, 1850 D
Rumania, responsible government demanded, 1928 E
remodelled, 1948 D
revised, 1952 J
Russia, support for a liberal, 1903 N
Zemstvo Congress demands Republican, 1904 L
Parliamentary institutions demanded, 1905 E
ratified by Soviet Congress, 1925 E
revised, 1936 M
commission to draft new, 1962 D
Sardinia, 1848 C
Saxe-Weimar, 1816 E
Saxony, 1830 J, 1831 J
Serbia, 1835 N, 1990 J
restored, 1894 E, 1903 F
Siam, 1932 F
Sierra Leone, conference, 1960 D
Singapore, conference, 1957 E
becomes self-governing, 1959 F
S. Africa, convention for drafting, 1908 K; approves new, 1983 L
South Vietnam, 1967 D
Spain, 1812 C, 1966 L
annulled, 1814 E
restored, 1820 A, C
powers demand abolition, 1823 A
republican, 1831 M
restored, 1936 B
Quadruple Alliance support for a liberal, 1834 D
liberal granted, 1837 F, 1845 E
re-established, 1856 J
annulled, 1856 K
revised, 1869 F
republican, 1873 B
Cortes provide for two-chamber legislature, 1876 A
Sri Lanka, 1977 G
Sudan, suppressed, 1958 L
Sweden, guaranteed by Russia and Prussia, 1764 D
revised, 1865 M, 1910 B
Switzerland, 1813 M, 1848 J, 1874 E
Syria, 1950 J
Tanganyika, 1955 L
internal self-government for, 1961 E
Tasmania, self-government for, 1856 N
Transvaal, agitation for self-government, 1905 A
granted, 1905 D, 1906 M
Transylvania, abrogated, 1784 G
Trinidad, cabinet government introduced, 1959 G
Turkey, partial autonomy for Serbs, 1817 L
revised, 1876 M
restored, 1908 G
republican, 1923 K
new, proposed, 1961 E
Tuscany, 1848 B
abolished, 1852 E
Uganda, conference, 1961 K
Union of Socialist Soviet Republics, 1977 F
United Arab Republic, 1962 J
United States of America, first, 1777 L
framed, 1787 E,
in force, 1788 F
first ten amendments to, 1789 C
ratified, 1791 M
11th amendment, 1794 M
12th amendment, on presidential ballots, 1804 J
13th amendment, 1865 M
14th amendment, 1866 F
states to draw up constitutions, 1867 C
15th amendment, not to revoke suffrage, 1870 C
presidential succession, 1886 E
Negro Rights and Force bill, 1892 L
17th amendment, on popular election of senators, 1913 E
18th amendment, on prohibition, 1919 A
19th amendment, on women's franchise, 1920 H
20th amendment, advancing president's inauguration, 1933 B
21st amendment, repeals prohibition, 1933 M

26th amendment extends voting rights, 1971 O
Equal Rights Amendment, 1982 O
Venezuela, 1811 G, 1821 F
Venice, 1797 E
Württemberg, 1819 J
Yugoslavia, suppressed, 1929 A, 1971 F, 1990 J, 1991 C
revision demanded, 1932 L
new, 1946 A
Zimbabwe, 1982 C, 1987 H
Constructivism, *Realistic Manifesto*, 1920 S
Consumers' Council, in Britain, 1963 C
Contadora Group, 1983 G, 1986 D, E
Contemplation de la nature (C. Bonnet), 1764 R
Contemplations, Les (V. Hugo), 1856 U
Contes Dôrlatiques (H. de Balzac), 1832 U
Contes d'Espagne et d'Italie (A. de Musset), 1829 U
Continental Drift, theory of, 1915 P
Continuity, Chance, and Change: The Character of the Industrial Revolution in England (E.A. Wrigley), 1988 Q
Contra rebels, 1989 L
covert US aid, 1983 G
Iran–Contra scandal, 1986 L, M, 1987 B, C, G, H, L, 1989 A, D
ceasefire agreement signed, 1988 C
'Continental System', Napoleon's: in operation, 1806 L; Prussia joins, 1807 G; Portugal refuses to enter, 1807 L; Austria joins, 1808 B; Sweden joins, 1810 A; Napoleon's annexations in Germany, to strengthen, 1810 M; pressure on Sweden to continue in, 1812 A; Prussia to adhere to, 1812 B
Contraband of War, defined, 1856 D
Contraband, British Black List, 1916 B, G
Contraception:
contraceptive pills
devised, 1952 P
Roman Catholics oppose use of, 1964 R
oral contraceptives connected to blood clotting, 1968 P
Humanae Vitae Papal Encyclical, 1968 R
House of Lords rules doctor can prescribe to girls under 16 without parents' consent, 1985 O
Irish Dail legalizes sale of contraceptives, 1985 O
See also under Birth Control
Contractor and Home, The (D. Storey), 1970 W
Control of Inflation, The (J. E. Meade), 1958 O
Controls:
Allied, of Bulgaria, abolished, 1928 A
Committee dissolved, 1931 A
Allied Control Commission for Germany, 1945 F
limits German protection, 1946 C
dissolves Wehrmacht, 1946 H
Russian delegates leave, 1948 C
British, of mines and shipping, 1916 M
of textile industries, 1918 O
of trade with China, removed, 1957 E
of trade with dollar area, removed, 1959 E
of office and industrial development, 1964 M
NATO countries, trade with Soviet block, relaxed, 1958 H
US, of food and fuel, 1917 G
of railways, 1917 M
ends, 1920 C
removed, 1946 L
See also under Currency; Rationing
Convention on International Trade in Endangered Species, 1989 K
Conventions (Diplomatic):
Akkerman, Russia with Turkey, 1826 K
Anglo-Russian, to prevent Baltic trade with France, 1793 C
Annapolis, under Madison and Hamilton, 1786 E
Bartenstein, between Russia and Prussia, 1807 D; Britain joins, 1807 F
Brussels, to control liquor traffic, 1911 O
Cintra, French army in Portugal with Britain, 1808 H
Graeco-Turkish, 1881 G
Hague, The, to fix limits of territorial waters, 1882 F
Irish, 1917 G
London on Transvaal, 1884 B
Marsa, between France and Tunis, 1883 F
Moss, between Sweden and Norway, 1814 H
Motor car, 1910 O
Philadelphia, 1787 E
Pretoria, between Britain and Transvaal, 1893 L
Slavery, 1826 J
Tauroggen, between Russia and Prussia, 1812 M
Uddevalla, between Denmark and Sweden, 1788 L
See also Treaties
Conventions, of US Political Parties (notable):
Democratic, first, 1832 L, 1912 G, 1916 F, 1920 G, 1924 F, 1980 H
Progressive Republican, 1912 H
Republican, 1912 F, 1916 F, 1920 F, 1924 F, 1976 H, 1980 G
Conversations (Anglican-Methodist), 1963 R
Conversations with Stalin (M. Djilas), 1962 E
Conversions, religious, notable:
Boris of Bulgaria, 1896 B
Newman, 1845 R
Conveyor-belts, 1913 P
Convicts, transportation of:
from Britain, to Botany Bay, 1823 G
to Cape Colony, forbidden, 1849 L
suspended, 1853 N
to Tasmania, 1849 L
from France, 1851 O
Convoy system, 1917 O
Convoys, notable:
British, to Malta, 1942 F, H
to Russia, 1942 E, J, M
Conway v. *Rimmer*, gives British courts power to inspect government documents privately, 1968 O
Conway, Henry Seymour, B. soldier and politician (1721–95), 1766 G
Conway, William Martin, lord Conway, B. explorer and art critic (1856–1937), 1896 P
Cook, James, B. navigator (1728–79), 1768 R, 1770 P, 1775 P, 1776 P, 1777 P, 1778 P, 1779 Z, 1970 C
Cook, Michael, Canad. dramatist (b. 1933), 1975 W
Cook, Thomas, B. travel agent (1808–92), 1841 W
Cooke, Deryck, B. musician (1919–76), completes Mahler symphony, 1964 T
Coolidge, Calvin, Am. Republican (1872–1933), 30th president of US (1923–92), 1872 Z, 1924 E, F, 1925 C; nominated vice-president, 1920 F; succeeds Harding as president, 1923 H; wins presidential election, 1924 L
Coomassie, Ghana, British capture, 1896 A
Cooper, Anthony Ashley, 7th earl of Shaftesbury, B. social reformer (1801–85), 1842 O
Cooper, Duff, lord Norwich, B. Conservative politician and diplomat (1890–1954), resigns ftom cabinet, 1938 K
Cooper, Gary, Am. film actor (1901–62), 1932 W
Cooper, Dame Gladys, B. actress (1889–1971), 1889 Z, 1971 Z
Cooper, Gordon, Am. astronaut, 1963 P
Cooper, James Fenimore, Am. novelist (1789–1851), 1789 Z, 1821 U, 1823 U, 1826 U, 1840 U, 1851 Z
Co-operative Movement:
Birmingham tailors, 1777 O
Rochdale pioneers, 1844 O
Sunday Citizen, The, 1967 V
Cooperstown, New York, US, baseball first played at, 1839 X
Coote, Sir Eyre, B. soldier (1726–83), 1781 G
Coover, Robert, Am. author (b. 1932), 1969 U
Copeland, Ralph, B. astronomer (1837–1905), 1882 P
Copenhagen, Denmark: Veterinary and Agricultural College, 1773 P; battle, 1801 D; Royal Navy bombards, 1807 J; Town Hall, 1893 S; SAS Building, 1959 S
Copland, Aaron, Am. musician (1900–90), 1900 Z, 1925 T, 1938 T, 1942 T, 1954 T, 1962 T, 1967 T, 1973 T, 1990 Z
Copley, John Singleton, B. artist (1737–1815), 1778 S, 1780 S
Copper deposits, in Katanga, 1891 D
Coppola, Francis Ford, Am. film director (b. 1939), 1972 W, 1974 W
Coptic Church. *See under* Religious Denominations
Copyright:
Berlin convention, 1908 O
British Act, 1911 O
revised international convention (U.C.C.), 1955 O
Coraës, Adamantios, Greek patriot (1748–1833), 1803 O
Corbeaux, Les (Becque), 1882 W
Corbett, Matthew Ridley, B. artist (1850–1902), 1894 S
Corbusier, Le (pseudonym of Charles Edouard Jeanneret), F. architect (1887–1965), 1887 Z, 1918 S, 1926 S, 1929 S, 1952 S, 1955 S, 1957 S, 1963 S, 1965 Z, 1967 S
retrospective (Hayward Gallery, London and Pompidou Centre, Paris), 1987 S
Corday d'Armont, Charlotte, F. revolutionary (1768–93), 1793 G
Cordeliers Club, Paris, 1790 N
Cordite, invented, 1889 P
Cordle, John Howard, B. politician (b. 1912), 1977 G
'Corelli, Marie'. *See* Mackay, Mary
Corfu, Greece: Pact, for union of Serbs, Croats and Slovenes, 1917 G; Italy occupies, 1923 H; Greece appeals to League, 1923 H; Albania held responsible for incidents in, 1949 D
Corigliano, John Paul, Am. musician (b. 1938), 1991 T
Corinne (A. de Staël), 1807 U
Corinth Canal, Greece, 1893 P
Cork, Eire, martial law in, 1920 M
Corn Law Rhymes (E. Elliott), 1831 O
Corn Laws, British: tracts on, 1777 O, 1831 O; revised, 1815 C; agitation for repeal, 1819 H; by Anti-Corn-Law league, 1838 C, J; amended, 1822 G, 1828 G, 1842 D; repealed, 1846 F
Corn Trade, in France, 1763 E, 1774 J, 1776 J
Corn is Green, The (E. Williams), 1938 W
Corn, treatise on, 1815 O
Corneau, Alain, F. film director, 1992 W
Cornelius, Peter von, G. artist (1783–1867), 1825 S, 1858 T
Cornwallis, Charles, marquess of Cornwallis, B. soldier and Governor-General of India

(1738–1805), 1780 H, 1781 A, C, J; capitulates at Yorktown, 1781 K; as Governor-General of India, 1786 B; defeats Tippoo at Seringapatam, 1791 E; reforms, 1793 N
Coro (L. Berio), 1976 T
Corona (P. Claudel), 1915 U
Coronel, S. America, naval battle, 1914 L
Corot, Jean Baptiste Camille, F. artist (1796–1875), 1796 Z, 1850 S, 1851 S, 1859 S, 1870 S, 1873 S, 1875 Z
Corporal Punishment, 1979 O
Corpus Inscriptionum Graecarum (ed. Böckh), 1824 Q
Corpus Juris Civilis, 1872 Q
Corregidor, Philippines, surrenders, 1942 E
Correspondence of John Locke, The (E.S. de Beer ed.), 1976 Q
Corridors of Power (C. P. Snow), 1964 U
Corruption, political:
  in Britain, sale of Parliamentary seats forbidden, 1809 F
    Lynskey tribunal to investigate, 1948 L
  in Sicily, 1848 A
  in US, by Tweed Ring in New York, 1871 G
    in Ohio, 1911 O
    judicial, 1913 O
    Sherman Adams affair, 1958 F
  See also Secret Societies
Corsair, The (Byron), 1814 U
Corsica, Island: France purchases, 1768 G; Paoli expelled, 1769 H; British occupy, 1793 G; British abandon, 1796 N; Italy claims, 1938 L; Daladier visits, 1939 A
Cort, Henry, B. iron-master (1740–1800), 1784 P
Cortege (C. Matthews), 1989 T
Corti, Ludovico, Count, It. diplomat (1823–88), 1878 F
Cortines, Ruiz, president of Mexico, 1952 G
Cortisone (Compound E), 1949 P
Corunna, Spain, 1809 A
Corvée, The, in France, 1776 A
Cosgrave, Liam, Prime Minister of Eire (b. 1920), 1973 C, J
Cosgrave, William Thomas, Sinn Fein leader, president of Eire (1880–1965), 1922 J, 1933 J
Cosmic radiation, 1945 P
Cosmic rays:
  analysis of, 1933 P
  observatory for, 1953 P
  studied by artificial satellite, 1958 P
Cosmic Rays and Nuclear Physics (L. Janossy), 1948 P
Cosmopolitanism and the National State (F. Meinecke), 1908 O
Cosmos (A. von Humboldt), 1845 P
Cossacks, revolt of, 1773 K, 1774 J
Costa Blanca, Spain, Basque separatist bomb attack, 1980 F
Costa Rica:
  enters Central American Federation, 1823 G
  frontier dispute with Panama, 1921 C
  Contadora peace treaty, 1986 E
  Arias Plan, 1987 H
Costa e Silva, Artur da, President of Brazil (1902–69), 1968 M, 1969 H
Costa, Charles de, Belg. author (1829–79), 1867 U
Costa, Gomes da, Port. politician, 1926 E, G
Costa, Lucio, Brazil, architect, 1957 S
Costa-Gavras, Kostantinos, F. film director (b. 1933), 1969 W
Costello, Elvis (stage name of Declan Patrick McManus), B. singer (b. 1955), 1977 W, 1979 W
Costello, John Aloysius, Ir. Fine Gael politician (1891–1976), premier, 1891 Z, 1951 F, 1954 F, 1976 Z
Cotman, John Sell, B. artist (1782–1842), 1803 S
Cotta, Johann Friedrich, G. publisher (1764–1832), 1798 V
Cotton gin, invented, 1793 P
Cotton industry:
  in Britain, trade in, 1772 Y, 1782 Y, 1792 Y, 1802 Y, 1812 Y, 1822 Y, 1832 Y, 1842 Y, 1852 Y, 1862 Y, 1872 Y, 1882 Y, 1892 Y, 1902 Y, 1912 Y, 1922 Y, 1932 Y
    statistics of weavers, 1806 Y
    spinners reduce productivity, 1935 A
    reorganisation of Lancashire industry, 1959 O
  in US, grants of exports, 1793 P, 1910 Y, 1940 Y, 1961 Y
Cotton, Thomas Henry, B. golfer (b. 1907), 1934 X
Cotton, raw production, 1910 Y, 1961 Y, 1984 Y
Cotton, sea-island, 1786 P
Cotton, spinning by steam, 1785 P
Cotton, tariffs, 1882 O, 1934 H
Coty, René, F. last president of 4th Republic (1882–1962), 1962 Z; elected president, 1953 M
Coubertin, Pierre de, F. re-founder of Olympic Games (1863–1937), 1863 Z
Coué, Emile, F. psychologist (1857–1926), 1857 Z, 1926 Z
Coulomb, Charles Augustin, F. natural philosopher (1736–1806), 1777 P, 1779 P, 1785 P
Council for Social Democracy, 1981 A
Council for the Encouragement of Music and the Arts (CEMA), 1941 T
Council of Churches for Britain and Ireland, 1990 R
Council of Europe:
  Assembly drafts constitution of European Political Community, 1953 A
  Cyprus joins, 1961 E
  Greek withdrawal, 1969 M
Count of Monte Cristo, The (A. Dumas), 1844 U
Country Doctor, The (F. Kafka), 1920 U
Country Party. *See under* Political Parties
Coupling, railway, automatic, 1906 P
Coups d'état, attempted
  in Afghanistan, 1990 C
  in Austria, by ex-Emperor Charles, 1921 C
    by Pfrimer, 1931 J
    Nazi, 1934 G
  in Chad, 1992 A
  in Ethiopia, 1989 E
  in France, by Louis Napoleon, 1840 H
    by Boulanger, 1887 K
    Fascist, 1937 L
  in Germany, by Kapp, 1920 C
    Black Reichwehr, 1923 K
    Hitler's in Munich, 1923 L
  in Haiti, 1989 D
  in Indonesia, 1965 K
  in Iraq, 1970 A
  in Morocco, 1971 G
  in Nigeria, 1976 B
  in Pakistan, 1980 C
  in Panama, 1989 K
  in Persia, royalist, 1953 H
  in Portugal, 1975 L
  in Spain, 1981 B
  in Syria, alleged, 1958 C, 1961 M
  in Trinidad and Tobago, 1990 G
Coups d'état:
  in Afghanistan, 1973 G
  in Argentina, 1976 C
  in Austria, Schuschnigg's 'bloodless', 1935 K
  in Bangladesh, military, 1982 C
  in Bolivia, 1934 M
  in Brazil, 1969 H
  in Bulgaria, 1923 F
  in Burkina Faso, 1987 K
  in Burma, 1962 C
  in Burundi, 1987 J
  in Czechoslovakia, Communist, 1948 B
  in Egypt, by King Fuad, 1928 G
    by Neguib, 1952 G
    by Nasser, 1954 B
  in Equatorial Guinea, 1979 H
  in Ethiopia, 1974 J
  in Fiji, 1987 E, J
  in Finland, Fascist, 1930 K
  in France, by Louis Napoleon, 1851 M
  in Ghana, 1966 B, 1978 G, 1979 F, 1981 M
  in Greece, 1925 F, 1967 D, E
  in Grenada, 1983 K
  in Guatamala, 1982 C, 1983 H
  in Haiti, 1988 F, J, 1991 J
  in Honduras, 1963 K
  in Iraq, 1958 G
  in Japan, 1936 B
  in Lesotho, 1991 D
  in Lithuania, Fascist, 1932 B
  in Nigeria, 1966 A, 1975 G, 1983 M, 1985 H
  in Pakistan, 1977 G
  in Paraguay, 1989 B
  in Persia, 1908 F, 1909 G
  in Poland, by Pilsudski, 1926 E
  in Portugal, 1828 F, 1926 E, 1974 D
  in Seychelles, 1977 F
  in Siam, military, 1933 F, 1958 K
  in Soviet Union, 1991 H
  in Sudan, 1985 D, 1989 F
  in Surinam, military, 1982 M
  in Syria, 1951 L, 1961 J, 1966 B
  in Thailand, 1957 J, 1971 L, 1977 K, 1976 K
  in Turkey, 1909 D, 1913 A, 1960 E, 1980 J
  in Uganda, 1985 G
  in Volta Upper, 1982 L
  in Venezuela, 1909 M
  in Viet-Nam, 1960 H, 1963 I
  in Yemen, 1962 J
Courbet, Gustave, F. artist (1819–77), 1819 Z, 1894 S, 1850 S, 1855 S, 1867 S, 1877 Z
Courland, now Russia, German offensive in, 1915 D
Cournot, Antoine Augustine, F. economist and mathematician (1801–77), 1888 O
Courrier Sud (St.-Exupéry), 1929 U
Course of Positive Philosophy (A. Comte), 1830 R
Court, Margaret, Austral. tennis player (b. 1942), 1970 X
Courteline, Georges, F. dramatist (1858–1929), 1893 W
Courtois, B., F. chemist, 1811 P
Courts:
  European
    European Court of First Instance, 1989 O
    European Court of Human Rights. *See* European Court of Human Rights
    European Court of Justice. *See* European Court of Justice
    International Court of Justice. *See* United Nations, The
  in Britain, Court of Appeal, 1873 C
    Court of Chivalry, 1954 O
    Crown Court, 1971 O
    Divorce, 1857 O
    Judicial Committee of Privy Council, 1876 L
      Canadian appeals to, discontinued, 1946 O
      Irish appeals to, made illegal, 1933 E
    House of Lords, jurisdiction of, 1876 L
    National Industrial Relations Court (NIRC), 1972 C, F, L, 1974 E, G

Supreme Court of Judicature, 1873 C
procedure revised, 1932 O
in Canada, 1978 A
in Germany, industrial, 1890 G
in Holland, feudal, suppressed, 1784 G
in Japan, reformed, 1875 D
International Court of arbitration, 1899 E. *See also* International Court
in US
press coverage of trials, 1976 V
Supreme Court, first woman Justice, 1981 J
Supreme Court overturns judgement on NAACP, 1982 O
See also Codes of Law; Judgments; Legislation
Cousine Bette, La (H. de Balzac), 1846 U
Cousins, Frank, B. trade unionist and Labour politician (1904–86), 1966 G
Couture, Thomas, F. artist (1815–79), 1847 S
Couve de Murville, Maurice, F. premier (b. 1907), 1968 G
Coventry, England:
bombing, 1941 D
cathedral, 1951 S, 1962 S
Belgrade Theatre, 1958 S
Coward, Noel, B. dramatist and composer (1899–1973), 1899 Z, 1924 W, 1925 W, 1929 W, 1931 W, 1941 W, 1943 W, 1973 Z
Cowpens, S. Carolina, US, battle, 1781 A
Cowper, Francis Thomas de Grey, earl Cowper, B. administrator (1834–1905), lord lieutenant of Ireland, 1882 E
Cowper, William, B. poet (1731–1800), 1779 R, 1782 U, 1800 Z
Cox, David, B. landscape artist (1783–1859), 1813 S
Cox, James Middleton, Am. Democrat (1870–1957), fights presidential election, 1920 G, L
Cozens, Alexander, B. landscape artist (c. 1717–86), treatise by, 1785 S
Crabbe, Commander, B. naval officer, disappearance of, 1955 K
Crabbe, George, B. poet (1754–1832), 1781 U, 1783 T, 1817 U, 1832 Z
Cracow, Poland: Austrians take, 1795 K; becomes independent republic, 1815 P, rising, 1846 B; occupied by Austrians and Russians, 1846 C; annexed by Austrians, 1846 L; Pan-Slav Conference, 1892 O; Russians hold line at, 1914 M; Russians take, 1945 A
Cradock, Sir Christopher George, B. admiral (1862–1914), 1914 L
Cragg, Tony (Anthony Douglas), B. sculptor (b. 1949), 1980 S, 1981 S, 1982 S, 1984 S, 1988 S
Turner Prize, 1988 S
Craig, James, Viscount Craigavon, United Ulster leader (1870–1940), 1921 B
Craig, Sir James Henry, B. general (1748–1812), 1795 J
Craik, Mrs. *See* Mulock, Dinah
Crane, Stephen, Am. author (1871–1900), 1871 Z, 1900 Z
Cranford (E. Gaskell), 1853 U
Cranko, John, B. choreographer 1927–73), 1949 T, 1951 T, 1952 T, 1959 T
Crankshaw, Edward, B. journalist and historian (1909–84), 1963 Q
Craythorne Committee on Sunday entertainment, 1964 W
Cream separator, invented, 1877 P
Cream, B. pop group, 1969 W
Crease-resisting fabric, 1929 P
Creche, the first, 1769 O
Creedence Clearwater Revival, Am. pop group, 1970 W
Creighton, Mandell, B. churchman and historian (1843–1901), 1886 Q
Creole incident, 1841 L
Creole, Der (Zshokke), 1830 U
Cresson, Edith, Prime Minister of France (b. 1934), 1991 E, 1992 D
Cressy, David, B. historian (b. 1946), 1987 Q
Crete (Candia), Island, Levant: Egyptians capture, 1824 D; Mehemet Ali surrenders, 1840 G, L; Turkish ultimatum to Greeks in, 1866 M; revolts against Turks, 1866 J, 1896 B, G, H, 1897 B; Greeks leave, 1869 B; proclaims union with Greece, 1897 B, M, 1908 K; Turks evacuate, 1898 L; Greek revolt, 1905 C; Greece annexes, 1913 M; Britain occupies, 1940 L; Germany invades, 1941 E; excavations in, 1900 Q
Creuzer, Georg Friedrich, G. philosopher (1771–1858), 1810 Q
Crève-cœur, Le (L. Aragon), 1941 U
Crichel Down Inquiry, 1953 O
Crichton, Michael, Am. author (b. 1942), 1969 U
Crick, Bernard, B. author (b. 1929), 1980 Q
Crick, Francis Henry Compton, B. chemist (b. 1916), 1961 P
Cricket:
MCC move to Lord's Cricket Ground, 1787 X
codifies Laws, 1788 X
English county championships, 1890 X
record scores:
Grace's triple centuries, 1876 X
Hobbs's record number of centuries, 1926 X
Hutton's test innings, 1938 X
English XI's tours of Australia:
first, 1862 X
first official tour, 1880 X
England *v.* Australia test matches, 1921 X, 1930 X, 1938 X, 1946 X, 1953 X
anti-apartheid campaigners raid grounds, 1970 A
South African tour cancelled by British Cricket Council, E, 1970 X
England regains Ashes, 1971 X, 1977 X, 1985 X
first one-day international, 1971 X
first women's World Cup, 1973 X
Headingley pitch damaged by protestors, 1975 H
Australia regains Ashes, 1975 X, 1983 X, 1989 X
first women's match at Lord's, 1976 X
record Test score, 1976 X
Centenary Test Match, Melbourne, 1977 X
Packer series, 1977 X, 1979 X
New Zealand victory over England, 1978 X
West Indies retain World Cup, 1979 X
Centenary Test Match, Lord's, 1980 X
England victory over Australia, 1981 X
Test ban for England players, 1982 X
Yorkshire lifts ban on players born outside county, 1990 X
English victory over West Indies, 1991 X
South Africa readmitted to International Cricket Conference, 1991 X
Cries from the Mammal House (T. Johnson), 1984 W
Crime and Punishment (F. Dostoievsky), 1866 U
Crime de Sylvestre Bonnard, Le (A. France), 1881 U
Crime, statistics of convictions for:
in Britain, 1873 Y, 1939 Y, 1950 Y, 1960 Y
in US, 1939 Y, 1950 Y, 1960 Y
Crimea, Russia: Russia conquers from Turkey, 1771 F; Turkey cedes, 1774 G; Turkey agrees to annexations, 1784 A; Allied landings, 1854 J. *See also under* War, Crimean. Red Army enters, 1919 D; independence, 1921 K; plans for film studios in, 1935 W; German attack in, 1942 E; Russians begin liberation, 1944 D
Criminal Law Revision Committee, 1972 O
Criminal, The (C. Lombroso), 1876 O
Criminals: identification of, 1890 O; First Offenders Act, 1958 O. *See also* Convicts
Criminology, science of, founded, 1876 O
Crippen, Hawley Harvey, Am. murderer (1861–1910), 1910 O
Cripps, Sir Stafford, B. Labour politician (1889–1952), 1889 Z, 1950 K; leads mission to USSR, 1940 E; becomes Leader of House, 1942 B; offers India self-government, 1942 D; replaced in war cabinet by Morrison, 1942 L
Crisis in the University, The (W. Moberley), 1949 O
Crisis of the Old Order (A. M. Schlesinger), 1957 Q
Crisis, agricultural, 1946 G
Crisis, economic:
in Australia, 1873 O
in Austria, 1811 B, 1873 E, 1931 E
in Belgium, 1926 G, 1932 J, 1935 C
in Brazil, 1928 O
in Britain, 1846 O, 1866 O, 1890 O, 1929 O, 1931 G, H, J,
through ending of Lend-Lease, 1945 K
over balance of payments, 1949 J, 1955 K
Butler's credit squeeze, 1955 K, 1961 G, 1964 K, 1964 L
pressure on pound, 1964 L; is eased, 1965 C
in Canada, 1849 K
in Europe, 1873 O, 1929 O, 1949 J
in France, 1788 H, 1926 G, H, 1935 G, 1936 K, 1949 K
in Germany, 1921 H, L, 1922 F, 1923 A, J, K, 1927 C, 1931 G, H
in Italy, 1936 K
in Japan, 1927 D
in Portugal, 1902 E
in US, 1784 N, 1873 J, O, 1920 O, 1929 O, 1933 C, 1957 O, 1958 O
World, 1929 U
Crisis, fuel, British, 1947 B, V
Crispi, Francesco, It. statesman (1819–1901), 1887 G, 1891 A, 1893 M, 1896 C
Cristiani, Alfredo, President of El Salvador (b. 1948), 1989 C
Cristina, Queen Regent of Spain, 1840 K
Critic, The (R. B. Sheridan), 1779 W
Critical Exposition of the Philosophy of Leibniz (B. Russell), 1900 R
Criticism of Political Economy (K. Marx), 1859 O
Critique of Judgment (Kant), 1790 R
Critique of Practical Reason (Kant), 1788 R
Critique of Pure Reason (Kant), 1781 R
attacks on, answered, 1783 R
Critique of Revelation (J. G. Fichte), 1792 R
Croatia
freed from effective government control, 1991 E
independence, 1991 F
Vukovar falls to Serb-dominated army, 1991 H
recognized by EC as independent republic, 1992 A
UN plan for deployment of peacekeeping forces, 1992 A
Yugoslavian civil war. *See* Civil Wars
Croats, boycott Yugoslav Parliament, 1928 H, 1935 F. *See also under* Political Parties
Croce, Benedetto, It. philosopher (1866–1952), 1866 Z, 1903 V, 1941 Q, 1952 Z
Crome, John Bernay, B. artist (1794–1842), 1803 S
Cromer, Lord. *See* Baring, Evelyn

Crompton, Samuel, B. inventor (1753–1827), 1779 P
Cromwell's Letters and Speeches (T. Carlyle), 1845 Q
Cronberg, Germany, 1906 H
Cronenberg, David, Canad. film director (b. 1943), 1988 W
Cronje, Piet Arnoldus, Boer general (1840–1911), 1899 M, 1900 B
Crookes, Sir William, B. scientist (1832–1919), 1832 Z, 1861 P, 1900 P, 1919 Z
Crosby, Brass, B. politician (1729–93), 1771 C
Crosby, Harry L. ('Bing'), Am. film actor (1904–77), 1904 Z, 1942 W, 1977 Z
Crosland, (Charles) Anthony Raven, B. Labour politician (1918–77), 1975 E, 1977 B
Cross, Charles Frederick, B. chemist (1885–1935), 1892 P
Cross, Jasper (James Richard), British Trade Commissioner in Canada (b. 1921), 1970 K
Cross, Richard Asheton, lord Cross, B. Conservative politician (1823–1914), 1874 B, 1885 F
Crosse, Gordon, B. musician (b. 1937), 1974 T
Crossman Diaries, The, 1975 K
Crossman, Richard Heward Stafford, B. Labour politician (1907–74), 1907 Z, 1974 Z
Crossroads squatter camp, S. Africa, 1986 E
Crotchet Castle (T. L. Peacock), 1831 U
Crow (E. Hughes), 1970 U
Crowley, Mart, Am. dramatist (b. 1935), 1969 W
'Crown' ethers, discovery, 1967 P
Crown Point, New York, US, 1775 E
Croydon, Surrey, England, tram-road at, 1801 P
Crucible, The (A. Miller), 1953 W
Cruel Sea, The (N. Monsarrat), 1951 U
Cruelle Enigme (P. Bourget), 1885 U
Cruise missile, 1981 L, 1982 M, 1983 G, K, L, 1984 C, E, F, 1985 B, C
  anti-nuclear demonstrations, 1985 B
  Belgian Parliament approves deployment, 1985 C
Crumb, George, Am. musician (b. 1929), 1977 T
Cruz Report on apartheid, 1955 L
Cry, the Beloved Country (A. Paton), 1948 U
Crying of Lot 49, The (T. Pynchon), 1966 U
Cryptates discovered, 1969 P
Crystallography, studies in, 1784 P, 1813 P, 1838 P; X-ray, 1912 P
Ctesiphon, Mesopotamia, battle, 1915 L
Cuba: US acquisition urged, 1854 K; risings, 1895 N; US war with, 1898 D, E, G, M; ceded by Spain, 1898 M; becomes virtually a protectorate of US, 1901 F; revolt, 1906 B; US marines land, 1912 F 1917 C; expropriation of sugar mills, 1959 F; US protests at, 1960 A; recognises Communist China 1960 J; Kennedy's broadcast on Russian bases, 1962 K; Russia's offer to withdraw missiles, 1962 K; US blockade, 1962 K, L; Kennedy announces Russia begins dismantling bases, 1962 L; Russia withdraws bombers, 1962 L; US places shipping restrictions on, 1963 B; Russia agrees to withdraw troops, 1963
  US ban on relations with lifted, 1975 G
  diplomatic exchange agreement with US, 1977 E
  Cubans seek political asylum in Peruvian Embassy, 1980 D
  military withdrawal from Angola, 1988 A, 1989 A
  phased withdrawal of forces from Namibia agreed, 1988 M
  withdrawal of Soviet troops, 1991 J
Cubism, 1907 S, 1912 S, 1914 S
Cubist Painters, The (Apollinaire), 1913 S
Cubitt, Joseph, B. civil engineer (1811–72), 1851 S
Cuddalore, off Madras, India, naval battle, 1782 G
Cugnot, Nicolas Joseph, F. engineer (1725–1804), 1762 P
Culham, England, Joint European Torus (JET), 1983 P, 1991 P
Cullen, William, B. physician (1710–90), 1774 P
Cultural Co-operation, International Union for, 1922 O
Culture and Anarchy (M. Arnold), 1869 O
Culture and Freedom (Dewey), 1939 R
Culture of Cities (L. Mumford), 1938 Q
Culture of Narcissism, The (C. Lasch), 1979 Q
Cummings, Edward Estlin, Am. poet (1874–1962), 1923 U, 1925 U
Cunard Company, 1963 K, 1964 M
  Queen Elizabeth II, 1967 J
Cuneiform inscriptions, 1837 Q
Cuno, Wilhelm, G. chancellor, 1922 L
Curie, Marie (*née* Sklodowska), F. scientist (1867–1934), 1867 Z, 1898 P, 1910 P, 1934 Z
Curie, Pierre, F. scientist (1860–1906), 1860 Z, 1898 P, 1906 Z
Curran, Father Charles, Am. theologian, 1986 R
Currency
  agreed exchange rates system (Bretton Woods Agreement), 1971 O
  floating exchange rate system, 1973 C
  gold market freed, 1967 A
  gold's remaining role abandoned by IMF, 1975 O
  International Union proposed, 1943 O
  in Australia, decimalization, 1966 O
  in Belgium, Franc devalued, 1926 G, 1935 C
  in Britain, bullion committee's report, 1810 J
    Bank of England resumes cash payments, 1817 K, 1820 E
    Bank Charter Act, limits fiduciary issue, 1844 G
    Treasury notes issued, 1914 O
    return to gold standard, 1925 D
    treatise on, 1930 O
    pound devalued, 1931 J, 1949 J
    dollar travel allowances increased, 1957 F
    convertibility of sterling for non-resident holders, 1958 M
    foreign support for pound, 1965 J
    bank rate, notable changes in, 1966 G, L, 1967 E, 1969 B, 1971 D, 1972 F
    devaluation, 1967 L
    interest rates cut, 1968 C
    London Gold Market closed, 1968 C
    decimalization, 1969 K, 1971 B
    50 pound limit abolished, 1970 A
    heavy selling of sterling, 1972 F
    pound floated, 1972 F
    falls in value of sterling, 1976 C, J, 1984 M
    exchange controls abolished, 1979 K
    sixpence abolished, 1980 F
    rise in value of sterling, 1980 K
    sterling withdrawn from ERM, 1992 J
  Commonwealth Declaration on monetary affairs, 1933 G
  in Europe, devaluation in, 1949 J
    markets close, 1968 L, 1971 E, H 1973 C
    European markets closed in face of currency crisis, 1973 C
    French franc forced out of European currency 'snake', 1976 C
    European Monetary System (EMS), 1978 D, 1978 M, 1979 C
    European Exchange Rate Mechanism (ERM), 1990 J, 1992 J
  in France, Assignats issued, 1788 M, 1967 A, 1968 L, 1969 H
    Franc notes issued, 1914 O
    Franc made convertible, 1958 M
    exchange controls abolished, 1967 A
    gold market, 1967 A
  in Germany, experts confer on, 1922 L
    rapid decline in Mark, 1923 K
    temporary stability, 1923 L
    suspension of cash transfers, 1934 G
    reformed, 1948 F
  in Iraq, withdrawal from sterling area, 1959 F
  in Italy, Lira devalued, 1936 K
    lira devalued within ERM, 1992 J
  in Japan, yen floated, 1971 H
  in Pakistan, devalued, 1955 G
  in Russia, devalued, 1947 M
  international speculation, 1969 E
  in US, specie payments resumed, 1879 A
    paper money redeemable in gold, 1900 C
    federal reserves reorganised, 1932 B
    president authorised to revalue, 1934 A
    Nixon suspends gold conversion, 1971 H
    dollar devalued, 1971 M, 1973 B
    Carter announces major support plan, 1978 L
    dollar reaches all-time low, 1987 M
  in West Germany, 1969 E
    two-tier system for gold agreed, 1968 O
    realignment of major currencies, 1971 M
  See also Coinage; Economy; Gold Standard
Currie, Mrs. Edwina, B. Conservative politician (b. 1946), 1986 J
  resignation as Under-Secretary of State for Health, 1988 M
Curtatone, Italy, Austrian victory, 1848 E
Curtin, John, Austral. Labour leader (1885–1945), 1945 G
Curtis, Lionel George, B. statesman (1872–1955), 1872 Z, 1916 O, 1934 R, 1945 O, 1955 Z
Curtiss, Glenn Hammond, Am. aviator (1878–1930), 1912 P
Curtius, Julius, G. diplomat, 1929 K, 1931 H
Curtius, T., G. chemist, 1890 P
Curzon, George Nathaniel, lord Curzon of Kedleston, B. diplomat (1859–1925), 1916 M, 1919 K
Curzon, the Last Phase (H. Nicolson), 1934 Q
'Curzon Line', Poland, Russians cross, 1944 G
Cushing, Harvey Williams, Am. neurological surgeon (1869–1939), 1902 P
Custom of the Country (E. Wharton), 1913 U
Customs Unions:
  Austro-German, projected, 1931 C
  Austro-Hungarian, 1850 O
  Benelux, 1947 K
  Ceylon and South India, 1964 M
  E. Pakistan, 1965 E
  European Economic Community, 1957 C, 1958 A. *See also* Common Market
  Franco-Italian, 1948 C
  German, 1888 K
  Prussia, with Hesse-Darmstadt, 1827 N. *See also* Zollverein
  US, 1789 G
Custozza, Italy, battles, 1848 G, 1866 F
Cuvier, Georges Léopold Chrétien, F. naturalist (1769–1832), 1769 Z, 1796 P, 1812 P, 1832 Z
Cuyper, P. J. H., Du. architect, 1877 S
Cyanide, used for extracting gold and silver, 1887 P
Cyclades Isles, 1827 K
Cycles of American History, The (A.M. Schlesinger Jnr), 1986 Q
Cycling Clubs, in England, 1878 X; in US, 1880 X

Cycling, World Cup, 1989 X
Cyclones
Bangladesh, 1985 E
Darwin, Australia, 1974 M
Cyclotron, the (or 'atom smasher'), 1931 P, 1934 P; giant, at California University, 1940 P; for Carnegie Institution, Washington, 1944 O; 'Nimrod', 1964 P
Cygnus constellation, X-ray emissions discovered, 1966 P
Cylinders, for steam engines, 1774 P
Cyprus:
British occupation, 1878 F, G
Britain annexes, 1914 L
declared a British colony, 1925 D
'Enosis' issue over, 1954 M, 1955 G, H
state of emergency, 1955 L
Athens broadcasts to, jammed, 1956 C
Makarios deported, 1956 C
Greece demands reference of problems to UN, 1956 C
EOKA rejects Harding's surrender terms 1956 H
UN calls for peaceful solution, 1957 B
EOKA offers to suspend terrorism, 1957 C
UN offers to mediate, 1957 C
Greek resolution fails in UN, 1957 M
British plan for Graeco-Turkish joint administration, 1958 F
agreement for independence signed, 1959 B
London Conference breaks down, 1960 A
agreement on bases, 1960 G
becomes independent Republic, 1960 H
fighting between Greeks and Turks, 1964 B, C, D
UN mediator appointed, 1964 C
UN peace force takes over, 1964 C
Greece rejects direct talks with Turkey, 1964 F
Turkish 'planes bomb, 1964 H
UN orders cease-fire, 1964 H
Gen. Grivas assmues command of Greek Cypriot forces, 1964 H
UN extends mandate for force, 1964 M
assassination attempt on Makarios, 1970 C
Greece demands Cyprus accept coalition government, 1972 B
Makarios returns, 1973 B, 1974 M
home of Israeli ambassador attacked by Palestinian terrorists, 1973 D
EOKA terrorist explosion in campaign for Enosis, 1973 G
Makarios deposed, 1973 R, 1974 G
Greeks to leave Cypriot National Guard, 1974 F
Sampson installed as leader, 1974 G
Britain, Turkey and Greece discuss future of, 1974 G
Northern Cyprus becomes Turkish Federated State, 1975 B
Turkish sector unilaterally declared independent, 1983 L
Israelis murdered, 1985 K
Kuwaiti airliner hijack, 1988 D 1992
merchant shipping tonnage statistics, Y
war. *See* Wars
Cyrano de Bergerac (E. Rostand), 1897 W
Cyrenaica: annexed by Italy, 1911 L; becomes autonomous under Italian suzerainty, 1912 K; Italian Egyptian agreement on, 1925 M
Czech Question, The (T. G. Masaryk), 1895 O
Czech Republic, Constitution, 1992 M
Czech language: studies in, 1818 Q; ordinances, 1897 D, L, 1899 K
Czechoslovak National Committee in London, 1940 G
Czechoslovakia: US recognises, 1918 J; independent republic proclaimed, 1918 K; irredentist agitation in, 1928 M; first crisis, 1938 E; second crisis, 1938 J; Hitler annexes, 1939 C
Prague Spring, 1968 E-K
National Assembly rehabilitates political prisoners, 1968 F
Soviet demand for meeting of Communist Party leaders rejected, 1968 G
withdrawal of Soviet troops halted, 1968 G
Warsaw Pact countries declare reforms unacceptable, 1968 G
Cierna-nad-Tisou talks, 1968 G
Soviet invasion, 1968 H, K
Dubček re-elected, 1968 H
Soviet occupation, 1969 A, C, H
created two-state federation, 1969 A
Husák succeeds Dubček as First Secretary, 1969 D
purge of reformers in Czechoslovak government, 1969 J
foreign travel restricted, 1969 K
Communist Party leader expelled, 1970 F
dissidents tried, 1972 G
diplomatic relations with W. Germany established, 1973 M
Munich Agreement of 1938 invalidated, 1973 M
dissidents convicted of subversion, 1979 K
British University lecturers expelled, 1980 R
political and economic reforms, 1987 C
divorce statistics, 1987 Y
major governmental and Communist party changes, 1988 K
demonstrations marking twentieth anniversary of Palach's suicide, 1989 A
Havel imprisoned, 1989 B
multi-party elections, 1989 D, F
demonstrations demanding end to Communist rule, 1989 L
general strike, 1989 L
Communist monopoly on power formally renounced, 1989 L
new government with non-Communist majority takes power, 1989 M
Havel elected President, 1989 M, R
USSR agrees to withdraw troops by July 1991, 1990 B
Civic Forum election victory, 1990 F
life expectancy, 1990 Y
illegitimacy rate, 1991 Y
pro-independence election victories in Slovakia, 1992 F
Slovak deputies vote for republic status, 1992 G
Czernowitz (now Chernovtsky), Russia, Russians take, 1916 F, 1917 H
Czolgosz, Léon, Am. anarchist, 1901 J

D

Da (H. Leonard), 1973 W
Da Nang, Vietnam, Buddhist rebellion, 1966 E
Dacko, David, Central Afr. Repub. leader (b. 1930), 1979 J
Dad's Army, television series, 1968 W
Dadaist Movement, 1915 S, 1916 S, 1920 S
Daedalus 88 sets new record for man-powered flight, 1988 P
Daffos, Fernand, 1983 P
Daguerre, Louis Jacques Mandé, F. pioneer of photography (1789–1851), 1789 Z, 1839 P, 1851 Z
Dahl, Vladimir Ivanovich, R. lexicographer (1802–1872), 1861 Q
Dahn, Julius Sophus Felix, G. author (1834–1900), 1876 U
Dahomey, West Africa: King of, 1892 N; French protectorate over, 1893 L; proclaimed a French colony, 1894 F; becomes an independent Republic, 1960 G
Daimler, Gottlieb, G. inventor of petrol engine (1834–1900), 1882 P, 1885 P
Dairen. *See* Dalny
Daisy Miller (H. James), 1878 U
Dakar, in Senegal, W. Africa, 1904 N, 1940 J
Dakota, North, State, US, becomes state, 1889 B
Dakota, South, State, US, becomes state, 1889 B
Daladier, Edouard, F. Radical Socialist politician (1884–1970), forms ministries, 1933 A, 1934 A, 1938 D; at Munich Conference, 1938 J; visits Algiers, 1939 A; empowered to rearm, 1939 C; attempts to negotiate with Hitler, 1939 N; reforms ministry, 1939 J; resigns, 1940 C
Dalai Lama of Tibet: appointed to prepare Tibet for regional autonomy, 1956 D; escapes, 1959 C; appeals to UN, 1961 C
Dale, Sir Henry Hallett, B. scientist (1875–1968), 1945 P
Daley, Richard Joseph, Am., Mayor of Chicago (1902–76), 1976 M
Daley, Steve, B. soccer player (b. 1953), 1979 X
Dalhousie, Earl of. *See* Ramsay, James
Dali, Salvador Felipe Jacinte, Sp. artist (1904–89), 1929 S, 1934 S, 1951 S, 1955 S
Dallapiccola, Luigi, It. musician (1904–75), 1968 T
Dallas, Tex., US, Kennedy assassinated at, 1963 L
Dallas, televsion series, 1978 W
Dalmatia: Austria obtains, 1797 K; ceded to Yugoslavia, 1920 L; Italy abandons claims in, 1924 C
Dalny (Dairen), Russia, Japanese occupy, 1904 E
Dalou, Jules, F. sculptor (1838–1902), 1898 S, 1899 S
Dalrymple, Sir Henry, B. soldier, 1808 H
Dalton, Hugh, B. Labour politician (1888–1962), as chancellor of Exchequer, 1945 G
Dalton, John, B. chemist and natural philosopher (1766–1844), 1766 Z, 1803 P, 1808 P, 1844 Z
Dam, Carl Peter Henrik, Dan. scientist (1895–1976), 1895 Z, 1976 Z
Damaged Goods (E. Brieux), 1917 W
Damaraland, exploration of, 1850 P
Damascus, Syria: Allies occupy, 1918 K; French occupy, 1920 G; French bombard, 1925 K, 1926 E, 1945 E; army *coup* in, 1961 J; terrorist bomb, 1981 L
Dame aux Camélias, La (A. Dumas), 1848 U
Damian, F., Aus. instrument maker, 1829 T
Dams:
Aswan, 1902 M
Aswan High, finance for, 1956 G, 1958 K; work begins, 1960 A; rescue of antiquities in area, 1960 Q; opened, 1964 E
Kariba, Rhodesia, 1960 E
Zola, France, 1843 P
Dana, James Dwight, Am. geologist (1813–95), 1837 P
Dance of Death (A. Strindberg), 1901 U
Dances:
Bebop, 1945 W, 1950 W
Cake-walk, 1900 W
Charleston, 1925 W
Foxtrot, 1913 W
Lambeth Walk, 1938 W
Lancers, 1836 X
Polka, 1835 W
Quadrille, 1815 W

Rock and Roll, 1956 W
Slow Foxtrot, 1927 W
Waltz, 1812 W
Dangerous Corner (J. B. Priestley), 1932 W
Daniloff, Nicholas, Am. journalist (b. 1934), 1986 H
Danish language, 1775 O
Dannecker, Johann Heinrich von, G. sculptor (1758–1841), 1794 S
Dans le labyrinthe (Robbe-Grillet), 1960 U
Danton's Death (G. Büchner), 1835 U
Danton, George Jacques, F. revolutionary (1759–94), 1790 N, 1792 L; leads Committee of Public Safety, 1793 D; executed, 1794 D
Danube, River: Napoleon crosses, 1809 E; Vienna Note demands free passage, 1854 H; freedom of navigation, 1856 C; crossed by Russians, 1877 F; open to navigation, 1919 C; convention for internationalisation, 1921 G; London Conference on, 1932 D; Italian designs on, 1936 L; Belgrade Conference on, 1948 G
Danubian *Bloc*, 1934 C; Italian and German rival interests in, 1934 F
Danubian Principalities. *See under* Moldavia and Wallachia
Danzig, Poland: as a free city, 1772 H; ceded to Prussia, 1790 C, 1793 E; Polish treaty with, 1920 K; declared a free city, 1920 L; Poland occupies, 1933 C; elections won by Nazis, 1933 E; Polish agreement with, 1933 H, 1937 A; Germany annexes, 1939 J; Russians take, 1945 C
Dar-es-Salaam, Tanganyika, British take, 1916 J
Darby, Sir Henry Clifford, B. historical geographer (1909–92), 1977 Q
Darby, John Nelson, B. founder of Plymouth Brethren (1800–82), 1827 R
Dardanelles, The: Royal Navy in, 1807 B; Treaty of, 1809 A; Turkey closes, to all except Russian warships, 1833 G; closed to warships in peace-time, 1841 G; British and French fleets off, 1853 F; Austria agrees to opening to Russian warships, 1908 J; Turkey closes, 1912 D, 1914 K; British and French bombard, 1915 B; Campaign, Allied attack fails, 1915 C; Fisher resigns over disagreement in Cabinet about, 1915 E; Report of Commission on, 1917 O; international control of, 1920 B; Turkey renounces sovereignty over, 1936 G
Dargomijsky, Alexander Sergeivich, R. musician (1813–69), 1856 T
Daring Young Man on the Flying Trapeze, The (W. Saroyan), 1935 U
Dark is Light Enough, The (C. Fry), 1954 W
Darlan, Jean François, F. admiral (1881–1942), agreement with Hitler, 1941 E; recognised by Eisenhower, 1942 L; assassinated, 1942 M
Darlington, Dur., England, railway opened, 1825 P
Darmesteter, James, F. antiquarian (1849–94), 1892 Q
Darmstadt, Germany, French occupy, 1920 C
Dartmouth, Devon, England, Royal Naval College, 1903 O
Dartmouth, Earl of. *See* Legge, W.
Darwin and After Darwinism (G. J. Romanes), 1892 R
Darwin, Australia, cyclone disaster, 1974 M
Darwin, Charles, B. scientist (1809–82), 1809 Z, 1831 O, 1839 P, 1858 P, 1859 P, 1868 P, 1871 P, 1882 Z
Darwin, Erasmus, B. scientist (1731–1802), 1794 P, 1802 Z
Dashwood, Edmée Elizabeth M., B. author under pseudonym of 'E. M. Delafield' (1890–1943), 1930 U
Dassin, Jules, F. film director, 1948 W, 1962 W
Daudet, Alphonse, F. author (1840–97), 1866 U, 1872 S, U, 1885 U
Daughters of the American Revolution, 1890 O
Daumier, Honoré, F. artist (1808–79), 1808 Z, 1830 S, 1841 S, 1879 Z
Daventry, Northants, England, transmitter, 1925 P
Davey, Grenville, B. artist, Turner Prize, 1992 S
David Copperfield (C. Dickens), 1849 U
David, Jacques Louis, F. artist (1749–1825), 1783 S, 1785 S, 1788 S, 1793 S, 1799 S, 1800 S, 1801 S, 1807 S, 1825 Z
Davidson, Donald, Am. philosopher (b. 1917), 1980 R, 1984 R, 1990 R
Davies, Sir Clement, B. Liberal politician (1895–1962), 1956 J
Davies, Harold, Am. diplomat (b. 1914), 1965 G
Davies, Laura, B. golfer (b. 1963), 1987 X
Davies, Sir Peter Maxwell, B. musician (b. 1934), 1959 T, 1969 T, 1972 T, 1980 T, 1985 T
Davies, R. L., B. architect, 1960 S
Davies, (Robert) Rees, B. historian (b. 1938), 1987 Q
Davies, Robertson, Canad. author (b. 1913), 1987 U, 1992 U
Davies, William Henry, B. poet (1871–1940), 1908 U
Daviot, Gordon, B. dramatist, 1933 W
Davis, D. F., B. tennis enthusiast, 1900 X
Davis, George, B. criminal, 1975 H, 1976 E, 1978 G
Davis, Jefferson, Am. Confederate (1808–89), Resolutions for federal slave trade, 1860 B; selected president of Confederate States, 1861 B
Davis, John W., Am. Democrat (1873–1955), in presidential election, 1924 F, L
Davis, Norman, B. literary scholar (1913–89), 1971 Q
Davis, Ralph Henry Carless, B. historian (1918–91), 1967 Q
Davis, Steve, B. snooker player (b. 1957), 1985 X
Davy, Sir Humphry, B. natural philosopher (1778–1829), 1778 Z, 1800 P, 1806 P, 1812 P, 1815 P, 1829 Z
Dawes, Charles Gates, Am. Republican (1865–1951), investigates German economy, 1923 L; Report on Reparations, 1924 D, G, H; nominated for vice-presidency, 1924 F
Dawes, Henry Laurence, Am. lawyner and Republican (1816–1903), 1887 B
Dawn (T. Dreiser), 1931 U
Dawson, Emily, N. magistrate, 1913 E
Dawson, Geoffrey, B. journalist (1874–1944), 1874 Z, 1912 V, 1941 V, 1944 Z
Day After, The, television programme, 1984 W
Day by the Sea, A. (N. C. Hunter), 1953 W
Day in the Death of Joe Egg, A (P. Nichols), 1967 W
Day of the Jackal, The (F. Forsyth), 1972 U
Day-Lewis, Cecil., Ir. poet (1904–72), 1904 Z, 1935 U, 1953 U, 1957 U, 1972 Z
Dayan, General Moshe, Isr. soldier and politician (1915–81), 1979 K, 1981 Z
Daylight Saving:
in Britain, introduced, 1916 O
Double Summer Time, 1941 U
in US, 1918 O
Daytona Beach, Florida, US, *Bluebird's* record at, 1935 P
Daza, Hilarión, Bolivian politician, 1876 N
DDT, invented, 1939 P
DDT pesticide, US ban, 1969 P
De Beers Mining Corporation, 1880, 1959 P
De Lorean Motor Company, 1982 B
Belfast factory, 1978 H, 1982 K
De Profundis (O. Wilde), 1905 U
De Statu Ecclesiae (J. Febronius), 1763 R
De Stijl, 1917 S
De l'Allemagne (Mme de Staël), 1810 U
De l'amour (Stendhal), 1822 U
De l'esprit de conquête et de l'usurpation dans les rapports avec la civilisation Européenne (B. Constant), 1813 O
De la défense de places fortes (L. Carnot), 1810 O
De la Démocratie en Amerique (A. de Tocqueville), 1835 O
De la littérature allemande (Frederick the Great), 1780 O
De mundi sensibilis et intelligibilis forma et principiis (I. Kant), 1770 R
Deacon, Richard, B. sculptor (b. 1949), 1980 S, 1982 S, 1983 S, 1987 S, 1989 S
Turner Prize, 1987 S
Dead Class, The (T. Cantor), 1982 W
Dead Sea Scrolls, 1947 S, 1960 Q
Dead Souls (N. Gogol), 1835 U
Deafness, treatment for, 1961 P
Deak Party, in Hungary, 1875 C
Deakin, Frederick William Dampier, B. historian (b. 1913), 1962 Q
Dean's December, The (S. Bellow), 1982 U
Dean, Basil, B. theatre manager, 1911 W, 1926 W
Dean, Brenda, B. trade unionist (b. 1943), 1984 O
Dean, Christopher Colin, B. ice dancer (b. 1958), 1984 X
Dean, John Wesley, Am. lawyer (b. 1938), 1973 F
Deane, Silas, Am. diplomat (1737–89), 1776 G
Dear Brutus (J. M. Barrie), 1917 W
Dearmer, Percy, B. hymnologist (1867–1936), 1906 R, 1925 R
Death Penalty:
in Britain, reduced for offences, 1823 G, O
abolition, bills introduced, 1956 F, 1964 M
in force, 1965 L
abolition in Britain, 1969 O
in S. Africa, imposed for sabotage, 1962 E
US Supreme Court rules death penalty contrary to Constitution, 1972 O
See also Capital Punishment
Death and Resurrection of Mr Roche (T. Kilroy), 1968 W
Death and the King's Horseman (W. Soyinka), 1975 W
Death and the Maiden (A. Dorfman), 1991 W
Death in Venice (T. Mann), 1913 U
Death in the Afternoon (E. Hemingway), 1932 U
Death of a Salesman (A. Miller), 1949 W
Death of the Heart, The (E. Bowen), 1938 U
Death on the Rock, television programme, 1989 W
Death, definition of, 1966 P
Deaths and Entrances (D. Thomas), 1946 U
Deaths, registrations of, in Britain, 1836 H
Débâcle, La (E. Zola), 1892 U
Debré, Michel, F. Radical, 1959 A, 1962 D
Debs, Eugene, Am. trade union leader (1855–1926), 1919 C
Debt, National, British, sinking fund for, 1786 C
Debts, Indonesian to Netherlands, repudiated, 1956 H
Debussy, Claude, F. musician (1862–1918), 1862 Z, 1892 W, 1894 T, 1902 T, 1905 T, 1918 Z
Debutantes, presentation of, discontinued, 1958 G
'Decadence', of Russian composers, alleged, 1931 T
Decazes, Elie, Duc de, F. foreign minister (1780–1860), 1818 M; 1820 B

Decazes, Louis Charles Elie, F. statesman (1819–86), 1875 D
Decimal System. The (J. Bowring), 1854 O
Declaration of Commonwealth on Monetary Affairs, 1933 G
Declaration of Frankfurt, for Allied invasion of France, 1813 M
Declaration of Grenada, 1971 G
Declaration of Independence, American, 1776 G
Declaration of Paris, defines blockade and contraband of war, 1856 D
Declaration of Rights of Man, in France, 1789 H
Declaration of Third International against Fascism, 1935 G
Declaration, 1957 O
Declaratory Act, 1766 C
Decline and Fall of the British Aristocracy, The (D. Cannadine), 1990 Q
Decline and Fall of the Roman Empire (E. Gibbon), 1776 Q
Decline of the West, The (O. Spengler), 1918 O
Decoration, interior, 1893 S
Decrees:
Berlin, revoked, 1810 L
Carlsbad, by the Frankfurt Diet, 1819 J
Fontainbleau, for confiscating British goods, 1810 K
Milan, 1807 M; revoked, 1810 L
Rambouillet, for sale of US ships seized by France, 1810 C
Deep Sea (F. Brett Young), 1914 U
Deep-freezing of food, 1925 P
Deep-sea exploration, 1960 P, 1964 P
Deephaven (S. O. Jewett), 1877 U
Deere, John, Am. inventor (1804–86), 1846 P
Defeat of the Armada, The (G. Mattingley), 1959 Q
Defence Committee, British, 1946 K
Defence Estimates, comparative, 1870 Y, 1910 Y, 1914 Y
Defence Ministry, in France, 1937 B
Defence White Paper, on Falklands War, 1982 M
Defence of Guenevere, The (W. Morris), 1958 U
Defence of Philosophic Doubt (A. J. Balfour), 1879 R
Defence of Usury (J. Bentham), 1787 O
Defence of the Constitution of Government of the US (J. Adams), 1787 O
Defence, British Minister of, given enlarged powers, 1957 A
Defence, British Ministry, unified, 1963 B
Defence, British spending on, 1951 D, 1974 M
Defense Department, US, establishment, 1949 H
Degas, Danse, Dessein (P. Valéry), 1938 U
Degli ultimi casa de Romagna (M. D'Azeglio), 1846 O
Dehaene, Jean-Luc, Prime Minister of Belgium, 1992 C
Deirdre of the Sorrows (J. M. Synge), 1907 U
Delacroix, Eugène, F. artist (1798–1863), 1798 Z, 1822 S, 1824 S, 1829 S, 1831 S, 1846 S, 1849 S, 1857 S, 1863 Z
Delafield, E. M. *See* Dashwood, E. E. M.
Delagoa Bay, S.E. Africa: Captured by Portuguese, 1781 N; Portuguese claim is upheld, 1875 N; railway concession in, 1883 M; railway to Transvaal, 1895 G; British designs on, 1898 H; munitions to Transvaal, prevented, 1899 K
Delane, John Thadeus, B. journalist (1817–79), 1817 Z, 1841 V, 1879 Z
Delavigne, Jean François, F. author (1793–1843), 1818 U
Delaware, State, US, 1777 L, 1778 G
River, steamboat on, 1787 P
Delcassé, Théophile, F. statesman (1852–1923), 1852 Z, 1898 G, 1899 H, 1903 G, 1905 F, 1915 K, 1923 Z
Delhi, India: British capture, 1857 J; Durbar, 1911 M; Hindu and Moslem riots in, 1924 G; Pact, between Viceroy and Gandhi, 1931 C; Central legislature at, 1935 H; Pact, on minorities, 1950 D; World Council of Churches meets, etc., 1961 R; food riots, 1966 C
Delibes, Léo, F. musician (1836–91), 1836 Z, 1870 T, 1876 T, 1891 Z
Delicate Balance, A. (E. Albee), 1966 W
Delisle, Léopold Victor, F. historian (1826–94), 1852 Q
Delititiae Sapientiae (E. Swedenborg), 1768 R
Delius, Frederick, B. musician (1863–1934), 1863 Z, 1902 T, 1903 T, 1904 T, 1905 T, 1907 T, 1912 T, 1934 Z, 1953 T
Dell, Ethel M. (Savage), B. novelist (1881–1939), 1881 Z, 1912 U, 1939 Z
Delors, Jacques Lucien Jean, F. President of European Commission (b. 1925), 1984 G
Delphic Oracle, The (Parke and Warmell), 1957 Q
Delphine (A. de Staël), 1802 U
Deluc, Jean André, Swi. geologist and meteorologist (1727–1817), 1771 P, 1778 P
Demerara, British Guiana:
British capture, 1796 N
British retain, 1814 H
Demetrios I, Patriarch of Constantinople, 1987 R
Demirel, Suleyman, Turkish politician, 1991 K
Demjanjuk, John, Am. citizen tried for war crimes (b. 1920), 1988 D
Democracy and Re-action (L. T. Hobhouse), 1904 O
Democracy and Sectarianism: A Political and Social History of Liverpool, 1868–1939 (P.J. Waller), 1981 Q
Democratic Parties. *See under* Political Parties
Democratic Republic of Hungary 1990 H. *See also* Hungary
Democratic Vistas (W. Whitman), 1871 U
Demonstrations:
against celebration of anniversary of arrival of Columbus in the Americas, 1992 K
anti-nuclear protests across Europe, 1983 K
in Algiers, by Europeans, 1948 E
in Baku, by Azerbaijani nationalists, 1990 A
in Bangui, Central African Empire, 1979 D
in Belgium, against Leopold III, 1950 G
in Britain, by Blanketeers, 1817 C
by Chartists, 1848 D
by Socialists in Trafalgar Square ('Bloody Sunday'), 1887 L
by ex-servicemen, 1923 D
by Fascists and anti-Fascists, 1934 J
for Second Front, 1942 G
CND Aldermaston March, 1956 O, 1963 D
CND sit-down, 1961 O
by unemployed, 1963 C
during visit of King and Queen of Hellenes, 1963 G
of aircraft-workers, 1965 A
against war in Viet-Nam, 1965 K
anti-Vietnam War, 1968 K
Red Lion Square, London, 1974 F
National Front in S. London, 1977 H
anti-nuclear protest by CND, London, 1980 K
anti-nuclear protests, 1980 K, 1983 F, L
anti-nuclear protests, Upper Heyford, 1983 F
anti-nuclear protests, Greenham Common, 1983 L
demonstrators outside Libyan People's Bureau fired on, 1984 D
against Poll Tax, 1990 C
in Bucharest, anti-government, 1990 F
in Budapest, calling for democracy and national independence, 1989 C
in Cairo, anti-government, 1981 J
in Chile, marking 10th anniversary of military coup, 1983 J
in China, against British possession of Hong Kong, 1967 E
in Czechoslovakia, 1969 C, 1989 A, L
in Dublin, British Embassy burnt down, 1972 B
in France, by Communists, 1952 E
in Germany, by Communist Youth, 1951 H
in E. Germany, demanding political reform, 1989 K, L
in India, by Socialists, 1951 F
in Ireland, for peace, 1976 H
in Jordan, against Eisenhower doctrine, 1957 D
in Kashmir, against incorporation with India, 1957 A
in Jerusalem, at Temple Mount, 1990 K
in Kenya, 1990 B, 1990 G
in Lithuania, demanding freedom, 1972 E
in Malta, celebrating 30 years of Mintoff's premiership, 1979 V
in Mietne, Poland, by students demanding restoration of crucifixes in classrooms, 1984 C
in Moscow , by opposition to Communist regime, 1990 E
in Northern Ireland, against IRA, 1971 C
in Nyasaland, against federation, 1953 H
in Philippines, demanding resignation of Marcos, 1983 J
in Poland, against Russian rule, 1861 B; 1982 E, H, 1983 E
in Russia, by students, 1901 B
in S. Africa, against pass-laws, 1960 C
in Spain, by students, 1929 C; 1966 D, 1970 M
in Tbilisi, for Georgian independence, 1989 D
in Teheran, 1978 J, 1980 M
in Tibet, against Chinese rule, 1987 K
in Timisoara, Roumania, 1989 M
in Turkey, by students, 1960 D
in US, by civil rights workers, 1963 H, 1965 C
against war in Viet-Nam, 1965 D, K
against US intervention in Cambodia, 1970 E
in W. Germany, anti-nuclear protests, 1984 D
See also Political Parties; Riots; Strikes
Demos (G. R. Gissing), 1886 U
Dempsey, Jack, Am. boxer (1895–1983), 1895 Z, 1919 X, 1983 Z
Dempsey, Sir Miles, B. general (1896–1969), 1945 C
Denby, Edwin, Am. politician, 1924 B
Denikin, Anton, R. general (1872–1947), 1919 B, J, M, 1920 C
Denison, George Anthony, B. churchman (1805–96), 1856 R
Denktas, Rauf, Turkish-Cypriot leader, 1985 A, 1986 G
Denmark: Struensee's rule in, 1770 J, M, 1772 A; cedes Oldenburg to Russia, 1773 K; invades Sweden, 1788 J; Germany invades, 1940 D
European Community membership, 1970 F, 1972 A, K
Danish trawlers banned from British waters, 1983 A
urbanization, 1985 Y
divorce statistics, 1987 Y
life expectancy, 1990 Y
illegitimacy rate, 1991 Y
European football championship victory, 1992 X
referendum over Maastricht Treaty, 1992 F

Dennett, Daniel Clement, Am. philosopher (b. 1942), 1978 R
Dennewitz, Germany, battle of, 1813 J
Denning, Alfred, lord Denning, B. lawyer (b. 1899), 1963 J
Deontology; or the Science of Morality (J. Bentham), 1834 O
Deoxyribonucleic acid (DNA), structure of, determined, 1961 P, 1962 P; 1970 P, 1973 P, 1977 P
  discovered in cells in the mitochondria, 1966 P
  The Double Helix (J.D. Watson), 1968 P
  synthetic, 1978 P
  genetic fingerprinting, 1984 P
  humans and chimpanzees, relationship between researched, 1984 P
Department of Scientific and Industrial Research (DSIR), 1956 O
Department of Trade and Industry, B., creation, 1970 K
Department of the Environment, B., creation, 1970 K
Deployment and Payment of the Clergy (L. Paul), 1964 R
Depositions of Monarchs:
  Alexander Cuza, of Rumania, 1866 B
  Isabella II, of Spain, 1868 J
  See also Abdications; Monarchies
Depressed areas, in Britain, 1934 L, 1936 G
Depretis, Agostino, It. politician (1813–87), 1876 C, 1887 G
Deptford, Kent, England, power station, 1890 P
  phosphate factory, 1843 P
Déracinés, Les (M. Barrs), 1897 U
Derain, André, F. artist (1880–1954), 1906 S, 1907 S
Derby, Earls of. *See under* Stanley
Derna, Tripoli: Wavell takes, 1941 A; British evacuate, 1942 B
Derrida, Jacques, F. philosopher (b. 1930), 1930 Z, 1967 R, 1987 R
Dervishes, in Sudan, 1885 G, 1894 G
Des Moines, Iowa, US, 1958 R
Des canyons aux étoiles (O. Messiaen), 1974 T
Desai, Morarji, Ind. Janata Party leader (b. 1896), 1975 F, 1977 C, 1979 G
Descent of Man, The (C. Darwin), 1871 P
Deschanel, Paul, F. statesman, president of France 1920 A, H
Deserted Village, The (O. Goldsmith), 1770 U
Design, US National Academy, 1826 S
Desio, M., It. mountaineer, 1954 P
Desmarest, Nicolas (1725–1815), F. geologist, 1774 P
Desmoulins, Lucie Simplice Camille Benoist, F. revolutionary (1760–94), 1794 D
Desolation of a City: Coventry and the Urban Crisis of the Late Middle Ages (C.V. Phythian-Adams), 1979 Q
Despair (V. Nabokov), 1966 U
Dessau, Germany, 1919 S, 1925 S
Destinée sociale (V. Considérant), 1836 O
Destinées, Les (A. de Vigny), 1864 U
Destiny (D. Edgar), 1976 W
Detective Stories, 1920 U, 1921 U
Deterding, Henry, 1907 O
Detergent, Synthetic, 1933 P
Detroit, Michigan, US: Indian rising, 1763 E; surrenders to British, 1812 H; US recapture, 1813 H; motor industry at, 1903 P
  race riots, 1967 G
Deutscher, Isaac, B. historian (1907–67), 1954 Q, 1963 Q
Deutschland ein Wintermärchen (H. Heine), 1844 U
Deux Sources de la monde et de la religion, Les (H. Bergson), 1932 R
Development Commission, British, 1910 O
Development Hypothesis, The (H. Spencer), 1852 P
Development of the Frog (R. Remak), 1850 P
Deviations, by Communists: Trotsky's, 1927 M; in Yugoslavia, 1948 J; in Poland, 1948 J; in China, 1955 C
Devil's Island, French Guiana, 1894 M
Devlin, Bernadette Josephine (Mrs. McAliskey), Irish civil rights activist and politician (b. 1947),1969 D, 1970 F
Devlin, Patrick, Lord Devlin, B. lawyer (b. 1905), 1905 Z, Chairman of Press Council, 1963 F; presides over Committee on Docks, 1965 H
Devonshire, Dukes of. *See under* Cavendish
Dewar, Sir James, B. chemist (1842–1923), 1894 P, 1914 P
Dewey, George, Am. colonial, 1898 E
Dewey, John, Am. philosopher (1859–1952), 1899 O, 1922 R, 1929 R, 1931 R, 1939 R
Dewey, Thomas E., Am. Republican (1902–71), 1944 L, 1948 L
Diabetes, treatment of, 1937 P
Diable et le Bon Dieu, Le (J.-P. Sartre), 1951 W
Diaghilev, Serge, R. choreographer (1872–1929), 1872 Z, 1909 T, 1917 S, 1918 T, 1919 T, 1926 T, 1929 Z
Diagnosis of Man, The (K. Walker), 1942 R
Dialogues des Carmélites (F. Poulenc), 1957 T
Dialogues of Natural Religion (D. Hume), 1779 R
Dialogues sur le Commerce des Blés (F. Galiani), 1770 O
Diamond Necklace Affair, 1785 F
Diamonds: discovered in Orange Free State, 1870 N; Kimberley diamond fields annexed by Britain, 1871 K; Rhodes amalgamates Rand companies, 1888 O; Williamson mine, Tanganyika, 1946 P; synthetic diamonds, 1959 P
Diana of the Crossways (G. Meredith), 1885 U
Diaries of Evelyn Waugh, The, 1976 U
Diary of Anne Frank, The 1955 U
Diary of Samuel Pepys, The (R.C. Latham and W. Matthews eds.), 1970 Q
Diary of a Provincial Lady (E. M. Delafield), 1930 U
Diary of a Witness of the War in Africa (P. Alarcón), 1859 U
Diastase, enzyme, separated from barley, 1832 P
Díaz, Jorge, Chilean dramatist, 1966 W
Díaz, Porfirio, president of Mexico (1830–1915), 1877 D, 1884 M, 1911 E, 1912 K
Dicey, Albert Venn, B. jurist (1835–1922), 1835 Z, 1860 O, 1922 Z
Dick, Sir William Reid, B. sculptor (1879–1961), 1879 Z, 1961 Z
Dickens (P. Ackroyd), 1990 Q
Dickens, Charles, B. novelist (1812–70), 1812 Z, 1836 U, 1837 U, 1838 U, 1840 U, 1843 U, 1849 U, 1859 U, 1861 U, 1864 U, 1870 U, Z
  edits *Daily News*, 1846 V
Dickinson, Goldsworthy Lowes (1862–1932), 1916 O
Dickinson, Michael, B. race-horse trainer (b. 1950), 1983 X
Dicksee, Sir Francis Bernard (Frank), B. artist (1853–1928), 1853 Z, 1928 Z
Dickson, J. T., Am. inventor of Terylene, 1941 P
Dictionaries:
  Classical (Lemprière), 1788 Q
  Etymological English (Skeat), 1879 Q
  French (Littré), 1863 Q
  German (Grimm), 1854 Q
  Grand Dictionnaire Universel du XIXe Siècle (Larousse), 1866 Q
  Greek–English Lexicon (Liddell and Scott), 1843 Q
  Hebrew and Chaldaic, 1812 Q
  Musique (Rousseau), 1767 T
  New English Dictionary (later known as *The Oxford Dictionary* (ed. Murray)), 1884 Q, 1928 Q, 1989 Q
  Philosophist (Voltaire), 1764 R
  Russian (Dahl's), 1861 Q
  Russian ('Imperial'), 1787 Q
  Sanskrit, 1819 Q, 1856 Q
  Tartare–Mantchou–français (Amiot), 1789 Q
  Totius Latinitatis Lexicon (Facciolati), 1771 Q
  Totius Latinitatis Lexicon (Forcellini), 1769 Q
  Webster's, 1828 Q
Dictionary of German Biography, 1875 Q
Dictionary of Labour Biography (J.M. Bellamy and J. Saville eds.), 1972 Q
Dictionary of National Biography, 1885 Q
Dictionary of the Khazars (M. Pavic), 1988 U
Diderot, Denis, F. philosopher (1713–84), 1766 R, 1775 R, 1784 Z
Didion, Joan, Am. author (b. 1934), 1977 U
Diefenbaker, John George, Canad. Progressive Conservative (1895–1979), 1895 Z, 1962 F; forms ministry, 1957 F; Macmillan visits, 1959 C; resigns, 1963 D; 1979 Z
Diem, Ngo Dinh, President of South Viet-Nam (1901–63), 1963 L
Dien Bien Phu, North Viet-Nam: US flies French battalion to defend, 1954 D; falls, 1954 E
Dieppe, France, raid on, 1942 H
Diesel, Rudolf, G. engineer (1857–1913), 1857 Z, 1892 P, 1913 Z
Diesel-electric railway, 1913 P
Diesel-electric vessel, 1936 P
Diet, treatise on, 1840 P
Dietrich, Marlene, G.-born, Am. singer and actress (1904–92), 1904 Z, 1930 W, 1932 W, 1992 Z
Diets. *See* Parliaments, etc.
Dieu et l'Etat (M. Bakunin), 1882 O
Diez, Friedrich Christian, G. philologist (1794–1876), 1836 Q
Diffusion of Useful Knowledge, Society for, 1827 O
Digestion, human, study of, 1822 P
Digging Up Jericho (K. Kenyon), 1957 Q
Digging Up the Past (L. Woolley), 1930 Q
Digital audio tape cassette, 1987 P
Dikko, (Alhaji) Umaru, Nig. politician (b. 1936), 1984 G
Dilemmas (G. Ryle), 1954 R
Dilettanti Society of London, 1764 Q
Dilke, Sir Charles Wentworth, B. Radical Liberal politician (1843–1911), 1872 C, 1884 O, 1886 U
Dillard, Annie, Am. author (b. 1945), 1989 U
Dillon, Clarence Douglas, Am. Rep. politician (b. 1909), 1960 L
Dillon, John, Ir. Nationalist leader (1851–1927), 1851 Z, 1886 L, 1927 Z
Dilthey, Wilhelm, G. philosopher, 1905 R
Dimbleby Lecture, BBC television, 1979 L
Dimitrios, Metropolitan of Imroz and Tenedos, 1972 R
Dimitrov, Filip, Prime Minister of Bulgaria (b. 1955), 1991 K
Dimitrov, Georgi, president of Bulgaria (1882–1949), 1946 L
Dimyes, Lajos, Hung., Smallholder Party leader, 1947 E
Dingle, Herbert, B. scientist (1890–1978), 1937 P

Dingley, Nelson, Am. politician (1832–99), 1897 G
Dingo (C. Wood), 1967 W
Dinkeloo, John Gerard, Am. architect (1918–81), 1975 S, 1976 S
Dinkins, David, Am. Mayor of New York (b. 1927), 1990 A
Dinner Party, The (J. Chicago), 1979 S
Diomedes, Alexander, Gr. premier, 1950 A
Dioxins
gas release, 1976 P
Netherlands research into, 1977 P
Diphtheria, immunity test, 1913 P
Diplock Commission, on Northern Ireland, 1972 M
Diplomatic Prelude, 1938–9 (L. B. Namier), 1948 Q
Diplomatic Service, British, 1965 A
Diplomatic, Science of, 1889 Q
Dirac, Paul Adrien Maurice, B. scientist (1902–84), 1937 P
Dire Straits, B. pop group, 1985 W
Disarmament Deadlock, The (J. Wheeler-Bennett), 1934 O
Disarmament:
Russian proposals, 1898 H
Washington Conferences on, 1921 H, L, M, 1922 F
by Denmark, 1926 C
Preparatory Conference on, 1926 E
Litvinov proposes immediate, 1927 L
Preparatory Commission on, 1930 D, M
British Plan for, fails, 1933 C
Germany leaves Conference on, 1933 K
Naval Conference on, 1934 K
Acheson's proposals to UN, 1951 L
Russia calls on West to reduce forces, 1956 F
Nehru appeals to Russia and US, 1957 L
Committee meets at Geneva, 1959 J, 1960 C
Washington discussions on, 1961 F
Russia proposes meeting at Summit level, 1962 B
Seventeen nations meet at Geneva, 1962 C, 1964 A
France boycotts, 1962 C
talks resumed, 1965 D
eighteen-nation talks, 1966 A, 1967 B, H, 1971 H
Strategic Arms Limitation Talks (SALT), 1969 L, 1972 K, 1979 F, 1983 C
British Labour Party votes for unilateral nuclear disarmament, 1980 K
Campaign for Nuclear Disarmament (CND), 1980 K, 1981 K
US-USSR talks, 1981 M, 1983 A, B, L, 1984 A, 1985 A, C, L, 1987 A, C, D, G, J, L, 1988 A
Brezhnev proposes freeze on strategic arms, 1982 E
USSR bargains with US, 1982 M
The Church and the Bomb, C. of E. report, 1982 R
Andropov's proposals, 1983 H
Gorbachev offers summit talks with Reagan, 1985 D
Intermediate-range Nuclear Forces (INF) Treaty, 1988 F
Gorbachev announces planned reductions in USSR armed forces and conventional weapons, 1988 M
Conference on Security and Cooperation in Europe (CSCE), 1990 L
Strategic Arms Reduction Treaty (START), 1991 G
anti-nuclear demonstrations. *See* Demonstrations
Disasters:
Aberfan, 1966 K
Airship R. 101, 1930 P
torrential rain in Brazil, 1988 B
Clapham Junction rail crash, 1988 M
Comet aircraft, 1954 P
Exxon Valdez accident, 1989 C
Flixborough, Nypro chemical plant blows up, 1974 F
Glasgow soccer stadium, 1971 A
Heysel Stadium riot, 1985 X
Hillsborough soccer stadium, 1989 X
Ibrox Park stadium disaster, 1971 A
S.S. *Lakonia*, 1963 M
at Lima football stadium, 1964 E
pilgrims crushed to death at Mecca, 1990 R
London Underground crashes, 1975 B, 1977 M
ferry disaster in Philippines, 1987 M
Piper Alpha explosion, 1988 G
contaminated cooking oil distributed in Spain, 1989 E
S.S. *Titanic* sunk, 1912 P
Union Carbide accident, Bhopal, India, 1984 M
Zeebrugge, *Herald of Free Enterprise* capsized, 1987 C, G, K
See also Air Crashes; Cyclones; Earthquakes; Famines; Fires; Floods; Hurricanes
Discipline and Punish (M. Foucault), 1975 R
Discourse Before the Congress Angostura (S. Bolívar), 1819 O
Discourse on Popular Education (P. Campanares), 1775 O
Discovery of the East (P. Claudel), 1900 Q
Discovery, voyages of, 1768 P, 1775 P, 1776 P, 1777 P, 1778 P, 1831 P, *See also under* Exploration
Discrimination:
Race Relations Act, B., 1968 D, O
Commission for Racial Equality, B., 1976 O
Supreme Court ruling, US, 1978 O
Charter of Rights and Freedoms, Can., 1985 D
Britain found guilty of sex discrimination in immigration policy, 1985 O
preferential minority hiring quotas, US, 1986 O
See also Racial Problems
Disease, Livestock, 1857 O, 1903 O
Disease, germ theory of, 1861 P
Diseases:
chronic, treated by penicillin, 1943 P
lung cancer, 1954 P
metabolic, cures for, 1946 P
pernicious anaemia, treatment for, 1955 P
streptococcus infections, treatment for, 1935 P
tetanus, controlled by serum, 1915 P
US Center for Disease Control, 1981 P
venereal, 1916 O, 1943 O
cure for, 1909 P
See also Epidemics, individual diseases and Medical Research
Disenchanted (C. E. Montague), 1927 O
Disestablishment, of Irish Church, 1869 G
of Welsh Church, proposed, 1891 K
effected, 1919 R
Dish-washer, mechanical, 1865 P
Disintegration of elements, 1921 P
Disney, Walt, Am. film director (1901–66), 1901 Z, 1928 W, 1938 W, 1950 W, 1966 Z
Displaced persons, aid to, 1945 O
Disquisitiones arithmeticae (K. F. Gauss), 1801 P
Disquisitions relating to Matter and Spirit (J. Priestley), 1777 R
Disraeli, Benjamin, Earl of Beaconsfield, B. Conservative statesman and author (1804–81), 1804 Z, 1873 C, 1874 R, 1875 J, 1879 L, 1881 Z
becomes leader of Conservatives, 1849 B
becomes Chancellor of Exchequer, 1852 A, M
Reform Bill introduced by, defeated, 1859 C
leads Commons, 1866 G
becomes prime minister, 1868 B, 1874 B
resigns, 1868 M, 1880 D
stand on Eastern Question, 1875 M, 1877 G
created Earl of Beaconsfield, 1876 H
at Berlin Conference, 1878 F
goes to country on Irish Home Rule issue, 1880 C
death, 1881 D
as a novelist, 1826 U, 1844 U, 1845 U, 1870 U 1880 U
Dissertation on Animal and Vegetable Science (Spallanzani), 1780 P
Dissertation on Miracles (J. Campbell), 1763 R
Distant Relations (C. Fuentes), 1982 U
Distiller's Company, compensation for thalidomide disablement, 1973 G
Dittersdorf, Karl Ditters von, Aus. musician (1739–1799), 1780 T, 1786 T
Dividend-stripping, 1958 D
Divine Trinity, The (D. Brown), 1985 R
Divorce:
in Austria, established, 1783 O
in Britain, 1857 O
royal commission on, 1912 O
women granted equality in litigation, 1923 G
Herbert's Act, 1937 G
legislation, 1971 O, 1989 O
in France, instituted, 1792 R
re-established, 1884 G
in Italy, 1970 O
statistics of 1987 Y; in Britain and US, 1913 Y, 1920 Y, 1940 Y, 1950 Y
Divorces, notable:
Napoleon, from Josephine, 1809 M
Dilke, 1886 O
Parnell, 1890 O
Dixieland Jazz Band, 1918 W
Dixmude, Belgium, 1918 J
Djibouti, independence, 1977 F
Djilas, Milovan, Yugoslav politician (b. 1911): expelled from Communist Party, 1954 A; sentence on, increased, 1957 K, 1962 E; released 1966 M
Dnieper River, Russia: ceded by Turkey, 1774 G; Russians cross, 1943 J
Dniester River, Russia: Russian boundary reaches, 1792 A; victory over Germans at, 1915 F; Russian withdrawal to, 1941 G; Russians force crossing, 1944 C
Dobell, William, Austral. artist (1899–1970), 1960 S
Dobrovsky, Joseph, Hung. philologist (1753–1829), 1783 U, 1818 Q
Dobrudja, Russia: Turkey cedes, 1878 G; Allies evacuate, 1917 A; Bulgaria acquires Southern area, 1947 B
Dobson, Austin, B. author (1840–1921), 1840 Z, 1914 Q, 1921 Z
Dobson, Frank, B. sculptor (1888–1963), 1888 Z, 1923 S, 1963 Z
Docks: Liverpool, radar installation at, 1948 P; Rochdale Committee on, 1962 D; workers' pay increased, 1962 E; Devlin Committee on, 1965 H
British dock workers strike, 1967 J, 1970 G, 1972 G, 1984 G, H
docks and depots 'blacked', B., 1972 C, F, G
Jones-Aldington proposals, 1972 G
Doctor Jekyll and Mr. Hyde (R. L. Stevenson), 1886 U
Doctor Zhivago (B. Pasternak), 1858 U

Doctorow, Edgar Lawrence, Am. author (b. 1931), 1971 U
Doctors:
in Belgium, strike, 1964 D
in Britain, advised by B.M.A. to leave Health Service, 1965 B
Doctrina numorum veterum (J. Eckhel), 1792 Q
Doctrines, Theological:
authority of Pentateuch denied, 1862 R
Eternal punishment, denied, 1863 R
Immaculate Conception, 1854 R
Real Presence, 1856 R
Documents of British Diplomatic History 1919–39, 1942 Q
Dodecanese Islands, Aegean: restored to Turkey, 1912 K; assigned to Greece, 1920 H; Italy transfers to Greece, 1946 F, 1947 B
Dodgson, Charles Lutwidge, B. author under pseudonym of 'Lewis Carroll' (1832–98), 1832 Z, 1865 U, 1871 U, 1898 Z
Dodsworth (S. Lewis), 1929 U
Doe, Samuel Kenyon, President of Liberia (1930–90), 1990 G, J
Doenitz, Karl G. admiral and chancellor (1891–1980), 1891 Z, 1980 Z
released from prison, 1956 T
Doesburg, Theo van, Du. artist (1883–1931), 1930 S
Dog Beneath the Skin, The (Auden and Isherwood), 1935 U
Dog Years (G. Grass), 1965 U
Dogger Bank, North Sea: incident, 1904 K; battle, 1915 A
Dogmatics in Outline (K. Barth), 1959 R
Dohnányi, Ernest, Hung. musician (1877–1960), 1877 Z, 1960 Z
Dolby noise-reduction system, 1967 P
Dolfus, Audouin, F. astronomer, 1955 P
Dolin, Sir Anton, B. dancer and choreographer (1904–83), 1904 Z, 1983 Z
D'Oliveira, Basil, B. cricketer (b. 1931), 1968 X
Doll Trilogy, The (K. Stakas), 1977 W
Doll's House, The (H. Ibsen), 1879 W
Dollfuss, Engelbert, Aus. Christian Socialist (1892–1934), 1934 B; becomes Chancellor, 1932 E; suspends Parliamentary government, 1933 C; murdered, 1934 G
Döllinger, Johann Joseph Ignaz von, G. theologian (1799–1890), 1799 Z, 1856 R, 1861 R, 1869 R, 1871 R, 1890 Z
Dolomite, for lining furnaces, 1878 P
Domagk, Gerhard, G. pathologist (1895–1965), 1935 P
Domaines (P. Boulez), 1968 T
Domesday England (H.C. Darby), 1977 Q
Dominica Island, W. Indies: ceded to Britain, 1763 B; seized by France, 1778 J
independence, 1978 L
Dominican Order, 1938 R
Dominican Republic, Hurricane David disaster, 1979 J
Dominion Office, 1925 O
Dominion Party. *See under* Political Parties
Dominion Status, 1931 M
Don Carlos (Schiller), 1787 W
Don Juan (Byron), 1818 U
Don Juan Tenorio (J. Zorilla Y Moral), 1844 U
Don Pacifico affair, 1850 A, D
Don, River, Russia, Italians routed on, 1942 M
Doña Luz (J. Valera), 1879 U
Doña Perfecta (Perez-Galdos), 1876 U
Doncaster, Yorks, England: St. Leger horse race, 1776 X; cotton factory, 1786 P
Donen, Stanley, Am. film director (b. 1924), 1963 W
Dongola, Sudan, Kitchener takes, 1896 J
Donizetti, Gaetano, It. musician (1798–1848), 1798 Z, 1832 T, 1835 T, 1840 T, 1843 T, 1848 Z, 1859 W
Donkin, Bryan, B. engineer, 1768 Z
Donleavy, James Patrick, Am. author (b. 1926), 1967 T
Données Immédiates et la conscience (H. Bergson), 1889 R
Donsokoi, Mark, R. film director, 1959 W
Donzère-Mondragon, France, power station at, 1952 P
Doom of Youth (W. Lewis), 1932 O
Doornkop, S. Africa, 1896 A
Doors, The, Am. pop group, 1967 W
Dorfman, Ariel, Chilean author (b. 1942), 1983 U, 1991 W
Dorpat (now Tartu), Estonia, university, 1802 O
Dorset South, English constituency, by-election, 1962 L
Dortmund–Ems Canal, Germany, 1899 P
Dos Passos, John, Am. author (1896–70), 1896 Z, 1921 U, 1925 U, 1930 U, 1970 Z
Dost Mohammed of Afghanistan, 1863 F
Dostoievsky, Feodor, R. novelist (1821–81), 1821 Z, 1846 U, 1866 U, 1868 U, 1870 U, 1880 U, 1881 Z
Double Helix (J.D. Watson), 1968 P
Double Negative (M. Heizer), 1969 S
Double Summer Time, 1941 O
Doughty, Charles Montagu, B. explorer (1843–1926), 1843 Z, 1888 P, 1926 Z
Douglas, James Buster, Am. boxer (b. 1960), 1990 X
Douglas, John Sholto, eighth marquess of Queensbery, B. sportsman (1844–1900), 1866 X, 1895 U
Douglas, Mary, B. anthropologist (b. 1921), 1921 Z, 1966 R
Douglas, Norman, B. author (1868–1952), 1917 U
Douglas, Stephen, Am. Northern Democrat (1813–1861), senatorial campaign with Lincoln, 1858 H; as presidential candidate, 1860 L
Doullens Agreement, 1918 C
Doumer, Paul, F. statesman (1857–1932), 1857 Z; elected president, 1931 E; assassinated, 1932 E
Doumergue, Gaston, president of France (1863–1937), 1924 F
Doumergue, Paul, F. politician, forms National Union ministry, 1934 B
Dover Road, The (A. A. Milne), 1922 W
Dover, Kent, England, submarine cable from, 1850 P
Down and Out in Paris and London (G. Orwell), 1933 U
Doyle, Sir Arthur Conan, B. novelist (1859–1930), 1859 Z, 1891 U, 1902 U, 1930 Z
Drabble, Margaret, B. author (b. 1939), 1972 U, 1985 Q
Draga, Queen of Serbia, 1903 F
Dragashen, Turkey, 1821 F
Drahtharfe, Die (W. Biermann), 1965 U
Drake, Edwin, L., Am. oil driller (1819–80), 1859 P
Drama, French classical, revival of, 1838 W
Dramatic criticism, 1767 W
Draper, Henry, Am. chemist (1837–82), 1881 P
Dreadnought, H.M.S., 1906 B
Dream of Gerontius, The (J. H. Newman), 1866 U
Dream on Monkey Mountain (D. Walcott), 1967 W
Dreams and Reality (N. Berdyaev), 1950 R
Drees, Willem, Du, Labour leader, 1948 G, 1951 A, 1952 J, 1958 M
Dreiser, Theodore, Am. author (1871–1945), 1871 Z, 1911 U, 1926 U, 1931 U, 1945 Z
Dresden, E. Germany: occupied by Russians and Prussians, 1813 C; battle, 1813 H; revolts in suppressed, 1849 E; Conference on German Unification, 1850 M, 1851 E; artists in, 1905 S
Dress, women's, reform of, 1849 O
Dresser, The (R. Harwood), 1980 W
Dreyfus, Alfred, F. soldier (1859–1935), 1896 C, 1897 L, 1898 A; arrested, 1894 K; convicted, 1894 M; retired, 1899 F; pardoned, 1899 J; rehabilitated, 1906 G
Dreyse, J. N. von, G. gunsmith (1787–1867), 1836 P
Drink and the Victorians (B. Harrison), 1971 Q
Drinkwater, John, B. poet (1882–1937), 1882 Z, 1913 W, 1923 U, 1937 Z
Driving Tests, in Britain, 1934 C
Droughts:
Ethiopia, 1983 C
Droysen, Johann Gustav, G. historian (1808–84), 1855 D
Drugs, legislation for controlling:
British, 1860 O, 1875 O
US, 1898 O, 1906 O; Food and Drug Administration, 1981 P
Drugs:
analgesic, 1887 P
antibiotic, 1946 P, 1960 P; side effects of, 1962 P
dangerous, 1839 G, H, L, 1958 F; taken by Beatniks, 1958 U
LSD withdrawn from sale, 1966 D
synthetic, 1886 P
Drum Taps (W. Whitman), 1866 U
Drummond, Thomas, B. engineer (1767–1840), 1796 O
Drums in the Night (B. Brecht), 1922 W
Drunkenness, statistics of convictions for, 1905 Y, 1920 Y
Druses, in Syria, revolt of, 1925 G, K
Druten, J. Van, B. dramatist, 1928 W, 1954 W
Druze Christians, Lebanese civil war, 1987 B
Drzezdzon, Jan, writer, 1984 U
Du Cubisme (Gleizes and Metzinger), 1912 S
Du Pape (de Maistre), 1817 R
Du côté de chez Swann (M. Proust), 1913 U
Du système industriel (St. Simon), 1821 O
Duala, Cameroons, 1914 J
Dubarry, Marie Jeanne Bécu, comtesse (1746–93), F. adventuress, 1769 D, 1770 M
Dubček, Alexander, Czech. statesman (1921–92), 1921 Z, 1969 D, 1992 Z
First Secretary of Czechoslovak Communist party, 1968 A, H
Prague Spring, 1968 G, H
Czechoslovak ambassador to Turkey, 1969 M
expelled by Communist Party, 1970 F
Dublin, Eire: Royal Irish Academy in, 1782 O; Bottle Riots in, 1822 M; University College, 1854 O Phoenix Park murders, 1882 E; Abbey Theatre, 1904 W; Sinn Fein riots in, 1917 F; Sinn Fein Congress, 1919 A; Four Courts, seizure of, by rebels, 1922 D, F
Trinity College Library, 1967 S
British Embassy burnt down, 1972 B
bomb explosions, 1974 E
EC summit meeting, 1979 L
Dubliners (J. Joyce), 1914 U
Dubrovnik, Yugoslavia, siege, 1991 K, L
Duca, Ion, Rum. Liberal, 1933 M
Duchamp, Marcel, F. artist (1887–1968), 1912 S, 1915 S
Ducis, Jean François, F. dramatist (1733–1816), 1769 W

Duck Hunting (A. Vampilov), 1976 W
Dudevin, Amandine. *See* Sand, George
Dudley, Staffs., England, riots in, 1874 B
Duet for One (T. Kempinski), 1981 W
Dufraure, Jules Armand Stanislas, F. Left-Centre politician (1728–1881), 1877 M
Dufferin, Lord. *See* Blackwood, Frederick
Duffy, Eamon, Ir. historian, 1992 Q
Dufrénoy, Ours Pierre Armand Petit, F. geologist (1792–1857), 1841 P
Dufy, Raoul, F. artist (1877–1953), 1937 S, 1938 S
Duhamel, Georges, F. author (1884–1966), 1884 Z, 1933 U
Duimo Elegies (R. M. Rilke), 1911 U
Dukakis, Michael, Am. Democrat politician (b. 1933), 1988 L
Dukas, Paul, F. musician (1865–1935), 1965 Z, 1907 T, 1935 Z
Dukes, Ashley, B. dramatist (1885–1959), 1925 W
Dulcigno, S. Yugoslavia, 1880 L
Dulles, John Foster, Am. secretary of state (1888–1959), 1955 L; visits Franco and Tito, 1955 L; Suez plan, 1956 H; Berlin speech, 1958 E; meets Macmillan, 1958 F; retires, 1959 D
Dulwich, Surrey, England, art gallery, 1814 S
Dumas, Alexander, pseudonym of Alexandre Davy de la Pailleterie, F. author (1802–70), 1802 Z, 1848 U
Dumas, Jean Baptiste André, F. chemist (1800–84), 1824 P, 1834 P
Dummett, Michael Anthony Eardley, B. philosopher (b. 1925), 1925 Z, 1973 R, 1991 R
Dumouriez, Charles François, F. general (1739–1823), 1792 C, L; defeated at Neerwinden, 1793 C; deserts to Allies, 1793 D
Dumping of manufactures, 1921 G
Dunant, Henri, Swi. founder of Red Cross (1828–1910), 1864 O
Duncan, Adam, Lord Camperdown, B. admiral (1731–1804), 1797 E, K
Duncan, Sir Andrew, B. administrator (b. 1905), 1961 O
Duncan, Ronald, B. dramatist (1914–82), 1945 W, 1955 W
Dundas, Henry, Lord Melville, B. Tory politician (1742–1811), 1782 E
Dungeness, Kent, England, atomic power station at, 1965 P
Dunkirk, France, British evacuation from, 1940 E account of, 1941 O
Dunlap, William, Am. artist (1766–1839), 1834 S
Dunlop, John Boyd, B. veterinary surgeon and inventor (1840–1921), 1888 P
Dunn, Geoffrey, B. actor, 1965 T
Dunn, Nell, 1981 W
Dunne, John William, B. philosopher (d. 1949), 1927 R
Dunning Tariff in US, 1930 E
Dunning, John, Lord Ashburton, B. Whig politician (1731–83), 1780 D
Dupont, Clifford, President of Rhodesia (b. 1905), 1970 C
Düppel, Schleswig, W. Germany, 1864 D
Dupuis, Charles François, F. author and politician (1742–1809), 1795 Q
Durban, S. Africa, 1908 K
Durey, Louis, F. musician (1888–1979), 1920 K
Durham Report on Canada, 1839 B
Durham, Lord. *See* Lampton, J. G.
Durham, N. Carolina, US, Johnston's surrender at, 1865 D
Durrant, Jennifer, B. artist (b. 1942), 1979 S
Durrell, Lawrence George, B. author (1912–90), 1958 U, 1960 U, 1968 U
Duruy, Jean Victor, F. statesman (1811–94), 1865 O
Duse, Eleonora, It. actress (1861–1924), 1861 Z, 1872 W, 1891 W, 1924 Z
Düsseldorf, Germany, 1971 S; French occupy, 1921 C; Art gallery, 1926 S
Dutra, Enrico, president of Brazil, 1945 M
Dutrochet, René Joachim Henri, F. physiologist (1776–1847), 1837 P
Dutschke, Rudi, G. student leader (b. 1940), 1968 D
Duvalier, François ('Papa Doc'), President of Haiti (1907–71), 1971 D
Duvalier, Jean-Claude ('Baby Doc'), President of Haiti (b. 1951), 1971 D, 1985 M, 1986 B
Dvina, River, Russia, 1772 H, 1795 K, 1920 A
Dvořák, Anton, Bohemian musician (1841–1904), 1841 Z, 1828 T, 1880 T, 1901 T, 1904 Z
  Stabat Mater, 1883 T
  Symphonies, 1882 T, 1893 T
  in US, 1892 T
Dworkin, Ronald Hyles, Am. legal theorist (b. 1931), 1977 R
Dyce, William, B. artist (1806–64), 1828 S
Dyer, Christopher, B. historian (b. 1944), 1989 Q
Dyer, H. G., B. chemist, 1838 P
Dyes:
  Aniline, 1856 P
  Ionamide, 1922 P
  Phthalacyamine, 1934 P
  Synthetic, 1869 P
Dylan, Bob (born Robert Zimmerman), Am. songwriter and singer (b. 1941), 1966 W, 1974 W, 1975 W, 1977 W
Dynamic Sociology (L. Ward), 1883 O
Dynamite, invented, 1866 P
Dynamo, with ring armature, 1870 P
Dynasts, The (T. Hardy), 1904 W
Dynasty, television series, 1981 W
Dyos, Harold James, B. historian (1921–78), 1973 Q
Dysentery bacillus, isolated, 1915 P

E

Eagles, The, Am. pop group, 1976 W
Eagleton, Thomas, Am. Democratic politician (b. 1929), 1972 G, H
Earl, Ralph, Am. artist (1751–1801), 1775 S
Early Bird, communications satellite, 1965 P
Early Church, The (H. Chadwick), 1967 Q
Early Oxford Schools, The (J. Catto), 1984 Q
Early Tudor Country House, The ... (M. Howard), 1987 Q
Earth, The:
  current, discovered, 1862 P
  density of, determined, 1798 P
  dynamic theory of, 1788 P
  magnetic field of, analysed, 1923 P
Earthly Paradise (W. Morris), 1868 U
Earthly Powers (A. Burgess), 1980 U
Earthquakes:
  Agadir, 1960 B
  Algeria, 1980 K
  California, 1892 O
  Chile, 1965 C
  Iran, 1968 H, 1978 J, 1990 F
  Mexico City, 1985 J
  Nicaragua, 1972 M
  Persia, 1962 J
  Peru, 1970 E
  Roumania, 1977 C
  San Francisco, 1989 K
  Sicily and S. Calabria, 1908 M
  Skopje, Yugoslavia, 1963 G
  Tangshan, China, 1976 G
  Tajikistan, 1989 A
  Turkey, 1966 H
East (S. Berkoff), 1977 W
East Africa Company, British: formed, 1887 E; occupies Uganda, 1890 M, 1893 C; treaty with Leopold II, 1890 E; dissolved, 1895 G
East Africa Company, German, 1885 B; cedes rights to Germany, 1890 K
East Africa, British: Anglo-German agreement on, 1886 L; Anglo–Italian agreement on, 1894 E; British protectorate in, 1895 G; settlement of uplands, 1902 J; frontier with Uganda, 1907 M; becomes Kenya, 1920 G; Central Legislature, 1948 D. *See also* Kenya
East Africa, German: Arab rising in, 1888 J; cleared of German troops, 1917 M; assigned as mandated territory to Britain, 1919 E. *See also* Tanganyika
East Galicia, 1772 H
East India Company, British: administration of India, 1767 A, 1772 C, D; regulating Act for 1773 E; Fox's Bill to reform, 1783 M; Pitt's Act, 1784 H; acquires Poona, 1802 M; monopoly in Indian trade abolished, 1813 O; Bentinck's reforms, 1829 O; powers transferred to Crown, 1858 H; end of rule in Straits Settlements, 1867 D
East Lynne (Mrs. Henry Wood), 1861 U
Eastenders, television series, 1985 W
Eastern Question, The: Napoleon's problem, 1808 K; Vienna note on, 1853 G; Congress of Berlin on, 1878 G. *See also* Russophobia
Eastern Schism, The (S. Runciman), 1955 Q
Eastman, George, Am. photographer (1854–1932), 1854 Z, 1885 P, 1888 P, 1889 P, 1932 Z
Eau de Javel (chlorine), 1785 P
Ebert, Friedrich, G. statesman (1871–1925), 1871 Z, 1925 B; as president of G. republic, 1919 B, 1922 K
Ecce Homo (J. R. Seeley), 1866 R
Eccles, David McAdam, lord Eccles, B. Conservative politician (b. 1904), dismissed from cabinet, 1962 G
Eccles, Sir John Carew, Austral. neurologist, 1963 P
Ecclesiastical Commissioners, 1836 R
Ecclesiastical Courts, proceedings in, notable, 1856 R, 1857 R, 1863 R, 1890 R
Ecclesiastics, imprisonment of notable, 1937 R
  Abp. Stephinac, 1946 J
  Card. Mindszenty, 1948 M
  Card. Wyszynski, 1953 J
  releases from, 1963 B, K
Ecdysone, structure determined, 1966 P
Eckhel, Joseph Hilarius, Aus. numismatist (1737–98), 1792 Q
Eclipses, solar, 1936 P
Eco, Umberto, It. author (b. 1932), 1980 U
Economic Affairs, British Ministry of, 1964 K
Economic Consequences of the Peace (J. M. Keynes), 1919 O
Economic Council, French National, 1925 O
Economic Council, German, 1947 F
Economic Reform, in Britain, 1780 E
Economic Studies (W. Bagehot), 1880 O
Economic Survey, British, 1948 O
Economic Warfare, US Office of, 1943 O
Economics of Imperfect Competition, The (J. Robinson), 1933 O
Economics, Ministry of, German, 1919 O
Economy:
  Arab Maghreb Union, 1989 B

Japanese Gross National Product exceeds that of West Germany, 1969 O
Third World debt mountain, 1988 J
in Africa
most African countries on verge of economic collapse, 1985 G
World Bank Fund for Africa, 1985 O
in Brazil, 1988 J
in Britain
credit squeeze tightened, 1966 B
Prices and Incomes Bill, 1966 B
wage and price standstill and other firm measures taken, 1966 G, K
bank rate, notable changes in, 1966 G, L, 1967 E, 1969 B, 1970 C, 1971 D, 1972 F
Wilson takes direct command of Department of Economic Affairs, 1967 H
Bank of International Settlements loan, 1967 L
International Monetary Fund (IMF) loans, 1967 L, 1976 J, M, 1977 A
capital spending cut, 1968 A
panic selling on London Stock Market, 1968 M
Department of Economic Affairs abolished, 1969 K
Bank of England attempts to control money supply, 1972 L
price, pay, rent and dividend increase freeze, 1972 L
fluctuating minimum lending rate tied to discount rate of Treasury bills, 1972 O
record fall in Financial Times Share Index, 1973 M
inflation rate, 1974 M, 1975 H, 1980 G, 1983 F, 1986 G
Financial Times Share Index at lowest level since 1954 , 1975 A
government spending statistics, 1976 Y
academics call for abandonment of hard-line monetarism, 1981 C
Monetary Trends in the United States and the United Kingdom (M.Friedman), 1981 O
Public Sector Borrowing Requirement, 1982 C, 1983 C, 1984 C
public expenditure cuts, 1983 G
FT 100 Share Index exceeds 1,000 points, 1985 A
borrowing requirement, 1985 C, 1986 C, 1987 C
increase in government spending, 1986 L
disagreement within government unsettles money markets, 1988 O
See also Budgets, Notable; Currency
in France, minimum wage raised, 1968 E
in India, 1991 G
in Italy, emergency legislation to prevent bankruptcy, 1992 G
in US, 1970 E
presidential proposals, 1981 B
record day's trading on New York Stock Exchange, 1982 K
in USSR, reforms, 1983 G
insider dealing, 1986 L, 1987 G
share price falls, 1986 J, 1987 K, 1988 A
share price panic, 1981 J
speculative flight from US dollar, 1968 C
Ecrits (J. Lacan), 1966 R
Ecstasy of Rita Joe, The (G. Ryga), 1967 W
Ecuador: Republic established, 1830 J; leaves Union of Colombia, 1831 L; becomes a theocracy, 1873 K; dispute with Peru, 1911 A
Eddington, Sir Arthur Stanley, B. scientist (1882–1944), 1882 Z, 1914 P, 1918 P, 1924 P, 1931 P, 1939 R, 1944 Z
Eddy, John Allen, Am. astronomer (b. 1931), 1979 P
Eddy, Mary Baker, Am. founder of Christian Science (1821–1910), 1821 Z, 1875 R, 1879 R, 1910 Z
Eden End (J. B. Priestley), 1934 W
Eden, Anthony, Viscount Avon, B. Conservative statesman (1897–1977), 1897 Z, 1977 Z; offers Mussolini concessions over Abyssinia, 1935 F; becomes foreign secretary, 1935 M; resigns, 1938 B; reappointed foreign secretary, 1940 M; in Moscow, 1941 M; at UN Conference, 1945 D; foreign secretary, 1951 K; plan for Europe, 1952 H; becomes premier, 1955 D; proposes reunification of Germany, 1955 G; reforms ministry, 1955 M; with Eisenhower issues Washington Declaration, 1956 B; recuperates, 1956 L; resigns, 1957 A
Eden, William, baron Auckland, B. diplomat (1744–1814), 1786 J
Edgar, David, B. playwright (b. 1948), 1976 W, 1980 W
Edge Island, Spitzbergen, expedition to, 1927 P
Edge of Darkness, television programme, 1985 W
Edge of the Union, At the, television programme, 1985 W
Edgeworth, Maria, B. novelist (1767–1849), 1800 U
Edinburgh Letter (Lord J. Russell), 1845 L
Edinburgh, Dukes of. *See* Alfred Ernest Albert; Philip
Edinburgh, Scotland:
Bank with 'women only' branch, 1964 O
European Community summit, 1992 M
Festival, 1947 W
Scott Museum, 1840 S
University, 1855 O
Edison, Thomas Alva, Am. inventor (1847–1931), 1847 Z, 1872 P, 1876 P, 1880 P, 1882 P, 1894 W, 1931 Z
Edo Bay, Japan, 1846 N
Education of Henry Adams (H. Adams), 1907 Q
Education sentimentale, L' (G. Flaubert), 1869 U
Education, Moral, Intellectual, Physical (H. Spencer), 1861 O
Education:
illiteracy statistics, 1983 Y
theories, co-education, 1922 O; Pestalozzi, 1781 O
treatises, 1775 O, 1803 O, 1806 O, 1861 O
for blind, 1784 O, 1791 O
in Austria, 1770 O, 1868 O
clerical control of, 1855 H
in Belgium, political crises over control of, 1880 F, 1895 H, 1912 F
primary, 1879 G
secondary, 1850 O
in Britain, adult, 1834 O, 1854 O, 1904 O
schools, monitorial system for, 1797 O
religious foundations, 1808 O, 1811 O
State grant for, 1833 O
reforms urged, 1867 O
board schools established, 1870 O
elementary, 1890 O
Board of Education, 1899 O
denominational schools brought within State system, 1902 M
school care committees, 1906 O
medical inspectors in, 1907 O
Fisher's Act, 1918 H
cuts in expenditure for, 1922 O
Butler's Act, 1944 O
Newsom Committee Report, 1963 O
proposal to raise leaving age to sixteen, 1963 O
Plowden Report, *Children and their Primary Schools*, 1967 O
teachers' pay talks break down, 1970 A
allocation of schools for primary closures, 1971 O
free milk abolished, 1971 F
Education: A Framework for Expansion White Paper, 1972 O
leaving age raised, 1973 O
abolition of 11-plus exam proposed, 1974 O
Callaghan's 'great debate', 1976 K
nation-wide testing, 1977 O, 1991 O
Waddell Committee recommends new examination, 1978 O
corporal punishment, 1979 O, 1986 O
General Certificate of Secondary Education (GCSE), 1984 O, 1988 O
Inner London Education Authority, abolition, 1987 O
Education Reform Act, 1988 O
National Curriculum, 1989 O, 1990 O, 1991 O
Chief Inspector of Schools report, 1990 O
schools, secondary
grants to 'direct grant' schools abolished, 1975 K
schools, secondary, girls', 1880 O
in Wales, 1889 O
in Britain, 1902 M
schools, comprehensive, circular about, 1965 O
comprehensive education, 1970 B, 1974 O, 1976 H, O, 1979 O
schools, independent, Fleming Report on, 1944 O
Commission on, 1965 M
Newsome Commission calls for integration of independent and state schools, 1968 O
Assisted Places Scheme, 1980 O
higher education, Robbins Report on, 1963 O
teaching of Russian in, 1962 O
student loans introduced, 1990 O
Polytechnics given university status, 1992 O
technological, increased spending on, 1956 O
teachers' training colleges, first, 1846 O
women's higher, 1849 O, 1869 O, 1871 O
in China, reformed, 1902 N
in Denmark, Veterinary and Agricultural College, 1773 P
reforms in, 1784 E
in France, compulsory, 1793 O, 1882 O
école Normale, 1794 O
école Polytechnique, 1795 O
écoles Centrales, 1795 O
clerical control of, 1822 F, 1833 F
primary, 1882 C
secondary, 1865 O
protests against reforms, 1986 L
in Germany, technical, 1884 O
university, 1909 O
in Ireland, Maynooth College, 1845 F
in Israel, religious, 1951 B
in Italy, 1877 O
in Prussia, elementary, 1763 O, 1765 O
secondary, 1859 O
religious, 1788 R, 1892 C
in S. Africa
Afrikaans education plan dropped after riots, 1976 F
in Spain, 1766 F
clerical control, 1851 C
Church schools closed, 1933 E
in US, degrees awarded to women, 1841 O
scientific and technological, 1862 O

graduate schools, 1876 O
Teaching of evolution forbidden in Tennessee, 1925 O
desegregation crisis, 1957 O, 1958 J
reading of prayers in New York unconstitutional, 1962 O
desegregated classes, 1970 O
desegration busing, 1974 K, 1975 J
See also Universities
Edward VII, King of Gt. Britain and Ireland (1901–1910), 1841 L, 1874 J, 1907 J, 1910 E; as Prince of Wales, visits India, 1875 H; witness in Tranby Croft case, 1891 O; accession, 1901 A; style, 1901 H; visits Paris, 1903 E, 1907 E; discussions with William II, 1906 H; visits Rome, 1907 D; meets Nicholas II, 1908 F; as race-horse owner, 1896 X, 1909 X
Edward VIII, King of Gt. Britain (1894–1972); 1894 Z, 1972 Z; as Prince of Wales, visits Canada and US, 1919 H; visits India, 1921 G; accession, 1936 A; relations with Mrs. Wallis Warfield Simpson, 1936 K, L; abdicates, 1936 M; becomes Duke of Windsor, 1936 M; marries Mrs. Simpson, 1937 F
Edwards, Robert Geoffrey, B. scientist (b. 1925), 1969 P
Egalitarianism and the Generation of Inequality (H. Phelps Brown), 1988 Q
Eggar, Samantha, B. film actress, 1965 W
Egmont (Goethe), 1788 W
Egoist, The (G. Meredith), 1879 U
Egypt: French interest in, 1795 Q; French expeditions to, 1798 E, G, H, 1799 E, G, H; Turks recover possession of, 1801 K; British and French armies leave, 1801 K; Turkey recognises independence, 1833 E; becomes possession of Mehemet Ali 1840 G, L, 1841 B; finances, 1875 M, 1876 C, 1884 F; Anglo-French control of, 1876 L, 1878 M, 1879 J, 1882 L; Gambetta Note on, 1882 A; Nationalist Movement in, 1881 B, J; British occupation, 1882 J, 1883 A; Anglo-French differences in, settled, 1904 D; Milner-Zaghlul conversations on, 1920 H; British Protectorate in, ends, 1922 B; Republic proclaimed, 1953 F; forms, with Syria, United Arab Republic, 1958 B
extends ceasefire and offers to re-open Suez Canal if Israel withdraws from Sinai, 1971 B
signs Benghazi Agreement, 1971 D
Soviet advisers expelled, 1972 G
Sudan and Egypt announce plans for full union, 1972 H
Constituent Assembly plan and unification with Libya, 1973 H
accepts US plan for ceasefire observance, 1973 L
border war with Libya, 1977 G
talks with Israel, 1978 A
signs peace treaty with Israel, 1979 C
ambassadors exchanged with Israel, 1980 B
on Palestinian autonomy, 1980 D, E
seeks USSR assistance for industry, 1982 A
economic relations with Jordan restored, 1983 M
illiteracy, 1983 Y
Islamic Conference Organization, 1984 A
diplomatic relations with Jordan restored, 1984 J
Jordan–Egypt peace initiative talks for West Bank, 1984 M
cotton production, 1984 Y
Achille Lauro hijack, 1985 K
hijacked Egyptian airliner stormed at Malta airport, 1985 L
urbanization, 1985 Y
diplomatic relations with Iran broken off, 1987 E
diplomatic relations with Algeria resumed, 1988 L
diplomatic relations with Syria resumed, 1989 M
See also Suez Canal; Suez Crisis; United Arab Republic
Egyptology, 1883 Q
Ehrenberg, Christian Gottfried, G. bacteriologist (1795–1876), 1854 P
Ehrenburg, Ilya Grigorievich, R. author (1891–1967), 1891 Z, 1941 U, 1955 U, 1967 Y
Ehrlich, Cyril, B. historian (b. 1925), 1985 Q
Ehrlich, Paul Ralph (b. 1932) and Anne Howard (b. 1933), Am. population biologists, 1970 P
Ehrlich, Paul, G. chemist (1854–1915), 1909 P
Ehrlichman, John Daniel, Am. presidential aide (b. 1925), 1975 A
Eichhorn, Johann Gottfried, G. theologian (1752–1827), 1783 R
Eichhorn, Karl Friedrich, G. jurist (1781–1854), 1808 Q
Eichmann, Adolf, G. Gestapo chief, arrested, 1960 E; trial, 1961 O; hanged, 1962 E
Eider River, Germany, linked by canal to Baltic, 1784 P
Eiffel, Gustav, F. engineer (1834–1923), 1834 Z, 1923 Z
Eight Songs for a Mad King (P. Maxwell Davies), 1969 T
Eighteenth-Century Studies (A. Dobson), 1914 Q
Eighth Day, The (T. Wilder), 1967 U
Eilat, Israel, Arab guerrilla attack, 1969 D
Einaudi, Luigi (1874–1961), president of Italian Republic (1948–55), 1948 E
Eindhoven, Holland, British airborne forces at, 1944 J
Einem, Gottfried von, Aus. musician (b. 1918), 1971 T
Einstein, Albert, Am. scientist and philosopher (1879–1955), 1879 Z, 1912 P, 1929 P, 1934 R, 1940 P, 1955 Z; theories of relativity, 1905 P, 1915 P, 1919 P; on Zionism, 1930 O
Einsturtzende Neubauten, G. pop group, 1984 W
Einthoven, Willem, Du. physiologist (1860–1927), 1860 Z, 1927 Z
Eire: Irish Free State proclaimed, 1922 M; name changed from Irish Free State, 1937 M; Republic formally proclaimed, 1949 D; Britain recognises, 1949 E; Prime Minister meets Northern Ireland premier, 1965 A
proposed federation with Northern Ireland, 1969 H
reserves mobilised and troops moved near Northern Irish frontier, 1969 H
European Community membership, 1970 F, 1972 A, E
Haughey dismissed as Finance Minister, 1970 E
refugee camps for Catholics, 1971 H
Fine Gael, 1973 C, 1977 F
first official visit by British PM, 1973 J
referendum supports legal ban on abortions, 1983 R
New Ireland Forum report, 1984 E
government enabled to seize Provisional IRA money, 1985 B
sale of contraceptives legalized, 1985 O
presidential elections, 1990 L
life expectancy, 1990 Y
illegitimacy rate, 1991 Y
Haughey resigns after allegations of telephone-tapping, 1992 A
referendum over Maastricht Treaty, 1992 F
See also Ireland; Irish Home Rule; Rebellions
Eirenicon (E. B. Pusey), 1865 R
Eisenach, Germany, Protestant Conference at, 1852 R
Eisenhower Doctrine, for US forces to protect independence of Middle East States, 1957 C, D
Eisenhower, Dwight David, Am. soldier and statesman, 34th president of US (1953–61), Republican (1890–1969), 1890 Z, 1954 E, 1955 A, 1958 E, J, 1969 Z
commands Allied landings in N. Africa, 1942 L
as supreme commander in N. Africa, 1943 B
on Italy's unconditional surrender, 1943 J
Jodl's capitulation to, 1945 E
retires from post of Supreme Allied Commander, 1952 D
elected president, 1952 L, inaugurated, 1953 A
visits Korea, 1952 M
meets Churchill, 1953 A, 1953 M, 1954 F
on principles of UN peace proposals for Korea, 1953 E
proposes control of atomic energy, 1953 M
broadcasts on Communist threat, 1954 D
message to Congress on Formosa, 1955 A
asks for foreign aid, 1955 D, F
heart attack, 1955 J
re-affirms joint policy in Middle East, 1956 B
re-elected, 1956 L
at Bermuda Conference, 1957 C
proposes mutual inspection for atom tests, 1958 D
meets Macmillan, 1958 F, 1959 H, L
admits S. Adams's imprudence, 1958 F
visits Germany and Britain, 1959 H
tours Europe, 1959 M
issues joint declaration on nuclear test negotiations, 1960 C
at Summit meeting, 1960 E
tours Far East, 1960 F
Eisenstein, Sergei, R. film director (1898–1948), 1928 W, 1938 W, 1945 W, 1959 W
Eisner, Kurt, Bavarian premier, 1919 B
Either-or (S. Kierkegaard), 1843 R
Ekman, Carl, Swe. Liberal politician, 1930 F
Eksund, arms haul on discovered, 1987 L
El Alamein, Egypt, battle, 1942 K
El Obeid, Sudan, British defeat at, 1883 L
El Salvador, forms union with Nicaragua and Honduras, 1895 F
Honduras–El Salvador border incidents following World Cup qualifying round, 1969 G
invasion of Honduras, 1969 G
guerrillas capture embassies, 1979 E
US accusations over, 1981 B
former National Guardsmen held pending murder investigations, 1982 B
US emergency assistance announced, 1982 B
civilians killed during anti-guerrilla campaign, 1982 J
murder of nuns and lay assistant, 1984 E
US military aid, 1984 E
US calls on Nicaragua to cease support for El Salvadorean rebels, 1984 F
Contadora peace treaty, 1986 E
Arias Plan, 1987 H
elections to National Assembly, 1988 C
presidential election, 1989 C
peace accord, 1991 J
UN-negotiated truce, 1992 B
El Wak, It. Somaliland, 1940 M
El Zanjn, Cuba, Convention of, 1878 B
El-Choufi, Hammoud, Syrian ambassador to UN (b. 1935), 1979 L
Elba, Isle of: Britain captures, 1796 G; Napoleon I banished to, 1814 D
Elbe, River, Germany, closed by Danes, 1801 C,

D; Canal to Trave, 1900 P; Allies cross, 1945 D
Elbing, Germany, Allies take, 1945 B
Elder Statesman, The (T. S. Eliot), 1958 W
Elders and Betters (I. Compton-Burnett), 1944 U
Election Court, in Britain, 1961 O
Elections:
in Albania, 1991 C, 1992 C
in Algeria, 1990 F, 1991 M, 1992 A
in Angola, 1992 J
in Argentina, 1973 B, 1983 K, 1987 J, 1989 E
in Australia, 1922 M, 1929 K, 1934 J, 1937 K, 1961 M, 1963 L, 1972 M, 1975 M, 1977 M, 1983 C, 1990 C
in Austria, 1911 F, 1945 L, 1949 K, 1953 B, 1959 E, 1970 C, 1983 D, 1990 K
presidential, 1920 M
in Bahamas, 1992 H
in Bangladesh, 1979 B, 1988 B
in Barbados, 1961 M
in Belgium, 1880 F, 1912 F, 1929 E, 1936 E, 1946 B, 1954 D, 1961 C, 1991 L
in Bermuda, 1989 B
in Brazil, 1989 M
in Britain:
By-elections, notable:
Clare (O'Connell), 1828 F
Barnard Castle (won byLabour), 1903 G
Bow (Lansbury), 1912 L
Brighton, 1944 B
Skipton (Commonwealth Party), 1944 A
Tonbridge, 1956 F
Lewisham, 1957 B
Rochdale, 1958 B
Torrington (Liberal), 1958 C
Orpington (Liberal), 1962 C
W. Lothian, 1962 F
Leicester, N., 1962 G
S. Dorset (Labour), 1962 L
Leyton (foreign secretary loses), 1965 A
Walthamstow, 1969 C
Mid-Ulster, 1969 D
Lincoln, 1972 K, 1973 C
Rochdale, 1972 K
Sutton and Cheam, 1972 K
Ripon, 1973 G
Govan and Berwick-on-Tweed, 1973 L
Workington and Walsall North, 1976 L
Ashfield and Grimsby, 1977 D
Warrington, 1981 G
Crosby, 1981 L
Glasgow Hillhead, 1982 C
Merton, Mitcham and Morden, 1982 F
Bermondsey, 1983 B
Chesterfield, 1984 C
Portsmouth, 1984 F
Brecon and Radnor, 1985 G
Fulham, 1986 D
Ryedale, 1986 E
Greenwich, 1987 B
Truro, 1987 C
Monmouth, 1991 E
General, 1784 C, 1790 L, 1806 K, M, 1807 D, F, 1818 F, 1820 B, 1831 D, 1868 M, 1874 B, 1880 C, D, 1885 L, 1886 G, 1892 G, ('Khaki') 1900 K, 1906 A, 1910 M, 1918 M, 1922 L, 1923 M, 1924 K, 1929 E, 1931 K, 1935 L, 1945 G, 1950 B, 1951 K, 1955 E, 1959 K, 1964 K, 1966 C, 1970 F, 1974 B, K, 1979 E, 1983 F, 1987 F, 1992 D
Act to prevent fraudulent votes in 1763 G
spending of parties and candidates in, limited, 1883 H
arrangements for National Service voters, 1945 A
pioneer study of, 1947 O
TV coverage of, 1959 O
local government, 1963 E, 1964 D, 1965 E, 1967 D, E, 1969 E, 1971 E, 1972 E, 1977 E, 1982 E, 1984 E, 1985 E, 1986 E, 1987 E
to European Parliament, 1979 F
deposit required from candidates increased, 1985 O
in British Guiana, 1953 D, 1957 H, 1961 H, 1964 M
in Bulgaria, 1945 L, 1991 K, 1992 A
in Burma, 1990 E
in Cameroon, 1992 K
in Canada, 1878 K, 1911 J, 1917 M, 1921 M, 1926 J, 1945 F, 1949 F, 1953 H, 1957 F, 1962 F, 1965 L, 1972 K, 1976 L, 1979 E, 1980 B, 1984 J, 1988 L
in Central African Federation, 1962 D
in Ceylon, 1952 F, 1956 D, 1960 C, 1965 C, 1970 E
in Chile, 1970 J, 1989 M
in Colombia, 1990 E
in Cuba, 1908 L
in Czechoslovakia, 1935 E, 1946 E, 1989 D, F, 1990 F, 1992 F
in Danzig, 1933 E
in Denmark, 1926 M, 1945 K, 1953 D, 1990 M
in Egypt, 1945 A, 1950 A
in Eire, 1922 F, 1923 H, 1927 J, 1932 B, 1933 A, 1938 F, 1973 C, 1987 B, 1990 L
presidential, 1932 C
in El Salvador, 1988 C, 1989 C
in Estonia, 1992 J
in Fiji, won by Indian-dominated coalition, 1987 D
in Finland, 1954 C
in France, 1967 C, 1978 C, 1981 F, 1986 C
General, 1816 J, 1817 J, 1818 M, 1827 L, 1830 G, 1848 E (on universal suffrage), 1879 A, 1889 D
multiple candidates forbidden in, 1889 G
proportional representation in, 1912 G, 1924 E, 1932 E, 1936 E, 1945 K, 1946 F, 1946 L, 1948 L, 1951 F, 1956 A, 1958 L
presidential, 1848 M, 1879 A, 1885 M, 1887 M, 1899 B, 1906 A, 1913 A, 1920 J, 1931 E, 1932 E, 1946 F, 1947 A, 1974 E, 1981 E, 1988 E
referendum for election by universal suffrage, 1962 K, 1965 K
municipal, 1947 K
regional, 1977 C, 1992 C
in Georgia, USSR, 1990 K, 1991 E
in Germany:
For Reichstag, 1874 A, 1878 G, 1906 M, 1912 A, 1919 A, 1924 E, 1924 M, 1928 E, 1930 J, 1932 G, 1932 L, 1933 C, L, 1936 C, 1953 J, 1957 J, 1961 J
presidential, 1925 D, 1932 C, D, 1959 G
holding of free, discussed, 1951 M, 1952 D, 1954 A, 1957 G
provincial, 1932 D
in East Germany, 1950 K, 1990 C
in West Germany, 1969 J, 1972 L, 1976 K, 1980 K, 1983 C, 1990 M
in Ghana, 1979 G
in Gibraltar, 1969 E
in Gold Coast, 1954 F, 1956 G
in Greece, 1952 L, 1981 K, 1989 F, L, 1990 D, 1990 E
in Guatemala, 1991 A
in Guyana, 1992 K
in Haiti, 1988 A, 1990 M
in Holland, 1946 E, 1952 J, 1977 E, 1989 J
in Honduras, 1954 D
in Hong Kong, for Legislative Council, 1985 J
in Hungary, 1990 D, 1947 H
in India, 1937 B, 1945 J, 1952 C, 1962 E, 1967 B, 1971 C, 1975 M, 1977 A, C, 1978 L, 1980 A, 1983 A, B, 1984 M, 1989 L, 1991E, 1992 B
in Indonesia, 1971 G
in Iran, 1981 G, 1981 K, 1989 G
in Israel, 1976 M, 1977 E, 1988 L, 1992 F
in Italy, 1976 F, 1979 F, 1987 F, 1992 D
General, 1904 K, 1921 E
single-party, 1929 C, 1948 D, 1953 F, 1958 E
presidential, 1946 F, 1948 E, 1962 E
in Jamaica, 1989 B
in Japan, 1890 G, 1946 D, 1964 J, 1976 M, 1979 K, 1989 G, 1990 B
in Jordan, 1989 L
in Lebanon, presidential, 1982 H
in Lithuania, nationalist victory, 1990 B
in Malta, 1987 E, 1992 B
in Mexico, 1988 G
in Mongolia, 1990 G
in Namibia, 1989 L, 1990 B, 1992 L
in Nepal, 1991 E
in New Zealand, 1890 D, 1919 M, 1928 L, 1946 L, 1954 L, 1969 L, 1972 L, 1981 L, 1984 G, 1990 K
in Nicaragua, 1927 E, 1984 L, 1990 B
in Northern Ireland, 1969 B, 1973 F, 1975 E, 1981 D, 1982 K, 1986 A
in Northern Rhodesia, 1959 D
in Norway, 1933 K, 1953 K, 1989 J
in Pakistan, presidential, 1965 A, 1970 M, 1977 C, 1983 H, 1988 L, 1990 K
cancelled, 1977 K, 1979 K
in Panama, 1989 E
in Paraguay, 1989 B
in Peru, 1990 F, 1992 L
in Philippines, 1907 G, 1984 E, 1986 B, 1992 F
in Poland
Solidarity wins landslide victory, 1989 F
presidential, 1989 G
Walesa elected President, 1990 M
parliamentary, 1991 K
in Portugal, 1934 M, 1945 L, 1953 L, 1969 K, 1975 D, 1991 A, K
in Rhodesia, 1979 D, 1980 B, C
in Roumania, 1990 E, 1992 B, K
in Russian Federation, 1990 E, 1991 F
in Serbia, 1990 M, 1992 M
white electorate votes for constitutional and political reform, 1992 C
in South Africa, 1910 J, 1924 F, 1933 E, 1938 E, 1948 E, 1953 D, 1958 D, 1966 C, 1977 L, 1987 E, 1988 K, 1989 J
in Southern Rhodesia, 1962 M, 1965 E
in South Vietnam, 1971 K
in Spain, 1914 C, 1933 L, 1934 A, 1936 B, 1977 F, 1982 K, 1989 K
in Sri Lanka, 1977 G
in Sudan, 1958 B
in Sweden, 1907 E, 1911 J, 1952 J, 1976 J, 1979 J, 1982 J, 1991 J
in Syria, 1953 K
in Thailand, 1976 D
in Tunisia, multi-party, 1981 L
in Turkey (single party), 1927 J, 1989 K, 1991 K
in Uganda, 1980 M
in Ukraine, 1990 F
in Union of Soviet Socialist Republics, 1987 F, 1989 C
in Uruguay, 1985 C
in US:
Congressional, 1914 L, 1918 L, 1922 L, 1938

L, 1946 L, 1950 L, 1958 L, 1962 L, 1966 L, 1968 L, 1970 L, 1972 L, 1974 L, 1976 L, 1978 L, 1980 K, 1982 L, 1986 L, 1988 L, 1992 L
presidential, 1796 L, 1800 L, 1804 J, 1812 L, 1824 L, 1827 L, 1832 L, 1844 L, 1852 L, 1856 L, 1860 L, 1872 L 1876 L, 1877 A, 1884 L, 1896 L, 1900 L, 1908 L, 1912 L, 1920 L, 1920 W, 1924 L, 1928 L, 1932 L, 1936 L, 1944 L, 1948 L, 1952 L, 1956 L, 1960 L, 1964 L; 1968 L, 1972 L, 1976 L, 1980 L, 1984 L, 1988 L, 1992 L
force bill to control, facts, 1890 F
expenses of, to be published, 1912 D
TV coverage of, 1960 O
senatorial, by direct system, 1911 D
State, disputed, 1874 E
voting in, by ballot, in Britain, 1872 G
in Canada, 1874 N
in US, 1804 J
in Yugoslavia, 1945 L
in Zambia, 1991 K
in Zanzibar, 1961 F
in Zimbabwe, 1990 D
Elective Affinities, The (Goethe), 1809 U
Electra (H. von Hofmannsthal), 1903 U
Electrical Consumer Goods, in Britain, 1965 Y
Electrical Engineers, British Institution of, 1889 P
Electrical Exhibition, Munich, 1883 P
Electrical Grids, linking of British and French, 1961 P
Electrical Industry, British, power station for, 1890 P; taken over by Electricity Authority, 1948 O; output, 1944 Y, 1957 Y
Electrical precipitation, 1884 P
Electrical Researches of the Hon. Henry Cavendish, 1879 P
Electrical Self-induction, 1834 P
Electrical Standards, 1861 P
Electrical Waves, detection of, 1896 P
Electricity Authority, British, 1948 O
Electricity Board, British, 1926 O
Electricity, Treatises on, 1789 P, 1814 P, 1820 P, 1826 P, 1839 P, 1843 P, 1873 P, 1879 P
Electricity, Uses of:
for lighthouses, 1858 P
for lighting, 1872 P, 1878 P, 1880 P, 1881 P
for lung pump, 1961 P
for motive power, 1879 P
to coat metals with nickel, 1843 P
to heat steel furnace, 1879 P
to power railways, 1879 P, 1895 P, 1904 P, 1910 P
to power submarine, 1896 P
to power washing-machine, 1869 P
to prepare potassium and sodium, 1806 P
Electricity:
A.C. motor for, 1888 P
accumulator for, 1859 P
blackout in New York, 1977 G
blackouts in Britain, 1977 K
carbon filament lamps, 1878 P
carbon-zinc battery, 1841 P
conduction of, through gases, 1903 P
Galvani's observations, 1789 P
generating station, 1882 P
hydro-electric power stations, 1882 P, 1952 P
produced from atomic energy, 1951 P
produced from steam turbine, 1884 P
tidal power, 1968 P
transformer for, 1831 P
Volta's cell, 1800 P
Voltaic pile, 1798 P
Electro-chemical analysis, 1822 P
Electro-magnetic Waves, 1887 P
Electro-magnetism, discoveries relating to, 1819 P, 1821 P
Electrodynamics (A. Ampère), 1826 P
Electrolytic process for making soda, 1894 P
Electron spin resonance spectroscopy, 1980 P
Electronic Power Production, comparative, 1959 Y
Electronic brain, 1942 P, 1946 P
Electronic music, 1959 T, 1964 T
Electrons: term first used, 1891 P; Bohr's theory, 1922 P; positive ('positrons'), 1933 P
Electroscope, 1903 P
Electroweak unification theory, 1967 P, 1973 P
Elegy Written in Spring (M. Bruce), 1767 U
Elegy on the Death of Pushkin (M. Y. Lermontov), 1837 U
Elektra (J. Giraudoux), 1937 W
Elements of Chemical Philosophy (H. Davy), 1812 P
Elements of Political Economy (James Mill), 1821 P
Elements of Psycho-Physics (G. T. Fechner), 1860 P
Elements of Systematic Morality (W. Whewell), 1846 R
Elements of the Philosophy of the Human Mind (D. Stewart), 1792 R
Elements, Named:
Californium (98), 1950 P
Germanium, 1886 P
Hafnium, 1922 P
Nobelium, 1957 P
Scandium, 1879 P
Elements:
Disintegration of, 1921 P
Law for classification of, 1869 P
Transmutation of, 1911 P, 1922 P
Eléments de Géomtérie (A. Legendre), 1794 P
Elenchus Zoophytorum (P. S. Pallas), 1767 P
Elevators, 1780 P, 1875 P
Elgar, Sir Edward, B. musician (1857–1934), 1857 Z, 1899 T, 1901 T, 1907 T, 1934 Z; *Dream of Gerontius*, 1900 T; symphonies, 1908 T, 1911 T; violin concerto, 1910 T; cello concerto, 1918 T
Elgin Marbles, 1801 S, 1816 S
Elgin Treaty, 1854 F
Eli Lilley and Co., 1981 P
Elias (W. Bilderdijck), 1786 U
Elias, Jorge Serrano, President of Guatemala (b. 1945), 1991 A
Elias, Ney, G. explorer, 1885 P
Elie de Baumont, Jean Baptiste Armand, F. geologist (1798–1858), 1841 P
Eliot, George. *See* Evans, Mary Ann
Eliot, Thomas Stearns, B. author (1888–1965), 1917 U, 1922 U, 1930 U, 1933 U, 1935 W, 1939 W, 1942 U, 1944 U, 1948 U, 1949 W, 1953 W, 1958 W, 1965 Z
Eliot, Valerie, B. scholar, 1971 Q
Elisabethville, Congo, UN troops occupy, 1962 M
Elixiere des Teufels, Die (E. Hoffmann), 1815 U
Elizabeth City, N. Carolina, US, taken by Unionists, 1826 B
Elizabeth II, Queen of Gt. Britain, since 1952; birth, 1926 Z; as Princess, marriage, 1947 L; accession, 1952 B; coronation, 1953 F, W, Commonwealth Tour, 1954 E; visits Canada and US, 1957 K, 1964 K; addresses UN, 1957 K; opens St. Lawrence Seaway, 1959 F; descendants not being Royal Highnesses, to bear name Mountbatten-Windsor, 1960 B; tours India, Pakistan and Cyprus, 1961 A; visits African territories, 1961 L; visits W. Germany, 1965 E; Awards to industry, 1965 O
death sentence on three Rhodesian Africans reprieved, 1968 C
abdication rumoured, 1968 M
visit to New Zealand and Australia, 1970 C
requests Civil List review, 1971 E
income, 1971 M
visit to Yugoslavia, 1972 K
Queen of Australia, 1973 O
formally opens North Sea Oil pumps, 1975 L
Jubilee week celebrations, 1977 F
Royal given Assent to Devolution Bill, 1978 G
visit to Vatican, 1980 K
proclaims new Canadian constitution, 1982 D
Australia Bill, 1986 C
visit to China, 1986 K
resignation of Sir Penaia Ganilau accepted, 1987 K
fortieth anniversary of accession, 1992 B
taxation of personal income, 1992 L
Elizabeth, Empress of Austria, 1898 J
Elizabethan House of Commons, The (J. E. Neale), 1949 Q
Elizabethan Puritan Movement, The (P. Collinson), 1967 Q
Elkin Park, Pa., US, Synagogue in, 1859 S
Elle et Lui (G. Sand), 1859 U
Ellegaård, Alvan, 1963 Q
Ellesworth, Lincoln, Am. explorer, 1939 P
Ellington, Duke, Am. jazz musician (1899–1974), 1899 Z, 1932 T, 1974 Z
Elliott, Ebenezer, B. author (1781–1849), 1831 O
Elliptic functions, study of, 1928 P
Ellis, Bret Easton, B. author (b. 1964), 1991 U
Ellis, Henry Havelock, B. psychologist (1859–1939), 1897 R, 1919 R
Ellis, Jimmy, Am. boxer (b. 1940), 1970 X
Ellis, Ruth, B. murderess, 1955 O
Ellman, Richard, Am. literary scholar (1918–87), 1987 Q
Elmer Gantry (S. Lewis), 1927 U
Elmira, N.Y., US, reformatory at, 1876 O
Elsie Venner (or *The Professor*) (O. W. Holmes), 1861 U
Elster, J.P.L.T., G. electrician, 1904 P
Eluard, Paul, F. author (1895–1952), 1949 U
Elton, Sir Geoffrey Rudolph, B. historian (b. 1921), 1921 Z, 1967 Q, 1972 Q, 1973 Q, 1986 Q
Elvin, Mark, B. historian (b. 1938), 1972 Q
Elytis, Odysseus, Greek author (b. 1911), 1979 U
Emancipation:
of serfs, in Russia, 1861 C
of Slaves in US, Lincoln's declaration, 1862 J
of women, Mill's treatise on, 1869 O. *See also under* Franchise
Emaux et Camées (T. Gautier), 1852 U
Embargoes:
by American Colonies, against British goods, 1774 M
by Britain, on oil for Rhodesia, 1965 M
by Russia, on British ships, 1800 L
by UN, on arms to S. Africa, 1977 L
by US, on British goods, 1812 D
by US, on shipments to Cuba, 1960 K
on trade with China, 1969 M, 1971 F
on Iranian oil, 1979 L
on Libya, 1982 C
Embarrassment of Riches, The (S. Schama), 1987 Q
Embryology, Comparative, science of, established, 1828 P
Emden and the Dutch Revolt: Exile and the Development of Reformed Protestantism (A. Pettegree), 1992 Q
Emergence of Penal Policy in Victorian and Edwardian England, The (L. Radzinowicz, R. Hood), 1986 Q

Emerson, Ralph Waldo, Am. author (1803–82), 1803 Z, 1836 R, 1840 R, 1850 U, 1882 Z
Emigration:
British, to US, 1830 Y, 1840 Y, 1850 Y, 1860 Y, 1870 Y, 1880 Y, 1890 Y, 1938 Y
of British scientists, 1963 B, 1964 P
Irish to US, 1830 Y, 1840 Y, 1850 Y, 1860 Y, 1870 Y, 1880 Y, 1890 Y
from USSR, US trade concessions linked with freedom of, 1974 K
Emigrés, French, 1789 K
Emile (Rousseau), attacks on, 1763 O
Emilia Galotti (Lessing), 1772 W
Eminent Victorians (L. Strachey), 1918 U
Emir Faisal, of Saudi Arabia, 1960 M
Emma (J. Austen), 1816 U
Emmet, Robert, Ir. politician (1778–1803), leader of United Irishmen, 1803 G
Empedocles on Etna (M. Arnold), 1852 U
Emperor Jones, The (E. O'Neill), 1921 W
Emperor in the Roman World, The, 31 B.C. – A.D. 337 (F. Millar), 1977 Q
Empire of the Sun, The (J.G. Ballard), 1984 U
Empirical Sociology (Neurath), 1931 R
Employment, in Britain
government aid, 1981 A
government funding for training schemes, 1981 G
Employment, in US
employers knowingly employing illegal aliens fined, 1986 O
preferential minority hiring quotas, 1986 O
Californian law obliging employers to grant pregnancy leave upheld, 1987 O
Empty House, The (A. Blackwood), 1906 U
Ems, Germany:
Punctation of, 1786 R
refuted by Pius VI, 1789 R
Telegram, 1870 G
En Route (J. K. Huysmans), 1895 U
Enahoro, Chief, of Nigeria, 1963 E
Enchanteur pourrissant, L' (G. Apollinaire), 1909 U
Encke, Johann Franz, G. astronomer (1791–1865), 1818 P
Encyclicals, Papal:
Aeterna Dei, 1961 R
Editio Saepe, 1910 E, F
Humanae Vitae, 1968 R
Humani Generis, 1950 R
Mortalium Animos, 1928 R
Pacem in Terris, 1963 R
Pascendi gregis, 1907 R
Quadragesimo Anno, 1931 R
Rerum novarum, 1891 R
on Atheistic Communism, 1937 R
Encyclopaedias:
Brockhaus, 1796 Q, 1935 Q
Encyclopaedia Britannica, 1771 Q, 1929 Q, 1974 Q
Penal Jurisprudence, 1800 O
Protestant Theology, 1853 R
End of Europe, The (Teatr Nowy), 1984 W
End of Laissez-Faire, The (J. M. Keynes), 1926 O
Endangered Species, Convention on International Trade in, 1989 K
Ender, Otto, Aus. Christian Socialist, 1930 M
Endgame (S. Beckett), 1957 W
Endorphins, dicovery, 1975 P
Ends and Means (A. Huxley), 1937 R
Endymion (J. Keats), 1818 U
Enemies of Promise (C. Connolly), 1938 U
Enemy of the People, An (H. Ibsen), 1882 U
Enemy, The (J. Green), 1955 U
Energie spirituelle, L' (H. Bergson), 1919 R
Energy Crisis:
in Britain
prompts state of emergency, 1973 K, L
petrol rationing and speed limit introduced, 1973 L
three day week for industry ordered, 1973 M
Department of Energy established, 1974 A
industry returns to five day week, 1974 C
state of emergency ends, 1974 C
in US
conservation plan, 1977 D
Department of Energy created, 1977 H
radical measures proposed, 1979 G
Energy, conservation of, laws of, 1837 P, 1842 P, 1851 P
Enfants terribles, Les (J. Cocteau), 1929 U
Enfranchisement. *See under* Franchise
Engels, Friedrich, G. Socialist (1820–95), 1820 Z, 1845 O, 1848 O, 1895 Z
Engerman, Stanley Lewis, Am. historian (b. 1936), 1974 Q
Enghien, Louis Antoine Henri de Bourbon Cond Duc d', F. (1722–1804), 1804 C
Engines:
internal combustion, 1885 P
jet, 1937 P
oil, 1873 P
petrol, 1882 P, 1892 P
for aeroplane, 1903 P
railway, atomic-powered, 1954 P
steam, 1814 P, 1825 P, 1829 P
single-cylinder, 1885 P
steam, 1765 P, 1774 P, 1775 P, 1800 P, 1811 P, 1813 P
for railway. *See above under* railway
for ships, 1803 P, 1807 P, 1812 P, 1815 P, 1818 P, 1820 P
England of Elizabeth, The (A. L. Rowse), 1950 Q
England under Queen Anne (G. M. Trevelyan), 1930 Q
England, Ireland and America (R. Cobden), 1835 O
English Alehouse, The: A Social History (P. Clark), 1983 Q
English Bards and Scots Reviewers (Byron), 1809 U
English Channel: Blériot flies across, 1909 P; hovercraft crosses, 1959 P
regular hovercraft service introduced, 1968 P
ports blockaded by French fishermen, 1980 H
English Constitution, The (W. Bagehot), 1867 O
English Culture and the Decline of the Industrial Spirit, 1850–1980 (M.J. Wiener), 1981 Q
English Drama 1900–1930: The Beginnings of the Modern Period (A. Nicoll), 1973 Q
English Patient, The (M. Ondaatje), 1992 U
English Peasantry in the Later Middle Ages, The (R.H. Hilton), 1975 Q
English Social History (G. M. Trevelyan), 1942 Q
English Society in the Eighteenth Century (R. Porter), 1982 Q
English Society in the Later Middle Ages (M. Keen), 1990 Q
English Society, 1580–1680 (K. Wrightson), 1982 Q
English Stage Company, 1955 W
English Towns in Transition, 1500–1700 (P. Clark and P. Slack), 1976 Q
English Water Colour Society, 1804 S
Englishman Abroad, An, television programme, 1983 W
Eniwetok Atoll, Pacific, hydrogen bomb tests at, 1952 P
Enniskillen, Northern Ireland, 1912 J IRA bomb attack, 1987 L
Eno, Brian (Brian Peter George St. Baptiste de la Salle Eno), B. pop musician (b. 1948), 1981 W
Enormous Room (E. E. Cummings), 1923 U
Enrile, Juan Ponce, Philippine politician (b. 1924), 1986 B
Ensor, James, Belg. artist (1860–1949), 1884 S, 1888 S
Entebbe, Uganda, hijack victims rescued, 1976 F
Entente Cordiale, between Britain and France, 1903 G, 1904 D
Entente, Little, between Czechoslovakia, Roumania and Yugoslavia, 1923 H, 1933 B; Balkan counterpart of, 1934 B; Rome Protocols counter, 1934 C
Entertainer, The (J. Osborne), 1957 W
Enthusiasm (R. A. Knox), 1950 R
Entomology, studies in, 1775 P
Environment
Torrey Canyon oil tanker accident, 1967 C
greenhouse effect, 1967 P
Red Book, The (J. Fisher), 1969 P
Rome summit to discuss pollution, 1969 P
chlorofluorocarbons (CFCs), action to limit damage caused by, 1974 P, 1978 A, P, 1987 P, 1992 P
Three Mile Island accident, 1979 P
Chernobyl accident, 1986 D
Dutch government resigns over financing of anti-pollution measures, 1989 E
Convention on International Trade in Endangered Species, 1989 K
environmental damage used as military tactic in Gulf War, 1991 A, B
Conference Environment and Development, 1992 P
Environs of London, The (D. Lysons), 1792 Q
Enzymes, the first, 1832 P; catalysis among, 1906 P
EOKA, in Cyprus, 1956 H
Eothen (A. W. Kinglake), 1844 U
Epaves, Les (C. Baudelaire), 1866 U
Epidemics:
Cholera, in Europe, 1830 O
Influenza, 1918 K, 1919 P
Typhoid, 1963 C, 1964 C
Epigonen (K. Immermann), 1836 U
Epirus, Greece, granted to Greece by Turkey, 1881 G
Episcopal Church. *See under* Religious Denominations
Episodios Nacionales (B. Pérez-Galdós), 1879 U
Epistola ad Episcopos Catholicos pro causa Italica (Passaglia), 1859 O
Epoques de la nature (G. Buffon), 1778 P
Epsom, Surrey, England, The Derby first run at, 1779 X
Epstein, Sir Jacob, B. sculptor (1880–1959), 1880 Z, 1908 S, 1911 S, 1913 S, 1925 S, 1926 S, 1927 S, 1928 S, 1929 S, 1931 S, 1935 S, 1937 S, 1939 S, 1949 S, 1952 S, 1957 S, 1959 S, 1962 S
Equality (R. H. Tawney), 1901 O
Equality and Partiality (T. Nagel), 1991 R
Equatorial Guinea:
independence, 1968 K
military coup, 1979 H
former president executed, 1979 J
Equivalent 8 (C. André), 1966 S, 1972 S
Equus (P. Shaffer), 1973 W
Erard, Sébastien, F. inventor of pianoforte (1752–1831), 1780 P, 1823 T
Erasmus of Christendom (R. Bainton), 1970 Q
Erasmus, Desiderius, letters of, edited, 1906 Q
Erasmus, Rudolf Phillip Botha, S. Afr. Justice (b. 1912), 1978 L
Erbförster, Die (O. Ludwig), 1850 W

Erdrich, (Karen) Louise, Am. author (b. 1954), 1986 U
Erewhon Revisited (S. Butler), 1901 U
Erewhon, or Over the Range (S. Butler), 1872 U
Erfurt, Germany: is incorporated in France, 1807 H; Congress, between Napoleon and his vassals, 1808 K; Parliament, 1850 C, D; Social Democrat Congress at, 1890 K; E. and W. German leaders meet at, 1970 C
Erhard, Ludwig, G. Christian Democrat (1879–1977), 1897 Z: Adenauer prevents candidature for presidential election, 1959 G; becomes Chancellor, 1963 K, 1966 M, 1977 Z
Erie, Lake, N. America, US actions on, 1813 J
Eriksen, Eric, Da. politician, forms ministry, 1945 K, 1950 K
Eritrea: as Italian Colony, 1890 E; Mahdist attack on, 1893 M; is federated with Ethiopia, 1952 J
Erivan, in Armenia, Russia: ceded to Russia, 1827 B; Persian defeat at, 1827 K
Erl King, The (M. Tournier), 1970 U
Erlander, Tage, Swe. Social Democrat, 1946 K
Ermland, Poland, 1772 H
Ernest Augustus, Duke of Cumberland (1771–1851), as King of Hanover, 1837 F, G, M, 1840 H, 1851 L
Ernest Bevin: Foreign Secretary (A. Bullock), 1983 Q
Ernesti, Johann August, G. theologian and philologist (1707–81), 1764 Q, 1768 Q
'ERNIE', used for premium bonds draws, 1957 F
Ernst und Falk (Lessing), 1777 R
Ernst, Max, G. artist (1891–1976), 1891 Z, 1925 S, 1976 Z
Eros and Civilization (H. Marcuse), 1955 R
Eros, sculpture by Gilbert, 1925 S
Ershad, Hossain Mohammad, President of Bangladesh (b. 1930), 1986 L
Erskine, John, B. lawyer (1695–1768), 1773 O
Erskine, Thomas, B. lawyer and theologian (1788–1870), 1820 R
Erzberger, Matthias, G. finance minister, 1921 H
Erzerum, Turkey, Russians take, 1916 B
Eschenburg, Johann Joachim, G. critic (1743–1820), 1775 W
Eschenmoser, Albert, Swiss chemist (b. 1925), 1976 P
Eshkol, Levi, Premier of Israel (1895–1969), 1969 B
Espaces du Sommeil, Les (W. Lutoslawski), 1975 T
Espartero, Baldomero, Sp. soldier and politician (1792–1879), 1840 F, 1840 K, 1841 E; risings against, 1842 K, M; defeated, 1843 G; recalled, 1847 J; becomes premier, 1854 H; replaced by O'Donnell, 1856 J
Espionage:
in Britain:
Fuchs, 1950 C
Blake, 1961 E, O, 1966 K
Lonsdale, 1961 O
Vassall, 1962 K
Radcliffe Tribunal Report on, 1963 D
Bossard and Allen, 1965 E
Brooke exchanged for 'Portland spies', 1969 G
Soviet diplomats and officials expelled, 1971 J, 1985 J
Blunt, 1979 L
Spycatcher affair, 1986 G, 1988 F
Security Services Act, 1989 O
Mrs. Stella Rimington appointed head of M.I.5, 1991 M
in Canada, 1946 G; Munsinger, 1966 C
in Egypt, 1957 F
in Russia, Wynne, 1962 L; concealed microphones, 1964 E
USSR accuses South Korean airliner of spying, 1983 J
Britons expelled, 1985 J
Daniloff, US journalist, arrested, 1986 H
KGB collegium disbanded, 1991 H
in US, the Rosenbergs, 1953 F
Republican Party finance chairman accused of, 1972 J
Zakharov, R. diplomat, arrested, 1986 H
members of USSR mission to UN ordered out of US, 1986 J
Iraq executes men accused of spying for Israel, 1969 A
Mehmet Shehu, Albanian Prime Minister, denounced as spy, 1981 M
in W. Germany, 1985 H, 1985 J
industrial, by Hitachi Ltd, 1983 B
Espiritu Santo, New Hebrides, rebellion, 1980 E
Espoir, L' (Malraux), 1937 U
Esquipulas, Guatemala, Contadora peace treaty summit, 1986 E
Essai d'une théorie sur la structure des cristaux (R. Haüy), 1784 P
Essai de Cristallographie (J. de l'Isle), 1772 P
Essai de Statique Chimique (C. Berthollet), 1803 P
Essai de monde et de critique (E. Renan), 1859 R
Essai historique, politique et moral sur les Révolutions (Chateaubriand), 1797 O
Essai sur l'Indifférence (H. F. R. de Lamennais), 1817 R
Essai sur la Peinture (D. Diderot), 1766 S
Essai sur la langue et la littérature chinoises (J. P. A. Rémusat), 1811 Q
Essai sur le Despotisme (Mirabeau), 1772 O
Essais de Psychologie contemporaine (P. Bourget), 1883 U
Essay on Beethoven (R. Wagner), 1870 T
Essay on Church Reforms (T. Arnold), 1832 R
Essay on Finance (R. Giffen), 1879 O
Essay on Goethe (T. Carlyle), 1828 Q
Essay on Liberation, An (H. Marcuse), 1969 R
Essay on Mind, with other poems (E. B. Browning), 1826 U
Essay on Slavery (Clarkson), 1786 O
Essay on the Development of Christian Doctrine (J. H. Newman), 1845 R
Essay on the First Principles of Government (J. Priestley), 1768 O
Essay on the History of Civil Society (A. Ferguson), 1766 O
Essay on the Nature and Immutability of Truth (J. Beattie), 1770 R
Essay on the Nature and Principles of Taste (A. Alison), 1790 S
Essay on the Principle of Population (T. R. Malthus), 1790 O
Essay on the Vedas (H. T. Colebrooke), 1805 Q
Essays and Reviews (F. Temple and M. Pattison), 1860 R
Essays Catholic and Critical, 1926 R
Essays in Criticism (M. Arnold), 1865 U
Essays in Liberality (A. Vidler), 1957 R
Essays in Musical Analysis (D. F. Tovey), 1935 T
Essays in Self-Criticism (L. Althusser), 1976 R
Essays of Elia (C. Lamb), 1820 U
Essays on Action and Events (D. Davidson), 1980 R
Essays on the Active Powers of the Human Mind (T. Reid), 1788 R
Essays on the Sociology of Culture (K. Mannheim), 1956 R
Essays Philosophical and Theological (R. Bultmann), 1956 R
Essen, P., Am. scientist, 1947 P
Essen, Germany, Krupps works at, 1810 P, 1903 P
Essence of Christianity (L. Feuerbach), 1841 R
Essential Tension, The (T. Kuhn), 1977 R
Essequibo, B. Guiana: British capture, 1796 N; Britain retains, 1814 H
Esso, withrawal from South Africa, 1986 M
Estaing, Charles Hector, Comte d', F. admiral (1729–94), 1778 G
Esterhazy, Marie Charles, F. soldier, 1897 L
Estes, Richard, Am. artist (b. 1932), 1973 S
Esther Waters (G. Moore), 1894 U
Estonia: Bolshevik rule in, 1918 M; Bolsheviks invade, 1919 B; declares independence, 1920 B
Popular Front, 1988 K
Estonian parliament gives itself rights to veto laws from Moscow, 1988 L
Soviet constitution suspended, 1990 C
independence, 1990 E, 1991 C, H, J
government resignation over food and fuel shortages, 1992 A
post-independence elections, 1992 J
Eternal City, The (H. Caine), 1901 U
Ethan Frome (E. Wharton), 1911 U
Ether Alcohol, constitution of, 1832 P
Ether, used as anaesthetic, 1842 P, 1846 P
Ethical Culture, Society for, 1876 R
Ethical Studies (F. H. Bradley), 1876 R
Ethics and the Limits of Philosophy (B. Williams), 1985 R
Ethics, Treatises on, 1785 R, 1874 R, 1876 R, 1879 R, 1882 R, 1903 R, 1947 R, 1957 R
Ethiopia (Abyssinia): exploration of, 1772 P; British expedition to, 1868 A; frontiers 1891 C, 1902 D; Italian claims to, 1889 E, 1891 B; Italian troops in, 1895 C; Italy withdraws protectorate, 1896 K; independence is guaranteed, 1906 B; Italy invades, 1935 K; Italy annexes, 1936 E; Allies liberate, 1941 C, E
UN reports on drought deaths, 1973 K
armed forces take control, 1974 F
Haile Selassie deposed, 1974 J
military government executions, 1974 L
Somali forces invade, 1977 G
drought, 1983 C
famine, 1983 C, 1984 L, 1985 O, 1987 L
illiteracy, 1983 Y
peace agreement with Somalia, 1988 D
attempted coup, 1989 E
civil war, 1991 E
Ethnographie moderne des races sauvages (L. A. Bertillon), 1883 P
Ethnological Society founded, 1843 O
Euler, Leonhard, Swi. mathematician (1707–83), 1770 P, 1772 P, 1783 Z
Eupen, Belgium, 1920 A
Euratom: resolution on, adopted by ECSC, 1956 E; Rome Treaty for, 1957 C; in force, 1958 E; Britain agrees to co-operate with, 1959 B; Britain applies to join, 1962 C; merger of executive authority, 1965 M; Commission of the European Communities, 1967 G
Euripides, works of, edited, 1802 Q
Europe, Council of: Statute of, 1949 E; W. Germany joins, 1950 F; adopts Eden Plan, 1952 J
European Advisory Commission, Allied, 1943 L
European Anarchy, The (G. Lowes Dickinson), 1916 O
European Bank for Reconstruction and Development, 1991 O
European Coal and Steel Community (ECSC): in force, 1952 G, 1953 A; resolution of, on Common Market, 1956 E; Britain applies to join, 1962 C; merger of executive authority, 1965 M

Commission of the European Communities, 1967 G
European Community (EC):
See also Common Market; European Economic Community.
France ends boycott of EC meetings, 1966 A
Common Agricultural Policy (CAP), 1966 G, 1988 O
British membership, 1966 L, 1967 A, E, M, 1969 M, 1970 F, 1971 E, F, G, J, K, 1972 A, B, K, 1973A, 1975 A, C, D, F, 1983 E
Danish membership, 1967 E, 1970 F, 1972 A, J, 1973 A
Irish membership, 1967 E, 1970 F, 1972 A, E, 1973 A
Commission of the European Communities, 1967 G, 1977 A, 1981 A
France disputes British account of talks on future of, 1969 B
Britain and the European Communities—An Economic Assessment, White
Paper, 1970 B
Norwegian membership, 1970 F, 1972 A, J
Paris talks between Heath and Pompidou, 1971 E
British deals with, 1971 F
The United Kingdom and the European Communities, White Paper, 1971 G
British Labour Party call for referendum on membership, 1972 D
economic and monetary union, 1972 K, 1988 J, 1990 K, 1991 M
British government defeated on new immigration rules favouring EC over Commonwealth citizens, 1972 L
British members nominated, 1972 M
French referendum on enlargement, 1972 D
butter surplus to USSR, 1973 E
Arab co-operation proposal, 1974 C
Paris summit on revized British contribution, 1974 M
EFTA agreement, 1977 O
VAT unified, 1977 O
trade agreement with China, 1978 B
Greek membership, 1979 E
Dublin summit, 1979 L
Luxembourg summit, 1980 D
rebate to Britain, 1980 E
trade sanctions against Iran, 1980 E
warns USSR against intervention in Poland, 1980 M
British Social Democratic Party supports membership, 1981 C
imposes economic sanctions on Argentina, 1982 D
British budget contribution, 1984 F
Fontainebleau summit, 1984 F
heads of government summit, 1985 C
Spanish membership, 1985 C, F, 1986 A
Portuguese membership, 1985 C, F, 1986 A
Comecon summit proposes links with, 1985 F
sanctions against South Africa, 1985 J
new investment in South Africa prohibited, 1986 J
Council of Ministers, qualified majority voting, 1987 G
Single European Act, 1987 G
Thatcher warns against political and economic union, 1988 J
Social Charter, 1989 O
European Exchange Rate Mechanism (ERM), entry of sterling, 1990 J
Rome summit, 1990 K
single currency, 1990 K
Yugoslavian civil war, 1991 G, J, K, L, 1992 A, D
Hague peace conference on Yugoslavia, 1991 J, K
Maastricht Treaty, 1991 M, 1992 F, J, M
Croatia and Slovenia recognized as independent republics, 1992 A
economic sanctions against South Africa lifted, 1992 A
Finland votes to apply for membership, 1992 C
Bosnia-Herzegovina formally recognized, 1992 D
Edinburgh summit, 1992 M
European Conference on Security and Co-operation, 1983 J
European Convention on Human Rights, 1954 E
European Court of First Instance, 1989 O
European Court of Human Rights, 1978 A
verdict on Northern Irish internees, 1978 A
verdict on Isle of Man birching, 1978 D
on trade union's 'closed shop', 1981 O
condemns use of tawse in Scottish schools, 1982 O
ruling on corporal punishment in British schools, 1982 O
Britain found guilty of sex discrimination in immigration policy, 1985 O
European Court of Justice
on Community law, 1978 O
France defies exports ruling, 1979 O
length of proceedings in, 1990 O
European Defence Community (EDC): NATO approves, 1952 B; Britain proposes defence treaty with, 1952 D; Paris Treaty signed, 1952 E
European Economic Co-operation, Organisation for (OEEC), 1948 D
European Economic Community (EEC) or 'Common Market': Foreign ministers of 'The Six', at Rome Conference, 1953 B; W. German Bundestag approves, 1953 C; Eisenhower pledges support to, 1954 D; Brussels negotiations founder, 1954 H Britain applies for membership, 1961 H; E. Heath's statement to, 1961 K; Agreement on agriculture, 1962 A; Commonwealth premiers endorse Britain's attempted entry, 1962 J; Britain resumes negotiations with, 1962 L; Britain is refused entry, 1963 A
European Exchange Rate Mechanism (ERM)
entry of sterling, 1990 J
lira devalued, 1992 J
sterling withdrawn, 1992 J
European Free Trade Association (EFTA): 'The Seven' sign a treaty, 1959 L; first meeting, 1960 A; in force, 1960 E
customs union created, 1966 O
EEC agreement, 1977 O
European Monetary System (EMS), 1978 D, M
European Nuclear Energy Agency, 1957 M
European Payments Union, 1950 J
European Political Systems (P. Feuerbach), 1800 O
European Recovery Programme, under Marshall Aid: formed, 1947 F; Paris discussions on, 1947 G, 1948 D; Marshall Aid, US Acts, 1948 F, 1949 D; German representation in, demanded, 1948 F; achieved, 1949 M
European Reformation, The (E. Cameron), 1991 Q
European Security Conference, 1972 L
European Space Agency:
Ariane rocket, 1979 P
ERS-1 satellite, 1991 P
European Trade Union Confederation, 1973 O
European Union: Hague Conference on, 1948 E; Strasbourg Conference on, 1950 H; Nine-power agreement on, 1954 D; Paris Treaty for, ratified, 1955 C, D; provokes Russia to annul treaties, 1955 E; Assembly meets at Strasbourg, 1955 G; Paris Assembly calls for single NATO nuclear force, 1962 M
Europera III/IV (J. Cage), 1989 T
Eurovision network, 1954 P
Euston Road School of Artists, 1937 S
Eutaw, N. Carolina, US, 1781 J
Euthanasia, Californian ruling on, 1976 O
Euzkadi, Spain, 1979 K
Eva Trout (E. Bowen), 1970 U
Evangelical Alliance, American, 1866 R
Evangelicals. *See under* Religious Denominations
Evans, Sir Arthur, B. archaeologist (1851–1941), 1851 Z, 1900 Q, 1910 Q, 1941 Z
Evans, Mary Ann, B. novelist under pseudonym 'George Eliot' (1819–80), 1819 Z, 1857 U, 1859 U, 1860 U, 1861 U, 1871 U, 1880 Z
Evans, Oliver, Am. wheelwright (1755–1819), 1780 P
Evaporated milk, 1847 P
Evatt, Herbert Vere, Aus. politician (1894–1965), 1894 Z, 1965 Z
Eve of St. Agnes, The (J. Keats), 1820 U
Evelina (F. Burney), 1778 U
Everest, Mount, climbed, 1953 P
Everitt, Alan Milner, B. historian (b. 1926), 1985 Q
Everlasting Mercy, The (J. Masefield), 1911 U
Everyman's Library, 1906 U
Evidence from Scripture of the Second Coming of Christ (W. Miller), 1842 R
Evidences of Christianity (W. Paley), 1794 R
Evolution créatrice, L' (H. Bergson), 1907 R
Evolution of Ethics (T. H. Huxley) 1893 P
Evolution of the Labour Party, The, 1910–24 (R. McKibbin), 1974 Q
Evolution, term coined, 1852 P
teaching of, forbidden, 1925 O
theories of, 1948 P
Evren, General Kenan, Turkish soldier and leader (b. 1918), 1980 J, 1989 K
Ewald, Johannes, Da. poet and dramatist (1743–81), 1770 W
Ewart, William, B. Whig politician (1798–1869), 1850 O
Ewart-Biggs, Christopher, B. diplomat (1921–76) assassinated by IRA, 1976 G
Ewins, Arthur James, B. biochemist (1882–1957), 1938 P
Examination of the British Doctrine which subjects to capture a Neutral Trade (J. Madison), 1806 O
Exchange (Y. Trifonov), 1990 W
Excited Pastoral (S. Chia), 1980 S
Exclusive Brethren. *See under* Religious Denominations
Exclusive Commercial State (J. G. Fichte), 1800 O
Excommunications, notable, 1871 R, 1885 O
Excursion, The (W. Wordsworth), 1814 U
Execution (G. Segal), 1967 S
Executioner's Song, The (N. Mailer), 1979 U
Exeter, Devon, England, bombed, 1942 D
Exhibitions and World Fairs:
Great Exhibition, Hyde Park, 1851 W
Paris, 1855 S
International, London, 1862 W
Paris, 1867 W
Chicago, 1893 W
British Empire, Wembley, 1924 W
Paris, 1937 W
Empire, Glasgow, 1938 W
New York, 1939 W
Swiss National, Zrich, 1939 W
Festival of Britain, 1951 S, W
Brussels, 1958 W

Expo 67, 1967 D
Expo 70, 1970 S
Exhibitions, Art:
in Britain:
Post-Impressionist, London, 1910 S
Ruskin, 1919 S
Sargent, 1926 S
Italian Art, 1930 S
Chinese Art, 1935 S
Augustus John, 1940 S
Sickert, 1941 S
Aid Russia, 1942 S
Mexican Art, 1953 S
Picasso, 1960 S
Goya, 1963 S
'Art of a Decade', 1964 S
Beckmann, 1965 S
Bonnard, 1965 S
Giacometti, 1965 S
Moore, Tate Gallery, London and elsewhere, 1968 S
'When Attitude Becomes Form', ICA, London, 1969 S
'Art in Revolution', Hayward Gallery, London, 1971 S
Arbus, Arts Council, London, 1974 S
'British Photography 1840–1950', Hayward Galley, London, 1975 S
'Sand Circles', Hayward Galley, London, 1976 S
unofficial Soviet art, ICA, London, 1977 S
'The State of British Art', ICA, London, 1978 S
'20th-Century British Sculpture', Whitechapel Gallery, London, 1981 S
'A New Spirit in Painting', Royal Academy, London, 1981 S
Tinguely retrospective, London and Switzerland, 1982 S
'Essential Cubism, The', Tate Gallery, London, 1983 S
'German Art in the Twentieth Century 1905–1985', Royal Academy, London, 1985 S
British Architecture, Royal Academy, London, 1986 S
'British Art of the Twentieth Century', Royal Academy, London, 1987 S
Le Corbusier retrospective, London and Paris, 1987 S
'Italian Art in the Twentieth Century', Royal Academy, London, 1989 S
'Monet in the '90s', Royal Academy, London, 1990 S
'Pop Art', Royal Academy, London, 1991 S
in France, Impressionist, 1874 S, 1877 S, 1886 S
van Gogh, 1891 S
Rodin, 1900 S
Cubist, paintings, 1907 S
multi-part homage to Picasso, 1966 S
Paris Biennale, 1971 S
Duchamp, Pompidou Centre, Paris, 1977 S
'Paris–Berlin', Pompidou Centre, Paris, 1978 S
'Paris–Moscou', Pompidou Centre, Paris, 1979 S
Le Corbusier retrospective, London and Paris, 1987 S
in Germany, Islamic Art, Munich, 1910 S
Nazi Exhibition of 'Degenerate Art' 1937 S
Prospect 71, Düsseldorf, 1971
'Inquiry into Reality: Images of Today' – 5th Documenta, 1972 S
'Zeitgeist', Martin Gropius Bau, Berlin, 1982 S
'Metropolis', Martin Gropius Bau, Berlin, 1991 S
Exhibitions, Art, in Italy
Venice Biennale, 1974 S, 1976 S, 1977 S, 1990 S
'Futurism and Futurisms', Palazzo Grassi, Venice, 1986 S
in US, Armoury of Post-Impressionists, 1913 S
Unknown American Painters, 1939 S
of *Mona Lisa*, 1963 S
'Art of the Real', MOMA, New York, 1968 S
Lichtenstein retrospective, Guggenheim Museum, New York, 1969 S
Smith retrospective, Guggenheim Museum, New York, 1969 S
6th Guggenheim International, New York, 1971 S
Beuys retrospective, Guggenheim Museum, New York, 1979 S
Picasso, MOMA, New York, 1980 S
'The Avant-Garde in Russia, The', Los Angeles County Museum, 1980 S
'Temporary Contemporary, The', Los Angeles Museum of Contemporary Art, 1983 S
'Primitivism in the Twentieth Century', MOMA, New York, 1984 S
'Deconstructivist Architecture', MOMA, New York, 1988 S
'High and Low', MOMA, New York, 1991 S
Matisse, MOMA, New York, 1992 S
Russian Utopia, Guggenheim Museum, New York, 1992 S
Exhibitions, Miscellaneous:
Electrical, Munich, 1883 P
Aeronautic, Vienna, 1888 P
Sweated Industries, London, 1906 O
Diaghilev, Edinburgh, 1954 S
Shakespeare Quatercentenary, 1964 S, W
'Treasures of Tutankhamun', British Museum, London, 1972 Q
'Particular Places', British Library, London, 1989 Q
Exiles, The (J. Joyce), 1918 W
Existence and Analogy (E. Mascall), 1949 R
Existentialism, Papal decree against, 1950 R
Existentialism (Ruggiero), 1947 R
Exit the King (E. Ionescu), 1963 W
Exorcismes (H. Michaud), 1943 U
Expansion of England, The (J. R. Seeley), 1883 Q
Expectancy of life, observations on, 1769 O
Expedition of Humphry Clinker, The (T. Smollett), 1771 U
Experience and Poetry (W. Dilthey), 1905 R
Experience of World War I, The (J.M. Winter), 1988 Q
Experimental Inquiry into the Nature and Properties of Heat (J. Leslie), 1804 P
Experiments and Instruments depending on the relations of Air to Heat and Moisture (J. Leslie), 1813 O
Experiment with Time (J. W. Dunne), 1927 R
Exploration:
Africa, 1772 P, 1795 P, 1799 P, 1850 P, 1852 P, 1854 P, 1855 P, 1856 P, 1871 P, 1875 P
N. America, 1790 P
N. Pole, 1871 P, 1888 P, 1893 P, 1900 P, 1906 P, 1909 P, 1926 P
N.W. Passage, 1850 P
Pacific, 1766 P, 1768 P, 1770 P, 1775 P, 1776 P, 1778 P
S. America, 1799 P
S. Pole, 1903 P, 1908 P, 1910 P, 1912 P, 1934 P, 1935 P
Spitzbergen, 1927 P
under water, 1934 P
... explosante-fixe ... (P. Boulez), 1973 T
Exposition des Droits de l'Homme (Sièyes), 1789 O
Exposition du système du monde (P. Laplace), 1796 P
Extradition Agreements
Eire–British, 1987 L
Extraterritorial privileges in China, agreement to abolish, 1930 A
Exxon Valdez accident, 1989 C
Eye of the Storm, The (P. White), 1973 U
Eyeless in Gaza (A. Huxley), 1936 U
Eylau, Russia, formerly E. Prussia, battle, 1807 B
Eyre, Richard, B. theatre director (b. 1943), 1988 W
Eyskens, Gaston, Belg. Christian Socialist, 1948 H

F

Faber, Frederick Williams, B. ecclesiastic (1814–63), 1849 R
Fabian Essays (G. B. Shaw), 1889 O
Fabian Society, 1884 O
Fabiola, Doña y Aragon, Sp. Princess, marries King Baudouin I of Belgium, 1960 M
Fabius, Laurent, French Socialist politician (b. 1946), 1985 H, J, 1992 A
Fables (J. Kriloff), 1809 U
Fabricius, Johann Christian. Da. entomologist (1745–1808), 1775 P
Facciolati, Jacopo, It. philologist (1682–1769), 1771 Q
Factories:
in Britain, cotton spinning, 1785 P, 1786 P
legislation for, 1825 F, 1833 H, 1844 F, 1847 F, O, 1867 O, 1906 O
munitions, 1917 O
Owen's model, 1800 O
women in, 1906 O, 1917 O
in Germany, employment of women, 1908 M
inspection of, 1891 F
Fahd, King of Saudi Arabia (b. 1923), Basic Law, 1992 O
Fair Stood the Wind for France (H. E. Bates), 1944 U
Fairbanks, Douglas Elton (Sr.), Am. film actor (1883–1939), 1915 W, 1920 W
Fairey Aviation Company, 1946 P; privatization, 1980 O
Fairs, World. *See under* Exhibitions
Fairy Tales (H. Andersen), 1835 U
Fairy Tales (J. and W. Grimm), 1812 U
Faisal, King of Saudi Arabia (1907–58), 1964 L; heads Arab Federation, 1958 B; murdered, 1958 G
Faisal, King of Saudi Arabia (1905–75), assassination, 1975 C
Faisal, King of Syria, 1920 C, G
Falaise Gap, France, defeat of Germans in, 1944 H
Falconer (J. Cheever), 1977 U
Falconet, Etienne Maurice, F. sculptor (1716–91), 1763 S, 1766 S
Falk, Paul Ludwig Adalbert, G. politician (1827–1900), 1873 E
Falkenhagen, Erich von, G. general, 1914 J
Falkland Isles, S. America: discovered by France, 1764 N; claimed by Britain, 1766 N; Anglo-Spanish dispute over, 1770 H; Spain sells to Britain, 1771 A; Britain proclaims sovereignty over, 1833 A; battle, 1914 M; Britain's dispute with Argentina and Chile, 1955 E

Argentina suspends diplomatic ties with Britain over, 1976 A
Falklands War. *See* Wars
Lord Shackleton's report on economic development, 1982 J
airport announced, 1983 F
Fall of Paris, The (I. Ehrenburg), 1941 A
Fall of Robespierre, The (Coleridge, Southey and Lovell), 1794 W
Fall of the British Monarchies, 1637–1642, The (C. Russell), 1991 Q
Fall of the House of Habsburg (E. Crankshaw), 1963 Q
Fall, The, B. pop group, 1983 W
Falla, Manuel de, Sp. musician (1876–1946), 1915 T, 1919 T, 1923 T
Fälldin, Thorbjörn, Prime Minister of Sweden, 1976 J
Fallières, Clément Armand, F. Republican (1841–1931), 1883 A; elected President, 1906 A
Falmer, near Brighton, Sussex, England, Sussex University, 1964 S
False Start (J. Johns), 1988 S
Family Reunion (T. S. Eliot), 1939 W
Family allowances, 1945 O
Family, Sex and Marriage, The, 1500–1800 (L. Stone), 1977 Q
Family, The, television documentary, 1974 W
Family, The: A Social History of the Twentieth Century (J. Harriss ed.), 1991 Q
Famine Relief. *See* Aid
Famines:
in China, 1920 L
in Ethiopia, 1973 K, 1983 C, 1984 L, 1985 O, 1987 L
in India, 1769 N, 1873 N, 1877 N, 1897 N, 1964 L
in Ireland, 1846 N
in Italy, 1898 E
in Japan, 1783 N
in Russia, 1892 N, 1932 N
world wheat shortage, 1946 G
Famished Road, The (B. Okri), 1991 U
Fanfani, Amintore, It. Christian Democrat (b. 1908), 1954 A; forms coalitions, 1958 F, 1960 B; resigns, 1959 A
Fanny Hill (Cleland), 1963 U
Fanny by Gaslight (M. Sadleir), 1940 U
Fantasias. *See under* Rhapsodies
Fantin-Latour, Henri, F. artist (1836–1904), 1870 S
Far East:
reduction in British defence commitments announced, 1967 G
British troops retained, 1970 K
Far Eastern Commission, terminates Japan's reparations payments, 1949 E
Far Eastern Republic, Siberia, votes for union with USSR, 1922 L
Far From the Madding Crowd (T. Hardy), 1874 U
Faraday, Michael, B. natural philosopher (1791–1867), 1791 Z, 1821 P, 1823 P, 1825 P, 1831 P, 1834 P, 1839 P, 1843 P, 1867 Z
Fareed, Abdul Sabbur, Prime Minister of Afghanistan, 1992 G
Farewell to Arms, A (E. Hemingway), 1929 U
Farm mortgage corporation, US, 1934 A
Farmer's Boy, The (R. Bloomfield), 1800 U
Farms credit act, US, 1933 F
Farms, collective, 1930 O
Farmyard (F. Kroetz), 1972 W
Farnborough, Surrey, England, prize fight at, 1860 X
Farouk I, King of Egypt (1920–65), 1952 G, 1965 Z
accession, 1936 D
abdicates, 1952 G
Farrell, James Gordon, B. author (1935–79), 1978 U
Farrell, Terry, B. architect (b. 1938), 1990 S
Fascism, studies in, 1943 O
Fascists. *See under* Political Parties
Fashoda, Sudan, 1896 F; French occupy, 1897 G; Kitchener reaches, 1898 J; French evacuate, 1898 L; crisis ends, 1899 C
Fassbinder, Rainer Werner, G. film director (1946–82), 1946 Z, 1972 W, 1973 W, 1982 Z
Fastnet Yacht Race, hurricane hits, 1979 H
Fatherland Front. *See under* Political Parties
Fathers and Sons (I. Turgeniev), 1862 U
Fats, liquid, process for hardening, 1901 P
Fauget, Emile, F. author (1847–1915), 1892 O
Faulkner, Arthur Brian Deane, Lord Faulkner of Downpatrick, Northern Ir. politician (1921–77), 1971 J
Prime Minister, 1971 C
Chief Executive of Northern Ireland, 1974 A
Faulkner, William, Am. author (1897–1961), 1926 U, 1929 U, 1930 U, 1932 U, 1953 U, 1959 U, 1962 U
Faure, Edgar, F. Radical politician, 1952 A, B, 1955 B
Faure, Félix, F. Moderate Republican politician (1841–99), elected president, 1895 A, 1899 B
Faust (Goethe), 1808 W, 1831 W
Faust (N. Lenau), 1836 U
Fauves, Les, group of French artists, 1905 S
Faux-Monnayeurs, Les (A. Gide), 1925 U
Favaloro, Rene, Am. surgeon, 1967 P
Faw, Iraq, Iran takes, 1986 B
Fawcett, Millicent Garrett, B. suffragette (1847–1929), 1847 Z, 1929 Z
Fawley, Hants, England, oil refinery at, 1951 P
Faya-Largeau, Chad, bombing and capture by Libya, 1983 H
Fayette, N.Y., US Mormon Church at, 1830 D
Fear of Flying (E. Jong), 1974 U
Fear of Freedom, The (E. Fromm), 1942 R
Fearful Joy, A (J. Cary), 1949 U
Feast of Reason, 1793 R
Feast of Supreme Being, 1794 R
Febronius, Justinus. *See* Hontheim
Fechner, Gustav Theodor, G. physicist (1801–87), 1860 P
Federal Republic of Germany (FRG). *See* Germany, West
Federal Union, advocated, 1929 J, 1939 O
Federation of Arab Republics, Benghazi Agreement establishes, 1971 D
Federation of Employers, British National, 1873 O
Federation of Labor, American, 1881 O
Fehrenbach, Konstantin, G. Chancellor, 1920 F
Feinstein, Charles Hilliard, B. historian (b. 1932), 1982 Q
Feldhoven Caves, near Hochdel, Germany, 1856 Q
Fellini, Federico, It. film director (1920–93), 1920 Z, 1953 W, 1954 W, 1960 W, 1969 W, 1974 W
Female Eunuch, The (G. Greer), 1971 R
Fences (A. Wilson), 1986 W
Fender, Percy George Herbert, B. cricketer (1892–1985), 1920 X, 1922 X, 1985 Z
Fenian outrages, 1857 K, 1866 B, 1867 B, J, M, 1883 C; in Quebec, 1870 E
Féodora (V. Sardou), 1882 U
Ferdinand I of Austria (1835–48), 1835 C; flees, 1848 E; returns to Vienna, 1848 H
Ferdinand I of Bulgaria (1887–1918), 1887 G, 1896 G, 1908 K, 1909 B
Ferdinand I of Naples (1759–1825), 1798 L, 1815 F, 1820 G, 1825 A
Ferdinand II of Naples (1830–59), 1830 L, 1859 E; grants constitution, 1848 B
Ferdinand VII of Spain (1814–33), 1814 E, 1822 L, 1833 J; as Crown Prince, renounces throne, 1808 E; Venezuela's allegiance to, 1810 D, 1811 G; Napoleon to restore, 1813 M; restored to throne 1815 F; fails to keep to constitution, 1820 A, C, L; refuses to leave Madrid, 1823 F; restored by French, 1823 K; abrogates Salic Law, 1830 C
Ferdinand and Isabella (W. H. Prescott), 1837 Q
Ferdinand of Saxe-Coburg, elected prince of Bulgaria, 1887 G
Ferguson, Adam, B. philosopher (1725–1816), 1766 O
Ferguson, Charles Wright, Am. historian (1901–87), 1971 Q
Ferguson, Sarah, *see* York, Duchess of
Fermentation, lactic, 1857 P
Fermi National Accelerator Laboratory (Fermilab), 1969 P
Fermi, Enrico, Am. atomic physicist (1901–54), 1934 P; splits the atom, 1942 P
Fermor, Patrick Leigh, B. author (b. 1915), 1977 U
Fernández-Armesto, Felipe, historian, 1991 Q
Fernando Po, Island, in Gulf of Guinea, ceded by Portugal to Spain, 1778 N
Fernau, Hermann, 1917 O
Ferneyhough, Brian John Peter, B. musician (b. 1943), 1979 T
Ferranti Ltd., profit on Bloodhound missile, 1964 D
government stake in, 1975 E
privatization, 1980 O
Ferrara, N. Italy, formerly a Papal State, 1797 G, 1801 G; ceded to France, 1797 B; Austrians occupy, 1847 G
Ferrari, Enzo, It. car designer (1898–1988), 1898 Z, 1939 X, 1988 Z
Ferrari, Giuseppe, It. philosopher (1812–76), 1847 R
Ferraro, Geraldine, Am. Democrat politician (b. 1935), 1984 G
Ferrer, Guardia Francisco, Sp. anti-clerical, 1909 K
Ferrer, José, Am. Film actor (1912–92), 1952 W
Ferry Jules, François Camille, F. Republican statesman (1832–93), 1883 B, 1885 C; Tunisian policy 1881 L, 1884 L; Egyptian policy, 1884 F
Ferstel, H. von, Aust. architect (1828–83), 1856 S
Fertilisation, study of, 1763 P, 1779 P
through krilium, 1951 P
through peat, 1914 P
Fertilisers, production of, statistics of, 1932 Y, 1940 Y, 1959 Y
Fertility Treatments
British woman gives birth to sextuplets, 1968 P
'Test Tube' baby, 1978 P
human embryo transferred, 1983 P
Warnock Report on Human Fertilization and Embryology, 1984 O
frozen embryos, 1984 P
in vitro fertilization, 1984 P
septuplets born in US, 1985 P
Vatican document, 1987 O
Fessenden, Reginald Aubrey, Am. scientist, 1900 P
F.E. Smith (J. Campbell), 1983 Q
Festivals:
of Britain, 1951 S, W
Champ de Mars, 1790 G
Edinburgh, 1947 W, 1954 T

Glyndebourne, 1934 T
Hambach, 1832 E
Reason, 1793 R
Salzburg, 1946 T, 1955 S
Wartburg, 1817 K
Fêtes galantes (P. Verlaine), 1869 U
Feuchtwanger, Lion, G. author (1884–1958), 1917 V
Feuerbach, Ludwig Andreas, G. theologian (1804–72), 1841 R
Feuerbach, Paul Johann Anslem, G. jurist (1775–1833), 1800 O
Feuillet, Octave, F. author (1821–90), 1858 U
Few Late Chrysanthemums, A (J. Betjeman), 1954 U
Fey, Emil, Aus. minister of interior, 1935 K
Feyerabend, Paul, Am. philosopher (b. 1924), 1975 R
Feynman, Richard, Am. physicist (1918–88), 1918 Z, 1949 P, 1988 Z
Fez, Arab summit on Middle East, 1981 L
Fianna Fail. *See under* Political Parties
Fibre optics, cable laid across Atlantic Ocean, 1987 P
Fichte, Immanuel Hermann von, G. philosopher (1797–1879), 1837 R
Fichte, Johann Gottlieb, G. philosopher and statesman (1762–1814), 1792 R, 1794 R, 1796 O, 1798 R, 1800 O, 1806 R, 1808 O, 1812 R, 1814 Z, 1818 R; as rector of Berlin University, 1810 O; Herder's attack on, 1799 R
Fick, Am. speculator, leader of the 'Erie Ring', 1872 A
Fiction:
English Romantic School, 1765 U
Gothic novel, 1794 U
historical novel, 1765 U
Field, John, B. musician (1782–1837), 1814 T
Field, Winston Joseph, Rhodesian Front politician (b. 1904), 1962 M, 1964 D
Fields, Dame Gracie, B. actress (1898–1979), 1898 Z, 1931 W, 1979 Z
Fielinger, Zdenek, Czech. National Front leader, 1945 D
Fierstein, Harvey, Am. actor and writer (b. 1954), 1981 W
Fieschi, Giuseppe, Corsican Radical (1790–1836), 1835 G
Fifth Dimension (Byrds), 1966 W
Fight for the Leadership of the Tory Party (R. Churchill), 1964 O
Figli, Leopold, Aust. People's Party leader, 1945 M, 1952 K
Figuration Libre movement, France, 1981 S
Fiji Islands, Britain annexes, 1874 K
independence within Commonwealth, 1970 K
election victory by Indian-dominated coalition, 1987 D
coups d'état, 1987 E, J
colonial links with Britain ended, 1987 K
declared Republic, 1987 K
Filangieri, Gaetano, It. Lawyer (1752–88), 1780 O
Filles du feu, Les (G. de Nerval), 1854 U
Fillmore, Millard, Am. Whig (1800–74), 13th president of US (1850–3), 1850 G, 1850 G, 1856 L
Film Censors, British Board of, 1920 W; introduces 'X' certificate, 1951 W
Film Institute, British, 1933 W
Film, roll, 1889 P
Filming machine, rapid, 1923 P
Films, sound, 1919 P, 1927 W, 1932 W
colour, 1924 W, 1928 W, 1929 P, W
Films:
Á Nous la Liberté, 1932 W
Accident, 1967 W
Accuse, J', 1919 W
Adventuress from Monte Carlo, The, 1921 W
Advice and Consent, 1962 W
African Queen, The, 1951 W
Alexander Newski, 1938 W
Alfie, 1966 W
Alien, 1979 W
All Quiet on the Western Front, 1930 W
All the King's Men, 1949 W
Amarcord, 1974 W
Anatomy of Murder, 1959 W
Andere Ich, Das, 1941 W
Andrei Rublev, 1966 W
Anna Karenina, 1911 W, 1935 W
Anne Boleyn, 1921 W
Année Dernière à Marienbad, L', 1961 W
Annie Hall, 1977 W
Aparajito, 1956 W
As You Like It, 1936 W
Ashes and Diamonds, 1958 W
Atlantic City, My Dinner with Andre, 1981 W
Au Revoir les Enfants, 1988 W
Avventura, L', 1960 W
B'wana Devil, 1953 W
Baby Doll, 1956 W
Back to the Future, 1985 W
Ballet Mécanique, Le, 1924 W
Barton Fink, 1991 W
Batman, 1989 W
Beauté du Diable, La, 1950 W
Beauty and the Beast, 1991 W
Becky Sharp, 1935 W
Belle et la Bête, La, 1946 W
Belle Noiseuse, Le, 1991 W
Ben Hur, 1926 W
Best Intentions, The, 1992 W
Best Years of Our Lives, The, 1946 W
Betty Blue, 1986 W
Bicycle Thieves, 1948 W
Big Chill, The, 1983 W
Big House, The, 1930 W
Big Store, The, 1941 W
Birds, The, 1962 W
Birth of a Nation, 1915 W
Bitter Tears of Petra Von Kant, The, 1972 W
Black Orpheus, 1960 W
Bladerunner, 1982 W
Blue Angel, The, 1930 W
Blue Light, The, 1932 W
Blue Velvet, 1986 W
Bonjour Tristesse, 1957 W
Bonnie and Clyde, 1967 W
Breakfast at Tiffany's, 1961 W
Bridge on the River Kwai, The, 1957 W
Bull-Dog Drummond, 1929 W
Butch Cassidy and the Sundance Kid, 1969 W
Cabaret, 1972 W
Cabinet of Dr. Caligari, The, 1920 W
Camille, 1937 W
Canterbury Tales, The, 1973 W
Cardinal, The, 1963 W
Carmen, 1909 W, 1915 W
Carnal Knowledge, 1971 W
Cavalcade, 1933 W
Celine and Julie Go Boating, 1974 W
Charade, 1963 W
Chariots of Fire, 1981 W
Child of the Ghetto, A, 1910 W
Chinatown, 1974 W
Cid, El, 1961 W
Cinema Paradiso, 1990 W
Circus, 1928 W
Citizen Kane, 1941 W
City Lights, 1931 W
City of Sorrows, 1990 W
Cleopatra, 1962 W
Cleopatra, 1963 W
Clockwork Orange, A, 1971 W
Close Encounters of the Third Kind, 1977 W
Coastal Command, 1942 W
Collector, The, 1965 W
Colonel Blimp, 1943 W
Colonel Redl, 1985 W
Congress Dances, The, 1931 W
Co-optimists, The, 1929 W
Court Jester, The, 1955 W
Cranes Are Flying, The, 1957 W
Crimes and Misdemeanours, 1989 W
Cyrano de Bergerac, 1935 W
Cyrano de Bergerac, 1990 W
Dance from the Volcano, 1938 W
Danton, 1983 W
David Copperfield, 1935 W
Dawn Patrol, The, 1939 W
Day for Night, 1973 W
Day in the New World, A, 1940 W
Dead Ringers, 1988 W
Death in Venice, 1971 W
Death of a Cyclist, 1955 W
Death of a Princess, 1980 R
Decameron, The, 1972 W
Deer Hunter, The, 1978 W
Dekalog, 1988 W
Delicatessen, 1991 W
Derrière la Façade, 1940 W
Diaboliques, Les, 1954 W
Diesel, 1942 W
Dirty Dozen, The, 1967 W
Discreet Charm of the Bourgeoisie, The, 1972 W
Diva, 1981 W
Divided Heart, The, 1954 W
Do the Right Thing, 1989 W
Dr. Mabuse, 1922 W
Dr. Strangelove, 1964 W
Dr. Who and the Daleks, 1965 W
Dog Day Afternoon, 1975 W
Dog's Life, A, 1918 W
Dolce Vita, La, 1960 W
Don Juan, 1926 W
Don't Look Now, 1973 W
Dona Herlinda and her Son, 1986 W
Double Life of Veronique, The, 1991 W
Edge of the World, The, 1937 W
Elektra, 1961 W
Elephant Man, 1980 W
Emil and the Detectives, 1931 W
Enfants terribles, Les, 1949 W
Enter the Dragon, 1973 W
Entertainer, The, 1960 W
ET, 1982 W
Europa Europa, 1991 W
Evening Visitor, The, 1942 W
Everyman for Himself and God Against All, 1975 W
Exodus, 1960 W
Fall of Troy, The, 1911 W
Fallen Idol, The, 1948 W
Fanny and Alexander, 1982 W
Fantasia, 1940 W
Far from the Madding Crowd, 1967 W
Farewell to Arms, A, 1932 W
Fatal Attraction, 1987 W
Faust, 1910 W
Fear Eats the Soul, 1973 W
First of the Few, The, 1941 W
Fish Called Wanda, A, 1988 W
Fitzcarraldo, 1982 W
Five Easy Pieces, 1970 W
Foma Gordeyev, 1959 W

For Whom the Bell Tolls, 1943 W
Forgotten Men, 1934 W
Forgotten Village, The, 1944 W
Forty-Ninth Parallel, 1941 W
Four Chimneys, 1953 W
Frankenstein, 1931 W
French Connection, The, 1971 W
French Lieutenant's Woman, The, 1981 W
Friedmann Bach, 1941 W
From Here to Eternity, 1953 W
Gandhi, 1982 W
Garden of the Finzi-Continis, The, 1971 W
Gaslight, 1940 W
Generallinie, Die, 1929 W
Generation, A, 1954 W
Gentler Sex, The, 1943 W
Georgy Girl, 1966 W
Getting of Wisdom, The, 1979 W
Gigi, 1959 W
Glorious Adventure, 1922 W
Go-Between, The, 1971 W
Godfather, The, 1972 W
Godfather II, 1974 W
Gold Rush, The, 1925 W
Goldfinger, 1964 W
Gone With the Wind, 1939 W
Good, The Bad and The Ugly, The, 1968 W
Goodbye Mr. Chipps, 1939 W
Graduate, The, 1968 W
Grand Hotel, 1932 W
Grandes Manoeuvres, Les, 1955 W
Grasshopper, The, 1955 W
Great Dictator, The, 1940 W
Great Expectations, 1946 W
Great Illusion, The, 1937 W
Great Train Robbery, The, 1905 W
Great Well, The, 1924 W
Great Ziegfeld, The, 1936 W
Greed, 1925 W
Hallelujah, 1930 W
Hamlet, 1948 W
Hannah and her Sisters, 1986 W
Hard Day's Night, A, 1964 W
Heaven's Gate, 1980 W
Hedda Gabler, 1919 W
Hell's Angels, 1930 W
Help! 1965 W
Henry V, 1944 W
Hiroshima Mon Amour, 1959 W
Holiday Inn, 1942 W
How Green Was My Valley, 1942 W
How the West Was Won, 1962 W
Howard's End, 1992 W
Hunger! Hunger! Hunger! 1921 W
I Vitelloni, 1953 W
I.N.R.I., 1923 W
If..., 1968 W
In the Heat of the Night, 1968 W
Irma La Douce, 1963 W
Iron Horse, The, 1924 W
It Always Rains on Sunday, 1947 W
It's A Wonderful World, 1946 W
Ivan the Terrible, 1945 W
Jane Eyre, 1943 W
Jaws, 1975 W
Jean de Florette, 1986 W
Jesus of Montreal, 1990 W
Journey's End, 1930 W
Jules et Jim, 1961 W
Julius Caesar, 1907 W
Juno and the Paycock, 1929 W
Justice is Coming, 1944 W
Kagemusha, 1980 W
Kes, 1970 W
Kid, The, 1921 W
Kind of Loving, A, 1962 W
King and I, The, 1956 W
King in New York, A, 1957 W
King Kong, 1933 W
King of Kings, 1927 W
Kings of the Road, 1976 W
Kipps, 1941 W
Kiss of the Spider Woman, 1985 W
Knack, The, 1965 W
Lacombe Lucien, 1974 W
Lady Vanishes, The, 1938 W
Lady With the Little Dog, The, 1960 W
Lamb, The, 1915 W
Last Days of Pompeii, The, 1926 W
Last Emperor, The, 1987 W
Last Millionaire, The, 1934 W
Last of the Mohicans, The, 1922 W
Last Tango in Paris, 1973 W, 1974 W, 1987 W
Last Temptation of Christ, The, 1988 R, 1988 W
Last Waltz, The, 1977 W
Lawrence of Arabia, 1962 W
Leopard, The, 1963 W
Lifeboat, 1944 W
Limelight, 1952 W
Little American, The, 1917 W
Little Angel, The, 1914 W
Lives of Bengal Lancer, 1935 W
Local Hero, 1983 W
Look Back in Anger, 1959 W
Lord of the Flies, 1964 W
Lost Horizon, The, 1937 W
Lost Week-end, The, 1945 W
Love on the Dole, 1923 W
Love Parade, The, 1929 W
Love Story, 1970 W
Love, 1927 W
Loveletter, 1942 W
Lucrezia Borgia, 1910 W
M, 1931 W
Mad Max, 1979 W
Madame Dubarry, 1919 W
Mädchen in Uniform, 1931 W
Making a Living, 1914 W
Malcolm X, 1992 W
Man and a Woman, A, 1966 W
Man for All Seasons, A, 1966 W
Man from the South, The, 1945 W
Man of Iron, 1981 W
Manchurian Candidate, The, 1962 W
Marathon Man, 1976 W
Mater dolorosa, 1917 W
Maternelle, La, 1932 W
Mean Streets, 1973 W
Messalina, 1910 W
Metropolis, 1926 W
Midnight Cowboy, 1969 W
Midnight Express, 1978 W
Mr. Deeds Comes to Town, 1936 W
Mrs. Miniver, 1942 W
Million, The, 1931 W
Miracle in Milan, 1951 W
Miracle of the Wolves, 1925 W
Modern Times, 1936 W
Mon Oncle, 1958 W
Monsieur Verdoux, 1947 W
Monty Python's Life of Brian, 1979 W
Morning Glory, 1932 W
Mother, The, 1920 W
Moulin Rouge, 1952 W
Murder, 1930 W
Muriel, 1964 W
My Beautiful Laundrette, 1986 W
My Brilliant Career, 1980 W
My Left Foot, 1989 W
Mystère Picasso, Le, 1955 W
Mystery Man, The, 1919 W
Naked City, The, 1948 W
Nana, 1926 W
Norte, El, 1983 W
Nostalgia, 1984 W
Notte, La, 1961 W
Nous les Gosses, 1941 W
Nuit et Brouillard, 1956 W
O Lucky Man, 1973 W
October, 1928 W
Odd Man Out, 1947 W
Oh! What a Lovely War, 1969 W
On Golden Pond, 1981 W
On the Waterfront, 1954 W
One Day of War, 1943 W
One Flew Over the Cuckoo's Nest, 1975 W
Only Way, The, 1925 W
Ordinary People, 1980 W
Orlando, 1992 W
Orphée, 1950 W
Othello, 1952 W
Our Man in Havana, 1959 W
Out of Africa, 1985 W
Outcast of the Islands, 1951 W
Outlaw Josey Wales, The, 1976 W
Owd Bob, 1925 W
Padre Padrone, 1977 W
Paisa, 1946 W
Pandora's Box, 1929 W
Paris, Texas, 1984 W
Passage to India,A, 1984 W
Passenger, The, 1964 W
Passion, 1982 W
Pather Panchali, 1955 W
Patriot, The, 1928 W
Payday, 1922 W
Pelle the Conqueror, 1987 W
Phaedra, 1962 W
Pharaoh's Wife, 1922 W
Pickpocket, 1959 W
Pilgrim, The, 1923 W
Pinocchio, 1911 W
Plaisir, 1951 W
Planet of the Apes, 1968 W
Platoon, 1986 W
Player, The, 1992 W
Polyanna, 1920 W
Porte des Lilas, 1957 W
Portes de la Nuit, Les, 1946 W
Postmaster, The, 1940 W
Prince and the Showgirl, The, 1957 W
Private Life of Henry VIII, 1933 W
Psycho, 1960 W
Public Opinion, 1923 W
Pumpkin Eater, The, 1964 W
Pygmalion, 1938 W
Quai des Orfèvres, 1947 W
Quatorze Juli, 1933 W
Queen Christina, 1933 W
Queen Elizabeth, 1912 W
Quiet Flows the Don, 1957 W
Quiet Man, The, 1952 W
Quo Vadis? 1912 W
Raging Bull, 1980 W
Rain Man, 1988 W
Ran, 1985 W
Rashomon, 1950 W
Rear Window, 1954 W
Rebecca, 1940 W
Rebel Without a Cause, 1955 W
Rembrandt, 1942 W
Return of Martin Guerre, The, 1982 W
Reveille, 1924 W
Rhapsody in Blue, 1945 W
Rickshaw Man, The, 1959 W

Rio Bravo, 1959 W
Rio Grande, 1950 W
Robe, The, 1953 W
Robin Hood, 1923 W
Rocco and his Brothers, 1960 W
Rock Around the Clock, 1955 W
Rocky, 1976 W
Roman Holiday, 1953 W
Rome, Open City, 1945 W
Ronde, La, 1950 W
Rue Cases Negres, 1983 W
Rules of the Game, The, 1939 W
Running Man, The, 1963 W
Sacrifice, 1986 W
Safety First, 1923 W
Sally in Our Alley, 1931 W
Saturday Night and Sunday Morning, 1960 W
Satyricon, 1969 W
Scarlet Pimpernel, The, 1934 W
Sebastiane, 1976 W
Seven Samurai, The, 1954 W
Seventh Seal, The, 1956 W
Sex, Lies and Videotape, 1989 W
Shadows, 1960 W
Shanghai Express, 1932 W
She Done Him Wrong, 1933 W
Shining, The, 1980 W
Shoeshine, 1946 W
Shoulder Arms, 1918 W
Silence, The, 1964 W
Silence est d'or, Le, 1947 W
Silence of the Lambs, 1991 W
Silken Skin, 1964 W
Skyscraper, 1923 W
Smiles of a Summer Night, 1955 W
Snow White and the Seven Dwarfs, 1938 W
Sous les Toits de Paris, 1930 W
Spartacus, 1911 W
Squaw Man, The, 1913 W
Stage-Door Canteen, 1943 W
Stagecoach, 1939 W
Stalingrad, 1943 W
Star is Born, A, 1937 W
Star Wars, 1977 W
State of the Union, The, 1948 W
Strada, La, 1954 W
Strangers on a Train, 1951 W
Strictly Ballroom, 1992 W
Student of Prague, The, 1913 W
Summer Light, 1943 W
Summer with Monika, 1952 W
Sunday Bloody Sunday, 1971 W
Sunday in August, 1950 W
Sunday in the Country, A, 1984 W
Sunset Boulevard, 1950 W
Superman, 1978 W
Taste of Honey, A, 1961 W
Ten Commandments, The, 1924 W
Terminator, 1984 W
Terminator 2, 1991 W
Testament d'Orphée, Le, 1959 W
Testament of Dr. Mabuse, The, 1933 W
That Obscure Object of Desire, 1977 W
Thelma and Louise, 1991 W
Theorem, 1969 W
Thin Man, The, 1934 W
Things to Come, 1936 W
Third Man, The, 1949 W
This is Cinerama, 1952 W
Tom Jones, 1963 W
Toni, 1935 W
Top Hat, 1935 W
Touch of Evil, 1958 W
Tout les Matins du Monde, 1992 W
Town Like Alice, A, 1956 W
Trader Horn, 1931 W
Trial, The, 1962 W
Tricheurs, Les, 1958 W
Tunnel Under the Canal, The, 1907 W
2001, A Space Odyssey, 1968 W
Underworld, 1927 W
Untouchables, The, 1987 W
Vampire, The, 1913 W
Veritas Vincit, 1918 W
Vertigo, 1958 W
Voyage in Italy, 1954 W
Wall Street, 1987 W
Wanderer of the Wasteland, 1924 W
Way Ahead, The, 1944 W
Whistle Down The Wind, 1961 W
White Christmas, 1954 W
White Cliffs of Dover, The, 1944 W
Whooping Cough, 1987 W
Wild Birds, 1955 W
Wild Bunch, The, 1969 W
Wild Strawberries, 1957 W
Wind Cannot Read, The, 1958 W
Wings of Desire, 1987 W
Winslow Boy, The, 1949 W
Winter Light, 1962 W
Woman in the Moon, The, 1928 W
Woman of Paris, A, 1923 W
Women in Love, 1969 W
World of Apu, The, 1959 W
Yol, 1981 W
Z, 1969 W
Zeebrugge, 1924 W
Zola, 1944 W
Finch-Hatton, George Williams, Earl of Winchilsea (1791–1858), 1829 C
Fine Arts, 1805 S, 1961 S, 1882 O, 1900 S
Fingerprints, 1885 P, 1890 O
Fink, Uwe, astronomer, 1980 P
Finland: invaded by Sweden, 1788 F; Russian territory in, 1790 H; Russian aggression in, 1807 G, 1812 D; liberties suppressed, 1899 B; Republic proclaimed, 1917 M; signs peace with Central Powers, 1918 C; Russia invades, 1939 C; Russian offensive against, 1944 F, J
East Germany recognized, 1972 L
divorce statistics, 1987 Y
life expectancy, 1990 Y
illegitimacy rate, 1991 Y
votes to apply for E.C. membership, 1992 C
Finley, Moses I, Am. historian (1912–86), 1973 Q
Finnegans Wake (J. Joyce), 1939 U
Finno-Karelian Republic, incorporated in USSR, 1956 G
Finzi, Gerald, B. musician (1901–1956), 1949 T
Fire Next Time, The (J. Baldwin), 1963 U
Fire, studies in, 1824 P
Fires, notable:
Bradford City soccer stadium, 1985 X
Crystal Palace, 1936 S
Hofburg, Vienna, 1992 L
Houses of Parliament, 1834 K
King's Cross Underground Station, 1987 L
Lisbon, 1988 H
Manchester Airport, 1985 H
Paris Bourse, 1968 E
Reichstag, 1933 B
Windsor Castle, 1992 L
First Lines of the Practice of Physic (W. Cullen), 1774 P
First Principles (H. Spencer), 1862 O
First World War, The: An Agrarian Interpretation (A. Offer), 1989 Q
Fischer, Abram, S. Afr. lawyer, 1964 L
Fischer, Bobby, Am. chess champion (b. 1943), 1972 X, 1975 X
Fischer, Emil, G. chemist (1852–1919), 1852 Z, 1887 P, 1907 P, 1919 Z
Fischer, Kuno, G. philosopher (1824–1907), 1852 R
Fisher, Andrew, Aus. Labour politician (1862–1928), 1908 E, 1911 B
Fisher, Geoffrey Francis, B. churchman (1887–1972), Archbishop of Canterbury, 1960 R, 1961 A
Fisher, Herbert Albert Laurens, B. historian and Liberal statesman (1865–1940), 1865 Z, 1918 H, 1936 Q, 1940 Z
Fisher, Irving, Am. economist (1867–1948), 1910 O, 1919 O
Fisher, James, scientist, 1969 P
Fisher, John, lord Fisher, B. admiral (1841–1920), 1841 Z, 1920 Z; as First Lord of Admiralty, 1914 K; resigns over Dardanelles policy, 1915 E
Fisheries, 'Cod War':
Anglo-Icelandic talks on fisheries dispute, 1972 L
Iceland shells British trawler *Everton*, 1973 E
escalation, 1973 F
Icelandic diplomatic relations threat, 1973 J
ends, 1973 K
starts again when Iceland increases territorial waters, 1975 J, K
British frigates protect trawlers in Icelandic waters, 1975 L
first shots fired, 1975 M
diplomatic relations broken off, 1976 B
Icelandic gunboat attacks British trawler, 1976 E
ends with agreement, 1976 F
Fisheries:
Bering Sea Seal, 1892 B
Danish trawlers banned from British waters, 1983 A
Icelandic, 1958 F, J, 1961 B
International Whaling Commission, 1982 G
in France, campaign for government aid, 1980 H
Newfoundland, 1763 B
US–Canadian agreement on, 1925 B
Fitch, John, Am. inventor (1743–98), 1787 P
FitzGerald, Dr. Garret, Prime Minister of Eire (b. 1926), 1926 Z, 1981 F, 1982 M
Anglo-Irish agreement, 1981 L
Fitzgerald, Edward, B. poet and translator (1809–83), 1809 W, 1859 U, 1883 Z
Fitzgerald, F. Scott, Am. author (1896–1940), 1923 U, 1925 U, 1934 U, 1941 U
Fiume, Italy: d'Annunzio attempts seizure, 1919 J; independence, 1919 M, 1920 L; agreement on, 1921 F; Italy annexes, 1924 C
Five Checks to Antinomianism (J. W. Fletcher), 1771 R
Five Great Monarchies of the Ancient Eastern World (H. Rawlinson), 1862 Q
Five Modular Units (Lewitt), 1970 S
Fixx, James Fuller, Am. author and jogger (1932–84), 1984 G
Fizeau, Armand Hippolyte Louis, F. physicist (1819–96), 1849 P
Flagg, Ernest, Am. architect (1857–1939), 1905 S
Flamandes, Les (E. Verhaeren), 1883 U
Flanagan, Barry, B. sculptor (b. 1941), 1968 S, 1973 S, 1978 S, 1982 S
Flandin, Pierre, F. Radical politician, 1934 L, 1935 E
Flannery, Kent Vaughan, Am. anthropologist, 1966 Q
Flare Path (T. Rattigan), 1942 W
Flash-light photography, 1898 P

Flaubert, Gustave, F. author (1821–80), 1821 Z, 1856 U, 1862 U, 1869 U, 1874 U, 1880 Z, 1881 U
Flaubert's Parrot (J. Barnes), 1985 U
Flavin, Dan, Am. sculptor (b. 1933), 1969 S
Flax, machine for spinning, 1812 P
Flaxman, John, B. designer and sculptor (1755–1826), 1775 S, 1824 S
Flecker, James Elroy, B. poet (1884–1915), 1884 Z, 1915 W, 1923 W
Fleet Air Arm, British, increase in, 1936 C
Flegeljahre (Jean Paul); 1804 U
Fleischmann, Martin, B. physicist (b. 1927), 1989 P
Fleming Report on independent schools, 1944 O
Fleming, Sir Alexander, B. scientist (1881–1955), 1881 Z, 1928 P, 1934 P, 1955 Z
Fleming, Ian Lancaster, B. author (1908–64), 1908 Z, 1953 U, 1964 Z
Flemish language, 1870 O; admitted in courts of Flanders, 1873 N; becomes official language of Flanders, 1932 G; campaign against French-speakers at University of Louvain brings down government, 1968 B; Flemish extremists make gains in Belgian election, 1991 L
Fletcher, Anthony John, B. historian (b. 1941), 1981 Q
Fletcher, John William, B. divine (1729–85), 1771 R
Fletcher, Yvonne, B. policewoman, 1984 D
Fleure, Herbert John, B. zoologist (1877–1969), 1948 P
Fleurs du Mal, Les (Baudelaire), 1857 U
Fleurus, S.W. Belgium, battle, 1794 F
Flights. *See* Aeronautics; Aeroplanes; Space
Flinders, Matthew, B. naval officer (1774–1814), 1774 Z
Floating World, The (J. Romeril), 1974 W
Flogging, in British forces, abolished, 1881 O
Flood, Henry, Ir. statesman (1732–91), 1779 M
Floods:
- Bangladesh, 1974 H, 1988 H
- China, 1991 G
- China, Szechuan province, 1981 G
- East Pakistan, 1970 L
- England, 1968 J
- Florence, 1966 S
- France, 1992 J
- Italy, 1966 L, S
- Philippines, 1991 L
- Roumania, 1970 E
- Sudan, 1988 H

Floquet, Charles Thomas, F. Republican (1828–96), 1888 Q
Florence, Italy: peace of, 1801 C; becomes Italian capital, 1864 J; riots in, 1921 B; Eighth Army takes, 1944 H; floods, 1966 S
Florey, Sir Howard Walter, Lord Florey of Adelaide, Austral. scientist (1898–1968), 1898 Z, 1940 P, 1968 Z
Florida, State, US: as a British colony, 1763 B, K; Spanish claims to, 1779 F; Spanish conquest of, 1782 F; restored to Spain, 1783 J; US boundary with, 1795 K; US obtains from Spain, 1819 B; becomes a US State, 1845 C; as a Confederate State, 1861 B; hurricane Andrew, 1992 H
Florin, the, introduced, 1854 O
Flotow, Friedrich von, G. musician (1812–83), 1847 T
Flowering Cherry, The (R. Bolt), 1957 W
Flowers and Salome (Lindsay Kemp Company), 1977 W
Fluorescent lamps, 1927 P
Fluorine, preparation of, 1886 P
Flushing, Holland, liberated, 1944 L
Fly Leaves (C. S. Calverley), 1872 U
Flying-bombs, 1944 F; launching sites for, 1944 J
'Flying-saucers', 1955 P
'Flying-spot' microscope, 1951 P
Fo, Dario, It. playwright (b. 1926), 1970 W, 1974 W
Foch, Ferdinand, F. soldier (1851–1929), 1851 Z, 1929 Z; as French Chief of Staff, 1917 E; as united commander on Western Front, 1918 C
Focshani, Rumania, Turkish defeat at, 1789 G
Fogazzaro, Antonio, It. author (1842–1911), 1842 Z, 1874 O, 1911 Z
Fogel, Robert, Am. historian (b. 1926), 1974 Q
Foinavon, racehorse, 1967 X
Fokine, Michael, R. dancer and choreographer (1880–1942), 1909 T
Fokker, Anthony, G. aircraft designer (1890–1939), 1890 Z, 1939 Z
Folklore, German, 1778 U, 1810 R
Follette, Robert La, Am. Republican politician (1855–1925), 1911 A, 1915 O; as Progressive presidential candidate, 1924 L
Foma Gordeyev (M. Gorki), 1899 U
Fommenah, Ghana, treaty of, 1874 B
Fonseca, Manoel Deodoro da, Brazil, general, 1891 L
Fontainebleau, France:
- Treaty, abrogates Barrier Treaty, 1715, 1784 K
- Treaty, between France and Spain against Portugal, 1807 K
- decree, for confiscating British goods, 1810 K
- EC summit, 1984 F

Fontane, Theodor, G. author (1818–98), 1878 U
Fonteyn, Margot. *See* Arias, Margot Fonteyn de
Food:
- canned, 1874 P, 1880 P, 1892 P
- frozen, 1925 P
- legislation relating to, British, 1860 O, 1875 O
  - American, 1898 O, 1906 O, 1917 G
- shortages and rationing, in Britain, 1918 O
  - in France, 1916 O
  - in Germany, 1916 O, 1917 D
  - in India, 1966 C, 1974 C
- US grain sales to USSR, 1972 G, 1983 D
- in Poland, 1970 M, 1980 M, 1981 D, G, H
  - Gdansk curfew following riots, 1982 A
  - price increases, 1982 A

Food Kitchens, 1918 O
Fool for Love (S. Shepard), 1983 W
Fool of Quality, The (H. Brooke), 1765 U
Fools of Fortune (W. Trevor), 1984 U
Foot, Hugh, lord Caradon, B. administrator and diplomat (1907–90), as governor of Cyprus, 1957 K; resigns as Britain's representative to U.N., 1962 K
Foot, Michael Mackintosh, B. Labour politician (b. 1913)
- Secretary for Employment, 1974 C
- Party leadership, 1976 C, 1980 L, 1983 F

Foot, Michael Richard Daniell, B. historian (b. 1919), 1968 Q
Foot-and-mouth epidemic, B., 1967 K
Football, Association, in Britain, 1863 X
- F.A. Cup, 1871 X
  - at Wembley, 1923 X
- first international match, 1872 W
- League, 1888 X
- Players convicted of fixing matches, 1965 X

For Coloured Girls who have Considered Suicide when the Rainbow is enuf (N. Shange), 1974 W
For Those Who Have ears (R. Deacon), 1983 S
For Whom the Bell Tolls (E. Hemingway), 1940 U
For the Sake of Heaven (M. Buber), 1945 R
Foraker, Joseph Benson, Am. Republican (1846–1917), 1900 E
Forbes, George W., New Zealand United Party leader, 1930 E
Forbes-Robertson, Sir Johnston, B. actor (1853–1937), 1897 W
Force of Habit, The (T. Berhard), 1974 W
Forced labour, of Belgians deported to Germany, 1916 L
Forcellini, Egidio, It. classical scholar (1688–1768), 1769 Q, 1771 Q
Ford Foundation, 1936 O
Ford Motor Company:
- strikes, 1969 B, 1978 J
- pay offer breaches pay policy, 1978 L
- commercial sanctions against, voted down in Parliament, 1978 M
- in US, fined for installing dangerous fuel tanks, 1978 O

Ford, Ford Madox (F. M. Hueffer), B. author and editor (1873–1939), 1873 Z, 1908 V, 1924 V, 1939 Z
Ford, Gerald Rudolph, Am. statesman, Republican (b. 1913), 38th President of US (1974–77), 1913 Z
- Vice-President, 1973 M
- Presidential victory, 1974 H
- pardons Nixon, 1974 J
- discusses arms control with Brezhnev, 1974 L
- State of the Union address, 1975 A
- renomination at Republican convention, 1976 H
- declaration on Eastern Europe, 1976 K

Ford, Henry, Am. motor-car manufacturer (1863–1947), 1863 Z, 1909 P, 1913 P, 1947 Z
Ford, John (born Sean Aloysius O'Fearna), Am. film director (1895–1973), 1895 Z, 1924 W, 1950 W, 1952 W, 1962 W, 1973 Z
Foreign Service, British, amalgamation of overseas staffs of Foreign Office and Commonwealth Relations Office, 1964 B, 1965 A
Foreign investments, statistics of comparative, 1914 Y
Foreman, George, Am. boxer (b. 1948), 1973 X
Foreskin's Lament (G. McGee), 1980 W
Forests, US National Commission, 1906 O
Forever Amber (K. Winsor), 1945 U
Forgery, notable, 1789 R
Forman, Milos, Am. film director (b. 1932), 1932 Z, 1975 W
Formosa (or Taiwan), S.E. China: rebellion in, 1787 N; ceded to Japan, 1895 D; China renounces sovereignty over, 1945 J; Chiang Kai-shek removes to, 1949 G, 1954 K; Britain supports US plan for, 1958 J
Formulary, National War, 1941 P
Fors Claviger (J. Ruskin), 1871 O
Forster, Edward Morgan, B. author (1879–1970), 1879 Z, 1908 U, 1910 U, 1924 U, 1970 Z
Forster, William Edward, B. Liberal statesman (1818–86), 1818 Z, 1870 O, 1886 Z
Forsyte Saga, The, television series, 1967 W
Forsyth, Bill, B. film director (b. 1947), 1983 W
Forsyth, Frederick, B. author (b. 1938), 1972 U
Fort Clark, N. Carolina, US, captured by Unionists, 1861 H
Fort Donelson, Tenn., US, taken by Grant, 1862 B
Fort Henry, Tenn., US, taken by Grant, 1862 B
Fort Hudson, Missouri, US, surrenders to Unionists, 1863 G
Fort Lee, New Jersey, US, 1776 L
Fort St. George, Canada, 1813 E

Fort Sumpter, in Charleston Harbour, S. Carolina, US, 1861 D
Fort Ticonderoga, New York, US, 1775 E
Fort Worth, Tex., US, Kimbell Art Museum, 1972 S
Forth Bridge, Scotland, 1890 P, 1964 P
Fortification, study of, 1810 O
Forty Years On (A. Bennett), 1968 W
Forty-Second Parallel (J. Dos Passos), 1930 U
Forty-hour week, in France, 1936 F
Forty-ninth parallel, as Canadian–US frontier, 1818 K
Forzano, Giovacchino, It. politician, 1931 O
Foscani, Italy: taken by Austrians, 1917 A; German offensive, 1917 H, M
Foscolo, Ugo, Niccolo Ugo, It. author (1778–1827), 1778 Z, 1797 W, 1798 U, 1807 U, 1827 Z
Fosse, Bob (Robert Louis), Am. film director (1927–87), 1972 W
Fossils, study of, 1837 P, 1846 P, 1962 P
Foster Associates, Willis, Faber, architects, 1975 S
Foster, Sir Norman, B. architect (b. 1935), 1935 Z, 1978 S, 1985 S, 1986 S, 1991 S
Foucault, Michel, F. philosopher (1926–84), 1926 Z, 1968 R, 1975 R, 1984 Z
Fouché, Joseph, duc de Otranto, F. politician (1763–1820), 1800 W
Foulness, Essex, England, proposed airport, 1971 D
Foundation's Edge (I. Asimov), 1983 U
Foundations of Belief, The (A. J. Balfour), 1895 R
Foundations of Empirical Knowledge (A. J. Ayer), 1940 R
Foundations of Political Economy (Cohn), 1885 O
Foundations of Psychology (Waitz), 1846 R
Foundations of the XIXth Century (H. S. Chamberlain), 1899 O
Foundations:
- Balzan International, 1964 B
- Carnegie Peace, 1911 O
- Ford, projects sponsored by, 1955 O
- Nuffield, 1943 O
- Pahlavi, 1961 K

Foundations: a Statement of Christian Belief ... (ed. Streeter), 1912 R
Fountain, The (C. Morgan), 1932 U
Fouqué, Friedrich Heinrich, Freiherr de la Motte, G. author (1777–1843), 1811 U
Four Essays on Liberty (I. Berlin), 1969 R
Four Horsemen of the Apocalypse, The (Ibáñez), 1919 U
Four Quartets (T. S. Eliot), 1944 U
Four-dimensional geometry, 1908 P
Four-minute mile, 1954 X
Fournier de Pescay, François, F. medical practitioner and scientific author (1771–1833), 1822 P
Fournier, Henri. *See* Alain-Fournier
Fourteen sonnets written chiefly on picturesque spots (W. Bowles), 1789 U
Fowles, John, B. author (b. 1926), 1966 U, 1969 U
Fox, Charles James, B. Whig politician (1749–1806), 1782 C, E, G, 1790 C, 1806 J; coalition with North, 1783 D, M; supports Parliamentary Reform, 1783 E; India Bill, 1783 M; welcomes French Revolution, 1790 B; leads Whig rump, 1794 G; excluded from Pitt's cabinet, 1804 E; becomes foreign secretary, 1806 B
Fox, Henry, baron Holland, B. Whig politician (1705–74), 1763 D
Fragment on Government, A (J. Bentham), 1776 O
Fragonard, Jean Honoré, F. artist (1733–1806), 1766 S, 1776 S, 1806 Z
Frampton, Sir George, B. architect and sculptor (1860–1928), 1912 S
Françaix, Jean, F. musician (b. 1912), 1957 T
France and England in the New World (F. Parkman), 1865 Q
France, 1848–1948, Vol. I (T. Zeldin), 1973 Q
France, Anatole. *See* Thibaut, J. A. A.
France:
- botanical survey, 1813 P
- geological map, 1841 P
- frontier with Spain, 1856 M
- student unrest, 1968 E
- population, 1971 Y, 1981 Y, 1991 Y
- neutron bomb capability, 1980 F
- Chad civil war, 1983 H, L
- agrees to withdraw forces from Chad, 1984 J
- urbanization, 1985 Y
- divorce statistics, 1987 Y
- Kanak separatists, New Caladonia, 1988 D
- 200th anniversary of French Revolution celebrated, 1989 G
- life expectancy, 1990 Y
- illegitimacy rate, 1991 Y
- floods, 1992 J
- Maastricht Treaty, 1992 J

Francesca da Rimini (G. D'Annunzio), 1902 W
Francesca da Rimini (S. Pellico), 1855 W
Franchini, Gio Franco, architect, 1977 S
Franchise, The:
- in Australia, for women, 1902 G
- in Austria, reformed, 1873 D
  - problem of women's, 1893 K
  - universal, 1907 A
- in Belgium, universal male, demanded, 1885 N; achieved, 1893 O
  - women's, 1948 O
- in Britain, attempts to widen, 1810 E, 1811 O, 1818 F, 1831 C, J
  - removal of Roman Catholic disabilities, 1829 D
  - widened by First Reform Bill, 1832 F
  - antiquated forms, eliminated, 1832 F
  - Chartists demand manhood, 1838 O
  - assimilation of county and borough, motion for, 1851 B
  - extended, 1867 D, 1884 M
  - plural voting abolished, 1891 K
  - for women, bills rejected, 1912 C, 1913 E, 1914 E
    - by-election on issue of, 1912 L
    - Suffragette demonstrations, 1913 A, D, 1914 C
    - at age of thirty, 1918 O
    - at age of twenty-one, 1928 E
  - abolition of university seats, 1948 O
  - reduction in age of majority, 1967 O, 1969 O
- in Denmark, women's 1915 F
  - age limit reduced, 1953 C
- in France, limited, 1817 B
  - electoral colleges regulated, 1820 F
  - plural voting introduced, 1820 F
  - extension, demanded, 1847 G
  - universal, 1848 E, L; abolished, 1850 E
  - women's, 1945 O
- in Germany:
  - universal, promised in Prussia, 1917 D
  - women's 1919 O
- in Holland, reformed, 1887 F
  - widened, 1896 F
  - proportional representation adopted, 1899 M
- in Hungary, universal, 1906 G
- in Italy, extended, 1881 N
  - reformed, 1882 A
  - reduced, 1928 E
  - women's, 1946 O
- in Japan, extended, 1925 C
- in Liechtenstein
  - women allowed to vote in elections to National Diet, 1986 O
- in New Zealand, manhood, 1889 N
  - women's, 1893 O
- in Northern Ireland, 1968 L, 1969 D
- in Norway, 1907 F
- in Russia, for propertied classes, 1907 F
- in S. Africa, controversy in Transvaal, 1899 C, G
  - for white women, 1930 E
  - law commission calls for universal, 1989 O
- in Spain, universal, 1890 C
- in Sweden, proportional representation, 1911 J
- in Switzerland, women ineligible to vote in federal elections, 1959 B
- in Turkey, women's 1934 M
- in US:
  - rights of Negro voters, attempts to protect, 1890 F
    - safeguarded by Civil Rights Bill, 1960 D
  - women's adopted in Arizona, Kansas and Wisconsin, 1912 L
    - proposal for, defeated, 1915 A
    - achieved, by 19th Amendment, 1920 H

Francis Ferdinand, archduke of Austria, assassinated, 1914 F
Francis I, Holy Roman Emperor (1745–65), 1765 H
Francis I, of Naples, King of the Two Sicilies (1825–1830), 1825 A, 1830 L
Francis II, Holy Roman Emperor (1792–1806), emperor of Austria (1804–35), 1792 C, 1804 H, 1809 B, 1835 C; resigns as Holy Roman Emperor, 1806 H
Francis II, King of the Two Sicilies (1859), 1859 E; flees, 1860 J; surrenders to Garibaldi, 1861 B
Francis Joseph I, emperor of Austria (1848–1916), 1848 M, 1900 A, 1916 L; concordat with Pius IX, 1855 R; crowned King of Hungary, 1867 F; army reforms, 1903 J
Francis, Trevor, B. soccer player (b. 1954), 1979 X
Franck, César, Belg. musician (1822–95), 1822 Z, 1858 T, 1872 T, 1880 T, 1884 T, 1885 T, 1889 T, 1895 Z
Franco, Francisco, Sp. general and dictator (1892–1975) 1955 L, 1969 A, 1973 F; leads army revolt, 1936 G, H; rebels elect chief of state, 1936 K; recognised by Germany and Italy, 1936 L; begins naval blockade, 1937 L; retakes Teruel, 1938 B; offensive in Catalonia, 1938 M; recognised by powers, 1939 B; Western powers appeal for overthrow of, 1946 L; proposes monarchy on death or resignation, 1947 G, 1957 G
- new Spanish constitution, 1966 L
- Prince Juan Carlos named as successor, 1969 G
- Spanish citizenship offered to all Gibraltarians, 1969 G death, 1975 L

Franco, Jono, Sp. politician, becomes premier, 1906 E
François Charles Joseph, King of Rome, 1811 C
Frank E. Evans, USS, collision with *Melbourne* aircraft carrier, 1969 F
Frankenau, formerly E. Prussia, Germany, 1914 M
Frankenheimer, John, Am. film director, 1962 W
Frankenstein (Mary Shelley), 1818 U
Frankfurt, Declaration of, 1813 M
Frankfurt-am-Main, Germany; Diet at, 1816 L;

Professors discuss Germany's reunification at, 1846 E; Vorparlement meets at, 1848 C; German National Assembly meets at, 1848 E; Princes meet to reform Confederation, 1863 H; annexed by Prussia, 1866 H, J; Franco-German Peace Treaty, 1871 E; French occupation, 1920 D; Museum für Kunsthandwerk, 1985 S
Frankie Goes to Hollywood, B. pop group, 1983 W
Frankland, Sir Edward, B. chemist (1825–99), 1849 P
Franklin, Benjamin, Am. diplomat and inventor (1706–90), 1776 G, 1782 E, L, 1790 Z
Franklin, Sir John, B. Arctic explorer (1786–1847), 1786 Z, 1845 P, 1847 Z; search for, 1850 P
Franks Committee, on reform of Official Secrets Act, 1972 O
Franks, Oliver Sherwell, lord Franks, B. economist and administrator (1905–92), 1947 O, 1960 C
appointed to chair Falklands invasion investigation, 1982 G
Franny and Zooey (J. D. Salinger), 1961 U
Franz Josef Land, discovered, 1873 P
Fraser, Malcolm, Prime Minister of Australia (b. 1930), 1975 L, 1977 M
Frau Sorge (H. Sudermann), 1887 U
Fraudulent mediums, legislation against, 1951 R
Frayn, Michael, B. playwright (b. 1933), 1982 W
Frazer, Sir James George, B. anthropologist (1854–1941), 1854 Z, 1890 Q, 1941 Z
Frazier, Joe, Am. boxer (b. 1944), 1970 X, 1971 X
retains World Heavy-weight title, 1971 X
beaten on points in championship fight, 1975 X
Frears, Stephen Arthur, B. film director (b. 1941), 1986 W
Frederick Augustus, duke of York and of Albany, B. soldier (1763–1827), 1793 J, 1799 J, K
Frederick Christian, renounces Norwegian throne, 1814 H
Frederick II ('The Great'), King of Prussia (1740–1786), 1763 B, O, 1767 D, 1769 H, K, 1770 J, R, 1786 H; as author, 1768 L, 1780 U; role in first Partition of Poland, 1772 H; forms League of German Princes, 1785 G; monument, 1851 S; remains re-interred in Potsdam, 1991 H
Frederick III, emperor of Germany (1888), as Crown Prince, 1870 H; as emperor, 1888 C, F
Frederick VI, of Denmark (1808–39), 1839 M
Frederick VII, of Denmark (1848–63), 1848 A, 1863 L
Frederick William II, of Prussia (1786–97), 1786 H, 1790 F, 1791 G, 1795 D, 1797 L
Frederick William III, of Prussia (1797–1840) 1797 L, 1812 M, 1840 F; open letter to, 1797 O; dismisses Stein, 1807 A; meets Napoleon, 1807 G; declares war on France, 1813 C; promises constitution, 1815 E
Frederick William IV, of Prussia (1840–61), 1840 F, 1850 R, 1861 A; summons Diet, 1847 B; grants constitution, 1848 C; refusal to be elected 'emperor', 1849 C, D; summons Erfurt Parliament, 1850 C; insanity, 1857 K, 1858 K
Frederick the Great (T. Carlyle), 1858 Q
Fredericksburg, Va., US, Lee's victory at, 1862 M
Frederik IX, King of Denmark (1899–1972), 1972 A
Frederikshavn, Treaty of, 1809 J, 1810 A
Free French Government, 1940 H
Committee of National Liberation, 1943 F
Free State, The (D. W. Brogan), 1945 O
Free Trade Association, Latin American, 1961 F
Free Trade:
Austro-German customs union projected, 1931 C
in Britain:
with Ireland, 1780 M
relaxation of navigation laws, 1821 E, 1822 F, 1823 E, G, D, 1825 G, 1894 F, K
Cobden's pamphlet, 1835 O. *See also* Anti-Corn Law League
The Times declares for, 1839 A
budgets, 1842 D, 1845 D
Russell's conversion to, 1845 L
repeal of Corn Laws, 1846 E
Gladstone's budget, 1853 O, 1861 D
treaty with France, 1860 A
in Prussia:
Gentz's plea, 1797 O
internal, 1805 O, 1818 E
'Zollverein', 1819 K, 1826 M, 1818 A, 1829 E, 1833 C, 1835 E
See also Common Market; EFTA; Tariff Questions
Freedom Parties. *See under* Political Parties
Freedom and Organisation (B. Russell), 1934 O
Freedom and Resentment (P.F. Strawson), 1974 R
Freedom from Hunger Campaign, 1960 G
Freedom of Necessity, The (J. D. Bernal), 1949 O
Freedom of Worship, *See* Religious Toleration
Freeman Etudes (J. Cage), 1977 T
Freeman, Edward Augustus, B. historian (1823–92), 1823 Z, 1867 Q, 1892 Z
Freemasonry
Masonic Lodge 'Propaganda 2', Italy, 1981 E
Methodist Conference takes anti-Masonic measures, 1985 R
Frege: Philosophy of Language (M. Dummett), 1973 R
Freiligrath, Ferdinand, G. poet (1810–76), 1846 U
Fréjus, S.E. France, 1799 K
Frémont, John Charles, Am. Republican (1813–90), 1856 L
French Committee of National Liberation, 1943 F
French Equatorial Africa, 1910 A
French Guiana, 1800 M, 1801 J
French Lieutenant's Woman, The (J. Fowles), 1969 U
French Revolution, The (J.M. Roberts), 1978 Q
French Revolution, The (J. M. Thompson), 1943 Q
French Revolution, The (T. Carlyle), 1837 Q
French Revolution. *See* Revolution, French
French Somaliland, referendum on independence, 1967 C
French Without Tears (T. Rattigan), 1936 W
French, David, Canad. dramatist (b. 1939), 1972 W
French, John, earl of Ypres, B. soldier (1852–1925), 1915 M
Frere, Sheppard Sunderland, B. historian (b. 1916), 1967 Q
Frere, Sir Henry Bartle Edward, B. colonial administrator (1815–84), 1877 C, 1878 M
Fresh Start for Britain, A, joint statement by Liberals and SDP, 1981 F
Fresnel, Augustin Jean, F. physicist (1788–1827), 1815 P, 1822 P
Fretilin, liberation movement, 1975 L
Freud, Lucien, B. artist (b. 1922), 1986 S
Freud, Sigmund, Aus. psychologist (1856–1939), 1856 Z, 1895 R, 1900 R, 1901 R, 1905 R, 1909 R, 1913 R, 1927 R, 1930 R; autobiography 1936 R
Freycinet, Charles Louis de Saulces de, F. Moderate Republican politician (1828–1912), 1882 A, 1886 A, M
Freyssinet, Eugène, F. architect, 1916 S, 1922 S
Freytag, Gustave, G. dramatist (1816–95), 1853 W
Frick, Wilhelm, G. Nazi, 1930 A, 1933 A
Friction: experiments, 1778 P, 1798 P; laws of, 1779 P
Friday (M. Tournier), 1967 U
Friedland, W. Germany, battle 1807 F
Friedman, Milton, Am. economist (b. 1912), 1981 O
Friedrich, Johann, G. theologian (1836–1912), 1869 R
Friedrich, Kaspar David, G. artist (1774–1840), 1808 S, 1809 S, 1835 S
Friel, Brian, Ir. author (b. 1929), 1980 W
Friendly Societies, in Britain, 1876 O
Fries, Jakob Friedrich, G. philosopher (1773–1843), 1808 R
Friesland, East, Germany, ceded to Hanover, 1815 F
Fringe of Leaves, A (P. White), 1976 U
Frisch, Otto, Aus. physicist (1904–79), 1904 Z, 1979 Z
Frith, William Powell, B. artist (1819–1909), 1858 S
Frithjofs Saga (E. Tegner), 1825 U
Frobel, Friedrich Wilhelm August, G. philosopher and educationalist (1782–1852), 1816 O, 1837 O
Frogs, treatise on, 1850 P
Fröhliche Wissenschaft, Die (F. Nietzsche), 1882 U
From Another Shore (A. Hertzen), 1850 U
From Bauhaus to Our House (T. Wolfe), 1981 S
From Memory to Written Record: England 1066–1307 (M.T. Clanchy), 1979 Q
From Sarajevo to Potsdam (A.J.P. Taylor), 1966 Q
From the Four Winds (J. Galsworthy), 1897 U
Fromm, Erich, Am. psychoanalyst (1900–80), 1900 Z, 1942 R, 1949 R, 1980 Z
Fromme, Lynette Alice,. 'Squeaky', Am. would-be assassin, 1975 J
Frost, Sir David Paradine, B. broadcaster (b. 1939), Nixon interviews, 1977 O
Frost, Robert, Am. poet (1874–1963), 1930 U, 1951 U
Frottage technique, 1925 S
Frou-frou (W. Halévy), 1869 W
Froude, James Anthony, B. historian (1818–94), 1818 Z, 1848 R, 1856 Q, 1894 Z
Fructose, synthesis of, 1887 P
Fruits, canned, 1892 P
Fry, Christopher, B. dramatist (b. 1907), 1947 W, 1948 W, 1951 W, 1954 W
Fry, E. M., B. architect, 1936 S
Fry, Elizabeth, B. prison-reformer (1780–1845), 1813 O
Fry, Roger Eliot, B. artist and critic (1866–1934), 1866 Z, 1910 S, 1934 Z
Fry, William Henry, Am. musician (1815–64), 1863 T
Fuad I, King of Egypt, 1922 C, 1928 G
Fuad II, King of Egypt, 1952 G
Fuchs, Klaus, Am. atomic spy, 1950 C, 1952 O
Fuchs, Sir Vivian Ernest, B. explorer (b. 1908), 1908 Z, 1958 P
Fuentes, Carlos, Mex. author (b. 1928), 1982 U
Fugard, Athol, S. Afr. dramatist (b. 1932), 1932 Z, 1970 W, 1972 W, 1975 W
Fujimori, Alberto Kenyo, President of Peru (b. 1939), 1990 F, 1992 D, 1992 L
Fukuda, Takeo, Jap. premier (b. 1905), 1976 M, 1978 L

Full Employment in a Free Society (W. Beveridge), 1944 O
Fuller, (Richard) Buckminster, Am. architect (1895–1983), 1895 Z, 1948 S, 1983 Z
Fuller, Charles, Am. playwright (b. 1939), 1981 W
Fuller, Sarah Margaret, Am. journalist and social reformer (1810–50), 1840 R
Fullerenes:
evidence found for existence of, 1985 P
isolated, 1991 P
Fulton Committee Report, on British civil service, 1968 O
Fulton, Missouri, US, Churchill's speech at, 1946 C
Fulton, Robert, Am. civil engineer (1765–1815), 1765 Z, 1801 P, 1803 P, 1807 P
Fumigators, chemical, 1920 P
Funck, Casimir, Pol. chemist (1884–1941), 1912 P
Fundamenta Astronomiae (F. W. Bessel), 1818 P
Fundamental particles, 1964 P
Fundamentalism, defined, 1895 R
Funk, Walter, H. economics minister (1891–1960), 1937 L, 1939 A, 1946 J
Furnaces, blast, 1829 P; gas-fired, 1861 P
Furniture, 'Utility', 1941 O
Fuseli, Henry, B. painter (1741–1825), 1782 S
Fussell, Paul, Am. author (b. 1924), 1975 Q, 1989 Q
Fustel de Coulanges, Numa Denis, F. archaeologist, (1830–89), 1864 Q
Future of An Illusion (Freud), 1927 R
Futurism, term coined, 1909 S
Futurist Manifesto, 1910 S
Fylingdales, Yorks, England, early warning station, 1960 B

G

G (J. Berger), 1972 U
Gabes Gap, Tunisia, Rommel retreats through, 1943 D
Gabo, Naum (born Naum Neemia Pevsner), R. sculptor (1890–1977), 1890 Z, 1920 S, 1977 Z
Gabon, now independent state of French Community, as French Equatorial Africa, 1888 M
Gabor, Dennis, B. physicist (1900–79), 1900 Z, 1947 P, 1979 Z
Gabriel, Ange Jacques, F. architect (1698–1782), 1765 S
Gabriel, Peter, B. singer (b. 1950), 1986 W
Gadamer, Hans Georg, German philosopher (b. 1900), 1975 R
Gaddis, William, Am. author (b. 1922), 1986 U
Gadsden Purchase, of US Far West territories, 1854 D
Gaeta, Cen. Italy, 1848 L, 1849 B; Francis II surrenders to Garibaldi, 1861 B
Gagarin, Yuri, R. cosmonaut (1934–68), 1961 P
Gage, Thomas, B. soldier (1721–87), 1775 D
Gageure imprévue, La (M. J. Sedaine), 1768 W
Gaillard, Félix, F. Radical Socialist (b. 1919), 1957 K, 1958 D
Gainsborough, Thomas, B. artist (1727–88), 1770 S, 1777 S, 1788 Z
Gaisford, Thomas, B. classical scholar (1779–1855), 1793 Q
Gaitskell, Hugh Todd Naylor, B. Labour Party leader (1906–63), 1906 Z, 1960 M, 1963 A; becomes Chancellor of Exchequer, 1950 K; elected Party leader, 1955 M; conflict with Labour unilateralists, 1960 K, 1961 F; defeats Wilson in election for leadership, 1960 K
Gaius, Institutes of, discovered, 1816 Q
Galanskov, Yuri, R. dissident (1939–72), 1968 A
Galapagos (K. Vonnegut), 1985 U
Galathea, deep-sea expedition by the, 1950 P
Galbraith, John Kenneth, Am. economist (b. 1908), 1958 O, 1977 Q
Galbraith, Thomas Galloway, B. Conservative politician (1917–82), 1962 L
Galiani, Ferdinando, It. economist (1728–87), 1770 O
Galicia, Poland, 1809 K; Polish designs on, 1790 C; taken by Austria, 1795 K; Russian offensive in, 1916 A; Germano-Austrian counter-attack, 1917 G; Poles defeated in, 1919 A; mandate over, assigned to Poland, 1919 L; recognised as Polish, 1923 C
Galilee, N. Israel, British district commissioner for, 1937 J
Galileo, Galilei, It. scientist (1564–1642)
Pope annuls 1633 condemnation of, 1980 K
formally rehabilitated by Vatican, 1992 K
Gall, Franz Joseph, G. anatomist and physiologist (1758–1828), 1810 P
Galle, Johann Gottfried, G. astronomer (1812–90), 1846 P
Gallegos, Rómulo, Venezuelan leader of Democratic Action Party, 1947 M
Galleries and Museums:
in Britain:
closure of, 1916 Q
Bethnal Green Museum, 1874 Q
British Museum, public admission to, 1879 W
Edward VII Gallery opened, 1914 Q
Reading Room, 1916 Q
See also under London
Buckingham Palace Gallery, 1962 S
Dulwich Art Gallery, 1814 S
entrance charges, 1971 E, 1974 A
Fitzwilliam Museum, Cambridge, 1837 S
Hayward Gallery, London, 1971 S, 1975 S, 1976 S
National Gallery, 1824 S, 1832 S
damage by Suffragettes, 1914 C
cleaning of pictures in, 1936 S, 1947 S
theft and return of Goya's *Wellington*, 1961 S, 1965 S
acquires Cézanne's *Les Grandes Baigneuses*, 1964 S
Sainsbury Wing, 1991 S
See also under Exhibitions, Art
National Maritime Museum, Greenwich, 1937 Q
National Portrait Gallery, 1857 S
Natural History Museum, S. Kensington, 1881 P, 1916 Q
Royal Academy, founded, 1768 S
Chantrey bequest to, 1841 S
sells Leonardo da Vinci cartoon, 1962 S
Sackler Galleries, 1991 S
See also under Exhibitions, Art
Saatchi Collection, London, 1985 S
Sainsbury Centre, University of East Anglia, 1978 S
Science Museum, S. Kensington, 1857 O
Tate Gallery, 1897 S
Turner Wing of, 1910 S
Duveen Gallery at, 1937 S
A. McAlpine gift, 1971 A
Clore Gallery, 1987 S
See also under Exhibitions, Art
Wallace Collection, 1900 S
Whitechapel Art Gallery, 1897 S
in Canada, Art Gallery of Ontario, Toronto, 1974 S
in France
'Art Nouveau', 1897 S
Louvre, The, 1793 S
theft of *Mona Lisa* from, 1911 S
Musée d'Orangerie, 1916 S
Musée d'Orsay, Paris, 1986 S
Museum of Science and Industry, Paris, 1986 P
Picasso Museum, Paris, 1985 S
Pyramid, 1989 S
in Germany:
Atlas Museum, Berlin, 1824 S
German Museum, Munich, 1903 O
Museum of Twentieth Century, Berlin, 1963 S
Neue Staatsgalerie, Stuttgart, 1984 S
in Holland, Rijksmuseum, Amsterdam, 1877 S
in Ireland, Lane bequest to, 1915 S
in Italy, Brera Gallery, Milan, 1806 S
Palazzo Grassi, Venice, 1986 S
Rome Museum, 1769 Q
in Japan
Gunma Prefectural Museum of Fine Arts, 1974 S
Tokio Museum, 1957 S
in Spain, Thyssen Collection, Madrid, 1991 S
in US
Guggenheim Art Museum, 1953 S, 1959 S
de Menil Museum, Houston, 1987 S
Museum of Contemporary Art, Los Angeles, 1986 S
Museum of Modern Art, New York, 1929 S
National Gallery of Art, Washington, 1937 S, 1978 S
Philadelphia Museum, 1769 Q
See also under Exhibitions, Art
Gallican Articles of Religion of 1682, observation enforced, 1766 R; adopted in Italy, 1786 R
Gallipoli, Turkey: Anglo-French landings, 1915 D, H; British withdrawal from Suvla and Anzac, 1915 M
Gallium, element, discovered, 1871 P
Gallup, George Horace, Am. pollster (1901–84), 1901 Z, 1935 O, 1984 Z
Galois, Evaniste, F. mathematician (1811–32), 1846 P
Galsworthy, John, B. novelist and dramatist (1867–1933), 1867 Z, 1933 Z; as novelist, 1879 U, 1906 U, 1920 U, 1921 U, 1924 U; as dramatist, 1920 W
Galt, John, B. novelist (1779–1839), 1821 U
Galtieri, General Leopoldo Fortunato, President of Argentina (b. 1926), 1981 M, 1982 F, 1985 D
Galton, Sir Francis, B. forensic scientist, 1850 P, 1869 P, 1885 P
Galvani, Luigi, It. physiologist (1737–98), 1771 P, 1789 P, 1798 Z
Galvanometer, invented, 1826 P; mirror, 1858 P
Gambaro, Griselda, Argent. dramatist (b. 1928), 1967 W
Gambetta, Léon, F. Moderate Republican statesman (1838–82), 1838 Z, 1870 J, 1882 Z; forms ministry, 1881 L; Note on Egypt, 1882 A; loses power, 1882 A
Gambia: taken over by Britain, 1821 E; becomes Crown Colony, separate from Sierra Leone, 1843 D; independence agreed, 1964 G; becomes independent, 1965 B; becomes republic within Commonwealth, 1970 D; federates with Senegal, 1981 L
Gamma rays, 1906 P, 1913 P, 1960 P
Gamsakhurdia, Zviad Konstantinovich, President of Georgia (1939–93), 1991 E, 1992 A
Gandamak, Afghanistan, treaty of, 1879 E
Gandhi, Indira, Prime Minister of India (1917–84), 1917 Z, 1971 C
appointed Prime Minister, 1966 A

ordinance to nationalize banks, 1969 G
accused of electoral corruption, 1975 F, L
declares state of emergency, 1975 F
calls election, 1977 A
loses election, 1977 C
returns to Lok Sabha in by-election, 1978 L
expelled from Lok Sabha for contempt and imprisoned, 1978 M
governor and police chief of Punjab dismissed, 1984 F
assassination, 1984 K, Z
death sentence announced for murderers of, 1986 A
Gandhi, Mohandas Karamchand, Ind. statesman and social reformer (1869–1948), 1869 Z; arrested, 1913 L; returns to India, 1914 N; imprisoned, 1922 C; opens civil disobedience campaign, 1930 C; released for discussions, 1931 A; signs Delhi Pact, 1931 C; at Round Table Conference, 1931 J; re-arrested, 1932 A; suspends civil disobedience campaign, 1934 D; withdraws from Indian National Congress, 1934 K; rejects proposals for self-government, 1945 J; assassinated, 1948 A
Gandhi, Rajiv, Prime Minister of India (1944–91), 1984 K, M
Sri Lankan–Indian summit to discuss violence in Sri Lanka, 1985 F
agreement announced to reduce tension in Punjab, 1985 G
attempted assassination, 1986 K
agreement aimed at ending communal violence in Sri Lanka, 1987 G
loses parliamentary majority, 1989 L
assassination, 1991 E
Ganganelli, Lorenzo, It. (1705–74), elected Pope Clement XIV, 1769 E
Ganilau, Ratu Sir Penaia Kanatabatu, Governor-General of Fiji (b. 1918), 1987 K
Garbo, Greta (born Greta Lovisa Gustafsson), Swe. film actress (1905–90), 1905 Z, 1927 W, 1933 W, 1935 W, 1990 Z
Garciá-Gutiérrez, Antonio, Sp. author (1812–84), 1836 U
García Márquez, Gabriel, Colombian author (b. 1928), 1967 U, 1983 U, 1988 U
Gard, R. M. du, F. author, 1922 U
Garden Party, The (K. Mansfield), 1922 U
Gardiner, Gerald, lord Gardiner, B. lawyer and Labour Party politician (1900–90), becomes Lord Chancellor, 1964 K
Gardiner, Samuel Rawson, B. historian (1829–1902), 1829 Z, 1863 Q, 1902 Z
Gardner, John, B. musician, 1957 T
Gardos, Peter, Hung. film director, 1987 W
Garfield, James Abraham, Am. Republican (1831–1881), inaugurated 20th president of US, 1881 C; assassinated, 1881 G
Garfunkel, Art, Am. singer and actor (b. 1941), 1982 W
Garibaldi, Giuseppe, It. statesman and soldier (1807–82), 1807 Z, 1882 Z; defends Rome, 1849 G; forms Italian National Association, 1857 H; proclaims Victor Emmanuel King of Italy, 1860 K; takes surrender of Francis II of Naples, 1861 B; is captured, 1862 H; March on Rome, 1867 K, L
Garnett, David, B. author (1892–1981), 1924 U, 1925 U
Garnier, Jean Louis Charles, F. architect (1825–98), 1861 S
Garrick, David, B. actor (1718–79), 1779 Z
Garrison, William Lloyd, Am. anti-slavery leader and journalist (1805–79), 1831 O
Garrod, Heathcote William, B. author and critic (1878–1960), 1947 Q
Garson, Greer, Am. film actress (b. 1908), 1942 W
Garvin, James Louis, B. journalist (1867–1947), 1868 Z, 1808 V, 1942 V, 1947 Z
Gas:
North Sea, 1967 O, 1971 H
Ukraine–W. Germany pipe-line opened, 1973 P
British Gas, conversion programme, 1977 P
natural, USSR to supply W. Germany, 1981 L
Euro-Siberian pipeline, US embargo on technology for, 1982 F, H
Gas—Collective Happening (A. Kaprow), 1966 S
Gas turbine, peat-fired, 1951 P
Gas, Coal, system of heating and lighting by, 1798 P; used for street-lighting, 1802 W, 1809 P, 1812 P, 1822 P
Gas, Poison: Hague Convention on, 1899 E; first used, 1915 D; banned by Washington Conference, 1922 B; Geneva Conference on, 1925 E; anti-gas school, British, 1936 C
Gas-mantle, 1886 P
Gascoigne, David. *See under* Sanderson, Cobden
Gascoigne, Paul John, B. soccer player (b. 1967), 1988 X
Gases, chemistry of, 1766 P
diffusion of, laws on, 1829 P
kinetic theory of, 1850 P
partial pressure, law of, 1803 P
separation of, 1863 P
Gases:
krypton, 1903 P
natural, 1963 P, 1964 P
xenon, 1903 P
Gaskell, Elizabeth Cleghorn (*ne* Stevenson), B. novelist (1810–65), 1810 Z, 1848 U, 1853 U, 1865 Z
Gasperi, Alcide de, It. statesman (1881–1954), Christian Democrat; forms coalitions, 1945 L, 1947 B, E, 1950 A, 1953 G; becomes provisional head of state, 1946 F
Gaspra asteroid, 1991 P
Gastein, Austria, Convention of, 1865 H
Gates, Horatio, Am. general (1728–1806), 1777 K, 1780 K
Gathering Storm, The (W. S. Churchill), 1948 Q
Gatling, Richard Jordan, Am. gunsmith (1818–1903), 1862 P
Gaudi, Antoni, Sp. architect (1852–1926), 1905 S, 1926 S
Gaughan, Michael, IRA member, 1974 F
Gauguin, Paul, F. artist (1848–1903), 1848 Z 1876 S, 1884 S, 1891 S, 1897 S, 1901 S, 1902 S, 1903 Z
Gaulle, Charles André Joseph Marie de, F. statesman and soldier (1890–1970), 1890 Z, 1962 L, 1963 A
becomes leader of Free French, 1940 H
enters Paris, 1944 H
heads French Provisional Government, 1944 K
orders cease-fire in Syria and Lebanon, 1945 E
visits Washington, 1945 H
elected president of Provisional Government, 1945 L
resigns, 1946 A
controls Rassemblement du Peuple Franais, 1947 D, 1948 L
forms government, 1958 E
is prepared to take office, 1958 E
meets Adenauer, 1958 J
elected president, 1958 M
proclaimed president of Fifth Republic, 1959 A
meets Macmillan, 1959 C, 1961 L
broadcasts on Algeria, 1959 J
at Summit meeting, 1960 E
offers terms to Algerian rebels, 1960 F
on Tunisian crisis, 1961 H
attempted assassination, 1962 H
asks Pompidou to remain in office, 1962 K
objects to Britain entering Common Market, 1963 A
rejects offer of Polaris missile, 1963 A
tours S. America, 1964 J
defeats Mitterrand in presidential election, 1965 M
fails to obtain clear majority for presidency, 1965 M
calls for dismantling of NATO, 1966 B
visits USSR, 1966 F
calls for US withdrawal from Vietnam, 1966 K
vetoes British entry to EC, 1967 E
visits Montreal, 1967 G
student unrest, 1968 E
refuses to devalue Franc, 1968 L
talks on future of EC, 1969 B
resignation as President, 1969 D
death, 1970 Z
Gauss, Karl Friedrich, G. mathematician and astronomer (1777–1855), 1772 Z, 1801 P, 1809 P, 1833 P, 1855 Z
Gautier, Théophile, F. author (1811–72), 1811 Z, 1925 U, 1852 U, 1872 Z
Gavarni. *See* Chevalier, Sulpice
Gavaskar, Sunil, Indian cricketer (b. 1949), 1987 X
Gay Lord Quex, The (A. W. Pinero), 1899 U
Gay-Lussac, Joseph Louis, F. Chemist (1778–1850), 1778 Z, 1807 P, 1808 P, 1850 Z
Gaye, Marvin, Am. pop singer (1939–84), 1971 W
Gaza, in Egyptian-controlled Sinai: Turks defeated at, 1917 C; battle, 1917 D; British take, 1917 L, 1956 L
Israel gains control, 1967 F
Israeli action against Palestinians criticized by UN, 1987 M
Gazala-Bir Hakeim Line, Western Desert, 1942 F
GBH, television series, 1991 W
Gdansk, Poland
rioting and strikes, 1970 M, 1980 H, M 1970
shipyard occupied by strikers, 1980 H
memorial to rioters unveiled, 1980 M
national congress of Solidarity, 1981 J
shipyard workers demand restoration of Solidarity union, 1983 C
Walesa returns to work, 1983 D
Solidarity demonstration, 1985 E
shipyard closed, 1988 K
Thatcher visits shipyard, 1988 L
Gear, speed-reducing, for turbines, 1910 P
Gebir (W. S. Landor), 1798 U
Geddes Committee, 1922 O
Gedo (K. Barth), 1935 R
Geiger Counter, 1928 P
Geiger, H., G. physicist (1882–1945), 1913 P, 1928 P
Gell-Man, Murray, Am. scientist (b. 1929), 1929 Z, 1972 P
Gemayel, Amin, Leban. politician (b. 1942), 1982 J, 1984 B
Gemayel, Bashir, Leban. politician (1947–82), 1982 H, J
Gemini (M. Tournier), 1975 U
Gendre de M. Poirier, Le (Angier and Sandeau), 1854 W
Genentech, Am. genetic engineering company, 1976 P
Genera Crustaceorum et Insectorum (P. A. Latreille), 1806 P
General Agreement on Tariffs and Trade (GATT), Geneva, Conferences on, 1963 E, 1964 E

Kennedy Round, 1967 F
Tokio Round, 1979 O
General Belgrano, Argentine cruiser sunk during Falklands War, 1985 B
General History of Africa (UNESCO), 1981 Q
General History of the Science and Practice of Music (J. Hawkins), 1776 T
General Motors, sit-down strike, 1937 O
South African subsidiary ceases operation, 1986 O
General Plantarum (A. de Jussieu), 1789 P
General Post Office, takes over British telephone system, 1912 O
General Song (P. Neruda), 1950 U
General Theory of Employment (J. M. Keynes), 1936 O
General Warrants, 1763 D
Generating Stations. *See under* Electricity
Generations (T. Cragg), 1988 S
Genetic Code, breaking of, 1961 P
Genetics:
research in, 1909 P, 1927 P
genetic code shown to common to all life forms, 1967 P
single gene isolated, 1969 P
gene assembled from its chemical components, 1970 P
rabbit cloned, 1975 P
first genetic engineering company, foundation of, 1976 P
microbe patented, 1980 P
patenting of genetically engineered microbe, 1980 P
US Supreme Court ruling, 1980 P
engineering products, 1981 P
gene transfer, 1981 P
growth gene transfer, 1982 P
artificial chromosome created, 1983 P
genes from extinct animal cloned, 1984 P
genetic fingerprinting, 1984 P
humans and chimpanzees, relationship between researched, 1984 P
gene marker for cystic fibrosis, 1985 P
gene marker for polycystic kidney disease, 1985 P
carrier of Duchenne muscular dystrophy located, 1986 P
growth inhibiting gene discovered, 1986 P
US government supervision of genetic engineering, 1986 P
virus produced by genetic engineering marketed, 1986 P
first suspect convicted by genetic fingerprinting, 1987 P
gene marker for cancer of colon, 1987 P
gene which initiates development of male features in mammals discovered, 1987 P
human growth hormone controllers inserted into fish, 1987 P
patenting of animals produced by genetic engineering, 1987 P, 1988 P
cattle produced by cloning embryos, 1988 P
human gene implanted into mouse, 1988 P
Human Genome Organization (HUGO), 1988 P
project to map human genes, 1988 P, 1990 P
gene responsible for cystic fibrosis identified, 1989 P
genetically engineered white blood cells introduced into cancer patients, 1989 P
gene which may be important in breast cancer discovered, 1990 P
human gene experiment, 1990 P
gene responsible for mental handicap discovered, 1991 P
Geneva, Switzerland:
Lemanic Republic in, 1798 A
Protestant revivalists in, 1810 R
Convention, on Red Cross, 1864 D
Court of Arbitration, 1872 J
League of Nations moves to, 1920 K
building for, 1938 S
Protocol, adopted by League of Nations, 1924 K
Britain refuses to sign, 1926 C
Conference on Arms Traffic, 1925 E
Conferences on Economic Affairs, 1927 E, 1930 L
Disarmament Conference, 1927 L
Protocol, on Germany's equality of rights, 1932 M
World Health Assembly, 1948 U
Conference on Korea and Indo-China, 1954 D
Summit Conference proposed, 1955 F, G
Conference on atomic energy,1955 H
Conference of foreign ministers on Germany, 1955 K, 1959 E
Conference on detection of nuclear explosions, 1958 G
Conference on surprise attack, 1958 L
Conference on law of the sea, 1958 O
Wheat agreement, 1959 C
Disarmament Committee, 1960 C
Conference on atomic weapon tests, 1962 A
negotiations on Laos, 1962 A, G
France boycotts, 1962 C
Disarmament Conference, 1962 C, 1964 A
eighteen-nation disarmament conference, 1966 A, 1967 B, H, 1971 H
SALT talks, 1972 K
US–USSR arms reduction talks, 1981 M, 1983 A, B, L, 1985 A, C, L, 1987 A, C, D, G, J, L, 1988 A
national reconciliation conference on Lebanon, 1983 K
Genghis Khan: His Life and Legacy (P. Ratchnevsky), 1983 Q
Génie du Christianisme, Le (Chateaubriand), 1802 U
Genius of Spain (de Madariaga), 1923 Q
Genius, The (H. Brenton), 1983 W
Genoa, Italy: sells Corsica to France, 1768 G; Ligurian Republic in, 1797 F; capitulates to French, 1800 F; under French domination, 1805 F; Conference on Economic Affairs, 1922 D; Convention, between Russia and Vatican, 1922 E; British bombard, 1941 B; Allies capture, 1945 D
Genocide, convention on prevention of, 1948 M
Gentz, Friedrich von, G. publicist (1764–1832), 1797 O
Geodesic Dome, 1948 S
Geographical Society, The Royal, London, 1830 P
Geography in its Relation to Nature and History (K. Ritter), 1817 P
Geology, studies in, 1775 P, 1815 P, 1816 P, 1830 P, 1839 P
Geometry, four-dimensional, 1908 P
line, invented, 1865 P
synthetic, founded, 1832 P
treatises on, 1794 P, 1854 P
Geophysical Year, International, 1957 P, 1958 P
George I, King of Greece (1863–1913), 1863 C; murdered, 1913 C
George II, King of Greece (1890–1947), 1935 L; as Crown Prince, 1898 L; deposed, 1923 M; returns to Athens, 1946 J
George III, King of Great Britain and Ireland (1738–1820), 1766 G, 1769 A, 1782 C, 1795 L; Dunning's motion on power of, 1780 D; derangement of, 1788 L; recovery of, 1789 B; insanity, 1811 B; death, 1820 A; library, 1923 Q
George IV, King of Great Britain and Ireland (1820–30), 1823 Q, 1830 F; as Prince of Wales, 1789 B; as Prince Regent, 1811 B, 1812 B, 1815 K, 1819 M; attack on, 1817 A; accession, 1820 A; relations with Caroline, Princess of Wales, 1820 F, G, 1821 G
George V, King of Great Britain, etc. (1910–36), accession, 1910 E; coronation, 1911 F; holds Delhi Durbar, 1911 M; Buckingham Palace Conference, 1914 G; adopts name of Windsor, 1917 F; Silver Jubilee celebrations, 1935 W; death, 1936 A
George V, King of Hanover (1851–66), 1851 L, 1855 E
George VI, King of Great Britain, etc. (1932–52), accession, 1936 M; visits Paris, 1938 G; visits Canada and US, 1939 F; peace feelers to, 1939 L; presents sword to Stalingrad, 1943 B; death, 1952 B
George Orwell: A Life (B. Crick), 1980 Q
George William Frederick, Duke of Cambridge (1819–1904), B. soldier, 1895 F
George XIII, Prince of Georgia, 1780 J
George, Henry, Am. political economist (1839–97), 1879 O
George, Stefan, G. author (1868–1933), 1868 Z, 1890 V, 1897 U, 1899 U, 1933 Z
Georgetown, B. Guiana, riots in, 1962 B
Georgi, Howard Mason, Am. scientist (b. 1947), 1974 P
Georgia, Russia: Russian intervention in, 1783 K, 1787 H; Russian annexation, 1801 J; independence proclaimed, 1918 E
pro-independence demonstrations, 1989 D
percentage of Georgians in Soviet population, 1989 Y
calls for independence and market economy, 1990 K
independence, 1991 D
presidential elections, 1991 E
rebel forces besiege government buildings in Tbilisi, 1992 A
war declared on rebel forces, 1992 A
Georgia, State, US: dispute with Cherokee Indians, 1830 E; as a Confederate State, 1861 B; Sherman's march through, 1864 E, J
Georgian Poetry (ed. E. Marsh), 1911 U
Gérard, François, F. artist (1770–1837), 1789 S
Gerettete Venedig, Das (H. von Hofmannsthal), 1905 W
Gerhardsen, Einar, Norw. Labour leader, as premier, 1945 F, 1955 A
Gerhardt, Charles Férdéric, F. chemist (1816–56), 1852 P
Géricault, Théodore, F. artist (1790–1824), 1790 Z, 1819 S, 1824 Z
Germ theory of disease, 1861 P
Germ warfare, China accuses US troops in Korea of using, 1952 C
Germain, George Sackville, Viscount, B. soldier and politician (1716–85), 1775 L
German (formerly Jones), Sir Edward, B. musician (1862–1936), 1902 T
German Catastrophe, The (F. Meinecke), 1946 O
German Confederation: established under Austria, 1815 F; Diet of, 1816 L; issues Carlsbad Decrees, 1819 J; to interfere in states unable to maintain public order, 1820 E; reserves rights in Schleswig-Holstein, 1846 F; suspended, 1848 E; replaced by the Reich, 1848 F; Prussia attempts revival through Erfurt Parliament, 1850 C, D; Austria revives Frankfurt Bundestag, 1850 E; Prussia

reorganises, 1851 E, 1866 H; Princes meet to reform, 1863 H; declared at an end, 1866 F
German Democratic Republic (GDR). *See* Germany, East
German Dictatorship, The (K.D. Bracher), 1969 Q
German Empire established, 1871 A, D
German Legal Antiquities (J. G. Grimm), 1828 Q
German Mythology (J. G. Grimm), 1835 Q
German literature, introduced to England by Carlyle, 1828 W
Germanium, element, discovered, 1886 P
Germantown, Pennsylvania, US, battle, 1777 K
Germany, Unification of: national revival against Napoleon, 1806 O; Prussian despatch on, 1849 A; by Parliamentary means fails, 1849 F; Dresden Conference fails, 1850 M; work of German National Association for, 1859 J; under Prussia's lead, 1865 K, 1866 H, 1871 A, D
Germany:
Allied military control ends, 1927 A
Allied occupation, 1945 F, 1954 K, 1955 E
economic fusion of British and US zones, 1946 M
problem of, differences between Russia and West on, 1952 C
Britain proposes four-power conference on, 1952 G, 1955 K
Russia rejects proposals for reunification through free elections, 1954 A
Russia refuses to discuss reunification, 1955 L
West German Bundestag asks for solution to problem, 1958 G
East Germany demands recognition, 1958 L
Russian proposals on Berlin rejected, 1958 M
Foreign ministers' conference on Berlin and peace treaty, 1959 E
Adenauer appeals for peace treaty based on self-determination, 1961 F
Khrushchev proposes a peace conference and Berlin as a free city, 1961 F
Berlin Wall, 1961 H
unification, 1990 G, H, K
vote to move government from Bonn to Berlin, 1991 F
illegitimacy rate, 1991 Y
population, 1991 Y
public service strike, 1992 D
asylum law, 1992 H, M
asylum seekers, 1992 H
emergency plan to support East German industry and jobs, 1992 J
See also Berlin; Germany, East; Germany, West
Germany and the Revolution (J. Görres), 1820 O
Germany, East: Democratic Republic established, 1949 K; frontier with Poland settled, 1950 L; demands recognition, 1958 L
new constitution adopted, 1968 D
visas required by West Berliners, 1968 F
diplomatic relations with West Germany proposed, 1969 M
recognized by Finland, 1972 L
Basic Treaty signed with West Germany, 1972 M
British Embassy opens, 1973 D
diplomatic relations established with US, 1974 J
anniversary of Berlin Wall celebrated, 1981 H
East German leader makes official visit to West Germany, 1987 J
Hungary allows East Germans to cross freely to West, 1989 J
New Forum, 1989 J
political reform demanded, 1989 K, L
Poland opens border and accepts refugees, 1989 K
Krenz replaces Honecker as Party leader, 1989 K
West German border opened, 1989 L
Berlin Wall demolished, 1989 L
Politburo and Communist Party Central Committee resign, 1989 M
Brandenburg Gate reopened, 1989 M
'Alliance for Germany', 1990 C
Maizière sworn in as Prime Minister, 1990 D
unification with West Germany, 1990 G, H, K
collapse of coalition government, 1990 H
Germany, West: federal constitution demanded, 1948 F; Federal Republic in force, 1949 E
USSR accuses of neo-Nazism and militarism, 1967 A
Soviet invasion threat, 1968 J
security review, 1968 K
relations with governments recognising East Germany, 1969 E
diplomatic relations with East Germany proposed, 1969 M
Soviet talks on mutual renunciation of force, 1969 M
Oder–Neisse Line frontier treaty with Poland, 1970 M, 1972 E
population, 1971 Y, 1981 Y
treaties with USSR and Poland ratified, 1972 E
Baader-Meinhof group rounded up, 1972 F
terrorism, 1972 J
Lufthansa flight hijacked by Palestinian terrorists, 1972 K
Basic Treaty signed with East Germany, 1972 M
establishes diplomatic relations with Czechoslovakia, 1973 M
dipomatic relations with Poland normalised, 1976 F
relations normalized with Poland, 1976 F
government collapses, 1982 J
Soviet foreign minister visits, 1983 A
general election, 1983 C
Bundestag votes for deployment of Pershing II missiles, 1983 L
anti-nuclear demonstrations, 1984 D
urbanisation, 1985 Y
US-Soviet plan to eliminate medium-range missiles from Europe endorsed, 1987 F
diplomatic realations established with Albania, 1987 J
divorce statistics, 1987 Y
unification with East Germany, 1990 G, H, K
life expectancy, 1990 Y
Germinal (E. Zola), 1885 U
Gernet, Jacques, F. historian, 1982 Q
Gerry, Elbridge Thomas, Am. lawyer and philanthropist (1837–1927), 1837 Z, 1874 O, 1927 Z
Gershwin, George, Am. musician (1898–1937), 1924 T, 1928 T, 1935 T, 1937 W
Gerstenberg, Heinrich Wilhelm von, G. poet and critic (1737–1823), 1766 U, 1767 U
Gertrude of Wyoming (T. Campbell), 1809 U
Geschichte der Poesie der Griechen und Römer (K. Schlegel), 1798 Q
Gesenius, Heinrich Friedrich, G. orientalist (1786–1842), 1812 Q
Gesner, Abraham, Canad. geologist (1797–1864), 1854 P
Getty Oil Company, 1949 O, 1984 O
Getty, Jean Paul, Am. businessman and art collector (1892–1976), 1892 Z, 1949 O, 1976 Z
Gettysburg, Pennsylvania, US, Lee's defeat at, 1863 G
Ghali, Butros, Egyptian premier, assassinated, 1910 B
Ghana: becomes independent, 1957 C; becomes a one-party state, 1964 B; *coups d'état*, 1966 B, 1978 F, G, 1981 M; immigrants expelled, 1969 L.*See also* Gold Coast
Ghent, Belgium: Treaty, between Britain and US, 1814 M; Peace, 1815 A; University, 1816 O; infants' welfare centre, 1903 O; Germans occupy, 1914 K
Ghetto (J. Sobol), 1989 W
Ghost Stories of An Antiquary (M. R. James), 1904 U
Ghost Writer, The (P. Roth), 1979 U
Ghosts (H. Ibsen), 1881 W
Giacometti, Alberto, Swi. sculptor (1901–66), 1933 S, 1947 S, 1950 S, 1965 S
Giaour, The (Byron), 1813 U
Gibb, Walter, B. aviator (b. 1919), 1955 P
Gibberd, Frederick, and Partners, architects, 1987 S
Gibberd, Sir Frederick, B. architect (1908–84), 1955 S, 1957 S, 1967 S
Gibbon, Edward, B. historian (1737–94), 1764 U, 1776 O, 1794 Z
Giberellin, hormone, 1957 P
Gibraltar: siege of, 1779 F; relief of, 1780 A, 1782 K
Spanish–British talks, 1966 E
frontier closed to all traffic except pedestrians, 1966 K
Gibraltarian passports refused by Spain, 1966 K
referendum on retaining links with Britain, 1967 J
access to restricted, 1968 E
constitution, 1969 E
frontier closed and ferry service suspended, 1969 F
Spanish citizenship offered to all Gibraltarians, 1969 G
border with Spain re-opened, 1980 D
Spanish frontier to be opened, 1982 A
Spanish frontier re-opened, 1985 B
suspected IRA terrorists shot dead, 1988 C
Gibson, Edward, Lord Ashbourne, Ir. attorney-general (1837–1913), 1885 H
Gibson, W. Am. scientist, 1978 P
Gide, André, F. author (1869–1951), 1899 U, 1902 U, 1909 U, 1919 U, 1925 U; *Journal*, 1889 U, 1946 U
Gierek, Edward, Pol. leader (b. 1913)
First Secretary of Polish Communist Party, 1970 M
visits Bonn, 1976 F
succeeded by Stanislaw Kania, 1980 J
Giffen, Sir Robert, B. administrator and economist (1837–1910), 1879 O
Gifford, William, B. author (1756–1826), 1794 U
Gigli, Benjamino, It. singer (1890–1957), 1930 T
Gijón, Spain, falls to rebels, 1937 K
Gilbert and Ellice Islands, S. Pacific, Britain annexes, 1915 L
Gilbert and George (Gilbert Proesch, b. 1943, George Passmore, b. 1942), B. artists, 1971 S
Turner Prize, 1986 S
Gilbert, Cass, Am. architect (1859–1934), 1859 Z, 1902 S, 1913 S, 1934 Z
Gilbert, Sir Alfred, B. sculptor (1854–1934), 1925 S
Gilbert, Sir Joseph Henry, B. Congregationalist minister and agriculturalist (1779–1852), 1843 P
Gilbert, Martin John, B. historian (b. 1936), 1988 Q
Gilbert, Walter, Am. scientist (1932), 1968 P
Gilbert, Sir William Schwenck, B. dramatist (1836–1911), 1836 Z, 1875 T, 1896 T, 1911 Z

Gilchrist, Percy, B. metallurgist (1851–1935), 1878 P
Gildea, Robert Nigel, B. historian (b. 1952), 1987 Q
Gill, Arthur Eric Rowton, B. stone-carver, engraver and typographer (1882–1940), 1882 Z, 1913 S, 1925 S, 1927 S, 1928 S, 1932 S, 1938 S, 1940 Z
Gillray, James, B. caricaturist (1757–1815), 1779 S
Gilman, Harold, B. artist (1876–1919), 1913 S
Gilmore, Gary, Am. criminal, 1977 A
Gilson, Etienne, F. historian and philosopher (1884–1978), 1922 R, 1941 R
Gin, cotton, invented, 1793 P
Ginsberg, Allen, Am. author (b. 1926), 1926 Z, 1968 U
Ginsburg, Alexander, R. dissident (b. 1936), 1968 A
Gioberti, Vincenzo, It. political author (1801–52), 1851 P
Giocanda Smile, The (A. Huxley), 1948 W
Giolitti, Giovanni, It. statesman (1842–1928), 1909 M, 1911 C; becomes premier, 1892 E; falls, 1893 M; forms second ministry, 1906 E
Giordano, Umberto, It. musician (1867–1934), 1898 T
Giotto space probe, 1986 P
Girard, Philippe Henri de, F. engineer (1775–1845), 1812 P
Giraudoux, Jean, F. dramatist (1882–1944), 1928 W, 1929 W, 1937 W
Girl Guides, 1909 O
Girodet de Roussy, Anne Louis, F. artist (1767–1824), 1793 S
Girondins in France: in power, 1792 L; overthrown, 1793 F; execution of prominent, 1793 K; survivors admitted to Convention, 1794 M
Girouard, Mark, B. historian (b. 1931), 1971 Q, 1977 Q, 1978 Q, 1981 Q
Girtin, Thomas, B. artist (1775–1802), 1797 S, 1800 S, 1802 S
Giscard d'Estaing, Valéry, F. Independent Republican politician (b. 1926), 1926 Z, 1974 E, 1981 E
publishes *La Démocratie Française*, 1976 O
discloses France's neutron bomb capability, 1980 F
Gissing, George Robert, B. author (1857–1903), 1886 U, 1891 U, 1903 U
Gitanjali (R. Tagore), 1912 U
Givenchy, France, battle, 1915 F
Gizenga, Antoine, Congolese politician, 1960 M
Gizikis, Phaidon, Greek general (b. 1917), 1973 L
Glaciers, treatise on, 1840 P
Gladstone Diaries (M.R.D. Foot and H.C.G. Matthew eds.), 1968 Q
Gladstone, William Ewart, B. statesman and Liberal (1809–98), 1809 Z, 1898 Z
becomes chancellor of Exchequer, 1852 M
Free Trade budget, 1853 D
leads House of Commons, 1865 K
forms first ministry, 1868 M
resigns after government defeat, but returns to office, 1872 C
both premier and chancellor of Exchequer, 1873 H, 1880 D
hopes to abolish income tax, 1874 B
resigns, 1874 B
attacks papal infallibility, 1874 R
resigns Liberal Party leadership, 1875 A
publishes *The Bulgarian Horrors*, 1876 J
conducts Midlothian campaign, 1879 L
forms second ministry, 1880 D
introduces Irish land act, 1881 H
Third Reform Bill, 1884 M
resigns, 1885 F
forms third ministry, 1886 B
introduces Irish Home Rule bill, 1886 D
defeated over, 1886 F
forms fourth ministry, 1892 H
delivers Romanes Lecture, 1892 Q
resigns, 1894 C
speeches on Armenian massacres, 1896 J
Glam Rock, 1971 W
Glasgow Celtic, Scot. soccer team, 1967 X
Glasgow, Scotland: School of Art, 1900 S; riots in, 1931 J; Empire Exhibition 1938 W; Ibrox Park stadium disaster, 1971 A
Glashow, Sheldon Lee, Am. physicist (b. 1932), 1967 P, 1974 P
Glasnost, Soviet policy of, 1985 C
Glass Menagerie, The (T. Williams), 1944 W
Glass, Philip, Am. musician (b. 1937), 1976 T. 1980 T, 1984 T, 1987 T, 1992 T
Glass, optical, 1916 P
Glassboro, N.J., US, 1967 F
Glatz (now Klodzkow), Poland, restored by Austria, 1763 B
Glazounov, Alexander, R. musician (1865–1936), 1865 Z, 1936 Z
Gleizes, Albert, F. artist (1881–1953), 1912 S
Glemp, Jozef, Pol. cardinal and primate (b. 1929)
attends crisis talks, 1981 L
calls for release of Lech Walesa, 1982 H
Glencoe, S. Africa, Boer defeat at, 1899 K
Glengarry Glen Ross (D. Mamet), 1983 W
Glenn, John, Am. cosmonaut (b. 1921), 1962 P
Glomar Challenger, Deep Sea Drilling Project, 1968 P
Gloucester, England, Sunday School at, 1780 R
Gloucestershire County Cricket Club, 1870 X
Glubb, Sir John Bagot, B. soldier (1897–1986), 1956 C
Gluck, Christoph Willibald von, G. musician (1714–1787), 1767 T, 1774 T, 1775 S, 1777 T, 1779 T, 1778 Z
Gluon, 1972 P
Glyndebourne, Sussex, England, operatic festival at, 1934 T
Gneisenau, August Wilhelm Anton, Count Neithandt von, Pruss. soldier (1760–1831), 1812 A
Gnesen, Poland, ceded to Prussia, 1793 E
Go-Between God, The (J.V. Taylor), 1972 R
Go-Karting, 1960 X
Goa, Indians invade, 1955 H, 1961 M
Gobbi, Tito, It. opera singer (1915–84), 1915 Z, 1984 Z
Goblet, René, F. Moderate Republican (1828–1905), 1886 M, 1887 E
God and Philosophy (E. Gilson), 1941 R
God that Failed, The (ed. A. Koestler), 1950 Q
God's Englishman: Oliver Cromwell and the English Revolution (C. Hill), 1970 Q
God's Face (J. Drzezdzon), 1984 U
Godard, Jean-Luc, F. film director (b. 1930), 1982 W
Goddard, Rayner, lord Goddard, B. judge (1877–1971), 1958 J
Gödel, Kurt, Am. mathematician (1906–78), 1906 Z, 1931 P, 1978 Z
Goderich, Viscount. *See* Robinson, F. J.
Godesberg, Germany, Chamberlain visits, 1938 J
Godoy, Alvarez de Faria Manuel de, Duke of El Alcudia, Sp. dictator (1767–1851), 1792 N, 1798 C, 1800 E
Godwin Austen, Mount (K2), in Himalayas, 1954 P
Godwin, William, B. political author (1756–1836), 1793 O, 1794 U
Goebbels, Joseph, G. Nazi leader (1897–1945), 1936 J
Goehr, Alexander, B. musician (b. 1932), 1967 T, 1970 T, 1985 T, 1990 T
Goethe, Johann Wolfgang, G. poet, dramatist and philosopher (1750–1832), 1774 U, 1775 U, 1794 U, 1809 U, 1811 U, 1819 U, 1821 U; *Faust*, 1808 W, 1832 W; other plays, 1773 W, 1787 W, 1788 W, 1791 W, 1792 W; scientific works, 1790 P, 1791 P, 1810 P; *Wilhelm Meister*, 1795 U; centenary medal, 1932 Q
Goetz von Berlichingen (Goethe), 1773 W
Goeze, Johann Melchior, G. pastor (1717–86), 1778 R
Goga, Octavian, Rum. anti-Semite, 1937 M
Gogh, Vincent van, Du. artist (1853–90), 1853 Z, 1884 T, 1888 T, 1889 T, 1890 Z, 1891 T
Irises sold for 30 million pounds, 1987 S
Gogol, Nicolai, R. author (1809–52), 1809 Z, 1833 U, 1835 U, 1842 U, 1952 Z
Goito, Italy, battles, 1848 D, E
Golan Heights, Israel–Syria:
Arab–Israeli conflict, 1970 A, 1972 L, 1973 K, 1974 D, E
Gold Coast: taken over by British government, 1821 E; Britain purchases forts from Denmark, 1850 G; Britain purchases Dutch trading-posts, 1872 B; frontiers with Togoland settled, 1886 G, 1899 L; frontiers defined, 1898 F; independence granted, 1956 H. *See also* Ghana
Gold Standard:
Britain returns to, 1925 D
abandons, 1931 J
Canada abandons, 1933 D
France returns to, 1926 O
abandons, 1936 J
Germany adopts, 1871 O
Holland abandons, 1936 J
Italy returns to, 1928 O
Japan adopts, 1897 C
abandons, 1931 M
S. Africa abandons, 1932 W
Sweden returns to, 1924 O
Switzerland abandons, 1936 J
US adopts, 1873 O
abandons, 1933 D
Gold, discoveries of:
in Australia, 1851 F, P
in Canada, 1897 P
in S. Africa, 1885 P
in US, 1847 P, 1866 P
Gold, extraction by cyanide, 1887 P; production, statistics of, 1944 Y
Goldberger, W., G. biochemist, 1925 P
Golden Age, The (L. Nowra), 1985 W
Golden Bough, The (J. G. Frazer), 1890 Q
Golden Bowl, The (H. James), 1914 U
Golden Gate, The (V. Seth), 1986 U
Golden Girls, The, television series, 1985 W
Golden Legend (H. W. Longfellow), 1851 U
Goldfine, Bernard, Am. businessman, 1958 F
Golding, William, B. author (1911–93), 1954 U, 1964 U, 1981 U
Goldmark, Karl, Hung. musician (1882–1911), 1875 T
Goldmark, Peter, Am. technologist, 1948 P
Goldsmith, Oliver, B. author (1728–74), 1766 U, 1767 U, 1767 W, 1770 U, 1773 W, 1774 Q, Z
Goldsmith, Sir James Michael, F.-B. financier (b. 1933), 1979 V
Goldstone Commission, on state dirty tricks campaign against ANC, 1992 L
Goldstücker, Theodor, G. scholar (1821–72), 1856 Q

Goldwater, Barry, Am. Republican Senator (b. 1909), 1909 Z; defeated by Johnson, 1964 L
Goldwyn, Samuel, Am. film producer (1882–1974), 1882 Z
Golf: British championships, 1860 X, 1886 X, 1904 X, 1934 X; Royal and Ancient Golf Club, St. Andrews, 1834 X
US Open Championship, 1970 X
Walker Cup, 1971 X
European golfers in Ryder Cup matches, 1978 X
Ryder Cup won by European golfers, 1985 X
British and Irish women golfers win Curtis Cup, 1986 X
Ryder Cup won by European golfers, 1987 X
first British and Irish Walker Cup victory in US, 1989 X
Gollancz, Victor, B. publisher (1893–1967), 1935 O
Goluchowski, Agenor, Aus. statesman (1849–1921), 1895 E
Gömbös, Julius, Hung. politician, anti-Semite Nationalist, 1932 K
Gombrich, Sir Ernst Hans Josef, B. art historian (b. 1909), 1909 Z, 1979 Q
Gomel, Russia, Russians take, 1943 L
Gomes, General Francisco Costa, President of Portugal (b. 1914), 1974 J
Gómez, José, Cuban president (1908–13), 1908 L, 1909 M
Gomulka, Wladyslaw, Pol. politician (1905–82), 1905 Z, 1970 M, 1982 Z
expelled for deviations, 1948 J
Goncalves, Vasco dos Santos, Port. leader (b. 1921), 1974 G
Goncharov, Ivan Alexandrovich, R. author (1812–1891), 1859 U, 1870 U
Göncz, Arpad, President of Hungary (b. 1922), 1990 H
Goncourt, Edmond de, F. author (1822–96), 1822 Z, 1896 Z
Goncourt, Jules de, F. author (1830–70), 1864 U
Gone With The Wind (M. Mitchell), 1936 U
Gone to Earth (M. Webb), 1917 U
Gooch, George Peabody, B. historian (1873–1968), 1913 Q
Good Companions, The (J. B. Priestley), 1929 U
Good Earth, The (P. Buck), 1931 U
Good Natur'd Man, The (O. Goldsmith), 1767 W
Good Society, The (W. Lippmann), 1937 O
Good Terrorist, The (D. Lessing), 1985 U
Good Time Was Had By All, A (S. Smith), 1937 U
Goodbye to All That (R. Graves), 1929 U
Goodbye to Berlin (C. Isherwood), 1938 U
Goodman, Benny, Am. band leader (1909–86), 1938 T
Goodman, Martin, B. author (b. 1956), 1992 U
Goodman, Nelson, Am. philosopher (b. 1906), 1978 R, 1984 R
Goodwood, Sussex, England, horse-racing at, 1802 X
Goodyear, Charles, Am. inventor (1800–60), 1839 P
Goon Show, radio series, 1972 W
Goonhilly Down, Cornwall, England, 1962 P
Goose Green, Falkland Islands, 1982 E
Gorani, Hajrullah, Yugoslavian trade union leader, 1990 J
Göransson, G. F., Swe. steelmaker (1819–1900), 1858 P
Gorbach, Alphons, Aus. People's Party leader, 1961 D
Gorbachev, Mikhail Sergeyevich, R. politician (b. 1931), 1931 Z
visits London, 1984 M
US–Soviet arms reduction talks, 1985 A, C, L, 1987 A, C, D, G
First Secretary of Communist Party, 1985 C
moratorium on missile deployments in Europe announced, 1985 D
offers summit talks with Reagan, 1985 D
timetable for elimination of all nuclear weapons proposed, 1986 A
reforms, 1987 A, 1988 F, 1990 H, 1991 C
secret ballots proposed for election of party officials, 1987 A
arms reduction proposals, 1987 B
criticism of Stalin for political errors, 1987 L
Intermediate-range Nuclear Forces (INF) Treaty, 1987 M, 1988 F
Soviet withdrawal from Afghanistan, 1988 B, E
appeals for calm in Armenia, 1988 B
changes in administrative structure of USSR planned, 1988 F
elected President, 1988 K
planned reductions in armed forces and conventional weapons announced, 1988 M
rehabilitation of victims of Stalinist purges, 1989 A, 1990 H
Bonn Document, 1989 F
end of Cold War declared, 1989 M
visits Vatican, 1989 R
sworn in as first executive president of USSR, 1990 C
citizenship restored to exiled dissidents, 1990 H
Nobel Peace Prize, 1990 K
emergency powers granted to, 1990 L
referendum on proposed renewed federation, 1991 C
Strategic Arms Reduction Treaty (START), 1991 G
coup against, 1991 H
resignation as First Secretary of Communist Party, 1991 H
resignation as President, 1991 M
Gorchakov, Prince Alexander Mikhailovich, R. diplomat (1798–1883), 1875 E
Gordimer, Nadine, S. Afr. author (b. 1923), 1979 U
Gordimer, Nadine, S. Afr. author (b. 1923), 1979 U
Gordon Walker, Patrick Chrestian, B. Labour politician (1907–80); appointed Foreign Secretary, 1964 K; resigns on by-election defeat, 1965 A
Gordon, Adam Lindsay, Austral. poet (1833–70), 1867 U
Gordon, Aloysius ('Lucky'), 1963 M
Gordon, Charles George, B. soldier (1833–85), 1884 B, 1885 A
Gordon, George Hamilton, Earl of Aberdeen, B. Whig statesman (1784–1860), 1784 Z, 1846 K, 1860 Z; forms coalition, 1852 M; resigns, 1855 B
Gordon, Lord George, B. agitator (1751–93), 1780 F
Gordonstoun School, Morayshire, Scotland, 1934 O
Gore, Mrs. Catherine Grace Frances, B. author (1799–1861), 1831 W, 1841 W
Gore, Charles, B. churchman (1853–1932), 1890 R, 1892 R, 1907 R
Gore, Spencer, B. lawn-tennis player, 1877 X
Goree, Island, West Indies: restored to France, 1763 B; France recovers, 1783 J; attack on, 1799 E
Goremykin, Ivan, R. Conservative, 1906 E
Gorham, George Cornelius, B. divine (1787–1857), 1850 R
Göring, Hermann, G. Nazi politician (1893–1946), 1893 Z, 1933 A; becomes economics minister, 1936 K; sentenced by Nuremberg tribunal, 1946 J
Gorki, Maxim, R. novelist (1868–1936), 1868 Z, 1899 U, 1900 U, 1902 U, 1907 U, 1934 U, 1936 Z
Gorky Park (M.C. Smith), 1981 U
Gorky, USSR, 1980 A
Gorman, Arthue Pue, Am. Democrat (1839–1906), 1894 H
Görres, Johann Joseph von, G. author (1776–1848), 1820 O, 1821 U, 1836 R
Gorst, Sir John Eldon, B. lawyer and Conservative politician (1835–1916), 1880 E
Gorton, Sir John Grey, Prime Minister of Australia (b. 1911), 1968 A, 1971 C
Goschen, George Joachim, Viscount Goschen, B. Liberal politician (1831–1907), 1876 L; as chancellor of Exchequer, 1887 A, 1888 D
Gospel of Christian Atheism, The (T.J.J. Altizer), 1966 R
Gota Canal, Sweden, 1832 P
Gotha, Sweden, 1874 E
Gothenberg, Sweden, system of liquor control, 1866 O
Gothic novel, the, 1794 U
Gothic style of architecture, 1845 S
Gothic type, abandoned by Germany, 1941 O
Gotti, John, Am. Mafia leader, 1992 O
Göttingen, Germany: *Hainbuch* in, 1772 U; telegraph at, 1833 P; brothers Grimm dismissed from University, 1837 M
Gottwald, Klement, Czech. Communist (1896–1953), 1896 Z, 1953 Z; becomes premier, 1946 E; becomes president of Republic, 1948 F
Gouda, Holland, 1787 F
Gough, Hugh, lord Gough, B. soldier (1779–1869), 1846 B
Gouin, Félix, F. Socialist, 1946 A
Goulart, João Belchior, Brazilian politician (1918–76), deposed from presidency, 1964 D
Gould, Sir Francis Carruthers, B. caricaturist (1844–1925), 1844 Z, 1925 Z
Gounod, Charles François, F. musician (1818–93), 1818 Z, 1859 T, 1882 T, 1893 Z
Gournaris, Demetrios, Gr. politician, 1915 C
Government Communication Headquarters (GCHQ), B., staff deprived of right to belong to trade unions,1984 A, G
Government Inspector, The (N. Gogol), 1833 U
Gow, Ian Reginald Edward, B. Conservative politician (1937–90), 1985 L, 1990 G
Gower, David Ivon, B. cricketer (b. 1957), 1992 X
Gowing, Sir Lawrence Burnett, B. artist (1918–91), 1937 S
Gowing, Margaret M. (b. 1921), B. historian, 1949 Q
Gowon, General Yakubu, Nigerian leader (b. 1934), 1966 G, 1969 C, 1975 G
Goya, Francisco y Lucientes, Sp. artist (1747–1828), 1795 S, 1796 S, 1799 S, 1800 S, 1805 S, 1808 S, 1810 S, 1814 S, 1815 S, 1816 S, 1819 S, 1828 S, 1850 S
portrait of Wellington, 1812 S, 1961 S, 1965 S
Grâce, La (G. Marcel), 1921 W
Grace, William Gilbert, B. cricketer (1848–1915), 1848 Z, 1865 X, 1870 X, 1876 X, 1915 Z
Graf, Steffi, German tennis player (b. 1969), 1988 X
Grafton, Augustus Henry Fitzroy, Duke of, B. Whig statesman (1735–1811), 1766 G, 1769 A, 1770 A, 1775 L, 1776 C
Graham, Thomas, B. chemist (1805–69), 1829 P, 1863 P
Graham, William Franklin ('Billy'), Am.

evangelist (b. 1918), 1918 Z, 1954 R
Greater London Crusade, 1966 R, 1984 R
Grahame, Kenneth, B. author (1859–1932), 1859 Z, 1908 U, 1932 Z
Gramido, Convention, 1847 G
Grammar of Assent (J. H. Newman), 1870 R
Grammar of Politics (H. Laski), 1925 O
Grammar of the Romance Languages (F. C. Dietz), 1836 Q
Gramme, Z. T., F. electrician (1826–1901), 1870 P
Gramophone, 1887 P; stereoscopic recordings for, 1958 P
Granadian Confederation, 1858 D
Grand Man, The (S.S. Bhoosnurmath), 1984 U
Grand Trunk Pacific Railway, 1919 C
Grand Unified Theory, 1974 P
Grande Peur des bien pensants, La (Bernanos), 1931 U
Grandi, Count Dino, It. politician (1895–1988), 1929 J
'Grandma Moses', Am. artist, 1939 S
Grandmaster Flash and the Furious Five, Am. pop group, 1981 W
Grant, Bernard Alexander Montgomery, 'Bernie', B. Labour politician (b. 1944), 1985 D
Grant, Ulysses Simpson, Am. Unionist general and Republican leader, president of US (1822–85), 1822 Z, 1862 B, 1864 E, 1872 A, 1876 M, 1885 Z; elected president, 1868 L, 1869 C; re-elected, 1872 L
Granville, lord. *See* Leveson-Gower, G. G.
Granville-Barker, Harley Granville, B. actor, producer and dramatist (1877–1946), 1877 Z, 1904 W, 1946 Z
Grapes of Wrath, The (J. Steinbeck), 1939 U
Graphology (Klarges), 1932 P
Grass, Günter, G. author (b. 1927), 1963 U, 1965 U, 1986 U
Grasse, François Joseph Paul, Comte de, F. naval officer (1722–88), 1781 D, H, 1782 D
Grateful Dead, The, Am. pop group, 1970 W
Gratry, Auguste Joseph Alphonse, F. author and theologian (1805–72), 1855 R
Grattan, Henry, Ir. statesman (1746–1820), 1779 M, 1780 D; makes Irish Declaration of Rights, 1782 D
Gravelet, Jean François. *See* Blondin
Gravellotte, France, battle, 1870 H
Graves, Robert Ranke, B. author (1895–1985), 1895 Z, 1929 U, 1934 U, 1939 U, 1985 Z
Gravitation and the Principle of Relativity (A. Eddington), 1918 P
Gravitation, theory of, 1964 P
Gravitations (Supervielle), 1925 U
Gravity's Rainbow (T. Pynchon), 1973 U
Gray, Alasdair James, B. author (b. 1934), 1981 U
Gray, Andy, B. soccer player (b. 1955), 1979 X
Gray, Thomas, B. poet (1716–1771), 1768 U, 1771 Z
Great Expectations (C. Dickens), 1861 U
Great Gatsby, The (S. Fitzgerald), 1925 U
Great Illusion, The (N. Angell), 1933 O
Great Lakes, N. America, agreement to limit naval forces on, 1817 D
Great Learning, The (C. Cardew), 1971 T
Great Railway Bazaar, The (P. Theroux), 1975 U
Great Salt Lake, Utah, Mormons' trail to, 1846 F
Great War and Modern Memory, The (P. Fussell), 1975 Q
Great War and the British People, The (J.M. Winter), 1985 Q
Great War in Germany, The (R. Huch), 1914 O
Great War, television series, 1964 W
Greater London Council, 1964 D, 1965 O
abolition proposed, 1983 O
Grechko, Andrei Antonovich, R. Defence Minister (1903–76), 1968 E
1952 constitution restored, 1974 H
Greece (W. M. Leake), 1812 O
Greece:
antiquities in, 1764 Q
restoration of empire, planned by Russia, 1781 B
independence, cause of, 1803 D
War of Independence from Turkey, 1821 C, D, F, K, 1822 F, G, 1824 D, G, K, 1827 D, F
proposals for British protection, 1825 F
Sultan rejects mediation, 1827 M
powers allow France to intervene in Morea, 1828 G
constitution adopted, 1822 A
independence proclaimed, 1822 A
guaranteed by powers, 1829 C, J, 1830 B
blockaded, for aiding Rumelian rebels, 1886 E
finances to be controlled by international commission, 1898 B
blockade of, 1916 F
Italy's demands to, 1940 K
German ultimatum to, 1941 D
British expedition to, 1941 D
Russia withdraws recognition of, 1941 F
military junta, 1967 D, E, L, M
arbitrary arrest abolished, 1969 K
military powers limited, 1969 K
press freedom restored, 1969 K
withdrawal from Council of Europe, 1969 M
martial law relaxed, 1970 D
political prisoners released, 1970 D
cabinet changes, 1971 H
naval mutiny foiled, 1973 E
formal abolition of monarchy, 1973 H
Gizikis ousts Papadopoulos, 1973 L
military government resigns, 1974 G
withdrawal from NATO, 1974 H
vote against restoration of monarchy, 1974 M
colonels found guilty of treason, 1975 H
European Community membership, 1979 E, 1981 A
first Socialist government, 1981 K
cotton production, 1984 Y
divorce statistics, 1987 Y
elections, 1989 F, L
New Democracy Party election victory, 1990 D
presidential elections, 1990 E
life expectancy, 1990 Y
illegitimacy rate, 1991 Y
Cabinet dismissed, 1992 M
merchant shipping tonnage statistics, 1992 Y
Greek, Classical, studies in, 1781 Q, 1802 Q
Greeley, Horace, Am. journalist and Democratic politician (1811–72), as presidential candidate, 1872 E, L
Green Belt, 1935 O
Green Mansions (W. H. Hudson), 1904 U
Green Pastures (M. Connelly), 1924 W
Green, Sir Allan David, B. Director of Public Prosecutions (b. 1935), 1991 K
Green, Henry, B. author (1905–1974), 1943 U, 1945 U
Green, John Richard, B. historian (1837–83), 1874 Q
Green, Julien, F. author (b. 1900), 1955 U
Green, Paul, Am. dramatist (1894–1981), 1926 W
Green, Thomas Hill, B. philosopher (1836–82), 1836 Z, 1882 Z, 1899 R
Greene, Graham, B. author (1904–91), 1904 Z, 1928 U, 1940 U, 1948 U, 1953 W, 1955 U, 1958 W, 1966 U, 1973 U, 1978 U, 1991 Z
Greene, Jack P., Am. historian (b. 1931), 1991 Q
Greene, Nathaniel, Am. soldier (1742–86), 1777 J, 1781 C, J
Greenham Common, Berkshire, England
Cruise missiles deployed at military base, 1980 F, 1982 M, 1983 G, L
women's peace camp, 1984 D, 1984 J
Greenhouse Effect, 1967 P
Greenland: discovery of interior, 1870 P; crossed by Nansen, 1888 P; Norway annexes East Greenland, 1931 G
Greenmantle (J. Buchan), 1916 U
Greenpeace:
founded, 1971 O
members detained in Siberia, 1983 G
Rainbow Warrior sunk by French agents, 1985 G, H, J, L, 1986 G
Greenwich Mean Time, adopted by France, 1911 C
Britain reverts to, 1971 K
Greenwich, Kent, England, National Maritime Museum at, 1937 Q
Greenwood, John, artist, 1990 S
Greer, Germaine, Aust. author (b. 1939), 1971 R
Gregory XVI, Pope (Bartolommeo Alberto Cappellari), It. (1765–1846), 1831 B, 1832 R
Grein, J. T., B. theatrical producer, 1891 W
Grenada, Declaration of, 1971 G
Grenada, W. Indies, 1763 B, K; captured by France, 1779 G; captured by Britain, 1796 N
independence, 1974 B
New Jewel movement seizes power, 1979 C
military coup and US invasion, 1983 K
state of emergency declared, 1983 L
Grenadines:
independence, 1979 K
Grenville, George, B. Whig statesman (1712–70), 1763 D, 1765 C, G
Grenville, Thomas, B. diplomat (1755–1846), 1782 E
Grenville, lord. *See* Wyndham, William
Grétry, André, Belg. musician (1741–1813), 1784 T
Greuze, Jean Baptiste, F. artist (1725–1805), 1765 S, 1777 S, 1805 Z
Grévy, Jules, F. Republican politician (1813–91), elected president, 1879 A; re-elected, 1885 M; resigns after scandals, 1887 K, M
Grey, Charles, Earl Grey, B. Whig statesman (1764–1845), 1794 G, 1832 E; becomes premier, 1830 L; dissolves Parliament, 1831 D; resigns, 1834 G
Grey, Edward, Viscount Grey of Fallodon, B. Liberal statesman (1862–1933), 1862 Z, 1895 C, 1933 Z; as foreign secretary, 1905 M, 1914 G; memoirs, 1925 Q
Griechen und Römer, Die (Schlegel), 1797 Q
Grieg, Edvard, Nor. musician (1843–1907), 1843 Z, 1868 T, 1907 Z
Griesbach, Johann Jakob, G. New Testament scholar (1745–1812), 1775 Q
Griffin, Bernard, Cardinal Archbishop of Westminster (1899–1956), 1943 R
Griffith, Arthur Ir. politician (1872–1922), 1922 J; as head of S. Ireland provisional government, 1922 A
Griffith, David Wark, Am. film director (1875–1948), 1909 W, 1915 W
Griffiths, Trevor, B. playwright (b. 1935), 1975 W
Grigg, Sir James, B. administrator and politician (1890–1964), becomes war secretary, 1942 B
Grillparzer, Franz, Aus. author (1791–1872), 1791 Z, 1817 U, 1818 U, 1834 U, 1872 Z
Grimm, Jakob, G. author and philologist (1785–1863), 1785 Z, 1812 U, 1819 Q, 1828 Q, 1835 Q, 1837 M, 1848 Q, 1854 Q, 1863 Z

Grimm, Wilhelm, G. author and philologist (1786–1859), 1786 Z, 1812 U, 1837 M, 1859 Z
Grimond, Joseph, Lord Grimond of Firth, B. Liberal politician (1913–93), 1956 J, 1967 A, 1976 E
Griqualand West, Cape Province, S. Africa, annexed by Cape Colony, 1872 K
Gris, Juan, Sp. artist (1887–1927), 1920 S
Grissom, Virgil, Am. astronaut, 1965 P
Grivas, George, Cypriot-born Greek general (1898–1974), as EOKA leader, 1957 L; returns to Athens, 1959 C; assumes command of Greek Cypriot forces, 1964 H
Groce, Cherry, B. woman wounded by London policeman, 1985 J
Groen, Alma de, N. Zeal. playwright (b. 1941) 1987 W
Gromyko, Andrei Andreevich, R. politician (1909–89), 1973 D, 1983 J; appointed foreign minister, 1957 B; holds discussions preliminary to Summit talks, 1958 F
  Foreign Minister, 1969 M, 1985 A
  named President of USSR, 1985 G
  retirement, 1988 J
Gronchi, Giovanni, It. Christian Democrat (1887–1978), elected president of Italy, 1955 D
Groningen, Holland, natural gas deposits in, 1963 P
Gropius, Walter Adolph, G. architect (1883–1969), 1883 Z, 1911 S, 1919 S, 1925 S, 1936 S, 1969 Z
Gross National Product statistics, 1975 Y
Grossbeeren, Germany, battle, 1813 H
Grosskhophta, Der (Goethe), 1792 W
Grossman, David, Israeli author (b. 1954), 1986 U, 1989 U
Grossmith, George, Junior (1874–1935), B. comedian and promoter of entertainment, 1922 W
Grósz, Károly, Prime Minister of Hungary (b. 1930), 1987 F
Grote, George, B. historian and Radical politician (1794–1871), 1794 Z, 1821 O, 1846 Q, 1871 Z
Grotefend, Georg Friedrich, G. epigraphist (1775–1853), 1837 Q
Grotewohl, Otto, E. Germ. Communist leader (d. 1964), 1964 Z
  becomes minister president, 1949 K
Group of Ten, 1983 A
Group, The (M. McCarthy), 1963 U
Grove, Sir George, B. musicologist (1820–1900), 1878 T, 1883 T
Growing Up in New Guinea (M. Mead), 1935 R
Growth of Political Stability in England, 1675–1725, The (J.H. Plumb), 1967 Q
Growth of the Soil (K. Hamsun), 1917 U
Groza, Petru, Rum. Communist, 1945 C
Gruenther, Aldred, Am. general (1899–1983), as Supreme Allied Commander Europe, 1953 E, 1956 L
Grüne, Heinrich, Der (G. Keller), 1851 U
Grunge Music, 1991 W
Grylls, inventor of rapid filming-machine, 1923 P
Guadalcanal Pacific: US task forces at, 1942 H, L; Japanese driven from, 1943 A
Guadaloupe, W. Indies, 1794 N; restored to France, 1763 B; British take, 1810 N
Gualdeloupe Hidalgo, Treaty, between US and Mexico, 1848 B
Guam, S. Pacific, ceded by Spain to US, 1898 M
Guarantees:
  by Britain and France, for independence of Rumania and Greece, 1939 D
  by Germany, for Belgium's inviolability, 1937 K
Guardi, Francesco, Venetian painter (1712–93), 1763 S, 1782 S
Guardian Angel (O. W. Holmes), 1867 U
Guare, John, Am. dramatist (b. 1938), 1971 W, 1992 W
Guatemala: independence declared, 1821 J; enters Central American Federation, 1823 G; movement for a federal Central America in, 1887 N; coffee production in, 1909 Y
  guerrillas kidnap West German Ambassador, 1970 C
  military coup, 1982 C
  coup, 1983 H
  Contadora peace treaty, 1986 E
  Esquipulas summit, 1986 E
  Arias Plan, 1987 H
Guerazzi, Francisco Domenico, It. publicist (1804–1873), 1834 U, 1854 U
Guernica (P. Picasso), 1937 P, 1981 S
Guernica, Spain, destroyed by rebels, 1937 D
  Basque regional parliament, 1980 C
Guerrero, Vincente, Mexic. leader, 1821 B
Guess, George. *See* Sequoyah
Guevara, Ernesto Che, Bolivian revolutionary (1928–67), 1928 Z, 1967 K, Z
Guiana, British. *See* British Guiana
Guides, railway, 1841 V
Guildford Cathedral, Surrey, 1961 S
Guildford Four, 1975 K
  cleared, 1989 O
Guildford, Surrey, England
  IRA bombings, 1974 K
Guilds, Religious, abolished in Tuscany, 1786 R
Guilford, Conn., US, battle, 1781 C
Guillaume, Günther, W. German spy, 1974 E
Guillebaud, Claude William, B. economist (1890–1971), as chairman of committee on Health Service, 1956 A; on railwaymen's pay, 1960 C
'Guillotine', use of, in Parliamentary procedure, 1904 C
Guin, Ursula Le, Am. author (b.1929), 1968 U
Guinea, French, W. Africa, 1882 F, 1893 C
Guinea, Spanish, protectorate in, 1885 A
Guinea, attempted invasion by Portuguese mercenaries, 1970 L
Guinea-Bissau, wins independence from Portugal, 1974 J
Guinness trial, 1990 O
Guinness, Sir Alec, B. actor (b. 1914), 1957 W, 1982 W
Guinness, Edward, lord Iveagh, B. brewer and philanthropist (1847–1927), 1928 S
Guipuzcoa, Spain, state of emergency declared, 1968 H
Guizot, François, F. politician and historian (1787–1874), 1787 Z, 1829 Q, 1846 K; becomes premier, 1847 J
Gujarat, India, Sikhs defeated at, 1849 B; Hindu–Muslim violence, 1969 J
Gulag Archipelago, The (A. Solzhenitsyn), 1974 U, 1990 U
Gulbenkian, Nubar Sarkis, Iran. financier and philanthropist (1896–1972), establishes Fund, 1958 S
Guldberg, Ove Höegh, Da. statesman (d. 1788), 1772 A
Gulf
  Gulf War. *See* Wars
  US offers naval protection to Kuwaiti tankers in Gulf, 1987 G
  US attacks on Iranian oil installations, 1987 K
  Iranian oil platforms destroyed in US attack, 1988 D
  Iranian civilian airliner shot down by US, 1988 G
  oil pumped into as military tactic, 1991 A
Gulf States, oil prices raised, 1971 B, 1973 M
Gun-cotton, 1846 P
Guney, Yilmaz, Turk. film director (b. 1937), 1981 W
Gunn, Thom, B. author (b. 1929), 1968 U
Gunpowder, experiments with, 1778 P
Guns n' Roses, Am. rock group, 1991 W
Guppy, Shusha, Iranian author (b. 1938), 1989 U
Gura, Ethiopia, 1876 C
Gurkhas, in Nepal, Indian warriors: conquer Nepal, 1768 N; British war with, 1814 K
Gurney, Sir Henry, B. high commissioner in Malaya (1898–1951), 1951 K
Gürsel, Cemal, Turk. soldier, 1960 E
Gustaf VI Adolf, King of Sweden (1882–1973), 1973 J
Gustafsson, Greta. *See* Garbo, Greta
Gustav Line, in Italy, 1944 E
Gustavus Adolphus Society, 1832 R
Gustavus III, King of Sweden (1746–92), 1772 G, H, 1784 O, 1789 B, 1791 M, 1792 C
Gustavus IV, King of Sweden (1792–1809), 1809 C
Gustavus V, King of Sweden (1907–50), 1907 M
Guston, Philip, Am. painter (1913–80), 1979 S
Guy Mannering (W. Scott), 1815 U
Guyana:
  becomes republic within Commonwealth, 1970 B
  independence, 1966 E
  mass suicide in People's Temple, Jim Jones cult centre, 1978 L
  election, 1992 K
Guys, Constantin, F. draughtsman (1802–92), 1863 S
Gwalior, Cen. India, 1802 K, 1803 H
Gyani, General, Ind., commands UN peace force in Cyprus, 1964 C
Gynnasium, the first, 1765 O
Gyro-compass, 1907 P

H

Haacke, Hans Christoph Carl, G. artist (b. 1936), 1984 S
Haakon VII, King of Norway (1905–57), 1905 L, 1957 J
Haas, Paul, B. chemist (1877–1960), 1933 P
Habeas Corpus Act, British, suspended, 1777 M, 1817 C
  suspension repealed, 1818 A
Haber, Fritz, G. chemist (1868–1934), 1908 P
Habermas, Jürgen, G. philosopher (b. 1929), 1968 R, 1981 R, 1985 R
Habib, Philip Charles, Am. diplomat (1920–92), tours Middle East as peace envoy, 1981 E
Habré, Hissène, President of Chad (b. 1942), 1983 H, 1990 M, 1992 A
Habsburg Empire, The (C.A. Macartney), 1969 Q
Hacha, Emil, Czech. president, 1938 L
Hackney, London, England, container depots 'blacked', 1972 G
Hadar, Ethiopia, ancient hominid discovery, 1975 Q
Hadlee, Richard John, N. Zeal. cricketer (b. 1951), 1990 X
Haeckel, Ernst Heinrich, G. biologist (1834–1919), 1868 P, 1874 P, 1899 P
Hafnium, element, discovered, 1922 P
Hagen, Friedrich Heinrich von der, G. philologist (1780–1856), 1810 U

Haggard, Sir Henry Rider, B. novelist (1856–1925), 1856 Z, 1886 U 1925 Z
Hague, The, Holland:
Treaty, for Britain to subsidise Allies, 1794 D
Communist Conference at, 1872 O
Convention, on territorial waters, 1882 F
international commission at, 1904 K
International Court of Arbitration, settlements by, 1903 B, 1910 J, 1911 A
Peace Conference at, 1907 F
International Court of Justice, Permanent, at, 1920 F, 1922 B
Iran *v.* Iranian Oil Company dispute outside jurisdiction, 1952 G
Congress on European Unity, at, 1948 E
Japanese Red Army terrorists take hostages, 1974 J
peace conference on Yugoslavia, 1991 J, L
Hahn, Kurt Matthias Robert Martin, G. educationalist (1886–1974), 1886 Z, 1934 O, 1974 Z
Hahn, Otto, G. atomic physicist (1879–1968), 1939 P
Hahnemann, Samuel, G. doctor (1755–1843), 1810 P
Haifa, Israel, pipelines to, 1935 P
Haig, Alexander Meigs, Am. soldier and Secretary of State (b. 1924)
Falklands plan rejected by Britain and Argentina, 1982 D
offers mediation in Falklands dispute, 1982 D
resigns, 1982 F
Haig, Douglas, Earl Haig, B. soldier (1861–1928), 1861 Z, 1915 M, 1917 G, 1928 Z
Hail and Farewell (G. Moore), 1914 U
Haile Selassie, Emperor of Ethiopia (1892–1975), 1892 Z, 1930 D, 1974 J, 1975 Z
Hailey, William Malcolm, Lord Hailey, B. administrator (1872–1969), 1957 O
Hain, Peter Gerald, B. politician (b. 1950), accused and acquitted of bank robbery, 1975 K, 1976 D
Hainan Tao, Island, Kwangtung, China: Japanese occupy, 1939 B; China regains sovereignty over, 1945 J
Hainault, Belgium, constitution revoked, 1789 K
Hainsich, Michael, Aus. statesman, Socialist (1858–1941), president of Austria, 1920 M, 1928 M
Haiphong, Vietnam, US bombing, 1966 F
Haiti: US marines land, 1914 A; US commission in, 1930 B
Jean-Claude Duvalier ('Baby Doc') succeeds his father, 1971 D
President Duvalier ('Papa Doc') dies, 1971 D
anti-government demonstrations, 1985 M
Duvalier flees and Namphy forms government, 1986 B
elections, 1988 A, 1990 M
military rule ended, 1988 B
military coups, 1988 F, J, 1991 J
attempted coup, 1989 D
Pascal-Triuillot replaces Avril as President, 1990 C
Haldane, John Burdon Sanderson, B. biochemist (1892–1964), 1935 R
Haldane, Richard Burdon, Viscount Haldane, B. Liberal statesman and lawyer (1856–1928), 1905 M
Haldeman, H.R., Am. presidential aide (b. 1926), 1975 A
Halévy, Ludovic, F. dramatist (1834–1908), 1869 W
Haley, Alex, Am. author (1921–92), 1976 U
Haley, Sir William John, B. journalist (1901–87), 1952 V
Haley, William ('Bill'), Am. singer (1927–81), 1955 W
Half-tone blocks, 1880 V
Halicarnassus, mausoleum of, discovered, 1857 Q
Halifax, Lord. *See* Wood
Hall, Albert W., Am. scientist, 1927 P
Hall, Alfred Rupert, B. historian of technology (b. 1920), 1955 P
Hall, Asaph, Am. astronomer (1829–1907), 1877 P
Hall, Harry Reginald Holland, B. archaeologist (1873–1930), 1918 Q
Hall, Marshall, B. physiologist (1790–1857), 1832 P
Hall, Sir Peter Reginald Frederick, B. theatre director (b. 1930), 1959 W, 1964 W, 1975 W, 1988 W
Hall, Robert, B. Baptist minister (1764–1831), 1791 R
Hallam, Henry, B. historian (1777–1859), 1777 Z, 1818 Q, 1827 Q, 1859 Z
Haller, Albrecht von, G. theologian (1708–77), 1772 R
Haller, Johannes, G. Catholic priest and historian, 1903 R
Halley's Comet, 1986 P
probes launched to rendezvous with, 1985 P
Halley, Peter, Am. artist (b. 1953), 1988 S
Ham, France, Louis Napoleon imprisoned in, 1840 H
Hamaguchi, Japanese premier, Minseito Party, assassinated, 1930 L
Hamah, Syria
anti-government rising, 1982 B
Hambach, Germany, Festival, 1832 E
Hamburg, Germany: Danes enter, 1801 C; annexed by Napoleon, 1810 M; Russians occupy, 1813 C; Communist riots in, 1921 C; R.A.F. bombs, 1942 G; Allies enter, 1945 E; Deutsches Elektron Synchroton (DESY), 1979 P
Hamburgische Dramaturgie (Lessing), 1767 W
Hamer, Robert, Am. film director, 1947 W
Hamilton, Alexander, Am. statesman (1757–1804), president of US, Federalist, 1786 E, 1789 D, 1790 B, 1792 N
Hamilton, Richard, B. artist (b. 1922), 1922 Z, 1968 S
Hammarskjöld, Dag (Hjalmar Agne Carl), Swe. statesman (1905–61), becomes UN Secretary-General, 1953 C; arranges Israel-Jordan ceasefire, 1956 D; visits Nasser, 1957 C; re-elected UN Secretary-General, 1957 J; enters Katanga, 1960 H; visits S. Africa, 1961 A; Khrushchev's campaign against, 1961 B; killed in air crash, 1961 J
Hammerstein, Oscar I, Am. composer and theatre manager (1847–1919), 1903 W
Hammerstein, Oscar II, Am. librettist (1895–1960), 1895 Z, 1960 Z
Hampden Clubs, 1811 O
Hampden, Viscount. *See* Brand, H. B. W.
Hampstead Garden Suburb, London, England, 1906 S
Hampton Roads, Virginia, US, naval action in, 1862 C
Hampton, Christopher James, B. dramatist (b. 1946), 1970 W, 1985 W
Hamrouche, Mouloud, President of Algeria (b. 1943), 1991 F
Hamsun, Knut. *See* Pederson, Knut
Hanafi Moslems, 1977 C
Hanau, Germany, French occupation, 1920 D
Hancock's Half-Hour, radio show, 1954 W
Hancock's Half-Hour, television show, 1956 W
Hancock, John, Am. statesman (1737–93), 1775 G
Hancock, Sir Keith, Austral. economic historian (1898–1988), 1949 Q
Hancock, Tony (Anthony John), B. comedian (1924–68), 1924 Z, 1954 W, 1956 W, 1968 Z
Handbook of Climatology (J. Hann), 1897 P
Handbook to the History of Graeco-Roman Philosophy (C. Brandis), 1835 Q
Handbuch der Urkundenlehre für Deutschland und Italien (H. Bresslau), 1889 Q
Handcuffs (*The Donnelly Trilogy*) (J. Reeney), 1975 W
Handel, George Frederick, G. musician (1685–1759), Messiah by, notable performances of, 1770 T, 1772 T; anniversary concert, 1959 T
Handicrafts Societies, National League of US, 1907 S
Handke, Peter, Aus. dramatist (b. 1942), 1968 W
Handley, Thomas ('Tommy'), B. comedian (1894–1949), 1942 W
Handmaid's Tale, The (M. Atwood), 1987 U
Hangchow, China, Japanese take, 1937 M
Hankey, Maurice, Lord Hankey, B. cabinet secretary (1877–1964), 1940 O, 1961 Q; becomes secretary of Committee of Imperial Defence, 1912 B
Hankow, China: Kuo Min Tang government at, 1927 A; reduction of British concessions at, 1927 B; Japanese take, 1938 K
Hanley, Gerald Anthony, B. author (b. 1916), 1953 U
Hanley, Staffs., England, riots at, 1874 B
Hann, Julius, Aus. meteorologist (1839–1921), 1897 P
Hanoi, North Vietnam: French reverses at, 1885 C; Communists occupy, 1954 K
US bombing raids, 1966 F, M
captured US airmen paraded, 1966 G
Hanover, Germany: Prussians overrun, 1801 D, 1805 M; French occupation of, 1803 F, 1806 D, K; Northern, annexed by Napoleon, 1810 M; proclaimed a Kingdom, 1814 K; Salic law in, 1837 F; invaded by Prussia, 1866 F; incorporated in Prussia, 1866 H, J; royal territory outside, confiscated by Prussia, 1868 C; US troops take, 1945 D; IRA car bomb attack, 1989 G
Hansen, T., Aus. architect (1813–91), 1861 S
'Hansom' cabs, 1834 P
Hansson, Per A., Swe. Social Democrat (1885–1946), 1945 G, 1946 K
Happy Days, television programme, 1974 W
Happy Death, A (A. Camus), 1971 U
Happy Mondays, B. pop group, 1990 W
Hara, Takashi, Jap. premier, 1921 L
Harald V, King of Norway (b. 1937), 1991 A
Harar, Ethiopia: assigned to Italy, 1894 E; British take, 1941 C
Harcourt, Sir William George Granville Venables Vernon, B. Liberal politician (1827–1904), 1886 B; 1892 H, 1899 A; becomes home secretary, 1880 D; becomes Liberal leader, 1896 K
Harden, Sir Arthur, B. chemist (1865–1940), 1906 P
Hardenberg, Friedrich von, G. author under pseudonym of 'Novalis' (1772–1801), 1772 Z, 1799 U, 1800 U, 1801 Z
Hardenberg, Karl August von, Prince, Pruss. statesman (1750–1822), 1810 F, 1811 J
Hardie, James Keir, B. Socialist leader (1856–1915), 1856 Z, 1893 A, 1915 Z
Harding, John, Lord Harding of Petherton, B. soldier and administrator (1896–1989), as governor of Cyprus, 1955 J, L, 1956 H, 1957 K

Harding, Warren Gamaliel, Am. statesman, Republican (1865–1923), president of US (1921–3), 1922 C, 1923 H; nominated, 1920 F; elected president, 1920 L; inaugurated, 1921 D; declares US could play no part in League of Nations, 1921 D
Hardinge, Charles, lord Hardinge, B. administrator (1858–1944), 1916 O
Hardtmann, Eduard von, G. philosopher (1842–1906), 1869 R
Hardy, Thomas, B. author (1840–1928), 1840 Z, 1928 Z
novels, 1872 U, 1874 U, 1878 U, 1887 U, 1891 U, 1896 U
plays, 1904 W
poems, 1898 U, 1919 U
Hare, David, B. dramatist (b. 1947), 1978 W, 1983 W, 1985 W
Hargreaves, James, B. inventor (d. 1778), 1764 P, 1778 Z
Harman, Gilbert Helms, Am. Philosopher (b. 1938), 1989 R
Harmonica, music for, 1952 T
Harmony (A. Panufnik), 1989 T
Harmony of the World (P. Hindemith), 1950 T
Harmsworth, Alfred, Viscount Northcliffe, B. journalist and newspaper proprietor (1865–1922), 1865 Z, 1896 V, 1904 V, 1922 Z; buys *The Times*, 1908 V
Harmsworth, Harold, Lord Rothermere, B. newspaper proprietor (1868–1940), 1868 Z, 1940 Z
Harnack, Adolf, G. theologian (1851–1912), 1886 R
Harper's Ferry, W. Virginia, US, John Brown's raid on, 1859 K
Harriman, Averell, Am. secretary of state, diplomat and Governor of New York (1891–1986), 1891 Z, 1941 J, 1986 Z; confers in Moscow, 1942 H; negotiates in Iran, 1951 G
Harris, Sir Arthur Travers, B. air marshal (1891–1980), 1892 Z, 1984 Z
Harris, Rt. Rev. Barbara, Am., suffragan Bishop of Massachusetts (b. 1930), 1988 R
Harris, Joel Chandler, Am. author under pseudonym of 'Uncle Remus' (1848–1908), 1848 Z, 1908 Z
Harris, José, B. historian, 1972 Q, 1977 Q
Harris, Roy, Am. musician (1898–1979), 1942 T
Harrison, Benjamin, Am. Republican (1833–1901), 23rd president of US (1889–93), 1833 Z, 1888 L, 1889 C; defeated in election, 1892 L
Harrison, Brian, B. historian (b. 1937), 1971 Q
Harrison, C. Ross, B. pathologist, 1907 P
Harrison, Michael R., Am. surgeon (b. 1943), 1989 P
Harrison, William Henry, Am. Whig (1773–1841), president of US, 1841 D
Harriss, John, B. historian and anthropologist, 1991 Q
Hart, J. C., Am. author, investigates Shakespeare–Bacon controversy, 1848 Q
Hart, Moss, Am. dramatist (1904–61), 1943 W
Hart, Robert, Am. inspector-general of Chinese Customs service (1863–1906), 1906 E
Harte, Bret, Am. author and editor (1836–1902), 1868 V, 1869 U
Hartford, Conn., US, Colt's armoury at, 1853 P
Hartington, Marquess of. *See* Cavendish, S. C.
Hartmann, H., G. philosopher, 1921 R, 1925 R
Haruki, Marukami, Jap. author (b. 1949), 1987 U
Harvey, P.J., 1992 W
Harwell, Berks, England, British nuclear research station at, 1947 P, 1956 P, 1961 P
Harwood, John, B. horologist, 1922 P
Harwood, Ronald, B. dramatist (b. 1934), 1980 W
Hashem, Ibrahim, Jordan Right-wing politician, 1957 D
Hassan (J. E. Flecker), 1923 W
Hassan II, King of Morocco (b. 1929), 1971 G
attempted assassination, 1972 H
Hastings, Adrian Christopher, B. historian (b. 1929), 1986 Q
Hastings, Warren, B. governor-general of India (1732–1818), 1772 D, 1773 J, 1774 O, 1775 N, 1778 N, 1781 F; plundering by, 1781 F; recalled, 1782 E; returns to England, 1785 F; is impeached, 1787 E; trial, 1788 B; acquittal, 1795 D
Hatteras, N. Carolina, US, Fort, captured by Unionists, 1861 H
Hattersley, Roy Sydney George, B. Labour politician (b. 1932), 1992 D
Haughey, Charles James, Eire politician (b. 1925), 1925 Z, 1970 E, 1992 A
Prime Minister, 1979 M, 1987 C
discusses Anglo–Irish links with Mrs. Thatcher, 1980 M
Hauptmann, Gerhart, G. author (1862–1946), 1862 Z, 1889 U, 1912 U, 1946 Z
Haussmann, Georges Eugène, baron, F. town-planner (1809–91), 1853 S
Haüy, René Just, F. mineralogist (1743–1822), 1784 P
Haüy, Valentin, F. founder of blind school (1745–1822), 1784 O
Havana, Cuba, West Indies, 1898 B, 1900 L; Spain exchanges Florida for, 1763 B; Russian exhibition in, 1960 B; 10,000 Cubans seek political asylum in Peruvian embassy, 1980 D
Have You Anything to Declare? (M. Baring), 1936 U
Havel, Václav, Czech. dissident playwright (b. 1936), 1936 Z
convicted of subversion, 1979 K
imprisonment, 1989 B
elected President of Czechoslovakia, 1989 M, R
resignation as President, 1992 G
Havelock, Sir Henry Marshman, B. soldier (1830–97), 1857 J
Havilland, Sir Geoffrey de, B. aircraft designer, 1965 Z
Hawaii Five-O, television programme, 1968 W
Hawaii: independence recognised, 1842 M, 1843 L; republic proclaimed, 1893 A; problem of US annexation, 1893 B; transferred to US, 1898 H; organised as US territory, 1900 D; becomes a US state, 1959 C
Hawke, Bob (Robert James Lee), Prime Minister of Australia (b. 1929), 1929 Z, 1991 M
Hawke, Edward, lord Hawke, B. admiral (1705–81), 1781 Z
Hawking, Stephen, B. scientist (b. 1942), 1942 Z, 1988 P
Hawkins, Anthony Hope, B. novelist under pseudonym of 'Anthony Hope' (1863–1933), 1863 Z, 1894 U, 1933 Z
Hawkins, Sir John, B. musicologist (1719–89), 1776 T
Hawks, Howard, Am. film director (1896–1977), 1959 W
Hawksmoor (P. Ackroyd), 1986 U
Hawthorne, Nathaniel, Am. author (1804–64), 1804 Z, 1850 U, 1851 U, 1853 U, 1864 Z
Haxthausen, August Franz Ludwig Maria von, G. political economist (1792–1866), 1843 O
Hay Fever (N. Coward), 1925 W
'Hay, Ian', B. author and dramatist, pseudonym of 'John Hay Beth' (1876–1952), 1936 W
Hay, John, Am. secretary of state (1838–1905), Note on 'Open-door' in China, 1899 J, 1900 G; treaty with Britain (Pauncefoote) on Panama, 1901 L; pact with Colombia (Herrán) on Panama Canal, 1903 A
Haydn, Joseph, Aus. musician (1732–1809), 1785 T, 1809 Z
Creation, The, 1798 T
Masses, 1766 T, 1796 T
Seasons, The, 1801 T
String quartets, 1771 T, 1781 T, 1797 T
Symphonies, 1764 T, 1772 T, 1777 T, 1780 T, 1784 T, 1788 T, 1791 T, 1794 T, 1795 T
anniversary concert, 1959 T
Haydon, Benjamin Robert, B. artist (1786–1846), 1786 Z, 1816 S, 1846 Z
Hayek, Friedrich August von (1899–1992), 1899 Z, 1944 R, 1992 Z
Hayes, Rutherford Birchard, Am. Republican (1822–1893), 19th president of US (1877–81), 1876 L, 1877 A, C
Hazlitt, William, B. essayist (1778–1830), 1778 Z, 1818 U, 1821 U, 1825 U, 1830 Z
Hazza-el-Majali, Jordan premier, assassinated, 1960 H
He Who Gets Slapped (L. Andreyev), 1916 W
Head of Catherine Lampert (F. Auerbach), 1986 S
Headingley Cricket Ground, Leeds, England Test Match, 1981 X
Headlong Hall (T. L. Peacock), 1816 U
Healey, Denis Winston, Lord Healey of Riddlesden, B. Labour politician (b. 1917), 1917 Z
becomes Chancellor of the Exchequer, 1974 C
currency crisis, 1976 J
announces wage increase guideline, 1978 G
loses Party leadership, 1980 L
wins Party deputy leadership, 1981 J
Healey-Kay, Patrick. *See* Dolin. Anton.
Health Service:
British, 1911 E, 1912 E, 1946 L
charges imposed, 1951 D
Guillebaud Committee on, 1956 A
charges increased, 1961 B
charges abolished, 1964 M
B.M.A. advises general practitioners to resign from, 1965 B
charges imposed, 1968 A, O
industrial action against hospital pay beds, 1974 G
family planning service, 1974 O
new management structure, 1974 O
consultants work-to-rule, 1975 A, D
government to abolish hospital pay beds, 1975 E
charges increased, 1981 M
pay dispute called off, 1982 M
opticians' monopoly on sale of spectacles ended, 1983 O
private contractors tender for services, 1983 O
National Health Service and Community Care Act, 1990 O
fears about future of, 1991 E
US, medical care for the aged, 1965 G
Health, World Assembly, 1948 O
Health, in Britain, report on, 1844 O
Healy, Timothy, Ir. politician, 1855 Z, 1931 Z
Heap 3 (B. Flanagan), 1968 S
Heape, A., Am. inventor of filming-machine, 1923 P
Hearing Secret Harmonies (*A Dance to the Music of Time*) (A. Powell), 1975 U
Hearst, Patricia Campbell, Am. heiress (b. 1954), 1975 J, 1976 C

Hearst, William Randolph, Am. newspaper proprietor (1863–1951), 1930 V
Heart of Midlothian (W. Scott), 1818 U
Heart of the Matter, The (G. Greene), 1948 U
Heat Rays, variability of, 1850 P
Heat of the Day, The (E. Bowen), 1949 U
Heat:
experiments concerning, 1778 P, 1840 P
generated by friction, 1798 P
radiant, discoveries in, 1831 P
treatises on, 1804 P, 1822 P, 1835 P, 1843 P
Heath, Sir Edward Richard George, B. Conservative leader (b. 1916), 1916 Z; statement on Britain's approach to the Common Market, 1961 K; elected Conservative leader, 1965 G
forms Conservative ministry, 1970 F
meeting with Pompidou, 1971 E
sharp exchanges with Eire Prime Minister Lynch, 1971 H
talks on Northern Ireland, 1971 J
use of 'intensive' interrogation techniques forbidden in Northern Ireland, 1972 C
Pay Board and Prices Commission, 1973 A
visits Eire and meets Cosgrave, 1973 J
three day week, 1973 M
government resignation after election defeat, 1974 C
visits China, 1974 E
resigns leadership, 1975 B
Heathcoat, John, B. manufacturer (1783–1861), 1809 P
Heathrow airport, bomb discovered in El Al passenger's luggage, 1986 D
Heating, by gas, devised, 1798 P
Heaviside Layer, measured, 1924 P
Heaviside, Oliver, B. mathematical physicist (1850–1925), 1902 P
Hébert, Jacques René, F. revolutionary (1757–94), 1793 R; partisans of, 1794 C
Hebrew, study of, 1812 Q
Hebron, Jordan, Israeli forces attack, 1966 L
Hecker, Isaac Thomas, Am. Catholic priest (1819–1888), 1858 R; opinions condemned by Pope Leo XIII, 1899 R
Hecuba (Euripides), 1802 Q
Hedda Gabler (H. Ibsen), 1890 W
Heenan, John C., Am. pugilist, 1860 X
Heeren, Arnold Hermann Ludwig, G. historian (1760–1842), 1800 O
Hegel, Georg Wilhelm Friedrich, G. philosopher (1770–1831), 1770 Z, 1801 R, 1807 R, 1812 R, 1817 R, 1821 R, 1831 Z; succeeds Fichte, 1818 R
Heidegger, Martin, G. philosopher (1889–1976), 1889 Z, 1927 R, 1929 R, 1976 Z
Heidelberg, Germany, European Molecular Biology Laboratory, inauguration, 1979 P
Heilmann, Josué, F. inventor (1796–1848), 1845 P
Heimat, television film, 1984 W
Heine, Heinrich, G. poet (1797–1856), 1797 Z, 1821 U, 1826 U, 1827 U, 1844 U, 1851 U, 1856 Z
Heinrich von Ofterdingen (Novalis), 1799 U
Heinse, Johann Jacob Wilhelm, G. author (1749–1803), 1787 U
Heir at Law, The (G. Colman), 1797 W
Heir of Redclyffe (C. M. Yonge), 1853 U
Heiress, The (J. Burgoyne), 1786 W
Heisenberg, Werner, G. physicist (1901–76), 1926 P, 1927 P
Heitler, Walter Heinrich, G. physicist (1904–81), 1927 P
Heizer, Michael, Am. sculptor (b. 1944), 1969 S
Hejaz (later Saudi Arabia): railway, 1900 N; Arab revolt in, 1916 F; Kingdom recognised, 1917 A; name changed to Saudi Arabia, 1926 A
Helicopter, 1917 P; first flight, 1939 P
Heligoland Bight, N. Sea, battle, 1914 H
Heligoland, Island, Germany: retained by Britain, 1814 A, 1815 F; exchanged with Germany for Zanzibar, 1890 G
Heliopolis, Turkey, Kléber's victory at, 1800 C
Helium, discovered, 1896 P
Hellman, Lillian, Am. playwright (1907–84), 1907 Z, 1939 W, 1960 W, 1984 Z
Helmholtz, Hermann, G. instrument-maker (1821–1894), 1847 P, 1850 P, 1851 P, 1856 P, 1858 P, 1862 P
Héloïse and Abelard (G. Moore), 1921 U
Helpmann, Sir Robert, Austral. actor and choreographer (1909–86), 1909 Z, 1986 Z
Helsinki (or Helsingfors), Finland: Bolsheviks occupy, 1918 A; Germans occupy, 1918 D
SALT talks, 1969 L
Conference on Security and Co-operation in Europe, 1972 L, 1973 G, 1975 H
World Athletics Championships, 1983 X
Israeli-Soviet talks on Russian Jews, 1986 H
'Helsinki process', 1983 J
Helvetian Republic, under Napoleon (Switzerland), 1798 C, H, 1801 B
Hemingway, Ernest Miller, Am. author (1900–61), 1927 U, 1929 U, 1932 U, 1937 U, 1940 U, 1950 U, 1952 U
Hemlock and After (A. Wilson), 1952 U
Hemming, J., B. chemist, 1838 P
Hempton, David, B. historian (b. 1952), 1984 Q
Hench, Philip Showalter, Am. physician (1896–1965), 1949 P
Henderson the Rain King (S. Bellow), 1959 U
Henderson, Arthur, B. Labour politician (1863–1935), 1903 G, 1916 M; becomes foreign minister, 1929 F; leads rump of Labour Party, 1931 H
Hendon, Middlesex, England, Police College, 1934 O
Hendrix, Jimi, Am. musician (1942–70), 1942 Z, 1967 W, 1970 W, Z
Henle, Friedrich, Gustav Jakob, G. pathologist and anatomist (1809–85), 1809 Z, 1846 P, 1885 Z
Henley, Oxfordshire, England, Regatta, 1839 X
Henry VIII (J. Chénier), 1791 W
Henry VIII (J.J. Scarisbrick), 1968 Q
Henry, Patrick, Am. statesman (1736–99), 1763 M, 1765 E
Henry, Prince of Prussia, 1771 A
Henty, George Alfred, B. author (1832–1902), 1832 Z, 1902 Z
Henze, Hans Werner, G. musician (b. 1926), 1956 T, 1958 T, 1960 T, 1961 T, 1966 T, 1974 T, 1976 T, 1983 T, 1990 T
Hepburn, Audrey, Belg. film actress (b. 1929), 1929 Z, 1953 W, 1959 W, 1961 W
Hepplewhite, George, B. cabinet-maker, 1786 Z
Hepworth, Dame (Jocelyn) Barbara, B. sculptor (1903–75), 1903 Z, 1953 S, 1954 S, 1955 S, 1959 S, 1975 Z
Heraclius II, of Georgia, recognises Russian sovereignty, 1783 K
Herald of Free Enterprise, capsized, 1987 C, G, K
Herat, Afghanistan, 1856 L
Herbart, Johann Friedrich, G. philosopher (1776–1841), 1806 O, 1813 R, 1824 R
Herbert, Sir Alan Patrick, B. author and lawyer (1890–1971), 1890 Z, 1937 G, 1971 Z
Herbert, George Edward Stanhope Molyneux, lord Carnarvon, B. archaeologist (1860–1923), 1922 Q
Herbert, Henry Howard Molyneux, lord Carnarvon, B. Conservative politician (1831–90), as colonial secretary, 1875 H
Herbison, Margaret McCrorie, B. Labour politician (b. 1907), 1967 G
Herder, Johann Gottfried von, G. author (1744–1803), 1769 U, 1772 Q, 1773 U, 1775 U, 1778 U, 1782 U, 1784 R, 1799 R, 1803 Z
Here Come the Clowns (P. Barry), 1938 W
Heredia, José Maria de, F. poet (1842–1905), 1893 U
Hereditary Genius, its Laws and Consequences (F. Galton), 1869 P
Heredity, laws of: established, 1866 P; rediscovered 1900 P; modified by Benoit, 1959 P
Hereros, in East Africa, rising of, 1904 K
Heresy: in Italy, Church's jurisdiction in, abolished, 1850 R
in Prussia, penalties for, 1788 R
Heritage and Its History (I. Compton-Burnett), 1959 U
Herman, Woody (Woodrow Charles), Am. jazz musician (1913–87), 1913 Z, 1936 T, 1987 Z
Hermann, K. S. L., G. chemical manufacturer, 1818 P
Hermes, Georg, G. Catholic theologian (1775–1831), 1819 R
Hermetic-sealing, 1765 P
Hermosillo, Jaime, Mexican film director (b. 1942), 1986 W
Hernani (V. Hugo), 1830 U
Herne Bay, Kent, England, church for Anglican–Methodist joint use, 1960 R
Hernu, Charles, F. Defence Minister (1923–1990), 1985 J
Hero of Our Time (M. Y. Lermontov), 1839 U
Hérold, Louis Joseph Ferdinand, F. musician (1791–1833), 1831 T
Herriot, Edouard, F. statesman, Radical Socialist (1872–1957), 1872 Z, 1957 D; as premier, 1924 F, G; ministry falls, 1925 D; forms new ministry, 1932 F; resigns, 1932 M
Herschel, Sir John Frederick William, B. astronomer (1792–1871), 1792 Z, 1825 P, 1834 P, 1871 Z
Herschel, Sir William, B. astronomer (1738–1822), 1781 P, 1783 P, 1786 P, 1789 P, 1800 P, 1802 P, 1822 Z
Herself Surprised (J. Cary), 1941 U
Hersey, John, Am. author (1914–93), 1945 U
Herstmonceux, Sussex, England, Royal Observatory moved to, 1953 P
Herter, Christian Archibald, Am. diplomat (1895–1966), 1895 Z, 1966 Z; succeeds Dulles as secretary of state, 1959 D
Hertling, Georg, Count von, G. Centre Party (1843–1919), becomes Chancellor, 1917 L
Hertz, Henrik, Da. author (1797–1870), 1845 W
Hertz, Rudolf, G. physicist (1857–94), 1887 P
Hertzberg, Ewald Friedrich, Count von, Pruss. minister (1725–95), 1791 G
Hertzen, Alexander, R. author (1812–70), 1850 U
Hertzog, James Barry Munnik, S. Afr. statesman, Nationalist and soldier (1866–1942), 1866 Z, 1942 Z; as Boer general, 1901 B; founds S. African party, 1910 D; is left out of Botha's cabinet, 1912 M; leads Nationalist Party to success, 1915 K; forms ministry, 1924 F; forms coalition, 1933 E; forms United S. African Nationalists, 1934 F; resigns premiership, 1938 E
Hervás y Panduro, Sp. philologist (1735–1809), 1800 Q

Herzegovina, Yugoslavia: rebellion, 1875 G, M; reforms, 1878 L. *See also* Bosnia and Herzegovina
Herzl, Theodor, Hung. founder of political Zionism (1860–1904), 1897 R
Herzog (S. Bellow), 1964 U
Herzog, Johann Jakob, G. Protestant theologian (1805–82), 1853 R
Herzog, Werner, G. film director (b. 1942), 1975 W, 1982 W
Heseltine, Michael Ray Dibdin, B. Conservative politician (b. 1933), 1992 P
causes Commons suspension, 1976 E
Defence Secretary, 1983 A, L
resignation over Westland affair, 1986 A
leadership challenge to Mrs. Thatcher, 1990 L
Hesperidin, phosphorated, as contraceptive tablet, 1952 P
Hesperus (Jean Paul), 1795 U
Hess, Dame Myra, B. pianist (1890–1965), 1939 T
Hess, Rudolf Walter Richmond, G. politician (1894–1987), 1894 Z, 1987 Z; lands in Scotland, 1941 E; sentenced by Nuremberg tribunal, 1946 J
Hesse, Grand Duchy, Germany: Prussia invades, 1866 F; Prussia incorporates, 1866 H, J
Hessian mercenaries, Britain recruits, 1776 H, M
Het Volk organisation in Transvaal, 1905 A
Heuss, Theodor, G. Free Democrat (1884–1963), 1954 G; becomes W. German president, 1949 J; retires, 1959 G
Hewett, Dorothy, Austral. dramatist (b. 1923), 1972 W, 1979 W
Hewish, Anthony, B. astronomer (b. 1924), 1967 P
Hey, Donald Holroyde, B. physicist (1904–87), 1946 P
Heydrich, Reinhard, G. Gestapo leader (1904–42), 1942 E
Heyerdahl, Thor. Nor. author and ethnologist (b. 1914), 1950 P
Heym, Stefan, G. writer (b. 1913), 1984 U
Heyne, Christian Gottlob, G. classical scholar (1729–1812), 1767 Q
Heyrowsky, J., Am. scientist, 1922 P
Heyse, Paul Johann Ludwig, G. author (1830–1915), 1873 U
Hibberd, Jack (John Charles), Austral. dramatist (b. 1940), 1972 W
Hibbert Lectures on Comparative Religion, 1878 Q
Hick, John Horwood, B. theologian (b. 1922), 1977 R
Hicks, William, B. general in Egyptian army (1830–1883), 1883 L
Hicks-Beach, Michael Edward, Earl of St. Aldwyn, B. Conservative politician (1837–1916), 1885 F; budget of, 1901 D
Hidalgo, planet, 1920 P
High Commission in Germany, Allied: takes over from Allied Military Government, 1949 J; makes concessions to Germany on joining Ruhr Authority, 1949 L
High Price of Bullion (D. Ricardo), 1809 O
High Priestess, The (A. Kiefer), 1985 S
High Tech architecture, 1984 S
High Technology, US bans sale of equipment to USSR, 1980 C
High Windows (P. Larkin), 1974 U
Highfield, John Roger Loxdale, B. historian (b. 1922), 1988 Q
Higuchi, Russell, Am. biologist (b. 1937), 1984 P
Hijackings:
Boeing 727 by Japanese students, 1970 C
attempted, at Leningrad airport, 1970 F
BOAC airliner by Palestinian terrorists, 1970 J
Palestinian terrorists hijack four aircraft, 1970 J
three aircraft blown up at Dawson's Field, 1970 J
Lufthansa flight hijacked by Palestinians, 1972 K
Dutch train by South Moluccan terrorists, 1975 M, 1977 E
Air France plane by Palestinian terrorists, 1976 F
hijacked plane in Mogadishu stormed, 1977 K
TWA jet by Shi'ite Moslem extremists, 1985 F
Achille Lauro cruise liner, 1985 K
hijacked Egyptian airliner stormed at Malta airport, 1985 L
Kuwaiti airliner by Shi'ite Moslem extremists, 1988 D
Hildesheim, Germany, ceded to Hanover, 1815 F
Hill Street Blues, television series, 1980 W
Hill, David, B. historian (b. 1937), 1981 Q
Hill, Geoffrey William, B. author (b. 1932), 1971 U
Hill, Graham, B. racing driver (1929–75), 1929 Z, 1962 X, 1969 X, 1975 Z
Hill, John Edward Christopher, B. historian (b. 1912), 1912 Z, 1967 Q, 1970 Q, 1972 Q
Hill, John, B. quack physician (?1716–75), 1770 P
Hill, Octavia, B. philanthropist (1838–1912), 1838 Z, 1864 O, 1912 Z
Hill, Sir Rowland, B. inventor of penny-postage (1795–1879), 1795 Z, 1840 O, 1879 Z
Hill, Ureli Corelli, Am. musician (1802–75), 1842 T
Hillary, Sir Edmund, N.Z. mountaineer (b. 1919), 1919 Z, 1953 P
Hiller, Johann Adam, G. musician (1728–1804), 1781 T
Hillery, Dr. Patrick John, Ir. Foreign Minister (b. 1923), 1970 G
Hills, Denis, B. lecturer (b. 1913), 1975 F
Hilton, John, B. socialist and economist (1883–1943), 1940 O
Hilton, Rodney Howard, B. historian (b. 1916) 1975 Q
Hindawi, Nezar, Arab terrorist, 1986 D
Hindemith, Paul, Swi. musician (1895–1963), 1922 T, 1924 T, 1929 T, 1938 T, 1944 T, 1950 T, 1957 T
Hindenburg Line, British break through, 1917 E
Hindenburg, Paul von, G. soldier and statesman (1847–1934), 1847 Z, 1914 J, 1934 H; as chief of general staff, 1916 M; demands peace offer, 1918 J; elected president of Germany, 1925 D; repudiates Germany's war guilt, 1927 J; authorises budget by decree, 1930 G; re-elected president, 1932 C, D
Hindi, becomes official language of India, 1965 O
Hindus. *See under* Religious Denominations
Hinsley, Arthur, B. Cardinal Archbishop of Westminster (1865–1943), 1935 R, 1943 R
Hinsley, Sir Francis Harry, B. historian (b. 1918), 1979 Q
Hirohito, Emperor of Japan (1901–89), 1901 Z, 1989 A, Z
visits Britain, 1971 K
Hiroshima (M. Oda), 1981 U
Hiroshima, Japan, atomic bomb on, 1945 H
Hirota, Koki, Japanese premier, 1936 A, 1937 F
Hirst, Damian, sculptor, 1990 S, 1992 S
His Eminence, Cardinal Basil Hume, O.S.B., Archbishop of Westminster (J. Stultiens), 1987 S
His House in Order (A. W. Pinero), 1906 W
Hiss, Alger, Am. Communist, 1950 A
Histoire contemporaine, L' (A. France), 1896 U
Histoire d'un fait divers (J. T. Gautier), 1946 U
Histoire de France (J. Michelet), 1833 Q
Histoire de Port-Royal (Sainte-Beuve), 1840 U
Histoire de dix ans (L. Blanc), 1841 O
Histoire de la Civilisation en France (F. Guizot), 1829 Q
Histoire de la Conquête d'Angleterre par les Normands (Thierry), 1825 Q
Histoire de la Révolution française (J. Michelet), 1847 Q
Histoire de la Révolution française (L. Thiers), 1823 Q
Histoire des Origines du christianisme (E. Renan), 1863 R
Histoire naturelle des animaux (Lamarck), 1815 P
Histoire naturelle des oiseaux (G. Buffon), 1786 P
Historic Buildings Council, grants by, 1954 S
Historical Association, The, 1917 Q
Historical Miniatures (A. Strindberg), 1905 U
Historical Research, Institute of, London, 1921 Q
Historismus (E. Troeltsch), 1922 R
History (E. Morante), 1974 U
History and Class Consciousness (G.S. von Lukacs), 1923 R
History and Historians of the Nineteenth Century (G. P. Gooch), 1913 Q
History and the Triune God (J. Moltmann), 1991 R
History as Literature (T. Roosevelt), 1914 Q
History as the Story of Liberty (B. Croce), 1941 Q
History of America (W. Robertson), 1771 Q
History of Ancient Art (J. J. Winckelmann), 1764 Q
History of Caliph Vathek, The (W. Beckford), 1786 U
History of Charles V (W. Robertson), 1769 Q
History of Chinese Civilization, A (J. Gernet), 1982 Q
History of Civilization (H. T. Buckle), 1857 Q
History of Creation, The (E. Haeckel), 1868 P
History of Dogma (Harnack), 1886 R
History of England (G. M. Trevelyan), 1926 Q
History of England (H. Belloc), 1925 Q
History of England (Lord Macaulay), 1848 Q
History of England Principally in the Seventeenth Century (L. von Ranke), 1859 Q
History of England from the Death of Wolsey to the Defeat of the Armada (J. A. Froude), 1856 Q
History of England from the Earliest Period (S. Turner), 1799 Q
History of England in the Eighteenth Century (W. E. H. Lecky), 1878 Q
History of England, 1603–56 (S. R. Gardiner), 1863 Q
History of English Christianity, 1920–1985, A (A. Hastings), 1986 Q
History of English Criminal Law and its Administration (L. Radzinowicz), 1986 Q
History of English Law (Pollock and Maitland), 1894 Q
History of English Poetry (T. Warton), 1774 U
History of Europe (H. A. L. Fisher), 1936 Q
History of European Morals, A (W. E. H. Lecky), 1869 Q
History of France, Principally in the Sixteenth and Seventeenth Centuries (L. von Ranke), 1852 Q
History of German Law (K. F. Eichhorn), 1808 Q
History of Germany in the Nineteenth Century (Treitschke), 1879 Q
History of Great Britain (D. Hume), 1763 Q
History of Greece (C. Thirlwall), 1835 Q
History of Greece (G. Grote), 1846 Q
History of Greece (W. Mitford), 1784 Q
History of Henry Esmond, The (W. M. Thackeray), 1852 Q
History of Herodotus, The (ed. H. Rawlinson), 1858 Q
History of Italian Literature (G. Tiraboschi), 1782 Q

History of Italy (C. Botta), 1824 Q
History of Latin Christianity (H. Milman), 1855 Q
History of Materialism (F. Lange), 1866 R
History of Medieval Political Theory in the West (A. J. Carlyle), 1936 Q
History of Mexico (I. Noguchi), 1936 S
History of Mr. Polly, The (H. G. Wells), 1910 U
History of Modern Philosophy (K. Fischer), 1852 R
History of Music (C. Burney), 1776 T
History of Protestant Dogma (G. J. Planck), 1781 R
History of Prussian Policy (J. Droysen), 1855 Q
History of Roman Law in the Middle Ages (F. Savigny), 1815 Q
History of Rome (T. Arnold), 1838 Q
History of Rome (T. Mommsen), 1853 Q
History of Soviet Russia (E. H. Carr), 1951 Q
History of Technology, A (Singer, Holymard and Hall), 1955 P
History of Thomas Friis, The (S. C. F. Schandorph), 1881 U
History of Trade Unionism (S. and B. Webb), 1894 O
History of Western Philosophy (B. Russell), 1946 R
History of the Anglo-Saxons (R. H. Hodgkin), 1935 Q
History of the Apostolic Church (P. Schaff), 1851 R
History of the Consulate and Empire (L. Thiers), 1845 Q
History of the Corruptions of Christianity, A (J. Priestley), 1782 R
History of the Countryside, The (O. Rackham), 1986 Q
History of the Crimean War (A. W. Kinglake), 1863 Q
History of the Crusades (S. Runciman), 1951 Q
History of the Czech Language (J. Dobrovsky), 1818 Q
History of the Earth and Animated Nature (O. Goldsmith), 1774 Q
History of the English Drama, 1660–1900 (A. Nicoll), 1973 Q
History of the English-Speaking Peoples (W. S. Churchill), 1956 Q
History of the French Revolution (H. von Sybel), 1853 Q
History of the French Revolution (L. Blanc), 1847 O
History of the German Languages (J. Grimm), 1848 Q
History of the Index of Forbidden Books (Reusch), 1883 R
History of the Inquisition in Spain (J. Llorente), 1817 R
History of the Italian Republics (J. Sismondi), 1807 Q
History of the Jews (H. H. Milman), 1829 Q
History of the Norman Conquest (E. A. Freeman), 1867 Q
History of the Oxford Movement (R. W. Church), 1891 R
History of the Peninsular War (W. Napier), 1828 Q
History of the Popes (L. von Ranke), 1834 Q
History of the Popes (Pastor), 1928 R
History of the Reformation in Germany (L. von Ranke), 1839 Q
History of the Revolt of the Netherlands under the Spanish Régime (F. Schiller), 1788 Q
History of the Rise and Influence of Rationalism in Europe, A (W. E. H. Lecky), 1865 Q
History of the Roman and Teutonic People (L. von Ranke), 1824 Q
History of the Russian Empire (N. Karamzin), 1816 Q
History of the Russian Revolution (L. Trotsky), 1933 O
History of the United Netherlands (J. R. Motley), 1860 Q
History of the United States (G. Bancroft), 1834 Q
History of the University of Oxford, The, 1984 Q
Hitachi Ltd, pleads guilty to conspiracy charges, 1983 B
Hitchcock, Sir Alfred Joseph, B. film director (1899–1980), 1899 Z, 1930 W, 1940 W, 1944 W, 1951 W, 1954 W, 1960 W, 1980 Z
Hitler Line, in Italy, 1944 E
Hitler, Adolf, G. dictator (1889–1945), 1889 Z 1931 K, 1943 V, 1945 D
  Munich *coup fails*, 1923 L
  imprisoned, 1924 D
  Mein Kampf, 1925 O, 1927 O
  opposes Hindenburg, 1932 C
  refuses to serve under von Papen, 1932 H
  rejects Chancellorship, 1932 L
  appointed Chancellor, 1933 A
  denounces Reichstag Fire as Communist plot, 1933 B
  is granted dictatorial powers, 1933 E
  meets Mussolini, 1934 F, 1938 E, 1940 K
  alleged plot against, 1934 F
  is vested with sole power as Führer, 1934 H
  Halifax visits, 1937 L
  becomes war minister, 1938 B
  annexes Austria, 1938 C
  attitude to Sudeten question, 1938 E, J
  Chamberlain's visits to, 1938 J
  dismisses Schacht, 1939 A
  dismembers Czechoslovakia, 1939 C
  denounces non-aggression pact with Poland, 1939 C
  denounces Anglo-German naval agreement, 1939 D
  pact with Mussolini, 1939 E
  invades Poland, 1939 J
  attempted assassination of, 1944 G
  study of last days of, 1947 Q
Hittite Language, The (Hrozny), 1917 Q
Hjeller, near Oslo, Norway, atomic research station, 1951 P
Ho Chi Minh, North Vietnamese leader (1892–1969), 1890 Z, 1945 J, 1965 M, 1967 B, 1969 J, Z
Hökfelt, Tomas G.M., research scientist, 1977 P
Hoare, Samuel John Gurney, Viscount Templewood, B. Conservative politician (1880–1959): becomes foreign secretary, 1935 F; resigns, following outcry at proposals on Abyssinia, 1935 M
Hoare–Laval Pact, with Mussolini on Abyssinia, proposed, 1935 M
Hoban, James, Am., formerly Ir., architect (1762–1831), 1792 G
Hobart, Tasmania, 1804 K
  Federal convention at, 1897 A
Hobbs, Sir John Berry, B. cricketer (1882–1964), 1882 Z, 1926 X
Hobhouse, Leonard Trelawny, B. philosopher and journalist (1864–1929), 1901 R, 1904 R
Hobson's Choice (Brighouse), 1916 W
Hobson, John Atkinson, B. economist and publicist (1858–1940), 1902 P
Hobson, Sir John Gardiner Sumner, B. lawyer and Conservative politician (1912–67), attorney-general, 1963 E
Hoche, Lazare, F. general (1768–97), 1794 G, 1796 M
Hochhuth, Rolf, G. dramatist, 1963 W
Höchstedt, Germany, battle, 1800 F
Hockney, David, B. artist (b. 1937), 1937 Z, 1967 S, 1970 S, 1971 S
Hodge, Merton (Horace Emerton), B. dramatist (1904–58), 1933 W
Hodgkin, Alan Lloyd, B. neurologist (b. 1914), 1963 P
Hodgkin, Dorothy Crowfoot, B. scientist (b. 1910), 1910 Z, 1955 P, 1964 P, 1969 P
Hodgkin, Robert H., B. historian (d. 1943), 1935 Q
Hodgkin, Sir Howard, B. painter (b. 1932), Turner Prize, 1985 S
Hodgkinson, Patrick, B. architect, 1973 S
Hodza, Milan, Czechoslovak politician, Agrarian party, 1935 L, 1938 J
Hoelderlin, Friedrich, G. author and translator (1770–1843), 1804 Q
Hoensbroech, Paul, G. churchman, 1902 R
Hofburg, Vienna, fire, 1992 L
Hoffmann, August Heinrich, G. author (1798–1874), 1841 T, 1847 U
Hoffmann, Ernst Theodor Wilhelm, G. author (1776–1822), 1776 Z, 1815 U, 1822 Z
Hofmann, K. H., G. chemist, 1960 P
Hofmann, Karl, G. chemist, 1909 P
Hofmannsthal, Hugo von, Aus. poet (1884–1929), 1884 Z, 1903 U, 1905 W, 1911 U, 1929 U, Z
Hogarth, William, B. artist (1697–1764), 1764 Z
Hogben, Lancelot, B. social biologist, 1936 O
Hogg, Quintin McGarel, Lord Hailsham, Conservative politician (b. 1907), appointed minister for North-East, 1963 A
Hoggart, Richard, B. author and critic (b. 1918), 1957 O
Hohenlinden, Bavaria, Germany, battle, 1800 M
Hohenlohe-Schillingsfürst, Chlodwig Karl Victor, Prince of, G. statesman (1819–1901); Chancellor, 1894 K; retires, 1900 K
Hola Camp, Kenya, deaths of Mau Mau prisoners in, 1959 C
Holbach, Paul Henri Thiry, Baron d', F. philosopher and natural historian (1723–89), 1770 R
Holden, William, B. architect, 1933 S
Hölderlin, Johann Christian Friedrich, G. author (1770–1843), 1797 U
Holford, Sir William Graham, B. town-planner (1907–75), 1956 S
Holiday camps, 1937 W
Holidays with pay, 1938 O
Holidays, Bank, in England and Wales, 1871 W, 1964 C
Holkar, Maharaja of Indore, 1802 K, 1804 D
Holkham, Norfolk, England, 1772 P
Holland (the Netherlands): sides with American Colonists, 1778 J; Britain declares war on, 1780 L; Germany invades, 1940 E.
  ministerial crisis, 1973 D
  Cruise missile, 1984 F
  urbanization, 1985 Y
  divorce statistics, 1987 Y
  life expectancy, 1990 Y
  illegitimacy rate, 1991 Y
  See also under Netherlands, The United
Holland, Agnieszka, Pol. film director (b. 1948), 1991 W
Holland, Edward Milner, B. lawyer (1902–69), reports on London housing, 1965 O
Holland, Sir Sidney George, N.Z. National Party leader (1893–1961), 1957 J
Hollandia, New Guinea, 1944 D
Holman Hunt, William, B. artist (1827–1910), 1827 Z, 1848 S, 1860 S, 1905 S, 1910 Z
Holmes, Colin, B. historian (b. 1938), 1988 Q
Holmes, Larry, Am. boxer (b. 1949), 1978 X
Holmes, Oliver Wendell, Am. author (1809–94), 1809 Z, 1858 U, 1861 U, 1867 U, 1894 Z

Holmyard, E. J., Am. historian of technology, 1955 P
Holocaust, television programme, 1978 W
Holography, 1947 P
Holst, Gustav, B. musician (1874–1934), 1874 Z, 1915 T, 1917 T, 1923 T, 1934 Z
Holstein, Duchy, W. Germany: Russia cedes claim to, 1776 D; Saxon and Hanoverian troops enter 1863 M; ceded to Austria and Prussia, 1864 K; acquired by Austria, 1865 H; Prussia annexes, 1866 F. *See also* Schleswig-Holstein Question
Holt, Harold, Prime Minister of Australia (1908–67), 1908 Z, 1966 A, 1967 M, 1967 Y
Holt, Richard, B. historian (b. 1948), 1989 Q
Holy Alliance, 1815 J, K, 1833 K; United Netherlands joins, 1816 F; Sweden joins, 1817 E
Holy Household, The: Women and Morals in Reformation Augsburg (L. Roper), 1989 Q
Holy Loch, Firth of Clyde, nr. Dunoon, Scotland, facilities for US Polaris submarines at, 1960 L
Holy Roman Empire, The (J. Bryce), 1864 Q
Holy Roman Empire: dismembered by Peace of Lunéville, 1801 B; reconstruction of, 1803 B; end of, 1806 H
Holy Shroud of Turin, carbon dating, 1988 R
Holyfield, Evander, boxer, 1990 X, 1992 W
Holyoake, Sir Keith Jacks, Prime Minister of New Zealand (1904–83), 1957 J, 1960 L, 1972 B
Holzer, Jenny, Am. artist (b. 1950), 1982 S, 1983 S, 1990 S
Homage to H. G. Wells (Brindle), 1963 T
Homage to Mistress Bradstreet (J. Berryman), 1956 U
Home Front (M. Walser), 1967 W
Home Guard, in Britain, 1940 E
Home Rule, for Ireland. *See* Ireland, Home Rule for
Home, Sir Alec (Alexander Frederick) Douglas-, Lord Home of the Hirsel, B. Conservative politician, 1903 Z, 1970 F, 1971 L, 1972 K; appointed foreign secretary, 1960 G; becomes premier, 1963 K; renounces peerage, 1963 K; resigns, 1964 K; resigns Conservative Party leadership, 1965 G
Home, William Douglas-, B. dramatist (1912–92), 1947 W
Homecoming, The (H. Pinter), 1967 W
Homeopathy, science of, founded, 1810 P
Homer, Winslow, Am. artist (1836–1910), 1865 S, 1877 S
Homeric studies, 1781 Q, 1795 Q
Homme approximatif, L' (T. Tzana), 1931 U
Homme comme les autres, Un (A. Salaam), 1936 W
Homme et ses fantmes, L' (Lenormand), 1924 W
Homme qui rit, L' (V. Hugo), 1869 U
Hommes de bonne volonté, Les (J. Romains), 1932 U
Homo Ludens (Huizinga), 1938 Q
Homosexual offences, Wolfenden Report on, 1957 J
Homosexuality:
Sexual Offences Act, 1967 O
General Synod of the Church of England report, 1987 R
Honderich, Ted (Edgar Dawn Ross), Canad. philosopher (b. 1933), 1988 R
Hondschoote, Belgium, 1793 J
Honduras: Britain takes, 1798 N; enters Central American Federation, 1823 G; union with Nicaragua and El Salvador, 1895 E; war with Nicaragua, 1907 B; civil war, 1909 M; becomes independent Republic, 1922 B; US troops in, 1924 B
Honduras–El Salvador border incidents following World Cup qualifying round, 1969 G
invasion by El Salvador, 1969 G
British, renamed Belize, 1973 F
hurricane Fifi, 1974 J
Contadora peace treaty, 1986 E
Arias Plan, 1987 H
Honecker, Erich, E. German leader (b. 1912), 1989 K
becomes Socialist Party leader, 1971 E
official visit to W. Germany, 1987 J
charged with abuse of office, 1989 M
trial on manslaughter charges, 1992 G
Honegger, Arthur, Swi., later Am., musician (1892–1955), 1920 T, 1921 T, 1923 T, 1926 T, 1927 T, 1934 T, 1945 T, 1950 T
Honest to God (J. Robinson), 1963 R
Hong Kong: British take, 1839; British sovereignty over, 1841 A; surrenders to Japan, 1941 M; typhoon strikes, 1960 F; hospital in, 1963 P
US warships, 1966 B
rioting following ferry toll increases, 1966 D
Chinese demonstrations against British possession, 1967 E
rioting, 1967 E
Communists arrested, 1967 G
emergency powers introduced, 1967 G
Communist bombing campaign, 1967 K
British sovereignty, 1968 A
share price panic, 1981 J
talks in Peking on future of, 1982 J
Sino-British talks on future of, 1983 G
China announces intention to declare unilateral policy on, 1983 L
draft agreement for return to China, 1984 J
elections for Legislative Council, 1985 J
Hong Kong and Shanghai Bank Headquarters, 1985 S
Britain rules out automatic right of abode to Hong Kong residents, 1989 G
Vietnamese boat people forcibly repatriated, 1989 M
Basic Law approved by Chinese People's Congress, 1990 D
Honolulu, Hawaii, meeting of Pacific Council, 1952 H
Honorary Consul, The (G. Greene), 1973 U
Honours and Awards:
in Britain:
Victoria Cross, 1856 A
Order of Merit, 1902 O
Garter Roll, Emperors of Germany and Austria removed from, 1915 E
Companion of Honour, 1917 O
Order of British Empire, 1917 O
George Cross, 1940, O, 1942 O
life peerages, 1958 G
Queen's Awards to Industry, 1965 O
New Year's Honours List, 1979 M
in France, Legion of Honour, 1802 E
in Germany, Goethe medal, 1932 Q
in US, Congressional Medal, awarded to Verdun, 1922 F
See also Nobel Prizes
Hontheim, Johann Nikolaus von (Justinus Febronius), G. Bishop of Treves (1701–90), 1763 R
Hood, Alexander, lord Bridport, B. admiral (1727–1814), occupies Toulon, 1793 H
Hood, John Bell, Am. Confederate general (1831–79), 1864 G
Hood, Raymond, Am. architect (1881–1934), 1923 S, 1930 S
Hood, Roger Grahame, B. historian (b. 1936), 1986 Q
Hooker, Sir William Jackson, B. director of Kew Gardens (1785–1865), 1835 P, 1841 P
Hoover, Herbert, Am. statesman, Republican (1874–1964), president of US (1929–33), 1874 Z, 1922 O, 1930 F, 1964 Z; as director of relief for Europe, 1919 A; election, 1928 L; proposes moratorium for war debts, 1931 F, H; Roosevelt defeats, 1932 L; vetoes Philippines independence, 1933 A
Hoover, John Edgar, Am. Director of FBI (1895–1972), 1895 Z, 1924 O, 1972 Z
'Hope, Anthony.' *See* Hawkins, Anthony Hope
Hopkins, Gerard Manley, B. poet (1844–89), 1918 U
Hopkins, Harry L., Am. Democrat statesman (1890–1946), 1890 Z, 1942 D, 1946 Z, 1948 Q
Hopper, Edward, Am. artist (1882–1967), 1931 S
Hoppner, John, B. artist (1758–1810), 1786 S
Horace (Corneille), produced, 1838 W
Horace Walpole's Correspondence (W.S. Lewis ed.), 1983 Q
Hore-Belisha, Leslie, lord Hore-Belisha, Conservative politician (1894–1957); war secretary, 1937 M, 1940 A
Horen (ed. F. Schiller), 1794 U
Hormones, discovered, 1902 P
Giberellin, 1957 P
pituitary, is synthesised, 1960 P
Horn, Rebecca, G. artist (b. 1944), 1975 S
Hornby, Charles Harry St. John, B. printer and connoisseur (1867–1946), 1894 S
Horos (I. Xenakis), 1987 T
Horovitz, Israel, Am. dramatist (b. 1939), 1968 W
Horror comics, 1952 V
Horse-racing:
in Britain, Ascot, grandstand rebuilt, 1964 S
Arkle, third successive Cheltenham Gold Cup victory, 1966 X
Cesarewitch, The (Newmarket), 1839 X
Derby, The (Epsom), 1779 X
won by Edward VII, 1896 X, 1909 X
Derby won by *Shergar*, 1981 X
Goodwood, 1802 X
Grand National, The (Aintree), 1839 X
Newmarket, 1809 X
Piggott wins The Derby on *Nijinsky*, 1970 X
Piggott wins Triple Crown, 1970 X
Red Rum wins Grand National, 1977 X
St. Leger, The (Doncaster), 1776 X
stable boys' pay dispute, 1975 X
women jockeys allowed to compete, 1972 X
in France, Grand Prix de Paris (Longchamp), 1863 X
Prix du Jockey Club, 1836 X
in US, 1818 X, 1894 X
Hort, Fenton John Anthony, B. churchman and New Testament scholar (1828–92), 1881 Q
Horthy de Nagybanya, Nicholas, Hung admiral and regent (1868–1957), 1920 C, 1957 Z
Hospitals:
in Britain, Elizabeth Garrett Anderson, 1866 O
in France, 1789 O
in Germany, epileptic, 1868 O
in Hong Kong, 1963 P
Hoskins, William George, B. historian (1908–92), 1908 Z, 1976 Q, 1992 Z
Hostage, The (B. Behan), 1959 W
Hostages:
Beirut, 1985 C, F, 1986 D, 1987 A
Kuwaiti airliner hijacked, 1988 D
Lebanon, French hostages in, 1988 E, 1990 D
Brian Keenan released, 1990 H
Western nationals in Kuwait rounded up and

used as 'human shields' in Gulf War, 1990 H, M
Alan Steen, 1991 M
John McCarthy released, 1991 H
Terry Waite released, 1991 L
Joseph Cicipio, 1991 M
Terry Anderson, 1991 M
'Hot line', White House–Kremlin, 1963 F
Hot Springs Conference, 1943 F
Hot-strip rolling of steel, 1923 P
Hotson, Leslie, Am. Shakespearean scholar (1897–1992), 1964 Q
Hottentots, E. Africa, rising of, 1904 K
Hou Xiaoxian, Chinese film director, 1990 W
'Houdini.' *See* Weiss, E.
Houdon, Jean Antoine, F. sculptor (1741–1828), 1764 S, 1771 S, 1775 S, 1779 S, 1781 S, 1783 S; visits US, 1785 S
Hound of the Baskervilles, The (A. C. Doyle), 1902 U
Hounsfield, Sir Godfrey Newbold, B. scientist (b. 1919), 1919 Z
Hourra l'Oural (L. Aragon), 1934 U
Hours of Idleness (Byron), 1807 U
House Fly, Disease Carrier, The (L. O. Howard), 1912 P
House and its Head, A (I. Compton-Burnett), 1935 U
House of Blue Leaves, The (J. Guare), 1971 W
House of Mirth, The (E. Wharton), 1905 U
House of Seven Gables (N. Hawthorne), 1851 U
House of Spirits, The (I. Allende), 1982 U
House of the Dead, The (F. Dostoievsky), 1870 U
House, Edward Mandell, Am. statesman (1858–1938), 1858 Z, 1926 O, 1938 Z
Housemaster, The (I. Hay), 1936 W
Housewife-Superstar! (B. Humphries), 1976 W
Housing:
in Britain, artisans, 1867 O, 1884 O, 1890 O
building under act of 1919, 1919 O, 1939 Y
slum clearance, 1932 D, 1950 S
landlord and tenant act, 1954 O
rent act, de-restricts previously controlled rents, 1957 F
rent riots, 1960 J
L.C.C. offers 100 per cent. loans for house purchase, 1963 B
'Rachmanism', 1963 O
rent act, 1965 M
Milner Holland report on rented accommodation in London, 1965 O
Leasehold Reform Act, 1967 O
Northern Ireland, proposed reforms, 1968 L
government subsidy prevents rise in mortgage rate, 1973 D
mortgage rate increase, 1973 J
Housing Act gives council tenants right to buy homes, 1980 O
See also Building Societies; New Towns
in India, protests at, 1951 F
in US, finance for, under Wagner-Steagall Act, 1937 J
Civil Rights Bill, 1968 D
Housman, Albert Edward, B. poet and classical scholar (1859–1936), 1859 Z, 1896 U, 1936 Z
Housman, Laurence, B. author (1865–1959), 1918 U, 1937 W
Houston, Tex., US:
Rothko Chapel, 1958 S
de Menil Museum, 1987 S
Hovaida, Amir Abbas, Prime Minister of Iran (1919–79), 1979 D
Hovercraft, regular service introduced in English Channel, 1968 P
How Gertrude Teaches her Children (J.H. Pestalozzi), 1801 O
How Green Was My Valley (R. Llewellyn), 1939 U
Howard's End (E. M. Forster), 1910 U
Howard, Henry Charles, earl of Surrey, later duke of Norfolk, B. Conservative politician (1791–1856), 1829 O
Howard, John, B. philanthropist (?1726–90), 1770 O
Howard, L. O., B. physician, 1912 P
Howard, Leslie, B. film actor (1893–1943), 1938 W, 1941 W
Howard, Maurice, B. architectural historian, 1987 Q
Howe, Elias, Am. inventor (1819–67), 1846 P
Howe, Julia Ward, Am. author (1819–1910), 1819 Z, 1910 Z
Howe, Richard, Earl Howe, B. admiral (1726–99), 1782 K, 1794 F
Howe, Sir (Richard Edward) Geoffrey, Lord Howe, B. Conservative politician (b. 1926), 1926 Z, 1981 M
first budget, 1979 F
exchange controls abolished, 1979 K
announces public spending cuts and taxation increases, 1980 L
Foreign Secretary, 1983 F
peace mission to South Africa, 1986 F, G
resignation as Leader of the House of Commons, 1990 L
Howe, Sir William, B. soldier (1729–1814), 1776 C, J, 1777 J
Howell, Denis Herbert, Lord Howell, B. Labour politician (b. 1923), 1976 H
Howells, William Dean, Am. author (1837–1920), 1837 Z, 1882 U, 1920 Z
Howick Committee on ecclesiastical appointments, 1964 R
Hoxha, Enver, Albanian leader (1908-85), 1945 L, 1966 L, 1985 D
Hoyle, Fred, B. astronomer (b. 1915), 1950 W, 1957 R, 1961 P, 1964 P
Hrawi, Elias, President of The Lebanon (b. 1930), 1989 L
Hrozny, Bedrich, Czech. archaeologist (1879–1952), 1917 Q
Hsi-an, China, 1974 Q
Hsu Shi-chang, president of China, 1918 J
Hua Kuo-feng, Ch. premier (b. 1920), 1976 A
succeeds Mao as Chairman, 1976 K
repudiates Soviet-bloc congratulations, 1976 K
Hubble Space Telescope placed in Earth orbit, 1990 P
Huber, Johann Nepomuk, G. philosopher and leader of Old Catholics (1830–79), 1869 R
Hubertusburg, Treaty of, 1763 B
Hübsch, Heinrich, G. architect (1795–1863), 1840 S
Huch, Richard, G. author, 1914 O
Huckleberry Finn (M. Twain), 1884 U
Huddleston, Trevor, B. churchman (b. 1913), 1957 O
Hudson River, New York, US, 1807 P
Hudson's Bay Company, territories of, purchased by Canada, 1869 L
Hudson, Rock (born Roy Harold Scherer), Am. film star (1925–85), 1985 P
Hudson, William Henry, B. author (1841–1922), 1904 U
Hué, Annam, 1884 F
Hueffer, Ford. *See* Ford, Ford Madox
Huerta, Adolfo de la, Mex. president, 1920 E
Huerta, Victoriano, Mex. general (1854–1916), 1913 K, L, 1914 G
Hufeland, Gottlieb, G. economist (1760–1817), 1807 O
Huggins, Godfrey, lord Malvern, premier of Central African Federation (1883–1971), 1953 M; retires, 1956 K
Hughes, Charles E., Am. Republican (1862–1948), nominated Republican candidate, 1916 F; as secretary of state, 1923 C, 1925 A
Hughes, David Edward, B. electrician (1831–1900), 1878 P
Hughes, Howard, Am. businessman, aviator and recluse (1905–76), 1905 Z, 1938 P, 1950 O, 1976 Z
Hughes, John Russell, Am. scientist (b. 1928), 1975 P
Hughes, Richard, B. author (1900–76), 1973 U
Hughes, Ted, B. poet (b. 1930), 1930 Z, 1970 U
appointed Poet Laureate, 1985 U
Hughes, Thomas B. author (1822–96), 1857 U
Hughes, William, Austral. politician, Labour, later Nationalist, as premier, 1917 B, 1921 M
Hugo, Victor, F. poet and dramatist (1802–85), 1802 Z, 1819 U, 1829 U, 1830 U, 1831 U, 1832 W, 1838 U, 1856 U, 1859 U, 1862 U, 1866 U, 1869 U, 1874 U, 1885 Z
Huis Clos (J.-P. Sartre), 1944 W
Huizinga, J. B., Du. historian, 1919 Q, 1938 Q
Hull, Cordell, Am. statesman (1871–1955), secretary of state (1933–44), 1944 L
Hull, Yorkshire, England, disturbances following Toxteth riots, 1981 G
Human Factor, The (G. Greene), 1978 U
Human Genome Organization (HUGO), 1988 P
Human Immunodeficiency Virus (HIV), 1981 P, 1983 P
Human Nature (J. Dewey), 1922 R
Human Nature in Politics (G. Wallas), 1908 U
Human Needs of Labour, The (S. Rowntree), 1937 O
Human Rights (ed. J. Maritain), 1949 O
Human Rights:
UN declaration on, 1948 M
European convention on, 1954 E
European court of, 1959 B
Czechoslovakian 'Charter 77' manifesto, 1977 A
violations in Uganda, 1977 B, F
Orlov, Soviet human rights campaigner, sentenced, 1978 E
violations in Nicaragua, 1979 B
violations in Argentina, 1983 H, 1985 M
European Conference on Security and Co-operation, 1983 J
violations in Chile, 1984 R
Britain found guilty of sex discrimination in immigration policy, 1985 O
European Court of. *See* European Court of Human Rights
Human Sacrifices:
in Ashanti, 1874 B
in Benin, 1879 N
Human Understanding (S. Toulmin), 1972 R
Humanae Vitae Papal Encyclical, 1968 R
Humanity Asleep (J. Schnabel), 1982 S
Humber, Lincolnshire–Yorkshire, England, bridge opens, 1981 P
Humbert I, King of Italy (1878–1900), 1878 A; assassinated, 1900 G
Humboldt, Alexander von, G. astronomer and explorer (1769–1859), 1769 Z, 1799 P, 1807 P, 1808 R, 1845 P
Humboldt's Gift (S. Bellow), 1975 U
Humboldt, Karl Wilhelm von, G. philologist and author (1767–1835), 1791 O; becomes Prussian education minister, 1810 O
Hume, (George) Basil, B. Roman Catholic Archbishop of Westminster (b. 1923), 1923 Z, 1976 R, 1987 S

Hume, David, Scot. philosopher and historian (1711–76), 1763 Q, 1776 Z, 1779 R
Hume, Joseph, B. Radical (1777–1855), 1824 O
Humperdinck, Engelbert, G. musician (1854–1921), 1854 Z, 1893 T, 1921 Z
Humphrey, Hubert Horatio, Am. Democrat politician (1911–78), 1911 Z, 1978 Z
Presidential election candidacy, 1968 D, H, L
Humphries, (John) Barry, Austral. comedian (b. 1934), 1976 W
Hun Sen, Prime Minister of Kampuchea, 1985 A
Hundred Days of Reform, by Te Tsung, 1898 F
Hundred Days, Napoleon's, 1815 C
Hundred Days, The (Mussolini and Forzano), 1931 O
Hung Siu-tsuen, Chin. rebel, 1850 K
Hungarian literature, 1783 U
Hungary: under Maria Theresa, 1765 H; serfdom abolished, 1780 K; Red Army advances in, 1944 K; republic proclaimed, 1946 B; crisis of 1956.
economy, 1987 F
political parties allowed, 1989 A
demonstration calling for democracy and national independence, 1989 C
Austrian border security fence dismantled, 1989 E
East Germans allowed to cross freely to West, 1989 J
Socialist Workers' Party votes for its own dissolution, 1989 K
Democratic Forum wins landslide victory, 1990 D
Democratic Republic of, 1990 H, K
illegitimacy rate, 1991 Y
See under Revolutions, Hungarian
Hunger (K. Hamsun), 1890 U
Hunger Marches, in Britain, 1922 K, L
Hungerford, Berkshire, England, Ryan kills 16 with automatic weapon, 1987 H
Hungerpastor, Der (W. Raabe), 1864 U
Hunt Committee report, on Northern Ireland policing, 1969 K
Hunt, Sir Henry Cecil John, B. mountaineer (b. 1910), 1910 Z, 1953 P
Hunt, Leigh, B. author (1785–1859), 1785 Z, 1808 V, 1816 U, 1859 Z
Hunt, William Holman. *See under* Holman Hunt
Hunter, John, B. surgeon and anatomist (1728–93), 1794 P
Hunter, Norman Charles, B. dramatist (1908–71), 1953 W
Hunter, William, B. anatomist (1718–83), 1774 P
Huntingdon, Selina Hastings, Countess of (1707–91), 1771 R, 1779 R
Huntingtower (J. Buchan), 1922 U
Hurd, Douglas Richard, B. Conservative politician (b. 1930)
Home Secretary, 1985 J
Conservative Party leadership election, 1990 L
Hurricanes, 1963 K
Fifi, 1974 J
Fastnet yacht race hit by, 1979 H
David, 1979 J
England, 1987 K
Hugo, 1989 J
Andrew, 1992 H
Hurry on Down (J. Wain), 1953 U
Husák, Gustáv, Czechoslovak General Secretary of Communist Party, 1913 Z, 1969 D, 1991 Z
political and economic reforms, 1987 C
resignation, 1987 M
Husker Du, 1986 W
Huskisson, William, B. Tory statesman (1770–1830), 1770 Z, 1830 J; as president of Board of Trade, 1823 A, O; resigns from Wellington's ministry, 1828 E
Hussein, Kemel, Khedive of Egypt, 1914 M
Hussein, King of Hejaz (1916–24), abdicates, 1924 K, 1970 F; expelled, 1926 A
Hussein, King of Jordan (b. 1935), 1952 H; dismisses General Glubb, 1956 C; proclaims martial law, 1957 D; as head of Arab Federation, 1958 G; dissolves Arab Federation, 1958 H; asks for British support, 1958 G
Middle East peace plan, 1969 D
ceasefire with Palestine agreed, 1970 F
Palestinian militia disbanded, 1970 J
signs Cairo agreement, 1970 J
autonomous Palestinian state proposed, 1972 C
talks with Arafat on proposed Palestinian state confederated with Jordan, 1982 K
peace initiative talks with Mubarak, 1984 M
meeting with President Assad of Syria, 1985 M
plans to cut legal and administrative ties with occupied West Bank announced, 1988 G
Hussein, Saddam, Iraqi leader (b. 1937), 1979 G, 1990 M
Husserl, Edmund, G. philosopher, 1913 R
Huston, John, Am. film director (1906–87), 1951 W
Hutchinson History of the World, The (J.M. Roberts), 1976 Q
Hutchinson, Horatio Gordon ('Horace'), B. golfer (1859–1932), 1886 X
Hutchinson, Thomas, B. governor of Massachusetts Colony (1711–80), 1774 B
Hutton, James, B. geologist (1726–97), 1788 P
Hutton, John, B. artist (b. 1927), 1962 S
Hutton, Sir Leonard, B. cricketer (b. 1916), 1938 X
Huvé, Jean Jacques, F. architect, 1845 S
Huxley, Aldous Leonard, B. author (1894–1963), 1894 Z, 1921 U, 1925 U, 1928 U, 1932 U, 1936 U, 1937 R, 1944 U, 1946 R, 1948 U, W, 1958 U
Huxley, Anthony Julian, B. author (b. 1920), 1992 Q
Huxley, Elspeth, B. traveller and author (b. 1907), 1944 O
Huxley, Sir Julian Sorell, B. biologist (1887–1975), 1887 Z, 1944 O, 1975 Z
Huxley, Thomas Henry, B. scientist (1825–95), 1825 Z, 1858 P, 1870 P, 1889 R, 1893 P
Huysmans, Joris Karl, F. novelist (1848–1907), 1848 Z, 1891 U, 1895 U, 1898 U, 1907 Z
Hwang, David Henry, Am. dramatist (b. 1957), 1988 W
Hyacinthe, Père. *See* Loyson. Hyacinthe
Hyatt, J. W., Am. inventor of celluloid (1837–1920), 1869 P
Hyde Park, London
IRA bomb, 1982 G
Hyde, Douglas, president of Eire (1860-1949), 1938 E, 1945 F
Hyder Ali, Ind. ruler (*c.* 1722–82), 1763 N, 1769 F, 1782 M; usurps throne of Mysore, 1764 N; conquers the Carnatic, 1780 J; defeated by Coote, 1781 G
Hyderabad, India: Nizam of, 1766 L, 1790 G, 1792 B, 1798 J, 1799 E; joins Indian Union, 1948 J
Hydraulic press, invented, 1795 P
Hydro-electric plant, 1882 P, 1886 P, 1935 P, 1952 P
Hydrogen Bomb:
Russia explodes, 1953 P
US development of, 1950 A, 1952 P, 1954 P
Hydrogen, density of, 1766 P
sulphuretted, 1777 P
Hydrography, studies in, 1855 P, 1872 P
Hydrophobia, cured, 1885 P
Hyer, Tom, Am. boxer, 1841 X
Hylton-Foster, Sir Harry, B. Conservative politician and Speaker of House of Commons (1905–1965), 1965 J
Hymn of Jesus (A. Holst), 1917 T
Hymnals:
English Hymnal, The, 1906 R
Olney Hymns (Cowper and Newton), 1779 R
Songs of Praise, 1925 R
Hymnen (K. Stockhausen), 1967 T
Hyndman, Henry Mayers, B. Socialist (1842–1921), 1886 B
Hyogo, Japan, Rokko Housing, 1983 S
Hypatia (C. Kingsley), 1853 U
Hyperion (J. Hölderlin), 1797 U
Hyperion (J. Keats), 1819 U
Hypnotism, 1842 P

I

I am a Camera (J. van Druten and C. Isherwood), 1954 W
I Am Still Alive (Kawara), 1970 S
I and Thou (M. Buber), 1837 R
I Know Why the Caged Bird Sings (M. Angelou), 1970 U
I like America and America Likes Me (J. Beuys), 1974 S
I'm Talking About Jerusalem (A. Wesker), 1960 W
I Promessi Sposi (A. Manzoni), 1825 U
I Shop Therefore I Am (B. Kruger), 1987 S
I, Claudius (R. Graves), 1934 U
I, Claudius, television series, 1976 W
I, Robot (I. Asimov), 1951 U
I, Too, Speak of the Rose *(E. Carballido), 1966 W*
Iambes, Les (H. Barbier), 1831 U
Ibánez, Cárlos, Chil. dictator, 1927 D, 1931 G, 1952 J
IBM, personal computer with built-in hard disc, 1983 P
Ibn Saud, King of Saudi Arabia (*c.* 1880–1953), 1926 A
Ibrahim Abboud, Sudan. politician, 1958 L
Ibrahim, son of Mohammed Ali of Egypt, 1826 D, 1832 E; routs Turks, 1839 F; evacuates Syria, 1840 L; viceroy of Egypt, 1848 L
Ibsen, Henrik, Nor. dramatist (1828–1906), 1828 Z, 1850 W, 1864 U, 1866 W, 1867 U, 1877 W, 1879 W, 1881 W, 1882 W, 1884 W, 1890 W, 1896 W, 1906 Z; plays of, introduced to London, 1891 W
Ice-breaker, nuclear-powered, 1958 P
Iceland: self-government granted, 1874 G; becomes a sovereign state, 1918 M; Allied occupation, 1941 G; demands withdrawal of US troops, 1956 C; US troops writhdraw, 1959 M
fishing limit extended, 1972 J
Anglo–Icelandic talks on fisheries break down, 1972 L
diplomatic relations with Britain, 1973 J, 1976 B
'Cod War'. *See* Fisheries
Ice Cube (born Oshea Jackson), Am. rap artist, 1990 W Iceland
Icelandic, study of, 1810 Q, 1811 Q
Iceman Cometh, The (O'Neill), 1946 W
Idaho, State, US: organised as US territory, 1863 C; becomes a US state, 1890 G; grants for irrigation in, 1894 H
Iddesleigh, Earl. *See* Northcote, Stafford

Idea of History, The (R. G. Collingwood), 1946 R
Idea of Nature, The (R. G. Collingwood), 1945 R
Ideals in Ireland (G. W. Russell and others), 1901 U
Ideas towards a Philosophy of History (J. G. von Herder), 1784 R
Ideological Origins of the American Revolution, The (B. Bailyn), 1967 Q
Ideologies of Class, The: Social Relations in England 1880–1950 (R. McKibbin), 1990 Q
Idris, King of Libya, 1969 J
Idiot, The (F. Dostoievsky), 1868 U
Idiots' Delight (R. Sherwood), 1936 W
Idlewild, N. York, US, Kennedy Airport, 1961 S
Idris I, King of Libya, 1951 M
Idstedt, Austria, 1850 G
Idylls of the King (Tennyson), 1859 U
If Christ Came to Chicago (W. T. Stead), 1893 R
If Not Now, When (P. Levi), 1982 U
If on a Winter's Night a Traveller (I. Calvino), 1979 U
If the Shoe Fits (R. Deacon), 1980 S
If This is a Man (P. Levi), 1947 U
Iffland, August, G. theatrical director (1759–1814), 1796 W
Igloo Fibonacci (Merz), 1970 S
Ignatiev, Nikolai Pavlovich, R. diplomat (1832–1908), 1878 C
Ikeda, Hayato, Jap. Liberal Democrat (1899–1965), 1960 G
Ikeya, M., Jap. scientist, 1980 P
Ikon of Light (J. Tavener), 1984 T
Ile de Bourbon, Indian Ocean, British take, 1810 G
Ile des pingouins, L' (A. France), 1908 U
Il fu Mattia Pascal (L. Pirandello), 1904 W
Ileo, Joseph, Congol. politician, 1960 J
Iliescu, Ion, President of Roumania (b. 1930), 1990 E, 1992 K
Ili Valley, N.W. China, Russia acquires posts in, 1879 J
Illegitimacy, statistics, 1991 Y
Illinois, state, US: becomes a US state, 1818 M; population, 1818 M; prohibition enforced in, 1851 O
Illiteracy, statistics of comparative, 1935 Y, 1983 Y
Illuminations, Les (A. Rimbaud), 1886 U
Illusion and Reality (Caudwell), 1937 U
Illustrated Man, The (R. Bradbury), 1952 U
Illustrated, half-tone block for, 1880 V
Illustrations ... of the Principles of Population (F. Place), 1822 P
Illustrator Was There, An (D. Salle), 1981 S
Illyria: Austria cedes to France, 1809 K; France promises restoration, 1812 C
Image Old and New (M. Ramsey), 1963 R
Image-dissector camera, 1956 P
Imaginary Conversations (W. S. Landor), 1824 U
Immermann, Karl Lebrecht, G. poet (1796–1840), 1836 U, 1838 U
Immigration:
  Rome Conference on, 1924 E
  Nigeria orders expulsion of illegal immigrants, 1983 A
  statistics in western Europe, 1969 Y
  to Australia, restricted, 1855 N, 1902 G
  colour bar abandoned, 1973 A
  to Austria, 1969 Y
  to Belgium, 1969 Y
  to Britain, statistics, 1938 Y, 1969 Y
    controlled by Commonwealth Immigration Act, 1961 L, 1962 O
    limit on Commonwealth immigrants imposed, 1965 H
    Kenyan Asians, emergency legislation to restrict, 1968 C
    Powell's 'river of blood' speech, 1968 D
    Powell calls for repatriation of coloured immigrants, 1969 F
    Immigration Bill, 1971 B
    government defeated on new rules favouring EC over Commonwealth citizens, 1972 L
    Ugandan Asians, 1972 H, J, L
    British fears expressed, 1978 A
  to Canada, by British schoolchildren, 1940 K
  to France, 1969 Y
  to Germany, 1969 Y
  to Ghana, 1969 L
  to Holland, 1969 Y
  to Luxembourg, 1969 Y
  to Sweden, 1969 Y
  to Switzerland, 1969 Y
  to New Zealand, of Japanese, restricted, 1881 F
  to Palestine, of Jews, 1930 K
    Jewish protests at restrictions, 1933 M
  to Transvaal, 1896 L
    of Chinese, 1903 L
  to US from Britain and Ireland, statistics, 1840 Y, 1850 Y, 1860 Y, 1870 Y, 1880 Y, 1890 Y
    of Chinese, banned, 1882 E
    restrictions on, 1907 O
    of Japanese, 1912 D
    literacy made a condition of, 1912 D
    bill for controlling, 1914 B
      vetoes, 1915 A
    bill for controlling, 1916 M
      curtailed, 1919 M
    emergency quota act, 1921 E
    limits on, 1924 E
    of Japanese, excluded, 1924 E
    employers knowingly employing illegal aliens fined, 1986 O
Immoralist, The (A. Gide), 1902 U
Impact of Plague in Tudor and Stuart England, The (P. Slack), 1985 Q
Imperial Chemical Industries (I.C.I.), 1931 P, 1935 P; endows fellowships, 1944 O
Imperial Conferences, London, 1907 E, 1911 E, 1926 K
Imperial Council (Reichrat), Austria, 1860 C
Imperial Defence, Committee of, British, 1902 M, 1912 B
Imperial Federation League, in Canada, 1884 D
Imperial Germany (von Bülow), 1913 O
Imperial Preference, 1903 J, 1932 G
Imperial War Cabinet, British, first meets, 1917 C
Imperialism (J. A. Hobson), 1902 P
Imphal, India, Japanese advance on, 1944 C
Impressionism, 1874 S, 1901 S
Impressionist Exhibitions, 1877 S, 1886 S
Improvements in Education as it respects the Industrious Classes (J. Lancaster), 1803 O
In Chancery (J. Galsworthy), 1920 U
In Cold Blood (T. Capote), 1966 U
In Darkest England and the Way Out (W. Booth), 1890 O
In Defence of Sensuality (J. C. Powys), 1930 U
In God's Way (B. Björnson), 1889 U
In Memoriam (Tennyson), 1850 U
In Place of Strife ..., White Paper, 1969 A, C
In Quest of the Historical Jesus (A. Schweitzer), 1910 R
In Search of Criminology (L. Radzinowycz), 1961 O
In a Free State (V.S. Naipaul), 1972 U
In a German Pension (K. Mansfield), 1911 U
In the Interlude (B. Pasternak), 1962 U
In the Skin of a Lion (M. Ondaatje), 1987 U
In't Wonderjaar (H. Conscience), 1837 U
Inadmissible Evidence (J. Osborne), 1964 W
Inchbald, Elizabeth, B. dramatist and actress (1753–1821), 1791 W
Inchon, Korea, 1950 J
Incident Book, The (F. Adcock), 1986 U
Incomes and wages, in Britain:
  railwaymen's pay, 1960 C
  wages pause, 1961 G, 1962 A; ends, 1962 C
  dockers, increased, 1962 E
  National Incomes Commission, 1963 D
  teachers' salaries, 1963 G
  Statement of Intent on productivity, prices and incomes, 1964 M
  doctors, new pay structure proposed for, 1965 B
  Prices and Incomes Board, 1965 C
  the norm for pay increases, 1965 D
  printers, wage claim, 1965 E
  See also Prices; Strikes
Incomes, pioneer study of, 1855 O
Indemnities:
  Burma, to Britain, 1826 B
  China, to Russia, 1881 B
    to powers, 1901 J
  France, to Allies, 1818 J, K
    to Germany, 1871 E
  Japan, to powers, 1864 J
  Turkey, to Russia, 1878 C
  US, to Mexico, 1848 E
Independent Labour Party. *See under* Political Parties
Independent Television Authority, 1954 O
Independent Theatre Society, London, 1891 W
Index, papal, 1814 R, 1883 R
India (V.S. Naipaul), 1990 U
India, British administration of. *See under* East India Company, British
  French settlements in, 1763 B, 1793 N
  Native states. *See* Delhi; Kanara; Mysore; Murshidabad; Oudh
  Mutiny, 1857 E, F, G, J, L, M
  Queen Victoria proclaimed Empress, 1877 A
  Indian National Congress, first, 1886 N
  tea production in, 1909 Y
  Simon Commission on, 1926 L
  All-party conference votes for dominion status, 1928 H
  Labour unrest in, 1929 D
  Round Table Conference on, 1929 M
  All-India Congress demands British withdrawal, 1945 J
  Independence, discussions on, 1946 M; achieved, 1947 M
  Hyderabad joins Indian Union, 1948 J
  Chinese invade, 1959 H, 1962 J, K, L
  Radhakrishnan elected President, 1962 E
  Eastern Assam rebellion, 1966 C
  food riots, 1966 C
  banks nationalized, 1969 G
  sectarian violence, 1969 J, 1990 K, 1992 M
  Congress Party formally split, 1969 L
  presidential decree, 1970 J
  Congress Party election victory, 1971 C
  East Pakistani refugees, 1971 E
  population, 1971 Y, 1981 Y, 1991 Y
  Bangladesh signs mutual defence pact, 1972 C
  India and Pakistan agree to renounce force in settlement of disputes, 1972 G
  Pakistan and India agree on truce line, 1972 M
  Ogdala Sioux protest at treatment, 1973 B
  becomes world's 6th nuclear power, 1974 E
  opposition leaders imprisoned, 1975 F
  state of emergency declared, 1975 F
  diplomatic relations with Pakistan normalized, 1976 D
  emergency powers assumed by government, 1980 J
  Parliament besieged by Sikhs, 1982 K

elections in Assam, 1983 A, B
illiteracy, 1983 Y
Amritsar Golden Temple stormed, 1984 F, R
Sikh soldiers mutiny, 1984 F
Union Carbide accident, 1984 M
general election, 1984 M
cotton production, 1984 Y
Sikh extremist attacks, 1985 E
urbanization, 1985 Y
militants expelled from Amritsar Golden Temple, 1986 D
Sikhs declare independent state of Khalistan, 1986 D
Sikh rebels occupying Amritsar Golden Temple surrender, 1988 E
Kashmir brought under direct rule and curfew imposed, 1990 A
army takes direct control in Kashmir, 1990 G
Hindu militants attack mosque built on Hindu holy site at Ayodhya, 1990 K
government resigns, 1990 L
economic reforms, 1991 G
Sikh militants attempt enforcement of election boycott, 1992 B
Ayodhya mosque destroyed, 1992 M
Punjab. *See* Punjab
India-rubber cloth, 1791 P
Indian Wants the Bronx, The (I. Horovitz), 1968 W
Indiana (G. Sand), 1832 U
Indiana, state, US, becomes a US state, 1816 M
Indianapolis, US, car-racing at, 1965 X
Indians (A. Kopit), 1969 W
Indians, in US: settlement of, 1830 E; Dawes Act for, 1887 B.
See also under Massacres
Indigo, synthetic, 1880 P
Indo-China, Japanese land in, 1941 G
international conference proposal, 1970 D
Indonesian Republic:
Dutch refuse to recognise, 1945 H
recognise, 1946 L
transfer sovereignty to, 1949 M
Britain suspends aid to, 1963 K
talks with Malaysia fail, 1964 F
anti-Chinese violence, 1966 D
general election, 1971 G
population, 1981 Y, 1991 Y
illiteracy, 1983 Y
Indore, Cen. India, 1802 K, 1818 A
Induction, magnetic-electric, laws of, 1851 P
Indus Civilization, The (M. Wheeler), 1954 Q
Indus, Waters, treaty for development, 1960 J
Industrial Archaeology of Northern Ireland, The (W. A. McCutcheon), 1980 Q
Industrial Democracy (S. and B. Webb), 1897 O
Industrial Development Executive, B., 1972 C
Industrial Health and Safety Centre, London, 1927 O
Industrial Output, comparative tables of increases in, 1913 Y
Industrial Psychology, National Institute of, London, 1921 O
Industrial Workers of the World, Political Branch of, 1909 O
Industry, in Britain:
Industrial Development Executive, 1972 C
interventionist policy, 1972 C, D
TUC and CBI agree to set up independent conciliation service, 1972 G
Indy, Vincent D', F. musician (1851–1931), 1851 Z, 1897 T, 1920 T, 1931 Z
Infallible? An Enquiry (H. Küng), 1971 R
Infanticide, in India, abolished, 1870 O
Infants' Welfare Centre, 1903 O. *See also* Crêche
Inferno (A. Strindberg), 1897 U
Influence of Sea Power on History (A. T. Mahan), 1890 Q
Influence of a Low Price of Corn on the Profits of Stock, The (D. Ricardo), 1815 O
Influenza epidemics, 1918 K, 1919 P
Information, Ministry of, British, 1939 O
Infra-red solar rays, 1800 P
Inge, William Ralph, B. churchman and author (1864–1954), 1919 R, 1948 R
Ingoldsby Legends, The (R. H. Barham), 1840 U
Ingres, Jean Auguste Dominique, F. artist (1780–1867), 1780 Z, 1808 S, 1823 S, 1824 S, 1842 S, 1856 S, 1859 S, 1867 Z
Injections, of insulin, 1922 P, 1937 P
Inkerman, Russia, battle, 1854 C
Inmos Microprocessor Factory, Gwent, Wales, 1982 S
Inn Quarter, Austria: acquired from Bavaria, 1779 E; ceded to Bavaria, 1809 K
Inni Sacri (A. Manzoni), 1813 U
Innocent, The (I. McEwan), 1990 U
Innocents Abroad, The (M. Twin), 1869 U
Innsbruck, Austria, 1848 E
Inoculations against anthrax, 1883 P
Inönü, Ismet, Turk, politician (1894–1973), 1938 L, 1964 B, 1973 Z
Inori (K. Stockhausen), 1974 T
Inquiries into Truth and Interpretation (D. Davidson), 1984 R
Inquiry Concerning Political justice, The (W. Godwin), 1793 O
Inquiry into the Human Mind (T. Reid), 1764 R
Inquiry into the Nature and Causes of the Wealth of Nations (A. Smith), 1776 U
Inquiry into the Nature and Progress of Rent, An (T. R. Malthus), 1815 U
Inquiry into the Relation of Cause and Effect (T. Brown), 1804 R
Inquisition, The:
in Italy, abolished in Tuscany, 1765 H
Napoleon abolishes in Italian States, 1808 R
revived, 1814 R
in Portugal, abolished, 1821 A
in Spain, seizes Goya's *Capriccios*, 1796 S
Napoleon abolishes, 1808 R
revived, 1814 R
abolished, 1820 C
account of, 1817 R
Inscape (A. Copeland), 1967 T
Inscriptiones Aegypticae (H. Brugsch), 1883 Q
Inscriptions, cuneiform, 1846 Q
Insecticides, 1924 P
Insects, classification of, 1775 P
Insider Dealing
Boesky, 1986 L
Morgan Grenfell, 1987 G
Insight and Outlook (A. Koestler), 1949 R
Inspections, medical, of schoolchildren, 1907 O
Inspector Morse, television series, 1986 W
Installation, for the Kassel Documenta (D. Buren), 1982 S
Institute of Advanced Legal Studies, London, 1948 O
Institute of Economic and Social Research, National, London, 1938 O
Institute of Historical Research, London, 1921 O
Institute of International Affairs, London, 1920 O
Institute of Mechanics, Liverpool, 1834 O
Institute of Technical Optics, S. Kensington, 1917 P
Institute of Technology, Chicago, 1939 O
Institute of Technology, Massachusetts, develops use of ultra-high-frequency waves, 1955 P
Institutes of the Law of Scotland (J. Erskine), 1773 O
Institutiones theologicae dogmaticae (J. Wegscheider), 1815 R
Instruction on Christian Freedom and Liberation, Vatican document, 1986 R
Instruction on Respect for Human Life in its Origin and on the Dignity of Procreation ..., Vatican document, 1987 O
Instrumentation, treatise on, 1844 T
Insulin, is isolated, 1922 P
structure of, 1955 P
zinc protamine, for treating diabetes, 1937 P
structure announced, 1969 P
Insurance Societies, British, 1769 O, 1963 M
in India, nationalised, 1956 E
in US, alleged corruption, 1905 O
Insurance:
old age, in Britain, 1909 A, 1913 O, 1940 B, 1964 L
in France, 1850 O
in Germany, 1883 E, 1889 E
sickness, in Britain, 1913 O
in France, 1930 D
in New Zealand, 1898 O
unemployment, in Britain, 1925 G
in Denmark, 1891 M
Intelligent Man's Guide to the Post-War World, The (G. D. H. Cole), 1947 O
Intelligent Woman's Guide to Socialism and Capitalism (G. B. Shaw), 1928 *O*
Inter-relations of Cultures (UNESCO), 1955 Q
Internal Evidence for the Truth of Revealed Religion *(T. Erskine), 1820 **R***
International Court of Justice. *See* United Nations, The
International Justice, Permanent Court of, The Hague, 1922 B; US Senate rejects proposal to join, 1923 C; US joins, 1929 J; decides against Austro-German customs union, 1931 C; ruling in Anglo-Iranian dispute, 1951 G; Britain submits Falkland Isles dispute to, 1955 E; to hear India's dispute with Portugal, 1957 L
International Labour Organisation, 1919 O
S. Africa leaves, 1964 C
US quits, 1977 L
International Monetary Fund (IMF), 1975 O
loans to Britain, 1967 L, 1976 J, M, 1977 A
loan to Mexico, 1982 L
foreign debts, 1982 M
General Agreements to Borrow unit funds increased, 1983 A
loan to Brazil, 1983 B
International Olympic Committee (IOC). *See* Olympic Games
International Red Cross. *See* Red Cross
International Whaling Commission, 1979 G, 1982 G
bans hunting of sperm whales, 1979 G
International Working-Men's Association, 1876 O
International, Communist, 1876 O; Bakunin expelled from, 1872 O; Third, 1919 O; French Socialists adhere to, 1920 M; Zinoviev Letter, 1924 K; declaration in support of governments against Fascism, 1935 G; dissolved, 1943 E
International, Labour and Socialist, 1923 O
Interpretation of Dreams, The (S. Freud), 1900 R
Interpretation of Personality, The (Jung), 1940 R
Intimate Papers of Colonel House, The, 1926 O
Introduction aux Travaux Scientifiques du XIXe Siècle (St. Simon), 1807 O
Introduction to Algebra (L. Euler), 1770 P
Introduction to English Historical Demography, An (E.A. Wrigley), 1966 Q
Introduction to Greek and Latin Palaeography (E. M. Thompson), 1912 Q
Introduction to Philosophy (J. F. Herbart), 1813 R

Introduction to the Law of Nature and Notions (Mackintosh), 1799 O
Introduction to the Principles of Morals and Legislation (J. Bentham), 1789 O
Inuit people, Nunavut, 1992 L
Inukai, Japanese premier, 1932 E
Invergordon, Scotland, mutiny at, 1931 J
Invisible Man (H. G. Wells), 1897 U
Invisible Writing, The (A. Koestler), 1954 O
Invitation au Château, L' (Anouilh), 1947 W
Invitation to the Waltz (R. Lehmann), 1932 U
Inwood, William, B. architect (1771–1843), 1819 S
Iodine, discovered, 1811 P
Ion microscope, 1956 P
Ionamide dyes, 1922 P
Ionesco, Eugène, F. dramatist (b. 1912), 1960 W, 1963 W
Ionian Islands: France occupies, 1797 F; conquered by Turks and Russians, 1788 C; independence recognised, 1801 K; British protectorate over, 1815 L; cede Parga, 1819 D; conference on, 1863 L; ceded by Britain to Greece, 1864 C
Iowa, US, becomes a US state, 1846 M
Iphigenie auf Tauris (Goethe), 1787 W
Ipsara, Island, Aegean, Turks capture, 1824 G
Ipswich, Suffolk, Dumas Building, 1975 S
Iran (formerly Persia): name changed from Persia, 1935 O; Allies invade, 1941 H
- Persian monarchy celebrations, 1971 K
- Tunbs Islands occupied, 1971 L
- becomes one-party state, 1975 C
- ban on political parties lifted, 1978 H
- violent demonstrations in Teheran, 1978 J
- earthquakes, 1978 J, 1990 F
- military government appointed, 1978 L
- Islamic revolutionary violence in Teheran, 1979 A
- Revolutionary Council, 1979 B, L
- Islamic republic declared, 1979 D
- industries nationalized, 1979 G
- US hostages taken in Teheran embassy seige, 1979 L
- US imposes oil embargo, 1979 L
- US hostages' release sought by UN, 1980 A
- US diplomats escape, 1980 A
- US breaks diplomatic relations, 1980 D
- US severs links with, 1980 D
- border attack by Iraq, 1980 D
- US commando mission fails, 1980 D
- London embassy siege, 1980 D
- conditions for release of US hostages, 1980 J, M
- US hostages released, 1981 A
- British missionaries released, 1981 B
- Bani-Sadr denounced by Khomeini, 1981 F
- Teheran bomb kills 74, 1981 F
- presidential elections, 1981 G, 1989 G
- Teheran bomb kills president and prime minister, 1981 H
- Soviet diplomats expelled, 1983 E
- Tudeh outlawed, 1983 E
- illiteracy, 1983 Y
- Islam declared 'religion of the sword', 1983 R
- cotton production, 1984 Y
- urbanization, 1985 Y
- control taken of Faw and Shatt al-Arab waterway, 1986 B
- arms for hostages deal, 1986 L
- Egypt breaks diplomatic relations, 1987 E
- Syria agrees to end political and military support, 1987 L
- Iranian oil platforms destroyed in US attack, 1988 D
- Kuwaiti airliner hijack, 1988 D
- diplomatic relations with Britain broken over Rushdie affair, 1989 C
- riots on Azerbaijani border, 1989 M
- diplomatic relations with Britain resumed, 1990 J
- population, 1991 Y
- Iran–Iraq War. *See* Wars

Iran–Contra scandal, 1986 L, M, 1987 B, C, G, H, L, 1989 A, D
Iraq Petroleum Company, pipeline seized by Syria, 1966 M
Iraq: independence recognised, 1927 M, 1930 F; massacre of Assyrian Christians, 1933 G; severs relations with France, 1938 M; demands withdrawal of British, 1941 E; forms, with Jordan, the Arab Federation, 1958 B; Arab Federation dissolved, 1958 H; petroleum company's dispute with Lebanon, 1959 F; federates with United Arab Republic, 1963 D
- war with Israel, 1967 F
- abortive coup, 1970 A
- Kurdish autonomy recognized, 1970 C
- closes Jordanian border, 1971 G
- alleges British-Iranian collusion, 1971 L
- Soviet treaty of friendship and co-operation, 1972 D
- airliner forced down by Israeli fighters, 1973 H
- joins war against Israel, 1973 K
- forces clash with Kurdish rebels, 1974 C
- Saddam Hussein becomes President, 1979 G
- Israel bombs Iraqi nuclear reactor under construction, 1981 F
- US restores diplomatic relations, 1984 L
- Iran takes control of Faw and Shatt al-Arab waterway, 1986 B
- 'supergun' parts destined for, detained in Britain, 1990 D
- UN sanctions, 1990 H
- Kurdish refugees, 1991 C, D
- popular revolt against Saddam Hussein, 1991 C
- UN inspects nuclear facilities, 1991 H
- air exclusion zone to protect Shi'ite Moslems, 1992 H
- Gulf War. *See* Wars
- Iran–Iraq War. *See* Wars

Ireland:
- Whiteboys Revolt in, 1763 G
- Protestant Volunteers in, 1779 C
- free trade with Britain, 1779 M, 1780 M
- Home Rule for, demanded, 1780 D, 1782 D granted, 1782 E
- Gratton's Parliament, 1782 E
- French attempt invasion, 1798 H, K
- Union with England, 1800 C, 1801 A
- Famine, 1845 N
- Coercion bill for, rejected, 1846 F
- Disestablishment of Church, 1869 G
- land legislation for, 1870 H
- Land League, 1880 L
- disturbances in, 1881 A, C, 1882 E, G
- Land Act, 1881 H, J
- eviction of tenants, 1882 N
- agrarian outrages, 1882 N
- loans to tenants, 1885 H
- Crimes Act, 1887 A
- Rebellion, 1916 O
- emigration to US, 1830 Y, 1840 Y, 1850 Y, 1860 Y, 1870 Y, 1880 Y, 1890 Y, 1900 Y
- *See also* Eire; Irish Free State; Irish Home Rule

Ireland Since the Famine (F.S.L. Lyons), 1971 Q
Ireland, John, B. musician (1879–1962), 1915 T
Ireland, Northern: first Parliament of, 1821 F; boundary settled, 1825 L, M; votes for non-inclusion in Irish Free State, 1922 M; Britain re-affirms position of, 1949 E; premier meets prime minister of Eire, 1965 A
- civil rights marches, Londonderry, 1968 K, L
- housing and local franchise reforms proposed, 1968 L
- Catholic and Protestant demonstrators clash, 1969 A
- general election, 1969 B
- Devlin elected to Parliament, 1969 D
- British military presence, 1969 D
- terrorist campaigns, 1969 D
- universal adult suffrage conceded, 1969 D
- amnesty of arrested rioters, 1969 E
- rioting, 1969 H, K
- Southern Irish troops mobilized, 1969 H
- Unionists rule out coalition government, 1969 H
- British army assumes full responsibility for security in, 1969 H
- federation with Eire proposed, 1969 H
- civil rights reforms, 1969 H
- barricades in Belfast and Londonderry dismantled, 1969 J
- 'B' specials, 1969 K
- Royal Ulster Constabulary (RUC), 1969 K
- Hunt Committee report, 1969 K
- British troop reinforcements, 1970 D, 1971 C, K
- Devlin imprisoned, 1970 F
- security forces search for arms, 1970 G
- British troops criticized by Dr. Hillery, 1970 G
- ban on marches, 1970 G
- first British soldier killed, 1971 B
- Belfast demonstrations, 1971 C, 1972 F
- Faulkner becomes Prime Minister, 1971 C
- East Belfast riots, 1971 D
- SDLP withdraws from Stormont Parliament, 1971 G
- internment and processions, new legislation on, 1971 H
- deaths from fighting between IRA and troops, 1971 H
- Anglo-Irish relations close to breaking point, 1971 H
- internees, British government inquiry, 1971 H
- emergency debate in House of Commons, 1971 J
- leaders discuss at Chequers, 1971 J
- border incidents, 1971 K
- Compton Report, 1971 L
- 'Bloody Sunday', 1972 A, D
- direct rule assumed by Britain, 1972 C
- Parker Report on security forces, 1972 C
- use of 'intensive' interrogation techniques forbidden, 1972 C
- internees released, 1972 D, 1975 M
- amnesty declared for illegal marchers, 1972 D
- ban on marches lifted, 1972 D
- Protestant 'no go' areas, 1972 E, G
- Ulster Defence Association (UDA), 1972 E
- battle in Belfast leaves six dead, 1972 F
- terrorist attacks, 1972 G
- Whitelaw holds secret talks with IRA, 1972 G
- British government offers reward for information on motiveless murders, 1972 H
- Darlington Conference, 1972 J
- internment ended, 1972 J
- Catholics promised greater political power, 1972 K
- death toll, 1972 M, 1974 D, 1977 M, 1980 A
- Diplock Commission, 1972 M
- civil disturbance after Protestant arrests, 1973 B
- referendum, 1973 C
- White Paper on, 1973 C
- Council of Ireland, 1973 M, 1974 E
- Ulster Freedom Fighters murder SDLP senator, 1973 F
- Northern Ireland Assembly election, 1973 F

militants disrupt Northern Ireland Assembly, 1973 G
agreement on power-sharing executive, 1973 K
Sunningdale talks with Irish government, 1973 M
Pope condemns violence, 1973 R
Protestant general strikes, 1974 E, 1977 E
Executive collapses, 1974 E
direct rule re-imposed, 1974 E
Constitutional Convention elections, 1975 E
nine bombings kill 15, 1975 J
sectarian murders in South Armagh, 1976 A
SAS sent, 1976 A
tanker drivers' strike causes state of emergency, 1979 A
'Carson trail' parade, 1981 B
riots follow death of hunger striker, 1981 E
De Lorean car plant closed, 1982 K
Sinn Fein election victories, 1982 K
SDLP and Sinn Fein boycott opening of Northern Ireland Assembly, 1982 L
Ballykelly bomb explosion, 1982 M
'supergrass' informer against IRA cell, 1983 H
IRA arms consignment seized, 1983 H
Republican prisoners escape from Maze Prison, 1983 J
Official Unionist Party withdraws from Northern Ireland Assembly, 1983 L
New Ireland Forum report, 1984 E
Anglo-Irish Agreement, 1985 L, M
Northern Ireland Assemby dissolved, 1986 F
broadcasts of interviews with terrorist organizations banned, 1988 K
life expectancy, 1990 Y
Irish Republican Army (IRA). *See* Irish Republican Army
Ireland, Southern. *See* Eire
Ireland, unification proposal, 1971 L
Irène (Voltaire), 1778 U
Irises (V. van Gogh), sold for 30 million pounds, 1987 S
Irish Free State: officially proclaimed, 1922 M; becomes Eire, 1937 M. *See also* Eire
Irish Home Rule:
Disraeli goes to country on issue of, 1880 C
Gladstone's bill, 1886 D
defeated, 1886 F
issue of, 1891 K
Lords reject bill, 1893 J
issue splits British Liberal Party, 1894 C
Campbell-Bannerman on, 1905 L
as election issue, 1910 A
Ulster Unionists resolve to repudiate, 1912 A, J
Liberals defeated over, 1912 L
Lords reject bill for, 1913 A, G
Ulster Unionists appoint provisional government, 1913 J
bill passes Commons, 1914 E
suspended for duration of war, 1914 J
Ulster determines to resist, 1914 G
Buckingham Palace Conference on, 1914 G
Rebellion, 1916 O
Iris Convention meets, 1917 G
Britain abandons, 1918 F
Sinn Fein Congress adopts declaration of independence, 1919 A
Carson demands repeal of, 1919 G
Ulster votes to accept bill, 1920 C
Belfast riots, 1920 G
under Government of Ireland Act, 1920 M, 1921 D
British truce with Sinn Fein, 1921 G
Dail rejects British peace offer, 1921 H
Anglo-Irish Peace treaty, 1921 M
Dail approves, 1922 A
Irish Free State, 1922 M
Irish National Liberation Army, Neave murdered, 1979 C
Irish Republican Army (IRA), 1933 G, 1955 H
Tooting bomb store, 1970 H
'Bloody Sunday', 1972 A, D
Aldershot bomb attack, 1972 B
calls ceasefire, 1972 F
Whitelaw holds secret talks with, 1972 G
London car bombs, 1973 C
letter-bomb incidents, IRA blamed for, 1973 H
Christmas bombing campaign in London, 1973 M
bus bomb kills, 12 1974 B
hunger-striker dies, 1974 F
Tower of London bomb, 1974 F
Westminster Hall bomb, 1974 F
terrorist prison escape, 1974 H
Guildford bombings, 1974 K
Birmingham pub bombings, 1974 L
ceasefire, 1975 B
Birmingham Six trial, 1975 F
Guildford Four sentenced, 1975 K
McWhirter murdered, 1975 L
Balcombe Street seige, London, 1975 M
British ambassador in Dublin assassinated, 1976 G
Balcombe Street gang imprisoned, 1977 B
British ambassador to Holland assassinated, 1979 C
Earl Mountbatten killed by bomb, 1979 H
attack at Warrenpoint, 1979 H
Maze prison hunger strikers demand political status, 1980 K
Bobby Sands wins by-election, 1981 D
Maze Prison hunger-strike ends, 1981 K
Unionist MP murdered, 1981 L
bomb attacks in Regents Park and Hyde Park, 1982 G
'supergrass' informer, 1983 H
arms consignment for seized, 1983 H
car bomb explosion outside Harrods, London, 1983 M
Conservative Party members killed in Brighton bomb attack, 1984 K
Irish Dail enabled to seize money from Provisional IRA bank accounts, 1985 B
Brighton hotel bombing, 1986 F
US senate approves treaty allowing extradition of suspected IRA terrorists to Britain, 1986 G
Lord Justice Gibson and Lady Gibson killed, 1987 D
nine IRA men killed in battle with police and troops, 1987 E
arms haul on trawler *Eksund* discovered, 1987 L
bomb attack at Enniskillen, 1987 L
Catholic bishops denounce violence, 1987 L
suspected terrorists shot dead on Gibraltar, 1988 C
attacks on British army personnel in West Germany, 1989 G
Guildford Four cleared, 1989 O
bomb attack at London Stock Exchange, 1990 G
Gow murdered, 1990 G
broadcasts of interviews with banned, 1990 O
bomb damage to 10 Downing Street, London, 1991 B
Birmingham Six cleared, 1991 C
London Bridge station bombed, 1992 B
Irish Republican Brotherhood, 1857 K. *See also under* Fenians
Iron Guard. *See under* Political Parties
Iron and Steel:
British Federation, 1934 O
Nationalisation, in force in Britain, 1949 L
denationalised, 1952 L
in France and Germany, Schuman Plan for, 1950 E
production of, in Austria, 1870 Y
in Belgium, 1938 Y, 1948 Y
in Britain, 1806 Y, 1818 Y, 1825 Y, 1835 Y, 1841 Y, 1851 Y, 1860 Y, 1861 Y, 1870 Y, 1871 Y, 1875 Y, 1880 Y, 1895 Y, 1913 Y, 1938 Y, 1941 Y, 1948 Y
in France, 1841 Y, 1851 Y, 1860 Y, 1861 Y, 1870 Y, 1871 Y, 1875 Y, 1880 Y, 1938 Y, 1948 Y
in Germany, 1861 Y, 1870 Y, 1871 Y, 1875 Y, 1880 Y, 1913 Y, 1938 Y, 1948 Y
in Russia, 1851 Y, 1880 Y, 1932 Y, 1938 Y, 1940 Y, 1948 Y
in US 1860 Y, 1861 Y, 1870 Y, 1880 Y, 1913 Y, 1938 Y, 1948 Y
Iron steamship, 1820 P
Iron, cast, building-frame of, 1851 P
Iron, wrought, Cort's process for, 1784 P
Ironsi, Major-General Johnson, Nigerian leader (1924–66), 1966 A, G
Ironside, television programme, 1967 W
Irredentist Movement in Italy, 1878 N
Irrigation works, 1894 H, 1902 O
Irving, Sir Henry, B. actor (1838–1917), 1838 Z, 1856 W, 1866 W, 1878 W, 1917 Z
Irving, John Winslow, Am. author (b. 1942), 1989 U
Irving, Washington, Am. author (1783–1859), 1783 Z, 1809 U, 1820 U, 1822 U, 1832 U, 1859 Z
Irwin Lord. *See* Wood, Edward
Isabella II, Queen of Spain (1833–68), 1833 J, 1843 L, 1868 J, 1870 F, 1874 L
Isandhlwana, Zululand, S. Africa, massacre at, 1879 A
Isernia, Italy, Eighth Army takes, 1943 L
Isherwood, Christopher William Bradshaw, B. author (1904–86), 1904 Z, 1928 U, 1935 U, 1937 U, 1938 U, 1954 U, 1964 U, 1986 Z
Ishiguro, Kazuo, B. author (b. 1954), 1987 U, 1989 U
Isidore decretals admitted as forgery, 1789 R
Islam, Holy Places, 1900 N
Islamabad, Pakistan:
Secretariat Buildings, 1966 S
explosion at army ammunition dump, 1988 D
Islamic Conference Organization, Egyptian membership, 1984 A
Islamic Jihad
bomb attack in Madrid, 1985 D
French hostages freed in Lebanon, 1988 E
Islamic fundamentalism, Iranian funding, 1987 E
Islamic summit meeting, Lahore, 1974 B
Ismail, Khedive of Egypt (1830–95), 1863 A, 1866 E, 1879 F
Ismail, Russia, captured from Turkey, 1790 M
Ismail, Sidky Pasha, becomes Egyptian premier, 1930 F
Isolation, British policy of, ends, 1902 A
Isomorphism, theory of, 1819 P
Isonzo, Italy, battles of, 1915, F, G, K, L, 1916 C, H, J, K, 1917 E
Isotope, term coined, 1913 P
235, possibility of splitting, 1939 P
radio-, 1952 P
Isotopy, phenomena of, established, 1919 P
Isozaki, Arata, Jap. architect, 1974 S, 1976 S, 1986 S
Israel: provisional government formed, 1948 E; recognised by Britain, 1950 D; W. Germany establishes relations with, 1965 E.

Israeli airliner in Athens attacked, 1968 M
Jews legally defined by Knesset, 1970 C
US supplies Phantom jets to, 1970 C
affirms Jewish settlement policy, 1971 B
Japanese terrorists kill 26 Israelis at Lod airport, 1972 E
Olympic team members murdered, 1972 J
invades Syria via Golan Heights, 1973 K
Yom Kippur War, 1973 K
nuclear weapons manufacture possible, 1974 M
Sinai peninsular, withdrawal from, 1975 J, K, 1980 A
talks with Egypt, 1978 A
invades Southern Lebanon, 1978 C
Knesset approves Camp David accord, 1978 J
signs peace treaty with Egypt, 1979 C
on Palestinian autonomy, 1979 K, 1980 D, E
ambassadors exchanged with Egypt, 1980 B
Golan Heights formally annexed, 1981 M
disbands Palestinian council of El Birah, 1982 C
to assert sovereignty over occupied West Bank, 1982 E
illiteracy, 1983 Y
Kahane Commission, on Beirut massacre, 1983 B
US halts sale of F-16 fighters to, 1983 C
withdrawal of Israeli forces from Lebanon, 1983 E, G, J
PLO and Israel exchange prisoners of war, 1983 L
government of national unity, 1984 H
urbanization, 1985 Y
UN Security Council criticizes Israeli action against Palestinians, 1987 M
diplomatic visit to USSR by Israeli representatives, 1988 G
elections, 1988 L
national unity coalition government collapses, 1990 C
police fire on demonstrators at Temple Mount, Jerusalem, 1990 K
right-wing coalition government formed, 1990 F
Iraq launches Scud missile against, 1991 A
general election, 1992 F
Palestinians deported, 1992 M
Arab–Israeli conflict. *See* Middle East
See also under Jerusalem; Middle East Crisis; Suez Crisis
Issigonis, Alec (Sir Alexander Arnold Constantine), B. car designer (1906–88), 1906 Z, 1988 Z
Istanbul, Turkey: name changed from Constantinople, 1930 C; riots in 1955 H, 1960 D
Istria, Italy: Austria obtains, 1797 K; Italy obtains, 1920 L
It is Never Too Late to Mend (C. Reade), 1856 U
Italian National Association, 1857 H
Italian Visit, An (C. Day-Lewis), 1953 U
Italian War and the Mission of Prussia (F. Lassalle), 1859 O
Italian, The (A. Radcliffe), 1795 U
Italy
Republic established, 1802 A
Unification of, Garibaldi's plans for, 1857 H, 1860 E, H, J
Napoleon III's designs, 1858 G
plebiscites for, 1860 C, K, L
British support for, 1860 H
Kingdom of Italy proclaimed, 1860 K, 1861 B
France and Prussia agree upon, 1865 K
achievements towards, 1866 K, 1870 K
Allies invade, 1943 J
cedes territory to France, 1946 F
population, 1971 Y, 1981 Y, 1991 Y
socialist government resigns, 1976 A
Christian Democrat government formed, 1976 B
Moro government collapses, 1976 D
Andreotti forms government, 1976 G
collapse of Andreotti government, 1978 A
'Historic Compromise', 1978 C, 1979 A
President Leone resigns, 1978 F
Andreotti government resigns, 1979 A
government falls after 'Propaganda 2' revelations, 1981 E
secret societies banned, 1981 E
urbanization, 1985 Y
divorce statistics, 1987 Y
life expectancy, 1990 Y
illegitimacy rate, 1991 Y
elections, 1992 D, E
emergency legislation to prevent bankruptcy, 1992 G
lira devalued within ERM, 1992 J
ITMA, radio series, 1942 W
Ito, Prince of Japan (1841–1909), 1892 F, 1901 L, 1909 K
Iturbide, Augustus, president of Mexico (1783–1824), 1822 E, 1823 C
Ituzaingo, Brazil, battle, 1827 B
Ivangorod, Russia, Russians break through at, 1914 K
Ivanhoe (W. Scott), 1820 U
Ivashko, Vladimir Antonovich, President of Ukraine (b. 1932), 1990 F
Iveagh, Lord. *See* Guinness, Edward
Ivory
Kenya bans trade in, 1973 H
international ban on trading in, 1989 K
Ivory Coast (French West Africa): French Protectorate over, 1889 A; French colony established, 1893 C
Ivory Coast Republic, independence for, 1960 G
world's largest cathedral, Yamoussoukro, 1990 R
Ivory, James Francis, Am. film director (b. 1928), 1992 W
Izmir, Turkey, riots in, 1955 J
Izvolski, Alexander, R. foreign minister (1856–1919), 1906 E, 1908 J; meets Edward VII, 1907 J; visits London, 1908 L

J

J'accuse (E. Zola), 1898 A
Jacaranda Tree, The (H. E. Bates), 1949 U
Jacklin, Tony, B. golfer (b. 1944), 1969 X, 1970 X, 1985 X
Jackson, Andrew, Am. statesman, Democrat (1767–1845), 1845 Z; 7th president of US (1828–37), 1767 Z, 1827 L, 1829 C, 1832 L, 1833 A, C, H
Jackson, Sir Barry, B. theatrical manager (1879–961), 1913 W
Jackson, Sir Geoffrey Holt Seymour, B. diplomat (1915–87), 1971 A
Jackson, Henry, Am. senator, 1974 K
Jackson, Sir Herbert, B. scientist (1863–1936), 1916 P
Jackson, Michael Joseph, Am. pop singer (b. 1958), 1982 W
Jackson, Miss., US, civil rights rally, 1966 F
Jackson, Thomas Jonathan ('Stonewall'), Am. Confederate general (1824–63), 1862 H, 1863 E
Jacksonville, Flor., US, 1862 C
Jacobins Club, 1790 N. *See also* Political Parties
Jacob's Wake *(M. Cook), 1975 W*
Jacobsen, Arne, Dan. architect (1902–71), 1902 Z, 1959 S, 1964 S, 1971 Z
Jacobsen, David, Am. hostage, 1986 L
Jacobsen, Jens Peter, Da. author (1847–85), 1880 U
Jadis et naguère (P. Verlaine), 1884 U
Jadotville, Katanga, Congo, UN force captures, 1963 A
Jaeger, Werner, G. philosopher (1888–1961), 1888 Z, 1961 Z
Jaenisch, Rudolf, G.-born Am. scientist, 1988 P
Jaffa (Yafo), Israel, British take, 1917 L
Jaffna peninsula, Sri Lankan forces seek to establish control, 1986 E
Jagan, Cheddi, B. Guian. People's Party leader (b. 1918), sentenced, 1954 D; forms ministry, 1957 H, 1961 H; dismissed, 1964 M
Jagow, Gottlieb von, G. foreign minister (1863–1917), 1913 A
Jahr der Seele, Das (S. George), 1897 U
Jakeš, Milos, General Secretary of Czechoslovak Communist Party (b. 1922), 1987 M
Jamaica, becomes independent, 1962 H
reggae music, 1972 W
election victory for People's National Party, 1989 B
James, Henry, Am. author (1843–1916), 1843 Z, 1876 U, 1877 U, 1878 U, 1881 U, 1886 U, 1895 U, 1898 U, 1903 U, 1913 S, 1914 U, 1916 Z, 1917 U
James, Montague Rhodes, B. scholar (1862–1936), 1904 U
James, Naomi, B. yachtswoman (b. 1949), 1978 X
James, William, Am. philosopher (1842–1910), 1842 Z, 1890 R, 1902 R, 1907 R, 1909 R, 1910 Z
Jameson Raid, Report on, 1897 G
Jameson, Sir Leander Starr, S. African statesman (1849–1912), 1849 Z, 1891 F, 1893 L, 1894 A, 1896 A, 1912 Z; raid into Transvaal, 1895 M; founds Unionist Party, 1910 E
Jammu, India, disturbances in, 1959 G
India and Pakistan agree on truce line, 1972 M
Janácek, Leos, Czech. musician (1854–1928), 1916 T
Jane Eyre (C. Brontë), 1847 U
Jane's Addiction, Am. pop group, 1990 W
Janissaries, Turkish, dissolved, 1826 F
Janossy, Lajos, Hung. scientist (b. 1912), 1948 P
Jansky, Karl, radio-astronomer, 1932 P
Janson, Paul, Belg. Liberal, 1937 K
Japan: extra-territorial concessions in, 1886 E; art of, introduced to West, 1867 S; US forces land in, 1945 H
Sato elected Prime Minister, 1964 J
US military bases, 1968 M
Okinawa, US agrees to return, 1969 L
economy, 1969 O
population, 1971 Y, 1981 Y, 1991 Y
Gunma Prefectural Museum of Fine Arts, 1974 S
refuses new credits to Poland, 1982 B
restrictions on women's work removed, 1985 O
urbanization, 1985 Y
railways privatized, 1987 O
divorce statistics, 1987 Y
general election, 1990 B
life expectancy, 1990 Y
Jardin de Bérénice (M. Barres), 1891 U
Jarman, Derek, B. film director (1942–94), 1942 Z, 1976 W
Jarring, Gunnar, Swe. UN mediator (b. 1907), 1970 H
Jarrow, Durham, England, development scheme, 1936 G
Jars, Plain of, Laotian offensive against North Vietnam, 1969 J
Jaruzelski, General Wojciech, Prime Minister of Poland (b. 1923), 1983 F, 1985 L, 1989 G
Prime Minister, 1981 B

government reconstruction, 1981 F
First Secretary of Communist Party, 1981 K
attends crisis talks, 1981 L
visits Moscow for talks, 1982 C
announces leadership changes in Polish Communist Party, 1982 G
resignation as Prime Minister, 1985 L
amnesty for 300 political prisoners announced, 1986 F
Jaspers, Karl, Swi. philosopher (1883–1968), 1883 Z, 1932 R, 1935 R, 1953 R, 1969 Z
Jassy, Moldavia, Russia, peace treaty of, 1792 A
Jauraie, La, Vende, France, treaty, 1795 B
Jaurès, Auguste Marie Joseph Jean-, F. Socialist leader (1859–1914), 1859 Z, 1911 D, 1914 G
Java: restored to Netherlands, 1816 M; Japanese land in, 1942 B; war in, 1947 G; Communists in, 1948 J
Jay, John, Am. diplomat (1745–1829), 1794 L
Jay, Peter, B. journalist and diplomat (b. 1937), 1977 E
Jayawardene, Junius, President of Sri Lanka (b. 1906), 1977 G, 1978 B, 1985 F, 1987 G
Jazz: sweeps US, 1916 T; Original Dixieland Band, 1948 W, becomes universal, 1920 W
Jean Calas (J. Chénier), 1791 W
Jean–Christophe (R. Rolland), 1904 U
Jeanneret, Charles Edouard. *See* Corbusier, Le
Jeans, Sir James, B. astronomer (1877–1946), 1877 Z, 1914 P, 1929 P, 1946 Z
Jebb, John, B. theologian (1736–86), 1771 R
Jebb, Sir Richard Claverhouse, B. classical scholar (1841–1905), 1841 Z, 1905 Z
Jedermann (H. von Hofmannsthal), 1911 U
Jeff and Ilona (Made in Heaven) *(J. Koons), 1990 S*
Jefferson, Thomas, Am. statesman (1743–1826), 3rd president of US, Republican (1801–9), 1776 G; 1778 N, 1784 D, 1792 N, 1798 N, 1801 C, 1807 F, 1817 S, 1826 Z; as secretary of state, 1789 D; defeated by John Adams, 1796 L; elected president, 1800 L; second term, 1805 C
Jeffreys, Sir Alec John, B. biochemist (b. 1950), 1950 Z, 1984 P
Jeffries, J. J., Am. boxer, 1910 X
Jeffries, John, Am. physician and scientist (1744–1818), 1785 P
Jehovah's Witnesses. *See under* Religious Denominations
Jellicoe, George Patrick John Rushworth, 2nd Earl of Jellicoe, B. politician (b. 1918), Lord Privy Seal, 1973 E
Jellicoe, John Rushworth, Earl Jellicoe, B. admiral (1859–1935), 1916 L
Jemappes, Hainault, Belgium, Austrian defeat at, 1792 L
Jena, Germany, Zeiss optical factory at, 1846 P
Jenkins, David Edward, B. churchman (b. 1925), Bishop of Durham, 1984 J, R
Jenkins, Roy Harris, Lord Jenkins of Hillhead, B. politician (b. 1920), 1964 Q
Chancellor of Exchequer, 1967 L
resignation as deputy leader of Labour Party, 1972 D
Home Secretary, 1974 C
President of European Commission, 1977 A
Dimbleby Lecture, 1979 L
suggests radical centre party, 1980 F
'Limehouse Declaration', 1981 A
loses by-election for SDP, 1981 G
elected SDP leader, 1982 G
wins Glasgow Hillhead by-election, 1982 C
resignation as leader of SDP, 1983 F
Jenkinson, Robert Banks, Earl of Liverpool, B. Tory politician (1770–1828), 1805 O; premier, 1812 E, 1827 A
Jenner, Edward, B. physician (1749–1823), 1796 P
Jennie Gerhardt (T. Dreiser), 1911 U
Jenyns, Soame, B. philosopher (1704–87), 1776 R
Jericho, Jordan: Australians occupy, 1918 B; Arab Congress of, 1948 M; excavations at, 1952 Q
Jerome, Jerome Klapka, B. author (1859–1927), 1859 Z, 1889 U, 1927 U
Jerusalem (M. Mendelssohn), 1783 R
Jerusalem (S. Lagerlöf), 1901 U
Jerusalem (W. Blake), 1804 U
Jerusalem, Israel: Russian Orthodox Church establishes monastery, 1860 R; excavations at, 1866 Q; surrenders to Allenby 1917 M; missionary conference at, 1928 R; Arab–Jew conflict over Wailing Wall, 1929 H; UN trusteeship for, 1947 L; Arabs enter, 1948 E; Israel attempts to found capital, 1949 M; Religious Centre for World Jewry, 1958 R
Israel gains control of Old Jerusalem, 1967 F, R
UN orders Israel to desist from unifying Jerusalem, 1967 G
Al-Aqsa Mosque damaged by fire, 1969 J, R
unified Jerusalem proclaimed capital of Israel, 1980 G
police fire on demonstrators at Temple Mount, 1990 K
Jerusalem Bible, The, *1966 R*
Jervis, John, lord St. Vincent, B. admiral (1735–1823), 1797 B
Jesuits (Society of Jesus):
dissolution demanded, 1769 A
dissolved, 1773 G
revived, 1814 R
in France, suppressed, 1764 L, 1879 F, 1880 C, R
allowed to return, 1826 N
attacked, 1828 F
in Germany, laws against, 1872 F, 1904 R
in Parma, expelled, 1768 N
in Poland, expelled, 1774 N
in Spain and Sicilies, expelled, 1767 C
Jesus and Mary Chain, pop group, 1985 W
Jesus Christ in Modern Thought (J. MacQuarrie), 1990 R
Jesus the Jew (G. Vermes), 1973 R
Jet engine, 1937 P
Jeu de paume (A. Chénier), 1790 O
Jeune captive (A. Chénier), 1794 O
Jeune parque, La (P. Valéry), 1917 U
Jeunes filles, Les (H. de Montherlant), 1936 U
Jeunesses musicales, 1958 T
Jeunet, F. film director, 1991 W
Jevons, William Stanley, B. economist (1835–82), 1865 O, 1871 O, 1874 P, 1882 O
Jew Süss (Feuchtwanger), 1917 U
Jewel in the Crown, The, television series, 1984 W
Jewett, Sarah Orme, Am. author (1849–1909), 1877 U
Jewkes, John, B. economist (1902–88), 1948 O
Jews, The:
disabilities of, tract on, 1781 R
statistics of, 1909 Y, 1980 W
World Conference, Montreux, 1948 R
Conference of Rabbis, 1957 R
Religious Centre for World Jewry, Jerusalem, 1958 R
Knesset's legal definition of, 1970 C
reactions to Israeli invasion of Lebanon, 1982 R
See also Anti-Semitism; Israel
in Britain, removal of disabilities, 1858 G, O
in France, admitted to civil liberties, 1790 R
consistorial organisation of, 1806 R
in Germany, Prussian, emancipated, 1812 R
seminary in Breslau, 1854 R
influence of, 1878 O
persecution of, 1933 D, 1935 J
in Israel
Eichmann's trial for crimes against, 1961 O
See also Israel; Jerusalem; Middle East
in Palestine, Balfour Declaration on national home for, 1917 L
protests at immigration restrictions, 1933 M
admission to Palestine demanded, 1945 H
in Poland, deported to Lublin, 1939 K
pogrom, 1946 G
in Russia
persecuted, 1881 R
closure of synagogues, 1961 R
Supreme Soviet offices occupied, 1971 C
Jews sentenced in Leningrad, 1971 E
Soviet Jews' transit camp in Austria closed, 1973 J
copies of the Torah taken to Moscow synagogue, 1977 R
Israeli–USSR talks on Russian Jews, 1986 H
in Spain, 1492 decree expelling Jews annulled, 1968 M
'Jindivik' pilotless plane, 1953 P
Jingoism, in Britain, 1878 A
Jinnah, Miss, Pakist., 1965 A
Joachim, Joseph, G. violinist (1831–1907), 1831 Z, 1844 T, 1879 T, 1907 Z
Jocelyn (A. de Lamartine), 1836 U
Jodl, General, G., capitulates to Eisenhower, 1945 E
Jodrell Bank, England, radio-telescope, 1957 P, 1991 P
Joffre, Joseph, F. general and statesman (1852–1931), 1852 Z, 1916 M, 1931 Z; takes offensive, 1915 J; as commander-in-chief, 1915 M
Johannes IV, King of Ethiopia (1872–89), 1888 M, 1889 L
Johannesburg, S. Africa, 1892 J, 1896 A; Uitlanders petition, 1899 C; Roberts occupies, 1900 H; strikes in, 1922 C; race riots in, 1950 A; Progressive Party established at 1959 L, trial in, 1964 L
John Brown's Body (S. V. Bent), 1928 U
John Bull's Island: Immigration and British Society, 1871–1971 (C. Holmes), 1988 Q
John Deth (E. Burra), 1952 S
John Gilpin (W. Cowper), 1785 U
John Halifax Gentleman (D. Muloch), 1857 U
John Inglesant (J. H. Shorthouse), 1880 U
John Paul I, Pope, It. (Cardinal Albino Luciani, Patriarch of Venice, 1912–78), 1978 H, 1978 J, R
John Paul II, Pope, Pol. (Karol Wojtyla, Archbishop of Cracow, b. 1920), 1920 Z, 1990 R
elected Pope, 1978 K, R
visits Ireland, 1979 J
assassination attempt on, 1981 E
celebrates Mass for Peace, 1982 E
visits Britain, 1982 E
visits Poland, 1983 F
visits South America, 1988 E
opposition to women priests, 1988 R
Gorbachev visits Vatican, 1989 R
John VI, King of Portugal (1816–26), 1792 N, 1816 A, C, 1820 B, M, 1821 D, J, 1823 F, 1824 D, 1826 C
John XXIII, Pope (Cardinal Angelo Roncalli), 1963 F; elected Pope, 1958 K, W; decides to call Vatican Council, 1959 R; appeals for world peace, 1961 J; insists on retention of Latin, 1962 R; encyclical, *Pacem in Terris*, 1963 R
John Gabriel Borkman (Ibsen), 1896 W

John, Augustus, B. artist (1879–1961), 1908 S, 1909 S, 1911 S, 1914 S, 1926 S, 1940 S
John, Elton Hercules (born Reginald Kennth Dwight), B. singer (b. 1947), 1973 W
libel action against *The Sun* newspaper, 1988 V
John, Gwen, B. artist (1876–1939), 1924 S
Johns, Jasper, Am. artist (b. 1930), 1930 Z, 1988 S
Johnson, Amy (later Mollison), B. airwoman (1903–1941), 1903 Z, 1930 O, P, 1936 P, 1941 Z
Johnson, Andrew, Am. statesman, Republican (1808–75), 17th president of US (1865–70), 1864 L, 1865 D
acquitted after impeachment, 1868 E
Johnson, Ben, Canadian athlete (b. 1961), 1988 X
Johnson, C. S., Am. author, 1930 O
Johnson, Jack, Am. boxer, 1908 X, 1910 X
Johnson, Louis Arthur (b. 1891), Am. defence secretary, 1950 J
Johnson, Lyndon Baines, Am. statesman, Democrat (1908–73), 36th President of US (1963–69), 1908 Z, 1965 A, 1973 Z
appointed vice-president, 1960 L
visits Berlin, 1961 H
succeeds as president, 1963 L
proposes reduced defence budget, 1964 A
submits poverty bill, 1964 C
signs Civil Rights Act, 1964 G
defeats Goldwater, 1964 L
meets H. Wilson, 1964 M
offers Panama a new Canal treaty, 1964 M
proposes aid for S.E. Asia, 1965 D
signs Medical Care for Aged bill, 1965 G
meets South Vietnamese leaders, 1966 B
civil rights legislation, 1966 D, 1968 B
tour of Far East and Pacific, 1966 K
war tax surcharge, 1967 A
offers to cease US bombing of North Vietnam, 1967 B
Glassboro talks with Kosygin, 1967 F
race riots, commission appointed to investigate, 1967 G
re-election as President not sought, 1968 C
US bombing of North Vietnam restricted and stopped, 1968 C, K
peace talks with North Vietnamese, 1968 K, L
Johnson, Philip Cortelyon, Am. architect (b. 1906), 1958 S, 1984 S
Johnson, Prince, President of Liberia, 1990 J
Johnson, Samuel, B. author, lexicographer and wit (1709–84), 1763 U, 1764 U, 1775 U, 1779 U, 1784 Z, 1785 R, 1796 S
Johnson, Terry, 1984 W
Johnston, Sir Harry Hamilton, B. explorer and administrator (1858–1927), 1858 Z, 1927 Z
Johnston, Joseph Eggleston, Am. Confederate general (1807–91), 1865 D
Joint European Torus (JET), Culham, England, 1983 P, 1991 P
Jókai, Maurus, Hung. novelist (1825–1904), 1846 U
Joliot-Curie, Frédéric, F. physicist, 1934 P, 1939 P
Jolson, Al, Am. singer (1886–1950), 1927 W
Jonas, Franz, president of Austria, 1965 E
Jonathan Livingston Seagull (R. Bach), 1970 U
Jones, Ann, B. tennis player (b. 1938), 1969 X
Jones, Arnold Hugh Martin, B. ancient historian (1904–1970), 1964 Q
Jones, Aubrey, B. Conservative politician (b. 1911), as Chairman of Prices and Incomes Board, 1965 C
Jones, Edith. *See* Wharton, Edith
Jones, Edward. *See* German, Sir Edward
Jones, Sir Harold Spencer, B. astronomer (1890–1960), 1890 Z
Jones, Henry Arthur, B. dramatist (1851–1929), 1882 U
Jones, John Paul, Am. naval officer (1747–92), 1779 J
Jones, Maldwyn Allen, B. historian (b. 1922), 1983 Q
Jones, Sir William, B. orientalist (1764–94), 1784 Q, 1789 Q
Jones–Aldington proposals to ease unemployment of dock workers, 1972 G
Jong, Erica Mann, Am. author (b. 1942), 1974 U
Joplin, Janis, Am. pop singer (1943–70), 1971 W
Jordan, Hashemite Kingdom of: name changed, from Transjordan, 1949 F; forms, with Iraq, Arab Federation, 1958 B; Arab Federation ended, 1958 H
war with Israel, 1967 F
battle between Israeli and Jordanian forces, 1968 A
tightens control on Palestinian guerrilla movement, 1970 B, J
army fights Palestinian guerrillas/ceasefire agreed, 1970 F
renewed conflict between army and Palestinians, 1971 C
Palestinians assassinate Prime Minister, 1971 L
joins war against Israel, 1973 K
Arafat-Jordanian talks on proposed Palestinian state confederated with Jordan, 1982 K, L
withdrawal from Middle East peace plan talks, 1983 D
economic relations with Egypt restored, 1983 M
diplomatic relations with Egypt restored, 1984 J
Jordan–Egypt peace initiative talks for West Bank, 1984 M
Arab summit, 1987 L
parliamentary election, 1989 L
Jorrocks's Jaunts and Jollities (R. S. Surtees), 1838 U
Jose, Francisco Sionil, Phil. author (b. 1924), 1984 U
Joseph (Bonaparte), King of Naples, 1806 C, 1810 D, J; becomes King of Spain, 1808 F; flees from Madrid, 1808 H; flees from Spain, 1813 F
Joseph Delorme (Sainte-Beuve), 1829 U
Joseph I, King of Portugal (1750–77), insanity of, 1774 N
Joseph II, Emperor of Austria (1765–90), 1768 M, 1769 H, K, 1770 J, 1780 F, L, 1783 F, 1784 K, 1787 A, 1788 B, K, 1790 B; as Archduke of Austria, 1763 B; elected emperor, 1765 H; claims Lower Bavaria, 1777 M, 1778 A; reforms, 1781 K, L, 1782 C; abrogates Barrier Treaty, 1782 D; attempts to exchange Bavaria for Netherlands, 1785 A, G, 1786 K
Joseph and His Brothers (T. Mann), 1933 U
Joseph, Archduke of Austria (1872–1931), as 'state governor' of Hungary, 1919 H
Joseph, Sir Keith Sinjohn, Lord Joseph of Portsoken, B. Conservative politician (b. 1918), 1974 J
Josephine (Marie Rose Josephine Tascher de la Pagenie) (1763–1814), F. empress, as Josephine Beauharnais, marries Napoleon Bonaparte, 1796 C; Napoleon divorces, 1809 M
Joubert, Barthélemy Catherine, F. general (1769–99), 1798 L, M
Joubert, M., F. financier, 1876 L
Joubert, Piet Jacobus, Boer general (1834–1900) 1899 K, L
Jouffroy d'Abbans, Claude François Dorothée Marquis de, F. pioneer of steam navigation (1751–1832), 1783 P
Jouhaud, Edouard, Alger, OAS leader, sentence reprieved, 1962 L
Joule, James Prescott, B. physicist (1818–89) 1818 Z, 1840 P, 1843 P, 1889 Z
Jourdan, Jean Baptiste, F. general (1762–1833) 1794 F, 1795 F, 1796 F, H, 1799 C
Journal Intime (H. F. Amiel), 1883 U
Journal of Transactions ... on the Coast of Labrador (G. Cartwright), 1792 P
Journal of a Country Priest (G. Bernanos), 1936 U
Journalist, The (G. Freytag), 1853 W
Journalists, Society of Women, 1884 V
Journals, scientific, development of, 1920 P
Journals:
Action française, 1899 V
Adelphi, The, *1923 V*
Aeronaute, L', 1963 P
Allgemeine Zeitung, 1798 V
American Historical Review, 1895 Q
Athenaeum, 1931 V
Atlantic Monthly, 1857 V
Blackwood's Magazine, 1817 V, 1857 V
Blätter fur die Kunst, 1890 V
Botanical Magazine, 1777 P
Caricature, La, 1830 S
Catholic, The, 1856 R
Children's Newspaper, The, 1919 V
Cinema Quarterly, The, 1932 W
Civiltà Cattolica, La, 1850 R
Constitutionnel, Le, 1849 V
Cornhill Magazine, The, 1860 V
Criterion, 1922 V
Critica, La, 1903 V
Critical Journal of Philosophy, 1801 R
Deutsche Museum, Das, 1810 V
Dial, The, 1840 R
Economic History Review, 1927 Q
Economist, The, 1843 V
Edinburgh Press, The, 1802 V, 1825 Q
Egyptian Archaeology, 1914 Q
English Historical Review, 1886 Q
English Review, The, 1908 V
Field, The, 1853 V
Fortnightly Review, The, 1865 V
Forward, is suppressed, 1916 V
Fraser's Magazine, 1838 U
Harper's Weekly, 1856 V
History Today, 1951 V
History, 1917 Q
Hochland, 1903 V
Illustrated London News, The, 1842 V
Industrial Syndecalist, the, 1910 O
John Bull, 1820 V
Knickerbocker Magazine, 1833 V
Lancet, The, 1823 P
Left Review, 1934 V
Liberator, The, 1831 O
Life magazine, 1972 V, 1978 V
Life and Letters, 1928 V
Listener, The, closure, 1991 V
London Magazine, The, 1954 W
Mind, 1876 R
Musical Times, The, 1844 T
National Reformer, The, 1860 V
National and Athenaeum, 1931 V
New Society merged into *New Statesman*, 1988 V
New Statesman, The, 1913 V, 1931 V
New Writing and Daylight, 1943 U
New Yorker, The, 1925 U
Nineteenth Century, The, 1877 U
Nouvelle Revue Française, 1909 V
Now! magazine, 1979 V, 1981 V
Overland Monthly, The, 1868 V
Pall Mall Gazette, 1865 V

Penny Magazine, 1832 V
Poetry Review, 1912 V
Political Register, 1816 V
Populaire, Le, 1916 V
Private Eye, 1962 V
Punch, 1841 V, 1896 V, closure, 1992 V
Quarterly Review, 1809 V
Review of Reviews, 1890 V
Revue des deux Mondes, 1829 V
Round Table, The, 1910 V
Saturday Review, The, 1855 V
Scrutiny, 1932 U
Sketch, The, 1893 V
Spectator, The, 1828 V, 1978 V
Speculum, 1926 Q
Spiegel, Der, 1962 K, L
Stern publishes extracts from *The Hitler Diaries*, 1983 V
Stijl, De, 1917 S
Strand Magazine, 1891 U
Studio, The, 1893 S
Symboliste, Le, 1886 V
Tablet, The, 1840 V
Tatler, The, 1901 V
Time Magazine, 1923 V
Time and Tide, 1920 V
Times Literary Supplement, 1902 V
Transatlantic Review, 1924 V
Truth, 1877 R
Westminster Review, 1824 V
Zeitschrift für Philosophie, 1837 R
See also under Newspapers
Journey from St. Petersburg to Moscow (A. Radistcheff), 1790 O
Journey to the Western Islands of Scotland, A (S. Johnson), 1775 U
Journey's End (R. C. Sherriff), 1929 W
Jouve, P. J., F. poet (1887–1976), 1945 U
Jowett, Benjamin, B. educationalist (1817–93), 1870 O
Joy Division, 1980 W
Joy Luck Club, The (A. Tan), 1989 U
Joyce, James, Ir. author (1882–1941), 1882 Z, 1914 U, 1916 U, 1918 W, 1922 U, 1939 U, 1941 Z, 1984 U
Juan Carlos I, King of Spain (b. 1938), 1938 Z
Franco names as successor, 1969 G
restoration of monarchy, 1975 L
denounces coup, 1981 B
Judd, Donald Clarence, Am. sculptor (b. 1928), 1969 S
Jude the Obscure (T. Hardy), 1896 U
Judea Lives Again (N. Bentwich), 1944 O
Judgments, Notable:
in Britain, Taff Vale, 1901 G
in US, in Dred Scott case, 1856 C
Puerto Ricans not US citizens, 1901 M
in Northern Securities case, 1904 C
Income Tax ruled unconstitutional, 1916 A
Debs's conviction for espionage upheld, 1919 L
National Industrial Recovery Act declared unconstitutional, 1935 E
Segregation of Negroes on buses declared unconstitutional, 1946 O
on loyalty oaths of New York tenants, 1955 O
for desegregation in Little Rock Schools, 1958 J
that Communist Party should register as foreign-dominated body, 1961 F
reading of prayers in schools ruled unconstitutional, 1962 O
Judiciary, British:
Court of Chivalry revived, 1954 O
Family Courts proposed, 1965 O
Judicial Committee of Privy Council, 1856 R
Canadian appeals to, discontinued, 1946 O
Judson, Egbert Putnam, Am. inventor (1812–93), 1893 P
Julian (G. Vidal), 1964 U
Juliana, Queen of Netherlands (Louise Emma Marie Wilhelmina Juliana, b. 1909), 1948 J
abdication, 1980 D
Jumblatt, Kamal, Lebanese Moslem leader (1919–77), assassination, 1977 C
Jumpers (T. Stoppard), 1972 W
Jung, Carl Gustav, Swi. psychologist (1876–1961), 1917 R, 1920 R, 1940 R, 1944 R
Jungfrau, Switzerland, mountain, 1811 P
Junghans, Siegfried, G. metallurgist, 1927 P
Jungle (U. Sinclair), 1906 O
Jungle Book, The (R. Kipling), 1894 U
Junin, Prince, 1824 H
Junius, Letters of, 1768 V, 1769 A, 1770 F
Juno and the Paycock (O'Casey), 1925 W
Junot, Androche, F. general (1771–1813), 1808 M
Junta de Defensa Nacional, in Spain, 1936 G
Jupiter, planet, emission of radio waves from, 1955 P,
reached by Pioneer XI, 1974 P
Galileo probe, 1989 P
Ulysses probe, 1992 P
Jurandes, privileged corporations in France, abolished, 1776 B
Jurgen (J. B. Cabell), 1919 U
Jussieu, Antoine Laurent de, F. botanist (1748–1836), 1789 P
Just So Stories (R. Kipling), 1902 U
Justice, La (Sully-Prudhomme), 1878 U
Justine (L. Durrell), 1858 U
Jutland, battle of, 1916 E
Juvenile offenders, 1854 O, 1964 C, E
courts for, 1965 O
reformatories for, 1851 O, 1876 O
Juveniles, employment of, 1819 O
in Britain, legislation to control, 1825 F, 1833 M, 1842 M, 1844 F, 1847 F
in Germany, regulated, 1908 M
in US, regulated, 1903 N
products of labour by, excluded from inter-state commerce, 1916 O
forbidden, 1938 P

K

Kabaka, The, of Buganda, recognition of, withdrawn 1954 L; returns to Uganda, 1955 K; becomes president of Uganda 1963 K
Kabale und Liebe (Schiller), 1784 W
Kabul, Afghanistan:
British capitulate at, 1842 A
British legation at, massacred, 1879 J
martial law proclaimed, 1980 B
Kádár, János, Hung. Communist, becomes leader of Central Committee of Workers' Party, 1956 K; defection of, 1956 L; refuses entry of UN observers, 1956 L
Kaffaria, Colony, S. Africa, united with Cape Colony, 1865 C
Kafi, Ali, President of Algeria (b. 1928), 1992 F
Kafka, Franz, Aus. author (1883–1924), 1920 U, 1925 U, 1926 U, 1956 T
Kagel, Mauricio Paul, Argent. musician (b. 1931), 1971 T, 1982 T
Kahane Commission, on Beirut massacre, 1983 B
Kahn, Gustave, F. poet (1859–1941), 1886 V
Kahn, Louis Isadore, Am. architect (1901–74), 1901 Z, 1960 S, 1972 S, 1974 Z, 1977 S
Kaifu, Toshiki, Prime Minister of Japan (b. 1931), 1989 H
Kaiser, Henry, Am. industrialist (1882–1967), 1943 O
Kajar dynasty, Persia, 1794 N
Kaleidoscope, invented, 1816 P
Kaletski, Alexander, Am. (formerly R.) author (b. 1946), 1985 U
Kalinin, Mikhail Ivanovich, R. statesman (1875–1946), 1875 Z, 1946 Z
Kalisch, Cen. Poland: Prussia acquires, 1793 E; treaty, between Prussia and Russia, 1813 B
Kallman, Chester, Am. librettist (1921–1975), 1951 T
Kalstozov, Mikhail, R. film director, 1957 W
Kaluga, Russia, Russians recapture, 1941 W
Kamishari, N. Japan, solar eclipse observed at, 1936 P
Kamitz, Wenzel Anton, Prince von, Aus. chancellor (1711–94), 1768 M
Kampala, Uganda, 1955 H
Nigerian–Biafran peace talks, 1968 E
falls to Tanzanian and rebel forces, 1979 D
attack by Ugandan Freedom Movement members, 1982 B
Kampf, Ein (J. Dahn), 1876 U
Kampuchea. *See Cambodia.*
Kanara, State, Bombay, India, 1763 N
Kandinsky, Wassily, R., later Am., artist (1866–1944), 1911 S, 1912 S, 1933 S, 1940 S
Kandy, King, of Ceylon, 1815 A
Kandyan Provinces, Ceylon, 1815 C
K'ang Yu-wei, Chin. reformer, 1898 F
Kangaroo (D. H. Lawrence), 1923 U
Kangaroo (Y. Aleshkovsky), 1986 U
Kania, Stanislaw, Pol. leader (b. 1927), 1980 J, 1981 K
Kansas, state, US: settlement of, 1854 E; Civil war on slavery issue, 1856 E; becomes a US state, 1861 A; adopts women's suffrage, 1912 L
Kant, Immanuel, G. philosopher (1724–1804), 1770 R, 1781 R, 1783 R, 1784 R, 1785 R, 1788 R, 1790 R, 1793 R, 1795 R, 1797 R, 1798 R, 1799 R, 1804 Z
Kapital, Das (K. Marx), Vol. I, 1867 O, Vol. II, 1885 O; Vol. III, 1895 O; English edition of Vol. I, 1886 O
Kapitza, Pyotr Leonidovich, R. scientist (1894–1984), 1894 Z, 1938 P, 1984 Z
Kapoor, Anish, B. artist (b. 1954), 1982 S, 1988 S
Turner Prize, 1991 S
Kapp, Wolfgang, G. politician (1868–1922), leader of attempted *coup*, 1920 C
followers of, pardoned, 1925 H
Kaprow, Allan, Am. artist (b. 1927), 1966 S
Karachi, Pakistan, riots in, 1953 A
ethnic clashes, 1990 E
Karamanlis, Constantine, Greek politician (b. 1907), 1961 K, 1963 F, 1974 G, 1990 E
Karami, Rashid Abdul Hamid, Prime Minister of The Lebanon (1921–87), 1987 F
Karamzin, Nikolai Mikhailovich, R. historian (1765–1826), 1793 U, 1816 Q
Karelia, Finland: Russians attack, 1940 B; ceded to Russia, 1940 C; Finns invade, 1941 F
Kariba Dam, Rhodesia, 1960 E
Karloff, Boris (W. H. Pratt), Am. film actor (1887–1969), 1931 W
Karlsruhe, Germany, chemical conference at, 1860 P
Karmal, Babrak, Afghan. leader (b. 1929), 1979 M, 1986 E
Karpov, Anatoly, R. chess player (b. 1951), 1975 X

Karrer, O. Paul, Swi. biochemist (b. 1889), 1931 P, 1938 P
Kars, Russia: Russian take, 1855 L; Turkey transfers to Russia 1877 L, 1878 C, G
Karume, Abdul Aman, president of Zanzibar, 1964 B
Kasavubu, Joseph, Congolese leader (1910–69), 1961 C; as president of Congolese Republic, 1960 F; dismisses Lumumba, 1960 J; dismisses Tshombe, 1965 K; is deposed, 1965 L
Kasdan, Lawrence Edward, Am. film director (b. 1949), 1983 W
Kashmir, India: admitted into Indian Union, 1947 K; problem of, referred to UN, 1947 M; fighting in, 1951 G; India's agreement with, 1952 G; votes for integration with India, 1956 L; is incorporated in India, 1957 A; disturbances, 1959 G; talks between India and Pakistan on, 1962 M; failure of, 1963 E
India and Pakistan agree on truce line, 1972 M
brought under direct rule and curfew imposed, 1990 A
army takes direct control, 1990 G
Kaspar (P. Handke), 1968 W
Kassala, Sudan: Dervishes take, 1885 G; Italians take, 1894 G; ceded to Egypt, 1897 M; British take, 1941 A
Kassel, E. and W. German leaders meet, 1970 C
Kassem, Abdul Kerim, general, premier of Iraq (1914–63), founds Palestinian Army, 1960 C; declares Kuwait part of Iraq, 1961 F; is assassinated, 1963 B
Kasserine Pass, Tunisia, 1943 B
Kästner, Erich, G. author (1899–1974), 1899 Z, 1974 Z
Katanga, Congo: settled by Company, 1891 D; UN troops enter, 1960 H; UN breaks off relations, 1961 J; cease fire in, 1961 M; Tshombe ends secession of, 1961 M; UN plans for, 1962 J, 1963 A
Kätchen von Heilbronn, Das, 1808 W
Katsura, Japanese Prince, 1906 A, 1912 M
Katzbach, Germany, battle, 1813 H
Kaufman, George S., Am. playwright (1889–1961), 1889 Z, 1939 W, 1961 Z
Kaunas, Lithuania, demonstrations demanding freedom for Lithuania, 1972 E
Kaunda, Kenneth David, President of Zambia (b. 1924), 1924 Z, 1969 H, 1991 K; premier of Northern Rhodesia, 1962 M, 1964 A; president of Zambia, 1964 K
Kavalla, Greece, Greeks surrender at, 1916 J
Kavanagh, Patrick Joseph Gregory, B. author (b. 1931), 1966 U
Kawabata, Yasunari, Jap. author (1899–1972), 1899 Z, 1948 U, 1972 Z
Nobel Prize, 1968 U
Kawara, On, Jap. artist (b. 1933), 1970 S
Kawawa, Rashidj, Tanzanian politician forms ministry, 1962 A
Kay, John, B. inventor (1704–64), 1764 Z
Kay-Shuttleworth, Sir T. P. *See under* Shuttleworth
Kaye, Danny (born David Daniel Kominski), Am. actor (1913–87), 1913 Z, 1954 W, 1955 W, 1987 Z
Kazakhs, percentage in Soviet population, 1989 Y
Kazan, Elia, Am. film director (b.1909), 1954 W, 1956 W
Kazhdan, Alexander P., R. author (b. 1922), 1991 Q
Kazviv, Persia, 1911 L
Kean, Edmund, B. actor (1787–1833), 1787 Z, 1814 W, 1820 W, 1833 W, Z
Keating, Paul John, Prime Minister of Australia (b. 1944), 1944 Z, 1991 M
Britain accused of abandoning Australia to Japan in World War II, 1992 B
Keats, John, B. poet (1795–1821), 1795 Z, 1818 U, 1819 U, 1820 U, 1821 Z
Keays, Sara, B. secretary (b. 1947), 1983 K
Keble, John, B. divine and poet (1792–1866), 1792 Z, 1827 R, 1833 R, 1866 Z
Kedah, N.W. Malaya: Rajah of, 1786 H; becomes Siamese territory, 1826 F
Keele, Staffordshire, England, University college at, 1949 O
Keeler, Christine, B. model, 1963 G, M
Keen, Maurice Hugh, B. historian (b. 1933), 1990 Q
Keenan, Brian, Irish hostage (b. 1950), 1986 D, 1990 H
Kefauver Committee on Crime in US inter-state commerce, 1951 C
Keilhau, Germany, Froebel's community at, 1816 O
Keillor, Garrison Edward, Am. broadcaster and author (b. 1942), 1986 U
(K)ein Sommernachtstraum (A. Schnittke), 1985 T
Keir, Gillian, B. historian, 1975 Q
Keitel, Wilhelm von, G. general (1882–1946), 1945 E
Keith, Sir Arthur, B. anthropologist (1866–1955), 1948 P
Kekulé, Friedrich August, G. chemist (1829–96), 1829 Z, 1865 P, 1896 Z
Keller, Gottfried, G. author (1819–90), 1819 Z, 1846 U, 1851 U, 1890 Z
Kellogg, Frank Billings, Am. statesman (1856–1937), 1856 Z, 1937 Z; becomes secretary of state, 1925 A; proposes pact for renunciation of war, 1927 M, 1928 D
Kellogg, William Pitt, Am. politician, Republican governor of Louisiana (1830–1918), 1874 F
Kellogg-Briand pact, 1928 D, F, H; embodied in Act of League Assembly, 1928 J; Germany accepts, 1929 B; in force, 1929 G; Rome Pact endorses, 1933 G
Kelly, Grace, Am. film actress (1929–82), 1928 Z, 1956 W, 1982 Z
Kelly, Sean, Ir. cyclist (b. 1956), 1989 X
Kelly, William, B. steel engineer (1811–88), 1851 P
Kelmscott Press, 1890 S
Kelvin, lord. *See* Thomson, William
Kemble, John Mitchell, B. historian (1807–57), 1833 Q, 1849 Q
Kemel Atatürk, Turk. statesman (1881–1938), 1881 Z, 1907 M, 1919 H, 1922 L, 1923 K, 1927 J, 1938 L, 1938 Z; elected president of Turkey, 1923 H; suppresses Communist propaganda, 1929 F; takes name Atatürk, 1935 A; as author, 1927 O
Kemp, George Meikle, Scot. architect (1795–1844), 1840 S
Kempinski, Tom, B. playwright (b. 1938), 1981 W
Kendall, Edward Calvin, Am. chemist (1886–1972), 1886 Z, 1935 P, 1972 Z
Kendall, James, B. chemist (1889–1978), 1915 P
Kendrew, John Cowdery, B. biophysicist (b. 1917), 1960 P
Keneally, Thomas Michael, Austral. author (b. 1935), 1982 U
Kenilworth (W. Scott), 1821 U
Kennan, George, Am. diplomat (b. 1904), Russia demands recall of, 1952 K
Kennedy, Edward Moore, Am. senator, Democrat (b. 1932)
Chappaquiddick incident, 1969 G, 1970 D
challenges Carter for presidential nomination, 1979 L
withdraws challenge to Carter, 1980 H
Kennedy, John Fitzgerald, Am. statesman, Democrat (1917–63), 35th president of US (1961–3), 1917 Z, wins presidential election, 1960 L
inaugurated, 1961 A
meets Macmillan, 1961 C, M, 1962 M, 1963 F
establishes Peace Corps, 1961 C
extra-ordinary State of Union message, 1961 E
visits Europe, 1961 E
sends L. B. Johnson to Berlin, 1961 H
envisages partnership with a United Europe, 1962 G
broadcast on installation of Russian missile base in Cuba, 1962 K
'Kennedy Round' tariff negotiations, 1963 E, 1964 E
speech on Civil Rights, 1963 F
is assassinated, 1963 L
Warren Report on assassination, 1964 O
US House of Representatives decision on assassination of, 1978 M
Kennedy, Margaret, B. author, 1926 W
Kennedy, Michael, B. musicologist (b. 1926), 1964 T
Kennedy, Robert Francis, US senator, Democrat (1925–68), 1925 Z
candidacy for Democratic Presidential nomination, 1968 C
assassination, 1968 F, Z
Kennicott, Benjamin, B. Biblical scholar (1718–83), 1776 Q
Kennington, Eric Henri, B. artist (1888–1960), 1917 S
Kenny, Dr. Anthony, B. philosopher (b. 1931), expulsion from Czechoslovakia, 1980 R
Kentucky, State, US: becomes a US state, 1792 F; legislature, 1798 N
Kenwood House, Middlesex, 1764 S, 1928 S, 1953 S
Kenya (formerly East African Protectorate), 1920 G; white settlers advocate closer ties with Uganda and Tanganyika, 1935 J; Italians driven from, 1941 A; emergency, 1953 D, 1959 L; becomes an independent Republic, 1963 M, 1964 M
hunting of elephants and trade in ivory banned, 1973 H
death of Kenyatta, 1978 H, Z
urbanization, 1985 Y
demonstrations demanding Moi's resignation and inquiry into murder of Foreign Minister, 1990 B
demonstrations against one-party rule, 1990 G
general assembly votes to end one-party state, 1991 M
Democratic Party, 1992 A
Kenyatta, Jomo, Kenyan leader (1889–1978), 1889 Z, 1978 H, Z; convicted of managing Mau Mau, 1953 D, G; released, 1961 D; becomes president of Kenya, 1964 M
Kenyon, Kathleen Mary, B. archaeologist (1906–78), 1957 Q
Keppel, Henry, B. naval officer (1809–1904), 1809 Z, 1904 Z
Kerala, India, riots in, 1964 L
Kerch Peninsula, Russia, Germans attack, 1942 E
Kerekou, Brigadier-General Mathieu Ahmed, President of Benin (b. 1933), 1991 C
Keren, Ethiopia, British take, 1941 C
Kerensky, Alexander, R. politician (1881–1970), 1881 Z, 1917 C, F, 1970 Z; becomes premier,

1917 G; proclaims Republic, 1917 J; falls, 1917 L
Kermadec Isles, Pacific, annexed by New Zealand, 1887 A
Kern, Jerome, Am. composer (1885–1945), 1939 W
Kerosene, first manufactured, 1854 P
Kerouac, Jack, Am. author (1923–69), 1957 U
Kerr, Deborah, B. film actress (b. 1921), 1956 W
Kerr, Sir John Robert, Governor-General of Australia (1914–91), 1975 L, 1977 G
Kerr, Malcolm, President of American University in Beirut, murdered, 1984 A
Kerr, Robert Schomberg, Marquess of Lothian, B. administrator and journalist (1874–1930), 1910 V
Kerry, Munster, Ireland, Fenian outrages in, 1867 B
Kesselring, Albert, G. soldier (1886–1960), 1960 Z
Ketteler, Wilhelm Emmanuel, G. bishop of Mainz (1811–77), 1856 R
Keuffel und Esser, G. company, makes last slide-rule, 1976 P
Kew Gardens, Surrey, England, 1835 P, 1840 P
Key West, Florida, US, 1961 C
Keyes, Roger, lord Keyes, B. naval officer (1872–1945), 1872 Z, 1945 Z
Keynes, John Maynard, B. economist (1883–1946), 1883 Z, 1919 O, 1926 O, 1930 O, 1936 O, 1943 O, 1946 Z
Khachaturian, Aram (1903–78), R. musician, 1943 T
Khaddhafi, Colonel Moamer, Libyan leader (b. 1942), 1942 Z
takes power, 1969 J
Egyptian–Libyan joint Constituent Assembly plan, 1973 H
partial reprieve for exiles, 1980 F
Khaled, Leila, Palestinian hijacker, arrest, 1970 J
Khaled, Sheikh Hassan, Grand Mufti of Lebanon, 1989 E
Khalid, King of Saudi Arabia (1913–82), 1975 C
Khalistan, Sikhs declare independent state of, 1986 D
Khama, Sir Seretse, President of Botswana (1921–80), 1965 C, 1966 J
Khameini, Hojatoleslam Ali, Iran. religious leader and politician (b. 1940), 1981 K
Kharg Island, Iran, oil terminal blockaded, 1984 B
Kharkov, Russia: Bolsheviks capture, 1919 M; Germans take, 1941 K; fighting near, 1942 E; Russians recapture, 1943 B, H; Russians evacuate, 1943 C
Khartoum, Sudan: Gordon at, 1884 B; Mahdi takes, 1885 A; riots in, 1964 M; floods, 1988 H
Khedda, Ben, Alger. leader, 1961 H
Khiva, Russia, Russians assume control of, 1873 H
Khmer Republic. *See* Cambodia
Khmer Rouge, 1975 D, 1976 D, 1979 A, 1985 J
Khomeini, Ayatollah Ruhollah, Iranian religious and political leader (1902–89), 1902 Z, 1989 F, Z
returns from exile, 1979 B
declares Iran an Islamic Republic, 1979 D
supporters of dominate new constituent assembly, 1979 H
Islamic Revolutionary Council takes power, 1979 L
makes conditions for US hostages' release, 1980 J
denounces President Bani-Sadr, 1981 F
declares Islam 'religion of the sword', 1983 R
fatwa against Salman Rushdie, 1989 B
Khorasan, in Khuzistan, Persia, 1796 N,
Khrushchev, Nikita, R. leader (1894–1971), 1894 Z, 1958 H, 1962 D, 1963 K, 1971 Z
appointed first secretary of Central Committee, 1953 J
visits Yugoslavia, 1955 E
visits E. Germany, 1955 G
denounces Stalin's policies, 1956 B
visits Britain, 1956 D
appeals to Labour and Socialist parties to prevent US aggression in Middle East, 1957 K
proposals for immediate summit meeting rejected, 1958 G
visits Peking, 1958 G
warns US against attacking China, 1958 J
visits Albania, 1959 E
reaffirms Oder–Neisse Line as German frontier, 1959 G
calls for denuclearised zone in Europe, 1959 G
addresses UN, 1959 J, 1960 J
visits Peking, 1959 J
invited to Summit Conference, 1959 M
visits India, Burma and Indonesia, 1960 B
protests against possibility of Spain providing bases for W. Germany, 1960 C
attends Summit Conference, 1960 E
wages campaign against Hammarskjöld, 1961 B
proposes a German peace conference, 1961 F
proposes disarmament and test-ban talks proceed simultaneously, 1961 F
proposes disarmament committee meet at summit level, 1962 B
in Cuban crisis, 1962 K
opens Aswan Dam, 1964 E
is replaced by Brezhnev and Kosygin, 1964 K
Khyber Pass, E. Afghanistan, British occupy, 1879 E
Kiamil Pasha, grand vizier of Turkey, 1909 B
Kiao-chow, Shantung, N. China: Germany occupies, 1897 L; Japan demands German withdrawal, 1914 H
Kibaki, Mwai, Kenyan politician (b. 1931), 1992 A
Kidd, Benjamin, B. sociologist (1858–1916), 1894 O
Kidnappings:
of Lindbergh's son, 1932 O
of English teacher from Lusaka, 1964 H
of Jasper Cross, British Trade Commissioner in Canada, 1970 K
of Pierre Laporte, Can. Minister of Labour, 1970 K
of W. German Ambassador to Guatemala, 1970 C
of Geoffrey Jackson, British Ambassador to Uruguay, 1971 A
from Rhodesian mission school, 1973 G
attempted, of Princess Anne, 1974 C
of Patricia Hearst, US heiress, 1975 J
of Peter Lorenz, Chairman of W. Berlin Christian Democratic Union, 1975 B
of US ambassador to Lebanon, then murdered, 1976 F
of Hans-Martin Schleyer, W. German business leader, 1977 J
of Aldo Moro, Italian Prime Minister, 1978 C, 1983 A
of two Britons and US journalist in Beirut, 1985 C, 1986 D
arms for hostages deal, 1986 L
of Brian Keenan in Beirut, 1986 D
of David Jacobsen, 1986 L
of John McCarthy in Beirut, 1986 D, 1991 H
of Mordechai Vanunu, 1986 K
of Terry Waite in Beirut, 1987 A, 1991 L
of French hostages in Lebanon, 1988 E
of Terry Anderson, 1991 M
of Joseph Cicipio, 1991 M
of Alan Steen, 1991 M
Kiefer, Anselm, G. sculptor (b. 1945), 1971 S, 1974 S, 1978 S, 1985 S
Kiel, Germany: acquired by Prussia, 1865 H; Canal, 1895 P; Treaty, between Denmark and Sweden, 1914 A, D; German naval mutiny at, 1918 L
Kielce, Poland, pogrom in, 1946 G
Kierkegaard, Soren, Dan. theologian (1813–55), 1813 Z, 1843 R, 1855 Z
Kiesinger, Kurt Georg, W. German Chancellor (1904–88), 1966 M
Kieslowski, Krzysztof, film director (b. 1941), 1988 W, 1991 W
Kiev, Russia: Germans occupy, 1918 C, Bolsheviks take, 1919 B; Denikin's force enters, 1919 J; Poles enter, 1920 E; Germans take, 1941 J; Russians recapture, 1943 L
Kikuyu, tribe in Kenya, 1953 D
Killing of Sister George, The (F. Marcus), 1965 W
Kilmainham Treaty, between Parnell and British government, 1882 E
Kilmartin, Terence Kevin, B. translator (b. 1922), 1981 U
Kilmuir, Lord. *See* Maxwell Fyfe, D.
Kiln, tunnel, 1839 P
Kilroy, Thomas, Ir. dramatist (b. 1934), 1968 W
Kim (R. Kipling), 1901 U
Kimberley, Earl of. *See* Wodehouse, John
Kimberley, Griqualand West, S. Africa: Britain annexes diamond fields, 1871 K; amalgamation of mining companies, 1888 O; railway reaches, 1885 L
Kinder der Welt (P. Heyse), 1873 U
Kindergarten, the first, 1837 O
Kindersley Report on UK doctors' pay, 1966 E
Kinetic theory of gases, 1850 P
Kinetoscope, the, 1894 W
King Cotton (T. Armstrong), 1947 U
King George V, His Life and Reign (H. Nicolson), 1952 Q
King George VI, His Life and Reign (J. Wheeler-Bennett), 1958 Q
King Henry III and the Lord Edward (F. M. Powicke), 1947 Q
King René's Daughter (H. Hertz), 1845 U
King Solomon's Mines (R. Haggard), 1886 U
King Steven (R.H.C. Davis), 1967 Q
King's Cross Underground Station fire, 1987 L
King's Mountain, N. Carolina, US, battle, 1780 K
King, Billie Jean, Am. tennis player (b. 1943), 1943 Z, 1968 X, 1969 X
King, Carole, Am. pop singer (b. 1942), 1971 W
King, Edward, B. churchman, Bishop of Lincoln (1829–1910), 1890 R
King, Horace Maybray, Lord Maybray-King, B. Labour politician (1901–86), 1971 A
elected Speaker, 1965 J
King, Martin Luther, Am. civil rights leader (1929–68), 1929 Z, 1964 K, 1965 C, 1969 C
civil disobedience campaign, 1967 H
assassination, 1968 D, Z
birthday made federal holiday, 1983 O
King, William Mackenzie, Can. statesman, Liberal (1874–1950), 1874 Z, 1919 H, 1937 H; becomes premier, 1921 M; maintains ministry with Labour support, 1925 K; resigns, 1926 F; forms ministry, 1926 J, 1935 K, 1945 F; confers with Churchill and Roosevelt, 1943 H
'King and Country' debate, in Oxford Union, 1933 O

Kinglake, Alexander William, B. traveller and author (1809–91), 1844 U, 1863 Q
Kingsley, Charles, B. author, churchman and social reformer (1819–75), 1819 Z, 1849 U, 1853 U, 1854 U, 1863 U, 1875 Z; founds Christian Socialism, 1849 R
Kinnock, Neil Gordon, B. Labour leader (b. 1942), 1942 Z, 1983 K, 1992 D
pledges to close all US nuclear bases in Britain, 1986 J
Kinsey, Alfred Charles, Am. psychologist (1894–1956), 1948 P
Kinshasa, Zaire, boxing championship, 1974 X
Kipling, Rudyard, B. author (1865–1936), 1865 Z, 1888 U, 1892 U, 1894 U, 1897 U, 1899 U, 1901 U, 1902 U, 1936 Z
Kipps (H. G. Wells), 1905 U
Kirchhoff, Johann Wilhelm Adolf, G. classical scholar (1826–1908), 1859 P
Kirchner, Ernst, G. artist (1880–1938), 1905 S
Kiribati (formerly the Gilbert Islands), independence, 1979 G
Kirk, Sir John, B. naturalist and administrator (1832–1922), 1873 F
Kirk, Captain Kent Sand, Dan. fisherman and MEP (b. 1948), 1983 A
Kirk, Norman Eric, Prime Minister of New Zealand (1923–74), 1972 L, 1974 H
Kirkuk, Iraq, pipelines from, 1935 P
Iraqi government forces bomb Kurdish rebels, 1991 C
Kirkwood, David, Lord Kirkwood, B. Labour politician (1872–1956), 1925 C
Kirov, Serge, R. politician (1886–1934), 1943 M
Kirstein, Lincoln Edward, Am. choreographer (b. 1907), 1933 T
Kiss and Tell (R. Deacon), 1989 S
Kiss, The (Rodin), 1898 S
Kissinger, Henry Alfred, Am. statesman (b. 1923)
Vietnam War, 1972 A, 1972 K
calls for new Atlantic Charter, 1973 D
Secretary of State, 1973 J
agrees Middle East plan with Brezhnev, 1973 K
tours Arab capitals, 1973 L
secures Israeli–Syrian agreement, 1974 E
proposes oil price reduction plan, 1974 L
Kitchener, Horatio, Lord Kitchener, B. soldier (1850–1916), 1850 Z, 1915 V, 1916 F, G; in Sudan, 1896 J, 1898 D; in S. Africa, 1900 A, 1901 A
Kiukiang, China, British concessions at, reduced, 1927 B
Kiwanuka, Benedicte, premier of Uganda, 1962 C
Kléber, Jean Baptiste, F. general (1753–1800), 1800 C
Klebs, Edwin, G. pathologist (1834–1913), 1834 Z
Klee, Paul, Swi. artist (1879–1940), 1918 S, 1921 S, 1922 S, 1929 S, 1933 S
Kleist, Heinrich von, G. author (1777–1811), 1808 W, 1811 U
Klemperer, Otto, G. musician (1885–1973), 1885 Z, 1927 T, 1973 Z
Klenk, Micheal de, Du. architect, 1921 S
Klenze, Les, G. architect (1784–1864), 1816 S, 1830 S, 1846 T
Klerk, Frederik Willem de, President of South Africa (b. 1936), 1936 Z, 1989 B, 1989 J, 1989 L
ban on ANC lifted, 1990 B
state of emergency lifted from all parts except Natal province, 1990 F
planned repeal of laws underpinning apartheid, 1991 B
Klima, Ivan, Czech. author (b. 1931), 1985 U
Klinger, Friedrich Maximilian von, G. dramatist (1752–1831), 1776 W
Klinger, Max, G. artist (1857–1920), 1857 Z, 1897 S, 1920 Z
Klinghoffer, Leon, Am. hostage, 1985 K
Klondyke, Yukon, Canada, gold rush, 1897 P
Klopstock, Friedrich Gottlieb, G. poet (1724–1803), 1771 U, 1773 U
'Kneel-in' campaigns in American churches, 1960 R
Knickerbocker's History of New York (W. Irving), 1809 U
Knight, Dame Laura, B. artist (1877–1970), 1936 S, 1939 S, 1965 S
Knott, Kathleen, B. poet, 1947 U
Knowledge and Human Interests (J. Habermas), 1968 R
Knowledge of the External World (B. Russell), 1914 R
Knowles, Sir James Thomas, B. journalist and architect (1831–1908), 1869 R, 1877 V
Knox peace resolution, 1920 E
Knox, Ronald Arbuthnot, B. Roman Catholic dignitary and Biblical scholar (1888–1957), 1888 Z, 1946 Q, 1950 R, 1957 Z
Knox-Johnston, Robin, B. yachtsman (b. 1939), 1969 X
Knussen, (Stuart) Oliver, B. musician (b. 1952), 1980 T, 1985 T
Köhler, Georges J.F., G. scientist (b. 1946), 1946 Z, 1975 P
Koc, Adam, Pol. politician, 1937 C
Koch, Ed, Am., Mayor of New York City (b. 1924), 1977 L
Koch, Robert, G. physician (1843–1910), 1877 P, 1883 P
Kodachrome film, 1935 P
Kodak box camera, 1888 P
Kodak company, 1929 P
Kodály, Zoltan, Hung. musician (1882–1967), 1923 T, 1961 T
Koestler, Arthur, Hung.-born B. author (1905–83), 1905 Z, 1949 R, 1950 O, 1954 O, 1964 R, 1983 Z
Koffee, King, of Ashanti, 1824 B
Kohl, Helmut, G. Chancellor (b. 1930), 1930 Z
forms coalition government, 1982 J
secretary in Kohl's office defects to E. Germany, 1985 J
Bonn Document, 1989 F
returned as Chancellor of united Germany, 1990 M
Kojak, television series, 1973 W
Koje Island, Korea, riots in prison camp, 1952 E
Kokkonen, Joonas, Fin. musician (b. 1921), 1975 T
Kokoschka, Oskar, Aus. painter (1886–1980), 1886 Z, 1909 S, 1914 S, 1926 S, 1955 S, 1962 S, 1980 Z
Kokovtsoff, Vladimir, R., becomes premier, 1911 J
Kolarov, Vassil, Bulg. politician, 1950 B
Kolbe, Adolphe Wilhelm Hermann, G. chemist (1818–84), 1845 P
Köller, Franz, Aus. inventor of tungsten-steel, 1855 P
Kölliker, Rudolph von, G. scientist (1817–1905), 1840 P
Kolozsvár, Hungary, diet at, 1865 M
Kölreuter, Joseph Gottlieb, G. botanist (1733–1806), 1763 P
Koltchak, Alexander (1874–1920), R. admiral, 1920 A
Kondylis, George, president of Greece, 1926 H
Königgratz, formerly Sadowa, Austria, battle, 1866 G
Konieh, Turkey, battle, 1832 M
Konoye, Jap. Prince (1891–1945), becomes premier, 1937 F
Kon-Tiki Expedition, The (T. Heyerdahl), 1950 P
Koons, Jeff, Am. artist (b. 1955), 1986 S, 1990 S
Kopechne, Mary Jo, Am., drowned, 1969 G
Kopit, Arthur, dramatist, 1969 W
Koralek, Paul, architect, 1967 S
Körber, Ernst von, Aust. politician (1860–1919), 1900 A
Korda, Sir Alexander, B. film producer (1893–1956), 1933 W
Korea, North, US naval intelligence plane shot down, 1969 D
Korea, South, president assassinated, 1979 K
Korea:
declared independent, 1876 B, 1895 L
US trading rights in, 1882 E
declares war on China, 1894 G
Queen assassinated, 1895 K
Russian position in, recognised, 1896 E
intervention of Russia and Japan in, 1897 K
Japan seeks concessions in, 1901 L
independence guaranteed, 1902 A
Russian concessions annulled, 1904 B
Japanese interests in, recognised by Russia, 1905 J
Japanese protectorate over, 1905 L, 1907 G
Japanese dictatorship in, 1909 K
Russo-Japanese agreement on, 1910 G
Japan annexes, 1910 H
is placed under US and USSR occupation, 1945 J
the Allies demand democratic government in, 1945 M
Republic proclaimed, 1948 H
Democratic Republic formed, 1948 J
US withdraws occupying force, 1949 F
See also under Wars, Korean
Korn (L. Lundkvist), 1985 U
Korngold, Erich Wolfgang, Aus. musician (1897–1957), 1916 T
Kornilov, Lavr, R. general, 1917 J
Korsákov, Alexander Mikhailovich, R. general, 1799 J
Korzeniowski, Josef Konrad. *See* Conrad, Joseph
Kosciuszko, Tadeusz Andrzej, Pol. Nationalist (1746–1817), 1794 C
Kosovo, Yugoslavia:
demonstrations calling for martial law, 1988 J
constitution stripping Kosovo of its autonomy, 1990 J
strike by ethnic Albanians, 1990 J
constitution suspended, 1991 C
Kössel, H., G. chemist, 1916 P
Kossuth, Louis, Hung. patriot (1802–94), 1848 J
Kostrowitsky, Wilhelm. *See* Apollinaire, Guillaume
Kosuth, Joseph, Am. artist (b. 1945), 1966 S
Kosygin, Alexei Nikolaevich, Sov. Premier (1904–80), 1904 Z, 1968 E, 1980 K, 1980 Z
becomes premier, 1964 K
visits Britain, 1967 B
Glassboro talks with Johnson, 1967 F
visits Peking, 1969 J
Kotalawala, Sir John, Ceyl. premier, 1953 K
Kötzebue, August, G. dramatist (1761–1819), 1797 W, 1819 C, H
Koussevitsky, Sergei, Am. musician (1874–1951), 1924 T
Kowal, Charles T., Am. astronomer, (b. 1940), 1974 P, 1975 P
Kowloon, China, leased to Britain, 1898 979

Krafft-Ebing, Richard, baron, G. psychologist (1840–1902), 1886 P
Kraftwerk, G. pop group, 1974 W
Kramer, Larry, Am. dramatist (b. 1935), 1986 W
Kraprayaon, General, Prime Minister of Thailand, 1992 E
Krasnoyarsk, Russia, 1920 A
Krassin, Leonid, R. trade delegate, 1920 E
Krause, Karl Christian Friedrich, G. philosopher (1781–1832), 1804 R
Kray de Krajof, Paul, Baron Kray, Aus. general (1735–1804), 1779 D, 1800 D
Kray, Reginald, B. gangster (b. 1933), 1969 C
Kray, Ronald, B. gangster (b. 1933), 1969 C
Krebs, Sir Hans Adolf, G.-born B. biochemist (1900–81), 1900 Z, 1932 P, 1981 Z
Křenek Ernst, Hung. musician (1900-91), 1927 T, 1941 T, 1960 T
Krenz, Egon, E. German Party leader (b. 1937), 1989 K
Kreutzer Sonata, The (L. Tolstoy), 1890 U
Krilium, synthetic chemical, 1951 P
Kriloff, Ivan, R. author (1768–1844), 1809 U
Kripke, Saul Aaron, Am. philosopher (b. 1940), 1973 R
Krishna Menon, Vengali Krishnan, Ind. statesman (1897–1974), 1897 Z, 1957 D, O
Kristin Lavransdatter (S. Undset), 1920 U
Kritische Wälder (Herder), 1769 U
Krivoy Rog, Ukraine, Russians recapture, 1944 B
Kroetz, Franz, G. dramatist (b. 1946), 1972 W
Kroger, Helen and Peter, B. spies, 1961 O, 1969 G
Kronstadt, Russia, French navy visits, 1891 G
Kropotkin, Peter Alexeivich, R. revolutionary (1842–1921), 1884 O
Kruger, Barbara, Am. artist (b. 1945), 1987 S
Kruger, Stephanus Johannes Paulus, S. African statesman (1825–1904), 1825 Z, 1880 M, 1899 C, G, 1904 Z; president of Transvaal, 1883 C, 1893 D, 1898 B; William II's telegram to, 1896 A; ultimatum to Britain, 1899 K; flight, 1900 K
Krumir Tribe, N. Africa, raids by, 1881 C
Krupp, Alfred, G. metallurgist (1812–87), 1812 Z, 1849 P, 1887 Z
Krypton, gas, 1903 P
Ktima, Cyprus, 1964 C
Ku-Klux-Klan, in US, 1922 O, 1965 C, K
Kuala Lumpur, Malaya, Japanese take, 1942 A
  Malay-Chinese violence, 1969 E
  Kampuchean leaders form opposition government-in-exile, 1982 F
Kuban, Russia: Russia annexation, 1783 G; agreed by Turkey, 1784 A; Russia's recapture, 1943 K
Kubla Khan (S. T. Coleridge), 1797 U, 1816 U
Kubrick, Stanley, Am. film director, (b. 1928), 1928 Z, 1964 W, 1968 W, 1971 W
Kühlmann, Richard von, G. foreign minister, 1917 H
Kuhmo Lake, Finland, Russian attack near, 1940 B
Kuhn, Thomas S., Am. philosopher (b. 1922), 1970 R, 1977 R
Kuibishev, Russia, government moved to, 1941 K
Kulturkampf, in Germany, 1871 G
Kumasi, Ghana, 1874 B
Kun, Bela, Hung. Socialist (1886–1938), 1919 H
Kundera, Milan, Czech. author (b. 1929), 1979 U, 1984 U
Küng, Hans, Swi. theologian (b. 1928), 1928 Z, 1971 R
Künstler, Die (F. Schiller), 1789 U
Kunstmythologie (K. A. Böttiger), 1811 Q
Kuo Min Tang. *See under* Political Parties
Kuo-feng, Hua, Chinese Communist Party Chairman (b. 1920), 1982 J
Kurak, Russia, Russians take, 1943 B
Kurdla, India, 1795 C
Kurds, tribe, rising by, 1930 G
  Kurdish autonomy recognized by Iraq, 1970 C
  Iraqi forces clash with Kurdish rebels, 1974 C
  rebellion in Iraq, 1991 C
  Iraqi forces bomb Kirkuk, 1991 C
  refugees, 1991 C, D
Kureishi, Hanif, B. playwright (b. 1934), 1986 W
Kurokawa, Kisho, Jap. architect (b. 1934), 1970 S, 1972 S, 1982 S
Kurosawa, Akira, Jap. film director (b. 1910), 1950 W, 1980 W, 1985 W
Kursk, Russia: Germans take, 1941 L; German offensive at, 1943 G
Kurtag, György, Hung. musician (b. 1926), 1981 T
Kushner, Tony, Am. playwright (b. 1956), 1992 W
Kut-el-Amara, Mesopotamia, 1915 J, 1916 D
Kutahia, Turkey, battle, 1921 G
Kutchuk-Kainardji, Bulgaria, peace signed at, 1774 G
Kutno, Russia, Germans break through at, 1914 L
Kuwait: admitted to Arab League, 1961 F; Kassem declares is part of Iraq, 1961 F; British troops sent to, 1961 F; US offers naval protection to Kuwaiti tankers in Gulf, 1987 G; Gulf War. *See* Wars
Kvetch (S. Berkoff), 1991 W
Kwang-su, Emperor of China (1875–1908), 1875 A
Kymograph, for measuring blood pressure, 1865 P
Kynoch, George, B. gunsmith (1834–91), 1882 P
Kynshu, Japan, US naval mutiny at, 1945 D
Kyprianu, Spyros, President of Cyprus (b. 1932), 1985 A
Kyrgyz, percentage in Soviet population, 1989 Y

L

Là-bas (J. Huysmans), 1891 U
La Fontaine et ses Fables (H. Taine), 1853 Q
Labiche, Eugène Maria, F. dramatist (1815–88), 1860 W
Labouchere, Henry du Pré, B. Liberal politician (1831–1912), 1831 Z, 1912 Z
Labour Day, May Day celebrations, 1890 O
Labour Department, German, founded, 1892 C
Labour Exchanges in Britain, 1910 O
Labour Parties. *See under* Political Parties
Labour codes:
  in France, 1912 O
  in Italy, 1927 D
Labour in Power, 1945–1951 (K.O. Morgan), 1984 Q
Labour, Ministry, British, 1917 O
  minister's powers for dealing with strikes, agitation against, 1944 D
Labour, Ministry, in Germany, 1918 O
Labour, treatise on, 1848 O
Labyrinth of Language (M. Black), 1968 R
Lacan, Jacques, 1966 R
Lachenmann, Helmut, G. musician (b. 1935), 1986 T
Lachmann, Karl Konrad Friedrich Wilhelm, G. classical scholar (1793–1851), 1850 Q
Lack, David Lamber, B. scientist (1910–73), 1966 P
Lacordaire, Jean Baptiste Henri, F. ecclesiastic (1802–61), 1838 R
Lacoste, Admiral Pierre, F. head of Foreign Service, 1985 J
Ladisla, J., Hung., inventor, 1938 P
Ladoga, Lake, Finland, shores of, ceded to Russia, 1940 C
Lady Chatterley's Lover (D. H. Lawrence), 1928 U; publication of, 1959 O
Lady Windermere's Fan (O. Wilde), 1892 W
Lady of Shalott, The (Tennyson), 1832 U
Lady of the Lake, The (W. Scott), 1810 U
Lady's Not for Burning (C. Fry), 1948 W
Ladysmith, Natal, S. Africa: surrenders to Joubert, 1899 L; relieved, 1900 B
Laetoli, Tanzania, archaeological find, 1978 Q
Lafayette, Marie Joseph Paul Yves du Motier, Marquis de, F. soldier (1757–1834), 1791 G; in America, 1777 D, 1781 J; commands National Guard, 1789 G; portrait, 1825 S
Laforgue, Jules, F. poet (1860–87), 1885 U
Lagerlöf, Selmar, Swe. author (1858–1940), 1858 Z
Lagos Charter for Pan-African Co-operation, 1962 A
Lagos, Nigeria, as a British Colony, 1886 A
Lagrange, Joseph Louis, Comte de, F. mathematician (1737–1813), 1788 P, 1797 P, 1813 Z
Laguardia, Fionello Henry, Am. mayor of New York (1882–1947), 1882 Z, 1947 Z
Lahore, Pakistan, Treaty, between Britain and Sikhs, 1846 C
  Islamic summit conference, 1974 B
Laibach, now Yugoslavia, Conference, 1820 M, 1821 A, B
Laienbrever (L. Schefer), 1834 U
Laing's Neck, Transvaal, S. Africa, British defeat at, 1881 A
Lakanal, Joseph, F. politician (1762–1845), 1795 O
Lakatos, Imre, Hung. philosopher (1922–74), 1976 R
Lake Wobegon Days (G. Keillor), 1986 U
Lake, Gerard, lord Lake, B. soldier (1744–1803), 1797 C, 1798 F
Laker Airways, 1977 J
Lallement, Pierre, F. inventor of 'bone-shaker' bicycle, 1865 P
Lamarck, Jean Baptiste Antoine de Monnel, Chevalier de, F. naturalist (1744–1829), 1803 P, 1809 P, 1815 P
Lamarque, General, F., 1832 F
Lamartine, Alphonse de, F. author (1790–1869), 1790 Z, 1820 U, 1823 U, 1836 U, 1869 Z; heads provisional government, 1848 B
Lamb, Charles, B. essayist (1775–1834), 1775 Z, 1807 U, 1820 U, 1834 Z
Lamb, Henry, B. artist (1883–1960), 1940 S
Lamb, Mary, B. author (1764–1847), 1807 U
Lamb, William, Viscount Melbourne, B. Whig statesman (1779–1848), 1779 Z, 1839 E; forms ministry, 1834 G; resigns, 1834 L; forms ministry, 1835 D; resigns, 1841 H
Lambert, Constant, B. musician (1905–1951), 1905 Z, 1926 T, 1929 T, 1936 T, 1951 Z
Lambeth Walk, The, 1938 W
Lambton, Antony Claud Frederick, Viscount Lambton, B. politician (b. 1922), resignation, 1973 E
Lambton, John George, Earl of Durham, B. colonial governor (1792–1840), 1838 E, K; report on Canada, 1839 B
Lamennais, Hughes, Félicité Robert de, F. author

(1782–1854), 1782 Z, 1817 R, 1830 O, 1834 R, 1854 Z
Lamont, Norman Stewart Hughson, B. Conservative politician (b. 1942), 1992 J
Lamp, acetylene, 1900 P
carbon filament, 1878 P
fluorescent, 1927 P
miner's safety (Davy), 1815 P
ultra violet, 1904 P
Lanark (A. Gray), 1981 U
Lanark, New, Scotland, 1800 O
Lancashire and the New Liberalism (P. F. Clarke), 1971 Q
Lancaster, Joseph, B. educationalist (1778–1838), 1778 Z, 1803 O, 1808 O, 1838 Z
Lance, Bert (Thomas Bertram), Am. politician (b. 1931), 1977 J
Land, Edwin, B. scientist, 1932 P
Land, use of, comparative statistics of, 1965 Y
Land:
in Britain, nationalisation advocated, 1775 O
Uthwatt Report on, 1942 O
Land Commission, 1965 O
in Ireland, Land League, 1878 K
land purchase, 1903 G
in S. Africa, land tenure legislation, 1946 F
in US, squatters' rights, 1841 N
minimum prices fixed, 1820 D
Lander, John, B. explorer of Africa (1807–39), 1830 P
Lander, Richard Lemon, B. explorer of Africa (1804–34), 1830 P
Landon, A. M., Am. Republican, 1936 L
Landor, Walter Savage, B. author (1775–1864), 1775 Z, 1798 U, 1824 U, 1864 Z
Landsbergis, Dr. Vitautis, President of Lithuania (b. 1932), 1990 C
Landscape and Community in England (A. M. Everitt), 1985 Q
Landscapes and Departures (K. Knott), 1947 U
Landseer, Sir Edwin Henry, B. artist (1802–73), 1818 S
Lane, Sir Allen, B. publisher (1902–70), 1936 U
Lane, Dame Elizabeth, B. judge (1905–88), 1965 O
Lane, Sir Hugh, bequest by, 1915 S
Lang Vei, Vietnam, accidental bombing by US, 1967 C
Lang, Fritz, Aus. film director (1890–1976), 1890 Z, 1926 W, 1931 W, 1976 Z lang, k d, (Karen Dawn), Canad. pop singer (b. 1962), 1988 W
Lange, David Russell, Prime Minister of New Zealand (b. 1942), 1989 H
Lange, Friedrich Albert, G. philosopher (1828–75), 1866 R
Langensalza, Germany, 1866 F
Langford, Paul, B. historian, 1989 Q
Langhans, Karl Gotthard, G. architect (1732–1808), 1791 S
Langley, Samuel Pierpont, Am. physicist and astronomer (1834–1906), 1881 P, 1896 P
Language and Wisdom of the Indians (F. Schlegel), 1808 Q
Language, Truth and Logic (A. J. Ayer), 1936 R
Languages:
Czech, in Bohemia, ordinances for, 1897 D, L; repealed, 1899 K
Dutch, in S. Africa, 1879 O
Basic English, 1932 O, 1947 O, 1949 R
Esperanto, 1887 O
Flemish, in Flanders provinces of Belgium, 1873 N, 1878 O, 1932 G
German, enforced in Bohemia, 1783 F
Hindi, official language of India, 1965 O
Latin, Pope John XXIII insists on retention of, 1962 R
Romanset, in Switzerland, 1937 O
Sinhalese, in Ceylon, 1956 G
Laniel, Joseph, French politician, 1953 F, M
Lankester, Edwin, B. scientist (1814–74), 1884 P
Lankester, Sir Edwin Ray, B. scientist (1847–1929), 1916 P
Lansbury, George, B. Labour politician (1859–1940), 1859 Z, 1912 L, 1935 A; resigns to fight by-election on issue of women's vote, 1912 L
Lansdowne, Marquess of. *See* Petty-Fitzmaurice
Lansing, Robert, Am. Secretary of State (1864–1928), 1915 F, 1920 B
Laocoön (Lessing), 1766 Q
Laon, France: battle, 1814 C; French take, 1918 K
Laos, Viet Nam, 1953 D French protectorate over, 1893 N; France pledges to respect inpependence, 1954 G; recognises UN as arbiter, 1959 B; emergency in, 1959 G; *coup* in, 1960 H; disturbances in, 1961 D; Princes, invited to Geneva talks, 1962 A; fighting resumed, 1962 D; Geneva Conference guarantees neutrality of, 1962 G; establishes relations with Communist China and Vietnam, 1962 J; Russia calls for conference on, 1964 G
conflict in, 1969 C, E, G
North Vietnamese offensive in, 1970 B
proposed international conference on, 1970 D
accidental US bombing, 1973 H
bombing ends after US funding cut, 1973 E
Communist forces take control, 1975 M
king abdicates, 1975 M
Laplace, Pierre Simon, Marquis de, F. mathematician and astronomer (1749–1827), 1788 P, 1796 P, 1812 P, 1827 Z
Laporte, Pierre, Canad. Minister of Labour, 1970 K
Larkin, Philip Arthur, B. author (1922–85), 1964 U, 1974 U, 1985 Z
Larousse, Pierre, F. lexicographer, 1866 Q
Las Vegas, Nevada, US, World boxing championship, 1980 X
Lasch, Christopher, Am. historian (b. 1932), 1979 Q
Lasdun, Sir Denys, B. architect (b. 1914), 1976 S, 1981 S
Laser:
carbon dioxide, 1970 P
typesetting, 1976 P
LaserVision video disc system, 1979 P
used to clean clogged arteries, 1985 P, 1987 P
removal of tissue from cornea, 1986 P
Laski, Harold Joseph, B. political scientist (1893–1950), 1893 Z, 1925 O, 1930 O, 1943 O, 1950 Z
Lassalle, Ferdinand, G. Socialist (1825–64), 1825 Z, 1859 O, 1861 O, 1862 O, 1864 Z
Last Chronicle of Barset, The (A. Trollope), 1867 U
Last Days of Hitler, The (H. R. Trevor-Roper), 1947 Q
Last Days of Pompeii, The (Lytton), 1834 U
Last Imam, The (I. Tahir), 1984 U
Last of the Barons, The (Lytton), 1843 U
Last of the Mohicans, The (J. F. Cooper), 1826 U
Last Puritan, The (G. Santayana), 1933 U
Last Supper in Dresden (G. Baselitz), 1982 S
Last Tycoon, The (S. Fitzgerald), 1941 U
Late George Apley, The (J. P. Marquand), 1937 U
Late Mattia Pascal, The (Pirandello), 1923 W
Later Roman Empire, The (A. H. M. Jones), 1964 Q
Later the Same Day (G. Paley), 1985 U
Lateran Treaty, for independence of Vatican City, 1929 B
Latey Committee, B., 1967 O
Latham, Peter, B. sportsman, 1895 X
Latham, Robert Clifford, B. historian (b. 1912), 1970 Q
Lathanum discovered, 1839 P
Lathe, carriage, 1797 P
screw-cutting, 1800 P
Latreille, Pierre André, F. naturalist (1762–1833), 1806 P
Latvia, independence of, 1918 D, L
Popular Front seeks independence from USSR, 1989 K
independence, 1990 E, 1991 H, J
referendum approving independence, 1991 C
Lauder, Sir Harry, B. comedian, 1870 Z, 1950 Z
Lauenberg, W. Germany: duchy, annexed by Napoleon, 1810 M; part of, returned to Denmark, 1815 F; ceded by Denmark to Austria and Prussia, 1864 K; purchased by Prussia, 1865 H
Laugh-In, television programme, 1967 W
Laughton, Charles, B. actor (1899–1965), 1899 Z, 1933 W, 1965 Z
Laurent, Auguste, F. chemist (1807–53), 1846 P
Laurier, Sir Wilfred, Can. statesman (1841–1919), 1896 G
Lausanne, Switzerland: Treaty, between Italy and Turkey, 1912 K; Conference, 1923 B, E; Treaty, between Greece, Turkey and Allies, 1923 G; Treaty, for establishing World Peace, 1924 H; Conference on Faith and Order, 1927 R; Anglo-French Treaty of friendship, 1932 F; Reparations Conference at, 1932 F
Lebanon reconciliation conference, 1984 C
Lauterbur, Paul, Am. nuclear physicist (b. 1929), 1973 P
Laval, Carl Gustaf Patrik de, Swe. engineer (1845–1913), 1877 P, 1887 P
Laval, Pierre, F. politician (1883–1945), 1883 Z, 1945 Z; as premier, 1931 A, 1935 F; proposals with Hoare, on Italy, 1935 M; falls, 1936 A
Lavater, Johann Kaspar, Swi. author (1741–1801), 1767 U
Laveleye, Emile Louis Victor de, Belg. author (1822–92), 1875 R
Lavengro (G. Borrow), 1851 U
Laver, Rod, Austral. tennis player (b. 1938), 1968 X, 1969 X
Lavigerie, Charles Martial Allemand, F. Cardinal (1825–92), 1890 L
Lavoisier, Antoine Laurent, F. chemist (1743–94), 1774 P, 1780 P, 1787 P, 1789 P, 1794 Z
Law of Conservation of Energy (J. Mayer), 1842 P
Law of the Constitution (A. V. Dicey), 1886 O
Law, Andrew Bonar, B. Conservative politician (1858–1923), 1858 Z, 1918 L, 1923 Z; becomes Unionist leader, 1911 L; resigns leadership, 1921 C; becomes premier, 1922 K; resigns, 1923 E
Law, International, Geneva Conference on law of the sea, 1958 O
Law, The (R. Vailland), 1957 U
Law, studies in, 1789 O, 1798 O, 1814 O, 1815 Q
Law:
in Britain, commission, 1965 O
in Russia, land, 1843 O
codified, 1830 O
See also Codes of law; Legislation
Lawes, Sir John Bennett, B. agriculturalist (1814–1900), 1843 P
Lawler, L. Austral. dramatist, 1955 W
Lawn-tennis. *See* Tennis

Lawrence Commission on MPs. salaries, 1964 L
Lawrence, David Herbert, B. author (1885–1930), 1885 Z, 1911 U, 1913 U, 1915 U, 1921 U, 1922 U, 1923 U, 1926 U, 1928 U, 1930 Z, 1959 O
Lawrence, Ernest O., Am. nuclear physicist (1901–1958), 1931 P, 1934 P, 1940 P
Lawrence, Richard Smith, Am. inventor (1817–92), 1855 P
Lawrence, Sir Thomas, B. artist (1769–1830), 1769 Z, 1811 S, 1830 Z
Lawrence, Thomas Edward ('Lawrence of Arabia', *alias* 'T. E. Shaw'), B. soldier and author (1888–1935), 1888 Z, 1926 U, 1927 O, 1935 Q, 1935 Z
Laws of Radiation (Max Planck), 1901 P
Laws of Thought on which are founded the Mathematical Theories of Logic and Probabilities, The (G. Boole), 1854 R
Lawson, Nigel, Lord Lawson, B. Conservative politician (b. 1932), 1983 F, 1986 L, 1988 C, O, 1989 K
Lay of the Last Minstrel, The (W. Scott), 1805 U
Lay patronage, issue of, in Scotland, 1843 R
Layard, Sir Austen Henry, B. archaeologist (1817–1894), 1845 Q
Lays of Ancient Rome (T. B. Macaulay), 1842 U
Layton-Wiggin Report on credit for Germany, 1931 H
Lazarus, Moritz, G. philosopher (1824–1903), 1859 R
Le Mans, France, 1793 M
Le Play, Pierre Guillaume Frédéric, F. engineer and economist (1800–82), 1855 O, 1864 O
Lévesque, René, Canad. politician (1922–87), 1976 L
Leach, Bernard Howell, B. potter (1887–1979), 1887 Z, 1920 S, 1979 Z
Leacock, Stephen, B. humorist, 1869 Z, 1944 Z
Leaden Wings (Zhang Jie), 1980 U
Leaflet Raids on Germany, 1939 J
League of Nations, The (A. F. Pollard), 1918 O
League of Nations, membership of:
  Abyssinia joins, 1923 J
  Albania joins, 1920 M
  Argentina joins, 1920 A
  Austria joins, 1920 M
  Bulgaria joins, 1920 M
  Costa Rica joins, 1920 M
  Denmark joins, 1920 C
  Egypt joins, 1937 E
  Estonia joins, 1921 J
  Finland joins, 1920 M
  Germany, gives terms for membership, 1924 J
    applies for membership, 1926 B
    membership prevented by Brazil and Spain, 1926 C
    joins, 1926 J
    leaves, 1933 K
  Holland, joins, 1920 C
  Hungary joins, 1922 J
    leaves, 1939 D
  Iraq joins, 1932 K
  Irish Free State joins, 1923 J
  Italy leaves, 1937 M
  Japan announces she will leave, 1933 E
    leaves, 1938 K
  Latvia joins, 1921 J
  Lithuania joins, 1921 J
  Mexico joins, 1932 M
  Norway joins, 1920 C
  Paraguay leaves, 1937 B
  Russia joins, 1934 J
    is expelled from, 1939 M
  Spain threatens withdrawal from, 1926 F, J
    leaves, 1939 E
  Switzerland joins, 1920 B
  Turkey joins, 1932 G
  US Senate rejects membership, 1920 A, C
League of Nations:
  Peace Conference adopts principle of, 1919 A
  Wilson presides at first meeting, 1919 B
  Covenant of, laid before Peace Conference, 1919 B
    campaign in US against, 1919 B, L, 1920 A, C
    comes into force, 1920 A
    is endorsed by Rome Pact, 1933 G
    is separated from Versailles Treaty, 1938 K
  Council first meets, 1920 A
  admissions to. *See above* under League Membership
  takes over Saar, 1920 B
  moves to Geneva, 1920 K
  Harding declared US could play no part in, 1921 D
  approves mandated territories, 1922 G
  Greece appeals to, over Corfu, 1923 J
  re-organises Hungarian finances, 1924 D
  Germany's terms for joining, 1924 J
  adopts Geneva protocol, 1924 K
  advises against partition of Mosul, 1925 H, M
  Bulgaria appeals to, over Greece, 1925 K, M
  Council, Canada acquires seat on, 1927 L
  decides Lithuanian–Polish dispute, 1927 M
  Act of, embodies Kellogg–Briand Pact, 1928 J
  rules against Norway's annexation of Greenland, 1931 G
  Council, US delegates attend, 1931 K
  orders Peru to withdraw from Columbia, 1932 J
  Lytton Report on Manchuria, to, 1932 K
    adopted, 1933 B
  holds Peace Ballot, 1935 F
  imposes sanctions against Italy, 1935 K, 1936 G
  Britain's role in, Labour Party view of, 1937 J
  pronounces Japan the aggressor, 1938 J
  separates Covenant from Versailles Treaty, 1938 K
  Assembly dissolved, 1946 D
Leake, William Martin, B. classical scholar and numismatist (1777–1860), 1812 O
Leakey, Louis Seymour Bazett, B. archaeologist (1903–72), 1903 Z, 1959 P, 1972 Z
Lean, Sir David, B. film director (1908–91), 1946 W, 1957 W, 1962 W, 1984 W
Lear (E. Bond), 1971 W
Lear, Edward, B. artist and humorist (1812–88), 1846 U
Leather, D., B. athlete, 1954 X
'Leatherstocking' novels of J. F. Cooper, 1823 U
Leaves of Grass (W. Whitman), 1855 U
Leaving Home (D. French), 1972 W
Leavis, Frank Raymond, B. author and critic (1895–1978), 1895 Z, 1930 O, 1932 U, 1952 U, 1962 U, 1978 Z
Lebanon, The: mandated to France, 1920 D; Republic proclaimed, 1926 E, cease-fire in, 1945 E; British and French evacuate, 1946 C; amnesty in, 1958 M
  war with Israel, 1967 F
  Israeli attack, 1972 B
  civil war, 1975 D
  fighting resumes, 1975 K
  Arab Protection Force takes control from Syrians, 1976 F
  ceasefire planned at Riyadh summit, 1976 K
  interim military council, 1976 C
  Syrian forces enter, 1976 E
  Syrians control Beirut, 1976 L
  US ambassador kidnapped and murdered, 1976 F
  Moslem leader's assassination provokes more violence, 1977 C
  first 'UNIFIL' troops arrive, 1978 C
  Israeli's pull out of South, as fighting erupts in North, 1978 F
  renewed fighting in Beirut, 1978 K, 1981 D
  South Lebanon invaded by Israel, 1978 C
  Britons advised to leave, 1981 D
  Israel and PLO agree ceasefire, 1981 G
  bomb attacks on Israeli military headquartes in Tyre, 1982 L, 1983 L
  Israeli armed forces invade, 1982 F
  Israeli jets bomb guerrilla targets, 1982 F
  UN peace-keeping force to be increased, 1982 B
  Arafat and supporters evacuated, 1983 M
  ceasefire, 1983 J
  civil war in Chouf mountains, 1983 J
  national reconciliation conference, Geneva, 1983 K
  PLO and Israel exchange prisoners of war, 1983 L
  Syrian tanks besiege PLO bases, 1983 F
  US plan for simultaneous withdrawal of Israeli and Syrian forces, 1983 E
  withdrawal of Israeli forces, 1983 E, G, J
  army takes over positions in Beirut from militias, 1984 G
  curfew imposed as Shi'a Muslim and Druze militia overrun W. Beirut, 1984 B
  Kerr shot dead in Beirut by pro-Iranian group, 1984 A
  national reconciliation conference, Lausanne, 1984 C
  US marines withdraw from Beirut, 1984 B
  Israeli Army removes Lebanese prisoners to Israel, 1985 D
  Israeli withdrawal, 1985 A, F
  two Britons and US journalist kidnapped, 1985 C
  President Muawad assassinated, 1989 L
  Brian Keenan released, 1990 H
  French hostages, 1988 E, 1990 D
  American hostages released, 1991 M
  Terry Waite released, 1991 L
  government resigns over economic situation, 1992 E
  refuses to accept Palestinians deported from Israel, 1992 M
Lebas, Louis Hippolyte, F. architect (1782–1860), 1823 S
Leben des Quintus Fixlein (Jean Paul), 1796 U
Leblanc, Nicholas, F. chemist (1742–1806), 1787 P
Lebon, Philippe, F. chemist (1769–1804), 1798 P
Lebrun, Albert, F. statesman (1871–1950), 1871 Z, 1932 E, 1950 Z
Lecky, William Edward Hartpole, B. historian (1838–1903), 1838 Z, 1865 Q, 1869 Q, 1878 Q, 1903 Z
Lecocq, Alexandre Charles, F. composer (1832–1918), 1872 T
Leçon de morale, Une (P. Eluard), 1949 U
Leconte de Lisle, Charles Marie, F. author (1818–1894), 1884 U
Lectures on Dramatic Art and Literature (A. Schlegel), 1809 U
Lectures on the Decorative Arts (O. Wilde), 1882 S
Lectures on the Eastern Church (A. P. Stanley), 1861 Q
Lectures on the English Poets (W. Hazlitt), 1818 U
Lectures on the Feudal and English Laws (F. S. Sullivan), 1772 O
Lectures on the Philosophy of the Human Mind (T. Brown), 1820 R

Led Zeppelin, B. rock group, 1971 W
Leda senza Cigno, La (D'Annunzio), 1916 U
Lederman, Leon, scientist, 1977 P
Lee Kuan Yew, Prime Minister of Singapore (b. 1923), 1990 L
Lee, Ann., B. revivalist (1736–84), 1774 R
Lee, Arthur Hamilton, Lord Lee of Fareham (1868–1947), 1921 O
Lee, Lawrence, B. artist, 1962 S
Lee, Richard Henry, Am. statesman (1732–94), 1776 E, F
Lee, Robert Edward, Am. Confederate general (1807–70), 1862 M, 1864 E; defeated at Gettysberg, 1863 G; capitulates at Appomattox, 1865 D
Lee, Sir Sidney, B. author and editor, 1859 Z, 1926 Z
Lee, Spike (Shelton Jackson), Am. film director (b. 1957), 1989 W, 1992 W
Leech, John, B. caricaturist (1817–64), 1817 Z, 1841 Z, 1864 Z
Leeds, Yorkshire, England: coal carriage at, 1811 P; Yorkshire college founded, 1874 O
Leeward Islands, Federation of, 1956 F
Lefebvre, Archbishop Marcel, F. churchman (1905–91), 1987 R
  excommunication, 1988 R
Left Book Club, 1935 O
Legacy, A (S. Bedford), 1957 U
Legal aid, in Britain, 1950 O
Legal decisions:
  House of Lords need not always be bound by own decision, ruling as to, 1966 O
  Miranda v. Arizona, decision in, US, 1966 O
  Conway v. *Rimmer*, gives British courts power to inspect government documents privately, 1968 O
Legal Studies, Institute of Advanced, London, 1948 O
Legendre, Adrien Marie, F. mathematician (1752–1833), 1794 P
Légende d'Uylenspiegel (C. de Coster), 1867 U
Légende des Siècles, La (V. Hugo), 1859 U
Legends of Flowers (M. Tompa), 1854 U
Léger, Fernand, F. artist (1881–1955). 1912 S, 1921 S, 1924 W, 1941 S, 1948 S, 1950 S
Legge, William, Earl of Dartmouth, B. politician (1731–1801), 1775 L
Leghorn, Italy: British raid, 1941 B; Allies take, 1944 G
Legion of Honour, 1802 E
Legislation:
  in Australia, Financial Agreement Enforcement, 1932 N
    Immigration restriction, 1902 G
    for troops to work mines during strike, 1949 H
  in Austria, anti-Hapsburg laws abolished, 1935 G
  in Belgium, Bill dividing country, 1980 H
  in Britain
    Administration of Justice, 1970 O
    Agricultural Holdings, 1875 O
    Air Raid Precautions, 1937 L
    Aliens, 1792 M
    Allotments, 1887 O
    Apothecaries, 1815 O
    Appellate Jurisdiction, 1876 L
    Apprentices (1563), repealed, 1814 O
    Artisans' Dwellings, 1867 O, 1890 O
    Ashbourne, for loans to Irish tenants, 1885 H
    Asylums, inspection of, 1842 O
    Australia Bill severs legal ties with Britain, 1986 C
    Australia Government, 1850 H
Ballot, 1872 G
Bank Charter, 1844 G
Bankruptcy, 1883 G
Benefices, 1898 R
Blasphemy Law, government decision not to extend to cover Islam, 1989 O
British Citizenship, 1948 G
British Nationality, 1981 O
British North America, 1867 C
British Possessions, 1846 H
British Steel Renationalization, 1966 G
Building Societies, 1874 O
Burials, 1880 R
Canada Constitution, 1791 E, 1840 G
Cash payments, 1819 G
Children, 1989 O
Chimney Sweeps, 1834 O
Cinematograph Licensing, 1909 W
Coal Mines, 1911 O
Colonial Welfare and Development, 1940 O
Combinations, 1800 O
  repealed, 1824 O, 1825 G
Commonwealth Immigration, 1961 L, 1962 O
Community Land Bill, 1975 K
community service introduced, 1972 O
Companies, 1980 O
Control of Office and Industrial Development, 1964 M
Conventicle, repealed, 1812 R
Copyhold, 1887 O
Copyright, 1911 O
Corn Laws, 1815 C
  amended, 1822 G, 1828 G
  repealed, 1846 E
Corrupt Practices in elections, 1883 H
Court of Appeal given power to review lenient sentences, 1989 O
criminal bankruptcy orders introduced, 1972 O
Criminal Justice, 1961 D, 1963 H, 1967 O, 1982 O, 1991 O
Criminal Law, 1977 O
Criminal Law Revision Committee, 1972 O
Curwen's, to prevent sale of Parliamentary seats, 1809 F
dangerous dogs, 1991 O
Data Protection, 1984 O
Death penalty, Abolition of, 1956 F, 1965 L
Defence of Realm, 1915 O
deferred sentences introduced, 1972 O
Department of Scientific and Industrial Research, 1956 O
Depressed Areas, 1934 L
Devolution Bill, 1977 B, 1978 A, G
divorce, 1984 O
Divorce Reform, 1971 O
Drought Bill, 1976 G
Ecclesiastical Titles, 1851 H
  repealed, 1871 R
Education, 1902 M
Education (Forster's), 1870 H, O
Education (Fisher's), 1918 H
Education (Butler's), 1944 O
Education for Wales, 1889 O
Education Reform, 1988 O
Emergency Powers, 1939 H
Employers' Liability, 1880 O
Employment, 1980 J
Enabling, for Church Assembly, 1919 R
Equal Opportunities Commission, 1975 O
Equal Pay, 1970 O
European Communities, 1972 B
Factory, 1833 H, 1844 F, 1847 F
Factory Inspection, 1867 H
Family Law Reform, age of Majority lowered, 1970 O
First Offenders, 1958 O
Food and Drugs, 1860 O, 1875 O
Fraudulent Mediums, 1951 R
Government of India, 1935 H
Government of Ireland, 1920 M, 1921 D
Habeas Corpus, suspended, 1793 C, 1801 D, 1817 C, 1818 A
  in Ireland, 1866 B, 1881 C
Health and Morals of Apprentices, 1802 O
Hire Purchase restrictions abolished, 1971 G
Horne Tooke, 1801 F
House of Lords ruling on marital rape, 1991 O
Housing, 1919 O, 1980 O
Hovering, against smuggling, 1784 G
Immigration Bill, 1971 B
Imperial Preference Provisions, 1919 H
Indian Councils, 1909 E
Industrial and Provident Societies, 1876 O
Industrial Relations, 1970 M, 1971 H, 1972 J, 1973 J, 1974 B, G, 1975 A
Irish Coercion, 1881 A
Irish Crimes, 1887 A
Irish Free State, 1924 K
Irish Land, 1870 H, 1881 H
Irish Land Purchase, 1903 G
Irish University, 1873 C
Jewish Disabilities, removal of, 1858 G
Judicature, 1873 O
Juvenile Offenders, 1854 O
Labourers' Dwellings, 1874 O
Landlord and Tenant, 1954 O
Leasehold Reform, 1967 O
Legitimisation, 1959 O
Libel, 1792 O
Local Government, 1888 H, 1972 O, 1988 O
Local Government Finance, 1982 O
Machinery of Government, 1964 M
Married Women's Property, 1870 H, 1882 O
Matrimonial Causes, 1857 O, 1923 G, 1937 G
Mental Health, 1959 O
Merchant Shipping, 1906 O
Military Service, 1916 B
Mines (Ashley's), 1842 H
Mines Inspection, 1850 O
Municipal Corporations, 1835 J
National Health Insurance, 1912 C
National Health Service, 1946 G
National Health Service and Community Care, 1990 O
National Insurance, 1946 G
National Registration, 1915 G
National Service, 1939 J
Nationalisation of Coal Mines, 1946 E
Nationalisation of Iron and Steel, 1949 L
  repealed, 1952 L
Nationalisation of Transport, 1946 L, 1951 O, 1953 E
Naval Construction, 1909 C
Naval Defence, 1889 E
Navigation, modified, 1822 F, 1823 G, 1825 G
  repealed, 1849 F
New Ministries, 1916 O
Obscene Publications, 1959 O
Official Secrets, 1911 O, 1972 O, 1989 O
Parliament, 1911 O, 1949 M
Patent, 1906 O
Peerage Renunciation, 1963 G
Plimsoll's Merchant Shipping, 1875 O
Police and Criminal Evidence ('PACE'), 1984 O
Poor Law Amendment, 1834 O

Prevention of Crimes, Ireland, 1882 G
Prevention of Terrorism, 1974 L
Prices and Incomes, 1966 B, 1966 K
Protection of Prince Regent, 1817 C
Public Exhibitions, 1866 S
Public Health, 1818 O, 1875 H, 1891 O
Public Libraries, 1850 O
Public Records, 1838 O, 1958 O
Public Worship, 1855 R, 1874 R
Race Relations, 1968 D, O, 1976 O
Reform, of Parliament, 1832 F, 1867 H, 1884 M
Regency, 1811 B
Regulation of Children and Women's Work, 1867 H
Rehabilitation of Offenders, 1974 O
Relief of Distress for Ireland, 1880 H
Remuneration of Teachers, 1863 G
Rent, 1957 F, 1965 M, 1974 O
Reparations Recovery, 1921 C
repealed, 1925 D
Representation of the People, 1945 A, 1969 O
Resale Prices, 1964 G
Restrictive Practices, 1956 G
Road Safety, 1967 O
Road Traffic, 1934 C
Roman Catholic Relief, 1829 D
Safeguarding of Industries, 1921 G
Security Services, 1989 O
Sedition, 1934 L
Seditious Meetings, 1795 L, 1817 C
Sex Discrimination, 1975 O
Sexual Offences, 1967 O
Shops, 1911 O
'Six Acts', 1817 M
Street Offences, 1959 O
Ten Hours, 1847 O
Test and Corporations, repealed, 1828 E
Theatres, 1843 W
Tithe Commutation, 1836 H
Trade Disputes, 1906 M, 1946 B
Trade Union and Labour Relations Bill, 1976 C
Trade Union law, 1983 G
Trade Unions, 1871 F, 1927 G
Traitorous Correspondence, 1793 C
Transport, 1980 K
Unemployment, 1934 E
Unemployment Insurance, 1925 G
University Test, abolition, 1871 F
Warehousing of Goods, 1823 E
Welsh Church Disestablishment, 1912 D
Westminster, Statute of, on Dominion Status, 1931 M
Witchcraft, repealed, 1951 R
Workmen's Compensation, 1897 O
in Canada, Elgin's Reciprocity, 1854 F
Emergency, in depression, 1930 J
in Egypt, Organic Law, 1883 E
in European Community
Single European Act, 1987 G
Court of First Instance, 1989 O
Social Charter, 1989 O
in Finland, against Communism, 1930 L
in France, amnesty for Communards, 1880 G
anti-Jesuit, 1879 F
Army, 1913 H
Association Law, 1880 C, 1901 G
Excluding Bourbons, and Bonapartists, 1832 D
Fixing Prices and Wages, 1793 L
Forbidding Multiple Candidates, 1889 G
Indemnity, to compensate nobles, 1825 D
Labour Code, cancelled, 1938 B
Press Laws, 1824 J, 1827 D, 1828 D
'September' Laws, 1835 J
in German Confederation, for interfering in states unable to maintain order, 1820 E
in Germany, anti-Jesuit, 1904 C, R
anti-Socialist, 1878 K, 1890 K
Army, 1886 M, 1893 G, 1911 B, 1913 H
Enabling Law, grants dictatorial powers, 1933 E
Labour regulations, 1916 O, 1934 O
'May Laws', against Ultramontane clergy, 1871 E, 1878 B
Navy, 1898 C, 1900 F, 1906 F, 1908 F
'Nuremberg Laws', 1935 J
Old-age insurance, 1889 E
Protection of Republic, repealed, 1929 F.
Protectionist, 1879 G
See also Prussia
in Hong Kong, Basic Law, 1990 D
in India, Public Safety, 1929 D
Trade Disputes, 1929 D
Untouchability outlawed, 1947 E
in Ireland, Abolition of Oath of Loyalty, 1932 E, 1933 E
Maynooth College, 1795 R
in Italy, against Anarchists and Socialists, 1894 G
Corporations, 1934 B
Electoral Reform, 1953 A
Law of Guarantees, 1871 E
in Mexico, anti-clerical, 1926 G
expropriations, 1936 L
petroleum, 1927 M
in New Zealand, Immigration, 1881 F
in Pakistan, Basic Democracies Order, 1959 K
in Prussia, 'May Laws' to control clergy, 1873 E
County Organisation, 1872 M. *See also* Germany
in Russia, Fundamental, 1906 E
in S.Africa, Aliens Immigration, in Transvaal, 1896 L
Asiatic Land Tenure, 1946 F
Bantu Amendment, 1964 E
Bantu self-government, 1960 F
Citizenship, 1949 F
General Law Amendment, 1962 E
Glen Grey, in Cape Colony, 1894 M
Group Areas, 1987 J, 1991 O
High Court of Parliament, 1952 D
Indian Representation, 1946 F
Land Acts, 1991 O
Native Representation, 1936 D
Population Registration, 1991 F, O
Public Safety, 1953 B
Separate Amenities, 1987 J, 1989 L
status, 1934 F
suppression of Communism, 1964 L
in Spain, Associations, 1933 E
Protection of Republic, 1931 K
Salic, abrogated, 1830 C
Succession, 1947 G
in Sweden, Unity and Security, 1789 B
in Switzerland, Mediation, 1803 B
revoked, 1813 M
in Turkey, Reform Edict, 1856 B
in US, Acts of Congress, resolutions to nullify in particular states, 1798 N, 1799 N
passed over president's veto, 1867 C, 1894 H, 1919 K, 1933 A, 1943 G, 1947 F
Agricultural Adjustments, 1933 E
Aliens, 1798 N
Anti-Strike, 1943 G
Anti-Trust, 1903 B, O
Basic Reconstruction, 1867 C
Bland-Allison, for silver standard, 1878 B
Burnett, Immigration, 1914 B
California State law obliging employers to grant pregnancy leave upheld, 1987 O
Carey, to encourage irrigation, 1894 H
Civil Rights, 1866 F, 1960 D, 1964 G
Civil Rights Bill, 1966 D, J
Civil Works Emergency Relief, 1934 B
Clay Tariff, 1833 C
Clayton, prohibiting injunction without notice, 1912
Clean Air, 1990 O
Coal Stabilization, 1935 H
Combat Poverty, 1964 C
Control of Communists, 1950 J
Control of Livestock Disease, 1903 O
Currency, 1900 C
Dawes, for dividing lands amongst Indians, 1887 B
Desert Land, 1877 C
Dillingham, Immigration, 1912 D
Elkins, Inter-state Commerce, 1903 N
Embargo, 1807 M, 1809 C
Emergency Quota Immigration, 1921 E
Emergency Relief, 1933 E
Excise, 1912 C
Farm Credit, 1933 F
Federal budget, emergency bill, 1990 K
Federal Reserve, 1913 O
Food and Drugs, 1898 O, 1906 O
Foraker, 1900 E
Force, for collecting revenue, 1833 C
Force, to control elections, 1890 F
Fordney-McComben, Tariff, 1922 O
Foreign Aid, 1952 F
Foreign Assistance, 1949 D
Fugitive Slaves, 1793 N, 1850 G
Funding, 1790 B
Georgia State law prohibiting oral and anal intercourse ruled not unconstitutional, 1986 O
Gold Reserve, 1934 A
Inter-state Commerce, 1887 B
Kansas–Nebraska, 1854 E, G
La Follette, Seamen's, 1915 O
Land, 1784 D, 1820 D
Lend–Lease, 1941 A, C
Limiting Butter Substitution, 1902 O
Marshall Aid, 1948 C
Medical Care for the Aged, 1965 G
Mutual Defense Assistance, 1949 K
Mutual Security, Russia demands revocation, 1951 M
National Banking, 1863 B, 1864 F
National Industrial Recovery, 1933 F
declared unconstitutional, 1935 E
National Labor Service, 1942 K
Neutrality, 1935 M, 1937 E
amended, 1939 L
New York State abortion laws, 1970 O
Non-Intercourse, 1809 C, 1811 B
Organic, for administration of Alaska, 1884 E
Overman, for re-organising departments, 1918 E
Pendleton, for reforming Civil Service, 1883 A, 1901 O
Pre-emption Distribution, 1841 N
Presidential Succession, 1886 E
Reciprocal Trade Agreements, 1958 J
Rural Credit, 1916 O
St. Lawrence Seaway, 1954 E
Securities, 1933 E
Seditions, 1798 N
Selective Training and Service, 1940 J, 1948 F
Sherman, anti-Trust, 1890 G
Sherman, for compulsory silver-purchase, 1893 L

Silver Purchase, 1934 F
Smoot, Pensions, 1912 L
Social Security, 1935 H, O
Taft-Hartley, for Union Funds, 1947 F
Tariff, 1832 G
Tenure of Office, 1867 C, 1868 B
Trade Agreement, 1955 A
Trade Expansion, 1962 K
Tydings–McDuffie, for Philippine independence, 1934 C
Volstead, Prohibition, 1919 K
Voting Rights, 1971 O
Wages and Hours, 1938 O
Wagner–Steagall, to finance housing, 1937 J
Water-power, 1920 F
Wealth Tax, 1935 N
Législation orientale (A. H. Anquetil Duperron), 1778 Q
Legitimation of child born before parents' marriage, 1959 O
Leguia, Augusto, Peruv. president (1863–1932), 1930 H
Léhar, Franz, Aus. musician (1870–1947), 1905 T, 1922 T, 1925 T
Lehmann, John, B. author (1907–87), 1936 V, 1943 U, 1955 U
Lehmann, Rosamund, B. author (1901–90), 1932 U, 1936 V, 1944 U
Lehrs, Karl, G. classical scholar (1802–78), 1869 Q
Leicester, North, Eng. constituency, by-election, 1962 G
Leighton, Frederick, Lord Stretton, B. artist (1830–1896), 1890 S, 1896 S
Leipzig, Germany, 1822 P: Gewandhaus concerts, 1781 T; 'Battle of The Nations', 1813 K, anniversary of, 1817 K; Conservatoire, 1843 T; railway station, 1915 P; war trials at, 1921 A, D; demonstration demanding political reform, 1989 K, L
Lekhanya, Major-General Justin, Lesotho military leader (b. 1938), 1991 D
Lélia (G. Sand), 1833 U
Lelouch, Claude, F. film director (b. 1937), 1966 W
Lemanic Republic (Switzerland), 1798 A
Lemass, Séan, Ir. politician (1899–1971), 1959 F
Lemberg, Poland: Austrian occupation, 1769 B; Austro-German force takes, 1915 E
Lemnitzer, Lyman L., Am. soldier (1899–1988), Supreme Allied Commander, Europe, 1963 A
Lemon, Mark, B. journalist (1809–70), edits *Punch*, 1841 V
Lemprière, John, B. classical scholar (1765–1824), 1788 Q
Lend-lease, by US, 1941 A, C; revised agreement with Russia, 1942 E; ends, 1945 H, K; total cost of 1945 H
Lenglen, Suzanne, F. tennis champion, 1919 X
Lenin, Nicolai (Vladimir Ilich, originally Oulianov) R. statesman (1870–1924), 1870 Z, 1903 H, 1924 A
writings, 1905 O, 1909 O
leaves Russia, 1907 N
seizes power, 1917 G
becomes chief of commissars, 1917 L
centenary celebrated, 1970 D
Leningrad (formerly St. Petersburg), Russia: Germans advance to outskirts, 1941 J
Russians relieve, 1941 M, 1944 A
attempted hijacking at airport, 1970 F
court sentences Jews, 1971 E
name reverts to St. Petersburg, 1991 K
Lennon, John, B. singer and songwriter (1940–80), 1940 Z, 1966 W, 1980 M, Z
Lennox, Charles, Duke of Richmond, B. sportsman (1735–1806), 1780 F, 1802 X
Lenormand, H. R., F. dramatist (1882–1951), 1924 W
Lens, Russia, Germans retire towards, 1915 J
Lenshina, Alice, Rhodes. religious fanatic, 1964 G, H
Lenz, Jacob Michael Reinhold, G. author (1751–92), 1776 W
Leo XII, Pope, Cardinal Annibal della Genga (1823–9), concordat with United Netherlands, 1827 F
Leo XIII, Pope, Cardinal Giocchino Pecci (1878–1903), 1878 B, 1891 R, 1899 R, 1903 G
Leoben, Styria, Austria, Peace, between France and Austria, 1797 D
Leonard and Gertrude (J. H. Pestalozzi), 1781 O
Leonard, Hugh, Ir. playwright (b. 1926), 1973 W
Leoncavallo, Ruggiero, It. musician (1858–1917), 1858 Z, 1892 T, 1917 Z
Leone, Giovanni, President of Italy (b. 1908), 1978 F
Leone, Sergio, It. film director (1921–89), 1968 W
Leonore (G. A. Bürger), 1773 U
Leonov, Alexei, R. cosmonaut, 1965 P
Leopardi, Giacomo, Count, It. author (1798–1837), 1793 Z, 1816 U, 1824 U, 1827 U, 1837 Z
Leopold I, of Belgium (Prince Leopold of Saxe–Coburg), 1831 F, 1865 M
Leopold II, Duke of Tuscany (1824–59) purchases Lucca, 1846 M; recalled, 1849 D; abolishes constitution, 1852 E
Leopold II, Holy Roman Emperor (1790–2), 1790 B, 1792 C; as grand duke of Tuscany, 1765 H, 1786 R; calls for support for Louis XVI, 1791 G
Leopold II, of Belgium (1865–1909), 1865 M, 1895 J, 1909 M; sends expedition to Congo, 1880 F; establishes Belgian Congo, 1885 B, 1891 D; plans for East Africa, 1890 E; claims land on Upper Nile, 1894 E, H; excused of Congolese atrocities, 1905 L; hands over Congo to Belgium, 1908 H
Leopold III, of Belgium (1901–83), referendum favours return, 1950 C; returns, 1950 G; abdicates, 1950 H
Leopold, Prince of Hohenzollern, 1870 G
Leopold, Prince of Saxe-Coburg, 1831 F
Léopoldville, Congo: disturbances in, 1959 A, 1960 G; conference of Independent African States in, 1960 H; becomes federal capital, 1961 E
Lepage, Robert, Canad. director, 1990 W
Lermontov, Mikhail Yurevich, R. poet and novelist (1814–41), 1837 U, 1839 U
Lerroux, Alejandro, Sp. Right-wing leader, 1934 K
Leslie, Sir John, B. mathematician and natural philosopher (1766–1832), 1804 P, 1813 P
Lesotho
independence, 1966 K
coup, 1991 D
Lespinasse, Jean de, F. author (1732–76), 1764 U
Lesseps, Ferdinand de, F. diplomat and maker of Suez Canal (1805–94): organises Canal Company, 1879 H; trial for corruption, 1892 L, 1893 C
Lessing, Doris, B. author (b. 1919), 1919 Z, 1952 U, 1985 U
Lessing, Gotthold Ephraim, G. author (1729–81), 1766 Q, 1767 W, 1769 U, 1772 W, 1777 R, 1778 R, 1779 W, 1781 Z
Leticia, Peru, dispute between Peru and Columbia over, 1832 J, 1934 E
Letter to a Member of the National Assembly (E. Burke), 1791 O
Letter to a Noble Lord, A (E. Burke) 1796 O
Letter to the Sheriffs of Bristol, A (E. Burke), 1777 O
Letters covering the Aesthetic Education of Mankind (Schiller), 1795 U
Letters of Jacopo Ortis (U. Foscolo), 1798 U
Letters of Janus (Döllinger, Huber and Friedrich), 1869 R
Letters of Samuel Johnson, The (B. Redford ed.), 1992 Q
Letters on a Regicide Peace (E. Burke), 1796 O
Letters on the Curiosities of Literature (H. Gernstenberg), 1766 U
Letters to His Son (Lord Chesterfield), 1774 U
Letters to Travis (R. Porson), 1788 R
Lettres à une princesse d'Allemagne (L. Euler), 1732 P
Lettres de la Montagne (J. J. Rousseau), 1763 O
Lettres de mon moulin (A. Daudet), 1866 W
Lettres physiques et morales sur les montagnes (J. A. Deluc), 1778 P
Leucotomy, 1961 P
Levana (Jean Paul), 1807 U
Lever, Charles James, Ir. author (1806–72), 1846 U
Leverrier, Urbain Jean Joseph, F. astronomer (1811–1877), 1846 P
Leveson-Gower, Granville George, Earl of Granville, B. Whig-Liberal statesman (1815–91), as foreign secretary, 1851 M, 1880 D, 1883 A
Levi, Carlo, It. author and artist (1902–75), 1945 U
Levi, Primo, It. author (1919–87), 1919 Z, 1947 U, 1975 U, 1982 U, 1987 Z
Lewis, Carl, 1984 X
Lewis, Christopher Piers, B. historian (b. 1957), 1989 Q
Lewis, Clive Staples, B. author (1893–63), 1942 R, 1947 R
Lewis, David Kellogg, Am. philosopher (b. 1941), 1986 R
Lewis, G. N., B. chemist, 1916 P
Lewis, Ltd., of Gt. Britain, 1937 O
Lewis, Matthew Gregory, B. author (1775–1818), 1795 U
Lewis, Sinclair, Am. author (1885–1951), 1920 U, 1922 U, 1927 U, 1929 U, 1945 U
Lewis, Ted 'Kid', B. boxer (1894–1970), 1980 X
Lewis, W.S., 1983 Q
Lewis, Wyndham, B. artist (1884–1957), 1913 S
Lewisham, Kent, England, by-election, 1957 B
Lewiston, Maine, US, 1965 X
Lewitt, Sol, Am. sculptor (b. 1928), 1968 S, 1970 S
Lexington, Mass., US, battle, 1775 D
Leyland Motors, merger with British Motor Corporation, 1968 A
Leyton, Essex, England, by-election, 1965 A
Lhasa, Tibet
demonstrations against Chinese rule, 1987 K
martial law imposed, 1989 C
Li P'eng, Prime Minister of China (b. 1928), 1987 L
Liaisons Dangereuses, Les (Choderlos de Laclos), 1772 U
Liaisons Dangereuses, Les (dramatization) (C. Hampton), 1985 W
Liao Tung, N.E. China, 1895 D, E
Liaoyang China, Russian defeat at, 1904 H
Liaquat Ali Khan, Pakis. premier, 1947 H
Libby, Willard Frank, Am. chemist (1908–80), 1908 Z, 1947 P, 1980 Z
Libel Act, British, 1792 O
Seditious, penalties increased, 1819 M
Libel Actions, notable: Wilkes (seditious), 1763

D; publishers of 'Junius' (seditious), 1770 F; Ruskin *v.* Whistler, 1878 S; G. Cumming *v.* Lycett Green (Tranby Croft), 1891 O; by Elton John *v. Sun* 1988 V
Liberace, (born Wladziu Valentino Liberace), Am. musician (1919–87), 1919 Z, 1952 W, 1987 Z
Liberals. *See under* Political Parties
Liberation Theology
  Instruction on Certain Aspects of the Theology of Liberation, An, 1984 R
Liberation, Union of, in Russia, founded, 1903 N
Liberia: founded, 1822 N; proclaimed an independent republic, 1847 H; independence recognised, 1862 F; boundary with Sierra Leone, 1885 L
  refugees massacred and US marines sent in, 1990 G
  civil war, 1990 H, J
  fighting in north-western, 1992 J
  merchant shipping tonnage statistics, 1992 Y
Liberté du travail, La (M. Baudrillant), 1865 O
Liberty and the Modern State (H. Laski), 1930 O
'Liberty' ship, 1943 O
Libraries:
  in Britain, Cambridge University, 1934 S
    circulating, 1842 O
    copyright, 1911 O
    John Rylands, Manchester, 1899 Q
    I. Newton's purchased, 1943 Q
    public, Ewart's Act for, 1850 P
    public lending right (PLR), 1984 U
    See also British Museum
  in Canada, National Library, Ottawa, 1967 T
  in France, Bibliothèque Impériale, Paris, 1852 Q
  in Germany, Berlin public, 1850 O
  in Spain, National, Madrid, 1796 Q
Library, The (G. Crabbe), 1781 U
Libya: self-government, revoked, 1927 C; frontier with Sudan, 1934 F; declared part of Italy, 1938 K; becomes an independent federation, 1951 M
  alliance with UAR and Sudan, 1969 M
  closure of British bases demanded, 1969 K
  Khaddhafi takes power, 1969 J
  federates with United Arab Republic (UAR), Sudan and Syria, 1970 L
  signs Benghazi Agreement, 1971 D
  airliner crashes after Israeli interception, 1973 B
  Constituent Assembly plan and unification with Egypt, 1973 H
  border war with Egypt, 1977 G
  proclaimed single state with Syria, 1980 J
  diplomats expelled from US, 1981 E
  fighters shot down by US air force, 1981 H
  diplomatic links with Saudi Arabia re-established, 1983 A
  Britain breaks diplomatic relations, 1984 D
  federation with Morocco, 1984 H
  Libyan forces in Chad, 1984 J, L
  suspected of involvement in international terrorism, 1986 A, D
  US bomb attack on targets in, 1986 D
  US sanctions imposed, 1986 A
  diplomatic relations with Tunisia restored, 1987 M
  war with Chad ended, 1988 K
  Arab Maghreb Union, 1989 B
  French arms deal with, leads to release of hostages in Lebanon, 1990 D
  UN sanctions imposed, 1992 C
Lichfield House Compact, 1835 C
Lichtenberg, Georg Christoph, G. physicist (1742–1799), 1777 P
Lichtenstein, Roy, Am. painter (b. 1923), 1967 S, 1969 S
Liddell, Henry Georg, B. churchman and Greek scholar (1811–98), 1843 Q
Lidice, Bohemia, Nazis burn, 1942 F
Lie of the Mind, A (S. Shepard), 1988 W
Lie, Trygve Haivdan, Nor. statesman (1896–1968), 1896 Z, 1968 Z; elected UN Secretary-General, 1946 B; second term, 1950 F; urges UN members to assist S. Korea, 1950 F
Lieber, Francis, Am., formerly G., publicist (1800–1872), 1838 O
Liebermann, Max, G. artist (1849–1935), 1849 Z, 1881 S, 1935 Z
Liebermann, Rolf, G. musician (b. 1910), 1955 T
Liebig, Justus von, baron, G. chemist (1803–73), 1803 Z, 1832 P, 1838 P, 1840 P, 1873 Z
Liechtenstein, women allowed to vote in elections to National Diet, 1986 O
Liège, Belgium, Germans occupy, 1914 H
Lifar, Serge, F. dancer and choreographer (1905–86), 1905 Z, 1986 Z
Life and Labour of the People of London (C. Booth), 1891 O
Life and Times of Michael K., The (J.M. Coetzee), 1984 U
Life expectancy at birth, statistics, 1990 Y
Life in the English Country House (M. Girouard), 1978 Q
Life in the Theatre, A (D. Mamet), 1989 W
Life of Jesus (D. F. Strauss), 1835 R
Life of Johnson (J. Boswell), 1791 U
Life of Nelson (R. Southey), 1813 U
Life of Reason (G. Santayana), 1905 R
Life of Savonarola (P. Villari), 1859 Q
Life of the Bee, The (M. Maeterlinck), 1901 U
Life on Earth, television series, 1979 W
Life peerages, 1958 G
Life-insurance, in India, nationalised, 1956 E
Lifts. *See* elevators
Ligeti, György Sándor, Aus. musician (b. 1923), 1966 T, 1973 T, 1974 T, 1978 T, 1988 T, 1990 T
Light in August (W. Faulkner), 1932 U
Light of Nature Pursued, The (A. Tucker), 1765 R
Light, defraction of, 1815 P
  experiments concerning, 1800 P
  polarisation of, discovered, 1809 P
  speed of, re-calculated, 1950 P
  velocity of, measured, 1849 P
Lightening Field (W. De Maria), 1977 S
Lighthouses:
  New Eddystone, 1878 P
  lenses for, 1822 P
  S. Foreland, lit by electricity, 1858 P
Lighting:
  electric, 1878 P, 1880 P
  gas, 1798 P, 1802 W, 1809 P, 1812 P
  'limelight', 1796 P
Lightning conductors, 1769 P
Ligurian Republic (Genoa), N.W. Italy, 1797 F, 1801 B; is united with France, 1805 F
Liki, T., Jap. scientist, 1980 P
Lilac Domino, The, 1918 W
Liliencron, Detley von, G. author (1844–1909), 1888 U
Lille, France: German occupation, 1914 H, K; British capture, 1918 K
Lilly, Simon J., Am. astronomer, 1988 P
Lima, Peru, riots at football match, 1964 E
Limann, Hilla, President of Ghana, 1979 G
Limanova, Italy, Austrian victory at, 1914 M
Limassol, Cyprus, 1964 B
Lime, 1862 P
Lime, chloride of, 1798 P
'Limelight' invented, 1796 P
Limewood Sculptors of Renaissance Germany (M. Baxandall), 1980 Q
Limits of Liberty, The: American History 1607–1980 (M. A. Jones), 1983 Q
Lin Piao, Chinese politician, 1966 K
Lincoln, Abraham, Am. statesman, Republican (1809–65), 16th president of US (1861–5), 1809 Z; senatorial campaign with Douglas, 1858 H; elected president, 1860 L; inaugurated, 1861 C; calls for militia, 1861 D; declares all slaves to be free, 1862 J, 1863 O; re-elected, 1864 L; assassinated, 1865 D
Lind, Jenny (*alias* Johanna Maria), B., formerly Swe. singer (1820–87), 1838 W, 1850 W
Lindbeck, G.A., 1984 R
Lindbergh, Charles Augustus, Am. aviator (1902–74), 1902 Z, 1927 P,
1974 Z; son of, kidnapped, 1932 O
Linde, C. von, G. inventor, 1898 P
Lindemann, Frederick Alexander, Lord Cherwell, B. scientist (1886–1957), 1923 P, 1926 P, 1957 Z
Linden Tree, The (J. B. Priestley), 1947 W
Lindman, Arvid, Swe. pol., Conservative, 1928 K
Lindsay Kemp Company, The, 1977 W
Lindsay, Alexander Dunlop, Lord Lindsay of Birker, B. author and administrator (1879–1952), 1943 O, 1949 O
Lindsay, Kenneth, B. educationalist and sociologist (b. 1897), 1926 Q
Lindstrand, Per, 1991 A
Line Made by Walking, A (R. Long), 1967 S
Line in Ireland, A (R. Long), 1974 S
Linear B, interpretation of, 1952 Q
Linear transformations, theory of, 1845 P
Linens: British exports, 1772 Y, 1782 Y, 1792 Y, 1802 Y, 1812 Y, 1822 Y, 1832 Y, 1842 Y, 1852 Y, 1862 Y, 1872 Y, 1882 Y, 1892 Y, 1902 Y, 1912 Y, 1922 Y, 1932 Y
Ling, Arthur George, B. architect (b. 1913), 1958 S
Linguistic Atlas of England, The (H. Orton, S. Sanderson, J. Widdowson eds.), 1977 Q
Linhares, José, Braz. president, 1945 K
Linnaeus (Carl von Linné), Swe, botanist (1707–78), 1778 Z
Linnean Society, founded, 1788 P
Linotype, 1886 V
Liola (L. Pirandello), 1917 W
Lionel Cranfield (R. H. Tawney), 1958 Q
Lipchitz, Jacques, F. sculptor (1891–1973), 1891 Z, 1973 Z
Lippmann, Walter, Am. journalist (1889–1974), 1929 R, 1937 O, 1943 O
Liquefaction of air, 1898 P
Liquid Crystal Display (LCD), 1975 P
Liquor traffic:
  Brussels Conference on suppressing traffic to undeveloped peoples, 1889 F
  Conventions to control traffic, 1890 G, 1911 O
  in Britain, licensing, local veto on, proposed, 1891 K
    hours, 1904 H
    Welsh counties vote on Sunday opening, 1961 O
  in France, sale of absinthe prohibited, 1915 O
  in Sweden, state control, 1866 O
  in US, Prohibition, in Maine, 1851 N
    Anti-Saloon League, 1893 N
    Volstead Act for, 1919 K, 1920 A
  See also Prohibition
Lisbon, Portugal:
  Royal Academy of Sciences, 1779 P
  National Library, 1796 Q

John VI agrees to remove government to, 1821 D
revolts in, 1824 D, 1921 K
British troops in, to support Q. Maria, 1827 A
occupied by Dom Pedro's followers, 1833 G
NATO Council meets in, 1952 B
Portuguese revolutionaries explode bombs, 1973 A
Gulbenkian Foundation for Modern Art, 1983 S
centre gutted by fire, 1988 H
Lisk, Calif., US, observatory, 1954 P
Lissa, Italy, naval battle off, 1866 G
List, Friedrich, G. economist (1789–1846), 1789 Z, 1841 O, 1846 Z
Lister, Joseph, Lord Lister, B. surgeon (1827–1912), 1817 Z, 1865 P, 1912 Z
Liston, Sonny, Am. boxer, 1964 X, 1965 X
Liszt, Franz, Hun. musician (1811–86), 1811 Z, 1822 T, 1845 T, 1846 T, 1849 T, 1850 T, 1854 T, 1857 T
Lithography, invented, 1798 P
Lithuania: Russia acquires, 1793 E; German offensive in, 1915 F; independence in, 1918 L; re-opens frontier with Poland, 1938 C
demonstrations demanding freedom for, 1972 E
Soviet tanks enter Vilnius, 1990 C
independence declared, 1990 C
independence suspended, 1990 F
nationalists defeat Communists in elections, 1990 B
USSR cuts off oil supplies, 1990 D
government resignation over price increases, 1991 A
independence formally granted, 1991 J
referendum approving independence, 1991 B
Soviet troops storm television station, 1991 A
Soviet troops withdrawn, 1992 C
Little Entente (of Czechoslovakia, Rumania and Yugoslavia). *See under* Entente
Little Foxes, The (L. Hellman), 1939 W
Little Gidding (T. S. Eliot), 1932 U
Little Minister, The (J. M. Barrie), 1891 U
Little Rock, Arkansas, US, 1982 R; desegregation crisis in, 1957 O, 1958 J
Little Women (L. A. Alcott), 1808 U
Littlewood, Joan, B. producer, 1964 W
Littré, Paul Emile, F. lexicographer (1801–81), 1863 Q
Litvinov Protocol, 1929 B, D
Litvinov, Maxim, R. politician (1876–1951), 1929 B, 1939 E
proposes disarmament, 1927 L
becomes foreign secretary, 1930 G
Liu Shao-chi, Chinese Premier (1898–1969), 1966 L, 1968 K; elected chairman of Republic, 1959 D
Liuzzo, Viola, Am. Civil Rights worker, 1965 C
Live-Aid concerts, 1985 W
Liver extract, 1926 P
Liver, glycogenic function of, 1850 P
Liverpool, Lancs., England: blind school, 1791 O; railway to Manchester, 1830 P; Mechanics' Institute, 1834 O; baths and wash-houses in, 1844 O; automatic signals at, 1893 P; cathedrals, 1903 S, 1932 S; Repertory Theatre, 1911 W; Radar installations in Docks, 1948 P; drive in bank, 1959 O
RC Cathedral of Christ the King, 1967 R, S
docks 'blacked', 1972 C
Toxteth riots, 1981 G
Democracy and Sectarianism: A Political and Social History of Liverpool, 1868–1939 (P. J. Waller), 1981 Q
Liverpool, Lord. *See* Jenkinson, Robert Banks
Lives of the Poets (S. Johnson), 1779 U
Living Corpse, The (L. Tolstoy), 1900 U
Living God, The (N. Söderblom), 1933 R
Living Planet, The, television series, 1984 W
Living Room, The (G. Greene), 1953 W
Livingstone, David, B. explorer and missionary (1813–73), 1813 Z, 1841 P, R, 1852 P, 1855 P, 1871 P, 1873 Z
meets Stanley, 1871 L
Llandaff, Wales, cathedral, 1957 S
Llanthony Abbey, Wales, 1862 R
Lleshi, Haxhi, Albanian head of state (b. 1913), 1982 L
'Llewellyn, Richard.' *See* Lloyd, R. D. V. L.
Llorente, Juan Antonio, Sp. Secretary of Inquisition (1756–1823), 1817 R
Lloyd's Register of Shipping, 1834 V
Lloyd, Harold Clayton, Am. film comedian (1893–1971), 1893 Z, 1923 W, 1971 Z
'Lloyd, Marie.' *See* Wood, Matilda
Lloyd, Richard Dafydd Vivian Llewellyn, B. author under pseudonym of 'Richard Llewellyn', 1939 U
Lloyd, Selwyn (John Selwyn Brooke), Lord Selwyn-Lloyd, B. Conservative politician (1904–78), 1957 A, 1971 A ; becomes foreign secretary, 1955 M; overseas tours, 1959 B, C; appointed chancellor of exchequer, 1960 G; begins wages pause, 1961 G; Macmillan dismisses, 1962 G
Lloyd-George and Co. (D. Low), 1922 S
Lloyd George, David, Earl Lloyd-George, B. statesman, Liberal (1863–1945), 1863 Z, 1938 O, 1945 Z
appointed chancellor of exchequer, 1908 D
budget of, rejected by Lords, 1909 L; election on issue of, 1910 A; passed, 1910 D
introduces health service bill, 1911 E
home attacked by suffragettes, 1913 D
acquitted of corruption over Marconi affair, 1913 E
as minister of munitions, 1915 F
as war secretary, 1916 G
resigns from Asquith's cabinet, 1916 M
forms war cabinet, 1916 M
leadership threatened, 1918 E
issues Coalition manifesto, 1918 L
Coalition falls, 1922 K
becomes leader of Liberal party, 1925 A
'New Deal' speech, 1935 A
forms Council of Action, 1935 F
Loach, Ken, B. film director (b. 1936), 1970 W
Loana, Italy, Austrian defeat at, 1795 L
Loans. *See* Aid
Lobengula, King of Matabele, 1888 B, K
Local Defence Volunteers (LDV), British, later Home Guard, 1940 E
Local Government:
in Britain, chartered boroughs reformed, 1835 J
boards created, 1871 H
county councils established, 1888 H
London County Council, 1889 O
Labour Party majority on, 1934 C
offers 100 per cent housing loans, 1963 B
parish councils, 1894 O
London Borough Councils, 1899 O, 1965 O
Royal Commission on Greater London, 1957 G
Greater London Council established, 1965 O
Ministry of Local Government and Regional Planning created, 1969 K
Redcliffe-Maud Report, 1969 O
re-organization, 1972 O
Greater London Council, Labour control, 1973 D
new metropolitan councils, 1973 D
county boundaries re-drawn, 1974 D
government halts welfare services expansion, 1975 E
Tameside, Manchester, defies directive over comprehensive schools, 1976 H
Conservative election gains, 1977 E
Greater London Council, strong National Front vote, 1977 E
House of Lords ruling on GLC public transport subsidies, 1981 M
GLC invitation to Sinn Fein leaders, 1982 M
Local Government Finance Act, 1982 O
in France, administrative departments, 1789 L
re-organised, 1790 B
in Ireland, 1840
in New Zealand, reformed through centralisation, 1875 K
in Prussia, municipal councils, 1808 L
provincial councils of state, 1817 C
provincial diets, 1823 N
remodelled, 1872 M
in Russia, reform of, 1820 F
provincial courts (Zemstvos) established, 1864 A
Local history, study of, 1900 Q, 1985 Q, 1987 Q, 1989 Q
Locarno Conference, 1925 K
Locarno treaties, 1925 M; Rome pact endorses, 1933 G; Belgium released from obligations under, 1937 D
Lock, Brahmah's patent, 1784 P
Lock-outs, in British printing industry, 1956 B
Lockerbie, B., Pan Am Boeing 747 crash, 1988 M
UN sanctions imposed on Libya, 1992 C
Lockheed, bribery scandal, 1976 B, G
Lockyer, Sir Joseph Norman, B. astronomer (1836–1912), 1887 P
Lod, Israel, Japanese terrorists kill 26 Israelis at airport, 1972 E
Lodge, Henry Cabot, Am. politician and diplomat (1902–85), 1902 Z, 1919 B, 1985 Z
Lodge, Sir Oliver, B. physicist (1851–1940), 1884 P
Lodomerica, Poland, 1772 H
Lodz, Poland, Germans take, 1914 M
Lofoten Islands, Royal Navy raids, 1941 C, M
Logical positivism, 1922 R, 1955 R, 1960 R
Logic (J. S. Mill), 1843 R
Logic on the Morphology of Thought (B. Bosanquet), 1888 R
Logic, studies in, 1843 R, 1854 R, 1883 R
Logical basis of Metaphysics, The (M. Dummett), 1991 R
Logical positivism, 1922 R, 1955 R, 1960 R
Lolita (V. Nabokov), 1955 U, 1959 O
Lomé Convention, EC markets access, 1975 B
Lombardy, Italy: ceded to France, 1797 K: Republic established, 1796 E; restored to Austria, 1815 F; Sardinia surrenders, 1848 H; ceded by Austria to France, 1859 G
Lombroso, Cesare, It. criminologist (1836–1909), 1876 O
Lonardi, Edouardo, Argentine general, president, 1955 J
London 800–1216: The Shaping of a City (C.N.L. Brooke and G. Keir), 1975 Q
London Fields (M. Amis), 1990 U
London, England,
events
riots in, 1764 A
street lighting in, 1812 P
Spa Fields riots, 1816 M
monopoly of theatre managements ended, 1843 W
medical school for women, 1875 P

political meetings in Trafalgar Square, 1886 B
on 'Bloody Sunday', 1887 L
London County Council, 1889 O
Borough Councils, 1899 O
Port of London Authority, 1908 O
Suffragette riots, 1911 G
Tower Hill riot, 1912 G
air attack on, 1917 J
television demonstrated in Soho, 1926 P
riots, 1931 J
London Passenger Transport Board, 1933 O
Fascist meetings, 1934 F, J
green-belt scheme, 1935 O
'bus strike, 1937 E
evacuation from, 1939 H
Blitz, 1940 H, J, 1941 C, E, 1943 A, 1944 B, F
Second Front demonstration, 1942 G
flying bombs on, 1944 F
UN General Assembly meets, 1946 A
racial disturbances at Notting Hill, 1958 H
rent riots at St. Pancras, 1960 J
CND sit-down demonstrations, 1961 O
Billy Graham's Greater London Crusade, 1966 R
British–Rhodesian talks, 1966 E
Commonwealth Conference, 1966 J
Anglo-Maltese conference on rundown of British forces in Malta, 1967 B
student protest at London School of Economics, 1967 C
anti-Vietnam War demonstrations, 1968 K
Notting Hill Carnival, 1976 H
Moorgate Underground Station crash, 1977 M
Iranian embassy seized by terrorists, 1980 D
Brixton riots, 1981 D
CND rally, 1981 K
Marathon, 1981 X
SDP national conference, 1981 K
share price panic, 1981 J
Falklands Thanksgiving Service, 1982 G
IRA bomb attacks in Regent's Park and Hyde Park, 1982 G
Greater London Council (GLC), proposed abolition, 1983 O
IRA car bomb explosion outside Harrods, 1983 M
demonstrators outside Libyan People's Bureau fired on, 1984 D
Greater London Council (GLC) and metropolitan counties abolished, 1986 C
Inner London Education Authority (ILEA) abolished, 1987 O
King's Cross Underground Station fire, 1987 L
anti-poll tax demonstration, 1990 C
IRA bomb attack at London Stock Exchange, 1990 G
IRA bomb attack on 10 Downing Street, 1991 B
IRA bomb attack at London Bridge station, 1992 B
places, buildings and institutions, in or near
Adam Smith Institute, 1977 O
Adelphi, The, 1769 S
Airport, 1955 S
Albert Hall, Royal, opened 1872 W
Albert Memorial, 1862 S
Aldwych Theatre, 1964 W
Almack's gaming house, 1763 W
Argyll Rooms, 1813 T
Bank of England, 1795 S, 1803 S
Barbican Theatre, 1982 W
Bedford College for Women, 1849 O
Bethnal Green Museum, 1874 Q
Bloomsbury, University moves to, 1936 O
Britannic House, Finsbury, 1924 S
British Museum, buildings, 1816 S, 1823 S, 1845 S, 1914 Q
as copyright library, 1911 O
public admission to, 1879 W
royal library, 1823 Q
Broadcasting House, 1932 S
Brooks' Club, 1763 W
Brunswick Centre, 1973 S
Buckingham Palace, Nash's building, 1825 S
Victoria Memorial at, 1905 S
Canary Wharf, 1987 S
Cenotaph, Whitehall, 1919 S
Central Criminal Court, 1907 S
Chamber of Commerce, 1882 O
Charing Cross redevelopment, 1990 S
City Temple, 1917 R
Cleopatra's Needle, 1878 S
Clerkenwell, 1867 M
Clore Gallery, Tate Gallery, 1987 S
Coal Exchange, 1846 S, 1963 S
Cobden Club, 1866 O
College of Chemistry, 1845 O
County Hall, 1922 S
Covent Garden Opera House, 1858 S, 1910 T
sculpture in, 1963 S
Crystal Palace, 1850 S
concerts at, 1855 T
Drury Lane Theatre, 1775 W
Economist buildings, 1961 S
Elizabeth Garrett Anderson Dispensary, 1866 O
Euston portico, demolished, 1961 S
Exeter Hall, 1853 R
Festival Hall, 1951 S
G.P.O. Building, St. Martin le Grand, 1823 S
G.P.O. Tower, 1954 S, 1965 S
Hammersmith Flyover, 1961 S
Hampton Court Palace, fire damage to, 1986 C
Hayward Gallery, 1968 S
Heathrow Airport, underground rail link, 1977 M
Highpoint I, Highgate, 1933 S
Houses of Parliament, destroyed by fire, 1834 K
rebuilt by Barry, 1840 S
destruction by bombs, 1941 E
Hyde Park, Great Exhibition in, 1851 W
Imperial Institute, 1893 O
Industrial Health and Safety Centre, 1927 O
Institute of Contemporary Art, 1953 S
Institute of Technical Optics, 1917 P
Kensington Gardens, 'Peter Pan' in, 1912 S
King's College, 1830 O
King's Cross Station, 1851 S
Lambeth Bridge, 1932 P
Literary Club, 1764 U
Lloyd's building, 1985 S
London Library, 1841 Q
London School of Economics, 1895 O
London Transport Building, St. James's Park, 1929 S
Lord's Cricket Ground, 1787 X
Lyceum Theatre, Irving's Company at, 1878 W
Mermaid Theatre, 1959 W
National Gallery, 1824 S, 1832 S, 1838 S
concerts in, 1939 T
National History Museum, 1881 P
National Portrait Gallery, 1857 S, 1896 S
National Theatre, South Bank Centre, 1976 S, W, 1980 W
Newgate Prison, 1813 O
Olympia, Barnum and Bailey's Show at, 1889 W
Oratory, The, 1849 R
Paddington Station, 1852 S
Pall Mall, lit by gas, 1809 P
Philosophical Society, 1869 R
Piccadilly Circus, 'Eros' (Shaftesbury Memorial) in, 1925 S
inquiry for development, 1959 S
Pimlico housing estate, 1950 S
Pioneer Club, 1892 O
Public Record Office, 1838 O
Queen's Hall, Promenade Concerts in, 1895 T
R.I.B.A. Building, 1933 S
Regent Street, Nash's improvements to, 1811 S
Polytechnic, 1882 O
Regent's Canal, 1820 P
Rose and Globe Theatres, remains discovered, 1989 Q
Royal Academy, 1768 S
Royal Academy of Music, 1822 T, 1861 T
Royal College of Music, 1883 T
Royal College of Surgeons, 1800 P
Royal Court Theatre, 1904 W
English Stage Company at, 1956 W
Royal Courts of Justice, 1868 S
Royal Geographical Society, 1830 P
Royal Institute of International Affairs, 1920 O
Saatchi Collection, 1985 S
Sackler Galleries, Royal Academy, 1991 S
Sadlers Wells Theatre, 1931 W
Sainsbury Wing, National Gallery, 1991 S
St. Marylebone, reform to tenements in, 1864 O
St. Pancras Church, 1819 S
St. Paul's Cathedral, notable monuments in, 1796 S, 1858 S
interior decorations for, 1891 S
New Barbican scheme, 1954 S, 1956 S
Savoy Theatre, 1881 W
Science Museum, 1857 O
Senate House, Bloomsbury, 1933 S
Skinners' Company Hall, 1904 S
Skyscrapers in, 1963 S
Somerset House, 1776 S
Spa Fields Chapel, 1779 R
Stansted Airport, 1967 E
Stock Exchange, 1992 O
compensation fund, 1950 O
public galleries, 1953 O
re-organised, 1962 O
Stratford East, Theatre Workshop, 1964 W
Swiss Cottage Library and Swimming Pool, 1964 S
Tate Gallery, 1897 S
McAlpine gift, 1971 S
Temple of Mithras, 1954 Q
Thames Flood Barrier, 1973 P
Times, The, Building, 1960 S
Underground railway development, 1905 P, 1963 P
University College, 1826 O
University, 1836 O, 1860 O, 1898 O
moves to Bloomsbury, 1936 O
Wallace Collection, 1900 S
Waterloo Bridge, 1811 S
Westminster Abbey, anniversary celebrations, 1965 R
Westminster Cathedral, 1895 R, 1903 S, 1913 S
Whitechapel Art Gallery, 1897 S
Windmill Theatre, closes, 1964 W
Wyndhams Theatre, 1910 W

Zoo, 1974 E
Aviary at, 1965 S
Zoological Society, Royal, 1826 P
population: 1801 Y, 1841 Y, 1881 Y, 1906 Y, 1950 Y, 1960 Y, 1970 Y
musical events in: 1785 T, 1813 T, 1825 T, 1844 T, 1855 T, 1876 T, 1895 T, 1916 T, 1918 T, 1923 T, 1940 T
London, F., B. scientist, 1927 P
London, Jack, Am. author (1876–1916), 1904 U
London, Treaties, Protocols, etc:
protocol recognises Greek independence, 1827 G, 1828 L, 1829 C
protocol on French intervention in Greece, 1828 G
Treaty, recognises Belgian independence, 1839 D
Treaty of Quadruple Alliance with Mehemet Ali, 1840 G, L
Treaty on Schleswig-Holstein, 1850 H
Treaty guarantees Denmark's integrity, 1852 E
protocol demands Turkish reforms, 1877 C, D
Naval convention, 1936 C
Londonderry, Northern Ireland
civil rights marches, 1968 K, L
rioting, 1969 H
Roman Catholic and Protestant demonstrators clash, 1969 A
troops dismantle barricades, 1969 J
police station attacked, 1970 C
rioters shot by troops, 1971 G
deaths from fighting between IRA and troops, 1971 H
'Bloody Sunday', 1972 A, D
Protestant 'no go' areas, 1972 G
Lonely Crowd, The (D. Riesman), 1951 R
Long Day's Journey into Night (O'Neill), 1940 U
Long Revolution, The (R. Williams), 1961 O
Long Week End, The (R. Graves), 1939 U
Long, Crawford, Am. surgeon (1815–78), 1842 P
Long, Huey Pierce, Am. politician (1893–1935), 1893 Z, 1935 Z
Long, Richard, B. artist (b. 1945), 1967 S, 1974 S, 1977 S, 1981 S
Turner Prize, 1989 S
Long-playing records, invented, 1948 P
Longchamps, France, horse-racing at, 1863 X
Longfellow, Henry Wadsworth, Am. poet (1807–82), 1807 Z, 1839 U, 1842 U, 1846 U, 1851 U, 1855 U, 1880 U, 1882 Z
Longman Companion to Victorian Fiction (J. Sutherland), 1988 Q
Longowal, Sant Harchand Singh, Punjabi Sikh leader (1928–85), 1985 G
Longwy, France, Prussians capture, 1792 J
Longwy, France, riots over steel plants closures, 1979 E
Lonsdale, Gordon, B. spy, 1961 O, 1964 D
Look Back in Anger (J. Osborne), 1956 W
Look Homeward Angel (T. Wolfe), 1929 U
Look Stranger (W. H. Auden), 1936 U
Looking Backwards, 2000–1887 (E. Bellamy), 1888 U
Loom: automatic, 1895 P; Brussels power, 1845 P
Loos, France, battle, 1915 J
Loot (J. Orton), 1966 W
Lord Byron: The Complete Poetical Works (J.J. McGann ed.), 1980 Q
Lord I was Afraid (N. Balchin), 1947 U
Lord Jim (J. Conrad), 1900 U
Lord of the Flies, The (W. Golding), 1954 U
Lord of the Rings, The (J. Tolkien), 1954 U
Lords, House of, Committee recommends an heir be able to disclaim peerage, 1962 M
Lore and Language of Schoolchildren, The (I. and P. Opie), 1959 Q
Lorean, John Zachary De, Am. businessman (b. 1925), 1982 K, 1984 H
Loren, Sophia, It. film actress (b. 1934), 1934 Z
Lorenz, Konrad Zacharias, Aus. scientist (1903–89), 1966 P
Lorenz, Peter, W. German politician, 1975 B
Loris-Melikov, Michael, Count, R. minister of Interior (1825–88), 1880 E
Lorna Doone (R. D. Blackmore), 1869 U
Lorraine, Duchy, France, 1766 B
Los Alamos, New Mex., US, laboratory at, 1956 P
Los Angeles, Calif., US: Olympic Games at, 1932 X; atomic research in, 1941 P; race riots in, 1965 H
assassination of Robert Kennedy, 1968 F
population, 1970 Y
Los Angeles County Museum, 1980 S
Olympic Games, 1984 X
Museum of Contemporary Art, 1986 S
riots, 1992 D
white policemen in Los Angeles acquitted of beating black motorist, 1992 D
Losey, Joseph, Am. film director (1909–84), 1909 Z, 1967 W, 1971 W, 1984 Z
Losing Battles (E. Welty), 1970 U
Lothair (B. Disraeli), 1870 U
Lothian, Lord, *See* Kerr
Lothian, West, Scotland, by-election, 1862 F
'Loti, Pierre.' *See* Viaud, Julien
Lotte in Weimar (T. Mann), 1939 U
Lottery, national, in US, 1776 O
Lotus-Eaters, The (Lord Tennyson), 1832 U
Lotze, Rudolf Hermann, G. philosopher (1817–81), 1841 R, 1856 R
Lou Grant, television programme, 1977 W
Loubet, Emile, F. statesman (1838–1929), 1838 Z, 1929 Z; elected president, 1899 B; visits London, 1903 G; visits Italy, 1904 D
Louis (Bonaparte), King of Holland, 1806 F; abdicates, 1810 G
Louis I, King of Portugal (1861–89), 1861 L
Louis Napoleon. *See* Napoleon III
Louis Philip Joseph, Duke d'Orléans ('Philippe Egalité', 1747–93), 1793 L
Louis Philippe Albert d'Orléans, Comte de Paris, 1848 B, 1850 G
Louis Philippe, Comte de Paris (1838–94), 1872 L, 1873 H
Louis Philippe, King of the French (1830–48), 1773 Z, 1830 G, 1831 B, 1835 G; elected King, 1830 H; abdicates, 1848 B; death, 1850 G
Louis XV, King of France (1715–74), 1769 D, 1774 E
Louis XVI, King of France (1774–93), 1774 E, H, 1781 E
as Dauphin, 1765 M
marriage, 1770 E
mediates in Scheldt crisis, 1784 K
banishes Parlement of Paris, 1787 H
summons Estates General, 1787 L, 1789 H
summons notables, 1788 L
dismisses Necker, 1789 G
moved from Versailles to Paris, 1789 K
accepts constitution, 1790 G
vetoes decree of Legislative Assembly, 1791 L
a prisoner, 1791 D
attempted flight, 1791 F
trial, 1792 M
execution, 1793 A
Louis XVIII, King of France (1814–24), 1816 J, 1824 J; enters Paris, 1814 E; issues Constitutional Charter, 1814 F, flees, 1815 C; returns to Paris, 1815 G
Louis, Joe, Am. boxer (1914–81), 1914 Z, 1936 X, 1946 X, 1981 Z
Louisiana, state, US: acquired by Spain from France, 1763 B; Spain sells to France, 1800 K, 1801 A; US purchases from France, 1803 D; Burr's expedition to, 1806 N; slavery to be abolished, except in Missouri, 1820 C; as a Confederate state, 1861 B; rival governors in, 1874 F
Lourdes, France, pilgrimages to, 1858 R
Louvain, Belgium: riots, 1787 A; seminary, 1786 K
Louw, Eric, S. African Nationalist (b. 1890), 1960 E
Love in Idleness (T. Rattigan), 1944 W
Love in a Cold Climate (N. Mitford), 1949 U
Love in the Time of Cholera (G. García Márquez), 1988 U
Love of Four Colonels, The (P. Ustinov), 1951 W
Love, Power and Justice (P. Tillich), 1954 R
Lovell, Sir Bernard, B. astronomer (b. 1913), 1957 P
Loving (H. Green), 1945 U
Low, Sir David, N. Zeal. cartoonist (1891–1965), 1891 Z, 1918 S, 1922 S
Lowe, Robert, Viscount Sherbrooke, B. Liberal (1811–92), 1868 M
Lowell, James Russell, Am. author and diplomat (1819–91), 1843 U, 1848 U, 1857 V
Lowell, John, Jnr., Am. businessman and philanthropist (1799–1836), 1839 Q
Lowell, Robert, Am. poet (1917–77), 1917 Z, 1965 U, 1967 T, 1977 Z
Lowell, Robert, B. poet (1770–96), 1794 W
Lowry, Laurence Stephen, B. artist (1887–1976), 1887 Z, 1927 S, 1976 Z
Lowth, Robert, B. divine (1710–87), 1779 R
Loyson, Hyacinthe, F. priest ('Père Hyacinthe'), 1872 R
Luanda, Angola, fighting in, 1992 L
Lubbers, Ruud (Rudolphus Frans Marie), Dutch politician (b. 1939), 1989 E, J
Lubbock, Eric Reginald, B. Liberal (b. 1928), 1962 C
Lübeck, E. Germany: Napoleon annexes, 1801 C, 1810 M, bombed, 1942 C
Lübke, Heinrich, W. German president (b. 1894), 1959 G
Lublin Committee of Polish Liberation in Moscow, 1944 G
Lublin, Poland, Jews deported to, 1939 K
Lucas, George, Am. film director (b. 1944), 1977 W
Lucca, Duchy, Italy, sold to Leopold of Tuscany, 1846 M
Lucerne Committee on broadcasting, 1934 O
Luciani, Albino, It. patriarch (1912–78), elected pope (as John Paul I), 1978 H
Luciano, S., It. film director, 1950 W
Lucinde (Schlegel), 1799 U
Lucknow, India, relief of, 1857 J, L
Lucky Jim (K. Amis), 1954 U
Luddites, in Britain, 1812 C
Ludendorff, Erich, G. soldier (1865–1937), 1865 Z, 1918 K; acquitted of breaches of rules of war, 1921 D
Ludwig, Karl Friedrich Wilhelm, G. physiologist (1816–95), 1865 P
Ludwig, Otto, G. dramatist (1813–65), 1850 W
Luganda, talks agree on Cuban military withdrawal from Angola, 1988 A
Lugard, Frederick, Lord Lugard, B. administrator in Africa (1858–1945), 1858 Z, 1890 M, 1900 A, 1945 Z
Lugard; The Years of Adventure (M. Perham), 1956 Q

Luhrmann, Baz, 1992 W
Luisa Fernanda, Sp. Princess (1832–95), marries Duc de Montpensier, 1846 K
Luise (J. H. Voss), 1795 U
Lukács, György Szegedy von, Hung. philosopher (1885–1971), 1885 Z, 1923 R, 1971 Z
Lule, Yusufu, President of Uganda, 1979 D, F
Lumet, Sidney, Am. film director (b. 1924), 1975 W
Lumière, Auguste, F. inventor (1862–1954), 1895 P, 1907 P
Lumière, Louis, F. inventor (1864–1948), 1895 P
Lumpa Church, N. Rhodesia, 1964 G
Lumumba, Patrice, Congol. leader (1925–61): becomes premier, 1960 F; dismissed, 1960 J; arrested, 1960 M; CIA plot to kill revealed, 1975 L
Lunéville, France, Treaty, 1801 B
Lunatics, treatment of, reformed, 1792 O. *See also* Asylums
Lundkvist, Lars, author, 1985 U
Lung cancer, connexion with smoking, 1954 P, 1962 P
Lung pump, electric, 1961 P
Luns, Dr. Joseph Marie Antoine Hubert, Dutch politician and diplomat (b. 1911), NATO Secretary-General, 1971 K, 1983 M
Lusaka, S. Africa, 1964 M; Commonwealth Conference, 1979 H
Lusitania, S.S., sinking of, 1915 E
Lusk, Mary, Scottish lay preacher, 1963 R
Luther (J. Osborne), 1961 W
Luther, Hans, G. Independent Socialist (1879–1934): as Chancellor, 1925 A, 1926 A; resigns, 1926 E
Lutoslawski, Witold, Pol. musician (1913–94), 1967 T, 1970 T, 1975 T, 1983 T, 1988 T
Lutyens, Sir Edwin, B. architect (1869–1944) 1869 Z, 1900 S, 1906 S, 1919 S, 1924 S, 1930 S, 1932 S, 1944 Z
Lutyens, Elizabeth, B. musician (1906–83), 1940 T
Lützen, Germany, battle, 1813 E
Luwum, Janani, Ugand. Archbishop (1922–77), murdered, 1977 B
Lux Aeterna (W. Mathias), 1982 T
Lux Mundi (ed. C. Gore), 1890 R
Luxemburg: capitulates to French, 1795 F; becomes independent Grand Duchy, 1839 D; neutrality guaranteed, 1867 E; is separated from Netherlands, 1890 L; Germans occupy, 1914 H; Germany invades, 1940 E; EC summit meeting, 1980 D; European Investment Bank, 1981 S
Luxor, Egypt, Tutankhamun's tomb at, 1922 Q
Luzon, Philippines, Japanese landings, 1941 M
Luzzatti, Luigi, It. premier (1841–1928), 1911 C, D
Lvov, Archbishop of, released, 1963 B
Lvov, Prince George of, R. premier, 1917 C, E, G
Lyakhov, Vladimir A., R. cosmonaut (b. 1941), 1979 P
Lyell, Sir Charles, B. geologist (1767–1849), 1830 P, 1863 P
Lyle, 'Sandy' (Alexander), B. golfer (b. 1958), 1988 X
Lynch, David, Am. film director (b. 1946), 1980 W, 1986 W, 1989 W
Lynch, John Mary, Prime Minister of Eire (b. 1917)
  proposes federation between Eire and Northern Ireland, 1969 H
  deterioration in Anglo-Irish relations, 1971 H
  Chequers meeting over Northern Ireland, 1971 J
  resignation, 1979 M
Lyne, Joseph Leycester ('Father Ignatius'), F. priest (1837–1908), 1862 R
Lynskey Tribunal, 1948 L
Lynton, Norbert Casper, B. art historian (b. 1927), 1980 Q
Lyons, France, riots of silk-weavers in, 1831 L, 1834 D
Lyons, Francis Stuart Leland, Ir. historian (1923–83), 1971 Q
Lyons, Joseph A., Austral. politician (1879–1939), 1939 D
  founds United Australian Party, 1931 N
  forms Coalition, 1934 L
Lyotard, Jean-François, F. philosopher (b. 1924), 1979 R
Lyrical Ballads (Wordsworth and Coleridge), 1798 U, 1800 U
Lys, The, south of Ypres, France, German attack at, 1918 D
Lysenko, Trofim Denisovich, R. geneticist (1898–1976), 1948 P
Lysons, David, B. antiquarian and topographer (1762–1834), 1792 Q
Lytton Report on Manchuria, 1932 K, 1933 B
Lytton, Lord. *See* Bulwer-Lytton

M

Maas, River, Holland, Canadian troops reach, 1944 K
Maastricht Treaty, 1991 M, 1992 F, J, M
MacArthur, Douglas, Am. soldier (1880–1964), 1880 Z, 1964 Z; enters Manila, 1945 B; orders trials of Japanese war criminals, 1946 N; commands UN force in Korea, 1950 G, L; China rejects offer of truce by, 1951 C; removed from Korean command, 1951 D; investigations on removal, 1951 E
MacDonald, James Ramsay, B. Labour leader (1866–1937), 1866 Z, 1937 Z
  appointed Labour Party Secretary, 1900 B
  elected Labour Party Chairman, 1911 B
  becomes premier, 1924 A
  refuses to sign treaty of Mutual Assistance, 1924 G
  on the immunity of the executive, 1924 O
  resigns, 1924 L
  becomes premier, 1929 F
  forms first National government, 1931 H
  is expelled from Labour Party, 1931 H
  forms second National government, 1931 L
  is ordered to rest, 1934 F
  serves under Baldwin, 1935 F
  defeated in election, 1935 L
MacDonald, Sir John Alexander, Can. Conservative leader (1815–91), 1878 K, 1891 F
MacGregor, Ian, B. Chairman of National Coal Board (b. 1912), 1983 C, E, J
MacGregor, John Roddick Russell, B. Conservative politician (b. 1937), 1990 O
MacIntyre, Alasdair Chalmers, B. philosopher (b. 1929), 1929 Z, 1971 R, 1981 R, 1988 R
MacKay, Mary, B. novelist under pseudonym of 'Marie Corelli' (1855–1924), 1855 Z, 1924 Z
MacMahon, William, Prime Minister of Australia (1908–88), 1971 C
MacNeice, Louis, B. author (1907–65), 1907 Z, 1963 U
MacQuarrie, John, B. theologian (b. 1919), 1990 R
Macadam, John Loudon, B. road-builder (1756–1836), 1815 P
Macao, S.E. China, Portugal acquires, 1887 M
  Portugal agrees to return to China in 1999, 1987 A
Macartney, Carlile Aylmer, B. historian (1895–1978), 1969 Q
Macaulay, Rose, B. author (1881–1958), 1932 U
Macaulay, Thomas Babbington, Lord Macaulay, B. historian and Liberal politician (1800–59), 1800 Z, 1825 Q, 1842 Q, 1848 Q, 1859 Z
Macdonald, Sharman, B. playwright (b. 1951), 1984 W
Macedonia:
  reforms in, 1878 G
  movement for independence, 1893 N
  raids into, 1895 F
  activities of External Revolutionary Organisation, 1895 F
  disturbances in, 1902 N
  reforms for pacification demanded, 1903 B
    Austro-Russian agreement on, 1903 K
  agitation in, 1905 N
  Nicholas II, agrees to reforms, 1908 F
  Young Turks revolt, 1908 G
  Turkey declines to undertake reforms, 1908 G
Macfarlane, Alan Donald James, B. historian (b. 1941), 1978 Q
Machado, Bernadino, president of Portugal, 1915 H
Machel, Samora Moises, President of Mozambique (1933–86), 1975 F, 1986 K
Machine infernale, La (J. Cocteau), 1934 W
Machine-tool industry:
  British, 1800 P, 1910 P, 1939 Y
  German, 1910 P, 1939 Y
  US, 1853 P, 1910 P, 1939 Y
Machine-tools:
  for small arms manufacture, 1853 P plane, 1776 P
  turret-lathe, 1855 P
Machinery, exports from Britain legalised, 1843 P
Machines:
  automatic computer, 1942 P
  bottle-making, 1898 P
  cable-making, 1792 P
  combing, 1845 P
  for liquefaction of air, 1898 P
  for manufacture of coated photographic paper, 1885 P
  for proving laws of accelerated motion, 1784 P
  logical, 1874 P
  nail-making, 1786 P, 1790 P, 1806 P
  rapid filming, 1923 P
  sewing, 1846 P, 1851 P
  sounding, 1872 P
  teaching, 1963 O
  threshing, 1784 P
  typesetting, 1897 P
  universal milling, 1862 P
  wood-working, 1793 P
  See also under Automation
Machoro, Eloi, New Caledonian separatist leader, 1985 A
Macintosh, Charles, B. chemist and inventor (1766–1843), 1766 Z, 1823 P
Mack von Leiberich, Karl, Baron, Aus. general (1752–1828), defeated at Ulm, 1805 K
Mackenzie, Sir Compton, B. author (1883–1972), 1883 Z, 1912 U, 1972 Z
Mackenzie, Thomas, N. Zeal. politician, 1912 G
Mackenzie, William Lyon, Canad. rebel, 1837 M, 1838 A
Mackenzie, William Warrender, Lord Amulree, B. administrator (1860–1942), 1938 O
Mackie, John Leslie, B. philosopher (1917–81), 1974 R
Mackinnon, Sir William Henry, B. general (1857–1929), 1890 E

Mackintosh, Charles Rennie, B. architect (1868–1928), 1900 S, 1904 S
Mackintosh, Sir James, B. philosopher (1765–1832), 1791 O, 1799 O
Maclean, Donald Duart, B. spy (1913–83), 1913 Z, 1983 Z; flees to Russia, 1951 F
Maclean, Sir Fitzroy, B. soldier and Conservative politician (b. 1911), 1943 K
Maclennan, Robert Adam Ross, B. Labour/SDP/Liberal Democrat politician (b. 1936), 1987 H
Macleod, Iain Norman, B. Conservative politician (1913–70), 1970 F, 1970 G; as Colonial Secretary, Lord Salisbury attacks policy of, 1961 C; refuses to serve under Douglas-Home, 1963 K
Maclure, William, B. merchant and geologist (1763–1840), 1809 P
Macmahon, Marie Edmé Patrice Maurice de, Duke of Magenta, F. Marshal (1809–93), 1875 N, 1877 E; defeated, 1870 H; elected president, 1873 E, L; resigns, 1879 A
Macmillan, Harold, Earl of Stockton, B. Conservative politician (1894–1986), 1894 Z, 1955 G L, 1958 K, 1986 Z
minister of defence, 1954 K
foreign secretary, 1955 D
chancellor of Exchequer, 1955 M
introduces premium savings bonds, 1956 D
forms ministry, 1957 A
at Bermuda Conference with Eisenhower, 1957 C
visits US and Canada, 1957 K
resignations from ministry, 1958 A
tours Commonwealth, 1958 A, 1959 C
meets Eisenhower, 1958 F
rejects Russian proposal for immediate Summit talks, 1958 G
visits Russia, 1959 B
leads Conservatives to victory in election, 1959 K
visits Africa, 1960 A
'Wind of change' speech, 1960 B
elected Chancellor of Oxford University, 1960 C
issues joint declaration on nuclear tests, 1960 C
at Summit meeting, 1960 E
addresses UN, 1960 J
announces facilities for US Polaris submarines, 1960 L
meets de Gaulle, 1961 L
meets Kennedy, 1961 C, M, 1962 M, 1963 F
dismisses seven cabinet ministers, 1962 G
appoints Radcliffe tribunal, 1962 L
resigns premiership, 1963 K
Macready, William Charles, B. actor (1793–1873), 1851 W
Madagascar: Anglo-French expedition to, 1845 F; French commercial treaty with, 1868 H; liberation of slaves in, 1877 K; French war with, 1883 F; French control of, 1885 M; French conquest of 1894 L; France annexes, 1896 H; Britain surrenders claims, 1904 D; British invade, 1942 E; Nationalist revolt in, 1947 C; becomes independent as Malagasy Republic, 1960 F
Madame Bovary (G. Flaubert), 1856 U
Madariaga, Salvador de, Sp. author (1886–1978), 1886 Z, 1923 Q, 1978 Z
Mademoiselle de Maupin (F. Gautier), 1835 U
Madero, Francisco, President of Mexico, 1911 L
Madison, James, Am. statesman (1751–1836), 4th president of US (1809–17), 1785 R, 1787 O, 1786 E, 1798 N, 1799 N, 1800 L, 1806 O; inaugurated, 1809 C; orders war preparations against Britain, 1811 L; presidential election, 1812 L
Madmen and Specialists (W. Soyinka), 1971 W
'Mad Mullah', in Somaliland, 1899 J
Madness of George III, The (A. Bennett), 1991 W
Madness, B. pop group, 1974 D
Madoc (R. Southey), 1805 U
Madonna, (Madonna Louise Veronica Ciccone), Am. pop singer and actress (b. 1958), 1984 W
Madras, India, East India Company at, 1769 F
Madrid, Spain: treaty, 1801 J, Murat occupies, 1808 C; capitulates to Napoleon, 1808 M; Nationalist rising against French, 1808 E; rebels in, 1808 H; Wellington enters, 1812 H; Prado Museum, 1818 S; Monarchists in, 1873 D; University, closed by government, 1929 C; siege, 1936 L; surrenders to Franco, 1939 C
The Bank, 1980 S
Prado, 1981 S
East–West talks suspended, 1982 B
European Conference on Security and Co-operation, 1983 J
bomb explosion, 1985 D
Thyssen Collection, 1991 S
Maestricht, Belgium, Joseph II renounces claim to, 1785 L
Maeterlinck, Maurice, Belg. author (1862–1949), 1862 Z, 1889 U, 1892 W, 1901 U, 1909 U, 1949 Z
Mafeking, Cape Province, S. Africa, relieved, 1900 E
Mafia, in Sicily, 1926 J
Magdala, Ethiopia, 1868 D
Magee, Patrick, Ir. terrorist, jailed for Brighton hotel bombing, 1986 F
Magenta, Italy, battle, 1859 F
Magersfontein, Orange Free State, S. Africa, 1899 M
Magic Mountain, The (T. Mann), 1924 U
Maginot Line, France, 1930 O; extended, 1937 B
Maginot, André, F. military expert, 1877 Z, 1932 Z
Magna Carta, 750th anniversary celebrations, 1965 O
Magnano, Italy, battle, 1799 D
Magnetic North Pole, 1946 P
Magnetic detection of electrical waves, 1896 P
Magnetic mines, 1939 L
Magnetic recordings, 1899 P; expedition to take, 1957 P
Magnetic tape, 1942 P
Magnetic waves, 1825 P
Magnetism, studies in, 1807 P, 1851 P, 1923 P
Magus, The (J. Fowles), 1966 U
Magyars, oppose Francis Joseph, 1903 J, 1904 C
Mahabharata, The (dramatization) (J.-C. Carrière and P. Brook), 1985 W
Mahan, Alfred Thayer, Am. admiral and naval historian (1840–1914), 1840 Z, 1890 Q, 1914 Z
Maharishi Mahesh Yogi, Iran. Transcendental Meditation guru (b. 1911), 1968 W
Mahdi, The, Egyptian revolutionary. *See* Mahommed Ahmed ibn Seyyid Abdullah
Mahdists, attack Eritrea, 1893 M
Mahfouz, Najob, Egypt. author (b. 1911), 1967 T
Mahiwa, E. Africa, German attack on, 1917 K
Mahler, Gustav, Aus. musician (1860–1911), 1860 Z, 1888 T, 1895 T, 1900 T, 1909 T, 1911 T, Z, 1964 T
Mahmud II, Sultan of Turkey (1808–39), 1808 G, 1839 F, dissolves Janissaries, 1826 F; rejects Allies' rights to mediate in Greek war, 1827 M
Mahommed Ahmed ibn Seyyid Abdullah, Dongolese leader of Egyptian revolutionaries ('The Mahdi'), (d. 1885), 1883 L, 1884 B, K, 1885 F
Mahommed Ali, Shah of Persia, deposed, 1909 G
Mahrattas, Indian tribe of W. and Central India, 1770 N, 1773 J, 1795 C; British alliance with, 1790 E; British war against, 1802 K, 1803 H
Mai, Angelo, It. cardinal and philologist (1782–1854), 1819 Q
Maid of Orleans, The (F. Schiller), 1801 U
Mail-train robbery, 1963 H, 1964 D
Mailer, Norman Kingsley, Am. author (b. 1923), 1948 U, 1959 U, 1965 U, 1979 U
Maillol, Aristide, F. sculptor (1861–1944), 1906 S
Main Street (S. Lewis), 1920 U
Maine, Sir Henry James Sumner, B. jurist (1822–1888), 1861 Q, 1885 O
Main Streams of XIXth Century Literature (G. Brandes), 1872 Q
Maine, state, US: enters Union, 1820 C; prohibition in, 1851 N, O; repeal of, defeated, 1911 J; remains Republican, 1936 L
Maisky, Ivan Mikhailovich, R. diplomat (1884–1975), 1884 Z, 1975 Z
Maison Tellier, Le (G. de Maupassant), 1881 U
Maistre, Joseph de, F. author (1755–1821), 1796 O, 1809 O, 1817 R
Maistre, Xavier de, F. author (1763–1852), 1763 Z, 1794 U
Maitland, Frederic William, B. historian (1850–1906), 1850 Z, 1887 Q, 1894 Q, 1906 Z
Maizière, Lothar de, Prime Minister of E. Germany (b. 1940), 1990 D, M
Major Barbara (G. B. Shaw), 1907 W
Major, John, B. Conservative politician (b. 1943), 1943 Z, 1992 L
Chancellor of the Exchequer, 1989 K
Conservative leader and Prime Minister, 1990 L
Citizen's Charter, 1991 O
Majuba Hill, Natal, S. Africa, B. defeat at, 1881 B
Makarios III, Archbishop of Cyprus (1913–77), 1913 Z; deported to Seychelles, 1956 C, released, 1957 C; returns to Cyprus, 1959 C; becomes president of Cyprus Republic, 1960 H; abrogates 1960 Treaty, 1964 D
re-election as President, 1968 B
assassination attempt on, 1970 C
returned unopposed, 1973 B
deposed, 1973 R
asks Greeks to leave Cypriot National Guard, 1974 F
overthrown by National Guard, 1974 G
returns from exile, 1974 M
death, 1977 Z
Makin, Gilbert Isles, Pacific, US occupy, 1943 L
Making of Americans, The (G. Stein), 1925 U
Making of the President, The (T. H. White), 1962 O
Malaga, Spain, falls to rebels, 1937 B
Malagasy Republic (formerly Madagascar), independence, 1960 F
Malan, Douglas François, S. Afr. Nationalist (1877–1955), 1934 F; forms ministry, 1948 F; race legislation invalidated by Supreme Court, 1952 C, D; retires, 1954 M
Malaria: parasite observed, 1880 P; bacillus discovered, 1897 P
Malawi, Republic (formerly Nyasaland), becomes an independent republic, 1964 G
Malay States, 1873 N
Malaya: Japanese attack on, 1941 M; independent federation proposed, 1956 A, 1957 H
Malaysian Federation: proposed, 1961 E, 1962 G; Singapore and N. Borneo vote to join, 1962 J; formed, 1963 J; illiteracy statistics, 1983 Y

Malcolm X, Am. Black Muslim leader (1925–65), 1965 B
Málek, Jaromír, Czech.-born B. Egyptologist, 1980 Q
Malenkov, George Maximilianovich, R. leader (1902–88), chairman of Council of Ministers, 1953 C; premier, 1954 D; resigns, 1955 B; visits Britain, 1956 C; expelled from Soviet Central Committee, 1957 G
Malesherbes, Chrétien Guillaume de Lamoignon de, F. statesman (1721–94), 1775 G, 1776 E
Malet conspiracy against Napoleon, 1812 K
Mali, Federated state of, 1959 A
  border conflict with Burkina Faso, 1985 M
Malik, Jacob, R. politician, 1950 H
Mallarmé, Stéphane, F. author (1842–98), 1842 Z, 1876 U, 1898 Z
Malle, Louis, F. film director (b. 1932), 1974 W, 1981 W, 1988 W
Malmédy is united with Belgium, 1920 A
Malmö, Sweden, truce between Denmark and Prussia, 1848 H
Malone, Edmund, B. literary critic (1714–1812), 1778 Q
Malouet, Pierre Victor, F. publicist and politician (1740–1814), 1789 O
Malraux, André, F. author (1901–76), 1901 Z, 1933 W, 1935 U, 1937 U, 1950 R, 1976 Z
Malta: captured by France, 1798 F; Britain takes, 1800 J, L; restored to Knights of St. John, 1801 K; restored to Britain, 1815 F; Indian troops sent to, 1878 C; air attack on, 1942 D; convoys to, 1942 F, H; awarded George Cross, 1942 O; legislative assembly demands employment for dockyard workers, 1957 M; governor assumes control, 1958 D; requests independence within Common-wealth, 1962 H; Britain agrees to grant independence, 1963 H; becomes independent, 1964 J
  Anglo-Maltese conference on rundown of British forces in, 1967 B
  British–Maltese defence agreement, 1971 F
  ultimatum on naval bases, 1971 M
  withdrawal of British forces suspended, 1972 A
  Britain and NATO agree to pay for use of military bases, 1972 C
  Malta demands increase in rent for for use of military bases, 1972 M
  cuts military links with Britain, 1979 C
  demonstrations, 1979 V
  hijacked Egyptian airliner stormed at Malta airport, 1985 L
  Nationalist Party election victory, 1987 E, 1992 B
  merchant shipping tonnage statistics, 1992 Y
Malthus, Thomas Robert, B. political economist (1766–1834), 1766 Z, 1798 O, 1815 O, 1820 P, 1834 Z
Malus, Etienne Louis, F. physicist (1775–1812), 1809 P
Malvern, Lord. *See* Huggins, Godfrey
Mälzel, Johann Nepomuk, G. inventor of metronome (1772–1838), 1814 T
Mamaloni, Solomon Sunaone, Prime Minister of The Solomon Islands (b. 1943), 1989 C
Mamelles de Tirésias, Les (G. Apollinaire), 1917 W
Mamelukes, massacre of, 1811 C
Mamet, David Alan, Am. playwright (b. 1947), 1975 W, 1983 W, 1988 W, 1989 W
Mammography, introduction, 1967 P
Man Born to be King, The (D. L. Sayers), 1943 W
Man Who Came to Dinner, The (G. S. Kaufman), 1939 W
Man Who was Thursday, The (G. K. Chesterton), 1908 U
Man With A Load of Mischief, The (A. Dukes), 1925 W
Man and Materialism (F. Hoyle), 1957 R
Man and Superman (G. B. Shaw), 1903 W
Man for All Seasons, A (R. Bolt), 1960 W
Man for Himself (Fromm), 1949 R
Man from Mukinupin, The (D. Hewett), 1979 W
Man of Property, The (J. Galsworthy), 1906 U
Man on His Nature (C. Sherrington), 1939 R
Man versus the State, The (H. Spencer), 1884 O
Man's Place in Nature (T. H. Huxley), 1863 P
Man, Isle of, fiscal rights in, 1765 J
Manabe, Syukuvo, Am. scientist (b. 1931), 1967 P
Managerial Revolution, The (J. Burnham), 1942 O
Managil Project, Sudan, 1958 G
Managua, Nicaragua
  earthquake, 1972 M
  Sandinista rebels, 1979 F, G
Manchester, England, 1774 R, 1817 C; Peterloo Massacre in, 1819 H; Anti-Corn Law League founded in, 1838 J, O; Owens College, 1851 O, 1880 O; Church Congress at, 1863 R; Fenianism in, 1867 J; University, 1880 O; Ship Canal, 1893 P; John Rylands Library, 1899 Q; Corporation's suit with Palace of Varieties, 1954 O; Jodrell Bank radio telescope, 1957 P
  disturbances following Toxteth riots, 1981 G
  Manchester Airport fire, 1985 H
  Strangeways Prison riot, 1990 D
Manchukuo: Republic proclaimed, 1932 A; Pi Yi becomes president, 1932 L; emperor of, 1934 C; Germany recognises, 1938 E; Japanese–Russian clash on borders, 1938 G
Manchuria: Russo-Chinese convention on, 1896 J; Russia's right to operate railway in Northern, 1896 F; Russian occupation, 1900 L; Russian evacuation, 1901 B, 1902 D, 1903 H; Russo-Japanese agreement on, 1910 G, 1912 H; Japanese leases in, 1915 A; Japanese occupation of, 1931 J; republic proclaimed, 1932 A; Lytton Report on, 1932 K, 1933 B; China regains sovereignty over, 1945 J; fighting for control of, 1945 K
Manchus, in China, expulsion of, demanded, 1905 N
Mancroft, Stormont Mancroft Samuel, Lord Mancroft, B. financier (1901–87), 1963 M
Mandalay, Upper Burma: British occupy, 1885 L; Japanese take, 1942 E; 14th Army enters, 1945 C
Mandated Territories:
  by Supreme Allied Council, 1919 L, 1920 D
  British in Iraq, ends, 1932 K
    in Palestine ends, 1948 E
  See also under League of Nations
'M. and B.' (sulphapyradine), 1938 P
Mandela, Nelson Rolihlahla, S. Afr. politician (b. 1918), 1918 Z, 1985 H, 1986 G
  sentenced, 1964 F
  refuses offer of freedom conditional on renunciation of violence, 1985 B
  release of called for on his 70th birthday, 1988 G
  Mandela birthday concert, London, 1988 W
  public statement made by, 1989 G
  release from prison, 1990 B, W
  announces separation from Winnie Mandela, 1992 D
Mandela, Winnie, S. Afr. politician (b. 1934), 1992 D
  forcibly removed from home, 1985 M
  charged with kidnapping and assault, 1990 J
  imprisonment, 1991 E
Manet, Edouard, F. artist (1832–83), 1832 Z, 1858 S, 1859 S, 1860 S, 1862 S, 1863 S, 1865 S, 1867 S, 1868 S, 1873 S, 1877 S, 1882 S, 1883 Z
Manfred (Byron), 1817 U
'Manhattan Project', for splitting atom, 1941 P
Manhattan Transfer (J. Dos Passos), 1925 U
Manifestos:
  African Charter, issued by Casablanca Conference, 1961 A
  Atlantic Charter, 1941 H, J
  Brunswick's, Duke of, 1792 G
  'Charter 77', on human rights, 1977 A
  Communist, 1848 O
  Fundamental Rights, German, 1848 M
    abolished, 1851 N
  Futurist, 1910 S
  Human Rights, UN declaration on, 1948 M
  Lagos Charter, for Pan-African Co-operation, 1962 A
  Lassalles Working-Class Programme, 1862 O
  Nationalisation, British Labour Party retains 'Clause 4', 1960 C
  October Manifesto, by Canadians for union with US, 1849 K
  October, in Russia, 1905 K
  Ostend, advises US acquisition of Cuba, 1854 K
  Peace, by German Social Democrats, 1915 F
  Pillnitz, Declaration, 1791 H
  Polish National Committee, 1863 A
  Potomac Charter, 1954 F
  Realistic Manifesto (European Constructivism), 1920 S
  Rights of Man, French Declaration of, 1789 H
  Russian Communist Party condemns Mao Tse-tung's dogmatism, 1960 H
  Scharnhorst's, for reforming Prussian army, 1807 N
  Spanish civil servants pro-democracy, 1975 B
  Spanish Liberal, 1854 G
  Surrealist, 1929 S
  Tamworth, by Peel, 1834 M
  Viborg, issued by Russian Cadets, 1906 G
  Washington Declaration, on Anglo-US policy in Middle East, 1956 B
  Western Powers, for German re-unification and free elections, 1957 G
Manigat, Leslie, President of Haiti (b. 1930), 1988 B, F
Manila Conference of Vietnam War allies, 1966 K
Manila, Philippines: Spain regains, 1763 B; Spanish fleet destroyed at, 1898 E; US captures, 1898 H; sterilisation of water in, 1912 P; US troops enter, 1945 B; chess championship, 1980 X
Manin, Daniele, It. revolutionary (1804–57), 1848 C
Man in the Zoo, A (D. Garnett), 1924 U
Manitoba, Province, Canada, 1870 E
Mankiewicz, Joseph L., Am. film director (1909–93), 1963 W
Mankind and Technology (O. Spengler), 1931 R
Manley, Michael Norman, Jamaican politician (b. 1924), 1989 B
Mann im Wald (Kiefer), 1971 S
Mann, Anthony, US. film director (1907-67), 1930 W, 1961 W
Mann, Horace, Am. educationalist (1796–1859), 1837 O
Mann, Thomas, G. author (1875–1955), 1901 U, 1913 U, 1924 U, 1933 U, 1939 U
Mann, Tom, B. syndicalist and trades union leader (1856–1941), 1910 O, 1912 C
Mannerheim Line, Finland, Russian attack on, 1940 B
Mannerheim, Carl, Baron, Fin. soldier (1868–1951), 1868 Z

Mannheim, Karl, G. sociologist (1893–1947), 1956 R
Mannheim, Germany, 1795 J, 1819 C
Manning, Henry Edward, B. cardinal (1808–92), 1850 R, 1869 R
Manry, Robert, Am. sailor, 1965 X
Mansbridge, Albert, B. founder of WEA (1876–1952), 1904 O
Mansell, Nigel, B. racing driver (b. 1953), 1992 W
Mansfield Park (J. Austen), 1814 U
Mansfield, Earl of, *See* Murray
'Mansfield, Katherine.' *See* Murry, Kathleen
Mansion, The (W. Faulkner), 1959 U
Manstein, Erich von, G. Field Marshal (1887–1973), fails to relieve Stalingrad, 1942 M
Mantes, Russian agent in US, 1921 A
Manteuffel, Otto von, Prussian premier, 1850 L
Mantoux, Etienne, F. historian, 1946 O
Mantua, Italy: attempted relief, 1796 H; surrenders to French, 1797 B
Manual of Rational Pathology (F. G. J. Henle), 1846 P
Manuel II of Portugal (1908–10), 1908 B, 1910 K
Manufactured goods, comparative statistics of increases in production, 1913 Y
Manufacturing, statistics of hours worked per week, 1978 Y
Manuscripts, discoveries, 1842 R, 1948 Q
Manxman, The (Hall Caine), 1894 U
Many Faces of Realism, The (H. Putnam), 1987 R
Manzoni, Alessandro, It. author (1785–1873), 1785 Z, 1813 U, 1821 U, 1825 U, 1873 Z
Mao Tse-tung, President of China (1893–1976), 1893 Z , 1949 K; negotiations with Chiang Kai-shek break down, 1945 K; resigns as chairman of Republic, 1959 D; dogmatism of, condemned by Russian Communist Party, 1960 H
  swims down Yangtse, 1966 G
  accusations against USSR, 1970 A
  USSR accused of complicity in assassination plot, 1972 H
  death, 1976 J 1976 Z
Maoris, in New Zealand: chiefs surrender to Britain, 1840 B, revolts, 1843 F, 1845 C, 1863 E; British wars with, 1860 C, 1861 C, 1865 J, 1868 F
Map of the World, A (D. Hare), 1983 W
Maps and Atlases: Bengal Atlas, 1779 P; aeronautical map of France, 1911 P; geological, 1841 P; the Vinland, 1965 Q
Marakeesh, Morocco, 1908
Marat, Jean Paul, F. revolutionary (1743–93), 1793 G
Marathon, London, 1981 X
Marc, Franz, G. artist (1880–1916), 1911 S, 1912 S, 1913 S
Marcel Proust (G. Painter), 1865 Q
Marcel, Gabriel, F. dramatist (1889–1973), 1921 W
Marchand, Leslie Alexis, Am. scholar (b. 1900), 1973 Q
Marchand, Major, F. soldier, 1896 F, 1897 G
Marciano, Rocky (born Rocco Francis Marchegiano), Am. boxer (1923–69), 1923 Z, 1952 X, 1969 Z
Marconi Scandal, 1913 F
Marconi, Guglielmo, It. inventor of wireless telegraphy (1874–1937), 1874 Z, 1895 P, 1901 P, 1920 W, 1937 Z
Marconiphone Company, 1933 P
Marcos, Ferdinand, President of the Philippines (1917–89), 1973 A, 1981 D
  Philippine sovereignty proclaimed over most of Sabah, 1968 J
  Philippine troops recalled from Vietnam, 1969 K
  demonstrations demanding resignation, 1983 J
  Presidential elections, 1986 B
  death, 1989 J
Marcos, Imelda Romualdez, Philippine politician (b. 1930), 1990 G
Marcus, Frank, B. dramatist (b. 1928), 1965 W
Marcuse, Herbert, Am. philosopher (1898–1979), 1898 Z, 1955 R, 1964 R, 1969 R, 1979 Z
Mare, Walter de la, B. poet (1873–1956), 1873 Z, 1935 U, 1956 Z
Mare au diable, La (G. Sand), 1846 U
Marengo, Italy, Napoleon's victory at, 1800 F
Mareth Line, N. Africa, Montgomery breaks through, 1943 C
Marey, Etienne Jules, P. physiologist and inventor (1830–1904), 1888 P
Margaret, Princess, Countess of Snowdon (b. 1930), 1960 E
Margarethe II, Queen of Denmark (b. 1940), 1972 A
Margarine, invented, 1869 P; substitution for butter, limited in US, 1912 O
Maria Christina, Queen Regent of Spain, 1854 H
Maria I, Queen of Portugal (1777–1816), 1777 B, 1816 C; as Regent, 1774 N
Maria II, Queen of Portugal (1826–53), 1831 D, 1853 L; accession as an infant, 1826 E; British support for, 1826 M, 1827 A; returns to Lisbon, 1833 G; restoration, 1834 E, J
Maria Nefeldi (O. Elytis), 1979 U
Maria Theresa, Archduchess of Austria, Queen of Hungary and Bohemia, wife of the Holy Roman Emperor Francis I (1717–80), 1765 H, 1780 L
Maria, Walter De, Am. sculptor (b. 1935), 1977 S
Mariage Blanc (T. Rosewicz), 1975 W
Mariage de Figaro (P. Beaumarchais), 1784 W
Marianne Island, Pacific, bought by Germany, 1899 B
Marie Alexandrovna, R. Princess, married Alfred, Duke of Edinburgh, 1874 A
Marie Antoinette, daughter of Empress Maria Theresa of Austria (1755–1793): marries Louis XVI, 1770 E; discredited by Diamond Necklace affair, 1785 H; executed, 1793 K
Marie-Louise, of Austria, married Napoleon I, 1810 B
Marienbad, now Czechoslovakia, 1907 J, 1922 H
Mariette, Auguste Ferdinand François, F. Egyptologist (1821–81), 1850 Q
Marilyn Monroe (A. Warhol), 1967 S
Marine Biological Association, 1884 P
Marinetti, F. T., F. poet (1876–1944), 1909 S
Marini, Marino, It. sculptor (1901–80), 1901 Z, 1936 S, 1952 S, 1980 Z
Marion, Ohio, US, 1898 P
Maritain, Jacques, Fr. philosopher (1882–1973), 1882 Z, 1920 R, 1943 R, 1949 U, 1973 Z
Marius the Epicurean (W. Pater), 1885 U
Markov, Georgi, Bulg. author and broadcaster (1929–78), unlawfully killed in London, 1978 J
Marković, Ante, Yugos. politician (b. 1924), 1989 A, 1991 M
Marlborough, His Life and Times (W. S. Churchill), 1933 Q
Marmion (W. Scott), 1808 U
Marmont, Auguste Frédéric Louis, Duke of Ragusa, F. general (1774–1852), 1812 G
Marmontel, Jean François, F. author (1723–99), 1767 R, 1770 U
Marne, River, France, battles, 1914 J, 1918 G
Marquand, David Ian, B. historian (b. 1934), 1977 Q
Marquand, John Phillips, B. author (1893–1960), 1937 U
Marquis, Frederick James, Lord Woolton, B. Conservative (1893–1964), 1941 D, 1943 L
Marriage:
  in Austria, civil, 1783 O, 1894 R
    Roman Catholic control of, 1855 H
  in Britain, of Nonconformists, 1833 R
    registration, 1836 H
    civil, in England and Wales, 1857 O
  in France, civil, 1792 R
  in Germany, mixed, in Prussia, 1837 R
    civil, 1874 O
  in Italy, minimum age of brides raised, 1892 O
  in Morocco, women permitted to choose husbands, 1958 O
  in S. Africa, mixed, forbidden, 1949 F
  in Turkey, civil, 1926 J
  in US, polygamy among Mormons, 1843 R
  See also under Divorce
Marriage, notable:
  King Baudouin, 1960 M
  Princess Elizabeth, 1947 L
  Luisa Fernanda with Duc de Montpensier, 1846 K
  Marie Antoinette, 1770 E
  Princess Margaret, 1960 E
  Napoleon, 1796 C, 1810 B
  Prince Rainer to Grace Kelly, 1956 W
  Duke of Windsor, 1937 F
Married Women's property act, in Britain, 1870 H, 1882 O
Marryat, Frederick, B, novelist (1792–1848), 1836 U
Mars, planet, 1971 P, 1976 P : satellites of discovered, 1877 P; photo-electric observations, 1955 P; conditions on, 1963 P; photographs of, 1964 P, 1965 P
  landing on, 1971 P
  photographed, 1971 P
  Viking I and II, 1976 P
Mars-la-Tour, France, Prussian victory at, 1870 H
Marsa, Tunisia, convention, 1883 F
Marseilles, France, Franco-Italian agreement, 1935 A
Marsh, Sir Edward, B. civil servant and promoter of literature (1872–1953), 1911 U, 1918 U
Marshall Plan, 1947 F, 1948 C; Germany becomes a full member of, 1949 M; aid to Britain ceases, 1950 M; replaced by Mutual Security Agency, 1951 M
Marshall, Alfred, B. economist (1842–1924), 1842 Z, 1890 O, 1923 O, 1924 Z
Marshall, George Catlett, Am. general and statesman (1880–1959), 1880 Z, 1942 D, 1951 E; commands Allied occupation of Japan, 1945 H; attempts mediation in China, 1945 M, becomes Secretary of State, 1947 A; calls for European Recovery Programme (Marshall Aid), 1947 F; retires, 1949 A; becomes defense secretary, 1950 J
Marshall, John, Am. jurist (1755–1835), 1819 O
Marshall, Sir John Ross, Prime Minister of New Zealand (1912–88), 1972 B
Martens, Georg Friedrich von, G. jurist and diplomat (1756–1821), 1791 Q
Martha Quest (D. Lessing), 1952 U
Martial Law:
  in Aleppo, 1980 C
  in Bangladesh, 1975 L, 1986 L
    ended, 1986 L
  in Belgium, 1936 K
  in Germany, 1923 J
  in Greece, 1970 D

in Kabul, 1980 B
in Kosovo, demonstrations calling for, 1988 J
in Lhasa, 1989 C
in Pakistan, 1969 C, 1983 H, 1985 M
in Spain, 1969 A
in Thailand, 1991 B
Martignac, Jean Baptiste Sylvere Gay, Vicomte de, F. Doctrinaire Royalist (1778–1832), becomes premier, 1828 A; attacks Jesuits, 1828 F; is dismissed, 1829 H
Martin, John, B. artist (1789–1854), 1822 S
Martin, (Basil) Kingsley, B. journalist (1897–1969), 1897 Z, 1931 V, 1969 Z
Martin, Sir John Leslie, B. architect (b. 1908), 1983 S
Martin, Pierre Emile, F. engineer (1824–1915), 1861 P
Martin, Troy Kennedy, B. author (b. 1932), 1985 W
Martineau, James, B. Unitarian divine (1805–1900), 1888 R
Martinique, West Indies: restored to France, 1763 B; Britain captures, 1794 N, 1809 N
Martinu, Botuslav, Czech. musician (1890–1959), 1956 T
Marx Brothers, Am. film actors, 1941 W
Marx, (Heinrich) Karl, G. Socialist (1818–83), 1818 Z, 1847 O, 1848 O, 1867 O, 1883 Z, 1885 O, 1886 O 1895 O
Marx, Wilhelm, G. Centre Party Chancellor (1863–1936), 1924 E, 1925 A, 1926 E, 1927 A, 1928 F
Mary Barton (E. Gaskell), 1848 U
Mary Stuart (F. Schiller), 1800 W
Mary Tyler Moore Show, The, television programme, 1970 W
Mary, Queen Consort of King George V of Gt. Britain (Princess Mary of Teck), 1867 Z, 1953 Z
Marylebone Cricket Club (M.C.C.), 1787 X, 1788 X, 1814 X, 1980 X
Marzeppa (Byron), 1819 U
Masampo, Korea, 1900 C
Masaryk, Thomas Garrigue, Czech, statesman (1850–1937), 1850 Z, 1895 O, 1935 M, 1937 Z; elected president of Czechoslovakia, 1918 L; re-elected, 1927 E
Mascall, Eric Lionel, B. churchman (b. 1905), 1949 R
Masefield, John, B. poet (1878–1967), 1878 Z, 1902 U, 1911 U, 1941 O, 1961 U, 1967 Y
Mash, television series, 1972 W
Mashonaland, Rhodesia, 1890 J
Mask of Time, The (M. Tippett), 1984 T
Maskelyne, Nevil, B. astronomer (1732–1811), 1767 P
Masks and Faces (C. Reade), 1852 W
Mass (Bernstein), 1970 T
Mass Civilization and Minority Culture (F. R. Leavis), 1930 O
Mass, Roman Catholic, in vernacular, 1786 R, 1964 R; musical settings of, notable, 1766 T, 1796 T, 1783 T, 1949 T
Mass-spectrograph, 1919 P
Massachusetts Institute of Technology, 1865 O; develops ultra-high-frequency waves, 1955 P
Massachusetts Spy, The, 1770 V
Massachusetts, state, US: Colonial assembly dissolved, 1768 G, committees of correspondence in, 1772 L; coercive acts against, 1774 C; educational reforms in, 1837 O
Massacres:
Boipatong, South Africa, 1992 F
My Lai, Vietnam, 1969 L
T'ien-an Men Square, Peking, China, 1989 D, F
in Mozambique, alleged by *The Times*, 1973 G
of Armenians by Turks, 1895 K, L, 1896 H
Gladstone on, 1896 J
of Assyrian Christians, 1933 G
of British by Afghans, 1841 L, 1879 J
by Indians, at Cawnpore, 1857 F, G
by Zulus, at Isandhlwana, 1879 A
of Bulgarians, by Turks, 1876 C
of Christians, by Druses in Syria, 1860 J
of French, during 'June Days', 1848 F
of Greeks, at Chios, by Turks, 1822 D
of Indians in US, at Wyoming, 1778 G
at Cherry Valley, 1778 L
of Anapahoe Indians, 1864 L
of Cheyenne Indians, 1864 L
of Irish family at Maamtrasna, 1882 H
of Poles, by Russians, at Warsaw, 1861 B
of Turks, by Greeks, 1821 K
of US pro-slavers at Pottawatomie Creek, 1856 E
Massawa, Eritrea: Italians occupy, 1885 B; British take, 1941 D
Masséna André, general, Duke of Rivoli (1756–1817), 1799 F, J
Massenet, Jules, F. musician (1842–1912), 1842 Z, 1884 T, 1894 T, 1906 T, 1912 Z
Massey, (Charles) Vincent, Canad. diplomat and statesman (1887–1967), 1887 Z; becomes Canadian minister to Washington, 1926 L; becomes Governor General of Canada, 1952 A; death, 1967 Z
Massey, William Ferguson, N. Zeal. politician (1856–1925), 1856 Z, 1925 E; becomes premier, 1912 G
Massie, Bob, Australian cricketer (b. 1947), 1972 X
Mastai-Ferretti, Giovanni Maria, It. cardinal, Pope Pius IX (1846–78), 1792 Z, 1878 Z; elected Pope, 1846 F. *See under* Pius IX
Masters, John, B. author (1914–83), 1954 U
Masters, The (C. P. Snow), 1950 U
Masuria, Poland (formerly East Prussia), battles, 1914 J, 1915 B
Matabeleland, Rhodesia: under British protection, 1888 B; mineral rights in, 1888 K; risings in, 1893 G; revolt in, crushed, 1893 L; British occupation, 1894 A
Matapan, Cape, Italy, naval battle off, 1941 C
Matches:
friction, invented, 1827 P
phosphorus, prohibited in Britain, 1908 O
safety, 1898 P
Mateos, Lópex, Mex. president, 1964 M
Materialism and Empiric Criticism (Lenin), 1909 O
Maternity benefits, in Germany, 1914 O
Mathematical Logic (G. Boole), 1847 P
Mathematics of Commerce (A. Cournot), 1838 O
Mathematics:
algebraic equations, 1846 P
bi-quaternions, 1873 P
calculus of forms, 1852 P
Gödel's proof, 1931 P
linear transformations, theory of, 1845 P
numbers, theory of, 1854 P
of relativity, 1908 P
primary numbers, treatise on, 1850 P
See also Geometry
Mathias, William, B. musician (1934–92), 1982 T, 1991 T
Matière et Mémoire (H. Bergson), 1896 R
Matisse, Henri, F. artist and sculptor (1869–1954), 1869 Z, 1905 S, 1907 S, 1909 S, 1911 S, 1914 S, 1916 S, 1920 S, 1927 S, 1928 S, 1930 S, 1931 S, 1940 S, 1954 S
Matteotti, Giacomo, It. Socialist (1885–1924), 1924 F
Matterhorn, The, Switzerland, ascents, 1865 X, 1965 X
Matthew, Henry Colin Gray, B. historian (1941), 1968 Q
Matthew, Robert, B. architect, 1951 S
Matthews, Sir Bryan, B. scientist (b. 1906), 1929 P
Matthews, Colin, B. musician (b. 1946), 1989 T
Matthews, John Frederick, historian (b. 1940), 1975 Q
Matthews, Robert Charles Oliver, B. economist (b. 1927), 1982 Q
Matthews, William, B. scholar (1905–75), 1970 Q
Matthiessen, Peter, Am. author (b. 1927), 1979 U
Mattingly, Garrett, Am. historian (1900–62), 1959 Q
Mattini, Il (G. Parini), 1763 U
Mau Mau terrorists in Kenya, 1952 K, 1953 D, H; Kenya government's terms for surrender, 1955 A; prisoners' deaths at Hola Camp, 1959 C
Mauberge, France, British take, 1918 L
Maud and Other Poems (Tennyson), 1855 U
Maude, Frederick Stanley, B. soldier (1864–1917), 1917 D
Maudling, Reginald, B. Conservative politician (1917–79), 1970 F, 1972 G; Chancellor of Exchequer, 1962 G, 1963 D
Maudslay, Henry, B. engineer (1771–1831), 1797 P, 1800 P
Maufe, Sir Edward, B. architect (1883–1974), 1961 S
Maugham, William Somerset, B. author (1874–1965), 1874 Z, 1915 U, 1919 U, 1926 U, 1930 W, 1944 U, 1965 Z; portrait, 1949 S
Maunsell, G., B. architect, 1961 S
Maupassant, Guy de, F. author (1850–93), 1850 Z, 1880 U, 1881 U, 1883 U, 1885 U, 1888 U, 1893 Z
Maupeon, René Nicolas Charles Augustin, F. statesman (1714–92), 1770 M, 1771 A
Maupin, Armistead, Am. author (b. 1944), 1978 U
Maurepas, Jean Frédéric Phéypeaux, Comte de, F. statesman (1701–81), 1774 E
Mauriac, François, F. author (1885–1970), 1885 Z, 1970 Z
Maurice, Frederick Denison, B. churchman (1805–1872),1849 R, 1853 R, 1854 O
Maurice, Sir Frederick (1871–1951), B. soldier and administrator, 1918 E
Maurier, Sir Gerald Hubert Edward Busson de, B. actor-manager (1873–1934), 1873 Z, 1910 W, 1934 Z
Mauritania, becomes an independent Islamic republic, 1960 L
anti-Senegalese violence, 1989 D, F
becomes republic within Commonwealth, 1992 C
agrees to pull out of Sahara, 1975 L
shares Western Sahara with Morocco, 1976 D
renounces claims to Western Sahara, 1979 H
Arab Maghreb Union, 1989 B
Mauritius, Indian Ocean: British take, 1810 G; constitutional conference promises independence, 1965 J
Mauroy, Pierre, French Socialist politician (b. 1928), 1981 E, 1992 A
Maury, Jean Giffrein, F. churchman (1746–87), Cardinal Archbishop of Paris, 1800 C
Maury, Matthew Fontaine, Am. hydrographer (1806–73), 1855 P
Mavor, Osborne Henry. *See* Bridie, James
Max, Prince of Baden, 1918 K, L
Max-Müller, Friedrich, B. orientalist and philologist (1823–1900), 1875 Q, 1878 R

Maxim, Sir Hiram, Am. gunsmith (1840–1916), 1884 P
Maxim, Hudson, Am. inventor, 1853 Z, 1927 Z
Maximilian III, King of Bavaria (1745–77), 1777 M
Maximilian, Archduke of Austria (1832–67), becomes Emperor of Mexico, 1864 D; loses French support, 1867 C; is executed, 1867 F
Maxwell, Robert, B. businessman and publisher (1923–91), 1923 Z, 1990 V
attempted purchase of *The News of the World*, 1968 V
buys Mirror group, 1984 V
London Daily News launched, 1987 V
death, 1991 L, Z
collapse of business empire, 1991 M
New York Daily News, 1991 V
Maxwell-Fyfe, David, Lord Kilmuir, Conservative politician, Lord Chancellor (1900–67), 1962 G
May Committee on Britain's budget deficit, 1931 G
May Day Labour celebrations, 1890 O
May, Nunn, B. atomic spy, 1952 O
May, Philip William ('Phil'), B. cartoonist (1864–1903), 1896 V
May, Princess of Teck. *See* Mary, Queen
Mayence, France, 1792 K, 1793 G, 1797 M
Mayer, Julius, G. physicist (1814–87), 1842 P
Mayer, Sir Robert, B. promoter of children's concerts (1879–1985), 1923 T
Mayerling, near Vienna, Austria, 1889 A
Mayhew, Christopher Paget, Lord Mayhew, B. Labour/Liberal politician (b. 1915), 1966 B
Maynooth College, Ireland: founded, 1795 R; British grant to, 1845 F
Mayo, Earl of. *See* Bourke, R. S.
Mayo, county, Eire, boycotting in, 1880 N
Mayr-Harting, Henry Maria Robert Egmont, B. historian (b. 1936), 1972 Q, 1991 Q
Mazowiecki, Tadeusz, Prime Minister of Poland (b. 1927), 1989 H, 1990 M
Mazzini, Giuseppe, It. statesman (1805–72), 1805 Z, 1832 O, 1834 B, 1872 Z; proclaims Roman Republic, 1849 B
Mboya, Tom, Kenyan politician (1930–69), 1930 Z, 1964 M, 1969 Z
McCallum, Ronald Buchanan, B. author and psephologist (1898–1973), 1947 O
McCarthy, John, B. journalist, 1986 D, 1991 H
McCarthy, Joseph, Am. Republican (1909–1957), 1909 Z; Senatorial Committee denies charges by, 1950 G; Senatorial Committee reports improper action by, 1954 J, M
McCarthy, Justin, Ir. politician and author (1830–1912), succeeds Parnell as Nationalist leader, 1890 M
McCarthy, Mary, Am. author (b. 1912), 1963 U
McCollum, Elmer Verner, B. biochemist (1879–1967), 1913 P
McConnochie, Catherine, Church of Scotland minister, 1969 R
McCormick, Cyrus, Am. engineer (1809–84), 1834 P
McCutcheon, W.A., 1980 Q
McEnery, Samuel Douglas, Am. Democrat (1837–1910), 1874 F
McEwan, Ian, B. writer (b. 1948), 1990 U, 1992 U
McFarlane, Robert Carl, Am. National Security Adviser (b. 1937), attempted suicide, 1987 B
MC5, The, Am. pop group, 1969 W
McGahey, Michael, B. union leader, 1974 A
McGann, Jerome John, Am. literary scholar (b. 1937), 1980 Q
McGee, Greg, N. Zeal. dramatist (b. 1950), 1980 W
McGovern, George Stanley, Am. Democrat (b. 1922), presidential nomination and candidacy, 1972 G, L
McGrath, John Peter, B. dramatist and director (b. 1935), 1973 W
McKenna, Reginald, B. Liberal (1863–1943), as Home Secretary, 1911 K; as Chancellor of Exchequer, 1915 E; investigates German economy, 1923 L; reports on reparations, 1924 D
McKibbin, Ross, Austral.-born B. historian, 1974 Q, 1990 Q
McKinley, William, Am. Republican (1843–1901), 25th president of US (1897–1901), 1900 B, F, 1901 J; wins presidential elections, 1896 L, 1900 L; inaugurated, 1897 C
tariff, 1890 K, 1892 L
repealed, 1894 E
McLuhan, (Herbert) Marshall, Canad. author (1911–80), 1911 Z, 1964 O, 1980 Z
McMahon Line, Indian frontier, Chinese troops cross, 1962 J
McMillan, Edwin, Am. scientist, 1940 P
McMillan, Margaret, B. educationalist, 1860 Z 1931 Z
McNamara, Robert Strange, Am. defense secretary (b. 1916), 1960 L
McNaught, William, B. engineer (1813–81), 1945 P
McPherson, James, Am. historian (b. 1936), 1988 Q
McWhirter, (Alan) Ross, B. publisher (1925–75), murdered by IRA, 1975 L
McWilliam, Frederick Edward, B. sculptor (b. 1909) 1961 S, 1963 S, 1964 S
Mead, Margaret, Am. anthropologist (1901–78), 1901 Z, 1935 R, 1950 R, 1953 Q, 1978 Z
Meade, George Gordon, Am. Unionist general (1815–72), 1863 G
Meade, James Edward, B. economist (b. 1907), 1935 A
Means-test, in Britain, 1935 A, 1936 G
Measles, vaccine for, 1963 P
Meat:
chilling process for, 1934 P
frozen, 1877 P, 1879 P
Mécanique analytique (Lagrange), 1788 P
Mecca, Saudi Arabia
Grand Mosque seized by militants, 1979 L
armed pilgrims sent, 1983 R
pilgrims crushed to death at, 1990 R
Mechanics, studies in, 1788 P
Medical Research:
venereal diseases, 1909 P, 1916 O, 1943 O
tetanus, 1915 P
steroid hormone cortisone isolated, 1935 P
streptococcus infections, treatment for, 1935 P
penicillin treatment for chronic diseases, 1943 P
metabolic diseases, 1946 P
hip replacement operation, 1954 P
pernicious anaemia, 1955 P
death, definition of, 1966 P
meningitis, 1968 P
artificial human heart, 1969 P
in vitro fertilization of human egg cells, 1969 P
fibre-optic endoscope, 1971 P
somnatotropin synthesized, 1971 P
CAT body-scanner, 1975 P
endorphins, 1975 P
monoclonal antibodies, 1975 P
Legionnaire's disease, 1976 P
Karposi's sarcoma, 1977 P
Cyclosporin A introduced in organ transplant surgery, 1978 P
smallpox eradicated, 1978 K
hepatitis B vaccine, 1980 P
laboratory production of interferon, 1980 P
lithotripter, 1980 P
artificial heart implant, 1982 P
Acquired Immunodeficiency Syndrome (AIDS), 1983 P
blood extracted from and disease diagnosed in foetus, 1983 P
hormone regulating blood pressure isolated and synthesized, 1983 P
human embryo transferred, 1983 P
Human Immunodeficiency Virus (HIV) isolated, 1983 P
embryo transplants, 1987 P
experiments on living embryos, Vatican document, 1987 O
sterilization of subnormal girl approved in Britain, 1987 O
surrogate motherhood, US ruling, 1987 O
RV486 abortion-inducing drug, 1988 P
abortion. *See* Abortion
cancer research. *See* Cancer Research
fertility treatments. *See* Fertility Treatments
genetics. *See* Genetics
Medical practitioners, unqualified, prohibited from practising, 1815 O. *See also* Health Service
Medieval Idea of Marriage, The (C.N.L. Brooke), 1989 Q
Medieval history, study of, 1866 Q
Médiations poètiques (A. de Lamartine), 1870 U
Mediterranean, Anglo-French agreement on, 1937 A
Medoff, Mark, Am. dramatist (b. 1940), 1980 W
Mee, Arthur, B. journalist (1875–1943), 1919 V
Meerut, India, mutiny of, 1857 E
Meetings: British act to prevent seditious, 1817 C; in Egypt, British ultimatum for free, 1928 D; political in Persia, banned, 1961 E
Mège-Mouries, H., F. chemist (1817–80), 1869 P
Mehemet Ali, Egypt. ruler (d. 1849), 1811 C; quits Greece, 1828 H; Turkey recognises independence in Egypt, 1833 E; powers reserve right to treat with, 1839 G; terms of Quadruple Alliance to, 1840 G, L; is forced to submit, 1840 J, K; death, 1849 H
Meier, Richard Alan, Am. architect (b. 1934), 1985 S
Meighen, Arthur, Can. politician (1874–1960), 1920 G, 1926 F
Meiji, dynasty in Japan, 1868 A
Meikle, Andrew, B. millwright and inventor (1719–1811), 1748 P
Mein Kampf (A. Hitler), 1925 O, 1927 O
Meinecke, Frederick, G. historian (1862–1959), 1908 O, 1936 Q
Meinhof, Ulrike Marie, G. terrorist leader (1934–76), suicide, 1976 E
Meir, Golda, Prime Minister of Israel (1898–1978), 1898 Z, 1969 B, 1973 R, 1978 Z
Melba, Nellie, Austral. operatic singer (1861–1931), 1861 Z, 1931 Z
Melbourne aircraft carrier, collision with USS *Frank E. Evans*, 1969 F
Melbourne, Australia, Olympic Games at, 1956 X
Melbourne, Viscount. *See* Lamb, William
Meline, Félix Jules, F. Conservative Republican (1838–1912), 1891 N, 1896 D
Mellers, Wilfrid, B. musicologist (b.1914), 1964 T
Mellini, Macedonio, It. physicist (1798–1854), 1831 P, 1850 P

Mello, Fernando Collor de, Brazilian politician (b. 1949), 1989 M, 1990 C
Mellon, Andrew William, Am. politician (1855–1937), 1923 F
Mellon, Paul, Am. executive art collector and benefactor (b. 1907), 1937 S
Mellor, David, B. Conservative politician (b. 1949), 1992 J
Melville, Herman, Am. author (1819–91), 1819 Z, 1846 U, 1851 U, 1891 Z
Melville, Jean, Am. film director, 1949 W
Memel, Lithuania: Germans capture, 1915 B; under Allied Control, 1920 B; seized from Allies by Lithuania, 1923 A, B; German–Lithuanian arbitration treaty, 1928 A; Germany annexes, 1939 C
Memento Mori (M. Spark), 1959 U
Mémoires d'Outre-tombe (Chateaubriand), 1848 U
Memoirs of an Aesthete (H. Acton), 1948 U
Memory of Snow and Dust (B. Breytenbach), 1989 U
Memphis, Tenn., US
  Martin Luther King assassinated, 1968 D
Men and Power (Lord Beaverbrook), 1956 Q
Men at Arms (E. Waugh), 1952 U
Men without Women (E. Hemingway), 1927 U
Menai Straits, England: suspension bridge, 1819 P; tubular railway bridge, 1849 P
Mencken, H. L., Am. critic (1880–1956), 1919 Q
Mendeléev, Dimitry Ivanovich, R. chemist (1834–1907), 1834 Z, 1869 P, 1907 Z
Mendel, Gregor, Aus. biologist (1822–82): establishes laws of heredity, 1866 P; work of, rediscovered, 1900 P
Mendelssohn, Erich, Am. architect (1887–1953), 1935 S
Mendelssohn, Moses, G. philosopher (1729–86), 1767 R, 1781 R, 1783 R, 1785 U
Mendelssohn-Bartholdy, Felix, G. musician (1809–1847), 1809 Z, 1826 T, 1829 T, 1833 T, 1842 T, 1846 T, 1844 T, 1847 Z; establishes Leipzig Conservatoire, 1843 T; as conductor, 1839 T
Menderes, Adnam, Turk. politician (1899–1961), 1955 M, 1960 E
Mendès-France, Pierre, F. politician (1907–1982), 1907 Z, 1982 Z; as premier, 1954 F; resigns, 1955 B
Mendoza, Eduardo, Sp. author (b. 1943), 1988 U
Meneghini, G. B. *See* Callas, Maria
Menelek, King of Ethiopia (1889–1911), 1889 L, 1891 B, 1897 E; as Menelek of Shoa revolts against Johannes IV, 1888 M; denounces Italian claims, 1891 B
Menem, Carlos Saul, President of Argentina (b. 1935), 1989 E
Mengele, Josef, G. doctor (1911–79), 1985 F
Mengistu Haile Mariam, Colonel, Ethiop. politician (b. 1937), 1977 B, 1991 E
Menon, Krishna. *See* Krishna Menon
Menotti, Gian Carlo, It. musician (b. 1911), 1942 T, 1950 T, 1954 T, 1968 T
Menschenhass und Reue (A. Kötzebue), 1797 W
Mensheviks. *See under* Political Parties
Menshikov, Prince Alexander, R. emissary to Turkey (1787–1869), 1853 D, E
Mental Evolution in Man (G. T. Romanes), 1888 R
Mental Health, treatment of, 1792 O, 1893 P, 1953 O, 1959 O. *See also* Asylums
Mental Patients, Royal Commission on, 1953 O
  system of detention reformed, 1959 O
Mentana, Italy, Garibaldi's defeat at, 1867 L
Mentone, France, purchased from Monaco, 1862 B
Menuhin, Yehudi, Lord Menuhin, Am.-born B. violinist (b. 1916), 1916 Z
Menzel, Adolph Friedrich Erdmann von, G. artist (1815–1905), 1815 Z, 1875 S, 1905 Z
Menzies, Sir Robert Gordon, Austral. Liberal statesman (1894–1978), 1894 Z, 1954 A, 1966 A, 1978 Z ; becomes premier, 1939 D; forms new coalition, 1949 M, 1954 E, 1961 M
Mephisto (A. Mnouchkine), 1981 W
Mercer, David, B. dramatist (1928–80), 1970 W
Merchant Shipping:
  in Britain, contract for Cunard Q4 liner, 1964 M
    control of, 1875 O
    construction in wartime, 1940 Y, 1941 Y, 1942 Y, 1943 Y
    convoy system for, 1917 O
    'Liberty' ships, 1943 O
    reforms in, 1906 O
    registered tonnage, 1786 Y, 1806 Y, 1826 Y 1836 Y, 1846 Y, 1856 Y, 1866 Y, 1876 Y, 1886 Y, 1896 Y, 1914 Y, 1919 Y, 1926 Y, 1939 Y, 1946 Y, 1951 Y, 1964 Y
    wartime losses, 1914 Y, 1915 Y, 1916 Y, 1917 Y, 1918 Y, 1939 L, Y, 1940 J, Y, 1941 Y, 1942 Y, 1943 Y, 1944 Y, 1945 A, Y
  in US, conditions in, improved, 1915 A
    Wilson arms, without Congressional authority, 1917 C
  world tonnages, 1914 Y, 1919 Y, 1939 Y, 1946 Y, 1951 Y, 1964 Y
  losses in war, 1918 Y, 1945 Y
  Japan launches *Nisseki Maru* supertanker, 1971 P
Merchant, Ismail, Ind. film producer (b. 1936), 1992 W
Mercian Hymns (G. Hill), 1971 U
Mercier, Cardinal, Belg., 1916 L
Merckx, Eddie, Belg. cyclist (b. 1945), 1972 X
Mercure, Paris journal, 1770 V
Mercury, Freddy (born Frederick Bulsara), B. rock star (1946–91), 1991 L, 1992 W
Mercury, planet, rotation of, 1889 P
  photographed, 1974 P
Meredith, George, B. author (1828–1909), 1828 Z, 1859 U, 1862 U, 1879 U, 1885 U, 1902 Z
Mérimée, Prosper, F. author (1803–70), 1803 Z, 1830 U, 1840 U, 1847 W, 1870 Z
Merrill, John Ogden, Am. architect, 1952 S
Mersah Matruh, Libya, British retreat to, 1942 F
Mery, Russia, Afghanistan cedes, 1884 A
Méryon, Charles, F. artist (1821–68), 1852 S
Merz, Mario, It. sculptor (b. 1925), 1970 S
Mesmer, Franz Anton, Aus. physician (1733–1815), 1778 O, 1815 Z
Mesopotamia, Syria: Anglo-German agreement on, 1914 F; surrenders to Britain, 1915 F; Allied offensive, 1916 H; British offensive, 1916 M; Report of Commission on, 1917 O; mandate of, to Britain, 1920 D
Messager, André, F. musician (1853–1929), 1919 T
Messages of the Late Miss R.V. Troussova (Kurtag), 1981 T
Messeniennes, Les (J. Delavigne), 1818 U
Messerschmitt, Willy, G. aircraft designer (1898–1978), 1898 Z, 1978 Z
Messiaen, Olivier, F. musician (1908–92), 1908 Z, 1969 T, 1983 T, 1992 Z
Messiah (G. F. Klopstock), 1773 U
Messina, Sicily, US troops occupy, 1943 H
Messines, France, battle, 1917 F
Messmer, Pierre Auguste Joseph, Prime Minister of France (b. 1916), 1972 G
Messner, Professor Zbigniew, Prime Minister of Poland (b. 1939), 1985 L
Metakritik (J. G. Herder), 1799 R
Metamorphose der Pflanzen (Goethe), 1790 O
Metamorphosis (R. Strauss), 1945 T
Metaphysical Foundations of the Theory of Right (Kant), 1797 R
Metaphysical School of painting, 1917 S
Metaphysics (R. Lotze), 1841 R
Metaphysics of Logical Positivism (Bergmann), 1955 R
Metargon, discovered, 1898 P
Metasinfonia (Panufnik), 1978 T
Metaxas, John, Greek general and politician (1871–1941), becomes premier, 1936 D
Meteorites, study of, 1961 P
Meteorological Society, Royal, 1850 P
Meteorological Stations, 1937 P
Meteorology, studies in, 1897 P
  ozone layer hole detected, 1985 P
Meteors, size of, investigated, 1923 P
Methene, British imports from Sahara, 1961 P
Methicillin, anti-biotic drug, 1960 P
Méthode de nomenclature chimique (A. Lavoisier), 1787 P
Methodism and Politics in British Society, 1750–1850 (D. Hempton), 1984 Q
Methodists. *See under* Religious Denominations
Methods of Ethics (H. Sidgwick), 1874 R
Methuen, Paul, lord Methuen, B. soldier (1845–1932), 1899 M
Metric system, Britain's proposed change to, 1965 O
Metrication Board in Britain, to be wound up, 1979 J
Metro, A Novel of the Moscow Underground (A. Kaletski), 1985 U
Metropolitan Police Force, London, founded, 1829 O
Metternich, Clemens, Prince, Aus. statesman (1773–1859), 1773 Z; as chief minister, 1809 H; agrees to peace conference, 1813 F; mediates Prussian armistice with France, 1813 F; presides over German confederation, 1816 L, 1819 J, L; presides at Vienna Conference, 1820 E; Six articles for reactionary government, 1832 F
Metz, Moselle, N.E. France, France surrenders, 1870 K
Metzinger, Jean, F. artist (1883–1956), 1912 S
Meuse, River, France: Germans cross, 1914 H; French offensive near, 1916 M
Mexico City, Mexico: US captures, 1847 J; occupied by Constitutionalist Party, 1914 H; University, 1952 S; population, 1960 Y, 1970 Y, 1990 Y
  treaty prohibiting nuclear weapons from Latin America, 1967 B
  Aztec great temple foundations discovered, 1978 Q
  earthquake, 1985 J
Mexico, New, US: US negotiations for purchase, 1846 D; US obtains, 1846 H, 1848 E; admitted to statehood on conditions, 1911 H
Mexico:
  revolt against Spain, 1810 J
  declares independence, 1813 L
  fresh proposals for independence, 1821 B
  Emperor of, elected, 1822 E
  becomes a republic, 1823 C
  Britain recognises independence, 1824 M
  Texas becomes independent of, 1836 C, D
  US war with, 1846 D, E
  Convention, following suspension of foreign debts, 1861 K
  withdrawal of French troops in, 1865 K
  coffee production in, 1909 Y
  US punitive expedition to, 1916 C, F
  Britain resumes diplomatic relations, 1941 K

population, 1971 Y, 1991 Y
international loans to, 1982 L, 1983 B
Contadora Group, 1983 G
illiteracy, 1983 Y
UN Conference on Population, 1984 O
cotton production, 1984 Y
urbanization, 1985 Y
Presidential election, 1988 G
Meyer, Harry Martin, Am. scientist (b. 1928), 1966 P
Meyer, John Rudolf, Swi. mountaineer, 1811 P
Meyer, Konrad Ferdinand, Swi. poet (1825–98), 1887 U
Meyer, Nathan, Lord Rothschild, B. financier (1840–1915), 1898 O
Meyerbeer, Giacomo (Jakob Liebmann Beer), G. musician (1791–1864), 1791 Z, 1820 T, 1836 T, 1849 T, 1851 T, 1864 Z, 1937 T
Meyrin, near Geneva, Switzerland, international nuclear research laboratory near, 1953 P
Miall, Edward, B. Liberal politician (1809–81), 1844 O
Miami Vice, television series, 1984 W
Michael II, King of Serbia (1839–42), 1839 F
Michael III, Prince of Serbia (1860–68), 1868 F
Michael, King of Roumania, abdicates, 1947 M
Michaelis, George, G. Chancellor (1857–1943), 1917 G
Michaux, Henri, F. author (1899–1984), 1927 U, 1932 U, 1943 U
Michaux, Pierre, F. manufacturer of bicycles (d. 1883), 1867 P
Michelangelo, It. artist (1475–1564)
Pietà attacked, 1972 S
500th anniversary of birth, 1975 S
Michelet, Jules, F. historian (1798–1874), 1798 Z, 1933 Q, 1847 Q, 1874 Z
Michigan, state, US, becomes a US state, 1837 A
Micklem, Nathaniel, B. theologian (1888–1976), 1941 R
Micro-wave laser, 1960 P
Microgeology (C. Ehrenberg), 1854 P
Microphone, invented, 1878 P
Microscopes:
'flying spot', 1951 P
ion, 1956 P
reflecting, 1947 P
study of, 1770 P
ultramicroscope, 1903 P
Microscopic Investigations in the Structure ... of Plants and Animals (T. Schwann), 1839 P
Microscopic study, 1770 P
Mid-Victorian Britain, 1851–1870 (G. Best), 1971 Q
Middle Age of Mrs. Eliot, The (A. Wilson), 1958 U
Middle East:
US 6th Fleet sails for Mediterranean, 1957 D
concentration of Turkish troops on Syrian borders, 1957 J
Syria declares state of emergency, 1957 K
Dulles warns Russia against attacking Turkey, 1957 K
Khrushchev appeals to Labour and Socialist Parties to prevent US aggression, 1957 K
Lebanon, amnesty in, 1958 M
Baghdad *coup*, 1958 G
Lebanon requests US troops, 1958 G
British paratroops land in Jordan, 1958 G
leave Jordan, 1958 L
Israeli jets raid Syria, 1966 G
Israeli and Syrian forces clash around Sea of Galilee, 1966 H
Israeli forces attack Hebron area of Jordan, 1966 L
UN censure of Israel, 1966 L
Arab Defence Council co-ordinates military response, 1966 M
border clashes around Lake Tiberias, 1967 D
UN peace-keeping force withdrawn from Israeli–Egyptian border, 1967 E
Arab League Council declares attack on one Arab state would be attack on all, 1967 E
army reserves called up, 1967 E
Gulf of Aqaba closed to Israeli shipping, 1967 E
ceasefire in Arab–Israeli war, 1967 F
Six-Day War, 1967 F
Israel wins control of Sinai Peninsula, Gaza strip and Old Jerusalem, 1967 F
USSR breaks off diplomatic relations with Israel, 1967 F
UN orders Israel to desist from unifying Jerusalem, 1967 G
battle between Israeli and Jordanian forces, 1968 A
Israel bombs Palestinian guerrilla bases in Jordan, 1968 H
potash plant on Dead Sea attacked, 1968 L
bridges in Jordan blown up, 1968 L
Iraqi artillery shells Israeli villages, 1968 M
Iraqi bases in Jordan bombed, 1968 M
Israeli airliner in Athens attacked, 1968 M
Beirut airport bombed by Israel, 1968 M
France bans sale of military supplies to Israel, 1969 A
Iraq executes men accused of spying for Israel, 1969 A
Arab guerrillas attack Eilat, 1969 D
Israeli attack on Aqaba, 1969 D
King Hussein of Jordan's peace plan, 1969 D
UN talks on Middle East, 1969 D
Arab League plans holy war against Israel, 1969 H
Israel attacks UAR military bases, 1969 J
US peace plan, 1969 K
Israeli positions in Sinai shelled, 1969 L
air battle over Suez Canal, 1969 L
US calls on Israel to withdraw from occupied territories, 1969 M
Israeli attack on UAR positions around Suez, 1969 M
severe fighting between Israel and Syria on Golan Heights, 1970 A
Israeli supply ship sunk by UAR, 1970 B
UAR minesweepers sunk by Israel, 1970 B
Israeli air raid near Cairo kills civilians, 1970 B
Nile delta bombing, 1970 D
Israeli school bus ambushed, 1970 E
clashes/ceasefire between Jordan and Palestine, 1970 F
'Rogers Plan' proposal, 1970 F
UAR and Israel accept 'Rogers Plan', 1970 F
90 day truce, 1970 H
representatives meet UN mediator, 1970 H
Syria invades Jordan, 1970 J
indirect peace talks resumed, 1971 A
Egypt extends ceasefire and offers to re-open Suez Canal if Israel withdraws from Sinai, 1971 B
Middle East ceasefire expires, 1971 C
heavy fighting between Jordanian army and Palestinian guerrillas, 1971 G
Israeli attack on Lebanon, 1972 B
autonomous Palestinian state proposed, 1972 C
Japanese terrorists kill 26 Israelis at Lod airport, 1972 E
Israeli Olympic team members murdered, 1972 J
battle on Golan Heights, 1972 L
air battle between Israel and Syria, 1973 J, 1974 D
full-scale war as Egypt and Syria attack Israel, 1973 K
Soviet military supplies airlifted to Arab states, 1973 K
Iraq, Saudi Arabia and Jordan join war against Israel, 1973 K
Israel invades Syria via Golan Heights, 1973 K
Israel invades Egypt, 1973 K
US military aid for Israel, 1973 K
Arab states put pressure on US Middle East policy, 1973 K
Moscow meeting agrees plan to stop Middle East war, 1973 K
UN ceasefire ignored, 1973 K
Syria accepts UN ceasefire, 1973 K
US forces on alert, 1973 K
Yom Kippur War, 1973 K
Israel and Egypt accept US plan for ceasefire observance, 1973 L
Geneva Peace Conference, 1973 M
Israeli-Syrian air battle over Golan Heights, 1974 D
Israeli troops storm school at Ma'alot, 1974 E
Israel bombs Palestinian refugee camps in Lebanon, 1974 E
Israel and Syria agree to Golan Heights ceasefire, 1974 E
Israeli withdrawal agreement with Egypt, 1975 J
part of Israeli-occupied Sinai returned to Egypt, 1975 K
Syrian forces enter Lebanon, 1976 E
Arabs call for Syrian withdrawal from Lebanon, 1976 F
Arab Protection Force controls Lebanon, 1976 F
Libya–Egypt border war, 1977 G
Israeli raid on Southern Lebanon, 1980 D
Syrian troops massed on Jordanian border, 1980 L
Britons advised to leave Lebanon, 1981 D
US peace envoy's tour, 1981 E
Syria shells Beirut, 1981 E
Israelis attack Palestinian areas in Beirut, 1981 G
Israel agrees to UN peace-keeping force in Sinai, 1982 A
Israeli forces invade Lebanon, 1982 F
Israeli and Syrian forces clash in Lebanon, 1982 F
Israeli forces defeat Syrian armour around Lake Karoun, 1982 F
Israeli forces surround PLO guerrillas in W. Beirut, 1982 F
Israel demands surrender of PLO guerrillas, 1982 F
UN Resolution 242 accepted by PLO, 1982 G
US refuses to recognize PLO, 1982 G
Israeli bombardment of Beirut intensifies, 1982 H
Israel accepts US plan to evacuate PLO guerrillas from Beirut, 1982 H
Brezhnev peace plan, 1982 J
Israel rejects US peace proposals, 1982 J
Israeli troops withdrawn from W. Beirut, 1982 J
French, Italian and US peace-keeping force in Beirut, 1982 J
Arafat–Jordanian talks on proposed Palestinian state confederated with Jordan, 1982 K
Lebanese army moves through Beirut, 1982 K
bomb attack on Israeli military headquarters in Tyre, 1982 L, 1983 L
Beirut massacre, 1983 B
US halts sale of F-16 fighters to Israel, 1983 C
US peace plan collapses, 1983 D

bomb explosion at US embassy in Beirut, 1983 D
US plan for simultaneous withdrawal of Israeli and Syrian forces from Lebanon, 1983 E
withdrawal of Israeli forces from Lebanon, 1983 E, G, J
Syrian tanks besiege PLO bases in Lebanon, 1983 F
civil war in Chouf mountains, 1983 J
ceasefire agreed in Lebanon, 1983 J
suicide attack on UN peace-keeping force in Beirut, 1983 K
National Reconciliation Conference on Lebanon, Geneva, 1983 K
PLO and Israel exchange prisoners of war, 1983 L
Arafat and supporters evacuated from Lebanon, 1983 M
Kerr shot dead in Beirut by pro-Iranian group, 1984 A
curfew imposed as Shi'a Muslim and Druze militia overrun W. Beirut, 1984 B
US marines withdraw from Beirut, 1984 B
Lebanon reconciliation conference, Lausanne, 1984 C
Lebanese army takes over positions in Beirut from militias, 1984 G
US embassy in Beirut bombed, 1984 J
Jordan–Egypt peace initiative talks for West Bank, 1984 M
Israeli withdrawal from occupied Lebanon, 1985 A, F
Israeli Army removes Lebanese prisoners to Israel, 1985 D
Palestinian prisoners and Israeli soldiers exchanged, 1985 E
Shi'ite Moslem gunmen hijack TWA jet, 1985 F
PLO headquarters attacked, 1985 K
Achille Lauro cruise liner hijacked, 1985 K
Shultz peace mission, 1988 B
Jordan announces plans to cut legal and administrative ties with occupied West Bank, 1988 G
PLO Parliament in exile declares independent state of Palestine, 1988 L
US resumes contacts with PLO, 1988 M
Lebanese government resigns over economic situation, 1992 E
Palestinians deported from Israel, 1992 M
See also Egypt; Israel; Jordan; Lebanon; Palestine; Suez
Middle Years, The (H. James), 1895 U, 1917 U
Middle-classes, British, survey of, 1949 O
Middleburg, S. Africa, 1901 B
Middlemarch (G. Eliot), 1871 U
Midhat Pasha, Turk. politician (1822–84), 1876 E, 1877 B
Midland Bank, taken over by Hong Kong and Shangai Banking Corporation, 1992 O
Midlothian campaign, Gladstone's, 1879 L
Midnight's Children (S. Rushdie), 1981 U
Midway Islands, Pacific, battle in, 1942 F
Mies van der Rohe, Ludwig, G. architect (1886–1969), 1886 Z, 1968 S, 1969 Z
Mietne, Poland, students demand restoration of crucifixes in classrooms, 1984 C
MI5 and MI6, Security Services Act, 1989 O
Mignet, François, F. historian (1796–1884), 1796 Z, 1884 Z
Miguel Street (V. S. Naipaul), 1959 U
Miguel, Dom Maria Evariste, Portug. pretender (1802–56), 1824 D, 1826 E, 1828 F, 1832 G; Spanish support for, 1826 M; as lieutenant in Portugal, 1827 G; as Regent, 1828 B; followers of, defeated, 1833 G; surrenders and abdicates, 1834 D; supporters of, rise, 1846 E
Miki, Takeo, Jap. Premier (b. 1907), 1974 L, 1976 M
Miklas, General, Hung. politician, 1945 A
Miklas, Wilhelm, Aus. president, 1928 M
Mikoyan, Anastas Ivanovich, R. politician (1895–1978), opens Havana exhibition, 1960 B; visits Cuba, 1962 L; becomes president of USSR, 1964 G; is replaced, 1965 M
Mikrokosmos (R. Lotze), 1856 R
Mikulic, Branko, Yugos. politician (b. 1928), 1988 M
Milan III, Prince of Serbia, 1839 F
Milan IV, Prince, later King, of Serbia (1868–89), 1868 F, 1882 C, 1889 C, 1901 B
Milan, Italy:
Napoleon enters, 1796 E
Murat occupies, 1800 F
Napoleon is crowned in, 1805 E
Brera Gallery in, 1806 S
Napoleon issues decrees against British trade, 1807 M
revoked, 1810 L
Peace, between Sardinia and Austria, 1849 H
liberated by French troops, 1859 F
People's Bank, 1866 O
Socialist International meets, 1952 K
Pirelli Building, 1958 S
Banco Ambrosiano, liquidation of, 1982 H
Mildenhall, Suffolk, England, Anglo-Saxon treasure hoard at, 1942 Q
Mile, The, Bannister's record, 1954 X
Miles, Bernard, Lord Miles, B. actor and producer (1907–91), 1959 W
Milhaud, Darius, F. musician (1892–1974), 1920 T, 1930 T, 1940 T, 1946 T, 1953 T, 1954 T
Milinkov, Paul, R. Liberal, 1905 E, 1917 C
Militant Tendency, 1980 C
Military Conventions:
Anglo-French, 1905 D, 1906 A
Franco-Belgian, 1920 J
Franco-Polish, 1922 J
Franco-Prussian discussions for, 1911 H
Germano-Turkish, 1913 K
opposed by Britain and France, 1913 M
Military and Political Consequences of Atomic Energy (P. Blackett), 1948 O
Militia:
in Britain, 1786 F. *See also* Local Defence Volunteers
in France, National Guard, 1789 G
Milk:
evaporated, 1847 P
powdered, 1855 P
Milky Way, The, 1892 P
Mill on the Floss, The (G. Eliot), 1860 U
Mill, James, B. utilitarian philosopher (1773–1836), 1821 O 1829 Q
Mill, John Stuart, B. philosopher (1806–73), 1806 Z, 1843 R, 1844 R, 1848 O, 1859 O, 1860 O, 1862 R, 1865 R, 1867 R, 1869 R, 1873 U, Z
Mill, boring, 1774 P
Millais, Sir John Everett, B. artist (1829–96), 1829 Z, 1848 S, 1850 S, 1896 Z
Millar, Fergus Graham Bartholomew, B. historian (b. 1935), 1977 Q
Mille, Agnes de, Am. choreographer, 1940 T
Mille, Cecil Blount de, Am. film director (1881–1959), 1881 Z, 1915 W, 1927 W
Miller, Arthur, Am. dramatist (b. 1915), 1915 Z, 1949 W, 1953 W, 1955 W, 1964 W, 1968 W
Miller, Henry Valentine, Am. author (1891–1980), 1891 Z, 1962 U, 1980 Z
Miller, Hugh, B. author and geologist (1802–56), 1838 P, 1846 U
Miller, Joachim, Am. author (?1841–1913), 1871 U
Miller, William, Am. leader of Second Adventists (1782–1849), 1831 R, 1842 R
Millerand, Alexandre, F. politician, President of France, 1920 H, 1924 F
Millesino, N. Italy, Austrian defeat at, 1796 D
Millet, Jean François, F. artist (1814–75), 1831 S, 1846 S, 1848 S, 1857 S, 1859 S
Millett, Kate, Am. author (b. 1934), 1970 R
Millikan, Robert Andrews, Am. physicist (1868–1953), 1925 P, 1933 P
Milling-machine, universal, 1862 P
Mills, C. Wright, Am. author (1916–62), 1959 O
Mills, Mrs. Barbara Jean Lyon, B. lawyer (b. 1940), 1992 O
Milman, Henry Hart, B. churchman and author (1791–1868), 1829 Q, 1855 Q
Milne, Alan Alexander, B. journalist and author (1882–1956), 1922 W, 1926 U
Milne, Edward Arthur, B. mathematician (1896–1950), 1937 P
Milner, Alfred, Lord Milner, B. administrator (1854–1925), 1899 C, 1916 M, 1918 C; as high commissioner for S. Africa, 1897 H; policy criticised, 1903 B; as war secretary, 1918 D; conversations with Zaghlul on Egypt, 1920 H
Milner, John, B. Roman Catholic priest, Bishop of Castabala (1752–1826), 1810 R
Milosh (Obrenovich), of Serbia, 1835 N; Sultan limits authority of, 1838 M; abdicates, 1839 F; restored, 1858 M
Milosevic, Slobodan, President of Serbia (b. 1941), 1990 M, 1992 M
Milosz, Czeslaw, Pol.-born Am. author (b. 1911), 1968 U
Milstein, Cesar, Argent.-born B. biologist (b. 1927), 1927 Z, 1975 P
Milton (W. Blake), 1804 U
Mimas, a satellite, discovered, 1789 P
Mind in Chains, The, 1937 O
Mind in Evolution (L. T. Hobhouse), 1901 R
Mindszenty, Cardinal, Hungarian (1892–1975), 1971 J; arrested, 1948 M; released, 1956 K
Mines, Coal:
in Britain, royal commission on, 1842 H
inspection, 1850 O
government control of, 1916 M
strikes, 1921 L, 1926 E, L
government enquiry, 1925 G
ballot, to press for wage increase, 1935 L
nationalisation of, 1946 E, 1947 A
in France, general strike, 1901 N
Mines, Diamond, in Tanganyika, 1946 P
in Transvaal, Chinese labour for, 1903 L
Mines, School of, London, 1850 O
Mines, explosive, 1915 P
magnetic, 1939 L
Minghetti, Marco, It. premier (1818–86), 1873 J, 1874 E, 1876 C
Mingus, Charlie, Am. jazz musician (1922–79), 1922 Z, 1979 Z
Minié, C. E., F. gunsmith, 1849 P
Minkowski, Herman, G. mathematician (1864–1909), 1908 P
Minna of Barnhelm (Lessing), 1767 W
Minneapolis, US, Institute of Art, 1974 S
Minnelieder, 1803 Q
Minnesota, state, US: becomes a US state, 1858 E; Sioux rising in, 1862 H
Minoan culture, discovery of, 1900 Q
Minorca, Island, Spain: ceded to Britain, 1763 B; Spanish capture, 1782 B; Spain retains, 1783 J; Britain captures, 1798 L
Minsk, Russia: Germans take, 1941 F; Russians recapture, 1944 G

Minter, Alan, B. boxer (b. 1951), World Middleweight title, 1980 X
Mintoff, 'Dom' (Dominic), Prime Minister of Malta (b. 1916), 1971 F, 1972 A, 1979 V, 1984 M
Mir Kasim, Nabwab of Murshidabad, 1763 G
Mirabeau, Gabriel Honoré de Riquetti, Comte de, F. statesman (1749–91), 1772 O; as Louis XVI's agent, 1790 E; elected President of Assembly, 1791 A; death, 1791 D, Z
Miracles (C. S. Lewis), 1947 R
Miracles in the New Testament (J. M. Thompson), 1911 R
Miraculous Story, A (Grupa Chwilowa), 1984 W
Miramar (N. Mahfouz), 1967 U
Miranda (Fogazzaro), 1874 U
Miranda v. Arizona, decision in, 1966 O
Miranda, Francisco de, Venez. politician (1750–1816), 1811 G, 1812 G
Miró, Joan, Sp. artist (1893–1983), 1893 Z, 1922 S, 1937 S, 1959 S, 1983 Z
Mirror on Which to Dwell, A (E. Carter), 1975 T
Mirza, Iskander, President of Pakistan, 1958 K
Misérables, Les (V. Hugo), 1862 U
Mishima, Yukio (born Hiraoka Kimitake, 1925–70), Jap. author, 1966 U, 1970 U
Miss Julie (Strindberg), 1888 W
Missiles:
  Argentine, sink British destroyer, 1982 E
  Bloodhound, 1964 D
  Blue Streak, 1960 D
    launched, 1964 P
  Cruise. *See* Cruise missile
  guided, vessels for, 1956 G
    US to make available to Britain, 1957 C
  Pershing. *See* Pershing missile
  pilotless, radio-controlled, 1946 P
  Polaris, bases in England, Bulganin's note on, 1958 C
    for Bundeswehr, Russia protests at, 1960 G
    agreement from US to provide to Britain, in place of Skybolt, 1962 M
    de Gaulle rejects offer of, 1963 A
    US recommends surface ships of NATO fleet should carry, 1963 B
    Anglo-US agreement on, 1963 D
  Russian, in Cuba, 1962 M, L
  USSR halts SS-20 deployment, 1982 C
  USSR medium-range, 1981 L
  V2 rockets, 1942 P, 1944 J, 1945 C
  See also Nuclear Warfare; Rockets
Missionary Societies:
  American Bible Society, 1816 R
  American Sunday School Union, 1824 R
  Baptist, British, 1792 R
  British and Foreign Bible Society, 1804 R
  China Inland Mission, 1865 R
  Church Army, 1882 R
  Church Missionary Society, 1799 R
  International Missionary Council, 1961 R
  Jerusalem conference on, 1928 R
  Methodist, British, 1813 R
  Missions to Africa, 1841 R
  Presbyterian, Britain, 1846 R
  Religious Tract Society, 1799 R
  World Conference, 1911 R
  World Student Christian Federation, 1895 R
Mississippi River, US, navigation rights, 1795 K
Mississippi state, US, 1955 O; is admitted to Union, 1817 M; as a Confederate state, 1861 B; arrest of sheriff in connexion with murder of Civil Rights workers, 1964 M
Missolonghi, Greece: Byron's death, 1824 D; falls to Ibrahim, 1826 D
Missouri Compromise, 1820 C; repealed, 1854 E
Missouri state, US, enters Union as a slave state, 1821 H
Mr and Mrs Ossie Clark and Percy (D. Hockney), 1970 S
Mister Behram (G. Patel), 1988 W
Mr. Bolfrey (J. Bridie), 1943 W
Mr. Midshipman Easy (F. Marryat), 1836 U
Mr. Norris Changes Trains (C. Isherwood), 1935 U
Mr. Perrin and Mr. Trail (H. Walpole), 1911 U
Mr. W. H. (L. Hotson), 1964 Q
Mr. Weston's Good Wine (T. F. Powys), 1928 U
Mistral, Frédéric, F. poet (1830–1914), 1830 Z, 1854 U, 1914 Z
Mrs. Dalloway (V. Woolf), 1925 U
Mrs. Minniver (Jan Struther), 1939 U
Mita, (Luigi) Ciriaco De, Prime Minister of Italy (b. 1928), 1989 E
Mitchell, John N., Am. presidential aide (1913–88), 1975 A
Mitchell, Joni, Canad. singer (b. 1943), 1970 W
Mitchell, Julian, B. author (b. 1935), 1982 W
Mitchell, Margaret, Am. author (1900–49), 1936 U
Mitford, Mary Russell, B. author (1787–1855), 1787 Z, 1824 U, 1855 Z
Mitford, Nancy, B. author (1904–73), 1949 W
Mitford, William, B. historian of Greece (1744–1827), 1784 Q
Mithridates (J. C. Adelung), 1806 Q
Mitscherlich, Eilhardt, G. chemist (1794–1863), 1819 P
Mitsotakis, Constantine, Prime Minister of Greece (b. 1918), 1990 D, 1992 M
Mitteleuropa (F. Neumann), 1915 U
Mitterrand, François Maurice Marie, F. politician and President (b. 1916), 1916 Z, 1965 M, 1974 E, 1984 L
  President, 1981 E, 1988 E
  appoints Mauroy as Premier, 1981 E
  indicates support for Palestine, 1982 C
  Channel Tunnel rail link, 1986 A, B
Mitylene, Greece: Greek victory at, 1824 K; Greece annexes, 1914 F
Mizo, India, Pakistan and China accused of aiding rebels, 1968 F
Mladenov, Petar Toshev, Bulgarian leader (b. 1936), 1989 L, 1990 G
Mnouchkine, Ariane, F. theatre director (b. 1934), 1981 W
Moberly, Sir Walter, B. administrator (1881–1974), 1949 O
Mobiles, invented, 1932 S
Mobulu, Congol. general, deposes Kasavubu, 1965 L
Mobutu Sese Seko (formerly Joseph-Desire Mobutu), President of Zaire (b. 1930), 1971 K, 1991 K
Moby Dick (H. Melville), 1851 U
Model for a Sculpture (G. Baselitz), 1980 S
Modena, Italy, 1797 G
Modern Democracies (J. Bryce), 1921 O
Modern Democratic State (A. D. Lindsay), 1943 O
Modern India: The Origins of an Asian Democracy (J.M. Brown), 1985 Q
Modern Instance, A (W. D. Howells), 1882 U
Modern Love (G. Meredith), 1862 U
Modern Predicament, The (H. J. Paton), 1955 R
Moderne Kapitalismus, Der (W. Sombart), 1920 O
Modernism, condemned, 1907 R
Modigliani, Amedeo, It. artist and sculptor (1884–1920), 1910 S, 1912 S, 1917 S, 1919 S, 1920 S
Modrow, Hans, Prime Minister of East Germany (b. 1928), 1989 L
Mods *v.* Rockers, 1964 C, E
Moeran, Ernest John, B. musician (1894–1950), 1944 T
Moffatt, James, B. translator of Bible (1870–1944), 1913 R
Mogadishu, Somalia:
  rebels overrun, 1991 A
  UN military observers arrive, 1992 G
  operation 'Restore Hope', 1992 M
Mohamed V, Sultan of Turkey (1909–18), 1909 D
Mohammed Ali, Khedive of Syria, 1832 D, F
Mohammed Ali, Pakis. premier, 1953 D
Mohammed Said, Khedive of Egypt (1822–63) 1854 G, 1863 A
Mohammed Said, Pers., forms government, 1950 A
Mohammed Zahir Shah, King of Afghanistan (b. 1914), 1973 G
Mohammed ben Abdullah, 'Mad Mullah', Somali chief, 1899 J
Mohammed, Ali Mahdi, Prime Minister of Somalia, 1991 A
Mohammed, Ali, Shah of Persia, 1908 F
Mohammed, General Murtala, Niger. leader (1938–76), 1975 G, 1976 B
Mohl, Hugo von, G. botanist (1805–72), 1846 P
Mohr, Karl Friedrich, G. pharmacist (1806–79), 1837 P
Moi, Daniel arap, President of Kenya (b. 1924), 1978 H, 1990 B
Moignan, Martine le, B. squash player, 1989 X
Moines de l'Occident (C. de Montalembert), 1860 Q
Moissan, Henri, F. chemist (1852–1907), 1886 P
Mola, Emilio, Sp. general, 1936 G
Moldavia *and* Wallachia, Danubian Principalities, 1858 H, L; become independent from Turkey, 1829 J; Russians quash revolts, 1848 G; Russo-Turkish joint occupation, 1849 E; Russia invades, 1853 G; Austrians occupy, during war, 1854 F, H, M; Vienna Four Points guarantee integrity of, 1854 H; Austria defends in return for guarantee of Italian possessions, 1854 M; guaranteed by powers, 1856 C; powers decide on union between Wallachia and Moldavia, 1858 H
Moldavia, 1812 E; Russians occupy, 1769 J; Russia restores conquests to Turkey, 1792 A; is united with Wallachia, to form Roumania, 1861 M; republic (Bessarabia), 1917 M. *See also* Bessarabia; Roumania; Wallachia
Moldavians, percentage in Soviet population, 1989 Y
Molecules, structure of, 1930 P
Molesworth, Cambridgeshire, England
  Cruise missiles deployed at military base, 1980 F, 1983 G
  anti-Cruise missile protest, 1985 B
Molinari, Ricardo, Argentin. poet (b. 1913), 1943 U
Mollet, Guy, F. Socialist (1905–75), serves under Pleven, 1950 G; forms ministry, 1956 B; resigns, 1957 E
Mollison, Amy. *See* Johnson, Amy
Molotov, Vaycheslay, R. diplomat and politician (1890–1986), 1890 Z, 1942 E, 1956 F, 1986 Z; as foreign minister, 1939 E; in Berlin, 1940 L; at UN Conference, 1945 D; replaced as foreign minister, 1949 C; presides at Prague Conference, 1950 K; refuses to discuss Germany's unification, 1955 L; is expelled from Soviet Central Committee, 1957 G
Molteno, Sir John Charles, S. Afr. politician (1814–1886), 1872 K
Moltke, Helmuth von, Count, G. soldier (1800–91), 1800 Z, 1891 Z

Moltke, Helmuth von, G. general (1848–1916), 1906 A, 1914 J
Moltmann, Jürgen, G. theologian (b. 1926), 1926 Z, 1978 R, 1991 R
Mombasa, Kenya, railway to, 1901 M
Mommsen, Theodor, G. historian (1817–1903), 1817 Z, 1853 Q, 1863 Q, 1871 Q, 1872 Q, 1903 Z
Mona Lisa, theft, 1911 S
Monaco, Principality:
 sells Mentone and Roquebrune to France, 1862 B
Monarchies:
 in Albania, 1828 J
 in Austria-Hungary, dual, 1867 B, F
  question of Hapsburg restoration, 1937 B
 in Belgium, 1830 L, 1831 B, F
  problems of, 1946 B
 in Britain, change in royal style, 1901 H
  renunciation of German titles, 1917 F
 in Bulgaria, 1879 D, 1886 L, 1887 G, 1946 J
 in China, 1912 B
 in France, July, 1830 H
  falls, 1848 B
  Second Empire, 1852 A, M
  hope of restoration ended, 1877 K
 in Greece, 1832 H, 1935 L
  candidates for, 1863 B, C
  plebiscite favours, 1946 J
 in Hanover, 1814 K, 1837 F
 in Hawaii, 1893 B
 in Hungary, 1784 G
 in Italy, under Napoleon, 1805 E, 1808 F
  under Victor Emmanuel, 1860 K
  ends, 1946 F
 in Japan, emperor's authority restored, 1868 A
 in Luxemburg, 1919 K
 in Mexico, 1864 D
 in Montenegro, 1901 H
 in Naples, 1808 F
 in The Netherlands,
  abdication of Queen Juliana, 1980 D
 in Norway, 1814 D, L, 1905 K, L
 in Poland, 1791 E
 in Portugal (Braganza), 1807 L, 1815 F, 1822 J, 1826 D, E, 1834 E, 1910 K, 1919 B
 in Roumania, 1866 B, 1930 F
 in Saxony, 1806 M
 in Serbia, 1882 C
 in Spain, 1802 E, F, 1812 C, 1873 B, D, 1874 L, M
  Duke of Aosta elected to, 1870 L
  Hohenzollern candidate for, 1870 G
  bill for succession, 1947 G
  Franco's announcement on, 1957 G
  restoration, 1975 L
 in Sweden, 1818 B
 in Syria, 1920 C
 in Turkey, 1924 B
 in Tuscany, proposed, 1800 K
 in Westphalia, 1807 H
 See also Abdications
Monasteries:
 Austrian Empire, dissolved, 1781 R
 in Britain, founded, 1862 R
 in France, regulated, 1778 R
 in Italy, dissolved, 1873 G
 in Portugal, suppressed, 1834 R
Monboddo, James Burnett, Lord, B. judge (1714–1799), 1773 Q
Monckton, Walter, Lord Monckton, B. lawyer (1891–1965), report on Rhodesia and Nyasaland, 1960 K
Moncrieff, (Charles Kenneth) Scott, B. translator (1889–1930), 1981 U
Mondale, Walter Frederick, Am. Democrat politician (b. 1928), 1980 H, 1984 L, 1984 G
Monde où l'on s'ennuie, Le (E. Pailleron), 1881 W
Mondovi, Piedmont, N. Italy, Napoleon's victory at, 1796 D
Mondrian, Piet, Du. artist (1872–1944), 1917 S, 1929 S, 1936 S; designs, 1965 S
Monet, Claude Oscar, F. artist (1840–1926), 1840 Z, 1866 S, 1869 S, 1875 S, 1881 S, 1892 S, 1900 S, 1902 S, 1908 S, 1916 S, 1926 Z
 Impression Sunrise, 1874 S
Monetary Trends in the United States and the United Kingdom (M. Friedman), 1981 O
Money, Credit and Commerce (A. Marshall), 1923 O
Mongolia: Russo-Japanese agreement on, 1912 H; declaration on Outer, 1913 L; Stein's expedition to South, 1915 Q; Russian treaty with, 1921 L; independence of Outer, 1945 H; Outer becomes under Soviet control, 1945 J; China regains Inner, 1945 J; free elections, 1990 G
Mongols, The (D. Morgan), 1986 Q
Monier, Joseph, F. gardener and inventor of reinforced concrete (1823–1906), 1849 P, 1877 P
Monitor, television programme, 1959 W
Monk, Meredith, Am. musician (b. 1943), 1988 T
Monk, The (M. G. Lewis), 1795 U
Monk, Thelonius, Am. jazz musician (1920–1982), 1920 Z, 1959 T, 1982 Z
Monkees, The, television series, 1966 W
Monmouth, New Jersey, US, battle, 1778 F
Monnet Plan for French industry, 1946 O
Monnet, Jean, F. statesman (1888–1979), 1888 Z, 1979 Z
Monod, Frédéric, F. Protestant leader (1810–49), 1848 R
Monod, Jacques L., F. biochemist (1910–76), 1910 Z, 1976 Z 1971 P
Monopolies, Mergers and Restrictive Practices (White Paper), 1964 O
Monopolies:
 East India Company's in Indian trade, abolished, 1813 O
 Commission recommends abolition of price maintenance in Britain, 1963 M
Monotype company, laser typesetting, 1976 P
Monotype typesetting machine, 1897 P
Monroe Doctrine, 1823 M; Canning counters, 1824 M; Britain declares is not binding, 1854 E; US resolves to extend, 1912 H; Clark memorandum on, 1930 C
Monroe, James, Am. statesman (1758–1831), 5th President of US (1817–25), 1758 Z; inaugurated, 1817 C; second term, 1821 C
Monroe, Marilyn, Am. film actress (1926–62), 1957 W
Monrovia Group, of heads of African state (Liberia, Togo, Nigeria and Cameroon), 1962 A
Monrovia, Liberia, refugees massacred and US marines sent in, 1990 G
Mons, France: battle, 1914 H; Allies retreat from, 1914 H
Monsarrat, Nicolas, B. author (1910–79), 1951 U
Monsieur Teste (P. Valéry), 1906 U
Mont Blanc, France, climbed, 1787 P
Mont Cenis tunnel, Switzerland, 1871 P
Mont St. Michel and Chartres (H. Adams), 1904 Q
Montagn, John, Earl of Sandwich, B. naval officer (1718–92), 1776 T
Montagu-Chelmsford Report on India, 1918 G
Montague, Charles Edward, B. author (1867–1928), 1922 O
Montale, Eugenio, Ital. poet (1896–1981), 1896 Z, 1981 Z
Montalembert, Charles de, F. author (1810–70), 1810 Z, 1860 Q, 1870 Z
Montana, state, US: becomes US territory, 1864 E; created a state, 1889 B; returns first woman member of Congress, 1916 L
Monte Bello Islands, N.W. Australia, British atom bomb tests at, 1952 P
Monte Cassino, Italy: monastery bombed, 1944 B; assault on, 1944 C; falls, 1944 E
Montenegro, Yugoslavia: Russian intrigues in, 1767 N; frontiers fixed, 1858 L; declares war on Turkey, 1876 G; enlargement and independence of, 1878 C, G; occupies Dulcigno, 1880 L; proclaimed an independent kingdom, 1910 H; Turkey is warned to withdraw troops from frontier, 1911 E; Turkish troops withdrawn, 1911 K; is united with Serbia, 1918 L; votes for union with Yugoslavia, 1919 D. *See also* Yugoslavia
Montero, Juan, Chil. president, 1931 G
Monte Video, Uruguay: Portuguese attack on, 1775 C; *Graf Spee* scuttled off, 1939 M
Montgolfier, Jacques Etienne, F. balloonist (1745–1799), 1783 P
Montgolfier, Michel, F. balloonist (1740–1810), 1783 P
Montgomery, Albama, US: Congresses at, to form Confederate states, 1861 B; Civil Rights procession to, 1965 C
Montgomery, Bernard Law, Viscount Montgomery, B. soldier (1887–1976), 1887 Z, 1976 Z; commands 8th Army, 1942 H; breaks through Mareth Line, 1943 C
Month in the Country, A (I. Turgeniev), 1872 U
Montherlant, Henry de, F. author (1896–1972), 1896 Z, 1936 U, 1963 W, 1972 Z
Montini, Giovanni, It. Cardinal (1897–1978), Pope Paul VI , 1897 Z, 1963 F, 1978 Z; *see* Paul VI
Montiori, Eugenio, It. architect, 1950 S
Montluçon, France, peace with Vendans at, 1800 A
Montmorin de St. Hérem, Armand Marc, Comte de, F. diplomat (1745–92), 1787 K; becomes foreign minister, 1787 B
Montpensier, Antoine Marie Philipe Louis, Duc de (1824–90), 1846 K
Montreal, Canada: rebellion in, 1849 D; Commonwealth trade conference at, 1958 J
 Expo 67, 1967 D
 de Gaulle visits, 1967 G
Montreux, Switzerland: Convention, 1937 E; World Jewish Congress at, 1948 R
Monty Python's Flying Circus, television series, 1969 W
Monument for V. Tatlin (D. Flavin), 1969 S
Monumenta Germaniae Historica (ed. Pertz), 1826 Q
Monumenti antichi inediti (J. J. Winckelmann), 1767 Q
Monywa, on Chindwin River, Burma, 14th Army takes, 1945 A
Moody, Dwight Lyman, Am. evangelist (1837–99), 1870 R, 1873 R
Moody, Helen Wills, Am. tennis player (b. 1905), 1990 X
Moon and Sixpence, The (W. S. Maugham), 1919 U
Moon is Down, The (J. Steinbeck), 1942 U
Moon, The (Wilkins and Moore), 1956 P
Moon, The:
 photographs, 1851 P
  by Lunik III, 1959 P
  by satellite, 1964 P
 volcanic eruption of, 1958 P

Lunik II reaches, 1959 P
space research for flights to, 1963 K
dark side photographed, 1966 P
first soft landing, 1966 P
Luna programme, 1966 P, 1970 P, 1975 P
Surveyor I, 1966 P
manned mission to, 1968 P
manned landing, 1969 G, P
Apollo XIII mission aborted, 1970 P
Moon, William Least-heat, author, 1983 U
Moonstone, The (W. Collins), 1868 U
Moore, Brian, Canad. author (b. 1921), 1988 U
Moore, George Augustus, B. novelist (1852–1933), 1852 Z, 1885 U, 1894 U, 1895 U, 1914 U, 1916 U, 1921 U, 1933 Z
Moore, George Edward, B. philosopher (1873–1958), 1903 B
Moore, Henry, B. sculptor (1898–1986), 1898 Z, 1926 S, 1940 S, 1941 S, 1943 S, 1945 S, 1947 S, 1948 S, 1953 S, 1957 S, 1958 S, 1968 S, 1974 S, 1986 Z
Moore, Michael Kenneth, Prime Minister of New Zealand (b. 1949), 1990 J
Moore, Patrick Alfred Caldwell, B. astronomer (b. 1923), 1956 P
Moore, Sara Jane, Am. citizen, attempts assassination of US President Ford, 1975 J
Moore, Sir John, B. soldier (1761–1809), 1809 A
Moore, Thomas, B. poet (1779–1852), 1779 Z, 1807 T, 1852 Z
Moorehead, Alan, B. historian (b. 1910), 1952 O
Moral Man and Immoral Society (K. Niebuhr), 1934 K
Moral Order and Progress (S. Alexander), 1889 R
Moral Philosophy, 1846 R
Moral Rearmament, 1939 R
Moral Thinking (R.M. Hare), 1981 R
Moran, Lord. *See* Wilson, Charles McMoran
Morante, Elsa, It. author (1918–85), 1974 U
Moras, Jean, F. poet (1856–1910), 1884 U, 1886 V
Moravia, Alberto (pseudonym of Alberto Pincherle), It. author (1907–90), 1907 Z, 1944 U, 1990 Z
Moravia, Germans occupy, 1939 C
Moravian Brethren, reform of, 1764 R
More Die of Heartbreak (S. Bellow), 1988 U
More, Hannah, B. author (1745–1833), 1788 O, 1809 U
Morea, The, Greece, 1781 B; guaranteed by the powers, 1828 L
Moreau, Gustave, F. painter (1826–98), 1866 S
Moreau, Jean, F. general (1763–1813), 1796 F, 1800 E, F
Moreau, Jeanne, F. actress (b. 1930), 1961 W
Morel, Edmund, D., B. Labour politician (1873–1924), 1903 E
Morgan Grenfell, directors fined for insider dealing, 1987 G
Morgan, Charles, B. author (1894–1958), 1929 U, 1932 U, 1949 W
Morgan, Daniel, Am. soldier (1736–1802), 1781 A
Morgan, David, B. historian (b. 1947), 1986 Q
Morgan, John Pierpont, Am. banker and connoisseur (1837–1913), 1837 Z, 1901 O, 1913 Z
Morgan, Kenneth Owen, B. historian (b. 1934), 1981 Q, 1984 Q, 1990 Q
Morgan, Thomas H., Am. geneticist (1866–1945), 1909 B, 1928 P
Morghen, Raffaello Sanzio, It. engraver (1758–1833), 1792 S
Mörike, Eduard Friedrich, G. poet (1804–75), 1838 U
Morillo, Pablo, defeats Bolívar, 1816 B
Moritz, Karl Philipp, G. author (1757–93), 1790 U
Morland, George, B. artist (1763–1804), 1791 S
Morley, John, Lord Morley (1838–1923), B. Liberal, 1838 Z, 1923 Z
Morley, Malcolm, B. artist (b. 1931), 1966 S
Turner Prize, 1984 S
Mormons. *See* Religious denominations
Moro, Aldo, It. politician (1916–78), 1976 A, B, D
kidnapped by Red Brigade terrorists, 1978 C
found dead in Rome, 1978 E
terrorists jailed, 1983 A
Morocco:
French war in, 1844 H, J
Spanish wars in, 1859 K, 1860 D
France advances interests in, 1900 B, M
Anglo-German pact on, is sought, 1901 F
France is granted control of frontier, 1901 G
Franco-Spanish agreements on, 1902 L, 1904 K
Anglo-French differences settled, 1904 D
Crisis, first, 1905 C, E
conference on, 1905 G, J
Crisis, second, 1906 D
Algeciras Conference, 1906 A, D
Franco-Spanish control in, 1906 D
Civil War, 1908 H
Germany recognises France's interests in, 1909 B
Agadir Crisis, 1911 F, G
Franco-German convention, 1911 L
French agreement on, 1912 B
becomes a French protectorate, 1912 C
pacification of, 1932 A
Berber revolt in S.W., 1934 B
France deposes Sultan, 1953 H
Sultan abdicates, 1955 K
independence recognised, 1956 C
Spanish troops leave, 1961 H
attempted assassination of King Hassan, 1972 H
agrees to pull out of Sahara, 1975 L
unarmed invasion of Spanish Sahara, 1975 L
shares Western Sahara with Mauritania, 1976 D
federation with Libya, 1984 H
Arab Maghreb Union, 1989 B
Morrill, Justin Smith, Am. financier (1810–98), tariff of, 1861 C
Morris, Colin, B. historian (b. 1928), 1989 Q
Morris, Desmond John, B. anthroplogist (b. 1928), 1967 P
Morris, Robert, Am. sculptor (b. 1931), 1967 S
Morris, William, B. poet, artist and Socialist (1834–96), 1834 Z, 1861 S, 1896 Z; as artist, 1890 S, 1896 S; as author, 1858 U, 1868 U, 1876 U
Morrison, Danny, Sinn Fein leader, 1982 M
Morrison, Herbert, Lord Morrison, B. Labour leader (1888–1965), 1965 Z; replaces Cripps in war cabinet, 1942 L; becomes foreign secretary, 1951 C
Morrison, Toni, Am. author (b. 1931), 1987 U
Morrison, Van, Ir. rock singer (b. 1945), 1968 W
Morse, Samuel Finley Breese, Am. artist and inventor (1791–1872), 1791 Z, 1825 S, 1832 P, 1844 P, 1872 Z
Mort dans l'âme, La (J. P. Sartre), 1950 R
Mort, T.S., Austral. pioneer of refrigeration (1816–1878), 1861 P
Mortal Questions (T. Nagel), 1979 R
Morte d'Arthur and other Idylls (Lord Tennyson), 1842 U
Mortimer, John, B. dramatist (b. 1923), 1960 W
Morton, William Thomas, Am. dentist (1819–68), 1846 P
Morts sans sépultures (J. P. Sartre), 1946 W
Mosaics, glass, 1891 S
Mosander, Karl Gustav, Swe. scientist (1797–1858), 1839 D
Moscicki, Ignace, Pol. premier, 1926 F, 1939 J
Moscow, Russia:
Napoleon's occupation, 1812 J
Napoleon's retreat from, 1812 K
Kremlin built, 1838 S
revolt of workers, 1905 M
riots in, 1915 F
British trade missions visit, 1921 C, 1940 E
Soviet Writers' Conference, 1934 U
purges in, 1937 A
failure of first German offensive towards, 1941 K
Stalin remains in, 1941 K
Second German offensive against, 1941 L
war leaders confer in, 1942 H
conference of Allied foreign ministers, 1943 K, 1945 M, 1947 C
Churchill visits, 1944 K
Council for Mutual Economic Assistance in, 1949 A
population, 1950 Y, 1960 Y, 1970 Y, 1990 Y
isolation of Western diplomats, 1952 K
conference of Soviet satellites in, 1954 L
concealed microphones in US embassy, 1964 E
World Communist Conference, 1969 F
Sino–Soviet talks, 1982 L
Rust lands in Red Square, 1987 E
arms reduction summit, 1988 F
1,000 years of Christianity in Russia celebrated, 1988 F
opposition demonstrations disrupt May Day parade, 1990 E
Moser, Justus, G. publicist (1720–94), 1775 O
Moshoeshoe II, King of Lesotho (b. 1938), 1966 K
Moslem League. *See under* Political Parties
Moslems. *See under* Religious Denominations
Mosley, Nicholas, Baron Ravensdale, B. author (b. 1923), 1991 U
Mosley, Sir Oswald Ernald, B. Fascist (1896–1980), 1896 Z, 1980 Z; founds New Party, 1931 B; founds British Union of Fascists, 1932 N; holds Fascist meetings, 1934 F, 1902 G; anti-Jewish activities, 1936 K, is released from detention, 1943 L
Mosquito Coast, The (P. Theroux), 1981 U
Moss, Convention of, between Sweden and Norway, 1814 H
Mössbauer, R. L., Am. scientist (b. 1929), 1960 P
Mostert, Anton, S. African lawyer, 1978 B, L
Mosul: controversy before League, 1924 J; question of Partition, 1925 H, M; Anglo-Turkish agreement on, 1926 F; pipe-line to Tripoli, 1934 G; revolt, 1959 C
Mother (M. Gorki), 1907 U
Mother Courage (B. Brecht), 1941 W
Motion, accelerated, laws of, 1784 P; theory of, 1858 P
Mother as Void (A. Kapoor), 1988 S
Mother, The (B. Brecht), 1932 W
Motion of the Solar System in Space (W. Herschel), 1783 P
Motley, John Lothrop, Am. historian (1814–77), 1814 Z, 1856 Q, 1860 Q, 1877 Z
Motor bicycle, 1901 P
Motor 'buses, in London, 1905 P
Motor car:
single-cylinder engine for, 1885 P
Benz's four-wheel, 1893 P
first Paris–Rouen trial run, 1894 X
'Ford model T', 1909 P
'Austin 7', 1922 P
companies:
Austin, 1905 P, 1922 P
Ford, 1909 P
Rolls-Royce, 1904 P

convention for, 1910 O
redundancies, 1979 J
regulations, in Britain:
speed limit, 1903 H, 1935 C
driving tests, 1934 C
parking meters, 1958 O
production, statistics of, 1906 Y, 1914 Y, 1957 Y, 1988 Y
vehicles licensed, statistics of, 1920 Y, 1938 Y, 1940 Y, 1941 Y, 1950 Y, 1960 Y, 1968 Y
wearing of seat belts for front-seat made compulsory in Britain, 1983 O
Motor scooter, 1919 P
Motor, electric, A.C., 1888 P
Motorways, M. I, 1959 P
Motown Music, 1966 W
Mots, Les (J. P. Sartre), 1964 U
Mott, Sir Frederick Walter, B. neurologist (1853–1926), 1916 P
Mouches, Les (J. P. Sartre), 1943 W
Mount Athos, Greece, 1842 R
Mount Palomar telescope, California, 1991 P
Mount Wilson, US telescope, 1910 P, 1918 P
Mountaineering:
ascent of Jungfrau, 1811 P
ascent of Matterhorn, 1865 X, 1965 X
ascent of Mt. Blanc, 1787 P
ascent of Mt. Everest, 1953 P
ascent of Mt. Godwin Austen, 1954 P
ascent of Nanga Parbat, 1953 P
Mountbatten, Louis, Lord, Earl Mountbatten (1900–79), 1900 Z, 1979 Z
killed by IRA bomb, 1979 H
involvement in anti-government coup denied by Wilson, 1981 C
Mountbatten-Windsor, surname to be borne by Elizabeth II's descendants, not being Royal Highnesses, 1960 B
Mountford, Edward, B. architect (1855–1908), 1907 S
Mourning Becomes Electra (E. O'Neill), 1931 W
Mouroux, Jean, F. philosopher, 1956 R
Mousetrap, The (A. Christie), 1952 W
Moussoursky, Modeste Petrovich, R. musician (1839–81), 1839 Z, 1874 T, 1881 Z
Mouth-organ, invented, 1829 T
Mouvement Républicain Populaire. *See under* Political Parties
Moveable Feast, A (E. Hemingway), 1964 U
Mowbray, Anne, Duchess of York (d. 1481), coffin of, 1965 Q
Mozambique, 1895 N, 1907 E; German designs on, 1898 H; Indian nationals required to leave, 1962 F
Portugal grants measure of autonomy, 1970 M
The Times alleges massacre, 1973 G
nationalist government takes office, 1974 J
independence, 1975 F
civil war, peace agreement, 1991 K
Mozart, Wolfgang Amadeus, G. musician (1756–91), 1791 Z
chamber music, 1795 T
Eine kleine Nachtmusik, 1787 T
mass, 1783 T
operas: *Cosí fan Tutti*, 1790 F
Don Giovanni, 1787 T
Figaro, 1786 T
Magic Flute, 1791 T
other operas, 1768 T, 1781 T, 1789 T
requiem, 1791 T
symphonies: 'Jupiter', 1788 T
'Prague', 1787 T
other symphonies, 1781 T, 1788 T
Salzburg festival, 1906 T
M'Taggart, John, B. philosopher (1866–1925), 1921 R
Müller, K. Alex, Swi. physicist (b. 1927), 1986 P
Muawad, Ren, President of The Lebanon (1925–89), assassination, 1989 L
Mubarak, Muhammad Hosni, President of Egypt (b. 1928), 1981 K, 1982 A
Jordan–Egypt peace initiative talks, 1984 M
Israeli–Egyptian talks with Peres, 1985 K, 1986 J
Mudie, Charles Edward, B. founder of circulating library (1818–90), 1842 O
Mugabe, Robert Gabriel, Zimbabwean leader (b. 1924), 1976 K, 1984 H, 1990 D
Patriotic Front, 1977 J
Patriotic Front excluded from power-sharing government, 1978 C
forms coalition government, 1980 C
orders new constitution, 1982 C
ZANU (PF) and ZAPU parties united, 1987 M
Mugwumps, The, or Reformist Republicans in US, 1884 L
Muhlenberg, William Augustus, Am. episcopalian (1796–1877), 1853 O
Muir, Karen, S. Afr. swimmer, 1965 X
Mukden, Manchuria: Russian defeat at, 1905 C; Japanese siege, 1931 J
Mulai Hafid, Sultan of Morocco, 1908 A, H
Mulberry Bush, The (A. Wilson), 1956 W
Mulder, C.P. ('Connie'), S. African politician (1925–88)
resigns from cabinet, 1978 L
expelled from National Party, 1979 D
Muldoon, Sir Robert David, Prime Minister of New Zealand (1921–92), 1975 L, 1978 L
Mulisch, Harry, D. author (b. 1927), 1982 U
Müller, F. W., Swi. scientist, 1956 P
Müller, Hermann, G. Socialist (b. 1890), becomes Chancellor, 1928 F; resigns, 1930 C
Müller, Paul, Swi. chemist, inventor of DDT, 1939 P
Müller, Wilhelm, G. scientist, 1927 P, 1928 P
Mulock, Dinah Maria (afterwards Mrs. Craik), B. author (1826–87), 1857 U
Mulroney, (Martin) Brian, Prime Minister of Canada (b. 1939), 1939 Z, 1988 L
Mumford, Lewis, Am. author (1895–1990), 1895 Z, 1934 O, 1938 Q, 1944 R, 1990 Z
Mummer's Wife (G. Moore), 1885 U
Munch, Edvard, Nor. artist (1863–1944), 1863 Z, 1897 S, 1901 S, 1907 S, 1909 S, 1919 S, 1921 S, 1928 S, 1935 S, 1944 Z
Münchengrätz Conference, between Russia, Prussia and Austria, 1833 J
Münchhausen (K. Immermann), 1838 U
Mundania Conference, between Allies and Turkey, 1922 K
Mundos de la Madrugada (R. Molinari), 1943 U
Mundoseer, India, treaty, 1818 A
Munich, Bavaria, Germany:
Glyptothek, 1816 S
Ludwigskirche, 1825 S
University, 1826 O
Propylaea, 1846 S
School of theologians, led by Döllinger, 1856 R
Archbishop of, 1871 R
electrical exhibition, 1883 P
German museum, 1903 O
'Blue Rider' school of artists, 1911 S
government troops regain from Communists, 1919 E
exhibition of 'Degenerate Art', 1937 S
conference on Czechoslovakia, 1938 J
Olympic Games, 1972 J, X
Munitions, Ministry, British, 1915 F, O
Munitions:
workers, 1916 V; women workers, 1917 O
in Britain, production, 1941 Y, 1942 Y, 1943 Y, 1944 Y
special weeks, 1941 J
in France, nationalised, 1937 B
in US, factories achieve maximum production, 1942 N
See also under Armaments
Munk, Andrzej, R. film director, 1964 W
Munnings, Sir Alfred, B. artist (1878–1959), 1919 S, 1925 S
Munro, Hector Hugh, B. author under pseudonym of 'Saki' (1870–1916), 1911 U, 1912 U
Munro, Sir Hector, B. soldier (1726–1805), 1764 K, 1778 N
Munsinger, Gerda, East German spy, 1966 C
Munth, Carl, G. Roman Catholic propagandist, 1903 V
Munthe, Axel, Swe. physician and author, 1857 Z, 1949 Z
Muppett Show, The, television series, 1976 W
Murad V, Sultan of Turkey, 1876 E, H
Murakami, Ryu, Jap. author (b. 1952), 1976 U
Murat, Joachim, King of Naples, F. general (1767–1815), 1800 F, 1806 L, 1812 M, 1915 D, E; becomes King of Naples, 1808 F; deserts Napoleon, 1814 A; is shot, 1815 K
Muraviev, Michael, Count, R. diplomat, 1900 B
Murchison, Sir Roderick Impey, B. geologist (1792–1871), 1839 P
Murder in the Cathedral (T. S. Eliot), 1935 W
Murders:
Ross McWhirter, 1975 L
Georgi Markov, 1978 J
El Salvador, murder of nuns and lay assistant, 1984 E
Father Jerzy Popieluszko, 1984 K
P.C. Keith Blakelock, 1985 K
Lord Justice Maurice Gibson and Lady Gibson, 1987 D
San Salvador, Jesuit priests and their household, 1989 R
Ian Gow, 1990 G
Murdoch, Dame (Jean) Iris, B. author (b. 1919), 1919 Z, 1957 U, 1961 U, 1963 U, 1970 U, 1973 U, 1978 U
Murdoch, (Keith) Rupert, Austral.-born Am. media tycoon (b. 1931), 1931 Z, 1977 V, 1981 V
buys 51 per cent stake in *The News of the World*, 1968 V
buys *The Sun*, 1969 V
buys *The Sunday Telegraph*, 1972 V
buys *The Sydney Daily Telegraph*, 1972 V
News International Plant, Wapping, 1986 V, 1987 A, B
buys *Today*, 1987 V
Murdock, William, B. engineer, inventor of coal gas lighting (1754–1839), 1802 W
Mure, Geoffrey Reginald Gilbert, B. philosopher (1893–1979), 1951 R
Murger, Henri, F. author (1822–61), 1822 Z, 1848 U, 1861 Z
Murmansk, Russia, British withdraw from 1919 K
Murray, Andrew W., geneticist, 1983 P
Murray, Archibald, B. soldier, 1917 C
Murray, George Gilbert Aim, B. author (1866–1957), 1921 O, 1942 O
Murray, Sir James Augustus Henry, B. lexicographer (1837–1915), 1884 O
Murray, William, Earl of Mansfield, B. judge (1705–1793), 1769 A, 1772 O
Murrell, John, Canad. dramatist (b. 1945), 1977 W

Murry, Kathleen, N. Zeal. author under pseudonym of 'Katherine Mansfield' (1888–1923), 1888 Z, 1911 U, 1920 U, 1922 U, 1923 Z
Murshidabad, India, Nabwab of, 1763 G
Murther and Walking Spirits (R. Davies), 1992 U
Mürzstag Agreement, between Austria and Russia on Macedonian reforms, 1903 K
Musachino City, Japan, Kaijima House, Kichijoji, 1976 S
Musaddiq, Dr. Z., Iran, politician: becomes premier, 1951 D; granted special powers, 1952 G; arrested, 1953 H; sentenced, 1953 M
Musäus, John Karl August, G. author (1735–87), 1786 U
Musavi, Hosein, Prime Minister of Iran, 1981 K
Museums. *See* Galleries and Museums
Museveni, Yoweri Kaguta, President of Uganda (b. 1944), 1986 A
  National Resistance Army leadership, 1985 M
Musgrave, Thea, B. musician (b. 1928), 1969 T, 1977 T
Music Profession in Britain since the Eighteenth Century, The: A Social History (C. Ehrlich), 1985 Q
Music for Chameleons (T. Capote), 1980 U
Music for Pieces of Wood (S. Reich), 1973 T
Music in a New Found Land (W. Mellors), 1964 T
Music, metaphysics of, 1870 T
Music, Royal College of, London, 1883 T
Musicals:
  audience statistics, 1989 W
  Aspects of Love, 1989 W
  Call Me Madam, 1950 W
  Evita, 1978 W
  Fings Ain't What they Used T'Be, 1960 W
  Hair, 1968 W
  Jesus Christ Superstar, 1972 W
  Lilac Time, 1922 W
  Me and My Girl, 1985 W
  Misérables, Les, 1985 W
  Miss Saigon, 1989 W
  My Fair Lady, 1957 W
  Oklahoma, 1943 W
  Oliver, 1961 W
  Phantom of the Opera, The, 1986 W
  South Pacific, 1951 W
  Starlight Express, 1984 W
  West Side Story, 1958 W
  See also Reviews
Musicians Union, London, 1921 T
Musicircus (J. Cage), 1967 T
'Musique concrète', 1954 T
Muskets, 1800 P
Muskie, Edmund Sixtus, US Democrat politician (b. 1914), 1972 D, 1980 D
Musset, Alfred de, F. author (1810–57), 1810 Z, 1829 U, 1833 U, 1857 U
Mussolini, Benito, It. dictator (1883–1945), 1883 Z, 1935 G
  founds Fascio di Combattimento, 1919 B
  march on Rome, 1922 K
  attempts on life, 1926 D
  autobiography, 1928 O
  champions revision of Versailles treaty, 1930 E
  The 100 Days, 1931 O
  proposes four-power pact, 1933 C
  meets Hitler, 1934 F, 1937 J, 1938 E, 1940 K
  rejects concessions over Abyssinia, 1935 F
  proclaims Rome–Berlin axis, 1936 L
  in Libya, 1937 C
  meets Schuschnigg, 1937 D
  in Berlin, 1937 J
  at Munich Conference, 1938 J
  demands colonies in N. Africa, 1939 A
  talks with Chamberlain and Halifax, 1939 A
  pact with Hitler, 1939 E
  falls, 1943 G
  is killed by partisans, 1945 D
Mustapha IV, Sultan of Turkey (1807–8), 1807 E, 1808 G
Mutinies, notable:
  Royal Navy, at Spithead, 1797 D
    at Nore, 1797 E, F
    at Invergordon, 1931 J
  Aden, 1967 F
  of Congolese National Army, 1960 G
  of French Army, 1917 E
  of German Fleet, 1917 G, 1918 L
  of Nigerian army, 1966 G
  of Russian Fleet, 1917 F
  of troops in Tanganyika, Uganda and Kenya, 1964 A
Mutual Economic Assistance, Council for, 1949 A
Mutual Security Agency, in US, 1951 M
Muzorewa, Abel Tendekayi, Zimb. churchman and politician (b. 1925), 1979 F
Mwinyi, Ali Hassan, President of Tanzania (b. 1925), 1985 K
My Apprenticeship (B. Webb), 1926 O
My Bloody Valentine, pop group, 1988 W
My First Loves (I. Klima), 1985 U
My Imprisonment (S. Pellico), 1832 O
My Lai, Vietnam, massacre, 1969 L
My Life, Poetry and Truth (Goethe), 1811 U
My Philosophy (A. Einstein), 1934 R
My Way (D. Hirst), 1990 S
Myoglobin, discoveries in 1960 P
Myra Breckinridge (G. Vidal), 1968 U
Mysore, India, 1763 N, 1769 F, 1782 M; Hyder Ali usurps throne, 1764 N; signs peace with Britain, 1784 C; to Britain, 1792 B; shared between Britain and Hyderabad, 1799 E; annexed by East India Company, 1831 N
Mystère de la charité de Jeanne d'Arc (Péguy), 1910 U
Mysteries of Udolpho, The (A. Radcliffe), 1794 U
Mysterious Affairs at Styles, The (A. Christie), 1921 U
Mystery of Edwin Drood (C. Dickens), 1870 U
Mysticism (E. Underhill), 1910 R
Mysticism in Religion (W. R. Inge), 1948 R
Mysticism of Logic (B. Russell), 1918 R
Myth of God Incarnate, The (J. Hick ed.), 1977 R
Mythologies (R. Barthes), 1957 R
Mythology, German, 1835 Q
Myths of the 20th Century (Rosenberg), 1930 U
Myxomatosis, 1953 P

N

Nabiyev, Rakhmon, President of Tajikistan (b. 1930), 1992 J
Nablus Congress on Palestine, 1922 H
Nabokov, Vladimir, R.-born Am. author (1899–1977), 1899 Z, 1955 U, 1959 O, 1966 U, 1977 Z
Nacht der Nacht (H. Pousseur), 1985 T
Nachtigal, Gustav, G. explorer of Central Africa (1834–85), 1869 P
Nadar, A., F. photographer and balloonist (1820–1910), 1863 P
Nadir Khan, King of Afghanistan, 1929 E
Nagaland, India, Pakistan and China accused of aiding rebels, 1968 F
Nagar, formerly Bednore, Mysore, India, 1783 D
Nagasaki, Japan, atomic Bomb on, 1945 H
Nagel, Thomas, Am. philosopher (b. 1937), 1979 R, 1986 R, 1991 R
Nagib, Mohammed, Egypt, general (b. 1900), 1954 B; seizes power, 1952 G; is voted dictatorial powers, 1953 B; becomes president of Egypt, 1953 F; falls, 1954 L
Nagorno-Karabakh, Azerbaijan:
  Regional Soviet votes for transfer from Azerbaijan to Armenia, 1988 B
  Soviet troops move in in response to ethnic violence, 1988 F, 1990 A
  state of emergency declared, 1988 J
  dispute over, 1992 J
Nagpur, India, 1817 L; Britain annexes, 1853 M
Nagy, Ferenc, Hung. politician, 1947 E
Nagy, Imre, Hung. leader (1896–1958), 1953 G; recall demanded, 1956 K; forms ministry, 1956 K; takes refuge, 1956 L
Nagy, P., Am. scientist, 1961 P
Nahas Pashas, Egypt. Wafd leader, 1927 H, 1936 E; as premier, 1928 C, 1930 A, 1950 A
Nail-making machine, 1786 P, 1790 P
Naipaul, Shiva, Trinidadian author (1945–85), 1980 U
Naipaul, Sir Vidiadhar Surajprasad, Trinidad-born B. author (b. 1932), 1932 Z, 1959 U, 1972 U, 1979 U, 1990 U
Nairobi, Kenya, East African legislature at, 1948 D
  conference to end UN Decade for Women, 1985 G
Najibullah, President of Afghanistan (b. 1947), 1986 E
  state of emergency imposed, 1989 B
  failed coup against, 1990 C
  overthrow, 1992 D
Naked Ape, The (D. Morris), 1967 P
Naked Lunch, The (Burroughs), 1964 U
Naked and the Dead, The (N. Mailer), 1948 U
Naktong, River, Korea, 1953 J
Name of the Rose, The (U. Eco), 1980 U
Names, family, obligatory in Turkey, 1935 A
Namibia:
  South Africa re-imposes direct rule, 1983 A
  South African control, 1984 L, 1985 F
  multi-racial administration announced, 1985 F
  independence agreed at UN, 1988 M
  election of first independent government, 1989 L
  Nujoma returns, 1989 J
  Republic of Namibia declared independent sovereign state, 1990 B
  SWAPO election victory, 1992 L
  See also Southwest Africa
Namibia Declaration, 1992 L
Namier, Sir Lewis Bernstein, B. historian (1888–1960), 1888 Z, 1942 O, 1948 Q, 1960 Z
Naming and Necessity (S. Kripke), 1973 R
Namphy, General Henri, President of Haiti (b. 1933), 1986 B, 1988 F, J
Namsos, Norway, British evacuate, 1940 E
Namur, Belgium, 1785 A battle; 1914 H
Nana (E. Zola), 1880 U
Nancy, France, mutiny in, 1790 H
Nanga Parbat, Himalayas, ascent of, 1953 P
Nanking, China: treaty, ends Opium War, 1842 H; confirmed, 1843 K; falls to rebels, 1850 K; bombed by revolutionaries, 1911 L; falls to Yüan Shih-Kai, 1913 J; National Convention in, 1931 E; Communists seize, 1927 C; Chiang Kai-shek at, 1927 D; Japanese take, 1937 M; puppet government at, 1938 C; National Assembly, 1948 C
Nansen, Fridtjof, Norw. explorer (1861–1930), 1861 Z, 1888 P, 1893 P, 1930 Z
Napier, Sir Charles, B. soldier (1782–1853), conquers Sund, 1843 A
Napier, Robert Cornelis, Lord Napier, B. soldier (1810–90), 1868 A, D

Napier, Sir William Francis Patrick, B. soldier and military historian (1785–1860), 1828 Q
Naples, Italy, 1768 N, 1815 K; British influence in, 1779 N; French overrun, 1798 M; Suvorov recaptures, 1799 F; French evacuate, 1801 K; French re-enter, 1806 B; San Carlos Opera House, 1810 S; Garibaldi enters, 1860 J; plebiscite supports union with Sardinia, 1860 K; Allies capture, 1943 J; NATO Headquarters, 1971 H
Napoleon I (Napoleon Bonaparte), F. emperor (1769–1821), 1769 Z, 1800 K, 1806 R, 1808 R
takes Toulon, 1793 M
'whiff of grapeshot', 1795 K
marries Josephine de Beauharnais, 1796 C
takes command in Italy, 1796 D
wins battle of Lodi, 1796 E
defeats Wurmser, 1796 H
wins battle of Rivoli, 1797 A
advances to Vienna, 1797 B
founds Ligurian Republic, 1797 F
given command of French forces invading England, 1797 K
occupies Alexandria, 1798 G
in Syria, 1799 A, C, E
defeats Turks, 1799 G
lands at Fréjus, 1799 K
overthrows Directory, 1799 L
becomes First Consul, 1799 M, 1800 B
crosses Great St. Bernard Pass, 1800 E
defeats Austrians at Marengo, 1800 F
becomes president of Italian Republic, 1802 A
creates Legion of Honour, 1802 E
becomes First Consul for life, 1802 H
conspiracies against, 1804 B, 1812 K
proclaimed Emperor, 1804 E, M
crowned King of Italy, 1805 E
occupies Berlin, 1806 K
meets Alexander I at Tilsit, 1807 G
imprisons Pope Pius VII, 1809 G
divorces Josephine, 1809 M
marries Marie-Louise, 1810 B
annexes Holland, 1810 G
disputes with Pius VII, 1811 F
invades Russia, 1812 F
occupies Moscow, 1812 J
retreats from Moscow, 1812 K
returns to Paris, 1812 M
victory at Lützen, 1813 E
victory at Dresden, 1813 H
banished to Elba, 1814 D
lands in France ('Hundred Days'), 1815 C
issues Constitutions of Le Champ de Mai, 1815 F
defeated at Waterloo, 1815 F
abdicates, 1815 F
banished to St. Helena, 1815 H
art treasures looted by, 1815 S
death, 1821 Z
remains brought to Paris, 1840 M
Napoleon III (Charles Louis Napoleon Bonaparte), F. emperor (1808–73), 1808 Z, 1860 L, 1863 S
is exiled, 1836 K
attempts rising at Boulogne, 1840 H
escapes to London, 1846 E
elected president of France, 1848 M
coup d'état, 1851 M
is granted monarchical powers, 1852 A
proclaimed Emperor, 1852 M
marries Eugénie de Montijo, 1853 A
birth of heir, 1856 C
meets Cavour, 1858 G
meets Bismarck, 1865 K
promises French neutrality in Austro-Prussian War, 1866 F
announces cession of Venezia to Italy, 1866 G
withdraws support from Maximilian of Mexico, 1867 C
attempts to buy Duchy of Luxemburg, 1867 E
adopts Parliamentary system, 1869 G
capitulates at Sedan, 1870 J
death, 1873 A
Napoleon of Notting Hill, The (G. K. Chesterton), 1904 U
Narasimha Rao, P.V., Prime Minister of India (b. 1921), 1991 F
Narayan, Rasipuram Krishnaswamy, Ind. author (b. 1906), 1983 U
Narlikar, Jayant Vishnu, B. scientist, 1964 P
Narva, Russia, Germans occupy, 1918 C
Narvarez, Ramon Maria, Sp. soldier and politician (1800–68), defeats Espartero, 1843 G; becomes premier, 1864 J; is dismissed, 1865 F
Nash, John Northcote, B. artist (1893–1977), 1918 S, 1940 S
Nash, John, B. architect (1752–1835), 1811 S, 1815 S, 1825 S
Nash, Malcolm, B. cricketer (b. 1945), 1968 X
Nash, Paul, B. artist (1889–1946), 1889 Z, 1918 S, 1940 S, 1941 S, 1946 S
Nasir Ud-Din, Shah of Persia (1848–96), 1848 K, 1896 E
Nasmyth, James, B. engineer (1808–90),1839 P
Nassau, Bahamas, Kennedy meets Macmillan at, 1962 M
Nassau, Duchy, annexed by Prussia, 1866 H, J
Nasser, Gamal Abdel, President of UAR and Egypt (1918–70), 1918 Z; usurps power, 1954 B; becomes premier, 1954 D; becomes head of state, 1954 L; meets Tito, 1956 A; elected president of Egypt, 1956 F; seizes Suez Canal, 1956 G; boycotts London Conference on Suez, 1956 H; rejects Dulles's proposals, 1956 J; Hammarskjöld visits, 1957 C; becomes president of United Arab Republic, 1958 B; confiscates property, 1961 K; Suez Canal closed, 1967 F; death, 1970 J, Z
Natal, S. Africa: Dutch settlers found Republic, 1837 F, British war with Boers in, 1842 N; is proclaimed a British colony, 1843 E; combined with Cape Colony, 1844 E; segregation in, 1846 N; becomes a Crown Colony, 1856 G; self-government for, 1893 E
Natalia (N. Karamzin), 1793 U
Nathan the Wise (Lessing), 1779 W
Nathan, Peter (b. 1914), B. author, 1943 O
National anthems:
French (La Marseillaise), 1792 T
Russian, 1944
S. African, 1957 U
National Apostasy (J. Keble), 1833 R
National Art Collections Fund, British, 1903 S
National Council of Churches of Christ, US, 1950 R
National Debt, British, interest on, reduced, 1888 D
National Development Bonds, 1964 D
National Economic Council, German, 1920 O
National Economic Development Council, T.U.C. joins, 1962 B
National Enterprise Board, B., 1975 A
National Express, B. coach company, 1980 K
National Forests Commission, US, 1906 O
National Freight Corporation, privatization, 1981 K
National Guard, French, 1789 J
dissolved, 1827 D
National Health Service. *See* Health Service, British
National Health, The (P. Nichols), 1970 W
National Incomes Commission, British, 1962 O
first report, 1963 D
National Industrial Relations Court (NIRC)
TGWU fined, 1972 C, F
AUEW fined for excluding member, 1972 L
AUEW funds sequestrated, 1974 E
abolished, 1974 G
National Insurance in Britain, 1946 L
National Liberation Front (Vietnam), 1969 A
National Life and Character; a Forecast (C. H. Pearson), 1893 O
National Parties. *See under* Political Parties
National Plan, The (British White Paper), 1965 O
National Registration, in Britain, 1915 G, 1938 M
National Savings Movement, 1916 O
National Socialists. *See under* Political Parties
National Society, The, for educating the poor, 1811 O
National System of Political Economy (F. List), 1841 O
National Theatre, British, 1951 W
National Trust, The, founded, 1895 O
Quorn Hunt banned from National Trust land, 1991 L
National Union of Mineworkers (NUM), 1973 K, L, 1974 C, 1982 L, 1984 K
National Vitality (I. Fisher), 1910 O
Nationalisation:
in Argentina, of oil, 1928 J
in Australia, of banks, 1947 L
of monopolies, proposed, 1911 B
in Britain, of land, advocated, 1775 O
of coal mines, 1946 E, 1947 A
of Bank of England, 1946 G
of railways, 1946 L, 1948 A
of iron and steel, 1949 L
repealed, 1952 L
of road transport, repealed, 1953 E
Labour Party retains 'Clause 4', 1960 C
British Steel renationalization, 1966 G
plans to sell nationalized industries, 1971 A
Rolls-Royce divisions, 1971 B
coal industry, 1972 M
Thomas Cook travel agency privatized, 1972 O
Labour Party proposals, 1973 F, 1980 G
government plans to exert greater control over industry defeated, 1974 F
shipbuilding industry, 1974 G, 1977 B, C, O
aircraft construction industry, 1975 A, 1977 B, C, O
British Telecom privatization, 1984 L
Trustee Savings Bank privatized, 1986 J
British Gas privatized, 1986 M
water service privatized, 1988 L
electricity service privatized, 1988 L
Local Government Act, 1988 O
in Canada, of Grand Trunk Pacific Railway, 1919 C
in France, of Bank of France, 1945 O; 1981 J
of Church property, 1789 L
of munitions industry, 1936 G, 1937 B
in Germany, of industries, demanded, 1918 M
in India, of life insurance, 1956 E; of banks, 1969 G
in Indonesia, of Dutch businesses, 1958 M
in Iran, of oil industry, 1951 G; 1979 G
in Japan, of railways, 1906 C; privatized, 1987 O
in Mexico, of oil and minerals, 1926 E
in New Zealand, of Reserve Bank, 1936 N
in Poland, 1946 F

in Russia, of industries, dismissals for incompetence, 1946 F
in Spain, of Church property, 1933 E
in Switzerland, of railways, 1910 N
in US, of silver, president empowered to order, 1934 F
in Venezuela, of oil industry, 1976 A
in Zambia, of copper mines, 1969 H
in Zimbabwe, of white-owned farms, 1990 M
Nationalism
Armenia, 1988 B, F
Azerbaijan, 1988 F,L
Baltic States, 1989 H
Basques, 1968 H
Belgium, Flemish campaign against French-speakers at University of Louvain brings down government, 1968 B
Bougainville Island, 1992 E
Estonia, 1988 K, L
Georgia, 1989 D
Kanak separatists, New Caledonia, 1988 D
Kashmir, 1990 A
Latvia, 1989 K
Lithuania, 1990 C, 1990 B
Nigerian–Biafran conflict, 1968 E, G-J
Palestinians, 1968 H
Rhodesia, African nationalists, 1968 C
Sri Lankan Tamils, 1983 G
Yugoslavia, 1988 J, 1990 B
Nationalist Parties. *See under* Political Parties
Native Realm (C. Milosz), 1968 U
Natural History of Selborne (G. White), 1789 P
Natural Religions and Christian Theology (C. Raven), 1954 R
Natural Theology (W. Paley), 1802 R
Naturalism and Agnosticism (J. Ward), 1899 R
Nature (R. W. Emerson), 1836 R
Nature and Destiny of Man, The (R. Niebuhr), 1941 R
Nature of Doctrine, The (G.A. Lindbeck), 1984 R
Nature of Existence, The (McTaggart), 1921 R
Nature of the Corn Laws (J. Anderson), 1777 O
Nature of the Universe, The (F. Hoyle), 1950 W
Nature, Man and God (W. Temple), 1934 R
Naught for Your Comfort (T. Huddleston), 1957 O
Nauman, Bruce, Am. sculptor (b. 1941), 1972 S
Nauru, independence, 1968 A
Nausée, La (J.P. Sartre), 1937 U
Nautical Almanac, 1767 P
Nauvoo City, Illinois, US, 1846 F
Nava, Gregory, Am. film director (b. 1949), 1983 W
Navarino Bay, Greece, battle, 1827 K
Navarre, France, Spain invades, 1793 C
Navarro, Raymon, Am. film actor, 1926 W
Navies:
Agreements: International, London Naval Convention, 1936 C
Russia accedes to, 1936 K
Britain with Germany, 1935 F, 1937 G
Hitler denounces, 1939 D
Britain with Russia, 1937 G
Russia with Turkey, on Black Sea, 1931 C
US with Japan, 1922 B
Conferences: London Naval, 1908 M
Washington, restricts submarine warfare, 1922 B
London Naval Disarmament, 1930 D, 1934 K
Japan leaves, 1936 A
Naval Strengths, comparative, 1838 Y, 1903 Y, 1914 Y, 1918 Y, 1945 Y
Argentine; *General Belgrano*, cruiser, sunk by British submarine, 1982 E
Austrian, *Wien* sunk, 1917 M
Brazilian, 1891 L
Royal:
actions, at Trafalgar, 1805 K
at Naravino Bay, 1827 K
off Dardanelles, 1853 F, 1895 K
sent into Black Sea, 1854 A
sent to Constantinople, 1878 A, B
bombards Alexandria, 1882 G
Cossack rescues prisoners from *Altmark*, 1940 B
sinks French Fleet in Oran, 1940 G
raids Lofoten Islands, 1941 C
sinks *Bismarck*, 1941 E
convoys to Malta, 1942 F, H; to Russia, 1942 J, M
construction, etc., increase in, 1791 C
extensive building programme, 1889 E
Spencer programme, 1894 N
Dartmouth R.N. College, 1903 E
battleships, 1903 Y
Dreadnought launched, 1906 P
bill for increasing, 1909 C
battleships, 1910 Y
George V launched, 1911 K
losses of capital ships, notable, *Formidable*, 1915 A
Hampshire, 1916 F
total in World War I, 1918 Y
Courageous, 1939 J
Royal Oak, 1939 K
Jervis Bay, 1940 L
Illustrious, 1941 A
Southampton, 1941 A
Hood, 1941 E
Ark Royal, 1941 L
Barnham, 1941 L
Prince of Wales, 1941 M
Repulse, 1941 M
losses in Bay of Bengal, 1942 D
Eagle, 1942 H
Manchester, 1942 H
total in World War II, 1945 Y
Sheffield, 1982 E
mutinies, 1797 D, E, F, 1931 J
miscellaneous, flogging abolished, 1881 O
paravanes used, 1915 P
acquires US destroyers, 1940 J
first guided-missile vessel, 1956 G
Canadian, Royal, formed, 1910 N
Canada rejects Navy bill, 1913 E
H.M.C.S. *Labrador*, 1957 P
Danish, surrenders to Britain, 1807 J
Egyptian, destroyed at Navarino Bay, 1827 K
French, visits Kronstadt, 1891 G
construction of battleships, 1903 Y, 1910 Y, 1911 B
losses, 1918 Y
in Oran, sunk, 1940 G
German, of 1848, auctioned, 1853 N
expansion under Tirpitz, 1898 C, 1900 F
battleship construction, 1903 Y, 1910 Y
increased under Navy bills, 1906 F, 1908 F
alarm at growth of, 1909 C
in World War I:
actions, etc.: *Breslau* and *Goeben* escape through Dardanelles, 1914 H
Emden sunk, 1914 L
Blücher sunk, 1915 A
Westfalen sunk, 1916 H
Breslau sunk, 1918 A
submarines, attack without warning, 1915 A, E, 1916 B
attacks intensified, 1915 B
not to attack merchantmen, 1915 J
unrestricted attacks, 1917 A
attacks suspended, 1918 K
Kiel mutinies, 1918 L
plebiscite against building battleships fails, 1928 K
not to exceed a third of tonnage of Royal Navy, 1935 F
bombards Almeira, 1937 E
in World War II:
Graf Spee scuttled, 1939 M
Bismarck sunk, 1941 E
Prinz Eugen escapes, 1941 E
Scharnhorst sunk, 1943 M
Tirpitz sunk, 1944 L
U-boats:
lay magnetic mines, 1939 L
attacks intensified, 1940 K, 1941 C
use homing torpedoes, 1945 A
losses, 1945 Y
W. German, agreement for building destroyers for firing nuclear weapons, 1961 E
Greek, is handed over to Allies, 1916 K
Indian, 1934 K
Italian, construction of battleships, 1910 Y, 1930 D
losses at Taranto, 1940 L
losses off Cape Matapan, 1941 C
Japanese: is attacked, 1864 J
battleships in, 1903 Y, 1910 Y
losses, 1945 Y
Merchant. *See* Merchant Navy.
NATO: US recommends surface ships in, to carry Polaris missiles, 1963 B
France withdraws Atlantic force from, 1963 F
mixed-manned nuclear fleet, discussed, 1963 K
Russian: in Bosphorus, 1833 B
visits Toulon, 1893 K
battleships in, 1903 Y, 1910 Y
crippled by Japanese, 1904 H
fires on British trawlers, 1904 K
mutinies, 1917 F, G
visits Portsmouth, 1955 K
Spanish, Britain fails to win contract for building warships for, 1964 F
Swedish, destroyed by Russians, 1788 G
Turkish, destruction at Navarino, 1827 K
destruction at Sinope, 1853 L
US, created, 1798 G
Chesapeake incident, 1807 F, M
first steam warship, 1815 P
battleships in, 1903 Y, 1910 Y
naval appropriations bill, 1912 E
contracts suspended, 1921 A
defeats Japanese at Kynshu, 1945 A
losses, 1945 Y
Nautilus atom-powered submarine, 1957 P
sails for E. Mediterranean, 1957 D
Gulf of Sirte, exercises in, 1981 D
Navigators Island, Pacific, 1766 P
Navratilova, Martina, Am. tennis player (b. 1956), 1990 X
Navy Lark, The, radio series, 1977 W
Nazarener group of German artists, 1810 S, 1828 S
Nazim Pasha, Turk. leader, murdered, 1913 A
Nazis. *See under* Political Parties
Ndjamene, Chad
rebel forces capture, 1982 F
Ne Win (Maung Shu Maung), Burmese general (b. 1911), 1962 C
Neale, Sir John Ernest, B. historian (1890–1975), 1949 Q
Neanderthal skull, discovered, 1856 Q
Near the Ocean (R. Lowell), 1967 U
Neat Lawn, A. (D. Hockney), 1967 S
Neave, Airey Middleton Sheffield, B.

Conservative politician (1916–79), murder, 1979 C
Nebraska, state, US: settlement of, 1854 E; becomes a US state, 1867 C
Nebular hypothesis, enunciated by Laplace, 1796 P
Necker, Jacques, Swi. financier (1732–1804), 1776 K, 1780 N, 1781 E, O, 1790 J, 1804 Z; is recalled as F. finance minister, 1788 H; Louis XVI dismisses, 1789 G
Necker, Suzanne, Swi. literary hostess (d. 1794), 1764 U
Needle's Eye, The (M. Drabble), 1972 U
Neerwinden, Belgium, battle, 1793 C
Negapatam, Madras, India: British capture, 1781 L; is ceded to Britain, 1784 C
Negative Dialectics (T. Adorno), 1966 R
Neglect of Science Committee, 1916 P
Negro in American Civilization, The (C. S. Johnson), 1930 O
Negroes, in US, emancipated, 1863 O. *See also under* Civil Rights
Nehru, Shri Jawahalal, Indian statesman, leader of Indian Congress (1889–1964), 1945 J
becomes premier, 1947 H, 1952 E
leads Congress Party to victory in election, 1952 C
plan for solving Algerian problem, 1956 E
plan for solving Suez Crisis, 1956 H
forms new ministry, 1957 D
appeals for disarmament, 1957 L
at Belgrade meeting of non-aligned powers, 1961 J
stand on Goa, 1961 M
death, 1964 E
Neill, Rt. Revd Stephen Charles, B. churchman (1900–84), 1961 R
Neisse, Germany, 1769 H
Nelson, Horatio, Lord Nelson, B. admiral (1758–1805), at Cape Vincent, 1797 B; at Nile, 1798 H; at Copenhagen, 1801 D; at Trafalgar, 1805 K
Nelson, James Beaumont, B. engineer (1792–1865), 1829 P
Nelson, Richard, Am. dramatist (b. 1950), 1986 W
Nemesis of Faith (J. A. Froude), 1848 R
Nemesis of Power (J. Wheeler-Bennett), 1953 Q
Nemon, Oscar, B. sculptor (1906–85), 1906 Z, 1985 Z
Nemours, Louis Charles Philippe Raphal, Duc de (1814–96), 1831 B
Neo-classicism, 1775 S
Neo-Geo movement, 1984 S
Neomycin, 1949 P
Neon, discovered, 1898 P; signs, 1905 P
'Neoprene' synthetic rubber process, 1931 P
Nepal: Gurkhas conquer, 1768 N; British war with, 1814 K; elections, 1991 E
Neptune, planet, 1846 P
partial ring around photographed, 1984 P
great dark spot discovered, 1989 P
Neptunium, element, 1940 P
Neruda, Pablo Neftali Reyes, Chilean poet (1904–73), 1904 Z, 1924 U, 1950 U, 1973 Z
Nerval, Gérard de, F. author (1808–55), 1854 U, 1855 U
Nerve-centres, reflex action of, discovered, 1832 P
Nerves, treatise on, 1873 P
Nervi, Pier Luigi, It. architect (1891–1979), 1948 S, 1953 S, 1956 S, 1958 S, 1970 S, 1971 S
Nervous System of the Human Body, The (C. Bell), 1830 P
Nervous System, studies in, 1830 P
Nervous impulses:
of single nerve fibres, 1929 P
speed of, established, 1850 P
transmission of, work in, 1963 P
Nesbit, Edith (Mrs. E. Bland), B. author of children's books (1858–1924), 1899 U
Nesselrode, Karl Robert von, R. diplomat (1814–96), 1844 F
Net Book Agreement in Britain upheld, 1962 O
Netherlands, Austrian, France conquers, 1792 L
Netherlands, Kingdom of. *See* Holland
Netherlands, The United, 1815 F, 1816 F; concordat with Pope Leo XII, 1827 F; is divided into Holland and Belgium, 1831 A, F, K
Neto, (Antonio) Agostinho, President of Angola (1922–79), 1975 L, 1979 J
Netto, Italy, Allied landings at, 1944 A
Nettuno Treaty, on Dalmatia, 1925 G
Neuchâtel, France, 1805 M
Neue Armadis, Der (C. M. Wieland), 1771 U
Neue Gedichte (R. M. Rilke) 1907 U
Neufchâtel, Switzerland: rising against Republic, 1856 J; Prussia renounces sovereignty, 1857 E
Neuilly Peace treaty, between Allies and Bulgaria, 1919 L
Neumann, Franz Ernest, G. physicist and mathematician (1798–1895), 1851 P
Neumann, Franz, G. author, 1915 U
Neun Bücher preussischer Geschichte (L. von Ranke), 1847 Q
Neurath, Constantin von, G. diplomat (1873–1956), as foreign minister, 1932 F, 1933 A; rules Bohemia and Moravia, 1939 C
Neurath, K., G. sociologist, 1931 R
Neurology, studies in, 1830 P, 1854 P
transplant, 1970 P
neurons, composition of, 1977 P
Neustadt, Germany, 1770 J
Neutral Nations, rights of, 1802 O, 1806 O
Neutrino, detection, 1956 P, 1967 P
Neutrons, research into, 1832 P
Neuve Chapelle, France, battle, 1915 C
Neuville, France, Allies take, 1915 F
Nevada, state, US, US obtains, 1848 E
Nevado del Ruiz, Colombia, volcanic eruption, 1985 L
Neville Brothers, Am. pop group, 1989 W
Nevinson, Henry Wood, B. essayist and journalist (1856–1941), 1856 Z, 1941 Z
New Bearings in English Poetry (F. R. Leavis), 1932 U
New Berne, N. Carolina, US, Unionist take, 1862 C
New Brunswick, enters Dominion of Canada, 1867 C
New Caledonia: France annexes, 1853 J; nickel ore deposits in, 1876 P
state of emergency declared, 1985 A
Kanak separatists, 1988 D
New Cambridge Modern History, 1957 Q
New Critique of Reason (J. F. Fries), 1808 R
New Deal:
in Britain, Lloyd George's proposed programme for, 1935 A
in Canada, legislation for, nullified, 1936 F
in USA, Roosevelt introduces, 1933 C
social security legislation, 1935 O
New Delhi, India, Asian Legal Consultative Committee at, 1957 D
Parliament besieged by Sikhs, 1982 K
New Economic Policy (NEP), in Russia, 1921 O
New English Art Club, 1886 S
New English Bible, 1970 R
New Forum, 1989 J
New Foundations of Political Economy (G. Hafeland), 1807 O
New Georgia Island, Japanese evacuate, 1943 G
New Granada: revolt against Spanish, 1810 E; Congress, 1816 B; with Venezuela, forms Colombia, 1819 M; leaves Union of Colombia, 1831 L; becomes independent, 1831 L. *See* Colombia.
New Grove Dictionary of Music and Musicians, The (S. Sadie ed.), 1980 Q
New Guinea, 1883 N; Northern, annexed by Germany, 1885 E, N; Southern, British protectorate in, 1885 N; Germans capitulate, 1914 J; US landings in, 1943 F; West, proclaimed as an Indonesian province, 1962 A, H; UN takes over administration, 1962 K
New Hampshire, state, US, 1788 F
New Haven, Ct., US, Yale Centre for British Art, 1977 S
New Hebrides, 1887 L
occupation, 1980 E
rebellion in Espiritu Santo, 1980 E
independence, 1980 G
New International Version of the Bible, The, 1979 R
New Jersey, state, US, 1776 L
New Leviathan, The (R. G. Collingwood), 1942 R
New Macchiavelli, The (H. G. Wells), 1911 U
New Men, The (C. P. Snow), 1954 U
New Mexico, US, Gadsden Purchase, 1854 D
New Order, B. pop group, 1987 W
New Orleans, La., US: US purchases from France, 1803 D; British defeat at, 1815 A; siege of, 1862 D; Court of Appeals orders desegregation of schools, 1967 C
New Oxford Book of Victorian Verse, The (C. Ricks ed.), 1987 U
New Royal Horticultural Society Dictionary of Gardening, The (A. Huxley at al. eds.), 1992 Q
New South Wales, Australia: opposes federation, 1891 C; role in federation, 1899 N; artificial rain in 1957 P
New Street (G. Gissing), 1891 U
New System of Chemical Philosophy (J. Dalton), 1808 P
New Testament and Mythology (R. Bultmann), 1941 R
New Testament and the People of God, The (N.T. Wright), 1992 R
New Theology and the Old Religion, The (C. Gore), 1907 R
New Theory of Human Evolution, A (A. Keith), 1948 P
New Theory of the Earth (J. Hutton), 1788 P
New Towns of the Middle Ages (M. Beresford), 1967 Q
New Turkey, The (Kemel Atatürk), 1927 O
New View of Society, A (R. Owen), 1813 O
New World of the Mind, The (Rhine), 1953 R
New Writing, 1936 V
New York City (J. Holzer), 1983 S
New York Dolls, The, Am. pop group, 1973 W
New York State, US, investigations of insurance houses in, 1905 O
abortion on demand, 1970 O
New York, N.Y., US:
Stamp Act Congress, 1765 K
assembly suspended, 1767 F
falls to Howe, 1776 J
becomes federal capital, 1788 J
trades unions in, 1833 N
corruption in, 1871 G
Tammany Hall in, 1888 L
Austrian ambassador recalled from, 1915 J
Wall Street Crash, 1929 K, O
World Fair, 1938 W
Exhibition, 1939 W
UN headquarters in, 1946 M

Harlem race riots, 1964 G
transport strike, 1966 A
United Nations talks on Middle East, 1969 D
Attica prison riots, 1971 J
Municipal Assistance Corporation, 1975 F
financial crisis, 1975 J, K
Mayoral election, 1977 L
first black mayor, 1990 A
World Summit for Children, 1990 J
places, buildings and institutions in or near:
AT&T Building, 1984 S
Brooklyn, Barnum and Bailey's Circus, 1871 W
Carnegie Music Hall, 1891 T
Chamber of Commerce, 1903 S
Customs House, 1902 S
Daily News Building, 1930 S
Drury Lane Theatre (later Manhattan Opera House), 1903 W
Empire State Building, 1930 S
Grand Central Station, 1912 S
Guggenheim Art Museum, 1959 S
Hudson Terminal Building, 1909 T
Idlewild Air Terminal, 1958 S
Jockey Club, 1894 X
Kinetoscope Parlour, 1894 W
Lever House, 1952 S
Lincoln Memorial, 1914 S
Manhattan bridge, 1910 P
Manhattan Opera House, 1903 P
Metropolitan Opera, 1883 T
Museum of Modern Art, 1929 S
National Conservatory, 1892 T
New Crotoun tunnel, 1893 P
One UN Plaza, 1976 S
Pan American Airlines Building, 1962 S
Pearl Street generating station, 1882 P
Philharmonic Society, 1842 T
Piscator's Studio Theatre, 1941 W
Rockefeller Center, 1931 S
Seagram Building, 1958 S
Singer Building, 1905 S
Stock Exchange, 1903 S, 1929 K, O
Subway, 1904 P, 1908 P
UN Building, 1950 S
Whitney Museum, 1966 S
Woolworth Building, 1913 S
World Trade Center, 1970 S, 1973 S
art in, 1825 S, 1913 S
drama in, 1820 W
music in, 1770 T, 1796 T, 1842 T, 1859 T
university extension lectures, 1850 O
population, 1801 Y, 1841 Y, 1881 Y, 1906 Y, 1950 Y, 1960 Y, 1970 Y
New Zealand: coast of, charted, 1768 P; proclaimed a British Colony, 1841 E; Maoris sign treaty of Waitangi, 1840 B; Maori revolt, 1843 F. *See also under* Wars, Maori; female franchise in, 1893 O
Queen's visit for Cook bi-centenary celebrations, 1970 C
elections, 1981 L, 1984 G, 1990 K
anti-nuclear policy espoused and access for US warships and military aircraft denied, 1986 H
US defence obligations to suspended, 1986 H
New towns, in Britain, 1946 O; Hatfield, 1952 S; Commission, 1961 O
Newark, Canada, 1913 M
'Newcastle Programme' of British Liberal Party, 1891 K
Newcastle-upon-Tyne, Northumb., England, railway bridge, 1850 P
Newfoundland: French fishing rights off, 1763 B; Anglo-French fishery dispute settled, 1904 D, 1910 J; loses Dominion status for mismanagement, 1933 M, bases in, leased to US, 1940 J; joins Dominion of Canada, 1949 C
Newman, John Henry, B. cardinal (1801–90), 1801 Z, 1845 R, 1870 R, 1890 Z; *Apologia*, 1864 R *Tract 90*, 1841 R
awarded title 'Venerable', 1991 R
Newman, Robert, B. concert promoter (1859–1926), 1895 T
Newmarket, Cambs., England, horse-races at, 1809 X, 1839 X
Newport, Mons., Wales, Chartist rising at, 1839 L
Newport, Rhode Island, US, 1778 H, 1780 G
Newry, Northern Ireland, deaths from fighting between IRA and troops, 1971 H
News International dispute, 1986 E, V, 1987 A, B
Newsfilms, 1912 W
Newsom, Sir John, B. publisher and educationalist (1910–71), 1963 O, 1965 M
Newsom Commission, on British public schools, 1968 O
Newspapers:
newsprint, worldwide shortage of, 1974 V
in Australia
consortium led by Conrad Black takes over Fairfax Group, 1991 V
in Britain:
circulation figures, 1991 V
Express Newspapers bought by United Newspapers, 1985 V
illustrated, 1890 V
industrial disputes, 1970 V, 1978 L, 1979 L, V, 1986 E, V, 1987 A, B
Lord Thomson's death, 1976 V
Maxwell buys Mirror group, 1984 V
Messenger group of free newspapers, 1983 V
Mirror Group taken into receivership, 1991 V
Murdoch buys *The Times*, 1981 V
national daily, circulation figures for, 1965 V
News International Plant, Wapping, 1986 E, V, 1987 A, B
News International dispute, 1986 E, 1987 A, B
non-union labour used, 1983 V
Press Complaints Commission replaces Press Council, 1990 V
provincial, affected by strike, 1959 F
Sunday, the first, 1780 V
taxes on, 1798 V, 1819 M; abolished, 1855 V
Telegraph newspapers controlled by Conrad Black, 1985 V
Thomson buys *The Times*, 1966 V
in US, New York strike, 1963 D
Supreme Court ruling on press coverage of trials, 1976 V
See also Journals; Press, freedom of
Asahi Shimbun, 1980 V
Berliner Tageblatt, 1882 V
Berlin Post, war-scare by, 1875 C
Birmingham Post, 1857 V
Boston Centinel, 1784 V
Catholic Times, The, 1860 V
Citizen, The, 1978 K
Collier's Weekly, 1888 V
Daily Chronicle, merges with *Daily News*, 1930 V
Daily Express, The, 1900 V, 1965 V; Beaverbrook buys, 1915 V; Christiensen becomes editor, 1933 V
Daily Graphic, The, 1890 V
Daily Herald, The, 1912 V; Russia attempts to subsidise, 1920 H; last appears, 1964 V
Daily Mail, The, 1896 V, 1965 V, 1981 R
merger, 1971 V
forged document published by, 1977 F
Daily Mirror, The, 1904 V, 1965 V, 1977 V, 1992 H
Daily News, The, 1846 V, 1906 O, 1930 V
Daily Sketch, The, 1909 V, 1965 V; merger, 1971 V
Daily Star, The, 1978 V
Daily Telegraph, The, 1855 V, 1965 V; interviews Kaiser, 1908 K, L; merger with *Morning Post*, 1937 V; new format, 1969
Daily Worker, The, 1930 V, 1965 V; suspended, 1941 V; 1966 V
European, The, 1990 V, 1991 V, 1992 V
Evening News, The, 1881 V, 1987 V; merged into *The Evening*
Standard, 1980 V
Evening Standard, The, 1827 V
Express group, 1977 V, 1985 V
Figaro, Le, 1854 V; charges against Caillaux, 1914 A; editor murdered, 1914 C
Financial Times, The, 1888 V, 1965 V, 1973 M
Frankfurter Zeitung, 1856 V; suppressed, 1943 V
Gay News, 1977 O
Globe, The, 1803 V, 1824 V; suppressed, 1915 V
Guardian, The (formerly *Manchester Guardian*), 1959 V, 1965 V, 1984 C; withdrawal from 'lobby' system, 1986 O
Il Hajja, offices destroyed, 1979 V
Independent, The, 1986 V
withdrawal from 'lobby' system, 1986 O
Independent on Sunday, The, 1990 V
London Daily News, The, 1987 V
Mail on Sunday, The, 1982 V
Manchester Guardian, The, 1821 V; Scott as editor, 1872 V; renamed, 1959 V
Matin, Le, 1884 V
Mattino, Il, 1891 V
Montreal Star, ceases publication, 1979 V
Morning Chronicle, The, 1769 V
Morning Post, The, 1772 V; merged in *Daily Telegraph*, 1937 V
Morning Star, The, 1966 V
Neue Freie Presse, 1864 V
News Chronicle, The, 1930 V
St. James's Chronicle, 1763 V
News of the World, The, 1843 V
Murdoch buys 51 per cent stake, 1968 V
relaunched as tabloid, 1984 V
Wapping plant opened, 1986 V
News on Sunday, The, 1987 V
New York Daily Graphic, 1880 V
New York Daily News, The, purchased by Maxwell, 1991 V
New York Evening Post, 1801 V
New York Herald, 1835 V
New York Post, The, 1977 V
New York Times, 1851 V, 1971 F
Pentagon Papers trial dismissal, 1973
New York Tribune, 1841 V; uses linotype, 1886 V; editor stands for presidency, 1872 E, L
Northern Star, 1838 V
Observer, The, 1791 V; Garvin as editor, 1908 V, 1942 V; under independent governing body, 1946 V, 1979 V
purchased by 'Tiny' Rowland's Lonrho company, 1981 V
People's Daily, 1984 M
Petit Journal, Le, 1863 V
Post, The, 1988 V
Presse, La, 1836 V
ceases publication, 1960 V
Red Star, 1976 A
Scotsman, The, 1817 V

Scottish Daily News, The, 1975 V
Siècle, Le, 1836 V
Sketch and *Mail* merge, 1971 V
Star, The, 1888 V, 1918 S; ceases publication, 1960 V
Stars and Stripes, 1942 V
Sun, The, 1964 V, 1965 V, 1977 V
purchased by Murdoch, 1969 V
industrial dispute, 1978 L, V, 1979 L, V
Wapping plant opened, 1986 V
Elton John libel claim, 1988 V
Sunday Citizen, The, 1967 V
Sunday Correspondent, 1989 V
Sunday Pictorial, The (late *Sunday Mirror*), 1915 V
Sunday Telegraph, The, 1960 V
Sunday Times, The, 1822 V; issues colour supplement, 1962 V
Jack the Ripper allegations, 1970 L
Sydney Daily Telegraph purchased by Murdoch, 1972 V
Sydney Sunday Telegraph purchased by Murdoch, 1972 V
Temps, Le, exonerated from charges of collaboration, 1946 V
Times, The, 1788 V
sends out first war correspondent, 1808 V
is printed by steam, 1814 V
Barnes appointed editor, 1817 V
declares for free trade, 1839 A
Delane appointed editor, 1841 V
on 'Parnellism and Crime', 1887 A
action regarding Parnell's letters, 1888 G
bought by Northcliffe, 1908 V
Dawson appointed editor, 1912 V
Barrington Ward appointed editor, 1941 V
Haley appointed editor, 1952 V
purchased by Thomson, 1966 V
new format, 1966 V
alleges Mozambique massacre, 1973 G
purchased by Murdoch, 1981 V
Times of Malta, offices fire-bombed, 1979 V
Times of India, The, 1838 V
Times Newspapers
industrial dispute, 1978 L, V, 1979 L V
News International dispute, 1986 E, 1987 A, B
Wapping plant opened, 1986 V
Today, 1986 V, 1987 V
Tribuna, La, 1883 V
Washington Star, The, 1981 V
Weekly Political Register, 1802 V
Workers' Weekly, prosecution of, 1924 K
World Journal Tribune, 1966 V
publication ceases, 1967 V
Newton, Sir Charles Thomas, B. archaeologist (1816–94), 1857 Q
Newton, Sir Isaac, B. scientist (1642–1727), library of, 1943 Q
Newton, John, B. divine (1725–1807), 1779 R
Ney, Michel, F. marshal (1769–1815), 1813 J; takes Cuidad Rodrigo, 1810 G; is shot, 1815 M
Nezib, Syria, Turks routed at, 1839 F
Ngami, Lake, Bechuanaland, Central Africa, 1802 P, 1841 P
Ngo Dinh Diem, S. Vietnam, 1955 K
Nguema, (Francisco) Macias, President of Equatorial Guinea (1922–79), deposed and executed, 1979 H, J
Niagara, N. America:
British capture Fort, 1813 M
Bible Conference at, 1895 R
Falls, suspension bridge, 1852 P
Blondin crosses, 1859 W
hydro-electric installations, 1886 P, 1896 P
Conference between US and Mexico, 1914 E, F
Niazi Bay, Young Turk leader, 1908 G
Nicaragua: enters American Federation, 1823 G; union with Honduras and El Salvador, 1895 F; war with Honduras, 1907 B; asks for protection against Costa Rica, 1919 F; US supervises elections in, 1927 E
US cuts off aid to Somoza regime, 1979 B
general strike, 1979 C
Sandinista rebels in Managua, 1979 F
Somoza flees as Sandinista rebels take over, 1979 G
constitution suspended, 1982 C
Reagan declares support for Contras, 1983 E
US consulates closed, 1983 F
US diplomats expelled, 1983 F
US aid to Contras, 1983 G, 1984 E
International Court of Justice ruling over US blockade of ports, 1984 E
US calls on Nicaragua to cease support for El Salvadorean rebels, 1984 F
Sandinista Front election victory, 1984 L
US financial and trade sanctions, 1985 E
Contadora peace treaty, 1986 E
Iran–Contra scandal, 1986 L, M, 1987 B, C, G, H, L, 1989 A, D
Arias Plan, 1987 H
civil war, 1988 C, 1989 L, 1990 D
US ambassador and diplomats expelled, 1988 G
Sandinista government, 1989 L
Sandinista government defeated in elections, 1990 B
Nice, France: France annexes, 1792 L; is ceded to France, 1796 E, 1860 C; Italy claims, 1938 L; bank robbery, 1976 G
Nicholas I, Tsar of Russia (1796–1855), 1796 Z, 1825 M, 1830 L, 1843 O, 1855 C; relations with Poland, 1831 A, 1832 B; suggests partition of Turkey, 1844 F; visits London, 1844 F; orders occupation of Danubian Principalities, 1853 E
Nicholas I, of Montenegro (1860–1918), 1910 H, 1913 E, 1918 L, 1919 D
Nicholas II, Tsar of Russia (1868–1918), 1894 L, 1899 B, E, 1904 K, 1905 M, 1916 B
visits London, 1896 K
promises reforms, 1905 C
signs treaty of mutual aid with Germany, 1905 G
suppresses Duma, 1905 H
capitulates to Duma's demand for legislative powers, 1905 K
dissolves Duma, 1907 F
meets William II, 1907 H
meets Edward VII, 1908 F
agrees to Macedonian reforms, 1908 F
ceases to oppose Baghdad Railway, 1910 L
takes over Russian command, 1915 J
abdicates, 1917 C
executed, 1918 G
Nicholas Nickleby (C. Dickens), 1838 U
Nicholas Nickleby (theatrical adaptation by D. Edgar), 1980 W
Nichols, Mike, Am. film director (b. 1931), 1968 W, 1971 W
Nichols, Peter Richard, B. dramatist (b. 1927), 1967 W, 1970 W, 1977 W
Nicholson's Well, Natal, S. Africa, battle, 1899 K
Nicholson, Ben, B. artist (1894–1982), 1894 Z, 1946 S, 1953 S, 1982 Z
Nicholson, Sir William Newzam Prior, B. artist (1872–1949), 1904 S
Nickel, metals coated with, 1843 P; deposits in New Caledonia, 1876 P
Nicola, Enrico, President of Italy, 1946 F
Nicolai, Carl Otto Ehrenfried, G. musician (1810–1849), 1848 T
Nicolai, Christoph Friedrich, G. author (1733–1811), 1765 R
Nicolaievich, Nicholas, R. grand duke, 1915 J
Nicoll, (John Ramsay) Allardyce, B. scholar (1894–1976), 1973 Q
Nicolson, Sir Harold, B. author (1883–1961), 1934 Q, 1952 Q
Nicosia, negotiations between Greek and Turkish Cypriots in, 1968 F
Niebla (Unamuno y Jugo), 1914 U
Niebuhr, Berthold, G. historian (1777–1831), 1777 Z, 1811 Q, 1814 O, 1816 Q, 1821 R, 1831 Z
Niebuhr, Reinhold, Am. theologian (1892–1971), 1934 R, 1941 R, 1961 R
Niels Lyhne (Jacobsen), 1880 U
Niemen, River, Russia, 1795 K; Napoleon crosses, 1812 F; battle, 1914 J
Niemeyer, Oscar, Brazil. architect (b. 1907), 1958 S, 1960 O
Niemöller, (Friedrich Gustav Emil) Martin, G. theologian (1892–1984), 1892 Z, 1984 Z
Niepce, Joseph, F. physicist (1765–1833), 1765 Z, 1827 P, 1833 Z
Nietzsche, Friedrich Wilhelm, G. philosopher (1844–1900), 1844 Z, 1882 U, 1883 U, 1886 U, 1900 Z
Nieuwland, Julius A., G. chemist, 1931 P
Niger Company, British, 1895 A; sells possessions to Britain, 1899 H; Niger Republic, independence of, 1960 G
Niger, River, Africa: M. Park explores, 1795 P; expeditions to, 1805 P, 1830 P; British protectorate over, 1885 F
Niger, Upper, French conquest, 1883 N
Nigeria: Presbyterian missions in, 1846 R; Anglo-French agreement on, 1890 H; boundaries defined, 1893 L, 1898 F, 1913 C; protectorate, 1899 H; North, British conquest of, 1903 C; amalgamation of North and South, 1914 A; becomes a republic within the Commonwealth, 1963 K
protests against creation of unitary state, 1966 E
mid-west declares independence as Benin, 1967 J
Biafran surrender accepted, 1970 A
population, 1971 Y, 1981 Y, 1991 Y
coups d'état, 1975 G, 1983 M, 1985 H
abortive coup, 1976 B
new constitution, 1978 J
military rule ends, 1979 K
orders expulsion of illegal immigrants, 1983 A
Supreme Military Council assumes power, 1984 A
Dikko affair, 1984 G
National Resistance Army signs peace accord, 1985 M
urbanization, 1985 Y
Nigerian Federation, independence of, 1960 K
Nigger of the Narcissus, The (J. Conrad), 1897 U
Night clubs, 1921 W
Night Fantasies (E. Carter), 1980 T
Night Music (T. Musgrave), 1969 T
Night Must Fall (E. Williams), 1935 W
'Night of the Barricades', Paris, France, 1968 E
Night Thoughts (A. Copland), 1973 T
Nightingale, Florence, B. pioneer of nursing (1820–1910), 1820 Z, 1910 Z
Nightmare Abbey (T. L. Peacock), 1818 U
Nights at the Circus (A. Carter), 1985 U
Nihilists. *See under* Political Parties
Nijinsky, race horse, 1970 X

Nikki, near Dahomey, W. Africa, 1895 A
Nikolaier, Arthur, G. physician (1862–1934), 1884 P
Nikolsburg, Austria, peace treaty, 1866 G, H
Nile, River:
expeditions to discover source of, 1772 P, 1790 P, 1856 P
battle, 1798 H
Upper, territory near, 1890 E
left bank of, assigned to Leopold II, 1894 E, H
Franco-Belgian co-operation on, 1895 J
White, British action on, 1899 L
waters of, Egyptian-Sudan agreements on, 1952 K, 1959 L
diversion of, 1958 G
Nimrod early-warning programme, scrapped by Britain, 1986 O
Nine Days' Wonder, The (J. Masefield), 1934 U
Nine Tailors, The (D. L. Sayers), 1934 U
Niner (C. Andre), 1981 S
Nineteen Eighty-Four (G. Orwell), 1949 W
Ninety-three (V. Hugo), 1874 O
Nineveh, ancient Assyrian capital, excavations of, 1845 Q
Nintendo computer games, 1991 W
Nippur, Iraq, excavations of Babylonian remains at, 1888 Q
Nirvana, pop group, 1991 W
Nissan:
pilot car assembly plant in England, 1984 B
single-union deal negotiated at British plant, 1985 O
Sunderland assembly plant, B., 1986 O
Nitrates, shipped from S. America, 1830 P
Nitric acid, composition of, discovered, 1785 P
Nitrogen, discovery of, 1772 P
Nitroglycerine, 1846 P
Nitrous oxide, Davy's researches concerning, 1800 P
Nitti, Francesco Saverio, It. premier (1868–1953), 1919 F
Nivelle, Robert George, F. soldier (1856–1924), 1916 M, 1917 E
Nixon, Richard Milhous, Am. statesman, Republican (b. 1913), 37th President of US (1969–74), 1913 Z, 1969 A
defeated in presidential election, 1960 L
presidential nomination and election, 1968 H, L
tour of Western European capitals, 1969 B
Vietnam War, 1969 E, F, L, 1972 A, E
visits southern Asia, Roumania and Britain, 1969 G
destruction of US germ warfare stocks ordered, 1969 L
presents US Foreign Policy document to Congress, 1970 B
US troops withdrawal from Vietnam, 1970 D, 1971 D
peace plan proposal, 1970 K
visit to China, 1971 G, 1972 B
blockade and mining of North Vietnamese ports ordered, 1972 E
visits USSR, 1972 E, 1974 F
Watergate affair, 1972 F, 1973 D, F, K, 1974 D, G, H
grain sales to USSR, 1972 G
presidential re-nomination and re-election, 1972 H, L, 1973 A
alleged secret tape-recordings, 1973 G
State of the Union address, 1974 A
pays income tax debt, 1974 D
tours Middle East, 1974 F
impeachment recommended by US House Judiciary Committee, 1974 G
resignation, 1974 H
pardoned by President Ford, 1974 J
Nkomo, Joshua, Rhod./Zimbabwean leader (b. 1917), 1976 K, 1981 B, 1983 B, 1987 M; placed under restriction, 1964 D; detention of, declared illegal, 1964 L
Patriotic Front, 1977 J
Patriotic Front excluded from power-sharing government, 1978 C
Minister of Home Affairs, 1980 C
dismissed from government, 1982 B
flees Zimbabwe, 1983 C
Nkrumah, Kwame, President of Ghana (1909–72), 1909 Z, 1966 B, 1972 Z
forms ministry, 1954 F
increases majority, 1956 G
demands independence for Gold Coast, 1956 H
founds mutual assistance in Africa, 1958 B
proposes conference of independent African states, 1959 G
takes over Convention People's Party, 1961 E
visits Russia, 1961 G
at Belgrade meeting of non-aligned powers, 1961 J
detains opposition leaders, 1961 J
attempted assassination, 1962 H
dismisses chief justice of Ghana, 1963 M
See also under Ghana; Gold Coast
No Force Declaration, 1932 M
No Man's Land (H. Pinter), 1975 W
Nobel Prizes, notable awards, 1920 M, 1964 P, K, 1968 U, 1971 K, 1972 D, 1979 R, 1988 J, 1990 K
Walesa awarded Peace Prize, 1983 K
Nobel, Alfred, Swe. inventor (1833–96), 1833 Z, 1866 P, 1896 Z; establishes prizes, 1896 O
Nobelium, element 102, 1957 P
Nobili, Leopoldo, It. physicist (1784–1835), 1826 P
Noble, Sir Fraser, B. administrator (b. 1918), reports on influence of TV on the young, 1963 O
Nocturne (F. Swinnerton), 1917 U
Nogaisk Steppes, Russia, Russians penetrate, 1943 K
Noguchi, Isamu, Am. sculptor (1904–88), 1904 Z, 1936 S, 1988 Z
Noises Off (M. Frayn), 1982 W
Nokrashy, Pasha, of Egypt, 1948 M
Nolan, Sidney Robert, Austral. artist (b. 1917), 1958 S, 1960 S, 1962 S
Non-Aligned Movement, calls for sanctions against South Africa, 1986 F
Non-aggression Pact, Russia with Persia, 1927 K
Russia with Germany, 1939 S
Non-intervention in Spanish Civil War, Germany and Japan withdraw from Committee, 1937 F
Nono, Luigi, It. musician (1924–90), 1961 T 1975 T, 1985 T
Nonsuch Palace, Surrey, England, site of, excavated, 1959 Q
Nootka Sound, British Columbia, Canada, Anglo-Spanish crisis concerning, 1789 F, 1790 E, K
Nordan, Max Simon, G. philosopher and Zionist (1849–1911), 1897 R
Nordenskjöld, Niels Adolfe Erik, Swe. explorer (1832–1901), 1870 P
Nore, The, England, naval mutiny at, 1797 E, F
Norette, Judge Joseph, President of Haiti, 1991 J
Noriega, Antonio, Panamanian soldier (b. 1940), 1989 E
survives attempted coup, 1989 K
US troops invade Panama to overthrow, 1989 M
surrender to US authorities, 1990 A
conviction for drug trafficking and racketeering, 1992 D
Norm and Ahmed (A. Buzo), 1974 W
Normal Heart, The (L. Kramer), 1986 W
Norman Conquests, The (A. Ayckbourn), 1973 W
Norman, Montagu, Lord Norman, B. economist and financier (1871–1950), 1871 Z, 1950 Z
Normandie, S.S., 1935 P
Normann, Wilhelm, G. chemist, 1901 P
Norse, Old, study of, 1811 Q
Norstad, Lauris, Am. soldier (1907–88), as supreme Allied Commander in Europe, 1956 L, 1963 A
North American Air Defense Council, 1958 E
North Atlantic Treaty, signed, 1949 D
North Atlantic Treaty Organization (NATO):
Eire refuses to participate in, 1949 B
US military aid for, 1949 K
bilateral agreement, 1950 A
Council decides to form European defence force, 1950 J
Turkey agrees to co-operate with, 1950 K
plans to use W. German troops, 1951 J
approval of European defence project, 1952 B
Morocco and Tunis to enter, 1952 B
Russia offers to join, 1954 C
conference on European unity agrees W. Germany should enter, 1954 K
W. Germany enters, 1955 E
offers to mediate in Cyprus, 1957 C
France leaves conference, 1957 L
missile bases in Greece, Russian threats over, 1958 A
W. German forces handed over to, 1958 A
Council rejects Russian proposal on Berlin, 1958 M
Parliamentarians Conference of, sponsors Atlantic Congress, 1959 F
Poland asks for acknowledgement of Oder–Neisse frontier, 1960 G
unified air defence council, 1960 J
exercises, *Der Spiegel's* articles on, 1962 K, L
W. European Union calls for a single nuclear force, 1962 M
US recommends surface ships of, to carry Polaris missiles, 1963 B
France withdraws force from fleet, 1963 F
mixed-manned nuclear fleet, discussed, 1963 K
Greece withdraws from, 1964 H
de Gaulle calls for dismantling, 1966 B
removal of bases from French territory requested, 1966 C
French withdrawal, 1966 G
headquarters moved to Casteau, Belgium, 1967 C
statistics, 1968 Y
headquarters moved from Malta to Naples, 1971 H
Secretary General, 1971 K
military bases in Malta, 1972 C
Greek withdrawal, 1974 H
British Social Democratic Party support for, 1981 C
Carrington succeeds Luns as Secretary-General, 1983 M
Danish Parliament votes to halt payments for deployment of Pershing II and Cruise missiles in Europe, 1984 E
Spain votes to remain in, but not in command structure, 1986 C
Brussels summit, 1989 E
Conference on Security and Cooperation in Europe, 1990 L
North Briton, The, 1763 D, 1764 B
'North, Christopher.' *See* Wilson, John
North German Confederation: formed, 1867 D; Baden seeks to enter, 1870 A; alliances with Bavaria and Wrttemburg, 1870 L

North Pole. *See* Polar Expeditions
North Sea Convention, 1908 H
North Sea gas, 1967 O
North Sea oil and gas concessions, auction of, 1971 H
North, Frederick, Lord North, Earl of Guildford, B. Tory (1732–92), 1767 J, 1778 B, 1782 C; appointed prime minister, 1770 A; resigns, 1782 C; declines to form ministry, 1783 B; opposes Parliamentary Reform, 1783 E; forms Coalition with Fox, 1783 D, M
North, Lieutenant-Colonel Oliver, Am. marine officer (b. 1943), 1986 L, G, 1989 A, D
North-West Passage: expeditions to discover, 1818 P, 1845 P, 1850 P; new passage discovered, 1957 P
North-West Territory, US, 1787 P
Northampton, Northants, England, Bradlaugh as M.P. for, 1880 E
Northanger Abbey (J. Austen), 1818 U
Northcliffe, Lord. *See* Harmsworth, Alfred
Northcote, Stafford Henry, Earl of Iddesleigh, B. Conservative (1818–87), 1854 O, 1874 B, 1881 D
Northern Circars, Madras, India, ceded to Britain, 1766 L
Northern Ireland: A Framework for Devolution, White Paper, 1982 O
Northern Securities case, US, 1904 C
Northrop, John Howard, Am. inventor (1891–1987), 1895 P, 1930 P
Norton, Ken, Am. boxer (b. 1943), 1978 X
Norway: Swedish annexation suggested, 1812 D; ceded by Denmark to Sweden, 1814 A; statholdership abolished, 1873 N; separated from Sweden, 1905 F, J, K; Germany invades, 1940 D
  European Community membership, 1970 F, 1972 A, J
  first woman Prime Minister, 1981 B
  divorce statistics, 1987 Y
  elections under system favouring small parties, 1989 J
  elections, 1990 K
  life expectancy, 1990 Y
  illegitimacy rate, 1991 Y
  merchant shipping tonnage statistics, 1992 Y
Norwegian National Theatre, 1899 W
Norwegian Wood (H. Marukami), 1987 U
Norwich School of Artists, 1803 S
Nostromo (J. Conrad), 1904 U
Not Honour More (J. Cary), 1955 U
Not I (S. Beckett), 1972 W
Notes Towards the Definition of Culture (T. S. Eliot), 1948 O
Notes of a Film Director (S. Eisenstein), 1959 W
Notes of a Native Son (J. Baldwin), 1955 U
Notion of a Universal History in a Cosmopolitan Sense (Kant), 1784 R
Notre-Dame de Paris (V. Hugo), 1831 U
Nott, Sir John William Frederic, B. Conservative politician (b. 1932), 1981 A
Notting Hill Carnival, London, B., 1976 H
Nottingham, Notts., England, racial disturbances in, 1958 H
Nouveau Christianisme (St. Simon), 1825 R
Nouveaux Principes d'Economie Politique (J. Sismondi), 1819 O
Nouvelles Méditations Poétiques (A. de Lamartine), 1823 U
Nouvelles génevoises (R. Töpffer), 1839 U
'Novalis.' *See* Hardenberg, Friedrich von
Nova Scotia: ceded to Britain, 1763 B; enters Dominion of Canada, 1867 C
Novara, Piedmont, Italy, battles, 1821 D, 1849 C
Novel on Yellow Paper (S. Smith), 1936 U
Novel, The:
  gothic, 1794 U
  historical, 1809 U
  romantic, 1765 U
Novello, Ivor, B. actor and composer (1893–1951), 1935 W, 1939 W
November Steps (T. Takemitsu), 1967 T
Novi, Italy, 1799 H
Novo-Georgievsk, Russia, Germans take, 1915 H
Novoroissik, on Black Sea, Russia, 1920 C
Novotny, Antonin, President of Czechoslovakia (1904–75), 1904 Z, 1968 C, 1975 Z
Nowra, Louis, Austral. writer (b. 1950), 1985 W
Nozick, Robert, Am. philosopher (b. 1938), 1974 R
Nu, U., Burmese leader (b. 1907), overthrown, 1962 L
Nubar Pasha, Egyptian Nationalist, 1878 H, 1879 B
Nuclear Energy: European Agency, 1957 M; Inter American Commission, 1959 K
  Tokomak experimental fusion reactors, 1968 P
  in Canada, cooling system, 1971 P
  Swedish government collapses over, 1978 K
  Windscale re-processing plant to be constructed, 1978 O
  Three Mile Island accident, 1979 P
  Israel bombs Iraqi reactor under construction, 1981 F
  Chernobyl accident, 1986 D
  research suggests link between radiation and leukaemia at Sellafield, 1990 B
  atomic fusion, 1991 P
Nuclear Ice-breaker, 1958 P
Nuclear Physics. *See* Atomic Physics
Nuclear Power Stations, 1956 P
Nuclear Radiation, fears of danger to health from, 1955 P
Nuclear Research: Meyrin International Laboratory, 1953 P; US provides Greece with information, 1959 F
Nuclear Submarines, 1958 P, 1963 P
Nuclear Tests
  Japan protests to Russia, 1957 D
  Schweitzer urges condemnation of, 1957 D
  British test bombs of megaton range, 1957 E
  Russia appeals to West to cease, 1957 E
  Geneva conference on detection of, 1958 G
  Russia resumes tests, 1958 J
  Anglo-US declaration on negotiations, 1960 C
  Three-power conference on, 1961 C
    fails, 1962 A
  Russia proposes ban talks should proceed simultaneously with disarmament talks, 1961 F
  UN Assembly demands end of tests, 1962 L
  Test Ban Treaty signed, 1963 H
  China tests guided nuclear missile, 1966 K
  China explodes hydrogen bomb, 1967 F, P
  in South Pacific, by France, 1968 H, 1973 G
  63 nations ban sea-bed atomic weapons, 1971 O
  in India, 1974 E
  Rainbow Warrior sunk by French agents, 1985 G, H, J, L, 1986 G
Nuclear Warfare:
  Conference on surprise attack, 1958 L
  W. German fleet for firing missiles approved by W. European Union, 1961 E
  US plan for multi-lateral force, 1963 A
  NATO mixed-manned fleet, discussed, 1963 K
  Denuclearised Zones:
    Rapacki Plan for, 1957 K; rejected by US and Britain, 1958 B
    negotiations for zone in Middle East, 1959 E
    Russia proposes zone in Balkans, 1959 F
    Russia calls for zone in Europe, 1959 G
    UN resolves to treat Africa as zone, 1961 L
  nuclear weapons prohibited from Latin America, 1967 B
  treaty banning from outer space, 1967 O
  France becomes fifth thermo-nuclear power, 1968 H
  Treaty on Non-Proliferation of Nuclear Weapons, 1968 G, 1969 L
  US agrees to remove from Japan, 1969 L
  mistaken US broadcast of attack, 1971 B
  international treaty banning nuclear weapons from sea-bed signed, 1971 O
  Israeli weapons capability, 1974 M
  SALT II Treaty limiting nuclear weapons, 1979 F
  computer error causes US alert, 1980 F
  cruise missile, 1980 F, 1981 L, 1982 M, 1983 G, K, L, 1984 C, E, F, 1985 B, C
  French neutron bomb capability, 1980 F
  Trident-I missile system, 1980 G
  anti-nuclear demonstrations, 1980 K, 1981 K, 1982 M, 1983 F, K, L, 1984 D, E, 1985 B
  British Labour Party votes for unilateral disarmament, 1980 K
  Chinese inter-continental ballistic missile, 1980 P
  Iraqi Osirak reactor bombed by Israelis, 1981 F
  US neutron bomb, 1981 H
  missiles deal between US and USSR, 1981 L
  Pershing missile, 1981 L, 1983 K, L, 1984 E
  Britain to replace Polaris with Trident II, 1982 C
  Trident-II missile system, 1982 C
  USSR halts SS-20 missile deployment, 1982 C
  US MX missiles funding refused, 1982 M
  USSR bargains with US over missiles, 1982 M
  The Church and the Bomb, C. of E. report, 1982 R
  central Europe nuclear-free zone proposed, 1983 A, B
  Church of England General Synod votes against unilateral nuclear disarmament, 1983 B
  deployment of US missiles in Europe, 1983 K, L
  Greenham Common women's peace camp, 1984 D
  Danish Parliament votes to halt payments to NATO for deployment of Pershing II and Cruise missiles in Europe, 1984 E
  US–USSR arms reduction talks, 1985 A, C, L, 1987 A, C, D, F, G
  Gorbachev proposes timetable for elimination of all nuclear weapons, 1986 A
  British Labour Party pledges to close all US nuclear bases in Britain, 1986 J
  Intermediate-range Nuclear Forces (INF) Treaty, 1987 J, L, M, 1988 F
  Strategic Arms Reduction Treaty (START), 1991 G
  Iraqi nuclear facilities inspected by UN, 1991 H
Nucleohelicates, creation, 1990 P
Nude, The (K. Clark), 1957 S
Nuffield Foundation, 1943 O
Nujoma, Sam Shafilshuna, SWAPO president (b. 1929), 1989 J
  elected President of Republic of Namibia, 1990 B
Numbers, Theory of, 1854 P
Numismatics, studies in, 1792 Q, 1840 Q
Nunavut, Canada, 1992 L
Nuncomar, Indian official (d. 1775), 1775 N
Nuremberg, Germany: Social Democrat rally, 1908 J; Laws, against Jews, 1935 J; Tribunal, of war criminals, 1946 J

Nuri-es-Said, Iraq. politician, 1958 C, G
'Nutcracker Man', 1959 P
Nyas, Lake, Cameroon, toxic gas eruption, 1986 H
Nyasaland: proclaimed a British protectorate, 1891 F; frontier settled, 1901 B; right to cede from Central African Federation, acknowledged, 1962 M; becomes self-governing, 1963 A; becomes independent republic as Malawi, 1964 G. *See also* Central African Federation; Malawi
Nyerere, Julius Kamharage, President of Tanzania (b. 1922), 1985 K; becomes premier of Tanganyika, 1961 E; resigns, 1962 A; elected President of Tanganyika, 1962 L; elected President of Tanzania, 1964 D
Nyers, Rezso, Hungarian politician (b. 1923), 1989 K
Nylon stockings, invented, 1937 P

O

Oakeshott, Michael, B. philosopher (1903–90), 1939 O
Oberland (D. Richardson), 1927 U
Oberlin, Jean Frédéric, G. pastor and philanthropist (1740–1826), 1769 O
Oberon (C. M. Wieland), 1780 U
Objections to Christian Belief (ed. A. Vidler), 1963 R
Oblomov (I. Goncharov), 1859 U
Obregón, Alvaro, president of Mexico (1880–1928), 1920 J, 1928 G
O'Brien, James, B. Chartist leader (1805–64), 1848 G
O'Brien, William Smith, Ir. Nationalist leader (1803–64), 1886 L
Obscenity and the Law (N. St. John-Stevas), 1956 O
Observations on Civil Liberty and the Justice and Policy of the War with America (R. Price), 1776 O
Observations on Magnetism (J. Gay-Lussac), 1807 P
Observations on a late Publication on the Present State of the Nation (E. Burke), 1769 O
Observations on the Geology of the U.S. (W. Maclure), 1809 P
Observations sur les hôpitaux (P. Cabanis), 1789 O
Observatories:
  in Britain, Mullard, Cambridge, 1957 P
    Royal, Herstmonceux, 1953 P
  in Russia, Central, of the USSR Academy of Sciences, 1954 P
  in US Lisk, California, 1954 P
    Mt. Wrangell, Alaska, 1953 P
Ocana, Spain, Spanish defeat at, 1809 L
O'Casey, Sean, Ir. dramatist (1884–1964), 1884 Z, 1925 W, 1926 W, 1934 W, 1942 W, 1964 Z
Oceanography:
  surveys, 1872 P, 1934 P, 1950 P, 1959
    through bathyscaphe, 1948 P, 1964 P
Ochakóv, on Black Sea, Russia: Russians capture, 1788 M, 1791 C; Turkey cedes, 1792 A
O'Connell, Daniel, Ir. Nationalist leader (1775–1847), 1775 Z, 1835 C; establishes Catholic Association, 1823 E; wins Clare election, 1828 F
O'Connor, Feargus, Ir. Chartist leader (1794–1855), 1838 O, V
Ode on the Intimations of Immortality (W. Wordsworth), 1807 U
Ode to a Nightingale (J. Keats), 1820 U
Ode to the West Wind (P. B. Shelley), 1820 U
Ödenburg, plebiscite for union with Hungary, 1921 M
Odeon cinema circuit in Britain, 1933 W
Oder, River, Cen. Europe, 1772 P, 1945 A
Oder–Neisse line, 1950 L; Poland asks for acknowledgment of, 1960 G
Odes (F. Klopstock), 1771 U
Odes (V. Hugo), 1819 U
Odessa, Russia: port founded, 1791 N; Turks bombard, 1914 K; Allies evacuate, 1919 D; Bolsheviks, capture, 1920 B; Germans take, 1941 K
Odets, Clifford, Am. dramatist (1906–63), 1935 W
Odom, Capt., Am. aviator, 1947 P
O'Donnell, Leopold, duke of Tetuan, Sp. general and Liberal politician (1809–67), 1854 G, 1856 J, K, 1865 F, 1867 L
O'Duffy, Eoin, Ir. politician (1892–1944), 1933 J
Odyssey of Homer, The (T. E. Lawrence's translation), 1935 Q
Oecumenical movement, 1928 R, 1959 R 1961 R
Oersted, Hans Christian, Da. physicist (1777–1851), 1819 P
Oesophagus, resection of, 1872 P
Offenbach, Jacques, F. musician (1819–80), 1819 Z, 1858 T, 1880 Z, 1881 T
Offenburg, Germany, French troops leave, 1924 H
Of Human Bondage (W. S. Maugham), 1915 U
Of Mice and Men (J. Steinbeck), 1937 U
Of Mind and Other Matters (N. Goodman), 1984 R
Of Spirit: Heidegger and the Question (J. Derrida), 1987 R
Ogaden, Ethiopia, Somali invasion, 1977 G
Ogden, Charles Kay, B. originator of Basic English (1889–1957), 1927 O, 1947 O
O'Gorman, Juan, Mexic. architect (b. 1905), 1952 S
O'Higgins, Kevin Christopher, Ir. Nationalist (1892–1927), 1927 G
Ohio: becomes a US state, 1803 C; steam engine to, 1829 P; abandons liquor licensing, 1851 O; corruption in, 1911 O; demonstrators shot at Kent State University, 1970 E
Ohira, Masayoshi, Prime Minister of Japan (1910–80), 1978 L
  death, 1980 F
Ohm, Georg Simon, G. physicist (1787–1854), 1787 Z, 1827 P, 1843 P, 1854 Z
Oil:
  petroleum consumption, comparative statistics, 1937 Y
  Arab oil embargo on Britain and US, 1967 F, J
  Suez oil refineries destroyed by Israeli artillery, 1967 K
  Deep Sea Drilling Project, 1968 P
  first supertanker, 1968 P
  price rises, 1971 B, 1973 M, 1978 M, 1979 M, 1980 M
  British government bargains with Iran, 1974 A
  Kissinger proposals for price reduction, 1974 L
  Organization of Petroleum Exporting Countries (OPEC), 1975 M, 1978 M, 1980 M, 1983 C
  Alexander Kielland platform collapses, 1980 C
  OPEC meeting in Vienna on production quotas, 1982 M
  price falls, 1983 C, 1986 D
  in Alaska, 1968 O
  in Algeria, 1977 Y
  in Argentine, nationalised, 1928 J
  in Britain, 1977
    refinery at Fawley, 1951 P
    licences to drill in N. Sea, 1964 P
    embargo placed on oil for Rhodesia, 1965 M
    airlift to Zambia in operation, 1965 M
    company strikes oil in N. Sea, 1965 P
    North Sea concessions auction, 1971 H
    first North Sea Oil pumped ashore, 1975 F
    net exports, 1980 O
    Piper Alpha explosion, 1988 G
  in Central and South America, 1946 Y
  in Dutch East Indies, 1937 Y
  in Iran, 1937 Y, 1977 Y
    agreement with Russia is nullified, 1947 L
    nationalised, 1951 G
    strike action by workers, 1978 K
    admits to production and export stoppage, 1978 M
    Kharg Island oil terminal blockaded by Iraq, 1984 B
    US attacks on Iranian oil installations in Gulf, 1987 K
    Iranian oil platforms destroyed in US attack, 1988 D
  in Iraq, 1977 Y
    Iraq Petroleum Company pipeline seized by Syria, 1966 M
    Iran takes Iraqi oil port of Faw, 1986 B
  in Kuwait, 1977 Y
    US offers naval protection to Kuwaiti tankers in Gulf, 1987 G
  in Libya, 1977 Y, 1982 C
  in Mexico, 1920 Y, 1937 Y, 1977 Y
    concessions in, 1923 D
    expropriations of British and US properties, 1938 C
  in Nigeria, 1977 Y
  in Norway, 1977 Y
  in Panama, 1946 Y
  in Roumania, 1860 Y, 1937 Y, 1946 Y
    seized by Germans, 1940 K
  in Russia and Soviet Union, 1903 Y, 1920 Y, 1932 Y, 1937 Y, 1940 Y, 1946 Y, 1951 Y, 1977 Y
  in Saudi Arabia, 1946 Y, 1949 O, 1977 Y, 1983 C
    Getty Oil Company, 1949 O
    rationing plan rejected, 1979 E
    oil tankers attacked by Iran, 1984 E
  in US, 1860 Y, 1863 Y, 1873 Y, 1883 Y, 1893 Y, 1901 Y, 1903 Y, 1906 Y, 1911 Y, 1916 Y, 1920 Y,1921 Y, 1926 Y, 1937 Y, 1946 Y, 1951 Y, 1961 Y, 1977 Y
    Congress rejects Carter's petrol rationing plan, 1979 E
    US embargo, 1979 L
  in Venezuela, 1937 Y, 1976 A, 1977 Y
  See also Petroleum
Oil Companies:
  Anglo-Persian agreement annulled by Persia, 1932 L
    dispute settled, 1933 B. *See also* Iranian Oil Co
  Iraq Petroleum, dispute with the Lebanon settled, 1959 F
  Royal Dutch Shell Oil, banned by Indonesia, 1958 F
  Shell Oil refinery, Havana, dispute with Cuba, 1960 G
  Standard Oil Co., 1922 D
  US leases for, scandal over, 1924 B
Oil pipe-lines:
  Mosul–Tripoli, 1934 G
  Kirkuk, Iraq, to Haifa and Tripolis, 1935 P
  from Texas ('big inch'), 1943 P
  Abadan–Teheran, completed, 1957 A
  Iraq Petroleum Company pipe-line seized by Syria, 1966 M
  trans-Alaska, 1977 P
Oil pollution of sea, 1954 O
  Amoco Cadiz tanker runs aground, 1978 C
  Exxon Valdez accident, 1989 C
  Torrey Canyon runs aground, 1967 C

Oil production. *See under* Petrol
Oil tanker fleets, comparative tonnages, 1964 Y
Oil wells, in Pennsylvania, 1859 P; in Baku, 1873 P
Oil-engine, 1873 P
Oise–Aisne Canal, France, Germans forced back to, 1917 K
Oiza, Francisco Saenz de, Sp. architect (b. 1918), 1980 S
Ojukwu, Colonel Chukwuemeka Odumegwu, Biafran leader (b. 1933), 1967 E, 1970 A
Okada, Keisuke, Jap. premier (1868–1952), 1934 G
Okello, Brigadier Tito, Ugandan leader (b. 1914), 1985 M, 1985 G
O'Kelly, Sean, president of Eire, 1945 F, 1959 F
Oken, Lorenz, G. scientist (1779–1851), 1822 P
Okinawa, Ryukyu Islands, Pacific, US take, 1945 D
returned to Japan, 1969 L
Oklahoma, state, US: opened to settlement, 1889 D; admitted as a US state, 1907 L
Okri, Ben, Nig. author (b. 1959), 1991 U
Olav V, King of Norway (1903–91), 1957 J, 1991 A
Olbers, Henrich Wilhelm Matthias, G. astronomer (1758–1840), 1797 P, 1801 L
Old Curiosity Shop, The (C. Dickens), 1840 U
Old Faith and the New, The (D. F. Strauss), 1872 R
Old Man and the Sea, The (E. Hemingway), 1952 U
Old Mortality (W. Scott), 1816 U
Old People (S. Rowntree), 1947 O
Old Red Sandstone (H. Miller), 1841 U
Old Wives' Tale, The (A. Bennett), 1908 U
Old-age pensions, in Britain, advocated, 1879 O
Rothschild's Committee on, 1898 O
increased, 1964 L
introduced, 1909 A
women to receive at 60, 1940 B
in France, 1850 O
in Germany, 1889 E
in New Zealand, 1898 O
Oldenburg, W. Germany, grand duchy: ceded by Denmark to Russia, 1773 K; Napoleon annexes, 1811 A
Oldfield, Mike, B. musician (b. 1953), 1974 W
Oleo-margarine, substitution for butter limited, 1902 P
Olga, dowager Queen of Greece, 1920 L
Olivenza, Spain, ceded to Spain, 1801 F
Oliver Twist (C. Dickens), 1837 U
Olivia, Achille Bonito, It. art critic, 1979 S
Olivier, Borg, Maltese Nationalist Party, 1953 G, 1962 C
Olivier, Laurence Kerr, Lord Olivier, B. actor (1907–89), 1907 Z, 1944 W, 1948 W, 1957 W, 1966 W, 1989 Z
Ollivier, Oliver Emile, F. statesman (1825–1912), 1870 A
Olmec culture studied, 1966 Q
Olmütz, Czechslovakia, Punctation of, 1850 L
Olney Hymns (Cowper and Newton), 1779 R
Olszewski, Jan, Prime Minister of Poland (b. 1930), 1992 F
Olympia and York, Canary Wharf development, 1987 S
Olympia, Greece, 'Hermes' of Praxiteles found at, 1875 S
Olympic Games: Athens, 1896 X; London, 1908 X; Stockholm, 1912 X; Antwerp, 1920 X; Paris, 1924 X; Los Angeles, 1932 X; Berlin, 1936 X; Melbourne, 1956 X; Rome, 1960 X; Tokio, 1964 P, X
Mexico, 1968 X
IOC expells South Africa, 1970 F
Israeli team members murdered, 1972 J
Munich, 1972 J, X
Montreal, 1976 X
IOC decision on China, 1979 X
IOC decision on Moscow, 1980 B
Moscow, 1980 C, G, R, X
Los Angeles, 1984 X
Seoul, 1988 X
IOC readmits South Africa, 1991 X
Barcelona, 1992 X
Omaha, Nebraska, US, Populist Convention at, 1892 G
Oman, Steppes, Arabia, 1948 P
Oman, revolt of the Imam, 1957 G
Ombudsman, The (or Parliamentary Commissioner) in Britain, 1965 O
Omdurman, Khartoum, Sudan, 1884 K; Kitchener's victory at, 1898 J
Omeros (D. Walcott), 1991 U
Ommanney, Erasmus, B. admiral (1810–75), 1850 P
Omnibus:
horse-drawn, 1892 P
motor, 1905 P
ordered by Cuba, 1964 A
Omsk, Siberia, Russia: Red Army takes, 1919 L; solar eclipse observed at, 1936 P
On American Taxation (E. Burke), 1774 O
On Bended Knees (M. Goodman), 1992 U
On Crimes and Punishments (C. Beccaria), 1764 O
On Discovery in Medicine (J. G. Zimmermann), 1764 P
On Heroes and Hero-Worship (T. Carlyle), 1841 U
On Labour (W. T. Thornton), 1869 O
On Laughter (H. Bergson), 1900 R
On Liberty (J. S. Mill), 1859 O
On Literature (A. de Staël), 1800 U
On Living in a Revolution (J. Huxley), 1944 O
On Primary Numbers (P. L. Chebichev), 1850 P
On Two Levels With Two Colours (D. Buren), 1976 S
On the Archetypes and Homologies of the Vertebrate Skeleton (Owen), 1848 P
On the Buses, television programme, 1970 W
On the Civil Amelioration of the ... Jews (M. Mendelssohn), 1781 R
On the Conservation of Energy (H. Helmholtz 1847 P
On the Eve (I. Turgeniev), 1860 U
On the Hypotheses forming the Foundation of Geometry (G. Riemann), 1854 P
On the Notion of the Theory of Science (J. G. Fichte), 1794 R
On the Origins of Speech (Herder), 1772 P
On the Plurality of Worlds (D.K. Lewis), 1986 R
On the Road (J. Kerouac), 1957 U
Onassis, Aristotle Socrates, Greek ship-owner (1906–75), 1906 Z, 1932 O, 1975 Z
Ondaatje, Michael, Canad. author (b. 1943), 1987 U, 1992 U
One Day in the Life of Ivan Denisovich (A. Solzhenitsyn), 1962 U
One Hundred Years of Solitude (G. García Márquez), 1967 U
One of Us (H. Young), 1989 Q
One-Dimensional Man (H. Marcuse), 1964 R
O'Neill, Eugene Gladstone, Am. dramatist (1888–1953), 1916 W, 1920 W, 1921 W, 1923 W, 1931 W, 1933 W, 1940 W, 1946 W
O'Neill, Terence Marne, Lord O'Neill, N. Ir. premier (1914–90) 1963 C, 1969 E
Only Fools and Horses, television series, 1981 W
Ontario, Canada, enters Dominion of Canada, 1867 C
OP Art, 1964 S
Open Society and Its Enemies, The (K. Popper), 1945 R
'Open-door' policy in China, 1907 F, 1922 B
Opera ballet: *Persephone* (Stravinsky), 1934 T
Opera:
Abu Hassan (Weber), 1811 T
Aïda (Verdi), 1871 T
Akhnaten (P. Glass), 1984 T
Al gran sole carico d'amore (L. Nono), 1975 T
Albert Herring (B. Britten), 1947 T
Alcestre (Gluck), 1767 T
Antigone (Honegger), 1927 T
Antigone (Piccinni), 1771 T
Antony and Cleopatra (S. Barber), 1966 T
Arabella (R. Strauss), 1933 T
Archers of Switzerland, The (B. Carr), 1796 T
Arden Must Die (A. Goehr), 1967 T
Ariadne and Bluebeard (P. Dukas), 1907 T
Ariane (Massenet), 1906 T
Armide (Gluck), 1777 T
Babel (Stravinsky), 1952 T
Barber of Baghdad (Cornelius), 1858 T
Barber of Seville (G. Paisiells), 1780 T
Barber of Seville (Rossini), 1816 T
Bartered Bride, The (Smetana), 1866 T
Bassarids, The (H.W. Henze), 1966 T
Bastien and Bastienne (Mozart), 1768 T
Behold the Sun (A. Goehr), 1985 T
Benvenuto Cellini (Berlioz), 1837 T
Besuch der Alten Dame, Der (G. von Einen), 1971 T
Billy Budd (Britten), 1951 T
Billy the Kid (A. Copland), 1938 T
Bluebeard's Castle (Bartók), 1918 T
Boatswain's Mate, The (E. Smyth), 1916 T
Bohème, La (Puccini), 1896 T
Bohemian Girl, The (Balfe), 1843 T
Boris Godunov (Moussorgski), 1874 T
Bride of Lammermoor (Donizetti), 1859 W
Burning Fiery Furnace, The (B. Britten), 1966 T
Caliph of Baghdad (Boieldieu), 1799 T
Cavalleria Rusticana (P. Mascagni), 1890 T
Cenerentola, La (Rossini), 1810 T
Christopher Columbus (D. Milhaud), 1930 T
Comte Dry, Le (Rossini), 1828 T
Consul, The (C. Menotti), 1950 T
Coppélia (Delibes), 1870 T
Corregidor, The (H. Wolf), 1896 T
Così fan tutte (Mozart), 1789 T, 1790 T
Crown Diamonds (Auber), 1841 T
Danaides, Les (A. Salieri), 1784 T
David (D. Milhaud), 1953 T
Death in Venice (B. Britten), 1973 T
Devils of Loudon, The (K. Penderecki), 1969 T
Diary of a Madman (H. Searle), 1958 T
Doctor and Apotheker (Dittersdorf), 1786 T
Dr. Faustus (Busoni), 1925 T
Don Carlos (Verdi), 1867 T
Don Giovanni (Mozart), 1787 T
Don Pasquale (Donizetti), 1843 T
Donnerstag aus Licht (K. Stockhausen), 1981 T
Duenna, The (Prokofiev), 1946 T
Einstein on the Beach (P. Glass), 1976 T
Electrification of the Soviet Union, The (N. Osborne), 1987 T
Elisir d'Amore, L' (Donizetti), 1832 T
Enchantress, The (Bliss), 1952 T
English Cat, The (H. W. Henze), 1983 T
Ernani (Verdi), 1844 T
Erwartung (Schoenberg), 1924 T
Eugene Onegin (Tchaikovsky), 1879 T
Fair Maid of Perth, The (Bizet), 1867 T
Falstaff (Verdi), 1893 T
Faust (Gounod), 1859 T

Fedora (U. Giordano), 1898 T
Ferdinand Cortez (Spontini), 1809 T
Fervaal (D'Indy), 1897 T
Fidelio (Beethoven), 1805 T, 1814 T
Fille du Régiment, La (Donizetti), 1840 T
Flaming Angel, The (Prokofiev), 1954 T
Fledermaus, Die (J. Strauss), 1874 T
Flying Dutchman, The (Wagner), 1843 T
Forgotten Rite, The (J. Ireland), 1915 T
Forza del Destino, La (Verdi), 1862 T
Fra Diavolo (Auber), 1830 S
Freischütz, Der (Weber), 1838 W
Gazza Ladra, La (Rossini), 1817 T
Ghosts of Versailles, The (J. Corigliano), 1991 T
Girl of the Golden West, The (Puccini), 1910 T
Gloriana (Britten), 1953 T
Glückliche Hand, Die (Schoenberg), 1924 T
Golden Cockerel, The (Rimsky-Korsakov), 1910 T
Gondoliers, The (Sullivan), 1889 T
Götterdämmerung (R. Wagner), 1874 T
Grand Duke, The (Sullivan), 1896 T
Grand Macabre, Le (G. Ligeti), 1978 T
Hansel and Gretel (Humperdinck), 1893 T
Harmony of the World, The (Hindemith), 1957 T
Hecube (Martinu), 1956 T
Help, Help, the Globolinks! (G.C. Menotti), 1968 T
H.M.S. Pinafore (Sullivan), 1878 T
Herodias (P. Hindemith), 1944 T
Higglety-Pigglety Pop (O. Knussen), 1985 T
Horseman, The (A. Sallinen), 1975 T
Hugenots, The (Meyerbeer), 1836 T
I Pagliacci (Leoncavallo), 1892 T
Ice Break, The (M. Tippett), 1977 T
Idomeneo (Mozart), 1781 T
Immortal Hour, The (R. Boughton), 1914 T
Intoleranza (L. Nono), 1961 T
Iolanthe (Sullivan), 1882 T
Iphigenia in Aulis (Gluck), 1774 T
Iphigenia in Tauris (Gluck), 1779 T
Irmelin (Delius), 1953 T
Island of God, The (C. Menotti), 1942 T
Italian in Algiers, The (Rossini), 1813 T
Ivan the Terrible (Rimsky-Korsakov), 1873 T
Jenufa (Janáček), 1916 T
Jewels of the Madonna, The (Wolf-Ferrari), 1911 T
Johnny Strikes Up (E. Křenek), 1927 T
Joseph (Méhul), 1807 T
Judith (Honegger), 1926 T
Julius Caesar Jones (Williamson), 1965 T
King David (Honegger), 1921 T
King Goes Forth to France, The (A. Sallinen), 1984 T
King Midas (Françaix), 1957 T
King Priam (M. Tippett), 1962 T
Knot Garden, The (M. Tippett), 1970 T
Koanga (Delius), 1904 T
Kullervo (A. Sallinen), 1992 T
Lady Macbeth of Mtsensk (Shostakovich), 1932 T
Last Temptations, The (J. Kokkonen), 1975 T
Lear (A. Reimann), 1978 T
Life for the Czar, A (Glinka), 1836 T
Life with an Idiot (A. Schnittle), 1992 T
Lighthouse, The (P. M. Davies), 1980 T
Lodoiska (Cherubini), 1791 T
Lohengrin (Wagner), 1850 T
Lorenzaccio (S. Busotti), 1972 T
Louise (G. Charpentier), 1900 T
Love for Three Oranges, The (Prokofiev), 1921 T
Lovespell, The (De Falla), 1915 T
Lucy of Lammermoor (Donizetti), 1835 T
Lulu (A. Berg), 1979 T
Macbeth (Verdi), 1847 T
Madam Angot's Daughter (Lecocq), 1872 T
Madame Butterfly (Puccini), 1904 T
Magic Flute (Mozart), 1791 T, 1955 T
Making of the Representative for Planet 8, The (P. Glass), 1987 T
Manon Lescaut (Puccini), 1893 T
Manon (Massenet), 1884 T
Margherita d'Anjou, 1820 T
Marriage of Figaro, The (Mozart), 1786 T
Martha (Flotow), 1847 T
Mary of Egypt (J. Tavener), 1992 T
Mary Queen of Scots (T. Musgrave), 1977 T
Masaniello (Auber), 1828 T
Mask of Orpheus, The (H. Birtwistle), 1983 T
Master Pédros (De Falla), 1923 T
Mastersingers, The (Wagner), 1868 T
Mathis der Maler (Hindemith), 1934 T
Mavra (Stravinsky), 1922 T
Médéa (D. Milhaud), 1940 T
Medea (Cherubini), 1797 T
Medium, The (Menotti), 1946 T
Merrie England (E. German), 1902 T
Merry Widow, The (Léhar), 1905 T
Merry Wives of Windsor, The (Nicolai), 1848 T
Midsummer Marriage, The (M. Tippett), 1955 T
Midsummer Night's Dream, A (Britten), 1961 T
Mignon (Thomas), 1866 T
Montag aus Licht (K. Stockhausen), 1988 T
Moon and Sixpence, The (J. Gardner), 1957 T
Moses and Aaron (Schoenberg), 1954 T, 1965 T
Nelson (L. Berkeley), 1954 T
Neues vom Tage (Hindemith), 1929 T
New Year (M. Tippett), 1989 T
Night at the Chinese Opera, A (J. Weir), 1987 T
Nixon in China (J. Adams), 1987 T
Norma (Bellini), 1831 T
Notre Dame de Paris (Fry), 1863 T
Oedipus Rex (Stravinsky), 1927 T
Opera (L. Berio), 1970 T
Orpheus in the Underworld (Offenbach), 1858 T
Othello (Verdi), 1887 T
Owen Wingrave (B. Britten), 1971 T
Palestrina (Pfitzner), 1917 T
Paradise Lost (K. Penderecki), 1978 T
Parsifal (Wagner), 1882 T
Pearl Fishers, The (Bizet), 1863 T
Pelléas et Mélisande (Debussy), 1902 T
Penny for a Song, A (R.R. Bennett), 1967 T
Perfect Fool, The (Holst), 1923 T
Perfect Lives (television opera) (R. Ashley), 1984 T
Peter Grimes (Britten), 1945 T
Pietra del Paragone, La, 1812 T
Pilgrim's Progress, A (Vaughan Williams), 1951 T
Pirata, Il (Bellini), 1827 T
Pirates of Penzance, The (Sullivan), 1880 T
Porgy and Bess (G. Gershwin), 1935 T
Prince Igor (Borodin), 1887 T, 1890 T
Prinz von Hamburg, Der (H. W. Henze), 1960 T
Prodigal Son, The (B. Britten), 1968 T
Punch and Judy (H. Birtwistle), 1968 T
Queen of Sheba (Goldmark), 1875 T
Queen of Spades (Tchaikovsky), 1890 T
Quiet Place, A (L. Bernstein), 1983 T
Rake's Progress, The (Stravinsky), 1951 T
Rape of Lucretia, The (Britten), 1946 T
Re in Ascolta, Un (L. Berio), 1984 T
Rhinegold, The (Wagner), 1869 T
Richard Coeur de Lion (Grétry), 1784 T
Rienzi (Wagner), 1842 T
Rigoletto (Verdi), 1851 T
Ring, The, Wagner's text of, 1853 T
first complete performance, 1876 T
broadcast without a break, 1962 W
Rip Van Winkle (Bristow), 1855 T
Rosenkavalier, Der (R. Strauss), 1911 T
Ruddigore (Sullivan), 1887 T
Russalka (Dargomijsky), 1856 T
Russalka (Dvorák), 1901 T
Russlan and Ludmilla (Glinka), 1842 T
Saint François d'Assise (O. Messiaen), 1983 T
St. Susanna (Hindemith), 1922 T
Saint of Bleecker Street, The (Menotti), 1954 T
Salome (R. Strauss), 1905 T
Samstag aus Licht (K. Stockhausen), 1984 T
Satyagraha (P. Glass), 1980 T
Savonarola (C. V. Stanford), 1884 T
School for Wives (Liebermann), 1955 T
Schwanda the Bagpiper (Weinberger), 1927 T
Schwarze Maske, Die (K. Penderecki), 1986 T
Secret Marriage, The (D. Cimarosa), 1792 T
Seraglio, Il (Mozart), 1782 T
Shadowplay-2 (A. Goehr), 1970 T
Sicilian Vespers (Berlioz), 1855 T
Siegfried (Wagner), 1876 T
Sir Gawain and the Green Knight (H. Birtwistle), 1991 T
Snow Maiden, The (Rimsky-Korsakov), 1882 T
Socratie (E. Satie), 1920 T
Sonnambula, La (Bellini), 1831 T
Staatstheater (M. Kagel), 1971 T
Story of Vasco, The (G. Crosse), 1974 T
Sylvia (Delibes), 1876 T
Tales of Hoffmann, The (Offenbach), 1881 T
Tancredi (Rossini), 1813 T
Tannhäuser (Wagner), 1845 T
Tarquin (Křenek), 1941 T
Taverner (P. M. Davies), 1972 T
Tender Land, The (A. Copland), 1954 T
Thais (Massenet), 1894 T
Threepenny Opera, The (Weill and Brecht), 1928 T
London production of, 1956 W
Tiefland (D'Albert), 1903 T
Tobias and the Angel (Britten), 1960 T
Tosca (Puccini), 1900 T
Traviata, La (Verdi), 1853 T
Trial by Jury (Sullivan), 1875 T
Tristan and Isolde (Wagner), 1859 T, 1865 R
Trittico, Il (Puccini), 1918 T
Troades (A. Reimann), 1986 T
Troilus and Cressida (Walton), 1954 T
Trojans, The, Part I (Berlioz), 1863 T
Part II (The Taking of Troy), 1899 T
Trovatore, Il (Verdi), 1853 T
Turandot (Puccini), 1924 T
Turn of the Screw, The (Britten), 1954 T
Ulisse (L. Dallapiccola), 1968 T
Vanessa (S. Barber), 1958 T
Vanishing Bridegroom, The (J. Weir), 1990 T
Vera Storia, La (L. Berio), 1982 T
verratene Meer, Das (H. W. Henze), 1990 T
Vestal Virgin, The (Spontini), 1807 T
Village Romeo and Juliet, A (Delius), 1907 T
Violanta (Korngold), 1916 T
Voie Humaine, La (Poulenc), 1959 T
Von Heute auf Morgen (Schoenberg), 1930 T
Voyage, The (P. Glass), 1992 T
Walkürie Die (Wagner), 1870 T
Wallenstein (Weinberger), 1937 T
War and Peace (Prokofiev), 1946 T
Water-Carrier, The (Cherubini), 1800 T
We Come to the River (H. W. Henze), 1976 T
Where the Wild Things Are (O. Knussen), 1980 T
William Tell (Rossini), 1829 T
Wozzeck (Berg), 1926 T
Wreckers, The (E. Smyth), 1906 T
Wundersame Schustersfrau, Die (U. Zimmerman), 1982 T

Yan Tan Tethera (H. Birtwistle), 1986 T
Zampa (Hérold), 1831 T
Zenobia (L. Coerne), 1905 T
Zweihunderttausend Thaler (B. Blacher), 1969 T
Operetta:
Frasquita (Léhar), 1922 T
Monsieur Beaucaire (Messager), 1919 T
Paganini (Léhar), 1925 T
See also under Musicals
Operette morali (Leopardi), 1827 U
Ophthalmoscope, 1851 P
Ophuls, Max, F. film director, 1950 W, 1951 W
Opie, Iona, B. author (b. 1923), 1959 Q
Opie, John, B. artist (1761–1807), 1781 S, 1783 S
Opie, Peter, B. author (1918–82), 1959 Q
Opinion Poll, first conducted, 1935 O
Opinions of Nature (A. von Humboldt), 1808 R
Opium: British war with China over, 1839, G, H, L; trade to China, legalised, 1858 F
Oporto, Portugal: battle, 1809 E; revolution in, 1820 H
Oppenheim, Denis, Am. artist (b. 1938), 1970 S
Oppenheimer, Robert, Am. physicist (1904–67), 1953 P
Optical glass, 1846 P, 1916 P
Optical instruments, 1846 P
Optical studies, 1791 P, 1856 P
Optics, principles of, discussed, 1772 P
Optimist's Daughter, The (E. Welty), 1972 U
Opuscules physiques et chimiques (A. Lavoisier), 1774 P
Oran, Algeria, French fleet sunk, 1940 G
Orange Free State, S. Africa: established, 1854 B; diamonds discovered in, 1870 N; supports Kruger, 1899 K; British annexes, 1900 E
Orange River Colony, S. Africa, 1848 H
Orangeburg, Sth. Carolina, US, black students killed after attempt to desegregate bowling alley,1968B
Orangemen, riot in Dublin, 1822 M
Oratorios:
Amadis de Gaule (J. C. Bach), 1779 T
Béatitudes, Les (C. Franck), 1872 T
Canticum sacrum and honorem Sancti Marci nominis, 1956 T
Chichester Psalms (L. Bernstein), 1965 T
Child of Our Time, A (M. Tippett), 1940 T
Childhood of Christ, The (Berlioz), 1854 T
Creation, The (Haydn), 1798 T
Damnation of Faust (Berlioz), 1846 T
Djinns, Les (C. Franck), 1884 T
Dream of Gerontius (Elgar), 1900 T
Elijah (Mendelssohn), 1846 T
German Requiem, A (Brahms), 1868 T
Israelities in the Wilderness, The (C. P. E. Bach), 1775 T
Job (C. H. H. Parry), 1892 T
Job (K. von Dittersdorf), 1780 T
Legend of St. Christopher, The (D'Indy), 1920 T
Mary of Magdala (Bliss), 1963 T
Messiah, The (Handel), notable performances of, 1770 T, 1772 T
Moses in Egypt (Rossini), 1818 T
Noye's Fludde (Britten), 1958 T
Passion Cantata (C. P. E. Bach), 1769 T
Prophet, The (Meyerbeer), 1849 T
Psalm 150 (Bruckner), 1802 T
Psalmus Hungarius (Kodály), 1923 T
Redemption, The (F. Gounod), 1882 T
Requiem (Verdi), 1874 T
St. Matthew Passion (Bach), revival of, 1829 T
Sampson and Delilah (C. Saint-Saëns), 1877 T
Stabat Mater (Dvořák), 1883 T
Stabat Mater (Rossini), 1841 T
Te Deum (Bruckner), 1884 T
Twelve, The (Walton), 1965 T
Whitsun Oratorio (E. Křenek), 1960 T
Orators, The (W. H. Auden), 1932 U
Oratory of St. Francis de Sales, 1841 R
Orb, The, B. pop group
Orchestras, notable:
Berlin Philharmonic, 1882 T
Boston Symphony, 1924 T
London Philharmonic, 1932 T
New York Philharmonic, 1929 T
Ordaz, Gustav, Mex. president, 1964 M
Ordeal by Planning (J. Jewkes), 1948 O
Ordeal of Richard Feverel, The (G. Meredith), 1859 U
Ordnance Survey, British, established, 1791 P
Örebro, Sweden, Treaty of, alliance between Sweden and Russia, 1812 G
Oregon, state, US: Canadian–US joint occupation, 1818 K; becomes a US state, 1859 B; laws of, applied to Alaska, 1884 E
Orel, Russia, Russian offensive at, 1943 G, H
Oreste, president of Haiti, 1914 A
Orfila, Mathieu, Joseph Bonaventure, F. chemist (1787–1853), 1814 P
Organic Compounds, theory of, 1852 P
Organisation Man, The (W. H. Whyte), 1956 O
Organisation du travail, L' (L. Blanc), 1839 O
Organisation of American States, Conference of, 1954 C
Organisation of European Economic Cooperation (OEEC): formed, 1948 D; Convention for Economic Cooperation signed, 1960 M
Organization of African Unity (OAU)
Britain urged to use force against Rhodesia, 1966 C
appeals to Biafra to abandon independence struggle, 1968 J
Chad civil war, 1983 G
Addis Ababa Conference, 1984 L, 1985 G
calls for sanctions against South Africa, 1986 F
Organization of American States
lifts ban on relations with Cuba, 1975 G
Organization of Petroleum Exporting Countries (OPEC). *See* Oil
Organon of Therapeutics (S. Hahnemann), 1810 P
Orient Express, 1883 P, 1961 E
Oriental and African Studies, School of, London, 1916 O
Oriental studies, 1778 Q, 1784 Q, 1789 Q, 1875 Q
Orientales, Les (V. Hugo), 1829 U
Origin and Progress of Language (Lord Monboddo), 1773 Q
Origin of Historismus, The (F. Meinecke), 1936 Q
Origin of Species by Natural Selection, The (C. Darwin), 1859 P
Origin of the Ovum (K. Baer), 1827 P
Origine de tous les cultes (C. F. Dupois), 1795 Q
Origines de la France contemporaine (H. Taine), 1873 O
Origins of Commerce, The (Anderson), 1764 Q
Origins of English Individualism, The (A. Macfarlane), 1978 Q
Orkney Wedding, An, with Sunrise (P. Maxwell Davies), 1985 T
Orlando (V. Woolf), 1928 U
Orlando, Vittorio, It. premier (1860–1936), 1917 K
Orléans family, banished from France, 1852 A, 1886 F
Orlov, Dr. Yuri Fedorovich, R. human rights campaigner (b. 1924), 1978 E, 1986 K
Orly, France, airship hangars at, 1916 S
Ornithology, studies in, 1786 P, 1830 P
Orpen, Sir William, B. artist (1878–1931), 1878 Z, 1900 S, 1909 S, 1917 S, 1931 Z
Orphanage, Dr. Barnardo's homes, 1866 O
Orpington, Kent, England, by-election, 1962 C
Orsini, Felice, It. anarchist (1819–58), 1858 A, B
Orsova, S. W. Rumania, ceded to Austria, 1791 H
Ortega y Gasset, José, Sp. philosopher and historian, 1930 O
Ortega, Daniel, President of Nicaragua (b. 1945), 1982 C, 1984 L, 1989 L, 1990 B
Orthological Institute, 1927 O
Orton, Arthur, B. impostor (1837–83), 1874 O
Orton, Harold, B. linguistic scholar (1898–1975), 1977 Q
Orton, 'Joe' (John Kingsley), B. dramatist (1933–67), 1933 Z, 1966 W, 1967 Z, 1969 W
Orvieto, Italy, Fifth Army takes, 1944 F
Orwell, George. *See* Blair, Eric
Osaka, Japan
Expo '70 exhibition, 1970 S
Row House Sumiyoshi, 1976 S
Osborne, John James, B. dramatist (b. 1929), 1929 Z, 1956 W, 1957 W, 1961 W, 1964 W, 1965 W
Osborne, Judgment, 1909 O
Osborne, Nigel, B. musician (b. 1948), 1987 T
Oscar I, King of Sweden (1844–59), 1844 C, 1859 G
Oscar II, King of Sweden (1872–1907), 1907 M; abdicates Norwegian Crown, 1905 K
Oscar Wilde (R. Ellman), 1987 Q
Oscar and Lucinda (P. Carey), 1988 U
O'Shea, William Henry, Ir. politician (1840–1905), 1890 O
Oslo, Norway (formerly Christiana): university, 1811 O; name changed from Christiana, 1925 A; agreement on tariffs, 1930 M; Convention on Scandinavian economic cooperation, 1932 B
Osnabrück, Germany, US army takes, 1945 D
Osobka-Morawski, Polish Communist, forms ministry, 1945 F
Ostend, Belgium; manifesto, advising US acquisition of Cuba, 1854 K; British take, 1918 E
Ostrolenke, Poland, Polish rebels defeated at, 1831 E
Ostrovsky, Alexander Nicolaievich, R. author (1823–86), 1847 W, 1860 W, 1872 W
Oswald, Lee, H., Am. assassin, 1963 L
Othello (Olivier's), 1966 W
Otis, E. G. Am. civil engineer (1811–61), 1857 P
Ottawa, Canada: becomes capital, 1858 O; Parliament House at, 1859 S; Colonial Conference in, 1894 F; Imperial Economic Conference in, 1932 G; Churchill visits, 1941 M; National Library, 1967 T
Otto I, King of Greece (1832–62), 1832 H, 1843 J, 1862 K
Otto, Archduke of Habsburg, refused to return to Austria, 1961 F
Otto, of Bavaria, Prince, elected King of Greece, 1832 H
Ottonian Book Illumination: An Historical Study (H. Mayr-Harting), 1991 Q
Oudh, India:
Nabwab of, defeated, 1764 K
alliance with E. India Company, 1773 J
treasures of, plundered, 1781 N
Britain annexes, 1856 B
Oudney, Walter, B. naval surgeon and explorer (1790–1824), 1823 P
Oueddei, Goukouni, President of Chad (b. 1944), 1982 F
'Ouida'. *See* Rame, Marie Louise de la
Oulianov. *See* Lenin
Oulton, Therese, B. artist, 1989 S

Our Changing Democracy, White Paper, proposing devolution for Scotland and Wales, 1975 L
Our Country's Good (T. Wertenbaker), 1988 W
Our Mutual Friend (C. Dickens), 1864 U
Our Town (T. Wilder), 1938 W
Our Village (M. Mitford), 1824 U
Outbreak of the English Civil War, The (A. Fletcher), 1981 Q
Outcasts of Poker Flat, The (B. Harte), 1869 U
Outline of History (H. G. Wells), 1920 Q
Outlines and Experiments respecting Sound and Light (T. Young), 1800 P
Outpourings of a Monk (W. Wackenroder), 1797 U
Outrages:
  in Belgium, by anarchists, 1901 N
  in Britain, attack on Prince Regent, 1817 A
    Peterloo massacre, 1819 H
    Cato Street Conspiracy, 1820 B
    sinking of *Lusitania*, 1915 E
    sinking of *Athenia*, 1939 E
    sinking of *Empress of Britain*, 1940 K
    See also under Fenianism; Suffragettes
  in Czechoslovakia, Nazi burning of Lidice, 1942 F
  in France, by anarchists, 1858 A, 1893 L, M
  in India, between Moslems and Hindus, 1947 H
    anti-Moslem violence, 1964 C
  in Korea, by Communists, alleged, 1953 K
  in S. Africa, Sharpeville shootings, 1960 C
  in US, against Negroes in Alabama, 1963 J
    murders of Civil Rights workers, 1964 H, M
  See also Assassinations; Kidnappings
Outram, Sir James, B. soldier (1805–64), 1857 J
Outsider, The (C. Wilson), 1956 R
Outspoken Essays (W. R. Inge), 1919 R
Outward Bound (S. Vane), 1923 W
Ouvriers européens, Les (P. Le Play), 1855 O
Over the Bridge (R. Church), 1955 U
Overbeck, Johann Friedrich, G. artist (1789–1869), 1810 S, 1824 S
Overend and Gurney, London firm of bill discounters, failure of, 1866 O
Overruled (G. B. Shaw), *Preface to*, 1916 U
Overtures, Symphonic Poems, etc.:
  Academic Festival (Brahms), 1881 T
  Après-midi d'un Faune, L' (Debussy), 1894 T
  Cockaigne (Elgar), 1901 T
  Coriolanus (Beethoven), 1807 T
  Dance Suite (Bartok), 1923 T
  Death and Transfiguration (R. Strauss), 1889 T
  Dieux dans l'ombre des cavernes, Les (A. Roussel), 1917 T
  Don Juan (R. Strauss), 1888 T
  1812 (Tchaikovsky), 1880 T
  Elegy for Young Lovers (Henze), 1961 T
  Enigma Variations (Elgar), 1899 T
  Faust Overture (Wagner), 1840 T
  Finlandia (Sibelius), 1900 T
  Firebird Suite (Stravinsky), 1910 T
  Fountains of Rome, The (Respighi), 1917 T
  Francesca da Rimini (Tchaikovsky), 1876 T
  Harold in Italy (Berlioz), 1834 T
  Háry János Suite (Kodály), 1923 T
  Italian Capriccio (Tchaikovsky), 1880 T
  Italian Serenade (H. Wolf), 1894 T
  Karelia Suite (Sibelius), 1893 T
  Leonora No. 3 (Beethoven), 1807 T
  Lincoln Portrait (A. Copland), 1942 T
  Mazeppa (Liszt), 1854 T
  Mer, La (Debussy), 1905 T
  My Fatherland (Smetana), 1874 T
  On Hearing the First Cuckoo of Spring (Delius), 1912 T
  Pacific 231 (Honegger), 1923 T
  Perfect Fool, The (Holst), 1923 T
  Pictures from an Exhibition (Moussorgski), 1874 T
  Planets, The, Suite (Holst), 1915 T
  Romeo and Juliet (Berlioz), 1838 T
  Romeo and Juliet (Tchaikovsky), 1864 T
  Rouet D'Omphale, Le (Saint-Saëns), 1871 T
  Scapino (Walton), 1941 T
  Scheherezade (Rimsky-Korsakov), 1888 T
  Symphonic Nocturne (Busoni), 1914 T
  Symphonic Variations (Franck), 1885 T
  Thus Spake Zarathustra (R. Strauss), 1896 T
  Till Eulenspiegel's Merry Pranks (R. Strauss), 1895 T
  Tintagel (Bax), 1917 T
  Tragic (Brahms), 1881 T
  Variations for Orchestra (E. Carter), 1957 T
  Variations on a Theme of Haydn (St. Anthony Chorale) (Brahms), 1873 T
Ovett, Stephen Michael, 'Steve', B. athlete (b. 1955), 1981 X
Oweisa, Iran, 1980 D
Owen, Dr. David Anthony Llewellyn, Lord Owen, B. Labour/SDP politician (b. 1938)
  Foreign Secretary, 1977 B
  peace plan proposal for Rhodesia, 1977 J
  Social Democratic Party, 1981 A, 1983 F, 1987 H, 1990 O
  'Limehouse Declaration', 1981 A
  breakaway 'continuing' Social Democratic Party, 1987 H
  chief mediator on Yugoslav crisis, 1992 H
Owen, Robert, B. Socialist and philanthropist (1771–1858), 1771 Z, 1800 O, 1813 O, 1834 A, C, 1858 Z
Owen, Sir Richard, B. naturalist (1804–92), 1846 P, 1848 P
Owens, Jesse James Cleveland, Am. athlete (1913–80), 1913 Z, 1936 X, 1980 Z
Owens, M. J., Am. inventor, 1898 P
Owings, Nathaniel Alexander, Am. architect (1903–84), 1952 S
Oxford and Asquith, earl and countess of. *See* Asquith
Oxford and Cambridge (C. Brooke, R. Highfield and W. Swaan), 1988 Q
Oxford and Cambridge boat race, 1829 W, 1978 X, 1984 X, 1986 X
Oxford Committee for Famine Relief (OXFAM), 1942 O
Oxford Companion to English Literature, The (5th edn., M. Drabble, ed.), 1985 Q
Oxford Conference on Church, Community and State, 1937 R
Oxford Dictionary of Byzantium, The (A.P. Kazhdan et al., eds.), 1991 Q
Oxford English Dictionary, The (J.A. Simpson, E.S.C. Weiner, eds.), 1989 Q
Oxford English Dictionary, The, Supplement, 1986 Q
Oxford Group, 1939 R
Oxford History of England (G. Clark ed.), 1934 Q
Oxford History of Music, 1929 T
Oxford History of South Africa, The (M. Wilson, L. Thompson, eds.), 1969 Q
Oxford Illustrated History of Britain, The (K.O. Morgan), 1984 Q
Oxford Movement, The, 1833 R, 1841 R, 1845 R
Oxford Union Society, 1823 W, 1933 O
Oxford University:
  Balliol College, under Jowett, 1870 O
  Bampton Lectures, 1780 R
  Conference on Industry, Duke of Edinburgh's, 1956 G
  Florey Building, The Queen's College, 1972 S
  Green College, 1979 O
  Keble College, founded, 1870 O
  Macmillan elected Chancellor, 1960 C
  music faculty founded, 1944 T
  Natural science honours school, 1850 O
  Pitt Rivers Museum, 1874 Q
  Professorship of modern history at, 1866 Q
  religious tests abolished, 1871 F, O
  Rewley House, 1990 O
  Roosevelt honoured by, at Harvard, 1941 O
  appoints Franks Commission, 1964 O
  St Catherine's College, 1964 S
  Wolfson College, 1966 O
Oxfordshire, Buildings of England series (J. Sherwood, N. Pevsner), 1974 Q
Oxygen, is liquefied, 1894 P
Özal, Turgot, President of Turkey (1927–93), 1989 K
Ozenfant, Amédée, F. artist (1886–1966), 1918 S, 1928 S
Ozone Layer, British Antarctic Survey detects hole in, 1985 P

P

Paardeberg, S. Africa, Cronje surrenders at, 1900 B
Pace-maker, the, for cardiac therapy, 1960 P
Pacific Charter, 1954 J
Pacific Council, under Security Treaty of 1951, 1952 H
Pacific Islands, US trusteeship for, 1947 D
Pacific Ocean, submarine current in, 1958 P
Pacific, Advisory Commission for, 1947 A
Packard, Vance Oakley, Am. author (b. 1914,) 1959 O
Packer, Kerry Francis Bullmore, Austral. businessman (b. 1937), 1977 X, 1979 X
Pacts:
  Anti-Comintern (Germany with Japan), 1936 L
    Italy joins, 1937 L
    Spain joins, 1939 D
    collapse of, 1939 H
  Baghdad (Turkey and Iraq), 1955 B
    Britain accedes to, 1955 D
    Iran joins, 1955 L
    end of boycott to Britain, 1957 C
    changes name to Central Treaty Organisation (CENTO), 1959 H
  Balkan (Roumania, Greece, Yugoslavia and Turkey), 1934 B
  Balkan, Greece prevents Rumania from joining, 1957 J
  Belgrade (armistice between Italy and Yugoslavia), 1937 C
  Central Treaty Organisation (CENTO), on defence, collapse, 1979 C
  Delhi (between British Viceroy and Gandhi), 1931 C
  Delhi (between India and Pakistan, in minorities), 1950 D
  Eastern (or Litvinov Protocol, between Estonia, Latvia, Poland, Rumania and Russia), 1929 B
    Iran joins, 1929 D
    Turkey joins, 1929 B
  Four-Power (Britain, France, Germany and Italy), 1932 C, G
  Kellogg–Briand, for international peace, 1928 F, H
    Germany accepts, 1929 B
    in force, 1929 G
    Rome Pact endorses, 1933 G
  Rome, four-power, 1933 G
  Rome (between Italy, Austria and Hungary), 1936 C

Rome–Berlin Axis, 1936 L
'Pact of Steel' (between Hitler and Mussolini), 1939 E
Warsaw. *See* Warsaw Pact
Afghanistan with Iran, Iraq and Turkey (non-aggression), 1937 G
Britain with Hungary (amity), 1941 B
Britain with Italy (over Ethiopia), 1938 D
Britain with Spain (over Spanish exports of wolfram to Germany), 1944 E
Britain with Turkey (mutual assistance), 1939 E
France with Germany (on inviolability of frontiers), 1938 M
France with Russia (non-aggression), 1932 L
Germany with Italy and Japan (economic and military), 1940 J
endorsed by Hungary and Rumania, 1940 L
Germany with Poland (non-aggression), 1934 A
Hitler denounces, 1939 C
Germany with Scandinavian and Baltic states, offered (non-aggression), 1939 E
Greece with Bulgaria (non-aggression), 1938 G
Greece with Turkey (non-aggression), 1933 J
India–Bangladesh defence, 1972 C
Italy with Austria and Hungary, 1937 L
Latin American states (non-aggression), 1933 K
Russia with Estonia, 1939 J
Russia with Finland (non-aggression), 1934 D
Russia with Germany (non-aggression), 1939 H
Russia with Japan (neutrality), 1941 D
denounced by Russia, 1945 D
Russia with Latvia, 1939 K
Russia with Poland (non-aggression), 1932 A, 1938 L
Turkey with Russia (1925), denounced, 1945 C
US with Nationalist China (mutual security), 1954 M
US with Japan (defence), 1954 C
US with Philippines (defence), 1951 H
Yugoslavia with Germany, 1941 C
Pacts, Trade, *See* Treaties, Commercial
Paderewski, Ignaz Jan, Pol. statesmen and pianist (1860–1941), 1860 Z, 1887 T, 1909 T, 1941 Z
becomes premier of Poland, 1919 A
Paes, Sidonio, president of Portugal, 1918 M
Paganini, Niccolò, It. violinist (1784–1840), 1784 Z, 1793 T, 1805 T, 1940 Z
Page and Steele, architects, 1966 S
Page, David C., scientist, 1987 P
Paik, Nam June Am. artist, 1972 S
Paik-Abe Video Synthesizer (Nam June Paik), 1972 S
Pailleron, Edouard Jules Henri, F. author (1834–90), 1881 W
Pailleterie, Alexandre Davy de la. *See* Dumas, Alexander
Paine, Thomas, B. radical and political pamphleteer (1737–1809), 1776 O, 1791 O, 1792 O, M, 1794 O, 1809 Z
Painlevé, Paul, F. premier, 1917 J, L, 1925 D
Painter's Credo, A (J. Bratby), 1956 S
Painter, George, B. author (b. 1915), 1965 Q
Painting and Experience in Fifteenth Century Italy (M. Baxandall), 1972 Q
Paisiello, Giovanni, It. musician (1741–1816), 1780 T
Paisley, Rev. Ian Richard Kyle, N. Ir. politician (b. 1926), 1973 G
'Carson trail' parade, 1981 B
Pajou, Augustin, F. sculptor (1730–1809), 1768 S, 1791 S
Pakistan: independence proclaimed, 1947 H; becomes and Islamic republic, 1956 B
East Pakistani demonstrators demand greater autonomy, 1966 F
military government takes over, 1969 C
cyclone disaster in East Pakistan, 1970 L
Awami League, 1970 M, 1971 A, C
general strike in East Pakistan, 1971 C
Pakistani Constituent Assembly postponed, 1971 C
troops fight separatists in West Pakistan, 1971 C
protests at India's support for East Pakistan separatism, 1971 D
independence of East Pakistan as Bangladesh, 1971 M
Zulfikar Ali Bhutto, 1971 M, 1977 C
population, 1971 Y, 1981 Y, 1991 Y
leaves Commonwealth in anticipation of British recognition of Bangladesh, 1972 A
India and Pakistan agree to renounce force in settlement of disputes, 1972 G
India and Pakistan agree on truce line, 1972 M
new constitution under leadership of Zulfikar Ali Bhutto, 1973 H
diplomatic relations with India normalized, 1976 D
post-election violence, 1977 C
coup d'état, 1977 G
Zulfikar Ali Bhutto executed, 1979 D
illiteracy, 1983 Y
cotton production, 1984 Y
martial law ended, 1985 M
urbanization, 1985 Y
explosion at army ammunition dump, 1988 D
Indian border sealed following violence in Punjab, 1988 D
Zia ul-Haq killed, 1988 H
state of emergency, 1988 H
general elections, 1988 L, 1990 K
ethnic clashes, 1990 E
Benazir Bhutto dismissed, 1990 H
Benazir Bhutto calls for fresh elections, 1992 L
See also Bangladesh
Palach, Jan, Czech. student (1948–69), death 1969 A
twentieth anniversary of suicide marked, 1989 A
Palacky, Francis, Czech. historian and politician (1798–1876), 1848 F
Palaeography, study of, 1852 Q, 1912 Q
Palatinate, Elector of, 1777 M
Palau, Luis, Am. (formerly Argent.) evangelist and author (b. 1934), 1984 R
Palermo, Sicily: revolt in, 1848 A; Neapolitans enter, 1849 E; Garibaldi takes, 1860 E; Allies occupy, 1943 G
Palestine Liberation Organization (PLO)
Arafat elected chairman, 1969 B
recognized by Arab nations, 1974 K
ceasefire agreed with Israel, 1981 G
scheme for Palestinian confederation with Jordan rejected, 1982 L
civilian members of Al fatah oppose Arafts's leadership, 1983 F
Syrian tanks besiege PLO bases in Lebanon, 1983 F
PLO and Israel exchange prisoners of war, 1983 L
Arafat and supporters evacuated from Lebanon, 1983 M
Tunis headquarters attacked by Israel, 1985 K
Arafat re-elected chairman, 1987 D
assassination of Abu Jihad, 1988 D
Parliament in exile declares independent state of Palestine, 1988 L
PLO Parliament in exile declares independent state of Palestine, 1988 L
US resumes contacts with, 1988 M
Palestine:
frontier with Egypt, 1906 E
Balfour declaration on, 1917 L
Turkish collapse in, 1918 J
mandate of, to Britain, 1920 D
boundary with Syria settled, 1920 M
League mandate for, 1922 G, H
Arab Congress rejects, 1922 H
Greece is warned against attempt to occupy, 1922 H
British mandate begins, 1923 J
Separatism in, 1923 K, L
unrest in, 1933 K
Jewish immigration to, restricted, 1933 M
Arab High Committee formed, 1936 D
end of mandate recommended, 1937 G
murder of district commissioner, 1937 J
Britain proposes partition, 1938 A
plan for independence, 1939 E
admission of Jews to, demanded, 1945 H
Arab states' warning to US, 1945 K
British proposal for partition under trusteeship is rejected, 1947 B
advice against partition, 1946 D
Britain refers problem to UN, 1947 D
UN plan for future of, 1947 L
Arabs invade, 1948 E
UN Conciliatory Commission discusses, 1951 J
Israel–Jordan raids, 1955 N
UN truce is accepted, 1956 A
Hammarskjöld arranges cease-fire, 1956 D, E
Israel withdraws from mixed armistice commission, 1956 K
Britain states she must assist Jordan if attacked, 1956 K
Israeli troops invade Sinai, 1956 K
withdrawal, 1957 A
Israel hands over Gaza strip to UN, 1957 C
See also; Israel; Jerusalem; Jordan
Palestinian Army, formed by Kassem, 1960 C
Palestinians:
Palestinian guerrilla bases in Jordan bombed, 1968 H
Palestinian terrorists attack El Al airliner, 1969 B
claim responsibilty for air crash, 1970 B
Jordan tightens control on guerrilla movement, 1970 B
Palestinian terrorists claim responsibilty for air crash, 1970 B
ambush Israeli school bus, 1970 E
fighting breaks out with Jordan/ceasefire agreed, 1970 F
Jordanian army ordered to disband Palestinian militia, 1970 H
Palestinian prisoners released for hijack hostages, 1970 J
militia disbanded by King Hussein, 1970 J
renewal of conflict with Jordanian army, 1971 C
Jordanian army captures guerrillas, 1971 G
suppression of guerillas prompts border closures, 1971 G
Hussein refuses talks with guerrillas, 1971 L
Palestinian terrorists murder Wasfi Tell, 1971 L
autonomous Palestinian state proposed, 1972 C
Palestinian terrorists hijack Lufthansa flight, 1972 K
Palestinian terrorists kill Israelis at Kiryat Shemona, 1974 D
El Birah disbanded by Israel, 1982 C
Arafat–Jordanian talks on proposed Palestinian state confederated with Jordan, 1982 K, L
Palestinian prisoners and Israeli soldiers exchanged, 1983 L, 1985 E
Shi'a Muslim militia attempts to drive Palestinians from refugee camps in Beirut, 1985 E

Palestinian terrorists hijack *Achille Lauro* cruise liner, 1985 K
Palestinian National Council, 1987 D
UN Security Council criticizes Israeli action against, 1987 M
US resumes contacts with PLO, 1988 M
deported from Israel, 1992 M
Paley, Grace, Am. author (b. 1922), 1985 U
Paley, William, B. theologian (1743–1805), 1785 R, 1794 R, 1802 R
Palin, Michael Edward, B. actor and writer (b. 1943), 1989 W, 1992 W
Pa-li-Chan, China, Chinese defeat at, 1860 J
Palingénésie philosophie (C. Bonnet), 1769 R
Palladium, discovered in platinum, 1804 P
Pallas, Peter Simon, G. naturalist (1741–1811), 1767 P, 1768 P
Palma, Brian de, Am. film director (b. 1940), 1987 W
Palmas Island, near Philippines, Pacific, awarded to Holland, 1928 D
Palme, (Sven) Olof, Prime Minister of Sweden (1927–86), assassination, 1986 B
Palmer, Sir Geoffrey Winston Russell, Prime Minister of New Zealand (b. 1942), 1989 H, 1990 J
Palmerston, Viscount. *See* Temple, Henry
Palo Alto, New Mexico, US, battle, 1846 E
Pamirs, mountain range, Central Asia, 1885 P
Pampeluna, Spain, surrenders to British, 1813 K
Pan African Congress. *See under* Political Parties
Pan American Airways, 1939 P; closure, 1991 M
Pan American Conferences, 1889 K, 1938 M
Pan American Congress, under Bolívar, 1826 F
Pan German League, 1891 O
Pan Slav Pact, of Corfu, for union of Serbs, Croats and Slovenes, 1917 G
Pan-Islam movement, 1900 N
Pan-Slav Conferences, 1848 F, 1892 O, 1908 G, 1918 D
Panama Canal:
concession for building, 1878 E
Lesseps organises French Company for building, 1879 H
Scandal in France concerning, 1892 L, 1893 C
reports on routes, 1899 F, 1903 L
treaty for US construction of, 1901 L
US purchases French company's rights, 1902 F, 1904 D
Hay–Herrán Pact of US acquisition, 1903 A
Canal Zone placed in US hands, 1903 M
construction begins, 1904 P
rates for, alleged to infringe 1901 Treaty, 1912 H
first vessel passes, 1913 L
civil government in Canal Zone, 1914 D
is officially open to traffic, 1914 P
alliance for defence of, 1926 G
statistics of ships using, 1939 Y, 1951 Y
US plans for a new canal, 1964 M
Panama: declares independence and joins Colombian Republic, 1821 L; is given federal status, 1855 A; becomes independent, 1903 L; Canal Zone placed in US hands, 1903 M; frontier dispute with Costa Rica, 1921 C; is invaded from Cuba, 1959 D
rejects US draft treaties on Canal Zone, 1970 J
signs Panama Canal Treaty, 1977 J
Treaty ratified by US Senate, 1978 D
Canal Zone handed over, 1979 K
Contadora Group, 1983 G
elections annulled by Noriega, 1989 E
US breaks off diplomatic relations, 1989 J
attempted coup, 1989 K
US invasion, 1989 M, 1990 A
merchant shipping tonnage statistics, 1992 Y
Pangalos, Theodore, Greek dictator, 1925 F, 1926 A; is overthrown, 1926 H
Pangkor, Isle, Malaysia, Britain acquires, 1826 F
Pani, Mario, It. architect, 1950 S
Pankhurst, Emeline, B. suffragette (1858–1928), 1903 P, 1913 D
Pankhurst, Estelle Sylvia, B. suffragette (1882–1960), 1882 Z, 1960 Z
Panmunjohn, Korea, 1951 K, 1953 K
Panopticon, Bentham's, 1791 O
Pantelleria, Island, Mediterranean, surrenders to Allies, 1943 F
Panufnik, Sir Andrzej, Pol.- born B. musician (1914–91), 1978 T, 1989 T, 1992 T
Paoli, Pasquale, Corsican general and patriot (1725–1807), 1769 H
Papacy and Church Reform, The (J. Haller), 1903 R
Papacy in its Social and Cultural Influence, The (P. Hoensbroech), 1902 R
Papacy, The:
concordat with Austria, 1855 H
revoked, 1870 G
concordat with France, 1801 R
ended, 1905 M
concordat with Prussia, 1821 R
concordat with Spain, 1851 C
Decree of Papal Infallability, 1870 R
law of guarantees for, 1871 E
undertakes arbitration, 1885 M
Papal primacy and the Church of England, 1977 R
See also under Vatican, The
Papadopoulos, Georgios, Greek army officer and politician (b. 1919)
cabinet changes increase power of, 1971 H
ousted by General Gizikis, 1973 L
President, 1973 H
imprisoned, 1975 M
Papagos, Greek field-marshal, forms ministry, 1952 L
Papal Bulls, notable:
condemning nationalism, 1835 R
Dominus ac Redemptor, 1773 G
Paschalis Mysterii, 1969 R
Quod Nunquam, 1874 E
Testem Benevolentiae, 1899 R
See also under Encyclicals
Papal Encyclical, *Humanae Vitae*, 1968 R
Papal Infallability, discussed, 1864 R, 1869 R; declared, 1870 R; Gladstone attacks, 1874 R
Papal Monarchy, The (C. Morris), 1989 Q
Papal States, 1763 R, 1766 R, 1781 L
Avignon is regained, 1773 M
annexed by France, 1809 E
Austria evacuates, 1838 K
French expedition to, 1849 D, G
Papandreou, Andreas George, Prime Minister of Greece (b. 1919), 1965 G, 1983 B, 1989 F
forms Socialist government, 1981 K
trial on bribery charges, 1991 C
Papen, Franz von, G. Socialist (1879–1969), forms ministry, 1932 F; removes Prussian premier, 1932 G; Hitler refuses to serve under, 1932 H; resigns, 1932 L; becomes Vice-Chancellor, 1933 A; is acquitted by Nuremberg Tribunal, 1946 J
Paper money:
in Britain, issue restricted, 1844 O
Treasury Notes are issued, 1914 O
in France, Assignats are issued, 1789 O
Franc Notes are issued, 1914 O
Paper, duties on, British, repealed, 1861 O
Paperbacks, 1936 U
Papineau, Louis Joseph, Can. rebel, 1837 L
Papplewick, Notts., England, cotton spinning factory at, 1785 P
Papua New Guinea
independence, 1975 J
peace agreement with secessionists on Bougainville Island, 1992 E
Paracelsus (R. Browning), 1835 U
Paradigm (F. Clemente), 1988 S
Paraguay, independence of, 1811 H
cotton production, 1984 Y
Pope John Paul II visits, 1988 E
state of siege allowed to lapse, 1987 D
military coup, 1989 B
Parathyroid gland, extract of, 1925 P
Paravanes, 1915 P
Parcy, Euzhan, film director, 1983 W
Pardoe, John Wentworth, B. Liberal politician (b. 1934), 1976 G
Parents terribles, Les (J. Cocteau), 1938 W
Pareto, G., It. sociologist (1848–1923), 1916 R
Parga, Greece, Italy obtains, 1819 D
Parini, Giuseppi, It. poet (1729–99), 1763 U
Paris Street Scene (R. Estes), 1973 S
Paris, Comte de. *See* Louis Philippe
Paris, France:
events:
Parlement, meets, 1785 N
demands summoning of Estates General, 1787 H
is banished to Troyes, 1787 H
is banished, 1788 A
Bastille is sacked, 1789 G
Champs de Mars festival, 1790 G
political clubs, 1790 N, 1794 L
Louis XVI attempts to go to St. Cloud, 1791 D
Massacre of Champs de Mars, 1791 G
Massacre of Swiss Guard at Les Tuileries, 1792 H
Revolutionary Commune, 1792 H, 1794 G
execution of Louis XVI, 1793 A
Napoleon installed in Tuileries, 1800 B
Allies enter, 1814 C
July Revolution, 1830 G
Napoleon I's remains removed to Les Invalides, 1840 M
street-lighting in, 1841 P
reform banquets are prohibited, 1848 B
Revolution in, 1848 B, E, F, M, L
reconstruction of, 1853 S
World Fair at, 1855 S, W
siege, 1870 J
capitulates to Prussians, 1871 A
Commune is established, 1871 C
defeated, 1871 E
anarchist outrages, 1893 C
Edward VII visits, 1903 E
postal strike, 1909 D
French government returns to, 1914 M
Zeppelin raids on, 1916 A
is shelled by Germans, 1918 C
riots in, 1934 B
World Fair, 1937 S, W
George VI visits, 1938 G
Germans enter, 1940 F
is liberated, 1944 H
French Provisional government is transferred from Algiers, 1944 H
Communist demonstrations, 1952 E
EFTA meeting, 1960 A
anti-OAS riots, 1962 B
multi-part exhibition in homage to Picasso, 1966 S
student unrest, 1968 E
'Night of the Barricades', 1968 E

Bourse set on fire, 1968 E
Vietnam peace talks, 1968 E, L, 1969 A, 1970 M
Saudi Arabian Embassy siege, 1973 J
EC summit, 1974 M
Jewish restaurant attacked, 1982 H
Pont Neuf wrapped by Christo, 1985 S
Conference on Security and Cooperation in Europe, 1990 L
buildings, institutions and places in or near:
Arc de Triomphe, 1806 S, 1836 S
Bibliothèque Impériale, 1852 Q
Bing's 'Art Nouveau' Gallery, 1897 S
blind school in, 1784 O
Bois de Boulogne, 1853 S
Centre National d'Art et de Culture Georges Pompidou, 1977 S, 1978 S, 1979 S, 1983 S
Champs de Mars, art exhibition in, 1890 S
Comédie Française, 1862 W, 1881 W
Conservatoire de Musique, 1795 T
Ecole des Chartes, 1821 Q
Ecole Polytechnique, 1795 O
Eiffel Tower, 1889 S, W
Hôtel de Ville, 1889 P
Institut National, 1795 O
Invalides, 1915 T
La Grande Arche, La Défense, 1989 S
Louvre, The, 1793 S, 1911 S
Louvre Pyramid, 1989 S
Salon d'Apollon in, 1849 S
Luxembourg, 1846 S, 1894 S
Madeleine, The, 1763 S, 1845 S
Metro, The, 1898 P
Montmartre music hails, 1891 S
Musée d'Orangerie, 1916 S
Musée d'Orsay, 1986 S
Museum of Science and Industry, 1986 P
Notre Dame, 1845 S
Notre Dame de Lorette, 1823 S
Opera House, 1861 S
Pantheon, 1764 S
Pasteur Institute, 1880 O
Picasso Museum, 1985 S
Place de la Concorde, 1765 S
St. Eustache Church, 1793 R
St. Sulpice, 1857 S
Salon, 1775 S, 1831 S, 1867 S, 1876 S, 1877 S
secession of artists from, 1890 S
Salon des Indépendants, 1891 S, 1901 S
Salon des Refusés, 1863 S
Théâtre des Champs-Elysées, 1912 S
Théâtre Français, 1838 W
Théâtre Libre, 1887 W
Unesco building, 1953 S, 1959 S
art in: Impressionist exhibitions, 1874 S, 1877 S, 1886 S
Gris's lectures on painting, 1924 S
ballet in: 1909 T
literary salons in, 1764 U
music in, 1943 T
public restaurants, 1770 O
the theatre in, 1775 W, 1875 W, 1881 W
population, 1801 Y, 1841 Y, 1881 Y, 1906 Y, 1990 Y
Treaties and Peace Negotiations at, 1763 B, 1782 E, 1814 E, 1815 L, 1856 C, D, 1857 C, 1951 D, 1955 C, D, E
Parisienne, La (H. F. Becque), 1885 W
Park Chung-Hee, S. Korean president (1917–79)
attempted assassination, 1968 A
assassinated, 1979 K
Park, Mungo, B. explorer of Africa (1771–1806), 1795 P, 1805 P
Park, W., of Musselburgh, B. golf champion, 1860 X
Parke, Herbert William, B. ancient historian (1903–86), 1957 Q
Parke-Bernet, of New York, fine art auctioneers, 1964 S
Parker Report, on Northern Irish security forces, 1972 C
Parker, Alan William, B. film director (b. 1944), 1978 W
Parker, Alton Brooks, Am. Democrat (1852–1926), 1904 L
Parker, Hubert Lister, Lord Parker of Waddington, B. judge (1900–72), 1957 M, 1958 J
Parkes, Sir Henry, Austral. statesman (1815–96), 1880 N, 1891 C
Parking meters, in London, 1958 O
Parkinson, Cecil Edward, Lord Parkinson, B. Conservative politician (b. 1931), 1983 F
resignation from cabinet, 1983 K
Parkman, Francis, Am. historian (1820–93), 1820 Z, 1851 Q, 1865 Q, 1893 Z
Parliament of England, The (G.R. Elton), 1986 Q
Parliamentary Commissioner for Administration (Ombudsman), B., 1967 D
Parliamentary Reform in Britain:
advocated, 1774 O, 1776 O, 1816 M, 1821 D
Yorkshire petition for, 1780 B
manhood suffrage proposed, 1780 F
Pitt's scheme for, 1783 E; defeated, 1785 D
issue of, splits Whig Party, 1794 G
sale of Parliamentary seats is forbidden, 1809 F
bills for, defeated, 1810 E, 1818 E, F, 1821 E, 1831 C, J
agitation for, 1819 H
Russell's campaign for, 1819 M
election on issue of, 1831 D
riots favour, 1831 K
new bill in Commons, 1831 M
1st Reform Bill passes Commons, 1832 C; Lords, 1832 F
in Scotland, 1832 G
in Ireland, 1832 H
Chartist demands for, 1838 O
bill introduced by Disraeli, defeated, 1859 C
2nd Reform Bill, 1867 H
Trevelyan's bill to extend franchise, 1874 E
3rd Reform Bill, 1884 M
re-distribution of seats, 1885 F
power of Lords, 1910 E
Quinquennial Parliaments proposed, 1910 E
Parliament Bill, progress accelerated by 'Kangaroo' clause, 1911 D
Lansdowne's reconstruction bill, 1911 E
Parliament Bill, passes Commons, 1911 E
Lords amendments to, 1911 G
passes Lords, 1911 H
in Ireland, 1790 K
Parliaments and other elected assemblies:
in Albania, Constituent Assembly, 1946 A
in Alsace-Lorraine, separate legislature granted, 1911 E
in Australia, federal, 1927 E
in Austria, States General promised, 1848 C
Reichstag meets, 1848 G
suspended, 1933 C
in Bohemia, committee of Diet suppressed, 1783 F
in Brazil, legislative assembly, 1824 C
in Britain, 700th anniversary celebrations, 1965 O
debates, printing of, 1771 C
emergency sessions, 1950 J
House of Commons, electors' rights, 1782 E
evacuation following tear-gas bomb attack, 1970 G
first woman speaker, 1992 O
members, Anglican clergy not eligible, 1801 F
Dissenters in, 1844 O
Jewish, first, 1858 O
property qualifications abolished, 1858 O
Roman Catholic, first, 1829 O
salaries for, 1911 H, 1964 L, 1983 O
university, abolished, 1948 O
women, first, 1919 L
ministers in, increase in, 1964 M
privilege, 1763 E, L, 1771 C
procedure, Kangaroo clause, 1911 D
obstruction to, by Irish members, 1881 A
Select Committees, 1979 O
televisation, 1985 L, 1988 O, 1989 O
tie in division, 1965 F
House of Lords, powers of, attempt to restrict, 1907 F, 1910 E
Parliament Bill, 1911 D, E, G, H
to veto legislation reduced, 1949 M
committee recommends an heir be able to disclaim peerage, 1962 M
composition, 1970 Y, 1978 Y
Poll Tax Bill passed, 1988 E
proposed reforms, 1968 F, L, 1969 D
televisation, 1983 M, 1985 O
in British East Africa, Central legislature, 1948 D
in Burma, constituent assembly, 1947 F
in Canada, special sessions of, 1930 J
resolution to 'patriate' constitution from Britain, 1981 M
in Cape Colony, 1853 G
in China, Nanking Revolutionary Assembly, 1912 B
Republican assembly, 1913 D
People's National Convention, 1931 E
Nanking Nationalist Assembly, 1948 L
in Czechoslovakia, Sudetens leave, 1937 L
in Egypt, legislative council, 1883 E
in Eire, Dail, rejects British peace offer, 1921 H, 1922 J
votes for abolition of loyalty oath, 1932 E
Senate abolished, 1936 E
passes constitution, 1937 F
in France: States-General, demand for summoning, 1783 G
meets, 1789 E
third estate declares it is a National Assembly, 1789 F
Journal des Débats of, 1789 O
proceedings of, 1790 E
National Assembly dissolves itself, 1791 J
Legislative Assembly, 1791 J, K
is suspended, 1792 H
National Convention, 1792 J
Senate is enlarged, 1802 H
Tribunate is suppressed by Napoleon, 1807 J
Senate, 1814 D
National Assembly, 1848 E
is dissolved, 1849 A
power of legislature is increased, 1860 L
financial powers extended, 1861 L
National Assembly, at Bordeaux, 1871 B
principle of elections to Chamber, 1912 G
Constituent Assembly, 1946 F
in Germany: Diet of Confederation, 1803 B, 1816 L, 1819 L, 1820 E
revolutionaries fail to take over, 1833 D
National Assembly, 1848 E, 1849 C, D
moves to Stuttgart and is dissolved, 1849 F
Erfurt, summoned by Frederick William IV, 1850 C, D
Frankfurt Bundestag, revived, 1850 E

Prussia recognises, 1850 L
votes for federal action against Denmark, 1863 K
North German Reichstag, 1867 H
Imperial Reichstag, rejects legislation against Radicals, 1878 E
conflict in, over army bill, 1886 M
Bismarck's speech on Russian designs, 1888 B
Weimar Republic National Assembly, 1919 F
Reichstag Fire, 1933 B
West German Bundestag, votes to resume relations with Russia, 1955 J
in Gold Coast, Africans secure majority on legislature, 1946 C
in Greece, National Assembly, 1832 H, 1843 J, 1924 A
Senate is restored, 1929 E
sets up representative Parliamentary Council with Yugoslavia and Turkey, 1955 C
in Holland, States-General, 1783 K
in Holstein, Estates resolve on independence, 1844 L
in Hungary, Diet re-opened, 1825 J
dissolved, 1861 H
at Kolozsvár, decrees for incorporation of Transylvania, 1865 M, 1867 B
Chamber, wild scenes in, 1912 E
Upper House re-established, 1926 L
in India, legislative council given greater powers, 1909 E
Lok Sabha, 1975 L, 1978 M, 1979 G
first Parliament, 1921 A
central legislature at Delhi, 1935 M
Constituent Assembly, 1946 M, 1947 E
dissolved, 1959 G
in Indonesia, suspended, 1960 C
Mutual Co-operation Parliament, 1960 F
in Iran, Majlis, 1980 E
in Iraq, first Parliament, 1925 G
in Ireland, Gratton's, 1782 E
passes Act of Union, 1800 C
See also Eire
in Northern Ireland, first, 1921 F
in Israel, Knesset, 1951 B, 1970 C, 1977 L, 1980 G
in Italy, first, 1860 D
proclaims Victor Emmanuel King, 1861 B
Chamber of Deputies is replaced by Fasces and Corporations, 1938 M
Senate to be popularly elected, 1947 M
is reformed, 1953 A
in Japan, first Diet, promise of calling, 1881 N; meets, 1890 L
Power of emperor transferred to Assembly, 1946 L
in Korea, N. Koreans boycott constitutional assembly, 1948 E
in Lebanon, Chamber of Deputies, 1982 H
in Mexico, Constitutional Congress, 1822 E
in Naples, suspended, 1849 C
in Nigeria, federal council, 1955 A
in Northern Ireland
Stormont, 1971 G
Assembly, SDLP and Sinn Fein boycott opening, 1982 L
in Norway, national assembly, 1814 D
Storting meets, 1905 F
in Pakistan, Constituent Assembly, loss of confidence in, 1954 K
Palestinian council of El Birah, Israel disbands, 1982 C
in Philippines, assembly, 1907 G
legislative reject independence, 1933 A
in Poland, Diet, 1812 F, 1831 A
referendum favours single-house assembly, 1946 F
in Portugal, Cortes established, 1821 A, 1826 D
in Prussia, Diet is summoned by Frederick William IV, 1847 B
national assembly, 1848 E
Upper House reconstituted, 1854 K
Diet rejects military budget, 1862 K
indemnifies Bismarck for unconstitutional rule, 1866 J
special creations of peers to pass legislation, 1872 M
in Russia, Decembrists demand summoning of assembly, 1825 M
assembly of notables is called, 1881 C
representative assembly is demanded, 1905 E
Duma, first, 1905 H, 1906 E
is dissolved, 1906 G
second, 1907 C
is dissolved, 1907 F
third, 1907 L
meeting of, 1916 B
Soviet two-chamber, 1936 M
in South Africa, Cape Assembly meets, 1853 G
reports on Jameson Raid, 1896 A
constitutional convention, 1908 K
native representation in Cape Parliament, 1936 D
in Spain, Cortes meets, 1812 C
Basque regional parliament, 1980 C
to meet annually, 1856 J
in Syria, constituent assembly, 1928 F
is prolonged indefinitely, 1934 L
in Tangier, Council of the Throne, 1955 K
in Transjordan, Arab Congress, 1948 M
in Turkey, first, 1908 M
national assembly at Ankara, 1920 D
abolishes Caliphate, 1924 B
constituent assembly, 1961 E
in US, New York Assembly, 1787 D
first Congress meets, 1789 C
extraordinary sessions of Congress, 1911 D, 1917 D, 1937 L
presidential messages to Congress, notable, 1918 A
presidential veto overturned by Congress, 1973 L
House of Representatives elects J. Q. Adams president, 1824 C
Speaker of, attempts to reduce power of, 1910 C
Senate, stops Force Bill, 1890 F
popular elections for, 1913 E
in S. Vietnam, Constituent Assembly for, 1956 L
in West European Union, Strasbourg assembly first meets, 1955 G
in Yugoslavia, Croats withdraw from, 1928 H, 1935 F
constituent assembly, 1945 L
Parma, Duchy, Italy, 1767 C; confiscated by Clement XIII, 1768 N; forms, with Tuscany, Kingdom of Etruria, 1801 B; Napoleon annexes, 1802 K; ceded by Austria, 1859 G
Parma, Duke of. *See* Cambacérès, Jean
Parman, Paul P., Am. scientist, 1966 P
Parnassus School of Poets, 1853 U
Parnell, Charles Stewart, Ir. Nationalist politician (1846–91), 1887 A; as president of Irish Land League, 1878 K; followers of, acquitted, 1880 L; imprisoned for inciting Irish, 1881 K; is party to Kilmainham 'treaty', 1882 E; calls on Irish in Britain to vote Conservative, 1885 L; dispute with *The Times*, 1888 G; resigns leadership of Irish Nationalists, 1890 M; divorce action, 1890 O
Paroles (J. Prévert), 1946 U
Paroles d'un Croyant (H. F. R. Lamennais), 1834 R
Paroles d'un Révolté (P. A. Kropotkin), 1884 O
Parri, Ferrucio, It. politician, resigns, 1945 L
Parry, Sir Charles Hubert Hastings, B. musician (1848–1918), 1848 Z, 1892 T, 1918 Z
Parsons, Sir Charles, B. marine engineer (1854–1931), 1884 P, 1910 P
Parsons, Talcott, Am. sociologist (1902–79), 1902 Z, 1937 O, 1951 R, 1979 Z
Pärt, Arvo, musician, 1971 T, 1981 T
Part of Speech, A (J. Brodsky), 1980 U
Partage de Midi (P. Claudel), 1906 W
Parthenopaen Republic, in Piedmont, 1798 A
Particular Places (C. Lewis), 1989 Q
Pasadena, Calif., US, atomic research at, 1950 P
Pascal-Trouillot, Ertha, President of Haiti (b. 1943), 1990 C
Pasmore, Victor, B. artist (b. 1908), 1949 S, 1950 S
Pasolini, Pier Paolo, It. film director (1922–75), 1969 W, 1972 W, 1973 W
Pasquier Chronicle, The (G. Duhamel), 1933 U
Passage (T. Oulton), 1989 S
Passage to India (E. M. Forster), 1924 U
Passaglia, Carlo, It. churchman (1812–87), 1859 O
Passchendaele, W. Flanders, Belgium: battle (or 3rd Battle of Ypres), 1917 G; British and Canadians capture Ridge, 1917 L
Passfield White Paper on Arabs and Palestine, 1930 K
Passfield, Lord and Lady. *See* Webb
Passio domini nostri Jesu Christi secundum Johannem (A. Pärt), 1981 T
Past and Present (T. Carlyle), 1843 U
Pasternak, Boris, R. author (1890–1960), 1890 Z, 1932 U, 1958 U, 1962 U
Pasteur, Louis, F. biologist and chemist (1822–95), 1857 P, 1861 P, 1864 P, 1880 P, 1881 P, 1885 P
Paston Letters and Papers of the 15th Century, Pt I (N. Davis), 1971 Q
Pastor, L., G. ecclesiastical historian, 1928 R
Pastrengo, Italy, Austrians defeated at, 1848 D
Patel, Gieve, 1988 W
Patent law:
in Britain, 1906 O
in Germany, 1877 O
in US, 1790 P
Pater, Walter Horatio, B. author (1839–94), 1839 Z, 1873 Q, 1885 U, 1849 Z
Pathé, Charles, F. photographer (1873–1957), 1912 W
Path to Rome, The (H. Belloc), 1902 U
Pathet Lao, 1969 C, E, 1970 D
Pathfinder, The (J.F. Cooper), 1840 U
Patmore, Coventry Kersey Dighton, B. poet (1823–1896), 1854 U
Paton, Alan (1903–88), 1903 Z, 1948 U, 1988 Z
Paton, Herbert James, B. philosopher (1887–1969), 1955 R
Patriot for Me, A (J. Osborne), 1965 W
Patriotic Phantasies (J. Moser), 1775 O
Patriots and Liberators (S. Schama), 1977 Q
Patriots. *See under* Political Parties
Patten, Christopher Francis, 'Chris', Conservative politician (b. 1944), B. Governor of Hong Kong, 1992 G
Pattern of the Chinese Past, The (M. Elvin), 1972 Q
Patti, Adelina, It. operatic singer (1843–1919), 1843 Z, 1859 W, 1919 Z

Pattison, Mark, B. churchman and author (1813–84), 1860 R, 1867 O
Patton, George Smith, Am. soldier, 1885 Z, 1945 Z
Paul I, King of Greece, 1964 C
visits Britain, 1963 F, G
Paul I, Tsar of Russia (1796–1801), 1796 L, 1797 N, 1801 C
Paul Report on Deployment of Clergy, 1964 R
Paul VI, Pope, It. (Cardinal Giovanni Montini, 1897–1978), 1897 Z; elected Pope, 1963 F; makes pilgrimage to Holy Land, 1964 R; addresses UN, 1965 R, closes Vatican Council, 1965 R
appeals for peace in Vietnam, 1966 A
Archbishop Ramsey pays official visit, 1966 R
inaugurates a Holy Year, 1974 R
death, 1978 H, R, Z
Paul et Virginie (St. Pierre), 1789 U
Paul, Jean. *See* Richter, Jean Paul
Paul, Prince, of Yugoslavia, is deposed, 1941 C
Paul, Wolfgang, G. physicist (b. 1918), 1978 P
Paul-Boncour, Joseph, F. politician (1873–1943), 1932 M
Pauline (R. Browning), 1833 U
Pavic, Milorad, Serb. author (b. 1929), 1988 U
Pavlov, Alexis Petrovich, R. pathologist (1849–1936), 1907 P
Pavlova, Anna, R. prima ballerina, 1931 Z
Pawlak, Waldemar, Prime Minister of Poland, 1992 F
Paxton, Joseph, B. architect (1803–65), 1803 Z, 1850 S, 1865 Z
Pay-as-you-earn Income Tax in Britain, 1944 B
Payer, Julius, Aus. explorer, 1873 P
Payne-Aldrich tariff in US, 1909 H
Paysans, Les (H. de Balzac), 1845 U
Pérez, Carlos Andrés, President of Venezuela (b. 1922), 1989 B
Peace Ballot, 1935 F
Peace Conference, Versailles: opens, 1919 A; German delegates at, 1919 D; US delegates leave, 1919 M. *See also under* Conferences, Versailles
Peace Corps of Young Americans, for overseas service, 1961 C
Peace Foundation, Carnegie, 1911 O
Peace Pledge Union, 1934 O
Peace That Was Left (E. Cammaerts), 1945 O
Peace Treaties. *See* Treaties of Peace
Peach, Blair, B. teacher, 1979 D
Peacock, Thomas Love, B. novelist (1785–1866), 1785 Z, 1816 U, 1818 U, 1831 U, 1866 Z
Pearce Commission, on Rhodesia, 1972 A, E
Pearce, Edward Holroyd, Lord Pearce, B. judge (1901–90), B., 1972 A
Pearl Harbor, Philippines, Japanese bomb, 1941 M
Pearson, Sir Arthur, B. newspaper owner (1866–1921), 1900 V
Pearson, Charles Henry, B. Colonial administrator and historian (1830–94), 1893 O
Pearson, Lester Bowles, Canad. Liberal leader (1897–1972), 1897 Z, 1963 D, 1965 L; 1968 D, 1972 Z
Peary, Robert Edwin, Am. explorer (1856–1920), 1856 Z, 1909 P, 1920 Z
Peasants Parties. *See under* Political Parties
Peasants of Languedoc, The (E. Le Roy Ladurie), 1966 Q
Peasants:
in Prussia, proprietorship, 1811 J
in Russia, services of, 1797 N
Peat:
fertilisation through, 1914 P
for firing gas turbine, 1951 P
Peau de Chagrin (H. de Balzac), 1931 U
Pecci, Joachim, It. Cardinal, Pope Leo XIII (1810–1903), 1891 R; elected Pope, 1878 B
Péché de M. Antoine, Le (G. Sand), 1847 U
Pêcheur d'ombres, Le (J. Sarment), 1921 W
Pêcheurs d'Islande (P. Loti), 1886 U
Peckinpah, Sam, Am. film director (1925–84), 1969 W
Pedersen, Charles John, Am. chemist (1904–89), 1967 P
Pederson, Knut, Norw. author under pseudonym of 'Knut Hamsun' (1859–1936), 1893 U, 1917 U
Pedro II, King of Brazil, 1889 L
Pedro, Dom, Emperor of Brazil, 1822 K, 1823 L, 1825 M, 1832 G, 1833 G; abdicates, 1831 D; becomes Peter IV of Portugal, 1826 C. *See* Peter IV
Peel, Samuel, B. inventor, 1791 P
Peel, Sir Robert, B. Conservative statesman (1788–1850), 1788 Z, 1819 G, 1829 O, 1850 Z; as Home Secretary, reforms, 1822 A, 1823 G, 1827 F; founds London Metropolitan Police, 1820 F; becomes premier, 1834 L; issues Tamworth Manifesto, 1834 M; resigns, 1835 D; fails to form ministry, 1839 E; forms ministry, 1841 H; free trade budgets, 1842 D, 1845 D; resigns on issue of free trade, but returns to office, 1845 M; repeals Corn Laws, 1846 E; resigns, 1846 F
Peenemünde, Germany, rocket research centre, 1938 P
Peer Gynt (H. Ibsen), 1867 W
Peerages, in Britain: life, introduced, 1958 G; Stansgate peerage, election court ruling, 1961 O; Lords Committee recommends an heir be able to disclaim, 1962 M; renunciations, 1963 G, K
Pegasus (C. Day-Lewis), 1957 U
Pegram, G. B., Am. scientist, 1941 P
Pegu, Lower Burma, Britain annexes, 1852 M
Péguy (R. Rolland), 1943 U
Péguy, Charles, F. author and critic (1873–1914), 1900 U, 1910 U, 1913 U
Pei, Ieoh Ming, Am. architect (b. 1917), 1975 S, 1978 S, 1979 S, 1989 S
Peiping, China, 1949 K
Peixoto, Floriano, Brazil, dictator, 1891 L
Peking Man ('Sinanthropus'), 1920 Q
Peking, China: Chinese rebels attack, 1850 K; treaty, ratifying earlier treaties between Britain, China and France, 1860 K; siege of legations in, 1900 F; relieved, 1900 H; treaty, ends Boxer rising, 1901 J; treaty, between Britain and China, 1925 A; British legation in, 1926 N; Japanese siege, 1937 G; All-China People's Congress at, 1954 J
Red Guards parade, 1966 H
churches closed, 1966 R
Soviet embassy besieged, 1967 A
military rule imposed, 1967 B
demonstrations against British possession of Hong Kong, 1967 E
British embassy set on fire, 1967 H
Kosygin's visit, 1969 J
'Gang of Four' trial opens, 1980 L
talks on Hong Kong, 1982 J
Sino-British talks on future of Hong Kong, 1983 G
T'ien-an Men Square demonstration and massacre, 1989 D, F
population, 1990 Y
Pele, (born Edson Arantes do Nascimento), Braz. footballer (b. 1940), 1940 Z
Pèlerin d'Angkor, Le (P. Loti), 1912 U
Pelew, Island, in Pacific, Germany purchases, 1899 B
Pella, Giuseppe, It. Christian Democrat (1902–81), 1953 H, 1954 A
Pelléas et Melisande (M. Maeterlinck), 1892 W
Pellechia and Myers, architects, 1977 S
Pelli, Cesar, Am. architect (b. 1926), 1987 S
Pellico, Silvio, It. author (1788–1854), 1832 O, 1855 W
Pelloux, Luigi, It. general and Moderate Left politician (1839–1924), 1898 F, 1900 F
Pemba, Island, off Zanzibar, Britain acquires, 1890 G, H
Pen:
ball-point, 1938 P
steel, 1780 P
P.E.N. (Poets, Essayists, Novelists), London, 1922 U
Penal Reform, tracts advocating, 1764 O. *See also under* Capital Punishment, Abolition of
Penal settlements, in Botany Bay, 1788 A
Penang, Malaya: ceded to Britain, 1786 H; British evacuate, 1941 M
Pendennis (W. M. Thackeray), 1850 U
Penderecki, Krzysztof, Pol. musician (b. 1933), 1969 T, 1970 T, 1973 T, 1978 T, 1980 T, 1986 T
Pendleton, George Hart, Am. lawyer (1825–89): reforms US Civil Service, 1883 A; reforms completed, 1901 O
Penguin Books, 1936 U
Penhaligon, David Charles, B. Liberal politician (1944–86), 1987 C
Penicillin: discovered, 1928 P; developed, 1940 P; used for treating chronic diseases, 1943 P
Peninsular War. *See under* Wars
Penjdeh, Afghanistan, Russians occupy, 1885 C
Penn, Arthur, Am. film director (b. 1922), 1967 W
Penney, William George, B. physicist (1909–91), 1909 Z, , 1991 Z
Pennies from Heaven, television programme, 1978 W
Pennsylvania, state, US: as British Colony, 1776 L
University, sends archaeological expedition, 1888 Q
builds electronic brain, 1946 P
research laboratory, 1960 S
Penny for the Poor, A (B. Brecht), 1937 W
Penobscot, Maine, US, 1779 H
Pensacola, Florida, US, Spanish capture, 1781 G
Pensions, old-age:
in Britain, advocated, 1879 O
Rothschild committee on, 1898 O
introduced, 1909 A
women, to receive at 60, 1940 B
increased, 1964 L, 1971 C, 1973 C, 1974 C, 1982 C
in France, 1850 D
in Germany, 1889 E
in New Zealand, 1898 O
People's Parties. *See under* Political Parties
People's Peace, The: British History 1945–1990 (K.O. Morgan), 1990 Q
People's Republic of South Yemen, 1967 L
People's War, The (A. Calder), 1969 Q
Pepita Jimenez (J. Valera), 1848 U
Pepsin, 1930 P
Perak, Malay, independence of, 1826 F
Perception, Physics and Psychical Research (C. D. Broad), 1914 R
Perceval, Spencer, B. Tory premier (1762–1812), 1809 K; assassinated, 1812 E

Percy, Lord Eustace, B. Conservative politician, minister without portfolio (1887–1958), resigns, 1936 C
Percy, Thomas, B. antiquarian and poet, Bishop of Dromore (1729–1811), 1765 U, 1811 Z
Père Duchesne (ed. J. Hébert), 1793 R
Père Goriot, Le (H. de Balzac), 1834 U
Perekop, on Sea of Azov, Russia, Germans take, 1941 K
Perennial Philosophy, The (A. Huxley), 1946 R
Peres, Shimon, Prime Minister of Israel (b. 1923)
government of national unity, 1984 H
Israeli–Egyptian talks with Mubarak, 1986 J
dismissal, 1990 C
Perestroika, Soviet policy of, 1985 C
Perez de Cuellar, Javier, UN Secretary-General (b. 1920), 1992 A
Pérez Galdós, Benito, Sp. poet (1845–1920), 1845 Z, 1876 U, 1879 U, 1920 Z
Perfect Stranger, The (P.J. Kavanagh), 1966 U
Perfume (P. Suskind), 1985 U
Perham, Dame Margery, B. historian of Africa (1895–1982), 1944 O, 1956 Q
Periodic Table, The (P. Levi), 1975 U
Perkin, Sir William Henry, B. chemist (1838–1907), 1856 P
Perlon, invented, 1938 P
Perón, Eva, Argent., 1922 Z, 1952 Z
Perón, (Maria Estela) Isabel (b. 1931), Argent. leader
Vice-President, 1973 J
President, 1974 G
deposed by military coup, 1976 C
Perón, Juan Domingo, Argent. leader (1895–1974), 1895 Z, 1946 B, K, 1973 C; re-elected President, 1951 L; resigns, 1955 J; detained in Brazil, 1964 M
returns from exile to riots, 1973 F
President, 1973 J
death, 1974 G
Péronne, France, British capture, 1917 C, 1918 J
Perot, (Henry) Ross, Am. businessman and politician (b. 1930), Independent, 1992 L
Perpetual Motion (S. Chia), 1978 S
Perry, Matthew Calbraith, Am. naval officer (1794–1858), 1854 C
Perryville Kentucky, US, battle, 1862 K
Perse, St. John, F. poet (Alexis St. Léger), 1924 U, 1947 U
Pershing missile, 1981 L, 1983 K, L, 1984 E
Pershing, John Joseph, Am. soldier (1860–1948), 1917 L
Persia (late Iran): Babist sect in, 1843 R; Russian advance into, 1849 N; Russian interests in, 1903 K, 1910 L; Anglo-Russian convention on, 1907 H; concessions to Russia, 1911 L; changes name to Iran, 1935 O. *See also under* Iran
Persia, Shah of: visits Britain, 1959 E; hands over properties for educational and charitable purposes, 1961 K
Persian Gulf, bases on, 1903 E
Perspex, invented, 1930 P
Persuasion (J. Austen), 1818 U
Perth, Scotland
first SDP national conference, 1981 K
Perthes, Friedrich Christoph, G. philosopher (1772–1843), 1810 V
Pertini, Alessandro, President of Italy (1896–1990), 1978 F
Pertz, Georg Heinrich, G. historian (1795–1876), 1826 Q
Peru: revolt in Upper, 1809 G; independence, 1821 G; nitrates' trade, 1830 P; federation with Bolivia, 1836 K, dissolved, 1839 A; independence recognised, 1865 A; declares war on Spain, 1866 A; Declaration of, 1938 M
earthquake, 1970 E
military rule ends, 1980 G
state of emergency declared, 1983 E
terrorism, 1983 E
illiteracy, 1983 Y
Pope John Paul II visits, 1988 E
elections, 1990 F, 1992 L cabinet resigns over economic crisis, 1991 B
constitution suspended and Congress dissolved, 1992 D
Perutz, Max Ferdinand, Aus.-born B. scientist (b. 1914), 1914 Z, 1962 P
Peshaw of Poona, 1802 K; surrenders independence to Britain, 1802 M
Peshawar, India: Sikhs capture, 1834 E; Treaty, between Britain and Afghanistan, 1855 C
Pest control, chemical, dangers of, 1963 P
Pestalozzi, C., Swi. educationalist, 1922 O
Pestalozzi, Johann Heinrich, Swi. educationalist (1746–1827), 1781 O, 1801 O
Pesth, Hungary, is united with Buda, 1873 L
Pesticides:
DDT banned in US, 1969 P
poisonous gas release from Seveso pesticide plant, Italy, 1976 P
Union Carbide accident, Bhopal, India, 1984 M
Pétain, Henri Philippe, F. marshal (1856–1951), 1925 H; as chief of staff, 1917 D; as commander in-chief, 1917 E; replaces Reynaud as head of administration, 1940 F; sentenced for collaboration, 1945 H; entombed body stolen by extremists, 1973 B
Peter Abelard (H. Waddell), 1933 U
Peter I of Serbia (1903–21), 1903 F, 1918 L
Peter IV of Portugal (Dom Pedro, 1826–8), 1826 C, D, 1834 J; abdicates, 1828 C. *See also under* Pedro, Dom
Peter Pan (J. M. Barrie), 1904 S, W
Peter Plymley's Letters (S. Smith), 1808 R
'Peter Porcupine' pamphlets (W. Cobbett), 1792 O
Peter Schlemihl (A. Chamisso), 1813 U
Peter V of Portugal (1853–61), 1853 L, 1861 L
Peter and the Wolf (Prokofiev), 1936 T
Peterloo (M. Arnold), 1968 T
'Peterloo Massacre', Manchester, 1819 H
Petrie, Sir William Flinders, B. archaeologist (1853–1942), 1853 Z, 1942 Z
Petrified Forest, The (R. Sherwood), 1935 W
Petrograd, Russia: name changed from St. Petersburg, 1914 J; Bolsheviks seize power, 1917 G; Kornilov's march on, 1917 J; October Revolution in, 1917 L; Bolsheviks attack British Embassy, 1918 H. *See also* St. Petersburg
Petrol engine, Daimler's, 1882 P
developed, 1892 P
for aeroplane, 1903 P
for tractor, 1898 P
Petrol: is produced from coal, 1931 P, 1935 P; is rationed in Britain, 1956 M; Mexican laws concerning, 1927 M
Petroleum
Mexican laws concerning, 1927 M
produced from coal, 1931 P, 1935 P
rationed in Britain, 1956 M
Petroleum production:
in America, Central and South, 1946 Y
in Dutch East Indies, 1937 Y
in Iran, 1937 Y
in Mexico, 1920 Y, 1937 Y
in Panama, 1946 Y
in Roumania, 1860 Y, 1937 Y, 1946 Y
in Russia, 1903 Y, 1920 Y, 1932 Y, 1937 Y, 1940 Y, 1946 Y, 1951 Y
in Saudi Arabia, 1946 Y
in US, 1860 Y, 1863 Y, 1873 Y, 1883 Y, 1893 Y, 1901 Y, 1903 Y, 1906 Y, 1911 Y, 1916 Y, 1920 Y, 1921 Y, 1926 Y, 1937 Y, 1946 Y, 1951 Y, 1961 Y
in Venezuela, 1937 Y
Petroleum, consumption, comparative statistics of, 1937 Y
Petroleum. *See* Oil
Petropolis, Treaty between Bolivia and Brazil, 1903 L
Petrov, Vladimir, R. diplomat, 1954 D
Petsumo, Russia, Finland cedes to Russia, 1947 B
Pettegree, Andrew David Mark, B. historian (b. 1957), 1992 Q
Petty, William, Earl of Shelburne, Marquess of Lansdowne, B. Tory stateman (1737–1805), 1763 J, 1766 G, 1768 K, 1782 C, 1783 B; becomes premier, 1782 G
Petty-Fitzmaurice, Henry Charles Keith, Marquess of Lansdowne, B. conservative (1845–1927), 1903 E, 1904 K; becomes foreign secretary, 1900 K; introduces reconstruction of House of Lords bill, 1911 E
Pevsner, Antoine, Russ.-born F. artist (1886–1962), 1920 S
Pevsner, Sir Niklaus Bernhard, G.-born B. art historian (1902–83), 1902 Z, 1974 Q, 1983 Z
Pfitzner, Hans Erich, G. musician (1869–1942), 1917 T, 1931 T
Pflimlin, Pierre, F. leader of M.R.P., 1958 E
Pfrimer, Dr. Aus. Fascist, 1931 J
Phaedon (M. Mendelssohn), 1767 R
Pharmaceutical Society, British, founded, 1841 P
Phenacetin, 1887 P
Phenomenon of Man, The (P. de Chardin), 1959 R
Phenomenology (E. Husserl), 1913 R
Phenomenology of Spirit (G. W. F. Hegel), 1807 R
Philadelphia, Pennsylvania, US:
museum, 1773 Q
Continental Congresses at, 1774 J, M, 1775 E, G
British occupy, 1777 J
British evacuate, 1778 F
mint, 1792 O
American Association for the Advancement of Science founded at, 1848 P
International Working Men's Association at, 1876 O
Philanthropist, The (C. Hampton), 1970 W
Philby, H. A. R., B. journalist (1912–88), defects to Russia, 1963 G
Philharmonic Society, London, 1813 T
Philip II (W. H. Prescott), 1855 Q
Philip, Prince, Duke of Edinburgh (b. 1921), marries Princess Elizabeth, 1947 L; Oxford Conference, 1954 E
Philippe Egalité, Duke of Orléans (d. 1793), 1793 L
Philippines, Islands:
recovered by Spain, 1763 B
Spain cedes to US, 1898 M
demand independence, 1899 B
Taft Commission for, 1900 B
appropriations for public works in, 1900 J
Spooner's amendment for civil government in, 1901 C
Civil government in, 1901 G
independence demanded, 1919 D
US votes for, 1933 A
Tydings-McDuffie Act for, 1934 C
as Commonwealth, 1935 L
US landings in, 1944 K
republic inaugurated, 1946 G
Vietnam War, 1969 K
new constitution, 1973 A

referendum on presidential powers, 1981 D
Benigno Aquino assassinated, 1983 H, 1984 K
demonstrations demanding resignation of Marcos, 1983 J
elections, 1984 E, 1992 F
Benigno Aquino's accused murderers tried, 1985 A, M
ferry diaster, 1987 M
Imelda Marcos accused of plotting to steal public funds, 1990 G
floods and landslides, 1991 L
population, 1991 Y
US military withdrawal, 1992 L
Philips Company, video system, 1979 P
Phillips, Captain Mark Antony Peter, B. soldier and horseman (b. 1948), 1973 L, 1989 H, 1992 D
Phillips, H., B. scientist, discovers 'M. and B.', 1938 P
Phillpotts, Henry, B. churchman (1778–1869), 1852 R
Philology, comparative, 1772 Q. *See also under* Dictionaries
Philosophe sans le savoir (M. J. Sedaine), 1765 W
Philosophes Français du XIX siècle, Les (H. Taine), 1856 R
Philosophical Discourse of Modernity, The (J. Habermas), 1985 R
Philosophical Foundation of Quantum Mechanics (Reichenbach), 1942 R
Philosophical Introduction to Christian Theology (A. Schopenhauer), 1919 R
Philosophical Society, London, founded, 1869 R
Philosophical Systems (K. C. F. Krause), 1804 R
Philosophie (K. Jaspers), 1932 R
Philosophie de la misère (P. J. Proudhon), 1846 O
Philosophy and Civilization (Dewey), 1931 R
Philosophy and the Mirror of Nature (R. Rorty), 1979 R, 1980 R
Philosophy in the Twentieth Century (A.J. Ayer), 1982 R
Philosophy of 'As If', The (Vaihingen), 1911 R
Philosophy of A Biologist (J. Haldane), 1935 R
Philosophy of Conflict (H. Ellis), 1919 R
Philosophy of History (G. Ferrari), 1847 R
Philosophy of Inductive Sciences (W. Whewell), 1840 P
Philosophy of Knowledge (H. Hardtmann), 1921 R
Philosophy of Law (F. J. Stahl), 1830 P
Philosophy of Logic (W. Quine), 1970 R
Philosophy of Nature (Schelling), 1797 R
Philosophy of Physical Science, The (A. Eddington), 1939 R
Philosophy of Religion (J. Caird), 1880 R
Philosophy of Right (G. W. Hegel), 1821 R
Philosophy of the Active and Moral Powers of Man (D. Stewart), 1818 Q
Philosophy of the Middle Ages, The (E. Gilson), 1922 R
Philosophy of the Unconscious, The (E. Hardtmann), 1869 R
Philosophy, studies in, 1764 R, 1783 R, 1798 R, 1799 R, 1854 R, 1856 R, 1866 R, 1900 R, 1929 R
political, survey of, 1939 O
scholastic, 1922 R
Phnom Penh, Cambodia
Pathet Lao advances on, 1970 D
captured by Khmer Rouge, 1975 D
captured from Khmer Rouge, 1979 A
Phoenix, Arizona, US, 1938 S
Phonograph, The, invented, 1876 P. *See also under* Gramophone
Phosphates, factory for, 1843 P
Phosphorus, matches, sale of, prohibited in Britain, 1908 O
Phosphorus, sesquisulphide of, discovered, 1898 P
Photo-electric cell, 1904 P
Photochemical equivalence, law of, 1912 P
Photographie judiciare (L. A. Bertillon), 1890 O
Photographs:
of comets, 1881 P
of dark side of moon, 1966 P
of Jupiter, by satellite, 1973 P
of Mars, by satellite, 1964 P, 1965 P, 1971 P, 1976 P
of the moon, 1840 P, 1951 P, 1964 P
of the night sky, composite, 1954 P
of Saturn, by US space probe, 1981 P
of Venus and Mercury, by satellite, 1974 P
Photography:
the first photograph, 1802 P
box camera, 1888 P
coated photographic paper, 1885 P
colour, 1873 P
Spier-Dufuy process for, 1931 P
daguerreotype, perfected, 1839 P
flash bulb for, 1930 P
Fox Talbot's negative, 1839 P
half-tone block used for daily newspaper, 1880 V
produced on metal plate, 1827 P
roll film, 1889 P
very rapid, by image-dissector camera, 1956 P
automatic focus, 1978 P
See also Camera; Cinematography
Photosynthesis of plants, 1857 P, 1898 P
Phtalacyamine dyes, 1934 P
Physical Geography of the Sea (M. Maury), 1855 P
Physical Impossibility of Death in the Mind of Someone Living, The (D. Hirst), 1992 S
Physical Laboratory, National, Teddington, 1914 P
Physical Significance of the Quantum Theory (Lindemann), 1926 P
Physics:
atomic. *See* Atomic Physics
wave mechanics, 1924 P
quantum electrodynamics (QED), 1949 P
quantum chromodynamics (QCD), 1972 P
superconductivity, 1986 P, 1987 P
Physics and Politics (W. Bagehot), 1869 O
Physics, Atomic, 1931 P, 1932 P, 1941 P, 1942 P, 1943 P, 1944 P, 1945 P
Physiological Optics (H. Helmholtz), 1856 P
Physiological Psychology (W. Wundt), 1874 R
Physiology, Institute of, Breslau, 1839 O
Phythian-Adams, Charles V., B. historian, 1979 Q, 1987 Q
Piacenza, N. Italy, Duchy, Napoleon annexes, 1802 K
Piaget, Jean, Swiss psychologist (1896–1980), 1896 Z, 1971 R, 1980 Z
Piano Tuner, The (C. Naishen), 1989 U
Piano, Renzo, It. architect (b. 1937), 1977 S, 1987 S
Pianoforte, the first, 1780 P
Piave, River, N. E. Italy, Italians retreat to, 1917 L
Piazzi, Giuseppe, It. astronomer (1746–1826), 1801 P
Pic du Midi, France, atomic research at, 1950 P
Picasso, Pablo Ruiz y, Sp. artist (1881–1973), 1881 Z, 1905 S, 1907 S, 1912 S, 1915 S, 1919 S, 1921 S, 1923 S, 1925 S, 1929 S, 1938 S, 1939 S, 1954 S, 1960 S
ballet sets by, 1917 S
'bone' period, 1928 S
mural, 1937 P
founds Vallauris pottery, 1946 S
as sculptor, 1950 S
multi-part homage to shown in Paris, 1966 S
death, 1973 S, Z
gift of works to French nation, 1979 S
Picasso Museum, Paris, 1985 S
Piccard, Auguste, Belg. marine biologist (1884–1962), 1948 P, 1960 P
Piccinni, Niccolò, It. musician (1728–1800), 1771 T; controversy with Gluck, 1779 T
Pichegru, Charles, F. general (1761–1804), 1794 E, M, 1795 J
captures Dutch fleet, 1795 A
Pickford, Mary (born Gladys Mary Smith), Am. film actress (1893–1979), 1893 Z, 1909 W, 1920 W, 1979 Z
Pickwick Papers (C. Dickens), 1836 U
Picture of Dorian Gray, The (O. Wilde), 1891 U
Picture-telegraphy, 1930 P
Pictures of Travel (H. Heine), 1826 U
Pictures, cleaning of, 1936 S, 1947 S
Pieck, Wilhelm, president of East German Republic (1875–1960), 1949 K
Piedmont, Italy: Joubert occupies, 1798 L; Parthenopaer Republic established in, 1799 A; Napoleon annexes, 1802 J; Austrian intervention in, 1821 D
Pierce, Franklin, Am. Democrat (1804–69), 14th president of US (1853–7), 1852 L, 1853 C
Pierre et Jean (G. de Maupassant), 1888 U
Piggott, Lester, B. jockey (b. 1935), 1935 Z, 1970 X, 1983 X, 1990 X
Pigtails, abolished in China, 1911 M
Pilgrim Trust, The, founded, 1930 O; benefaction through, 1943 Q
Pilgrims, The, founded, 1902 O
Pilkington Report on Broadcasting in Britain, 1962 W
Pillars of Society, The (H. Ibsen), 1877 W
Pillnitz, near Dresden, E. Germany, Declaration of, 1791 H
Pilotless aircraft, 1950 P, 1953 P
missiles, 1946 P. *See also* Rockets
Pilsudski, Jozef Clemens, Pol. statesman (1867–1935), 1920 D, 1922 M, 1926 E, 1930 H
Piltdown Man, 1912 P; proved to be a hoax, 1953 P
Pinay, Antoine, F. politician, 1952 B, M, 1955 L
Pinckney, Charles Cotesworth, Am. lawyer and Federalist (1746–1825), 1800 L
Pinckney, Thomas, Am. diplomat (1750–1828), 1795 K
Pindling, Sir Lynden Oscar, President of The Bahamas (b. 1930), 1992 H
Pinel, Philippe, F. alienist (1745–1826), 1791 P
Pinero, Sir Arthur Wing, B. dramatist (1855–1934), 1855 Z, 1888 W, 1893 W, 1899 W, 1906 W, 1934 Z
Pink Floyd, B. pop group, 1973 W, 1990 W
Pinkowski, Jozef, Pol. politician, 1981 B
Pinochet, Augusto, Chilean general and politician (b. 1915)
seizes power, 1973 J
eight-year extension of government, 1980 J
assassination attempt, 1986 J
Pinsk, in Pripet Marshes, Russia, Russians take, 1920 G
Pinter, Harold, B. dramatist (b. 1930), 1930 Z, 1958 W, 1960 W, 1961 W, 1967 W, 1975 W, 1978 W
Pioneers, The (J. F. Cooper), 1823 U
Piper Alpha explosion, 1988 G
Piper, John, B. artist (1903–92), 1903Z, 1934 S, 1940 S, 1942 S, 1962 S, 1992 Z
Piracy:
Algerian, 1775 G

arising from Spanish Civil War, 1937 J
Piraeus, Greece: Royal Navy blockades, 1850 A; French and British occupation, 1854 E; blockade of, 1897 B, C
Pirandello, Luigi, It. dramatist (1867–1936), 1867 Z, 1904 W, 1913 W, 1917 W, 1918 W, 1923 W, 1936 Z
Pirot, Serbia, 1885 L
Pirquet, Charles, F. physician, 1907 P
Piss Christ (A. Serrano), 1987 S
Pissarro, Camille, F. artist (1831–1903), 1831 Z, 1872 S, 1874 S, 1807 S, 1903 Z
Pissarro, Lucien, F. artist (1863–1944), 1863 Z, 1944 Z
Pithecanthropus, skull of, 1937 P
Pitman, Sir Isaac, B. inventor of shorthand (1813–97), 1837 P
Pitt, William (The Younger), B. Tory statesman (1759–1806), 1790 L, 1792 M
  as Chancellor of Exchequer, 1782 G
  declines to form ministry, 1783 B
  proposes Parliamentary Reform, 1783 E
  becomes premier, 1783 M
  opposition to dwindles, 1784 C
  gains support through elections, 1784 C
  reduces excise duties, 1784 F
  India Bill, 1784 H
  motion for Parliamentary Reform defeated, 1785 D
  establishes Sinking Fund, 1786 C
  excise scheme, 1786 F
  policy over Belgian independence, 1790 A
  seeks to maintain neutrality, 1791 H
  subsidies Allies, 1793 C
  begins peace negotiations, 1796 C
  increases newspaper tax, 1798 V
  advocates Catholic Emancipation, 1800 J
  resigns from premiership, 1801 C
  forms second ministry, 1804 E
  death, 1806 A
Pitt, William, Earl of Chatham, B. statesman (1708–1778), 1766 G, 1769 B, 1778 Z, 1780 S; illness, 1767 C; proposes conciliation with America, 1775 B, 1778 D
Pitt-Rivers, Augustus Henry Lane Fox, B. anthropologist and archaeologist (1827–1900), 1874 Q
Pittsburgh, East, Pennsylvania, US, broadcasting station at, 1920 W
Pittsburgh, West, Pennsylvania, US, 1881 O; early cinema in, 1905 W; university, 1955 P
Pituitary body, study of, 1902 P
Pius VI, Pope (Cardinal Giovanni Angelo Braschi), It. (1717–99), elected Pope 1775, 1782 C; admits forged decretals, 1789 R; refutes Ems articles, 1789 R; cedes Romagna and Bologna to France, 1797 B; leaves Romes, 1798 B
Pius VII, Pope (Cardinal Luigi Barnaba Chiaramonti), It. (1740–1823), 1808 B, 1811 F, 1815 S; elected Pope, 1800 C; concordat with Napoleon, 1801 G; crowns Napoleon, 1804 M; Napoleon imprisons, 1809 G; restores Inquisition and Index, 1814 R; restored to Papal Estates, 1815 F
Pius IX, Pope (Cardinal Giovanni Maria Mastai-Ferretti), It. (1792–1878), 1792 Z, 1847 G, 1854 R, 1867 R, 1881 R; elected Pope, 1846 F; disassociates himself from Italian Nationalism, 1848 D; flees to Gaeta, 1848 L; is restored by French, 1849 G, 1850 D; revokes Constitution, 1850 D; concordat with Francis Joseph of Austria, 1855 R; issues Syllabus of Errors, 1864 R; temporal power is attacked, 1859 O; calls Vatican Council, 1870 R; annuls German May Laws, 1874 E
Pius X, Pope (Cardinal Giuseppe Sarto), It. (1835–1914), elected Pope, 1903 G; condemns Modernism, 1907 R; encyclical *Editio Saepe*, 1910 E, F
Pius XI, Pope (Cardinal Achille Ratti), It. (1857–1939), 1922 B, 1928 R; leaves Vatican, 1929 G
Pius, XII, Pope (Cardinal Eugene Pacelli), It. (1876–1958), 1876 Z; elected 1939, 1946 R; pronounces on bodily assumption, 1950 R; death, 1958 K
Pixies, The, Am. pop group, 1988 W
Place, Francis, B. Radical reformer and pioneer of birth control (1771–1854), 1822 P, 1824 O
Plague, The (A. Camus), 1947 U
Plain Tales from the Hills (R. Kipling), 1888 U
Planck, Gottlieb Jakob, G. Protestant divine (1751–1833), 1781 R
Planck, Max Karl Ernst Ludwig, G. physicist (1858–1947), 1858 Z, 1900 P, 1901 P, 1947 Z
Plane, machine, 1776 P
Planetary system, laws of, 1788 P
Planets, The:
  Hidalgo, 1920 P
  Jupiter, emission of radio waves from, 1955 P
  Mars, satellites of, discovered, 1877 P
    photo-electric observations, 1955 P
    data on, from space research, 1963 P
    photographs of, 1964 P, 1965 P
  Mercury, rotation of, 1889 P
  Neptune, 1846 P
  Pallas, 1801 P
  Pluto, 1930 P
  Uranus, discovered, 1781 P
  Venus, observations of transit of, 1768 P, 1882 P
    is explored by satellites, 1962 P, 1963 P
Plans:
  Acheson, to increase powers of UN to resist aggression, 1950 K
  Colombo, to aid S.E. Asia, 1950 A, 1951 B
  Eden, for Council of Europe, 1952 H
  Germany's 4-year, 1946 K
  Marshall, for European recovery, 1947 A, F, 1948 C, 1949 M, 1950 M, 1951 M
  Rapacki, for denuclearised military zone, 1957 K, 1958 B
  Russia's first 5-year, 1928 P
    subsequent 5-year, 1932 A, 1946 C, 1952 K, 1971 B
  Schuman, for iron and steel community, 1950 E
  Turkey's 5-year, 1928 P
Plante, Linda La, B. author (b. 1946), 1991 W
Planté, R. L. Gaston, F. electrical engineer (1834–1889), 1859 P
Plants, cellular theory of, 1838 P
  classification of, 1789 P
  fertility of, 1793 P
  growth of, chemicals needed for, 1843 P
Plastic Palette I (T. Cragg), 1980 S
Plata, La, United Provinces of (Argentina), independence, 1816 G. *See also* Argentina
Plate River, S. America, vice-royalty, 1776 N
  naval battle, 1939 M
Plath, Sylvia, Am. author (1932–63), 1932 Z, 1966 U
Platinum, found in Urals, 1820 P
  palladium discovered in, 1804 P
Platt, Orville Hitchcock, Am. Republican (1827–1905), 1901 C
Playboy of the Western World (J. M. Synge), 1907 W
Playfair, Sir Nigel Ross, B. producer (1874–1934), 1919 W
Playing Fields Association, National, 1933 X
Pleasures of Hope, The (T. Campbell), 1799 U
Pleasures of Memory, The (S. Rogers), 1792 U
Plebiscites:
  in British Togoland, for integration with Gold Coast, 1956 E
  in Cameroons, 1961 B
  in Carinthia, 1920 H
  in France, for Louis Napoleon's constitution, 1851 M
    for revival of French Empire, 1852 L
  in Germany, against battleships, 1928 K
    vesting Hitler with power as *Führer*, 1934 H
  in Greece, for King Constantine's return, 1920 M
    for George II, 1935 L
    favouring monarchy, 1946 J
  in Naples, favouring union with Sardinia, 1860 K
  in Norway, for separation from Sweden, 1905 F
  in Ödenburg, for union with Hungary, 1921 M
  in Philippines, demanded, 1926 G
  in Prussia, 1920 G
  in Saar, for incorporation in Germany, 1935 A
  in Salzburg, for union with Germany, 1921 E
  in North Schleswig, annulled, 1878 K
  in Schleswig, 1920 B
  in Upper Silesia, for incorporation in Germany, 1921 C
  in Sudan, 1951 L
  in Taca and Arica, S. America, 1883 K
  in Tuscany, etc., favouring union with Sardinia, 1860 C
  in Tyrol, favouring Germany, 1921 D
  in Umbria, for union with Sardinia, 1860 L
  in United Arab Republic, for Nasser to be head of state, 1958 B
  in Venezia, 1866 K
  See also Referenda
Plecharoff, G. V., R. politician, 1903 H
Plehve, Viacheslav, R. minister of interior, 1902 D, 1904 G
Pléiade, La, formed to finance performance of French music, 1943 T
Plenty (D. Hare), 1978 W
Pleven, René, F. statesman (b. 1901), 1950 G, 1951 B, H, 1952 A
Plevna, Bulgaria, 1877 M
Plimsoll, Samuel, B. politician and social reformer (1824–98), 1875 O
Plombières, France, Napoleon III meets Cavour at, 1858 G
Plough and the Stars, The (O'Casey), 1926 W
Plowden Committee on British Aircraft Industry, 1965 M
Plowden Committee on Public Expenditure, 1964 B
Plowden Report, *Children and their Primary Schools*, 1967 O
Plückner, Julius, G. mathematician (1801–68), 1865 P
Plumb, Sir John Harold, B. historian (b. 1911), 1967 Q
Plumed Serpent, The (D. H. Lawrence), 1926 U
Plunckett, Sir Horace Curzon, Ir. statesman (1854–1932), 1917 G
Pluralistic Universe, A (W. James), 1909 R
Pluto, planet, 1930 P
  moon discovered, 1978 P
  atmosphere discovered, 1980 P
Plutonium:
  manufacture, 1944 P
  separation from pitchblende concentrates, 1950 P
  Sellafield Pile, 1951 P

Plymouth Brethren. *See under* Religious Denominations
Pneumatic tyre, 1888 P
Po, River, Italy, Allies reach, 1945 D
Po-on (F. Sionil Jose), 1984 U
Pobédonostev, Constantine Petrovich, R. jurist (1827–1907), 1881 R
Podgorny, Nikolai Viktorovich, President of the Soviet Union (1903–83), 1965 M, 1967 F, 1971 A, 1972 F
Poe, Edgar Allan, Am. author (1809–49), 1809 Z, 1827 U, 1838 U, 1850 U, 1849 Z
Poelaert, Joseph, Belg. architect (1816–79), 1866 S
Poèmes Antiques (de Lisle), 1853 U
Poèmes saturniens (P. Verlaine), 1866 U
Poems Chiefly Lyrical (Lord Tennyson), 1830 U
Poems Chiefly in the Scottish Dialect (R. Burns), 1786 U
Poems and Ballads (A. C. Swinburne), 1866 U
Poems by Two Brothers (A. and C. Tennyson), 1827 U
Poems of the English Roadside (G. Meredith), 1862 U
Poetical Studies (W. Blake), 1783 U
Pogues, The, B. pop group, 1985 W
Poher, Alain Emile Louis Marie, F. politician (b. 1909), 1969 D, 1974 D
Pöhl, Karl Otto, G. economist (b. 1929), President of the Bundesbank, 1991 E
Poincaré, Raymond, F. statesman (1860–1934), 1860 Z; forms ministry, 1912 A; visits Russia, 1912 H, 1914 G; elected President of France, 1913 A; visits Britain, 1913 F; as premier, 1922 A; of National Union ministry, 1926 G; resigns, 1919 G
Poindexter, Vice-Admiral John, Am. National Security Adviser (b. 1936), 1986 L, 1987 G
Point Counter Point (A. Huxley), 1928 U
Poischwitz, Germany, armistice between Prussia and France at, 1813 F
Poison Gas: first used, 1915 D; banned by Washington Conference, 1922 B; Geneva Conference on, 1925 E
Poisson, Siméon Denis, F. mathematician (1781–1840), 1811 P, 1835 P
Pol Pot, Commander in Chief of Khmer Rouge Army (b. 1928), resignation, 1985 J
Poland:
constitution in, 1764 D
Russian intrigues in, 1766 N, 1767 D, L
Civil War in, 1768 H
Partition of, proposed, 1768 M, 1769 B, H, 1771 H
first, 1772 H
Russians invade, 1792 E
Second Partition, 1793, A, E
Third Partition, 1795 A, K, 1797 A
becomes independent, 1812 F
Russian designs on, 1814 L
East Poland is ceded to Russia, 1815 F, L
West Poland is ceded to Prussia, 1815 F
independence proclaimed, 1831 A
Russian, is divided into provinces, 1863 C
Russian provinces autonomy to, 1914 H
Kingdom is proclaimed by Central Powers, 1916 L
Russia guarantees independence, 1917 C
Republic proclaimed, 1918 L
Germany invades, 1939 J
Russia invades, 1939 J
Polish government in London, 1940 H
Russia severs relations with, 1943 D
Lublin Committee for Polish Liberation, in Moscow, 1944 G
frontier with East Germany agreed, 1950 L
student demonstrations against political censorship, 1968 A
Gierek replaces Gomulka, 1970 M
Oder–Neisse Line frontier treaty, 1970 M, 1972 E
price increases cause strikes and riots, 1970 M
West German treaty ratified, 1972 E
price rises announced, 1976 F
relations between Poland and West Germany normalised, 1976 F
wage rises approved, 1980 G
Solidarity registered, 1980 K
Warsaw Pact manoeuvres, 1981 C, J
Solidarity branded counter-revolutionary by USSR, 1981 C
food rationing introduced, 1981 D
farmers trade union, 1981 D
Communists approve reforms, 1981 D
government reconstructed, 1981 F
ration cuts and food price increases planned, 1981 G
Solidarity blockades Warsaw city centre, 1981 H
USSR increases supplies to, 1981 H
Leninist principles encouraged by USSR, 1981 H
Solidarity, 1981 J, 1983 C, 1985 E
crisis talks, 1981 L
martial law imposed, 1981 M
martial law denounced by EC, 1982 A
massive food increases announced, 1982 A
debts covered by US, 1982 A
Gdansk curfew following riots over food increases, 1982 A
arrests in security service raids, 1982 B
refused new credits by Japan, 1982 B
Moscow talks on, 1982 C
Military Council of National Salvation releases detainees, 1982 D
Solidarity supporters demonstrate against martial law, 1982 E
detainees released, 1982 G
Solidarity demonstrators broken up by riot police, 1982 H
Cardinal Glemp calls for release of Lech Walesa, 1982 H
Solidarity anniversary demonstrations, 1982 H
Solidarity banned, 1982 K
new trade unions banned, 1982 K
US trade sanctions imposed, 1982 K
military law enforced, 1982 K
strikes in Polish shipyards, 1982 K
martial law suspended by Council of State, 1982 M
Walesa returns to work at Lenin Shipyard, Gdansk, 1983 D
May Day demonstrations across Poland broken up, 1983 E
Pope visits, 1983 F
Church warned to stay out of politics, 1983 F
martial law ended and amnesty for political prisoners announced, 1983 G
US trade sanctions partialiy lifted, 1984 A
students demand restoration of crucifixes in classrooms, 1984 C
agreement reached on display of crucifixes in public places, 1984 D
Popieluszko murdered, 1984 K
secret police officers sentenced for murder of Popieluszko, 1985 B
amnesty for 300 political prisoners announced, 1986 F
shipyard workers strike, 1988 E
Solidarity leaders detained, 1988 E
Walesa holds talks with government, 1988 H
Gdansk shipyard closed, 1988 K
Thatcher visits, 1988 L
political and economic reforms agreed, 1989 D
Solidarity legalized, 1989 D
Roman Catholic Church given increased status and powers, 1989 E
Solidarity wins landslide victory in parliamentary elections, 1989 F
presidential election, 1989 G
state price controls abolished, 1989 H
coalition government led by Solidarity, 1989 H, J
border with East Germany opened, 1989 K
parliamentary elections, 1989 F, 1991 K
Bielicki nominated Prime Minister, 1990 M
Walesa elected President, 1990 M
parliament votes government out of office, 1992 F
Polanski, Roman, F. film director (b. 1933), 1974 W
Polanyi, Michael, B. formerly Czech., chemist and philosopher (1891–1976), 1947 R
Polar Discovery:
Scott Polar Research Institute, Cambridge, 1926 P
North Pole, Nansen's expedition, 1893 P
Peary reaches, 1909 P
flights over, 1926 P
observation station near, 1937 P
magnetic N. Pole, position of, 1946 P
Nautilus passes under ice cap, 1958 P
Arctic submarine plateau discovered, 1959 P
South Pole, Amundsen at, 1911 P
Scott at, 1912 P
Shackleton's expedition, 1914 P
flights over, 1929 P
survey of East Antarctica, 1939 P
Commonwealth Transantarctic expedition, 1957 P, 1958 P
Polaris submarines, facilities for, at Holy Loch, 1960 L. *See also under* Missiles
Polariser, synthetic light, 1932 P
Pole to Pole, television series, 1992 W
Pole, Jack Richon, B. historian (b. 1922), 1991 Q
Police and the People, The (R.Cobb), 1970 Q
Police forces:
international, proposed, 1932 B
Hendon Police College, 1934 O
Metropolitan, Peel founds, 1829 O
Obscene Publications Squad, corruption charges, 1977 E
Police Complaints Board established, 1976 O
Police, The, B. pop group, 1979 W
Policy and Police ... (G.R. Elton), 1972 Q
Policy for the Arts, A, 1965 O
Polignac, Prince Jules de, F. Ultra Royalist (1780–1847), 1829 H
Poliomyelitis, Salk vaccine against, 1955 P
Polite and Commercial People, A: England 1727–1783 (P. Langford), 1989 Q
Political Arithmetic (A. Young), 1774 O
Political Arithmetic; Mathematics for the Million (L. Hogben), 1936 O
Political Economy, treatises on, 1844 O, 1848 O, 1885 O
Political Ethics (F. Lieber), 1838 O
Political Parties:
in Albania
Communist Party of Labour, 1991 C
Democrat, 1992 C
in Algeria
Front de la libération nationale, 1960 F, 1962 C

Islamic Salvation Front, 1990 F, 1991 M, 1992 A, G
National Liberation Front, 1991 M
Nationalist movement for the Triumph of Democratic Liberties, dissolved, 1953 L
in Angola, Popular Movement for Liberation of Angola Workers' Party, 1992 J
in Argentina
Civic Union, 1987 J
Labour, 1983 C, 1990 C, 1991 M
Liberal and National, 1975 K
Peronists, 1989 E
Radical, 1983 K, 1989 E
in Australia
Country, forms coalition with United Australia, 1934 L
election success, 1937 K
Labour, 1908 E, 1929 K, 1983 C, 1990 C, 1991 M
losses to United Australia, 1931 N
election defeat, 1937 K
Liberal and National, 1975 K
Liberal–Country, in power, 1961 M
Nationalist, 1922 M, 1931 M
United Australia founded, 1931 N
in power, 1934 J
election success, 1937 K
in Austria, Agrarian joins coalition with Christian Socialist, 1932 E
reversal for, 1911 F
in power, 1926 K, 1930 M, 1931 F
supports Schober, 1929, J
forfeits support of working classes, 1934 B
Fatherland Front, becomes sole party, 194 B
under Schuschnigg's leadership, 1936 E, K
Nationalist Socialist (Nazi), 1931 J
is dissolved, 1933 F
attempted *coup*, 1934 G
Schuschnigg's *coup* against, 1935 K
amnesty for, 1937 A
release of members, forced, 1938 B
People's, 1945 L, M
in power, 1953 B, D
forms coalition with Socialists, 1959 E
Socialist, 1970 C, 1983 D, 1990 K
split in, 1897 N
election losses, 1949 K
election success, 1953 B
forms coalition with People's, 1959 E
in Barbados, Labour, election losses, 1961 M
in Bavaria, Communist, *coup* by, 1919 D
expelled from Munich, 1919 E
in Belgium, Catholic, in power, 1929 E
Christian Democrat, in power, 1950 H
Christian Socialist, in power, 1946 B, 1952 A
forms coalition with Liberals, 1949 H
loses majority, 1954 D
forms coalition with Christian Socialists, 1942 H
Clerical, unites with Liberals, 1928 G
in power, 1880 F, 1912 F
Democrat (or Vonckists), lose power, 1790 C
Green, 1991 L
Labour, 1885 N
Liberals, 1846 F
unite with Clericals, 1828 G
defeated, 1880 F
in power, 1937 K
forms coalition with Christian Socialists, 1942 H
Rexist (Fascist) 1936, E, K
Socialist, demonstrate against Leopold III, 1950 G
Vonckist, *See* Democrat
uniformed parties, prohibited, 1934 G
in Bermuda, United Bermuda, 1989 B
in Brazil, Conservative, 1989 M
Liberal, 1945 K
political parties banned, 1937 M
in Britain, British Union of Fascists, founded, 1932 N
mass meetings and demonstrations, 1934 F, J, 1962 G
Commonwealth, 1943 C
by-election success, 1944 A
Communist, application for affiliation with Labour Party rejected, 1936 K
supports Pacifist People's Convention, 1941 C
Conservative (and Unionist), based on Tamworth manifesto, 1834 M
in power, 1841 H
split by repeal of Corn Laws, 1846 E
Disraeli elected leader, 1849 B
in power, 1852 B, 1858 B,1866 F, 1874 B
defeated, 1880 D
leadership, under Northcote, 1881 D
in power, 1885 F
electoral success, 1886 G
defeated, 1892 G
in power, 1895 F
divided on issue of Imperial Preference, 1903 E
out of office, 1905 M
defeated in election, 1906 A
Bonar Law succeeds to leadership, 1911 L
A. Chamberlain elected leader, 1921 C
in power, 1922 L
defeated in election, 1923 M
in power, 1924 L
defeated in election, 1929 E
in power, 1945 E
defeated in election, 1945 G
successes in local elections, 1947 L
in power, 1951 K
losses in by-elections, 1958 B, C, 1962 C, F, G
Macmillan becomes leader, 1957 A
wins general election, 1959 K
back-bench revolt, 1961 D
Home elected leader, 1963 J
account of struggle for leadership, 1964 O
defeated in election, 1964 K
by-election success, 1965 A
local election successes, 1965 E
Heath elected leader, 1965 G
divisions between leadership and Powellites, 1968 K
London borough election victories, 1968 E
election victories, 1970 F, 1979 E, 1983 F, 1987 F, 1992 D
governmental re-organisation, 1970 K
mini-budget, 1970 K
seats lost, 1971 E
votes in favour of EC entry, 1971 K
Cabinet statistics, 1976 Y, 1979 Y
spending cuts announced, 1979 L
Monetarist policies, 1980 K
Cabinet reshuffle, 1981 J
election manifesto, 1983 E
Brighton bomb attack, 1984 K
Thatcher challenged and resigns as leader, 1990 L
fourth–term election victory, 1992 D
Democratic Labour, 1973 C
Ecology
founded, 1975 O
name changed to Green Party, 1985 O
'Fourth, The', a Conservative splinter-group, 1880 E
Green, 1985 O
Independent Labour (I.L.P.), founded 1892 G, 1893 A
refuses affiliation with Communists, 1921 C
forms United Front, 1937 A
'King's Friends', 1770 A
Labour, founded, 1900 B
wins by-election, 1903 G
elects MacDonald Chairman, 1911 B
against conscription, 1916 A
newspaper suppressed, 1916 V
secedes from Coalition, 1918 L, 1919 A
appoints Council of Action, 1920 H
refuses affiliation with Communists, 1921 F, 1922 F, 1936 K
defeated, 1924 A
in power, 1924 L
leaves Commons on Kirkwood's suspension, 1925 C
in power, 1929 E
expels MacDonald and those serving with him, 1931 H
rump of, led by Henderson, 1931 H
wins majority on L.C.C., 1934 C
declares that war is not inevitable, 1937 J
sends delegations to Finland, 1940 B
divided by Mosley's release, 1943 L
in power, 1945 G
majority reduced, 1950 B
split by Bevanite revolt, 1951 D
defeated in election, 1951 K
Gaitskell elected leader, 1955 M
by-election successes, 1957 B, 1958 B
hostility to Rent Act, 1957 F
retains 'Clause 4' on nationalisation, 1960 C
censures government over 'Blue Streak' missile, 1960 D
unilateralist conflict in, 1960 K
back-bench refuse to follow Gaitskell on defence, 1960 M
Gaitskell's victory over unilateralists, 1961 F
by-election successes, 1962 L
Wilson elected leader on Gaitskell's death 1963 B
wins first G.L.C. election, 1964 D
wins general election, 1964 K
election defeats, 1970 F, 1979 E
proposes compulsory comprehensive education, 1970 B
revises rules for pay increases, 1970 A
statutory incomes policy, practical end of, 1970 A
National Executive votes against EC membership, 1971 G
resolution against EC entry, 1971 K
referendum on EC membership called form 1972 D
nationalisation plans repudiated by Wilson, 1973 F
wins control of GLC, 1973 B
forms minority government, 1974 C
forms majority government, 1974 K
social and educational composition of Cabinet, 1974 Y
conference supports incomes policy, 1975 J
Callaghan becomes leader, 1976 C
loses overall majority, 1976 D
Lib–Lab Pact, 1977 C, 1978 E

conference votes against pay policy, 1978 K
Callaghan calls general election, 1979 C
loses no confidence motion, 1979 C
mandatory reselection of sitting MPs, 1979 K, 1980 K
calls for British withdrawal from EC, 1980 K, 1983 E
Foot elected leader, 1980 L
infiltration by Militant Tendency, 1980 C
radical proposals, 1980 G
unilateral nuclear disarmament, 1980 K, 1983 E
electoral college of MPs, 1981 A
Healey elected deputy leader, 1981 J
election manifesto, 1983 E
Foot resigns as leader, 1983 F
Kinnock elected leader, 1983 K
pledges to close all US nuclear bases in Britain, 1986 J
Monmouth by-election victory, 1991 E
Kinnock and Hattersley resign as leader and deputy leader, 1992 D
Smith and Beckett elected leader and deputy-leader, 1992 G
Liberal, in power, 1830 L. *See also* Whig.
out of office, 1841 H
in power, 1846 F
out of office, 1852 B
in power, 1852 M, 1855 B
defeated, 1858 B
in power, 1859 F
defeated, 1866 F
in power, 1868 M
back bench revolt, 1873 C
electoral defeat, 1874 B
Hartington elected leader, 1875 B
wins election, 1880 D
out of office, 1885 F
returns to power, 1886 B
back bench revolt over Home Rule, 1886 F
falls from power, 1886 G
adopts Newcastle Programme, 1891 K
wins election, 1892 G
defeated, being split by Home Rule, 1894 C
falls from power, 1886 G
adopts Newcastle Programme, 1891 K
wins election, 1892 G
defeated, being split by Home Rule, 1894 C
Rosebery resigns leadership, 1896 K
Campbell Bannerman as leader, 1899 A
closes ranks over Irish Home Rule, 1905 L
in power, 1905 M
electoral landslide, 1906 A
majority is reduced, 1910 A
Lloyd George becomes leader, 1925 A
joins opposition to National government, 1933 L
downfall, 1945 G
Grimond elected leader, 1956 J
wins Torrington by-election, 1958 C
by-election successes, 1962 C
holds balance between major parties, 1964 K
Thorpe elected leader, 1967 A
refuses to enter coalition with Conservatives, 1974 C
Grimond as interim leader, 1976 E
Steel elected leader, 1976 G
Thorpe resigns leadership, 1976 E
Lib–Lab Pact, 1977 C, J, 1978 E
electoral alliance with SDP, 1981 J
issues joint statement with SDP, 1981 F
Brecon and Radnor by-election victory, 1985 G
merger with SDP, 1987 H, J, 1988 O
Liberal–SDP Alliance, 1981 J
County Council election gains, 1985 E
Liberal Unionist, under J. Chamberlain, 1891 M
Rosebery becomes premier, 1894 C
unites with Conservatives, 1914 E
Municipal Reform, 1934 C
National Front, 1977 E, H, L
election meeting violence, 1979 D
supporters clash with Asians, 1981 G
National Liberal, 1932 J
New Party, Mosley's, 1931 B
Scottish Labour (SLP):
launched, 1976 A
breaks from Labour, 1976 G
Social Democratic (SDP):
Limehouse Declaration, 1981 A
official launch, 1981 C
issues joint statement with Liberals, 1981 F
by-election loss, 1981 G
electoral alliance with Liberals, 1981 J, 1985 E
national conference, 1981 K
by-election victory, 1981 L
Owen replaces Jenkins as leader, 1983 F
votes against merger with Liberal Party, 1983 J
Portsmouth South by-election victory, 1984 F
Greenwich by-election victory, 1987 B
breakaway 'continuing', 1987 H
merger with Liberal Party, 1987 H, 1988 O
Owen resigns leadership, 1987 H
wound up, 1990 O
Social Democratic Federation, 1886 B
Socialist, mass meeting, 1887 L. *See* Labour Party
Socialist League, forms United Front, 1937 A
Syndicalist, 1912 C
Tory, in power, 1807 C
out of office, 1830 L
attempts to form government, 1834 L, M
Peel refounds, on Tamworth Manifesto, 1834 M
Peelites coalesce with Whigs, 1852 M. *See* Conservative Party
Unionist. *See under* Conservative
United Front, 1937 A
Whig, led by Bedford, 1763 J
led by Rockingham, 1776 K
split on issue of Reform, 1794 G
fall from power, 1807 C
in power, 1830 L
defeated, 1841 H
coalesce with Peelites, 1852 M
in British Guiana, People's National Congress, 1964 M
People's Progressive, 1953 D, 1957 H
in Bulgaria, are banned, 1934 F
Communist, excluded from amnesty, 1926 A
Fatherland Front (Communist), 1945 L
is unopposed, 1953 M
Socialist, 1991 K
in Burma, National League for Democracy, 1990 E
in Canada, Conservative in power, 1878 K, 1911 K, 1925 K, 1930 H
Liberal, 1979 E, 1980 B, 1984 J
adopts reciprocity, 1890 K
in power, 1896 G
defeated, 1911 J
elect Mackenzie King as leader, 1919 H
in power, 1921 M
defeated, 1925 K
in power, 1925 K
defeated, 1930 H
in power, 1945 F, 1949 F, 1953 H
defeated, 1957 F
Parti Québecois, 1976 L
Progressive Conservative, in power, 1957 F, 1979 E, 1984 J, 1988 L
loses overall majority, 1962 F
Unionist, 1917 M
in Ceylon, Freedom Party, in power, 1960 G
People's United Front, 1956 C
United National, in power, 1952 E
in Chile, Socialist, in power, 1932 F
Christian Democrats, 1989 M
parties banned, 1977 C
in China, Communist, 1936 J, 1977, G, H
is purged, 1955 C
Kuo Min Tang (Nationalist), 1924 A
British Sympathy with, 1926 N
split in, 1927 D
See also under Civil Wars, in China
in Cuba, Liberal, 1908 L
in Czechoslovakia, Agrarian, 1935 L
Civic Forum, 1990 F
Communist, 1946 E, 1970 F, 1988 K
stages *coup*, 1948 B
is purged, 1951 C
National Front, 1945 D
Sudeten (Nazi), 1935 E
in Danzig, 1933 E
in Denmark, Liberal, in power, 1901 G, 1926 M
Social Democrats, electoral success, 1945 K
in power, 1947 L, 1953 D, J, 1990 M
Socialist, in power, 1924 D, 1929 D
in Egypt, dissolution of all, 1953 A
legalised, 1976 L
Liberal Constitution, in power, 1937 M
Nationalist, 1882 A, B, 1907 M, 1909 C, 1910 B, 1919 C, 1921 E
demands constitutional reform, 1935 L
Wafd, boycotts elections, 1945 A
in power, 1936 E, 1950 A
leadership of, 1927 H
in Eire, Fianna Fail, founded, 1926 C, 1938 F, 1981 F, 1987 B
gains majority, 1933 A
Fine Gael–Labour coalition, 1973 B, C, 1981 F, 1982 M
Irish Republican Army (IRA), 1933 G
National Guard (Blue Shirts), 1933 G
forms United Ireland Party, 1933 J
Nationalist, 1923 H
Republican, 1922 C
tactics of, denounced, 1927 G
agrees to take seets in Dail, 1927 H
in power, 1932 B
Sinn Fein, adopts declaration of independence, 1919 A
elects de Valera president of Dail executive, 1919 D
de Valera resigns from leadership, 1926 C
United Ireland, founded, 1933 J
See also under Ireland
in El Salvador
Arena, 1989 C
Christian Democrat, 1989 C
Nationalist Republican Alliance, 1988 C
in Europe, Communist, meeting of French, Italian and Spanish leaders, 1977 C
in Finland, Fascist, 1930 K, 1932 B

in France, Communist League, 1836 O, 1848 E
Communist Party, 1925 O, 1946 F
electoral successes, 1946 L, 1956 A
stages demonstrations, 1952 E
Communist and Socialist alliance, 1972 F, 1977 J
Dantonist, 1794 G
Democratic Republications, 1800 M
Fascist, suppressed, 1936 F
plot by, 1937 L
Gaullist, 1968 F
Girondist, 1791 K, 1792 C, 1794 M
fall of, 1792 L, 1793 F
Hébertistes, 1794 C
Jacobins, in power, 1792 L
Liberal, electoral success, 1830 G
Monarchist, 1877 E
'Mountain, The' (Moderates), 1794 G
Mouvement Républican Populaire (MRP), success in elections to Constituent Assembly, 1946 F
National Union of Left, electoral success, 1928 D
Popular Front, 1935 L
dominates elections, 1936 E
forms ministry, 1936 F
ends, 1938 K
Progressive, 1896 D
Radical, 1895 L
in power, 1948 J
Radical Socialist, 1938 A
Rassemblement du peuple Français (RPF), 1947 D
success in local elections, 1947 K
success in elections, 1948 L
Rassemblement pour la République (RPR), 1976 M
Republican, 1832 F, 1876 C, 1879 A
Republican *bloc*, 1900 D
electoral success, 1889 D
Socialist, 1916 V, 1972 F, 1977 J, 1981 E, F, 1992 A, C
votes to adhere to Moscow International, 1920 M
leave Chautemps's Cabinet, 1938 A
in power, 1946 M, 1956 B
adverse vote of, on social security policy, 1952 A
Socialist and Republican Union, 1935 L
Third Party, 1863 L, 1869 G
Ultra Conservative, in power, 1821 M
defeated, 1827 L
Ultra Royalist, 1817 J
Union de la Gauche Socialiste, formed, 1957 M
Union et Fraternité Française (Poujadist), electoral successes, 1956 A
Union for a New Republic (UNR), electoral successes, 1958 L
Youthful Patriot, 1925 O
in Germany, Catholic (Centre), 1870 M, 1874 A, 1921 E
revolts, 1906 M
Christian Democrats, 1940 J, 1957 J
loses overall majority, 1961 J
Communist, 1916 A, 1930 J
('Spartacist'), 1919 A
electoral successes, 1924 E
loses seats to Socialists, 1924 M
Conservative, 1876 O, 1878 G
Democrats (South German), 1832 E
Free Democrat, 1949 J
Independent Labour Party, 1917 D
Labour Front, 1934 K
Liberal (Prussia), 1856 O
Liberal (North German), split in, 1866 L
Liberal, split by protection, 1879 G
attempts to control army appropriations, 1886 M
National Liberal (North German), 1866 L
National Socialist (Nazi), formed, 1919 A
electoral successes, 1924 E, 1932 D
through denouncing Versailles Treaty, 1930 J
excluded from Von Papen's ministry, 1932 F
Storm Troopers of, 1932 F, 1933 C
refuses to enter coalition with Socialists, 1932 G
in power, 1933 A
engineers Reichstag Fire, 1933 B
becomes sole party, 1933 G, L
is purged, 1934 F
dominates elections, 1936 C
leading Nazis sentenced by Nuremberg Tribunal, 1946 J
neo-Nazi groups banned, 1960 O
time limit for trials of members, extended, 1965 C
Revisionist Social Democrats, 1899 N
Social Democrat, adopts Marxist Programme, 1890 K
holds rally, 1908 J
demands peace negotiations, 1915 F
Socialist, 1867 H
is driven underground, 1878 K
electoral losses, 1906 M
becomes strongest party, 1912 E
attacks Kaiser, 1912 E
in power, 1919 A
wins elections, 1924 M, 1930 J
loses power, 1930 C
will not enter coalition with Nazis, 1932 G
Socialist Workingmen's, 1874 E
lose seats to Socialists, 1924 M
in East Germany, Communist, merges with Social Democrats, 1946 D
National Front (Communist), 1950 K
New Forum, 1989 J
Social Democrat, merges with Communists, 1946 D
Socialist Unity, 1971 E
in West Germany
Bavarian Christian Social Union, 1979 G
Christian Democrat, 1983 C
Christian Democrat–Free Democrat coalition, 1982 J
Green, 1983 C
Social Democrat, 1976 K, 1980 K
in Ghana (or Gold Coast), Convention People's, 1954 F, 1956 G
Nkrumah takes over, 1961 E
becomes one party state, 1964 B
in Greece, Communist, dissolved by government, 1947 M
Communist, 1989 F
E.A.M. (Republican), 1944 M
dissolved by government, 1947 M
Greek Rally, 1952 L
Military League, 1910 A
National Radical Union, 1961 K
New Democracy, 1989 F, 1990 D
Panhellenic Socialist Movement, 1981 K
Pasok, 1989 F
in Guyana
People's National Congress, 1992 K
People's Progressive, 1992 K
in Holland, Calvinist, 1889 M
Catholic, 1889 M
Catholic People's Party, 1946 E
in power, 1959 C
Christian Democrat, 1989 J
Clerical, in power, 1901 G
Labour, 1989 J
is supported by Protestant Parties, 1960 M
Liberal Democrat, 1989 E
Liberal, fall of, 1889 M, 1896 F
Patriot, 1786 N
in Hungary, Communist, electoral successes, 1947 H
is purged, 1949 F
Deak, 1875 C
Democratic Forum, 1990 D
Liberal, in power, 1847 C
Nationalist, anti-Semite, 1932 K
National Socialist (Fascist), 1937 K
Smallholders, 1945 L, 1946 B
in power, 1947 E
Socialist, 1989 K
Socialist Workers', votes for its own dissolution, 1989 K
in India, National (or All-India) Congress, 1886 N, 1969 L, 1971 C, 1977 C, 1978 A, 1980 A, 1984 M, 1989 L
boycotts Prince of Wales's visit, 1921 G
President of, arrested, 1921 M
recognises Round Table Conference, 1931 C
declared illegal, 1932 A
electoral success, 1937 B
demands independence, 1937 D
refuses to serve on War Council, 1940 H
rejects terms for self-government, 1942 D, 1945 J
electoral success, 1945 J, 1952 C
Independence of India League, 1928 H
Janata, 1977 C, 1979 G
Moslem League, 1906 N
electoral success, 1945 J
boycotts constituent assembly, 1946 M
Socialist, protests at food and housing policies, 1951 F
in Indonesia, National Front, 1960 A
in Iran
ban on lifted, 1978 H
Islamic Republican, 1981 F
Tudeh, 1983 E
in Ireland, Nationalist, under O'Connell, make compact with Whigs, 1835 C
in House of Commons, 1880 D, 1881 A, 1886 G, 1887 L, 1892 G, 1895 G, 1900 K
McCarthy succeeds Parnell as leader, 1890 M
Sinn Fein, 1905 L
United Irishmen, 1790 K
Ulster Unionists, 1912 A, 1913 J
agree to exclude Ulster from Government of Ireland Act, 1916 F
leadership of, 1921 B
See also under Eire
in Israel
Islamic Democratic Alliance, 1990K
Likud, 1977 E, 1992 F
Labour, 1992 F
Moledet, 1992 B
Tehiya, 1992 B
in Italy, Christian Democrats, 1948 D, 1976 B, 1979 A
electoral success, 1953 F, 1958 E
dissensions among, 1959 A
form coalition with Independents, 1947 E

Communist, 1978 C, 1979 A, 1979 F
Fascist, founded, 1919 B
electoral success, 1921 E
forms government, 1922 K
founds *Balilla* Youth organisation, 1926 D
grand Council of, becomes embedded in Constitution, 1928 L
Green, 1992 D
La Rete, 1992 D
Liberal, withdraw support from Government, 1950 A
supports Segni's ministry, 1959B
Lombard League, 1992 D
Monarchist, supports Segni's ministry, 1959 B
Radical, 1896 C
Socialist, uses strike action, 1901 N
is discredited by strikes, 1904 K
in Jamaica, Labour, in power, 1962 D
People's National, 1989 B
in Japan, parties are founded, 1881 N
Democratic–Liberal, 1948 K, 1960 G, 1976 M, 1979 K, 1989 G, 1990 B
National Union, 1937 F
in Kenya, Kenya–African Union, members are arrested, 1952 K
party is proscribed, 1953 F
forms government, 1961 D
Democatic Party, 1992 A
becomes a single–party state, 1964 L
in Latvia, Conservative, in power, 1928 A
Popular Front, 1989 K
in Liberia, True Whig, 1959 E
in Lithuania, National Union (Fascist), 1932 M
in Malawi, Nyasaland African Congress, 1953 H, 1959 B
in Malta, Labour, ministry resigns, 1958 D
Nationalist, 1987 E, 1992 B
in Mexico, Institutional Revolutionary, 1988 G
in Nepal, Congress, 1991 E
in Morocco, Nationalist, 1934 L
in New Zealand, Conservative, defeated, 1890 D
Labour, in power, 1890 D, 1935 L, 1946 L, 1984 G
Liberal, 1890 D
defeated, 1919 M
National, in power, 1960 L, 1975 L, 1978 L, 1981 L, 1990 K
Reform, 1925 E
forms coalition with United Party, 1931 J
Social Credit, electoral success, 1954 L
United (Liberal), in power, 1928 L
in Nicaragua, Sandanista Front, 1984 L
in Northern Ireland
power-sharing Executive, 1973 L
Sinn Fein, 1982 K, L, 1988 K, 1990 O
Social Democratic and Labour (SDLP), 1982 L
Official Unionist, 1983 L
Ulster Unionist, 1975 E, 1981 C, 1985 M
in Norway, Labour, in power, 1927 K, 1933 K, 1935 C, 1955 A, 1957 K, 1990 K
electoral success, 1953 K
Liberal, in power, 1933 A
in Pakistan
Awami League, 1979 M
Islamic Democratic Alliance, 1990 K
Pakistan People's, 1988 L, 1990 K
in Palestine, Higher Arab Committee, delcared illegal, 1937 K
in Poland, Communist, 1948 J, 1970 M, 1980 J, 1981 D, 1982 G
National Unity Camp, 1937 C, 1945 F
Peasants', in power, 1926 E
Solidarity, 1989 F, G, H
United Workers' is purged of Titoists, 1949 L
Workers'; and Peasants' Camp, 1937 C
in Portugal, National Union (neo Fascist), 1930 G
becomes the sole party, 1934 M, 1945 L, 1953 L
Opposition parties are formed, 1945 K
Republican, 1882 O
Social Democratic, 1991 K
in Rhodesia, African Nationalist Congress, is suppressed, 1959 D
People's Caretaker Council, is banned, 1964 H
Rhodesian Front, electoral success, 1962 M, 1965 E
Rhodesia New Africa, formed, 1961 L
United Federal Party, 1953 M, 1958 B
electoral success, 1959 D, 1962 D
electoral defeat, 1962 M
United Nationalist Independent, 1964 A
United Rhodesia, formed, 1958 D
Zimbabwe African People's Union declared unlawful, 1962 J, 1964 H
See also under Zimbabwe
in Rumania, Iron Guard (Fascist), 1933 M, 1938 L, 1939 J
National Peasants', 1926 K, 1928 E
in power, 1928 M
is dissolved, 1947 G
National Salvation Front, 1989 M, 1990 E
Socialist Party of Labour, 1990 L
in Russia, Cadets, 1906 E, G
Communist (formerly Bolshevist), 1903 L
seizes power, 1917 G
Trotsky expelled from, 1927 M
purges of, 1933 N, 1937 A
O.G.P.U. purge of, 1934 M
holds Congress, 1952 K
condemns Mao Tse-tung's dogmatism, 1960 M
Menshevist, 1903 L
Nihilist, 1880 E
Populist, 1876 N
Social Democratic, splits, 1903 L
Social Revolutionary, 1901 N
in Serbia, Nationalist, 1904 M
Nationalist Radical, 1883 L
Socialist, 1990 M, 1992 M
in South Africa, National Congress is banned, 1960 D
African National Congress (ANC). *See* African National Congress
Conservative, 1987 E
Dominion, withdraws from coalition, 1945 K
Inkatha, 1992 F
Labour, withdraws from coalition, 1945 K
National, 1915 K, 1977 L, 1979 D, 1987 E, 1989 B, J, 1990 K
in power, 1924 F
is reformed under Malan, 1934 F
secure clear majority, 1953 D
sweeping electoral victory, 1958 D
Nationalist–Afrikaner *bloc*, in power, 1948 E
Pan African Congress, demonstrates against pass laws, 1960 D
is banned, 1960 D
Progressive, 1959 L
South Africa Party, 1910 D, 1915 K
Unionist, 1910 E, J
United S. African, Nationalist, 1934 F, 1938 E
in power, 1945 K
in Spain, Liberal, in power, 1909 K
Communist, legalised, 1977 D
Monarchist, in power, 1914 C
Popular Front, electoral success, 1936 B
proposed lifting of ban on parties, 1976 A
Socialist, 1934 D, 1982 K
Socialist Workers', 1989 K
in Sri Lanka, Tamil, 1977 G
in Sudan, Umma, in power, 1958 B
in Sweden, Conservative, 1928 K, 1976 J
Liberal, in power, 1926 F, 1930 F, 1978 K
non-socialists retain power, 1979 J
Social Democrat, in power, 1945 G, 1976 J, 1982 J, 1990 B, 1991 J
in Switzerland, Liberal, 1847 K
in Syria, Arab Liberation, in power, 1953 K
Nationalist, 1928 F
Syrian Popular, 1961 M
in Taiwan, opposition parties legalised, 1987 G
in Trinidad, People's National Movement, in power, 1961 M
in Tunisia, Neo-Destour, 1959 L
in Turkey, Communist, propaganda by, suppressed, 1929 F
Liberal, 1877 B
Mohammedan Union, revolt against, 1902 D
Nationalist, 1909 B, 1919 H
breaks with Sultan's government, 1920 H
People's, has monopoly, 1927 J
True Path, 1991 K
Young Turk, 1896 N, 1908 G
dominates first Ottoman Parliament, 1908 M
Opposition parties are founded, 1930 E
in US, parties are formed, 1792 N
Communist, is outside scope of deportation laws, 1920 E
leaders of, are convicted of conspiracy, 1949 K
McCarthy's charges of infiltration by, denied, 1950 G
Control of Communists bill, 1950 J
supreme court rules must register as a foreign–dominated body, 1961 F
Constitutional Union, 1860 L
Democrat, landslides, 1932 L, 1964 L
in power, 1948 L
electoral successes, 1958 L
in control of Senate and House of Representatives, 1962 L
retains large majority in Congress, 1976 L
small losses in Congress, 1978 L
Cabinet reshuffle, 1979 G
convention, New York, 1980 H
rules committee vote, 1980 H
Mondale and Ferraro selected as presidential and vice-presidential candidates, 1984 G
Federal, 1792 N
fall of, 1800 L
Labour, repudiates Communis, 1923
Liberal Democrat, 1872 E
Mugwumps (Reformist Republican), 1884 L
National Progressive Republican League, 1911 A
National Prohibition, 1869 J

National Republican, is absorbed by Whigs, 1833 N
Northern Democrat, 1860 L
Populist, 1892 B, G, L, 1986 L
Progressive, 1924 L
Progressive Republican, 1912 F, H
Republican, is established, 1854 G
electoral successes, 1914 L, 1946 L, 1950 L
electoral landslide, 1952 L
Party finance chairman accused of political espionage, 1972 J
convention, Kansas City, 1976 H
convention, Detroit, 1980 G
presidential election victory, 1980 L
Southern Democrat, 1860 L
Tammany Hall (Democrat Organisation in New York), 1888 L
Whig, 1833 N
Working Men's, 1827 N
See also under Conventions
in Venezuela, Democratic Action, 1947 M
in Yugoslavia, Communist, is purged of Cominform supporters, 1948 G
Croat, is dissolved, 1929 A
is reformed, 1932 L
National Front, 1945 L
in Zimbabwe
African National Council, 1971 M
Patriotic Front, 1977 H
Rhodesian Front, 1977 H
ZANU, 1969 B, 1980 C, 1987 M
ZAPU, 1987 M
See also under Administrations; Elections; Parliaments
Political Survey of Great Britain, A (J. Campbell), 1774 O
Politicians and the Press (Lord Beaverbrook), 1925 O
Politics of Influence (G. Wooton), 1963 O
Politiques et Moralistes françaises du XIX siècle (E. Faguet), 1892 O
Polk, James Knox, Am. Democrat (1795–1849), 11th president of US (1845–9), 1844 L, 1845 C; sends troops to Mexico, 1846 D
Pollard, Albert Frederick, B. historian (1869–1948), 1918 O, 1921 Q
Pollard, Graham, B. bibliographer (1903–1976), 1948 Q
Pollock, Sir Frederick, B. jurist (1845–1937), 1845 Z, 1894 Q, 1937 Z
Pollock, F., Am. sociologist, 1956 O
Pollock, Jackson, Am. artist (1912–56), 1948 S, 1952 S
Pollock, Sharon, Canad. playwright (b. 1936), 1981 W
Pollution. *See* Environment
Polonium, discovered, 1898 P
Polyethylene, 1935 P
Polygamy:
in Africa, condoned, 1863 R
in Morocco, restricted, 1958 O
in US, authorised among Mormons, 1843 R
Polypropylene, world production tops 1 million tons per annum, 1969 P
Polythene, invented, 1939 P
Pombal, Sebastiano Jose de Carvalho E. Mello, Marquess, Port. statesman (1699–1782), 1774 N, 1777 B
Pomerania, Swedish, Sweden recovers, 1810 A; France re-occupies, 1812 A
Pomerania, Western (or Hither), France annexes, 1807 J; Prussia obtains, 1814 A, 1815 F
Pomp and Circumstance, March, No. 4 (Elgar), 1907 T
Pompadour, Jeanne Antoinette Poisson Le Normant D'Etioles, Marquis de, F. mistress of Louis XV (1721–65), 1765 S
Pompidou, Georges, Jean Raymond, F. politician (1911–74), 1911 Z, 1962 d, k, 1968 G, 1969 F, 1971 E, 1974 D, 1974 Z
Poncelet, Jean Victor, F. mathematician (1788–1867), 1822 P
Pondicherry, India, French settlement, 1778 N
Pondoland, S. Africa, Britain annexes, 1894 J
Pons, Stanley, Am. physicist (b. 1943), 1989 P
Pontecorvo affair, 1952 O
Ponti, Gio, It. architect (1891–1979), 1958 S, 1966 S
Pontiac, Indian chief of Ottawa tribe (1720–69), 1763 E
Ponting, Clive, B. Ministry of Defence official and author (b. 1946), 1985 B
Pontoise, France, artists at, 1872 S
Poona, Central India, 1802 K, M, 1817 L; comes under British control, 1818 F; plague in, 1897 N
Poor Bitos (J. Anouilh), 1956 W
Poor Folk (F. Dostoievsky), 1846 U
Poor Lisa (N. Karamzin), 1793 U
Poor Relief:
in Britain, Speenhamland system, 1795 O
out-door relief prohibited by Poor Law Amendment Act, 1834 O
in Ireland, 1838 G
in Italy, by religious bodies, 1841 R
in US, bill to combat poverty, 1964 C
Pope, Albert Augustus, Am. engineer (1843–1909), 1878 P
Pop, Iggy, (born James Newell Osterberg), Am. punk rock singer (b. 1947), 1977 W
Popieluszko, Father Jerzy, Pol. priest (1947–84), murder, 1984 K
Popov, Leonid I., R. cosmonaut, 1980 P
Popper, Sir Karl Raimund, B. philosopher (b. 1902), 1902 Z, 1945 R, 1972 R, 1983 R, 1990 R
'Pop Stars', 1943 W, 1963 W
Popular Front. *See under* Political Parties
Popular Government (H. Maine), 1885 O
Popular Movement for the Liberation of Angola (MPLA), 1975 L
Popular Music:
rock festivals, 1957 W, 1970 W, 1974 H
Motown, 1966 W
Woodstock Music and Arts Fair, 1969, W
glam rock, 1971 W
Concert for Bangladesh, 1972 W
reggae, 1972 W
disco music, 1978 W
Ska revival by British bands, 1980 W
Simon and Garfunkel's reunion concert, 1982 W
Live-Aid concerts, 1985 W
Mandela birthday concert, 1988 W
world wide tour of rock concerts in aid of Amnesty International, 1988 W
Acid-house rave parties, 1989 W
Mandela release concert, 1990 W
grunge, 1991 W
AIDS awareness benefit concert, 1992 W
Population History of England, The, 1541–1871: A Reconstruction (E.A. Wrigley and R.S. Schofield), 1981 Q
Population Statistics, of Countries:
Austria, 1821 Y, 1851 Y, 1891 Y, 1901 Y
Bangladesh, 1971 Y, 1981 Y, 1991 Y
Brazil, 1941 Y, 1946 Y, 1961 Y, 1971 Y, 1981 Y, 1991 Y
Britain, 1801 Y, 1811 Y, 1821 Y, 1831 Y, 1841 Y, 1851 Y, 1861 Y, 1871 Y, 1881 Y, 1891 Y, 1901 Y, 1911 Y, 1921 Y, 1926 Y, 1931 Y, 1936 Y, 1941 Y, 1946 Y, 1951 Y, 1961 Y, 1971 Y, 1981 Y, 1991 Y
China, 1911 Y, 1931 Y, 1936 Y, 1941 Y, 1946 Y, 1951 Y, 1961 Y, 1971 Y, 1981 Y, 1991 Y
Egypt, 1946 Y
France, 1801 Y, 1811 Y, 1821 Y, 1831 Y, 1841 Y, 1851 Y, 1861 Y, 1871 Y, 1881 Y, 1891 Y, 1901 Y, 1906 Y, 1911 Y, 1921 Y, 1926 Y, 1931 Y, 1936 Y, 1941 Y, 1946 Y, 1951 Y, 1961 Y, 1971 Y, 1981 Y, 1991 Y
Germany, 1801 Y, 1811 Y, 1821 Y, 1831 Y, 1841 Y, 1851 Y, 1861 Y, 1871 Y, 1881 Y, 1891 Y, 1901 Y, 1906 Y, 1911 Y, 1921 Y, 1926 Y, 1931 Y, 1936 Y, 1941 Y, 1946 Y, 1951 Y, 1961 Y
India, 1901 Y, 1911 Y, 1931 Y, 1946 Y, 1951 Y, 1961 Y, 1971 Y, 1981 Y, 1991 Y
Indonesia, 1981 Y, 1991 Y
Iran, 1991 Y
Ireland, 1801 Y, 1821 Y, 1831 Y, 1841 Y, 1851 Y, 1861 Y, 1871 Y, 1881 Y, 1891 Y, 1901 Y, 1906 Y, 1911 Y, 1921 Y, 1926 Y, 1931 Y
Italy, 1801 Y, 1821 Y, 1851 Y, 1861 Y, 1871 Y, 1881 Y, 1891 Y, 1901 Y, 1911 Y, 1921 Y, 1926 Y, 1946 Y, 1951 Y, 1961 Y, 1971 Y, 1981 Y, 1991 Y
Japan, 1871 Y, 1891 Y, 1901 Y, 1911 Y, 1921 Y, 1926 Y, 1931 Y, 1936 Y, 1941 Y, 1946 Y, 1951 Y, 1971 Y, 1981 Y, 1991 Y
Korea, 1946 Y
Mexico, 1946 Y, 1971 Y, 1981 Y, 1991 Y
Nigeria, 1971 Y, 1981 Y, 1991 Y
Pakistan, 1961 Y, 1971 Y, 1981 Y, 1991 Y
Philippines, 1991 Y
Poland, 1946 Y
Russia, 1861 Y, 1901 Y, 1906 Y, 1911 Y, 1921 Y, 1926 Y, 1931 Y, 1936 Y, 1941 Y, 1946 Y, 1951 Y, 1961 Y
South Africa, 1951 Y
Spain, 1946 Y
Turkey, 1991 Y
US, 1801 Y, 1831 Y, 1851 Y, 1861 Y, 1871 Y, 1881 Y, 1891 Y, 1901 Y, 1906 Y, 1911 Y, 1921 Y, 1926 Y, 1931 Y, 1936 Y, 1941 Y, 1946 Y, 1951 Y, 1961 Y, 1971 Y, 1981 Y, 1991 Y
USSR, 1971 Y, 1981 Y, 1991 Y
Vietnam, 1991 Y
West Germany, 1971 Y, 1981 Y,
Population Study of Birds (D. Lack), 1966 P
Population, Economy, and Society in Pre-Industrial England (J.D. Chambers), 1972 Q
Population, Resources and Experimental Issues in Human Ecology (P.R. and A.H. Ehrlich), 1970 P
Population:
observations on, 1769 O
treatises on, 1798 P, 1936 O
first census, 1801 Y
world, report on, 1955 O
movements in Britain, 1964 C
European, working in agriculture, 1970 Y
of cities, statistics, 1970 Y, 1980 Y, 1990 Y
British, census provisional results, 1971 O
statistics, 1971 Y, 1976 A, 1981 Y, 1987 O, 1991 Y
UN Conference, Mexico, 1984 O
Populations of Chief Cities. *See Index under entries for places concerned*
Populists. *See Under* Political Parties
Porridge, television series, 1974 W
Porson, Richard B., Greek scholar (1759–1808), 1788 R, 1793 Q, 1802 Q

Port Arthur, China: Japanese victory at, 1894 L; agreements over, 1895 D, E; Russians occupy, 1897 M; Russians lease, 1898 C; railway to, 1901 P; Japanese siege, 1904 B; Russian fleet defeated off, 1904 H; surrenders to Japanese, 1905 A; ceded to Japan, 1905 J
Port Darwin, Falkland Islands, 1982 E
Port Egmont, Falkland Isles, 1766 N
Port Elizabeth, S. Africa, riots, 1976 H
Port Hamilton, Korea, British occupy, 1885 D
Port Said, Egypt, British troops land, 1956 L
Port San Carlos, Falkland Islands, 1982 E
Port Stanley, Falkland Islands
RAF bombs airport, 1982 E
Argentine forces surrender, 1982 F
Port Talbot steel works, Wales, strike action, 1969 F
Portal, Sir Gerald Herbert, B. diplomat (1858–94), 1893 C
Porte Etroite, La (Gide), 1909 U
Porter, Cole, Am. composer of popular songs, 1893 Z, 1964 Z
Porter, Roy, B. historian (b. 1946), 1982 Q
Portes Gil, Emilio, Mex. leader, 1928 G
Portland, Duke of. *See* Bentinck, W. H. C.
Portman, John Calvin, Am. architect (b. 1924), 1973 S
Portnoy's Complaint (P. Roth), 1969 U
Porto Novo, Coromandel Coast, Madras, India, 1781 G
Portrait in Miniature (Lytton Strachey), 1931 U
Portrait in a Mirror (C. Morgan), 1929 U
Portrait of Mallarmé (P. Boulez), 1960 T
Portrait of a Lady (H. James), 1881 U
Portrait of the Artist as a Young Dog (D. Thomas), 1940 U
Portrait of the Artist as a Young Man (J. Joyce), 1916 U
Portsmouth, Hampshire, England, Treaty of, between Russia and Japan, 1905 J
Portugal: attacks Monte Video, 1775 C; re-organises S. American colonies, 1776 N; joins League of Armed Neutrality, 1782 G; suppression of monasteries in, 1834 R; separation of Church and State, 1911 D
contested elections, 1969 K
opposition dissolved, 1969 K
military coup, 1974 D
censorship ends, 1974 E
political prisoners released, 1974 E
left-wing government, 1974 G
Socialists win free elections, 1975 D
new constitution, 1976 D
new constitution enforced and military influence in government ended, 1982 K
coalition government, 1983 F
Gulbenkian Foundation for Modern Art, 1983 S
European Community membership, 1985 C, F, 1986 A
agrees to return Macao to China in 1999, 1987 A
Lisbon fire, 1988 H
elections, 1991 K
Posen, Poland: Prussia acquires, 1793 E; Treaty of, Saxony with France, 1806 M; Archbishop of, 1837 R; expropriation of Polish landowners, 1886 D; Polish occupation, 1918 M
Positivism, 1830 R, 1855 R, 1865 R
'Positrons' (positive electrons), 1933 P
Possession (A.S. Byatt), 1990 U
Post Office
telephone division, 1979 J
Post-Impressionism, 1913 S
Post-modern Condition, The (J.-F. Lyotard), 1979 R
Postal Services:
in Britain, penny post, 1840 O
airmail to Australia, 1934 P
parcel post, 1880 O
second class mail, 1968 O
in Germany, letter post, 1800 O
in US, parcel post, 1912 O
postal savings banks, 1910 O
Posters, notable, 1891 S
Potassium: electrical preparation of, 1806 P; deposits, exploited, 1860 P
Potemkin, Grigory Aleksandrovich, R. statesman (1739–91), favourite of Catherine II, 1776 N, 1788 M
Potemkin, Russian battleship, mutiny aboard, 1905 K
Potomak Charter, 1954 F
Potsdam signatories, USSR accuses W. Germany of neo-Nazism and militarism, 1967 A
Potsdam, Germany, Conference of Allied leaders at, 1945 G
remains of Frederick the Great of Prussia re-interred, 1991 H
Potter, Dennis Christopher George, B. playwright (b. 1935), 1986 W
Potter, Sally, B. film director, 1992 W
Potter, Thomas Bayley, B. politician (1817–98), 1866 O
Potthast, August, G. historian (1824–98), 1862 Q
Potting Shed, The (G. Greene), 1958 W
Pottle, Frederick Albert, Am. scholar (1897–1987), 1950 Q
Pouce, Le (César), 1976 S
Poujade, M., F. politician, founder of Union et Fraternité Française, 1956 A
Poulenc, François, F. musician (1899–1963), 1899 Z, 1920 T, 1923 T, 1957 T, 1959 T
Poulson scandal, 1974 B
report on, 1977 G
Poulson, Frederick, Am. electrician, 1902 P
Poulson, John, B. architect, 1972 G, 1974 B
Pound, Ezra Loomis, Am. poet (1885–1972), 1885 Z, 1915 U, 1950 W, 1972 Z
Pound, Roscoe, Am. lawyer (1870–1965), 1870 Z, 1965 Z
Pousseur, Henri, Belg. musician (b. 1929), 1959 T, 1985 T
Poverty and Progress (B. S. Rowntree), 1941 O
Poverty and Public Health (M'Gonighe and Kirby), 1936 O
Poverty of Philosophy, The (P. J. Proudhon), 1847 O
Poverty: a Study of Town Life (B. S. Rowntree), 1901 O
Powder, bleaching, 1870 P
Powdered milk, 1855 P
Powell, Anthony Dymoke, B. author (b. 1905), 1905 Z, 1950 U, 1975 U
Powell, Felix, B. musician, 1915 W
Powell, (John) Enoch, B. Conservative/Unionist politician (b. 1912), 1968 K, 1974 B; resigns from Cabinet, 1958 A; becomes Minister of Health, 1961 B; refuses to serve under Home, 1963 K
'river of blood' speech, 1968 D
dismissal from Shadow Cabinet, 1968 D
calls for repatriation of coloured immigrants, 1969 F
fails to be re-elected to seat in Northern Ireland, 1986 A
Powell, Michael Anthony, 'Mike', Am. athlete (b. 1963), 1991 X
Power
Nuclear. *See* Nuclear Energy
energy crisis. *See* Energy Crisis
tidal power station, F., 1968 P
Power and the Glory, The (G. Greene), 1940 U
Power and the State (Lord Radcliffe), 1951 O
Power of Darkness, The (L. Tolstoy), 1885 U
Power, electric, produced from atomic energy, 1951 P
plants. *See under* electricity
Powers, Francis, Am. pilot, 1960 E
Powicke, Sir Frederick Maurice, B. medieval historian (1879–1963), 1947 Q
Powys, John Cowper, B. author (1872–1963), 1930 U
Powys, Theodore Francis, B. author (1875–1953), 1928 U
Poznan, Poland, riots in, 1956 F
Practical View of the Religious System (W. Wilberforce), 1797 R
Practice of History, The (G.R. Elton), 1967 Q
Pragmatism (W. Jones), 1907 R
Prague Spring, 1968 E-K
Prague, Czechoslovakia: Congress, 1813 G; Czech revolt in, 1848 F; music school in, 1848 T; Peace of, 1866 H; University, 1882 O; Pan Slav Conference in, 1908 G; Russians take, 1945 E; purge of collaborators in, 1945 E; Conference of Soviet Satellites in, 1950 K
anti-Soviet demonstrations, 1969 C
protestors mark anniversary of Soviet invasion, 1969 H
dissidents tried, 1972 G
demonstrations marking twentieth anniversary of Palach's suicide, 1989 A
demonstrations demanding end to Communist rule, 1989 L
thanksgiving mass after Havel's inauguration as President, 1989 R
protocol signed marking formal end of Warsaw Pact, 1991 G
Prairie (A. Caro), 1967 S
Prairie Home Companion, The (G. Keillor), 1974 W
Prasad, Rajendra, Indian president (1884–1963), 1952 E
Pratt, Charles, Earl of Camden, B. judge (1714–94), 1763 E
Pratt, David, S. African, wounds Verwoerd, 1960 D
Pratt, Orsen, Am. Mormon leader (1811–81), 1833 R
Pravda (H. Brenton and D. Hare), 1985 W
Praxiteles, *The Hermes* of, found at Olympia, 1875 S
Prayer Books:
Church of England, revised, 1928 R; *Alternative Service Book 1980*, 1980 R
Church of Scotland, revised, 1912 R
vernacular liturgies approved by Vatican Council, 1963 R
Prayer for Owen Meany, A (J. Irving), 1989 U
Pré, Jacqueline Mary du, B. musician (1945–87), 1945 Z, 1961 T, 1987 Z
Prévert, Jacques, F. poet and screenwriter (1900–77), 1900 Z, 1946 U, 1977 Z
Pre-Raphaelite Brotherhood, 1848 S
Pre-Raphaelitism (W. Holman Hunt), 1905 S
Precious Bane (M. Webb), 1924 U
Precipice, The (I. Goncharov), 1870 U
Precipitation, electrical, 1884 P
Preface to Morals (W. Lippmann), 1929 R
Prehistoric Settlement of Britain, The (R. Bradley), 1978 Q
Preliminary Sketch of Bi-quarternions (W. K. Clifford), 1873 P
Prelude, The (W. Wordsworth), 1805 U

Premadasa, Ranasinghe, Sri Lankan President, 1989 A
Preminger, Otto, Am. film director (1906-1986), 1957 W, 1959 W, 1960 W, 1963 W
Premium Savings Bonds, 1956 D, 1957 F
Prempeh, King of Ashanti, 1896 A
Prentice, Reginald Ernest, Lord Prentice, B. Labour/Conservative politician (b. 1923), 1974 O, 1975 G, 1976 M
defects to Conservatives, 1977 K
Presbyterians. *See under* Religious Denominations
Prescott, William Hickling, Am. historian (1796–1859), 1796 Z, 1837 Q, 1846 Q, 1855 Q, 1859 Z
Present Condition of Civilisation in Greece (A. Cores), 1803 O
Present State of Music in Germany, the Netherlands and the United Provinces (C. Burney), 1773 T
Presentations of débutantes at Court, ends in Britain, 1958 G
Preservation of Rural England, Council for, 1926 O
Preserving, process of, 1765 P
Presley, Elvis Aaron, Am. singer (1935–77), death, 1977 H
Press, The, Censorship of:
advocated by Pope Gregory XVI, 1837 R
in Austria, abolished, 1781 K
clerical control in force 1855, H
in Belgium, abolished, 1831 B
in Britain, seditious publications suppressed, 1817 C
Daily Worker suspended, 1941 V
relaxations through Obscene Publications Act, 1959 O
newspapers banned from publishing extracts from *Spycatcher*, 1986 G
in Ceylon, imposed, 1960 H
in Czechoslovakia, press freedom promised, 1968 D
in Denmark, abolished, 1770 M, 1784 E
in Egypt, imposed, 1909 C, 1928 G
in France, relaxed, 1796 C, 1819 E, 1830 H, 1868 E, 1881 O
re-imposed, 1800 V, 1820 C, 1822 C, 1824 J, 1827 D, F, 1828 D, 1830 G, 1835 J, 1850 J, 1852 B
in Germany, imposed, 1819 J, 1851 E, 1933 B, 1943 V
Gentz's plan for freedom, 1797 O
in Greece, press freedom restored, 1969 K
in Ireland, abolished, 1919 H
in Philippines, political censorship, 1983 J
in Poland, student demonstrations against, 1968 A
in Portugal, imposed, 1945 K
in Spain, 1966 D
in Transvaal, restrictions imposed, 1896 L
in Turkey, abolished, 1876 M
Press, The:
in Britain, cheap, 1816 V, 1846 V
press campaigns, to reform sweated industries, 1906 O
on neglect of science, 1916 P
Royal Commission on, 1961 B
Press Council, 1963 F
journalists imprisoned for refusing to reveal sources of information, 1963 V
national strike, 1970 V
freedom of, 1975 L
Reuters, stock market flotation, 1984 V
lobby system, 1986 O
Press Complaints Commission replaces Press Council, 1990 V
in France, cheap, 1836 V
in US, cheap, 1835 V
See also under Journals; Newspapers
Pressburg, Germany, Peace between Austria and France, 1805 M
Presses, Private:
Ashendene, 1894 S
Kelmscott, 1896 S
Pressure-cooking, for canned foods, 1874 P
Pretender, Young. *See* Charles Edward Louis Philip Casimir
Pretenders, The (H. Ibsen), 1864 W
Pretenders, The (F. Sionil Jose), 1984 U
Pretoria, Transvaal, S. Africa: becomes capital of Transvaal, 1860 D; Treaty, between Britain and Boers, 1881 D; Convention, over Swaziland annexation, 1893 L; is fortified, 1896 A; Buller takes, 1900 F; Britain annexes Transvaal at, 1900 K; Rivonia trial in, 1964 F; Anglo–Rhodesian settlement talks, 1970 L
Pretorius, Marthinius, President of Transvaal (1819–1901), 1856 M
Prevention of Cruelty to Children, Society for, 1864 O
Prevost, Constant, F. geologist (1787–1856), 1824 P
Price, Richard, B. Nonconformist minister and author (1723–91), 1769 O, 1771 O, 1776 O
Price, The (A. Miller), 1968 W
Prices, Wages and Incomes:
in Britain, minimum wage, 1912 B, C
comprehensive wages agreement, 1937 O
electrical workers wage increase, 1961 L
National Incomes Commission, 1962 O
printers' wage claim referred to, 1965 E
resale price maintenance on electrical equipment, etc., abolition recommended, 1963 M
resale prices act, in force, 1964 G
Prices and Incomes Board, National, 1965 C
wages and price freeze, 1966 G, K
Royal Commission on Trade Unions and Employers' Associations recommendations, 1968 O
statutory incomes policy rejected by TUC, 1968 J
voluntary wage restraint, 1968 J
statutory incomes policy ends, 1970 A
Prices and Incomes Board abolished, 1970 L
tripartite talks on wages and price restraints, 1972 J
price, pay, rent and dividend increases freeze, 1972 L
Pay Board and Prices Commission, 1973 A
anti-inflation programme, pay rise limits, 1973 D, L
statistics, 1974 M
government pay policy, 1976 E, 1977 G, 1978 G
pay talks between unions and government break down, 1978 K
government pay policy breached, 1978 L, M
Prices Commission and price controls abolished, 1979 E
Clegg Commission on pay for public sector workers, 1979 H
Labour Party proposals, 1980 G
NUM vote on wage increase, 1982 A
in France, prices are fixed, 1793 J
minimum wage raised, 1968 E
freeze follows devaluation, 1982 F
in Germany, courts for adjusting wages, 1890 B
in Poland
price rises suspended, 1976 F
massive increases in food prices announced, 1982 A
in US, minimum wage, 1938 O
trade deficit, 1971 H
minimum wage rise, 1977 L
Pricksongs and Descants (R. Coover), 1969 U
Pride and Prejudice (J. Austen), 1813 U
Priestley, John Boynton, B. author (1894–1984), 1894 Z, 1984 Z ; *The Good Companions*, 1929 W; plays, 1932 W, 1934 W, 1937 W, 1947 W
Priestley, Joseph, B. Nonconformist minister and chemist (1733–1804), 1767 P, 1768 O, 1772 P, 1777 R, 1782 R, 1804 Z; discovers oxygen, 1774 P; rioters attack, 1791 G
Prim, Juan, Marquis de los Castillejas, Sp. general and statesman (1814–70), 1868 J
Primal Scream, B. pop group, 1991 W
Prime Suspect, television programme, 1991 W
Primrose League, founded, 1882 O
Primrose, Archibald Philip, Lord Rosebery, B. Liberal statesman and historian (1847–1929), 1847 Z, 1889 O, 1905 L, 1929 Z; as foreign secretary, 1886 B, 1892 H; becomes premier, 1894 C; seeks *entente* with Germany, 1894 F; resigns, 1895 F; resigns Liberal leadership, 1896 K
Prince (born Prince Rogers Nelson), Am. pop singer and actor (b. 1958), 1982 W, 1984 W
Prince Edward Island, joins Dominion of Canada, 1873 G
Prince William Sound, Alaska
Exxon Valdez accident, 1989 C
Princess Casamassima, The (H. James), 1886 U
Princeton, New Jersey, US, battle, 1777 A
Principe Générateur des Constitutions Politiques (de Maistre), 1809 O
Principe des moeurs chez toutes les nations ou catechisme universel (St. Lambert), 1798 R
Principes fondamenteux de l'equilibre et du movement (L. Carnot), 1803 P
Principia Ethica (G. E. Moore), 1903 R
Principia Mathematica (Russell and Whitehead), 1910 R
Principia Scriptoriae (R. Nelson), 1986 W
Principles of Economics (A. Marshall), 1890 O
Principles of Ethics (H. Spencer), 1879 R
Principles of Geology (C. Lyell), 1830 P
Principles of Logic, The (F. H. Bradley), 1883 R
Principles of Moral and Political Philosophy (W. Paley), 1785 R
Principles of Political Economy and Taxation (D. Ricardo), 1817 O
Principles of Political Economy (J. S. Mill), 1848 O
Principles of Political Economy (T. R. Malthus), 1820 O
Principles of Psychology (W. James), 1890 R
Principles of Psychology (H. Spencer), 1855 R
Principles of Social Service (H. Carey), 1858 D
Pringsheim, Nathaniel, G. botanist (1823–1904), 1856 P
Printing industry, in Britain, lock-out in, 1956 B
Printing of calicoes, machine for, 1783 P
Printing:
printing press, improved, 1813 P
hydraulic, 1795 P
Staples' iron, 1800 P
steam, 1814 V
linotype, 1886 V
monotype type-setting machine, 1897 P
type-casting machine, 1838 P
See also Presses, Private

Prior, James Michael Leathes, Lord Prior, B. Conservative politician (b. 1927), 1972 L, 1981 J
Prison Reform, advocated, 1777 O, 1813 O
  in Britain, 1823 G, 1958 O, 1963 H
  in Turkey, 1856 B
Prisoner of Zenda, The (A. Hope), 1894 U
Prisoner, The, television series, 1967 W
Prisons, Maze, Northern Ireland
  hunger-strike ends, 1981 K
  Republican prisoners escape, 1983 J
Prisons: panopticon designed, 1791 O
  escapes, notable, 1964 H
  statistics of criminals in, 1960 Y
  Parkhurst, England, 1974 F
  Portlaoise, Eire, 1974 H
  Spandau, E. Germany, 1966 J
  Strangeways, England, riot, 1990 D
  See also Convicts; Transportation
Pritchett, Sir Victor Sawdon, B. literary critic (b. 1900), 1982 U
Private Lives (N. Coward), 1930 W
Private Papers of Henry Rycroft (G. R. Gissing), 1903 U
Privateering, abolished, 1856 D
Privates on Parade (P. Nichols), 1977 W
Privatisation. *See* Nationalization
Privy Council. *See under* Judicature, in Britain
Probabilities, studies in the theory of, 1854 R
Probate of wills, civil, in Britain, 1857 O
Problem of Foreign Policy (G. Murray), 1921 O
Problem of Knowledge, The (A. J. Ayer), 1957 R
Problem of the Commonwealth, The (L. Curtis), 1916 O
Problem, The (A. Schweitzer), 1954 T
Problems in Astrophysics (A. M. Clerke), 1903 P
Production of Heat by Voltaic Electricity (J. P. Joule), 1843 P
Production:
  census of, in Britain, 1907 O
  values of world, comparative percentages, 1888 Y, 1929 Y
  war, in Britain, 1939 Y, 1940 Y, 1941 Y, 1942 Y, 1943 Y, 1944 Y
Professional Foul (T. Stoppard), 1977 W
Professor, The (or *Elsie Venner*; O. W. Holmes), 1861 U
Profumo, John Dennis, B. Conservative politician (b. 1915), Secretary of State for war, misleads Commons, 1963 C; resigns, 1963 F
Progress and Poverty (H. George), 1879 O
Progress of Metaphysical, Ethical and Political Philosophy (D. Stewart), 1815 R
Progressives. *See under* Political Parties
Prohibition:
  in Canada, 1917 M
  in India, proposal for, 1977 H
  in New Zealand, referendum against, 1919 D
  in Norway, 1919 K
  in US, in Illinois, 1851 O
    in Maine, 1851 O, 1911 I
    National Prohibition Party formed, 1869 J
    Anti-Saloon League founded, 1893 N
    Volstead Act, 1919 A
      passes over president's veto, 1919 K
      in force, 1920 A, O
    liquor running, 1922 O
    'Prohibition Navy', 1922 O
    repealed in New York state, 1923 G
    repealed, 1933 M
Projet de Code Civil (J. Cambacérès), 1796 O
Prokofiev, Serge, R. musician (1891–1953), 1917 T, 1921 T, 1936 T, 1945 T, 1946 T, 1952 T, 1954 T
Prolegomena to Ethics (T. H. Green), 1899 R
Prolegomena to Homer (F. Wolf), 1795 Q
Prolegomena to any Possible Metaphysic (I. Kant), 1783 R
Prometeo-Tragedia dell'ascolto (L. Nono), 1985 T
Promethée mal enchainé, Le (A. Gide), 1899 U
Prometheus (A. Scriabin), 1913 T
Prometheus Unbound (P. B. Shelley), 1820 U
Proofs and Refutations (I. Lakatos), 1976 R
Propaganda as a Political Weapon (Stern-Rubarth), 1921 O
Property and Politics 1870–1914 (A. Offer), 1981 Q
Prophet Armed, The (I. Deutscher), 1954 Q
Prophet Outcast, The (I. Deutscher), 1963 Q
Proportional Representation: adopted in Netherlands, 1899 M; adopted in Sweden, 1907 E
Prospects of Industrial Civilization (B. Russell), 1921 O
Prostitution in Britain, 1904 O; Wolfenden Report on, 1957 J; Street Offences Act, 1959 O
Protactinium, radio-active element, 1918 P
Protecting Veil, The (J. Tavener), 1989 T
Protection of Ancient Buildings, Society for, 1877 S
Protection. *See under* Tariff Questions
Protée (P. Claudel), 1927 W
Proteins, chemistry of, 1907 P
Protestant Ethic and the Birth of Capitalism, The (M. Weber), 1901 Q
Protestants, *See under* Religious Denominations
Protocols:
  London, on French intervention in Greece, 1828 G
    recognises Greek independence, 1828 L, 1929 C
    on Belgium, 1831 A
  St. Petersburg, between Britain and Russia, over Greece, 1826 D
  non-intervention in Spanish Civil War, 1936 M
Protoplasm, term first used, 1840 P; Mohl's discovery, 1846 P
Proudhon, Pierre Joseph, F. political philosopher (1809–65), 1809 Z, 1840 P, 1846 O, 1847 O, 1865 Z
Proust, Louis Joseph, F. chemist (1754–1826), 1815 P
Proust, Marcel, F. novelist (1871–1922), 1871 Z, 1913 U, 1922 Z, 1927 U
Provençal culture, revived by Mistral, 1854 U
Providence, Rhode island, US, Brown University, 1764 O
Prufrock and other Observations (T. S. Eliot), 1917 U
Prunskiene, Kazimiera, Lithuanian leader (b. 1943), 1991 A
Prussia's Right to Saxony (B. Niebuhr), 1814 O
Prussia, East, Germany: Russians evacuate, 1914 H, 1915 B; plebiscite in, 1920 G
Prussia, West, Germany: Polish landowners expropriated, 1886 D; plebiscite in, 1920 G
Prussia: education in, 1763 O; acquires rights in Ansbach and Bayreuth, 1769 K, 1779 E; gains through first partition of Poland, 1772 H; joins League of Armed Neutrality, 1781 E; gymnasia reformed, 1810 O; historiographer of, 1841 Q
  See also Germany
Prussianism and Socialism (O. Spengler), 1920 U
Pruth, River, Russia, 1853 G
Przemysl, Russia: Russians take, 1915 C; Germans recapture, 1915 F
Psephology, 1947 O, 1948 L, 1962 O
Psychical Research, Society for, 1882 P
Psychical research, studies in, 1914 R
Psycho-analysis, science of, founded, 1895 R
  Freud's lectures on, 1909 R
Psychological Types (C. Jung), 1920 R
Psychology and Religion (C. Jung), 1944 R
Psychology and the Church (Hardtmann), 1925 R
Psychology of Art (A. Malraux), 1950 R
Psychology of Everyday Life (S. Freud), 1901 R
Psychology of Fascism, The (P. Nathan), 1943 O
Psychology of Imagination, The (J. P. Sartre), 1951 R
Psychology of Sex, 1886 P, 1897 R
Psychology, Comparative, 1859 R
Psychology, Industrial, Institute of, 1921 O
Psychology, studies in, 1824 R, 1846 R, 1855 R, 1890 R, 1900 R, 1913 R
Psychopathia Sexualis (Krafft-Ebing), 1886 P
Ptashne, Mark Stephen, Am. scientist (b. 1940), 1968 P
Pu Yi (1906–67), Emperor of China (to 1912), installed as Emperor of Manchukuo, 1932 C, 1934 C
Public Economy of Athens, The (P. Böckh), 1817 Q
Public Enemy, Am. pop group, 1989 W
Public Health, legislation for, 1891 O
Public Holidays, in Britain, 1974 O, 1978 E
Public Lectures, free, 1839 Q
Public Meetings, Right of holding:
  in Britain, curtailed, 1795 L, 1819 M
  in France, 1868 F
  in Germany, restricted, 1878 K
  in Transvaal, restricted, 1896 L
Public Opinion Polls, confounded by Truman's presidential election, 1948 L
Puccini, Giacomo, It. musician (1858–1924), 1858 Z, 1893 T, 1896 T, 1900 T, 1904 T, 1910 T, 1918 T, 1924 T, Z
Puddling process, Cort's, 1784 P
Pueblo, US, intelligence ship, seized bu North Korea, 1968 A
Puerto Rico: US invades, 1898 G; Spain cedes to US, 1898 M; Foraker Act for, 1900 E; decision on US citizenship, 1901 M; nationalist Rising in, 1950 K
Pugachoff, Emel'yon Ivanovich, R. pretender (?1741–75), 1773 K, 1774 J
Pugilism. *See* Boxing
Puissance motrice de Feu (N. Carnot), 1824 P
Pulitzer Prizes, 1917 U
Pullman dining-car, first, 1879 P
Pulsar, discovery, 1967 P
Pump, lung, 1961 P
Pump, steam, 1841 P
Punjab, India, 1985 G, 1987 E
  attacks on Sikhs, 1982 K
  direct rule imposed, 1983 K, 1987 E
  constitution amended to acknowledge Sikhism as religion distinct from Hinduism, 1984 C
  declared dangerously disturbed area, 1984 D
  detention without trial imposed, 1984 D
  governor and police chief dismissed, 1984 F
  agreement aimed at reducing tension, 1985 G
  Sikh agreement aimed at reducing tension in, 1985 G
  Sikhs declare independent state of Khalistan, 1986 D
  militants expelled from Amritsar Golden Temple, 1986 D
  Sikhs arrested while protesting on second anniversary of army attack on Golden Temple, 1986 F
  violence by Sikh extremists, 1988 D
  Indian border with Pakistan sealed, 1988 D
  militants surrender after occupying Amritsar

Golden Temple, 1988 E
Sikh militants boycott elections, 1992 B
Purcell Society, founded, 1876 T
Purcell, Henry, B. musician (1658–1695), anniversary concert, 1959 T
Purges:
in China, 1955 C
in Czechoslovakia, 1951 C
in Germany, 1934 F
in Hungary, 1949 F
in Russia, 1933 N, 1934 M, 1937 A, F of Scientific Committees, 1948 F
'Purism', in art, 1918 S, 1928 S
Purity and Danger (M. Douglas), 1966 R
Purkinje, Johannes Evangelista, G. biologist (1781–1869), 1840 P
Pursuit of Truth (W. Quine), 1989 R
Pusey, Edward Bouverie, B. churchman (1800–82), 1836 R, 1865 R
Pushkin, Alexander, R. author (1799–1837), 1799 Z, 1820 U, 1822 U, 1825 U, 1828 U, 1832 U, 1837 Z
Putnam, Hilary, Am. philosopher (b. 1926), 1987 R
Putumayo, Peru, atrocities in rubber industry in, Casement's Report on, 1912 G
Puvis de Chavannes, Pierre, F. artist (1824–98), 1878 S, 1889 S, 1890 S
Pygmalion, Preface to (G. B. Shaw), 1916 U
Pym, Francis Leslie, Lord Pym, B. Conservative politician (b. 1922), 1973 M, 1981 A, 1982 D
Pynchon, Thomas, Am. author (b. 1937), 1966 U, 1973 U, 1990 U
Pyramids, The, Egypt, battle of, 1798 G

Q

'Q'. *See* Quiller-Couch
Quakers. *See under* Religious Denominations
Quantum theory, 1900 P
report on, 1914 P
studies in, 1926 P, 1942 P
uncertainty principle, 1927 P
Quasimodo, Salvatore (1901–1968), It. poet, 1930 U
Quay, J. E. de, Du. Catholic People's Party leader, 1959 C, 1960 M
Quebec, Canada: assigned to Britain, 1763 K; attack on, 1775 M; enters Dominion of Canada, 1867 C; Fenianism in, 1870 E;
Conference of Allied leaders at, 1943 H; Churchill meets Roosevelt in, 1944 J; Nationalist riots in, 1964 E; Queen Elizabeth's visit, 1964 K
Queen Elizabeth, S. S., launched, 1938 P
Queen Elizabeth II, launched, 1967 J
Queen Mab (P. B. Shelley), 1813 U
Queen Mary, S. S., launched, 1934 P
Queen Victoria (G. Lytton Sprachey), 1921 Q
Queen and the Rebels, The (U. Betti), 1955 W
Queensbury, Marquess of. *See* Douglas, John Sholto
Queensland, Australia: is separated from N. S. Wales, 1859 A; requests to annex New Guinea, 1883 N; boycotts Hobart Convention, 1897 A; artificial rain in, 1957 P
Queenston Heights, US, battle, 1812 K
Queitulle, Henri, F. Radical, 1950 G; forms ministry, 1948 J; resigns, 1949 K; forms ministry, 1951 C
Quemoy: Chinese bombard, 1958 H; US concern over, 1962 F
Qu'est-ce-que la Propriété? (P. J. Proudhon), 1840 O
Qu'est-ce-que le Tiers Etat? (Sieyès), 1789 O
Quest for Certainty, The (Dewey), 1929 R
Question of Upbringing, A (A. Powell), 1950 U
Quetelet, Lambert Adolphe Jacques, F. philosopher (1796–1874), 1835 P
Qui je fus (H. Michaux), 1927 U
Quiberon Bay, France, Emigres defeated at, 1794 G
Quiberon, France, British aid to insurgents in, 1795 F
Quiet American, The (G. Greene), 1955 U
Quiller-Couch, Sir Arthur, B. novelist and critic under pseudonym of 'Q' (1863–1944), 1863 Z, 1888 U, 1916 U, 1944 U
Quincey, Thomas de, B. author (1785–1859), 1785 Z, 1821 U, 1959 Z
Quinine, is synthesised, 1944 O
Quintana, Marcel, Sp. poet (1772–1857), 1772 Z
Quisling, Vidkun, Norw. puppet premier, 1942 B
sentenced for collaboration, 1945 J
Quiz programmes, 1935 W
Quo Vadis? (H. Sienkiewicz), 1895 U
Quoinez, François, F. author under pseudonym of 'Françoise Sagan' (b. 1935), 1935 Z, 1950 U, 1958 T
Quorn Hunt, Leicestershire, England, banned from National Trust land, B., 1991 L

R

Raab, Julius, Aus. People's Party leader (1892–1964), 1964 Z; forms coalitions, 1953 D, 1956 F, 1959 E; retires, 1961 D
Raabe, Wilhelm, G. author (1831–1910), 1864 C
Rabbit (J. Koons), 1986 S
Rabbit Run (J. Updike), 1960 U
Rabbit is Rich (J. Updike), 1982 U
Rabbit quartet (J. Updike), 1991 U
Rabbits, in Britain, killed by myxomatosis, 1953 P
Rabe, David, Am. dramatist (b. 1940), 1972 W
Rabin, Yitzhak, Prime Minister of Israel (b. 1922), 1974 F, 1976 M, 1977 D
Rabuka, Colonel Sitiveni Ligamamada, Fijian soldier and politician (b. 1948), 1987 E, J
Racconigi agreement, Russia with Italy, on Balkans, 1909 K
Race Relations (E. Huxley and M. Perham), 1944 O
Rachel, Elisa, F. actress (1820–58), 1838 W
Rachid Ali, of Iraq, flees, 1941 E
Rachmaninoff, Sergei, R. musician (1873–1943), 1873 Z, 1901 T, 1935 S, 1943 Z; music is banned in Russia, 1931 T
'Rachmanism', exploitation of tenants of rented dwellings, campaign against, 1963 O
Racial Problems:
UN condemns discrimination, 1959 L
in Britain, disturbances, 1958 H
Powell's 'river of blood' speech, 1968 D
Race Relations Act, 1968 D, O
Commission for Racial Equality established, 1976 O
Notting Hill Carnival violence, 1976 H
St Paul's riots, Bristol, 1980 D
in Rhodesia, racial discrimination in public places to be scrapped, 1978 H
in South Africa
bill for segretation rejected, 1925 G
discrimination over franchise, 1930 E
alleged discrimination against Indians, 1949 E
riots in Johannesburg, 1950 A
Malan's aparthied legislation invalidated by courts, 1952 C
in force, 1952 D
Sharpeville shooting, 1960 C
protests and riots, 1976 F, H
deaths in clashes with police, 1980 F
See also under Apartheid; Treason trials
in US, riots in Chicago, 1919 G
segregation on 'buses ruled unconstitutional, 1946 O
Negro lynching, 1955 O
Harlem riots, 1964 G
Los Angeles riots, 1965 H
desegregation of schools, 1956 O, 1967 C
crisis in Arkansas, 1957 O
Little Rock High School required to admit Negroes, 1958 J
crisis in Birmingham 1963 J
discrimination against Negroes, in Mormon priesthood, 1962 R
lunch-counter sit-in, 1960 B
'kneel-in' campaign in churches, 1960 R
freedom rides, 1961 O
Negro voting rights safeguarded in Civil Rights Bill, 1960 D
Kennedy's speech on Civil Rights, 1963 F
Negro peaceful demonstrations, 1963 H
Negro petition on grievances, delivered at Montgomery, 1965 C
race riots, 1966 G, J, 1967 F, G
black students killed in Orangeburg after attempt to desegregate bowling alley, 1968 B
Martin Luther King assassinated, 1968 D
Supreme Court ruling over discrimination, 1978 O
deaths in clashes with police, 1980 F
Los Angeles riots, 1992 D
white policemen in Los Angeles acquitted of beating black motorist, 1992 D
See also under Civil Rights Campaign
Racine et Shakespeare (Stendhal), 1823 U
Racine, Wiscon., US, 1936 S
Racing, horse. *See* horse-racing
Rackham, Arthur, B. illustrator, 1867 Z, 1939 Z
Rackham, Oliver, 1986 Q
Racquets, championship, 1895 X
Radar, equipment devised, 1935 P; developments are publicised, 1945 P; port installation, 1948 P
Radcliffe, Mrs. Anne, B. author (1764–1823), 1794 U, 1795 U
Radcliffe, Cyril John, lord Radcliffe, B. judge (1899–1977), 1951 O; proposals for Cyprus Constitution, 1961 E; reviews security procedures, 1961 E; heads tribunal on security, 1962 L, 1963 D, V
Radek, Karl, R. politician (1885–1941), 1937 A
Radetsky, Joseph, Count of Radetz, Aus. soldier (1766–1858), 1832 A, 1848 C, D, G
Radford, Rev. Robert John, Ir. Unionist MP (1941–81), murder, 1981 L
Radhakrishnan, Sarvepalli, President of India (1888–1975), 1888 Z, 1962 E, 1975 Z
Radiant heat, discoveries in, 1831 P
Radiation:
Geiger counter for measure of, 1927 P
'Positrons' discovered, 1933 P
Report on, 1914 P
researches in, 1913 P, 1927 P
Radiation, Cosmic, studies in, 1925 P, 1953 P, 1962 P
Radiation, Nuclear, disposal of radio-active waste, 1954 P, 1955 P, 1956 O

Radio, Transistor, is banned in Capri, 1963 W
is invented, 1948 P
'pirate' radio stations become illegal in Britain, 1967 W
local radio broadcasts, BBC, 1967 W
programmes. *See* individual titles
Radio Caroline, pirate radio station, 1965 W
Radio communication, global, test for, 1963 P
Radio Newsreel, 1940 W
Radio Waves:
emitted from Jupiter, 1955 P
speed of, 1947 P
speed of light through, 1950 P
sunspots emitted from, 1946 P
Radio-activity: theory of, 1904 P, 1918 P; induced, 1934 P; carbon tests, for dating archaeological finds, 1952 Q
Radio-isotopes, extended use of, 1952 P
Radio-reflector satellite, 1958 P, 1960 P
Radio-telescopes:
Jodrell Bank, 1957 P
Mullard Observatory, Cambridge, 1957 P
Radiography, Treatise on, 1910 P
Radistcheff, Alexander, R. author (1749–1802), 1790 O
Radium: discovered, 1898 P; testing of preparations of, 1914 P
Radstadt Conference, 1797 M, 1799 D
Radzinowicz, Sir Leon, Pol.-born B. historian (b. 1906), 1961 O, 1986 Q
Raeburn, Sir Henry, B. portrait painter (1756–1823), 1803 S, 1809 S
Raffles, Sir Thomas Stamford, B. colonial governor (1781–1826), 1819 B, 1826 P
Rafsanjani, Hojatoleslam Ali Akhbar Hashemi, President of Iran (b. 1934), 1989 G
Ragged School Union, 1844 O
Rahman, Mujibur, President of Bangladesh (1920–75), 1971 M, 1971 A, 1972 A
murdered, 1975 H
Raikes, Robert, B. promoter of Sunday Schools (1735–1811), 1780 R
Railways
corridor-train, 1890 P
couplings, automatic, 1906 P
diesel electric system, 1913 P
electric, 1879 P, 1895 P
Pullman dining car, 1879 P
signals, automatic, 1893 P
train ferry, 1934 P
truck, refrigerated, 1888 P
tunnel, first, 1826 P
Railways:
in Africa, first trans-African, 1931 G
in Australia, Sydney–Melbourne, 1883 P
in Austria, Budweis–Linz, 1832 P
mileage in operation, 1907 Y
in Britain, Beeching Report, 1963 O
City and S. London, 1890 P
Clapham Junction crash, 1988 M
drivers' over-time ban, 1973 M
drivers' strikes, 1974 A
Great Western, 1842 P
Heathrow Airport extension to London Underground, 1977 M
Liverpool–Manchester, 1826 P, 1829 P, 1830 J, P
London, the first train into, 1836 P
London Metropolitan, 1864 P
Underground, 1890 P, 1898 P, 1905 P, 1963 P
amalgamated with Metropolitan, 1911 L
London Midland and Scottish, *Coronation Scot*, 1937 P
mileage in operation, 1840 Y, 1850 Y, 1860 Y, 1870 Y, 1880 Y, 1890 Y, 1935 Y, 1945 Y, 1955 Y
Moorgate London Underground train crash, 1975 B
nationalisation, in force, 1948 A
season tickets, 1910 O
standard gauge on, 1942 P
Stockton and Darlington, 1825 P
Channel Tunnel. *See* Channel Tunnel
in Canada, the first, 1836 P
Canadian Grand Trunk, 1914 P, 1919 L
Canadian Pacific Railway, 1881 M, 1886 P
in China, 1888 P
Chinese Eastern, agreement on, 1929 M
Russia sells interest in, 1935 C
mileage in operation, 1955 Y
North Manchurian, 1896 F
in East Africa, 1928 N
in Ethiopia, finance for, 1902 B
in France, Paris Metro, 1898 P
mileage in operation, 1880 Y, 1890 Y, 1935 Y, 1945 Y
Train à Grande Vitesse (TGV), 1981 P
in Germany, electric, 1910 R
Leipzig station, 1915 P
mileage in operation, 1907 Y, 1935 Y, 1945 Y
in Greece, railway to Salonika, proposed, 1908 A
in India, mileage in operation, 1907 Y
in Iran, Trans-Iranian, 1939 P
in Iraq, Baghdad Railway, German interests in, 1888 K, 1898 L, 1899 M, 1903 D
discussions on, 1907 H, 1909 L, 1910 L
international agreements on, 1914 B, F
British army administers, 1919 A
in Italy, Rome Station, 1950 S
mileage in operation, 1955 Y
in Japan, nationalisation of, 1906 C
privatisation, 1987 O
in Russia, Trans-Siberian, 1891 G, 1891 P, 1901 P
Turkestan–Siberian, 1930 P
mileage in operation, 1860 Y, 1880 Y, 1890 Y, 1907 Y, 1925 Y, 1935 Y, 1945 Y
In Saudi Arabia, Hejaz Railway, 1900 N
in South Africa, Cape Railway, 1885 L, 1892 J
to Rhodesia, 1897 L
from Delagoa Bay to Transvaal, 1883 M, 1895 G
in South America, 1894 P, 1911 P
in Sweden, 1913 P
in Switzerland, Trans-Alpine, 1853 P
nationalisation of, 1910 N
in Turkey, Orient Express, 1883 P, 1961 E
in Uganda, 1901 M
in US, first steam locomotive, 1829 P
New York Subway, 1904 P, 1908 P
mileage in operation, 1840 Y, 1850 Y, 1860 Y, 1870 Y, 1880 Y, 1890 Y, 1907 Y, 1925 Y, 1935 Y, 1945 Y, 1955 Y
regulation of, by Elkins Act, 1903 N
by Interstate Commerce Act, 1887 B
mergers of, judged to violate anti-Trust laws, 1904 C, 1912 M
rates for, 1913 F
strike, military control during, 1951 B
war-time control of, 1917 M, 1920 C
in Zambia, 'TanZam', Chinese loan for, 1970 G
Rain, artificial, 1957 P
Rainbow Warrior sunk by French agents, 1985 G, H, J, L
agents released into French custody, 1986 G
Rainbow in Curved Air, A (Riley), 1970 T
Rainbow, The (D. H. Lawrence), 1915 U
Raine, Kathleen (Mrs. Madge), B. poet (b. 1908), 1956 U
Ruines, ou méditations sur les révolutions des empires, Les (C. Volney), 1791 Q
Rainier, Prince of Monaco (b. 1923), 1956 W
Rajai, Muhammad Ali, President of Iran (1933–81), 1981 G, H
Rajput States, India, under British protection, 1818 A
Rakósi, Matyas, Hungarian Communist, 1952 H
Rama I, King of Siam (1782–1809), 1782 N
Ramadier, Paul, F. Socialist (1888–1961), 1947 A, L
Ramaema, Colonel Elias Phisoana, Lesotho politician (b. 1933), 1991 D
Rambert, Dame Marie (born Cyvia Rambam, 1888–1982), 1888 Z, 1920 T, 1982 Z
Rambouillet Decrees, for sale of US ships seized by French, 1810 C
Rameau, Jean Philippe, F. musician (1683–1764), 1764 Z
Ramé, Marie Louise de la, B. novelist under pseudonym of 'Ouida' (1839–1908), 1839 Z, 1867 U, 1908 Z
Ramek, Rudolf, Aus. politician, 1926 K
Ramones, The, Am. pop group, 1976 W
Ramos, Fidel, Philippines army officer (b. 1928), 1986 B, 1992 F
Ramsay MacDonald (D. Marquand), 1977 Q
Ramsay, Allan, B. artist (1713–84), 1767 S
Ramsay, James, earl of Dalhousie, B. administrator (1812–60), as governor-general of India, 1848 A
Ramsay, Sir William, B. scientist (1852–1916), 1896 P, 1898 P, 1903 P.
Ramsden, Jesse, B. engineer (1735–1800), 1770 P, 1800 Z
Ramsey, (Arthur) Michael, Lord Ramsey of Canterbury, B. churchman (1904–88), 1904 Z, 1963 R, 1966 R, 1974 R, 1988 Z; appointed Archbishop of Canterbury, 1961 A; speaks on use of force in Rhodesia, 1965 K
Rand, S. Africa: gold mines in, Chinese labour for, 1903 L; strike in, 1922 A
Randall Commission, on US foreign economic policy, 1954 A
Rangoon, Burma: British capture, 1824 E; falls to Japanese, 1942 C; Allies enter, 1945 E; Asian Socialist Conference at, 1953 A; Buddhist Council meets at, 1956 R
Ranke, Leopold von, G. historian (1795–1886), 1795 Z, 1824 Q, 1834 Q, 1839 Q, 1841 Q, 1847 Q, 1852 Q, 1859 Q, 1886 Z
Rankin, Jeanette, Am. Irish woman member of Congress, 1916 L
Rapacki Plan, for denuclearised zone in Europe, 1957 K
rejected by Britain and US, 1958 B
Rapallo, Italy: Allied Conference at, 1917 L; Treaty, Italy with Yugoslavia, 1920 L; Italy abrogates, 1924 J; Treaty, German with Russia, 1922 D
Rappeneau, Jean-Paul, F. film director (b. 1932), 1990 W
Ras Tafari. *See* Haile Selassie
Rask, Rasmus Christian, Dan. philologist (1787–1832), 1811 Q
Rasmussen, Steen Eiler, Dan. architect (1898–1990), 1898 Z, 1990 Z
Rat, The (G. Grass), 1986 U
Ratchnevsky, Paul, 1983 Q
Rates of Exchange (M. Bradbury), 1983 U

Rates, in Britain:
church abolished, 1868 R
industrial, raised, 1957 B
Rathenau, Walter, G. industrialist and economist (1867–1922), 1867 Z; becomes minister for Reparation, 1921 E; as Chancellor, 1921 E, 1922 A; is murdered, 1922 F
Rationing:
in Britain, bread, 1917 B, 1946 G, 1948 O
clothes, 1941 O, 1949 B
food, 1918 B, 1940 A
penalties for black-marketeers, 1941 M
petrol, 1956 M
in Germany, food, 1916 O
in Russia, abolished, 1947 O
Ratisbon, Germany, Diet, reconstructs German states, 1803 B
Ratti, Achille, It. cardinal (1857–1939), elected Pope Pius XI, 1922 B
Rattigan, Sir Terence Mervyn, B. dramatist (1911–1977), 1936 W, 1942 W, 1944 W, 1946 W, 1948 W, 1960 W
Räuber, Die (Schiller), 1781 W
Rauch, Christian Daniel, G. sculptor (1727–1857), 1851 S
Ravel, Maurice, F. musician (1875–1937), 1875 Z, 1901 T, 1907 T, 1911 T, 1922 T, 1927 T, 1928 T, 1932 T, 1937 Z
Raven, Charles Earle, B. theologian (1885–1963), 1943 R, 1954 R
Ravenna, Italy, falls to Allies, 1944 M
Ravilious, Eric, B. artist (d. 1942), 1940 S
Rawalpindi, Pakistan: Sikhs surrender at, 1849 C; and Afghanistan Peace Conference, 1919 G; designated provisional capital, 1959 K
Rawlings, Flight-Lieutenant Jerry, Ghanaian military officer and politician (b. 1947)
leads military coup in Ghana, 1979 F
stages 2nd military coup in Ghana, 1981 M
Rawlinson, Sir Henry Creswiek, B. orientalist and soldier (1810–95), 1846 Q, 1858 Q, 1862 Q
Rawls, John, Am. philosopher (b. 1921), 1971 R
Rawsthorne, Alan, B. musician (1905–1971), 1949 T, 1950 T
Ray, James Earl, Am. assassin (b. 1928), 1969 C
Ray, Man (born Emanuel Rahivovich), Am. painter and photographer (1890–1976), 1890 Z, 1916 S,1976 Z
Ray, Nicholas, B. film director, (1911–1979), 1955 W
Ray, Satyajit, Ind. film director (1921–92), 1921 Z, 1955 W, 1956 W, 1959 W, 1992 Z
Rayleigh, Lord. *See* Strutt, J. W.
Rayon, manufacture of, 1892 P
Rays of Positive Electricity and Their Application to Chemical Analysis (J. J. Thomson), 1913 P
Rays, cosmic observatory for, 1953 P
Razor blades, safety, 1904 P
Razor's Edge, The (W. S. Maugham), 1944 U
Répons (P. Boulez), 1983 T
Re-armament:
in France, 1939 C
in Germany, 1935 B
See also under Conferences
Re-thinking English Local History (C. Phythian-Adams), 1987 Q
Reaction Committee, appointed by German Diet, 1851 N
Reactors, atomic, statistics of, 1862 P
Read, Sir Herbert, B. artist and critic (1863–1949), 1933 S
Reade, Charles, B. author (1814–84), 1852 U, 1856 U, 1861 U
Reading Position for a Second Degree Burn (Oppenheim), 1970 S
Reading, Berks, University, 1926 O
disturbances following Toxteth riots, 1981 G
Reading, colour, finger-tip, 1964 P
Readman, Alison, B. psephologist, 1947 O
Reagan, Ronald Wilson, Am. actor and statesman, Republican (b. 1911), 40th President of US (1981–89), 1911 Z
challenges Ford at Republican convention, 1976 H
presidential nomination and election victory, 1980 G, L
presidential inauguration, 1981 A
proposals on economy, 1981 B
assassination attempt on, 1981 C
missiles deal with USSR, 1981 L
economic sanctions against USSR, 1981 M
emergency assistance for El Salvador, 1982 B
request for defence funding refused, 1982 M
proposes summit meeting with Andropov, 1983 A
Strategic Defense Initiative (Star Wars programme), 1983 C, 1985 B, M, 1986 K, 1987 B
halts sale of F-16 fighters to Israel, 1983 C
US marines in Beirut, 1983 K, 1984 B
presidential re-nomination and re-election, 1984 H, L
Gorbachev offers summit talks with, 1985 D
arms for hostages deal, 1986 L
Iran–Contra scandal, 1986 L, M, 1987 B, C, G, H, L
Intermediate-range Nuclear Forces (INF) Treaty, 1987 M, 1988 F
Real Thing, The (T. Stoppard), 1982 W
Realism and the Aim of Science (K. Popper), 1983 R
Realization of the Possible (A. Bain), 1899 R
Realm of Spirit (G. Santayana), 1940 R
Reaping-machine, 1834 P
Rebellions and Revolutions:
nations undergoing, to be expelled from Concert of Europe, 1820 L
in Albania, suppressed, 1910 D, 1915 A
in Algeria, 1961 D, 1965 F
in American Colonies. *See* Wars, War of American Independence
of Arabs, in Turkey, 1916 F, L, 1917 A
in Argentina, against Joseph Bonaparte, 1810 E, 1930 J
by army officers, 1987 D
in Austria, 1848 C, E, K
in Austrian Empire, of Peasants in Bohemia, 1775 B
in Transylvania, 1784 G
by Czechs, 1848 F
in Bohemia, 1908 M
in Austrian Netherlands, 1789 K, 1790 M
in Belgium, 1830 H, L, M, 1831 H
in Brazil, 1930 K, 1932 G
in Brunei, 1962 M
in Brunswick, 1830 J
in Canada, under Papineau, 1837 L, M
under Mackenzie, 1837 M, 1838 A
Lord Durham's leniency towards rebels criticised, 1838 K
Red River Rebellion, 1869 K, 1870 E
in Ceylon, 1971 D
in Chile, 1810 J, 1932 F
in China, by White Lotus Society in Shantung, 1774 N
Taiping, 1850 K, 1855 K, 1911 K, L, M, 1912 B, 1913 J
Cultural Revolution, 1966 H
in Congo, 1905 B, 1965 F
in Crete, 1866 J, 1896 B, G, H, 1905 C
in Cuba, 1906 B
by Castro, 1958 D
in Dutch East Indies, 1894 N
in Eastern Assam, 1966 C
in Eastern Rumelia, 1886 D, E
in Ecuador, 1925 G
in Espiritu Santo, 1980 E
in Ethiopia, 1930 C
in Finland, by Nazis, 1932 B
in France:
Revolution of, 1789:
Third Estate declares itself to be National Assembly, 1789 F
takes Tennis Court Oath, 1789 F
sack of Bastille, 1789 G
abolition of feudal system, 1789 H
March of women to Versailles, 1789 H
Declaration of Rights of Man, adopted, 1789 H
nationalisation of church property, 1789 L
civil constitution of clergy, 1790 L, R
English views of, 1790 B, 1791 G
Paris Commune, 1792 H, 1794 G
sack of Tuileries, 1792 H
Republic proclaimed, 1792 J
Revolutionary Calendar, 1792 J
Convention offers assistance to all peoples for overthrowing governments, 1792 L
decree for revolutional institutes to be adopted in lands occupied by French armies, 1792 M
abolition of Christianity, 1793 K
execution of Louis XVI, 1793 A
Committee of Public Safety, 1793 D, G
Reign of terror, 1793 F
Marie Antoinette executed, 1793 K
Rising of royalists in La Vendée, 1793 C, K, M, 1796 C
Feast of Reason, 1793 R
mass execution, 1794 F
Terror ends, 1794 G
White Terror, 1795 E
'Day of the Sections', 1795 K
Directory established, 1795 L
Royalist re-action prevented, 1797 J
Consulate established, 1799 M
See also under Wars
July Revolution, 1830 G
influence of, 1831 B
by Republicans, 1832 F
1848 Revolution:
Lamartine's provisional government, 1848 B
Communists rise, 1848 E
'June Days', 1848 F
Republican constitution, 1848 L
Paris, rising, 1870 J
in Geneva, 1792 M
in Georgia, 1992 A
in Germany, crushed, 1833 D, 1848 C
in Berlin, 1918 L
Spartacist, 1919 A
in Haiti, 1915 G
in Hesse, 1830 J
in Hesse–Cassel, 1850 J, L
in Hungary, 1848, J, K
Revolution of, 1956:
demonstrations call for democratic government, 1956 K
Nagy forms ministry, 1956 K
Russian troops intervene, 1956 K
Hungarian government renounces Warsaw treaty and appeals to UN, 1956 L
Kádár's deflection, 1956 L
Soviet attack on Budapest, 1956 L

Nagy seeks refuge, 1956 L
mass arrests, 1956 M
UN report on, 1957 J
demonstrations call for democratic government, 1956 K
in Iraq, 1963 B
in Ireland, Whiteboys Rebellion, 1763 G
Ulster Rebellion, 1797 C
1798 A, F
Emmet's rebellion, 1803 G
Sinn Fein Easter Rebellion, 1916 D, O
amnesty for rebels, 1917 F
Sinn Fein, 1922 D, F, G
amnesty for rebels, 1923 D
in Japan, Satsuma Rebellion, 1877 J
in Java, Communist Revolt, 1926 L
in Macedonia, Young Turk revolt, 1908 G
in Madagascar, against French, 1947 C
in Matabeleland, 1893 L
in Mexico, against Spain, 1810 J
in Milan, 1848 C
in Modena, 1831 B, 1859 D
in Moldavia, against Turks, 1821 C, 1907 C
in Mosul, 1959 L
in Naples, 1820 G, 1821 B, C, 1848 E
in New Grenada, 1810 E
in Nicaragua, 1926 E
in Papal States, 1831 B, 1832 A
in Parma, 1831 B, 1848 C, 1859 D
in Persia, 1905 M
by Kurds, 1930 G
in Peru, 1809 G, 1930 H
in Philippines, against Spain, 1872 N, 1948 G
in Poland, against Russia, 1830 L, 1831 A
suppressed, 1831 E, J, 1848 E, 1863 A, B
in Portugal, 1820 H, 1910 K, 1921 K
against Carmona, 1927 B
in Rhodesia, 1965 L
in Roumania, 1989 M, R
in Russia, Cossack Rebellion, 1773 K, 1774 J
Peasants' Revolt, 1902 D
Revolution of 1905:
Bloody Sunday, 1905 A
Tsar promises to call assembly, 1905 C, 1905 H, K
General Strike, 1905 K
Potemkin mutiny, 1905 K
General Strike, 1905 K
October manifesto, 1905 K
Moscow workers revolt, 1905 M
revolutionary outbreak suppressed, 1907 L
Revolution of 1917, February:
separation of Church and State, 1917 B
beginnings, 1917 C
all-Russia congress of Soviets, 1917 F
Lenin and Bolsheviks seize power, 1917 G
all-Russia conference, 1917 H
Kornilov's counter-revolution, 1917 J
Republic proclaimed, 1917 J
Soviet Congress resolves on armistice, 1917 K
Revolution of 1917, October:
outbreak, 1917 L
armistice with Germany, 1917 M
Bolsheviks dissolve constituent assembly, 1918 A
in San Domingo, 1791 H, 1865 E, 1912 J
in Saxony, 1830 J
in Serbia, revolt of Nationalist Radicals, 1883 L
in Sicily, 1848 A, D
in South Africa, Boer revolt, 1914 K
in South Vietnam, by Buddhists, 1966 E, F
in Spain, 1820 A, L
crushed by French troops, 1823 K, 1840 K
O'Donnell's revolt, 1854 G, 1868 J
for Catalonian home rule, 1917 H, 1931 D
Sanjurjo's revolt in Seville, 1932 H
in Syria, Revolt of Druses, 1925 G, K, 1927 F
army revolt, 1954 B, 1962 C
in Transvaal, of Boers against British, 1881 A, B, D
in Transylvania, 1784 G
in Turkish Empire, by sheriff of Mecca, 1916 F
in Tuscany, 1859 D
in US, Pontiac's Rebellion, 1763 E
Whiskey Insurrection in Pennsylvania, 1794 M
Shay's Rebellion, in Massachusetts, 1786 J
Whiskey Insurrection in Pennsylvania, 1794 M
Dore Rebellion, in Rhode Island, 1841 K
in Venezuela, 1902 M
in Venice, 1848 C
in Wallachia, against Turks, 1821 C
in Zanzibar, 1964 A, B
See also Civil Wars; *Coup d'États*; Riots and Risings; Wars
Rebirth of a Nation: Wales 1880–1980 (K.O. Morgan), 1981 Q
Recent Advances in Vaccine and Serum Therapy (Fleming and Petrie), 1934 P
Recessional (R. Kipling), 1897 W
Recherche de L'Absolu, La (H. de Balzac), 1834 U
Recherches Chimiques sur la Végétation (N. de Saussure), 1797 P
Recherches Théoriques et expérimentals sur la force de torsion ... (C. A. Coulomb), 1785 P
Recherches sur les ossements fossiles de quadrupèdes (G. Cuvier), 1812 P
Reciprocity. *See* Tariff Questions
Recits des temps mérovingiens (A. Thierry), 1850 Q
Reclamation force, US, 1902 P
Reconstruction, Ministry, in Britain, 1943 L
Recording, magnetic, 1899 P
Dolby noise-reduction system, 1967 P
quadrophonic sound, 1971 P
Sony 'Walkman', personal tape recorder/player, 1980 P
compact disc player (CD), 1982 P
digital audio system, 1987 P
Records, Public, in Britain, 1838 O, 1958 O
access to, 1958 O
Records, gramophone, long-playing, 1948 P
Recueil des traités (G. Martens), 1791 Q
Red Book, The (J. Fisher), 1969 P
Red Brigade, kidnap of Aldo Moro, 1978 C, 1983 A
Red Cell (P. Halley), 1988 S
Red Cross League, 1864 O
Red Cross, British, funds for, 1915 S, T
Nigeria forbids relief supplies to be flown to Biafra, 1968 H
Red Flag, The, 1899 T
Red Guards, 1966 H, L, R
Soviet embassy in Peking besieged, 1967 A
British embassy, Peking, set on fire, 1967 H
Red Pope I, II, III (A. Serrano), 1990 S
Red River Rebellion, in Canada, 1869 K, 1870 E
Red Room, The (A. Strindberg), 1879 W
Red Roses for Me (O'Carey), 1942 W
Red Sea, Italian domination of east coast of, 1926 J
Redcliffe-Maud Report, on Local Government reform, 1969 O
Reden über die Religion (F. Schleiermarcher), 1799 R
Redford, Bruce, Am. literary scholar (b. 1953), 1992 Q
Redgauntlet (W. Scott), 1824 O
Redgrave, Vanessa, B. actress (b. 1937), 1937 Z
Redhouse and Softly, architects, 1981 S
Reed, Sir Carol, B. film director (1906–1976), 1947 W, 1948 W, 1949 W, 1951 W, 1959 W, 1963 W
Reed, Ezekiel, Am. inventor, 1786 P
Reed, Lou, Am. singer (b. 1942), 1973 W, 1989 W
Reeney, James, 1975 W
Referenda:
See also under Plebiscites
in Austria, halts opening of nuclear power station, 1978 L
in Belgium, for return of Leopold III, 1950 C
in Bosnia-Herzegovina, on independence, 1992 C
in Britain, for Parliament Bill, proposal for, rejected, 1911 D
on revised terms for British EC membership, 1975 C, 1975 A
on devolution in Scotland and Wales, 1979 C
in Bulgaria, against monarchy, 1946 J
in Canada
on Charlottetown reform agreement, 1992 K
on creation of Nunavut, 1992 L
in Chile, on military government, 1980 J
in Denmark, on Maastricht Treaty, 1992 F
in Eire
on EC membership, 1972 E
on Maastricht Treaty, 1992 F
in Estonia, approving independence, 1991 C
in France, rejects draft constitution, 1946 E
approves Constitution of Fifth Republic, 1958 J
favours president's election by universal suffrage, 1962 K
on Algiers, 1961 A, 1962 G
on constitutional reform, 1969 D
on enlargement of EC, 1972 D
on Maastricht Treaty, 1992 J
in French Somaliland, on independence, 1967 C
in Germany, on Young Plan for reparations, 1929 M
in Gibraltar, on retaining links with Britain, 1967 J
in Greece, on restoration of monarchy, 1974 M
in Iran, Khomeini declares Islamic Republic, 1979 D
in Italy, favours republic, 1946 F
in Jamaica, to secede from West Indies Federation, 1961 J
in Latvia, approving independence, 1991 C
in Lithuania, approving independence, 1991 B
in Luxembourg, on monarchy, 1919 K
in Malta, favours union with Britain, 1956 B
in New Zealand against Prohibition, 1919 D
in Northern Ireland, on remaining within UK, 1973 C
in Norway, on EC membership, 1972 J
in Philippines, grants presidential powers, 1981 D
in Poland, for single-house assembly, 1946 F
for wide nationalisation, 1946 F
in Quebec, on possible separation from Canada, 1980 E
in S. Africa, for a Republic, 1960 K
approves new constitution, 1983 L
in S. Rhodesia, for new constitution, 1961 G

favours independence, 1964 L
in S. Vietnam, for a republic, 1955 K
in Spain
on constitution, 1966 L
on transition to democracy, 1976 M
on devolution of power to Basque provinces, 1979 K
in Switzerland, against female suffrage, 1959 B
against import or manufacture of atomic weapons, 1962 D
on female suffrage, 1971 O
in US, on California property taxes, 1978 F
in USSR, on proposed renewed federation, 1991 C
Reflecting microscope, 1947 P
Reflections and Memoirs (Otto von Bismarck), 1898 O
Reflections on Language (N. Chomsky), 1976 R
Reflections on Violence (G. Sorel), 1908 O
Reflections on the Revolution in France (E. Burke), 1790 O
Reflections on the Revolution of our Time (H. Laski), 1943 O
Reflex-action, of nerve-centres, discovered, 1832 P
Reflexes, conditioned, 1907 P
Réflexions sur la formation et le distribution des richesses (A. Turgot), 1765 O
Reform Parties. *See under* Political Parties
Reform and Renewal: Thomas Cromwell and the Common Weal (G.R. Elton), 1973 Q
Reform:
in Britain, of Church, essay on, 1832 R
of Parliament. *See* Parliamentary Reform
in Russia, shelved, 1880 E
Reformation and the English People, The (J.J. Scarisbrick), 1985 Q
Reformation to Industrial Revolution (C. Hill), 1967 Q
Reformatories, proposed for juvenile offenders, 1851 O
founded, 1876 O
Reformatory Schools for ... Juvenile Offenders (M. Carpenter), 1851 O
Réforme Sociale, La (Le Play), 1864 O
Refrigeration: early development, 1850 P; cold store, 1861 P; railway truck, 1888 P; Chilling process for meat, 1934 P
Refrigerators, domestic, statistics, 1937 Y, 1965 Y
Refugees
Refugees: Bermuda Conference on, 1943 D; UNRRA established, 1943 O; World Refugee Year, 1959 O
Vietnamese boat people, 1979 J, 1989 M
Palestinian, 1985 E, 1987 D
Tamil, 1986 H
E. German accepted by Poland, 1989 K
in Liberia, massacre of, 1990 G
Albanian, 1991 A, C
Iraqi Kurds, 1991 C, D
Regan, Donald Bromas, Am. White House Chief of Staff (b. 1918), 1987 B
Regencies, in Britain:
bills for, 1765 G, 1811 B, 1812 B
in force, 1788 M, 1789 B, 1811 B
Prince Regent. *See under* George IV
Regensberg, Bavaria, W. Germany, the Walhalla near, 1830 S
Reger, Max, G. musician (1873–1916), 1915 T
Reggae music, 1972 W
Regional economic planning councils, British, 1965 B
Registration, national, British, 1939 J
Registrations of births, deaths and marriages, in Britain, 1836 H
Reich, Steve, Am. musician (b. 1936), 1973 T
Reichenbach, Germany: Conference and treaty, 1790 F; Treaty, Austria with Russia and Prussia, 1813 F
Reichstag Fire, 1933 B
Reichstein, Tadeus, Swi. chemist (b. 1897), 1934 P
Reid, Thomas, B. philosopher (1710–96), 1764 R, 1788 R
Reigen (A. Schnitzler), 1903 W
Reign of Grace (A. Booth), 1768 Q
Reimann, Aribert, G. musician (b. 1936), 1978 T, 1986 T
Reinecke Fuchs (Goethe), 1794 U
Reis, Philipp, G. scientist, 1861 P
Reiske, Johann Jacob, G. Arabic scholar (1716–74), 1789 Q
Reisz, Karel, B. film director (b. 1926), 1960 W, 1981 W
Reith, John Charles Walstam, Lord Reith, B. broadcaster and administrator (1889–1971), 1889 Z, 1922 W, 1971 Z
Reith Lectures, 1949 O, 1950 W, 1951 O, 1952 O, 1953 P, 1956 P, 1963 R, 1978 R
Reitz, Edgar, G. film director (b. 1932), 1984 W
Reivers, The (W. Faulkner), 1962 U
Réjane, Gabrielle (Charlotte Réju), F. actress (1857–1923), 1875 W
Relativity:
Einstein's first theory of, 1905 P
general theory of, 1915 P
mathematics of, 1908 P
studies in, 1918 P, 1919 P
Relief for Europe, 1919 A
Religion and the Decline of Magic (K. Thomas), 1971 Q
Religion and the Rise of Capitalism (R. H. Tawney), 1926 R
Religion in America (Sperry), 1945 R
Religion within the Boundaries of Reason (I. Kant), 1793 R
Religious Denominations:
Eglise Libre, French, 1848 R
African sects, statistics of, 1962 Y
Anglican Communion, first colonial bishop appointed, 1814 R
Pan Anglican synod, first, 1867 R
ordination of women, 1971 R, 1992 R
See also Church of England
Baptist World Alliance, 1905 R
Baptists, British, form Baptist Union, 1812 R
US, statistics, 1840 Y, 1905 Y, 1936 Y, 1947 Y, 1967 Y, 1986 Y
statistics, 1905 Y, 1930 Y, 1950 Y
union of, 1891 R
Black Muslims, US, 1965 B
Buddhists, Indian, 1963 Y
in S. Vietnam, arrested, 1963 H
Chile, state religion in, 1833 E
Christadelphians, 1844 R
Christian Scientists, 1879 R, 1936 Y, 1947 Y
Church of England, advowsons, sale of prohibited, 1898 R
advised by Anglican–Roman Catholic Ccommission, 1977 R
Alternative Service Book 1980, 1980 R
Anglican orders, validity of, 1891 R
Anglo–Catholic party in, 1846 R, 1860 R
appointments, Howick Committee on, 1964 R
bishops, powers of, increased, 1898 R
Suffragan, revival of, 1869 R
Carey, George, Archbishop of Canterbury, 1990 G, 1991 D, R
Christian Socialist party in, 1849 R
Church and the Bomb report, 1982 R
Church Assembly, 1919 R
communion rules, changes in, 1971 R
Congress, 1863 R
Convocation, revived, 1852 R, 1860 R
appoints Committee to prepare Revised Version of Bible, 1870 R
Crockford's Clerical Directory preface critical of church leaders, 1987 R
Doctrine Commission report, 1976 R
ecclesiastical discipline, commission on, 1903 R
English Church Union,1860 R
Evangelical Party in, 1783 R, 1846 R
Faith in the City report, 1985 M
General Synod, 1970 R
homosexuality debated by General Synod, 1987 R
Lambeth Conference, 1968 R, 1988 R
Methodists, relations with, 1958 R, 1960 R, 1963 R
ordination of women to diaconate, 1985 R
ordination of women, 1978 R, 1979 R, 1981 R, 1992 R
Oxford Movement in, 1833 R, 1846 R, 1860 R, 1891 R
Paul Report, on deployment of clergy, 1964 R
Prayer Book of 1928, rejected by Parliament, 1928 R
ritualistic practices in, 1857 R, 1874 R
proceedings against, 1890 R
Roman Catholic Church, relations with, 1894 R
statistics, 1905 Y, 1930 Y, 1945 Y, 1950 Y
We Believe in God report, 1987 R
See also Anglican Communion
Church of Ireland, revenues of, 1835 D
is disestablished, 1869 R
Church of Jesus Christ of Latter-Day Saints (Mormons), founded, 1825 R
in England, 1962 R
in US, 1830 D, R, 1833 R, 1843 R
leave for Salt Lake City, 1846 F, 1847 R
Negroes refused admission to priesthood in, 1962 R
statistics, 1967 Y, 1986 Y
Church of Scotland, Free, 1843 R
Church of Scotland, Presbyterian, General Assembly deposes Campbell, 1831 R
appeal of woman for ordination in, 1963 R
first woman minister, 1969 R
Prayer Book revised, 1912 R
re-grouping of, 1847 R, 1929 R, 1930 T
statistics, 1905 Y, 1945 Y, 1950 Y
unconfirmed children allowed to receive communion, 1992 R
Church of Wales, disestablishment, proposed, 1891 K
legislation for, opposed, 1912 D, 1913 B,
bill suspended for duration of war, 1914 J
Church of the Brethren, US, 1958 R
Congregationalists, in Britain, 1905 Y, 1930 Y, 1945 Y, 1950 Y
formation of United Reformed Church, 1972 R
in US, 1950 Y, 1936 Y, 1945 Y, 1947 Y, 1958 R
Coptic, in Africa, 1962 Y
in Egypt, 1910 B
Dutch Reformed Church, racism declared a sin, 1968 R
Episcopal Church in US, 1801 R, 1853 R
ordination of women, 1976 R, 1977 A
first woman bishop, 1988 R
statistics, 1905 Y, 1936 Y, 1945 Y, 1947 Y, 1967 Y, 1986 Y
Episcopal Church of Scotland, ministers

ordained in, permitted to hold English benefices, 1864 R
re-grouping, 1930 T
statistics, 1905 Y, 1930 Y, 1945 Y, 1950 Y
Evangelicals, in Germany, revived, 1809 R, 1850 R
Union, formed by Lutheran and Reformed, 1817 R
angered by papal encyclical, 1910 E, F
in Palatinate, 1958 R
statistics, 1945 Y
in US, Evangelical Association (or 'New Methodists'), 1807 R
Evangelical Alliance, 1866 R, 1958 R
defines Fundamentalism, 1895 R
Billy Graham's revivals, 1954 R
statistics, 1905 Y, 1936 Y, 1945 Y, 1947 Y
Exclusive Brethren, British, expulsions from, 1962 R
French National Church, 1848 R, 1872 R
separation of Church and State, 1905 R
Greek Orthodox Church
military junta takes control, 1967 E
Hindus, Indian, 1924 G, 1945 Y, 1947 H, 1963 Y, 1966 L
Hindu–Moslem violence, 1969 J, 1992 M
militants attack mosque built on Hindu holy site at Ayodhya, 1990 K
Illuminati, Bavarian, 1776 R
Islam, 1945 Y
Al-Aqsa Mosque, Jerusalem, damaged by fire, 1969 J, R
British Blasphemy Law not extened to cover, 1989 O
fatwa issued against Rushdie, 1989 B, 1989 O
Hanafi gunmen sieze buildings in Washington, US, 1977 C
Hindu–Muslim violence in India, 1969 J, 1992 M
in Syria, Moslem Brotherhood, 1982 B
Iran breaks off diplomatic relations with Britain over Rushdie affair, 1989 C, 1990 J
Islamic fundamentalism, 1981 J, 1982 D
Islamic 'Parliament', London, 1992 O
Islamic Salvation Front, Algeria, 1990 F
Khomeini declares Islam 'religion of the sword',1983 R
Lebanese Moslem leader assassinated, 1977 C
Moslem extremists attempt coup in Trinidad and Tobago, 1990 G
pilgrims crushed to death at Mecca, 1990 R
no longer state religion in Turkey, 1928 D
Jehovah's Witnesses, founded, 1871 R
Jews, statistics of, 1905 Y, 1909 Y, 1936 Y, 1947 Y, 1950 Y, 1967 Y, 1986 Y
See also main index under Jews
Lebanese Christian Phalangists, 1982 H, J
Lumpar Church, N. Rhodesia, 1964 G
Lutherans, World Conference, 1929 Y
German. *See under* Evangelicals
Swedish, 1958 R
admit women to pastorate, 1960 R
US. *See under* Evangelicals
statistics, 1905 Y, 1936 Y, 1945 Y, 1967 Y, 1986 Y
Mennonites, in Canada, 1786 R
Methodists, British, Wesleyan, deed of declaration for, 1784 R
New Connexion leaves, 1797 R
founds missionary Society, 1813 R
statistics, 1837 Y, 1905 Y, 1930 Y, 1950 Y
re-union of, 1932 R
conversations with Church of England, 1958 R, 1963 R
scheme for Anglican–Methodist union fails, 1969 R
proposed covenant of unity, 1982 R
anti-Masonic measures, 1985 R
sanctions against South Africa supported, 1986 R
patriarchy condemned as sin, 1992 R
US, Wesleyan, presbyters ordained, 1784 R
statistics, 1837 Y, 1840 Y, 1905 Y, 1936 Y, 1947 Y, 1967 Y, 1986 Y
Moravians, 1982 R
Mormons. *See* Church of Latter Day Saints
Moslems, 1886 M
in Albania, rising by, 1937 E
in India, 1924 G, 1947 H
violence against, 1964 C
in Indonesia, 1955 H
statistics, 1945 Y, 1963 Y
multi-faith Commonwealth Day service in Westminster Abbey, 1991 R
Old Catholics, 1871 R, 1874 R
Orthodox Church, annuls excommunication of Church of Rome, 1965 R
Patriarch of Constantinople joins Pope to bless crowds in St Peter's Square, 1987 R
in Africa, statistics, 1962 R
in Armenia, despoiled, 1902 D
in Russia, claims protectorate over Ottoman Christians, 1853 E, 1860 R
separation of Church and State, 1917 B
election of Patriarch of All-Russia, 1943 J
attends World Council of Churches meeting, 1961 R
in Turkish Empire, civil power of heads of, abolished, 1856 B
statistics, 1945 Y
in US, statistics, 1967 Y, 1986 Y
Pentecostal Churches, in Chile, attend World Council of Churches meeting, 1961 R
Plymouth Brethren, 1827 R
Presbyterian, in Britain, 1846 R
invited Congregations of, 1876 R
statistics, 1905 Y, 1930 Y, 1950 Y
formation of United Reformed Church, 1972 R
in Scotland, United Church, 1847 R
separate churches unite, 1929 R
statistics, 1905 Y, 1950 Y
See also Church of Scotland
in South Africa
mixed race marriages in, 1981 K
in US, revision of Catechism, 1788 R, 1810 Q, 1837 R
United Church formed, 1958 R
statistics, 1840 Q, 1905 Y, 1947 Y
Protestants, French (Huguenot), General Assembly of, revived, 1872 R
German, Eisenach, Conference of, 1852 R. *See also under* Evangelicals; Lutherans
Welsh, leave Anglican Church, 1811 R
Quakers. *See* Society of Friends
Relief Church of Scotland, 1847 R
Roman Catholic, catechism, 1992 R
Council of Churches for Britain and Ireland, 1990 R
Curran declared unfit to teach Catholic theology, 1986 R
demonstrations against human rights violations in Chile backed by, 1984 R
diplomatic relations between USSR and the Vatican, agreement to reestablish, 1989 R
Freemasonry permitted, 1974 R
Gorbachev visits Vatican, 1989 R
Humanae Vitae Papal Encyclical, 1968 R
impact of Second Vatican Council assessed, 1985 L
index of prohibited books abolished, 1966 R
Instruction on Respect for Human Life in its Origin and on the Dignity of Procreation ..., 1987 O
Instruction on Christian Freedom and Liberation, 1986 R
Instruction on Certain Aspects of the Theology of Liberation, An, 1984 R
Jesuit priests and their household tortured and murdered in San Salvador, 1989 R
Lefebvre, 1987 R, 1988 R
liberation theology, 1985 R
Office of Inquisitor abolished, 1966 R
order of deacons revived, 1967 R
Pope condemns Ulster violence, 1973 R
Pope John Paul II reiterates his opposition to women priests, 1988 R
primacy of Pope, 1977 R
RCs forbidden to attend prayers for unity in Anglican Church, Rome, 1967 R
sends observers to World Council of Churches meeting, 1961 R
statistics, 1945 Y
Vatican Councils, 1870 R, 1962 R
See also main index under Encyclical, papal; Papacy; Papal Bulls; Vatican
in Africa, statistics, 1962 Y
in Belgium, 1895 H
in Britain, penal laws against, eased, 1778 E, 1780 F
Catholic emancipation for, advocated, 1800 R
achieved, 1828 R
first M.P., 1829 O
appointment of Archbishop Hume, 1976 R
appointment of bishops, 1810 R
hierarchy established, 1850 R
ecclesiastical titles act, 1851 R
repealed, 1871 R
converts to, 1845 R, 1850 R
joint prayers authorised, 1964 R
martyrs canonised, 1887 R
ruling on contraceptive pill, 1964 R
statistics, 1780 Y, 1869 Y, 1905 Y, 1930 Y, 1950 Y
in China, 1966 R
in France, civil constitution of clergy, 1790 R
non-juring priests threatened with death penalty, 1793 R
concordat with Papacy, 1801 G
repealed, 1905 R
repealed, 1905 R
no longer state religion, 1830 H, R
worker-priest movement, 1943 R, 1965 R
statistics, 1945 Y
in Germany, aims at a national church, 1786 R
Ems articles rejected by Pius VI, 1789 R
Kulturkampf against, 1871 G
Ultramontane clergy, 1856 R, 1874 E
in Holland, hierarchy established, 1853 R
in Hungary, refuse concessions to government, 1948 M
in Italy, 1976 L, 1984 R; vernacular liturgy, 1786 R
in Poland, concordat is denounced, 1947 J
given increased status and powers, 1989 E
in Scotland, hierarchy is restored, 1878 R
statistics, 1905 Y, 1950 Y
in Spain, to be sole faith, 1851 C
property is nationalised, 1933 E
separation of Church and State called for, 1971 B
in Sweden, combated by Gustavus Adolphus

Society, 1832 R
in Switzerland, protected by *Sonderbund*, 1845 M
in US, first bishopric:
plenary council, 1852, R
Sulpician seminary, 1791 R
statistics, 1840 Y, 1905 Y, 1936 Y, 1947 Y, 1967 Y, 1986 Y
Salvation Army, in Britain, founded, 1865 R 1878 R
Second Adventists, in US, 1831 R, 1842 R
Shakers, the in US, 1774 R
Sikhs
British, 1975 O
Indian, 1984 C, F, R, 1985 E, 1986 D, F, 1988 D, E
Société des Amis, Geneva, 1810 R
Society of Friends (Quakers), statistics, 1905 Y, 1936 Y, 1945 Y, 1947 Y, 1950 Y
Stundists, in Russia, 1858 R
Swedenborgians, in US, 1792 R
Templeton Prize, 1973 R, 1974 R, 1976 R
US Federal Council of Churches, 1908 R
Unification Church ('Moonies'), 1981 R
Unitarians, statistics, 1905 Y, 1936 Y, 1945 Y, 1947 Y, 1950 Y
United Brethren in Christ, US, 1800 R
United Church of Canada, 1925 R
United Church of Christ (Congregationalist and Evangelical), in US, 1958 R
United Free Church of Scotland, 1843 R
United Presbyterian Church, US, formed, 1958 R
United Reformed Church, 1972 R, 1982 R
supports unilateral nuclear disarmament, 1983 R
United Secession Church of Scotland, 1847 R
in US
federal court's ruling on creationism and evolutionary theory, 1982 R
statistics, 1967 Y, 1977 Y, 1986 Y
Religious Experience (C. J. Webb), 1945 R
Religious Houses. *See* Monasteries
Religious Orders and Committees:
Dominicans, 1838 R
Jesuits. *See main index under* Jesuits, The
in Austria, made independent of Rome, 1781 L
in Belgium, Louvain Seminary, 1786 K
in Britain, revived, 1862 R
Community of the Resurrection (Anglican), 1892 R
in France, orders, disolved, 1950 J
Communities, decree for non-authorised, 1800 C
prohibited from teaching, 1828 F
abolished, 1875 E, 1903 C
Protestant Community of Taizé, 1944 R
in Hungary, dissolved, 1950 J
in Sardinia, contemplative orders dissolved, 1855 R
in US, Paulist Fathers, 1858 R
Sisters of Charity of St. Joseph, 1809 R
Religious Toleration:
is condemned by Gregory XVI, 1832 R
in Austria, 1781 K, 1782 C, 1894 R
in Belgium, 1831 B
in Bosnia and Herzegovina, demanded, 1875 M
in Britain, relief for Protestant Dissenting ministers, 1778 E
Saville's Act modifies penal laws for Roman Catholics, 1778 E, 1780 F
registration of Dissenters' Chapels, 1779 R
position of Protestant Dissenters eased, 1812 R
Test and Corporation Acts, repealed, 1828 E
Catholic Emancipation, 1828 R
religious tests, for office, abolished, 1867 R
in universities, abolished, 1871 O
in Denmark, 1770 M
in France, opposed, 1767 R
for Protestants, 1787 R, 1795 B
toleration advocated, 1830 O
achieved, 1905 M
in Germany, advocated, 1777 R, 1783 R
emancipation of Jews, 1812 R
in Russia, 1766 R
in Turkey, 1856 B, 1876 M
in Virginia, 1785 R
principles of, advocated by Presbyterians, 1788 R
Reliques of Ancient English Poetry (T. Percy), 1765 U
R.E.M., Am. pop group, 1983 W, 1992 W
Remains of the Day (K. Ishiguro), 1989 U
Remak, Robert, G. biologist and naturalist (1815–1892), 1850 P
Remaking of Christian Doctrine, The (M. Wiles), 1974 R
Remarque, Erich, G. author (1898–1970), 1929 U
Rembrandt, picture by, cleaning of, 1947 S
Remembrance (D. Walcott), 1990 W
Remembrance of Things Past (Proust), 1981 U
Remington, Philo, Am. manufacturer (1816–89), 1873 P
Removalists, The (D. Williamson), 1971 W
'Remus, Uncle', *See* Harris, Joel Chandler
Rémuset, Jean Pierre Abel, F. orientalist (1788–1832), 1811 Q
Renan, Ernest, F. philosopher (1823–92), 1823 Z, 1857 R, 1859 R, 1863 R, 1883 R, 1892 Z
Rendez-Vous, Le (A. Robbe-Grillet), 1979 U
René, (France) Albert, Seychelles leader (b. 1935), 1977 F
René (Chateaubriand), 1805 U
Renée Mauperin (J. Goncourt), 1864 U
Renfrew, (Andrew) Colin, Lord Renfrew, B. archaeologist and historian (b.1937), 1974 Q
Rennell, James, B. geographer (1742–1830), 1779 P
Renner, Karl, Aus. Socialist (1870–1950), 1919 C, 1945 D
elected president of Austria, 1945 M
Rennie, John, B. civil engineer (1761–1821), 1811 S
Renoir, Jean, F. film director (1894–1979), 1926 W, 1935 W, 1937 W, 1939 W, 1945 W
Renoir, Pierre Auguste, F. artist (1841–1919), 1841 Z, 1868 S, 1874 S, 1876 S, 1879 S, 1883 S, 1911 S, 1917 S, 1919 Z
Rent, treatise on, 1815 O
Reparations:
Bulgarian, to Allies, further payments renounced, 1932 B
China, to Japan, not honoured, 1913 J
Finland, to Russia, 1952 J
Germany, to Allies, Supreme Allied Council agrees on payments, 1920 F
Spa Conference, on, 1920 G
Brussels Conference on, 1920 M
Allies fix payments, 1921 A
US representative is recalled from commission, 1921 B
Germany announces default, 1921 C
British Reparation Recovery Act, 1921 C
repealed, 1925 D
Germany's failure to pay leads to occupation of Ruhr, 1921 C, E
US declines to mediate in controversy, 1921 D
Commission fixes liability, 1921 D
Germany accepts Allies' ultimatum, 1921 E
to supply France with reparations in kind, 1921 K
Germany applies for moratorium, 1921 M
payments postponed by decision at Cannes Conference, 1922 A
to pay with raw materials, 1922 C
Bankers' Committee declines to recommend loan, 1922 F
Balfour Note on, 1922 H
Commission permits payments by instalments on Treasury bills, 1922 H
Commission declares Germany defaulted voluntarily, 1922 M
Ruhr is occupied, 1923 A
Commission appoints Dawes and McKenna Committees, 1923 L
Britain reduces reparations import duty, 1924 B
Reports of Dawes and McKenna Committees, 1924 D
approved, 1924 G
London Conference, 1924 G
Stresemann's discussions with Briand, 1926 J
Young Committee, 1928 M, 1929 F
Hague Conference, 1929 H
Young Plan, 1929 H
upheld by referendum, 1929 M
in force, 1930 E
to be made through Basle Bank, 1929 L
Hoover proposes moratorium, 1931 F
London protocol on, 1931 H
Brüning declares Germany will pay no more, 1932 A
Layton–Wiggin Report, for extending credit, 1931 H
Lausanne Conference, requires final payment, 1932 F
demanded by Russia, 1947 L
Russia cancels East German, 1953 H
Italy, Allies impose, 1947 B
Japan, terminated, 1949 E
See also War debts
Repentant Thief, The (J. Tavener), 1991 T
Répétition, La (J. Anouilh), 1950 W
Report on Radiation and the Quantum Theory (Jeans), 1914 P
Reports, notable:
Annan Committee, on teaching of Russian, 1962 O
Annan, on British broadcasting, 1977 O
Barlow, on location of industry, 1940 O
Beeching, on reshaping British railways, 1963 O
Berrill, on representation overseas, 1976 A
Beveridge, on social security, 1942 O, 1943 B
Bingham, on oil sanctions against Rhodesia, 1978 J
Brandt, *North–South: A Programme for Survival*, 1980 O
Bryce Committee, on German Atrocities, 1916 O
Buchanan, on traffic in towns, 1963 O
Bullock, on industrial democracy, 1977 O
Capital Punishment, royal commission, 1953 O
Chadwick, on sanitary reform, 1842 O
Chief Inspector of Schools, 1990 O
Church and the Bomb, The Church of England report, 1982 R
Compton, on Northern Ireland, 1971 L
Cruz, on apartheid, 1955 L
Dardanelles Commission, 1917 O
Denning, on the Profumo Affair, 1963 O
Durham, on Canada, 1839 B
Erasmus, 1978 M, 1979 D, F
Faith in the City, Church of England, 1985 M

Fleming, on independent schools, 1944 O
Franks, on Falklands War, 1983 A
Fulton Committee, on British civil service, 1968 O
Geddes Economy Committee, 1922 O
Health of Towns, 1844 O
on homosexuality, General Synod of the Church of England, 1987 R
Irish Rebellion, Commission, 1916 O
Kilbrandon, on Scotland and Wales, 1973 O
Kindersley, on UK doctors' pay, 1966 E
Layfield, on local government finance, 1976 O
Lytton, on Manchuria, 1932 K, 1933 B
Mesopotamia Campaign, 1917 O
Milner Holland, on London housing, 1965 O
Monckton, on Rhodesia and Nyasaland, 1960 K
Montagu-Chelmsford, on India, 1918 G
New Ireland Forum, 1984 E
Newsom, on education, 1963 O
Northcote-Trevelyan, on Civil Service, 1854 O
Parker, on Northern Irish security forces, 1972 C
Pilkington, on broadcasting, 1962 W
Plowden, *Children and their Primary Schools*, 1967 O
Radcliffe Tribunal, on security procedure, 1963 D
Randall Commission, on US foreign economic policy, 1954 A
Redcliffe–Maud, on Local Government reform, 1969 O
Robbins Committee, on higher education, 1963 O
rejected by government, 1965 B
Rochdale Committee, on British docks, 1962 O
Rockefeller Commission, on CIA activities, 1975 F
Sankey Coal Commission, 1919 B, O
Scarman, on Grunwick strike, 1977 H
Seebohm, on local welfare services, 1968 O
Simon, on India, 1930 F
Smoking and Health, by Royal College of Physicians, 1962 P
Venereal Disease, Royal Commission on, 1916 O
Warnock, on Human Fertilizatiaon and Embryology, 1984 O
Warren, on Kennedy's assassination, 1964 O
We believe in God, Doctrine Commission of the Church of England, 1987 R
Wheatley, on football stadia, 1971 E
Widgery, on 'Bloody Sunday', 1972 D
Williams, on obscenity, 1979 O
Wolfenden, on homosexual offences and prostitution, 1957 J
of US Surgeon-general, on cigarette smoking, 1979 P
Yarmolinsky, on US security precautions, 1955 O
See also under Committees and Commissions; Plans
Reppe, J., inventor of artificial fabrics, 1930 P
Representative, The (R. W. Emerson), 1850 U
Representative, The (R. Hochhuth), 1963 W
Republic of Namibia 1990 B. *See also* Namibia
Republicans. *See under* Political Parties
République universelle, La (J.B. Cloots), 1792 O
Requiem for a Nun (W. Faulkner), 1953 U
Resaca de la Palma, New Mexico, battle, 1846 E
Resale price maintenance, in Britain, 1964 G
Researches in Electricity (M. Faraday), 1839 P
Researches on the Chemistry of Proteins (E. Fisher), 1907 P
Researches, Chemical and Philosophical, Chiefly Concerning Nitrous Oxide (H. Davy), 1800 P
Resection of oesophagus, 1872 P
Reshaping of British Railways, The (Dr. R. Beeching), 1963 O
Resina, Macedonia, 1908 G
Resnais, Alain, F. film director (b. 1922), 1956 W, 1959 W, 1961 W, 1964 W
Respighi, Ottorino, It. musican (1879–1936), 1917 T, 1922 T, 1924 T
Respiration, study of, 1780 P
Ressel, Joseph, Aus. enginner (1793–1857), 1827 P
Restaurants, public, first, 1770 U
Restoration (E. Bond), 1981 W
Restrictive Practices in Britain:
Court, is established, 1956 G
first case before, 1958 O
upholds net book agreement, 1962 O
White Paper, 1964 O
Resumptio (A. Kiefer), 1974 S
Resurrection (L. Tolstoy), 1899 U
Retailing, bar codes, 1973 P
Rethel, Alfred, G. wood-engraver (1816–59), 1849 S
Retirement Age, in US, 1978 D
Retraite Sentimentale, La (Colette), 1908 U
Retreat from Truth (G. R. Mure), 1959 R
Return of the Native, The (T. Hardy), 1878 U
Return to Camelot, The: Chivalry and the English Gentleman (M. Girouard), 1981 Q
Réunion, Isle, Indian Ocean, becomes a French Colony, 1764 N
Reusch, Franz Heinrich, G. theologian (Old Catholic) (1823–1900), 1883 R
Reuter, Ernst, G. Social Democrat, Chief Bürgermeister of Berlin (1889–1953), 1948 M
Reuters, stock market flotation, 1984 V
Reval, Estonia, 1908 F
Revel, Riot and Rebellion: Popular Politics and Culture in England, 1603–60 (D.E. Underdown),1986Q
Rêve et la Vie, La (G. de Nerval), 1855 U
Revett, Nicholas, B. architect and draughtsman (1720–1804), 1794 Q
Reviews (Theatrical):
Beyond the Fringe, 1961 W
Bing Boys of Broadway, The, 1918 W
Boy Friend, The, 1945 W
Bubbly, 1917 W
Dancing Years, The, 1939 W
Glamorous Nights, 1935 W
Pins and Needles, 1937 W
Salad Days, 1954 W
Reviews (publications). *See* Journals
Revolt in the Desert (T. E. Lawrence), 1927 O
Revolt of Islam (P. B. Shelley), 1817 U
Revolt of the Masses (Ortega y Gasset), 1930 O
Revolution Society, The (London), 1789 L
Revolution in Philosophy, The (A. J. Ayer), 1956 R
Revolution in Tanner's Lane, The (M. Rutherford), 1888 U
Revolution of the Robots (F. Pollock and A. Weber), 1956 O
Revolutions, *See* Rebellions and Revolutions
Revolver, Colt's, 1835 P. *See also under* Arms
Reyes, Rafael, Colombian dictator, 1904 G
Reykjavik, Iceland
World Chess Championship, 1972 X
summit talks on arms control, 1986 K
Reynaud, Paul, F. politician (1878–1966), 1878 Z, 1940 C, F, 1966 Z
Reynolds, Albert, Prime Minister of Eire (b. 1935), 1992 A
Reynolds, Sir Joshua, B. artist (1723–92), 1764 U, 1768 S, 1773 S, 1775 S, 1780 S, 1784 S, 1786 S, 1787 S, 1892 Z
statue of, 1931 S
Reza Khan, usurps Persian Throne, 1925 K
Reza Shah Pahlevi, Mohammed, Shah of Iran (1919–80), 1919 Z, 1967 K
announces oil price increase, 1973 M
flees to Egypt with family, 1979 A
purge of former officials, 1979 D
flown to US for medical treatment, 1979 K
return and trial demanded, 1979 L
Rhapsodies:
Bolero (Ravel), 1928 T
Brigg Fair (Delius), 1907 T
Capriccio (Stravinsky), 1928 T
España (Chabrier), 1883 T
Fantasia on a theme by Tallis (R. Vaughan Williams), 1909 T
On a theme of Paganini (S. Rachmaninoff), 1935 T
Rhapsody in Blue (G. Gershwin), 1924 T
Spanish Rhapsody (M. Ravel), 1907 T
Rhee, Syngman, Korean president (1871–1965), 1948 H, 1960 D
Rheims, France: Germans occupy, 1914 J; Allies recapture, 1914 J; Germans take, 1918 E
Rheumatism, cure for, 1949 R
Rhine, Confederation of, 1815 F
Rhine, Joseph Banks, Am. philosopher (1895–1919), 1935 R
Rhine, River, Europe:
French army reaches, 1794 K
France cedes conquests on right bank, 1795 D
Austrian conquests on right bank, 1795 J
Moreau's campaign, 1796 F
Prussia yields land on left bank to France, 1796 H
cession of left bank to France agreed upon, 1797 K
free navigation, 1797 K
France annexes left bank, 1798 C
France is assigned left bank, 1801 B
British troops reach, 1945 B
Dempsey crosses, 1945 C
Rhineland, The: ceded to Prussia, 1815 F; US troops evacuate, 1922 C; costs of US army in, 1923 E; French troops evacuate, 1925 G; Franco–German discussions on, 1926 J; Allied evacuation of 1929 H, L, 1930 F; Germany occupies demilitarized zone, 1936 C
Rhinoceros, The (E. Ionescu), 1960 W
Rhinoscope, invented, 1860 P
Rhode Island, state, US ; as British Colony, 1772 F; Howe captures, 1776 J; Dorr Rebellion, 1841 K
Rhodes James, Sir Robert Vidal, B. historian and Conservative politician (b. 1933), 1986 Q
Rhodes, Cecil John, B. imperialist and benefactor (1853–1902), 1853 Z, 1888 K, O, 1902 Z; heads S. Africa Company, 1889 K; becomes premier of Cape Province, 1890 G; resigns premiership, 1896 A; connexion with Jameson Raid, 1897 G
Rhodes, Wilfred, B. cricketer (1877–1973), 1877 Z, 1930 X, 1973 Z
Rhodesia (formerly S. Rhodesia):
is organised by British S. Africa Company, 1895 E
votes against joining Union of S. Africa, 1922 K
constitution for, 1923 K
Federation of N. and S. Rhodesia, 1953 K
state of emergency, 1959 B
UN Trusteeship Committee resolves to consider whether full self-government is attained, 1962 B
asks Britain not to transfer Federation forces to, 1963 K
Nationalist Movement in, is banned, 1964 H
Wilson warns that a UDI would be an act of defiance, 1964 K

Nkomo placed in a restriction area, 1964 L
referendum favours independence, 1964 L
Smith rejects visit by Commonwealth Secretary, 1964 L
appoints 'accredited' representative to Lisbon, 1965 J
Wilson's talks with Smith, 1965 K
Archbishop Ramsey's remarks on the use of force, 1965 K
Smith makes UDI, 1965 L
Britain declares Smith regime illegal, 1965 L
Britain imposes trade and exchange restrictions, 1965 L
nine African states sever relations with Britain for not using force against rebels, 1965 M
Britain imposes oil embargo, 1965 M
British trade ban, 1966 A, C, D
UN authorizes Britain to prevent oil shipments to, 1966 D
withdrawal of British diplomats demanded, 1966 D
Salisbury talks, 1966 E, 1971 L
UN mandatory sanctions against, 1966 J, M
High Court ruling on Smith regime, 1966 J
Tiger talks, 1966 M
British demands for black majority rule, 1966 M
republic declared, 1966 M, 1970 C
UN condemns British failure to overthrow Smith regime, 1967 K
Smith–Thomson talks, 1967 L
three Africans hanged despite reprieve by Elizabeth II, 1968 C
Wilson–Smith talks, 1968 K, L
British links cut, 1969 F
votes to become republic, 1969 F
Dupont becomes President, 1970 C
Anglo–Rhodesian settlement talks in Pretoria, 1970 L
new constitution, 1971 L
Zimbabwe leaders from African National Council, 1971 M
Pearce Commission, 1972 A, E
Zambian border closed, 1973 A
mission school kidnapping, 1973 G
Smith calls constitutional conference, 1974 M
Smith accepts principle of majority rule, 1976 J
Smith rejects British proposals, 1977 A
parliamentary victory for Rhodesian Front, 1977 H
Smith's equal votes proposal, 1977 L
agreement on power-sharing government, 1978 C
forces kill at black political meeting, 1978 E
racial discrimination in public places to be scrapped, 1978 H
black conscripts to fight Patriotic Front, 1978 J
air attacks on Zambia, 1979 B
Lancaster House conference and agreement, 1979 J, M
Unilateral Declaration of Independence (UDI) ended, 1979 M
gains legal independence as Zimbabwe, 1980 D
See also Zimbabwe
Rhodesia, Northern:
German troops surrender, 1918 L
Federation of N. and S. Rhodesia and Nyasaland in force, 1953 K. *See also* Central African Federation
becomes independent republic, 1964 K
is renamed Zambia, 1964 K
See also under Zambia
Rhodesian Sanctions Order, rejection by House of Lords, 1968 F
Rhondda, Margaret, Lady (1883–1958), B. Liberal, attempts to take seat as peer, 1922 O
Rhoodie, Eschel Mostert, S. African politician (b. 1933), 1978 F, 1979 K
Rhymes from Various Sonorous Sources (Pousseur), 1959 T
Rhys, Jean (born Ella Gwendolen Williams), B. author (1894–1979), 1966 U
Ribbentrop, Joachim von, G. diplomat, national Socialist (1893–1946), 1893 Z
as foreign minister, 1938 B
sentenced by Nuremberg Tribunal, 1946 J
Ribonucleic acid (RNA), 1967 P, 1970 P
Ribot, Alexandre Félix Joseph, F. politician (1842–1927), 1895 A, L, 1917 C
Ricardo, David, B. economist (1772–1823), 1772 Z, 1809 O, 1817 O
Ricci, Lorenzo, It. bishop of Pistoria and Prata, 1786 R
Rice, Elmer, Am. dramatist (1892–1967), 1923 W, 1929 W, 1930 W
Riceyman Steps (A. Bennett), 1923 U
Rich Man, Poor Man (J. Hilton), 1944 O
Richard of Bordeaux (G. Daviot), 1933 W
Richards, Isaac Vivian Alexander, 'Viv', W. Indian cricketer (b. 1952), 1976 X
Richardson, Dorothy (Mrs. Alan Odle), B. author (1873–1957), 1927 U
Richardson, Elliot Lee, Am. lawyer (b. 1920), 1973 K
Richardson, Tony, B. stage and film director (b. 1928), 1959 W
Richelieu, Armand Emmanuel Sophie Septemanie du Plessis, Duc de, F. royalist politician (1766–1822), 1818 M, 1820 B, C, 1821 M
Richet, Charles, F. physician, 1902 P
Richler, Mordechai, Canad. author (b. 1931), 1990 U
Richmond, Sir William Blake, B. artist (1842–1921), 1891 S
Richmond, Virginia, US surrenders to Grant, 1865 D
Richmond, duke of, *See* Lennox
Richter, Burton, Am. physicist (b. 1931), 1974 P
Richter, Hans, G. musician (1843–1912), 1876 T
Richter, Jean Paul Friedrich, G. author under pseudonym 'Jean Paul' (1763–1825), 1763 Z, 1793 U, 1795 U, 1796 U, 1800 U, 1804 U, 1807 U, 1825 Z
Ricks, Christopher Bruce, B. author (b. 1933), 1987 U
Riddle of the Universe, The (E. Haeckel), 1899 P
Ride, Sally, Am. astronaut (b. 1951), 1983 P
Riders to the Sea (J.M. Synge), 1904 W
Ridgway, Matthew Bunker, Am. general (b. 1895), succeeds MacArthur in Korea, 1951 D; breaks off Korea armistice talks, 1951 H; becomes supreme Allied Commander in Europe, 1952 D
Ried, Austria, Treaty, Bavaria with Austria, 1813 K
Riel, Louis, Can. insurgent (1844–85), 1869 K
Riemann, Georg Friedrich Bernhard, G. mathematician (1826–66), 1854 P
Rienzi (Lytton), 1835 O
Riesman, David, Am. sociologist, 1951 R
Rieti, Naples, Italy, Austrians crush rebels at, 1821 C
Riga, Latvia: Germans attack, 1917 H, J; Bolsheviks take, 1919 A; Treaty, between Russia and Poland, 1921 B, C
Right Stuff, The (T. Wolfe), 1980 U
Right of Search, British, countered by Armed Neutrality, 1780 C, L
Rights of Man, The (T. Paine), 1791 O, 1792 M, O
Rights of Neutral Nations in Time of War, The (D. Webster), 1802 O
Rights of Passage (W. Golding), 1981 U
Riley, Terry Mitchell, Am. musician (b. 1935), 1970 T
Rilke, Rainer Maria, G. poet (1875–1926), 1875 Z, 1907 U, 1911 U, 1922 U, 1926 Z
Rimbaud, Arthur, F. author (1854–91), 1854 Z, 1873 U, 1886 U, 1891 Z, 1895 U
Rime of the Ancient Mariner (S. T. Coleridge), 1798 U
Rimington, Stella, B. head of M.I.5 (b. 1935), 1991 M
Rimnik, near Martinesti, Wallachia, Turkish defeat at, 1789 J
Rimsky-Korsakov, Nicholas, R. musician (1844–1908), 1844 Z, 1865 T, 1873 T, 1882 T, 1888 T, 1908 Z, 1910 T
Ring Round the Moon (C. Fry—J. Anouilh), 1947 W
Ring and the Book, The (R. Browning), 1868 U
Ringed with Vision (O. Kokoschka), 1962 S
Rinnovamente Civile d'Italia, Il (V. Gioberti), 1851 O
Rio Grande, US troops sent to, 1911 A
Rio de Janeiro, Brazil: as capital of Portuguese colonies in S. America, 1776 N; non-aggression pact, 1933 K; treaty of Mutual Assistance, by American Republics, 1947 J
Conference on Environment and Development, 1992 P
Rio de la Plata (Argentina), revolts against Joseph Bonaparte, 1810 E
Riots and Risings:
See also under Coup d'états; Rebellions and Revolutions
in Aegean Isles, against Turks, in Samos, 1912 J
in Aden, 1967 B
in Albania, by Moslems, 1937 E
in Algeria, against rising prices and unemployment, 1988 K
in Algiers, 1846 A
against French, 1881 G
by Nationalists, 1945 E, 1954 L, M, 1955 A
by Europeans, 1960 A
by Islamic Salvation Front, 1991 F
in Argentina, at Córdoba, 1955 H
at return of Perón, 1973 F
in Armenia, by Nationalist Revolutionaries, 1890 M
in Ashanti, suppressed, 1900 L
in Austria, by Socialists, 1927 G
in Austrian Netherlands, 1787 A
Azerbaijan–Iran border, 1989 M
in Bangkok, 1992 E
in Bosnia and Herzegovina, against Turks, 1875 G, M
in Brazil, 1914 C
in Britain, pro-Wilkes riots, 1764 A, 1768 E
Gordon Riots, 1780 F
against sympathisers with French Revolution, 1791 G
Spa Fields Riots, 1816 M
in Derbyshire, 1817 F
in Bristol, 1831 K
by Chartists, 1839 G, L, 1842 H
election riots, 1874 B
in Wales, 1911 C
by Suffragettes, 1911 L
at London Docks, 1912 G
provoked by government economies, 1931 J
Bristol, St Paul's district, 1980 D
Brixton, London, 1981 D, G, 1985 J
Toxteth, Liverpool, 1981 G
Birmingham, 1985 J
Tottenham, London, 1985 K
Strangeways Prison, Manchester, 1990 D
in British Guiana, 1962 B, 1963 D, 1964 C

in Brussels, at Heysel Stadium, 1985 X
in Bulgaria, 1876 A, E
in Canada, in Montreal, against British, 1849 D
in Quebec, by Nationalists, 1964 E
in China, Boxer Rising, 1900 F, 1901 J
over removal of Chou En-lai wreaths, 1976 D
in Congo, by Arab Slave-holders, 1892 L
of Bartebelas, 1897 J
anti-Belgian, 1959 A
in Crete, of Christians, against Turks, 1894 N, 1896 G, 1897 B
in Cuba, 1875 J, 1895 N
in Cyprus, between Greeks and Turks, 1963 M
in Czechoslovakia, 1937 K
in Eastern Rumelia, 1885 J
in Egypt, Nationalist Risings, 1881 J, 1882 F, 1919 C, 1921 E
anti-British, 1952 A, 1964 M
in Ethiopia, pro-British, 1941 A
in Formosa, 1787 N
in France, bread riots in Paris, 1795 D
by Lions silk-weavers, 1831 L, 1834 D
by Republicans, in Paris, 1834 D
by Communists, in Paris, 1849 F
anti-government, in Paris, 1934 B
anti-OAS, in Paris, 1962 B
over steel plants closures, 1979 E
in German East Africa, by Arabs, 1888 J
by Moslems, 1905 N
in German South West Africa, 1904 K, 1907 J
in Germany, by students, 1817 K
in Hamburg, by Communists, 1921 C
in Rhineland, by Separatists, 1923 L
anti-Communist, in East Berlin, 1953 F
at Rostock reception centre for asylum seekers, 1992 H
in Greece, in Thessaly, 1878 A
pro-Venizelos rising, suppressed, 1935 C
in Athens, about Cyprus issue, 1954 M
in Holland, 1787 F, J
in Hong Kong, 1966 D, 1967 E
in India, by Mohammedans, in Calcutta, 1918 J
in Delhi, 1924 G
anti-Muslim riots, 1964 C
food riots, 1964 L
food riots in Delhi, 1966 C
over cow slaughter laws, 1966 L
over food, 1974 C
in Iran, by Communists, in Aberdaijan, 1945 L
in Ireland, at Dublin, 1822 M
in Tipperary, 1848 G
Sinn Fein, in Dublin, 1914 G, 1917 F
and Unionist Riots in Belfast, 1935 G
anti-Roman Catholic, in Belfast, 1935 G
in Israel, occupied West Bank, over disbanding of El Birah, 1982 C
in Italy, riots in Sicily, 1894 N
between Communists and Fascists, in Florence, 1921 B
between Fascists and Socialists, 1922 H
in Jakarta, against Japanese premier's visit, 1974 A
in Jamaica, riots, 1839 E
in Japan, by students, against treaty with US, 1960 F
in Korea, anti-Chinese, 1931 G
of Communist prisoners at Koje Camp, 1952 E
in Matabeleland, against British Africa Company, 1893 G, 1896 K
in Morocco, 1955 H
in Mozambique, 1895 N
in New Zealand, Maori Risings, 1845 C, 1863 E
in Northern Ireland, 1969 H, K, 1971 D, G, 1974 K, 1981 E
in Nyasaland, 1959 B
in Pakistan, riots in Karachi, 1953 A
in Panama, 1964 A
in Peru, at Lima, 1964 E
in Philippines, 1896 H
against US, 1899 B, C
in Poland, 1794 C, L
in Cracow, 1846 B, C, L
Warsaw Rising, 1944 H
Labour riots at Poznan, 1956 F
over price rises, 1970 M, 1976 F, 1982 A
in Portugal, Miguelist Rising, 1846 F
Royalist rising, 1913 K, 1915 E, 1919 D
in Puerto Rico, Nationalist rising, 1950 K
in Qom, Iran, by Islamic fundamentalists, 1978 E
in Rhodesia, rising by Matabeles, 1893 G, 1896 C, K
in N. Rhodesia, 1964 G
in S. Rhodesia, 1964 A
at University, 1973 H
in Rumania, by Serbs in Belgrade, 1862 F
agrarian rising, 1888 D
by miners, 1991 J
in Russia, Decembrist rising, 1825 M
riots in Moscow, 1915 F
risings in Georgia, by Stalinists, 1956 L
African students riot in Moscow, 1963 M
in South Africa, race riots, 1950 A, 1976 H, 1984 J
in Spain, risings against Espartero, 1842 K
Carlist risings, 1873 D, J
in Catalonia, 1909 G
by anarchists and Syndicalists, in Barcelona, 1933 A
by Radicals, 1933 M
in Switzerland, of Prussian royalist, against Neufchatel republic, 1856 J
in Syria, 1925 K
anti-government, by Moslem Brotherhood, 1982 B
in Tangier, anti-French, 1952 C
in Tibet, against China, 1959 L
in Turkey, by Janissaries, 1826 F
Army, 1909 D
anti-Greek, in Istanbul, 1955 J
by students, 1960 D
in US, by Sioux, in Minnesota, 1862 H
by Knights of Labor, in Chicago, 1886 E
race riots in Chicago, 1919 G
over desegregation in schools, 1963 J
race riots, in Harlem, 1964 G
in Los Angeles, 1965 H
race riots, 1966 G, J, 1967 F, G, 1992 D
Attica prison, New York, 1971 J
over busing for desegregation in Louisville, Kentucky, 1975 J
Los Angeles, following acquittal of policemen acused of beating black motorist, 1992 D
in Viet Nam, riots in Saigon, 1964 L
in Zaire, 1991 K
in Zambia, against food price rises, 1986 M
in Zanzibar, 1961 F
Rip Van Winkle (W. Irving), 1809 U
Rise and Fall of Little Voice, The (J. Cartwright), 1992 W
Rise and Fall of the Political Press, The Vol. I (S. Koss), 1981 Q
Rise and Progress of the Arts of Design in the U.S. (W. Dunlap), 1834 S
Rise of Christianity, The (E. W. Barnes), 1947 R
Rise of the Dutch Republic, The (J. R. Motley), 1856 Q
Risings. *See* Riots and Risings
Ristich, Jovan, Serb. regent (1831–99), 1876 F, 1889 C
Ristori, Adelaide, It. actress (1822–1906), 1855 W
Ritter, Karl, G. geographer, 1817 P
Rituel (P. Boulez), 1975 T
Rivals, The (R. B. Sheridan), 1775 W
River Line, The (C. Morgan), 1949 W
Rivera, Miguel de Primo, Sp. dictator (1870–1930), 1923 J, 1930 A
Riverrun (T. Takemitsu), 1985 T
Rivers of China, The (A. de Groen), 1987 W
Rivette, Jacques, F. film director (b. 1928), 1974 W, 1991 W
Riviera, French, British land in, 1944 H
Rivière Endormie, La (D. Milhaud), 1954 T
Rivoli, Italy, Austrian defeat at, 1797 A
Rivonia trial, S. Africa, 1964 F, L
Riyadh, Saudi Arabia, Arab summit, 1976 K
Road Traffic, Buchanan Report on, 1963 P
Road carriage, steam, 1769 P
Road to 1945, The (P. Addison), 1975 Q
Road to Serfdom, The (F.A. von Hayek), 1944 R
Road to Wigan Pier, The (G. Orwell), 1937 U
Roads:
Autobahn, in Germany, 1932 P
construction of, 1764 P, 1815 P
Hammersmith, flyover, 1961 S
M. I motorway, 1959 P
road surface-heating cables, 1961 S
speed limit, in Britain, 1935 C
Telford's, in Scotish Highlands, 1802 P
Roanoke Island, N. Carolina, US, Unionists take, 1862 B
Roaratorio (Cage), 1979 T
Rob Roy (W. Scott), 1818 U
Robbe-Grillet, Alain, F. author (b. 1922), 1960 U, 1979 U
Robbery Under Arms (R. Boldrewood), 1888 U
Robbins, Jerome, Am. choreographer (b. 1918), 1946 T, 1950 T, 1959 T
Robbins, Lionel, Lord Robbins, B. economist (1898–1984), 1963 O
Robert N. L. F., inventor, 1798 P
Robens, Alfred, Lord Robens (b. 1910), National Coal Board Chairman, 1971 A
Robert Kennedy and his Times (A. Schlesinger Jnr), 1978 Q
Roberts, Frederick, lord Roberts, B. soldier (1832–1914), as C-in-C in S. Africa, 1900 A, C, G,
Roberts, John Morris, B. historian (b. 1928), 1976 Q, 1978 Q, 1985 W
Robertson, Anna M. ('Grandma Moses'), Am. artist (1860–1961), 1939 S
Robertson, John, B. Labour/Scottish Labour politician (1913–87), 1976 A
Robertson William, B. historian (1721–93), 1769 Q, 1771 Q, 1793 Z
Robertson, Sir William, B. soldier (1860–1933), 1915 M
Robeson, Paul, Am. singer (1898–1976), 1898 Z, 1976 Z
Robespierre, Maxmilien François Marie Isadore de, F. revolutionary (1758–94), 1790 N, 1793 G, 1794 G, R
Robey, Sir George, B. comedian (1869–1954), 1917 W
Robinson, Derek ('Red Robbo'), B. union shop steward, 1979 L
Robinson, Frederick John, viscount Goderich, earl of Ripon, B. Tory (1782–1859), 1827 H, 1828 A
Robinson, G. N., B. chemist, 1960 P

Robinson, Heath, B. humorist (1872–1944), 1872 Z, 1944 Z
Robinson, Henry Crabb, B. journalist (1775–1867), 1808 V
Robinson, Joan Violet, B. economist (1903–83), 1903 Z, 1933 O, 1983 Z
Robinson, John, B. bishop of Woolwich (1919–1983), 1963 R
Robinson, Mary ('Perdita'), B. actress (1758–1800), 1780 S
Robinson, Mary, President of Eire (b. 1944), 1990 L
Rocard, Michel Louis Léon, Prime Minister of France (b. 1930), 1988 E, 1991 E
Rochambeau, Jean Baptiste Donation de Vimeur, F. soldier (1725–1807), 1780 G
Rochdale Committee on British Docks, 1962 O
Rochdale pioneers of co-operation, 1844 O
Rochdale, Lancs, England, by-election, 1958 B
Roche, Eamonn Kevin, Am. architect (b. 1922), 1975 S 1976 S
Roche, Stephen, Irish cyclist (b. 1959), 1987 X
Rochebouet, Gaetan de Grimaudet de, F. politician, 1877 L
Rochefort, Henri, Marquis de Rochefort Lucay, F. Communard (1830–1912), 1871 G
Rock Pool, The (C. Connolly), 1935 U
Rock and Roll dancing, 1956 W
Rockall, annexed by Britain, 1971 L
Rockefeller Commission, 1975 F
Rockefeller, Foundation, 1913 O, 1940 P
Rockefeller, John Davison, Am. industrialist and philanthropist (1839–1937), 1839 Z, 1870 P, 1937 Z
Rockefeller, Nelson Aldrich, Am. politician, Republican (1908–79), 1908 Z, 1968 D, 1979 Z
'Rockers', hooliganism by, 1964 C, E
Rockets:
  artillery, 1805 P
  ballistic, 1959 F
  German V2, 1942 P, 1944 J, 1945 C
  pilotless, 1946 P
  space, 1958 P, 1959 P, 1963 P
  See also under Atomic weapons; Aviation
Rockingham, marquess of. *See* Watson-Wentworth
Roderick Hudson (H. James), 1876 U
Rodesian Front. *See under* Political Parties
Rodgers, Richard, Am. musician (1902–79), 1902 Z, 1943 W, 1979 Z
Rodgers, William Thomas, Lord Rodgers, B. Labour/SDP/Liberal Democrat politician (b. 1928), 1981 A
Rodin, Auguste, F. sculptor (1840–1917), 1840 Z, 1864 S, 1877 S, 1879 S, 1884 S, 1898 S, 1900 S, 1902 S
Rodney, George Brydges, B. admiral (1719–92), 1780 A, D, 1782 D
Rodríguez, General Andrés, President of Paraguay (b. 1924), 1989 B
Roebuck, John, B. chemist and inventor (1718–94), 1794 Z
Roeg, Nicolas Jack, B. film director (b. 1928), 1973 W
Roehan, Ernst, G. Politician, executed, 1934 F
Rogers, Ginger (born Virginia Katherine McMath), Am. actress and dancer (b. 1911), 1935 W
Rogers, Samuel, B. poet (1763–1855), 1792 U
Rogers, Sir Richard George, B. architect (b. 1933), 1933 Z, 1977 S, 1982 S, 1985 S, 1986 S
Rogue Herries (H. Walpole), 1930 U
Rohan, Louis René Edouard de, F. Cardinal Archbishop of Strasbourg (1734–1803), 1785 H
Rohe, Ludwig, Mies van der, Am. architect (1886–1969), 1958 S, 1963 S
Rohilkland (now Bareilly), India, 1774 D
Rohillas, tribe of Afghan marauders, 1774 D
Roi s'amuse, Le (V. Hugo), 1832 W
Rokeby Venus (of Velázquez), damaged by Suffragettes, 1914 C
Roland de la Platière, Jean Marie, F. Girondin leader (1734–93), 1792 L
Roland, Manon Jean, F. author (1754–93), 1793 U
Rolf Krage (J. Ewald), 1770 W
Roll-film, celluloid 1889 P
Rolland, Romain, F. author (1866–1944), 1866 Z, 1904 U, 1943 U, 1944 Z
Roller-bearings, 1910 P
Rolling Stones, The, B. pop group, 1968 W, 1972 W
Rolling-mill, steam, 1790 P
Rolls Royce Ltd, 1970 L
  nationalization of divisions, 1971 B
Rolls-Royce motor company, 1904 P
'Rolls, Series', of Chronicles and Memorials of the Middle Ages, 1857 Q
Romagna, Italy, 1797 B, G, 1801 G
Romains, Jules, F. author (1885–1972), 1932 U
Roman alphabet, Turkey adopts, 1928 L
Roman Britain (P. Salway), 1981 Q
Roman Catholicism. *See* Religious Denominations
Roman Constitutional Law (T. Mommsen), 1871 Q
Roman d'un jeune homme pauvre (O. Feuillet), 1858 U
Roman de l'énergie nationale, Le (M. Barrès), 1897 U
Roman History (B. Niebuhr), 1811 Q
Roman Law, in Canada, 1774 D
Roman Republic established, 1798 B, 1849 B
Roman Russe, Le (E. Vogué), 1886 U
Roman, Petre, Prime Minister of Roumania (b. 1946), 1991 J
Romances sans Paroles (P. Verlaine), 1874 U
Romanenko, Yuri V., R. cosmonaut (b. 1944), 1987 P
Romanes Lectures, at Oxford, notable, 1892 Q, 1958 S
Romanes, George John, Can. scientist (1848–94), 1878 R, 1888 R, 1892 R
Romans in Britain, The (H. Brenton), 1980 W
Romanset language, 1937 O
Romantic Movement in England, 1765 U, 1800 U
Romany Rye, The (G. Borrow), 1857 U
Romanzero (H. Heine), 1851 U
Rome, Italy:
  French take, 1798 B
  Republic established, 1798 B
  Ferdinand IV enters, 1798 L
  French recapture, 1798 M
  French occupation, 1808 B
  restoration of art treasures to, 1815 S
  Republic proclaimed, 1849 E
  French troops restore Pius IX, 1849 G
  Pius IX revokes constitution, 1850 D
  French garrison in, 1850 D
  Italy renounces claim on, 1864 J
  Garibaldi's march on, 1867 K
  Italian troops enter, 1870 H
  becomes capital of Italy, 1870 K
  Conference of criminal anthropologists at, 1887 O
  Mussolini's march on, 1922 K
  Conference on Immigration, 1924 E
  Protocol, Italy with Austria and Hungary, 1934 C
  Pact, between Italy, Austria and Hungary, 1936 C
  Air raids on, 1943 G
  Fifth Army enters, 1944 F
  Conference of EDC foreign ministers, 1953 B
  Treaties, for Common Market and Euratom, 1957 C
  Olympic Games at, 1960 X
  summit to discuss pollution, 1969 P
  Arab terrorists attack airport, 1973 M
  Pope John Paul II wounded in assassination attempt, 1981 E
  Mass for Peace celebrated, 1982 E
  European Community summit, 1990 K
Rome, Italy, buildings and institutions in:
  Archaeological Institute, 1829 Q
  Braccio Nuova, Vatican Museum, 1817 S
  Catacombs, The, 1864 Q
  International Agricultural Institute, 1905 O
  Palazzo dello Sport, 1956 S
  Pio-Clementiano Museum, 1769 Q
  Railway Station, 1950 S
  Vatican Audience Hall, 1971 S
  Vatican Library, discovery in, 1819 Q
Rome de L'Isle, Jean Baptiste Louis, F, mineralogist (1736–90), 1772 P
Romeril, John, Austral. playwright (b. 1945), 1974 W
Romero, Oscar Arnulfo, El Salvadorean Archbishop (1917–80), 1980 C
Rommel, Erwin, G. general (1891–1944), 1941 B, D; retreats in, N. Africa, 1941 M; new offensives, 1942 A, E; takes Tobruk, 1942 F; retreats after El Alamein, 1942 L; replaced by von Arnim, 1943 D
Romney, George, B. artist (1734–1802), 1775 S
Roncalli, Angelo, It. Cardinal (1881–1963), elected Pope John XXII, 1958 K. *See also under* John XXIII
Röntgen, Wilhelm, G. Physicist (1845–1923), 1895 P
Room Temperature (N. Baker), 1990 U
Room With a View, A (E. M. Forster), 1908 U
Room at the Top (J. Braine), 1957 U
Room of One's Own (V. Woolf), 1929 U
Roon, Albert von, Prussian minister of war, 1859 M
Roosevelt, Anna Eleanor, Am., wife of F. D. Roosevelt, chairman of UNESCO Commission on human rights (1884–1962), 1962 Z
Roosevelt, Franklin Delano, Am. statemen, Democrat (1882–1945), 32nd president of US (1933–45), 1882 Z, 1934 F, 1941 O
  nominated vice-president, 1920 G
  asks Hitler and Mussolini for assurances against aggression, 1932 D
  elected president, 1932 L
  inauguration, 1933 C
  New Deal, 1933 C, 1937 J
  Congress grants wide powers to, 1933 C
  opposes currency stabilization, 1933 F
  signs Social Security Act, 1935 H
  re-elected, 1936 L
  signs Neutrality Act, 1937 E
  defence budget, 1939 A
  'Cash and Carry' bill, 1939 L
  re-elected, 1940 L
  sends Lend-Lease bill to Congress, 1941 A
  meets Churchill in W. Atlantic, 1941 H
  vetoes anti-strike act, 1943 G
  at Quebec Conference, 1943 H
  at Cairo Conference, 1943 L
  at Teheran Conference, 1943 L
  at Yalta Conference, 1945 B
  death, 1945 D
Roosevelt, Theodore, Am. stateman, Republican (1859–1919), 26th president of US (1901–9), 1859 Z, 1900 F, 1902 F, 1907 F, 1919 Z

succeeds as president on McKinley's death, 1901 J
ends coal strike, 1902 K
re-elected, 1904 L
mediates between Russia and Japan, 1905 J
intervenes in Cuba, 1906 B
on 'the New Nationalism', 1910 H
proposes new Progressive Republican Party, 1912 F, H
as author, 1914 Q
declines nomination, 1916 F
Root, Elihu, Am. lawyer and statesman (1845–1937), 1845 Z, 1917 F, 1937 Z
Roots (A. Haley), 1976 U
Roots (A. Wesker), 1959 W
Roots, television programme, 1977 W
Rope Dancer Accompanies Herself with Her Shadow, The, 1916 S
Roper, Lyndal Anne, Austral.-born B. historian (b. 1956), 1989 Q
Roquebrune, France, purchased from Monaco, 1862 B
Rorty, Richard Mckay, Am. philosopher (b. 1931), 1979 R, 1980 R, 1982 R
Rosas, Juan de, Argent. dictator, 1835 N, 1852 B
Rose and the Ring, The (W. M. Thackeray), 1855 U
Rosebery, Lord. *see* Primrose, Archibald
Rosenberg, Arthur, G. author, 1930 O
Rosenbergs, Am. atomic spies (Julius, 1918–53; Ethel, 1915–53), 1953 F
Rosencrantz and Guildenstern are Dead (T. Stoppard), 1967 W
Rosmersholm (H. Ibsen), 1886 W
Ross (T. Rattigan), 1960 W
Ross, Sir James Clark, B. admiral and explorer (1800–62), 1841 P
Ross, Sir John, B. Arctic navigator (1777–1856), 1818 P
Ross, Mrs. Nellie Tayloe of Wyoming (1876–1977), Am. first woman governor of a state, 1925 A
Ross, Sir Ronald, B. discoverer of the mosquito cycle in malaria (1857–1932), 1857 Z, 1879 P, 1932 Z
Rossellini, Roberto, It. film director (1906–77), 1945 W, 1946 W
Rossen, Robert, Am. film director (1908–66), 1949 W
Rossetti, Dante Gabriel, B. artist and poet (1828–82), 1828 Z, 1882 Z
as artist, 1848 S, 1863 S
as poet, 1870 U, 1881 U
Rossi, Aldo, It. architect (b. 1931), 1979 S
Rossi, Michele de, It. archaeologist, 1864 Q
Rossini, Gioacchino, It. musician (1792–1868), 1792 Z, 1810 T, 1812 R, 1813 T, 1816 T, 1817 T, 1818 T, 1828 T, 1829 T, 1841 T, 1868 Z
Rossiter, Clinton, Am. political scientist, 1956 O
Rostand, Edmond, F. author (1868–1918), 1868 Z, 1879 U, 1900 U, 1918 Z
Rostock, Germany, rioting at reception centre for asylum seekers, 1992 H
Rostov on Don, Russia: Germans evacuate, 1941 L; Germans take, 1942 G; Russians recapture, 1943 B
Rostovziev, M., R. later Am. historian (1870–1952), 1926 Q
Roth, Philip, Am. author (b. 1933), 1933 Z, 1969 U, 1979 U
Rothamsted, Herts., England, experimental plant station at, 1843 P
Rothenstein, Sir William, B. artist (1872–1945), 1917 S, 1924 S
Rothermere, lord. *See* Harmsworth, Harold
Rothière, La, France, battle, 1814 B
Rothko, Marc (born Marcus Rothkovitch), Latvian-born, Am. artist (1903–70), 1903 Z, 1958 S, 1970 Z
Rothschild, lord. *See* Meyer, Nathan
Rôtisserie de la Reine Pédauque (A. France), 1893 U
Rotocycle, invented, 1958 P
Rouaud, Jean, author, 1991 U
Rouault, Georges, F. artist (1871–1958), 1906 S, 1916 S, 1925 S, 1938 S
Rouge et le Noir, Le (Stendhal), 1830 U
Rouget de Lisel, Claude Joseph, F. author (1760–1836), 1792 T, 1915 T
Rougon-Macquart, Les, series of novels (E. Zola), 1871 U
Roumania:
created by unification of Moldavia and Wallachia, 1861 M
monarchy in, 1866 B
Russians invade, 1877 D
declares war on Turkey, 1877 E
to be independent, 1878 C, G
union with Transylvania proclaimed, 1918 L
Russia invades, 1940 F
asks for German protection, 1940 G
Russians enter, 1944 D, H
armistice with Russia, 1944 J
Soviet invasion of Czechoslovakia condemned, 1968 H
Brezhnev doctrine refuted, 1969 B
extensive flood damage, 1970 E
earthquake, 1977 D
state of emergency declared, 1989 M
Revolution, 1989 M, R
National Salvation Front, 1989 M
reforms and free elections promised, 1989 M
elections, 1990 E, 1992 K
anti-government demonstrations, 1990 F
Socialist Party of Labour, 1990 L
miners riot demanding higher wages, 1991 J
government resigns, 1991 J
local elections, 1992 B
one-party rule ended, 1992 B
Round the World in Eighty Days, television series, 1989 W
Rousseau, Henri, F. artist (1844–1910), 1904 S, 1905 S, 1907 S, 1909 S 1910 S
Rousseau, Jean Jacques, F. philosopher (1712–78), 1763 O, 1767 T, 1781 U, 1778 Z
Rousseau, Pierre Etienne Théodore, F. artist (1812–1867), 1831 S
Roussel, Albert, F. musician (1869–1937), 1917 T, 1923 T, 1928 T
Roussillon, S. France, Spain invades, 1793 C
Rouvier, Maurice, F. Republican (1842–1930), 1887 E, 1905 E
Rover car group, sale to British Aerospace, 1988 C
Rowing:
Oxford and Cambridge Boat Race, 1829 X
Henley Royal Regatta, 1839 X
Cambridge sinks during University Boat Race, 1978 X
Henley Royal Regatta, 1979 X
Cambridge collides with stationary barge before University Boat Race, 1984 X
Cambridge wins University Boat Race, 1986 X
Rowland, Roland W. ('Tiny', born R.W. Fuhrhop), Ind.-born B. businessman (b. 1917), 1981 V
Rowlandson, Thomas, B. artist and caricaturist (1756–1827), 1784 S
Rowling, Sir Wallace, Prime Minister of New Zealand (b. 1927), 1974 H
Rowntree, Joseph, B. manufacturer and philanthropist, 1836 Z, 1925 Z
Rowntree, Seebohm B., B. chocolate manufacturer and sociologist (1871–1954), 1901 O, 1937 O, 1941 O, 1947 O
Rowse, Alfred Leslie, B. historian (b. 1903), 1950 Q
Roy Ladurie, Emmanuel Le, F. historian (b. 1929), 1966 Q
Royal Academy of Music, London, founded, 1861 T
Royal Academy, London, founded, 1768 S
Royal Dutch Shell Oil Group, formed, 1907 O
operations in Indonesia, banned, 1958 F
Royal Flying Corps, formed, 1912 O; replaced by Royal Air Force, 1918 D
Royal Historical Society, founded, 1868 Q
Royal Hunt of the Sun, The (P. Shaffer), 1964 W
Royal Institute, The, founded, 1799 P
Royal Literary Fund, founded, 1790 U
Royal Marriage Act, in Britain, 1772 C
Royal Niger Company, British, 1886 G
Royal Shakespeare Company (RSC), 1982 W
London theatres closed temporarily, 1990 W
Royal Society, sponsors board of scientific studies, 1916 P
committee on emigration of scientists, 1963 B
Royalists. *See under* Political Parties
Royce, Sir Frederick Henry, B. automobile engineer (1863–1933), 1863 Z, 1933 Z
Royden, Agnes Maude (Mrs. G. W. H. Shaw), B. Congregational minister (1876–1956), 1917 R
Rozewicz, Tadeusz, Pol. playwright (b. 1921), 1975 W
Rrrrrr.... (M. Kagel), 1982 T
Ruanda, East Africa: is ceded to Britain, 1921 C; republic proclaimed, 1961 A; UN calls for elections, 1961 D; independence, 1962 G
Rubaiyát of Omar Khayyam (E. Fitzgerald), 1859 U
Rubber Ring Floating in a Swimming Pool (D. Hockney), 1971 S
Rubber production, comparative statistics, 1911 Y, 1957 Y
Rubber tyre, 1888 P
Rubber, synthetic, 1902 Y, 1931 P
production, comparative statistics, 1944 Y, 1957 Y
Rubber, vulcanised, 1839 P
Rubbra, Edmund, B. musician (1901–86), 1942 T, 1949 T, 1954 T, 1986 Z
Rubella vaccine developed, 1966 P
Rubidium, an element, is isolated, 1861 P
Rubinstein, Artur, Pol.-born Am. pianist (1887–1982), 1887 Z, 1937 T, 1982 Z
Ruby, Jack, Am. strip-tease parlour proprietor, shoots Kennedy's assassin, 1963 L
Ruckert, Friedrich, G. poet (1788–1866), 1814 U
Rudin (I. Turgeniev), 1855 U
Rudini, Antonio Starabba, marquis di, It. statesman (1839–1908), 1896 C, 1891 A, 1892 E, 1898 F
Rudolf, Crown Prince, Archduke of Austria (1857–1889), 1889 A
Ruff's Guide to the Turf, 1842 X
Rug, The (P. Guston), 1979 S
Rugby Football, 1924 X
British Lions win Test series in New Zealand, 1971 X
British Lions win first Test series in South Africa, 1974 X
New Zealand tour of South Africa, 1976 X
Wales wins Triple Crown and Five Nations Championship, 1979 X
Rugby League
Australian tour of Britain and France, 1982 X

Runcorn Highfield win match after 75 matches without victory 1991 X
Rugby, Warwickshire, England, School, under Arnold, 1828 O
Rügen, E. Germany: French occupation, 1812 A; Prussians enter, 1814 A; ceded to Prussia, 1815 F
Ruggiero, Guido de, It. philosopher, 1947 R
Ruhr, Germany: German evacuation, demanded, 1920 D; French occupation, 1921 C, E, J; Franco-Belgian occupation, 1923 A; evacuation, 1924 L, H; bombing, 1943 D, E; International Authority constituted, 1948 M, Germany joins, 1949 L
Ruines, ou méditations sur les révolutions des empires, Les (C. Volney), 1791 Q
Rulers, Townsmen and Bazaars: North Indian Society in the Age of British Expansionism, 1770–1870 (C.A. Bayly), 1983 Q
Ruling Class, The (P. Barnes), 1968 W
Rumelia, Eastern, 1878 G; disturbances in, 1885 J, L, 1886 D, E
Rumford, Count. *See* Thompson, Benjamin
Run From Fear / Fun From Rear (B. Nauman), 1972 S
Runaway Soul, The (H. Brodkey), 1992 U
Runcie, Robert Alexander Kennedy, Lord Runcie, B. churchman, (b. 1921), 1921 Z, 1979 R, 1982 G
Runciman, Sir Stephen, B. historian (b. 1903), 1951 Q, 1955 Q, 1958 Q
Runciman, Walter, viscount Runciman, B. Liberal National (1870–1949), visits Prague, 1938 G
Runge, Philipp Otto, G. artist (1777–1810), 1805 S
Running Fence (Christo), 1976 S
Runyon, Alfred Damon, Am. author and journalist, 1884 Z, 1946 Z
R.U.R. (Capek), 1923 W
Rural Rides (W. Cobbett), 1830 U
Rural credits, US, 1916 O
Rush–Bagot agreement, 1817 D
Rushdie, (Ahmed) Salman, Ind.-born B. author (b. 1947), 1947 Z, 1981 U, 1983 U, 1988 U
  fatwa issued against, 1989 B, 1989 O
  Iran breaks off diplomatic relations with Britain over Rushdie affair, 1989 C, 1990 J
Rusk, Dean, Am. diplomat (b. 1909), 1909 Z, 1966 B
Ruskin, John, B. author, artist and social reformer (1819–1900), 1819 Z, 1900 Z; as author, 1865 U, 1871 O; as artist, 1843 S, 1849 S, 1851 S, 1919 S; Whistler's libel action against, 1878 S
Ruslan and Ludmila (A. Pushkin), 1820 U
Russell, Bertrand Arthur William, third Earl Russell, B. philosopher (1871–1970), 1872 Z, 1900 R, 1910 R, 1914 R, 1918 R, 1921 O, 1927 R, 1934 O, 1946 R, 1949 O, 1970 Z
  Bertrand Russell International War Crimes Tribunal, 1967 E
Russell, Conrad Sebastian Robert, fifth Earl Russell, B. historian and Liberal Democrat politician (b. 1937), 1990 Q, 1991 Q
Russell, Francis, fifth duke of Bedford, B. Whig (1765–1805), 1796 O
Russell, George William, B. poet under pseudonym 'AE' (1867–1935), 1867 Z, 1901 U, 1935 Z
Russell, John, duke of Bedford, B. Whig politician (1710–71), 1763 R
Russell, Ken, B. film director (b. 1927), 1969 W
Russell, lord John, B. Whig-Liberal statesman (1792–1878), 1792 Z, 1845 M, 1864 D, 1878 Z
  campaigns for Parliamentary Reform, 1819 M, 1821 E, 1831 C
  William IV refuses his appointment as leader of Commons, 1834 L
  is converted to free trade, 1845 L
  becomes prime minister, 1846 F
  resigns, but returns to premiership, 1851 B
  resigns, 1852 B
  forms second ministry, 1865 K
  resigns, 1866 F
Russia (R. Cobden), 1835 O
Russia (Union of Soviet Socialist Republics):
  intrigues in Poland, 1767 D, 1768 H
  share in first partition of Poland, 1772 H
  acquires Oldenburg, 1773 K
  acquires the Crimea and mouth of R. Dnieper, 1774 G
  Russia plans to restore Greek empire, 1781 B
  share in second partition of Poland, 1793 A, E
  share in third partition of Poland, 1795 H, K
  Russia America Company, 1799 O
  frontier treaty with US, over Alaska, 1824 D
  USSR recognised as a 'great power', 1922 D
  Union is formally established, 1923 A
  Britain recognises USSR, 1924 B
  US recognises USSR, 1933 L
  Germany invades, 1941 F
  Chinese students expelled, 1966 K
  50th anniversary of Bolshevik Revolution celebrated, 1967 L
  political dissent, 1968 A
  bomb explosion at Soviet embassy in US, 1968 B
  West German talks on mutual renunciation of force, 1969 M
  celebrates Lenin's centenary, 1970 D
  Soviet–West German treaty on mutual renunciation of force, 1970 H, 1972 E
  ninth Five Year Plan, 1971 B
  population, 1971 Y, 1991 Y
  Iraqi treaty of friendship and co-operation, 1972 D
  Nixon visits, 1972 E
  US treaty limiting anti-ballistic missile sites, 1972 E
  Politburo reshuffle, 1973 D
  Politburo exhorts Polish government to adhere to Leninist principles, 1981 H
  population, 1981 Y
  Sino–Soviet talks, 1982 L, 1983 C
  US grain sales to, 1983 D
  US ban on export of pipe-laying equipment to, lifted, 1983 H
  cotton production, 1984 Y
  urbanization, 1985 Y
  Communist Party Central Committee membership changes, 1986 C
  Politburo membership changes, 1986 C
  Helsinki talks on plight of Soviet Jews, 1986 H
  140 political dissidents released, 1987 B
  multi-candidate lists in local elections, 1987 F
  1,000 years of Christianity in Russia celebrated, 1988 F
  major changes in Politburo, 1988 J
  victims of Stalinist purges rehabilitated, 1989 A, 1990 H
  elections to Congress of People's Deputies, 1989 C
  human chain in Baltic republics marks 50th anniversary of USSR–German non-aggression pact, 1989 H
  strikes in key industries banned, 1989 K
  ethnic composition, 1989 Y
  Central Committee of Communist Party votes to end Party's monopoly on power, 1990 B
  Gorbachev sworn in as first executive president, 1990 C
  opposition demonstrations disrupt May Day parade, 1990 E
  first official British royal visit since 1917 Revolution, 1990 E
  Russian Federation declared sovereign state, 1990 F
  Yeltsin and others resign from Communist Party, 1990 G
  citizenship restored to exiled dissidents, 1990 H
  emergency powers granted to Gorbachev, 1990 L
  US airlift of food to, 1990 L
  referendum on proposed renewed federation, 1991 C
  coup against Gorbachev, 1991 H
  Communist Party suspended and assets seized, 1991 H
  government dismissed, 1991 H
  KGB collegium disbanded, 1991 H
  central government suspended, 1991 J
  Commonwealth of Independent States (CIS) founded, 1991 M
  USSR officially ceases to exist, 1991 M
  illegitimacy rate, 1991 Y
  religious affiliations, 1991 Y
  Black Sea fleet divided with Ukraine, 1992 A
  price controls lifted, 1992 A
  Russia and Ukraine agree on joint control of Black Sea fleet, 1992 H
  merchant shipping tonnage statistics, 1992 Y
Russia America Company, 1799 O
Russia at War (A. Werth), 1964 Q
Russian Federation:
  presidential elections, 1990 E
  declared sovereign state, 1990 F
  Yeltsin elected leader, 1991 F
Russian literature, introduced to England, 1821 U
Russophobia:
  in Britain, 1835 O, 1838 K, 1878 A, C, F, 1904 K, 1923 E. *See also* Wars, Crimean War
  in Germany, 1770 J, 1771 G, 1772 H, 1882 B, 1888 B
  in Roumania, 1883 K
Rust, Mathias, G. aviator (b. 1968), lands in Moscow's Red Square, 1987 E
Rutan, Richard Glenn, 'Dick', Am. aviator (b. 1938), 1986 P
Ruthenia: annexed by Hungary, 1939 C; ceded to Russia, 1945 F
Rutherford, Ernest, lord Rutherford, B. scientist (1871–1937), 1871 Z, 1896 P, 1904 P, 1911 P, 1919 P, 1921 P, 1937 Z
Rutherford, John, B. physician (1695–1779), 1772 P
'Rutherford, Mark,' *See* White, W. H.
Ruy Blas (V. Hugo), 1838 U
Rwanda, Ugandan invasion, 1990 K
Ryan, Michael, B. gunman, Hungerford shootings, 1987 H
Rybakov, Anatoli Naumovich, R. author (b. 1911), 1988 U
Ryga, George, Canad. dramatist (1932–87), 1967 W
Rykoff, Alexei, R. politician (1881–1938), 1924 B
Ryle, Gilbert, B. philosopher (1900–76), 1900 Z, 1950 R, 1954 R, 1976 Z
Ryle, Sir Martin, B. astronomer (1918–84), 1918 Z, 1961 P, 1984 Z
Ryumin, Valery V., R. cosmonaut, 1979 P, 1980 P

S

Saar, The, Germany:
League of Nations takes over, 1920 B
last Allied troops leave, 1930 M
plebiscite for incorporation in Germany, 1935 A
restored to Germany, 1935 C
autonomy of, 1950 C
crisis over administration of, 1952 A
Franco–German agreement on, 1956 K
incorporated in W. German economic system, 1959 G
Saarinen, Eero, Am. architect (1910–61), 1955 S, 1956 S, 1958 S, 1961 S
Sabbatarianism in England, 1835 R
Sabri el Assali, Syrian leader, 1954 B
Saburov, Pierre Alexandrovich, R. diplomat, 1879 K
Sachs, Julius Wilhelm, G. botanist (1832–97), 1862 P
Sacks, Dr. Jonathan, B. Chief Rabbi (b. 1948), 1991 R
Sackville-West, Victoria Mary, B. author (1892–1964), 1931 U
Sacred Heart, celebration of, sanctioned, 1766 R
Sacrilege, made a capital offence in France, 1825 O
Sadi-Carnot, Marie François, F. statesman (1837–1894), elected president of France, 1887 M; assassinated, 1894 F
Sadie, Stanley John, B. musicologist (b. 1930), 1980 Q
Sadleir, Michael, B. author and publisher (1888–1957), 1940 U
Sadowa, Czech Republic, Austria, battle, 1866 G
Sadras, Madras, India, battle, 1782 B
Safety legislation in factories, earliest, 1802 O
Safety-match, invented, 1898 P
Sagan, Françoise, *See* Quoirez, Françoise
Sagerre (P. Verlaine), 1881 U
Saghalein, Russia, Japanese evacuate, 1925 D
Sahara, N. Africa: exploration, 1869 P; concessions to France in, 1899 C; French company to exploit resources, 1957 C; methane from, 1961 P; Sahel-Benin Union formed, 1959 D
Sahara, Western, N. Africa
Spain, Morroco and Mauritania agree to pull out, 1975 L
unarmed Morrocan invasion of Spanish, 1975 L
Polisario Front, 1976 B, 1979 H
chiefs vote for union with Morroco, 1976 B
declared independent by Polisario Front, 1976 B
divided between Morroco and Mauritania, 1976 D
Sa'id el-Mufti, Jordan leader, 1955 E, 1956 E
Said Pasha, premier of Persia, 1912 G
Said Zaghlul Pasha, Egypt-Nationalist, deposed, 1919 C
Saigon, Viet Nam: treaty between France and Annam, 1862 F; becomes capital, 1949 F; headquarters of Armistice Commission wrecked, 1955 G; riots in, 1964 L; bomb explodes in US embassy in, 1965 C
anti-government protests, 1966 D
Sailing:
solo round-the-world voyages, 1967 X, 1978 X
first single-handed round-the-world yacht race, 1969 X
America's Cup won by Australia, 1983 X
Sailor who fell from Grace with the Sea, The (Y. Mishima), 1966 U
Sainsbury Centre, University of East Anglia, 1978 S
St. Aldwyn, earl. *See* Hicks-Beach, M.E.
St. Andrews, Fife, Scotland, Royal and Ancient Golf Club, 1834 X
St. Bernard Pass, Great, Switzerland, Napoleon's army crosses, 1800 E
St. Christopher (or St Kitts), Island, W. Indies, 1782 B
St. Claire Deville, Etienne Henri, F. chemist (1818–1881), 1855 P
St. Elsewhere, television programme, 1982 W
St. Eustacius, Island, W. Indies, 1781 L
St. Exupéry, Antoine de, F. author (1900–44), 1929 U, 1931 U
St. Germain, France, Treaty of, Allies with Austria, 1919 J, 1920 G
Austria ratifies, 1919 K
St. George and the Dragon (T. Cragg), 1984 S
St. Gotthard tunnel, through Alps, 1882 P
St. Helena, Napoleon banished to, 1815 H
Saint Jean, General Alfredo, President of Argentina, 1982 F
St. Joan (G. B. Shaw), 1924 W
St. John-Stevas, Norman Antony Francis, Lord St John, B. Conservative politician and author (b. 1927), 1956 O, 1981 A, 1986 Q
St. Juan, N. W. America, adjudication over, 1872 K
St. Julien, France, battle, 1915 D
St. Just, Antoine Louis Léon de Richebourg de, F. revolutionary (1767–94), 1793 G, 1794 G
St. Kitts. *See* St Christopher
St. Kitts–Nevis Islands, W. Indies, independence, 1983 J
St. Lambert, Jean François de. F. poet (1716–1803), 1768 U, 1798 U
St. Laurent, Louis Stephen, Can. Liberal (1882–1973), 1957 F
St. Lawrence River, Canada, improvements to, 1847 P
St. Lawrence Seaway, N. America, 1954 E, 1959 F
St. Leger, Anthony, B. soldier and sportsman, 1776 X
St. Louis, Missouri, US: Populist Party founded at, 1892 B:democratic convention at, 1916 F
Pruitt Igoe housing blocks destroyed, 1971 S
Washington University School of Medicine, 1980 P
St. Lucia Bay, S. Africa, annexed by Britain to Natal, 1884 L
St. Lucia, W. Indies: restored to France, 1763 B; Britain captures, 1778 L; France recovers, 1783 J; changes hands in Napoleonic wars, 1794N, 1795 F, 1796 N, 1803 F; independence, 1979 B
St. Martin, Louis Claude de, F. philosopher (1743–1803), 1775 R
St. Mihiel, France. US offensive at, 1918 J
St. Nazaire, France, Britain raids, 1942 C
St. Petersburg (later Leningrad), Russia:
monument to Peter the Great, 1766 S
Alliance, Allies against France, 1794 J
Treaty, 1801 F
Bourse, 1804 S
Alliance between Britain and Russia to liberate N. Germany, 1805 D
Austria joins, 1805 H
Theological Seminary founded, 1809 R
St. Isaac's Cathedral, 1817 S
Protocol, between Britain and Russia over Greek independence, 1826 D
docks in, electrically lit, 1872 P
Treaty, China with Russia, 1881 B
population, 1881 Y, 1906 Y
revolution in, 1905 A
first Soviet formed in, 1905 K
name changed to Petrograd, 1914 J
name reverts from Leningrad to, 1991 K
See also Leningrad
Saint Phalle, Niki de, F. artist (b. 1930), 1983 S
St. Pierre, Jacques Henri Bernardin de, F. author (1737–1814), 1784 R, 1789 U
St. Privat, Corrèze, France, French defeat at, 1870 H
St. Quentin, Aisne, France: French defeat at, 1871 A; French take, 1918 K
St. Saëns, Charles Camille, F. musician (1835–1921), 1835 Z, 1871 T, 1877 T, 1921 Z
Saint Simon, Claude Henri de Rouvray, comte de, F. Socialist (1760–1825), 1807 O, 1821 O, 1823 O, 1825 R
St. Vincent, Cape, Portugal, naval battles, 1780 A, 1797 B
St Vincent, Island, in Windward Islands: ceded to Britain, 1763 B; French capture, 1779 F; independence, 1979 K
Saint's Day (J. Whitney), 1951 W
Sainte-Beuve, Charles Augustin, F. author (1804–1869), 1804 Z, 1829 U, 1840 U, 1849 U, 1869 Z
Saints, The Battle of the, off Dominica, W. Indies, 1782 D
Saipan, Island, Marianas, Pacific, US take, 1944 F
Saison en Enfer, Une (A. Rimbaud), 1873 U
Saisons, Les (J. de St. Lambert), 1768 U
Sakhalin, North, Japan, mineral concessions in, 1944 C
Sakharov, Andrei Dimitrievich, R. dissident physicist (1921–89), 1984 E, 1986 M
internal exile, 1980 A
hunger strike, 1981 M
Sakkaria, Turkey, battle, 1921 H
Sakuntalà (trans. W. Jones), 1789 Q
Salacrou, Armand, F. dramatist (1895–1989), 1936 W
Salam, Abdus, Pak. physicist (b. 1926), 1967 P
Salamanca, Danielo, president of Bolivia (1869–1935), 1934 M
Salamanca, Spain, Wellington's victory, 1812 G
Salammbô (G. Flaubert), 1862 U
Salan, Raoul, F. Algerian rebel, leader of O.A.S. (1899–1984), 1958 M, 1961 D, 1962 D
Salazar, Antonio de Oliviera, Portuguese dictator (1889–1970), 1889 Z, 1928 D, 1945 K, L, 1953 L, 1968 J, 1970 Z ; elected premier, 1932 G
Salbai, Madras, India, Treaty of, 1782 E
Sale of St. Thomas (L. Abercrombie), 1931 U
Salerno, Italy, Allied landings at, 1943 J
Salic Law: in Hanover, 1837 F; in Spain, abrogated, 1830 C
Salieri, Antonio, It. musician (1750–1825), 1784 T
Salinas de Gortari, Carlos, President of Mexico (b. 1948), 1988 G
Salinger, Jerome David, Am. author (b. 1919), 1951 U, 1961 U
Salisbury, Rhodesia: founded, 1890 J; riots in, 1964 A
British–Rhodesian talks, 1966 E
Salk, Jonas Edward, Am. scientist (b. 1914), 1914 Z, 1955 P
Salle, David, Am. artist (b. 1952), 1981 S
Sallinen, Aulis Heikki, Fin. musician (b. 1935), 1975 T, 1984 T, 1992 T
Salonika, Macedonia, Greece: railway to, proposed, 1908 A; Allied landings, 1915 K; Venizelos government at, 1916 K
Salt Lake City, Utah, US, 1847 R
Salt Water Ballads (J. Masefield), 1902 U
Saltash, Cornwall, bridge, 1853 P
Salvarsan, prepared, 1909 P
Salvation Army, 1865 R, 1878 R, 1981 R
Salway, Peter, B. historian, 1981 Q
Salzburg, Austria: archbishopric of, Austrian designs on, 1797 K; Austria cedes to Bavaria, 1809 K; plebiscite favours union with

Germany, 1921 E; Mozart Festival, 1906 T, 1946 T
Salzedo, Leonard Lopes, Am. choreographer (b. 1921), 1958 T
Samarkand, Uzbek, Russia, occupied by Russians, 1868 E
Samoa (formerly Navigator's Isles), S. W. Pacific: US treaty with, 1878 A; commercial treaty with Germany, 1879 A; King of, recognised by powers, 1880 C; Washington Conference on, 1887 F; unrest in 1927 G; Anglo-German settlement on, 1899 L; West Samoa becomes independent, 1962 A
Samphan, Khieu, Cambodian head of state (b. 1932), 1976 D
Sampson, Anthony, B. journalist (b. 1926), 1962 O
Sampson, Nicos, Cypriot leader (b. 1935), 1974 G
Samsonov, Sergei, R. film director, 1955 W
Samuel, Herbert, viscount Samuel, B. Liberal statesman (1870–1963), 1870 Z, 1932 J, 1963 Z
San Domingo, East Hispaniola, W. Indies: part ceded to France, 1795; independent republic established, 1821 M; annexed by Spain, 1861 C; revolt in, 1865 E
San Francisco Polyphony (G. Ligeti), 1974 T
San Francisco, US , UN Conference at, 1945 D
race riots. 1966 J
Hyatt Regency Hotel, 1970 S
Roman Catholic Cathedral, 1970 S
earthquake, 1989 K
San Ildefonso, Old Castile, Spain:
Treaty, Spain with France, 1796 H
Treaty, Spain with US, 1800 K
San Jacinto, Mexico, battle, 1836 D
San Salvador, El Salvador, 1980 C
rebel guerrillas win over parts of city, 1989 L
Jesuits tortured and murdered, 1989 R
San Salvador: asks for incorporation in US 1822 M; enters Central American Federation, 1823 G
San Sebastian, Spain, capitulates to Wellington, 1813 J
San Vicente province, El Salvador, anti-guerrilla campaign, 1982 J
San Vittore, Italy, US troops take, 1944 A
Sanctions:
by League of Nations against Italy, 1935 K; raised, 1936 G
Russia threatens Greece with, 1958 A
UN calls for, against S. Africa, 1963 J
against Rhodesia, 1965 L
Commonwealth calls for sanctions against Rhodesia, 1966 J
UN sanctions against Rhodesia, 1966 J, M, 1973 E
Rhodesian Sanctions Order rejected by House of Lords, 1968 F
Bingham Report on oil sanctions against Rhodesia, 1978 J
EC sanctions against Iran, 1980 E
US economic sanctions against USSR, 1981 M
EC sanctions against Argentina, 1982 D, E
US sanctions against Argentina, 1982 D
US sanctions against Poland, 1982 K, 1984 A
US sanctions against Nicaragua, 1985 E
EC sanctions against South Africa, 1985 J, 1986 J, 1992 A
international sanctions against South Africa, 1985 J, 1986 F, H, J, K, R
US sanctions against Libya, 1986 A, 1992 C
Commonwealth calls for sanctions against South Africa, 1986 F, G
US sanctions against South Africa, 1986 K
Churches support sanctions against South Africa, 1986 R
UN sanctions against Iraq, 1990 H
EC sanctions against Yugoslvia, 1991 L
UN sanctions against Libya, 1992 C
See also Embargoes
Sand Creek, Colorado, US, massacre at, 1864 L
Sand River Convention, establishing Transvaal, 1852 A; violated, 1877 D
Sand, George, pseudonym of Amandine Dudevin (née Dupin), F. author (1804–76), 1804 Z, 1832 U, 1833 U, 1846 U, 1847 U, 1859 U
Sandcastle, The (I. Murdoch), 1957 U
Sandeau, Léonard Sylvain Julien (*alias* Jules), F. novelist and dramatist (1811–83), 1854 W
Sanderson, Cobden, B. art critic (under pseudonym of 'David Gascoigne'), 1935 S
Sanderson, Stewart Forsen, B. linguistic scholar (b. 1924), 1977 Q
Sandinistas, Nicaragua, 1989 L, 1990 B
Sandoz Pharmaceuticals Inc., 1966 D
Sands, Bobby, N. Ir. IRA member (1954–81)
by-election victory, 1981 D
death causes riots, 1981 E
Sandwich Islands, S. Seas, 1775 P
Sandwich, Kent, golf course, championship at, 1934 X
Sandwich, earl of. *See* Montagu, John
Sandys, Duncan, Lord Duncan-Sandys, B. Conservative politician (1908–87), visits Cyprus, 1963 M
Sanger's Circus, 1941 W
Sanger, Frederick, B. scientist (b. 1918), 1955 P, 1977 P
Sanguinetti, Julio Maria, President of Uruguay (b. 1936), 1985 C
Sanitation, in Britain:
Chadwick's report, 1842 O
legislation, 1848 O
London's main drainage completed, 1875 P
See also Health, Public
Sanjurjo, José, Sp. general, 1932 H
Sankey, Ira David, Am. evangelist (1840–1908), 1870 R, 1873 R
Sankey, John, lord Sankey, Labour politician and lawyer (1866–1948), reports on coal industry, 1919 B
Sans-serif alphabet, Gill's, 1927 S
Sanskrit, study of, 1784 Q, 1819 Q
Santa Fé, New Mexico, US captures, 1846 H
Santander, Spain, falls to rebels, 1937 F
Santayana, George, Sp. - born Am. author (1863–1952), 1905 R, 1933 U, 1940 R
Santerno River, Italy, 8th Army reaches, 1945 D
Santiago, Chile: US Navy at, 1898 G; US marines land, 1917 C
Santis, Giuseppe de, It. film director, 1948 W
Santos, José Eduardo dos, President of Angola (b. 1942), 1979 J, 1989 F, 1991 E, 1992 L
Saône River, France, 1783 P
São Paulo, Brazil, population, 1990 Y
São Tom e Principe, independence, 1975 G
Sap, circulation of, in plants, 1846 P
Sappho (F. Grillparzer), 1818 U
Saracco, Giuseppe, It. politician, 1901 B
Saragat, Giuseppe, It. president (1898–1988), 1964 M
Sarajevo, Yugoslavia, assassination at, 1914 F
clashes between Serbs, Croats and Muslims, 1992 C
bombardment, 1992 D
Sarassin, Pote, Thai, Secretary-general of SEATO, and premier of Thailand, 1957 J
Sarawak, N.W. Borneo, British protectorate over, 1888 C
agreement to decide status by referendum, 1966 H
Sardou, Victorien, F. dramatist (1831–1908), 1882 U, 1887 W, 1891 W
Sargent, John Singer, Am. artist (1856–1925), 1856 Z, 1882 S, 1886 S, 1900 S, 1902 S, 1905 S, 1913 S, 1917 S, 1925 Z, 1926 S
Sargent, W., Am. author, 1957 O
Sarment, Jean, F. dramatist (b. 1897), 1921 W
Sarotoga, New York, British capitulate at, 1777 K
Saroyan, William, Am. author (b. 1908), 1935 U
Sarraut, Albert, F. politician (1872–1962), 1933 K, 1936 A
Sarto, Giuseppe, It. cardinal (1835–1914), elected Pope Pius X, 1903 G
Sartor Resartus (T. Carlyle), 1833 U
Sartre, Jean-Paul, F. philosopher and author (1905–80), 1905 Z, 1937 U, 1943 R, W, 1944 W, 1945 U, 1980 Z
Saskatchewan, Canada, becomes a province, 1905 J
Satanic Verses, The (S. Rushdie), 1988 U, 1989 B, 1989 O
Satellites, artificial:
Aerial, to study cosmic radiation, 1962 P
Atlas, to investigate radio relay, 1958 P
ball of copper needles in orbit, 1963 P
COBE (Cosmic Background Explorer), 1989 P
Cosmic Background Explorer (COBE), 1992 P
Discoverer, recovered, 1960 P
ERS-1, 1991 P
Early Bird, for tele-communications, 1965 P
earth's resources surveyed from space, 1972 P
Explorer I, to study cosmic rays, 1958 P
French launch first, 1965 P
Gagarin's flight, 1961 P
Hipparcos, 1989 P
Infrared Astronomical Satellite, 1983 P
Intelsat-V, 1980 P
Intelsat-VI, 1992 P
Israel launches satellite for geophysical studies, 1988 P
Japan and China launch, 1970 P
Japanese moon satellite launched, 1990 P
Landsat I, 1972 P
launching of first, anticipated, 1955 P
Mariner IV, for photographing Mars, 1964 P, 1965 P
Nimbus, for meteorological survey, 1964 P
Pioneer IV, 1959 P
radio-reflector, 1960 P
Ranger VII, for photographing moon's surface, 1964 P
satellite television, 1979 P, 1989 W
Sputnik I and II launched, 1957 P
Sputnik III launched, 1958 P
Star Wars defence system, 1983 C
Syncom, for relaying TV pictures, 1964 P
Telstar, for tele-communications, 1962 P
Vanguard I, to test solar cells, 1958 P
Zone Z, for photographing Mars, 1964 P
See also under Aviation; Rockets
Satellites, cosmic, 1789 P
Satie, Erik, F. musician (1866–1925), 1916 T, 1920 T
Sato, Eisaku, Prime Minister of Japan (1901–75), 1901 Z, 1964 J, 1972 G, 1975 Z
Sattar, Abdus, President of Bangladesh (1906–85), 1981 E
Saturn, planet, 1980 P, 1981 P
probe travels through rings of, 1979 P
additional rings discovered, 1984 P
18th moon discovered, 1990 P
Saud, King of Saudi Arabia (1905–69), 1957 D; attempted *coup* in Syria, 1958 C; takes over government, 1960 M; is deposed, 1964 L

Saudi Arabia (formerly Hejaz): name changed from Hejaz, 1926 A; independence recognised, 1927 E
hostages held by Jordanian terrorists in Paris Embassy, 1973 J
joins war against Israel, 1973 K
militants seize Grand Mosque in Mecca, 1979 L
expels British ambassador following television showing of *Death of Princess*, 1980 D
peace plan for Middle East, 1981 L
diplomatic links with Libya re-established, 1983 A
illiteracy, 1983 Y
Iranian war planes attack oil tankers, 1984 E
US missiles sent, 1984 E
pilgrims crushed to death at Mecca, 1990 R
Basic Law, 1992 O
Gulf War. *See* Wars
Saussure, Horace Bénédict de, Swi. physicist (1740–99), 1787 P, 1797 P
Savage Islands, Pacific, Britain acquires, 1899 L
Savage, Ethel. *See* Dell, Ethel M
Savage, Michael Joseph, N. Zeal. Labour leader (1872–1940), 1935 L
Savannah, Georgia, US: British capture, 1778 H; British evacuate, 1781 K; Sherman occupies, 1864 M
Savigny, Friedrich Karl von, G. jurist (1779–1861), 1779 Z, 1814 O, 1815 O
Savile, Sir George, B. politician (1726–84), 1778 E
Saville, John, B. historian (b. 1916), 1972 Q
Savimbi, Dr. Jonas, Angolan politician (b. 1934), 1989 F, 1991 E, 1992 L
Savings, National, 1916 O
Savonarole (N. Lenau), 1837 U
Savoy: serfdom abolished, 1770 O; France annexes, 1792 L; is ceded to France, 1796 E, 1860 C
Saw circular, invented, 1780 P
Sax, Antoine (*alias* Adolphe), Joseph, Belg. maker of musical instruments (1814–94), 1840 T
Saxe-Weimar, Germany, constitution in, 1816 E
Saxony, Germany: evacuated by Prussians, 1763 B; elector of, becomes King of Poland, 1791 E; becomes a Kingdom, 1866 M; King of, rules Duchy of Warsaw, 1807 G; flees, 1813 L; Prussia invades, 1866 F; cedes territory to Prussia, 1866 H
Saxophone, invented, 1840 T
Say, Jean Baptiste, F. economist (1767–1832), 1803 O
Sayers, Dorothy Leigh (Mrs. A. Fleming), B. author (1893–1957), 1893 Z, 1923 U, 1934 U, 1943 W, 1957 Z
Sayers, Tom, B. boxer (1826–65), 1860 X
Sazonov, Sergei, R. diplomat (1866–1937), 1913 L, 1916 G
Scale, twelve-tone, 1911 T
Scalfaro, Oscar Luigi, President of Italy (b. 1918), 1992 E
Scandal (E. Shusaku), 1986 U
Scandals:
in Belgium, financial corruption, 1937 K
in Britain, Lynskey tribunal investigates charges of corruption, 1948 L
Profumo affair, 1963 C, F, G, J
footballers fix match results, 1965 X
in France, trafficking in Legion of Honour medals, 1887 M
Panama, 1892 L
Dreyfus, 1894 K, 1899 J
in Italy, bank, 1893 M
in US, oil companies' leases, 1924 B
Sherman Adams affair, 1958 F
TV Quiz, 1959 W
Scandium, the element, 1879 P
Scarborough, Yorks, England, Labour Party Conference at, 1960 K
Scargill, Arthur, B. trade unionist (b. 1938), 1984 D, E, J
Scarisbrick, John Joseph, B. historian (b. 1928), 1968 Q, 1985 Q
Scarlet Letter, The (N. Hawthorne), 1850 U
Scarman, Sir Leslie George, B. judge (b. 1911), 1965 O
Scelba, Mario, It. People's Party leader, 1954 B, 1955 F
Scènes de la Vie Bohème (H. Murger), 1848 U
Scenes from Clerical Life (G. Eliot), 1857 U
Scepticism and Naturalism (P.F. Strawson), 1985 R
Schacht, Hjalmar Horace Greely, G. economist (1877–1970), 1877 Z, 1970 Z; plans to control Germany's foreign trade, 1934 O; Funk replaces him, as economics minister, 1937 L; dismissed from Reichsbank, 1939 A; Nuremberg tribunal acquits, 1946 J
Schadow, Friedrich Wilhelm, G. artist (1789–1862), 1876 S, 1842 S
Schaff, Philip, Am., formerly Swi., theologian (1819–93), 1851 R
Schama, Simon Michael, B. historian (b. 1945), 1977 Q, 1987 Q, 1989 Q
Schandorph, Sophus Christian Frederick, Dan. author (1836–1901), 1881 U
Schärf, Adolf, Aust., elected president, 1957 E
Scharnhorst, Gerhard Johann David von, Pruss. general (1755–1813), 1807 N, 1812 B
Schatz, A., Am., scientist, 1943 P
Scheele, Karl Wilhelm, Swe. chemist (1742–86), 1774 P, 1775 P, 1777 P, 1781 P, 1786 Z
Schefer, Leopold, G. Poet and novelist (1784–1862), 1834 U
Scheidermann, Philipp, G. Socialist (1865–1942), 1919 B, F
Scheldt, River, Europe: navigation of, 1783 K, 1784 K, 1785 L; is opened to commerce, 1792 L; British expedition to, 1809 D, G; agreement to open to commerce, 1839 D; Belgo–Dutch agreements on, 1919 L, 1925 D
Schelling, Friedrich Wilhelm Joseph, G. philosopher (1775–1854), 1775 Z, 1797 R, 1800 R, 1801 R, 1802 P, 1854 Z, 1856 R
Schenectady, US, atomic power station at, 1955 P
Schérer, Barthlemy Louis Joseph, F. general (1747–1804), 1795 L, 1799 D
expounds 12-tone scale, 1911 T
Schiaparelli, Giovanni Virginio, It. astronomer (1835–1910), 1889 P
Schick, Bela, Hun. scientist (b. 1877), 1913 P
Schiller, Friedrich, G. author (1759–1805), as dramatist, 1781 W, 1784 W, 1787 W, 1799 W, 1800 W, 1801 W, 1804 W
other works, 1788 Q, 1789 U, 1794 U, 1795 U, 1803 U
bust of, 1794 S
death, 1805 Z
Schindler's Ark (T. Keneally), 1982 U
Schinkel, Karl Friedrich, G. architect and artist (1781–1841), 1819 S, 1824 S, 1851 S
Schirach, Baldur von, G. politician (1907–74), 1966 J
Schizophrenia, 1852 H
Schlegel, August, G. author (1767–1845), 1767 Z, 1809 U
Schlegel, Karl Wilhelm Friedrich von, G. critic and scholar (1772–1829), 1797 Q, 1799 U, 1808 Q
Schleicher, Kurt von, G. politician (1882–1934), 1932 M, 1933 A, 1934 F
Schleiden, Matthias Jacob, G. biologist (1804–81), 1838 P, 1846 P
Schleiermacher, Friedrich Ernst Daniel, G. theologian (1768–1834), 1799 R, 1823 R
Schlesinger, Arthur Meier, Jr., Am. historian (b. 1917), 1957 Q, 1965 Q, 1978 Q, 1986 Q
Schlesinger, John Richard, B. film director (b. 1926), 1967 W, 1969 W, 1971 W, 1976 W
Schleswig-Holstein Question: Holstein Estates resolve on independence, 1844 L; German Confederation reserves rights in Duchies, 1846 G, J; Frederick VII announces Denmark will incorporate Holstein, 1848 C; Prussia invades Denmark, 1848 E; Frederick VII decides to incorporate Schleswig Duchy in Denmark, 1848 L; settled by Treaty of Berlin, 1850 G; position guaranteed by Treaty of London, 1850 H; Schleswig is incorporated in Denmark, 1863 C, L; ultimatum to Denmark, 1864 A; Austrian and Prussian troops enter, 1864 B; War, 1864 D, F; Denmark cedes to Austria and Prussia, 1864 K; convention of Gastein re-arranges conquests, 1865 H; Prussia acquires, 1865 H; Duchies are incorporated in Prussia, 1866 M; plebiscite in, 1920 B; is transferred to Denmark, 1920 G
Schleyer, Hans-Martin, W. Germ. businessman (1915–77), kidnap, 1977 J
Schliemann, Heinrich, G. archaeologist (1822–90), 1870 O
Schlüter, Poul Holmskov, Danish Prime Minister (b. 1929), 1990 M
Schmeling, Max, G. boxer, 1930 X, 1936 X
Schmidt, Helmut, W. German Chancellor (b. 1918), 1918 Z, 1976 K, 1980 K
talks with Brezhnev in Moscow, 1974 K
proposes European Monetary System (EMS), 1978 D
Schnabel, Julian, Am. artist (b. 1951), 1982 S
Schnaebelé, F. frontier official, incident concerning, 1887 D
Schnittke, Alfred, R. musician, 1981 T, 1984 T, 1985 T, 1989 T, 1990 T, 1992 T
Schnitzler, Arthur, Aus. dramatist (1862–1931), 1903 W
Schnuschnigg, Kurt von, Aus. politician (1897–1977), 1897 Z, 1977 Z
Schober, Johann, Aus. Moderate (1874–1946), 1929 J
Schoenberg, Arnold, Am., formerly Aus, Musician (1874–1951), 1874 Z, 1912 T, 1924 T, 1930 T, 1954 T, 1965 T
Schofield, Roger Snowden, B. historian (b. 1937), 1981 Q
Scholar Gipsy: The (M. Arnold), 1853 U
Scholarship: Its Meaning and Value (H. W. Garrod), 1947 Q
Scholes, Christopher Latham, Am. printer and inventor (1819–90), 1873 P
Schönbein, Christian Friedrich, G. chemist (1799–1868), 1799 Z, 1846 P, 1848 Z
Schönbrunn, Germany, Treaties, between France and Prussia, 1805 M, 1809 K
School and Society (J. Dewey), 1899 O
School for Coquettes (C. Gore), 1831 W
School for Scandal, The (R. B. Sheridan), 1778 W
Schools. *See under* Education
Schopenhauer, Arthur, G. philosopher (1788–1860) 1788 Z, 1819 R, 1860 Z, 1870 T
Schubart, Christian Friedrich Daniel, G. poet (1739–91), 1785 U
Schubert, Franz, G. musician (1797–1828), 1797 Z, 1814 T, 1816 T, 1818 T, 1820 T, 1823 T, 1825 T, 1827 T, 1828 Z
Erl King, 1816 T
'Great C. Major' Symphony, 1828 T, 1839 T
Trout Quintet, 1819 T

'Unfinished' Symphony, 1822 T
Schuler, Marx, G. scientist, 1907 P
Schultze, Marx Johann Sigismund, G. microscopic anatomist (1825–74), 1863 P
Schumacher, Ernst Friedrich, G.-born B. economist (1911–77), 1911 Z, 1973 O, 1977 Z
Schumacher, Kurt, G. Social Democrat (1895–1952), 1952 H
Schuman, Robert, F. statesman (1886–1963), 1947 L, 1948 J
Plan, 1950 E
embodied in Paris Treaty, 1951 D
ratified by France, 1951 M
Schumann, Robert, G. musician (1810–56), 1810 Z, 1834 T, 1838 T, 1840 T, 1849 T, 1850 T, 1853 T
Schurman, Jacob Gould, Am. administrator and educationalist (1854–1942), leads Philippines Commission 1899 C
Schuschnigg, Kurt von, Aus. politician (1897–1977), 1937 B; appointed Chancellor, 1934 G; *coup* in Vienna, 1935 K; becomes leader of Fatherland Front, 1936 E; dissolves Heimwehr, 1936 K; meets Mussolini, 1937 D; promises release of Nazi prisoners, 1938 B
Schuster, Sir Arthur, B. physicist (1851–1934), 1851 Z, 1934 Z
Schutz, Brother Roger, F. monk, 1944 R, 1974 R
Schutzenberger, Paul, F. chemist (1829–97), 1865 P
Schwann, Theodor, G. botanist (1810–82), 1810 Z, 1839 P, 1882 Z
Schwanzenberg, Prince Karl, Philipp zu, Aus. general (1771–1820), 1813 M, 1814 B
Schwarzenberg, Prince Friedrich zu (1800–70), 1850 L
Schweitzer, Albert, F. missionary-surgeon, theologian and musician (1875–1965), 1875 Z, 1905 T, 1910 R, 1954 R, 1957 D, 1965 Z
Schwind, Moritz, G. artist (1804–71), 1854 S
Sciascia, Leonardo, It. author (1921–89), 1977 U
Science and Health (M. B. Eddy), 1875 R
Science and Human Behaviour (Skinner), 1953 R
Science and the Common Understanding (R. Oppenheim), 1953 P
Science and the Modern World (A. N. Whitehead), 1925 P
Science and the Nation, 1956 P
Science of Antiquity (F. Wolf), 1807 Q
Science of Ethics (L. Stephen), 1882 R
Science of Legislation (G. Filangieri), 1780 O
Science of Rights (J. G. Fichte), 1796 O
Science, Faith and Society (M. Polanyi), 1947 R
Science, Religion and the Future (C. E. Raven), 1943 R
Science:
American Association for the Advancement of, 1848 P
British Association for the Advancement of, 1831 P
British Committee on the Neglect of, 1916 P
degrees at London University, 1860 O
Sciences Were Never at War, The (G. de Beer), 1960 Q
Scientific Advisory Committee, British, 1940 O
Scientific Papers (Lord Rayleigh), 1900 P
Scientific Policy, British Advisory Committee on, 1947 P
Scientific Studies, British Board of, 1916 P
Scientific Theory and Religion (E. W. Barnes), 1933 R
Scientific and Industrial Research, Department of, in Britain (DISR), 1916 P
Scoon, Sir Paul, Governor-General of Grenada (b. 1935), 1983 K
Scooter, motor, 1919 P
Scorsese, Martin, Am. film director (b. 1942), 1942 Z, 1973 W, 1980 W, 1988 W
Scotland:
Highlands of, roads in, 1802 P
Secretary of State, for, first appointed, 1885 H; legislation for, 1894 N
Scottish Development Agency, 1975 L
White Paper on devolution, 1975 L
Scottish Labour Party launched, 1976 A
bill for devolution published, 1976 L
referendum on devolution, 1979 C
Scott Brown, Denise, Am. architect (b. 1931), 1991 S
Scott Polar Research Institute, Cambridge, 1926 P
Scott, Charles Prestwich, B. journalist (1846–1932), 1872 V
Scott, Mrs. Dawson, B. founder of P. E. N., 1922 U
Scott, E., B. architect, 1928 S
Scott, Sir Francis Clayton, B. soldier (1834–1902), 1896 A
Scott, Sir George Albert, B. architect (1811–78), 1862 S
Scott, Sir Giles Gilbert, B. architect (1880–1960), 1903 S
Scott, Norman, B. model, 1976 B, 1977 K, 1978 H, 1979 E
Scott, Paul Mark, B. author (1920–78), 1977 U
Scott, Ridley, B. film director (b. 1939), 1979 W, 1982 W, 1991 W
Scott, Robert, B. churchman and Greek scholar (1811–87), 1843 Q
Scott, Robert Falcon, B. Polar explorer (1868–1912), 1868 Z, 1912 Z
reaches S. Pole, 1912 P
Scott, Sir Walter, B. novelist and poet (1771–1832), 1771 Z, 1805 U, 1808 U, 1809 V, 1810 U, 1814 U, 1815 U, 1816 U, 1818 U, 1820 U, 1821 U, 1824 U, 1826 U
Museum for, in Edinburgh, 1840 S
Scott, Winfield, Am. Whig (1786–1866), 1852 L
Scouting Movement, 1907 O
Scramble for Africa:
Britain warns Germany against infringement of rights, 1883 D
Belgium drive in Congo region, 1884 B, 1885 B
Berlin Conference, 1884 L
See also under Congo; Nigeria; Rhodesia; Somaliland; South West Africa
Screw, ship's, invented, 1827 P
Screwtape Letters (C. S. Lewis), 1942 R
Scriabin, Alexander, R. musician (1872–1915), 1872 Z, 1913 T, 1915 Z
Scriptores rerum Bohemicarum (J. Dobrovsky), 1783 U
Scudamore, Peter, B. jockey (b. 1958), 1989 X
Scullin, James Henry, Austral. Labour leader (1876–1953), 1929 K
Scurvy, is conquered, 1775 P
Se non così (L. Pirandello), 1913 W
Sea Spray and Smoke Drift (A. L. Gordon), 1867 U
Sea, The Sea, The (I. Murdoch), 1978 U
Sea Wolf (J. London), 1904 U
Sea of Galilee, Israel:
Israeli and Syrian forces clash around, 1966 H
battle between Israeli and Jordanian forces, 1968 A
Sea-island cotton, 1786 P
Seaborg, Glenn Theodore, Am. chemist (b. 1912), 1950 P
Seagull, The (A. Chekhov), 1896 W
Seaham, Harbour, Co. Durham, England, election in, 1935 L
'Sealab', 1964 P
Seaplanes, 1912 P
Search, right of, at sea, 1850 M
Searle, Humphrey, B. musician (1915–1982), 1915 Z, 1956 T, 1960 T, 1982 Z
Searle, John R., Am. philosopher (b. 1932), 1969 R
Sears, R. D., Am. lawn-tennis player (1861–1943), 1881 X
Season Tickets on railways, 1910 O
Season in the Congo, A (A. Césaire), 1966 W
Seattle, Wash., US, grunge music, 1991 W
Sebastopol, Russia: harbour begun, 1776 N; siege of 1854 K; storm at, 1854 L; allies enter, 1855 J; Turks bombard, 1914 K; Germans occupy, 1918 E; Red Army takes, 1920 L, Germans enter, 1942 G
Second Adventists. *See under* Religious Denominations
Second Birth (B. Pasternak), 1932 U
Second Front, movement for, 1941 J; Anglo-US talks on, 1942 D; British demonstrations favouring, 1942 G
Second Mrs. Tanqueray, The (A. W. Pinero), 1893 U
Second Sex, The (S. de Beauvoir), 1949 U
Second World War, The: An Illustrated History (A.J.P. Taylor), 1975 Q
Secret Agent (J. Conrad), 1907 U
Secret Societies:
in China, Boxers, 1898 N
White Lotus, in Shantung, 1774 N
union of, organised, 1905 N
in Ireland, Irish Republican Brotherhood, 1857 K
The Invincibles, 1882 H
in Italy, the Carbonari, 1820 G, 1821 C
Mafia, in Sicily, 1926 J
in Macedonia, revolutionary organisations, 1893 N, 1895 F
in Russia, Land and Liberty, 1876 O
Will of the People, 1879 O
in US, Ku-Klux Klan, 1922 O
shoot Civil Rights worker, 1965 C
before Un-American Committee, 1965 K
See also under Armies, private
Secret ballot, in Britain, 1872 G
Secrets Act, Official, British, 1911 O
Security Pacts:
Arab League, 1952 H
France, with Czechoslovakia and Poland, 1925 K
Germany's proposals for, 1925 F, K
See also under Pacts
Security Services, British, alleged plot by, 1977 G
Security procedures, Radcliffe review of, 1961 E
Sedaine, Michel Jean, F. dramatist (1719–97), 1765 W, 1768 W
Sedan, Ardennes, N. E. France: French defeat at 1870 J; US troops occupy, 1918 L; Germans break through near, 1940 E
Seditious meetings. *See under* Public Assembly
Seditious publications. *See under* Censorship
See Naples and Die (E. Rice), 1929 W
See Under: Love (D. Grossman), 1989 U
Seebeck, Thomas Johann, G. scientist (1770–1839), 1821 P
Seebohm Report, B., 1968 O
Seeley, Sir John Robert, B. historian (1834–95), 1883 Q
Seferis, George (born George Seferiades), Greek poet (1900–71), 1900 Z, 1931 U, 1971 Z
Sega computer games, 1991 W
Segal, George, Am. sculptor (b. 1924), 1967 S
Segantini, Giovanni, It. artist (1858–99), 1891 S
Segni, Antonio, It. Christian Democrat (1891–1972), forms ministry, 1955 F; resigns,

1957 E; forms ministry, 1959 B; resigns, 1960 B; elected president of Italy, 1962 E; resigns presidency, 1964 M
Segovia, Andrés, Sp. musician (1893–1987), 1893 Z, 1913 T, 1987 Z
Segregation. *See* Apartheid; Racial Problems
Sein und Zeit (Heidegger), 1927 R
Seipel, Ignaz, Aus. Christian Socialist (1876–1932), 1926 K
Selangor, Malay: independence, 1826 F; Sultan of, heads Malaysian Federation, 1960 D
Self and the Dramas of History, The (R. Niebuhr), 1961 R
Self-winding watch, 1922 P
Selfridge, Harry Gordon, B. formerly Am. businessman, 1858 Z, 1947 Z
Selim III, Sultan of Turkey (1789–1807), 1789 D, 1807 E
Sella, Quintius, It. politician and financier (1827–84), 1874 E
Sellafield, Cumb, England, atomic power station at, 1951 P
  nuclear re-processing plant, 1978 O
  research suggests link between radiation and leukaemia at Sellafield, 1990 B
Sellers, Peter, B. actor (1925–80), 1925 Z, 1980 Z
Selma, Alabama, US: violence in, 1965 C; Civil Rights procession from, 1965 C
Selznick, David Oliver, Am. film director (1902–65), 1935 W
Semaphore (or optical telegraph), 1793 P
Sembilan, Islands, Malaysia, B. acquires, 1826 F
Seminaries:
  in France, closed, 1791 R
  in Ireland, Maynooth established, 1795 R
  in Russia, established at St. Petersburg, 1809 R
  See also under Monasteries; Religious Communities
Semler, Johann Salomo, G. Biblical critic (1725–91), 1771 R
Senanayake, Dudley Stetton Ceyl. United National Party leader (1911–73), 1952 F, 1960 C, 1965 C
Senanayake, Stephen, Ceyl. United Party leader (1884–1952), 1947 J
Senefelde, Alois, G. inventor (1771–1834), 1798 R
Senegal, West Africa: ceded to Britain, 1763 B; captured by France, 1779 A; France recovers, 1783 J; forms, with Sudan, Mali Republic, 1959 A
  federates with Gambia, 1981 L
  revenge killings for anti-Senegalese violence in Mauritius, 1989 D, F
Senegambia, 1981 L
Senior, Nassau William, B. economist (1790–1864), 1790 Z, 1864 Z
Sensations of Tones (H. Helmholtz), 1862 P
Sense and Sensibilia (J. L. Austin), 1962 R
Sense and Sensibility (J. Austen), 1811 U
Sense and the Intellect (A. Bain), 1855 R
Sense of Order, The: A Study in the Psychology of Decorative Art (E.H. Gombrich), 1979 Q
Sentences, criminal: first offenders act, 1958 O; 42 years imprisonment, 1961 E. *See also under* Death penalty; Penal Reform
Sentimental Journey, A (L. Sterne), 1768 U
Seoul, Korea: incidents against Japanese in, 1882 G; palace, seized by Japanese, 1894 G; Japanese occupy, 1904 B; Constituent Assembly, boycotted by N. Korea, 1948 E; N. Koreans capture, 1950 F; UN force recaptures, 1950 J
  North Korean raid, 1968 A
  Olympics, 1988 X
  population, 1990 Y
Separator, cream, invented, 1877 P
Sequoyah (*alias* George Guess), Am. Indian (1770–1843), invents Cherokee alphabet, 1824 Q
Serbia: Russian ultimatum to Turkey about, 1826 D; Russian influence in, 1826 K; independence, 1829 J; declares war on Turkey, 1876 G, 1877 M; independence guaranteed, 1878 C; monarchy in, 1903 F; to have canal access to Adriatic, 1912 M
  constitution stripping Kosovo of its autonomy, 1990 J
  ethnic Albanians, 1990 J
  elections, 1990 M
  Kosovo provincial constitution suspended, 1991 C
  UN plan for deployment of peacekeeping forces, 1992 A
  announces plan to create new Yugoslav state, 1992 A
  UN peace plan, 1992 B
  Socialist Party of Serbia election victory, 1992 M
  Yugoslavian civil war. *See* Civil Wars
Serbo-Croat-Slovene Kingdom. *See* Yugoslavia
Serbs:
  gain partial autonomy, 1817 L
  rising of, in Belgrade, 1862 F
  nationalism, 1990 B
Serfdom:
  emancipation of, plea for, 1790 O
  in Austria, abolished, 1781 L, 1848 J
  in Bohemia, abolished, 1780 K
    revolts against, 1775 B
  in Denmark, abolished, 1784 E
  in Hungary, abolished, 1780 K
  in Prussia, emancipated, 1807 K
  in Russia, problem studied, 1857 L
    emancipation of, 1858 O, 1861 C
  in Savoy, abolished, 1771 O
  See also Slaves
Sergeant Pepper's Lonely Hearts Club Band album (The Beatles), 1967 W
Seringapatam, Mysore, S. India, battles, 1791 E, 1799 E
Serious Money (C. Churchill), 1987 W
Serra, Richard, Am. artist (b. 1939), 1972 S
Serrano y Dominguez, Francisco, duke de la Torre, Sp. statesman (1810–85), 1874 A
Serrano, Andres, artist, 1987 S, 1990 S
Serres Chaudes (M. Maeterlinck), 1889 U
Serum:
  anti-diphtheria, 1902 P
  for tetanus, 1915 P
  Salk, for poliomyelitis, 1955 P
  See also Vaccines
Servitude et grandeur militaires (A. de Vigny), 1835 U
Sesame Street, television series, 1969 W
Sesame and Lilies (J. Ruskin), 1865 U
Seth, Vikram, Ind. author (b. 1952), 1986 U
Seton, Elizabeth Ann Bayley, Am. founder of the Sisters of Charity of St. Joseph (1774–1821), 1809 R
Seurat, Georges, F. artist (1859–91), 1884 S, 1886 S
Seven Men (M. Beerbohm), 1919 U
'Seven, The' (EFTA), 1959 L; *See also* European Free Trade Association
77 Dream Songs (J. Berryman), 1964 U
Severed Head, A (I. Murdoch), 1961 U
Severini, Gino, It. artist (1883–1966), 1910 S
Severn, River, England, tunnel, 1886 P
Seville, Spain, revolt in, 1932 H
Sèvres, France, treaty of, 1920 H
Sewing-machine, 1846 P, 1851 P
Sex Abuse, child, in Britain, 1986 O
Sex Education in Schools, 1943 O
Sex Pistols, The, punk group, 1977 W
Sex, Treatise on, 1905 R
Sexual Behaviour in the Human Male (Kinsey), 1948 P
Sexual Politics (K. Millett), 1970 R
Seychelles Islands: Britain captures, 1794 N; Makarios deported to, 1956 C
  gain independence, 1976 F
  coup d'état, 1977 F
Seymour, Horatio, Am. Democrat (1810–86), 1868 L
Sfax, Tunisia, British occupy, 1943 O
Shackleton, Sir Ernest Henry, B. explorer (1874–1922), 1874 Z, 1914 P, 1919 P, 1922 Z
Shackleton, Lord, (b. 1911) report on Falkland Islands, 1982 J
Shaffer, Peter Levin, B. playwright (b. 1926), 1926 Z, 1964 W, 1973 W, 1979 W
Shagari, Alhaji Shehu Usman Aliu, President of Nigeria (b. 1925), 1983 M
Shah, Eddie, B. newspaper proprietor (b. 1944), 1983 V, 1988 V
Shahn, Benn, Lithuanian artist (1898–1969), 1945 S
Shaikh Abdullah, Kashmir premier, 1964 D
Shakers, The, Sect, 1774 R
Shakespeare, William, B. dramatist (1564–1616):
  Complete Works (ed. S. Wells and G. Taylor), 1986 Q
  Plays, production of, notable, 1769 W, 1814 W, 1820 W, 1833 W, 1897 W, 1914 W
    filmed, 1944 W, 1948 W, 1952 W
    televised, 1961 W
  quatercentenary exhibition, 1964 S, W
  studies, 1778 Q
  translations, 1775 W
Shakespeare–Bacon controversy, 1848 Q
Shaking of the Foundations, The (P. Tillich), 1949 R
Shame (S. Rushdie), 1983 U
Shamir, Yitzhak, Prime Minister of Israel (b. 1915), 1983 H, 1986 K, 1990 C, F
  government of national unity, 1984 H
  loses parliamentary majority, 1992 B
Shange, Ntozake (born Paulette Williams), Am. playwright (b. 1948), 1974 W
Shanghai, China: is opened to British commerce, 1842 H; falls to rebels, 1850 K; anti-British incidents in, 1925 E; Japanese occupy, 1932 A; Chinese driven from, 1932 C; Japanese take, 1937 L; population, 1950 Y, 1960 Y, 1970 Y, 1990 Y
Shanhaikwan, China, Japanese troops reach, 1932 A
Shankar, Ramsewak, President of Surinam, 1988 A
Shantung, China: rebellion in, 1774 N; Japanese ultimatum on rights in, 1915 A; German concession in, granted to Japan, 1919 D; US Senate rejects clause of Versailles treaty about, 1919 H; restored to China, 1922 B; Japanese intervention in, 1927 E, 1928 D; evacuate, 1929 E
Share-pushing, 1937 O
Sharett, Moshé, Israel leader (b. 1894), 1953 M, 1954 A
Sharif, Nawaz, Prime Minister of Pakistan (b. 1949), 1990 K
Sharif-Emami, Jafar, Iranian politician (b. 1910), 1978 H
Sharman, Helen, B. astronaut (b. 1963), 1991 P
Sharon, Ariel, Israeli Defence Minister (b. 1928), 1983 B

Sharp, Thomas, B. town-planner (1901–78), 1944 O
Sharpeville, S. Africa, shooting of demonstrators at, 1960 C
deaths during rioting, 1984 J
Sharples, Sir Richard, Governor of Bermuda (1916–73), assassination, 1973 C
Shastri, Lal Bahandra, Prime Minister of India (1904–66), 1966 A; succeeds Nehru, 1964 E
Shatila refugee camp, Lebanon, 1985 E, 1987 D
Shatt al-Arab waterway, Iran takes control, 1986 B
Shatt-el-Adhaim, Mesopotamia, Turks defeated at, 1917 D
Shaw, George Bernard, B. author (1856–1950), 1856 Z, 1900 U, 1932 U, 1950 Z
as dramatist, 1892 W, 1894 W, 1897 W, 1898 W, 1903 W, 1907 W, 1919 W, 1923 W, 1924 W, 1929 W
political works, 1898 O, 1928 O
portrait, 1914 S
Prefaces to published plays, 1916 U
Shaw, Robert, B. author (1927–78), 1962 U
Shawe, T. E. *See* Lawrence, T. E.
Shays, Daniel, Am. insurgent (1747–1825), 1786 J
Shcharansky, Anatoly, Sov. dissident (b. 1948), 1978 G, 1986 B
She Stoops to Conquer (O. Goldsmith), 1773 W
Shearman, Sir Harold, B. Labour politician (1896–1984), first chairman of Greater London Council, 1965 O
Sheehan, Neil, Am. author (b. 1936), 1988 Q
Sheepfold, The (L. Housman), 1918 U
Sheffield, England, Hillsborough soccer stadium disaster, 1989 X
Shehu, Mehmet, Prime Minister of Albania (1913–81), reported suicide, 1981 M
Shekhar, Chandra, Prime Minister of India (b. 1927), 1991 C
Shelburne, earl of. *See* Petty, William
Shell Oil Company, dispute with Cuba over Havana refinery, 1960 G
Shell-shock, 1916 P
Shelley, Mary Wollstonecroft, B. author (1797–1851), 1797 Z, 1818 U
Shelley, Percy Bysshe, B. poet (1792–1822), 1792 Z, 1813 U, 1816 U, 1817 U, 1820 U, 1821 U, 1822 Z
Shenkunsk, Russia, Allies withdraw from, 1919 A
Shenstone, William, B. poet (1714–63), 1765 U
Shepard, Alan, Am. astronaut (b. 1923), 1961 P
Shepard, Sam, Am. actor and playwright (b. 1943), 1972 W, 1980 W, 1983 W, 1988 W
Shepherd's Calendar, The (J. Clare), 1827 U
Shepilov, Dmitri Trofimovitch, R. leader: becomes foreign minister, 1956 F; is superseded, 1957 B; is expelled from Soviet Central Committee, 1957 G
Shepstone, Sir Theophilis, S. African statesman (1817–93), 1877 D
Sheridan, Richard Brinsley, B. dramatist (1751–1816), 1775 W, 1778 W, 1779 W, 1816 Z
Sheriff, Robert Cedric, B. author (b. 1896), 1929 W
Sherman, Cindy, Am. artist (b. 1954), 1980 S, 1983 S, 1985 S
Sherman, John, Am. financier and statesman (1823–1900), introduces Anti-Trust law, 1890 G
Sherman, Martin, Am. playwright (b. 1938), 1979 W
Sherman, William Tecumseh, Am. Unionist general (1820–91), 1864 G, M, 1865 D; march through Georgia, 1864 E
Sherrington, Sir Charles Scott, B. physiologist (1857–1952), 1857 Z, 1939 R, 1952 Z
Sherwood, Jennifer, B. architectural historian, 1974 Q
Sherwood, Robert Emmet, Am. dramatist (1896–1955), 1935 W, 1936 W
Shevardnadze, Edvard Amvrosiyevich, R./Georgian politician (b. 1928), 1985 G, 1987 J, L, 1990 M
Shevket Pasha, Turk, leader, forms ministry, 1913 A
Shi'a Muslims, Lebanese civil war, 1987 B, D
Shi'ite Moslem gunmen
TWA jet hijacked, 1985 F
Kuwaiti airliner hijacked, 1988 D
Shift (R. Serra), 1972 S
Shiloh, Tenn., US, Confederate success at, 1862 D
Shimonoseki, Japan, Treaty, 1895 D; fleet attacked in, 1864 J
Shimuzu, Kuniu, 1991 W
Shintoism, disestablished in Japan, 1945 O
Shinwell, Emmanuel, B. Labour politician (1884–1986), defeats MacDonald in Seaham Harbour election, 1935 L
Shipka Pass, Central Bulgaria, Turks capitulate at, 1878 A
Shipping:
control of Black See fleet, 1992 A, H
embargoes on, 1800 M, 1801 A, C, 1803 E
Exxon Valdez accident, 1989 C
Gulf of Aqaba closed to Israeli shipping, 1967 E
Herald of Free Enterprise capsizes, 1987 C, G, K
in Britain, modification of navigation laws, 1822 F, 1825 G
Lloyd's Register, 1834 V
government control, 1916 M
loan to Cunard Company, 1963 K
merchant shipping tonnage statistics, 1992 Y
supertanker, 1968 P, 1971 P
in US, note to Britain on use of US flag, 1915 B
note to Germany on sinking of neutral ships, 1915 B
Shipping Board, 1916 O
Ships:
atomic powered, 1959 P
guided-missiles, 1956 G
iron, 1820 P
iron-clad, 1861 P
non-magnetic, 1957 P
screw for, invented, 1827 P
steam, 1783 P, 1803 P, 1807 P, 1812 P
Shipton, Eric Earle, B. mountaineer (1907–77), 1907 Z, 1977 Z
Sholokov, Mikhail Aleksandrovich, R. author (1905–84), 1905 Z, 1934 U, 1984 Z
Shops, early-closing of British, 1911 O
Short History of the English People (J. R. Green), 1874 Q
Short Survey of Surrealism (D. Gascoigne), 1935 S
Short, Nigel, B. chess player (b. 1965), 1980 X
Shorthand, invented, 1837 P
Shorthouse, Joseph Henry, B. author (1834–1903), 1880 U
Shostakovich, Dmitry Dmitrievich, R. musician (1906–75), 1906 Z, 1927 T, 1932 T, 1937 T, 1942 T, 1944 T, 1946 T, 1954 T, 1969 T, 1971 T, 1975 Z
Showalter, Mark R., Am. astronomer, 1990 P
Shrapnel, Henry, B. soldier and inventor (1761–1842), 1803 P
Shreveport, Louisiana, US, Confederates surrender at, 1865 E
Shriver, (Robert) Sargent Jnr, Am. Democratic politician (b. 1915), 1972 H
Shropshire Lad, A (A. E. Housman), 1896 U
Shultz, George, Am. Secretary of State (b. 1920), 1982 F, 1983 J, F, 1985 A
US–USSR arms reduction talks, 1987 J, L
Middle East peace mission, 1988 B
Shumla, Bulgaria, battle, 1774 G
Shusaku, Endu, author, 1986 U
Shuttleworth, Sir Thomas Phillips Kay, B. educationalist (1804–77), 1840 O
Shuvalov, Peter Andreivich, R. diplomat (1827–89), 1878 E, F
Si le grain ne meurt (Gide), 1926 U
Siam: Burmese invade, 1767 H; France maintains as buffer state, 1893 G; Anglo-French agreements on, 1893 M, 1896 A; independence confirmed, 1907 D; changes name to Thailand, 1949 E. *See also under* Thailand
Siameses, Los (G. Gambaro), 1967 W
Sibelius, Jean Julius Christian, Fin. musician (1865–1957), 1865 Z, 1893 T, 1899 T, 1900 T, 1957 Z
Siberia: Japanese advance into 1918 H; East, British, US, and Japanese agreement on, 1919 M
Siberian Highway, 1781 P
Sibley, Charles Gald (b. 1917), 1984 P
Sica, Vittorio de, It. film director (1902–74), 1901 Z, 1946 W, 1948 W, 1951 W, 1971 W
Sicilian Vespers (S. Runciman), 1958 Q
Sicily, Italy: Kingdom of Two Sicilies (Sicily and Naples), 1767 C; declared independent of Naples, 1848 D; forced to submit to Naples, 1849 E; plebiscite supports union with Sardinia, 1860 K; Allies land in, 1943 G
Sickel, Theodor von, G. historian (1826–1908), 1867 Q
Sickert, Walter Richard, B. artist (1860–1942), 1860 Z, 1886 S, 1913 S, 1941 S, 1942 Z
Siddons, Sarah (née Kemble), B. actress (1755–1831), 1775 W, 1784 S, 1812 W, 1831 Z
Sidgwick, Henry, B. philosopher (1838–1900), 1874 R, 1882 P
Sidi Barrani, Cyrenaica, N. Africa, 1940 J, M
Sidi Omar, Cyrenaica, N. Africa, British withdrawal to, 1942 F
Sidmouth, Viscount. *See* Addington
Sidon, Lebanon, Israeli air attacks, 1982 F
Sidqi, Bakr, Iraq. premier, 1937 H
Siege of Corinth (Byron), 1816 U
Siegfried (J. Giraudoux), 1928 W
Siegfried Line, Germany, Germans retreat to, 1918 J
Siemens, Ernst Werner von, G. electrician (1816–92), 1816 Z, 1879 P, 1892 Z
Siemens, Sir William, B. metallurgist and electrician (1823–83), 1856 P, 1861 P
Siemkiewicz, Henryk, Pol. author (1849–1916), 1895 U
Sierra Leone, W. Africa: is settled as asylum for slaves, 1788 H; Sierra Leone Company is formed, 1792 N; becomes Crown Colony, 1808 A; taken over by Britain, 1821 E; boundaries defined, 1882 F, 1885 L; becomes independent, 1961 D; becomes republic within Commonwealth, 1971 D
Sieyès, Emmanuel Joseph, F. abbé and politician (1758–1836), 1789 O, 1836 Z
Signals, railway, automatic, 1893 P
Signs of the Times (C. von Bunsen), 1856 O
Sigurid the Volsung (W. Morris), 1876 U
Sigwart, Christoph, G. philosopher (1830–94), 1873 R
Sihanouk, (Samdech Preah) Norodom, King of Cambodia (b. 1922), 1976 D, 1991 L
overthrow, 1970 C
Sikhs: British treaty with, 1809 D; British wars

against, 1834 E, 1845 M, 1846 A, B, C, 1848 C, 1849 A, B, C
Sikorsky, Igor Ivan, R.-born Am. aircraft designer (1889–1972), 1889 Z, 1939 P, 1972 Z
Silas Marner (G. Eliot), 1861 U
Silent Spring, The (R. Carson), 1963 P
Silesia, Germany: Austria renounces claim to, 1768 K; ceded to Prussia, 1866 H
Upper, plebiscite for incorporation in Germany, 1921 C; future of, referred to League, 1921 H, K; partition of, 1921 K; cession to Poland, 1922 E
Silestria, Rumania, battle, 1809 J
Silk manufactures, British exports, 1772 Y, 1782 Y, 1792 Y, 1802 Y, 1822 Y, 1842 Y, 1852 Y, 1862 Y, 1872 Y, 1882 Y, 1892 Y, 1902 Y, 1912 Y, 1922 Y, 1932 Y
production, comparative statistics, 1910 Y
Silk, artificial, 1887 P
Sillars, James, B. Labour/Scottish Labour/Scottish Nationalist politician (b. 1937), 1976 A
Silver King, The (H. A. Jones), 1882 W
Silver:
compulsory purchase repealed, 1893 L
extraction by cyanide, 1887 P
Roosevelt empowered to nationalise, 1934 F
standard in US, 1878 B
Silverman, Sydney, B. Labour politician (1895–1968), advocates abolition of death penalty, 1956 F
introduces new death penalty abolition bill, 1964 M
Simeon, Charles, B. evangelical churchman (1759–1836), 1783 R
Simon and Garfunkel, Am. singers, 1970 W
Simon, John, viscount Simon, B. National Liberal politician (1873–1954), 1873 Z, 1935 F, 1954 Z; leads commission on India, 1926 L; becomes foreign secretary, 1931 L; elected National Liberal Leader, 1932 J; as chancellor of Exchequer, 1937 E
Simon, Jules, F. philosopher and statesman (1814–1896), 1877 E
Simon, Neil, Am. playwright (b. 1927), 1982 W, 1984 W
Simon, Paul, Am. singer (b. 1942), 1970 W, 1982 W, 1986 W
Simonstown, S. Africa, naval base, returned by Britain to S. Africa, 1955 G
Simple Story, A (E. Inchbald), 1791 W
Simplon Pass, Alps: carriage-road, 1800 P; tunnel, 1906 P
Simpson, Sir James Young, B. physician (1811–70), 1811 Z, 1847 P, 1870 Z
Simpson, John Andrew, B. lexicographer, 1989 Q
Simpson, Mrs. Wallis Warfield (later duchess of Windsor), Am. (1896–1986), 1936 K, L, 1967 F
marries duke of Windsor, 1937 F
Sinai Peninsula, 1975 J, K, 1980 A
Israel gains control, 1967 F
UN peace-keeping force, 1982 A
'Sinanthropus' (Peking Man), 1920 Q
Sinatra, Francis Albert (Frank), Am. singer and film actor (b. 1917), 1943 W
Since Cézanne (C. Bell), 1922 S
Sinclair, Sir Clive Marles, B. inventor and businessman (b. 1940), 1981 P
Sinclair, Sir John, B. administrator and economist (1754–1835), 1791 O
Sinclair, Upton Beall, Am. author (1878–1968), 1878 Z, 1906 O, 1928 U, 1940 U, 1968 Z
Sind, India, Napier conquers, 1843 A, H
Sindhia, India, peace signed with East India Company, 1805 L
Sindhia, of Gwalior, Ind. ruler, 1802 K, 1803 H, J, M
Sinecures, proposals for abolition in Britain, 1780 E
Sinfonie Liturgique (P. Honegger), 1945 T
Singapore Grip, The (J.G. Farrell), 1978 U
Singapore: East India Company's settlement at, 1819 B; falls to Japanese, 1942 B; votes to join Malaysian Federation, 1962 J; Overseas Chinese Banking Corporation HQ, 1979 S
Singer, Charles, E., B. historian of technology (1876–1960), 1955 P
Singer, Isaac Merritt, Am. inventor (1811–75); 1851 P
Singh, (Chandhuri) Charan, Prime Minister of India (1902–87), 1979 G
Singh, Vishwanath Pratap, Prime Minister of India (b. 1931), 1989 L, 1990 L
Singing Detective, The, television programme, 1986 W
'Singing-Mice', 1937 W
Single Man, A (C. Isherwood), 1964 U
Sinhalese;
amnity talks between Tamil and Sinhalese representatives, 1984 A
clashes with Tamils in Sri Lanka, 1984 H
Sinhalese, becomes official language of Ceylon, 1956 G
Sinkiang, China, USSR forces cross border at, 1969 H
Sinn Fein, 1982 K, L, 1988 K, 1990 O. *See under* Political Parties
Sinope, Turkey, battle of, 1853 L, P
Sinowatz, Dr. Fred, Aus. politician (b. 1929), 1983 D
Sioux rising in Minnesota, 1862 H
Siphon recorder, 1867 P
Sipyengin, R. minister of interior, 1902 D
Siroky, Vilian, Czech. Communist (1902–71), 1954 M, 1963 J
Sirte, Gulf of, Libya, 1981 H
Sisley, Alfred, F. artist (1840–99), 1874 S
Sismondi, Jean Charles Leonard de, Swi. historian (1773–1842), 1773 Z, 1807 Q, 1819 O, 1842 Z
Sisters-in-Law, The (M. Tremblay), 1968 W
Sistova, Bulgaria, peace of, 1791 H
Sithole, Ndabaningi, Zimbabwean politician (b. 1920), 1969 B
Sitwell, Dame Edith, B. author, 1887 Z, 1964 Z
Six Characters in Search of an Author (L. Pirandello), 1918 W
Six Degrees of Separation (J. Guare), 1992 W
Six Scenes from a Marriage, television programme, 1972 W
Six, Les, French school of musicians, 1920 T
'Six, The' (France, W. Germany, Italy, Belgium, Netherlands and Luxembourg forming the Common Market), signs Paris Treaty, 1951 D
Sizwe Banzi is Dead (A. Fugard), 1972 W
Ska revival by British bands, 1980 W
Skeat, Walter William, B. philologist (1835–1912), 1879 Q
Skegness, Lincs., England, holiday camp at, 1937 W
Skepticism and the Definition of Knowledge (G. Harman), 1989 R
Sketch Book of Geoffrey Crayon, Gent, The (W. Irving), 1820 U
Sketches by Boz (C. Dickens), 1836 U
Skidmore, Owings and Merrill, Am. architects, 1968 S
Skiing, water, 1958 X
Skinner, Burrhus, Am. psychologist (1904–90), 1953 R
Skipton, Yorks., England, by-election, 1944 A
Sklodowska, Marie. *See* Curie, Marie
Skobelev, Mikhail Dimitrivich, R. general and diplomat (1843–82), 1882 B
Skopje, Yugoslavia, earthquake at, 1963 G
Skouloudis, Sophocles, Greek premier, 1915 L
Skutari, Turkey, 1913 E
Skyscrapers, 1857 P, 1883 P, 1930 S, 1964 S
Slab Boys, The (J. Byrne), 1982 W
Slack, Paul Alexander, B. historian (b. 1943), 1976 Q, 1985 Q
Slade, Julian, B. composer and dramatist (b. 1930), 1954 W
Slansky, Rudolf, Czech. Communist (1901–52), 1952 L
Slaughterhouse Five (K. Vonnegut), 1969 U
Slav influence in Austria-Hungary, 1879 H
Slave Trade:
Brussels Conference on abolition, 1889 F
Africa–US, prohibited, 1808 A
African, abolished, 1884 L
Brussels convention to eradicate, 1890 G
in Britain, Parliamentary motion for abolition, 1788 E
in Denmark, abolished, 1792 N, O
in Spain, ended, 1817 J
in US, forbidden in District of Columbia, 1850 J
Dredd Scott case, 1856 C
J. Davis's resolutions, 1860 B
in Zanzibar, abolished, 1873 F
Slavery:
Anti-Slavery Congress, 1890 O
International Convention for abolition, 1926 J
tract advocating abolition, 1786 O
in Africa, abolished, 1884 L
in Brazil, abolished, 1888 E
in Britain, Lord Mansfield's decision in Somerset's case, 1772 O
in British Empire, abolished, 1834 O
Creole incident with US, 1841 L
decision over restoration of fugitive slaves, 1875 J
Jamaican riots following emancipation, 1839 E
in French Colonies, abolished, 1794 N
in Liberia, colony established for freed US slaves, 1822 N
reported to persist, 1930 C
in Madagascar, liberation of, 1877 K
in Russia, pleas for emancipation, 1790 O
in Sierra Leone, asylum for slaves, 1788 H
in US, Jefferson champions rights of slaves, 1778 N
in part of Louisiana purchase, abolished, 1820 C
fugitive slaves, legislation about, 1793 N, 1850 G
Abolition Society founded, 1832 O
Wilmot Proviso on, 1846 H
Clay's compromise resolution on, 1850 A
pro-slavers massacred, 1856 E
Lincoln's declaration against slavery, 1862 J
Lincoln declares emancipation of negro slaves, 1863 O
Slavery abolished by 13th Amendement, 1865 M
in Zanzibar, abolished, 1897 D
Sleep of Prisoners, A (C. Fry), 1951 W
Sleep of Reason, The (A. Buero Vallejo), 1970 W
Sleeping Clergyman (J. Briche), 1933 W
Slivnitza, Bulgaria, Serbs defeated at, 1885 L
Slogans, 'Buy British' campaign, 1933 F
Slovak Republic, Slovak deputies vote for republic status, 1992 G

Slovakia: Southern, Hungary annexes, 1938 L; is placed under German 'protection', 1939 C. *See also* Czechoslovakia
Slovenia:
secession from Yugoslavia and independence, 1989 J, 1990 M, 1991 F
EC recognition as independent republic, 1992 A
Slum clearance, in Britain, 1864 O, 1867 O, 1932 D. *See also under* Housing
Small House at Allington, The (A. Trollope), 1864 U
Small is Beautiful; a Study of Economics as if People Mattered (E.F. Schumacher), 1973 O
Smallholders. *See under* Political Parties
Smallpox, vaccination against, 1796 P
Smeaton, John, B. engineer (1724–92), 1792 Z
Smeatonian Club, 1771 P
Smetana, Friedrich, Bohemian musician (1824–84), 1824 Z, 1848 T, 1866 T, 1874 T, 1884 Z
Smethwick, Warwicks., England, election, 1964 K
Smile of the Lamb (D. Grossman), 1986 U
Smiles, Samuel, B. author (1812–1904), 1812 Z, 1904 Z
Smiley's People (J. le Carré), 1980 U
Smiley's People, television programme, 1982 W
Smirke, Sir Robert, B. architect (1780–1867), 1780 Z, 1823 S, 1845 S, 1867 Z
Smith, Adam, B. political economist (1723–90), 1776 O, 1790 Z
Smith, Albert Emanuel, Am. Democrat (1873–1947), 1928 L
Smith, Mrs. Burnett, B. novelit, under pseudonym of 'Annie S. Swan' (1872–1943), 1872 Z, 1943 Z
Smith, Sir Cyril, B. Liberal politician (b. 1928), 1972 K
Smith, David Roland, Am. artist (1906–65), 1969 S
Smith, Dodie (Mrs. Alec Beesley; pseudonym of C. L. Anthony), B. dramatist (1896–1990), 1931 W
Smith, Frederick Edwin, B. Earl of Birkenhead, lawyer and Conservative politician, (1872–1930), 1872 Z, 1930 Z
Smith, F. E. (J. Campbell), 1983 Q
Smith, Gladys. *See* Pickford, Mary
Smith, Goldwin, B. controversionalist (1823–1910), 1823 Z, 1891 O, 1910 Z
Smith, Hamilton, architect, 1966 S, 1971 S
Smith, Sir Harry George Wakelyn, B. soldier (1787–1860), 1846 A, 1848 B
Smith, Henry John Stephen, B. mathematician (1826–83), 1954 P
Smith, Ian Douglas, Rhodesian politician (b. 1919), 1969 B, 1971 L, 1976 J, 1977 H; forms ministry, 1964 D; rejects visit by Commonwealth Secretary, 1964 L; talks with Wilson, 1965 K; proclaims U.D.I., 1965 L
Rhodesian Republic declared, 1966 M
Tiger talks with Wilson, 1966 M
talks with Thomson, 1967 L
talks with Wilson, 1968 K, L
Smith, John, B. Labour politician (b. 1938), 1992 G
Smith, Joseph, Am. Mormon leader (1805–44), 1825 R, 1830 R, 1843 R
Smith, Lloyd Logan Pearsall, B., formerly Am., author (1865–1946), 1865 Z, 1946 Z
Smith, Martin Cruz, Am. author (b. 1942), 1981 U
Smith, Patti, Am. pop singer (b. 1946), 1975 W
Smith, Sir Ross Macpherson, B. aviator (1892–1922), 1919 P
Smith, Stevie (born Florence Margaret Smith), B. poet (1902–71), 1902 Z, 1936 U, 1937 U, 1971 Z
Smith, Sydney, B. ecclesiastic (1771–1845), 1771 Z, 1808 R
Smith, William Henry, B. Conservative politician and newsagent (1825–91), 1887 A
Smith, William, B. geologist (1769–1839), 1815 P, 1816 P
Smith, Sir William Sidney, B. naval officer (1764–1840), 1799 C
Smiths, The, B. pop group, 1985 W, 1986 W
Smithson, Alison, and Peter Denham (b. 1923), B. architects, 1961 S
Smithson, Robert, Am. sculptor (1938–73), 1970 S, 1973 S
'Smog', in London, 1952 P
Smoke (I. Turgeniev), 1867 U
Smoking of Cigarettes: connexion with lung cancer, 1954 P; report of Royal College of Physicians on, 1962 P
Smolensk, Russia: Russian defeat at, 1812 H; German capture, 1941 G; Germans advance from, 1941 K; Russians recapture, 1943 J
Smollett, Tobias, B. author (1721–71), 1771 U, Z
Smoot, Reed, Am., Senator for Utah (1862–1947), 1912 C
Smooth-Hawley tariff, 1930 F
Smrkovsky´, Josef, Czechoslovak National Assembly Chairman, 1968 D
Smuggling in Britain, checked, 1784 G. *See also under* Free Trade
Smuts, Jan Christian, S. Afr. statesman (1870–1950), 1870 Z, 1916 F, 1950 Z; electoral defeat, 1924 F; joins Hertzog's cabinet, 1933 E; unites with Hertzog's followers to form United South African Nationalists, 1934 F; becomes premier, 1939 J; addresses British Parliament, 1942 K; at UN Conference, 1945 D; heads United Party ministry, 1945 K; refuses to place South-West Africa under UN trusteeship, 1947 A; coalition led by, defeated by Nationalist-Afrikander *Bloc*, 1948 E
Smyth, Dame Ethel Mary, B. musician (1858–1944), 1906 T, 1916 T
Snooker
Thorburn wins world championship, 1980 X
televisation, 1985 X
Snow Country (Y. Kawabata), 1948 U
Snow Leopard, The (P. Matthiessen), 1979 U
Snow Maiden, The (A. Ostrovsky), 1872 W
Snow, Charles Percy, lord Snow, B. novelist and scientist (1905–80), 1905 Z, 1950 Z, 1950 U, 1954 U, 1962 U, 1964 U, 1980 Z; delivers Richmond Lecture, 1959 U
Snowden, Sir Philip, B. Labour politician (1864–1937), as chancellor of Exchequer, 1924 A, 1929 F; is expelled from Labour Party, 1931 H
Snowden, lord. *See* Armstrong-Jones, Anthony
Soames, Sir (Arthur) Christopher John, Lord Soames, B. Conservative politician (1920–87), 1972 K, 1979 M
Soane, Sir John, B. architect (1753–1837), 1795 S, 1803 S
Soares, Mario Alberto Nobve Lopes, Port. politician (b. 1924), 1983 F, 1991 A
Sobers, Sir Garfield St Auburn, 'Garry', W. Ind. cricketer (b. 1936), 1936 Z, 1968 X, 1974 X
Sobhuza II, King of Swaziland (1899–1982), 1968 J
Soblen, Robert, Am. spy (d. 1962), asylum for, refused in Britain, 1962 G
Sobol, Joshua, Israeli playwright (b. 1939), 1989 W
Sobrahan, India, battle, 1846 B
Sobrero, Ascacio, It. chemist (1811–70), 1846 P
Soccer:
transfer fees, 1966 X, 1979 X, 1988 X
World Cup, 1966 X, 1969 G, 1970 X, 1974 X, 1978 X, 1982 X, 1986 X, 1990 X
first Scottish team to win European Cup, 1967 X
Queen's Park Rangers, 1967 X, 1981 X
Third Division side win cup final, 1967 X
Manchester United, 1968 X
Honduras-El Salvador border incidents following World Cup qualifying round, 1969 G
Rimet Trophy, 1970 X
Ibrox Park stadium disaster, 1971 A
Sunderland win FA Cup, 1973 X
Ramsey sacked as English manager, 1974 X
West Germany wins World Cup, 1974 X
Liverpool's League Championship record, 1976 X, 1980 X
hooliganism, 1979 X, 1980 X
AC Milan relegated by disciplinary commission, 1980 X
EUFA fines British Football Association, 1980 X
first League match on artificial turf, 1981 X
Bradford City fire, 1985 X
English clubs banned from European competitions, 1985 X
Heysel Stadium riot, 1985 X
Hillsborough disaster, 1989 X
English clubs form premier league, 1991 X
Liverpool returns to European football, 1991 X
Social Anthropology (M. Mead), 1950 R
Social Democrats. *See under* Political Parties
Social Progress and Educational Waste (K. Lindsay), 1926 O
Social Question, The (A. Wagner), 1871 O
Social Revolution (B. Kidd), 1894 O
Social Security:
in Belgium, 1936 F
in Britain, Beveridge Plan, 1942 O. *See also under* legislation
supplementary benefit, 1966 O
National Insurance benefits increased, 1972 C
child allowance, 1973 G
National Insurance changes proposed, 1985 C
in Canada, 1936 F
in France, 1952 A
in Germany, 1903 D
in US, 1935 H. *See also under* New Deal
Social Statics (H. Spencer), 1850 O
Social System, The (T. Parsons), 1951 R
Social and Economic History of the Roman Empire (Rostovziev), 1926 Q
Social and Political Doctrines of Contemporary Europe, The (M. Oakeshott), 1939 O
Socialism and the Christian Church (E. Troeltsch), 1912 R
Socialism:
condemned by Pius IX, 1849 R
state, advocated, 1862 O
Jaurès advocates, 1911 D
studies in, 1936 O, 1937 O
Socialist Parties. *See under* Political Parties
Socialist Party, in Britain. *See under* Political Parties, Labour Party
Society Islands, Pacific, explored, 1768 P
Society of Jesus. *See* Jesuits
Sociology (W. Sombart), 1936 R
Sociology, studies in, 1846 O, 1850 O, 1853 R, 1858 O, 1873 O, 1916 R
Socorro, New Mexico, US, Very Large Array (VLA) satellite, 1980 P
Soda manufacturing processes for, 1787 P, 1838 P, 1861 P, 1894 P

Soddy, Frederick, B. scientist (1877–1956), 1877 Z, 1904 P, 1911 P, 1913 P, 1956 Z
Soderbergh, Steven, Am. film director (b. 1963), 1989 W
Söderblom, Nathan Swe, theologian (1866–1947), 1933 R
Sodium, electrical preparation of, 1806 P
Sofia, Bulgaria: military *coup* in, 1886 H; Macedonian revolutionaries in, 1895 F
SOGAT , picket of News International Plant, Wapping, 1987 A, B
SOGAT '82, Dean elected leader, 1984 O
Soglo, Nicephore, President of Benin (b. 1934), 1991 C
Sohab and Rustrum (M. Arnold), 1853 U
Soissons, France: battles near, 1915 A; German withdrawal from, 1917 B; Germans take, 1918 E; French recapture, 1918 H
Sol Senn, Commander in Chief of Khmer Rouge Army, 1985 J
Solar battery, 1954 P
Solar cells tested by satellite, 1958 P
Soldaten, Die (J. Lenz), 1776 W
Soldier's Play, A (C. Fuller), 1981 W
Soldiers' Pay (W. Faulkner), 1926 U
Solferino, Italy, Austrian defeat at, 1859 F
Solid Mandala, The (P. White), 1966 U
Solidarity, Pol. trade union:
- registered, 1980 K
- delegation received by Pope, 1981 A
- branded counter-revolutionary by USSR, 1981 C
- blockades Warsaw city centre, 1981 H
- national congress of, 1981 J
- supporters demonstrate against martial law, 1982 E
- banned, 1982 K
- Walesa released from detention, 1982 L
- Gdansk shipyard workers demand Solidarity's restoration, 1983 C
- Walesa returns to work at Lenin Shipyard, Gdansk, 1983 D
- demonstrations, 1983 E, 1985 E
- leaders detained, 1988 E
- Walesa talks with Polish authorities, 1988 H
- legalized, 1989 D
- landslide victory in parliamentary elections, 1989 F
- government led by, 1989 H, J

Soloman, H., Am. manufacturer of canned foods, 1874 P
Solomon Gursky Was Here (M. Richler), 1990 U
Solomon Islands, Pacific, US recovers, 1944 B
- independence, 1978 G
- intention to change status to republic announced, 1989 C

Solomon, (born Solomon Cutner), B. pianist (1902–88), 1902 Z, 1910 T, 1988 Z
Solvay, Ernest, Belg. chemist (1838–1922), 1861 P
Solzhenitsyn, Alexander Isayevich, R. author and dissident (b. 1918), 1918 Z, 1962 U, 1971 U 1974 U, 1990 H
- Nobel Prize for Literature, 1972 D
- deportation, 1974 B
- Russian State Literature Prize, 1990 U

Somalia, 1960 F
- peace agreement with Ethiopia, 1988 D
- civil war, 1991 A, 1992 B
- United Somali Congress, 1991 A
- Somali National Movement declares north independent, 1991 E
- operation 'Restore Hope', 1992 M
- UN military observers, 1992 G

Somaliland, British: exploration, 1854 P; protectorate established, 1884 N; Mad Mullah raids on, 1899 J; Italian advance into, 1940 H; becomes independent, 1960 F; joins Somalia, 1960 F
Somaliland, French, boundary defined, 1897 C
Somaliland, Italian: Mad Mullah raids on, 1899 J; occupation completed, 1925 K; becomes protectorate, 1925 K; clashes on Abyssinian frontier with, 1934 M; British troops invade, 1941 B; trusteeship is transferred to Italy, 1950 D
Sombart, Werner, G. economist (1863–1934), 1863 Z, 1920 O, 1936 R
Some Aspects of British Civilization (H. L. Fleure), 1948 P
Somerville, William, B. physician and explorer of Africa (1771–1860), 1802 P
Somme, River, France, battles, 1916 G, 1918 C
Sömmering, Samuel Thomas, G. anatomist and inventor, 1809 P
Somoza, General Anastasio, Jnr, President of Nicaragua (1925–80), 1967 B, 1979 G
Son of a Servant, The (A. Strindberg), 1886 U
Sonatas, notable:
- by Beethoven, *Appassionata*, 1807 T
  - *Les Adieux*, 1811 T
  - *Moonlight*, 1802 T
  - *Pathétique*, 1799 T
  - *Kreutzer*, 1803 T
- *St. Michael* for wind instruments (P. M. Davies), 1959 T
- by Ravel, 1922 T, 1927 T
- by Walton, 1950 T

Sonderbund, The, in Switzerland, 1845 M; War of, 1847 K
Sonette am Orpheus (R. M. Rilke), 1922 U
Song of Bernadette, The (F. Werfel), 1941 U
Song of Hiawatha, The (H. W. Longfellow), 1855 U
Song-cycles:
- Heiss, *Expression K*, 1956 T
- Hindemith, *Das Marienleben*, 1924 T
- Schoenberg, *Pierrot Lunaire*, 1912 T

Songlines (B. Chatwin), 1987 U
Songs of Experience (W. Blake), 1794 U
Songs of Innocence (W. Blake), 1789 U
Songs of Praise (hymnal), 1925 R
Songs of the Fleet (H. Newbolt), 1910 U
Songs, Popular:
- *Alexander's Ragtime Band* (I. Berlin), 1911 T
- *Hang Out the Washing on the Siegfried Line*, 1939 W
- *Last Time I Saw Paris, The* (J. Kern), 1939 W
- *Lili Marlene*, 1940 W
- *Pack Up Your Troubles*, 1915 W
- *Roll Out the Barrel*, 1939 W
- *Tar-ra-ra-boom-de-ay*, 1892 W

Sonic Youth, Am. pop group, 1985 W, 1988 W
Sonnets from the Portuguese (E. B. Browning), 1850 U
Sonnino, Sidney, baron (1847–1922), It. statesman, 1902 M
Sons and Lovers (D. H. Lawrence), 1913 U
Sony 'Walkman', personal tape recorder/player, 1980 P
Sophie's Choice (W. Styron), 1979 U
Sophocles, tragedies of, translated into German, 1804 Q
Sorel, Albert, F. historian (1842–1906), 1842 Z, 1885 Q, 1906 Z, 1908 O
Sorrell and Son (W. Deeping), 1925 U
Sorrows of Werther (Goethe), 1774 U
Sotheby's, auctioneers, 1983 S
Soubirous, Bernadette, of Lourdes, 1858 R
Soulie de satin (P. Claudel), 1929 W
Soult, Nicholas Jean, F. soldier (1769–1851), 1769 Z, 1809 E, 1811 E, L, 1851 Z
Sound films, 1919 P, 1927 W
Sound, experiments concerning, 1800 P; treatise on, 1877 P
Sounding-machine, Kelvin, 1872 P
Sound and the Fury, The (W. Faulkner), 1929 U
Sous l'Oeil des Barberes (M. Barrès), 1808 U
Soustelle, Jacques, F. Left Republican (1912–90), governor-general of Algeria, 1955 A
South Africa:
- Smith annexes country between Orange and Vaal rivers, 1848 B
- problems of federation in, 1875 H, 1877 C, 1880 F
- War. *See under* Wars, Britain with Boers
- becomes a dominion, 1910 G
- Portuguese labour in, regulated, 1928 J
- becomes an independent republic outside the Commonwealth, 1961 E
- International Court of Justice ruling, 1971 F
- 'petty apartheid' measures abolished, 1975 D
- Transkei first nominally independent 'homeland', 1975 K
- riots, 1976 F, 1984 J
- National Party election victory, 1977 L
- Bophuthatswana becomes nominally independent, 1977 M
- information scandal, 1978 B, L, M, 1979 D, F
- Information Department abolished, 1978 F
- *The Citizen*, funding of, 1978 K
- Erasmus Commission report, 1978 M, 1979 D, F
- inter-racial marriage and sexual intercourse, 1981 K, 1985 D, F
- new constitution approved, 1983 L
- Botha visits Britain, 1984 F
- three-chamber Parliament, 1985 A
- Mandela refuses offer of freedom conditional on renunciation of violence, 1985 B
- police fire on crowds at Uitenhage, 1985 C
- withdrawal from Angola announced, 1985 D
- Namibia, 1985 F
- state of emergency, 1985 G, H, 1986 C, F, 1990 F
- Parliamentary representation for blacks ruled out, 1985 H
- Boesak arrested, 1985 H
- sanctions against, 1985 J, 1986 F, H, J, K, R, 1992 A
- emergency restrictions put on reporting of unrest, 1985 L
- Congress of South African Trade Unions, 1985 L
- Winnie Mandela removed from her home, 1985 M
- urbanization, 1985 Y
- pass laws abolished, 1986 D
- blacks expelled from Crossroads squatter camp, 1986 E
- Howe peace mission, 1986 F, G
- Esso announces withdrawal from, 1986 M
- American subsidiaries closed or sold off, 1986 O
- racism declared sin by Dutch Reformed Church, 1986 R
- National Party election victory, 1987 E
- relaxation of Group Areas Act recommended, 1987 J
- Separate Amenities Act, 1987 J, 1989 L
- Commonwealth Conference declaration, 1987 K
- clergy detained following protest, 1988 B
- simultaneous elections to white, black and coloured local councils, 1988 K
- South African Council of Churches bombed, 1988 R

sporting contacts severed, 1988 X
law commission calls for abolition of apartheid and introduction of universal franchise, 1989 O
clashes between ANC and Zulu Inkatha movement, 1990 H
National Party membership opened to all races, 1990 K
UN ends ban on sporting, academic and scientific links with, 1991 M
readmitted to International Olympic Committee and International Cricket Conference, 1991 X
constititutional and political reform, 1992 C
Boipatong massacre, 1992 F
Inkatha Movement, 1992 F
troops fire on ANC demonstrators, 1992 J
Goldstone Commission on state dirty tricks campaign against ANC, 1992 L
See also under Cape of Good Hope; Transvaal
South African Company, British: is chartered, 1889 K; founds Salisbury, 1890 J; organises Rhodesia, 1895 E
South African Republic, of Transvaal, established, 1852 A
See under Transvaal.
South Arabia, negotiations on transfer of power, 1967 L
South Carolina, State, US: rejects tariff act, 1832 G; as Confederate state, 1861 B
South East Asia Treaty Organization (SEATO) Conference at Bangkok, 1955 B; Sarassin appointed Secretary-General, 1957 J; dissolution 1977 F
South Foreland lighthouse, Kent, England, 1858 P
South Georgia:
Argentinian flag raised on, 1982 C
recaptured by British forces, 1982 D
South Pole. *See under* Polar Exploration
South Seas, discoveries in, 1775 P
South Wind (N. Douglas), 1917 U
South Yemen, president assassinated, 1978 F
South-East England, study on development of, 1964 C
South-West Africa People's Organization (SWAPO), 1992 L
Nujoma returns to Namibia, 1989 J
Nujoma elected first president of Namibia, 1990 B
Southall, London, National Front, 1979 D, 1981 G
Southcott, Joanna, B. fanatic (1750–1814), 1814 Z
Southey, Robert, B. author (1774–1843), 1774 Z, 1794 W, 1801 U, 1805 U, 1813 Q, 1814 U
Southwest Africa: German colonies in, 1883 D; German occupation, 1884 D; boundary with Angola, 1886 M; risings in, 1904 K; German forces surrender to British, 1915 G; assigned as mandated territory to S. Africa and Belgium, 1919 E; political activities by foreigners in, prohibited, 1937 D; UN rejects S. African proposal for incorporation, 1946 M; Smuts refuses to place under UN trusteeship, 1947 A, 1950 M; South African mandate over ended by UN, 1966 K; UN demands South African withdrawal, 1967 M; terrorism, 1968 B; *See also* Namibia
Souvenirs d'enfance et de jeunesse (Renan), 1883 U
Soviet Communism: A New Civilization (S. and B. Webb), 1935 O
Soweto, S. Africa
riots, 1976 F 1976 H
Winnie Mandela removed from her home, 1985 M
Soyinka, Wole, Nig. dramatist (b. 1934), 1971 W, 1975 W
Spa, Belgium: beauty contest at, 1888 V; Conference on Reparations at, 1920 G
Spaak, Paul, Belg. statesman Socialist (1899–1972), 1899 Z, 1972 Z; forms coalition, 1938 E; president of U.N. General Assembly, 1946 A; Secretary-general of NATO, 1956 M
Space flights:
dogs sent in orbit in, 1958 P, 1959 P
monkeys sent in orbit in, 1959 P
Y. Gagarin, 1961 P
A. Shepard, 1961 P
J. Glenn, 1962 P
M. Scott Carpenter, 1962 P
G. Cooper, 1963 P
V. Tereshkova, 1963 P
A. Leonov, 1965 P
link-up of manned space craft, 1966 P
Soviet cosmonaut dies during descent of Soyuz I spacecraft, 1967 P
US astronauts die in training exercise, 1967 P
manned mission to moon, 1968 P
manned moon landing, 1969 G, P
Soviet cosmonauts die, 1971 P
record times spent in space, 1978 P, 1979 P, 1980 P
first US woman astronaut in space, 1983 P
Challenger space shuttle explodes, 1986 A, P
record 326 days spent in space station, 1987 P
Space Research: Programmes for launching satellites, 1955 P; Sputniks I and II, launched, 1957 P; Lunik I, launched, 1959 P; Lunik II, reaches moon, 1959 P; Lunik III, photographs moon, 1959 P; Gemini III–VI launched, 1965 P
Agena rocket, 1966 P
Cygnus constellation, X-ray emissions discovered, 1966 P
dark side of moon photographed, 1966 P
first soft moon landing, 1966 P
Gemini VIII, 1966 P
Gemini XII, 1966 P
Luna XIII, 1966 P
Luna IX, 1966 P Luna XI, 1966 P
Lunar Orbiter I, 1966 P
man-made object lands on another planet, 1966 P
Surveyor I, 1966 P
Venera probes, 1966 P, 1967 P, 1975 P, 1978 P, 1982 P, 1983 P
nuclear weapons from outer space, 1967 O
first soft landing on another planet, 1967 P
Apollo VII, 1968 P
Apollo VIII, 1968 P
Zond V mission, 1968 P
Apollo X, 1969 P
Apollo IX, 1969 P
Apollo XI, 1969 P
experimental space station, 1969 P
Apollo XIII moon landing aborted, 1970 P
Luna XVI moon landing, 1970 P
Luna XVII deploys Lunokhod I moon vehicle, 1970 P
Apollo XIV, 1971 P
Apollo XV lunar rover, 1971 P
Mariner IX photographs Mars, 1971 P
Mars II orbits Mars, 1971 P
Mars III capsule lands on Mars, 1971 P
Salyut I space station, 1971 P
Apollo XVI, 1972 P
Apollo XVII, 1972 P
first man-made object to leave solar system, 1972 P, 1983 P
Pioneer X, 1972 P, 1973 P, 1983 P
soft landing on Venus, 1972 P
Venus VIII, 1972 P
Skylab, 1973 P, 1979 P
Jupiter reached, 1974 P
Mariner X photographs Venus and Mercury, 1974 P
Pioneer XI, 1974 P, 1979 P
Apollo XVIII docks with Soyuz XIX, 1975 P
European Space Agency, 1975 P, 1979 P
Helios I space probe, 1975 P
Soyuz XIX docks with US Apollo XVIII, 1975 P
Viking I and II transmit Mars data, 1976 P
Voyagers I and II, 1977 P, 1979 P, 1980 P, 1981 P
moon of Pluto discovered, 1978 P
Pioneer I and II, orbit Venus, 1978 P
Seasat I launched for ocean monitoring, 1978 P
Ariane rocket, 1979 P
High Energy Astronomy Observatory (HEAO2; later renamed the Einstein Observatory), 1979 P
Saturn, rings of, 1979 P
Sun, data on, 1979 P
atmosphere discovered on Pluto, 1980 P
US shuttle with orbiter *Columbia,* 1981 P
US space shuttle, 1981 P, 1982 P, 1983 P, 1985 P, 1986 A, 1986 P, 1988 P, 1989 P, 1990 P, 1991 P,1992 P
Columbia space shuttle, 1982 P, 1991 P
Challenger space shuttle, 1983 P, 1986 A, 1986 P
untethered space walk, 1984 P
Atlantis space shuttle, 1985 P
Discovery space shuttle, 1985 P, 1990 P
probes launched to rendezvous with Halley's comet, 1985 P
Giotto space probe, 1986 P
Mir space station, 1986 P, 1987 P
satellites of Uranus discovered, 1986 P
Voyager II space probe, 1986 P
Energia superbooster space launcher, 1987 P
Buran space shuttle, 1988 P
Phobos space probes, 1988 P
Soviet space shuttle, 1988 P
US–USSR draft space defence treaty, 1988 A
COBE (Cosmic Background Explorer), 1989 P, 1992 P
Galileo probe, 1989 P, 1991 P
Hipparcos satellite, 1989 P
Magellan probe, 1989 P, 1990 P
surface of Venus mapped, 1989 P
Voyager II, 1989 P
Hubble Space Telescope placed in Earth orbit, 1990 P
Japanese moon probe, 1990 P
Röntgensatellite, 1990 P
Voyager II, 1990 P
Arthur Holly Gamma Ray Observatory, 1991 P
Space Life Sciences-1, 1991 P
Endeavour space shuttle, 1992 P
Ulysses probe, 1992 P
See also Astronomy; Satellites, artificial
Space Research Organisation, European, 1962 F
Space, Outer, US–Russian agreement on peaceful use of, 1962 M
Space, Time and Deity (S. Alexander), 1920 R
Space, scale of, 1953 P
Space, walks in, 1965 P
Spain: Social classes in, 1773 N; troops finally leave South America, 1824 M; frontier with France, defined, 1856 M
young 'technocrats' take office, 1969 K
Church and State separation called form, 1971 B
agrees to pull out of Sahara, 1975 L
monarchy restored, 1975 L
amnesty for political prisoners, 1976 G
abolishes death penalty in peacetime, 1978 H

Basque separatists demand for autonomy recognized, 1978 J
devolution of power to Basque provinces approved, 1979 K
Basque regional parliament, 1980 C
border with Gibralter re-opened, 1980 D
coup d'état, 1981 B
replacement of armed forces' chiefs, 1982 A
agrees to end blockade of Gibralter, 1982 A
court martial of officers involved in coup, 1982 B
general election, 1982 K
EC membership, 1985 C, F, 1986 A
NATO membership, 1986 C
general strike, 1988 M
contaminated cooking oil kills over 600 people, 1989 E
Spain, 1808–1939 (R. Carr), 1966 Q
Spallanzani, Lazaro, It. scientist (1729–99), 1765 P, 1779 P, 1780 P
Spandau Prison, Berlin:
Speer and von Schirach released, 1966 J
Spangenberg, August Gottlieb, G. theologian (1704–92), bishop of Moravian Brethren, 1764 R
Spark, Muriel, B. author, 1959 U
Sparkenbrook (C. Morgan), 1936 U
'Spartacus' Communist group in Berlin, 1916 A, 1919 A
Spassky, Boris Vasiliyevich, R. chess player (b. 1937), 1972 X
Special Air Service (SAS):
sent to Northern Ireland, 1976 A
storms Iranian embassy in London, 1980 D
Species, origin of, propounded by Darwin, 1859 P
Species, variation of, 1858 P
Specimens of the Russian Poets (J. Bowring), 1821 U
Spectrum analysis, 1859 P, 1861 P
Speech Acts (J.R. Searle), 1969 R
Speech, transmission of first, 1861 P; by telephone, 1876 P; by wireless, 1900 P
Speeches, notable:
Acheson, at West Point, 1962 M
Balfour, in Washington, 1917 E
Bismarck's 'Blood and Iron', 1862 J
Burke, on Conciliation with America, 1775 O; on French Revolution, 1790 B
J. Chamberlain, at Leicester, 1899 L
Lord R. Churchill, at Dartford, 1886 K
W. S. Churchill, 'Blood and Toil', 1940 E; at Fulton, 1946 C
Dulles, in Berlin, 1958 E
Eisenhower, on Communist threat, 1954 D
Kennedy, on Cuba, 1962 K
Lavigerie's 'Algiers Toast', 1890 L
Lloyd George's 'New Deal' at Bangor, 1935 A
H. Macmillan's 'Wind of Change', in Capetown, 1960 B
G. Marshall, at Harvard, 1947 F
Palmerston's, 'Civis Romanus Sum', 1850 F
F. D. Roosevelt, on 'Policy of the Good Neighbour', 1933 C
Speed limit, in Britain, for motor vehicles, 1903 H, 1935 C
Speed records:
ground, by Campbell, 1935 P
by Cobb, 1939 P, 1947 P
locomotive, 1939 P
water, by Campbell, 1939 P
by Cobb, 1952 P
Speed-reducing gear, for turbines, 1910 P
Speed-the-Plow (D. Mamet), 1988 W
Speenhamland, Berks., England, system of poor relief, 1795 O
Speer, Albert, G. architect and politician (1905–81), 1966 J
Speke, John Hanning, B. explorer (1827–64), 1854 P, 1856 P
Spellman, Francis Joseph, Am. Cardinal (1889–1967), Archbishop of New York, 1966 M
Spence, Sir Basil, B. architect (1907–76), 1907 Z, 1951 S, 1959 S, 1962 S, 1964 S, 1976 Z
Spence, Thomas, B. bookseller and author (1750–1814), 1775 O
Spencer, Herbert, B. philosopher (1820–1903), 1850 O, 1852 P, 1855 R, 1861 O, 1862 O, 1873 O, 1879 R, 1884 O
Spencer, John Poyntz, earl Spencer, B. Liberal politician (1835–1910), as first lord of Admiralty, 1894 N
Spencer, Lady Diana Frances (b. 1961), 1961 Z
marriage, 1981 G
See also Wales, Princess of
Spencer, Sir Stanley, B. artist (1891–1959), 1891 Z, 1913 S, 1920 S, 1922 S, 1923 S, 1926 S, 1934 S, 1935S, 1939 S, 1941 S, 1945 S, 1959 Z
Spender, Sir Stephen, B. poet and critic (b. 1909), 1909 Z, 1937 O
Spengler, Oswald, G. philosopher (1880–1936), 1880 Z, 1918 O, 1920 O, 1931 R, 1936 Z
Speranski, Mikhail Mikhailovich, Count, R. statesman (1772–1839), 1830 U
Sperry, Elmer Ambrose, Am. inventor (1861–1930), 1861 Z, 1930 Z
Sperry, William Learoyd, Am. author (1882–1954), 1945 R
Spezia, N. W. Italy, 1888 B
Sphinx Rock, Bernese Oberland, meteorological station, 1937 P
Sphymograph, 1878 P
Spicer-Dufuy process for colour photography, 1931 P
Spicheren, Alsace-Lorraine, France, German victory at, 1870 H
Spielberg, Steven, Am. film director (b. 1947), 1975 W, 1982 W
Spinks, Leon, Am. boxer, 1978 X
Spinning jenny, 1864 P
Spinning machine, for cotton, 1762 P; for flax, 1812 P
Spinning mule, Crompton's, 1779 P
Spinola, Antonio Sebastiao Ribesvo de, Port. army officer and politician (b. 1910), 1974 D, J
Spiral Jetty (Smithson), 1970 S
Spire, The (W. Golding), 1964 U
Spirit of Hebrew Poetry, The (Herder), 1782 U
Spirit of '76, The: The Growth of American Patriotism Before Independence, 1607–1776 (C.Bridenbaugh), 1975 Q
Spirit of the Age (E. Arndt), 1806 O
Spirit of the Age; or Contemporary Portraits (W. Hazlitt), 1825 U
Spiritualism, in US, 1848 R
Spithead, Hampshire, England, naval mutiny at, 1797 D
Spitzbergen, Norway: assigned to Norway, 1919 J; ceded to Norway, 1920 B; Norway annexes, 1925 H; expedition to, 1927 P
Splitting the atom, 1942 P
Spontaneous generation, 1765 P, 1870 P
Spontini, Gasparo Luigi Pacificio, It. musician (1774–1851), 1809 T
Spooner, John Coit, Am. Republican (1843–1919), 1901 C
Sport
Sportaid's 'Race Against Time', 1986 X
drug abuse, 1988 X
Sport and the British (R. Holt), 1989 Q
Sportsman's Sketches, A (I. Turgeniev), 1852 U
Sportsylvania Courthouse, Virginia, US battle, 1864 E
Spratly Islands, China and Vietnam clash over, 1988 C
Spreckelsen, Johann Otto von, architect, 1989 S
Sprengel, Kurt, G. botanist (1766–1833), 1793 P
Spreti, Count von, W. Germ. diplomat, 1970 C
Spring's Awakening (F. Wedekind), 1891 U
Spring, Howard, B. author (1889–1966), 1948 U
Springsteen, Bruce, Am. pop singer (b. 1949), 1975 W, 1984 W
Spurgeon, Charles Haddon, B. nonconformist preacher (1834–92), 1852 R, 1900 R
Spurzheim, Johann, G. phrenologist (1776–1832), 1810 P
'Spy', cartoonist, *See* Ward, Leslie
Spy, The (J. F. Cooper), 1821 U
Spycatcher (P. Wright), 1986 G, 1988 F
Squeaker, The (E. Wallace), 1928 U
Sri Lanka:
republic of, 1972 E
government defeat in elections, 1977 G
Jayawardene becomes President, 1978 B
curfew imposed and political parties advocating partition banned, 1983 G
illiteracy, 1983 Y
amity talks between Tamil and Sinhalese representatives, 1984 A
clashes between Tamils and Sinhalese, 1984 H
Tamil terrorists attack Sri Lankan army convoy, 1984 M
attack on Anuradhapura, 1985 E
Sri Lankan–Indian summit to discuss violence in, 1985 F
Tamils, 1986 H
Tamil terrorists ambush buses near Trincomala, 1987 D
civil war, ceasefire, 1989 F
SS 'Amsterdam' in Front of Rotterdam (M. Morley), 1966 S
Stabiles, 1932 S
Stabilising the Dollar in Purchasing Power (I. Fisher), 1919 O
Stack, Sir Lee, B. governor of Sudan (1868–1924), 1924 O
Stack, Tommy, jockey, 1977 X
Staël, Anne Louis Germaine Necker, baronne de Staël-Holstein, F. author (1766–1817), 1766 Z, 1800 U, 1802 U, 1807 U, 1810 U, 1817 Z, 1818 U
Stahl, Friedrich Julius, G. ecclesiastical lawyer (1802–61), 1830 O
Staines, Surrey, England, BEA Trident crashes, 1972 F
Stainless steel, invented, 1912 P
Stakas, Kid, 1977 W
Stalin, Joseph, R. dictator (1879–1953), 1879 Z, 1926 K, 1934 M, 1947 C, 1953 C
victorious at All-Union Congress, 1927 M
makes neutrality pact with Japan, 1941 D
becomes head of USSR government, 1941 E
meets Churchill, in Moscow, 1942 H
and Roosevelt at Teheran, 1943 L
Ode to, 1943 T
at Yalta Conference, 1945 B
at Potsdam Conference, 1945 G
as Chairman of Council of Ministers, 1946 C
policies of, denounced by Khrushchev, 1956 B
Stalingrad, Russia: Germans reach, 1942 H; sword presented to, 1943 B
'Stalin Line', Russia, Russian troops retire to, 1941 G
Stalky and Co. (R. Kipling), 1899 U
Stambolisky, Alexander, Bulgarian politician (1879–1923), 1923 F

Stambulov, Stephen, Bulgarian Nationalist (1854–95), 1886 J, 1895 G
Stamp Act, Britain, imposes on American Colonies, 1765 C
repealed, 1766 B
Stamp Act Congress, in America, 1765 K
Stamp duties, in Britain, reduced, 1836 H
Stamps, postage. *See under* Postal services
Stamps, trading, campaign against, 1963 O
Standard Oil Company: Rockefeller founds, 1870 P;
dissolution ordered, 1911 E; rights in Palestine, 1922 D
Standards of Living in the Later Middle Ages: Social Change in England, c. *1200–1520* (C. Dyer), 1989 Q
Standards, electrical, 1861 P
Standing Man (De Andrea), 1970 S
Stanford, Sir Charles Villiers, B. musician (1852–1924), 1852 Z, 1884 T, 1924 Z
Stanhope, Charles, third earl Stanhope, B. Whig politician and scientist (1753–1816), 1774 O, 1800 P
Stanhope, Philip Dormer Stanhope, earl of Chesterfield (1694–73), 1773 Z, 1774 U
Stanislaus II (Pontiatowski), King of Poland (1764–1795), 1768 H, 1791 E; elected King, 1764 J; abdicates, 1795 L
Stanislaus Lesczcynski, King of Poland (1733–6), ruler of Lorraine (1730–66), 1766 B
Stanislavsky, Constantin, R. Choreographer (1863–1938), 1863 Z, 1938 Z
Stanley, Arthur Penrhyn, B. churchman and scholar (1815–81), 1861 Q
Stanley, Edward, 14th earl of Derby, B. Conservative statesman (1799–1869), 1799 Z, 1851 B, 1859 C, 1869 Z
becomes premier, 1852 B, 1858 B, 1866 G
resigns, 1852 M, 1859 F, 1868 B
Stanley, Edward Henry, 15th earl of Derby, B. Conservative (1826–93), 1878 D; as foreign secretary, 1874 B; protests against Jingoism, 1878 A
Stanley, Sir Henry Morton, B. explorer of Africa (1840–1904), 1840 Z, 1875 P, 1880 F, 1887 P; meets Livingstone, 1871 P
Stanley, James, B. machinist (1831–81), 1885 P
Stanley, Oliver Frederick George, B. Conservative politician (1896–1950), War Secretary, 1940 A
Stanleyville, Congo: rebels capture, 1964 H; is recaptured, 1964 L
Stans, Maurice Hubert, Am. Republican politician (b. 1908), 1972 J
Stansgate, peerage, election court ruling on, 1961 O
Stansgate, viscount. *See* Benn, A. N. W.
Stanstead Airport, Essex, England, 1967 E, 1991 S
Star Child (G. Crumb), 1977 T
Star Trek, 1966 W
Star Wars programme. *See* Strategic Defense Initiative
Starch, discovery concerning, 1862 P
Starhemberg, Prince, Aus. (1899–1956), 1935 K
Starik (Y. Trifonov), 1978 U
Stark, USS, hit by Iraqi Exocet missile, 1987 E
Starlight Express (A. Blackwood), 1916 W
Starling, Ernest Henry, B. physiologist (1866–1927), 1902 P
Stars:
See also Astronomy
codification of, 1818 P, 1862 P
Cygnus constellation, X-ray emissions discovered, 1966 P
luminosity of, 1924 P
measurements of, 1837 P
revolutions of, 1802 P
Starsky and Hutch, television series, 1975 W
State in Relation to Labour, The (W. S. Jevons), 1882 O
State of the Arts, The (Lord Bridges), 1958 S
State of the Prisons of England, The (J. Howard), 1770 O
Statement of the Question of Parliamentary Reform (G. Grote), 1821 O
Statements (A. Fugard), 1975 W
Statistical Account of Scotland, The (J. Sinclair), 1791 O
Statistical Method for Determining Authorship (A. Ellegärd), 1963 Q
Statute of Liberty, 1886 S
Stavisky, Serge, R. promoter (d. 1934), 1933 M
Staying On (P. Scott), 1977 U
Stead, William Thomas, B. journalist (1849–1912), 1890 V, 1893 R
'Steady-State' theory, 1961 P
Steam engine:
compound, 1845 P
early constructions, 1765 P, 1774 P
for cotton spinning, 1785 P
in US, first engine, 1829 P
invention perfected, 1775 P
Puffing Billy, 1812 P
Rocket, The, 1829 P
rotary motion, 1785 P
Stephenson's first effective, 1814 P
Trevithick's, 1800 P
Westinghouse brakes for, 1868 P
Steam, measurement of heat of, 1764 P
Steam road-carriage, 1769 P
Steam rolling-mill, 1790 P
Steam-hammer, Nasmyth's, 1839 P
Steam-pump, 1841 P
Steam-roller, 1859 P
Steaming (N. Dunn), 1981 W
Steamship Companies, 'Castle' and 'Union' lines amalgamate, 1900 O
Cunard, loan to, 1964 M
Steamships, notable:
Great Eastern, 1859 P
Lusitania, 1907 P, 1915 E
Mauritania, 1907 P
Normandie, 1935 P
Queen Mary, 1934 P
Savannah, 1818 P
Titanic, 1912 P
Steamships: paddle-wheel, 1783 P, Fitch's, 1787 P; early vessels, 1803 P, 1807 P, 1812 P; iron, 1820 P; screw for, 1839 P. *See also under* Merchant Shipping
Steel Corporation, US, Morgan founds, 1901 O
Steel Production:
in Austria, 1890 Y, 1911 Y
in Britain, 1820 Y, 1875 Y, 1885 Y, 1890 Y, 1896 Y, 1901 Y, 1911 Y, 1913 Y, 1924 Y, 1938 Y,
1941 Y, 1948 Y
in France, 1875 Y, 1885 Y, 1890 Y, 1896 Y, 1901 Y, 1911 Y, 1913 Y, 1924 Y, 1938 Y, 1948 Y
in Germany, 1801 Y, 1811 Y, 1821 Y, 1831 Y, 1841 Y, 1851 Y, 1861 Y, 1871 Y, 1881 Y, 1891 Y, 1901 Y, 1906 Y, 1911 Y, 1921 Y, 1926 Y, 1931 Y, 1936 Y, 1941 Y, 1946 Y, 1951 Y, 1961 Y
in Russia, 1890 Y, 1911 Y, 1913 Y, 1932 Y, 1938 Y, 1940 Y, 1948 Y
in US, 1890 Y, 1896 Y, 1901 Y, 1911 Y, 1924 Y, 1938 Y, 1942 Y, 1948 Y
Steel pens, 1780 P
Steel, Sir David Martin Scott, B. Liberal leader (b. 1938)
wins leadership election, 1976 G
'Lib–Lab' Pact, 1977 C, 1978 E
Steel-framed buildings, 1890 P
Steel:
'basic' process for, 1878 P
Bessemer's process, 1856 P
Carnegie's large furnace, 1880 P
cheap, 1856 P, 1857 P, 1861 P
continous hot-strip rolling, 1923 P
ductile, 1856 P
electric arc to heat, 1879 P
furnace lined with dolomite, 1877 P
open-hearth process, 1861 P
stainless, invented, 1912 P
steel-making converter, 1851 P
tungsten, 1855 P
See also Iron.
Steely Dan, Am. pop group, 1974 W
Steen, Alan, Am. hostage, 1991 M
Steer, Philip Paul Wilson, B. artist (1860–1942), 1860 Z, 1886 S, 1903 S, 1922 S, 1942 Z
Stein, Sir Aurel, B. archaeologist (1862–1943), 1915 Q
Stein, Gertrude, Am. author (1874–1946), 1874 Z, 1925 U, 1933 U, 1946 Z
Stein, Heinrich Friedrich Karl, baron von und zum, G. statesman (1757–1831), 1804 K, 1807 A, G, 1808 M, 1810 F, 1826 Q
Steinbeck, John, Am. author (1902–68), 1902 Z, 1939 U, 1942 U, 1968 Z
Steiner, Jakob, Swe. mathematician (1796–1863), 1832 P
Steinheim skull, 1933 P
Steintal, Alsace, France, Crêche at, 1769 O
Steinthal, Heymann, G. philosopher (1823–99), 1859 R
Steinway, William, Am. formerly G. piano manufacturer (1835–96), 1853 T
Stella, Frank Philip, Am. artist (b. 1936), 1936 Z
Charles Eliot Norton Professor of Poetry, Harvard University, 1984 S
Stellaland Republic, in Bechuanaland, S. Africa, 1873 J, 1885 C
Stellar Movement and the Structure of the Universe (Eddington), 1914 P
Stendhal. *see* Beyle, Marie Henri
Stenton, Sir Frank Merry, B. historian (1880–1967), 1944 Q
Stephanopoulos, Stephanhos, Greek leader of Social Populist Party (1893–1982), 1965 G
Stephen, Sir Leslie, B. author and philosopher (1832–1904), 1832 Z, 1882 R, 1885 Q, 1893 R, 1900 O, 1904 Z
Stephens, Alexander Hamilton, Am. Confederate, 1868 O
Stephens, Uriah, Smith, Am. garment cutter, founder of Knights of Labor (1821–82), 1869 O
Stephenson, George, B. engineer (1781–1848), 1781 Z, 1814 P, 1848 Z, 1850 P
Rocket, 1829 P
Stephinac, Aloizje, Yugoslav Cardinal (1898–1960), Archbishop of Zagreb and primate of Yugoslavia, imprisoned, 1946 J
Stereophonic gramophone recordings, 1958 P
Sterilisation of water, by ultra-violet rays, 1912 P
Stern-Rubath, G. political scientist, 1921 O
Sterne, Lawrence, B. author (1713–68), 1767 U, 1768 O, Z

Stettinius, Edward, Am. Secretary of state, (1900–1949), appointed secretary of state, 1944 L; at UN Conference, 1945 D; retires, 1945 G
Stevenage New Town, Herts., England, 1948 S
Stevens, Alfred, B. artist (1818–75), 1858 S
Stevenson, Adlai, Am. Democrat (1900–65), defeated in presidential elections, 1952 L, 1956 L
Stevenson, Elizabeth. *See* Gaskell, Elizabeth
Stevenson, Sir John Andrew, Ir. musician (1760–1833), 1807 T
Stevenson, Robert Louis, B. author (1850–94), 1850 Z, 1879 U, 1881 U, 1883 U, 1886 U, 1894 Z, 1896 U
Steward, J. D., B. author, 1958 O
Stewart, Dugald, B. philosopher (1753–1828), 1782 R, 1792 R, 1815 R, 1828 R
Stewart, (Robert) Michael Maitland, Lord Stewart, B. Labour politician (1906–90), 1966 H, 1968 C; becomes foreign secretary, 1965 A
Stewart, Robert, viscount Castlereagh, marquess of Londonderry, B. statesman, Tory (1769–1822), 1769 Z, 1807 C; fights duel with Canning, 1809 J; becomes foreign secretary, 1812 C; suicide, 1822 H
Stewart, Roderick David, 'Rod', B. pop singer (b. 1945), 1971 W
Stijl, De, 1917 S
Stimpson Doctrine, 1932 A
Stimpson, Henry Lewis, Am. secretary of state, Republican (1867–1950), 1927 E
Stirling, James, B. architect (b. 1926), 1968 S, 1972 S, 1984 S, 1986 S, 1987 S
Stock Exchange, London: compensation fund, 1950 O; public galleries opened, 1953 O; reorganisation of, 1962 O; requires companies to supply information, 1964 O
Stock Exchange, New York: built, 1903 S; crash, 1929 O
Stock, James, 1991 W
Stockach, Baden, Germany, 1799 C
Stockhausen, Karlheinz, G. musician (b. 1928), 1967 T, 1971 T, 1974 T, 1981 T, 1984 T, 1988 T
Stockholm, Sweden: national theatre, 1773 W; treaty, Britain with Sweden, 1813 C; music in, 1838 W; Town Hall, 1909 O; Olympic Games in, 1912 X; Confederation of Free Trade Union meets at, 1953 G
  Bertrand Russell International War Crimes Tribunal, 1967 E
  disarmament conference, 1984 A
Stockton-on-Tees, Durham, England, railway opened, 1825 P
Stolojan, Teodor, Prime Minister of Roumania (b. 1943), 1991 J
Stolypin, Peter, R. premier (1862–1911), 1906 F; agrarian reforms of, 1906 L; assassinated, 1911 J
Stone, Lawrence, B.-born Am. historian (b. 1919), 1977 Q
Stone, Oliver, Am. film director (b. 1946), 1986 W
Stonehenge, Wiltshire, England, excavations at, 1957 Q, 1964 Q
Stonehouse, John Thompson, B. Labour/English National/SDP politician (1925–88), 1974 L
  defects to English National Party, 1976 D
  trial, 1976 D
Stoney, Johnstone, B. physicist (1826–1911), 1891 P
Stonyhurst College, England, 1794 O
Stooges, The, Am. pop group, 1969 W
Stopes, Marie Carmichael, B. pioneer of birth control (1890–1958), 1890 Z, 1922 O, 1958 Z
Stoph, Willi, E. German politician (b. 1914), 1970 C, 1989 L
Stoppard, Tom (born Thomas Straussler), B. dramatist, 1937 Z, 1967 W, 1972 W, 1974 W 1977 W, 1982 W
Storey, David Malcolm, B. author (b. 1933), 1970 W
Storm-Troopers, Nazi, 1932 F, 1933 C
Story of Agathon, The (C. M. Wieland), 1766 U
Story of Modern Art, The (N. Lynton), 1980 Q
Story of Rimini, The (L. Hunt), 1816 U
Story of the Treasure Seekers, The (E. Nesbitt), 1899 U
Stowe, Harriet Beecher, Am. author (1811–96), 1811 Z, 1896 Z
Strachey, Giles Lytton, B. author (1880–1932), 1880 Z, 1918 U, 1921 Q, 1931 U, 1932 Z
Strachey, John, B. Labour politician and author (1902–63), 1932 O, 1936 O
Straits Settlements: becomes Crown Colony, 1867 D; under Clarke's governorship, 1873 N; treaty of federation of, 1896 G
Stranger, The (A. Kötzebue), 1797 W
Strasbourg, Bas-Rhin, France: Napoleon III's revolt at, fails, 1836 K; surrenders to Prussians, 1870 K; University, 1872 O; Allies recapture, 1944 L; becomes seat of Council of Europe, 1949 E; Congress of European Unity at, 1950 H; Assembly of W. European Union meets at, 1955 G; European Court of Human Rights meets at, 1959 B; Louis Pasteur University, 1990 P
Strassfurt, near Magdeburg, Germany, 1860 P
Strassman, W., atomic physicist, 1939 P
Strata Identified by Organised Fossils, 1816 P
Strategic Arms Limitation Talks (SALT), 1969 L, 1972 K, 1979 F, 1983 C
Strategic Defense Initiative (Star Wars programme), 1983 C, 1985 B, M, 1986 K, 1987 B
Stratford upon Avon, Warwickshire, England, Shakespeare Memorial Theatre at, 1928 S, 1932 W, 1959 W
Strauss, David Friedrich, G. theologian (1808–74), 1835 R, 1872 R
Strauss, Franz Josef, W. German politician (1915–88), 1979 G; dismissed from Ministry of Defence over *Der Spiegel* affair, 1962 L
Strauss, Johann, the younger, Aus. musician (1825–1899), 1867 T, 1874 T
Strauss, Richard, G. musician (1864–1949), 1888 T, 1889 T, 1895 T, 1896 T, 1905 T, 1907 T, 1911 T, 1912 T, 1933 T, 1945 T
Straussfedern (J. Musäus), 1786 U
Stravinsky, Igor Fyodorovich, R.-born Am. musician (1882–1971), 1882 Z, 1910 T, 1912 T, 1913 T, 1920 T, 1922 T, 1924 T, 1927 T, 1928 T, 1930 T, 1934 T, 1935 T, 1940 T, 1945 T, 1951 T, 1952 T, 1956 T, 1957 T, 1971 Z
Strawson, Sir Peter Frederick, B. philosopher (b. 1919), 1919 Z, 1974 R, 1985 R
Strayed Reveller, The (M. Arnold), 1849 U
Streeruwitz, Ernst, Aus. Chancellor, 1929 D
Street Scene (E. Rice), 1930 W
Street of Crocodiles (Théâtre de Complicité), 1992 W
Street, George Edmund, B. architect (1824–88), 1868 S
Street-lighting:
  by gas, in London, 1822 P
  by electricity, in Paris, 1841 P
    in London, 1878 P
    in New York, 1880 P
Streetcar Named Desire, A (T. Williams), 1947 W
Streeter, Burnett Hillman, B. theologian (1874–1937), 1912 R
Strehlenau, Nikolas Franz Niembsch von, Aus. poet under pseudonym 'Nikolas Lenau' (1802–50), 1836 U, 1837 U, 1842 U
Strell, Martin, G. chemist (b. 1916), 1960 P
Streptococcal injections, treatment for, 1935 P
Streptococcus, discovery of, 1880 P
Streptomycine, 1943 P, 1946 P
Stresa, Italy Conference, between Britain, France and Italy, 1935 D
Stresemann, Gustave, G. statesman (1878–1929), 1878 Z, 1925 A, 1929 K; becomes Chancellor, 1923 H; as foreign minister, 1925 A; meets Briand, 1926 J
Stretch of the Imagination, A (J. Hibberd), 1972 W
Strife of the Faculties (I. Kant), 1798 R
Strijdom, Johannes Gerhardus, S. African Nationalist (1893–1958), 1954 M, 1958 J
Strikes:
  See also under Trade Unions
  in Aden, general, 1967 D
  in Albania, general, 1991 F
  in Australia, coal miners, 1949 H
  in Austria, in Vienna, 1918 A
    general, 1927 G, 1953 K
  in Belgium, general, 1893 D, 1901 N; doctors, 1964 D
  in Britain, tailors, 1777 O
    strikes effectively prohibited, 1825 G
    general, plan for, fails, 1834 A
    agricultural workers, 1874 B
    London dockers, 1889 H, T
    peaceful picketing permitted, 1906 M
    South Wales miners, 1911 C, H
    London dockers, 1911 H, 1912 E, G
    railwaymen, 1911 H, M
    coal miners, 1912 A, B, C
    transport workers, 1912 F
    munition workers, 1916 C
    South Wales miners, 1916 L
    statistics of working days lost, 1919 Y, 1920 Y, 1921 Y, 1922 Y, 1923 Y, 1924 Y
    general strike to be called if Britain declares war on USSR, 1920 H
    coal miners, 1921 C, 1922 D
    London dockers, 1923 G
    dockers, 1924 B
    coal miners, 1926 E, L
    general strike, 1926 E
    statistics of working days lost, 1926 Y
    illegality of certain strikes under Trade Unions Act, 1927 G
    London busmen, 1937 E
    South Wales coal miners, 1944 B
    power of Minister of Labour in, agitation against, 1944 D
    repeal of Trades Disputes Act, 1946 B
    statistics of working days lost, 1946 N
    dockers, 1949 F, 1950 D
    railwaymen, 1955 E
    dockers, 1955 G
    'busmen' 1957 G, 1958 E
    printers, 1959 F
    seamen, 1966 E
    car industry, 1966 J, 1969 B, 1971 B, 1978 J, 1979 L
    dock workers, 1967 J, 1970 G, 1972 G, 1984 G, H
    steel workers, 1969 F
    teachers, 1970 A
    power station workers, work-to-rule, 1970 M
    newspaper workers, 1970 V, 1978 L
    postal workers, 1971 A

coal miners, 1972 A, B, 1973 L, 1974 B, 1981 B, 1984 C-F, H, J-L, 1985 B, C
British Rail, work-to-rule, 1972 D
civil servants, 1973 B, 1981 C
gas workers, 1973 B
hospital ancillary workers, 1973 C
TUC calls for pay policy, 1973 E
British Rail train drivers over-time ban, 1973 M
picket line ruling, 1973 O
British Rail train drivers, 1974 A
health workers, 1974 G, 1979 A, 1982 M, 1988 B
hospital consultants, work-to-rule, 1975 A, D
Glasgow refuse collectors, 1975 C
stable boys picket Ascot, 1975 X
Grunwick photographic plant, London, 1977 F
bakery workers, 1977 J, 1978 L
power station workers, 1977 K
firemen, 1977 L, 1978 A, 1980 L
petrol tanker drivers, over-time ban, 1978 L, 1979 A
'winter of discontent', 1979 A, B
lorry drivers, 1979 A
public sector workers, 1979 A
engineering workers, 1979 H-K
ITV closed down, 1979 H
Department of Employment report, 1980 A
national steel workers, 1980 A
Employment Bill, 1980 B
prison officers, work-to-rule, 1980 K
ASLEF members, over 'flexible rosters', 1982 G
compulsory ballots, legislation as to, 1983 G
television journalists, 1985 W
News International dispute, 1986 E, V, 1987 A, B
in British Guiana, general strike, 1963 D, 1964 G
sugar workers, 1964 C, G
in Canada, in Winnipeg, 1919 E
sit-down, in motor industry, 1937 C, O
in Czechoslovakia, general strike calls for end to Communist rule, 1989 L
in Denmark, statistics, 1925 Y
in France, principle of general strike, 1895 A
at Le Creusot, 1899 J
coal miners, 1901 N
postal workers, 1909 D
general strike averted, 1910 K
railwaymen, 1910 K
statistics of working days lost, 1919 Y, 1920 Y, 1921 Y, 1922 Y
strike action, 1947 E, 1953 H
1968 strikes, 1968 E
in Germany, food strike in Berlin, 1917 D
in Berlin, 1918 A
general, 1923 A, Y
public service workers, 1992 D
in Gold Coast, 1950 A
in Holland, dockers, 1903 D
railwaymen, 1903 D
statistics, 1923 Y
in Iceland, of women, 1975 K
in India, 1928 N
national rail, 1974 E
in Iran, oil workers, 1978 K
in Italy, in Genoa, 1901 B
in chief cities, 1901 N
general, prevented, 1902 B
general, 1904 J
in Japan, 1974 D
in Kosovo, Yugoslavia, by ethnic Albanians, 1990 J
in Nicaragua, 1978 A, 1979 C
in Northern Ireland, 1974 E, 1977 E, 1981 L
in Poland, 1970 M, 1980 H, 1988 E
in Russia, general, 1905 K
in South Africa, 1922 C by miners, 1985 H
in Spain, 1968 G, 1970 M, 1988 M
general, in Barcelona, 1909 G
by Socialists in Barcelona, 1934 D
frequent, 1934 K
in Sweden, 1980 E
in US, iron and steel workers, 1892 F
coal miners, 1902 E, K
steel workers, 1919 J
New York dockers, 1919 K
statistics of working days lost, 1919 Y, 1920 Y, 1921 Y, 1922 Y, 1923 Y, 1924 Y
coal miners, 1923 H
sit-down, in motor industry, 1937 O
widespread, 1945 L
steel and electrical workers, 1946 B
federal government takes over mines and railways, 1946 E
statistics of working days lost, 1946 N
position under Taft-Hartley Act, 1947 F
military control during railway strike, 1951 B
steel workers, averted, 1952 D
New York newspaper men, 1963 D
New York transport strike, 1966 A
coal miners, 1977 M, 1978 A, C
air traffic controllers, 1981 H
in USSR
Parliament bans, in key industries, 1989 K
in Uruguay, call for general strike, 1956 M
Strindberg, August, Swe. author (1849–1912), 1849 Z, 1879 W, 1886 U, 1888 W, 1897 U, 1901 U, 1905 U, 1912 Z
Stripping of the Altars, The: Traditional Religion in England, 1400–1580 (E. Duffy), 1992 Q
Stroesner, Alfredo, President of Paraguay (b. 1912), 1989 B
Stromberg, S. Africa, British defeat at, 1899 M
Stromeyer, F., Swe. chemist, 1818 P
Štrougal, Lubomir, Prime Minister of Czechoslovakia (b. 1924), 1988 K
Structuralism (J. Piaget), 1971 R
Structure Which Eats Salad (Anselmo), 1968 S
Structure and Content of Truth (D. Davison), 1990 R
Structure of Scientific Revolution, The (T.S. Kuhn), 1970 R
Structure of Social Action, The (T. Parsons), 1937 O
Structure of the Atom, The (E. Andrade), 1923 P
Struensee, Johann Frederick, Dan. politician (1731–1772), 1770 J, M, 1772 A
Struther, Jan, pseudonym of Mrs. A. K. Plazeck (née Joyce Anstruther), Am. author (1901–53), 1939 U
Strutt, John William, lord Rayleigh, B. scientist (1842–1919), 1877 P, 1894 P, 1900 P
Struve, Friedrich Georg Wilhelm, G. astronomer (1793–1864), 1837 P
Struwwelpeter (A. H. Hoffmann), 1847 U
Stuart, James, B. artist and architect (1713–88), 1794 Q
Stubbs, George, B. artist (1724–1806), 1766 S
Stubbs, William, B. medieval historian and bishop of Oxford (1825–1901), 1825 Z, 1866 Q, 1874 Q, 1901 Z
Studien über Hysterie (S. Freud), 1895 R
Studies in History and Jurisprudence (J. Bryce), 1901 Q
Studies in the Psychology of Sex (H. Ellis), 1897 R
Studies of Glaciers (Agassiz), 1840 P
Study of History, A (A. Toynbee), 1934 Q
Study of Religion, A (J. Martineau), 1888 R
Study of Sociology (H. Spencer), 1873 P
Stultiens, Jeff, artist, 1987 S
Sturdee, Sir Frederick Charles Doveton, B. admiral (1859–1925), 1914 M
Stürgkh, Carl, Count, Aus. premier (1859–1916), 1916 K
Sturm und Drang (F. M. von Klinger), 1776 W
Sturm und Drang in literature, 1766 U
Stürmer, Boris, R. premier (1848–1917), 1916 B
Stuttgart, Germany, Neue Staatsgalerie, 1984 S
Styron, William, Am. author, 1979 U
Suarez, Adolfo, Sp. politician (b. 1932), 1976 G, 1977 F, 1981 A
Subjection of Women, The (J. S. Mill), 1869 O
Submarine Warfare:
by Germany; in World War I, sinkings without warning, 1915 A, E
intensified, 1915 B
undertaking not to attack merchant shipping, 1915 J
sinkings of merchant shipping without warning, 1916 B
unrestricted warfare, 1917 A
suspended, 1918 K
losses, 1918 Y
restricted by Washington Conference, 1922 B
regulated by London Conference, 1930 D
in World War II, lay magnetic mines, 1939 L
warfare intensified, 1940 K, 1941 C
use homing torpedoes, 1945 A
losses, 1945 Y
Submarine cables, 1850 P, 1866 P
Submarines:
atomic powered, 1952 P, 1959 P
commercial, 1916 G
electric, 1896 P
the first, 1801 P
nuclear, *Nautilus*, passes under Polar ice-cap, 1958 P
Polaris, facilities for, at Holy Loch, 1960 L
Subsidies, bread, in Britain, 1956 J
mortgage loans in Britain, 1973 D
food, paid by British government, 1973 E, 1974 C
Subsidies, paid by Britain to Allies, 1809 D, 1813 C, F. *See also under* Loans
Substitution, chemical law of, 1834 P
Such is Life (F. Wedekind), 1907 W
Sudan:
exploration of, 1869 P
British occupation, 1882 J
British evacuation, 1883 L, 1885 A
under Dervish control, 1885 G
British campaigns in, 1896 G, J, 1897 G, H, 1898 D, J, L, 1899 L
Anglo-Egyptian convention on, 1899 A
frontier settlements, 1901 M, 1902 D, 1934 F
Anglo-Egyptian joint sovereignty over, 1922 C
Britain refuses Egyptian demands to evacuate, 1924 F
Anglo-Egyptian talks on, 1930 E
military operations in, end, 1945 J
preparation for self-government, 1947 A
Egypt abrogates 1899 convention, 1951 K
Anglo-Egyptian agreement on, 1953 B
proclaimed an independent republic, 1956 A
forms, with Egypt, United Arab Republic, 1958 B
alliance with UAR and Libya, 1969 M
federates with UAR, Libya and Syria, 1970 L
Egypt and Sudan announce plans for full union, 1972 H
Palestinian terrorists murder US ambassador, 1973 C

illiteracy, 1983 Y
cotton production, 1984 Y
coups, 1985 D, 1989 F
floods, 1988 H
civil war, 1989 C
Sudermann, Hermann, G. author (1857–1938), 1857 Z, 1887 U, 1938 U
Sudetenland, Czechoslovakia: riots in, 1937 K; S. Germans leave Czech Parliament, 1937 L; Halifax discusses problem with Hitler, 1937 L; Germans in demand autonomy, 1938 D; France and Britain oppose Germany, 1938 E; Runciman's role in talks, 1938 G; is transferred to Germany, 1938 J
Sue, Eugène, F. novelist (1804–57), 1844 U
Suenens, Leo Jozef, Belg. cardinal (b. 1904), awarded Templeton Prize, 1976 R
Suez Canal, Egypt:
opened, 1869 L
statistics of shipping using, 1870 Y, 1880 Y, 1939 Y, 1951 Y
Britain purchases shares in, 1875 L
Russia is warned against attempting blockade of, 1877 E
Constantinople Convention declares open to all nations, 1888 K
Convention on, 1904 D
Turks are repulsed from, 1915 B
Britain occupies Canal Zone, 1936 H
Anglo-Egyptian agreement on evacuation of Canal Zone, 1954 K
Egypt not to extend Canal Company's concession, 1956 F
last British troops leave Canal Zone, 1956 F
Nasser seizes, 1956 G
air lift of British families from Canal Zone, 1956 H
Canal-Users Association established, 1956 H
London Conferences on, 1956 H, J
Nehru's plan for, 1956 H
Britain and France refer dispute to UN, 1956 J
Dulles Plan for, rejected by Nasser, 1956 J
Anglo-French bombing of Egypt, 1956 K
Anglo-French ultimatum to Egypt and Israel, 1956 K
Israel invades Sinai, 1956 K
Israel accepts demands for cease-fire, 1956 K
Anglo-French cease-fire, 1956 L
Britain and France accept cease-fire if UN force will keep peace, 1956 L
British paratroops land at Port Said, 1956 L
UN sends force, 1956 L
Anglo-French withdrawal, 1956 M
UN fleet clears Canal, 1956 M
is re-opened to shipping, 1957 C
Anglo-Egyptian settlement of claims, 1959 B
compensation for British subjects, 1962 H
closed, 1967 F
Egypt offers to re-open if Israel withdraws from Sinai, 1971 B
ceasefire retained along, 1971 C
forces disengaged along, 1974 A
reopened, 1975 F
Suez, British commitments east of, 1966 B, 1968 A, B
Suez, Gulf of, UAR minesweepers sunk by Israeli jets, 1970 B
Suffering and Existence (K. Jaspers), 1935 R
Suffolk Convention, Massachusetts, US, 1774 H
Suffrage, The. *See under* Franchise, The
Suffragettes, in Britain, 1903 O; riots by, 1911 L; forcible feeding, of, 1912 F; demonstrations by, 1913 A: outrages by, 1913 D, 1914 C
Suffren St. Tropez, Pierre André de, F. admiral (1729–88), 1781 D
Sugarcubes, The, Icelandic pop group, 1987 W
Suhard, Archbishop of Paris, 1943 R
Suharto, General Raden, Indonesian soldier and politician (b. 1921), 1966 C
Suicide for Love (M. Akimoto), 1989 W
Suicide, Am. pop group, 1981 W
Sukarno, Achmed, Indonesian president (1901–70), 1901 Z, 1945 L, 1948 M, 1956 M, 1966 C, 1970 Z; attempted assassination, 1957 M; dissolves Constituent assembly, 1959 G; forms National Front, 1960 A; suspends Parliament, 1960 C; proclaims West New Guinea an Indonesian province, 1962 A; increases hostility to Malaysia, 1963 J
Sullivan, Sir Arthur Seymour, B. musician (1842–1900), 1842 Z, 1875 T, 1878 T, 1880 T, 1882 T, 1887 T, 1889 T, 1900 Z; ends partnership with Gilbert, 1896 T; music arranged as ballet, 1951 T
Sullivan, Francis Stoughton, B. jurist (1719–76), 1772 Q
Sully-Prudhomme, René François Armand, F. poet (1839–1907), 1878 U
Sulphapyridine ('M and B'), 1938 P
Sumgait, Azerbaijan, curfew imposed, 1988 C
Summer of the Seventeenth Doll, The (Lawler), 1955 W
Summertime, 1916 O
Summit meeting: proposed, 1958 A; preliminary talks, 1958 B, F; Khrushchev's proposals for immediate meeting rejected, 1958 G; Western powers invite Russia to, 1959 M; meeting in Paris achieved, 1960 E
Summoned by Bells (J. Betjeman), 1960 U
Sumner, Benedict Humphrey, B. historian (1893–1951), 1944 Q
Sumter, Thomas, Am. soldier (1736–1832), 1780 H
Sun Doctor, The (R. Shaw), 1962 U
Sun Yat-Sen, Chi. statesman (1867–1925), 1867 Z, 1905 N, 1911 M, 1925 Z
Sun, The:
eclipses of, 1919 P, 1936 P
rays of, measurement of heat of, 1825 P
infra-fed, 1800 P
spots, 1946 P
Sunday Schools:
in Britain, 1780 R
London Society for establishing, 1785 R
in US, 1824 R
Sunday rest:
in Austria, 1850 O
in Britain, revival of Sabbatarianism, 1835 R
Superconductivity, new superconductors discovered, 1986 P, 1987 P
Supermarkets, bar codes, 1973 P
Supernova observed, 1987 P
Supervielle, Jules, F. author (1884–1961), 1925 U
Supply, British Ministry of, 1939 O
Supports/Surfaces movement, F., 1968 S
Supreme Allied War Council, 1917 L, 1921 E
Supreme Command, The (Lord Hankey), 1961 Q
Supreme Council of National Economy, Russian, 1963 O
Supreme War Council of Central Powers, 1916 J
Sur l'homme et le développement de ses faculties (L. A. J. Quetelet), 1835 P
Surgeons, Royal College of, London, 1800 P
Surgery:
Coronary bypass operation, 1967 P
artificial human heart, 1969 P
on baby in womb, 1984 P, 1990 P
clogged arteries unblocked by laser, 1985 P, 1987 P
tissue removed from cornea by laser, 1986 P
foetus temporarily removed from womb for, 1989 P
heart repair technique, 1991 P
Surgery, transplant, 1980 P
heart, 1967 P, 1968 P
nerve transplant, 1970 P
of insulin-producing pancreatic islets, 1980 P
human embryo, 1983 P
baboon's heart tranplanted into human, 1984 P
heart, lung and liver, 1986 P
monoclonal antibody OKT3, 1986 P
five-organ, 1987 P
knee, 1987 P
bowel and liver, 1990 P
baboon liver transplanted into human, 1992 P
Surinam (formerly Dutch Guyana)
independence, 1975 L
military coup, 1982 M
military rule ended, 1988 A
Surrealism, 1917 S, 1929 S, 1935 S
Surrey, earl of. *See* Howard, Henry
Surrogate Motherhood, Warnock Report on Human Fertilization and Embryology, 1984 O
Surtees, Robert Smith, B. sporting novelist (1803–1864), 1838 U
Survey of Russian History (B. H. Sumner), 1944 Q
Süskind, Patrick, G. author (b. 1949), 1985 U
Sutcliffe, Peter, B. criminal ('the Yorkshire Ripper', b. 1946), 1981 E
Sutherland, Graham Vivian, B. artist (1903–80), 1903 Z, 1939 S, 1942 S, 1944 S, 1946 S, 1949 S, 1951 S, 1954 S, 1957 S, 1962 S, 1980 Z
Sutherland, John, B. literary critic (b. 1938), 1988 Q
Sutlej River, W. Pakistan, British gains beyond, 1846 C
Suvla, Gallipoli, Turkey: Allied landings, 1915 H; withdrawal, 1915 M
Suvorov, Alexander Vasilievich, Count Suvarov Rimniksy, R. soldier (1729–1800), 1789 G, 1790 M, 1799 D, F, H, J
Suzuki, Zenko, Prime Minister of Japan (b. 1911), 1980 F
Svevo, Italo, It. author (1861–1928), 1921 U
Svoboda, General Ludvik, President of Czechoslovakia (1895–1979), 1968 C
Swaan, Wim, Am. architect and photographer (b. 1927), 1988 Q
Swakopmund, S. W. Africa, occupied, 1915 A
Swan, Annie, S. *See* Smith, Mrs. Burnett
Swan, Sir John William, B. physicist and electrician (1828–1914), 1878 P, 1880 P
Swar al-Dahab, General Abdul Rahman, Sudanese leader (b. 1934), 1985 D
Swart, Charles Roberts, S. Afri. Natioanlist (1901–82), president of Republic, 1961 E
Swastika, becomes German flag, 1935 J
Swaziland, S. Africa, annexed by Transvaal, 1893 L
Swaziland, independence, 1968 J
Sweated industries, campaign to reform British, 1906 O
legislation to end, 1909 O
Sweden: Constitution in, 1764 D, 1769 K, M; monarchy in, 1772 G, H; union with Norway, 1813 C; acquiesces in Norway's independence, 1905 J
death of Gustaf VI Adolf, 1973 J
Carl XVI Gustaf succeeds, 1973 J
all powers removed from monarchy, 1974 B
Davis Cup victory, 1984 X
urbanization, 1985 Y
divorce statistics, 1987 Y
government resignation, 1990 B
life expectancy, 1990 Y

general election, 1991 J
illegitimacy rate, 1991 Y
policy of neutrality ended, 1992 B
Swedenborg, Emanuel, Swe. theologian (1688–1772), 1768 R, 1772 Z
Swedenborgians. *See under* Religious Denominations
Sweet Lavender (A. W. Pinero), 1888 W
Sweetness and Light: The 'Queen Anne' Movement, 1860–1900 (M. Girouard), 1977 Q
Swift, Graham Colin, B. author (b. 1949), 1984 U
Swimming records, 1927 X, 1965 X
Swinburn, Walter Robert John, B. jockey (b. 1961), 1981 X
Swinburne, Algernon Charles, B. poet (1837–1909), 1837 Z, 1865 U, 1866 U, 1878 U, 1909 Z
Swinemunde, Poland, emperors meet at, 1907 H
'Swing', term coined, 1935 T
Swinging London (R. Hamilton), 1968 S
Swinnerton, Frank Arthur, B. author (1884–1982), 1917 U
Swiss Songs (J. K. Lavater), 1767 U
Switchboard, telephone, automatic, 1892 P
Switzerland: Cantons regain independence, 1803 B; single coinage in, 1850 P
referendum approves female suffrage, 1971 O
40 hour week proposal rejected, 1976 M
Sword in the Stone, The (T. H. White), 1958 U
Sybel, Heinrich von, G. historian (1817–95), 1853 Q
Sybil, or the Two Nations (B. Disraeli), 1845 U
Sybilline Leaves (S. T. Coleridge), 1817 U
Sydney, N. S. Wales, Australia: cold store, at 1861 P; railway to Melbourne, 1883 P; convention for federation at, 1891 C; harbour, bridge, 1932 P; Commonwealth finance ministers meet at, 1954 A; Opera House, 1956 S, 1973 S, L; bicentenary of arrival of European settlers celebrated, 1988 A
Syllabus of Errors, issued by Pius IX, 1864 R; Döllinger opposes, 1869 R
Sylt, Isle of, Germany, 1940 C
Sylvain (J. F. Marmontel), 1770 U
Sylvania Waters, television documentary, 1992 W
Sylvester, James Joseph, B. mathematician (1814–1897), 1852 P
'Symbionese Liberation Army', 1976 C
Symbolism of the Ancients (G. F. Creuzer), 1810 Q
Symbolist Movement, 1855 U, 1886 V
Symphonic Poems and Suites. *See* Overtures, etc.
Symphonie Pastorale, La (A. Gide), 1919 U
Symphonies, named:
Choral (Beethoven), 1824 T, 1825 T
Classical (Prokofiev), 1917 T
Clock (Haydn), 1794 T
Colour (Bliss), 1922 T
Drum Roll (Haydn), 1795 T
Eroica (Beethoven), 1804 T
Fantastique (Berlioz), 1830 T
Farewell (Haydn), 1772 T
Faust (Liszt), 1857 T
From the New World (Dvořák), 1893 T
Great C Major (Schubert), 1839 T
Haffner (Mozart), 1782 T
Italian (Mendelssohn), 1833 T
Jupiter (Mozart), 1788 T
Kaddish (Bernstein), 1964 T
Leningrad (Shostakovich), 1942 T
London (Haydn), 1795 T
London (Vaughan Williams), 1914 T
Oxford (Haydn), 1788 T
Paris (Haydn), 1784 T
Pastoral (Beethoven), 1808 T
Pastoral (Vaughan Williams), 1922 T
Pathétique (Tchaikovsky), 1893 T
Philosopher, The (Haydn), 1764 T
Prague (Mozart), 1787 T
Rhenish (Schumann), 1850 T
Roxolane, La (Haydn), 1777 T
Scottish (Mendelssohn), 1842 T
Sea (Vaughan Williams), 1910 T
Surprise (Haydn), 1791 T
Symphony for Three Orchestras, A (Carter), 1977 T
Toy (Haydn), 1780 T
Unfinished (Schubert), 1822 T
Youth (Prokofiev), 1952 T
Symphonies, other notable:
Arnold, 1957 T, 1973 T, 1991 T
Bax, 1928 T
van Beethoven, 1800 T, 1802 T, 1804 T, 1806 T, 1808 T, 1810 T, 1812 T, 1824 T, 1825 T
Borodin, 1877 T
Brahms, 1876 T, 1877 T, 1883 T, 1885 T
Britten, 1964 T
Bruckner, 1884 T
Copland, 1925 T
Dvořák, 1889 T
Elgar, 1908 T, 1911 T
Franck, 1889 T
Harris, 1942 T
Honegger, 1950 T
Kodály, 1961 T
Lutoslawski, 1967 T, 1983 T
Mahler, 1895 T, 1900 T, 1909 T, 1964 T
Mathias, 1991 T
Milhaud, 1946 T
Pärt, 1971 T
Penderecki, 1973 T, 1980 T
Rawsthorne, 1950 T
Rubbra, 1942 T, 1954 T
Schnittke, 1981 T, 1984 T
Searle, 1960 T
Shostakovich, 1927 T, 1937 T, 1944 T, 1946 T, 1954 T, 1971 T
Sibelius, 1899 T
Stravinsky, 1940 T, 1945 T
Tchaikovsky, 1877 T, 1889 T
Tippett, 1972 T
Vaughan Williams, 1943 T, 1953 T, 1958 T
Walton, 1935 T
Syndicalism, British T.U.C. votes against, 1912 J
Syndicalists. *See* Political Parties
Synge, John Millington, Ir. dramatist (1871–1909), 1904 W, 1907 W, 1909 W
Synnöve Solbakken (B. Björnson), 1857 U
Synthetic diamonds, 1959 P
Synthetic fibres:
artificial silk, 1887 P
nylon, 1937 P
rayon, 1892 P
terylene, 1941 P
Synthetic rubber, 1909 P, 1944 Y
Syria: ceded by Turkey to Egypt, 1833 E; Turks invade, 1839 D; Ibrahim evacuates, 1840 L; is assigned to Mehemet Ali, 1840 G, L; massacres in, 1860 J; independence, 1920 C; mandated to France, by League, 1920 D, G, 1922 G; boundary with Palestine settled, 1920 M; Allied invasion of, 1941 F; cease fire in, 1941 G, 1945 E; France and Britain pledge to evacuate, 1945 M; Arab Republic formed, 1961 J; alleges UAR interference, 1962 H; federated with UAR, 1963 D
Arab–Israeli conflict, 1967 F, 1972 L
severe fighting on Golan Heights, 1970 A
federates with UAR, Libya and Sudan, 1970 L
closes Jordanian border, 1971 G
accepts ceasefire, 1973 K
Syrian forces enter Lebanon, 1976 E
martial law in Aleppo, 1980 C
proclaimed single state with Libya, 1980 J
bomb attack in Damascus, 1981 L
US plan for simultaneous withdrawal of Israeli and Syrian forces from Lebanon, 1983 E
Syrian tanks besiege PLO bases in Lebanon, 1983 F
Arafat ordered out, 1983 F
cotton production, 1984 Y
diplomats expelled from Britain for alleged involvement in terrorism, 1986 E
Britain breaks off diplomatic relations, 1986 K
Lebanese civil war, 1987 D
US diplomatic relations restored, 1987 H
agrees to end political and military support of Iran, 1987 L
diplomatic relations with Egypt resumed, 1989 M
Syrtes, Les (J. Moras), 1884 U
Système de la Nature (P. Holbach), 1770 R
Système des animaux sans vertèbres (Lamarck), 1809 P
System der Sittenlehre (J. G. Fichte), 1798 R
System of Assigned Rights (F. Lassalle), 1861 O
System of Comparative Surgery (C. Bell), 1807 P
System of Conjugation (F. Bopp), 1816 Q
System of Minerology (J. Dana), 1837 P
System of Transcendental Idealism (F. W. Schelling), 1800 R
Systema Entomologiae (J. C. Fabricius), 1775 P
Szabo, Istvan, Hung. film director (b. 1938), 1985 W
Szostak, Jack W., B.-born Am. geneticist (b. 1952), 1983 P

T

Taaffe, Eduard Franz Joseph von, Count, Aus. statesman (1833–95), 1879 H, 1893 K
Taaffe, Pat, Ir. jockey (1930–92), 1966 X
Table Talk (W. Cowper), 1782 U
Table Talk (W. Hazlitt), 1821 U
Table Tennis, US team visit China, 1971 D
Tableau du Progrès de l'Esprit humain (Condorcet), 1793 O
Tablets, contraceptive, 1952 P
Tacna-Arica dispute, S. America, 1883 K, 1922 G
Taff Vale judgment, 1901 G
Taft, William Howard, Am. Republican statesman (1857–1930), 27th president of US (1909–13), 1857 Z, 1911 G, H, 1912 C, F, 1930 Z; heads commission on Philippines, 1900 B, J; governor of Philippines, 1901 G; elected president, 1908 L; inaugurated, 1909 C; vetoes army bill, 1912 F; loses presidential election to Wilson, 1912 L
Taggart, television series, 1985 W
Tagore, Rabindranath, Ind. poet (1861–1941), 1861 Z, 1912 U, 1941 Z
Tahir, Ibrahim, writer, 1984 U
Tahiti, Society Islands, Pacific: France annexes, 1880 F; Gauguin settles in, 1891 S
Tailleferre, Germaine, F. musician (1892–1983), 1920 T
Taine, Hippolyte, F. author (1828–93), 1828 Z, 1853 Q, 1856 R, 1865 R, 1873 O, 1893 Z
Taiping Rebellion in China, 1851 N, 1855 C
Tait, Archibald Campbell, B. churchman (1811–82), 1867 R
Taiwan (formerly Formosa)
Japan acknowledges China's territorial rights over, 1972 B

British consulate closed, 1972 C
Chiang Kai-shek dies, 1975 D
Yen Chia-kan succeeds as president, 1975 D
US arms sales to, 1982 H
opposition parties legalized, 1987 G
See also Formosa
Taizé, near Cluny, France, Protestant community at, 1944 R
Tajikistan
Nabiyev forced to resign, 1992 J
earthquake, 1989 A
Take Your Choice (J. Cartwright), 1776 O
Takemitsu, Toru, Jap. musician (b. 1930), 1967 T, 1985 T
Takeshita, Noboru, Prime Minister of Japan (b. 1924), 1989 D
Taking Rights Seriously (R. Dworkin), 1977 R
Taking Stock (H. Haacke), 1984 S
Talal I, King of Jordan (1911–72), reign of, is terminated, 1952 H
Talbot, William Henry Fox, B. pioneer of photography (1800–77), 1800 Z, 1839 P, 1877 Z
Tale of Two Cities, A (C. Dickens), 1859 U
Tales from Shakespeare (C. and M. Lamb), 1807 U
Tales of Jacob (T. Mann), 1933 U
Tales of Peter Lebrecht (L. Tieck), 1797 U
Tales of the City (A. Maupin), 1978 U
Tales of the Grotesque and Arabesque (E. A. Poe), 1840 U
Tales of the Hall (G. Crabbe), 1817 U
Tales of the Jazz Age (S. Fitzgerald), 1923 U
Tales of the Unexpected, television programme, 1979 W
Talienwan, China, is ceded to Japan, 1905 J
Talking Heads, Am. pop group, 1978 W
Talleyrand-Périgord, Charles Maurice de, F. diplomat (1754–1838), 1797 G, 1799 L, L, 1814 D, 1838 Z
Tallinn, Russia, Germans take, 1941 G
Tam O'Shanter (R. Burns), 1790 U
Tamerlane (E. A. Poe), 1827 U
Tamils
attacks on, 1983 G
amity talks between Tamil and Sinhalese representatives, 1984 A
clashes with Sinhalese in Sri Lanka, 1984 H
Tamil terrorists attack Sri Lankan army convoy, 1984 M
separatists attack Anuradhapura, 1985 E
Sri Lankan forces seek to establish control over Jaffna pninsula, 1986 E
refugees, 1986 H
buses ambushed near Trincomale, 1987 D
Indian–Sri Lankan agreement aimed at ending communal violence in Sri Lanka, 1987 G
arms surrendered to Indian peacekeeping force, 1987 H
Tamil Tigers agree ceasefire, 1989 F
Rajiv Gandhi assassinated by Tamil suicide bomber, 1991 E
Tampico, Mexico, US troops sent to, 1914 D
Tamworth Manifesto, Peel issues, 1834 M
Tan, Amy, Am. author (b. 1952), 1989 U
Tanaka, Kakuei, Prime Minister of Japan (b. 1918), 1972 G
resignation, 1974 L
charged with accepting bribes, 1976 G
Tanganyika, Lake, Africa: exploration of, 1856 P; British Africa Company acquires land near, 1890 E
Tanganyika: Germany annexes, 1885 B; League mandate for, 1922 G; internal self-government for, 1961 E; becomes republic within Commonwealth, 1962 M; is united with Zanzibar, 1964 D; changes name to Tanzania, 1964 D. *See also under* Tanzania
Tange, Kenzo, Jap. architect (b. 1913), 1974 S
Tangier, Morocco: William II visits, 1905 C; convention on, 1923 B; Spanish control in, 1928 G; Sultan of Morocco visits, 1955 K; North African Nationalists meet at, 1958 D
Tanglewood Tales (N. Hawthorne), 1853 U
Tango at the End of Winter (K. Shimuzu), 1991 W
Tangshan, China, earthquake, 1976 G
Tankara ministry in Japan, falls, 1929 G
Tanks, military: first used in warfare, 1916 J, P; used in British advance on Cambrai, 1917 L; notable battles in Western Desert, 1942 E, F; British production of, 1939 Y, 1940 Y, 1941 J, Y, 1942 Y, 1943 Y
Tannenburg, Poland: Russians defeated at, 1914 E; memorial, 1927 J
Tanner, Beatrice. *See* Campbell, Mrs. Patrick
'TanZam' railway, Chinese loan for, 1970 G
Tanzania, formed by union of Tanganyika and Zanzibar, 1964 D
Ugandan exiles attempt to invade Uganda from, 1972 J
border clashes with Uganda, 1978 K
troops move into Ugandan border areas, 1978 L
Uganda drops territorial claims on, 1978 L
troops invade Uganda, 1979 A
Tape, magnetic, 1942 P
Tapestries, Morris's, 1861 S
Tapisserie de Notre-Dame, La (C. Péguy), 1913 U
Taraki, Nur Mohammad, President of Afghanistan (1917–79), 1979 J
Taranto, Italy, British attack on, 1940 L; falls to Eighth Army, 1943 J
Tarare (P. Beaumarchais), 1787 W
Tardieu, André, F. premier, 1932 B
Tariff Questions:
Pan-American plans for reciprocity, 1889 K
Geneva Conference on, 1930 B
Oslo agreement on, 1930 M
General Agreement on Trade and Tariffs (GATT), negotiations on (Kennedy Round'), 1963 E, 1964 E
EFTA countries abolish tariffs on industrial goods, 1966 O
Canadian–US agreement to reduce, 1987 K
See also under General Agreement on Tariffs and Trade, Treaties, Treaties of Commerce
in Australia, duty on Lancashire cottons, 1934 H
in Belgium and Luxembourg, customs union, 1912 O
in Belgium, Holland, Luxembourg, customs union ('Benelux'), formed, 1947 K
Anglo-Irish pact on coal and cattle, 1934 M
duties on German Reparation goods, 1921 C; reduced, 1924 B
in Britain: free trade, beginnings of, 1821 E; completed, 1849 F, H
imperial preference, issue of, 1897 G, 1902 F, 1903 E
Chamberlain resigns to test feeling on, 1903 J
Act passed, 1919 H
Britain rejects, with Canada, 1930 K
protection is introduced, 1932 C
favoured by Ottawa Conference, 1932 G
Samuel resigns on issue of, 1932 J
tariff war with Ireland ended, 1936 B
import surcharge imposed, 1964 L; reduced, 1965 D
in Canada, right to fix tariffs, 1846 H
protection, 1878 H
reciprocity with US urged, 1890 K
protectionist in force, 1904 O
preferential agreement with W. Indies, 1912 D
customs scandals, 1926 F
Britain rejects preference, 1930 K
Dunning tariff, 1930 E
gives Britain preference, 1930 E
reciprocal trade agreement with US, 1935 L
See also under US
in Central and S. America, Latin American Free Trade Association, 1961 F
in China, boycott of US goods, 1905 G
Japan recognises right of China to fix, 1930 E
in Egypt, economic union with Syria, 1957 J
in Europe, high tariffs introduced, 1921 O
See Common Market; European Economic Community; European Free Trade Association
in France, Trianon tariff, 1810 H
protection, 1891 N
tariff war with Switzerland, 1893 N
with Italy, 1898 L
Franco-Canadian agreement, 1933 E
Franco-Italian customs union, 1948 C
in Germany, protectionist, 1879 G, 1902 M
See also under Prussia *and main index under* Zollverein
in New Zealand, protectionist, 1888 N
favours Britain, 1903 N
in Persia, discriminatory, 1902 L
in Prussia, internal duties abolished, 1818 E
treaty with Schwarzburg-Sonderhausen, 1819 K
See also Zollverein
in Russia, 1810 M
in Siberia, tariff was with Austria, 1905 N
in Sweden, protective, 1888 N
in Switzerland, customs union with Liechtenstein, 1923 F
in US, protectionist, 1816 O
'Tariff of Abominations' (protectionist), 1828 E; revised, 1832 G
Clay Tariff appeases S. Carolina, 1833 C
New Whig Tariff (protective), 1842 N
reciprocity with Canada, 1854 F
Morrill Tariff, 1861 C
as issue in presidential election, 1888 L
Mackinley Tariff, 1890 K, 1892 L
repealed, 1894 E
Wilson-Gorman Tariff, 1894 H
Dindley's Tariff (protective), 1897 G
Payne-Aldrich Tariff, maintains protection, 1909 H
reciprocity with Canada, 1911 D, G; annulled, 1911 J
revised, 1913 E
treaty with China, 1920 K
protectionist tariff, 1922 J, O
agricultural produce bill, defeated, 1926 F
Smoot-Hawley Tariff (high duty), 1930 F, O
Agricultural Adjustment tariff, 1933 O
president's power to reduce tariffs, 1934 F
Reciprocal Trade Agreements Act, 1958 J
Tarka the Otter (H. Williamson), 1927 U
Tarkovsky, Andrei, R. film director (1932–86), 1966 W, 1984 W, 1986 W
Tarleton, Sir Banastre, B. general (1754–1833), 1780 H, 1781 A
Tartarescu, George, Rum. leader (1892–1957), 1933 M
Tartarin the Mountaineer (A. Daudet), 1885 U
Tartu, Estonia, peace of, 1920 K

Tarzan films, 1932 W
Tashkent peace agreement, 1966 A
Task forces. *See* Commandos
Task, The (W. Cowper), 1785 U
Tasmania, proved to be an island, 1798 P
Tasso (Goethe), 1789 W
Tatar people, percentage in Soviet population, 1989 Y
Tate, John, Am. boxer (b. 1955), 1979 X
Tati, Jacques (born Jacques Tatischeff), F. film director and actor (1908–82), 1908 Z, 1958 W, 1982 Z
Taubman, Alfred, Am. entrepreneur (b. 1925), 1983 S
Tauroggen, Roumania convention of, 1812 M
Tavener, John, B. musician (b. 1944), 1968 T, 1984 T, 1989 T, 1991 T, 1992 T
Taverne, Richard, B. Labour/Democratic Labour politician (b. 1928), 1972 K, 1973 C
Tavernier, Bertrand René Maurice, F. film director (b. 1941), 1984 W
Taviani, Paolo (b. 1931) and Vittorio (b. 1929), It. film directors, 1977 W
Tawfiq Abul-Huda, Jordan. leader (1864–1956), 1955 E
Tawney, Richard Henry, B. historian (1880–1962), 1880 Z, 1926 R, 1931 O, 1958 Q, 1962 Z
Taxation, treatise on, 1817 O
Taxation:
in Britain: advertisements tax, repealed, 1853 O
capital allowances raised, 1971 G
capital gains tax, 1964 L, 1965 D
capital transfer tax, 1974 H
Community Charge or 'poll tax', 1986 O, 1988 E, 1990 C, 1991 D
corporation tax, 1964 L, 1965 F, 1966 E, 1969 D, 1970 K, 1984 C
council tax, 1966 E, 1971 C, 1991 D
customs duties, repealed, 1821 E, 1842 D, 1945 D
death duties, 1894 D
duties increased, 1968 C, 1969 D, 1981 C, 1982 C, 1986 C
employers' National Insurance Insurance surcharge abolished, 1984 C
employment tax, 1969 D
entertainment tax, doubled, 1942 D
reduced, 1948 W
abolished on living theatre, 1957 W
excise scheme, Pitt's, 1786 F
excise, on tea and spirits, reduced, 1784 F
import deposits, 1968 L
import surcharge abolished, 1966 L
imports surcharge, 1964 K
reduced, 1965 D
income tax, 1970 K, 1971 C, 1972 C, 1974 C, 1975 D, 1977 C, G, 1978 E, 1979 F, 1981 C, 1982 C, 1984 C, 1985 C, 1986 C, 1987 C, 1988 C
introduced, 1798 E
revived, 1842 D
Gladstone aims to abolish, 1874 B
standard rate raised to 7*s*. 6*d*. in, 1939 J
10s. in, 1941 D
PAYE, introduced, 1944 B
Schedule 'A' abolished, 1963 D
increased, 1964 L
increases in, 1980 L
indirect taxation increased, 1968 L
land tax, reduced, 1767 B
levy on unearned income, 1968 C
mortgage tax relief, 1983 C
National Insurance contributions, 1972 C, 1981 M, 1982 C, 1985 C
newspaper, 1789 V, 1819 M
abolished, 1855 R, V
paper duties, repealed, 1861 O
personal pension scheme, 1987 C
profits, tax, increased, 1960 D
purchase tax, 1940 G, 1971 G
rates, 1981 M
revenue from direct exceeds that from indirect taxation, 1901 D
separate taxation for married women introduced, 1990 O
speculative gains tax, 1962 D
system revised, 1940 G, 1971 O
threshold for higher tax rates of income tax raised, 1978 E
Value Added Tax, 1973 C, 1974 G, 1977 O, 1979 F
wealth tax, 1974 H
White Papers proposals, 1974 H
See also Rates
in France, reform of, 1780 N
duties on colonial imports, 1810 H
duties on wine, reduced, 1900 G
National Assembly witholds increases in, 1952 B
in Russia, poll tax, abolished, 1884 A
in US, Britain's taxation of American Colonies, 1764 E, 1765 E, 1766 C, 1767 E, 1768 G, 1769 E, 1770 D
customs duties, 1787 D
excise, 1794 N
Stamp duties, 1819 M
reduced, 1836 H
Force Act enables collection of revenue, 1833 C
Window tax, abolished, 1851 G
income tax, imposed, 1894 N
declared unconstitutional, 1895 E, 1916 A
net income taxed from business sources, 1912 C
federal income tax, 1913 B
surtax, 1935 H
Surtax, starting point of, raised, 1961 D
poll tax ruled unconstitutional as voting requirement, 1966 O
war tax surcharge, 1967 A
'Proposition 13' to cut property taxes in California, 1978 F
Taxi, motor, 1903 P
Taxi, television programme, 1978 W
Taylor, Alan John Percivale, B. historian (1906–90), 1906 Z, 1966 Q, 1969 Q, 1972 Q, 1975 Q, 1990 Z
Taylor, Dennis, Ir. snooker player (b. 1949), 1985 X
Taylor, Elizabeth, B.-born Am. actress (b. 1932), 1962 W, 1963 W
Taylor, Gary, Am. literary critic (b. 1953), 1986 Q
Taylor, John Vernon, B. theologian and churchman (b. 1914), 1972 R
Taylor, Zachary, Am. Whig (1784–1850), 12th president of US (1849–50), 1850 G; in Mexican War, 1846 E; inaugurated, 1849 C
Tbilisi, Georgia
pro-independence demonstrations, 1989 D
rebel forces besiege government buildings, 1992 A
Tchaikovsky, Peter Iljitch, R. musician (1840–93), 1840, Z, 1893 Z
ballet music, 1878 T, 1891 T
operas, 1864 T, 1876 T, 1880 T
overtures, 1864 T, 1876 T, 1880 T
piano concerto, 1875 T
symphonies, 1877 T, 1889 T, 1893 T
Tchesme, Turkey, battle, 1770 G
Te Tsung, Emperor of China (1875–1908), reforms under, 1898 F
Tea: Boston Tea Party, 1773 M; production statistics, 1909 Y
Teach-Ins, 1965 O
Teaching machines, 1963 O
Teaching. *see under* Education; Universities
Teatr Nowy, 1984 W
Tebbit, Norman Beresford, Lord Tebbit, B. Conservative politician (b. 1931), 1981 J, 1983 K
Technics and Civilization (L. Mumford), 1934 O
Technology:
history of, 1955 P
in Britain, professorship at Edinburgh University, 1855 O
Regent Street Polytechnic, 1882 O
agreement for pooling knowledge with US, 1940 L
increased spending on, 1956 O
Ministry of, 1964 O
in Ceylon, agreement with Russia, 1958 B
in Germany, Berlin School of Technology, 1884 O
in US, Massachusetts Institute of Technology, 1865 O
Tectonic Plates (R. Lepage), 1990 W
Teddington, Middlesex, England, National Physical Laboratory at, 1950 P
Tegnér, Esaias, Swe. author (1782–1846), 1822 U, 1825 U
Teheran, Iran:
Anglo-Persian agreement of, 1919 H
University, 1935 O
Conference of Allied leaders at, 1943 B, L
Reza Shah crowned, 1967 K
violent demonstrations, 1978 J
Islamic revolutionary violence, 1979 A
US embassy seized, 1979 B, L
US hostages, 1980 A, L
British embassy closes, 1980 J
anti-USSR demonstrations, 1980 M
bomb kills president and prime minister, 1981 H
Islamic Republican Party offices bombed, 1981 F
Teilhard de Chardin, Pierre, F. theologian (1881–1955), 1959 R
Tel Aviv, Israel, 1949 M
Tel-el-Kebir, Egypt, battle, 1882 J
Telegraph:
optical, 1793 P
invented, 1809 P
water volta-meter, 1809 P
Morse, invented, 1832 P
electric, 1833 P
first message transmitted in US, 1844 P
cross-Channel, 1846 P
London–Balaclava, 1855 P
trans-Atlantic, 1866 P
duplex, 1872 P
wireless, 1895 P
trans-Atlantic transmissions, 1901 P
picture, 1930 P
Telepathy and Clairvoyance (Teschner), 1921 R
Telephone, The: invented, 1876 P; automatic switchboard for, 1892 P; exchange, London's first, 1879 P; public, first, 1877 P; G.P.O. takes over B. System, 1912 O; Trans-Atlantic service, 1956 P; visual, 1956 P; direct dialling from New York to Paris and London, 1967 P
Telephones, statistics of subscribers:
in Britain, 1910 Y, 1930 Y, 1940 Y, 1965 Y
in US, 1880 Y, 1940 Y

Telescopes:
Jodrell Bank radio telescope, 1957 P
Mount Wilson, 1910 P, 1918 P
Mullard Observatory, Cambridge, 1957 P
reflecting, 1789 P
See also Observatories
Television:
Baird demonstrates, 1926 P
colour, demonstrated, 1928 P
Trans-Atlantic transmission, 1928 P
experiments with, 1953 P
Eurovision network, 1954 P
Telstar relays pictures, 1962 P
Early Bird relays pictures, 1965 P
colour broadcasts, 1967 W
ownership, statistics, 1970 Y
video-cassette recorder, 1972 P, 1974 W, 1979 P
fibre optics, 1977 P
4th channel proposed in White Paper, 1978 O
LaserVision video disc system, 1979 P
satellite, 1979 P, 1989 W
technological development in Japan, 1979 P
pocket-size, 1981 P
Live-Aid concerts, 1985 W
cable, 1992 W
programmes. *See* individual titles
Television Services:
in Britain, BBC develops, 1932 O
BBC opens regular service, 1936 W
BBC service resumed, 1946 W
statistics of viewers, 1946 W, 1959 Y, 1960 Y, 1965 Y
Independent Television Authority, 1954 O
starts commercial programmes, 1955 W
Pilkington Committee's Report, 1962 W
Noble Committee's Report, 1963 O
BBC2, alternative programme, 1964 W
cigarette advertising on, banned, 1965 W
Opening of Parliament televised, 1966 O
CEEFAX, 1972 P
licences, 1976 K
ITV closed by strike, 1979 H
Channel 4 station, 1982 W
TV AM, 1983 W
British House of Lords televised, 1985 O
British House of Commons televised, 1988 O
Sky TV, 1989 W
in Cuba, regular colour TV, 1959 W
in France, statistics of viewers, 1959 Y, 1960 Y
in Germany, regular service, 1935 W
statistics of viewers, 1960 Y
in Japan, regular colour TV, 1960 W
in S. Africa, decision against introducing TV, 1959 W
in US, Quiz scandal, 1959 W
statistics of viewers, 1959 Y, 1960 Y
confrontation of presidential candidates on, 1960 O
Television, Am. pop group, 1977 W
Telford, Thomas, B. engineer (1757–1834), 1802 P, 1805 P, 1819 P
Tell Mardikh, Syria, ancient texts discovered, 1975 Q
Tell, Wasfi, Jordanian politician (1920–71), 1971 L
Telstar, communications satellite, 1962 P
Temin, Howard, Am. virologist (b. 1934), 1970 P
Temperance, 1869 J. *See also under* Prohibition
Temperatures:
bolometer for determining changes, 1881 P
very low, research into, 1933 P
Tempest, Marie, B. actress, 1864 Z, 1942 Z
Tempest, The (A. Ostrovsky), 1860 W
Temple, Frederick, B. Churchman, Archbishop of Canterbury (1821–1902), 1860 R
Temple, Henry John, Viscount Palmerston, B. Whig-Liberal statesman (1784–1865), 1784 Z, 1865 Z; becomes foreign secretary, 1830 L, 1846 F; '*Civis Romanus Sum*' speech, 1850 F; resigns, 1851 M; forms ministry, 1855 B; resigns, following Orsini affair, 1858 B; forms ministry, 1859 F
Temple, Shirley, Am. film actress (b. 1928), 1932 W, 1936 W
Temple, William, B. churchman, Archbishop of Canterbury (1881–1944), 1881 Z, 1934 R, 1944 R, Z; appointed Archbishop of Canterbury, 1942 R
Templewood, Viscount. *See* Hoare, Samuel
Temporal power of Pope, attacked, 1859 O
Temps du mepris, Le (A. Malraux), 1935 U
Temps retrouvé, Le (M. Proust), 1927 U
Temptation of Pescara (K. Meyer), 1887 U
Tenant Right League, Ireland, 1850 F
Tender is the Night (S. Fitzgerald), 1934 U
Ténébreuse Affaire, Une (H. de Balzac), 1841 U
Tenedos, Isle, Asia Minor, battle off, 1913 A
Tenerife, air disaster, 1977 C
Teng Hsiao-p'ing, Chinese politician (b. 1904), 1904 Z, 1966 L, 1987 K
reinstated, 1977 G
consolidates power, 1980 H
Chairman of Central Military Commission, 1989 L
Tennant, Charles, B. chemist (1768–1838), 1798 P
Tennant, Margot. *See* Asquith, M
Tennessee Valley Authority, 1933 E
Tennessee, State, US: becomes US state, 1796 F; forbids teaching of evolution, 1925 O
Tenniel, Sir John, B. artist (1820–1914), 1820 Z, 1851 S, 1914 Z
Tennis:
invented, 1874 X
Wimbledon championships, 1877 X, 1895 X, 1919 X, 1920 X, 1927 X
US championships, 1881 X
Lawn Tennis Association founded, 1888 X
Davis Cup, 1900 X
Davis Cup victory for Australia, 1966 X
distinction between amateur and professional abolished, 1967 X
Wimbledon, first open championships, 1968 X
Grand Slam win for Margaret Court, 1970 X
professional players boycott Wimbledon, 1973 X
Ashe wins Wimbledon Men's Singles, 1975 X
French Open Championships, 1976 X
Wade wins Wimbledon Women's Singles, 1977 X
Borg wins Wimbledon Men's Singles, 1980 X
fault-finding equipment, 1980 X
Davis Cup victory for Sweden, 1984 X
restoration to Olympic Games, 1988 X
Tennyson, Alfred, Lord Tennyson, B. poet (1809–1892), 1809 Z, 1827 U, 1830 U, 1832 U, 1842 U, 1850 U, 1855 U, 1859 U, 1892 Z
Tennyson, C. *See* Turner, Charles Tennyson
Tentation de St. Antoine, La (G. Flaubert), 1874 U
Tenzing, Norkey, Sherpa mountaineer (1914–86), 1953 P
Teplitz, Czechoslovakia Treaty, 1813 J
Teppich des Lebens, Der (S. George), 1899 U
Teresa, Mother (born Agnes Gonxha Bojaxhiu), Albanian missionary (b. 1910), 1910 Z, 1973 R
Nobel Peace Prize, 1979 R
Tereshkova, Valentina, R. cosmonaut (b. 1937), first woman in space, 1963 P
Terracotta Circle (R. Long), 1981 S
Terre est un homme, La (Ferneyhough), 1979 T
Terre, La (E. Zola), 1888 U
Territorial Waters: limit of, fixed by Hague Convention, 1882 F; Iceland extends fishery limit, 1958 F, J; Indonesia extends, 1958 A; US, violated by Britain, 1811 L
Terrorism:
See also Atrocities; Massacres
in Aden, 1965 J
in Algeria, 1953 L, M
in Angola, 1961 B
in Britain and Ireland, by Fenians, 1882 E, H, 1883 C
British government measures in fight against, 1980 O
Britain bans broadcasts of interviews with 11 terrorist organizations, 1988 K
in British Guina, 1963 D
in Cyprus, by EOKA, 1957 C
in Kenya, by Mau Mau, 1952 K, 1953 D, H, 1955 A
in US, by Ku-Klux-Klan, 1964 H, M, 1965 C
Libya suspected of involvement in international, 1981 E, 1986 A, D
UN sanctions imposed on Libya following Lockerbie bombing, 1992 C
Terry, Ellen, B. actress (1848–1928), 1848 Z, 1878 W, 1928 Z
Terry, Fernando Belaunde, President of Peru, 1980 G
Terson, Peter, B. dramatist (b. 1932), 1968 W
Teruel, Spain, battles, 1937 M, 1938 B
Terylene, invention of, 1941 P
Teschen, Austria: Peace signed at, 1779 E; Agreement, between Czechoslovakia and Poland, 1920 G; ceded to Poland, 1938 K
Tesla, Nikola, Am. engineer (1856–1943), 1888 P
Tess of the D'Urbervilles (T. Hardy), 1891 U
Test ban treaty, 1963 H
'Test Tube' baby, first in England, 1978 P
Testament of Beauty, The (R. Bridges), 1929 U
Testament of Youth, television programme, 1979 W
Tet offensive, 1968 A
Tetanus: bacillus discovered, 1884 P; is controlled by injections, 1915 P; treatment of, 1925 P
Tewfik Pasha, Grand Vizier of Persia, 1912 G
Tewfik, Khedive of Egypt (1879–92), 1879 F, 1882 A; appoints Nationalist ministry, 1882 B
Texaco Inc. acquires Getty Oil Co., 1984 O
Texas, State, US: declares itself independent of Mexico, 1836 C, D; US treaty for annexation of, defeated, 1844 D; US Congress agrees to annexation, 1845 C; becomes a US state, 1845 M; US obtains, 1848 E; surrenders claim to New Mexico, 1850 H
Texel, Holland, River, 1795 A, 1797 E
Textiles Trade, British, 1772 Y, 1782 Y, 1812 Y, 1822 Y, 1832 Y, 1842 Y, 1852 Y, 1862 Y, 1872 Y, 1882 Y, 1892 Y, 1902 Y, 1912 Y, 1922 Y, 1932 Y
Teyte, Dame Maggie, B. prima donna (1888–1976), 1919 T
Thackeray, William Makepeace, B. novelist (1811–1863), 1811 Z, 1838 U, 1846 U, 1847 U, 1850 U, 1852 U, 1855 U, 1857 U, 1863 Z
edits *Cornhill*, 1860 V
Thailand, King of, 1992 E
Thailand: name changed from Siam, 1949 E; state of emergency in, 1957 C
military coup, 1971 L
government defeated in general election, 1976 D
incursion into, by Khmer Rouge, 1977 B
martial law declared, 1991 B, 1977 K

See also under Siam
Thalaba, the Destroyer (R. Southey), 1801 U
Thalidomide, compensation for victims, 1973 G
Thallium, discovery of, 1861 P
Thames, River, England, tunnels under, 1843 P, 1890 P
 Flood Barrier, 1973 P
Thames, River, Ontario, Canada, US victory at, 1813 K
Thanatopsis (W. C. Bryant), 1817 U
Thant, U, Burm. statesman (1909–74), Secretary-General of UN, 1966 M, 1967 C; plans for Congo, 1962 J; elected UN secretary, 1962 L
Thark (B. Travers), 1927 W
That Was The Week That Was television series, 1962 W
That's My Bus (J. Greenwood), 1990 S
Thatcher, Mrs. Margaret Hilda, Lady Thatcher, B. Conservative politician (b. 1925), 1925 Z, 1971 F, 1984 K, M, 1988 A
 elected Conservative Party leader, 1975 B
 branded 'Iron Lady' by USSR paper *Red Star*, 1976 A
 views on immigration, 1978 A
 becomes Prime Minister, 1979 E
 persists with monetarist policies, 1980 K
 Dublin meeting with Haughey on Anglo-Irish links, 1980 M
 assigns funds for job training schemes, 1981 G
 Anglo-Irish agreement, 1981 L
 attends talks on Hong Kong, 1982 J
 meeting with Botha, 1984 F
 refused honorary doctorate by Oxford University, 1985 A
 Channel Tunnel rail link, 1986 A, B
 Bruges speech on European political and economic union, 1988 J
 visits Poland, 1988 L
 economic policy, 1988 O
 attitude towards EC, 1990 L
 Howe resigns, 1990 L
 resignation as leader of Conservative Party, 1990 L
Thaw, The (I. Ehrenburg), 1955 W
Théâtre de Complicité, 1992 W
Theatre of Cruelty, 1964 W
Thefts of works of art:
 Cézanne paintings, 1961 S
 Goya's *Wellington*, 1961 S, 1965 S
 Mona Lisa, 1911 S
Theodorakis, Mikis, Gk. musician (b. 1925), 1959 T
Theogony of Hesiod, illustrated edition, 1931 S
Theological Essays (F. D. Maurice), 1853 R
Theology and Politics (N. Micklem), 1941 R
Theoria motus corporum coelestium (K. F. Gauss), 1809 P
Théorie Analytique de la Chaleur (Fournier de Pescay), 1822 P
Théorie Analytique (P. Laplace), 1812 P
Théorie des fonctions analytiques (J. L. Lagrange), 1797 O
Théorie du pouvoir politique et religieux (L. de Bonald), 1796 O
Théorie mathématique de la Chaleur (S. D. Poisson), 1835 P
Theory and Practice of Socialism, The (J. Strachey), 1936 O
Theory of Beauty (E. F. Carritt), 1914 S
Theory of Chemical Proportions (J. J. Berzelius), 1814 P
Theory of Colours (Goethe), 1810 P
Theory of Communicative Action, The (J. Habermas), 1981 R
Theory of Justice, A (J. Rawls), 1971 R
Theory of Linear Transformations (A. Cayley), 1845 P
Theory of Political Economy (W. S. Jevons), 1871 O
Theory of Sex (T. H. Morgan), 1928 O
Theosophical Society, founded, 1875 R
Theotokis, A., Greek premier (b. 1908), 1950 A
Therapeutic Research Council, British, 1941 P
There is No Armour (H. Spring), 1948 U
Thérèse Raquin (E. Zola), 1867 U
Thermidor (V. Sardou), 1891 W
Thermo-electricity, discovered, 1821 P
Thermodynamics, second law of, 1850 P
Thermomultiplier, used for discoveries in radiant heat, 1831 P
Theroux, Paul Edward, Am. author (b. 1941), 1975 U, 1981 U
Thesiger, Wilfred, B. explorer (b. 1910), 1948 P
Thessaly, Greece: risings in, 1878 A; granted by Turkey to Greece, 1881 G; Turkish defeat at, 1879 E; Allies demand Greek withdrawalfrom, 1916 M
They Were Defeated (R. Macaulay), 1932 U
Thibaut, Anton Friedrich Justus, G. jurist (1774–1840), 1798 O
Thibaut, Jacques, Antoine Anatole, F. novelist under pseudonym of 'Anatole France' (1844–1924), 1881 U, 1888 U, 1893 U, 1896 U, 1908 U
Thibault, Les (R. M. du Gard), 1922 U
Thibaw, King of Burma (1858–1916), 1885 K
Thierry, Augustin, F. historian (1795–1856), 1795 Z, 1825 Q, 1840 Q, 1856 Z
Thiers, Louis Adolphe, F. statesman and historian (1797–1877), 1797 Z, 1823 Q, 1845 Q, 1873 E, 1877 Z; crushes Paris rising, 1834 D; becomes premier, 1836 B; resigns, 1836 J; becomes premier, 1840 B; resigns, 1840 K; holds Reform banquets, 1847 G; forms Third Party, 1863 L; becomes head of executive, 1871 B; elected President of France, 1871 H
Thieu, Nguyen van, President of South Vietnam (b. 1923), 1967 D, 1969 J, 1971 K, 1972 L
Third February 1973 (B. Flanagan), 1973 S
Third Policeman, The (F. O'Brien), 1967 U
Thirlwall, Connor, B. churchman and historian (1797–1875), 1835 Q
Thirty-Nine Steps, The (J. Buchan), 1915 U
This Happy Breed (N. Coward), 1943 W
This Island Now (G. M. Carstairs), 1963 R
This Way to the Tomb (R. Duncan), 1945 W
Thoiry, France, Briand meets Stresemann at, 1926 J
Thomas Cook travel agency privatized, 1972 O
Thomas J. Wise in the Original Cloth (Carter and Pollard), 1948 Q
Thomas, Charles Louis Ambroise, F. musician (1811–96), 1866 T
Thomas, Donald Michael, B. author (b. 1935), 1981 U
Thomas, Dylan Marlais, B. poet (1914–53), 1936 U, 1940 U, 1946 U, 1952 U, 1954 W
Thomas, James Henry, B. Trade-Union leader and Labour politician (1874–1949), 1874 Z, 1949 Z; is expelled from Labour Party, 1931 H; resigns over budget leakage, 1936 E
Thomas, John, Am. founder of Christadelphians (1805–71), 1844 R
Thomas, Sidney Gilchrist, B. metallurgist (1850–85), 1878 P
Thomas, Sir Keith Vivian, B. historian (b. 1933), 1933 Z, 1971 Q
Thompson, Benjamin, Count Rumford, B. scientist (1753–1814), 1798 P, 1799 P
Thompson, Daley (b. 1958), B. athlete, 1982 X
Thompson, Dorothy, Am. author (1894–1961), 1894 Z, 1961 Z
Thompson, Sir Edward Maunde, B. palaeographer, (1840–1929), 1912 Q
Thompson, Edward Palmer, B. historian (1924–93), 1975 Q
Thompson, Francis Michael Longstreth, B. historian (b. 1925), 1990 Q
Thompson, Francis, B. poet (1860–1907), 1860 Z, 1880 U, 1907 Z
Thompson, James Matthew, B. historian and theologian (1878–1956), 1911 R, 1943 Q
Thompson, Sir John Sparrow David, Canadian Conservative (1844–94), becomes premier, 1892 M; dies, 1894 M
Thompson, John Taliaferno, Am. gunsmith (1860–1940), 1920 P
Thompson, Joseph John, B. physicist (1856–1940), 1856 Z, 1903 P, 1906 P, 1913 P, 1940 Z
Thompson, Leonard Monteath, B. historian (b. 1916), 1969 Q
Thompson, Linda, 1982 W
Thompson, Paul Richard, B. historian (b. 1935), 1978 Q
Thompson, Richard, 1982 W
Thompson, Thomas, B. chemist (1773–1852), 1807 P
Thompson, William, lord Kelvin, B. scientist (1824–1907), 1824 Z, 1851 P, 1857 P, 1861P, 1867 P, 1872 P, 1879 P, 1882 P, 1897 P, 1907 Z
Thomson, George Morgan, Lord Thomson of Monifieth, B. Labour politician (b. 1921), 1967 L, 1972 K
Thomson, Roy Herbert, Lord Thomson of Fleet, Canad.-born B. newspaper proprietor (1894–1976), 1966 V, 1976 V
Thorburn, Archibald (1860–1935), B. naturalist, 1915 P
Thorburn, Clifford Charles Devlin, 'Cliff', Can. snooker player (b. 1948), 1980 X
Thoreau, Henry David, Am. author (1817–62), 1817 Z, 1854 U, 1862 Z
Thorkelin, Grim Johnson, Dan. scholar (1752–1829), 1815 Q
Thorn, Gaston, Luxembourg politician (b. 1928), President of European Commission, 1981 A, 1984 G
Thorn, N. Poland, ceded to Prussia, 1790 C, 1793 E
Thorneycroft, Peter, B. Conservative politician (b. 1909), appointed Chancellor of Exchequer, 1957 A; resigns, 1958 A
Thornton, William Thomas, B. author (1813–80), 1869 O
Thornton, William, Am. architect (1759–1828), 1793 S
Thornycroft, Sir William Hambro, B. sculptor (1850–1925), 1899 S
Thorpe, Adam, B. author (b. 1956), 1992 U
Thorpe, (John) Jeremy, B. Liberal leader (b. 1929), 1929 Z
 Liberal Party leadership, 1967 A
 accusations against, 1976 A
 resigns, 1976 E
 Norman Scott plot, 1977 K
 charged, 1978 H
 committal hearings in Minehead, 1978 L
 trial, 1979 E
Thorwaldsen, Bertel, Dan. sculptor (1770–1844), 1770 Z, 1797 S, 1811 S, 1819 S, 1820 S, 1844 Z
Those Barren Leaves (A. Huxley), 1925 U
Thoughts on Hunting (P. Beckford), 1781 X

Thoughts on the Cause of the Present Discontents (E. Burke), 1770 O
Thoughts on the Constitution (L. S. Amery), 1947 O
Thoughts on the Importance of the Manners of the Great to General Society (H. More), 1788 O
Thousand Days (A. Schlesinger), 1965 Q
Thrace, Greece: Greeks evacuate, 1922 K; frontier settled, 1913 J
Three-Cornered Hat (P. Alarcón), 1874 U
Threads, television programme, 1984 W
Three Emperors' League, 1881 F, 1884 C
Three Men in a Boat (J. K. Jerome), 1889 U
Three Mile Island nuclear power station, Penn., US, accident, 1979 P
Three Musketeers, The (A. Dumas), 1844 U
Three People (M. Gorki), 1900 U
Three Plays for Puritans (G. B. Shaw), 1900 U
Three Sisters (A. Chekhov), 1902 W
Three Soldiers (J. Dos Passos), 1921 U
Three Treaties on the Theory of Sex (S. Freud), 1905 R
Three-dimensional films, 1953 W
Through the Looking-Glass (L. Carroll), 1871 U
Throwing a Stone Around MacGillycuddy's Rocks (R. Long), 1977 S
Thunder Rock (R. Ardrey), 1940 W
Thunderbirds, television series, 1966 W
Thurber, Charles, Am. inventor of typewriter (1803–86), 1843 P
Thurber, James, Am. humorist (1894–1961), 1894 Z, 1859 U
Thus Spake Zarathustra (F. Nietzsche), 1883 R
Thyroxine, 1915 P, 1928 P
Tiberias, Lake, Syrian–Israeli border clashes, 1967 D
Tibet–Sikkim frontier, Indian and Chinese troops clash, 1967 J
Tibet: Anglo-Chinese convention on, 1906 H; Chinese Republic proclaimed in, 1912 D; Britain restrains China from sending expedition to, 1912 H; China offers regional autonomy to, 1950 E; China occupies, 1950 K; Tibet appeals to UN for restoration of independence, 1961 C demonstrations against Chinese rule, 1987 K martial law imposed in Lhasa, 1989 C
Tichborne claimant, 1874 O
Tieck, Ludwig, G. author (1773–1854), 1773 Z, 1795 U, 1797 U, 1803 Q, 1854 Z
Tiedge, Hans Joachim, West German counter-espionage official, 1985 H
T'ien-an Men Square, Peking, China, demonstration and massacre, 1989 D, R
Tientsin, China: treaty, ends Anglo-Chinese War, 1858 F; Anglo-French troops take, 1860 H; commercial treaties, 1861 J, 1885 F; taken by international force, 1900 G; Japanese seize, 1937 G; Japanese blockade British concession at, 1939 F; falls to Communists, 1949 A
Tiepolo, Giovanni, It. artist (1692–1769), 1769 Z
Tieste (U. Foscolo), 1797 W
Tiflis, Georgia, Russia, sacked by Persian chief, 1783 K
Tiger for Malgudi, A (R.K. Narayan), 1983 U
Tiger, HMS, Smith/Wilson talks on Rhodesia, 1966 M
Tight-rope walking, 1859 Q
Tigre, Ethiopia, famine, 1984 L
Tikhivin, Russia, Russians recapture, 1941 M
Tikhonov, Nikolay Aleksandrovich, R. Prime Minister (b. 1905), 1980 K, 1983 B
Tilden, Samuel Jones, Am. Democrat (1814–86), 1876 L
Tilden, William, Am. lawn-tennis player (1893–1953), 1920 X
Tildy, Zoltan, Hung. leader of Smallholders Party (1889–1961), 1945 L, 1946 B, 1948 G
Tiller Girls, The, dancing troupe, 1908 W
Tillet, Ben, B. Trades Union leader (1860–1943), 1912 G
Tillich, Paul, Am. form. G., theologian (1886–1965), 1949 R, 1954 R
Tilsit, Russia: consequences of Treaty between Napoleon and Russia, for Britain, 1807 L; Treaty of 1807; violated, 1810 M, 1811 A; Russians take, 1945 A
Time Machine, The (H. G. Wells), 1895 U
Time Must Have a Stop (A. Huxley), 1944 U
Time and Freewill, Matter and Memory (H. Bergson), 1909 R
Time and the Conways (J. B. Priestley), 1937 W
Time for Decision, The (S. Welles), 1944 O
Time of Gifts, A (P.L. Fermor), 1977 U
Time on the Cross: The Economics of American Negro Slavery (R. Fogel and S. Engerman), 1974 Q
Time to Dance, A (C. Day Lewis), 1935 U
Times Atlas of World History, The (G. Barraclough ed.), 1978 Q
Times Square (J. Holzer), 1982 S
Timisoara, Roumania, army fires on demonstration, 1989 M
Timor, Portuguese (East)
declared independent, 1975 L
Indonesian forces invade, 1975 M
Timoshenko, Semyon, R. general (1895–1970), 1895 Z, 1941 L, 1942 G, 1970 Z
Tin Drum, The (G. Grass), 1963 U
Ting, Samuel Chao Chung, Am. physicist (b. 1936), 1974 P
Tinguely, Jean, Swi. sculptor (1925–91), 1983 S
Tinker, Tailor, Soldier, Spy (J. le Carré), 1974 U
Tinned food, 1880 P, 1892 P
Tipperary, Ireland: rising in, 1848 G; captured by Nationalists, 1922 G
Tippett, Sir Michael Kemp, B. musician (b. 1905), 1905 Z, 1940 T, 1955 T, 1962 T, 1963 T, 1970 T, 1972 T, 1977 T, 1979 T, 1984 T, 1989 T, 1992 T
Tippoo Sahib, ruler of Mysore (1782–99), 1782 M, 1783 D, 1784 C, 1789 M, 1791 E, 1792 B, 1799 E
Tiraboschi, Girolamo, It. author (1731–94), 1782 Q
Tirana, treaty between Italy and Albania, 1926 L
Tirannide, La (V. Alfieri), 1777 O
Tirard, Pierre Emanuel, F. politician (1827–93), 1889 B
Tirol, Austria, Austrians evacuate Southern, 1916 F
Tirpitz, Alfred von, G. minister of marine (1849–1930), 1849 Z, 1897 F, 1930 Z; expands navy, 1898 C; resigns, 1916 C
Tischendorf, Lobegott Friedrich Konstantin von, G. Biblical critic (1815–74), 1844 Q, 1859 Q
Tisdall, Sarah, B. Foreign Office clerk, 1984 C
Tiso, Joseph, Czech. politician (1887–1947), 1939 C, 1947 D
Tissue culture, 1907 P
Tisza, Kálmán, Hung. statesman (1830–1902), 1875 C
Tisza, Stephen, Count, Hung. leader (1861–1918), elected president of Hungarian Chamber, 1912 E; resigns, 1917 E; assassinated, 1918 K
Titan (Jean Paul), 1800 U
Titanic disaster, 1912 P
Tithes, commutation of, in England, 1836 H, R
Titled (Art as an Idea) (J. Kosuth), 1966 S
Titles, in Turkey, abolished, 1934 L
Tito (Josip Broz), Yugo. soldier and statesman (1892–1980), 1892 Z, 1945 L, 1955 L 1980 E, Z; Maclean's mission to, 1943 K; Yugoslav Communists give vote of confidence to, 1948 G; elected president, 1953 A; visits London, 1953 C; visits Greece, 1954 E; visits Delhi, 1954 M; meets Nasser, 1956 A; visits Moscow, 1956 F
purges Croat leadership of nationalists, 1971 M
received by Pope, 1971 R
Titulescu, Nicholas, Rum. leader, falls, 1937 M
Titusville, Pa., US, oil well at, 1859 P
Tizard, Sir Henry, B. scientist and administrator, 1885 Z, 1959 Z
To Have or Have Not (E. Hemingway), 1937 U
To Let (J. Galsworthy), 1921 U
To the Finland Station (E. Wilson), 1941 O
To the Lighthouse (V. Woolf), 1927 U
To the Night (Novalis), 1800 U
Tobago, Island, West Indies: ceded to Britain, 1763 B; France captures, 1781 D; France recovers, 1783 J; British capture, 1803 F. *See also* Trinidad and Tobago
Tobias and the Angel (J. Bridie), 1952 W
Tobruk, Libya: Rommel attacks, 1941 D
Rommel takes, 1942 F
British recapture, 1942 L
Tocqueville, Charles Alexis de, F. author (1805–59), 1805 Z, 1835 O, 1856 Q, 1859 Z
Todd, Garfield, Rhodesian politician (b. 1908), ousted from leadership of United Federal Party, 1958 B; forms United Rhodesian Party, 1958 D; founds Rhodesian New Africa Party, 1961 L
Togo (formerly Togoland), becomes an independent republic, 1960 D
Togoland, South-west Africa: German occupation, 1884 D; frontier with Gold Coast settled, 1886 G, 1899 L; British and French forces occupy, 1914 H; League of Nations mandate for, 1922 G; UN agrees on independence for, 1959 M; becomes an independent republic, as Togo, 1960 D
Tojo, Hideki, Jap. general and premier (1884–1948), resigns, 1944 G; sentenced for war crimes, 1948 L
Tökes, Pastor Lázló, Roumanian cleric (b. 1952), 1989 R
Tokio, Japan:
Conference to discuss extra-territorial concessions, 1886 E
population, 1881 Y, 1906 Y, 1950 Y, 1960 Y
US air raids on, 1945 B
population overtakes London's, 1960 Y
anti-US demonstrations, 1968 K
population, 1970 Y, 1990 Y
Nagakin Capsule Tower, 1972 S
share price panic, 1981 J
Tokomak experimental fusion reactors, 1968 P
Tolentino, Italy: Treaty, between France and Papacy, 1797 B; Austrians defeat Murat at, 1815 E
Tolkein, John Ronald Reuel, B. literary scholar and author (1892–1973), 1892 Z, 1954 U, 1973 Z
Toller, Ernst, G. revolutionary and dramatist, 1893 Z, 1939 Z
Tolpuddle Martyrs, 1834 C
Tolstoy, Leo, R. novelist and social reformer (1828–1910), 1828 Z, 1864 U, 1873 U, 1885 U, 1890 U, 1899 U, 1900 U, 1910 Z
Tom Brown's Schooldays (T. Hughes), 1857 U
Tomin, Dr. Julius, Czech. philosopher and dissident, 1980 R
Tommy rock opera (The Who), 1969 W
Tompa, Mihály, Hung. poet (1817–68), 1854 U

Ton Dac Thang, President of North Vietnam (1888–1980), 1969 J
Tonbridge, Kent, England, by-election, 1956 F
Tone poems. *See* Overtures, Symphonic Poems, etc.
Tone, Theobald Wolfe, Ir. politician (1763–98), 1790 K
Tonegawa, Susumu, Jap. molecular biologist (b. 1939), 1976 P
Tonga Islands, S. Pacific, Britain annexes, 1899 L, 1900 E
Tonkin, Gulf of, US fleet attacked in, 1972 D
Tonkin, Viet-Nam: French protectorate in, 1883 H; becomes part of French Union Indo-Chinese, 1887 N
Tono Bungay (H. G. Wells), 1909 U
Tooke, John Horne, B. politician and philologist (1736–1812), 1801 F
Tootal Company, Ltd., makes crease-resisting fabric, 1929 P
Tooth of the Crime, The (S. Shepard), 1972 W
Toothache (F. Clemente), 1981 S
Toothbrush, The (J. Diaz), 1966 W
Top Girls (C. Churchill), 1982 W
Topete, Juan Bauptista, Sp. naval officer and politician (1821–85), 1868 J
Töpffer, Rodolphe, Sw. author (1799–1846), 1838 U
Topolski, Felix, B. formerly Pol. artist (1907–89), 1941 S
Torah, The, 1977 R
Torch Song Trilogy (H. Fierstein), 1981 W
Torgau, Germany, juncture of US and Russian armies at, 1945 D
Tories. *See under* Political Parties
Tornadoes and typhoons:
  in Hong Kong, 1960 F
  in US Middle West, 1965 D
Tornatore, Giuseppe, It. film director (b. 1956), 1990 W
Toron of the Prairie, A (W. Irving), 1832 U
Toronto (formerly York Town), Canada, US force takes, 1813 D
  Scarborough College building, 1966 S
  Art Gallery of Toronto, 1974 S
  Canadian National Tower, 1974 S
Torpedoes: invented, 1777 P; Whitehead's, 1864 P; homing, 1945 A
Torrens, William Torrens McCullagh, B. politician (1813–94), 1867 O
Torres Vedras, Spain, Wellington holds line of, 1819 K
Torrey Canyon oil tanker accident, 1967 C
Torrington, Devon, England, by-election, 1958 C
Torsion balance invented, 1777 P
Torture, in Turkey, suppressed, 1856 B
Torvill, Jayne, B. ice dancer (b. 1957), 1984 X
Tosca, La (Sardou), 1887 W
Toscanini, Arturo, Am. formerly It. musician (1867–1957), 1867 Z, 1929 T, 1957 Z
Totem and Taboo (S. Freud), 1913 R
Tottenham, London
  riots, 1985 K
Touch (T. Gunn), 1968 U
Toulmin, Stephen Edelston, B. philosopher (b. 1922), 1972 R
Toulon, France, Bonaparte takes, 1793 M
Toulouse-Lautrec, Henri Marie Raymond de, F. artist (1864–1901), 1864 Z, 1891 S, 1892 S, 1900 S, 1901 Z
Tourcoing, N. France, battle, 1794 E
Tourism, statistics, 1973 Y
Tournier, Michel, F. author (b. 1924), 1967 T, 1970 U, 1975 U
Tous les hommes sont mortels (S. de Beauvoir), 1946 U
Tovey, Sir Donald Francis, B. musicologist (1875–1940), 1935 T
Tower, John, Am. Republican politician (1925–91), 1986 L
Tower, The (W. B. Yeats), 1928 U
Town planning:
  in Britain, *County of London Plan*, 1943 O
    Sharpe's plan for Greater London, 1944 O
    Reith Committee on new towns, 1946 O
    New Towns Commission, 1961 O
    Holford's plan for St. Paul's precinct, London, 1966 S
  in France, Haussmann rebuilds Paris, 1853 S
  in Germany, model dwellings, 1853 O
Town, City, and Nation: England 1850–1914 (P.J. Waller), 1983 Q
Townsend Thorensen ferry *Herald of Free Enterprise* capsizes, 1987 C, G, K
Townshend, Charles, B. Tory politician (1725–67), 1766 G, 1767 E, J
Toxicologie générale (M. Orfila), 1814 P
Toxteth, Liverpool, England, riots, 1981 G
Toynbee, Arnold Joseph, B. historian (1889–1975), 1889 Z, 1934 Q, 1952 O, 1975 Z
Toys in the Attic (L. Hellman), 1960 W
Tractatus Logico-Philosophicus (Wittgenstein), 1922 R
Tractor, petrol-driven, 1898 P
Tracts for the Times, 1833 R
Trade:
  European Free Trade Association customs union, 1966 O
  US agrees to export high-technology items to China, 1983 E
  US-USSR, 1983 H
  US trade sanctions on Poland partially lifted, 1984 A
  bill to deregulate Sunday trading in England and Wales rejected, 1986 D
  Canadian–US agreement to reduce tariffs and economic barriers, 1987 K
  Canadian–US free trade agreement signed, 1988 A
  See also Embargoes; Sanctions
Trade, Council of, in Britain, 1786 N
Trades Union Congress (TUC), Britain:
  pledges to deal with unofficial strikes, 1969 F
  rejects EC membership terms, 1971 J
  government proposes wage and price restraints, 1972 J
  independent conciliation service with CBI, 1972 H
  unions suspended for registering under Industrial Relations Act, 1972 J
  calls for pay policies strike, 1973 E
  expels 20 unions, 1973 J
  talks on miners' break down, 1974 A
  endorses 'social contract', 1974 J
  government incomes policy supported by, 1975 J
  approves new incomes policy, 1976 F
  votes against 5% pay policy, 1978 G
  Concordat with government, 1979 B
  Brighton Conference deplores Employment Act, 1980 J
Trade Unions:
  Industrial Workers of the World, Detroit, 1909 O
  World Conference, London, 1945 B
  in Britain, forbidden by Combinations Act, 1800 O
    permitted, with repeal of Combinations Acts, 1824 O
    expansion of, 1825 O
    strike action prohibited, 1825 G
    Grand National Consolidated Union formed, 1834 A, C
    legalised, 1871 F, O
    National Agricultural Labourers Union, 1872 O
    statistics of membership, 1892 Y, 1902 Y, 1912 Y, 1922 Y, 1932 Y
    Taff Vale, judgment, 1901 G
    peaceful picketing permitted, 1906 M
    Osborne judgment rules levies illegal, 1909 O
    TUC votes against Syndicalism, 1912 J
    Act declares certain strikes and lock-outs illegal, 1927 G
      repealed, 1946 B
    Closed shop dispute, 1946 H
    TUC agrees to join National Economic Development Council, 1962 B
    decision in Rookes *v.* Barnard 1964 O
    TUC sells *Daily Herald*, 1964 V
    TUC signs statement of intent on productivity, prices and incomes, 1964 M
    Royal Commission on, 1965 B
    Royal Commission on Trade Unions and Employers' Associations, 1968 O
    Trade Union Reform Bill abandoned, 1969 F
    TGWU fined for blacking Liverpool docks, 1972 C, F
    AUEW fined for excluding member, 1972 L
    European Trade Union Confederation, 1973 O, 1973 P
    AUEW funds sequestrated, 1974 E
    closed shops for journalists, 1975 L
    pay talks with government break down, 1978 K
    'day of action' against government policies, 1980 E
    NUM vote on wage increase, 1982 A
    ASLEF members strike over 'flexible rosters', 1982 G
    reforms in Trade Union law, 1983 G
    GCHQ staff deprived of right to belong to union, 1984 A, G
    miners' strike, 1984 C-K,L
    'day of action' in support of miner's strike, 1984 F
    NUM fined for contempt of court, 1984 K
    first woman to lead major union, 1984 O
    Nissan negotiates single-union deal at British plant, 1985 O
    Union of Democratic Mineworkers (UDM), 1985 K
    News International dispute, 1986 V, 1987 A, B
    See also Trades Union Congress
  in France, government attempts to suppress, 1834 D
    legalised, 1884 C
    Congress adopts strike principle, 1895 A
  in Germany, suppressed, 1933 E
  in Italy, Confederazione Generale del Lavaro, 1906 O
    non-Fascist, abolished, 1924 A
  in Poland
    independent, 1980 H
    farmers, 1981 D
    curbs on, 1981 M
    new trade unions banned, 1982 K
    Solidarity. *See* Solidarity
  in South Africa, 1985 L
  in Spain
    Spanish bishops proclaim workers' right to form, 1968 G
  in US, General Trades Union, 1833 N
    Knights of Labor, founded, 1869 O

American Federation of Labor, 1881 O, 1886 O
excommunicated, 1885 O
stage Chicago riot, 1886 E
statistics of membership, 1902 Y
Closed Shop outlawed, 1947 F
levies for political purposes prohibited, 1947 F
See also under Strikes
Trading Stamps, in Britain, campaign against, 1963 O
Trafalgar House, B. business conglomerate, 1977 V
Trafalgar, Spain, battle of, 1805 K
Traffic in Towns (Buchanan Report), 1963 O
Traffic lights, in New York, 1918 P
Tragedy is Not Enough (K. Jaspers), 1953 R
Tragedy of Agis (G. Bessenyei), 1772 W
Traité d'Economique politique (J. B. Saye), 1803 O
Traité de Mécanique (S. D. Poisson), 1811 P
Traité des Propriétés projectives des figures (J. V. Poncelet), 1822 P
Traité élmentaire de chimie (A. L. Lavoisier), 1789 P
Traité medico-philosophique de l'aliénation mentale (P. Pinel), 1791 P
Traitors, The (A. Moorehead), 1952 O
Tram-road, iron, 1801 P
Trams, last London, 1952 P
Trans (Stockhausen), 1971 T
Trans-Iranian pipe-line, 1957 A
Trans-Siberian Railway, 1891 G, 1901 P
Transatlantic cable, 1857 P, 1865 P
Transatlantic telephone service, 1956 P
'Transavanguardia,', 1979 S
Transcaucasia, Russia, Russian war with Persia over 1826 J
Transcendental Meditation, US tour by Maharishi Mahesh Yogi and The Beach Boys, 1968 W
Transcendental Philosophy (J. G. Fichte), 1812 R
Transcendentalism, 1836 R, 1840 R
Transfer of Power in India (V. P. Menon), 1957 O
Transfiguration of Our Lord Jesus Christ, The (O. Messiaen), 1969 T
Transformer, electric, 1831 P
Transistor radio, invented, 1948 P
Transjordan: becomes independent, 1923 E; independence recognised, 1928 B, 1946 C; Arab Legion of, invades Palestine, 1948 E; is renamed Jordan, 1949 F. *See also* Jordan; Middle East
Translations (B. Friel), 1980 W
Transmutation of atoms, 1919 P, 1922 P
Transport
transport strike in New York, 1966 A
breath test introduced in Britain, 1967 O
Sweden changes to drive on the right, 1967 O
hot-air balloon crossing of Pacific Ocean, 1991 A
See also Aircraft; Channel Tunnel; Motor Car; Railways; Shipping
Transport and General Workers' Union (TGWU), B. trade union, fined for blacking Liverpool docks, 1972 C, F
Transport industry, in Britain: nationalisation of 1946 L; closed-shop dispute in, 1946 H; road transport denationalised, 1953 E
Transportation of Convicts:
from Britain, 1823 G, 1834 C
to Tasmania, suspended, 1853 N
from France, 1851 O
Transvaal (or South African Republic), S. Africa: established, 1852 A; Pretorius organises, 1856 M; Britain annexes, 1877 D; Republic proclaimed, 1879 M, 1880 M; declares itself independent, 1880 K; Britain recognises independence, 1881 D; Kruger becomes president, 1883 D; status of, regulated, 1884 B; gold discovered in, 1885 P; communication with coast is blocked, 1887 F; relations with British S. Africa Company, 1889 K; Britain blocks coastal access, 1895 F; Jameson Raid into, 1895 M; franchise in, 1899 C, G; Britain annexes, 1900 K
Transylvania, now in Rumania and Russia: incorporated in Hungary, 1865 M, union with Russia proclaimed, 1918 L; Rumania annexes, 1919 A; Russian gains in, 1947 B
Traum, ein Leben, Der (F. Grillparzer), 1834 U
Travailleurs de la mer (V. Hugo), 1866 U
Travancore, India, Rajah of, attacked by Tippoo of Mysore, 1789 M
Travel-tours, 1841 W
Traveller, The (O. Goldsmith), 1764 U
Travelling North (D. Williamson), 1979 W
Travels in Arabia Deserta (C. M. Doughty), 1888 P
Travels in Asia Minor (R. Chandler), 1775 P
Travels in France (A. Young), 1792 O
Travels in the Interior of Africa (M. Park), 1799 P
Travels to Discover the Source of the Nile (J. Bruce), 1790 P
Travers, Ben, B. dramatist (1886–1980), 1927 W
Travers, Morris William, B. chemist (1872–1947), 1898 P
Travesties (T. Stoppard), 1974 W
Travis, Walter John, Am. golfer (1862–1927), 1904 X
Treason Trials:
in Czechoslovakia, 1952 L
in Ghana, 1963 M
in South Africa, 1956 M, 1959 A, 1961 C, 1964 F
in Turkey, 1960 K
in US trials removed from Colonial courts to Westminster, 1769 G
Treasure Island (R. L. Stevenson), 1883 U
Treaties of Alliance, Leagues, etc.:
Afghanistan with Persia, 1921 F
Albania with Italy, 1927 L
Armenia with Turkey (Alexandropol), 1920 M
Austria with Britain and France, against Prussia and Russia, 1815 A
Austria with Britain, Prussia and Russia, against France, 1815 C
Austria with Britain and France, over Danubian Provinces, 1854 M
Austria with France, 1812 C
Austria with Germany, 1879 K
joined by Italy, 1882 E
Austria with Prussia, against France, 1792 B
Austria with Prussia, against Russia, 1854 D
Austria with Roumania, 1883 K
Austria with Russia, against Turkey, 1781 B
Austria with Serbia, 1881 F
Austria with Turkey, 1771 G
Balkan Alliance (Greece, Yugoslavia and Turkey), 1954
dissolved, 1960 F
Baltic States treaty of collaboration, 1934 J
Bavaria with Austria (Reid), 1813 K
Benghazi Agreement establishes Federation of Arab Republics, 1971 D
Britain with Afghanistan, against Persia (Peshawar), 1855 C
Britain with Egypt, 1899 A
Egypt abrogates, 1951 K
Britain with Egypt, to end occupation, 1936 H
Egypt demands revision, 1945 J
proposed British revision referred by Egypt to UN, 1947 A
Britain with France (Entente Cordiale), 1904 D
Britain with France, 1947 C
Britain with France and Italy, 1915 D
Britain with France and Turkey, 1947 C
Britain with Germany, proposed, rejected, 1899 L, M
Britain with Germany, negotiations for, founder, 1901 K
Britain with Holland, 1788 D
joined by Prussia, 1788 H
Britain with Hyderabad, 1790 G
Britain with Iraq, 1955 D
Britain with Japan, negotiations for, 1901 G, K, M
signed, 1902 A
Franco–Russian declaration on, 1902 C
renewed, 1905 H, 1911 G
Britain with Jordan, 1948 D
expires on, 1957 C
Britain with Libya, 1953 G
Britain with Persia, against Russian interests in Near East, 1905 C
Britain with Russia, against France, 1798 M
Britain with Russia, talks founder, 1903 K
Britain with Russia, 1907
Russia denounces, 1918 A
Britain with Russia, urged, 1939 D, G
negotiations for, 1939 H
Britain with Russia, 1942 E
Russia threatens to annul, 1954 M
Britain with Russia and Iran, 1942 A
Britain with Sweden and Russia (Örebro), 1812 G, 1813 C
Brussels, against armed attack in Europe, 1948 C
Bulgaria with Austria–Hungary, 1913 F
Bulgaria with Germany and Turkey, 1915 J
China with Russia, 1896 F
Czechoslovakia with Rumania, 1921 D
Czechoslovakia with Yugoslavia, 1922 H
Egypt with Saudi Arabia and Yemen, 1956 D
Egypt with Syria, 1955 C
European Defence Community (Paris), 1952 E
France and Britain with Serbia, 1915 K
France with Czechoslovakia, 1924 A
France with Holland, 1785 L
France with Prussia, against Britain, 1806 B
France with Rumania, 1926 F
France with Russia, 1808 K
France with Russia, 1893 A, 1897 H
extended, 1899 H
France with Sardinia, 1859 A
France with Spain (San Ildefonso), 1796 M
France with Spain, against Portugal (Fontainebleau), 1807 K
France with US, 1778 B
Franco–African to form French-speaking commonwealth, 1980 E
Fürstenbund, Die (League of German Princes), 1785 G
Germany with Austria, 1879 K
terms published, 1888 B
Germany with Italy ('Pact of Steel'), 1939 E
Germany with Russia (Re-insurance Treaty), 1887 F
lapses, 1890 F
terms published, 1896 K
Germany with Russia, negotiations founder, 1904 L
Germany with Turkey, 1914 H
Holland with US, 1778 J
Holy Alliance, between Austria, Prussia and Russia, 1815 J
Bavaria joins, 1816 H
Holland joins, 1816 H
Sweden joins, 1817 E
terms extended, 1833 K

Italy with France, 1902 L
Italy with Prussia, against Austria, 1866 D
Italy with Roumania, 1926 J
Little Entente, of Yugoslavia, Czechoslovakia and Roumania, 1920 H
London, between Allies, against separate peace, 1914 J
 Japan a signatory to, 1915 K
North Atlantic, 1949 D. See also under NATO
North German Confederation with Bavaria and Württemberg, 1870 L
Prussia with Baden, against France, 1866 H
Prussia with Bavaria, against France, 1866 H
Prussia with Hanover and Saxony (Three Kings' League), 1849 E
 Hanover leaves, 1850 B
Prussia with Russia, against France (Kalisch), 1813 B
Prussia with Württemberg, against France, 1866 H
Quadruple Alliance, between Austria, Prussia, Russia and Britain, 1815 L
 renewed, 1818 L
 joined by Mehemet Ali, 1840 G, L
 joined by France, 1841 G
Quadruple Alliance, between Britain, France, Spain and Portugal, 1834 D
 Britain sends squadron to Portugal under terms of, 1846 E
Roumania with Poland, 1926 C
Roumania with Yugoslavia, 1921 F
Russia with Austria, 1787 A
Russia with Britain (St. Petersburg), 1805 D
 Austria joins, 1805 H
Russia proposes defence alliance with Britain, 1939 D
Russia with Nationalist China, 1945 H
Russia with China, 1950 B
Russia with Czechoslovakia, for defeating Germany, 1943 M
Russia with Denmark, 1769 M, 1774 H, 1776 D
Russia with France (Tilsit), 1807 L
 violated, 1810 M, 1811 A
Russia with Germany, attempt to renew, 1879 K
Russia with Germany, 1939 H
Russia with Japan, 1925 A
Russia with Latvia (Riga), 1920 H
Russia with Mongolia, 1920 L
Russia with Prussia, 1767 D, 1769 K
Russia with Turkey and Britain, 1799 A
Russia with Turkey, 1921 M, 1925 M
Serbia with Greece, Serbia refused aid under, 1915 K
Sweden with Allies, against Russia, 1855 L
Sweden with Russia (Abo), 1812 D
Switzerland with France, 1777 N
Teplitz, uniting Russia, Prussia and Austria against France, 1813 J
Three Emperors' League, of Germany, Russia and Austria–Hungary, 1873 K, 1881 F
 renewed, 1884 C
 Russia refuses extension, 1887 F
Transvaal with Orange Free State, 1896 C
Triple Alliance, of Britain, Holland and Prussia, 1788 H, L
Triple Alliance, of Germany, Austria and Italy, 1882 E
 renewed, 1887 B, 1891 E, 1902 F, 1907 G
 Italy denounces, 1915 E
 naval convention of, 1913 L
Turkey with Afghanistan, 1923 B
Turkey with Russia (Unkiai-Skelessi), 1833 G
 overthrown, 1841 G
US with Panama, 1926 G
UAR, Libya, Sudan and Syria, federation, 1970 L
Yugoslavia with Czechoslovakia and Roumania (Little Entente), 1920 H
Treaties of Arbitration in Disputes:
 Britain with US, 1911 G
 France with US, 1913 B
 Germany with Lithuania, 1928 A
 Washington Treaty for inter-American arbitration, 1929 A
 among Scandinavian States, 1930 F
Treaties of Commerce, Trade Pacts, etc.:
 Austria with Serbia, 1910 H
 Bavaria with Württemberg, 1828 A
 Belgium with Luxembourg, 1921 G
 Belgium, Holland and Luxembourg (Benelux), 1958 B
 Britain with Belgium, denounced, 1897 G
 Britain with China, 1843 K, 1902 J
 Britain with France (Eden Treaty), 1786 J
 Britain with France (Cobden-Chevalier Treaty), 1860 A
 Britain with France, 1872 L, 1959 D
 Britain with Germany, denounced, 1897 G
 Britain with Germany, 1924 M, 1933 D, 1959 A
 Britain with India, 1935 A
 Britain with Ireland, 1936 B
 Britain with Japan, 1858 H, 1911 D
 Britain with Madagascar, 1877 K
 Britain with Persia, 1959 C
 Britain with Russia, 1921 C, J, 1922 J
 annulled, 1927 E
 Britain with Russia, 1934 B, 1941 H, 1959 E
 Britain with Scandinavian States, for economic co-operation, 1950 A
 Britain with Siam, 1826 F
 Britain with South Africa, to supply arms, 1970 G
 Britain with Spain, 1958 B, 1959 B
 Britain with Zollverein, 1865 E
 Canada with US, reciprocal, 1935 L
 China with Ceylon, 1959 F
 Convention on International Trade in Endangered Species, 1989 K
 Europe, Organization for Economic Co-operation and Development (OED), 1960 M
 European Community–China, 1978 B
 European Economic Community ('The Six' member states of the Common Market), Rome Treaty for, 1957 C
 European Free Trade Association ('The Seven' member states of EFTA), 1959 L
 Finland with Russia, 1854 G
 France with Canada, 1922 M
 France with Egypt, 1958 M
 France with W. Germany, 1954 K, 1963 A
 France with Italy, 1898 L
 France with Madagascar, 1868 H
 France with Prussia, 1862 H
 France with Russia, 1857 F. 1893 F, 1957 B
 France with US, 1778 B
 General Agreement on Tariffs and Trade (GATT). See General Agreement on Tariffs and Trade
 Germany with Austria, 1892 B, 1904 G
 Germany with Balkan States, 1893 N
 Germany with Belgium, 1892 B, 1904 G
 Germany with Estonia, 1923 F
 Germany with Italy, 1892 B
 Germany with Poland, 1935 L
 Germany with Russia, 1894 B
 unpopularity in Germany, 1894 K
 Germany with Samoa, 1879 A
 Germany with Sweden, 1904 G
 Germany with Switzerland, 1892 B, 1904 G
 Hungary with China, 1858 C
 India with China, 1954 D
 India with Pakistan, on Indus Waters development, 1960 J
 Italy with Russia, 1921 M, 1922 E
 Japan with powers, 1866 F
 Japan with France, 1911 F
 Lomé Convention, EC markets access, 1975 B
 Oslo-Convention on Scandinavian economic cooperation, 1932 B
 Pakistan with Russia, 1956 F
 Pan-American reciprocity plan, rejected, 1889 K
 Paris Treaty, embodying Schuman Plan, 1951 D
 Prussia with Austria, 1953 B
 Prussia with China, 1861 J
 Prussia with Hanover, 1851 J
 Prussia with Mecklenburg-Schwerin, 1826 M
 Prussia with Poland, 1775 C
 Prussia with US, 1785 J
 Rome Treaty for Common Market, 1957 C
 Russia with Austria, 1955 D
 Russia with Cuba, 1962 A
 Russia with Germany, 1939 H
 Russia with Italy, 1961 F
 Russia with Mongolian Republic, 1956 D
 Russia with Poland, 1931 F
 Russia with Sweden, 1922 C
 Russia with US, 1935 G
 Spain with Argentina, 1946 K
 US with Britain. See under Lend Lease
 US with China, 1920 K
 US with Italy, 1948 B
 US with Japan, 1911 B
 US denounces, 1911 G
 US with Russia, 1937 G
 See also under Tariff Questions
Treaties–Conventions:
 Austria with Germany, for Austrian independence, 1936 G
 Balta-Liman, Russia with Turkey, 1849 E
 Baltic, for maintaining status quo, 1908 H
 Bloemfontein, for Orange Free State, 1854 B
 Britain with Belgium, on Ruanda, 1921 C
 Britain with Egypt, on Sudan, 1899 A
 Britain with France, on Tripoli, 1899 C
 Britain with China, on Tibet, 1906 H
 Britain with Russia, on Persia, 1907 H
 Britain with Turkey, 1938 E
 Constantinople, declaring Suez Canal open to all nations, 1888 K
 Drummond-Wolff, Britain with Egypt, 1887 E
 Egypt with Sudan, over Nile, 1952 K
 France with Belgium, 1920 H
 France with Italy, over Tunis, 1896 J
 France with Japan, on 'open door' in China, 1907 F
 France with Spain, to break Portugal's allegiance to Britain, 1801 A
 France with Spain, to enforce neutrality of Portugal, 1803 K
 France with Syria, 1837 M
 Genoa, Russia with Vatican, 1922 E
 Helsinki, between Scandinavian States, 1962 C
 Intermediate-range Nuclear Forces (INF), 1988 F
 Latin American nations, to prohibit nuclear weapons, 1967 B
 London, defines the aggressor, 1933 G
 London, naval, 1936 C, K
 Mediterranean, Britain, Italy and Austria, 1887 B, C, E
 Montreux, for Turkish sovereignty over Dardanelles, 1936 G
 Montreux, abolishes Egyptian capitulations, 1937 E

Mozambique, denounced by S. Africa, 1922 D
Nicaragua, Honduras with Costa Rica, 1920 L
North Sea, for maintaining status quo, 1908 H
nuclear weapons banned from outer space, 1967 O
Preventing pollution of sea by oil, 1954 O
prohibiting stock-piling of biological weapons, 1972 D
Russia with China, on Manchuria, 1896 J
Russia with Japan, on China, 1907 G
SALT II, limiting nuclear weapons, 1979 F
Sand River, establishes Transvaal, 1852 A
Straits, guarantees Ottoman independence, 1841 G
Strategic Arms Reduction Treaty (START), 1991 G
Treaty on Non-Proliferation of Nuclear Weapons, 1968 G, 1969 L
UN Convention on the Prevention and Punishment of the Crime of Genocide, 1986 O
US–USSR, draft treaty to ban biological weapons, 1971 H
USSR–US, limiting anti-ballistic missile sites, 1972 E
Treaties of Friendship:
Austria with Italy, 1930 B
Balkan, Entente, origins of, 1930 K
Britain with Eire, 1938 D
Britain with France (Entente Cordiale), 1904 D
Britain with France (Lausanne), 1932 F
Britain with Sikhs, 1809 D
Bulgaria with Turkey, 1929 C
Bulgaria with Yugoslavia (Treaty of Perpetual Peace), 1937 A
Burma with China, 1960 A
Central American States, 1887 N
Central American States (Washington), 1923 B
China with Mongolia, 1952 K
China with US, 1946 L
Egypt with Iraq, 1931 D
Egypt–USSR, 1971 E
France with Lebanon, 1936 J
France with Russia, 1891 H
France with Syria, 1936 J
France with Yugoslavia, 1927 L
Germany with Russia (Berlin), 1926 D
Germany with Transvaal, 1885 A
Germany with Turkey, 1924 C
Greece with Turkey, 1938 D
Greece with Turkey and Yugoslavia, 1953 B
Greece with Yugoslavia, 1926 H, 1929 C
Iraq with Iran, 1929 H
Iraq with Transjordan, 1931 C
Italy with Ethiopia, 1928 H
Italy with Greece, 1928 J
Italy with Hungary, 1927 D
Japan with Korea, 1875 N
Malaya with Indonesia, 1959 D
Pan-American, 1924 E
Roumania with Yugoslavia, 1947 M
Russia with E. Germany, 1964 F
Russia with Poland, 1931 F
Russia with Yugoslavia, 1941 D
Russia denounces, 1949 J
Russia with Yugoslavia, 1955 E
Saudi Arabia with Persia, 1929 H
Saudi Arabia with Transjordan, 1933 G
Saudi Arabia with Turkey, 1929 H
Turkey with Greece, 1930 K
Turkey with Spain, 1959 D
US with Germany, 1923 M
US with Italy, 1949 B
USSR–Iraq, 1972 D
Yugoslavia with Bulgaria, denounced, 1949 K
Yugoslavia with Poland, 1926 J
Yugoslavia with Roumania, denounced, 1949 K
Treaties of Mutual Assistance and Military Aid:
American Republics, 1947 J
Britain with Poland, 1939 H
Britain with Russia, 1941 G
Cuba with US, Cuba denounces, 1960 J
France with Belgium, Belgium denounces, 1936 K
France with Russia, 1935 E
Germany with Russia, 1905 G
Greece with Yugoslavia and Turkey, 1954 H
India with Indonesia, 1956 B
Persia with Turkey and Afghanistan, 1926 D
Russia with Czechoslovakia, 1935 E
Russia with Finland, 1948 D
Russia with Mongolia, 1936 D
South East Asia, 1954 J
United Arab Republic with Iraq, 1958 G
US with Japan, 1960 A
Japan ratifies, despite protests, 1960 F
US with S. Korea, 1953 H
US with Liberia, 1959 G
See also under Aid
Treaties of Peace:
Adrianople, ends Russo–Turkish War, 1829 J
Allies with Austria, note by Western powers to Russia on, 1952 J
Allies with Germany, Russia proposes Conference for, 1959 A
Amiens, between Britain and France, 1802 C
Ancór, between Peru and Chile, 1883 K
Arab leaders agree to end Jordanian civil war, 1970 J
Basle, between France and Prussia, 1795 D
Bassein, between East India Company and Poona, 1802 M
Berlin, between Prussia and Denmark, 1850 G
Berlin, on Eastern Question, 1878 G
adjustment to, 1880 L
Turkey denounces, 1917 A
Berlin, Germany with Latvia, 1920 E
Bolivia with Chile, 1866 H
Brest-Litovsk, between Russia and Central Powers, 1918 C
Soviet government annuls, 1918 L
Britain with Ireland, 1921 M
Britain with Mysore, 1784 C
Bucharest, between Turkey and Russia, 1812 E
Bucharest, between Serbia and Bulgaria, 1886 C
Bulgaria with Turkey, 1913 J
Burma with Japan, 1954 L
Campo Formio, between France and Austria, 1797 K
Cherasco, between Sardinia and France, 1796 E
Constantinople, between Turkey and Russia, 1784 A
Constantinople, between Greece and Turkey, 1897 M
Contadora peace treaty, 1986 E
Dardanelles, between Britain and Turkey, 1809 A
Estonia with Russia, 1920 B
Finland with Russia, 1940 C
Florence, between France and Naples, 1801 C
Fommenah, between Britain and Ashanti, 1874 B
Frankfurt, between France and Germany, 1871 E
Frederikshavn, between Russia and Sweden, 1810 A
France recognises, 1810 A
Germany with Russia, 1921 E
Ghent, Britain with US, 1814 M, 1815 A
Gramido, ends Portuguese Civil War, 1847 G
Greece with Turkey, 1913 L
Guadeloupe-Hidalgo, between US and Mexico, 1848 B
ratified, 1848 E
Hubertusburg, Prussia with Austria, 1763 B
India with Afghanistan, 1919 G
Israel–Egypt, 1978 J, 1979 C
Japan–China, 1978 H
Jassy, between Russia and Turkey, 1792 A
Jaunaie, La, ends Vendéan revolt, 1795 B
Kutchuk-Kainardji, between Russia and Turkey, 1774 G
Lahore, Britain with Sikhs, 1846 L
Lausanne, between Greece, Turkey and the Allies, 1823 G
Lausanne, between Italy and Turkey, 1912 K
Leoben, between France and Austria, 1797 D
Lunéville, between Austria and France, 1801 B
Milan, between Sardinia and Austria, 1849 H
Montlucon, between France and Vendéans, 1800 A
Nanking, between Britain and China, 1842 H
confirmed, 1843 K
Neuilly, between Allies and Bulgaria, 1919 L
Nikolsburg, between Prussia and Austria, 1866 G
Paris, ends Seven Years War, 1763 B
Paris, between Allies and France, 1814 E, 1815 L
Paris, ends Crimean War, 1856 L
Turkey denounces, 1917 A
Paris, Britain with Persia, 1857 C
Paris, between Spain and US, 1898 M
Paris, Allies with Bulgaria, Finland, Hungary and Roumania, 1946 G, 1947 B
Peking, ends Boxer Rising, 1901 J
Portsmouth, between Russia and Japan, 1905 J
Posen, between Saxony and France, 1806 M
Prague, between Austria and Prussia, 1866 H
clause of annulled, 1878 K
Pressburg, between Austria and France, 1805 M
Prussia, Russia and Austria, with Saxony, 1815 E
Prussia with German States, 1866 H
Prussia with Saxony, 1866 K
Riga, between Russia and Poland, 1921 B
Russia with Afghanistan, 1921 B
Russia with Central Powers, 1918 E
Russia with Lithuania, 1920 G
Russia with Persia, 1921 B
St. Germain, Allies with Austria, 1919 J, 1920 G
Salbai, between East India Company and Mahrattas, 1782 E
San Francisco, Allies with Japan, 1951 C, J
San Stefano, between Russia and Turkey, 1878 C
Austria not reconciled to, 1878 C
Schönbrunn, between Austria and France, 1809 K
Schönbrunn, between France and Prussia, 1805 M
Sèvres, between Allies and Turkey, 1920 H
Shimonoseki, between China and Japan, 1895 D
Sistova, between Turkey and Austria, 1791 H
Austria ratifies, 1919 K
Tartu, between Russia and Poland, 1920 K
Teschen, ends War of Bavarian Succession, 1792 A
Tientsin, Britain with China, 1858 F
Tilsit, France with Prussia, 1807 G
Tilsit, France with Russia, 1807 G
Tolentino, between France and Papacy, 1797 B
Trianon, between Allies and Hungary, 1920 F
Turin, between France and Sardinia, 1860 C

Turkey with Afghanistan, 1921 C
Turkey with Serbia, 1914 C
Turkmanchai, between Persia and Russia, 1827 B
US with Austria, 1921 H
US with Germany, 1921 H
US with Hungary, 1921 H
US with Mexico, 1914 F, 1916 L
Valparaiso, between Bolivia and Chile, 1884 D
Vereeniging, ends Boer War, 1902 E
Verela, between Sweden and Russia, 1790 H
Versailles, between Britain and France, 1783 J
Versailles, between Britain and Holland, 1784 C
Versailles, between France and Germany, 1871 B
Versailles, between Allies and Germany, 1919 F
Austria protests at, 1919 F
US Senate rejects, 1920 L
Mussolini champions revision of, 1930 E
Nazis in Germany denounce, 1930 J
Germany repudiates disarmament clauses of, 1935 C
Germany violates, 1936 C
Germany denounces, 1936 L
League Covenant is separated from, 1938 K
Vienna, between Allies and France, 1815 F
Austria violates, 1846 L
Vienna, between Denmark, Austria and Prussia, 1864 K
Villafranca, between Austria and France, 1859 G
treaty of Zurich confirms, 1859 L
Waitangi, Britain with Maoris, 1840 B
Yandaba, Britain with Burma, 1826 B
Zurich, confirms treaty of Villafranca between Austria and France, 1859 L
Treaties, Other Treaties and International Agreements:
Adams–Onis, on Florida, 1819 B
Addis Ababa, Italy withdraws protectorate over Ethiopia, 1896 K
Afghanistan with Russia, 1926 G
Ankara, between France and Turkey, 1920 K
Aranjuez, Spain with France, for cessation of Louisiana, 1801A
Armed Neutrality of the North, 1800 M
Atlantic Charter, new charter called for, 1973 B
Austria with France, secret, 1866 F
Badajoz, Spain with Portugal, 1801 F
Bardo, between France and Tunis, 1881 E
Barrier, between Austria and Holland (1715), abrogated, 1782 D
Basic Treaty, East–West Germany, 1972 M
Berlin, on West German–West Berlin communications, 1971 J
Britain with Austria and Italy, for status quo in Near East, 1887 M
Britain with China, on extra-territorial rights, 1943 A
Britain with Ethiopia, on Somaliland, 1897 E
Britain with France, on W. African colonial boundaries, 1882 E
Britain with Germany, on Portuguese Africa, 1898 H
Britain with Russia, on N. W. America, 1825 B
Britain with Russia, secret, on Bulgaria, 1878E
Britain with US, on W. Indian bases (1941), US relinquishes rights in, 1961 B
Britain with Uganda, 1900 C
Calhoun's, for US annexation of Texas, 1844 D
Chaumont, for Allies not to make separate peace with Napoleon, 1814 C
Chile–USSR, on economic co-operation, 1971 E
China–US, high-level liaison agreement, 1973 B
Clayton-Bulwer, on Panama Canal, 1850 D
Corfu Pact, for union of Serbs, Croats and Slovenes, 1917 G
Elgin, between Britain and US, on Canada, 1854 F
Family Compact, between France and Spain, French obligations under, 1790 E
Fontainbleau, between Austria and Netherlands, 1785 L
France with Italy, over Florence and Rome, 1864 J
France with Italy, on Middle East, 1900 M
France with Prussia, for exchange of lands, 1796 H
France with Russia, military, 1892 H
France with Spain, on Morocco, 1904 K
Gandamak, between Britain and Afghanistan, 1879 E
Germany with Italy, military, 1888 A
Germany with Russia, military, 1873 E
Greece signs Treaty of Accession to EC, 1979 E
Greece with Italy, on Dodecanese Isles, 1920 H
Greece with Turkey and Cyprus (1960), Makarios abrogates, 1964 D
Hague, The, for Britain to subsidise Allies, 1794 D
Hay-Pauncefoote, on Panama, 1901 L
infringement of, alleged, 1912 H
Hué, between Annam and France, 1884 F
Hyderabad, between Britain and the Nizam, 1798 J
Jay, US with Britain, on boundaries, 1794 L
Jeddah, on independence of Saudi Arabia, 1927 E
Kiel, between Denmark and Sweden, 1814 A, D
Lancaster House agreement on Rhodesia, 1979 M
Lateran, for independence of Vatican City, 1929 B
Lausanne, for establishing world peace, 1924 H
Livadia, between Russia and China, on Ili Valley, 1879 J
Locarno, on mutual guarantees in Europe, 1925 M
Rome Pact endorses, 1933 G
Belgium is released from obligations under, 1937 D
London, between Britain, France and Russia, recognising Greek autonomy, 1827 G
London, for separation of Holland and Belgium, 1831 L
London, for Belgian independence, 1839 D
London, Schleswig-Holstein, 1850 H
London, guarantees integrity of Denmark, 1852 E
London, between France, Russia and Britain against a separate peace, 1914 J
Japan, a signatory to, 1915 K
London, naval, 1936 C
Russia accedes to, 1936 K
Maastricht Treaty, on European economic and political union, 1991 M, 1992 F, J, M
Mackinnon, between British East Africa Company and Leopold II, 1890 E
Madrid, between France and Portugal, 1801 J
Mundoseer, between Britain and Indore, 1818 A
Munich Agreement of 1938 invalidated, 1973 M
Nettuno, on Dalmatia, 1925 G
New States Treaty, 1920 H
Paris, for Western European Union, ratified, 1955 C, D
ratification provokes Russia to annul treaties with France and Britain, 1955 E
Peking, China with Britain and France, ratifying earlier treaties, 1860 K
Peking, Britain with China, 1925 A
Petropolis, Bolivar with Brazil, 1903 L
Portugal grants measure of autonomy to Angola and Mozambique, 1970 M
Pretoria, Britain with Boers, on independence of Transvaal, 1881 D
Rapallo, between Italy and Yugoslavia, 1920 L
Italy abrogates, 1924 J
Rapallo, Germany with Russia, 1922
Reichenbach, between Prussia and Austria, 1790 F
cessation of Orsova, in defiance of, 1791 F
Reichenbach, Austria with Russia and Prussia, 1813 F
Russia with Afghanistan, neutrality, 1931 F
Russia with Poland, on Ukraine (Riga), 1921 C
St. Petersburg, Britain with the powers of the Armed Neutrality of the North, 1801 F
St. Petersburg, between China and Russia, 1881 B
San Ildefonso, between Spain and France, for sale of Louisiana, 1800 K
San Lorenzo, between US and Spain, 1795 K
Serbia with Austria, 1881 G
Spain with Peru, 1865 A
Straits Settlements federation, 1896 G
Test Ban, 1963 H
Tientsin, between France and China, on Annam, 1885 F
Tirana, between Italy and Albania, 1926 L
Ucciali, between Italy and Ethiopia, 1889 E
UN convention governing use of sea and seabed, 1982 O
US with Japan, 1854 C
US with Panama, on Canal Zone, 1903 M, 1970 J
US with Panama, new canal treaty offered by US, 1964 M
US with Russia, on N. W. frontier, 1824 D
Valençay, between France and Spain, for restoration of Ferdinand VII, 1813 M
Vienna, Britain with France, US and Russia for restoring Austria's independence, 1955 E
Washington, fixing Oregon–Canadian frontier, 1846 F
Washington, on Pacific, 1921 M
Japan denounces, 1934 M
Washington, on submarine warfare and use of gas, 1922 B
Washington, to settle differences between US and Britain, 1871 E
Webster–Ashburton, on US–Canadian frontier, 1842 H
West Germany–Poland, on Oder–Neisse Line frontier, 1970 M, 1972 E
West Germany–USSR, renouncing use of force, 1970 H, 1972 E
Windsor, Britain and Portugal, to prevent arms from passing from Delagoa Bay to Transvaal, 1899 K
See also under Pacts
Treaties, collection of, 1791 Q
Treatise of General Sociology (Pareto), 1916 R
Treatise on Differential and Integral Calculus (J. Bertrand), 1864 P
Treatise on Electricity and Magnetism, A (J. Clerk-Maxwell), 1879 P
Treatise on Magnetic Waves (W. and E. Weber), 1825 P
Treatise on Money (J. M. Keynes), 1930 O
Treatise on Radiography (M. Curie), 1910 P
Treatise on Representative Government (J. S. Mill), 1860 O
Treatise on Sound (Lord Rayleigh), 1877 P
Treatise on Tolerance (Voltaire), 1763 R

Treatise on the Blood, Inflammation and Gunshot Wounds (J. Hunter), 1794 P
Treatise on the Coins of the Realm (Lord Liverpool), 1805 O
Trebbia, The, Naples, Italy, battle, 1799 F
Treblinka concentration camp, 'Ivan the Terrible', 1988 D
Tree, Sir Herbert Beerbohm, B. actor-manager, 1853 Z, 1956 Z
Tree-ring chronology, 1971 Q
Treebizond, Turkey, Russians take, 1916 D
Treitschke, Heinrich von, G. historian (1834–96), 1834 Z, 1878 O, 1879 Q, 1896 Z
Tremblay, Michel, Canad. dramatist (b. 1942), 1968 W
Trenchard, Hugh, Viscount Trenchard, B. Air-Marshal, 1873 Z, 1956 Z
Trent affair, 1861 L
Trenton, New Jersey, US, 1776 M
Trésaguet, P. M. J., F. engineer (1716–94), 1764 P
Trevelyan, Sir Charles Edward, B. administrator (1807–86), 1954 O
Trevelyan, George Macaulay, B. historian (1876–1962), 1876 Z, 1926 Q, 1930 Q, 1942 Q, 1962 Z
Trevelyan, Sir George Otto, B. author and Liberal politician (1838–1928), 1874 E
Treviranus, Gottfried Reinhold, G. naturalist (1776–1837), 1802 P
Trevithick, Richard, B. engineer (1771–1833), 1771 Z, 1800 P
Trevor, William, Ir. writer (b. 1928), 1984 U
Trevor-Roper, Hugh Redwald, Lord Dacre of Glanton, B. historian (b. 1914), 1947 O, 1983 V
T. Rex, B. pop group, 1971 W
Trial, The (F. Kafka), 1925 U
Trials of Life, The, television programme, 1991 W
Trials, notable:
- in Britain, of CND Committee of a Hundred members for breaches of Secrets Acts, 1962 B
  - of Warren Hastings, 1788 B, 1795 D
  - of C. Keeler, for perjury, 1963 M
  - of Lonsdale and Blake, for espionage, 1961 O
  - of A. Orton, the Tichborne claimant, 1874 O
  - of T. Paine, 1792 M
  - of W. Vassall, for espionage, 1962 K
  - of O. Wilde, 1895 U
- in Czechoslovakia, for treason, 1952 L
- in Egypt, for espionage, 1957 F
- in France, of de Lesseps, for corruption, 1892 L
  - of Louis XVI, 1792 M
- in Germany, of Auschwitz prison camp officials, 1965 H
  - of Nazis in W. Germany, time limit for, extended, 1965 C. See also Tribunals, Allied
- in Ghana, for treason, 1963 M
- in Russia, for political offences, 1938 C
- in South Africa, for treason, 1956 M, 1959 A, 1961 C, 1964 F
- in Syria, for conspiracy, 1957 A
- in Turkey, of members of Menderes' regime, 1960 K
- in US, of Alger Hiss, 1950 A
  - of New York Times, The, Pentagon Papers trial, 1973 D

Tribunals:
- Allied, for war criminals:
  - German, Nuremberg, verdicts, 1946 J
  - Japanese, 1946 M, 1948 L
- Bertrand Russell International War Crimes Tribunal, 1967 E
- in Britain, Bank Rate, 1957 M
  - Lynski, 1948 L
  - Radcliffe, 1963 V

Trident missile system, 1980 G, 1982 C
Trier, Germany, US troops near, 1944 J
Trieste, Italy: ceded by Austria to France, 1809 K; railway, from Vienna, 1853 P; Italian agitation for acquiring, 1878 N; loss of Austrian battleship in, 1917 M; established as free territory, 1947 B; administration of Zone A, to be handed to Italy, 1953 K; agreement for free territory to be divided into Italian and Yugoslav Zones, 1954 K
Trifonov, Yuri Valentinovich (1925–81), 1978 U, 1990 W
Trincomalee, Ceylon/Sri Lanka, surrendered by Holland to Britain, 1782 A
- Tamil terrorists ambush buses near, 1987 D

Trinidad and Tobago, Islands, W. Indies, become independent within Commonwealth, 1962 H, 1976 H; attempted coup, 1990 G. See also Tobago
Trinidad, Island, W. Indies: Abercromby captures, 1797 B; Britain retains, 1801 K
Triplepatte (T. Bernard), 1905 W
Tripoli, N. Africa: expeditions from, 1823 P; Italian interests in, 1900 M; Italian bombardment of, 1911 J; Italian victory in, 1911 J; Italy annexes, 1911 L; becomes autonomous under Italian suzerainty, 1912 K; pipe-line from Mosul, 1934 G; Eighth Army enters, 1943 A; US embassy attacked, 1979 M
Tripolitza, Morea, Greece, Greeks capture, 1821 K
Tripura, India, tribal violence, 1980 F
Tristan (H.W. Henze), 1974 T
Tristan da Cunha, eruption in, 1961 K
Tristram Shandy (L. Sterne), 1767 U
Tristram, Ernest William, B. art historian (1882–1952), 1945 S
Triumph of Time, The (H. Birtwistle), 1972 S
Triumph of the West, The, television programme, 1985 W
Triumphant Democracy (A. Carnegie), 1886 O
Trocadero, Spain, French take, 1823 H
Troeltsch, Ernst, G. philosopher (1865–1923), 1912 R, 1922 R
Trois Villes, Les (E. Zola), 1894 U
Trolley-buses, 1938 P
Trollope, Anthony, B. novelist (1815–82), 1815 Z, 1855 U, 1857 U, 1864 U, 1867 U, 1882 Z
Trondheim, Norway, British expedition to, 1940 D
Trophées, Les (J. de Heredia), 1893 U
Tropic of Capricorn (H. Miller), 1962 U
Tropical medicine, studies in, 1897 P
Troppau, Austria, conference, 1820 K, L, M
Trotsky, Lev, R. politician (1877–1940), 1877 Z, 1903 H, 1940 Z; becomes premier, 1917 L; dismissed from chairmanship of Revolutionary Council, 1925 A; expelled from Politbureau 1926 K; expelled from Communist Party, 1927 M expelled from Russia, 1929 A, O; autobiography, 1930 O; biography of, 1954 Q, 1963 Q; History, by, 1933 O
Trotskyite Revolutionary League, 1980 C
Trovador, El (A. Garciá-Gutiérrez), 1836 U
Troy, excavations at, 1870 Q
Troyes, France, Parlement of Paris banished to, 1787 H
Trudeau, Pierre Elliott, Prime Minister of Canada (b. 1919), 1919 Z, 1968 D, 1972 K, 1979 E, M, 1980 B
True West (S. Shepard), 1980 W
True Whig. See Political Parties
Truffaut, François, F. film director (1932–84), 1932 Z, 1961 W, 1964 W, 1973 W, 1984 Z
Trujillo, Cesar Gaviria, Colombian politician, 1990 E
Truman, Harry S., Am. statesman, Democrat (1884–1972), 32nd president of US (1945–53), 1884 Z, 1952 P, 1972 Z
- succeeds to presidency, 1945 D
- at Potsdam Conference 1945 G
- orders end of Lend-Lease, 1945 H
- gives bill of credit to Britain, 1946 G
- removes controls, 1946 L
- Doctrine, of economic and military aid, 1947 C
- vetoes Taft-Hartley Act, 1947 F
- Four-point programme, 1949 A
- signs Mutual Defense Assistance Act, 1949 K
- message to Congress on spending for Korean War, 1950 G
- orders army to control railways, 1951 B
- relieves MacArthur of command, 1951 D
- urges compromise in Anglo-Iranian dispute, 1951 G
- indicates retirement, 1952 C
- orders seizure of steel industry, 1952 D
- signs Foreign Aid bill, 1952 F
- orders development of hydrogen bomb, 1959 A

Trustee Savings Bank (TSB), privatization, 1984 M
Trusts in US, Anti-Trust Laws, 1903 O, 1904 Y
Truter, Sir John Andreas, B. Cape of Good Hope judge and African explorer (d. 1826), 1802 P
Truth About the Peace Treaties, The (D. Lloyd George), 1938 O
Truth and Method (H.G. Gadamer), 1975 R
Trypsin, 1930 P
Tsaldaris, Panyoti, Gk. moderate Royalist (1868–1936), 1932 K
Tsao Kun, president of China (1862–1938), 1924 K
Tschokke, Johann Henrich Daniel, G. author (1771–1848), 1830 U
Tshisekedi, Etienne, Prime Minister of Zaire, 1991 K
Tshombe, Moise Kapenda, Congolese politician (1920–69), leader of Conakat Party as premier of Katanga, 1960 G; imprisoned, 1961 F; ends Katanga secession, 1961 M; accepts UN plan on Katanga, 1963 A; resigns from premiership, 1963 F; becomes Congo premier, 1964 G; debarred from attending Cairo Conference, 1964 K; is dismissed, 1965 K
Tsinan, China, Chinese–Japanese clashes at, 1928 E
Tsingtao, China, Japanese take, 1938 A
TSR-2, military aircraft, contract cancelled, 1965 D
Tsushima Strait, Korea, Japanese victory at, 1905 E
Tuan Ch'i-Jui, Chinese premier (1865–1936), 1917 E, G
Tubbs, Ralph, B. architect (b. 1912), 1951 S
Tube Investment, Ltd., high energy plant, 1956 P
Tuberculosis, diagnosis of, 1907 P
Tubman, William Vacanavat Shadvach, Liberian President (1895–1971), 1895 Z, 1959 E, 1971 Z; conference of independent African states, 1959 G
Tucker, Abraham, B. philosopher (1705–74), 1765 R
Tucuman, Congress of, 1816 G
Tugenbund, German patriotic organisation, formed, 1808 O
Tuke, William, B. chemist (1732–1822), 1792 O
Tumbledown, television programme, 1989 W
Tumioja, Sakari, Finn., appointed mediator in Cyprus, 1964 C
Tunc (L. Durrell), 1968 U

Tungsten, 1781 P, 1855 P
Tunis, Tunisia: accepts control by powers, 1869 N; Franco–Italian rivalry in, 1880 E; French occupation, 1881 C, D; Franco–Italian convention on, 1896 J; Allies take, 1943 E
PLO headquarters attacked, 1985 K
assassination of Abu Jihad, 1988 D
Tunisia: French in, 1881 L; French control of 1883 F; demands autonomy, 1952 A; independence is recognised, 1956 C; France's dispute with, 1958 B, D; clashes between French and Tunisians, 1961 G
multi-party elections, 1981 L
illiteracy, 1983 Y
diplomatic relations with Libya restored, 1987 M
Arab Maghreb Union, 1989 B
Tunnels:
Channel. See Channel Tunnel
Mont Cenis, 1871 P
New Croutown aqueduct, New York, 1871 P
railway, the first, 1826 P
St. Gotthard, 1882 P
Severn, 1886 P
Simplon, 1906 P
Thames railway, 1890 P
Tupolev, Andrei Nikolaevich, R. aeronautical engineer (1888–1972), 1888 Z, 1955 P, 1972 Z
Turbine, gas, 1951 P; steam, 1884 P
Turf, Ruff's Guide to The, 1842 X
Turgeniev, Ivan, R. novelist (1818–83), 1818 Z, 1852 U, 1855 U, 1860 U, 1862 U, 1867 U, 1872 U, 1883 Z
Turgot, Anne Robert Jacques, F. economist and statesman (1727–81), 1765 O, 1774 H, J, 1775 J, 1776 A, E, 1781 Z, 1787 O
Turin, Italy: Suvorov occupies, 1799 D; Piazzo Vittorio Veneto in, 1818 S; supplanted as capital of Italy by Florence, 1864 J; Exhibition Hall, 1948 S; soccer hooliganism, 1980 X
Turkestan, Russia: Russian control over, 1867 G
Turkey: Austria and Russia aim to maintain Ottoman Empire, 1804 L; integrity of Ottoman Empire guaranteed, 1833 K, 1856 C; financial collapse, 1874 N; reforms advocated, 1876 A, E, 1877 C; partition of Empire, proposed, 1895 H; Allies agree on, 1916 C; proclaimed a republic, 1922 L
military coup, 1980 J
leading politicians banned, 1983 D
political parties permitted, 1983 D
military rule ended, 1983 M
cotton production, 1984 Y
presidential elections, 1989 K
True Path Party election victory, 1991 K
population, 1991 Y
Turkmen, percentage in Soviet population, 1989 Y
Turks and Caicos islands
advisory council appointed to administer, 1986 G
Turn of the Screw, The (H. James), 1898 U
Turn of the Tide, The (A. Bryant), 1957 Q
Turner Prize for Painting, 1984 S
Turner, Charles Tennyson, B. poet (1808–79), 1827 U
Turner, Joseph Mallord William, B. artist (1775–1851), 1775 Z, 1797 S, 1801 S, 1805 S, 1807 S, 1813 S, 1815 S, 1819 S, 1827 S, 1839 S, 1843 S, 1851 Z
Turner, Sharon, B. historian (1768–1847), 1799 Q
Turning Point, The (G. Seferis), 1931 U
Turret-lathe, 1855 P
Tuscany, Italy: Grand Duchy, 1765 H; French occupy, 1799 C; is ceded to Parma, 1810 B; Napoleon annexes, 1808 E; Grand Duke flees, 1849 B; plebiscite supports union with Sardinia, 1860 K
Tushingham Rita (b. 1942), B. actress, 1965 W
Tutu, Desmond Mpilo, S. Afr. churchman (b. 1931), 1931 Z, 1986 J
passport withdrawn, 1980 R
detained following protest, 1988 B
Tuvalu (formerly Ellice Islands), independence, 1978 J
TV AM breakfast time station, 1983 W
Twain, Mark. See Clemens, Samuel Langhorne
Tweed, William Mancy, Am. political boss (1823–78), 1871 G
Tweedsmuir, lord. See Buchan, John
Twelve, The (A. Blok), 1918 U
Twenty-Five Years (Lord Grey of Falloden), 1925 Q
Twenty Love Poems and a Song of Despair (P. Neruda), 1924 U
Twenty Thousand Leagues Under the Sea (J. Verne), 1869 U
Twenty Years' Crisis, The (E. H. Carr), 1939 U
Twilight of the Gods (R. Garnett), 1925 U
Twin Peaks, television series, 1989 W
Twiss, Peter, B. test pilot (b. 1921), 1956 P
Two Cultures and the Sciences, The (C. P. Snow), 1959 U
Two Minutes' Silence, 1919 L
Two Tactics (Lenin), 1905 O
Twyborn Affair, The (P. White), 1980 U
Tydings–McDuffie Act, for Philippines, 1934 C
Tyler, John, Am. Whig (1773–1841), president of US (1841), 1841 D
Tylor, Sir Edward Burnett, B. anthropologist (1832–1917), 1881 P
Typewriter, the:
forerunner of, 1843 P
Scholes's, 1873 P
Typhoid epidemics, 1963 C, 1964 E
Typhoons. See Tornadoes
Typography:
Gill's, 1927 S
Gothic, abandoned in Germany, 1941
Tyre, Lebanon:
Israeli air attacks on, 1982 F
bomb attacks on Israeli military headquartes in, 1982 L, 1983 L
Tyres:
balloon for tractors, 1932 P
pneumatic, 1888 P
Tyrol, Austrian, ceded to France, 1805 M; Germanisation of, 1926 B
Tyson, Mike, Am. boxer (b. 1966), 1986 X, 1990 X
Tytus, John, B. metallurgist, 1923 P
Tzannetakis, Tzannis, Greek leader, 1989 F
Tzara, Tristan, artist (1896–1963), 1916 S, 1931 U
Tzu-hsi, dowager empress of China (1835–1908), 1898 J

U

Ucciali, Ethiopia, treaty, 1889 E
Uddevalla, Sweden, convention between Denmark and Sweden, 1788 L
Ufa, Russia, Red Army takes, 1919 F
Uganda: Lugard occupies, 1890 M; East Africa Company hands over to Britain, 1893 C; becomes a British Protectorate, 1894 D; mutiny in, 1897 J; Britain regulates government, 1900 C; frontier with East Africa, 1907 M; attains full internal self-government, 1962 C; becomes independent within the Commonwealth, 1962 K
Obote deposed by Amin, 1971 A
Ugandan Asians expelled, 1972 H, J, L
Ugandan exiles attempt to invade from Tanzania, 1972 J
Callaghan secures release of B. lecturer, Denis Hills, 1975 F
Amin declared president for life, 1976 F
Britain breaks off relations, 1976 G
Archbishop Luwum assassinated, 1977 B
border clashes with Tanzania, 1978 K
drops territorial claim on Tanzania, 1978 L
Tanzanian troops move into border area, 1978 L
Tanzanian troops invade, 1979 A
Amin flees, 1979 D
Kampala falls to Tanzanian and rebel forces, 1979 D
Lule inaugurated as President, 1979 D
Lule replaced as President, 1979 F
Obote elected President, 1980 M
coup d'état, 1985 G
National Resistance Army, 1985 M, 1986 A
invasion of Rwanda, 1990 K
Uitenhage, S. Afr., crowds fired on by police, 1985 C
Ujiji, Africa, Stanley meets Livingstone at, 1871 L, P
Ukhrul, Burma, British take, 1944 G
Ukraine, Russia: Russia acquires Western Ukraine, 1793 E; republic proclaimed, 1917 L; Poland abandons claim to, 1921 C; Germans enter, 1941 G
percentage of Ukrainians in USSR population, 1989 Y
Communist hardliner elected President, 1990 G
percentage of Ukrainians in USSR population, 1990 Y
Commonwealth of Independent States (CIS), 1991 M
price controls lifted, 1992 A
Ulbricht, Walter, E. Germ. politician (1893–1973), 1893 Z, 1971 E 1973 Z
Ullsten, Ola, Swe. Liberal leader (b. 1931), 1978 K
Ulm, Bad-Württemberg, Germany, battle, 1805 K
Ulmanis, Karlis, Latvian dictator (1877–1942), 1934 E
Ulster Defence Association (UDA), 1972 E
Ulster Unionists. See under Political Parties
Ulster, N. Ireland: rebellion in, 1797 C; exclusion from Government of Ireland Act, insisted upon, 1916 F; votes to accept Home Rule Bill, 1920 C.
See also Ireland, Northern
Ultima Thule (Longfellow), 1880 U
Ultra Royalists. *See under* Political Parties
Ultra-high-frequency waves, 1955 P
Ultra-microscope, 1903 P
Ultra-violet lamp, 1904 P
Ultra-violet rays, for sterilising water, 1912 P
Ulverton (A. Thorpe), 1992 U
Ulysses (J. Joyce), 1922 U, 1984 U
Umberto II, King of Italy (1946), 1946 E
leaves Italy, 1946 F
Umuahia, Biafra, Nigerian forces capture, 1969 D
Unamuno y Jugo, Miguel de, Sp. poet (1864–1936), 1914 U
Unbearable Lightness of Being, The (M. Kundera), 1984 U
Uncle Tom's Cabin (H. Beecher-Stowe), 1852 U
Uncle Vanya (Chekhov), 1900 W
Unconscious, The (Jung), 1917 R
Under Milk Wood (D. Thomas), 1954 W
Under Two Flags (Onida), 1867 U
Under the Greenwood Tree (T. Hardy), 1872 U
Under the Red Robe (S. Weyman), 1894 U

Underdown, David Edward, historian (b. 1925), 1986 Q
Underhill, Evelyn, B. religious author (1875–1941), 1875 Z, 1910 R
Underhill, Henry Reginald, Lord Underhill, B. Labour politician (b. 1914), 1980 C
Underneath the Arches (Gilbert and George), 1971 S
Understanding the Media (M. McLuhan), 1964 O
Undine (F. Fowqué), 1811 U
Undset, Fru Sigrid, Da. Author (1882–1949), 1920 U, 1930 U
Unemployment (W. A. Appleton), 1923 O (W. Beveridge), 1909 O
Unemployment and Politics: A Study in English Social Policy, 1886–1914 (J. Harris), 1972 Q
Unemployment, world statistics, 1982 Y
Unemployment:
world, 1929 O; statistics, 1982 Y
in Britain, 1817 F, 1919 Y, 1921 Y, 1932 Y, 1971 D, 1975 K, 1980 H, 1981 D, 1987 F
Hunger marches, 1922 K, L
legislation to ameliorate, 1925 G, 1934 E
Labour Party censure motion, 1933 D
means test, 1935 A, 1936 G
demonstrations, 1963 C
exceeds 1 million, 1972 A
government statistics on, 1982 A
in France, national workshops for easing, 1848 B, F
in Germany, 1932 Y
commissioner for, 1932 O
four-year plan for, 1933 O
in Palestine, of Arabs, 1930 K
in USA, 1932 Y, 1958 O
Unfinished Novels:
Mystery of Edwin Drood (C. Dickens), 1870 U
Weir of Hermiston, The (R. L. Stevenson), 1896 O
Unicorn (R. Horn), 1975 S
Unicorn, The (I. Murdoch), 1963 U
Unicorn, The (M. Walser), 1966 U
Union Dead (R. Lowell), 1965 U
Union Générale des postes, 1874 O
Union Indo-Chinoise, S.E. Asia, 1887 N
Union de la Gauche Socialiste. *See under* Political Parties
Union of Democratic Mineworkers (UDM), 1985 K
Union of Soviet Socialist Republic (USSR), formally established, 1923 A. *See under* Russia
Union of Unions, Russian, 1909 E
Unionists. *See under* Political Parties
UNITA
declaration signed ending Angola civil war, 1989 F
senior figures in killed, 1992 L
Unitarians. *See under* Religious Denominations
Unitary Field Theory (Einstein), 1929 P
'Unité d'Habitation', near Marseilles, France, 1952 B
United Arab Emirates, formation of, 1971 M
United Arab Republic (UAR):
formed by union of Egypt and Sudan, 1958 B
diplomatic relations with Jordan, 1959 H
with Britain, 1959 M
Syria secedes from, 1961 J
Syria and Iraq agree to federate with, 1963 D
war with Israel, 1967 E, F, K
alliance with Sudan and Libya, 1969 M
frogmen sink Israeli supply ship, 1970 B
minesweepers sunk by Israel, 1970 B
accepts 'Rogers Plan', 1970 F
federates with Libya, Sudan and Syria, 1970 L
United Irishmen, Society of, 1790 K
United Kingdom
British Standard Time adopted, 1968 B
Ministerial mergers, 1968 K, L
population, 1971 Y, 1981 Y
urbanization, 1985 Y
United Kingdom and the European Communities, The, White Paper, 1971 G
United Nations, The (UN):
preliminaries:
Bretton Woods monetary and financial conference, 1944 G
San Fransisco Conference of, 1945 B, D
foundation of, 1945 K
charter is ratified, 1945 K
permanent headquarters for, 1946 M
U Thant's peace plan for Vietnam, 1967 C
diplomatic mission to Aden, 1967 D
Israel ordered to desist from unifying Jerusalem, 1967 G
Trusteeship Committee condemns British failure to overthrow Rhodesian Smith regime, 1967 K
Nauru trust territory, independence, 1968 A
colonial rule in Gibraltar declared incompatible with UN Charter, 1968 M
talks on Middle East, New York, 1969 D
admission of Communist China rejected, 1969 L, 1970 L
Middle East peace talks mediation, 1970 H, 1971 A
Waldheim appointed as Secretary General, 1971 M
Bangladeshi admission vetoed by China, 1972 H
Britain, France and US veto motion to expel South Africa, 1974 K
South African arms embargo, 1977 L
Commission visits Iran, 1980 B
Law of Sea Conference, 1982 O
Chad–Libya border dispute, 1983 C
US vetos motion deploring US invasion of Grenada, 1983 K
Educational, Scientific and Cultural Organization (UNESCO), US withdrawal, 1983
Iran–Iraq War, 1984 F, 1987 G, J
Conference on Population, Mexico, 1984 O
Special Committee against Apartheid, 1986 F
members of USSR mission to UN ordered out of US, 1986 J
Convention on the Prevention and Punishment of the Crime of Genocide, US ratification, 1986 O
Israeli action against Palestinians criticised, 1987 M
Peacekeeping Force, Nobel Peace Prize, 1988 J
conditions for Namibian independence agreed, 1988 M
inspection of Iraqi nuclear facilities, 1991 H
Yugoslavian civil war, 1991 J, L, 1992 E, H
Somalian civil war, 1992 A
El Salvadorean civil war, 1992 B
sanctions imposed on Libya, 1992 C
Yugoslavia, peace plan, 1992 B
UN military observers in Mogadishu, 1992 G
Acheson Plan, to increase powers of, 1950 K, 1951 L
Apartheid Committee calls for sanctions against S. Africa, 1963 J
Atomic Energy Commission, 1946 M
suspends meetings, 1949 G
Balzan International Foundation Peace Prize awarded to, 1964 B
Educational, Scientific and Cultural Organisation (UNESCO) symposium on human rights, 1949 O
Food and Agricultural Organization, launches Freedom from Hunger Campaign, 1960 G
Forces in, Congo, 1960 G, H, 1961 J, 1962 M, 1963 A, 1964 F
in Cyprus, 1964 C, H, M
in Korea. See under Wars, Korean
in Middle East, ocupies Gaza Strip, 1957 C
on Israeli–Egyptian border, 1967 E
in Cyprus, 1972 B
Interim Force in Lebanon (UNIFIL), 1978 C
in Sinai, 1982 A
in Southern Lebanon, 1982 B
suicide attack on peace-keeping force in Beirut, 1983 K
in Cambodia, 1992 B
General Assembly, first session, in London, 1946 A
meets in New York, 1946 K
rules on Siam's return of territory to Indo-China, 1946 K
rejects S. Africa's proposal for incorporating S.W. Africa, 1946 M
bans Spain from activities, 1946 M
calls on Greece and Balkan countries to settle disputes, 1947 K
recognises Korea's claim to independence, 1947 L
adopts convention on human rights, 1948 M
discusses alleged racial discrimination in S. Africa, 1949 E
votes for ultimate independence of Italy's former colonies, 1949 L
requires information on arms and forces, 1949 M
calls for recognition of China, 1949 M
revokes resolution on Spain, 1950 L
Acheson presents disarmament proposals to, 1951 L
adopts Indian armistice proposals for Korea, 1952 M
control of atomic energy proposed to, 1953 M
Greece proposes to lay Cyprus problems before, 1955 G, 1956 C
France leaves meeting on Algeria, 1955 K
withdraws inspection teams from Korea, 1956 E
censures Russia over Hungary, 1956 L
demands withdrawal of Soviet troops from Hungary, 1956 L
adopts Canadian resolution to send force to Middle East, 1956 L
calls on S. Africa to reconsider Apartheid, 1957 A
calls for peaceful solution of Cyprus problem, 1957 B
Elizabeth II addresses, 1957 K
adopts report on Hungary, 1957 J
meeting on Middle East, 1958 H
Khruschchev addresses, 1959 J, 1960 J
considers Apartheid in S. Africa, 1959 L
condemns all racial discrimination, 1959 L
resolves on independence for Togoland, 1959 M
Macmillan addresses, 1960 J
condemns S. African policies in S.W. Africa, 1961 D
calls for elections in Ruanda and Urundi, 1961 D
calls on Portugal to cease repression in Angola, 1961 F
resolution to treat Africa as a denuclearised zone, 1961 L
calls for independence of colonial peoples, 1961 L

requests Britain to suspend enforcement of new constitution in Rhodesia, 1962 K
demands end to nuclear tests, 1962 L
condemns repression in S. Africa, 1963 K
Pope John Paul VI addresses, 1965 R
Rhodesia, sanctions against, 1966 D, 1973 E
South African mandate over South-West Africa ended, 1966 K
Israel censured, 1966 L
South African withdrawal from South-West Africa demanded, 1967 M
addressed by PLO leader, Yassir Arafat, 1974 L
International Court of Justice, first decision by, 1940 D
ruling on S. African administration, 1971 F
ruling over US blockade of Nicaraguan ports, 1984 E
Membership, changes in, since foundation,
Albania, 1955 M
Argentina, 1955 M
Bulgaria, 1955 M
Cambodia, 1955 M
Ceylon, 1955 M
China's admission rejected, 1958 J, 1961 M, 1962 K
Peking delegates attend as observers, 1950 L
admitted, 1971 K
East and West Germany, 1973 J
Eire, 1955 M
Finland, 1955 M
Ghana, 1957 C
Hungary, 1955 M
Indonesia, 1950 J
withdraws, 1965 A
Israel, 1949 E
Italy, 1955 M
Japan, 1956 M
Jordan, 1955 M
Kuwait's admission vetoed, 1961 F
Laos, 1955 M
Libya, 1955 M
Mauritania, 1916 K
Mongolia, 1961 K
Nepal, 1955 M
Pakistan, 1947 J
Portugal, 1955 M
Roumania, 1955 M
S. Africa withdraws, 1955 L
resumes membership, 1958 G
Spain, excluded, 1945 F
elected, 1955 M
Taiwan expelled, 1971 K
US participation approved by Senate, 1945 M
Yemen, The, 1947 J
Palestine, conciliatary commission for, 1951 J
mixed armistice commission for, Israel withdraws from, 1954 C
truce accepted, 1956 A
Relief and Rehabilitation Administration (UNRRA), 1943 O
Secretary General, T. Lie appointed, 1946 B
second term, 1950 F
D. Hammarskjöld appointed, 1953 C
killed, 1961 J
U Thant, as acting, 1961 J
elected, 1962 L
Security Council, Egypt refers revision of 1936 Treaty with Britain to, 1947 A
Palestine question referred to, 1947 D
appoints Trusteeship for Pacific Isles, 1947 D
calls for Indonesian cease fire, 1947 H
Kashmir problem referred to, 1947 M
orders truce in Palestine, 1948 G
Russia vetoes plan for ending Berlin blockade, 1948 K
calls for end of war in Burma, 1949 A
discusses Korea, 1950 H
Tibet appeals to, 1950 L
India complains to, over Pakistan, 1951 G
to supervise Sudan plebiscite, 1951 L
Greece elected to, 1951 M
Tunisia appeals to, 1952 A
proposals for supervised German elections rejected by Russia, 1952 D
Thailand complains her security is threatened, 1954 E
China appeals to, over Formosa, 1954 K
Vietnam appeals to, over actions of Viet Minh, 1955 D
Britain and France refer Suez dispute to, 1956 J, K
Hungary appeals to, 1956 L
considers Cyprus problems, 1957 M
Russia asks for action to end flights of military aircraft, 1958 D
Laos recognises, as sole arbiter, 1959 B
Dalai Lama appeals to, 1959 C, 1961 C
Lumumba appeals for aid, 1960 G
demands enquiry into Lumumba's death, 1961 B
supervises Cameroons plebscite, 1961 B
orders ceasefire in Tunisia, 1961 G
votes for embargo on arms to S. Africa, 1963 M
mandatory sanctions against Rhodesia, 1966 J, M
Cyprus asks for prevention of Turkish invasion, 1967 L
bombing of Iraqi nuclear reactor under construction condemned, 1981 F
calls for halt to fighting in Lebanon, 1982 F
Resolution 502 demands Argentinian withdrawal from Falkland Islands, 1982 D
Resolution 242 accepted by PLO, 1982 G
Resolution 541 on Cyprus, 1983 L
votes to send peacekeeping force to Cambodia, 1992 B
Trusteeship, S. Africa refuses to place S. W. Africa under, 1947 A, 1950 M
for Pacific Isles, 1947 D
for Jerusalem, proposed, 1947 L
for Far East, China rejects proposal, 1951 A
for Ruanda Republic, 1961 A
Committee resolves to consider whether S. Rhodesia has obtained self-government, 1962 B
takes over administration of West New Guinea, 1962 K
asks Britain not to transfer Rhodesian Federation forces to S. Rhodesia, 1963
United Parties. *See under* Political Parties
United States of America (US):
Congress resolves on suppression of British authority, 1776 C
Congress passes Declaration of Independence, 1776 G
Confederation Articles of Perpetual Union, Congress adopts, 1777 L
Britain recognises independence, 1783 J
frontier treaty with Russia, over Alaska, 1824 D
frontier with Canada, defined, 1818 K, 1842 H
geology of, 1809 P
Western States, opening up of, 1902 O
resolution not to commit troops to foreign countries without Congressional approval, 1969 F
United States Foreign Policy (W. Lippmann), 1943 O
Universe Around US, The (J. Jeans), 1929 P
Universities:
in Belgium, Ghent, 1816 O
Louvain, Flemish campaign against French-speakers, 1968 B
in Britain, Robbins Report on, 1963 O
proposals for further foundations rejected by government, 1965 B
overseas students, 1979 O
government grant reduction, 1981 O
Cambridge, Churchill College, 1960 C
Clare Hall, 1966 O
Fitzwilliam College, 1966 O
Girton College, 1869 O
Professorship of American history, 1943 O
Professorship of Experimental Physics, 1871 P
religious tests abolished, 1871 F, O
residence for women students (later Newnham College), 1871 O
University College, 1965 O
University extension lectures, 1870 O
East Anglia
Sainsbury Centre, 1978 S
Edinburgh, chair of technology, 1855 O
Kent, 1965 O
Leeds (formerly Yorkshire College), 1874 P
London, founded, 1836 O
science degrees at, 1860 O
established as a teaching university, 1898 O
moves to Bloomsbury, 1936 O
Bedford College, 1849 O
Imperial College of Science and Technology, 1850 O
Imperial Institute, 1893 O
King's College, 1830 O, 1853 R
London School of Economics and Political Science, 1895 O
student protest, 1967 C, 1969 A
School of Mines, 1850 O
School of Oriental and African Studies, 1916 O
University College, 1826 O
Warburg Institute, 1933 S
Manchester (Owen's College), 1851 O, 1880 O
North Staffordshire, 1949 O
Oxford, appoints Franks Commission, 1964 O
artist in residence, 1979 S
Balliol College, 1870 O, 1980 R
Bampton Lectures, 1780 R
Green College founded, 1979 O
Keble College, 1870 O
Macmillan elected chancellor, 1960 C
music faculty, 1944 T
natural science honours shcool, 1850 O
Pitt Rivers Museum, 1874 Q
Professorship of modern history under Stubbs, 1866 Q
Queen's College, Florey Building, 1972 S
religious tests ended, 1871 F, O
Rewley House, 1990 O
Roosevelt honoured, at Harvard, 1941 O
St. Catherine's College, 1964 S
St. Hilda's, 1980 R
Thatcher refused honorary doctorate, 1985 A
Wolfson College, 1966 O
Reading, 1926 O
Sussex, 1961 O, 1964 S
Wales, 1893 O
Warwick, 1965 O
in Canada
Toronto, Scarborough College, 1966 S
in Czechoslovakia, Prague, 1882 O

in El Salvador, University of Central America, San Salvador, Jesuits tortured and murdered, 1989 R
in Europe, Cambridge Conference of European Vice-Chancellors, 1955 O
in France, clerical control, 1822 F
in Germany, placed under state supervision, 1819 J
women admitted, 1909 O
Berlin, 1810 O, 1818 R
Bonn, 1818 O
Göttingen, dismissals from, 1837 M
Munich, 1826 O
Strasburg, 1872 O
in Iran, Teheran, 1935 O
in Ireland, Gladstone's bill for, defeated, 1873 C
Dublin University College, 1854 O
in Japan
Yamaguchi, scientific research, 1980 P
in Mexico, Mexico University City, 1950 S, 1952 S
in Norway, Christiania, 1811 O
in Rhodesia, race riots, 1973 H
in Rumania, Bucharest, 1864 O
in Russia, Odessa, 1865 O
in Spain, Madrid, closed by government, 1929 C
in Switzerland, Zurich, 1832 O
in US, women awarded degrees, 1841 O
State colleges for science and technology, 1862 O
Alabama, desegregation crisis in, 1956 O
Brown, Rhode Island, 1764 O
California Medical School, discrimination ruling by Supreme Court, 1978 O
Harvard, Carpenter Center for Visual Arts at, 1963 S
John Hopkins, 1876 O
Kent State University, demonstrators shot, 1970 E
Massachusetts Institute of Technology, 1865 O
Pennsylvania, archaeological expedition from, 1888 Q
Pittsburgh, scientific research at, 1955 P
Utah, 1954 P
Virginia, 1817 S
Yale, Beinecke Library at, 1963 S
Washington Catholic University, 1889 Q
in Yugoslavia, Belgrade, 1864 O
University Extension Lectures, 1850 O, 1870 O
Unkiar Skelessi, treaty, between Turkey and Russia, 1833 G
overthrown by Straits Convention, 1841 G
'Unknown Political Prisoner, The', sculpture competition, 1953 S
Uno, Sosuke, Prime Minister of Japan (b. 1922), 1989 D, H
Unsettled Questions of Political Economy (J. S. Mill), 1844 O
Unsichtbare Loge, Die (Jean Paul), 1793 U
Untitled (Felt sculpture, soft) (R. Morris), 1967 S
Untitled Vitrine (J. Beuys), 1983 S
Unto This Last (J. Ruskin), 1862 O
Untouchability, outlawed in India, 1947 E
Untouchables, in Bombay, disabilities removed, 1946 O
Updike, John Hoyer, Am. author (b. 1932), 1932 Z, 1960 U, 1963 U, 1982 U, 1991 U
Upper Heyford, Oxfordshire, England, anti-nuclear protest, 1983 F
Upper Volta:
military coup, 1982 L
renamed Burkina Faso, 1984 H
Uppsala, Sweden, Fourth Assembly of World Council of Churches, 1968 R
Upstairs Downstairs, television series, 1970 W
Ur, discoveries at, 1927 Q
Ural Mountains, Russia, 1820 P
Ural Regional Council, orders execution of Nicholas II, 1918 G
Uranium, separation of, 1900 P; pile, 1944 P
Uranus, discovery of, 1781 P; satellites of discovered, 1986 P
Urbanization, statistics, 1985 Y
Urea, synthesis of, 1828 P
Urey, Harold Clayton, Am. chemist (1893–1981), 1893 Z, 1932 P, 1941 P, 1981 Z
Uriburu, José, Argent. president (1868–1932), 1930 J
Urrutia, Manuel, Cuban premier (1901–81), 1959 A
Uruguay: becomes independent of Brazil, 1825 H, 1828 H; Brazil's war with Argentina over, 1825 M
Tupamaros guerrillas kidnap ambassador, 1971 A
Pope John Paul II visits, 1988 E
Urundi, S.E. Cen. Africa, UN calls for elections, 1961 D
Use of Poetry and the Use of Criticism (T. S. Eliot), 1933 U
Uses of Literacy, The (R. Hoggart), 1957 U
Ussuri River, Soviet–Chinese border conflict, 1969 C
Ustinov, Peter Alexander, B. actor (b. 1921), 1951 W
Usury, tract on, 1787 O
Utah, State, US: US obtains, 1848 E; becomes a US state, 1896 A, 1906 N
Uthwatt Report, 1942 O
Utilitarianism (J. S. Mill), 1862 O
Utilitarianism, 1802 O, 1862 O
Utilitarians, The (L. Stephen), 1900 O
Utility clothing, in Britain, 1941 O
Utrenia (Penderecki), 1970 T
Utrillo, Maurice, F. artist (1883–1955), 1908 S, 1923 S
U2 aircraft, US, incident, 1960 E
U2, Ir. pop group. 1987 W
Utzon, Jorn, Dan. architect (b. 1918), 1956 S, 1973 S
Uyl, Joop Marten den, Dutch leader (b. 1919), 1973 E
Uzbekistan
percentage of Uzbekis in USSR population, 1989 Y
independence declared, 1990 F

V

Vaagno, near Trondheim, Norway, British commando raids on, 1941 M
Vaccination against smallpox, 1796 P
Vaccines:
for anthrax, 1881 P
for measles, 1963 P
for poliomyelitis (Salk's), 1955 P
Vacuum-cleaners, statistics, 1965 Y
Vaihinger, Hans, G. philosopher (1852–1933), 1911 R
Vailland, Auguste, F. anarchist, 1893 M
Vailland, Roger François, F. author (b. 1907), 1957 U
Valençay, France, treaty, 1813 M
Valencia, Spain, government moves to, 1936 L
Valency:
theory, 1916 P
wave mechanics of, 1927 P
Valentino, Rudolph, Am. film actor (1895–1926), 1926 W
Valera, Eamon de, Ir. statesman (1882–1975), 1919 D 1922 A, C, 1933 A, 1966 F, 1973 E, 1975 Z; proclamation of terms for amnesty to rebels, 1923 D; is arrested 1923 H; resigns from Sinn Fein, 1926 C; founds Fianna Fail, 1926 C; agrees to take seat in Dail, 1927 H; elected premier of Irish Free State, 1932 C; founds Republican Army, 1933 G; is again premier, 1937 G; retains power, 1951 F; vote of confidence in, 1953 G; resigns premiership, 1959 F; becomes president of Eire, 1959 F
Valera, Juan, Sp. novelist (1824–1905), 1848 U, 1879 U
Valéry, Paul, F. author (1871–1945), 1871 Z, 1906 U, 1917 U, 1920 U, 1921 U, 1938 U, 1945 Z
Vallauris, France, pottery, 1946 S
Valley (R. Whiteread), 1990 S
Valley Curtain, Colorado (Christo), 1972 S
Valmy, Marne, France, canonade, 1792 J
Valois, Dame Ninette de, B. ballerina (b. 1898), 1950 T
Valparaiso, Chile: Treaty, 1884 D; railway to, 1911 D
Valsarno, Italy, Austrian victory at, 1813 K
Valteline, Switzerland, France annexes, 1797 K
Value of world production, 1888 Y, 1929 Y
Valves, wireless, all-metal, 1933 P
Vampilov, Alexander Valentinovich, R. playwright (1937–72), 1976 W
Van der Noot, Henry, Du. patriot, 1787 A, 1789 K, 1790 C
Vance, Cyrus Roberts, Am. Secretary of State (b. 1917), 1977 J, 1980 D
Vancouver Island, British Columbia, Canada, Spain abandons claim to, 1790 K
Vancouver, George, B. naval officer and explorer (1758–98), 1790 P
Vane, Sutton, B. dramatist (1888–1963), 1923 W
Vanity Fair (W. M. Thackeray), 1847 U
Vanuatu (formerly New Hebrides), independence, 1980 G
Vanunu, Mordechai, Israeli nuclear technician, 1986 K
Varennes, Meuse, France, Louis XVI stopped at, 1791 E
Varieties of Goodness (G. H. von Wright), 1963 R
Vargas Llosa, Mario, Peruvian author and politician (b. 1936), 1981 U, 1990 F
Vargas, Getúlio, Braz. leader (1883–1954), becomes president, 1930 K; given dictatorial powers, 1933 L; resigns, 1945 K
Variations of Animals and Plants under Domesticisation (C. Darwin), 1868 P
Variations, orchestral. *See under* Symphonic Suites
Varieties of Religious Experience (W. James), 1902 R
Varna, Turkey, Russians occupy, 1828 K
Vassall, William, B. spy, 1962 K, L, 1963 D, V
Vatican Council:
Pius IX calls, 1867 R; meets, 1869 R, 1870 R
John XXIII calls, 1959 R; preparations for, 1961 R; opens, 1962 R; approves principle of fixed Easter, 1963 K; approves use of vernacular liturgies, 1963 R; ends, 1964 J
Vatican Decrees, The (W. E. Gladstone), 1874 R
Vatican Decrees, of Pius IX, refusal to accept leads to excommunication, 1871 R
Vatican, The: Pope allowed possession, of, 1870 E; Prussian legation at, 1882 D; relations with Italy, 1889 G; French ambassador to, recalled, 1904 E; independence of Vatican City, 1929 B, G
Meir visits, 1973 R
State visit by Queen Elizabeth II, 1980 K
Britain resumes full diplomatic relations, 1982 A

Galileo formally rehabilitated, 1992 K
Vaughan Williams, Ralph, The Works of (M. Kennedy), 1964 T
Vaughan Williams, Ralph, B. musician (1872–1958), 1872 Z, 1952 T, 1958 Z
as musical editor of *English Hymnal,* 1906 R
Choral works, 1907 T, 1914 T
Fantasia, 1909 T
opera. 1951 T
Symphonies, 1910 T, 1914 T, 1922 T, 1943 T, 1953 T, 1958 T
Vaughan, Herbert Alfred, B. cardinal (1832–1903) 1891 R, 1895 R
Vauxcelles, Louis, F. art critic, 1905 S
Vedic Concordance (M. Bloomfield), 1907 Q
Vedrenne, John E. (1867–1930), B. theatre manager, 1904 W
Veidt, Conrad, G. film actor (1893–1943), 1920 W
Velázquez, Don Diego de Silva y, Sp. painter (1599–1660)
Juan de Pareja achieves record auction price for art work, 1979 S
Velocipede, or fore-runner of bicycle, invented, 1779 P
See also Bicycle.
Velvet Underground, Am. rock group, 1966 W
Vendée, La, Poitou, France, Royalist revolt in, 1793 C, K, M
Venereal disease; cure for, 1909 P; in Britain, 1916 O, 1943 O
Venetia, Italy: restored to Austria, 1815 F; Prussia promises to restore to Italy, 1866 D; Austrian cession of, announced, 1866 G, plebiscites for union with Italy, 1866 K
Venezia Giulia, Yugoslavia, 1947 B
Venezuela: refuses allegiance to Joseph Bonaparte, 1810 D; independence proclaimed, 1811 G; Republic, falls, 1812 G; independence, proclamations of, 1813 G, 1818 L; forms, with New Granada, Colombia, 1819 M; independence guaranteed, 1821 F; leaves Colombia Union, 1830 J, 1831 L; boundary with British Guiana, 1899 K; blockade by powers, 1902 M; blockade lifted, 1903 B; US severs diplomatic relations with, 1908 F; coffee production in, 1909 Y
Contadora Group, 1983 G
oil industry nationalized, 1989 B
Pérez sworn in as President, 1989 B
Venice, Italy: Austria obtains, 1797 K; Republic proclaimed, 1848 C; submits to Austria, 1894 P, H; to remain an Austrian possession, 1859 G; Hitler meets Mussolini at, 1934 F; falls to Allies, 1945 D
Biennale cancelled, 1974 S
Teatro del Mondo, 1979 S
Palazzo Grassi, 1986 S
Venizelos, Eleutherios, Greek statesman (1864–1942), 1935 C; as premier, 1910 K, 1915 C, 1916 K, 1924 A, 1928 E; resigns as premier, 1933 A; 'becomes' premier, 1933 A
Venn, Henry, B. Evangelical divine (1725–97), 1763 R
Ventris, Michael, B. Minoan scholar (1922–56), 1952 Q
Vents (St. J. Perse), 1947 U
Venturi, Robert, Am. architect (b. 1925), 1991 S
Venus, planet:
transit of, observations of, 1768 P, 1882 P
space research gives data on, 1962 P, 1963 P
Venera probes, 1966 P, 1967 P, 1975 P, 1978 P, 1982 P, 1983 P
soft landings on, 1967 P, 1972 P
photographed, 1974 P
orbited by probes, 1978 P
Magellan radar mapper, 1989 P, 1990 P
Venus de Milo, discovery of, 1820 S
Vera Cruz, Mexico: French troops occupy, 1838 L; Diaz occupies, 1912 K; US troops land at, 1914 D; withdraw from, 1914 J
Verdi, Giuseppe, It. musician (1813–1901), 1813 Z, 1844 T, 1847 T, 1851 T, 1853 T, 1862 T, 1867 T, 1871 T, 1874 T, 1887 T, 1893 T, 1901 Z
Verdun, Meuse, France: Austrian attack, 1792 J; battles, 1916 B, D, 1917 H; receives Congressional medal 1922 F
Vereeniging, S. Africa, Peace of, 1902 E
Verela, Sweden, Treaty of, 1790 H
Vergennes, Charles Gravier, Comte de, F. statesman (1717–87), 1774 E, 1782 E, 1787 B
Vergina, Greece, archaeological excavation, 1978 Q
Verhaeren, Emile, Belg. author (1855–1916), 1883 U, 1902 U
Verlaine, Paul, F. author (1844–96), 1844 Z, 1866 U, 1869 U, 1874 U, 1881 U, 1884 U, 1888 U, 1896 Z
Vermes, Geza, B. scholar (b. 1924), 1973 R
Vermont, State, US: becomes a US state, 1791 C; Fenians in 1870 E; remains Republican, 1936 L
Verne, Jules, F. author (1828–1905), 1869 U, 1872 U
Verona, Italy: discoveries in, 1816 Q; Congress at, 1822 K, L, M; Fifth Army takes, 1945 D
Verranzano-Narrows Bridge, US, 1964 P
Versailles, France:
Treaty ends War of American Independence, 1783 J, 1784 C
Notables meet at, 1787 B
Edict, for religious freedom for Protestants, 1787 R
States General meet at, 1789 E
March of women to, 1789 K
Peace between France and Germany, 1871 B
French Chamber is moved from, 1879 L
Peace Conference, 1918 L, 1919 A
Leage of Nations Covenant is laid before, 1919 B
German delegates attend, 1919 D
China leaves, 1919 D
disposes of Germany's Colonies, 1919 E
US delegates leave, 1919 M
Treaty of Peace, ending World War I:
Austria protests at terms, 1919 F
Germany signs, 1919 F
US Senate rejects Shantung Clause, 1919 H
US Senate virtually rejects treaty, 1919 L
Clause 231, on Germany's war guilt, repudiated, 1927 J
Mussolini champions revision, 1930 E
denounced by Nazis, 1930 J
Germany repudiates disarmament clauses, 1935 C
Germany violates, 1936 C
Germany denounces, 1936 L
League Covenant is separated from Treaty, 1938 K
See also League of Nations
Verses and Sonnets (H. Belloc), 1895 U
Versuche über einzelne Theile der Theorie des Rechts, 1798 O
Vertebrate skulls, theory of, 1858 P
Verwoerd, Hendrik Frensch, Prime Minister of South Africa (1901–66), 1966 J; becomes premier, 1958 J; attempted assassination, 1960 D; states S. Africa will leave Commonwealth, 1961 C
Vessels, steam, 1803 P, 1812 P, 1818 P. *See also under* Ships
Vestiges of the National History of Creation, The (R. Chambers), 1844 P
Vetus Testamentum Hebraicum cum variis lectionibus (B. Kennicott), 1776 Q
Vexed and Troubled Englishmen (C. Bridenbaugh), 1968 Q
Viallat, Claude, F. artist (b. 1936), 1976 S
Viaud, Julien, F. author under pseudonym of 'Pierre Loti' (1850–1923), 1850 Z, 1886 U, 1912 U, 1923 Z
Viborg, Finland: manifesto, 1906 G; Russia takes, 1940 C
Vibrations, harmonic, analysis of, 1843 P
Vicar of Wakefield, The (O. Goldsmith), 1776 U
Vicenza, Italy, battle, 1848 F
Vices of the Political System of the United States, The (Madison), 1787 O
Vichy, France, French government at, breaks off relations with Britain, 1940 G
Vicksburg, Missouri, US, Confederate defeat at, 1863 G
Victor Emmanuel I, King of Sardinia (1802–5 and 1814–21), abdicates, 1821 C
Victor Emmanuel II, King of Sardinia (1849–61), King of Italy (1861–78), 1849 C, 1850 R, 1878 A; invades Papal States, 1860 J; proclaimed King of Italy, 1860 K, 1861 B
Victor Emmanuel III, King of Italy (1900–1943), 1904 D, 1943 G; abdicates, 1946 E
Victoria Falls, Cen. Africa, discovered, 1855 P
Victoria History of the Counties of England, The, 1900 Q, 1989 Q
Victoria Nyanza, Lake, Cen. Africa, discovered, 1856 P
Victoria Regina (L. Housman), 1937 W
Victoria, Australia: is separated from New South Wales, 1850 H; proclaimed a British Colony, 1851 G
Victoria, Lake, Cen. Africa, railway to, 1901 M
Victoria, Queen of Great Britain and Ireland (1837–1901), 1819 Z, 1837 F, 1895 F; Bedchamber Question, 1839 E; marriage, 1840 B; statue of, 1869 S; expenditure, enquiry into, 1872 C; proclaimed Empress of India, 1877 A; Golden Jubilee, 1887 F; Diamond
Jubilee, 1897 W; Uitlanders petition to, 1899 C
Victorian Church, The (O. Chadwick), 1966 Q
Victorian City, The: Images and Realities (H.J. Dyos and M. Wolff eds.), 1973 Q
Victorian Country House, The (M. Girouard), 1971 Q
Victorian Countryside, The (G.E. Mingay ed.), 1981 Q
Victorian Society, The, 1958 S
Victory (H. Barker), 1983 W
Victory (J. Conrad), 1915 U
Vidal, Gore, Am. author (b. 1925), 1925 Z, 1964 U, 1968 U
Video:
video-cassette recorder, 1972 P
video-cassettes in US, 1974 W
LaserVision video disc system, 1979 P
Vidler, Alexander Roper, B. theologian (1899–1991), 1957 R, 1963 R
Vie de Jésus (E. Renan), 1863 R
Vie littéraire, La (A. Francc), 1888 U
Vie, Une (G. de Maupassant), 1883 U
Vienna, Austria:
events:
Pius VI visits, 1782 C
Hungarian crown removed to, 1784 G
Moreau advances on, 1800 M
French capture, 1809 E
Congress, 1814 L, 1815 F
Treaty of Peace, 1815 F

Conference at, under Metternich, 1820 E
Ferdinand I flees from, 1848 E
Note, on Eastern Question, 1853 G
railway from, to Trieste, 1853 P
Four Points, to Russia, 1854 H
Austrian ultimatum to Russia on, 1855 M
Peace Treaty of, 1864 K
Treaty of, 1866 K
financial crisis in, 1873 E
strike in, 1918 A
Socialist riots and strikes in, 1927 G
Schuschnigg's coup in, 1935 K
Conference, on Danube basin, 1936 L
Communist Conference at, 1952 M
Treaty, restores Austria's independence, 1955 E
World Peace Council offices at, closed by government, 1957 B
places and institutions in:
aeronautical exhibition, 1888 P
Heinrichshof, 1861 S
Ringstrasse in, 1858 S
Votivkirche in, 1856 S
music in, 1887 T
population of, 1801 Y, 1841 Y, 1881 Y, 1906 Y
the theatre in, 1891 W
Vientiane, Laos, Laos and Pathet Lao sign ceasefire, 1973 B
Vierge de Paris, La (P. J. Jouve), 1945 U
Viet Cong, 1969 E
Tet offensive, 1968 A
major assaults on South Vietnam, 1970 C
Viet Nam:
republic formed, 1945 J
France recognises as a free state within the Indo-Chinese Federation, 1946 L
Nationalists, under Bao Dai, recognised by France, 1949 L
state, established under Bao Dai, 1949 F
France transfers sovereignty to Republic, 1949 M
French evacuate N. Viet Nam, 1954 G
Communists evacuate S. Viet Nam, 1954 G
Republic proclaimed in S. Viet Nam, 1955 K
disturbances in, 1959 J
US military council in S. Viet Nam, 1962 B
martial law in S. Viet Nam, 1963 H
H. Davies attempts to open peace talks, 1965 G
Russia admits supplying arms to Hanoi, 1965 J
N. Viet Nam recognized by Sweden, 1969 A
proposed international conference on, 1970 D
Podgorny visits N. Viet Nam, 1972 F 1988 C
South and North formally unified, 1976 G
begins full-scale invasion of Cambodia, 1978 M
China makes punitive incursions, 1979 B
'boat people', 1979 J, 1989 M
victory over Kampuchean rebels claimed, 1983 D
clash with China over Spratly Islands, 1988 C
withdrawal from Kampuchea, 1989 J
population, 1991 Y
war. See Wars
View from Nowhere, The (T. Nagel), 1986 R
View from the Bridge, The (A. Miller), 1955 W
View of the Internal Evidence of the Christian Religion (S. Jenyns), 1776 R
View of the State of Europe in the Middle Ages, The (H. Hallam), 1818 Q
Vigevano, Italy, Peace, between Austria and Sardinia, 1848 H
Vigny, Alfred de, F. author (1797–1863), 1797 Z, 1826 U, 1835 U, 1864 U, 1863 Z
Vigne, Daniel, F. film director (b. 1942), 1982 W
Vilàgos, Hungary, Hungarians capitulate at, 1849 H
Vile Bodies (E. Waugh), 1930 U
Villafranca, Italy, Peace Treaty, Austria with France, 1859 G; confirmed by Treaty of Zurich, 1859 L
Village trust, Bournville, 1900 O
Village, The (T. Crabbe), 1783 U
Villari, Pasquale, It. historian (1827–1910), 1859 Q
Villèle, Jean Baptiste comte de, F. politician, Royalist (1773–1854), 1821 M, 1927 F, 1828 A
Villers-Bretonneux, France, British victory at, 1918 D
Villiers, George William Frederick, earl of Clarendon, B. foreign secretary (1800–70), 1868 M
Vilna, Lithuania: Germans take, 1915 J; Poles annex, 1920 K; recognised as Polish, 1923 C; Russia cedes to Lithuania, 1939 K
Vilna, River, Russia, Napoleon crosses, 1812 F
Vilnius, Lithuania:
Soviet tanks enter, 1990 C
Soviet troops storm television station, 1991 A
Vimiero, Portugal, Wellington's victory at, 1808 H
Vimy Ridge, France, Canadian troops take, 1917 D
Vincennes, Indiana, US, 1779 B
Vincennes, USS, Iranian civilian airliner shot down, 1988 G
Vincent, Stenio, president of Haiti (1874–1959), 1930 B
Vindications of the Rights of Women (M. Wollstonecraft), 1792 O
Vindiciae Gallicae (J. MacKintosh), 1791 O
Vinegar Hill, Wexford, Ireland, rebels routed at, 1798 F
Vineland (T. Pynchon), 1990 U
'Vingt, Les', artists, 1884 S
Vinland Map, 1965 Q
Vionville, France, falls to Prussians, 1870 H
Virgin Isles, US takes over, 1917 C
Virginia, State, US: Colonial Assembly, 1765 E; dissolved, 1769 G; Provincial Committee of correspondence, 1773 C; Convention, 1776 E; Bill of Rights, 1776 F; legislature, 1798 M
Virginians, The (W. M. Thackeray), 1857 U
Virginibus Puerisque (R. L. Stevenson), 1881 U
Vischer, Friedrich Theodor, G. philosopher (1807–1887), 1846 R
Visconti, Luchino, Count Don Luchino Visconti di Modrone, It. film director (1906–76), 1906 Z, 1960 W, 1963 W, 1971 W, 1976 Z
Viscose, discovered, 1892 P
Vision of Bernadette Soubirous, 1858 R
Vision of Britain, A: A Personal View of Architecture (H.R.H. The Prince of Wales), 1989 S
Vision of Judgment (R. Southey), 1814 U
Visser't Hooft, Willem Adolf, Dutch theologian and churchman (1900–92), 1900 Z, 1992 Z
Vistula River, Poland, 1772 P
Vitamine, Funck coins term, 1912 P
Vitamins:
A, is isolated, 1931 P
A, crytalline, 1937 P
A, synthesis of, 1945 P
B, isolated, 1925 P
B.1, synthesis of, 1937 P
B.2, isolated, 1925 P
B12, composition of, 1955 P
C, pure, 1934 P
D, discovered, 1932 P
E, synthesis of, 1938 P
K, concentrate, 1937 P
Vitebsk, Russia, Germans trapped at, 1944 F
Vittoria, Spain, battle, 1813 F
Vivian Grey (B. Disraeli), 1826 U
Viviani, René, F. politician (1863–1925), 1914 F, 1915 K
Vivisection, royal commission on, 1912 O
Vladivostok, Russia: founded, 1860 G, O; British force lands, 1918 H
Vlakfontein, S. Africa, 1950 G
Vlaminck, Maurice, F. artist (1876–1958), 1908 S, 1947 S
Vocation of a Scholar (J. G. Fichte), 1794 R
Vogel, Sir Julius, premier of New Zealand (1835–99), 1875 K
Vogt, Hans, G. inventor of sound films, 1919 P
Vogué, Eugène Melchior, comte de, F. author (1848–1910), 1886 U
Voice of the Past, The: Oral History (P. Thompson), 1978 Q
Voices of Freedom (J. G. Whittier), 1846 U
Voices of the Night (H. W. Longfellow), 1839 U
Vol de Nuit (St. Exupéry), 1931 U
Volcanic eruptions:
Tristan da Cunha, 1961 K
Nevado del Ruiz, Colombia, 1985 L
Lake Nyas gas eruption, 1986 H
Volcanoes, study of, 1774 P
Volney, Constantin François, comte de, F. author (1757–1820), 1791 Q
Volta, Alessandro, comte, It. physicist (1745–1827), 1789 P, 1800 P, 1827 Z
Volta River Project, Ghana, 1961 M
Volta, Upper, Republic, becomes independent, 1960 G
Voltaic pile, 1798 P
Voltaire, François Marie Arouet de, F. philosopher (1694–1778), 1763 R, 1764 R, 1770 R, 1778 U, Z
Volturno, River, Italy, Germans retire from, 1943 K
Von deutscher Art und Kunst (Herder), 1773 U
Vonnegut, Kurt, Am. author (b. 1922), 1969 U, 1985 U
Vor dem Sturm (T. Fontane), 1878 U
Voronezh, Russia, Russian victory at, 1943 A
Voroshilov, Kliment Efremovich, R. marshal (1881–1969), 1950 C, 1960 E
Vorovski, Vaslav, R. diplomat, 1923 E
Vorster, Balthazar Johannes, S. Afr. politician (1915–83), 1966 J, 1978 E
Information Department abolished, 1978 F
allegations against, ignored by Erasmus Commission, 1978 M
resigns as Prime Minister; becomes President, 1978 J
resigns as President, 1979 F
Vortex motion theory, 1858 P
Vortex, The (N. Coward), 1924 W
Voss (P. White), 1957 U
Voss, Johann Heinrich, G. poet and translator (1751–1826), 1781 G, 1795 U, 1826 Z
Voyage au bout de la nuit (L. Céline), 1932 U
Voyage autour de ma chambre (X. de Maistre), 1794 U
Voyage aux régions équinoxiales (A. von Humboldt and A. Bonpland), 1807 P
Voyage de M. Perrichon, Le (E. Labiche), 1860 W
Voyage du jeune Anarcharsis en Grèce (J. Barthélney) 1787 Q
Voyage en Icarie (E. Cabet), 1842 O
Voyage of the Beagle (C. Darwin), 1839 P
Voyager aircraft flies round world without refuelling, 1986 P
Voyageur sans bagage (J. Anouilh), 1938 W
'V' particles, 1950 P
Vranitzky, Franz, Aus. politician (b. 1937), 1987 A

Vries, Hugo de, F. botanist (1848–1935), 1900 P
V2 rockets, 1942 P, 1944 J
Vukovar, Croatia, falls to Serb-dominated army, 1991 H
Vyshinsky, Andrei Yanuarievich, R. marshal and diplomat (1883–1954), 1951 M
becomes foreign minister, 1949 C

W

Wackenroder, Wilhelm Heinrich, G. author (1773–1798), 1797 U
Waddell, Helen, B. author and translator (1889–1965), 1933 U
Waddington, William Henry, F. statesman (1826–94), 1878 P, 1879 B
Wafd. *See under* Political Parties
Wage, Labour and Capital (K. Marx), 1848 O
Wages. *See* Prices, Wages and Incomes
Wagner, Adolph, G. economist (1835–1912), 1871 O
Wagner, Richard, G. musician (1813–83), 1813 Z, 1883 Z
Essay on Beethoven, 1870 T
Operas, 1840 T, 1842 T, 1843 T, 1845 T, 1850 T, 1851 T, 1855 T, 1859 T, 1865 T, 1868 T, 1869 T, 1870 T, 1874 T, 1876 T, 1882 T
text of *The Ring,* 1853 T
complete broadcast performance of *The Ring,* 1962 W
Wagner-Steagall Act in US, to finance housing, 1937 J
Wagram, Austria, battle, 1809 G
Wailers, Bob Marley and The, Jamaican reggae group, 1972 W
Wain, John Barrington, B. author (b. 1935), 1953 U
Waitangi, New Zealand, Treaty between Britain and Maoris, 1840 B
Waite, Terence Hardy, 'Terry', B. envoy of the Archbishop of Canterbury (b. 1939), 1986 L, 1991 L
kidnapped in Beirut, 1987 A
Waiting for Godot (S. Beckett), 1955 W
Waiting for Lefty (C. Odets), 1935 W
Waiting for the Parade (J. Murrell), 1977 W
Waits, Tom, Am. pop singer (b. 1949), 1976 W
Waitz, Theodor, G. psychologist (1821–64), 1846 R
Wajda, Andrzej, Pol. film director (b. 1926), 1954 W, 1958 W, 1981 W, 1983 W
Wakatsuki, Reijiro, Jap. premier (1866–1949), 1927 D
Wakefield, Edward Gibbon, B. colonial statesman (1796–1862), 1796 Z, 1862 Z
Waksman, Selman A., Am. formerly R. microbiologist (1888–1973), 1913 P, 1949 P
Walcheren, Holland, British expedition to, fails, 1809 G, J
Walcott, Derek, W. Ind. author (b. 1930), 1930 Z, 1967 W, 1973 U, 1990 W, 1991 U
Walcott, Jersey Joe, Am. boxer (b. 1914), 1952 X
Waldeck Rousseau, René, F. Moderate Republican (1846–1904), 1899 F, 1902 F
Pardons Dreyfus, 1899 J
Walden, or Life in the Woods (H. D. Thoreau), 1854 U
Waldermar, Prince of Denmark, refuses to serve as King of Belgians, 1886 L
Waldheim, Kurt, Aus. diplomat and politician (b. 1918)
UN Secretary-General, 1971 M
visits Teheran, 1980 A
elected President of Austria, 1986 F
alleged involvement in Nazi atrocities, 1987 D
cleared of war crimes by International Commission, 1988 B
Waldorf, William, viscount Astor, B. newspaper owner (1848–1919), 1848 Z, 1919 Z
Wales, Princess of, 1992 H, M
See also Spencer, Lady Diana Frances
Wales:
bill for devolution published, 1976 L
education in, 1889 O
liquor licensing in, 1961 O
national extremists, 1980 L
referendum on devolution, 1979 C
schism in, 1811 R
University of, 1893 O
White Paper on devolution, 1975 L
Walesa, Lech, Pol. trade unionist and politician (b. 1943), 1943 Z
reforms agreed with government, 1980 H, 1989 D
leads 'Solidarity' delegation, 1981 A
talks held with government, 1981 L, 1988 H
release called for, 1982 H
release from detention, 1982 L
returns to work at Lenin Shipyard, Gdansk, 1983 D
talks with Pope, 1983 F
Nobel Peace Prize, 1983 K
meeting with Thatcher, 1988 L
elected President, 1990 M
Walfish Bay, South West Africa, Britain annexes, 1877 C
Walhalla, The, near Regensberg, Germany, 1830 S
Walker, Alice Malsenior, Am. author (b. 1944), 1983 U
Walker, Kenneth Macfarlane, B. surgeon and author (1888–1966), 1942 R
Walker, Peter Edward, Lord Walker, B. Conservative politician (b. 1932), 1972 L, M
Wall Street Crash, 1929 K, O
Wall-Painting, English Medieval (E. W. Tristram), 1945 S
Wall-paintings, 1842 S
Wallace Collection, Manchester Square, London, 1900 S
Wallace, Alfred Russell, B. naturalist (1823–1910), 1858 P
Wallace, Edgar, B. author and journalist (1875–1932), 1875 Z, 1928 U, 1932 Z
Wallace, George Corley, Am. politician (b. 1919), 1968 L, 1972 E
Wallace, Lewis, A. soldier and author (1827–1905), 1880 U
Wallace-Hadrill, (John) Michael, B. historiam (1916–85), 1916 Z, 1952 Q, 1985 Z
Wallachia, is united with Moldavia to form Roumania, 1861 M
Wallas, Graham, B. Socialist (1858–1932), 1858 Z, 1908 O, 1932 Z
Wallenstein (Schiller), 1709 W
Waller, Fred, Am. inventor of 'Cinerama', 1951 W
Waller, Philip John, B. historian (b. 1946), 1981 Q, 1983 Q
Wallis, Sir Barnes Neville, B. engineer (1887–1979), 1887 Z, 1943 E, 1979 Z
Wallpapers, Morris's, 1861 S
Walpole, Horace, 4th earl of Orford, B. author and wit (1717–97), 1763 S, 1765 U, 1771 S, 1797 Z
Walpole, Sir Hugh Seymour, B. author (1884–1941), 1911 U, 1922 U, 1930 U
Walser, Margin, G. author (b. 1927), 1966 U, 1967 W
Walsh, James, Am. missionary, 1970 G
Walsh, Lawrence Edward, Am. lawyer (b. 1912), 1986 M
Walter, John, B. founder of *The Times* (1739–1812), 1788 V
Walter, John, II, B. proprietor of *The Times* (1776–1847), 1814 V
Walter, Thomas Ustrick, A. architect (1804–87), 1839 S, 1851 S
Walton, Sir William Turner, B. musician (1902–83), 1902 Z, 1923 T, 1929 T, 1931 T, 1935 T, 1939 T, 1941 T, 1947 T, 1950 T, 1954 T, 1957 T, 1965 T, 1983 Z
Waltons, The, television series, 1972 W
Waltz of the Toreadors, The (J. Anouilh), 1956 W
Wandering Jews, The (S. Heym), 1984 U
Wandering Jew, The (E. Sue), 1844 U
Wanderings of Oisin, The (W. B. Yeats), 1889 U
Wandsbeck Messenger, 1771 U
Wandsworth, Surrey, England, tram road at, 1801 P
Waning of the Middle Ages, The (J. Huizinga), 1919 Q
War Artists, 1918 S, 1941 S
War Game, The, television programme, 1985 W
War Office, British, reformed, 1870 F
War Production, 1939 Y, 1940 Y, 1941 Y, 1942 Y, 1943 Y, 1944 N, Y
War Raw Materials Department, German, 1914 O
War and Peace (L. Tolstoy), 1864 U
War by Timetable (A. J. P. Taylor), 1969 Q
War correspondent, the first, 1808 V
War criminals, trials of:
in World War I, at Leipzig, 1921 A
in World War II, at Nuremburg, 1946 J
of Japanese, 1946 N, 1948 L
War debts (of World War I):
Balfour Note on, 1922 H
Belgium to US, 1925 H
Britain to US, is funded, 1923 A, F
final payment, 1933 M
France, to US, Herrick defeated over, 1932 M
Germany, US Congress resolves against cancellation, 1932 M
Hoover moratorium, 1932 F, H
Italy to US, agreement on, 1925 L
See also Reparations
War of the End of the World, The (M. V. Llosa), 1981 U
War of the Worlds (H. G. Wells), 1898 U
Warburg Institute, 1933 S
Ward, Artemus, *See* Browne, C. F.
Ward, Mrs. Humphrey (Mary Augusta Arnold), B. novelist (1851–1920), 1851 Z, 1883 U, 1920 Z
Ward, James, B. philosopher and psychologist (1843–1925), 1899 R
Ward, Joseph, N. Zeal. United Party leader (1856–1930), 1919 H, 1928 L, 1930 E
Ward, Sir Leslie, B. cartoonist as 'Spy' (1851–1922), 1851 Z, 1922 Z
Ward, Lester, Frank, Am. sociologist and geologist (1841–1912), 1883 O
Ward, Stephen, B. osteopath (d. 1963), 1963 G
Warden, The (A. Trollope), 1855 U
Warhol, Andy (born Andrew Warhola), A. artist (c. 1928-87), 1966 W, 1967 S, 1970 S
Warmerdam, Am. pole-jumper, 1942 X
Warner Brothers, film company, 1929 W
Warnock, (Helen) Mary, Lady Warnock (b. 1924), 1984 O
Warren, Earl, Am. Chief Justice of Supreme Court (1891–1974), 1891 Z, 1964 O, 1968 F, 1974 Z
Warren, Robert Penn, Am. author (1905–89), 1946 U, 1969 U

Warrenpoint, N. Ireland, IRA attack, 1979 H
Wars:
Afghanistsan
Soviet withdrawal, 1988 B, E
American Civil, opens, 1861 D
ends, 1865 E
for campaign. *See under* Civil Wars
American War of Independence (1775–83):
opens, 1775 D
tract defending, 1776 O
Lafayette's volunteers for, 1777 D
French alliance with Americans, 1778 B
Britain declares war on France, 1778 B
Dutch alliance with America, 1778 J
Spain declares war on Britain, 1779 F
League of Armed Neutrality against Britain, 1780 C, 1781 E
Britain declares war on Holland, 1780 L
Rodney saves W. Indies, 1782 D
continuation of, deprecated, 1782 B
peace negotiations, 1782 E, L
armistice signed, 1783 B
Arab–Israeli conflict. See Middle East
Austria against Sardinia, 1849 C, H
Austria with Prussia, against Denmark, 1864 D, K
Azerbaijan against Armenia, 1990 A
Balkan wars:
First, Turkey against Bulgaria, Serbia, Montenegro and Greece, 1912 K, L, M, 1913 C, E
Bulgaria renews, 1913 B
Second, Bulgaria against Serbia and Greece, 1913 F
Russia and Turkey declare against Bulgaria, 1913 G
Bavarian Succession, Prussia against Austria and Saxony, 1778 G, 1779 E
Bolivia against Paraguay (Chaco War), 1928 M, 1919 J, 1932 G
Brazil against Argentina, 1925 M, 1828 H
Britain against Afghanistan, 1838 K, 1840 C, 1841 C, 1842 A, K, 1919 E, G
Britain against Ashanti, 1873 D, 1874 B, 1896 A
Britain against Boers, in Natal, 1842 N
S. African war, opens, 1899 K
operations, 1899 K–M, 1900 passim, 1901 A, B
ends, 1902 E
casualities, 1902 E
Britain against Burma, 1824 B, E, 1826 B, 1852 D, M, 1853 F, 1885 K
Britain against China, 'Opium War', 1839 G, H, L, 1842 H
Second, 1856 K, L, 1957 F, M, 1858 F, 1860 H, J
Britain against Kaffirs, 1850 C, 1877 H
Britain against Maoris, 1860 C, 1861 C, 1865 J, 1868 F
Britain against Persia, 1856 L, 1857 C
Britain against US, 1812 F, 1814 M
operations, 1813 D, E, F, J, K, L, M, 1814 G, J, 1815 A
burning of Washington, 1814 H
Britain against Zulus, 1877 D, 1879 A, H, J
Britain in India:
against Gurkhas, 1814 K
against Indore, 1804 D, L
against Mahrattas, 1782 E, 1802 K, 1803 H, 1817 L, 1818 F
against Nepalese, 1815 M
against Sikhs, 1834 E, 1845 M, 1846 A, B, E, 1848 C, 1849 A, B, C
against Sind, 1843 A
See also under Mutinies
Britain in Sudan, 1884 B, F, K
Cambodia
US admits shelling, 1966 E
US ground troops withdrawn, 1970 F
navy seizes USS *Mayaguez,* 1975 E
UN votes to send peacekeeping force, 1992 B
Chaco. *See* Bolivia against Paraguay
Chad with Libya, 1988 K
Chile against Peru and Bolivia, 1836 L, 1880 N
China against India, 1959 H
Crimean War (1854–6):
Britain and France declare war on Russia, 1854 C
Greece promises neutrality, 1854 E
Austrian treaty with Turkey, for occupying Danubian provinces, 1854 F
Vienna Four Points, 1854 H
battle of the Alma, 1854 J
siege of Sebastool opens, 1854 K
battle of Balaclava, 1854 K
Charge of Light Brigade, 1854 K
Battle of Inkerman, 1854 L
Piedmont joins Allies against Russia, 1855 A
Russians capitulate at Sebastopol, 1855 J
British muddles and disasters, 1855 O
history of, 1863 Q
Cuba against Spain, 1878 B
France against Austria, 1859 E, F, G
Cyprus, 1967 D, L
negotiations between Greek and Turkish Cypriots in Nicosia, 1968 F
arms yielded to UN peace-keepers, 1972 B
Turkish invasion, 1974 G
Turkish ultimatum, 1974 H
Turkish forces resume offensive, 1974 H
ceasefire, 1974 H
summit conference at UN, 1985 A
UN request for talks on border re-opening refused by Denktas, 1986 G
Falklands (1982):
Argentine troops invade, 1982 D
UN Security Council Resolution 502, 1982 D
Royal Navy Task Force, first ships sail for, 1982 D
US offers mediation, 1982 D
exclusion zone declared by Britain, 1982 D
Haig plan rejected by Britain and Argentina, 1982 D
US backs Britain, 1982 D
RAF bombs Port Stanley airport, 1982 E
HMS *Conqueror* sinks *General Belgrano*, 1982 E
HMS *Sheffield* sunk by Argentine missiles, 1982 E
Britain warns Argentine forces, 1982 E
British troops land on East Island, 1982 E
Britain recaptures Port Darwin and Goose Green, 1982 E
British landing ships attacked at Bluff Cove, 1982 F
Argentine forces surrender, 1982 F
death toll, 1982 F
Argentina recognizes de facto cessation of hostilities with Britain, 1982 G
inquiry by Privy Councillors, 1982 G
equipment losses proposal, 1982 M
Franks Report, 1983 A
sinking of *General Belgrano,* 1985 B
formal cessation of hostilities, 1989 K
France against Austria, 1859 E, F, G
France against China, 1860 H, J, 1885 C, F
France against King Dahomey in W. Africa, 1892 N
French and Indian (Seven Years), ends, 1763 B
France in Indo–China, 1954 D, E, G
France against Madagascar, 1883 F
France in Morocco, 1844 H, J, 1925 D, H, 1926 F
France against Prussia, 1870–1):
opens, 1870 G
French defeats, 1870 H
Belgian neutrality is guaranteed, 1870 H
Napoleon III capitulates at Sedan, 1870 J
siege of Paris opens, 1870 J
Strasbourg falls to Prussians, 1870 K
Paris capitulates, 1871 A
armistice signed, 1871 A
French revenge for, 1886 A
France against Spain, 1823 D, K
French Revolutionary wars (1792–1801):
War of First Coalition: France declares war on Austria, 1792 D
France declares war on Prussia and Sardinia, 1792 G
battles of Longwy and Verdun, 1792 J
French check invaders at Valmy, 1792 J
battle of Jemappes, 1792 L
France declares war on Britain and Holland, 1793 B
First Coalition is formed, 1793 B
France declares war on Spain, 1793 C
US neutrality, 1773 D
French victory at Tourcoing, 1794 E
Austrian defeat at Fleurus, 1795 F
French invasion of Spain, 1794 F
Prussia enters war against France, 1794 J
French troops reach Rhine, 1794 K
Prussia withdraws from war, 1794 K
French invade Holland, 1794 M
Spain signs peace with France, 1795 G
Prussia signs peace with France, 1795 D
Austrian defeat at Loano, 1795 L
Austria signs armistice with France, 1795 M
Bonaparte's Italian campaign, 1796 C, D, E, F, L, 1797 A, B
Jourdan's defeat at Würzburg, 1796 J
Spain declares war against Britain, 1796 K
British conquests in W. Indies, 1796
battle of Cape St. Vincent, 1797 B
Austria signs peace of Leoben with France, 1797 D
Peace of Campo Formio, 1797 K
US negotiations for preserving peace with France, 1797 K
French take Rome, 1798 B
Bonaparte conquers Egypt, 1798 G
Nelson's victory at battle of the Nile, 1788 H
Turkey declares war on France, 1798 J
French overrun Naples, 1798 M
Austria declares war on France, 1799 C
Siege of Acre, 1799 C, E
War of Second Coalition: coalition of Britain, Russia, Austria, Turkey, Portugal and Naples is formed by Pitt, 1798 F
Bonaparte leaves Egypt, 1799 H
Russia abandons coalition, 1799 K
Bonaparte reconquers Italy through battle of Marengo, 1800 F
Moreau advances on Vienna, 1800 M
Armed Neutrality of North, against Britain's right of search, 1800 CM, 1801 C, F
Peace of Lunéville, 1801 B
Nelson's victory at Copenhagen, 1801 D
British take Cairo, 1801 F
Peace of Amiens, between Britain and France, 1801 K, 1802 C
Greece with Turkey, 1878 B, 1897 D, E, M, 1921 F, G, H, 1922 G, H, K
Greek Independence, 1821 C, D, F, K, 1822 D, F, G, 1823 C, 1824 D, G, K, 1825 B,

1827 D, F, G, H, M
Gulf War (1990–1), 1991 A, B
Iraqi troops mass on Kuwaiti border, 1990 G, H
Iraq announces annexation of Kuwait, 1990 H
UN sanctions imposed against Iraq, 1990 H
US forces sent to Saudi Arabia, 1990 H
Western nationals in Kuwait rounded up and used as 'human shields', 1990 H, M
Iraq fails to meet UN deadline for withdrawal from Kuwait, 1991 A
'Operation Desert Storm', 1991 A
Iraq launches Scud missile against Israel, 1991 A
oil pumped into Gulf, 1991 A
Kuwait oil wells set alight, 1991 B
Kuwait liberated, 1991 B
ticker-tape parade in New York celebrates victory, 1991 F
Holland against Belgium, 1833 E
Holland in North Sumatra, 1873 D
Honduras with Nicaragua, 1907 B
India with Pakistan, over Kashmir, 1965 D, F
Pakistani troops cross cease-fire line, 1965 J
Indian troops invade Pakistan, 1965 J
Indian 'planes bomb Lahore, 1965 J
cease-fire, 1965 J
Indonesian War of Independence from Holland, opens, 1945 J
truce, 1948 A
is renewed, 1948 M
ends with Dutch transfer of sovereignty, 1949 M
Indonesia with Malaya, incidents, 1963 D, 1966 M
Malaysia breaks off relations with Indonesia, 1963 J
Indonesian landings in Malaya, 1964 J, K, 1965 A
Commonwealth troops move in, 1964 J
Iran–Iraq (1980–8):
Iraq invades Iran, 1980 J
Iranian troops enter Iraq, 1982 G
Iran commences bombing non-military targets in Iran, 1984 B
Iraq blockades Kharg Island oil terminal, 1984 B
chemical weapons, 1984 C
UN supervision of Iranian agreement sought by Iran, 1984 F
'war of the cities', 1987 B
USS *Stark* hit by Iraqi Exocet missile, 1987 E
UN calls for ceasefire, 1987 G
UN peace mission, 1987 J
Iranian oil platforms destroyed in US attack, 1988 D
Iranian civilian airliner shot down by US, 1988 G
ceasefire, 1988 H
Iraq makes peace with Iran, 1990 H
Italy with Austria, 1866 F
Italy with Ethiopia, 1896 C
Mussolini's war, 1935 K, L, 1936 E
Italy with Turkey, 1911 J, 1912 C, K
Japan with China. See Sino–Japanese War
legal state of war ended, 1972 J
Korea with China, 1894 G
Korean (1950–3):
opens, 1950 F
UN appoints force to assist S. Koreans, 1950 G
UN Security Council discusses, 1950 H
UN troops land, 1950 J
N. Koreans attack across Naktong River, 1950 J
UN force recaptures Seoul, 1950 J
S. Koreans cross 38th parallel, 1950 K
massing of Chinese Communists in, 1950 L
UN troops forced to withdraw, 1950 L
emergency in US, following UN reverses, 1950 M
Chinese cross 38th parallel, 1950 M
Communists take Seoul, 1951 A
truce is urged, 1951 C
N. Korean offensive, 1951 E
attempts at armistice, 1951 F
Ridgway breaks off armistice talks, 1951 H
UN force takes Heartbreak Ridge, 1951 J
armistice talks resumed, 1951 K, M
allegations of killing prisoners of war, 1951 L
China accuses US of using germ warfare, 1952 C
Clark succeeds Ridgway as UN commander, 1952 D
Communists riot at Koje Prison Camp, 1952 E
UN air force bomb plants, 1952 F
UN adopts Indian proposals on armistice, 1952 M
China rejects, 1952 M
Eisenhower states principles of UN peace proposals, 1953 E
exchange of prisoners, 1953 D, F
armistice signed, 1953 G
withdrawal of all foreign troops from Korea, 1958 B
Laos, 1969 CV, E, G
Plain of Jars offensive, 1969 J
North Vietnamese offensive, 1970 B
S. Vietnam invades then withdraws from Laos, 1971 B
Latvia with Germany, 1919 L
Mexico with France, 1838 L, 1839 C
Napoleonic (1803–15):
Anglo–French hostilities renewed, 1803 E
neutrality of Spain and Portugal, 1803 K
Austro–Russian declaration on maintenance of Ottoman Empire, 1804 L
Spain declares war on Britain, 1804 M
Britain and Russia form 3rd Coalition against France, 1805 D
Austria joins Coalition, 1805 H
battle of Trafalgar, 1805 K
battle of Ulm, 1805 K
Napoleon's victory at Austerlitz, 1805 M
Austria signs Peace of Pressburg with France, 1805 M
end of Holy Roman Empire, 1806 H
Prussia declares war on France, 1806 K
Napoleon enters Warsaw, 1806 M
Russia and Prussia sign peace treaties with Napoleon at Tilsit, 1807 G
French invade Spain, 1808 B
Britain sends expedition to Portugal, 1808 H
battle of Corunna, 1809 A
Austria declares war on France, 1809 B
Wellington takes command in Peninsula, 1809 D
Napoleon defeats Austrians at Wagram, 1809 G
British expedition to Walcheren, 1809 G
Austria signs peace of Schönbrunn with France, 1809 K
Wellington holds lines of Torres Vedras, 1810 K
Wellington takes Cuidad Rodrigo, 1812 A
Napoleon invades Russia, 1812 F
Wellington enters Madrid, 1812 H
Napoleon enters Moscow, 1812 J
Napoleon retreats from Moscow, 1812 K
Prussia declares war on France, 1813 C
Wellington routs French at Vittoria, 1813 F
Austria declares war on France, 1813 H
Napoleon is defeated at battle of Leipzig, 1813 K
Wellington enters France, 1813 K
Allies offer peace proposals to Napoleon, 1813 L
Murat deserts Napoleon, 1814 A
Allies enter Paris, 1814 C
Napoleon is banished to Elba, 1814 D
Congress of Vienna opens, 1814 L
Napoleon's Hundred Days, 1815 C
battle of Waterloo, 1815 F
Congress of Vienna closes, 1815 F
Allies re-enter Paris, 1815 G
Nigeria with Biafra, 1968 G, 1969 D
Kampala peace talks break down, 1968 E
Nigeria forbids Red Cross to fly relief supplies to Biafra, 1968 H
OAU appeals to Biafra to abandon independence struggle, 1968 J
Nigerian government takes control of relief operations, 1969 F
North and South Yemen, 1979 B
Oranges (Spain with Portugal), 1801 C
Palestine, between Arabs and Jews, 1948 E
See also main Index under Middle East; Palestine
UN orders truce, 1948 G
Paraguay against Argentina, Brazil and Uruguay (1865–70), 1865 C, 1870 C
Paraguay with Bolivia, 1933 E
Peninsular War. See under Napoleonic Wars, entries 1808–13
history of, 1828 Q
Peru with Columbia, 1932 J
Peru with Spain 1866 A
Poland with Russia, 1920 D, G, H, K
Prussia with Denmark, 1848 E, H, 1850 G
Prussia with France, 1870 G–K, 1871 A, B
Russia with Finland, 1919 F; 1939 L, 1940 B, C
Russia with Japan, 1904 B, E, H, 1905 A, C, E, J–
Russia with Persia, over Transcaucasia, 1826 J, 1828 B
Russia with Turkey, 1768 K, 1774 G, 1787 H, 1788 B, K, 1790 A, 1792 A
1806 K, 1809 E, 1810 N
1827 D, K, 1829 J
1853 K. See also Crimean War
1877 D, E, M, 1878 A
Sardinia with Austria, 1848 C, D, H
Saudi Arabia with the Yemen, 1934 F
Serbia with Bulgaria, 1885 L, 1886 C
Serbia with Turkey, 1876 F, 1877 B
Seven Years (or French and Indian) ends, 1763 B
Sino-Japanese, 1894 H, L, 1895 B, D, E, 1933 B, 1936 M, 1937 G, L, M, 1938 A, C, J, K, 1939 B, 1940 G
Japanese take Nanking, 1937 M
League pronounces Japan the aggressor, 1938 J
South Africa. See Britain against Boers
Spain against Moors, 1859 K, 1860 D
Spain against Portugal (War of the Oranges), 1801 C
Sweden against Denmark, 1809 C
Sweden against Russia, 1788 F, G
Turkey against Egypt, 1832 D, E, M
Russia supports Turkey 1833 B
Turkey against Greece, 1828 B, 1897 D, E, M, 1921 F, G, H, 1922 G, H, K
Turkey against Mehemet Ali, 1839 D, F, G
Turkey against Russia. See under Russia

US against Spanish in Cuba, 1898 D, E, G, H, M, O
Uruguay against Argentina, 1839 B
Vietnam (1954–75):
escalation of fighting between N. and S. Vietnamese, 1965 B
US aircraft bomb N. Vietnam, 1965 B, D
shot down by Russian 'planes, 1965 D
US marines land, 1965 C
demonstrations in Washington against war, 1965 D
Australian troops sent, 1965 D
S. Vietnam severs relations with France, 1965 F
US troops are authorised to take offensive, 1965 F
demonstrations in Britain against war, 1965 K
Ho Chi Minh rejects peace talks with US, 1965 K
Pope appeals for peace, 1966 A
'Iron Triangle', 1966 A
US bombing campaign, 1966 A, F, K, M, 1967 B, 1968 C, K, 1970 E, 1972 H, M
Johnson and South Vietnamese leaders meet in Honolulu, 1966 B
Australian forces, 1966 C
South Vietnam promises elections, 1966 D
Buddhist rebellion in South Vietnam, 1966 E, F
Britain dissociates itself from bombing of populated areas, 1966 F
captured US airmen paraded through Hanoi, 1966 G
Soviet aid to N. Vietnam, 1966 G
US bill to penalise US citizens aiding Viet Cong, 1966 H
US accused of bombing Chinese territory, 1966 J
defoliation, 1966 J
Chinese accuse USSR and US of plotting together, 1996 K
Manila Conference, 1966 K
de Gaulle calls for US withdrawal, 1966 K
Archbishop Spellman's sermon, 1966 M
British initiative to arrange ceasefire, 1966 M
US–South Vietnamese offensive, 1967 A
US war tax surcharge, 1967 A
Johnson offers to cease bombing campaigns, 1967 B
Operation Junction City, 1967 B
accidental US bombing of Lang Vei, 1967 C
Bertrand Russell International War Crimes Tribunal, 1967 E
U Thant's peace plan, 1967 C
anti-war demonstrations, 1967 K, M, 1968 H, K, 1969 K, 1970 E, 1971 D
Stop the Draft Week, 1967 M
number of US troops in Vietnam reaches 486,000, 1968 A
Tet offensive, 1968 A
US–South Vietnamese offensive in Saigon area, 1968 C
US bombing of North Vietnam restricted, 1968 C
direct contact between US and North Vietnam established, 1968 D
Paris peace talks, 1968 E, 1969 A, 1970 M
General Abrams takes over US command, 1968 F
total US combat deaths exceed 25,000, 1968 F
US bombing of North Vietnam halted, 1968 K
Viet Cong offensive, 1969 E
American and North Vietnamese withdrawal proposed, 1969 E
Laos, 1969 E, G, J, 1970 B
US withdrawal, 1969 F, L, 1970 D, 1971 D, L, 1972 H, 1973 C
Philippine troops recalled, 1969 K
My Lai massacre, 1969 L
North Vietnamese offensive in Laos, 1970 B
Viet Cong assaults on S. Vietnam, 1970 D
US–South Vietnamese offensive in Cambodia, 1970 D
anti-war demonstrators shot in US, 1970 E
Nixon proposes peace plan for Indo–China, 1970 K
N. Vietnam rejects peace plan, 1970 K
Ho Chi Minh Trail closed, 1971 B
S. Vietnam invades then withdraws from Laos, 1971 B
US Lieutenant sentenced for MyLai massacre, 1971 C
US combat death figures, 1971 D
Pentagon Papers published, 1971 F
Australia and New Zealand withdraw forces, 1971 H
US offensive role ends with troop withdrawal, 1971 L
Kissinger peace negotiations, 1972 A
Quang Tri offensive, 1972 C
US fleet attacked in Gulf of Tonkin, 1972 D
Quang Tri city falls and is recaptured, 1972 E
blockade and mining of North Vietnamese ports ordered, 1972 E
Korean withdrawal, 1972 J
ceasefire plan, 1972 K, L
US suspends all military action, 1973 A
Paris ceasefire agreement, 1973 A
first US prisoners of war released, 1973 B
last US prisoners of war released, 1973 C
second official ceasefire, 1973 F
Phuoc Province of S. Vietnam falls to N. Vietnamese, 1975 A
N. Vietnam forces capture Da Nang, 1975 C
US personnel flee embassy in Saigon, 1975 D
Saigon surrendered to Communist forces, 1975 D
Carter pardons draft evaders, 1977 A
Vietnamese withdrawal from Kampuchea, 1989 J
World War I (1914–18):
Political Events:
Austria–Hungary declares war on Serbia, 1914 G
on Russia, 1914 H
Germany declares war on Russia, 1914 H
on France, 1914 H
Britain declares war on Germany, 1914 H
Serbia and Montenegro declare war on Germany, 1914 H
France and Britain declare war on Austria, 1914 H
Russia declares war on Turkey, 1914 L
Britain and France declare war on Turkey, 1914 L
Italy declares war on Austria, 1915 E
on Turkey, 1915 H
Britain declares war on Bulgaria, 1915 K
Germany declares war on Portugal, 1916 C
Italy declares war on Germany, 1916 H
Turkey declares war on Russia, 1916 H
Roumania declares war on Austria, 1916 H
Bulgaria declares war on Roumania, 1916 J
Germany's peace note, 1916 M
President Wilson's peace note, 1916 M
Reichstag motion on peace talks, 1917 G
US declares war on Germany, 1917 D
on Austria, 1917 M
Cuba declares war on Germany, 1917 D
Brazil declares war on Germany, 1917 F
Greece severs connexion with Central Powers, 1917 F
China declares war on Germany and Austria, 1917 H
Soviets offer armistice, 1917 L, M
Peace of Brest-Litovsk, 1917 M
Roumania signs armistice with Central Powers, 1917 M
Ukraine signs peace with Central Powers, 1918 B
Roumania's peace treaty with Central Powers, 1918 E
Russia and US severs relations, 1918 H
Austro–Hungarian peace talk offer, 1918 J
Bulgaria signs armistice, 1918 J
Hindenburg's peace-offer, 1918 J
Germany and Austria make peace offer, 1918 K
agree to Wilson's terms, 1918 K
Turkey signs armistice, 1918 K
Allied armistice with Central Powers, 1918 L
Britain and France authorise resumption of relations with Germany, 1919 G
Wilson vetoes Knox peace resolution, 1920 E
Operations – Western Front:
Germany invades Belgium, 1914 H
battle of Mons, 1914 H
first battle of Marne, 1914 J
battle of Aisne, 1914 J
Antwerp surrenders, 1914 K
battle of Yser, 1914 K
first battle of Ypres, 1914 K
battle of Neuve Chapelle, 1915 C
second battle of Ypres, 1915 D
battle of St. Julien, 1915 D
Allies take Neuville, 1915 F
E. Cavell's execution, 1915 K
Haig succeeds French, 1915 M
battle of Berdun, 1916 B
Allies begin Somme offensive, 1916 G
tanks first used, 1916 J
German withdrawal, 1917 C
battle of Arras, 1917 D
battle of Vimy Ridge, 1917 D
Pétain becomes French C.-in-C., 1917 E
mutinies in French army, 1917 E
US troops land in France, 1917 F
third battle of Ypres (Passchendaele), 1917 G
second battle of Verdun, 1917 H
second battle of Somme, 1918 C
intensive German offensive, 1918 E
second battle of Marne, 1918 G
British offensive opens, 1918 H
Germans withdraw to Siegfried Line, 1918 J
British take Cambrai, 1918 K
Bruges is recaptured, 1918 K
Operations – Eastern Front:
Russians invade East Prussia, 1914 H
battle of Frankenau, 1914 H
German victory at Tannenberg, 1914 H
battle of Masurian Lakes, 1914 H
battle of Masurian Lakes, 1914 J
Russians invade Hungary, 1914 J
Russian break-through at Ivangorod, 1914 K
Germans take Lódz, 1914 M
second battle of Masuria, 1915 B
Russians evacuate East Prussia, 1915 B
German victory at Przemysl, 1915 F
Germans take Brest-Litovsk, 1915 H
Russians take Erzurum, 1916 B
Russian offensive checked, 1916 J
Kerensky's counter-attack, 1917 F
Russians break German line, 1917 G
armistice at Brest-Litovsk, 1917 M

Operations – Turkish Front:
Gallipoli landings, 1915 D
British defeat Turks at Kut-el-Amara, 1915 J
Allied landings at Salonika, 1915 K
battle of Ctesiphon, 1915 L
withdrawal of allies from Gallipoli, 1915 M
Turks take Kut-el-Amara, 1916 D
Arab revolt begins, 1916 F
Turks defeated at Gaza, 1917 C
British take Gaza and Jaffa, 1917 L
Australians occupy Jericho, 1918 B
collapse of Turkish army in Palestine, 1918 J
Allies take Beirut and Damascus, 1918 K
Operations – Italian Front:
Italians routed in Caporetto campaign, 1917 K
Operations – in Colonies:
Allied occupation of Togoland, 1914 H
Germans capitulate in New Guinea, 1914 J
de Wet's rebellion in S. Africa, 1914 K
S. Africans occupy Swakopmund, South West Africa, 1915 A
Botha occupies Windhoeck, 1915 E
Germans in South West Africa surrender, 1915 G
British take Dar-es-Salaam, 1916 J
German East Africa is cleared of German troops, 1917 M
Germans in N. Rhodesia surrender, 1918 L
Operations – at sea:
battle of Heligoland Bight, 1914 H
battle of Coronel, 1914 L
battle of Falkland Islands, 1914 M
Formidable sunk, 1915 A
Blücher sunk, 1915 A
S.S. Lusitania sunk, 1915 E
battle of Jutland, 1916 E
Hampshire sunk, 1916 F
Westfalen sunk, 1916 H
mutinies in German fleet, 1917 G
Breslau sunk, 1918 A
Zeebrugge raid, 1918 D
Germany mutiny at Kiel, 1918 L
Submarine warfare, German:
sinking without warning, 1915 A
sinkings of armed merchantmen, 1916 B
unrestricted warfare on neutrals, 1917 A
suspended, 1918 K
See also under Navies
Operations – in the air:
Zeppelin raids on London, first, 1915 F
on Paris, first, 1916 A
on English industrial areas, 1917 G
intensified, on London, 1917 J
See also under Air Forces
World War II (1939–45):
Political events:
Germany invades Poland, 1939 J
Britain and France declare war on Germany, 1939 J
Russia invades Poland, 1939 J
Russia invades Finland, 1939 L
Germany invades Norway and Denmark, 1940 D
Germany invades Holland and Britain, 1940 F
Italy declares war on France and Britain, 1940 F
France signs armistice with Germany and Italy, 1940 F
Russia invades Roumania, 1940 F
Vichy government breaks off relations with Britain, 1940 G
Britain aids Greece, 1940 K, 1941 D
Allies invade Iran, 1941 J
Britain declares war on Finland, 1941 M
on Hungary, 1941 M
on Roumania, 1941 M
Germany invades Russia, 1941 F
Hungary declares war on Russia, 1941 F
Finland invades Karelia, 1941 F
Japanese bomb Pearl Harbour, 1941 M
Britain and US declare war on Japan, 1941 M
US declares war on Germany and Italy, 1941 M
Allies pledge not to make separate peace, 1942 A
Second Front demonstrations, 1942 G
Italy surrenders to Allies, 1943 J
Italy declares war on Germany, 1943 K
Russia declares war on Bulgaria, 1944 J
Hungary signs armistice, 1945 A
Egypt declares war on Germany, 1945 B,
Germany capitulates, 1945 E
Japan capitulates, 1945 H, J
Russia decrees end of state of war with Germany, 1955 A
casualties, comparative, 1945 Y
See also under Conferences of Allied leaders
Early Campaigns:
fall of Poland, 1939 J
Russia's Finnish campaign, 1939 L, 1940 A, B
Germany's campaign in Norway and Denmark, 1940 D
Germany's campaign in Belgium, Holland and France, 1940 E
evacuation of Dunkirk, 1940 E
Germans enter PAris, 1940 F
Abyssinian campaign, 1940 H, 1941 A, D, E
British campaign in Greece, 1940 K, 1941 A, D
raids on Lofoten islands, 1942 C
St. Nazaire raid, 1942 C
Dieppe raid, 1942 H
North African Campaign:
British offensive under Wavell, 1940 M
German troops cross to N. Africa from Italy, 1941 B
German counter–offensive, 1941 C
British attack, 1941 L
British recapture Bardia, 1941 L
Benghazi, 1941 M
Rommel's offensive, 1942 A, E
British withdrawal, 1942 F
Rommel takes Tobruk, 1942 F
Eighth Army retreats to El Alamein, 1942 F
Alexander succeeds to C-in-C, 1942 H
Montgomery commands Eighth Army, 1942 H
battle of El Alamein, 1942 K
British take Tobruk, 1942 L
British re-occupy Benghazi, 1942 M
Eighth Army enters Tripoli, 1943 A
Eisenhower is appointed supreme allied commander, 1943 B
Montgomery breaks Mareth line, 1943 C
British and US armies link up, 1943 D
Von Arnim replaces Rommel, 1943 D
Allies take Tunis and Bizerta, 1943 E
German army in Tunisia surrenders, 1943 E
Italian Campaign:
Pantelleria surrenders to British, 1943 F
Allies land in Sicily, 1943 G
Allies occupy Palermo, 1943 G
Allies invade Italy, 1943 J
Italy surrenders, 1943 J
Naples falls, 1943 J
Italy declares war on Germany, 1943 K
Germans retire from Volturno River, 1943 K
Allies land at Nettuno and Anzio, 1944 A
Allies attack Monte Cassino, 1944 B, C, E
Allies attack Gustav line, 1944 E
Hitler line, 1944 E
Fifth Army enters Rome, 1944 F
Allies take Leghorn and Florence, 1944 G
Ravenna, 1944 M
Eighth Army reaches Salerno, 1945 D
Bologna falls, 1945 D
Allies reach river Po, 1945 D
Fifth Army takes Genoa and Verona, 1945 D
death of Mussolini, 1945 D
surrender of German army in Italy, 1945 E
Liberation of Europe:
'D' Day landings in Normandy, 1944 F
Cherbourg falls, 1944 F
US troops break through at Avranches, 1944 H
Allies land in French Riviera, 1944 H
Paris is liberated, 1944 H
Antwerp is liberated, 1944 J
Brussels is liberated, 1944 J
US troops cross into Germany, 1944 J
British airborne forces land at Eindhoven and Arnhem, 1944 J
Canadians reach river Maas, 1944 K
Antwerp is re-opened, 1944 L
Strasbourg falls, 1944 L
'Battle of the Bulge' in Ardennes, 1944 M, 1945 A
Allies take Colmar, 1945 B
British reach river Rhine, 1945 B
Cologne falls, 1945 C
US take Osnabrück and Hanover, 1945 D
Allies take Arnhem, 1945 D
Bremen surrenders, 1945 D
juncture of US and Russian forces at Torgau, 1945 D
Allies cross R. Elbe, 1945 D
death of Hitler, 1945 D
Allies enter Hamburg, 1945 D
Berlin surrenders, 1945 D
Jodl capitulates to Eisenhower, 1945 E
Russian Front:
Germany invades Russia, 1941 F
German offensives against Moscow, 1941 K, L, M
Timoshenko's counter-offensive, 1941 L
Leningrad is saved, 1941 M
Germans attack Kerch peninsula, 1942 E
German counter-offensive in Kharkov region, 1942 F
Germans take Rostov and overrun N. Caucasus, 1942 G
Germans reach Stalingrad, 1942 H
Russian counter-offensive from Stalingrad surrounds Germans, 1942 L
Germans withdraw from Caucasus, 1943 A
Russian victory at Voronezh, 1943 A
German defeat south-west of Stalingrad, 1943 A
Russians recapture Rostov and Kharkov, 1943 B
Russians evacuate Kharkov, 1943 L
German offensive at Kursk, 1943 G
Russians recapture Orel, 1943 H
Kharkov, 1943 H
Russians cross R. Dnieper, 1943 J
Russians recapture Smolensk, 1943 J
Kiev, 1943 L
Russians relieve Leningrad, 1944 A
Russians force R. Dniester, 1944 C
Russians enter Roumania, 1944 D
Russians recapture Sebastopol, 1944 E

Russians encircle Germans at Vitebsk, 1944 F
Russian offensive against Finland, 1944 F
Russians recapture Minsk, 1944 G
Russians cross 'Curzon line' 1944 G
Russians take Brest-Litovsk, 1944 G
Russians enter Bucharest, 1944 H
Finnish cease-fire, 1944 J
Russians invade Yugoslavia, 1944 J
Belgrade is liberated, 1944 K
Russians invade Hungary, 1944 K
Russians surround Budapest, 1944 M
Russian offensive in Silesia, 1945 A
Russians take Warsaw and Cracow, 1945 A
Russians reach R. Oder, 1945 A
Russians cross Austrian frontier, 1945 C
Russians reach Berlin, 1945 D
juncture of Russian and UN forces at Torgau, 1945 D
Berlin surrenders, 1945 E
von Keitel surrenders to Zhukov, 1945 E
Russians take Prague, 1945 E
Campaign in South East Asia:
Japanese invade Burma, 1942 A
Rangoon falls, 1942 C
Mandalay falls to Japanese,. 1942 E
British operations in Burma, 1942 M
Wingate's commandoes in Burma Jungle, 1943 D
British offensive, 1944 B
Japanese advance on Imphal, 1944 C
British capture Ukhrul, 1944 G
North Burma is cleared of Japanese, 1944 M
Fourteenth Army launches offensive, 1945 A
enters Mandalay, 1945 C
enters Rangoon, 1945 E
Campaign in Far East:
Japanese bomb Pearl Harbor, 1941 M
Japanese invade Dutch East Indies, 1942 A
Japanese invade Java, 1942 B
Singapore falls, 1942 B
US forces land in Guadalcanal, 1942 H
Japanese are driven from Guadalcanal, 1943 A
US landings in Aleutian Islands, 1943 E
in New Guinea, 1943 F
at Bougainville, 1943 L
US force occupies Makin, Gilbert Isles, 1943 L
US force recapture Solomon Isles, 1944 B
Allied landings in New Guinea, 1944 D
Saipan falls to US, 1944 F
US landings in Philippines, 1944 K
MacArthur enters Manila, 1945 B
air raids on Tokio, 1945 B
US force take Okinawa, 1945 D
Russia invades Manchuria, 1945 H
US drops atomic bombs, 1945 H
Japan surrenders, 1945 H
Japan signs capitulation, 1945 J
War at Sea:
S.S. *Athenia* sunk, 1939 J
Courageous sunk, 1939 J
Royal Oak sunk, 1939 K
magnetic mines, 1939 L
Graf Spee scuttled, 1939 M
Altmark incident. 1940 B
Germany's intensified U-boat warfare, 1940 K
S.S. *Empress of Britain* sunk, 1940 K
Jervis Bay sunk, 1940 L
Southampton and *Illustrious* sunk, 1941 A
Italian cruisers sunk off Cape Matapan, 1941 C
Hood sunk, 1941 E
Bismarck sunk, 1941 E
Ark Royal sunk, 1941 L
Barham sunk, 1941 L
Prince of Wales and *Repulse* sunk, 1941 M
British losses in Bay of Bengal, 1942 D
convoys to Russia, 1942 E, J, M
convoys to Malta, 1942 F, H
Eagle and *Manchester* sunk, 1942 H
Scharnhorst sunk, 1943 M
Tirpitz sunk, 1944 L
Germans use homing-torpedoes, 1945 A
naval battle off Kyushu, 1945 D
naval losses, 1945 Y
losses of merchant shipping, 1939 Y, 1940 Y, 1941 Y, 1942 Y, 1943 Y, 1944 Y, 1945 Y
See also under Navies
War in the Air:
R.A.F. begins night bombing of Germany, 1940 G
Battle of Britain, 1940 G, H, J
'Blitz' begins in Britain, 1940 J, L, 1941 E, 1943 A
heavy raids on London, etc., 1940 J, L, 1941 E, 1943 A
raid on Coventry, 1941 D
German 'Baedeker' raids, 1942 D
R.A.F. raids Cologne, 1942 E
R.A.F. first 1000–bomber raid, 1942 F
R.A.F. bombs European railway system, 1943 C
heavy raids on Berlin, 1944 A, D
flying bombs on London, 1944 F
V2 rockets in England, 1944 J, 1945 L
atomic bombs on Japan, 1945 H
See also under Air Forces
War Production, 1939 Y, 1940 Y, 1941 Y, 1942 Y, 1943 Y, 1944 N, Y
Warsaw, Poland:
Russians enter, 1794 L
Prussians take, 1975 K
French take, 1806 L
Napoleon enters, 1806 M
Duchy of, established, 1807 G
Austrians occupy, 1809 D
Russians take, 1831 J
rising in, 1848 E
massacre by Russian troops, 1861 B
Conservatory, 1909 T
Germans advance towards, 1914 J
battle for, 1914 K
Germans enter, 1915 H
Russians defeated at, 1920 H
Germans reach, 1939 J
rising, 1944 H
falls to Russians, 1945 A
Communist Conference at, 1947 K
Communist Youth Congress at, 1955 H
student demonstrations against political censorship, 1968 A
Solidarity blockades city centre, 1981 H
Warsaw Pact:
Albania leaves, 1968 J
statistics, 1968 Y
manoeuvres, 1981 C, J
leaders to agree to renew military alliance, 1985 D
Conference on Security and Cooperation in Europe, 1990 L
dissolution, 1990 L, 1991 C, G
Warships. *See under* Navies
Wartburg: Castle, frescoes at, 1854 S; Festival, 1817 K
Wartime (P. Fussell), 1989 Q
Warton, Thomas, B. author (1728–90), 1774 U, 1784 S
Was Ist Das Deutsche Vaterland? (E. Arndt), 1813 U
Washburn, J., Am. atomic physicist, 1932 P
Washing–machines, electric, invented, 1869 P; statistics of ownership, 1965 Y
Washington, D.C., US:
events:
is laid out, 1791 N
becomes seat of government, 1800 F, 1801 C
British burn, 1814 M
Treaty, fixes Oregon–Canada boundary, 1846 F
Peace convention, to attempt to preserve Union, 1861 B
Treaty between Britain and US, 1871 E
Conference on Samoa, 1887 F
Pan–American Conference, 1889 K
Treaty between US and Japan, 1911 B
Conference on disarmament, 1921 L, 1927 F
Treaty on Pacific, 1921 M
Treaty, on naval warfare, 1922 B
Treaty, to secure China's independence, 1922 B
Japan denounces, 1934 M
Canadian minister to, first appointed, 1926 L
Churchill visits, 1941 M
Vietnam War demonstrations, 1970 E, 1971 D
Watergate trial opens, 1973 A
Moslems seize buildings, 1977 C
assassination attempt on Reagan, 1981 C
US–USSR summit agrees to eliminate intermediate nuclear forces, 1987 M
buildings and institutions in:
Capitol, 1793 S, 1851 S
Carnegie Institution, Dept. of Terrestrial Magnetism, 1944 P
Catholic University, 1889 O
Folger Library, 1932 Q
Lincoln Memorial, 1917 S
National Gallery of Art, 1937 S, 1978 S
Observatory, observations from, 1877 P
White House, The, 1792 S
Washington, George, Am. soldier and statesman, Federalist (1732–99), first president of US (1789–97), 1785 S, 1799 Z; appointed C.-in-C. of American forces, 1775 F; as general, 1776 C, M, 1777 A, K, 1778 F, 1781 J; at Philadelphia Convention 1787 E; inaugurated president, 1789 D; farewell address, 1796 J
Washington, Harold, Am. Mayor of Chicago (1922–87), 1983 D
Washington State,US, created a US state, 1889 B
Washkansky, Louis, S. Afr. transplant patient (d. 1967), 1967 P
Waste Land, The (T. S. Eliot), 1922 U
Waste Land, The: A Facsimile and Transcript of the Original Drafts (V. Eliot ed.),1971 Q
Waste, radio-active, disposal of, 1954 P, 1955 P, 1956 P
Waste-Makers, The (V. Packard), 1959 O
Watch, self-winding, 1922 P
Water closet, Bramah's, 1778 P
Water skiing, 1958 X
Water Babies, The (C.Kingsley), 1863 U
Water:
compound nature of, discovered, 1784 P
electrolysed, 1932 P
sterilised by ultra-violet rays, 1912 P
Watergate affair, 1972 F, 1973 A, D, F, K, 1974 D, G, H, 1975 A, 1977 O
Waterland (G. Swift), 1984 U
Waterloo, battle of, 1815 F
Watership Down (R. Adams), 1973 U

Watkins, Henry George (Gino), B. explorer (1907–30), 1927 P
Watkinson, Harold, Lord Watkinson, B. Conservative (b. 1910), dismissed from cabinet, 1962 G
Watson, James Dewey, Am. scientist (b. 1928), 1968 P
Watson, Joshua, B. philanthropist (1771–1855), 1811 O
Watson, Richard, B. Methodist minister (1781–1833), 1796 R
Watson-Watt, Sir Robert, B. physicist (1892–1973), 1892 Z, 1935 P, 1973 Z
Watson-Wentworth, Charles, Marquess of Rockingham, B. Tory premier (1730–82), 1765 G, 1766 G, 1782 C, G
Watt, James, B. engineer (1736–1819), 1765 P, 1775 P, 1785 P, 1807 P, 1819 Z
Watts, Sir George Frederick, B. artist (1817–1904), 1817 Z, 1904 Z
Waugh, Evelyn, B. novelist (1903–66), 1903 Z, 1930 U, 1945 U, 1952 U, 1976 U
Wave Mechanics, 1924 P
Wavell, Archibald, Lord Wavell, B. soldier (1883–1950), 1883 Z, 1940 M, 1941 A, D, G
Waverley (W. Scott), 1814 U
Waverley Committee, on export of works of art, 1952 S
Waves, electrical, magnetic detection of, 1896 P
waves, radio, 1902 P, 1955 P. *See also under* Wireless
waves, ultra-high-frequency, 1955 P
Way of All Flesh, The (S. Butler), 1903 U
Way of an Eagle, The (E. M. Dell), 1912 U
Wayne, John (born Marion Morrison), Am. film actor (1907–79), 1907 Z, 1939 W, 1952 W, 1959 W, 1979 Z
Ways of Worldmaking (N. Goodman), 1978 R
We Believe in God report, Doctrine Commission of the Church of England, 1987 R
Wealth (E. Cannan), 1914 Q
Wealth of Nations, The (A. Smith), 1776 O
Weather forecasting. *See* Meteorology
Weather: Abnormally dry, 1959 Q; extreme cold, 1963 P
Weaver, James Baird, Am. Populist (1833–1912), stands as presidential candidate, 1892 G, L
Weaver, Robert, A. statesman (b. 1907), 1966 A
Webb, Sir Aston, B. architect (1849–1930), 1849 Z, 1905 S
Webb, Beatrice, Lady Passfield (née Potter), B. Socialist and author (1858–1943), 1858 Z, 1894 O, 1897 O, 1913 V, 1926 O, 1935 O, 1943 Z
Webb, Clement Charles, John, B. philosopher (1865–1954), 1945 R
Webb, Mary Gladys, B. author (1881–1927), 1917 U, 1924 U
Webb, Sidney, Lord Passfield, B. Socialist and author (1859–1947), 1894 O, 1897 O, 1913 V, 1935 O
Weber, A., 1956 O
Weber, Carl Maria von, G. musician (1786–1826), 1786 Z, 1811 T, 1821 T, 1823 T, 1826 T, Z, 1838 W
Weber, Ernst Heinrich, G. anatomist (1795–1878), 1825 P
Webe, Max, G. economist (1864–1920), 1901 Q
Weber, Wilhelm Edward, G. physicist (1804–91), 1825 P, 1833 P
Webern, Anton, Aus. musician (1883–1945), 1924 T
Webster, Daniel, Am. lawyer and Diplomat (1782–1852), 1802 O, 1830 A, 1842 H
Webster, Noah, Am. lexicographer (1758–1843), 1828 Q
Wedekind, Franz, G. author (1864–1918), 1864 Z, 1891 U, 1907 W, 1918 Z
Wedgwood, Josiah, B. potter (1730–95), 1769 P, 1775 S, 1795 Z
Wedgwood, Thomas, B. photographer (1771–1805), 1802 P
Wegener, Anton, G. geographer, 1915 P
Wegscheider, Julius August Ludwig, G. theologian (1771–1849), 1815 R
Wei-hai-we, China: Japanese victory at, 1895 B; is leased to Britain, 1898 C; Britain restores to China, 1930 K
Weil, Kurt, G. musician (1900–50), 1928 T
Weimar, Germany: Herder at, 1775 U; theatre at, under Goethe, 1791 W; German national assembly at, authorises signing of Versailles Treaty, 1919 F; Republican Constitution agreed at, 1919 G
Weinberg, Steven, Am. physicist (b. 1933), 1967 P
Weinberger, Jaromir, Czech. musician (1896–1967), 1927 T, 1937 T
Weiner, Edmund Simon Christopher, B. lexicographer (b. 1950), 1989 Q
Weir of Hermiston, The (R. L. Stevenson), 1896 U
Weir, Judith, B. musician (b. 1954), 1987 T, 1990 T
Weiss, Ernst, Hun. magician under pseudonym of 'Houdini' (1874–1936), 1936 Z
Weissenburg, Germany: French victory at, 1793 M; MacMahon defeated by Prussians at, 1870 H
Weissmuller, Johnny, Am. swimmer and actor (1904–84), 1904 Z, 1927 X, 1984 Z
Weizmann, Chaim, president of Israel (1874–1952)., 1948 E, 1952 M
Welding, friction 1963 P
Weldon, Walter, B. chemist (1832–85), 1870 P
Welensky, Sir Roy (Roland), Rhodesian (b. 1907), premier of Central African Federation, 1956 K
Welfare centre, infants', 1903 O
Welle, Congo, revolt in, 1905 B
Welles, Orson, Am. actor and director (1915–85), 1941 W, 1943 W, 1949 W, 1952 W, 1958 W, 1962 W
Welles, Sumner, Am. statesman (1892–1961), 1892 Z, 1944 O, 1961 Z
Wellesley, Arthur, Duke of Wellington, B. soldier and Tory statesman (1769–1852), 1769 Z, 1809 D, 1814 C, 1828 D, 1832 E, 1852 A
in India, 1803 J, 1805 B
wins battle of Vimeiro, 1808 H
wins battle of Talavera, 1809 G
created duke, 1809 G
defeats Soult at Oporto, 1809 E
holds lines of Torres Vedras, 1810 K
defeats Marmont, 1812 G
enters Madrid, 1812 H
at Fuentes d'Onoro, 1911 E
wins battle of Vittoria, 1913 P
invades France, 1813 K
defeats Napoleon at Waterloo, 1815 F
at Verona Congress, 1822 K
becomes premier, 1828 A
duel with Winchilsea, 1829 C
resigns, 1830 L
Wellesley, Richard Colley, Marquess of Wellesley, B. and Tory (1760–1842), as governor-general of India, 1798 E
as foreign secretary, 1812 C
Wellington, Duke of. See Wellesley, Arthur
Wellington, New Zealand, supplants Auckland as capital, 1865 N
wins Olympic 100 metres gold, 1980 X
Wells, Herbert George, B. author (1866–1946), 1866 Z, 1895 U, 1897 U, 1898 U, 1905 U, 1909 U, 1910 U, 1911 U, 1920 Q, 1964 Z
Wells, Stanley William, B. literary scholar (b. 1930), 1986 Q
Welsbach, C. A. von G. inventor of gas mantle (1858–1929), 1886 P
Welty, Eudora, Am. author (b. 1909), 1970 U, 1972 U
Welwyn Garden City, Herts., England, 1920 O
Wembley, Middlesex, England: Cup Final at, 1923 X; Empire Exhibition at, 1924 W
Wenders, Wim. G. film director (b. 1945), 1976 W, 1984 W, 1987 W
Wenzel, Karl Friedrich, G. metallurgist (1740–93), 1777 P
Werfel, Franz, Czech. author (1890–1945), 1941 U
Werner, Abraham Gottlob, G.geologist (1750–1817), 1775 P
Wertenbaker, Timberlake, Am.-born B. playwright, 1988 W
Werth, Alexander, B. author and journalist (1901–69), 1964 Q
Wesker, Arnold, B. playwright (b. 1932), 1932 Z, 1959 W, 1960 W, 1962 W, 1981 W
Wesley, John, B. evangelist, founder of Methodism (1703–91), 1771 R; signs Methodist deedof declaration, 1784 R; *Sermons,* 1787 R
Wessex Poems (T. Hardy), 1898 U
West Africa States, Union of, proposed, 1958 L
West Africa, Archbishop of, expelled from Ghana, 1962 H
West Africa, British, Colony formed from lands of former African Company, 1821 E
West Africa, French, re-organised, 1904 N
West Bank, Israeli action against Palestinians criticized by UN, 1987 M
West Indian Island, sold by Denmark to US, 1919 H
West Indies Federation, British: federation in force, 1958 A; Jamaican referendum to secede from 1961 J; federation ends, 1962 D; 'Little Eight' propose to form new federation, 1962 E
West Indies: US trade with, closed down by Britain, 1805 N; Coffee production in, 1909 Y
West Point, New York, US, fort, plot to surrender, 1780 L
West Virginia, created a US state, 1863 F
West, Benjamin, B. artist (1738–1820), 1771 S, 1803 S
West, Dame Rebecca (born Cicily Isabel Fairfield), B. author (1892–1983), 1892 Z, 1941 U,1983 Z
West, Mae, Am. actress (1892–1980), 1892 Z, 1933 W, 1980 Z
Westcott, Brooke Foss, B. churchman and New Testament Scholar (1825–1901), 1881 Q
Western Aristocracies and Imperial Court, A.D. 364–425 (J. Matthews), 1975 Q
Western Australia: representative government in, 1870 H; responsible government in, 1890 K
Western European Union, France ends boycott of, 1970 F
Westinghouse Company, US, 1920 W
Westinghouse, George, Am. inventor (1846–1914), 1846 Z, 1868P, 1888 P, 1914 Z
'Westland affair', 1986 A
Westmoreland, William Childs, Am. soldier (b. 1914), 1968 F
West-östlicher Divan (Goethe), 1819 U

Westphalia, Germany, Kingdom of, under Jerome Bonaparte, 1807 H
Westward Ho! (C. Kingsley), 1854 U
Wet, Christian Rudolph de, Boer general (1854–1922), 1901 B; rebels, 1914 K, 1915 F, M
Wetherald, R. T., scientist, 1967 P
Wette, Wilhelm Martin Leberecht de, G. theologian (1780–1849), 1806 Q
Weyman, Stanley John, B. novelist (1855–1928), 1855 Z, 1894 U, 1928 Z
Weyprecht, Karl, Aus. explorer (1838–81), 1873 P
Whaam (R. Lichtenstein), 1967 S
Whale, The (J. Tavener), 1968 T
Whaling:
  Greenpeace members detained in Siberia, 1983 G
  International Whaling Commission bans commeercial whaling, 1985 O
Wharton, Edith (née Jones), Am. author (1862–1937), 1862 Z, 1905 U, 1911 U, 1913 U, 1937 Z
What is Philosophy? (Heidegger), 1929 R
What the Butler Saw (J. Orton), 1969 W
What's Bred in the Bone (R. Davies), 1987 U
Wheat:
  international agreement, 1933 H, 1959 C
  world shortage, 1946 G
  See also under Corn Laws
Wheatstone, Sir Charles, B. inventor and makere of musical instruments (1802–75), 1829 T
Wheeler, Sir Charles, B. sculptor (b. 1892), 1924 S
Wheeler, Sir Mortimer, B. archaeologist (1890–1976), 1954 Q
Wheeler-Bennett, Sir John, B. historian (1902–75), 1934 O, 1953 Q, 1958 Q
When I was a Girl I used to Scream and Shout (S. Macdonald), 1984 W
Whewell, William, B. moral philosopher (1774–1858), 1840 P, 1846 R
Whigs and Hungers (E.P. Thompson), 1975 Q
Whigs. *See under* Political Parties
Whinfield, J. R., Am. inventor of Terylene, 1941 P
Whipsnade, Beds., England, Zoo, 1931 O
Whispering Gallery, The (J. Lehmann), 1955 U
Whistler, James, Abbott McNeill, B. artist (1834–1903), 1863 S, 1871 S, 1886 S
Libel action with Ruskin, 1878 S
Whistler, Reginald John (Rex), B. artist (1905–44), 1927 S, 1930 S, 1936 S, 1940 S, 1957 S
White Doe of Rylstone (W. Wordsworth), 1815 U
White Hotel, The (D.M. Thomas), 1981 U
White House Papers of Harry L. Hopkins, 1948 Q
White Lotus Society, China, 1774 N
White Monkey, The (J. Galsworthy), 1924 U
White Peacock, The (D. H. Lawrence), 1911 U
White Sand, Red Millett, Many Flowers (A. Kapoor), 1982 S
White Slave trade, Conference on, 1904 O
White Terror, in France, 1815 G
White, Edmund, Am. author (b. 1940), 1982 U
White, Edward, Am. astronaut (1930–67), walks in space, 1965 P
White, Sir George,, B. soldier (1835–1911), Joubert defeats, 1899 K
White, Gilbert, B. naturalist (1720–93), 1789 P, 1793 Z
White Patrick Victor Martindale, Aust. author (1912–90), 1912 Z, 1957 U, 1966 U, 1973 U, 1976 U, 1980 U, 1990 Z
White, Terence, Hamburg, B. author (1906 64), 1958 U
White, Theodore Harold, Am. author (1915–86), 1962 O
White, William Hale, B. novelist under pseudonym of 'Mark Rutherford' (1829–1913), 1888 U, 1893 U
Whitehead, Alfred North, B. mathematician and philosopher (1861–1947), 1861 Z, 1910 R, 1925 P, 1933 P, 1947 Z
Whitehead, Sir Edgar Cuthbert, Rhodes, United Federal Party leader (1905–71), 1958 B, 1962 M
Whitehead, Robert, B. inventor (1823–1905), 1864 P
Whitehouse, Mary, B. campaigner (b. 1910), 1977 O
Whitelaw, William Stephen Ian, Lord Whitelaw (b. 1918), B. Conservative politician
  Secretary of State for Northern Ireland, 1972 C, G, J
  Secretary of State for Employment, 1973 M
  speech to House as Home Secretary, 1980 O
Whiteman, Paul, Am. band-leader (1890–1967), 1920 W
Whiteread, Rachel, B. artist, 1988 S, 1990 S
Whitlam, Edward Gough, Prime Minister of Australia (b. 1916), 1972 M, 1975 L
Whitman, Walt, Am. poet (1819–92), 1819 Z, 1855 U, 1866 U, 1871 U, 1892 Z
Whitney, Eli, Am. inventor (1765–1825), 1765 Z, 1793 P, 1800 P
Whitney, John, B. dramatist (1904–82), 1951 W
Whitsun Weddings, The (P. Larkin), 1964 U
Whittam-Smith, Andreas (b. 1937), B. journalist, 1986 V
Whittier, John Greenleaf, Am. poet (1807–92), 1846 U, 1862 U, 1890 U
Whittle, Sir Frank, B. aeronautical engineer (b. 1907). 1907 Z, 1937 P
Who's Afraid of Virginia Woolf? (E. Albee), 1962 W
Who, The, B. pop group, 1969 W, 1979 W
Whose Body? (D. L. Sayers), 1923 U
Whose Justice? Which Rationality? (A. MacIntyre), 1988 R
Whose Life is it Anyway (B. Clark), 1978 W
Whymper, Edward, B. mountaineer (1840–1911), 1840 Z, 1865 X, 1911 Z
Whyte, William Hollingsworth, Jr., Am. author (b. 1917), 1956 O
Widdowson, John David Allison, B. linguistic scholar (b. 1935), 1977 Q
Wide Sargasso Sea, The (J. Rhys), 1966 U
Widgery Report, on 'Bloody Sunday', 1972 D
Widowers' Houses (G. B. Shaw), 1892 W
Widows (A. Dorfman), 1983 U
Wie die Alten den Tod gebildet (Lessing), 1769 U
Wieck, Dorothea, G. film actress, 1931 W
Wieland, Christopher Martin, G. author (1733–1813), 1765 U, 1766 U, 1771 I, 1773 V, 1774 U, 1780 U
Wieland; or the Transformation (C. Brockden Brown), 1798 U
Wiener, Martin J., Am. historian (b. 1941), 1981 Q
Wilberforce Commission, on miners' pay, 1972 B
Wilberforce, Samuel, B. churchman (1805–73), 1852 R
Wilberforce, William, B. anti-slavery leader and philanthropist (1759–1833), 1797 R
Wild Duck, The (H. Ibsen), 1884 W
Wild Swans (Jung Chang), 1992 U
Wild life, African, conference for preservation, 1961 P
Wilde, Oscar O'Flahertie Willis, B. author (1856–1900), 1856 Z, 1882 S, 1891 U, 1892 W, 1893 W, 1895 U, 1898 U, 1905 U; trial, 1895 P; tomb of, 1911 S
Wilder, Billy, Am. film director (b. 1906), 1945 W, 1950 W, 1963 W
Wilder, Thornton Niven dramatist (1897–1975), 1927 W, 1938 W, 1967 U
Wilderness, The, Virginia, US battle, 1864 E
Wiles, Maurice Frank, B. theologian (b. 1923), 1974 R
Wilhelm Meister (Goethe), 1795 U
Wilhelm Meisters Wanderjahre (Goethe), 1821 U
Wilhelm Tell (F. Schiller), 1804 W
Wilhelmina, Princess of Orange, consort of William V, 1786 H, 1787 F
Wilhelmina, Queen of Netherlands (1890–1948), 1890 L, 1948 J, 1962 Z
Wilhelmsthal, E. Africa, Smuts captures, 1916 F
Wilkes, John, B. Radical (1727–97), 1763 D, L, 1764 A, B, 1768 C, E, 1769 A, B, 1782 E, 1787Z
  elected lord mayor of London, 1774 L
Wilkes, Dr. Kathleen, B. philosopher (b. 1946), expelled from Czechoslovakia, 1980 R
Wilkie, Sir David, B. artist (1785–1841), 1785 Z, 1800 S, 1841 Z
Wilkie, Wendell, Am. Republican (1892–1944), opposes Roosevelt in presidential election 1940 L
Wilkins, Hugh Percival, B. astronomer (b. 1896), 1956 P
Wilkins, William, B. architect (1778–1839), 1832 S
Wilkinson, John, B. engineer (1728–1808), 1774 P
Willard, Jess, Am. boxer (1881–1968), 1919 X
Willford, Michael, architect, 1987 S
William Beveridge: A Biography (J. Harris), 1977 Q
William I of Holland (1772–40), as King of United Netherlands, 1828 G, accepts treaty of London on Belgian independence, 1839 D; abdicates, 1840 K
William I, King of Prussia (1861–71), emperor of Germany (1871–88), as regent, 1858 K; accession, 1861 A; proclaimed emperor at Versailles, 1871 A; death, 1888 C
William II, emperor of Germany (1888–1918), (b. 1859, d. 1941), 1888 K, 1900 K, 1910 L
  accession, 1888 F
  dismisses Bismarck, 1890 C
  meets Alexander II at Narva, 1890 H
  visits England, 1891 G, 1895 H, 1899 L, 1901 A
  sends 'Kruger Telegram', 1896 A
  visits Tangier, 1905 C
  signs treaty of mutual aid with Russia, 1905 G
  dismisses Holstein, 1906 D
  meets Nicholas II, 1907 H
  Daily Telegraph interview, 1908 K, L
  speaks on Germany's place in the sun, 1911 H
  Socialists attack, 1912 E
  promises universal suffrage, 1917 D
  abdicates, 1918 L
  Holland refuses to surrender, 1920 A
William III, King of Holland (1840–9), 1840 K, 1848 C
William IV, King of Great Britain and Ireland (1830–7), accession, 1830 F, 1834 X, 1837 F; forces Grey's resignation, 1832 E; agrees to create Whig peers, 1832 F; as King of Hanover, 1833 J
William Lovell (L. Tieck), 1795 U
William Shakespeare (R. W. Chambers), 1930 Q

William Shakespeare: The Complete Works (S. Wells, G. Taylor eds.), 1986 Q
William V, Prince of Orange (1748–1806), deposed from command of army, 1786 N; in England, 1795 J; restored, 1797 J; second restoration, 1813 L
William, Prince of Denmark (1856–1913), becomes King of Greece, 1863 C
Williams, Bernard Arthur Owen, B. philosopher (b. 1929), 1985 R
Williams, David, B. dissenting minister (1738–1816), 1790 U
Williams, Emlyn, B. dramatist and actor (1905–87), 1935 W, 1938 W
Williams, Eric Eustace, Trinid. politician (1911–81), 1961 M
Williams, Raymond Henry, B. critic (1921–88), 1961 O
Williams, Shirley, Lady Williams of Crosby, B. Labour/SDP/Liberal Democrat politician (b. 1930), 1981 L
'Limehouse Declaration', 1981 A
Williams, Tennessee (born Thomas Lanier Williams), Am. playwright (1911–83), 1944 W, 1947 W, 1954 W, 1956 W, 1983 Z
Williamson, David Keith, Austral. playwright (b. 1942), 1971 W, 1979 W
Williamson, Henry, B. author (1895–1977), 1895 Z1977 Z
Williamson, Malcolm, B. musician (b. 1933), 1965 T
Wills, Helen, A, lawn-tennis player (b. 1905), 1927 X
Willstätter, Richard, G. chemist (1872–1942), 1913 P
Wilmot, David, Am. politician (1814–65), introduces proviso on slavery, 1846 H
Wilson, Allan, N. Zeal.-born Am. geneticist, 1984 P
Wilson, Sir Angus Frank Johnstone, B. author (1913–91), 1913 Z, 1952 U, 1956 U, 1958 U, 1986 W, 1991 Z
Wilson, Sir Charles, B. soldier and archaeologist (1836–1905), 1886 Q
Wilson, Charles McMoran, Lord Moran, B. medical practitioner (1882–1977), 1945 O
Wilson, Sir Charles Rivers, B. financier and civil servant (1831–1916), 1878 H
Wilson, Charles Thomas Rees, B. inventor (1879–1956), 1903 P
Wilson, Charles, B. mail-train robber, escapes, 1964 H
Wilson, Colin Henry, B. author (b. 1931), 1956 R
Wilson, Daniel, F., son-in-law of Jules Grévy, scandals connected with, 1887 K, M
Wilson, David Clive, Lord Wilson of Tillyorn (b. 1935), B. Governor of Hong Kong, 1992 G
Wilson, Edmund, Am. author (1895–1972), 1941 O
Wilson, Horace Hayam, B. orientalist (1786–1860), 1819 Q
Wilson, James Harold, Lord Wilson of Rievaulx, B. Labour Party leader (b. 1916), 1916 Z, 1967 B, 1970 F; resigns from Attlee's cabinet, 1951 D; unsuccessful candidate for leadership of Parliamentary Labour Party, 1960 K; defeated in election for deputy leadership, 1962 L; elected leader of Labour Party, 1963 B; forms ministry, 1964 K; states Rhodesian UDI would be open act of defiance, 1964 K; meets L. B. Johnson, 1964 M
British EC membership, 1966 L, 1967 A
Tiger talks on Rhodesia, 1966 M
Smith–Wilson on Rhodesia problem, 1966 M, 1968 K, L
takes direct command of Department of Economic Affairs, 1967 H
radical reform of Upper House promised, 1968 F
talks with General Gowon, 1969 C
Irish unification proposal, 1971 L
repudiates nationalization plans, 1973 F
announces social contract with TUC, 1974 B
forms minority Labour government, 1974 C
condemns National Industrial Relations Court, 1974 E
alleges S. African participation in Thorpe scandal, 1976 C
resignation, 1976 C
resignation Honours List, 1976 E
alleged plot against, 1977 G
confirms coup reports, 1981 C
Wilson, John, B. journalist (1785–1854), under pseudonym of 'Christopher North', 1817 V
Wilson, Lanford, Am. playwright (b. 1937), 1987 W
Wilson, Monica, S. Afr. anthropologist (1908–82), 1969 Q
Wilson, Patrick, Ir. politician, 1973 F
Wilson, Richard, B. artist (1715–82), 1782 Z
Wilson, Sandy, B. composer (b. 1924), 1954 W
Wilson, William Lyne, Am. Confederate soldier and Democrat (1843–1900), 1894 H
Wilson, Woodrow, Am. statesman, Democrat (1856–1924), 27th president of US (1913–21), 1856 Z, 1914 D, 1920 E, 1924 Z
nominated, 1912 G
wins presidential election, 1912 L
inaugurated, 1913 L
vetoes immigration bill, 1915 A
re-elected, 1916 L
declaration of war on Germany, 1917 B, C, D
propounds Fourteen Points, 1918 A
suggests peace terms, 1918 K
attends Versailles Peace Conference, 1918 M
lays League Covenant before Peace Conference, 1919 B
presides at first League of Nations meeting, 1919 B
vetoes Volstead Act on prohibition, 1919 K
vetoes Knox peace proposals, 1920 E
awarded Nobel Peace prize, 1920 M
Wimbledon Championship, Surrey, England, All-England lawn tennis championships, 1877 X, 1968 X
Winchilsea, Earl of. See Finch-Hatton, George
Winckelmann, Johann Joachim, G. archaeologist (1717–68), 1764 Q, 1767 Q
Winckler, Hugo, G. archaeologist (1863–1913), 1906 Q
Wind and the Rain, The (M. Hodge), 1933 W
Wind in the Willows (K. Grahame), 1908 E
Windhoek, South-west Africa, Botha occupies, 1915 E
Windischgratz, Prince Alfred, Aust. (1787–1862), 1848 F, K
Window in Tahiti, Homage to Matisse (C. Viallat), 1976 S
Window in Thrums (J. M. Barrie), 1889 U
Window tax, abolished, 1851 G
Windowless building, 1963 S
Winds of War, The, television programme, 1983 W
Windscale, Cumbria, England: see Sellafield
Windsor Great Park, England, pop festival, 1974 H
Windsor, Berkshire, England:
Castle, royal apartments in, 1824 S
statue at, 1869 S
fire, 1992 L
Treaty, between Britain and Portugal, 1899 K
Windsor, House of, British royal family adopt name, 1917 F
Windsor, duke of. *See under* Edward VIII
Wine industry, French, crisis in, 1906 N
Wine-growers, French, aided, 1900 G
Winesburg, Ohio (S. Anderson), 1919 T
Wingate, Orde Charles, B. soldier (1903–44), 1943 D
Wingate, Sir Reginald, B. soldier (1861–1953), 1899 L
Wingfield, Walter Clapton, B. inventor of Lawn Tennis (1833–1912), 1874 Y
Winnie the Pooh (A. A. Milne), 1926 U
Winnipeg, Manitoba, Canada: Riel's rebellion near, 1869 K; strike in, 1919 E
Winslow Boy, The (T. Rattigan), 1946 W
Winsor, Kathleen, Am. author, 1945 U
Winter, Jay Murray, Am.-born B. historian (b. 1945), 1985 Q, 1988 Q
'Winter of Discontent', B., 1979 A
Wireless telegraphy: Marconi invents, 1895 P; trans-Atlantic messages, 1901 P
Wireless, waves, studies in, 1902 P
Wireless-valves, all-metal, 1933 P
Wireless:
first transmission of speech by, 1900 P
broadcasting by amateurs, 1919 W
medium wave broadcasts, 1921 P
2LO broadcasts in Britain, 1922 W
licences issued in Britain, statistics, 1925 Y, 1930 Y, 1940 Y
Conference on re-distribution of wave-lengths, 1948 P
See also under Broadcasting; B.B.C.
Wirth, Karl Joseph, G. Centre Party leader (1879–1943), becomes Chancellor, 1921 E
Wirth, Niklaus, Swi. scientist (b. 1934), 1971 P
Wisconsin, state, US: becomes a US state, 1848 E; adopts women's suffrage, 1912 L
Wise Children (A. Carter), 1991 U
Wise, Thomas, James, B. collector of manuscripts (1859–1937), 1948 Q
Wiseman, Nicholas Patrick Stephen, B. cardinal (1802–65), 1802 Z, 1865 Z
Witchcraft, legislation against, 1951 R
Within the Gates (O. Casey), 1934 W
Witos, Vincent, Pol. Peasants' Party leader (1874–1945), 1926 E
Witte, Sergei, Count, R. statesman (1849–1915), as finance minister, 1892 J, 1903 H; becomes premier, 1905 L; falls, 1906 E
Wittgenstein, Ludwig, B. philosopher (1889–1951), 1922 R, 1958 R
Wizard of Earthsea, A (U. Le Guin), 1968 U
Wodehouse, John, Earl of Kimberley, B. Liberal (1826–1902), 1896 K
Wodehouse, Sir Pelham Grenville, B. author (1881–1975), 1881 Z, 1925 U, 1975 Z
knighted, 1975 U
Woëvre Plain, Belgium, French offensive near, 1916 M
Wöhler, Friedrich, G. chemist (1800–82), 1800 Z, 1827 P, 1828 P, 1862 P, 1882 Z
Wojtiyla, Karol, Pol. Archbishop. *See* John Paul II, Pope
Wolf, Friedrichc Augustus, G. philosopher (1759–1824), 1795 Q, 1807 Q, 1824 Z
Wolf, Hugo, Aus. musician (1860–1903), 1860 Z, 1888 T, 1894 Tm 1896 T, 1903 Z
Wolf-Ferrari, Ermanno, It. musician (1876–1948), 1911 T
Wolfe, Thomas Kennedy, 'Tom', Am. author (b. 1931), 1980 U, 1981 S
Wolfe, Thomas, Am. author (1900–38), 1929 U

Wolfenden Report on homosexual offences and prostitution, 1975 J
Wolff, Sir Henry Drummond Charles, B. Conservative (1830–1908), 1880 E, 1887 E
Wolff, Michael, B. historian (b. 1930), 1973 Q
Wolfram, Spanish exports to Germany, reduced, 1944 E
Wollaston, William Hyde, B. scientist (1766–1828), 1804 P
Wollstonecraft, Mary, B. political author (1759–1797), 1792 O
Wolseley, Garnet, Lord Wolseley, B. soldier (1833–1913), 1833 Z, 1874 B, 1882 J, 1913 Z
Wolverhampton, Staffs., England, riots in, 1874 B
Woman in Bed (J. De Andrea), 1975 S
Woman in White, The (W. Collins), 1860 U
Woman of No Importance, A (O. Wilde), 1893 W
Women:
  Jockey club allows women to be licensed racehorse trainers, 1966 X
  Jockey club allows women to participate in horse races, 1972 X
  one-day strike of women in Iceland, 1975 K
  protest at Greenham Common air base, 1982 M, 1984 D
  UN Decade for Women, 1985 G
  Britain found guilty of sex discrimination in immigration policy, 1985 O
  Japan removes restrictions on women's work, 1985 O
  Californian law obliging employers to grant pregnancy leave upheld, 1987 O
  separate taxation of married women in Britain, 1990 O
  allowed to succeed to Belgian throne, 1991 O
  franchise. *See* Franchise
Women, achievements of:
  first British magistrate, 1913 E
  first British M.B., 1919 L
  first British prime miniser, 1979 E
  first High Court Judge, 1965 O
  first leader of major British union, 1984 O
  first Minister in Church of Scotland, 1969 R
  first prime minister of Norway, 1981 B
  first Privy Councillor, 1929 O
  first US woman in space, 1983 P
  first vice-presidential candidate in US, 1984 G
  first woman artist in residence at Oxford University, 1979 S
  first woman bishop in US Episcopal Church, 1988 R
  first woman Director of Public Prosecutions, 1992 O
  first woman in space, 1963 P
  first woman justice of US Supreme Court, 1981 J
  first woman member of US Congress, 1916 L
  first woman preacher in England, 1917 R
  first woman premier of Commonwealth, 1960 G
  first woman president of Eire, 1990 L
  first woman speaker of British House of Commons, 1992 O
  first woman to represent US at Venice Biennale, 1990 S
  first women priests in Australia, 1992 R
  first women priests in US Episcopal Church, 1977 A
  first woman state governor in US, 1925 A
  first woman to climb Matterhorn north wall, 1965 Z
  first women's Cricket World Cup, 1973 X
  first women's cricket match at Lord's, 1976 X
  first women's races at Henley regatta, 1979 X
Women, enfranchisement of:
  advocated, 1869 O
  in Australia, 1902 G
  in Belgium, 1948 O
  in Britain, bills for, rejected, 1912 C, 1914 E, 1915 A
    Bow by-election, on issue of, 1912 L
    gain vote at age of 30, 1918 O
    first woman M.P., 1919 L
    Lady Rhondda attempts to take seat in Lords, 1922 O
    gain vote at age of 21, 1928 E
    See also Suffragettes
  in Denmark, 1915 F
  in France, 1945 O
  in Germany, 1919 O
  in Italy, 1946 O
  in Liechtenstein, 1986 O
  in New Zealand, 1893 O
  Norway, 1907 F
  in South Africa, for white women, 1930 E
  in Switzerland, ineligible to vote in federal elections, 1959 B
  in Turkey, 1929 M, 1934 M
  in US, in Wyoming, 1869 O
    in Arizona, Kansas and Wisconsin, 1912 L
    achieved by 19th Amendment, 1920 H
Women, equal pay for, proposed in Britain, 1946 L
Women Journalists, Society of, 1844 V
Women in Love (D. H. Lawrence), 1921 U
Women, Married, Property Acts, in Britain, 1882 O
Women's Institutes, 1915 P
Women's Social and Political Union, 1903 P
Women's Voluntary Service, 1938 O
Women's clubs, 1892 O
Women, the ordination of, 1958 R, 1960 R, 1963 R, 1969 R, 1976 R, 1977 A, 1978 R, 1979 R, 1981 R, 1985 R, 1988 R, 1992 R
Women, war work:
  employed in British munitions factories, 1917 O
  liability for military service (aged 20–30), 1941 M
Women, working conditions in factories, 1844 F, 1847 F, 1906 O
Wonder, Stevie (born Steveland Judkins Morris), Am. singer (b. 1950), 1972 W
Wood on its Head, The (G. Baselitz), 1969 S
Wood, Charles Gerald, B. playwright (b. 1932), 1967 W
Wood, Charles Lindley, Viscount Halifax (1839–1934), 1894 R
Wood, Edward Frederick Lindley, Viscount Halifax, B. statesman, Conservative (1881–1959), as Lord Irwin, Viceroy of India, 1931 C; visits Hitler, 1937L; becomes foreign secretary, 1938 B; meets Mussolini, 1939 A; as British ambassador in Washington, 1940 M
Wood, Ellen (Mrs Henry Wood), B. author (1814–87), 1861 U
Wood, Grant, Am. artist (1892–1942), 1929 S, 1930 S
Wood, Mrs Henry. See Wood, Ellen
Wood, Sir Henry Joseph, B. musician, conductor (1869–1944), 1869 Z, 1895 T, 1944 Z
Wood, Matilda, b. musical hall artiste, under name of 'Marie Lloyd' (1870–1922), 1870 Z, 1922 Z
Wood, Wilfred Denniston, B. churchman (b. 1936), 1985 D
Wood-working machinery, 1793 P
Woodcock, George, B. T.U.C. Secretary, (1904–79), 1960 J
Wooden Shepherdess, The (R. Hughes), 1973 U
Woodhead, Sir John Ackroyd, B. administrator (1881–1973), 1938 A
Woodlanders, The (T. Hardy), 1887 U
Woodrow, William Robert, 'Bill', B. sculptor (b. 1948), 1982 S
Woodstock (W. Scott), 1826 U
Woodstock Music and Arts Fair, US, 1969 W
Woodward, Robert Burns, Am. chemist (1917–79), 1960 P, 1976 P
Wool production, comparative statistics of, 1910 Y
Woolf, Virginia (née Stephen), B. author (1882-1941), 1882 Z, 1925 U, 1927 U, 1928 U, 1929 U, 1941 Z
Woollen goods, British exports, 1822 Y, 1832 Y, 1842 Y, 1852 Y, 1862 Y, 1872 Y, 1882 Y, 1892 Y, 1902 Y, 1912 Y, 1922 Y
Woolley, Sir Leonard, B. archaeologist (1880–1960), 1918 Q, 1927 Q, 1930 Q
Woolton, Lord. See Marquis, F. J.
Woomera, Australia, space rocket launched at, 1959 P
Wooton, Graham, B. author (b. 1897), 1963 O
Wordsworth, William, B. poet (1770–1850), 1770 Z, 1798 U, 1800 U, 1805 U, 1807 U, 1814 U, 1815 U, 1835 U, 1850 Z; appointed poet laureate, 1843 U
Workers' Educational Association, 1904 O
Workers' Party. See under Political Parties
Workhouse Donkey, The (J. Arden), 1963 W
Working Days (M. Jokai), 1846 U
Working Men's Association, London, 1836 F, 1838 O
Working Men's Association, International, 1864 O
Working men's club, 1847 R
Workmen's compensation, 1880 J, O, 1897 O
Workshops, national, Blanc proposes, 1839 O
  in France, 1848 B
World Bank sets up Fund for Africa, 1985 O
World Climate Research Program launched, 1980 P
World Council of Churches, 1968 R, 1970 R, 1981 R; scheme for, 1946 R; founded 1948 R; Dehli meeting of, attended by Roman Catholic observers, 1961 R
World Health Organization (WHO), announces eradication of small-pox, 1978 K
World Journal Tribune, Am. newspaper, 1966 V
World Monetary Conference, London, 1933 F
World Ocean Experiment (WOCE), 1991 P
World Peace Council, in East Berlin, 1951 O
  in Vienna, offices closed, 1957 B
World Population (A. Carr-Saunders), 1936 O
World Population and Resources, (PEP Report), 1955 O
World Student Christian Federation, 1895 R
World Summit for Children, New York, 1990 J
World Turned Upside Down, The: Radical Ideas during the English Revolution. (C. Hill), 1972 Q
World War: Its Cause and Cure (L. Curtis
World and the West, The (A. Toynbee), 1952 O
World at War, The, television programme, 1975 W
World of Late Antiquity, The (P. Brown), 1971 Q
World of Physics, The (A. Eddington), 1931 P
World of Propensities, A (K. Popper), 1990 R
World, end of, predicted, 1831 R
Wormell, Donald Ernest Wilson, B. ancient historian (1908–90), 1957 Q
Wornum, George Grey, B. architect (1888–1957), 1933 S
Worship, freedom of. See Religious Toleration
Worth, France, Prussian victory at, 1870H

Worthington, Henry Rossiter, Am. Hydraulic engineer (1817–80), 1841 P
Wouk, Herman, Am. author (b. 1915), 1951 U
Wrangell, Mount, Alaska, observatory, 1953 P
Wrapped Walkways (Christo), 1978 S
Wright, Frank Lloyd, Am. architect (1869–1959), 1869 Z, 1909 S, 1936 S, 1938 S, 1949 S, 1959 S, Z
Wright, George Henrik von, Fin. philosopher, 1963 R
Wright, Harold, B. economist, 1931 O
Wright, Nicholas Thomas, B. theologian (b. 1948), 1992 R
Wright, Orville, Am. aviator (1871–1948), 1871 Zm 1903 P, 1948 Z
Wright, Peter, B. M.I.5 officer (b. 1916), *Spycatcher,* 1986 G, 1988 F
Wright, Richard Robert, Am. author, 1954 O
Wright, Wilbur, Am. aviator (1867–1912), 1903 P
Wrightson, Keith, 1982 Q
Wrigley, Edward Anthony, B. historian (b. 1931), 1931 Z, 1966 Q, 1981 Q, 1988 Q
Writing Life, The (A. Dillard), 1989 U
Writtle, Essex, England, first British broadcasting station at, 1920 W
Wrong Side of the Park, The (J. Mortimer), 1960 W
Wundt, Wilhelm Max, G. physiologist and philospher (1832–1920), 1832 Z, 1874 R, 1900 R, 1920 Z
Wurmser, Dagobert Sigismond, Count of, Aus. general (1724–97), 1796 H
Württemberg, Germany: becomes a Kingdom, 1805 M; merged in N. German Confederation, 1870 L
Wuthering Heights (E. Bronte), 1847 U
Wyatt, Thomas Henry, B. architect (1807–80), 1852 S
Wyatville, Sir Jeffry, B. architect (1766–1840), 1824 S
Wylam, Staffs., England, colliery, 1813 P
Wyler, William, Am. film director (1902–81), 1946 W, 1953 W
Wyndham, William, B. Whig (1750–1810), 1794 G
Wyndham, William, Lord Granville, B. Whig statesman (1759–1834), 1806 B, K, M, 1807 C
Wynne, Greville, B. businessman, arrested in Budapest oncharge of espionage, 1962 L; released from Moscow imprisonment, on exchange, 1964 D
Wyoming, Penna, US: massacre by Indians, 1778 G; reprisals for, 1779 H
Wyoming, state, US: gold discovered, 1866 P; enfranchises women, 1869 O; becomes a US state, 1890 G; has first woman state governor, 1925 A
Wyszynski, Stefan, Pol. Cardinal, primate of Poland (1901–81), arrested, 1953 J; released, 1956 K

X

X certificate films, 1951 W
X-Ray crystallography, 1912 P, 1964 P
X-Rays:
invention of, 1895 P
diffraction of, 1915 P
XLI Poems (e.e. cummings), 1925 U
XYZ Affairs, 1797 K, 1798 D
Xenakis, Iannis, F. (formerly Greek) musician (b. 1922), 1974 T, 1987 T
Xenon, gas, discovered, 1903 P
Xerography, invented, 1946P
Xi-particles, 1959 P

Y

Yachting, 1964 X
Yahya Khan, General Agha Muhammad (1917–80), Pakistani military ruler, 1969 C
Yakub, Amir of Afghanistan, 1879 E, K
Yale University, New Haven, Conn., US,
Beinecke, Library at, 1963 S
Hockey Rink, 1958 S
Yalta Conference of Allied leaders, 1954 B
Yamasaki, Minoru, Am. architect (b. 1912), 1970 S, 1971 S, 1973 S
Yamoussoukro, Ivory Coast, world's largest cathedral, 1990 R
Yandabu Treaty, between Britain and Burma, 1826 B
Yanggn, Korea, 1951 J
Yangtze Agreement, between Britain and Germany, 1900 K
Yangtze River, China, Japanese flotilla on, 1913 J; Mao Tse-tung swims in, 1966 G
Yamolinsky Report on US security precautions, 1955 O
Yarrow Revisited (W. Wordsworth), 1835 U
Yeager, Jeana, Am. pilot, 1986 P
Year of the Lion, The (G. Hanley), 1953 U
Year with Ross, The (J.Thurber), 1959 U
Yeats, William Butler, Ir. poet (1865–1939), 1865 Z, 1889 U, 1895 U, 1901 U, 1928 U, 1939 Z
Yellow Book, The 1894 S
Yellow Plus Papers (W. M. Thackeray), 1838 U
Yeltsin, Boris Nikolayevich, R. politician (b. 1931), 1931 Z
dismissed as chief of Moscow Communist Party, 1987 L
elected to Congress of People's Deputies, 1989 C
elected President of Russian Federation, 1990 E
resignation from Communist Party, 1990 G
elected leader of Russian Federation, 1991 F
leads popular resistance to coup, 1991 H
Yemen Republic, North and South Yemen merge to form, 1990 E
Yemen, South
People's Republic of, 1967 L
border fighting, 1972 J
president assassinated, 1978 F
Yemen: Italian agreement with, 1926 J; Britain accused of plotting to overthrow regime, 1962 L; cease-fire in, 1964 L; signs cease-fire with United Arab Republic, 1965 H; border fighting, 1972 J; President killed by S. Yemeni parcel bomb, 1978 F
Yonge, Charlotte Mary, B. author (1823–1901), 1823 Z, 1853 U, 1901 Z
York, von Wartenburg, Hans David Ludwig, Count, Pruss. general, 1812 M
York, Duchess of, (Sarah Margaret Ferguson, B. 1959), 1992 C, H
York, Duke of: *See* Andrew, Prince; Frederick Augustus
York, England; Retreat, 1792 O; Social survey of, 1941 O
lightning strikes Minster, 1984 R
York, now Toronto, Canada, US forces take, 1813 D
Yorktown, Va. US, siege, 1781 J, K
Yoshida, Shigeru, Hap. Democrat (1878–1967), 1948 K, 1953 E
Young, Andrew, Am. diplomat (b. 1932), resigns as UN ambassador, 1979 H
Young, Arthur, B. agriculturalist (1741–1820), 1774 O, 1792 O
appointed secretary of Board of Agriculture, 1846 P
Young, Brigham, Am. Mormon leader (1801–77), 1846 F
Young, David Ivor, Lord Young of Graffham, B. Conservative politician (b. 1932), 1988 C
Young, Edward, B. author (1783–1865), 1865 U
Young, Francis Brett, B. author (1884–1954), 1914 U
Young, Hugo John Smelter, B. journalist and author (b. 1938), 1989 Q
'Young Italy' movement (Mazzini's) founded, 1832 O; attempt on Savoy, 1834 B
Young, John, Am. astronaut (b. 1930), 1965 P
Young, Neil, Canad. pop singer (b. 1945), 1979 W
Young, Owen, D., Am. financier (1874–1957), 1928 M
reports on Reparations, 1929 F, H
upheld by German referendum, 1929 M
in force, 1930 E
Young, Thomas, B. physician, physicist and Egyptologist (1773-1829), 1800 P
'Young Turk' movement, 1896 N. See also Political Parties
Young, William John, B. chemist (1878–1942), 1906 P
Young Woodley (J. Van Druten), 1928 W
Younger, George Kenneth Hoson, Lord Younger of Pretwick, B. Conservative politician (b. 1931), 1986 A
Younghusband, Sir Francis, B. soldier and explorer (1863–194), 1863 Z, 1904 J, 1942 Z
Yourcenar, Marguerite (pseudonym of Marguerite de Crayencour), F. author (1903–87), 1968 U
Youth (J. Conrad), 1902 U
Youth Hostels Association, 1930 O
Ypres, Belg. battles, 1914 K, 1915 D, 1916 F, 1917 G, J
Yser, Belgium, battle, 1914 K
Yuan Shih-kai, Chin. leader (1859–1916), 1909 A; forms cabinet, 1911 L; proposes constitutional reform, 1912 B; takes Nanking, 1913 J; elected president, 1913 K; governs without Parliament, 1914 A; is proposed as emperor, 1915 L; dies, 1916 C
Yudenitch, Nicolai, R. counter-revolutionary, 1919 K
Yugoslavia:
republic established, 1918 K
Serbo-Croat-Slovene Kingdom proclaimed, 1918 M
Croat separatism in, 1928 H
Yugoslavia adopted as name of Serbo-Croat-Slovene Kingdom, 1929 K
German ultimatum to, 1941 D
opposition to Germany collapses, 1941 D
Russia withdraws recognition, 1941 D
Russians invade, 1944 J
Federal People's Republic proclaimed, 1945 L
recognised, 1946 D
Soviet invasion of Czechoslovakia condemned, 1968 H
Brezhnev doctrine refused, 1969 B
constitutional amendments, 1971 F
Croat leadership purged of nationalists, 1971 M
British state visit, 1972 K
collective presidency, 1980 E
Albanian separatists, 1988 J, 1990 B, 1991 C
nationalism, 1988 J
Mikulic government reigns, 1988 M

Slovenia's secession, 1989 J
Communist Party votes to abolish Party's monopoly on power, 1990 A
clashes between ethnic Albanians and Serbs, 1990 B
Slovenia, independence, 1990 M, 1991 F
Croatia freed from effective government control, 1991 E
Croatia declares independence, 1991 F
Bosnia-Herzegovina votes in favour of independence, 1991 K, 1992 C
Marković resigns as federal Prime Minister, 1991 M
Slovenia recognized by EC as independent republic, 1992 A
Croatia recognized by EC as independent republic, 1992 A
Serbia announces plan to create new Yugoslavia state, 1992 A
UN ban on trade, air and sporting links, 1992 E
civil war. *See* Civil Wars
Yungay, Peru, battle, 1839 A

Z

Z Cars, television series, 1978 W
Zabern incident, 1913 L
Zachariae von Lingerthal, Karl Salomo, G. jurist (1769–1843), 1806 O
Zagreb, Croatia, Croat separatist assembly in, 1928 H; air attack, 1991 K
Zahedi, General Fazlo'llah, premier of Iran (1897–1963), 1954 D
Zaire (formerly Congo), 1971 K
Zakharov, Gennady, F. USSR diplomat, 1986 H
Zambesi River, Africa: exploration of, 1852 P, 1855 P; Anglo–Portuguese agreements on, 1890 L, 1891 F; bridge over, 1935 P
Zambia (formerly Northern Rhodesia), becomes an independent republic, 1964 K
copper mines nationalised, 1969 H
Rhodesian border closed, 1973 A
Rhodesian air attacks, 1979 B
urbanization, 1985 Y
Kaunda defeated in presidential elections, 1991 K
Zamenhof, Ludwig, F. founder of Esperanto (1859–1917), 1887 O
Zamon, General Oreste, president of Haiti (d. 1915), 1914 A
Zamora, Alcalá, Sp. politician (1877–1949), 1931 D, 1936 D
elected president, 1931 M
Zanardelli, Giuseppe, It. premier (1826–1903), 1901 B
Zangwill, Israel, B. author (1864–1926), 1864 Z, 1892 U, 1926 Z
Zanzibar: independence recognised, 1862 C; Sultan of, abolishes slave traffic, 1873 F; annexed by Germany, 1885 B; exchanged with Britain for Heligoland, 1890 G; slavery in, abolished, 1897 D; incorporated with British East Africa, 1913 G; becomes independent within the Commonwealth, 1963 M; declared republic, 1964 A; is united with Tanganyika to form Tanzania, 1964 D. *See also* Tanzania.
Zappa, Frank, Am. musician (b. 1940), 1969 W
Zhorov, on R. Dniester, Russia, Russian break through at, 1917 G
Zeebrugge, Belgium: R. Navy bombards, 1914 L; air attack on, 1916 C; R, Navy raids, 1918 D; Admiralty film on, 1924 W; Belgians recapture, 1918 K; *Herald of Free Enterprise* capsizes, 1987 C, G, K
Zeeland, Paul Van, Belg. financier (1893–1973), premier of National Unity Ministry, 1935 C, 1936 F, 1937 K; forms Social Democrat, ministry, 1950 H
Zeila, British Somaliland, 1884 N
Zeiss optical glass, Jackson's substitute for, 1916 P
Zeldin, Theodore, B. historian (b. 1933), 1973 Q
Zemstvo Congress, 1904 L
Zeppelin, Ferdinand, Count, G. inventor (1838–1905), 1838 Z, 1898 P, 1900 P
Zeppelins, used for bombardment, 1915 F, 1916 A, 1917 G
Zerata, Webb, architect, 1974 S
Zermatt, Switzerland, typhoid at, 1963 C
Zhang Jie, Chinese author (b. 197), 1980 U
Zhelev, Zhelyu, Bulg. leader (b. 1935), 1992 A
Zhivkov, Todor, Bulg. leader (b. 1911), 1989 L, 1992 J
Zhukov, Georgi Konstantinovich (1896–1974), R. general, 1896 Z, 1974 Z; replaces Timoshenko, 1942 G; von Keitel surrenders to, 1945 E; relieved of post as defence minister, 1957 K
Zia ul-Haq, Mohaammed, President of Pakistan (1924–88), 1985 M
takes power, 1977 G
cancels elections, 1977 K, 1979 K
bans political activity, 1979 K
crushes attempted military coup, 1980 C
attempts mediation on Iran–Iraq war, 1980 J
elections and lifting of martial law announced, 1983 H
death, 1988 H
Zia ur-Rahman, President of Bangladesh (1936–81), 1936 Z, 1977 D, 1979 B, 1981 Z
assassinated, 1981 E
Zigger Zagger (P. Terson), 1968 W
Zimbabwe, Africa:
Commonwealth Conference on, 1979 H
British rule ended, 1979 M
clashes between ex-guerilla forces, 1981 B
Nkomo dismissed from government, 1982 B
one-party state planned, 1984 H
seats reserved for whites abolished, 1987 H
ZANU (PF) and ZAPU parties united, 1987 M
nationalization of white-owned farms, 1990 M
See also Rhodesia
Zimbabwe African National Union (ZANU), 1969 B, 1980 C, 1987 M, 1990 D
Zimbabwe African People's Party. *See under* Political Parties
Zimmermann, Arthur, G. foreign minister (1864–1940), 1916 L
Zimmermann, Johann Georg, Swi. philosopher and physician (1728–95), 1764 P
Zimmermann, Udo, G. musician (b. 1943), 1982 T
Zinc protamine insulin, 1937 P
Zinnermann, Fred, Am. film director, 1953 W
Zinoviev letter, 1924 K
Zinoviev, Grigori, R. diplomat (1883–1936), expelled from Politbureau, 1926 K; convicted of treason, 1935 A
Zionism, 1897 R, 1930 O, 1946 J. *See also* Israel
Zip fastener, invented, 1893 P
Zips, Poland, occupied by Austria, 1769 B
Zog I, King of Albania, 1928 J
Zola Dam, near Aix en Provence, France, 1843 P
Zola, Emile, F. author (1840–1902), 1840 Z, 1867 U, 1871 U, 1877 U, 1880 U, 1885 U, 1888 U, 1892 U, 1894 U, 1902 Z; writes J'accuse, 1898 A
Zoli, Adone, It. premier (1887–1960), 1957 E, 1958 F
Zollverein (Customs Union): origin of Prussia's, 1819 K; development of 1826 M, 1827 N; formally established, 1833 C; Baden joins, 1835 E; Hanover joins, 1853 D; commercial treaty with Britain, 1865 E
Zolotas, Professor Xenophon, Greek economist and politician (b. 1904), 1989 L
Zoological Society, The Royal, 1826 P
Zoonomia, on the Laws of Organic Life (E. Darwin), 1794 P
Zorilla y Moral, José, S. author (1817–93), 1844 U
Zsigmondy, Richard Adolf, G. scientist (1865–1929), 1903 P
Zuider Zee, Holland, drainage scheme, 1906 P, 1932 P
Zululand, S. Africa, 1884 L; Britain annexes, 1887 F; annexed to Natal, 1897 M
Zulus: Boers defeat, 1838 M; are segregated in Natal, 1846 N; Britain's wars with, 1877 D, 1889 A, H, J; Inkatha movement, clashes with ANC, 1990 H
Zum ewigen Frieden (I. Kant), 1795 R
Zurich, Switzerland, 1799 J; Masséna's defeat at, 1799 F; University, 1832 O; treaty, confirms treaty of Villafranca, 1859 L; art in, 1916 S
Centre Le Corbusier, 1967 S
Palestinian terrorists attack El Al airliner at airport, 1969 B
Zvend-Avesta (ed. Darmesteter), 1892 Q
Zwentersdorf, Austria
nuclear power station, 1978 L